القرآن

The Meaning of THE GLORIOUS QUR'AN

An explanatory translation by

Marmaduke Pickthall

The Meaning of The Glorious Qur'an

Translated By: Mohammed Marmaduke Pickthall

ISBN 81-7101-139-X

Edition 1998

Published by:
Idara Isha'at-e-Diniyat (P) Ltd.
168/2, Jha House, Hazrat Nizamuddin
New Delhi-110 013 (India)
Fax: +91-11-693-2787 & 463-2786
Email: idara@idara.com
Website: www.idara.com

Printed at:
Johar Offset Printers, New Delhi

TRANSLATOR'S FOREWORD

THE aim of this work is to present to English readers what Muslims the world over hold to be the meaning of the words of the Qur'an and the nature of that Book, in not unworthy language and concisely, with a view to the requirements of English Muslims. It may be reasonably claimed that no Holy Scripture can be fairly presented by one who disbelieves its inspiration and its message; and this is the first English translation of the Qur'an by an Englishman who is a Muslim. Some of the translations include commentation offensive to Muslims, and almost all employ a style of language which Muslims at once recognise as unworthy The Qur'an cannot be translated. That is the belief of old-fashioned Sheykhs and the view of the present writer. The Book is here rendered almost literally and every effort has been made to choose befitting language. But the result is not the Glorious Qur'an, that inimitable symphony, the very sounds of which move men to tears and ecstasy. It is only an attempt to present the meaning of the Qur'an—and peradventure something of the charm—in English. It can never take the place of the Qur'an in Arabic, nor is it meant to do so.

Before publication the work has been scrutinised word by word and thoroughly revised in Egypt with the help of one whose mother-tongue is Arabic, who has studied the Qur'an and who knows English; and when difficulties were encountered the translator had recourse to perhaps the greatest living authority on the subject. Every care has thus been taken to avoid unwarrantable renderings. On the one or two occasions where there is departure from the traditional interpretation, the traditional rendering will be found in a footnote.

The translator's thanks are due to Lord Lloyd for an introduction of great use in Egypt; to Dr. F. Krenkow for supplying him with old meanings of Arabic words not to be found in dictionaries; to Muhammad Ahmad Al-Ghamrawi Bey of the Cairo College of Medicine for his invaluable and patient help with the revision of the manuscript, a work which occupied three months; to the Sheykh Mustafa Al-Maraghi, former Rector of Al-Azhar University, for his advice and guidance in the revision; and to His Excellency Fuad Bey Salim Al-Hijazi, by whose effort such revision was made possible.

The *mushaf* (copy of the Qur'an) which has been used throughout is lithograph copy of that written by Al-Hajj Muhammad Shakarzadeh at the command of Sultan Mahmud of Turkey in 1246 A.H In the Introduction and the notes to individual surahs, Ibn Hisham (Bulaqed 1295 A.H.) has been followed, with occasional reference to the much later, much abbreviated, but more critical Life of the Prophet by Ibn Khaldun (published as an appendix to his *Tarikh,* Bulaqed.) Other *Surahs,* like that of Abu'l-Fida, late in date and uncritical, have been read but not followed. Of commentators Al-Beydawi and Zamakshari must be mentioned, while for reference during the work of revision, the brief commentary of Al-Jalaleyn was kept at hand. Wahidi's *Asbabu'n-Nuzul* has been largely consulted, and for the authenticity of Traditions the translator has relied upon Bukhari.

INTRODUCTION

PART 1

(*At Mecca*)

The Prophet's birth

MUHAMMAD, son of Abdullah, son of Abdul Muttalib, of the tribe of Qureysh, was born at Mecca fifty-three years before the Hijrah His father died before he was born, and he was protected first by his grandfather, Abdul Muttalib, and, after his grandfather's death, by his uncle, Abu Talib. As a young boy he travelled with his uncle in the merchants' caravan to Syria, and some years afterwards made the same journey in the service of a wealthy widow named Khadijah. So faithfully did he transact the widow's business, and so excellent was the report of his behaviour which she received from her old servant who had accompanied him, that she soon afterwards married her young agent; and the marriage proved a very happy one, though she was fifteen years older than he was. Throughout the twenty-six years of their life together he remained devoted to her; and after her death, when he took other wives, he always mentioned her with the greatest love and reverence. This marriage gave him rank among the notables of Mecca, while his conduct earned for him the surname *Al-Amin*, the "trustworthy."

His marriage

The Meccans claimed descent from Abraham through Ishmael, and tradition stated that their temple, the Ka'bah, had been built by Abraham for the worship of the One God. It was still called the House of Allah, but the chief objects of worship there were a number of idols wich were called daughters of Allah and intercessors. The few who felt disgust at this idolatry, which had prevailed for centuries, longed for the religion of Abraham and tried to find out what had been its teaching. Such seekers of the truth were known as *Hunafa* (sing. *Hanif*), a word originally meaning "those who turn away" (from the existing idol-worship), but coming in the end to have the sense of "upright" or "by nature upright" because such persons held the way of truth to be right conduct. These *Hunafa* did not form a community. They were the agnostics of their day, each seeking truth by the light of his own inner consciousness. Muhammad son of Abdullah became one of these. It was his practice to retire with his family for a month of every year to a cave in the desert for meditation. His place of retreat was *Hira*, a desert hill not far from Mecca, and his chosen month was *Ramadan*, the month of heat. It was there one night toward the end of his quiet month that the first revelation came to him when he was forty years old. He was asleep or in a trance when he heard a voice say: "Read" ! He said: "I cannot Read." The voice again said: "Read" He said: I cannot read." A third time the voice, more terrible, commanded: "Read" ! He said 'What can I read?" The voice said:

The *Hunafa*

The first revelation

"Read: In the name of thy Lord Who createth.
"Createth man from a clot.
"Read: And it is thy Lord the Most Bountiful
"Who teacheth by pen,
"Teacheth man that which he knew not."[1]

When he awoke the words remained "as if inscribed upon his heart." He went out of the cave on to the hillside and heard the same awe-inspring voice say: "O Muhammad! Thou art Allah's messenger,

1. Surah XCVI 1...5.

and I am Gabriel." Then he raised his eyes and saw the angel, in the likeness of a man, standing in the sky above the horizon: And again the dreadful voice said: "O Muhammad! Thou art Allah's messenger, and I am Gabriel." Muhammad (God bless and keep him!) stood quite still turning away his face from the brightness of the vision, but whithersoever he might turn his face, there, always stood the angel confronting him. He remained thus a long while till at length the angel vanished, when he returned in great distress of mind to his wife Khadijah. She did her best to reassure him, saying that his conduct had been such that Allah would not let a harmful spirit come to him and that it was her hope that he was to become the Prophet of his people. On their return to Mecca she took him to her cousin Waraqa ibn Naufal, a very old man, "who knew the Scriptures of the Jews and Christians," who declared his belief that the heavenly messenger who came to Moses of old had come to Muhammad, and that he was chosen as the Prophet of his people.

The vision of Mt. *Hira*

To understand the reason of the Prophet's diffidence and his extreme distress of of mind after the vision of Mt. Hira, it must be remembered that the *Hunafa*, of whom he had been one, sought true religion in the natural and regarded with distrust the intercourse with spirits of which men "avid of the Unseen,"[1] sorcerers and soothsayers and even poets, boasted in those days. Moreover, he was a man of humble and devout intelligence, a lover of quiet and solitude, and the very thought of being chosen out of all mankind to face mankind, alone, with such a Message, appalled him at the first. Recognition of the Divine nature of the call he had received involved a change in his whole mental outlook sufficiently disturbing to a sensitive and honest mind, and also the forsaking of his quiet, honoured way of life. The early biographers tell how his wife Khadijah "tried the spirit" which came to him and proved it to be good, and how, with the continuance of the revelations and the conviction that they brought, he, at length, accepted the tremendous task imposed on him, becoming filled with an enthusiasm of obedience which justifies his proudest title of "The Slave of Allah."

His distress of mind.

The words which came to him when in a state of trance are held sacred by the Muslims and are never confounded with those which he uttered when no physical change was apparent in him. The former are the Sacred Book; the latter the *Hadith* or *Sunnah* of the Prophet. And because the angel on Mt. Hira bade him "Read!"—insisted on his "Reading" though he was illiterate—the Sacred Book is known as *Al-Qur'an*, "The Reading,"[2] the Reading of the man who knew not how to read.

The Qur'an or "Reading"

For the first three years, or rather less, of his Mission, the Prophet preached only to his family and his intimate friends, while the people of Mecca as a whole regarded him as one who had become a little mad. The first of all his converts was his wife Khadijah, the second his first cousin Ali, whom he had adopted, the third his servant Zeyd, a former slave. His old friend Abu Bakr also was among those early converts with some of his slaves and dependents.

First converts

At the end of third year the Prophet received the command to "arise and warn,"[3] whereupon he began to preach in public,

Beginning of persecution.

1 XXXI, 24.

2 Or "The lecture," as it is here translated in passages where the term will bear translation on the analogy of "Scripture," used for sacred "writing,"

3 LXXIV. 2.

pointng out the wretched folly of idolatry in face of the tremendous laws of day and night, of life and death, of growth and decay, which manifest the power of Allah and attest His Sovereignty. It was then, when he began to speak against their gods, that Qureysh became actively hostile, persecuting his poorer disciples, mocking and insulting him. The one consideration which prevented them from killing him was fear of the blood-vengeance of the clan to which his family belonged. Strong in his inspiration, the Prophet went on warning, pleading, threatening, while Qureysh did all they could to ridicule his teaching, and deject his followers.

The flight to Abyssinia

The converts of the first four years ware mostly humble folk unable to defend themselves against oppression. So crucl was the persecution they endured that the Prophet advised all who could possibly contrive to do so to emigrate to a Christain country, Abyssinia.[1] And still in spite of persecution and emigration the little company of Muslims grew in number. Qureysh were seriously alarmed. The idol-worship at the Ka'bah, the holy place to which all Arabia made pilgrimage, ranked for them as guardians of the Ka'bah as first among their vested interests. At the season of the pilgrimage they posted men on all the roads to warn the tribes against the madman who was preaching in their midst. They tried to bring the Prophet to a compromise, offering to accept his religion if he would so modify it as to make room for their gods as intercessors with Allah, offering to make him their king if he would give up attacking idolatry; and, when their efforts at negotiation failed, they went to his uncle Abu Talib, offering to give him the best of their young men in place of Muhammad, to give him all that he desired, if only he would let them kill Muhammad and have done with him. Abu Talib refused. The exasperation of the idolaters was increased by the conversion of Umar,[2] one of their stalwarts. They grew more and more embittered, till things came to such a pass that they decided to ostracise the Prophet's whole clan, idolaters who protected him as well as Muslims who believed in him. Their chief men caused a document to be drawn up to the effect that none of them or those belonging to them would hold any intercourse with that clan or sell to them or buy from them. This they all signed, and it was deposited in the Ka'bah. Then for three years, the Prophet was shut up with all his kinsfolk in their stronghold which was situated in one of the gorges which run down to Mecca. Only at the time of pilgrimage could he go out and preach, or did any of his kinsfolk dare to go into the city.

Conversion of Umar

The *Sahifah* or deed of ostracism

At length some kinder hearts among Qureysh grew weary of the boycott of old friends and neighbours. They managed to have the document which had been placed in the Ka'bah brought out for reconsideration ; when it was found that all the writing had been destroyed by white ants, except the words *Bismika Allahumma* ("In Thy name, O Allah"). When the elders saw that marvel the ban was removed, and the Prophet was again free to go about the city. But meanwhile the opposition to his preaching had grown rigid. He had little success among the Meccans, and any attempt which he made to preach in the city of Ta'if was a failure. His Misson was a failure, judged by worldly standards, when, at the season of the yearly pilgrimage, he came upon a little group of men who heard him gladly.

Destruction of the *Sahifah*

The men from Yathrib

1 See XIX, introductory note.
2 See XX, introductory note.

They came from Yathrib, a city more than two hundred miles away, which has since become world-famous *Al-Madinah,* "the City" *par excellence.* At Yathrib there were Jewish tribes with learned rabbis, who had often spoken to the pagans of a Prophet soon to come among the Arabs, with whom, when he came, the Jews would destroy the pagans as the tribes of A'ad and Thamud had been destroyed of old for their idolatry. When the men from Yathrib saw Muhammad they recognised him as the Prophet whom the Jewish rabbis had described to them. On their return to Yathrib they told what they had seen and heard, with the result that at the next season of pilgrimage a deputation came from Yathrib purposely to meet the Prophet. These swore allegiance to him in the first pact of Al-'Aqabah, the oath they took being that which was afterwards exacted from women converts, with no mention of fighting. They then returned to Yathrib with a Muslim teacher in their company, and soon "there was not a house in Yathrib wherein there was not mention of the messenger of Allah."

First Pact of Al-'Aqbah

In the following year, at the time of pilgrimage, seventy-three Muslims from Yathrib came to Mecca to vow allegiance to the Prophet and invite him to their city. At Al-'Aqabah, by night, they swore to defend him as they would defend their own wives and children. I was then that the Hijrah, the Flight to Yathrib, was decided.

Second pact of Al-'Aqbah

Soon the Muslims who were in a position to do so began to sell their property and to leave Mecca unobtrusively. Qureysh had wind of what was going on. They hated Muhammad in their midst, but dreaded what he might become if he escaped from them. It would be better, they considred, to destroy him now. The death of Abu Talib had removed his chief protector; but still they had to reckon with the vengeance of his clan upon the murderer. They cast lots and chose a slayer out of every clan. All those were to attack the Prophet simultaneously and strike together, as one man. Thus his blood would be on all Qureysh. It was at this time (Ibn Khaldun asserts, and it is the only satisfactory explanation of what happened afterwards) that the Prophet received the first revelation ordering him to make war upon his persecutors "until persecution is no more and religion is Allah only."[1]

Plot to murdur the Prophet

The last of the able Muslims to remain in Mecca were Abu Bakr, Ali and the Prophet himself. Abu Bakr, a man of wealth, had bought two riding-camels and retained a guide in readiness for the Flight. The Prophet only waited God's command. It came at length. It was the night appointed for his murder. The slayers were before his house. He gave his cloak to Ali, bidding him lie down on the bed so that anyone looking in might think Muhammad lay there. The slayers were to strike him as he came out of the house. whether in the night or early morning. He knew they would not injure Ali. Then he let the house and, it is said, a blindness fell upon the would be murderers so that he put dust on their heads as he pased by—without their knowing it. He went to Abu Bakr's house and called to him, and they two went together to a cavern in the desert hills and hid there till the hue and cry was past. Abu Bakr's son and daughter and his herdsman bringing them food and tidings after nightfall. Once a search-party came quite near them in their hiding-place. and Abu Bakr was afraid; but the Prophet said;

1 VIII, 39

THE HIJRAH (June 20th, 622 A D.)

"Fear not! Allah is with us"[1] Then, when, the coast was clear, Abu Bakr had the riding camels and the guide brought to the cave one night and they set out on the long ride to Yathrib.

After travelling for manys days by unfrequented paths, the fugitives reached a suburb of Yathrib, whither, for weeks past, the people of the city had been going every morning, watching for the Prophet till heat drove them to shelter. The travellers arrived in the heat of the day, after the watchers had retired. It was a Jew who called out to the Muslims in derisive tones that he whom they expected had at last arrived.

Such was the Hijrah, the Flight from Mecca to Yathrib, which counts as the beginning of the Muslim era. The thirteen years of humiliation, of persecution, of seeming failure, of prophecy still unfulfilled, were over. The ten years of success, thc fullest that has ever crowned one man's endeavour, had begun. The Hijrah makes a clear division in the story of the Prophet's Mission, which is evident in the Qur'an. Till then he had been a preacher only. Thenceforth he was the ruler of a State, at first a very small one, which grew in ten years to be the empire of Arabia. The kind of guidance which he and his people needed after the Hijrah was not the same as that which they had before needed. The Madinah surahs differ, therefore, from the Meccan surahs. The latter give guidance to the individual soul and to the Prophet as warner; the former give guidance to a growing social and political community and to the Prophet as exemplar, lawgiver and reformer.

Classification of Meccan Surahs

For classification the Meccan surahs are here subdivided into four groups: Very Early, Early, Middle and Late. Though the historical data and traditions are insufficient for a strict chronological grouping, the very early surahs are, roughly, speaking, those revealed before the beginning of the persecution; the early surahs those revealed between the beginning of the persecution and the conversion of Umar; the middle surahs those revealed between the conversion of Umar and the destruction of the deed of ostracism; and the late surahs those revealed between the raising of the ban of ostracism and the Hijrah.

PART II

At Al-Madinah

In the first year of his reign at Yathrib the Prophet made a solemn treaty with the Jewish tribes, which secured to them equal rights of citizenship and full religious liberty in return for their support of the new State. But their idea of a Prophet was one who would give them dominion, not one who made the Jews who followed him as brothers of every Arab who might happen to believe as they did. When they found that they could not use the Prophet for their own ends, they tried to shake his faith in his Mission and to seduce his followers; behaviour in which they were encouraged secretly by some professing Muslims who considered they had reason to resent the Prophet's coming, since it robbed them of their local influence. In the Madinah surahs there is frequent mention of these Jews and Hypocrites.

The Jews and Hypocrites

The *Qiblah*

Till then the *Qiblah* (the place toward which the Muslims turn their faces in prayer) had been Jerusalem. The Jews imag-

[1] IX, 40

ined that the choice implied a leaning toward Judaism and that the Prophet stood in need of their instruction. He received command to change the Qiblah[1] from Jerusalem to the Ka'bah at Mecca. The whole first part of surah II relates to this Jewish controversy.

The Prophet's first concern as a ruler was to establish public worship and lay down the constitution of the State; but he did not forget that Qureysh had sworn to make an end of his religion, nor that he had received command to fight against them till they ceased from persecution. After he had been twelve months in Yathrib several small expeditions went out, led either by the Prophet himself or some other of the fugitives from Mecca, for the purpose of reconnoitring and of dissuading other tribes from siding with Qureysh. These are generally represented as warlike but, considering their weakness and the fact that they did not result in fighting, they can hardly have been that, though it is certain that they went out ready to resist attack. It is noteworthy that in those expeditions only fugitives from Mecca were employed, never natives of Yathrib; the reason being (if we accept Ibn Khaldun's theory, and there is no other explanation) that the command to wage war had been revealed to the Prophet at Mecca after the Yathrib men had sworn their oath of allegiance at Al-'Aqabah, and in their absence. Their oath foresaw fighting in mere defence, not fighting in the field. Blood was shed and booty taken in only one of those early expeditions, and then it was against the Prophet's orders. One purpose of those expeditions may have been to accustom the Meccan Muslims to going out in warlike trim. For thirteen years they had been strict pacifists, and it is clear, from several passages of the Qur'an[2] that many of them, including, it may be, the Prophet himself, hated the idea of fighting even in self-defence and had to be inured to it

The First Expedition

In the second year of the Hijrah the Meccan merchants' caravan was returning from Syria as usual by a road which passed not far from Yathrib. As its leader Abu Sufyan approached the territory of Yathrib he heard of the Prophet's design to capture the caravan. At once he sent a camel-rider on to Mecca, who arrived in a worn-out state and shouted frantically from the valley to Qureysh to hasten to the rescue unless they wished to lose both wealth and honour. A force a thousand strong was soon on its way to Yathrib; less, it would seem, with the hope of saving the caravan than with the idea of punishing the raiders, since the Prophet might have taken the caravan before the relief force started from Mecca. Did the Prophet ever intend to raid the caravan? In Ibn Hisham, in the account of the Tabuk expedition, it is stated that the Prophet on that one occasion did not hide his real objeetive as had been his custom in other campaigns. The caravan was the pretext in the campaign of Badr, the real objective was the Meccan army. He had received command to fight his persecutors, and promise of victory; he was prepared to venture against any odds, as was well seen at Badr. But the Muslims, disinclined and ill-equipped for war, would have despaired if they had known from the first that they were to face a well armed force three times their number.

The campaign of Badr

1 II, 144, 149, 150

2 e.g. II, 216

The army of Qureysh had advanced more than half to Yathrib before the Prophet set out. All three parties—the army of Qureysh, the Muslim army and the caravan—were heading for the water of Badr. Abu Sufyan, the leader of the caravan, heard from one of his scouts that the Muslims were near the water, and turned back to the coast-plain. And the Muslims met the army of Qureysh by the water of Badr. Before the battle the Prophet was prepared still further to increase the odds against him. He gave leave to all the Ansar (natives of Yathrib) to return to their homes unreproached, since their oath did not include the duty of fighting in the field; but the Ansar were only hurt by the suggestion that they could possibly desert him in a time of danger. The battle went at first against the Muslims, but ended in a signal victory for them.[1]

The victory of Badr gave the Prophet new prestige among the Arab tribes; but thenceforth there was the feud of blood between Qureysh and the Islamic State in addition to the old religious hatred. Those passages of the Qur'an which refer to the battle of Badr give warning of much greater struggles yet to come.

In fact in the following year, an army of three thousand came from Mecca to destroy Yathrib. The Prophet's first idea was merely to defend the city, a plan of which Abdullah ibn Ubeyy, the leader of " Hypocrites " (or lukewarm Muslims), strongly approved. But the men who had fought at Badr and believed that God would help them against any odds thought it a shame that they should linger behind walls. The Prophet, approving of their faith and zeal, gave way to them, and set out with an army of one thousand men toward Mt. Uhud, where the enemy were encamped. Abdullah ibn Ubeyy was much offended by the change of plan. He thought it unlikely that the Prophet really meant to give battle in conditions so adverse to the Muslims, and was unwilling to take part in a mere demonstration designed to flatter the fenatical extremists. So he withdrew with his men, a fourth of the army.

The battle on Mt. *Uhud*

Despite the heavy odds, the battle on Mt. Uhud would have been an even greater victory than that at Badr for the Muslims but for the disobedience of a band of fifty archers whom the Prophet set to guard a pass against the enemy cavalry. Seeing their comrades victorious, these men left their post, fearing to lose their share of the spoils. The cavalry of Qureysh rode through the gap and fell on the exultant Muslims. The Prophet himself was wounded and the cry arose that he was slain, till someone recognised him and shouted that he was still living a shout to which the Muslims rallied. Gathering round the Prophet, they retreated, leaving many dead on the hillside.[2]

On the following day the Prophet again sallied forth with what remained of the army, that Qureysh might hear that he was in the field and so might perhaps be deterred from attacking the city. The stratagem succeeded, thanks to the behaviour of a friendly Bedawi, who met the Muslims and conversed with them and afterwads met the army of Qureysh. Questioned by Abu Sufyan, he said that

1 See also Surah VIII, introductory note.

2 See also III, introductory note.

Muhammad was in the field, stronger than ever, and thirsting for fevenge for yesterday's affair. On that information, Abu Sufyan decided to return to Mecca

Massacre of Muslims

The reverse which they had suffered on Mt. Uhud lowered the prestige of the Muslims with the Arab tribes and also with the Jews of Yathrib. Tribes which had inclined toward the Muslims now inclined toward Qureysh. The Prophet's followers were attacked and murdered when they went abroad in little companies. Khubeyb, one of his envoys, was captured by a desert tribe and sold to Qureysh, who tortured him to death in Mecca publicly. And the Jews, despite their treaty, now hardly concealed their hostility. They even went so far in flattery of Qureysh as to declare the religion of the pagan Arabs superior to Al-Islam.[1] The Prophet was obliged to take punitive action against some of them. The tribe of Bani Nadir were besieged in their strong towers, subdued and forced to emigrate. The Hypocrites had sympathised with the Jews and secretly egged them on.[2]

Expulsion of the *Bani Nadir*

The War of the Trench

In the fifth years of the Hijrah the idolaters made a great effort to destroy Al-Islam in the War of the Clans or War of the Trench, as it is variously called; when Qureysh with all their clans and the great desert tribe of Ghatafan with all their clans, an army of ten thousand men rode aginst Al-Madinah (Yathrib). The Prophet (by the advice of Salman the Persian, it is said) caused a deep trench to be dug before the city. and himself led the work of digging it. The army of the clans was stopped by the trench, a novelty in Arab warfare. It seemed impassable for cavalry, which formed their strength. They camped in sight of it and daily showered their arrows on its defenders. While the Muslims were awaiting the assault, news came that Bani Qureyzah, a Jewish tribe of Yathrib which had till then been loyal, had gone over to the enemy. The case seemed desperate. But the delay caused by the trench had damped the ardour of the clans, and one who was secretly a Muslim managed to sow distrust between Qureysh and their Jewish allies, so that both hesitated to act. Then came a bitter wind from the sea, which blew for three days and nights so terribly that not a tent could be kept standing, not a fire lighted, not a pot boiled. The tribesmen were in utter misery. At length, one night the leader of Qureysh decided that the torment could be borne no longer and gave the order to retire.[3] When Ghatafan awoke next morning they found Qureysh had gone and they took up their baggage and retreated.

Punishment of *Bani Qureyzah*

On the day of the return from the trench the Prophet ordered war on the treacherous Bani Qureyzah, who, conscious of their guilt, had already taken to their towers of refuge. After a siege of nearly a month they had to surrender unconditionally. They only begged that they might be judged bo a member of the Arab tribe of which they were adherents. The Prophet granted their request. But the judge, upon whose favour they had counted, condemned their men to death, their women and children to slavery.

The salander against Ayeshah

Early in the sixth year of the Hijrah the Prophet led a compaign against the Bani'l-Mustaliq, a tribe who were preparing to attack the Muslims. It was during the return from that campaign that Ayeshah, his young wife, was left behind and brought back to camp

1 IV, 51 2 LIX

3 See also XXXII, introductory note

by a young soldier, an incident which gave rise to the scandal denounced in Surah XXIV.[1] It was on this campaign also that Abdullah Ibn Ubeyy, the "Hippocrite" chief, said: "When we return to the city the mightier will soon expel the weaker"[2] at sight of a quarrel between Muhajrin (immigrants from Mecca) and Ansar (natives of Yathrib).

In the same year the Prophet had a vision in which he found himself entering the holy place at Mecca unopposed ; therefore he determined to attempt the pilgrimage.[3] Besides a number of Muslims from Yathrib (which we shall henceforth call Al-Madinah) he called upon the friendly Arabs, whose numbers had increased since the miraculous (as it was considered) discomfiture of the clans, to accompany him, hut most of them did not respond,[4] Attired as pilgrims, and taking with them the customary offerings, a company of fourteen hundred journeyed to Mecca. As they drew near the holy valley they were met by a friend from the city who warned the Prophet that Qureysh had put on their leopard-skins (the badge of valour) and had sworn to prevent his entering the sanctuary; their cavalry was on the road before him. On that, the Prophet ordered a detour through mountain gorges and the Muslims were tired out when they came down at last into the valley of Mecca and encamped at a spot called Al-Hudeybiyah; from whence he tried to open negotiations with Qureysh, explaining that he came only as a pilgrim. The first messenger he sent towards the city was maltreated and his camel hamstrung. He returned without delivering his message. Qureysh on their side sent an envoy who was threatening in tone, and very arrogant. Another of their envoys was too familiar and had to be reminded sternly of the respect due to the Prophet. It was he who, on his return to the city, said: "I have seen Cæsar and Chosroes in their pomp, but never have I seen a man honoured as Muhammad is honoured by his comrades."

Al-Hudeybiyah

The Prophet sought some messenger who would impose respect. Uthman was finally chosen because of his kinship with the powerful Umayyad family. While the Muslims were awaiting his return the news came that he had been murdered. It was then that the Prophet sitting under a tree[5] in Al-Hudeybiyah, took an oath from all his comrades that they would stand or fall together. After a while, however, it became known that Uthman had not been murdered. A troop which came out from the city to molest the Muslims in their camp were captured before they could do any hurt[6] and brought before the Prophet, who forgave them on their promise to renounce hostility. Then proper envoys came from Qureysh. After some negotiation, truce of Al-Hudeybiyah was signed. For ten years there were to be no hostilities between the parties. The Prophet was to return to Al-Madinah without visiting the Ka'bah, but in the following year he might perform the pilgrimage with his comrades, Qureysh promising to evacuate Mecca for three days to allow of his doing so. Deserters from Qureysh to the Muslims during the period of the truce were to be returned; not so deserters from the Muslims to Qureysh. Any tribe or clan who wished to share in the treaty as allies of the Prophet might do so, and any tribe or clan who wished to share in the treaty as allies of Qureysh might do so.

1 XXIV, 11 ff. 2 LXIII, 8 3 XLVIII, 27 4 XLVIII, 11 ff. 5 XLVIII, 13. 6 XLVIII, 24.

There was dismay among the Muslims at these terms. They asked one another: "Where is the victory that we were promised?" It was during the return journey from Al-Hudeybiyah that the surah entitled "Victory"[1] was revealed. This truce proved, in fact, to be the greatest victory that the Muslims had till then achieved. War had been a barrier between them and the idolaters, but now both parties met and talked together, and the new religion spread more rapidly. In the two years which elapsed between the signing of the truce and the fall of Mecca the number of converts was greater than the total number of all previous converts. The Prophet travelled to Al-Hudebiyah with 1,000 men. Two years later, when the Meccans broke the truce, he marched against them with an army of 10,000.

The campaign of Kheaybar

In the seventh year of the Hijrah the Prophet led a campaign against Khaybar, the stronghold of the Jewish tribes in North Arabia, which had become a hornet's nest of his enemies. The forts of Kheybar were reduced one by one, and the Jews of Kheybar became thenceforth tenants of the Muslims until the expulsion of the Jews from Arabia in the Caliphate of Umar. On the day when the last fort surrendered, Ja'far, son of Abu Talib, the Prophet's first cousin, arrived with all who remained of the Muslims, who had fled to Abyssinia to escape from persecution in the early days. They had been absent from Arabia fifteen years. It was at Khaybar that a Jewess prepared for the Prophet poisoned meat, of which he only tasted a morsel without swallowing it, then warned his comrades that it was poisoned. One Muslim, who had already swallowed a mouthful, died immediately, and the Prophet himself from the mere taste of it, derived the illness which eventually caused his death. The woman who cooked the meat was brought before him. When she said that she had done it on account of humiliation of her people, he forgave her.

Pilgrimage to Mecca

In the same year the Prophet's vision was fulfilled: he visited the holy place at Mecca unopposed. In accordance with the terms of the truce idolaters evacuated the city, and from the surrounding heights watched the procedure of the Muslims. At the end of the stipulated three days the chiefs of Qureysh sent word to remind the Prophet that the time was up. He then withdrew, and the idolaters reoccupied the city.

Mutah expedition

In the eighth year of the Hijrah, hearing that the Byzantine emperor was gathering a force in Syria for the destruction of Al-Islam, the Prophet sent three thousand men to Syria under the command of his freedman Zeyd. The campaign was unsuccessful except that it impressed the Syrians with a notion of the reckless valour of the Muslims. The three thousand did not hesitate to join battle with a hundred thousand. When all the three leaders appointed by the Prophet had been killed, the survivors obeyed Khalid ibn al-Walid, who, by his strategy and courage, managed to preserve a remnant and return with them to Al-Madinah.

Truce broken by Qureysh

In the same year Qureysh broke the truce by attacking a tribe that was in alliance with the Prophet and massacring them even in the sanctuary at Mecca. Afterwards they were afraid because of

1 XLVIII.

what they had done. They sent Abu Sufyan to Al-Madinah to ask for the existing treaty to be renewed and its term prolonged. They hoped Sat he would arrive before the tidings of the massacre. But a massenger from the injured tribe had been before him, and his embassy was fruitless.

Conquest of Mecca

Then the Prophet summoned all the Muslims capable of bearing arms and marched to Mecca. Qureysh were overawed. Their cavalry put up a show of defence before the town, but were routed without bloodshed; and the Prophet entered his native city as conqueror. The inhabitants expected vengeance for their past misdeeds. The Prophet proclaimed a general amnesty. Only a few known criminals were prorsribed, and most of those were in the end forgiven. In their relief and surprise, the whole population of Mecca hastened to swear allegiance. The Prophet caused all the idols which were in the sanctuary to be destroyed, saying; "Truth hath come; darkness hath vanished away;[1] and the Muslim call to prayer was heard in Mecca.

Battle of *Huneyn*

In the same year there was angry gathering of pagan tribes eager to regain the Ka'bah. The Prophet led twelve thousand men against them. At Huneyn, in a deep ravine, hir troops were ambushed by the enemy and almost put to flight. It was with difficulty that they were rallied to the Prophet and his bodyguard of faithful comrades who alone stood firm. But the victory, when it came, was complete and the booty enormous, for many of the hostile tribes had brought out with them everything that they possessed.

Consequent of *Ta'if*

The tribe of Thaqif were among the enemy at Huneyn. After that victory their city of Ta'if was besieged by the Muslims, and finally reduced. Then the Prophet appointed a governor of Mecca, and himself returned to Al-Madinah to the bundless joy of the Ansar, who had feared lest, now that he had regained his native city, he might forsake them and make Mecca the capital.

The Tabuk expedition

In the ninth year of the Hijrah, hearing that an army was again being mustered in Syria, the Prophet called on all the Muslims to support him in a great campaign. The far distance, the hot season, the fact that it was harvest time and the prestige of the enemy caused many to excuse themseves and many more to stay behind without excuse. Those defaulters are denounced in the Qur'an[2] But the campaign ended peacefully. The army advanced to Tabuk, on the confines of Syria, and there learnt that the enemy had not yet gathered.

Declaration of Immunity

Although Mecca had been conquered and its people were now Muslims, the official order of the pilgrimage had been changed; the pagan Arabs performing it in their manner and the Muslims in their manner. It was only after the pilgrims' caravan had left Al-Madinah in the ninth year of the Hijrah, when Al-Islam was dominant in North Arabia, that the Declaration of Immunity,[3] as it is called, was revealed. The Prophet sent a copy of it by messenger to Abu Bakar, leader of the pilgrimaeg, with the instruction that Ali was to read it to the multitudes at Mecca. Its purport was that after that year Muslims only were to make the pilgrimage, exception being made for such of the idolaters as had a

1 XVII, 18. 2 XVII 81. 3 IX, 38—98

treaty with the Muslims and had never broken their treaty nor supported anyone against them. Such were to enjoy the privileges of their treaty for the term thereof, but when their treaty expired they would be as other idolaters. That proclamation marks the end of idol-worship in Arabia.

The year of Deputations

The ninth year of the Hijrah is called the Year of Deputations, because from all parts of Arabia deputations came to Al-Madinah to swear allegiance to the Prophet and to hear the Qur'an. The Prophet had become, in fact, the emperor of Arabia, but his way of life remained as simple as before.

The number of the campaigns which he led in person during the last years of his life is twenty-seven, in nine of which there was hard fighting. The number of the expeditions which he planned and sent out under other leaders is thirty-eight. He personally controlled every detail of organisation, judged every case and was accessible to every suppliant. In those ten years he destroyed idolatry in Arabia; raised woman from the status of a chattel to complete legal equality with man; effectually stopped the drunkenness and immorality which had till then disgraced the Arabs; made men to live with faith, sincerity and honest dealing; transformed tribes who had been for centuries content with ignorance into a people with the greatest thirst for knowledge; and for the first time in history made universal human brotherhood a fact and principle of common law. And his support and guide in all that work was the Qur'an.

The Farewell Pilgrimage

In the tenth year of the Hijrah he went to Mecca as a pilgrim for the last time—his "pilgrimage of farewell," it is called—when from Mt. 'Arafat he preached to an enormous throng of pilgrims. He reminded them of all the duties Al-Islam enjoined upon them, and that they would one day have to meet their Lord, who would judge each one of them according to his work. At the end of the discourse, he asked: "Have I not conveyed the message?" And from that great multitude of men who a few months or years before had all been conscienceless idolaters, the shout went up: "O Allah! Yes!" The Prophet said: "O Allah! Be Thou witness!"

Illness and death of the Prophet

It was during that last pigrimage that the Surah entitled "Succour"[1] was revealed, which he received as an announcement of approaching death. Soon after his return to Al-Madinah he fell ill. The tidings of his illness caused dismay throughout Arabia and anguish to the folk of Al-Madinah, Mecca and Ta'if, the hometowns. At early dawn on the last day of his earthly life he came out from his room beside the mosque at Al-Madinah and joined the public prayer, which Abu Bakr had been leading since his illness. And there was great relief among the people who supposed him well again. When, later in the day, the rumour grew that he was dead, Umar theratened those who spread the rumour with dire punishment, declaring it a crime to think that the messenger of God could die. He was storming at the people in this strain when Abu Bakr came into the mosque and overheard him. Abu Bakr went to the chamber of his daughter Ayeshah, where the Prophet lay. Having ascertained the fact, and kissed the dead man's forehead, he went back into the mosque. The people were still listening to Umar, who was saying that the rumour was a wicked lie, that the Prophet who was all in all to them could not be dead. Abu Bakr went up to Umar

1 XLIX.

and tried to stop him by a whispered word. Then, finding he would pay no heed, Abu Bakr called to the people, who, recognising his voice, left Umar and came crowding round him. He first gave praise to Allah, and then said: "O people! Lo! as for him who used to worship Muhammad, Muhammad is dead But as for him who used to worship Allah, Allah is Alive and dieth not. He then recited the verse of the Qur'an:

"And Muhammad is but a messenger, messengers the like of whom have passed away before him. Will it be that, when he dieth or is slain, ye will turn back on your heels? He who turneth back doth no hurt to Allah, and Allah will reward the thankful."[1]

"And," says the narrator, an eye-witness, "it was as if the people had not known that such a verse had been revealed till Abu Bakr recited it." And another witness tells how Umar used to say: "Directly I heard Abu Bakr recite that verse my feet were cut from beneath me and I fell to the ground, for I knew that Allah's messenger was dead. May Allah bless and keep him!"

All the surahs of the Qur'an had been recorded in writing before the Prophet's death, and many Muslims had committed the whole Qur'an to memory. But the written surahs were dispersed among the people; and when, in a battle which took place during the Caliphate of Abu Bakr—that is to say, within two years of the Prophet's death—a large number of those who knew the whole Qur'an by heart were killed, a collection of the whole Qur'an was made and put in writing. In the Caliphate of Uthman, all existing copies of surahs were called in, and an authoritative version, based on Abu Bakr's collection and the testimony of those who had the whole Qur'an by heart, was compiled exactly in the present form and order, which is regarded as traditional and as the arrangement of the Prophet himself, the Caliph Uthman and his helpers being Comrades of the Prophet and the most devout students of the revelation. The Qur'an has thus been very carefully preserved.

The arrangement is not easy to understand. Revelations of various dates and on different subjects are to be found together in surahs; some of the Madinah surahs, though of late revelation, are placed first and the very early Meccan surahs at the end. But the arrangement is not haphazard, as some have hastily supposed. Closer study will reveal a sequence and significance—as, for instance, with regard to the placing of the very early Meccan surahs at the end. The inspiration of the Prophet progressed from inmost things to outward things, whereas most people find their way through outward things to things within.

There is another peculiarity which is disconcerting in translation though it proceeds from one of the beauties of the original, and is unavoidable without abolishing the verse-division of great importance for reference. In Arabic the verses are divided according to the rhythm of the language. When a certain sound which marks the rhythm recurs there is a strong pause and the verse ends naturally, although the sentence may go on to the next verse or to several subsequent verses. That is of the spirit of the Arabic language; but attempts to reproduce such rhythm in English have the opposite effect to that produced by the Arabic. Here only the division is preserved, the verses being divided as in the Qur'an and numbered.

[1] CX

SURAH INDEX
قرآن مجید کی سورتوں کی فہرست

Al-Fātiḥah, "The Opening," or *Fātiḥatu'l-Kitāb*, "The Opening of the Scripture" or *Ummu'l-Qurān*, "The Essence of the Koran," as it is variously named, has been called the Lord's Prayer of the Muslims. It is an essential part of all Muslim worship, public and private, and no solemn contract or transaction is complete unless it is recited. The date of revelation is uncertain, but the fact that it has always, from the very earliest times, formed a part of Muslim worship, there being no record or remembrance of its introduction, or of public prayer without it, makes it clear that it was revealed before the fourth year of the Prophet's Mission (the tenth year before the Hijrah); because we know for certain that by that time regular congregational prayers were offered by the little group of Muslims in Mecca. In that year, as the result of insult and attack[1] by the idolaters, the Prophet arranged for the services, which had till then been held out of doors, to take place in a private house.

This sūrah is also often called *Saba'an min al-Mathāni*, "Seven of the Oft-repeated" ("verses" being understood), S. XV, 87, words which are taken as referring to this sūrah.[2]

1. Ibn Hishām *Sīrah* (Cairo Ed.), Part 1, p. 88.
2. See Nöldeke, *Geschichte des Qorâns*, Zweite Auflage, bearbeitet von Fr. Schwally, Part 1, pp. 110 *seq*.

TRANSLATOR'S NOTE: I have retained the word Allah throughout, because there is no corresponding word in English. The word *Allâh* (the stress is on the last syllable) has neither feminine nor plural, and has never been applied to anything other than the unimaginable Supreme Being. I use the word "God" only where the corresponding word *ilâh* is found in the Arabic.

The words in backets are interpolated to explain the meaning.

THE OPENING

Revealed at Mecca

1. In the name of Allah, the Beneficent, the Merciful.

2. Praise be to Allah, Lord of the Worlds:

3. The Beneficent, the Merciful:

4. Owner of the Day of Judgement.

5. Thee (alone) we worship; Thee (alone) we ask for help.

6. Show us the straight path:

7. The path of those whom Thou hast favoured; Not (the path) of those who earn Thine anger nor of those who go astray.

اٰيَاتُهَا ٧ سُوْرَةُ الْفَاتِحَةِ مَكِّيَّةٌ رُكُوْعُهَا ١

المنزل ١

بِسْمِ اللّٰهِ الرَّحْمٰنِ الرَّحِيْمِ ﴿١﴾

اَلْحَمْدُ لِلّٰهِ رَبِّ الْعٰلَمِيْنَ ﴿٢﴾

الرَّحْمٰنِ الرَّحِيْمِ ﴿٣﴾

مٰلِكِ يَوْمِ الدِّيْنِ ﴿٤﴾

اِيَّاكَ نَعْبُدُ وَاِيَّاكَ نَسْتَعِيْنُ ﴿٥﴾

اِهْدِنَا الصِّرَاطَ الْمُسْتَقِيْمَ ﴿٦﴾

صِرَاطَ الَّذِيْنَ اَنْعَمْتَ عَلَيْهِمْ ۙ غَيْرِ الْمَغْضُوْبِ

عَلَيْهِمْ وَلَا الضَّآلِّيْنَ ﴿٧﴾ ع

Al-Baqarah (The Cow) is so named from the story of the yellow heifer (vv. 67-71). As is the case with many other sūrahs, the title is taken from some word or incident which surprised the listeners. All suggestions to the contrary notwithstanding, it seems probable that the whole of this sūrah was revealed during the first four years after the Hijrah, and that by far the greater portion of it was revealed in the first eighteen months of the Prophet's reign at Al-Madînah—that is to say, before the battle of Badr.[1]

The Jewish tribes, once paramount in Yathrib, had, not very long before the coming of Al-Islām, been reduced by the pagan Arab tribes of Aus and Khazraj, each Jewish tribe becoming an adherent of one or the other. But they had preserved a sort of intellectual ascendancy owing to their possession of the Scripture and their fame for occult science, the pagan Arabs consulting their rabbis on occasions and paying heed to what they said. Before the coming of Al-Islām,[2] these Jewish rabbis had often told their neighbours that a Prophet was about to come, and had often threatened them that, when he came, they (the Jews) would destroy the pagan Arabs as the tribes of 'Aād and Thamūd had been destroyed of old.[3] So plainly did they describe the coming Prophet that pilgrims from Yathrib recognised the Prophet, when he addressed them in Mecca, as the same whom the Jewish doctors had described to them. But the Jewish idea of a Prophet was one who would give them dominion, not one who would make them brethren of every pagan Arab who chose to accept Al-Islām. When they found that they could not make use of the newcomer, they opposed him and tried to bewilder him with questions from their theology, speaking to him as men who possessed superior wisdom; failing to perceive that, from a Prophet's stand-point, theology is childish nonsense, the very opposite of religion, and its enemy; religion, for the Prophet, being not a matter of conjecture and speech, but of fact and conduct.

Ibn Isḥāq[4] states definitely that vv. 1-141 were revealed concerning these Jewish rabbis and such of the new converts to Al-Islām as were half-hearted and inclined to them. There follows the order to change the *Qiblah* (the place toward which the Muslims turn their face in prayer) from Jerusalem to the Ka'bah at Mecca, which was built by Abraham, the choice of Jerusalem having led to a misunderstanding on the part of the Jews that the Prophet was groping his way toward their religion and stood in need of their guidance and instruction.

All through the sūrah runs the note of warning, which sounds indeed throughout the whole Koran, that it is not the mere profession of a creed, but righteous conduct, which is true religion. There is the repeated announcement that the religion of Abraham, to which Judaism and Christianity (which springs from Judaism) trace their origin, is the only true religion, and that that religion consists in the surrender of man's will and purpose to the Will and Purpose of the Lord of Creation as manifested in His creation and revealed by way of guidance through successive Prophets. Of sincerity in that religion the one test is conduct, and the standard of that religion is for all alike.

At the time when this sūrah was revealed at Al-Madînah, the Prophet's own tribe, the pagan Qureysh at Mecca, were preparing to attack the Muslims in their place of refuge. Cruel persecution was the lot of Muslims who had stayed in Meccan territory or who journeyed thither, and Muslims were being prevented from performing the pilgrimage. The possible necessity of fighting had been foreseen in the terms of the oath, taken at Al-'Aqabah by the Muslims of Yathrib before the Flight, to defend the Prophet as they would their own wives and children, and the first commandment to fight was revealed to the Prophet before his flight from Mecca; but there was no

1. Th. Nöldeke, *Geschichte des Qorâns*, Zweite Auflage, bearbeitet von Fr. Schwally, Part I, pp. 173 *seq.*
2. *Al-Islām* means "The Surrender"—*i.e.* man's surrender to God's will and purpose.
3. Ibn Hishām (Cairo ed.), Part I, pp. 180 *seq.*
4. *Apud* Ibn Hishām, *Sirah* (Cairo Ed.), pp. 189 *seq.*

actual fighting by the Muslims until the battle of Badr. Many of them were reluctant, having before been subject to a rule of strict non-violence. It was with difficulty that they could accept the idea of fighting even in self-defence, as can be seen from several verses in this sūrah, which contains also rules for fasting and the pilgrimage, bequests, almsgiving, divorce and contracts, and verses which discountenance usury, strong drink and gambling. It concludes with a statement of the universal character of Al-Islām, the religion of Allah's sovereignty, and a prayer for the forgiveness of shortcomings.

This sūrah might be described as the Koran in little. It contains mention of all the essential points of the Revelation, which are elaborated elsewhere. This accounts for the precedence given to it in the arrangement of the Book.

The period of revelation is the years 1 and 2 A.H. for the most part, certain verses of legislation being considered as of later date.

THE COW

Revealed at Al-Madinah

In the name of Allah, the Beneficent, the Merciful.

1. Alif. Lām. Mīm.[1]

2. This is the Scripture whereof there is no doubt, a guidance unto those who ward off (evil):

3. Who believe in the unseen, and establish worship, and spend of that We have bestowed upon them;

4. And who believe in that which is revealed unto thee (Muhammad) and that which was revealed before thee, and are certain of the Hereafter.

5. These depend on guidance from their Lord. These are the successful.

6. As for the disbelievers, whether thou warn them or thou warn them not it is all one for them; they believe not.

7. Allah hath sealed their hearing and their hearts, and on their eyes there is a covering. Theirs will be an awful doom.

8. And of mankind are some who say, We believe in Allah and the Last Day, when they believe not.

9. They think to beguile Allah and those who believe, and they beguile none save themselves; but they perceive not.

10. In their hearts is a disease, and Allah increaseth their disease. A painful doom is theirs because they lie.

آياتها ٢٨٦ (٢) سُورَةُ الْبَقَرَةِ مَدَنِيَّةٌ رُكُوعَاتُهَا ٤٠

بِسْمِ اللّٰهِ الرَّحْمٰنِ الرَّحِيْمِ ○

الٓمّٓ ①

ذٰلِكَ الْكِتٰبُ لَا رَيْبَ ۚۛ فِيْهِ ۚۛ هُدًى لِّلْمُتَّقِيْنَ ②

الَّذِيْنَ يُؤْمِنُوْنَ بِالْغَيْبِ وَيُقِيْمُوْنَ الصَّلٰوةَ وَمِمَّا
رَزَقْنٰهُمْ يُنْفِقُوْنَ ③

وَالَّذِيْنَ يُؤْمِنُوْنَ بِمَآ اُنْزِلَ اِلَيْكَ وَمَآ اُنْزِلَ مِنْ
قَبْلِكَ ۚ وَبِالْاٰخِرَةِ هُمْ يُوْقِنُوْنَ ④

اُولٰٓئِكَ عَلٰى هُدًى مِّنْ رَّبِّهِمْ ۗ وَاُولٰٓئِكَ هُمُ
الْمُفْلِحُوْنَ ⑤

اِنَّ الَّذِيْنَ كَفَرُوْا سَوَآءٌ عَلَيْهِمْ ءَاَنْذَرْتَهُمْ اَمْ
لَمْ تُنْذِرْهُمْ لَا يُؤْمِنُوْنَ ⑥

خَتَمَ اللّٰهُ عَلٰى قُلُوْبِهِمْ وَعَلٰى سَمْعِهِمْ ۗ وَعَلٰٓى
اَبْصَارِهِمْ غِشَاوَةٌ ۫ وَّلَهُمْ عَذَابٌ عَظِيْمٌ ⑦ ع

وَمِنَ النَّاسِ مَنْ يَّقُوْلُ اٰمَنَّا بِاللّٰهِ وَبِالْيَوْمِ
الْاٰخِرِ وَمَا هُمْ بِمُؤْمِنِيْنَ ⑧ وقف لازم

يُخٰدِعُوْنَ اللّٰهَ وَالَّذِيْنَ اٰمَنُوْا ۚ وَمَا يَخْدَعُوْنَ
اِلَّآ اَنْفُسَهُمْ وَمَا يَشْعُرُوْنَ ⑨

فِيْ قُلُوْبِهِمْ مَّرَضٌ ۙ فَزَادَهُمُ اللّٰهُ مَرَضًا ۚ وَلَهُمْ
عَذَابٌ اَلِيْمٌ ۢ بِمَا كَانُوْا يَكْذِبُوْنَ ⑩

1. Three letters of the Arabic alphabet: Many sūrahs begin thus with letters of the alphabet. Opinions differ as to their significance, the prevalent view being that they indicate some mystic words. Some have opined that they are merely the initials of the scribe. They are always included in the text and recited as part of it.

11. And when it is said unto them: Make not mischief in the earth, they say: We are peacemakers only.

12. Are not they indeed the mischief-makers? But they perceive not.

13. And when it is said unto them: Believe as the people[1] believe, they say: Shall we believe as the foolish believe? Are not they indeed the foolish? But they know not.

14. And when they fall in with those who believe, they say: We believe; but when they go apart to their devils they declare: Lo! we are with you; verily we did but mock.

15. Allah (Himself) doth mock them, leaving them to wander blindly on in their contumacy.

16. These are they who purchase error at the price of guidance, so their commerce doth not prosper, neither are they guided.

17. Their likeness is as the likeness of one who kindleth fire, and when it sheddeth its light around him Allah taketh away their light and leaveth them in darkness, where they cannot see.

18. Deaf, dumb and blind; and they return not:

19. Or like a rainstorm from the sky wherein is darkness, thunder and the flash of lightning. They thrust their fingers in their ears by reason of the thunder-claps, for fear of death. Allah encompasseth the disbelievers (in His guidance).

20. The lightning almost snatcheth away their sight from them. As often as it flasheth forth for them they walk therein, and when it darkeneth against them they stand still. If Allah willed, He could destroy their hearing and their sight. Lo! Allah is Able to do all things.

وَاِذَا قِيْلَ لَهُمْ لَا تُفْسِدُوْا فِي الْاَرْضِ قَالُوْٓا اِنَّمَا
نَحْنُ مُصْلِحُوْنَ ﴿١١﴾
اَلَآ اِنَّهُمْ هُمُ الْمُفْسِدُوْنَ وَلٰكِنْ لَّا يَشْعُرُوْنَ ﴿١٢﴾
وَاِذَا قِيْلَ لَهُمْ اٰمِنُوْا كَمَآ اٰمَنَ النَّاسُ قَالُوْٓا
اَنُؤْمِنُ كَمَآ اٰمَنَ السُّفَهَآءُ اَلَآ اِنَّهُمْ هُمُ السُّفَهَآءُ وَ
لٰكِنْ لَّا يَعْلَمُوْنَ ﴿١٣﴾
وَاِذَا لَقُوا الَّذِيْنَ اٰمَنُوْا قَالُوْٓا اٰمَنَّا وَاِذَا خَلَوْا اِلٰى
شَيٰطِيْنِهِمْ قَالُوْٓا اِنَّا مَعَكُمْ اِنَّمَا نَحْنُ مُسْتَهْزِءُوْنَ ﴿١٤﴾
اَللّٰهُ يَسْتَهْزِئُ بِهِمْ وَيَمُدُّهُمْ فِيْ طُغْيَانِهِمْ
يَعْمَهُوْنَ ﴿١٥﴾
اُولٰٓئِكَ الَّذِيْنَ اشْتَرَوُا الضَّلٰلَةَ بِالْهُدٰى فَمَا
رَبِحَتْ تِّجَارَتُهُمْ وَمَا كَانُوْا مُهْتَدِيْنَ ﴿١٦﴾
مَثَلُهُمْ كَمَثَلِ الَّذِي اسْتَوْقَدَ نَارًا فَلَمَّآ اَضَآءَتْ
مَا حَوْلَهٗ ذَهَبَ اللّٰهُ بِنُوْرِهِمْ وَتَرَكَهُمْ فِيْ ظُلُمٰتٍ
لَّا يُبْصِرُوْنَ ﴿١٧﴾
صُمٌّۢ بُكْمٌ عُمْيٌ فَهُمْ لَا يَرْجِعُوْنَ ﴿١٨﴾
اَوْ كَصَيِّبٍ مِّنَ السَّمَآءِ فِيْهِ ظُلُمٰتٌ وَّرَعْدٌ وَّبَرْقٌ
يَجْعَلُوْنَ اَصَابِعَهُمْ فِيْٓ اٰذَانِهِمْ مِّنَ الصَّوَاعِقِ
حَذَرَ الْمَوْتِ وَاللّٰهُ مُحِيْطٌۢ بِالْكٰفِرِيْنَ ﴿١٩﴾
يَكَادُ الْبَرْقُ يَخْطَفُ اَبْصَارَهُمْ كُلَّمَآ اَضَآءَ لَهُمْ مَّشَوْا
فِيْهِ وَاِذَآ اَظْلَمَ عَلَيْهِمْ قَامُوْا وَلَوْ شَآءَ اللّٰهُ لَذَهَبَ
بِسَمْعِهِمْ وَاَبْصَارِهِمْ اِنَّ اللّٰهَ عَلٰى كُلِّ شَيْءٍ قَدِيْرٌ ﴿٢٠﴾ ع ٢

1. *i.e.* the people of Al-Madīnah, most of whom were Muslims, vv. 8 to 19 refer to the "Hypocrites," or lukewarm Muslims of Al-Madīnah, whose leader was Abdullah ibn Ubeyy. They pretended that their aim was to make peace between the Muslims and the Jewish rabbis, but they only embittered the controversy.

21. O mankind! Worship your Lord, Who hath created you and those before you, so that ye may ward off (evil):

22. Who hath appointed the earth a resting-place for you, and the sky a canopy; and causeth water to pour down from the sky, thereby producing fruits as food for you. And do not set up rivals to Allah when ye know (better).

23. And if ye are in doubt concerning that which We reveal unto Our slave[1] (Muhammad), then produce a sūrah of the like thereof, and call your witnesses beside Allah if ye are truthful.

24. And if ye do it not—and ye can never do it—then guard yourselves against the fire prepared for disbelievers, whose fuel is of men and stones.

25. And give glad tidings (O Muhammad) unto those who believe and do good works; that theirs are Gardens underneath which rivers flow; as often as they are regaled with food of the fruit thereof, they say: This is what was given us aforetime;[2] and it is given to them in resemblance. There for them are pure companions; there for ever they abide.

26. Lo! Allah disdaineth not to coin the similitude even of a gnat. Those who believe know that it is the truth from their Lord; but those who disbelieve say: What doth Allah wish (to teach) by such a similitude? He misleadeth many thereby, and He guideth many thereby; and He misleadeth thereby only miscreants;

27. Those who break the covenant of Allah after ratifying it, and sever that which Allah ordered to be joined, and (who) make mischief in the earth: Those are they who are the losers.

يَٰٓأَيُّهَا ٱلنَّاسُ ٱعْبُدُوا۟ رَبَّكُمُ ٱلَّذِى خَلَقَكُمْ وَٱلَّذِينَ
مِن قَبْلِكُمْ لَعَلَّكُمْ تَتَّقُونَ ﴿٢١﴾
ٱلَّذِى جَعَلَ لَكُمُ ٱلْأَرْضَ فِرَٰشًا وَٱلسَّمَآءَ بِنَآءً وَ
أَنزَلَ مِنَ ٱلسَّمَآءِ مَآءً فَأَخْرَجَ بِهِۦ مِنَ ٱلثَّمَرَٰتِ رِزْقًا
لَّكُمْ ۖ فَلَا تَجْعَلُوا۟ لِلَّهِ أَندَادًا وَأَنتُمْ تَعْلَمُونَ ﴿٢٢﴾
وَإِن كُنتُمْ فِى رَيْبٍ مِّمَّا نَزَّلْنَا عَلَىٰ عَبْدِنَا فَأْتُوا۟
بِسُورَةٍ مِّن مِّثْلِهِۦ وَٱدْعُوا۟ شُهَدَآءَكُم مِّن دُونِ
ٱللَّهِ إِن كُنتُمْ صَٰدِقِينَ ﴿٢٣﴾
فَإِن لَّمْ تَفْعَلُوا۟ وَلَن تَفْعَلُوا۟ فَٱتَّقُوا۟ ٱلنَّارَ ٱلَّتِى وَقُودُهَا
ٱلنَّاسُ وَٱلْحِجَارَةُ ۖ أُعِدَّتْ لِلْكَٰفِرِينَ ﴿٢٤﴾
وَبَشِّرِ ٱلَّذِينَ ءَامَنُوا۟ وَعَمِلُوا۟ ٱلصَّٰلِحَٰتِ أَنَّ لَهُمْ
جَنَّٰتٍ تَجْرِى مِن تَحْتِهَا ٱلْأَنْهَٰرُ ۖ كُلَّمَا رُزِقُوا۟ مِنْهَا مِن
ثَمَرَةٍ رِّزْقًا ۙ قَالُوا۟ هَٰذَا ٱلَّذِى رُزِقْنَا مِن قَبْلُ ۖ وَأُتُوا۟ بِهِۦ
مُتَشَٰبِهًا ۖ وَلَهُمْ فِيهَآ أَزْوَٰجٌ مُّطَهَّرَةٌ ۖ وَهُمْ فِيهَا خَٰلِدُونَ ﴿٢٥﴾
إِنَّ ٱللَّهَ لَا يَسْتَحْىِۦٓ أَن يَضْرِبَ مَثَلًا مَّا بَعُوضَةً
فَمَا فَوْقَهَا ۚ فَأَمَّا ٱلَّذِينَ ءَامَنُوا۟ فَيَعْلَمُونَ أَنَّهُ ٱلْحَقُّ
مِن رَّبِّهِمْ ۖ وَأَمَّا ٱلَّذِينَ كَفَرُوا۟ فَيَقُولُونَ مَاذَآ أَرَادَ
ٱللَّهُ بِهَٰذَا مَثَلًا ۘ يُضِلُّ بِهِۦ كَثِيرًا وَيَهْدِى بِهِۦ كَثِيرًا ۚ وقف لازم
وَمَا يُضِلُّ بِهِۦٓ إِلَّا ٱلْفَٰسِقِينَ ﴿٢٦﴾
ٱلَّذِينَ يَنقُضُونَ عَهْدَ ٱللَّهِ مِنۢ بَعْدِ مِيثَٰقِهِۦ وَ
يَقْطَعُونَ مَآ أَمَرَ ٱللَّهُ بِهِۦٓ أَن يُوصَلَ وَيُفْسِدُونَ
فِى ٱلْأَرْضِ ۚ أُو۟لَٰٓئِكَ هُمُ ٱلْخَٰسِرُونَ ﴿٢٧﴾

1. To be the slave of Allah is the proudest boast of the Muslim, bondage to Allah liberating from all other servitudes. In the Koran mankind are often called God's slaves or bondmen, a stronger and more just expression than the word "servants" generally substituted in translations.

2. The joys of Paradise will recall, in a rapturous degree, the joys the righteous tasted in their life on earth.

28. How disbelieve ye in Allah when ye were dead and He gave life to you! Then he will give you death, then life again, and then unto Him ye will return.

كيف تكفرون بالله وكنتم امواتا فاحياكم ثم
يميتكم ثم يحييكم ثم اليه ترجعون ﴿٢٨﴾

29. He it is Who created for you all that is in the earth. Then turned He to the heaven, and fashioned it as seven heavens. And He is Knower of all things.

هو الذي خلق لكم ما في الارض جميعا ثم
استوى الى السماء فسوىهن سبع سموت وهو
بكل شيء عليم ﴿٢٩﴾ ع ٣

30. And when thy Lord said unto the angels: Lo! I am about to place a viceroy in the earth, they said: Wilt Thou place therein one who will do harm therein and will shed blood, while we, we hymn Thy praise and sanctify Thee? He said: Surely I know that which ye know not.

واذ قال ربك للملئكة اني جاعل في الارض
خليفة قالوا اتجعل فيها من يفسد فيها ويسفك
الدماء ونحن نسبح بحمدك ونقدس لك قال
اني اعلم ما لا تعلمون ﴿٣٠﴾

31. And He taught Adam all the names,[1] then showed them to the angels, saying: Inform me of the names of these if ye are truthful.

وعلم ادم الاسماء كلها ثم عرضهم على الملئكة
فقال انبئوني باسماء هؤلاء ان كنتم
صدقين ﴿٣١﴾

32. They said: Be glorified! We have no knowledge saving that which Thou hast taught us. Lo! Thou, only Thou, art the Knower, the Wise.

قالوا سبحنك لا علم لنا الا ما علمتنا انك انت
العليم الحكيم ﴿٣٢﴾

33. He said: O Adam! Inform them of their names, and when he had informed them of their names, He said: Did I not tell you that I know the secret of the heavens and the earth? And I know that which ye disclose and which ye hide.

قال يادم انبئهم باسمائهم فلما انباهم باسمائهم
قال الم اقل لكم اني اعلم غيب السموت والارض
واعلم ما تبدون وما كنتم تكتمون ﴿٣٣﴾

34. And when We said unto the angels: Prostrate yourselves before Adam, they fell prostrate, all save Iblīs. He demurred through pride, and so became a disbeliever.

واذ قلنا للملئكة اسجدوا لادم فسجدوا الا ابليس
ابى واستكبر وكان من الكفرين ﴿٣٤﴾

35. And We said: O Adam! Dwell thou and thy wife in the Garden, and eat ye[2] freely (of the fruits) thereof where ye will; but come not nigh this tree lest ye become wrongdoers.

وقلنا يادم اسكن انت وزوجك الجنة وكلا منها
رغدا حيث شئتما ولا تقربا هذه الشجرة فتكونا من
الظلمين ﴿٣٥﴾

1. Some, especially Sufis, hold "the names" to be the attributes of Allah: others, the names of animals and plants.

2. Here the command is in the dual, as addressed to Adam and his wife.

36. But Satan caused them to deflect therefrom and expelled them from the (happy) state in which they were; and We said: Fall down,[1] one of you a foe unto the other! There shall be for you on earth a habitation and provision for a time.

37. Then Adam received from his Lord words (of revelation), and He relented toward him. Lo! He is the Relenting, the Merciful.

38. We said: Go down, all of you, from hence; but verily there cometh unto you from Me a guidance; and whoso followed My guidance, there shall no fear come upon them neither shall they grieve.

39. But they who disbelieve, and deny Our revelations, such are rightful owners of the Fire. They will abide therein.

40. O Children of Israel! Remember My favour wherewith I favoured you, and fulfil your (part of the) covenant, I shall fulfil My (part of the) covenant, and fear Me.

41. And believe in that which I reveal, confirming that which ye possess already (of the Scripture), and be not first to disbelieve therein, and part not with My revelations for a trifling price, and keep your duty unto Me.

42. Confound not truth with falsehood, nor knowingly conceal the truth.

43. Establish worship, pay the poor-due,[2] and bow your heads with those who bow (in worship).

44. Enjoin ye righteousness upon mankind while ye yourselves forget (to practise it)? And ye are readers of the Scripture! Have ye then no sense?

45. Seek help in patience and prayer; and truly it is hard save for the humble-minded,

49. Who know that they will have to meet their Lord, and that unto Him they are returning.

فأزلهما الشيطن عنها فأخرجهما مما كانا فيه
وقلنا اهبطوا بعضكم لبعض عدو ولكم في
الأرض مستقر ومتاع إلى حين ﴿٣٦﴾
فتلقى آدم من ربه كلمت فتاب عليه إنه هو
التواب الرحيم ﴿٣٧﴾
قلنا اهبطوا منها جميعا فإما يأتينكم مني هدى
فمن تبع هداي فلا خوف عليهم ولا هم يحزنون ﴿٣٨﴾
والذين كفروا وكذبوا بآيتنا أولئك أصحب النار
هم فيها خلدون ﴿٣٩﴾ ع
يبني إسرائيل اذكروا نعمتي التي أنعمت عليكم و
أوفوا بعهدي أوف بعهدكم وإياي فارهبون ﴿٤٠﴾
وآمنوا بما أنزلت مصدقا لما معكم ولا تكونوا
أول كافر به ولا تشتروا بآيتي ثمنا قليلا و
إياي فاتقون ﴿٤١﴾
ولا تلبسوا الحق بالبطل وتكتموا الحق و
أنتم تعلمون ﴿٤٢﴾
وأقيموا الصلوة وآتوا الزكوة واركعوا مع الركعين ﴿٤٣﴾
أتأمرون الناس بالبر وتنسون أنفسكم وأنتم
تتلون الكتب أفلا تعقلون ﴿٤٤﴾
واستعينوا بالصبر والصلوة وإنها لكبيرة إلا
على الخشعين ﴿٤٥﴾
الذين يظنون أنهم ملقوا ربهم وأنهم إليه رجعون ﴿٤٦﴾ ع

1. Here the command is in the plural, as addressed to Adam's race.

2. *Az-Zakāh*; A tax at a fixed rate in proportion to the worth of property, collected from the well-to-do and distributed among the poor Muslims.

47. O Children of Israel! Remember My favour wherewith I favoured you and how I preferred you to (all) creatures.

48. And guard yourselves against a day when no soul will in aught avail another, nor will intercession be accepted from it, nor will compensation be received from it, nor will they be helped.

49. And (remember) when We did deliver you from Pharaoh's folk, who were afflicting you with dreadful torment, slaying your sons and sparing your women: That was a tremendous trial from your Lord.

50. And when We brought you through the sea and rescued you, and drowned the folk of Pharaoh in your sight.

51. And when We did appoint for Moses forty nights (of solitude), and then ye chose the calf, when he had gone from you, and were wrongdoers.

52. Then, even after that, We pardoned you in order that ye might give thanks.

53. And when We gave unto Moses the Scripture and the Criterion (of right and wrong), that ye might be led aright.

54. And when Moses said unto his people: O my people! Ye have wronged yourselves by your choosing of the calf (for worship) so turn in penitence to your Creator, and kill (the guilty) yourselves. That will be best for you with your Creator and He will relent toward you. Lo! He is the Relenting, the Merciful.

55. And when ye said: O Moses! We will not believe in thee till we see Allah plainly; and even while ye gazed the lightning seized you.

56. Then We revived you after your extinction, that ye might give thanks.

يٰبَنِيٓ إِسْرَآءِيلَ اذْكُرُوا نِعْمَتِيَ الَّتِيٓ أَنْعَمْتُ عَلَيْكُمْ
وَأَنِّي فَضَّلْتُكُمْ عَلَى الْعٰلَمِينَ ﴿٤٧﴾
وَاتَّقُوا يَوْمًا لَّا تَجْزِي نَفْسٌ عَنْ نَّفْسٍ شَيْـًٔا وَّلَا
يُقْبَلُ مِنْهَا شَفٰعَةٌ وَّلَا يُؤْخَذُ مِنْهَا عَدْلٌ وَّلَا
هُمْ يُنْصَرُونَ ﴿٤٨﴾
وَإِذْ نَجَّيْنٰكُمْ مِّنْ اٰلِ فِرْعَوْنَ يَسُومُونَكُمْ سُوٓءَ الْعَذَابِ
يُذَبِّحُونَ أَبْنَآءَكُمْ وَيَسْتَحْيُونَ نِسَآءَكُمْ وَفِي ذٰلِكُمْ
بَلَآءٌ مِّنْ رَّبِّكُمْ عَظِيمٌ ﴿٤٩﴾
وَإِذْ فَرَقْنَا بِكُمُ الْبَحْرَ فَأَنْجَيْنٰكُمْ وَأَغْرَقْنَآ اٰلَ فِرْعَوْنَ
وَأَنْتُمْ تَنْظُرُونَ ﴿٥٠﴾
وَإِذْ وٰعَدْنَا مُوسٰىٓ أَرْبَعِينَ لَيْلَةً ثُمَّ اتَّخَذْتُمُ الْعِجْلَ
مِنْ بَعْدِهِۦ وَأَنْتُمْ ظٰلِمُونَ ﴿٥١﴾
ثُمَّ عَفَوْنَا عَنْكُمْ مِّنْ بَعْدِ ذٰلِكَ لَعَلَّكُمْ تَشْكُرُونَ ﴿٥٢﴾
وَإِذْ اٰتَيْنَا مُوسَى الْكِتٰبَ وَالْفُرْقَانَ لَعَلَّكُمْ
تَهْتَدُونَ ﴿٥٣﴾
وَإِذْ قَالَ مُوسٰى لِقَوْمِهِۦ يٰقَوْمِ إِنَّكُمْ ظَلَمْتُمْ أَنْفُسَكُمْ
بِاتِّخَاذِكُمُ الْعِجْلَ فَتُوبُوٓا إِلٰى بَارِئِكُمْ فَاقْتُلُوٓا أَنْفُسَكُمْ
ذٰلِكُمْ خَيْرٌ لَّكُمْ عِنْدَ بَارِئِكُمْ فَتَابَ عَلَيْكُمْ إِنَّهُۥ هُوَ
التَّوَّابُ الرَّحِيمُ ﴿٥٤﴾
وَإِذْ قُلْتُمْ يٰمُوسٰى لَنْ نُّؤْمِنَ لَكَ حَتّٰى نَرَى اللّٰهَ جَهْرَةً
فَأَخَذَتْكُمُ الصّٰعِقَةُ وَأَنْتُمْ تَنْظُرُونَ ﴿٥٥﴾
ثُمَّ بَعَثْنٰكُمْ مِّنْ بَعْدِ مَوْتِكُمْ لَعَلَّكُمْ تَشْكُرُونَ ﴿٥٦﴾

57. And We caused the white cloud to overshadow you and sent down on you the manna and the quails, (saying): Eat of the good things wherewith We have provided you—We wronged them not, but they did wrong themselves.

وَظَلَّلْنَا عَلَيْكُمُ الْغَمَامَ وَاَنْزَلْنَا عَلَيْكُمُ الْمَنَّ وَ
السَّلْوٰى ؕ كُلُوْا مِنْ طَيِّبٰتِ مَا رَزَقْنٰكُمْ ؕ وَمَا ظَلَمُوْنَا وَ
لٰكِنْ كَانُوْٓا اَنْفُسَهُمْ يَظْلِمُوْنَ ﴿٥٧﴾

58. And when We said: Go into this township and eat freely of that which is therein, and enter the gate prostrate, and say: "Repentance."[1] We will forgive you your sins and will increase (reward) for the right-doers.

وَاِذْ قُلْنَا ادْخُلُوْا هٰذِهِ الْقَرْيَةَ فَكُلُوْا مِنْهَا حَيْثُ
شِئْتُمْ رَغَدًا وَّادْخُلُوا الْبَابَ سُجَّدًا وَّقُوْلُوْا حِطَّةٌ
نَّغْفِرْ لَكُمْ خَطٰيٰكُمْ ؕ وَسَنَزِيْدُ الْمُحْسِنِيْنَ ﴿٥٨﴾

59. But those who did wrong changed the word which had been told them for another saying,[1] and We sent down upon the evil-doers wrath from Heaven for their evildoing.

فَبَدَّلَ الَّذِيْنَ ظَلَمُوْا قَوْلًا غَيْرَ الَّذِيْ قِيْلَ لَهُمْ
فَاَنْزَلْنَا عَلَى الَّذِيْنَ ظَلَمُوْا رِجْزًا مِّنَ السَّمَآءِ بِمَا
كَانُوْا يَفْسُقُوْنَ ﴿٥٩﴾

60. And when Moses asked for water for his people, We said: Smite with thy staff the rock. And there gushed out therefrom twelve springs (so that) each tribe knew their drinking-place. Eat and drink of that which Allah hath provided, and do not act corruptly, making mischief in the earth.

وَاِذِ اسْتَسْقٰى مُوْسٰى لِقَوْمِهٖ فَقُلْنَا اضْرِبْ بِّعَصَاكَ
الْحَجَرَ ؕ فَانْفَجَرَتْ مِنْهُ اثْنَتَا عَشْرَةَ عَيْنًا ؕ قَدْ
عَلِمَ كُلُّ اُنَاسٍ مَّشْرَبَهُمْ ؕ كُلُوْا وَاشْرَبُوْا مِنْ رِّزْقِ
اللّٰهِ وَلَا تَعْثَوْا فِى الْاَرْضِ مُفْسِدِيْنَ ﴿٦٠﴾

61. And when ye said: O Moses! We are weary of one kind of food; so call upon thy Lord for us that He bring forth for us of that which the earth groweth—of its herbs and its cucumbers and its corn and its lentils and its onions. He said: Would ye exchange that which is higher for that which is lower? Go down to settled country, thus ye shall get that which ye demand. And humiliation and wretchedness were stamped upon them and they were visited with wrath from Allah. That was because they disbelieved in Allah's revelations and slew the prophets wrongfully. That was for their disobedience and transgression.

وَاِذْ قُلْتُمْ يٰمُوْسٰى لَنْ نَّصْبِرَ عَلٰى طَعَامٍ وَّاحِدٍ فَادْعُ
لَنَا رَبَّكَ يُخْرِجْ لَنَا مِمَّا تُنْۢبِتُ الْاَرْضُ مِنْۢ بَقْلِهَا وَ
قِثَّآئِهَا وَفُوْمِهَا وَعَدَسِهَا وَبَصَلِهَا ؕ قَالَ اَتَسْتَبْدِلُوْنَ
الَّذِىْ هُوَ اَدْنٰى بِالَّذِىْ هُوَ خَيْرٌ ؕ اِهْبِطُوْا مِصْرًا فَاِنَّ
لَكُمْ مَّا سَاَلْتُمْ ؕ وَضُرِبَتْ عَلَيْهِمُ الذِّلَّةُ وَالْمَسْكَنَةُ
وَبَآءُوْ بِغَضَبٍ مِّنَ اللّٰهِ ؕ ذٰلِكَ بِاَنَّهُمْ كَانُوْا
يَكْفُرُوْنَ بِاٰيٰتِ اللّٰهِ وَيَقْتُلُوْنَ النَّبِيّٖنَ
بِغَيْرِ الْحَقِّ ؕ ذٰلِكَ بِمَا عَصَوْا وَّكَانُوْا
يَعْتَدُوْنَ ﴿٦١﴾

1. According to a tradition of the Prophet, *Hittatun* is a word implying submission to Allah and repentance. The evil-doers changed it for a word of rebellion—*i.e.* they were disobedient.

62. Lo! those who believe (in that which is revealed unto thee, Muhammad), and those who are Jews, and Christians, and Sabaeans—whoever believeth in Allah and the Last Day and doth right—surely their reward is with their Lord, and there shall no fear come upon them neither shall they grieve.

63. And (remember, O children of Israel) when We made a covenant with you and caused the Mount to tower above you, (saying): Hold fast that which We have given you, and remember that which is therein, that ye may ward off (evil).

64. Then, even after that, ye turned away, and if it had not been for the grace of Allah and His mercy ye had been among the losers.

65. And ye know of those of you who broke the Sabbath, how We said unto them: Be ye apes, despised and hated!

66. And We made it an example to their own and to succeeding generations, and an admonition to the Godfearing.

67. And when Moses said unto his people: Lo! Allah commandeth you that ye sacrifice a cow, they said: Dost thou make game of us? He answered: Allah forbid that I should be among the foolish!

68. They said: Pray for us unto thy Lord that He make clear to us what (cow) she is. (Moses) answered: Lo! He saith, Verily she is a cow neither with calf nor immature; (she is) between the two conditions; so do that which ye are commanded.

69. They said: Pray for us unto thy Lord that He make clear to us of what colour she is. (Moses) answered: Lo! He saith: Verily she is a yellow cow. Bright is her colour, gladdening beholders.

70. They said: Pray for us unto thy Lord that He make clear to us what (cow) she is. Lo! cows are much alike to us; and lo! if Allah wills, we may be led aright.

إِنَّ الَّذِينَ آمَنُوا وَالَّذِينَ هَادُوا وَالنَّصَارَىٰ وَ
الصَّابِئِينَ مَنْ آمَنَ بِاللَّهِ وَالْيَوْمِ الْآخِرِ وَعَمِلَ
صَالِحًا فَلَهُمْ أَجْرُهُمْ عِنْدَ رَبِّهِمْ وَلَا خَوْفٌ عَلَيْهِمْ
وَلَا هُمْ يَحْزَنُونَ ﴿٦٢﴾
وَإِذْ أَخَذْنَا مِيثَاقَكُمْ وَرَفَعْنَا فَوْقَكُمُ الطُّورَ خُذُوا
مَا آتَيْنَاكُمْ بِقُوَّةٍ وَاذْكُرُوا مَا فِيهِ لَعَلَّكُمْ تَتَّقُونَ ﴿٦٣﴾
ثُمَّ تَوَلَّيْتُمْ مِنْ بَعْدِ ذَٰلِكَ فَلَوْلَا فَضْلُ اللَّهِ عَلَيْكُمْ
وَرَحْمَتُهُ لَكُنْتُمْ مِنَ الْخَاسِرِينَ ﴿٦٤﴾
وَلَقَدْ عَلِمْتُمُ الَّذِينَ اعْتَدَوْا مِنْكُمْ فِي السَّبْتِ
فَقُلْنَا لَهُمْ كُونُوا قِرَدَةً خَاسِئِينَ ﴿٦٥﴾
فَجَعَلْنَاهَا نَكَالًا لِمَا بَيْنَ يَدَيْهَا وَمَا خَلْفَهَا وَ
مَوْعِظَةً لِلْمُتَّقِينَ ﴿٦٦﴾
وَإِذْ قَالَ مُوسَىٰ لِقَوْمِهِ إِنَّ اللَّهَ يَأْمُرُكُمْ أَنْ تَذْبَحُوا
بَقَرَةً قَالُوا أَتَتَّخِذُنَا هُزُوًا قَالَ أَعُوذُ بِاللَّهِ أَنْ
أَكُونَ مِنَ الْجَاهِلِينَ ﴿٦٧﴾
قَالُوا ادْعُ لَنَا رَبَّكَ يُبَيِّنْ لَنَا مَا هِيَ قَالَ إِنَّهُ يَقُولُ
إِنَّهَا بَقَرَةٌ لَا فَارِضٌ وَلَا بِكْرٌ عَوَانٌ بَيْنَ ذَٰلِكَ
فَافْعَلُوا مَا تُؤْمَرُونَ ﴿٦٨﴾
قَالُوا ادْعُ لَنَا رَبَّكَ يُبَيِّنْ لَنَا مَا لَوْنُهَا قَالَ إِنَّهُ يَقُولُ
إِنَّهَا بَقَرَةٌ صَفْرَاءُ فَاقِعٌ لَوْنُهَا تَسُرُّ النَّاظِرِينَ ﴿٦٩﴾
قَالُوا ادْعُ لَنَا رَبَّكَ يُبَيِّنْ لَنَا مَا هِيَ إِنَّ الْبَقَرَ تَشَابَهَ
عَلَيْنَا وَإِنَّا إِنْ شَاءَ اللَّهُ لَمُهْتَدُونَ ﴿٧٠﴾

71. (Moses) answered: Lo! He saith: Verily she is a cow unyoked; she plougheth not the soil nor watereth the tilth; whole and without mark. They said: Now thou bringest the truth. So they sacrificed her, though almost they did not.

72. And (remember) when ye slew a man and disagreed concerning it and Allah brought forth that which ye were hiding.

73. And We said: Smite him with some of it. Thus Allah bringeth the dead to life and showeth you His portents so that ye may understand.[1]

74. Then, even after that, your hearts were hardened and became as rocks, or worse than rocks, for hardness. For indeed there are rocks out of which rivers gush, and indeed there are rocks which split asunder so that water floweth from them. And indeed there are rocks which fall down for the fear of Allah. Allah is not unaware of what ye do.

75. Have ye any hope that they will be true to you when a party of them used to listen to the Word of Allah, then used to change it, after they had understood it, knowingly?

76. And when they fall in with those who believe, they say: We believe. But when they go apart one with another they say: Prate ye to them of that which Allah hath disclosed to you that they may contend with you before your Lord concerning it? Have ye then no sense?

77. Are they then unaware that Allah knoweth that which they keep hidden and that which they proclaim?

78. Among them are unlettered folk who know the Scripture not except from hearsay. They but guess.

79. Therefore woe be unto those who write the Scripture with their hands and then say, "This is from Allah," that they may purchase a small gain therewith. Woe unto them for that their hands have written, and woe unto them for that they earn thereby.

قَالَ اِنَّهٗ يَقُوْلُ اِنَّهَا بَقَرَةٌ لَّا ذَلُوْلٌ تُثِيْرُ الْاَرْضَ
وَلَا تَسْقِي الْحَرْثَ ۚ مُسَلَّمَةٌ لَّا شِيَةَ فِيْهَا ۚ قَالُوا الْـٰٔنَ
جِئْتَ بِالْحَقِّ ۚ فَذَبَحُوْهَا وَمَا كَادُوْا يَفْعَلُوْنَ ﴿٧١﴾ ع ٨
وَاِذْ قَتَلْتُمْ نَفْسًا فَادّٰرَءْتُمْ فِيْهَا ۚ وَاللّٰهُ مُخْرِجٌ مَّا كُنْتُمْ تَكْتُمُوْنَ ﴿٧٢﴾
فَقُلْنَا اضْرِبُوْهُ بِبَعْضِهَا ۚ كَذٰلِكَ يُحْيِ اللّٰهُ الْمَوْتٰى وَ
يُرِيْكُمْ اٰيٰتِهٖ لَعَلَّكُمْ تَعْقِلُوْنَ ﴿٧٣﴾
ثُمَّ قَسَتْ قُلُوْبُكُمْ مِّنْ بَعْدِ ذٰلِكَ فَهِيَ كَالْحِجَارَةِ
اَوْ اَشَدُّ قَسْوَةً ۚ وَاِنَّ مِنَ الْحِجَارَةِ لَمَا يَتَفَجَّرُ مِنْهُ
الْاَنْهٰرُ ۚ وَاِنَّ مِنْهَا لَمَا يَشَّقَّقُ فَيَخْرُجُ مِنْهُ الْمَآءُ ۚ وَاِنَّ مِنْهَا
لَمَا يَهْبِطُ مِنْ خَشْيَةِ اللّٰهِ ۚ وَمَا اللّٰهُ بِغَافِلٍ عَمَّا تَعْمَلُوْنَ ﴿٧٤﴾
اَفَتَطْمَعُوْنَ اَنْ يُّؤْمِنُوْا لَكُمْ وَقَدْ كَانَ فَرِيْقٌ مِّنْهُمْ
يَسْمَعُوْنَ كَلٰمَ اللّٰهِ ثُمَّ يُحَرِّفُوْنَهٗ مِنْ بَعْدِ مَا عَقَلُوْهُ
وَهُمْ يَعْلَمُوْنَ ﴿٧٥﴾
وَاِذَا لَقُوا الَّذِيْنَ اٰمَنُوْا قَالُوْٓا اٰمَنَّا ۚ وَاِذَا خَلَا بَعْضُهُمْ
اِلٰى بَعْضٍ قَالُوْٓا اَتُحَدِّثُوْنَهُمْ بِمَا فَتَحَ اللّٰهُ عَلَيْكُمْ
لِيُحَآجُّوْكُمْ بِهٖ عِنْدَ رَبِّكُمْ ۚ اَفَلَا تَعْقِلُوْنَ ﴿٧٦﴾
اَوَلَا يَعْلَمُوْنَ اَنَّ اللّٰهَ يَعْلَمُ مَا يُسِرُّوْنَ وَمَا يُعْلِنُوْنَ ﴿٧٧﴾
وَمِنْهُمْ اُمِّيُّوْنَ لَا يَعْلَمُوْنَ الْكِتٰبَ اِلَّآ اَمَانِيَّ وَاِنْ هُمْ
اِلَّا يَظُنُّوْنَ ﴿٧٨﴾ النصف
فَوَيْلٌ لِّلَّذِيْنَ يَكْتُبُوْنَ الْكِتٰبَ بِاَيْدِيْهِمْ ۗ ثُمَّ يَقُوْلُوْنَ
هٰذَا مِنْ عِنْدِ اللّٰهِ لِيَشْتَرُوْا بِهٖ ثَمَنًا قَلِيْلًا ۚ فَوَيْلٌ
لَّهُمْ مِّمَّا كَتَبَتْ اَيْدِيْهِمْ وَوَيْلٌ لَّهُمْ مِّمَّا يَكْسِبُوْنَ ﴿٧٩﴾

1. The old commentators tell various stories by way of explaining vv. 72 and 73; one of them concerning a miracle that happened at Al-Madinah. For Maulvi Muhammad Ali's exposition of them as referring to the martyrdom of Jesus Christ (on whom be peace) see the footnote to v. 72 in his translation.

80. And they say: The fire (of punishment) will not touch us save for a certain number of days. Say: Have ye received a covenant from Allah—truly Allah will not break His covenant—or tell ye concerning Allah that which ye know not?

وقالوا لن تمسنا النار إلا أياما معدودة قل
أتخذتم عند الله عهدا فلن يخلف الله عهده
أم تقولون على الله ما لا تعلمون ٨٠

81. Nay, but whosoever hath done evil and his sin surroundeth him, such are rightful owners of the Fire; they will abide therein.

بلى من كسب سيئة وأحاطت به خطيئته فأولئك
أصحب النار هم فيها خلدون ٨١

82. And those who believe and do good works: such are rightful owners of the Garden. They will abide therein.

والذين آمنوا وعملوا الصلحت أولئك أصحب
ع ٩ الجنة هم فيها خلدون ٨٢

83. And (remember) when We made a covenant with the Children of Israel, (saying) : Worship none save Allah (only), and be good to parents and to kindred and to orphans and the needy, and speak kindly to mankind; and establish worship and pay the poor-due. Then, after that, ye slid back save a few of you, being averse.

وإذ أخذنا ميثاق بني إسرآءيل لا تعبدون إلا
الله وبالوالدين إحسانا وذي القربى واليتمى
والمسكين وقولوا للناس حسنا وأقيموا الصلوة
وآتوا الزكوة ثم توليتم إلا قليلا منكم وأنتم
معرضون ٨٣

84. And when We made with you a covenant (saying): Shed not the blood of your people nor turn (a party of) your people out of your dwellings. Then ye ratified (Our covenant) and ye were witnesses (thereto).[1]

وإذ أخذنا ميثاقكم لا تسفكون دماءكم ولا
تخرجون أنفسكم من دياركم ثم أقررتم وأنتم
تشهدون ٨٤

85. Yet ye it is who slay each other and drive out a party of your people from their homes, supporting one another against them by sin and transgression[2]—and if they came to you as captives ye would ransom them, whereas their expulsion was itself unlawful for you—Believe ye in part of the Scripture and disbelieve ye in part thereof? And what is the reward of those who do so save ignominy in the life of the world, and on the Day of Resurrection they will be consigned to the most grievous doom. For Allah is not unaware of what ye do.

ثم أنتم هؤلاء تقتلون أنفسكم وتخرجون فريقا
منكم من ديارهم تظهرون عليهم بالإثم و
العدوان وإن يأتوكم أسرى تفدوهم وهو
محرم عليكم إخراجهم أفتؤمنون ببعض
الكتب وتكفرون ببعض فما جزاء من يفعل
ذلك منكم إلا خزي في الحيوة الدنيا ويوم القيمة
يردون إلى أشد العذاب وما الله بغافل عما تعملون ٨٥

1. v. 83 is generally taken as referring to the Biblical covenant and v. 84 as referring to the solemn treaty which the Jews of Al-Madinah made with the Prophet in the year 1 A.H.

2. The reference is to the wars between the Arab tribes of Al-Madinah in which the Jews used to take part as allies of one and the other, Jew waging war upon Jew.

86. Such are those who buy the life of the world at the price of the Hereafter. Their punishment will not be lightened, neither will they have support.

أُولٰٓئِكَ الَّذِينَ اشْتَرَوُا الْحَيٰوةَ الدُّنْيَا بِالْاٰخِرَةِ فَلَا
يُخَفَّفُ عَنْهُمُ الْعَذَابُ وَلَا هُمْ يُنْصَرُونَ ﴿٨٦﴾ ع

87. And verily We gave unto Moses the Scripture and We caused a train of messengers to follow after him, and We gave unto Jesus, son of Mary, clear proofs (of Allah's sovereignty), and We supported him with the holy Spirit.[1] Is it ever so, that, when there cometh unto you a messenger (from Allah) with that which ye yourselves desire not, ye grow arrogant, and some ye disbelieve and some ye slay?

وَلَقَدْ اٰتَيْنَا مُوسَى الْكِتٰبَ وَقَفَّيْنَا مِنْ بَعْدِهٖ بِالرُّسُلِ
وَاٰتَيْنَا عِيسَى ابْنَ مَرْيَمَ الْبَيِّنٰتِ وَاَيَّدْنٰهُ بِرُوحِ الْقُدُسِ
اَفَكُلَّمَا جَآءَكُمْ رَسُولٌ بِمَا لَا تَهْوٰٓى اَنْفُسُكُمُ اسْتَكْبَرْتُمْ
فَفَرِيقًا كَذَّبْتُمْ وَفَرِيقًا تَقْتُلُونَ ﴿٨٧﴾

88. And they say: Our hearts are hardened. Nay, but Allah hath cursed them for their unbelief. Little is that which they believe.

وَقَالُوا قُلُوبُنَا غُلْفٌ بَلْ لَّعَنَهُمُ اللّٰهُ بِكُفْرِهِمْ
فَقَلِيلًا مَّا يُؤْمِنُونَ ﴿٨٨﴾

89. And when there cometh unto them a Scripture from Allah, confirming that in their possession—though before that they were asking for a signal triumph over those who disbelieved—and when there cometh unto them that which they know (to be the Truth) they disbelieve therein. The curse of Allah is on disbelievers.

وَلَمَّا جَآءَهُمْ كِتٰبٌ مِّنْ عِنْدِ اللّٰهِ مُصَدِّقٌ لِّمَا
مَعَهُمْ وَكَانُوا مِنْ قَبْلُ يَسْتَفْتِحُونَ عَلَى الَّذِينَ
كَفَرُوا فَلَمَّا جَآءَهُمْ مَّا عَرَفُوا كَفَرُوا بِهٖ فَلَعْنَةُ
اللّٰهِ عَلَى الْكٰفِرِينَ ﴿٨٩﴾

90. Evil is that for which they sell their souls: that they should disbelieve in that which Allah hath revealed, grudging that Allah should reveal of His bounty unto whom He will of His bondmen.[2] They have incurred anger upon anger. For disbelievers is a shameful doom.

بِئْسَمَا اشْتَرَوْا بِهٖٓ اَنْفُسَهُمْ اَنْ يَّكْفُرُوا بِمَآ اَنْزَلَ
اللّٰهُ بَغْيًا اَنْ يُّنَزِّلَ اللّٰهُ مِنْ فَضْلِهٖ عَلٰى مَنْ يَّشَآءُ
مِنْ عِبَادِهٖ فَبَآءُوْ بِغَضَبٍ عَلٰى غَضَبٍ وَلِلْكٰفِرِينَ
عَذَابٌ مُّهِينٌ ﴿٩٠﴾

91. And when it is said unto them: Believe in that which Allah hath revealed, they say: We believe in that which was revealed unto us. And they disbelieve in that which cometh after it, though it is the truth confirming that which they possess. Say (unto them, O Muhammad): Why then slew ye the Prophets of Allah aforetime, if ye are (indeed) believers?

وَاِذَا قِيلَ لَهُمْ اٰمِنُوا بِمَآ اَنْزَلَ اللّٰهُ قَالُوا نُؤْمِنُ بِمَآ
اُنْزِلَ عَلَيْنَا وَيَكْفُرُونَ بِمَا وَرَآءَهٗ وَهُوَ الْحَقُّ
مُصَدِّقًا لِّمَا مَعَهُمْ قُلْ فَلِمَ تَقْتُلُونَ اَنْبِيَآءَ اللّٰهِ
مِنْ قَبْلُ اِنْ كُنْتُمْ مُّؤْمِنِينَ ﴿٩١﴾

92. And Moses came unto you with clear proofs (of Allah's sovereignty), yet, while he was away, ye chose the calf (for worship) and ye were wrong-doers.

وَلَقَدْ جَآءَكُمْ مُّوسٰى بِالْبَيِّنٰتِ ثُمَّ اتَّخَذْتُمُ الْعِجْلَ
مِنْ بَعْدِهٖ وَاَنْتُمْ ظٰلِمُونَ ﴿٩٢﴾

1. "The holy Spirit" is a term for the angel of Revelation, Gabriel (on whom be peace).
2. See v. 23, footnote.

93. And when We made with you a covenant and caused the Mount to tower above you, (saying): Hold fast by that which We have given you, and hear (Our Word), they said: We hear and we rebel. And (worship of) the calf was made to sink into their hearts because of their rejection (of the Covenant). Say (unto them): Evil is that which your belief enjoineth on you, if ye are believers.

94. Say (unto them): If the abode of the Hereafter in the providence of Allah is indeed for you alone and not for others of mankind (as ye pretend), then long for death (for ye must long for death) if ye are truthful.

95. But they will never long for it, because of that which their own hands have sent before them. Allah is Aware of evildoers.

96. And thou wilt find them greediest of mankind for life and (greedier) than the idolaters. (Each) one of them would like to be allowed to live a thousand years. And to live (a thousand years) would by no means remove him from the doom. Allah is Seer of what they do.

97. Say (O Muhammad, to mankind:) Who is an enemy to Gabriel! For he it is who hath revealed (this Scripture) to thy heart by Allah's leave, confirming that which was (revealed) before it, and a guidance and glad tidings to believers;

98. Who is an enemy to Allah, and His angels and His messengers, and Gabriel and Michael! Then, lo! Allah (Himself) is an enemy to the disbelievers.

99. Verily We have revealed unto thee clear tokens, and only miscreants will disbelieve in them.

100. Is it ever so that when ye make a covenant a party of you set it aside? The truth is, most of them believe not.

وَاِذْ اَخَذْنَا مِيْثَاقَكُمْ وَرَفَعْنَا فَوْقَكُمُ الطُّوْرَ خُذُوْا
مَآ اٰتَيْنٰكُمْ بِقُوَّةٍ وَّاسْمَعُوْا قَالُوْا سَمِعْنَا وَعَصَيْنَا
وَاُشْرِبُوْا فِيْ قُلُوْبِهِمُ الْعِجْلَ بِكُفْرِهِمْ قُلْ بِئْسَمَا
يَاْمُرُكُمْ بِهٖٓ اِيْمَانُكُمْ اِنْ كُنْتُمْ مُّؤْمِنِيْنَ ﴿٩٣﴾
قُلْ اِنْ كَانَتْ لَكُمُ الدَّارُ الْاٰخِرَةُ عِنْدَ اللّٰهِ خَالِصَةً
مِّنْ دُوْنِ النَّاسِ فَتَمَنَّوُا الْمَوْتَ اِنْ كُنْتُمْ
صٰدِقِيْنَ ﴿٩٤﴾
وَلَنْ يَّتَمَنَّوْهُ اَبَدًا بِمَا قَدَّمَتْ اَيْدِيْهِمْ وَاللّٰهُ
عَلِيْمٌ بِالظّٰلِمِيْنَ ﴿٩٥﴾
وَلَتَجِدَنَّهُمْ اَحْرَصَ النَّاسِ عَلٰى حَيٰوةٍ وَمِنَ الَّذِيْنَ
اَشْرَكُوْا يَوَدُّ اَحَدُهُمْ لَوْ يُعَمَّرُ اَلْفَ سَنَةٍ وَمَا هُوَ
بِمُزَحْزِحِهٖ مِنَ الْعَذَابِ اَنْ يُّعَمَّرَ وَاللّٰهُ بَصِيْرٌ
بِمَا يَعْمَلُوْنَ ﴿٩٦﴾
قُلْ مَنْ كَانَ عَدُوًّا لِّجِبْرِيْلَ فَاِنَّهٗ نَزَّلَهٗ عَلٰى قَلْبِكَ
بِاِذْنِ اللّٰهِ مُصَدِّقًا لِّمَا بَيْنَ يَدَيْهِ وَهُدًى وَّبُشْرٰى
لِلْمُؤْمِنِيْنَ ﴿٩٧﴾
مَنْ كَانَ عَدُوًّا لِّلّٰهِ وَمَلٰٓئِكَتِهٖ وَرُسُلِهٖ وَجِبْرِيْلَ وَ
مِيْكٰلَ فَاِنَّ اللّٰهَ عَدُوٌّ لِّلْكٰفِرِيْنَ ﴿٩٨﴾
وَلَقَدْ اَنْزَلْنَآ اِلَيْكَ اٰيٰتٍۭ بَيِّنٰتٍ وَمَا يَكْفُرُ بِهَآ اِلَّا
الْفٰسِقُوْنَ ﴿٩٩﴾
اَوَكُلَّمَا عٰهَدُوْا عَهْدًا نَّبَذَهٗ فَرِيْقٌ مِّنْهُمْ بَلْ
اَكْثَرُهُمْ لَا يُؤْمِنُوْنَ ﴿١٠٠﴾

101. And when there cometh unto them a messenger from Allah, confirming that which they possess, a party of those who have received the Scripture fling the Scripture of Allah behind their backs as if they knew not:

وَلَمَّا جَآءَهُمْ رَسُوْلٌ مِّنْ عِنْدِ اللّٰهِ مُصَدِّقٌ لِّمَا مَعَهُمْ نَبَذَ فَرِيْقٌ مِّنَ الَّذِيْنَ أُوْتُوا الْكِتٰبَ كِتٰبَ اللّٰهِ وَرَآءَ ظُهُوْرِهِمْ كَاَنَّهُمْ لَا يَعْلَمُوْنَ ۝

102. And follow that which the devils falsely related against the kingdom of Solomon. Solomon disbelieved not; but the devils disbelieved, teaching mankind magic and that which was revealed to the two angels in Babel, Hārūt and Mārūt. Nor did they (the two angels) teach it to anyone till they had said: We are only a temptation, therefore disbelieve not (in the guidance of Allah). And from these two (angels) people learn that by which they cause division between man and wife; but they injure thereby no-one save by Allah's leave. And they learn that which harmeth them and profiteth them not. And surely they do know that he who trafficketh therein will have no (happy) portion in the Hereafter; and surely evil is the price for which they sell their souls, if they but knew.[1]

وَاتَّبَعُوْا مَا تَتْلُوا الشَّيٰطِيْنُ عَلٰى مُلْكِ سُلَيْمٰنَ وَ مَا كَفَرَ سُلَيْمٰنُ وَلٰكِنَّ الشَّيٰطِيْنَ كَفَرُوْا يُعَلِّمُوْنَ النَّاسَ السِّحْرَ وَمَا اُنْزِلَ عَلَى الْمَلَكَيْنِ بِبَابِلَ هَارُوْتَ وَمَارُوْتَ وَمَا يُعَلِّمٰنِ مِنْ اَحَدٍ حَتّٰى يَقُوْلَآ اِنَّمَا نَحْنُ فِتْنَةٌ فَلَا تَكْفُرْ فَيَتَعَلَّمُوْنَ مِنْهُمَا مَا يُفَرِّقُوْنَ بِهٖ بَيْنَ الْمَرْءِ وَزَوْجِهٖ وَمَا هُمْ بِضَآرِّيْنَ بِهٖ مِنْ اَحَدٍ اِلَّا بِاِذْنِ اللّٰهِ وَيَتَعَلَّمُوْنَ مَا يَضُرُّهُمْ وَلَا يَنْفَعُهُمْ وَلَقَدْ عَلِمُوا لَمَنِ اشْتَرٰىهُ مَا لَهٗ فِى الْاٰخِرَةِ مِنْ خَلَاقٍ وَلَبِئْسَ مَا شَرَوْا بِهٖٓ اَنْفُسَهُمْ لَوْ كَانُوْا يَعْلَمُوْنَ ۝

103. And if they had believed and kept from evil, a recompense from Allah would be better, if they only knew.

وَلَوْ اَنَّهُمْ اٰمَنُوْا وَاتَّقَوْا لَمَثُوْبَةٌ مِّنْ عِنْدِ اللّٰهِ خَيْرٌ لَوْ كَانُوْا يَعْلَمُوْنَ ۝

104. O ye who believe, say not (unto the Prophet): "Listen to us" but say "Look upon us,"[2] and be ye listeners. For disbelievers is a painful doom.

يٰٓاَيُّهَا الَّذِيْنَ اٰمَنُوْا لَا تَقُوْلُوْا رَاعِنَا وَقُوْلُوا انْظُرْنَا وَاسْمَعُوْا وَلِلْكٰفِرِيْنَ عَذَابٌ اَلِيْمٌ ۝

105. Neither those who disbelieve among the people of the Scripture[3] nor the idolaters love that there should be sent down unto you any good thing from your Lord. But Allah chooseth for His mercy whom He will, and Allah is of Infinite bounty.

مَا يَوَدُّ الَّذِيْنَ كَفَرُوْا مِنْ اَهْلِ الْكِتٰبِ وَلَا الْمُشْرِكِيْنَ اَنْ يُّنَزَّلَ عَلَيْكُمْ مِّنْ خَيْرٍ مِّنْ رَّبِّكُمْ وَاللّٰهُ يَخْتَصُّ بِرَحْمَتِهٖ مَنْ يَّشَآءُ وَاللّٰهُ ذُو الْفَضْلِ الْعَظِيْمِ ۝

106. Such of Our revelations as We abrogate or cause to be forgotten, We bring (in place) one better or the like thereof. Knowest thou not that Allah is Able to do all things?

مَا نَنْسَخْ مِنْ اٰيَةٍ اَوْ نُنْسِهَا نَاْتِ بِخَيْرٍ مِّنْهَآ اَوْ مِثْلِهَا اَلَمْ تَعْلَمْ اَنَّ اللّٰهَ عَلٰى كُلِّ شَيْءٍ قَدِيْرٌ ۝

1. The reference is to the occult science practised by the Jews, the origin of which was ascribed to Solomon.
2. The first word which the Muslims used to call the Prophet's attention respectfully. Rā'ina, the Jews could change into an insult by a slight mispronunciation. 3. *i.e.* Jews and Christians.

107. Knowest thou not that it is Allah unto Whom belongeth the sovereignty of the heavens and earth; and ye have not, beside Allah, any friend or helper?

108. Or would ye question your messenger as Moses was questioned aforetime? He who chooseth disbelief instead of faith, verily he hath gone astray from a plain road.

109. Many of the People of the Scripture long to make you disbelievers after your belief, through envy on their own account, after the truth hath become manifest unto them. Forgive and be indulgent (toward them) until Allah give command. Lo! Allah is Able to do all things.

110. Establish worship, and pay the poor-due;[1] and whatever of good ye send before (you) for your souls, ye will find it with Allah. Lo! Allah is Seer of what ye do.

111. And they say: None entereth Paradise unless he be a Jew or a Christian. These are their own desires. Say: Bring your proof (of what ye state) if ye are truthful.

112. Nay, but whosoever surrendereth his purpose to Allah while doing good, his reward is with his Lord; and there shall no fear come upon them neither shall they grieve.

113. And the Jews say the Christians follow nothing (true), and the Christians say the Jews follow nothing (true); yet both are readers of the Scripture. Even thus speak those who know not. Allah will judge between them on the Day of Resurrection concerning that wherein they differ.

الم تعلم ان الله له ملك السموت والارض ۗ و
ما لكم من دون الله من ولي ولا نصير ﴿١٠٧﴾
ام تريدون ان تسـٔلوا رسولكم كما سئل موسى
من قبل ۗ ومن يتبدل الكفر بالايمان فقد
ضل سواء السبيل ﴿١٠٨﴾
ود كثير من اهل الكتب لو يردونكم من بعد
ايمانكم كفارا ۚ حسدا من عند انفسهم من بعد
ما تبين لهم الحق ۚ فاعفوا واصفحوا حتى
يأتي الله بامره ۗ ان الله على كل شيء قدير ﴿١٠٩﴾
واقيموا الصلوة واتوا الزكوة ۚ وما تقدموا لانفسكم
من خير تجدوه عند الله ۗ ان الله بما تعملون
بصير ﴿١١٠﴾
وقالوا لن يدخل الجنة الا من كان هودا او
نصرى ۗ تلك امانيهم ۗ قل هاتوا برهانكم ان
كنتم صدقين ﴿١١١﴾
بلى من اسلم وجهه لله وهو محسن فله اجره
عند ربه ۖ ولا خوف عليهم ولا هم يحزنون ﴿١١٢﴾
وقالت اليهود ليست النصرى على شيء ۖ وقالت
النصرى ليست اليهود على شيء ۙ وهم يتلون الكتب ۗ
كذلك قال الذين لا يعلمون مثل قولهم ۚ فالله
يحكم بينهم يوم القيمة فيما كانوا فيه
يختلفون ﴿١١٣﴾

1. *Az-Zakāh*, a tax at a fixed rate in proportion to the worth of property, collected from the well-to-do and distributed among the poor Muslims.

114. And who doth greater wrong than he who forbiddeth the approach to the sanctuaries of Allah lest His name should be mentioned therein, and striveth for their ruin? As for such, it was never meant that they should enter them except in fear. Theirs in the world is ignominy and theirs in the Hereafter is an awful doom.

115. Unto Allah belong the East and the West, and whithersoever ye turn, there is Allah's countenance. Lo! Allah is All-Embracing, All-Knowing.

116. And they say: Allah hath taken unto Himself a Son. Be He glorified! Nay, but whatsoever is in the heaven and the earth is His. All are subservient unto Him.

117. The Originator of the heavens and the earth! When He decreeth a thing, He saith unto it only: Be! and it is.

118. And those who have no knowledge say: Why doth not Allah speak unto us, or some sign come unto us? Even thus, as they now speak, spake those (who were) before them. Their hearts are all alike. We have made clear the revelations for people who are sure.

119. Lo! We have sent thee (O Muhammad) with the truth, a bringer of glad tidings and a warner. And thou wilt not be asked about the owners of hell-fire.

120. And the Jews will not be pleased with thee, nor will the Christians, till thou follow their creed. Say: Lo! the guidance of Allah (Himself) is Guidance. And if thou shouldst follow their desires after the knowledge which hath come unto thee, then wouldst thou have from Allah no protecting friend nor helper.

121. Those unto whom We have given the Scripture, who read it with the right reading, those believe in it. And whoso disbelieveth in it, those are they who are the losers.

ومن اظلم ممن منع مسجد الله ان يذكر فيها
اسمه وسعى في خرابها اولئك ما كان لهم ان
يدخلوها الا خائفين لهم في الدنيا خزي و
لهم في الاخرة عذاب عظيم ١١٤
ولله المشرق والمغرب فاينما تولوا فثم وجه
الله ان الله واسع عليم ١١٥
وقالوا اتخذ الله ولدا سبحنه بل له ما في السموت
والارض كل له قنتون ١١٦
بديع السموت والارض واذا قضى امرا فانما
يقول له كن فيكون ١١٧
وقال الذين لا يعلمون لولا يكلمنا الله او تاتينا
اية كذلك قال الذين من قبلهم مثل قولهم
تشابهت قلوبهم قد بينا الايت لقوم يوقنون ١١٨
انا ارسلنك بالحق بشيرا ونذيرا ولا تسئل
عن اصحب الجحيم ١١٩
ولن ترضى عنك اليهود ولا النصرى حتى تتبع
ملتهم قل ان هدى الله هو الهدى ولئن
اتبعت اهواءهم بعد الذي جاءك من العلم
ما لك من الله من ولي ولا نصير ١٢٠ وقف منزل
الذين اتينهم الكتب يتلونه حق تلاوته اولئك
يؤمنون به ومن يكفر به فاولئك هم
الخسرون ١٢١ ع

122. O Children of Israel! Remember My favour wherewith I favoured you and how I preferred you to (all) creatures.

123. And guard (yourselves) against a day when no soul will in aught avail another, nor will compensation be accepted from it, nor will intercession be of use to it; nor will they be helped.

124. And (remember) when his Lord tried Abraham with (His) commands, and he fulfilled them, He said: Lo! I have appointed thee a leader for mankind. (Abraham) said: And of my offspring (will there be leaders)? He said: My covenant includeth not wrong-doers.

125. And when We made the House (at Mecca) a resort for mankind and a sanctuary, (saying): Take as your place of worship the place where Abraham stood (to pray). And We imposed a duty upon Abraham and Ishmael, (saying): Purify My House for those who go around and those who meditate therein and those who bow down and prostrate themselves (in worship).

126. And when Abraham prayed: My Lord! Make this a region of security and bestow upon its people fruits, such of them as believe in Allah and the Last Day, He answered: As for him who disbelieveth, I shall leave him in contentment for a while, then I shall compel him to the doom of fire—a hapless journey's end!

127. And when Abraham and Ishmael were raising the foundations of the House, (Abraham prayed): Our Lord! Accept from us (this duty). Lo! Thou, only Thou, art the Hearer, the Knower.

128. Our Lord! and make us submissive unto Thee and of our seed a nation submissive unto Thee, and show us our ways of worship, and relent toward us. Lo! Thou, only Thou, art the Relenting, the Merciful.

يٰبَنِيٓ اِسْرَآءِيْلَ اذْكُرُوْا نِعْمَتِيَ الَّتِيْٓ اَنْعَمْتُ عَلَيْكُمْ
وَاَنِّيْ فَضَّلْتُكُمْ عَلَى الْعٰلَمِيْنَ ﴿١٢٢﴾
وَاتَّقُوْا يَوْمًا لَّا تَجْزِيْ نَفْسٌ عَنْ نَّفْسٍ شَيْـًٔا وَّ
لَا يُقْبَلُ مِنْهَا عَدْلٌ وَّلَا تَنْفَعُهَا شَفَاعَةٌ وَّلَا هُمْ
يُنْصَرُوْنَ ﴿١٢٣﴾
وَاِذِ ابْتَلٰٓى اِبْرٰهٖمَ رَبُّهٗ بِكَلِمٰتٍ فَاَتَمَّهُنَّ ۭ قَالَ اِنِّيْ
جَاعِلُكَ لِلنَّاسِ اِمَامًا ۭ قَالَ وَمِنْ ذُرِّيَّتِيْ ۭ قَالَ لَا
يَنَالُ عَهْدِي الظّٰلِمِيْنَ ﴿١٢٤﴾
وَاِذْ جَعَلْنَا الْبَيْتَ مَثَابَةً لِّلنَّاسِ وَاَمْنًا ۭ وَاتَّخِذُوْا
مِنْ مَّقَامِ اِبْرٰهٖمَ مُصَلًّى ۭ وَعَهِدْنَآ اِلٰٓى اِبْرٰهٖمَ وَ
اِسْمٰعِيْلَ اَنْ طَهِّرَا بَيْتِيَ لِلطَّاۗىِٕفِيْنَ وَالْعٰكِفِيْنَ
وَالرُّكَّعِ السُّجُوْدِ ﴿١٢٥﴾
وَاِذْ قَالَ اِبْرٰهٖمُ رَبِّ اجْعَلْ ھٰذَا بَلَدًا اٰمِنًا وَّارْزُقْ
اَھْلَهٗ مِنَ الثَّمَرٰتِ مَنْ اٰمَنَ مِنْهُمْ بِاللّٰهِ وَالْيَوْمِ
الْاٰخِرِ ۭ قَالَ وَمَنْ كَفَرَ فَاُمَتِّعُهٗ قَلِيْلًا ثُمَّ اَضْطَرُّهٗٓ
اِلٰى عَذَابِ النَّارِ ۭ وَبِئْسَ الْمَصِيْرُ ﴿١٢٦﴾
وَاِذْ يَرْفَعُ اِبْرٰهٖمُ الْقَوَاعِدَ مِنَ الْبَيْتِ وَاِسْمٰعِيْلُ ۭ
رَبَّنَا تَقَبَّلْ مِنَّا ۭ اِنَّكَ اَنْتَ السَّمِيْعُ
الْعَلِيْمُ ﴿١٢٧﴾
رَبَّنَا وَاجْعَلْنَا مُسْلِمَيْنِ لَكَ وَمِنْ ذُرِّيَّتِنَآ اُمَّةً
مُّسْلِمَةً لَّكَ ۠ وَاَرِنَا مَنَاسِكَنَا وَتُبْ عَلَيْنَا ۚ اِنَّكَ اَنْتَ
التَّوَّابُ الرَّحِيْمُ ﴿١٢٨﴾

129. Our Lord! And raise up in their midst a messenger from among them who shall recite unto them Thy revelations, and shall instruct them in the Scripture and in wisdom and shall make them grow. Lo! Thou, only Thou, art the Mighty, Wise.

130. And who forsaketh the religion of Abraham save him who befooleth himself? Verily We chose him in the world, and lo! in the Hereafter he is among the righteous.

131. When his Lord said unto him: Surrender! he said: I have surrendered to the Lord of the Worlds.

132. The same did Abraham enjoin upon his sons, and also Jacob, (saying): O my sons! Lo! Allah hath chosen for you the (true) religion; therefore die not save as men who have surrendered (unto Him).

133. Or were ye present when death came to Jacob, when he said unto his sons: What will ye worship after me? They said: We shall worship thy God, the God of thy fathers, Abraham and Ishmael and Isaac, One God, and unto Him we have surrendered.

134. Those are a people who have passed away. Theirs is that which they earned, and yours is that which ye earn. And ye will not be asked of what they used to do.

135. And they say: Be Jews or Christians, then ye will be rightly guided. Say (unto them, O Muhammad): Nay, but (we follow) the religion of Abraham, the upright, and he was not of the idolaters.

136. Say (O Muslims): We believe in Allah and that which is revealed unto us and that which was revealed unto Abraham and Ishmael, and Isaac, and Jacob, and the tribes, and that which Moses and Jesus received, and that which the Prophets received from their Lord. We make no distinction between any of them, and unto Him we have surrendered.

رَبَّنَا وَابْعَثْ فِيْهِمْ رَسُوْلًا مِّنْهُمْ يَتْلُوْا عَلَيْهِمْ
اٰيٰتِكَ وَيُعَلِّمُهُمُ الْكِتٰبَ وَالْحِكْمَةَ وَيُزَكِّيْهِمْ
اِنَّكَ اَنْتَ الْعَزِيْزُ الْحَكِيْمُ ﴿۱۲۹﴾ ع
وَمَنْ يَّرْغَبُ عَنْ مِّلَّةِ اِبْرٰهٖمَ اِلَّا مَنْ سَفِهَ نَفْسَهٗ
وَلَقَدِ اصْطَفَيْنٰهُ فِي الدُّنْيَا وَاِنَّهٗ فِي الْاٰخِرَةِ لَمِنَ
الصّٰلِحِيْنَ ﴿۱۳۰﴾
اِذْ قَالَ لَهٗ رَبُّهٗٓ اَسْلِمْ قَالَ اَسْلَمْتُ لِرَبِّ الْعٰلَمِيْنَ ﴿۱۳۱﴾
وَوَصّٰى بِهَآ اِبْرٰهٖمُ بَنِيْهِ وَيَعْقُوْبُ يٰبَنِيَّ اِنَّ اللّٰهَ
اصْطَفٰى لَكُمُ الدِّيْنَ فَلَا تَمُوْتُنَّ اِلَّا وَ
اَنْتُمْ مُّسْلِمُوْنَ ﴿۱۳۲﴾
اَمْ كُنْتُمْ شُهَدَآءَ اِذْ حَضَرَ يَعْقُوْبَ الْمَوْتُ اِذْ قَالَ
لِبَنِيْهِ مَا تَعْبُدُوْنَ مِنْ بَعْدِيْ قَالُوْا نَعْبُدُ اِلٰهَكَ
وَاِلٰهَ اٰبَآئِكَ اِبْرٰهٖمَ وَاِسْمٰعِيْلَ وَاِسْحٰقَ اِلٰهًا وَّاحِدًا
وَّنَحْنُ لَهٗ مُسْلِمُوْنَ ﴿۱۳۳﴾
تِلْكَ اُمَّةٌ قَدْ خَلَتْ لَهَا مَا كَسَبَتْ وَلَكُمْ مَّا
كَسَبْتُمْ وَلَا تُسْـَٔلُوْنَ عَمَّا كَانُوْا يَعْمَلُوْنَ ﴿۱۳۴﴾
وَقَالُوْا كُوْنُوْا هُوْدًا اَوْ نَصٰرٰى تَهْتَدُوْا قُلْ بَلْ مِلَّةَ
اِبْرٰهٖمَ حَنِيْفًا وَمَا كَانَ مِنَ الْمُشْرِكِيْنَ ﴿۱۳۵﴾
قُوْلُوْٓا اٰمَنَّا بِاللّٰهِ وَمَآ اُنْزِلَ اِلَيْنَا وَمَآ اُنْزِلَ اِلٰٓى اِبْرٰهٖمَ
وَاِسْمٰعِيْلَ وَاِسْحٰقَ وَيَعْقُوْبَ وَالْاَسْبَاطِ وَمَآ
اُوْتِيَ مُوْسٰى وَعِيْسٰى وَمَآ اُوْتِيَ النَّبِيُّوْنَ مِنْ رَّبِّهِمْ
لَا نُفَرِّقُ بَيْنَ اَحَدٍ مِّنْهُمْ وَنَحْنُ لَهٗ مُسْلِمُوْنَ ﴿۱۳۶﴾

137. And if they believe in the like of that which ye believe, then are they rightly guided. But if they turn away, then are they in schism, and Allah will suffice thee (for defence) against them. He is the Hearer, the Knower.

فَإِنْ آمَنُوا بِمِثْلِ مَآ آمَنْتُمْ بِهِ فَقَدِ اهْتَدَوْا وَّإِنْ تَوَلَّوْا فَإِنَّمَا هُمْ فِىْ شِقَاقٍ فَسَيَكْفِيكَهُمُ اللّٰهُ وَهُوَ السَّمِيْعُ الْعَلِيْمُ ۞

138. (We take our) colour from Allah, and who is better than Allah at colouring? We are His worshippers.

صِبْغَةَ اللّٰهِ وَمَنْ أَحْسَنُ مِنَ اللّٰهِ صِبْغَةً وَّنَحْنُ لَهٗ عٰبِدُوْنَ ۞

139. Say (unto the People of the Scripture): Dispute ye with us concerning Allah when He is our Lord and your Lord? Ours are our works and yours your works. We look to Him alone:

قُلْ أَتُحَآجُّوْنَنَا فِى اللّٰهِ وَهُوَ رَبُّنَا وَرَبُّكُمْ وَلَنَآ أَعْمَالُنَا وَلَكُمْ أَعْمَالُكُمْ وَنَحْنُ لَهٗ مُخْلِصُوْنَ ۞

140. Or say ye that Abraham, and Ishmael, and Isaac, and Jacob, and the tribes were Jews or Christians? Say: Do ye know best, or doth Allah? And who is more unjust than he who hideth a testimony which he hath received from Allah? Allah is not unaware of what ye do.

أَمْ تَقُوْلُوْنَ إِنَّ إِبْرٰهٖمَ وَإِسْمٰعِيْلَ وَإِسْحٰقَ وَيَعْقُوْبَ وَالْأَسْبَاطَ كَانُوْا هُوْدًا أَوْ نَصٰرٰى قُلْ ءَأَنْتُمْ أَعْلَمُ أَمِ اللّٰهُ وَمَنْ أَظْلَمُ مِمَّنْ كَتَمَ شَهَادَةً عِنْدَهٗ مِنَ اللّٰهِ وَمَا اللّٰهُ بِغَافِلٍ عَمَّا تَعْمَلُوْنَ ۞

141. Those are a people who have passed away; theirs is that which they earned and yours that which ye earn, and ye will not be asked of what they used to do.

تِلْكَ أُمَّةٌ قَدْ خَلَتْ لَهَا مَا كَسَبَتْ وَلَكُمْ مَّا كَسَبْتُمْ وَلَا تُسْأَلُوْنَ عَمَّا كَانُوْا يَعْمَلُوْنَ ۞

142. The foolish of the people will say: What hath turned them from the *qiblah*[1] which they formerly observed? Say: Unto Allah belong the East and the West. He guideth whom He will unto a Straight path.

سَيَقُوْلُ السُّفَهَآءُ مِنَ النَّاسِ مَا وَلّٰهُمْ عَنْ قِبْلَتِهِمُ الَّتِىْ كَانُوْا عَلَيْهَا قُلْ لِّلّٰهِ الْمَشْرِقُ وَالْمَغْرِبُ يَهْدِىْ مَنْ يَّشَآءُ إِلٰى صِرَاطٍ مُّسْتَقِيْمٍ ۞

143. Thus We have appointed you a middle nation, that ye may be witnesses against mankind, and that the messenger may be a witness against you. And We appointed the *qiblah* which ye formerly observed only that We might know him who followeth the messenger, from him who turneth on his heels. In truth it was a hard (test) save for those whom Allah guided. But it was not Allah's purpose that your faith should be in vain, for Allah is full of pity, Merciful! toward mankind.

وَكَذٰلِكَ جَعَلْنَاكُمْ أُمَّةً وَّسَطًا لِّتَكُوْنُوْا شُهَدَآءَ عَلَى النَّاسِ وَيَكُوْنَ الرَّسُوْلُ عَلَيْكُمْ شَهِيْدًا وَمَا جَعَلْنَا الْقِبْلَةَ الَّتِىْ كُنْتَ عَلَيْهَا إِلَّا لِنَعْلَمَ مَنْ يَّتَّبِعُ الرَّسُوْلَ مِمَّنْ يَّنْقَلِبُ عَلٰى عَقِبَيْهِ وَإِنْ كَانَتْ لَكَبِيْرَةً إِلَّا عَلَى الَّذِيْنَ هَدَى اللّٰهُ وَمَا كَانَ اللّٰهُ لِيُضِيْعَ إِيْمَانَكُمْ إِنَّ اللّٰهَ بِالنَّاسِ لَرَؤُوْفٌ رَّحِيْمٌ ۞

1. *i.e.* the place towards which the face is turned at prayer. The first *qiblah* of the Muslims was Jerusalem, which gave rise to a misunderstanding on the part of the Jews of Al-Madinah, who wished to draw the Muslims into Judaism. This was the cause of the Prophet's anxiety mentioned in the next verse but one.

144. We have seen the turning of thy face to heaven (for guidance, O Muhammad). And now verily We shall make thee turn (in prayer) toward a *qiblah* which is dear to thee. So turn thy face toward the Inviolable Place of Worship,[1] and ye (O Muslims), wheresoever ye may be, turn your faces (when ye pray) toward it. Lo! those who have received the Scripture know that (this Revelation) is the Truth from their Lord. And Allah is not unaware of what they do.

145. And even if thou broughtest unto those who have received the Scripture all kinds of portents, they would not follow thy *qiblah*, nor canst thou be a follower of their *qiblah*; nor are some of them followers of the *qiblah* of others. And if thou shouldst follow their desires after the knowledge which hath come unto thee, then surely wert thou of the evil-doers.

146. Those unto whom We gave the Scripture recognise (this Revelation) as they recognise their sons. But lo! a party of them knowingly conceal the truth.

147. It is the Truth from thy Lord (O Muhammad), so be not thou of those who waver.

148. And each one hath a goal toward which he turneth; so vie with one another in good works. Wheresoever ye may be, Allah will bring you all together. Lo! Allah is Able to do all things.

149. And whencesoever thou comest forth (for prayer, O Muhammad) turn thy face toward the Inviolable Place of Worship. Lo! it is the Truth from thy Lord. Allah is not unaware of what ye do.

150. Whencesoever thou comest forth turn thy face toward the Inviolable Place of Worship; and wheresoever ye may be (O Muslims) turn your faces toward it (when ye pray) so that men may have no argument against you, save such of them as do injustice—Fear them not, but fear Me!—and so that I may complete My grace upon you, and that ye may be guided.

1. The Ka'bah at Mecca.

قَدْ نَرَىٰ تَقَلُّبَ وَجْهِكَ فِي السَّمَاءِ ۖ فَلَنُوَلِّيَنَّكَ
قِبْلَةً تَرْضَاهَا ۚ فَوَلِّ وَجْهَكَ شَطْرَ الْمَسْجِدِ الْحَرَامِ ۚ
وَحَيْثُ مَا كُنْتُمْ فَوَلُّوا وُجُوهَكُمْ شَطْرَهُ ۗ وَإِنَّ
الَّذِينَ أُوتُوا الْكِتَابَ لَيَعْلَمُونَ أَنَّهُ الْحَقُّ مِنْ رَبِّهِمْ ۗ
وَمَا اللَّهُ بِغَافِلٍ عَمَّا يَعْمَلُونَ ١٤٤
وَلَئِنْ أَتَيْتَ الَّذِينَ أُوتُوا الْكِتَابَ بِكُلِّ آيَةٍ مَا تَبِعُوا
قِبْلَتَكَ ۚ وَمَا أَنْتَ بِتَابِعٍ قِبْلَتَهُمْ ۚ وَمَا بَعْضُهُمْ بِتَابِعٍ
قِبْلَةَ بَعْضٍ ۚ وَلَئِنِ اتَّبَعْتَ أَهْوَاءَهُمْ مِنْ بَعْدِ مَا
جَاءَكَ مِنَ الْعِلْمِ ۙ إِنَّكَ إِذًا لَمِنَ الظَّالِمِينَ ١٤٥ وقف لازم
الَّذِينَ آتَيْنَاهُمُ الْكِتَابَ يَعْرِفُونَهُ كَمَا يَعْرِفُونَ أَبْنَاءَهُمْ ۖ
وَإِنَّ فَرِيقًا مِنْهُمْ لَيَكْتُمُونَ الْحَقَّ وَهُمْ يَعْلَمُونَ ١٤٦
الْحَقُّ مِنْ رَبِّكَ ۖ فَلَا تَكُونَنَّ مِنَ الْمُمْتَرِينَ ١٤٧
وَلِكُلٍّ وِجْهَةٌ هُوَ مُوَلِّيهَا ۖ فَاسْتَبِقُوا الْخَيْرَاتِ ۚ أَيْنَ
مَا تَكُونُوا يَأْتِ بِكُمُ اللَّهُ جَمِيعًا ۚ إِنَّ اللَّهَ عَلَىٰ كُلِّ شَيْءٍ قَدِيرٌ ١٤٨
وَمِنْ حَيْثُ خَرَجْتَ فَوَلِّ وَجْهَكَ شَطْرَ الْمَسْجِدِ
الْحَرَامِ ۖ وَإِنَّهُ لَلْحَقُّ مِنْ رَبِّكَ ۗ وَمَا اللَّهُ بِغَافِلٍ
عَمَّا تَعْمَلُونَ ١٤٩
وَمِنْ حَيْثُ خَرَجْتَ فَوَلِّ وَجْهَكَ شَطْرَ الْمَسْجِدِ
الْحَرَامِ ۚ وَحَيْثُ مَا كُنْتُمْ فَوَلُّوا وُجُوهَكُمْ شَطْرَهُ
لِئَلَّا يَكُونَ لِلنَّاسِ عَلَيْكُمْ حُجَّةٌ إِلَّا الَّذِينَ ظَلَمُوا
مِنْهُمْ فَلَا تَخْشَوْهُمْ وَاخْشَوْنِي وَلِأُتِمَّ نِعْمَتِي
عَلَيْكُمْ وَلَعَلَّكُمْ تَهْتَدُونَ ١٥٠

151. Even as We have sent unto you a messenger from among you, who reciteth unto you Our revelations and causeth you to grow, and teacheth you the Scripture and wisdom, and teacheth you that which ye knew not.[1]

152. Therefore remember Me, I will remember you. Give thanks to Me, and reject not Me.

153. O ye who believe! Seek help in steadfastness and prayer. Lo! Allah is with the steadfast.

154. And call not those who are slain in the way of Allah "dead." Nay, they are living, only ye perceive not.

155. And surely We shall try you with something of fear and hunger, and loss of wealth and lives and crops; but give glad tidings to the steadfast,

156. Who say, when a misfortune striketh them: Lo! we are Allah's and lo! unto Him we are returning.

157. Such are they on whom are blessings from their Lord, and mercy. Such are the rightly guided.

158. Lo! (the mountains) As-Safā and Al-Marwah are among the indications of Allah. It is therefore no sin for him who is on pilgrimage to the House (of God) or visiteth it, to go around them (as the pagan custom is). And he who doth good of his own accord (for him), lo! Allah is Responsive, Aware.

159. Those who hide the proofs and the guidance which We revealed, after We had made it clear in the Scripture: such are accursed of Allah and accursed of those who have the power to curse:

160. Except such of them as repent and amend and make manifest (the truth). These it is toward whom I relent. I am the Relenting, the Merciful.

1. See Abraham's prayer, v. 129.

كَمَآ اَرْسَلْنَا فِيْكُمْ رَسُوْلًا مِّنْكُمْ يَتْلُوْا عَلَيْكُمْ اٰيٰتِنَا
وَيُزَكِّيْكُمْ وَيُعَلِّمُكُمُ الْكِتٰبَ وَالْحِكْمَةَ وَيُعَلِّمُكُمْ
مَّا لَمْ تَكُوْنُوْا تَعْلَمُوْنَ ﴿١٥١﴾
فَاذْكُرُوْنِيْٓ اَذْكُرْكُمْ وَاشْكُرُوْا لِيْ وَلَا تَكْفُرُوْنِ ﴿١٥٢﴾
يٰٓاَيُّهَا الَّذِيْنَ اٰمَنُوا اسْتَعِيْنُوْا بِالصَّبْرِ وَالصَّلٰوةِ ۭ اِنَّ
اللّٰهَ مَعَ الصّٰبِرِيْنَ ﴿١٥٣﴾
وَلَا تَقُوْلُوْا لِمَنْ يُّقْتَلُ فِيْ سَبِيْلِ اللّٰهِ اَمْوَاتٌ ۭ بَلْ
اَحْيَاۗءٌ وَّلٰكِنْ لَّا تَشْعُرُوْنَ ﴿١٥٤﴾
وَلَنَبْلُوَنَّكُمْ بِشَيْءٍ مِّنَ الْخَوْفِ وَالْجُوْعِ وَنَقْصٍ مِّنَ
الْاَمْوَالِ وَالْاَنْفُسِ وَالثَّمَرٰتِ ۭ وَبَشِّرِ الصّٰبِرِيْنَ ﴿١٥٥﴾
الَّذِيْنَ اِذَآ اَصَابَتْهُمْ مُّصِيْبَةٌ ۙ قَالُوْٓا اِنَّا لِلّٰهِ وَاِنَّآ
اِلَيْهِ رٰجِعُوْنَ ﴿١٥٦﴾
اُولٰۗىِٕكَ عَلَيْهِمْ صَلَوٰتٌ مِّنْ رَّبِّهِمْ وَرَحْمَةٌ ۣ وَ
اُولٰۗىِٕكَ هُمُ الْمُهْتَدُوْنَ ﴿١٥٧﴾
اِنَّ الصَّفَا وَالْمَرْوَةَ مِنْ شَعَاۗىِٕرِ اللّٰهِ ۚ فَمَنْ حَجَّ
الْبَيْتَ اَوِ اعْتَمَرَ فَلَا جُنَاحَ عَلَيْهِ اَنْ يَّطَّوَّفَ
بِهِمَا ۭ وَمَنْ تَطَوَّعَ خَيْرًا ۙ فَاِنَّ اللّٰهَ شَاكِرٌ عَلِيْمٌ ﴿١٥٨﴾
اِنَّ الَّذِيْنَ يَكْتُمُوْنَ مَآ اَنْزَلْنَا مِنَ الْبَيِّنٰتِ وَالْهُدٰى
مِنْۢ بَعْدِ مَا بَيَّنّٰهُ لِلنَّاسِ فِي الْكِتٰبِ ۙ اُولٰۗىِٕكَ يَلْعَنُهُمُ
اللّٰهُ وَيَلْعَنُهُمُ اللّٰعِنُوْنَ ﴿١٥٩﴾
اِلَّا الَّذِيْنَ تَابُوْا وَاَصْلَحُوْا وَبَيَّنُوْا فَاُولٰۗىِٕكَ اَتُوْبُ
عَلَيْهِمْ ۚ وَاَنَا التَّوَّابُ الرَّحِيْمُ ﴿١٦٠﴾

161. Lo! those who disbelieve, and die while they are disbelievers; on them is the curse of Allah and of angels and of men combined:

162. They ever dwell therein. The doom will not be lightened for them, neither will they be reprieved.

163. Your God is One God; there is no God save Him, the Beneficent, the Merciful.

164. Lo! in the creation of the heavens and the earth, and the difference of night and day, and the ships which run upon the sea with that which is of use to men, and the water which Allah sendeth down from the sky, thereby reviving the earth after its death, and dispersing all kinds of beasts therein, and (in) the ordinance of the winds, and the clouds obedient between heaven and earth: are signs (of Allah's sovereignty) for people who have sense.

165. Yet of mankind are some who take unto themselves (objects of worship which they set as) rivals to Allah, loving them with a love like (that which is the due) of Allah (only)—Those who believe are stauncher in their love for Allah—Oh, that those who do evil had but known, (on the day) when they behold the doom, that power belongeth wholly to Allah, and that Allah is severe in punishment!

166. (On the day) when those who were followed disown those who followed (them), and they behold the doom, and all their aims collapse with them.

167. And those who were but followers will say: If a return were possible for us, we would disown them even as they have disowned us. Thus will Allah show them their own deeds as anguish for them, and they will not emerge from the Fire.

168. O mankind! Eat of that which is lawful and wholesome in the earth, and follow not the footsteps of the devil. Lo! he is an open enemy for you.

إن الذين كفروا وماتوا وهم كفار أولئك عليهم لعنة الله والملائكة والناس أجمعين ﴿١٦١﴾

خالدين فيها لا يخفف عنهم العذاب ولا هم ينظرون ﴿١٦٢﴾

وإلهكم إله واحد لا إله إلا هو الرحمن الرحيم ﴿١٦٣﴾ ع

إن في خلق السماوات والأرض واختلاف الليل والنهار والفلك التي تجري في البحر بما ينفع الناس وما أنزل الله من السماء من ماء فأحيا به الأرض بعد موتها وبث فيها من كل دابة وتصريف الرياح والسحاب المسخر بين السماء والأرض لآيات لقوم يعقلون ﴿١٦٤﴾

ومن الناس من يتخذ من دون الله أندادا يحبونهم كحب الله والذين آمنوا أشد حبا لله ولو يرى الذين ظلموا إذ يرون العذاب أن القوة لله جميعا وأن الله شديد العذاب ﴿١٦٥﴾

إذ تبرأ الذين اتبعوا من الذين اتبعوا ورأوا العذاب وتقطعت بهم الأسباب ﴿١٦٦﴾

وقال الذين اتبعوا لو أن لنا كرة فنتبرأ منهم كما تبرءوا منا كذلك يريهم الله أعمالهم حسرات عليهم وما هم بخارجين من النار ﴿١٦٧﴾ ع

يا أيها الناس كلوا مما في الأرض حلالا طيبا ولا تتبعوا خطوات الشيطان إنه لكم عدو مبين ﴿١٦٨﴾

169. He enjoineth upon you only the evil and the foul, and that ye should tell concerning Allah that which ye know not.

إنما يأمركم بالسوء والفحشاء وأن تقولوا على
الله ما لا تعلمون ﴿١٦٩﴾

170. And when it is said unto them: Follow that which Allah hath revealed, they say: We follow that wherein we found our fathers. What! Even though their fathers were wholly unintelligent and had no guidance?

وإذا قيل لهم اتبعوا ما أنزل الله قالوا بل
نتبع ما ألفينا عليه آباءنا أولو كان آباؤهم
لا يعقلون شيئا ولا يهتدون ﴿١٧٠﴾

171. The likeness of those who disbelieve (in relation to the messenger) is as the likeness of one who calleth unto that which heareth naught except a shout and cry. Deaf, dumb, blind, therefore they have no sense.

ومثل الذين كفروا كمثل الذي ينعق بما لا
يسمع إلا دعاء ونداء صم بكم عمي فهم لا
يعقلون ﴿١٧١﴾

172. O ye who believe! Eat of the good things wherewith We have provided you, and render thanks to Allah if it is (indeed) He whom ye worship.

يا أيها الذين آمنوا كلوا من طيبات ما رزقناكم
واشكروا لله إن كنتم إياه تعبدون ﴿١٧٢﴾

173. He hath forbidden you only carrion, and blood, and swineflesh, and that which hath been immolated to (the name of) any other than Allah. But he who is driven by necessity, neither craving nor transgressing, it is no sin for him. Lo! Allah is Forgiving, Merciful.

إنما حرم عليكم الميتة والدم ولحم الخنزير
وما أهل به لغير الله فمن اضطر غير باغ ولا
عاد فلا إثم عليه إن الله غفور رحيم ﴿١٧٣﴾

174. Lo! those who hide aught of the Scripture which Allah hath revealed, and purchase a small gain therewith, they eat into their bellies nothing else than fire. Allah will not speak to them on the Day of Resurrection, nor will He make them grow. Theirs will be a painful doom.

إن الذين يكتمون ما أنزل الله من الكتاب و
يشترون به ثمنا قليلا أولئك ما يأكلون في
بطونهم إلا النار ولا يكلمهم الله يوم القيامة و
لا يزكيهم ولهم عذاب أليم ﴿١٧٤﴾

175. Those are they who purchase error at the price of guidance, and torment at the price of pardon. How constant are they in their strife to reach the Fire!

أولئك الذين اشتروا الضلالة بالهدى والعذاب
بالمغفرة فما أصبرهم على النار ﴿١٧٥﴾

176. That is because Allah hath revealed the Scripture with the truth. Lo! those who find (a cause of) disagreement in the Scripture are in open schism.

ذلك بأن الله نزل الكتاب بالحق وإن
الذين اختلفوا في الكتاب لفي شقاق
بعيد ﴿١٧٦﴾ ع

177. It is not righteousness that ye turn faces to the East and the West; but righteous is he who believeth in Allah and the Last Day and the angels and the Scripture and the Prophets; and giveth his wealth, for love of Him, to kinsfolk and to orphans and the needy and the wayfarer and to those who ask, and to set slaves free; and observeth proper worship and payeth the poor-due.[1] And those who keep their treaty when they make one, and the patient in tribulation and adversity and time of stress. Such are they who are sincere. Such are the God-fearing.

178. O ye who believe! Retaliation is prescribed for you in the matter of the murdered; the freeman for the freeman, and the slave for the slave, and the female for the female. And for him who is forgiven somewhat by his (injured) brother, prosecution according to usage and payment unto him in kindness. This is an alleviation and a mercy from your Lord. He who transgresseth after this will have a painful doom.

179. And there is life for you in retaliation, O men of understanding, that ye may ward off (evil).

180. It is prescribed for you, when one of you approacheth death, if he leave wealth, that he bequeath unto parents and near relatives in kindness. (This is) a duty for all those who ward off (evil).

181. And whoso changeth (the will) after he hath heard it— the sin thereof is only upon those who change it. Lo! Allah is Hearer, Knower.

182. But he who feareth from a testator some unjust or sinful clause, and maketh peace between the parties, (it shall be) no sin for him. Lo! Allah is Forgiving, Merciful.

183. O ye who believe! Fasting is prescribed for you, even as it was prescribed for those before you, that ye may ward off (evil);

1. See v. 43, footnote.

لَيْسَ الْبِرَّ اَنْ تُوَلُّوْا وُجُوْهَكُمْ قِبَلَ الْمَشْرِقِ وَ
الْمَغْرِبِ وَلٰكِنَّ الْبِرَّ مَنْ اٰمَنَ بِاللّٰهِ وَالْيَوْمِ الْاٰخِرِ
وَالْمَلٰٓئِكَةِ وَالْكِتٰبِ وَالنَّبِيّٖنَ ۚ وَاٰتَى الْمَالَ عَلٰى حُبِّهٖ
ذَوِي الْقُرْبٰى وَالْيَتٰمٰى وَالْمَسٰكِيْنَ وَابْنَ السَّبِيْلِ ۙ
وَالسَّآئِلِيْنَ وَفِي الرِّقَابِ ۚ وَاَقَامَ الصَّلٰوةَ وَاٰتَى الزَّكٰوةَ ۚ
وَالْمُوْفُوْنَ بِعَهْدِهِمْ اِذَا عٰهَدُوْا ۚ وَالصّٰبِرِيْنَ فِي
الْبَاْسَآءِ وَالضَّرَّآءِ وَحِيْنَ الْبَاْسِ ؕ اُولٰٓئِكَ الَّذِيْنَ
صَدَقُوْا ؕ وَاُولٰٓئِكَ هُمُ الْمُتَّقُوْنَ ﴿١٧٧﴾
يٰٓاَيُّهَا الَّذِيْنَ اٰمَنُوْا كُتِبَ عَلَيْكُمُ الْقِصَاصُ فِي الْقَتْلٰى ؕ
اَلْحُرُّ بِالْحُرِّ وَالْعَبْدُ بِالْعَبْدِ وَالْاُنْثٰى بِالْاُنْثٰى ؕ فَمَنْ
عُفِيَ لَهٗ مِنْ اَخِيْهِ شَيْءٌ فَاتِّبَاعٌ بِالْمَعْرُوْفِ وَاَدَآءٌ
اِلَيْهِ بِاِحْسَانٍ ؕ ذٰلِكَ تَخْفِيْفٌ مِّنْ رَّبِّكُمْ وَرَحْمَةٌ ؕ
فَمَنِ اعْتَدٰى بَعْدَ ذٰلِكَ فَلَهٗ عَذَابٌ اَلِيْمٌ ﴿١٧٨﴾
وَلَكُمْ فِي الْقِصَاصِ حَيٰوةٌ يّٰاُولِي الْاَلْبَابِ لَعَلَّكُمْ تَتَّقُوْنَ ﴿١٧٩﴾
كُتِبَ عَلَيْكُمْ اِذَا حَضَرَ اَحَدَكُمُ الْمَوْتُ اِنْ تَرَكَ خَيْرَا ۨ الْوَصِيَّةُ
لِلْوَالِدَيْنِ وَالْاَقْرَبِيْنَ بِالْمَعْرُوْفِ ۚ حَقًّا عَلَى الْمُتَّقِيْنَ ﴿١٨٠﴾
فَمَنْۢ بَدَّلَهٗ بَعْدَمَا سَمِعَهٗ فَاِنَّمَآ اِثْمُهٗ عَلَى الَّذِيْنَ
يُبَدِّلُوْنَهٗ ؕ اِنَّ اللّٰهَ سَمِيْعٌ عَلِيْمٌ ﴿١٨١﴾
فَمَنْ خَافَ مِنْ مُّوْصٍ جَنَفًا اَوْ اِثْمًا فَاَصْلَحَ بَيْنَهُمْ
فَلَآ اِثْمَ عَلَيْهِ ؕ اِنَّ اللّٰهَ غَفُوْرٌ رَّحِيْمٌ ﴿١٨٢﴾ ع
يٰٓاَيُّهَا الَّذِيْنَ اٰمَنُوْا كُتِبَ عَلَيْكُمُ الصِّيَامُ كَمَا كُتِبَ
عَلَى الَّذِيْنَ مِنْ قَبْلِكُمْ لَعَلَّكُمْ تَتَّقُوْنَ ﴿١٨٣﴾ ۙ

184. (Fast) a certain number of days; and (for) him who is sick among you, or on a journey, (the same) number of other days; and for those who can afford it there is a ransom: the feeding of a man in need—But whoso doth good of his own accord, it is better for him: and that ye fast is better for you if ye did but know—

185. The month of Ramadān in which was revealed the Qur'ān, a guidance for mankind, and clear proofs of the guidance, and the Criterion (of right and wrong). And whosoever of you is present, let him fast the month, and whosoever of you is sick or on a journey, (let him fast the same) number of other days. Allah desireth for you ease; He desireth not hardship for you; and (He desireth) that ye should complete the period, and that ye should magnify Allah for having guided you, and that peradventure ye may be thankful.

186. And when My servants question thee concerning Me, then surely I am nigh. I answer the prayer of the suppliant when he crieth unto Me. So let them hear My call and let them trust in Me, in order that they may be led aright.

187. It is made lawful for you to go unto your wives on the night of the fast. They are raiment for you and ye are raiment for them. Allah is aware that ye were deceiving yourselves[1] in this respect and He hath turned in mercy toward you and relieved you. So hold intercourse with them and seek that which Allah hath ordained for you, and eat and drink until the white thread becometh distinct to you from the black thread of the dawn. Then strictly observe the fast till nightfall and touch them not, but be at your devotions in the mosques. These are the limits imposed by Allah, so approach them not. Thus Allah expoundeth His revelations to mankind that they may ward off (evil).

أَيَّامًا مَّعْدُودَٰتٍ ۚ فَمَن كَانَ مِنكُم مَّرِيضًا أَوْ عَلَىٰ
سَفَرٍ فَعِدَّةٌ مِّنْ أَيَّامٍ أُخَرَ ۚ وَعَلَى ٱلَّذِينَ يُطِيقُونَهُۥ
فِدْيَةٌ طَعَامُ مِسْكِينٍ ۖ فَمَن تَطَوَّعَ خَيْرًا فَهُوَ خَيْرٌ
لَّهُۥ ۚ وَأَن تَصُومُوا۟ خَيْرٌ لَّكُمْ ۖ إِن كُنتُمْ تَعْلَمُونَ ١٨٤

شَهْرُ رَمَضَانَ ٱلَّذِىٓ أُنزِلَ فِيهِ ٱلْقُرْءَانُ هُدًى
لِّلنَّاسِ وَبَيِّنَٰتٍ مِّنَ ٱلْهُدَىٰ وَٱلْفُرْقَانِ ۚ فَمَن شَهِدَ
مِنكُمُ ٱلشَّهْرَ فَلْيَصُمْهُ ۖ وَمَن كَانَ مَرِيضًا أَوْ عَلَىٰ
سَفَرٍ فَعِدَّةٌ مِّنْ أَيَّامٍ أُخَرَ ۗ يُرِيدُ ٱللَّهُ بِكُمُ ٱلْيُسْرَ
وَلَا يُرِيدُ بِكُمُ ٱلْعُسْرَ وَلِتُكْمِلُوا۟ ٱلْعِدَّةَ وَلِتُكَبِّرُوا۟
ٱللَّهَ عَلَىٰ مَا هَدَىٰكُمْ وَلَعَلَّكُمْ تَشْكُرُونَ ١٨٥

وَإِذَا سَأَلَكَ عِبَادِى عَنِّى فَإِنِّى قَرِيبٌ ۖ أُجِيبُ دَعْوَةَ
ٱلدَّاعِ إِذَا دَعَانِ ۖ فَلْيَسْتَجِيبُوا۟ لِى وَلْيُؤْمِنُوا۟ بِى لَعَلَّهُمْ
يَرْشُدُونَ ١٨٦

أُحِلَّ لَكُمْ لَيْلَةَ ٱلصِّيَامِ ٱلرَّفَثُ إِلَىٰ نِسَآئِكُمْ ۚ هُنَّ
لِبَاسٌ لَّكُمْ وَأَنتُمْ لِبَاسٌ لَّهُنَّ ۗ عَلِمَ ٱللَّهُ أَنَّكُمْ
كُنتُمْ تَخْتَانُونَ أَنفُسَكُمْ فَتَابَ عَلَيْكُمْ وَعَفَا عَنكُمْ ۖ
فَٱلْـَٔـٰنَ بَٰشِرُوهُنَّ وَٱبْتَغُوا۟ مَا كَتَبَ ٱللَّهُ لَكُمْ ۚ وَ
كُلُوا۟ وَٱشْرَبُوا۟ حَتَّىٰ يَتَبَيَّنَ لَكُمُ ٱلْخَيْطُ ٱلْأَبْيَضُ
مِنَ ٱلْخَيْطِ ٱلْأَسْوَدِ مِنَ ٱلْفَجْرِ ۖ ثُمَّ أَتِمُّوا۟ ٱلصِّيَامَ
إِلَى ٱلَّيْلِ ۚ وَلَا تُبَٰشِرُوهُنَّ وَأَنتُمْ عَٰكِفُونَ فِى ٱلْمَسَٰجِدِ ۗ
تِلْكَ حُدُودُ ٱللَّهِ فَلَا تَقْرَبُوهَا ۗ كَذَٰلِكَ يُبَيِّنُ ٱللَّهُ
ءَايَٰتِهِۦ لِلنَّاسِ لَعَلَّهُمْ يَتَّقُونَ ١٨٧

1. Until this verse was revealed, the Muslims used to fast completely from the evening meal of one day till the evening meal of the next, and if they fell asleep before they had taken their meal they had considered it their duty to abstain from it, with the result that men fainted and came near to death. Intercourse with their wives had been similarly restricted.

188. And eat not up your property among yourselves in vanity, nor seek by it to gain the hearing of the judges that ye may knowingly devour a portion of the property of others wrongfully.

189. They ask thee, (O Muhammad), of new moons. Say: They are fixed seasons for mankind and for the pilgrimage. It is not righteousness that ye go to houses by the backs thereof (as do the idolaters at certain seasons), but the righteous man is he who wardeth off (evil). So go to houses by the gates thereof, and observe your duty to Allah, that ye may be successful.

190. Fight in the way of Allah against those who fight against you, but begin not hostilities. Lo! Allah loveth not aggressors.

191. And slay them wherever ye find them, and drive them out of the places whence they drove you out, for persecution is worse than slaughter. And fight not with them at the Inviolable Place of Worship until they first attack you there, but if they attack you (there) then slay them. Such is the reward of disbelievers.

192. But if they desist, then lo! Allah is Forgiving, Merciful.

193. And fight them until persecution is no more, and religion is for Allah. But if they desist, then let there be no hostility except against wrongdoers.

194. The forbidden month for the forbidden month, and forbidden things in retaliation. And one who attacketh you, attack him in like manner as he attacked you. Observe your duty to Allah, and know that Allah is with those who ward off (evil).

195. Spend your wealth for the cause of Allah, and be not cast by your own hands to ruin; and do good. Lo! Allah loveth the beneficent.

ولا تأكلوا اموالكم بينكم بالباطل وتدلوا بها
الى الحكام لتأكلوا فريقا من اموال الناس
بالاثم وانتم تعلمون ﴿١٨٨﴾ ع ٢٣

يسئلونك عن الاهلة قل هي مواقيت للناس
والحج وليس البر بان تأتوا البيوت من ظهورها
ولكن البر من اتقى واتوا البيوت من ابوابها
واتقوا الله لعلكم تفلحون ﴿١٨٩﴾

وقاتلوا في سبيل الله الذين يقاتلونكم ولا
تعتدوا ان الله لا يحب المعتدين ﴿١٩٠﴾

واقتلوهم حيث ثقفتموهم واخرجوهم من
حيث اخرجوكم والفتنة اشد من القتل و
لا تقتلوهم عند المسجد الحرام حتى يقتلوكم فيه
فان قتلوكم فاقتلوهم كذلك جزاء الكفرين ﴿١٩١﴾

فان انتهوا فان الله غفور رحيم ﴿١٩٢﴾

وقتلوهم حتى لا تكون فتنة ويكون الدين لله
فان انتهوا فلا عدوان الا على الظلمين ﴿١٩٣﴾

الشهر الحرام بالشهر الحرام والحرمت قصاص
فمن اعتدى عليكم فاعتدوا عليه بمثل ما اعتدى
عليكم واتقوا الله واعلموا ان الله مع
المتقين ﴿١٩٤﴾

وانفقوا في سبيل الله ولا تلقوا بايديكم الى التهلكة
واحسنوا ان الله يحب المحسنين ﴿١٩٥﴾

196. Perform the pilgrimage[1] and the visit (to Mecca) for Allah. And if ye are prevented, then send such gifts as can be obtained with ease, and shave not your heads until the gifts have reached their destination. And whoever among you is sick or hath an ailment of the head must pay a ransom of fasting or almsgiving or offering. And if ye are in safety, then whosoever contenteth himself with the Visit for the Pilgrimage (shall give) such gifts as can be had with ease. And whosoever cannot find (such gifts), then a fast of three days, while on the pilgrimage, and of seven when ye have returned; that is, ten in all. That is for him whose folk are not present at the Inviolable Place of Worship. Observe your duty to Allah, and know that Allah is severe in punishment.

197. The pilgrimage is (in) the well-known months, and whoever is minded to perform the pilgrimage therein (let him remember that) there is (to be) no lewdness nor abuse nor angry conversation on the pilgrimage. And whatsoever good ye do Allah knoweth it. So make provision for yourselves (hereafter); for the best provision is to ward off evil. Therefore keep your duty unto Me, O men of understanding.

198. It is no sin for you that ye seek the bounty of your Lord (by trading). But, when ye press on in the multitude from 'Arafāt, remember Allah by the sacred monument. Remember Him as He hath guided you, although before ye were of those astray.

199. Then hasten onward from the place whence the multitude hasteneth onward, and ask forgiveness of Allah. Lo! Allah is Forgiving, Merciful.

200. And when ye have completed your devotions, then remember Allah as ye remember your fathers[2] or with a more lively remembrance. But of mankind is he who saith: "Our Lord! Give unto us in the world," and he hath no portion in the Hereafter.

وَأَتِمُّوا الْحَجَّ وَالْعُمْرَةَ لِلَّهِ فَإِنْ أُحْصِرْتُمْ فَمَا اسْتَيْسَرَ
مِنَ الْهَدْيِ وَلَا تَحْلِقُوا رُءُوسَكُمْ حَتَّىٰ يَبْلُغَ الْهَدْيُ
مَحِلَّهُ فَمَنْ كَانَ مِنْكُمْ مَرِيضًا أَوْ بِهِ أَذًى مِنْ رَأْسِهِ
فَفِدْيَةٌ مِنْ صِيَامٍ أَوْ صَدَقَةٍ أَوْ نُسُكٍ فَإِذَا أَمِنْتُمْ
فَمَنْ تَمَتَّعَ بِالْعُمْرَةِ إِلَى الْحَجِّ فَمَا اسْتَيْسَرَ مِنَ الْهَدْيِ
فَمَنْ لَمْ يَجِدْ فَصِيَامُ ثَلَاثَةِ أَيَّامٍ فِي الْحَجِّ وَسَبْعَةٍ
إِذَا رَجَعْتُمْ تِلْكَ عَشَرَةٌ كَامِلَةٌ ذَٰلِكَ لِمَنْ لَمْ
يَكُنْ أَهْلُهُ حَاضِرِي الْمَسْجِدِ الْحَرَامِ وَاتَّقُوا اللَّهَ
ع ٢٤ وَاعْلَمُوا أَنَّ اللَّهَ شَدِيدُ الْعِقَابِ ١٩٦
الْحَجُّ أَشْهُرٌ مَعْلُومَاتٌ فَمَنْ فَرَضَ فِيهِنَّ الْحَجَّ
فَلَا رَفَثَ وَلَا فُسُوقَ وَلَا جِدَالَ فِي الْحَجِّ وَمَا
تَفْعَلُوا مِنْ خَيْرٍ يَعْلَمْهُ اللَّهُ وَتَزَوَّدُوا فَإِنَّ خَيْرَ
الزَّادِ التَّقْوَىٰ وَاتَّقُونِ يَا أُولِي الْأَلْبَابِ ١٩٧
لَيْسَ عَلَيْكُمْ جُنَاحٌ أَنْ تَبْتَغُوا فَضْلًا مِنْ رَبِّكُمْ
فَإِذَا أَفَضْتُمْ مِنْ عَرَفَاتٍ فَاذْكُرُوا اللَّهَ عِنْدَ الْمَشْعَرِ
الْحَرَامِ وَاذْكُرُوهُ كَمَا هَدَاكُمْ وَإِنْ كُنْتُمْ مِنْ
قَبْلِهِ لَمِنَ الضَّالِّينَ ١٩٨
ثُمَّ أَفِيضُوا مِنْ حَيْثُ أَفَاضَ النَّاسُ وَاسْتَغْفِرُوا
اللَّهَ إِنَّ اللَّهَ غَفُورٌ رَحِيمٌ ١٩٩
فَإِذَا قَضَيْتُمْ مَنَاسِكَكُمْ فَاذْكُرُوا اللَّهَ كَذِكْرِكُمْ
آبَاءَكُمْ أَوْ أَشَدَّ ذِكْرًا فَمِنَ النَّاسِ مَنْ يَقُولُ رَبَّنَا
آتِنَا فِي الدُّنْيَا وَمَا لَهُ فِي الْآخِرَةِ مِنْ خَلَاقٍ ٢٠٠

وقف النبي صلى الله عليه وسلم

1. See also S. XXII, vv. 26 ff.
2. It was the custom of the pagan Arabs to praise their forefathers at the conclusion of the Pilgrimage.

201. And of them (also) is he who saith: "Our Lord! Give unto us in the world that which is good and in the Hereafter that which is good, and guard us from the doom of Fire."

202. For them there is in store a goodly portion out of that which they have earned. Allah is swift at reckoning.

203. Remember Allah through the appointed days. Then whoso hasteneth (his departure) by two days, it is no sin for him, and whoso delayeth, it is no sin for him; that is for him who wardeth off (evil). Be careful of your duty to Allah, and know that unto Him ye will be gathered.

204. And of mankind there is he whose conversation on the life of this world pleaseth thee (Muhammad), and he calleth Allah to witness as to that which is in his heart; yet he is the most rigid of opponents.

205. And when he turneth away (from thee) his effort in the land is to make mischief therein and to destroy the crops and the cattle; and Allah loveth not mischief.

206. And when it is said unto him: Be careful of thy duty to Allah, pride taketh him to sin. Hell will settle his account, an evil resting-place.

207. And of mankind is he who would sell himself, seeking the pleasure of Allah; and Allah hath compassion on (His) bondmen.

208. O ye who believe! Come, all of you, into submission (unto Him); and follow not the footsteps of the devil. Lo! he is an open enemy for you.

209. And if ye slide back after the clear proofs have come unto you, then know that Allah is Mighty, Wise.

210. Wait they for naught else than that Allah should come unto them in the shadows of the clouds with the angels? Then the case would be already judged. All cases go back to Allah (for judgment).

وَمِنْهُمْ مَّنْ يَّقُوْلُ رَبَّنَآ اٰتِنَا فِي الدُّنْيَا حَسَنَةً وَّفِي
الْاٰخِرَةِ حَسَنَةً وَّقِنَا عَذَابَ النَّارِ ﴿٢٠١﴾ النصف
اُولٰٓئِكَ لَهُمْ نَصِيْبٌ مِّمَّا كَسَبُوْا ۭ وَاللّٰهُ سَرِيْعُ
الْحِسَابِ ﴿٢٠٢﴾
وَاذْكُرُوا اللّٰهَ فِيْٓ اَيَّامٍ مَّعْدُوْدٰتٍ ۭ فَمَنْ تَعَجَّلَ فِيْ
يَوْمَيْنِ فَلَآ اِثْمَ عَلَيْهِ ۚ وَمَنْ تَاَخَّرَ فَلَآ اِثْمَ عَلَيْهِ ۙ
لِمَنِ اتَّقٰى ۭ وَاتَّقُوا اللّٰهَ وَاعْلَمُوْٓا اَنَّكُمْ اِلَيْهِ تُحْشَرُوْنَ ﴿٢٠٣﴾
وَمِنَ النَّاسِ مَنْ يُّعْجِبُكَ قَوْلُهٗ فِي الْحَيٰوةِ الدُّنْيَا
وَيُشْهِدُ اللّٰهَ عَلٰي مَا فِيْ قَلْبِهٖ ۙ وَهُوَ اَلَدُّ الْخِصَامِ ﴿٢٠٤﴾
وَاِذَا تَوَلّٰى سَعٰى فِي الْاَرْضِ لِيُفْسِدَ فِيْهَا وَيُهْلِكَ
الْحَرْثَ وَالنَّسْلَ ۭ وَاللّٰهُ لَا يُحِبُّ الْفَسَادَ ﴿٢٠٥﴾
وَاِذَا قِيْلَ لَهُ اتَّقِ اللّٰهَ اَخَذَتْهُ الْعِزَّةُ بِالْاِثْمِ
فَحَسْبُهٗ جَهَنَّمُ ۭ وَلَبِئْسَ الْمِهَادُ ﴿٢٠٦﴾
وَمِنَ النَّاسِ مَنْ يَّشْرِيْ نَفْسَهُ ابْتِغَاۗءَ مَرْضَاتِ
اللّٰهِ ۭ وَاللّٰهُ رَءُوْفٌۢ بِالْعِبَادِ ﴿٢٠٧﴾
يٰٓاَيُّهَا الَّذِيْنَ اٰمَنُوا ادْخُلُوْا فِي السِّلْمِ كَاۗفَّةً ۠ وَلَا
تَتَّبِعُوْا خُطُوٰتِ الشَّيْطٰنِ ۭ اِنَّهٗ لَكُمْ عَدُوٌّ مُّبِيْنٌ ﴿٢٠٨﴾
فَاِنْ زَلَلْتُمْ مِّنْۢ بَعْدِ مَا جَاۗءَتْكُمُ الْبَيِّنٰتُ فَاعْلَمُوْٓا
اَنَّ اللّٰهَ عَزِيْزٌ حَكِيْمٌ ﴿٢٠٩﴾
هَلْ يَنْظُرُوْنَ اِلَّآ اَنْ يَّاْتِيَهُمُ اللّٰهُ فِيْ ظُلَلٍ مِّنَ
الْغَمَامِ وَالْمَلٰۗىِٕكَةُ وَقُضِيَ الْاَمْرُ ۭ وَاِلَى اللّٰهِ تُرْجَعُ
الْاُمُوْرُ ﴿٢١٠﴾ ع

211. Ask of the Children of Israel how many a clear revelation We gave them! He who altereth the grace of Allah after it hath come unto him (for him), lo! Allah is severe in punishment.

212. Beautified is the life of the world for those who disbelieve; they make a jest of the believers. But those who keep their duty to Allah will be above them on the Day of Resurrection. Allah giveth without stint to whom He will.

213. Mankind were one community, and Allah sent (unto them) Prophets as bearers of good tidings and as warners, and revealed therewith the Scripture with the truth that it might judge between mankind concerning that wherein they differed. And only those unto whom (the Scripture) was given differed concerning it, after clear proofs had come unto them, through hatred one of another. And Allah by His will guided those who believe unto the truth of that concerning which they differed. Allah guideth whom He will unto a Straight path.

214. Or think ye that ye will enter Paradise while yet there hath not come unto you the like of (that which came to) those who passed away before you? Affliction and adversity befell them, they were shaken as with earthquake, till the messenger (of Allah) and those who believed along with him said: When cometh Allah's help? Now surely Allah's help is nigh.

215. They ask thee, (O Muhammad), what they shall spend. Say: That which ye spend for good (must go) to parents and near kindred and orphans and the needy and the wayfarer. And whatsoever good ye do, lo! Allah is Aware of it.

سل بني اسراءيل كم اتينهم من اية بينة
ومن يبدل نعمة الله من بعد ما جاءته فان
الله شديد العقاب ٢١١
زين للذين كفروا الحيوة الدنيا ويسخرون من
الذين امنوا والذين اتقوا فوقهم يوم القيمة
والله يرزق من يشاء بغير حساب ٢١٢
كان الناس امة واحدة فبعث الله النبين
مبشرين ومنذرين وانزل معهم الكتب بالحق
ليحكم بين الناس فيما اختلفوا فيه وما اختلف
فيه الا الذين اوتوه من بعد ما جاءتهم البينت
بغيا بينهم فهدى الله الذين امنوا لما اختلفوا
فيه من الحق باذنه والله يهدي من يشاء
الى صراط مستقيم ٢١٣
ام حسبتم ان تدخلوا الجنة ولما ياتكم مثل
الذين خلوا من قبلكم مستهم البأساء
والضراء وزلزلوا حتى يقول الرسول و
الذين امنوا معه متى نصر الله الا ان
نصر الله قريب ٢١٤
يسئلونك ماذا ينفقون قل ما انفقتم من
خير فللوالدين والاقربين واليتمى والمسكين
وابن السبيل وما تفعلوا من خير فان الله به
عليم ٢١٥

216. Warfare is ordained for you, though it is hateful unto you; but it may happen that ye hate a thing which is good for you, and it may happen that ye love a thing which is bad for you. Allah knoweth, ye know not.

217. They question thee (O Muhammad) with regard to warfare in the sacred month. Say: Warfare therein is a great (transgression), but to turn (men) from the Way of Allah, and to disbelieve in Him and in the Inviolable Place of Worship, and to expel its people thence, is a greater with Allah; for persecution is worse than killing. And they will not cease from fighting against you till they have made you renegades from your religion, if they can. And whoso becometh a renegade and dieth in his disbelief: such are they whose works have fallen both in the world and the Hereafter. Such are rightful owners of the Fire: they will abide therein.

218. Lo! those who believe, and those who emigrate (to escape the persecution) and strive in the Way of Allah, these have hope of Allah's mercy. Allah is Forgiving, Merciful.

219. They question thee about strong drink and games of chance. Say: In both is great sin, and (some) utility for men; but the sin of them is greater than their usefulness. And they ask thee what they ought to spend. Say: That which is superfluous. Thus Allah maketh plain to you (His) revelations, that haply ye may reflect—

220. Upon the world and the Hereafter. And they question thee concerning orphans. Say: To improve their lot is best. And if ye mingle your affairs with theirs, then (they are) your brothers. Allah knoweth him who spoileth from him who improveth. Had Allah willed He could have overburdened you. Allah is Mighty, Wise.

كُتِبَ عَلَيْكُمُ الْقِتَالُ وَهُوَ كُرْهٌ لَّكُمْ ۚ وَعَسَىٰ أَن
تَكْرَهُوا شَيْئًا وَهُوَ خَيْرٌ لَّكُمْ ۖ وَعَسَىٰ أَن تُحِبُّوا
ع شَيْئًا وَهُوَ شَرٌّ لَّكُمْ ۗ وَاللَّهُ يَعْلَمُ وَأَنتُمْ لَا تَعْلَمُونَ ﴿٢١٦﴾
يَسْأَلُونَكَ عَنِ الشَّهْرِ الْحَرَامِ قِتَالٍ فِيهِ ۖ قُلْ قِتَالٌ
فِيهِ كَبِيرٌ ۖ وَصَدٌّ عَن سَبِيلِ اللَّهِ وَكُفْرٌ بِهِ وَ
الْمَسْجِدِ الْحَرَامِ وَإِخْرَاجُ أَهْلِهِ مِنْهُ أَكْبَرُ عِندَ
اللَّهِ ۚ وَالْفِتْنَةُ أَكْبَرُ مِنَ الْقَتْلِ ۗ وَلَا يَزَالُونَ يُقَاتِلُونَكُمْ
حَتَّىٰ يَرُدُّوكُمْ عَن دِينِكُمْ إِنِ اسْتَطَاعُوا ۚ وَمَن
يَرْتَدِدْ مِنكُمْ عَن دِينِهِ فَيَمُتْ وَهُوَ كَافِرٌ فَأُولَٰئِكَ
حَبِطَتْ أَعْمَالُهُمْ فِي الدُّنْيَا وَالْآخِرَةِ ۖ وَأُولَٰئِكَ
أَصْحَابُ النَّارِ ۖ هُمْ فِيهَا خَالِدُونَ ﴿٢١٧﴾
إِنَّ الَّذِينَ آمَنُوا وَالَّذِينَ هَاجَرُوا وَجَاهَدُوا فِي
سَبِيلِ اللَّهِ أُولَٰئِكَ يَرْجُونَ رَحْمَتَ اللَّهِ ۚ وَاللَّهُ
غَفُورٌ رَّحِيمٌ ﴿٢١٨﴾
يَسْأَلُونَكَ عَنِ الْخَمْرِ وَالْمَيْسِرِ ۖ قُلْ فِيهِمَا إِثْمٌ
كَبِيرٌ وَمَنَافِعُ لِلنَّاسِ وَإِثْمُهُمَا أَكْبَرُ مِن نَّفْعِهِمَا ۗ
وَيَسْأَلُونَكَ مَاذَا يُنفِقُونَ قُلِ الْعَفْوَ ۗ كَذَٰلِكَ
يُبَيِّنُ اللَّهُ لَكُمُ الْآيَاتِ لَعَلَّكُمْ تَتَفَكَّرُونَ ﴿٢١٩﴾
فِي الدُّنْيَا وَالْآخِرَةِ ۗ وَيَسْأَلُونَكَ عَنِ الْيَتَامَىٰ ۖ قُلْ
إِصْلَاحٌ لَّهُمْ خَيْرٌ ۖ وَإِن تُخَالِطُوهُمْ فَإِخْوَانُكُمْ ۚ وَاللَّهُ
يَعْلَمُ الْمُفْسِدَ مِنَ الْمُصْلِحِ ۚ وَلَوْ شَاءَ اللَّهُ لَأَعْنَتَكُمْ ۚ
إِنَّ اللَّهَ عَزِيزٌ حَكِيمٌ ﴿٢٢٠﴾

221. Wed not idolatresses till they believe; for lo! a believing bondwoman is better than an idolatress though she please you; and give not your daughters in marriage to idolaters till they believe, for lo! a believing slave is better than an idolater though he please you. These invite unto the Fire, and Allah inviteth unto the Garden, and unto forgiveness by His grace, and expoundeth thus His revelations to mankind that haply they may remember.

222. They question thee (O Muhammad) concerning menstruation. Say: It is an illness, so let women alone at such times and go not in unto them till they are cleansed. And when they have purified themselves, then go in unto them as Allah hath enjoined upon you. Truly Allah loveth those who turn unto Him, and loveth those who have a care for cleanness.

223. Your women are a tilth for you (to cultivate) so go to your tilth as ye will, and send (good deeds) before you for your souls, and fear Allah, and know that ye will (one day) meet Him. Give glad tidings to believers, (O Muhammad).

224. And make not Allah, by your oaths, a hindrance to your being righteous and observing your duty unto Him and making peace among mankind. Allah is Hearer, Knower.

225. Allah will not take you to task for that which is unintentional in your oaths. But He will take you to task for that which your hearts have garnered. Allah is Forgiving, Clement.

226. Those who forswear their wives must wait four months; then, if they change their mind, lo! Allah is Forgiving, Merciful.

227. And if they decide upon divorce (let them remember that) Allah is Hearer, Knower.

وَلَا تَنْكِحُوا الْمُشْرِكٰتِ حَتّٰى يُؤْمِنَّ ۚ وَلَاَمَةٌ مُّؤْمِنَةٌ
خَيْرٌ مِّنْ مُّشْرِكَةٍ وَّلَوْ اَعْجَبَتْكُمْ ۚ وَلَا تُنْكِحُوا الْمُشْرِكِيْنَ
حَتّٰى يُؤْمِنُوْا ۚ وَلَعَبْدٌ مُّؤْمِنٌ خَيْرٌ مِّنْ مُّشْرِكٍ وَّلَوْ
اَعْجَبَكُمْ ۚ اُولٰٓئِكَ يَدْعُوْنَ اِلَى النَّارِ ۖ وَاللّٰهُ يَدْعُوْٓا
اِلَى الْجَنَّةِ وَالْمَغْفِرَةِ بِاِذْنِهٖ ۚ وَيُبَيِّنُ اٰيٰتِهٖ لِلنَّاسِ
لَعَلَّهُمْ يَتَذَكَّرُوْنَ ﴿٢٢١﴾ ع ٢٧
وَيَسْـَٔلُوْنَكَ عَنِ الْمَحِيْضِ ۗ قُلْ هُوَ اَذًى ۙ فَاعْتَزِلُوا
النِّسَآءَ فِى الْمَحِيْضِ ۙ وَلَا تَقْرَبُوْهُنَّ حَتّٰى يَطْهُرْنَ ۚ
فَاِذَا تَطَهَّرْنَ فَاْتُوْهُنَّ مِنْ حَيْثُ اَمَرَكُمُ اللّٰهُ ۗ اِنَّ
اللّٰهَ يُحِبُّ التَّوَّابِيْنَ وَيُحِبُّ الْمُتَطَهِّرِيْنَ ﴿٢٢٢﴾
نِسَآؤُكُمْ حَرْثٌ لَّكُمْ ۖ فَاْتُوْا حَرْثَكُمْ اَنّٰى شِئْتُمْ ۖ وَ
قَدِّمُوْا لِاَنْفُسِكُمْ ۚ وَاتَّقُوا اللّٰهَ وَاعْلَمُوْٓا اَنَّكُمْ مُّلٰقُوْهُ ۗ
وَبَشِّرِ الْمُؤْمِنِيْنَ ﴿٢٢٣﴾
وَلَا تَجْعَلُوا اللّٰهَ عُرْضَةً لِّاَيْمَانِكُمْ
اَنْ تَبَرُّوْا وَتَتَّقُوْا وَتُصْلِحُوْا بَيْنَ النَّاسِ ۗ
وَاللّٰهُ سَمِيْعٌ عَلِيْمٌ ﴿٢٢٤﴾
لَا يُؤَاخِذُكُمُ اللّٰهُ بِاللَّغْوِ فِىْٓ اَيْمَانِكُمْ
وَلٰكِنْ يُّؤَاخِذُكُمْ بِمَا كَسَبَتْ قُلُوْبُكُمْ ۗ وَاللّٰهُ
غَفُوْرٌ حَلِيْمٌ ﴿٢٢٥﴾
لِلَّذِيْنَ يُؤْلُوْنَ مِنْ نِّسَآئِهِمْ تَرَبُّصُ اَرْبَعَةِ اَشْهُرٍ ۚ
فَاِنْ فَآءُوْ فَاِنَّ اللّٰهَ غَفُوْرٌ رَّحِيْمٌ ﴿٢٢٦﴾
وَاِنْ عَزَمُوا الطَّلَاقَ فَاِنَّ اللّٰهَ سَمِيْعٌ عَلِيْمٌ ﴿٢٢٧﴾

228. Women who are divorced shall wait, keeping themselves apart, three (monthly) courses. And it is not lawful for them that they should conceal that which Allah hath created in their wombs if they are believers in Allah and the Last Day. And their husbands would do better to take them back in that case if they desire a reconciliation. And they (women) have rights similar to those (of men) over them in kindness, and men are a degree above them. Allah is Mighty, Wise.

وَالْمُطَلَّقٰتُ يَتَرَبَّصْنَ بِاَنْفُسِهِنَّ ثَلٰثَةَ قُرُوْٓءٍ ۭ وَلَا
يَحِلُّ لَهُنَّ اَنْ يَّكْتُمْنَ مَا خَلَقَ اللّٰهُ فِيْٓ اَرْحَامِهِنَّ
اِنْ كُنَّ يُؤْمِنَّ بِاللّٰهِ وَالْيَوْمِ الْاٰخِرِ ۭ وَبُعُوْلَتُهُنَّ اَحَقُّ
بِرَدِّهِنَّ فِيْ ذٰلِكَ اِنْ اَرَادُوْٓا اِصْلَاحًا ۭ وَلَهُنَّ مِثْلُ
الَّذِيْ عَلَيْهِنَّ بِالْمَعْرُوْفِ ۠ وَلِلرِّجَالِ عَلَيْهِنَّ دَرَجَةٌ ۭ
وَاللّٰهُ عَزِيْزٌ حَكِيْمٌ ﴿٢٢٨﴾ ع ٢٨ ١٢

229. Divorce must be pronounced twice and then (a woman) must be retained in honour or released in kindness. And it is not lawful for you that ye take from women aught of that which ye have given them; except (in the case) when both fear that they may not be able to keep within the limits (imposed by) Allah. And if ye fear that they may not be able to keep the limits of Allah, in that case it is no sin for either of them if the woman ransom herself. These are the limits (imposed by) Allah. Transgress them not. For whoso transgresseth Allah's limits: such are wrongdoers.

اَلطَّلَاقُ مَرَّتٰنِ ۠ فَاِمْسَاكٌۢ بِمَعْرُوْفٍ اَوْ تَسْرِيْحٌۢ بِاِحْسَانٍ ۭ
وَلَا يَحِلُّ لَكُمْ اَنْ تَاْخُذُوْا مِمَّآ اٰتَيْتُمُوْھُنَّ شَيْـًٔا اِلَّآ
اَنْ يَّخَافَآ اَلَّا يُقِيْمَا حُدُوْدَ اللّٰهِ ۭ فَاِنْ خِفْتُمْ اَلَّا يُقِيْمَا
حُدُوْدَ اللّٰهِ ۙ فَلَا جُنَاحَ عَلَيْهِمَا فِيْمَا افْتَدَتْ بِهٖ ۭ تِلْكَ
حُدُوْدُ اللّٰهِ فَلَا تَعْتَدُوْھَا ۚ وَمَنْ يَّتَعَدَّ حُدُوْدَ اللّٰهِ
فَاُولٰۗىِٕكَ ھُمُ الظّٰلِمُوْنَ ﴿٢٢٩﴾

230. And if he hath divorced her (the third time), then she is not lawful unto him thereafter until she hath wedded another husband. Then if he (the other husband) divorce her it is no sin for both of them that they come together again if they consider that they are able to observe the limits of Allah. These are the limits of Allah. He manifesteth them for people who have knowledge.

فَاِنْ طَلَّقَهَا فَلَا تَحِلُّ لَهٗ مِنْۢ بَعْدُ حَتّٰى تَنْكِحَ زَوْجًا
غَيْرَهٗ ۭ فَاِنْ طَلَّقَهَا فَلَا جُنَاحَ عَلَيْهِمَآ اَنْ يَّتَرَاجَعَآ
اِنْ ظَنَّآ اَنْ يُّقِيْمَا حُدُوْدَ اللّٰهِ ۭ وَتِلْكَ حُدُوْدُ اللّٰهِ
يُبَيِّنُهَا لِقَوْمٍ يَّعْلَمُوْنَ ﴿٢٣٠﴾

231. When ye have divorced women, and they have reached their term, then retain them in kindness or release them in kindness. Retain them not to their hurt so that ye transgress (the limits). He who doth that hath wronged his soul. Make not the revelations of Allah a laughing-stock (by your behaviour), but remember Allah's grace upon you and that which He hath revealed unto you of the Scripture and of wisdom, whereby He doth exhort you. Observe your duty to Allah and know that Allah is Aware of all things.

وَاِذَا طَلَّقْتُمُ النِّسَاۗءَ فَبَلَغْنَ اَجَلَهُنَّ فَاَمْسِكُوْھُنَّ
بِمَعْرُوْفٍ اَوْ سَرِّحُوْھُنَّ بِمَعْرُوْفٍ ۠ وَلَا تُمْسِكُوْھُنَّ
ضِرَارًا لِّتَعْتَدُوْا ۚ وَمَنْ يَّفْعَلْ ذٰلِكَ فَقَدْ ظَلَمَ نَفْسَهٗ ۭ
وَلَا تَتَّخِذُوْٓا اٰيٰتِ اللّٰهِ ھُزُوًا ۡ وَاذْكُرُوْا نِعْمَتَ اللّٰهِ عَلَيْكُمْ
وَمَآ اَنْزَلَ عَلَيْكُمْ مِّنَ الْكِتٰبِ وَالْحِكْمَةِ يَعِظُكُمْ بِهٖ ۭ
وَاتَّقُوا اللّٰهَ وَاعْلَمُوْٓا اَنَّ اللّٰهَ بِكُلِّ شَيْءٍ عَلِيْمٌ ﴿٢٣١﴾ ع ٢٩ ١٣

232. And when ye have divorced women and they reach their term, place not difficulties in the way of their marrying their husbands if it is agreed between them in kindness. This is an admonition for him among you who believeth in Allah and the Last Day. That is more virtuous for you, and cleaner. Allah knoweth: ye know not.

233. Mothers shall suckle their children for two whole years; (that is) for those who wish to complete the suckling. The duty of feeding and clothing nursing mothers in a seemly manner is upon the father of the child. No one should be charged beyond one's capacity. A mother should not be made to suffer because of her child, nor should he to whom the child is born (be made to suffer) because of his child. And on the (father's) heir is incumbent the like of that (which was incumbent on the father). If they desire to wean the child by mutual consent and (after) consultation, it is no sin for them; and if ye wish to give your children out to nurse, it is no sin for you, provided that ye pay what is due from you in kindness. Observe your duty to Allah, and know that Allah is Seer of what ye do.

234. Such of you as die and leave behind them wives, they (the wives) shall wait, keeping themselves apart, four months and ten days. And when they reach the term (prescribed for them) then there is no sin for you in aught that they may do with themselves in decency. Allah is Informed of what ye do.

235. There is no sin for you in that which ye proclaim or hide in your minds concerning your troth with women. Allah knoweth that ye will remember them. But plight not your troth with women except by uttering a recognised form of words. And do not consummate the marriage until (the term) prescribed is run. Know that Allah knoweth what is in your minds, so beware of Him; and know that Allah is Forgiving, Clement.

وَإِذَا طَلَّقْتُمُ النِّسَاءَ فَبَلَغْنَ أَجَلَهُنَّ فَلَا تَعْضُلُوهُنَّ
أَنْ يَنْكِحْنَ أَزْوَاجَهُنَّ إِذَا تَرَاضَوْا بَيْنَهُمْ بِالْمَعْرُوفِ
ذَٰلِكَ يُوعَظُ بِهِ مَنْ كَانَ مِنْكُمْ يُؤْمِنُ بِاللَّهِ وَالْيَوْمِ
الْآخِرِ ذَٰلِكُمْ أَزْكَىٰ لَكُمْ وَأَطْهَرُ وَاللَّهُ يَعْلَمُ وَأَنْتُمْ لَا تَعْلَمُونَ ﴿٢٣٢﴾
وَالْوَالِدَاتُ يُرْضِعْنَ أَوْلَادَهُنَّ حَوْلَيْنِ كَامِلَيْنِ
لِمَنْ أَرَادَ أَنْ يُتِمَّ الرَّضَاعَةَ وَعَلَى الْمَوْلُودِ لَهُ
رِزْقُهُنَّ وَكِسْوَتُهُنَّ بِالْمَعْرُوفِ لَا تُكَلَّفُ نَفْسٌ
إِلَّا وُسْعَهَا لَا تُضَارَّ وَالِدَةٌ بِوَلَدِهَا وَلَا مَوْلُودٌ
لَهُ بِوَلَدِهِ وَعَلَى الْوَارِثِ مِثْلُ ذَٰلِكَ فَإِنْ أَرَادَا
فِصَالًا عَنْ تَرَاضٍ مِنْهُمَا وَتَشَاوُرٍ فَلَا جُنَاحَ عَلَيْهِمَا
وَإِنْ أَرَدْتُمْ أَنْ تَسْتَرْضِعُوا أَوْلَادَكُمْ فَلَا جُنَاحَ
عَلَيْكُمْ إِذَا سَلَّمْتُمْ مَا آتَيْتُمْ بِالْمَعْرُوفِ وَاتَّقُوا
اللَّهَ وَاعْلَمُوا أَنَّ اللَّهَ بِمَا تَعْمَلُونَ بَصِيرٌ ﴿٢٣٣﴾
وَالَّذِينَ يُتَوَفَّوْنَ مِنْكُمْ وَيَذَرُونَ أَزْوَاجًا يَتَرَبَّصْنَ بِأَنْفُسِهِنَّ
أَرْبَعَةَ أَشْهُرٍ وَعَشْرًا فَإِذَا بَلَغْنَ أَجَلَهُنَّ فَلَا جُنَاحَ عَلَيْكُمْ فِيمَا
فَعَلْنَ فِي أَنْفُسِهِنَّ بِالْمَعْرُوفِ وَاللَّهُ بِمَا تَعْمَلُونَ خَبِيرٌ ﴿٢٣٤﴾
وَلَا جُنَاحَ عَلَيْكُمْ فِيمَا عَرَّضْتُمْ بِهِ مِنْ خِطْبَةِ النِّسَاءِ
أَوْ أَكْنَنْتُمْ فِي أَنْفُسِكُمْ عَلِمَ اللَّهُ أَنَّكُمْ سَتَذْكُرُونَهُنَّ وَ
لَٰكِنْ لَا تُوَاعِدُوهُنَّ سِرًّا إِلَّا أَنْ تَقُولُوا قَوْلًا مَعْرُوفًا
وَلَا تَعْزِمُوا عُقْدَةَ النِّكَاحِ حَتَّىٰ يَبْلُغَ الْكِتَابُ أَجَلَهُ
وَاعْلَمُوا أَنَّ اللَّهَ يَعْلَمُ مَا فِي أَنْفُسِكُمْ فَاحْذَرُوهُ
ع ٣٠ ١٤ وَاعْلَمُوا أَنَّ اللَّهَ غَفُورٌ حَلِيمٌ ﴿٢٣٥﴾

236. It is no sin for you if ye divorce women while yet ye have not touched them, nor appointed unto them a portion. Provide for them, the rich according to his means, and the straitened according to his means, a fair provision. (This is) a bounden duty for those who do good.

لَا جُنَاحَ عَلَيْكُمْ إِنْ طَلَّقْتُمُ النِّسَاءَ مَا لَمْ تَمَسُّوهُنَّ
أَوْ تَفْرِضُوا لَهُنَّ فَرِيضَةً ۚ وَمَتِّعُوهُنَّ عَلَى الْمُوسِعِ
قَدَرُهُ وَعَلَى الْمُقْتِرِ قَدَرُهُ ۚ مَتَاعًا بِالْمَعْرُوفِ ۖ
حَقًّا عَلَى الْمُحْسِنِينَ ﴿٢٣٦﴾

237. If ye divorce them before ye have touched them and ye have appointed unto them a portion, then (pay the) half of that which ye appointed, unless they (the women) agree to forgo it, or he agreeth to forgo it in whose hand is the marriage tie.[1] To forgo is nearer to piety. And forget not kindness among yourselves. Allah is Seer of what ye do.

وَإِنْ طَلَّقْتُمُوهُنَّ مِنْ قَبْلِ أَنْ تَمَسُّوهُنَّ وَقَدْ
فَرَضْتُمْ لَهُنَّ فَرِيضَةً فَنِصْفُ مَا فَرَضْتُمْ إِلَّا أَنْ
يَعْفُونَ أَوْ يَعْفُوَ الَّذِي بِيَدِهِ عُقْدَةُ النِّكَاحِ ۚ وَ
أَنْ تَعْفُوا أَقْرَبُ لِلتَّقْوَىٰ ۚ وَلَا تَنْسَوُا الْفَضْلَ بَيْنَكُمْ ۚ
إِنَّ اللَّهَ بِمَا تَعْمَلُونَ بَصِيرٌ ﴿٢٣٧﴾

238. Be guardians of your prayers, and of the midmost prayer,[2] and stand up with devotion to Allah.

حَافِظُوا عَلَى الصَّلَوَاتِ وَالصَّلَاةِ الْوُسْطَىٰ وَقُومُوا
لِلَّهِ قَانِتِينَ ﴿٢٣٨﴾

239. And if ye go in fear, then (pray) standing or on horseback. And when ye are again in safety, remember Allah, as He hath taught you that which (heretofore) ye knew not.

فَإِنْ خِفْتُمْ فَرِجَالًا أَوْ رُكْبَانًا ۖ فَإِذَا أَمِنْتُمْ فَاذْكُرُوا
اللَّهَ كَمَا عَلَّمَكُمْ مَا لَمْ تَكُونُوا تَعْلَمُونَ ﴿٢٣٩﴾

240. (In the case of) those of you who are about to die and leave behind them wives, they should bequeath unto their wives a provision for the year without turning them out, but if they go out (of their own accord) there is no sin for you in that which they do of themselves within their rights. Allah is Mighty, Wise.

وَالَّذِينَ يُتَوَفَّوْنَ مِنْكُمْ وَيَذَرُونَ أَزْوَاجًا وَصِيَّةً
لِأَزْوَاجِهِمْ مَتَاعًا إِلَى الْحَوْلِ غَيْرَ إِخْرَاجٍ ۚ فَإِنْ
خَرَجْنَ فَلَا جُنَاحَ عَلَيْكُمْ فِي مَا فَعَلْنَ
فِي أَنْفُسِهِنَّ مِنْ مَعْرُوفٍ ۗ وَاللَّهُ عَزِيزٌ
حَكِيمٌ ﴿٢٤٠﴾

241. For divorced women a provision in kindness: a duty for those who ward off (evil).

وَلِلْمُطَلَّقَاتِ مَتَاعٌ بِالْمَعْرُوفِ ۖ حَقًّا عَلَى
الْمُتَّقِينَ ﴿٢٤١﴾

242. Thus Allah expoundeth unto you His revelations so that ye may understand.

كَذَٰلِكَ يُبَيِّنُ اللَّهُ لَكُمْ آيَاتِهِ لَعَلَّكُمْ
تَعْقِلُونَ ﴿٢٤٢﴾ ع

1. *i.e.* the bridegroom.
2. Meaning, probably, the best amid all forms of prayer; but some authorities think the reference is to the 'Asr (afternoon) prayer which Muslim are most apt to forget.

243. Bethink thee (O Muhammad) of those of old, who went forth from their habitations in their thousands, fearing death,[1] and Allah said unto them: Die, and then He brought them back to life. Lo! Allah is the Lord of Kindness to mankind, but most of mankind give not thanks.

244. Fight in the way of Allah, and know that Allah is Hearer, Knower.

245. Who is it that will lend unto Allah a goodly loan,[2] so that He may give it increase manifold? Allah straiteneth and enlargeth. Unto Him ye will return.

246. Bethink thee of the leaders of the Children of Israel after Moses, how they said unto a Prophet whom they had: Set up for us a king and we will fight in Allah's way. He said: Would ye then refrain from fighting if fighting were prescribed for you? They said: Why should we not fight in Allah's way when we have been driven from our dwellings with our children? Yet, when fighting was prescribed for them, they turned away, all save a few of them. Allah is Aware of evil-doers.

247. Their Prophet said unto them: Lo! Allah hath raised up Saul to be a king for you. They said: How can he have kingdom over us when we are more deserving of the kingdom than he is, since he hath not been given wealth enough? He said: Lo! Allah hath chosen him above you, and hath increased him abundantly in wisdom and stature. Allah bestoweth His sovereignty on whom He will. Allah is All-Embracing, All-Knowing.

1. The reference is to the Exodus.
2. A loan without interest—*i.e.* without thought of gain.

أَلَمْ تَرَ إِلَى الَّذِينَ خَرَجُوا مِنْ دِيَارِهِمْ وَهُمْ أُلُوفٌ
حَذَرَ الْمَوْتِ فَقَالَ لَهُمُ اللهُ مُوتُوا ثُمَّ أَحْيَاهُمْ
إِنَّ اللهَ لَذُو فَضْلٍ عَلَى النَّاسِ وَلٰكِنَّ أَكْثَرَ
النَّاسِ لَا يَشْكُرُونَ ﴿٢٤٣﴾
وَقَاتِلُوا فِي سَبِيلِ اللهِ وَاعْلَمُوا أَنَّ اللهَ سَمِيعٌ
عَلِيمٌ ﴿٢٤٤﴾
مَنْ ذَا الَّذِي يُقْرِضُ اللهَ قَرْضًا حَسَنًا فَيُضٰعِفَهُ
لَهُ أَضْعَافًا كَثِيرَةً وَاللهُ يَقْبِضُ وَيَبْصُطُ وَ
إِلَيْهِ تُرْجَعُونَ ﴿٢٤٥﴾
أَلَمْ تَرَ إِلَى الْمَلَإِ مِنْ بَنِي إِسْرَآءِيلَ مِنْ بَعْدِ مُوسٰى وقف لازم
إِذْ قَالُوا لِنَبِيٍّ لَهُمُ ابْعَثْ لَنَا مَلِكًا نُقَاتِلْ فِي سَبِيلِ
اللهِ قَالَ هَلْ عَسَيْتُمْ إِنْ كُتِبَ عَلَيْكُمُ الْقِتَالُ
أَلَّا تُقَاتِلُوا قَالُوا وَمَا لَنَا أَلَّا نُقَاتِلَ فِي سَبِيلِ اللهِ
وَقَدْ أُخْرِجْنَا مِنْ دِيَارِنَا وَأَبْنَآئِنَا فَلَمَّا كُتِبَ
عَلَيْهِمُ الْقِتَالُ تَوَلَّوْا إِلَّا قَلِيلًا مِنْهُمْ وَاللهُ
عَلِيمٌ بِالظّٰلِمِينَ ﴿٢٤٦﴾
وَقَالَ لَهُمْ نَبِيُّهُمْ إِنَّ اللهَ قَدْ بَعَثَ لَكُمْ طَالُوتَ
مَلِكًا قَالُوا أَنّٰى يَكُونُ لَهُ الْمُلْكُ عَلَيْنَا وَنَحْنُ
أَحَقُّ بِالْمُلْكِ مِنْهُ وَلَمْ يُؤْتَ سَعَةً مِنَ الْمَالِ
قَالَ إِنَّ اللهَ اصْطَفٰهُ عَلَيْكُمْ وَزَادَهُ بَسْطَةً فِي
الْعِلْمِ وَالْجِسْمِ وَاللهُ يُؤْتِي مُلْكَهُ مَنْ يَشَآءُ
وَاللهُ وَاسِعٌ عَلِيمٌ ﴿٢٤٧﴾

248. And their Prophet said unto them: Lo! the token of his kingdom is that there shall come unto you the ark wherein is peace of reassurance from your Lord, and a remnant of that which the house of Moses and the house of Aaron left behind, the angels bearing it. Lo! herein shall be a token for you if (in truth) ye are believers.

249. And when Saul set out with the army, he said: Lo! Allah will try you by (the ordeal of) a river. Whosoever therefore drinketh thereof he is not of me, and whosoever tasteth it not he is of me, save him who taketh (thereof) in the hollow of his hand. But they drank thereof, all save a few of them. And after he had crossed (the river), he and those who believed with him, they said: We have no power this day against Goliath and his hosts. But those who knew that they would meet their Lord exclaimed: How many a little company hath overcome a mighty host by Allah's leave! Allah is with the steadfast.

250. And when they went into the field against Goliath and his hosts they said: Our Lord! Bestow on us endurance, make our foothold sure, and give us help against the disbelieving folk.

251. So they routed them by Allah's leave and David slew Goliath; and Allah gave him the kingdom and wisdom, and taught him of that which He willeth. And if Allah had not repelled some men by others the earth would have been corrupted. But Allah is the Lord of Kindness to (His) creatures.

252. These are the portents of Allah which We recite unto thee (Muhammad) with truth, and lo! thou art of a number of (Our) messengers;

وَقَالَ لَهُمْ نَبِيُّهُمْ إِنَّ آيَةَ مُلْكِهِ أَنْ يَأْتِيَكُمُ التَّابُوتُ
فِيهِ سَكِينَةٌ مِنْ رَبِّكُمْ وَبَقِيَّةٌ مِمَّا تَرَكَ آلُ
مُوسَىٰ وَآلُ هَارُونَ تَحْمِلُهُ الْمَلَائِكَةُ ۚ إِنَّ فِي ذَٰلِكَ
لَآيَةً لَكُمْ إِنْ كُنْتُمْ مُؤْمِنِينَ ﴿٢٤٨﴾ ع ٣٢ ١٦
فَلَمَّا فَصَلَ طَالُوتُ بِالْجُنُودِ قَالَ إِنَّ اللَّهَ مُبْتَلِيكُمْ
بِنَهَرٍ فَمَنْ شَرِبَ مِنْهُ فَلَيْسَ مِنِّي وَمَنْ لَمْ
يَطْعَمْهُ فَإِنَّهُ مِنِّي إِلَّا مَنِ اغْتَرَفَ غُرْفَةً بِيَدِهِ ۚ
فَشَرِبُوا مِنْهُ إِلَّا قَلِيلًا مِنْهُمْ ۚ فَلَمَّا جَاوَزَهُ هُوَ
وَالَّذِينَ آمَنُوا مَعَهُ قَالُوا لَا طَاقَةَ لَنَا الْيَوْمَ بِجَالُوتَ
وَجُنُودِهِ ۚ قَالَ الَّذِينَ يَظُنُّونَ أَنَّهُمْ مُلَاقُو اللَّهِ
كَمْ مِنْ فِئَةٍ قَلِيلَةٍ غَلَبَتْ فِئَةً كَثِيرَةً بِإِذْنِ اللَّهِ ۗ
وَاللَّهُ مَعَ الصَّابِرِينَ ﴿٢٤٩﴾
وَلَمَّا بَرَزُوا لِجَالُوتَ وَجُنُودِهِ قَالُوا رَبَّنَا أَفْرِغْ
عَلَيْنَا صَبْرًا وَثَبِّتْ أَقْدَامَنَا وَانْصُرْنَا عَلَى
الْقَوْمِ الْكَافِرِينَ ﴿٢٥٠﴾
فَهَزَمُوهُمْ بِإِذْنِ اللَّهِ وَقَتَلَ دَاوُودُ جَالُوتَ وَ
آتَاهُ اللَّهُ الْمُلْكَ وَالْحِكْمَةَ وَعَلَّمَهُ مِمَّا يَشَاءُ ۗ وَ
لَوْلَا دَفْعُ اللَّهِ النَّاسَ بَعْضَهُمْ بِبَعْضٍ لَفَسَدَتِ
الْأَرْضُ وَلَٰكِنَّ اللَّهَ ذُو فَضْلٍ عَلَى
الْعَالَمِينَ ﴿٢٥١﴾
تِلْكَ آيَاتُ اللَّهِ نَتْلُوهَا عَلَيْكَ بِالْحَقِّ ۚ وَإِنَّكَ لَمِنَ
الْمُرْسَلِينَ ﴿٢٥٢﴾

253. Of those messengers, some of whom We have caused to excel others, and of whom there are some unto whom Allah spake, while some of them He exalted (above others) in degree; and We gave Jesus, son of Mary, clear proofs (of Allah's sovereignty) and We supported him with the holy Spirit.[1] And if Allah had so willed it, those who followed after them would not have fought one with another after the clear proofs had come unto them. But they differed, some of them believing and some disbelieving. And if Allah had so willed it, they would not have fought one with another; but Allah doth what He will.

254. O ye who believe! Spend of that wherewith We have provided you ere a day come when there will be no trafficking, nor friendship, nor intercession. The disbelievers, they are the wrong-doers.

255. Allah! There is no God save Him, the Alive, the Eternal. Neither slumber nor sleep overtaketh Him. Unto Him belongeth whatsoever is in the heavens and whatsoever is in the earth. Who is he that intercedeth with Him save by His leave? He knoweth that which is in front of them and that which is behind them, while they encompass nothing of His knowledge save what He will. His throne includeth the heavens and the earth, and He is never weary of preserving them. He is the Sublime, the Tremendous.

256. There is no compulsion in religion. The right direction is henceforth distinct from error. And he who rejecteth false deities and believeth in Allah hath grasped a firm handhold which will never break. Allah is Hearer, Knower.

257. Allah is the Protecting Friend of those who believe. He bringeth them out of darkness into light. As for those who disbelieve, their patrons are false deities. They bring them out of light into darkness. Such are rightful owners of the Fire. They will abide therein.

1. *i.e.* the angel Gabriel.

تِلْكَ الرُّسُلُ فَضَّلْنَا بَعْضَهُمْ عَلٰى بَعْضٍ مِنْهُمْ
مَنْ كَلَّمَ اللّٰهُ وَرَفَعَ بَعْضَهُمْ دَرَجٰتٍ وَاٰتَيْنَا عِيْسَى
ابْنَ مَرْيَمَ الْبَيِّنٰتِ وَاَيَّدْنٰهُ بِرُوْحِ الْقُدُسِ وَ
لَوْ شَآءَ اللّٰهُ مَا اقْتَتَلَ الَّذِيْنَ مِنْ بَعْدِهِمْ مِنْ
بَعْدِ مَا جَآءَتْهُمُ الْبَيِّنٰتُ وَلٰكِنِ اخْتَلَفُوْا فَمِنْهُمْ مَنْ
اٰمَنَ وَمِنْهُمْ مَنْ كَفَرَ وَلَوْ شَآءَ اللّٰهُ مَا اقْتَتَلُوْا
وَلٰكِنَّ اللّٰهَ يَفْعَلُ مَا يُرِيْدُ ﴿٢٥٣﴾
يٰٓاَيُّهَا الَّذِيْنَ اٰمَنُوْٓا اَنْفِقُوْا مِمَّا رَزَقْنٰكُمْ مِنْ قَبْلِ
اَنْ يَّاْتِيَ يَوْمٌ لَّا بَيْعٌ فِيْهِ وَلَا خُلَّةٌ وَّلَا شَفَاعَةٌ
وَالْكٰفِرُوْنَ هُمُ الظّٰلِمُوْنَ ﴿٢٥٤﴾
اَللّٰهُ لَآ اِلٰهَ اِلَّا هُوَ الْحَيُّ الْقَيُّوْمُ لَا تَاْخُذُهٗ سِنَةٌ
وَّلَا نَوْمٌ لَهٗ مَا فِي السَّمٰوٰتِ وَمَا فِي الْاَرْضِ مَنْ
ذَا الَّذِيْ يَشْفَعُ عِنْدَهٗٓ اِلَّا بِاِذْنِهٖ يَعْلَمُ مَا بَيْنَ
اَيْدِيْهِمْ وَمَا خَلْفَهُمْ وَلَا يُحِيْطُوْنَ بِشَيْءٍ مِّنْ
عِلْمِهٖٓ اِلَّا بِمَا شَآءَ وَسِعَ كُرْسِيُّهُ السَّمٰوٰتِ وَالْاَرْضَ
وَلَا يَـُٔوْدُهٗ حِفْظُهُمَا وَهُوَ الْعَلِيُّ الْعَظِيْمُ ﴿٢٥٥﴾
لَآ اِكْرَاهَ فِي الدِّيْنِ قَدْ تَّبَيَّنَ الرُّشْدُ مِنَ الْغَيِّ
فَمَنْ يَّكْفُرْ بِالطَّاغُوْتِ وَيُؤْمِنْ بِاللّٰهِ فَقَدِ اسْتَمْسَكَ
بِالْعُرْوَةِ الْوُثْقٰى لَا انْفِصَامَ لَهَا وَاللّٰهُ سَمِيْعٌ عَلِيْمٌ ﴿٢٥٦﴾
اَللّٰهُ وَلِيُّ الَّذِيْنَ اٰمَنُوْا يُخْرِجُهُمْ مِّنَ الظُّلُمٰتِ اِلَى النُّوْرِ
وَالَّذِيْنَ كَفَرُوْٓا اَوْلِيٰٓـُٔهُمُ الطَّاغُوْتُ يُخْرِجُوْنَهُمْ مِّنَ
النُّوْرِ اِلَى الظُّلُمٰتِ اُولٰٓئِكَ اَصْحٰبُ النَّارِ هُمْ فِيْهَا خٰلِدُوْنَ ﴿٢٥٧﴾

258. Bethink thee of him who had an argument with Abraham about his Lord, because Allah had given him the kingdom; how, when Abraham said: My Lord is He who giveth life and causeth death, he answered: I give life and cause death. Abraham said: Lo! Allah causeth the sun to rise in the East, so do thou cause it to come up from the West. Thus was the disbeliever abashed. And Allah guideth not wrong-doing folk.

259. Or (bethink thee of) the like of him who, passing by a township which had fallen into utter ruin, exclaimed: How shall Allah give this township[1] life after its death? And Allah made him die a hundred years, then brought him back to life. He said: How long hast thou tarried? (The man) said: I have tarried a day or part of a day. (He) said: Nay, but thou hast tarried for a hundred years. Just look at thy food and drink which have rotted! Look at thine ass! And, that We may make thee a token unto mankind, look at the bones, how We adjust them and then cover them with flesh! And when (the matter) became clear unto him, he said: I know now that Allah is Able to do all things.

260. And when Abraham said (unto his Lord): My Lord! Show me how Thou givest life to the dead, He said: Dost thou not believe? Abraham said: Yea, but (I ask) in order that my heart may be at ease. (His Lord) said: Take four of the birds and cause them to incline unto thee, then place a part of them on each hill, then call them, they will come to thee in haste. And know that Allah is Mighty, Wise.

261. The likeness of those who spend their wealth in Allah's way is as the likeness of a grain which groweth seven ears, in every ear a hundred grains. Allah giveth increase manifold to whom He will. Allah is All-Embracing, All-Knowing.

الم تر إلى الذي حاج إبرهم في ربه أن اتىه
الله الملك إذ قال إبرهم ربي الذي يحي ويميت
قال أنا أحي وأميت قال إبرهم فإن الله يأتي
بالشمس من المشرق فأت بها من المغرب
فبهت الذي كفر والله لا يهدي القوم الظلمين ﴿٢٥٨﴾
أو كالذي مر على قرية وهي خاوية على عروشها
قال أنى يحي هذه الله بعد موتها فأماته الله
مائة عام ثم بعثه قال كم لبثت قال لبثت
يوما أو بعض يوم قال بل لبثت مائة عام
فانظر إلى طعامك وشرابك لم يتسنه وانظر
إلى حمارك ولنجعلك اية للناس وانظر إلى العظام
كيف ننشزها ثم نكسوها لحما فلما تبين له
قال أعلم أن الله على كل شيء قدير ﴿٢٥٩﴾
وإذ قال إبرهم رب أرني كيف تحي الموتى قال
أولم تؤمن قال بلى ولكن ليطمئن قلبي قال
فخذ أربعة من الطير فصرهن إليك ثم
اجعل على كل جبل منهن جزءا ثم ادعهن
يأتينك سعيا واعلم أن الله عزيز حكيم ﴿٢٦٠﴾
مثل الذين ينفقون أمولهم في سبيل الله كمثل
حبة أنبتت سبع سنابل في كل سنبلة مائة حبة
والله يضعف لمن يشاء والله وسع
عليم ﴿٢٦١﴾

1. Most of the commentators agree that the reference here is to Jerusalem in ruins, while the following words tell of the vision of Ezekiel.

262. Those who spend their wealth for the cause of Allah and afterward make not reproach and injury to follow that which they have spent; their reward is with their Lord, and there shall no fear come upon them, neither shall they grieve

اَلَّذِيْنَ يُنْفِقُوْنَ اَمْوَالَهُمْ فِيْ سَبِيْلِ اللّٰهِ ثُمَّ لَا
يُتْبِعُوْنَ مَآ اَنْفَقُوْا مَنًّا وَّلَآ اَذًى لَّهُمْ اَجْرُهُمْ
عِنْدَ رَبِّهِمْ ۚ وَلَا خَوْفٌ عَلَيْهِمْ وَلَا هُمْ
يَحْزَنُوْنَ ﴿٢٦٢﴾

263. A kind word with forgiveness is better than almsgiving followed by injury. Allah is Absolute, Clement.

قَوْلٌ مَّعْرُوْفٌ وَّمَغْفِرَةٌ خَيْرٌ مِّنْ صَدَقَةٍ يَّتْبَعُهَآ
اَذًى ۭ وَاللّٰهُ غَنِيٌّ حَلِيْمٌ ﴿٢٦٣﴾

264. O ye who believe! Render not vain your almsgiving by reproach and injury, like him who spendeth his wealth only to be seen of men and believeth not in Allah and the Last Day. His likeness is as the likeness of a rock whereon is dust of earth; a rainstorm smiteth it, leaving it smooth and bare. They have no control of aught of that which they have gained. Allah guideth not the disbelieving folk.

يٰٓاَيُّهَا الَّذِيْنَ اٰمَنُوْا لَا تُبْطِلُوْا صَدَقٰتِكُمْ بِالْمَنِّ وَ
الْاَذٰى ۙ كَالَّذِيْ يُنْفِقُ مَالَهٗ رِئَاۗءَ النَّاسِ وَلَا
يُؤْمِنُ بِاللّٰهِ وَالْيَوْمِ الْاٰخِرِ ۭ فَمَثَلُهٗ كَمَثَلِ صَفْوَانٍ
عَلَيْهِ تُرَابٌ فَاَصَابَهٗ وَابِلٌ فَتَرَكَهٗ صَلْدًا ۭ لَا
يَقْدِرُوْنَ عَلٰي شَيْءٍ مِّمَّا كَسَبُوْا ۭ وَاللّٰهُ لَا يَهْدِي
الْقَوْمَ الْكٰفِرِيْنَ ﴿٢٦٤﴾

265. And the likeness of those who spend their wealth in search of Allah's pleasure, and for the strengthening of their souls, is as the likeness of a garden on a height. The rainstorm smiteth it and it bringeth forth its fruit twofold. And if the rainstorm smite it not, then the shower. Allah is Seer of what ye do.

وَمَثَلُ الَّذِيْنَ يُنْفِقُوْنَ اَمْوَالَهُمُ ابْتِغَاۗءَ مَرْضَاتِ
اللّٰهِ وَتَثْبِيْتًا مِّنْ اَنْفُسِهِمْ كَمَثَلِ جَنَّةٍۢ بِرَبْوَةٍ
اَصَابَهَا وَابِلٌ فَاٰتَتْ اُكُلَهَا ضِعْفَيْنِ ۚ فَاِنْ لَّمْ
يُصِبْهَا وَابِلٌ فَطَلٌّ ۭ وَاللّٰهُ بِمَا تَعْمَلُوْنَ
بَصِيْرٌ ﴿٢٦٥﴾

266. Would any of you like to have a garden of palm-trees and vines, with rivers flowing underneath it, with all kinds of fruit for him therein; and old age hath stricken him and he hath feeble offspring; and a fiery whirlwind striketh it and it is (all) consumed by fire. Thus Allah maketh plain His revelations unto you, in order that ye may give thought.

اَيَوَدُّ اَحَدُكُمْ اَنْ تَكُوْنَ لَهٗ جَنَّةٌ مِّنْ نَّخِيْلٍ وَّ
اَعْنَابٍ تَجْرِيْ مِنْ تَحْتِهَا الْاَنْهٰرُ ۙ لَهٗ فِيْهَا مِنْ كُلِّ
الثَّمَرٰتِ ۙ وَاَصَابَهُ الْكِبَرُ وَلَهٗ ذُرِّيَّةٌ ضُعَفَاۗءُ ښ
فَاَصَابَهَآ اِعْصَارٌ فِيْهِ نَارٌ فَاحْتَرَقَتْ ۭ كَذٰلِكَ يُبَيِّنُ
اللّٰهُ لَكُمُ الْاٰيٰتِ لَعَلَّكُمْ تَتَفَكَّرُوْنَ ﴿٢٦٦﴾ ع

267. O ye who believe! Spend of the good things which ye have earned, and of that which We bring forth from the earth for you, and seek not the bad (with intent) to spend thereof (in charity) when ye would not take it for yourselves save with disdain; and know that Allah is Absolute Owner of Praise.

268. The devil promiseth you destitution and enjoineth on you lewdness. But Allah promiseth you forgiveness from Himself with bounty. Allah is All-Embracing. All-Knowing.

269. He giveth wisdom unto whom He will, and he unto whom wisdom is given, he truly hath received abundant good. But none remember except men of understanding.

270. Whatever alms ye spend or vow ye vow, lo! Allah knoweth it. Wrong-doers have no helpers.

271. If ye publish your almsgiving, it is well, but if ye hide it and give it to the poor, it will be better for you, and will atone for some of your ill-deeds. Allah is Informed of what ye do.

272. The guiding of them is not thy duty (O Muhammad), but Allah guideth whom He will. And whatsoever good thing ye spend, it is for yourselves, when ye spend not save in search of Allah's countenance; and whatsoever good thing ye spend, it will be repaid to you in full, and ye will not be wronged.

273. (Alms are) for the poor who are straitened for the cause of Allah, who cannot travel in the land (for trade). The unthinking man accounteth them wealthy because of their restraint. Thou shalt know them by their mark: They do not beg of men with importunity. And whatsoever good thing ye spend, lo! Allah knoweth it.

يٰٓاَيُّهَا الَّذِيْنَ اٰمَنُوْٓا اَنْفِقُوْا مِنْ طَيِّبٰتِ مَا كَسَبْتُمْ وَ
مِمَّآ اَخْرَجْنَا لَكُمْ مِّنَ الْاَرْضِ ۪ وَلَا تَيَمَّمُوا الْخَبِيْثَ
مِنْهُ تُنْفِقُوْنَ وَلَسْتُمْ بِاٰخِذِيْهِ اِلَّآ اَنْ تُغْمِضُوْا
فِيْهِ ؕ وَاعْلَمُوْٓا اَنَّ اللّٰهَ غَنِيٌّ حَمِيْدٌ ﴿٢٦٧﴾
اَلشَّيْطٰنُ يَعِدُكُمُ الْفَقْرَ وَيَاْمُرُكُمْ بِالْفَحْشَآءِ ۚ وَاللّٰهُ
يَعِدُكُمْ مَّغْفِرَةً مِّنْهُ وَفَضْلًا ؕ وَاللّٰهُ وَاسِعٌ عَلِيْمٌ ۖۙ ﴿٢٦٨﴾
يُّؤْتِي الْحِكْمَةَ مَنْ يَّشَآءُ ۚ وَمَنْ يُّؤْتَ الْحِكْمَةَ فَقَدْ
اُوْتِيَ خَيْرًا كَثِيْرًا ؕ وَمَا يَذَّكَّرُ اِلَّآ اُولُوا الْاَلْبَابِ ﴿٢٦٩﴾
وَمَآ اَنْفَقْتُمْ مِّنْ نَّفَقَةٍ اَوْ نَذَرْتُمْ مِّنْ نَّذْرٍ فَاِنَّ
اللّٰهَ يَعْلَمُهٗ ؕ وَمَا لِلظّٰلِمِيْنَ مِنْ اَنْصَارٍ ﴿٢٧٠﴾
اِنْ تُبْدُوا الصَّدَقٰتِ فَنِعِمَّا هِيَ ۚ وَاِنْ تُخْفُوْهَا وَ
تُؤْتُوْهَا الْفُقَرَآءَ فَهُوَ خَيْرٌ لَّكُمْ ؕ وَيُكَفِّرُ عَنْكُمْ مِّنْ سَيِّاٰتِكُمْ ؕ
وَاللّٰهُ بِمَا تَعْمَلُوْنَ خَبِيْرٌ ﴿٢٧١﴾
لَيْسَ عَلَيْكَ هُدٰىهُمْ وَلٰكِنَّ اللّٰهَ يَهْدِيْ مَنْ يَّشَآءُ ؕ
وَمَا تُنْفِقُوْا مِنْ خَيْرٍ فَلِاَنْفُسِكُمْ ؕ وَمَا تُنْفِقُوْنَ اِلَّا
ابْتِغَآءَ وَجْهِ اللّٰهِ ؕ وَمَا تُنْفِقُوْا مِنْ خَيْرٍ يُّوَفَّ اِلَيْكُمْ
وَاَنْتُمْ لَا تُظْلَمُوْنَ ﴿٢٧٢﴾
لِلْفُقَرَآءِ الَّذِيْنَ اُحْصِرُوْا فِيْ سَبِيْلِ اللّٰهِ لَا
يَسْتَطِيْعُوْنَ ضَرْبًا فِي الْاَرْضِ ؗ يَحْسَبُهُمُ الْجَاهِلُ
اَغْنِيَآءَ مِنَ التَّعَفُّفِ ۚ تَعْرِفُهُمْ بِسِيْمٰهُمْ ۚ لَا يَسْـَٔلُوْنَ
النَّاسَ اِلْحَافًا ؕ وَمَا تُنْفِقُوْا مِنْ خَيْرٍ فَاِنَّ اللّٰهَ بِهٖ
عَلِيْمٌ ﴿٢٧٣﴾ ع

274. Those who spend their wealth by night and day, by stealth and openly, verily their reward is with their Lord, and there shall no fear come upon them neither shall they grieve.

الذين ينفقون اموالهم بالليل والنهار سرا و
علانية فلهم اجرهم عند ربهم ولا خوف
عليهم ولا هم يحزنون ٢٧٤

275. Those who swallow usury cannot rise up save as he ariseth whom the devil hath prostrated by (his) touch. That is because they say: Trade is just like usury; whereas Allah permitteth trading and forbiddeth usury. He unto whom an admonition from his Lord cometh, and (he) refraineth (in obedience thereto), he shall keep (the profits of) that which is past, and his affair (henceforth) is with Allah. As for him who returneth (to usury)—Such are rightful owners of the Fire. They will abide therein.

الذين ياكلون الربوا لا يقومون الا كما يقوم الذي
يتخبطه الشيطن من المس ذلك بانهم قالوا انما
البيع مثل الربوا واحل الله البيع وحرم الربوا
فمن جاءه موعظة من ربه فانتهى فله ما سلف
وامره الى الله ومن عاد فاولئك اصحب النار
هم فيها خلدون ٢٧٥

276. Allah hath blighted usury and made almsgiving fruitful. Allah loveth not the impious and guilty.

يمحق الله الربوا ويربي الصدقت والله لا
يحب كل كفار اثيم ٢٧٦

277. Lo! those who believe and do good works and establish worship and pay the poor-due, their reward is with their Lord and there shall no fear come upon them neither shall they grieve.

ان الذين امنوا وعملوا الصلحت واقاموا
الصلوة واتوا الزكوة لهم اجرهم عند ربهم و
لا خوف عليهم ولا هم يحزنون ٢٧٧

278. O ye who believe! Observe your duty to Allah, and give up what remaineth (due to you) from usury, if ye are (in truth) believers.

يايها الذين امنوا اتقوا الله وذروا ما بقي من
الربوا ان كنتم مؤمنين ٢٧٨

279. And if ye do not, then be warned of war (against you) from Allah and His messenger. And if ye repent, then ye have your principal (without interest). Wrong not, and ye shall not be wronged.

فان لم تفعلوا فاذنوا بحرب من الله ورسوله
وان تبتم فلكم رءوس اموالكم لا تظلمون ولا تظلمون ٢٧٩

280. And if the debtor is in straitened circumstances, then (let there be) postponement to (the time of) ease; and that ye remit the debt as almsgiving would be better for you if ye did but know.

وان كان ذو عسرة فنظرة الى ميسرة وان
تصدقوا خير لكم ان كنتم تعلمون ٢٨٠

281. And guard yourselves against a day in which ye will be brought back to Allah. Then every soul will be paid in full that which it hath earned, and they will not be wronged.

واتقوا يوما ترجعون فيه الى الله ثم توفى
كل نفس ما كسبت وهم لا يظلمون ٢٨١

282. O ye who believe! When ye contract a debt for a fixed term, record it in writing. Let a scribe record it in writing between you in (terms of) equity. No scribe should refuse to write as Allah hath taught him, so let him write, and let him who incurreth the debt dictate, and let him observe his duty to Allah his Lord, and diminish naught thereof. But if he who oweth the debt is of low understanding, or weak, or unable himself to dictate, then let the guardian of his interests dictate in (terms of) equity. And call to witness, from among your men, two witnesses. And if two men be not (at hand) then a man and two women, of such as ye approve as witnesses, so that if the one erreth (through forgetfulness) the other will remember. And the witnesses must not refuse when they are summoned. Be not averse to writing down (the contract) whether it be small or great, with (record of) the term thereof. That is more equitable in the sight of Allah and more sure for testimony, and the best way of avoiding doubt between you; save only in the case when it is actual merchandise which ye transfer among yourselves from hand to hand. In that case it is no sin for you if ye write it not. And have witnesses when ye sell one to another, and let no harm be done to scribe or witness. If ye do (harm to them) lo! it is a sin in you. Observe your duty to Allah. Allah is teaching you. And Allah is Knower of all things.

283. If ye be on a journey and cannot find a scribe, then a pledge in hand (shall suffice). And if one of you entrusteth to another let him who is trusted deliver up that which is entrusted to him (according to the pact between them) and let him observe his duty to Allah. Hide not testimony. He who hideth it, verily his heart is sinful. Allah is Aware of what ye do.

يٰٓاَيُّهَا الَّذِيْنَ اٰمَنُوْٓا اِذَا تَدَايَنْتُمْ بِدَيْنٍ اِلٰٓى اَجَلٍ
مُّسَمًّى فَاكْتُبُوْهُ ۭ وَلْيَكْتُبْ بَّيْنَكُمْ كَاتِبٌۢ بِالْعَدْلِ ۠ وَ
لَا يَاْبَ كَاتِبٌ اَنْ يَّكْتُبَ كَمَا عَلَّمَهُ اللّٰهُ فَلْيَكْتُبْ ۚ
وَلْيُمْلِلِ الَّذِيْ عَلَيْهِ الْحَقُّ وَلْيَتَّقِ اللّٰهَ رَبَّهٗ وَلَا
يَبْخَسْ مِنْهُ شَيْـًٔا ۭ فَاِنْ كَانَ الَّذِيْ عَلَيْهِ الْحَقُّ سَفِيْهًا
اَوْ ضَعِيْفًا اَوْ لَا يَسْتَطِيْعُ اَنْ يُّمِلَّ ھُوَ فَلْيُمْلِلْ وَلِيُّهٗ
بِالْعَدْلِ ۭ وَاسْتَشْهِدُوْا شَهِيْدَيْنِ مِنْ رِّجَالِكُمْ ۚ
فَاِنْ لَّمْ يَكُوْنَا رَجُلَيْنِ فَرَجُلٌ وَّامْرَاَتٰنِ مِمَّنْ تَرْضَوْنَ
مِنَ الشُّهَدَاۗءِ اَنْ تَضِلَّ اِحْدٰىهُمَا فَتُذَكِّرَ اِحْدٰىهُمَا
الْاُخْرٰى ۭ وَلَا يَاْبَ الشُّهَدَاۗءُ اِذَا مَا دُعُوْا ۭ وَلَا تَسْـَٔمُوْٓا
اَنْ تَكْتُبُوْهُ صَغِيْرًا اَوْ كَبِيْرًا اِلٰٓى اَجَلِهٖ ۭ ذٰلِكُمْ اَقْسَطُ
عِنْدَ اللّٰهِ وَاَقْوَمُ لِلشَّهَادَةِ وَاَدْنٰٓى اَلَّا تَرْتَابُوْٓا اِلَّآ
اَنْ تَكُوْنَ تِجَارَةً حَاضِرَةً تُدِيْرُوْنَهَا بَيْنَكُمْ فَلَيْسَ
عَلَيْكُمْ جُنَاحٌ اَلَّا تَكْتُبُوْھَا ۭ وَاَشْهِدُوْٓا اِذَا تَبَايَعْتُمْ ۠
وَلَا يُضَاۗرَّ كَاتِبٌ وَّلَا شَهِيْدٌ ڛ وَاِنْ تَفْعَلُوْا فَاِنَّهٗ
فُسُوْقٌۢ بِكُمْ ۭ وَاتَّقُوا اللّٰهَ ۭ وَيُعَلِّمُكُمُ اللّٰهُ ۭ وَاللّٰهُ
بِكُلِّ شَيْءٍ عَلِيْمٌ ٢٨٢
وَاِنْ كُنْتُمْ عَلٰي سَفَرٍ وَّلَمْ تَجِدُوْا كَاتِبًا فَرِھٰنٌ
مَّقْبُوْضَةٌ ۭ فَاِنْ اَمِنَ بَعْضُكُمْ بَعْضًا فَلْيُؤَدِّ الَّذِي
اؤْتُمِنَ اَمَانَتَهٗ وَلْيَتَّقِ اللّٰهَ رَبَّهٗ ۭ وَلَا تَكْتُمُوا
الشَّهَادَةَ ۭ وَمَنْ يَّكْتُمْهَا فَاِنَّهٗٓ اٰثِمٌ قَلْبُهٗ ۭ وَاللّٰهُ بِمَا
تَعْمَلُوْنَ عَلِيْمٌ ٢٨٣ ع ٣٩ ع ٧

284. Unto Allah (belongeth) whatsoever is in the heavens and whatsoever is in the earth; and whether ye make known what is in your minds or hide it, Allah will bring you to account for it. He will forgive whom He will and He will punish whom He will. Allah is Able to do all things.

285. The messenger believeth in that which hath been revealed unto him from his Lord and (so do) the believers. Each one believeth in Allah and His angels and His scriptures and His messengers—We make no distinction between any of His messengers—and they say: We hear, and we obey. (Grant us) Thy forgiveness, our Lord! Unto Thee is the journeying.

286. Allah tasketh not a soul beyond its scope. For it (is only) that which it hath earned, and against it (only) that which it hath deserved. Our Lord! Condemn us not if we forget, or miss the mark! Our Lord! Lay not on us such a burden as Thou didst lay on those before us! Our Lord! Impose not on us that which we have not the strength to bear! Pardon us, absolve us and have mercy on us! Thou, our Protector, and give us victory over the disbelieving folk.

لِلّٰهِ مَا فِي السَّمٰوٰتِ وَمَا فِي الْاَرْضِ ؕ وَاِنْ تُبْدُوْا
مَا فِيْٓ اَنْفُسِكُمْ اَوْ تُخْفُوْهُ يُحَاسِبْكُمْ بِهِ اللّٰهُ ؕ فَيَغْفِرُ
لِمَنْ يَّشَآءُ وَيُعَذِّبُ مَنْ يَّشَآءُ ؕ وَاللّٰهُ عَلٰى كُلِّ
شَيْءٍ قَدِيْرٌ ﴿۲۸۴﴾
اٰمَنَ الرَّسُوْلُ بِمَآ اُنْزِلَ اِلَيْهِ مِنْ رَّبِّهٖ وَ
الْمُؤْمِنُوْنَ ؕ كُلٌّ اٰمَنَ بِاللّٰهِ وَمَلٰٓئِكَتِهٖ وَكُتُبِهٖ وَرُسُلِهٖ ۟
لَا نُفَرِّقُ بَيْنَ اَحَدٍ مِّنْ رُّسُلِهٖ ۟ وَقَالُوْا سَمِعْنَا وَ
اَطَعْنَا ۫ غُفْرَانَكَ رَبَّنَا وَاِلَيْكَ الْمَصِيْرُ ﴿۲۸۵﴾
لَا يُكَلِّفُ اللّٰهُ نَفْسًا اِلَّا وُسْعَهَا ؕ لَهَا مَا كَسَبَتْ وَعَلَيْهَا
مَا اكْتَسَبَتْ ؕ رَبَّنَا لَا تُؤَاخِذْنَآ اِنْ نَّسِيْنَآ اَوْ اَخْطَاْنَا ۚ
رَبَّنَا وَلَا تَحْمِلْ عَلَيْنَآ اِصْرًا كَمَا حَمَلْتَهٗ عَلَى الَّذِيْنَ
مِنْ قَبْلِنَا ۚ رَبَّنَا وَلَا تُحَمِّلْنَا مَا لَا طَاقَةَ لَنَا بِهٖ ۚ وَ
اعْفُ عَنَّا ۫ وَاغْفِرْ لَنَا ۫ وَارْحَمْنَا ۫ اَنْتَ مَوْلٰىنَا
فَانْصُرْنَا عَلَى الْقَوْمِ الْكٰفِرِيْنَ ﴿۲۸۶﴾ ع

Āli 'Imrān takes its title from v. 32, where "the family of 'Imrān" (the father of Moses) occurs as a generic name for all the Hebrew prophets from Moses to John the Baptist and Jesus Christ. This, with the mention of the mother of Mary as "the wife of 'Imrān" (v. 34), and the words "sister of Aaron" addressed to Mary (XIX, 28), have given rise to a charge of anachronism—absurd because the whole of the rest of the Koran is against it—by Muir and other non-Muslim writers, who say that the Prophet confused Mary, the mother of Jesus, with Miriam, the sister of Moses. Most Muslims believe, on the authority of the Koran, that the grandfather of Jesus Christ was named 'Imrān, which may also have been the name of the father of Moses. In Sūrah, xix. 28, where Mary is addressed as "sister of Aaron," they hold the ancestral sense to be the more probable, while denying that there is any reason to suppose that the Virgin Mary had not a brother named Aaron.

If vv. 1 to 32 were, as tradition states, revealed on the occasion of the deputation from the Christians of Najrān, which took place in the tenth year of the Hijrah ("the year of deputations," as it is called), then they are of much later date than the rest of the Sūrah, but it seems possible that they were only recited by the Prophet on that occasion, having been revealed before.

The Jews have become bolder and more bitter in opposition which, as Nöldeke points out, cannot have been the case, after the signal victory of Badr, until after the Muslims suffered a reverse at Uḥud; a battle to which vv. 120 to 188 largely refer.

In the third year of the Hijrah the Meccans came against Al-Madînah, with an army of 3000 men to avenge their defeat at Badr in the previous year, and to wipe out the Muslims. The Prophet, against his own first plan, which was to defend Al-Madînah, at the instance of his companions, went out to meet them on Mt. Uḥud, posting his men carefully. He led an army of 1000 men, a third of whom under Abdullah ibn Ubeyy (the "Hypocrite" leader) deserted him before the battle, and said afterwards that they did not think there would be any fighting that day. The battle began well for the Muslims but was changed to something near defeat by the disobedience of a band of fifty archers placed to guard a certain point. Seeing the Muslims winning, they feared that they might lose their share of the spoils, and ran to join the others leaving a way open for the Meccan cavalry. The idolaters then rallied and inflicted considerable loss upon the Muslims, the Prophet himself being wounded in the struggle. A cry arose that the Prophet had been slain, and the Muslims were in despair till someone recognized the Prophet and cried out that he was living. The Muslims then rallied to his side, and retired in some sort of order. The army of Qureysh also retired after the battle.

In this battle the wives of the leaders of Qureysh, who had been brought with the army to give courage by their presence and their chanting, mutilated the Muslim slain, making necklaces and bracelets of ears and noses. Hind, the wife of Abū Sufyān, plucked out the liver of the Prophet's uncle, Hamzah, publicly, and tried to eat it. The Prophet, when he saw the condition of the slain, was moved to vow reprisals. But he was relieved of his vow by a revelation, and mutilation was forbidden to the Muslims.

On the day after the battle of Mt. Uḥud, the Prophet again went out with such of the army as survived, in order that Qureysh might hear that he was in the field and haply be deterred from any project of attacking Al-Madînah in its weakened state. On that occasion many wounded men went out with him. Tradition tells how a friendly nomad met the Muslims and afterwards met the army of Qureysh. Questioned by Abū Sufyān, he said that the Prophet was seeking vengeance with an overwhelming force; and that report determined Abū Sufyān to march back to Mecca.

The period of revelation is the third and fourth years of the Hijrah.

THE FAMILY OF 'IMRĀN

Revealed at Al-Madînah

In the name of Allah, the Beneficent, the Merciful.

1. Alif. Lām. Mîm.[1]

2. Allah! There is no God save Him, the Alive, the Eternal.

3. He hath revealed unto thee (Muhammad) the Scripture with truth, confirming that which was (revealed) before it, even as He revealed the Torah and the Gospel:

4. Aforetime, for a guidance to mankind; and hath revealed the Criterion (of right and wrong). Lo! those who disbelieve the revelations of Allah, theirs will be a heavy doom. Allah is Mighty, Able to Requite (the wrong).

5. Lo! nothing in the earth or in the heavens is hidden from Allah.

6. He it is who fashioneth you in the wombs as pleaseth Him. There is no God save Him, the Almighty, the Wise.

7. He it is Who hath revealed unto thee (Muhammad) the Scripture wherein are clear revelations—They are the substance of the Book—and others (which are) allegorical. But those in whose hearts is doubt pursue, forsooth, that which is allegorical seeking (to cause) dissension by seeking to explain it. None knoweth its explanation save Allah. And those who are of sound instruction say: We believe therein; the whole is from our Lord; but only men of understanding really heed.

8. Our Lord! Cause not our hearts to stray after Thou hast guided us, and bestow upon us mercy from Thy Presence. Lo! Thou, only Thou art the Bestower.

1. See Sūrah II, v. 1, footnote.

اٰياتها (٢٠٠) سُورَةُ اٰلِ عِمْرٰنَ مَدَنِيَّةٌ رُكُوعَاتُها (٢٠)

بِسْمِ اللّٰهِ الرَّحْمٰنِ الرَّحِيْمِ

الٓمّٓ ۝١

اَللّٰهُ لَآ اِلٰهَ اِلَّا هُوَ الْحَيُّ الْقَيُّوْمُ ۝٢

نَزَّلَ عَلَيْكَ الْكِتٰبَ بِالْحَقِّ مُصَدِّقًا لِّمَا بَيْنَ يَدَيْهِ

وَاَنْزَلَ التَّوْرٰىةَ وَالْاِنْجِيْلَ ۝٣

مِنْ قَبْلُ هُدًى لِّلنَّاسِ وَاَنْزَلَ الْفُرْقَانَ

اِنَّ الَّذِيْنَ كَفَرُوْا بِاٰيٰتِ اللّٰهِ لَهُمْ عَذَابٌ شَدِيْدٌ

وَاللّٰهُ عَزِيْزٌ ذُو انْتِقَامٍ ۝٤

اِنَّ اللّٰهَ لَا يَخْفٰى عَلَيْهِ شَيْءٌ فِي الْاَرْضِ وَلَا

فِي السَّمَآءِ ۝٥

هُوَ الَّذِيْ يُصَوِّرُكُمْ فِي الْاَرْحَامِ كَيْفَ يَشَآءُ لَآ

اِلٰهَ اِلَّا هُوَ الْعَزِيْزُ الْحَكِيْمُ ۝٦

هُوَ الَّذِيْٓ اَنْزَلَ عَلَيْكَ الْكِتٰبَ مِنْهُ اٰيٰتٌ مُّحْكَمٰتٌ

هُنَّ اُمُّ الْكِتٰبِ وَاُخَرُ مُتَشٰبِهٰتٌ فَاَمَّا الَّذِيْنَ فِيْ

قُلُوْبِهِمْ زَيْغٌ فَيَتَّبِعُوْنَ مَا تَشَابَهَ مِنْهُ ابْتِغَآءَ

الْفِتْنَةِ وَابْتِغَآءَ تَاْوِيْلِهٖ وَمَا يَعْلَمُ تَاْوِيْلَهٗٓ اِلَّا اللّٰهُ

وَالرّٰسِخُوْنَ فِي الْعِلْمِ يَقُوْلُوْنَ اٰمَنَّا بِهٖ كُلٌّ مِّنْ

عِنْدِ رَبِّنَا وَمَا يَذَّكَّرُ اِلَّآ اُولُوا الْاَلْبَابِ ۝٧

رَبَّنَا لَا تُزِغْ قُلُوْبَنَا بَعْدَ اِذْ هَدَيْتَنَا وَهَبْ لَنَا مِنْ

لَّدُنْكَ رَحْمَةً اِنَّكَ اَنْتَ الْوَهَّابُ ۝٨

9. Our Lord! it is Thou Who gatherest mankind together to a Day of which there is no doubt. Lo! Allah faileth not to keep the tryst.

10. (On that day) neither the riches nor the progeny of those who disbelieve will aught avail them with Allah. They will be fuel for fire:

11. Like Pharaoh's folk and those who were before them, they disbelieved Our revelations and so Allah seized them for their sins. And Allah is severe in punishment.

12. Say (O Muhammad) unto those who disbelieve: Ye shall be overcome and gathered unto Hell, an evil resting place.

13. There was a token for you in two hosts which met:[1] one army fighting in the Way of Allah, and another disbelieving, whom they saw as twice their number, clearly, with their very eyes. Thus Allah strengtheneth with His succour whom He will. Lo! herein verily is a lesson for those who have eyes.

14. Beautified for mankind is love of the joys (that come) from women and offspring, and stored-up heaps of gold and silver, and horses branded (with their mark), and cattle and land. That is comfort of the life of the world. Allah! With Him is a more excellent abode.

15. Say: Shall I inform you of something better than that? For those who keep from evil, with their Lord are Gardens underneath which rivers flow, and pure companions, and contentment from Allah. Allah is Seer of His bondmen.

رَبَّنَآ إِنَّكَ جَامِعُ النَّاسِ لِيَوْمٍ لَّا رَيْبَ فِيهِ ۚ إِنَّ
اللَّهَ لَا يُخْلِفُ الْمِيعَادَ ﴿٩﴾ ع
إِنَّ الَّذِينَ كَفَرُوا لَن تُغْنِيَ عَنْهُمْ أَمْوَالُهُمْ وَلَآ
أَوْلَادُهُم مِّنَ اللَّهِ شَيْـًٔا ۖ وَأُولَٰٓئِكَ هُمْ وَقُودُ
النَّارِ ﴿١٠﴾
كَدَأْبِ آلِ فِرْعَوْنَ وَالَّذِينَ مِن قَبْلِهِمْ ۚ كَذَّبُوا
بِآيَاتِنَا فَأَخَذَهُمُ اللَّهُ بِذُنُوبِهِمْ ۗ وَاللَّهُ شَدِيدُ
الْعِقَابِ ﴿١١﴾
قُل لِّلَّذِينَ كَفَرُوا سَتُغْلَبُونَ وَتُحْشَرُونَ إِلَىٰ جَهَنَّمَ ۚ
وَبِئْسَ الْمِهَادُ ﴿١٢﴾
قَدْ كَانَ لَكُمْ آيَةٌ فِي فِئَتَيْنِ الْتَقَتَا ۖ فِئَةٌ تُقَاتِلُ فِي
سَبِيلِ اللَّهِ وَأُخْرَىٰ كَافِرَةٌ يَرَوْنَهُم مِّثْلَيْهِمْ رَأْيَ
الْعَيْنِ ۚ وَاللَّهُ يُؤَيِّدُ بِنَصْرِهِ مَن يَشَاءُ ۗ إِنَّ فِي ذَٰلِكَ
لَعِبْرَةً لِّأُولِي الْأَبْصَارِ ﴿١٣﴾
زُيِّنَ لِلنَّاسِ حُبُّ الشَّهَوَاتِ مِنَ النِّسَاءِ وَالْبَنِينَ
وَالْقَنَاطِيرِ الْمُقَنطَرَةِ مِنَ الذَّهَبِ وَالْفِضَّةِ وَ
الْخَيْلِ الْمُسَوَّمَةِ وَالْأَنْعَامِ وَالْحَرْثِ ۗ ذَٰلِكَ مَتَاعُ
الْحَيَاةِ الدُّنْيَا ۖ وَاللَّهُ عِندَهُ حُسْنُ الْمَآبِ ﴿١٤﴾
قُلْ أَؤُنَبِّئُكُم بِخَيْرٍ مِّن ذَٰلِكُمْ ۚ لِلَّذِينَ اتَّقَوْا عِندَ
رَبِّهِمْ جَنَّاتٌ تَجْرِي مِن تَحْتِهَا الْأَنْهَارُ خَالِدِينَ
فِيهَا وَأَزْوَاجٌ مُّطَهَّرَةٌ وَرِضْوَانٌ مِّنَ اللَّهِ ۗ وَاللَّهُ
بَصِيرٌ بِالْعِبَادِ ﴿١٥﴾ ع

1. The reference is to the battle of Badr.

16. Those who say: Our Lord! Lo! we believe. So forgive us our sins and guard us from the punishment of Fire!

17. The steadfast, and the truthful, and the obedient, those who spend (and hoard not), those who pray for pardon in the watches of the night.

18. Allah (Himself) is witness that there is no God save Him. And the angels and the men of learning (too are witness). Maintaining His creation in justice, there is no God save Him, the Almighty, the Wise.

19. Lo! religion with Allah (is) The Surrender[1] (to His will and guidance). Those who (formerly) received the Scripture differed only after knowledge came unto them, through transgression among themselves. Whoso disbelieveth the revelations of Allah (will find that) lo! Allah is swift at reckoning.

20. And if they argue with thee, (O Muhammad), say: I have surrendered my purpose to Allah and (so have) those who follow me. And say unto those who have received the Scripture and those who read not: Have ye (too) surrendered? If they surrender, then truly they are rightly guided, and if they turn away, then it is thy duty only to convey the message (unto them), Allah is Seer of (His) bondmen.

21. Lo! those who disbelieve the revelations of Allah, and slay the Prophets wrongfully, and slay those of mankind who enjoin equity: announce them a painful doom.

22. Those are they, whose works have failed in the world and the Hereafter; and they have no helpers.

23. Hast thou not seen how those who have received the Scripture invoke the Scripture of Allah (in their disputes) that it may judge between them: then a faction of them turn away, being opposed (to it)?

1. Ar. *Al-Islām*.

الذين يقولون ربنا اننا امنا فاغفر لنا ذنوبنا
وقنا عذاب النار ١٦
الصبرين والصدقين والقنتين والمنفقين
والمستغفرين بالاسحار ١٧
شهد الله انه لا اله الا هو والملئكة واولوا العلم
النصف قائما بالقسط لا اله الا هو العزيز الحكيم ١٨
ان الدين عند الله الاسلام وما اختلف الذين
اوتوا الكتب الا من بعد ما جاءهم العلم بغيا
بينهم ومن يكفر بايت الله فان الله سريع
الحساب ١٩
فان حاجوك فقل اسلمت وجهي لله ومن اتبعن
وقل للذين اوتوا الكتب والامين ءاسلمتم
فان اسلموا فقد اهتدوا وان تولوا فانما عليك
ع ٢ البلغ والله بصير بالعباد ٢٠
ان الذين يكفرون بايت الله ويقتلون النبين
بغير حق ويقتلون الذين يامرون بالقسط
من الناس فبشرهم بعذاب اليم ٢١
اولئك الذين حبطت اعمالهم في الدنيا و
الاخرة وما لهم من نصرين ٢٢
الم تر الى الذين اوتوا نصيبا من الكتب يدعون
الى كتب الله ليحكم بينهم ثم يتولى فريق منهم
وهم معرضون ٢٣

24. That is because they say: The Fire will not touch us save for a certain number of days. That which they used to invent hath deceived them regarding their religion.

25. How (will it be with them) when We have brought them all together to a Day of which there is no doubt, when every soul will be paid in full what it hath earned, and they will not be wronged.

26. Say: O Allah! Owner of Sovereignty! Thou givest sovereignty unto whom Thou wilt, and Thou withdrawest sovereignty from whom Thou wilt. Thou exaltest whom Thou wilt and Thou abasest whom Thou wilt . In Thy hand is the good. Lo! Thou art Able to do all things.

27. Thou causest the night to pass into the day, and Thou causest the day to pass into the night. And Thou bringest forth the living from the dead, and Thou bringest forth the dead from the living. And Thou givest sustenance to whom Thou choosest, without stint.

28. Let not the believers take disbelievers for their friends in preference to believers. Whoso doth that hath no connection with Allah unless (it be) that ye but guard yourselves against them, taking (as it were) security. Allah biddeth you beware (only) of Himself. Unto Allah is the journeying.

29. Say (O Muhammad): Whether ye hide that which is in your breasts or reveal it, Allah knoweth it. He knoweth that which is in the heavens and that which is in the earth, and Allah is Able to do all things.

30. On the Day when every soul will find itself confronted with all that it hath done of good and all that it hath done of evil (every soul) will long that there might be a mighty space of distance between it and that (evil). Allah biddeth you beware of Him. And Allah is full of pity for (His) bondmen.

31. Say, (O Muhammad, to mankind): If ye love Allah, follow me; Allah will love you and forgive you your sins. Allah is Forgiving, Merciful.

ذٰلِكَ بِاَنَّهُمْ قَالُوْا لَنْ تَمَسَّنَا النَّارُ اِلَّآ اَيَّامًا مَّعْدُوْدٰتٍ
وَّغَرَّهُمْ فِيْ دِيْنِهِمْ مَّا كَانُوْا يَفْتَرُوْنَ ﴿٢٤﴾
فَكَيْفَ اِذَا جَمَعْنٰهُمْ لِيَوْمٍ لَّا رَيْبَ فِيْهِ وَوُفِّيَتْ
كُلُّ نَفْسٍ مَّا كَسَبَتْ وَهُمْ لَا يُظْلَمُوْنَ ﴿٢٥﴾
قُلِ اللّٰهُمَّ مٰلِكَ الْمُلْكِ تُؤْتِي الْمُلْكَ مَنْ تَشَآءُ وَ
تَنْزِعُ الْمُلْكَ مِمَّنْ تَشَآءُ وَتُعِزُّ مَنْ تَشَآءُ وَتُذِلُّ
مَنْ تَشَآءُ بِيَدِكَ الْخَيْرُ اِنَّكَ عَلٰى كُلِّ شَيْءٍ قَدِيْرٌ ﴿٢٦﴾
تُوْلِجُ الَّيْلَ فِي النَّهَارِ وَتُوْلِجُ النَّهَارَ فِي الَّيْلِ وَ
تُخْرِجُ الْحَيَّ مِنَ الْمَيِّتِ وَتُخْرِجُ الْمَيِّتَ مِنَ الْحَيِّ
وَتَرْزُقُ مَنْ تَشَآءُ بِغَيْرِ حِسَابٍ ﴿٢٧﴾
لَا يَتَّخِذِ الْمُؤْمِنُوْنَ الْكٰفِرِيْنَ اَوْلِيَآءَ مِنْ دُوْنِ
الْمُؤْمِنِيْنَ وَمَنْ يَّفْعَلْ ذٰلِكَ فَلَيْسَ مِنَ اللّٰهِ فِيْ
شَيْءٍ اِلَّآ اَنْ تَتَّقُوْا مِنْهُمْ تُقٰىةً وَيُحَذِّرُكُمُ اللّٰهُ
نَفْسَهٗ وَاِلَى اللّٰهِ الْمَصِيْرُ ﴿٢٨﴾
قُلْ اِنْ تُخْفُوْا مَا فِيْ صُدُوْرِكُمْ اَوْ تُبْدُوْهُ يَعْلَمْهُ
اللّٰهُ وَيَعْلَمُ مَا فِي السَّمٰوٰتِ وَمَا فِي الْاَرْضِ وَاللّٰهُ عَلٰى
كُلِّ شَيْءٍ قَدِيْرٌ ﴿٢٩﴾
يَوْمَ تَجِدُ كُلُّ نَفْسٍ مَّا عَمِلَتْ مِنْ خَيْرٍ مُّحْضَرًا
وَّمَا عَمِلَتْ مِنْ سُوْٓءٍ تَوَدُّ لَوْ اَنَّ بَيْنَهَا وَبَيْنَهٗ
اَمَدًا بَعِيْدًا وَيُحَذِّرُكُمُ اللّٰهُ نَفْسَهٗ وَاللّٰهُ رَءُوْفٌ بِالْعِبَادِ ﴿٣٠﴾
قُلْ اِنْ كُنْتُمْ تُحِبُّوْنَ اللّٰهَ فَاتَّبِعُوْنِيْ يُحْبِبْكُمُ
اللّٰهُ وَيَغْفِرْ لَكُمْ ذُنُوْبَكُمْ وَاللّٰهُ غَفُوْرٌ رَّحِيْمٌ ﴿٣١﴾

32. Say: Obey Allah and the messenger. But if they turn away, lo! Allah loveth not the disbelievers (in His guidance).

33. Lo! Allah preferred Adam and Noah and the Family of Abraham and the family of 'Imrān above (all His) creatures.

34. They were descendants one of another. Allah is Hearer, Knower.

35. (Remember) when the wife of 'Imrān said: My Lord! I have vowed unto Thee that which is in my belly as a consecrated (offering). Accept it from me, Lo! Thou, only Thou, art the Hearer, the Knower!

36. And when she was delivered she said: My Lord! Lo! I am delivered of a female—Allah knew best of what she was delivered—the male is not as the female; and lo! I have named her Mary, and lo! I crave Thy protection for her and for her offspring from Satan the outcast.

37. And her Lord accepted her with full acceptance and vouchsafed to her a goodly growth: and made Zachariah her guardian. Whenever Zachariah went into the sanctuary where she was, he found that she had food. He said: O Mary! Whence cometh unto thee this (food)? She answered: It is from Allah. Allah giveth without stint to whom He will.

38. Then Zachariah prayed unto his Lord and said: My Lord! Bestow upon me of Thy bounty goodly offspring. Lo! Thou art the Hearer of Prayer.

39. And the angels called to him as he stood praying in the sanctuary: Allah giveth thee glad tidings of (a son whose name is) John,[1] (who cometh) to confirm a word from Allah, lordly, chaste, a Prophet of the righteous.

1. Ar. *Yahya.*

قُلْ أَطِيعُوا اللّٰهَ وَالرَّسُولَ فَإِنْ تَوَلَّوْا فَإِنَّ اللّٰهَ
لَا يُحِبُّ الْكٰفِرِينَ ٣٢
إِنَّ اللّٰهَ اصْطَفٰى آدَمَ وَنُوحًا وَآلَ إِبْرٰهِيمَ وَآلَ
عِمْرٰنَ عَلَى الْعٰلَمِينَ ٣٣
ذُرِّيَّةً بَعْضُهَا مِنْ بَعْضٍ وَاللّٰهُ سَمِيعٌ عَلِيمٌ ٣٤
إِذْ قَالَتِ امْرَأَتُ عِمْرٰنَ رَبِّ إِنِّي نَذَرْتُ لَكَ مَا
فِي بَطْنِي مُحَرَّرًا فَتَقَبَّلْ مِنِّي إِنَّكَ أَنْتَ السَّمِيعُ
الْعَلِيمُ ٣٥
فَلَمَّا وَضَعَتْهَا قَالَتْ رَبِّ إِنِّي وَضَعْتُهَا أُنْثٰى وَاللّٰهُ
أَعْلَمُ بِمَا وَضَعَتْ وَلَيْسَ الذَّكَرُ كَالْأُنْثٰى وَإِنِّي
سَمَّيْتُهَا مَرْيَمَ وَإِنِّي أُعِيذُهَا بِكَ وَذُرِّيَّتَهَا
مِنَ الشَّيْطٰنِ الرَّجِيمِ ٣٦
فَتَقَبَّلَهَا رَبُّهَا بِقَبُولٍ حَسَنٍ وَأَنْبَتَهَا نَبَاتًا حَسَنًا
وَكَفَّلَهَا زَكَرِيَّا كُلَّمَا دَخَلَ عَلَيْهَا زَكَرِيَّا الْمِحْرَابَ
وَجَدَ عِنْدَهَا رِزْقًا قَالَ يٰمَرْيَمُ أَنّٰى لَكِ هٰذَا
قَالَتْ هُوَ مِنْ عِنْدِ اللّٰهِ إِنَّ اللّٰهَ يَرْزُقُ مَنْ يَشَاءُ
بِغَيْرِ حِسَابٍ ٣٧
هُنَالِكَ دَعَا زَكَرِيَّا رَبَّهُ قَالَ رَبِّ هَبْ لِي مِنْ
لَدُنْكَ ذُرِّيَّةً طَيِّبَةً إِنَّكَ سَمِيعُ الدُّعَاءِ ٣٨
فَنَادَتْهُ الْمَلٰئِكَةُ وَهُوَ قَائِمٌ يُصَلِّي فِي الْمِحْرَابِ
أَنَّ اللّٰهَ يُبَشِّرُكَ بِيَحْيٰى مُصَدِّقًا بِكَلِمَةٍ مِنَ اللّٰهِ
وَسَيِّدًا وَحَصُورًا وَنَبِيًّا مِنَ الصّٰلِحِينَ ٣٩

40. He said: My Lord! How can I have a son when age hath overtaken me already and my wife is barren? (The angel) answered: So (it will be). Allah doth what He will.

41. He said: My Lord! Appoint a token for me. (The angel) said: The token unto thee (shall be) that thou shalt not speak unto mankind three days except by signs. Remember thy Lord much, and praise (Him) in the early hours of night and morning.

42. And when the angels said: O Mary! Lo! Allah hath chosen thee and made thee pure, and hath preferred thee above (all) the women of creation.

43. O Mary! Be obedient to thy Lord, prostrate thyself and bow with those who bow (in worship).

44. This is of the tidings of things hidden. We reveal it unto thee (Muhammad). Thou wast not present with them when they threw their pens (to know) which of them should be the guardian of Mary, nor wast thou present with them when they quarrelled (thereupon).

45. (And remember) when the angels said: O Mary! Lo! Allah giveth thee glad tidings of a word from Him, whose name is the Messiah, Jesus, son of Mary, illustrious in the world and the Hereafter, and one of those brought near (unto Allah).

46. He will speak unto mankind in his cradle and in his manhood, and he is of the righteous.

47. She said: My Lord! How can I have a child when no mortal hath touched me? He said: So (it will be). Allah createth what He will. If He decreeth a thing, He saith unto it only: Be! and it is.

48. And He will teach him the Scripture and wisdom, and the Torah and the Gospel.

قَالَ رَبِّ اَنّٰى يَكُوْنُ لِىْ غُلٰمٌ وَّقَدْ بَلَغَنِىَ الْكِبَرُ وَ
امْرَاَتِىْ عَاقِرٌ ؕ قَالَ كَذٰلِكَ اللّٰهُ يَفْعَلُ مَا يَشَآءُ ﴿۴۰﴾
قَالَ رَبِّ اجْعَلْ لِّىْۤ اٰيَةً ؕ قَالَ اٰيَتُكَ اَلَّا تُكَلِّمَ
النَّاسَ ثَلٰثَةَ اَيَّامٍ اِلَّا رَمْزًا ؕ وَاذْكُرْ رَّبَّكَ كَثِيْرًا وَّ
سَبِّحْ بِالْعَشِىِّ وَالْاِبْكَارِ ﴿۴۱﴾ ع
وَاِذْ قَالَتِ الْمَلٰٓئِكَةُ يٰمَرْيَمُ اِنَّ اللّٰهَ اصْطَفٰكِ وَ
طَهَّرَكِ وَاصْطَفٰكِ عَلٰى نِسَآءِ الْعٰلَمِيْنَ ﴿۴۲﴾
يٰمَرْيَمُ اقْنُتِىْ لِرَبِّكِ وَاسْجُدِىْ وَارْكَعِىْ مَعَ
الرّٰكِعِيْنَ ﴿۴۳﴾
ذٰلِكَ مِنْ اَنْۢبَآءِ الْغَيْبِ نُوْحِيْهِ اِلَيْكَ ؕ وَمَا كُنْتَ
لَدَيْهِمْ اِذْ يُلْقُوْنَ اَقْلَامَهُمْ اَيُّهُمْ يَكْفُلُ مَرْيَمَ ۪
وَمَا كُنْتَ لَدَيْهِمْ اِذْ يَخْتَصِمُوْنَ ﴿۴۴﴾
اِذْ قَالَتِ الْمَلٰٓئِكَةُ يٰمَرْيَمُ اِنَّ اللّٰهَ يُبَشِّرُكِ بِكَلِمَةٍ
مِّنْهُ ۖ اسْمُهُ الْمَسِيْحُ عِيْسَى ابْنُ مَرْيَمَ وَجِيْهًا
فِى الدُّنْيَا وَالْاٰخِرَةِ وَمِنَ الْمُقَرَّبِيْنَ ﴿۴۵﴾ ۙ
وَيُكَلِّمُ النَّاسَ فِى الْمَهْدِ وَكَهْلًا وَّمِنَ
الصّٰلِحِيْنَ ﴿۴۶﴾
قَالَتْ رَبِّ اَنّٰى يَكُوْنُ لِىْ وَلَدٌ وَّلَمْ يَمْسَسْنِىْ بَشَرٌ ؕ
قَالَ كَذٰلِكِ اللّٰهُ يَخْلُقُ مَا يَشَآءُ ؕ اِذَا قَضٰۤى اَمْرًا
فَاِنَّمَا يَقُوْلُ لَهٗ كُنْ فَيَكُوْنُ ﴿۴۷﴾
وَيُعَلِّمُهُ الْكِتٰبَ وَالْحِكْمَةَ وَالتَّوْرٰىةَ
وَالْاِنْجِيْلَ ﴿۴۸﴾

49. And will make him a messenger unto the children of Israel, (saying): Lo! I come unto you with a sign from your Lord. Lo! I fashion for you out of clay the likeness of a bird, and I breathe into it and it is a bird, by Allah's leave. I heal him who was born blind, and the leper, and I raise the dead, by Allah's leave. And I announce unto you what ye eat and what ye store up in your houses. Lo! herein verily is a portent for you, if ye are to be believers.

50. And (I come) confirming that which was before me of the Torah, and to make lawful some of that which was forbidden unto you. I come unto you with a sign from your Lord, so keep your duty to Allah and obey me.

51. Lo! Allah is my Lord and your Lord, so worship Him. That is a Straight path.

52. But when Jesus became conscious of their disbelief, he cried: Who will be my helpers in the cause of Allah? The disciples said: We will be Allah's helpers, We believe in Allah, and bear thou witness that we have surrendered[1] (unto Him).

53. Our Lord! We believe in that which Thou hast revealed and we follow him whom Thou hast sent. Enroll us among those who witness (to the truth).

54. And they (the disbelievers) schemed, and Allah schemed (against them): and Allah is the best of schemers.

55. (And remember) when Allah said: O Jesus! Lo! I am gathering thee and causing thee to ascend unto Me, and am cleansing thee of those who disbelieve and am setting those who follow thee above those who disbelieve until the Day of Resurrection. Then unto Me ye will (all) return, and I shall judge between you as to that wherein ye used to differ.

56. As for those who disbelieve I shall chastise them with a heavy chastisement in the world and the Hereafter; and they will have no helpers.

1. Or "*are Muslims.*"

وَرَسُولًا إِلَىٰ بَنِىٓ إِسْرَٰٓءِيلَ أَنِّى قَدْ جِئْتُكُم بِـَٔايَةٍ
مِّن رَّبِّكُمْ أَنِّىٓ أَخْلُقُ لَكُم مِّنَ ٱلطِّينِ كَهَيْـَٔةِ ٱلطَّيْرِ
فَأَنفُخُ فِيهِ فَيَكُونُ طَيْرًۢا بِإِذْنِ ٱللَّهِ ۖ وَأُبْرِئُ ٱلْأَكْمَهَ
وَٱلْأَبْرَصَ وَأُحْىِ ٱلْمَوْتَىٰ بِإِذْنِ ٱللَّهِ ۖ وَأُنَبِّئُكُم
بِمَا تَأْكُلُونَ وَمَا تَدَّخِرُونَ فِى بُيُوتِكُمْ ۚ إِنَّ فِى
ذَٰلِكَ لَءَايَةً لَّكُمْ إِن كُنتُم مُّؤْمِنِينَ ﴿٤٩﴾
وَمُصَدِّقًا لِّمَا بَيْنَ يَدَىَّ مِنَ ٱلتَّوْرَىٰةِ وَلِأُحِلَّ
لَكُم بَعْضَ ٱلَّذِى حُرِّمَ عَلَيْكُمْ ۚ وَجِئْتُكُم بِـَٔايَةٍ
مِّن رَّبِّكُمْ فَٱتَّقُوا۟ ٱللَّهَ وَأَطِيعُونِ ﴿٥٠﴾
إِنَّ ٱللَّهَ رَبِّى وَرَبُّكُمْ فَٱعْبُدُوهُ ۗ هَٰذَا صِرَٰطٌ مُّسْتَقِيمٌ ﴿٥١﴾
فَلَمَّآ أَحَسَّ عِيسَىٰ مِنْهُمُ ٱلْكُفْرَ قَالَ مَنْ أَنصَارِىٓ
إِلَى ٱللَّهِ ۖ قَالَ ٱلْحَوَارِيُّونَ نَحْنُ أَنصَارُ ٱللَّهِ ءَامَنَّا
بِٱللَّهِ وَٱشْهَدْ بِأَنَّا مُسْلِمُونَ ﴿٥٢﴾
رَبَّنَآ ءَامَنَّا بِمَآ أَنزَلْتَ وَٱتَّبَعْنَا ٱلرَّسُولَ فَٱكْتُبْنَا
مَعَ ٱلشَّٰهِدِينَ ﴿٥٣﴾
وَمَكَرُوا۟ وَمَكَرَ ٱللَّهُ ۖ وَٱللَّهُ خَيْرُ ٱلْمَٰكِرِينَ ﴿٥٤﴾
إِذْ قَالَ ٱللَّهُ يَٰعِيسَىٰٓ إِنِّى مُتَوَفِّيكَ وَرَافِعُكَ إِلَىَّ وَ
مُطَهِّرُكَ مِنَ ٱلَّذِينَ كَفَرُوا۟ وَجَاعِلُ ٱلَّذِينَ ٱتَّبَعُوكَ
فَوْقَ ٱلَّذِينَ كَفَرُوٓا۟ إِلَىٰ يَوْمِ ٱلْقِيَٰمَةِ ۖ ثُمَّ إِلَىَّ
مَرْجِعُكُمْ فَأَحْكُمُ بَيْنَكُمْ فِيمَا كُنتُمْ فِيهِ تَخْتَلِفُونَ ﴿٥٥﴾
فَأَمَّا ٱلَّذِينَ كَفَرُوا۟ فَأُعَذِّبُهُمْ عَذَابًا شَدِيدًا فِى
ٱلدُّنْيَا وَٱلْءَاخِرَةِ وَمَا لَهُم مِّن نَّٰصِرِينَ ﴿٥٦﴾

57. And as for those who believe and do good works, He will pay them their wages in full Allah loveth not wrong-doers.

58. This (which) We recite unto thee is a revelation and a wise reminder.

59. Lo! the likeness of Jesus with Allah is as the likeness of Adam. He created him of dust, then He said unto him: Be! and he is.

60. (This is) the truth from thy Lord (O Muhammad), so be not thou of those who waver.

61. And whoso disputeth with thee concerning him, after the knowledge which hath come unto thee, say (unto him): Come! We will summon our sons and your sons, and our women and your women, and ourselves and yourselves, then we will pray humbly (to our Lord) and (solemnly) invoke the curse of Allah upon those who lie!

62. Lo! This verily is the true narrative. There is no God save Allah, and lo! Allah is the Mighty, the Wise.

63. And if they turn away, then lo! Allah is Aware of (who are) the corrupters.

64. Say: O people of the Scripture![1] Come to an agreement between us and you: that we shall worship none but Allah, and that we shall ascribe no partner unto Him, and that none of us shall take others for Lords beside Allah. And if they turn away, then say: Bear witness that we are they who have surrendered[2] (unto Him).

65. O People of the Scripture! Why will ye argue about Abraham, when the Torah and the Gospel were not revealed till after him? Have ye then no sense?

66. Lo! ye are those who argue about that whereof ye have some knowledge: Why then argue ye concerning that whereof ye have no knowledge? Allah knoweth. Ye know not.

1. Jews and Christians.
2. Ar. *muslimūn*.

وَأَمَّا الَّذِينَ آمَنُوا وَعَمِلُوا الصَّالِحَاتِ فَيُوَفِّيهِمْ
أُجُورَهُمْ وَاللَّهُ لَا يُحِبُّ الظَّالِمِينَ ﴿٥٧﴾
ذَٰلِكَ نَتْلُوهُ عَلَيْكَ مِنَ الْآيَاتِ وَالذِّكْرِ الْحَكِيمِ ﴿٥٨﴾
إِنَّ مَثَلَ عِيسَىٰ عِنْدَ اللَّهِ كَمَثَلِ آدَمَ خَلَقَهُ مِنْ
تُرَابٍ ثُمَّ قَالَ لَهُ كُنْ فَيَكُونُ ﴿٥٩﴾
الْحَقُّ مِنْ رَبِّكَ فَلَا تَكُنْ مِنَ الْمُمْتَرِينَ ﴿٦٠﴾
فَمَنْ حَاجَّكَ فِيهِ مِنْ بَعْدِ مَا جَاءَكَ مِنَ الْعِلْمِ
فَقُلْ تَعَالَوْا نَدْعُ أَبْنَاءَنَا وَأَبْنَاءَكُمْ وَنِسَاءَنَا وَ
نِسَاءَكُمْ وَأَنْفُسَنَا وَأَنْفُسَكُمْ ثُمَّ نَبْتَهِلْ فَنَجْعَلْ
لَعْنَتَ اللَّهِ عَلَى الْكَاذِبِينَ ﴿٦١﴾
إِنَّ هَٰذَا لَهُوَ الْقَصَصُ الْحَقُّ وَمَا مِنْ إِلَٰهٍ إِلَّا اللَّهُ
وَإِنَّ اللَّهَ لَهُوَ الْعَزِيزُ الْحَكِيمُ ﴿٦٢﴾
ع ١٤ فَإِنْ تَوَلَّوْا فَإِنَّ اللَّهَ عَلِيمٌ بِالْمُفْسِدِينَ ﴿٦٣﴾
قُلْ يَا أَهْلَ الْكِتَابِ تَعَالَوْا إِلَىٰ كَلِمَةٍ سَوَاءٍ بَيْنَنَا وَ
بَيْنَكُمْ أَلَّا نَعْبُدَ إِلَّا اللَّهَ وَلَا نُشْرِكَ بِهِ شَيْئًا وَلَا
يَتَّخِذَ بَعْضُنَا بَعْضًا أَرْبَابًا مِنْ دُونِ اللَّهِ فَإِنْ تَوَلَّوْا
فَقُولُوا اشْهَدُوا بِأَنَّا مُسْلِمُونَ ﴿٦٤﴾
يَا أَهْلَ الْكِتَابِ لِمَ تُحَاجُّونَ فِي إِبْرَاهِيمَ وَمَا أُنْزِلَتِ
التَّوْرَاةُ وَالْإِنْجِيلُ إِلَّا مِنْ بَعْدِهِ أَفَلَا تَعْقِلُونَ ﴿٦٥﴾
هَا أَنْتُمْ هَٰؤُلَاءِ حَاجَجْتُمْ فِيمَا لَكُمْ بِهِ عِلْمٌ فَلِمَ
تُحَاجُّونَ فِيمَا لَيْسَ لَكُمْ بِهِ عِلْمٌ وَاللَّهُ يَعْلَمُ وَ
أَنْتُمْ لَا تَعْلَمُونَ ﴿٦٦﴾

67. Abraham was not a Jew, nor yet a Christian; but he was an upright man who had surrendered (to Allah), and he was not of the idolaters.

68. Lo! those of mankind who have the best claim to Abraham are those who followed him, and this Prophet and those who believe (with him); and Allah is the Protecting Friend of the believers.

69. A party of the people of the Scripture long to make you go astray; and they make none to go astray except themselves, but they perceive not.

70. O People of the Scripture! Why disbelieve ye in the revelations of Allah, when ye (yourselves) bear witness (to their truth)?

71. O People of the Scripture! Why confound ye truth with falsehood and knowingly conceal the truth!

72. And a party of the People of the Scripture say: Believe in that which hath been revealed, unto those who believe at the opening of the day, and disbelieve at the end thereof, in order that they may return;[1]

73. And believe not save in one who followeth your religion—Say (O Muhammad): Lo! the guidance is Allah's guidance—that any one is given the like of that which was given unto you or that they may argue with you in the presence of their Lord. Say (O Muhammad): Lo! the bounty is in Allah's hand. He bestoweth it on whom He will. Allah is All-Embracing, All-Knowing.

74. He selecteth for His mercy whom He will. Allah is of Infinite bounty.

75. Among the People of the Scripture there is he who, if thou trust him with a weight of treasure, will return it to thee. And among them there is he who, if thou trust him with a piece of gold, will not return it to thee unless thou keep standing over him. That is because they say: We have no duty to the Gentiles. They speak a lie concerning Allah knowingly.

مَا كَانَ إِبْرٰهِيمُ يَهُودِيًّا وَّلَا نَصْرَانِيًّا وَّلٰكِن كَانَ
حَنِيفًا مُّسْلِمًا وَّمَا كَانَ مِنَ الْمُشْرِكِينَ ﴿٦٧﴾
إِنَّ أَوْلَى النَّاسِ بِإِبْرٰهِيمَ لَلَّذِينَ اتَّبَعُوهُ وَهٰذَا
النَّبِيُّ وَالَّذِينَ اٰمَنُوا وَاللّٰهُ وَلِيُّ الْمُؤْمِنِينَ ﴿٦٨﴾
وَدَّت طَّآئِفَةٌ مِّنْ أَهْلِ الْكِتٰبِ لَوْ يُضِلُّونَكُمْ وَمَا
يُضِلُّونَ إِلَّا أَنفُسَهُمْ وَمَا يَشْعُرُونَ ﴿٦٩﴾
يٰأَهْلَ الْكِتٰبِ لِمَ تَكْفُرُونَ بِاٰيٰتِ اللّٰهِ وَأَنتُمْ تَشْهَدُونَ ﴿٧٠﴾
يٰأَهْلَ الْكِتٰبِ لِمَ تَلْبِسُونَ الْحَقَّ بِالْبٰطِلِ وَ
تَكْتُمُونَ الْحَقَّ وَأَنتُمْ تَعْلَمُونَ ﴿٧١﴾
وَقَالَت طَّآئِفَةٌ مِّنْ أَهْلِ الْكِتٰبِ اٰمِنُوا بِالَّذِي
أُنزِلَ عَلَى الَّذِينَ اٰمَنُوا وَجْهَ النَّهَارِ وَاكْفُرُوا اٰخِرَهُ
لَعَلَّهُمْ يَرْجِعُونَ ﴿٧٢﴾
وَلَا تُؤْمِنُوا إِلَّا لِمَن تَبِعَ دِينَكُمْ قُلْ إِنَّ الْهُدٰى
هُدَى اللّٰهِ أَن يُؤْتٰى أَحَدٌ مِّثْلَ مَا أُوتِيتُمْ أَوْ
يُحَآجُّوكُمْ عِندَ رَبِّكُمْ قُلْ إِنَّ الْفَضْلَ بِيَدِ اللّٰهِ
يُؤْتِيهِ مَن يَشَآءُ وَاللّٰهُ وَاسِعٌ عَلِيمٌ ﴿٧٣﴾
يَخْتَصُّ بِرَحْمَتِهِ مَن يَشَآءُ وَاللّٰهُ ذُو الْفَضْلِ الْعَظِيمِ ﴿٧٤﴾
وَمِنْ أَهْلِ الْكِتٰبِ مَنْ إِن تَأْمَنْهُ بِقِنطَارٍ يُؤَدِّهِ
إِلَيْكَ وَمِنْهُم مَّنْ إِن تَأْمَنْهُ بِدِينَارٍ لَّا يُؤَدِّهِ
إِلَيْكَ إِلَّا مَا دُمْتَ عَلَيْهِ قَآئِمًا ذٰلِكَ بِأَنَّهُمْ قَالُوا
لَيْسَ عَلَيْنَا فِي الْأُمِّيِّينَ سَبِيلٌ وَيَقُولُونَ عَلَى اللّٰهِ
الْكَذِبَ وَهُمْ يَعْلَمُونَ ﴿٧٥﴾

1. The reference is to some Jews of Al-Madinah, who feigned an interest in Al-Islam only in the hope of detaching some of the Muslims by their subtle arguments.

76. Nay, but (the chosen of Allah is) he who fulfilleth his pledge and wardeth off (evil); for lo! Allah loveth those who ward off (evil).

77. Lo! those who purchase a small gain at the cost of Allah's covenant and their oaths,[1] they have no portion in the Hereafter. Allah will neither speak to them nor look upon them on the Day of Resurrection, nor will He make them grow. Theirs will be a painful doom.

78. And lo! there is a party of them who distort the Scripture with their tongues, that ye may think that what they say is from the Scripture, when it is not from the Scripture. And they say, It is from Allah, when it is not from Allah; and they speak a lie concerning Allah knowingly.

79. It is not (possible) for any human being unto whom Allah had given the Scripture and wisdom and the Prophethood that he should afterwards have said unto mankind: Be slaves of me instead of Allah; but (what he said was): Be ye faithful servants of the Lord by virtue of your constant teaching of the Scripture and of your constant study thereof.

80. And he commanded you not that ye should take the angels and the Prophets for lords. Would he command you to disbelieve after ye had surrendered (to Allah)?

81. When Allah made (His) covenant with the Prophets, (He said): Behold that which I have given you of the Scripture and knowledge. And afterward there will come unto you a messenger, confirming that which ye possess. Ye shall believe in him and ye shall help him. He said: Do ye agree, and will ye take up My burden (which I lay upon you) in this (matter)? They answered: We agree. He said: Then bear ye witness. I will be a witness with you.

بَلٰى مَنْ اَوْفٰى بِعَهْدِهٖ وَاتَّقٰى فَاِنَّ اللّٰهَ يُحِبُّ
الْمُتَّقِيْنَ ﴿٧٦﴾

اِنَّ الَّذِيْنَ يَشْتَرُوْنَ بِعَهْدِ اللّٰهِ وَاَيْمَانِهِمْ ثَمَنًا
قَلِيْلًا اُولٰٓئِكَ لَا خَلَاقَ لَهُمْ فِي الْاٰخِرَةِ وَلَا يُكَلِّمُهُمُ
اللّٰهُ وَلَا يَنْظُرُ اِلَيْهِمْ يَوْمَ الْقِيٰمَةِ وَلَا يُزَكِّيْهِمْ
وَلَهُمْ عَذَابٌ اَلِيْمٌ ﴿٧٧﴾

وَاِنَّ مِنْهُمْ لَفَرِيْقًا يَّلْوٗنَ اَلْسِنَتَهُمْ بِالْكِتٰبِ
لِتَحْسَبُوْهُ مِنَ الْكِتٰبِ وَمَا هُوَ مِنَ الْكِتٰبِ وَيَقُوْلُوْنَ
هُوَ مِنْ عِنْدِ اللّٰهِ وَمَا هُوَ مِنْ عِنْدِ اللّٰهِ وَيَقُوْلُوْنَ
عَلَى اللّٰهِ الْكَذِبَ وَهُمْ يَعْلَمُوْنَ ﴿٧٨﴾

مَا كَانَ لِبَشَرٍ اَنْ يُّؤْتِيَهُ اللّٰهُ الْكِتٰبَ وَالْحُكْمَ وَ
النُّبُوَّةَ ثُمَّ يَقُوْلَ لِلنَّاسِ كُوْنُوْا عِبَادًا لِّيْ مِنْ
دُوْنِ اللّٰهِ وَلٰكِنْ كُوْنُوْا رَبّٰنِيّٖنَ بِمَا كُنْتُمْ تُعَلِّمُوْنَ
الْكِتٰبَ وَبِمَا كُنْتُمْ تَدْرُسُوْنَ ﴿٧٩﴾

وَلَا يَاْمُرَكُمْ اَنْ تَتَّخِذُوا الْمَلٰٓئِكَةَ وَالنَّبِيّٖنَ اَرْبَابًا
ع ١٦ اَيَاْمُرُكُمْ بِالْكُفْرِ بَعْدَ اِذْ اَنْتُمْ مُّسْلِمُوْنَ ﴿٨٠﴾

وَاِذْ اَخَذَ اللّٰهُ مِيْثَاقَ النَّبِيّٖنَ لَمَآ اٰتَيْتُكُمْ مِّنْ
كِتٰبٍ وَّحِكْمَةٍ ثُمَّ جَآءَكُمْ رَسُوْلٌ مُّصَدِّقٌ لِّمَا
مَعَكُمْ لَتُؤْمِنُنَّ بِهٖ وَلَتَنْصُرُنَّهٗ قَالَ ءَاَقْرَرْتُمْ
وَاَخَذْتُمْ عَلٰى ذٰلِكُمْ اِصْرِيْ قَالُوْٓا
اَقْرَرْنَا قَالَ فَاشْهَدُوْا وَاَنَا مَعَكُمْ مِّنَ
الشّٰهِدِيْنَ ﴿٨١﴾

1. The Jews of Al-Madinah had made a solemn treaty with the Prophet in the year 1 A.H.

82. Then whosoever after this shall turn away: they will be miscreants.

83. Seek they other than the religion of Allah, when unto Him submitteth whosoever is in the heavens and the earth, willingly, or unwillingly, and unto Him they will be returned.

84. Say (O Muhammad): We believe in Allah and that which is revealed unto us and that which was revealed unto Abraham and Ishmael and Isaac and Jacob and the tribes, and that which was vouchsafed unto Moses and Jesus and the Prophets from their Lord. We make no distinction between any of them, and unto Him we have surrendered.[1]

85. And whoso seeketh as religion other than the Surrender[2] (to Allah) it will not be accepted from him, and he will be a loser in the Hereafter.

86. How shall Allah guide a people who disbelieved after their belief and (after) they bore witness that the messenger is true and after clear proofs (of Allah's sovereignty) had come unto them And Allah guideth not wrong-doing folk.

87. As for such, their guerdon is that on them rests the curse of Allah and of angels and of men combined.

88. They will abide therein. Their doom will not be lightened, neither will they be reprieved;

89. Save those who afterward repent and do right. Lo! Allah is Forgiving, Merciful.

90. Lo! those who disbelieve after their (profession of) belief, and afterward grow violent in disbelief: their repentance will not be accepted. And such are those who are astray.

فَمَنْ تَوَلّٰى بَعْدَ ذٰلِكَ فَاُولٰٓئِكَ هُمُ
الْفٰسِقُوْنَ ﴿٨٢﴾
اَفَغَيْرَ دِيْنِ اللّٰهِ يَبْغُوْنَ وَلَهٗٓ اَسْلَمَ مَنْ فِي السَّمٰوٰتِ
وَالْاَرْضِ طَوْعًا وَّكَرْهًا وَّاِلَيْهِ يُرْجَعُوْنَ ﴿٨٣﴾
قُلْ اٰمَنَّا بِاللّٰهِ وَمَآ اُنْزِلَ عَلَيْنَا وَمَآ اُنْزِلَ عَلٰٓى اِبْرٰهِيْمَ
وَاِسْمٰعِيْلَ وَاِسْحٰقَ وَيَعْقُوْبَ وَالْاَسْبَاطِ وَمَآ اُوْتِيَ
مُوْسٰى وَعِيْسٰى وَالنَّبِيُّوْنَ مِنْ رَّبِّهِمْ لَا نُفَرِّقُ
بَيْنَ اَحَدٍ مِّنْهُمْ وَنَحْنُ لَهٗ مُسْلِمُوْنَ ﴿٨٤﴾
وَمَنْ يَّبْتَغِ غَيْرَ الْاِسْلَامِ دِيْنًا فَلَنْ يُّقْبَلَ مِنْهُ وَ
هُوَ فِي الْاٰخِرَةِ مِنَ الْخٰسِرِيْنَ ﴿٨٥﴾
كَيْفَ يَهْدِي اللّٰهُ قَوْمًا كَفَرُوْا بَعْدَ اِيْمَانِهِمْ وَ
شَهِدُوْٓا اَنَّ الرَّسُوْلَ حَقٌّ وَّجَآءَهُمُ الْبَيِّنٰتُ وَ
اللّٰهُ لَا يَهْدِي الْقَوْمَ الظّٰلِمِيْنَ ﴿٨٦﴾
اُولٰٓئِكَ جَزَآؤُهُمْ اَنَّ عَلَيْهِمْ لَعْنَةَ اللّٰهِ وَالْمَلٰٓئِكَةِ
وَالنَّاسِ اَجْمَعِيْنَ ﴿٨٧﴾
خٰلِدِيْنَ فِيْهَا لَا يُخَفَّفُ عَنْهُمُ الْعَذَابُ وَلَا
هُمْ يُنْظَرُوْنَ ﴿٨٨﴾
اِلَّا الَّذِيْنَ تَابُوْا مِنْ بَعْدِ ذٰلِكَ وَاَصْلَحُوْا فَاِنَّ
اللّٰهَ غَفُوْرٌ رَّحِيْمٌ ﴿٨٩﴾
اِنَّ الَّذِيْنَ كَفَرُوْا بَعْدَ اِيْمَانِهِمْ ثُمَّ
ازْدَادُوْا كُفْرًا لَّنْ تُقْبَلَ تَوْبَتُهُمْ وَاُولٰٓئِكَ
هُمُ الضَّآلُّوْنَ ﴿٩٠﴾

1. Almost identical with II, 136.
2. Ar. *Al-Islam*.

91. Lo! those who disbelieve, and die in disbelief, the (whole) earth full of gold would not be accepted from such a one if it were offered as a ransom (for his soul). Theirs will be a painful doom and they will have no helpers.

92. Ye will not attain unto piety until ye spend of that which ye love. And whatsoever ye spend, Allah is aware thereof.

93. All food was lawful unto the children of Israel, save that which Israel forbade himself, (in days) before the Torah was revealed. Say: Produce the Torah and read it (unto us) if ye are truthful.

94. And whoever shall invent a falsehood after that concerning Allah, such will be wrong-doers.

95. Say: Allah speaketh truth. So follow the religion of Abraham, the upright. He was not of the idolaters.

96. Lo! the first Sanctuary appointed for mankind was that at Becca,[1] a blessed place, a guidance to the peoples;

97. Wherein are plain memorials (of Allah's guidance); the place where Abraham stood up to pray; and whosoever entereth it is safe. And pilgrimage to the House is a duty unto Allah for mankind, for him who can find a way thither. As for him who disbelieveth, (let him know that) lo! Allah is Independent of (all) creatures.

98. Say: O People of the Scripture! Why disbelieve ye in the revelations of Allah, when Allah (Himself) is Witness of what ye do?

99. Say: O People of the Scripture! Why drive ye back believers from the way of Allah, seeking to make it crooked, when ye are witnesses (to Allah's guidance) Allah is not unaware of what ye do.

[1]. Mecca.

اِنَّ الَّذِيْنَ كَفَرُوْا وَمَاتُوْا وَهُمْ كُفَّارٌ فَلَنْ يُّقْبَلَ مِنْ اَحَدِهِمْ مِّلْءُ الْاَرْضِ ذَهَبًا وَّلَوِ افْتَدٰى بِهٖ ؕ اُولٰٓئِكَ لَهُمْ عَذَابٌ اَلِيْمٌ وَّمَا لَهُمْ مِّنْ نّٰصِرِيْنَ ۝

لَنْ تَنَالُوا الْبِرَّ حَتّٰى تُنْفِقُوْا مِمَّا تُحِبُّوْنَ ؕ وَمَا تُنْفِقُوْا مِنْ شَيْءٍ فَاِنَّ اللّٰهَ بِهٖ عَلِيْمٌ ۝

كُلُّ الطَّعَامِ كَانَ حِلًّا لِّبَنِيْ اِسْرَآءِيْلَ اِلَّا مَا حَرَّمَ اِسْرَآءِيْلُ عَلٰى نَفْسِهٖ مِنْ قَبْلِ اَنْ تُنَزَّلَ التَّوْرٰىةُ ؕ قُلْ فَأْتُوْا بِالتَّوْرٰىةِ فَاتْلُوْهَآ اِنْ كُنْتُمْ صٰدِقِيْنَ ۝

فَمَنِ افْتَرٰى عَلَى اللّٰهِ الْكَذِبَ مِنْ بَعْدِ ذٰلِكَ فَاُولٰٓئِكَ هُمُ الظّٰلِمُوْنَ ۝

قُلْ صَدَقَ اللّٰهُ ۛ فَاتَّبِعُوْا مِلَّةَ اِبْرٰهِيْمَ حَنِيْفًا ؕ وَمَا كَانَ مِنَ الْمُشْرِكِيْنَ ۝

اِنَّ اَوَّلَ بَيْتٍ وُّضِعَ لِلنَّاسِ لَلَّذِيْ بِبَكَّةَ مُبٰرَكًا وَّهُدًى لِّلْعٰلَمِيْنَ ۝

فِيْهِ اٰيٰتٌ بَيِّنٰتٌ مَّقَامُ اِبْرٰهِيْمَ ۛ وَمَنْ دَخَلَهٗ كَانَ اٰمِنًا ؕ وَلِلّٰهِ عَلَى النَّاسِ حِجُّ الْبَيْتِ مَنِ اسْتَطَاعَ اِلَيْهِ سَبِيْلًا ؕ وَمَنْ كَفَرَ فَاِنَّ اللّٰهَ غَنِيٌّ عَنِ الْعٰلَمِيْنَ ۝

قُلْ يٰٓاَهْلَ الْكِتٰبِ لِمَ تَكْفُرُوْنَ بِاٰيٰتِ اللّٰهِ ۖ وَاللّٰهُ شَهِيْدٌ عَلٰى مَا تَعْمَلُوْنَ ۝

قُلْ يٰٓاَهْلَ الْكِتٰبِ لِمَ تَصُدُّوْنَ عَنْ سَبِيْلِ اللّٰهِ مَنْ اٰمَنَ تَبْغُوْنَهَا عِوَجًا وَّاَنْتُمْ شُهَدَآءُ ؕ وَمَا اللّٰهُ بِغَافِلٍ عَمَّا تَعْمَلُوْنَ ۝

100. O ye who believe! If ye obey a party of those who have received the Scripture they will make you disbelievers after your belief.

101. How can ye disbelieve, when Allah's revelations are recited unto you, and His messenger is in your midst? He who holdeth fast to Allah, he indeed is guided unto a right path.

102. O ye who believe! Observe your duty to Allah with right observance, and die not save as those who have surrendered (unto Him);

103. And hold fast, all of you together, to the cable of Allah, and do not separate. And remember Allah's favour unto you: how ye were enemies and He made friendship between your hearts so that ye became as brothers by His grace; and (how) ye were upon the brink of an abyss of fire, and He did save you from it. Thus Allah maketh clear His revelations unto you that haply ye may be guided;

104. And there may spring from you a nation who invite to goodness, and enjoin right conduct and forbid indecency. Such are they who are successful.

105. And be ye not as those who separated and disputed after the clear proofs had come unto them. For such there is an awful doom,

106. On the day when (some) faces will be whitened and (some) faces will be blackened; and as for those whose faces have been blackened, it will be said unto them: Disbelieved ye after your (profession of) belief? Then taste the punishment for that ye disbelieved.

يٰۤاَيُّهَا الَّذِيْنَ اٰمَنُوْۤا اِنْ تُطِيْعُوْا فَرِيْقًا مِّنَ الَّذِيْنَ
اُوْتُوا الْكِتٰبَ يَرُدُّوْكُمْ بَعْدَ اِيْمَانِكُمْ كٰفِرِيْنَ ١٠٠
وَكَيْفَ تَكْفُرُوْنَ وَاَنْتُمْ تُتْلٰى عَلَيْكُمْ اٰيٰتُ اللّٰهِ وَ
فِيْكُمْ رَسُوْلُهٗ ؕ وَمَنْ يَّعْتَصِمْ بِاللّٰهِ فَقَدْ هُدِيَ
ع اِلٰى صِرَاطٍ مُّسْتَقِيْمٍ ١٠١
يٰۤاَيُّهَا الَّذِيْنَ اٰمَنُوا اتَّقُوا اللّٰهَ حَقَّ تُقٰتِهٖ وَلَا
تَمُوْتُنَّ اِلَّا وَاَنْتُمْ مُّسْلِمُوْنَ ١٠٢
وَاعْتَصِمُوْا بِحَبْلِ اللّٰهِ جَمِيْعًا وَّلَا تَفَرَّقُوْا ۪
وَاذْكُرُوْا نِعْمَتَ اللّٰهِ عَلَيْكُمْ اِذْ كُنْتُمْ اَعْدَآءً
فَاَلَّفَ بَيْنَ قُلُوْبِكُمْ فَاَصْبَحْتُمْ بِنِعْمَتِهٖۤ اِخْوَانًا ۚ
وَكُنْتُمْ عَلٰى شَفَا حُفْرَةٍ مِّنَ النَّارِ فَاَنْقَذَكُمْ
مِّنْهَا ؕ كَذٰلِكَ يُبَيِّنُ اللّٰهُ لَكُمْ اٰيٰتِهٖ لَعَلَّكُمْ
تَهْتَدُوْنَ ١٠٣
وَلْتَكُنْ مِّنْكُمْ اُمَّةٌ يَّدْعُوْنَ اِلَى الْخَيْرِ وَيَاْمُرُوْنَ
بِالْمَعْرُوْفِ وَيَنْهَوْنَ عَنِ الْمُنْكَرِ ؕ وَاُولٰٓئِكَ هُمُ
الْمُفْلِحُوْنَ ١٠٤
وَلَا تَكُوْنُوْا كَالَّذِيْنَ تَفَرَّقُوْا وَاخْتَلَفُوْا مِنْ بَعْدِ مَا
جَآءَهُمُ الْبَيِّنٰتُ ؕ وَاُولٰٓئِكَ لَهُمْ عَذَابٌ عَظِيْمٌ ١٠٥
يَّوْمَ تَبْيَضُّ وُجُوْهٌ وَّتَسْوَدُّ وُجُوْهٌ ۚ فَاَمَّا الَّذِيْنَ
اسْوَدَّتْ وُجُوْهُهُمْ ۟ اَكَفَرْتُمْ بَعْدَ
اِيْمَانِكُمْ فَذُوْقُوا الْعَذَابَ بِمَا كُنْتُمْ
تَكْفُرُوْنَ ١٠٦

107. As for those whose faces have been whitened, lo! in the mercy of Allah they dwell for ever.

وَاَمَّا الَّذِيْنَ ابْيَضَّتْ وُجُوْهُهُمْ فَفِىْ رَحْمَةِ اللّٰهِ هُمْ فِيْهَا خَٰلِدُوْنَ ۝

108. These are revelations of Allah. We recite them unto thee in truth. Allah willeth no injustice to (His) creatures.

تِلْكَ اٰيٰتُ اللّٰهِ نَتْلُوْهَا عَلَيْكَ بِالْحَقِّ ۚ وَمَا اللّٰهُ يُرِيْدُ ظُلْمًا لِّلْعٰلَمِيْنَ ۝

109. Unto Allah belongeth whatsoever is in the heavens and whatsoever is in the earth; and unto Allah all things are returned.

وَلِلّٰهِ مَا فِى السَّمٰوٰتِ وَمَا فِى الْاَرْضِ ۚ وَاِلَى اللّٰهِ تُرْجَعُ الْاُمُوْرُ ۝

110. Ye are the best community that hath been raised up for mankind. Ye enjoin right conduct and forbid indecency; and ye believe in Allah. And if the People of the Scripture had believed it had been better for them. Some of them are believers; but most of them are evil-livers.

كُنْتُمْ خَيْرَ اُمَّةٍ اُخْرِجَتْ لِلنَّاسِ تَأْمُرُوْنَ بِالْمَعْرُوْفِ وَتَنْهَوْنَ عَنِ الْمُنْكَرِ وَتُؤْمِنُوْنَ بِاللّٰهِ ۚ وَلَوْ اٰمَنَ اَهْلُ الْكِتٰبِ لَكَانَ خَيْرًا لَّهُمْ ۚ مِنْهُمُ الْمُؤْمِنُوْنَ وَاَكْثَرُهُمُ الْفٰسِقُوْنَ ۝

111. They will not harm you save a trifling hurt, and if they fight against you they will turn and flee. And afterward they will not be helped.

لَنْ يَّضُرُّوْكُمْ اِلَّا اَذًى ۚ وَاِنْ يُّقَاتِلُوْكُمْ يُوَلُّوْكُمُ الْاَدْبَارَ ۖ ثُمَّ لَا يُنْصَرُوْنَ ۝

112. Ignominy shall be their portion wheresoever they are found save (where they grasp) a rope from Allah and a rope from men.[1] They have incurred anger from their Lord, and wretchedness is laid upon them. That is because they used to disbelieve the revelations of Allah, and slew the Prophets wrongfully. That is because they were rebellious and used to transgress.

ضُرِبَتْ عَلَيْهِمُ الذِّلَّةُ اَيْنَ مَا ثُقِفُوْٓا اِلَّا بِحَبْلٍ مِّنَ اللّٰهِ وَحَبْلٍ مِّنَ النَّاسِ وَبَآءُوْ بِغَضَبٍ مِّنَ اللّٰهِ وَضُرِبَتْ عَلَيْهِمُ الْمَسْكَنَةُ ۚ ذٰلِكَ بِاَنَّهُمْ كَانُوْا يَكْفُرُوْنَ بِاٰيٰتِ اللّٰهِ وَيَقْتُلُوْنَ الْاَنْۢبِيَآءَ بِغَيْرِ حَقٍّ ۚ ذٰلِكَ بِمَا عَصَوْا وَّكَانُوْا يَعْتَدُوْنَ ۝

113. They are not all alike. Of the People of the Scripture there is a staunch community who recite the revelations of Allah in the night season, falling prostrate (before Him).

لَيْسُوْا سَوَآءً ۗ مِنْ اَهْلِ الْكِتٰبِ اُمَّةٌ قَآئِمَةٌ يَّتْلُوْنَ اٰيٰتِ اللّٰهِ اٰنَآءَ الَّيْلِ وَهُمْ يَسْجُدُوْنَ ۝

114. They believe in Allah and the Last Day, and enjoin right conduct and forbid indecency, and vie one with another in good works. They are of the righteous.

يُؤْمِنُوْنَ بِاللّٰهِ وَالْيَوْمِ الْاٰخِرِ وَيَأْمُرُوْنَ بِالْمَعْرُوْفِ وَيَنْهَوْنَ عَنِ الْمُنْكَرِ وَيُسَارِعُوْنَ فِى الْخَيْرٰتِ ۖ وَاُولٰٓئِكَ مِنَ الصّٰلِحِيْنَ ۝

115. And whatever good they do, they will not be denied the meed thereof. Allah is Aware of those who ward off (evil).

وَمَا يَفْعَلُوْا مِنْ خَيْرٍ فَلَنْ يُّكْفَرُوْهُ ۗ وَاللّٰهُ عَلِيْمٌۢ بِالْمُتَّقِيْنَ ۝

1. *i.e.* when they keep the covenant which the Prophet had made with the Jews of Al-Madīnah.

110. Lo! the riches and the progeny of those who disbelieve will not avail them aught against Allah; and such are rightful owners of the Fire. They will abide therein.

إِنَّ الَّذِينَ كَفَرُوا لَن تُغْنِيَ عَنْهُمْ أَمْوَالُهُمْ وَلَا
أَوْلَادُهُم مِّنَ اللَّهِ شَيْئًا ۖ وَأُولَٰئِكَ أَصْحَابُ النَّارِ ۚ
هُمْ فِيهَا خَالِدُونَ ﴿١١٦﴾

117. The likeness of that which they spend in this life of the world is as the likeness of a biting, icy wind which smiteth the harvest of a people who have wronged themselves, and devastateth it. Allah wronged them not, but they did wrong themselves.

مَثَلُ مَا يُنفِقُونَ فِي هَٰذِهِ الْحَيَاةِ الدُّنْيَا كَمَثَلِ
رِيحٍ فِيهَا صِرٌّ أَصَابَتْ حَرْثَ قَوْمٍ ظَلَمُوا أَنفُسَهُمْ
فَأَهْلَكَتْهُ ۚ وَمَا ظَلَمَهُمُ اللَّهُ وَلَٰكِنْ أَنفُسَهُمْ
يَظْلِمُونَ ﴿١١٧﴾

118. O ye who believe! Take not for intimates others than your own folk, who would spare no pains to ruin you; they love to hamper you. Hatred is revealed by (the utterance of) their mouths, but that which their breasts hide is greater. We have made plain for you the revelations if ye will understand.

يَا أَيُّهَا الَّذِينَ آمَنُوا لَا تَتَّخِذُوا بِطَانَةً مِّن
دُونِكُمْ لَا يَأْلُونَكُمْ خَبَالًا وَدُّوا مَا عَنِتُّمْ قَدْ
بَدَتِ الْبَغْضَاءُ مِنْ أَفْوَاهِهِمْ ۖ وَمَا تُخْفِي
صُدُورُهُمْ أَكْبَرُ ۚ قَدْ بَيَّنَّا لَكُمُ الْآيَاتِ ۖ إِن كُنتُمْ
تَعْقِلُونَ ﴿١١٨﴾

119. Lo! ye are those who love them though they love you not, and ye believe in all the Scripture. When they fall in with you they say: We believe; but when they go apart they bite their finger tips at you, for rage. Say: Perish in your rage! Lo! Allah is Aware of what is hidden in (your) breasts.

هَا أَنتُمْ أُولَاءِ تُحِبُّونَهُمْ وَلَا يُحِبُّونَكُمْ وَتُؤْمِنُونَ بِالْكِتَابِ
كُلِّهِ وَإِذَا لَقُوكُمْ قَالُوا آمَنَّا ۖ وَإِذَا خَلَوْا عَضُّوا
عَلَيْكُمُ الْأَنَامِلَ مِنَ الْغَيْظِ ۚ قُلْ مُوتُوا بِغَيْظِكُمْ ۗ
إِنَّ اللَّهَ عَلِيمٌ بِذَاتِ الصُّدُورِ ﴿١١٩﴾

120. If a lucky chance befall you, it is evil unto them, and if disaster strike you they rejoice thereat. But if ye persevere and keep from evil their guile will never harm you. Lo! Allah is Surrounding what they do.

إِن تَمْسَسْكُمْ حَسَنَةٌ تَسُؤْهُمْ وَإِن تُصِبْكُمْ
سَيِّئَةٌ يَفْرَحُوا بِهَا ۖ وَإِن تَصْبِرُوا وَتَتَّقُوا لَا
يَضُرُّكُمْ كَيْدُهُمْ شَيْئًا ۗ إِنَّ اللَّهَ بِمَا يَعْمَلُونَ
مُحِيطٌ ﴿١٢٠﴾ ع ١٢

121. And remember when thou settedst forth at daybreak from thy housefolk to assign to the believers their positions for the battle,[1] Allah was Hearer, Knower.

وَإِذْ غَدَوْتَ مِنْ أَهْلِكَ تُبَوِّئُ الْمُؤْمِنِينَ مَقَاعِدَ
لِلْقِتَالِ ۗ وَاللَّهُ سَمِيعٌ عَلِيمٌ ﴿١٢١﴾

1. The battle of Mt. Uḥud near Al-Madīnah in the third year of the Hijrah. (See Introduction to this Sūrah).

122. When two parties of you almost fell away, and Allah was their Protecting Friend. In Allah do believers put their trust.

123. Allah had already given you the victory at Badr, when ye were contemptible. So observe your duty to Allah in order that ye may be thankful.

124. And when thou didst say unto the believers: Is it not sufficient for you that your Lord should support you with three thousand angels sent down (to your help)?

125. Nay, but if ye persevere, and keep mess evil, and (the enemy) attack you suddenly, your Lord will help you with five thousand angels sweeping on.

126. Allah ordained this only as a message of good cheer for you, and that thereby your hearts might be at rest— Victory cometh only from Allah, the Mighty, the Wise—

127. That He may cut off a part of those who disbelieve, or overwhelm them so that they retire, frustrated.

128. It is no concern at all of thee (Muhammad) whether He relent toward them or punish them; for they are evil-doers.

129. Unto Allah belongeth whatsoever is in the heavens and whatsoever is in the earth. He forgiveth whom He will, and punisheth whom He will. Allah is Forgiving, Merciful.

130. O ye who believe! Devour not usury, doubling and quadrupling (the sum lent). Observe your duty to Allah, that ye may be successful.

131. And ward off (from yourselves) the Fire prepared for disbelievers.

132. And obey Allah and the messenger, that ye may find mercy.

إذ همت طائفتان منكم أن تفشلا والله وليهما
وعلى الله فليتوكل المؤمنون ﴿١٢٢﴾
ولقد نصركم الله ببدر وأنتم أذلة فاتقوا
الله لعلكم تشكرون ﴿١٢٣﴾
إذ تقول للمؤمنين ألن يكفيكم أن يمدكم
ربكم بثلاثة آلاف من الملائكة منزلين ﴿١٢٤﴾
بلى إن تصبروا وتتقوا ويأتوكم من فورهم
هذا يمددكم ربكم بخمسة آلاف من الملائكة
مسومين ﴿١٢٥﴾
وما جعله الله إلا بشرى لكم ولتطمئن قلوبكم به
وما النصر إلا من عند الله العزيز الحكيم ﴿١٢٦﴾
ليقطع طرفا من الذين كفروا أو يكبتهم فينقلبوا
خائبين ﴿١٢٧﴾
ليس لك من الأمر شيء أو يتوب عليهم أو يعذبهم
فإنهم ظالمون ﴿١٢٨﴾
ولله ما في السماوات وما في الأرض يغفر لمن
يشاء ويعذب من يشاء والله غفور
رحيم ﴿١٢٩﴾ ع ١٣
يا أيها الذين آمنوا لا تأكلوا الربا أضعافا مضاعفة
واتقوا الله لعلكم تفلحون ﴿١٣٠﴾
واتقوا النار التي أعدت للكافرين ﴿١٣١﴾
وأطيعوا الله والرسول لعلكم ترحمون ﴿١٣٢﴾

133. And vie one with another for forgiveness from your Lord, and for a Paradise as wide as are the heavens and the earth, prepared for those who ward off (evil);

134. Those who spend (of that which Allah hath given them) in ease and in adversity, those who control their wrath and are forgiving toward mankind; Allah loveth the good;

135. And those who, when they do an evil thing or wrong themselves, remember Allah and implore forgiveness for their sins-- Who forgiveth sins save Allah only? -- and will not knowingly repeat (the wrong) they did. .

136. The reward of such will be forgiveness from their Lord, and Gardens underneath which rivers flow, wherein they will abide for ever -- a bountiful reward for workers!

137. Systems have passed away before you. Do but travel in the land and see the nature of the consequence for those who did deny (the messengers).

138. This is a declaration for mankind, a guidance and an admonition unto those who ward off (evil).

139. Faint not nor grieve, for ye will overcome them if ye are (indeed) believers.

140. If ye have received a blow, the (disbelieving) people have received a blow the like thereof.[1] These are (only) the vicissitudes which We cause to follow one another for mankind, to the end that Allah may know those who believe and may choose witnesses[2] from among you: and Allah loveth not wrong doers:

141. And that Allah may prove those who believe, and may blight the disbelievers.

142. Or deemed ye that ye would enter Paradise while yet Allah knoweth not those of you who really strive, not knoweth those (of you) who are steadfast?

1. At Badr.
2. Or *martyrs.*

وسارعوا الى مغفرة من ربكم وجنة عرضها
السموت والارض اعدت للمتقين ﴿١٣٣﴾
الذين ينفقون في السراء والضراء والكظمين
الغيظ والعافين عن الناس والله يحب المحسنين ﴿١٣٤﴾
والذين اذا فعلوا فاحشة او ظلموا انفسهم ذكروا الله
فاستغفروا لذنوبهم ومن يغفر الذنوب الا الله
ولم يصروا على ما فعلوا وهم يعلمون ﴿١٣٥﴾
اولئك جزاؤهم مغفرة من ربهم وجنت تجري
من تحتها الانهر خلدين فيها ونعم اجر
العملين ﴿١٣٦﴾
قد خلت من قبلكم سنن فسيروا في الارض
فانظروا كيف كان عاقبة المكذبين ﴿١٣٧﴾
هذا بيان للناس وهدى وموعظة للمتقين ﴿١٣٨﴾
ولا تهنوا ولا تحزنوا وانتم الاعلون ان كنتم
مؤمنين ﴿١٣٩﴾
ان يمسسكم قرح فقد مس القوم قرح مثله و
تلك الايام نداولها بين الناس وليعلم الله
الذين امنوا ويتخذ منكم شهداء والله لا
يحب الظلمين ﴿١٤٠﴾
وليمحص الله الذين امنوا ويمحق الكفرين ﴿١٤١﴾
ام حسبتم ان تدخلوا الجنة ولما يعلم الله الذين
جهدوا منكم ويعلم الصبرين ﴿١٤٢﴾

143. And verily ye used to wish for death before ye met it (in the field). Now ye have seen it with your eyes!

وَلَقَدْ كُنْتُمْ تَمَنَّوْنَ الْمَوْتَ مِنْ قَبْلِ أَنْ تَلْقَوْهُ
فَقَدْ رَأَيْتُمُوهُ وَأَنْتُمْ تَنْظُرُونَ ﴿١٤٣﴾

144. Muhammad is but a messenger, messengers (the like of whom) have passed away before him. Will it be that, when he dieth or is slain, ye will turn back on your heels? He who turneth back doth no hurt to Allah, and Allah will reward the thankful.[1]

وَمَا مُحَمَّدٌ إِلَّا رَسُولٌ قَدْ خَلَتْ مِنْ قَبْلِهِ
الرُّسُلُ أَفَإِنْ مَاتَ أَوْ قُتِلَ انْقَلَبْتُمْ عَلَىٰ
أَعْقَابِكُمْ وَمَنْ يَنْقَلِبْ عَلَىٰ عَقِبَيْهِ فَلَنْ يَضُرَّ
اللَّهَ شَيْئًا وَسَيَجْزِي اللَّهُ الشَّاكِرِينَ ﴿١٤٤﴾

145. No soul can ever die except by Allah's leave and at a term appointed. Whoso desireth the reward of the world, We bestow on him thereof; and whoso desireth the reward of the Hereafter, We bestow on him thereof. We shall reward the thankful.

وَمَا كَانَ لِنَفْسٍ أَنْ تَمُوتَ إِلَّا بِإِذْنِ اللَّهِ كِتَابًا
مُؤَجَّلًا وَمَنْ يُرِدْ ثَوَابَ الدُّنْيَا نُؤْتِهِ مِنْهَا
وَمَنْ يُرِدْ ثَوَابَ الْآخِرَةِ نُؤْتِهِ مِنْهَا وَسَنَجْزِي
الشَّاكِرِينَ ﴿١٤٥﴾

146. And with how many a prophet have there been a number of devoted men who fought (beside him). They quailed not for aught that befell them in the way of Allah, nor did they weaken, nor were they brought low. Allah loveth the steadfast.

وَكَأَيِّنْ مِنْ نَبِيٍّ قُتِلَ مَعَهُ رِبِّيُّونَ كَثِيرٌ
فَمَا وَهَنُوا لِمَا أَصَابَهُمْ فِي سَبِيلِ اللَّهِ
وَمَا ضَعُفُوا وَمَا اسْتَكَانُوا وَاللَّهُ يُحِبُّ
الصَّابِرِينَ ﴿١٤٦﴾

147. Their cry was only that they said: Our Lord! Forgive us for our sins and wasted efforts, make our foothold sure, and give us victory over the disbelieving folk.

وَمَا كَانَ قَوْلَهُمْ إِلَّا أَنْ قَالُوا رَبَّنَا اغْفِرْ لَنَا
ذُنُوبَنَا وَإِسْرَافَنَا فِي أَمْرِنَا وَثَبِّتْ أَقْدَامَنَا
وَانْصُرْنَا عَلَى الْقَوْمِ الْكَافِرِينَ ﴿١٤٧﴾

148. So Allah gave them the reward of the world and the good reward of the Hereafter. Allah loveth those whose deeds are good.

فَآتَاهُمُ اللَّهُ ثَوَابَ الدُّنْيَا وَحُسْنَ ثَوَابِ
الْآخِرَةِ وَاللَّهُ يُحِبُّ الْمُحْسِنِينَ ﴿١٤٨﴾

149. O ye who believe! If ye obey those who disbelieve, they will make you turn back on your heels, and ye turn back as losers.

يَا أَيُّهَا الَّذِينَ آمَنُوا إِنْ تُطِيعُوا الَّذِينَ كَفَرُوا
يَرُدُّوكُمْ عَلَىٰ أَعْقَابِكُمْ فَتَنْقَلِبُوا خَاسِرِينَ ﴿١٤٩﴾

150. But Allah is your Protector, and He is the best of helpers.

بَلِ اللَّهُ مَوْلَاكُمْ وَهُوَ خَيْرُ النَّاصِرِينَ ﴿١٥٠﴾

1. On the morning when the Prophet died, Abû Bakr came into the mosque at Al-Madinah and found the people all distracted, and Omar telling them that it was a sin to say that he was dead. Abû Bakr went and ascertained the truth, and coming back into the mosque, cried: "Lo! as for him who worshipped Muhammad, Muhammad is dead, but as for him who worshippeth Allah, Allah is alive and dieth not." Then he recited this verse "and it was as if the people had not known till then that such a verse had been revealed."

151. We shall cast terror into the hearts of those who disbelieve because they ascribe unto Allah partners, for which no warrant hath been revealed. Their habitation is the Fire, and hapless the abode of the wrong-doers.

152. Allah verily made good His promise unto you when ye routed them by His leave, until (the moment) when your courage failed you, and ye disagreed about the order and ye disobeyed, after He had shown you that for which ye long.[1] Some of you desired the world, and some of you desired the Hereafter. Therefore He made you flee from them, that He might try you. Yet now He hath forgiven you. Allah is Lord of Kindness to believers.

153. When ye climbed (the hill) and paid no heed to anyone, while the messenger, in your rear, was calling you (to fight). Therefore He rewarded you grief for (his) grief, that (He might teach) you not to sorrow either for that which ye missed or for that which befell you. Allah is Informed of what ye do.

154. Then, after grief, He sent down security for you. As slumber did it overcome a party of you, while (the other) party, who were anxious on their own account, thought wrongly of Allah, the thought of ignorance. They said: Have we any part in the cause? Say (O Muhammad): The cause belongeth wholly to Allah. They hide within themselves (a thought) which they reveal not unto thee, saying: Had we had any part in the cause we should not have been slain here. Say: Even though ye had been in your houses, those appointed to be slain would have gone forth to the places where they were to lie. (All this hath been) in order that Allah might try what is in your breasts and prove what is in your hearts. Allah is Aware of what is hidden in the breasts (of men).

سَنُلْقِي فِي قُلُوبِ الَّذِينَ كَفَرُوا الرُّعْبَ بِمَا
أَشْرَكُوا بِاللَّهِ مَا لَمْ يُنَزِّلْ بِهِ سُلْطَانًا ۚ وَمَأْوَاهُمُ
النَّارُ ۚ وَبِئْسَ مَثْوَى الظَّالِمِينَ ﴿١٥١﴾
وَلَقَدْ صَدَقَكُمُ اللَّهُ وَعْدَهُ إِذْ تَحُسُّونَهُم بِإِذْنِهِ ۖ
حَتَّىٰ إِذَا فَشِلْتُمْ وَتَنَازَعْتُمْ فِي الْأَمْرِ وَعَصَيْتُم
مِّن بَعْدِ مَا أَرَاكُم مَّا تُحِبُّونَ ۚ مِنكُم مَّن يُرِيدُ الدُّنْيَا
وَمِنكُم مَّن يُرِيدُ الْآخِرَةَ ۚ ثُمَّ صَرَفَكُمْ عَنْهُمْ
لِيَبْتَلِيَكُمْ ۖ وَلَقَدْ عَفَا عَنكُمْ ۗ وَاللَّهُ ذُو فَضْلٍ
عَلَى الْمُؤْمِنِينَ ﴿١٥٢﴾
إِذْ تُصْعِدُونَ وَلَا تَلْوُونَ عَلَىٰ أَحَدٍ وَالرَّسُولُ
يَدْعُوكُمْ فِي أُخْرَاكُمْ فَأَثَابَكُمْ غَمًّا بِغَمٍّ لِّكَيْلَا
تَحْزَنُوا عَلَىٰ مَا فَاتَكُمْ وَلَا مَا أَصَابَكُمْ ۗ وَاللَّهُ
خَبِيرٌ بِمَا تَعْمَلُونَ ﴿١٥٣﴾
ثُمَّ أَنزَلَ عَلَيْكُم مِّن بَعْدِ الْغَمِّ أَمَنَةً نُّعَاسًا يَغْشَىٰ
طَائِفَةً مِّنكُمْ ۖ وَطَائِفَةٌ قَدْ أَهَمَّتْهُمْ أَنفُسُهُمْ
يَظُنُّونَ بِاللَّهِ غَيْرَ الْحَقِّ ظَنَّ الْجَاهِلِيَّةِ ۖ يَقُولُونَ
هَل لَّنَا مِنَ الْأَمْرِ مِن شَيْءٍ ۗ قُلْ إِنَّ الْأَمْرَ كُلَّهُ لِلَّهِ ۗ
يُخْفُونَ فِي أَنفُسِهِم مَّا لَا يُبْدُونَ لَكَ ۖ يَقُولُونَ لَوْ
كَانَ لَنَا مِنَ الْأَمْرِ شَيْءٌ مَّا قُتِلْنَا هَاهُنَا ۗ قُل لَّوْ
كُنتُمْ فِي بُيُوتِكُمْ لَبَرَزَ الَّذِينَ كُتِبَ عَلَيْهِمُ الْقَتْلُ
إِلَىٰ مَضَاجِعِهِمْ ۖ وَلِيَبْتَلِيَ اللَّهُ مَا فِي صُدُورِكُمْ
وَلِيُمَحِّصَ مَا فِي قُلُوبِكُمْ ۗ وَاللَّهُ عَلِيمٌ بِذَاتِ الصُّدُورِ ﴿١٥٤﴾

1. **When the archers deserted their post to share in the spoils, thinking that the day was won.**

155. Lo! those of you who turned back on the day when the two hosts met, Satan alone it was who caused them to backslide, because of some of that which they have earned. Now Allah hath forgiven them. Lo! Allah is Forgiving, Clement.

156. O ye who believe! Be not as those who disbelieved and said of their brethren who went abroad in the land or were fighting in the field: If they had been (here) with us they would not have died or been killed; that Allah may make it anguish in their hearts. Allah giveth life and causeth death; and Allah is Seer of what ye do.

157. And what though ye be slain in Allah's way or die therein? Surely pardon from Allah and mercy are better than all that they amass.

158. What though ye be slain or die, when unto Allah ye are gathered?

159. It was by the mercy of Allah that thou wast lenient with them (O Muhammad), for if thou hadst been stern and fierce of heart they would have dispersed from round about thee. So pardon them and ask forgiveness for them and consult with them upon the conduct of affairs. And when thou art resolved, then put thy trust in Allah. Lo! Allah loveth those who put their trust (in Him).

160. If Allah is your helper none can overcome you, and if He withdraw His help from you, who is there who can help you? In Allah let believers put their trust.

161. It is not for any Prophet to deceive (mankind). Whoso deceiveth will bring his deceit with him on the Day of Resurrection. Then every soul will be paid in full what it hath earned; and they will not be wronged.

إِنَّ الَّذِينَ تَوَلَّوْا مِنكُمْ يَوْمَ الْتَقَى الْجَمْعَانِ إِنَّمَا
اسْتَزَلَّهُمُ الشَّيْطَانُ بِبَعْضِ مَا كَسَبُوا ۖ وَلَقَدْ عَفَا
اللَّهُ عَنْهُمْ ۗ إِنَّ اللَّهَ غَفُورٌ حَلِيمٌ ﴿١٥٥﴾ ع
يَا أَيُّهَا الَّذِينَ آمَنُوا لَا تَكُونُوا كَالَّذِينَ كَفَرُوا وَقَالُوا
لِإِخْوَانِهِمْ إِذَا ضَرَبُوا فِي الْأَرْضِ أَوْ كَانُوا غُزًّى لَّوْ
كَانُوا عِندَنَا مَا مَاتُوا وَمَا قُتِلُوا لِيَجْعَلَ اللَّهُ
ذَٰلِكَ حَسْرَةً فِي قُلُوبِهِمْ ۗ وَاللَّهُ يُحْيِي وَيُمِيتُ ۗ وَ
اللَّهُ بِمَا تَعْمَلُونَ بَصِيرٌ ﴿١٥٦﴾
وَلَئِن قُتِلْتُمْ فِي سَبِيلِ اللَّهِ أَوْ مُتُّمْ لَمَغْفِرَةٌ مِّنَ
اللَّهِ وَرَحْمَةٌ خَيْرٌ مِّمَّا يَجْمَعُونَ ﴿١٥٧﴾
وَلَئِن مُّتُّمْ أَوْ قُتِلْتُمْ لَإِلَى اللَّهِ تُحْشَرُونَ ﴿١٥٨﴾
فَبِمَا رَحْمَةٍ مِّنَ اللَّهِ لِنتَ لَهُمْ ۖ وَلَوْ كُنتَ فَظًّا
غَلِيظَ الْقَلْبِ لَانفَضُّوا مِنْ حَوْلِكَ ۖ فَاعْفُ عَنْهُمْ
وَاسْتَغْفِرْ لَهُمْ وَشَاوِرْهُمْ فِي الْأَمْرِ ۖ فَإِذَا عَزَمْتَ
فَتَوَكَّلْ عَلَى اللَّهِ ۚ إِنَّ اللَّهَ يُحِبُّ
الْمُتَوَكِّلِينَ ﴿١٥٩﴾
إِن يَنصُرْكُمُ اللَّهُ فَلَا غَالِبَ لَكُمْ ۖ وَإِن يَخْذُلْكُمْ
فَمَن ذَا الَّذِي يَنصُرُكُم مِّن بَعْدِهِ ۗ وَعَلَى اللَّهِ
فَلْيَتَوَكَّلِ الْمُؤْمِنُونَ ﴿١٦٠﴾
وَمَا كَانَ لِنَبِيٍّ أَن يَغُلَّ ۚ وَمَن يَغْلُلْ يَأْتِ بِمَا
غَلَّ يَوْمَ الْقِيَامَةِ ۚ ثُمَّ تُوَفَّىٰ كُلُّ نَفْسٍ مَّا كَسَبَتْ
وَهُمْ لَا يُظْلَمُونَ ﴿١٦١﴾

162. Is one who followeth the pleasure of Allah as one who hath earned condemnation from Allah, whose habitation is the Fire, a hapless journey's end?

163. There are degrees (of grace and reprobation) with Allah, and Allah is Seer of what ye do.

164. Allah verily hath shown grace to the believers by sending unto them a messenger of their own who reciteth unto them His revelations, and causeth them to grow, and teacheth them the Scripture and wisdom;[1] although before (he came to them) they were in flagrant error.

165. And was it so, when a disaster smote you, though ye had smitten (them with a disaster) twice (as great),[2] that ye said: How is this ? Say (unto them, O Muhammad): It is from yourselves. Lo! Allah is Able to do all things.

166. That which befell you, on the day when the two armies met, was by permission of Allah; that He might know the true believers;

167. And that He might know the hypocrites, unto whom it was said: Come, fight in the way of Allah, or defend yourselves. They answered: if we knew aught of fighting we would follow you. On that day they were nearer disbelief than faith. They utter with their mouths a thing which is not in their hearts. Allah is best aware of what they hide.

168. Those who, while they sat at home, said of their brethren (who were fighting for the cause of Allah): If they had been guided by us they would not have been slain. Say (unto them, O Muhammad): Then avert death from yourselves if ye are truthful.

169. Think not of those who are slain in the way of Allah, as dead. Nay, they are living. With their Lord they have provision :

أَفَمَنِ اتَّبَعَ رِضْوَانَ اللّٰهِ كَمَنْ بَآءَ بِسَخَطٍ مِّنَ اللّٰهِ
وَمَأْوٰىهُ جَهَنَّمُ وَبِئْسَ الْمَصِيْرُ ﴿١٦٢﴾
هُمْ دَرَجٰتٌ عِنْدَ اللّٰهِ وَاللّٰهُ بَصِيْرٌ بِمَا يَعْمَلُوْنَ ﴿١٦٣﴾
لَقَدْ مَنَّ اللّٰهُ عَلَى الْمُؤْمِنِيْنَ اِذْ بَعَثَ فِيْهِمْ رَسُوْلًا
مِّنْ اَنْفُسِهِمْ يَتْلُوْا عَلَيْهِمْ اٰيٰتِهٖ وَيُزَكِّيْهِمْ وَ
يُعَلِّمُهُمُ الْكِتٰبَ وَالْحِكْمَةَ وَاِنْ كَانُوْا مِنْ قَبْلُ
لَفِيْ ضَلٰلٍ مُّبِيْنٍ ﴿١٦٤﴾
اَوَلَمَّآ اَصَابَتْكُمْ مُّصِيْبَةٌ قَدْ اَصَبْتُمْ مِّثْلَيْهَا
قُلْتُمْ اَنّٰى هٰذَا قُلْ هُوَ مِنْ عِنْدِ اَنْفُسِكُمْ اِنَّ
اللّٰهَ عَلٰى كُلِّ شَيْءٍ قَدِيْرٌ ﴿١٦٥﴾
وَمَآ اَصَابَكُمْ يَوْمَ الْتَقَى الْجَمْعٰنِ فَبِاِذْنِ اللّٰهِ
وَلِيَعْلَمَ الْمُؤْمِنِيْنَ ﴿١٦٦﴾
وَلِيَعْلَمَ الَّذِيْنَ نَافَقُوْا وَقِيْلَ لَهُمْ تَعَالَوْا قَاتِلُوْا
فِيْ سَبِيْلِ اللّٰهِ اَوِ ادْفَعُوْا قَالُوْا لَوْ نَعْلَمُ قِتَالًا
لَّاتَّبَعْنٰكُمْ هُمْ لِلْكُفْرِ يَوْمَئِذٍ اَقْرَبُ مِنْهُمْ لِلْاِيْمَانِ
يَقُوْلُوْنَ بِاَفْوَاهِهِمْ مَّا لَيْسَ فِيْ قُلُوْبِهِمْ وَاللّٰهُ اَعْلَمُ
بِمَا يَكْتُمُوْنَ ﴿١٦٧﴾
اَلَّذِيْنَ قَالُوْا لِاِخْوَانِهِمْ وَقَعَدُوْا لَوْ اَطَاعُوْنَا
مَا قُتِلُوْا قُلْ فَادْرَءُوْا عَنْ اَنْفُسِكُمُ الْمَوْتَ اِنْ
كُنْتُمْ صٰدِقِيْنَ ﴿١٦٨﴾
وَلَا تَحْسَبَنَّ الَّذِيْنَ قُتِلُوْا فِيْ سَبِيْلِ اللّٰهِ اَمْوَاتًا
بَلْ اَحْيَآءٌ عِنْدَ رَبِّهِمْ يُرْزَقُوْنَ ﴿١٦٩﴾

1. In fulfilment of the prayer of Abraham (Sûrah II, v. 129).
2. At Badr.

170. Jubilant (are they) because of that which Allah hath bestowed upon them of His bounty, rejoicing for the sake of those who have not joined them but are left behind: that there shall no fear come upon them neither shall they grieve.

فرحين بما اتاهم الله من فضله ويستبشرون
بالذين لم يلحقوا بهم من خلفهم الا خوف
عليهم ولا هم يحزنون ﴿١٧٠﴾ وقف لازم

171. They rejoice because of favour from Allah and kindness, and that Allah wasteth not the wage of the believers.

يستبشرون بنعمة من الله وفضل وان الله لا
ع ١٧ يضيع اجر المؤمنين ﴿١٧١﴾

172. As for those who heard the call of Allah and His messenger after the harm befell them (in the fight); for such of them as do right and ward off (evil), there is great reward.

الذين استجابوا لله والرسول من بعد ما اصابهم
مع ٢ القرح للذين احسنوا منهم واتقوا اجر عظيم ﴿١٧٢﴾

173. Those unto whom men said: Lo! the people have gathered against you, therefor fear them. (The threat of danger) but increased the faith of them and they cried: Allah is sufficient for us! Most Excellent is He in Whom we trust!

الذين قال لهم الناس ان الناس قد جمعوا
لكم فاخشوهم فزادهم ايمانا وقالوا حسبنا
الله ونعم الوكيل ﴿١٧٣﴾

174. So they returned with grace and favour from Allah, and no harm touched them. They followed the good pleasure of Allah, and Allah is of Infinite bounty.

فانقلبوا بنعمة من الله وفضل لم يمسسهم سوء
واتبعوا رضوان الله والله ذو فضل عظيم ﴿١٧٤﴾

175. It is only the devil who would make (men) fear his partisans. Fear them not; fear Me, if ye are true believers.

انما ذلكم الشيطن يخوف اولياءه فلا تخافوهم
وخافون ان كنتم مؤمنين ﴿١٧٥﴾

176. Let not their conduct grieve thee, who run easily to disbelief, for lo! they injure Allah not at all. It is Allah's will to assign them no portion in the Hereafter, and theirs will be an awful doom.

ولا يحزنك الذين يسارعون في الكفر انهم
لن يضروا الله شيئا يريد الله الا يجعل لهم
حظا في الاخرة ولهم عذاب عظيم ﴿١٧٦﴾

177. Those who purchase disbelief at the price of faith harm Allah not at all, but theirs will be a painful doom.

ان الذين اشتروا الكفر بالايمان لن يضروا
الله شيئا ولهم عذاب اليم ﴿١٧٧﴾

178. And let not those who disbelieve imagine that the rein We give them bodeth good unto their souls. We only give them rein that they may grow in sinfulness. And theirs will be a shameful doom.

ولا يحسبن الذين كفروا انما نملي لهم خير
لانفسهم انما نملي لهم ليزدادوا اثما ولهم
عذاب مهين ﴿١٧٨﴾

179. It is not (the purpose) of Allah to leave you in your present state till He shall separate the wicked from the good. And it is not (the purpose of) Allah to let you know the unseen. But Allah chooseth of His messengers whom He will, (to receive knowledge thereof). So believe in Allah and His messengers. If ye believe and ward off (evil), yours will be a vast reward.

180. And let not those who hoard up that which Allah hath bestowed upon them of His bounty think that it is better for them. Nay, it is worse for them. That which they hoard will be their collar on the Day of Resurrection. Allah's is the heritage of the heavens and the earth, and Allah is Informed of what ye do.

181. Verily Allah heard the saying of those who said, (when asked for contributions to the war): "Allah, forsooth, is poor, and we are rich!"[1] We shall record their saying with their slaying of the Prophets wrongfully and We shall say: Taste ye the punishment of burning!

182. This is on account of that which your own hands have sent before (you to the judgement). Allah is no oppressor of (His) bondmen.

183. (The same are) those who say: Lo! Allah hath charged us that we believe not in any messenger until he bring us an offering which fire (from heaven) shall devour. Say (unto them, O Muhammad): Messengers came unto you before me with miracles, and with that (very miracle) which ye describe. Why then did ye slay them? (Answer that) if ye are truthful!

184. And if they deny thee, even so did they deny messengers who were before thee, who came with miracles and with the Psalms and with the Scripture giving light.

185. Every soul will taste of death. And ye will be paid on the Day of Resurrection only that which ye have fairly earned. Whoso is removed from the Fire and is made to enter Paradise, he indeed is triumphant. The life of this world is but comfort of illusion.

1. A saying of some Jews of Al-Madinah.

ما كان الله ليذر المؤمنين على ما انتم عليه حتى
يميز الخبيث من الطيب وما كان الله ليطلعكم على
الغيب ولكن الله يجتبي من رسله من يشاء فامنوا
بالله ورسله وان تؤمنوا وتتقوا فلكم اجر عظيم ﴿١٧٩﴾
ولا يحسبن الذين يبخلون بما اتىهم الله من
فضله هو خيرا لهم بل هو شر لهم سيطوقون
ما بخلوا به يوم القيمة ولله ميراث السموت و
الارض والله بما تعملون خبير ﴿١٨٠﴾ ع
لقد سمع الله قول الذين قالوا ان الله فقير و
نحن اغنياء سنكتب ما قالوا وقتلهم الانبياء
بغير حق ونقول ذوقوا عذاب الحريق ﴿١٨١﴾
ذلك بما قدمت ايديكم وان الله ليس بظلام
للعبيد ﴿١٨٢﴾
الذين قالوا ان الله عهد الينا الا نؤمن لرسول
حتى ياتينا بقربان تاكله النار قل قد جاءكم
رسل من قبلي بالبينت وبالذي قلتم فلم قتلتموهم
ان كنتم صدقين ﴿١٨٣﴾
فان كذبوك فقد كذب رسل من قبلك جاءو
بالبينت والزبر والكتب المنير ﴿١٨٤﴾
كل نفس ذائقة الموت وانما توفون اجوركم يوم
القيمة فمن زحزح عن النار وادخل الجنة
فقد فاز وما الحيوة الدنيا الا متاع الغرور ﴿١٨٥﴾

186. Assuredly ye will be tried in your property and in your persons, and ye will hear much wrong from those who were given the Scripture before you, and from the idolaters. But if ye persevere and ward off (evil), then that is of the steadfast heart of things.

لَتُبْلَوُنَّ فِىۤ اَمْوَالِكُمْ وَاَنْفُسِكُمْ وَلَتَسْمَعُنَّ مِنَ الَّذِيْنَ اُوْتُوا الْكِتٰبَ مِنْ قَبْلِكُمْ وَمِنَ الَّذِيْنَ اَشْرَكُوْۤا اَذًى كَثِيْرًا وَاِنْ تَصْبِرُوْا وَتَتَّقُوْا فَاِنَّ ذٰلِكَ مِنْ عَزْمِ الْاُمُوْرِ ۝

187. And (remember) when Allah laid a charge on those who had received the Scripture (He said): Ye are to expound it to mankind and not to hide it. But they flung it behind their backs and bought thereby a little gain. Verily evil is that which they have gained thereby.

وَاِذْ اَخَذَ اللّٰهُ مِيْثَاقَ الَّذِيْنَ اُوْتُوا الْكِتٰبَ لَتُبَيِّنُنَّهٗ لِلنَّاسِ وَلَا تَكْتُمُوْنَهٗ فَنَبَذُوْهُ وَرَآءَ ظُهُوْرِهِمْ وَاشْتَرَوْا بِهٖ ثَمَنًا قَلِيْلًا فَبِئْسَ مَا يَشْتَرُوْنَ ۝

188. Think not that those who exult in what they have given, and love to be praised for what they have not done—Think not they are in safety from the doom. A painful doom is theirs.

لَا تَحْسَبَنَّ الَّذِيْنَ يَفْرَحُوْنَ بِمَاۤ اَتَوْا وَّيُحِبُّوْنَ اَنْ يُّحْمَدُوْا بِمَا لَمْ يَفْعَلُوْا فَلَا تَحْسَبَنَّهُمْ بِمَفَازَةٍ مِّنَ الْعَذَابِ وَلَهُمْ عَذَابٌ اَلِيْمٌ ۝

189. Unto Allah belongeth the Sovereignty of the heavens and the earth. Allah is Able to do all things.

وَلِلّٰهِ مُلْكُ السَّمٰوٰتِ وَالْاَرْضِ وَاللّٰهُ عَلٰى كُلِّ شَىْءٍ قَدِيْرٌ ۝

190. Lo! In the creation of the heavens and the earth and (in) the difference of night and day are tokens (of His sovereignty) for men of understanding,

اِنَّ فِىْ خَلْقِ السَّمٰوٰتِ وَالْاَرْضِ وَاخْتِلَافِ الَّيْلِ وَالنَّهَارِ لَاٰيٰتٍ لِّاُولِى الْاَلْبَابِ ۝

191. Such as remember Allah, standing, sitting, and reclining, and consider the creation of the heavens and the earth, (and say): Our Lord! Thou createdst not this in vain. Glory be to Thee! Preserve us from the doom of Fire:

الَّذِيْنَ يَذْكُرُوْنَ اللّٰهَ قِيَامًا وَّقُعُوْدًا وَّعَلٰى جُنُوْبِهِمْ وَيَتَفَكَّرُوْنَ فِىْ خَلْقِ السَّمٰوٰتِ وَالْاَرْضِ رَبَّنَا مَا خَلَقْتَ هٰذَا بَاطِلًا سُبْحٰنَكَ فَقِنَا عَذَابَ النَّارِ ۝

192. Our Lord! Whom Thou causest to enter the Fire: him indeed Thou hast confounded. For evil-doers there will be no helpers.

رَبَّنَاۤ اِنَّكَ مَنْ تُدْخِلِ النَّارَ فَقَدْ اَخْزَيْتَهٗ وَمَا لِلظّٰلِمِيْنَ مِنْ اَنْصَارٍ ۝

193. Our Lord! Lo! we have heard a crier calling unto Faith: "Believe ye in your Lord!" So we believed. Our Lord! Therefor forgive us our sins, and remit from us our evil deeds, and make us die the death of the righteous.

رَبَّنَاۤ اِنَّنَا سَمِعْنَا مُنَادِيًا يُّنَادِيْ لِلْاِيْمَانِ اَنْ اٰمِنُوْا بِرَبِّكُمْ فَاٰمَنَّا رَبَّنَا فَاغْفِرْ لَنَا ذُنُوْبَنَا وَكَفِّرْ عَنَّا سَيِّاٰتِنَا وَتَوَفَّنَا مَعَ الْاَبْرَارِ ۝

194. Our Lord! And give us that which Thou hast promised to us by Thy messengers. Confound us not upon the Day of Resurrection. Lo! Thou breakest not the tryst.

195. And their Lord hath heard them (and He saith): Lo! I suffer not the work of any worker, male or female, to be lost. Ye proceed one from another.[1] So those who fled and were driven forth from their homes and suffered damage for My cause, and fought and were slain, verily I shall remit their evil deeds from them and verily I shall bring them into Gardens underneath which rivers flow—A reward from Allah. And with Allah is the fairest of rewards.

196. Let not the vicissitude (of the success) of those who disbelieve, in the land, deceive thee (O Muhammad).

197. It is but a brief comfort. And afterward their habitation will be hell, an ill abode.

198. But those who keep their duty to their Lord, for them are Gardens underneath which rivers flow, wherein they will be safe for ever. A gift of welcome from their Lord. That which Allah hath in store is better for the righteous.

199. And lo! of the People of the Scripture there are some who believe in Allah and that which is revealed unto you and that which was revealed unto them, humbling themselves before Allah. They purchase not a trifling gain at the price of the revelations of Allah. Verily their reward is with their Lord, and lo! Allah is swift to take account.

200. O ye who believe! Endure, outdo all others in endurance, be ready, and observe your duty to Allah, in order that ye may succeed.

ربنا وآتنا ما وعدتنا على رسلك ولا تخزنا يوم
القيامة إنك لا تخلف الميعاد ﴿١٩٤﴾
فاستجاب لهم ربهم أني لا أضيع عمل عامل
منكم من ذكر أو أنثى بعضكم من بعض
فالذين هاجروا وأخرجوا من ديارهم وأوذوا
في سبيلي وقاتلوا وقتلوا لأكفرن عنهم سيئاتهم
ولأدخلنهم جنات تجري من تحتها الأنهار ثوابا
من عند الله والله عنده حسن الثواب ﴿١٩٥﴾
لا يغرنك تقلب الذين كفروا في البلاد ﴿١٩٦﴾
متاع قليل ثم مأواهم جهنم وبئس المهاد ﴿١٩٧﴾
لكن الذين اتقوا ربهم لهم جنات تجري من تحتها
الأنهار خالدين فيها نزلا من عند الله وما عند
الله خير للأبرار ﴿١٩٨﴾
وإن من أهل الكتاب لمن يؤمن بالله وما أنزل
إليكم وما أنزل إليهم خاشعين لله لا يشترون
بآيات الله ثمنا قليلا أولئك لهم أجرهم عند
ربهم إن الله سريع الحساب ﴿١٩٩﴾
يا أيها الذين آمنوا اصبروا وصابروا ورابطوا
واتقوا الله لعلكم تفلحون ﴿٢٠٠﴾

1. This expression, which recurs in the Koran, is a reminder to men that women are of the same human status as themselves.

An-Nisā, "Women," is so-called because it deals largely with women's rights. The period of revelation is the months following the bettle of Uḥud, or, as Nöldeke, a careful critic, puts it, "between the end of the third year and the end of the fifth year"[1] of the Prophet's reign at Al-Madīnah. As the Sūrah contains no reference to the siege of Al-Madīnah ("The War of the Trench") by the allied tribes, which took place in the fifth year, I should rather say, between the end of the third year and the beginning of the fifth year.

Many Muslims were killed at the battle of Uḥud, hence the concern for orphans and widows in the opening verses which lead on to a declaration of some rights of women of which they were deprived among the pagan Arabs. The defection of the Hypocrites—as the lukewarm or purely time-serving adherents were called—had been the chief cause of the reverse at Uḥud; and after that reverse some of the Jewish tribes, who had till then observed the letter of their treaty with the Prophet, became avowed supporters of the enemy, even going so far as to declare that the old Arab idolatry was preferable to Al-Islām as a religion, and giving help and information to Qureysh, so that in the end the Muslims were obliged to make war on them. Both the Hypocrites and the rebellious Jews are dealt with incidentally in this Sūrah, the former at some length. There is a reference to Christian beliefs in vv. 171-2.

The period of revelation is the fourth year of the Hijrah.

1 Nöldeke, *Geschichte des Qorâns* (2nd ed.), Part I, p. 195.

WOMEN

Revealed at Al-Madinah

In the name of Allah the Beneficent, the Merciful.

1. O mankind! Be careful of your duty to your Lord Who created you from a single soul and from it created its mate and from them twain hath spread abroad a multitude of men and women. Be careful of your duty toward Allah in Whom ye claim (your rights) of one another, and toward the wombs (that bare you). Lo! Allah hath been a Watcher over you.

2. Give unto orphans their wealth. Exchange not the good for the bad (in your management thereof) nor absorb their wealth into your own wealth. Lo! that would be a great sin.

3. And if ye fear that ye will not deal fairly by the orphans, marry of the women, who seem good to you, two or three or four; and if ye fear that ye cannot do justice (to so many) then one (only) or (the captives) that your right hands possess. Thus it is more likely that ye will not do injustice.

4. And give unto the women, (whom ye marry) free gift of their marriage portions; but if they of their own accord remit unto you a part thereof, then ye are welcome to absorb it (in your wealth).

5. Give not unto the foolish (what is in) your (keeping of their) wealth, which Allah hath given you to maintain; but feed and clothe them from it, and speak kindly unto them.

اياتها ١٧٦ (٤) سُوۡرَةُ النِّسَآءِ مَدَنِيَّةٌ ركوعاتها ٢٤

بِسۡمِ اللّٰهِ الرَّحۡمٰنِ الرَّحِيۡمِ

يٰۤاَيُّهَا النَّاسُ اتَّقُوۡا رَبَّكُمُ الَّذِىۡ خَلَقَكُمۡ
مِّنۡ نَّفۡسٍ وَّاحِدَةٍ وَّخَلَقَ مِنۡهَا زَوۡجَهَا وَ
بَثَّ مِنۡهُمَا رِجَالًا كَثِيۡرًا وَّنِسَآءً ۚ وَاتَّقُوا اللّٰهَ
الَّذِىۡ تَسَآءَلُوۡنَ بِهٖ وَالۡاَرۡحَامَ ؕ اِنَّ اللّٰهَ كَانَ
عَلَيۡكُمۡ رَقِيۡبًا ﴿١﴾
وَاٰتُوا الۡيَتٰمٰٓى اَمۡوَالَهُمۡ وَلَا تَتَبَدَّلُوا الۡخَبِيۡثَ
بِالطَّيِّبِ وَلَا تَاۡكُلُوۡۤا اَمۡوَالَهُمۡ اِلٰٓى اَمۡوَالِكُمۡ ؕ
اِنَّهٗ كَانَ حُوۡبًا كَبِيۡرًا ﴿٢﴾
وَاِنۡ خِفۡتُمۡ اَلَّا تُقۡسِطُوۡا فِى الۡيَتٰمٰى فَانۡكِحُوۡا
مَا طَابَ لَكُمۡ مِّنَ النِّسَآءِ مَثۡنٰى وَثُلٰثَ وَرُبٰعَ
فَاِنۡ خِفۡتُمۡ اَلَّا تَعۡدِلُوۡا فَوَاحِدَةً اَوۡ مَا مَلَكَتۡ اَيۡمَانُكُمۡ
ذٰلِكَ اَدۡنٰٓى اَلَّا تَعُوۡلُوۡا ﴿٣﴾
وَاٰتُوا النِّسَآءَ صَدُقٰتِهِنَّ نِحۡلَةً ؕ فَاِنۡ طِبۡنَ
لَكُمۡ عَنۡ شَىۡءٍ مِّنۡهُ نَفۡسًا فَكُلُوۡهُ هَنِيۡٓـًٔا
مَّرِيۡٓـًٔا ﴿٤﴾
وَلَا تُؤۡتُوا السُّفَهَآءَ اَمۡوَالَكُمُ الَّتِىۡ جَعَلَ اللّٰهُ
لَكُمۡ قِيٰمًا وَّارۡزُقُوۡهُمۡ فِيۡهَا وَاكۡسُوۡهُمۡ وَقُوۡلُوۡا
لَهُمۡ قَوۡلًا مَّعۡرُوۡفًا ﴿٥﴾

6. Prove orphans till they reach the marriageable age; then, if ye find them of sound judgement, deliver over unto them their fortune; and devour it not by squandering and in haste lest they should grow up. Whoso (of the guardians) is rich, let him abstain generously (from taking of the property of orphans); and whoso is poor let him take thereof in reason (for his guardianship). And when ye deliver up their fortune unto orphans, have (the transaction) witnessed in their presence. Allah sufficeth as a Reckoner.

7. Unto the men (of a family) belongeth a share of that which parents and near kindred leave, and unto the women a share of that which parents and near kindred leave, whether it be little or much—a legal share.

8. And when kinsfolk and orphans and the needy are present at the division (of the heritage), bestow on them therefrom and speak kindly unto them.

9. And let those fear (in their behaviour toward orphans) who if they left behind them weak offspring would be afraid for them. So let them mind their duty to Allah, and speak justly.

10. Lo! Those who devour the wealth of orphans wrongfully, they do but swallow fire into their bellies, and they will be exposed to burning flame.

11. Allah chargeth you concerning (the provision for) your children: to the male the equivalent of the portion of two females, and if there be women more than two, then theirs is two-thirds of the inheritance, and if there be one (only) then the half. And to his[1] parents a sixth of the inheritance if he have a son; and if he have no son and his parents are his heirs, then to his mother appertaineth the third; and if he have brethren, then to his mother appertaineth the sixth, after any legacy he may have bequeathed, or debt (hath been paid). Your parent or syour children: Ye know not which of them is nearer unto you in usefulness. It is an injunction from Allah. Lo! Allah is Knower, Wise.

1. The deceased.

وَابْتَلُوا الْيَتٰمٰى حَتّٰىٓ اِذَا بَلَغُوا النِّكَاحَ ۚ فَاِنْ اٰنَسْتُمْ مِّنْهُمْ
رُشْدًا فَادْفَعُوْٓا اِلَيْهِمْ اَمْوَالَهُمْ ۚ وَلَا تَاْكُلُوْهَآ اِسْرَافًا
وَّبِدَارًا اَنْ يَّكْبَرُوْا ۗ وَمَنْ كَانَ غَنِيًّا فَلْيَسْتَعْفِفْ ۚ وَمَنْ
كَانَ فَقِيْرًا فَلْيَاْكُلْ بِالْمَعْرُوْفِ ۚ فَاِذَا دَفَعْتُمْ اِلَيْهِمْ
اَمْوَالَهُمْ فَاَشْهِدُوْا عَلَيْهِمْ ۗ وَكَفٰى بِاللّٰهِ حَسِيْبًا ﴿٦﴾
لِلرِّجَالِ نَصِيْبٌ مِّمَّا تَرَكَ الْوَالِدٰنِ وَالْاَقْرَبُوْنَ ۠ وَلِلنِّسَآءِ
نَصِيْبٌ مِّمَّا تَرَكَ الْوَالِدٰنِ وَالْاَقْرَبُوْنَ مِمَّا قَلَّ مِنْهُ اَوْ
كَثُرَ ۚ نَصِيْبًا مَّفْرُوْضًا ﴿٧﴾
وَاِذَا حَضَرَ الْقِسْمَةَ اُولُوا الْقُرْبٰى وَالْيَتٰمٰى وَالْمَسٰكِيْنُ
فَارْزُقُوْهُمْ مِّنْهُ وَقُوْلُوْا لَهُمْ قَوْلًا مَّعْرُوْفًا ﴿٨﴾
وَلْيَخْشَ الَّذِيْنَ لَوْ تَرَكُوْا مِنْ خَلْفِهِمْ ذُرِّيَّةً ضِعٰفًا
خَافُوْا عَلَيْهِمْ ۠ فَلْيَتَّقُوا اللّٰهَ وَلْيَقُوْلُوْا قَوْلًا سَدِيْدًا ﴿٩﴾
اِنَّ الَّذِيْنَ يَاْكُلُوْنَ اَمْوَالَ الْيَتٰمٰى ظُلْمًا اِنَّمَا يَاْكُلُوْنَ
ع ١٢ فِيْ بُطُوْنِهِمْ نَارًا ۗ وَسَيَصْلَوْنَ سَعِيْرًا ﴿١٠﴾
يُوْصِيْكُمُ اللّٰهُ فِيْٓ اَوْلَادِكُمْ ۖ لِلذَّكَرِ مِثْلُ حَظِّ الْاُنْثَيَيْنِ ۚ
فَاِنْ كُنَّ نِسَآءً فَوْقَ اثْنَتَيْنِ فَلَهُنَّ ثُلُثَا مَا تَرَكَ ۚ وَاِنْ
كَانَتْ وَاحِدَةً فَلَهَا النِّصْفُ ۗ وَلِاَبَوَيْهِ لِكُلِّ وَاحِدٍ
مِّنْهُمَا السُّدُسُ مِمَّا تَرَكَ اِنْ كَانَ لَهٗ وَلَدٌ ۚ فَاِنْ لَّمْ يَكُنْ
لَّهٗ وَلَدٌ وَّوَرِثَهٗٓ اَبَوٰهُ فَلِاُمِّهِ الثُّلُثُ ۚ فَاِنْ كَانَ لَهٗٓ اِخْوَةٌ
فَلِاُمِّهِ السُّدُسُ مِنْۢ بَعْدِ وَصِيَّةٍ يُّوْصِيْ بِهَآ اَوْ دَيْنٍ ۗ
اٰبَآؤُكُمْ وَاَبْنَآؤُكُمْ لَا تَدْرُوْنَ اَيُّهُمْ اَقْرَبُ لَكُمْ نَفْعًا ۚ
فَرِيْضَةً مِّنَ اللّٰهِ ۗ اِنَّ اللّٰهَ كَانَ عَلِيْمًا حَكِيْمًا ﴿١١﴾

12. And unto you belongeth a half of that which your wives leave, if they have no child; but if they have a child then unto you the fourth of that which they leave, after any legacy they may have bequeathed, or debt (they may have contracted, hath been paid). And unto them belongeth the fourth of that which ye leave if ye have no child, but if ye have a child then the eighth of that which ye leave, after any legacy ye may have bequeathed, or debt (ye may have contracted, hath been paid). And if a man or a woman have a distant heir (having left neither parent nor child), and he (or she) have a brother or a sister (only on the mother's side) then to each of them twain (the brother and the sister) the sixth, and if they be more than two, then they shall be sharers in the third, after any legacy that may have been bequeathed or debt (contracted) not injuring (the heirs by willing away more than a third of the heritage) hath been paid. A commandment from Allah. Allah is Knower, Indulgent.

13. These are the limits (imposed by) Allah. Whoso obeyeth Allah and His messenger, He will make him enter Gardens underneath which rivers flow, where such will dwell for ever. That will be the great success.

14. And whoso disobeyeth Allah and His messenger and transgresseth His limits, He will make him enter Fire, where such will dwell for ever; his will be a shameful doom.

15. As for those of your women who are guilty of lewdness, call to witness four of you against them. And if they testify (to the truth of the allegation) then confine them to the houses until death take them or (until) Allah appoint for them a way (through new legislation).[1]

16. And as for the two of you who are guilty thereof, punish them both. And if they repent and improve, then let them be. Lo! Allah is Relenting, Merciful.

وَلَكُمْ نِصْفُ مَا تَرَكَ أَزْوَاجُكُمْ إِنْ لَمْ يَكُنْ لَهُنَّ
وَلَدٌ ۚ فَإِنْ كَانَ لَهُنَّ وَلَدٌ فَلَكُمُ الرُّبُعُ مِمَّا تَرَكْنَ
مِنْ بَعْدِ وَصِيَّةٍ يُوصِينَ بِهَا أَوْ دَيْنٍ ۚ وَلَهُنَّ
الرُّبُعُ مِمَّا تَرَكْتُمْ إِنْ لَمْ يَكُنْ لَكُمْ وَلَدٌ ۚ فَإِنْ
كَانَ لَكُمْ وَلَدٌ فَلَهُنَّ الثُّمُنُ مِمَّا تَرَكْتُمْ مِنْ بَعْدِ
وَصِيَّةٍ تُوصُونَ بِهَا أَوْ دَيْنٍ ۗ وَإِنْ كَانَ رَجُلٌ
يُورَثُ كَلَالَةً أَوِ امْرَأَةٌ وَلَهُ أَخٌ أَوْ أُخْتٌ فَلِكُلِّ
وَاحِدٍ مِنْهُمَا السُّدُسُ ۚ فَإِنْ كَانُوا أَكْثَرَ مِنْ ذَٰلِكَ
فَهُمْ شُرَكَاءُ فِي الثُّلُثِ مِنْ بَعْدِ وَصِيَّةٍ يُوصَىٰ
بِهَا أَوْ دَيْنٍ غَيْرَ مُضَارٍّ ۚ وَصِيَّةً مِنَ اللَّهِ ۗ وَاللَّهُ
عَلِيمٌ حَلِيمٌ ﴿١٢﴾
تِلْكَ حُدُودُ اللَّهِ ۚ وَمَنْ يُطِعِ اللَّهَ وَرَسُولَهُ يُدْخِلْهُ
جَنَّاتٍ تَجْرِي مِنْ تَحْتِهَا الْأَنْهَارُ خَالِدِينَ فِيهَا ۚ وَ
ذَٰلِكَ الْفَوْزُ الْعَظِيمُ ﴿١٣﴾
وَمَنْ يَعْصِ اللَّهَ وَرَسُولَهُ وَيَتَعَدَّ حُدُودَهُ يُدْخِلْهُ
نَارًا خَالِدًا فِيهَا وَلَهُ عَذَابٌ مُهِينٌ ﴿١٤﴾ ع ١٣
وَاللَّاتِي يَأْتِينَ الْفَاحِشَةَ مِنْ نِسَائِكُمْ فَاسْتَشْهِدُوا
عَلَيْهِنَّ أَرْبَعَةً مِنْكُمْ ۖ فَإِنْ شَهِدُوا فَأَمْسِكُوهُنَّ
فِي الْبُيُوتِ حَتَّىٰ يَتَوَفَّاهُنَّ الْمَوْتُ أَوْ يَجْعَلَ اللَّهُ
لَهُنَّ سَبِيلًا ﴿١٥﴾
وَاللَّذَانِ يَأْتِيَانِهَا مِنْكُمْ فَآذُوهُمَا ۖ فَإِنْ تَابَا وَأَصْلَحَا
فَأَعْرِضُوا عَنْهُمَا ۗ إِنَّ اللَّهَ كَانَ تَوَّابًا رَحِيمًا ﴿١٦﴾

1. See XXIV, 2-10.

17. Forgiveness is only incumbent on Allah toward those who do evil in ignorance (and) then turn quickly (in repentance) to Allah. These are they toward whom Allah relenteth. Allah is ever Knower, Wise.

إِنَّمَا التَّوْبَةُ عَلَى اللّٰهِ لِلَّذِيْنَ يَعْمَلُوْنَ
السُّوْٓءَ بِجَهَالَةٍ ثُمَّ يَتُوْبُوْنَ مِنْ قَرِيْبٍ
فَاُولٰٓئِكَ يَتُوْبُ اللّٰهُ عَلَيْهِمْ ۗ وَكَانَ اللّٰهُ عَلِيْمًا
حَكِيْمًا ١٧

18. The forgiveness is not for those who do ill deeds until, when death attendeth upon one of them, he saith: Lo! I repent now; nor yet for those who die while they are disbelievers. For such We have prepared a painful doom.

وَلَيْسَتِ التَّوْبَةُ لِلَّذِيْنَ يَعْمَلُوْنَ السَّيِّاٰتِ ۚ حَتّٰٓى
اِذَا حَضَرَ اَحَدَهُمُ الْمَوْتُ قَالَ اِنِّيْ تُبْتُ الْـٰٔنَ وَلَا
الَّذِيْنَ يَمُوْتُوْنَ وَهُمْ كُفَّارٌ ۚ اُولٰٓئِكَ اَعْتَدْنَا لَهُمْ
عَذَابًا اَلِيْمًا ١٨

19. O ye who believe! It is not lawful for you forcibly to inherit the women (of your deceased kinsmen), nor (that) ye should put constraint upon them that ye may take away a part of that which ye have given them, unless they be guilty of flagrant lewdness. But consort with them in kindness, for if ye hate them it may happen that ye hate a thing wherein Allah hath placed much good.

يٰٓاَيُّهَا الَّذِيْنَ اٰمَنُوْا لَا يَحِلُّ لَكُمْ اَنْ تَرِثُوا
النِّسَآءَ كَرْهًا ۗ وَلَا تَعْضُلُوْهُنَّ لِتَذْهَبُوْا بِبَعْضِ
مَآ اٰتَيْتُمُوْهُنَّ اِلَّآ اَنْ يَّاْتِيْنَ بِفَاحِشَةٍ مُّبَيِّنَةٍ ۚ
وَعَاشِرُوْهُنَّ بِالْمَعْرُوْفِ ۚ فَاِنْ كَرِهْتُمُوْهُنَّ
فَعَسٰٓى اَنْ تَكْرَهُوْا شَيْئًا وَّيَجْعَلَ اللّٰهُ فِيْهِ
خَيْرًا كَثِيْرًا ١٩

20. And if ye wish to exchange one wife for another and ye have given unto one of them a sum of money (however great), take nothing from it. Would ye take it by the way of calumny and open wrong?

وَاِنْ اَرَدْتُّمُ اسْتِبْدَالَ زَوْجٍ مَّكَانَ زَوْجٍ ۙ وَّ
اٰتَيْتُمْ اِحْدٰىهُنَّ قِنْطَارًا فَلَا تَاْخُذُوْا مِنْهُ شَيْئًا ۚ
اَتَاْخُذُوْنَهٗ بُهْتَانًا وَّاِثْمًا مُّبِيْنًا ٢٠

21. How can ye take it (back) after one of you hath gone in unto the other, and they have taken a strong pledge from you?

وَكَيْفَ تَاْخُذُوْنَهٗ وَقَدْ اَفْضٰى بَعْضُكُمْ اِلٰى بَعْضٍ
وَّاَخَذْنَ مِنْكُمْ مِّيْثَاقًا غَلِيْظًا ٢١

22. And marry not those women whom your fathers married, except what hath already happened (of that nature) in the past. Lo! it was ever lewdness and abomination, and an evil way.

وَلَا تَنْكِحُوْا مَا نَكَحَ اٰبَآؤُكُمْ مِّنَ النِّسَآءِ اِلَّا مَا
قَدْ سَلَفَ ۗ اِنَّهٗ كَانَ فَاحِشَةً وَّمَقْتًا ۗ وَسَآءَ
سَبِيْلًا ٢٢ ٣ ع ١٤

23. Forbidden unto you are your mothers, and your daughters, and your sisters, and your father's sisters, and your mother's sisters, and your brother's daughters and your sister's daughters, and your foster-mothers, and your foster-sisters, and your mothers-in-law, and your step-daughters who are under your protection (born) of your women unto whom ye have gone in—but if ye have not gone in unto them, then it is no sin for you (to marry their daughters)—and the wives of your sons who (spring) from your own loins. And (it is forbidden unto you) that ye should have two sisters together, except what hath already happened (of that nature) in the past. Lo! Allah is ever Forgiving, Merciful:

24. And all married women (are forbidden unto you save those (captives) whom your right hands possess. It is a decree of Allah for you. Lawful unto you are all beyond those mentioned, so that ye seek them with your wealth in honest wedlock, not debauchery. And those of whom ye seek content (by marrying them), give unto them their portions as a duty. And there is no sin for you in what ye do by mutual agreement after the duty (hath been done). Lo! Allah is ever Knower, Wise.

25. And whoso is not able to afford to marry free, believing women, let them marry from the believing maids whom your right hands possess. Allah knoweth best (concerning) your faith. Ye (proceed) one from another;[1] so wed them by permission of their folk, and give unto them their portions in kindness, they being honest, not debauched nor of loose conduct. And if when they are honourably married, they commit lewdness they shall incur the half of the punishment (prescribed) for free women (in that case). This is for him among you who feareth to commit sin. But to have patience would be better for you. Allah is Forgiving, Merciful.

حُرِّمَتْ عَلَيْكُمْ أُمَّهٰتُكُمْ وَبَنٰتُكُمْ وَأَخَوٰتُكُمْ وَعَمّٰتُكُمْ
وَخٰلٰتُكُمْ وَبَنٰتُ الْأَخِ وَبَنٰتُ الْأُخْتِ وَأُمَّهٰتُكُمُ
الّٰتِيٓ أَرْضَعْنَكُمْ وَأَخَوٰتُكُمْ مِّنَ الرَّضٰعَةِ وَأُمَّهٰتُ
نِسَآئِكُمْ وَرَبٰٓئِبُكُمُ الّٰتِي فِي حُجُورِكُمْ مِّنْ نِّسَآئِكُمُ
الّٰتِي دَخَلْتُمْ بِهِنَّ فَإِنْ لَّمْ تَكُونُوا دَخَلْتُمْ بِهِنَّ فَلَا
جُنَاحَ عَلَيْكُمْ وَحَلٰٓئِلُ أَبْنَآئِكُمُ الَّذِينَ مِنْ
أَصْلٰبِكُمْ وَأَنْ تَجْمَعُوا بَيْنَ الْأُخْتَيْنِ إِلَّا مَا قَدْ
سَلَفَ إِنَّ اللّٰهَ كَانَ غَفُورًا رَّحِيمًا ﴿٢٣﴾
وَالْمُحْصَنٰتُ مِنَ النِّسَآءِ إِلَّا مَا مَلَكَتْ أَيْمٰنُكُمْ
كِتٰبَ اللّٰهِ عَلَيْكُمْ وَأُحِلَّ لَكُمْ مَّا وَرَآءَ ذٰلِكُمْ أَنْ
تَبْتَغُوا بِأَمْوٰلِكُمْ مُّحْصِنِينَ غَيْرَ مُسٰفِحِينَ فَمَا
اسْتَمْتَعْتُمْ بِهِ مِنْهُنَّ فَآتُوهُنَّ أُجُورَهُنَّ فَرِيضَةً
وَلَا جُنَاحَ عَلَيْكُمْ فِيمَا تَرٰضَيْتُمْ بِهِ مِنْ بَعْدِ
الْفَرِيضَةِ إِنَّ اللّٰهَ كَانَ عَلِيمًا حَكِيمًا ﴿٢٤﴾
وَمَنْ لَّمْ يَسْتَطِعْ مِنْكُمْ طَوْلًا أَنْ يَّنْكِحَ الْمُحْصَنٰتِ
الْمُؤْمِنٰتِ فَمِنْ مَّا مَلَكَتْ أَيْمٰنُكُمْ مِّنْ فَتَيٰتِكُمُ الْمُؤْمِنٰتِ
وَاللّٰهُ أَعْلَمُ بِإِيمٰنِكُمْ بَعْضُكُمْ مِّنْ بَعْضٍ فَانْكِحُوهُنَّ
بِإِذْنِ أَهْلِهِنَّ وَآتُوهُنَّ أُجُورَهُنَّ بِالْمَعْرُوفِ مُحْصَنٰتٍ
غَيْرَ مُسٰفِحٰتٍ وَّلَا مُتَّخِذٰتِ أَخْدَانٍ فَإِذَا أُحْصِنَّ
فَإِنْ أَتَيْنَ بِفٰحِشَةٍ فَعَلَيْهِنَّ نِصْفُ مَا عَلَى الْمُحْصَنٰتِ
مِنَ الْعَذَابِ ذٰلِكَ لِمَنْ خَشِيَ الْعَنَتَ مِنْكُمْ وَأَنْ
تَصْبِرُوا خَيْرٌ لَّكُمْ وَاللّٰهُ غَفُورٌ رَّحِيمٌ ﴿٢٥﴾

1. This expression, which recurs in the Koran, is a reminder to men that women are of the same human status as themselves.

26. Allah would explain to you and guide you by the examples of those who were before you, and would turn to you in mercy. Allah is Knower, Wise.

27. And Allah would turn to you in mercy; but those who follow vain desires would have you go tremendously astray.

28. Allah would make the burden light for you, for man was created weak.

29. O ye who believe! Squander not your wealth among yourselves in vanity, except it be a trade by mutual consent, and kill not one another. Lo! Allah is ever Merciful unto you.

30. Whoso doth that through aggression and injustice, We shall cast him into Fire, and that is ever easy for Allah.

31. If ye avoid the great (things) which ye are forbidden, We will remit from you your evil deeds and make you enter at a noble gate.

32. And covet not the thing in which Allah hath made some of you excel others. Unto men a fortune from that which they have earned, and unto women a fortune from that which they have earned. (Envy not one another) but ask Allah of His bounty. Lo! Allah is ever Knower of all things.

33. And unto each We have appointed heirs of that which parents and near kindred leave; and as for those with whom your right hands have made a covenant, give them their due. Lo! Allah is ever Witness over all things.

يُرِيدُ اللّٰهُ لِيُبَيِّنَ لَكُمْ وَيَهْدِيَكُمْ
سُنَنَ الَّذِينَ مِنْ قَبْلِكُمْ وَيَتُوبَ عَلَيْكُمْ وَاللّٰهُ
عَلِيمٌ حَكِيمٌ ﴿٢٦﴾
وَاللّٰهُ يُرِيدُ أَنْ يَتُوبَ عَلَيْكُمْ وَيُرِيدُ
الَّذِينَ يَتَّبِعُونَ الشَّهَوٰتِ أَنْ تَمِيلُوا مَيْلًا
عَظِيمًا ﴿٢٧﴾
يُرِيدُ اللّٰهُ أَنْ يُخَفِّفَ عَنْكُمْ وَخُلِقَ الْإِنْسَانُ
ضَعِيفًا ﴿٢٨﴾
يٰٓأَيُّهَا الَّذِينَ اٰمَنُوا لَا تَأْكُلُوٓا أَمْوَالَكُمْ بَيْنَكُمْ بِالْبَاطِلِ
إِلَّآ أَنْ تَكُونَ تِجَارَةً عَنْ تَرَاضٍ مِنْكُمْ وَلَا
تَقْتُلُوٓا أَنْفُسَكُمْ إِنَّ اللّٰهَ كَانَ بِكُمْ رَحِيمًا ﴿٢٩﴾
وَمَنْ يَفْعَلْ ذٰلِكَ عُدْوَانًا وَظُلْمًا فَسَوْفَ نُصْلِيهِ
نَارًا وَكَانَ ذٰلِكَ عَلَى اللّٰهِ يَسِيرًا ﴿٣٠﴾
إِنْ تَجْتَنِبُوا كَبَآئِرَ مَا تُنْهَوْنَ عَنْهُ نُكَفِّرْ عَنْكُمْ سَيِّاٰتِكُمْ
وَنُدْخِلْكُمْ مُدْخَلًا كَرِيمًا ﴿٣١﴾
وَلَا تَتَمَنَّوْا مَا فَضَّلَ اللّٰهُ بِهِ بَعْضَكُمْ عَلٰى بَعْضٍ
لِلرِّجَالِ نَصِيبٌ مِمَّا اكْتَسَبُوا وَلِلنِّسَآءِ نَصِيبٌ مِمَّا
اكْتَسَبْنَ وَسْئَلُوا اللّٰهَ مِنْ فَضْلِهِ إِنَّ اللّٰهَ كَانَ
بِكُلِّ شَيْءٍ عَلِيمًا ﴿٣٢﴾
وَلِكُلٍّ جَعَلْنَا مَوَالِيَ مِمَّا تَرَكَ الْوَالِدٰنِ وَالْأَقْرَبُونَ
وَالَّذِينَ عَقَدَتْ أَيْمَانُكُمْ فَاٰتُوهُمْ نَصِيبَهُمْ إِنَّ
ع اللّٰهَ كَانَ عَلٰى كُلِّ شَيْءٍ شَهِيدًا ﴿٣٣﴾

34. Men are in charge of women, because Allah hath made the one of them to excel the other, and because they spend of their property (for the support of women). So good women are the obedient, guarding in secret that which Allah hath guarded. As for those from whom ye fear rebellion, admonish them and banish them to beds apart, and scourge them. Then, if they obey you, seek not a way against them. Lo! Allah is ever High Exalted, Great.

35. And if ye fear a breach between them twain (the man and wife), appoint an arbiter from his folk and an arbiter from her folk. If they desire amendment Allah will make them of one mind. Lo! Allah is ever Knower, Aware.

36. And serve Allah. Ascribe nothing as partner unto Him. (Show) kindness unto parents, and unto near kindred, and orphans, and the needy, and unto the neighbour who is of kin (unto you) and the neighbour who is not of kin, and the fellow-traveller and the wayfarer and (the slaves) whom your right hands possess. Lo! Allah loveth not such as are proud and boastful,

37. Who hoard their wealth and enjoin avarice on others, and hide that which Allah hath bestowed upon them of His bounty. For disbelievers We prepare a shameful doom;

38. And (also) those who spend their wealth in order to be seen of men, and believe not in Allah nor the Last Day. Whoso taketh Satan for a comrade, a bad comrade hath he.

39. What have they (to fear) if they believe in Allah and the Last Day and spend (aright) of that which Allah hath bestowed upon them, when Allah is ever Aware of them (and all they do)?

الرِّجَالُ قَوّٰمُونَ عَلَى النِّسَآءِ بِمَا فَضَّلَ اللّٰهُ بَعْضَهُمْ
عَلٰى بَعْضٍ وَّبِمَآ أَنْفَقُوا مِنْ أَمْوٰلِهِمْ فَالصّٰلِحٰتُ
قٰنِتٰتٌ حٰفِظٰتٌ لِّلْغَيْبِ بِمَا حَفِظَ اللّٰهُ وَالّٰتِي تَخَافُونَ
نُشُوزَهُنَّ فَعِظُوهُنَّ وَاهْجُرُوهُنَّ فِي الْمَضَاجِعِ
وَاضْرِبُوهُنَّ فَإِنْ أَطَعْنَكُمْ فَلَا تَبْغُوا عَلَيْهِنَّ
سَبِيلًا إِنَّ اللّٰهَ كَانَ عَلِيًّا كَبِيرًا ﴿٣٤﴾
وَإِنْ خِفْتُمْ شِقَاقَ بَيْنِهِمَا فَابْعَثُوا حَكَمًا مِّنْ أَهْلِهِ
وَحَكَمًا مِّنْ أَهْلِهَا إِنْ يُّرِيدَآ إِصْلٰحًا يُّوَفِّقِ اللّٰهُ
بَيْنَهُمَا إِنَّ اللّٰهَ كَانَ عَلِيمًا خَبِيرًا ﴿٣٥﴾
وَاعْبُدُوا اللّٰهَ وَلَا تُشْرِكُوا بِهِ شَيْـًٔا وَّبِالْوٰلِدَيْنِ
إِحْسٰنًا وَّبِذِي الْقُرْبٰى وَالْيَتٰمٰى وَالْمَسٰكِينِ وَالْجَارِ
ذِي الْقُرْبٰى وَالْجَارِ الْجُنُبِ وَالصَّاحِبِ بِالْجَنْبِ وَ
ابْنِ السَّبِيلِ وَمَا مَلَكَتْ أَيْمَانُكُمْ إِنَّ اللّٰهَ لَا يُحِبُّ
مَنْ كَانَ مُخْتَالًا فَخُورًا ﴿٣٦﴾
الَّذِينَ يَبْخَلُونَ وَيَأْمُرُونَ النَّاسَ بِالْبُخْلِ وَيَكْتُمُونَ
مَآ اٰتٰهُمُ اللّٰهُ مِنْ فَضْلِهِ وَأَعْتَدْنَا لِلْكٰفِرِينَ
عَذَابًا مُّهِينًا ﴿٣٧﴾
وَالَّذِينَ يُنْفِقُونَ أَمْوٰلَهُمْ رِئَآءَ النَّاسِ وَلَا
يُؤْمِنُونَ بِاللّٰهِ وَلَا بِالْيَوْمِ الْاٰخِرِ وَمَنْ يَّكُنِ الشَّيْطٰنُ
لَهُ قَرِينًا فَسَآءَ قَرِينًا ﴿٣٨﴾
وَمَاذَا عَلَيْهِمْ لَوْ اٰمَنُوا بِاللّٰهِ وَالْيَوْمِ الْاٰخِرِ وَأَنْفَقُوا
مِمَّا رَزَقَهُمُ اللّٰهُ وَكَانَ اللّٰهُ بِهِمْ عَلِيمًا ﴿٣٩﴾

40. Lo! Allah wrongeth not even of the weight of an ant; and if there is a good deed, He will double it and will give (the doer) from His presence an immense reward.

إن الله لا يظلم مثقال ذرة وإن تك حسنة
يضعفها ويؤت من لدنه أجرا عظيما ﴿٤٠﴾

41. But how (will it be with them) when We bring of every people a witness, and We bring thee (O Muhammad) a witness against these?

فكيف إذا جئنا من كل أمة بشهيد وجئنا بك
على هؤلاء شهيدا ﴿٤١﴾

42. On that day those who disbelieved and disobeyed the messenger will wish that they were level with the ground, and they can hide no fact from Allah.

يومئذ يود الذين كفروا وعصوا الرسول لو تسوى
بهم الأرض ولا يكتمون الله حديثا ﴿٤٢﴾

43. O ye who believe! Draw not near unto prayer when ye are drunken, till ye know that which ye utter, nor when ye are polluted save when journeying upon the road, till ye have bathed. And if ye be ill, or on a journey, or one of you cometh from the closet, or ye have touched women, and ye find not water, then go to high clean soil and rub your faces and your hands (therewith). Lo! Allah is Benign, Forgiving.

يأيها الذين آمنوا لا تقربوا الصلوة وأنتم سكرى
حتى تعلموا ما تقولون ولا جنبا إلا عابري سبيل
حتى تغتسلوا وإن كنتم مرضى أو على سفر أو جاء
أحد منكم من الغائط أو لمستم النساء فلم تجدوا
ماء فتيمموا صعيدا طيبا فامسحوا بوجوهكم و
أيديكم إن الله كان عفوا غفورا ﴿٤٣﴾

44. Seest thou not those unto whom a portion of the Scripture hath been given, how they purchase error, and seek to make you (Muslims) err from the right way?

ألم تر إلى الذين أوتوا نصيبا من الكتب يشترون
الضللة ويريدون أن تضلوا السبيل ﴿٤٤﴾

45. Allah knoweth best (who are) your enemies. Allah is sufficient as a Friend, and Allah is sufficient as a Helper.

والله أعلم بأعدائكم وكفى بالله وليا وكفى
بالله نصيرا ﴿٤٥﴾

46. Some of those who are Jews change words from their context and say: "We hear and disobey; hear thou as one who heareth not" and "Listen to us!"[1] distorting with their tongues and slandering religion. If they had said: "We hear and we obey; hear thou, and look at us" it had been better for them, and more upright. But Allah hath cursed them for their disbelief, so they believe not, save a few.

من الذين هادوا يحرفون الكلم عن مواضعه
ويقولون سمعنا وعصينا واسمع غير مسمع و
راعنا ليا بألسنتهم وطعنا في الدين ولو أنهم
قالوا سمعنا وأطعنا واسمع وانظرنا لكان خيرا
لهم وأقوم ولكن لعنهم الله بكفرهم فلا
يؤمنون إلا قليلا ﴿٤٦﴾

1. Devices of some of the Jews of Al-Madīnah to annoy the Muslims by distorting words of Scripture. *Rā'inā* (meaning "listen to us"), by which the Muslims used to call the Prophet's notice, they turned by slight mispronunciation into a Hebrew word of insult (cf. S. II, v. 104, footnote).

47. O ye unto whom the Scripture hath been given! Believe in what We have revealed confirming that which ye possess, before We destroy countenances so as to confound them, or curse them as We cursed the Sabbathbreakers (of old time). The Commandment of Allah is always executed.

يٰٓاَيُّهَا الَّذِيْنَ اُوْتُوا الْكِتٰبَ اٰمِنُوْا بِمَا نَزَّلْنَا مُصَدِّقًا
لِّمَا مَعَكُمْ مِّنْ قَبْلِ اَنْ نَّطْمِسَ وُجُوْهًا فَنَرُدَّهَا عَلٰٓى
اَدْبَارِهَآ اَوْ نَلْعَنَهُمْ كَمَا لَعَنَّآ اَصْحٰبَ السَّبْتِ ۭ وَكَانَ
اَمْرُ اللّٰهِ مَفْعُوْلًا ﴿٤٧﴾

48. Lo! Allah forgiveth not that a partner should be ascribed unto Him. He forgiveth (all) save that to whom He will. Whoso ascribeth partners to Allah, he hath indeed invented a tremendous sin.

اِنَّ اللّٰهَ لَا يَغْفِرُ اَنْ يُّشْرَكَ بِهٖ وَيَغْفِرُ مَا دُوْنَ ذٰلِكَ
لِمَنْ يَّشَاۗءُ ۚ وَمَنْ يُّشْرِكْ بِاللّٰهِ فَقَدِ افْتَرٰٓى اِثْمًا عَظِيْمًا ﴿٤٨﴾

49. Hast thou not seen those who praise themselves for purity? Nay, Allah purifieth whom He will, and they will not be wronged even the hair upon a date-stone.

اَلَمْ تَرَ اِلَى الَّذِيْنَ يُزَكُّوْنَ اَنْفُسَهُمْ ۭ بَلِ اللّٰهُ يُزَكِّيْ مَنْ
يَّشَاۗءُ وَلَا يُظْلَمُوْنَ فَتِيْلًا ﴿٤٩﴾

50. See, how they invent lies about Allah! That of itself is flagrant sin.

اُنْظُرْ كَيْفَ يَفْتَرُوْنَ عَلَي اللّٰهِ الْكَذِبَ ۭ وَكَفٰى بِهٖٓ
ع اِثْمًا مُّبِيْنًا ﴿٥٠﴾

51. Hast thou not seen those unto whom a portion of the Scripture hath been given, how they believe in idols and false deities, and how they say of those (idolaters) who disbelieve: "These are more rightly guided than those who believe?"

اَلَمْ تَرَ اِلَى الَّذِيْنَ اُوْتُوْا نَصِيْبًا مِّنَ الْكِتٰبِ
يُؤْمِنُوْنَ بِالْجِبْتِ وَالطَّاغُوْتِ وَيَقُوْلُوْنَ لِلَّذِيْنَ
كَفَرُوْا هٰٓؤُلَاۗءِ اَهْدٰى مِنَ الَّذِيْنَ اٰمَنُوْا سَبِيْلًا ﴿٥١﴾

52. Those are they whom Allah hath cursed, and he whom Allah hath cursed, thou (O Muhammad) wilt find for him no helper.

اُولٰۗىِٕكَ الَّذِيْنَ لَعَنَهُمُ اللّٰهُ ۭ وَمَنْ يَّلْعَنِ اللّٰهُ فَلَنْ
تَجِدَ لَهٗ نَصِيْرًا ﴿٥٢﴾

53. Or have they even a share in the Sovereignty? Then in that case, they would not give mankind even the speck on a date-stone:

اَمْ لَهُمْ نَصِيْبٌ مِّنَ الْمُلْكِ فَاِذًا لَّا يُؤْتُوْنَ النَّاسَ
نَقِيْرًا ﴿٥٣﴾

54. Or are they jealous of mankind because of that which Allah of His bounty hath bestowed upon them? For We bestowed upon the house of Abraham (of old) the Scripture and Wisdom, and We bestowed on them a mighty kingdom.

اَمْ يَحْسُدُوْنَ النَّاسَ عَلٰي مَآ اٰتٰىهُمُ اللّٰهُ مِنْ فَضْلِهٖ ۚ
فَقَدْ اٰتَيْنَآ اٰلَ اِبْرٰهِيْمَ الْكِتٰبَ وَالْحِكْمَةَ وَاٰتَيْنٰهُمْ
مُّلْكًا عَظِيْمًا ﴿٥٤﴾

55. And of them were (some) who believed therein and of them were (some) who disbelieved therein. Hell is sufficient for (their) burning.

فَمِنْهُمْ مَّنْ اٰمَنَ بِهٖ وَمِنْهُمْ مَّنْ صَدَّ عَنْهُ ۭ وَ
كَفٰى بِجَهَنَّمَ سَعِيْرًا ﴿٥٥﴾

56. Lo! Those who disbelieve Our revelations, We shall expose them to the Fire. As often as their skins are consumed We shall exchange them for fresh skins that they may taste the torment. Lo! Allah is ever Mighty, Wise.

57. And as for those who believe and do good works, We shall make them enter Gardens underneath which rivers flow to dwell therein for ever; there for them are pure companions—and We shall make them enter plenteous shade.

58. Lo! Allah commandeth you that ye restore deposits to their owners, and if ye judge between mankind that ye judge justly. Lo! comely is this which Allah admonisheth you. Lo! Allah is ever Hearer, Seer.

59. O ye who believe! Obey Allah, and obey the messenger and those of you who are in authority; and if ye have a dispute concerning any matter, refer it to Allah and the messenger if ye are (in truth) believers in Allah and the Last Day. That is better and more seemly in the end.

60. Hast thou not seen those who pretend that they believe in that which is revealed unto thee and that which was revealed before thee, how they would go for judgement (in their disputes) to false deities when they have been ordered to abjure them? Satan would mislead them far astray.

61. And when it is said unto them: Come unto that which Allah hath revealed and unto the messenger, thou seest the hypocrites turn from thee with aversion.

62. How would it be if a misfortune smote them because of that which their own hands have sent before (them)? Then would they come unto thee, swearing by Allah that they were seeking naught but harmony and kindness.

إن الذين كفروا بايتنا سوف نصليهم نارا كلما
نضجت جلودهم بدلنهم جلودا غيرها ليذوقوا
العذاب إن الله كان عزيزا حكيما ﴿٥٦﴾
والذين امنوا وعملوا الصلحت سندخلهم جنت
تجري من تحتها الانهر خلدين فيها ابدا لهم
فيها ازواج مطهرة وندخلهم ظلا ظليلا ﴿٥٧﴾
إن الله يأمركم أن تؤدوا الامنت إلى أهلها وإذا
حكمتم بين الناس أن تحكموا بالعدل إن الله نعما
يعظكم به إن الله كان سميعا بصيرا ﴿٥٨﴾
يايها الذين امنوا أطيعوا الله وأطيعوا الرسول و
أولي الأمر منكم فإن تنازعتم في شيء فردوه إلى
الله والرسول إن كنتم تؤمنون بالله واليوم
الاخر ذلك خير وأحسن تأويلا ﴿٥٩﴾
ألم تر إلى الذين يزعمون أنهم امنوا بما أنزل
إليك وما أنزل من قبلك يريدون أن يتحاكموا
إلى الطاغوت وقد أمروا أن يكفروا به ويريد
الشيطن أن يضلهم ضللا بعيدا ﴿٦٠﴾
وإذا قيل لهم تعالوا إلى ما أنزل الله وإلى الرسول
رأيت المنفقين يصدون عنك صدودا ﴿٦١﴾
فكيف إذا أصابتهم مصيبة بما قدمت أيديهم
ثم جاءوك يحلفون بالله إن أردنا إلا إحسانا
وتوفيقا ﴿٦٢﴾

63. Those are they, the secrets of whose hearts Allah knoweth. So oppose them and admonish them, and address them in plain terms about their souls.

64. We sent no messenger save that he should be obeyed by Allah's leave. And if, when they had wronged themselves, they had but come unto thee and asked forgiveness of Allah, and asked forgiveness of the messenger, they would have found Allah Forgiving, Merciful.

65. But nay, by thy Lord, they will not believe (in truth) until they make thee judge of what is in dispute between them and find within themselves no dislike of that which thou decidest, and submit with full submission.

66. And if We had decreed for them: Lay down your lives or go forth from your dwellings, but few of them would have done it; though if they did what they are exhorted to do it would be better for them, and more strengthening:

67. And then We should bestow upon them from Our presence an immense reward,

68. And should guide them unto a Straight path.

69. Whoso obeyeth Allah and the messenger, they are with those unto whom Allah hath shown favour, of the Prophets and the saints and the martyrs and the righteous. The best of company are they!

70. Such is the bounty of Allah, and Allah sufficeth as Knower.

71. O ye who believe! Take your precautions, then advance the proven ones, or advance all together.

72. Lo! among you there is he who loitereth; and if disaster overtook you, he would say: Allah hath been gracious unto me since I was not present with them!

أُولٰٓئِكَ الَّذِيْنَ يَعْلَمُ اللّٰهُ مَا فِيْ قُلُوْبِهِمْ ۗ فَاَعْرِضْ
عَنْهُمْ وَعِظْهُمْ وَقُلْ لَّهُمْ فِيْٓ اَنْفُسِهِمْ قَوْلًاۢ بَلِيْغًا ﴿٦٣﴾
وَمَآ اَرْسَلْنَا مِنْ رَّسُوْلٍ اِلَّا لِيُطَاعَ بِاِذْنِ اللّٰهِ ۭ وَلَوْ
اَنَّهُمْ اِذْ ظَّلَمُوْٓا اَنْفُسَهُمْ جَآءُوْكَ فَاسْتَغْفَرُوا اللّٰهَ وَ
اسْتَغْفَرَ لَهُمُ الرَّسُوْلُ لَوَجَدُوا اللّٰهَ تَوَّابًا رَّحِيْمًا ﴿٦٤﴾
فَلَا وَرَبِّكَ لَا يُؤْمِنُوْنَ حَتّٰى يُحَكِّمُوْكَ فِيْمَا شَجَرَ بَيْنَهُمْ
ثُمَّ لَا يَجِدُوْا فِيْٓ اَنْفُسِهِمْ حَرَجًا مِّمَّا قَضَيْتَ وَيُسَلِّمُوْا
تَسْلِيْمًا ﴿٦٥﴾
وَلَوْ اَنَّا كَتَبْنَا عَلَيْهِمْ اَنِ اقْتُلُوْٓا اَنْفُسَكُمْ اَوِ
اخْرُجُوْا مِنْ دِيَارِكُمْ مَّا فَعَلُوْهُ اِلَّا قَلِيْلٌ مِّنْهُمْ ۭ
وَلَوْ اَنَّهُمْ فَعَلُوْا مَا يُوْعَظُوْنَ بِهٖ لَكَانَ خَيْرًا لَّهُمْ
وَاَشَدَّ تَثْبِيْتًا ﴿٦٦﴾
وَّاِذًا لَّاٰتَيْنٰهُمْ مِّنْ لَّدُنَّآ اَجْرًا عَظِيْمًا ﴿٦٧﴾
وَّلَهَدَيْنٰهُمْ صِرَاطًا مُّسْتَقِيْمًا ﴿٦٨﴾
وَمَنْ يُّطِعِ اللّٰهَ وَالرَّسُوْلَ فَاُولٰٓئِكَ مَعَ الَّذِيْنَ اَنْعَمَ
اللّٰهُ عَلَيْهِمْ مِّنَ النَّبِيّٖنَ وَالصِّدِّيْقِيْنَ وَالشُّهَدَآءِ
وَالصّٰلِحِيْنَ ۚ وَحَسُنَ اُولٰٓئِكَ رَفِيْقًا ﴿٦٩﴾
ع ذٰلِكَ الْفَضْلُ مِنَ اللّٰهِ ۭ وَكَفٰى بِاللّٰهِ عَلِيْمًا ﴿٧٠﴾
يٰٓاَيُّهَا الَّذِيْنَ اٰمَنُوْا خُذُوْا حِذْرَكُمْ فَانْفِرُوْا ثُبَاتٍ
اَوِ انْفِرُوْا جَمِيْعًا ﴿٧١﴾
وَاِنَّ مِنْكُمْ لَمَنْ لَّيُبَطِّئَنَّ ۚ فَاِنْ اَصَابَتْكُمْ مُّصِيْبَةٌ قَالَ
قَدْ اَنْعَمَ اللّٰهُ عَلَيَّ اِذْ لَمْ اَكُنْ مَّعَهُمْ شَهِيْدًا ﴿٧٢﴾

73. And if a bounty from Allah befell you, he would surely cry, as if there had been no love between you and him: Oh, would that I had been with them, then should I have achieved a great success!

ولئن اصابكم فضل من الله ليقولن كان لم
تكن بينكم وبينه مودة يليتني كنت معهم
فافوز فوزا عظيما ﴿٧٣﴾

74. Let those fight in the way of Allah who sell the life of this world for the other. Whoso fighteth in the way of Allah, be he slain or be he victorious, on him We shall bestow a vast reward.

فليقاتل في سبيل الله الذين يشرون الحيوة
الدنيا بالاخرة ومن يقاتل في سبيل الله فيقتل
او يغلب فسوف نؤتيه اجرا عظيما ﴿٧٤﴾

75. How should ye not fight for the cause of Allah and of the feeble among men and of the women and the children who are crying: Our Lord! Bring us forth from out this town[1] of which the people are oppressors! Oh, give us from Thy presence some protecting friend! Oh, give us from Thy presence some defender!

وما لكم لا تقاتلون في سبيل الله والمستضعفين
من الرجال والنسآء والولدان الذين يقولون
ربنا اخرجنا من هذه القرية الظالم اهلها و
اجعل لنا من لدنك وليا واجعل لنا من
لدنك نصيرا ﴿٧٥﴾

76. Those who believe do battle for the cause of Allah; and those who disbelieve do battle for the cause of idols. So fight the minions of the devil. Lo! the devil's strategy is ever weak.

الذين امنوا يقاتلون في سبيل الله والذين
كفروا يقاتلون في سبيل الطاغوت فقاتلوا
اوليآء الشيطن ان كيد الشيطن كان
ضعيفا ﴿٧٦﴾ ع

77. Hast thou not seen those unto whom it was said: Withhold your hands, establish worship and pay the poor-due, but when fighting was prescribed for them behold! a party of them fear mankind even as their fear of Allah or with greater fear, and say: Our Lord! Why hast Thou ordained fighting for us? If only Thou wouldst give us respite yet a while! Say (unto them, O Muhammad): The comfort of this world is scant; the Hereafter will be better for him who wardeth off (evil); and ye will not be wronged the down upon a date-stone.

الم تر الى الذين قيل لهم كفوا ايديكم واقيموا
الصلوة واتوا الزكوة فلما كتب عليهم القتال اذا
فريق منهم يخشون الناس كخشية الله او اشد
خشية وقالوا ربنا لم كتبت علينا القتال لو
لا اخرتنا الى اجل قريب قل متاع الدنيا
قليل والاخرة خير لمن اتقى ولا تظلمون
فتيلا ﴿٧٧﴾

1. Mecca

78. Wheresoever ye may be, death will overtake you, even though ye were in lofty towers. Yet if a happy thing befalleth them they say: This is from Allah; and if an evil thing befalleth them they say: This is of thy doing (O Muhammad). Say (unto them): All is from Allah. What is amiss with these people that they come not nigh to understand a happening?[1]

79. Whatever of good befalleth thee (O man) it is from Allah, and whatever of ill befalleth thee it is from thyself. We have sent thee (Muhammad) as a messenger unto mankind and Allah is sufficient as Witness.

80. Whoso obeyeth the messenger, obeyeth Allah, and whoso turneth away: We have not sent thee as a warder over them.

81. And they say: (It is) obedience; but when they have gone forth from thee a party of them spend the night in planning other than what thou sayest. Allah recordeth what they plan by night. So oppose them and put thy trust in Allah. Allah is sufficient as Trustee.

82. Will they not then ponder on the Qur'ān? If it had been from other than Allah they would have found therein much incongruity.

83. And if any tidings, whether of safety or fear, come unto them, they noise it abroad, whereas if they had referred it to the messenger and such of them as are in authority, those among them who are able to think out the matter would have known it. If it had not been for the grace of Allah and His mercy ye would have followed Satan, save a few (of you).

84. So fight (O Muhammad) in the way of Allah—Thou art not taxed (with the responsibility for anyone) except for thyself—and urge on the believers. Peradventure Allah will restrain the might of those who disbelieve. Allah is stronger in might and stronger in inflicting punishment.

أَيْنَ مَا تَكُونُوا يُدْرِكْكُمُ الْمَوْتُ وَلَوْ كُنْتُمْ فِي بُرُوجٍ
مُشَيَّدَةٍ ۗ وَإِنْ تُصِبْهُمْ حَسَنَةٌ يَقُولُوا هٰذِهٖ مِنْ
عِنْدِ اللّٰهِ ۚ وَإِنْ تُصِبْهُمْ سَيِّئَةٌ يَقُولُوا هٰذِهٖ مِنْ
عِنْدِكَ ۚ قُلْ كُلٌّ مِنْ عِنْدِ اللّٰهِ ۖ فَمَالِ هٰؤُلَآءِ الْقَوْمِ
لَا يَكَادُونَ يَفْقَهُونَ حَدِيثًا ﴿٧٨﴾
مَا أَصَابَكَ مِنْ حَسَنَةٍ فَمِنَ اللّٰهِ ۖ وَمَا أَصَابَكَ مِنْ
سَيِّئَةٍ فَمِنْ نَفْسِكَ ۚ وَأَرْسَلْنٰكَ لِلنَّاسِ رَسُولًا ۗ
وَكَفٰى بِاللّٰهِ شَهِيدًا ﴿٧٩﴾
مَنْ يُطِعِ الرَّسُولَ فَقَدْ أَطَاعَ اللّٰهَ ۚ وَمَنْ تَوَلّٰى فَمَآ
أَرْسَلْنٰكَ عَلَيْهِمْ حَفِيظًا ﴿٨٠﴾
وَيَقُولُونَ طَاعَةٌ ۡ فَإِذَا بَرَزُوا مِنْ عِنْدِكَ بَيَّتَ
طَآئِفَةٌ مِنْهُمْ غَيْرَ الَّذِي تَقُولُ ۗ وَاللّٰهُ يَكْتُبُ مَا يُبَيِّتُونَ ۚ
فَأَعْرِضْ عَنْهُمْ وَتَوَكَّلْ عَلَى اللّٰهِ ۗ وَكَفٰى بِاللّٰهِ وَكِيلًا ﴿٨١﴾
أَفَلَا يَتَدَبَّرُونَ الْقُرْآنَ ۗ وَلَوْ كَانَ مِنْ عِنْدِ غَيْرِ اللّٰهِ
لَوَجَدُوا فِيهِ اخْتِلَافًا كَثِيرًا ﴿٨٢﴾
وَإِذَا جَآءَهُمْ أَمْرٌ مِنَ الْأَمْنِ أَوِ الْخَوْفِ أَذَاعُوا
بِهٖ ۗ وَلَوْ رَدُّوهُ إِلَى الرَّسُولِ وَإِلٰٓى أُولِي الْأَمْرِ مِنْهُمْ
لَعَلِمَهُ الَّذِينَ يَسْتَنْبِطُونَهُ مِنْهُمْ ۗ وَلَوْلَا فَضْلُ اللّٰهِ
عَلَيْكُمْ وَرَحْمَتُهُ لَاتَّبَعْتُمُ الشَّيْطٰنَ إِلَّا قَلِيلًا ﴿٨٣﴾
فَقَاتِلْ فِي سَبِيلِ اللّٰهِ ۚ لَا تُكَلَّفُ إِلَّا نَفْسَكَ وَحَرِّضِ
الْمُؤْمِنِينَ ۚ عَسَى اللّٰهُ أَنْ يَكُفَّ بَأْسَ الَّذِينَ
كَفَرُوا ۗ وَاللّٰهُ أَشَدُّ بَأْسًا وَأَشَدُّ تَنْكِيلًا ﴿٨٤﴾

1. The reference is to the reverse which the Muslims suffered at Mt. Uḥud which was caused by their own disobedience to the Prophet's orders.

85. Whoso interveneth in a good cause will have the reward thereof, and whoso interveneth in an evil cause will bear the consequence thereof. Allah overseeth all things.

86. When ye are greeted with a greeting, greet ye with a better than it or return it. Lo! Allah taketh count of all things.

87. Allah! There is no God save Him. He gathereth you all unto a Day of Resurrection whereof there is no doubt. Who is more true in statement than Allah?

88. What aileth you that ye are become two parties regarding the hypocrites,[1] when Allah cast them back (to disbelief) because of what they earned? Seek ye to guide him whom Allah hath sent astray? He whom Allah sendeth astray, for him thou (O Muhammad) canst not find a road.

89. They long that ye should disbelieve even as they disbelieve, that ye may be upon a level (with them). So choose not friends from them till they forsake their homes in the way of Allah: If they turn back (to enmity) then take them and kill them wherever ye find them, and choose no friend nor helper from among them:

90. Except those who seek refuge with a people between whom and you there is a covenant, or (those who) come unto you because their hearts forbid them to make war on you or make war on their own folk. Had Allah willed He could have given them power over you so that assuredly they would have fought you. So, if they hold aloof from you and wage not war against you and offer you peace, Allah alloweth you no way against them.

91. Ye will find others who desire that they should have security from you, and security from their own folk. So often as they are returned to hostility they are plunged therein. If they keep not aloof from you nor offer you peace nor hold their hands, then take them and kill them wherever ye find them. Against such We have given you clear warrant.

من يشفع شفاعة حسنة يكن له نصيب منها
ومن يشفع شفاعة سيئة يكن له كفل منها
وكان الله على كل شيء مقيتا ﴿٨٥﴾
وإذا حييتم بتحية فحيوا بأحسن منها أو ردوها
إن الله كان على كل شيء حسيبا ﴿٨٦﴾ النصف
الله لا إله إلا هو ليجمعنكم إلى يوم القيمة لا
ع ريب فيه ومن أصدق من الله حديثا ﴿٨٧﴾
فما لكم في المنفقين فئتين والله أركسهم بما كسبوا أتريدون
أن تهدوا من أضل الله ومن يضلل الله فلن تجد له سبيلا ﴿٨٨﴾
ودوا لو تكفرون كما كفروا فتكونون سواء فلا
تتخذوا منهم أولياء حتى يهاجروا في سبيل الله
فإن تولوا فخذوهم واقتلوهم حيث وجدتموهم
ولا تتخذوا منهم وليا ولا نصيرا ﴿٨٩﴾
إلا الذين يصلون إلى قوم بينكم وبينهم ميثاق
أو جاءوكم حصرت صدورهم أن يقاتلوكم أو
يقاتلوا قومهم ولو شاء الله لسلطهم عليكم
فلقتلوكم فإن اعتزلوكم فلم يقاتلوكم وألقوا
إليكم السلم فما جعل الله لكم عليهم سبيلا ﴿٩٠﴾
ستجدون آخرين يريدون أن يأمنوكم ويأمنوا قومهم
كلما ردوا إلى الفتنة أركسوا فيها فإن لم يعتزلوكم ويلقوا
إليكم السلم ويكفوا أيديهم فخذوهم واقتلوهم حيث
ع ثقفتموهم وأولئكم جعلنا لكم عليهم سلطنا مبينا ﴿٩١﴾

1. According to Tradition, the reference here is not to the lukewarm section of the Muslims of Al-Madinah, but to a particular group of alleged converts from among the Arabs, who afterwards relapsed into idolatry, and concerning whom there were two opinions among the Muslims.

92. It is not for a believer to kill a believer unless (it be) by mistake. He who hath killed a believer by mistake, must set free a believing slave, and pay the blood-money to the family of the slain, unless they remit it as a charity. If he (the victim) be of a people hostile unto you, and he is a believer, then (the penance is) to set free a believing slave. And if he cometh of a folk between whom and you there is a covenant, then the blood-money must be paid unto his folk and (also) a believing slave must be set free. And whoso hath not the wherewithal must fast two consecutive months. A penance from Allah. Allah is Knower, Wise.

93. Whoso slayeth a believer of set purpose, his reward is Hell for ever. Allah is wroth against him and He hath cursed him and prepared for him an awful doom.

94. O ye who believe! When ye go forth (to fight) in the way of Allah, be careful to discriminate, and say not unto one who offereth you peace: "Thou art not a believer," seeking the chance profits of this life (so that ye may despoil him). With Allah are plenteous spoils. Even thus (as he now is) were ye before; but Allah hath since then been gracious unto you. Therefore take care to discriminate. Allah is ever Informed of what ye do.

95. Those of the believers who sit still, other than those who have a (disabling) hurt, are not on an equality with those who strive in the way of Allah with their wealth and lives. Allah hath conferred on those who strive with their wealth and lives a rank above the sedentary. Unto each Allah hath promised good, but He hath bestowed on those who strive a great reward above the sedentary;

96. Degrees of rank from Him, and forgiveness and mercy. Allah is ever Forgiving, Merciful.

وما كان لمؤمن أن يقتل مؤمنا إلا خطأ ۚ ومن
قتل مؤمنا خطأ فتحرير رقبة مؤمنة ودية مسلمة
إلى أهله إلا أن يصدقوا ۚ فإن كان من قوم عدو
لكم وهو مؤمن فتحرير رقبة مؤمنة ۖ وإن كان
من قوم بينكم وبينهم ميثاق فدية مسلمة
إلى أهله وتحرير رقبة مؤمنة ۖ فمن لم يجد
فصيام شهرين متتابعين توبة من الله ۗ وكان
الله عليما حكيما ﴿٩٢﴾
ومن يقتل مؤمنا متعمدا فجزاؤه جهنم خالدا فيها
وغضب الله عليه ولعنه وأعد له عذابا عظيما ﴿٩٣﴾
يا أيها الذين آمنوا إذا ضربتم في سبيل الله فتبينوا
ولا تقولوا لمن ألقى إليكم السلام لست مؤمنا
تبتغون عرض الحياة الدنيا فعند الله مغانم
كثيرة ۚ كذلك كنتم من قبل فمن الله عليكم
فتبينوا ۚ إن الله كان بما تعملون خبيرا ﴿٩٤﴾
لا يستوي القاعدون من المؤمنين غير أولي الضرر
والمجاهدون في سبيل الله بأموالهم وأنفسهم ۚ
فضل الله المجاهدين بأموالهم وأنفسهم على
القاعدين درجة ۚ وكلا وعد الله الحسنى ۚ وفضل
الله المجاهدين على القاعدين أجرا عظيما ﴿٩٥﴾
درجات منه ومغفرة ورحمة ۚ وكان الله
ع ١٣ غفورا رحيما ﴿٩٦﴾ ١٠

97. Lo! as for those whom the angels take (in death) while they wrong themselves, (the angels) will ask: In what were ye engaged? They will say: We were oppressed in the land (The angels) will say: Was not Allah's earth spacious that ye could have migrated therein? As for such, their habitation will be Hell, an evil journey's end;

إِنَّ الَّذِينَ تَوَفَّاهُمُ الْمَلَائِكَةُ ظَالِمِي أَنفُسِهِمْ قَالُوا
فِيمَ كُنتُمْ ۖ قَالُوا كُنَّا مُسْتَضْعَفِينَ فِي الْأَرْضِ ۚ قَالُوا
أَلَمْ تَكُنْ أَرْضُ اللَّهِ وَاسِعَةً فَتُهَاجِرُوا فِيهَا ۚ فَأُولَٰئِكَ
مَأْوَاهُمْ جَهَنَّمُ ۖ وَسَاءَتْ مَصِيرًا ٩٧

98. Except the feeble among men, and the women, and the children, who are unable to devise a plan and are not shown a way:

إِلَّا الْمُسْتَضْعَفِينَ مِنَ الرِّجَالِ وَالنِّسَاءِ وَالْوِلْدَانِ
لَا يَسْتَطِيعُونَ حِيلَةً وَلَا يَهْتَدُونَ سَبِيلًا ٩٨

99. As for such, it may be that Allah will pardon them. Allah is ever Clement, Forgiving.

فَأُولَٰئِكَ عَسَى اللَّهُ أَن يَعْفُوَ عَنْهُمْ ۚ وَكَانَ اللَّهُ عَفُوًّا غَفُورًا ٩٩

100. Whoso migrateth for the cause of Allah will find much refuge and abundance in the earth, and whoso forsaketh his home, a fugitive unto Allah and His messenger, and death overtaketh him, his reward is then incumbent on Allah. Allah is ever Forgiving, Merciful.

وَمَن يُهَاجِرْ فِي سَبِيلِ اللَّهِ يَجِدْ فِي الْأَرْضِ مُرَاغَمًا
كَثِيرًا وَسَعَةً ۚ وَمَن يَخْرُجْ مِن بَيْتِهِ مُهَاجِرًا إِلَى
اللَّهِ وَرَسُولِهِ ثُمَّ يُدْرِكْهُ الْمَوْتُ فَقَدْ وَقَعَ أَجْرُهُ
ع عَلَى اللَّهِ ۗ وَكَانَ اللَّهُ غَفُورًا رَّحِيمًا ١٠٠

101. And when ye go forth in the land, it is no sin for you to curtail (your) worship if ye fear that those who disbelieve may attack you. In truth the disbelievers are an open enemy to you.

وَإِذَا ضَرَبْتُمْ فِي الْأَرْضِ فَلَيْسَ عَلَيْكُمْ جُنَاحٌ أَن
تَقْصُرُوا مِنَ الصَّلَاةِ إِنْ خِفْتُمْ أَن يَفْتِنَكُمُ الَّذِينَ
كَفَرُوا ۚ إِنَّ الْكَافِرِينَ كَانُوا لَكُمْ عَدُوًّا مُّبِينًا ١٠١

102. And when thou (O Muhammad) art among them and arrangest (their) worship for them, let only a party of them stand with thee (to worship) and let them take their arms. Then when they have performed their prostrations let them fall to the rear and let another party come that hath not worshipped and let them worship with thee, and let them take their precaution and their arms. Those who disbelieve long for you to neglect your arms and your baggage that they may attack you once for all. It is no sin for you to lay aside your arms, if rain impedeth you or ye are sick. But take your precaution. Lo! Allah prepareth for the disbelievers shameful punishment.

وَإِذَا كُنتَ فِيهِمْ فَأَقَمْتَ لَهُمُ الصَّلَاةَ فَلْتَقُمْ طَائِفَةٌ
مِّنْهُم مَّعَكَ وَلْيَأْخُذُوا أَسْلِحَتَهُمْ فَإِذَا سَجَدُوا فَلْيَكُونُوا
مِن وَرَائِكُمْ وَلْتَأْتِ طَائِفَةٌ أُخْرَىٰ لَمْ يُصَلُّوا فَلْيُصَلُّوا
مَعَكَ وَلْيَأْخُذُوا حِذْرَهُمْ وَأَسْلِحَتَهُمْ ۗ وَدَّ الَّذِينَ كَفَرُوا
لَوْ تَغْفُلُونَ عَنْ أَسْلِحَتِكُمْ وَأَمْتِعَتِكُمْ فَيَمِيلُونَ عَلَيْكُم
مَّيْلَةً وَاحِدَةً ۚ وَلَا جُنَاحَ عَلَيْكُمْ إِن كَانَ بِكُمْ أَذًى مِّن
مَّطَرٍ أَوْ كُنتُم مَّرْضَىٰ أَن تَضَعُوا أَسْلِحَتَكُمْ ۖ وَخُذُوا
حِذْرَكُمْ ۗ إِنَّ اللَّهَ أَعَدَّ لِلْكَافِرِينَ عَذَابًا مُّهِينًا ١٠٢

103. When ye have performed the act of worship, remember Allah, standing, sitting and reclining. And when ye are in safety, observe proper worship. Worship at fixed hours hath been enjoined on the believers.

104. Relent not in pursuit of the enemy. If ye are suffering, lo! they suffer even as ye suffer and ye hope from Allah that for which they cannot hope. Allah is ever Knower, Wise.

105. Lo! We reveal unto thee the Scripture with the truth, that thou mayst judge between mankind by that which Allah showeth thee. And be not thou a pleader for the treacherous;

106. And seek forgiveness of Allah. Lo! Allah is ever Forgiving, Merciful.

107. And plead not on behalf of (people) who deceive themselves. Lo! Allah loveth not one who is treacherous and sinful.

108. They seek to hide from men and seek not to hide from Allah. He is with them when by night they hold discourse displeasing unto Him. Allah ever surroundeth what they do.

109. Lo! ye are they who pleaded for them in the life of the world. But who will plead with Allah for them on the Day of Resurrection, or who will then be their defender?

110. Yet whoso doth evil or wrongeth his own soul, then seeketh pardon of Allah, will find Allah Forgiving, Merciful.

111. Whoso committeth sin committeth it only against himself. Allah is ever Knower, Wise.

فَاِذَا قَضَيْتُمُ الصَّلٰوةَ فَاذْكُرُوا اللّٰهَ قِيٰمًا وَّقُعُوْدًا وَّ
عَلٰى جُنُوْبِكُمْ ۚ فَاِذَا اطْمَاْنَنْتُمْ فَاَقِيْمُوا الصَّلٰوةَ ۚ
اِنَّ الصَّلٰوةَ كَانَتْ عَلَى الْمُؤْمِنِيْنَ كِتٰبًا
مَّوْقُوْتًا ﴿١٠٣﴾
وَلَا تَهِنُوْا فِى ابْتِغَآءِ الْقَوْمِ ؕ اِنْ تَكُوْنُوْا تَاْلَمُوْنَ
فَاِنَّهُمْ يَاْلَمُوْنَ كَمَا تَاْلَمُوْنَ ۚ وَتَرْجُوْنَ مِنَ اللّٰهِ مَا
لَا يَرْجُوْنَ ؕ وَكَانَ اللّٰهُ عَلِيْمًا حَكِيْمًا ﴿١٠٤﴾
اِنَّآ اَنْزَلْنَآ اِلَيْكَ الْكِتٰبَ بِالْحَقِّ لِتَحْكُمَ بَيْنَ النَّاسِ
بِمَآ اَرٰىكَ اللّٰهُ ؕ وَلَا تَكُنْ لِّلْخَآئِنِيْنَ خَصِيْمًا ﴿١٠٥﴾
وَّاسْتَغْفِرِ اللّٰهَ ؕ اِنَّ اللّٰهَ كَانَ غَفُوْرًا رَّحِيْمًا ﴿١٠٦﴾
وَلَا تُجَادِلْ عَنِ الَّذِيْنَ يَخْتَانُوْنَ اَنْفُسَهُمْ ؕ اِنَّ اللّٰهَ
لَا يُحِبُّ مَنْ كَانَ خَوَّانًا اَثِيْمًا ﴿١٠٧﴾
يَّسْتَخْفُوْنَ مِنَ النَّاسِ وَلَا يَسْتَخْفُوْنَ مِنَ اللّٰهِ وَ
هُوَ مَعَهُمْ اِذْ يُبَيِّتُوْنَ مَا لَا يَرْضٰى مِنَ الْقَوْلِ ؕ وَ
كَانَ اللّٰهُ بِمَا يَعْمَلُوْنَ مُحِيْطًا ﴿١٠٨﴾
هٰٓاَنْتُمْ هٰٓؤُلَآءِ جٰدَلْتُمْ عَنْهُمْ فِى الْحَيٰوةِ الدُّنْيَا ۟
فَمَنْ يُّجَادِلُ اللّٰهَ عَنْهُمْ يَوْمَ الْقِيٰمَةِ اَمْ مَّنْ يَّكُوْنُ
عَلَيْهِمْ وَكِيْلًا ﴿١٠٩﴾
وَمَنْ يَّعْمَلْ سُوْٓءًا اَوْ يَظْلِمْ نَفْسَهٗ ثُمَّ يَسْتَغْفِرِ اللّٰهَ
يَجِدِ اللّٰهَ غَفُوْرًا رَّحِيْمًا ﴿١١٠﴾
وَمَنْ يَّكْسِبْ اِثْمًا فَاِنَّمَا يَكْسِبُهٗ عَلٰى نَفْسِهٖ ؕ وَ
كَانَ اللّٰهُ عَلِيْمًا حَكِيْمًا ﴿١١١﴾

112. And whoso committeth a delinquency or crime, then throweth (the blame) thereof upon the innocent, hath burdened himself with falsehood and a flagrant crime.

ومن يكسب خطيئة او اثما ثم يرم به بريئا
ع ١٦ فقد احتمل بهتانا واثما مبينا ﴿١١٢﴾

113. But for the grace of Allah upon thee (Muhammad), and His mercy, a party of them had resolved to mislead thee, but they will mislead only themselves and they will hurt thee not at all. Allah revealeth unto thee the Scripture and wisdom, and teacheth thee that which thou knewest not. The grace of Allah toward thee hath been infinite.

ولولا فضل الله عليك ورحمته لهمت طآئفة
منهم ان يضلوك وما يضلون الا انفسهم
وما يضرونك من شيء وانزل الله عليك
الكتب والحكمة وعلمك ما لم تكن تعلم و
النصف كان فضل الله عليك عظيما ﴿١١٣﴾

114. There is no good in much of their secret conferences save (in) him who enjoineth almsgiving and kindness and peace-making among the people. Whoso doth that, seeking the good pleasure of Allah, We shall bestow on him a vast reward.

لا خير في كثير من نجوىهم الا من امر بصدقة
او معروف او اصلاح بين الناس ومن يفعل
ذلك ابتغآء مرضات الله فسوف نؤتيه
اجرا عظيما ﴿١١٤﴾

115. And whoso opposeth the messenger after the guidance (of Allah) hath been manifested unto him, and followeth other than the believer's way, We appoint for him that unto which he himself hath turned, and expose him unto Hell—a hapless journey's end!

ومن يشاقق الرسول من بعد ما تبين
له الهدى ويتبع غير سبيل المؤمنين
نوله ما تولى ونصله جهنم وسآءت
ع ١٧ مصيرا ﴿١١٥﴾

116. Lo! Allah pardoneth not that partners should be ascribed unto Him. He pardoneth all save that to whom He will. Whoso ascribeth partners unto Allah hath wandered far astray.

ان الله لا يغفر ان يشرك به ويغفر ما دون
ذلك لمن يشآء ومن يشرك بالله فقد ضل
ضللا بعيدا ﴿١١٦﴾

117. They invoke in His stead only females;[1] they pray to none else than Satan, a rebel—

ان يدعون من دونه الا انثا وان يدعون
الا شيطنا مريدا ﴿١١٧﴾

118. Whom Allah cursed, and he said: Surely I will take of Thy bondmen an appointed portion.

لعنه الله وقال لاتخذن من عبادك نصيبا
مفروضا ﴿١١٨﴾

1. The idols which the pagan Arabs worshipped were all female.

119. And surely I will lead them astray, and surely I will arouse desires in them, and surely I will command them and they will cut the cattle's ears, and surely I will command them and they will change Allah's creation. Whoso chooseth Satan for a patron instead of Allah is verily a loser and his loss is manifest.

120. He promiseth them and stirreth up desires in them, and Satan promiseth them only to beguile.

121. For such, their habitation will be hell, and they will find no refuge therefrom.

122. But as for those who believe and do good works, We shall bring them into gardens underneath which rivers flow, wherein they will abide for ever. It is a promise from Allah in truth; and who can be more truthful than Allah in utterance?

123. It will not be in accordance with your desires, nor the desires of the People of the Scripture.[1] He who doth wrong will have the recompense thereof, and will not find against Allah any protecting friend or helper.

124. And whoso doth good works, whether of male or female, and he (or she) is a believer such will enter Paradise and they will not be wronged the dint in a date-stone.

125. Who is better in religion than he who surrendereth his purpose to Allah while doing good (to men) and followeth the tradition of Abraham, the upright? Allah (Himself) chose Abraham for Friend.

126. Unto Allah belongeth whatsoever is in the heavens and whatsoever is in the earth. Allah ever surroundeth all things.

وَّلَاُضِلَّنَّهُمْ وَلَاُمَنِّيَنَّهُمْ وَلَاٰمُرَنَّهُمْ فَلَيُبَتِّكُنَّ
اٰذَانَ الْاَنْعَامِ وَلَاٰمُرَنَّهُمْ فَلَيُغَيِّرُنَّ خَلْقَ اللّٰهِ
وَمَنْ يَّتَّخِذِ الشَّيْطٰنَ وَلِيًّا مِّنْ دُوْنِ اللّٰهِ فَقَدْ
خَسِرَ خُسْرَانًا مُّبِيْنًا ﴿١١٩﴾
يَعِدُهُمْ وَيُمَنِّيْهِمْ وَمَا يَعِدُهُمُ الشَّيْطٰنُ اِلَّا
غُرُوْرًا ﴿١٢٠﴾
اُولٰٓئِكَ مَاْوٰىهُمْ جَهَنَّمُ وَلَا يَجِدُوْنَ عَنْهَا
مَحِيْصًا ﴿١٢١﴾
وَالَّذِيْنَ اٰمَنُوْا وَعَمِلُوا الصّٰلِحٰتِ سَنُدْخِلُهُمْ جَنّٰتٍ
تَجْرِيْ مِنْ تَحْتِهَا الْاَنْهٰرُ خٰلِدِيْنَ فِيْهَآ اَبَدًا
وَعْدَ اللّٰهِ حَقًّا وَمَنْ اَصْدَقُ مِنَ اللّٰهِ قِيْلًا ﴿١٢٢﴾
لَيْسَ بِاَمَانِيِّكُمْ وَلَآ اَمَانِيِّ اَهْلِ الْكِتٰبِ مَنْ يَّعْمَلْ
سُوْٓءًا يُّجْزَ بِهٖ وَلَا يَجِدْ لَهٗ مِنْ دُوْنِ اللّٰهِ وَلِيًّا
وَّلَا نَصِيْرًا ﴿١٢٣﴾
وَمَنْ يَّعْمَلْ مِنَ الصّٰلِحٰتِ مِنْ ذَكَرٍ اَوْ اُنْثٰى وَهُوَ
مُؤْمِنٌ فَاُولٰٓئِكَ يَدْخُلُوْنَ الْجَنَّةَ وَلَا يُظْلَمُوْنَ
نَقِيْرًا ﴿١٢٤﴾
وَمَنْ اَحْسَنُ دِيْنًا مِّمَّنْ اَسْلَمَ وَجْهَهٗ لِلّٰهِ وَهُوَ
مُحْسِنٌ وَّاتَّبَعَ مِلَّةَ اِبْرٰهِيْمَ حَنِيْفًا وَاتَّخَذَ
اللّٰهُ اِبْرٰهِيْمَ خَلِيْلًا ﴿١٢٥﴾
وَلِلّٰهِ مَا فِي السَّمٰوٰتِ وَمَا فِي الْاَرْضِ وَكَانَ اللّٰهُ
ع بِكُلِّ شَيْءٍ مُّحِيْطًا ﴿١٢٦﴾

1. Jews and Christians.

127. They consult thee concerning women. Say: Allah giveth you decree concerning them, and the Scripture which hath been recited unto you (giveth decree), concerning female orphans unto whom ye give not that which is ordained for them though ye desire to marry them, and (concerning) the weak among children, and that ye should deal justly with orphans. Whatever good ye do, lo! Allah is ever Aware of it.

128. If a woman feareth ill-treatment from her husband, or desertion, it is no sin for them twain if they make terms of peace between themselves Peace is better. But greed hath been made present in the minds (of men). If ye dó good and keep from evil, lo! Allah is ever Informed of what ye do.

129. Ye will not be able to deal equally between (your) wives, however much ye wish (to do so). But turn not altogether away (from one), leaving her as in suspense. If ye do good and keep from evil, lo! Allah is ever Forgiving, Merciful.

130. But if they separate, Allah will compensate each out of His abundance. Allah is ever All-Embracing, All-Knowing.

131. Unto Allah belongeth whatsoever is in the heavens and whatsoever is in the earth. And We charged those who received the Scripture before you, and (We charge) you, that ye keep your duty toward Allah. And if ye disbelieve, lo! unto Allah belongeth whatsoever is in the heavens and whatsoever is in the earth, and Allah is ever Absolute, Owner of Praise.

132. Unto Allah belongeth whatsoever is in the heavens and whatsoever is in the earth. And Allah is sufficient as Defender.

133. If He will, He can remove you, O people and produce others (in your, stead). Allah is Able to do that.

وَيَسْتَفْتُونَكَ فِي النِّسَآءِ قُلِ اللّٰهُ يُفْتِيكُمْ فِيهِنَّ وَ
مَا يُتْلٰى عَلَيْكُمْ فِي الْكِتٰبِ فِي يَتٰمَى النِّسَآءِ الّٰتِي لَا
تُؤْتُونَهُنَّ مَا كُتِبَ لَهُنَّ وَتَرْغَبُونَ اَنْ تَنْكِحُوهُنَّ
وَالْمُسْتَضْعَفِينَ مِنَ الْوِلْدَانِ وَاَنْ تَقُومُوا لِلْيَتٰمٰى
بِالْقِسْطِ وَمَا تَفْعَلُوا مِنْ خَيْرٍ فَاِنَّ اللّٰهَ كَانَ بِهٖ عَلِيمًا ﴿١٢٧﴾
وَاِنِ امْرَاَةٌ خَافَتْ مِنْ بَعْلِهَا نُشُوزًا اَوْ اِعْرَاضًا
فَلَا جُنَاحَ عَلَيْهِمَآ اَنْ يُّصْلِحَا بَيْنَهُمَا صُلْحًا وَالصُّلْحُ
خَيْرٌ وَاُحْضِرَتِ الْاَنْفُسُ الشُّحَّ وَاِنْ تُحْسِنُوا وَ
تَتَّقُوا فَاِنَّ اللّٰهَ كَانَ بِمَا تَعْمَلُونَ خَبِيرًا ﴿١٢٨﴾
وَلَنْ تَسْتَطِيعُوٓا اَنْ تَعْدِلُوا بَيْنَ النِّسَآءِ وَلَوْ حَرَصْتُمْ
فَلَا تَمِيلُوا كُلَّ الْمَيْلِ فَتَذَرُوهَا كَالْمُعَلَّقَةِ وَاِنْ
تُصْلِحُوا وَتَتَّقُوا فَاِنَّ اللّٰهَ كَانَ غَفُورًا رَّحِيمًا ﴿١٢٩﴾
وَاِنْ يَّتَفَرَّقَا يُغْنِ اللّٰهُ كُلًّا مِّنْ سَعَتِهٖ وَكَانَ اللّٰهُ
وَاسِعًا حَكِيمًا ﴿١٣٠﴾
وَلِلّٰهِ مَا فِي السَّمٰوٰتِ وَمَا فِي الْاَرْضِ وَلَقَدْ وَصَّيْنَا
الَّذِينَ اُوتُوا الْكِتٰبَ مِنْ قَبْلِكُمْ وَاِيَّاكُمْ اَنِ اتَّقُوا اللّٰهَ
وَاِنْ تَكْفُرُوا فَاِنَّ لِلّٰهِ مَا فِي السَّمٰوٰتِ وَمَا فِي الْاَرْضِ
وَكَانَ اللّٰهُ غَنِيًّا حَمِيدًا ﴿١٣١﴾
وَلِلّٰهِ مَا فِي السَّمٰوٰتِ وَمَا فِي الْاَرْضِ وَكَفٰى بِاللّٰهِ
وَكِيلًا ﴿١٣٢﴾
اِنْ يَّشَاْ يُذْهِبْكُمْ اَيُّهَا النَّاسُ وَيَاْتِ بِاٰخَرِينَ
وَكَانَ اللّٰهُ عَلٰى ذٰلِكَ قَدِيرًا ﴿١٣٣﴾

134. Whoso desireth the reward of the world, (let him know that) with Allah is the reward of the world and the Hereafter. Allah is ever Hearer, Seer.

135. O ye who believe! Be ye staunch in justice, witnesses for Allah, even though it be against yourselves or (your) parents or (your) kindred, whether (the case be of) a rich man or a poor man, for Allah is nearer unto both (than ye are). So follow not passion lest ye lapse (from truth) and if ye lapse or fall away, then lo! Allah is ever Informed of what ye do.

136. O ye who believe! Believe in Allah and His messenger and the Scripture which He hath revealed unto His messenger, and the Scripture which He revealed aforetime. Whoso disbelieveth in Allah and His angels and His scriptures and His messengers and the Last Day, he verily hath wandered far astray.

137. Lo! those who believe, then disbelieve and then (again) believe, then disbelieve, and then increase in disbelief, Allah will never pardon them, nor will He guide them unto a way.

138. Bear unto the hypocrites the tidings that for them there is a painful doom;

139. Those who choose disbelievers for their friends instead of believers! Do they look for power at their hands? Lo! all power appertaineth to Allah.

140. He hath already revealed unto you in the Scripture that, when ye hear the revelations of Allah rejected and derided, (ye) sit not with them (who disbelieve and mock) until they engage in some other conversation. Lo! in that case (if ye stayed) ye would be like unto them. Lo! Allah will gather hypocrites and disbelievers, all together, into Hell;

مَن كَانَ يُرِيدُ ثَوَابَ الدُّنْيَا فَعِندَ اللَّهِ ثَوَابُ الدُّنْيَا
وَالْآخِرَةِ ۚ وَكَانَ اللَّهُ سَمِيعًا بَصِيرًا ﴿١٣٤﴾
يَا أَيُّهَا الَّذِينَ آمَنُوا كُونُوا قَوَّامِينَ بِالْقِسْطِ شُهَدَاءَ
لِلَّهِ وَلَوْ عَلَىٰ أَنفُسِكُمْ أَوِ الْوَالِدَيْنِ وَالْأَقْرَبِينَ ۚ إِن
يَكُنْ غَنِيًّا أَوْ فَقِيرًا فَاللَّهُ أَوْلَىٰ بِهِمَا ۖ فَلَا تَتَّبِعُوا
الْهَوَىٰ أَن تَعْدِلُوا ۚ وَإِن تَلْوُوا أَوْ تُعْرِضُوا فَإِنَّ اللَّهَ
كَانَ بِمَا تَعْمَلُونَ خَبِيرًا ﴿١٣٥﴾
يَا أَيُّهَا الَّذِينَ آمَنُوا آمِنُوا بِاللَّهِ وَرَسُولِهِ وَالْكِتَابِ
الَّذِي نَزَّلَ عَلَىٰ رَسُولِهِ وَالْكِتَابِ الَّذِي أَنزَلَ مِن
قَبْلُ ۚ وَمَن يَكْفُرْ بِاللَّهِ وَمَلَائِكَتِهِ وَكُتُبِهِ وَرُسُلِهِ وَ
الْيَوْمِ الْآخِرِ فَقَدْ ضَلَّ ضَلَالًا بَعِيدًا ﴿١٣٦﴾
إِنَّ الَّذِينَ آمَنُوا ثُمَّ كَفَرُوا ثُمَّ آمَنُوا ثُمَّ كَفَرُوا ثُمَّ
ازْدَادُوا كُفْرًا لَّمْ يَكُنِ اللَّهُ لِيَغْفِرَ لَهُمْ وَلَا لِيَهْدِيَهُمْ
سَبِيلًا ﴿١٣٧﴾
بَشِّرِ الْمُنَافِقِينَ بِأَنَّ لَهُمْ عَذَابًا أَلِيمًا ﴿١٣٨﴾
الَّذِينَ يَتَّخِذُونَ الْكَافِرِينَ أَوْلِيَاءَ مِن دُونِ
الْمُؤْمِنِينَ ۚ أَيَبْتَغُونَ عِندَهُمُ الْعِزَّةَ فَإِنَّ الْعِزَّةَ
لِلَّهِ جَمِيعًا ﴿١٣٩﴾
وَقَدْ نَزَّلَ عَلَيْكُمْ فِي الْكِتَابِ أَنْ إِذَا سَمِعْتُمْ آيَاتِ اللَّهِ
يُكْفَرُ بِهَا وَيُسْتَهْزَأُ بِهَا فَلَا تَقْعُدُوا مَعَهُمْ حَتَّىٰ
يَخُوضُوا فِي حَدِيثٍ غَيْرِهِ ۚ إِنَّكُمْ إِذًا مِّثْلُهُمْ ۗ إِنَّ اللَّهَ
جَامِعُ الْمُنَافِقِينَ وَالْكَافِرِينَ فِي جَهَنَّمَ جَمِيعًا ﴿١٤٠﴾

141. Those who wait upon occasion in regard to you and, if a victory cometh unto you from Allah, say: Are we not with you? and if the disbelievers meet with a success, say: Had we not the mastery of you, and did we not protect you from the believers?—Allah will judge between you at the Day of Resurrection, and Allah will not give the disbelievers any way (of success) against the believers.

142. Lo! the hypocrites seek to beguile Allah, but it is Allah who beguileth them. When they stand up to worship they perform it languidly and to be seen of men, and are mindful of Allah but little;

143. Swaying between this (and that), (belonging) neither to these nor to those. He whom Allah causeth to go astray, thou (O Muhammad) wilt not find a way for him:

144. O ye who believe! Choose not disbelievers for (your) friends in place of believers. Would ye give Allah a clear warrant against you?

145. Lo! the hypocrites (will be) in the lowest deep of the fire, and thou wilt find no helper for them;

146. Save those who repent and amend and hold fast to Allah and make their religion pure for Allah (only). Those are with the believers. And Allah will bestow on the believers an immense reward.

147. What concern hath Allah for your punishment if ye are thankful (for His mercies) and believe (in Him)? Allah was ever Responsive, Aware.

148. Allah loveth not the utterance of harsh speech save by one who hath been wronged. Allah is ever Hearer, Knower.

الَّذِيْنَ يَتَرَبَّصُوْنَ بِكُمْ ۚ فَاِنْ كَانَ لَكُمْ فَتْحٌ مِّنَ اللّٰهِ
قَالُوْٓا اَلَمْ نَكُنْ مَّعَكُمْ ۖ وَاِنْ كَانَ لِلْكٰفِرِيْنَ نَصِيْبٌ ۙ
قَالُوْٓا اَلَمْ نَسْتَحْوِذْ عَلَيْكُمْ وَنَمْنَعْكُمْ مِّنَ الْمُؤْمِنِيْنَ ؕ
فَاللّٰهُ يَحْكُمُ بَيْنَكُمْ يَوْمَ الْقِيٰمَةِ ؕ وَلَنْ يَّجْعَلَ اللّٰهُ
لِلْكٰفِرِيْنَ عَلَى الْمُؤْمِنِيْنَ سَبِيْلًا ﴿١٤١﴾

اِنَّ الْمُنٰفِقِيْنَ يُخٰدِعُوْنَ اللّٰهَ وَهُوَ خَادِعُهُمْ ۚ وَاِذَا
قَامُوْٓا اِلَى الصَّلٰوةِ قَامُوْا كُسَالٰى ۙ يُرَآءُوْنَ النَّاسَ وَلَا
يَذْكُرُوْنَ اللّٰهَ اِلَّا قَلِيْلًا ﴿١٤٢﴾

مُّذَبْذَبِيْنَ بَيْنَ ذٰلِكَ ۖ لَآ اِلٰى هٰٓؤُلَآءِ وَلَآ اِلٰى هٰٓؤُلَآءِ ؕ
وَمَنْ يُّضْلِلِ اللّٰهُ فَلَنْ تَجِدَ لَهٗ سَبِيْلًا ﴿١٤٣﴾

يٰٓاَيُّهَا الَّذِيْنَ اٰمَنُوْا لَا تَتَّخِذُوا الْكٰفِرِيْنَ اَوْلِيَآءَ
مِنْ دُوْنِ الْمُؤْمِنِيْنَ ؕ اَتُرِيْدُوْنَ اَنْ تَجْعَلُوْا لِلّٰهِ
عَلَيْكُمْ سُلْطٰنًا مُّبِيْنًا ﴿١٤٤﴾

اِنَّ الْمُنٰفِقِيْنَ فِى الدَّرْكِ الْاَسْفَلِ مِنَ النَّارِ ۚ وَلَنْ
تَجِدَ لَهُمْ نَصِيْرًا ﴿١٤٥﴾

اِلَّا الَّذِيْنَ تَابُوْا وَاَصْلَحُوْا وَاعْتَصَمُوْا بِاللّٰهِ وَ
اَخْلَصُوْا دِيْنَهُمْ لِلّٰهِ فَاُولٰٓئِكَ مَعَ الْمُؤْمِنِيْنَ ؕ وَسَوْفَ
يُؤْتِ اللّٰهُ الْمُؤْمِنِيْنَ اَجْرًا عَظِيْمًا ﴿١٤٦﴾

مَا يَفْعَلُ اللّٰهُ بِعَذَابِكُمْ اِنْ شَكَرْتُمْ وَاٰمَنْتُمْ ؕ وَ
كَانَ اللّٰهُ شَاكِرًا عَلِيْمًا ﴿١٤٧﴾

لَا يُحِبُّ اللّٰهُ الْجَهْرَ بِالسُّوْٓءِ مِنَ الْقَوْلِ اِلَّا
مَنْ ظُلِمَ ؕ وَكَانَ اللّٰهُ سَمِيْعًا عَلِيْمًا ﴿١٤٨﴾

149. If ye do good openly or keep it secret, or forgive evil, lo! Allah is Forgiving, Powerful.

إِنْ تُبْدُوا خَيْرًا أَوْ تُخْفُوهُ أَوْ تَعْفُوا عَنْ سُوٓءٍ
فَإِنَّ اللّٰهَ كَانَ عَفُوًّا قَدِيرًا ﴿١٤٩﴾

150. Lo! those who disbelieve in Allah and His messengers, and seek to make distinction between Allah and His messengers, and say: We believe in some and disbelieve in others, and seek to choose a way in between;

إِنَّ الَّذِينَ يَكْفُرُونَ بِاللّٰهِ وَرُسُلِهِ وَيُرِيدُونَ أَنْ
يُفَرِّقُوا بَيْنَ اللّٰهِ وَرُسُلِهِ وَيَقُولُونَ نُؤْمِنُ بِبَعْضٍ
وَّنَكْفُرُ بِبَعْضٍ وَّيُرِيدُونَ أَنْ يَتَّخِذُوا بَيْنَ
ذٰلِكَ سَبِيلًا ﴿١٥٠﴾

151. Such are disbelievers in truth; and for disbelievers We prepare a shameful doom.

أُولٰٓئِكَ هُمُ الْكٰفِرُونَ حَقًّا ۚ وَأَعْتَدْنَا لِلْكٰفِرِينَ
عَذَابًا مُّهِينًا ﴿١٥١﴾

152. But those who believe in Allah and His messengers and make no distinction between any of them, unto them Allah will give their wages; and Allah is ever Forgiving, Merciful.

وَالَّذِينَ اٰمَنُوا بِاللّٰهِ وَرُسُلِهِ وَلَمْ يُفَرِّقُوا بَيْنَ أَحَدٍ
مِّنْهُمْ أُولٰٓئِكَ سَوْفَ يُؤْتِيهِمْ أُجُورَهُمْ ۗ وَكَانَ اللّٰهُ
ع غَفُورًا رَّحِيمًا ﴿١٥٢﴾

153. The People of the Scripture ask of thee that thou shouldst cause an (actual) Book to descend upon them from heaven. They asked a greater thing of Moses aforetime, for they said: Show us Allah plainly. The storm of lightning seized them for their wickedness. Then (even after that) they chose the calf (for worship) after clear proofs (of Allah's Sovereignty) had come unto them. And We forgave them that! And We bestowed on Moses evident authority.

يَسْـَٔلُكَ أَهْلُ الْكِتٰبِ أَنْ تُنَزِّلَ عَلَيْهِمْ كِتٰبًا مِّنَ
السَّمَآءِ فَقَدْ سَأَلُوا مُوسٰٓى أَكْبَرَ مِنْ ذٰلِكَ فَقَالُوٓا
أَرِنَا اللّٰهَ جَهْرَةً فَأَخَذَتْهُمُ الصّٰعِقَةُ بِظُلْمِهِمْ ۚ ثُمَّ
اتَّخَذُوا الْعِجْلَ مِنْ بَعْدِ مَا جَآءَتْهُمُ الْبَيِّنٰتُ فَعَفَوْنَا
عَنْ ذٰلِكَ ۚ وَاٰتَيْنَا مُوسٰى سُلْطٰنًا مُّبِينًا ﴿١٥٣﴾

154. And We caused the Mount to tower above them at (the taking of) their covenant: and We bade them: Enter the gate, prostrate! and we bade them: Transgress not the Sabbath! and We took from them a firm covenant.

وَرَفَعْنَا فَوْقَهُمُ الطُّورَ بِمِيثَاقِهِمْ وَقُلْنَا لَهُمُ
ادْخُلُوا الْبَابَ سُجَّدًا وَّقُلْنَا لَهُمْ لَا تَعْدُوا فِي
السَّبْتِ وَأَخَذْنَا مِنْهُمْ مِّيثَاقًا غَلِيظًا ﴿١٥٤﴾

155. Then because of their breaking of their covenant, and their disbelieving in the revelations of Allah, and their slaying of the Prophets wrongfully, and thier saying: Our hearts are hardened—Nay, but Allah hath set a seal upon them for their disbelief, so that they believe not save a few—

فَبِمَا نَقْضِهِمْ مِّيثَاقَهُمْ وَكُفْرِهِمْ بِاٰيٰتِ اللّٰهِ وَقَتْلِهِمُ
الْأَنْۢبِيَآءَ بِغَيْرِ حَقٍّ وَّقَوْلِهِمْ قُلُوبُنَا غُلْفٌ ۚ بَلْ طَبَعَ
اللّٰهُ عَلَيْهَا بِكُفْرِهِمْ فَلَا يُؤْمِنُونَ إِلَّا قَلِيلًا ﴿١٥٥﴾

156. And because of their disbelief and of their speaking against Mary a tremendous calumny;

157. And because of their saying: We slew the Messiah Jesus son of Mary, Allah's messenger—They slew him not nor crucified, but it appeared so unto them; and lo! those who disagree concerning it are in doubt thereof; they have no knowledge thereof save pursuit of a conjecture; they slew him not for certain.

158. But Allah took him up unto Himself. Allah was ever Mighty, Wise.

159. There is not one of the People of the Scripture but will believe in him before his death, and on the Day of Resurrection he will be a witness against them—

160. Because of the wrongdoing of the Jews We forbade them good things which were (before) made lawful unto them, and because of their much hindering from Allah's way,

161. And of their taking usury when they were forbidden it, and of their devouring people's wealth by false pretences. We have prepared for those of them who disbelieve a painful doom.

162. But those of them who are firm in knowledge and the believers believe in that which is revealed unto thee, and that which was revealed before thee, especially the diligent in prayer and those who pay the poor-due, the believers in Allah and the Last Day. Upon these We shall bestow immense reward.

163. Lo! We inspire thee as We inspired Noah and the prophets after him, as We inspired Abraham and Ishmael and Isaac and Jacob and the tribes, and Jesus and Job and Jonah and Aaron and Solomon, and as we imparted unto David the Psalms;

وَبِكُفْرِهِمْ وَقَوْلِهِمْ عَلَى مَرْيَمَ بُهْتَانًا عَظِيمًا ۝

وَقَوْلِهِمْ اِنَّا قَتَلْنَا الْمَسِيحَ عِيْسَى ابْنَ مَرْيَمَ رَسُوْلَ اللّٰهِ ۚ وَمَا قَتَلُوْهُ وَمَا صَلَبُوْهُ وَلٰكِنْ شُبِّهَ لَهُمْ ۚ وَاِنَّ الَّذِيْنَ اخْتَلَفُوْا فِيْهِ لَفِيْ شَكٍّ مِّنْهُ ۚ مَا لَهُمْ بِهٖ مِنْ عِلْمٍ اِلَّا اتِّبَاعَ الظَّنِّ ۚ وَمَا قَتَلُوْهُ يَقِيْنًا ۝

بَلْ رَّفَعَهُ اللّٰهُ اِلَيْهِ ۚ وَكَانَ اللّٰهُ عَزِيْزًا حَكِيْمًا ۝

وَاِنْ مِّنْ اَهْلِ الْكِتٰبِ اِلَّا لَيُؤْمِنَنَّ بِهٖ قَبْلَ مَوْتِهٖ ۚ وَيَوْمَ الْقِيٰمَةِ يَكُوْنُ عَلَيْهِمْ شَهِيْدًا ۝

فَبِظُلْمٍ مِّنَ الَّذِيْنَ هَادُوْا حَرَّمْنَا عَلَيْهِمْ طَيِّبٰتٍ اُحِلَّتْ لَهُمْ وَبِصَدِّهِمْ عَنْ سَبِيْلِ اللّٰهِ كَثِيْرًا ۝

وَّاَخْذِهِمُ الرِّبٰوا وَقَدْ نُهُوْا عَنْهُ وَاَكْلِهِمْ اَمْوَالَ النَّاسِ بِالْبَاطِلِ ۚ وَاَعْتَدْنَا لِلْكٰفِرِيْنَ مِنْهُمْ عَذَابًا اَلِيْمًا ۝

لٰكِنِ الرّٰسِخُوْنَ فِي الْعِلْمِ مِنْهُمْ وَالْمُؤْمِنُوْنَ يُؤْمِنُوْنَ بِمَا اُنْزِلَ اِلَيْكَ وَمَا اُنْزِلَ مِنْ قَبْلِكَ وَالْمُقِيْمِيْنَ الصَّلٰوةَ وَالْمُؤْتُوْنَ الزَّكٰوةَ وَالْمُؤْمِنُوْنَ بِاللّٰهِ وَالْيَوْمِ الْاٰخِرِ ۚ اُولٰٓئِكَ سَنُؤْتِيْهِمْ اَجْرًا عَظِيْمًا ۝

اِنَّا اَوْحَيْنَا اِلَيْكَ كَمَا اَوْحَيْنَا اِلٰى نُوْحٍ وَّالنَّبِيّٖنَ مِنْ بَعْدِهٖ ۚ وَاَوْحَيْنَا اِلٰى اِبْرٰهِيْمَ وَاِسْمٰعِيْلَ وَاِسْحٰقَ وَيَعْقُوْبَ وَالْاَسْبَاطِ وَعِيْسٰى وَاَيُّوْبَ وَيُوْنُسَ وَهٰرُوْنَ وَسُلَيْمٰنَ ۚ وَاٰتَيْنَا دَاوٗدَ زَبُوْرًا ۝

164. And messengers We have mentioned unto thee before and messengers We have not mentioned unto thee; and Allah spake directly unto Moses;

165. Messengers of good cheer and of warning, in order that mankind might have no argument against Allah after the messengers. Allah was ever Mighty, Wise.

166. But Allah (Himself) testifieth concerning that which He hath revealed unto thee; in His knowledge hath He revealed it; and the Angels also testify. And Allah is sufficient Witness.

167. Lo! those who disbelieve and hinder (others) from the way of Allah, they verily have wandered far astray.

168. Lo! those who disbelieve and deal in wrong, Allah will never forgive them, neither will He guide them unto a road,

169. Except the road of Hell, wherein they will abide for ever. And that is ever easy for Allah.

170. O mankind! The messenger hath come unto you with the Truth from your Lord. Therefor believe; (it is) better for you. But if ye disbelieve, still, lo! unto Allah belongeth whatsoever is in the heavens and the earth. Allah is ever Knower, Wise.

171. O People of the Scripture! Do not exaggerate in your religion nor utter aught concerning Allah save the truth. The Messiah, Jesus son of Mary, was only a messenger of Allah, and His word which He conveyed unto Mary, and a spirit from Him. So believe in Allah and His messengers, and say not "Three"—Cease! (it is) better for you!—Allah is only One God. Far is it removed from His transcendent majesty that He should have a son. His is all that is in the heavens and all that is in the earth. And Allah is sufficient as Defender.

وَرُسُلًا قَدْ قَصَصْنٰهُمْ عَلَيْكَ مِنْ قَبْلُ وَرُسُلًا لَّمْ
نَقْصُصْهُمْ عَلَيْكَ ۚ وَكَلَّمَ اللّٰهُ مُوْسٰى تَكْلِيْمًا ﴿١٦٤﴾
رُسُلًا مُّبَشِّرِيْنَ وَمُنْذِرِيْنَ لِئَلَّا يَكُوْنَ لِلنَّاسِ عَلَى
اللّٰهِ حُجَّةٌ بَعْدَ الرُّسُلِ ۚ وَكَانَ اللّٰهُ عَزِيْزًا حَكِيْمًا ﴿١٦٥﴾
لٰكِنِ اللّٰهُ يَشْهَدُ بِمَا أَنْزَلَ إِلَيْكَ أَنْزَلَهٗ بِعِلْمِهٖ ۚ وَ
الْمَلٰٓئِكَةُ يَشْهَدُوْنَ ۚ وَكَفٰى بِاللّٰهِ شَهِيْدًا ﴿١٦٦﴾
إِنَّ الَّذِيْنَ كَفَرُوْا وَصَدُّوْا عَنْ سَبِيْلِ اللّٰهِ قَدْ
ضَلُّوْا ضَلٰلًا بَعِيْدًا ﴿١٦٧﴾
إِنَّ الَّذِيْنَ كَفَرُوْا وَظَلَمُوْا لَمْ يَكُنِ اللّٰهُ لِيَغْفِرَ لَهُمْ
وَلَا لِيَهْدِيَهُمْ طَرِيْقًا ﴿١٦٨﴾
إِلَّا طَرِيْقَ جَهَنَّمَ خٰلِدِيْنَ فِيْهَآ أَبَدًا ۚ وَكَانَ ذٰلِكَ
عَلَى اللّٰهِ يَسِيْرًا ﴿١٦٩﴾
يٰٓأَيُّهَا النَّاسُ قَدْ جَآءَكُمُ الرَّسُوْلُ بِالْحَقِّ مِنْ
رَّبِّكُمْ فَاٰمِنُوْا خَيْرًا لَّكُمْ ۚ وَإِنْ تَكْفُرُوْا فَإِنَّ لِلّٰهِ مَا فِي
السَّمٰوٰتِ وَالْأَرْضِ ۚ وَكَانَ اللّٰهُ عَلِيْمًا حَكِيْمًا ﴿١٧٠﴾
يٰٓأَهْلَ الْكِتٰبِ لَا تَغْلُوْا فِيْ دِيْنِكُمْ وَلَا تَقُوْلُوْا عَلَى
اللّٰهِ إِلَّا الْحَقَّ ۚ إِنَّمَا الْمَسِيْحُ عِيْسَى ابْنُ مَرْيَمَ رَسُوْلُ
اللّٰهِ وَكَلِمَتُهٗ ۚ أَلْقٰهَآ إِلٰى مَرْيَمَ وَرُوْحٌ مِّنْهُ ۖ فَاٰمِنُوْا
بِاللّٰهِ وَرُسُلِهٖ ۚ وَلَا تَقُوْلُوْا ثَلٰثَةٌ ۚ اِنْتَهُوْا خَيْرًا
لَّكُمْ ۚ إِنَّمَا اللّٰهُ إِلٰهٌ وَّاحِدٌ ۚ سُبْحٰنَهٗٓ أَنْ يَّكُوْنَ لَهٗ
وَلَدٌ ۘ لَهٗ مَا فِي السَّمٰوٰتِ وَمَا فِي الْأَرْضِ ۚ وَكَفٰى
بِاللّٰهِ وَكِيْلًا ﴿١٧١﴾

172. The Messiah will never scorn to be a slave unto Allah, nor will the favoured angels. Whoso scorneth His service and is proud, all such will He assemble unto Him;

لَنْ يَّسْتَنْكِفَ الْمَسِيْحُ اَنْ يَّكُوْنَ عَبْدًا لِّلّٰهِ وَلَا
الْمَلٰٓئِكَةُ الْمُقَرَّبُوْنَ ۭ وَمَنْ يَّسْتَنْكِفْ عَنْ عِبَادَتِهٖ
وَيَسْتَكْبِرْ فَسَيَحْشُرُهُمْ اِلَيْهِ جَمِيْعًا ﴿١٧٢﴾

173. Then, as for those who believed and did good works, unto them will He pay their wages in full, adding unto them of His bounty; and as for those who were scornful and proud, them will He punish with a painful doom. And they will not find for them, against Allah, any protecting friend or helper.

فَاَمَّا الَّذِيْنَ اٰمَنُوْا وَعَمِلُوا الصّٰلِحٰتِ فَيُوَفِّيْهِمْ
اُجُوْرَهُمْ وَيَزِيْدُهُمْ مِّنْ فَضْلِهٖ ۚ وَاَمَّا الَّذِيْنَ اسْتَنْكَفُوْا
وَاسْتَكْبَرُوْا فَيُعَذِّبُهُمْ عَذَابًا اَلِيْمًا ۙ وَّلَا يَجِدُوْنَ
لَهُمْ مِّنْ دُوْنِ اللّٰهِ وَلِيًّا وَّلَا نَصِيْرًا ﴿١٧٣﴾

174. O mankind! Now hath a proof from your Lord come unto you, and We have sent down unto you a clear Light;

يٰٓاَيُّهَا النَّاسُ قَدْ جَاۗءَكُمْ بُرْهَانٌ مِّنْ رَّبِّكُمْ وَ
اَنْزَلْنَآ اِلَيْكُمْ نُوْرًا مُّبِيْنًا ﴿١٧٤﴾

175. As for those who believe in Allah, and hold fast unto Him, them He will cause to enter into His mercy and grace, and will guide them unto Him by a straight road.

فَاَمَّا الَّذِيْنَ اٰمَنُوْا بِاللّٰهِ وَاعْتَصَمُوْا بِهٖ فَسَيُدْخِلُهُمْ
فِيْ رَحْمَةٍ مِّنْهُ وَفَضْلٍ ۙ وَّيَهْدِيْهِمْ اِلَيْهِ صِرَاطًا
مُّسْتَقِيْمًا ۭ ﴿١٧٥﴾

176. They ask thee for a pronouncement. Say: Allah hath pronounced for you concerning distant kindred. If a man die childless and he have a sister, hers is half the heritage, and he would have inherited from her had she died childless. And if there be two sisters, then theirs are two-thirds of the heritage, and if they be brethren, men and women, unto the male is the equivalent of the share of two females. Allah expoundeth unto you, so that ye err not. Allah is Knower of all things.

يَسْتَفْتُوْنَكَ ۭ قُلِ اللّٰهُ يُفْتِيْكُمْ فِي الْكَلٰلَةِ ۭ اِنِ امْرُؤٌا
هَلَكَ لَيْسَ لَهٗ وَلَدٌ وَّلَهٗٓ اُخْتٌ فَلَهَا نِصْفُ مَا تَرَكَ ۚ
وَهُوَ يَرِثُهَآ اِنْ لَّمْ يَكُنْ لَّهَا وَلَدٌ ۭ فَاِنْ كَانَتَا اثْنَتَيْنِ
فَلَهُمَا الثُّلُثٰنِ مِمَّا تَرَكَ ۭ وَاِنْ كَانُوْٓا اِخْوَةً رِّجَالًا
وَّنِسَاۗءً فَلِلذَّكَرِ مِثْلُ حَظِّ الْاُنْثَيَيْنِ ۭ يُبَيِّنُ اللّٰهُ
لَكُمْ اَنْ تَضِلُّوْا ۭ وَاللّٰهُ بِكُلِّ شَيْءٍ عَلِيْمٌ ﴿١٧٦﴾ ع ٢٤

Al Mā'idah, "The Table Spread," derives its name from vv. 112ff., where it is told how the disciples of Jesus asked that a table spread with food might be sent down from Heaven and their prayer was granted, a passage in which some have seen an allusion to the Eucharist. Many authorities regard it as the last Sūrah in order of revelation, and Rodwell has so placed it in his chronological arrangement; but the claim can only be established in the case of verse 3, which announces the completion of their religion for the Muslims, and the choice for them of Al-Islām (the Surrender to Allah) as their religion. That verse is undoubtedly the latest of the whole Koran. It was revealed during the Prophet's last pilgrimage ("The Farewell Pilgrimage," as it is called) to Mecca, and spoken by him in the course of his address to the assembled thousands at 'Arafāt, when all Arabia had embraced Al-Islām, only a little while before his death. It is possible that as Nöldeke supposes, two other verses near to it are of the same date, but the remainder of the revelations contained in this Sūrah belong rather to the period between the fourth and seventh years of the Hijrah. Its subject is observance of religious duties. The followers of former prophets had failed through breaking their covenant, and so the Muslims are adjured to keep their covenant with God and all their obligations watchfully, because God's covenant is only with those who do right. There is more mention of the Christians here than in the former Sūrahs, from which some writers infer that this Sūrah must have been revealed at the time when the Prophet was at war with certain Christian tribes belonging to the Eastern Roman Empire. But there is no evidence for that either in Tradition or in the text itself.

The period of revelation is between the fifth and tenth years of the Hijrah.

THE TABLE SPREAD

Revealed at Al-Madinah

آياتها ١٢٠ (٥) سُورَةُ الْمَآئِدَةِ مَدَنِيَّةٌ ١١٢ رُكُوعَاتُهَا ١٦

In the name of Allah, the Beneficent, the Merciful.

بِسْمِ اللّٰهِ الرَّحْمٰنِ الرَّحِيْمِ ○

1. O ye who believe! Fulfil your undertakings. The beast of cattle is made lawful unto you (for food) except that which is announced unto you (herein), game being unlawful when ye are on pilgrimage. Lo! Allah ordaineth that which pleaseth Him.

يٰۤاَيُّهَا الَّذِيْنَ اٰمَنُوْۤا اَوْفُوْا بِالْعُقُوْدِ ۬ اُحِلَّتْ لَكُمْ
بَهِيْمَةُ الْاَنْعَامِ اِلَّا مَا يُتْلٰى عَلَيْكُمْ غَيْرَ مُحِلِّي الصَّيْدِ
وَاَنْتُمْ حُرُمٌ ؕ اِنَّ اللّٰهَ يَحْكُمُ مَا يُرِيْدُ ①

2. O ye who believe! Profane not Allah's monuments nor the Sacred Month nor the offerings nor the garlands, nor those repairing to the Sacred House,[1] seeking the grace and pleasure of Allah. But when ye have left the sacred territory, then go hunting (if ye will). And let not your hatred of a folk who (once) stopped your going to the Inviolable Place of Worship seduce you to transgress; but help ye one another unto righteousness and pious duty. Help not one another unto sin and transgression, but keep your duty to Allah. Lo! Allah is severe in punishment.

يٰۤاَيُّهَا الَّذِيْنَ اٰمَنُوْا لَا تُحِلُّوْا شَعَآئِرَ اللّٰهِ وَلَا الشَّهْرَ
الْحَرَامَ وَلَا الْهَدْيَ وَلَا الْقَلَآئِدَ وَلَاۤ آٰمِّيْنَ الْبَيْتَ
الْحَرَامَ يَبْتَغُوْنَ فَضْلًا مِّنْ رَّبِّهِمْ وَرِضْوَانًا ؕ وَاِذَا
حَلَلْتُمْ فَاصْطَادُوْا ؕ وَلَا يَجْرِمَنَّكُمْ شَنَاٰنُ قَوْمٍ اَنْ
صَدُّوْكُمْ عَنِ الْمَسْجِدِ الْحَرَامِ اَنْ تَعْتَدُوْا ۘ وَتَعَاوَنُوْا
عَلَى الْبِرِّ وَالتَّقْوٰى ۪ وَلَا تَعَاوَنُوْا عَلَى الْاِثْمِ وَالْعُدْوَانِ ۪
وَاتَّقُوا اللّٰهَ ؕ اِنَّ اللّٰهَ شَدِيْدُ الْعِقَابِ ②

3. Forbidden unto you (for food) are carrion and blood and swine-flesh, and that which hath been dedicated unto any other than Allah, and the strangled, and the dead through beating, and the dead through falling from a height, and that which hath been killed by (the goring of) horns, and the devoured of wild beasts, saving that which ye make lawful (by the death-stroke), and that which hath been immolated unto idols. And (forbidden is it) that ye swear by the divining arrows. This is an abomination. This day are those who disbelieve in despair of (ever harming) your religion; so fear them not, fear Me! This day have I perfected your religion for you and completed My favour unto you, and have chosen for you as religion AL-ISLĀM.[2] Whoso is forced by hunger, not by will, to sin: (for him) lo! Allah is Forgiving, Merciful.

حُرِّمَتْ عَلَيْكُمُ الْمَيْتَةُ وَالدَّمُ وَلَحْمُ الْخِنْزِيْرِ وَ
مَاۤ اُهِلَّ لِغَيْرِ اللّٰهِ بِهٖ وَالْمُنْخَنِقَةُ وَالْمَوْقُوْذَةُ وَ
الْمُتَرَدِّيَةُ وَالنَّطِيْحَةُ وَمَاۤ اَكَلَ السَّبُعُ اِلَّا مَا ذَكَّيْتُمْ ۫
وَمَا ذُبِحَ عَلَى النُّصُبِ وَاَنْ تَسْتَقْسِمُوْا بِالْاَزْلَامِ ؕ
ذٰلِكُمْ فِسْقٌ ؕ اَلْيَوْمَ يَئِسَ الَّذِيْنَ كَفَرُوْا مِنْ دِيْنِكُمْ
فَلَا تَخْشَوْهُمْ وَاخْشَوْنِ ؕ اَلْيَوْمَ اَكْمَلْتُ لَكُمْ دِيْنَكُمْ وَ
اَتْمَمْتُ عَلَيْكُمْ نِعْمَتِيْ وَرَضِيْتُ لَكُمُ الْاِسْلَامَ
دِيْنًا ؕ فَمَنِ اضْطُرَّ فِيْ مَخْمَصَةٍ غَيْرَ مُتَجَانِفٍ لِّاِثْمٍ ۙ
فَاِنَّ اللّٰهَ غَفُوْرٌ رَّحِيْمٌ ③

1. *i.e.* the Ka'bah at Mecca.
2. *i.e.* "The Surrender" to Allah. Thus solemnly the religion which the Prophet had established received its name.

4. They ask thee (O Muhammad) what is made lawful for them. Say: (all) good things are made lawful for you. And those beasts and birds of prey which ye have trained as hounds are trained, ye teach them that which Allah taught you; so eat of that which they catch for you and mention Allah's name upon it, and observe your duty to Allah. Lo! Allah is swift to take account.

5. This day are (all) good things made lawful for you. The food of those who have received the Scripture is lawful for you, and your food is lawful for them. And so are the virtuous women of the believers and the virtuous women of those who received the Scripture before you (lawful for you) when ye give them their marriage portions and live with them in honour, not in fornication, nor taking them as secret concubines. Whoso denieth the faith, his work is vain and he will be among the losers in the Hereafter.

6. O ye who believe! When ye rise up for prayer, wash your faces, and your hands up to the elbows, and lightly rub your heads and (wash) your feet up to the ankles. And if ye are unclean, purify yourselves. And if ye are sick or on a journey, or one of you cometh from the closet, or ye have had contact with women, and ye find not water, then go to clean, high ground and rub your faces and your hands with some of it. Allah would not place a burden on you, but He would purify you and would perfect His grace upon you, that ye may give thanks.

7. Remember Allah's grace upon you and His covenant by which He bound you when ye said: We hear and we obey; and keep your duty to Allah. Lo! Allah knoweth what is in the breasts (of men).

يَسْـَٔلُونَكَ مَاذَآ أُحِلَّ لَهُمْ قُلْ أُحِلَّ لَكُمُ الطَّيِّبٰتُ وَمَا
عَلَّمْتُمْ مِّنَ الْجَوَارِحِ مُكَلِّبِيْنَ تُعَلِّمُوْنَهُنَّ مِمَّا عَلَّمَكُمُ
اللّٰهُ فَكُلُوْا مِمَّآ اَمْسَكْنَ عَلَيْكُمْ وَاذْكُرُوا اسْمَ اللّٰهِ عَلَيْهِ
وَاتَّقُوا اللّٰهَ اِنَّ اللّٰهَ سَرِيْعُ الْحِسَابِ ٤
اَلْيَوْمَ اُحِلَّ لَكُمُ الطَّيِّبٰتُ وَطَعَامُ الَّذِيْنَ اُوْتُوا
الْكِتٰبَ حِلٌّ لَّكُمْ وَطَعَامُكُمْ حِلٌّ لَّهُمْ وَالْمُحْصَنٰتُ
مِنَ الْمُؤْمِنٰتِ وَالْمُحْصَنٰتُ مِنَ الَّذِيْنَ اُوْتُوا
الْكِتٰبَ مِنْ قَبْلِكُمْ اِذَآ اٰتَيْتُمُوْهُنَّ اُجُوْرَهُنَّ
مُحْصِنِيْنَ غَيْرَ مُسٰفِحِيْنَ وَلَا مُتَّخِذِيْٓ اَخْدَانٍ
وَمَنْ يَّكْفُرْ بِالْاِيْمَانِ فَقَدْ حَبِطَ عَمَلُهٗ وَهُوَ
ع فِي الْاٰخِرَةِ مِنَ الْخٰسِرِيْنَ ٥
يٰٓاَيُّهَا الَّذِيْنَ اٰمَنُوْٓا اِذَا قُمْتُمْ اِلَى الصَّلٰوةِ فَاغْسِلُوْا
وُجُوْهَكُمْ وَاَيْدِيَكُمْ اِلَى الْمَرَافِقِ وَامْسَحُوْا بِرُءُوْسِكُمْ وَ
اَرْجُلَكُمْ اِلَى الْكَعْبَيْنِ وَاِنْ كُنْتُمْ جُنُبًا فَاطَّهَّرُوْا وَ
اِنْ كُنْتُمْ مَّرْضٰٓى اَوْ عَلٰى سَفَرٍ اَوْ جَآءَ اَحَدٌ مِّنْكُمْ مِّنَ
الْغَآئِطِ اَوْ لٰمَسْتُمُ النِّسَآءَ فَلَمْ تَجِدُوْا مَآءً فَتَيَمَّمُوْا
صَعِيْدًا طَيِّبًا فَامْسَحُوْا بِوُجُوْهِكُمْ وَاَيْدِيْكُمْ مِّنْهُ
مَا يُرِيْدُ اللّٰهُ لِيَجْعَلَ عَلَيْكُمْ مِّنْ حَرَجٍ وَّلٰكِنْ يُّرِيْدُ
لِيُطَهِّرَكُمْ وَلِيُتِمَّ نِعْمَتَهٗ عَلَيْكُمْ لَعَلَّكُمْ تَشْكُرُوْنَ ٦
وَاذْكُرُوْا نِعْمَةَ اللّٰهِ عَلَيْكُمْ وَمِيْثَاقَهُ الَّذِيْ وَاثَقَكُمْ
بِهٖٓ اِذْ قُلْتُمْ سَمِعْنَا وَاَطَعْنَا وَاتَّقُوا اللّٰهَ اِنَّ اللّٰهَ
عَلِيْمٌۢ بِذَاتِ الصُّدُوْرِ ٧

8. O ye who believe! Be steadfast witnesses for Allah in equity, and let not hatred of any people seduce you that ye deal not justly. Deal justly, that is nearer to your duty. Observe your duty to Allah. Lo! Allah is Informed of what ye do.

9. Allah hath promised those who believe and do good works: Theirs will be forgiveness and immense reward.

10. And they who disbelieve and deny Our revelations, such are rightful owners of hell.

11. O ye who believe! Remember Allah's favour unto you, how a people were minded to stretch out their hands against you but He withheld their hands from you; and keep your duty to Allah. In Allah let believers put their trust.

12. Allah made a covenant of old with the Children of Israel and We raised among them twelve chieftains, and Allah said: Lo! I am with you. If ye establish worship and pay the poor-due, and believe in My messengers and support them, and lend unto Allah a kindly loan,[1] surely I shall remit your sins, and surely I shall bring you into gardens underneath which rivers flow. Whoso among you disbelieveth after this, will go astray from a plain road.

13. And because of their breaking their covenant, We have cursed them and made hard their hearts. They change words from their context and forget a part of that whereof they were admonished. Thou wilt not cease to discover treachery from all save a few of them. But bear with them and pardon them. Lo! Allah loveth the kindly.

1. *i.e.* a loan without interest or thought of gain.

يا أيها الذين آمنوا كونوا قوامين لله شهداء بالقسط
ولا يجرمنكم شنآن قوم على ألا تعدلوا اعدلوا
هو أقرب للتقوى واتقوا الله إن الله خبير بما
تعملون ﴿٨﴾
وعد الله الذين آمنوا وعملوا الصالحات لهم
مغفرة وأجر عظيم ﴿٩﴾
والذين كفروا وكذبوا بآياتنا أولئك أصحاب
الجحيم ﴿١٠﴾
يا أيها الذين آمنوا اذكروا نعمت الله عليكم إذ هم
قوم أن يبسطوا إليكم أيديهم فكف أيديهم عنكم
واتقوا الله وعلى الله فليتوكل المؤمنون ﴿١١﴾ ع
ولقد أخذ الله ميثاق بني إسرائيل وبعثنا منهم
اثني عشر نقيبا وقال الله إني معكم لئن أقمتم
الصلاة وآتيتم الزكاة وآمنتم برسلي وعزرتموهم
وأقرضتم الله قرضا حسنا لأكفرن عنكم سيئاتكم
ولأدخلنكم جنات تجري من تحتها الأنهار فمن
كفر بعد ذلك منكم فقد ضل سواء السبيل ﴿١٢﴾
فبما نقضهم ميثاقهم لعناهم وجعلنا قلوبهم
قاسية يحرفون الكلم عن مواضعه ونسوا حظا
مما ذكروا به ولا تزال تطلع على خائنة منهم
إلا قليلا منهم فاعف عنهم واصفح إن الله
يحب المحسنين ﴿١٣﴾

14. And with those who say: "Lo! we are Christians," We made a covenant, but they forgot a part of that whereof they were admonished. Therefore We have stirred up enmity and hatred among them till the Day of Resurrection, when Allah will inform them of their handiwork.

15. O People of the Scripture ! Now hath Our messenger come unto you, expounding unto you much of that which ye used to hide in the Scripture, and forgiving much. Now hath come unto you Light from Allah and a plain Scripture,

16. Whereby Allah guideth him who seeketh His good pleasure unto paths of peace. He bringeth them out of darkness unto light by His decree, and guideth them unto a straight path.

17. They indeed have disbelieved who say: Lo! Allah is the Messiah, son of Mary. Say: Who then can do aught against Allah, if He had willed to destroy the Messiah, son of Mary, and his mother and everyone on earth? Allah's is the Sovereignty of the heavens and the earth and all that is between them. He createth what He will. And Allah is Able to do all things.

18. The Jews and Christians say: We are sons of Allah and His loved ones. Say: Why then doth He chastise you for your sins? Nay, ye are but mortals of His creating. He forgiveth whom He will, and chastiseth whom He will. Allah's is the Sovereignty of the heavens and the earth and all that is between them, and unto Him is the journeying.

19. O People of the Scripture! Now hath Our messenger come unto you to make things plain after an interval (of cessation) of the messengers, lest ye should say: There came not unto us a messenger of cheer nor any warner. Now hath a messenger of cheer and a warner come unto you. Allah is Able to do all things.

وَمِنَ الَّذِينَ قَالُوٓا إِنَّا نَصٰرٰٓى أَخَذْنَا مِيثَاقَهُمْ فَنَسُوا
حَظًّا مِّمَّا ذُكِّرُوا بِهٖ فَأَغْرَيْنَا بَيْنَهُمُ الْعَدَاوَةَ وَالْبَغْضَآءَ
إِلٰى يَوْمِ الْقِيٰمَةِ وَسَوْفَ يُنَبِّئُهُمُ اللّٰهُ بِمَا كَانُوا يَصْنَعُونَ ﴿١٤﴾
يٰٓأَهْلَ الْكِتٰبِ قَدْ جَآءَكُمْ رَسُولُنَا يُبَيِّنُ لَكُمْ كَثِيرًا
مِّمَّا كُنْتُمْ تُخْفُونَ مِنَ الْكِتٰبِ وَيَعْفُوا عَنْ كَثِيرٍ
قَدْ جَآءَكُمْ مِّنَ اللّٰهِ نُورٌ وَّكِتٰبٌ مُّبِينٌ ﴿١٥﴾
يَّهْدِي بِهِ اللّٰهُ مَنِ اتَّبَعَ رِضْوَانَهٗ سُبُلَ السَّلٰمِ وَ
يُخْرِجُهُمْ مِّنَ الظُّلُمٰتِ إِلَى النُّورِ بِإِذْنِهٖ وَيَهْدِيهِمْ
إِلٰى صِرَاطٍ مُّسْتَقِيمٍ ﴿١٦﴾
لَقَدْ كَفَرَ الَّذِينَ قَالُوٓا إِنَّ اللّٰهَ هُوَ الْمَسِيحُ ابْنُ مَرْيَمَ
قُلْ فَمَنْ يَّمْلِكُ مِنَ اللّٰهِ شَيْئًا إِنْ أَرَادَ أَنْ يُّهْلِكَ
الْمَسِيحَ ابْنَ مَرْيَمَ وَأُمَّهٗ وَمَنْ فِي الْأَرْضِ جَمِيعًا
وَلِلّٰهِ مُلْكُ السَّمٰوٰتِ وَالْأَرْضِ وَمَا بَيْنَهُمَا يَخْلُقُ
مَا يَشَآءُ وَاللّٰهُ عَلٰى كُلِّ شَيْءٍ قَدِيرٌ ﴿١٧﴾
وَقَالَتِ الْيَهُودُ وَالنَّصٰرٰى نَحْنُ أَبْنٰٓؤُا اللّٰهِ وَأَحِبَّآؤُهٗ
قُلْ فَلِمَ يُعَذِّبُكُمْ بِذُنُوبِكُمْ بَلْ أَنْتُمْ بَشَرٌ مِّمَّنْ
خَلَقَ يَغْفِرُ لِمَنْ يَّشَآءُ وَيُعَذِّبُ مَنْ يَّشَآءُ وَلِلّٰهِ
مُلْكُ السَّمٰوٰتِ وَالْأَرْضِ وَمَا بَيْنَهُمَا وَإِلَيْهِ الْمَصِيرُ ﴿١٨﴾
يٰٓأَهْلَ الْكِتٰبِ قَدْ جَآءَكُمْ رَسُولُنَا يُبَيِّنُ لَكُمْ عَلٰى
فَتْرَةٍ مِّنَ الرُّسُلِ أَنْ تَقُولُوا مَا جَآءَنَا مِنْ بَشِيرٍ
وَّلَا نَذِيرٍ فَقَدْ جَآءَكُمْ بَشِيرٌ وَّنَذِيرٌ وَاللّٰهُ عَلٰى كُلِّ
شَيْءٍ قَدِيرٌ ﴿١٩﴾ ع

20. And (remember) when Moses said unto his people: O my people! Remember Allah's favour unto you, how He placed among you Prophets, and He made you kings, and gave you that (which) He gave not to any (other) of (His) creatures.

وَاِذْ قَالَ مُوْسٰى لِقَوْمِهٖ يٰقَوْمِ اذْكُرُوْا نِعْمَةَ اللّٰهِ عَلَيْكُمْ
اِذْ جَعَلَ فِيْكُمْ اَنْۢبِيَآءَ وَجَعَلَكُمْ مُّلُوْكًا ۖ وَّاٰتٰىكُمْ مَّا
لَمْ يُؤْتِ اَحَدًا مِّنَ الْعٰلَمِيْنَ ﴿٢٠﴾

21. O my people! Go into the holy land which Allah hath ordained for you. Turn not in flight, for surely ye turn back as losers:

يٰقَوْمِ ادْخُلُوا الْاَرْضَ الْمُقَدَّسَةَ الَّتِيْ كَتَبَ اللّٰهُ
لَكُمْ وَلَا تَرْتَدُّوْا عَلٰٓى اَدْبَارِكُمْ فَتَنْقَلِبُوْا خٰسِرِيْنَ ﴿٢١﴾

22. They said: O Moses! Lo! a giant people (dwell) therein, and lo! we go not in till they go forth from thence. When they go forth, then we will enter (not till then).

قَالُوْا يٰمُوْسٰٓى اِنَّ فِيْهَا قَوْمًا جَبَّارِيْنَ ۖ وَاِنَّا لَنْ
نَّدْخُلَهَا حَتّٰى يَخْرُجُوْا مِنْهَا ۚ فَاِنْ يَّخْرُجُوْا مِنْهَا
فَاِنَّا دٰخِلُوْنَ ﴿٢٢﴾

23. Then outspake two of those who feared (their Lord, men) unto whom Allah had been gracious: Enter in upon them by the gate, for if ye enter by it, lo! ye will be victorious. So put your trust (in Allah) if ye are indeed believers.

قَالَ رَجُلٰنِ مِنَ الَّذِيْنَ يَخَافُوْنَ اَنْعَمَ اللّٰهُ عَلَيْهِمَا
ادْخُلُوْا عَلَيْهِمُ الْبَابَ ۚ فَاِذَا دَخَلْتُمُوْهُ فَاِنَّكُمْ غٰلِبُوْنَ ۚ
وَعَلَى اللّٰهِ فَتَوَكَّلُوْٓا اِنْ كُنْتُمْ مُّؤْمِنِيْنَ ﴿٢٣﴾

24. They said: O Moses! We will never enter (the land) while they are in it. So go thou and thy Lord and fight! We will sit here.

قَالُوْا يٰمُوْسٰٓى اِنَّا لَنْ نَّدْخُلَهَآ اَبَدًا مَّا دَامُوْا فِيْهَا
فَاذْهَبْ اَنْتَ وَرَبُّكَ فَقَاتِلَآ اِنَّا هٰهُنَا قٰعِدُوْنَ ﴿٢٤﴾

25. He said: My Lord! I have control of none but myself and my brother, so distinguish between us and the wrong-doing folk.

قَالَ رَبِّ اِنِّيْ لَآ اَمْلِكُ اِلَّا نَفْسِيْ وَاَخِيْ فَافْرُقْ بَيْنَنَا
وَبَيْنَ الْقَوْمِ الْفٰسِقِيْنَ ﴿٢٥﴾

26. (Their Lord) said: For this the land will surely be forbidden them for forty years that they will wander in the earth, bewildered. So grieve not over the wrong-doing folk.

قَالَ فَاِنَّهَا مُحَرَّمَةٌ عَلَيْهِمْ اَرْبَعِيْنَ سَنَةً ۚ يَتِيْهُوْنَ
فِي الْاَرْضِ ۭ فَلَا تَاْسَ عَلَى الْقَوْمِ الْفٰسِقِيْنَ ﴿٢٦﴾

27. But recite unto them with truth the tale of the two sons of Adam, how they offered each a sacrifice, and it was accepted from the one of them and it was not accepted from the other. (The one) said: I will surely kill thee. (The other) answered: Allah accepteth only from those who ward off (evil).

وَاتْلُ عَلَيْهِمْ نَبَاَ ابْنَيْ اٰدَمَ بِالْحَقِّ ۘ اِذْ قَرَّبَا قُرْبَانًا
فَتُقُبِّلَ مِنْ اَحَدِهِمَا وَلَمْ يُتَقَبَّلْ مِنَ الْاٰخَرِ ۭ قَالَ
لَاَقْتُلَنَّكَ ۭ قَالَ اِنَّمَا يَتَقَبَّلُ اللّٰهُ مِنَ الْمُتَّقِيْنَ ﴿٢٧﴾

28. Even if thou stretch out thy hand against me to kill me, I shall not stretch out my hand against thee to kill thee, lo! I fear Allah, the Lord of the Worlds.

لَىِٕنْۢ بَسَطْتَّ اِلَيَّ يَدَكَ لِتَقْتُلَنِيْ مَآ اَنَا بِبَاسِطٍ يَّدِيَ
اِلَيْكَ لِاَقْتُلَكَ ۚ اِنِّيْٓ اَخَافُ اللّٰهَ رَبَّ الْعٰلَمِيْنَ ﴿٢٨﴾

29. Lo! I would rather thou shouldst bear the punishment of the sin against me and thine own sin and become one of the owners of the Fire. That is the reward of evil-doers.

30. But (the other's) mind imposed on him the killing of his brother, so he slew him and became one of the losers.

31. Then Allah sent a raven scratching up the ground, to show him how to hide his brother's naked corpse. He said: Woe unto me! Am I not able to be as this raven and so hide my brother's naked corpse? And he became repentant.

32. For that cause We decreed for the Children of Israel that whosoever killeth a human being for other than manslaughter or corruption in the earth, it shall be as if he had killed all mankind, and whoso saveth the life of one, it shall be as if he had saved the life of all mankind. Our messengers came unto them of old with clear proofs (of Allah's sovereignty), but afterwards, lo! many of them became prodigals in the earth.

33. The only reward of those who make war upon Allah and His messenger and strive after corruption in the land will be that they will be killed or crucified, or have their hands and feet on alternate sides cut off, or will be expelled out of the land. Such will be their degradation in the world, and in the Hereafter theirs will be an awful doom;

34. Save those who repent before ye overpower them. For know that Allah is Forgiving, Merciful.

35. O ye who believe! Be mindful of your duty to Allah, and seek the way of approach unto Him, and strive in His way in order that ye may succeed.

إِنِّيٓ أُرِيدُ أَن تَبُوٓأَ بِإِثْمِى وَإِثْمِكَ فَتَكُونَ مِنْ
أَصْحَٰبِ ٱلنَّارِ ۚ وَذَٰلِكَ جَزَٰٓؤُا۟ ٱلظَّٰلِمِينَ ﴿٢٩﴾
فَطَوَّعَتْ لَهُۥ نَفْسُهُۥ قَتْلَ أَخِيهِ فَقَتَلَهُۥ فَأَصْبَحَ
مِنَ ٱلْخَٰسِرِينَ ﴿٣٠﴾
فَبَعَثَ ٱللَّهُ غُرَابًا يَبْحَثُ فِى ٱلْأَرْضِ لِيُرِيَهُۥ كَيْفَ
يُوَٰرِى سَوْءَةَ أَخِيهِ ۚ قَالَ يَٰوَيْلَتَىٰٓ أَعَجَزْتُ أَنْ
أَكُونَ مِثْلَ هَٰذَا ٱلْغُرَابِ فَأُوَٰرِىَ سَوْءَةَ أَخِى ۖ
فَأَصْبَحَ مِنَ ٱلنَّٰدِمِينَ ﴿٣١﴾
مِنْ أَجْلِ ذَٰلِكَ كَتَبْنَا عَلَىٰ بَنِىٓ إِسْرَٰٓءِيلَ أَنَّهُۥ مَن
قَتَلَ نَفْسًۢا بِغَيْرِ نَفْسٍ أَوْ فَسَادٍ فِى ٱلْأَرْضِ فَكَأَنَّمَا
قَتَلَ ٱلنَّاسَ جَمِيعًا وَمَنْ أَحْيَاهَا فَكَأَنَّمَآ أَحْيَا ٱلنَّاسَ
جَمِيعًا ۚ وَلَقَدْ جَآءَتْهُمْ رُسُلُنَا بِٱلْبَيِّنَٰتِ ثُمَّ إِنَّ كَثِيرًا
مِّنْهُم بَعْدَ ذَٰلِكَ فِى ٱلْأَرْضِ لَمُسْرِفُونَ ﴿٣٢﴾
إِنَّمَا جَزَٰٓؤُا۟ ٱلَّذِينَ يُحَارِبُونَ ٱللَّهَ وَرَسُولَهُۥ وَيَسْعَوْنَ
فِى ٱلْأَرْضِ فَسَادًا أَن يُقَتَّلُوٓا۟ أَوْ يُصَلَّبُوٓا۟ أَوْ تُقَطَّعَ
أَيْدِيهِمْ وَأَرْجُلُهُم مِّنْ خِلَٰفٍ أَوْ يُنفَوْا۟ مِنَ ٱلْأَرْضِ ۚ
ذَٰلِكَ لَهُمْ خِزْىٌ فِى ٱلدُّنْيَا ۖ وَلَهُمْ فِى ٱلْءَاخِرَةِ عَذَابٌ
عَظِيمٌ ﴿٣٣﴾
إِلَّا ٱلَّذِينَ تَابُوا۟ مِن قَبْلِ أَن تَقْدِرُوا۟ عَلَيْهِمْ ۖ فَٱعْلَمُوٓا۟
أَنَّ ٱللَّهَ غَفُورٌ رَّحِيمٌ ﴿٣٤﴾
يَٰٓأَيُّهَا ٱلَّذِينَ ءَامَنُوا۟ ٱتَّقُوا۟ ٱللَّهَ وَٱبْتَغُوٓا۟ إِلَيْهِ ٱلْوَسِيلَةَ
وَجَٰهِدُوا۟ فِى سَبِيلِهِۦ لَعَلَّكُمْ تُفْلِحُونَ ﴿٣٥﴾

36. As for those who disbelieve, lo! if all that is in the earth were theirs, and as much again therewith, to ransom them from the doom on the Day of Resurrection, it would not be accepted from them. Theirs will be a painful doom.

إِنَّ الَّذِينَ كَفَرُوا لَوْ أَنَّ لَهُم مَّا فِي الْأَرْضِ جَمِيعًا
وَمِثْلَهُ مَعَهُ لِيَفْتَدُوا بِهِ مِنْ عَذَابِ يَوْمِ الْقِيَامَةِ
مَا تُقُبِّلَ مِنْهُمْ ۖ وَلَهُمْ عَذَابٌ أَلِيمٌ ٣٦

37. They will wish to come forth from the Fire, but they will not come forth from it. Theirs will be a lasting doom.

يُرِيدُونَ أَن يَخْرُجُوا مِنَ النَّارِ وَمَا هُم بِخَارِجِينَ
مِنْهَا ۖ وَلَهُمْ عَذَابٌ مُّقِيمٌ ٣٧

38. As for the thief, both male and female, cut off their hands. It is the reward of their own deeds, an exemplary punishment from Allah. Allah is Mighty, Wise.

وَالسَّارِقُ وَالسَّارِقَةُ فَاقْطَعُوا أَيْدِيَهُمَا جَزَاءً بِمَا
كَسَبَا نَكَالًا مِّنَ اللَّهِ ۗ وَاللَّهُ عَزِيزٌ حَكِيمٌ ٣٨

39. But whoso repenteth after his wrongdoing and amendeth, lo! Allah will relent toward him. Lo! Allah is Forgiving, Merciful.

فَمَن تَابَ مِن بَعْدِ ظُلْمِهِ وَأَصْلَحَ فَإِنَّ اللَّهَ يَتُوبُ
عَلَيْهِ ۗ إِنَّ اللَّهَ غَفُورٌ رَّحِيمٌ ٣٩

40. Knowest thou not that unto Allah belongeth the Sovereignty of the heavens and the earth? He punisheth whom He will, and forgiveth whom He will. Allah is Able to do all things.

أَلَمْ تَعْلَمْ أَنَّ اللَّهَ لَهُ مُلْكُ السَّمَاوَاتِ وَالْأَرْضِ
يُعَذِّبُ مَن يَشَاءُ وَيَغْفِرُ لِمَن يَشَاءُ ۗ وَاللَّهُ عَلَىٰ
كُلِّ شَيْءٍ قَدِيرٌ ٤٠

41. O Messenger! Let not them grieve thee who vie one with another in the race to disbelief, of such as say with their mouths: "We believe," but their hearts believe not, and of the Jews: listeners for the sake of falsehood, listeners on behalf of other folk who come not unto thee, changing words from their context and saying: If this be given unto you, receive it, but if this be not given unto you, then beware! He whom Allah doometh unto sin, thou (by thine efforts) wilt avail him naught against Allah. Those are they for whom the will of Allah is that He cleanse not their hearts. Theirs in the world will be ignominy, and in the Hereafter an awful doom;

يَا أَيُّهَا الرَّسُولُ لَا يَحْزُنكَ الَّذِينَ يُسَارِعُونَ
فِي الْكُفْرِ مِنَ الَّذِينَ قَالُوا آمَنَّا بِأَفْوَاهِهِمْ وَلَمْ
تُؤْمِن قُلُوبُهُمْ ۛ وَمِنَ الَّذِينَ هَادُوا ۛ سَمَّاعُونَ
لِلْكَذِبِ سَمَّاعُونَ لِقَوْمٍ آخَرِينَ لَمْ يَأْتُوكَ ۖ يُحَرِّفُونَ
الْكَلِمَ مِن بَعْدِ مَوَاضِعِهِ ۖ يَقُولُونَ إِنْ أُوتِيتُمْ
هَٰذَا فَخُذُوهُ وَإِن لَّمْ تُؤْتَوْهُ فَاحْذَرُوا ۚ وَمَن يُرِدِ
اللَّهُ فِتْنَتَهُ فَلَن تَمْلِكَ لَهُ مِنَ اللَّهِ شَيْئًا ۚ
أُولَٰئِكَ الَّذِينَ لَمْ يُرِدِ اللَّهُ أَن يُطَهِّرَ قُلُوبَهُمْ ۚ
لَهُمْ فِي الدُّنْيَا خِزْيٌ ۖ وَلَهُمْ فِي الْآخِرَةِ عَذَابٌ
عَظِيمٌ ٤١

42. Listeners for the sake of falsehood! Greedy for illicit gain! If then they have recourse unto thee (Muhammad), judge between them or disclaim jurisdiction. If thou disclaimest jurisdiction, then they cannot harm thee at all. But if thou judgest, judge between them with equity. Lo! Allah loveth the equitable.

43. How come they unto thee for judgement when they have the Torah, wherein Allah hath delivered judgement (for them)? Yet even after that they turn away. Such (folk) are not believers.

44. Lo! We did reveal the Torah, wherein is guidance and a light, by which the Prophets who surrendered (unto Allah) judged the Jews and the rabbis and the priests (judged) by such of Allah's Scripture as they were bidden to observe, and thereunto were they witnesses. So fear not mankind, but fear Me. And barter not My revelations for a little gain. Whoso judgeth not by that which Allah hath revealed: such are disbelievers.

45. And We prescribed for them therein: The life for the life, and the eye for the eye, and the nose for the nose, and the ear for the ear, and the tooth for the tooth, and for wounds retaliation. But whoso forgoeth it (in the way of charity) it shall be expiation for him. Whoso judgeth not by that which Allah hath revealed: such are wrong-doers.

46. And We caused Jesus, son of Mary, to follow in their footsteps, confirming that which was (revealed) before him, and We bestowed on him the Gospel wherein is guidance and a light, confirming that which was (revealed) before it in the Torah—a guidance and an admonition unto those who ward off (evil).

سَمّٰعُوْنَ لِلْكَذِبِ اَكّٰلُوْنَ لِلسُّحْتِ فَاِنْ جَآءُوْكَ
فَاحْكُمْ بَيْنَهُمْ اَوْ اَعْرِضْ عَنْهُمْ وَاِنْ تُعْرِضْ عَنْهُمْ
فَلَنْ يَّضُرُّوْكَ شَيْئًا وَاِنْ حَكَمْتَ فَاحْكُمْ بَيْنَهُمْ
بِالْقِسْطِ اِنَّ اللّٰهَ يُحِبُّ الْمُقْسِطِيْنَ ﴿٤٢﴾
وَكَيْفَ يُحَكِّمُوْنَكَ وَعِنْدَهُمُ التَّوْرٰىةُ فِيْهَا حُكْمُ
اللّٰهِ ثُمَّ يَتَوَلَّوْنَ مِنْ بَعْدِ ذٰلِكَ وَمَآ اُولٰٓئِكَ
ع بِالْمُؤْمِنِيْنَ ﴿٤٣﴾
اِنَّآ اَنْزَلْنَا التَّوْرٰىةَ فِيْهَا هُدًى وَّنُوْرٌ يَحْكُمُ بِهَا
النَّبِيُّوْنَ الَّذِيْنَ اَسْلَمُوْا لِلَّذِيْنَ هَادُوْا وَالرَّبّٰنِيُّوْنَ
وَالْاَحْبَارُ بِمَا اسْتُحْفِظُوْا مِنْ كِتٰبِ اللّٰهِ وَكَانُوْا
عَلَيْهِ شُهَدَآءَ فَلَا تَخْشَوُا النَّاسَ وَاخْشَوْنِ
وَلَا تَشْتَرُوْا بِاٰيٰتِيْ ثَمَنًا قَلِيْلًا وَمَنْ لَّمْ يَحْكُمْ بِمَآ
اَنْزَلَ اللّٰهُ فَاُولٰٓئِكَ هُمُ الْكٰفِرُوْنَ ﴿٤٤﴾
وَكَتَبْنَا عَلَيْهِمْ فِيْهَآ اَنَّ النَّفْسَ بِالنَّفْسِ وَالْعَيْنَ
بِالْعَيْنِ وَالْاَنْفَ بِالْاَنْفِ وَالْاُذُنَ بِالْاُذُنِ وَالسِّنَّ
بِالسِّنِّ وَالْجُرُوْحَ قِصَاصٌ فَمَنْ تَصَدَّقَ بِهٖ
فَهُوَ كَفَّارَةٌ لَّهٗ وَمَنْ لَّمْ يَحْكُمْ بِمَآ اَنْزَلَ اللّٰهُ
فَاُولٰٓئِكَ هُمُ الظّٰلِمُوْنَ ﴿٤٥﴾
وَقَفَّيْنَا عَلٰٓى اٰثَارِهِمْ بِعِيْسَى ابْنِ مَرْيَمَ مُصَدِّقًا
لِّمَا بَيْنَ يَدَيْهِ مِنَ التَّوْرٰىةِ وَاٰتَيْنٰهُ الْاِنْجِيْلَ
فِيْهِ هُدًى وَّنُوْرٌ وَّمُصَدِّقًا لِّمَا بَيْنَ يَدَيْهِ مِنَ
التَّوْرٰىةِ وَهُدًى وَّمَوْعِظَةً لِّلْمُتَّقِيْنَ ﴿٤٦﴾

47. Let the People of the Gospel judge by that which Allah hath revealed therein. Whoso judgeth not by that which Allah hath revealed; such are evil-livers.

وَلْيَحْكُمْ أَهْلُ الْإِنْجِيلِ بِمَا أَنْزَلَ اللَّهُ فِيهِ ۚ وَمَنْ لَمْ
يَحْكُمْ بِمَا أَنْزَلَ اللَّهُ فَأُولَٰئِكَ هُمُ الْفَاسِقُونَ ﴿٤٧﴾

48. And unto thee have We revealed the Scripture with the truth, confirming whatever Scripture was before it, and a watcher over it. So judge between them by that which Allah hath revealed, and follow not their desires away from the truth which hath come unto thee. For each We have appointed a divine law and a traced-out way. Had Allah willed He could have made you one community. But that He may try you by that which He hath given you (He hath made you as ye are). So vie one with another in good works. Unto Allah ye will all return, and He will then inform you of that wherein ye differ.

وَأَنْزَلْنَا إِلَيْكَ الْكِتَابَ بِالْحَقِّ مُصَدِّقًا لِمَا بَيْنَ
يَدَيْهِ مِنَ الْكِتَابِ وَمُهَيْمِنًا عَلَيْهِ ۖ فَاحْكُمْ بَيْنَهُمْ بِمَا
أَنْزَلَ اللَّهُ ۖ وَلَا تَتَّبِعْ أَهْوَاءَهُمْ عَمَّا جَاءَكَ مِنَ الْحَقِّ ۚ
لِكُلٍّ جَعَلْنَا مِنْكُمْ شِرْعَةً وَمِنْهَاجًا ۚ وَلَوْ شَاءَ اللَّهُ
لَجَعَلَكُمْ أُمَّةً وَاحِدَةً وَلَٰكِنْ لِيَبْلُوَكُمْ فِي مَا آتَاكُمْ ۖ
فَاسْتَبِقُوا الْخَيْرَاتِ ۚ إِلَى اللَّهِ مَرْجِعُكُمْ جَمِيعًا فَيُنَبِّئُكُمْ
بِمَا كُنْتُمْ فِيهِ تَخْتَلِفُونَ ﴿٤٨﴾

49. So judge between them by that which Allah hath revealed, and follow not their desires, but beware of them lest they seduce thee from some part of that which Allah hath revealed unto thee. And if they turn away, then know that Allah's will is to smite them for some sin of theirs. Lo! many of mankind are evil-livers.

وَأَنِ احْكُمْ بَيْنَهُمْ بِمَا أَنْزَلَ اللَّهُ وَلَا تَتَّبِعْ أَهْوَاءَهُمْ
وَاحْذَرْهُمْ أَنْ يَفْتِنُوكَ عَنْ بَعْضِ مَا أَنْزَلَ اللَّهُ إِلَيْكَ ۖ
فَإِنْ تَوَلَّوْا فَاعْلَمْ أَنَّمَا يُرِيدُ اللَّهُ أَنْ يُصِيبَهُمْ بِبَعْضِ
ذُنُوبِهِمْ ۗ وَإِنَّ كَثِيرًا مِنَ النَّاسِ لَفَاسِقُونَ ﴿٤٩﴾

50. Is it a judgement of the time of (pagan) ignorance that they are seeking? Who is better than Allah for judgement to a people who have certainty (in their belief)?

أَفَحُكْمَ الْجَاهِلِيَّةِ يَبْغُونَ ۚ وَمَنْ أَحْسَنُ مِنَ اللَّهِ
حُكْمًا لِقَوْمٍ يُوقِنُونَ ﴿٥٠﴾

51. O ye who believe! Take not the Jews and Christians for friends. They are friends one to another. He among you who taketh them for friends is (one) of them. Lo! Allah guideth not wrongdoing folk.

يَا أَيُّهَا الَّذِينَ آمَنُوا لَا تَتَّخِذُوا الْيَهُودَ وَالنَّصَارَىٰ
أَوْلِيَاءَ ۘ بَعْضُهُمْ أَوْلِيَاءُ بَعْضٍ ۚ وَمَنْ يَتَوَلَّهُمْ مِنْكُمْ
فَإِنَّهُ مِنْهُمْ ۗ إِنَّ اللَّهَ لَا يَهْدِي الْقَوْمَ الظَّالِمِينَ ﴿٥١﴾

52. And thou seest those in whose heart is a disease race toward them, saying: We fear lest a change of fortune befall us. And it may happen that Allah will vouchsafe (unto thee) the victory, or a commandment from His presence. Then will they repent of their secret thoughts.

فَتَرَى الَّذِينَ فِي قُلُوبِهِمْ مَرَضٌ يُسَارِعُونَ فِيهِمْ
يَقُولُونَ نَخْشَىٰ أَنْ تُصِيبَنَا دَائِرَةٌ ۚ فَعَسَى اللَّهُ أَنْ
يَأْتِيَ بِالْفَتْحِ أَوْ أَمْرٍ مِنْ عِنْدِهِ فَيُصْبِحُوا عَلَىٰ مَا
أَسَرُّوا فِي أَنْفُسِهِمْ نَادِمِينَ ﴿٥٢﴾

53. Then will the believers say (unto the people of the Scripture): Are these they who swore by Allah their most binding oath that they were surely with you? Their works have failed, and they have become the losers.

54. O ye who believe! Whoso of you becometh a renegade from his religion, (know that in his stead) Allah will bring a people whom He loveth and who love Him, humble toward believers, stern toward disbelievers, striving in the way of Allah, and fearing not the blame of any blamer. Such is the grace of Allah which He giveth unto whom He will. Allah is All-Embracing, All-Knowing.

55. Your friend can be only Allah; and His messenger and those who believe, who establish worship and pay the poor-due, and bow down (in prayer).

56. And whoso taketh Allah and His messenger and those who believe for friend (will know that), lo! the party of Allah, they are the victorious.

57. O ye who believe! Choose not for friends such of those who received the Scripture before you, and of the disbelievers, as make a jest and sport of your religion. But keep your duty to Allah if ye are true believers.

58. And when ye call to prayer they take it for a jest and sport. That is because they are a folk who understand not.

59. Say: O People of the Scripture! Do ye blame us for aught else than that we believe in Allah and that which is revealed unto us and that which was revealed aforetime, and because most of you are evil-livers?

60. Shall I tell thee of a worse (case) than theirs for retribution with Allah? Worse (is the case of him) whom Allah hath cursed, him on whom His wrath hath fallen! Worse is he of whose sort Allah hath turned some to apes and swine, and who serveth idols. Such are in worse plight and further astray from the plain road.

وَيَقُولُ الَّذِينَ آمَنُوٓا أَهٰٓؤُلَآءِ الَّذِينَ أَقْسَمُوا بِاللّٰهِ جَهْدَ
أَيْمَانِهِمْ إِنَّهُمْ لَمَعَكُمْ حَبِطَتْ أَعْمَالُهُمْ فَأَصْبَحُوا خٰسِرِينَ ﴿٥٣﴾
يٰٓأَيُّهَا الَّذِينَ آمَنُوا مَنْ يَرْتَدَّ مِنْكُمْ عَنْ دِينِهِ فَسَوْفَ
يَأْتِي اللّٰهُ بِقَوْمٍ يُحِبُّهُمْ وَيُحِبُّونَهُٓ أَذِلَّةٍ عَلَى الْمُؤْمِنِينَ
أَعِزَّةٍ عَلَى الْكٰفِرِينَ يُجَاهِدُونَ فِي سَبِيلِ اللّٰهِ وَ
لَا يَخَافُونَ لَوْمَةَ لَآئِمٍ ذٰلِكَ فَضْلُ اللّٰهِ يُؤْتِيهِ
مَنْ يَشَآءُ وَاللّٰهُ وَاسِعٌ عَلِيمٌ ﴿٥٤﴾
إِنَّمَا وَلِيُّكُمُ اللّٰهُ وَرَسُولُهُ وَالَّذِينَ آمَنُوا الَّذِينَ يُقِيمُونَ
الصَّلٰوةَ وَيُؤْتُونَ الزَّكٰوةَ وَهُمْ رٰكِعُونَ ﴿٥٥﴾
وَمَنْ يَتَوَلَّ اللّٰهَ وَرَسُولَهُ وَالَّذِينَ آمَنُوا فَإِنَّ حِزْبَ
اللّٰهِ هُمُ الْغٰلِبُونَ ﴿٥٦﴾ ع
يٰٓأَيُّهَا الَّذِينَ آمَنُوا لَا تَتَّخِذُوا الَّذِينَ اتَّخَذُوا دِينَكُمْ
هُزُوًا وَلَعِبًا مِنَ الَّذِينَ أُوتُوا الْكِتٰبَ مِنْ قَبْلِكُمْ وَ
الْكُفَّارَ أَوْلِيَآءَ وَاتَّقُوا اللّٰهَ إِنْ كُنْتُمْ مُؤْمِنِينَ ﴿٥٧﴾
وَإِذَا نَادَيْتُمْ إِلَى الصَّلٰوةِ اتَّخَذُوهَا هُزُوًا وَلَعِبًا
ذٰلِكَ بِأَنَّهُمْ قَوْمٌ لَا يَعْقِلُونَ ﴿٥٨﴾
قُلْ يٰٓأَهْلَ الْكِتٰبِ هَلْ تَنْقِمُونَ مِنَّآ إِلَّآ أَنْ آمَنَّا بِاللّٰهِ وَ
مَآ أُنْزِلَ إِلَيْنَا وَمَآ أُنْزِلَ مِنْ قَبْلُ وَأَنَّ أَكْثَرَكُمْ فٰسِقُونَ ﴿٥٩﴾
قُلْ هَلْ أُنَبِّئُكُمْ بِشَرٍّ مِنْ ذٰلِكَ مَثُوبَةً عِنْدَ اللّٰهِ
مَنْ لَعَنَهُ اللّٰهُ وَغَضِبَ عَلَيْهِ وَجَعَلَ مِنْهُمُ الْقِرَدَةَ
وَالْخَنَازِيرَ وَعَبَدَ الطّٰغُوتَ أُولٰٓئِكَ شَرٌّ مَكَانًا
وَأَضَلُّ عَنْ سَوَآءِ السَّبِيلِ ﴿٦٠﴾

61. When they come unto you (Muslims), they say: We believe; but they came in in unbelief and they went out in the same; and Allah knoweth best what they were hiding.

وإذا جاءوكم قالوا آمنا وقد دخلوا بالكفر وهم قد
خرجوا به ۚ والله أعلم بما كانوا يكتمون ٦١

62. And thou seest many of them vying one with another in sin and transgression and their devouring of illicit gain. Verily evil is what they do.

وترى كثيرا منهم يسارعون في الإثم والعدوان
وأكلهم السحت ۚ لبئس ما كانوا يعملون ٦٢

63. Why do not the rabbis and the priests forbid their evil-speaking and their devouring of illicit gain? Verily evil is their handiwork.

لولا ينهاهم الربانيون والأحبار عن قولهم الإثم
وأكلهم السحت ۚ لبئس ما كانوا يصنعون ٦٣

64. The Jews say: Allah's hand is fettered. Their hands are fettered and they are accursed for saying so. Nay, but both His hands are spread out wide in bounty. He bestoweth as He will. That which hath been revealed unto thee from thy Lord is certain to increase the contumacy and disbelief of many of them, and We have cast among them enmity and hatred till the Day of Resurrection. As often as they light a fire for war, Allah existinguisheth it. Their effort is for corruption in the land, and Allah loveth not corrupters.

وقالت اليهود يد الله مغلولة ۚ غلت أيديهم و
لعنوا بما قالوا ۘ بل يداه مبسوطتان ينفق كيف
يشاء ۚ وليزيدن كثيرا منهم ما أنزل إليك من
ربك طغيانا وكفرا ۚ وألقينا بينهم العداوة و
البغضاء إلى يوم القيامة ۚ كلما أوقدوا نارا
للحرب أطفأها الله ۚ ويسعون في الأرض فسادا ۚ
والله لا يحب المفسدين ٦٤

65. If only the People of the Scripture would believe and ward off (evil), surely We should remit their sins from them and surely We should bring them into Gardens of Delight.

ولو أن أهل الكتاب آمنوا واتقوا لكفرنا عنهم
سيئاتهم ولأدخلناهم جنات النعيم ٦٥

66. If they had observed the Torah and the Gospel and that which was revealed unto them from their Lord, they would surely have been nourished from above them and from beneath their feet. Among them there are people who are moderate, but many of them are of evil conduct.

ولو أنهم أقاموا التوراة والإنجيل وما أنزل
إليهم من ربهم لأكلوا من فوقهم ومن تحت
أرجلهم ۚ منهم أمة مقتصدة ۖ وكثير منهم ساء
ما يعملون ٦٦

67. O Messenger! Make known that which hath been revealed unto thee from thy Lord, for if thou do it not, thou wilt not have conveyed His message. Allah will protect thee from mankind. Lo! Allah guideth not the disbelieving folk.

يا أيها الرسول بلغ ما أنزل إليك من ربك ۖ وإن
لم تفعل فما بلغت رسالته ۚ والله يعصمك من
الناس ۗ إن الله لا يهدي القوم الكافرين ٦٧

68. Say: O People of the Scripture! Ye have naught (of guidance) till ye observe the Torah and the Gospel and that which was revealed unto you from your Lord. That which is revealed unto thee (Muhammad) from thy Lord is certain to increase the contumacy and disbelief of many of them. But grieve not for the disbelieving folk.

قُلْ يٰٓاَهْلَ الْكِتٰبِ لَسْتُمْ عَلٰى شَيْءٍ حَتّٰى تُقِيْمُوا التَّوْرٰىةَ
وَالْاِنْجِيْلَ وَمَآ اُنْزِلَ اِلَيْكُمْ مِّنْ رَّبِّكُمْ ؕ وَلَيَزِيْدَنَّ
كَثِيْرًا مِّنْهُمْ مَّآ اُنْزِلَ اِلَيْكَ مِنْ رَّبِّكَ طُغْيَانًا وَّكُفْرًا ۚ
فَلَا تَاْسَ عَلَى الْقَوْمِ الْكٰفِرِيْنَ ﴿٦٨﴾

69. Lo! those who believe, and those who are Jews, and Sabaeans, and Christians—whosoever believeth in Allah and the Last Day and doth right—there shall no fear come upon them neither shall they grieve.[1]

اِنَّ الَّذِيْنَ اٰمَنُوْا وَالَّذِيْنَ هَادُوْا وَالصّٰبِـُٔوْنَ وَالنَّصٰرٰى
مَنْ اٰمَنَ بِاللّٰهِ وَالْيَوْمِ الْاٰخِرِ وَعَمِلَ صَالِحًا فَلَا
خَوْفٌ عَلَيْهِمْ وَلَا هُمْ يَحْزَنُوْنَ ﴿٦٩﴾

70. We made a covenant of old with the Children of Israel and We sent unto them messengers. As often as a messenger came unto them with that which their souls desired not (they became rebellious). Some (of them) they denied and some they slew.

لَقَدْ اَخَذْنَا مِيْثَاقَ بَنِيْٓ اِسْرَآءِيْلَ وَاَرْسَلْنَآ اِلَيْهِمْ
رُسُلًا ؕ كُلَّمَا جَآءَهُمْ رَسُوْلٌۢ بِمَا لَا تَهْوٰٓى اَنْفُسُهُمْ ۙ
فَرِيْقًا كَذَّبُوْا وَفَرِيْقًا يَّقْتُلُوْنَ ﴿٧٠﴾

71. They thought no harm would come of it, so they were wilfully blind and deaf. And afterward Allah turned (in mercy) toward them. Now (even after that) are many of them wilfully blind and deaf. Allah is Seer of what they do.

وَحَسِبُوْٓا اَلَّا تَكُوْنَ فِتْنَةٌ فَعَمُوْا وَصَمُّوْا ثُمَّ تَابَ اللّٰهُ
عَلَيْهِمْ ثُمَّ عَمُوْا وَصَمُّوْا كَثِيْرٌ مِّنْهُمْ ؕ وَاللّٰهُ بَصِيْرٌۢ
بِمَا يَعْمَلُوْنَ ﴿٧١﴾

72. They surely disbelieve who say: Lo! Allah is the Messiah, son of Mary. The Messiah (himself) said: O Children of Israel, worship Allah, my Lord and your Lord. Lo! whoso ascribeth partners unto Allah, for him Allah hath forbidden Paradise. His abode is the Fire. For evil-doers there will be no helpers.

لَقَدْ كَفَرَ الَّذِيْنَ قَالُوْٓا اِنَّ اللّٰهَ هُوَ الْمَسِيْحُ ابْنُ مَرْيَمَ ؕ
وَقَالَ الْمَسِيْحُ يٰبَنِيْٓ اِسْرَآءِيْلَ اعْبُدُوا اللّٰهَ رَبِّيْ وَ
رَبَّكُمْ ؕ اِنَّهٗ مَنْ يُّشْرِكْ بِاللّٰهِ فَقَدْ حَرَّمَ اللّٰهُ عَلَيْهِ الْجَنَّةَ
وَمَاْوٰىهُ النَّارُ ؕ وَمَا لِلظّٰلِمِيْنَ مِنْ اَنْصَارٍ ﴿٧٢﴾

73. They surely disbelieve who say: Lo! Allah is the third of three; when there is no God save the One God. If they desist not from so saying a painful doom will fall on those of them who disbelieve.

لَقَدْ كَفَرَ الَّذِيْنَ قَالُوْٓا اِنَّ اللّٰهَ ثَالِثُ ثَلٰثَةٍ ۘ وَمَا مِنْ وقف لازم
اِلٰهٍ اِلَّآ اِلٰهٌ وَّاحِدٌ ؕ وَاِنْ لَّمْ يَنْتَهُوْا عَمَّا يَقُوْلُوْنَ
لَيَمَسَّنَّ الَّذِيْنَ كَفَرُوْا مِنْهُمْ عَذَابٌ اَلِيْمٌ ﴿٧٣﴾

74. Will they not rather turn unto Allah and seek forgiveness of Him? For Allah is Forgiving, Merciful.

اَفَلَا يَتُوْبُوْنَ اِلَى اللّٰهِ وَيَسْتَغْفِرُوْنَهٗ ؕ وَاللّٰهُ غَفُوْرٌ
رَّحِيْمٌ ﴿٧٤﴾

1. Almost identical with Sûr. II, v. 62.

75. The Messiah, son of Mary, was no other than a messenger, messengers (the like of whom) had passed away before him. And his mother was a saintly woman. And they both used to eat (earthly) food. See how we make the revelations clear for them, and see how they are turned away!

ما المسيح ابن مريم إلا رسول قد خلت من
قبله الرسل وأمه صديقة كانا يأكلان الطعام
انظر كيف نبين لهم الآيات ثم انظر أنى يؤفكون ﴿٧٥﴾

76. Say: Serve ye in place of Allah that which possesseth for you neither hurt nor use? Allah it is Who is the Hearer, the Knower.

قل أتعبدون من دون الله ما لا يملك لكم ضرا
ولا نفعا والله هو السميع العليم ﴿٧٦﴾

77. Say: O People of the Scripture! Stress not in your religion other than the truth, and follow not the vain desires of folk who erred of old and led many astray, and erred from a plain road.

قل يا أهل الكتاب لا تغلوا في دينكم غير الحق ولا
تتبعوا أهواء قوم قد ضلوا من قبل وأضلوا كثيرا
وضلوا عن سواء السبيل ﴿٧٧﴾ ع ١٤

78. Those of the children of Israel who went astray were cursed by the tongue of David, and of Jesus, son of Mary. That was because they rebelled and used to transgress.

لعن الذين كفروا من بني إسرائيل على لسان
داود وعيسى ابن مريم ذلك بما عصوا وكانوا
يعتدون ﴿٧٨﴾

79. They restrained not one another from the wickedness they did. Verily evil was that they used to do!

كانوا لا يتناهون عن منكر فعلوه لبئس ما كانوا
يفعلون ﴿٧٩﴾

80. Thou seest many of them making friends with those who disbelieve. Surely ill for them is that which they themselves send on before them: that Allah will be wroth with them and in the doom they will abide.

ترى كثيرا منهم يتولون الذين كفروا لبئس ما
قدمت لهم أنفسهم أن سخط الله عليهم و
في العذاب هم خالدون ﴿٨٠﴾

81. If they believed in Allah and the Prophet and that which is revealed unto him, they would not choose them for their friends. But many of them are of evil conduct.

ولو كانوا يؤمنون بالله والنبي وما أنزل إليه ما
اتخذوهم أولياء ولكن كثيرا منهم فاسقون ﴿٨١﴾

82. Thou wilt find the most vehement of mankind in hostility to those who believe (to be) the Jews, and the idolaters. And thou wilt find the nearest of them in affection to those who believe (to be) those who say: Lo! We are Christians. That is because there are among them priests and monks,[1] and because they are not proud.

لتجدن أشد الناس عداوة للذين آمنوا اليهود
والذين أشركوا ولتجدن أقربهم مودة للذين
آمنوا الذين قالوا إنا نصارى ذلك بأن منهم
قسيسين ورهبانا وأنهم لا يستكبرون ﴿٨٢﴾

1. *i.e.* persons entirely devoted to the service of God, as were the Muslims.

83. When they listen to that which hath been revealed unto the messenger, thou seest their eyes overflow with tears because of their recognition of the Truth. They say: Our Lord, we believe. Inscribe us as among the witnesses.

84. How should we not believe in Allah and that which hath come unto us of the Truth. And (how should we not) hope that our Lord will bring us in along with righteous folk?

85. Allah hath rewarded them for that their saying—Gardens underneath which rivers flow, wherein they will abide for ever. That is the reward of the good.

86. But those who disbelieve and deny Our revelations, they are owners of hell-fire.

87. O ye who believe! Fobid not the good things which Allah hath made lawful for you, and transgress not. Lo! Allah loveth not transgressors.

88. Eat of that which Allah hath bestowed on you as food lawful and good, and keep your duty to Allah in Whom ye are believers.

89. Allah will not take you to task for that which is unintentional in your oaths, but He will take you to task for the oaths which ye swear in earnest. The expiation thereof is the feeding of ten of the needy with the average of that wherewith ye feed your own folk, or the clothing of them, or the liberation of a slave, and for him who findeth not (the wherewithal to do so) then a three days' fast. This is the expiation of your oaths when ye have sworn; and keep your oaths. Thus Allah expoundeth unto you His revelations in order that ye may give thanks.

90. O ye who believe! Strong drink and games of chance and idols and divining arrows are only an infamy of Satan's handiwork. Leave it aside in order that ye may succeed.

وإذا سمعوا ما أنزل إلى الرسول ترى أعينهم
تفيض من الدمع مما عرفوا من الحق يقولون
ربنا آمنا فاكتبنا مع الشاهدين ﴿٨٣﴾
وما لنا لا نؤمن بالله وما جاءنا من الحق و
نطمع أن يدخلنا ربنا مع القوم الصالحين ﴿٨٤﴾
فأثابهم الله بما قالوا جنات تجري من تحتها
الأنهار خالدين فيها وذلك جزاء المحسنين ﴿٨٥﴾
والذين كفروا وكذبوا بآياتنا أولئك أصحاب
الجحيم ﴿٨٦﴾
يا أيها الذين آمنوا لا تحرموا طيبات ما أحل الله لكم
ولا تعتدوا إن الله لا يحب المعتدين ﴿٨٧﴾
وكلوا مما رزقكم الله حلالا طيبا واتقوا الله الذي
أنتم به مؤمنون ﴿٨٨﴾
لا يؤاخذكم الله باللغو في أيمانكم ولكن يؤاخذكم
بما عقدتم الأيمان فكفارته إطعام عشرة مساكين
من أوسط ما تطعمون أهليكم أو كسوتهم أو تحرير
رقبة فمن لم يجد فصيام ثلاثة أيام ذلك كفارة
أيمانكم إذا حلفتم واحفظوا أيمانكم كذلك يبين
الله لكم آياته لعلكم تشكرون ﴿٨٩﴾
يا أيها الذين آمنوا إنما الخمر والميسر والأنصاب
والأزلام رجس من عمل الشيطان فاجتنبوه
لعلكم تفلحون ﴿٩٠﴾

91. Satan seeketh only to cast among you enmity and hatred by means of strong drink and games of chance, and to turn you from remembrance of Allah and from (His) worship. Will ye then have done?

92. Obey Allah and obey the messenger, and beware! But if ye turn away, then know that the duty of Our messenger is only plain conveyance (of the message).

93. There shall be no sin (imputed) unto those who believe and do good works for what they may have eaten (in the past). So be mindful of your duty (to Allah), and do good works; and again: be mindful of your duty, and believe; and once again: be mindful of your duty, and do right. Allah loveth the good.

94. O ye who believe! Allah will surely try you somewhat (in the matter) of the game which ye take with your hands and your spears, that Allah may know him who feareth Him in secret. Whoso transgresseth after this, for him there is a painful doom.

95. O ye who believe! Kill no wild game while ye are on the pilgrimage. Whoso of you killeth it of set purpose he shall pay its forfeit in the equivalent of that which he hath killed, of domestic animals, the judge to be two men among you known for justice, (the forfeit) to be brought as an offering to the Ka'bah; or, for expiation, he shall feed poor persons, or the equivalent thereof in fasting, that he may taste the evil consequences of his deed. Allah forgiveth whatever (of this kind) may have happened in the past, but whoso relapseth, Allah will take retribution from him. Allah is Mighty, Able to Requite (the wrong).

96. To hunt and to eat the fish of the sea is made lawful for you, a provision for you and for seafarers; but to hunt on land is forbidden you so long as ye are on the pilgrimage. Be mindful of your duty to Allah, unto Whom ye will be gathered.

إِنَّمَا يُرِيدُ الشَّيْطٰنُ أَنْ يُّوْقِعَ بَيْنَكُمُ الْعَدَاوَةَ
وَالْبَغْضَآءَ فِي الْخَمْرِ وَالْمَيْسِرِ وَيَصُدَّكُمْ عَنْ
ذِكْرِ اللهِ وَعَنِ الصَّلٰوةِ فَهَلْ أَنْتُمْ مُّنْتَهُوْنَ ﴿٩١﴾
وَأَطِيْعُوا اللهَ وَأَطِيْعُوا الرَّسُوْلَ وَاحْذَرُوْا فَإِنْ
تَوَلَّيْتُمْ فَاعْلَمُوْٓا أَنَّمَا عَلٰى رَسُوْلِنَا الْبَلٰغُ الْمُبِيْنُ ﴿٩٢﴾
لَيْسَ عَلَى الَّذِيْنَ اٰمَنُوْا وَعَمِلُوا الصّٰلِحٰتِ جُنَاحٌ
فِيْمَا طَعِمُوْٓا إِذَا مَا اتَّقَوْا وَّاٰمَنُوْا وَعَمِلُوا الصّٰلِحٰتِ
ثُمَّ اتَّقَوْا وَّاٰمَنُوْا ثُمَّ اتَّقَوْا وَّأَحْسَنُوْا وَاللهُ يُحِبُّ
الْمُحْسِنِيْنَ ﴿٩٣﴾ ع ١٢ ٢
يٰٓأَيُّهَا الَّذِيْنَ اٰمَنُوْا لَيَبْلُوَنَّكُمُ اللهُ بِشَيْءٍ مِّنَ الصَّيْدِ
تَنَالُهٗٓ أَيْدِيْكُمْ وَرِمَاحُكُمْ لِيَعْلَمَ اللهُ مَنْ
يَّخَافُهٗ بِالْغَيْبِ فَمَنِ اعْتَدٰى بَعْدَ ذٰلِكَ
فَلَهٗ عَذَابٌ أَلِيْمٌ ﴿٩٤﴾
يٰٓأَيُّهَا الَّذِيْنَ اٰمَنُوْا لَا تَقْتُلُوا الصَّيْدَ وَأَنْتُمْ حُرُمٌ
وَمَنْ قَتَلَهٗ مِنْكُمْ مُّتَعَمِّدًا فَجَزَآءٌ مِّثْلُ مَا قَتَلَ مِنَ
النَّعَمِ يَحْكُمُ بِهٖ ذَوَا عَدْلٍ مِّنْكُمْ هَدْيًا بٰلِغَ الْكَعْبَةِ
أَوْ كَفَّارَةٌ طَعَامُ مَسٰكِيْنَ أَوْ عَدْلُ ذٰلِكَ صِيَامًا
لِّيَذُوْقَ وَبَالَ أَمْرِهٖ عَفَا اللهُ عَمَّا سَلَفَ وَمَنْ
عَادَ فَيَنْتَقِمُ اللهُ مِنْهُ وَاللهُ عَزِيْزٌ ذُو انْتِقَامٍ ﴿٩٥﴾
أُحِلَّ لَكُمْ صَيْدُ الْبَحْرِ وَطَعَامُهٗ مَتَاعًا لَّكُمْ وَ
لِلسَّيَّارَةِ وَحُرِّمَ عَلَيْكُمْ صَيْدُ الْبَرِّ مَا دُمْتُمْ حُرُمًا
وَاتَّقُوا اللهَ الَّذِيْٓ إِلَيْهِ تُحْشَرُوْنَ ﴿٩٦﴾

97. Allah hath appointed the Ka'bah, the Sacred House, a standard for mankind, and the Sacred Month and the offerings and the garlands. That is so that ye may know that Allah knoweth whatsoever is in the heavens and whatsoever is in the earth, and that Allah is Knower of all things.

جَعَلَ اللّٰهُ الْكَعْبَةَ الْبَيْتَ الْحَرَامَ قِيٰمًا لِّلنَّاسِ
وَالشَّهْرَ الْحَرَامَ وَالْهَدْيَ وَالْقَلَآئِدَ ؕ ذٰلِكَ لِتَعْلَمُوْٓا
اَنَّ اللّٰهَ يَعْلَمُ مَا فِي السَّمٰوٰتِ وَمَا فِي الْاَرْضِ وَ
اَنَّ اللّٰهَ بِكُلِّ شَيْءٍ عَلِيْمٌ ۝٩٧

98. Know that Allah is severe in punishment, but that Allah (also) is Forgiving, Merciful.

اِعْلَمُوْٓا اَنَّ اللّٰهَ شَدِيْدُ الْعِقَابِ وَاَنَّ اللّٰهَ غَفُوْرٌ
رَّحِيْمٌ ۝٩٨

99. The duty of the messenger is only to convey (the message). Allah knoweth what ye proclaim and what ye hide.

مَا عَلَى الرَّسُوْلِ اِلَّا الْبَلٰغُ ؕ وَاللّٰهُ يَعْلَمُ مَا تُبْدُوْنَ
وَمَا تَكْتُمُوْنَ ۝٩٩

100. Say: The evil and the good are not alike even though the plenty of the evil attract thee. So be mindful of your duty to Allah, O men of understanding, that ye may succeed.

قُلْ لَّا يَسْتَوِي الْخَبِيْثُ وَالطَّيِّبُ وَلَوْ اَعْجَبَكَ
كَثْرَةُ الْخَبِيْثِ ۚ فَاتَّقُوا اللّٰهَ يٰٓاُولِي الْاَلْبَابِ لَعَلَّكُمْ
تُفْلِحُوْنَ ۝١٠٠ ع ١٣

101. O ye who believe! Ask not of things which, if they were made known unto you, would trouble you; but if ye ask of them when the Qur'ān is being revealed, they will be made known unto you. Allah pardoneth this, for Allah is Forgiving, Clement.

يٰٓاَيُّهَا الَّذِيْنَ اٰمَنُوْا لَا تَسْـَٔلُوْا عَنْ اَشْيَآءَ اِنْ تُبْدَ
لَكُمْ تَسُؤْكُمْ ۚ وَاِنْ تَسْـَٔلُوْا عَنْهَا حِيْنَ يُنَزَّلُ الْقُرْاٰنُ
تُبْدَ لَكُمْ ؕ عَفَا اللّٰهُ عَنْهَا ؕ وَاللّٰهُ غَفُوْرٌ حَلِيْمٌ ۝١٠١

102. A folk before you asked (for such disclosures) and then disbelieved therein.

قَدْ سَاَلَهَا قَوْمٌ مِّنْ قَبْلِكُمْ ثُمَّ اَصْبَحُوْا بِهَا
كٰفِرِيْنَ ۝١٠٢

103. Allah hath not appointed anything in the nature of a *Bāḥirah* or a *Sā'ibah* or a *Waṣilah* or a *Hami*,[1] but those who disbelieve invent a lie against Allah. Most of them have no sense.

مَا جَعَلَ اللّٰهُ مِنْ بَحِيْرَةٍ وَّلَا سَآئِبَةٍ وَّلَا وَصِيْلَةٍ
وَّلَا حَامٍ ۙ وَّلٰكِنَّ الَّذِيْنَ كَفَرُوْا يَفْتَرُوْنَ عَلَى اللّٰهِ
الْكَذِبَ ؕ وَاَكْثَرُهُمْ لَا يَعْقِلُوْنَ ۝١٠٣

104. And when it is said unto them: Come unto that which Allah hath revealed and unto the messenger, they say: Enough for us is that wherein we found our fathers. What! even though their fathers had no knowledge whatsoever, and no guidance?

وَاِذَا قِيْلَ لَهُمْ تَعَالَوْا اِلٰى مَآ اَنْزَلَ اللّٰهُ وَاِلَى
الرَّسُوْلِ قَالُوْا حَسْبُنَا مَا وَجَدْنَا عَلَيْهِ اٰبَآءَنَا ؕ اَوَلَوْ
كَانَ اٰبَآؤُهُمْ لَا يَعْلَمُوْنَ شَيْـًٔا وَّلَا يَهْتَدُوْنَ ۝١٠٤

1. Different classes of cattle liberated in honour of idols and reverenced by the pagan Arabs.

105. O ye who believe! Ye have charge of your own souls. He who erreth cannot injure you if ye are rightly guided. Unto Allah ye will all return; and then He will inform you of what ye used to do.

يٰۤاَيُّهَا الَّذِيْنَ اٰمَنُوْا عَلَيْكُمْ اَنْفُسَكُمْ ۚ لَا يَضُرُّكُمْ مَّنْ
ضَلَّ اِذَا اهْتَدَيْتُمْ ؕ اِلَى اللّٰهِ مَرْجِعُكُمْ جَمِيْعًا
فَيُنَبِّئُكُمْ بِمَا كُنْتُمْ تَعْمَلُوْنَ ۝١٠٥

106. O ye who believe! Let there be witnesses between you when death draweth nigh unto one of you, at the time of bequest—two witnesses, just men from among you, or two others from another tribe, in case ye are campaigning in the land and the calamity of death befall you. Ye shall empanel them both after the prayer, and, if ye doubt, they shall be made to swear by Allah (saying): We will not take a bribe, even though it were (on behalf of) a near kinsman nor will we hide the testimony of Allah, for then indeed we should be of the sinful.

يٰۤاَيُّهَا الَّذِيْنَ اٰمَنُوْا شَهَادَةُ بَيْنِكُمْ اِذَا حَضَرَ
اَحَدَكُمُ الْمَوْتُ حِيْنَ الْوَصِيَّةِ اثْنٰنِ ذَوَا
عَدْلٍ مِّنْكُمْ اَوْ اٰخَرٰنِ مِنْ غَيْرِكُمْ اِنْ اَنْتُمْ
ضَرَبْتُمْ فِى الْاَرْضِ فَاَصَابَتْكُمْ مُّصِيْبَةُ الْمَوْتِ ؕ
تَحْبِسُوْنَهُمَا مِنْۢ بَعْدِ الصَّلٰوةِ فَيُقْسِمٰنِ بِاللّٰهِ
اِنِ ارْتَبْتُمْ لَا نَشْتَرِىْ بِهٖ ثَمَنًا وَّلَوْ كَانَ ذَا
قُرْبٰى ۙ وَلَا نَكْتُمُ شَهَادَةَ اللّٰهِ اِنَّاۤ اِذًا لَّمِنَ
الْاٰثِمِيْنَ ۝١٠٦

107. But then, if it is afterwards ascertained that both of them merit (the suspicion of) sin, let two others take their place of those nearly concerned, and let them swear by Allah, (saying): Verily our testimony is truer than their testimony and we have not transgressed (the bounds of duty), for then indeed we should be of the evil-doers.

فَاِنْ عُثِرَ عَلٰۤى اَنَّهُمَا اسْتَحَقَّاۤ اِثْمًا فَاٰخَرٰنِ
يَقُوْمٰنِ مَقَامَهُمَا مِنَ الَّذِيْنَ اسْتَحَقَّ عَلَيْهِمُ
الْاَوْلَيٰنِ فَيُقْسِمٰنِ بِاللّٰهِ لَشَهَادَتُنَاۤ اَحَقُّ
مِنْ شَهَادَتِهِمَا وَمَا اعْتَدَيْنَاۤ ۖ اِنَّاۤ اِذًا لَّمِنَ
الظّٰلِمِيْنَ ۝١٠٧

108. Thus it is more likely that they will bear true witness or fear that after their oath the oath (of others) will be taken. So be mindful of your duty (to Allah) and hearken. Allah guideth not the froward folk.

ذٰلِكَ اَدْنٰۤى اَنْ يَّاْتُوْا بِالشَّهَادَةِ عَلٰى وَجْهِهَاۤ
اَوْ يَخَافُوْۤا اَنْ تُرَدَّ اَيْمَانٌۢ بَعْدَ اَيْمَانِهِمْ ؕ وَاتَّقُوا
اللّٰهَ وَاسْمَعُوْا ؕ وَاللّٰهُ لَا يَهْدِى الْقَوْمَ
الْفٰسِقِيْنَ ۝١٠٨ ع

109. In the day when Allah gathereth together the messengers, and saith: What was your response (from mankind)? they say: We have no knowledge. Lo! Thou, only Thou art the Knower of Things Hidden.

يَوْمَ يَجْمَعُ اللّٰهُ الرُّسُلَ فَيَقُوْلُ مَاذَاۤ اُجِبْتُمْ ؕ
قَالُوْا لَا عِلْمَ لَنَا ؕ اِنَّكَ اَنْتَ عَلَّامُ الْغُيُوْبِ ۝١٠٩

110. When Allah saith: O Jesus, son of Mary! Remember My favour unto thee and unto thy mother; how I strengthened thee with the holy Spirit, so that thou spakest unto mankind in the cradle as in maturity; and how I taught thee the Scripture and Wisdom and the Torah and the Gospel; and how thou didst shape of clay as it were the likeness of a bird by My permission, and didst blow upon it and it was a bird by My permission, and thou didst heal him who was born blind and the leper by My permission; and how thou didst raise the dead, by My permission; and how I restrained the Children of Israel from (harming) thee when thou camest unto them with clear proofs, and those of them who disbelieved exclaimed: This is naught else than mere magic;

111. And when I inspired the disciples, (saying): Believe in Me and in My messenger, they said: We believe. Bear witness that we have surrendered[1] (unto Thee).

112. When the disciples said: O Jesus, son of Mary! Is thy Lord able to send down for us a table spread with food from heaven? He said: Observe your duty to Allah, if ye are true believers.

113. (They said): We wish to eat thereof, that we may satisfy our hearts and know that thou hast spoken truth to us, and that thereof we may be witnesses.

114. Jesus, son of Mary, said: O Allah, Lord of us! Send down for us a table spread with food from heaven, that it may be a feast for us, for the first of us and for the last of us, and a sign from Thee. Give us sustenance, for Thou art the Best of Sustainers.

115. Allah said: Lo! I send it down for you. And whoso disbelieveth of you afterward, him surely will I punish with a punishment wherewith I have not punished any of (My) creatures.

1. Or "are Muslims."

إِذْ قَالَ اللّٰهُ يَا عِيْسَى ابْنَ مَرْيَمَ اذْكُرْ نِعْمَتِيْ عَلَيْكَ وَعَلٰى وَالِدَتِكَ إِذْ اَيَّدْتُّكَ بِرُوْحِ الْقُدُسِ تُكَلِّمُ النَّاسَ فِي الْمَهْدِ وَكَهْلًا وَإِذْ عَلَّمْتُكَ الْكِتٰبَ وَالْحِكْمَةَ وَالتَّوْرٰةَ وَالْإِنْجِيْلَ وَإِذْ تَخْلُقُ مِنَ الطِّيْنِ كَهَيْئَةِ الطَّيْرِ بِإِذْنِيْ فَتَنْفُخُ فِيْهَا فَتَكُوْنُ طَيْرًا بِإِذْنِيْ وَتُبْرِئُ الْأَكْمَهَ وَالْأَبْرَصَ بِإِذْنِيْ وَإِذْ تُخْرِجُ الْمَوْتٰى بِإِذْنِيْ وَإِذْ كَفَفْتُ بَنِيْ إِسْرَآءِيْلَ عَنْكَ إِذْ جِئْتَهُمْ بِالْبَيِّنٰتِ فَقَالَ الَّذِيْنَ كَفَرُوْا مِنْهُمْ إِنْ هٰذَآ إِلَّا سِحْرٌ مُّبِيْنٌ ۝

وَإِذْ اَوْحَيْتُ إِلَى الْحَوَارِيّنَ اَنْ اٰمِنُوْا بِيْ وَبِرَسُوْلِيْ قَالُوْا اٰمَنَّا وَاشْهَدْ بِاَنَّنَا مُسْلِمُوْنَ ۝

إِذْ قَالَ الْحَوَارِيُّوْنَ يَا عِيْسَى ابْنَ مَرْيَمَ هَلْ يَسْتَطِيْعُ رَبُّكَ اَنْ يُّنَزِّلَ عَلَيْنَا مَآئِدَةً مِّنَ السَّمَآءِ قَالَ اتَّقُوا اللّٰهَ اِنْ كُنْتُمْ مُّؤْمِنِيْنَ ۝

قَالُوْا نُرِيْدُ اَنْ نَّأْكُلَ مِنْهَا وَتَطْمَئِنَّ قُلُوْبُنَا وَنَعْلَمَ اَنْ قَدْ صَدَقْتَنَا وَنَكُوْنَ عَلَيْهَا مِنَ الشّٰهِدِيْنَ ۝

قَالَ عِيْسَى ابْنُ مَرْيَمَ اللّٰهُمَّ رَبَّنَآ اَنْزِلْ عَلَيْنَا مَآئِدَةً مِّنَ السَّمَآءِ تَكُوْنُ لَنَا عِيْدًا لِّأَوَّلِنَا وَاٰخِرِنَا وَاٰيَةً مِّنْكَ وَارْزُقْنَا وَاَنْتَ خَيْرُ الرّٰزِقِيْنَ ۝

قَالَ اللّٰهُ اِنِّيْ مُنَزِّلُهَا عَلَيْكُمْ فَمَنْ يَّكْفُرْ بَعْدُ مِنْكُمْ فَاِنِّيْ اُعَذِّبُهُ عَذَابًا لَّآ اُعَذِّبُهُ اَحَدًا مِّنَ الْعٰلَمِيْنَ ۝

116. And when Allah saith: O Jesus, son of Mary! Didst thou say unto mankind: Take me and my mother for two gods beside Allah? he saith: Be glorified! It was not mine to utter that to which I had no right. If I used to say it, then Thou knewest it. Thou knowest what is in my mind, and I know not what is in Thy mind. Lo! Thou, only Thou art the Knower of Things Hidden.

117. I spake unto them only that which Thou commandedst me, (saying): Worship Allah, my Lord and your Lord. I was a witness of them while I dwelt among them, and when Thou tookest me Thou wast the Watcher over them. Thou art Witness over all things.

118. If Thou punish them, lo! they are Thy slaves, and if Thou forgive them (lo! they are Thy slaves). Lo! Thou, only Thou art the Mighty, the Wise.

119. Allah saith: This is a day in which their truthfulness profiteth the truthful, for theirs are Gardens underneath which rivers flow, wherein they are secure for ever, Allah taking pleasure in them and they in Him. That is the great triumph.

120. Unto Allah belongeth the Sovereignty of the heavens and the earth and whatsoever is therein, and He is Able to do all things.

وَإِذْ قَالَ اللَّهُ يَٰعِيسَى ابْنَ مَرْيَمَ ءَأَنتَ قُلْتَ
لِلنَّاسِ اتَّخِذُونِي وَأُمِّيَ إِلَٰهَيْنِ مِن دُونِ اللَّهِ ۖ قَالَ
سُبْحَٰنَكَ مَا يَكُونُ لِي أَنْ أَقُولَ مَا لَيْسَ لِي بِحَقٍّ ۚ إِن
كُنتُ قُلْتُهُ فَقَدْ عَلِمْتَهُ ۚ تَعْلَمُ مَا فِي نَفْسِي وَلَا
أَعْلَمُ مَا فِي نَفْسِكَ ۚ إِنَّكَ أَنتَ عَلَّٰمُ الْغُيُوبِ ﴿١١٦﴾
مَا قُلْتُ لَهُمْ إِلَّا مَا أَمَرْتَنِي بِهِ أَنِ اعْبُدُوا اللَّهَ
رَبِّي وَرَبَّكُمْ ۚ وَكُنتُ عَلَيْهِمْ شَهِيدًا مَّا دُمْتُ
فِيهِمْ ۖ فَلَمَّا تَوَفَّيْتَنِي كُنتَ أَنتَ الرَّقِيبَ عَلَيْهِمْ ۚ
وَأَنتَ عَلَىٰ كُلِّ شَيْءٍ شَهِيدٌ ﴿١١٧﴾
إِن تُعَذِّبْهُمْ فَإِنَّهُمْ عِبَادُكَ ۖ وَإِن تَغْفِرْ لَهُمْ
فَإِنَّكَ أَنتَ الْعَزِيزُ الْحَكِيمُ ﴿١١٨﴾
قَالَ اللَّهُ هَٰذَا يَوْمُ يَنفَعُ الصَّٰدِقِينَ صِدْقُهُمْ ۚ
لَهُمْ جَنَّٰتٌ تَجْرِي مِن تَحْتِهَا الْأَنْهَٰرُ خَٰلِدِينَ
فِيهَا أَبَدًا ۚ رَّضِيَ اللَّهُ عَنْهُمْ وَرَضُوا عَنْهُ ۚ ذَٰلِكَ
الْفَوْزُ الْعَظِيمُ ﴿١١٩﴾
لِلَّهِ مُلْكُ السَّمَٰوَٰتِ وَالْأَرْضِ وَمَا فِيهِنَّ ۚ وَ
هُوَ عَلَىٰ كُلِّ شَيْءٍ قَدِيرٌ ﴿١٢٠﴾ ع

وقف النبي صلى الله عليه وسلم

Al-An'ām "Cattle," takes its name from a word in v. 137, repeated in vv. 139, 140, where cattle are mentioned in connection with superstitious practices condemned by Al-Islām.

With the possible exception of nine verses, which some authorities—*e.g.* Ibn Salāmah—ascribe to the Madînah period, the whole of this Sūrah belongs to the year before the Hijrah. It is related, on the authority of Ibn 'Abbās, that it was revealed in a single visitation. It is placed here on account of the subject, vindication of the Divine Unity, which fitly follows, on the subjects of the previous Sūrahs. The note of certain triumph is remarkable in the circumstances of its revelation, when the Prophet, after thirteen years of effort, saw himself obliged to flee from Mecca and seek help from strangers.

A late Meccan Sūrah.

CATTLE

Revealed at Mecca

In the name of Allah, the Beneficent, the Merciful.

1. Praise be to Allah, Who hath created the heavens and the earth, and hath appointed darkness and light. Yet those who disbelieve ascribe rivals unto their Lord.

2. He it is Who hath created you from clay, and hath decreed a term for you. A term is fixed with Him. Yet still ye doubt!

3. He is Allah in the heavens and in the earth. He knoweth both your secret and your utterance, and He knoweth what ye earn.

4. Never came there unto them a revelation of the revelations of Allah but they did turn away from it.

5. And they denied the truth when it came unto them. But there will come unto them the tidings of that which they used to deride.

6. See they not how many a generation We destroyed before them, whom We had established in the earth more firmly than We have established you, and We shed on them abundant showers from the sky, and made the rivers flow beneath them. Yet We destroyed them for their sins, and created after them another generation.

7. Had we sent down unto thee (Muhammad) (actual) writing upon parchment, so that they could feel it with their hands, those who disbelieve would have said: This is naught else than mere magic.

8. They say: Why hath not an angel been sent down unto him? If We sent down an angel, then the matter would be judged; no further time would be allowed them (for reflection).

آياتها ١٦٥ (٦) سورة الانعام مكية ركوعاتها ٢٠

بسم الله الرحمن الرحيم

الحمد لله الذي خلق السموت والارض
وجعل الظلمت والنور ثم الذين كفروا
بربهم يعدلون (١)
هو الذي خلقكم من طين ثم قضى اجلا و
اجل مسمى عنده ثم انتم تمترون (٢)
وهو الله في السموت وفي الارض يعلم سركم
وجهركم ويعلم ما تكسبون (٣)
وما تأتيهم من اية من ايت ربهم الا كانوا
عنها معرضين (٤)
فقد كذبوا بالحق لما جاءهم فسوف يأتيهم
انبؤا ما كانوا به يستهزءون (٥)
الم يروا كم اهلكنا من قبلهم من قرن مكنهم
في الارض ما لم نمكن لكم وارسلنا السماء عليهم
مدرارا وجعلنا الانهر تجري من تحتهم فاهلكنهم
بذنوبهم وانشأنا من بعدهم قرنا اخرين (٦)
ولو نزلنا عليك كتبا في قرطاس فلمسوه بايديهم
لقال الذين كفروا ان هذا الا سحر مبين (٧)
وقالوا لولا انزل عليه ملك ولو انزلنا ملكا
لقضي الامر ثم لا ينظرون (٨)

9. Had We appointed an angel (Our messenger), We assuredly had made him (as) a man (that he might speak to men); and (thus) obscured for them (the truth) they (now) obscure.

10. Messengers (of Allah) have been derided before thee, but that whereat they scoffed surrounded such of them as did deride.

11. Say (unto the disbelievers): Travel in the land, and see the nature of the consequence for the rejecters!

12. Say: Unto whom belongeth whatsoever is in the heavens and the earth? Say: Unto Allah. He hath prescribed for Himself mercy, that He may bring you all together to a Day whereof there is no doubt. Those who ruin their own souls will not believe.

13. Unto Him belongeth whatsoever resteth in the night and the day. He is Hearer, the Knower.

14. Say: Shall I choose for a protecting friend other than Allah, the Originator of the heavens and the earth who feedeth and is never fed? Say: I am ordered to be the first to surrender (unto Him). And be not thou (O Muhammad) of the idolaters.

15. Say: I fear, if I rebel against my Lord, the retribution of an Awful Day.

16. He from whom (such retribution) is averted on that day, (Allah) hath in truth had mercy on him. That will be the signal triumph.

17. If Allah touch thee with affliction, there is none that can relieve therefrom save Him, and if He touch thee with good fortune (there is none that can impair it); for He is Able to do all things.

18. He is the Omnipotent over His slaves, and He is the Wise, the Knower.

وَلَوْ جَعَلْنٰهُ مَلَكًا لَّجَعَلْنٰهُ رَجُلًا وَّلَلَبَسْنَا عَلَيْهِمْ
مَّا يَلْبِسُوْنَ ﴿٩﴾
وَلَقَدِ اسْتُهْزِئَ بِرُسُلٍ مِّنْ قَبْلِكَ فَحَاقَ بِالَّذِيْنَ
ع سَخِرُوْا مِنْهُمْ مَّا كَانُوْا بِهٖ يَسْتَهْزِءُوْنَ ﴿١٠﴾
قُلْ سِيْرُوْا فِي الْاَرْضِ ثُمَّ انْظُرُوْا كَيْفَ كَانَ
عَاقِبَةُ الْمُكَذِّبِيْنَ ﴿١١﴾
قُلْ لِّمَنْ مَّا فِي السَّمٰوٰتِ وَالْاَرْضِ قُلْ لِّلّٰهِ كَتَبَ
عَلٰى نَفْسِهِ الرَّحْمَةَ لَيَجْمَعَنَّكُمْ اِلٰى يَوْمِ الْقِيٰمَةِ لَا
رَيْبَ فِيْهِ اَلَّذِيْنَ خَسِرُوْٓا اَنْفُسَهُمْ فَهُمْ لَا يُؤْمِنُوْنَ ﴿١٢﴾
وَلَهٗ مَا سَكَنَ فِي الَّيْلِ وَالنَّهَارِ وَهُوَ السَّمِيْعُ
الْعَلِيْمُ ﴿١٣﴾
قُلْ اَغَيْرَ اللّٰهِ اَتَّخِذُ وَلِيًّا فَاطِرِ السَّمٰوٰتِ وَالْاَرْضِ
وَهُوَ يُطْعِمُ وَلَا يُطْعَمُ قُلْ اِنِّيْٓ اُمِرْتُ اَنْ اَكُوْنَ
اَوَّلَ مَنْ اَسْلَمَ وَلَا تَكُوْنَنَّ مِنَ الْمُشْرِكِيْنَ ﴿١٤﴾
قُلْ اِنِّيْٓ اَخَافُ اِنْ عَصَيْتُ رَبِّيْ عَذَابَ
يَوْمٍ عَظِيْمٍ ﴿١٥﴾
مَنْ يُّصْرَفْ عَنْهُ يَوْمَئِذٍ فَقَدْ رَحِمَهٗ وَذٰلِكَ
الْفَوْزُ الْمُبِيْنُ ﴿١٦﴾
وَاِنْ يَّمْسَسْكَ اللّٰهُ بِضُرٍّ فَلَا كَاشِفَ لَهٗٓ اِلَّا هُوَ
وَاِنْ يَّمْسَسْكَ بِخَيْرٍ فَهُوَ عَلٰى كُلِّ شَيْءٍ قَدِيْرٌ ﴿١٧﴾
وَهُوَ الْقَاهِرُ فَوْقَ عِبَادِهٖ وَهُوَ الْحَكِيْمُ
الْخَبِيْرُ ﴿١٨﴾

19. Say, (O Muhammad): What thing is of most weight in testimony? Say: Allah is witness between you and me. And this Qur'ān hath been inspired in me, that I may warn therewith you and whomsoever it may reach. Do ye in sooth bear witness that there are Gods beside Allah? Say: I bear no such witness. Say: He is only One God. Lo! I am innocent of that which ye associate (with Him).

20. Those unto whom We gave the Scripture recognise (this Revelation) as they recognise their sons. Those who ruin their own souls will not believe.

21. Who doth greater wrong than he who inventeth a lie against Allah and denieth His revelations? Lo! the wrong-doers will not be successful.

22. And on the day We gather them together We shall say unto those who ascribed partners (unto Allah): Where are (now) those partners of your make-believe?

23. Then will they have no contention save that they will say, By Allah, our Lord, we never were idolaters.

24. See how they lie against themselves, and (how) the thing which they devised hath failed them!

25. Of them are some who listen unto thee, but We have placed upon their hearts veils, lest they should understand, and in their ears a deafness. If they saw every token they would not believe therein; to the point that, when they come unto thee to argue with thee, the disbelievers say: This is naught else than fables of the men of old.

26. And they forbid (men) from it and avoid it, and they ruin none save themselves, though they perceive not.

27. If thou couldst see when they are set before the Fire and say: Oh, would that we might return! Then would we not deny the revelations of our Lord but we would be of the believers!

قُلْ اَيُّ شَيْءٍ اَكْبَرُ شَهَادَةً ۭ قُلِ اللّٰهُ ۣ شَهِيْدٌۢ

بَيْنِيْ وَبَيْنَكُمْ ۣ وَاُوْحِيَ اِلَيَّ هٰذَا الْقُرْاٰنُ لِاُنْذِرَكُمْ

بِهٖ وَمَنْۢ بَلَغَ ۭ اَىِٕنَّكُمْ لَتَشْهَدُوْنَ اَنَّ مَعَ اللّٰهِ اٰلِهَةً

اُخْرٰى ۭ قُلْ لَّآ اَشْهَدُ ۚ قُلْ اِنَّمَا هُوَ اِلٰهٌ وَّاحِدٌ وَّ

اِنَّنِيْ بَرِيْۗءٌ مِّمَّا تُشْرِكُوْنَ ﴿١٩﴾

اَلَّذِيْنَ اٰتَيْنٰهُمُ الْكِتٰبَ يَعْرِفُوْنَهٗ كَمَا يَعْرِفُوْنَ

اَبْنَاۗءَهُمْ ۘ اَلَّذِيْنَ خَسِرُوْٓا اَنْفُسَهُمْ فَهُمْ لَا يُؤْمِنُوْنَ ﴿٢٠﴾

وَمَنْ اَظْلَمُ مِمَّنِ افْتَرٰى عَلَى اللّٰهِ كَذِبًا اَوْ كَذَّبَ

بِاٰيٰتِهٖ ۭ اِنَّهٗ لَا يُفْلِحُ الظّٰلِمُوْنَ ﴿٢١﴾

وَيَوْمَ نَحْشُرُهُمْ جَمِيْعًا ثُمَّ نَقُوْلُ لِلَّذِيْنَ اَشْرَكُوْٓا

اَيْنَ شُرَكَاۗؤُكُمُ الَّذِيْنَ كُنْتُمْ تَزْعُمُوْنَ ﴿٢٢﴾

ثُمَّ لَمْ تَكُنْ فِتْنَتُهُمْ اِلَّآ اَنْ قَالُوْا وَاللّٰهِ رَبِّنَا مَا كُنَّا مُشْرِكِيْنَ ﴿٢٣﴾

اُنْظُرْ كَيْفَ كَذَبُوْا عَلٰٓي اَنْفُسِهِمْ وَضَلَّ عَنْهُمْ مَّا كَانُوْا

يَفْتَرُوْنَ ﴿٢٤﴾

وَمِنْهُمْ مَّنْ يَّسْتَمِعُ اِلَيْكَ ۚ وَجَعَلْنَا عَلٰي قُلُوْبِهِمْ

اَكِنَّةً اَنْ يَّفْقَهُوْهُ وَفِيْٓ اٰذَانِهِمْ وَقْرًا ۭ وَاِنْ يَّرَوْا كُلَّ

اٰيَةٍ لَّا يُؤْمِنُوْا بِهَا ۭ حَتّٰٓي اِذَا جَاۗءُوْكَ يُجَادِلُوْنَكَ

يَقُوْلُ الَّذِيْنَ كَفَرُوْٓا اِنْ هٰذَآ اِلَّآ اَسَاطِيْرُ الْاَوَّلِيْنَ ﴿٢٥﴾

وَهُمْ يَنْهَوْنَ عَنْهُ وَيَنْــــَٔـوْنَ عَنْهُ ۚ وَاِنْ يُّهْلِكُوْنَ

اِلَّآ اَنْفُسَهُمْ وَمَا يَشْعُرُوْنَ ﴿٢٦﴾

وَلَوْ تَرٰٓي اِذْ وُقِفُوْا عَلَي النَّارِ فَقَالُوْا يٰلَيْتَنَا نُرَدُّ وَلَا

نُكَذِّبَ بِاٰيٰتِ رَبِّنَا وَنَكُوْنَ مِنَ الْمُؤْمِنِيْنَ ﴿٢٧﴾

28. Nay, but that hath become clear unto them which before they used to hide. And if they were sent back they would return unto that which they are forbidden. Lo! they are liars.

29. And they say: There is naught save our life of the world, and we shall not be raised (again).

30. If thou couldst see when they are set before their Lord! He will say: Is not this real? They will say; Yea, verily, by our Lord! He will say: Taste now the retribution for that ye used to disbelieve.

31. They indeed are losers who deny their meeting with Allah until, when the hour cometh on them suddenly, they cry: Alas for us, that we neglected it! They bear upon their backs their burdens. Ah, evil is that which they bear!

32. Naught is the life of the world save a pastime and a sport. Better far is the abode of the Hereafter for those who keep their duty (to Allah). Have ye then no sense?

33. We know well how their talk grieveth thee, though in truth they deny not thee (Muhammad) but evil-doers flout the revelations of Allah.

34. Messengers indeed have been denied before thee, and they were patient under the denial and the persecution till Our succour reached them. There is none to alter the decisions of Allah. Already there hath reached thee (somewhat) of the tidings of the messengers (We sent before).

35. And if their aversion is grievous unto thee, then, if thou canst, seek a way down into the earth or a ladder unto the sky that thou mayst bring unto them a portent (to convince them all)!--If Allah willed, He could have brought them all together to the guidance—So be not thou among the foolish ones.

بل بدا لهم ما كانوا يخفون من قبل ولو ردوا
لعادوا لما نهوا عنه وانهم لكذبون (٢٨)
وقالوا ان هي الا حياتنا الدنيا وما نحن
بمبعوثين (٢٩)
ولو ترى اذ وقفوا على ربهم قال اليس هذا
بالحق قالوا بلى وربنا قال فذوقوا العذاب
بما كنتم تكفرون (٣٠)
قد خسر الذين كذبوا بلقاء الله حتى اذا جاءتهم
الساعة بغتة قالوا يحسرتنا على ما فرطنا فيها
وهم يحملون اوزارهم على ظهورهم الا ساء ما
يزرون (٣١)
وما الحيوة الدنيا الا لعب ولهو وللدار الاخرة
خير للذين يتقون افلا تعقلون (٣٢)
قد نعلم انه ليحزنك الذي يقولون فانهم لا
يكذبونك ولكن الظلمين بايت الله يجحدون (٣٣)
ولقد كذبت رسل من قبلك فصبروا على ما
كذبوا واوذوا حتى اتهم نصرنا ولا مبدل لكلمت
الله ولقد جاءك من نبائ المرسلين (٣٤)
وان كان كبر عليك اعراضهم فان استطعت
ان تبتغي نفقا في الارض او سلما في السماء
فتاتيهم باية ولو شاء الله لجمعهم على
الهدى فلا تكونن من الجهلين (٣٥)

36. Only those can accept who hear. As for the dead, Allah will raise them up; then unto Him they will be returned.

فَتِّنْقَبَّلُ اِنَّمَا يَسْتَجِيْبُ الَّذِيْنَ يَسْمَعُوْنَ وَالْمَوْتٰى يَبْعَثُهُمُ اللّٰهُ ثُمَّ اِلَيْهِ يُرْجَعُوْنَ ۞

37. They say: Why hath no portent been sent down upon him from his Lord? Say: Lo! Allah is Able to send down a portent. But most of them know not.

وَقَالُوْا لَوْلَا نُزِّلَ عَلَيْهِ اٰيَةٌ مِّنْ رَّبِّهٖ ۚ قُلْ اِنَّ اللّٰهَ قَادِرٌ عَلٰٓى اَنْ يُّنَزِّلَ اٰيَةً وَّلٰكِنَّ اَكْثَرَهُمْ لَا يَعْلَمُوْنَ ۞

38. There is not an animal in the earth nor a flying creature flying on two wings, but they are peoples like unto you. We have neglected nothing in the Book (of Our decrees). Then unto their Lord they will be gathered.

وَمَا مِنْ دَابَّةٍ فِى الْاَرْضِ وَلَا طٰٓئِرٍ يَّطِيْرُ بِجَنَاحَيْهِ اِلَّآ اُمَمٌ اَمْثَالُكُمْ ۚ مَا فَرَّطْنَا فِى الْكِتٰبِ مِنْ شَيْءٍ ثُمَّ اِلٰى رَبِّهِمْ يُحْشَرُوْنَ ۞

39. Those who deny our revelations are deaf and dumb in darkness. Whom Allah will He sendeth astray, and whom He will He placeth on a straight path.

وَالَّذِيْنَ كَذَّبُوْا بِاٰيٰتِنَا صُمٌّ وَّبُكْمٌ فِى الظُّلُمٰتِ ۚ مَنْ يَّشَإِ اللّٰهُ يُضْلِلْهُ ۚ وَمَنْ يَّشَأْ يَجْعَلْهُ عَلٰى صِرَاطٍ مُّسْتَقِيْمٍ ۞

40. Say: Can ye see yourselves, if the punishment of Allah come upon you or the Hour come upon you, calling upon other than Allah? Do ye then call (for help) to any other than Allah? (Answer that) if ye are truthful.

قُلْ اَرَاَيْتَكُمْ اِنْ اَتٰكُمْ عَذَابُ اللّٰهِ اَوْ اَتَتْكُمُ السَّاعَةُ اَغَيْرَ اللّٰهِ تَدْعُوْنَ ۚ اِنْ كُنْتُمْ صٰدِقِيْنَ ۞

41. Nay, but unto Him ye call, and He removeth that because of which ye call unto Him. If He will, and ye forget whatever partners ye ascribed unto Him.

بَلْ اِيَّاهُ تَدْعُوْنَ فَيَكْشِفُ مَا تَدْعُوْنَ اِلَيْهِ اِنْ شَآءَ وَتَنْسَوْنَ مَا تُشْرِكُوْنَ ۞

42. We have sent already unto peoples that were before thee, and We visited them with tribulation and adversity, in order that they might grow humble.

وَلَقَدْ اَرْسَلْنَآ اِلٰٓى اُمَمٍ مِّنْ قَبْلِكَ فَاَخَذْنٰهُمْ بِالْبَأْسَآءِ وَالضَّرَّآءِ لَعَلَّهُمْ يَتَضَرَّعُوْنَ ۞

43. If only, when our disaster came on them, they had been humble! But their hearts were hardened and the devil made all that they used to do seem fair unto them!

فَلَوْلَآ اِذْ جَآءَهُمْ بَأْسُنَا تَضَرَّعُوْا وَلٰكِنْ قَسَتْ قُلُوْبُهُمْ وَزَيَّنَ لَهُمُ الشَّيْطٰنُ مَا كَانُوْا يَعْمَلُوْنَ ۞

44. Then, when they forgot that whereof they had been reminded, We opened unto them the gates of all things till, even as they were rejoicing in that which they were given, We seized them unawares, and lo! they were dumbfounded.

فَلَمَّا نَسُوْا مَا ذُكِّرُوْا بِهٖ فَتَحْنَا عَلَيْهِمْ اَبْوَابَ كُلِّ شَيْءٍ ۚ حَتّٰٓى اِذَا فَرِحُوْا بِمَآ اُوْتُوْا اَخَذْنٰهُمْ بَغْتَةً فَاِذَا هُمْ مُّبْلِسُوْنَ ۞

45. So of the people who did wrong the last remnant was cut off. Praise be to Allah, Lord of the Worlds!

46. Say: Have ye imagined, if Allah should take away your hearing and your sight and seal your hearts, who is the God who could restore it to you save Allah? See how We display the revelations unto them? Yet still they turn away.

47. Say: Can ye see yourselves, if the punishment of Allah come upon you unawares or openly? Would any perish save wrongdoing folk?

48. We send not the messengers save as bearers of good news and warners. Whoso believeth and doth right, there shall no fear come upon them neither shall they grieve.

49. But as for those who deny Our revelations, torment will afflict them for that they used to disobey.

50. Say (O Muhammad, to the disbelievers): I say not unto you (that) I possess the treasures of Allah, nor that I have knowledge of the Unseen; and I say not unto you: Lo! I am an angel. I follow only that which is inspired in me. Say: Are the blind man and the seer equal? Will ye not then take thought?

51. Warn hereby those who fear (because they know) that they will be gathered unto their Lord, for whom there is no protecting friend nor intercessor beside Him, that they may ward off (evil).

52. Repel not those who call upon their Lord at morn and evening, seeking His countenance. Thou art not accountable for them in aught, nor are they accountable for thee in aught, that thou shouldst repel them and be of the wrong-doers.

فَقُطِعَ دَابِرُ الْقَوْمِ الَّذِيْنَ ظَلَمُوْا ۗ وَالْحَمْدُ لِلّٰهِ
رَبِّ الْعٰلَمِيْنَ ﴿۴۵﴾
قُلْ اَرَءَيْتُمْ اِنْ اَخَذَ اللّٰهُ سَمْعَكُمْ وَاَبْصَارَكُمْ وَ
خَتَمَ عَلٰى قُلُوْبِكُمْ مَّنْ اِلٰهٌ غَيْرُ اللّٰهِ يَاْتِيْكُمْ بِهٖ ؕ اُنْظُرْ
كَيْفَ نُصَرِّفُ الْاٰيٰتِ ثُمَّ هُمْ يَصْدِفُوْنَ ﴿۴۶﴾
قُلْ اَرَءَيْتَكُمْ اِنْ اَتٰىكُمْ عَذَابُ اللّٰهِ بَغْتَةً اَوْ
جَهْرَةً هَلْ يُهْلَكُ اِلَّا الْقَوْمُ الظّٰلِمُوْنَ ﴿۴۷﴾
وَمَا نُرْسِلُ الْمُرْسَلِيْنَ اِلَّا مُبَشِّرِيْنَ وَمُنْذِرِيْنَ ۚ
فَمَنْ اٰمَنَ وَاَصْلَحَ فَلَا خَوْفٌ عَلَيْهِمْ وَلَا هُمْ
يَحْزَنُوْنَ ﴿۴۸﴾
وَالَّذِيْنَ كَذَّبُوْا بِاٰيٰتِنَا يَمَسُّهُمُ الْعَذَابُ بِمَا
كَانُوْا يَفْسُقُوْنَ ﴿۴۹﴾
قُلْ لَّاۤ اَقُوْلُ لَكُمْ عِنْدِيْ خَزَآئِنُ اللّٰهِ وَلَاۤ
اَعْلَمُ الْغَيْبَ وَلَاۤ اَقُوْلُ لَكُمْ اِنِّيْ مَلَكٌ ۚ اِنْ اَتَّبِعُ
اِلَّا مَا يُوْحٰۤى اِلَيَّ ؕ قُلْ هَلْ يَسْتَوِي الْاَعْمٰى وَ
الْبَصِيْرُ ؕ اَفَلَا تَتَفَكَّرُوْنَ ﴿۵۰﴾ ع
وَاَنْذِرْ بِهِ الَّذِيْنَ يَخَافُوْنَ اَنْ يُّحْشَرُوْۤا اِلٰى رَبِّهِمْ
لَيْسَ لَهُمْ مِّنْ دُوْنِهٖ وَلِيٌّ وَّلَا شَفِيْعٌ لَّعَلَّهُمْ يَتَّقُوْنَ ﴿۵۱﴾
وَلَا تَطْرُدِ الَّذِيْنَ يَدْعُوْنَ رَبَّهُمْ بِالْغَدٰوةِ وَالْعَشِيِّ
يُرِيْدُوْنَ وَجْهَهٗ ؕ مَا عَلَيْكَ مِنْ حِسَابِهِمْ مِّنْ شَيْءٍ
وَّمَا مِنْ حِسَابِكَ عَلَيْهِمْ مِّنْ شَيْءٍ فَتَطْرُدَهُمْ
فَتَكُوْنَ مِنَ الظّٰلِمِيْنَ ﴿۵۲﴾

53. And even so do We try some of them by others, that they say: Are these they whom Allah favoureth among us? Is not Allah best aware of the thanksgivers?

54. And when those who believe in Our revelations come unto thee, say: Peace be unto you! Your Lord hath prescribed for Himself mercy, that, whoso of you doth evil and repenteth afterward thereof and doeth right, (for him) lo! Allah is Forgiving, Merciful.

55. Thus do We expound the revelations that the way of the unrighteous may be manifest.

56. Say: I am forbidden to worship those on whom ye call instead of Allah. Say: I will not follow your desires, for then should I go astray and I should not be of the rightly guided.

57. Say: I am (relying) on clear proof from my Lord, while ye deny Him. I have not that for which ye are impatient. The decision is for Allah only. He telleth the truth and He is the Best of Deciders.

58. Say: If I had that for which ye are impatient, then would the case (ere this) have been decided between me and you. Allah is best aware of the wrong-doers.

59. And with Him are the keys of the Invisible. None but He knoweth them. And He knoweth what is in the land and the sea. Not a leaf falleth but He knoweth it, not a grain amid the darkness of the earth, naught of wet or dry but (it is noted) in a clear Record.

60. He it is Who gathereth you at night and knoweth that which ye commit by day. Then He raiseth you again to life therein, that the term appointed (for you) may be accomplished. And afterward unto Him is your return. Then He will proclaim unto you what ye used to do.

وَكَذٰلِكَ فَتَنَّا بَعْضَهُمْ بِبَعْضٍ لِّيَقُولُوٓا أَهٰٓؤُلَآءِ مَنَّ
اللّٰهُ عَلَيْهِمْ مِّنْ بَيْنِنَا ۗ أَلَيْسَ اللّٰهُ بِأَعْلَمَ بِالشّٰكِرِينَ ﴿٥٣﴾
وَإِذَا جَآءَكَ الَّذِينَ يُؤْمِنُونَ بِاٰيٰتِنَا فَقُلْ سَلٰمٌ
عَلَيْكُمْ كَتَبَ رَبُّكُمْ عَلٰى نَفْسِهِ الرَّحْمَةَ ۙ أَنَّهُ مَنْ
عَمِلَ مِنْكُمْ سُوٓءًا بِجَهَالَةٍ ثُمَّ تَابَ مِنْ بَعْدِهِ
وَأَصْلَحَ فَأَنَّهُ غَفُورٌ رَّحِيمٌ ﴿٥٤﴾
وَكَذٰلِكَ نُفَصِّلُ الْاٰيٰتِ وَلِتَسْتَبِينَ سَبِيلُ الْمُجْرِمِينَ ﴿٥٥﴾ ع ٦ ١٢
قُلْ إِنِّي نُهِيتُ أَنْ أَعْبُدَ الَّذِينَ تَدْعُونَ مِنْ
دُونِ اللّٰهِ ۗ قُلْ لَّآ أَتَّبِعُ أَهْوَآءَكُمْ ۙ قَدْ ضَلَلْتُ إِذًا
وَّمَآ أَنَا مِنَ الْمُهْتَدِينَ ﴿٥٦﴾
قُلْ إِنِّي عَلٰى بَيِّنَةٍ مِّنْ رَّبِّي وَكَذَّبْتُمْ بِهِ ۚ مَا عِنْدِي
مَا تَسْتَعْجِلُونَ بِهِ ۗ إِنِ الْحُكْمُ إِلَّا لِلّٰهِ ۖ يَقُصُّ الْحَقَّ
وَهُوَ خَيْرُ الْفٰصِلِينَ ﴿٥٧﴾
قُلْ لَّوْ أَنَّ عِنْدِي مَا تَسْتَعْجِلُونَ بِهِ لَقُضِيَ الْأَمْرُ
بَيْنِي وَبَيْنَكُمْ ۗ وَاللّٰهُ أَعْلَمُ بِالظّٰلِمِينَ ﴿٥٨﴾
وَعِنْدَهُ مَفَاتِحُ الْغَيْبِ لَا يَعْلَمُهَآ إِلَّا هُوَ ۚ وَيَعْلَمُ
مَا فِي الْبَرِّ وَالْبَحْرِ ۚ وَمَا تَسْقُطُ مِنْ وَّرَقَةٍ إِلَّا يَعْلَمُهَا
وَلَا حَبَّةٍ فِي ظُلُمٰتِ الْأَرْضِ وَلَا رَطْبٍ وَّلَا يَابِسٍ
إِلَّا فِي كِتٰبٍ مُّبِينٍ ﴿٥٩﴾
وَهُوَ الَّذِي يَتَوَفّٰكُمْ بِالَّيْلِ وَيَعْلَمُ مَا جَرَحْتُمْ
بِالنَّهَارِ ثُمَّ يَبْعَثُكُمْ فِيهِ لِيُقْضٰٓى أَجَلٌ مُّسَمًّى ۚ ثُمَّ
إِلَيْهِ مَرْجِعُكُمْ ثُمَّ يُنَبِّئُكُمْ بِمَا كُنْتُمْ تَعْمَلُونَ ﴿٦٠﴾ ع ٧ ١٣

61. He is the Omnipotent over His slaves. He sendeth guardians over you until, when death cometh unto one of you, Our messengers[1] receive him, and they neglect not.

62. Then are they restored unto Allah, their Lord, the Just. Surely His is the judgement. And He is the most swift of reckoners.

63. Say: Who delivereth you from the darkness of the land and the sea? Ye call upon Him humbly and in secret, (saying): If we are delivered from this (fear) we truly will be of the thankful.

64. Say: Allah delivereth you from this and from all affliction. Yet ye attribute partners unto Him.

65. Say: He is able to send punishment upon you from above you or from beneath your feet, or to bewilder you with dissension and make you taste the tyranny one of another. See how We display the revelations so that they may understand.

66. Thy people (O Muhammad) have denied it, though it is the Truth. Say: I am not put in charge of you.

67. For every announcement there is a term, and ye will come to know.

68. And when thou seest those who meddle with Our revelations, withdraw from them until they meddle with another topic. And if the devil cause thee to forget, sit not, after the remembrance, with the congregation of wrong-doers.

69. Those who ward off (evil) are not accountable for them in aught, but the Reminder (must be given them) that haply they (too) may ward off (evil).

1. *i.e.* angels. The same word *rusul* is used for angels and for prophets.

وَهُوَ الْقَاهِرُ فَوْقَ عِبَادِهٖ وَيُرْسِلُ عَلَيْكُمْ حَفَظَةً ۭ
حَتّٰٓى اِذَا جَاۗءَ اَحَدَكُمُ الْمَوْتُ تَوَفَّتْهُ رُسُلُنَا وَهُمْ
لَا يُفَرِّطُوْنَ ﴿٦١﴾
ثُمَّ رُدُّوْٓا اِلَى اللّٰهِ مَوْلٰىهُمُ الْحَقِّ ۭ اَلَا لَهُ الْحُكْمُ ۣ وَهُوَ
اَسْرَعُ الْحٰسِبِيْنَ ﴿٦٢﴾
قُلْ مَنْ يُّنَجِّيْكُمْ مِّنْ ظُلُمٰتِ الْبَرِّ وَالْبَحْرِ تَدْعُوْنَهٗ
تَضَرُّعًا وَّخُفْيَةً ۚ لَىِٕنْ اَنْجٰىنَا مِنْ هٰذِهٖ لَنَكُوْنَنَّ
مِنَ الشّٰكِرِيْنَ ﴿٦٣﴾
قُلِ اللّٰهُ يُنَجِّيْكُمْ مِّنْهَا وَمِنْ كُلِّ كَرْبٍ ثُمَّ اَنْتُمْ
تُشْرِكُوْنَ ﴿٦٤﴾
قُلْ هُوَ الْقَادِرُ عَلٰٓى اَنْ يَّبْعَثَ عَلَيْكُمْ عَذَابًا مِّنْ
فَوْقِكُمْ اَوْ مِنْ تَحْتِ اَرْجُلِكُمْ اَوْ يَلْبِسَكُمْ شِيَعًا وَّ
يُذِيْقَ بَعْضَكُمْ بَاْسَ بَعْضٍ ۭ اُنْظُرْ كَيْفَ نُصَرِّفُ
الْاٰيٰتِ لَعَلَّهُمْ يَفْقَهُوْنَ ﴿٦٥﴾
وَكَذَّبَ بِهٖ قَوْمُكَ وَهُوَ الْحَقُّ ۭ قُلْ لَّسْتُ عَلَيْكُمْ بِوَكِيْلٍ ﴿٦٦﴾
لِكُلِّ نَبَاٍ مُّسْتَقَرٌّ ۡ وَّسَوْفَ تَعْلَمُوْنَ ﴿٦٧﴾
وَاِذَا رَاَيْتَ الَّذِيْنَ يَخُوْضُوْنَ فِيْٓ اٰيٰتِنَا فَاَعْرِضْ
عَنْهُمْ حَتّٰى يَخُوْضُوْا فِيْ حَدِيْثٍ غَيْرِهٖ ۭ وَاِمَّا
يُنْسِيَنَّكَ الشَّيْطٰنُ فَلَا تَقْعُدْ بَعْدَ الذِّكْرٰى مَعَ
الْقَوْمِ الظّٰلِمِيْنَ ﴿٦٨﴾
وَمَا عَلَى الَّذِيْنَ يَتَّقُوْنَ مِنْ حِسَابِهِمْ مِّنْ شَيْءٍ
وَّلٰكِنْ ذِكْرٰى لَعَلَّهُمْ يَتَّقُوْنَ ﴿٦٩﴾

70. And forsake those who take their religion for a pastime and a jest, and whom the life of the world beguileth. Remind (mankind) hereby lest a soul be destroyed by what it earneth. It hath beside Allah no friend nor intercessor, and though it offer every compensation it will not be accepted from it. Those are they who perish by their own deserts. For them is drink of boiling water and a painful doom, because they disbelieved.

وذر الذين اتخذوا دينهم لعبا ولهوا وغرتهم
الحيوة الدنيا وذكر به ان تبسل نفس بما كسبت
ليس لها من دون الله ولي ولا شفيع وان تعدل
كل عدل لا يؤخذ منها اولئك الذين ابسلوا
بما كسبوا لهم شراب من حميم وعذاب
اليم بما كانوا يكفرون ﴿٧٠﴾

71. Say: Shall we cry, instead of unto Allah, unto that which neither profiteth us nor hurteth us, and shall we turn back after Allah hath guided us, like one bewildered whom the devils have infatuated in the earth, who hath companions who invite him to the guidance (saying): Come unto us? Say: Lo! the guidance of Allah is Guidance, and we are ordered to surrender to the Lord of the Worlds,

قل اندعوا من دون الله ما لا ينفعنا ولا يضرنا
ونرد على اعقابنا بعد اذ هدىنا الله كالذي
استهوته الشيطين في الارض حيران له
اصحب يدعونه الى الهدى ائتنا قل ان
هدى الله هو الهدى وامرنا لنسلم لرب
العلمين ﴿٧١﴾

72. And to establish worship and ward off (evil), and He it is unto Whom ye will be gathered.

وان اقيموا الصلوة واتقوه وهو الذي اليه
تحشرون ﴿٧٢﴾

73. He it is Who created the heavens and the earth in truth. In that day when He saith: Be! it is. His word is the truth, and His will be the Sovereignty on the day when the trumpet is blown. Knower of the invisible and the visible, He is the Wise, the Aware.

وهو الذي خلق السموت والارض بالحق و
يوم يقول كن فيكون قوله الحق وله
الملك يوم ينفخ في الصور علم الغيب والشهادة
وهو الحكيم الخبير ﴿٧٣﴾

74. (Remember) when Abraham said unto his father Azar: Takest thou idols for gods? Lo! I see thee and thy folk in error manifest.

واذ قال ابرهيم لابيه ازر اتتخذ اصناما
الهة اني ارىك وقومك في ضلل مبين ﴿٧٤﴾

75. Thus did We show Abraham the kingdom of the heavens and the earth that he might be of those possessing certainty:

وكذلك نري ابرهيم ملكوت السموت والارض
وليكون من الموقنين ﴿٧٥﴾

76. When the night grew dark upon him he beheld a star. He said: This is my Lord. But when it set, he said: I love not things that set.

77. And when he saw the moon uprising, he exclaimed: This is my Lord. But when it set, he said: Unless my Lord guide me, I surely shall become one of the folk who are astray.

78. And when he saw the sun uprising, he cried: This is my Lord! This is greater! And when it set he exclaimed: O my people! Lo! I am free from all that ye associate (with Him).

79. Lo! I have turned my face toward Him Who created the heavens and the earth, as one by nature upright, and I am not of the idolaters.

80. His people argued with him. He said: Dispute ye with me concerning Allah when He hath guided me? I fear not at all that which ye set beside Him unless my Lord willeth. My Lord includeth all things in His knowledge. Will ye not then remember?

81. How should I fear that which ye set up beside Him, when ye fear not to set up beside Allah that for which He hath revealed unto you no warrant? Which of the two factions hath more right to safety? (Answer me that) if ye have knowledge.

82. Those who believe and obscure not their belief by wrongdoing, theirs is safety; and they are rightly guided.

83. That is Our argument. We gave it unto Abraham against his folk. We raise unto degrees of wisdom whom We will. Lo! thy Lord is Wise, Aware.

84. And We bestowed upon him Isaac and Jacob: each of them We guided; and Noah did We guide aforetime; and of his seed (We guided) David and Solomon and Job and Joseph and Moses and Aaron. Thus do We reward the good.

فَلَمَّا جَنَّ عَلَيْهِ الَّيْلُ رَاٰ كَوْكَبًا ۚ قَالَ هٰذَا رَبِّيْ ۚ
فَلَمَّآ اَفَلَ قَالَ لَآ اُحِبُّ الْاٰفِلِيْنَ ﴿٧٦﴾
فَلَمَّا رَاَ الْقَمَرَ بَازِغًا قَالَ هٰذَا رَبِّيْ ۚ فَلَمَّآ اَفَلَ قَالَ لَئِنْ
لَّمْ يَهْدِنِيْ رَبِّيْ لَاَكُوْنَنَّ مِنَ الْقَوْمِ الضَّآلِّيْنَ ﴿٧٧﴾
فَلَمَّا رَاَ الشَّمْسَ بَازِغَةً قَالَ هٰذَا رَبِّيْ هٰذَآ اَكْبَرُ ۚ فَلَمَّآ
اَفَلَتْ قَالَ يٰقَوْمِ اِنِّيْ بَرِيْٓءٌ مِّمَّا تُشْرِكُوْنَ ﴿٧٨﴾
اِنِّيْ وَجَّهْتُ وَجْهِيَ لِلَّذِيْ فَطَرَ السَّمٰوٰتِ وَالْاَرْضَ
حَنِيْفًا وَّمَآ اَنَا مِنَ الْمُشْرِكِيْنَ ﴿٧٩﴾
وَحَآجَّهٗ قَوْمُهٗ ۭ قَالَ اَتُحَاۗجُّوْٓنِّيْ فِي اللّٰهِ وَقَدْ هَدٰىنِ ۭ
وَلَآ اَخَافُ مَا تُشْرِكُوْنَ بِهٖٓ اِلَّآ اَنْ يَّشَاۗءَ رَبِّيْ شَيْـــًٔا ۭ
وَسِعَ رَبِّيْ كُلَّ شَيْءٍ عِلْمًا ۭ اَفَلَا تَتَذَكَّرُوْنَ ﴿٨٠﴾
وَكَيْفَ اَخَافُ مَآ اَشْرَكْتُمْ وَلَا تَخَافُوْنَ اَنَّكُمْ اَشْرَكْتُمْ
بِاللّٰهِ مَا لَمْ يُنَزِّلْ بِهٖ عَلَيْكُمْ سُلْطٰنًا ۭ فَاَيُّ الْفَرِيْقَيْنِ
اَحَقُّ بِالْاَمْنِ ۚ اِنْ كُنْتُمْ تَعْلَمُوْنَ ﴿٨١﴾
اَلَّذِيْنَ اٰمَنُوْا وَلَمْ يَلْبِسُوْٓا اِيْمَانَهُمْ بِظُلْمٍ اُولٰۗىِٕكَ
لَهُمُ الْاَمْنُ وَهُمْ مُّهْتَدُوْنَ ﴿٨٢﴾
وَتِلْكَ حُجَّتُنَآ اٰتَيْنٰهَآ اِبْرٰهِيْمَ عَلٰي قَوْمِهٖ ۭ نَرْفَعُ
دَرَجٰتٍ مَّنْ نَّشَاۗءُ ۭ اِنَّ رَبَّكَ حَكِيْمٌ عَلِيْمٌ ﴿٨٣﴾
وَوَهَبْنَا لَهٗٓ اِسْحٰقَ وَيَعْقُوْبَ ۭ كُلًّا هَدَيْنَا ۚ وَنُوْحًا
هَدَيْنَا مِنْ قَبْلُ وَمِنْ ذُرِّيَّتِهٖ دَاوٗدَ وَسُلَيْمٰنَ
وَاَيُّوْبَ وَيُوْسُفَ وَمُوْسٰي وَهٰرُوْنَ ۭ وَكَذٰلِكَ
نَجْزِي الْمُحْسِنِيْنَ ﴿٨٤﴾

85. And Zachariah and John and Jesus and Elias. Each one (of them) was of the righteous.

86. And Ishmael and Elisha and Jonah and Lot. Each one of them did We prefer above (Our) creatures,

87. With some of their forefathers and their offspring and their brethren; and We chose them and guided them unto a Straight path.

88. Such is the guidance of Allah wherewith He guideth whom He will of His bondmen. But if they had set up (for worship) aught beside Him, (all) that they did would have been vain.

89. Those are they unto whom We gave the Scripture and command and prophethood. But if these disbelieve therein, then indeed We shall entrust it to a people who will not be disbelievers therein.

90. Those are they whom Allah guideth, so follow their guidance. Say (O Muhammad, unto mankind): I ask of you no fee for it. Lo! it is naught but a Reminder to (His) creatures.

91. And they measure not the power of Allah its true measure when they say: Allah hath naught revealed unto a human being. Say (unto the Jews who speak thus): Who revealed the Book which Moses brought, a light and guidance for mankind, which ye have put on parchments which ye show, but ye hide much (thereof), and by which ye were taught that which ye knew not yourselves nor (did) your fathers (know it)? Say: Allah. Then leave them to their play of cavilling.

92. And this is a blessed Scripture which We have revealed, confirming that which (was revealed) before it, that thou mayst warn the Mother of Villages[1] and those around her. These who believe in the Hereafter believe herein, and they are careful of their worship.

1. *i.e.* Mecca.

وَزَكَرِيَّا وَيَحْيٰى وَعِيْسٰى وَاِلْيَاسَ ۭ كُلٌّ مِّنَ الصّٰلِحِيْنَ ۝٨٥
وَاِسْمٰعِيْلَ وَالْيَسَعَ وَيُوْنُسَ وَلُوْطًا ۭ وَكُلًّا فَضَّلْنَا
عَلَي الْعٰلَمِيْنَ ۝٨٦
وَمِنْ اٰبَاۗىِٕهِمْ وَذُرِّيّٰتِهِمْ وَاِخْوَانِهِمْ ۚ وَاجْتَبَيْنٰهُمْ
وَهَدَيْنٰهُمْ اِلٰى صِرَاطٍ مُّسْتَقِيْمٍ ۝٨٧
ذٰلِكَ هُدَى اللّٰهِ يَهْدِيْ بِهٖ مَنْ يَّشَاۗءُ مِنْ عِبَادِهٖ ۭ
وَلَوْ اَشْرَكُوْا لَحَبِطَ عَنْهُمْ مَّا كَانُوْا يَعْمَلُوْنَ ۝٨٨
اُولٰۗىِٕكَ الَّذِيْنَ اٰتَيْنٰهُمُ الْكِتٰبَ وَالْحُكْمَ وَالنُّبُوَّةَ ۚ
فَاِنْ يَّكْفُرْ بِهَا هٰٓؤُلَاۗءِ فَقَدْ وَكَّلْنَا بِهَا قَوْمًا لَّيْسُوْا
بِهَا بِكٰفِرِيْنَ ۝٨٩
اُولٰۗىِٕكَ الَّذِيْنَ هَدَى اللّٰهُ فَبِهُدٰىهُمُ اقْتَدِهْ ۭ قُلْ لَّآ
ع ١٦ اَسْــَٔـلُكُمْ عَلَيْهِ اَجْرًا ۭ اِنْ هُوَ اِلَّا ذِكْرٰي لِلْعٰلَمِيْنَ ۝٩٠
وَمَا قَدَرُوا اللّٰهَ حَقَّ قَدْرِهٖٓ اِذْ قَالُوْا مَآ اَنْزَلَ اللّٰهُ
عَلٰي بَشَرٍ مِّنْ شَيْءٍ ۭ قُلْ مَنْ اَنْزَلَ الْكِتٰبَ الَّذِيْ
جَاۗءَ بِهٖ مُوْسٰي نُوْرًا وَّهُدًى لِّلنَّاسِ تَجْعَلُوْنَهٗ
قَرَاطِيْسَ تُبْدُوْنَهَا وَتُخْفُوْنَ كَثِيْرًا ۚ وَعُلِّمْتُمْ مَّا لَمْ
تَعْلَمُوْٓا اَنْتُمْ وَلَآ اٰبَاۗؤُكُمْ ۭ قُلِ اللّٰهُ ۙ ثُمَّ ذَرْهُمْ فِيْ
خَوْضِهِمْ يَلْعَبُوْنَ ۝٩١
وَهٰذَا كِتٰبٌ اَنْزَلْنٰهُ مُبٰرَكٌ مُّصَدِّقُ الَّذِيْ بَيْنَ
يَدَيْهِ وَلِتُنْذِرَ اُمَّ الْقُرٰى وَمَنْ حَوْلَهَا ۭ وَالَّذِيْنَ
يُؤْمِنُوْنَ بِالْاٰخِرَةِ يُؤْمِنُوْنَ بِهٖ وَهُمْ عَلٰي
صَلَاتِهِمْ يُحَافِظُوْنَ ۝٩٢

93. Who is guilty of more wrong than he who forgeth a lie against Allah, or saith: I am inspired, when he is not inspired in aught; and who saith: I will reveal the like of that which Allah hath revealed? If thou couldst see, when the wrong-doers reach the pangs of death and the angels stretch their hands out, saying: Deliver up your souls. This day ye are awarded doom of degradation for that ye spake concerning Allah other than the truth, and scorned His portents.

وَمَنْ أَظْلَمُ مِمَّنِ افْتَرَى عَلَى اللهِ كَذِبًا أَوْ قَالَ
أُوْحِىَ إِلَيَّ وَلَمْ يُوحَ إِلَيْهِ شَيْءٌ وَّمَنْ قَالَ سَأُنْزِلُ
مِثْلَ مَا أَنْزَلَ اللهُ وَلَوْ تَرَى إِذِ الظَّالِمُوْنَ فِيْ غَمَرَاتِ
الْمَوْتِ وَالْمَلَئِكَةُ بَاسِطُوٓا أَيْدِيْهِمْ أَخْرِجُوٓا
أَنْفُسَكُمُ الْيَوْمَ تُجْزَوْنَ عَذَابَ الْهُوْنِ بِمَا كُنْتُمْ
تَقُوْلُوْنَ عَلَى اللهِ غَيْرَ الْحَقِّ وَكُنْتُمْ عَنْ اٰيٰتِهِ
تَسْتَكْبِرُوْنَ ۝

94. Now have ye come unto Us solitary as We did create you at the first, and ye have left behind you all that We bestowed upon you, and We behold not with you those your intercessors, of whom ye claimed that they possessed a share in you. Now is the bond between you severed, and that which ye presumed hath failed you.

وَلَقَدْ جِئْتُمُوْنَا فُرَادَى كَمَا خَلَقْنٰكُمْ أَوَّلَ مَرَّةٍ
وَّتَرَكْتُمْ مَّا خَوَّلْنٰكُمْ وَرَاءَ ظُهُوْرِكُمْ وَمَا نَرَى
مَعَكُمْ شُفَعَاءَكُمُ الَّذِيْنَ زَعَمْتُمْ أَنَّهُمْ فِيْكُمْ
شُرَكٰٓؤُا لَقَدْ تَقَطَّعَ بَيْنَكُمْ وَضَلَّ عَنْكُمْ مَّا
كُنْتُمْ تَزْعُمُوْنَ ۝

95. Lo! Allah (it is) who splitteth the grain of corn and the date-stone (for sprouting). He bringeth forth the living from the dead, and is the bringer-forth of the dead from the living. Such is Allah. How then are ye perverted?

إِنَّ اللهَ فَالِقُ الْحَبِّ وَالنَّوَى يُخْرِجُ الْحَيَّ
مِنَ الْمَيِّتِ وَمُخْرِجُ الْمَيِّتِ مِنَ الْحَيِّ ذٰلِكُمُ
اللهُ فَأَنّٰى تُؤْفَكُوْنَ ۝

96. He is the Cleaver of the Daybreak, and He hath appointed the night for stillness, and the sun and the moon for reckoning. That is the measuring of the Mighty, the Wise.

فَالِقُ الْإِصْبَاحِ وَجَعَلَ الَّيْلَ سَكَنًا وَّالشَّمْسَ وَ
الْقَمَرَ حُسْبَانًا ذٰلِكَ تَقْدِيْرُ الْعَزِيْزِ الْعَلِيْمِ ۝

97. And He it is Who hath set for you the stars that ye may guide your course by them amid the darkness of the land and the sea. We have detailed our revelations for a people who have knowledge.

وَهُوَ الَّذِيْ جَعَلَ لَكُمُ النُّجُوْمَ لِتَهْتَدُوْا بِهَا فِيْ
ظُلُمٰتِ الْبَرِّ وَالْبَحْرِ قَدْ فَصَّلْنَا الْاٰيٰتِ لِقَوْمٍ
يَعْلَمُوْنَ ۝

98. And He it is Who hath produced you from a single being, and (hath given you) a habitation and a repository. We have detailed Our revelations for a people who have understanding.

وَهُوَ الَّذِيْ أَنْشَأَكُمْ مِّنْ نَّفْسٍ وَّاحِدَةٍ فَمُسْتَقَرٌّ
وَّمُسْتَوْدَعٌ قَدْ فَصَّلْنَا الْاٰيٰتِ لِقَوْمٍ يَفْقَهُوْنَ ۝

99. He it is Who sendeth down water from the sky, and therewith We bring forth buds of every kind. We bring forth the green blade from which we bring forth the thick-clustered grain; and from the date-palm, from the pollen thereof, spring pendant bunches, and (We bring forth) gardens of grapes, and the olive and the pomegranate, alike and unlike. Look upon the fruit thereof, when they bear fruit, and upon its ripening. Lo! herein verily are portents for a people who believe.

100. Yet they ascribe as partners unto Him the jinn, although He did create them, and impute falsely, without knowledge, sons and daughters unto Him. Glorified be He and high exalted above (all) that they ascribe (unto Him)!

101. The Originator of the heavens and the earth! How can He have a child, when there is for Him no consort, when He created all things and is Aware of all things?

102. Such is Allah, your Lord. There is no God save Him, the Creator of all things, so worship Him. And He taketh care of all things.

103. Vision comprehendeth Him not, but He comprehendeth (all) vision. He is the Subtile, the Aware.

104. Proofs have come unto you from your Lord so whoso seeth, it is for his own good, and whoso is blind is blind to his own hurt. And I am not a keeper over you.

105. Thus do We display Our revelations that they may say (unto thee, Muhammad): "Thou hast studied," and that We may make (it) clear for people who have knowledge.

106. Follow that which is inspired in thee from thy Lord; there is no God save Him; and turn away from the idolaters.

وَهُوَ الَّذِيٓ أَنْزَلَ مِنَ السَّمَآءِ مَآءً فَأَخْرَجْنَا بِهٖ
نَبَاتَ كُلِّ شَيْءٍ فَأَخْرَجْنَا مِنْهُ خَضِرًا نُّخْرِجُ مِنْهُ
حَبًّا مُّتَرَاكِبًا وَمِنَ النَّخْلِ مِنْ طَلْعِهَا قِنْوَانٌ دَانِيَةٌ
وَّجَنّٰتٍ مِّنْ أَعْنَابٍ وَّالزَّيْتُوْنَ وَالرُّمَّانَ مُشْتَبِهًا
وَّغَيْرَ مُتَشَابِهٍ انْظُرُوْٓا إِلٰى ثَمَرِهٖٓ إِذَآ أَثْمَرَ وَيَنْعِهٖ
إِنَّ فِيْ ذٰلِكُمْ لَاٰيٰتٍ لِّقَوْمٍ يُّؤْمِنُوْنَ ﴿٩٩﴾
وَجَعَلُوْا لِلّٰهِ شُرَكَآءَ الْجِنَّ وَخَلَقَهُمْ وَخَرَقُوْا لَهٗ
بَنِيْنَ وَبَنٰتٍ بِغَيْرِ عِلْمٍ سُبْحٰنَهٗ وَتَعٰلٰى عَمَّا
ع ١٢ يَصِفُوْنَ ﴿١٠٠﴾
١٨
بَدِيْعُ السَّمٰوٰتِ وَالْأَرْضِ أَنّٰى يَكُوْنُ لَهٗ وَلَدٌ وَّ
لَمْ تَكُنْ لَّهٗ صَاحِبَةٌ وَخَلَقَ كُلَّ شَيْءٍ وَهُوَ بِكُلِّ
شَيْءٍ عَلِيْمٌ ﴿١٠١﴾
ذٰلِكُمُ اللّٰهُ رَبُّكُمْ لَآ إِلٰهَ إِلَّا هُوَ خَالِقُ كُلِّ شَيْءٍ
فَاعْبُدُوْهُ وَهُوَ عَلٰى كُلِّ شَيْءٍ وَّكِيْلٌ ﴿١٠٢﴾
لَا تُدْرِكُهُ الْأَبْصَارُ وَهُوَ يُدْرِكُ الْأَبْصَارَ وَهُوَ
اللَّطِيْفُ الْخَبِيْرُ ﴿١٠٣﴾
قَدْ جَآءَكُمْ بَصَآئِرُ مِنْ رَّبِّكُمْ فَمَنْ أَبْصَرَ فَلِنَفْسِهٖ وَ
مَنْ عَمِيَ فَعَلَيْهَا وَمَآ أَنَا عَلَيْكُمْ بِحَفِيْظٍ ﴿١٠٤﴾
وَكَذٰلِكَ نُصَرِّفُ الْاٰيٰتِ وَلِيَقُوْلُوْا دَرَسْتَ وَلِنُبَيِّنَهٗ
لِقَوْمٍ يَّعْلَمُوْنَ ﴿١٠٥﴾
اِتَّبِعْ مَآ أُوْحِيَ إِلَيْكَ مِنْ رَّبِّكَ لَآ إِلٰهَ إِلَّا هُوَ وَ
أَعْرِضْ عَنِ الْمُشْرِكِيْنَ ﴿١٠٦﴾

107. Had Allah willed, they had not been idolatrous. We have not set thee as a keeper over them, nor art thou responsible for them.

108. Revile not those unto whom they pray beside Allah lest they wrongfully revile Allah through ignorance. Thus unto every nation have We made their deed seem fair. Then unto their Lord is their return, and He will tell them what they used to do.

109. And they swear a solemn oath by Allah that if there come unto them a portent they will believe therein. Say: Portents are with Allah and (so is) that which telleth you that if such came unto them they would not believe.

110. We confound their hearts and their eyes. As they believed not therein at the first, We let them wander blindly on in their contumacy.

111. And though We should send down the angels unto them, and the dead should speak unto them, and We should gather against them all things in array, they would not believe unless Allah so willed. Howbeit, most of them are ignorant.

112. Thus have We appointed unto every Prophet an adversary—devils of humankind and jinn who inspire in one another plausible discourse through guile. If thy Lord willed, they would not do so; so leave them alone with their devising;

113. That the hearts of those who believe not in the Hereafter may incline thereto, and that they may take pleasure therein, and that they may earn what they are earning.

114. Shall I seek other than Allah for judge, when He it is who hath revealed unto you (this) Scripture, fully explained? Those unto whom We gave the Scripture (aforetime) know that it is revealed from thy Lord in truth. So be not thou (O Muhammad) of the waverers.

وَلَوْ شَاءَ اللَّهُ مَا أَشْرَكُوا ۗ وَمَا جَعَلْنَاكَ عَلَيْهِمْ حَفِيظًا ۖ
وَمَا أَنْتَ عَلَيْهِمْ بِوَكِيلٍ ﴿١٠٧﴾
وَلَا تَسُبُّوا الَّذِينَ يَدْعُونَ مِنْ دُونِ اللَّهِ فَيَسُبُّوا
اللَّهَ عَدْوًا بِغَيْرِ عِلْمٍ ۗ كَذَٰلِكَ زَيَّنَّا لِكُلِّ أُمَّةٍ عَمَلَهُمْ
ثُمَّ إِلَىٰ رَبِّهِمْ مَرْجِعُهُمْ فَيُنَبِّئُهُمْ بِمَا كَانُوا
يَعْمَلُونَ ﴿١٠٨﴾
وَأَقْسَمُوا بِاللَّهِ جَهْدَ أَيْمَانِهِمْ لَئِنْ جَاءَتْهُمْ آيَةٌ
لَيُؤْمِنُنَّ بِهَا ۚ قُلْ إِنَّمَا الْآيَاتُ عِنْدَ اللَّهِ ۖ وَمَا يُشْعِرُكُمْ
أَنَّهَا إِذَا جَاءَتْ لَا يُؤْمِنُونَ ﴿١٠٩﴾
وَنُقَلِّبُ أَفْئِدَتَهُمْ وَأَبْصَارَهُمْ كَمَا لَمْ يُؤْمِنُوا بِهِ أَوَّلَ
مَرَّةٍ وَنَذَرُهُمْ فِي طُغْيَانِهِمْ يَعْمَهُونَ ﴿١١٠﴾ ع ١٣ ١٩
وَلَوْ أَنَّنَا نَزَّلْنَا إِلَيْهِمُ الْمَلَائِكَةَ وَكَلَّمَهُمُ الْمَوْتَىٰ وَ الجزء ٨
حَشَرْنَا عَلَيْهِمْ كُلَّ شَيْءٍ قُبُلًا مَا كَانُوا لِيُؤْمِنُوا إِلَّا
أَنْ يَشَاءَ اللَّهُ وَلَٰكِنَّ أَكْثَرَهُمْ يَجْهَلُونَ ﴿١١١﴾
وَكَذَٰلِكَ جَعَلْنَا لِكُلِّ نَبِيٍّ عَدُوًّا شَيَاطِينَ الْإِنْسِ وَ
الْجِنِّ يُوحِي بَعْضُهُمْ إِلَىٰ بَعْضٍ زُخْرُفَ الْقَوْلِ غُرُورًا ۚ
وَلَوْ شَاءَ رَبُّكَ مَا فَعَلُوهُ ۖ فَذَرْهُمْ وَمَا يَفْتَرُونَ ﴿١١٢﴾
وَلِتَصْغَىٰ إِلَيْهِ أَفْئِدَةُ الَّذِينَ لَا يُؤْمِنُونَ بِالْآخِرَةِ
وَلِيَرْضَوْهُ وَلِيَقْتَرِفُوا مَا هُمْ مُقْتَرِفُونَ ﴿١١٣﴾
أَفَغَيْرَ اللَّهِ أَبْتَغِي حَكَمًا وَهُوَ الَّذِي أَنْزَلَ إِلَيْكُمُ الْكِتَابَ
مُفَصَّلًا ۚ وَالَّذِينَ آتَيْنَاهُمُ الْكِتَابَ يَعْلَمُونَ أَنَّهُ مُنَزَّلٌ
مِنْ رَبِّكَ بِالْحَقِّ ۖ فَلَا تَكُونَنَّ مِنَ الْمُمْتَرِينَ ﴿١١٤﴾

115. Perfected is the Word of thy Lord in truth and justice. There is naught that can change His words. He is the Hearer, the Knower.

وتمت كلمت ربك صدقا وعدلا لا مبدل
لكلمته وهو السميع العليم ﴿١١٥﴾

116. If thou obeyedst most of those on earth they would mislead thee far from Allah's way, They follow naught but an opinion, and they do but guess.

وان تطع اكثر من في الارض يضلوك عن
سبيل الله ان يتبعون الا الظن وان هم الا
يخرصون ﴿١١٦﴾

117. Lo! thy Lord, He knoweth best who erreth from His way; and He knoweth best (who are) the rightly guided.

ان ربك هو اعلم من يضل عن سبيله وهو
اعلم بالمهتدين ﴿١١٧﴾

118. Eat of that over which the name of Allah hath been mentioned, if ye are believers in His revelations.

فكلوا مما ذكر اسم الله عليه ان كنتم بايته
مؤمنين ﴿١١٨﴾

119. How should ye not eat of that over which the name of Allah hath been mentioned, when He hath explained unto you that which is forbidden unto you, unless ye are compelled thereto. But lo! many are led astray by their own lusts through ignorance. Lo! thy Lord, He is best aware of the transgressors.

وما لكم الا تاكلوا مما ذكر اسم الله عليه وقد
فصل لكم ما حرم عليكم الا ما اضطررتم اليه
وان كثيرا ليضلون باهوائهم بغير علم ان
ربك هو اعلم بالمعتدين ﴿١١٩﴾

120. Forsake the outwardness of sin and the inwardness thereof. Lo! those who garner sin will be awarded that which they have earned.

وذروا ظاهر الاثم وباطنه ان الذين يكسبون
الاثم سيجزون بما كانوا يقترفون ﴿١٢٠﴾

121. And eat not of that whereon Allah's name hath not been mentioned, for lo! it is abomination. Lo! the devils do inspire their minions to dispute with you. But if ye obey them, ye will be in truth idolaters.

ولا تاكلوا مما لم يذكر اسم الله عليه وانه لفسق
وان الشيطين ليوحون الى اوليئهم ليجادلوكم و
ان اطعتموهم انكم لمشركون ﴿١٢١﴾ ع

122. Is he who was dead and We have raised him unto life. and set for him a light wherein he walketh among men, as him whose similitude is in utter darkness whence he cannot emerge? Thus is their conduct made fair-seeming for the disbelievers.

او من كان ميتا فاحيينه وجعلنا له نورا
يمشي به في الناس كمن مثله في الظلمت ليس
بخارج منها كذلك زين للكفرين ما كانوا
يعملون ﴿١٢٢﴾

123. And thus have We made in every city great ones of its wicked ones, that they should plot therein. They do but plot against themselves, though they perceive not.

وَكَذٰلِكَ جَعَلْنَا فِي كُلِّ قَرْيَةٍ اَكٰبِرَ مُجْرِمِيْهَا لِيَمْكُرُوْا
فِيْهَا ۭ وَمَا يَمْكُرُوْنَ اِلَّا بِاَنْفُسِهِمْ وَمَا يَشْعُرُوْنَ ﴿١٢٣﴾

124. And when a token cometh unto them, they say: We will not believe till we are given that which Allah's messengers are given. Allah knoweth best with whom to place His message. Humiliation from Allah and heavy punishment will smite the guilty for their scheming.

وَاِذَا جَاۗءَتْهُمْ اٰيَةٌ قَالُوْا لَنْ نُّؤْمِنَ حَتّٰى نُؤْتٰى
مِثْلَ مَاۗ اُوْتِيَ رُسُلُ اللّٰهِ ۘ اَللّٰهُ اَعْلَمُ حَيْثُ يَجْعَلُ وقف لازم
رِسَالَتَهٗ ۭ سَيُصِيْبُ الَّذِيْنَ اَجْرَمُوْا صَغَارٌ عِنْدَ
اللّٰهِ وَعَذَابٌ شَدِيْدٌۢ بِمَا كَانُوْا يَمْكُرُوْنَ ﴿١٢٤﴾

125. And whomsoever it is Allah's will to guide, He expandeth his bosom unto the Surrender,[1] and whomsoever it is His will to send astray, He maketh his bosom close and narrow as if he were engaged in sheer ascent. Thus Allah layeth ignominy upon those who believe not.

فَمَنْ يُّرِدِ اللّٰهُ اَنْ يَّهْدِيَهٗ يَشْرَحْ صَدْرَهٗ لِلْاِسْلَامِ ۚ
وَمَنْ يُّرِدْ اَنْ يُّضِلَّهٗ يَجْعَلْ صَدْرَهٗ ضَيِّقًا حَرَجًا
كَاَنَّمَا يَصَّعَّدُ فِي السَّمَاۗءِ ۭ كَذٰلِكَ يَجْعَلُ اللّٰهُ الرِّجْسَ
عَلَى الَّذِيْنَ لَا يُؤْمِنُوْنَ ﴿١٢٥﴾

126. This is the path of thy Lord, a Straight path. We have detailed Our revelations for a people who take heed.

وَهٰذَا صِرَاطُ رَبِّكَ مُسْتَقِيْمًا ۭ قَدْ فَصَّلْنَا الْاٰيٰتِ
لِقَوْمٍ يَّذَّكَّرُوْنَ ﴿١٢٦﴾

127. For them is the abode of Peac- with their Lord. He will be their Protece ting Friend because of what they used to do.

لَهُمْ دَارُ السَّلٰمِ عِنْدَ رَبِّهِمْ وَهُوَ وَلِيُّهُمْ بِمَا كَانُوْا
يَعْمَلُوْنَ ﴿١٢٧﴾

128. In the day when He will gather them together (He will say): O ye assembly of the jinn! Many of humankind did ye seduce. And their adherents among humankind will say: Our Lord! We enjoyed one another, but now we have arrived at the appointed term which Thou appointedst for us. He will say: Fire is your home. Abide therein for ever, save him whom Allah willeth (to deliver). Lo! thy Lord is Wise, Aware.

وَيَوْمَ يَحْشُرُهُمْ جَمِيْعًا ۚ يٰمَعْشَرَ الْجِنِّ قَدِ
اسْتَكْثَرْتُمْ مِّنَ الْاِنْسِ ۚ وَقَالَ اَوْلِيٰۗؤُهُمْ مِّنَ
الْاِنْسِ رَبَّنَا اسْتَمْتَعَ بَعْضُنَا بِبَعْضٍ وَّبَلَغْنَاۗ
اَجَلَنَا الَّذِيْٓ اَجَّلْتَ لَنَا ۭ قَالَ النَّارُ مَثْوٰىكُمْ
خٰلِدِيْنَ فِيْهَاۗ اِلَّا مَا شَاۗءَ اللّٰهُ ۭ اِنَّ رَبَّكَ حَكِيْمٌ
عَلِيْمٌ ﴿١٢٨﴾

129. Thus We let some of the wrong-doers have power over others because of what they are wont to earn.

وَكَذٰلِكَ نُوَلِّيْ بَعْضَ الظّٰلِمِيْنَ بَعْضًۢا بِمَا كَانُوْا
يَكْسِبُوْنَ ﴿١٢٩﴾ ع ١٥ ٢

1. Al-Islam.

130. O ye assembly of the jinn and humankind! Came there not unto you messengers of your own who recounted unto you My tokens and warned you of the meeting of this your Day? They will say: We testify against ourselves. And the life of the world beguiled them. And they testify against themselves that they were disbelievers.

يمعشر الجن والانس الم ياتكم رسل منكم
يقصون عليكم ايتي وينذرونكم لقاء يومكم هذا
قالوا شهدنا على انفسنا وغرتهم الحيوة الدنيا
وشهدوا على انفسهم انهم كانوا كفرين ١٣٠

131. This is because thy Lord destroyeth not the townships arbitrarily while their people are unconscious (of the wrong they do).

ذلك ان لم يكن ربك مهلك القرى بظلم و
اهلها غفلون ١٣١

132. For all there will be ranks from what they did. Thy Lord is not unaware of what they do.

ولكل درجت مما عملوا وما ربك بغافل
عما يعملون ١٣٢

133. Thy Lord is the Absolute, the Lord of Mercy. If He will, He can remove you and can cause what He will to follow after you, even as He raised you from the seed of other folk.

وربك الغني ذو الرحمة ان يشا يذهبكم
ويستخلف من بعدكم ما يشاء كما انشاكم
من ذرية قوم اخرين ١٣٣

134. Lo! that which ye are promised will surely come to pass, and ye cannot escape.

ان ما توعدون لات وما انتم بمعجزين ١٣٤

135. Say (O Muhammad): O my people! Work according to your power. Lo! I too am working. Thus ye will come to know for which of us will be the happy sequel. Lo! the wrongdoers will not be successful.

قل يقوم اعملوا على مكانتكم اني عامل فسوف
تعلمون من تكون له عاقبة الدار انه لا
يفلح الظلمون ١٣٥

136. They assign unto Allah, of the crops and cattle which He created, a portion, and they say: "This is Allah's" —in their make-believe—"and this is for (His) partners in regard to us." Thus that which (they assign) unto His partners in them reacheth not Allah and that which (they assign) unto Allah goeth to their (so-called) partners. Evil is their ordinance.

وجعلوا لله مما ذرا من الحرث والانعام نصيبا
فقالوا هذا لله بزعمهم وهذا لشركائنا فما كان
لشركائهم فلا يصل الى الله وما كان لله فهو
يصل الى شركائهم ساء ما يحكمون ١٣٦

137. Thus have their (so-called) partners (of Allah) made the killing of their children to seem fair unto many of the idolaters, that they may ruin them and make their faith obscure for them. Had Allah willed (it otherwise), they had not done so. So leave them alone with their devices.

وكذلك زين لكثير من المشركين قتل اولادهم
شركاؤهم ليردوهم وليلبسوا عليهم دينهم و
لو شاء الله ما فعلوه فذرهم وما يفترون ١٣٧

138. And they say: Such cattle and crops are forbidden. No one is to eat of them save whom We will—in their make-believe—cattle whose backs are forbidden, cattle over which they mention not the name of Allah. (All that is) a lie against Him. He will repay them for that which they invent.

وقالوا هذه انعام وحرث حجر لا يطعمها الا
من نشاء بزعمهم وانعام حرمت ظهورها وانعام
لا يذكرون اسم الله عليها افتراء عليه سيجزيهم
بما كانوا يفترون ١٣٨

139. And they say: That which is in the bellies of such cattle is reserved for our males and is forbidden to our wives; but if it be born dead, then they (all) may be partakers thereof. He will reward them for their attribution (of such ordinances unto Him).[1] Lo, He is Wise, Aware.

وقالوا ما في بطون هذه الانعام خالصة لذكورنا
ومحرم على ازواجنا وان يكن ميتة فهم فيه
شركاء سيجزيهم وصفهم انه حكيم عليم ١٣٩

140. They are losers who besottedly have slain their children without knowledge,[2] and have forbidden that which Allah bestowed upon them, inventing a lie against Allah. They indeed have gone astray and are not guided.

قد خسر الذين قتلوا اولادهم سفها بغير علم
وحرموا ما رزقهم الله افتراء على الله قد ضلوا
وما كانوا مهتدين ١٤٠ ع

141. He it is Who produceth gardens trellised and untrellised, and the date-palm, and crops of divers flavour, and the olive and the pomegranate, like and unlike. Eat ye of the fruit thereof when it fruiteth, and pay the due thereof upon the harvest day, and be not prodigal. Lo! Allah loveth not the prodigals:

وهو الذي انشا جنت معروشت وغير معروشت
والنخل والزرع مختلفا اكله والزيتون والرمان
متشابها وغير متشابه كلوا من ثمره اذا اثمر
واتوا حقه يوم حصاده ولا تسرفوا انه لا يحب
المسرفين ١٤١

142. And of the cattle (He produceth) some for burdens, some for food. Eat of that which Allah hath bestowed upon you, and follow not the footsteps of the devil, for lo! he is an open foe to you.

ومن الانعام حمولة وفرشا كلوا مما رزقكم
الله ولا تتبعوا خطوت الشيطن انه لكم عدو
مبين ١٤٢

143. Eight pairs: Of the sheep twain, and of the goats twain. Say: Hath He forbidden the two males or the two females, or that which the wombs of the two females contain? Expound to me (the case) with knowledge, if ye are truthful:[3]

ثمنية ازواج من الضان اثنين ومن المعز
اثنين قل ءالذكرين حرم ام الانثيين اما
اشتملت عليه ارحام الانثيين نبئوني بعلم
ان كنتم صدقين ١٤٣

1. vv. 138 and 139 refer to customs of the pagan Arabs.
2. The reference is to the burial alive of female children who were deemed superfluous, and the practice of human sacrifice to idols.
3. This and the following verses relate to superstitions of the pagan Arabs with regard to cattle used for food.

144. And of the camels twain and of the oxen twain. Say: Hath He forbidden the two males or the two females, or that which the wombs of the two females contain; or were ye by to witness when Allah commanded you (all) this? Then who doth greater wrong than he who deviseth a lie concerning Allah, that he may lead mankind astray without knowledge. Lo! Allah guideth not wrongdoing folk.

145. Say: I find not in that which is revealed unto me aught prohibited to an eater that he eat thereof except it be carrion, or blood poured forth, or swineflesh—for that verily is foul or the abomination which was immolated to the name of other than Allah. But who so is compelled (thereto), neither craving nor transgressing, (for him) lo! your Lord is Forgiving, Merciful.

146. Unto those who are Jews We forbade every animal with claws. And of the oxen and the sheep forbade We unto them the fat thereof save that upon the backs or the entrails, or that which is mixed with the bone. That We awarded them for their rebellion. And lo! We verily are Truthful.

147. So if they give the lie to thee (Muhammad), say, Your Lord is a Lord of all-embracing mercy, and His wrath will never be withdrawn from guilty folk.

148. They who are idolaters will say: Had Allah willed, we had not ascribed (unto Him) partners neither had our fathers, nor had we forbidden aught. Thus did those who were before them give the lie (to Allah's messengers) till they tasted of the fear of Us. Say: Have ye any knowledge that ye can adduce for us? Lo! ye follow naught but an opinion, Lo! ye do but guess.

149. Say—For Allah's is the final argument—Had He willed He could indeed have guided all of you.

وَمِنَ الْإِبِلِ اثْنَيْنِ وَمِنَ الْبَقَرِ اثْنَيْنِ ۗ قُلْ
آٰلذَّكَرَيْنِ حَرَّمَ أَمِ الْأُنْثَيَيْنِ أَمَّا اشْتَمَلَتْ عَلَيْهِ أَرْحَامُ
الْأُنْثَيَيْنِ ۖ أَمْ كُنْتُمْ شُهَدَاءَ إِذْ وَصَّاكُمُ اللَّهُ بِهَٰذَا ۚ
فَمَنْ أَظْلَمُ مِمَّنِ افْتَرَىٰ عَلَى اللَّهِ كَذِبًا لِيُضِلَّ
ع ١٧ النَّاسَ بِغَيْرِ عِلْمٍ ۗ إِنَّ اللَّهَ لَا يَهْدِي الْقَوْمَ الظَّالِمِينَ ﴿١٤٤﴾
قُلْ لَا أَجِدُ فِي مَا أُوحِيَ إِلَيَّ مُحَرَّمًا عَلَىٰ طَاعِمٍ يَطْعَمُهُ
إِلَّا أَنْ يَكُونَ مَيْتَةً أَوْ دَمًا مَسْفُوحًا أَوْ لَحْمَ خِنْزِيرٍ
فَإِنَّهُ رِجْسٌ أَوْ فِسْقًا أُهِلَّ لِغَيْرِ اللَّهِ بِهِ ۚ فَمَنِ اضْطُرَّ
غَيْرَ بَاغٍ وَلَا عَادٍ فَإِنَّ رَبَّكَ غَفُورٌ رَحِيمٌ ﴿١٤٥﴾
وَعَلَى الَّذِينَ هَادُوا حَرَّمْنَا كُلَّ ذِي ظُفُرٍ ۖ وَمِنَ الْبَقَرِ
وَالْغَنَمِ حَرَّمْنَا عَلَيْهِمْ شُحُومَهُمَا إِلَّا مَا حَمَلَتْ
ظُهُورُهُمَا أَوِ الْحَوَايَا أَوْ مَا اخْتَلَطَ بِعَظْمٍ ۚ ذَٰلِكَ
جَزَيْنَاهُمْ بِبَغْيِهِمْ ۖ وَإِنَّا لَصَادِقُونَ ﴿١٤٦﴾
فَإِنْ كَذَّبُوكَ فَقُلْ رَبُّكُمْ ذُو رَحْمَةٍ وَاسِعَةٍ ۚ وَلَا
يُرَدُّ بَأْسُهُ عَنِ الْقَوْمِ الْمُجْرِمِينَ ﴿١٤٧﴾
سَيَقُولُ الَّذِينَ أَشْرَكُوا لَوْ شَاءَ اللَّهُ مَا أَشْرَكْنَا وَلَا
آبَاؤُنَا وَلَا حَرَّمْنَا مِنْ شَيْءٍ ۚ كَذَٰلِكَ كَذَّبَ الَّذِينَ
مِنْ قَبْلِهِمْ حَتَّىٰ ذَاقُوا بَأْسَنَا ۗ قُلْ هَلْ عِنْدَكُمْ
مِنْ عِلْمٍ فَتُخْرِجُوهُ لَنَا ۖ إِنْ تَتَّبِعُونَ إِلَّا الظَّنَّ وَ
إِنْ أَنْتُمْ إِلَّا تَخْرُصُونَ ﴿١٤٨﴾
قُلْ فَلِلَّهِ الْحُجَّةُ الْبَالِغَةُ ۖ فَلَوْ شَاءَ لَهَدَاكُمْ
أَجْمَعِينَ ﴿١٤٩﴾

150. Say: Come, bring your witnesses who can bear witness that Allah forbade (all) this. And, if they bear witness, do not thou bear witness with them. Follow thou not the whims of those who deny Our revelations, those who believe not in the Hereafter and deem (others) equal with their Lord.

قُلْ هَلُمَّ شُهَدَآءَكُمُ الَّذِيْنَ يَشْهَدُوْنَ اَنَّ اللّٰهَ
حَرَّمَ هٰذَا ۚ فَاِنْ شَهِدُوْا فَلَا تَشْهَدْ مَعَهُمْ ۚ
وَلَا تَتَّبِعْ اَهْوَآءَ الَّذِيْنَ كَذَّبُوْا بِاٰيٰتِنَا
وَالَّذِيْنَ لَا يُؤْمِنُوْنَ بِالْاٰخِرَةِ وَهُمْ بِرَبِّهِمْ
يَعْدِلُوْنَ ﴿١٥٠﴾

151. Say: Come, I will recite unto you that which your Lord hath made a sacred duty for you: that ye ascribe nothing as partner unto Him and that ye do good to parents, and that ye slay not your children because of penury—We provide for you and for them—and that ye draw not nigh to lewd things whether open or concealed. And that ye slay not the life which Allah hath made sacred, save in the course of justice. This He hath commanded you, in order that ye may discern.

قُلْ تَعَالَوْا اَتْلُ مَا حَرَّمَ رَبُّكُمْ عَلَيْكُمْ اَلَّا تُشْرِكُوْا
بِهٖ شَيْـًٔا وَّبِالْوَالِدَيْنِ اِحْسَانًا ۚ وَلَا تَقْتُلُوْا اَوْلَادَكُمْ
مِّنْ اِمْلَاقٍ ؕ نَحْنُ نَرْزُقُكُمْ وَاِيَّاهُمْ ۚ وَلَا تَقْرَبُوا
الْفَوَاحِشَ مَا ظَهَرَ مِنْهَا وَمَا بَطَنَ ۚ وَلَا تَقْتُلُوا
النَّفْسَ الَّتِيْ حَرَّمَ اللّٰهُ اِلَّا بِالْحَقِّ ؕ ذٰلِكُمْ
وَصّٰىكُمْ بِهٖ لَعَلَّكُمْ تَعْقِلُوْنَ ﴿١٥١﴾

152. And approach not the wealth of the orphan save with that which is better, till he reach maturity. Give full measure and full weight, in justice. We task not any soul beyond its scope. And if ye give your word, do justice thereunto, even though it be (against) a kinsman; and fulfil the covenant of Allah. This He commandeth you that haply ye may remember.

وَلَا تَقْرَبُوْا مَالَ الْيَتِيْمِ اِلَّا بِالَّتِيْ هِيَ اَحْسَنُ حَتّٰى
يَبْلُغَ اَشُدَّهٗ ۚ وَاَوْفُوا الْكَيْلَ وَالْمِيْزَانَ بِالْقِسْطِ ۚ لَا
نُكَلِّفُ نَفْسًا اِلَّا وُسْعَهَا ۚ وَاِذَا قُلْتُمْ فَاعْدِلُوْا وَلَوْ
كَانَ ذَا قُرْبٰى ۚ وَبِعَهْدِ اللّٰهِ اَوْفُوْا ؕ ذٰلِكُمْ وَصّٰىكُمْ
بِهٖ لَعَلَّكُمْ تَذَكَّرُوْنَ ﴿١٥٢﴾

153. And (He commandeth you, saying): This is My Straight path, so follow it. Follow not other ways, lest ye be parted from His way. This hath He ordained for you, that ye may ward off (evil).

وَاَنَّ هٰذَا صِرَاطِيْ مُسْتَقِيْمًا فَاتَّبِعُوْهُ ۚ وَلَا تَتَّبِعُوا
السُّبُلَ فَتَفَرَّقَ بِكُمْ عَنْ سَبِيْلِهٖ ؕ ذٰلِكُمْ وَصّٰىكُمْ بِهٖ
لَعَلَّكُمْ تَتَّقُوْنَ ﴿١٥٣﴾

154. Again, We gave the Scripture unto Moses, complete for him who would do good, an explanation of all things, a guidance and a mercy, that they might believe in the meeting with their Lord.

ثُمَّ اٰتَيْنَا مُوْسَى الْكِتٰبَ تَمَامًا عَلَى الَّذِيْۤ اَحْسَنَ
وَتَفْصِيْلًا لِّكُلِّ شَيْءٍ وَّهُدًى وَّرَحْمَةً لَّعَلَّهُمْ
بِلِقَآءِ رَبِّهِمْ يُؤْمِنُوْنَ ﴿١٥٤﴾

155. And this is a blessed Scripture which We have revealed. So follow it and ward off (evil), that ye may find mercy.

156. Lest ye should say: The Scripture was revealed only to two sects before us, and we in sooth were unaware of what they read;

157. Or lest ye should say: If the Scripture had been revealed unto us, we surely had been better guided than are they. Now hath there come unto you a clear proof from your Lord, a guidance and a mercy; and who doeth greater wrong than he who denieth the revelations of Allah and turneth away from them? We award unto those who turn away from Our revelations an evil doom because of their aversion.

158. Wait they, indeed, for nothing less than that the angels should come unto them, or thy Lord should come, or there should come one of the portents from thy Lord? In the day when one of the portents from thy Lord cometh, its belief availeth naught a soul which theretofore believed not, nor in its belief earned good (by works). Say: Wait ye! Lo! We (too) are waiting.

159. Lo! As for those who sunder their religion and become schismatics, no concern at all hast thou with them. Their case will go to Allah, who then will tell them what they used to do.

160. Whoso bringeth a good deed will receive tenfold the like thereof, while whoso bringeth an ill deed will be awarded but the like thereof; and they will not be wronged.

161. Say: Lo! As for me, my Lord hath guided me unto a straight path, a right religion, the community of Abraham, the upright, who was no idolater.

وَهٰذَا كِتٰبٌ اَنْزَلْنٰهُ مُبٰرَكٌ فَاتَّبِعُوْهُ وَاتَّقُوْا
لَعَلَّكُمْ تُرْحَمُوْنَ ﴿١٥٥﴾
اَنْ تَقُوْلُوْٓا اِنَّمَآ اُنْزِلَ الْكِتٰبُ عَلٰى
طَآئِفَتَيْنِ مِنْ قَبْلِنَا وَاِنْ كُنَّا عَنْ دِرَاسَتِهِمْ
لَغٰفِلِيْنَ ﴿١٥٦﴾
اَوْ تَقُوْلُوْا لَوْ اَنَّآ اُنْزِلَ عَلَيْنَا الْكِتٰبُ لَكُنَّآ اَهْدٰى
مِنْهُمْ فَقَدْ جَآءَكُمْ بَيِّنَةٌ مِّنْ رَّبِّكُمْ وَهُدًى وَّ
رَحْمَةٌ فَمَنْ اَظْلَمُ مِمَّنْ كَذَّبَ بِاٰيٰتِ اللّٰهِ وَصَدَفَ
عَنْهَا سَنَجْزِى الَّذِيْنَ يَصْدِفُوْنَ عَنْ اٰيٰتِنَا سُوْٓءَ
الْعَذَابِ بِمَا كَانُوْا يَصْدِفُوْنَ ﴿١٥٧﴾
هَلْ يَنْظُرُوْنَ اِلَّآ اَنْ تَاْتِيَهُمُ الْمَلٰٓئِكَةُ اَوْ يَاْتِىَ
رَبُّكَ اَوْ يَاْتِىَ بَعْضُ اٰيٰتِ رَبِّكَ يَوْمَ يَاْتِىْ بَعْضُ
اٰيٰتِ رَبِّكَ لَا يَنْفَعُ نَفْسًا اِيْمَانُهَا لَمْ تَكُنْ اٰمَنَتْ
مِنْ قَبْلُ اَوْ كَسَبَتْ فِىْٓ اِيْمَانِهَا خَيْرًا قُلِ انْتَظِرُوْٓا
اِنَّا مُنْتَظِرُوْنَ ﴿١٥٨﴾
اِنَّ الَّذِيْنَ فَرَّقُوْا دِيْنَهُمْ وَكَانُوْا شِيَعًا لَّسْتَ مِنْهُمْ
فِىْ شَىْءٍ اِنَّمَآ اَمْرُهُمْ اِلَى اللّٰهِ ثُمَّ يُنَبِّئُهُمْ بِمَا
كَانُوْا يَفْعَلُوْنَ ﴿١٥٩﴾
مَنْ جَآءَ بِالْحَسَنَةِ فَلَهٗ عَشْرُ اَمْثَالِهَا وَمَنْ جَآءَ
بِالسَّيِّئَةِ فَلَا يُجْزٰٓى اِلَّا مِثْلَهَا وَهُمْ لَا يُظْلَمُوْنَ ﴿١٦٠﴾
قُلْ اِنَّنِىْ هَدٰىنِىْ رَبِّىْٓ اِلٰى صِرَاطٍ مُّسْتَقِيْمٍ دِيْنًا
قِيَمًا مِّلَّةَ اِبْرٰهِيْمَ حَنِيْفًا وَمَا كَانَ مِنَ الْمُشْرِكِيْنَ ﴿١٦١﴾

162. Say: Lo! my worship and my sacrifice and my living and my dying are for Allah, Lord of the Worlds.

قُلْ إِنَّ صَلَاتِي وَنُسُكِي وَمَحْيَايَ وَمَمَاتِي لِلّٰهِ
رَبِّ الْعٰلَمِيْنَ ﴿١٦٢﴾

163. He hath no partner. This am I commanded, and I am first of those who surrender (unto Him).

لَا شَرِيْكَ لَهٗ ۚ وَبِذٰلِكَ أُمِرْتُ وَأَنَا أَوَّلُ
الْمُسْلِمِيْنَ ﴿١٦٣﴾

164. Say: Shall I seek another than Allah for Lord, when He is Lord of all things? Each soul earneth only on its own account, nor doth any laden bear another's load. Then unto your Lord is your return and He will tell you that wherein ye differed.

قُلْ أَغَيْرَ اللّٰهِ أَبْغِيْ رَبًّا وَّهُوَ رَبُّ كُلِّ شَيْءٍ ۚ وَلَا
تَكْسِبُ كُلُّ نَفْسٍ إِلَّا عَلَيْهَا ۚ وَلَا تَزِرُ وَازِرَةٌ وِّزْرَ
أُخْرٰى ۚ ثُمَّ إِلٰى رَبِّكُمْ مَّرْجِعُكُمْ فَيُنَبِّئُكُمْ بِمَا
كُنْتُمْ فِيْهِ تَخْتَلِفُوْنَ ﴿١٦٤﴾

165. He it is who hath placed you as viceroys of the earth and hath exalted some of you in rank above others, that He may try you by (the test of) that which He hath given you. Lo! Thy Lord is swift in prosecution, and lo! He is Forgiving, Merciful.

وَهُوَ الَّذِيْ جَعَلَكُمْ خَلٰٓئِفَ الْأَرْضِ وَرَفَعَ
بَعْضَكُمْ فَوْقَ بَعْضٍ دَرَجٰتٍ لِّيَبْلُوَكُمْ فِيْ مَآ
اٰتٰىكُمْ ۗ إِنَّ رَبَّكَ سَرِيْعُ الْعِقَابِ ۖ وَإِنَّهٗ لَغَفُوْرٌ
رَّحِيْمٌ ﴿١٦٥﴾

Al-A'rāf, "The Heights," takes its name from a word in v. 46, "And on the Heights are men who know them all, by their marks." The best authorities assign the whole of it to about the same period as Sūrah VI, *i.e.* the Prophet's last year in Mecca, though some consider vv. 163-167 to have been revealed at Al-Madînah. The subject may be said to be the opponents of God's will and purpose, from Satan onward, through the history of Divine Guidance.

A late Meccan Sūrah.

THE HEIGHTS

Revealed at Mecca

اياتها ٢٠٦ (٧) سورة الاعراف مكية (٣٩) ركوعاتها ٢٤

In the name of Allah, the Beneficent, the Merciful.

بسم الله الرحمن الرحيم

1. Alif. Lām. Mīm. Sād.[1]

المص ١

2. (It is) a Scripture that is revealed unto thee (Muhammad)—so let there be no heaviness in thy heart therefrom—that thou mayest warn thereby, and (it is) a Reminder unto believers!

كتب انزل اليك فلا يكن في صدرك حرج منه
لتنذر به وذكرى للمؤمنين ٢

3. (Saying): Follow that which is sent down unto you from your Lord, and follow no protecting friends beside Him. Little do ye recollect!

اتبعوا ما انزل اليكم من ربكم ولا تتبعوا من
دونه اولياء قليلا ما تذكرون ٣

4. How many a township have We destroyed! As a raid by night, or while, they slept at noon. Our terror came unto them.

وكم من قرية اهلكنها فجاءها باسنا بياتا او
هم قائلون ٤

5. No plea had they, when Our terror came unto them, save that they said: Lo! We were wrong-doers.

فما كان دعوىهم اذ جاءهم باسنا الا ان قالوا
انا كنا ظلمين ٥

6. Then verily We shall question those unto whom (Our message) hath been sent, and verily We shall question the messengers.

فلنسئلن الذين ارسل اليهم ولنسئلن المرسلين ٦

7. Then verily We shall narrate unto them (the event) with knowledge, for verily We were not absent (when it came to pass).

فلنقصن عليهم بعلم وما كنا غائبين ٧

8. The weighing on that day is the true (weighing). As for those whose scale is heavy, they are the successful.

والوزن يومئذ الحق فمن ثقلت موازينه
فاولئك هم المفلحون ٨

9. And as for those whose scale is light: those are they who lose their souls because they disbelieved Our revelations.

ومن خفت موازينه فاولئك الذين خسروا
انفسهم بما كانوا باياتنا يظلمون ٩

10. And We have given you (mankind) power in the earth, and appointed for you therein a livelihood. Little give ye thanks!

ولقد مكنكم في الارض وجعلنا لكم فيها
ع معايش قليلا ما تشكرون ١٠

11. And We created you, then fashioned you, then told the angels: Fall ye prostrate before Adam! And they fell prostrate, all save Iblīs, who was not of those who make prostration.

ولقد خلقنكم ثم صورنكم ثم قلنا للملئكة اسجدوا
لادم فسجدوا الا ابليس لم يكن من السجدين ١١

1. See Sūr. II, v. 1, footnote.

12. He said: What hindered thee that thou didst not fall prostrate when I bade thee? (Iblîs) said: I am better than him. Thou createdst me of fire while him Thou didst create of mud.

13. He said: Then go down hence! It is not for thee to show pride here, so go forth! Lo! thou art of those degraded.

14. He said: Reprieve me till the day when they are raised (from the dead).

15. He said: Lo! thou art of those reprieved.

16. He said: Now, because Thou hast sent me astray, verily I shall lurk in ambush for them on Thy Right Path.

17. Then I shall come upon them from before them and from behind them and from their right hands and from their left hands, and Thou wilt not find most of them beholden (unto Thee).

18. He said: Go forth from hence, degraded, banished. As for such of them as follow thee, surely I will fill hell with all of you.

19. And (unto man): O Adam! Dwell thou and thy wife in the Garden and eat from whence ye will, but come not nigh this tree lest ye become wrong-doers.

20. Then Satan whispered to them that he might manifest unto them that which was hidden from them of their shame, and he said: Your Lord forbade you from this tree only lest ye should become angels or become of the immortals.

21. And he swore unto them (saying): Lo! I am a sincere adviser unto you.

قال ما منعك الا تسجد اذ امرتك قال
انا خير منه خلقتني من نار وخلقته
من طين ﴿١٢﴾
قال فاهبط منها فما يكون لك ان تتكبر فيها
فاخرج انك من الصغرين ﴿١٣﴾
قال انظرني الى يوم يبعثون ﴿١٤﴾
قال انك من المنظرين ﴿١٥﴾
قال فبما اغويتني لاقعدن لهم صراطك
المستقيم ﴿١٦﴾
ثم لاتينهم من بين ايديهم ومن خلفهم
وعن ايمانهم وعن شمائلهم ولا تجد اكثرهم
شكرين ﴿١٧﴾
قال اخرج منها مذءوما مدحورا لمن تبعك
منهم لاملئن جهنم منكم اجمعين ﴿١٨﴾
ويادم اسكن انت وزوجك الجنة فكلا من
حيث شئتما ولا تقربا هذه الشجرة فتكونا
من الظلمين ﴿١٩﴾
فوسوس لهما الشيطن ليبدي لهما ما وري
عنهما من سوءتهما وقال ما نهكما ربكما عن
هذه الشجرة الا ان تكونا ملكين او تكونا من
الخلدين ﴿٢٠﴾
وقاسمهما اني لكما لمن النصحين ﴿٢١﴾

22. Thus did he lead them on with guile. And when they tasted of the tree their shame was manifest to them and they began to hide (by heaping) on themselves some of the leaves of the Garden. And their Lord called them, (saying): Did I not forbid you from that tree and tell you: Lo! Satan is an open enemy to you?

23. They said: Our Lord! We have wronged ourselves. If Thou forgive us not and have not mercy on us, surely we are of the lost!

24. He said: Go down (from hence), one of you a foe unto the other. There will be for you on earth a habitation and provision for a while.

25. He said: There shall ye live, and there shall ye die, and thence shall ye be brought forth.

26. O Children of Adam! We have revealed unto you raiment to conceal your shame, and splendid vesture, but the raiment of restraint from evil, that is best. This is of the revelations of Allah, that they may remember.

27. O Children of Adam! Let not Satan seduce you as he caused your (first) parents to go forth from the Garden and tore off from them their robe (of innocence) that he might manifest their shame to them. Lo! he seeth you, he and his tribe, from whence ye see him not. Lo! We have made the devils protecting friends for those who believe not.

28. And when they do some lewdness they say: We found our fathers doing it and Allah hath enjoined it on us, say: Allah, verily, enjoineth not lewdness. Tell ye concerning Allah that which ye know not?

فَدَلّٰىهُمَا بِغُرُوْرٍ ۚ فَلَمَّا ذَاقَا الشَّجَرَةَ بَدَتْ لَهُمَا
سَوْاٰتُهُمَا وَطَفِقَا يَخْصِفٰنِ عَلَيْهِمَا مِنْ وَّرَقِ
الْجَنَّةِ ۖ وَنَادٰىهُمَا رَبُّهُمَآ اَلَمْ اَنْهَكُمَا عَنْ تِلْكُمَا
الشَّجَرَةِ وَاَقُلْ لَّكُمَآ اِنَّ الشَّيْطٰنَ لَكُمَا عَدُوٌّ
مُّبِيْنٌ ﴿٢٢﴾

قَالَا رَبَّنَا ظَلَمْنَآ اَنْفُسَنَا ۫ وَاِنْ لَّمْ تَغْفِرْ لَنَا وَ
تَرْحَمْنَا لَنَكُوْنَنَّ مِنَ الْخٰسِرِيْنَ ﴿٢٣﴾

قَالَ اهْبِطُوْا بَعْضُكُمْ لِبَعْضٍ عَدُوٌّ ۚ وَلَكُمْ فِي
الْاَرْضِ مُسْتَقَرٌّ وَّمَتَاعٌ اِلٰى حِيْنٍ ﴿٢٤﴾

قَالَ فِيْهَا تَحْيَوْنَ وَفِيْهَا تَمُوْتُوْنَ وَمِنْهَا
ع تُخْرَجُوْنَ ﴿٢٥﴾

يٰبَنِيْٓ اٰدَمَ قَدْ اَنْزَلْنَا عَلَيْكُمْ لِبَاسًا يُّوَارِيْ سَوْاٰتِكُمْ
وَرِيْشًا ۗ وَلِبَاسُ التَّقْوٰى ۙ ذٰلِكَ خَيْرٌ ۗ ذٰلِكَ مِنْ
اٰيٰتِ اللّٰهِ لَعَلَّهُمْ يَذَّكَّرُوْنَ ﴿٢٦﴾

يٰبَنِيْٓ اٰدَمَ لَا يَفْتِنَنَّكُمُ الشَّيْطٰنُ كَمَآ اَخْرَجَ اَبَوَيْكُمْ
مِّنَ الْجَنَّةِ يَنْزِعُ عَنْهُمَا لِبَاسَهُمَا لِيُرِيَهُمَا
سَوْاٰتِهِمَا ۗ اِنَّهٗ يَرٰىكُمْ هُوَ وَقَبِيْلُهٗ مِنْ حَيْثُ لَا
تَرَوْنَهُمْ ۗ اِنَّا جَعَلْنَا الشَّيٰطِيْنَ اَوْلِيَآءَ لِلَّذِيْنَ لَا
يُؤْمِنُوْنَ ﴿٢٧﴾

وَاِذَا فَعَلُوْا فَاحِشَةً قَالُوْا وَجَدْنَا عَلَيْهَآ اٰبَآءَنَا
وَاللّٰهُ اَمَرَنَا بِهَا ۗ قُلْ اِنَّ اللّٰهَ لَا يَاْمُرُ بِالْفَحْشَآءِ ۗ
اَتَقُوْلُوْنَ عَلَى اللّٰهِ مَا لَا تَعْلَمُوْنَ ﴿٢٨﴾

29. Say: My Lord enjoineth justice. And set your faces, upright (toward Him) at every place of worship and call upon Him, making religion pure for Him (only). As He brought you into being, so return ye (unto Him).

قل امر ربي بالقسط واقيموا وجوهكم عند كل
مسجد وادعوه مخلصين له الدين كما بداكم
تعودون ٢٩

30. A party hath He led aright, while error hath just hold over (another) party, for lo! they choose the devils for protecting friends instead of Allah and deem that they are rightly guided.

فريقا هدى وفريقا حق عليهم الضللة انهم
اتخذوا الشيطين اولياء من دون الله ويحسبون
انهم مهتدون ٣٠

31. O Children of Adam! Look to your adornment at every place of worship, and eat and drink, but be not prodigal. Lo! He loveth not the prodigals.

يبني ادم خذوا زينتكم عند كل مسجد وكلوا
واشربوا ولا تسرفوا انه لا يحب المسرفين ٣١

32. Say: Who hath forbidden the adornment of Allah which He hath brought forth for His bondmen, and the good things of His providing? Say: Such, on the Day of Resurrection, will be only for those who believed during the life of the world. Thus do We detail Our revelations for people who have knowledge.

قل من حرم زينة الله التي اخرج لعباده
والطيبت من الرزق قل هي للذين امنوا في
الحيوة الدنيا خالصة يوم القيمة كذلك نفصل
الايت لقوم يعلمون ٣٢

33. Say: My Lord forbiddeth only indecencies, such of them as are apparent and such as are within, and sin and wrongful oppression, and that ye associate with Allah that for which no warrant hath been revealed, and that ye tell concerning Allah that which ye know not.

قل انما حرم ربي الفواحش ما ظهر منها وما بطن
والاثم والبغي بغير الحق وان تشركوا بالله ما لم
ينزل به سلطنا وان تقولوا على الله ما لا تعلمون ٣٣

34. And every nation hath its term, and when its term cometh, they cannot put it off an hour nor yet advance (it).

ولكل امة اجل فاذا جاء اجلهم لا يستاخرون
ساعة ولا يستقدمون ٣٤

35. O Children of Adam! If messengers of your own come unto you who narrate unto you My revelations, then whosoever refraineth from evil and amendeth—there shall no fear come upon them neither shall they grieve.

يبني ادم اما ياتينكم رسل منكم يقصون عليكم
ايتي فمن اتقى واصلح فلا خوف عليهم ولا
هم يحزنون ٣٥

36. But they who deny Our revelations and scorn them—such are rightful owners of the Fire; they will abide therein.

والذين كذبوا بايتنا واستكبروا عنها اولئك
اصحب النار هم فيها خلدون ٣٦

37. Who doth greater wrong than he who inventeth a lie concerning Allah or denieth Our tokens. (For such) their appointed portion of the Book (of destiny) reacheth them till, when Our messengers[1] come to gather them, they say: Where (now) is that to which ye cried beside Allah? They say: They have departed from us. And they testify against themselves that they were disbelievers.

38. He saith: Enter into the Fire among nations of the jinn and humankind who passed away before you. Every time a nation entereth, it curseth its sister (nation) till, when they have all been made to follow one another thither, the last of them saith unto the first of them: Our Lord! These led us astray, so give them double torment of the Fire. He saith: For each one there is double (torment), but ye know not.

39. And the first of them saith unto the last of them: Ye were no whit better than us, so taste the doom for what ye used to earn.

40. Lo! they who deny Our revelations and scorn them, for them the gates of Heaven will not be opened nor will they enter the Garden until the camel goeth through the needle's eye. Thus do We requite the guilty.

41. Theirs will be a bed of Hell, and over them coverings (of Hell). Thus do We requite wrong-doers.

42. But (as for) those who believe and do good works—We tax not any soul beyond its scope—Such are rightful owners of the Garden. They abide therein.

1. *i.e.* angels.

فمن اظلم ممن افترى على الله كذبا او كذب
بايته اولئك ينالهم نصيبهم من الكتب حتى
اذا جاءتهم رسلنا يتوفونهم قالوا اين ما كنتم
تدعون من دون الله قالوا ضلوا عنا وشهدوا
على انفسهم انهم كانوا كفرين ﴿٣٧﴾
قال ادخلوا في امم قد خلت من قبلكم من
الجن والانس في النار كلما دخلت امة لعنت
اختها حتى اذا اداركوا فيها جميعا قالت اخرىهم
لاولىهم ربنا هؤلاء اضلونا فاتهم عذابا
ضعفا من النار قال لكل ضعف ولكن لا
تعلمون ﴿٣٨﴾
وقالت اولىهم لاخرىهم فما كان لكم علينا من
ع فضل فذوقوا العذاب بما كنتم تكسبون ﴿٣٩﴾
ان الذين كذبوا بايتنا واستكبروا عنها لا
تفتح لهم ابواب السماء ولا يدخلون الجنة
حتى يلج الجمل في سم الخياط وكذلك
نجزي المجرمين ﴿٤٠﴾
لهم من جهنم مهاد ومن فوقهم غواش و
كذلك نجزي الظلمين ﴿٤١﴾
والذين امنوا وعملوا الصلحت لا نكلف نفسا
الا وسعها اولئك اصحب الجنة هم فيها
خلدون ﴿٤٢﴾

43. And We remove whatever rancour may be in their hearts. Rivers flow beneath them. And they say: The praise to Allah, Who hath guided us to this. We could not truly have been led aright if Allah had not guided us. Verily the messengers of our Lord did bring the Truth. And it is cried unto them: This is the Garden. Ye inherit it for what ye used to do.

44. And the dwellers of the Garden cry unto the dwellers of the Fire: We have found that which our Lord promised us (to be) the Truth. Have ye (too) found that which your Lord promised the Truth? They say: Yea, verily. And a crier in between them crieth: The curse of Allah is on evil-doers,

45. Who debar (men) from the path of Allah and would have it crooked, and who are disbelievers in the Last Day.

46. Between them is a veil. And on the Heights are men who know them all by their marks. And they call unto the dwellers of the Garden: Peace be unto you! They enter it not although they hope (to enter).

47. And when their eyes are turned toward the dwellers of the Fire, they say: Our Lord! Place us not with the wrong-doing folk.

48. And the dwellers on the Heights call unto men whom they know by their marks, (saying): What did your multitude and that in which ye took your pride avail you?

49. Are these they of whom ye swore that Allah would not show them mercy? (Unto them it hath been said): Enter the Garden. No fear shall come upon you nor is it ye who will grieve.

50. And the dwellers of the Fire cry out unto the dwellers of the Garden; Pour on us some water or some of that wherewith Allah hath provided you. They say: Lo! Allah hath forbidden both to disbelievers (in His guidance),

وَنَزَعْنَا مَا فِي صُدُورِهِم مِّنْ غِلٍّ تَجْرِي مِن تَحْتِهِمُ
الْأَنْهَارُ ۚ وَقَالُوا الْحَمْدُ لِلَّهِ الَّذِي هَدَانَا لِهَٰذَا وَمَا
كُنَّا لِنَهْتَدِيَ لَوْلَا أَنْ هَدَانَا اللَّهُ ۚ لَقَدْ جَاءَتْ رُسُلُ
رَبِّنَا بِالْحَقِّ ۚ وَنُودُوا أَن تِلْكُمُ الْجَنَّةُ أُورِثْتُمُوهَا
بِمَا كُنتُمْ تَعْمَلُونَ ﴿٤٣﴾
وَنَادَىٰ أَصْحَابُ الْجَنَّةِ أَصْحَابَ النَّارِ أَن قَدْ وَجَدْنَا
مَا وَعَدَنَا رَبُّنَا حَقًّا فَهَلْ وَجَدتُّم مَّا وَعَدَ رَبُّكُمْ حَقًّا ۖ قَالُوا
نَعَمْ ۚ فَأَذَّنَ مُؤَذِّنٌ بَيْنَهُمْ أَن لَّعْنَةُ اللَّهِ عَلَى الظَّالِمِينَ ﴿٤٤﴾
الَّذِينَ يَصُدُّونَ عَن سَبِيلِ اللَّهِ وَيَبْغُونَهَا عِوَجًا ۚ
وَهُم بِالْآخِرَةِ كَافِرُونَ ﴿٤٥﴾
وَبَيْنَهُمَا حِجَابٌ ۚ وَعَلَى الْأَعْرَافِ رِجَالٌ يَعْرِفُونَ
كُلًّا بِسِيمَاهُمْ ۚ وَنَادَوْا أَصْحَابَ الْجَنَّةِ أَن سَلَامٌ عَلَيْكُمْ ۚ
لَمْ يَدْخُلُوهَا وَهُمْ يَطْمَعُونَ ﴿٤٦﴾
وَإِذَا صُرِفَتْ أَبْصَارُهُمْ تِلْقَاءَ أَصْحَابِ النَّارِ قَالُوا رَبَّنَا
لَا تَجْعَلْنَا مَعَ الْقَوْمِ الظَّالِمِينَ ﴿٤٧﴾
وَنَادَىٰ أَصْحَابُ الْأَعْرَافِ رِجَالًا يَعْرِفُونَهُم بِسِيمَاهُمْ
قَالُوا مَا أَغْنَىٰ عَنكُمْ جَمْعُكُمْ وَمَا كُنتُمْ تَسْتَكْبِرُونَ ﴿٤٨﴾
أَهَٰؤُلَاءِ الَّذِينَ أَقْسَمْتُمْ لَا يَنَالُهُمُ اللَّهُ بِرَحْمَةٍ ۚ ادْخُلُوا
الْجَنَّةَ لَا خَوْفٌ عَلَيْكُمْ وَلَا أَنتُمْ تَحْزَنُونَ ﴿٤٩﴾
وَنَادَىٰ أَصْحَابُ النَّارِ أَصْحَابَ الْجَنَّةِ أَنْ أَفِيضُوا عَلَيْنَا
مِنَ الْمَاءِ أَوْ مِمَّا رَزَقَكُمُ اللَّهُ ۚ قَالُوا إِنَّ اللَّهَ حَرَّمَهُمَا
عَلَى الْكَافِرِينَ ﴿٥٠﴾

51. Who took their religion for a sport and pastime, and whom the life of the world beguiled. So this day We have forgotten them even as they forgot the meeting of this Day and as they used to deny Our tokens.

الذين اتخذوا دينهم لهوا ولعبا وغرتهم الحيوة
الدنيا فاليوم ننسهم كما نسوا لقاء يومهم هذا
وما كانوا بايتنا يجحدون ٥١

52. Verily We have brought them a Scripture which We expound with knowledge, a guidance and a mercy for a people who believe.

ولقد جئنهم بكتب فصلنه على علم هدى و
رحمة لقوم يؤمنون ٥٢

53. Await they aught save the fulfilment thereof? On the day when the fulfilment thereof cometh, those who were before forgetful thereof will say: The messengers of our Lord did bring the Truth! Have we any intercessors, that they may intercede for us? Or can we be returned (to life on earth), that we may act otherwise than we used to act? They have lost their souls, and that which they devised hath failed them.

هل ينظرون الا تاويله يوم ياتي تاويله يقول
الذين نسوه من قبل قد جاءت رسل ربنا
بالحق فهل لنا من شفعاء فيشفعوا لنا او نرد
فنعمل غير الذي كنا نعمل قد خسروا انفسهم و
ضل عنهم ما كانوا يفترون ٥٣ ع ٦ ١٢

54. Lo! your Lord is Allah Who created the heavens and the earth in six Days, then mounted He the Throne. He covereth the night with the day, which is in haste to follow it, and hath made the sun and the moon and the stars subservient by His command. His verily is all creation and commandment. Blessed be Allah, the Lord of the Worlds!

ان ربكم الله الذي خلق السموت والارض في
ستة ايام ثم استوى على العرش يغشي اليل
النهار يطلبه حثيثا والشمس والقمر والنجوم
مسخرت بامره الا له الخلق والامر تبرك
الله رب العلمين ٥٤

55. (O mankind!) Call upon your Lord humbly and in secret. Lo! He loveth not aggressors.

ادعوا ربكم تضرعا وخفية انه لا يحب المعتدين ٥٥

56. Work not confusion in the earth after the fair ordering (thereof), and call on Him in fear and hope. Lo! the mercy of Allah is nigh unto the good.

ولا تفسدوا في الارض بعد اصلاحها وادعوه
خوفا وطمعا ان رحمت الله قريب من المحسنين ٥٦

57. And He it is Who sendeth the winds as tidings heralding His mercy, till, when they bear a cloud heavy (with rain), We lead it to a dead land, and then cause water to descend thereon and thereby bring forth fruits of every kind. Thus bring We forth the dead. Haply ye may remember.

وهو الذي يرسل الريح بشرا بين يدي رحمته
حتى اذا اقلت سحابا ثقالا سقنه لبلد ميت فانزلنا
به الماء فاخرجنا به من كل الثمرت كذلك
نخرج الموتى لعلكم تذكرون ٥٧

58. As for the good land, its vegetation cometh forth by permission of its Lord; while as for that which is bad, only evil cometh forth (from it). Thus do We recount the tokens for people who give thanks.

وَالْبَلَدُ الطَّيِّبُ يَخْرُجُ نَبَاتُهُ بِإِذْنِ رَبِّهِ ۚ وَالَّذِي
خَبُثَ لَا يَخْرُجُ إِلَّا نَكِدًا ۚ كَذَٰلِكَ نُصَرِّفُ الْآيَاتِ
لِقَوْمٍ يَشْكُرُونَ ﴿٥٨﴾

59. We sent Noah (of old) unto his people, and he said: O my people! Serve Allah. Ye have no other God save Him. Lo! I fear for you the retribution of an Awful Day.

لَقَدْ أَرْسَلْنَا نُوحًا إِلَىٰ قَوْمِهِ فَقَالَ يَا قَوْمِ اعْبُدُوا
اللَّهَ مَا لَكُمْ مِنْ إِلَٰهٍ غَيْرُهُ إِنِّي أَخَافُ عَلَيْكُمْ
عَذَابَ يَوْمٍ عَظِيمٍ ﴿٥٩﴾

60. The chieftains of his people said: Lo! we see thee surely in plain error.

قَالَ الْمَلَأُ مِنْ قَوْمِهِ إِنَّا لَنَرَاكَ فِي ضَلَالٍ مُبِينٍ ﴿٦٠﴾

61. He said: O my people! There is no error in me, but I am a messenger from the Lord of the Worlds.

قَالَ يَا قَوْمِ لَيْسَ بِي ضَلَالَةٌ وَلَٰكِنِّي رَسُولٌ مِنْ
رَبِّ الْعَالَمِينَ ﴿٦١﴾

62. I convey unto you the messages of my Lord and give good counsel unto you, and know from Allah that which ye know not.

أُبَلِّغُكُمْ رِسَالَاتِ رَبِّي وَأَنْصَحُ لَكُمْ وَأَعْلَمُ مِنَ اللَّهِ
مَا لَا تَعْلَمُونَ ﴿٦٢﴾

63. Marvel ye that there should come unto you a Reminder from your Lord by means of a man among you, that he may warn you, and that ye may keep from evil, and that haply ye may find mercy.

أَوَعَجِبْتُمْ أَنْ جَاءَكُمْ ذِكْرٌ مِنْ رَبِّكُمْ عَلَىٰ رَجُلٍ
مِنْكُمْ لِيُنْذِرَكُمْ وَلِتَتَّقُوا وَلَعَلَّكُمْ تُرْحَمُونَ ﴿٦٣﴾

64. But they denied him, so We saved him and those with him in the ship, and We drowned those who denied Our tokens. Lo! they were blind folk.

فَكَذَّبُوهُ فَأَنْجَيْنَاهُ وَالَّذِينَ مَعَهُ فِي الْفُلْكِ وَأَغْرَقْنَا
الَّذِينَ كَذَّبُوا بِآيَاتِنَا ۚ إِنَّهُمْ كَانُوا قَوْمًا عَمِينَ ﴿٦٤﴾

65. And unto (the tribe of) 'Aād (We sent) their brother, Hūd.[1] He said: O my people! Serve Allah, Ye have no other God save Him. Will ye not ward off (evil)?

وَإِلَىٰ عَادٍ أَخَاهُمْ هُودًا ۗ قَالَ يَا قَوْمِ اعْبُدُوا اللَّهَ مَا
لَكُمْ مِنْ إِلَٰهٍ غَيْرُهُ ۚ أَفَلَا تَتَّقُونَ ﴿٦٥﴾

66. The chieftains of his people, who were disbelieving, said: Lo! we surely see thee in foolishness, and lo! we deem thee of the liars.

قَالَ الْمَلَأُ الَّذِينَ كَفَرُوا مِنْ قَوْمِهِ إِنَّا لَنَرَاكَ فِي
سَفَاهَةٍ وَإِنَّا لَنَظُنُّكَ مِنَ الْكَاذِبِينَ ﴿٦٦﴾

67. He said: O my people; There is no foolishness in me, but I am a messenger from the Lord of the Worlds.

قَالَ يَا قَوْمِ لَيْسَ بِي سَفَاهَةٌ وَلَٰكِنِّي رَسُولٌ مِنْ
رَبِّ الْعَالَمِينَ ﴿٦٧﴾

68. I convey unto you the messages of my Lord and am for you a true adviser.

أُبَلِّغُكُمْ رِسَالَاتِ رَبِّي وَأَنَا لَكُمْ نَاصِحٌ أَمِينٌ ﴿٦٨﴾

1. An ancient Arab prophet.

69. Marvel ye that there should come unto you a Reminder from your Lord by means of a man among you, that he may warn you? Remember how He made you viceroys after Noah's folk, and gave you growth of stature. Remember (all) the bounties of your Lord, that haply ye may be successful.

اوعجبتم ان جاءكم ذكر من ربكم على رجل منكم
لينذركم ۚ واذكروا اذ جعلكم خلفاء من بعد قوم
نوح وزادكم في الخلق بصطة ۚ فاذكروا آلاء
الله لعلكم تفلحون ٦٩

70. They said: Hast come unto us that we should serve Allah alone, and forsake what our fathers worshipped? Then bring upon us that wherewith thou threatenest us if thou art of the truthful!

قالوا اجئتنا لنعبد الله وحده ونذر ما كان
يعبد آباؤنا ۚ فأتنا بما تعدنا ان كنت من
الصدقين ٧٠

71. He said: Terror and wrath from your Lord have already fallen on you. Would ye wrangle with me over names which ye have named, ye and your fathers, for which no warrant from Allah hath been revealed? Then await (the consequence), lo! I (also) am of those awaiting (it).

قال قد وقع عليكم من ربكم رجس وغضب ۖ
اتجادلونني في اسماء سميتموها انتم واباؤكم
ما نزل الله بها من سلطن ۚ فانتظروا اني معكم
من المنتظرين ٧١

72. And We saved him and those with him by a mercy from Us, and We cut the root of those who denied Our revelations and were not believers.

فانجينه والذين معه برحمة منا وقطعنا دابر
ع ٩ الذين كذبوا بايتنا وما كانوا مؤمنين ٧٢

73. And to (the tribe of) Thamūd (We sent) their brother Ṣāliḥ.[1] He said: O my people! Serve Allah. Ye have no other God save Him. A wonder from your Lord hath come unto you. Lo! this is the camel of Allah, a token unto you; so let her feed in Allah's earth, and touch her not with hurt lest painful torment seize you.

والى ثمود اخاهم صلحا ۘ قال يقوم اعبدوا الله
ما لكم من اله غيره ۖ قد جاءتكم بينة من
ربكم ۖ هذه ناقة الله لكم اية فذروها تأكل
في ارض الله ولا تمسوها بسوء فيأخذكم
عذاب اليم ٧٣

74. And remember how He made you viceroys after 'Aād and gave you station in the earth. Ye choose castles in the plains and hew the mountains into dwellings, So remember (all) the bounties of Allah and do not evil, making mischief in the earth.

واذكروا اذ جعلكم خلفاء من بعد عاد وبوأكم
في الارض تتخذون من سهولها قصورا وتنحتون
الجبال بيوتا ۖ فاذكروا آلاء الله ولا تعثوا
في الارض مفسدين ٧٤

1. An ancient Arab prophet.

75. The chieftains of his people, who were scornful, said unto those whom they despised, unto such of them as believed: Know ye that Ṣāliḥ is one sent from his Lord? They said: Lo! In that wherewith he hath been sent we are believers.

76. Those who were scornful said: Lo! in that which ye believe we are disbelievers.

77. So they hamstrung the she-camel, and they flouted the commandment of their Lord, and they said: O Ṣāliḥ! Bring upon us that thou threatenest if thou art indeed of those sent (from Allah).

78. So the earthquake seized them, and morning found them prostrate in their dwelling-place.

79. And Ṣāliḥ turned from them and said: O my people! I delivered my Lord's message unto you and gave you good advice, but ye love not good advisers.

80. And Lot! (Remember) when he said unto his folk: Will ye commit abomination such as no creature ever did before you?

81. Lo! ye come with lust unto men instead of women. Nay, but ye are wanton folk.

82. And the answer of his people was only that they said (one to another): Turn them out of your township.[1] They are folk, forsooth, who keep pure.

83. And We rescued him and his household, save his wife, who was of those who stayed behind.

84. And We rained a rain upon them. See now the nature of the consequence for evil-doers!

85. And unto Midian (We sent) their brother, Shu'eyb.[2] He said: O my people! Serve Allah. Ye have no other God save Him. Lo! a clear proof hath come unto you from your Lord; so give full measure and full weight and wrong not mankind in their goods, and work not confusion in the earth after the fair ordering thereof. That will be better for you, if ye are believers.

قال الملا الذين استكبروا من قومه للذين استضعفوا
لمن امن منهم اتعلمون ان صلحا مرسل من
ربه قالوا انا بما ارسل به مؤمنون ﴿٧٥﴾
قال الذين استكبروا انا بالذي امنتم به كفرون ﴿٧٦﴾
فعقروا الناقة وعتوا عن امر ربهم وقالوا يصلح
ائتنا بما تعدنا ان كنت من المرسلين ﴿٧٧﴾
فاخذتهم الرجفة فاصبحوا في دارهم جثمين ﴿٧٨﴾
فتولى عنهم وقال يقوم لقد ابلغتكم رسالة ربي
ونصحت لكم ولكن لا تحبون النصحين ﴿٧٩﴾
ولوطا اذ قال لقومه اتاتون الفاحشة ما سبقكم
بها من احد من العلمين ﴿٨٠﴾
انكم لتاتون الرجال شهوة من دون النساء
بل انتم قوم مسرفون ﴿٨١﴾
وما كان جواب قومه الا ان قالوا اخرجوهم من
قريتكم انهم اناس يتطهرون ﴿٨٢﴾
فانجينه واهله الا امراته كانت من الغبرين ﴿٨٣﴾
ع ١٧ وامطرنا عليهم مطرا فانظر كيف كان عاقبة المجرمين ﴿٨٤﴾
والى مدين اخاهم شعيبا قال يقوم اعبدوا الله
ما لكم من اله غيره قد جاءتكم بينة من ربكم
فاوفوا الكيل والميزان ولا تبخسوا الناس اشياءهم
ولا تفسدوا في الارض بعد اصلاحها ذلكم خير
لكم ان كنتم مؤمنين ﴿٨٥﴾

1. The Arabic word *Qariah* means originally a settled community, polity or civilisation.
2. Identified with Jethro.

86. Lurk not on every road to threaten (wayfarers), and to turn away from Allah's path him who believeth in Him, and to seek to make it crooked. And remember, when ye were but few, how He did multiply you. And see the nature of the consequence for the corrupters!

87. And if there is a party of you which believeth in that wherewith I have been sent, and there is a party which believeth not, then have patience until Allah judge between us. He is the best of all who deal in judgment.

88. The chieftains of his people, who were scornful, said: Surely we will drive thee out, O Shu'eyb, and those who believe with thee, from our township, unless ye return to our religion. He said: Even though we hate it?

89. We should have invented a lie against Allah if we returned to your religion after Allah hath rescued us from it. It is not for us to return to it unless Allah should (so) will. Our Lord comprehendeth all things in knowledge. In Allah do we put our trust. Our Lord! Decide with truth between us and our folk, for Thou art the best of those who make decision.

90. But the chieftains of his people, who were disbelieving, said: If ye follow Shu'eyb, then truly we shall be the losers.

91. So the earthquake seized them, and morning found them prostrate in their dwelling-place.

92. Those who denied Shu'eyb became as though they had not dwelt there. Those who denied Shu'eyb, they were the losers.

93. So he turned from them and said: O my people! I delivered my Lord's messages unto you and gave you good advice; then how can I sorrow for a people that rejected (truth)?

وَلَا تَقْعُدُوا بِكُلِّ صِرَاطٍ تُوعِدُونَ وَتَصُدُّونَ
عَنْ سَبِيلِ اللّٰهِ مَنْ اٰمَنَ بِهٖ وَتَبْغُونَهَا عِوَجًا
وَاذْكُرُوا اِذْ كُنْتُمْ قَلِيلًا فَكَثَّرَكُمْ وَانْظُرُوا كَيْفَ كَانَ
عَاقِبَةُ الْمُفْسِدِينَ ﴿٨٦﴾
وَاِنْ كَانَ طَآئِفَةٌ مِّنْكُمْ اٰمَنُوا بِالَّذِيْٓ اُرْسِلْتُ بِهٖ
وَطَآئِفَةٌ لَّمْ يُؤْمِنُوا فَاصْبِرُوا حَتّٰى يَحْكُمَ اللّٰهُ
بَيْنَنَا وَهُوَ خَيْرُ الْحٰكِمِيْنَ ﴿٨٧﴾
قَالَ الْمَلَاُ الَّذِيْنَ اسْتَكْبَرُوا مِنْ قَوْمِهٖ لَنُخْرِجَنَّكَ
يٰشُعَيْبُ وَالَّذِيْنَ اٰمَنُوا مَعَكَ مِنْ قَرْيَتِنَآ اَوْ لَتَعُوْدُنَّ
فِيْ مِلَّتِنَا قَالَ اَوَلَوْ كُنَّا كٰرِهِيْنَ ﴿٨٨﴾
قَدِ افْتَرَيْنَا عَلَى اللّٰهِ كَذِبًا اِنْ عُدْنَا فِيْ مِلَّتِكُمْ بَعْدَ
اِذْ نَجّٰىنَا اللّٰهُ مِنْهَا وَمَا يَكُوْنُ لَنَآ اَنْ نَّعُوْدَ فِيْهَآ اِلَّآ
اَنْ يَّشَآءَ اللّٰهُ رَبُّنَا وَسِعَ رَبُّنَا كُلَّ شَيْءٍ عِلْمًا
عَلَى اللّٰهِ تَوَكَّلْنَا رَبَّنَا افْتَحْ بَيْنَنَا وَبَيْنَ قَوْمِنَا
بِالْحَقِّ وَاَنْتَ خَيْرُ الْفٰتِحِيْنَ ﴿٨٩﴾
وَقَالَ الْمَلَاُ الَّذِيْنَ كَفَرُوْا مِنْ قَوْمِهٖ لَئِنِ اتَّبَعْتُمْ
شُعَيْبًا اِنَّكُمْ اِذًا لَّخٰسِرُوْنَ ﴿٩٠﴾
فَاَخَذَتْهُمُ الرَّجْفَةُ فَاَصْبَحُوْا فِيْ دَارِهِمْ جٰثِمِيْنَ ﴿٩١﴾
الَّذِيْنَ كَذَّبُوْا شُعَيْبًا كَاَنْ لَّمْ يَغْنَوْا فِيْهَا الَّذِيْنَ
كَذَّبُوْا شُعَيْبًا كَانُوْا هُمُ الْخٰسِرِيْنَ ﴿٩٢﴾
فَتَوَلّٰى عَنْهُمْ وَقَالَ يٰقَوْمِ لَقَدْ اَبْلَغْتُكُمْ رِسٰلٰتِ رَبِّيْ
وَنَصَحْتُ لَكُمْ فَكَيْفَ اٰسٰى عَلٰى قَوْمٍ كٰفِرِيْنَ ﴿٩٣﴾

94. And We sent no prophet unto any township but We did afflict its folk with tribulation and adversity that haply they might grow humble.

95. Then changed We the evil plight for good till they grew affluent and said: Tribulation and distress did touch our fathers. Then We seized them unawares, when they perceived not.

96. And if the people of the townships had believed and kept from evil, surely We should have opened for them blessings from the sky and from the earth. But (unto every messenger) they gave the lie, and so We seized them on account of what they used to earn.

97. Are the people of the townships then secure from the coming of Our wrath upon them as a night-raid while they sleep?

98. Or are the people of the townships then secure from the coming of Our wrath upon them in the daytime while they play?

99. Are they then secure from Allah's scheme? None deemeth himself secure from Allah's scheme save folk that perish.

100. Is it not an indication to those who inherit the land after its people (who thus reaped the consequence of evil-doing) that, if We will, We can smite them for their sins and print upon their hearts so that they hear not?

101. Such were the townships. We relate some tidings of them unto thee (Muhammad). Their messengers verily came unto them with clear proofs (of Allah's Sovereignty), but they could not believe because they had before denied. Thus doth Allah print upon the hearts of disbelievers (that they hear not).

102. We found no (loyalty to any) covenant in most of them. Nay, most of them We found wrong-doers.

103. Then, after them, We sent Moses with our tokens unto Pharaoh and his chiefs, but they repelled them. Now, see the nature of the consequence for the corrupters!

وَمَآ أَرْسَلْنَا فِى قَرْيَةٍ مِّن نَّبِىٍّ إِلَّآ أَخَذْنَآ أَهْلَهَا
بِالْبَأْسَآءِ وَالضَّرَّآءِ لَعَلَّهُمْ يَضَّرَّعُونَ ﴿٩٤﴾
ثُمَّ بَدَّلْنَا مَكَانَ السَّيِّئَةِ الْحَسَنَةَ حَتّٰى عَفَوْا وَّقَالُوْا
قَدْ مَسَّ اٰبَآءَنَا الضَّرَّآءُ وَالسَّرَّآءُ فَأَخَذْنٰهُمْ بَغْتَةً وَّ
هُمْ لَا يَشْعُرُوْنَ ﴿٩٥﴾
وَلَوْ أَنَّ أَهْلَ الْقُرٰٓى اٰمَنُوْا وَاتَّقَوْا لَفَتَحْنَا عَلَيْهِمْ
بَرَكٰتٍ مِّنَ السَّمَآءِ وَالْأَرْضِ وَلٰكِنْ كَذَّبُوْا فَأَخَذْنٰهُمْ
بِمَا كَانُوْا يَكْسِبُوْنَ ﴿٩٦﴾
أَفَأَمِنَ أَهْلُ الْقُرٰٓى أَنْ يَّأْتِيَهُمْ بَأْسُنَا بَيَاتًا وَّهُمْ نَآئِمُوْنَ ﴿٩٧﴾
أَوَأَمِنَ أَهْلُ الْقُرٰٓى أَنْ يَّأْتِيَهُمْ بَأْسُنَا ضُحًى وَّ
هُمْ يَلْعَبُوْنَ ﴿٩٨﴾
ع أَفَأَمِنُوْا مَكْرَ اللّٰهِ فَلَا يَأْمَنُ مَكْرَ اللّٰهِ إِلَّا الْقَوْمُ الْخٰسِرُوْنَ ﴿٩٩﴾
أَوَلَمْ يَهْدِ لِلَّذِيْنَ يَرِثُوْنَ الْأَرْضَ مِنْ بَعْدِ أَهْلِهَآ
أَنْ لَّوْ نَشَآءُ أَصَبْنٰهُمْ بِذُنُوْبِهِمْ وَنَطْبَعُ عَلٰى قُلُوْبِهِمْ
فَهُمْ لَا يَسْمَعُوْنَ ﴿١٠٠﴾
تِلْكَ الْقُرٰى نَقُصُّ عَلَيْكَ مِنْ أَنْبَآئِهَا وَلَقَدْ جَآءَتْهُمْ
رُسُلُهُمْ بِالْبَيِّنٰتِ فَمَا كَانُوْا لِيُؤْمِنُوْا بِمَا كَذَّبُوْا مِنْ
قَبْلُ كَذٰلِكَ يَطْبَعُ اللّٰهُ عَلٰى قُلُوْبِ الْكٰفِرِيْنَ ﴿١٠١﴾
وَمَا وَجَدْنَا لِأَكْثَرِهِمْ مِّنْ عَهْدٍ وَإِنْ وَّجَدْنَآ أَكْثَرَهُمْ
لَفٰسِقِيْنَ ﴿١٠٢﴾
ثُمَّ بَعَثْنَا مِنْ بَعْدِهِمْ مُّوْسٰى بِاٰيٰتِنَآ إِلٰى فِرْعَوْنَ وَمَلَا۟ئِهٖ
فَظَلَمُوْا بِهَا فَانْظُرْ كَيْفَ كَانَ عَاقِبَةُ الْمُفْسِدِيْنَ ﴿١٠٣﴾

104. Moses said: O Pharaoh! Lo! I am a messenger from the Lord of the Worlds,

105. Approved upon condition that I speak concerning Allah nothing but the truth. I come unto you (lords of Egypt) with a clear proof from your Lord. So let the Children of Israel go with me.

106. (Pharaoh) said: If thou comest with a token, then produce it, if thou art of those who speak the truth.

107. Then he flung down his staff and lo! it was a serpent manifest;

108. And he drew forth his hand (from his bosom), and lo! it was white for the beholders.

109. The chiefs of Pharaoh's people said: Lo! this is some knowing wizard,

110. Who would expel you from your land. Now what do ye advise?

111. They said (unto Pharaoh): Put him off (a while)—him and his brother—and send into the cities summoners,

112. To bring each knowing wizard unto thee.

113. And the wizards came to Pharaoh, saying: Surely there will be a reward for us if we are victors.

114. He answered: Yea, and surely ye shall be of those brought near (to me).

115. They said: O Moses! Either throw (first) or let us be the first throwers?

116. He said: Throw! And when they threw they cast a spell upon the people's eyes, and overawed them, and produced a mighty spell.

117. And We inspired Moses (saying): Throw thy staff! And lo! is swallowed up their lying show.

118. Thus was the Truth vindicated and that which they were doing was made vain.

وَقَالَ مُوْسٰى يٰفِرْعَوْنُ اِنِّيْ رَسُوْلٌ مِّنْ رَّبِّ
الْعٰلَمِيْنَ ﴿١٠٤﴾
حَقِيْقٌ عَلٰٓى اَنْ لَّآ اَقُوْلَ عَلَى اللّٰهِ اِلَّا الْحَقَّ قَدْ جِئْتُكُمْ
بِبَيِّنَةٍ مِّنْ رَّبِّكُمْ فَاَرْسِلْ مَعِيَ بَنِيْٓ اِسْرَآءِيْلَ ﴿١٠٥﴾
قَالَ اِنْ كُنْتَ جِئْتَ بِاٰيَةٍ فَاْتِ بِهَآ اِنْ كُنْتَ مِنَ
الصّٰدِقِيْنَ ﴿١٠٦﴾
فَاَلْقٰى عَصَاهُ فَاِذَا هِيَ ثُعْبَانٌ مُّبِيْنٌ ﴿١٠٧﴾
وَّنَزَعَ يَدَهٗ فَاِذَا هِيَ بَيْضَآءُ لِلنّٰظِرِيْنَ ﴿١٠٨﴾
قَالَ الْمَلَاُ مِنْ قَوْمِ فِرْعَوْنَ اِنَّ هٰذَا لَسٰحِرٌ عَلِيْمٌ ﴿١٠٩﴾
يُّرِيْدُ اَنْ يُّخْرِجَكُمْ مِّنْ اَرْضِكُمْ فَمَاذَا تَاْمُرُوْنَ ﴿١١٠﴾
قَالُوْٓا اَرْجِهْ وَاَخَاهُ وَاَرْسِلْ فِي الْمَدَآئِنِ حٰشِرِيْنَ ﴿١١١﴾
يَاْتُوْكَ بِكُلِّ سٰحِرٍ عَلِيْمٍ ﴿١١٢﴾
وَجَآءَ السَّحَرَةُ فِرْعَوْنَ قَالُوْٓا اِنَّ لَنَا لَاَجْرًا اِنْ كُنَّا
نَحْنُ الْغٰلِبِيْنَ ﴿١١٣﴾
قَالَ نَعَمْ وَاِنَّكُمْ لَمِنَ الْمُقَرَّبِيْنَ ﴿١١٤﴾
قَالُوْا يٰمُوْسٰٓى اِمَّآ اَنْ تُلْقِيَ وَاِمَّآ اَنْ نَّكُوْنَ نَحْنُ
الْمُلْقِيْنَ ﴿١١٥﴾
قَالَ اَلْقُوْا فَلَمَّآ اَلْقَوْا سَحَرُوْٓا اَعْيُنَ النَّاسِ وَ
اسْتَرْهَبُوْهُمْ وَجَآءُوْ بِسِحْرٍ عَظِيْمٍ ﴿١١٦﴾
وَاَوْحَيْنَآ اِلٰى مُوْسٰٓى اَنْ اَلْقِ عَصَاكَ فَاِذَا هِيَ
تَلْقَفُ مَا يَاْفِكُوْنَ ﴿١١٧﴾
فَوَقَعَ الْحَقُّ وَبَطَلَ مَا كَانُوْا يَعْمَلُوْنَ ﴿١١٨﴾

119. Thus were they there defeated and brought low.

120. And the wizards fell down prostrate,

121. Crying: We believe in the Lord of the Worlds,

122. The Lord of Moses and Aaron.

123. Pharaoh said: Ye believe in Him before I give you leave! Lo! this is the plot that ye have plotted in the city that ye may drive its people hence. But ye shall come to know!

124. Surely I shall have your hands and feet cut off upon alternate sides. Then I shall crucify you every one.

125. They said: Lo! We are about to return unto our Lord!

126. Thou takest vengeance on us only forasmuch as we believed the tokens of our Lord when they came unto us. Our Lord! Vouchsafe unto us steadfastness and make us die as men who have surrendered (unto Thee).

127. The chiefs of Pharaoh's people said: (O King), wilt thou suffer Moses and his people to make mischief in the land, and flout thee and thy gods? He said: We will slay their sons and spare their women, for lo! we are in power over them.

128. And Moses said unto his people: Seek help in Allah and endure. Lo! the earth is Allah's. He giveth it for an inheritance to whom He will. And lo! the sequel is for those who keep their duty (unto Him).

129. They said: We suffered hurt before thou camest unto us, and since thou hast come unto us. He said: It may be that your Lord is going to destroy your adversary and make you viceroys in the eatrh, that He may see how ye behave

فَغُلِبُوْا هُنَالِكَ وَانْقَلَبُوْا صٰغِرِيْنَ ﴿١١٩﴾
وَاُلْقِيَ السَّحَرَةُ سٰجِدِيْنَ ﴿١٢٠﴾
قَالُوْٓا اٰمَنَّا بِرَبِّ الْعٰلَمِيْنَ ﴿١٢١﴾
رَبِّ مُوْسٰى وَهٰرُوْنَ ﴿١٢٢﴾
قَالَ فِرْعَوْنُ اٰمَنْتُمْ بِهٖ قَبْلَ اَنْ اٰذَنَ لَكُمْ ۚ اِنَّ هٰذَا
لَمَكْرٌ مَّكَرْتُمُوْهُ فِي الْمَدِيْنَةِ لِتُخْرِجُوْا مِنْهَآ اَهْلَهَا ۚ
فَسَوْفَ تَعْلَمُوْنَ ﴿١٢٣﴾
لَاُقَطِّعَنَّ اَيْدِيَكُمْ وَاَرْجُلَكُمْ مِّنْ خِلَافٍ ثُمَّ
لَاُصَلِّبَنَّكُمْ اَجْمَعِيْنَ ﴿١٢٤﴾
قَالُوْٓا اِنَّآ اِلٰى رَبِّنَا مُنْقَلِبُوْنَ ﴿١٢٥﴾
وَمَا تَنْقِمُ مِنَّآ اِلَّآ اَنْ اٰمَنَّا بِاٰيٰتِ رَبِّنَا لَمَّا جَآءَتْنَا ۭ
رَبَّنَآ اَفْرِغْ عَلَيْنَا صَبْرًا وَّتَوَفَّنَا مُسْلِمِيْنَ ﴿١٢٦﴾
وَقَالَ الْمَلَاُ مِنْ قَوْمِ فِرْعَوْنَ اَتَذَرُ مُوْسٰى وَقَوْمَهٗ
لِيُفْسِدُوْا فِي الْاَرْضِ وَيَذَرَكَ وَاٰلِهَتَكَ ۭ قَالَ
سَنُقَتِّلُ اَبْنَآءَهُمْ وَنَسْتَحْيٖ نِسَآءَهُمْ ۚ وَاِنَّا
فَوْقَهُمْ قٰهِرُوْنَ ﴿١٢٧﴾
قَالَ مُوْسٰى لِقَوْمِهِ اسْتَعِيْنُوْا بِاللّٰهِ وَاصْبِرُوْا ۚ اِنَّ
الْاَرْضَ لِلّٰهِ ڐ يُوْرِثُهَا مَنْ يَّشَآءُ مِنْ عِبَادِهٖ ۭ وَ
الْعَاقِبَةُ لِلْمُتَّقِيْنَ ﴿١٢٨﴾
قَالُوْٓا اُوْذِيْنَا مِنْ قَبْلِ اَنْ تَاْتِيَنَا وَمِنْۢ بَعْدِ مَا
جِئْتَنَا ۭ قَالَ عَسٰى رَبُّكُمْ اَنْ يُّهْلِكَ عَدُوَّكُمْ وَ
يَسْتَخْلِفَكُمْ فِي الْاَرْضِ فَيَنْظُرَ كَيْفَ تَعْمَلُوْنَ ﴿١٢٩﴾

130. And We straitened Pharaoh's folk with famine and the dearth of fruits, that peradventure they might heed.

131. But whenever good befell them, they said: This is ours; and whenever evil smote them they ascribed it to the evil auspices of Moses and those with him. Surely their evil auspice was only with Allah. But most of them knew not.

132. And they said: Whatever portent thou bringest wherewith to bewitch us, we shall not put faith in thee.

133. So We sent them the flood and the locusts and the vermin and the frogs and the blood—a succession of clear signs. But they were arrogant and became guilty.

134. And when the terror fell on them they cried: O Moses! Pray for us unto thy Lord, because He hath a covenant with thee. If thou removest the terror from us we verily will trust thee and will let the Children of Israel go with thee.

135. But when We did remove from them the terror for a term which they must reach, behold! they broke their covenant.

136. Therefore We took retribution from them; therefore We drowned them in the sea: because they denied Our revelations and were heedless of them.

137. And We caused the folk who were despised to inherit the eastern parts of the land and the western parts thereof which We had blessed. And the fair word of the Lord was fulfilled for the Children of Israel because of their endurance; and We annihilated (all) that Pharaoh and his folk had done and that they had contrived.

وَلَقَدْ اَخَذْنَآ اٰلَ فِرْعَوْنَ بِالسِّنِيْنَ وَنَقْصٍ مِّنَ
الثَّمَرٰتِ لَعَلَّهُمْ يَذَّكَّرُوْنَ ﴿١٣٠﴾
فَاِذَا جَآءَتْهُمُ الْحَسَنَةُ قَالُوْا لَنَا هٰذِهٖ ۚ وَاِنْ تُصِبْهُمْ
سَيِّئَةٌ يَّطَّيَّرُوْا بِمُوْسٰى وَمَنْ مَّعَهٗ ۗ اَلَآ اِنَّمَا طٰٓئِرُهُمْ
عِنْدَ اللّٰهِ وَلٰكِنَّ اَكْثَرَهُمْ لَا يَعْلَمُوْنَ ﴿١٣١﴾
وَقَالُوْا مَهْمَا تَاْتِنَا بِهٖ مِنْ اٰيَةٍ لِّتَسْحَرَنَا بِهَا ۙ فَمَا
نَحْنُ لَكَ بِمُؤْمِنِيْنَ ﴿١٣٢﴾
فَاَرْسَلْنَا عَلَيْهِمُ الطُّوْفَانَ وَالْجَرَادَ وَالْقُمَّلَ وَ
الضَّفَادِعَ وَالدَّمَ اٰيٰتٍ مُّفَصَّلٰتٍ ۫ فَاسْتَكْبَرُوْا وَ
كَانُوْا قَوْمًا مُّجْرِمِيْنَ ﴿١٣٣﴾
وَلَمَّا وَقَعَ عَلَيْهِمُ الرِّجْزُ قَالُوْا يٰمُوْسَى ادْعُ لَنَا رَبَّكَ
بِمَا عَهِدَ عِنْدَكَ ۚ لَئِنْ كَشَفْتَ عَنَّا الرِّجْزَ لَنُؤْمِنَنَّ
لَكَ وَلَنُرْسِلَنَّ مَعَكَ بَنِيْٓ اِسْرَآءِيْلَ ﴿١٣٤﴾ ۚ
فَلَمَّا كَشَفْنَا عَنْهُمُ الرِّجْزَ اِلٰٓى اَجَلٍ هُمْ بٰلِغُوْهُ
اِذَا هُمْ يَنْكُثُوْنَ ﴿١٣٥﴾
فَانْتَقَمْنَا مِنْهُمْ فَاَغْرَقْنٰهُمْ فِى الْيَمِّ بِاَنَّهُمْ كَذَّبُوْا
بِاٰيٰتِنَا وَكَانُوْا عَنْهَا غٰفِلِيْنَ ﴿١٣٦﴾
وَاَوْرَثْنَا الْقَوْمَ الَّذِيْنَ كَانُوْا يُسْتَضْعَفُوْنَ مَشَارِقَ
الْاَرْضِ وَمَغَارِبَهَا الَّتِيْ بٰرَكْنَا فِيْهَا ۗ وَتَمَّتْ كَلِمَتُ
رَبِّكَ الْحُسْنٰى عَلٰى بَنِيْٓ اِسْرَآءِيْلَ ۙ بِمَا صَبَرُوْا ۗ وَ
دَمَّرْنَا مَا كَانَ يَصْنَعُ فِرْعَوْنُ وَقَوْمُهٗ وَمَا كَانُوْا
يَعْرِشُوْنَ ﴿١٣٧﴾

138. And We brought the Children of Israel across the sea, and they came unto a people who were given up to idols which they had. They said: O Moses! Make for us a god even as they have gods. He said: Lo! ye are a folk who know not.

وَجٰوَزْنَا بِبَنِيْٓ اِسْرَآءِيْلَ الْبَحْرَ فَاَتَوْا عَلٰى قَوْمٍ
يَّعْكُفُوْنَ عَلٰٓى اَصْنَامٍ لَّهُمْ ۚ قَالُوْا يٰمُوْسَى اجْعَلْ لَّنَآ
اِلٰهًا كَمَا لَهُمْ اٰلِهَةٌ ۗ قَالَ اِنَّكُمْ قَوْمٌ تَجْهَلُوْنَ ﴿١٣٨﴾

139. Lo! as for these, their way will be destroyed and all that they are doing is in vain.

اِنَّ هٰٓؤُلَآءِ مُتَبَّرٌ مَّا هُمْ فِيْهِ وَبٰطِلٌ مَّا كَانُوْا
يَعْمَلُوْنَ ﴿١٣٩﴾

140. He said: Shall I seek for you a god other than Allah when He hath favoured you above (all) creatures?

قَالَ اَغَيْرَ اللّٰهِ اَبْغِيْكُمْ اِلٰهًا وَّهُوَ فَضَّلَكُمْ عَلَى
الْعٰلَمِيْنَ ﴿١٤٠﴾

141. And (remember) when We did deliver you from Pharaoh's folk who were afflicting you with dreadful torment, slaughtering your sons and sparing your women. That was a tremendous trial from your Lord.

وَاِذْ اَنْجَيْنٰكُمْ مِّنْ اٰلِ فِرْعَوْنَ يَسُوْمُوْنَكُمْ سُوْٓءَ
الْعَذَابِ ۚ يُقَتِّلُوْنَ اَبْنَآءَكُمْ وَيَسْتَحْيُوْنَ نِسَآءَكُمْ ۗ
وَفِيْ ذٰلِكُمْ بَلَآءٌ مِّنْ رَّبِّكُمْ عَظِيْمٌ ﴿١٤١﴾ ع

142. And when We did appoint for Moses thirty nights (of solitude), and added to them ten, and he completed the whole time appointed by his Lord of forty nights; and Moses said unto his brother: Take my place among the people. Do right, and follow not the way of mischief-makers:

وَوٰعَدْنَا مُوْسٰى ثَلٰثِيْنَ لَيْلَةً وَّاَتْمَمْنٰهَا بِعَشْرٍ فَتَمَّ
مِيْقَاتُ رَبِّهٖٓ اَرْبَعِيْنَ لَيْلَةً ۚ وَقَالَ مُوْسٰى لِاَخِيْهِ
هٰرُوْنَ اخْلُفْنِيْ فِيْ قَوْمِيْ وَاَصْلِحْ وَلَا تَتَّبِعْ سَبِيْلَ
الْمُفْسِدِيْنَ ﴿١٤٢﴾

143. And when Moses came to Our appointed tryst and his Lord had spoken unto him, he said: My Lord! Show me (Thy self), that I may gaze upon Thee. He said: Thou wilt not see Me, but gaze upon the mountain! If it stand still in its place, then thou wilt see Me. And when his Lord revealed (His) glory to the mountain He sent it crashing down. And Moses fell down senseless. And when he woke he said: Glory unto Thee! I turn unto Thee repentant, and I am the first of (true) believers.

وَلَمَّا جَآءَ مُوْسٰى لِمِيْقَاتِنَا وَكَلَّمَهٗ رَبُّهٗ ۙ قَالَ رَبِّ
اَرِنِيْٓ اَنْظُرْ اِلَيْكَ ۗ قَالَ لَنْ تَرٰىنِيْ وَلٰكِنِ انْظُرْ
اِلَى الْجَبَلِ فَاِنِ اسْتَقَرَّ مَكَانَهٗ فَسَوْفَ تَرٰىنِيْ ۚ فَلَمَّا
تَجَلّٰى رَبُّهٗ لِلْجَبَلِ جَعَلَهٗ دَكًّا وَّخَرَّ مُوْسٰى صَعِقًا ۚ
فَلَمَّآ اَفَاقَ قَالَ سُبْحٰنَكَ تُبْتُ اِلَيْكَ وَاَنَا اَوَّلُ
الْمُؤْمِنِيْنَ ﴿١٤٣﴾

144. He said: O Moses! I have preferred thee above mankind by My messages and by My speaking (unto thee). So hold that which I have given thee, and be among the thankful.

قَالَ يٰمُوْسٰٓى اِنِّى اصْطَفَيْتُكَ عَلَى النَّاسِ بِرِسٰلٰتِيْ
وَبِكَلَامِيْ ۖ فَخُذْ مَآ اٰتَيْتُكَ وَكُنْ مِّنَ الشّٰكِرِيْنَ ﴿١٤٤﴾

145. And We wrote for him, upon the tablets, the lesson to be drawn from all things and the explanation of all things, then (bade him): Hold it fast; and command thy people (saying): Take the better (course made clear) therein. I shall show thee the abode of evil-livers.

وَكَتَبْنَا لَهُ فِي الْأَلْوَاحِ مِنْ كُلِّ شَيْءٍ مَّوْعِظَةً وَتَفْصِيلًا
لِّكُلِّ شَيْءٍ فَخُذْهَا بِقُوَّةٍ وَأْمُرْ قَوْمَكَ يَأْخُذُوا بِأَحْسَنِهَا
سَأُورِيكُمْ دَارَ الْفَاسِقِينَ ﴿١٤٥﴾

146. I shall turn away from My revelations those who magnify themselves wrongfully in the earth, and if they see each token believe it not, and if they see the way of righteousness choose it not for (their) way, and if they see the way of error choose it for (their) way. That is because they deny Our revelations and are used to disregard them.

سَأَصْرِفُ عَنْ آيَاتِيَ الَّذِينَ يَتَكَبَّرُونَ فِي الْأَرْضِ
بِغَيْرِ الْحَقِّ وَإِن يَرَوْا كُلَّ آيَةٍ لَّا يُؤْمِنُوا بِهَا وَإِن يَرَوْا
سَبِيلَ الرُّشْدِ لَا يَتَّخِذُوهُ سَبِيلًا وَإِن يَرَوْا سَبِيلَ
الْغَيِّ يَتَّخِذُوهُ سَبِيلًا ذَٰلِكَ بِأَنَّهُمْ كَذَّبُوا بِآيَاتِنَا
وَكَانُوا عَنْهَا غَافِلِينَ ﴿١٤٦﴾

147. Those who deny Our revelations and the meeting of the Hereafter, their works are fruitless. Are they requited aught save what they used to do?

وَالَّذِينَ كَذَّبُوا بِآيَاتِنَا وَلِقَاءِ الْآخِرَةِ حَبِطَتْ أَعْمَالُهُمْ
ع هَلْ يُجْزَوْنَ إِلَّا مَا كَانُوا يَعْمَلُونَ ﴿١٤٧﴾

148. And the folk of Moses, after (he had left them), chose a calf…(for worship), (made) out of their ornaments, of saffron hue,[1] which gave a lowing sound. Saw they not that it spake not unto them nor guided them to any way? They chose it, and became wrong-doers.

وَاتَّخَذَ قَوْمُ مُوسَىٰ مِن بَعْدِهِ مِنْ حُلِيِّهِمْ عِجْلًا
جَسَدًا لَّهُ خُوَارٌ أَلَمْ يَرَوْا أَنَّهُ لَا يُكَلِّمُهُمْ وَلَا يَهْدِيهِمْ
سَبِيلًا اتَّخَذُوهُ وَكَانُوا ظَالِمِينَ ﴿١٤٨﴾ وقف لازم

149. And when they feared the consequences thereof and saw that they had gone astray, they said: Unless our Lord have mercy on us and forgive us, we verily are of the lost.

وَلَمَّا سُقِطَ فِي أَيْدِيهِمْ وَرَأَوْا أَنَّهُمْ قَدْ ضَلُّوا قَالُوا
لَئِن لَّمْ يَرْحَمْنَا رَبُّنَا وَيَغْفِرْ لَنَا لَنَكُونَنَّ مِنَ
الْخَاسِرِينَ ﴿١٤٩﴾

150. And when Moses returned unto his people, angry and grieved, he said: Evil is that (course) which ye took after I had left you. Would ye hasten on the judgement of your Lord? And he cast down the tablets, and he seized his brother by the head, dragging him toward him. He said: Son of my mother! Lo! the folk did judge me weak and almost killed me. Oh, make not mine enemies to triumph over me and place me not among the evil-doers!

وَلَمَّا رَجَعَ مُوسَىٰ إِلَىٰ قَوْمِهِ غَضْبَانَ أَسِفًا قَالَ
بِئْسَمَا خَلَفْتُمُونِي مِن بَعْدِي أَعَجِلْتُمْ أَمْرَ رَبِّكُمْ
وَأَلْقَى الْأَلْوَاحَ وَأَخَذَ بِرَأْسِ أَخِيهِ يَجُرُّهُ إِلَيْهِ
قَالَ ابْنَ أُمَّ إِنَّ الْقَوْمَ اسْتَضْعَفُونِي وَكَادُوا
يَقْتُلُونَنِي فَلَا تُشْمِتْ بِيَ الْأَعْدَاءَ وَلَا تَجْعَلْنِي
مَعَ الْقَوْمِ الظَّالِمِينَ ﴿١٥٠﴾

1. Or a *body*. But, as the word in the Arabic (*Jasad*) can only mean a body of flesh and blood, the meaning "saffron-coloured" better fits the context.

151. He said: My Lord! Have mercy on me and on my brother; bring us into Thy mercy, Thou the Most Merciful of all who show mercy.

قَالَ رَبِّ اغْفِرْ لِي وَلِأَخِي وَأَدْخِلْنَا فِي
رَحْمَتِكَ ۖ وَأَنْتَ أَرْحَمُ الرّٰحِمِينَ ﴿١٥١﴾ ع ٨

152. Lo! those who chose the calf (for worship), terror from their Lord and humiliation will come upon them in the life of the world. Thus do We requite those who invent a lie.

إِنَّ الَّذِينَ اتَّخَذُوا الْعِجْلَ سَيَنَالُهُمْ غَضَبٌ
مِّنْ رَّبِّهِمْ وَذِلَّةٌ فِي الْحَيٰوةِ الدُّنْيَا ۚ وَكَذٰلِكَ
نَجْزِي الْمُفْتَرِينَ ﴿١٥٢﴾

153. But those who do ill deeds and afterward repent and believe—lo! for them, afterward, Allah is Forgiving, Merciful.

وَالَّذِينَ عَمِلُوا السَّيِّاٰتِ ثُمَّ تَابُوا مِنْ
بَعْدِهَا وَاٰمَنُوْٓا إِنَّ رَبَّكَ مِنْ بَعْدِهَا لَغَفُورٌ
رَّحِيمٌ ﴿١٥٣﴾

154. Then, when the anger of Moses abated, he took up the tablets, and in their inscription there was guidance and mercy for all those who fear their Lord.

وَلَمَّا سَكَتَ عَنْ مُّوسَى الْغَضَبُ أَخَذَ الْأَلْوَاحَ ۖ
وَفِي نُسْخَتِهَا هُدًى وَّرَحْمَةٌ لِّلَّذِينَ هُمْ
لِرَبِّهِمْ يَرْهَبُونَ ﴿١٥٤﴾

155. And Moses chose of his people seventy men for Our appointed tryst and, when the trembling came on them, he said: My Lord! If thou hadst willed Thou hadst destroyed them long before, and me with them. Wilt thou destroy us for that which the ignorant among us did? It is but Thy trial (of us). Thou sendest whom Thou wilt astray and guidest whom Thou wilt. Thou art our Protecting Friend, therefore forgive us and have mercy on us, Thou, the Best of all who show forgiveness.

وَاخْتَارَ مُوسٰى قَوْمَهُ سَبْعِينَ رَجُلًا لِّمِيقَاتِنَا ۚ فَلَمَّآ
أَخَذَتْهُمُ الرَّجْفَةُ قَالَ رَبِّ لَوْ شِئْتَ أَهْلَكْتَهُمْ مِّنْ
قَبْلُ وَإِيَّايَ ۖ أَتُهْلِكُنَا بِمَا فَعَلَ السُّفَهَآءُ مِنَّا ۚ إِنْ
هِيَ إِلَّا فِتْنَتُكَ ۖ تُضِلُّ بِهَا مَنْ تَشَآءُ وَتَهْدِي مَنْ
تَشَآءُ ۖ أَنْتَ وَلِيُّنَا فَاغْفِرْ لَنَا وَارْحَمْنَا وَأَنْتَ
خَيْرُ الْغٰفِرِينَ ﴿١٥٥﴾

156. And ordain for us in this world that which is good, and in the Hereafter (that which is good), Lo! We have turned unto Thee. He said: I smite with My punishment whom I will, and My mercy embraceth all things, therefore I shall ordain it for those who ward off (evil) and pay the poor-due, and those who believe Our revelations;

وَاكْتُبْ لَنَا فِي هٰذِهِ الدُّنْيَا حَسَنَةً وَّفِي الْاٰخِرَةِ
إِنَّا هُدْنَآ إِلَيْكَ ۚ قَالَ عَذَابِيْٓ أُصِيبُ بِهِ مَنْ أَشَآءُ ۚ
وَرَحْمَتِي وَسِعَتْ كُلَّ شَيْءٍ ۚ فَسَأَكْتُبُهَا لِلَّذِينَ
يَتَّقُونَ وَيُؤْتُونَ الزَّكٰوةَ وَالَّذِينَ هُمْ بِاٰيٰتِنَا
يُؤْمِنُونَ ﴿١٥٦﴾

157. Those who follow the messenger, the Prophet who can neither read nor write, whom they will find described in the Torah and the Gospel (which are) with them. He will enjoin on them that which is right and forbid them that which is wrong. He will make lawful for them all good things and prohibit for them only the foul; and he will relieve them of their burden and the fetters that they used to wear. Then those who believe in him, and honour him, and help him, and follow the light which is sent down with him: they are the successful.

158. Say (O Muhammad): O mankind! Lo! I am the messenger of Allah to you all—(the messenger of) Him unto whom belongeth the Sovereignty of the heavens and the earth. There is no God save Him. He quickeneth and He giveth death. So believe in Allah and His messenger, the Prophet who can neither read nor write,[1] who believeth in Allah and in His words and follow him that haply ye may be led aright.

159. And of Moses' folk there is a community who lead with truth and establish justice therewith.

160. We divided them into twelve tribes, nations; and We inspired Moses, when his people asked him for water, saying: Smite with thy staff the rock! And there gushed forth therefrom twelve springs, so that each tribe knew their drinking-place. And we caused the white cloud to overshadow them and sent down for them the manna and the quails (saying): Eat of the good things wherewith We have provided you. They wronged Us not, but they were wont to wrong themselves.

161. And when it was said unto them: Dwell in this township and eat therefrom whence ye will, and say "Repentance,"[2] and enter the gate prostrate; We shall forgive you your sins; We shall increase (reward) for the right-doers.

ٱلَّذِينَ يَتَّبِعُونَ ٱلرَّسُولَ ٱلنَّبِىَّ ٱلْأُمِّىَّ ٱلَّذِى يَجِدُونَهُ
مَكْتُوبًا عِندَهُمْ فِى ٱلتَّوْرَىٰةِ وَٱلْإِنجِيلِ يَأْمُرُهُم
بِٱلْمَعْرُوفِ وَيَنْهَىٰهُمْ عَنِ ٱلْمُنكَرِ وَيُحِلُّ لَهُمُ ٱلطَّيِّبَٰتِ
وَيُحَرِّمُ عَلَيْهِمُ ٱلْخَبَٰٓئِثَ وَيَضَعُ عَنْهُمْ إِصْرَهُمْ وَ
ٱلْأَغْلَٰلَ ٱلَّتِى كَانَتْ عَلَيْهِمْ فَٱلَّذِينَ ءَامَنُوا بِهِۦ وَ
عَزَّرُوهُ وَنَصَرُوهُ وَٱتَّبَعُوا ٱلنُّورَ ٱلَّذِىٓ أُنزِلَ مَعَهُۥٓ
ع أُولَٰٓئِكَ هُمُ ٱلْمُفْلِحُونَ ﴿١٥٧﴾
قُلْ يَٰٓأَيُّهَا ٱلنَّاسُ إِنِّى رَسُولُ ٱللَّهِ إِلَيْكُمْ جَمِيعًا ٱلَّذِى
لَهُۥ مُلْكُ ٱلسَّمَٰوَٰتِ وَٱلْأَرْضِ لَآ إِلَٰهَ إِلَّا هُوَ يُحْىِۦ وَ
يُمِيتُ فَـَٔامِنُوا بِٱللَّهِ وَرَسُولِهِ ٱلنَّبِىِّ ٱلْأُمِّىِّ ٱلَّذِى
يُؤْمِنُ بِٱللَّهِ وَكَلِمَٰتِهِۦ وَٱتَّبِعُوهُ لَعَلَّكُمْ تَهْتَدُونَ ﴿١٥٨﴾
وَمِن قَوْمِ مُوسَىٰٓ أُمَّةٌ يَهْدُونَ بِٱلْحَقِّ وَبِهِۦ يَعْدِلُونَ ﴿١٥٩﴾
وَقَطَّعْنَٰهُمُ ٱثْنَتَىْ عَشْرَةَ أَسْبَاطًا أُمَمًا وَأَوْحَيْنَآ إِلَىٰ
مُوسَىٰٓ إِذِ ٱسْتَسْقَىٰهُ قَوْمُهُۥٓ أَنِ ٱضْرِب بِّعَصَاكَ
ٱلْحَجَرَ فَٱنۢبَجَسَتْ مِنْهُ ٱثْنَتَا عَشْرَةَ عَيْنًا قَدْ عَلِمَ
كُلُّ أُنَاسٍ مَّشْرَبَهُمْ وَظَلَّلْنَا عَلَيْهِمُ ٱلْغَمَٰمَ وَ
أَنزَلْنَا عَلَيْهِمُ ٱلْمَنَّ وَٱلسَّلْوَىٰ كُلُوا مِن طَيِّبَٰتِ مَا
رَزَقْنَٰكُمْ وَمَا ظَلَمُونَا وَلَٰكِن كَانُوٓا أَنفُسَهُمْ
يَظْلِمُونَ ﴿١٦٠﴾
وَإِذْ قِيلَ لَهُمُ ٱسْكُنُوا هَٰذِهِ ٱلْقَرْيَةَ وَكُلُوا مِنْهَا
حَيْثُ شِئْتُمْ وَقُولُوا حِطَّةٌ وَٱدْخُلُوا ٱلْبَابَ سُجَّدًا
نَّغْفِرْ لَكُمْ خَطِيٓـَٰٔتِكُمْ سَنَزِيدُ ٱلْمُحْسِنِينَ ﴿١٦١﴾

1. I give the usual rendering. Some modern criticism, while not denying the comparative illiteracy of the Prophet, would prefer the rendering "who is not of those who read the Scriptures" or "Gentile."
2. Sur. II, v. 58, footnote.

162. But those of them who did wrong changed the word which had been told them for another saying, and We sent down upon them wrath from heaven for their wrongdoing.

فَبَدَّلَ الَّذِيْنَ ظَلَمُوْا مِنْهُمْ قَوْلًا غَيْرَ الَّذِيْ قِيْلَ لَهُمْ فَاَرْسَلْنَا عَلَيْهِمْ رِجْزًا مِّنَ السَّمَاءِ بِمَا كَانُوْا يَظْلِمُوْنَ ۞

163. Ask them (O Muhammad) of the township that was by the sea, how they did break the sabbath, how their big fish came unto them visibly upon their sabbath day and on a day when they did not keep sabbath came they not unto them. Thus did We try them for that they were evil-livers.

وَسْـَٔلْهُمْ عَنِ الْقَرْيَةِ الَّتِيْ كَانَتْ حَاضِرَةَ الْبَحْرِ اِذْ يَعْدُوْنَ فِي السَّبْتِ اِذْ تَأْتِيْهِمْ حِيْتَانُهُمْ يَوْمَ سَبْتِهِمْ شُرَّعًا وَيَوْمَ لَا يَسْبِتُوْنَ لَا تَأْتِيْهِمْ ۚ كَذٰلِكَ ۚ نَبْلُوْهُمْ بِمَا كَانُوْا يَفْسُقُوْنَ ۞

164. And when a community among them said: Why preach ye to a folk whom Allah is about to destroy and punish with an awful doom, they said: In order to be free from guilt before your Lord, and that haply they may ward off (evil).

وَاِذْ قَالَتْ اُمَّةٌ مِّنْهُمْ لِمَ تَعِظُوْنَ قَوْمًا ۙ اللّٰهُ مُهْلِكُهُمْ اَوْ مُعَذِّبُهُمْ عَذَابًا شَدِيْدًا ۗ قَالُوْا مَعْذِرَةً اِلٰى رَبِّكُمْ وَلَعَلَّهُمْ يَتَّقُوْنَ ۞

165. And when they forgot that whereof they had been reminded, We rescued those who forbade wrong, and visited those who did wrong with dreadful punishment because they were evil-livers.

فَلَمَّا نَسُوْا مَا ذُكِّرُوْا بِهٖ اَنْجَيْنَا الَّذِيْنَ يَنْهَوْنَ عَنِ السُّوْءِ وَاَخَذْنَا الَّذِيْنَ ظَلَمُوْا بِعَذَابٍ بَئِيْسٍ ۭ بِمَا كَانُوْا يَفْسُقُوْنَ ۞

166. So when they took pride in that which they had been forbidden, We said unto them: Be ye apes despised and loathed!

فَلَمَّا عَتَوْا عَنْ مَّا نُهُوْا عَنْهُ قُلْنَا لَهُمْ كُوْنُوْا قِرَدَةً خَاسِئِيْنَ ۞

167. And (remember) when thy Lord proclaimed that He would raise against them till the Day of Resurrection those who would lay on them a cruel torment. Lo! verily thy Lord is swift in prosecution and lo! verily He is Forgiving, Merciful.

وَاِذْ تَاَذَّنَ رَبُّكَ لَيَبْعَثَنَّ عَلَيْهِمْ اِلٰى يَوْمِ الْقِيٰمَةِ مَنْ يَّسُوْمُهُمْ سُوْءَ الْعَذَابِ ۭ اِنَّ رَبَّكَ لَسَرِيْعُ الْعِقَابِ ۚ وَاِنَّهٗ لَغَفُوْرٌ رَّحِيْمٌ ۞

168. And We have sundered them in the earth as (separate) nations. Some of them are righteous, and some far from that. And We have tried them with good things and evil things that haply they might return.

وَقَطَّعْنٰهُمْ فِي الْاَرْضِ اُمَمًا ۚ مِنْهُمُ الصّٰلِحُوْنَ وَمِنْهُمْ دُوْنَ ذٰلِكَ ۖ وَبَلَوْنٰهُمْ بِالْحَسَنٰتِ وَالسَّيِّاٰتِ لَعَلَّهُمْ يَرْجِعُوْنَ ۞

169. And a generation hath succeeded them who inherited the Scriptures. They grasp the goods of this low life (as the price of evil-doing) and say: It will be forgiven us. And if there came to them, (again) the offer of the like, they would accept it (and would sin again). Hath not the covenant of the Scripture been taken on their behalf that they should not speak aught concerning Allah save the truth? And they have studied that which is therein. And the abode of the Hereafter is better, for those who ward off (evil). Have ye then no sense?

170. And as for those who make (men) keep the Scripture, and establish worship—lo! We squander not the wages of reformers.

171. And when We shook the Mount above them as it were a covering, and they supposed that it was going to fall upon them (and We said): Hold fast that which We have given you, and remember that which is therein, that ye may ward off (evil).

172. And (remember) when thy Lord brought forth from the Children of Adam, from their reins, their seed, and made them testify of themselves, (saying): Am I not your Lord? They said: Yea, verily. We testify. (That was) lest ye should say at the Day of Resurrection: Lo! of this we were unaware;

173. Or lest ye should say: (It is) only (that) our fathers ascribed partners to Allah of old and we were (their) seed after them. Wilt Thou destroy us on account of that which those who follow falsehood did?

174. Thus We detail our revelations, that haply they may return.

175. Recite unto them the tale of him to whom We gave Our revelations, but he sloughed them off, so Satan overtook him and he became of those who lead astray.

176. And had We willed We could have raised him by their means, but he clung to the earth and followed his own lust. Therefor his likeness is as the likeness of a dog; if thou attackest him he panteth with his tongue out, and if thou leavest him he panteth with his tongue out. Such is the likeness of the people who deny Our revelations. Narrate unto them the history (of the men of old), that haply they may take thought.

فَخَلَفَ مِنْ بَعْدِهِمْ خَلْفٌ وَّرِثُوا الْكِتٰبَ يَأْخُذُوْنَ
عَرَضَ هٰذَا الْاَدْنٰى وَيَقُوْلُوْنَ سَيُغْفَرُ لَنَا ۚ وَاِنْ
يَّاْتِهِمْ عَرَضٌ مِّثْلُهٗ يَاْخُذُوْهُ ؕ اَلَمْ يُؤْخَذْ عَلَيْهِمْ مِّيْثَاقُ
الْكِتٰبِ اَنْ لَّا يَقُوْلُوْا عَلَى اللّٰهِ اِلَّا الْحَقَّ وَدَرَسُوْا مَا فِيْهِ ؕ وَ
الدَّارُ الْاٰخِرَةُ خَيْرٌ لِّلَّذِيْنَ يَتَّقُوْنَ ؕ اَفَلَا تَعْقِلُوْنَ ﴿١٦٩﴾
وَالَّذِيْنَ يُمَسِّكُوْنَ بِالْكِتٰبِ وَاَقَامُوا الصَّلٰوةَ ؕ اِنَّا
لَا نُضِيْعُ اَجْرَ الْمُصْلِحِيْنَ ﴿١٧٠﴾
وَاِذْ نَتَقْنَا الْجَبَلَ فَوْقَهُمْ كَاَنَّهٗ ظُلَّةٌ وَّظَنُّوْٓا اَنَّهٗ وَاقِعٌۢ
بِهِمْ ۚ خُذُوْا مَآ اٰتَيْنٰكُمْ بِقُوَّةٍ وَّاذْكُرُوْا مَا فِيْهِ
ع لَعَلَّكُمْ تَتَّقُوْنَ ﴿١٧١﴾
وَاِذْ اَخَذَ رَبُّكَ مِنْۢ بَنِيْٓ اٰدَمَ مِنْ ظُهُوْرِهِمْ ذُرِّيَّتَهُمْ
وَاَشْهَدَهُمْ عَلٰٓى اَنْفُسِهِمْ ۚ اَلَسْتُ بِرَبِّكُمْ ؕ قَالُوْا بَلٰى ۛۚ شَهِدْنَا ۛۚ
اَنْ تَقُوْلُوْا يَوْمَ الْقِيٰمَةِ اِنَّا كُنَّا عَنْ هٰذَا غٰفِلِيْنَ ﴿١٧٢﴾
اَوْ تَقُوْلُوْٓا اِنَّمَآ اَشْرَكَ اٰبَآؤُنَا مِنْ قَبْلُ وَكُنَّا ذُرِّيَّةً
مِّنْۢ بَعْدِهِمْ ۚ اَفَتُهْلِكُنَا بِمَا فَعَلَ الْمُبْطِلُوْنَ ﴿١٧٣﴾
وَكَذٰلِكَ نُفَصِّلُ الْاٰيٰتِ وَلَعَلَّهُمْ يَرْجِعُوْنَ ﴿١٧٤﴾
وَاتْلُ عَلَيْهِمْ نَبَاَ الَّذِيْٓ اٰتَيْنٰهُ اٰيٰتِنَا فَانْسَلَخَ مِنْهَا
فَاَتْبَعَهُ الشَّيْطٰنُ فَكَانَ مِنَ الْغٰوِيْنَ ﴿١٧٥﴾
وَلَوْ شِئْنَا لَرَفَعْنٰهُ بِهَا وَلٰكِنَّهٗٓ اَخْلَدَ اِلَى الْاَرْضِ وَ
اتَّبَعَ هَوٰىهُ ۚ فَمَثَلُهٗ كَمَثَلِ الْكَلْبِ ۚ اِنْ تَحْمِلْ عَلَيْهِ يَلْهَثْ
اَوْ تَتْرُكْهُ يَلْهَثْ ؕ ذٰلِكَ مَثَلُ الْقَوْمِ الَّذِيْنَ كَذَّبُوْا
بِاٰيٰتِنَا ۚ فَاقْصُصِ الْقَصَصَ لَعَلَّهُمْ يَتَفَكَّرُوْنَ ﴿١٧٦﴾

177. Evil as an example are the folk who denied Our revelations, and were wont to wrong themselves.

178. He who Allah leadeth, he indeed is led aright, while he whom Allah sendeth astray—they indeed are losers.

179. Already have We urged unto hell many of the jinn and humankind, having hearts wherewith they understand not, and having eyes wherewith they see not, and having ears wherewith they hear not. These are as the cattle—nay, but they are worse! These are the neglectful.

180. Allah's are the fairest names. Invoke Him by them. And leave the company of those who blaspheme His names. They will be requited what they do.

181. And of those whom We created there is a nation who guide with the Truth and establish justice therewith.

182. And those who deny Our revelations—step by step We lead them on from whence they know not.

183. I give them rein (for) lo! My scheme is strong.

184. Have they not bethought them (that) there is no madness in their comrade? He is but a plain warner.

185. Have they not considered the dominion of the heavens and the earth, and what things Allah hath created, and that it may be that their own term draweth nigh? In what fact after this will they believe?

186. Those whom Allah sendeth astray, there is no guide for them. He leaveth them to wander blindly on in their contumacy.

سَاءَ مَثَلًا الْقَوْمُ الَّذِينَ كَذَّبُوا بِآيَاتِنَا وَأَنفُسَهُمْ
كَانُوا يَظْلِمُونَ ﴿١٧٧﴾
مَن يَهْدِ اللَّهُ فَهُوَ الْمُهْتَدِي وَمَن يُضْلِلْ فَأُولَٰئِكَ
هُمُ الْخَاسِرُونَ ﴿١٧٨﴾
وَلَقَدْ ذَرَأْنَا لِجَهَنَّمَ كَثِيرًا مِّنَ الْجِنِّ وَالْإِنسِ لَهُمْ
قُلُوبٌ لَّا يَفْقَهُونَ بِهَا وَلَهُمْ أَعْيُنٌ لَّا يُبْصِرُونَ
بِهَا وَلَهُمْ آذَانٌ لَّا يَسْمَعُونَ بِهَا أُولَٰئِكَ كَالْأَنْعَامِ
بَلْ هُمْ أَضَلُّ أُولَٰئِكَ هُمُ الْغَافِلُونَ ﴿١٧٩﴾
وَلِلَّهِ الْأَسْمَاءُ الْحُسْنَىٰ فَادْعُوهُ بِهَا وَذَرُوا الَّذِينَ
يُلْحِدُونَ فِي أَسْمَائِهِ سَيُجْزَوْنَ مَا كَانُوا يَعْمَلُونَ ﴿١٨٠﴾
وَمِمَّنْ خَلَقْنَا أُمَّةٌ يَهْدُونَ بِالْحَقِّ وَبِهِ
ع ٢٢ ١٢ يَعْدِلُونَ ﴿١٨١﴾
وَالَّذِينَ كَذَّبُوا بِآيَاتِنَا سَنَسْتَدْرِجُهُم مِّنْ حَيْثُ
لَا يَعْلَمُونَ ﴿١٨٢﴾
وَأُمْلِي لَهُمْ إِنَّ كَيْدِي مَتِينٌ ﴿١٨٣﴾
أَوَلَمْ يَتَفَكَّرُوا مَا بِصَاحِبِهِم مِّن جِنَّةٍ إِنْ هُوَ
إِلَّا نَذِيرٌ مُّبِينٌ ﴿١٨٤﴾
أَوَلَمْ يَنظُرُوا فِي مَلَكُوتِ السَّمَاوَاتِ وَالْأَرْضِ وَمَا
خَلَقَ اللَّهُ مِن شَيْءٍ وَأَنْ عَسَىٰ أَن يَكُونَ قَدِ اقْتَرَبَ
أَجَلُهُمْ فَبِأَيِّ حَدِيثٍ بَعْدَهُ يُؤْمِنُونَ ﴿١٨٥﴾
مَن يُضْلِلِ اللَّهُ فَلَا هَادِيَ لَهُ وَيَذَرُهُمْ فِي
طُغْيَانِهِمْ يَعْمَهُونَ ﴿١٨٦﴾

187. They ask thee of the (destined) Hour, when will it come to port. Say: Knowledge thereof is with my Lord only. He alone will manifest it at its proper time. It is heavy in the heavens and the earth. It cometh not to you save unawares. They question thee as if thou couldst be well informed thereof. Say: Knowledge thereof is with Allah only, but most of mankind know not.

يَسْـَٔلُونَكَ عَنِ السَّاعَةِ أَيَّانَ مُرْسٰهَا ۖ قُلْ إِنَّمَا عِلْمُهَا
عِنْدَ رَبِّي ۖ لَا يُجَلِّيهَا لِوَقْتِهَا إِلَّا هُوَ ۚ ثَقُلَتْ فِي وقف لازم / وقف منزل
السَّمٰوٰتِ وَالْأَرْضِ ۚ لَا تَأْتِيكُمْ إِلَّا بَغْتَةً ۗ يَسْـَٔلُونَكَ
كَأَنَّكَ حَفِيٌّ عَنْهَا ۖ قُلْ إِنَّمَا عِلْمُهَا عِنْدَ اللّٰهِ وَ
لٰكِنَّ أَكْثَرَ النَّاسِ لَا يَعْلَمُونَ ﴿١٨٧﴾

188. Say: For myself I have no power to benefit, nor power to hurt, save that which Allah willeth. Had I knowledge of the Unseen, I should have abundance of wealth, and adversity would not touch me. I am but a warner, and a bearer of good tidings unto folk who believe.

قُلْ لَا أَمْلِكُ لِنَفْسِي نَفْعًا وَلَا ضَرًّا إِلَّا مَا شَاءَ اللّٰهُ ۚ
وَلَوْ كُنْتُ أَعْلَمُ الْغَيْبَ لَاسْتَكْثَرْتُ مِنَ الْخَيْرِ ۛ
وَمَا مَسَّنِيَ السُّوءُ ۚ إِنْ أَنَا إِلَّا نَذِيرٌ وَبَشِيرٌ لِقَوْمٍ وقف النبي
يُؤْمِنُونَ ﴿١٨٨﴾ ع ٢٣ ١٣

189. He it is Who did create you from a single soul, and therefrom did make his mate that he might take rest in her. And when he covered her she bore a light burden, and she passed (unnoticed) with it, but when it became heavy they cried unto Allah, their Lord, saying: If thou givest unto us aright we shall be of the thankful.

هُوَ الَّذِي خَلَقَكُمْ مِنْ نَفْسٍ وَاحِدَةٍ وَجَعَلَ مِنْهَا
زَوْجَهَا لِيَسْكُنَ إِلَيْهَا ۖ فَلَمَّا تَغَشّٰهَا حَمَلَتْ حَمْلًا
خَفِيفًا فَمَرَّتْ بِهِ ۖ فَلَمَّا أَثْقَلَتْ دَعَوَا اللّٰهَ رَبَّهُمَا
لَئِنْ آتَيْتَنَا صَالِحًا لَنَكُونَنَّ مِنَ الشّٰكِرِينَ ﴿١٨٩﴾

190. But when He gave unto them aright, they ascribed unto Him partners in respect of that which He had given them. High is He exalted above all that they associate (with Him).

فَلَمَّا آتٰهُمَا صَالِحًا جَعَلَا لَهُ شُرَكَاءَ فِيمَا آتٰهُمَا ۚ
فَتَعٰلَى اللّٰهُ عَمَّا يُشْرِكُونَ ﴿١٩٠﴾

191. Attribute they as partners to Allah those who created naught, but are themselves created,

أَيُشْرِكُونَ مَا لَا يَخْلُقُ شَيْـًٔا وَهُمْ يُخْلَقُونَ ﴿١٩١﴾

192. And cannot give them help, nor can they help themselves?

وَلَا يَسْتَطِيعُونَ لَهُمْ نَصْرًا وَلَا أَنْفُسَهُمْ يَنْصُرُونَ ﴿١٩٢﴾

193. And if ye call them to the Guidance, they follow you not. Whether ye call them or are silent is all one to them.

وَإِنْ تَدْعُوهُمْ إِلَى الْهُدٰى لَا يَتَّبِعُوكُمْ ۚ سَوَاءٌ عَلَيْكُمْ
أَدَعَوْتُمُوهُمْ أَمْ أَنْتُمْ صَامِتُونَ ﴿١٩٣﴾

194. Lo! those on whom ye call beside Allah are slaves like unto you. Call on them now, and let them answer you, if ye are truthful!

إِنَّ الَّذِينَ تَدْعُونَ مِنْ دُونِ اللّٰهِ عِبَادٌ أَمْثَالُكُمْ ۖ
فَادْعُوهُمْ فَلْيَسْتَجِيبُوا لَكُمْ إِنْ كُنْتُمْ
صٰدِقِينَ ﴿١٩٤﴾

195. Have they feet wherewith they walk, or have they hands wherewith they hold, or have they eyes wherewith they see, or have they ears wherewith they hear? Say: Call upon your (so-called) partners (of Allah), and then contrive against me, spare me not!

196. Lo! my Protecting Friend is Allah Who revealeth the Scripture. He befriendeth the righteous.

197. They on whom ye call beside Him have no power to help you, nor can they help themselves.

198. And if ye (Muslims) call them to the Guidance they hear not; and thou (Muhammad) seest them looking toward thee, but they see not.

199. Keep to forgiveness (O Muhammad), and enjoin kindness, and turn away from the ignorant.

200. And if a slander from the devil wound thee, then seek refuge in Allah. Lo! He is Hearer, Knower.

201. Lo! those who ward off (evil), when a glamour from the devil troubleth them, they do but remember (Allah's guidance) and behold them seers!

202. Their brethren plunge them further into error and cease not.

203. And when thou bringest not a verse for them they say: Why hast thou not chosen it? Say: I follow only that which is inspired in me from my Lord. This (Qur'ān) is insight from your Lord, and a guidance and a mercy for a people that believe.

204. And when the Qur'ān is recited, give ear to it and pay heed, that ye may obtain mercy.

205. And do thou (O Muhammad) remember thy Lord within thyself humbly and with awe, below thy breath, at morn and evening. And be thou not of the neglectful.

206. Lo! those who are with thy Lord are not too proud to do Him service, but they praise Him and adore Him.

ألهم أرجل يمشون بها أم لهم أيد يبطشون بها
أم لهم أعين يبصرون بها أم لهم آذان يسمعون
بها قل ادعوا شركاءكم ثم كيدون فلا تنظرون ﴿١٩٥﴾
إن ولي الله الذي نزل الكتب وهو يتولى الصلحين ﴿١٩٦﴾
والذين تدعون من دونه لا يستطيعون نصركم
ولا أنفسهم ينصرون ﴿١٩٧﴾
وإن تدعوهم إلى الهدى لا يسمعوا وترىهم
ينظرون إليك وهم لا يبصرون ﴿١٩٨﴾
خذ العفو وأمر بالعرف وأعرض عن الجهلين ﴿١٩٩﴾
وإما ينزغنك من الشيطن نزغ فاستعذ بالله
إنه سميع عليم ﴿٢٠٠﴾
إن الذين اتقوا إذا مسهم طئف من الشيطن
تذكروا فإذا هم مبصرون ﴿٢٠١﴾
وإخوانهم يمدونهم في الغي ثم لا يقصرون ﴿٢٠٢﴾
وإذا لم تأتهم بآية قالوا لولا اجتبيتها قل إنما
أتبع ما يوحى إلي من ربي هذا بصائر من ربكم
وهدى ورحمة لقوم يؤمنون ﴿٢٠٣﴾
وإذا قرئ القرآن فاستمعوا له وأنصتوا لعلكم ترحمون ﴿٢٠٤﴾
واذكر ربك في نفسك تضرعا وخيفة ودون الجهر
من القول بالغدو والآصال ولا تكن من الغفلين ﴿٢٠٥﴾
إن الذين عند ربك لا يستكبرون عن عبادته
ويسبحونه وله يسجدون ﴿٢٠٦﴾ السجدة

Al-Anfāl, "The Spoils," takes its name from the first verse by which it is proclaimed that property in war belongs "to Allah and His messenger"—that is to say, to the theocratic State, to be used for the common weal. The date of the revelation of this Sūrah is established, from the nature of the contents, as the time that elapsed between the battle of Badr and the division of the spoils—a space of only one month—in the second year of the Hijrah. The concluding verses are of later date and lead up to the subject of Sūrah IX.

A Meccan caravan was returning from Syria, and its leader, Abū Sufyān, fearing an attack from Al-Madīnah, sent a camel-rider on to Mecca with a frantic appeal for help; which must have come too late, considering the distances, if, as some writers even among Muslims have alleged, the Prophet had always intended to attack the caravan. Ibn Ishāq (*apud* Ibn Hishām) when treating of the Tabūk expedition, says that the Prophet announced the destination on that occasion, whereas it was his custom to hide his real objective. Was not the real objective hidden in this first campaign? It is a fact that he only advanced when the army sent to protect the caravan, or rather (it is probable) to punish the Muslims for having plundered it, was approaching Al-Madīnah. His little army of three hundred and thirteen men, ill-armed and roughly equipped, traversed the desert for three days till, when they halted near the water of Badr, they had news that the army of Qureysh was approaching on the other side of the valley. Then rain fell heavily upon Qureysh so that they could not advance further on account of the muddy state of the ground, lightly on the Muslims, who were able to advance to the water and secure it. At the same time Abū Sufyān, the leader of the caravan, which was also heading for the water of Badr, was warned by one of his scouts of the advance of the Muslims and turned back to the coast-plain. Before the battle against what must have appeared to all men overwhelming odds, the Prophet gave the Anṣār, the men of Al-Madīnah, whose oath of allegiance had not included fighting in the field, the chance of returning if they wished; but they were only hurt by the suggestion that they could possibly forsake him. On the other hand, several of Qureysh, including the whole Zuhri clan, returned to Mecca when they heard the caravan was safe, having no grudge otherwise against the Prophet and his followers, whom they regarded as men who had been wronged.

Still the army of Qureysh outnumbered the Muslims by more than two to one, and was much better mounted and equipped, so that their leaders counted on an easy victory. When the Prophet saw them streaming down the sandhills, he cried: "O Allah! Here are Qureysh with all their chivalry and pomp, who oppose Thee and deny Thy messenger. O Allah! Thy help which Thou hast promised me! O Allah! Make them bow this day!"

The Muslims were successful in the single combats with which Arab battles opened. But the mêlée at first went hard against them; and the Prophet stood and prayed under the shelter which they had put up to screen him from the sun, and cried: "O Allah! If this little company is destroyed, there will be none left in the land to worship Thee." Then he fell into a trance and, when he spoke again, he told Abū Bakr, who was with him, that the promised help had come. Thereupon he went out to encourage his people. Taking up a handful of gravel, he ran towards Qureysh and flung it at them, saying: "The faces are confounded!" on which the tide of battle turned in favour of the Muslims. The leader of Qureysh and several of their greatest men were killed, many were taken prisoner, and their baggage and camels were captured by the Muslims. It was indeed a day to be remembered in the early history of Al-Islām, and there was great rejoicing in Al-Madīnah. But the Muslims are warned in this Sūrah that it is only the beginning of their struggle against heavy odds. In fact, in the following year at Mt. Uḥud (referred to in Sūr. III), the enemy came against them with an army of three thousand, and in the fifth year of the Hijrah, an allied army of the pagan clans, amounting to 10,000, besieged Al-Madīnah in the "War of the Trench" (see Sūr. XXXIII, "The Clans").

The date of revelation is the second year of the Hijrah for the most part. Some good Arabic authorities hold that vv. 30-40, or some of them, were revealed at Mecca just before the Hijrah.

SPOILS OF WAR

Revealed at Al-Madīnah

In the name of Allah, the Beneficent, the Merciful.

1. They ask thee (O Muhammad) of the spoils of war. Say: The spoils of war belong to Allah and the messenger, so keep your duty to Allah, and adjust the matter of your difference, and obey Allah and His messenger, if ye are (true) believers.

2. They only are the (true) believers whose hearts feel fear when Allah is mentioned, and when the revelations of Allah are recited unto them they increase their faith, and who trust in their Lord;

3. Who establish worship and spend of that We have bestowed on them.

4. Those are they who are in truth believers. For them are grades (of honour) with their Lord, and pardon, and a bountiful provision.

5. Even as thy Lord caused thee (Muhammad) to go forth from thy home with the Truth, and lo! a party of the believers were averse (to it):

6. Disputing with thee of the Truth after it had been made manifest, as if they were being driven to death visible.

7. And when Allah promised you one of the two bands[1] (of the enemy) that it should be yours, and ye longed that other than the armed one might be yours. And Allah willed that He should cause the Truth to triumph by His words, and cut the root of the disbelievers;

8. That He might cause the Truth to triumph and bring vanity to naught, however much the guilty might oppose;

1. Either the army or the caravan.

ایاتها ٧٥ (٨) سورة الانفال مدنية ركوعاتها ١٠

بسم الله الرحمن الرحيم

يسئلونك عن الانفال قل الانفال لله والرسول
فاتقوا الله واصلحوا ذات بينكم واطيعوا الله و
رسوله ان كنتم مؤمنين ①
انما المؤمنون الذين اذا ذكر الله وجلت قلوبهم
واذا تليت عليهم ايته زادتهم ايمانا وعلى
ربهم يتوكلون ②
الذين يقيمون الصلوة ومما رزقنهم ينفقون ③
اولئك هم المؤمنون حقا لهم درجت عند ربهم
ومغفرة ورزق كريم ④
كما اخرجك ربك من بيتك بالحق وان فريقا
من المؤمنين لكرهون ⑤
يجادلونك في الحق بعد ما تبين كانما
يساقون الى الموت وهم ينظرون ⑥
واذ يعدكم الله احدى الطائفتين انها
لكم وتودون ان غير ذات الشوكة تكون
لكم ويريد الله ان يحق الحق بكلمته ويقطع
دابر الكفرين ⑦
ليحق الحق ويبطل الباطل ولو كره
المجرمون ⑧

9. When ye sought help of your Lord and He answered you (saying): I will help you with a thousand of the angels, rank on rank.

10. Allah appointed it only as good tidings, and that your hearts thereby might be at rest. Victory cometh only by the help of Allah. Lo! Allah is Mighty, Wise.

11. When he made the slumber fall upon you as a reassurance from Him and sent down water from the sky upon you, that thereby He might purify you, and remove from you the fear of Satan, and make strong your hearts and firm (your) feet thereby.

12. When thy Lord inspired the angels, (saying:) I am with you. So make those who believe stand firm. I will throw fear into the hearts of those who disbelieve. Then smite the necks and smite of them each finger.

13. That is because they opposed Allah and His messenger. Whoso opposeth Allah and His messenger, (for him) lo! Allah is severe in punishment.

14. That (is the award), so taste it, and (know) that for disbelievers is the torment of the Fire.

15. O ye who believe! When ye meet those who disbelieve in battle, turn not your backs to them.

16. Whoso on that day turneth his back to them, unless manoeuvring for battle or intent to join a company, he truly hath incurred wrath from Allah, and his habitation will be hell, a hapless journey's end.

17. Ye (Muslims) slew them not, but Allah slew them. And thou (Muhammad) threwest not when thou didst throw, but Allah threw, that He might test the believers by a fair test from Him. Lo! Allah is Hearer, Knower.

18. That (is the case): and (know) that Allah (it is) Who maketh weak the plan of disbelievers.

إِذْ تَسْتَغِيثُونَ رَبَّكُمْ فَاسْتَجَابَ لَكُمْ أَنِّي مُمِدُّكُمْ
بِأَلْفٍ مِّنَ الْمَلَائِكَةِ مُرْدِفِينَ ٩
وَمَا جَعَلَهُ اللَّهُ إِلَّا بُشْرَىٰ وَلِتَطْمَئِنَّ بِهِ قُلُوبُكُمْ وَمَا
ع النَّصْرُ إِلَّا مِنْ عِندِ اللَّهِ إِنَّ اللَّهَ عَزِيزٌ حَكِيمٌ ١٠
إِذْ يُغَشِّيكُمُ النُّعَاسَ أَمَنَةً مِّنْهُ وَيُنَزِّلُ عَلَيْكُم مِّنَ
السَّمَاءِ مَاءً لِّيُطَهِّرَكُم بِهِ وَيُذْهِبَ عَنكُمْ رِجْزَ الشَّيْطَانِ
وَلِيَرْبِطَ عَلَىٰ قُلُوبِكُمْ وَيُثَبِّتَ بِهِ الْأَقْدَامَ ١١
إِذْ يُوحِي رَبُّكَ إِلَى الْمَلَائِكَةِ أَنِّي مَعَكُمْ فَثَبِّتُوا الَّذِينَ
آمَنُوا سَأُلْقِي فِي قُلُوبِ الَّذِينَ كَفَرُوا الرُّعْبَ فَاضْرِبُوا
فَوْقَ الْأَعْنَاقِ وَاضْرِبُوا مِنْهُمْ كُلَّ بَنَانٍ ١٢
ذَٰلِكَ بِأَنَّهُمْ شَاقُّوا اللَّهَ وَرَسُولَهُ وَمَن يُشَاقِقِ
اللَّهَ وَرَسُولَهُ فَإِنَّ اللَّهَ شَدِيدُ الْعِقَابِ ١٣
ذَٰلِكُمْ فَذُوقُوهُ وَأَنَّ لِلْكَافِرِينَ عَذَابَ النَّارِ ١٤
يَا أَيُّهَا الَّذِينَ آمَنُوا إِذَا لَقِيتُمُ الَّذِينَ كَفَرُوا زَحْفًا
فَلَا تُوَلُّوهُمُ الْأَدْبَارَ ١٥
وَمَن يُوَلِّهِمْ يَوْمَئِذٍ دُبُرَهُ إِلَّا مُتَحَرِّفًا لِّقِتَالٍ أَوْ
مُتَحَيِّزًا إِلَىٰ فِئَةٍ فَقَدْ بَاءَ بِغَضَبٍ مِّنَ اللَّهِ وَمَأْوَاهُ
جَهَنَّمُ وَبِئْسَ الْمَصِيرُ ١٦
فَلَمْ تَقْتُلُوهُمْ وَلَٰكِنَّ اللَّهَ قَتَلَهُمْ وَمَا رَمَيْتَ إِذْ رَمَيْتَ
وَلَٰكِنَّ اللَّهَ رَمَىٰ وَلِيُبْلِيَ الْمُؤْمِنِينَ مِنْهُ بَلَاءً حَسَنًا
إِنَّ اللَّهَ سَمِيعٌ عَلِيمٌ ١٧
ذَٰلِكُمْ وَأَنَّ اللَّهَ مُوهِنُ كَيْدِ الْكَافِرِينَ ١٨

19. (O Qureysh!) If ye sought a judgement, now hath the judgement come unto you. And if ye cease (from persecuting the believers) it will be better for you, but if ye return (to the attack) We also shall return. And your host will avail you naught, however numerous it be, and (know) that Allah is with the believers (in His guidance).

20. O ye who believe! Obey Allah and His messenger, and turn not away from him when ye hear (him speak).

21. Be not as those who say, We hear, and they hear not.

22. Lo! the worst of beasts in Allah's sight are the deaf, the dumb, who have no sense.

23. Had Allah known of any good in them He would have made them hear, but had He made them hear they would have turned away, averse.

24. O ye who believe; Obey Allah, and the messenger when He calleth you to that which quickeneth you, and know that Allah cometh in between the man and his own heart, and that He it is unto Whom ye will be gathered.

25. And guard yourselves against a chastisement which cannot fall exclusively on those of you who are wrong-doers, and know that Allah is severe in punishment.

26. And remember, when ye were few and reckoned feeble in the land, and were in fear lest men should extirpate you, how He gave you refuge, and strengthened you with His help, and made provision of good things for you, that haply ye might be thankful.

27. O ye who believe! Betray not Allah and His messenger, nor knowingly betray your trusts.

28. And know that your possessions and your children are a test, and that with Allah is immense reward.

إن تستفتحوا فقد جاءكم الفتح وإن تنتهوا فهو
خير لكم وإن تعودوا نعد ولن تغني عنكم فئتكم
ع شيئا ولو كثرت وأن الله مع المؤمنين ﴿١٩﴾
يا أيها الذين آمنوا أطيعوا الله ورسوله ولا تولوا
عنه وأنتم تسمعون ﴿٢٠﴾
ولا تكونوا كالذين قالوا سمعنا وهم لا يسمعون ﴿٢١﴾
إن شر الدواب عند الله الصم البكم الذين لا
يعقلون ﴿٢٢﴾
ولو علم الله فيهم خيرا لأسمعهم ولو أسمعهم
لتولوا وهم معرضون ﴿٢٣﴾
يا أيها الذين آمنوا استجيبوا لله وللرسول إذا
دعاكم لما يحييكم واعلموا أن الله يحول بين
المرء وقلبه وأنه إليه تحشرون ﴿٢٤﴾
واتقوا فتنة لا تصيبن الذين ظلموا منكم
خاصة واعلموا أن الله شديد العقاب ﴿٢٥﴾
واذكروا إذ أنتم قليل مستضعفون في الأرض
تخافون أن يتخطفكم الناس فآواكم وأيدكم
بنصره ورزقكم من الطيبات لعلكم تشكرون ﴿٢٦﴾
يا أيها الذين آمنوا لا تخونوا الله والرسول وتخونوا
أماناتكم وأنتم تعلمون ﴿٢٧﴾
واعلموا أنما أموالكم وأولادكم فتنة وأن الله
ع عنده أجر عظيم ﴿٢٨﴾

29. O ye who believe! If ye keep your duty to Allah, He will give you discrimination (between right and wrong) and will rid you of your evil thoughts and deeds, and will forgive you. Allah is of Infinite bounty.

30. And when those who disbelieve plot against thee (O Muhammad) to wound thee fatally, or to kill thee or to drive thee forth; they plot, but Allah (also) plotteth; and Allah is the best of plotters.

31. And when Our revelations are recited unto them they say: We have heard. If we wish we can speak the like of this. Lo! this is naught but fables of the men of old.

32. And when they said: O Allah! If this be indeed the truth from Thee, then rain down stones on us or bring on us some painful doom!

33. But Allah would not punish them while thou wast with them, nor will He punish them while they seek forgiveness.

34. What (plea) have they that Allah should not punish them, when they debar (His servants) from the Inviolable Place of Worship, though they are not its fitting guardians. Its fitting guardians are those only who keep their duty to Allah. But most of them know not.

35. And their worship at the (holy) House is naught but whistling and hand-clapping. Therefore (it is said unto them): Taste of the doom because ye disbelieve.

36. Lo! those who disbelieve spend their wealth in order that they may debar (men) from the way of Allah. They will spend it, then it will become an anguish for them, then they will be conquered. And those who disbelieve will be gathered unto hell:

يَٰٓأَيُّهَا ٱلَّذِينَ ءَامَنُوٓا إِن تَتَّقُوا ٱللَّهَ يَجْعَل لَّكُمْ
فُرْقَانًا وَيُكَفِّرْ عَنكُمْ سَيِّـَٔاتِكُمْ وَيَغْفِرْ لَكُمْ ۗ وَٱللَّهُ
ذُو ٱلْفَضْلِ ٱلْعَظِيمِ ﴿٢٩﴾
وَإِذْ يَمْكُرُ بِكَ ٱلَّذِينَ كَفَرُوا لِيُثْبِتُوكَ أَوْ يَقْتُلُوكَ
أَوْ يُخْرِجُوكَ ۚ وَيَمْكُرُونَ وَيَمْكُرُ ٱللَّهُ ۖ وَٱللَّهُ خَيْرُ
ٱلْمَٰكِرِينَ ﴿٣٠﴾
وَإِذَا تُتْلَىٰ عَلَيْهِمْ ءَايَٰتُنَا قَالُوا قَدْ سَمِعْنَا لَوْ نَشَآءُ
لَقُلْنَا مِثْلَ هَٰذَآ ۙ إِنْ هَٰذَآ إِلَّآ أَسَٰطِيرُ ٱلْأَوَّلِينَ ﴿٣١﴾
وَإِذْ قَالُوا ٱللَّهُمَّ إِن كَانَ هَٰذَا هُوَ ٱلْحَقَّ مِنْ عِندِكَ
فَأَمْطِرْ عَلَيْنَا حِجَارَةً مِّنَ ٱلسَّمَآءِ أَوِ ٱئْتِنَا بِعَذَابٍ
أَلِيمٍ ﴿٣٢﴾
وَمَا كَانَ ٱللَّهُ لِيُعَذِّبَهُمْ وَأَنتَ فِيهِمْ ۚ وَمَا كَانَ
ٱللَّهُ مُعَذِّبَهُمْ وَهُمْ يَسْتَغْفِرُونَ ﴿٣٣﴾
وَمَا لَهُمْ أَلَّا يُعَذِّبَهُمُ ٱللَّهُ وَهُمْ يَصُدُّونَ عَنِ
ٱلْمَسْجِدِ ٱلْحَرَامِ وَمَا كَانُوٓا أَوْلِيَآءَهُ ۚ إِنْ أَوْلِيَآؤُهُ
إِلَّا ٱلْمُتَّقُونَ وَلَٰكِنَّ أَكْثَرَهُمْ لَا يَعْلَمُونَ ﴿٣٤﴾
وَمَا كَانَ صَلَاتُهُمْ عِندَ ٱلْبَيْتِ إِلَّا مُكَآءً وَتَصْدِيَةً ۚ
فَذُوقُوا ٱلْعَذَابَ بِمَا كُنتُمْ تَكْفُرُونَ ﴿٣٥﴾
إِنَّ ٱلَّذِينَ كَفَرُوا يُنفِقُونَ أَمْوَٰلَهُمْ لِيَصُدُّوا عَن
سَبِيلِ ٱللَّهِ ۚ فَسَيُنفِقُونَهَا ثُمَّ تَكُونُ عَلَيْهِمْ حَسْرَةً
ثُمَّ يُغْلَبُونَ ۗ وَٱلَّذِينَ كَفَرُوٓا إِلَىٰ جَهَنَّمَ
يُحْشَرُونَ ﴿٣٦﴾

37. That Allah may separate the wicked from the good. The wicked will He place piece upon piece, and heap them all together, and consign them unto hell. Such verily are the losers.

38. Tell those who disbelieve that if they cease (from persecution of believers) that which is past will be forgiven them; but if they return (thereto) then the example of the men of old hath already gone (before them, for a warning).

39. And fight them until persecution is no more, and religion is all for Allah. But if they cease, then lo! Allah is Seer of what they do.

40. And if they turn away, then know that Allah is your Befriender—a transcendent Patron, a transcendent Helper!

41. And know that whatever ye take as spoils of war, lo! a fifth thereof is for Allah, and for the messenger[1] and for the kinsman (who hath need) and orphans and the needy and the wayfarer, if ye believe in Allah and that which We revealed unto Our slave on the Day of Discrimination, the day when the two armies met. And Allah is Able to do all things.

42. When ye were on the near bank (of the valley) and they were on the yonder bank, and the caravan was below you (on the coast plain). And had ye trysted to meet one another ye surely would have failed to keep the tryst, but (it happened, as it did, without the forethought of either of you) that Allah might conclude a thing that must be done; that he who perished (on that day) might perish by a clear proof (of His sovereignty) and he who survived might survive by a clear proof (of His sovereignty). Lo! Allah in truth is Hearer, Knower:

43. When Allah showed them unto thee (O Muhammad) in thy dream as few in number, and if He had shown them to thee as many, ye (Muslims) would have faltered and would have quarrelled over the affair. But Allah saved (you). Lo! He knoweth what is in the breasts (of men).

1. *i.e.* for the State, to be used for the common weal.

لِيَمِيزَ اللَّهُ الْخَبِيثَ مِنَ الطَّيِّبِ وَيَجْعَلَ الْخَبِيثَ
بَعْضَهُ عَلَىٰ بَعْضٍ فَيَرْكُمَهُ جَمِيعًا فَيَجْعَلَهُ فِي
جَهَنَّمَ ۚ أُولَٰئِكَ هُمُ الْخَاسِرُونَ ﴿٣٧﴾ ع ١٨
قُل لِّلَّذِينَ كَفَرُوا إِن يَنتَهُوا يُغْفَرْ لَهُم مَّا قَدْ سَلَفَ
وَإِن يَعُودُوا فَقَدْ مَضَتْ سُنَّتُ الْأَوَّلِينَ ﴿٣٨﴾
وَقَاتِلُوهُمْ حَتَّىٰ لَا تَكُونَ فِتْنَةٌ وَيَكُونَ الدِّينُ كُلُّهُ
لِلَّهِ ۚ فَإِنِ انتَهَوْا فَإِنَّ اللَّهَ بِمَا يَعْمَلُونَ بَصِيرٌ ﴿٣٩﴾
وَإِن تَوَلَّوْا فَاعْلَمُوا أَنَّ اللَّهَ مَوْلَاكُمْ ۚ نِعْمَ الْمَوْلَىٰ وَ
نِعْمَ النَّصِيرُ ﴿٤٠﴾
وَاعْلَمُوا أَنَّمَا غَنِمْتُم مِّن شَيْءٍ فَأَنَّ لِلَّهِ خُمُسَهُ
وَلِلرَّسُولِ وَلِذِي الْقُرْبَىٰ وَالْيَتَامَىٰ وَالْمَسَاكِينِ وَ
ابْنِ السَّبِيلِ إِن كُنتُمْ آمَنتُم بِاللَّهِ وَمَا أَنزَلْنَا عَلَىٰ
عَبْدِنَا يَوْمَ الْفُرْقَانِ يَوْمَ الْتَقَى الْجَمْعَانِ ۗ وَاللَّهُ
عَلَىٰ كُلِّ شَيْءٍ قَدِيرٌ ﴿٤١﴾
إِذْ أَنتُم بِالْعُدْوَةِ الدُّنْيَا وَهُم بِالْعُدْوَةِ الْقُصْوَىٰ
وَالرَّكْبُ أَسْفَلَ مِنكُمْ ۚ وَلَوْ تَوَاعَدتُّمْ لَاخْتَلَفْتُمْ فِي
الْمِيعَادِ ۙ وَلَٰكِن لِّيَقْضِيَ اللَّهُ أَمْرًا كَانَ مَفْعُولًا
لِّيَهْلِكَ مَنْ هَلَكَ عَن بَيِّنَةٍ وَيَحْيَىٰ مَنْ حَيَّ عَن
بَيِّنَةٍ ۗ وَإِنَّ اللَّهَ لَسَمِيعٌ عَلِيمٌ ﴿٤٢﴾
إِذْ يُرِيكَهُمُ اللَّهُ فِي مَنَامِكَ قَلِيلًا ۖ وَلَوْ أَرَاكَهُمْ كَثِيرًا
لَّفَشِلْتُمْ وَلَتَنَازَعْتُمْ فِي الْأَمْرِ وَلَٰكِنَّ اللَّهَ سَلَّمَ ۗ إِنَّهُ
عَلِيمٌ بِذَاتِ الصُّدُورِ ﴿٤٣﴾

44. And when He made you (Muslims), when ye met (them), see them with your eyes as few, and lessened you in their eyes, (it was) that Allah might conclude a thing that must be done. Unto Allah all things are brought back.

45. O ye who believe! When ye meet an army, hold firm and think of Allah much, that ye may be successful.

46. And obey Allah and His messenger, and dispute not one with another lest ye falter and your strength depart from you; but be steadfast! Lo! Allah is with the steadfast.

47. Be not as those who came forth from their dwellings boastfully and to be seen of men, and debar (men) from the way of Allah, while Allah is surrounding all they do.

48. And when Satan made their deeds seem fair to them and said: No one of mankind can conquer you this day, for I am your protector. But when the armies came in sight of one another, he took flight, saying: Lo! I am guiltless of you. Lo! I see that which ye see not. Lo! I fear Allah. And Allah is severe in punishment.

49. When the hypocrites and those in whose hearts is a disease said: Their religion hath deluded these. Whoso putteth his trust in Allah (will find that) lo! Allah is Mighty, Wise.

50. If thou couldst see how the angels receive those who disbelieve, smiting their faces and their backs and (saying): Taste the punishment of burning!

51. This is for that which your own hands have sent before (to the Judgement), and (know) that Allah is not a tyrant to His slaves.

وإذ يريكموهم إذ التقيتم في أعينكم قليلا ويقللكم
في أعينهم ليقضي الله أمرا كان مفعولا وإلى
الله ترجع الأمور ﴿٤٤﴾
يا أيها الذين آمنوا إذا لقيتم فئة فاثبتوا واذكروا
الله كثيرا لعلكم تفلحون ﴿٤٥﴾
وأطيعوا الله ورسوله ولا تنازعوا فتفشلوا و
تذهب ريحكم واصبروا إن الله مع الصابرين ﴿٤٦﴾
ولا تكونوا كالذين خرجوا من ديارهم بطرا ورئاء
الناس ويصدون عن سبيل الله والله بما
يعملون محيط ﴿٤٧﴾
وإذ زين لهم الشيطان أعمالهم وقال لا غالب لكم
اليوم من الناس وإني جار لكم فلما تراءت الفئتان
نكص على عقبيه وقال إني بريء منكم إني أرى
ما لا ترون إني أخاف الله والله شديد
العقاب ﴿٤٨﴾
إذ يقول المنافقون والذين في قلوبهم مرض
غر هؤلاء دينهم ومن يتوكل على الله فإن الله
عزيز حكيم ﴿٤٩﴾
ولو ترى إذ يتوفى الذين كفروا الملائكة يضربون
وجوههم وأدبارهم وذوقوا عذاب الحريق ﴿٥٠﴾
ذلك بما قدمت أيديكم وأن الله ليس بظلام
للعبيد ﴿٥١﴾

52. (Their way is) as the way of Pharaoh's folk and those before them; they disbelieved the revelations of Allah, and Allah took them in their sins. Lo! Allah is Strong, severe in punishment.

53. That is because Allah never changeth the grace He hath bestowed on any people until they first change that which is in their hearts, and (that is) because Allah is Hearer, Knower,

54. (Their way is) as the way of Pharaoh's folk and those before them; they denied the revelations of their Lord, so We destroyed them in their sins. And We drowned the folk of Pharaoh. All were evil-doers.

55. Lo! the worst of beasts in Allah's sight are the ungrateful who will not believe;

56. Those of them with whom thou madest a treaty, and then at every opportunity they break their treaty, and they keep not duty (to Allah).

57. If thou comest on them in the war, deal with them so as to strike fear in those who are behind them, that haply they may remember.

58. And if thou fearest treachery from any folk, then throw back to them (their treaty) fairly. Lo! Allah loveth not the treacherous.

59. And let not those who disbelieve suppose that they can outstrip (Allah's purpose). Lo! they cannot escape.

60. Make ready for them all thou canst of (armed) force and of horses tethered, that thereby ye may dismay the enemy of Allah and your enemy, and others beside them whom ye know not. Allah knoweth them. Whatsoever ye spend in the way of Allah it will be repaid to you in full, and ye will not be wronged.

كَدَاْبِ اٰلِ فِرْعَوْنَ ۙ وَالَّذِيْنَ مِنْ قَبْلِهِمْ ؕ كَفَرُوْا
بِاٰيٰتِ اللّٰهِ فَاَخَذَهُمُ اللّٰهُ بِذُنُوْبِهِمْ ؕ اِنَّ اللّٰهَ
قَوِيٌّ شَدِيْدُ الْعِقَابِ ﴿٥٢﴾
ذٰلِكَ بِاَنَّ اللّٰهَ لَمْ يَكُ مُغَيِّرًا نِّعْمَةً اَنْعَمَهَا عَلٰى قَوْمٍ
حَتّٰى يُغَيِّرُوْا مَا بِاَنْفُسِهِمْ ۙ وَاَنَّ اللّٰهَ سَمِيْعٌ عَلِيْمٌ ﴿٥٣﴾
كَدَاْبِ اٰلِ فِرْعَوْنَ ۙ وَالَّذِيْنَ مِنْ قَبْلِهِمْ ؕ كَذَّبُوْا
بِاٰيٰتِ رَبِّهِمْ فَاَهْلَكْنٰهُمْ بِذُنُوْبِهِمْ وَاَغْرَقْنَاۤ اٰلَ
فِرْعَوْنَ ۚ وَكُلٌّ كَانُوْا ظٰلِمِيْنَ ﴿٥٤﴾
اِنَّ شَرَّ الدَّوَآبِّ عِنْدَ اللّٰهِ الَّذِيْنَ كَفَرُوْا فَهُمْ لَا
يُؤْمِنُوْنَ ﴿٥٥﴾
اَلَّذِيْنَ عٰهَدْتَّ مِنْهُمْ ثُمَّ يَنْقُضُوْنَ عَهْدَهُمْ
فِيْ كُلِّ مَرَّةٍ وَّهُمْ لَا يَتَّقُوْنَ ﴿٥٦﴾
فَاِمَّا تَثْقَفَنَّهُمْ فِى الْحَرْبِ فَشَرِّدْ بِهِمْ مَّنْ خَلْفَهُمْ
لَعَلَّهُمْ يَذَّكَّرُوْنَ ﴿٥٧﴾
وَاِمَّا تَخَافَنَّ مِنْ قَوْمٍ خِيَانَةً فَانْۢبِذْ اِلَيْهِمْ عَلٰى
ع سَوَآءٍ ؕ اِنَّ اللّٰهَ لَا يُحِبُّ الْخَآئِنِيْنَ ﴿٥٨﴾
وَلَا يَحْسَبَنَّ الَّذِيْنَ كَفَرُوْا سَبَقُوْا ؕ اِنَّهُمْ لَا يُعْجِزُوْنَ ﴿٥٩﴾
وَاَعِدُّوْا لَهُمْ مَّا اسْتَطَعْتُمْ مِّنْ قُوَّةٍ وَّمِنْ رِّبَاطِ
الْخَيْلِ تُرْهِبُوْنَ بِهٖ عَدُوَّ اللّٰهِ وَعَدُوَّكُمْ وَاٰخَرِيْنَ
مِنْ دُوْنِهِمْ ۚ لَا تَعْلَمُوْنَهُمْ ۚ اَللّٰهُ يَعْلَمُهُمْ ؕ وَمَا
تُنْفِقُوْا مِنْ شَيْءٍ فِيْ سَبِيْلِ اللّٰهِ يُوَفَّ اِلَيْكُمْ وَ
اَنْتُمْ لَا تُظْلَمُوْنَ ﴿٦٠﴾

61. And if they incline to peace, incline thou also to it, and trust in Allah. Lo! He is the Hearer, the Knower.

62. And if they would deceive thee, then lo! Allah is sufficient for thee. He it is Who supporteth thee with His help and with the believers,

63. And (as for the believers) hath attuned their hearts. If thou hadst spent all that is in the earth thou couldst not have attuned their hearts, but Allah hath attuned them. Lo! He is Mighty, Wise.

64. O Prophet! Allah is sufficient for thee and those who follow thee of the believers.

65. O Prophet! Exhort the believers to fight. If there be of you twenty steadfast they shall overcome two hundred, and if there be of you a hundred steadfast they shall overcome a thousand of those who disbelieve, because they (the disbelievers) are a folk without intelligence.

66. Now hath Allah lightened your burden, for He knoweth that there is weakness in you. So if there be of you a steadfast hundred they shall overcome two hundred, and if there be of you a thousand (steadfast) they shall overcome two thousand by permission of Allah. Allah is with the steadfast.

67. It is not for any Prophet to have captives until he hath made slaughter in the land. Ye desire the lure of this world and Allah desireth (for you) the Hereafter, and Allah is Mighty, Wise.

68. Had it not been for an ordinance of Allah which had gone before, an awful doom had come upon you on account of what ye took.

69. Now enjoy what ye have won, as lawful and good, and keep your duty to Allah. Lo! Allah is Forgiving, Merciful.[1]

وان جنحوا للسلم فاجنح لها وتوكل على الله انه
هو السميع العليم ﴿٦١﴾
وان يريدوا ان يخدعوك فان حسبك الله هو
الذي ايدك بنصره وبالمؤمنين ﴿٦٢﴾
والف بين قلوبهم لو انفقت ما في الارض جميعا
ما الفت بين قلوبهم ولكن الله الف بينهم انه
عزيز حكيم ﴿٦٣﴾
ع يايها النبي حسبك الله ومن اتبعك من المؤمنين ﴿٦٤﴾
يايها النبي حرض المؤمنين على القتال ان يكن
منكم عشرون صبرون يغلبوا مائتين وان يكن
منكم مائة يغلبوا الفا من الذين كفروا بانهم
قوم لا يفقهون ﴿٦٥﴾
الئن خفف الله عنكم وعلم ان فيكم ضعفا فان يكن
منكم مائة صابرة يغلبوا مائتين وان يكن منكم
الف يغلبوا الفين باذن الله والله مع الصبرين ﴿٦٦﴾
ما كان لنبي ان يكون له اسرى حتى يثخن في
الارض تريدون عرض الدنيا والله يريد
الاخرة والله عزيز حكيم ﴿٦٧﴾
لولا كتب من الله سبق لمسكم فيما اخذتم
عذاب عظيم ﴿٦٨﴾
فكلوا مما غنمتم حللا طيبا واتقوا الله ان
ع الله غفور رحيم ﴿٦٩﴾ ع

1. vv. 67-69 were revealed when the Prophet had decided to spare the lives of the prisoners taken at Badr and hold them to ransom, against the wish of Omar, who would have executed them for their past crimes. The Prophet took the verses as a reproof, and they are generally understood to mean that no quarter ought to have been given in that first battle.

70. O Prophet! Say unto those captives who are in your hands: If Allah knoweth any good in your hearts He will give you better than that which hath been taken from you, and will forgive you. Lo! Allah is Forgiving, Merciful.

يٰٓأَيُّهَا النَّبِيُّ قُلْ لِّمَنْ فِيٓ أَيْدِيكُمْ مِّنَ الْأَسْرٰٓى
إِنْ يَّعْلَمِ اللّٰهُ فِي قُلُوبِكُمْ خَيْرًا يُّؤْتِكُمْ خَيْرًا مِّمَّآ أُخِذَ
مِنْكُمْ وَيَغْفِرْ لَكُمْ ۗ وَاللّٰهُ غَفُورٌ رَّحِيمٌ ﴿٧٠﴾

71. And if they would betray thee, they betrayed Allah before, and He gave (thee) power over them. Allah is Knower, Wise.

وَإِنْ يُّرِيدُوا خِيَانَتَكَ فَقَدْ خَانُوا اللّٰهَ مِنْ قَبْلُ
فَأَمْكَنَ مِنْهُمْ ۗ وَاللّٰهُ عَلِيمٌ حَكِيمٌ ﴿٧١﴾

72. Lo! those who believed and left their homes and strove with their wealth and their lives for the cause of Allah, and those who took them in and helped them: these are protecting friends one of another. And those who believed but did not leave their homes, ye have no duty to protect them till they leave their homes; but if they seek help from you in the matter of religion then it is your duty to help (them) except against a folk between whom and you there is a treaty. Allah is Seer of what ye do.

إِنَّ الَّذِينَ اٰمَنُوا وَهَاجَرُوا وَجٰهَدُوا بِأَمْوَالِهِمْ وَ
أَنْفُسِهِمْ فِي سَبِيلِ اللّٰهِ وَالَّذِينَ اٰوَوْا وَّنَصَرُوٓا أُولٰٓئِكَ
بَعْضُهُمْ أَوْلِيَآءُ بَعْضٍ ۗ وَالَّذِينَ اٰمَنُوا وَلَمْ يُهَاجِرُوا
مَا لَكُمْ مِّنْ وَّلَايَتِهِمْ مِّنْ شَيْءٍ حَتّٰى يُهَاجِرُوا ۚ وَ
إِنِ اسْتَنْصَرُوكُمْ فِي الدِّينِ فَعَلَيْكُمُ النَّصْرُ إِلَّا عَلٰى
قَوْمٍ بَيْنَكُمْ وَبَيْنَهُمْ مِّيثَاقٌ ۗ وَاللّٰهُ بِمَا تَعْمَلُونَ
بَصِيرٌ ﴿٧٢﴾

73. And those who disbelieve are protectors one of another—If ye do not so, there will be confusion in the land, and great corruption.

وَالَّذِينَ كَفَرُوا بَعْضُهُمْ أَوْلِيَآءُ بَعْضٍ ۗ إِلَّا تَفْعَلُوهُ
تَكُنْ فِتْنَةٌ فِي الْأَرْضِ وَفَسَادٌ كَبِيرٌ ﴿٧٣﴾

74. Those who believed and left their homes and strove for the cause of Allah, and those who took them in and helped them—these are the believers in truth. For them is pardon, and a bountiful provision.

وَالَّذِينَ اٰمَنُوا وَهَاجَرُوا وَجٰهَدُوا فِي سَبِيلِ اللّٰهِ وَ
الَّذِينَ اٰوَوْا وَّنَصَرُوٓا أُولٰٓئِكَ هُمُ الْمُؤْمِنُونَ حَقًّا ۗ
لَهُمْ مَّغْفِرَةٌ وَّرِزْقٌ كَرِيمٌ ﴿٧٤﴾

75. And those who afterwards believed and left their homes and strove along with you, they are of you; and those who are akin are nearer one to another in the ordinance of Allah. Lo! Allah is Knower of all things.

وَالَّذِينَ اٰمَنُوا مِنْ بَعْدُ وَهَاجَرُوا وَجٰهَدُوا مَعَكُمْ
فَأُولٰٓئِكَ مِنْكُمْ ۗ وَأُولُوا الْأَرْحَامِ بَعْضُهُمْ أَوْلٰى بِبَعْضٍ
فِي كِتٰبِ اللّٰهِ ۗ إِنَّ اللّٰهَ بِكُلِّ شَيْءٍ عَلِيمٌ ﴿٧٥﴾ ع

At-Taubah, "Repentance," takes its name from v. 104. It is often called Al-Barā'at. (The Immunity), from the first word. It is the only Sūrah which is without the *Bi'smi'llāhi'r-Raḥmāni'r-Rāḥîm* ("In the name of Allah, the Beneficent, the Merciful") which is generally considered to be on account of the stern commandments against idolaters which it contains. Vv. 1-12, forming the proclamation of immunity from obligation toward the idolaters, were revealed after the pilgrims had started for Mecca in the ninth year of the Hijrah and sent by special messenger to Abū Bakr, leader of the pilgrimage, to be read out by Ali to the multitudes at Mecca. It signified the end of idolatry in Arabia. The Christian Byzantine Empire had begun to move against the growing Muslim power, and this Sūrah contains mention of a greater war to come, and instructions with regard to it. Vv. 38-99 refer to the Tabūk campaign, and especially to those Arab tribes who failed to join the Muslims in that campaign. The "Hypocrites," as the half-hearted supporters of Al-Islām, were called, had long been a thorn, in the side of the Muslims. They had even at one time gone the length in dissent of forming a congregation and building a mosque of their own surreptitiously. On the Prophet's return from Tabūk they invited him to visit that mosque. This is referred to in vv. 107 ff.

The date of revelation is the ninth year of the Hijrah.

REPENTANCE

Revealed at Al-Madinah

1. Freedom from obligation (is proclaimed) from Allah and His messenger toward those of the idolaters with whom ye made a treaty:

2. Travel freely in the land four months, and know that ye cannot escape Allah and that Allah will confound the disbelievers (in His guidance).

3. And a proclamation from Allah and His messenger to all men on the day of the Greater Pilgrimage that Allah is free from obligation to the idolaters, and (so is) His messenger. So, if ye repent, it will be better for you; but if ye are averse, then know that ye cannot escape Allah. Give tidings (O Muhammad) of a painful doom to those who disbelieve.

4. Excepting those of the idolaters with whom ye (Muslims) have a treaty, and who have since abated nothing of your right nor have supported anyone against you. (As for these), fulfil their treaty to them till their term. Lo! Allah loveth those who keep their duty (unto Him).

5. Then, when the sacred months have passed, slay the idolaters wherever ye find them, and take them (captive), and besiege them, and prepare for them each ambush. But if they repent and establish worship and pay the poor-due, then leave their way free. Lo! Allah is Forgiving, Merciful.

6. And if anyone of the idolaters seeketh thy protection (O Muhammad), then protect him so that he may hear the word of Allah, and afterward convey him to his place of safety. That is because they are a folk who know not.

آياتها ١٢٩ (٩) سُورَةُ التَّوْبَةِ مَدَنِيَّةٌ رُكُوعَاتُهَا ١٦

بَرَآءَةٌ مِّنَ اللّٰهِ وَرَسُوْلِهٖٓ اِلَى الَّذِيْنَ عٰهَدْتُّمْ
مِّنَ الْمُشْرِكِيْنَ ①
فَسِيْحُوْا فِي الْاَرْضِ اَرْبَعَةَ اَشْهُرٍ وَّاعْلَمُوْٓا اَنَّكُمْ
غَيْرُ مُعْجِزِي اللّٰهِ ۙ وَاَنَّ اللّٰهَ مُخْزِي الْكٰفِرِيْنَ ②
وَاَذَانٌ مِّنَ اللّٰهِ وَرَسُوْلِهٖٓ اِلَى النَّاسِ يَوْمَ الْحَجِّ
الْاَكْبَرِ اَنَّ اللّٰهَ بَرِيْٓءٌ مِّنَ الْمُشْرِكِيْنَ ۙ وَرَسُوْلُهٗ
فَاِنْ تُبْتُمْ فَهُوَ خَيْرٌ لَّكُمْ ۚ وَاِنْ تَوَلَّيْتُمْ فَاعْلَمُوْٓا
اَنَّكُمْ غَيْرُ مُعْجِزِي اللّٰهِ ؕ وَبَشِّرِ الَّذِيْنَ كَفَرُوْا
بِعَذَابٍ اَلِيْمٍ ③
اِلَّا الَّذِيْنَ عٰهَدْتُّمْ مِّنَ الْمُشْرِكِيْنَ ثُمَّ لَمْ
يَنْقُصُوْكُمْ شَيْـًٔا وَّلَمْ يُظَاهِرُوْا عَلَيْكُمْ اَحَدًا فَاَتِمُّوْٓا
اِلَيْهِمْ عَهْدَهُمْ اِلٰى مُدَّتِهِمْ ؕ اِنَّ اللّٰهَ يُحِبُّ
الْمُتَّقِيْنَ ④
فَاِذَا انْسَلَخَ الْاَشْهُرُ الْحُرُمُ فَاقْتُلُوا الْمُشْرِكِيْنَ
حَيْثُ وَجَدْتُّمُوْهُمْ وَخُذُوْهُمْ وَاحْصُرُوْهُمْ وَ
اقْعُدُوْا لَهُمْ كُلَّ مَرْصَدٍ ۚ فَاِنْ تَابُوْا وَاَقَامُوا الصَّلٰوةَ وَ
اٰتَوُا الزَّكٰوةَ فَخَلُّوْا سَبِيْلَهُمْ ؕ اِنَّ اللّٰهَ غَفُوْرٌ رَّحِيْمٌ ⑤
وَاِنْ اَحَدٌ مِّنَ الْمُشْرِكِيْنَ اسْتَجَارَكَ فَاَجِرْهُ حَتّٰى
يَسْمَعَ كَلٰمَ اللّٰهِ ثُمَّ اَبْلِغْهُ مَاْمَنَهٗ ؕ ذٰلِكَ بِاَنَّهُمْ
قَوْمٌ لَّا يَعْلَمُوْنَ ⑥ ع

7. How can there be a treaty with Allah and with His messenger for the idolaters save those with whom ye made a treaty at the Inviolable Place of Worship? So long as they are true to you, be true to them. Lo! Allah loveth those who keep their duty.

8. How (can there be any treaty for the others) when, if they have the upperhand of you, they regard not pact nor honour in respect of you? They satisfy you with their mouths the while their hearts refuse And most of them are wrong-doers.

9. They have purchased with the revelations of Allah a little gain, so they debar (men) from His way. Lo! evil is that which they are wont to do.

10. And they observe toward a believer neither pact nor honour. These are they who are transgressors.

11. But if they repent and establish worship and pay the poor-due, then are they your brethren in religion. We detail Our revelations for a people who have knowledge.

12. And if they break their pledges after their treaty (hath been made with you) and assail your religion, then fight the heads of disbelief —Lo! they have no binding oaths—in order that they may desist.

13. Will ye not fight a folk who broke their solemn pledges, and purposed to drive out the messenger and did attack you first? What! Fear ye them? Now Allah hath more right that ye should fear Him, if ye are believers.

14. Fight them! Allah will chastise them at your hands, and He will lay them low and give you victory over them, and He will heal the breasts of folk who are believers.

15. And He will remove the anger of their hearts. Allah relenteth toward whom He will. Allah is Knower, Wise.

كَيْفَ يَكُونُ لِلْمُشْرِكِيْنَ عَهْدٌ عِنْدَ اللهِ وَعِنْدَ رَسُوْلِهٖٓ اِلَّا الَّذِيْنَ عَاهَدْتُّمْ عِنْدَ الْمَسْجِدِ الْحَرَامِ ۚ فَمَا اسْتَقَامُوْا لَكُمْ فَاسْتَقِيْمُوْا لَهُمْ ۗ اِنَّ اللهَ يُحِبُّ الْمُتَّقِيْنَ ۞

كَيْفَ وَاِنْ يَّظْهَرُوْا عَلَيْكُمْ لَا يَرْقُبُوْا فِيْكُمْ اِلًّا وَّلَا ذِمَّةً ۗ يُرْضُوْنَكُمْ بِاَفْوَاهِهِمْ وَتَاْبٰى قُلُوْبُهُمْ ۚ وَاَكْثَرُهُمْ فٰسِقُوْنَ ۞

اِشْتَرَوْا بِاٰيٰتِ اللهِ ثَمَنًا قَلِيْلًا فَصَدُّوْا عَنْ سَبِيْلِهٖ ۗ اِنَّهُمْ سَاءَ مَا كَانُوْا يَعْمَلُوْنَ ۞

لَا يَرْقُبُوْنَ فِيْ مُؤْمِنٍ اِلًّا وَّلَا ذِمَّةً ۗ وَاُولٰٓئِكَ هُمُ الْمُعْتَدُوْنَ ۞

فَاِنْ تَابُوْا وَاَقَامُوا الصَّلٰوةَ وَاٰتَوُا الزَّكٰوةَ فَاِخْوَانُكُمْ فِى الدِّيْنِ ۗ وَنُفَصِّلُ الْاٰيٰتِ لِقَوْمٍ يَّعْلَمُوْنَ ۞

وَاِنْ نَّكَثُوْٓا اَيْمَانَهُمْ مِّنْ بَعْدِ عَهْدِهِمْ وَطَعَنُوْا فِيْ دِيْنِكُمْ فَقَاتِلُوْٓا اَئِمَّةَ الْكُفْرِ ۙ اِنَّهُمْ لَآ اَيْمَانَ لَهُمْ لَعَلَّهُمْ يَنْتَهُوْنَ ۞

اَلَا تُقَاتِلُوْنَ قَوْمًا نَّكَثُوْٓا اَيْمَانَهُمْ وَهَمُّوْا بِاِخْرَاجِ الرَّسُوْلِ وَهُمْ بَدَءُوْكُمْ اَوَّلَ مَرَّةٍ ۚ اَتَخْشَوْنَهُمْ ۚ فَاللهُ اَحَقُّ اَنْ تَخْشَوْهُ اِنْ كُنْتُمْ مُّؤْمِنِيْنَ ۞

قَاتِلُوْهُمْ يُعَذِّبْهُمُ اللهُ بِاَيْدِيْكُمْ وَيُخْزِهِمْ وَيَنْصُرْكُمْ عَلَيْهِمْ وَيَشْفِ صُدُوْرَ قَوْمٍ مُّؤْمِنِيْنَ ۞

وَيُذْهِبْ غَيْظَ قُلُوْبِهِمْ ۗ وَيَتُوْبُ اللهُ عَلٰى مَنْ يَّشَاءُ ۗ وَاللهُ عَلِيْمٌ حَكِيْمٌ ۞

16. Or deemed ye that ye would be left (in peace) when Allah yet knoweth not those of you who strive, choosing for familiar none save Allah and His messenger and the believers? Allah is Informed of what ye do.

17. It is not for the idolaters to tend Allah's sanctuaries, bearing witness against themselves of disbelief. As for such, their works are vain and in the Fire they will abide.

18. He only shall tend Allah's sanctuaries who believeth in Allah and the Last Day and observeth proper worship and payeth the poor-due and feareth none save Allah. For such (only) is it possible that they can be of the rightly guided.

19. Count ye the slaking of a pilgrim's thirst and tendance of the Inviolable Place of Worship as (equal to the worth of him) who believeth in Allah and the Last Day, and striveth in the way of Allah? They are not equal in the sight of Allah. Allah guideth not wrongdoing folk.

20. Those who believe, and have left their homes and striven with their wealth and their lives in Allah's way are of much greater worth in Allah's sight. These are they who are triumphant.

21. Their Lord giveth them good tidings of mercy from Him, and acceptance, and Gardens where enduring pleasure will be theirs;

22. There they will abide for ever. Lo! with Allah there is immense reward.

23. O ye who believe! Choose not your fathers nor your brethren for friends if they take pleasure in disbelief rather than faith. Whoso of you taketh them for friends, such are wrong-doers.

أم حسبتم أن تتركوا ولما يعلم الله الذين جاهدوا
منكم ولم يتخذوا من دون الله ولا رسوله ولا
المؤمنين وليجة والله خبير بما تعملون ﴿١٦﴾
ما كان للمشركين أن يعمروا مساجد الله شاهدين
على أنفسهم بالكفر أولئك حبطت أعمالهم و
في النار هم خالدون ﴿١٧﴾
إنما يعمر مساجد الله من آمن بالله واليوم الآخر
وأقام الصلوة وآتى الزكوة ولم يخش إلا الله فعسى
أولئك أن يكونوا من المهتدين ﴿١٨﴾
أجعلتم سقاية الحاج وعمارة المسجد الحرام
كمن آمن بالله واليوم الآخر وجاهد في سبيل
الله لا يستوون عند الله والله لا يهدي القوم
الظالمين ﴿١٩﴾
الذين آمنوا وهاجروا وجاهدوا في سبيل الله
بأموالهم وأنفسهم أعظم درجة عند الله و
أولئك هم الفائزون ﴿٢٠﴾
يبشرهم ربهم برحمة منه ورضوان وجنات لهم
فيها نعيم مقيم ﴿٢١﴾
خالدين فيها أبدا إن الله عنده أجر عظيم ﴿٢٢﴾
يا أيها الذين آمنوا لا تتخذوا آباءكم وإخوانكم
أولياء إن استحبوا الكفر على الإيمان ومن يتولهم
منكم فأولئك هم الظالمون ﴿٢٣﴾

24. Say: If your fathers, and your sons, and your brethren, and your wives, and your tribe, and the wealth ye have acquired, and merchandise for which ye fear that there will be no sale,[1] and dwellings ye desire are dearer to you than Allah and His messenger and striving in His way: then wait till Allah bringeth His command to pass. Allah guideth not wrongdoing folk.

25. Allah hath given you victory on many fields and on the day of Ḥuneyn,[2] when ye exulted in your multitude but it availed you naught, and the earth, vast as it is, was straitened for you: then ye turned back in flight;

26. Then Allah sent His peace of reassurance down upon His messenger and upon the believers, and sent down hosts ye could not see, and punished those who disbelieved. Such is the reward of disbelievers.

27. Then afterward Allah will relent toward whom He will; for Allah is Forgiving, Merciful.

28. O ye who believe! The idolaters only are unclean. So let them not come near the Inviolable Place of Worship after this their year. If ye fear poverty (from the loss of their merchandise) Allah shall preserve you of His bounty if He will. Lo! Allah is Knower, Wise.

29. Fight against such of those who have been given the Scripture as believe not in Allah nor the Last Day, and forbid not that which Allah hath forbidden by His messenger, and follow not the religion of truth, until they pay the tribute readily, being brought low.

قُلْ إِنْ كَانَ آبَاؤُكُمْ وَأَبْنَاؤُكُمْ وَإِخْوَانُكُمْ وَأَزْوَاجُكُمْ
وَعَشِيرَتُكُمْ وَأَمْوَالٌ اقْتَرَفْتُمُوهَا وَتِجَارَةٌ تَخْشَوْنَ
كَسَادَهَا وَمَسَاكِنُ تَرْضَوْنَهَا أَحَبَّ إِلَيْكُمْ مِنَ اللَّهِ
وَرَسُولِهِ وَجِهَادٍ فِي سَبِيلِهِ فَتَرَبَّصُوا حَتَّىٰ يَأْتِيَ
ع اللَّهُ بِأَمْرِهِ ۗ وَاللَّهُ لَا يَهْدِي الْقَوْمَ الْفَاسِقِينَ ﴿٢٤﴾
لَقَدْ نَصَرَكُمُ اللَّهُ فِي مَوَاطِنَ كَثِيرَةٍ ۙ وَيَوْمَ حُنَيْنٍ ۙ
إِذْ أَعْجَبَتْكُمْ كَثْرَتُكُمْ فَلَمْ تُغْنِ عَنْكُمْ شَيْئًا وَضَاقَتْ
عَلَيْكُمُ الْأَرْضُ بِمَا رَحُبَتْ ثُمَّ وَلَّيْتُمْ
مُدْبِرِينَ ﴿٢٥﴾
ثُمَّ أَنْزَلَ اللَّهُ سَكِينَتَهُ عَلَىٰ رَسُولِهِ وَعَلَى الْمُؤْمِنِينَ
وَأَنْزَلَ جُنُودًا لَمْ تَرَوْهَا وَعَذَّبَ الَّذِينَ كَفَرُوا ۚ وَ
ذَٰلِكَ جَزَاءُ الْكَافِرِينَ ﴿٢٦﴾
ثُمَّ يَتُوبُ اللَّهُ مِنْ بَعْدِ ذَٰلِكَ عَلَىٰ مَنْ يَشَاءُ ۗ وَ
اللَّهُ غَفُورٌ رَحِيمٌ ﴿٢٧﴾
يَا أَيُّهَا الَّذِينَ آمَنُوا إِنَّمَا الْمُشْرِكُونَ نَجَسٌ فَلَا يَقْرَبُوا
الْمَسْجِدَ الْحَرَامَ بَعْدَ عَامِهِمْ هَٰذَا ۚ وَإِنْ خِفْتُمْ
عَيْلَةً فَسَوْفَ يُغْنِيكُمُ اللَّهُ مِنْ فَضْلِهِ إِنْ شَاءَ ۚ
إِنَّ اللَّهَ عَلِيمٌ حَكِيمٌ ﴿٢٨﴾
قَاتِلُوا الَّذِينَ لَا يُؤْمِنُونَ بِاللَّهِ وَلَا بِالْيَوْمِ الْآخِرِ وَلَا
يُحَرِّمُونَ مَا حَرَّمَ اللَّهُ وَرَسُولُهُ وَلَا يَدِينُونَ دِينَ
الْحَقِّ مِنَ الَّذِينَ أُوتُوا الْكِتَابَ حَتَّىٰ يُعْطُوا الْجِزْيَةَ
ع عَنْ يَدٍ وَهُمْ صَاغِرُونَ ﴿٢٩﴾

1. It was objected that, if idolaters were forbidden to make the pilgrimage, the trade of Mecca would decline.
2. The Muslim army, ambushed at Ḥuneyn, gained a great victory after being nearly routed.

30. And the Jews say: Ezra is the son of Allah, and the Christians say: The Messiah is the son of Allah. That is their saying with their mouths. They imitate the saying of those who disbelieved of old. Allah (Himself) fighteth against them. How perverse are they!

31. They have taken as lords beside Allah their rabbis and their monks and the Messiah son of Mary, when they were bidden to worship only One God. There is no god save Him. Be He glorified from all that they ascribe as partner (unto Him)!

32. Fain would they put out the light of Allah with their mouths, but Allah disdaineth (aught) save that He shall perfect His light, however much the disbelievers are averse.

33. He it is Who hath sent His messenger with the guidance and the Religion of Truth, that He may cause it to prevail over all religion, however much the idolaters may be averse.

34. O ye who believe! Lo! many of the (Jewish) rabbis and the (Christian) monks devour the wealth of mankind wantonly and debar (men) from the way of Allah. They who hoard up gold and silver and spend it not in the way of Allah, unto them give tidings (O Muhammad) of a painful doom,

35. On the day when it will (all) be heated in the fire of hell, and their foreheads and their flanks and their backs will be branded therewith (and it will be said unto them): Here is that which ye hoarded for yourselves. Now taste of what ye used to hoard.

36. Lo! the number of the months with Allah is twelve months by Allah's ordinance in the day that He created the heavens and the earth. Four of them are sacred: that is the right religion. So wrong not yourselves in them. And wage war on all the idolaters as they are waging war on all of you. And know that Allah is with those who keep their duty (unto Him).

وَقَالَتِ الْيَهُوْدُ عُزَيْرُ ابْنُ اللّٰهِ وَقَالَتِ النَّصٰرَى الْمَسِيْحُ
ابْنُ اللّٰهِ ذٰلِكَ قَوْلُهُمْ بِاَفْوَاهِهِمْ يُضَاهِـُٔوْنَ قَوْلَ
الَّذِيْنَ كَفَرُوْا مِنْ قَبْلُ قٰتَلَهُمُ اللّٰهُ اَنّٰى يُؤْفَكُوْنَ ﴿٣٠﴾
اِتَّخَذُوْا اَحْبَارَهُمْ وَرُهْبَانَهُمْ اَرْبَابًا مِّنْ دُوْنِ اللّٰهِ
وَالْمَسِيْحَ ابْنَ مَرْيَمَ وَمَا اُمِرُوْا اِلَّا لِيَعْبُدُوْا اِلٰهًا
وَّاحِدًا لَا اِلٰهَ اِلَّا هُوَ سُبْحٰنَهٗ عَمَّا يُشْرِكُوْنَ ﴿٣١﴾
يُرِيْدُوْنَ اَنْ يُّطْفِـُٔوْا نُوْرَ اللّٰهِ بِاَفْوَاهِهِمْ وَيَاْبَى اللّٰهُ
اِلَّا اَنْ يُّتِمَّ نُوْرَهٗ وَلَوْ كَرِهَ الْكٰفِرُوْنَ ﴿٣٢﴾
هُوَ الَّذِيْ اَرْسَلَ رَسُوْلَهٗ بِالْهُدٰى وَدِيْنِ الْحَقِّ
لِيُظْهِرَهٗ عَلَى الدِّيْنِ كُلِّهٖ وَلَوْ كَرِهَ الْمُشْرِكُوْنَ ﴿٣٣﴾ النصف
يٰۤاَيُّهَا الَّذِيْنَ اٰمَنُوْۤا اِنَّ كَثِيْرًا مِّنَ الْاَحْبَارِ وَالرُّهْبَانِ
لَيَاْكُلُوْنَ اَمْوَالَ النَّاسِ بِالْبَاطِلِ وَيَصُدُّوْنَ عَنْ
سَبِيْلِ اللّٰهِ وَالَّذِيْنَ يَكْنِزُوْنَ الذَّهَبَ وَالْفِضَّةَ وَ
لَا يُنْفِقُوْنَهَا فِيْ سَبِيْلِ اللّٰهِ فَبَشِّرْهُمْ بِعَذَابٍ اَلِيْمٍ ﴿٣٤﴾
يَّوْمَ يُحْمٰى عَلَيْهَا فِيْ نَارِ جَهَنَّمَ فَتُكْوٰى بِهَا جِبَاهُهُمْ
وَجُنُوْبُهُمْ وَظُهُوْرُهُمْ هٰذَا مَا كَنَزْتُمْ لِاَنْفُسِكُمْ
فَذُوْقُوْا مَا كُنْتُمْ تَكْنِزُوْنَ ﴿٣٥﴾
اِنَّ عِدَّةَ الشُّهُوْرِ عِنْدَ اللّٰهِ اثْنَا عَشَرَ شَهْرًا فِيْ كِتٰبِ
اللّٰهِ يَوْمَ خَلَقَ السَّمٰوٰتِ وَالْاَرْضَ مِنْهَاۤ اَرْبَعَةٌ حُرُمٌ
ذٰلِكَ الدِّيْنُ الْقَيِّمُ فَلَا تَظْلِمُوْا فِيْهِنَّ اَنْفُسَكُمْ
وَقَاتِلُوا الْمُشْرِكِيْنَ كَاۤفَّةً كَمَا يُقَاتِلُوْنَكُمْ كَاۤفَّةً وَ
اعْلَمُوْۤا اَنَّ اللّٰهَ مَعَ الْمُتَّقِيْنَ ﴿٣٦﴾

37. Postponement (of a sacred month)[1] is only an excess of disbelief whereby those who disbelieve are misled, they allow it one year and forbid it (another) year, that they may make up the number of the months which Allah hath hallowed, so that they allow that which Allah hath forbidden. The evil of their deeds is made fair-seeming unto them. Allah guideth not the disbelieving folk.

38. O ye who believe! What aileth you that when it is said unto you: Go forth in the way of Allah, ye are bowed down to the ground with heaviness. Take ye pleasure in the life of the world rather than in the Hereafter? The comfort of the life of the world is but little than in the Hereafter.

39. If ye go not forth He will afflict you with a painful doom, and will choose instead of you a folk other than you. Ye cannot harm Him at all. Allah is Able to do all things.

40. If ye help him not, still Allah helped him when those who disbelieve drove him forth, the second of two; when they two[2] were in the cave, when he said unto his comrade: Grieve not. Lo! Allah is with us. Then Allah caused His peace of reassurance to descend upon him and supported him with hosts ye cannot see, and made the word of those who disbelieved the nethermost, while Allah's word it was that became the uppermost. Allah is Mighty, Wise.

41. Go forth, light-armed and heavy-armed, and strive with your wealth and your lives in the way of Allah! That is best for you if ye but knew.

42. Had it been a near adventure and an easy journey they had followed thee, but the distance seemed too far for them.[3] Yet will they swear by Allah (saying): If we had been able we would surely have set out with you. They destroy their souls, and Allah knoweth that they verily are liars.

إِنَّمَا النَّسِيٓءُ زِيَادَةٌ فِي الْكُفْرِ يُضَلُّ بِهِ الَّذِينَ كَفَرُوا
يُحِلُّونَهُ عَامًا وَيُحَرِّمُونَهُ عَامًا لِّيُوَاطِـُٔوا عِدَّةَ مَا حَرَّمَ
اللَّهُ فَيُحِلُّوا مَا حَرَّمَ اللَّهُ ۚ زُيِّنَ لَهُمْ سُوٓءُ أَعْمَالِهِمْ ۗ
ع وَاللَّهُ لَا يَهْدِي الْقَوْمَ الْكَافِرِينَ ﴿٣٧﴾
يَا أَيُّهَا الَّذِينَ آمَنُوا مَا لَكُمْ إِذَا قِيلَ لَكُمُ انفِرُوا فِي
سَبِيلِ اللَّهِ اثَّاقَلْتُمْ إِلَى الْأَرْضِ ۚ أَرَضِيتُم بِالْحَيَاةِ
الدُّنْيَا مِنَ الْآخِرَةِ ۚ فَمَا مَتَاعُ الْحَيَاةِ الدُّنْيَا فِي
الْآخِرَةِ إِلَّا قَلِيلٌ ﴿٣٨﴾
إِلَّا تَنفِرُوا يُعَذِّبْكُمْ عَذَابًا أَلِيمًا وَيَسْتَبْدِلْ قَوْمًا
غَيْرَكُمْ وَلَا تَضُرُّوهُ شَيْئًا ۗ وَاللَّهُ عَلَىٰ كُلِّ شَيْءٍ قَدِيرٌ ﴿٣٩﴾
إِلَّا تَنصُرُوهُ فَقَدْ نَصَرَهُ اللَّهُ إِذْ أَخْرَجَهُ الَّذِينَ
كَفَرُوا ثَانِيَ اثْنَيْنِ إِذْ هُمَا فِي الْغَارِ إِذْ يَقُولُ لِصَاحِبِهِ
لَا تَحْزَنْ إِنَّ اللَّهَ مَعَنَا ۖ فَأَنزَلَ اللَّهُ سَكِينَتَهُ عَلَيْهِ
وَأَيَّدَهُ بِجُنُودٍ لَّمْ تَرَوْهَا وَجَعَلَ كَلِمَةَ الَّذِينَ
كَفَرُوا السُّفْلَىٰ ۗ وَكَلِمَةُ اللَّهِ هِيَ الْعُلْيَا ۗ وَاللَّهُ عَزِيزٌ
حَكِيمٌ ﴿٤٠﴾
انفِرُوا خِفَافًا وَثِقَالًا وَجَاهِدُوا بِأَمْوَالِكُمْ وَأَنفُسِكُمْ
فِي سَبِيلِ اللَّهِ ۚ ذَٰلِكُمْ خَيْرٌ لَّكُمْ إِن كُنتُمْ تَعْلَمُونَ ﴿٤١﴾
لَوْ كَانَ عَرَضًا قَرِيبًا وَسَفَرًا قَاصِدًا لَّاتَّبَعُوكَ وَ
لَٰكِن بَعُدَتْ عَلَيْهِمُ الشُّقَّةُ ۚ وَسَيَحْلِفُونَ بِاللَّهِ
لَوِ اسْتَطَعْنَا لَخَرَجْنَا مَعَكُمْ يُهْلِكُونَ أَنفُسَهُمْ ۚ
ع وَاللَّهُ يَعْلَمُ إِنَّهُمْ لَكَاذِبُونَ ﴿٤٢﴾

1. The idolaters would postpone a sacred month in which war was forbidden, when they wanted to make war, and make up for it by hallowing another month.
2. The Prophet and Abū Bakr during the Flight from Mecca to Al-Madīnah.
3. The reference is to the Tabūk expedition. Tabūk is half-way between Al-Madīnah and Damascus.

43. Allah forgive thee (O Muhammad)! Wherefor didst thou grant them leave ere those who told the truth were manifest to thee and thou didst know the liars?

عَفَا اللّٰهُ عَنۡكَ لِمَ اَذِنۡتَ لَهُمۡ حَتّٰى يَتَبَيَّنَ لَكَ الَّذِيۡنَ صَدَقُوۡا وَتَعۡلَمَ الۡكٰذِبِيۡنَ ۞

44. Those who believe in Allah and the Last Day ask no leave of thee lest they should strive with their wealth and their lives. Allah is Aware of those who keep their duty (unto Him).

لَا يَسۡتَاۡذِنُكَ الَّذِيۡنَ يُؤۡمِنُوۡنَ بِاللّٰهِ وَالۡيَوۡمِ الۡاٰخِرِ اَنۡ يُّجَاهِدُوۡا بِاَمۡوَالِهِمۡ وَاَنۡفُسِهِمۡ ؕ وَاللّٰهُ عَلِيۡمٌ بِالۡمُتَّقِيۡنَ ۞

45. They alone ask leave of thee who believe not in Allah and the Last Day, and whose hearts feel doubt, so in their doubt they waver.

اِنَّمَا يَسۡتَاۡذِنُكَ الَّذِيۡنَ لَا يُؤۡمِنُوۡنَ بِاللّٰهِ وَالۡيَوۡمِ الۡاٰخِرِ وَارۡتَابَتۡ قُلُوۡبُهُمۡ فَهُمۡ فِىۡ رَيۡبِهِمۡ يَتَرَدَّدُوۡنَ ۞

46. And if they had wished to go forth they would assuredly have made ready some equipment, but Allah was averse to their being sent forth and held them back and (it was said unto them): Sit ye with the sedentary!

وَلَوۡ اَرَادُوا الۡخُرُوۡجَ لَاَعَدُّوۡا لَهٗ عُدَّةً وَّلٰكِنۡ كَرِهَ اللّٰهُ انۡبِعَاثَهُمۡ فَثَبَّطَهُمۡ وَقِيۡلَ اقۡعُدُوۡا مَعَ الۡقٰعِدِيۡنَ ۞

47. Had they gone forth among you they had added to you naught save trouble and had hurried to and fro among you, seeking to cause sedition among you, and among you there are some who would have listened to them. Allah is Aware of evil-doers.

لَوۡ خَرَجُوۡا فِيۡكُمۡ مَّا زَادُوۡكُمۡ اِلَّا خَبَالًا وَّلَاَ اَوۡضَعُوۡا خِلٰلَكُمۡ يَبۡغُوۡنَكُمُ الۡفِتۡنَةَ ۚ وَفِيۡكُمۡ سَمّٰعُوۡنَ لَهُمۡ ؕ وَاللّٰهُ عَلِيۡمٌۢ بِالظّٰلِمِيۡنَ ۞

48. Aforetime they sought to cause sedition and raised difficulties for thee till the Truth came and the decree of Allah was made manifest, though they were loth.

لَقَدِ ابۡتَغَوُا الۡفِتۡنَةَ مِنۡ قَبۡلُ وَقَلَّبُوۡا لَكَ الۡاُمُوۡرَ حَتّٰى جَآءَ الۡحَقُّ وَظَهَرَ اَمۡرُ اللّٰهِ وَهُمۡ كٰرِهُوۡنَ ۞

49. Of them is he who saith: Grant me leave (to stay at home) and tempt me not.[1] Surely it is into temptation that they (thus) have fallen. Lo! hell is all around the disbelievers.

وَمِنۡهُمۡ مَّنۡ يَّقُوۡلُ ائۡذَنۡ لِّىۡ وَلَا تَفۡتِنِّىۡ ؕ اَلَا فِى الۡفِتۡنَةِ سَقَطُوۡا ؕ وَاِنَّ جَهَنَّمَ لَمُحِيۡطَةٌۢ بِالۡكٰفِرِيۡنَ ۞

50. If good befalleth thee (O Muhammad) it afflicteth them, and if calamity befalleth thee, they say: We took precaution, and they turn away well pleased.

اِنۡ تُصِبۡكَ حَسَنَةٌ تَسُؤۡهُمۡ ۚ وَاِنۡ تُصِبۡكَ مُصِيۡبَةٌ يَّقُوۡلُوۡا قَدۡ اَخَذۡنَاۤ اَمۡرَنَا مِنۡ قَبۡلُ وَيَتَوَلَّوۡا وَّهُمۡ فَرِحُوۡنَ ۞

51. Say: Naught befalleth us save that which Allah hath decreed for us. He is our Protecting Friend. In Allah let believers put their trust!

قُلۡ لَّنۡ يُّصِيۡبَنَاۤ اِلَّا مَا كَتَبَ اللّٰهُ لَنَا ۚ هُوَ مَوۡلٰٮنَا ۚ وَعَلَى اللّٰهِ فَلۡيَتَوَكَّلِ الۡمُؤۡمِنُوۡنَ ۞

1. The temptation here referred to is generally explained as being the beauty of the women of Syria, the country against which the campaign was directed.

52. Say: Can ye await for us aught save one of two good things (death or victory in Allah's way)? while we await for you that Allah will afflict you with a doom from Him or at our hands. Await then! Lo! we are awaiting with you.

53. Say: Pay (your contribution), willingly or unwillingly, it will not be accepted from you. Lo! ye were ever froward folk.

54. And naught preventeth that their contributions should be accepted from them save that they have disbelieved in Allah and in His messenger, and they come not to worship save as idlers, and pay not (their contribution) save reluctantly.

55. So let not their riches nor their children please thee (O Muhammad). Allah thereby intendeth but to punish them in the life of the world and that their souls shall pass away while they are disbelievers.

56. And they swear by Allah that they are in truth of you, when they are not of you, but they are folk who are afraid.

57. Had they but found a refuge, or caverns, or a place to enter, they surely had resorted thither swift as runaways.

58. And of them is he who defameth thee in the matter of the alms. If they are given thereof they are content, and if they are not given thereof, behold! they are enraged.

59. (How much more seemly) had they been content with that which Allah and His messenger had given them and had said: Allah sufficeth us. Allah will give us of His bounty, and (also) His messenger. Unto Allah we are suppliants.

قُلْ هَلْ تَرَبَّصُونَ بِنَآ إِلَّآ إِحْدَى الْحُسْنَيَيْنِ
وَنَحْنُ نَتَرَبَّصُ بِكُمْ أَنْ يُصِيبَكُمُ اللّٰهُ بِعَذَابٍ
مِّنْ عِنْدِهٖٓ أَوْ بِأَيْدِينَا فَتَرَبَّصُوٓا إِنَّا مَعَكُمْ
مُّتَرَبِّصُونَ ﴿٥٢﴾
قُلْ أَنْفِقُوا طَوْعًا أَوْ كَرْهًا لَّنْ يُّتَقَبَّلَ مِنْكُمْ إِنَّكُمْ
كُنْتُمْ قَوْمًا فٰسِقِينَ ﴿٥٣﴾
وَمَا مَنَعَهُمْ أَنْ تُقْبَلَ مِنْهُمْ نَفَقٰتُهُمْ إِلَّآ أَنَّهُمْ
كَفَرُوا بِاللّٰهِ وَبِرَسُولِهٖ وَلَا يَأْتُونَ الصَّلٰوةَ إِلَّا وَ
هُمْ كُسَالٰى وَلَا يُنْفِقُونَ إِلَّا وَهُمْ كٰرِهُونَ ﴿٥٤﴾
فَلَا تُعْجِبْكَ أَمْوَالُهُمْ وَلَآ أَوْلَادُهُمْ إِنَّمَا يُرِيدُ
اللّٰهُ لِيُعَذِّبَهُمْ بِهَا فِي الْحَيٰوةِ الدُّنْيَا وَتَزْهَقَ
أَنْفُسُهُمْ وَهُمْ كٰفِرُونَ ﴿٥٥﴾
وَيَحْلِفُونَ بِاللّٰهِ إِنَّهُمْ لَمِنْكُمْ وَمَا هُمْ مِّنْكُمْ وَ
لٰكِنَّهُمْ قَوْمٌ يَّفْرَقُونَ ﴿٥٦﴾
لَوْ يَجِدُونَ مَلْجَـًٔا أَوْ مَغٰرٰتٍ أَوْ مُدَّخَلًا لَّوَلَّوْا
إِلَيْهِ وَهُمْ يَجْمَحُونَ ﴿٥٧﴾
وَمِنْهُمْ مَّنْ يَّلْمِزُكَ فِي الصَّدَقٰتِ فَإِنْ أُعْطُوا
مِنْهَا رَضُوا وَإِنْ لَّمْ يُعْطَوْا مِنْهَآ إِذَا هُمْ
يَسْخَطُونَ ﴿٥٨﴾
وَلَوْ أَنَّهُمْ رَضُوا مَآ اٰتٰىهُمُ اللّٰهُ وَرَسُولُهٗ وَقَالُوا
حَسْبُنَا اللّٰهُ سَيُؤْتِينَا اللّٰهُ مِنْ فَضْلِهٖ وَرَسُولُهٗٓ
إِنَّآ إِلَى اللّٰهِ رٰغِبُونَ ﴿٥٩﴾

60. The alms are only for the poor and the needy, and those who collect them, and those whose hearts are to be reconciled,[1] and to free the captives and the debtors, and for the cause of Allah, and (for) the wayfarers; a duty imposed by Allah. Allah is Knower, Wise.

61. And of them are those who vex the Prophet and say: He is only a hearer. Say: A hearer of good for you, who believeth in Allah and is true to the believers, and a mercy for such of you as believe. Those who vex the messenger of Allah, for them there is a painful doom.

62. They swear by Allah to you (Muslims) to please you, but Allah, with His messenger, hath more right that they should please Him if they are believers.

63. Know they not that whoso opposeth Allah and His messenger, his portion verily is hell, to abide therein? That is the extreme abasement.

64. The hypocrites fear lest a sūrah should be revealed concerning them, proclaiming what is in their hearts. Say: Scoff (your fill)! Lo! Allah is disclosing what ye fear.

65. And if thou ask them (O Muhammad) they will say: We did but talk and jest. Say: Was it at Allah and His revelations and His messenger that ye did scoff?

66. Make no excuse. Ye have disbelieved after your (confession of) belief. If We forgive a party of you, a party of you We shall punish because they have been guilty.

67. The hypocrites, both men and women, proceed one from another. They enjoin the wrong, and they forbid the right, and they withhold their hands (from spending for the cause of Allah). They forget Allah, so He hath forgotten them. Lo! the hypocrites, they are the transgressors.

إنما الصدقت للفقراء والمسكين والعملين عليها
والمؤلفة قلوبهم وفي الرقاب والغرمين وفي
سبيل الله وابن السبيل فريضة من الله
والله عليم حكيم ﴿٦٠﴾
ومنهم الذين يؤذون النبي ويقولون هو أذن
قل أذن خير لكم يؤمن بالله ويؤمن للمؤمنين
ورحمة للذين امنوا منكم والذين يؤذون رسول
الله لهم عذاب أليم ﴿٦١﴾
يحلفون بالله لكم ليرضوكم والله ورسوله أحق
أن يرضوه إن كانوا مؤمنين ﴿٦٢﴾
ألم يعلموا أنه من يحادد الله ورسوله فأن له نار
جهنم خالدا فيها ذلك الخزي العظيم ﴿٦٣﴾
يحذر المنفقون أن تنزل عليهم سورة تنبئهم
بما في قلوبهم قل استهزءوا إن الله مخرج
ما تحذرون ﴿٦٤﴾
ولئن سألتهم ليقولن إنما كنا نخوض ونلعب
قل أبالله وايته ورسوله كنتم تستهزءون ﴿٦٥﴾
لا تعتذروا قد كفرتم بعد إيمانكم إن نعف عن
طائفة منكم نعذب طائفة بأنهم كانوا مجرمين ﴿٦٦﴾
المنفقون والمنفقت بعضهم من بعض يأمرون
بالمنكر وينهون عن المعروف ويقبضون أيديهم
نسوا الله فنسيهم إن المنفقين هم الفسقون ﴿٦٧﴾

1. A special portion of the Alms was allotted to the people of Mecca, the former enemies of Al-Islām, who were converted *en masse* after the capture of the city, and whose "hearts were to be reconciled."

68. Allah promiseth the hypocrites, both men and women, and the disbelievers fire of hell for their abode. It will suffice them. Allah curseth them, and theirs is lasting torment.

وَعَدَ اللّٰهُ الْمُنٰفِقِيْنَ وَالْمُنٰفِقٰتِ وَالْكُفَّارَ نَارَ جَهَنَّمَ
خٰلِدِيْنَ فِيْهَا ۗ هِيَ حَسْبُهُمْ ۚ وَلَعَنَهُمُ اللّٰهُ ۚ وَلَهُمْ
عَذَابٌ مُّقِيْمٌ ۙ ﴿٦٨﴾

69. Even as those before you were mightier than you in strength, and more affluent than you in wealth and children. They enjoyed their lot awhile, so ye enjoy your lot awhile even as those before you did enjoy their lot awhile. And ye prate even as they prated. Such are they whose works have perished in the world and the Hereafter. Such are they who are the losers.

كَالَّذِيْنَ مِنْ قَبْلِكُمْ كَانُوْٓا اَشَدَّ مِنْكُمْ قُوَّةً وَّاَكْثَرَ
اَمْوَالًا وَّاَوْلَادًا ۗ فَاسْتَمْتَعُوْا بِخَلَاقِهِمْ فَاسْتَمْتَعْتُمْ
بِخَلَاقِكُمْ كَمَا اسْتَمْتَعَ الَّذِيْنَ مِنْ قَبْلِكُمْ
بِخَلَاقِهِمْ وَخُضْتُمْ كَالَّذِيْ خَاضُوْا ۗ اُولٰٓئِكَ
حَبِطَتْ اَعْمَالُهُمْ فِي الدُّنْيَا وَالْاٰخِرَةِ ۚ وَاُولٰٓئِكَ
هُمُ الْخٰسِرُوْنَ ﴿٦٩﴾

70. Hath not the fame of those before them reached them—the folk of Noah, 'Aād, Thamūd, the folk of Abraham, the dwellers of Midian and the disasters (which befell them)? Their messengers (from Allah) came unto them with proofs (of Allah's sovereignty). So Allah surely wronged them not, but they did wrong themselves.

اَلَمْ يَاْتِهِمْ نَبَاُ الَّذِيْنَ مِنْ قَبْلِهِمْ قَوْمِ نُوْحٍ وَّعَادٍ وَّ
ثَمُوْدَ ۙ وَقَوْمِ اِبْرٰهِيْمَ وَاَصْحٰبِ مَدْيَنَ وَالْمُؤْتَفِكٰتِ ۗ
اَتَتْهُمْ رُسُلُهُمْ بِالْبَيِّنٰتِ ۚ فَمَا كَانَ اللّٰهُ لِيَظْلِمَهُمْ
وَلٰكِنْ كَانُوْٓا اَنْفُسَهُمْ يَظْلِمُوْنَ ﴿٧٠﴾

71. And the believers, men and women, are protecting friends one of another; they enjoin the right and forbid the wrong, and they establish worship and they pay the poor-due, and they obey Allah and His messenger. As for these, Allah will have mercy on them. Lo! Allah is Mighty, Wise.

وَالْمُؤْمِنُوْنَ وَالْمُؤْمِنٰتُ بَعْضُهُمْ اَوْلِيَاۤءُ بَعْضٍ ۘ ربع
يَاْمُرُوْنَ بِالْمَعْرُوْفِ وَيَنْهَوْنَ عَنِ الْمُنْكَرِ وَ
يُقِيْمُوْنَ الصَّلٰوةَ وَيُؤْتُوْنَ الزَّكٰوةَ وَيُطِيْعُوْنَ اللّٰهَ
وَرَسُوْلَهٗ ۗ اُولٰٓئِكَ سَيَرْحَمُهُمُ اللّٰهُ ۗ اِنَّ اللّٰهَ عَزِيْزٌ
حَكِيْمٌ ﴿٧١﴾

72. Allah promiseth to the believers, men and women, Gardens underneath which rivers flow, wherein they will abide—blessed dwellings in Gardens of Eden. And—greater (far)!—acceptance from Allah. That is the Supreme triumph.

وَعَدَ اللّٰهُ الْمُؤْمِنِيْنَ وَالْمُؤْمِنٰتِ جَنّٰتٍ تَجْرِيْ مِنْ
تَحْتِهَا الْاَنْهٰرُ خٰلِدِيْنَ فِيْهَا وَمَسٰكِنَ طَيِّبَةً فِيْ
جَنّٰتِ عَدْنٍ ۗ وَرِضْوَانٌ مِّنَ اللّٰهِ اَكْبَرُ ۗ ذٰلِكَ هُوَ
الْفَوْزُ الْعَظِيْمُ ﴿٧٢﴾ ع

73. O Prophet! Strive against the disbelievers and the hypocrites! Be harsh with them. Their ultimate abode is hell, a hapless journey's-end.

74. They swear by Allah that they said nothing (wrong), yet they did say the word of disbelief, and did disbelieve after their Surrender (to Allah). And they purposed that which they could not attain, and they sought revenge only that Allah by His messenger should enrich them of His bounty. If they repent it will be better for them; and if they turn away, Allah will afflict them with a painful doom in the world and the Hereafter, and they have no protecting friend nor helper in the earth.

75. And of them is he who made a covenant with Allah (saying): If He give us of His bounty We will give alms and become of the righteous.

76. Yet when He gave them of His bounty, they hoarded it and turned away, averse;

77. So He hath made the consequence (to be) hypocrisy in their hearts until the day when they shall meet Him, because they broke their word to Allah that they promised Him, and because they lied.

78. Know they not that Allah knoweth both their secret and the thought that they confide, and that Allah is the Knower of Things Hidden?

79. Those who point at such of the believers as give the alms willingly and such as can find naught to give but their endeavours, and deride them—Allah (Himself) derideth them. Theirs will be a painful doom.

80. Ask forgiveness for them (O Muhammad), or ask not forgiveness for them; though thou ask forgiveness for them seventy times Allah will not forgive them. That is because they disbelieved in Allah and His messenger, and Allah guideth not wrongdoing folk.

يٰٓاَيُّهَا النَّبِيُّ جَاهِدِ الْكُفَّارَ وَالْمُنٰفِقِيْنَ وَاغْلُظْ عَلَيْهِمْ ۚ
وَمَاْوٰىهُمْ جَهَنَّمُ ۗ وَبِئْسَ الْمَصِيْرُ ﴿٧٣﴾
يَحْلِفُوْنَ بِاللّٰهِ مَا قَالُوْا ۗ وَلَقَدْ قَالُوْا كَلِمَةَ الْكُفْرِ وَ
كَفَرُوْا بَعْدَ اِسْلَامِهِمْ وَهَمُّوْا بِمَا لَمْ يَنَالُوْا ۚ وَمَا
نَقَمُوْٓا اِلَّآ اَنْ اَغْنٰىهُمُ اللّٰهُ وَرَسُوْلُهٗ مِنْ فَضْلِهٖ ۚ فَاِنْ
يَّتُوْبُوْا يَكُ خَيْرًا لَّهُمْ ۚ وَاِنْ يَّتَوَلَّوْا يُعَذِّبْهُمُ اللّٰهُ
عَذَابًا اَلِيْمًا ۙ فِي الدُّنْيَا وَالْاٰخِرَةِ ۚ وَمَا لَهُمْ فِي
الْاَرْضِ مِنْ وَّلِيٍّ وَّلَا نَصِيْرٍ ﴿٧٤﴾
وَمِنْهُمْ مَّنْ عٰهَدَ اللّٰهَ لَئِنْ اٰتٰىنَا مِنْ فَضْلِهٖ
لَنَصَّدَّقَنَّ وَلَنَكُوْنَنَّ مِنَ الصّٰلِحِيْنَ ﴿٧٥﴾
فَلَمَّآ اٰتٰىهُمْ مِّنْ فَضْلِهٖ بَخِلُوْا بِهٖ وَتَوَلَّوْا وَّهُمْ
مُّعْرِضُوْنَ ﴿٧٦﴾
فَاَعْقَبَهُمْ نِفَاقًا فِيْ قُلُوْبِهِمْ اِلٰى يَوْمِ يَلْقَوْنَهٗ بِمَآ
اَخْلَفُوا اللّٰهَ مَا وَعَدُوْهُ وَبِمَا كَانُوْا يَكْذِبُوْنَ ﴿٧٧﴾
اَلَمْ يَعْلَمُوْٓا اَنَّ اللّٰهَ يَعْلَمُ سِرَّهُمْ وَنَجْوٰىهُمْ وَاَنَّ اللّٰهَ
عَلَّامُ الْغُيُوْبِ ﴿٧٨﴾
اَلَّذِيْنَ يَلْمِزُوْنَ الْمُطَّوِّعِيْنَ مِنَ الْمُؤْمِنِيْنَ فِي
الصَّدَقٰتِ وَالَّذِيْنَ لَا يَجِدُوْنَ اِلَّا جُهْدَهُمْ فَيَسْخَرُوْنَ
مِنْهُمْ ۗ سَخِرَ اللّٰهُ مِنْهُمْ ۖ وَلَهُمْ عَذَابٌ اَلِيْمٌ ﴿٧٩﴾
اِسْتَغْفِرْ لَهُمْ اَوْ لَا تَسْتَغْفِرْ لَهُمْ ۗ اِنْ تَسْتَغْفِرْ لَهُمْ
سَبْعِيْنَ مَرَّةً فَلَنْ يَّغْفِرَ اللّٰهُ لَهُمْ ۗ ذٰلِكَ بِاَنَّهُمْ كَفَرُوْا
بِاللّٰهِ وَرَسُوْلِهٖ ۗ وَاللّٰهُ لَا يَهْدِي الْقَوْمَ الْفٰسِقِيْنَ ﴿٨٠﴾ ع ١٦

81. Those who were left behind rejoiced at sitting still behind the messenger of Allah, and were averse to striving with their wealth and their lives in Allah's way. And they said: Go not forth in the heat! Say: The heat of hell is more intense of heat, if they but understood.

82. Then let them laugh a little: they will weep much, as the reward of what they used to earn.

83. If Allah bring thee back (from the campaign) unto a party of them and they ask of thee leave to go out (to fight) then say unto them: Ye shall never more go out with me nor fight with me against a foe. Ye were content with sitting still the first time. So sit still, with the useless.

84. And never (O Muhammad) pray for one of them who dieth, nor stand by his grave. Lo! they disbelieved in Allah and His messenger, and they died while they were evil-doers.

85. Let not their wealth nor their children astonish thee! Allah purposeth only to punish them thereby in the world, and that their souls shall pass away while they are disbelievers.

86. And when a sūrah is revealed (which saith): Believe in Allah and strive along with His messenger, the men of wealth among them still ask leave of thee and say: Suffer us to be with those who sit (at home).

87. They are content that they should be with the useless and their hearts are sealed, so that they apprehend not.

فرح المخلفون بمقعدهم خلف رسول الله
وكرهوا أن يجاهدوا بأموالهم وأنفسهم
في سبيل الله وقالوا لا تنفروا في الحر
قل نار جهنم أشد حرا لو كانوا
يفقهون ٨١
فليضحكوا قليلا وليبكوا كثيرا جزاء بما
كانوا يكسبون ٨٢
فإن رجعك الله إلى طائفة منهم فاستأذنوك
للخروج فقل لن تخرجوا معي أبدا ولن
تقاتلوا معي عدوا إنكم رضيتم بالقعود أول
مرة فاقعدوا مع الخالفين ٨٣
ولا تصل على أحد منهم مات أبدا ولا تقم
على قبره إنهم كفروا بالله ورسوله وماتوا و
هم فاسقون ٨٤
ولا تعجبك أموالهم وأولادهم إنما يريد
الله أن يعذبهم بها في الدنيا وتزهق أنفسهم
وهم كافرون ٨٥
وإذا أنزلت سورة أن آمنوا بالله وجاهدوا مع
رسوله استأذنك أولوا الطول منهم وقالوا ذرنا
نكن مع القاعدين ٨٦
رضوا بأن يكونوا مع الخوالف وطبع على قلوبهم
فهم لا يفقهون ٨٧

88. But the messenger and those who believe with him strive with their wealth and their lives. Such are they for whom are the good things. Such are they who are the successful.

لٰكِنِ الرَّسُوْلُ وَالَّذِيْنَ اٰمَنُوْا مَعَهٗ جٰهَدُوْا بِاَمْوَالِهِمْ
وَاَنْفُسِهِمْ ۚ وَاُولٰٓئِكَ لَهُمُ الْخَيْرٰتُ ۡ وَاُولٰٓئِكَ هُمُ
الْمُفْلِحُوْنَ ﴿٨٨﴾

89. Allah hath made ready for them Gardens underneath which rivers flow, wherein they will abide. That is the Supreme triumph.

اَعَدَّ اللّٰهُ لَهُمْ جَنّٰتٍ تَجْرِيْ مِنْ تَحْتِهَا الْاَنْهٰرُ خٰلِدِيْنَ
فِيْهَا ۚ ذٰلِكَ الْفَوْزُ الْعَظِيْمُ ﴿٨٩﴾ ع

90. And those among the wandering Arabs who had an excuse came in order that permission might be granted them. And those who lied to Allah and His messenger sat at home. A painful doom will fall on those of them who disbelieve.

وَجَآءَ الْمُعَذِّرُوْنَ مِنَ الْاَعْرَابِ لِيُؤْذَنَ لَهُمْ وَقَعَدَ
الَّذِيْنَ كَذَبُوا اللّٰهَ وَرَسُوْلَهٗ ۚ سَيُصِيْبُ الَّذِيْنَ
كَفَرُوْا مِنْهُمْ عَذَابٌ اَلِيْمٌ ﴿٩٠﴾

91. Not unto the weak nor unto the sick nor unto those who can find naught to spend is any fault (to be imputed though they stay at home) if they are true to Allah and His messenger. Not unto the good is there any road (of blame). Allah is Forgiving ,Merciful.

لَيْسَ عَلَى الضُّعَفَآءِ وَلَا عَلَى الْمَرْضٰى وَلَا عَلَى
الَّذِيْنَ لَا يَجِدُوْنَ مَا يُنْفِقُوْنَ حَرَجٌ اِذَا نَصَحُوْا
لِلّٰهِ وَرَسُوْلِهٖ ۚ مَا عَلَى الْمُحْسِنِيْنَ مِنْ سَبِيْلٍ ۚ وَ
اللّٰهُ غَفُوْرٌ رَّحِيْمٌ ﴿٩١﴾

92. Nor unto those whom, when they came to thee (asking) that thou shouldst mount them, thou didst tell: I cannot find whereon to mount you. They turned back with eyes flowing with tears, for sorrow that they could not find the means to spend.

وَّلَا عَلَى الَّذِيْنَ اِذَا مَآ اَتَوْكَ لِتَحْمِلَهُمْ قُلْتَ لَآ اَجِدُ
مَآ اَحْمِلُكُمْ عَلَيْهِ ۠ تَوَلَّوْا وَّاَعْيُنُهُمْ تَفِيْضُ مِنَ
الدَّمْعِ حَزَنًا اَلَّا يَجِدُوْا مَا يُنْفِقُوْنَ ﴿٩٢﴾

93. The road (of blame) is only against those who ask for leave of thee (to stay at home) when they are rich. They are content to be with the useless. Allah hath sealed their hearts so that they know not.

اِنَّمَا السَّبِيْلُ عَلَى الَّذِيْنَ يَسْتَاْذِنُوْنَكَ وَهُمْ اَغْنِيَآءُ ۚ
رَضُوْا بِاَنْ يَّكُوْنُوْا مَعَ الْخَوَالِفِ ۙ وَطَبَعَ اللّٰهُ عَلٰى
قُلُوْبِهِمْ فَهُمْ لَا يَعْلَمُوْنَ ﴿٩٣﴾

94. They will make excuse to you (Muslims) when ye return unto them. Say: Make no excuse, for we shall not believe you. Allah hath told us tidings of you. Allah and His messenger will see your conduct, and then ye will be brought back unto Him Who knoweth the invisible as well as the visible, and He will tell you what ye used to do.

يَعْتَذِرُوْنَ اِلَيْكُمْ اِذَا رَجَعْتُمْ اِلَيْهِمْ ۚ قُلْ لَّا
تَعْتَذِرُوْا لَنْ نُّؤْمِنَ لَكُمْ قَدْ نَبَّاَنَا اللّٰهُ مِنْ اَخْبَارِكُمْ ۚ
وَسَيَرَى اللّٰهُ عَمَلَكُمْ وَرَسُوْلُهٗ ثُمَّ تُرَدُّوْنَ اِلٰى عٰلِمِ
الْغَيْبِ وَالشَّهَادَةِ فَيُنَبِّئُكُمْ بِمَا كُنْتُمْ تَعْمَلُوْنَ ﴿٩٤﴾

95. They will swear by Allah unto you, when ye return unto them, that ye may let them be. Let them be, for lo! they are unclean, and their abode is hell as the reward for what they used to earn.

96. They swear unto you, that ye may accept them. Though ye accept them, Allah verily accepteth not wrongdoing folk.

97. The wandering Arabs are more hard in disbelief and hypocrisy, and more likely to be ignorant of the limits which Allah hath revealed unto His messenger. And Allah is Knower, Wise.

98. And of the wandering Arabs there is he who taketh that which he expendeth (for the cause of Allah), as a loss, and awaiteth (evil) turns of fortune for you (that he may be rid of it). The evil turn of fortune will be theirs. Allah is Hearer, Knower.

99. And of the wandering Arabs there is he who believeth in Allah and the Last Day, and taketh that which he expendeth and also the prayers of the messenger as acceptable offerings in the sight of Allah. Lo! verily it is an acceptable offering for them. Allah will bring them into His mercy. Lo! Allah is Forgiving, Merciful.

100. And the first to lead the way, of the Muhājirīn [1] and the Anṣār,[2] and those who followed them in goodness—Allah is well pleased with them and they are well pleased with Him, and He hath made ready for them Gardens underneath which rivers flow, wherein they will abide for ever. That is the supreme triumph.

101. And among those around you of the wandering Arabs there are hypocrites, and among the townspeople of Al-Madînah (there are some who) persist in hypocrisy whom thou (O Muhammad) knowest not. We, We know them, and We shall chastise them twice; then they will be relegated to a painful doom.

سَيَحْلِفُوْنَ بِاللّٰهِ لَكُمْ اِذَا انْقَلَبْتُمْ اِلَيْهِمْ لِتُعْرِضُوْا
عَنْهُمْ فَاَعْرِضُوْا عَنْهُمْ اِنَّهُمْ رِجْسٌ وَّمَاْوٰىهُمْ
جَهَنَّمُ جَزَآءًۢ بِمَا كَانُوْا يَكْسِبُوْنَ ٩٥
يَحْلِفُوْنَ لَكُمْ لِتَرْضَوْا عَنْهُمْ فَاِنْ تَرْضَوْا عَنْهُمْ
فَاِنَّ اللّٰهَ لَا يَرْضٰى عَنِ الْقَوْمِ الْفٰسِقِيْنَ ٩٦
اَلْاَعْرَابُ اَشَدُّ كُفْرًا وَّنِفَاقًا وَّاَجْدَرُ اَلَّا يَعْلَمُوْا حُدُوْدَ
مَآ اَنْزَلَ اللّٰهُ عَلٰى رَسُوْلِهٖ وَاللّٰهُ عَلِيْمٌ حَكِيْمٌ ٩٧
وَمِنَ الْاَعْرَابِ مَنْ يَّتَّخِذُ مَا يُنْفِقُ مَغْرَمًا وَّ
يَتَرَبَّصُ بِكُمُ الدَّوَآئِرَ عَلَيْهِمْ دَآئِرَةُ السَّوْءِ وَاللّٰهُ
سَمِيْعٌ عَلِيْمٌ ٩٨
وَمِنَ الْاَعْرَابِ مَنْ يُّؤْمِنُ بِاللّٰهِ وَالْيَوْمِ الْاٰخِرِ
وَيَتَّخِذُ مَا يُنْفِقُ قُرُبٰتٍ عِنْدَ اللّٰهِ وَصَلَوٰتِ
الرَّسُوْلِ اَلَآ اِنَّهَا قُرْبَةٌ لَّهُمْ سَيُدْخِلُهُمُ اللّٰهُ فِيْ
رَحْمَتِهٖ اِنَّ اللّٰهَ غَفُوْرٌ رَّحِيْمٌ ٩٩ ع ١٢
وَالسّٰبِقُوْنَ الْاَوَّلُوْنَ مِنَ الْمُهٰجِرِيْنَ وَالْاَنْصَارِ
وَالَّذِيْنَ اتَّبَعُوْهُمْ بِاِحْسَانٍ رَّضِيَ اللّٰهُ عَنْهُمْ
وَرَضُوْا عَنْهُ وَاَعَدَّ لَهُمْ جَنّٰتٍ تَجْرِيْ تَحْتَهَا الْاَنْهٰرُ
خٰلِدِيْنَ فِيْهَآ اَبَدًا ذٰلِكَ الْفَوْزُ الْعَظِيْمُ ١٠٠
مع وَمِمَّنْ حَوْلَكُمْ مِّنَ الْاَعْرَابِ مُنٰفِقُوْنَ وَمِنْ اَهْلِ
الْمَدِيْنَةِ مَرَدُوْا عَلَى النِّفَاقِ لَا تَعْلَمُهُمْ نَحْنُ وقف منزل
نَعْلَمُهُمْ سَنُعَذِّبُهُمْ مَّرَّتَيْنِ ثُمَّ يُرَدُّوْنَ اِلٰى
عَذَابٍ عَظِيْمٍ ١٠١

[1] The fugitives from Mecca to Al-Madînah.
[2] The Muslims of Al-Madînah who welcomed the fugitives from Mecca and helped the Prophet with their wealth and defended him with their lives.

102. And (there are) others who have acknowledged their faults. They mixed a righteous action with another that was bad. It may be that Allah will relent toward them. Lo! Allah is Relenting, Merciful.

103. Take alms of their wealth, wherewith thou mayst purify them and mayst make them grow, and pray for them. Lo! thy prayer is an assuagement for them. Allah is Hearer, Knower.

104. Know they not that Allah is He Who accepteth repentance from His bondmen and taketh the alms, and that Allah is He Who is the Relenting, the Merciful.

105. And say (unto them): Act! Allah will behold your actions, and (so will) His messenger and the believers, and ye will be brought back to the Knower of the invisible and the visible, and He will tell you what ye used to do.

106. And (there are) others who await Allah's decree, whether He will punish them or will forgive them. Allah is Knower, Wise.

107. And as for those who chose a place of worship out of opposition and disbelief, and in order to cause dissent among the believers, and as an outpost for those who warred against Allah and His messenger aforetime, they will surely swear: We purposed naught save good. Allah beareth witness that they verily are liars.

108. Never stand (to pray) there. A place of worship which was founded upon duty (to Allah) from the first day is more worthy that thou shouldst stand (to pray) therein, wherein are men who love to purify themselves. Allah loveth the purifiers.

109. Is he who founded his building upon duty to Allah and His good pleasure better; or he who founded his building on the brink of a crumbling, overhanging precipice so that it toppled with him into the fire of hell? Allah guideth not wrongdoing folk.

وَاٰخَرُوْنَ اعْتَرَفُوْا بِذُنُوْبِهِمْ خَلَطُوْا عَمَلًا صَالِحًا
وَّاٰخَرَ سَيِّئًا ؕ عَسَى اللّٰهُ اَنْ يَّتُوْبَ عَلَيْهِمْ ؕ اِنَّ اللّٰهَ
غَفُوْرٌ رَّحِيْمٌ ﴿١٠٢﴾
خُذْ مِنْ اَمْوَالِهِمْ صَدَقَةً تُطَهِّرُهُمْ وَتُزَكِّيْهِمْ بِهَا وَ
صَلِّ عَلَيْهِمْ ؕ اِنَّ صَلٰوتَكَ سَكَنٌ لَّهُمْ ؕ وَاللّٰهُ سَمِيْعٌ عَلِيْمٌ ﴿١٠٣﴾
اَلَمْ يَعْلَمُوْۤا اَنَّ اللّٰهَ هُوَ يَقْبَلُ التَّوْبَةَ عَنْ عِبَادِهٖ وَ
يَاْخُذُ الصَّدَقٰتِ وَاَنَّ اللّٰهَ هُوَ التَّوَّابُ الرَّحِيْمُ ﴿١٠٤﴾
وَقُلِ اعْمَلُوْا فَسَيَرَى اللّٰهُ عَمَلَكُمْ وَرَسُوْلُهٗ
وَالْمُؤْمِنُوْنَ ؕ وَسَتُرَدُّوْنَ اِلٰى عٰلِمِ الْغَيْبِ وَالشَّهَادَةِ
فَيُنَبِّئُكُمْ بِمَا كُنْتُمْ تَعْمَلُوْنَ ﴿١٠٥﴾
وَاٰخَرُوْنَ مُرْجَوْنَ لِاَمْرِ اللّٰهِ اِمَّا يُعَذِّبُهُمْ وَاِمَّا يَتُوْبُ
عَلَيْهِمْ ؕ وَاللّٰهُ عَلِيْمٌ حَكِيْمٌ ﴿١٠٦﴾
وَالَّذِيْنَ اتَّخَذُوْا مَسْجِدًا ضِرَارًا وَّكُفْرًا وَّتَفْرِيْقًا
بَيْنَ الْمُؤْمِنِيْنَ وَاِرْصَادًا لِّمَنْ حَارَبَ اللّٰهَ وَرَسُوْلَهٗ
مِنْ قَبْلُ ؕ وَلَيَحْلِفُنَّ اِنْ اَرَدْنَاۤ اِلَّا الْحُسْنٰى ؕ وَاللّٰهُ
يَشْهَدُ اِنَّهُمْ لَكٰذِبُوْنَ ﴿١٠٧﴾
لَا تَقُمْ فِيْهِ اَبَدًا ؕ لَمَسْجِدٌ اُسِّسَ عَلَى التَّقْوٰى مِنْ
اَوَّلِ يَوْمٍ اَحَقُّ اَنْ تَقُوْمَ فِيْهِ ؕ فِيْهِ رِجَالٌ يُّحِبُّوْنَ
اَنْ يَّتَطَهَّرُوْا ؕ وَاللّٰهُ يُحِبُّ الْمُطَّهِّرِيْنَ ﴿١٠٨﴾
اَفَمَنْ اَسَّسَ بُنْيَانَهٗ عَلٰى تَقْوٰى مِنَ اللّٰهِ وَرِضْوَانٍ
خَيْرٌ اَمْ مَّنْ اَسَّسَ بُنْيَانَهٗ عَلٰى شَفَا جُرُفٍ هَارٍ فَانْهَارَ
بِهٖ فِيْ نَارِ جَهَنَّمَ ؕ وَاللّٰهُ لَا يَهْدِى الْقَوْمَ الظّٰلِمِيْنَ ﴿١٠٩﴾

110. The building which they built will never cease to be a misgiving in their hearts unless their hearts be torn to pieces. Allah is Knower, Wise.

111. Lo! Allah hath bought from the believers their lives and their wealth because the Garden will be theirs: they shall fight in the way of Allah and shall slay and be slain. It is a promise which is binding on Him in the Torah and the Gospel and the Qur'ān. Who fulfilleth his covenant better than Allah? Rejoice then in your bargain that ye have made, for that is the supreme triumph.

112. (Triumphant) are those who turn repentant (to Allah), those who serve (Him), those who praise (Him), those who fast, those who bow down, those who fall prostrate (in worship), those who enjoin the right and who forbid the wrong and those who keep the limits (ordained) of Allah—And give glad tidings to believers!

113. It is not for the Prophet, and those who believe, to pray for the forgiveness of idolaters even though they may be near of kin (to them) after it hath become clear that they are people of hell-fire.

114. The prayer of Abraham for the forgiveness of his father was only because of a promise he had promised him, but when it had become clear unto him that he (his father) was an enemy to Allah he (Abraham) disowned him. Lo! Abraham was soft of heart, long-suffering.

115. It was never Allah's (part) that he should send a folk astray after He had guided them until He had made clear unto them what they should avoid. Lo! Allah is Aware of all things.

116. Lo! Allah! Unto Him belongeth the sovereignty of the heavens and the earth. He quickeneth and He giveth death. And ye have, instead of Allah, no protecting friend nor helper.

لَا يَزَالُ بُنْيَانُهُمُ الَّذِي بَنَوْا رِيبَةً فِي قُلُوبِهِمْ إِلَّا
ع ١٣/٣ أَنْ تَقَطَّعَ قُلُوبُهُمْ ۚ وَاللَّهُ عَلِيمٌ حَكِيمٌ ﴿١١٠﴾
إِنَّ اللَّهَ اشْتَرَىٰ مِنَ الْمُؤْمِنِينَ أَنْفُسَهُمْ وَأَمْوَالَهُمْ
بِأَنَّ لَهُمُ الْجَنَّةَ ۚ يُقَاتِلُونَ فِي سَبِيلِ اللَّهِ فَيَقْتُلُونَ
وَيُقْتَلُونَ ۖ وَعْدًا عَلَيْهِ حَقًّا فِي التَّوْرَاةِ وَالْإِنْجِيلِ وَ
الْقُرْآنِ ۚ وَمَنْ أَوْفَىٰ بِعَهْدِهِ مِنَ اللَّهِ ۚ فَاسْتَبْشِرُوا
بِبَيْعِكُمُ الَّذِي بَايَعْتُمْ بِهِ ۚ وَذَٰلِكَ هُوَ الْفَوْزُ الْعَظِيمُ ﴿١١١﴾
التَّائِبُونَ الْعَابِدُونَ الْحَامِدُونَ السَّائِحُونَ الرَّاكِعُونَ
السَّاجِدُونَ الْآمِرُونَ بِالْمَعْرُوفِ وَالنَّاهُونَ عَنِ
الْمُنْكَرِ وَالْحَافِظُونَ لِحُدُودِ اللَّهِ ۗ وَبَشِّرِ
الْمُؤْمِنِينَ ﴿١١٢﴾
مَا كَانَ لِلنَّبِيِّ وَالَّذِينَ آمَنُوا أَنْ يَسْتَغْفِرُوا
لِلْمُشْرِكِينَ وَلَوْ كَانُوا أُولِي قُرْبَىٰ مِنْ بَعْدِ مَا تَبَيَّنَ
لَهُمْ أَنَّهُمْ أَصْحَابُ الْجَحِيمِ ﴿١١٣﴾
وَمَا كَانَ اسْتِغْفَارُ إِبْرَاهِيمَ لِأَبِيهِ إِلَّا عَنْ مَوْعِدَةٍ
وَعَدَهَا إِيَّاهُ فَلَمَّا تَبَيَّنَ لَهُ أَنَّهُ عَدُوٌّ لِلَّهِ تَبَرَّأَ
مِنْهُ ۚ إِنَّ إِبْرَاهِيمَ لَأَوَّاهٌ حَلِيمٌ ﴿١١٤﴾
وَمَا كَانَ اللَّهُ لِيُضِلَّ قَوْمًا بَعْدَ إِذْ هَدَاهُمْ حَتَّىٰ
يُبَيِّنَ لَهُمْ مَا يَتَّقُونَ ۚ إِنَّ اللَّهَ بِكُلِّ شَيْءٍ عَلِيمٌ ﴿١١٥﴾
إِنَّ اللَّهَ لَهُ مُلْكُ السَّمَاوَاتِ وَالْأَرْضِ ۖ يُحْيِي
وَيُمِيتُ ۚ وَمَا لَكُمْ مِنْ دُونِ اللَّهِ مِنْ وَلِيٍّ وَ
لَا نَصِيرٍ ﴿١١٦﴾

117. Allah hath turned in mercy to the Prophet, and to the Muhājirīn and the Anṣār[1] who followed him in the hour of hardship. After the hearts of a party of them had almost swerved aside, then turned He unto them in mercy. Lo! He is Full of Pity, Merciful for them:

118. And to the three also (did He turn in mercy) who were left behind, when the earth, vast as it is, was straitened for them, and their own souls were straitened for them till they bethought them that there is no refuge from Allah save toward Him. Then turned He unto them in mercy that they (too) might turn (repentant unto Him).[2] Lo! Allah! He is the Relenting, the Merciful.

119. O ye who believe! Be careful of your duty to Allah, and be with the truthful.

120. It is not for the townsfolk of Al-Madīnah and for those around them of the wandering Arabs to stay behind the messenger of Allah and prefer their lives to his life. That is because neither thirst nor toil nor hunger afflicteth them in the way of Allah, nor step they any step that angereth the disbelievers, nor gain they from the enemy a gain, but a good deed is recorded for them therefor. Lo! Allah loseth not the wages of the good:

121. Nor spend they any spending, small or great, nor do they cross a valley, but it is recorded for them, that Allah may repay them the best of what they used to do.

122. And the believers should not all go out to fight. Of every troop of them, a party only should go forth, that they (who are left behind) may gain sound knowledge in religion, and that they may warn their folk when they return to them, so that they may beware.

لَقَدْ تَّابَ اللّٰهُ عَلَى النَّبِيِّ وَالْمُهٰجِرِيْنَ وَالْاَنْصَارِ
الَّذِيْنَ اتَّبَعُوْهُ فِيْ سَاعَةِ الْعُسْرَةِ مِنْۢ بَعْدِ مَا كَادَ
يَزِيْغُ قُلُوْبُ فَرِيْقٍ مِّنْهُمْ ثُمَّ تَابَ عَلَيْهِمْ اِنَّهٗ
بِهِمْ رَءُوْفٌ رَّحِيْمٌ ﴿١١٧﴾
وَّعَلَى الثَّلٰثَةِ الَّذِيْنَ خُلِّفُوْا حَتّٰٓى اِذَا ضَاقَتْ عَلَيْهِمُ
الْاَرْضُ بِمَا رَحُبَتْ وَضَاقَتْ عَلَيْهِمْ اَنْفُسُهُمْ وَظَنُّوْٓا
اَنْ لَّا مَلْجَاَ مِنَ اللّٰهِ اِلَّآ اِلَيْهِ ثُمَّ تَابَ عَلَيْهِمْ لِيَتُوْبُوْا
ع اِنَّ اللّٰهَ هُوَ التَّوَّابُ الرَّحِيْمُ ﴿١١٨﴾
يٰٓاَيُّهَا الَّذِيْنَ اٰمَنُوا اتَّقُوا اللّٰهَ وَكُوْنُوْا مَعَ الصّٰدِقِيْنَ ﴿١١٩﴾
مَا كَانَ لِاَهْلِ الْمَدِيْنَةِ وَمَنْ حَوْلَهُمْ مِّنَ الْاَعْرَابِ
اَنْ يَّتَخَلَّفُوْا عَنْ رَّسُوْلِ اللّٰهِ وَلَا يَرْغَبُوْا بِاَنْفُسِهِمْ عَنْ
نَّفْسِهٖ ذٰلِكَ بِاَنَّهُمْ لَا يُصِيْبُهُمْ ظَمَاٌ وَّلَا نَصَبٌ وَّلَا
مَخْمَصَةٌ فِيْ سَبِيْلِ اللّٰهِ وَلَا يَطَـُٔوْنَ مَوْطِئًا يَّغِيْظُ
الْكُفَّارَ وَلَا يَنَالُوْنَ مِنْ عَدُوٍّ نَّيْلًا اِلَّا كُتِبَ لَهُمْ بِهٖ
عَمَلٌ صَالِحٌ اِنَّ اللّٰهَ لَا يُضِيْعُ اَجْرَ الْمُحْسِنِيْنَ ﴿١٢٠﴾
وَلَا يُنْفِقُوْنَ نَفَقَةً صَغِيْرَةً وَّلَا كَبِيْرَةً وَّلَا
يَقْطَعُوْنَ وَادِيًا اِلَّا كُتِبَ لَهُمْ لِيَجْزِيَهُمُ اللّٰهُ اَحْسَنَ
مَا كَانُوْا يَعْمَلُوْنَ ﴿١٢١﴾
وَمَا كَانَ الْمُؤْمِنُوْنَ لِيَنْفِرُوْا كَآفَّةً فَلَوْلَا نَفَرَ مِنْ
كُلِّ فِرْقَةٍ مِّنْهُمْ طَآئِفَةٌ لِّيَتَفَقَّهُوْا فِي الدِّيْنِ
وَلِيُنْذِرُوْا قَوْمَهُمْ اِذَا رَجَعُوْٓا اِلَيْهِمْ لَعَلَّهُمْ
ع يَحْذَرُوْنَ ﴿١٢٢﴾

[1] See v. 100, footnotes.
[2] The reference is to three men of Al-Madinah who were ostracised on account of a misdeed, but afterwards repented and were forgiven.

123. O ye who believe! Fight those of the disbelievers who are near to you, and let them find harshness in you, and know that Allah is with those who keep their duty (unto Him).

124. And whenever a sūrah is revealed there are some of them who say: Which one of you hath thus increased in faith? As for those who believe, it hath increased them in faith and they rejoice (therefor).

125. But as for those in whose hearts is disease, it only addeth wickedness to their wickedness, and they die while they are disbelievers.

126. See they not that they are tested once or twice in every year? Still they turn not in repentance, neither pay they heed.

127. And whenever a sūrah is revealed, they look one at another (as who should say): Doth anybody see you? Then they turn away. Allah turneth away their hearts because they are a folk who understand not.

128. There hath come unto you a messenger, (one) of yourselves, unto whom aught that ye are overburdened is grievous, full of concern for you, for the believers full of pity, merciful.

129. Now, if they turn away (O Muhammad) say: Allah sufficeth me. There is no God save Him. In Him have I put my trust, and He is Lord of the Tremendous Throne.

يٰٓأَيُّهَا الَّذِينَ ءَامَنُوا قَٰتِلُوا الَّذِينَ يَلُونَكُم مِّنَ
الْكُفَّارِ وَلْيَجِدُوا فِيكُمْ غِلْظَةً ۚ وَاعْلَمُوٓا أَنَّ اللَّهَ
مَعَ الْمُتَّقِينَ ﴿١٢٣﴾
وَإِذَا مَآ أُنزِلَتْ سُورَةٌ فَمِنْهُم مَّن يَقُولُ أَيُّكُمْ
زَادَتْهُ هَٰذِهِۦٓ إِيمَٰنًا ۚ فَأَمَّا الَّذِينَ ءَامَنُوا فَزَادَتْهُمْ
إِيمَٰنًا وَهُمْ يَسْتَبْشِرُونَ ﴿١٢٤﴾
وَأَمَّا الَّذِينَ فِى قُلُوبِهِم مَّرَضٌ فَزَادَتْهُمْ رِجْسًا
إِلَىٰ رِجْسِهِمْ وَمَاتُوا وَهُمْ كَٰفِرُونَ ﴿١٢٥﴾
أَوَلَا يَرَوْنَ أَنَّهُمْ يُفْتَنُونَ فِى كُلِّ عَامٍ مَّرَّةً أَوْ
مَرَّتَيْنِ ثُمَّ لَا يَتُوبُونَ وَلَا هُمْ يَذَّكَّرُونَ ﴿١٢٦﴾
وَإِذَا مَآ أُنزِلَتْ سُورَةٌ نَّظَرَ بَعْضُهُمْ إِلَىٰ بَعْضٍ هَلْ
يَرَىٰكُم مِّنْ أَحَدٍ ثُمَّ انصَرَفُوا ۚ صَرَفَ اللَّهُ قُلُوبَهُم
بِأَنَّهُمْ قَوْمٌ لَّا يَفْقَهُونَ ﴿١٢٧﴾
لَقَدْ جَآءَكُمْ رَسُولٌ مِّنْ أَنفُسِكُمْ عَزِيزٌ عَلَيْهِ مَا
عَنِتُّمْ حَرِيصٌ عَلَيْكُم بِالْمُؤْمِنِينَ رَءُوفٌ رَّحِيمٌ ﴿١٢٨﴾
فَإِن تَوَلَّوْا فَقُلْ حَسْبِىَ اللَّهُ لَآ إِلَٰهَ إِلَّا هُوَ ۖ عَلَيْهِ
تَوَكَّلْتُ ۖ وَهُوَ رَبُّ الْعَرْشِ الْعَظِيمِ ﴿١٢٩﴾

Derives its title from v. 99. "If only there had been a community (of those that were) destroyed of old that believed and profited by its belief as did the folk of Jonah!" As is the case with nearly all the Meccan Sūrahs, the date of revelation is uncertain, on account of the dearth of historical allusion. All that can with certainty be said is, that it belongs to the latest group of Meccan Sūrahs, and must therefore have been revealed at some time during the last four years before the Hijrah.

A late Meccan Sūrah, with the exception of three verses revealed at Al-Madinah.

110. And (O Muhammad) follow that which is inspired in thee, and forbear until Allah give judgement. And He is the Best of Judges.

JONAH
Revealed at Mecca

In the name of Allah, the Beneficent, the Merciful.

1. Alif. Lām. Rā.[1] These are verses of the wise Scripture.

2. Is it a wonder for mankind that We have inspired a man among them, saying: Warn mankind and bring unto those who believe the good tidings that they have a sure footing with their Lord? The disbelievers say: Lo! this is a mere wizard.

3. Lo! your Lord is Allah Who created the heavens and the earth in six Days,[2] then He established Himself upon the Throne, directing all things. There is no intercessor (with Him) save after His permission. That is Allah, your Lord, so worship Him. Oh, will ye not remember?

4. Unto Him is the return of all of you; it is a promise of Allah in truth. Lo! He produceth creation, then reproduceth it, that He may reward those who believe and do good works with equity; while, as for those who disbelieve, theirs will be a boiling drink and painful doom because they disbelieved.

5. He it is Who appointed the sun a splendour and the moon a light, and measured for her stages, that ye might know the number of the years, and the reckoning. Allah created not (all) that save in truth. He detaileth the revelations for people who have knowledge.

6. Lo! in the difference of day and night and all that Allah hath created in the heavens and the earth are portents, verily, for folk who ward off (evil).

[1] See Sūr. II, v. 1, footnote.

[2] See XXII, 47, XXXII, 5 and LXX, 4.

اٰياتها ١٠٩ (١٠) سُوْرَةُ يُوْنُسَ مَكِّيَّةٌ رُكُوْعَاتُهَا ١١

بِسْمِ اللّٰهِ الرَّحْمٰنِ الرَّحِيْمِ ○

الٓرٰ تِلْكَ اٰيٰتُ الْكِتٰبِ الْحَكِيْمِ ①
اَكَانَ لِلنَّاسِ عَجَبًا اَنْ اَوْحَيْنَآ اِلٰى رَجُلٍ مِّنْهُمْ اَنْ
اَنْذِرِ النَّاسَ وَبَشِّرِ الَّذِيْنَ اٰمَنُوْٓا اَنَّ لَهُمْ قَدَمَ
صِدْقٍ عِنْدَ رَبِّهِمْ ۗ قَالَ الْكٰفِرُوْنَ اِنَّ هٰذَا لَسٰحِرٌ
مُّبِيْنٌ ②
اِنَّ رَبَّكُمُ اللّٰهُ الَّذِيْ خَلَقَ السَّمٰوٰتِ وَالْاَرْضَ فِيْ
سِتَّةِ اَيَّامٍ ثُمَّ اسْتَوٰى عَلَى الْعَرْشِ يُدَبِّرُ الْاَمْرَ ۗ مَا
مِنْ شَفِيْعٍ اِلَّا مِنْۢ بَعْدِ اِذْنِهٖ ۗ ذٰلِكُمُ اللّٰهُ رَبُّكُمْ
فَاعْبُدُوْهُ ۗ اَفَلَا تَذَكَّرُوْنَ ③
اِلَيْهِ مَرْجِعُكُمْ جَمِيْعًا ۗ وَعْدَ اللّٰهِ حَقًّا ۗ اِنَّهٗ يَبْدَؤُا
الْخَلْقَ ثُمَّ يُعِيْدُهٗ لِيَجْزِيَ الَّذِيْنَ اٰمَنُوْا وَعَمِلُوا
الصّٰلِحٰتِ بِالْقِسْطِ ۗ وَالَّذِيْنَ كَفَرُوْا لَهُمْ شَرَابٌ مِّنْ
حَمِيْمٍ وَّعَذَابٌ اَلِيْمٌۢ بِمَا كَانُوْا يَكْفُرُوْنَ ④
هُوَ الَّذِيْ جَعَلَ الشَّمْسَ ضِيَآءً وَّالْقَمَرَ نُوْرًا وَّ
قَدَّرَهٗ مَنَازِلَ لِتَعْلَمُوْا عَدَدَ السِّنِيْنَ وَالْحِسَابَ ۗ مَا
خَلَقَ اللّٰهُ ذٰلِكَ اِلَّا بِالْحَقِّ ۚ يُفَصِّلُ الْاٰيٰتِ لِقَوْمٍ
يَّعْلَمُوْنَ ⑤
اِنَّ فِي اخْتِلَافِ الَّيْلِ وَالنَّهَارِ وَمَا خَلَقَ اللّٰهُ فِي
السَّمٰوٰتِ وَالْاَرْضِ لَاٰيٰتٍ لِّقَوْمٍ يَّتَّقُوْنَ ⑥

7. Lo! those who expect not the meeting with Us but desire the life of the world and feel secure therein, and those who are neglectful of Our revelations,

8. Their home will be the Fire because of what they used to earn.

9. Lo! those who believe and do good works, their Lord guideth them by their faith. Rivers will flow beneath them in the Gardens of Delight.

10. Their prayer therein will be: Glory be to Thee, O Allah! and their greeting therein will be: Peace! And the conclusion of their prayer will be: Praise be to Allah, Lord of the Worlds!

11. If Allah were to hasten on for men the ill (that they have earned) as they would hasten on the good, their respite would already have expired. But We suffer those who look not for the meeting with Us to wander blindly on in their contumacy.

12. And if misfortune touch a man he crieth unto Us, (while reclining) on his side, or sitting or standing, but when We have relieved him of the misfortune he goeth his way as though he had not cried unto Us because of a misfortune, that afflicted him. Thus is what they do made (seeming) fair unto the prodigal.

13. We destroyed the generations before you when they did wrong; and their messengers (from Allah) came unto them with clear proofs (of His Sovereignty) but they would not believe. Thus do We reward the guilty folk.

14. Then We appointed you viceroys in the earth after them, that We might see how ye behave.

15. And when Our clear revelations are recited unto them, they who look not for the meeting with Us say: Bring a Lecture[1] other than this, or change it Say (O Muhammad): It is not for me to change it of my own accord. I only follow that which is inspired in me. Lo! if I disobey my Lord I fear the retribution of an awful Day.

1. Ar. *Qur'ān*

إِنَّ الَّذِينَ لَا يَرْجُونَ لِقَاءَنَا وَرَضُوا بِالْحَيَاةِ الدُّنْيَا
وَاطْمَأَنُّوا بِهَا وَالَّذِينَ هُمْ عَنْ آيَاتِنَا غَافِلُونَ ﴿٧﴾
أُولَٰئِكَ مَأْوَاهُمُ النَّارُ بِمَا كَانُوا يَكْسِبُونَ ﴿٨﴾
إِنَّ الَّذِينَ آمَنُوا وَعَمِلُوا الصَّالِحَاتِ يَهْدِيهِمْ رَبُّهُمْ
بِإِيمَانِهِمْ ۖ تَجْرِي مِنْ تَحْتِهِمُ الْأَنْهَارُ فِي جَنَّاتِ النَّعِيمِ ﴿٩﴾
دَعْوَاهُمْ فِيهَا سُبْحَانَكَ اللَّهُمَّ وَتَحِيَّتُهُمْ فِيهَا سَلَامٌ ۚ
وَآخِرُ دَعْوَاهُمْ أَنِ الْحَمْدُ لِلَّهِ رَبِّ الْعَالَمِينَ ﴿١٠﴾
وَلَوْ يُعَجِّلُ اللَّهُ لِلنَّاسِ الشَّرَّ اسْتِعْجَالَهُمْ بِالْخَيْرِ
لَقُضِيَ إِلَيْهِمْ أَجَلُهُمْ ۖ فَنَذَرُ الَّذِينَ لَا يَرْجُونَ لِقَاءَنَا
فِي طُغْيَانِهِمْ يَعْمَهُونَ ﴿١١﴾
وَإِذَا مَسَّ الْإِنْسَانَ الضُّرُّ دَعَانَا لِجَنْبِهِ أَوْ قَاعِدًا أَوْ
قَائِمًا فَلَمَّا كَشَفْنَا عَنْهُ ضُرَّهُ مَرَّ كَأَنْ لَمْ يَدْعُنَا
إِلَىٰ ضُرٍّ مَسَّهُ ۚ كَذَٰلِكَ زُيِّنَ لِلْمُسْرِفِينَ مَا كَانُوا يَعْمَلُونَ ﴿١٢﴾
وَلَقَدْ أَهْلَكْنَا الْقُرُونَ مِنْ قَبْلِكُمْ لَمَّا ظَلَمُوا ۙ وَ
جَاءَتْهُمْ رُسُلُهُمْ بِالْبَيِّنَاتِ وَمَا كَانُوا لِيُؤْمِنُوا ۚ
كَذَٰلِكَ نَجْزِي الْقَوْمَ الْمُجْرِمِينَ ﴿١٣﴾
ثُمَّ جَعَلْنَاكُمْ خَلَائِفَ فِي الْأَرْضِ مِنْ بَعْدِهِمْ لِنَنْظُرَ
كَيْفَ تَعْمَلُونَ ﴿١٤﴾
وَإِذَا تُتْلَىٰ عَلَيْهِمْ آيَاتُنَا بَيِّنَاتٍ ۙ قَالَ الَّذِينَ لَا يَرْجُونَ
لِقَاءَنَا ائْتِ بِقُرْآنٍ غَيْرِ هَٰذَا أَوْ بَدِّلْهُ ۚ قُلْ مَا يَكُونُ لِي
أَنْ أُبَدِّلَهُ مِنْ تِلْقَاءِ نَفْسِي ۖ إِنْ أَتَّبِعُ إِلَّا مَا يُوحَىٰ إِلَيَّ ۖ
إِنِّي أَخَافُ إِنْ عَصَيْتُ رَبِّي عَذَابَ يَوْمٍ عَظِيمٍ ﴿١٥﴾

16. Say: If Allah had so willed I should not have recited it to you nor would He have made it known to you. I dwelt among you a whole lifetime before it (came to me). Have ye then no sense?

17. Who doth greater wrong than he who inventeth a lie concerning Allah and denieth His revelations? Lo! the guilty never are successful.

18. They worship beside Allah that which neither hurteth them nor profiteth them, and they say: These are our intercessors with Allah. Say: Would ye inform Allah of (something) that He knoweth not in the heavens or in the earth? Praised be He and high exalted above all that ye associate (with Him)!

19. Mankind were but one community; then they differed; and had it not been for a word that had already gone forth from thy Lord, it had been judged between them in respect of that wherein they differ.

20. And they will say: If only a portent were sent down upon him from his Lord! Then say (O Muhammad): The unseen belongeth to Allah. So wait! Lo, I am waiting with you.

21. And when We cause mankind to taste of mercy after some adversity which had afflicted them, behold! they have some plot against Our revelations. Say: Allah is more swift in plotting. Lo! Our messengers write down that which ye plot.

22. He it is Who maketh you to go on the land and the sea till, when ye are in the ships and they sail with them with a fair breeze and they are glad therein, a storm-wind reacheth them and the wave cometh unto them from every side and they deem that they are overwhelmed therein; (then) they cry unto Allah, making their faith pure for Him only: If Thou deliver us from this, we truly will be of the thankful.

قُل لَّوْ شَاءَ اللَّهُ مَا تَلَوْتُهُ عَلَيْكُمْ وَلَا أَدْرَاكُم بِهِ ۖ فَقَدْ
لَبِثْتُ فِيكُمْ عُمُرًا مِّن قَبْلِهِ ۚ أَفَلَا تَعْقِلُونَ ﴿١٦﴾
فَمَنْ أَظْلَمُ مِمَّنِ افْتَرَىٰ عَلَى اللَّهِ كَذِبًا أَوْ كَذَّبَ
بِآيَاتِهِ ۚ إِنَّهُ لَا يُفْلِحُ الْمُجْرِمُونَ ﴿١٧﴾
وَيَعْبُدُونَ مِن دُونِ اللَّهِ مَا لَا يَضُرُّهُمْ وَلَا يَنفَعُهُمْ
وَيَقُولُونَ هَٰؤُلَاءِ شُفَعَاؤُنَا عِندَ اللَّهِ ۚ قُلْ أَتُنَبِّئُونَ
اللَّهَ بِمَا لَا يَعْلَمُ فِي السَّمَاوَاتِ وَلَا فِي الْأَرْضِ ۚ سُبْحَانَهُ
وَتَعَالَىٰ عَمَّا يُشْرِكُونَ ﴿١٨﴾
وَمَا كَانَ النَّاسُ إِلَّا أُمَّةً وَاحِدَةً فَاخْتَلَفُوا ۚ وَلَوْلَا
كَلِمَةٌ سَبَقَتْ مِن رَّبِّكَ لَقُضِيَ بَيْنَهُمْ فِيمَا فِيهِ
يَخْتَلِفُونَ ﴿١٩﴾
وَيَقُولُونَ لَوْلَا أُنزِلَ عَلَيْهِ آيَةٌ مِّن رَّبِّهِ ۖ فَقُلْ إِنَّمَا
ع الْغَيْبُ لِلَّهِ فَانتَظِرُوا إِنِّي مَعَكُم مِّنَ الْمُنتَظِرِينَ ﴿٢٠﴾
وَإِذَا أَذَقْنَا النَّاسَ رَحْمَةً مِّن بَعْدِ ضَرَّاءَ مَسَّتْهُمْ
إِذَا لَهُم مَّكْرٌ فِي آيَاتِنَا ۚ قُلِ اللَّهُ أَسْرَعُ مَكْرًا ۚ إِنَّ
رُسُلَنَا يَكْتُبُونَ مَا تَمْكُرُونَ ﴿٢١﴾
هُوَ الَّذِي يُسَيِّرُكُمْ فِي الْبَرِّ وَالْبَحْرِ ۖ حَتَّىٰ إِذَا كُنتُمْ
فِي الْفُلْكِ وَجَرَيْنَ بِهِم بِرِيحٍ طَيِّبَةٍ وَفَرِحُوا بِهَا
جَاءَتْهَا رِيحٌ عَاصِفٌ وَجَاءَهُمُ الْمَوْجُ مِن كُلِّ
مَكَانٍ وَظَنُّوا أَنَّهُمْ أُحِيطَ بِهِمْ ۙ دَعَوُا اللَّهَ مُخْلِصِينَ
لَهُ الدِّينَ لَئِنْ أَنجَيْتَنَا مِنْ هَٰذِهِ لَنَكُونَنَّ مِنَ
الشَّاكِرِينَ ﴿٢٢﴾

23. Yet when He hath delivered them, behold! they rebel in the earth wrongfully. O mankind! Your rebellion is only against yourselves. (Ye have) enjoyment of the life of the world: then unto Us is your return and We shall proclaim unto you what ye used to do.

فَلَمَّآ أَنجَىٰهُمْ إِذَا هُمْ يَبْغُونَ فِى ٱلْأَرْضِ بِغَيْرِ ٱلْحَقِّ
يَٰٓأَيُّهَا ٱلنَّاسُ إِنَّمَا بَغْيُكُمْ عَلَىٰٓ أَنفُسِكُم مَّتَٰعَ ٱلْحَيَوٰةِ
ٱلدُّنْيَا ثُمَّ إِلَيْنَا مَرْجِعُكُمْ فَنُنَبِّئُكُم بِمَا كُنتُمْ
تَعْمَلُونَ ﴿٢٣﴾

24. The similitude of the life of the world is only as water which We send down from the sky, then the earth's growth of that which men and cattle eat mingleth with it till, when the earth hath taken on her ornaments and is embellished, and her people deem that they are masters of her, Our commandment cometh by night or by day and We make it as reaped corn as if it had not flourished yesterday. Thus do We expound the revelations for people who reflect.

إِنَّمَا مَثَلُ ٱلْحَيَوٰةِ ٱلدُّنْيَا كَمَآءٍ أَنزَلْنَٰهُ مِنَ ٱلسَّمَآءِ
فَٱخْتَلَطَ بِهِۦ نَبَاتُ ٱلْأَرْضِ مِمَّا يَأْكُلُ ٱلنَّاسُ وَ
ٱلْأَنْعَٰمُ حَتَّىٰٓ إِذَآ أَخَذَتِ ٱلْأَرْضُ زُخْرُفَهَا وَ
ٱزَّيَّنَتْ وَظَنَّ أَهْلُهَآ أَنَّهُمْ قَٰدِرُونَ عَلَيْهَآ أَتَىٰهَآ
أَمْرُنَا لَيْلًا أَوْ نَهَارًا فَجَعَلْنَٰهَا حَصِيدًا كَأَن لَّمْ تَغْنَ
بِٱلْأَمْسِ كَذَٰلِكَ نُفَصِّلُ ٱلْءَايَٰتِ لِقَوْمٍ يَتَفَكَّرُونَ ﴿٢٤﴾

25. And Allah summoneth to the abode of Peace, and leadeth whom He will to a straight path.

وَٱللَّهُ يَدْعُوٓا۟ إِلَىٰ دَارِ ٱلسَّلَٰمِ وَيَهْدِى مَن يَشَآءُ
إِلَىٰ صِرَٰطٍ مُّسْتَقِيمٍ ﴿٢٥﴾

26. For those who do good is the best (reward) and more (thereto). Neither dust nor ignominy cometh near their faces. Such are rightful owners of the Garden; they will abide therein.

لِّلَّذِينَ أَحْسَنُوا۟ ٱلْحُسْنَىٰ وَزِيَادَةٌ وَلَا يَرْهَقُ
وُجُوهَهُمْ قَتَرٌ وَلَا ذِلَّةٌ أُو۟لَٰٓئِكَ أَصْحَٰبُ ٱلْجَنَّةِ
هُمْ فِيهَا خَٰلِدُونَ ﴿٢٦﴾

27. And those who earn ill deeds, (for them) requital of each ill deed by the like thereof; and ignominy overtaketh them—They have no protector from Allah—as if their faces had been covered with a cloak of darkest night. Such are rightful owners of the Fire; they will abide therein.

وَٱلَّذِينَ كَسَبُوا۟ ٱلسَّيِّـَٔاتِ جَزَآءُ سَيِّئَةٍۭ بِمِثْلِهَا وَ
تَرْهَقُهُمْ ذِلَّةٌ مَّا لَهُم مِّنَ ٱللَّهِ مِنْ عَاصِمٍ كَأَنَّمَآ
أُغْشِيَتْ وُجُوهُهُمْ قِطَعًا مِّنَ ٱلَّيْلِ مُظْلِمًا أُو۟لَٰٓئِكَ
أَصْحَٰبُ ٱلنَّارِ هُمْ فِيهَا خَٰلِدُونَ ﴿٢٧﴾

28. On the Day when We gather them all together, then We say unto those who ascribed partners (unto Us): Stand back, ye and your (pretended) partners (of Allah)! And We separate them, the one from the other, and their (pretended) partners say: It was not us ye worshipped.

وَيَوْمَ نَحْشُرُهُمْ جَمِيعًا ثُمَّ نَقُولُ لِلَّذِينَ أَشْرَكُوا۟
مَكَانَكُمْ أَنتُمْ وَشُرَكَآؤُكُمْ فَزَيَّلْنَا بَيْنَهُمْ وَقَالَ
شُرَكَآؤُهُم مَّا كُنتُمْ إِيَّانَا تَعْبُدُونَ ﴿٢٨﴾

29. Allah sufficeth as a witness between us and you, that we were unaware of your worship.

فَكَفٰى بِاللّٰهِ شَهِيْدًاۢ بَيْنَنَا وَبَيْنَكُمْ اِنْ كُنَّا عَنْ
عِبَادَتِكُمْ لَغٰفِلِيْنَ ﴿٢٩﴾

30. There doth every soul experience that which it did aforetime, and they are returned unto Allah, their rightful Lord, and that which they used to invent hath failed them.

هُنَالِكَ تَبْلُوْا كُلُّ نَفْسٍ مَّاۤ اَسْلَفَتْ وَرُدُّوْۤا اِلَى اللّٰهِ
مَوْلٰىهُمُ الْحَقِّ وَضَلَّ عَنْهُمْ مَّا كَانُوْا يَفْتَرُوْنَ ﴿٣٠﴾

31. Say (unto them, O Muhammad): Who provideth for you from the sky and the earth, or Who owneth hearing and sight; and Who bringeth forth the living from the dead and bringeth forth the dead from the living; and Who directeth the course? They will say: Allah. Then say: Will ye not then keep your duty (unto Him)?

قُلْ مَنْ يَّرْزُقُكُمْ مِّنَ السَّمَآءِ وَالْاَرْضِ اَمَّنْ يَّمْلِكُ
السَّمْعَ وَالْاَبْصَارَ وَمَنْ يُّخْرِجُ الْحَيَّ مِنَ الْمَيِّتِ
وَيُخْرِجُ الْمَيِّتَ مِنَ الْحَيِّ وَمَنْ يُّدَبِّرُ الْاَمْرَ
فَسَيَقُوْلُوْنَ اللّٰهُ فَقُلْ اَفَلَا تَتَّقُوْنَ ﴿٣١﴾

32. Such then is Allah, your rightful Lord. After the Truth what is there saving error? How then are ye turned away!

فَذٰلِكُمُ اللّٰهُ رَبُّكُمُ الْحَقُّ فَمَاذَا بَعْدَ الْحَقِّ اِلَّا
الضَّلٰلُ فَاَنّٰى تُصْرَفُوْنَ ﴿٣٢﴾

33. Thus is the Word of thy Lord justified concerning those who do wrong that they believe not.

كَذٰلِكَ حَقَّتْ كَلِمَتُ رَبِّكَ عَلَى الَّذِيْنَ فَسَقُوْۤا
اَنَّهُمْ لَا يُؤْمِنُوْنَ ﴿٣٣﴾

34. Say: Is there of your partners (whom ye ascribe unto Allah) one that produceth Creation and then reproduceth it? Say: Allah produceth Creation, then reproduceth it. How, then, are ye misled!

قُلْ هَلْ مِنْ شُرَكَآئِكُمْ مَّنْ يَّبْدَؤُا الْخَلْقَ ثُمَّ
يُعِيْدُهٗ قُلِ اللّٰهُ يَبْدَؤُا الْخَلْقَ ثُمَّ يُعِيْدُهٗ فَاَنّٰى
تُؤْفَكُوْنَ ﴿٣٤﴾

35. Say: Is there of your partners (whom ye ascribe unto Allah) one that leadeth to the Truth? Say: Allah leadeth to the Truth. Is He Who leadeth to the Truth more deserving that He should be followed, or he who findeth not the way unless he (himself) be guided? What aileth ye? How judge ye?

قُلْ هَلْ مِنْ شُرَكَآئِكُمْ مَّنْ يَّهْدِيْۤ اِلَى الْحَقِّ
قُلِ اللّٰهُ يَهْدِيْ لِلْحَقِّ اَفَمَنْ يَّهْدِيْۤ اِلَى الْحَقِّ
اَحَقُّ اَنْ يُّتَّبَعَ اَمَّنْ لَّا يَهِدِّيْۤ اِلَّاۤ اَنْ يُّهْدٰى
فَمَا لَكُمْ كَيْفَ تَحْكُمُوْنَ ﴿٣٥﴾

36. Most of them follow naught but conjecture. Assuredly conjecture can by no means take the place of truth. Lo! Allah is Aware of what they do.

وَمَا يَتَّبِعُ اَكْثَرُهُمْ اِلَّا ظَنًّا اِنَّ الظَّنَّ لَا
يُغْنِيْ مِنَ الْحَقِّ شَيْـًٔا اِنَّ اللّٰهَ عَلِيْمٌۢ بِمَا
يَفْعَلُوْنَ ﴿٣٦﴾

37. And this Qur'ān is not such as could ever be invented in despite of Allah; but it is a confirmation of that which was before it and an exposition of that which is decreed for mankind—Therein is no doubt—from the Lord of the Worlds.

وما كان هذا القرآن أن يفترى من دون الله
ولكن تصديق الذي بين يديه وتفصيل الكتب
لا ريب فيه من رب العلمين ﴿٣٧﴾

38. Or say they: He hath invented it? Say: Then bring a sūrah like unto it, and call (for help) on all ye can besides Allah, if ye are truthful.

أم يقولون افترىه قل فأتوا بسورة مثله
وادعوا من استطعتم من دون الله إن كنتم
صدقين ﴿٣٨﴾

39. Nay, but they denied that, the knowledge whereof they could not compass, and whereof the interpretation (in events) hath not yet come unto them. Even so did those before them deny. Then see what was the consequence for the wrong-doers!

بل كذبوا بما لم يحيطوا بعلمه ولما يأتهم
تأويله كذلك كذب الذين من قبلهم
فانظر كيف كان عقبة الظلمين ﴿٣٩﴾

40. And of them is he who believeth therein, and of them is he who believeth not therein, and thy Lord is best aware of the corrupters.

ومنهم من يؤمن به ومنهم من لا يؤمن به
ع وربك أعلم بالمفسدين ﴿٤٠﴾

41. And if they deny thee, say: Unto me my work, and unto you your work. Ye are innocent of what I do, and I am innocent of what ye do.

وإن كذبوك فقل لي عملي ولكم عملكم أنتم
بريئون مما أعمل وأنا بريء مما تعملون ﴿٤١﴾

42. And of them are some who listen unto thee. But canst thou make the deaf to hear even though they apprehend not?

ومنهم من يستمعون إليك أفأنت تسمع الصم و
لو كانوا لا يعقلون ﴿٤٢﴾

43. And of them is he who looketh toward thee. But canst thou guide the blind even though they see not?

ومنهم من ينظر إليك أفأنت تهدي العمي
ولو كانوا لا يبصرون ﴿٤٣﴾

44. Lo! Allah wrongeth not mankind in aught; but mankind wrong themselves.

إن الله لا يظلم الناس شيئا ولكن الناس
أنفسهم يظلمون ﴿٤٤﴾

45. And on the day when He shall gather them together, (when it will seem) as though they had tarried but an hour of the day, recognising one another, those will verily have perished who denied the meeting with Allah and were not guided.

ويوم يحشرهم كأن لم يلبثوا إلا ساعة من
النهار يتعارفون بينهم قد خسر الذين كذبوا
بلقاء الله وما كانوا مهتدين ﴿٤٥﴾

46. Whether We let thee (O Muhammad) behold something of that which We promise them[9] or (whether We) cause thee to die, still unto Us is their return, and Allah, moreover, is Witness over what they do.

47. And for every nation there is a messenger. And when their messenger cometh (on the Day of Judgement) it will be judged between them fairly, and they will not be wronged.

48. And they say: When will this promise be fulfilled, if ye are truthful?

49. Say: I have no power to hurt or benefit myself, save that which Allah willeth. For every nation there is an appointed time. When their time cometh, then they cannot put it off an hour, nor hasten (it).

50. Say: Have ye thought: When His doom cometh unto you as a raid by night, or in the (busy) day, what is there of it that the guilty ones desire to hasten?

51. Is it (only) then, when it hath befallen you, that ye will believe? What! (Believe) now, when (until now) ye have been hastening it on (through disbelief)?

52. Then will it be said unto those who dealt unjustly: Taste the torment of eternity. Are ye requited aught save what ye used to earn?

53. And they ask thee to inform them (saying): Is it true? Say: Yea, by my Lord, verily it is true, and ye cannot escape.

54. And if each soul that doth wrong had all that is in the earth it would seek to ransom itself therewith: and they will feel remorse within them, when they see the doom. But it hath been judged between them fairly and they are not wronged.

55. Lo! verily all that is in the heavens and the earth is Allah's. Lo! verily Allah's promise is true. But most of them know not.

56. He quickeneth and giveth death, and unto Him ye will be returned.

وَإِمَّا نُرِيَنَّكَ بَعْضَ الَّذِي نَعِدُهُمْ أَوْ نَتَوَفَّيَنَّكَ فَإِلَيْنَا
مَرْجِعُهُمْ ثُمَّ اللَّهُ شَهِيدٌ عَلَىٰ مَا يَفْعَلُونَ ﴿٤٦﴾
وَلِكُلِّ أُمَّةٍ رَسُولٌ فَإِذَا جَاءَ رَسُولُهُمْ قُضِيَ بَيْنَهُمْ
بِالْقِسْطِ وَهُمْ لَا يُظْلَمُونَ ﴿٤٧﴾
وَيَقُولُونَ مَتَىٰ هَٰذَا الْوَعْدُ إِنْ كُنْتُمْ صَادِقِينَ ﴿٤٨﴾
قُلْ لَا أَمْلِكُ لِنَفْسِي ضَرًّا وَلَا نَفْعًا إِلَّا مَا شَاءَ اللَّهُ
لِكُلِّ أُمَّةٍ أَجَلٌ إِذَا جَاءَ أَجَلُهُمْ فَلَا يَسْتَأْخِرُونَ
سَاعَةً وَلَا يَسْتَقْدِمُونَ ﴿٤٩﴾
قُلْ أَرَأَيْتُمْ إِنْ أَتَاكُمْ عَذَابُهُ بَيَاتًا أَوْ نَهَارًا مَاذَا
يَسْتَعْجِلُ مِنْهُ الْمُجْرِمُونَ ﴿٥٠﴾
أَثُمَّ إِذَا مَا وَقَعَ آمَنْتُمْ بِهِ آلْآنَ وَقَدْ كُنْتُمْ بِهِ
تَسْتَعْجِلُونَ ﴿٥١﴾
ثُمَّ قِيلَ لِلَّذِينَ ظَلَمُوا ذُوقُوا عَذَابَ الْخُلْدِ هَلْ
تُجْزَوْنَ إِلَّا بِمَا كُنْتُمْ تَكْسِبُونَ ﴿٥٢﴾
وَيَسْتَنْبِئُونَكَ أَحَقٌّ هُوَ قُلْ إِي وَرَبِّي إِنَّهُ لَحَقٌّ
وَمَا أَنْتُمْ بِمُعْجِزِينَ ﴿٥٣﴾
وَلَوْ أَنَّ لِكُلِّ نَفْسٍ ظَلَمَتْ مَا فِي الْأَرْضِ لَافْتَدَتْ
بِهِ وَأَسَرُّوا النَّدَامَةَ لَمَّا رَأَوُا الْعَذَابَ وَقُضِيَ
بَيْنَهُمْ بِالْقِسْطِ وَهُمْ لَا يُظْلَمُونَ ﴿٥٤﴾
أَلَا إِنَّ لِلَّهِ مَا فِي السَّمَاوَاتِ وَالْأَرْضِ أَلَا إِنَّ وَعْدَ
اللَّهِ حَقٌّ وَلَٰكِنَّ أَكْثَرَهُمْ لَا يَعْلَمُونَ ﴿٥٥﴾
هُوَ يُحْيِي وَيُمِيتُ وَإِلَيْهِ تُرْجَعُونَ ﴿٥٦﴾

57. O mankind! There hath come unto you an exhortation from your Lord, a balm for that which is in the breasts, a guidance and a mercy for believers.

58. Say: In the bounty of Allah and in His mercy: therein let them rejoice. It is better than what they hoard.

59. Say: Have ye considered what provision Allah hath sent down for you, how ye have made of it lawful and unlawful? Say: Hath Allah permitted you, or do ye invent a lie concerning Allah?

60. And what think those who invent a lie concerning Allah (will be their plight) upon the Day of Resurrection? Lo! Allah truly is Bountiful toward mankind, but most of them give not thanks.

61. And thou (Muhammad) art not occupied with any business and thou recitest not a lecture[1] from this (Scripture), and ye (mankind) perform no act, but We are Witness of you when ye are engaged therein. And not an atom's weight in the earth or in the sky escapeth your Lord, nor what is less than that or greater than that, but it is (written) in a clear Book.

62. Lo! verily the friends of Allah are (those) on whom fear (cometh) not, nor do they grieve.

63. Those who believe and keep their duty (to Allah),

64. Theirs are good tidings in the life of the world and in the Hereafter—There is no changing the Words of Allah—that is the Supreme Triumph.

65. And let not their speech grieve thee (O Muhammad). Lo! power belongeth wholly to Allah. He is the Hearer, the Knower.

1. Ar. *Qur'ān*.

يٰۤاَيُّهَا النَّاسُ قَدْ جَآءَتْكُمْ مَّوْعِظَةٌ مِّنْ رَّبِّكُمْ وَ
شِفَآءٌ لِّمَا فِي الصُّدُوْرِ ۙ وَهُدًى وَّرَحْمَةٌ
لِّلْمُؤْمِنِيْنَ ﴿٥٧﴾

قُلْ بِفَضْلِ اللّٰهِ وَبِرَحْمَتِهٖ فَبِذٰلِكَ فَلْيَفْرَحُوْا ؕ
هُوَ خَيْرٌ مِّمَّا يَجْمَعُوْنَ ﴿٥٨﴾
قُلْ اَرَءَيْتُمْ مَّاۤ اَنْزَلَ اللّٰهُ لَكُمْ مِّنْ رِّزْقٍ فَجَعَلْتُمْ
مِّنْهُ حَرَامًا وَّحَلٰلًا ؕ قُلْ آٰللّٰهُ اَذِنَ لَكُمْ اَمْ عَلَى
اللّٰهِ تَفْتَرُوْنَ ﴿٥٩﴾

وَمَا ظَنُّ الَّذِيْنَ يَفْتَرُوْنَ عَلَى اللّٰهِ الْكَذِبَ يَوْمَ
الْقِيٰمَةِ ؕ اِنَّ اللّٰهَ لَذُوْ فَضْلٍ عَلَى النَّاسِ وَلٰكِنَّ
ع اَكْثَرَهُمْ لَا يَشْكُرُوْنَ ﴿٦٠﴾

وَمَا تَكُوْنُ فِيْ شَاْنٍ وَّمَا تَتْلُوْا مِنْهُ مِنْ قُرْاٰنٍ وَّ
لَا تَعْمَلُوْنَ مِنْ عَمَلٍ اِلَّا كُنَّا عَلَيْكُمْ شُهُوْدًا اِذْ تُفِيْضُوْنَ
فِيْهِ ؕ وَمَا يَعْزُبُ عَنْ رَّبِّكَ مِنْ مِّثْقَالِ ذَرَّةٍ فِي
الْاَرْضِ وَلَا فِي السَّمَآءِ وَلَاۤ اَصْغَرَ مِنْ ذٰلِكَ وَلَاۤ
اَكْبَرَ اِلَّا فِيْ كِتٰبٍ مُّبِيْنٍ ﴿٦١﴾

اَلَاۤ اِنَّ اَوْلِيَآءَ اللّٰهِ لَا خَوْفٌ عَلَيْهِمْ وَلَا هُمْ يَحْزَنُوْنَ ﴿٦٢﴾ ۚ
الَّذِيْنَ اٰمَنُوْا وَكَانُوْا يَتَّقُوْنَ ﴿٦٣﴾ ؕ
لَهُمُ الْبُشْرٰى فِي الْحَيٰوةِ الدُّنْيَا وَفِي الْاٰخِرَةِ ؕ لَا
تَبْدِيْلَ لِكَلِمٰتِ اللّٰهِ ؕ ذٰلِكَ هُوَ الْفَوْزُ الْعَظِيْمُ ﴿٦٤﴾ ؕ
وَلَا يَحْزُنْكَ قَوْلُهُمْ ۘ اِنَّ الْعِزَّةَ لِلّٰهِ جَمِيْعًا ؕ هُوَ السَّمِيْعُ وقف لازم
الْعَلِيْمُ ﴿٦٥﴾

66. Lo! is it not unto Allah that belongeth whosoever is in the heavens and whosoever is in the earth? Those who follow aught instead of Allah follow not (His) partners. They follow only a conjecture, and they do but guess.

67. He it is Who hath appointed for you the night that ye should rest therein and the day giving sight. Lo! herein verily are portents for a folk that heed.

68. They say: Allah hath taken (unto Him) a son—Glorified be He! He hath no needs! His is all that is in the heavens and all that is in the earth. Ye have no warrant for this. Tell ye concerning Allah that which ye know not?

69. Say: Verily those who invent a lie concerning Allah will not succeed.

70. This world's portion (will be theirs), then unto Us is their return. Then We make them taste a dreadful doom because they used to disbelieve.

71. Recite unto them the story of Noah, when he told his people: O my people! If my sojourn (here) and my reminding you by Allah's revelations are an offence unto you, in Allah have I put my trust, so decide upon your course of action, you and your partners. Let not your course of action be in doubt for you. Then have at me, give me no respite.

72. But if ye are averse I have asked of you no wage. My wage is the concern of Allah only, and I am commanded to be of those who surrender (unto Him).

73. But they denied him, so We saved him and those with him in the ship, and made them viceroys (in the earth), while We drowned those who denied Our revelations. See then the nature of the consequence for those who had been warned.

أَلَآ إِنَّ لِلّٰهِ مَنْ فِي السَّمٰوٰتِ وَمَنْ فِي الْأَرْضِ ۗ وَ
مَا يَتَّبِعُ الَّذِينَ يَدْعُونَ مِنْ دُونِ اللّٰهِ شُرَكَآءَ ۗ إِنْ
يَتَّبِعُونَ إِلَّا الظَّنَّ وَإِنْ هُمْ إِلَّا يَخْرُصُونَ ﴿٦٦﴾
هُوَ الَّذِي جَعَلَ لَكُمُ الَّيْلَ لِتَسْكُنُوا فِيهِ وَالنَّهَارَ
مُبْصِرًا ۗ إِنَّ فِي ذٰلِكَ لَآيٰتٍ لِقَوْمٍ يَسْمَعُونَ ﴿٦٧﴾
قَالُوا اتَّخَذَ اللّٰهُ وَلَدًا سُبْحٰنَهُ ۖ هُوَ الْغَنِيُّ ۗ لَهُ مَا فِي
السَّمٰوٰتِ وَمَا فِي الْأَرْضِ ۗ إِنْ عِنْدَكُمْ مِنْ سُلْطٰنٍ
بِهٰذَا ۗ أَتَقُولُونَ عَلَى اللّٰهِ مَا لَا تَعْلَمُونَ ﴿٦٨﴾
قُلْ إِنَّ الَّذِينَ يَفْتَرُونَ عَلَى اللّٰهِ الْكَذِبَ لَا
يُفْلِحُونَ ﴿٦٩﴾ ۗ
مَتَاعٌ فِي الدُّنْيَا ثُمَّ إِلَيْنَا مَرْجِعُهُمْ ثُمَّ نُذِيقُهُمُ
الْعَذَابَ الشَّدِيدَ بِمَا كَانُوا يَكْفُرُونَ ﴿٧٠﴾ ع
وَاتْلُ عَلَيْهِمْ نَبَأَ نُوحٍ ۘ إِذْ قَالَ لِقَوْمِهِ يٰقَوْمِ إِنْ
كَانَ كَبُرَ عَلَيْكُمْ مَقَامِي وَتَذْكِيرِي بِآيٰتِ اللّٰهِ
فَعَلَى اللّٰهِ تَوَكَّلْتُ فَأَجْمِعُوا أَمْرَكُمْ وَشُرَكَآءَكُمْ
ثُمَّ لَا يَكُنْ أَمْرُكُمْ عَلَيْكُمْ غُمَّةً ثُمَّ اقْضُوا إِلَيَّ وَ
لَا تُنْظِرُونِ ﴿٧١﴾
فَإِنْ تَوَلَّيْتُمْ فَمَا سَأَلْتُكُمْ مِنْ أَجْرٍ ۗ إِنْ أَجْرِيَ
إِلَّا عَلَى اللّٰهِ ۙ وَأُمِرْتُ أَنْ أَكُونَ مِنَ الْمُسْلِمِينَ ﴿٧٢﴾
فَكَذَّبُوهُ فَنَجَّيْنٰهُ وَمَنْ مَعَهُ فِي الْفُلْكِ وَجَعَلْنٰهُمْ
خَلٰٓئِفَ وَأَغْرَقْنَا الَّذِينَ كَذَّبُوا بِآيٰتِنَا ۚ فَانْظُرْ كَيْفَ
كَانَ عَاقِبَةُ الْمُنْذَرِينَ ﴿٧٣﴾

74. Then, after him, We sent messengers unto their folk, and they brought them clear proofs. But they were not ready to believe in that which they before denied. Thus print We on the hearts of the transgressors.

75. Then, after them, We sent Moses and Aaron unto Pharaoh and his chiefs with Our revelations, but they were arrogant and were a guilty folk.

76. And when the Truth from Our presence came unto them, they said: This is mere magic.

77. Moses said: Speak ye (so) of the Truth when it hath come unto you? Is this magic? Now magicians thrive not.

78. They said: Hast thou come unto us to pervert us from that (faith) in which we found our fathers, and that you two may own the place of greatness in the land? We will not believe you two.

79. And Pharaoh said: Bring every cunning wizard unto me.

80. And when the wizards came, Moses said unto them: Cast your cast!

81. And when they had cast, Moses said: That which ye have brought is magic. Lo! Allah will make it vain. Lo! Allah upholdeth not the work of mischief makers.

82. And Allah will vindicate the Truth by His words, however much the guilty be averse.

83. But none trusted Moses, save some scions of his people, (and they were) in fear of Pharaoh and their chiefs, that they would persecute them. Lo! Pharaoh was verily a tyrant in the land, and lo! he verily was of the wanton.

84. And Moses said: O my people! If ye have believed in Allah then put trust in Him, if ye have indeed surrendered (unto Him)!

ثُمَّ بَعَثْنَا مِنْ بَعْدِهِ رُسُلًا إِلَىٰ قَوْمِهِمْ فَجَاءُوهُمْ
بِالْبَيِّنٰتِ فَمَا كَانُوا لِيُؤْمِنُوا بِمَا كَذَّبُوا بِهِ مِنْ قَبْلُ
كَذٰلِكَ نَطْبَعُ عَلَىٰ قُلُوبِ الْمُعْتَدِينَ ﴿٧٤﴾
ثُمَّ بَعَثْنَا مِنْ بَعْدِهِمْ مُوسَىٰ وَهٰرُونَ إِلَىٰ فِرْعَوْنَ
وَمَلَائِهِ بِاٰيٰتِنَا فَاسْتَكْبَرُوا وَكَانُوا قَوْمًا مُجْرِمِينَ ﴿٧٥﴾
فَلَمَّا جَاءَهُمُ الْحَقُّ مِنْ عِنْدِنَا قَالُوا إِنَّ هٰذَا
لَسِحْرٌ مُبِينٌ ﴿٧٦﴾
قَالَ مُوسَىٰ أَتَقُولُونَ لِلْحَقِّ لَمَّا جَاءَكُمْ أَسِحْرٌ
هٰذَا وَلَا يُفْلِحُ السّٰحِرُونَ ﴿٧٧﴾
قَالُوا أَجِئْتَنَا لِتَلْفِتَنَا عَمَّا وَجَدْنَا عَلَيْهِ اٰبَاءَنَا وَ
تَكُونَ لَكُمَا الْكِبْرِيَاءُ فِي الْأَرْضِ وَمَا نَحْنُ لَكُمَا بِمُؤْمِنِينَ ﴿٧٨﴾
وَقَالَ فِرْعَوْنُ ائْتُونِي بِكُلِّ سٰحِرٍ عَلِيمٍ ﴿٧٩﴾
فَلَمَّا جَاءَ السَّحَرَةُ قَالَ لَهُمْ مُوسَىٰ أَلْقُوا مَا أَنْتُمْ
مُلْقُونَ ﴿٨٠﴾
فَلَمَّا أَلْقَوْا قَالَ مُوسَىٰ مَا جِئْتُمْ بِهِ السِّحْرُ إِنَّ اللّٰهَ
سَيُبْطِلُهُ إِنَّ اللّٰهَ لَا يُصْلِحُ عَمَلَ الْمُفْسِدِينَ ﴿٨١﴾
وَيُحِقُّ اللّٰهُ الْحَقَّ بِكَلِمٰتِهِ وَلَوْ كَرِهَ الْمُجْرِمُونَ ﴿٨٢﴾ ع
فَمَا اٰمَنَ لِمُوسَىٰ إِلَّا ذُرِّيَّةٌ مِنْ قَوْمِهِ عَلَىٰ خَوْفٍ
مِنْ فِرْعَوْنَ وَمَلَائِهِمْ أَنْ يَفْتِنَهُمْ وَإِنَّ فِرْعَوْنَ
لَعَالٍ فِي الْأَرْضِ وَإِنَّهُ لَمِنَ الْمُسْرِفِينَ ﴿٨٣﴾
وَقَالَ مُوسَىٰ يٰقَوْمِ إِنْ كُنْتُمْ اٰمَنْتُمْ بِاللّٰهِ فَعَلَيْهِ
تَوَكَّلُوا إِنْ كُنْتُمْ مُسْلِمِينَ ﴿٨٤﴾

85. They said: In Allah we put trust. Our Lord! Oh, make us not a lure for the wrongdoing folk;

86. And, of Thy mercy, save us from the folk that disbelieve!

87. And We inspired Moses and his brother, (saying): Appoint houses for your people in Egypt and make your houses oratories, and establish worship. And give good news to the believers.

88. And Moses said: Our Lord! Lo! Thou hast given Pharaoh and his chiefs splendour and riches in the life of the world. Our Lord! that they may lead men astray from Thy way. Our Lord! Destroy their riches and harden their hearts so that they believe not till they see the painful doom.

89. He said: Your prayer is heard. Do ye twain keep to the straight path, and follow not the road of those who have no knowledge.

90. And We brought the Children of Israel across the sea, and Pharaoh with his hosts pursued them in rebellion and transgression, till, when the (fate of) drowning overtook him, he exclaimed: I believe that there is no God save Him in Whom the Children of Israel believe, and I am of those who surrender (unto Him).

91. What! Now! When hitherto thou hast rebelled and been of the wrong-doers?

92. But this day We save thee in thy body that thou mayest be a portent for those after thee. Lo! most of mankind are heedless of Our portents.

93. And We verily did allot unto the Children of Israel a fixed abode, and did provide them with good things; and they differed not until knowledge came unto them. Lo! thy Lord will judge between them on the Day of Resurrection concerning that wherein they used to differ.

فَقَالُوا عَلَى اللّٰهِ تَوَكَّلْنَا رَبَّنَا لَا تَجْعَلْنَا فِتْنَةً لِّلْقَوْمِ
الظّٰلِمِيْنَ ﴿٨٥﴾
وَنَجِّنَا بِرَحْمَتِكَ مِنَ الْقَوْمِ الْكٰفِرِيْنَ ﴿٨٦﴾
وَاَوْحَيْنَآ اِلٰى مُوْسٰى وَاَخِيْهِ اَنْ تَبَوَّاٰ لِقَوْمِكُمَا بِمِصْرَ
بُيُوْتًا وَّاجْعَلُوْا بُيُوْتَكُمْ قِبْلَةً وَّاَقِيْمُوا الصَّلٰوةَ ؕ وَ
بَشِّرِ الْمُؤْمِنِيْنَ ﴿٨٧﴾
وَقَالَ مُوْسٰى رَبَّنَآ اِنَّكَ اٰتَيْتَ فِرْعَوْنَ وَمَلَاَهٗ زِيْنَةً
وَّاَمْوَالًا فِى الْحَيٰوةِ الدُّنْيَا ۙ رَبَّنَا لِيُضِلُّوْا عَنْ سَبِيْلِكَ ۚ
رَبَّنَا اطْمِسْ عَلٰٓى اَمْوَالِهِمْ وَاشْدُدْ عَلٰى قُلُوْبِهِمْ فَلَا
يُؤْمِنُوْا حَتّٰى يَرَوُا الْعَذَابَ الْاَلِيْمَ ﴿٨٨﴾
قَالَ قَدْ اُجِيْبَتْ دَّعْوَتُكُمَا فَاسْتَقِيْمَا وَلَا تَتَّبِعٰٓنِّ
سَبِيْلَ الَّذِيْنَ لَا يَعْلَمُوْنَ ﴿٨٩﴾
وَجٰوَزْنَا بِبَنِيْٓ اِسْرَآءِيْلَ الْبَحْرَ فَاَتْبَعَهُمْ فِرْعَوْنُ
وَجُنُوْدُهٗ بَغْيًا وَّعَدْوًا ؕ حَتّٰٓى اِذَآ اَدْرَكَهُ الْغَرَقُ ۙ قَالَ
اٰمَنْتُ اَنَّهٗ لَآ اِلٰهَ اِلَّا الَّذِيْٓ اٰمَنَتْ بِهٖ بَنُوْٓا اِسْرَآءِيْلَ
وَاَنَا مِنَ الْمُسْلِمِيْنَ ﴿٩٠﴾
آٰلْـٰٔنَ وَقَدْ عَصَيْتَ قَبْلُ وَكُنْتَ مِنَ الْمُفْسِدِيْنَ ﴿٩١﴾
فَالْيَوْمَ نُنَجِّيْكَ بِبَدَنِكَ لِتَكُوْنَ لِمَنْ خَلْفَكَ اٰيَةً ؕ
وَاِنَّ كَثِيْرًا مِّنَ النَّاسِ عَنْ اٰيٰتِنَا لَغٰفِلُوْنَ ﴿٩٢﴾ ع
وَلَقَدْ بَوَّاْنَا بَنِيْٓ اِسْرَآءِيْلَ مُبَوَّاَ صِدْقٍ وَّرَزَقْنٰهُمْ
مِّنَ الطَّيِّبٰتِ ۚ فَمَا اخْتَلَفُوْا حَتّٰى جَآءَهُمُ الْعِلْمُ ؕ اِنَّ
رَبَّكَ يَقْضِيْ بَيْنَهُمْ يَوْمَ الْقِيٰمَةِ فِيْمَا كَانُوْا فِيْهِ يَخْتَلِفُوْنَ ﴿٩٣﴾

94. And if thou (Muhammad) art in doubt concerning that which We reveal unto thee, then question those who read the Scripture (that was) before thee. Verily the Truth from thy Lord hath come unto thee. So be not thou of the waverers:

95. And be not thou of those who deny the revelations of Allah, for then wert thou of the losers.

96. Lo! those for whom the word of thy Lord (concerning sinners) hath effect will not believe,

97. Though every token come unto them, till they see the painful doom.

98. If only there had been a community (of all those that were destroyed of old) that believed and profited by its belief as did the folk of Jonah! When they believed We drew off from them the torment of disgrace in the life of the world and gave them comfort for a while.

99. And if thy Lord willed, all who are in the earth would have believed together. Wouldst thou (Muhammad) compel men until they are believers?

100. It is not for any soul to believe save by the permission of Allah. He hath set uncleanness upon those who have no sense.

101. Say: Behold what is in the heavens and the earth! But revelations and warnings avail not folk who will not believe.

102. What expect they save the like of the days of those who passed away before them? Say: Expect then! I am with you among the expectant.

103. Then shall We save Our messengers and the believers, in like manner (as of old). It is incumbent upon Us to save believers.

فَإِنْ كُنْتَ فِي شَكٍّ مِمَّا أَنْزَلْنَا إِلَيْكَ فَسْئَلِ الَّذِينَ
يَقْرَءُونَ الْكِتٰبَ مِنْ قَبْلِكَ لَقَدْ جَاءَكَ الْحَقُّ مِنْ
رَبِّكَ فَلَا تَكُونَنَّ مِنَ الْمُمْتَرِينَ ٩٤
وَلَا تَكُونَنَّ مِنَ الَّذِينَ كَذَّبُوا بِآيٰتِ اللّٰهِ فَتَكُونَ
مِنَ الْخٰسِرِينَ ٩٥
إِنَّ الَّذِينَ حَقَّتْ عَلَيْهِمْ كَلِمَتُ رَبِّكَ لَا
يُؤْمِنُونَ ٩٦
وَلَوْ جَاءَتْهُمْ كُلُّ آيَةٍ حَتّٰى يَرَوُا الْعَذَابَ
الْأَلِيمَ ٩٧
فَلَوْلَا كَانَتْ قَرْيَةٌ آمَنَتْ فَنَفَعَهَا إِيمَانُهَا إِلَّا قَوْمَ
يُونُسَ لَمَّا آمَنُوا كَشَفْنَا عَنْهُمْ عَذَابَ الْخِزْيِ
فِي الْحَيٰوةِ الدُّنْيَا وَمَتَّعْنٰهُمْ إِلٰى حِينٍ ٩٨
وَلَوْ شَاءَ رَبُّكَ لَآمَنَ مَنْ فِي الْأَرْضِ كُلُّهُمْ جَمِيعًا
أَفَأَنْتَ تُكْرِهُ النَّاسَ حَتّٰى يَكُونُوا مُؤْمِنِينَ ٩٩
وَمَا كَانَ لِنَفْسٍ أَنْ تُؤْمِنَ إِلَّا بِإِذْنِ اللّٰهِ وَيَجْعَلُ
الرِّجْسَ عَلَى الَّذِينَ لَا يَعْقِلُونَ ١٠٠
قُلِ انْظُرُوا مَاذَا فِي السَّمٰوٰتِ وَالْأَرْضِ وَمَا تُغْنِي
الْآيٰتُ وَالنُّذُرُ عَنْ قَوْمٍ لَا يُؤْمِنُونَ ١٠١
فَهَلْ يَنْتَظِرُونَ إِلَّا مِثْلَ أَيَّامِ الَّذِينَ خَلَوْا مِنْ قَبْلِهِمْ
قُلْ فَانْتَظِرُوا إِنِّي مَعَكُمْ مِنَ الْمُنْتَظِرِينَ ١٠٢
ثُمَّ نُنَجِّي رُسُلَنَا وَالَّذِينَ آمَنُوا كَذٰلِكَ حَقًّا
عَلَيْنَا نُنْجِ الْمُؤْمِنِينَ ١٠٣

104. Say (O Muhammad): O mankind! If ye are in doubt of my religion, then (know that) I worship not those whom ye worship instead of Allah, but I worship Allah Who causeth you to die, and I have been commanded to be of the believers.

105. And (O Muhammad) set thy purpose resolutely for religion, as a man by nature upright, and be not of those who ascribe partners (to Allah).

106. And cry not, beside Allah, unto that which cannot profit thee nor hurt thee, for if thou didst so then wert thou of the wrong-doers.

107. If Allah afflicteth thee with some hurt there is none who can remove it save Him; and if He desireth good for thee, there is none who can repel His bounty. He striketh with it whom He will of his bondmen. He is the Forgiving, the Merciful.

108. Say: O mankind! Now hath the Truth from your Lord come unto you. So whosoever is guided, is guided only for (the good of) his soul, and whosoever erreth, erreth only against it. And I am not a warder over you.

109. And (O Muhammad) follow that which is inspired in thee, and forbear until Allah give judgement. And He is the Best of Judges.

قُلْ يٰٓاَيُّهَا النَّاسُ اِنْ كُنْتُمْ فِيْ شَكٍّ مِّنْ دِيْنِيْ
فَلَآ اَعْبُدُ الَّذِيْنَ تَعْبُدُوْنَ مِنْ دُوْنِ اللّٰهِ وَلٰكِنْ
اَعْبُدُ اللّٰهَ الَّذِيْ يَتَوَفّٰىكُمْ ۚ وَاُمِرْتُ اَنْ اَكُوْنَ مِنَ
الْمُؤْمِنِيْنَ ﴿١٠٤﴾
وَاَنْ اَقِمْ وَجْهَكَ لِلدِّيْنِ حَنِيْفًا ۚ وَلَا تَكُوْنَنَّ مِنَ
الْمُشْرِكِيْنَ ﴿١٠٥﴾
وَلَا تَدْعُ مِنْ دُوْنِ اللّٰهِ مَا لَا يَنْفَعُكَ وَلَا يَضُرُّكَ ۚ
فَاِنْ فَعَلْتَ فَاِنَّكَ اِذًا مِّنَ الظّٰلِمِيْنَ ﴿١٠٦﴾
وَاِنْ يَّمْسَسْكَ اللّٰهُ بِضُرٍّ فَلَا كَاشِفَ لَهٗٓ اِلَّا هُوَ ۚ وَ
اِنْ يُّرِدْكَ بِخَيْرٍ فَلَا رَآدَّ لِفَضْلِهٖ ۗ يُصِيْبُ بِهٖ مَنْ
يَّشَآءُ مِنْ عِبَادِهٖ ۗ وَهُوَ الْغَفُوْرُ الرَّحِيْمُ ﴿١٠٧﴾
قُلْ يٰٓاَيُّهَا النَّاسُ قَدْ جَآءَكُمُ الْحَقُّ مِنْ رَّبِّكُمْ ۚ
فَمَنِ اهْتَدٰى فَاِنَّمَا يَهْتَدِيْ لِنَفْسِهٖ ۚ وَمَنْ ضَلَّ
فَاِنَّمَا يَضِلُّ عَلَيْهَا ۚ وَمَآ اَنَا عَلَيْكُمْ بِوَكِيْلٍ ﴿١٠٨﴾
وَاتَّبِعْ مَا يُوْحٰٓى اِلَيْكَ وَاصْبِرْ حَتّٰى يَحْكُمَ اللّٰهُ ۚ
وَهُوَ خَيْرُ الْحٰكِمِيْنَ ﴿١٠٩﴾ ع

Takes its name from v. 50, which begins the story of Hūd, of the tribe of 'Aād, one of the prophets of Arabia who is not mentioned in the Hebrew Scriptures. The Sūrah also contains the stories of two other Arab prophets, Ṣālih, of the tribe of Thamūd, and Shu'eyb of Midian (identified with Jethro), which, with those of Noah and Moses, are quoted as part of the history of Divine Revelation, the truth of which is here vindicated in a manner supplementary to Sūrah X.

A late Meccan Sūrah, except v. 114 f., revealed at Al-Madīnah.

H Ū D

Revealed at Mecca

In the name of Allah, the Beneficent, the Merciful.

1. Alif. Lām. Rā.[1] (This is) a Scripture the revelations whereof are perfected and then expounded. (It cometh) from One Wise, Informed,

2. (Saying): Serve none but Allah. Lo! I am unto you from Him a warner and a bringer of good tidings.

3. And (bidding you): Ask pardon of your Lord and turn to Him repentant. He will cause you to enjoy a fair estate until a time appointed. He giveth His bounty unto every bountiful one. But if ye turn away, lo! (then) I fear for you the retribution of an Awful day.

4. Unto Allah is your return, and He is Able to do all things.

5. Lo! now they fold up their breasts that they may hide (their thoughts) from Him. At the very moment when they cover themselves with their clothing, Allah knoweth that which they keep hidden and that which they proclaim. Lo! He is Aware of what is in the breast (of men).

6. And there is not a beast in the earth but the sustenance thereof dependeth on Allah. He knoweth its habitation and its repository. All is in a clear record.

7. And He it is Who created the heavens and the earth in six Days[2]—and His Throne was upon the water—that He might try you, which of you is best in conduct. Yet if thou (O Muhammad) sayest: Lo! ye will be raised again after death! those who disbelieve will surely say: This is naught but mere magic.

1. See Sûr. II, v. 1, footnote.
2. V. XXII, 47, XXXII, 5, and LXX, 4.

اٰياتها (١١) سُورَةُ هُودٍ مَكِّيَّةٌ ركوعاتها

بِسْمِ اللّٰهِ الرَّحْمٰنِ الرَّحِيْمِ

الٓرٰ كِتٰبٌ اُحْكِمَتْ اٰيٰتُهٗ ثُمَّ فُصِّلَتْ مِنْ لَّدُنْ
حَكِيْمٍ خَبِيْرٍ ١
اَلَّا تَعْبُدُوْٓا اِلَّا اللّٰهَ اِنَّنِيْ لَكُمْ مِّنْهُ نَذِيْرٌ وَّبَشِيْرٌ ٢
وَّاَنِ اسْتَغْفِرُوْا رَبَّكُمْ ثُمَّ تُوْبُوْٓا اِلَيْهِ يُمَتِّعْكُمْ
مَّتَاعًا حَسَنًا اِلٰٓى اَجَلٍ مُّسَمًّى وَّيُؤْتِ كُلَّ ذِيْ
فَضْلٍ فَضْلَهٗ وَاِنْ تَوَلَّوْا فَاِنِّيْٓ اَخَافُ عَلَيْكُمْ
عَذَابَ يَوْمٍ كَبِيْرٍ ٣
اِلَى اللّٰهِ مَرْجِعُكُمْ وَهُوَ عَلٰى كُلِّ شَيْءٍ قَدِيْرٌ ٤
اَلَآ اِنَّهُمْ يَثْنُوْنَ صُدُوْرَهُمْ لِيَسْتَخْفُوْا مِنْهُ اَلَا
حِيْنَ يَسْتَغْشُوْنَ ثِيَابَهُمْ يَعْلَمُ مَا يُسِرُّوْنَ وَمَا
يُعْلِنُوْنَ اِنَّهٗ عَلِيْمٌ بِذَاتِ الصُّدُوْرِ ٥
وَمَا مِنْ دَآبَّةٍ فِي الْاَرْضِ اِلَّا عَلَى اللّٰهِ رِزْقُهَا
وَيَعْلَمُ مُسْتَقَرَّهَا وَمُسْتَوْدَعَهَا كُلٌّ فِيْ كِتٰبٍ
مُّبِيْنٍ ٦
وَهُوَ الَّذِيْ خَلَقَ السَّمٰوٰتِ وَالْاَرْضَ فِيْ سِتَّةِ
اَيَّامٍ وَّكَانَ عَرْشُهٗ عَلَى الْمَآءِ لِيَبْلُوَكُمْ اَيُّكُمْ
اَحْسَنُ عَمَلًا وَلَئِنْ قُلْتَ اِنَّكُمْ مَّبْعُوْثُوْنَ مِنْ
بَعْدِ الْمَوْتِ لَيَقُوْلَنَّ الَّذِيْنَ كَفَرُوْٓا اِنْ هٰذَآ اِلَّا
سِحْرٌ مُّبِيْنٌ ٧

8. And if We delay for them the doom until a reckoned time, they will surely say: What withholdeth it? Verily on the day when it cometh unto them, it cannot be averted from them, and that which they derided will surround them.

9. And if We cause man to taste some mercy from Us and afterward withdraw it from him, lo! he is despairing, thankless.

10. And if We cause him to taste grace after some misfortune that had befallen him, he saith: The ills have gone from me. Lo! he is exultant, boastful;

11. Save those who persevere and do good works. Theirs will be forgiveness and a great reward.

12. A likely thing, that thou wouldst forsake aught of that which hath been revealed unto thee, and that thy breast should be straitened for it, because they say: Why hath not a treasure been sent down for him, or an angel come with him? Thou art but a warner, and Allah is in charge of all things.

13. Or they say: He hath invented it. Say: Then bring ten sūrahs, the like thereof, invented, and call on everyone ye can beside Allah, if ye are truthful!

14. And if they answer not your prayer, then know that it is revealed only in the knowledge of Allah; and that there is no God save Him. Will ye then be (of) those who surrender?[1]

15. Whoso desireth the life of the world and its pomp, We shall repay them their deeds herein, and therein they will not be wronged.

16. Those are they for whom is naught in the Hereafter save the Fire. (All) that they contrive here is vain and (all) that they are wont to do is fruitless.

1. Ar. *Muslimīn*.

وَلَئِنْ أَخَّرْنَا عَنْهُمُ الْعَذَابَ إِلَىٰ أُمَّةٍ مَّعْدُودَةٍ
لَّيَقُولُنَّ مَا يَحْبِسُهُ ۗ أَلَا يَوْمَ يَأْتِيهِمْ لَيْسَ مَصْرُوفًا
عَنْهُمْ وَحَاقَ بِهِم مَّا كَانُوا بِهِ يَسْتَهْزِئُونَ ﴿٨﴾ ع
وَلَئِنْ أَذَقْنَا الْإِنسَانَ مِنَّا رَحْمَةً ثُمَّ نَزَعْنَاهَا مِنْهُ
إِنَّهُ لَيَئُوسٌ كَفُورٌ ﴿٩﴾
وَلَئِنْ أَذَقْنَاهُ نَعْمَاءَ بَعْدَ ضَرَّاءَ مَسَّتْهُ لَيَقُولَنَّ
ذَهَبَ السَّيِّئَاتُ عَنِّي ۚ إِنَّهُ لَفَرِحٌ فَخُورٌ ﴿١٠﴾
إِلَّا الَّذِينَ صَبَرُوا وَعَمِلُوا الصَّالِحَاتِ أُولَٰئِكَ لَهُم
مَّغْفِرَةٌ وَأَجْرٌ كَبِيرٌ ﴿١١﴾
فَلَعَلَّكَ تَارِكٌ بَعْضَ مَا يُوحَىٰ إِلَيْكَ وَضَائِقٌ بِهِ
صَدْرُكَ أَن يَقُولُوا لَوْلَا أُنزِلَ عَلَيْهِ كَنزٌ أَوْ جَاءَ
مَعَهُ مَلَكٌ ۚ إِنَّمَا أَنتَ نَذِيرٌ ۚ وَاللَّهُ عَلَىٰ كُلِّ شَيْءٍ
وَكِيلٌ ﴿١٢﴾
أَمْ يَقُولُونَ افْتَرَاهُ ۖ قُلْ فَأْتُوا بِعَشْرِ سُوَرٍ مِّثْلِهِ
مُفْتَرَيَاتٍ وَادْعُوا مَنِ اسْتَطَعْتُم مِّن دُونِ اللَّهِ
إِن كُنتُمْ صَادِقِينَ ﴿١٣﴾
فَإِلَّمْ يَسْتَجِيبُوا لَكُمْ فَاعْلَمُوا أَنَّمَا أُنزِلَ بِعِلْمِ اللَّهِ
وَأَن لَّا إِلَٰهَ إِلَّا هُوَ ۖ فَهَلْ أَنتُم مُّسْلِمُونَ ﴿١٤﴾
مَن كَانَ يُرِيدُ الْحَيَاةَ الدُّنْيَا وَزِينَتَهَا نُوَفِّ
إِلَيْهِمْ أَعْمَالَهُمْ فِيهَا وَهُمْ فِيهَا لَا يُبْخَسُونَ ﴿١٥﴾
أُولَٰئِكَ الَّذِينَ لَيْسَ لَهُمْ فِي الْآخِرَةِ إِلَّا النَّارُ ۖ وَ
حَبِطَ مَا صَنَعُوا فِيهَا وَبَاطِلٌ مَّا كَانُوا يَعْمَلُونَ ﴿١٦﴾

17. Is he (to be counted equal with them) who relieth on a clear proof from his Lord, and a witness from Him reciteth it, and before it was the Book of Moses, an example and a mercy? Such believe therein, and whoso disbelieveth therein of the clans, the Fire is his appointed place. So be not thou in doubt concerning it. Lo! it is the Truth from thy Lord; but most of mankind believe not.

أَفَمَنْ كَانَ عَلَىٰ بَيِّنَةٍ مِّنْ رَّبِّهٖ وَيَتْلُوْهُ شَاهِدٌ مِّنْهُ
وَمِنْ قَبْلِهٖ كِتٰبُ مُوْسٰٓى اِمَامًا وَّرَحْمَةً ۭ اُولٰۗىِٕكَ
يُؤْمِنُوْنَ بِهٖ ۭ وَمَنْ يَّكْفُرْ بِهٖ مِنَ الْاَحْزَابِ فَالنَّارُ
مَوْعِدُهٗ ۚ فَلَا تَكُ فِيْ مِرْيَةٍ مِّنْهُ ۤ اِنَّهُ الْحَقُّ مِنْ رَّبِّكَ
وَلٰكِنَّ اَكْثَرَ النَّاسِ لَا يُؤْمِنُوْنَ ﴿١٧﴾

18. Who doth greater wrong than he who inventeth a lie concerning Allah? Such will be brought before their Lord, and the witnesses will say: These are they who lied concerning their Lord. Now the curse of Allah is upon wrong-doers,

وَمَنْ اَظْلَمُ مِمَّنِ افْتَرٰى عَلَى اللّٰهِ كَذِبًا ۭ اُولٰۗىِٕكَ
يُعْرَضُوْنَ عَلٰي رَبِّهِمْ وَيَقُوْلُ الْاَشْهَادُ هٰٓؤُلَاۗءِ
الَّذِيْنَ كَذَبُوْا عَلٰي رَبِّهِمْ ۚ اَلَا لَعْنَةُ اللّٰهِ عَلَي
الظّٰلِمِيْنَ ﴿١٨﴾

19. Who debar (men) from the way of Allah and would have it crooked, and who are disbelievers in the Hereafter.

الَّذِيْنَ يَصُدُّوْنَ عَنْ سَبِيْلِ اللّٰهِ وَيَبْغُوْنَهَا عِوَجًا ۭ
وَهُمْ بِالْاٰخِرَةِ هُمْ كٰفِرُوْنَ ﴿١٩﴾

20. Such will not escape in the earth, nor have they any protecting friends beside Allah, For them the torment will be double. They could not bear to hear, and they used not to see.

اُولٰۗىِٕكَ لَمْ يَكُوْنُوْا مُعْجِزِيْنَ فِي الْاَرْضِ وَمَا كَانَ
لَهُمْ مِّنْ دُوْنِ اللّٰهِ مِنْ اَوْلِيَاۗءَ ۘ يُضٰعَفُ لَهُمُ
الْعَذَابُ ۭ مَا كَانُوْا يَسْتَطِيْعُوْنَ السَّمْعَ وَمَا كَانُوْا
يُبْصِرُوْنَ ﴿٢٠﴾

21. Such are they who have lost their souls, and that which they used to invent hath failed them.

اُولٰۗىِٕكَ الَّذِيْنَ خَسِرُوْٓا اَنْفُسَهُمْ وَضَلَّ عَنْهُمْ مَّا
كَانُوْا يَفْتَرُوْنَ ﴿٢١﴾

22. Assuredly in the Hereafter they will be the greatest losers.

لَا جَرَمَ اَنَّهُمْ فِي الْاٰخِرَةِ هُمُ الْاَخْسَرُوْنَ ﴿٢٢﴾

23. Lo! those who believe and do good works and humble themselves before their Lord: such are rightful owners of the Garden: they will abide therein.

اِنَّ الَّذِيْنَ اٰمَنُوْا وَعَمِلُوا الصّٰلِحٰتِ وَاَخْبَتُوْٓا اِلٰى
رَبِّهِمْ ۙ اُولٰۗىِٕكَ اَصْحٰبُ الْجَنَّةِ ۚ هُمْ فِيْهَا خٰلِدُوْنَ ﴿٢٣﴾

24. The similitude of the two parties is as the blind and the deaf and the seer and the hearer. Are they equal in similitude? Will ye not then be admonished?

مَثَلُ الْفَرِيْقَيْنِ كَالْاَعْمٰى وَالْاَصَمِّ وَالْبَصِيْرِ وَ
السَّمِيْعِ ۭ هَلْ يَسْتَوِيٰنِ مَثَلًا ۭ اَفَلَا تَذَكَّرُوْنَ ﴿٢٤﴾

25. And We sent Noah unto his folk (and he said): Lo! I am a plain warner unto you.

26. That ye serve none, save Allah. Lo! I fear for you the retribution of a painful Day.

27. The chieftains of his folk, who disbelieved, said: We see thee but a mortal like us, and we see not that any follow thee save the most abject among us, without reflection. We behold in you no merit above us—nay, we deem you liars.

28. He said: O my people! Bethink you, if I rely on a clear proof from my Lord and there hath come unto me a mercy from His presence, and it hath been made obscure to you, can we compel you to accept it when ye are averse thereto?

29. And O my people! I ask of you no wealth therefor. My reward is the concern only of Allah, and I am not going to thrust away those who believe—Lo! they have to meet their Lord—but I see you a folk that are ignorant.

30. And, O my people! who would deliver me from Allah if I thrust them away? Will ye not then reflect?

31. I say not unto you: "I have the treasures of Allah" nor "I have knowledge of the Unseen," nor say I: "Lo! I am an angel!" Nor say I unto those whom your eyes scorn that Allah will not give them good—Allah knoweth best what is in their hearts—Lo! then indeed I should be of the wrong-doers.

32. They said: O Noah! Thou hast disputed with us and multiplied disputation with us; now bring upon us that wherewith thou threatenest us, if thou art of the truthful.

وَلَقَدْ اَرْسَلْنَا نُوحًا اِلٰى قَوْمِهٖۤ اِنِّىْ لَكُمْ نَذِيْرٌ مُّبِيْنٌۙ ۞

اَنْ لَّا تَعْبُدُوْۤا اِلَّا اللّٰهَ ؕ اِنِّىْۤ اَخَافُ عَلَيْكُمْ عَذَابَ يَوْمٍ اَلِيْمٍ ۞

فَقَالَ الْمَلَاُ الَّذِيْنَ كَفَرُوْا مِنْ قَوْمِهٖ مَا نَرٰىكَ اِلَّا بَشَرًا مِّثْلَنَا وَمَا نَرٰىكَ اتَّبَعَكَ اِلَّا الَّذِيْنَ هُمْ اَرَاذِلُنَا بَادِىَ الرَّاْىِ ۚ وَمَا نَرٰى لَكُمْ عَلَيْنَا مِنْ فَضْلٍۭ بَلْ نَظُنُّكُمْ كٰذِبِيْنَ ۞

قَالَ يٰقَوْمِ اَرَءَيْتُمْ اِنْ كُنْتُ عَلٰى بَيِّنَةٍ مِّنْ رَّبِّىْ وَاٰتٰىنِىْ رَحْمَةً مِّنْ عِنْدِهٖ فَعُمِّيَتْ عَلَيْكُمْ ؕ اَنُلْزِمُكُمُوْهَا وَاَنْتُمْ لَهَا كٰرِهُوْنَ ۞

وَيٰقَوْمِ لَاۤ اَسْـَٔلُكُمْ عَلَيْهِ مَالًا ؕ اِنْ اَجْرِىَ اِلَّا عَلَى اللّٰهِ وَمَاۤ اَنَا بِطَارِدِ الَّذِيْنَ اٰمَنُوْا ؕ اِنَّهُمْ مُّلٰقُوْا رَبِّهِمْ وَلٰكِنِّىْۤ اَرٰىكُمْ قَوْمًا تَجْهَلُوْنَ ۞

وَيٰقَوْمِ مَنْ يَّنْصُرُنِىْ مِنَ اللّٰهِ اِنْ طَرَدْتُّهُمْ ؕ اَفَلَا تَذَكَّرُوْنَ ۞

وَلَاۤ اَقُوْلُ لَكُمْ عِنْدِىْ خَزَآئِنُ اللّٰهِ وَلَاۤ اَعْلَمُ الْغَيْبَ وَلَاۤ اَقُوْلُ اِنِّىْ مَلَكٌ وَّلَاۤ اَقُوْلُ لِلَّذِيْنَ تَزْدَرِىْۤ اَعْيُنُكُمْ لَنْ يُّؤْتِيَهُمُ اللّٰهُ خَيْرًا ؕ اَللّٰهُ اَعْلَمُ بِمَا فِىْۤ اَنْفُسِهِمْ ۚ اِنِّىْۤ اِذًا لَّمِنَ الظّٰلِمِيْنَ ۞

قَالُوْا يٰنُوْحُ قَدْ جَادَلْتَنَا فَاَكْثَرْتَ جِدَالَنَا فَاْتِنَا بِمَا تَعِدُنَاۤ اِنْ كُنْتَ مِنَ الصّٰدِقِيْنَ ۞

33. He said: Only Allah will bring it upon you if He will, and ye can by no means escape.

قَالَ إِنَّمَا يَأْتِيكُم بِهِ اللَّهُ إِن شَاءَ وَمَا أَنتُم
بِمُعْجِزِينَ ﴿٣٣﴾

34. My counsel will not profit you if I were minded to advise you, if Allah's will is to keep you astray. He is your Lord and unto Him ye will be brought back.

وَلَا يَنفَعُكُمْ نُصْحِي إِنْ أَرَدتُّ أَنْ أَنصَحَ لَكُمْ
إِن كَانَ اللَّهُ يُرِيدُ أَن يُغْوِيَكُمْ هُوَ رَبُّكُمْ وَإِلَيْهِ
تُرْجَعُونَ ﴿٣٤﴾

35. Or say they (again): He hath invented it? Say: If I have invented it, upon me be my crimes, but I am innocent of (all) that ye commit.

أَمْ يَقُولُونَ افْتَرَاهُ قُلْ إِنِ افْتَرَيْتُهُ فَعَلَيَّ إِجْرَامِي
ع وَأَنَا بَرِيءٌ مِّمَّا تُجْرِمُونَ ﴿٣٥﴾

36. And it was inspired in Noah, (saying): No one of thy folk will believe save him who hath believed already. Be not distressed because of what they do.

وَأُوحِيَ إِلَىٰ نُوحٍ أَنَّهُ لَن يُؤْمِنَ مِن قَوْمِكَ إِلَّا مَن
قَدْ آمَنَ فَلَا تَبْتَئِسْ بِمَا كَانُوا يَفْعَلُونَ ﴿٣٦﴾

37. Build the ship under Our Eyes and by Our inspiration, and speak not unto Me on behalf of those who do wrong. Lo! they will be drowned.

وَاصْنَعِ الْفُلْكَ بِأَعْيُنِنَا وَوَحْيِنَا وَلَا تُخَاطِبْنِي فِي
الَّذِينَ ظَلَمُوا إِنَّهُم مُّغْرَقُونَ ﴿٣٧﴾

38. And he was building the ship, and every time that chieftains of his people passed him, they made mock of him. He said: Though ye make mock of us, yet we mock at you even as ye mock;

وَيَصْنَعُ الْفُلْكَ وَكُلَّمَا مَرَّ عَلَيْهِ مَلَأٌ مِّن قَوْمِهِ
سَخِرُوا مِنْهُ قَالَ إِن تَسْخَرُوا مِنَّا فَإِنَّا نَسْخَرُ
مِنكُمْ كَمَا تَسْخَرُونَ ﴿٣٨﴾

39. And ye shall know to whom a punishment that will confound him cometh, and upon whom a lasting doom will fall.

فَسَوْفَ تَعْلَمُونَ مَن يَأْتِيهِ عَذَابٌ يُخْزِيهِ وَ
يَحِلُّ عَلَيْهِ عَذَابٌ مُّقِيمٌ ﴿٣٩﴾

40. (Thus it was) till, when Our commandment came to pass and the oven gushed forth water,[1] We said: Load therein two of every kind, a pair (the male and female), and thy household, save him against whom the word hath gone forth already, and those who believe. And but a few were they who believed with him.

حَتَّىٰ إِذَا جَاءَ أَمْرُنَا وَفَارَ التَّنُّورُ قُلْنَا احْمِلْ فِيهَا
مِن كُلٍّ زَوْجَيْنِ اثْنَيْنِ وَأَهْلَكَ إِلَّا مَن سَبَقَ
عَلَيْهِ الْقَوْلُ وَمَنْ آمَنَ وَمَا آمَنَ مَعَهُ إِلَّا
قَلِيلٌ ﴿٤٠﴾

41. And he said: Embark therein! In the name of Allah be its course and its mooring. Lo! my Lord is Forgiving, Merciful.

وَقَالَ ارْكَبُوا فِيهَا بِسْمِ اللَّهِ مَجْرَاهَا وَمُرْسَاهَا
إِنَّ رَبِّي لَغَفُورٌ رَّحِيمٌ ﴿٤١﴾

1. This was a sign of the deluge, water gushing up from underground as well as falling from the sky.

42. And it sailed with them amid waves like mountains, and Noah cried unto his son—and he was standing aloof—O my son! Come ride with us, and be not with the disbelievers.

43. He said: I shall betake me to some mountain that will save me from the water. (Noah) said: This day there is none that saveth from the commandment of Allah save him on whom He hath had mercy. And the wave came in between them, so he was among the drowned.

44. And it was said: O earth! Swallow thy water and, O sky! be cleared of clouds! And the water was made to subside. And the commandment was fulfilled. And it (the ship) came to rest upon (the mount) Al-Jūdī and it was said: A far removal for wrongdoing folk!

45. And Noah cried unto his Lord and said: My Lord! Lo! my son is of my household! Surely Thy promise is the Truth and Thou art the Most Just of Judges.

46. He said: O Noah! Lo! he is not of thy household; lo! he is of evil conduct, so ask not of Me that whereof thou hast no knowledge. I admonish thee lest thou be among the ignorant.

47. He said: My Lord! Lo! in Thee do I seek refuge (from the sin) that I should ask of Thee that whereof I have no knowledge. Unless Thou forgive me and have mercy on me I shall be among the lost.

48. It was said (unto him): O Noah! Go thou down (from the mountain) with peace from Us and blessings upon thee and some nations (that will spring) from those with thee. (There will be other) nations unto whom We shall give enjoyment a long while and then a painful doom from Us will overtake them.

49. This is of the tidings of the Unseen which We inspire in thee (Muhammad). Thou thyself knewest it not, nor did thy folk (know it) before this. Then have patience. Lo! the sequel is for those who ward off (evil).

وَهِيَ تَجْرِيْ بِهِمْ فِيْ مَوْجٍ كَالْجِبَالِ ۚ وَنَادٰى
نُوْحُ ابْنَهٗ وَكَانَ فِيْ مَعْزِلٍ يّٰبُنَيَّ ارْكَبْ مَّعَنَا
وَلَا تَكُنْ مَّعَ الْكٰفِرِيْنَ ﴿٤٢﴾
قَالَ سَاٰوِيْۤ اِلٰى جَبَلٍ يَّعْصِمُنِيْ مِنَ الْمَآءِ ؕ قَالَ
لَا عَاصِمَ الْيَوْمَ مِنْ اَمْرِ اللّٰهِ اِلَّا مَنْ رَّحِمَ ۚ وَحَالَ
بَيْنَهُمَا الْمَوْجُ فَكَانَ مِنَ الْمُغْرَقِيْنَ ﴿٤٣﴾
وَقِيْلَ يٰۤاَرْضُ ابْلَعِيْ مَآءَكِ وَيٰسَمَآءُ اَقْلِعِيْ وَ
غِيْضَ الْمَآءُ وَقُضِيَ الْاَمْرُ وَاسْتَوَتْ عَلَى الْجُوْدِيِّ
وَقِيْلَ بُعْدًا لِّلْقَوْمِ الظّٰلِمِيْنَ ﴿٤٤﴾ ربع
وَنَادٰى نُوْحٌ رَّبَّهٗ فَقَالَ رَبِّ اِنَّ ابْنِيْ مِنْ اَهْلِيْ
وَاِنَّ وَعْدَكَ الْحَقُّ وَاَنْتَ اَحْكَمُ الْحٰكِمِيْنَ ﴿٤٥﴾
قَالَ يٰنُوْحُ اِنَّهٗ لَيْسَ مِنْ اَهْلِكَ ۚ اِنَّهٗ عَمَلٌ غَيْرُ
صَالِحٍ ۖ فَلَا تَسْـَٔلْنِ مَا لَيْسَ لَكَ بِهٖ عِلْمٌ ؕ اِنِّيْۤ
اَعِظُكَ اَنْ تَكُوْنَ مِنَ الْجٰهِلِيْنَ ﴿٤٦﴾
قَالَ رَبِّ اِنِّيْۤ اَعُوْذُ بِكَ اَنْ اَسْـَٔلَكَ مَا لَيْسَ لِيْ بِهٖ
عِلْمٌ ؕ وَاِلَّا تَغْفِرْ لِيْ وَتَرْحَمْنِيْۤ اَكُنْ مِّنَ الْخٰسِرِيْنَ ﴿٤٧﴾
قِيْلَ يٰنُوْحُ اهْبِطْ بِسَلٰمٍ مِّنَّا وَبَرَكٰتٍ عَلَيْكَ وَعَلٰۤى
اُمَمٍ مِّمَّنْ مَّعَكَ ؕ وَاُمَمٌ سَنُمَتِّعُهُمْ ثُمَّ يَمَسُّهُمْ
مِّنَّا عَذَابٌ اَلِيْمٌ ﴿٤٨﴾
تِلْكَ مِنْ اَنْۢبَآءِ الْغَيْبِ نُوْحِيْهَاۤ اِلَيْكَ ۚ مَا كُنْتَ
تَعْلَمُهَاۤ اَنْتَ وَلَا قَوْمُكَ مِنْ قَبْلِ هٰذَا ۛؕ فَاصْبِرْ ۛؕ
اِنَّ الْعَاقِبَةَ لِلْمُتَّقِيْنَ ﴿٤٩﴾ ع

50. And unto (the tribe of) 'Aād (We sent) their brother, Hūd. He said: O my people! Serve Allah! Ye have no other God save Him. Lo! ye do but invent!

51. O my people! I ask of you no reward for it. Lo! my reward is the concern only of Him who made me. Have ye then no sense?

52. And, O my people! Ask forgiveness of your Lord, then turn unto Him repentant; He will cause the sky to rain abundance on you and will add unto you strength to your strength. Turn not away, guilty!

53. They said: O Hūd! Thou hast brought us no clear proof and we are not going to forsake our gods on thy (mere) saying, and we are not believers in thee.

54. We say naught save that one of our gods hath possessed thee in an evil way. He said: I call Allah to witness, and do ye (too) bear witness, that I am innocent of (all) that ye ascribe as partners (to Allah):

55. Beside Him. So (try to) circumvent me, all of you, give me no respite.

56. Lo! I have put my trust in Allah, my Lord and your Lord. Not an animal but He doth grasp it by the forelock! Lo! my Lord is on the Straight path.

57. And if ye turn away, still I have conveyed unto you that wherewith I was sent unto you, and my Lord will set in place of you a folk other than you. Ye cannot injure Him at all. Lo! my Lord is Guardian over all things.

58. And when Our commandment came to pass We saved Hūd and those who believed with him by a mercy from Us; We saved them from a harsh doom.

59. And such were 'Aād. They denied the revelations of their Lord and flouted His messengers and followed the command of every froward potentate.

وَإِلَىٰ عَادٍ أَخَاهُمْ هُودًا ۚ قَالَ يَٰقَوْمِ اعْبُدُوا اللَّهَ مَا
لَكُم مِّنْ إِلَٰهٍ غَيْرُهُ ۖ إِنْ أَنتُمْ إِلَّا مُفْتَرُونَ ﴿٥٠﴾
يَٰقَوْمِ لَا أَسْأَلُكُمْ عَلَيْهِ أَجْرًا ۖ إِنْ أَجْرِيَ إِلَّا عَلَى الَّذِي
فَطَرَنِي ۚ أَفَلَا تَعْقِلُونَ ﴿٥١﴾
وَيَٰقَوْمِ اسْتَغْفِرُوا رَبَّكُمْ ثُمَّ تُوبُوا إِلَيْهِ يُرْسِلِ
السَّمَاءَ عَلَيْكُم مِّدْرَارًا وَيَزِدْكُمْ قُوَّةً إِلَىٰ قُوَّتِكُمْ
وَلَا تَتَوَلَّوْا مُجْرِمِينَ ﴿٥٢﴾
قَالُوا يَٰهُودُ مَا جِئْتَنَا بِبَيِّنَةٍ وَمَا نَحْنُ بِتَارِكِي آلِهَتِنَا
عَن قَوْلِكَ وَمَا نَحْنُ لَكَ بِمُؤْمِنِينَ ﴿٥٣﴾
إِن نَّقُولُ إِلَّا اعْتَرَاكَ بَعْضُ آلِهَتِنَا بِسُوءٍ ۗ قَالَ
إِنِّي أُشْهِدُ اللَّهَ وَاشْهَدُوا أَنِّي بَرِيءٌ مِّمَّا تُشْرِكُونَ ﴿٥٤﴾
مِن دُونِهِ ۖ فَكِيدُونِي جَمِيعًا ثُمَّ لَا تُنظِرُونِ ﴿٥٥﴾
إِنِّي تَوَكَّلْتُ عَلَى اللَّهِ رَبِّي وَرَبِّكُم ۚ مَّا مِن دَابَّةٍ
إِلَّا هُوَ آخِذٌ بِنَاصِيَتِهَا ۚ إِنَّ رَبِّي عَلَىٰ صِرَاطٍ
مُّسْتَقِيمٍ ﴿٥٦﴾
فَإِن تَوَلَّوْا فَقَدْ أَبْلَغْتُكُم مَّا أُرْسِلْتُ بِهِ إِلَيْكُمْ ۚ وَ
يَسْتَخْلِفُ رَبِّي قَوْمًا غَيْرَكُمْ وَلَا تَضُرُّونَهُ شَيْئًا ۚ
إِنَّ رَبِّي عَلَىٰ كُلِّ شَيْءٍ حَفِيظٌ ﴿٥٧﴾
وَلَمَّا جَاءَ أَمْرُنَا نَجَّيْنَا هُودًا وَالَّذِينَ آمَنُوا مَعَهُ
بِرَحْمَةٍ مِّنَّا وَنَجَّيْنَاهُم مِّنْ عَذَابٍ غَلِيظٍ ﴿٥٨﴾
وَتِلْكَ عَادٌ ۖ جَحَدُوا بِآيَاتِ رَبِّهِمْ وَعَصَوْا رُسُلَهُ
وَاتَّبَعُوا أَمْرَ كُلِّ جَبَّارٍ عَنِيدٍ ﴿٥٩﴾

60. And a curse was made to follow them in the world and on the Day of Resurrection. Lo! 'Aād disbelieved in their Lord. A far removal for 'Aād, the folk of Hūd!

61. And unto (the tribe of) Thamūd (We sent) their brother Ṣāliḥ. He said: O my people! Serve Allah, ye have no other God save Him. He brought you forth from the earth and hath made you husband it. So ask forgiveness of Him and turn unto Him repentant. Lo, my Lord is Nigh, Responsive.

62. They said: O Ṣāliḥ! Thou hast been among us hitherto as that wherein our hope was placed. Dost thou ask us not to worship what our fathers worshipped? Lo! we verily are in grave doubt concerning that to which thou callest us.

63. He said: O my people! Bethink ye if I am (acting) on clear proof from my Lord and there hath come unto me a mercy from Him, who will save me from Allah if I disobey Him? Ye would add to me naught save perdition.

64. O my people! This is the camel of Allah, a token unto you, so suffer her to feed in Allah's earth, and touch her not with harm lest a near torment seize you.

65. But they hamstrung her, and then he said: Enjoy life in your dwelling-place three days! This is a threat that will not be belied.

66. So, when Our commandment came to pass, We saved Ṣāliḥ, and those who believed with him, by a mercy from Us, from the ignominy of that day. Lo, thy Lord! He is the Strong, the Mighty.

67. And the (Awful) Cry overtook those who did wrong, so that morning found them prostrate in their dwellings,

واتبعوا في هذه الدنيا لعنة ويوم القيمة الا ان
عادا كفروا ربهم الا بعدا لعاد قوم هود ﴿٦٠﴾
والى ثمود اخاهم صلحا قال يقوم اعبدوا الله
ما لكم من اله غيره هو انشاكم من الارض و
استعمركم فيها فاستغفروه ثم توبوا اليه ان
ربي قريب مجيب ﴿٦١﴾
قالوا يصلح قد كنت فينا مرجوا قبل هذا اتنهنا
ان نعبد ما يعبد اباؤنا واننا لفي شك مما
تدعونا اليه مريب ﴿٦٢﴾
قال يقوم ارءيتم ان كنت على بينة من ربي
واتىني منه رحمة فمن ينصرني من الله ان
عصيته فما تزيدونني غير تخسير ﴿٦٣﴾
ويقوم هذه ناقة الله لكم اية فذروها تاكل
في ارض الله ولا تمسوها بسوء فياخذكم عذاب
قريب ﴿٦٤﴾
فعقروها فقال تمتعوا في داركم ثلثة ايام
ذلك وعد غير مكذوب ﴿٦٥﴾
فلما جاء امرنا نجينا صلحا والذين امنوا معه
برحمة منا ومن خزي يومئذ ان ربك هو
القوي العزيز ﴿٦٦﴾
واخذ الذين ظلموا الصيحة فاصبحوا في ديارهم
جثمين ﴿٦٧﴾

68. As though they had not dwelt there. Lo! Thamūd disbelieved in their Lord: A far removal for Thamūd!

69. And Our messengers came unto Abraham with good news. They said: Peace! He answered: Peace! and delayed not to bring a roasted calf.

70. And when he saw their hands reached not to it, he mistrusted them and conceived a fear of them. They said: Fear not! Lo! we are sent unto the folk of Lot.

71. And his wife, standing by, laughed when We gave her good tidings (of the birth) of Isaac, and, after Isaac, of Jacob.

72. She said: Oh, woe is me! Shall I bear a child when I am an old woman, and this my husband is an old man? Lo! this is a strange thing!

73. They said: Wonderest thou at the commandment of Allah? The mercy of Allah and His blessings be upon you, O people of the house! Lo! He is Owner of Praise, Owner of Glory!

74. And when the awe departed from Abraham, and the glad news reached him, he pleaded with Us on behalf of the folk of Lot.

75. Lo! Abraham was mild, imploring, penitent.

76. (It was said) O Abraham! Forsake this! Lo! thy Lord's commandment hath gone forth, and lo! there cometh unto them a doom which cannot be repelled.

77. And when Our messengers came unto Lot, he was distressed and knew not how to protect them. He said: This is a distressful day!

كَأَن لَّمْ يَغْنَوْا فِيهَا ۗ أَلَآ إِنَّ ثَمُودَا۟ كَفَرُوا۟ رَبَّهُمْ
ع أَلَا بُعْدًا لِّثَمُودَ ﴿٦٨﴾
وَلَقَدْ جَآءَتْ رُسُلُنَآ إِبْرَٰهِيمَ بِٱلْبُشْرَىٰ قَالُوا۟
سَلَٰمًا ۖ قَالَ سَلَٰمٌ ۖ فَمَا لَبِثَ أَن جَآءَ بِعِجْلٍ
حَنِيذٍ ﴿٦٩﴾
فَلَمَّا رَءَآ أَيْدِيَهُمْ لَا تَصِلُ إِلَيْهِ نَكِرَهُمْ وَ
أَوْجَسَ مِنْهُمْ خِيفَةً ۚ قَالُوا۟ لَا تَخَفْ إِنَّآ أُرْسِلْنَآ
إِلَىٰ قَوْمِ لُوطٍ ﴿٧٠﴾
وَٱمْرَأَتُهُۥ قَآئِمَةٌ فَضَحِكَتْ فَبَشَّرْنَٰهَا بِإِسْحَٰقَ وَ
مِن وَرَآءِ إِسْحَٰقَ يَعْقُوبَ ﴿٧١﴾
قَالَتْ يَٰوَيْلَتَىٰٓ ءَأَلِدُ وَأَنَا۠ عَجُوزٌ وَهَٰذَا بَعْلِى
شَيْخًا ۖ إِنَّ هَٰذَا لَشَىْءٌ عَجِيبٌ ﴿٧٢﴾
قَالُوٓا۟ أَتَعْجَبِينَ مِنْ أَمْرِ ٱللَّهِ ۖ رَحْمَتُ ٱللَّهِ وَبَرَكَٰتُهُۥ
عَلَيْكُمْ أَهْلَ ٱلْبَيْتِ ۚ إِنَّهُۥ حَمِيدٌ مَّجِيدٌ ﴿٧٣﴾
فَلَمَّا ذَهَبَ عَنْ إِبْرَٰهِيمَ ٱلرَّوْعُ وَجَآءَتْهُ
ٱلْبُشْرَىٰ يُجَٰدِلُنَا فِى قَوْمِ لُوطٍ ﴿٧٤﴾
إِنَّ إِبْرَٰهِيمَ لَحَلِيمٌ أَوَّٰهٌ مُّنِيبٌ ﴿٧٥﴾
يَٰٓإِبْرَٰهِيمُ أَعْرِضْ عَنْ هَٰذَآ ۖ إِنَّهُۥ قَدْ جَآءَ
أَمْرُ رَبِّكَ ۖ وَإِنَّهُمْ ءَاتِيهِمْ عَذَابٌ غَيْرُ
مَرْدُودٍ ﴿٧٦﴾
وَلَمَّا جَآءَتْ رُسُلُنَا لُوطًا سِىٓءَ بِهِمْ وَضَاقَ بِهِمْ
ذَرْعًا وَقَالَ هَٰذَا يَوْمٌ عَصِيبٌ ﴿٧٧﴾

78. And his people came unto him, running towards him—and before then they, used to commit abominations—He said: O my people! Here are my daughters! They are purer for you. Beware of Allah, and degrade me not in (the presence of) my guests. Is there not among you any upright man?

79. They said: Well thou knowest that we have no right to thy daughters, and well thou knowest what we want.

80. He said: Would that I had strength to resist you or had some strong support (among you)!

81. (The messengers) said: O Lot! Lo! we are messengers of thy Lord: they shall not reach thee. So travel with thy people in a part of the night, and let not one of you turn round—(all) save thy wife. Lo! that which smiteth them will smite her (also). Lo! their tryst is (for) the morning. Is not the morning nigh?

82. So when Our commandment came to pass We overthrew (that township) and rained upon it stones of clay, one after another,

83. Marked with fire in the providence of thy Lord (for the destruction of the wicked). And they are never far from the wrong-doers.

84. And unto Midian (We sent) their brother Shu'eyb. He said: O my people! Serve Allah. Ye have no other God save Him! and give not short measure and short weight. Lo! I see you well-to-do, and lo! I fear for you the doom of a besetting Day.

85. O my people! Give full measure and full weight in justice, and wrong not people in respect of their goods. And do not evil in the earth, causing corruption.

وَجَآءَهُ قَوْمُهُ يُهْرَعُونَ إِلَيْهِ وَمِن قَبْلُ كَانُوا
يَعْمَلُونَ السَّيِّـَٔاتِ قَالَ يٰقَوْمِ هٰٓؤُلَآءِ بَنَاتِي هُنَّ
أَطْهَرُ لَكُمْ فَاتَّقُوا اللّٰهَ وَلَا تُخْزُونِ فِي ضَيْفِي أَلَيْسَ
مِنكُمْ رَجُلٌ رَّشِيدٌ ﴿٧٨﴾
قَالُوا لَقَدْ عَلِمْتَ مَا لَنَا فِي بَنَاتِكَ مِنْ حَقٍّ وَإِنَّكَ
لَتَعْلَمُ مَا نُرِيدُ ﴿٧٩﴾
قَالَ لَوْ أَنَّ لِي بِكُمْ قُوَّةً أَوْ ءَاوِي إِلَىٰ رُكْنٍ شَدِيدٍ ﴿٨٠﴾
قَالُوا يٰلُوطُ إِنَّا رُسُلُ رَبِّكَ لَن يَصِلُوا إِلَيْكَ فَأَسْرِ
بِأَهْلِكَ بِقِطْعٍ مِّنَ الَّيْلِ وَلَا يَلْتَفِتْ مِنكُمْ أَحَدٌ
إِلَّا امْرَأَتَكَ إِنَّهُ مُصِيبُهَا مَا أَصَابَهُمْ إِنَّ مَوْعِدَهُمُ
الصُّبْحُ أَلَيْسَ الصُّبْحُ بِقَرِيبٍ ﴿٨١﴾
فَلَمَّا جَآءَ أَمْرُنَا جَعَلْنَا عَالِيَهَا سَافِلَهَا وَأَمْطَرْنَا
عَلَيْهَا حِجَارَةً مِّن سِجِّيلٍ مَّنضُودٍ ﴿٨٢﴾
مُّسَوَّمَةً عِندَ رَبِّكَ وَمَا هِيَ مِنَ الظّٰلِمِينَ
بِبَعِيدٍ ﴿٨٣﴾ ع
وَإِلَىٰ مَدْيَنَ أَخَاهُمْ شُعَيْبًا قَالَ يٰقَوْمِ اعْبُدُوا
اللّٰهَ مَا لَكُم مِّنْ إِلٰهٍ غَيْرُهُ وَلَا تَنقُصُوا الْمِكْيَالَ
وَالْمِيزَانَ إِنِّي أَرٰىكُم بِخَيْرٍ وَإِنِّي أَخَافُ عَلَيْكُمْ
عَذَابَ يَوْمٍ مُّحِيطٍ ﴿٨٤﴾
وَيٰقَوْمِ أَوْفُوا الْمِكْيَالَ وَالْمِيزَانَ بِالْقِسْطِ وَلَا
تَبْخَسُوا النَّاسَ أَشْيَآءَهُمْ وَلَا تَعْثَوْا فِي الْأَرْضِ
مُفْسِدِينَ ﴿٨٥﴾

86. That which Allah leaveth with you is better for you if ye are believers; and I am not a keeper over you.

87. They said: O Shu'eyb! Doth thy way of prayer command thee that we should forsake that which our fathers (used to) worship, or that we (should leave off) doing what we will with our own property. Lo! thou art the mild, the guide to right behaviour.

88. He said: O my people! Bethink you: if I am (acting) on a clear proof from my Lord and He sustaineth me with fair sustenance from Him (how can I concede aught to you)? I desire not to do behind your backs that which I ask you not to do. I desire naught save reform so far as I am able. My welfare is only in Allah. In Him I trust and unto Him I turn (repentant).

89. And, O my people! Let not the schism with me cause you to sin so that there befall you that which befell the folk of Noah and the folk of Hūd, and the folk of Ṣāliḥ; and the folk of Lot are not far off from you!

90. Ask pardon of your Lord and then turn unto Him (repentant). Lo! my Lord is Merciful, Loving.

91. They said: O Shu'eyb! We understand not much of that thou tellest, and lo! we do behold thee weak among us. But for thy family, we should have stoned thee, for thou art not strong against us.

92. He said: O my people! Is my family more to be honoured by you than Allah? And ye put Him behind you, neglected! Lo! my Lord surroundeth what ye do.

93. And, O my people! Act according to your power, lo, I (too) am acting. Ye will soon know on whom there cometh a doom that will abase him, and who it is that lieth. And watch! Lo! I am a watcher with you.

بَقِيَّتُ اللّٰهِ خَيْرٌ لَّكُمْ اِنْ كُنْتُمْ مُّؤْمِنِيْنَ ۚ وَمَآ اَنَا
عَلَيْكُمْ بِحَفِيْظٍ ﴿٨٦﴾
قَالُوْا يٰشُعَيْبُ اَصَلٰوتُكَ تَاْمُرُكَ اَنْ نَّتْرُكَ مَا
يَعْبُدُ اٰبَآؤُنَآ اَوْ اَنْ نَّفْعَلَ فِيْٓ اَمْوَالِنَا مَا نَشٰٓؤُا ۭ
اِنَّكَ لَاَنْتَ الْحَلِيْمُ الرَّشِيْدُ ﴿٨٧﴾
قَالَ يٰقَوْمِ اَرَءَيْتُمْ اِنْ كُنْتُ عَلٰى بَيِّنَةٍ مِّنْ رَّبِّيْ وَ
رَزَقَنِيْ مِنْهُ رِزْقًا حَسَنًا ۭ وَمَآ اُرِيْدُ اَنْ اُخَالِفَكُمْ اِلٰى
مَآ اَنْهٰىكُمْ عَنْهُ ۭ اِنْ اُرِيْدُ اِلَّا الْاِصْلَاحَ مَا اسْتَطَعْتُ ۭ وَمَا
تَوْفِيْقِيْٓ اِلَّا بِاللّٰهِ ۭ عَلَيْهِ تَوَكَّلْتُ وَاِلَيْهِ اُنِيْبُ ﴿٨٨﴾
وَيٰقَوْمِ لَا يَجْرِمَنَّكُمْ شِقَاقِيْٓ اَنْ يُّصِيْبَكُمْ مِّثْلُ مَآ
اَصَابَ قَوْمَ نُوْحٍ اَوْ قَوْمَ هُوْدٍ اَوْ قَوْمَ صٰلِحٍ ۭ وَمَا
قَوْمُ لُوْطٍ مِّنْكُمْ بِبَعِيْدٍ ﴿٨٩﴾
وَاسْتَغْفِرُوْا رَبَّكُمْ ثُمَّ تُوْبُوْٓا اِلَيْهِ ۭ اِنَّ رَبِّيْ رَحِيْمٌ
وَّدُوْدٌ ﴿٩٠﴾
قَالُوْا يٰشُعَيْبُ مَا نَفْقَهُ كَثِيْرًا مِّمَّا تَقُوْلُ وَاِنَّا
لَنَرٰىكَ فِيْنَا ضَعِيْفًا ۚ وَلَوْلَا رَهْطُكَ لَرَجَمْنٰكَ ۡ
وَمَآ اَنْتَ عَلَيْنَا بِعَزِيْزٍ ﴿٩١﴾
قَالَ يٰقَوْمِ اَرَهْطِيْٓ اَعَزُّ عَلَيْكُمْ مِّنَ اللّٰهِ ۭ وَاتَّخَذْتُمُوْهُ
وَرَآءَكُمْ ظِهْرِيًّا ۭ اِنَّ رَبِّيْ بِمَا تَعْمَلُوْنَ مُحِيْطٌ ﴿٩٢﴾
وَيٰقَوْمِ اعْمَلُوْا عَلٰى مَكَانَتِكُمْ اِنِّيْ عَامِلٌ ۭ سَوْفَ
تَعْلَمُوْنَ ۙ مَنْ يَّاْتِيْهِ عَذَابٌ يُّخْزِيْهِ وَمَنْ هُوَ
كَاذِبٌ ۭ وَارْتَقِبُوْٓا اِنِّيْ مَعَكُمْ رَقِيْبٌ ﴿٩٣﴾

94. And when Our commandment came to pass We saved Shu'eyb and those who believed with Him by a mercy from Us; and the (Awful) Cry seized those who did injustice, and morning found them prostrate in their dwellings,

وَلَمَّا جَآءَ أَمْرُنَا نَجَّيْنَا شُعَيْبًا وَّالَّذِينَ آمَنُوا مَعَهُ بِرَحْمَةٍ مِّنَّا وَأَخَذَتِ الَّذِينَ ظَلَمُوا الصَّيْحَةُ فَأَصْبَحُوا فِي دِيَارِهِمْ جٰثِمِينَ ﴿٩٤﴾

95. As though they had not dwelt there. A far removal for Midian, even as Thamūd had been removed afar!

كَأَن لَّمْ يَغْنَوْا فِيهَا أَلَا بُعْدًا لِّمَدْيَنَ كَمَا بَعِدَتْ ثَمُودُ ﴿٩٥﴾

96. And verily We sent Moses with Our revelations and a clear warrant

وَلَقَدْ أَرْسَلْنَا مُوسٰى بِآيٰتِنَا وَسُلْطٰنٍ مُّبِينٍ ﴿٩٦﴾

97. Unto Pharaoh and his chiefs, but they did follow the command of Pharaoh, and the command of Pharaoh was no right guide.

إِلٰى فِرْعَوْنَ وَمَلَإِيْهِ فَاتَّبَعُوا أَمْرَ فِرْعَوْنَ وَمَآ أَمْرُ فِرْعَوْنَ بِرَشِيدٍ ﴿٩٧﴾

98. He will go before his people on the Day of Resurrection and will lead them to the Fire for watering-place. Ah, hapless is the watering-place (whither they are) led!

يَقْدُمُ قَوْمَهُ يَوْمَ الْقِيٰمَةِ فَأَوْرَدَهُمُ النَّارَ وَبِئْسَ الْوِرْدُ الْمَوْرُودُ ﴿٩٨﴾

99. A curse is made to follow them in the world and on the Day of Resurrection. Hapless is the gift (that will be) given (them).

وَأُتْبِعُوا فِي هٰذِهِ لَعْنَةً وَّيَوْمَ الْقِيٰمَةِ بِئْسَ الرِّفْدُ الْمَرْفُودُ ﴿٩٩﴾

100. That is (something) of the tidings of the townships[1] (which were destroyed of old). We relate it unto thee (Muhammad). Some of them are standing and some (already) reaped.

ذٰلِكَ مِنْ أَنۢبَآءِ الْقُرٰى نَقُصُّهُ عَلَيْكَ مِنْهَا قَآئِمٌ وَّحَصِيدٌ ﴿١٠٠﴾

101. We wronged them not, but they did wrong themselves; and their gods on whom they call beside Allah availed them naught when came thy Lord's command; they added to them naught save ruin.

وَمَا ظَلَمْنٰهُمْ وَلٰكِن ظَلَمُوا أَنفُسَهُمْ فَمَآ أَغْنَتْ عَنْهُمْ آلِهَتُهُمُ الَّتِي يَدْعُونَ مِن دُونِ اللّٰهِ مِن شَيْءٍ لَّمَّا جَآءَ أَمْرُ رَبِّكَ وَمَا زَادُوهُمْ غَيْرَ تَتْبِيبٍ ﴿١٠١﴾

102. Even thus is the grasp of thy Lord when he graspeth the township[1] while they are doing wrong. Lo! His grasp is painful, very strong.

وَكَذٰلِكَ أَخْذُ رَبِّكَ إِذَآ أَخَذَ الْقُرٰى وَهِيَ ظٰلِمَةٌ إِنَّ أَخْذَهُ أَلِيمٌ شَدِيدٌ ﴿١٠٢﴾

103. Lo! herein verily there is a portent for those who fear the doom of the Hereafter. That is a day unto which mankind will be gathered, and that is a day that will be witnessed.

إِنَّ فِي ذٰلِكَ لَآيَةً لِّمَنْ خَافَ عَذَابَ الْآخِرَةِ ذٰلِكَ يَوْمٌ مَّجْمُوعٌ لَّهُ النَّاسُ وَذٰلِكَ يَوْمٌ مَّشْهُودٌ ﴿١٠٣﴾

104. And We defer it only as a term already reckoned.

وَمَا نُؤَخِّرُهُ إِلَّا لِأَجَلٍ مَّعْدُودٍ ﴿١٠٤﴾

1. Or *communities*.

105. On the day when it cometh no soul will speak except by His permission, some among them will be wretched; (others) glad.

يوم يأت لا تكلم نفس إلا بإذنه فمنهم شقي
وسعيد ١٠٥

106. As for those who will be wretched (on that day) they will be in the Fire; sighing and wailing will be their portion therein,

فأما الذين شقوا ففي النار لهم فيها زفير
وشهيق ١٠٦

107. Abiding there so long as the heavens and the earth endure save for that which thy Lord willeth. Lo! thy Lord is Doer of what He will.

خلدين فيها ما دامت السموت والأرض إلا ما
شاء ربك إن ربك فعال لما يريد ١٠٧

108. And as for those who will be glad (that day) they will be in the Garden, abiding there so long as the heavens and the earth endure save for that which thy Lord willeth: a gift unfailing.

وأما الذين سعدوا ففي الجنة خلدين فيها
ما دامت السموت والأرض إلا ما شاء ربك
عطاء غير مجذوذ ١٠٨

109. So be not thou in doubt concerning that which these (folk) worship. They worship only as their fathers worshipped aforetime. Lo! We shall pay them their whole due unabated.

فلا تك في مرية مما يعبد هؤلاء ما يعبدون إلا
كما يعبد آباؤهم من قبل وإنا لموفوهم نصيبهم
غير منقوص ١٠٩

110. And We verily gave unto Moses the Scripture, and there was strife thereupon; and had it not been for a Word that had already gone forth from thy Lord, the case would have been judged between them, and lo! they are in grave doubt concerning it.

ولقد آتينا موسى الكتب فاختلف فيه ولولا
كلمة سبقت من ربك لقضي بينهم وإنهم
لفي شك منه مريب ١١٠

111. And lo! unto each thy Lord will verily repay his works in full, Lo! He is Informed of what they do.

وإن كلا لما ليوفينهم ربك أعمالهم إنه بما
يعملون خبير ١١١

112. So tread thou the Straight path as thou art commanded, and those who turn (unto Allah) with thee, and transgress not. Lo! He is Seer of what ye do.

فاستقم كما أمرت ومن تاب معك ولا تطغوا
إنه بما تعملون بصير ١١٢

113. And incline not toward those who do wrong lest the Fire touch you, and ye have no protecting friends against Allah, and afterward ye would not be helped.

ولا تركنوا إلى الذين ظلموا فتمسكم النار
وما لكم من دون الله من أولياء ثم لا
تنصرون ١١٣

114. Establish worship at the two ends of the day and in some watches of the night. Lo! good deeds annul ill deeds. This is a reminder for the mindful.

وَاَقِمِ الصَّلٰوةَ طَرَفَيِ النَّهَارِ وَزُلَفًا مِّنَ الَّيْلِ ؕ
اِنَّ الْحَسَنٰتِ يُذْهِبْنَ السَّيِّاٰتِ ؕ ذٰلِكَ ذِكْرٰى
لِلذّٰكِرِيْنَ ۚ ﴿١١٤﴾

115. And have patience, (O Muhammad), for lo! Allah loseth not the wages of the good.

وَاصْبِرْ فَاِنَّ اللّٰهَ لَا يُضِيْعُ اَجْرَ الْمُحْسِنِيْنَ ﴿١١٥﴾

116. If only there had been among the generations before you men possessing a remnant (of good sense) to warn (their people) from corruption in the earth, as did a few of those whom We saved from them! The wrong-doers followed that by which they were made sapless, and were guilty

فَلَوْلَا كَانَ مِنَ الْقُرُوْنِ مِنْ قَبْلِكُمْ اُولُوْا بَقِيَّةٍ
يَّنْهَوْنَ عَنِ الْفَسَادِ فِى الْاَرْضِ اِلَّا قَلِيْلًا مِّمَّنْ
اَنْجَيْنَا مِنْهُمْ ۚ وَاتَّبَعَ الَّذِيْنَ ظَلَمُوْا مَاۤ اُتْرِفُوْا فِيْهِ
وَكَانُوْا مُجْرِمِيْنَ ﴿١١٦﴾

117. In truth thy Lord destroyed not the townships tyrannously while their folk were doing right.

وَمَا كَانَ رَبُّكَ لِيُهْلِكَ الْقُرٰى بِظُلْمٍ وَّاَهْلُهَا
مُصْلِحُوْنَ ﴿١١٧﴾

118. And if thy Lord had willed, He verily would have made mankind one nation, yet they cease not differing,

وَلَوْ شَآءَ رَبُّكَ لَجَعَلَ النَّاسَ اُمَّةً وَّاحِدَةً وَّلَا
يَزَالُوْنَ مُخْتَلِفِيْنَ ۙ ﴿١١٨﴾

119. Save him on whom thy Lord hath mercy; and for that He did create them. And the Word of thy Lord hath been fulfilled: Verily I shall fill hell with the jinn and mankind together.

اِلَّا مَنْ رَّحِمَ رَبُّكَ ؕ وَلِذٰلِكَ خَلَقَهُمْ ؕ وَتَمَّتْ كَلِمَةُ رَبِّكَ
لَاَمْلَئَنَّ جَهَنَّمَ مِنَ الْجِنَّةِ وَالنَّاسِ اَجْمَعِيْنَ ﴿١١٩﴾

120. And all that We relate unto thee of the story of the messengers is in order that thereby We may make firm thy heart. And herein hath come unto thee the Truth and an exhortation and a reminder for believers.

وَكُلًّا نَّقُصُّ عَلَيْكَ مِنْ اَنْۢبَآءِ الرُّسُلِ مَا نُثَبِّتُ بِهٖ
فُؤَادَكَ ۚ وَجَآءَكَ فِىْ هٰذِهِ الْحَقُّ وَمَوْعِظَةٌ وَّذِكْرٰى
لِلْمُؤْمِنِيْنَ ﴿١٢٠﴾

121. And say unto those who believe not: Act according to your power. Lo! we (too) are acting.

وَقُلْ لِّلَّذِيْنَ لَا يُؤْمِنُوْنَ اعْمَلُوْا عَلٰى مَكَانَتِكُمْ ؕ
اِنَّا عٰمِلُوْنَ ۙ ﴿١٢١﴾

122. And wait! Lo! we (too) are waiting.

وَانْتَظِرُوْا ۚ اِنَّا مُنْتَظِرُوْنَ ﴿١٢٢﴾

123. And Allah's is the Invisible of the heavens and the earth, and unto Him the whole matter will be returned. So worship Him and put thy trust in Him. Lo! thy Lord is not unaware of what ye (mortals) do.

وَلِلّٰهِ غَيْبُ السَّمٰوٰتِ وَالْاَرْضِ وَاِلَيْهِ يُرْجَعُ الْاَمْرُ كُلُّهٗ
ع فَاعْبُدْهُ وَتَوَكَّلْ عَلَيْهِ ؕ وَمَا رَبُّكَ بِغَافِلٍ عَمَّا تَعْمَلُوْنَ ﴿١٢٣﴾

Yūsuf takes its name from its subject which is the life-story of Joseph. It differs from all other Sūrahs in having only one subject. The differences from the Bible narrative are striking. Jacob is here a Prophet, who is not deceived by the story of his son's death, but is distressed because, through a suspension of his clairvoyance, he cannot see what has become of Joseph. The real importance of the narrative, its psychic burden, is emphasised throughout, and the manner of narration, though astonishing to Western readers, is vivid.

Tradition says that it was recited by the Prophet at Mecca to the first converts from Yathrib (Al-Madīnah), *i.e.* in the second year before the Hijrah; but that, as Nöldeke points out, does not mean that it was not revealed till then, but that it had been revealed by then.

A late Meccan Sūrah.

JOSEPH

Revealed at Mecca

In the name of Allah, the Beneficent, the Merciful.

1. Alif. Lām. Rā. [1] These are verses of the Scripture that maketh plain.

2. Lo! We have revealed it, a Lecture [2] in Arabic, that ye may understand.

3. We narrate unto thee (Muhammad) the best of narratives in that We have inspired in thee this Qur'ān, though aforetime thou wast of the heedless.

4. When Joseph said unto his father: O my father! Lo! I saw in a dream eleven planets and the sun and the moon, I saw them prostrating themselves unto me.

5. He said: O my dear son! Tell not thy brethren of thy vision, lest they plot a plot against thee. Lo! Satan is for man an open foe.

6. Thus thy Lord will prefer thee and will teach thee the interpretation of events, and will perfect His grace upon thee and upon the family of Jacob as He perfected it upon thy forefathers, Abraham and Isaac. Lo! thy Lord is Knower, Wise.

7. Verily in Joseph and his brethren are signs (of Allah's Sovereignty) for the inquiring.

8. When they said: Verily Joseph and his brother are dearer to our father than we are, many though we be. Lo! our father is in plain aberration.

9. (One said): Kill Joseph or cast him to some (other) land, so that your father's favour may be all for you, and (that) ye may afterward be righteous folk.

1 See footnote, Sūrah II, v. 1.
2 Ar. *Qur'ān*.

اٰیاتها ١١١ (١٢) سُوْرَةُ يُوْسُفَ مَكِّيَّةٌ رُكُوْعَاتُهَا ١٢

بِسْمِ اللّٰهِ الرَّحْمٰنِ الرَّحِيْمِ

الٓرٰ تِلْكَ اٰيٰتُ الْكِتٰبِ الْمُبِيْنِ ﴿١﴾
اِنَّآ اَنْزَلْنٰهُ قُرْءٰنًا عَرَبِيًّا لَّعَلَّكُمْ تَعْقِلُوْنَ ﴿٢﴾
نَحْنُ نَقُصُّ عَلَيْكَ اَحْسَنَ الْقَصَصِ بِمَآ اَوْحَيْنَآ
اِلَيْكَ هٰذَا الْقُرْاٰنَ ۖ وَاِنْ كُنْتَ مِنْ قَبْلِهٖ لَمِنَ
الْغٰفِلِيْنَ ﴿٣﴾
اِذْ قَالَ يُوْسُفُ لِاَبِيْهِ يٰٓاَبَتِ اِنِّيْ رَاَيْتُ اَحَدَ عَشَرَ
كَوْكَبًا وَّالشَّمْسَ وَالْقَمَرَ رَاَيْتُهُمْ لِيْ سٰجِدِيْنَ ﴿٤﴾
قَالَ يٰبُنَيَّ لَا تَقْصُصْ رُءْيَاكَ عَلٰٓى اِخْوَتِكَ فَيَكِيْدُوْا
لَكَ كَيْدًا ۭ اِنَّ الشَّيْطٰنَ لِلْاِنْسَانِ عَدُوٌّ مُّبِيْنٌ ﴿٥﴾
وَكَذٰلِكَ يَجْتَبِيْكَ رَبُّكَ وَيُعَلِّمُكَ مِنْ تَاْوِيْلِ
الْاَحَادِيْثِ وَيُتِمُّ نِعْمَتَهٗ عَلَيْكَ وَعَلٰٓى اٰلِ يَعْقُوْبَ
كَمَآ اَتَمَّهَا عَلٰٓى اَبَوَيْكَ مِنْ قَبْلُ اِبْرٰهِيْمَ وَاِسْحٰقَ
ع اِنَّ رَبَّكَ عَلِيْمٌ حَكِيْمٌ ﴿٦﴾
لَقَدْ كَانَ فِيْ يُوْسُفَ وَاِخْوَتِهٖٓ اٰيٰتٌ لِّلسَّآئِلِيْنَ ﴿٧﴾
اِذْ قَالُوْا لَيُوْسُفُ وَاَخُوْهُ اَحَبُّ اِلٰٓى اَبِيْنَا مِنَّا وَ
نَحْنُ عُصْبَةٌ ۭ اِنَّ اَبَانَا لَفِيْ ضَلٰلٍ مُّبِيْنِ ﴿٨﴾
اقْتُلُوْا يُوْسُفَ اَوِ اطْرَحُوْهُ اَرْضًا يَّخْلُ لَكُمْ
وَجْهُ اَبِيْكُمْ وَتَكُوْنُوْا مِنْ بَعْدِهٖ قَوْمًا
صٰلِحِيْنَ ﴿٩﴾

10. One among them said: Kill not Joseph but, if ye must be doing, fling him into the depth of the pit; some caravar will find him.

11. They said: O our father! Why wilt thou not trust us with Joseph, when lo! we are good friends to him?

12. Send him with us to-morrow that he may enjoy himself and play. And lo! we shall take good care of him.

13. He said: Lo! in truth it saddens me that ye should take him with you, and I fear lest the wolf devour him while ye are heedless of him.

14. They said: If the wolf should devour him when we are (so strong) a band, then surely we should have already perished.

15. Then, when they led him off, and were of one mind that they should place him in the depth of the pit, We inspired in him: Thou wilt tell them of this deed of theirs when they know (thee) not.

16. And they came weeping to their father in the evening.

17. Saying: O our father! We went racing one with another, and left Joseph by our things, and the wolf devoured him, and thou believest not our sayings even when we speak the truth.

18. And they came with false blood on his shirt. He said: Nay, but your minds have beguiled you into something. (My course is) comely patience. And Allah it is Whose help is to be sought in that (predicament) which ye describe.

19. And there came a caravan, and they sent their water-drawer. He let down his pail (into the pit). He said: Good luck! Here is a youth. And they hid him as a treasure; and Allah was Aware of what they did.

قَالَ قَآئِلٌ مِّنْهُمْ لَا تَقْتُلُوا يُوسُفَ وَأَلْقُوهُ فِي
غَيٰبَتِ الْجُبِّ يَلْتَقِطْهُ بَعْضُ السَّيَّارَةِ إِنْ كُنْتُمْ
فٰعِلِينَ ﴿١٠﴾

قَالُوا يٰٓأَبَانَا مَا لَكَ لَا تَأْمَنَّا عَلٰى يُوسُفَ وَإِنَّا
لَهُ لَنٰصِحُونَ ﴿١١﴾

أَرْسِلْهُ مَعَنَا غَدًا يَرْتَعْ وَيَلْعَبْ وَإِنَّا لَهُ لَحٰفِظُونَ ﴿١٢﴾

قَالَ إِنِّي لَيَحْزُنُنِي أَنْ تَذْهَبُوا بِهِ وَأَخَافُ أَنْ
يَأْكُلَهُ الذِّئْبُ وَأَنْتُمْ عَنْهُ غٰفِلُونَ ﴿١٣﴾

قَالُوا لَئِنْ أَكَلَهُ الذِّئْبُ وَنَحْنُ عُصْبَةٌ إِنَّا إِذًا لَّخٰسِرُونَ ﴿١٤﴾

فَلَمَّا ذَهَبُوا بِهِ وَأَجْمَعُوا أَنْ يَجْعَلُوهُ فِي غَيٰبَتِ الْجُبِّ
وَأَوْحَيْنَا إِلَيْهِ لَتُنَبِّئَنَّهُمْ بِأَمْرِهِمْ هٰذَا وَهُمْ لَا
يَشْعُرُونَ ﴿١٥﴾

وَجَآءُوا أَبَاهُمْ عِشَآءً يَبْكُونَ ﴿١٦﴾

قَالُوا يٰٓأَبَانَا إِنَّا ذَهَبْنَا نَسْتَبِقُ وَتَرَكْنَا يُوسُفَ
عِنْدَ مَتٰعِنَا فَأَكَلَهُ الذِّئْبُ وَمَآ أَنْتَ بِمُؤْمِنٍ
لَّنَا وَلَوْ كُنَّا صٰدِقِينَ ﴿١٧﴾

وَجَآءُوا عَلٰى قَمِيصِهِ بِدَمٍ كَذِبٍ قَالَ بَلْ سَوَّلَتْ
لَكُمْ أَنْفُسُكُمْ أَمْرًا فَصَبْرٌ جَمِيلٌ وَاللّٰهُ الْمُسْتَعَانُ
عَلٰى مَا تَصِفُونَ ﴿١٨﴾

وَجَآءَتْ سَيَّارَةٌ فَأَرْسَلُوا وَارِدَهُمْ فَأَدْلٰى دَلْوَهُ
قَالَ يٰبُشْرٰى هٰذَا غُلٰمٌ وَأَسَرُّوهُ بِضٰعَةً وَاللّٰهُ
عَلِيمٌ بِمَا يَعْمَلُونَ ﴿١٩﴾

20. And they sold him for a low price, a number of silver coins; and they attached no value to him.

21. And he of Egypt who purchased him said unto his wife: Receive him honourably. Perchance he may prove useful to us or we may adopt him as a son. Thus We established Joseph in the land that We might teach him the interpretation of events. And Allah was predominant in his career, but most of mankind know not.

22. And when he reached his prime We gave him wisdom and knowledge. Thus We reward the good.

23. And she, in whose house he was, asked of him an evil act. She bolted the doors and said: Come! He said: I seek refuge in Allah! Lo! he is my lord, who hath treated me honourably. Wrong-doers never prosper.

24. She verily desired him, and he would have desired her if it had not been that he saw the argument of his lord. Thus it was, that We might ward off from him evil and lewdness. Lo! he was of Our chosen slaves.

25. And they raced with one another to the door, and she tore his shirt from behind, and they met her lord and master at the door. She said: What shall be his reward, who wisheth evil to thy folk, save prison or a painful doom?

26. (Joseph) said: She it was who asked of me an evil act. And a witness of her own folk testified: If his shirt is torn from front, then she speaketh truth and he is of the liars.

وَشَرَوْهُ بِثَمَنٍ بَخْسٍ دَرَاهِمَ مَعْدُودَةٍ وَكَانُوا

فِيهِ مِنَ الزَّاهِدِينَ ﴿٢٠﴾ ع

وَقَالَ الَّذِي اشْتَرَاهُ مِنْ مِصْرَ لِامْرَأَتِهِ أَكْرِمِي

مَثْوَاهُ عَسَىٰ أَنْ يَنْفَعَنَا أَوْ نَتَّخِذَهُ وَلَدًا وَكَذَٰلِكَ

مَكَّنَّا لِيُوسُفَ فِي الْأَرْضِ وَلِنُعَلِّمَهُ مِنْ تَأْوِيلِ

الْأَحَادِيثِ وَاللَّهُ غَالِبٌ عَلَىٰ أَمْرِهِ وَلَٰكِنَّ أَكْثَرَ

النَّاسِ لَا يَعْلَمُونَ ﴿٢١﴾

وَلَمَّا بَلَغَ أَشُدَّهُ آتَيْنَاهُ حُكْمًا وَعِلْمًا وَكَذَٰلِكَ

نَجْزِي الْمُحْسِنِينَ ﴿٢٢﴾

وَرَاوَدَتْهُ الَّتِي هُوَ فِي بَيْتِهَا عَنْ نَفْسِهِ وَ

غَلَّقَتِ الْأَبْوَابَ وَقَالَتْ هَيْتَ لَكَ قَالَ مَعَاذَ

اللَّهِ إِنَّهُ رَبِّي أَحْسَنَ مَثْوَايَ إِنَّهُ لَا يُفْلِحُ

الظَّالِمُونَ ﴿٢٣﴾

وَلَقَدْ هَمَّتْ بِهِ وَهَمَّ بِهَا لَوْلَا أَنْ رَأَىٰ بُرْهَانَ رَبِّهِ

كَذَٰلِكَ لِنَصْرِفَ عَنْهُ السُّوءَ وَالْفَحْشَاءَ إِنَّهُ مِنْ

عِبَادِنَا الْمُخْلَصِينَ ﴿٢٤﴾

وَاسْتَبَقَا الْبَابَ وَقَدَّتْ قَمِيصَهُ مِنْ دُبُرٍ وَأَلْفَيَا

سَيِّدَهَا لَدَى الْبَابِ قَالَتْ مَا جَزَاءُ مَنْ أَرَادَ بِأَهْلِكَ

سُوءًا إِلَّا أَنْ يُسْجَنَ أَوْ عَذَابٌ أَلِيمٌ ﴿٢٥﴾

قَالَ هِيَ رَاوَدَتْنِي عَنْ نَفْسِي وَشَهِدَ شَاهِدٌ

مِنْ أَهْلِهَا إِنْ كَانَ قَمِيصُهُ قُدَّ مِنْ قُبُلٍ

فَصَدَقَتْ وَهُوَ مِنَ الْكَاذِبِينَ ﴿٢٦﴾

27. And if his shirt is torn from behind, then she hath lied and he is of the truthful.

28. So when he saw his shirt torn from behind, he said: Lo! this is of the guile of you women. Lo! the guile of you is very great.

29. O Joseph! Turn away from this, and thou, (O woman), ask forgiveness for thy sin. Lo! thou art of the sinful.

30. And women in the city said: The ruler's wife is asking of her slave-boy an ill deed. Indeed he has smitten her to the heart with love. We behold her in plain aberration.

31. And when she heard of their sly talk, she sent for them and prepared for them a cushioned couch (to lie on at the feast) and gave to every one of them a knife and said (to Joseph): Come out unto them! And when they saw him they exalted him and cut their hands, exclaiming: Allah Blameless! This is not a human being. This is no other than some gracious angel!

32. She said: This is he on whose account ye blamed me. I asked of him an evil act, but he proved continent, but if he do not my behest he verily shall be imprisoned, and verily shall be of those brought low.

33. He said: O my Lord! Prison is more dear than that unto which they urge me, and if Thou fend not off their wiles from me I shall incline unto them and become of the foolish.

34. So his Lord heard his prayer and fended off their wiles from him. Lo! He is Hearer, Knower.

وَاِنۡ كَانَ قَمِيۡصُهٗ قُدَّ مِنۡ دُبُرٍ فَكَذَبَتۡ وَهُوَ مِنَ
الصّٰدِقِيۡنَ ﴿۲۷﴾
فَلَمَّا رَاٰ قَمِيۡصَهٗ قُدَّ مِنۡ دُبُرٍ قَالَ اِنَّهٗ مِنۡ كَيۡدِكُنَّ
اِنَّ كَيۡدَكُنَّ عَظِيۡمٌ ﴿۲۸﴾
يُوۡسُفُ اَعۡرِضۡ عَنۡ هٰذَا وَاسۡتَغۡفِرِىۡ لِذَنۡۢبِكِ
اِنَّكِ كُنۡتِ مِنَ الۡخٰطِـئِيۡنَ ﴿۲۹﴾ ع
وَقَالَ نِسۡوَةٌ فِى الۡمَدِيۡنَةِ امۡرَاَتُ الۡعَزِيۡزِ تُرَاوِدُ
فَتٰٮهَا عَنۡ نَّـفۡسِهٖ قَدۡ شَغَفَهَا حُبًّا اِنَّا لَـنَرٰٮهَا
فِىۡ ضَلٰلٍ مُّبِيۡنٍ ﴿۳۰﴾
فَلَمَّا سَمِعَتۡ بِمَكۡرِهِنَّ اَرۡسَلَتۡ اِلَيۡهِنَّ وَاَعۡتَدَتۡ
لَهُنَّ مُتَّكَـاً وَّاٰتَتۡ كُلَّ وَاحِدَةٍ مِّنۡهُنَّ سِكِّيۡنًا وَّ
قَالَتِ اخۡرُجۡ عَلَيۡهِنَّ فَلَمَّا رَاَيۡنَهٗۤ اَكۡبَرۡنَهٗ وَقَطَّعۡنَ
اَيۡدِيَهُنَّ وَقُلۡنَ حَاشَ لِلّٰهِ مَا هٰذَا بَشَرًا اِنۡ هٰذَاۤ
اِلَّا مَلَكٌ كَرِيۡمٌ ﴿۳۱﴾
قَالَتۡ فَذٰلِكُنَّ الَّذِىۡ لُمۡتُنَّنِىۡ فِيۡهِ وَلَقَدۡ رَاوَدْتُّهٗ
عَنۡ نَّـفۡسِهٖ فَاسۡتَعۡصَمَ وَلَـئِنۡ لَّمۡ يَفۡعَلۡ مَاۤ اٰمُرُهٗ
لَيُسۡجَنَنَّ وَلَيَكُوۡنًا مِّنَ الصّٰغِرِيۡنَ ﴿۳۲﴾
قَالَ رَبِّ السِّجۡنُ اَحَبُّ اِلَىَّ مِمَّا يَدۡعُوۡنَنِىۡۤ اِلَيۡهِ
وَاِلَّا تَصۡرِفۡ عَنِّىۡ كَيۡدَهُنَّ اَصۡبُ اِلَيۡهِنَّ وَاَكُنۡ
مِّنَ الۡجٰهِلِيۡنَ ﴿۳۳﴾
فَاسۡتَجَابَ لَهٗ رَبُّهٗ فَصَرَفَ عَنۡهُ كَيۡدَهُنَّ اِنَّهٗ
هُوَ السَّمِيۡعُ الۡعَلِيۡمُ ﴿۳۴﴾

35. And it seemed good to them (the men-folk) after they had seen the signs (of his innocence) to imprison him for a time.

36. And two young men went to prison with him. One of them said: I dreamed that I was pressing wine. The other said: I dreamed that I was carrying upon my head bread whereof the birds were eating. Announce unto us the interpretation, for we see thee of those good (at interpretation).

37. He said: The food which ye are given (daily) shall not come unto you but I shall tell you the interpretation ere it cometh unto you. This is of that which my Lord hath taught me. Lo! I have forsaken the religion of folk who believe not in Allah and are disbelievers in the Hereafter.

38. And I have followed the religion of my fathers, Abraham and Isaac and Jacob. It never was for us to attribute aught as partner to Allah. This is of the bounty of Allah unto us (the seed of Abraham) and unto mankind; but most men give not thanks.

39. O my two fellow-prisoners! Are divers lords better, or Allah the One, the Almighty?

40. Those whom ye worship beside Him are but names which ye have named, ye and your fathers. Allah hath revealed no sanction for them. The decision rests with Allah only, Who hath commanded you that ye worship none save Him. This is the right religion, but most men know not.

41. O my two fellow-prisoners! As for one of you, he will pour out wine for his lord to drink; and as for the other, he will be crucified so that the birds will eat from his head. Thus is the case judged concerning which ye did inquire.

ثُمَّ بَدَا لَهُمْ مِّنْۢ بَعْدِ مَا رَاَوُا الْاٰيٰتِ لَيَسْجُنُنَّهٗ
حَتّٰى حِيْنٍ ٣٥ ع
وَدَخَلَ مَعَهُ السِّجْنَ فَتَيٰنِ قَالَ اَحَدُهُمَآ اِنِّيْٓ
اَرٰىنِيْٓ اَعْصِرُ خَمْرًا وَقَالَ الْاٰخَرُ اِنِّيْٓ اَرٰىنِيْٓ
اَحْمِلُ فَوْقَ رَاْسِيْ خُبْزًا تَاْكُلُ الطَّيْرُ مِنْهُ نَبِّئْنَا
بِتَاْوِيْلِهٖ اِنَّا نَرٰىكَ مِنَ الْمُحْسِنِيْنَ ٣٦
قَالَ لَا يَاْتِيْكُمَا طَعَامٌ تُرْزَقٰنِهٖٓ اِلَّا نَبَّاْتُكُمَا بِتَاْوِيْلِهٖ
قَبْلَ اَنْ يَّاْتِيَكُمَا ذٰلِكُمَا مِمَّا عَلَّمَنِيْ رَبِّيْ اِنِّيْ تَرَكْتُ
مِلَّةَ قَوْمٍ لَّا يُؤْمِنُوْنَ بِاللّٰهِ وَهُمْ بِالْاٰخِرَةِ هُمْ كٰفِرُوْنَ ٣٧
وَاتَّبَعْتُ مِلَّةَ اٰبَآءِيْٓ اِبْرٰهِيْمَ وَاِسْحٰقَ وَيَعْقُوْبَ
مَا كَانَ لَنَآ اَنْ نُّشْرِكَ بِاللّٰهِ مِنْ شَيْءٍ ذٰلِكَ مِنْ
فَضْلِ اللّٰهِ عَلَيْنَا وَعَلَى النَّاسِ وَلٰكِنَّ اَكْثَرَ النَّاسِ
لَا يَشْكُرُوْنَ ٣٨
يٰصَاحِبَيِ السِّجْنِ ءَاَرْبَابٌ مُّتَفَرِّقُوْنَ خَيْرٌ اَمِ
اللّٰهُ الْوَاحِدُ الْقَهَّارُ ٣٩
مَا تَعْبُدُوْنَ مِنْ دُوْنِهٖٓ اِلَّآ اَسْمَآءً سَمَّيْتُمُوْهَآ اَنْتُمْ
وَاٰبَآؤُكُمْ مَّآ اَنْزَلَ اللّٰهُ بِهَا مِنْ سُلْطٰنٍ اِنِ الْحُكْمُ
اِلَّا لِلّٰهِ اَمَرَ اَلَّا تَعْبُدُوْٓا اِلَّآ اِيَّاهُ ذٰلِكَ الدِّيْنُ الْقَيِّمُ
وَلٰكِنَّ اَكْثَرَ النَّاسِ لَا يَعْلَمُوْنَ ٤٠
يٰصَاحِبَيِ السِّجْنِ اَمَّآ اَحَدُكُمَا فَيَسْقِيْ رَبَّهٗ خَمْرًا
وَاَمَّا الْاٰخَرُ فَيُصْلَبُ فَتَاْكُلُ الطَّيْرُ مِنْ رَّاْسِهٖ قُضِيَ
الْاَمْرُ الَّذِيْ فِيْهِ تَسْتَفْتِيٰنِ ٤١

42. And he said unto him of the twain who he knew would be released: Mention me in the presence of thy lord. But Satan caused him to forget to mention it to his lord, so he (Joseph) stayed in prison for some years.

وَقَالَ لِلَّذِىْ ظَنَّ اَنَّهٗ نَاجٍ مِّنْهُمَا اذْكُرْنِىْ عِنْدَ رَبِّكَ فَاَنْسَاهُ الشَّيْطٰنُ ذِكْرَ رَبِّهٖ فَلَبِثَ فِى السِّجْنِ بِضْعَ سِنِيْنَ ۞

43. And the king said: Lo! I saw in a dream seven fat kine which seven lean were eating, and seven green ears of corn and other (seven) dry. O notables! Expound for me my vision, if ye can interpret dreams.

وَقَالَ الْمَلِكُ اِنِّىْ اَرٰى سَبْعَ بَقَرٰتٍ سِمَانٍ يَّأْكُلُهُنَّ سَبْعٌ عِجَافٌ وَّسَبْعَ سُنْبُلٰتٍ خُضْرٍ وَّاُخَرَ يٰبِسٰتٍ يٰاَيُّهَا الْمَلَاُ اَفْتُوْنِىْ فِىْ رُءْيَاىَ اِنْ كُنْتُمْ لِلرُّءْيَا تَعْبُرُوْنَ ۞

44. They answered: Jumbled dreams! And we are not knowing in the interpretation of dreams.

قَالُوْا اَضْغَاثُ اَحْلَامٍ وَمَا نَحْنُ بِتَأْوِيْلِ الْاَحْلَامِ بِعٰلِمِيْنَ ۞

45. And he of the two who was released, and (now) at length remembered, said: I am going to announce unto you the interpretation, therefore send me forth.

وَقَالَ الَّذِىْ نَجَا مِنْهُمَا وَادَّكَرَ بَعْدَ اُمَّةٍ اَنَا اُنَبِّئُكُمْ بِتَأْوِيْلِهٖ فَاَرْسِلُوْنِ ۞

46. (And when he came to Joseph in the prison, he exclaimed): Joseph! O thou truthful one! Expound for us the seven fat kine which seven lean were eating and the seven green ears of corn and other (seven) dry, that I may return unto the people, so that they may know.

يُوْسُفُ اَيُّهَا الصِّدِّيْقُ اَفْتِنَا فِىْ سَبْعِ بَقَرٰتٍ سِمَانٍ يَّأْكُلُهُنَّ سَبْعٌ عِجَافٌ وَّسَبْعِ سُنْبُلٰتٍ خُضْرٍ وَّاُخَرَ يٰبِسٰتٍ لَّعَلِّىْ اَرْجِعُ اِلَى النَّاسِ لَعَلَّهُمْ يَعْلَمُوْنَ ۞

47. He said: Ye shall sow seven years as usual, but that which ye reap, leave it in the ear, all save a little which ye eat.

قَالَ تَزْرَعُوْنَ سَبْعَ سِنِيْنَ دَاَبًا فَمَا حَصَدْتُّمْ فَذَرُوْهُ فِىْ سُنْبُلِهٖ اِلَّا قَلِيْلًا مِّمَّا تَأْكُلُوْنَ ۞

48. Then after that will come seven hard years which will devour all that ye have prepared for them, save a little of that which ye have stored.

ثُمَّ يَأْتِىْ مِنْ بَعْدِ ذٰلِكَ سَبْعٌ شِدَادٌ يَّأْكُلْنَ مَا قَدَّمْتُمْ لَهُنَّ اِلَّا قَلِيْلًا مِّمَّا تُحْصِنُوْنَ ۞

49. Then, after that, will come a year when the people will have plenteous crops and when they will press (wine and oil).

ثُمَّ يَأْتِىْ مِنْ بَعْدِ ذٰلِكَ عَامٌ فِيْهِ يُغَاثُ النَّاسُ وَفِيْهِ يَعْصِرُوْنَ ۞

50. And the king said: Bring him unto me. And when the messenger came unto him, he (Joseph) said: Return unto thy lord and ask him what was the case of the women who cut their hands. Lo! my Lord knoweth their guile.

وَقَالَ الْمَلِكُ ائْتُوْنِىْ بِهٖ فَلَمَّا جَاءَهُ الرَّسُوْلُ قَالَ ارْجِعْ اِلٰى رَبِّكَ فَسْئَلْهُ مَا بَالُ النِّسْوَةِ الّٰتِىْ قَطَّعْنَ اَيْدِيَهُنَّ اِنَّ رَبِّىْ بِكَيْدِهِنَّ عَلِيْمٌ ۞

51. He (the king) (then sent for those women and) said: What happened when ye asked an evil act of Joseph? They answered: Allah Blameless! We know no evil of him. Said the wife of the ruler: Now the truth is out. I asked of him an evil act, and he is surely of the truthful.

52. (Then Joseph said: I asked for) this, that he (my lord) may know that I betrayed him not in secret, and that surely Allah guideth not the snare of the betrayers.

53. I do not exculpate myself. Lo! the (human) soul enjoineth unto evil, save that whereon my Lord hath mercy. Lo! my Lord is Forgiving, Merciful.

54. And the king said: Bring him unto me that I may attach him to my person. And when he had talked with him he said: Lo! thou art to-day in our presence established and trusted.

55. He said: Set me over the storehouses of the land. Lo! I am a skilled custodian.

56. Thus gave We power to Joseph in the land. He was the owner of it where he pleased. We reach with Our mercy whom We will. We lose not the reward of the good.

57. And the reward of the Hereafter is better, for those who believe and ward off (evil).

58. And Joseph's brethren came and presented themselves before him, and he knew them but they knew him not.

59. And when he provided them with their provision he said: Bring unto me a brother of yours from your father. See ye not that I fill up the measure and I am the best of hosts?

60. And if ye bring him not unto me, then there shall be no measure for you with me, nor shall ye draw near.

قَالَ مَا خَطْبُكُنَّ اِذْ رَاوَدْتُّنَّ يُوْسُفَ عَنْ نَّفْسِهٖ ۚ قُلْنَ حَاشَ لِلّٰهِ مَا عَلِمْنَا عَلَيْهِ مِنْ سُوْٓءٍ ۚ قَالَتِ امْرَاَتُ الْعَزِيْزِ الْـٰٔنَ حَصْحَصَ الْحَقُّ ۫ اَنَا رَاوَدْتُّهٗ عَنْ نَّفْسِهٖ وَاِنَّهٗ لَمِنَ الصّٰدِقِيْنَ ۝٥١

ذٰلِكَ لِيَعْلَمَ اَنِّيْ لَمْ اَخُنْهُ بِالْغَيْبِ وَاَنَّ اللّٰهَ لَا يَهْدِيْ كَيْدَ الْخَآئِنِيْنَ ۝٥٢

وَمَآ اُبَرِّئُ نَفْسِيْ ۚ اِنَّ النَّفْسَ لَاَمَّارَةٌۢ بِالسُّوْٓءِ اِلَّا مَا رَحِمَ رَبِّيْ ۭ اِنَّ رَبِّيْ غَفُوْرٌ رَّحِيْمٌ ۝٥٣

وَقَالَ الْمَلِكُ ائْتُوْنِيْ بِهٖٓ اَسْتَخْلِصْهُ لِنَفْسِيْ ۚ فَلَمَّا كَلَّمَهٗ قَالَ اِنَّكَ الْيَوْمَ لَدَيْنَا مَكِيْنٌ اَمِيْنٌ ۝٥٤

قَالَ اجْعَلْنِيْ عَلٰى خَزَآئِنِ الْاَرْضِ ۚ اِنِّيْ حَفِيْظٌ عَلِيْمٌ ۝٥٥

وَكَذٰلِكَ مَكَّنَّا لِيُوْسُفَ فِي الْاَرْضِ ۚ يَتَبَوَّاُ مِنْهَا حَيْثُ يَشَآءُ ۭ نُصِيْبُ بِرَحْمَتِنَا مَنْ نَّشَآءُ وَلَا نُضِيْعُ اَجْرَ الْمُحْسِنِيْنَ ۝٥٦

وَلَاَجْرُ الْاٰخِرَةِ خَيْرٌ لِّلَّذِيْنَ اٰمَنُوْا وَكَانُوْا يَتَّقُوْنَ ۝٥٧

وَجَآءَ اِخْوَةُ يُوْسُفَ فَدَخَلُوْا عَلَيْهِ فَعَرَفَهُمْ وَهُمْ لَهٗ مُنْكِرُوْنَ ۝٥٨

وَلَمَّا جَهَّزَهُمْ بِجَهَازِهِمْ قَالَ ائْتُوْنِيْ بِاَخٍ لَّكُمْ مِّنْ اَبِيْكُمْ ۚ اَلَا تَرَوْنَ اَنِّيْٓ اُوْفِي الْكَيْلَ وَاَنَا خَيْرُ الْمُنْزِلِيْنَ ۝٥٩

فَاِنْ لَّمْ تَاْتُوْنِيْ بِهٖ فَلَا كَيْلَ لَكُمْ عِنْدِيْ وَلَا تَقْرَبُوْنِ ۝٦٠

61. They said: We will try to win him from his father: that we will surely do.

62. He said unto his young men: Place their merchandise in their saddlebags, so that they may know it when they go back to their folk, and so will come again.

63. So when they went back to their father they said: O our father! The measure is denied us, so send with us our brother that we may obtain the measure, surely we will guard him well.

64. He said: Can I entrust him to you save as I entrusted his brother to you aforetime? Allah is better at guarding, and He is the Most Merciful of those who show mercy.

65. And when they opened their belongings they discovered that their merchandise had been returned to them. They said: O our father! What (more) can we ask? Here is our merchandise returned to us. We shall get provision for our folk and guard our brother, and we shall have the extra measure of a camel (load). This (that we bring now) is a light measure.

66. He said: I will not send him with you till ye give me an undertaking in the name of Allah that ye will bring him back to me, unless ye are surrounded. And when they gave him their undertaking he said: Allah is the Warden over what we say.

67. And he said: O my sons! Go not in by one gate; go in by different gates. I can naught avail you as against Allah. Lo! the decision rests with Allah only. In Him do I put my trust, and in Him let all the trusting put their trust.

68. And when they entered in the manner which their father had enjoined, it would have naught availed them as against Allah; it was but a need of Jacob's soul which he thus satisfied; [1] and lo! he was a lord of knowledge because We had taught him; but most of mankind know not.

قَالُوا سَنُرَاوِدُ عَنْهُ أَبَاهُ وَإِنَّا لَفَاعِلُونَ ﴿٦١﴾
وَقَالَ لِفِتْيَانِهِ اجْعَلُوا بِضَاعَتَهُمْ فِي رِحَالِهِمْ
لَعَلَّهُمْ يَعْرِفُونَهَا إِذَا انْقَلَبُوا إِلَىٰ أَهْلِهِمْ لَعَلَّهُمْ
يَرْجِعُونَ ﴿٦٢﴾
فَلَمَّا رَجَعُوا إِلَىٰ أَبِيهِمْ قَالُوا يَا أَبَانَا مُنِعَ مِنَّا الْكَيْلُ
فَأَرْسِلْ مَعَنَا أَخَانَا نَكْتَلْ وَإِنَّا لَهُ لَحَافِظُونَ ﴿٦٣﴾
قَالَ هَلْ آمَنُكُمْ عَلَيْهِ إِلَّا كَمَا أَمِنْتُكُمْ عَلَىٰ أَخِيهِ
مِنْ قَبْلُ فَاللَّهُ خَيْرٌ حِفْظًا وَهُوَ أَرْحَمُ الرَّاحِمِينَ ﴿٦٤﴾
وَلَمَّا فَتَحُوا مَتَاعَهُمْ وَجَدُوا بِضَاعَتَهُمْ رُدَّتْ
إِلَيْهِمْ قَالُوا يَا أَبَانَا مَا نَبْغِي هَٰذِهِ بِضَاعَتُنَا رُدَّتْ
إِلَيْنَا وَنَمِيرُ أَهْلَنَا وَنَحْفَظُ أَخَانَا وَنَزْدَادُ كَيْلَ
بَعِيرٍ ذَٰلِكَ كَيْلٌ يَسِيرٌ ﴿٦٥﴾
قَالَ لَنْ أُرْسِلَهُ مَعَكُمْ حَتَّىٰ تُؤْتُونِ مَوْثِقًا مِنَ
اللَّهِ لَتَأْتُنَّنِي بِهِ إِلَّا أَنْ يُحَاطَ بِكُمْ فَلَمَّا آتَوْهُ
مَوْثِقَهُمْ قَالَ اللَّهُ عَلَىٰ مَا نَقُولُ وَكِيلٌ ﴿٦٦﴾
وَقَالَ يَا بَنِيَّ لَا تَدْخُلُوا مِنْ بَابٍ وَاحِدٍ وَادْخُلُوا
مِنْ أَبْوَابٍ مُتَفَرِّقَةٍ وَمَا أُغْنِي عَنْكُمْ مِنَ اللَّهِ مِنْ شَيْءٍ
إِنِ الْحُكْمُ إِلَّا لِلَّهِ عَلَيْهِ تَوَكَّلْتُ وَعَلَيْهِ فَلْيَتَوَكَّلِ الْمُتَوَكِّلُونَ ﴿٦٧﴾
وَلَمَّا دَخَلُوا مِنْ حَيْثُ أَمَرَهُمْ أَبُوهُمْ مَا كَانَ يُغْنِي
عَنْهُمْ مِنَ اللَّهِ مِنْ شَيْءٍ إِلَّا حَاجَةً فِي نَفْسِ
يَعْقُوبَ قَضَاهَا وَإِنَّهُ لَذُو عِلْمٍ لِمَا عَلَّمْنَاهُ وَ
لَٰكِنَّ أَكْثَرَ النَّاسِ لَا يَعْلَمُونَ ﴿٦٨﴾

1 There is a prevalent superstition in the East that the members of a large family ought not to appear all together, for fear of the ill luck that comes from envy in the hearts of others.

69. And when they went in before Joseph, he took his brother unto himself, saying: Lo! I, even I, am thy brother, therefore sorrow not for what they did.

70. And when he provided them with their provision, he put the drinking-cup in his brother's saddlebag, and then a crier cried: O camel-riders! Ye are surely thieves!

71. They cried, coming toward them: What is it ye have lost?

72. They said: We have lost the king's cup, and he who bringeth it shall have a camel-load, and I (said Joseph) am answerable for it.

73. They said: By Allah, well ye know we came not to do evil in the land, and are no thieves.

74. They said: And what shall be the penalty for it, if ye prove liars?

75. They said: The penalty for it! He in whose bag (the cup) is found, he is the penalty for it. Thus we requite wrong-doers.

76. Then he (Joseph) began the search with their bags before his brother's bag, then he produced it from his brother's bag. Thus did We contrive for Joseph. He could not have taken his brother according to the king's law unless Allah willed. We raise by grades (of mercy) whom We will, and over every lord of knowledge there is one more knowing.

77. They said: If he stealeth, a brother of his stole before. But Joseph kept it secret in his soul and revealed it not unto them. He said (within himself): Ye are in worse case and Allah knoweth best (the truth of) that which ye allege.

78. They said: O ruler of the land! Lo! he hath an aged father, so take one of us instead of him. Lo! we behold thee of those who do kindness.

وَلَمَّا دَخَلُوا عَلَىٰ يُوسُفَ آوَىٰ إِلَيْهِ أَخَاهُ قَالَ إِنِّي
أَنَا أَخُوكَ فَلَا تَبْتَئِسْ بِمَا كَانُوا يَعْمَلُونَ ٦٩
فَلَمَّا جَهَّزَهُم بِجَهَازِهِمْ جَعَلَ السِّقَايَةَ فِي رَحْلِ
أَخِيهِ ثُمَّ أَذَّنَ مُؤَذِّنٌ أَيَّتُهَا الْعِيرُ إِنَّكُمْ
لَسَارِقُونَ ٧٠
قَالُوا وَأَقْبَلُوا عَلَيْهِم مَّاذَا تَفْقِدُونَ ٧١
قَالُوا نَفْقِدُ صُوَاعَ الْمَلِكِ وَلِمَن جَاءَ بِهِ حِمْلُ
بَعِيرٍ وَأَنَا بِهِ زَعِيمٌ ٧٢
قَالُوا تَاللَّهِ لَقَدْ عَلِمْتُم مَّا جِئْنَا لِنُفْسِدَ فِي الْأَرْضِ وَ
مَا كُنَّا سَارِقِينَ ٧٣
قَالُوا فَمَا جَزَاؤُهُ إِن كُنتُمْ كَاذِبِينَ ٧٤
قَالُوا جَزَاؤُهُ مَن وُجِدَ فِي رَحْلِهِ فَهُوَ جَزَاؤُهُ
كَذَٰلِكَ نَجْزِي الظَّالِمِينَ ٧٥
فَبَدَأَ بِأَوْعِيَتِهِمْ قَبْلَ وِعَاءِ أَخِيهِ ثُمَّ اسْتَخْرَجَهَا
مِن وِعَاءِ أَخِيهِ كَذَٰلِكَ كِدْنَا لِيُوسُفَ مَا كَانَ
لِيَأْخُذَ أَخَاهُ فِي دِينِ الْمَلِكِ إِلَّا أَن يَشَاءَ اللَّهُ نَرْفَعُ
دَرَجَاتٍ مَّن نَّشَاءُ وَفَوْقَ كُلِّ ذِي عِلْمٍ عَلِيمٌ ٧٦
قَالُوا إِن يَسْرِقْ فَقَدْ سَرَقَ أَخٌ لَّهُ مِن قَبْلُ فَأَسَرَّهَا
يُوسُفُ فِي نَفْسِهِ وَلَمْ يُبْدِهَا لَهُمْ قَالَ أَنتُمْ شَرٌّ
مَّكَانًا وَاللَّهُ أَعْلَمُ بِمَا تَصِفُونَ ٧٧
قَالُوا يَا أَيُّهَا الْعَزِيزُ إِنَّ لَهُ أَبًا شَيْخًا كَبِيرًا فَخُذْ
أَحَدَنَا مَكَانَهُ إِنَّا نَرَاكَ مِنَ الْمُحْسِنِينَ ٧٨

79. He said: Allah forbid that we should seize save him with whom we found our property; then truly we should be wrong-doers.

80. So, when they despaired of (moving) him, they conferred together apart. The eldest of them said: Know ye not how your father took an undertaking from you in Allah's name and how ye failed in the case of Joseph aforetime? Therefore I shall not go forth from the land until my father giveth leave or Allah judgeth for me. He is the Best of Judges.

81. Return unto your father and say: O our father! Lo! thy son hath stolen. We testify only to that which we know; we are not guardians of the unseen.

82. Ask the township where we were, and the caravan with which we travelled hither. Lo! we speak the truth.

83. (And when they came unto their father and had spoken thus to him) he said: Nay, but your minds have beguiled you into something. (My course is) comely patience! It may be that Allah will bring them all unto me. Lo! He, only He, is the Knower, the Wise.

84. And he turned away from them and said: Alas, my grief for Joseph! And his eyes were whitened with the sorrow that he was suppressing.

85. They said: By Allah, thou wilt never cease remembering Joseph till thy health is ruined or thou art of those who perish!

86. He said: I expose my distress and anguish only unto Allah, and I know from Allah that which ye know not.

87. Go, O my sons, and ascertain concerning Joseph and his brother, and despair not of the Spirit of Allah. Lo! none despaireth of the Spirit of Allah save disbelieving folk.

قَالَ مَعَاذَ اللّٰهِ اَنْ نَّاْخُذَ اِلَّا مَنْ وَّجَدْنَا مَتَاعَنَا
عِنْدَهٗۤ ۙ اِنَّاۤ اِذًا لَّظٰلِمُوْنَ ﴿٧٩﴾ ع
فَلَمَّا اسْتَيْـَٔسُوْا مِنْهُ خَلَصُوْا نَجِيًّا ؕ قَالَ كَبِيْرُهُمْ اَلَمْ
تَعْلَمُوْۤا اَنَّ اَبَاكُمْ قَدْ اَخَذَ عَلَيْكُمْ مَّوْثِقًا مِّنَ اللّٰهِ وَمِنْ
قَبْلُ مَا فَرَّطْتُّمْ فِيْ يُوْسُفَ ۚ فَلَنْ اَبْرَحَ الْاَرْضَ حَتّٰى
يَاْذَنَ لِيْۤ اَبِيْۤ اَوْ يَحْكُمَ اللّٰهُ لِيْ ۚ وَهُوَ خَيْرُ الْحٰكِمِيْنَ ﴿٨٠﴾
اِرْجِعُوْۤا اِلٰۤى اَبِيْكُمْ فَقُوْلُوْا يٰۤاَبَانَاۤ اِنَّ ابْنَكَ سَرَقَ ۚ وَمَا
شَهِدْنَاۤ اِلَّا بِمَا عَلِمْنَا وَمَا كُنَّا لِلْغَيْبِ حٰفِظِيْنَ ﴿٨١﴾
وَسْـَٔلِ الْقَرْيَةَ الَّتِيْ كُنَّا فِيْهَا وَالْعِيْرَ الَّتِيْۤ اَقْبَلْنَا
فِيْهَا ؕ وَاِنَّا لَصٰدِقُوْنَ ﴿٨٢﴾
قَالَ بَلْ سَوَّلَتْ لَكُمْ اَنْفُسُكُمْ اَمْرًا ؕ فَصَبْرٌ جَمِيْلٌ ؕ
عَسَى اللّٰهُ اَنْ يَّاْتِيَنِيْ بِهِمْ جَمِيْعًا ؕ اِنَّهٗ هُوَ
الْعَلِيْمُ الْحَكِيْمُ ﴿٨٣﴾
وَتَوَلّٰى عَنْهُمْ وَقَالَ يٰۤاَسَفٰى عَلٰى يُوْسُفَ وَابْيَضَّتْ
عَيْنٰهُ مِنَ الْحُزْنِ فَهُوَ كَظِيْمٌ ﴿٨٤﴾
قَالُوْا تَاللّٰهِ تَفْتَؤُا تَذْكُرُ يُوْسُفَ حَتّٰى تَكُوْنَ
حَرَضًا اَوْ تَكُوْنَ مِنَ الْهٰلِكِيْنَ ﴿٨٥﴾
قَالَ اِنَّمَاۤ اَشْكُوْا بَثِّيْ وَحُزْنِيْۤ اِلَى اللّٰهِ وَاَعْلَمُ
مِنَ اللّٰهِ مَا لَا تَعْلَمُوْنَ ﴿٨٦﴾
يٰبَنِيَّ اذْهَبُوْا فَتَحَسَّسُوْا مِنْ يُّوْسُفَ وَاَخِيْهِ وَلَا
تَايْـَٔسُوْا مِنْ رَّوْحِ اللّٰهِ ؕ اِنَّهٗ لَا يَايْـَٔسُ مِنْ رَّوْحِ
اللّٰهِ اِلَّا الْقَوْمُ الْكٰفِرُوْنَ ﴿٨٧﴾

88. And when they came (again) before him (Joseph) they said: O ruler! Misfortune hath touched us and our folk, and we bring but poor merchandise, so fill for us the measure and be charitable unto us. Lo! Allah will requite the charitable.

89. He said: Know ye what ye did unto Joseph and his brother in your ignorance?

90. They said: Is it indeed thou who art Joseph? He said: I am Joseph and this is my brother. Allah hath shown us favour. Lo! he who wardeth off (evil) and endureth (findeth favour) for verily Allah loseth not the wages of the kindly.

91. They said: By Allah, verily Allah hath preferred thee above us, and we were indeed sinful.

92. He said: Have no fear this day! May Allah forgive you, and He is the Most Merciful of those who show mercy.

93. Go with this shirt of mine and lay it on my father's face, he will become (again) a seer; and come to me with all your folk.

94. When the caravan departed their father had said: Truly I am conscious of the breath of Joseph, though ye call me dotard.

95. (Those around him) said: By Allah, lo! thou art in thine old aberration.

96. Then, when the bearer of glad tidings came, he laid it on his face and he became a seer once more. He said: Said I not unto you that I know from Allah that which ye know not?

97. They said: O our father! Ask forgiveness of our sins for us, for lo! we were sinful.

فَلَمَّا دَخَلُوا عَلَيْهِ قَالُوا يَا أَيُّهَا الْعَزِيزُ مَسَّنَا وَأَهْلَنَا
الضُّرُّ وَجِئْنَا بِبِضَاعَةٍ مُزْجَاةٍ فَأَوْفِ لَنَا الْكَيْلَ
وَتَصَدَّقْ عَلَيْنَا إِنَّ اللَّهَ يَجْزِي الْمُتَصَدِّقِينَ ٨٨
قَالَ هَلْ عَلِمْتُمْ مَا فَعَلْتُمْ بِيُوسُفَ وَأَخِيهِ إِذْ
أَنْتُمْ جَاهِلُونَ ٨٩
قَالُوا أَإِنَّكَ لَأَنْتَ يُوسُفُ قَالَ أَنَا يُوسُفُ وَهَٰذَا
أَخِي قَدْ مَنَّ اللَّهُ عَلَيْنَا إِنَّهُ مَنْ يَتَّقِ وَيَصْبِرْ
فَإِنَّ اللَّهَ لَا يُضِيعُ أَجْرَ الْمُحْسِنِينَ ٩٠
قَالُوا تَاللَّهِ لَقَدْ آثَرَكَ اللَّهُ عَلَيْنَا وَإِنْ كُنَّا
لَخَاطِئِينَ ٩١
قَالَ لَا تَثْرِيبَ عَلَيْكُمُ الْيَوْمَ يَغْفِرُ اللَّهُ لَكُمْ وَ
هُوَ أَرْحَمُ الرَّاحِمِينَ ٩٢
اذْهَبُوا بِقَمِيصِي هَٰذَا فَأَلْقُوهُ عَلَىٰ وَجْهِ أَبِي
يَأْتِ بَصِيرًا وَأْتُونِي بِأَهْلِكُمْ أَجْمَعِينَ ٩٣
وَلَمَّا فَصَلَتِ الْعِيرُ قَالَ أَبُوهُمْ إِنِّي لَأَجِدُ رِيحَ
يُوسُفَ لَوْلَا أَنْ تُفَنِّدُونِ ٩٤
قَالُوا تَاللَّهِ إِنَّكَ لَفِي ضَلَالِكَ الْقَدِيمِ ٩٥
فَلَمَّا أَنْ جَاءَ الْبَشِيرُ أَلْقَاهُ عَلَىٰ وَجْهِهِ فَارْتَدَّ
بَصِيرًا قَالَ أَلَمْ أَقُلْ لَكُمْ إِنِّي أَعْلَمُ مِنَ اللَّهِ مَا
لَا تَعْلَمُونَ ٩٦
قَالُوا يَا أَبَانَا اسْتَغْفِرْ لَنَا ذُنُوبَنَا إِنَّا كُنَّا
خَاطِئِينَ ٩٧

98. He said: I shall ask forgiveness for you of my Lord. Lo! He is the Forgiving, the Merciful.

99. And when they came in before Joseph, he took his parents unto him, and said: Come into Egypt safe, if Allah will !

100. And he placed his parents on the dais and they fell down before him prostrate, and he said: O my father! This is the interpretation of my dream of old. My Lord hath made it true, and He hath shown me kindness, since He took me out of the prison and hath brought you from the desert after Satan had made strife between me and my brethren. Lo! my Lord is tender unto whom He will. He is the Knower, the Wise.

101. O my Lord! Thou hast given me (something) of sovereignty and hast taught me (something) of the interpretation of events—Creator of the heavens and the earth! Thou art my Protecting Friend in the world and the Hereafter. Make me to die submissive (unto Thee), and join me to the righteous.

102. This is of the tidings of the Unseen which We inspire in thee (Muhammad). Thou wast not present with them when they fixed their plan and they were scheming.

103. And though thou try much, most men will not believe.

104. Thou askest them no fee for it. It is naught else than a reminder unto the peoples.

105. How many a portent is there in the heavens and the earth which they pass by with face averted!

106. And most of them believe not in Allah except that they attribute partners (unto Him).

قَالَ سَوْفَ أَسْتَغْفِرُ لَكُمْ رَبِّيْ ۚ إِنَّهٗ هُوَ الْغَفُوْرُ
الرَّحِيْمُ ﴿۹۸﴾
فَلَمَّا دَخَلُوْا عَلٰى يُوْسُفَ اٰوٰۤى إِلَيْهِ أَبَوَيْهِ وَقَالَ
ادْخُلُوْا مِصْرَ إِنْ شَآءَ اللّٰهُ اٰمِنِيْنَ ﴿۹۹﴾
وَرَفَعَ أَبَوَيْهِ عَلَى الْعَرْشِ وَخَرُّوْا لَهٗ سُجَّدًا ۚ وَ
قَالَ يٰۤأَبَتِ هٰذَا تَأْوِيْلُ رُءْيَايَ مِنْ قَبْلُ ۡ قَدْ
جَعَلَهَا رَبِّيْ حَقًّا ۖ وَقَدْ أَحْسَنَ بِيْۤ إِذْ أَخْرَجَنِيْ
مِنَ السِّجْنِ وَجَآءَ بِكُمْ مِّنَ الْبَدْوِ مِنْۢ
بَعْدِ أَنْ نَّزَغَ الشَّيْطٰنُ بَيْنِيْ وَبَيْنَ إِخْوَتِيْ ۭ
إِنَّ رَبِّيْ لَطِيْفٌ لِّمَا يَشَآءُ ۭ إِنَّهٗ هُوَ الْعَلِيْمُ
الْحَكِيْمُ ﴿۱۰۰﴾
رَبِّ قَدْ اٰتَيْتَنِيْ مِنَ الْمُلْكِ وَعَلَّمْتَنِيْ مِنْ تَأْوِيْلِ
الْأَحَادِيْثِ ۚ فَاطِرَ السَّمٰوٰتِ وَالْأَرْضِ ۟ أَنْتَ
وَلِيّٖ فِي الدُّنْيَا وَالْاٰخِرَةِ ۚ تَوَفَّنِيْ مُسْلِمًا وَّ
أَلْحِقْنِيْ بِالصّٰلِحِيْنَ ﴿۱۰۱﴾
ذٰلِكَ مِنْ أَنْۢبَآءِ الْغَيْبِ نُوْحِيْهِ إِلَيْكَ ۚ وَمَا كُنْتَ
لَدَيْهِمْ إِذْ أَجْمَعُوْۤا أَمْرَهُمْ وَهُمْ يَمْكُرُوْنَ ﴿۱۰۲﴾
وَمَآ أَكْثَرُ النَّاسِ وَلَوْ حَرَصْتَ بِمُؤْمِنِيْنَ ﴿۱۰۳﴾
ع وَمَا تَسْـَٔلُهُمْ عَلَيْهِ مِنْ أَجْرٍ ۭ إِنْ هُوَ إِلَّا ذِكْرٌ لِّلْعٰلَمِيْنَ ﴿۱۰۴﴾ ع
وَكَأَيِّنْ مِّنْ اٰيَةٍ فِي السَّمٰوٰتِ وَالْأَرْضِ يَمُرُّوْنَ
عَلَيْهَا وَهُمْ عَنْهَا مُعْرِضُوْنَ ﴿۱۰۵﴾
وَمَا يُؤْمِنُ أَكْثَرُهُمْ بِاللّٰهِ إِلَّا وَهُمْ مُّشْرِكُوْنَ ﴿۱۰۶﴾

107. Deem they themselves secure from the coming on them of a pall of Allah's punishment, or the coming of the Hour suddenly while they are unaware?

108. Say: This is my Way: I call on Allah with sure knowledge, I and whosoever followeth me—Glory be to Allah!—and I am not of the idolaters.

109. We sent not before thee (any messengers) save men whom We inspired from among the folk of the townships—Have they not travelled in the land and seen the nature of the consequence for those who were before them? And verily the abode of the Hereafter, for those who ward off (evil), is best. Have ye then no sense?—

110. Till, when the messengers despaired and thought that they were denied, then came unto them Our help, and whom We would was saved. And Our wrath cannot be warded from the guilty.

111. In their history verily there is a lesson for men of understanding. It is no invented story but a confirmation of the existing (Scripture) and a detailed explanation of everything, and a guidance and a mercy for folk who believe.

أفأمنوا أن تأتيهم غاشية من عذاب الله أو
تأتيهم الساعة بغتة وهم لا يشعرون ﴿١٠٧﴾
قل هذه سبيلي أدعوا إلى الله على بصيرة أنا
ومن اتبعني وسبحن الله وما أنا من المشركين ﴿١٠٨﴾
وما أرسلنا من قبلك إلا رجالا نوحي إليهم من
أهل القرى أفلم يسيروا في الأرض فينظروا كيف
كان عاقبة الذين من قبلهم ولدار الآخرة
خير للذين اتقوا أفلا تعقلون ﴿١٠٩﴾
حتى إذا استيئس الرسل وظنوا أنهم قد كذبوا
جاءهم نصرنا فنجي من نشاء ولا يرد بأسنا
عن القوم المجرمين ﴿١١٠﴾
لقد كان في قصصهم عبرة لأولي الألباب ما
كان حديثا يفترى ولكن تصديق الذي بين
يديه وتفصيل كل شيء وهدى ورحمة
ع لقوم يؤمنون ﴿١١١﴾

Ar-Ra'd, "The Thunder," takes its name from a word in v. 13. The subject is Divine guidance in relation to the law of consequences, it being explained here, as elsewhere in the Koran, that there is no partiality or aversion on the part of God, but that reward and punishment are the result of obeying or rejecting natural (or Divine) laws. According to some ancient authorities, it is a Meccan Sūrah with the exception of two verses revealed at Al-Madînah; according to others, a Madînan Sūrah with the exception of two verses revealed at Mecca. The very fact of such wholesale difference of opinion favours the Meccan attribution because there could be no such doubt about a complete Madînan Sūrah, owing to the great number of witnesses. The Madînan ascription may have arisen from the recognition of some verses by those witnesses as having been revealed at Al-Madînah on a certain occasion.

A late Meccan Sūrah for the most part.

THE THUNDER

Revealed at Mecca

In the name of Allah, the Beneficent, the Merciful.

1. Alif, Lām. Mīm. Rā.[1] These are verses of the Scripture. That which is revealed unto thee from thy Lord is the Truth, but most of mankind believe not.

2. Allah it is Who raised up the heavens without visible supports, then mounted the Throne, and compelled the sun and the moon to be of service, each runneth unto an appointed term; He ordereth the course; He detaileth the revelations, that haply ye may be certain of the meeting with your Lord.

3. And He it is Who spread out the earth and placed therein firm hills and flowing streams, and of all fruits he placed therein two spouses (male and female). He covereth the night with the day. Lo! herein verily are portents for people who take thought.

4. And in the Earth are neighbouring tracts, vineyards and ploughed lands, and date-palms, like and unlike,[2] which are watered with one water. And We have made some of them to excel others in fruit. Lo! herein verily are portents for people who have sense.

5. And if thou wonderest, then wondrous is their saying: When we are dust, are we then forsooth (to be raised) in a new creation? Such are they who disbelieve in their Lord; such have carcans on their necks; such are rightful owners of the Fire, they will abide therein.

6. And they bid thee hasten on the evil rather than the good, when exemplary punishments have indeed occurred before them. But lo! thy Lord is rich in pardon for mankind despite their wrong, and lo! thy Lord is strong in punishment.

1 See Sūrah II, v. 1. footnote.
2 Or it may be, "growing thickly or alone."

اياتها ٤٣ (١٣) سورة الرعد مدنية ركوعاتها ٦

بسم الله الرحمن الرحيم

المر تلك ايت الكتب والذي انزل اليك
من ربك الحق ولكن اكثر الناس لا يؤمنون ١
الله الذي رفع السموت بغير عمد ترونها ثم
استوى على العرش وسخر الشمس والقمر كل
يجري لاجل مسمى يدبر الامر يفصل الايت
لعلكم بلقاء ربكم توقنون ٢
وهو الذي مد الارض وجعل فيها رواسي وانهرا
ومن كل الثمرت جعل فيها زوجين اثنين يغشي
اليل النهار ان في ذلك لايت لقوم يتفكرون ٣
وفي الارض قطع متجورت وجنت من اعناب
وزرع ونخيل صنوان وغير صنوان يسقى بماء
واحد ونفضل بعضها على بعض في الاكل ان
في ذلك لايت لقوم يعقلون ٤
وان تعجب فعجب قولهم ءاذا كنا تربا ءانا لفي
خلق جديد اولئك الذين كفروا بربهم واولئك
الاغلل في اعناقهم واولئك اصحب النار هم
فيها خلدون ٥
ويستعجلونك بالسيئة قبل الحسنة وقد خلت
من قبلهم المثلت وان ربك لذو مغفرة للناس
على ظلمهم وان ربك لشديد العقاب ٦

7. Those who disbelieve say: If only some portent were sent down upon him from his Lord! Thou art a warner only, and for every folk a guide.

8. Allah knoweth that which every female beareth and that which the wombs absorb and that which they grow. And everything with Him is measured.

9. He is the Knower of the invisible and the visible, the Great, the High Exalted.

10. Alike of you is he who hideth the saying and he who noiseth it abroad, he who lurketh in the night and he who goeth freely in the daytime.

11. For him are angels ranged before him and behind him, who guard him by Allah's command.[1] Lo! Allah changeth not the condition of a folk until they (first) change that which is in their hearts; and if Allah willeth misfortune for a folk there is none that can repel it, nor have they a defender beside Him.

12. He it is Who showeth you the lightning, a fear and a hope,[2] and raiseth the heavy clouds.

13. The thunder hymneth His praise and (so do) the angels for awe of Him. He launcheth the thunderbolts and smiteth with them whom He will while they dispute (in doubt) concerning Allah, and He is mighty in wrath.

14. Unto Him is the real prayer. Those unto whom they pray beside Allah respond to them not at all, save as (is the response to) one who stretcheth forth his hands toward water (asking) that it may come unto his mouth, and it will never reach it. The prayer of disbelievers goeth (far) astray.

15. And unto Allah falleth prostrate whosoever is in the heavens and the earth, willingly or unwillingly, as do their shadows in the morning and the evening hours.

ويقول الذين كفروا لولا انزل عليه اية من
ع ربه انما انت منذر ولكل قوم هاد (٧)
الله يعلم ما تحمل كل انثى وما تغيض الارحام
وما تزداد وكل شيء عنده بمقدار (٨)
علم الغيب والشهادة الكبير المتعال (٩)
سواء منكم من اسر القول ومن جهر به ومن هو
مستخف باليل وسارب بالنهار (١٠)
له معقبت من بين يديه ومن خلفه يحفظونه
من امر الله ان الله لا يغير ما بقوم حتى يغيروا
ما بانفسهم واذا اراد الله بقوم سوءا فلا مرد له
وما لهم من دونه من وال (١١)
هو الذي يريكم البرق خوفا وطمعا وينشئ
السحاب الثقال (١٢)
ويسبح الرعد بحمده والملئكة من خيفته و
يرسل الصواعق فيصيب بها من يشاء وهم
يجادلون في الله وهو شديد المحال (١٣)
له دعوة الحق والذين يدعون من دونه لا
يستجيبون لهم بشيء الا كباسط كفيه الى الماء
ليبلغ فاه وما هو ببالغه وما دعاء الكفرين الا
في ضلل (١٤)
ولله يسجد من في السموت والارض طوعا و
كرها وظللهم بالغدو والاصال (١٥) السجدة
السجدة ٣

1 This is taken by some commentators to refer to "him who goeth freely in the daytime" in the previous verse. In that case it would read: "for whom are guards before him and behind him as if to gourd him against Allah's commandment."
2 The fear is of the lightning, and the hope is of the rain.

16. Say (O Muhammad): Who is Lord of the heavens and the earth? Say: Allah ! Say: Take ye then (others) beside Him for protectors, which, even for themselves, have neither benefit nor hurt? Say: Is the blind man equal to the seer, or is darkness equal to light? Or assign they unto Allah partners who created the like of His creation so that the creation (which they made and His creation) seemed alike to them? Say: Allah is the Creator of all things, and He is the One, the Almighty.

قُلْ مَنْ رَّبُّ السَّمٰوٰتِ وَالْاَرْضِ ۭ قُلِ اللّٰهُ ۭ قُلْ
اَفَاتَّخَذْتُمْ مِّنْ دُوْنِهٖٓ اَوْلِيَاۗءَ لَا يَمْلِكُوْنَ لِاَنْفُسِهِمْ
نَفْعًا وَّلَا ضَرًّا ۭ قُلْ هَلْ يَسْتَوِي الْاَعْمٰى وَالْبَصِيْرُ ڏ
اَمْ هَلْ تَسْتَوِي الظُّلُمٰتُ وَالنُّوْرُ ڬ اَمْ جَعَلُوْا لِلّٰهِ
شُرَكَاۗءَ خَلَقُوْا كَخَلْقِهٖ فَتَشَابَهَ الْخَلْقُ عَلَيْهِمْ ۭ
قُلِ اللّٰهُ خَالِقُ كُلِّ شَيْءٍ وَّهُوَ الْوَاحِدُ الْقَهَّارُ ﴿١٦﴾

17. He sendeth down water from the sky, so that valleys flow according to their measure, and the flood beareth (on its surface) swelling foam—from that which they smelt in the fire in order to make ornaments and tools riseth a foam like unto it—thus Allah coineth (the similitude of) the true and the false. Then, as for the foam, it passeth away as scum upon the banks, while, as for that which is of use to mankind, it remaineth in the earth. Thus Allah coineth the similitudes.

اَنْزَلَ مِنَ السَّمَاۗءِ مَاۗءً فَسَالَتْ اَوْدِيَةٌۢ بِقَدَرِهَا
فَاحْتَمَلَ السَّيْلُ زَبَدًا رَّابِيًا ۭ وَمِمَّا يُوْقِدُوْنَ عَلَيْهِ
فِي النَّارِ ابْتِغَاۗءَ حِلْيَةٍ اَوْ مَتَاعٍ زَبَدٌ مِّثْلُهٗ ۭ كَذٰلِكَ
يَضْرِبُ اللّٰهُ الْحَقَّ وَالْبَاطِلَ ڛ فَاَمَّا الزَّبَدُ فَيَذْهَبُ
جُفَاۗءً ۚ وَاَمَّا مَا يَنْفَعُ النَّاسَ فَيَمْكُثُ فِي الْاَرْضِ ۭ
كَذٰلِكَ يَضْرِبُ اللّٰهُ الْاَمْثَالَ ﴿١٧﴾

18. For those who answered Allah's call is bliss; and for those who answered not His call, if they had all that is in the earth, and therewith the like thereof, they would proffer it as ransom. Such will have a woeful reckoning, and their habitation will be hell, a dire abode.

لِلَّذِيْنَ اسْتَجَابُوْا لِرَبِّهِمُ الْحُسْنٰى ڼ وَالَّذِيْنَ لَمْ
يَسْتَجِيْبُوْا لَهٗ لَوْ اَنَّ لَهُمْ مَّا فِي الْاَرْضِ جَمِيْعًا وَّ
مِثْلَهٗ مَعَهٗ لَافْتَدَوْا بِهٖ ۭ اُولٰۗىِٕكَ لَهُمْ سُوْۗءُ الْحِسَابِ ڏ
وَمَاْوٰىهُمْ جَهَنَّمُ ۭ وَبِئْسَ الْمِهَادُ ﴿١٨﴾ ع

وقف النبي صلى الله عليه وسلم

19. Is he who knoweth that what is revealed unto thee from thy Lord is the truth like him who is blind? But only men of understanding heed;

اَفَمَنْ يَّعْلَمُ اَنَّمَآ اُنْزِلَ اِلَيْكَ مِنْ رَّبِّكَ الْحَقُّ
كَمَنْ هُوَ اَعْمٰى ۭ اِنَّمَا يَتَذَكَّرُ اُولُوا الْاَلْبَابِ ﴿١٩﴾

20. Such as keep the pact of Allah, and break not the covenant;

الَّذِيْنَ يُوْفُوْنَ بِعَهْدِ اللّٰهِ وَلَا يَنْقُضُوْنَ
الْمِيْثَاقَ ﴿٢٠﴾

21. Such as unite that which Allah hath commanded should be joined, and fear their Lord, and dread a woeful reckoning;

وَالَّذِيْنَ يَصِلُوْنَ مَآ اَمَرَ اللّٰهُ بِهٖٓ اَنْ يُّوْصَلَ وَ
يَخْشَوْنَ رَبَّهُمْ وَيَخَافُوْنَ سُوْۗءَ الْحِسَابِ ﴿٢١﴾

22. Such as persevere in seeking their Lord's countenance and are regular in prayer and spend of that which We bestow upon them secretly and openly, and overcome evil with good. Theirs will be the sequel of the (heavenly) Home,

23. Gardens of Eden which they enter, along with all who do right of their fathers and their helpmates and their seed. The angels enter unto them from every gate,

24. (Saying): Peace be unto you because ye persevered. Ah, passing sweet will be the sequel of the (heavenly) Home.

25. And those who break the covenant of Allah after ratifying it, and sever that which Allah hath commanded should be joined, and make mischief in the earth: theirs is the curse and theirs the ill abode.

26. Allah enlargeth livelihood for whom He will, and straiteneth (it for whom He will); and they rejoice in the life of the world, whereas the life of the world is but brief comfort as compared with the Hereafter.

27. Those who disbelieve say: If only a portent were sent down upon him from his Lord! Say: Lo! Allah sendeth whom He will astray, and guideth unto Himself all who turn (unto Him),

28. Who have believed and whose hearts have rest in the remembrance of Allah. Verily in the remembrance of Allah do hearts find rest!

29. Those who believe and do right: Joy is for them, and bliss (their) journey's end.

وَالَّذِيْنَ صَبَرُوا ابْتِغَآءَ وَجْهِ رَبِّهِمْ وَاَقَامُوا
الصَّلٰوةَ وَاَنْفَقُوْا مِمَّا رَزَقْنٰهُمْ سِرًّا وَّعَلَانِيَةً وَّ
يَدْرَءُوْنَ بِالْحَسَنَةِ السَّيِّئَةَ اُولٰٓئِكَ لَهُمْ عُقْبَى
الدَّارِ ﴿٢٢﴾
جَنّٰتُ عَدْنٍ يَّدْخُلُوْنَهَا وَمَنْ صَلَحَ مِنْ اٰبَآئِهِمْ
وَاَزْوَاجِهِمْ وَذُرِّيّٰتِهِمْ وَالْمَلٰٓئِكَةُ يَدْخُلُوْنَ عَلَيْهِمْ
مِّنْ كُلِّ بَابٍ ﴿٢٣﴾
سَلٰمٌ عَلَيْكُمْ بِمَا صَبَرْتُمْ فَنِعْمَ عُقْبَى الدَّارِ ﴿٢٤﴾
وَالَّذِيْنَ يَنْقُضُوْنَ عَهْدَ اللّٰهِ مِنْۢ بَعْدِ مِيْثَاقِهٖ وَ
يَقْطَعُوْنَ مَآ اَمَرَ اللّٰهُ بِهٖٓ اَنْ يُّوْصَلَ وَيُفْسِدُوْنَ
فِي الْاَرْضِ اُولٰٓئِكَ لَهُمُ اللَّعْنَةُ وَلَهُمْ سُوْٓءُ
الدَّارِ ﴿٢٥﴾
اَللّٰهُ يَبْسُطُ الرِّزْقَ لِمَنْ يَّشَآءُ وَيَقْدِرُ وَفَرِحُوْا
بِالْحَيٰوةِ الدُّنْيَا وَمَا الْحَيٰوةُ الدُّنْيَا فِي الْاٰخِرَةِ
اِلَّا مَتَاعٌ ﴿٢٦﴾
وَيَقُوْلُ الَّذِيْنَ كَفَرُوْا لَوْلَآ اُنْزِلَ عَلَيْهِ اٰيَةٌ مِّنْ
رَّبِّهٖ قُلْ اِنَّ اللّٰهَ يُضِلُّ مَنْ يَّشَآءُ وَيَهْدِيْٓ
اِلَيْهِ مَنْ اَنَابَ ﴿٢٧﴾
اَلَّذِيْنَ اٰمَنُوْا وَتَطْمَئِنُّ قُلُوْبُهُمْ بِذِكْرِ اللّٰهِ اَلَا
بِذِكْرِ اللّٰهِ تَطْمَئِنُّ الْقُلُوْبُ ﴿٢٨﴾
اَلَّذِيْنَ اٰمَنُوْا وَعَمِلُوا الصّٰلِحٰتِ طُوْبٰى لَهُمْ وَ
حُسْنُ مَاٰبٍ ﴿٢٩﴾

30. Thus We send thee (O Muhammad) unto a nation, before whom other nations have passed away, that thou mayst recite unto them that which We have inspired in thee, while they are disbelievers in the Beneficent. Say: He is my Lord; there is no God save Him. In Him do I put my trust and unto Him is my recourse.

31. Had it been possible for a Lecture[1] to cause the mountains to move, or the earth to be torn asunder, or the dead to speak, (this Qur'ān would have done so). Nay, but Allah's is the whole command. Do not those who believe know that, had Allah willed, He could have guided all mankind? As for those who disbelieve, disaster ceaseth not to strike them because of what they do, or it dwelleth near their home until the threat of Allah come to pass. Lo! Allah faileth not to keep the tryst.

32. And verily messengers (of Allah) were mocked before thee, but long I bore with those who disbelieved. At length I seized them, and how (awful) was My punishment!

33. Is He Who is aware of the deserts of every soul (as he who is aware of nothing)? Yet they ascribe unto Allah partners. Say: Name them. Is it that ye would inform Him of something which He knoweth not in the earth? Or is it but a way of speaking? Nay, but their contrivance is made seeming fair for those who disbelieve and they are kept from the right road. He whom Allah sendeth astray, for him there is no guide.

34. For them is torment in the life of the world, and verily the doom of the Hereafter is more painful, and they have no defender from Allah.

35. A similitude of the Garden which is promised unto those who keep their duty (to Allah): Underneath it rivers flow; its food is everlasting, and its shade; this is the reward of those who keep their duty, while the reward of disbelievers is the Fire.

1 Ar. *Qur'ān*.

كَذٰلِكَ اَرْسَلْنٰكَ فِيْٓ اُمَّةٍ قَدْ خَلَتْ مِنْ قَبْلِهَآ اُمَمٌ
لِّتَتْلُوَا۠ عَلَيْهِمُ الَّذِيْٓ اَوْحَيْنَآ اِلَيْكَ وَهُمْ يَكْفُرُوْنَ
بِالرَّحْمٰنِ ۭ قُلْ هُوَ رَبِّيْ لَآ اِلٰهَ اِلَّا هُوَ ۚ عَلَيْهِ تَوَكَّلْتُ
وَاِلَيْهِ مَتَابِ ﴿٣٠﴾
وَلَوْ اَنَّ قُرْاٰنًا سُيِّرَتْ بِهِ الْجِبَالُ اَوْ قُطِّعَتْ بِهِ
الْاَرْضُ اَوْ كُلِّمَ بِهِ الْمَوْتٰى ۭ بَلْ لِّلّٰهِ الْاَمْرُ جَمِيْعًا ۭ
اَفَلَمْ يَايْـَٔسِ الَّذِيْنَ اٰمَنُوْٓا اَنْ لَّوْ يَشَاۗءُ اللّٰهُ لَهَدَى
النَّاسَ جَمِيْعًا ۭ وَلَا يَزَالُ الَّذِيْنَ كَفَرُوْا تُصِيْبُهُمْ
بِمَا صَنَعُوْا قَارِعَةٌ اَوْ تَحُلُّ قَرِيْبًا مِّنْ دَارِهِمْ حَتّٰى
يَاْتِيَ وَعْدُ اللّٰهِ ۭ اِنَّ اللّٰهَ لَا يُخْلِفُ الْمِيْعَادَ ﴿٣١﴾
وَلَقَدِ اسْتُهْزِئَ بِرُسُلٍ مِّنْ قَبْلِكَ فَاَمْلَيْتُ لِلَّذِيْنَ
كَفَرُوْا ثُمَّ اَخَذْتُهُمْ ۣ فَكَيْفَ كَانَ عِقَابِ ﴿٣٢﴾
اَفَمَنْ هُوَ قَاۗىِٕمٌ عَلٰي كُلِّ نَفْسٍۢ بِمَا كَسَبَتْ ۚ وَجَعَلُوْا
لِلّٰهِ شُرَكَاۗءَ ۭ قُلْ سَمُّوْهُمْ ۭ اَمْ تُنَبِّـُٔـوْنَهٗ بِمَا لَا يَعْلَمُ
فِي الْاَرْضِ اَمْ بِظَاهِرٍ مِّنَ الْقَوْلِ ۭ بَلْ زُيِّنَ لِلَّذِيْنَ
كَفَرُوْا مَكْرُهُمْ وَصُدُّوْا عَنِ السَّبِيْلِ ۭ وَمَنْ يُّضْلِلِ اللّٰهُ
فَمَا لَهٗ مِنْ هَادٍ ﴿٣٣﴾
لَهُمْ عَذَابٌ فِي الْحَيٰوةِ الدُّنْيَا وَلَعَذَابُ الْاٰخِرَةِ
اَشَقُّ ۚ وَمَا لَهُمْ مِّنَ اللّٰهِ مِنْ وَّاقٍ ﴿٣٤﴾
مَثَلُ الْجَنَّةِ الَّتِيْ وُعِدَ الْمُتَّقُوْنَ ۭ تَجْرِيْ مِنْ تَحْتِهَا
الْاَنْهٰرُ ۭ اُكُلُهَا دَاۗىِٕمٌ وَّظِلُّهَا ۭ تِلْكَ عُقْبَى الَّذِيْنَ
اتَّقَوْا ڰ وَّعُقْبَى الْكٰفِرِيْنَ النَّارُ ﴿٣٥﴾

36. Those unto whom We gave the Scripture rejoice in that which is revealed unto thee. And of the clans there are who deny some of it. Say: I am commanded only that I serve Allah and ascribe unto Him no partner. Unto Him I cry, and unto Him is my return.

37. Thus have We revealed it, a decisive utterance in Arabic; and if thou shouldst follow their desires after that which hath come unto thee of knowledge, then truly wouldst thou have from Allah no protecting friend nor defender.

38. And verily We sent messengers (to mankind) before thee, and We appointed for them wives and offspring, and it was not (given) to any messenger that he should bring a portent save by Allah's leave. For everything there is a time prescribed.

39. Allah effaceth what He will, and establisheth (what He will), and with Him is the source of ordinance.

40. Whether We let thee see something of that which We have promised them, or make thee die (before its happening), thine is but conveyance (of the message), Ours the reckoning.

41. See they not how We visit the land, reducing it of its outlying parts? [1](When) Allah doometh there is none that can postpone His doom, and He is swift at reckoning.

42. Those who were before them plotted; but all plotting is Allah's. He knoweth that which each soul earneth. The disbelievers will come to know for whom will be the sequel of the (heavenly) Home.

43. They who disbelieve say: Thou art no messenger (of Allah). Say: Allah, and whosoever hath true knowledge of the Scripture, is sufficient witness between me and you.

وَالَّذِينَ آتَيْنٰهُمُ الْكِتٰبَ يَفْرَحُونَ بِمَا أُنْزِلَ إِلَيْكَ
وَمِنَ الْأَحْزَابِ مَنْ يُنْكِرُ بَعْضَهُ ۚ قُلْ إِنَّمَا أُمِرْتُ
أَنْ أَعْبُدَ اللّٰهَ وَلَا أُشْرِكَ بِهِ ۚ إِلَيْهِ أَدْعُوا وَإِلَيْهِ
مَآبِ ﴿٣٦﴾
وَكَذٰلِكَ أَنْزَلْنٰهُ حُكْمًا عَرَبِيًّا ۚ وَلَئِنِ اتَّبَعْتَ
أَهْوَاءَهُمْ بَعْدَمَا جَاءَكَ مِنَ الْعِلْمِ ۙ مَا لَكَ مِنَ
اللّٰهِ مِنْ وَلِيٍّ وَلَا وَاقٍ ﴿٣٧﴾ ع ١١
وَلَقَدْ أَرْسَلْنَا رُسُلًا مِنْ قَبْلِكَ وَجَعَلْنَا لَهُمْ أَزْوَاجًا
وَذُرِّيَّةً ۚ وَمَا كَانَ لِرَسُولٍ أَنْ يَأْتِيَ بِآيَةٍ إِلَّا
بِإِذْنِ اللّٰهِ ۗ لِكُلِّ أَجَلٍ كِتَابٌ ﴿٣٨﴾
يَمْحُوا اللّٰهُ مَا يَشَاءُ وَيُثْبِتُ ۖ وَعِنْدَهُ أُمُّ الْكِتٰبِ ﴿٣٩﴾
وَإِنْ مَا نُرِيَنَّكَ بَعْضَ الَّذِي نَعِدُهُمْ أَوْ نَتَوَفَّيَنَّكَ
فَإِنَّمَا عَلَيْكَ الْبَلٰغُ وَعَلَيْنَا الْحِسَابُ ﴿٤٠﴾
أَوَلَمْ يَرَوْا أَنَّا نَأْتِي الْأَرْضَ نَنْقُصُهَا مِنْ أَطْرَافِهَا ۚ وَ
اللّٰهُ يَحْكُمُ لَا مُعَقِّبَ لِحُكْمِهِ ۚ وَهُوَ سَرِيعُ الْحِسَابِ ﴿٤١﴾
وَقَدْ مَكَرَ الَّذِينَ مِنْ قَبْلِهِمْ فَلِلّٰهِ الْمَكْرُ جَمِيعًا ۖ
يَعْلَمُ مَا تَكْسِبُ كُلُّ نَفْسٍ ۗ وَسَيَعْلَمُ الْكُفّٰرُ لِمَنْ
عُقْبَى الدَّارِ ﴿٤٢﴾
وَيَقُولُ الَّذِينَ كَفَرُوا لَسْتَ مُرْسَلًا ۚ قُلْ كَفٰى
بِاللّٰهِ شَهِيدًا بَيْنِي وَبَيْنَكُمْ وَمَنْ عِنْدَهُ عِلْمُ
الْكِتٰبِ ﴿٤٣﴾ ع ٦ ١٢

1 If this is a Madinan verse, the reference would be to the spread of Al-Islām, if a Meccan verse, it would be to the Persian and Eastern Roman empires encroaching on Arabia.

Ibrāhîm, so-called from Abraham's prayer in vv. 35-41, at the time when he was establishing his son Ishmael, the ancestor of the Arabs, in the "uncultiv able valley" of Mecca. Otherwise the subject of the Sūrah is the same as that of other Meccan Sūrahs revealed during the last three years before the Hijrah. The reference in v. 46 to the plot of the idolaters makes it probable that it is among the last of the Meccan revelations.

A late Meccan Sūrah; except vv. 28-30, revealed at Al-Madînah.

ABRAHAM

Revealed at Mecca

In the name of Allah, the Beneficent, the Merciful.

1. Alif. Lām. Rā.[1] (This is) a Scripture which We have revealed unto thee (Muhammad) that thereby thou mayst bring forth mankind from darkness unto light, by the permission of their Lord, unto the path of the Mighty, the Owner of Praise,

2. Allah, unto Whom belongeth whatsoever is in the heavens and whatsoever is in the earth. And woe unto the disbelievers from an awful doom;

3. Those who love the life of the world more than the Hereafter, and debar (men) from the Way of Allah and would have it crooked: such are far astray.

4. And We never sent a messenger save with the language of his folk, that he might make (the message) clear for them. Then Allah sendeth whom He will astray, and guideth whom He will. He is the Mighty, the Wise.

5. We verily sent Moses with Our revelations, saying: Bring thy people forth from darkness unto light. And remind them of the days of Allah. Lo! therein are revelations for each steadfast, thankful (heart).

6. And (remind them) how Moses said unto his people: Remember Allah's favour unto you when He delivered you from Pharaoh's folk who were afflicting you with dreadful torment, and were slaying your sons and sparing your women; that was a tremendous trial from your Lord.

1 See Sūr. II, v. 1, footnote.

اٰيَاتُهَا ٥٢ (١٤) سُوْرَةُ اِبْرٰهِيْمَ مَكِّيَّةٌ ٧٢ رُكُوْعَاتُهَا ٧

بِسْمِ اللّٰهِ الرَّحْمٰنِ الرَّحِيْمِ

الٓرٰ كِتٰبٌ اَنْزَلْنٰهُ اِلَيْكَ لِتُخْرِجَ النَّاسَ مِنَ
الظُّلُمٰتِ اِلَى النُّوْرِ بِاِذْنِ رَبِّهِمْ اِلٰى صِرَاطِ
الْعَزِيْزِ الْحَمِيْدِ ﴿١﴾
اللّٰهِ الَّذِيْ لَهٗ مَا فِي السَّمٰوٰتِ وَمَا فِي الْاَرْضِ وَوَيْلٌ
لِّلْكٰفِرِيْنَ مِنْ عَذَابٍ شَدِيْدِ ﴿٢﴾
الَّذِيْنَ يَسْتَحِبُّوْنَ الْحَيٰوةَ الدُّنْيَا عَلَى الْاٰخِرَةِ وَ
يَصُدُّوْنَ عَنْ سَبِيْلِ اللّٰهِ وَيَبْغُوْنَهَا عِوَجًا اُولٰٓئِكَ
فِيْ ضَلٰلٍ بَعِيْدٍ ﴿٣﴾
وَمَا اَرْسَلْنَا مِنْ رَّسُوْلٍ اِلَّا بِلِسَانِ قَوْمِهٖ لِيُبَيِّنَ
لَهُمْ فَيُضِلُّ اللّٰهُ مَنْ يَّشَآءُ وَيَهْدِيْ مَنْ يَّشَآءُ
وَهُوَ الْعَزِيْزُ الْحَكِيْمُ ﴿٤﴾
وَلَقَدْ اَرْسَلْنَا مُوْسٰى بِاٰيٰتِنَآ اَنْ اَخْرِجْ قَوْمَكَ مِنَ
الظُّلُمٰتِ اِلَى النُّوْرِ وَذَكِّرْهُمْ بِاَيّٰىمِ اللّٰهِ اِنَّ فِيْ ذٰلِكَ
لَاٰيٰتٍ لِّكُلِّ صَبَّارٍ شَكُوْرٍ ﴿٥﴾
وَاِذْ قَالَ مُوْسٰى لِقَوْمِهِ اذْكُرُوْا نِعْمَةَ اللّٰهِ عَلَيْكُمْ
اِذْ اَنْجٰىكُمْ مِّنْ اٰلِ فِرْعَوْنَ يَسُوْمُوْنَكُمْ
سُوْٓءَ الْعَذَابِ وَيُذَبِّحُوْنَ اَبْنَآءَكُمْ وَ
يَسْتَحْيُوْنَ نِسَآءَكُمْ وَفِيْ ذٰلِكُمْ بَلَآءٌ مِّنْ
رَّبِّكُمْ عَظِيْمٌ ﴿٦﴾ ع

7. And when your Lord proclaimed: If ye give thanks, I will give you more; but if ye are thankless, lo! My punishment is dire.

8. And moses said: though ye and all who are in the earth prove thankless, lo! Allah verily is Absolute Owner of Praise.

9. Hath not the history of those before you reached you: the folk of Noah, and (the tribes of) Aad and Thamud, and those after them? None save Allah knoweth them. Their messengers came unto them with clear proofs, but they thrust their hands into their mouths, and said: Lo! we disbelieve in that where -- with ye have been sent, and lo! we are grave doubt concerning that to which ye call us.

10. Their messengers said: Can there be doubt concerning Allah, the Creator of the heavens and the earth? He calleth you that He may forgive you your sins and reprieve you unto an appointed term. They said: Ye are but mortals like us, who whould fain trun us away from what our fathers used to worship. Then bring some clear warrant.

11. Their messengers said unto them: We are but mortals like you, but Allah giveth grace unto whom He will of His slaves. It is not ours to bring you a warrant unless by the permission of Allah. In Allah let believers put their trust!

12. How should we not put our trust in Allah when He hath shown us our ways? We surely will endure what hurt ye do us. In Allah let the trusting put their trust!

وَاِذْ تَاَذَّنَ رَبُّكُمْ لَىِٕنْ شَكَرْتُمْ لَاَزِيْدَنَّكُمْ وَلَىِٕنْ
كَفَرْتُمْ اِنَّ عَذَابِيْ لَشَدِيْدٌ ⑦
وَقَالَ مُوْسٰٓى اِنْ تَكْفُرُوْٓا اَنْتُمْ وَمَنْ فِي الْاَرْضِ جَمِيْعًا
فَاِنَّ اللّٰهَ لَغَنِيٌّ حَمِيْدٌ ⑧

اَلَمْ يَاْتِكُمْ نَبَؤُا الَّذِيْنَ مِنْ قَبْلِكُمْ قَوْمِ نُوْحٍ وَّعَادٍ
وَّثَمُوْدَ ۛ وَالَّذِيْنَ مِنْ بَعْدِهِمْ ۛ لَا يَعْلَمُهُمْ اِلَّا اللّٰهُ ۭ
جَاۗءَتْهُمْ رُسُلُهُمْ بِالْبَيِّنٰتِ فَرَدُّوْٓا اَيْدِيَهُمْ فِيْٓ
اَفْوَاهِهِمْ وَقَالُوْٓا اِنَّا كَفَرْنَا بِمَآ اُرْسِلْتُمْ بِهٖ
وَاِنَّا لَفِيْ شَكٍّ مِّمَّا تَدْعُوْنَنَآ اِلَيْهِ
مُرِيْبٍ ⑨

قَالَتْ رُسُلُهُمْ اَفِي اللّٰهِ شَكٌّ فَاطِرِ السَّمٰوٰتِ وَ
الْاَرْضِ ۭ يَدْعُوْكُمْ لِيَغْفِرَ لَكُمْ مِّنْ ذُنُوْبِكُمْ وَيُؤَخِّرَكُمْ
اِلٰٓى اَجَلٍ مُّسَمًّى ۭ قَالُوْٓا اِنْ اَنْتُمْ اِلَّا بَشَرٌ مِّثْلُنَا ۭ
تُرِيْدُوْنَ اَنْ تَصُدُّوْنَا عَمَّا كَانَ يَعْبُدُ اٰبَاۗؤُنَا
فَاْتُوْنَا بِسُلْطٰنٍ مُّبِيْنٍ ⑩
قَالَتْ لَهُمْ رُسُلُهُمْ اِنْ نَّحْنُ اِلَّا بَشَرٌ مِّثْلُكُمْ وَلٰكِنَّ
اللّٰهَ يَمُنُّ عَلٰي مَنْ يَّشَاۗءُ مِنْ عِبَادِهٖ ۭ وَمَا كَانَ
لَنَآ اَنْ نَّاْتِيَكُمْ بِسُلْطٰنٍ اِلَّا بِاِذْنِ اللّٰهِ ۭ وَعَلَي اللّٰهِ
فَلْيَتَوَكَّلِ الْمُؤْمِنُوْنَ ⑪
وَمَا لَنَآ اَلَّا نَتَوَكَّلَ عَلَي اللّٰهِ وَقَدْ هَدٰىنَا سُبُلَنَا ۭ
وَلَنَصْبِرَنَّ عَلٰي مَآ اٰذَيْتُمُوْنَا ۭ وَعَلَي اللّٰهِ فَلْيَتَوَكَّلِ
الْمُتَوَكِّلُوْنَ ⑫

13. And those who disbelieved said unto their messengers: Verily we will drive you out from our land, unless ye return to our religion. Then their Lord inspired them, (saying): Verily We shall destroy the wrong-doers,

14. And verily We shall make you to dwell in the land after them. This is for him who feareth My Majesty and feareth My threats.

15. And they sought help (from their Lord) and every froward potentate was brought to naught;

16. Hell is before him, and he is made to drink a festering water,

17. Which he sippeth but can hardly swallow, and death cometh unto him from every side while yet he cannot die, and before him is a harsh doom.

18. A similitude of those who disbelieve in their Lord: Their works are as ashes which the wind bloweth hard upon a stormy day. They have no control of aught that they have earned. That is the extreme failure.

19. Hast thou not seen that Allah hath created the heavens and the earth with truth? If He will, He can remove you and bring (in) some new creation;

20. And that is no great matter for Allah.

21. They all come forth unto their Lord. Then those who were despised say unto those who were scornful: We were unto you a following, can ye then avert from us aught of Allah's doom? They say: Had Allah guided us, we should have guided you. Whether we rage or patiently endure is (now) all one for us; we have no place of refuge.

وقال الذين كفروا لرسلهم لنخرجنكم من
أرضنا أو لتعودن في ملتنا فأوحى إليهم ربهم
لنهلكن الظلمين ﴿١٣﴾
ولنسكننكم الأرض من بعدهم ذلك لمن
خاف مقامي وخاف وعيد ﴿١٤﴾
واستفتحوا وخاب كل جبار عنيد ﴿١٥﴾
من ورآئه جهنم ويسقى من مآء صديد ﴿١٦﴾
يتجرعه ولا يكاد يسيغه ويأتيه الموت من
كل مكان وما هو بميت ومن ورآئه عذاب
غليظ ﴿١٧﴾
مثل الذين كفروا بربهم أعمالهم كرماد
اشتدت به الريح في يوم عاصف لا
يقدرون مما كسبوا على شيء ذلك هو
الضلل البعيد ﴿١٨﴾
ألم تر أن الله خلق السموت والأرض بالحق
إن يشأ يذهبكم ويأت بخلق جديد ﴿١٩﴾
وما ذلك على الله بعزيز ﴿٢٠﴾
وبرزوا لله جميعا فقال الضعفؤا للذين
استكبروا إنا كنا لكم تبعا فهل أنتم مغنون عنا
من عذاب الله من شيء قالوا لو هدىنا الله
لهدينكم سوآء علينا أجزعنا أم صبرنا ما لنا
ع من محيص ﴿٢١﴾

22. And Satan saith, when the matter hath been decided: Lo! Allah promised you a promise of truth; and I promised you, then failed you. And I had no power over you save that I called unto you and ye obeyed me. So blame me not, but blame yourselves. I cannot help you, nor can ye help me. Lo! I disbelieved in that which ye before ascribed to me. Lo! for wrong-doers is a painful doom.

23. And those who believed and did good works are made to enter Gardens underneath which rivers flow, therein abiding by permission of their Lord, their greeting therein: Peace!

24. Seest thou not how Allah coineth a similitude: A goodly saying, as a goodly tree, its root set firm, its branches reaching into heaven,

25. Giving its fruit at every season by permission of its Lord? Allah coineth the similitudes for mankind in order that they may reflect.

26. And the similitude of a bad saying is as a bad tree, uprooted from upon the earth, possessing no stability.

27. Allah confirmeth those who believe by a firm saying in the life of the world and in the Hereafter, and Allah sendeth wrong-doers astray. And Allah doth what He will.

28. Hast thou not seen those who gave the grace of Allah in exchange for thanklessness and led their people down to the Abode of Loss,

29. (Even to) hell? They are exposed thereto. A hapless end!

وَقَالَ الشَّيْطٰنُ لَمَّا قُضِيَ الْاَمْرُ اِنَّ اللّٰهَ وَعَدَكُمْ
وَعْدَ الْحَقِّ وَوَعَدْتُّكُمْ فَاَخْلَفْتُكُمْ وَمَا كَانَ لِيَ
عَلَيْكُمْ مِّنْ سُلْطٰنٍ اِلَّاۤ اَنْ دَعَوْتُكُمْ فَاسْتَجَبْتُمْ
لِيْ فَلَا تَلُوْمُوْنِيْ وَلُوْمُوْۤا اَنْفُسَكُمْ مَاۤ اَنَا بِمُصْرِخِكُمْ
وَمَاۤ اَنْتُمْ بِمُصْرِخِيَّ اِنِّيْ كَفَرْتُ بِمَاۤ
اَشْرَكْتُمُوْنِ مِنْ قَبْلُ اِنَّ الظّٰلِمِيْنَ لَهُمْ
عَذَابٌ اَلِيْمٌ ﴿٢٢﴾
وَاُدْخِلَ الَّذِيْنَ اٰمَنُوْا وَعَمِلُوا الصّٰلِحٰتِ جَنّٰتٍ
تَجْرِيْ مِنْ تَحْتِهَا الْاَنْهٰرُ خٰلِدِيْنَ فِيْهَا بِاِذْنِ
رَبِّهِمْ تَحِيَّتُهُمْ فِيْهَا سَلٰمٌ ﴿٢٣﴾
اَلَمْ تَرَ كَيْفَ ضَرَبَ اللّٰهُ مَثَلًا كَلِمَةً طَيِّبَةً كَشَجَرَةٍ
طَيِّبَةٍ اَصْلُهَا ثَابِتٌ وَّفَرْعُهَا فِي السَّمَآءِ ﴿٢٤﴾
تُؤْتِيْۤ اُكُلَهَا كُلَّ حِيْنٍۢ بِاِذْنِ رَبِّهَا وَيَضْرِبُ اللّٰهُ
الْاَمْثَالَ لِلنَّاسِ لَعَلَّهُمْ يَتَذَكَّرُوْنَ ﴿٢٥﴾
وَمَثَلُ كَلِمَةٍ خَبِيْثَةٍ كَشَجَرَةٍ خَبِيْثَةِ اِجْتُثَّتْ
مِنْ فَوْقِ الْاَرْضِ مَا لَهَا مِنْ قَرَارٍ ﴿٢٦﴾
يُثَبِّتُ اللّٰهُ الَّذِيْنَ اٰمَنُوْا بِالْقَوْلِ الثَّابِتِ فِي الْحَيٰوةِ
الدُّنْيَا وَفِي الْاٰخِرَةِ وَيُضِلُّ اللّٰهُ الظّٰلِمِيْنَ وَ
يَفْعَلُ اللّٰهُ مَا يَشَآءُ ﴿٢٧﴾ ع
اَلَمْ تَرَ اِلَى الَّذِيْنَ بَدَّلُوْا نِعْمَتَ اللّٰهِ كُفْرًا وَّ
اَحَلُّوْا قَوْمَهُمْ دَارَ الْبَوَارِ ﴿٢٨﴾
جَهَنَّمَ يَصْلَوْنَهَا وَبِئْسَ الْقَرَارُ ﴿٢٩﴾

30. And they set up rivals to Allah that they may mislead (men) from His way. Say: Enjoy life (while ye may) for lo! your journey's end will be the Fire.

31. Tell My bondmen who believe to establish worship and spend of that which We have given them, secretly and publicly, before a day cometh wherein there will be neither traffick nor befriending.

32. Allah is He Who created the heavens and the earth, and causeth water to descend from the sky, thereby producing fruits as food for you, and maketh the ships to be of service unto you, that they may run upon the sea at His command, and hath made of service unto you the rivers;

33. And maketh the sun and the moon, constant in their courses, to be of service unto you, and hath made of service unto you the night and the day.

34. And He giveth you of all ye ask of Him, and if ye would count the bounty of Allah ye cannot reckon it. Lo! man is verily a wrong-doer, an ingrate.

35.. And when Abraham said: My Lord! Make safe this territory, and preserve me and my sons from serving idols.

36. My Lord! Lo! they have led many of mankind astray. But whoso followeth me, he verily is of me. And whoso disobeyeth me—Still Thou art Forgiving, Merciful.

37. Our Lord: Lo! I have settled some of my posterity in an uncultivable valley near unto Thy holy House,[1] our Lord! that they may establish proper worship; so incline some hearts of men that they may yearn toward them, and provide Thou them with fruits in order that they may be thankful.

1 The valley of Mecca.

وَجَعَلُوا لِلّٰهِ اَنْدَادًا لِّيُضِلُّوْا عَنْ سَبِيْلِهٖ ۭ قُلْ
تَمَتَّعُوْا فَاِنَّ مَصِيْرَكُمْ اِلَى النَّارِ (٣٠)
قُلْ لِّعِبَادِيَ الَّذِيْنَ اٰمَنُوْا يُقِيْمُوا الصَّلٰوةَ وَيُنْفِقُوْا
مِمَّا رَزَقْنٰهُمْ سِرًّا وَّعَلَانِيَةً مِّنْ قَبْلِ اَنْ يَّاْتِيَ
يَوْمٌ لَّا بَيْعٌ فِيْهِ وَلَا خِلٰلٌ (٣١)
اَللّٰهُ الَّذِيْ خَلَقَ السَّمٰوٰتِ وَالْاَرْضَ وَاَنْزَلَ مِنَ
السَّمَاۤءِ مَاۤءً فَاَخْرَجَ بِهٖ مِنَ الثَّمَرٰتِ رِزْقًا لَّكُمْ ۚ
وَسَخَّرَ لَكُمُ الْفُلْكَ لِتَجْرِيَ فِي الْبَحْرِ بِاَمْرِهٖ ۚ وَ
سَخَّرَ لَكُمُ الْاَنْهٰرَ (٣٢)
وَسَخَّرَ لَكُمُ الشَّمْسَ وَالْقَمَرَ دَاۤىِٕبَيْنِ ۚ وَسَخَّرَ لَكُمُ
الَّيْلَ وَالنَّهَارَ (٣٣)
وَاٰتٰىكُمْ مِّنْ كُلِّ مَا سَاَلْتُمُوْهُ ۭ وَاِنْ تَعُدُّوْا نِعْمَتَ
ع اللّٰهِ لَا تُحْصُوْهَا ۭ اِنَّ الْاِنْسَانَ لَظَلُوْمٌ كَفَّارٌ (٣٤)
وَاِذْ قَالَ اِبْرٰهِيْمُ رَبِّ اجْعَلْ هٰذَا الْبَلَدَ اٰمِنًا
وَّاجْنُبْنِيْ وَبَنِيَّ اَنْ نَّعْبُدَ الْاَصْنَامَ (٣٥)
رَبِّ اِنَّهُنَّ اَضْلَلْنَ كَثِيْرًا مِّنَ النَّاسِ ۚ فَمَنْ تَبِعَنِيْ
فَاِنَّهٗ مِنِّيْ ۚ وَمَنْ عَصَانِيْ فَاِنَّكَ غَفُوْرٌ رَّحِيْمٌ (٣٦)
رَبَّنَآ اِنِّيْٓ اَسْكَنْتُ مِنْ ذُرِّيَّتِيْ بِوَادٍ غَيْرِ ذِيْ
زَرْعٍ عِنْدَ بَيْتِكَ الْمُحَرَّمِ ۙ رَبَّنَا لِيُقِيْمُوا
الصَّلٰوةَ فَاجْعَلْ اَفْـِٕدَةً مِّنَ النَّاسِ تَهْوِيْٓ
اِلَيْهِمْ وَارْزُقْهُمْ مِّنَ الثَّمَرٰتِ لَعَلَّهُمْ
يَشْكُرُوْنَ (٣٧)

38. Our Lord! Lo! Thou knowest that which we hide and that which we proclaim. Nothing in the earth or in the heaven is hidden from Allah.

ربنا انك تعلم ما نخفي وما نعلن ۗ وما يخفى على
الله من شيء في الارض ولا في السماء ﴿٣٨﴾

39. Praise be to Allah Who hath given me, in my old age, Ishmael and Isaac! Lo! my Lord is indeed the Hearer of Prayer.

الحمد لله الذي وهب لي على الكبر اسمعيل
واسحق ۗ ان ربي لسميع الدعاء ﴿٣٩﴾

40. My Lord! Make me to establish proper worship, and some of my posterity (also); our Lord! and accept the prayer.

رب اجعلني مقيم الصلوة ومن ذريتي ۖ ربنا
وتقبل دعاء ﴿٤٠﴾

41. Our Lord! Forgive me and my parents and believers on the day when the account is cast.

ربنا اغفر لي ولوالدي وللمؤمنين يوم يقوم
ع ٦ ١٨ الحساب ﴿٤١﴾

42. Deem not that Allah is unaware of what the wicked do. He but giveth them a respite till a day when eyes will stare (in terror),

ولا تحسبن الله غافلا عما يعمل الظلمون ۗ انما
يؤخرهم ليوم تشخص فيه الابصار ﴿٤٢﴾

43. As they come hurrying on in fear, their heads upraised, their gaze returning not to them, and their hearts as air.

مهطعين مقنعي رءوسهم لا يرتد اليهم
طرفهم ۖ وافدتهم هواء ﴿٤٣﴾

44. And warn mankind of a day when the doom will come upon them, and those who did wrong will say: Our Lord! Reprieve us for a little while. We will obey Thy call and will follow the messengers. (It will be answered): Did ye not swear before that there would be no end for you?

وانذر الناس يوم ياتيهم العذاب فيقول
الذين ظلموا ربنا اخرنا الى اجل قريب ۙ نجب
دعوتك ونتبع الرسل ۗ اولم تكونوا اقسمتم
من قبل ما لكم من زوال ﴿٤٤﴾

45. And (have ye not) dwelt in the dwellings of those who wronged themselves (of old) and (hath it not) become plain to you how We dealt with them, and made examples for you?

وسكنتم في مسكن الذين ظلموا انفسهم وتبين
لكم كيف فعلنا بهم وضربنا لكم الامثال ﴿٤٥﴾

46. Verily they have plotted their plot, and their plot is with Allah, though their plot were one whereby the mountains should be moved.

وقد مكروا مكرهم وعند الله مكرهم ۗ وان
كان مكرهم لتزول منه الجبال ﴿٤٦﴾

47. So think not that Allah will fail to keep His promise to His messengers. Lo! Allah is Mighty, Able to Requite (the wrong).

فلا تحسبن الله مخلف وعده رسله ۗ ان الله
عزيز ذو انتقام ﴿٤٧﴾

48. On the day when the earth will be changed to other than the earth, and the heavens (also will be changed) and they will come forth unto Allah, the One, the Almighty,

يَوْمَ تُبَدَّلُ الْاَرْضُ غَيْرَ الْاَرْضِ وَالسَّمٰوٰتُ وَبَرَزُوْا
لِلّٰهِ الْوَاحِدِ الْقَهَّارِ ﴿٤٨﴾

49. Thou wilt see the guilty on that day linked together in chains.

وَتَرَى الْمُجْرِمِيْنَ يَوْمَئِذٍ مُّقَرَّنِيْنَ فِي الْاَصْفَادِ ﴿٤٩﴾

50. Their raiment of pitch, and the Fire covering their faces.

سَرَابِيْلُهُمْ مِّنْ قَطِرَانٍ وَّتَغْشٰى وُجُوْهَهُمُ النَّارُ ﴿٥٠﴾

51. That Allah may repay each soul what it hath earned. Lo! Allah is swift at reckoning.

لِيَجْزِيَ اللّٰهُ كُلَّ نَفْسٍ مَّا كَسَبَتْ اِنَّ اللّٰهَ سَرِيْعُ
الْحِسَابِ ﴿٥١﴾

52. This is a clear message for mankind in order that they may be warned thereby, and that they may know that He is only One God, and that men of understanding may take heed.

هٰذَا بَلٰغٌ لِّلنَّاسِ وَلِيُنْذَرُوْا بِهٖ وَلِيَعْلَمُوْٓا اَنَّمَا
هُوَ اِلٰهٌ وَّاحِدٌ وَّلِيَذَّكَّرَ اُولُوا الْاَلْبَابِ ﴿٥٢﴾

Al-Ḥijr (which I take to be a place-name) is so called from vv. 80-84, where the fate of the dwellers at that place is described. The date of revelation is earlier than that of any of the Meccan Sūrahs which precede it in the arrangement of the Book, though the subject and the tone are similar, which accounts for its position. Nöldeke places it in his middle group of Meccan Sūrahs, that is (as far as one can judge from the inclusions), those revealed after the eighth year and before the third year before the Hijrah, and in so doing confirms the judgment of the best Muslim authorities, though some Muslim authorities would place it among the earliest revelations.

It belongs to the middle group of Meccan Sūrahs.

AL-ḤIJR

Revealed at Mecca

In the name of Allah, the Beneficent, the Merciful.

1. Alif. Lām. Rā.[1] These are verses of the Scripture and a plain Reading.[2]

2. It may be that those who disbelieve wish ardently that they were Muslims.[3]

3. Let them eat and enjoy life, and let (false) hope beguile them. They will come to know!

4. And We destroyed no township but there was a known decree for it.

5. No nation can outstrip its term nor can they lag behind.

6. And they say: O thou unto whom the Reminder is revealed, lo! thou art indeed a madman!

7. Why bringest thou not angels unto us, if thou art of the truthful?

8. We send not down the angels save with the Fact, and in that case (the disbelievers) would not be tolerated.

9. Lo! We, even We, reveal the Reminder, and lo! We verily are its Guardian.

10. We verily sent (messengers) before thee among the factions of the men of old.

11. And never came there unto them a messenger but they did mock him.

12. Thus do We make it traverse the hearts of the guilty:

13. They believe not therein, though the example of the men of old hath gone before.

14. And even if We opened unto them a Gate of Heaven and they kept mounting through it,

15. They would say: Our sight is wrong —nay, but we are folk bewitched.

16. And verily in the heaven We have set mansions of the stars, and We have beautified it for beholders;

17. And We have guarded it from every outcast devil,

اٰياتها ٩٩ (١٥) سُوْرَةُ الْحِجْرِ مَكِّيَّةٌ رُكُوعَاتُهَا ٦

بِسْمِ اللّٰهِ الرَّحْمٰنِ الرَّحِيْمِ

الٓرٰ تِلْكَ اٰيٰتُ الْكِتٰبِ وَقُرْاٰنٍ مُّبِيْنٍ ﴿١﴾

رُبَمَا يَوَدُّ الَّذِيْنَ كَفَرُوْا لَوْ كَانُوْا مُسْلِمِيْنَ ﴿٢﴾

ذَرْهُمْ يَاْكُلُوْا وَيَتَمَتَّعُوْا وَيُلْهِهِمُ الْاَمَلُ فَسَوْفَ يَعْلَمُوْنَ ﴿٣﴾

وَمَاۤ اَهْلَكْنَا مِنْ قَرْيَةٍ اِلَّا وَلَهَا كِتَابٌ مَّعْلُوْمٌ ﴿٤﴾

مَا تَسْبِقُ مِنْ اُمَّةٍ اَجَلَهَا وَمَا يَسْتَاْخِرُوْنَ ﴿٥﴾

وَقَالُوْا يٰۤاَيُّهَا الَّذِيْ نُزِّلَ عَلَيْهِ الذِّكْرُ اِنَّكَ لَمَجْنُوْنٌ ﴿٦﴾

لَوْ مَا تَاْتِيْنَا بِالْمَلٰۤىِٕكَةِ اِنْ كُنْتَ مِنَ الصّٰدِقِيْنَ ﴿٧﴾

مَا نُنَزِّلُ الْمَلٰۤىِٕكَةَ اِلَّا بِالْحَقِّ وَمَا كَانُوْۤا اِذًا مُّنْظَرِيْنَ ﴿٨﴾

اِنَّا نَحْنُ نَزَّلْنَا الذِّكْرَ وَاِنَّا لَهٗ لَحٰفِظُوْنَ ﴿٩﴾

وَلَقَدْ اَرْسَلْنَا مِنْ قَبْلِكَ فِيْ شِيَعِ الْاَوَّلِيْنَ ﴿١٠﴾

وَمَا يَاْتِيْهِمْ مِّنْ رَّسُوْلٍ اِلَّا كَانُوْا بِهٖ يَسْتَهْزِءُوْنَ ﴿١١﴾

كَذٰلِكَ نَسْلُكُهٗ فِيْ قُلُوْبِ الْمُجْرِمِيْنَ ﴿١٢﴾

لَا يُؤْمِنُوْنَ بِهٖ وَقَدْ خَلَتْ سُنَّةُ الْاَوَّلِيْنَ ﴿١٣﴾

وَلَوْ فَتَحْنَا عَلَيْهِمْ بَابًا مِّنَ السَّمَآءِ فَظَلُّوْا فِيْهِ يَعْرُجُوْنَ ﴿١٤﴾

لَقَالُوْۤا اِنَّمَا سُكِّرَتْ اَبْصَارُنَا بَلْ نَحْنُ قَوْمٌ مَّسْحُوْرُوْنَ ﴿١٥﴾

وَلَقَدْ جَعَلْنَا فِي السَّمَآءِ بُرُوْجًا وَّزَيَّنّٰهَا لِلنّٰظِرِيْنَ ﴿١٦﴾

وَحَفِظْنٰهَا مِنْ كُلِّ شَيْطٰنٍ رَّجِيْمٍ ﴿١٧﴾

1 See Sūr. II, v. 1, footnote. 2 Ar. *Qur'ān.* 3 Or "those who have surrendered".

18. Save him who stealeth the hearing, and them doth a clear flame pursue.

إِلَّا مَنِ اسْتَرَقَ السَّمْعَ فَأَتْبَعَهُ شِهَابٌ مُّبِينٌ ﴿١٨﴾

19. And the earth have We spread out, and placed therein firm hills, and caused each seemly thing to grow therein.

وَالْأَرْضَ مَدَدْنَاهَا وَأَلْقَيْنَا فِيهَا رَوَاسِيَ وَأَنبَتْنَا فِيهَا مِن كُلِّ شَيْءٍ مَّوْزُونٍ ﴿١٩﴾

20. And We have given unto you livelihoods therein, and unto those for whom ye provide not.

وَجَعَلْنَا لَكُمْ فِيهَا مَعَايِشَ وَمَن لَّسْتُمْ لَهُ بِرَازِقِينَ ﴿٢٠﴾

21. And there is not a thing but with Us are the stores thereof. And We send it not down save in appointed measure.

وَإِن مِّن شَيْءٍ إِلَّا عِندَنَا خَزَائِنُهُ وَمَا نُنَزِّلُهُ إِلَّا بِقَدَرٍ مَّعْلُومٍ ﴿٢١﴾

22. And We send the winds fertilising, and cause water to descend from the sky, and give it you to drink. It is not ye who are the holders of the store thereof.

وَأَرْسَلْنَا الرِّيَاحَ لَوَاقِحَ فَأَنزَلْنَا مِنَ السَّمَاءِ مَاءً فَأَسْقَيْنَاكُمُوهُ وَمَا أَنتُمْ لَهُ بِخَازِنِينَ ﴿٢٢﴾

23. Lo! and it is We, even We, Who quicken and give death, and We are the Inheritor.

وَإِنَّا لَنَحْنُ نُحْيِي وَنُمِيتُ وَنَحْنُ الْوَارِثُونَ ﴿٢٣﴾

24. And verily We know the eager among you and verily We know the laggards.

وَلَقَدْ عَلِمْنَا الْمُسْتَقْدِمِينَ مِنكُمْ وَلَقَدْ عَلِمْنَا الْمُسْتَأْخِرِينَ ﴿٢٤﴾

25. Lo! thy Lord will gather them together. Lo! He is Wise, Aware.

وَإِنَّ رَبَّكَ هُوَ يَحْشُرُهُمْ إِنَّهُ حَكِيمٌ عَلِيمٌ ﴿٢٥﴾ ع ٢

26. Verily We created man of potter's clay of black mud altered,

وَلَقَدْ خَلَقْنَا الْإِنسَانَ مِن صَلْصَالٍ مِّنْ حَمَإٍ مَّسْنُونٍ ﴿٢٦﴾

27. And the Jinn did We create aforetime of essential fire.

وَالْجَانَّ خَلَقْنَاهُ مِن قَبْلُ مِن نَّارِ السَّمُومِ ﴿٢٧﴾

28. And (remember) when thy Lord said unto the angels: Lo! I am creating a mortal out of potter's clay of black mud altered.

وَإِذْ قَالَ رَبُّكَ لِلْمَلَائِكَةِ إِنِّي خَالِقٌ بَشَرًا مِّن صَلْصَالٍ مِّنْ حَمَإٍ مَّسْنُونٍ ﴿٢٨﴾

29. So, when I have made him and have breathed unto him of My spirit, do ye fall down, prostrating yourselves unto him.

فَإِذَا سَوَّيْتُهُ وَنَفَخْتُ فِيهِ مِن رُّوحِي فَقَعُوا لَهُ سَاجِدِينَ ﴿٢٩﴾

30. So the angels fell prostrate, all of them together

فَسَجَدَ الْمَلَائِكَةُ كُلُّهُمْ أَجْمَعُونَ ﴿٣٠﴾

31. Save Iblīs. He refused to be among the prostrate.

إِلَّا إِبْلِيسَ أَبَىٰ أَن يَكُونَ مَعَ السَّاجِدِينَ ﴿٣١﴾

32. He said: O Iblîs! What aileth thee that thou art not among the prostrate?

33. He said: Why should I prostrate myself unto a mortal whom Thou hast created out of potter's clay of black mud altered?

34. He said: Then go thou forth from hence, for verily thou art outcast,

35. And lo! the curse shall be upon thee till the Day of Judgement.

36. He said: My Lord! Reprieve me till the Day when they are raised.

37. He said: Then lo! thou art of those reprieved

38. Till an appointed time.

39. He said: My Lord! Because Thou has sent me astray, I verily shall adorn the path of error for them in the earth, and shall mislead them every one,

40. Save such of them as are Thy perfectly devoted slaves.

41. He said: This is a right course incumbent upon Me:

42. Lo! as for My slaves, thou hast no power over any of them save such of the froward as follow thee,

43. And lo! for all such, hell will be the promised place.

44. It hath seven gates, and each gate hath an appointed portion.

45. Lo! those who ward off (evil) are among gardens and watersprings.

46. (And it is said unto them): Enter them in peace, secure.

47. And We remove whatever rancour may be in their breasts. As brethren, face to face, (they rest) on couches raised.

48. Toil cometh not unto them there, nor will they be expelled from thence.

49. Announce, (O Muhammad), unto My slaves that verily I am the Forgiving, the Merciful,

قَالَ يٰٓاِبْلِيْسُ مَا لَكَ اَلَّا تَكُوْنَ مَعَ السّٰجِدِيْنَ ٣٢

قَالَ لَمْ اَكُنْ لِّاَسْجُدَ لِبَشَرٍ خَلَقْتَهٗ مِنْ صَلْصَالٍ

مِّنْ حَمَاٍ مَّسْنُوْنٍ ٣٣

قَالَ فَاخْرُجْ مِنْهَا فَاِنَّكَ رَجِيْمٌ ٣٤

وَّاِنَّ عَلَيْكَ اللَّعْنَةَ اِلٰى يَوْمِ الدِّيْنِ ٣٥

قَالَ رَبِّ فَاَنْظِرْنِيْٓ اِلٰى يَوْمِ يُبْعَثُوْنَ ٣٦

قَالَ فَاِنَّكَ مِنَ الْمُنْظَرِيْنَ ٣٧

اِلٰى يَوْمِ الْوَقْتِ الْمَعْلُوْمِ ٣٨

قَالَ رَبِّ بِمَآ اَغْوَيْتَنِيْ لَاُزَيِّنَنَّ لَهُمْ فِي الْاَرْضِ

وَلَاُغْوِيَنَّهُمْ اَجْمَعِيْنَ ٣٩

اِلَّا عِبَادَكَ مِنْهُمُ الْمُخْلَصِيْنَ ٤٠

قَالَ هٰذَا صِرَاطٌ عَلَيَّ مُسْتَقِيْمٌ ٤١

اِنَّ عِبَادِيْ لَيْسَ لَكَ عَلَيْهِمْ سُلْطٰنٌ اِلَّا مَنِ

اتَّبَعَكَ مِنَ الْغٰوِيْنَ ٤٢

وَاِنَّ جَهَنَّمَ لَمَوْعِدُهُمْ اَجْمَعِيْنَ ٤٣

لَهَا سَبْعَةُ اَبْوَابٍ لِكُلِّ بَابٍ مِّنْهُمْ جُزْءٌ مَّقْسُوْمٌ ٤٤ ع ٣

اِنَّ الْمُتَّقِيْنَ فِيْ جَنّٰتٍ وَّعُيُوْنٍ ٤٥

اُدْخُلُوْهَا بِسَلٰمٍ اٰمِنِيْنَ ٤٦

وَنَزَعْنَا مَا فِيْ صُدُوْرِهِمْ مِّنْ غِلٍّ اِخْوَانًا عَلٰى

سُرُرٍ مُّتَقٰبِلِيْنَ ٤٧

لَا يَمَسُّهُمْ فِيْهَا نَصَبٌ وَّمَا هُمْ مِّنْهَا بِمُخْرَجِيْنَ ٤٨

نَبِّئْ عِبَادِيْٓ اَنِّيْٓ اَنَا الْغَفُوْرُ الرَّحِيْمُ ٤٩

50. And that My doom is the dolorous doom.

51. And tell them of Abraham's guests,

52. (How) when they came in unto him, and said: Peace. He said: Lo! we are afraid of you.

53. They said: Be not afraid! Lo! we bring thee good tidings of a boy possessing wisdom.

54. He said: Bring ye me good tidings (of a son) when old age hath overtaken me? Of what then can ye bring good tidings?

55. They said: We bring thee good tidings in truth. So be not thou of the despairing.

56. He said: And who despaireth of the mercy of his Lord save those who are astray?

57. He said: And afterward what is your business, O ye messengers (of Allah) ?

58. They said: We have been sent unto a guilty folk,

59. (All) save the family of Lot. Them we shall deliver everyone,

60. Except his wife, of whom We had decreed that she should be of those who stay behind.

61. And when the messengers came unto the family of Lot,

62. He said: Lo! ye are folk unknown (to me).

63. They said: Nay, but we bring thee that concerning which they keep disputing,

64. And bring thee the Truth, and lo! we are truth-tellers.

65. So travel with thy household in a portion of the night, and follow thou their backs. Let none of you turn round, but go whither ye are commanded.

66. And We made plain the case to him, that the root of them (who did wrong) was to be cut at early morn.

67. And the people of the city came, rejoicing at the news (of new arrivals).

68. He said: Lo! they are my guests. Affront me not!

69. And keep your duty to Allah, and shame me not!

وَأَنَّ عَذَابِي هُوَ الْعَذَابُ الْأَلِيمُ ٥٠

وَنَبِّئْهُمْ عَنْ ضَيْفِ إِبْرَٰهِيمَ ٥١

إِذْ دَخَلُوا عَلَيْهِ فَقَالُوا سَلَٰمًا قَالَ إِنَّا مِنْكُمْ وَجِلُونَ ٥٢

قَالُوا لَا تَوْجَلْ إِنَّا نُبَشِّرُكَ بِغُلَٰمٍ عَلِيمٍ ٥٣

قَالَ أَبَشَّرْتُمُونِي عَلَىٰ أَنْ مَسَّنِيَ الْكِبَرُ فَبِمَ تُبَشِّرُونَ ٥٤

قَالُوا بَشَّرْنَٰكَ بِالْحَقِّ فَلَا تَكُنْ مِنَ الْقَٰنِطِينَ ٥٥

قَالَ وَمَنْ يَقْنَطُ مِنْ رَحْمَةِ رَبِّهِ إِلَّا الضَّالُّونَ ٥٦

قَالَ فَمَا خَطْبُكُمْ أَيُّهَا الْمُرْسَلُونَ ٥٧

قَالُوا إِنَّا أُرْسِلْنَا إِلَىٰ قَوْمٍ مُجْرِمِينَ ٥٨

إِلَّا آلَ لُوطٍ إِنَّا لَمُنَجُّوهُمْ أَجْمَعِينَ ٥٩

إِلَّا امْرَأَتَهُ قَدَّرْنَا إِنَّهَا لَمِنَ الْغَٰبِرِينَ ٦٠

فَلَمَّا جَاءَ آلَ لُوطٍ الْمُرْسَلُونَ ٦١

قَالَ إِنَّكُمْ قَوْمٌ مُنْكَرُونَ ٦٢

قَالُوا بَلْ جِئْنَٰكَ بِمَا كَانُوا فِيهِ يَمْتَرُونَ ٦٣

وَأَتَيْنَٰكَ بِالْحَقِّ وَإِنَّا لَصَٰدِقُونَ ٦٤

فَأَسْرِ بِأَهْلِكَ بِقِطْعٍ مِنَ الَّيْلِ وَاتَّبِعْ أَدْبَٰرَهُمْ وَلَا
يَلْتَفِتْ مِنْكُمْ أَحَدٌ وَامْضُوا حَيْثُ تُؤْمَرُونَ ٦٥

وَقَضَيْنَا إِلَيْهِ ذَٰلِكَ الْأَمْرَ أَنَّ دَابِرَ هَٰؤُلَاءِ مَقْطُوعٌ
مُصْبِحِينَ ٦٦

وَجَاءَ أَهْلُ الْمَدِينَةِ يَسْتَبْشِرُونَ ٦٧

قَالَ إِنَّ هَٰؤُلَاءِ ضَيْفِي فَلَا تَفْضَحُونِ ٦٨

وَاتَّقُوا اللَّهَ وَلَا تُخْزُونِ ٦٩

70. They said: Have we not forbidden you from (entertaining) anyone?

قَالُوٓا أَوَلَمْ نَنْهَكَ عَنِ الْعٰلَمِينَ ﴿٧٠﴾

71. He said: Here are my daughters, if ye must be doing (so).

قَالَ هٰٓؤُلَآءِ بَنٰتِىٓ إِن كُنتُمْ فٰعِلِينَ ﴿٧١﴾

72. By thy life (O Muhammad) they moved blindly in the frenzy of approaching death.

لَعَمْرُكَ إِنَّهُمْ لَفِى سَكْرَتِهِمْ يَعْمَهُونَ ﴿٧٢﴾

73. Then the (Awful) Cry overtook them at the sunrise.

فَأَخَذَتْهُمُ الصَّيْحَةُ مُشْرِقِينَ ﴿٧٣﴾

74. And We utterly confounded them, and We rained upon them stones of heated clay.

فَجَعَلْنَا عَالِيَهَا سَافِلَهَا وَأَمْطَرْنَا عَلَيْهِمْ حِجَارَةً
مِّن سِجِّيلٍ ﴿٧٤﴾

75. Lo! therein verily are portents for those who read the signs.

إِنَّ فِى ذٰلِكَ لَاٰيٰتٍ لِّلْمُتَوَسِّمِينَ ﴿٧٥﴾

76. And lo! it is upon a road still uneffaced.

وَإِنَّهَا لَبِسَبِيلٍ مُّقِيمٍ ﴿٧٦﴾

77. Lo! therein is indeed a portent for believers.

إِنَّ فِى ذٰلِكَ لَاٰيَةً لِّلْمُؤْمِنِينَ ﴿٧٧﴾

78. And the dwellers in the wood [1] indeed were evil-doers.

وَإِن كَانَ أَصْحٰبُ الْأَيْكَةِ لَظٰلِمِينَ ﴿٧٨﴾

79. So We took vengeance on them; and lo! they both are on a high road plain to see.

فَانتَقَمْنَا مِنْهُمْ وَإِنَّهُمَا لَبِإِمَامٍ مُّبِينٍ ﴿٧٩﴾

80. And the dwellers in Al-Ḥijr indeed denied (Our) messengers.

وَلَقَدْ كَذَّبَ أَصْحٰبُ الْحِجْرِ الْمُرْسَلِينَ ﴿٨٠﴾

81. And We gave them Our revelations, but they were averse to them.

وَاٰتَيْنٰهُمْ اٰيٰتِنَا فَكَانُوا عَنْهَا مُعْرِضِينَ ﴿٨١﴾

82. And they used to hew out dwellings from the hills, (wherein they dwelt) secure.

وَكَانُوا يَنْحِتُونَ مِنَ الْجِبَالِ بُيُوتًا اٰمِنِينَ ﴿٨٢﴾

83. But the (Awful) Cry overtook them at the morning hour.

فَأَخَذَتْهُمُ الصَّيْحَةُ مُصْبِحِينَ ﴿٨٣﴾

84. And that which they were wont to count as gain availed them not.

فَمَآ أَغْنٰى عَنْهُم مَّا كَانُوا يَكْسِبُونَ ﴿٨٤﴾

85. We created not the heavens and the earth and all that is between them save with truth, and lo! the Hour is surely coming. So forgive, O Muhammad, with a gracious forgiveness.

وَمَا خَلَقْنَا السَّمٰوٰتِ وَالْأَرْضَ وَمَا بَيْنَهُمَآ إِلَّا
بِالْحَقِّ وَإِنَّ السَّاعَةَ لَاٰتِيَةٌ فَاصْفَحِ الصَّفْحَ
الْجَمِيلَ ﴿٨٥﴾

86. Lo! Thy Lord! He is the All-Wise Creator.

إِنَّ رَبَّكَ هُوَ الْخَلّٰقُ الْعَلِيمُ ﴿٨٦﴾

87. We have given thee seven of the oft-repeated (verses)[2] and the great Qur'ān.

وَلَقَدْ اٰتَيْنٰكَ سَبْعًا مِّنَ الْمَثَانِى وَالْقُرْاٰنَ
الْعَظِيمَ ﴿٨٧﴾

1 Another name for Midian.
2 According to a strong tradition, the reference is to Sûr. I, which consists of seven verses and forms a part of every Muslim prayer.

88. Strain not thine eyes toward that which We cause some wedded pairs among them to enjoy, and be not grieved on their account, and lower thy wing (in tenderness) for the believers.

لَا تَمُدَّنَّ عَيْنَيْكَ إِلَىٰ مَا مَتَّعْنَا بِهِۦٓ أَزْوَٰجًا مِّنْهُمْ
وَلَا تَحْزَنْ عَلَيْهِمْ وَٱخْفِضْ جَنَاحَكَ لِلْمُؤْمِنِينَ ٨٨

89. And say: Lo! I, even I, am a plain warner,

وَقُلْ إِنِّىٓ أَنَا ٱلنَّذِيرُ ٱلْمُبِينُ ٨٩

90. Such as We send down for those who make division,

كَمَآ أَنزَلْنَا عَلَى ٱلْمُقْتَسِمِينَ ٩٠

91. Those who break the Qur'ān into parts.

ٱلَّذِينَ جَعَلُوا۟ ٱلْقُرْءَانَ عِضِينَ ٩١

92. Them, by thy Lord, We shall question, every one,

فَوَرَبِّكَ لَنَسْـَٔلَنَّهُمْ أَجْمَعِينَ ٩٢

93. Of what they used to do.

عَمَّا كَانُوا۟ يَعْمَلُونَ ٩٣

94. So proclaim that which thou art commanded, and withdraw from the idolaters.

فَٱصْدَعْ بِمَا تُؤْمَرُ وَأَعْرِضْ عَنِ ٱلْمُشْرِكِينَ ٩٤

95. Lo! We defend thee from the scoffers,

إِنَّا كَفَيْنَٰكَ ٱلْمُسْتَهْزِءِينَ ٩٥

96. Who set some other god along with Allah. But they will come to know.

ٱلَّذِينَ يَجْعَلُونَ مَعَ ٱللَّهِ إِلَٰهًا ءَاخَرَ ۚ فَسَوْفَ
يَعْلَمُونَ ٩٦

97. Well know We that thy bosom is at times oppressed by what they say,

وَلَقَدْ نَعْلَمُ أَنَّكَ يَضِيقُ صَدْرُكَ بِمَا يَقُولُونَ ٩٧

98. But hymn the praise of thy Lord, and be of those who make prostration (unto Him),

فَسَبِّحْ بِحَمْدِ رَبِّكَ وَكُن مِّنَ ٱلسَّٰجِدِينَ ٩٨

99. And serve thy Lord till the inevitable [1] cometh unto thee.

وَٱعْبُدْ رَبَّكَ حَتَّىٰ يَأْتِيَكَ ٱلْيَقِينُ ٩٩

1 *i.e.* death.

An-Naḥl, "The Bee", takes its name from v. 68, where the activities of the Bee are mentioned as a type of duty and of usefulness. It calls attention to God's providence for creation, and to His guidance to mankind as a necessary part of it, and warns disbelievers in that guidance of a folly in rejecting it as great as would be the rejection of food and drink. The Sūrah is ascribed to the last Meccan group, though some ancient authorities regard the ascription as valid only for vv. 1—40, and consider the whole latter portion as revealed at Al-Madînah. The only verse in the Sūrah which is self-evidently of Madînan revelation is v. 110, where the fugitives from persecution are said to have fought; for in the Meccan period fighting was unlawful for the Muslims, though many of them fled from persecution, taking refuge in Abyssinia.

A late Meccan Sūrah, with the exception of v. 110, which must have been revealed at Al-Madînah not earlier than the year 2 A.H., and possibly many other verses toward the end.

THE BEE

Revealed at Mecca

In the name of Allah, the Beneficent, the Merciful.

1. The commandment of Allah will come to pass, so seek not ye to hasten it. Glorified and Exalted be He above all that they associate (with Him).

2. He sendeth down the angels with the Spirit of His command unto whom He will of His bondmen, (saying), Warn mankind that there is no God save Me, so keep your duty unto Me.

3. He hath created the heavens and the earth with truth. High be He exalted above all that they associate (with Him)!

4. He hath created man from a drop of fluid, yet behold! he is an open opponent.

5. And the cattle hath He created, whence ye have warm clothing and uses, and whereof ye eat;

6. And wherein is beauty for you, when ye bring them home, and when ye take them out to pasture.

7. And they bear your loads for you unto a land ye could not reach save with great trouble to yourselves. Lo! your Lord is Full of Pity, Merciful:

8. And horses and mules and asses (hath He created) that ye may ride them, and for ornament. And He createth that which ye know not.

9. And Allah's is the direction of the way, and some (roads) go not straight. And had He willed He would have led you all aright.

10. He it is Who sendeth down water from the sky, whence ye have drink, and whence are trees on which ye send your beasts to pasture.[1]

اٰيَاتُهَا ١٢٨ (١٦) سُوْرَةُ النَّحْلِ مَكِّيَّةٌ رُكُوْعَاتُهَا ١٦

بِسْمِ اللّٰهِ الرَّحْمٰنِ الرَّحِيْمِ

اَتٰۤى اَمْرُ اللّٰهِ فَلَا تَسْتَعْجِلُوْهُ ؕ سُبْحٰنَهٗ وَتَعٰلٰى عَمَّا
يُشْرِكُوْنَ (١)
يُنَزِّلُ الْمَلٰٓئِكَةَ بِالرُّوْحِ مِنْ اَمْرِهٖ عَلٰى مَنْ
يَّشَآءُ مِنْ عِبَادِهٖۤ اَنْ اَنْذِرُوْۤا اَنَّهٗ لَاۤ اِلٰهَ اِلَّاۤ اَنَا
فَاتَّقُوْنِ (٢)
خَلَقَ السَّمٰوٰتِ وَالْاَرْضَ بِالْحَقِّ ؕ تَعٰلٰى عَمَّا
يُشْرِكُوْنَ (٣)
خَلَقَ الْاِنْسَانَ مِنْ نُّطْفَةٍ فَاِذَا هُوَ خَصِيْمٌ مُّبِيْنٌ (٤)
وَالْاَنْعَامَ خَلَقَهَا ۚ لَكُمْ فِيْهَا دِفْءٌ وَّمَنَافِعُ وَمِنْهَا
تَاْكُلُوْنَ (٥)
وَلَكُمْ فِيْهَا جَمَالٌ حِيْنَ تُرِيْحُوْنَ وَحِيْنَ تَسْرَحُوْنَ (٦)
وَتَحْمِلُ اَثْقَالَكُمْ اِلٰى بَلَدٍ لَّمْ تَكُوْنُوْا بٰلِغِيْهِ اِلَّا
بِشِقِّ الْاَنْفُسِ ؕ اِنَّ رَبَّكُمْ لَرَءُوْفٌ رَّحِيْمٌ (٧)
وَّالْخَيْلَ وَالْبِغَالَ وَالْحَمِيْرَ لِتَرْكَبُوْهَا وَزِيْنَةً ؕ وَ
يَخْلُقُ مَا لَا تَعْلَمُوْنَ (٨)
وَعَلَى اللّٰهِ قَصْدُ السَّبِيْلِ وَمِنْهَا جَآئِرٌ ؕ وَلَوْ شَآءَ
لَهَدٰىكُمْ اَجْمَعِيْنَ (٩) ع
هُوَ الَّذِيْۤ اَنْزَلَ مِنَ السَّمَآءِ مَآءً لَّكُمْ مِّنْهُ شَرَابٌ
وَّمِنْهُ شَجَرٌ فِيْهِ تُسِيْمُوْنَ (١٠)

1 There being hardly any herbage in Arabia, the cattle eat the leaves of trees and shrub.

11. Therewith He causeth crops to grow for you, and the olive and the date-palm and grapes and all kinds of fruit. Lo! herein is indeed a portent for people who reflect.

12. And he hath constrained the night and the day and the sun and the moon to be of service unto you, and the stars are made subservient by His command. Lo! herein indeed are portents for people who have sense:

13. And whatsoever He hath created for you in the earth of divers hues, lo! therein is indeed a portent for people who take heed.

14. And He it is Who hath constrained the sea to be of service that ye eat fresh meat from thence, and bring forth from thence ornaments which ye wear. And thou seest the ships ploughing it that ye (mankind) may seek of His bounty, and that haply ye may give thanks.

15. And He hath cast into the earth firm hills that it quake not with you, and streams and roads that ye may find a way,

16. And landmarks (too), and by the star they find a way.

17. Is He then Who createth as him who createth not? Will ye not then remember?

18. And if ye would count the favour of Allah ye cannot reckon it. Lo! Allah is indeed Forgiving, Merciful.

19. And Allah knoweth that which ye keep hidden and that which ye proclaim.

20. Those unto whom they cry beside Allah created naught, but are themselves created.

21. (They are) dead, not living. And they know not when they will be raised.

يُنۢبِتُ لَكُمۡ بِهِ الزَّرۡعَ وَالزَّيۡتُوۡنَ وَالنَّخِيۡلَ وَالۡاَعۡنَابَ وَمِنۡ كُلِّ الثَّمَرٰتِؕ اِنَّ فِيۡ ذٰلِكَ لَاٰيَةً لِّقَوۡمٍ يَّتَفَكَّرُوۡنَ ۞

وَسَخَّرَ لَكُمُ الَّيۡلَ وَالنَّهَارَۙ وَالشَّمۡسَ وَالۡقَمَرَؕ وَالنُّجُوۡمُ مُسَخَّرٰتٌۢ بِاَمۡرِهٖؕ اِنَّ فِيۡ ذٰلِكَ لَاٰيٰتٍ لِّقَوۡمٍ يَّعۡقِلُوۡنَ ۞

وَمَا ذَرَاَ لَكُمۡ فِى الۡاَرۡضِ مُخۡتَلِفًا اَلۡوَانُهٗؕ اِنَّ فِيۡ ذٰلِكَ لَاٰيَةً لِّقَوۡمٍ يَّذَّكَّرُوۡنَ ۞

وَهُوَ الَّذِىۡ سَخَّرَ الۡبَحۡرَ لِتَاۡكُلُوۡا مِنۡهُ لَحۡمًا طَرِيًّا وَّتَسۡتَخۡرِجُوۡا مِنۡهُ حِلۡيَةً تَلۡبَسُوۡنَهَاؕ وَتَرَى الۡفُلۡكَ مَوَاخِرَ فِيۡهِ وَلِتَبۡتَغُوۡا مِنۡ فَضۡلِهٖ وَلَعَلَّكُمۡ تَشۡكُرُوۡنَ ۞

وَاَلۡقٰى فِى الۡاَرۡضِ رَوَاسِىَ اَنۡ تَمِيۡدَ بِكُمۡ وَاَنۡهٰرًا وَّسُبُلًا لَّعَلَّكُمۡ تَهۡتَدُوۡنَ ۞

وَعَلٰمٰتٍؕ وَبِالنَّجۡمِ هُمۡ يَهۡتَدُوۡنَ ۞

اَفَمَنۡ يَّخۡلُقُ كَمَنۡ لَّا يَخۡلُقُؕ اَفَلَا تَذَكَّرُوۡنَ ۞

وَاِنۡ تَعُدُّوۡا نِعۡمَةَ اللّٰهِ لَا تُحۡصُوۡهَاؕ اِنَّ اللّٰهَ لَغَفُوۡرٌ رَّحِيۡمٌ ۞

وَاللّٰهُ يَعۡلَمُ مَا تُسِرُّوۡنَ وَمَا تُعۡلِنُوۡنَ ۞

وَالَّذِيۡنَ يَدۡعُوۡنَ مِنۡ دُوۡنِ اللّٰهِ لَا يَخۡلُقُوۡنَ شَيۡئًا وَّهُمۡ يُخۡلَقُوۡنَ ۞

اَمۡوَاتٌ غَيۡرُ اَحۡيَآءٍۚ وَمَا يَشۡعُرُوۡنَۙ اَيَّانَ يُبۡعَثُوۡنَ ۞

22. Your God is One God. But as for those who believe not in the Hereafter their hearts refuse to know, for they are proud.

23. Assuredly Allah knoweth that which they keep hidden and that which they proclaim. Lo! He loveth not the proud.

24. And when it is said unto them: What hath your Lord revealed? they say: (Mere) fables of the men of old,

25. That they may bear their burdens undiminished on the Day of Resurrection, with somewhat of the burdens of those whom they mislead without knowledge. Ah! evil is that which they bear!

26. Those before them plotted, so Allah struck at the foundations of their building, and then the roof fell down upon them from above them, and the doom came on them whence they knew not.

27. Then on the Day of Resurrection He will disgrace them and will say: Where are My partners, for whose sake ye opposed (My Guidance)? Those who have been given knowl dge will say: Disgrace this day and evil are upon the disbelievers,

28. Whom the angels cause to die while they are wronging themselves. Then will they make full submission (saying): We used not to do any wrong. Nay! Surely Allah is Knower of what ye used to do.

29. So enter the gates of hell, to dwell therein for ever. Woeful indeed will be the lodging of the arrogant.

30. And it is said unto those who ward off (evil): What hath your Lord revealed? They say: Good. For those who do good in this wo ld there is a good (reward) and the home of the Hereafter will be better. Pleasant indeed will be the home of those who ward off (evil)—

إِلٰهُكُمْ إِلٰهٌ وَّاحِدٌ فَالَّذِينَ لَا يُؤْمِنُونَ بِالْاٰخِرَةِ
قُلُوبُهُمْ مُّنْكِرَةٌ وَّهُمْ مُّسْتَكْبِرُونَ ﴿٢٢﴾
لَا جَرَمَ أَنَّ اللّٰهَ يَعْلَمُ مَا يُسِرُّونَ وَمَا يُعْلِنُونَ
إِنَّهُ لَا يُحِبُّ الْمُسْتَكْبِرِينَ ﴿٢٣﴾
وَإِذَا قِيلَ لَهُمْ مَّاذَا أَنْزَلَ رَبُّكُمْ قَالُوا أَسَاطِيرُ
الْأَوَّلِينَ ﴿٢٤﴾
لِيَحْمِلُوا أَوْزَارَهُمْ كَامِلَةً يَوْمَ الْقِيٰمَةِ وَمِنْ أَوْزَارِ
الَّذِينَ يُضِلُّونَهُمْ بِغَيْرِ عِلْمٍ أَلَا سَاءَ مَا يَزِرُونَ ﴿٢٥﴾ ع
قَدْ مَكَرَ الَّذِينَ مِنْ قَبْلِهِمْ فَأَتَى اللّٰهُ بُنْيَانَهُمْ مِّنَ
الْقَوَاعِدِ فَخَرَّ عَلَيْهِمُ السَّقْفُ مِنْ فَوْقِهِمْ وَأَتٰىهُمُ
الْعَذَابُ مِنْ حَيْثُ لَا يَشْعُرُونَ ﴿٢٦﴾
ثُمَّ يَوْمَ الْقِيٰمَةِ يُخْزِيهِمْ وَيَقُولُ أَيْنَ شُرَكَاءِيَ
الَّذِينَ كُنْتُمْ تُشَاقُّونَ فِيهِمْ قَالَ الَّذِينَ أُوتُوا
الْعِلْمَ إِنَّ الْخِزْيَ الْيَوْمَ وَالسُّوءَ عَلَى الْكٰفِرِينَ ﴿٢٧﴾
الَّذِينَ تَتَوَفّٰهُمُ الْمَلٰٓئِكَةُ ظَالِمِي أَنْفُسِهِمْ فَأَلْقَوُا
السَّلَمَ مَا كُنَّا نَعْمَلُ مِنْ سُوءٍ بَلٰى إِنَّ اللّٰهَ عَلِيمٌ
بِمَا كُنْتُمْ تَعْمَلُونَ ﴿٢٨﴾
فَادْخُلُوا أَبْوَابَ جَهَنَّمَ خٰلِدِينَ فِيهَا فَلَبِئْسَ
مَثْوَى الْمُتَكَبِّرِينَ ﴿٢٩﴾
وَقِيلَ لِلَّذِينَ اتَّقَوْا مَاذَا أَنْزَلَ رَبُّكُمْ قَالُوا خَيْرًا
لِلَّذِينَ أَحْسَنُوا فِي هٰذِهِ الدُّنْيَا حَسَنَةٌ وَلَدَارُ
الْاٰخِرَةِ خَيْرٌ وَلَنِعْمَ دَارُ الْمُتَّقِينَ ﴿٣٠﴾

31. Gardens of Eden which they enter, underneath which rivers flow, wherein they have what they will. Thus Allah repayeth those who ward off (evil),

32. Those whom the angels cause to die (when they are) good. They say: Peace be unto you! Enter the Garden because of what ye used to do.

33. Await they aught save that the angels should come unto them or thy Lord's command should come to pass? Even so did those before them. Allah wronged them not, but they did wrong themselves,

34. So that the evil of what they did smote them, and that which they used to mock surrounded them.

35. And the idolaters say: Had Allah willed, we had not worshipped aught beside Him, we and our fathers, nor had we forbidden aught without (command from) Him. Even so did those before them. Are the messengers charged with aught save plain conveyance (of the message)?

36. And verily We have raised in every nation a messenger, (proclaiming): Serve Allah and shun false gods. Then some of them (there were) whom Allah guided, and some of them (there were) upon whom error had just hold. Do but travel in the land and see the nature of the consequence for the deniers!

37. Even if thou (O Muhammad) desirest their right guidance, still Allah assuredly will not guide him who misleadeth. Such have no helpers.

38. And they swear by Allah their most binding oaths (that) Allah will not raise up him who dieth. Nay, but it is a promise (binding) upon Him in truth, but most of mankind know not,

جَنّٰتُ عَدْنٍ يَّدْخُلُوْنَهَا تَجْرِيْ مِنْ تَحْتِهَا الْاَنْهٰرُ
لَهُمْ فِيْهَا مَا يَشَآءُوْنَ كَذٰلِكَ يَجْزِي اللّٰهُ الْمُتَّقِيْنَ ﴿٣١﴾
الَّذِيْنَ تَتَوَفّٰىهُمُ الْمَلٰٓئِكَةُ طَيِّبِيْنَ يَقُوْلُوْنَ سَلٰمٌ
عَلَيْكُمُ ادْخُلُوا الْجَنَّةَ بِمَا كُنْتُمْ تَعْمَلُوْنَ ﴿٣٢﴾
هَلْ يَنْظُرُوْنَ اِلَّآ اَنْ تَاْتِيَهُمُ الْمَلٰٓئِكَةُ اَوْ يَاْتِيَ اَمْرُ
رَبِّكَ كَذٰلِكَ فَعَلَ الَّذِيْنَ مِنْ قَبْلِهِمْ وَمَا ظَلَمَهُمُ
اللّٰهُ وَلٰكِنْ كَانُوْٓا اَنْفُسَهُمْ يَظْلِمُوْنَ ﴿٣٣﴾
فَاَصَابَهُمْ سَيِّاٰتُ مَا عَمِلُوْا وَحَاقَ بِهِمْ مَّا كَانُوْا
بِهٖ يَسْتَهْزِءُوْنَ ﴿٣٤﴾ ع
وَقَالَ الَّذِيْنَ اَشْرَكُوْا لَوْ شَآءَ اللّٰهُ مَا عَبَدْنَا مِنْ
دُوْنِهٖ مِنْ شَيْءٍ نَّحْنُ وَلَآ اٰبَآؤُنَا وَلَا حَرَّمْنَا مِنْ
دُوْنِهٖ مِنْ شَيْءٍ كَذٰلِكَ فَعَلَ الَّذِيْنَ مِنْ قَبْلِهِمْ
فَهَلْ عَلَى الرُّسُلِ اِلَّا الْبَلٰغُ الْمُبِيْنُ ﴿٣٥﴾
وَلَقَدْ بَعَثْنَا فِيْ كُلِّ اُمَّةٍ رَّسُوْلًا اَنِ اعْبُدُوا اللّٰهَ
وَاجْتَنِبُوا الطَّاغُوْتَ فَمِنْهُمْ مَّنْ هَدَى اللّٰهُ وَ
مِنْهُمْ مَّنْ حَقَّتْ عَلَيْهِ الضَّلٰلَةُ فَسِيْرُوْا فِي الْاَرْضِ
فَانْظُرُوْا كَيْفَ كَانَ عَاقِبَةُ الْمُكَذِّبِيْنَ ﴿٣٦﴾
اِنْ تَحْرِصْ عَلٰى هُدٰىهُمْ فَاِنَّ اللّٰهَ لَا يَهْدِيْ
مَنْ يُّضِلُّ وَمَا لَهُمْ مِّنْ نّٰصِرِيْنَ ﴿٣٧﴾
وَاَقْسَمُوْا بِاللّٰهِ جَهْدَ اَيْمَانِهِمْ لَا يَبْعَثُ اللّٰهُ مَنْ
يَّمُوْتُ بَلٰى وَعْدًا عَلَيْهِ حَقًّا وَّلٰكِنَّ اَكْثَرَ النَّاسِ
لَا يَعْلَمُوْنَ ﴿٣٨﴾

39. That he may explain unto them that wherein they differ, and that those who disbelieved may know that they were liars.

40. And Our word unto a thing, when We intend it, is only that We say unto it: Be! and it is.

41. And those who became fugitives for the cause of Allah after they had been oppressed, We verily shall give them goodly lodging in the world, and surely the reward of the Hereafter is greater, if they but knew;

42. Such as are steadfast and put their trust in Allah.

43. And We sent not (as Our messengers) before thee other than men whom We inspired—Ask the followers of the Remembrance if ye know not!—

44. With clear proofs and writings; and We have revealed unto thee the Remembrance that thou mayst explain to mankind that which hath been revealed for them, and that haply they may reflect.

45. Are they who plan ill deeds then secure that Allah will not cause the earth to swallow them, or that the doom will not come on them whence they know not?

46. Or that He will not seize them in their going to and fro so that there by no escape for them?

47. Or that He will not seize them with a gradual wasting? Lo! thy Lord is indeed Full of Pity, Merciful.

48. Have they not observed all things that Allah hath created, how their shadows incline to the right and to the left, making prostration unto Allah, and they are lowly?

49. And unto Allah maketh prostration whatsoever is in the heavens and whatsoever is in the earth of living creatures, and the angels (also), and they are not proud.

50. They fear their Lord above them, and do what they are bidden.

لِيُبَيِّنَ لَهُمُ الَّذِى يَخْتَلِفُوْنَ فِيْهِ وَلِيَعْلَمَ الَّذِيْنَ كَفَرُوْۤا اَنَّهُمْ كَانُوْا كَاذِبِيْنَ ۝

اِنَّمَا قَوْلُنَا لِشَىْءٍ اِذَاۤ اَرَدْنٰهُ اَنْ نَّقُوْلَ لَهٗ كُنْ فَيَكُوْنُ ۝

وَالَّذِيْنَ هَاجَرُوْا فِى اللّٰهِ مِنْۢ بَعْدِ مَا ظُلِمُوْا لَنُبَوِّئَنَّهُمْ فِى الدُّنْيَا حَسَنَةً ۖ وَلَاَجْرُ الْاٰخِرَةِ اَكْبَرُ ۘ لَوْ كَانُوْا يَعْلَمُوْنَ ۝

الَّذِيْنَ صَبَرُوْا وَعَلٰى رَبِّهِمْ يَتَوَكَّلُوْنَ ۝

وَمَاۤ اَرْسَلْنَا مِنْ قَبْلِكَ اِلَّا رِجَالًا نُّوْحِيْۤ اِلَيْهِمْ فَسْئَلُوْۤا اَهْلَ الذِّكْرِ اِنْ كُنْتُمْ لَا تَعْلَمُوْنَ ۝

بِالْبَيِّنٰتِ وَالزُّبُرِ ۗ وَاَنْزَلْنَاۤ اِلَيْكَ الذِّكْرَ لِتُبَيِّنَ لِلنَّاسِ مَا نُزِّلَ اِلَيْهِمْ وَلَعَلَّهُمْ يَتَفَكَّرُوْنَ ۝

اَفَاَمِنَ الَّذِيْنَ مَكَرُوا السَّيِّاٰتِ اَنْ يَّخْسِفَ اللّٰهُ بِهِمُ الْاَرْضَ اَوْ يَاْتِيَهُمُ الْعَذَابُ مِنْ حَيْثُ لَا يَشْعُرُوْنَ ۝

اَوْ يَاْخُذَهُمْ فِىْ تَقَلُّبِهِمْ فَمَا هُمْ بِمُعْجِزِيْنَ ۝

اَوْ يَاْخُذَهُمْ عَلٰى تَخَوُّفٍ ۚ فَاِنَّ رَبَّكُمْ لَرَءُوْفٌ رَّحِيْمٌ ۝

اَوَلَمْ يَرَوْا اِلٰى مَا خَلَقَ اللّٰهُ مِنْ شَىْءٍ يَّتَفَيَّؤُا ظِلٰلُهٗ عَنِ الْيَمِيْنِ وَالشَّمَآئِلِ سُجَّدًا لِّلّٰهِ وَهُمْ دٰخِرُوْنَ ۝

وَلِلّٰهِ يَسْجُدُ مَا فِى السَّمٰوٰتِ وَمَا فِى الْاَرْضِ مِنْ دَآبَّةٍ وَّالْمَلٰئِكَةُ وَهُمْ لَا يَسْتَكْبِرُوْنَ ۝

يَخَافُوْنَ رَبَّهُمْ مِّنْ فَوْقِهِمْ وَيَفْعَلُوْنَ مَا يُؤْمَرُوْنَ ۩ ۝

51. Allah hath said: Choose not two gods. There is only One God. So of Me, Me only, be in awe.

52. Unto Him belongeth whatsoever is in the heavens and the earth, and religion is His for ever. Will ye then fear any other than Allah?

53. And whatever of comfort ye enjoy, it is from Allah. Then, when misfortune reacheth you, unto Him ye cry for help.

54. And afterward, when He hath rid you of the misfortune, behold! a set of you attribute partners to their Lord,

55. So as to deny that which We have given them. Then enjoy life (while ye may), for ye will come to know.

56. And they assign a portion of that which We have given them unto what they know not. By Allah! but ye will indeed be asked concerning (all) that ye used to invent.

57. And they assign unto Allah daughters —Be He glorified!—and unto themselves what they desire;

58. When if one of them receiveth tidings of the birth of a female, his face remaineth darkened, and he is wroth inwardly.

59. He hideth himself from the folk because of the evil of that whereof he hath had tidings, (asking himself): Shall he keep it in contempt, or bury it beneath the dust! Verily evil is their judgment.

60. For those who believe not in the Hereafter is an evil similitude, and Allah's is the Sublime Similitude. He is the Mighty, the Wise.

61. If Allah were to take mankind to task for their wrong-doing, he would not leave hereon a living creature, but He reprieveth them to an appointed term, and when their term cometh they cannot put (it) off an hour nor (yet) advance (it).

وَقَالَ اللّٰهُ لَا تَتَّخِذُوْٓا اِلٰهَيْنِ اثْنَيْنِ ۚ اِنَّمَا هُوَ اِلٰهٌ
وَّاحِدٌ ۚ فَاِيَّايَ فَارْهَبُوْنِ ﴿٥١﴾
وَلَهٗ مَا فِي السَّمٰوٰتِ وَالْاَرْضِ وَلَهُ الدِّيْنُ وَاصِبًا ؕ
اَفَغَيْرَ اللّٰهِ تَتَّقُوْنَ ﴿٥٢﴾
وَمَا بِكُمْ مِّنْ نِّعْمَةٍ فَمِنَ اللّٰهِ ثُمَّ اِذَا مَسَّكُمُ
الضُّرُّ فَاِلَيْهِ تَجْئَرُوْنَ ﴿٥٣﴾
ثُمَّ اِذَا كَشَفَ الضُّرَّ عَنْكُمْ اِذَا فَرِيْقٌ مِّنْكُمْ
بِرَبِّهِمْ يُشْرِكُوْنَ ﴿٥٤﴾
لِيَكْفُرُوْا بِمَآ اٰتَيْنٰهُمْ ؕ فَتَمَتَّعُوْا ۫ فَسَوْفَ تَعْلَمُوْنَ ﴿٥٥﴾
وَيَجْعَلُوْنَ لِمَا لَا يَعْلَمُوْنَ نَصِيْبًا مِّمَّا رَزَقْنٰهُمْ ؕ
تَاللّٰهِ لَتُسْـَٔلُنَّ عَمَّا كُنْتُمْ تَفْتَرُوْنَ ﴿٥٦﴾
وَيَجْعَلُوْنَ لِلّٰهِ الْبَنٰتِ سُبْحٰنَهٗ ۙ وَلَهُمْ مَّا يَشْتَهُوْنَ ﴿٥٧﴾
وَاِذَا بُشِّرَ اَحَدُهُمْ بِالْاُنْثٰى ظَلَّ وَجْهُهٗ مُسْوَدًّا
وَّهُوَ كَظِيْمٌ ﴿٥٨﴾
يَتَوَارٰى مِنَ الْقَوْمِ مِنْ سُوْٓءِ مَا بُشِّرَ بِهٖ ؕ اَيُمْسِكُهٗ
عَلٰى هُوْنٍ اَمْ يَدُسُّهٗ فِي التُّرَابِ ؕ اَلَا سَآءَ مَا
يَحْكُمُوْنَ ﴿٥٩﴾
لِلَّذِيْنَ لَا يُؤْمِنُوْنَ بِالْاٰخِرَةِ مَثَلُ السَّوْءِ ۚ وَلِلّٰهِ
ع الْمَثَلُ الْاَعْلٰى ؕ وَهُوَ الْعَزِيْزُ الْحَكِيْمُ ﴿٦٠﴾
وَلَوْ يُؤَاخِذُ اللّٰهُ النَّاسَ بِظُلْمِهِمْ مَّا تَرَكَ عَلَيْهَا
مِنْ دَآبَّةٍ وَّلٰكِنْ يُّؤَخِّرُهُمْ اِلٰٓى اَجَلٍ مُّسَمًّى ۚ فَاِذَا
جَآءَ اَجَلُهُمْ لَا يَسْتَاْخِرُوْنَ سَاعَةً وَّلَا يَسْتَقْدِمُوْنَ ﴿٦١﴾

62. And they assign unto Allah that which they (themselves) dislike, and their tongues expound the lie that the better portion will be theirs. Assuredly theirs will be the Fire, and they will be abandoned.

63. By Allah, We verily sent messengers unto the nations before thee, but the devil made their deeds fair-seeming unto them. So he is their patron this day, and theirs will be a painful doom.

64. And We have revealed the Scripture unto thee only that thou mayst explain unto them that wherein they differ, and (as) a guidance and a mercy for a people who believe.

65. Allah sendeth down water from the sky and therewith reviveth the earth after her death. Lo! herein is indeed a portent for a folk who hear.

66. And lo! in the cattle there is a lesson for you. We give you to drink of that which is in their bellies, from betwixt the refuse and the blood, pure milk palatable to the drinkers.

67. And of the fruits of the date-palm, and grapes, whence ye derive strong drink and (also) good nourishment. Lo! therein, is indeed a portent for people who have sense.

68. And thy Lord inspired the bee, saying: Choose thou habitations in the hills and in the trees and in that which they thatch;

69. Then eat of all fruits, and follow the ways of thy Lord, made smooth (for thee). There cometh forth from their bellies a drink diverse of hues, wherein is healing for mankind. Lo! herein is indeed a portent for people who reflect.

70. And Allah createth you, then causeth you to die, and among you is he who is brought back to the most abject stage of life, so that he knoweth nothing after (having had) knowledge. Lo! Allah is Knower, Powerful.

وَيَجْعَلُونَ لِلّٰهِ مَا يَكْرَهُونَ وَتَصِفُ أَلْسِنَتُهُمُ
الْكَذِبَ أَنَّ لَهُمُ الْحُسْنٰى ۖ لَا جَرَمَ أَنَّ لَهُمُ النَّارَ
وَأَنَّهُمْ مُّفْرَطُونَ ﴿٦٢﴾
تَاللّٰهِ لَقَدْ أَرْسَلْنَا إِلٰى أُمَمٍ مِّنْ قَبْلِكَ فَزَيَّنَ
لَهُمُ الشَّيْطٰنُ أَعْمَالَهُمْ فَهُوَ وَلِيُّهُمُ الْيَوْمَ وَ
لَهُمْ عَذَابٌ أَلِيمٌ ﴿٦٣﴾
وَمَا أَنْزَلْنَا عَلَيْكَ الْكِتٰبَ إِلَّا لِتُبَيِّنَ لَهُمُ الَّذِي
اخْتَلَفُوا فِيهِ ۙ وَهُدًى وَّرَحْمَةً لِّقَوْمٍ يُّؤْمِنُونَ ﴿٦٤﴾
وَاللّٰهُ أَنْزَلَ مِنَ السَّمَآءِ مَآءً فَأَحْيَا بِهِ الْأَرْضَ بَعْدَ
مَوْتِهَا ۚ إِنَّ فِي ذٰلِكَ لَآيَةً لِّقَوْمٍ يَّسْمَعُونَ ﴿٦٥﴾ ع ٨ ١٤
وَإِنَّ لَكُمْ فِي الْأَنْعَامِ لَعِبْرَةً ۖ نُّسْقِيكُمْ مِّمَّا فِي بُطُونِهِ
مِنْ بَيْنِ فَرْثٍ وَّدَمٍ لَّبَنًا خَالِصًا سَآئِغًا لِّلشّٰرِبِينَ ﴿٦٦﴾
وَمِنْ ثَمَرٰتِ النَّخِيلِ وَالْأَعْنَابِ تَتَّخِذُونَ مِنْهُ سَكَرًا
وَّرِزْقًا حَسَنًا ۗ إِنَّ فِي ذٰلِكَ لَآيَةً لِّقَوْمٍ يَّعْقِلُونَ ﴿٦٧﴾
وَأَوْحٰى رَبُّكَ إِلَى النَّحْلِ أَنِ اتَّخِذِي مِنَ الْجِبَالِ
بُيُوتًا وَّمِنَ الشَّجَرِ وَمِمَّا يَعْرِشُونَ ﴿٦٨﴾
ثُمَّ كُلِي مِنْ كُلِّ الثَّمَرٰتِ فَاسْلُكِي سُبُلَ رَبِّكِ
ذُلُلًا ۚ يَخْرُجُ مِنْ بُطُونِهَا شَرَابٌ مُّخْتَلِفٌ أَلْوَانُهُ فِيهِ
شِفَآءٌ لِّلنَّاسِ ۗ إِنَّ فِي ذٰلِكَ لَآيَةً لِّقَوْمٍ يَّتَفَكَّرُونَ ﴿٦٩﴾
وَاللّٰهُ خَلَقَكُمْ ثُمَّ يَتَوَفّٰكُمْ ۚ وَمِنْكُمْ مَّنْ يُّرَدُّ إِلٰى
أَرْذَلِ الْعُمُرِ لِكَيْ لَا يَعْلَمَ بَعْدَ عِلْمٍ شَيْئًا ۗ إِنَّ اللّٰهَ
عَلِيمٌ قَدِيرٌ ﴿٧٠﴾ ع ٩ ١٥

71. And Allah hath favoured some of you above others in provision. Now those who are more favoured will by no means hand over their provision to those (slaves) whom their right hands possess, so that they may be equal with them in respect thereof. Is it then the grace of Allah that they deny?

72. And Allah hath given you wives of your own kind, and hath given you, from your wives, sons and grandsons, and hath made provision of good things for you. Is it then in vanity that they believe and in the grace of Allah that they disbelieve?

73. And they worship beside Allah that which owneth no provision whatsoever for them from the heavens or the earth, nor have they (whom they worship) any power.

74. So coin not similitudes for Allah. Lo! Allah knoweth; ye know not.

75. Allah coineth a similitude: (on the one hand) a (mere) chattel slave, who hath control of nothing, and (on the other hand) one on whom We have bestowed a fair provision from Us, and he spendeth thereof secretly and openly. Are they equal? Praise be to Allah! But most of them know not.

76. And Allah coineth a similitude. Two men, one of them dumb, having control of nothing, and he is a burden on his owner; whithersoever he directeth him to go, he bringeth no good. Is he equal with one who enjoineth justice and followeth a straight path (of conduct)?

77. And unto Allah belongeth the Unseen of the heavens and the earth, and the matter of the Hour (of Doom) is but as a twinkling of the eye, or it is nearer still. Lo! Allah is Able to do all things.

وَاللّٰهُ فَضَّلَ بَعْضَكُمْ عَلٰى بَعْضٍ فِي الرِّزْقِ فَمَا
الَّذِيْنَ فُضِّلُوْا بِرَآدِّيْ رِزْقِهِمْ عَلٰى مَا مَلَكَتْ اَيْمَانُهُمْ
فَهُمْ فِيْهِ سَوَآءٌ اَفَبِنِعْمَةِ اللّٰهِ يَجْحَدُوْنَ ﴿٧١﴾
وَاللّٰهُ جَعَلَ لَكُمْ مِّنْ اَنْفُسِكُمْ اَزْوَاجًا وَّجَعَلَ لَكُمْ
مِّنْ اَزْوَاجِكُمْ بَنِيْنَ وَحَفَدَةً وَّرَزَقَكُمْ مِّنَ
الطَّيِّبٰتِ اَفَبِالْبَاطِلِ يُؤْمِنُوْنَ وَبِنِعْمَتِ اللّٰهِ
هُمْ يَكْفُرُوْنَ ﴿٧٢﴾
وَيَعْبُدُوْنَ مِنْ دُوْنِ اللّٰهِ مَا لَا يَمْلِكُ لَهُمْ رِزْقًا
مِّنَ السَّمٰوٰتِ وَالْاَرْضِ شَيْئًا وَّلَا يَسْتَطِيْعُوْنَ ﴿٧٣﴾
فَلَا تَضْرِبُوْا لِلّٰهِ الْاَمْثَالَ اِنَّ اللّٰهَ يَعْلَمُ وَاَنْتُمْ
لَا تَعْلَمُوْنَ ﴿٧٤﴾
ضَرَبَ اللّٰهُ مَثَلًا عَبْدًا مَّمْلُوْكًا لَّا يَقْدِرُ عَلٰى
شَيْءٍ وَّمَنْ رَّزَقْنٰهُ مِنَّا رِزْقًا حَسَنًا فَهُوَ يُنْفِقُ
مِنْهُ سِرًّا وَّجَهْرًا هَلْ يَسْتَوٗنَ اَلْحَمْدُ لِلّٰهِ بَلْ
اَكْثَرُهُمْ لَا يَعْلَمُوْنَ ﴿٧٥﴾
وَضَرَبَ اللّٰهُ مَثَلًا رَّجُلَيْنِ اَحَدُهُمَآ اَبْكَمُ لَا يَقْدِرُ
عَلٰى شَيْءٍ وَّهُوَ كَلٌّ عَلٰى مَوْلٰىهُ اَيْنَمَا يُوَجِّهْهُّ لَا يَاْتِ
بِخَيْرٍ هَلْ يَسْتَوِيْ هُوَ وَمَنْ يَّاْمُرُ بِالْعَدْلِ وَهُوَ
عَلٰى صِرَاطٍ مُّسْتَقِيْمٍ ﴿٧٦﴾ ع ٦ ١٦
وَلِلّٰهِ غَيْبُ السَّمٰوٰتِ وَالْاَرْضِ وَمَآ اَمْرُ السَّاعَةِ
اِلَّا كَلَمْحِ الْبَصَرِ اَوْ هُوَ اَقْرَبُ اِنَّ اللّٰهَ عَلٰى كُلِّ
شَيْءٍ قَدِيْرٌ ﴿٧٧﴾

78. And Allah brought you forth from the wombs of your mothers knowing nothing, and gave you hearing and sight and hearts that haply ye might give thanks.

وَاللّٰهُ اَخْرَجَكُمْ مِّنْ بُطُوْنِ اُمَّهٰتِكُمْ لَا تَعْلَمُوْنَ
شَيْـًٔا ۙ وَّجَعَلَ لَكُمُ السَّمْعَ وَالْاَبْصَارَ وَالْاَفْـِٕدَةَ ۙ
لَعَلَّكُمْ تَشْكُرُوْنَ ﴿٧٨﴾

79. Have they not seen the birds obedient[1] in mid-air? None holdeth them save Allah. Lo! herein, verily, are portents for a people who believe.

اَلَمْ يَرَوْا اِلَى الطَّيْرِ مُسَخَّرٰتٍ فِيْ جَوِّ السَّمَآءِ ؕ مَا يُمْسِكُهُنَّ
اِلَّا اللّٰهُ ؕ اِنَّ فِيْ ذٰلِكَ لَاٰيٰتٍ لِّقَوْمٍ يُّؤْمِنُوْنَ ﴿٧٩﴾

80. And Allah hath given you in your houses an abode, and hath given you (also), of the hides of cattle, houses[2] which ye find light (to carry) on the day of migration and on the day of pitching camp; and of their wool and their fur and their hair, caparison and comfort for a while.

وَاللّٰهُ جَعَلَ لَكُمْ مِّنْۢ بُيُوْتِكُمْ سَكَنًا وَّجَعَلَ لَكُمْ مِّنْ
جُلُوْدِ الْاَنْعَامِ بُيُوْتًا تَسْتَخِفُّوْنَهَا يَوْمَ ظَعْنِكُمْ وَ
يَوْمَ اِقَامَتِكُمْ ۙ وَمِنْ اَصْوَافِهَا وَاَوْبَارِهَا وَاَشْعَارِهَآ
اَثَاثًا وَّمَتَاعًا اِلٰى حِيْنٍ ﴿٨٠﴾

81. And Allah hath given you, of that which He hath created, shelter from the sun; and hath given you places of refuge in the mountains, and hath given you coats to ward off the heat from you, and coats (of armour) to save you from your own foolhardiness. Thus doth He perfect His favour unto you, in order that ye may surrender (unto Him).

وَاللّٰهُ جَعَلَ لَكُمْ مِّمَّا خَلَقَ ظِلٰلًا وَّجَعَلَ لَكُمْ مِّنَ
الْجِبَالِ اَكْنَانًا وَّجَعَلَ لَكُمْ سَرَابِيْلَ تَقِيْكُمُ
الْحَرَّ وَسَرَابِيْلَ تَقِيْكُمْ بَاْسَكُمْ ؕ كَذٰلِكَ يُتِمُّ
نِعْمَتَهٗ عَلَيْكُمْ لَعَلَّكُمْ تُسْلِمُوْنَ ﴿٨١﴾

82. Then, if they turn away, thy duty (O Muhammad) is but plain conveyance (of the message).

فَاِنْ تَوَلَّوْا فَاِنَّمَا عَلَيْكَ الْبَلٰغُ الْمُبِيْنُ ﴿٨٢﴾

83. They know the favour of Allah and then deny it. Most of them are ingrates.

ع يَعْرِفُوْنَ نِعْمَتَ اللّٰهِ ثُمَّ يُنْكِرُوْنَهَا وَاَكْثَرُهُمُ الْكٰفِرُوْنَ ﴿٨٣﴾

84. And (be think you of) the day when We raise up of every nation a witness, then there is no leave for disbelievers, nor are they allowed to make amends.

وَيَوْمَ نَبْعَثُ مِنْ كُلِّ اُمَّةٍ شَهِيْدًا ثُمَّ لَا يُؤْذَنُ
لِلَّذِيْنَ كَفَرُوْا وَلَا هُمْ يُسْتَعْتَبُوْنَ ﴿٨٤﴾

85. And when those who did wrong behold the doom, it will not be made light for them, nor will they be reprieved.

وَاِذَا رَاَ الَّذِيْنَ ظَلَمُوا الْعَذَابَ فَلَا يُخَفَّفُ عَنْهُمْ
وَلَا هُمْ يُنْظَرُوْنَ ﴿٨٥﴾

86. And when those who ascribed partners to Allah behold those partners of theirs, they will say: Our Lord! these are our partners unto whom we used to cry instead of Thee. But they will fling to them saying: Lo! ye verily are liars!

وَاِذَا رَاَ الَّذِيْنَ اَشْرَكُوْا شُرَكَآءَهُمْ قَالُوْا رَبَّنَا
هٰٓؤُلَآءِ شُرَكَآؤُنَا الَّذِيْنَ كُنَّا نَدْعُوْا مِنْ دُوْنِكَ ۚ
فَاَلْقَوْا اِلَيْهِمُ الْقَوْلَ اِنَّكُمْ لَكٰذِبُوْنَ ﴿٨٦﴾

1 Lit. made subservient—*i.e.* to the Law of Allah.

2. *i.e.* tents.

87. And they proffer unto Allah submission on that day, and all that they used to invent hath failed them.

وَالْقَوْاۤ اِلَى اللّٰهِ يَوْمَئِذٍ السَّلَمَ وَضَلَّ عَنْهُمْ مَّا كَانُوْا يَفْتَرُوْنَ ۞

88. For those who disbelieve and debar (men) from the way of Allah, We add doom to doom because they wrought corruption.

اَلَّذِيْنَ كَفَرُوْا وَصَدُّوْا عَنْ سَبِيْلِ اللّٰهِ زِدْنٰهُمْ عَذَابًا فَوْقَ الْعَذَابِ بِمَا كَانُوْا يُفْسِدُوْنَ ۞

89. And (bethink you of) the day when We raise in every nation a witness against them of their own folk, and We bring thee (Muhammad) as a witness against these. And We reveal the Scripture unto thee as an exposition of all things, and a guidance and a mercy and good tidings for those who have surrendered (to Allah).

وَيَوْمَ نَبْعَثُ فِيْ كُلِّ اُمَّةٍ شَهِيْدًا عَلَيْهِمْ مِّنْ اَنْفُسِهِمْ وَجِئْنَا بِكَ شَهِيْدًا عَلٰى هٰٓؤُلَاءِ وَنَزَّلْنَا عَلَيْكَ الْكِتٰبَ تِبْيَانًا لِّكُلِّ شَيْءٍ وَّهُدًى وَّرَحْمَةً وَّبُشْرٰى لِلْمُسْلِمِيْنَ ۞

90. Lo! Allah enjoineth justice and kindness, and giving to kinsfolk, and forbiddeth lewdness and abomination and wickedness. He exhorteth you in order that ye may take heed.[1]

اِنَّ اللّٰهَ يَأْمُرُ بِالْعَدْلِ وَالْاِحْسَانِ وَاِيْتَآئِ ذِى الْقُرْبٰى وَيَنْهٰى عَنِ الْفَحْشَآءِ وَالْمُنْكَرِ وَالْبَغْيِ يَعِظُكُمْ لَعَلَّكُمْ تَذَكَّرُوْنَ ۞

91. Fulfil the covenant of Allah when ye have covenanted, and break not your oaths after the asseveration of them, and after ye have made Allah surety over you. Lo! Allah knoweth what ye do.

وَاَوْفُوْا بِعَهْدِ اللّٰهِ اِذَا عَاهَدْتُّمْ وَلَا تَنْقُضُوا الْاَيْمَانَ بَعْدَ تَوْكِيْدِهَا وَقَدْ جَعَلْتُمُ اللّٰهَ عَلَيْكُمْ كَفِيْلًا اِنَّ اللّٰهَ يَعْلَمُ مَا تَفْعَلُوْنَ ۞

92. And be not like unto her who unravelleth the thread, after she hath made it strong, to thin filaments, making your oaths a deceit between you because of a nation being more numerous than (another) nation. Allah only trieth you thereby, and He verily will explain to you on the Day of Resurrection that wherein ye differed.

وَلَا تَكُوْنُوْا كَالَّتِيْ نَقَضَتْ غَزْلَهَا مِنْ بَعْدِ قُوَّةٍ اَنْكَاثًا تَتَّخِذُوْنَ اَيْمَانَكُمْ دَخَلًا بَيْنَكُمْ اَنْ تَكُوْنَ اُمَّةٌ هِيَ اَرْبٰى مِنْ اُمَّةٍ اِنَّمَا يَبْلُوْكُمُ اللّٰهُ بِهِ وَلَيُبَيِّنَنَّ لَكُمْ يَوْمَ الْقِيٰمَةِ مَا كُنْتُمْ فِيْهِ تَخْتَلِفُوْنَ ۞

93. Had Allah willed He could have made you (all) one nation, but He sendeth whom He will astray and guideth whom He will, and ye will indeed be asked of what ye used to do.

وَلَوْ شَآءَ اللّٰهُ لَجَعَلَكُمْ اُمَّةً وَّاحِدَةً وَّلٰكِنْ يُّضِلُّ مَنْ يَّشَآءُ وَيَهْدِيْ مَنْ يَّشَآءُ وَلَتُسْـَٔلُنَّ عَمَّا كُنْتُمْ تَعْمَلُوْنَ ۞

1 Since the time of Omar II the Omayyad, this verse has been recited at the end of every weekly sermon in all Sunni congregations.

94. Make not your oaths a deceit between you, lest a foot should slip after being firmly planted and ye should taste evil forasmuch as ye debarred (men) from the way of Allah, and yours should be an awful doom.

وَلَا تَتَّخِذُوٓا أَيْمَانَكُمْ دَخَلًا بَيْنَكُمْ فَتَزِلَّ قَدَمٌۢ
بَعْدَ ثُبُوتِهَا وَتَذُوقُوا السُّوٓءَ بِمَا صَدَدتُّمْ عَنْ
سَبِيلِ اللَّهِ ۚ وَلَكُمْ عَذَابٌ عَظِيمٌ ﴿٩٤﴾

95. And purchase not a small gain at the price of Allah's covenant. Lo! that which Allah hath is better for you, if ye did but know.

وَلَا تَشْتَرُوا بِعَهْدِ اللَّهِ ثَمَنًا قَلِيلًا ۚ إِنَّمَا عِنْدَ
اللَّهِ هُوَ خَيْرٌ لَّكُمْ إِنْ كُنْتُمْ تَعْلَمُونَ ﴿٩٥﴾

96. That which ye have wasteth away, and that which with Allah remaineth. And verily We shall pay those who are steadfast a recompense in proportion to the best of what they used to do.

مَا عِنْدَكُمْ يَنْفَدُ وَمَا عِنْدَ اللَّهِ بَاقٍ ۗ وَلَنَجْزِيَنَّ
الَّذِينَ صَبَرُوٓا أَجْرَهُمْ بِأَحْسَنِ مَا كَانُوا
يَعْمَلُونَ ﴿٩٦﴾

97. Whosoever doth right, whether male or female, and is a believer, him verily We shall quicken with good life, and We shall pay them a recompense in proportion to the best of what they used to do.

مَنْ عَمِلَ صَالِحًا مِّنْ ذَكَرٍ أَوْ أُنْثَىٰ وَهُوَ مُؤْمِنٌ
فَلَنُحْيِيَنَّهُ حَيٰوةً طَيِّبَةً ۚ وَلَنَجْزِيَنَّهُمْ أَجْرَهُمْ
بِأَحْسَنِ مَا كَانُوا يَعْمَلُونَ ﴿٩٧﴾

98. And when thou recitest the Qur'ān, seek refuge in Allah from Satan the outcast.

فَإِذَا قَرَأْتَ الْقُرْاٰنَ فَاسْتَعِذْ بِاللَّهِ مِنَ الشَّيْطٰنِ
الرَّجِيمِ ﴿٩٨﴾

99. Lo! he hath no power over those who believe and put trust in their Lord.

إِنَّهُ لَيْسَ لَهُ سُلْطٰنٌ عَلَى الَّذِينَ اٰمَنُوا وَعَلٰى
رَبِّهِمْ يَتَوَكَّلُونَ ﴿٩٩﴾

100. His power is only over those who make a friend of him, and those who ascribe partners unto Him (Allah).

إِنَّمَا سُلْطٰنُهُ عَلَى الَّذِينَ يَتَوَلَّوْنَهُ وَالَّذِينَ هُمْ
بِهِ مُشْرِكُونَ ﴿١٠٠﴾ ع ١٣ ١١ ١٩

101. And when We put a revelation in place of (another) revelation,—and Allah knoweth best what He revealeth—they say: Lo! thou art but inventing. Most of them know not.

وَإِذَا بَدَّلْنَا اٰيَةً مَّكَانَ اٰيَةٍ ۙ وَاللَّهُ أَعْلَمُ بِمَا
يُنَزِّلُ قَالُوٓا إِنَّمَا أَنْتَ مُفْتَرٍ ۚ بَلْ أَكْثَرُهُمْ
لَا يَعْلَمُونَ ﴿١٠١﴾

102. Say: The holy Spirit[1] hath revealed it from thy Lord with truth, that it may confirm (the faith of) those who believe, and as guidance and good tidings for those who have surrendered[2] (to Allah).

قُلْ نَزَّلَهُ رُوحُ الْقُدُسِ مِنْ رَّبِّكَ بِالْحَقِّ لِيُثَبِّتَ
الَّذِينَ اٰمَنُوا وَهُدًى وَّبُشْرٰى لِلْمُسْلِمِينَ ﴿١٠٢﴾

1 *i.e.* Gabriel. 2 Ar. *Muslimīn*.

103. And We know well that they say: Only a man teacheth him. The speech of him at whom they falsely hint is outlandish, and this is clear Arabic speech.[1]

ولقد نعلم انهم يقولون انما يعلمه بشر ط
لسان الذي يلحدون اليه اعجمي وهذا
لسان عربي مبين ١٠٣

104. Lo! those who disbelieve the revelations of Allah, Allah guideth them not and theirs will be a painful doom.

ان الذين لا يؤمنون بايت الله لا يهديهم
الله ولهم عذاب اليم ١٠٤

105. Only they invent falsehood who oelieve not Allah's revelations, and (only) they are the liars.

انما يفتري الكذب الذين لا يؤمنون بايت
الله واولئك هم الكذبون ١٠٥

106. Whoso disbelieveth in Allah after his belief—save him who is forced thereto and whose heart is still content with Faith—but whoso findeth ease in disbelief: on them is wrath from Allah. Theirs will be an awful doom.

من كفر بالله من بعد ايمانه الا من اكره و
قلبه مطمئن بالايمان ولكن من شرح
بالكفر صدرا فعليهم غضب من الله و
لهم عذاب عظيم ١٠٦

107. That is because they have chosen the life of the world reather than the Hereafter, and because Allah guideth not the disbelieving folk.

ذلك بانهم استحبوا الحيوة الدنيا
على الاخرة وان الله لا يهدي القوم
الكفرين ١٠٧

108. Such are they whose hearts and ears and eyes Allah hath sealed. And such are the heedless.

اولئك الذين طبع الله على قلوبهم وسمعهم
وابصارهم واولئك هم الغفلون ١٠٨

109. Assuredly in the Hereafter they are the losers.

لا جرم انهم في الاخرة هم الخسرون ١٠٩

110. Then lo! thy Lord—for those who become fugitives after they had been persecuted, and then fought and were steadfast—lo! thy Lord afterward is (for them) indeed Forgiving, Merciful,

ثم ان ربك للذين هاجروا من بعد ما فتنوا
ثم جهدوا وصبروا ان ربك من بعدها
ع لغفور رحيم ١١٠

111. On the Day when every soul will come pleading for itself, and every soul will be repaid what it did, and they will not be wronged.

يوم تاتي كل نفس تجادل عن نفسها وتوفى
كل نفس ما عملت وهم لا يظلمون ١١١

1 Among the various attempts of the idolaters to deride the Koran was the charge that a Christian slave among the earliest converts taught it to the Prophet. The same slave suffered cruel persecution for his belief in the divine inspiration of the Koran.

112. Allah coineth a similitude: a township that dwelt secure and well content, its provision coming to it in abundance from every side, but it disbelieved in Allah's favours, so Allah made it experience the garb of dearth and fear because of what they used to do.

113. And verily there had come unto them a messenger from among them, but they had denied him, and so the torment seized them while they were wrong-doers.

114. So eat of the lawful and good food which Allah hath provided for you, and thank the bounty of your Lord if it is Him ye serve.

115. He hath forbidden for you only carrion and blood and swine-flesh and that which hath been immolated in the name of any other than Allah; but he who is driven thereto, neither craving nor transgressing, lo! then Allah is Forgiving, Merciful.

116. And speak not, concerning that which your own tongues qualify (as clean or unclean), the falsehood: "This is lawful, and this is forbidden," so that ye invent a lie against Allah. Lo! those who invent a lie against Allah will not succeed.

117. A brief enjoyment (will be theirs); and theirs a painful doom.

118. And unto those who are Jews We have forbidden that which We have already related unto thee. And We wronged them not, but they were wont to wrong themselves.

119. Then lo! thy Lord—for those who do evil in ignorance and afterward repent and amend—lo! (for them) thy Lord is afterward indeed Forgiving, Merciful.

120. Lo! Abraham was a nation obedient to Allah, by nature upright, and he was not of the idolaters;

وَضَرَبَ اللّٰهُ مَثَلًا قَرْيَةً كَانَتْ اٰمِنَةً مُّطْمَىِٕنَّةً يَّاْتِيْهَا
رِزْقُهَا رَغَدًا مِّنْ كُلِّ مَكَانٍ فَكَفَرَتْ بِاَنْعُمِ اللّٰهِ فَاَذَاقَهَا
اللّٰهُ لِبَاسَ الْجُوْعِ وَالْخَوْفِ بِمَا كَانُوْا يَصْنَعُوْنَ ﴿١١٢﴾
وَلَقَدْ جَآءَهُمْ رَسُوْلٌ مِّنْهُمْ فَكَذَّبُوْهُ فَاَخَذَهُمُ
الْعَذَابُ وَهُمْ ظٰلِمُوْنَ ﴿١١٣﴾
فَكُلُوْا مِمَّا رَزَقَكُمُ اللّٰهُ حَلٰلًا طَيِّبًا وَّاشْكُرُوْا نِعْمَتَ
اللّٰهِ اِنْ كُنْتُمْ اِيَّاهُ تَعْبُدُوْنَ ﴿١١٤﴾
اِنَّمَا حَرَّمَ عَلَيْكُمُ الْمَيْتَةَ وَالدَّمَ وَلَحْمَ الْخِنْزِيْرِ وَمَآ
اُهِلَّ لِغَيْرِ اللّٰهِ بِهٖ فَمَنِ اضْطُرَّ غَيْرَ بَاغٍ وَّلَا عَادٍ
فَاِنَّ اللّٰهَ غَفُوْرٌ رَّحِيْمٌ ﴿١١٥﴾
وَلَا تَقُوْلُوْا لِمَا تَصِفُ اَلْسِنَتُكُمُ الْكَذِبَ هٰذَا حَلٰلٌ
وَّهٰذَا حَرَامٌ لِّتَفْتَرُوْا عَلَى اللّٰهِ الْكَذِبَ اِنَّ الَّذِيْنَ
يَفْتَرُوْنَ عَلَى اللّٰهِ الْكَذِبَ لَا يُفْلِحُوْنَ ﴿١١٦﴾
مَتَاعٌ قَلِيْلٌ وَّلَهُمْ عَذَابٌ اَلِيْمٌ ﴿١١٧﴾
وَعَلَى الَّذِيْنَ هَادُوْا حَرَّمْنَا مَا قَصَصْنَا عَلَيْكَ
مِنْ قَبْلُ وَمَا ظَلَمْنٰهُمْ وَلٰكِنْ كَانُوْٓا اَنْفُسَهُمْ
يَظْلِمُوْنَ ﴿١١٨﴾
ثُمَّ اِنَّ رَبَّكَ لِلَّذِيْنَ عَمِلُوا السُّوْٓءَ بِجَهَالَةٍ ثُمَّ
تَابُوْا مِنْۢ بَعْدِ ذٰلِكَ وَاَصْلَحُوْٓا اِنَّ رَبَّكَ مِنْۢ
ع بَعْدِهَا لَغَفُوْرٌ رَّحِيْمٌ ﴿١١٩﴾
اِنَّ اِبْرٰهِيْمَ كَانَ اُمَّةً قَانِتًا لِّلّٰهِ حَنِيْفًا وَلَمْ يَكُ
مِنَ الْمُشْرِكِيْنَ ﴿١٢٠﴾

121. Thankful for His bounties; He chose him and He guided him unto a straight path.

122. And We gave him good in the world, and in the Hereafter he is among the righteous.

123. And afterward We inspired thee (Muhammad, saying): Follow the religion of Abraham, as one by nature upright. He was not of the idolaters.

124. The Sabbath was appointed only for those who differed concerning it, and lo! thy Lord will judge between them on the Day of Resurrection concerning that wherein they used to differ.

125. Call unto the way of thy Lord with wisdom and fair exhortation, and reason with them in the better way. Lo! thy Lord is best aware of him who strayeth from His way, and He is Best Aware of those who go aright.

126. If ye punish, then punish with the like of that wherewith ye were afflicted. But if ye endure patiently, verily it is better for the patient.

127. Endure thou patiently (O Muhammad). Thine endurance is only by (the help of) Allah. Grieve not for them, and be not in distress because of that which they devise.

128. Lo! Allah is with those who keep their duty unto Him and those who are doers of good.

شَاكِرًا لِّأَنْعُمِهِ ۚ اجْتَبَاهُ وَهَدَاهُ إِلَىٰ صِرَاطٍ
مُّسْتَقِيمٍ ﴿١٢١﴾
وَآتَيْنَاهُ فِي الدُّنْيَا حَسَنَةً ۖ وَإِنَّهُ فِي الْآخِرَةِ لَمِنَ
الصَّالِحِينَ ﴿١٢٢﴾
ثُمَّ أَوْحَيْنَا إِلَيْكَ أَنِ اتَّبِعْ مِلَّةَ إِبْرَاهِيمَ حَنِيفًا ۖ
وَمَا كَانَ مِنَ الْمُشْرِكِينَ ﴿١٢٣﴾
إِنَّمَا جُعِلَ السَّبْتُ عَلَى الَّذِينَ اخْتَلَفُوا فِيهِ ۚ وَ
إِنَّ رَبَّكَ لَيَحْكُمُ بَيْنَهُمْ يَوْمَ الْقِيَامَةِ فِيمَا كَانُوا
فِيهِ يَخْتَلِفُونَ ﴿١٢٤﴾
ادْعُ إِلَىٰ سَبِيلِ رَبِّكَ بِالْحِكْمَةِ وَالْمَوْعِظَةِ الْحَسَنَةِ ۖ
وَجَادِلْهُم بِالَّتِي هِيَ أَحْسَنُ ۚ إِنَّ رَبَّكَ هُوَ أَعْلَمُ
بِمَن ضَلَّ عَن سَبِيلِهِ ۖ وَهُوَ أَعْلَمُ بِالْمُهْتَدِينَ ﴿١٢٥﴾
وَإِنْ عَاقَبْتُمْ فَعَاقِبُوا بِمِثْلِ مَا عُوقِبْتُم بِهِ ۖ وَ
لَئِن صَبَرْتُمْ لَهُوَ خَيْرٌ لِّلصَّابِرِينَ ﴿١٢٦﴾
وَاصْبِرْ وَمَا صَبْرُكَ إِلَّا بِاللَّهِ ۚ وَلَا تَحْزَنْ عَلَيْهِمْ
وَلَا تَكُ فِي ضَيْقٍ مِّمَّا يَمْكُرُونَ ﴿١٢٧﴾
إِنَّ اللَّهَ مَعَ الَّذِينَ اتَّقَوا وَّالَّذِينَ هُم
مُّحْسِنُونَ ﴿١٢٨﴾ ع ١٦ ٢٢

Banî Isrāîl, "The Children of Israel," begins and ends with references to the Israelites. V. 1 relates to the Prophet's vision, in which he was carried by night upon a heavenly steed to the Temple of Jerusalem, whence he was caught up through the seven heavens to the very presence of God. The Sūrah may be taken as belonging to the middle group of Meccan Sūrahs, except v. 81, or, according to other commentators, vv. 76-82, revealed at Al-Madînah.

THE CHILDREN OF ISRAEL

Revealed at Mecca

In the name of Allah, the Beneficent, the Merciful.

1. Glorified be He Who carried His servant by night from the Inviolable Place of Worship[1] to the Far Distant Place of Worship[2] the neighbourhood whereof We have blessed, that We might show him of Our tokens! Lo! He, only He, is the Hearer, the Seer.

2. We gave unto Moses the Scripture, and We appointed it a guidance for the Children of Israel, saying: Choose no guardian beside Me.

3. (They were) the seed of those whom We carried (in the ship) along with Noah. Lo! he was a grateful slave.

4. And We decreed for the Children of Israel in the Scripture: Ye verily will work corruption in the earth twice, and ye will become great tyrants.

5. So when the time for the first of the two came, We roused against you slaves of Ours of great might who ravaged (your) country, and it was a threat performed.

6. Then We gave you once again your turn against them, and We aided you with wealth and children and made you more in soldiery,

7. (Saying): If ye do good, ye do good for your own souls, and if ye do evil, it is for them (in like manner). So when the time for the second (of the judgements) came (We roused against you others of Our slaves) to ravage you, and to enter the Temple even as they entered it the first time, and to lay waste all that they conquered with an utter wasting.

8. It may be that your Lord will have mercy on you, but if ye repeat (the crime) We shall repeat (the punishment), and We have appointed hell a dungeon for the disbelievers.

1 Mecca.
2 Jerusalem.

المنزل ٤

اياتها ١١١ (١٧) سُوْرَةُ الْاِسْرَاۗءِ مَكِّيَّةٌ رُكُوْعَاتُهَا ١٢

بِسْمِ اللّٰهِ الرَّحْمٰنِ الرَّحِيْمِ

الجزء ١٥

سُبْحٰنَ الَّذِيْٓ اَسْرٰى بِعَبْدِهٖ لَيْلًا مِّنَ الْمَسْجِدِ
الْحَرَامِ اِلَى الْمَسْجِدِ الْاَقْصَا الَّذِيْ بٰرَكْنَا حَوْلَهٗ
لِنُرِيَهٗ مِنْ اٰيٰتِنَا ۭ اِنَّهٗ هُوَ السَّمِيْعُ الْبَصِيْرُ (١)
وَاٰتَيْنَا مُوْسَى الْكِتٰبَ وَجَعَلْنٰهُ هُدًى لِّبَنِيْٓ
اِسْرَاۗءِيْلَ اَلَّا تَتَّخِذُوْا مِنْ دُوْنِيْ وَكِيْلًا (٢)
ذُرِّيَّةَ مَنْ حَمَلْنَا مَعَ نُوْحٍ ۭ اِنَّهٗ كَانَ عَبْدًا شَكُوْرًا (٣)
وَقَضَيْنَآ اِلٰى بَنِيْٓ اِسْرَاۗءِيْلَ فِي الْكِتٰبِ لَتُفْسِدُنَّ
فِي الْاَرْضِ مَرَّتَيْنِ وَلَتَعْلُنَّ عُلُوًّا كَبِيْرًا (٤)
فَاِذَا جَاۗءَ وَعْدُ اُوْلٰىهُمَا بَعَثْنَا عَلَيْكُمْ عِبَادًا لَّنَآ اُولِيْ
بَاْسٍ شَدِيْدٍ فَجَاسُوْا خِلٰلَ الدِّيَارِ ۭ وَكَانَ وَعْدًا
مَّفْعُوْلًا (٥)
ثُمَّ رَدَدْنَا لَكُمُ الْكَرَّةَ عَلَيْهِمْ وَاَمْدَدْنٰكُمْ بِاَمْوَالٍ
وَّبَنِيْنَ وَجَعَلْنٰكُمْ اَكْثَرَ نَفِيْرًا (٦)
اِنْ اَحْسَنْتُمْ اَحْسَنْتُمْ لِاَنْفُسِكُمْ ۣ وَاِنْ اَسَاْتُمْ فَلَهَا ۭ
فَاِذَا جَاۗءَ وَعْدُ الْاٰخِرَةِ لِيَسُوْۗءٗا وُجُوْهَكُمْ وَلِيَدْخُلُوا
الْمَسْجِدَ كَمَا دَخَلُوْهُ اَوَّلَ مَرَّةٍ وَّلِيُتَبِّرُوْا مَا عَلَوْا
تَتْبِيْرًا (٧)
وقف لازم
عَسٰى رَبُّكُمْ اَنْ يَّرْحَمَكُمْ ۚ وَاِنْ عُدْتُّمْ عُدْنَا ۘ وَجَعَلْنَا
جَهَنَّمَ لِلْكٰفِرِيْنَ حَصِيْرًا (٨)

9. Lo! this Qur'ān guideth unto that which is straightest, and giveth tidings unto the believers who do good works that theirs will be a great reward;

إِنَّ هَٰذَا الْقُرْآنَ يَهْدِي لِلَّتِي هِيَ أَقْوَمُ وَيُبَشِّرُ الْمُؤْمِنِينَ الَّذِينَ يَعْمَلُونَ الصَّالِحَاتِ أَنَّ لَهُمْ أَجْرًا كَبِيرًا ٩

10. And that those who believe not in the Hereafter, for them We have prepared a painful doom.

وَأَنَّ الَّذِينَ لَا يُؤْمِنُونَ بِالْآخِرَةِ أَعْتَدْنَا لَهُمْ عَذَابًا أَلِيمًا ١٠ ع

11. Man prayeth for evil as he prayeth for good; for man was ever hasty.

وَيَدْعُ الْإِنْسَانُ بِالشَّرِّ دُعَاءَهُ بِالْخَيْرِ ۖ وَكَانَ الْإِنْسَانُ عَجُولًا ١١

12. And We appoint the night and the day two portents. Then We make dark the portent of the night, and We make the portent of the day sight-giving, that ye may seek bounty from your Lord, and that ye may know the computation of the years, and the reckoning; and everything have We expounded with a clear expounding.

وَجَعَلْنَا اللَّيْلَ وَالنَّهَارَ آيَتَيْنِ ۖ فَمَحَوْنَا آيَةَ اللَّيْلِ وَجَعَلْنَا آيَةَ النَّهَارِ مُبْصِرَةً لِتَبْتَغُوا فَضْلًا مِنْ رَبِّكُمْ وَلِتَعْلَمُوا عَدَدَ السِّنِينَ وَالْحِسَابَ ۚ وَكُلَّ شَيْءٍ فَصَّلْنَاهُ تَفْصِيلًا ١٢

13. And every man's augury have We fastened to his own neck, and We shall bring forth for him on the Day of Resurrection a book which he will find wide open.

وَكُلَّ إِنْسَانٍ أَلْزَمْنَاهُ طَائِرَهُ فِي عُنُقِهِ ۖ وَنُخْرِجُ لَهُ يَوْمَ الْقِيَامَةِ كِتَابًا يَلْقَاهُ مَنْشُورًا ١٣

14. (And it will be said unto him): Read thy book. Thy soul sufficeth as reckoner against thee this day.

اقْرَأْ كِتَابَكَ كَفَىٰ بِنَفْسِكَ الْيَوْمَ عَلَيْكَ حَسِيبًا ١٤

15. Whosoever goeth right, it is only for (the good of) his own soul that he goeth right, and whosoever erreth, erreth only to its hurt. No laden soul can bear another's load. We never punish until We have sent a messenger.

مَنِ اهْتَدَىٰ فَإِنَّمَا يَهْتَدِي لِنَفْسِهِ ۖ وَمَنْ ضَلَّ فَإِنَّمَا يَضِلُّ عَلَيْهَا ۚ وَلَا تَزِرُ وَازِرَةٌ وِزْرَ أُخْرَىٰ ۗ وَمَا كُنَّا مُعَذِّبِينَ حَتَّىٰ نَبْعَثَ رَسُولًا ١٥

16. And when We would destroy a township We send commandment to its folk who live at ease, and afterward they commit abomination therein, and so the Word (of doom) hath effect for it, and We annihilate it with complete annihilation.

وَإِذَا أَرَدْنَا أَنْ نُهْلِكَ قَرْيَةً أَمَرْنَا مُتْرَفِيهَا فَفَسَقُوا فِيهَا فَحَقَّ عَلَيْهَا الْقَوْلُ فَدَمَّرْنَاهَا تَدْمِيرًا ١٦

17. How many generations have We destroyed since Noah! And Allah sufficeth as Knower and Beholder of the sins of His slaves.

وَكَمْ أَهْلَكْنَا مِنَ الْقُرُونِ مِنْ بَعْدِ نُوحٍ ۗ وَكَفَىٰ بِرَبِّكَ بِذُنُوبِ عِبَادِهِ خَبِيرًا بَصِيرًا ١٧

18. Whoso desireth that (life) which hasteneth away, We hasten for him therein that We will for whom We please. And afterward We have appointed for him hell; they will endure the heat thereof, condemned, rejected.

19. And whoso desireth the Hereafter and striveth for it with the effort necessary, being a believer; for such, their effort findeth favour (with their Lord).

20. Each do We supply, both these and those, from the bounty of thy Lord. And the bounty of thy Lord can never be walled up.

21. See how We prefer one above another, and verily the Hereafter will be greater in degrees and greater in preferment.

22. Set not up with Allah any other god (O man) lest thou sit down reproved, forsaken.

23. Thy Lord hath decreed, that ye worship none save Him, and (that ye show) kindness to parents. If one of them or both of them attain to old age with thee, say not "Fie" unto them nor repulse them, but speak unto them a gracious word.

24. And lower unto them the wing of submission through mercy, and say: My Lord! Have mercy on them both as they did care for me when I was little.

25. Your Lord is best aware of what is in your minds. If ye are righteous, then lo! He was ever Forgiving unto those who turn (unto Him).

26. Give the kinsman his due, and the needy, and the wayfarer, and squander not (thy wealth) in wantonness.

27. Lo! the squanderers were ever brothers of the devils, and the devil was ever an ingrate to his Lord.

مَنْ كَانَ يُرِيدُ الْعَاجِلَةَ عَجَّلْنَا لَهُ فِيهَا مَا نَشَاءُ

لِمَنْ نُرِيدُ ثُمَّ جَعَلْنَا لَهُ جَهَنَّمَ يَصْلٰىهَا مَذْمُومًا

مَدْحُورًا ﴿١٨﴾

وَمَنْ أَرَادَ الْاٰخِرَةَ وَسَعٰى لَهَا سَعْيَهَا وَهُوَ مُؤْمِنٌ

فَأُولٰٓئِكَ كَانَ سَعْيُهُمْ مَشْكُورًا ﴿١٩﴾

كُلًّا نُمِدُّ هٰٓؤُلَآءِ وَهٰٓؤُلَآءِ مِنْ عَطَآءِ رَبِّكَ وَ

مَا كَانَ عَطَآءُ رَبِّكَ مَحْظُورًا ﴿٢٠﴾

اُنْظُرْ كَيْفَ فَضَّلْنَا بَعْضَهُمْ عَلٰى بَعْضٍ وَلَلْاٰخِرَةُ

أَكْبَرُ دَرَجٰتٍ وَأَكْبَرُ تَفْضِيلًا ﴿٢١﴾

لَا تَجْعَلْ مَعَ اللّٰهِ إِلٰهًا اٰخَرَ فَتَقْعُدَ مَذْمُومًا مَخْذُولًا ﴿٢٢﴾ ع

وَقَضٰى رَبُّكَ أَلَّا تَعْبُدُوٓا إِلَّآ إِيَّاهُ وَبِالْوَالِدَيْنِ

إِحْسَانًا إِمَّا يَبْلُغَنَّ عِنْدَكَ الْكِبَرَ أَحَدُهُمَآ أَوْ

كِلٰهُمَا فَلَا تَقُلْ لَهُمَآ أُفٍّ وَلَا تَنْهَرْهُمَا وَقُلْ لَهُمَا

قَوْلًا كَرِيمًا ﴿٢٣﴾

وَاخْفِضْ لَهُمَا جَنَاحَ الذُّلِّ مِنَ الرَّحْمَةِ وَ

قُلْ رَبِّ ارْحَمْهُمَا كَمَا رَبَّيٰنِي صَغِيرًا ﴿٢٤﴾

رَبُّكُمْ أَعْلَمُ بِمَا فِي نُفُوسِكُمْ إِنْ تَكُونُوا صٰلِحِينَ

فَإِنَّهُ كَانَ لِلْأَوَّابِينَ غَفُورًا ﴿٢٥﴾

وَاٰتِ ذَا الْقُرْبٰى حَقَّهُ وَالْمِسْكِينَ وَابْنَ

السَّبِيلِ وَلَا تُبَذِّرْ تَبْذِيرًا ﴿٢٦﴾

إِنَّ الْمُبَذِّرِينَ كَانُوٓا إِخْوَانَ الشَّيٰطِينِ وَكَانَ

الشَّيْطٰنُ لِرَبِّهِ كَفُورًا ﴿٢٧﴾

28. But if thou turn away from them, seeking mercy from the Lord, for which thou hopest, then speak unto them a reasonable word.

29. And let not thy hand be chained to thy neck nor open it with a complete opening, lest thou sit down rebuked, denuded.

30. Lo! thy Lord enlargeth the provision for whom He will, and straiteneth (it for whom He will). Lo, He was ever Knower, Seer of His slaves.

31. Slay not your children, fearing a fall to poverty. We shall provide for them and for you. Lo! the slaying of them is great sin.

32. And come not near unto adultery. Lo! it is an abomination and an evil way.

33. And slay not the life which Allah hath forbidden save with right. Whoso is slain wrongfully, We have given power unto his heir, but let him not commit excess in slaying. Lo! he will be helped.

34. Come not near the wealth of the orphan save with that which is better till he come to strength; and keep the covenant. Lo! of the covenant it will be asked.

35. Fill the measure when ye measure, and weigh with a right balance; that is meet, and better in the end.

36. (O man), follow not that whereof thou hast no knowledge. Lo! the hearing and the sight and heart—of each of these it will be asked.

37. And walk not in the earth exultant. Lo! thou canst not rend the earth, nor canst thou stretch to the height of the hills.

38. The evil of all that is hateful in the sight of thy Lord.

وَاِمَّا تُعۡرِضَنَّ عَنۡهُمُ ابۡتِغَآءَ رَحۡمَةٍ مِّنۡ رَّبِّكَ
تَرۡجُوۡهَا فَقُلۡ لَّهُمۡ قَوۡلًا مَّيۡسُوۡرًا ﴿٢٨﴾
وَلَا تَجۡعَلۡ يَدَكَ مَغۡلُوۡلَةً اِلٰى عُنُقِكَ وَلَا تَبۡسُطۡهَا
كُلَّ الۡبَسۡطِ فَتَقۡعُدَ مَلُوۡمًا مَّحۡسُوۡرًا ﴿٢٩﴾
اِنَّ رَبَّكَ يَبۡسُطُ الرِّزۡقَ لِمَنۡ يَّشَآءُ وَيَقۡدِرُ ؕ اِنَّهٗ
كَانَ بِعِبَادِهٖ خَبِيۡرًۢا بَصِيۡرًا ﴿٣٠﴾
وَلَا تَقۡتُلُوۡۤا اَوۡلَادَكُمۡ خَشۡيَةَ اِمۡلَاقٍ ؕ نَحۡنُ نَرۡزُقُهُمۡ
وَاِيَّاكُمۡ ؕ اِنَّ قَتۡلَهُمۡ كَانَ خِطۡاً كَبِيۡرًا ﴿٣١﴾
وَلَا تَقۡرَبُوا الزِّنٰٓى اِنَّهٗ كَانَ فَاحِشَةً ؕ وَسَآءَ سَبِيۡلًا ﴿٣٢﴾
وَلَا تَقۡتُلُوا النَّفۡسَ الَّتِىۡ حَرَّمَ اللّٰهُ اِلَّا بِالۡحَقِّ ؕ وَ
مَنۡ قُتِلَ مَظۡلُوۡمًا فَقَدۡ جَعَلۡنَا لِوَلِيِّهٖ سُلۡطٰنًا فَلَا
يُسۡرِفْ فِّى الۡقَتۡلِ ؕ اِنَّهٗ كَانَ مَنۡصُوۡرًا ﴿٣٣﴾
وَلَا تَقۡرَبُوۡا مَالَ الۡيَتِيۡمِ اِلَّا بِالَّتِىۡ هِىَ اَحۡسَنُ
حَتّٰى يَبۡلُغَ اَشُدَّهٗ ۖ وَاَوۡفُوۡا بِالۡعَهۡدِ ۚ اِنَّ الۡعَهۡدَ
كَانَ مَسۡـُٔوۡلًا ﴿٣٤﴾
وَاَوۡفُوا الۡكَيۡلَ اِذَا كِلۡتُمۡ وَزِنُوۡا بِالۡقِسۡطَاسِ الۡمُسۡتَقِيۡمِ ؕ
ذٰلِكَ خَيۡرٌ وَّاَحۡسَنُ تَاۡوِيۡلًا ﴿٣٥﴾
وَلَا تَقۡفُ مَا لَيۡسَ لَكَ بِهٖ عِلۡمٌ ؕ اِنَّ السَّمۡعَ وَالۡبَصَرَ
وَالۡفُؤَادَ كُلُّ اُولٰٓئِكَ كَانَ عَنۡهُ مَسۡـُٔوۡلًا ﴿٣٦﴾
وَلَا تَمۡشِ فِى الۡاَرۡضِ مَرَحًا ۚ اِنَّكَ لَنۡ تَخۡرِقَ
الۡاَرۡضَ وَلَنۡ تَبۡلُغَ الۡجِبَالَ طُوۡلًا ﴿٣٧﴾
كُلُّ ذٰلِكَ كَانَ سَيِّئُهٗ عِنۡدَ رَبِّكَ مَكۡرُوۡهًا ﴿٣٨﴾

39. This is (part) of that wisdom wherewith thy Lord hath inspired thee (O Muhammad). And set not up with Allah any other god, lest thou be cast into hell, reproved, abandoned.

ذٰلِكَ مِمَّآ اَوْحٰٓى اِلَيْكَ رَبُّكَ مِنَ الْحِكْمَةِ ۗ وَلَا تَجْعَلْ مَعَ
اللّٰهِ اِلٰهًا اٰخَرَ فَتُلْقٰى فِىْ جَهَنَّمَ مَلُوْمًا مَّدْحُوْرًا ﴿۳۹﴾

40. Hath your Lord then distinguished you (O men of Mecca) by giving you sons, and hath chosen for Himself females from among the angels? Lo! verily ye speak an awful word!

اَفَاَصْفٰىكُمْ رَبُّكُمْ بِالْبَنِيْنَ وَاتَّخَذَ مِنَ الْمَلٰٓئِكَةِ
ع اِنَاثًا ۭ اِنَّكُمْ لَتَقُوْلُوْنَ قَوْلًا عَظِيْمًا ﴿۴۰﴾

41. We verily have displayed (Our warnings) in this Qur'ān that they may take heed, but it increaseth them in naught save aversion.

وَلَقَدْ صَرَّفْنَا فِىْ هٰذَا الْقُرْاٰنِ لِيَذَّكَّرُوْا ۭ وَمَا
يَزِيْدُهُمْ اِلَّا نُفُوْرًا ﴿۴۱﴾

42. Say (O Muhammad, to the disbelievers): If there were other gods along with Him, as they say, then had they sought a way against the Lord of the Throne.

قُلْ لَّوْ كَانَ مَعَهٗٓ اٰلِهَةٌ كَمَا يَقُوْلُوْنَ اِذًا لَّابْتَغَوْا
اِلٰى ذِى الْعَرْشِ سَبِيْلًا ﴿۴۲﴾

43. Glorified is He, and High Exalted above what they say!

سُبْحٰنَهٗ وَتَعٰلٰى عَمَّا يَقُوْلُوْنَ عُلُوًّا كَبِيْرًا ﴿۴۳﴾

44. The seven heavens and the earth and all that is therein praise Him, and there is not a thing but hymneth His praise; but ye understand not their praise. Lo! He is ever Clement, Forgiving.

تُسَبِّحُ لَهُ السَّمٰوٰتُ السَّبْعُ وَالْاَرْضُ وَمَنْ فِيْهِنَّ ۭ
وَاِنْ مِّنْ شَىْءٍ اِلَّا يُسَبِّحُ بِحَمْدِهٖ وَلٰكِنْ لَّا تَفْقَهُوْنَ
تَسْبِيْحَهُمْ ۭ اِنَّهٗ كَانَ حَلِيْمًا غَفُوْرًا ﴿۴۴﴾

45. And when thou recitest the Qur'ān We place between thee and those who believe not in the Hereafter a hidden barrier;

وَاِذَا قَرَاْتَ الْقُرْاٰنَ جَعَلْنَا بَيْنَكَ وَبَيْنَ الَّذِيْنَ
لَا يُؤْمِنُوْنَ بِالْاٰخِرَةِ حِجَابًا مَّسْتُوْرًا ﴿۴۵﴾

46. And We place upon their hearts veils lest they should understand it, and in their ears a deafness; and when thou makest mention of thy Lord alone in the Qur'ān, they turn their backs in aversion.

وَّجَعَلْنَا عَلٰى قُلُوْبِهِمْ اَكِنَّةً اَنْ يَّفْقَهُوْهُ وَفِىْٓ
اٰذَانِهِمْ وَقْرًا ۭ وَاِذَا ذَكَرْتَ رَبَّكَ فِى الْقُرْاٰنِ وَحْدَهٗ
وَلَّوْا عَلٰٓى اَدْبَارِهِمْ نُفُوْرًا ﴿۴۶﴾

47. We are best aware of what they wish to hear when they give ear to thee and when they take secret counsel, when the evil-doers say: Ye follow but a man bewitched.

نَحْنُ اَعْلَمُ بِمَا يَسْتَمِعُوْنَ بِهٖٓ اِذْ يَسْتَمِعُوْنَ اِلَيْكَ
وَاِذْ هُمْ نَجْوٰٓى اِذْ يَقُوْلُ الظّٰلِمُوْنَ اِنْ تَتَّبِعُوْنَ
اِلَّا رَجُلًا مَّسْحُوْرًا ﴿۴۷﴾

48. See what similitudes they coin for thee, and thus are all astray, and cannot find a road!

اُنْظُرْ كَيْفَ ضَرَبُوْا لَكَ الْاَمْثَالَ فَضَلُّوْا فَلَا
ع يَسْتَطِيْعُوْنَ سَبِيْلًا ﴿۴۸﴾

49. And they say: When we are bones and fragments, shall we, forsooth, be raised up as a new creation?

50. Say: Be ye stones or iron

51. Or some created thing that is yet greater in your thoughts! Then they will say: Who shall bring us back (to life)? Say: He Who created you at the first. Then will they shake their heads at thee, and say: When will it be? Say: It will perhaps be soon;

52. A day when He will call you and ye will answer with His praise, and ye will think that ye have tarried but a little while.

53. Tell My bondmen to speak that which is kindlier. Lo! the devil soweth discord among them. Lo! the devil is for man an open foe.

54. Your Lord is best aware of you. If He will, He will have mercy on you, or if He will, He will punish you. We have not sent thee (O Muhammad) as a warden over them.

55. And thy Lord is best aware of all who are in the heavens and the earth. And We preferred some of the Prophets above others, and unto David We gave the Psalms.

56. Say: Cry unto those (saints and angels) whom ye assume (to be gods) beside Him, yet they have no power to rid you of misfortune nor to change.

57. Those unto whom they cry seek the way of approach to their Lord, which of them shall be the nearest; they hope for His mercy and they fear His doom. Lo! the doom of thy Lord is to be shunned.

وَقَالُوْٓا ءَاِذَا كُنَّا عِظَامًا وَّرُفَاتًا ءَاِنَّا لَمَبْعُوْثُوْنَ
خَلْقًا جَدِيْدًا ﴿۴۹﴾
قُلْ كُوْنُوْا حِجَارَةً اَوْ حَدِيْدًا ﴿۵۰﴾
اَوْ خَلْقًا مِّمَّا يَكْبُرُ فِيْ صُدُوْرِكُمْ فَسَيَقُوْلُوْنَ
مَنْ يُّعِيْدُنَا قُلِ الَّذِيْ فَطَرَكُمْ اَوَّلَ مَرَّةٍ
فَسَيُنْغِضُوْنَ اِلَيْكَ رُءُوْسَهُمْ وَيَقُوْلُوْنَ مَتٰى
هُوَ قُلْ عَسٰٓى اَنْ يَّكُوْنَ قَرِيْبًا ﴿۵۱﴾
يَوْمَ يَدْعُوْكُمْ فَتَسْتَجِيْبُوْنَ بِحَمْدِهٖ وَتَظُنُّوْنَ
اِنْ لَّبِثْتُمْ اِلَّا قَلِيْلًا ﴿۵۲﴾
وَقُلْ لِّعِبَادِيْ يَقُوْلُوا الَّتِيْ هِيَ اَحْسَنُ اِنَّ الشَّيْطٰنَ
يَنْزَغُ بَيْنَهُمْ اِنَّ الشَّيْطٰنَ كَانَ لِلْاِنْسَانِ عَدُوًّا
مُّبِيْنًا ﴿۵۳﴾
رَبُّكُمْ اَعْلَمُ بِكُمْ اِنْ يَّشَاْ يَرْحَمْكُمْ اَوْ اِنْ يَّشَاْ
يُعَذِّبْكُمْ وَمَآ اَرْسَلْنٰكَ عَلَيْهِمْ وَكِيْلًا ﴿۵۴﴾
وَرَبُّكَ اَعْلَمُ بِمَنْ فِي السَّمٰوٰتِ وَالْاَرْضِ وَلَقَدْ
فَضَّلْنَا بَعْضَ النَّبِيّٖنَ عَلٰى بَعْضٍ وَّاٰتَيْنَا
دَاوٗدَ زَبُوْرًا ﴿۵۵﴾
قُلِ ادْعُوا الَّذِيْنَ زَعَمْتُمْ مِّنْ دُوْنِهٖ فَلَا
يَمْلِكُوْنَ كَشْفَ الضُّرِّ عَنْكُمْ وَلَا تَحْوِيْلًا ﴿۵۶﴾
اُولٰٓئِكَ الَّذِيْنَ يَدْعُوْنَ يَبْتَغُوْنَ اِلٰى رَبِّهِمُ الْوَسِيْلَةَ
اَيُّهُمْ اَقْرَبُ وَيَرْجُوْنَ رَحْمَتَهٗ وَيَخَافُوْنَ عَذَابَهٗ
اِنَّ عَذَابَ رَبِّكَ كَانَ مَحْذُوْرًا ﴿۵۷﴾

58. There is not a township[1] but We shall destroy it ere the Day of Resurrection, or punish it with dire punishment. That is set forth in the Book (of Our decrees).

59. Naught hindereth Us from sending portents save that the folk of old denied them. And We gave Thamūd the she-camel—a clear portent—but they did wrong in respect of her. We send not portents save to warn.

60. And (it was a warning) when We told thee: Lo! thy Lord encompasseth mankind, and We appointed the vision[2] which We showed thee as an ordeal for mankind, and (likewise) the Accursed Tree in the Qur'ān[3]. We warn them, but it increaseth them in naught save gross impiety.

61. And when We said unto the angels: Fall down prostrate before Adam and they fell prostrate all save Iblis, he said: Shall I fall prostrate before that which Thou hast created of clay?

62. He said: Seest Thou this (creature) whom Thou hast honoured above me, if Thou give me grace until the Day of Resurrection I verily will seize his seed, save but a few.

63. He said: Go, and whosoever of them followeth thee—lo! hell will be your payment, ample payment.

64. And excite any of them whom thou canst with thy voice, and urge thy horse and foot against them, and be a partner in their wealth and children, and promise them. Satan promiseth them only to deceive.

65. Lo! My (faithful) bondmen—over them thou hast no power, and thy Lord sufficeth as (their) guardian.

66. (O mankind), your Lord is He Who driveth for you the ship upon the sea that ye may seek of His bounty. Lo! He was ever Merciful toward you.

وَإِنْ مِّنْ قَرْيَةٍ إِلَّا نَحْنُ مُهْلِكُوهَا قَبْلَ يَوْمِ
الْقِيٰمَةِ أَوْ مُعَذِّبُوهَا عَذَابًا شَدِيدًا ۚ كَانَ ذٰلِكَ
فِي الْكِتٰبِ مَسْطُورًا ﴿٥٨﴾
وَمَا مَنَعَنَا أَنْ نُّرْسِلَ بِالْاٰيٰتِ إِلَّا أَنْ كَذَّبَ بِهَا
الْأَوَّلُونَ ۚ وَاٰتَيْنَا ثَمُودَ النَّاقَةَ مُبْصِرَةً فَظَلَمُوا
بِهَا ۚ وَمَا نُرْسِلُ بِالْاٰيٰتِ إِلَّا تَخْوِيفًا ﴿٥٩﴾
وَإِذْ قُلْنَا لَكَ إِنَّ رَبَّكَ أَحَاطَ بِالنَّاسِ ۚ وَمَا جَعَلْنَا الرُّءْيَا
الَّتِي أَرَيْنٰكَ إِلَّا فِتْنَةً لِّلنَّاسِ وَالشَّجَرَةَ الْمَلْعُونَةَ فِي
ع الْقُرْاٰنِ ۚ وَنُخَوِّفُهُمْ فَمَا يَزِيدُهُمْ إِلَّا طُغْيَانًا كَبِيرًا ﴿٦٠﴾
وَإِذْ قُلْنَا لِلْمَلٰٓئِكَةِ اسْجُدُوا لِاٰدَمَ فَسَجَدُوا إِلَّا
إِبْلِيسَ ۚ قَالَ ءَأَسْجُدُ لِمَنْ خَلَقْتَ طِينًا ﴿٦١﴾
قَالَ أَرَءَيْتَكَ هٰذَا الَّذِي كَرَّمْتَ عَلَيَّ لَئِنْ أَخَّرْتَنِ
إِلٰى يَوْمِ الْقِيٰمَةِ لَأَحْتَنِكَنَّ ذُرِّيَّتَهُ إِلَّا قَلِيلًا ﴿٦٢﴾
قَالَ اذْهَبْ فَمَنْ تَبِعَكَ مِنْهُمْ فَإِنَّ جَهَنَّمَ جَزَآؤُكُمْ
جَزَآءً مَّوْفُورًا ﴿٦٣﴾
وَاسْتَفْزِزْ مَنِ اسْتَطَعْتَ مِنْهُمْ بِصَوْتِكَ وَأَجْلِبْ
عَلَيْهِمْ بِخَيْلِكَ وَرَجِلِكَ وَشَارِكْهُمْ فِي الْأَمْوَالِ وَ
الْأَوْلَادِ وَعِدْهُمْ ۚ وَمَا يَعِدُهُمُ الشَّيْطٰنُ إِلَّا غُرُورًا ﴿٦٤﴾
إِنَّ عِبَادِي لَيْسَ لَكَ عَلَيْهِمْ سُلْطٰنٌ ۚ وَكَفٰى بِرَبِّكَ
وَكِيلًا ﴿٦٥﴾
رَبُّكُمُ الَّذِي يُزْجِي لَكُمُ الْفُلْكَ فِي الْبَحْرِ لِتَبْتَغُوا
مِنْ فَضْلِهِ ۚ إِنَّهُ كَانَ بِكُمْ رَحِيمًا ﴿٦٦﴾

1 Or *community*.
2 The Prophet's vision of his ascent through the seven heavens.
3 See Sûr. XLIV, vv. 43-49.

67. And when harm toucheth you upon the sea, all unto whom ye cry (for succour) fail save Him (alone), but when He bringeth you safe to land, ye turn away, for man was ever thankless.

68. Feel ye then secure that He will not cause a slope of the land to engulf you, or send a sand-storm upon you, and then ye will find that ye have no protector?

69. Or feel ye secure that He will not return you to that (plight) a second time, and send against you a hurricane of wind and drown you for your thanklessness, and then ye will not find therein that ye have any avenger against Us?

70. Verily We have honoured the children of Adam. We carry them on the land and the sea, and have made provision of good things for them, and have preferred them above many of those whom We created with a marked preferment.

71. On the day when We shall summon all men with their record, whoso is given his book in his right hand—such will read their book and they will not be wronged a shred.

72. Whoso is blind here will be blind in the Hereafter, and yet further from the road.

73. And they indeed strove hard to beguile thee (Muhammad) away from that wherewith We have inspired thee, that thou shouldst invent other than it against Us; and then would they have accepted thee as a friend.[1]

74. And if We had not made thee wholly firm thou mightest almost have inclined unto them a little.

75. Then had We made thee taste a double (punishment) of living and a double (punishment) of dying, then hadst thou found no helper against Us.

وَإِذَا مَسَّكُمُ الضُّرُّ فِي الْبَحْرِ ضَلَّ مَنْ تَدْعُونَ
إِلَّا إِيَّاهُ ۚ فَلَمَّا نَجّٰكُمْ إِلَى الْبَرِّ أَعْرَضْتُمْ ۚ وَكَانَ
الْإِنْسَانُ كَفُورًا ﴿٦٧﴾
أَفَأَمِنْتُمْ أَنْ يَخْسِفَ بِكُمْ جَانِبَ الْبَرِّ أَوْ يُرْسِلَ
عَلَيْكُمْ حَاصِبًا ثُمَّ لَا تَجِدُوا لَكُمْ وَكِيلًا ﴿٦٨﴾
أَمْ أَمِنْتُمْ أَنْ يُعِيدَكُمْ فِيهِ تَارَةً أُخْرٰى فَيُرْسِلَ
عَلَيْكُمْ قَاصِفًا مِنَ الرِّيحِ فَيُغْرِقَكُمْ بِمَا كَفَرْتُمْ
ثُمَّ لَا تَجِدُوا لَكُمْ عَلَيْنَا بِهِ تَبِيعًا ﴿٦٩﴾
وَلَقَدْ كَرَّمْنَا بَنِيٓ اٰدَمَ وَحَمَلْنٰهُمْ فِي الْبَرِّ وَالْبَحْرِ
وَرَزَقْنٰهُمْ مِنَ الطَّيِّبٰتِ وَفَضَّلْنٰهُمْ عَلٰى كَثِيرٍ
ع مِمَّنْ خَلَقْنَا تَفْضِيلًا ﴿٧٠﴾
يَوْمَ نَدْعُوا كُلَّ أُنَاسٍ بِإِمَامِهِمْ ۚ فَمَنْ أُوتِيَ
كِتٰبَهُ بِيَمِينِهِ فَأُولٰٓئِكَ يَقْرَءُونَ كِتٰبَهُمْ وَلَا
يُظْلَمُونَ فَتِيلًا ﴿٧١﴾
وَمَنْ كَانَ فِي هٰذِهٖٓ أَعْمٰى فَهُوَ فِي الْاٰخِرَةِ
أَعْمٰى وَأَضَلُّ سَبِيلًا ﴿٧٢﴾
وَإِنْ كَادُوا لَيَفْتِنُونَكَ عَنِ الَّذِيٓ أَوْحَيْنَآ إِلَيْكَ
لِتَفْتَرِيَ عَلَيْنَا غَيْرَهُ ۖ وَإِذًا لَّاتَّخَذُوكَ خَلِيلًا ﴿٧٣﴾
وَلَوْلَآ أَنْ ثَبَّتْنٰكَ لَقَدْ كِدْتَّ تَرْكَنُ إِلَيْهِمْ شَيْئًا
قَلِيلًا ﴿٧٤﴾
إِذًا لَّأَذَقْنٰكَ ضِعْفَ الْحَيٰوةِ وَضِعْفَ الْمَمَاتِ
ثُمَّ لَا تَجِدُ لَكَ عَلَيْنَا نَصِيرًا ﴿٧٥﴾

1 The idolaters more than once offered to compromise with the Prophet.

76. And they indeed wished to scare thee from the land that they might drive thee forth from thence, and then they would have stayed (there) but a little after thee.

77. (Such was Our) method in the case of those whom we sent before thee (to mankind), and thou will not find for Our method aught of Power to change.

78. Establish worship at the going down of the sun until the dark of night, and (the recital of) the Qur'an at dawn, Lo! (the recital of) the Qur'an at dawn is ever witnessed.

79. And some part of the night awake for it, a largess for thee. It may be that thy Lord will raise there to a praised estate.

80. And Say: My Lord! Cause me to come in with a firm incomming and to go out with a firm outgoing. And give me from Thy presence a sustaining Power.

81. And say: Truth hath come and falsehood hath vanished away. Lo! falsehood is ever bound to vanish.

82. And We reveal of the Qur'an that which is a healing and a mercy for believers though it increase the evil-doers in naught save ruin.

83. And when We make life pleasant unto man, he turneth away and is averse; and when ill toucheth him he is in despair.

84. Say: Each one doth according to his rule of conduct, and thy Lord is best aware of him whose way is right.

85. They wil ask thee concerning the Spirit say: The Spirit is by command of my Lord, and of knowledge ye hae been vouchsafed but little.

86. And if We willed We could withdraw that which we have revealed unto thee, then wouldst thou find no guardian for thee against Us in respect thereof.

وَإِنْ كَادُوْا لَيَسْتَفِزُّوْنَكَ مِنَ الْأَرْضِ لِيُخْرِجُوْكَ
مِنْهَا وَإِذًا لَّا يَلْبَثُوْنَ خِلٰفَكَ إِلَّا قَلِيْلًا ﴿٧٦﴾
سُنَّةَ مَنْ قَدْ أَرْسَلْنَا قَبْلَكَ مِنْ رُّسُلِنَا وَلَا تَجِدُ
ع لِسُنَّتِنَا تَحْوِيْلًا ﴿٧٧﴾
أَقِمِ الصَّلٰوةَ لِدُلُوْكِ الشَّمْسِ إِلٰى غَسَقِ الَّيْلِ وَ
قُرْاٰنَ الْفَجْرِ ۖ إِنَّ قُرْاٰنَ الْفَجْرِ كَانَ مَشْهُوْدًا ﴿٧٨﴾
وَمِنَ الَّيْلِ فَتَهَجَّدْ بِهٖ نَافِلَةً لَّكَ ۖ عَسٰٓى أَنْ يَّبْعَثَكَ
رَبُّكَ مَقَامًا مَّحْمُوْدًا ﴿٧٩﴾
وَقُلْ رَّبِّ أَدْخِلْنِيْ مُدْخَلَ صِدْقٍ وَّأَخْرِجْنِيْ مُخْرَجَ
صِدْقٍ وَّاجْعَلْ لِّيْ مِنْ لَّدُنْكَ سُلْطٰنًا نَّصِيْرًا ﴿٨٠﴾
وَقُلْ جَآءَ الْحَقُّ وَزَهَقَ الْبَاطِلُ ۚ إِنَّ الْبَاطِلَ
كَانَ زَهُوْقًا ﴿٨١﴾
وَنُنَزِّلُ مِنَ الْقُرْاٰنِ مَا هُوَ شِفَآءٌ وَّرَحْمَةٌ
لِّلْمُؤْمِنِيْنَ ۙ وَلَا يَزِيْدُ الظّٰلِمِيْنَ إِلَّا خَسَارًا ﴿٨٢﴾
وَإِذَآ أَنْعَمْنَا عَلَى الْإِنْسَانِ أَعْرَضَ وَنَاٰ بِجَانِبِهٖ ۚ
وَإِذَا مَسَّهُ الشَّرُّ كَانَ يَـُٔوْسًا ﴿٨٣﴾
قُلْ كُلٌّ يَّعْمَلُ عَلٰى شَاكِلَتِهٖ ۖ فَرَبُّكُمْ أَعْلَمُ بِمَنْ
ع هُوَ أَهْدٰى سَبِيْلًا ﴿٨٤﴾
وَيَسْـَٔلُوْنَكَ عَنِ الرُّوْحِ ۖ قُلِ الرُّوْحُ مِنْ أَمْرِ رَبِّيْ
وَمَآ أُوْتِيْتُمْ مِّنَ الْعِلْمِ إِلَّا قَلِيْلًا ﴿٨٥﴾
وَلَئِنْ شِئْنَا لَنَذْهَبَنَّ بِالَّذِيْٓ أَوْحَيْنَآ إِلَيْكَ ثُمَّ
لَا تَجِدُ لَكَ بِهٖ عَلَيْنَا وَكِيْلًا ﴿٨٦﴾

1. If, as the jalgleyn declare, w. 76-82 were revealed at Al-Madinah the reference here is to the ploting of the jews and Hypocrites.
2. These words were recited by the Pro[het when he witnessed the destruction of the idols round the Kabah after the conquest of Makkah.

87. (It is naught) save mercy from thy Lord. Lo! His kindness unto thee was ever great.[1]

88. Say: Verily, though mankind and Jinn should assemble to produce the like of this Qur'ān, they could not produce the like thereof though they were helpers one of another.

89. And verily We have displayed for mankind in this Qur'ān all kinds of similitudes, but most of mankind refuse aught save disbelief.

90. And they say: We will not put faith in thee till thou cause a spring to gush forth from the earth for us;

91. Or thou have a garden of date-palms and grapes, and cause rivers to gush forth therein abundantly;

92. Or thou cause the heaven to fall upon us piecemeal, as thou has pretended, or bring Allah and the angels as a warrant;

93. Thou have a house of gold; or thou ascend up into heaven, and even then we will put no faith in thine ascension till thou bring down for us a book that we can read. Say (O Muhammad): My Lord be glorified! Am I naught save a mortal messenger?

94. And naught prevented mankind from believing when the guidance came unto them save that they said: Hath Allah sent a mortal as (His) messenger?

95. Say: If there were in the earth angels walking secure, We had sent down for them from heaven an angel as messenger.

96. Say: Allah sufficeth for a witness between me and you. Lo! He is Knower, Seer of His slaves.

إِلَّا رَحْمَةً مِّن رَّبِّكَ إِنَّ فَضْلَهُ كَانَ عَلَيْكَ
كَبِيرًا ﴿٨٧﴾
قُل لَّئِنِ اجْتَمَعَتِ الْإِنسُ وَالْجِنُّ عَلَىٰ أَن يَأْتُوا
بِمِثْلِ هَٰذَا الْقُرْآنِ لَا يَأْتُونَ بِمِثْلِهِ وَلَوْ كَانَ
بَعْضُهُمْ لِبَعْضٍ ظَهِيرًا ﴿٨٨﴾
وَلَقَدْ صَرَّفْنَا لِلنَّاسِ فِي هَٰذَا الْقُرْآنِ مِن كُلِّ
مَثَلٍ فَأَبَىٰ أَكْثَرُ النَّاسِ إِلَّا كُفُورًا ﴿٨٩﴾
وَقَالُوا لَن نُّؤْمِنَ لَكَ حَتَّىٰ تَفْجُرَ لَنَا مِنَ
الْأَرْضِ يَنبُوعًا ﴿٩٠﴾
أَوْ تَكُونَ لَكَ جَنَّةٌ مِّن نَّخِيلٍ وَعِنَبٍ فَتُفَجِّرَ
الْأَنْهَارَ خِلَالَهَا تَفْجِيرًا ﴿٩١﴾
أَوْ تُسْقِطَ السَّمَاءَ كَمَا زَعَمْتَ عَلَيْنَا كِسَفًا أَوْ تَأْتِيَ
بِاللَّهِ وَالْمَلَائِكَةِ قَبِيلًا ﴿٩٢﴾
أَوْ يَكُونَ لَكَ بَيْتٌ مِّن زُخْرُفٍ أَوْ تَرْقَىٰ فِي السَّمَاءِ
وَلَن نُّؤْمِنَ لِرُقِيِّكَ حَتَّىٰ تُنَزِّلَ عَلَيْنَا كِتَابًا نَّقْرَؤُهُ
قُلْ سُبْحَانَ رَبِّي هَلْ كُنتُ إِلَّا بَشَرًا رَّسُولًا ﴿٩٣﴾ ع
وَمَا مَنَعَ النَّاسَ أَن يُؤْمِنُوا إِذْ جَاءَهُمُ الْهُدَىٰ
إِلَّا أَن قَالُوا أَبَعَثَ اللَّهُ بَشَرًا رَّسُولًا ﴿٩٤﴾
قُل لَّوْ كَانَ فِي الْأَرْضِ مَلَائِكَةٌ يَمْشُونَ مُطْمَئِنِّينَ
لَنَزَّلْنَا عَلَيْهِم مِّنَ السَّمَاءِ مَلَكًا رَّسُولًا ﴿٩٥﴾
قُلْ كَفَىٰ بِاللَّهِ شَهِيدًا بَيْنِي وَبَيْنَكُمْ إِنَّهُ كَانَ
بِعِبَادِهِ خَبِيرًا بَصِيرًا ﴿٩٦﴾

1 Vv. 85, 86 and 87 are said to have been revealed in answer to the third question which some Jewish rabbis prompted the idolaters to ask, the first two questions being answered in the following Sûrah.

97. And he whom Allah guideth, he is led aright; while, as for him whom He sendeth astray, for them thou wilt find no protecting friends beside Him, and We shall assemble them on the Day of Resurrection on their faces, blind, dumb and deaf; their habitation will be hell; whenever it abateth, We increase the flame for them.

98. That is their reward because they disbelieved Our revelations and said: When we are bones and fragments shall we, forsooth, be raised up as a new creation?

99. Have they not seen that Allah Who created the heavens and the earth is Able to create the like of them, and hath appointed for them an end whereof there is no doubt? But the wrong-doers refuse aught save disbelief.

100. Say (unto them): If ye possessed the treasures of the mercy of my Lord, ye would surely hold them back for fear of spending, for man was ever grudging.

101. And verily We gave unto Moses nine tokens, clear proofs (of Allah's Sovereignty). Do but ask the Children of Israel how he came unto them, then Pharaoh said unto him: Lo! I deem thee one bewitched, O Moses.

102. He said: In truth thou knowest that none sent down these (portents) save the Lord of the heavens and the earth as proofs, and lo! (for my part) I deem thee lost, O Pharaoh.

103. And he wished to scare them from the land, but We drowned him and those with him, all together:

104. And We said unto the Children of Israel after him: Dwell in the land; but when the promise of the Hereafter cometh to pass we shall bring you as a crowd gathered out of various nations.[1]

105. With truth have We sent it down, and with truth hath it descended. And We have sent thee as naught else save a bearer of good tidings and a warner.

وَمَن يَهْدِ اللّٰهُ فَهُوَ الْمُهْتَدِ ۚ وَمَن يُضْلِلْ فَلَن
تَجِدَ لَهُمْ أَوْلِيَاءَ مِن دُونِهِ ۖ وَنَحْشُرُهُمْ يَوْمَ
الْقِيٰمَةِ عَلٰى وُجُوهِهِمْ عُمْيًا وَّبُكْمًا وَّصُمًّا ۖ مَّأْوٰىهُمْ
جَهَنَّمُ ۖ كُلَّمَا خَبَتْ زِدْنٰهُمْ سَعِيرًا ﴿٩٧﴾
ذٰلِكَ جَزَاؤُهُم بِأَنَّهُمْ كَفَرُوا بِآيٰتِنَا وَقَالُوا أَءِذَا
كُنَّا عِظٰمًا وَّرُفٰتًا أَءِنَّا لَمَبْعُوثُونَ خَلْقًا جَدِيدًا ﴿٩٨﴾
أَوَلَمْ يَرَوْا أَنَّ اللّٰهَ الَّذِي خَلَقَ السَّمٰوٰتِ وَالْأَرْضَ
قَادِرٌ عَلٰى أَن يَخْلُقَ مِثْلَهُمْ وَجَعَلَ لَهُمْ أَجَلًا لَّا
رَيْبَ فِيهِ فَأَبَى الظّٰلِمُونَ إِلَّا كُفُورًا ﴿٩٩﴾
قُل لَّوْ أَنتُمْ تَمْلِكُونَ خَزَائِنَ رَحْمَةِ رَبِّي إِذًا لَّأَمْسَكْتُمْ
ع خَشْيَةَ الْإِنفَاقِ ۚ وَكَانَ الْإِنسَانُ قَتُورًا ﴿١٠٠﴾
وَلَقَدْ آتَيْنَا مُوسٰى تِسْعَ آيٰتٍ بَيِّنٰتٍ فَسْئَلْ بَنِي
إِسْرَائِيلَ إِذْ جَاءَهُمْ فَقَالَ لَهُ فِرْعَوْنُ إِنِّي لَأَظُنُّكَ
يٰمُوسٰى مَسْحُورًا ﴿١٠١﴾
قَالَ لَقَدْ عَلِمْتَ مَا أَنزَلَ هٰؤُلَاءِ إِلَّا رَبُّ السَّمٰوٰتِ وَ
الْأَرْضِ بَصَائِرَ ۖ وَإِنِّي لَأَظُنُّكَ يٰفِرْعَوْنُ مَثْبُورًا ﴿١٠٢﴾
فَأَرَادَ أَن يَسْتَفِزَّهُم مِّنَ الْأَرْضِ فَأَغْرَقْنٰهُ وَمَن
مَّعَهُ جَمِيعًا ﴿١٠٣﴾
وَّقُلْنَا مِن بَعْدِهِ لِبَنِي إِسْرَائِيلَ اسْكُنُوا الْأَرْضَ
فَإِذَا جَاءَ وَعْدُ الْآخِرَةِ جِئْنَا بِكُمْ لَفِيفًا ﴿١٠٤﴾
وَبِالْحَقِّ أَنزَلْنٰهُ وَبِالْحَقِّ نَزَلَ ۗ وَمَا أَرْسَلْنٰكَ إِلَّا
مُبَشِّرًا وَّنَذِيرًا ﴿١٠٥﴾

1 A reference to the dispersal of the Jews as the consequence of their own deeds after God had established them in the land.

106. And (it is) a Qur'ān that We have divided, that thou mayest recite it unto mankind at intervals, and We have revealed it by (successive) revelation.

وَقُرْاٰنًا فَرَقْنٰهُ لِتَقْرَاَهٗ عَلَى النَّاسِ عَلٰى مُكْثٍ وَّ
نَزَّلْنٰهُ تَنْزِيْلًا ﴿١٠٦﴾

107. Say: Believe therein or believe not, lo! those who were given knowledge before it, when it is read unto them, fall down prostrate on their faces, adoring,

قُلْ اٰمِنُوْا بِهٖٓ اَوْ لَا تُؤْمِنُوْا ۭ اِنَّ الَّذِيْنَ اُوْتُوا الْعِلْمَ
مِنْ قَبْلِهٖٓ اِذَا يُتْلٰى عَلَيْهِمْ يَخِرُّوْنَ لِلْاَذْقَانِ
سُجَّدًا ﴿١٠٧﴾

108. Saying: Glory to our Lord! Verily the promise of our Lord must be fulfilled.

وَّيَقُوْلُوْنَ سُبْحٰنَ رَبِّنَآ اِنْ كَانَ وَعْدُ رَبِّنَا
لَمَفْعُوْلًا ﴿١٠٨﴾

109. They fall down on their faces, weeping, and it increaseth humility in them.

سجدة وَيَخِرُّوْنَ لِلْاَذْقَانِ يَبْكُوْنَ وَيَزِيْدُهُمْ خُشُوْعًا ﴿١٠٩﴾ السجدة

110. Say (unto mankind): Cry unto Allah, or cry unto the Beneficent,[1] unto whichsoever ye cry (it is the same). His are the most beautiful names. And thou (Muhammad), be not loud voiced in thy worship nor yet silent therein, but follow a way between.

قُلِ ادْعُوا اللّٰهَ اَوِ ادْعُوا الرَّحْمٰنَ ۭ اَيًّا مَّا تَدْعُوْا فَلَهُ
الْاَسْمَاۗءُ الْحُسْنٰى ۚ وَلَا تَجْهَرْ بِصَلَاتِكَ وَلَا تُخَافِتْ
بِهَا وَابْتَغِ بَيْنَ ذٰلِكَ سَبِيْلًا ﴿١١٠﴾

111. And say: Praise be to Allah, Who hath not taken unto Himself a son, and Who hath no partner in the Sovereignty, nor hath He any protecting friend through dependence. And magnify Him with all magnificence.

وَقُلِ الْحَمْدُ لِلّٰهِ الَّذِيْ لَمْ يَتَّخِذْ وَلَدًا وَّلَمْ يَكُنْ
لَّهٗ شَرِيْكٌ فِي الْمُلْكِ وَلَمْ يَكُنْ لَّهٗ وَلِيٌّ مِّنَ الذُّلِّ
ع ١٢ ١٢ وَكَبِّرْهُ تَكْبِيْرًا ﴿١١١﴾

1. The idolaters had a peculiar objection to the name of *Ar-Rahman*, "The Beneficent," in the Koran. They said: "We do not know this Rahmān." Some of them thought that Ar-Rahman was a man living in Yamamah!

Al-Kahf, "The Cave," takes its name from the story of the youths who took refuge from persecution in a cave (vv. 10—27) and were preserved there as if asleep for a long period—a story which is generally identified by Western writers (*e.g.* Gibbon) with the legend of the Seven Sleepers of Ephesus. But a strong tradition in the Muslim world asserts that this story and that of Dhū'l Qarneyn ("The Two-Horned One"), vv. 83—98, possibly also that of Moses and the angel, vv. 60—82, were revealed to the Prophet to enable him to answer the questions which the Jewish doctors of Yathrib had instructed the idolaters to ask him, as a test of Prophethood.

The questions were three: "Ask him", said the Rabbis, " of some youth who were of old, what was their fate, for they have a strange story; and ask him of a much-travelled man who reached the sunrise regions of the earth and the sunset regions thereof, what was his history; and ask him of the Spirit, what it is."

The tormentors of the Prophet, who had been to Yathrib to get hints from the Jews, on their return to Mecca put these questions to the Prophet, after having told the people that it was to be a crucial test. The Prophet said that he would surely answer them upon the morrow, without adding "if God will," as though he could command God's revelation. As a reproof for that omission, the wished-for revelation was withheld from him for some days, and when it came included the rebuke contained in verse 24.[1] There is no reason whatever to doubt the truth of the tradition which connects this chapter with three questions set by Jewish rabbis, and the answers must have been considered satisfying, or at least silencing, or the Jews would certainly have made fun of them when they were taunting the Prophet daily after his flight to Yathrib (Al-Madînah). That being so, it would seem rash to identify the story with that of the Christian Seven Sleepers; it must belong, as the story of the "Two-Horned One" actually does belong, to rabbinical lore. The third of the question is answered in Sūrah XVII, vv. 85ff.

It belongs to the middle group of Meccan Sūrahs.

1. Ibn Hisham (Cairo edition), Part I, pp. 102, 103.

THE CAVE

Revealed at Mecca

In the name of Allah, the Beneficent, the Merciful.

1. Praise be to Allah Who hath revealed the Scripture unto His slave, and hath not placed therein any crookedness,

2. (But hath made it) straight, to give warning of stern punishment from Him, and to bring unto the believers who do good works the news that theirs will be a fair reward,

3. Wherein they will abide for ever;

4. And to warn those who say: Allah hath chosen a son,

5. (A thing) whereof they have no knowledge, nor (had) their fathers. Dreadful is the word that cometh out of their mouths. They speak naught but a lie.

6. Yet it may be, if they believe not in this statement, that thou (Muhammad) wilt torment thy soul with grief over their footsteps.

7. Lo! We have placed all that is in the earth as an ornament thereof that We may try them: which of them is best in conduct.

8. And lo! We shall make all that is therein a barren mound.

9. Or deemest thou that the People of the Cave and the Inscription are a wonder among Our portents?

10. When the young men fled for refuge to the Cave and said: Our Lord! Give us mercy from Thy presence, and shape for us right conduct in our plight.

اٰياتها ١١٠ (١٨) سُوْرَةُ الْكَهْفِ مَكِّيَّةٌ رُكُوْعَاتُهَا ١٢

بِسْمِ اللّٰهِ الرَّحْمٰنِ الرَّحِيْمِ

اَلْحَمْدُ لِلّٰهِ الَّذِیْٓ اَنْزَلَ عَلٰی عَبْدِهِ الْكِتٰبَ وَلَمْ
يَجْعَلْ لَّهٗ عِوَجًا ﴿١﴾
قَيِّمًا لِّيُنْذِرَ بَاْسًا شَدِيْدًا مِّنْ لَّدُنْهُ وَيُبَشِّرَ
الْمُؤْمِنِيْنَ الَّذِيْنَ يَعْمَلُوْنَ الصّٰلِحٰتِ اَنَّ لَهُمْ
اَجْرًا حَسَنًا ﴿٢﴾
مَّاكِثِيْنَ فِيْهِ اَبَدًا ﴿٣﴾
وَّيُنْذِرَ الَّذِيْنَ قَالُوا اتَّخَذَ اللّٰهُ وَلَدًا ﴿٤﴾
مَا لَهُمْ بِهٖ مِنْ عِلْمٍ وَّلَا لِاٰبَآئِهِمْ كَبُرَتْ
كَلِمَةً تَخْرُجُ مِنْ اَفْوَاهِهِمْ اِنْ يَّقُوْلُوْنَ اِلَّا
كَذِبًا ﴿٥﴾
فَلَعَلَّكَ بَاخِعٌ نَّفْسَكَ عَلٰٓی اٰثَارِهِمْ اِنْ لَّمْ يُؤْمِنُوْا
بِهٰذَا الْحَدِيْثِ اَسَفًا ﴿٦﴾
اِنَّا جَعَلْنَا مَا عَلَی الْاَرْضِ زِيْنَةً لَّهَا لِنَبْلُوَهُمْ
اَيُّهُمْ اَحْسَنُ عَمَلًا ﴿٧﴾
وَاِنَّا لَجٰعِلُوْنَ مَا عَلَيْهَا صَعِيْدًا جُرُزًا ﴿٨﴾
اَمْ حَسِبْتَ اَنَّ اَصْحٰبَ الْكَهْفِ وَالرَّقِيْمِ كَانُوْا
مِنْ اٰيٰتِنَا عَجَبًا ﴿٩﴾
اِذْ اَوَی الْفِتْيَةُ اِلَی الْكَهْفِ فَقَالُوْا رَبَّنَآ اٰتِنَا مِنْ
لَّدُنْكَ رَحْمَةً وَّهَيِّئْ لَنَا مِنْ اَمْرِنَا رَشَدًا ﴿١٠﴾

11. Then We sealed up their hearing in the Cave for a number of years;

12. And afterward We raised them up that We might know which of the two parties would best calculate the time that they had tarried.

13. We narrate unto thee their story with truth. Lo! they were young men who believed in their Lord, and We increased them in guidance.

14. And We made firm their hearts when they stood forth and said: Our Lord is the Lord of the heavens and the earth. We cry unto no god beside Him, for then should we utter an enormity.

15. These, our people, have chosen (other) gods beside Him though they bring no clear warrant (vouchsafed) to them. And who doth greater wrong than he who inventeth a lie concerning Allah?

16. And when ye withdraw from them and that which they worship except Allah, then seek refuge in the Cave; your Lord will spread for you of His mercy and will prepare for you a pillow in your plight.

17. And thou mightest have seen the sun when it rose move away from their cave to the right, and when it set go past them on the left, and they were in the cleft thereof. That was (one) of the portents of Allah. He whom Allah guideth, he indeed is led aright, and he whom He sendeth astray, for him thou wilt not find a guiding friend.

18. And thou wouldst have deemed them waking though they were asleep, and We caused them to turn over to the right and the left, and their dog stretching out his paws on the threshold. If thou hadst observed them closely thou hadst assuredly turned away from them in flight, and hadst been filled with awe of them.

فَضَرَبْنَا عَلَىٰٓ اٰذَانِهِمْ فِي الْكَهْفِ سِنِيْنَ عَدَدًا ﴿١١﴾
ثُمَّ بَعَثْنٰهُمْ لِنَعْلَمَ اَيُّ الْحِزْبَيْنِ اَحْصٰى لِمَا لَبِثُوْٓا اَمَدًا ﴿١٢﴾ ع
نَحْنُ نَقُصُّ عَلَيْكَ نَبَاَهُمْ بِالْحَقِّ اِنَّهُمْ فِتْيَةٌ
اٰمَنُوْا بِرَبِّهِمْ وَزِدْنٰهُمْ هُدًى ﴿١٣﴾
وَّرَبَطْنَا عَلٰى قُلُوْبِهِمْ اِذْ قَامُوْا فَقَالُوْا رَبُّنَا رَبُّ
السَّمٰوٰتِ وَالْاَرْضِ لَنْ نَّدْعُوَا مِنْ دُوْنِهٖٓ اِلٰهًا
لَّقَدْ قُلْنَآ اِذًا شَطَطًا ﴿١٤﴾
هٰٓؤُلَآءِ قَوْمُنَا اتَّخَذُوْا مِنْ دُوْنِهٖٓ اٰلِهَةً لَوْلَا يَاْتُوْنَ
عَلَيْهِمْ بِسُلْطٰنٍ بَيِّنٍ فَمَنْ اَظْلَمُ مِمَّنِ افْتَرٰى
عَلَى اللّٰهِ كَذِبًا ﴿١٥﴾
وَاِذِ اعْتَزَلْتُمُوْهُمْ وَمَا يَعْبُدُوْنَ اِلَّا اللّٰهَ فَاْوٗٓا
اِلَى الْكَهْفِ يَنْشُرْ لَكُمْ رَبُّكُمْ مِّنْ رَّحْمَتِهٖ وَيُهَيِّئْ
لَكُمْ مِّنْ اَمْرِكُمْ مِّرْفَقًا ﴿١٦﴾
وَتَرَى الشَّمْسَ اِذَا طَلَعَتْ تَّزٰوَرُ عَنْ كَهْفِهِمْ
ذَاتَ الْيَمِيْنِ وَاِذَا غَرَبَتْ تَّقْرِضُهُمْ ذَاتَ
الشِّمَالِ وَهُمْ فِيْ فَجْوَةٍ مِّنْهُ ذٰلِكَ مِنْ اٰيٰتِ
اللّٰهِ مَنْ يَّهْدِ اللّٰهُ فَهُوَ الْمُهْتَدِ وَمَنْ يُّضْلِلْ
ع فَلَنْ تَجِدَ لَهٗ وَلِيًّا مُّرْشِدًا ﴿١٧﴾
وَتَحْسَبُهُمْ اَيْقَاظًا وَّهُمْ رُقُوْدٌ وَّنُقَلِّبُهُمْ ذَاتَ
الْيَمِيْنِ وَذَاتَ الشِّمَالِ وَكَلْبُهُمْ بَاسِطٌ ذِرَاعَيْهِ
بِالْوَصِيْدِ لَوِ اطَّلَعْتَ عَلَيْهِمْ لَوَلَّيْتَ مِنْهُمْ فِرَارًا وَّ
لَمُلِئْتَ مِنْهُمْ رُعْبًا ﴿١٨﴾

19. And in like manner We awakened them that they might question one another. A speaker from among them said: How long have ye tarried? They said: We have tarried a day or some part of a day, (Other) said: Your Lord best knoweth what ye have tarried. Now send one of you with this your silver coin unto the city, and let him see what food is purest there and bring you a supply thereof. Let him be courteous and let no man know of you.

20. For they, if they should come to know of you, will stone you or turn you back to their religion; then ye will never prosper.

21. And in like manner We disclosed them (to the people of the city) that they might know that the promise of Allah is true, and that, as for the Hour, there is no doubt concerning it. When (the people of the city) disputed of their case among themselves, they said: Build over them a building; their Lord knoweth best concerning them. Those who won their point said: We verily shall build a place of worship over them.

22. (Some) will say: They were three, their dog the fourth, and (some) say: Five, their dog the sixth, guessing at random; and (some) say: Seven, and their dog the eighth. Say (O Muhammad): My Lord is best aware of their number. None knoweth them save a few. So contend not concerning them except with an outward contending, and ask not any of them to pronounce concerning them.

23. And say not of anything: Lo! I shall do that tomorrow,

24. Except if Allah will. And remember thy Lord when thou forgettest, and say: It may be that my Lord guideth me unto a nearer way of truth than this.

وَكَذٰلِكَ بَعَثْنٰهُمْ لِيَتَسَآءَلُوْا بَيْنَهُمْ قَالَ قَآئِلٌ مِّنْهُمْ
كَمْ لَبِثْتُمْ قَالُوْا لَبِثْنَا يَوْمًا اَوْ بَعْضَ يَوْمٍ قَالُوْا
رَبُّكُمْ اَعْلَمُ بِمَا لَبِثْتُمْ فَابْعَثُوْٓا اَحَدَكُمْ بِوَرِقِكُمْ
هٰذِهٖٓ اِلَى الْمَدِيْنَةِ فَلْيَنْظُرْ اَيُّهَآ اَزْكٰى طَعَامًا
فَلْيَاْتِكُمْ بِرِزْقٍ مِّنْهُ وَلْيَتَلَطَّفْ وَلَا يُشْعِرَنَّ
بِكُمْ اَحَدًا ﴿١٩﴾
اِنَّهُمْ اِنْ يَّظْهَرُوْا عَلَيْكُمْ يَرْجُمُوْكُمْ اَوْ يُعِيْدُوْكُمْ
فِيْ مِلَّتِهِمْ وَلَنْ تُفْلِحُوْٓا اِذًا اَبَدًا ﴿٢٠﴾
وَكَذٰلِكَ اَعْثَرْنَا عَلَيْهِمْ لِيَعْلَمُوْٓا اَنَّ وَعْدَ اللّٰهِ
حَقٌّ وَّاَنَّ السَّاعَةَ لَا رَيْبَ فِيْهَا ۚ اِذْ يَتَنَازَعُوْنَ
بَيْنَهُمْ اَمْرَهُمْ فَقَالُوا ابْنُوْا عَلَيْهِمْ بُنْيَانًا رَبُّهُمْ
اَعْلَمُ بِهِمْ قَالَ الَّذِيْنَ غَلَبُوْا عَلٰٓى اَمْرِهِمْ لَنَتَّخِذَنَّ
عَلَيْهِمْ مَّسْجِدًا ﴿٢١﴾
سَيَقُوْلُوْنَ ثَلٰثَةٌ رَّابِعُهُمْ كَلْبُهُمْ ۚ وَيَقُوْلُوْنَ خَمْسَةٌ
سَادِسُهُمْ كَلْبُهُمْ رَجْمًۢا بِالْغَيْبِ ۚ وَيَقُوْلُوْنَ
سَبْعَةٌ وَّثَامِنُهُمْ كَلْبُهُمْ قُلْ رَّبِّيْٓ اَعْلَمُ
بِعِدَّتِهِمْ مَّا يَعْلَمُهُمْ اِلَّا قَلِيْلٌ فَلَا تُمَارِ
فِيْهِمْ اِلَّا مِرَآءً ظَاهِرًا وَّلَا تَسْتَفْتِ فِيْهِمْ
مِّنْهُمْ اَحَدًا ﴿٢٢﴾ ع
وَلَا تَقُوْلَنَّ لِشَايْءٍ اِنِّيْ فَاعِلٌ ذٰلِكَ غَدًا ﴿٢٣﴾
اِلَّآ اَنْ يَّشَآءَ اللّٰهُ وَاذْكُرْ رَّبَّكَ اِذَا نَسِيْتَ وَقُلْ
عَسٰٓى اَنْ يَّهْدِيَنِ رَبِّيْ لِاَقْرَبَ مِنْ هٰذَا رَشَدًا ﴿٢٤﴾

نصف القرآن باعتبار عدد الحروف بأن التاء بعد الياء من النصف الاول و اللام الثانية من النصف الآخر ١٢

25. And (it is said) they tarried in their Cave three hundred years and add nine.

26. Say: Allah is best aware how long they tarried. His is the invisible of the heavens and the earth. How clear of sight is He and keen of hearing! They have no protecting friend beside Him, and He maketh none to share in His government.

27. And recite that which hath been revealed unto thee of the Scripture of thy Lord. There is none who can change His words, and thou wilt find no refuge beside Him.

28. Restrain thyself along with those who cry unto their Lord at morn and evening, seeking His countenance; and let not thine eyes overlook them, desiring the pomp of the life of the world; and obey not him whose heart We have made heedless of Our remembrance, who followeth his own lust and whose case hath been abandoned.

29. Say: (It is) the truth from the Lord of you (all). Then whosoever will, let him believe, and whosoever will, let him disbelieve. Lo! We have prepared for disbelievers Fire. Its tent encloseth them. If they ask for showers, they will be showered with water like the molten lead which burneth the faces. Calamitous the drink and ill the resting-place!

30. Lo! as for those who believe and do good works—Lo! We suffer not the reward of one whose work is goodly to be lost.

31. As for such, theirs will be Gardens of Eden, wherein rivers flow beneath them; therein they will be given armlets of gold and will wear green robes of finest silk and gold embroidery, reclining upon thrones therein. Blest the reward, and fair the resting-place!

وَلَبِثُوْا فِيْ كَهْفِهِمْ ثَلٰثَ مِائَةٍ سِنِيْنَ وَازْدَادُوْا
تِسْعًا ﴿٢٥﴾
قُلِ اللّٰهُ اَعْلَمُ بِمَا لَبِثُوْا ۚ لَهٗ غَيْبُ السَّمٰوٰتِ وَ
الْاَرْضِ ۭ اَبْصِرْ بِهٖ وَاَسْمِعْ ۭ مَا لَهُمْ مِّنْ دُوْنِهٖ مِنْ
وَّلِيٍّ وَّلَا يُشْرِكُ فِيْ حُكْمِهٖٓ اَحَدًا ﴿٢٦﴾
وَاتْلُ مَآ اُوْحِيَ اِلَيْكَ مِنْ كِتَابِ رَبِّكَ ۚ لَا مُبَدِّلَ
لِكَلِمٰتِهٖ ۚ وَلَنْ تَجِدَ مِنْ دُوْنِهٖ مُلْتَحَدًا ﴿٢٧﴾
وَاصْبِرْ نَفْسَكَ مَعَ الَّذِيْنَ يَدْعُوْنَ رَبَّهُمْ بِالْغَدٰوةِ
وَالْعَشِيِّ يُرِيْدُوْنَ وَجْهَهٗ وَلَا تَعْدُ عَيْنٰكَ عَنْهُمْ ۚ تُرِيْدُ
زِيْنَةَ الْحَيٰوةِ الدُّنْيَا ۚ وَلَا تُطِعْ مَنْ اَغْفَلْنَا قَلْبَهٗ عَنْ
ذِكْرِنَا وَاتَّبَعَ هَوٰىهُ وَكَانَ اَمْرُهٗ فُرُطًا ﴿٢٨﴾
وَقُلِ الْحَقُّ مِنْ رَّبِّكُمْ ۣ فَمَنْ شَآءَ فَلْيُؤْمِنْ وَّمَنْ شَآءَ
فَلْيَكْفُرْ ۙ اِنَّآ اَعْتَدْنَا لِلظّٰلِمِيْنَ نَارًا ۙ اَحَاطَ بِهِمْ سُرَادِقُهَا ۭ
وَاِنْ يَّسْتَغِيْثُوْا يُغَاثُوْا بِمَآءٍ كَالْمُهْلِ يَشْوِي الْوُجُوْهَ ۭ
بِئْسَ الشَّرَابُ ۭ وَسَآءَتْ مُرْتَفَقًا ﴿٢٩﴾
اِنَّ الَّذِيْنَ اٰمَنُوْا وَعَمِلُوا الصّٰلِحٰتِ اِنَّا لَا نُضِيْعُ
اَجْرَ مَنْ اَحْسَنَ عَمَلًا ﴿٣٠﴾
اُولٰۗىِٕكَ لَهُمْ جَنّٰتُ عَدْنٍ تَجْرِيْ مِنْ تَحْتِهِمُ
الْاَنْهٰرُ يُحَلَّوْنَ فِيْهَا مِنْ اَسَاوِرَ مِنْ ذَهَبٍ
وَّيَلْبَسُوْنَ ثِيَابًا خُضْرًا مِّنْ سُنْدُسٍ وَّ
اِسْتَبْرَقٍ مُّتَّكِـِٕيْنَ فِيْهَا عَلَى الْاَرَاۗىِٕكِ ۭ نِعْمَ
الثَّوَابُ ۭ وَحَسُنَتْ مُرْتَفَقًا ﴿٣١﴾

32. Coin for them a similitude: Two men, unto one of whom we had assigned two gardens of grapes, and We had surrounded both with date palms and had put between them tillage.

33. Each of the gardens gave its fruit and withheld naught thereof. And we caused a river to gush forth therein!

34. And he had fruits. And he said unto his comrade, when he spake with him: I am more than thee in wealth, and stronger in respect of men.

35. And he went into his garden, while he (thus) wronged himself. He said: I think not that all this will ever perish;

36. I think not that Hour will ever come, and if indeed I am brought back unto my Lord I surely shall find better than this as a resort.

37. And his comrade, while he disputed with him, exclaimed: Disbelievest thou in Him Who created thee of dust, then of a drop (of seed), and then fashioned thee a man?

38. But He is Allah, My Lord, and I ascribe unto my Lord no partner.

39. If only, when thou enteredst thy garden, thou hadst said; that which Allah willeth (will come to pass)! There is no strength save in Allah! Though thou seest me as less than thee in wealth and children.

40. Yet It may be that my Lord will give me better than thy garden, and will send on it a bolt from heaven, and some morning it will be a smooth hillside.

وَاضْرِبْ لَهُمْ مَثَلًا رَّجُلَيْنِ جَعَلْنَا لِأَحَدِهِمَا
جَنَّتَيْنِ مِنْ أَعْنَابٍ وَحَفَفْنَاهُمَا بِنَخْلٍ وَجَعَلْنَا
بَيْنَهُمَا زَرْعًا ﴿٣٢﴾
كِلْتَا الْجَنَّتَيْنِ آتَتْ أُكُلَهَا وَلَمْ تَظْلِمْ مِّنْهُ شَيْئًا
وَفَجَّرْنَا خِلَالَهُمَا نَهَرًا ﴿٣٣﴾
وَكَانَ لَهُ ثَمَرٌ فَقَالَ لِصَاحِبِهِ وَهُوَ يُحَاوِرُهُ أَنَا
أَكْثَرُ مِنكَ مَالًا وَأَعَزُّ نَفَرًا ﴿٣٤﴾
وَدَخَلَ جَنَّتَهُ وَهُوَ ظَالِمٌ لِّنَفْسِهِ قَالَ مَا أَظُنُّ
أَن تَبِيدَ هَٰذِهِ أَبَدًا ﴿٣٥﴾
وَمَا أَظُنُّ السَّاعَةَ قَائِمَةً وَلَئِن رُّدِدتُّ إِلَىٰ
رَبِّي لَأَجِدَنَّ خَيْرًا مِّنْهَا مُنقَلَبًا ﴿٣٦﴾
قَالَ لَهُ صَاحِبُهُ وَهُوَ يُحَاوِرُهُ أَكَفَرْتَ بِالَّذِي
خَلَقَكَ مِن تُرَابٍ ثُمَّ مِن نُّطْفَةٍ ثُمَّ سَوَّاكَ
رَجُلًا ﴿٣٧﴾
لَّٰكِنَّا هُوَ اللَّهُ رَبِّي وَلَا أُشْرِكُ بِرَبِّي
أَحَدًا ﴿٣٨﴾
وَلَوْلَا إِذْ دَخَلْتَ جَنَّتَكَ قُلْتَ مَا شَاءَ اللَّهُ
لَا قُوَّةَ إِلَّا بِاللَّهِ إِن تَرَنِ أَنَا أَقَلَّ مِنكَ مَالًا
وَوَلَدًا ﴿٣٩﴾
فَعَسَىٰ رَبِّي أَن يُؤْتِيَنِ خَيْرًا مِّن جَنَّتِكَ وَ
يُرْسِلَ عَلَيْهَا حُسْبَانًا مِّنَ السَّمَاءِ فَتُصْبِحَ صَعِيدًا
زَلَقًا ﴿٤٠﴾

41. Or some morning the water thereof will be lost in the earth so that thou canst not make search for it.

42. And his fruit was beset (with destruction). Then began he to wring his hands for all that he had spent upon it, when (now) it was all ruined on its trellises, and to say: Would that I had ascribed no partner to my Lord!

43. And he had no troop of men to help him as against Allah, nor could he save himself.

44. In this case protection is only from Allah, the True. He is best for reward, and best for consequence.

45. And coin for them the similitude of the life of the world as water We send down from the sky, and the vegetation of the earth mingleth with it and then becometh dry twigs that the winds scatter. Allah is Able to do all things.

46. Wealth and children are an ornament of life of the world. But the good deeds which endure are better in thy Lord's sight for reward, and better in respect of hope.

47. And (bethink you of) the Day when We remove the hills and ye see the earth emerging, and We gather them together so as to leave not one of them behind.

48. And they are set before thy Lord in ranks (and it is said unto them): Now verily have ye come unto Us as We created you at the first. But ye thought that We had set no tryst for you.

49. And the Book is placed, and thou seest the guilty fearful of that which is therein, and they say: What kind of a book is this that leaveth not a small thing nor a great thing but hath counted it! And they find all that they did confronting them, and thy Lord wrongeth no one.

اَوْ يُصْبِحَ مَاۤؤُهَا غَوْرًا فَلَنْ تَسْتَطِيْعَ لَهٗ طَلَبًا ﴿٤١﴾
وَاُحِيْطَ بِثَمَرِهٖ فَاَصْبَحَ يُقَلِّبُ كَفَّيْهِ عَلٰى مَاۤ اَنْفَقَ
فِيْهَا وَهِيَ خَاوِيَةٌ عَلٰى عُرُوْشِهَا وَيَقُوْلُ يٰلَيْتَنِيْ
لَمْ اُشْرِكْ بِرَبِّيْۤ اَحَدًا ﴿٤٢﴾
وَلَمْ تَكُنْ لَّهٗ فِئَةٌ يَّنْصُرُوْنَهٗ مِنْ دُوْنِ اللّٰهِ وَمَا
كَانَ مُنْتَصِرًا ﴿٤٣﴾
هُنَالِكَ الْوَلَايَةُ لِلّٰهِ الْحَقِّ هُوَ خَيْرٌ ثَوَابًا وَّخَيْرٌ
ع عُقْبًا ﴿٤٤﴾
وَاضْرِبْ لَهُمْ مَّثَلَ الْحَيٰوةِ الدُّنْيَا كَمَاۤءٍ اَنْزَلْنٰهُ
مِنَ السَّمَاۤءِ فَاخْتَلَطَ بِهٖ نَبَاتُ الْاَرْضِ فَاَصْبَحَ
هَشِيْمًا تَذْرُوْهُ الرِّيٰحُ وَكَانَ اللّٰهُ عَلٰى كُلِّ
شَيْءٍ مُّقْتَدِرًا ﴿٤٥﴾
اَلْمَالُ وَالْبَنُوْنَ زِيْنَةُ الْحَيٰوةِ الدُّنْيَا وَالْبٰقِيٰتُ
الصّٰلِحٰتُ خَيْرٌ عِنْدَ رَبِّكَ ثَوَابًا وَّخَيْرٌ اَمَلًا ﴿٤٦﴾
وَيَوْمَ نُسَيِّرُ الْجِبَالَ وَتَرَى الْاَرْضَ بَارِزَةً وَّ
حَشَرْنٰهُمْ فَلَمْ نُغَادِرْ مِنْهُمْ اَحَدًا ﴿٤٧﴾
وَعُرِضُوْا عَلٰى رَبِّكَ صَفًّا لَقَدْ جِئْتُمُوْنَا كَمَا خَلَقْنٰكُمْ
اَوَّلَ مَرَّةٍ بَلْ زَعَمْتُمْ اَلَّنْ نَّجْعَلَ لَكُمْ مَّوْعِدًا ﴿٤٨﴾
وَوُضِعَ الْكِتٰبُ فَتَرَى الْمُجْرِمِيْنَ مُشْفِقِيْنَ مِمَّا
فِيْهِ وَيَقُوْلُوْنَ يٰوَيْلَتَنَا مَالِ هٰذَا الْكِتٰبِ لَا يُغَادِرُ
صَغِيْرَةً وَّلَا كَبِيْرَةً اِلَّاۤ اَحْصٰىهَا وَوَجَدُوْا مَا عَمِلُوْا
ع حَاضِرًا وَلَا يَظْلِمُ رَبُّكَ اَحَدًا ﴿٤٩﴾

50. And (remember) when We said unto the angels: Fall prostrate before Adam, and they fell prostrate, all save Iblis. He was of the Jinn, so he rebelled against his Lord's command. Will ye choose him and his seed for your protecting friends instead of Me, when they are an enemy unto you? Calamitous is the exchange for evil-doers!

51. I made them not to witness the creation of the heavens and the earth, nor their own creation; choose I misleaders for (My) helpers?

52. And (be mindful of) the Day when He will say: Call those partners of Mine whom ye pretended. Then they will cry unto them, but they will not hear their prayer, and We shall set a gulf of doom between them.

53. And the guilty behold the Fire and know that they are about to fall therein, and they find no way of escape thence.

54. And verily We have displayed for mankind in this Qur'an all manner of similitudes, but man is more than anything contentious.

55. And naught hindereth mankind from believing when the guidance cometh unto them, and from asking forgiveness of their Lord, unless (it be that they wish) that the judgement of the men of old should come upon them or (that) they should be confronted with the Doom.

56. We send not the messengers save as bearers of good news and warners. Those who disbelieve contend with falsehood in order to refute the Truth thereby. And they take Our revelations and that wherewith they are threatened as a jest.

57. And who doth greater wrong than he who hath been reminded of the revelations of his Lord, yet turneth away from them and forgetteth what his hands send forward (to the Judgement)? Lo! on their hearts We have placed coverings so that they understand not, and in their ears a deafness. And though thou call them to the guidance, in that case they can never be led aright.

وَاِذْ قُلْنَا لِلْمَلٰٓئِكَةِ اسْجُدُوْا لِاٰدَمَ فَسَجَدُوْٓا اِلَّآ اِبْلِيْسَ
كَانَ مِنَ الْجِنِّ فَفَسَقَ عَنْ اَمْرِ رَبِّهٖ اَفَتَتَّخِذُوْنَهٗ
وَذُرِّيَّتَهٗٓ اَوْلِيَآءَ مِنْ دُوْنِيْ وَهُمْ لَكُمْ عَدُوٌّ بِئْسَ
لِلظّٰلِمِيْنَ بَدَلًا ۝٥٠
مَآ اَشْهَدْتُّهُمْ خَلْقَ السَّمٰوٰتِ وَالْاَرْضِ وَلَا خَلْقَ
اَنْفُسِهِمْ وَمَا كُنْتُ مُتَّخِذَ الْمُضِلِّيْنَ عَضُدًا ۝٥١
وَيَوْمَ يَقُوْلُ نَادُوْا شُرَكَآءِيَ الَّذِيْنَ زَعَمْتُمْ فَدَعَوْهُمْ
فَلَمْ يَسْتَجِيْبُوْا لَهُمْ وَجَعَلْنَا بَيْنَهُمْ مَّوْبِقًا ۝٥٢
وَرَاَ الْمُجْرِمُوْنَ النَّارَ فَظَنُّوْٓا اَنَّهُمْ مُّوَاقِعُوْهَا وَلَمْ
يَجِدُوْا عَنْهَا مَصْرِفًا ۝٥٣ ع ١٩
وَلَقَدْ صَرَّفْنَا فِيْ هٰذَا الْقُرْاٰنِ لِلنَّاسِ مِنْ كُلِّ
مَثَلٍ وَكَانَ الْاِنْسَانُ اَكْثَرَ شَيْءٍ جَدَلًا ۝٥٤
وَمَا مَنَعَ النَّاسَ اَنْ يُّؤْمِنُوْٓا اِذْ جَآءَهُمُ الْهُدٰى
وَيَسْتَغْفِرُوْا رَبَّهُمْ اِلَّآ اَنْ تَاْتِيَهُمْ سُنَّةُ الْاَوَّلِيْنَ
اَوْ يَاْتِيَهُمُ الْعَذَابُ قُبُلًا ۝٥٥
وَمَا نُرْسِلُ الْمُرْسَلِيْنَ اِلَّا مُبَشِّرِيْنَ وَمُنْذِرِيْنَ
وَيُجَادِلُ الَّذِيْنَ كَفَرُوْا بِالْبَاطِلِ لِيُدْحِضُوْا بِهِ
الْحَقَّ وَاتَّخَذُوْٓا اٰيٰتِيْ وَمَآ اُنْذِرُوْا هُزُوًا ۝٥٦
وَمَنْ اَظْلَمُ مِمَّنْ ذُكِّرَ بِاٰيٰتِ رَبِّهٖ فَاَعْرَضَ عَنْهَا
وَنَسِيَ مَا قَدَّمَتْ يَدٰهُ اِنَّا جَعَلْنَا عَلٰى قُلُوْبِهِمْ اَكِنَّةً
اَنْ يَّفْقَهُوْهُ وَفِيْٓ اٰذَانِهِمْ وَقْرًا وَاِنْ تَدْعُهُمْ اِلَى
الْهُدٰى فَلَنْ يَّهْتَدُوْٓا اِذًا اَبَدًا ۝٥٧

1. The fact that Iblis or Satan is of the Jinn and not of the angels, though he was among the latter, explains his disobedience; since Jinn, like men, can choose their path of conduct.

58. Thy Lord is the Forgiver, Full of Mercy. If He took them to task (now) for what they earn, He would hasten on the doom for them; but theirs is an appointed term from which they will find no escape.

59. And (all) those townships! We destroyed them when they did wrong, and We appointed a fixed time for their destruction.

60. And when Moses said unto his servant: I will not give up until I reach the point where the two rivers meet, though I march on for ages.

61. And when they reached the point where the two met, they forgot their fish, and it took its way into the waters, being free.

62. And when they had gone further, he said unto his servant: Bring us our breakfast. Verily we have found fatigue in this our journey.

63. He said: Didst thou see, when we took refuge on the rock, and I forgot the fish—and none but Satan caused me to forget to mention it—it took its way into the waters by a marvel.

64. He said: This is that which we have been seeking. So they retraced their steps again.

65. Then found they one of Our slaves, unto whom We had given mercy from Us, and had taught him knowledge from Our presence.

66. Moses said unto him: May I follow thee, to the end that thou mayst teach me right conduct of that which thou hast been taught?

67. He said: Lo! thou canst not bear with me.

68. How canst thou bear with that whereof thou canst not compass any knowledge?

وَرَبُّكَ الْغَفُوْرُ ذُو الرَّحْمَةِ لَوْ يُؤَاخِذُهُمْ بِمَا كَسَبُوْا لَعَجَّلَ لَهُمُ الْعَذَابَ بَلْ لَهُمْ مَّوْعِدٌ لَّنْ يَّجِدُوْا مِنْ دُوْنِهٖ مَوْئِلًا ۝

وَتِلْكَ الْقُرٰى اَهْلَكْنٰهُمْ لَمَّا ظَلَمُوْا وَجَعَلْنَا لِمَهْلِكِهِمْ مَّوْعِدًا ۝

وَاِذْ قَالَ مُوْسٰى لِفَتٰهُ لَاۤ اَبْرَحُ حَتّٰى اَبْلُغَ مَجْمَعَ الْبَحْرَيْنِ اَوْ اَمْضِيَ حُقُبًا ۝

فَلَمَّا بَلَغَا مَجْمَعَ بَيْنِهِمَا نَسِيَا حُوْتَهُمَا فَاتَّخَذَ سَبِيْلَهٗ فِى الْبَحْرِ سَرَبًا ۝

فَلَمَّا جَاوَزَا قَالَ لِفَتٰهُ اٰتِنَا غَدَآءَنَا لَقَدْ لَقِيْنَا مِنْ سَفَرِنَا هٰذَا نَصَبًا ۝

قَالَ اَرَءَيْتَ اِذْ اَوَيْنَاۤ اِلَى الصَّخْرَةِ فَاِنِّيْ نَسِيْتُ الْحُوْتَ وَمَاۤ اَنْسٰنِيْهُ اِلَّا الشَّيْطٰنُ اَنْ اَذْكُرَهٗ وَاتَّخَذَ سَبِيْلَهٗ فِى الْبَحْرِ عَجَبًا ۝

قَالَ ذٰلِكَ مَا كُنَّا نَبْغِ فَارْتَدَّا عَلٰۤى اٰثَارِهِمَا قَصَصًا ۝

فَوَجَدَا عَبْدًا مِّنْ عِبَادِنَاۤ اٰتَيْنٰهُ رَحْمَةً مِّنْ عِنْدِنَا وَعَلَّمْنٰهُ مِنْ لَّدُنَّا عِلْمًا ۝

قَالَ لَهٗ مُوْسٰى هَلْ اَتَّبِعُكَ عَلٰۤى اَنْ تُعَلِّمَنِ مِمَّا عُلِّمْتَ رُشْدًا ۝

قَالَ اِنَّكَ لَنْ تَسْتَطِيْعَ مَعِيَ صَبْرًا ۝

وَكَيْفَ تَصْبِرُ عَلٰى مَا لَمْ تُحِطْ بِهٖ خُبْرًا ۝

69. He said: Allah willing, thou shalt find me patient and I shall not in aught gainsay thee.

70. He said: Well, if thou go with me, ask me not concerning aught till I myself mention of it unto thee.

71. So the twain set out till, when they were in the ship, he made a hole therein. (Moses) said: Hast thou made a hole therein to drown the folk thereof? Thou verily hast done a dreadful thing.

72. He said: Did I not tell thee thou couldst not bear with me?

73. (Moses) said: Be not wroth with me that I forgot, and be not hard upon me for my fault.

74. So the twain journeyed on till, when they met a lad, he slew him. (Moses) said: What! Hast thou slain an innocent soul who hath slain no man? Verily thou hast done a horrid thing!

75. He said: Did I not tell thee that thou couldst not bear with me?

76. (Moses) said: If I ask thee after this concerning aught, keep not company with me. Thou hast received an excuse from me.

77. So the twain journeyed on till, when came unto the folk of a certain township, they asked its folk for food, but they refused to make them guests. And they found therein a wall upon the point of falling into ruin, and he repaired it. (Moses) said: If thou hadst wished, thou couldst have taken payment for it.

78. He said: This is the parting between thee and me! I will announce unto thee the interpretation of that thou couldst not bear with patience.

قَالَ سَتَجِدُنِيٓ إِن شَآءَ ٱللَّهُ صَابِرًا وَلَآ أَعۡصِي
لَكَ أَمۡرًا ﴿٦٩﴾
قَالَ فَإِنِ ٱتَّبَعۡتَنِي فَلَا تَسۡـَٔلۡنِي عَن شَيۡءٍ حَتَّىٰٓ
ع ٩ ١١ أُحۡدِثَ لَكَ مِنۡهُ ذِكۡرًا ﴿٧٠﴾
فَٱنطَلَقَا حَتَّىٰٓ إِذَا رَكِبَا فِي ٱلسَّفِينَةِ خَرَقَهَا
قَالَ أَخَرَقۡتَهَا لِتُغۡرِقَ أَهۡلَهَا لَقَدۡ جِئۡتَ شَيۡـًٔا
إِمۡرًا ﴿٧١﴾
قَالَ أَلَمۡ أَقُلۡ إِنَّكَ لَن تَسۡتَطِيعَ مَعِيَ صَبۡرًا ﴿٧٢﴾
قَالَ لَا تُؤَاخِذۡنِي بِمَا نَسِيتُ وَلَا تُرۡهِقۡنِي مِنۡ
أَمۡرِي عُسۡرًا ﴿٧٣﴾
فَٱنطَلَقَا حَتَّىٰٓ إِذَا لَقِيَا غُلَٰمًا فَقَتَلَهُۥ قَالَ أَقَتَلۡتَ
نَفۡسًا زَكِيَّةَۢ بِغَيۡرِ نَفۡسٍ لَّقَدۡ جِئۡتَ شَيۡـًٔا
نُّكۡرًا ﴿٧٤﴾
الجزء ١٦ قَالَ أَلَمۡ أَقُل لَّكَ إِنَّكَ لَن تَسۡتَطِيعَ مَعِيَ صَبۡرًا ﴿٧٥﴾
قَالَ إِن سَأَلۡتُكَ عَن شَيۡءِۢ بَعۡدَهَا فَلَا تُصَٰحِبۡنِي
قَدۡ بَلَغۡتَ مِن لَّدُنِّي عُذۡرًا ﴿٧٦﴾
فَٱنطَلَقَا حَتَّىٰٓ إِذَآ أَتَيَآ أَهۡلَ قَرۡيَةٍ ٱسۡتَطۡعَمَآ
أَهۡلَهَا فَأَبَوۡاْ أَن يُضَيِّفُوهُمَا فَوَجَدَا فِيهَا جِدَارًا
يُرِيدُ أَن يَنقَضَّ فَأَقَامَهُۥ قَالَ لَوۡ شِئۡتَ
لَتَّخَذۡتَ عَلَيۡهِ أَجۡرًا ﴿٧٧﴾
قَالَ هَٰذَا فِرَاقُ بَيۡنِي وَبَيۡنِكَ سَأُنَبِّئُكَ بِتَأۡوِيلِ
مَا لَمۡ تَسۡتَطِع عَّلَيۡهِ صَبۡرًا ﴿٧٨﴾

79. As for the ship, it belonged to poor people working on the river,[1] and I wished to mar it, for there was a king behind them who was taking every ship by force.

80. And as for the lad, his parents were believers and we feared lest he should oppress them by rebellion and disbelief.

81. And we intended that their Lord should change him for them for one better in purity and nearer to mercy.

82. And as for the wall, it belonged to two orphan boys in the city, and there was beneath it a treasure belonging to them, and their father had been righteous, and thy Lord intended that they should come to their full strength and should bring forth their treasure as a mercy from their Lord; and I did it not upon my own command. Such is the interpretation of that wherewith thou couldst not bear.

83. They will ask thee of Dhū'l-Qarneyn. Say: I shall recite unto you a remembrance of him.

84. Lo! We made him strong in the land and gave him unto everything a road.

85. And he followed a road

86. Till, when he reached the setting-place of the sun, he found it setting in a muddy spring, and found a people thereabout: We said: O Dhū'l-Qarneyn! Either punish or show them kindness.

1. Or, it might be, "sea."

أَمَّا السَّفِينَةُ فَكَانَتْ لِمَسٰكِينَ يَعْمَلُونَ فِي الْبَحْرِ
فَأَرَدْتُّ أَنْ أَعِيبَهَا وَكَانَ وَرَآءَهُمْ مَّلِكٌ يَأْخُذُ
كُلَّ سَفِينَةٍ غَصْبًا ٧٩
وَأَمَّا الْغُلٰمُ فَكَانَ أَبَوٰهُ مُؤْمِنَيْنِ فَخَشِينَآ
أَنْ يُّرْهِقَهُمَا طُغْيٰنًا وَّكُفْرًا ٨٠
فَأَرَدْنَآ أَنْ يُّبْدِلَهُمَا رَبُّهُمَا خَيْرًا مِّنْهُ زَكٰوةً
وَّأَقْرَبَ رُحْمًا ٨١
وَأَمَّا الْجِدَارُ فَكَانَ لِغُلٰمَيْنِ يَتِيمَيْنِ فِي الْمَدِينَةِ
وَكَانَ تَحْتَهُ كَنْزٌ لَّهُمَا وَكَانَ أَبُوهُمَا صٰلِحًا
فَأَرَادَ رَبُّكَ أَنْ يَّبْلُغَآ أَشُدَّهُمَا وَيَسْتَخْرِجَا
كَنْزَهُمَا رَحْمَةً مِّنْ رَّبِّكَ وَمَا فَعَلْتُهُ
عَنْ أَمْرِي ذٰلِكَ تَأْوِيلُ مَا لَمْ تَسْطِعْ عَّلَيْهِ
صَبْرًا ٨٢
وَيَسْـَٔلُونَكَ عَنْ ذِي الْقَرْنَيْنِ قُلْ سَأَتْلُوا
عَلَيْكُمْ مِّنْهُ ذِكْرًا ٨٣
إِنَّا مَكَّنَّا لَهُ فِي الْأَرْضِ وَآتَيْنٰهُ مِنْ كُلِّ
شَيْءٍ سَبَبًا ٨٤
فَأَتْبَعَ سَبَبًا ٨٥
حَتّٰى إِذَا بَلَغَ مَغْرِبَ الشَّمْسِ وَجَدَهَا تَغْرُبُ
فِي عَيْنٍ حَمِئَةٍ وَّوَجَدَ عِنْدَهَا قَوْمًا قُلْنَا يٰذَا
الْقَرْنَيْنِ إِمَّآ أَنْ تُعَذِّبَ وَإِمَّآ أَنْ تَتَّخِذَ فِيهِمْ
حُسْنًا ٨٦

87. He said: As for him who doth wrong, we shall punish him, and then he will be brought back unto his Lord, who will punish him with awful punishment!

88. But as for him who believeth and doth right, good will be his reward, and We shall speak unto him a mild command.

89. Then he followed a road

90. Till, when he reached the rising-place of the sun, he found it rising on a people for whom We had appointed no shelter therefrom,

91. So (it was). And We knew all concerning him.

92. Then he followed a road

93. Till, when he came between the two mountains, he found upon their hither side a folk that scarce could understand a saying.

94. They said: O Dhū'l-Qarneyn! Lo! Gog and Magog are spoiling the land. So may we pay thee tribute on condition that thou set a barrier between us and them?

95. He said: That wherein my Lord hath established me is better (than your tribute). Do but help me with strength (of men), I will set between you and them a bank:

96. Give me pieces of iron—till, when he had levelled up (the gap) between the cliffs, he said: Blow!—till, when he had made it a fire, he said: Bring me molten copper to pour thereon.

97. And (Gog and Magog) were not able to surmount, nor could they pierce (it)

قَالَ اَمَّا مَنْ ظَلَمَ فَسَوْفَ نُعَذِّبُهٗ ثُمَّ يُرَدُّ اِلٰى
رَبِّهٖ فَيُعَذِّبُهٗ عَذَابًا نُّكْرًا ﴿٨٧﴾
وَاَمَّا مَنْ اٰمَنَ وَعَمِلَ صَالِحًا فَلَهٗ جَزَآءَ اِلْحُسْنٰى
وَسَنَقُوْلُ لَهٗ مِنْ اَمْرِنَا يُسْرًا ﴿٨٨﴾
ثُمَّ اَتْبَعَ سَبَبًا ﴿٨٩﴾
حَتّٰٓى اِذَا بَلَغَ مَطْلِعَ الشَّمْسِ وَجَدَهَا
تَطْلُعُ عَلٰى قَوْمٍ لَّمْ نَجْعَلْ لَّهُمْ مِّنْ دُوْنِهَا
سِتْرًا ﴿٩٠﴾
كَذٰلِكَ وَقَدْ اَحَطْنَا بِمَا لَدَيْهِ خُبْرًا ﴿٩١﴾
ثُمَّ اَتْبَعَ سَبَبًا ﴿٩٢﴾
حَتّٰٓى اِذَا بَلَغَ بَيْنَ السَّدَّيْنِ وَجَدَ مِنْ دُوْنِهِمَا
قَوْمًا لَّا يَكَادُوْنَ يَفْقَهُوْنَ قَوْلًا ﴿٩٣﴾
قَالُوْا يٰذَا الْقَرْنَيْنِ اِنَّ يَاْجُوْجَ وَمَاْجُوْجَ مُفْسِدُوْنَ
فِى الْاَرْضِ فَهَلْ نَجْعَلُ لَكَ خَرْجًا عَلٰٓى اَنْ تَجْعَلَ
بَيْنَنَا وَبَيْنَهُمْ سَدًّا ﴿٩٤﴾
قَالَ مَا مَكَّنِّىْ فِيْهِ رَبِّىْ خَيْرٌ فَاَعِيْنُوْنِىْ بِقُوَّةٍ
اَجْعَلْ بَيْنَكُمْ وَبَيْنَهُمْ رَدْمًا ﴿٩٥﴾
اٰتُوْنِىْ زُبَرَ الْحَدِيْدِ حَتّٰٓى اِذَا سَاوٰى بَيْنَ الصَّدَفَيْنِ
قَالَ انْفُخُوْا حَتّٰٓى اِذَا جَعَلَهٗ نَارًا قَالَ اٰتُوْنِىْٓ اُفْرِغْ
عَلَيْهِ قِطْرًا ﴿٩٦﴾
فَمَا اسْطَاعُوْٓا اَنْ يَّظْهَرُوْهُ وَمَا اسْتَطَاعُوْا لَهٗ
نَقْبًا ﴿٩٧﴾

98. He said: This is a mercy from my Lord; but when the promise of my Lord cometh to pass, He will lay it low, for the promise of my Lord is true.

99. And on that day We shall let some of them surge against others, and the Trumpet will be blown. Then We shall gather them together in one gathering;

100. On that day We shall present hell to the disbelievers, plain to view,

101. Those whose eyes were hoodwinked from My reminder, and who could not bear to hear.

102. Do the disbelievers reckon that they can choose My bondmen as protecting friends beside Me? Lo! We have prepared hell as a welcome for the disbelievers.

103. Say: Shall We inform you who will be the greatest losers by their works?

104. Those whose effort goeth astray in the life of the world, and yet they reckon that they do good work.

105. Those are they who disbelieve in the revelations of their Lord and in the meeting with Him. Therefor their works are vain, and on the Day of Resurrection We assign no weight to them.

106. That is their reward: hell, because they disbelieved, and made a jest of Our revelations and Our messengers.

107. Lo! those who believe and do good works, theirs are the Gardens of Paradise for welcome,

108. Wherein they will abide, with no desire to be removed from thence.

قَالَ هٰذَا رَحْمَةٌ مِّنْ رَّبِّيْ ۚ فَإِذَا جَآءَ وَعْدُ
رَبِّيْ جَعَلَهٗ دَكَّآءَ ۚ وَكَانَ وَعْدُ رَبِّيْ
حَقًّا ﴿٩٨﴾
وَتَرَكْنَا بَعْضَهُمْ يَوْمَئِذٍ يَّمُوْجُ فِيْ بَعْضٍ وَّنُفِخَ
فِي الصُّوْرِ فَجَمَعْنٰهُمْ جَمْعًا ﴿٩٩﴾
وَّعَرَضْنَا جَهَنَّمَ يَوْمَئِذٍ لِّلْكٰفِرِيْنَ عَرْضًا ﴿١٠٠﴾
الَّذِيْنَ كَانَتْ اَعْيُنُهُمْ فِيْ غِطَآءٍ عَنْ ذِكْرِيْ وَكَانُوْا
لَا يَسْتَطِيْعُوْنَ سَمْعًا ﴿١٠١﴾
اَفَحَسِبَ الَّذِيْنَ كَفَرُوْٓا اَنْ يَّتَّخِذُوْا عِبَادِيْ مِنْ
دُوْنِيْٓ اَوْلِيَآءَ ۚ اِنَّآ اَعْتَدْنَا جَهَنَّمَ لِلْكٰفِرِيْنَ
نُزُلًا ﴿١٠٢﴾
قُلْ هَلْ نُنَبِّئُكُمْ بِالْاَخْسَرِيْنَ اَعْمَالًا ﴿١٠٣﴾
اَلَّذِيْنَ ضَلَّ سَعْيُهُمْ فِي الْحَيٰوةِ الدُّنْيَا وَهُمْ
يَحْسَبُوْنَ اَنَّهُمْ يُحْسِنُوْنَ صُنْعًا ﴿١٠٤﴾
اُولٰٓئِكَ الَّذِيْنَ كَفَرُوْا بِاٰيٰتِ رَبِّهِمْ وَلِقَآئِهٖ
فَحَبِطَتْ اَعْمَالُهُمْ فَلَا نُقِيْمُ لَهُمْ يَوْمَ الْقِيٰمَةِ
وَزْنًا ﴿١٠٥﴾
ذٰلِكَ جَزَآؤُهُمْ جَهَنَّمُ بِمَا كَفَرُوْا وَاتَّخَذُوْٓا
اٰيٰتِيْ وَرُسُلِيْ هُزُوًا ﴿١٠٦﴾
اِنَّ الَّذِيْنَ اٰمَنُوْا وَعَمِلُوا الصّٰلِحٰتِ كَانَتْ لَهُمْ
جَنّٰتُ الْفِرْدَوْسِ نُزُلًا ﴿١٠٧﴾
خٰلِدِيْنَ فِيْهَا لَا يَبْغُوْنَ عَنْهَا حِوَلًا ﴿١٠٨﴾

109. Say: Though the sea became ink for the Words of my Lord, verily the sea would be used up before the Words of my Lord were exhausted, even though We brought the like thereof to help.

قُل لَّوْ كَانَ الْبَحْرُ مِدَادًا لِّكَلِمٰتِ رَبِّيْ لَنَفِدَ الْبَحْرُ
قَبْلَ اَنْ تَنْفَدَ كَلِمٰتُ رَبِّيْ وَلَوْ جِئْنَا بِمِثْلِهٖ
مَدَدًا ١٠٩

110. Say: I am only a mortal like you. My Lord inspireth in me that your God is only One God. And whoever hopeth for the meeting with his Lord, let him do righteous work, and make none sharer of the worship due unto his Lord.

قُلْ اِنَّمَآ اَنَا بَشَرٌ مِّثْلُكُمْ يُوْحٰٓى اِلَيَّ اَنَّمَآ اِلٰهُكُمْ
اِلٰهٌ وَّاحِدٌ فَمَنْ كَانَ يَرْجُوْا لِقَآءَ رَبِّهٖ
فَلْيَعْمَلْ عَمَلًا صَالِحًا وَّلَا يُشْرِكْ بِعِبَادَةِ
ع ١٢ ٣ رَبِّهٖٓ اَحَدًا ١١٠

Maryam takes its name from v. 16 ff. That it is of quite early Meccan revelations is established by the following tradition:

In the fifth year of the Prophet's mission (the ninth before the Hijrah, or Flight, to Al-Madînah) a number of the poorer converts were allowed by the Prophet to emigrate to Abyssinia, a Christian country where they would not be subject to persecution for their worship of the One God. This is known as the first Hijrah. The rulers of Mecca sent ambassadors to ask the Negus for their extradition, accusing them of having left the religion of their own people without entering the Christian religion, and of having done wrong to their own country. The Negus (against the wish of the envoys) sent for the spokesmen of the refugees and, in the presence of the bishops of his realm, questioned them of their religion. Ja'far ibn Abî Ṭālib, cousin of the Prophet, answered: (I translate from the account given by Ibn Isḥaq):—

"We were folk immersed in ignorance, worshipping idols, eating carrion, given to lewdness, severing the ties of kinship, bad neighbours, the strong among us preying the weak; thus were we till Allah sent to us a messenger of our own, whose lineage, honesty, trustworthiness and chastity we knew, and he called us to Allah that we should acknowledge His unity and worship Him and eschew all the stones and idols that we and our fathers used to worship beside Him; and ordered us to be truthful and to restore the pledge and observe the ties of kinship, and be good neighbours, and to abstain from things forbidden, and from blood, and forbade us lewdness and false speech, and to prey upon the wealth of orphans, and to accuse good women; and commanded us to worship Allah only, ascribing nothing unto Him as partner, and enjoined upon us prayer and legal alms and fasting. (And he enumerated for him the teachings of Islām.)

"So we trusted him and we believed in him and followed that which he had brought from Allah, and we worshipped Allah only, and ascribed nothing as partner unto Him. And we refrained from that which was forbidden to us, and indulged in that which was made lawful for us. And our people became hostile to us and tormented us and sought to turn us from our religion that they might bring us back to the worship of idols from the worship of Allah Most High, and that we might indulge in those inequities which before we had deemed lawful.

"And when they persecuted and oppressed us, and hemmed us in, and kept us from the practice of our religion, we came forth to thy land, and chose thee above all others, and sought thy protection, and hoped that we should not be troubled in thy land, O King!"

Then the Negus asked him: Hast with thee aught of that which he brought from Allah? Ja'far answered: Yes. Then the Negus said: Relate it to me, and Ja'far recited to him the beginning of Kāf, Hā, Yā, Ain, Ṣād"—the Arabic letters with which this Sūrah begins, such letters being generally used instead of titles by the early Muslims. Therefore this Sūrah must have been revealed and well known before the departure of the emigrants for Abyssinia.

An early Meccan Sūrah, with the possible exception of vv. 59 and 60, which, according to some authorities, were revealed at Al-Madînah.

1. Ibn Hisham Sîrah (Cairo edition), Part I, p. 116.

MARY

Revealed at Mecca

In the name of Allah, the Beneficent, the Merciful.

1. Kāf. Hā. Yā. 'Aīn. Ṣād.[1]

2. A mention of the mercy of thy Lord unto His servant Zachariah:—

3. When he cried unto his Lord a cry in secret,

4. Saying: My Lord! Lo! the bones of me wax feeble and my head is shining with grey hair, and I have never been unblest in prayer to Thee, my Lord.

5. Lo! I fear my kinsfolk after me, since my wife is barren. Oh, give me from Thy presence a successor

6. Who shall inherit of me and inherit (also) of the house of Jacob. And make him, my Lord, acceptable (unto Thee).

7. (It was said unto him): O Zachariah! Lo! We bring thee tidings of a son whose name is John[2]; We have given the same name to none before (him).

8. He said: My Lord! How can I have a son when my wife is barren and I have reached infirm old age?

9. He said: So (it will be). Thy Lord saith: It is easy for Me, even as I created thee before, when thou wast naught.

10. He said: My Lord! Appoint for me some token. He said: Thy token is that thou, with no bodily defect, shalt not speak unto mankind three nights.

11. Then he came forth unto his people from the sanctuary, and signified to them: Glorify your Lord at break of day and fall of night.

1. See Sûr. II, v. 1, footnote. 2. Ar. *Yahya*.

آياتها ٩٨ (١٩) سُورَةُ مَرْيَمَ مَكِّيَّةٌ رُكُوعَاتُهَا ٦

بِسْمِ اللّٰهِ الرَّحْمٰنِ الرَّحِيْمِ

كٓهٰيٰعٓصٓ (١)

ذِكْرُ رَحْمَتِ رَبِّكَ عَبْدَهٗ زَكَرِيَّا (٢)

إِذْ نَادٰى رَبَّهٗ نِدَآءً خَفِيًّا (٣)

قَالَ رَبِّ إِنِّيْ وَهَنَ الْعَظْمُ مِنِّيْ وَاشْتَعَلَ الرَّأْسُ

شَيْبًا وَّلَمْ أَكُنْ بِدُعَآئِكَ رَبِّ شَقِيًّا (٤)

وَإِنِّيْ خِفْتُ الْمَوَالِيَ مِنْ وَّرَآءِيْ وَكَانَتِ امْرَأَتِيْ

عَاقِرًا فَهَبْ لِيْ مِنْ لَّدُنْكَ وَلِيًّا (٥)

يَّرِثُنِيْ وَيَرِثُ مِنْ اٰلِ يَعْقُوْبَ وَاجْعَلْهُ رَبِّ

رَضِيًّا (٦)

يٰزَكَرِيَّآ إِنَّا نُبَشِّرُكَ بِغُلٰمِ ٱِسْمُهٗ يَحْيٰى لَمْ نَجْعَلْ

لَّهٗ مِنْ قَبْلُ سَمِيًّا (٧)

قَالَ رَبِّ أَنّٰى يَكُوْنُ لِيْ غُلٰمٌ وَّكَانَتِ امْرَأَتِيْ عَاقِرًا

وَّقَدْ بَلَغْتُ مِنَ الْكِبَرِ عِتِيًّا (٨)

قَالَ كَذٰلِكَ قَالَ رَبُّكَ هُوَ عَلَيَّ هَيِّنٌ وَّقَدْ

خَلَقْتُكَ مِنْ قَبْلُ وَلَمْ تَكُ شَيْئًا (٩)

قَالَ رَبِّ اجْعَلْ لِّيْ اٰيَةً قَالَ اٰيَتُكَ أَلَّا تُكَلِّمَ

النَّاسَ ثَلٰثَ لَيَالٍ سَوِيًّا (١٠)

فَخَرَجَ عَلٰى قَوْمِهٖ مِنَ الْمِحْرَابِ فَأَوْحٰى إِلَيْهِمْ

أَنْ سَبِّحُوْا بُكْرَةً وَّعَشِيًّا (١١)

12. (And it was said unto his son): O John ! Hold fast the Scripture. And We gave him wisdom when a child,

13. And compassion from Our presence, and purity; and he was devout,

14. And dutiful toward his parents. And he was not arrogant, rebellious.

15. Peace on him the day he was born, and the day he dieth and the day he shall be raised alive!

16. And make mention of Mary in the Scripture, when she had withdrawn from her people to a chamber looking East,

17. And had chosen seclusion from them. Then We sent unto her Our Spirit and it assumed for her the likeness of a perfect man.

18. She said: Lo! I seek refuge in the Beneficent One from thee, if thou art Godfearing.

19. He said: I am only a messenger of thy Lord, that I may bestow on thee a faultless son.

20. She said: How can I have a son when no mortal hath touched me, neither have I been unchaste?

21. He said: So (it will be). Thy Lord saith: It is easy for Me. And (it will be) that We may make of him a revelation for mankind and a mercy from Us, and it is a thing ordained.

22. And she conceived him, and she withdrew with him to a far place.

23. And the pangs of childbirth drove her unto the trunk of the palm tree. She said: Oh, would that I had died ere this and had become a thing of naught, forgotten!

24. Then (one) cried unto her from below her, saying: Grieve not! Thy Lord hath placed a rivulet beneath thee,

يٰيَحْيٰى خُذِ الْكِتٰبَ بِقُوَّةٍ ۗ وَاٰتَيْنٰهُ الْحُكْمَ
صَبِيًّا ﴿١٢﴾
وَّحَنَانًا مِّنْ لَّدُنَّا وَزَكٰوةً ۗ وَكَانَ تَقِيًّا ﴿١٣﴾
وَّبَرًّا بِوَالِدَيْهِ وَلَمْ يَكُنْ جَبَّارًا عَصِيًّا ﴿١٤﴾
وَسَلٰمٌ عَلَيْهِ يَوْمَ وُلِدَ وَيَوْمَ يَمُوْتُ وَيَوْمَ
يُبْعَثُ حَيًّا ﴿١٥﴾
وَاذْكُرْ فِي الْكِتٰبِ مَرْيَمَ ۘ إِذِ انْتَبَذَتْ مِنْ أَهْلِهَا
مَكَانًا شَرْقِيًّا ﴿١٦﴾
فَاتَّخَذَتْ مِنْ دُوْنِهِمْ حِجَابًا ۖ فَأَرْسَلْنَآ إِلَيْهَا
رُوْحَنَا فَتَمَثَّلَ لَهَا بَشَرًا سَوِيًّا ﴿١٧﴾
قَالَتْ إِنِّيْٓ أَعُوْذُ بِالرَّحْمٰنِ مِنْكَ إِنْ كُنْتَ تَقِيًّا ﴿١٨﴾
قَالَ إِنَّمَآ أَنَا رَسُوْلُ رَبِّكِ ۖ لِأَهَبَ لَكِ غُلٰمًا
زَكِيًّا ﴿١٩﴾
قَالَتْ أَنّٰى يَكُوْنُ لِيْ غُلٰمٌ وَّلَمْ يَمْسَسْنِيْ بَشَرٌ وَّلَمْ
أَكُ بَغِيًّا ﴿٢٠﴾
قَالَ كَذٰلِكِ ۚ قَالَ رَبُّكِ هُوَ عَلَيَّ هَيِّنٌ ۚ وَلِنَجْعَلَهٗٓ اٰيَةً
لِّلنَّاسِ وَرَحْمَةً مِّنَّا ۚ وَكَانَ أَمْرًا مَّقْضِيًّا ﴿٢١﴾
فَحَمَلَتْهُ فَانْتَبَذَتْ بِهٖ مَكَانًا قَصِيًّا ﴿٢٢﴾
فَأَجَآءَهَا الْمَخَاضُ إِلٰى جِذْعِ النَّخْلَةِ ۚ قَالَتْ
يٰلَيْتَنِيْ مِتُّ قَبْلَ هٰذَا وَكُنْتُ نَسْيًا مَّنْسِيًّا ﴿٢٣﴾
فَنَادٰىهَا مِنْ تَحْتِهَآ أَلَّا تَحْزَنِيْ قَدْ جَعَلَ رَبُّكِ
تَحْتَكِ سَرِيًّا ﴿٢٤﴾

25. And shake the trunk of the palm-tree toward thee; thou wilt cause ripe dates to fall upon thee.

وَهُزِّيٓ إِلَيْكِ بِجِذْعِ النَّخْلَةِ تُسٰقِطْ عَلَيْكِ رُطَبًا
جَنِيًّا ﴿٢٥﴾

26. So eat and drink and be consoled. And if thou meetest any mortal, say: Lo! I have vowed a fast unto the Beneficent, and may not speak this day to any mortal.

فَكُلِيْ وَاشْرَبِيْ وَقَرِّيْ عَيْنًا ۚ فَاِمَّا تَرَيِنَّ مِنَ الْبَشَرِ
اَحَدًا ۙ فَقُوْلِيْٓ اِنِّيْ نَذَرْتُ لِلرَّحْمٰنِ صَوْمًا فَلَنْ
اُكَلِّمَ الْيَوْمَ اِنْسِيًّا ﴿٢٦﴾

27. Then she brought him to her own folk, carrying him. They said: O Mary! Thou hast come with an amazing thing.

فَاَتَتْ بِهٖ قَوْمَهَا تَحْمِلُهٗ ۭ قَالُوْا يٰمَرْيَمُ لَقَدْ جِئْتِ
شَيْـًٔا فَرِيًّا ﴿٢٧﴾

28. Oh sister of Aaron[1] ! Thy father was not a wicked man nor was thy mother a harlot.

يٰٓاُخْتَ هٰرُوْنَ مَا كَانَ اَبُوْكِ امْرَاَ سَوْءٍ وَّمَا
كَانَتْ اُمُّكِ بَغِيًّا ﴿٢٨﴾

29. Then she pointed to him. They said: How can we talk to one who is in the cradle, a young boy?

فَاَشَارَتْ اِلَيْهِ ۭ قَالُوْا كَيْفَ نُكَلِّمُ مَنْ كَانَ فِي
الْمَهْدِ صَبِيًّا ﴿٢٩﴾

30. He spake: Lo! I am the slave of Allah. He hath given me the Scripture and hath appointed me a Prophet,

قَالَ اِنِّيْ عَبْدُ اللّٰهِ ۣ اٰتٰىنِيَ الْكِتٰبَ وَجَعَلَنِيْ
نَبِيًّا ﴿٣٠﴾

31. And hath made me blessed wheresoever I may be, and hath enjoined upon me prayer and almsgiving so long as I remain alive,

وَّجَعَلَنِيْ مُبٰرَكًا اَيْنَ مَا كُنْتُ ۠ وَاَوْصٰنِيْ بِالصَّلٰوةِ
وَالزَّكٰوةِ مَا دُمْتُ حَيًّا ﴿٣١﴾

32. And (hath made me) dutiful toward her who bore me, and hath not made me arrogant, unblest.

وَّبَرًّۢا بِوَالِدَتِيْ ۡ وَلَمْ يَجْعَلْنِيْ جَبَّارًا شَقِيًّا ﴿٣٢﴾

33. Peace on me the day I was born, and the day I die, and the day I shall be raised alive!

وَالسَّلٰمُ عَلَيَّ يَوْمَ وُلِدْتُّ وَيَوْمَ اَمُوْتُ وَيَوْمَ
اُبْعَثُ حَيًّا ﴿٣٣﴾

34. Such was Jesus, son of Mary, (this is) a statement of the truth concerning which they doubt.

ذٰلِكَ عِيْسَى ابْنُ مَرْيَمَ ۚ قَوْلَ الْحَقِّ الَّذِيْ
فِيْهِ يَمْتَرُوْنَ ﴿٣٤﴾

35. It befitteth not (the Majesty of) Allah that He should take unto Himself a son. Glory be to Him! When He decreeth a thing, He saith unto it only: Be! and it is.

مَا كَانَ لِلّٰهِ اَنْ يَّتَّخِذَ مِنْ وَّلَدٍ ۙ سُبْحٰنَهٗ ۭ اِذَا
قَضٰٓى اَمْرًا فَاِنَّمَا يَقُوْلُ لَهٗ كُنْ فَيَكُوْنُ ﴿٣٥﴾

1. See Sûr. III, introduction.

36. And lo! Allah is my Lord and your Lord. So serve Him. That is the right path.

وَإِنَّ اللّٰهَ رَبِّي وَرَبُّكُمْ فَاعْبُدُوهُ ۚ هٰذَا صِرَاطٌ
مُّسْتَقِيمٌ ٣٦

37. The sects among them differ: but woe unto the disbelievers from the meeting of an awful Day.

فَاخْتَلَفَ الْأَحْزَابُ مِنْ بَيْنِهِمْ ۖ فَوَيْلٌ لِّلَّذِينَ
كَفَرُوا مِن مَّشْهَدِ يَوْمٍ عَظِيمٍ ٣٧

38. See and hear them on the Day they come unto Us! Yet the evil-doers are to-day in error manifest.

أَسْمِعْ بِهِمْ وَأَبْصِرْ يَوْمَ يَأْتُونَنَا ۖ لٰكِنِ الظّٰلِمُونَ
الْيَوْمَ فِي ضَلٰلٍ مُّبِينٍ ٣٨

39. And warn them of the Day of anguish when the case hath been decided. Now they are in a state of carelessness, and they believe not.

وَأَنذِرْهُمْ يَوْمَ الْحَسْرَةِ إِذْ قُضِيَ الْأَمْرُ وَهُمْ
فِي غَفْلَةٍ وَهُمْ لَا يُؤْمِنُونَ ٣٩

40. Lo! We inherit the earth and all who are thereon, and unto Us they are returned.

إِنَّا نَحْنُ نَرِثُ الْأَرْضَ وَمَنْ عَلَيْهَا وَإِلَيْنَا
يُرْجَعُونَ ٤٠

41. And make mention (O Muhammad) in the Scripture of Abraham. Lo! he was a saint, a Prophet.

وَاذْكُرْ فِي الْكِتٰبِ إِبْرٰهِيمَ ۚ إِنَّهُ كَانَ صِدِّيقًا
نَّبِيًّا ٤١

42. When he said unto his father: O my father! Why worshippest thou that which heareth not nor seeth, nor can in aught avail thee?

إِذْ قَالَ لِأَبِيهِ يٰأَبَتِ لِمَ تَعْبُدُ مَا لَا يَسْمَعُ وَلَا
يُبْصِرُ وَلَا يُغْنِي عَنكَ شَيْئًا ٤٢

43. O my father! Lo! there hath come unto me of knowledge that which came not unto thee. So follow me, and I will lead thee on a right path.

يٰأَبَتِ إِنِّي قَدْ جَاءَنِي مِنَ الْعِلْمِ مَا لَمْ يَأْتِكَ
فَاتَّبِعْنِي أَهْدِكَ صِرَاطًا سَوِيًّا ٤٣

44. O my father! Serve not the devil. Lo! the devil is a rebel unto the Beneficent.

يٰأَبَتِ لَا تَعْبُدِ الشَّيْطٰنَ ۖ إِنَّ الشَّيْطٰنَ كَانَ
لِلرَّحْمٰنِ عَصِيًّا ٤٤

45. O my father! Lo! I fear lest a punishment from the Beneficent overtake thee so that thou become a comrade of the devil.

يٰأَبَتِ إِنِّي أَخَافُ أَن يَمَسَّكَ عَذَابٌ مِّنَ الرَّحْمٰنِ
فَتَكُونَ لِلشَّيْطٰنِ وَلِيًّا ٤٥

46. He said: Rejectest thou my gods, O Abraham? If thou cease not, I shall surely stone thee. Depart from me a long while!

قَالَ أَرَاغِبٌ أَنتَ عَنْ آلِهَتِي يٰإِبْرٰهِيمُ ۖ لَئِن لَّمْ
تَنتَهِ لَأَرْجُمَنَّكَ ۖ وَاهْجُرْنِي مَلِيًّا ٤٦

47. He said: Peace be unto thee! I shall ask forgiveness of my Lord for thee. Lo! He was ever gracious unto me.

قَالَ سَلَامٌ عَلَيْكَ سَأَسْتَغْفِرُ لَكَ رَبِّيْ اِنَّهُ كَانَ بِيْ حَفِيًّا ۟

48. I shall withdraw from you and that unto which ye pray beside Allah, and I shall pray unto my Lord. It may be that, in prayer unto my Lord, I shall not be unblest.

وَاَعْتَزِلُكُمْ وَمَا تَدْعُوْنَ مِنْ دُوْنِ اللّٰهِ وَاَدْعُوْا رَبِّيْ عَسٰۤى اَلَّا اَكُوْنَ بِدُعَآءِ رَبِّيْ شَقِيًّا ۟

49. So, when he had withdrawn from them and that which they were worshipping beside Allah, We gave him Isaac and Jacob. Each of them We made a Prophet.

فَلَمَّا اعْتَزَلَهُمْ وَمَا يَعْبُدُوْنَ مِنْ دُوْنِ اللّٰهِ وَهَبْنَا لَهُ اِسْحٰقَ وَيَعْقُوْبَ ۚ وَكُلًّا جَعَلْنَا نَبِيًّا ۟

50. And We gave them of Our mercy, and assigned to them a high and true renown.

وَوَهَبْنَا لَهُمْ مِنْ رَّحْمَتِنَا وَجَعَلْنَا لَهُمْ لِسَانَ صِدْقٍ عَلِيًّا ۟

51. And make mention in the Scripture of Moses. Lo! he was chosen, and he was a messenger (of Allah), a Prophet.

وَاذْكُرْ فِي الْكِتٰبِ مُوْسٰۤى اِنَّهُ كَانَ مُخْلَصًا وَّكَانَ رَسُوْلًا نَّبِيًّا ۟

52. We called him from the right slope of the Mount, and brought him nigh in communion.

وَنَادَيْنٰهُ مِنْ جَانِبِ الطُّوْرِ الْاَيْمَنِ وَقَرَّبْنٰهُ نَجِيًّا ۟

53. And We bestowed upon him of Our mercy his brother Aaron, a Prophet (likewise).

وَوَهَبْنَا لَهُ مِنْ رَّحْمَتِنَا اَخَاهُ هٰرُوْنَ نَبِيًّا ۟

54. And make mention in the Scripture of Ishmael. Lo! he was a keeper of his promise, and he was a messenger (of Allah), a Prophet.

وَاذْكُرْ فِي الْكِتٰبِ اِسْمٰعِيْلَ اِنَّهُ كَانَ صَادِقَ الْوَعْدِ وَكَانَ رَسُوْلًا نَّبِيًّا ۟

55. He enjoined upon his people worship and almsgiving, and was acceptable in the sight of his Lord.

وَكَانَ يَأْمُرُ اَهْلَهُ بِالصَّلٰوةِ وَالزَّكٰوةِ ۪ وَكَانَ عِنْدَ رَبِّهٖ مَرْضِيًّا ۟

56. And make mention in the Scripture of Idris.[1] Lo! he was a saint, a Prophet;

وَاذْكُرْ فِي الْكِتٰبِ اِدْرِيْسَ اِنَّهُ كَانَ صِدِّيْقًا نَّبِيًّا ۟

57. And We raised him to high station.

وَرَفَعْنٰهُ مَكَانًا عَلِيًّا ۟

1. Identified with Enoch.

58. These are they unto whom Allah showed favour from among the Prophets, of the seed of Adam and of those whom We carried (in the ship) with Noah, and of the seed of Abraham and Israel, and from among those whom We guided and chose. When the revelations of the Beneficent were recited unto them, they fell down, adoring and weeping.

59. Now there hath succeeded them a later generation who have ruined worship and have followed lusts. But they will meet deception,

60. Save him who shall repent and believe and do right. Such will enter the Garden, and they will not be wronged in aught—

61. Gardens of Eden, which the Beneficent hath promised to His slaves in the Unseen. Lo! His promise is ever sure of fulfilment—

62. They hear therein no idle talk, but only Peace! and therein they have food for morn and evening.

63. Such is the Garden which We cause the devout among Our bondmen to inherit.

64. We (angels) come not down save by commandment of thy Lord. Unto Him belongeth all that is before us and all that is behind us and all that is between those two, and thy Lord was never forgetful—

65. Lord of the heavens and the earth and all that is between them! Therefore, worship thou Him and be thou steadfast in His service. Knowest thou one that can be named along with Him?

66. And man saith: When I am dead, shall I forsooth be brought forth alive?

67. Doth not man remember that We created him before, when he was naught?

أُولَٰئِكَ الَّذِينَ أَنْعَمَ اللَّهُ عَلَيْهِم مِّنَ النَّبِيِّينَ مِن
ذُرِّيَّةِ آدَمَ وَمِمَّنْ حَمَلْنَا مَعَ نُوحٍ وَمِن ذُرِّيَّةِ
إِبْرَاهِيمَ وَإِسْرَائِيلَ وَمِمَّنْ هَدَيْنَا وَاجْتَبَيْنَا إِذَا
تُتْلَىٰ عَلَيْهِمْ آيَاتُ الرَّحْمَٰنِ خَرُّوا سُجَّدًا وَبُكِيًّا ۩ ٥٨ [السجدة]
فَخَلَفَ مِن بَعْدِهِمْ خَلْفٌ أَضَاعُوا الصَّلَاةَ وَاتَّبَعُوا
الشَّهَوَاتِ فَسَوْفَ يَلْقَوْنَ غَيًّا ٥٩
إِلَّا مَن تَابَ وَآمَنَ وَعَمِلَ صَالِحًا فَأُولَٰئِكَ
يَدْخُلُونَ الْجَنَّةَ وَلَا يُظْلَمُونَ شَيْئًا ٦٠
جَنَّاتِ عَدْنٍ الَّتِي وَعَدَ الرَّحْمَٰنُ عِبَادَهُ بِالْغَيْبِ
إِنَّهُ كَانَ وَعْدُهُ مَأْتِيًّا ٦١
لَّا يَسْمَعُونَ فِيهَا لَغْوًا إِلَّا سَلَامًا وَلَهُمْ رِزْقُهُمْ فِيهَا
بُكْرَةً وَعَشِيًّا ٦٢
تِلْكَ الْجَنَّةُ الَّتِي نُورِثُ مِنْ عِبَادِنَا مَن كَانَ
تَقِيًّا ٦٣
وَمَا نَتَنَزَّلُ إِلَّا بِأَمْرِ رَبِّكَ لَهُ مَا بَيْنَ أَيْدِينَا وَمَا
خَلْفَنَا وَمَا بَيْنَ ذَٰلِكَ وَمَا كَانَ رَبُّكَ نَسِيًّا ٦٤
رَّبُّ السَّمَاوَاتِ وَالْأَرْضِ وَمَا بَيْنَهُمَا فَاعْبُدْهُ
وَاصْطَبِرْ لِعِبَادَتِهِ هَلْ تَعْلَمُ لَهُ سَمِيًّا ٦٥ [ع]
وَيَقُولُ الْإِنسَانُ أَإِذَا مَا مِتُّ لَسَوْفَ أُخْرَجُ
حَيًّا ٦٦
أَوَلَا يَذْكُرُ الْإِنسَانُ أَنَّا خَلَقْنَاهُ مِن قَبْلُ وَلَمْ
يَكُ شَيْئًا ٦٧

68. And, by thy Lord, verily We shall assemble them and the devils, then We shall bring them, crouching, around hell.

69. Then We shall pluck out from every sect whichever of them was most stubborn in rebellion to the Beneficent.

70. And surely We are best aware of those most worthy to be burned therein.

71. There is not one of you but shall approach it. That is a fixed ordinance of thy Lord.

72. Then We shall rescue those who kept from evil, and leave the evil-doers crouching there.

73. And when Our clear revelations are recited unto them, those who disbelieve say unto those who believe: Which of the two parties (yours or ours) is better in position, and more imposing as an army?

74. How many a generation have We destroyed before them, who were more imposing in respect of gear and outward seeming!

75. Say: As for him who is in error, the Beneficent will verily prolong his span of life until, when they behold that which they were promised, whether it be punishment (in the world), or the Hour of Doom), they will know who is worse in position and who is weaker as an army.

76. Allah increaseth in right guidance those who walk aright, and the good deeds which endure are better in thy Lord's sight for reward, and better for resort.

77. Hast thou seen him who disbelieveth in Our revelations and saith: Assuredly I shall be given wealth and children?

فَوَرَبِّكَ لَنَحْشُرَنَّهُمْ وَالشَّيٰطِيْنَ ثُمَّ لَنُحْضِرَنَّهُمْ
حَوْلَ جَهَنَّمَ جِثِيًّا ﴿٦٨﴾
ثُمَّ لَنَنْزِعَنَّ مِنْ كُلِّ شِيْعَةٍ اَيُّهُمْ اَشَدُّ عَلَى
الرَّحْمٰنِ عِتِيًّا ﴿٦٩﴾
ثُمَّ لَنَحْنُ اَعْلَمُ بِالَّذِيْنَ هُمْ اَوْلٰى بِهَا صِلِيًّا ﴿٧٠﴾
وَاِنْ مِّنْكُمْ اِلَّا وَارِدُهَا كَانَ عَلٰى رَبِّكَ حَتْمًا
مَّقْضِيًّا ﴿٧١﴾
ثُمَّ نُنَجِّي الَّذِيْنَ اتَّقَوْا وَّنَذَرُ الظّٰلِمِيْنَ فِيْهَا
جِثِيًّا ﴿٧٢﴾
وَاِذَا تُتْلٰى عَلَيْهِمْ اٰيٰتُنَا بَيِّنٰتٍ قَالَ الَّذِيْنَ كَفَرُوْا
لِلَّذِيْنَ اٰمَنُوْٓا اَيُّ الْفَرِيْقَيْنِ خَيْرٌ مَّقَامًا وَّاَحْسَنُ
نَدِيًّا ﴿٧٣﴾
وَكَمْ اَهْلَكْنَا قَبْلَهُمْ مِّنْ قَرْنٍ هُمْ اَحْسَنُ اَثَاثًا
وَّرِءْيًا ﴿٧٤﴾
قُلْ مَنْ كَانَ فِي الضَّلٰلَةِ فَلْيَمْدُدْ لَهُ الرَّحْمٰنُ
مَدًّا حَتّٰٓى اِذَا رَاَوْا مَا يُوْعَدُوْنَ اِمَّا الْعَذَابَ وَ
اِمَّا السَّاعَةَ فَسَيَعْلَمُوْنَ مَنْ هُوَ شَرٌّ مَّكَانًا وَّ
اَضْعَفُ جُنْدًا ﴿٧٥﴾
وَيَزِيْدُ اللّٰهُ الَّذِيْنَ اهْتَدَوْا هُدًى وَالْبٰقِيٰتُ
الصّٰلِحٰتُ خَيْرٌ عِنْدَ رَبِّكَ ثَوَابًا وَّخَيْرٌ مَّرَدًّا ﴿٧٦﴾
اَفَرَءَيْتَ الَّذِيْ كَفَرَ بِاٰيٰتِنَا وَقَالَ لَاُوْتَيَنَّ مَالًا
وَّوَلَدًا ﴿٧٧﴾

78. Hath he perused the Unseen, or hath he made a pact with the Beneficent?

79. Nay, but We shall record that which he saith and prolong for him a span of torment,

80. And We shall inherit from him that whereof he spake, and he will come unto Us, alone (without his wealth and children).

81. And they have chosen (other) gods beside Allah that they may be a power for them:

82. Nay, but they will deny their worship of them, and become opponents unto them.

83. Seest thou not that We have set the devils on the disbelievers to confound them with confusion?

84. So make no haste against them (O Muhammad). We do but number unto them a sum (of days).

85. On the Day when We shall gather the righteous unto the Beneficent, a goodly company,

86. And drive the guilty unto Hell, a weary herd,

87. They will have no power of intercession, save him who hath made a covenant with his Lord.

88. And they say: The Beneficent hath taken unto Himself a son.

89. Assuredly ye utter a disastrous thing,

90. Whereby almost the heavens are torn, and the earth is split asunder and the mountains fall in ruins,

91. That ye ascribe unto the Beneficent a son,

92. When it is not meet for (the Majesty of) the Beneficent that He should choose a son.

93. There is none in the heavens and the earth but cometh unto the Beneficent as a slave.

أَطَّلَعَ الْغَيْبَ أَمِ اتَّخَذَ عِنْدَ الرَّحْمٰنِ عَهْدًا ٧٨
كَلَّا سَنَكْتُبُ مَا يَقُولُ وَنَمُدُّ لَهُ مِنَ الْعَذَابِ مَدًّا ٧٩
وَنَرِثُهُ مَا يَقُولُ وَيَأْتِينَا فَرْدًا ٨٠
وَاتَّخَذُوا مِنْ دُونِ اللّٰهِ آلِهَةً لِيَكُونُوا لَهُمْ
عِزًّا ٨١
كَلَّا سَيَكْفُرُونَ بِعِبَادَتِهِمْ وَيَكُونُونَ عَلَيْهِمْ
ع ضِدًّا ٨٢
أَلَمْ تَرَ أَنَّا أَرْسَلْنَا الشَّيٰطِينَ عَلَى الْكٰفِرِينَ
تَؤُزُّهُمْ أَزًّا ٨٣
فَلَا تَعْجَلْ عَلَيْهِمْ إِنَّمَا نَعُدُّ لَهُمْ عَدًّا ٨٤
يَوْمَ نَحْشُرُ الْمُتَّقِينَ إِلَى الرَّحْمٰنِ وَفْدًا ٨٥
وقف لازم وَنَسُوقُ الْمُجْرِمِينَ إِلَىٰ جَهَنَّمَ وِرْدًا ٨٦
لَا يَمْلِكُونَ الشَّفَاعَةَ إِلَّا مَنِ اتَّخَذَ عِنْدَ
وقف لازم الرَّحْمٰنِ عَهْدًا ٨٧
وَقَالُوا اتَّخَذَ الرَّحْمٰنُ وَلَدًا ٨٨
لَقَدْ جِئْتُمْ شَيْئًا إِدًّا ٨٩
تَكَادُ السَّمٰوٰتُ يَتَفَطَّرْنَ مِنْهُ وَتَنْشَقُّ الْأَرْضُ وَ
تَخِرُّ الْجِبَالُ هَدًّا ٩٠
أَنْ دَعَوْا لِلرَّحْمٰنِ وَلَدًا ٩١
وَمَا يَنْبَغِي لِلرَّحْمٰنِ أَنْ يَتَّخِذَ وَلَدًا ٩٢
إِنْ كُلُّ مَنْ فِي السَّمٰوٰتِ وَالْأَرْضِ إِلَّا آتِي الرَّحْمٰنِ
عَبْدًا ٩٣

94. Verily He knoweth them and numbereth them with (right) numbering.

لَقَدْ أَحْصٰهُمْ وَعَدَّهُمْ عَدًّا ۞

95. And each one of them will come unto Him on the Day of Resurrection, alone.

وَكُلُّهُمْ اٰتِيْهِ يَوْمَ الْقِيٰمَةِ فَرْدًا ۞

96. Lo! those who believe and do good works, the Beneficent will appoint for them love.

اِنَّ الَّذِيْنَ اٰمَنُوْا وَعَمِلُوا الصّٰلِحٰتِ سَيَجْعَلُ لَهُمُ الرَّحْمٰنُ وُدًّا ۞

97. And We make (this Scripture) easy in thy tongue, (O Muhammad) only that thou mayst bear good tidings therewith unto those who ward off (evil), and warn therewith the froward folk.

فَاِنَّمَا يَسَّرْنٰهُ بِلِسَانِكَ لِتُبَشِّرَ بِهِ الْمُتَّقِيْنَ وَ تُنْذِرَ بِهِ قَوْمًا لُّدًّا ۞

98. And how many a generation before them have We destroyed! Canst thou (Muhammad) see a single man of them, or hear from them the slightest sound?

وَكَمْ اَهْلَكْنَا قَبْلَهُمْ مِّنْ قَرْنٍ هَلْ تُحِسُّ مِنْهُمْ مِّنْ اَحَدٍ اَوْ تَسْمَعُ لَهُمْ رِكْزًا ۞

Tā Hā takes its name from the Arabic letters which form the first verse. As in the case of Sūrah XIX, the early date of revelation is established by a strong tradition.

Omar ibn al-Khattāb, who afterwards became Caliph, was among the bitterest opponents of Islām in early days. He set out one day, sword in hand, with the intention of killing the Prophet—"this Sabaean who has split the unity of Qureysh, calls their ideals foolish and their religion shameful, and blasphemes their gods"—when a friend who met him dissuaded him, reminding him that if he slew the Prophet he would have to reckon with the vengeance of a powerful clan: "Thinkest thou that the Banū 'Abd Munāf would let thee walk on the earth if thou hadst slain Muhammad?" for tribal pride survived religious difference. "Is it not better for thee to return to the folk of thine own house and keep them straight?" Omar asked: "Which of the folk of my house?" "Thy brother-in-law and cousin, Sa'id ibn Zeyd, and thy sister, Fātimah, daughter of Al-Khattāb, for, by Allah, they are become Muslims and followers of Muhammad in his religion, so look thou to them." Then Omar returned, enraged against his sister and brother-in-law, and there was with them in the house Khabāb ibn 'Arit, having with him a leaf on which was written Ṭā Hā (this Sūrah) which he was reading aloud to them. When they heard the noise of Omar's coming, Khabāb hid in a closet that they had in the house and Fātimah took the leaf and hid it under her thigh. But Omar had heard the sound of Khabāb's reading as he drew near the house, and when he entered he said: "What was that mumbling which I heard?" They said: "Thou heardest nothing." Omar said: "Yea, by Allah! And I have already been informed that ye are become followers of Muhammad in his religion." Then he attacked his brother-in-law Sa'id ibn Zeyd, but Fātimah sprang to keep him off her husband and he struck and wounded her. And when he had done that, his sister and his brother-in-law said to him: "Yes, we are Muslims and we believe in Allah and His messenger, so do what thou wilt!" But when Omar saw the blood upon his sister he was sorry for what he had done, and he said to his sister: "Give me that leaf from which I heard you reading just now, that I may see what this is that Muhammad has brought." And Omar was a scribe. When he said that, his sister said: "We fear to trust thee with it." He said: "Fear not!" and swore by his gods that he would return it to her when he had read it. And when he said that, she hoped for his conversion to Al-Islam, but said: "O my brother, thou art unclean on account of thine idolatry and none may touch it save the purified." Then Omar went out and washed himself, and she gave him the leaf on which Ṭā Hā was written and he read it. And when he had read it he said: "How excellent are these words!" and praised it highly. And when he heard that, Khabāb came out to him and said: "O Omar, I hope that Allah has brought you in answer to the prayer of the Prophet, for only yesterday I heard him saying: O Allah! Strengthen Al-Islām with Abū'l-Hukm ibn Hishām or Omar ibn al-Khattāb; and Allah is Allah, O Omar!" At that he said: "O Khabāb, direct me to Muhammad that I may go to him and make surrender."[1]

The conversion of Omar took place in the fifth year of the Prophet's mission (ninth before the Hijrah) soon after the departure of the emigrants to Abyssinia. At that time this Sūrah was already written down and in circulation.

An early Meccan Sūrah.

1. Ibn Hisham, Part I, pp. 119 and 120.

ṬĀ HĀ

Revealed at Mecca

In the name of Allah, the Beneficent, the Merciful.

1. Ṭā Hā.

2. We have not revealed unto thee (Muhammad) this Qur'ān that thou shouldst be distressed,

3. But as a reminder unto him who feareth,

4. A revelation from Him Who created the earth and the high heavens,

5. The Beneficent One, Who is established on the Throne.

6. Unto Him belongeth whatsoever is in the heavens and whatsoever is in the earth, and whatsoever is between them, and whatsoever is beneath the sod.

7. And if thou speakest aloud, then lo! He knoweth the secret (thought) and (that which is yet) more hidden.

8. Allah! There is no God save Him. His are the most beautiful names.

9. Hath there come unto thee the story of Moses?

10. When he saw a fire and said unto his folk: Wait! Lo! I see a fire afar off. Peradventure I may bring you a brand therefrom or may find guidance at the fire.

11. And when he reached it, he was called by name: O Moses!

12. Lo! I, even I, am thy Lord. So take off thy shoes, for lo! thou art in the holy valley of Ṭuwa.

13. And I have chosen thee, so hearken unto that which is inspired.

14. Lo! I, even I, am Allah. There is no God save Me. So serve Me and establish worship for My remembrance.

آياتها ١٣٥ (٢٠) سُورَةُ طٰهٰ مَكِّيَّةٌ ركوعاتها ٨

بِسْمِ اللّٰهِ الرَّحْمٰنِ الرَّحِيْمِ

طٰهٰ ﴿١﴾

مَآ اَنْزَلْنَا عَلَيْكَ الْقُرْاٰنَ لِتَشْقٰٓى ﴿٢﴾

اِلَّا تَذْكِرَةً لِّمَنْ يَّخْشٰى ﴿٣﴾

تَنْزِيْلًا مِّمَّنْ خَلَقَ الْاَرْضَ وَالسَّمٰوٰتِ الْعُلٰى ﴿٤﴾

اَلرَّحْمٰنُ عَلَى الْعَرْشِ اسْتَوٰى ﴿٥﴾

لَهٗ مَا فِى السَّمٰوٰتِ وَمَا فِى الْاَرْضِ وَمَا بَيْنَهُمَا وَ
مَا تَحْتَ الثَّرٰى ﴿٦﴾

وَاِنْ تَجْهَرْ بِالْقَوْلِ فَاِنَّهٗ يَعْلَمُ السِّرَّ وَ
اَخْفٰى ﴿٧﴾

اَللّٰهُ لَآ اِلٰهَ اِلَّا هُوَ لَهُ الْاَسْمَآءُ الْحُسْنٰى ﴿٨﴾

وَهَلْ اَتٰىكَ حَدِيْثُ مُوْسٰى ﴿٩﴾

اِذْ رَاٰ نَارًا فَقَالَ لِاَهْلِهِ امْكُثُوْٓا اِنِّىْٓ اٰنَسْتُ نَارًا
لَّعَلِّىْٓ اٰتِيْكُمْ مِّنْهَا بِقَبَسٍ اَوْ اَجِدُ عَلَى النَّارِ هُدًى ﴿١٠﴾

فَلَمَّآ اَتٰىهَا نُوْدِىَ يٰمُوْسٰى ﴿١١﴾

اِنِّىْٓ اَنَا رَبُّكَ فَاخْلَعْ نَعْلَيْكَ اِنَّكَ بِالْوَادِ الْمُقَدَّسِ
طُوًى ﴿١٢﴾

وَاَنَا اخْتَرْتُكَ فَاسْتَمِعْ لِمَا يُوْحٰى ﴿١٣﴾

اِنَّنِىْٓ اَنَا اللّٰهُ لَآ اِلٰهَ اِلَّآ اَنَا فَاعْبُدْنِىْ وَاَقِمِ
الصَّلٰوةَ لِذِكْرِىْ ﴿١٤﴾

15. Lo! the Hour is surely coming. But I will to keep it hidden, that every soul may be rewarded for that which it striveth (to achieve).

16. Therefor, let not him turn thee aside from (the thought of) it who believeth not therein but followeth his own desire, lest thou perish.

17. And what is that in thy right hand, O Moses?

18. He said: This is my staff whereon I lean, and wherewith I beat down branches for my sheep, and wherein I find other uses.

19. He said: Cast it down, O Moses!

20. So he cast it down, and lo! it was a serpent, gliding.

21. He said: Grasp it and fear not. We shall return it to its former state.

22. And thrust thy hand within thine armpit, it will come forth white without hurt. (That will be) another token,

23. That We may show thee (some) of Our greater portents,

24. Go thou unto Pharaoh! Lo! he hath transgressed (the bounds).

25. (Moses) said: My Lord! Relieve my mind

26. And ease my task for me;

27. And loose a knot from my tongue,

28. That they may understand my saying.

29. Appoint for me a henchman from my folk,

30. Aaron, my brother.

31. Confirm my strength with him.

إِنَّ السَّاعَةَ اٰتِيَةٌ أَكَادُ أُخْفِيهَا لِتُجْزٰى كُلُّ
نَفْسٍ بِمَا تَسْعٰى ١٥
فَلَا يَصُدَّنَّكَ عَنْهَا مَن لَّا يُؤْمِنُ بِهَا وَاتَّبَعَ
هَوٰىهُ فَتَرْدٰى ١٦
وَمَا تِلْكَ بِيَمِينِكَ يٰمُوسٰى ١٧
قَالَ هِيَ عَصَايَ أَتَوَكَّؤُا عَلَيْهَا وَأَهُشُّ بِهَا
عَلٰى غَنَمِي وَلِيَ فِيهَا مَاٰرِبُ أُخْرٰى ١٨
قَالَ أَلْقِهَا يٰمُوسٰى ١٩
فَأَلْقٰىهَا فَإِذَا هِيَ حَيَّةٌ تَسْعٰى ٢٠
قَالَ خُذْهَا وَلَا تَخَفْ سَنُعِيدُهَا سِيرَتَهَا
الْأُولٰى ٢١
وَاضْمُمْ يَدَكَ إِلٰى جَنَاحِكَ تَخْرُجْ بَيْضَاءَ مِنْ
غَيْرِ سُوْءٍ اٰيَةً أُخْرٰى ٢٢
لِنُرِيَكَ مِنْ اٰيٰتِنَا الْكُبْرٰى ٢٣
ع اِذْهَبْ إِلٰى فِرْعَوْنَ إِنَّهُ طَغٰى ٢٤
قَالَ رَبِّ اشْرَحْ لِي صَدْرِي ٢٥
وَيَسِّرْ لِي أَمْرِي ٢٦
وَاحْلُلْ عُقْدَةً مِّن لِّسَانِي ٢٧
يَفْقَهُوا قَوْلِي ٢٨
وَاجْعَل لِّي وَزِيرًا مِّنْ أَهْلِي ٢٩
هٰرُونَ أَخِي ٣٠
اشْدُدْ بِهِ أَزْرِي ٣١

32. And let him share my task,

33. That we may glorify Thee much,

34. And much remember Thee.

35. Lo! Thou art ever Seeing us.

36. He said: Thou art granted thy request, O Moses.

37. And indeed, another time, already We have shown thee favour,

38. When We inspired in thy mother that which is inspired,

39. Saying: Throw him into the ark, and throw it into the river, then the river shall throw it on to the bank, and there an enemy to Me and an enemy to him shall take him. And I endued thee with love from Me that thou mightest be trained according to My will,

40. When thy sister went and said: Shall I show you one who will nurse him? and We restored thee to thy mother that her eyes might be refreshed and might not sorrow. And thou didst kill a man and We delivered thee from great distress, and tried thee with a heavy trial. And thou didst tarry years among the folk of Midian. Then camest thou (hither) by (My) providence, O Moses,

41. And I have attached thee to Myself.

42. Go, thou and thy brother, with My tokens, and be not faint in remembrance of Me.

43. Go, both of you, unto Pharaoh. Lo! he hath transgressed (the bounds).

44. And speak unto him a gentle word, that peradventure he may heed or fear.

45. They said: Our Lord! Lo! we fear that he may be beforehand with us or that he may play the tyrant.

46. He said: Fear not. Lo! I am with you twain, Hearing and Seeing.

وَأَشْرِكْهُ فِي أَمْرِي ﴿٣٢﴾

كَيْ نُسَبِّحَكَ كَثِيرًا ﴿٣٣﴾

وَنَذْكُرَكَ كَثِيرًا ﴿٣٤﴾

إِنَّكَ كُنْتَ بِنَا بَصِيرًا ﴿٣٥﴾

قَالَ قَدْ أُوتِيتَ سُؤْلَكَ يَا مُوسَىٰ ﴿٣٦﴾

وَلَقَدْ مَنَنَّا عَلَيْكَ مَرَّةً أُخْرَىٰ ﴿٣٧﴾

إِذْ أَوْحَيْنَا إِلَىٰ أُمِّكَ مَا يُوحَىٰ ﴿٣٨﴾

أَنِ اقْذِفِيهِ فِي التَّابُوتِ فَاقْذِفِيهِ فِي الْيَمِّ فَلْيُلْقِهِ
الْيَمُّ بِالسَّاحِلِ يَأْخُذْهُ عَدُوٌّ لِي وَعَدُوٌّ لَهُ وَأَلْقَيْتُ
عَلَيْكَ مَحَبَّةً مِنِّي وَلِتُصْنَعَ عَلَىٰ عَيْنِي ﴿٣٩﴾ وقف لازم

إِذْ تَمْشِي أُخْتُكَ فَتَقُولُ هَلْ أَدُلُّكُمْ عَلَىٰ مَنْ
يَكْفُلُهُ فَرَجَعْنَاكَ إِلَىٰ أُمِّكَ كَيْ تَقَرَّ عَيْنُهَا وَلَا
تَحْزَنَ وَقَتَلْتَ نَفْسًا فَنَجَّيْنَاكَ مِنَ الْغَمِّ وَ
فَتَنَّاكَ فُتُونًا فَلَبِثْتَ سِنِينَ فِي أَهْلِ مَدْيَنَ
ثُمَّ جِئْتَ عَلَىٰ قَدَرٍ يَا مُوسَىٰ ﴿٤٠﴾

وَاصْطَنَعْتُكَ لِنَفْسِي ﴿٤١﴾

اذْهَبْ أَنْتَ وَأَخُوكَ بِآيَاتِي وَلَا تَنِيَا فِي ذِكْرِي ﴿٤٢﴾

اذْهَبَا إِلَىٰ فِرْعَوْنَ إِنَّهُ طَغَىٰ ﴿٤٣﴾

فَقُولَا لَهُ قَوْلًا لَيِّنًا لَعَلَّهُ يَتَذَكَّرُ أَوْ يَخْشَىٰ ﴿٤٤﴾

قَالَا رَبَّنَا إِنَّنَا نَخَافُ أَنْ يَفْرُطَ عَلَيْنَا أَوْ أَنْ
يَطْغَىٰ ﴿٤٥﴾

قَالَ لَا تَخَافَا إِنَّنِي مَعَكُمَا أَسْمَعُ وَأَرَىٰ ﴿٤٦﴾

47. So go ye unto him and say: Lo! we are two messengers of thy Lord. So let the Children of Israel go with us, and torment them not. We bring thee a token from thy Lord. And peace will be for him who followeth right guidance.

48. Lo! it hath been revealed unto us that the doom will be for him who denieth and turneth away.

49. (Pharaoh) said: Who then is the Lord of you twain, O Moses?

50. He said: Our Lord is He Who gave unto everything its nature, then guided it aright.

51. He said: What then is the state of the generations of old?

52. He said: The knowledge thereof is with my Lord in a Record. My Lord neither erreth nor forgetteth,

53. Who hath appointed the earth as a bed and hath threaded roads for you therein and hath sent down water from the sky and thereby We have brought forth divers kinds of vegetation,

54. (Saying): Eat ye and feed your cattle. Lo! herein verily are portents for men of thought.

55. Thereof We created you, and thereunto We return you, and thence We bring you forth a second time.

56. And We verily did show him all Our tokens, but he denied them and refused.

57. He said: Hast come to drive us out from our land by thy magic, O Moses?

58. But we surely can produce magic the like thereof; so appoint a tryst between us and you, which neither we nor thou shall fail to keep, at a place convenient (to us both).

59. (Moses) said: Your tryst shall be the day of the feast, and let the people assemble when the sun hath risen high.

فَأْتِيَاهُ فَقُولَا إِنَّا رَسُولَا رَبِّكَ فَأَرْسِلْ مَعَنَا بَنِي
إِسْرَاءِيلَ وَلَا تُعَذِّبْهُمْ قَدْ جِئْنَاكَ بِآيَةٍ مِنْ
رَبِّكَ وَالسَّلَامُ عَلَىٰ مَنِ اتَّبَعَ الْهُدَىٰ ﴿٤٧﴾
إِنَّا قَدْ أُوحِيَ إِلَيْنَا أَنَّ الْعَذَابَ عَلَىٰ مَنْ كَذَّبَ
وَتَوَلَّىٰ ﴿٤٨﴾
قَالَ فَمَنْ رَبُّكُمَا يَا مُوسَىٰ ﴿٤٩﴾
قَالَ رَبُّنَا الَّذِي أَعْطَىٰ كُلَّ شَيْءٍ خَلْقَهُ ثُمَّ هَدَىٰ ﴿٥٠﴾
قَالَ فَمَا بَالُ الْقُرُونِ الْأُولَىٰ ﴿٥١﴾
قَالَ عِلْمُهَا عِنْدَ رَبِّي فِي كِتَابٍ لَا يَضِلُّ رَبِّي وَ
لَا يَنْسَى ﴿٥٢﴾
الَّذِي جَعَلَ لَكُمُ الْأَرْضَ مَهْدًا وَسَلَكَ لَكُمْ
فِيهَا سُبُلًا وَأَنْزَلَ مِنَ السَّمَاءِ مَاءً فَأَخْرَجْنَا
بِهِ أَزْوَاجًا مِنْ نَبَاتٍ شَتَّىٰ ﴿٥٣﴾
كُلُوا وَارْعَوْا أَنْعَامَكُمْ إِنَّ فِي ذَٰلِكَ لَآيَاتٍ لِأُولِي
النُّهَىٰ ﴿٥٤﴾ ع
مِنْهَا خَلَقْنَاكُمْ وَفِيهَا نُعِيدُكُمْ وَمِنْهَا نُخْرِجُكُمْ
تَارَةً أُخْرَىٰ ﴿٥٥﴾
وَلَقَدْ أَرَيْنَاهُ آيَاتِنَا كُلَّهَا فَكَذَّبَ وَأَبَىٰ ﴿٥٦﴾
قَالَ أَجِئْتَنَا لِتُخْرِجَنَا مِنْ أَرْضِنَا بِسِحْرِكَ يَا مُوسَىٰ ﴿٥٧﴾
فَلَنَأْتِيَنَّكَ بِسِحْرٍ مِثْلِهِ فَاجْعَلْ بَيْنَنَا وَبَيْنَكَ
مَوْعِدًا لَا نُخْلِفُهُ نَحْنُ وَلَا أَنْتَ مَكَانًا سُوًى ﴿٥٨﴾
قَالَ مَوْعِدُكُمْ يَوْمُ الزِّينَةِ وَأَنْ يُحْشَرَ النَّاسُ ضُحًى ﴿٥٩﴾

60. Then Pharaoh went and gathered his strength, then came (to the appointed tryst).

61. Moses said unto them: Woe unto you! Invent not a lie against Allah, lest He extirpate you by some punishment. He who lieth faileth miserably.

62. Then they debated one with another what they must do, and they kept their counsel secret.

63. They said: Lo! these are two wizards who would drive you out from your country by their magic, and destroy your best traditions;

64. So arrange your plan, and come in battle line. Whoso is uppermost this day will be indeed successful.

65. They said: O Moses! Either throw first, or let us be the first to throw?

66. He said: Nay, do ye throw! Then lo! their cords and their staves, by their magic, appeared to him as though they ran.

67. And Moses conceived a fear in his mind.

68. We said: Fear not! Lo! thou art the higher.

69. Throw that which is in thy right hand! It will eat up that which they have made. Lo! that which they have made is but a wizard's artifice, and a wizard shall not be successful to whatever point of (skill) he may attain.

70. Then the wizards were (all) flung down prostrate, crying: We believe in the Lord of Aaron and Moses.

71. (Pharaoh) said: Ye put faith in him before I give you leave. Lo! he is your chief who taught you magic. Now surely I shall cut off your hands and your feet alternately, and I shall crucify you on the trunks of palm trees, and ye shall know for certain which of us hath sterner and more lasting punishment.

فَتَوَلّٰى فِرْعَوْنُ فَجَمَعَ كَيْدَهٗ ثُمَّ اَتٰى ﴿٦٠﴾
قَالَ لَهُمْ مُّوْسٰى وَيْلَكُمْ لَا تَفْتَرُوْا عَلَى اللّٰهِ كَذِبًا
فَيُسْحِتَكُمْ بِعَذَابٍ ۚ وَقَدْ خَابَ مَنِ افْتَرٰى ﴿٦١﴾
فَتَنَازَعُوْٓا اَمْرَهُمْ بَيْنَهُمْ وَاَسَرُّوا النَّجْوٰى ﴿٦٢﴾
قَالُوْٓا اِنْ هٰذٰنِ لَسٰحِرٰنِ يُرِيْدٰنِ اَنْ يُّخْرِجٰكُمْ مِّنْ
اَرْضِكُمْ بِسِحْرِهِمَا وَيَذْهَبَا بِطَرِيْقَتِكُمُ الْمُثْلٰى ﴿٦٣﴾
فَاَجْمِعُوْا كَيْدَكُمْ ثُمَّ ائْتُوْا صَفًّا ۚ وَقَدْ اَفْلَحَ
الْيَوْمَ مَنِ اسْتَعْلٰى ﴿٦٤﴾
قَالُوْا يٰمُوْسٰٓى اِمَّآ اَنْ تُلْقِيَ وَاِمَّآ اَنْ نَّكُوْنَ اَوَّلَ
مَنْ اَلْقٰى ﴿٦٥﴾
قَالَ بَلْ اَلْقُوْا ۚ فَاِذَا حِبَالُهُمْ وَعِصِيُّهُمْ يُخَيَّلُ
اِلَيْهِ مِنْ سِحْرِهِمْ اَنَّهَا تَسْعٰى ﴿٦٦﴾
فَاَوْجَسَ فِيْ نَفْسِهٖ خِيْفَةً مُّوْسٰى ﴿٦٧﴾
قُلْنَا لَا تَخَفْ اِنَّكَ اَنْتَ الْاَعْلٰى ﴿٦٨﴾
وَاَلْقِ مَا فِيْ يَمِيْنِكَ تَلْقَفْ مَا صَنَعُوْا ۚ اِنَّمَا صَنَعُوْا
كَيْدُ سٰحِرٍ ۚ وَلَا يُفْلِحُ السّٰحِرُ حَيْثُ اَتٰى ﴿٦٩﴾
فَاُلْقِيَ السَّحَرَةُ سُجَّدًا قَالُوْٓا اٰمَنَّا بِرَبِّ هٰرُوْنَ
وَمُوْسٰى ﴿٧٠﴾
قَالَ اٰمَنْتُمْ لَهٗ قَبْلَ اَنْ اٰذَنَ لَكُمْ ۚ اِنَّهٗ لَكَبِيْرُكُمُ
الَّذِيْ عَلَّمَكُمُ السِّحْرَ ۚ فَلَاُقَطِّعَنَّ اَيْدِيَكُمْ وَ
اَرْجُلَكُمْ مِّنْ خِلَافٍ وَّلَاُصَلِّبَنَّكُمْ فِيْ جُذُوْعِ
النَّخْلِ وَلَتَعْلَمُنَّ اَيُّنَآ اَشَدُّ عَذَابًا وَّاَبْقٰى ﴿٧١﴾

72. They said: We choose thee not above the clear proofs that have come unto us, and above Him Who created us. So decree what thou wilt decree. Thou wilt end for us only the life of the world.

73. Lo! we believe in our Lord, that He may forgive us our sins and the magic unto which thou didst force us. Allah is better and more lasting.

74. Lo! whoso cometh guilty unto his Lord, verily for him is hell. There he will neither die nor live.

75. But whoso cometh unto Him a believer, having done good works, for such are the high stations;

76. Gardens of Eden underneath which rivers flow, wherein they will abide for ever. That is the reward of one who groweth.

77. And verily We inspired Moses, saying: Take away My slaves by night and strike for them a dry path in the sea, fearing not to be overtaken, neither being afraid (of the sea).

78. Then Pharaoh followed with his hosts and there covered them that which did cover them of the sea.

79. And Pharaoh led his folk astray, he did not guide them.

80. O Children of Israel! We delivered you from your enemy, and We made a covenant with you on the holy mountain's side, and sent down on you the manna and the quails,

81. (Saying): Eat of the good things wherewith We have provided you, and transgress not in respect thereof lest My wrath come upon you; and he on whom My wrath cometh, he is lost indeed.

قَالُوْا لَنْ نُّؤْثِرَكَ عَلٰى مَا جَآءَنَا مِنَ الْبَيِّنٰتِ وَالَّذِيْ
فَطَرَنَا فَاقْضِ مَآ اَنْتَ قَاضٍ ۭ اِنَّمَا تَقْضِيْ هٰذِهِ
الْحَيٰوةَ الدُّنْيَا ۝٧٢
اِنَّآ اٰمَنَّا بِرَبِّنَا لِيَغْفِرَ لَنَا خَطٰيٰنَا وَمَآ اَكْرَهْتَنَا
عَلَيْهِ مِنَ السِّحْرِ ۭ وَاللّٰهُ خَيْرٌ وَّاَبْقٰى ۝٧٣
اِنَّهٗ مَنْ يَّاْتِ رَبَّهٗ مُجْرِمًا فَاِنَّ لَهٗ جَهَنَّمَ ۭ لَا
يَمُوْتُ فِيْهَا وَلَا يَحْيٰى ۝٧٤
وَمَنْ يَّاْتِهٖ مُؤْمِنًا قَدْ عَمِلَ الصّٰلِحٰتِ فَاُولٰۗىِٕكَ
لَهُمُ الدَّرَجٰتُ الْعُلٰى ۝٧٥
جَنّٰتُ عَدْنٍ تَجْرِيْ مِنْ تَحْتِهَا الْاَنْهٰرُ خٰلِدِيْنَ
فِيْهَا ۭ وَذٰلِكَ جَزٰۗؤُا مَنْ تَزَكّٰى ۝٧٦
وَلَقَدْ اَوْحَيْنَآ اِلٰى مُوْسٰٓى ڏ اَنْ اَسْرِ بِعِبَادِيْ فَاضْرِبْ
لَهُمْ طَرِيْقًا فِي الْبَحْرِ يَبَسًا ۙ لَّا تَخٰفُ دَرَكًا وَّلَا تَخْشٰى ۝٧٧
فَاَتْبَعَهُمْ فِرْعَوْنُ بِجُنُوْدِهٖ فَغَشِيَهُمْ مِّنَ الْيَمِّ
مَا غَشِيَهُمْ ۝٧٨
وَاَضَلَّ فِرْعَوْنُ قَوْمَهٗ وَمَا هَدٰى ۝٧٩
يٰبَنِيْٓ اِسْرَاۗءِيْلَ قَدْ اَنْجَيْنٰكُمْ مِّنْ عَدُوِّكُمْ
وَوٰعَدْنٰكُمْ جَانِبَ الطُّوْرِ الْاَيْمَنَ وَنَزَّلْنَا عَلَيْكُمُ
الْمَنَّ وَالسَّلْوٰى ۝٨٠
كُلُوْا مِنْ طَيِّبٰتِ مَا رَزَقْنٰكُمْ وَلَا تَطْغَوْا فِيْهِ
فَيَحِلَّ عَلَيْكُمْ غَضَبِيْ ۚ وَمَنْ يَّحْلِلْ عَلَيْهِ
غَضَبِيْ فَقَدْ هَوٰى ۝٨١

82. And lo! verily I am Forgiving toward him who repenteth and believeth and doth good, and afterward walketh aright.

83. And (it was said): What hath made thee hasten from thy folk, O Moses?

84. He said: They are close upon my track. I hastened unto Thee that Thou mightest be well pleased.

85. He said: Lo! We have tried thy folk in thine absence, and As-Sāmiri hath misled them.

86. Then Moses went back unto his folk, angry and sad. He said: O my people! Hath not your Lord promised you a fair promise? Did the time appointed then appear too long for you, or did ye wish that wrath from your Lord should come upon you, that ye broke tryst with me?

87. They said: We broke not tryst with thee of our own will, but we were laden with burdens of ornaments of the folk, then cast them (in the fire), for thus As-Sāmiri proposed;

88. Then he produced for them a calf, of saffron hue,[1] which gave forth a lowing sound. And they cried: This is your God and the God of Moses, but he hath forgotten.

89. See they not, then, that it returneth no saying unto them and possesseth for them neither hurt nor use?

90. And Aaron indeed had told them beforehand: O my people! Ye are but being seduced therewith, for lo! your Lord is the Beneficent, so follow me and obey my order.

91. They said: We shall by no means cease to be its votaries till Moses return unto us.

وَإِنِّي لَغَفَّارٌ لِّمَن تَابَ وَآمَنَ وَعَمِلَ صَالِحًا
ثُمَّ اهْتَدَىٰ ٨٢
وَمَا أَعْجَلَكَ عَن قَوْمِكَ يَا مُوسَىٰ ٨٣
قَالَ هُمْ أُولَاءِ عَلَىٰ أَثَرِي وَعَجِلْتُ إِلَيْكَ رَبِّ لِتَرْضَىٰ ٨٤
قَالَ فَإِنَّا قَدْ فَتَنَّا قَوْمَكَ مِن بَعْدِكَ وَأَضَلَّهُمُ
السَّامِرِيُّ ٨٥
فَرَجَعَ مُوسَىٰ إِلَىٰ قَوْمِهِ غَضْبَانَ أَسِفًا قَالَ يَا قَوْمِ
أَلَمْ يَعِدْكُمْ رَبُّكُمْ وَعْدًا حَسَنًا أَفَطَالَ عَلَيْكُمُ
الْعَهْدُ أَمْ أَرَدتُّمْ أَن يَحِلَّ عَلَيْكُمْ غَضَبٌ مِّن
رَّبِّكُمْ فَأَخْلَفْتُم مَّوْعِدِي ٨٦
قَالُوا مَا أَخْلَفْنَا مَوْعِدَكَ بِمَلْكِنَا وَلَٰكِنَّا حُمِّلْنَا
أَوْزَارًا مِّن زِينَةِ الْقَوْمِ فَقَذَفْنَاهَا فَكَذَٰلِكَ
أَلْقَى السَّامِرِيُّ ٨٧
فَأَخْرَجَ لَهُمْ عِجْلًا جَسَدًا لَّهُ خُوَارٌ فَقَالُوا هَٰذَا
إِلَٰهُكُمْ وَإِلَٰهُ مُوسَىٰ فَنَسِيَ ٨٨
أَفَلَا يَرَوْنَ أَلَّا يَرْجِعُ إِلَيْهِمْ قَوْلًا وَلَا يَمْلِكُ لَهُمْ
ضَرًّا وَلَا نَفْعًا ٨٩ ع ٤ ١٤
وَلَقَدْ قَالَ لَهُمْ هَارُونُ مِن قَبْلُ يَا قَوْمِ إِنَّمَا
فُتِنتُم بِهِ وَإِنَّ رَبَّكُمُ الرَّحْمَٰنُ فَاتَّبِعُونِي وَ
أَطِيعُوا أَمْرِي ٩٠
قَالُوا لَن نَّبْرَحَ عَلَيْهِ عَاكِفِينَ حَتَّىٰ يَرْجِعَ
إِلَيْنَا مُوسَىٰ ٩١

1. Or "a body." See VII, 148, footnote.

92. He (Moses) said: O Aaron! What held thee back when thou didst see them gone astray,

93. That thou followedst me not? Hast thou then disobeyed my order?

94. He said: O son of my mother! Clutch not my beard nor my head! I feared lest thou shouldst say: Thou hast caused division among the Children of Israel, and has not waited for my word.[1]

95. (Moses) said: And what has thou to say, O Samiri?

96. He said: I perceived what they perceive not, so I seized a handful from the footsteps of the messenger, and then threw it in. Thus my soul commended to me.[2]

97. (Moses) said: Then go! And lo! in this life it is for thee to say: Touch me not! and lo! there is for thee a tryst thou canst not break. Now look upon thy god of which thou hast remained a votary. Verily we will burn it and will scatter its dust over the sea.

98. Your God is only Allah, than Whom there is no other God. He embraceth all things in His knowledge.

99. Thus do We relate unto thee (Muhammad) some tidings of that which happened of old, and We have given thee from Our presence a Reminder.

100. Whoso turneth away from it, he verily will bear a burden on the Day of Resurrection,

101. Abiding under it—an evil burden for them on the Day of Resurrection,

102. The day when the Trumpet is blown. On that day We assemble the guilty white-eyed (with terror),

103. Murmuring among themselves: Ye have tarried but ten (days).

قَالَ يٰهٰرُونُ مَا مَنَعَكَ إِذْ رَأَيْتَهُمْ ضَلُّوٓا ﴿٩٢﴾
أَلَّا تَتَّبِعَنِ أَفَعَصَيْتَ أَمْرِى ﴿٩٣﴾
قَالَ يَبْنَؤُمَّ لَا تَأْخُذْ بِلِحْيَتِى وَلَا بِرَأْسِى إِنِّى
خَشِيتُ أَن تَقُولَ فَرَّقْتَ بَيْنَ بَنِىٓ إِسْرَآءِيلَ
وَلَمْ تَرْقُبْ قَوْلِى ﴿٩٤﴾
قَالَ فَمَا خَطْبُكَ يٰسَامِرِىُّ ﴿٩٥﴾
قَالَ بَصُرْتُ بِمَا لَمْ يَبْصُرُوا بِهٖ فَقَبَضْتُ
قَبْضَةً مِّنْ أَثَرِ الرَّسُولِ فَنَبَذْتُهَا وَكَذٰلِكَ
سَوَّلَتْ لِى نَفْسِى ﴿٩٦﴾
قَالَ فَاذْهَبْ فَإِنَّ لَكَ فِى الْحَيٰوةِ أَن تَقُولَ لَا
مِسَاسَ وَإِنَّ لَكَ مَوْعِدًا لَّن تُخْلَفَهٗ وَانْظُرْ إِلٰى
إِلٰهِكَ الَّذِى ظَلْتَ عَلَيْهِ عَاكِفًا لَّنُحَرِّقَنَّهٗ ثُمَّ
لَنَنْسِفَنَّهٗ فِى الْيَمِّ نَسْفًا ﴿٩٧﴾
إِنَّمَآ إِلٰهُكُمُ اللّٰهُ الَّذِى لَآ إِلٰهَ إِلَّا هُوَ وَسِعَ كُلَّ
شَىْءٍ عِلْمًا ﴿٩٨﴾
كَذٰلِكَ نَقُصُّ عَلَيْكَ مِنْ أَنْبَآءِ مَا قَدْ سَبَقَ
وَقَدْ اٰتَيْنٰكَ مِنْ لَّدُنَّا ذِكْرًا ﴿٩٩﴾
مَنْ أَعْرَضَ عَنْهُ فَإِنَّهٗ يَحْمِلُ يَوْمَ الْقِيٰمَةِ وِزْرًا ﴿١٠٠﴾
خٰلِدِينَ فِيهِ وَسَآءَ لَهُمْ يَوْمَ الْقِيٰمَةِ حِمْلًا ﴿١٠١﴾
يَوْمَ يُنْفَخُ فِى الصُّورِ وَنَحْشُرُ الْمُجْرِمِينَ يَوْمَئِذٍ
زُرْقًا ﴿١٠٢﴾
يَتَخَافَتُونَ بَيْنَهُمْ إِنْ لَّبِثْتُمْ إِلَّا عَشْرًا ﴿١٠٣﴾

1 The explanation usually given is that As-Sāmiri had seen the angel Gabriel pass by, and had taken some of the dust which he had hallowed, and thrown it into the image of the calf, thus giving it a semblance of life. Others say that As-Sāmiri was an adept of the Egyptian idolatry who had believed for a little while and half-heartedly in the God of Moses.

104. We are best aware of what they utter when their best in conduct say: Ye have tarried but a day.

105. They will ask thee of the mountains (on that day). Say: My Lord will break them into scattered dust,

106. And leave it as an empty plain,

107. Wherein thou seest neither curve nor ruggedness.

108. On that day they follow the summoner who deceiveth not, and voices are hushed for the Beneficent, and thou hearest but a faint murmur.

109. On that Day no intercession availeth save (that of) him unto whom the Beneficent hath given leave and whose He accepteth.

110. He knoweth (all) that is before them and (all) that is behind them, while they cannot compass it in knowledge.

111. And faces humble themselves before the Living, the Eternal. And he who beareth (a burden of) wrongdoing is indeed a failure (on that Day).

112. And he who hath done some good works, being a believer, he feareth not injustice nor begrudging (of his wage).

113. Thus We have revealed it as a Lecture[1] in Arabic, and have displayed therein certain threats, that peradventure they may keep from evil or that it may cause them to take heed.

114. Then exalted be Allah, the True King! And hasten not (O Muhammad) with the Qur'ān ere its revelation hath been perfected unto thee, and say: My Lord! Increase me in knowledge.

115. And verily We made a covenant of old with Adam, but he forgot, and We found no constancy in him.

1. Ar. *Qur'ān*.

نَحْنُ أَعْلَمُ بِمَا يَقُولُونَ إِذْ يَقُولُ أَمْثَلُهُمْ طَرِيقَةً
إِنْ لَبِثْتُمْ إِلَّا يَوْمًا ﴿١٠٤﴾ ع ٥ ١٤
وَيَسْأَلُونَكَ عَنِ الْجِبَالِ فَقُلْ يَنْسِفُهَا رَبِّي نَسْفًا ﴿١٠٥﴾
فَيَذَرُهَا قَاعًا صَفْصَفًا ﴿١٠٦﴾
لَا تَرَىٰ فِيهَا عِوَجًا وَلَا أَمْتًا ﴿١٠٧﴾
يَوْمَئِذٍ يَتَّبِعُونَ الدَّاعِيَ لَا عِوَجَ لَهُ وَخَشَعَتِ
الْأَصْوَاتُ لِلرَّحْمَٰنِ فَلَا تَسْمَعُ إِلَّا هَمْسًا ﴿١٠٨﴾
يَوْمَئِذٍ لَا تَنْفَعُ الشَّفَاعَةُ إِلَّا مَنْ أَذِنَ لَهُ الرَّحْمَٰنُ
وَرَضِيَ لَهُ قَوْلًا ﴿١٠٩﴾
يَعْلَمُ مَا بَيْنَ أَيْدِيهِمْ وَمَا خَلْفَهُمْ وَلَا
يُحِيطُونَ بِهِ عِلْمًا ﴿١١٠﴾
وَعَنَتِ الْوُجُوهُ لِلْحَيِّ الْقَيُّومِ وَقَدْ خَابَ مَنْ
حَمَلَ ظُلْمًا ﴿١١١﴾
وَمَنْ يَعْمَلْ مِنَ الصَّالِحَاتِ وَهُوَ مُؤْمِنٌ فَلَا يَخَافُ
ظُلْمًا وَلَا هَضْمًا ﴿١١٢﴾
وَكَذَٰلِكَ أَنْزَلْنَاهُ قُرْآنًا عَرَبِيًّا وَصَرَّفْنَا فِيهِ مِنَ
الْوَعِيدِ لَعَلَّهُمْ يَتَّقُونَ أَوْ يُحْدِثُ لَهُمْ ذِكْرًا ﴿١١٣﴾
فَتَعَالَى اللَّهُ الْمَلِكُ الْحَقُّ وَلَا تَعْجَلْ بِالْقُرْآنِ
مِنْ قَبْلِ أَنْ يُقْضَىٰ إِلَيْكَ وَحْيُهُ وَقُلْ رَبِّ
زِدْنِي عِلْمًا ﴿١١٤﴾
وَلَقَدْ عَهِدْنَا إِلَىٰ آدَمَ مِنْ قَبْلُ فَنَسِيَ وَلَمْ
نَجِدْ لَهُ عَزْمًا ﴿١١٥﴾ ع ٦ ١٥

116. And when We said unto the angels: Fall prostrate before Adam, they fell prostrate (all) save Iblis; he refused.

117. Therefor We said: O Adam! This is an enemy unto thee and unto thy wife, so let him not drive you both out of the Garden so that thou come to toil.

118. It is (vouchsafed) unto thee that thou hungerest not therein nor art naked,

119. And thou thirstest not therein nor art exposed to the sun's heat.

120. But the Devil whispered to him, saying: O Adam! Shall I show thee the tree of immortality and power that wasteth not away?

121. Then they twain ate thereof, so that their shame became apparent unto them, and they began to hide by heaping on themselves some of the leaves of the Garden. And Adam disobeyed his Lord, so went astray.[1]

122. Then his Lord chose him, and relented toward him, and guided him.

123. He said: Go down hence, both of you, one of you a foe unto the other. But if there come unto you from Me a guidance, then whoso followeth My guidance, he will not go astray nor come to grief.[2]

124. But he who turneth away from remembrance of Me, his will be a narrow life, and I shall bring him blind to the assembly on the Day of Resurrection.

125. He will say: My Lord! Wherefor hast Thou gathered me (hither) blind, when I was wont to see?

126. He will say: So (it must be). Our revelations came unto thee but thou didst forget them. In like manner thou art forgotten this Day!

127. Thus do We reward him who is prodigal and believeth not the revelations of his Lord; and verily the doom of the Hereafter will be sterner and more lasting.

1. Cf. Sûr. VII, 20 ff.
2. Cf. Sûr. II, and the passage leading up to it.

وإذ قلنا للملٰئكة اسجدوا لآدم فسجدوا إلا
إبليس أبى ﴿١١٦﴾
فقلنا يا آدم إن هذا عدو لك ولزوجك فلا
يخرجنكما من الجنة فتشقى ﴿١١٧﴾
إن لك ألا تجوع فيها ولا تعرى ﴿١١٨﴾
وأنك لا تظمؤا فيها ولا تضحى ﴿١١٩﴾
فوسوس إليه الشيطن قال يا آدم هل أدلك على
شجرة الخلد وملك لا يبلى ﴿١٢٠﴾
فأكلا منها فبدت لهما سوآتهما وطفقا يخصفن
عليهما من ورق الجنة وعصى آدم ربه
فغوى ﴿١٢١﴾
ثم اجتبه ربه فتاب عليه وهدى ﴿١٢٢﴾
قال اهبطا منها جميعا بعضكم لبعض عدو فإما
يأتينكم مني هدى فمن اتبع هداي فلا
يضل ولا يشقى ﴿١٢٣﴾
ومن أعرض عن ذكري فإن له معيشة ضنكا
ونحشره يوم القيمة أعمى ﴿١٢٤﴾
قال رب لم حشرتني أعمى وقد كنت بصيرا ﴿١٢٥﴾
قال كذلك أتتك آيتنا فنسيتها وكذلك اليوم
تنسى ﴿١٢٦﴾
وكذلك نجزي من أسرف ولم يؤمن بآيت
ربه ولعذاب الآخرة أشد وأبقى ﴿١٢٧﴾

128. Is it not a guidance for them (to know) how many a generation We destroyed before them, amid whose dwellings they walk? Lo! therein verily are signs for men of thought.

اَفَلَمْ يَهْدِ لَهُمْ كَمْ اَهْلَكْنَا قَبْلَهُمْ مِّنَ الْقُرُوْنِ يَمْشُوْنَ فِيْ مَسَاكِنِهِمْ ؕ اِنَّ فِيْ ذٰلِكَ لَاٰيٰتٍ لِّاُولِى النُّهٰى ۞

129. And but for a decree that had already gone forth from thy Lord, and a term already fixed, the judgement would (have) been inevitable (in this world).

وَلَوْلَا كَلِمَةٌ سَبَقَتْ مِنْ رَّبِّكَ لَكَانَ لِزَامًا وَّ اَجَلٌ مُّسَمًّى ۞

130. Therefor (O Muhammad), bear with what they say, and celebrate the praises of thy Lord ere the rising of the sun and ere the going down thereof. And glorify Him some hours of the night and at the two ends of the day, that thou mayst find acceptance.

فَاصْبِرْ عَلٰى مَا يَقُوْلُوْنَ وَسَبِّحْ بِحَمْدِ رَبِّكَ قَبْلَ طُلُوْعِ الشَّمْسِ وَقَبْلَ غُرُوْبِهَا ۚ وَمِنْ اٰنَآئِ الَّيْلِ فَسَبِّحْ وَاَطْرَافَ النَّهَارِ لَعَلَّكَ تَرْضٰى ۞

131. And strain not thine eyes toward that which We cause some wedded pairs among them to enjoy the flower of the life of the world, that We may try them thereby. The provision of thy Lord is better and more lasting.

وَلَا تَمُدَّنَّ عَيْنَيْكَ اِلٰى مَا مَتَّعْنَا بِهٖۤ اَزْوَاجًا مِّنْهُمْ زَهْرَةَ الْحَيٰوةِ الدُّنْيَا ۙ لِنَفْتِنَهُمْ فِيْهِ ؕ وَرِزْقُ رَبِّكَ خَيْرٌ وَّاَبْقٰى ۞

132. And enjoin upon thy people worship, and be constant therein. We ask not of thee a provision: We provide for thee. And the sequel is for righteousness.

وَاْمُرْ اَهْلَكَ بِالصَّلٰوةِ وَاصْطَبِرْ عَلَيْهَا ؕ لَا نَسْـَٔلُكَ رِزْقًا ؕ نَحْنُ نَرْزُقُكَ ؕ وَالْعَاقِبَةُ لِلتَّقْوٰى ۞

133. And they say: If only he would bring us a miracle from his Lord! Hath there not come unto them the proof of what is in the former Scriptures?

وَقَالُوْا لَوْلَا يَاْتِيْنَا بِاٰيَةٍ مِّنْ رَّبِّهٖ ؕ اَوَلَمْ تَاْتِهِمْ بَيِّنَةُ مَا فِى الصُّحُفِ الْاُوْلٰى ۞

134. And if We had destroyed them with some punishment before it, they would assuredly have said: Our Lord! If only Thou hadst sent unto us a messenger, so that we might have followed Thy revelations before we were (thus) humbled and disgraced!

وَلَوْ اَنَّآ اَهْلَكْنٰهُمْ بِعَذَابٍ مِّنْ قَبْلِهٖ لَقَالُوْا رَبَّنَا لَوْلَا اَرْسَلْتَ اِلَيْنَا رَسُوْلًا فَنَتَّبِعَ اٰيٰتِكَ مِنْ قَبْلِ اَنْ نَّذِلَّ وَنَخْزٰى ۞

135. Say: Each is awaiting; so await ye! Ye will come to know who are the owners of the path of equity, and who is right.

قُلْ كُلٌّ مُّتَرَبِّصٌ فَتَرَبَّصُوْا ۚ فَسَتَعْلَمُوْنَ مَنْ اَصْحٰبُ الصِّرَاطِ السَّوِيِّ وَمَنِ اهْتَدٰى ۞

Al-Anbiyā, "The Prophets," is named from its subject, the history of the former Prophets. The speaker in v. 4 and v. 112 is every Prophet. There is no historical reference or tradition to enable us to fix the date. It is undoubtedly of Meccan revelation, and lacks the characteristics of the latest and earliest Meccan Sūrahs. It may, therefore, be taken as belonging to the middle group of Meccan Sūrahs.

THE PROPHETS

Revealed at Mecca

In the name of Allah, the Beneficent, the Merciful.

1. Their reckoning draweth nigh for mankind, while they turn away in heedlessness.

2. Never cometh there unto them a new reminder from their Lord but they listen to it while they play:

3. With hearts preoccupied. And they confer in secret. The wrong-doers say: Is this other than a mortal like you? Will ye then succumb to magic when ye see (it)?

4. He saith: My Lord knoweth what is spoken in the heaven and the earth. He is the Hearer, the Knower.

5. Nay, say they, (these are but) muddled dreams; nay, he hath but invented it; nay, he is but a poet. Let him bring us a portent even as those of old (who were God's messengers) were sent (with portents).

6. Not a township believed of those which We destroyed before them (though We sent them portents): would they then believe?

7. And We sent not (as Our messengers) before thee other than men whom We inspired. Ask the followers of the Reminder[1] if ye know not.

8. We gave them not bodies that would not eat food, nor were they immortals.

9. Then We fulfilled the promise unto them. So We delivered them and whom We would, and We destroyed the prodigals.

10. Now We have revealed unto you a Scripture wherein is your Reminder. Have ye then no sense?

1. *i.e.* the Jewish Scripture.

ايَاتُهَا ١١٢ (٢١) سُوْرَةُ الْاَنْبِيَاءِ مَكِّيَّةٌ رُكُوْعَاتُهَا ٧

الجزء ١٧

بِسْمِ اللّٰهِ الرَّحْمٰنِ الرَّحِيْمِ

اِقْتَرَبَ لِلنَّاسِ حِسَابُهُمْ وَهُمْ فِيْ غَفْلَةٍ
مُّعْرِضُوْنَ ۚ (١)
مَا يَاْتِيْهِمْ مِّنْ ذِكْرٍ مِّنْ رَّبِّهِمْ مُّحْدَثٍ اِلَّا اسْتَمَعُوْهُ
وَهُمْ يَلْعَبُوْنَ (٢)
لَاهِيَةً قُلُوْبُهُمْ ۭ وَاَسَرُّوا النَّجْوَى ۖ الَّذِيْنَ ظَلَمُوْا ۖ
هَلْ هٰذَآ اِلَّا بَشَرٌ مِّثْلُكُمْ ۚ اَفَتَاْتُوْنَ السِّحْرَ وَاَنْتُمْ
تُبْصِرُوْنَ (٣)
قٰلَ رَبِّيْ يَعْلَمُ الْقَوْلَ فِي السَّمَاۗءِ وَالْاَرْضِ ۡ وَهُوَ
السَّمِيْعُ الْعَلِيْمُ (٤)
بَلْ قَالُوْٓا اَضْغَاثُ اَحْلَامٍ بَلِ افْتَرٰىهُ بَلْ هُوَ شَاعِرٌ ۚ
فَلْيَاْتِنَا بِاٰيَةٍ كَمَآ اُرْسِلَ الْاَوَّلُوْنَ (٥)
مَآ اٰمَنَتْ قَبْلَهُمْ مِّنْ قَرْيَةٍ اَهْلَكْنٰهَا ۚ اَفَهُمْ يُؤْمِنُوْنَ (٦)
وَمَآ اَرْسَلْنَا قَبْلَكَ اِلَّا رِجَالًا نُّوْحِيْٓ اِلَيْهِمْ فَسْــَٔلُوْٓا
اَهْلَ الذِّكْرِ اِنْ كُنْتُمْ لَا تَعْلَمُوْنَ (٧)
وَمَا جَعَلْنٰهُمْ جَسَدًا لَّا يَاْكُلُوْنَ الطَّعَامَ وَمَا
كَانُوْا خٰلِدِيْنَ (٨)
ثُمَّ صَدَقْنٰهُمُ الْوَعْدَ فَاَنْجَيْنٰهُمْ وَمَنْ نَّشَاۗءُ وَ
اَهْلَكْنَا الْمُسْرِفِيْنَ (٩)
ع لَقَدْ اَنْزَلْنَآ اِلَيْكُمْ كِتٰبًا فِيْهِ ذِكْرُكُمْ ۭ اَفَلَا تَعْقِلُوْنَ (١٠) ع

11. How many a community that dealt unjustly have We shattered, and raised up after them another folk!

12. And, when they felt Our might, behold them fleeing from it!

13. (But it was said unto them): Flee not, but return to that (existence) which emasculated you and to your dwellings, that ye may be questioned.

14. They cried: Alas for us! Lo! we were wrongdoers.

15. And this their crying ceased not till We made them as reaped corn, extinct.

16. We created not the heaven and the earth and all that is between them in play.

17. If We had wished to find a pastime, We could have found it in Our presence— if We ever did.

18. Nay, but We hurl the true against the false, and it doth break its head and lo! it vanisheth. And yours will be woe for that which ye ascribe (unto Him).

19. Unto Him belongeth whosoever is in the heavens and the earth. And those who dwell in His presence are not too proud to worship Him, nor do they weary.

20. They glorify (Him) night and day; they flag not.

21. Or have they chosen Gods from the earth who raise the dead?

22. If there were therein Gods beside Allah, then verily both (the heavens and the earth) had been disordered. Glorified be Allah, the Lord of the Throne, from all that they ascribe (unto Him).

23. He will not be questioned as to that which He doth, but they will be questioned.

24. Or have they chosen other gods beside Him? Say: Bring your proof (of their godhead). This is the Reminder of those with me and those before me, but most of them know not the Truth and so they are averse.

وَكَمْ قَصَمْنَا مِنْ قَرْيَةٍ كَانَتْ ظَالِمَةً وَّأَنْشَأْنَا بَعْدَهَا قَوْمًا اٰخَرِيْنَ ۞

فَلَمَّا اَحَسُّوْا بَأْسَنَا اِذَا هُمْ مِّنْهَا يَرْكُضُوْنَ ۞

لَا تَرْكُضُوْا وَارْجِعُوْا اِلٰى مَا اُتْرِفْتُمْ فِيْهِ وَمَسٰكِنِكُمْ لَعَلَّكُمْ تُسْئَلُوْنَ ۞

قَالُوْا يٰوَيْلَنَا اِنَّا كُنَّا ظٰلِمِيْنَ ۞

فَمَا زَالَتْ تِّلْكَ دَعْوٰىهُمْ حَتّٰى جَعَلْنٰهُمْ حَصِيْدًا خٰمِدِيْنَ ۞

وَمَا خَلَقْنَا السَّمَآءَ وَالْاَرْضَ وَمَا بَيْنَهُمَا لٰعِبِيْنَ ۞

لَوْ اَرَدْنَا اَنْ نَّتَّخِذَ لَهْوًا لَّاتَّخَذْنٰهُ مِنْ لَّدُنَّآ اِنْ كُنَّا فٰعِلِيْنَ ۞

بَلْ نَقْذِفُ بِالْحَقِّ عَلَى الْبَاطِلِ فَيَدْمَغُهُ فَاِذَا هُوَ زَاهِقٌ وَلَكُمُ الْوَيْلُ مِمَّا تَصِفُوْنَ ۞

وَلَهُ مَنْ فِى السَّمٰوٰتِ وَالْاَرْضِ وَمَنْ عِنْدَهُ لَا يَسْتَكْبِرُوْنَ عَنْ عِبَادَتِهِ وَلَا يَسْتَحْسِرُوْنَ ۞

يُسَبِّحُوْنَ الَّيْلَ وَالنَّهَارَ لَا يَفْتُرُوْنَ ۞

اَمِ اتَّخَذُوْا اٰلِهَةً مِّنَ الْاَرْضِ هُمْ يُنْشِرُوْنَ ۞

لَوْ كَانَ فِيْهِمَا اٰلِهَةٌ اِلَّا اللّٰهُ لَفَسَدَتَا فَسُبْحٰنَ اللّٰهِ رَبِّ الْعَرْشِ عَمَّا يَصِفُوْنَ ۞

لَا يُسْئَلُ عَمَّا يَفْعَلُ وَهُمْ يُسْئَلُوْنَ ۞

اَمِ اتَّخَذُوْا مِنْ دُوْنِهِ اٰلِهَةً قُلْ هَاتُوْا بُرْهَانَكُمْ هٰذَا ذِكْرُ مَنْ مَّعِىَ وَذِكْرُ مَنْ قَبْلِىْ بَلْ اَكْثَرُهُمْ لَا يَعْلَمُوْنَ الْحَقَّ فَهُمْ مُّعْرِضُوْنَ ۞

25. And We sent no messenger before thee but We inspired him, (saying): There is no God save Me (Allah), so worship Me.

26. And they say: The Beneficent hath taken unto Himself a son. Be He glorified! Nay, but (those whom they call sons) are honoured slaves;

27. They speak not until He hath spoken, and they act by His command.

28. He knoweth what is before them and what is behind them, and they cannot intercede except for him whom He accepteth, and they quake for awe of Him.

29. And one of them who should say: Lo! I am a God beside Him, that one We should repay with hell. Thus We repay wrongdoers.

30. Have not those who disbelieve known that the heavens and the earth were of one piece, then We parted them, and We made every living thing of water? Will they not then believe?

31. And We have placed in the earth firm hills lest it quake with them, and We have placed therein ravines as roads that haply they may find their way.

32. And We have made the sky a roof withheld (from them). Yet they turn away from its portents.

33. And He it is Who created the night and the day, and the sun and the moon. They float, each in an orbit.

34. We appointed immortality for no mortal before thee. What if thou diest, can they be immortal?

35. Every soul must taste of death, and We try you with evil and with good, for ordeal. And unto Us ye will be returned.

وما ارسلنا من قبلك من رسول الا نوحي اليه انه
لا اله الا انا فاعبدون ٢٥
وقالوا اتخذ الرحمن ولدا سبحنه بل عباد
مكرمون ٢٦
لا يسبقونه بالقول وهم بامره يعملون ٢٧
يعلم ما بين ايديهم وما خلفهم ولا يشفعون الا
لمن ارتضى وهم من خشيته مشفقون ٢٨
ومن يقل منهم اني اله من دونه فذلك نجزيه
جهنم كذلك نجزي الظلمين ٢٩ ع ٢
اولم ير الذين كفروا ان السموت والارض كانتا
رتقا ففتقنهما وجعلنا من الماء كل شيء حي
افلا يؤمنون ٣٠
وجعلنا في الارض رواسي ان تميد بهم وجعلنا
فيها فجاجا سبلا لعلهم يهتدون ٣١
وجعلنا السماء سقفا محفوظا وهم عن
ايتها معرضون ٣٢
وهو الذي خلق اليل والنهار والشمس و
القمر كل في فلك يسبحون ٣٣
وما جعلنا لبشر من قبلك الخلد افاين مت
فهم الخلدون ٣٤
كل نفس ذائقة الموت ونبلوكم بالشر والخير
فتنة والينا ترجعون ٣٥

36. And when those who disbelieve behold thee, they but choose thee out for mockery, (saying) Is this he who maketh mention of your gods? And they would deny all mention of the Beneficent.

وإذا رآك الذين كفروا إن يتخذونك إلا هزوا
أهذا الذي يذكر آلهتكم وهم بذكر الرحمن
هم كافرون ٣٦

37. Man is made of haste. I shall show you My portents, but ask Me not to hasten.

خلق الإنسان من عجل سأوريكم آياتي فلا
تستعجلون ٣٧

38. And they say: When will this promise (be fulfilled), if ye are truthful?

ويقولون متى هذا الوعد إن كنتم صادقين ٣٨

39. If those who disbelieved but knew the time when, they will not be able to drive off the fire from their faces and from their backs, and they will not be helped!

لو يعلم الذين كفروا حين لا يكفون عن
وجوههم النار ولا عن ظهورهم ولا هم
ينصرون ٣٩

40. Nay, but it will come upon them unawares so that it will stupefy them, and they will be unable to repel it, neither will they be reprieved.

بل تأتيهم بغتة فتبهتهم فلا يستطيعون ردها
ولا هم ينظرون ٤٠

41. Messengers before thee, indeed, were mocked, but that whereat they mocked surrounded those who scoffed at them.

ولقد استهزئ برسل من قبلك فحاق بالذين
سخروا منهم ما كانوا به يستهزءون ٤١

42. Say: Who guardeth you in the night or in the day from the Beneficent? Nay, but they turn away from mention of their Lord!

قل من يكلؤكم بالليل والنهار من الرحمن بل
هم عن ذكر ربهم معرضون ٤٢

43. Or have they gods who can shield them from Us? They cannot help themselves nor can they be defended from Us.

أم لهم آلهة تمنعهم من دوننا لا يستطيعون
نصر أنفسهم ولا هم منا يصحبون ٤٣

44. Nay, but We gave these and their fathers ease until life grew long for them. See they not how We visit the land, reducing it of its outlying parts?[1] Can they then be the victors?

بل متعنا هؤلاء وآباءهم حتى طال عليهم
العمر أفلا يرون أنا نأتي الأرض ننقصها من
أطرافها أفهم الغالبون ٤٤

45. Say (O Muhammad, unto mankind): I warn you only by the Inspiration. But the deaf hear not the call when they are warned.

قل إنما أنذركم بالوحي ولا يسمع الصم
الدعاء إذا ما ينذرون ٤٥

1. See XIII, 41, note.

46. And if a breath of thy Lord's punishment were to touch them, they assuredly would say: Alas for us! Lo! we were wrongdoers.

47. And We set a just balance for the Day of Resurrection so that no soul is wronged in aught. Though it be of the weight of a grain of mustard seed, We bring it. And We suffice for reckoners.

48. And We verily gave Moses and Aaron the Criterion (of right and wrong) and a light and a Reminder for those who keep from evil—

49. Those who fear their Lord in secret and who dread the Hour (of doom).

50. This is a blessed Reminder that We have revealed: Will ye then reject it?

51. And We verily gave Abraham of old his proper course, and We were Aware of him,

52. When he said unto his father and his folk: What are these images unto which ye pay devotion?

53. They said: We found our fathers worshippers of them.

54. He said: Verily ye and your fathers were in plain error.

55. They said: Bringest thou unto us the truth, or art thou some jester?

56. He said: Nay, but your Lord is the Lord of the heavens and the earth, Who created them; and I am of those who testify unto that.

57. And, by Allah, I shall circumvent your idols after ye have gone away and turned your backs.

وَلَئِن مَّسَّتْهُمْ نَفْحَةٌ مِّنْ عَذَابِ رَبِّكَ لَيَقُولُنَّ
يَا وَيْلَنَا إِنَّا كُنَّا ظَالِمِينَ ﴿٤٦﴾
وَنَضَعُ الْمَوَازِينَ الْقِسْطَ لِيَوْمِ الْقِيَامَةِ فَلَا تُظْلَمُ
نَفْسٌ شَيْئًا وَإِن كَانَ مِثْقَالَ حَبَّةٍ مِّنْ خَرْدَلٍ
أَتَيْنَا بِهَا وَكَفَىٰ بِنَا حَاسِبِينَ ﴿٤٧﴾
وَلَقَدْ آتَيْنَا مُوسَىٰ وَهَارُونَ الْفُرْقَانَ وَضِيَاءً
وَذِكْرًا لِّلْمُتَّقِينَ ﴿٤٨﴾
الَّذِينَ يَخْشَوْنَ رَبَّهُم بِالْغَيْبِ وَهُم مِّنَ
السَّاعَةِ مُشْفِقُونَ ﴿٤٩﴾
وَهَٰذَا ذِكْرٌ مُّبَارَكٌ أَنزَلْنَاهُ أَفَأَنتُمْ لَهُ
مُنكِرُونَ ﴿٥٠﴾ ع
وَلَقَدْ آتَيْنَا إِبْرَاهِيمَ رُشْدَهُ مِن قَبْلُ وَكُنَّا
بِهِ عَالِمِينَ ﴿٥١﴾
إِذْ قَالَ لِأَبِيهِ وَقَوْمِهِ مَا هَٰذِهِ التَّمَاثِيلُ الَّتِي
أَنتُمْ لَهَا عَاكِفُونَ ﴿٥٢﴾
قَالُوا وَجَدْنَا آبَاءَنَا لَهَا عَابِدِينَ ﴿٥٣﴾
قَالَ لَقَدْ كُنتُمْ أَنتُمْ وَآبَاؤُكُمْ فِي ضَلَالٍ مُّبِينٍ ﴿٥٤﴾
قَالُوا أَجِئْتَنَا بِالْحَقِّ أَمْ أَنتَ مِنَ اللَّاعِبِينَ ﴿٥٥﴾
قَالَ بَل رَّبُّكُمْ رَبُّ السَّمَاوَاتِ وَالْأَرْضِ الَّذِي
فَطَرَهُنَّ وَأَنَا عَلَىٰ ذَٰلِكُم مِّنَ الشَّاهِدِينَ ﴿٥٦﴾
وَتَاللَّهِ لَأَكِيدَنَّ أَصْنَامَكُم بَعْدَ أَن تُوَلُّوا
مُدْبِرِينَ ﴿٥٧﴾

58. Then he reduced them to fragments, all save the chief of them, that haply they might have recourse to it.

59. They said: Who hath done this to our gods? Surely it must be some evil-doer.

60. They said: We heard a youth make mention of them, who is called Abraham.

61. They said: Then bring him (hither) before the people's eyes that they may testify.

62. They said: Is it thou who hast done this to our gods, O Abraham?

63. He said: But this, their chief hath done it. So question them, if they can speak.

64. Then gathered they apart and said: Lo! ye yourselves are the wrongdoers.

65. And they were utterly confounded, and they said: Well thou knowest that these speak not.

66. He said: Worship ye then instead of Allah that which cannot profit you at all, nor harm you?

67. Fie on you and all that ye worship instead of Allah! Have ye then no sense?

68. They cried: Burn him and stand by your gods, if ye will be doing.

69. We said: O fire, be coolness and peace for Abraham!

70. And they wished to set a snare for him, but We made them the greater losers.

71. And We rescued him and Lot (and brought them) to the land which We have blessed for (all) peoples.

72. And We bestowed upon him Isaac, and Jacob as a grandson. Each of them We made righteous.

فَجَعَلَهُمْ جُذٰذًا إِلَّا كَبِيرًا لَّهُمْ لَعَلَّهُمْ إِلَيْهِ
يَرْجِعُونَ ٥٨

قَالُوا مَنْ فَعَلَ هٰذَا بِآلِهَتِنَا إِنَّهُ لَمِنَ الظّٰلِمِينَ ٥٩

قَالُوا سَمِعْنَا فَتًى يَذْكُرُهُمْ يُقَالُ لَهُ إِبْرٰهِيمُ ٦٠

قَالُوا فَأْتُوا بِهِ عَلٰى أَعْيُنِ النَّاسِ لَعَلَّهُمْ يَشْهَدُونَ ٦١

قَالُوا ءَأَنْتَ فَعَلْتَ هٰذَا بِآلِهَتِنَا يٰإِبْرٰهِيمُ ٦٢

قَالَ بَلْ فَعَلَهُ كَبِيرُهُمْ هٰذَا فَسْئَلُوهُمْ إِنْ
كَانُوا يَنْطِقُونَ ٦٣

فَرَجَعُوا إِلٰى أَنْفُسِهِمْ فَقَالُوا إِنَّكُمْ أَنْتُمُ الظّٰلِمُونَ ٦٤

ثُمَّ نُكِسُوا عَلٰى رُءُوسِهِمْ لَقَدْ عَلِمْتَ مَا هٰؤُلَاءِ
يَنْطِقُونَ ٦٥

قَالَ أَفَتَعْبُدُونَ مِنْ دُونِ اللّٰهِ مَا لَا يَنْفَعُكُمْ شَيْئًا
وَلَا يَضُرُّكُمْ ٦٦

أُفٍّ لَكُمْ وَلِمَا تَعْبُدُونَ مِنْ دُونِ اللّٰهِ أَفَلَا
تَعْقِلُونَ ٦٧

قَالُوا حَرِّقُوهُ وَانْصُرُوا آلِهَتَكُمْ إِنْ كُنْتُمْ فٰعِلِينَ ٦٨

قُلْنَا يٰنَارُ كُونِي بَرْدًا وَسَلٰمًا عَلٰى إِبْرٰهِيمَ ٦٩

وَأَرَادُوا بِهِ كَيْدًا فَجَعَلْنٰهُمُ الْأَخْسَرِينَ ٧٠

وَنَجَّيْنٰهُ وَلُوطًا إِلَى الْأَرْضِ الَّتِي بٰرَكْنَا فِيهَا
لِلْعٰلَمِينَ ٧١

وَوَهَبْنَا لَهُ إِسْحٰقَ وَيَعْقُوبَ نَافِلَةً وَكُلًّا
جَعَلْنَا صٰلِحِينَ ٧٢

73. And we made them chiefs who guide by Our command, and We inspired in them the doing of good deeds arnd the right establishment of worship and the giving of alms, and they were worshippers of Us (alone).

74. And unto Lot we gave judgement and knowledge, and We delivered him from the community that did abominations. Lo! they were folk of evil, lewd;

75. And We brought him in unto Our mercy. Lo! he was of the righteous.

76. And Noah, when he cried of old, We heard his prayer and saved him and his household from the great affliction.

77. And delivered him from the people who denied our revelations. Lo! they were folk of evil, therefor did We drown them all.

78. And David and Solomon, when they gave judgement concerning the field, when people's sheep had strayed and browsed therein by night; and we were witnesses to their judgement.

79. And we made Solomon to understand (the case); and unto each of them We gave judgement and knowledge. And We subdued the hills and the birds to hymn (His) praise along with David, We were the doers (thereof).

80. And we taught him the art of making garments (of mail) to protect you in your daring. Are ye then thankful?

81. And unto Solomon (We subdued) the wind in its raging. It set by his command toward the land which We had blessed. And of everything we are Aware.

82. And of the evil one's (subdued we unto him) some who dived (for pearls) for him and did other work, and we were warders unto them:

1. Ar. *Shyastin*, lit." devils"

وَجَعَلْنٰهُمْ اَئِمَّةً يَّهْدُوْنَ بِاَمْرِنَا وَاَوْحَيْنَآ
اِلَيْهِمْ فِعْلَ الْخَيْرٰتِ وَاِقَامَ الصَّلٰوةِ وَاِيْتَآءَ الزَّكٰوةِ
وَكَانُوْا لَنَا عٰبِدِيْنَ ﴿٧٣﴾
وَلُوْطًا اٰتَيْنٰهُ حُكْمًا وَّعِلْمًا وَّنَجَّيْنٰهُ مِنَ الْقَرْيَةِ
الَّتِيْ كَانَتْ تَّعْمَلُ الْخَبٰٓئِثَ ۭ اِنَّهُمْ كَانُوْا قَوْمَ سَوْءٍ
فٰسِقِيْنَ ﴿٧٤﴾
ع وَاَدْخَلْنٰهُ فِيْ رَحْمَتِنَا ۭ اِنَّهٗ مِنَ الصّٰلِحِيْنَ ﴿٧٥﴾
وَنُوْحًا اِذْ نَادٰى مِنْ قَبْلُ فَاسْتَجَبْنَا لَهٗ فَنَجَّيْنٰهُ
وَاَهْلَهٗ مِنَ الْكَرْبِ الْعَظِيْمِ ﴿٧٦﴾
وَنَصَرْنٰهُ مِنَ الْقَوْمِ الَّذِيْنَ كَذَّبُوْا بِاٰيٰتِنَا ۭ اِنَّهُمْ
كَانُوْا قَوْمَ سَوْءٍ فَاَغْرَقْنٰهُمْ اَجْمَعِيْنَ ﴿٧٧﴾
وَدَاوٗدَ وَسُلَيْمٰنَ اِذْ يَحْكُمٰنِ فِي الْحَرْثِ اِذْ نَفَشَتْ
فِيْهِ غَنَمُ الْقَوْمِ ۚ وَكُنَّا لِحُكْمِهِمْ شٰهِدِيْنَ ﴿٧٨﴾
فَفَهَّمْنٰهَا سُلَيْمٰنَ ۚ وَكُلًّا اٰتَيْنَا حُكْمًا وَّعِلْمًا ۡ وَّ
سَخَّرْنَا مَعَ دَاوٗدَ الْجِبَالَ يُسَبِّحْنَ وَالطَّيْرَ ۭ وَكُنَّا
فٰعِلِيْنَ ﴿٧٩﴾
وَعَلَّمْنٰهُ صَنْعَةَ لَبُوْسٍ لَّكُمْ لِتُحْصِنَكُمْ مِّنْۢ بَاْسِكُمْ ۚ
فَهَلْ اَنْتُمْ شٰكِرُوْنَ ﴿٨٠﴾
وَلِسُلَيْمٰنَ الرِّيْحَ عَاصِفَةً تَجْرِيْ بِاَمْرِهٖٓ اِلَى الْاَرْضِ
الَّتِيْ بٰرَكْنَا فِيْهَا ۭ وَكُنَّا بِكُلِّ شَيْءٍ عٰلِمِيْنَ ﴿٨١﴾
وَمِنَ الشَّيٰطِيْنِ مَنْ يَّغُوْصُوْنَ لَهٗ وَيَعْمَلُوْنَ
عَمَلًا دُوْنَ ذٰلِكَ ۚ وَكُنَّا لَهُمْ حٰفِظِيْنَ ﴿٨٢﴾

83. And Job, when he cried unto his Lord, (saying): Lo! adversity afflicteth me, and Thou art Most Merciful of all who show mercy.

84. Then We heard his prayer and removed that adversity from which he suffered, and We gave him his household (that he had lost) and the like thereof along with them, a mercy from Our store, and a remembrance for the worshippers.

85. And (mention) Ishmael, and Idris, and Dhū'l-Kifl.[1] All were of the steadfast.

86. And We brought them in unto Our mercy. Lo! they are among the righteous.

87. And (mention) Dhū'n-Nūn, when he went off in anger and deemed that We had no power over him, but he cried out in the darkness, saying: There is no God save Thee. Be Thou glorified! Lo! I have been a wrongdoer.

88. Then We heard his prayer and saved him from the anguish. Thus We save believers.

89. And Zachariah, when he cried unto his Lord: My Lord! Leave me not childless, though Thou art the best of inheritors.

90. Then We heard his prayer, and bestowed upon him John, and adjusted his wife (to bear a child) for him. Lo! they used to vie one with the other in good deeds, and they cried unto Us in longing and in fear, and were submissive unto Us.

91. And she who was chaste,[3] therefor We breathed into her (something) of Our spirit and made her and her son a token for (all) peoples.

92. Lo! this, your religion, is one religion, and I am your Lord, so worship Me.

وَأَيُّوبَ إِذْ نَادَىٰ رَبَّهُ أَنِّي مَسَّنِيَ الضُّرُّ وَأَنْتَ
أَرْحَمُ الرَّاحِمِينَ ﴿٨٣﴾
فَاسْتَجَبْنَا لَهُ فَكَشَفْنَا مَا بِهِ مِنْ ضُرٍّ وَآتَيْنَاهُ
أَهْلَهُ وَمِثْلَهُمْ مَعَهُمْ رَحْمَةً مِنْ عِنْدِنَا وَ
ذِكْرَىٰ لِلْعَابِدِينَ ﴿٨٤﴾
وَإِسْمَاعِيلَ وَإِدْرِيسَ وَذَا الْكِفْلِ ۖ كُلٌّ مِنَ
الصَّابِرِينَ ﴿٨٥﴾
وَأَدْخَلْنَاهُمْ فِي رَحْمَتِنَا ۖ إِنَّهُمْ مِنَ الصَّالِحِينَ ﴿٨٦﴾
وَذَا النُّونِ إِذْ ذَهَبَ مُغَاضِبًا فَظَنَّ أَنْ لَنْ نَقْدِرَ
عَلَيْهِ فَنَادَىٰ فِي الظُّلُمَاتِ أَنْ لَا إِلَٰهَ إِلَّا أَنْتَ
سُبْحَانَكَ إِنِّي كُنْتُ مِنَ الظَّالِمِينَ ﴿٨٧﴾
فَاسْتَجَبْنَا لَهُ وَنَجَّيْنَاهُ مِنَ الْغَمِّ ۚ وَكَذَٰلِكَ
نُنْجِي الْمُؤْمِنِينَ ﴿٨٨﴾
وَزَكَرِيَّا إِذْ نَادَىٰ رَبَّهُ رَبِّ لَا تَذَرْنِي فَرْدًا وَ
أَنْتَ خَيْرُ الْوَارِثِينَ ﴿٨٩﴾
فَاسْتَجَبْنَا لَهُ وَوَهَبْنَا لَهُ يَحْيَىٰ وَأَصْلَحْنَا لَهُ
زَوْجَهُ ۚ إِنَّهُمْ كَانُوا يُسَارِعُونَ فِي الْخَيْرَاتِ وَ
يَدْعُونَنَا رَغَبًا وَرَهَبًا ۖ وَكَانُوا لَنَا خَاشِعِينَ ﴿٩٠﴾
وَالَّتِي أَحْصَنَتْ فَرْجَهَا فَنَفَخْنَا فِيهَا مِنْ رُوحِنَا
وَجَعَلْنَاهَا وَابْنَهَا آيَةً لِلْعَالَمِينَ ﴿٩١﴾
إِنَّ هَٰذِهِ أُمَّتُكُمْ أُمَّةً وَاحِدَةً وَأَنَا رَبُّكُمْ
فَاعْبُدُونِ ﴿٩٢﴾

1. A prophet famous among the Arabs, whose story resembles that of Ezekiel.
2. Lit. "Lord of the Fish" = Jonah.
3. The reference here is to the Virgin Mary.

93. And they have broken their religion (into fragments) among them, (yet) all are retruning unto us.

ع وَتَقَطَّعُوٓا أَمْرَهُمْ بَيْنَهُمْ ۖ كُلٌّ إِلَيْنَا رٰجِعُونَ ﴿٩٣﴾

94. Then whoso doth good works and is a believer, there will be no rejection of his effort. Lo! We record (it) for him.

فَمَنْ يَعْمَلْ مِنَ الصّٰلِحٰتِ وَهُوَ مُؤْمِنٌ فَلَا كُفْرَانَ لِسَعْيِهٖ ۚ وَإِنَّا لَهٗ كٰتِبُونَ ﴿٩٤﴾

95. And there is a ban upon any community which We have destroyed: that they shall not return,

وَحَرٰمٌ عَلٰى قَرْيَةٍ أَهْلَكْنٰهَآ أَنَّهُمْ لَا يَرْجِعُونَ ﴿٩٥﴾

96. Until, when Gog and Magog are let loose, and they hasten out of every mound.

حَتّٰٓى إِذَا فُتِحَتْ يَأْجُوجُ وَمَأْجُوجُ وَهُمْ مِّنْ كُلِّ حَدَبٍ يَّنْسِلُونَ ﴿٩٦﴾

97. And the True Promise draweth nigh; then behold them. staring wide (in terror), the eyes of those who disbelieve! (They say): Alas for us! We (lived) in forgetfulness of this. Ah, but we were wrongdoers!

وَاقْتَرَبَ الْوَعْدُ الْحَقُّ فَإِذَا هِيَ شَاخِصَةٌ أَبْصٰرُ الَّذِيْنَ كَفَرُوْا ۖ يٰوَيْلَنَا قَدْ كُنَّا فِيْ غَفْلَةٍ مِّنْ هٰذَا بَلْ كُنَّا ظٰلِمِيْنَ ﴿٩٧﴾

98. Lo! ye (idolaters) and that which ye worship besides Allah are fuel of hell. There--unto ye will come.

إِنَّكُمْ وَمَا تَعْبُدُوْنَ مِنْ دُوْنِ اللّٰهِ حَصَبُ جَهَنَّمَ ۖ أَنْتُمْ لَهَا وٰرِدُوْنَ ﴿٩٨﴾

99. If these had been gods they would not have come thither, but all will abide therein.

لَوْ كَانَ هٰٓؤُلَآءِ اٰلِهَةً مَّا وَرَدُوْهَا ۖ وَكُلٌّ فِيْهَا خٰلِدُوْنَ ﴿٩٩﴾

100 Therein wailing is their portion, and therein they hear not.

لَهُمْ فِيْهَا زَفِيْرٌ وَّهُمْ فِيْهَا لَا يَسْمَعُوْنَ ﴿١٠٠﴾

10.1 Lo! those unto whom kindness hath gone forth before from Us, they will be far removed from thence;

إِنَّ الَّذِيْنَ سَبَقَتْ لَهُمْ مِّنَّا الْحُسْنٰىٓ ۙ أُولٰٓئِكَ عَنْهَا مُبْعَدُوْنَ ﴿١٠١﴾

102 They will not hear the slightest sound thereof, while they abide in that which their souls desire.

لَا يَسْمَعُوْنَ حَسِيْسَهَا ۚ وَهُمْ فِيْ مَا اشْتَهَتْ أَنْفُسُهُمْ خٰلِدُوْنَ ﴿١٠٢﴾

103 The Supreme Horror will not grieve them, and the angels will welcome them, (saying): This is your day which ye were promised.

لَا يَحْزُنُهُمُ الْفَزَعُ الْأَكْبَرُ وَتَتَلَقّٰىهُمُ الْمَلٰٓئِكَةُ ۖ هٰذَا يَوْمُكُمُ الَّذِيْ كُنْتُمْ تُوْعَدُوْنَ ﴿١٠٣﴾

104 The Day when We shall roll up the heavens as a recorder rolleth up a written scroll. As We began the first creation, We shall repeat it (it is a promise binding) upon Us. Lo! We are to perform it.

يَوْمَ نَطْوِي السَّمَآءَ كَطَيِّ السِّجِلِّ لِلْكُتُبِ ۚ كَمَا بَدَأْنَآ أَوَّلَ خَلْقٍ نُّعِيْدُهٗ ۚ وَعْدًا عَلَيْنَا ۚ إِنَّا كُنَّا فٰعِلِيْنَ ﴿١٠٤﴾

105. And verily We have written in the Scripture, after the Reminder My righteous slaves will inherit the earth.

106. Lo! there is a plain statement for folk who are devout.

107. We sent thee not save as a mercy for the peoples.

108. Say: It is only inspired in me that your God is One God. Will ye then surrender (unto Him)?

109. But if they are averse, then say: I have warned you all alike, although I know not whether nigh or far is that which ye are promised.

110. Lo! He knoweth that which is said openly, and that which ye conceal.

111. And I know not but that this may be a trial for you, and enjoyment for a while.

112. He saith: My Lord! Judge Thou with truth. Our Lord is the Beneficent, Whose help is to be implored against that which ye ascribe (unto Him).

وَلَقَدْ كَتَبْنَا فِي الزَّبُورِ مِنْ بَعْدِ الذِّكْرِ أَنَّ
الْأَرْضَ يَرِثُهَا عِبَادِيَ الصّٰلِحُونَ ﴿١٠٥﴾
إِنَّ فِي هٰذَا لَبَلٰغًا لِّقَوْمٍ عٰبِدِينَ ﴿١٠٦﴾
وَمَا أَرْسَلْنٰكَ إِلَّا رَحْمَةً لِّلْعٰلَمِينَ ﴿١٠٧﴾
قُلْ إِنَّمَا يُوحٰى إِلَيَّ أَنَّمَا إِلٰهُكُمْ إِلٰهٌ وَّاحِدٌ فَهَلْ
أَنْتُمْ مُّسْلِمُونَ ﴿١٠٨﴾
فَإِنْ تَوَلَّوْا فَقُلْ اٰذَنْتُكُمْ عَلٰى سَوَآءٍ وَإِنْ أَدْرِيْ
أَقَرِيبٌ أَمْ بَعِيدٌ مَّا تُوعَدُونَ ﴿١٠٩﴾
إِنَّهُ يَعْلَمُ الْجَهْرَ مِنَ الْقَوْلِ وَيَعْلَمُ مَا
تَكْتُمُونَ ﴿١١٠﴾
وَإِنْ أَدْرِيْ لَعَلَّهُ فِتْنَةٌ لَّكُمْ وَمَتَاعٌ إِلٰى
حِينٍ ﴿١١١﴾
قٰلَ رَبِّ احْكُمْ بِالْحَقِّ وَرَبُّنَا الرَّحْمٰنُ الْمُسْتَعَانُ
عَلٰى مَا تَصِفُونَ ﴿١١٢﴾

Al-Ḥajj, "The Pilgrimage," takes its name from vv. 26-38 relating to the pilgrimage to Mecca. This Sūrah is ascribed by some authorities to the Meccan, by others to the Madînah period. The copy of the Koran which I have followed throughout has the Madînah ascription, and, as it was copied long before the days of "higher" criticism, and was authorised for use throughout the Ottoman Empire, I retain that ascription. Vv. 11-13, 25-30, 39-41 and 58-60 were, according to all authorities, revealed at Al-Madînah. Nöldeke, greatest of the "higher" critics, says that the ascription is justified on account of the importance of the verses in this Sūrah which must, from the nature of their contents, have been revealed at Al-Madînah, while holding that much of the Sūrah belongs to the last Meccan period.

THE PILGRIMAGE

Revealed at Al-Madinah

In the name of Allah, the Beneficent, the Merciful.

1. O mankind! Fear your Lord. Lo! the earthquake of the Hour (of Doom) is a tremendous thing:

2. On the day when ye behold it, every nursing mother will forget her nursling and every pregnant one will be delivered of her burden, and thou (Muhammad) wilt see mankind as drunken, yet they will not be drunken, but the Doom of Allah will be strong (upon them).

3. Among mankind is he who disputeth concerning Allah without knowledge, and followeth each froward devil;

4. For him it is decreed that whoso taketh him for friend, he verily will mislead him and will guide him to the punishment of the Flame.

5. O mankind! If ye are in doubt concerning the Resurrection, then lo! We have created you from dust, then from a drop of seed, then from a clot, then from a little lump of flesh shapely and shapeless, that We may make (it) clear for you. And We cause what We will to remain in the wombs for an appointed time, and afterward We bring you forth as infants, then (give you growth) that ye attain your full strength. And among you there is he who dieth (young), and among you there is he who is brought back to the most abject time of life, so that, after knowledge, he knoweth naught. And thou (Muhammad) seest the earth barren, but when We send down water thereon, it doth thrill and swell and put forth every lovely kind[1] (of growth).

اياتها ٧٨ (٢٢) سورة الحج مدنية (١٠) ركوعاتها

بسم الله الرحمن الرحيم

يايها الناس اتقوا ربكم ان زلزلة الساعة
شيء عظيم ﴿١﴾
يوم ترونها تذهل كل مرضعة عما ارضعت
وتضع كل ذات حمل حملها وترى الناس
سكرى وما هم بسكرى ولكن عذاب الله
شديد ﴿٢﴾
ومن الناس من يجادل في الله بغير علم و
يتبع كل شيطن مريد ﴿٣﴾
كتب عليه انه من تولاه فانه يضله ويهديه
الى عذاب السعير ﴿٤﴾
يايها الناس ان كنتم في ريب من البعث فانا
خلقنكم من تراب ثم من نطفة ثم من علقة
ثم من مضغة مخلقة وغير مخلقة لنبين لكم
ونقر في الارحام ما نشاء الى اجل مسمى ثم
نخرجكم طفلا ثم لتبلغوا اشدكم ومنكم من
يتوفى ومنكم من يرد الى ارذل العمر لكيلا يعلم
من بعد علم شيئا وترى الارض هامدة فاذا
انزلنا عليها الماء اهتزت وربت وانبتت من
كل زوج بهيج ﴿٥﴾

1. Or "every lovely pair." Prof. Ghamrawi who helped me in the revision of the text kept exclaiming on the subtlety and wealth of meaning of every expression used in the Koran concerning natural phenomena. Thus the word "pair" occurs often in the sense of "species," commemorating the fact that word "pair" of the earth exists as male and female. See particularly XXXVI, 35.—Tr.

6. That is because Allah, He is the Truth. Lo! He quickeneth the dead, and lo! He is Able to do all things;

ذٰلِكَ بِاَنَّ اللّٰهَ هُوَ الْحَقُّ وَاَنَّهٗ يُحْيِ الْمَوْتٰى وَ
اَنَّهٗ عَلٰى كُلِّ شَيْءٍ قَدِيْرٌ ﴿٦﴾

7. And because the Hour will come, there is no doubt thereof; and because Allah will raise those who are in the graves.

وَّاَنَّ السَّاعَةَ اٰتِيَةٌ لَّا رَيْبَ فِيْهَا ۙ وَاَنَّ اللّٰهَ يَبْعَثُ
مَنْ فِي الْقُبُوْرِ ﴿٧﴾

8. And among mankind is he who disputeth concerning Allah without knowledge or guidance or a Scripture giving light,

وَمِنَ النَّاسِ مَنْ يُّجَادِلُ فِي اللّٰهِ بِغَيْرِ عِلْمٍ وَّلَا
هُدًى وَّلَا كِتٰبٍ مُّنِيْرٍ ﴿٨﴾

9. Turning away in pride to beguile (men) from the way of Allah. For him in this world is ignominy, and on the Day of Resurrection We make him taste the doom of burning.

ثَانِيَ عِطْفِهٖ لِيُضِلَّ عَنْ سَبِيْلِ اللّٰهِ ؕ لَهٗ فِي
الدُّنْيَا خِزْيٌ وَّنُذِيْقُهٗ يَوْمَ الْقِيٰمَةِ عَذَابَ
الْحَرِيْقِ ﴿٩﴾

10. (And unto him it will be said): This is for that which thy two hands have sent before, and because Allah is no oppressor of His slaves.

ذٰلِكَ بِمَا قَدَّمَتْ يَدٰكَ وَاَنَّ اللّٰهَ لَيْسَ بِظَلَّامٍ
لِّلْعَبِيْدِ ﴿١٠﴾ ع

11. And among mankind is he who worshippeth Allah upon a narrow marge so that if good befalleth him he is content therewith, but if a trial befalleth him, he falleth away utterly. He loseth both the world and the Hereafter. That is the sheer loss.[1]

وَمِنَ النَّاسِ مَنْ يَّعْبُدُ اللّٰهَ عَلٰى حَرْفٍ ۚ فَاِنْ
اَصَابَهٗ خَيْرُ اطْمَاَنَّ بِهٖ ۚ وَاِنْ اَصَابَتْهُ فِتْنَةُ
انْقَلَبَ عَلٰى وَجْهِهٖ ۚ خَسِرَ الدُّنْيَا وَالْاٰخِرَةَ ؕ ذٰلِكَ
هُوَ الْخُسْرَانُ الْمُبِيْنُ ﴿١١﴾

12. He calleth, beside Allah, unto that which hurteth him not nor benefiteth him. That is the far error.

يَدْعُوْا مِنْ دُوْنِ اللّٰهِ مَا لَا يَضُرُّهٗ وَمَا لَا يَنْفَعُهٗ ؕ
ذٰلِكَ هُوَ الضَّلٰلُ الْبَعِيْدُ ﴿١٢﴾

13. He calleth unto him whose harm is nearer than his benefit; verily an evil patron and verily an evil friend!

يَدْعُوْا لَمَنْ ضَرُّهٗ اَقْرَبُ مِنْ نَّفْعِهٖ ؕ لَبِئْسَ
الْمَوْلٰى وَلَبِئْسَ الْعَشِيْرُ ﴿١٣﴾

14. Lo! Allah causeth those who believe and do good works to enter the Gardens underneath which rivers flow. Lo! Allah doth what He intendeth.

اِنَّ اللّٰهَ يُدْخِلُ الَّذِيْنَ اٰمَنُوْا وَعَمِلُوا الصّٰلِحٰتِ
جَنّٰتٍ تَجْرِيْ مِنْ تَحْتِهَا الْاَنْهٰرُ ؕ اِنَّ اللّٰهَ
يَفْعَلُ مَا يُرِيْدُ ﴿١٤﴾

1. Tradition says that the reference is to certain Arabs who came to the the Prophet at Al-Madīnah and professed Al-Islām; then, if they prospered in a worldly sense, they were content, but if they had to suffer at all they relapsed to idolatry.

15. Whoso is wont to think (through envy) that Allah will not give him (Muhammad) victory in the world and the Hereafter (and is enraged at the thought of his victory), let him stretch a rope up to the roof (of his dwelling), and let him hang himself. Then let him see whether his strategy dispelleth that whereat he rageth![1]

16. Thus We reveal it as plain revelations, and verily Allah guideth whom He will.

17. Lo! those who believe (this Revelation), and those who are Jews, and the Sabaeans and the Christians and the Magians and the idolaters—Lo! Allah will decide between them on the Day of Resurrection. Lo! Allah is Witness over all things.

18. Hast thou not seen that unto Allah payeth adoration whosoever is in the heavens and whosoever is in the earth, and the sun, and the moon, and the stars, and the hills, and the trees, and the beasts, and many of mankind, while there are many unto whom the doom is justly due. He whom Allah scorneth, there is none to give him honour. Lo! Allah doth what He will.

19. These twain (the believers and the disbelievers) are two opponents who contend concerning their Lord. But as for those who disbelieve, garments of fire will be cut out for them; boiling fluid will be poured down on their heads.

20. Whereby that which is in their bellies, and their skins too, will be melted;

21. And for them are hooked rods of iron.

22. Whenever, in their anguish, they would go forth from thence they are driven back therein and (it is said unto them): Taste the doom of burning.

مَنْ كَانَ يَظُنُّ اَنْ لَّنْ يَّنْصُرَهُ اللّٰهُ فِي الدُّنْيَا
وَالْاٰخِرَةِ فَلْيَمْدُدْ بِسَبَبٍ اِلَى السَّمَآءِ
ثُمَّ لْيَقْطَعْ فَلْيَنْظُرْ هَلْ يُذْهِبَنَّ كَيْدُهٗ
مَا يَغِيْظُ ﴿١٥﴾

وَكَذٰلِكَ اَنْزَلْنٰهُ اٰيٰتٍۢ بَيِّنٰتٍ ۙ وَّاَنَّ اللّٰهَ يَهْدِيْ
مَنْ يُّرِيْدُ ﴿١٦﴾

اِنَّ الَّذِيْنَ اٰمَنُوْا وَالَّذِيْنَ هَادُوْا وَالصّٰبِـِٕيْنَ وَ
النَّصٰرٰى وَالْمَجُوْسَ وَالَّذِيْنَ اَشْرَكُوْٓا ۖ اِنَّ اللّٰهَ
يَفْصِلُ بَيْنَهُمْ يَوْمَ الْقِيٰمَةِ ؕ اِنَّ اللّٰهَ عَلٰى كُلِّ
شَيْءٍ شَهِيْدٌ ﴿١٧﴾

اَلَمْ تَرَ اَنَّ اللّٰهَ يَسْجُدُ لَهٗ مَنْ فِي السَّمٰوٰتِ وَمَنْ
فِي الْاَرْضِ وَالشَّمْسُ وَالْقَمَرُ وَالنُّجُوْمُ وَالْجِبَالُ
وَالشَّجَرُ وَالدَّوَآبُّ وَكَثِيْرٌ مِّنَ النَّاسِ ؕ وَكَثِيْرٌ
حَقَّ عَلَيْهِ الْعَذَابُ ؕ وَمَنْ يُّهِنِ اللّٰهُ فَمَا لَهٗ مِنْ
مُّكْرِمٍ ؕ اِنَّ اللّٰهَ يَفْعَلُ مَا يَشَآءُ ۩ ﴿١٨﴾ السجدة

هٰذٰنِ خَصْمٰنِ اخْتَصَمُوْا فِيْ رَبِّهِمْ ۫ فَالَّذِيْنَ
كَفَرُوْا قُطِّعَتْ لَهُمْ ثِيَابٌ مِّنْ نَّارٍ ؕ يُصَبُّ مِنْ
فَوْقِ رُءُوْسِهِمُ الْحَمِيْمُ ﴿١٩﴾
يُصْهَرُ بِهٖ مَا فِيْ بُطُوْنِهِمْ وَالْجُلُوْدُ ؕ ﴿٢٠﴾
وَلَهُمْ مَّقَامِعُ مِنْ حَدِيْدٍ ﴿٢١﴾
كُلَّمَآ اَرَادُوْٓا اَنْ يَّخْرُجُوْا مِنْهَا مِنْ غَمٍّ اُعِيْدُوْا
فِيْهَا ۗ وَذُوْقُوْا عَذَابَ الْحَرِيْقِ ﴿٢٢﴾ ع

1. The meaning is that Allah will undoubtedly cause the Prophet to triumph in both worlds, and therefore his opponents have no strategy save that of despair.

23. Lo! Allah will cause those who believe and do good works to enter Gardens underneath which rivers flow, wherein they will be allowed armlets of gold, and pearls, and their raiment therein will be silk.

24. They are guided unto gentle speech; they are guided unto the path of the Glorious One.

25. Lo! those who disbelieve and bar (men) from the way of Allah and from the Inviolable Place of Worship, which We have appointed for mankind together, the dweller therein and the nomad; whosoever seeketh wrongful partiality therein, him We shall cause to taste a painful doom.

26. And (remember) when We prepared for Abraham the place of the (holy) House, saying: Ascribe thou nothing as partner unto Me, and purify My House for those who make the round (thereof) and those who stand and those who bow and make prostration.

27. And proclaim unto mankind the Pilgrimage.[1] They will come unto thee on foot and on every lean camel; they will come from every deep ravine:

28. That they may witness things that are of benefit to them, and mention the name of Allah on appointed days over the beast of cattle that He hath bestowed upon them. Then eat thereof and feed therewith the poor unfortunate.

29. Then let them make an end of their unkemptness and pay their vows and so and go around the ancient House.

30. That (is the command). And whoso magnifieth the sacred things of Allah, it will be well for him in the sight of his Lord. The cattle are lawful unto you save that which hath been told you. So shun the filth of idols, and shun lying speech:

1. II, 196 ff.

إِنَّ اللَّهَ يُدْخِلُ الَّذِينَ آمَنُوا وَعَمِلُوا الصَّالِحَاتِ
جَنَّاتٍ تَجْرِي مِنْ تَحْتِهَا الْأَنْهَارُ يُحَلَّوْنَ فِيهَا مِنْ
أَسَاوِرَ مِنْ ذَهَبٍ وَلُؤْلُؤًا وَلِبَاسُهُمْ فِيهَا حَرِيرٌ ﴿٢٣﴾
وَهُدُوا إِلَى الطَّيِّبِ مِنَ الْقَوْلِ وَهُدُوا إِلَىٰ
صِرَاطِ الْحَمِيدِ ﴿٢٤﴾
إِنَّ الَّذِينَ كَفَرُوا وَيَصُدُّونَ عَنْ سَبِيلِ اللَّهِ
وَالْمَسْجِدِ الْحَرَامِ الَّذِي جَعَلْنَاهُ لِلنَّاسِ سَوَاءً
الْعَاكِفُ فِيهِ وَالْبَادِ وَمَنْ يُرِدْ فِيهِ بِإِلْحَادٍ
ع بِظُلْمٍ نُذِقْهُ مِنْ عَذَابٍ أَلِيمٍ ﴿٢٥﴾
وَإِذْ بَوَّأْنَا لِإِبْرَاهِيمَ مَكَانَ الْبَيْتِ أَنْ لَا تُشْرِكْ
بِي شَيْئًا وَطَهِّرْ بَيْتِيَ لِلطَّائِفِينَ وَالْقَائِمِينَ
وَالرُّكَّعِ السُّجُودِ ﴿٢٦﴾
وَأَذِّنْ فِي النَّاسِ بِالْحَجِّ يَأْتُوكَ رِجَالًا وَعَلَىٰ كُلِّ
ضَامِرٍ يَأْتِينَ مِنْ كُلِّ فَجٍّ عَمِيقٍ ﴿٢٧﴾
لِيَشْهَدُوا مَنَافِعَ لَهُمْ وَيَذْكُرُوا اسْمَ اللَّهِ فِي
أَيَّامٍ مَعْلُومَاتٍ عَلَىٰ مَا رَزَقَهُمْ مِنْ بَهِيمَةِ الْأَنْعَامِ
فَكُلُوا مِنْهَا وَأَطْعِمُوا الْبَائِسَ الْفَقِيرَ ﴿٢٨﴾
ثُمَّ لْيَقْضُوا تَفَثَهُمْ وَلْيُوفُوا نُذُورَهُمْ وَلْيَطَّوَّفُوا
بِالْبَيْتِ الْعَتِيقِ ﴿٢٩﴾
ذَٰلِكَ وَمَنْ يُعَظِّمْ حُرُمَاتِ اللَّهِ فَهُوَ خَيْرٌ لَهُ
عِنْدَ رَبِّهِ وَأُحِلَّتْ لَكُمُ الْأَنْعَامُ إِلَّا مَا يُتْلَىٰ عَلَيْكُمْ
فَاجْتَنِبُوا الرِّجْسَ مِنَ الْأَوْثَانِ وَاجْتَنِبُوا قَوْلَ الزُّورِ ﴿٣٠﴾

31. Turning unto Allah (only), not ascribing partners unto Him; for whoso ascribeth partners unto Allah, it is as if he had fallen from the sky and the birds had snatched him or the wind had blown him to a far-off place.

32. That (is the command). And whoso magnifieth the offerings consecrated to Allah, it surely is from devotion of the hearts.

33. Therein are benefits for you for an appointed term; and afterward they are brought for sacrifice[1] unto the ancient House.

34. And for every nation have We appointed a ritual, that they may mention the name of Allah over the beast of cattle that He hath given them for food;[2] and your God is One God, therefor surrender unto Him. And give good tidings (O Muhammad) to the humble;

35. Whose hearts fear when Allah is mentioned, and the patient of whatever may befall them, and those who establish worship and who spend of that We have bestowed on them.

36. And the camels! We have appointed them among the ceremonies of Allah. Therein ye have much good. So mention the name of Allah over them when they are drawn up in lines. Then when their flanks fall (dead), eat thereof and feed the beggar and the suppliant. Thus have We made them subject unto you, that haply ye may give thanks.

37. Their flesh and their blood reach not Allah, but the devotion from you reacheth Him. Thus have We made them subject unto you that ye may magnify Allah that He hath guided you. And give good tidings (O Muhammad) to the good.

38. Lo! Allah defendeth those who are true. Lo! Allah loveth not each treacherous ingrate.

حُنَفَآءَ لِلّٰهِ غَيْرَ مُشْرِكِيْنَ بِهٖ ؕ وَمَنْ يُّشْرِكْ بِاللّٰهِ
فَكَاَنَّمَا خَرَّ مِنَ السَّمَآءِ فَتَخْطَفُهُ الطَّيْرُ اَوْ تَهْوِيْ
بِهِ الرِّيْحُ فِيْ مَكَانٍ سَحِيْقٍ ﴿٣١﴾
ذٰلِكَ ۗ وَمَنْ يُّعَظِّمْ شَعَآئِرَ اللّٰهِ فَاِنَّهَا مِنْ تَقْوَى
الْقُلُوْبِ ﴿٣٢﴾
لَكُمْ فِيْهَا مَنَافِعُ اِلٰٓى اَجَلٍ مُّسَمًّى ثُمَّ مَحِلُّهَآ
اِلَى الْبَيْتِ الْعَتِيْقِ ﴿٣٣﴾
وَلِكُلِّ اُمَّةٍ جَعَلْنَا مَنْسَكًا لِّيَذْكُرُوا اسْمَ اللّٰهِ عَلٰى
مَا رَزَقَهُمْ مِّنْۢ بَهِيْمَةِ الْاَنْعَامِ ؕ فَاِلٰهُكُمْ اِلٰهٌ
وَّاحِدٌ فَلَهٗٓ اَسْلِمُوْا ؕ وَبَشِّرِ الْمُخْبِتِيْنَ ﴿٣٤﴾
الَّذِيْنَ اِذَا ذُكِرَ اللّٰهُ وَجِلَتْ قُلُوْبُهُمْ وَالصّٰبِرِيْنَ
عَلٰى مَآ اَصَابَهُمْ وَالْمُقِيْمِي الصَّلٰوةِ ۙ وَمِمَّا
رَزَقْنٰهُمْ يُنْفِقُوْنَ ﴿٣٥﴾
وَالْبُدْنَ جَعَلْنٰهَا لَكُمْ مِّنْ شَعَآئِرِ اللّٰهِ لَكُمْ فِيْهَا
خَيْرٌ ۖ فَاذْكُرُوا اسْمَ اللّٰهِ عَلَيْهَا صَوَآفَّ ۚ فَاِذَا وَجَبَتْ
جُنُوْبُهَا فَكُلُوْا مِنْهَا وَاَطْعِمُوا الْقَانِعَ وَالْمُعْتَرَّ ؕ
كَذٰلِكَ سَخَّرْنٰهَا لَكُمْ لَعَلَّكُمْ تَشْكُرُوْنَ ﴿٣٦﴾
لَنْ يَّنَالَ اللّٰهَ لُحُوْمُهَا وَلَا دِمَآؤُهَا وَلٰكِنْ يَّنَالُهُ
التَّقْوٰى مِنْكُمْ ؕ كَذٰلِكَ سَخَّرَهَا لَكُمْ لِتُكَبِّرُوا اللّٰهَ
عَلٰى مَا هَدٰىكُمْ ؕ وَبَشِّرِ الْمُحْسِنِيْنَ ﴿٣٧﴾
اِنَّ اللّٰهَ يُدٰفِعُ عَنِ الَّذِيْنَ اٰمَنُوْا ؕ اِنَّ اللّٰهَ لَا يُحِبُّ
كُلَّ خَوَّانٍ كَفُوْرٍ ﴿٣٨﴾

1. The slaughter of animals for food for the poor which is one of the ceremonies of the Muslim pilgrimage is not a propitiatory sacrifice, but is in commemoration of the sacrifice of Abraham which marked the end of human sacrifices for the Semitic race, and which made it clear that the only sacrifice which God requires of man is the Surrender of his will and purpose—*i.e.* Al-Islām.

2. In order that they may realise the awfulness of taking life, and the solemn nature of the trus which Allah has imposed on them in the permission to eat animal food.

39. Sanction is given unto those who fight because they have been wronged; and Allah is indeed Able to give them victory;

40. Those who have been driven from their homes unjustly only because they said: Our Lord is Allah—For had it not been for Allah's repelling some men by means of others, cloisters and churches and oratories and mosques, wherein the name of Allah is oft mentioned, would assuredly have been pulled down. Verily Allah helpeth one who helpeth Him. Lo! Allah is Strong, Almighty—

41. Those who, if We give them power in the land, establish worship and pay the poor-due and enjoin kindness and forbid iniquity. And Allah's is the sequel of events.

42. If they deny thee (Muhammad), even so the folk of Noah, and (the tribes of) 'Aad and Thamūd, before thee, denied (Our messengers);

43. And the folk of Abraham and the folk of Lot;

44. (And) the dwellers in Midian. And Moses was denied; but I indulged the disbelievers a long while, then I seized them, and how (terrible) was My abhorrence!

45. How many a township have We destroyed while it was sinful, so that it lieth (to this day) in ruins, and (how many) a deserted well and lofty tower!

46. Have they not travelled in the land, and have they hearts wherewith to feel and ears wherewith to hear? For indeed it is not the eyes that grow blind, but it is the hearts, which are within the bosoms, that grow blind.

أُذِنَ لِلَّذِينَ يُقٰتَلُونَ بِأَنَّهُمْ ظُلِمُوا وَإِنَّ اللّٰهَ عَلٰى
نَصْرِهِمْ لَقَدِيرٌ ﴿٣٩﴾
الَّذِينَ أُخْرِجُوا مِنْ دِيٰرِهِمْ بِغَيْرِ حَقٍّ إِلَّآ أَنْ
يَقُولُوا رَبُّنَا اللّٰهُ وَلَوْلَا دَفْعُ اللّٰهِ النَّاسَ بَعْضَهُمْ
بِبَعْضٍ لَهُدِّمَتْ صَوٰمِعُ وَبِيَعٌ وَصَلَوٰتٌ وَمَسٰجِدُ
يُذْكَرُ فِيهَا اسْمُ اللّٰهِ كَثِيرًا وَلَيَنْصُرَنَّ اللّٰهُ مَنْ
يَنْصُرُهُ إِنَّ اللّٰهَ لَقَوِيٌّ عَزِيزٌ ﴿٤٠﴾
اَلَّذِينَ إِنْ مَكَّنّٰهُمْ فِي الْأَرْضِ أَقَامُوا الصَّلٰوةَ
وَاٰتَوُا الزَّكٰوةَ وَأَمَرُوا بِالْمَعْرُوفِ وَنَهَوْا عَنِ
الْمُنْكَرِ وَلِلّٰهِ عٰقِبَةُ الْأُمُورِ ﴿٤١﴾
وَإِنْ يُكَذِّبُوكَ فَقَدْ كَذَّبَتْ قَبْلَهُمْ قَوْمُ نُوحٍ
وَعَادٌ وَثَمُودُ ﴿٤٢﴾
وَقَوْمُ إِبْرٰهِيمَ وَقَوْمُ لُوطٍ ﴿٤٣﴾
وَأَصْحٰبُ مَدْيَنَ وَكُذِّبَ مُوسٰى فَأَمْلَيْتُ
لِلْكٰفِرِينَ ثُمَّ أَخَذْتُهُمْ فَكَيْفَ كَانَ نَكِيرِ ﴿٤٤﴾
فَكَأَيِّنْ مِنْ قَرْيَةٍ أَهْلَكْنٰهَا وَهِيَ ظَالِمَةٌ فَهِيَ
خَاوِيَةٌ عَلٰى عُرُوشِهَا وَبِئْرٍ مُعَطَّلَةٍ وَقَصْرٍ
مَشِيدٍ ﴿٤٥﴾
أَفَلَمْ يَسِيرُوا فِي الْأَرْضِ فَتَكُونَ لَهُمْ قُلُوبٌ
يَعْقِلُونَ بِهَآ أَوْ اٰذَانٌ يَسْمَعُونَ بِهَا فَإِنَّهَا لَا
تَعْمَى الْأَبْصٰرُ وَلٰكِنْ تَعْمَى الْقُلُوبُ الَّتِي
فِي الصُّدُورِ ﴿٤٦﴾

47. And they will bid thee hasten on the Doom, and Allah faileth not His promise, but lo! a Day with Allah is as a thousand years of what ye reckon.

48. And how many a township did I suffer long though it was sinful! Then I grasped it. Unto Me is the return.

49. Say: O mankind! I am only a plain warner unto you.

50. Those who believe and do good works, for them is pardon and a rich provision;

51. While those who strive to thwart Our revelations, such are rightful owners of the Fire.

52. Never sent We a messenger or a Prophet before thee but when he recited (the message) Satan proposed (opposition) in respect of that which he recited thereof. But Allah abolisheth that which Satan proposeth. Then Allah establisheth His revelations. Allah is Knower, Wise;

53. That He may make that which the devil proposeth a temptation for those in whose hearts is a disease, and those whose hearts are hardened—Lo! the evil-doers are in open schism—

54. And that those who have been given knowledge may know that it is the truth from thy Lord, so that they may believe therein and their hearts may submit humbly unto Him. Lo! Allah verily is guiding those who believe unto a right path.

55. And those who disbelieve will not cease to be in doubt thereof until the Hour come upon them unawares, or there come unto them the doom of a disastrous day.

وَيَسْتَعْجِلُوْنَكَ بِالْعَذَابِ وَلَنْ يُّخْلِفَ اللّٰهُ وَعْدَهٗ
وَاِنَّ يَوْمًا عِنْدَ رَبِّكَ كَاَلْفِ سَنَةٍ مِّمَّا تَعُدُّوْنَ ﴿٤٧﴾
وَكَاَيِّنْ مِّنْ قَرْيَةٍ اَمْلَيْتُ لَهَا وَهِيَ ظَالِمَةٌ ثُمَّ
ع ١٢ اَخَذْتُهَا ۚ وَاِلَيَّ الْمَصِيْرُ ﴿٤٨﴾
قُلْ يٰۤاَيُّهَا النَّاسُ اِنَّمَاۤ اَنَا لَكُمْ نَذِيْرٌ مُّبِيْنٌ ﴿٤٩﴾
فَالَّذِيْنَ اٰمَنُوْا وَعَمِلُوا الصّٰلِحٰتِ لَهُمْ مَّغْفِرَةٌ
وَّرِزْقٌ كَرِيْمٌ ﴿٥٠﴾
وَالَّذِيْنَ سَعَوْا فِيْۤ اٰيٰتِنَا مُعٰجِزِيْنَ اُولٰٓئِكَ
اَصْحٰبُ الْجَحِيْمِ ﴿٥١﴾
وَمَاۤ اَرْسَلْنَا مِنْ قَبْلِكَ مِنْ رَّسُوْلٍ وَّلَا نَبِيٍّ اِلَّاۤ
اِذَا تَمَنّٰۤى اَلْقَى الشَّيْطٰنُ فِيْۤ اُمْنِيَّتِهٖ ۚ فَيَنْسَخُ اللّٰهُ
مَا يُلْقِي الشَّيْطٰنُ ثُمَّ يُحْكِمُ اللّٰهُ اٰيٰتِهٖ ۗ وَاللّٰهُ عَلِيْمٌ
حَكِيْمٌ ﴿٥٢﴾
لِّيَجْعَلَ مَا يُلْقِي الشَّيْطٰنُ فِتْنَةً لِّلَّذِيْنَ فِيْ
قُلُوْبِهِمْ مَّرَضٌ وَّالْقَاسِيَةِ قُلُوْبُهُمْ ۗ وَاِنَّ الظّٰلِمِيْنَ
لَفِيْ شِقَاقٍ بَعِيْدٍ ﴿٥٣﴾
وَّلِيَعْلَمَ الَّذِيْنَ اُوْتُوا الْعِلْمَ اَنَّهُ الْحَقُّ مِنْ رَّبِّكَ
فَيُؤْمِنُوْا بِهٖ فَتُخْبِتَ لَهٗ قُلُوْبُهُمْ ۗ وَاِنَّ اللّٰهَ لَهَادِ
الَّذِيْنَ اٰمَنُوْۤا اِلٰى صِرَاطٍ مُّسْتَقِيْمٍ ﴿٥٤﴾
وَلَا يَزَالُ الَّذِيْنَ كَفَرُوْا فِيْ مِرْيَةٍ مِّنْهُ حَتّٰى
تَاْتِيَهُمُ السَّاعَةُ بَغْتَةً اَوْ يَاْتِيَهُمْ عَذَابُ يَوْمٍ
عَقِيْمٍ ﴿٥٥﴾

56. The Sovereignty on that day will be Allah's. He will judge between them. Then those who believed and did good works will be in Gardens of Delight.

الملك يومئذ لله يحكم بينهم فالذين آمنوا
وعملوا الصالحات في جنات النعيم ٥٦

57. While those who disbelieved and denied Our revelations, for them will be a shameful doom.

والذين كفروا وكذبوا بآياتنا فأولئك لهم
عذاب مهين ٥٧

58. Those who fled their homes for the cause of Allah and then were slain or died, Allah verily will provide for them a good provision. Lo! Allah, He verily is Best of all who make provision.

والذين هاجروا في سبيل الله ثم قتلوا أو ماتوا
ليرزقنهم الله رزقا حسنا وإن الله لهو
خير الرازقين ٥٨

59. Assuredly He will cause them to enter by an entry that they will love. Lo! Allah verily is Knower, Indulgent.

ليدخلنهم مدخلا يرضونه وإن الله لعليم
حليم ٥٩

60. That (is so). And whoso hath retaliated with the like of that which he was made to suffer and then hath (again) been wronged, Allah will succour him. Lo! Allah verily is Mild, Forgiving.

ذلك ومن عاقب بمثل ما عوقب به ثم
بغي عليه لينصرنه الله إن الله لعفو
غفور ٦٠

61. That is because Allah maketh the night to pass into the day and maketh the day to pass into the night, and because Allah is Hearer, Seer.

ذلك بأن الله يولج الليل في النهار ويولج
النهار في الليل وأن الله سميع بصير ٦١

62. That is because Allah, He is the True, and that whereon they call instead of Him, it is the False, and because Allah, He is the High, the Great.

ذلك بأن الله هو الحق وأن ما يدعون
من دونه هو الباطل وأن الله هو العلي
الكبير ٦٢

63. Seest thou not how Allah sendeth down water from the sky and then the earth becometh green upon the morrow? Lo! Allah is Subtile, Aware.

ألم تر أن الله أنزل من السماء ماء
فتصبح الأرض مخضرة إن الله لطيف
خبير ٦٣

64. Unto Him belongeth all that is in the heavens and all that is in the earth. Lo! Allah, He verily is the Absolute, the Owner of Praise.

له ما في السماوات وما في الأرض وإن الله
لهو الغني الحميد ٦٤

65. Hast thou not seen how Allah hath made all that is in the earth subservient unto you? And the ship runneth upon the sea by His command, and He holdeth back the heaven from falling on the earth unless by His leave. Lo! Allah is, for mankind, Full of Pity, Merciful.

66. And He it is Who gave you life, then He will cause you to die, and then will give you life (again). Lo! man is verily an ingrate.

67. Unto each nation have We given sacred rites which they are to perform; so let them not dispute with thee of the matter, but summon thou unto thy Lord. Lo! thou indeed followest right guidance.

68. And if they wrangle with thee, say: Allah is best aware of what ye do.

69. Allah will judge between you on the Day of Resurrection concerning that wherein ye used to differ.

70. Hast thou not known that Allah knoweth all that is in the heaven and the earth? Lo! it is in a record. Lo! that is easy for Allah.

71. And they worship instead of Allah that for which no warrant hath been revealed unto them, and that whereof they have no knowledge. For evil-doers there is no helper.

72. And when Our revelations are recited unto them, thou knowest the denial in the faces of those who disbelieve; they all but attack those who recite Our revelations unto them. Say: Shall I proclaim unto you worse than that? The Fire! Allah hath promised it for those who disbelieve. A hapless journey's end!

ألم تر أن الله سخر لكم ما في الأرض والفلك
تجري في البحر بأمره ويمسك السماء أن
تقع على الأرض إلا بإذنه إن الله بالناس
لرءوف رحيم ٦٥
وهو الذي أحياكم ثم يميتكم ثم يحييكم إن
الإنسان لكفور ٦٦
لكل أمة جعلنا منسكا هم ناسكوه فلا ينازعنك
في الأمر وادع إلى ربك إنك لعلى هدى
مستقيم ٦٧
وإن جادلوك فقل الله أعلم بما تعملون ٦٨
الله يحكم بينكم يوم القيامة فيما كنتم فيه
تختلفون ٦٩
ألم تعلم أن الله يعلم ما في السماء والأرض
إن ذلك في كتاب إن ذلك على الله يسير ٧٠
ويعبدون من دون الله ما لم ينزل به
سلطانا وما ليس لهم به علم وما للظالمين
من نصير ٧١
وإذا تتلى عليهم آياتنا بينات تعرف في وجوه
الذين كفروا المنكر يكادون يسطون بالذين
يتلون عليهم آياتنا قل أفأنبئكم بشر من
ذلكم النار وعدها الله الذين كفروا وبئس
ع المصير ٧٢
١٦

73. O mankind! A similitude is coined, so pay ye heed to it: Lo! those on whom ye call beside Allah will never create a fly though they combine together for the purpose. And if the fly took something from them, they could not rescue it from him. So weak are (both) the seeker and the sought!

74. They measure not Allah His rightful measure. Lo! Allah is Strong, Almighty.

75. Allah chooseth from the angels messengers, and (also) from mankind. Lo! Allah is Hearer, Seer.

76. He knoweth all that is before them and all that is behind them, and unto Allah all things are returned.

77. O, ye who believe! Bow down and prostrate yourselves, and worship your Lord, and do good, that haply ye may prosper.

78. And strive for Allah with the endeavour which is His right. He hath chosen you and hath not laid upon you in religion any hardship; the faith of your father Abraham (is yours). He hath named you Muslims[1] of old time and in this (Scripture), that the messenger may be a witness against you, and that ye may be witnesses against mankind. So establish worship, pay the poor-due, and hold fast to Allah. He is your Protecting Friend. A blessed Patron and a blessed Helper!

1. "Those who have surrendered."

يٰۤاَيُّهَا النَّاسُ ضُرِبَ مَثَلٌ فَاسْتَمِعُوْا لَهٗ اِنَّ
الَّذِيْنَ تَدْعُوْنَ مِنْ دُوْنِ اللّٰهِ لَنْ يَّخْلُقُوْا
ذُبَابًا وَّلَوِ اجْتَمَعُوْا لَهٗ وَاِنْ يَّسْلُبْهُمُ الذُّبَابُ
شَيْـًٔا لَّا يَسْتَنْقِذُوْهُ مِنْهُ ضَعُفَ الطَّالِبُ وَ
الْمَطْلُوْبُ ﴿٧٣﴾
مَا قَدَرُوا اللّٰهَ حَقَّ قَدْرِهٖ اِنَّ اللّٰهَ لَقَوِىٌّ عَزِيْزٌ ﴿٧٤﴾
اَللّٰهُ يَصْطَفِىْ مِنَ الْمَلٰٓئِكَةِ رُسُلًا وَّمِنَ النَّاسِ
اِنَّ اللّٰهَ سَمِيْعٌۢ بَصِيْرٌ ﴿٧٥﴾
يَعْلَمُ مَا بَيْنَ اَيْدِيْهِمْ وَمَا خَلْفَهُمْ وَاِلَى اللّٰهِ
تُرْجَعُ الْاُمُوْرُ ﴿٧٦﴾
يٰۤاَيُّهَا الَّذِيْنَ اٰمَنُوا ارْكَعُوْا وَاسْجُدُوْا وَاعْبُدُوْا
رَبَّكُمْ وَافْعَلُوا الْخَيْرَ لَعَلَّكُمْ تُفْلِحُوْنَ ﴿٧٧﴾
وَجَاهِدُوْا فِى اللّٰهِ حَقَّ جِهَادِهٖ هُوَ اجْتَبٰىكُمْ
وَمَا جَعَلَ عَلَيْكُمْ فِى الدِّيْنِ مِنْ حَرَجٍ مِلَّةَ
اَبِيْكُمْ اِبْرٰهِيْمَ هُوَ سَمّٰىكُمُ الْمُسْلِمِيْنَ مِنْ
قَبْلُ وَفِىْ هٰذَا لِيَكُوْنَ الرَّسُوْلُ شَهِيْدًا عَلَيْكُمْ
وَتَكُوْنُوْا شُهَدَآءَ عَلَى النَّاسِ فَاَقِيْمُوا الصَّلٰوةَ وَ
اٰتُوا الزَّكٰوةَ وَاعْتَصِمُوْا بِاللّٰهِ هُوَ مَوْلٰىكُمْ فَنِعْمَ
الْمَوْلٰى وَنِعْمَ النَّصِيْرُ ﴿٧٨﴾

Al Mu'minūn, "The Believers," is so named from a word occurring in the first verse or, it may be said, from its subject, which is the triumph of believers. It is considered to be the last of the Sūrahs revealed at Mecca, immediately before the Prophet's flight to Yathrib (Al-Madīnah).

A late Meccan Sūrah.

THE BELIEVERS

Revealed at Mecca

In the name of Allah, the Beneficent, the Merciful.

1. Successful indeed are the believers

2. Who are humble in their prayers,

3. And who shun vain conversation,

4. And who are payers of the poor-due

5. And who guard their modesty—

6. Save from their wives or the (slaves) that their right hands possess, for then they are not blameworthy.

7. But whoso craveth beyond that, such are transgressors—

8. And who are shepherds of their pledge and their covenant,

9. And who pay heed to their prayers.

10. These are the heirs

11. Who will inherit Paradise. There they will abide.

12. Verily We created man from a product of wet earth;

13. Then placed him as a drop (of seed) in a safe lodging;

14. Then fashioned We the drop a clot, then fashioned We the clot a little lump, then fashioned We the little lump bones, then clothed the bones with flesh, and then produced it as another creation. So blessed be Allah, the Best of Creators!

15. Then lo! after that ye surely die.

16. Then lo! on the Day of Resurrection ye are raised (again).

اٰيَاتُهَا ١١٨ (٢٣) سُوْرَةُ الْمُؤْمِنُوْنَ مَكِّيَّةٌ رُكُوْعَاتُهَا ٦

بِسْمِ اللّٰهِ الرَّحْمٰنِ الرَّحِيْمِ

الجزء ١٨

قَدْ اَفْلَحَ الْمُؤْمِنُوْنَ ﴿١﴾

الَّذِيْنَ هُمْ فِيْ صَلَاتِهِمْ خٰشِعُوْنَ ﴿٢﴾

وَالَّذِيْنَ هُمْ عَنِ اللَّغْوِ مُعْرِضُوْنَ ﴿٣﴾

وَالَّذِيْنَ هُمْ لِلزَّكٰوةِ فٰعِلُوْنَ ﴿٤﴾

وَالَّذِيْنَ هُمْ لِفُرُوْجِهِمْ حٰفِظُوْنَ ﴿٥﴾

اِلَّا عَلٰٓى اَزْوَاجِهِمْ اَوْ مَا مَلَكَتْ اَيْمَانُهُمْ فَاِنَّهُمْ
غَيْرُ مَلُوْمِيْنَ ﴿٦﴾

فَمَنِ ابْتَغٰى وَرَآءَ ذٰلِكَ فَاُولٰٓئِكَ هُمُ الْعٰدُوْنَ ﴿٧﴾

وَالَّذِيْنَ هُمْ لِاَمٰنٰتِهِمْ وَعَهْدِهِمْ رٰعُوْنَ ﴿٨﴾

وقف لازم

وَالَّذِيْنَ هُمْ عَلٰى صَلَوٰتِهِمْ يُحَافِظُوْنَ ﴿٩﴾

اُولٰٓئِكَ هُمُ الْوٰرِثُوْنَ ﴿١٠﴾

الَّذِيْنَ يَرِثُوْنَ الْفِرْدَوْسَ هُمْ فِيْهَا خٰلِدُوْنَ ﴿١١﴾

وَلَقَدْ خَلَقْنَا الْاِنْسَانَ مِنْ سُلٰلَةٍ مِّنْ طِيْنٍ ﴿١٢﴾

ثُمَّ جَعَلْنٰهُ نُطْفَةً فِيْ قَرَارٍ مَّكِيْنٍ ﴿١٣﴾

ثُمَّ خَلَقْنَا النُّطْفَةَ عَلَقَةً فَخَلَقْنَا الْعَلَقَةَ مُضْغَةً
فَخَلَقْنَا الْمُضْغَةَ عِظٰمًا فَكَسَوْنَا الْعِظٰمَ لَحْمًا ثُمَّ
اَنْشَاْنٰهُ خَلْقًا اٰخَرَ فَتَبٰرَكَ اللّٰهُ اَحْسَنُ الْخٰلِقِيْنَ ﴿١٤﴾

ثُمَّ اِنَّكُمْ بَعْدَ ذٰلِكَ لَمَيِّتُوْنَ ﴿١٥﴾

ثُمَّ اِنَّكُمْ يَوْمَ الْقِيٰمَةِ تُبْعَثُوْنَ ﴿١٦﴾

17. And We have created above you seven paths, and We are never unmindful of creation.

18. And We send down from the sky water in measure, and We give it lodging in the earth, and lo! We are able to withdraw it.

19. Then We produce for you therewith gardens of date-palms and grapes, wherein is much fruit for you and whereof ye eat;

20. And a tree that springeth forth from Mount Sinai that groweth oil and relish for the eaters.

21. And lo! in the cattle there is verily a lesson for you We give you to drink of that which is in their bellies, and many uses have ye in them, and of them do ye eat;

22. And on them and on the ship ye are carried.

23. And We verily sent Noah unto his folk, and he said: O my people! Serve Allah. Ye have no other god save Him. Will ye not ward off (evil)?

24. But the chieftains of his folk, who disbelieved, said: This is only a mortal like you who would make himself superior to you. Had Allah willed, He surely could have sent down angels. We heard not of this in the case of our fathers of old.

25. He is only a man in whom is a madness, so watch him for a while.

26. He said: My Lord! Help me because they deny me.

27. Then We inspired in him, saying: Make the ship under Our eyes and Our inspiration. Then, when Our command cometh and the oven gusheth water, introduce therein of every (kind) two spouses, and thy household save him thereof against whom the Word hath already gone forth. And plead not with Me on behalf of those who have done wrong. Lo! they will be drowned,

وَلَقَدْ خَلَقْنَا فَوْقَكُمْ سَبْعَ طَرَآئِقَ ۖ وَمَا كُنَّا عَنِ الْخَلْقِ
غٰفِلِينَ ﴿١٧﴾
وَأَنْزَلْنَا مِنَ السَّمَآءِ مَآءً بِقَدَرٍ فَأَسْكَنّٰهُ فِي الْأَرْضِ ۖ
وَإِنَّا عَلٰى ذَهَابٍ بِهِ لَقٰدِرُونَ ﴿١٨﴾
فَأَنْشَأْنَا لَكُمْ بِهِ جَنّٰتٍ مِنْ نَخِيلٍ وَأَعْنَابٍ لَكُمْ وقف لازم
فِيهَا فَوٰكِهُ كَثِيرَةٌ وَمِنْهَا تَأْكُلُونَ ﴿١٩﴾
وَشَجَرَةً تَخْرُجُ مِنْ طُورِ سَيْنَآءَ تَنْبُتُ بِالدُّهْنِ
وَصِبْغٍ لِلْآكِلِينَ ﴿٢٠﴾
وَإِنَّ لَكُمْ فِي الْأَنْعَامِ لَعِبْرَةً ۖ نُسْقِيكُمْ مِمَّا فِي بُطُونِهَا
وَلَكُمْ فِيهَا مَنَافِعُ كَثِيرَةٌ وَمِنْهَا تَأْكُلُونَ ﴿٢١﴾
ع وَعَلَيْهَا وَعَلَى الْفُلْكِ تُحْمَلُونَ ﴿٢٢﴾
وَلَقَدْ أَرْسَلْنَا نُوحًا إِلٰى قَوْمِهِ فَقَالَ يٰقَوْمِ اعْبُدُوا
اللّٰهَ مَا لَكُمْ مِنْ إِلٰهٍ غَيْرُهُ ۖ أَفَلَا تَتَّقُونَ ﴿٢٣﴾
فَقَالَ الْمَلَؤُا الَّذِينَ كَفَرُوا مِنْ قَوْمِهِ مَا هٰذَآ إِلَّا بَشَرٌ
مِثْلُكُمْ يُرِيدُ أَنْ يَتَفَضَّلَ عَلَيْكُمْ ۖ وَلَوْ شَآءَ اللّٰهُ لَأَنْزَلَ
مَلٰئِكَةً ۚ مَا سَمِعْنَا بِهٰذَا فِي آبَآئِنَا الْأَوَّلِينَ ﴿٢٤﴾
إِنْ هُوَ إِلَّا رَجُلٌ بِهِ جِنَّةٌ فَتَرَبَّصُوا بِهِ حَتّٰى حِينٍ ﴿٢٥﴾
قَالَ رَبِّ انْصُرْنِي بِمَا كَذَّبُونِ ﴿٢٦﴾
فَأَوْحَيْنَآ إِلَيْهِ أَنِ اصْنَعِ الْفُلْكَ بِأَعْيُنِنَا وَوَحْيِنَا فَإِذَا
جَآءَ أَمْرُنَا وَفَارَ التَّنُّورُ ۙ فَاسْلُكْ فِيهَا مِنْ كُلٍّ زَوْجَيْنِ
اثْنَيْنِ وَأَهْلَكَ إِلَّا مَنْ سَبَقَ عَلَيْهِ الْقَوْلُ مِنْهُمْ ۖ وَلَا
تُخَاطِبْنِي فِي الَّذِينَ ظَلَمُوا ۚ إِنَّهُمْ مُغْرَقُونَ ﴿٢٧﴾

28. And when thou art on board the ship, thou and whoso is with thee, then say: Praise be to Allah Who hath saved us from the wrongdoing folk!

29. And say: My Lord! Cause me to land at a blessed landing-place, for Thou art best of all who bring to land.

30. Lo! herein verily are portents, for lo! We are ever putting (mankind) to the test.

31. Then, after them, We brought forth another generation;

32. And We sent among them a messenger of their own, saying: Serve Allah. Ye have no other god save Him. Will ye not ward off (evil)?

33. And the chieftains of his folk, who disbelieved and denied the meeting of the Hereafter, and whom We had made soft in the life of the world, said: This is only a mortal like you, who eateth of that whereof ye eat and drinketh of that ye drink.

34. If ye were to obey a mortal like yourselves, ye surely would be losers:

35. Doth he promise you that you, when ye are dead and have become dust and bones, will (again) be brought forth?

36. Begone, begone, with that which ye are promised!

37. There is naught but our life of the world; we die and we live, and we shall not be raised (again).

38. He is only a man who hath invented a lie about Allah. We are not going to put faith in him.

39. He said: My Lord! Help me because they deny me.

40. He said: In a little while they surely will become repentant.

فَاِذَا اسْتَوَيْتَ اَنْتَ وَمَنْ مَّعَكَ عَلَى الْفُلْكِ فَقُلِ
الْحَمْدُ لِلّٰهِ الَّذِيْ نَجّٰنَا مِنَ الْقَوْمِ الظّٰلِمِيْنَ ﴿٢٨﴾
وَقُلْ رَّبِّ اَنْزِلْنِيْ مُنْزَلًا مُّبٰرَكًا وَّاَنْتَ خَيْرُ
الْمُنْزِلِيْنَ ﴿٢٩﴾
اِنَّ فِيْ ذٰلِكَ لَاٰيٰتٍ وَّاِنْ كُنَّا لَمُبْتَلِيْنَ ﴿٣٠﴾
ثُمَّ اَنْشَاْنَا مِنْ بَعْدِهِمْ قَرْنًا اٰخَرِيْنَ ﴿٣١﴾
فَاَرْسَلْنَا فِيْهِمْ رَسُوْلًا مِّنْهُمْ اَنِ اعْبُدُوا اللّٰهَ مَا
ع لَكُمْ مِّنْ اِلٰهٍ غَيْرُهٗ اَفَلَا تَتَّقُوْنَ ﴿٣٢﴾
وَقَالَ الْمَلَاُ مِنْ قَوْمِهِ الَّذِيْنَ كَفَرُوْا وَكَذَّبُوْا
بِلِقَاۗءِ الْاٰخِرَةِ وَاَتْرَفْنٰهُمْ فِي الْحَيٰوةِ الدُّنْيَا مَا
هٰذَاۤ اِلَّا بَشَرٌ مِّثْلُكُمْ يَاْكُلُ مِمَّا تَاْكُلُوْنَ مِنْهُ وَ
يَشْرَبُ مِمَّا تَشْرَبُوْنَ ﴿٣٣﴾
وَلَىِٕنْ اَطَعْتُمْ بَشَرًا مِّثْلَكُمْ اِنَّكُمْ اِذًا لَّخٰسِرُوْنَ ﴿٣٤﴾
اَيَعِدُكُمْ اَنَّكُمْ اِذَا مِتُّمْ وَكُنْتُمْ تُرَابًا وَّعِظَامًا اَنَّكُمْ
مُّخْرَجُوْنَ ﴿٣٥﴾
هَيْهَاتَ هَيْهَاتَ لِمَا تُوْعَدُوْنَ ﴿٣٦﴾
اِنْ هِيَ اِلَّا حَيَاتُنَا الدُّنْيَا نَمُوْتُ وَنَحْيَا وَمَا نَحْنُ
بِمَبْعُوْثِيْنَ ﴿٣٧﴾
اِنْ هُوَ اِلَّا رَجُلُ ۨافْتَرٰى عَلَى اللّٰهِ كَذِبًا وَّمَا نَحْنُ
لَهٗ بِمُؤْمِنِيْنَ ﴿٣٨﴾
قَالَ رَبِّ انْصُرْنِيْ بِمَا كَذَّبُوْنِ ﴿٣٩﴾
قَالَ عَمَّا قَلِيْلٍ لَّيُصْبِحُنَّ نٰدِمِيْنَ ﴿٤٠﴾

41. So the (Awful) Cry overtook them rightfully, and We made them like as wreckage (that a torrent hurleth). A far removal for wrongdoing folk!

42. Then after them We brought forth other generations.

43. No nation can outstrip its term, nor yet postpone it.

44. Then We sent Our messengers one after another. Whenever its messenger came unto a nation they denied him; so We caused them to follow one another (to disaster) and We made them bywords. A far removal for folk who believe not!

45. Then We sent Moses and his brother Aaron with Our tokens and a clear warrant

46. Unto Pharaoh and his chiefs, but they scorned (them) and they were despotic folk.

47. And they said: Shall we put faith in two mortals like ourselves, and whose folk are servile unto us?

48. So they denied them, and became of those who were destroyed.

49. And We verily gave Moses the Scripture, that haply they might go aright.

50. And We made the son of Mary and his mother a portent, and We gave them refuge on a height, a place of flocks and water-springs.

51. O ye messengers! Eat of the good things, and do right. Lo! I am Aware of what ye do.

52. And lo! this your religion is one religion and I am your Lord, so keep your duty unto Me.

53. But they (mankind) have broken their religion among them into sects, each sect rejoicing in its tenets.

فَأَخَذَتْهُمُ الصَّيْحَةُ بِالْحَقِّ فَجَعَلْنٰهُمْ غُثَآءً ۚ
فَبُعْدًا لِّلْقَوْمِ الظّٰلِمِيْنَ ﴿٤١﴾
ثُمَّ أَنْشَأْنَا مِنْۢ بَعْدِهِمْ قُرُوْنًا اٰخَرِيْنَ ﴿٤٢﴾
مَا تَسْبِقُ مِنْ أُمَّةٍ أَجَلَهَا وَمَا يَسْتَأْخِرُوْنَ ﴿٤٣﴾
ثُمَّ أَرْسَلْنَا رُسُلَنَا تَتْرَا ۖ كُلَّمَا جَآءَ أُمَّةً رَّسُوْلُهَا
كَذَّبُوْهُ فَأَتْبَعْنَا بَعْضَهُمْ بَعْضًا وَّجَعَلْنٰهُمْ أَحَادِيْثَ ۚ
فَبُعْدًا لِّقَوْمٍ لَّا يُؤْمِنُوْنَ ﴿٤٤﴾
ثُمَّ أَرْسَلْنَا مُوْسٰى وَأَخَاهُ هٰرُوْنَ ۙ بِاٰيٰتِنَا وَسُلْطٰنٍ
مُّبِيْنٍ ﴿٤٥﴾ ۙ
إِلٰى فِرْعَوْنَ وَمَلَا۟ئِهٖ فَاسْتَكْبَرُوْا وَكَانُوْا قَوْمًا عَالِيْنَ ﴿٤٦﴾ ۚ
فَقَالُوْٓا أَنُؤْمِنُ لِبَشَرَيْنِ مِثْلِنَا وَقَوْمُهُمَا لَنَا
عٰبِدُوْنَ ﴿٤٧﴾ ۚ
فَكَذَّبُوْهُمَا فَكَانُوْا مِنَ الْمُهْلَكِيْنَ ﴿٤٨﴾
وَلَقَدْ اٰتَيْنَا مُوْسَى الْكِتٰبَ لَعَلَّهُمْ يَهْتَدُوْنَ ﴿٤٩﴾
وَجَعَلْنَا ابْنَ مَرْيَمَ وَأُمَّهٗٓ اٰيَةً وَّاٰوَيْنٰهُمَآ إِلٰى رَبْوَةٍ
ذَاتِ قَرَارٍ وَّمَعِيْنٍ ﴿٥٠﴾ ع
يٰٓأَيُّهَا الرُّسُلُ كُلُوْا مِنَ الطَّيِّبٰتِ وَاعْمَلُوْا صَالِحًا ۖ
إِنِّيْ بِمَا تَعْمَلُوْنَ عَلِيْمٌ ﴿٥١﴾ ۗ
وَإِنَّ هٰذِهٖٓ أُمَّتُكُمْ أُمَّةً وَّاحِدَةً وَّأَنَا رَبُّكُمْ
فَاتَّقُوْنِ ﴿٥٢﴾
فَتَقَطَّعُوْٓا أَمْرَهُمْ بَيْنَهُمْ زُبُرًا ۖ كُلُّ حِزْبٍۭ بِمَا
لَدَيْهِمْ فَرِحُوْنَ ﴿٥٣﴾

54. So leave them in their error till a time.

55. Think they that in the wealth and sons wherewith We provide them,

56. We hasten unto them with good things? Nay, but they perceive not.

57. Lo! those who go in awe for fear of their Lord,

58. And those who believe in the revelations of their Lord,

59. And those who ascribe not partners unto their Lord,

60. And those who give that which they give with hearts afraid because they are about to return unto their Lord,

61. These race for the good things, and they shall win them in the race.

62. And We task not any soul beyond its scope, and with Us is a Record which speaketh the truth, and they will not be wronged.

63. Nay, but their hearts are in ignorance of this (Qur'ān), and they have other works, besides, which they are doing;

64. Till when We grasp their luxurious ones with the punishment, behold! they supplicate.

65. Supplicate not this day! Assuredly ye will not be helped by Us.

66. My revelations were recited unto you, but ye used to turn back on your heels,

67. In scorn thereof. Nightly did ye rave together.

68. Have they not pondered the Word, or hath that come unto them which came not unto their fathers of old?

فَذَرْهُمْ فِي غَمْرَتِهِمْ حَتّٰى حِيْنٍ ﴿٥٤﴾
اَيَحْسَبُوْنَ اَنَّمَا نُمِدُّهُمْ بِهٖ مِنْ مَّالٍ وَّبَنِيْنَ ﴿٥٥﴾
نُسَارِعُ لَهُمْ فِي الْخَيْرٰتِ ؕ بَلْ لَّا يَشْعُرُوْنَ ﴿٥٦﴾
اِنَّ الَّذِيْنَ هُمْ مِّنْ خَشْيَةِ رَبِّهِمْ مُّشْفِقُوْنَ ﴿٥٧﴾
وَالَّذِيْنَ هُمْ بِاٰيٰتِ رَبِّهِمْ يُؤْمِنُوْنَ ﴿٥٨﴾
وَالَّذِيْنَ هُمْ بِرَبِّهِمْ لَا يُشْرِكُوْنَ ﴿٥٩﴾
وَالَّذِيْنَ يُؤْتُوْنَ مَاۤ اٰتَوْا وَّقُلُوْبُهُمْ وَجِلَةٌ اَنَّهُمْ اِلٰى
رَبِّهِمْ رٰجِعُوْنَ ﴿٦٠﴾
اُولٰٓئِكَ يُسٰرِعُوْنَ فِي الْخَيْرٰتِ وَهُمْ لَهَا
سٰبِقُوْنَ ﴿٦١﴾
وَلَا نُكَلِّفُ نَفْسًا اِلَّا وُسْعَهَا وَلَدَيْنَا كِتٰبٌ يَّنْطِقُ
بِالْحَقِّ وَهُمْ لَا يُظْلَمُوْنَ ﴿٦٢﴾
بَلْ قُلُوْبُهُمْ فِيْ غَمْرَةٍ مِّنْ هٰذَا وَلَهُمْ اَعْمَالٌ
مِّنْ دُوْنِ ذٰلِكَ هُمْ لَهَا عٰمِلُوْنَ ﴿٦٣﴾
حَتّٰىۤ اِذَاۤ اَخَذْنَا مُتْرَفِيْهِمْ بِالْعَذَابِ اِذَا هُمْ
يَجْئَرُوْنَ ﴿٦٤﴾
لَا تَجْئَرُوا الْيَوْمَ اِنَّكُمْ مِّنَّا لَا تُنْصَرُوْنَ ﴿٦٥﴾
قَدْ كَانَتْ اٰيٰتِيْ تُتْلٰى عَلَيْكُمْ فَكُنْتُمْ عَلٰىۤ اَعْقَابِكُمْ
تَنْكِصُوْنَ ﴿٦٦﴾
مُسْتَكْبِرِيْنَ بِهٖ سٰمِرًا تَهْجُرُوْنَ ﴿٦٧﴾
اَفَلَمْ يَدَّبَّرُوا الْقَوْلَ اَمْ جَآءَهُمْ مَّا لَمْ يَاْتِ
اٰبَآءَهُمُ الْاَوَّلِيْنَ ﴿٦٨﴾

69. Or know they not their messenger, and so reject him?

أَمْ لَمْ يَعْرِفُوا رَسُولَهُمْ فَهُمْ لَهُ مُنكِرُونَ ﴿٦٩﴾

70. Or say they : There is a madness in him? Nay,but he bringeth them the Truth; and most ot them are haters of the Truth.

أَمْ يَقُولُونَ بِهِ جِنَّةٌ ۚ بَلْ جَاءَهُم بِالْحَقِّ وَ
أَكْثَرُهُمْ لِلْحَقِّ كٰرِهُونَ ﴿٧٠﴾

71. And if the truth had followed their desires, verily the heavens and the earth and whosoever is therein had been corrupted. Nay we have brought them their Reminder, but from their Reminder they now turn away.

وَلَوِ اتَّبَعَ الْحَقُّ أَهْوَاءَهُمْ لَفَسَدَتِ السَّمٰوٰتُ وَ
الْأَرْضُ وَمَن فِيهِنَّ ۚ بَلْ أَتَيْنٰهُم بِذِكْرِهِمْ فَهُمْ
عَن ذِكْرِهِم مُّعْرِضُونَ ﴿٧١﴾

72. Or dost thou ask of them (O Muhammad) any tribute?. But the bounty of thy Lord is better, for He is best of all who make provision.

أَمْ تَسْـَٔلُهُمْ خَرْجًا فَخَرَاجُ رَبِّكَ خَيْرٌ ۖ وَهُوَ
خَيْرُ الرّٰزِقِينَ ﴿٧٢﴾

73. And lo! thou summonest them indeed unto a right path.

وَإِنَّكَ لَتَدْعُوهُمْ إِلٰى صِرٰطٍ مُّسْتَقِيمٍ ﴿٧٣﴾

74. And lo! those who believe not in the Hereafter are indeed astray from the path.

وَإِنَّ الَّذِينَ لَا يُؤْمِنُونَ بِالْاٰخِرَةِ عَنِ الصِّرٰطِ
لَنٰكِبُونَ ﴿٧٤﴾

75. Though we had mercy on them and relieved them of the harm afflicting them, they still would wander blindly on in their contumacy.

وَلَوْ رَحِمْنٰهُمْ وَكَشَفْنَا مَا بِهِم مِّن ضُرٍّ لَّلَجُّوا فِي
طُغْيٰنِهِمْ يَعْمَهُونَ ﴿٧٥﴾

76. Already have We grasped them with punishment, but they humble not themselves unto their Lord, nor do they pray.

وَلَقَدْ أَخَذْنٰهُم بِالْعَذَابِ فَمَا اسْتَكَانُوا لِرَبِّهِمْ
وَمَا يَتَضَرَّعُونَ ﴿٧٦﴾

77. Until, when We open for them the gate of extreme punishment, behold! they are aghast thereat.

حَتّٰى إِذَا فَتَحْنَا عَلَيْهِم بَابًا ذَا عَذَابٍ شَدِيدٍ إِذَا
هُمْ فِيهِ مُبْلِسُونَ ﴿٧٧﴾

78. He it is Who hath created for you ears and eyes and hearts. Small thanks give ye!

وَهُوَ الَّذِي أَنشَأَ لَكُمُ السَّمْعَ وَالْأَبْصٰرَ وَالْأَفْـِٔدَةَ ۚ
قَلِيلًا مَّا تَشْكُرُونَ ﴿٧٨﴾

79. And He it is Who hath sown you broadcast in the earth, and unto Him ye will be gathered.

وَهُوَ الَّذِي ذَرَأَكُمْ فِي الْأَرْضِ وَإِلَيْهِ تُحْشَرُونَ ﴿٧٩﴾

80. And He it is Who giveth life and causeth death, and His is the difference of night and day. Have ye then no sense?

وَهُوَ الَّذِي يُحْيِي وَيُمِيتُ وَلَهُ اخْتِلَافُ الَّيْلِ وَ
النَّهَارِ ۚ أَفَلَا تَعْقِلُونَ ﴿٨٠﴾

81. Nay, but they say the like of that which said the men of old;

82. They say: When we are dead and have become (mere) dust and bones, shall we then, forsooth, be raised again?

83. We were already promised this, we and our forefathers. Lo! this is naught but fables of the men of old.

84. Say: Unto Whom (belongeth) the earth and whosoever is therein, if ye have knowledge?

85. They will say: Unto Allah. Say: Will ye not then remember?

86. Say: Who is Lord of the seven Heavens, and Lord of the Tremendous Throne?

87. They will say: Unto Allah (all that belongeth). Say: Will ye not then keep duty (unto Him)?

88. Say: In Whose hand is the dominion over all things and He protecteth, while against Him there is no protection, if ye have knowledge?

89. They will say: Unto Allah (all that belongeth). Say: How then are ye bewitched?

90. Nay, but We have brought them the Truth, and lo! they are liars.

91. Allah hath not chosen any son, nor is there any God along with Him; else would each God have assuredly championed that which he created, and some of them would assuredly have overcome others. Glorified be Allah above all that they allege:

92. Knower of the invisible and the visible! and exalted be He over all that they ascribe as partners (unto Him)!

93. Say: My Lord! If Thou shouldst show me that which they are promised,

94. My Lord! then set me not among the wrongdoing folk.

95. And verily We are Able to show thee that which We have promised them.

بَلْ قَالُوْا مِثْلَ مَا قَالَ الْاَوَّلُوْنَ ﴿٨١﴾
قَالُوْٓا ءَاِذَا مِتْنَا وَكُنَّا تُرَابًا وَّعِظَامًا ءَاِنَّا
لَمَبْعُوْثُوْنَ ﴿٨٢﴾
لَقَدْ وُعِدْنَا نَحْنُ وَاٰبَآؤُنَا هٰذَا مِنْ قَبْلُ اِنْ
هٰذَآ اِلَّآ اَسَاطِيْرُ الْاَوَّلِيْنَ ﴿٨٣﴾
قُلْ لِّمَنِ الْاَرْضُ وَمَنْ فِيْهَآ اِنْ كُنْتُمْ
تَعْلَمُوْنَ ﴿٨٤﴾
سَيَقُوْلُوْنَ لِلّٰهِ قُلْ اَفَلَا تَذَكَّرُوْنَ ﴿٨٥﴾
قُلْ مَنْ رَّبُّ السَّمٰوٰتِ السَّبْعِ وَرَبُّ الْعَرْشِ
الْعَظِيْمِ ﴿٨٦﴾
سَيَقُوْلُوْنَ لِلّٰهِ قُلْ اَفَلَا تَتَّقُوْنَ ﴿٨٧﴾
قُلْ مَنْ بِيَدِهٖ مَلَكُوْتُ كُلِّ شَيْءٍ وَّهُوَ يُجِيْرُ وَلَا
يُجَارُ عَلَيْهِ اِنْ كُنْتُمْ تَعْلَمُوْنَ ﴿٨٨﴾
سَيَقُوْلُوْنَ لِلّٰهِ قُلْ فَاَنّٰى تُسْحَرُوْنَ ﴿٨٩﴾
بَلْ اَتَيْنٰهُمْ بِالْحَقِّ وَاِنَّهُمْ لَكٰذِبُوْنَ ﴿٩٠﴾
مَا اتَّخَذَ اللّٰهُ مِنْ وَّلَدٍ وَّمَا كَانَ مَعَهٗ مِنْ اِلٰهٍ اِذًا
لَّذَهَبَ كُلُّ اِلٰهٍ بِمَا خَلَقَ وَلَعَلَا بَعْضُهُمْ عَلٰى
بَعْضٍ سُبْحٰنَ اللّٰهِ عَمَّا يَصِفُوْنَ ﴿٩١﴾
ع عٰلِمِ الْغَيْبِ وَالشَّهَادَةِ فَتَعٰلٰى عَمَّا يُشْرِكُوْنَ ﴿٩٢﴾
قُلْ رَّبِّ اِمَّا تُرِيَنِّيْ مَا يُوْعَدُوْنَ ﴿٩٣﴾
رَبِّ فَلَا تَجْعَلْنِيْ فِي الْقَوْمِ الظّٰلِمِيْنَ ﴿٩٤﴾
وَاِنَّا عَلٰٓى اَنْ نُّرِيَكَ مَا نَعِدُهُمْ لَقٰدِرُوْنَ ﴿٩٥﴾

96. Repel evil with that which is better. We are best Aware of that which they allege.

97. And say: My Lord! I seek refuge in Thee from suggestions of the evil ones,

98. And I seek refuge in Thee, my Lord, lest they be present with me,

99. Until, when death cometh unto one of them, he saith: My Lord! Send me back,

100. That I may do right in that which I have left behind! But nay! It is but a word that he speaketh; and behind them is a barrier until the day when they are raised.

101. And when the Trumpet is blown there will be no kinship among them that day, nor will they ask of one another.

102. Then those whose scales are heavy, they are the successful.

103. And those whose scales are light are those who lose their souls, in hell abiding.

104. The fire burneth their faces, and they are glum therein.

105. (It will be said): Were not My revelations recited unto you, and then ye used to deny them?

106. They will say: Our Lord! Our evil fortune conquered us, and we were erring folk.

107. Our Lord! Oh, bring us forth from hence! If we return (to evil) then indeed we shall be wrongdoers.

108. He saith: Begone therein, and speak not unto Me.

109. Lo! there was a party of My slaves who said: Our Lord! We believe, therefor forgive us and have mercy on us for Thou art best of all who show mercy;

ادفع بالتي هي احسن السيئة نحن اعلم بما
يصفون ٩٦
وقل رب اعوذ بك من همزت الشيطين ٩٧
واعوذ بك رب ان يحضرون ٩٨
حتى اذا جاء احدهم الموت قال رب ارجعون ٩٩
لعلي اعمل صالحا فيما تركت كلا انها كلمة
هو قائلها ومن ورائهم برزخ الى يوم
يبعثون ١٠٠
فاذا نفخ في الصور فلا انساب بينهم يومئذ
ولا يتساءلون ١٠١
فمن ثقلت موازينه فاولئك هم المفلحون ١٠٢
ومن خفت موازينه فاولئك الذين خسروا
انفسهم في جهنم خلدون ١٠٣
تلفح وجوههم النار وهم فيها كلحون ١٠٤
الم تكن ايتي تتلى عليكم فكنتم بها
تكذبون ١٠٥
قالوا ربنا غلبت علينا شقوتنا وكنا قوما
ضالين ١٠٦
ربنا اخرجنا منها فان عدنا فانا ظلمون ١٠٧
قال اخسئوا فيها ولا تكلمون ١٠٨
انه كان فريق من عبادي يقولون ربنا امنا
فاغفر لنا وارحمنا وانت خير الرحمين ١٠٩

110. But ye chose them for a laughing-stock until they caused you to forget remembrance of Me, while ye laughed at them.

111. Lo! I have rewarded them this day forasmuch as they were steadfast; and they verily are the triumphant.

112. He will say: How long tarried ye in the earth, counting by years?

113. They will say: We tarried but a day or part of a day. Ask of those who keep count!

114. He will say: Ye tarried but a little if ye only knew.

115. Deemed ye then that We had created you for naught, and that ye would not be returned unto Us?

116. Now Allah be exalted, the True King! There is no God save Him, the Lord of the Throne of Grace.

117. He who crieth unto any other god along with Allah hath no proof thereof. His reckoning is only with his Lord. Lo! disbelievers will not be successful.

118. And (O Muhammad) say: My Lord! Forgive and have mercy, for Thou art best of all who show mercy.

فاتخذتموهم سخريا حتى أنسوكم ذكري وكنتم
منهم تضحكون ﴿١١٠﴾
إني جزيتهم اليوم بما صبروا أنهم هم
الفائزون ﴿١١١﴾
قال كم لبثتم في الأرض عدد سنين ﴿١١٢﴾
قالوا لبثنا يوما أو بعض يوم فسئل العادين ﴿١١٣﴾
قل إن لبثتم إلا قليلا لو أنكم كنتم تعلمون ﴿١١٤﴾
أفحسبتم أنما خلقناكم عبثا وأنكم إلينا لا
ترجعون ﴿١١٥﴾
فتعلى الله الملك الحق لا إله إلا هو رب
العرش الكريم ﴿١١٦﴾
ومن يدع مع الله إلها آخر لا برهان له به
فإنما حسابه عند ربه إنه لا يفلح الكفرون ﴿١١٧﴾
وقل رب اغفر وارحم وأنت خير الرحمين ﴿١١٨﴾

An-Nūr, "Light," takes its name from vv. 35-40, descriptive of the Light of God as it should shine in the homes of believers, the greater part of the Sūrah being legislation for the purifying of home life. All its verses were revealed at Al-Madînah. Tradition says that vv. 11—20 relate to the slanderers of Ayeshah in connecti on with an incident which occurred in the fifth year of the Hijrah when the Prophet was returning from the campaign against the Banî'l-Muṣṭaliq, Ayeshah, having been left behind on a march, and found and brought back by a young soldier who let her mount his camel and himself led the camel. A weaker tradition places the revelation of vv. 1-10 as late as the ninth year of the Hijrah.

The period of revelation is the fifth and sixth years of the Hijrah.

LIGHT

Revealed at Al-Madinah

In the name of Allah, the Beneficent, the Merciful.

1. (Here is) a Sūrah which We have revealed and enjoined, and wherein We have revealed plain tokens, that haply we may take heed.

2. The adulterer and the adulteress, scourge ye each one of them (with) a hundred stripes. And let not pity for the twain withhold you from obedience to Allah, if ye believe in Allah and the Last Day. And let a party of believers witness their punishment.

3. The adulterer shall not marry save an adulteress or an idolatress, and the adulteress none shall marry save an adulterer or an idolater. All that is forbidddn unto believers.

4. And those who accuse honourable women but bring not four witnesses, scourge them (with) eighty stripes and never (afterward) accept their testimony—They indeed are evil-doers—

5. Save those who afterward repent and make amends. (For such) lo! Allah is Forgiving, Merciful.

6. As for those who accuse their wives but have no witnesses except themselves; let the testimony of one of them be four testimonies, (swearing) by Allah that he is of those who speak the truth;

ایاتہا ٦٤ (٢٤) سُورَةُ النُّورِ مَدَنِيَّةٌ رکوعاتہا ٩

بِسْمِ اللّٰهِ الرَّحْمٰنِ الرَّحِيْمِ

سُوْرَةٌ اَنْزَلْنٰهَا وَفَرَضْنٰهَا وَاَنْزَلْنَا فِيْهَآ اٰيٰتٍ
بَيِّنٰتٍ لَّعَلَّكُمْ تَذَكَّرُوْنَ ①
اَلزَّانِيَةُ وَالزَّانِيْ فَاجْلِدُوْا كُلَّ وَاحِدٍ مِّنْهُمَا مِائَةَ
جَلْدَةٍ وَّلَا تَاْخُذْكُمْ بِهِمَا رَاْفَةٌ فِيْ دِيْنِ اللّٰهِ اِنْ
كُنْتُمْ تُؤْمِنُوْنَ بِاللّٰهِ وَالْيَوْمِ الْاٰخِرِ وَلْيَشْهَدْ
عَذَابَهُمَا طَآئِفَةٌ مِّنَ الْمُؤْمِنِيْنَ ②
اَلزَّانِيْ لَا يَنْكِحُ اِلَّا زَانِيَةً اَوْ مُشْرِكَةً وَّالزَّانِيَةُ
لَا يَنْكِحُهَآ اِلَّا زَانٍ اَوْ مُشْرِكٌ وَحُرِّمَ ذٰلِكَ عَلَى
الْمُؤْمِنِيْنَ ③
وَالَّذِيْنَ يَرْمُوْنَ الْمُحْصَنٰتِ ثُمَّ لَمْ يَاْتُوْا بِاَرْبَعَةِ
شُهَدَآءَ فَاجْلِدُوْهُمْ ثَمٰنِيْنَ جَلْدَةً وَّلَا
تَقْبَلُوْا لَهُمْ شَهَادَةً اَبَدًا وَاُولٰٓئِكَ هُمُ
الْفٰسِقُوْنَ ④
اِلَّا الَّذِيْنَ تَابُوْا مِنْۢ بَعْدِ ذٰلِكَ وَاَصْلَحُوْا فَاِنَّ
اللّٰهَ غَفُوْرٌ رَّحِيْمٌ ⑤
وَالَّذِيْنَ يَرْمُوْنَ اَزْوَاجَهُمْ وَلَمْ يَكُنْ
لَّهُمْ شُهَدَآءُ اِلَّآ اَنْفُسُهُمْ فَشَهَادَةُ
اَحَدِهِمْ اَرْبَعُ شَهٰدٰتٍ بِاللّٰهِ اِنَّهٗ لَمِنَ
الصّٰدِقِيْنَ ⑥

7. And yet a fifth, invoking the curse of Allah on him if he is of those who lie.

8. And it shall avert the punishment from her if she bear witness before Allah four times that the thing he saith is indeed false,

9. And a fifth (time) that the wrath of Allah be upon her if he speaketh truth.

10. And had it not been for the grace of Allah and His mercy unto you, and that Allah is Clement, Wise, (ye had been undone).

11. Lo! they who spread the slander are a gang among you. Deem it not a bad thing for you; nay, it is good for you. Unto every man of them (will be paid) that which he hath earned of the sin; and as for him among them who had the greater share therein, his will be an awful doom.

12. Why did not the believers, men and women, when ye heard it, think good of their own folk, and say: It is a manifest untruth?

13. Why did they not produce four witnesses? Since they produce not witnesses, they verily are liars in the sight of Allah.

14. Had it not been for the grace of Allah and His mercy unto you in the world and the Hereafter, an awful doom had overtaken you for that whereof ye murmured.

15. When ye welcomed it with your tongues, and uttered with your mouths that whereof ye had no knowledge, ye counted it a trifle. In the sight of Allah it is very great.

وَالْخَامِسَةَ أَنَّ لَعْنَتَ اللّٰهِ عَلَيْهِ إِنْ كَانَ مِنَ الْكَاذِبِيْنَ ۞

وَيَدْرَؤُا عَنْهَا الْعَذَابَ أَنْ تَشْهَدَ أَرْبَعَ شَهٰدٰتٍ بِاللّٰهِ اِنَّهُ لَمِنَ الْكَاذِبِيْنَ ۞

وَالْخَامِسَةَ أَنَّ غَضَبَ اللّٰهِ عَلَيْهَا إِنْ كَانَ مِنَ الصّٰدِقِيْنَ ۞

وَلَوْلَا فَضْلُ اللّٰهِ عَلَيْكُمْ وَرَحْمَتُهُ وَأَنَّ اللّٰهَ تَوَّابٌ حَكِيْمٌ ۞

اِنَّ الَّذِيْنَ جَآءُوْ بِالْاِفْكِ عُصْبَةٌ مِّنْكُمْ لَا تَحْسَبُوْهُ شَرًّا لَّكُمْ بَلْ هُوَ خَيْرٌ لَّكُمْ لِكُلِّ امْرِئٍ مِّنْهُمْ مَّا اكْتَسَبَ مِنَ الْاِثْمِ وَالَّذِيْ تَوَلّٰى كِبْرَهُ مِنْهُمْ لَهُ عَذَابٌ عَظِيْمٌ ۞

لَوْلَا اِذْ سَمِعْتُمُوهُ ظَنَّ الْمُؤْمِنُوْنَ وَالْمُؤْمِنٰتُ بِأَنْفُسِهِمْ خَيْرًا ۙ وَّقَالُوْا هٰذَا اِفْكٌ مُّبِيْنٌ ۞

لَوْلَا جَآءُوْ عَلَيْهِ بِأَرْبَعَةِ شُهَدَآءَ ۚ فَاِذْ لَمْ يَأْتُوْا بِالشُّهَدَآءِ فَأُولٰئِكَ عِنْدَ اللّٰهِ هُمُ الْكَاذِبُوْنَ ۞

وَلَوْلَا فَضْلُ اللّٰهِ عَلَيْكُمْ وَرَحْمَتُهُ فِي الدُّنْيَا وَالْاٰخِرَةِ لَمَسَّكُمْ فِيْ مَا اَفَضْتُمْ فِيْهِ عَذَابٌ عَظِيْمٌ ۞

اِذْ تَلَقَّوْنَهُ بِأَلْسِنَتِكُمْ وَتَقُوْلُوْنَ بِأَفْوَاهِكُمْ مَّا لَيْسَ لَكُمْ بِهِ عِلْمٌ وَّتَحْسَبُوْنَهُ هَيِّنًا ۖ وَّهُوَ عِنْدَ اللّٰهِ عَظِيْمٌ ۞

16. Wherefor, when ye heard it, said ye not: It is not for us to speak of this. Glory be to Thee (O Allah)! This is awful calumny.

وَلَوْلَآ إِذْ سَمِعْتُمُوهُ قُلْتُم مَّا يَكُونُ لَنَآ أَن نَّتَكَلَّمَ
بِهَٰذَا سُبْحَٰنَكَ هَٰذَا بُهْتَٰنٌ عَظِيمٌ ﴿١٦﴾

17. Allah admonisheth you that ye repeat not the like thereof ever, if ye are (in truth) believers.

يَعِظُكُمُ ٱللَّهُ أَن تَعُودُوا۟ لِمِثْلِهِۦٓ أَبَدًا إِن كُنتُم
مُّؤْمِنِينَ ﴿١٧﴾

18. And He expoundeth unto you His revelations. Allah is Knower, Wise.

وَيُبَيِّنُ ٱللَّهُ لَكُمُ ٱلْءَايَٰتِ وَٱللَّهُ عَلِيمٌ حَكِيمٌ ﴿١٨﴾

19. Lo! those who love that slander should be spread concerning those who believe, theirs will be a painful punishment in the world and the Hereafter. Allah knoweth. Ye know not.

إِنَّ ٱلَّذِينَ يُحِبُّونَ أَن تَشِيعَ ٱلْفَٰحِشَةُ فِى ٱلَّذِينَ
ءَامَنُوا۟ لَهُمْ عَذَابٌ أَلِيمٌ فِى ٱلدُّنْيَا وَٱلْءَاخِرَةِ وَٱللَّهُ
يَعْلَمُ وَأَنتُمْ لَا تَعْلَمُونَ ﴿١٩﴾

20. Had it not been for the grace of Allah and His mercy unto you, and that Allah is Clement, Merciful, (ye had been undone).

وَلَوْلَا فَضْلُ ٱللَّهِ عَلَيْكُمْ وَرَحْمَتُهُۥ وَأَنَّ ٱللَّهَ رَءُوفٌ
رَّحِيمٌ ﴿٢٠﴾ ع

21. O ye who believe! Follow not the footsteps of the devil. Unto whomsoever followeth the footsteps of the devil, lo! he commandeth filthiness and wrong. Had it not been for the grace of Allah and His mercy unto you, not one of you would ever have grown pure. But Allah causeth whom He will to grow. And Allah is Hearer, Knower.

يَٰٓأَيُّهَا ٱلَّذِينَ ءَامَنُوا۟ لَا تَتَّبِعُوا۟ خُطُوَٰتِ ٱلشَّيْطَٰنِ وَمَن
يَتَّبِعْ خُطُوَٰتِ ٱلشَّيْطَٰنِ فَإِنَّهُۥ يَأْمُرُ بِٱلْفَحْشَآءِ وَ
ٱلْمُنكَرِ وَلَوْلَا فَضْلُ ٱللَّهِ عَلَيْكُمْ وَرَحْمَتُهُۥ مَا زَكَىٰ
مِنكُم مِّنْ أَحَدٍ أَبَدًا وَلَٰكِنَّ ٱللَّهَ يُزَكِّى مَن يَشَآءُ وَ
ٱللَّهُ سَمِيعٌ عَلِيمٌ ﴿٢١﴾

22. And let not those who possess dignity and ease among you swear not to give to the near of kin and to the needy, and to fugitives for the cause of Allah.[1] Let them forgive and show indulgence. Yearn ye not that Allah may forgive you? Allah is Forgiving, Merciful.

وَلَا يَأْتَلِ أُو۟لُوا۟ ٱلْفَضْلِ مِنكُمْ وَٱلسَّعَةِ أَن يُؤْتُوٓا۟
أُو۟لِى ٱلْقُرْبَىٰ وَٱلْمَسَٰكِينَ وَٱلْمُهَٰجِرِينَ فِى سَبِيلِ ٱللَّهِ
وَلْيَعْفُوا۟ وَلْيَصْفَحُوٓا۟ أَلَا تُحِبُّونَ أَن يَغْفِرَ ٱللَّهُ لَكُمْ
وَٱللَّهُ غَفُورٌ رَّحِيمٌ ﴿٢٢﴾

23. Lo! as for those who traduce virtuous, believing women (who are) careless, cursed are they in the world and the Hereafter. Theirs will be an awful doom.

إِنَّ ٱلَّذِينَ يَرْمُونَ ٱلْمُحْصَنَٰتِ ٱلْغَٰفِلَٰتِ ٱلْمُؤْمِنَٰتِ
لُعِنُوا۟ فِى ٱلدُّنْيَا وَٱلْءَاخِرَةِ وَلَهُمْ عَذَابٌ
عَظِيمٌ ﴿٢٣﴾

1. Tradition says that Abû Bakr, when he heard that a kinsman of his own whom he had supported had been among the slanderers of his daughter Ayeshah, swore no longer to support him, and that this verse was revealed on that occasion.

24. On the day when their tongues and their hands and their feet testify against them as to what they used to do,

25. On that day Allah will pay them their just due, and they will know that Allah, He is the Manifest Truth.

26. Vile women are for vile men, and vile men for vile women. Good women are for good men, and good men for good women; such are innocent of that which people say: For them is pardon and a bountiful provision.

27. O ye who believe! Enter not houses other than your own without first announcing your presence and invoking peace upon the folk thereof. That is better for you, that ye may be heedful.

28. And if ye find no one therein, still enter not until permission hath been given. And if it be said unto you: Go away again, then go away, for it is purer for you. Allah knoweth what ye do.

29. (It is) no sin for you to enter uninhabited houses wherein is comfort for you. Allah knoweth what ye proclaim and what ye hide.

30. Tell the believing men to lower their gaze and be modest. That is purer for them. Lo! Allah is Aware of what they do.

يَوْمَ تَشْهَدُ عَلَيْهِمْ أَلْسِنَتُهُمْ وَأَيْدِيهِمْ وَ
أَرْجُلُهُمْ بِمَا كَانُوا يَعْمَلُونَ ﴿٢٤﴾
يَوْمَئِذٍ يُوَفِّيهِمُ اللَّهُ دِينَهُمُ الْحَقَّ وَيَعْلَمُونَ
أَنَّ اللَّهَ هُوَ الْحَقُّ الْمُبِينُ ﴿٢٥﴾
الْخَبِيثَاتُ لِلْخَبِيثِينَ وَالْخَبِيثُونَ لِلْخَبِيثَاتِ ۖ وَ
الطَّيِّبَاتُ لِلطَّيِّبِينَ وَالطَّيِّبُونَ لِلطَّيِّبَاتِ ۚ أُولَٰئِكَ
مُبَرَّءُونَ مِمَّا يَقُولُونَ ۖ لَهُمْ مَغْفِرَةٌ وَرِزْقٌ
كَرِيمٌ ﴿٢٦﴾
يَا أَيُّهَا الَّذِينَ آمَنُوا لَا تَدْخُلُوا بُيُوتًا
غَيْرَ بُيُوتِكُمْ حَتَّىٰ تَسْتَأْنِسُوا وَتُسَلِّمُوا
عَلَىٰ أَهْلِهَا ۚ ذَٰلِكُمْ خَيْرٌ لَكُمْ لَعَلَّكُمْ
تَذَكَّرُونَ ﴿٢٧﴾
فَإِنْ لَمْ تَجِدُوا فِيهَا أَحَدًا فَلَا تَدْخُلُوهَا
حَتَّىٰ يُؤْذَنَ لَكُمْ ۖ وَإِنْ قِيلَ لَكُمُ ارْجِعُوا
فَارْجِعُوا ۖ هُوَ أَزْكَىٰ لَكُمْ ۚ وَاللَّهُ بِمَا تَعْمَلُونَ
عَلِيمٌ ﴿٢٨﴾
لَيْسَ عَلَيْكُمْ جُنَاحٌ أَنْ تَدْخُلُوا بُيُوتًا غَيْرَ
مَسْكُونَةٍ فِيهَا مَتَاعٌ لَكُمْ ۚ وَاللَّهُ يَعْلَمُ مَا
تُبْدُونَ وَمَا تَكْتُمُونَ ﴿٢٩﴾
قُلْ لِلْمُؤْمِنِينَ يَغُضُّوا مِنْ أَبْصَارِهِمْ وَيَحْفَظُوا
فُرُوجَهُمْ ۚ ذَٰلِكَ أَزْكَىٰ لَهُمْ ۗ إِنَّ اللَّهَ خَبِيرٌ بِمَا
يَصْنَعُونَ ﴿٣٠﴾

31. And tell the believing women to lower their gaze and be modest, and to display of their adornment only that which is apparent, and to draw their veils over their bosoms, and not to reveal their adornment save to their own husbands or fathers or husbands' fathers, or their sons or their husbands' sons, or their brothers or their brothers' sons or sisters' sons, or their women, or their slaves, or male attendants who lack vigour, or children who know naught of women's nakedness. And let them not stamp their feet so as to reveal what they hide of their adornment. And turn unto Allah together, O believers, in order that ye may succeed.

32. And marry such of you as are solitary and the pious of your slaves and maid-servants. If they be poor, Allah will enrich them of His bounty. Allah is of ample means, Aware.

33. And let those who cannot find a match keep chaste till Allah give them independence by His grace. And such of your slaves as seek a writing (of emancipation), write it for them if ye are aware of aught of good in them, and bestow upon them of the wealth of Allah which He hath bestowed upon you. Force not your slave-girls to whoredom that ye may seek enjoyment of the life of the world, if they would preserve their chastity. And if one force them, then (unto them), after their compulsion, Lo! Allah will be Forgiving, Merciful.

34. And verily We have sent down for you revelations that make plain, and the example of those who passed away before you. An admonition unto those who ward off (evil).

وقل للمؤمنت يغضضن من ابصارهن ويحفظن
فروجهن ولا يبدين زينتهن الا ما ظهر منها
وليضربن بخمرهن على جيوبهن ولا يبدين
زينتهن الا لبعولتهن او ابآئهن او ابآء بعولتهن
او ابنآئهن او ابنآء بعولتهن او اخوانهن او بني
اخوانهن او بني اخوتهن او نسآئهن او ما ملكت
ايمانهن او التبعين غير اولي الاربة من الرجال
او الطفل الذين لم يظهروا على عورت النسآء ولا
يضربن بارجلهن ليعلم ما يخفين من زينتهن و
توبوا الى الله جميعا ايه المؤمنون لعلكم تفلحون ٣١
وانكحوا الايامى منكم والصلحين من عبادكم
وامآئكم ان يكونوا فقرآء يغنهم الله من فضله
والله واسع عليم ٣٢
وليستعفف الذين لا يجدون نكاحا حتى يغنيهم
الله من فضله والذين يبتغون الكتب مما ملكت
ايمانكم فكاتبوهم ان علمتم فيهم خيرا و
اتوهم من مال الله الذي اتكم ولا تكرهوا
فتيتكم على البغآء ان اردن تحصنا لتبتغوا عرض
الحيوة الدنيا ومن يكرههن فان الله من بعد
اكراههن غفور رحيم ٣٣
ولقد انزلنآ اليكم ايت مبينت ومثلا من الذين
خلوا من قبلكم وموعظة للمتقين ٣٤

35. Allah is the Light of the heavens and the earth. The similitude of His light is as a niche wherein is a lamp. The lamp is in a glass. The glass is as it were a shining star. (This lamp is) kindled from a blessed tree, an olive neither of the East nor of the West, whose oil would almost glow forth (of itself) though no fire touched it. Light upon light, Allah guideth unto His light whom He will. And Allah speaketh to mankind in allegories, for Allah is Knower of all things:

36. (This lamp is found) in houses which Allah hath allowed to be exalted and that His name shall be remembered therein. Therein do offer praise to Him at morn and evening—

37. Men whom neither merchandise nor sale beguileth from remembrance of Allah and constancy in prayer and paying to the poor their due; who fear a day when hearts and eyeballs will be overturned;

38. That Allah may reward them with the best of what they did, and increase reward for them of His bounty. Allah giveth blessings without stint to whom He will.

39. As for those who disbelieve, their deeds are as a mirage in a desert. The thirsty one supposeth it to be water till he cometh unto it and findeth it naught, and findeth, in the place thereof, Allah, Who payeth him his due; and Allah is swift at reckoning;

40. Or as darkness on a vast, abysmal sea. There covereth him a wave, above which is a wave, above which is a cloud. Layer upon layer of darkness. When he holdeth out his hand he scarce can see it. And he for whom Allah hath not appointed light, for him there is no light.

اَللّٰهُ نُوْرُ السَّمٰوٰتِ وَالْاَرْضِ ؕ مَثَلُ نُوْرِهٖ كَمِشْكٰوةٍ فِيْهَا
مِصْبَاحٌ ؕ اَلْمِصْبَاحُ فِيْ زُجَاجَةٍ ؕ اَلزُّجَاجَةُ كَاَنَّهَا كَوْكَبٌ
دُرِّيٌّ يُّوْقَدُ مِنْ شَجَرَةٍ مُّبٰرَكَةٍ زَيْتُوْنَةٍ لَّا شَرْقِيَّةٍ
وَّلَا غَرْبِيَّةٍ ۙ يَّكَادُ زَيْتُهَا يُضِيْٓءُ وَلَوْ لَمْ تَمْسَسْهُ نَارٌ ؕ
نُوْرٌ عَلٰى نُوْرٍ ؕ يَهْدِي اللّٰهُ لِنُوْرِهٖ مَنْ يَّشَآءُ ؕ وَيَضْرِبُ
اللّٰهُ الْاَمْثَالَ لِلنَّاسِ ؕ وَاللّٰهُ بِكُلِّ شَيْءٍ
عَلِيْمٌ ۙ ﴿٣٥﴾
فِيْ بُيُوْتٍ اَذِنَ اللّٰهُ اَنْ تُرْفَعَ وَيُذْكَرَ فِيْهَا اسْمُهٗ ۙ
يُسَبِّحُ لَهٗ فِيْهَا بِالْغُدُوِّ وَالْاٰصَالِ ۙ ﴿٣٦﴾
رِجَالٌ ۙ لَّا تُلْهِيْهِمْ تِجَارَةٌ وَّلَا بَيْعٌ عَنْ ذِكْرِ اللّٰهِ
وَاِقَامِ الصَّلٰوةِ وَاِيْتَآءِ الزَّكٰوةِ ۙ يَخَافُوْنَ يَوْمًا
تَتَقَلَّبُ فِيْهِ الْقُلُوْبُ وَالْاَبْصَارُ ۙ ﴿٣٧﴾
لِيَجْزِيَهُمُ اللّٰهُ اَحْسَنَ مَا عَمِلُوْا وَيَزِيْدَهُمْ مِّنْ
فَضْلِهٖ ؕ وَاللّٰهُ يَرْزُقُ مَنْ يَّشَآءُ بِغَيْرِ حِسَابٍ ﴿٣٨﴾
وَالَّذِيْنَ كَفَرُوْٓا اَعْمَالُهُمْ كَسَرَابٍ بِقِيْعَةٍ يَّحْسَبُهُ
الظَّمْاٰنُ مَآءً ؕ حَتّٰٓى اِذَا جَآءَهٗ لَمْ يَجِدْهُ شَيْـًٔا وَّ
وَجَدَ اللّٰهَ عِنْدَهٗ فَوَفّٰىهُ حِسَابَهٗ ؕ وَاللّٰهُ سَرِيْعُ
الْحِسَابِ ۙ ﴿٣٩﴾
اَوْ كَظُلُمٰتٍ فِيْ بَحْرٍ لُّجِّيٍّ يَّغْشٰىهُ مَوْجٌ مِّنْ فَوْقِهٖ
مَوْجٌ مِّنْ فَوْقِهٖ سَحَابٌ ؕ ظُلُمٰتٌ ۢ بَعْضُهَا فَوْقَ بَعْضٍ ؕ
اِذَآ اَخْرَجَ يَدَهٗ لَمْ يَكَدْ يَرٰىهَا ؕ وَمَنْ لَّمْ يَجْعَلِ اللّٰهُ
لَهٗ نُوْرًا فَمَا لَهٗ مِنْ نُّوْرٍ ﴿٤٠﴾ ع

41. Hast thou not seen that Allah, He it is Whom all who are in the heavens and the earth praise, and the birds in their flight? Of each He knoweth verily the worship and the praise; and Allah is Aware of what they do.

42. And unto Allah belongeth the sovereignty of the heavens and the earth, and unto Allah is the journeying.

43. Hast thou not seen how Allah wafteth the clouds, then gathereth them, then maketh them layers, and thou seest the rain come forth from between them; He sendeth down from the heaven mountains wherein is hail, and smiteth therewith whom He will, and averteth it from whom He will. The flashing of His lightning all but snatcheth away the sight.

44. Allah causeth the revolution of the day and the night. Lo! herein is indeed a lesson for those who see.

45. Allah hath created every animal of water. Of them is (a kind) that goeth upon its belly and (a kind) that goeth upon two legs and (a kind) that goeth upon four. Allah createth what He will. Lo! Allah is Able to do all things.

46. Verily We have sent down revelations and explained them. Allah guideth whom He will unto a straight path.

47. And they say: We believe in Allah and the messenger, and we obey; then after that a faction of them turn away. Such are not believers.

48. And when they appeal unto Allah and His messenger to judge between them, lo! a faction of them are averse;

49. But if right had been with them they would have come unto him willingly.

الم تر ان الله يسبح له من في السموت والارض
والطير صفت كل قد علم صلاته وتسبيحه
والله عليم بما يفعلون ﴿٤١﴾
ولله ملك السموت والارض والى الله المصير ﴿٤٢﴾
الم تر ان الله يزجي سحابا ثم يؤلف بينه ثم
يجعله ركاما فترى الودق يخرج من خلله وينزل
من السماء من جبال فيها من برد فيصيب به من
يشاء ويصرفه عن من يشاء يكاد سنا برقه يذهب
بالابصار ﴿٤٣﴾
يقلب الله اليل والنهار ان في ذلك لعبرة
لاولي الابصار ﴿٤٤﴾
والله خلق كل دابة من ماء فمنهم من يمشي
على بطنه ومنهم من يمشي على رجلين ومنهم
من يمشي على اربع يخلق الله ما يشاء ان
الله على كل شيء قدير ﴿٤٥﴾
لقد انزلنا ايت مبينت والله يهدي من يشاء
الى صراط مستقيم ﴿٤٦﴾
ويقولون امنا بالله وبالرسول واطعنا ثم يتولى
فريق منهم من بعد ذلك وما اولئك بالمؤمنين ﴿٤٧﴾
واذا دعوا الى الله ورسوله ليحكم بينهم اذا فريق
منهم معرضون ﴿٤٨﴾
وان يكن لهم الحق ياتوا اليه مذعنين ﴿٤٩﴾

50. Is there in their hearts a disease, or have they doubts, or fear they lest Allah and His messenger should wrong them in judgement? Nay, but such are evil-doers.

افي قلوبهم مرض ام ارتابوا ام يخافون ان يحيف
الله عليهم ورسوله بل اولئك هم الظلمون ﴿٥٠﴾ ع ٦ ١٢

51. The saying of (all true) believers when they appeal unto Allah and His messenger to judge between them is only that they say: We hear and we obey. And such are the successful.

انما كان قول المؤمنين اذا دعوا الى الله ورسوله
ليحكم بينهم ان يقولوا سمعنا واطعنا واولئك هم
المفلحون ﴿٥١﴾

52. He who obeyeth Allah and His messenger, and feareth Allah, and keepeth duty (unto Him); such indeed are the victorious.

ومن يطع الله ورسوله ويخش الله ويتقه فاولئك
هم الفائزون ﴿٥٢﴾

53. They swear by Allah solemnly that, if thou order them, they will go forth. Say: Swear not; known obedience (is better). Lo! Allah is Informed of what ye do.

واقسموا بالله جهد ايمانهم لئن امرتهم ليخرجن
قل لا تقسموا طاعة معروفة ان الله خبير بما
تعملون ﴿٥٣﴾

54. Say: Obey Allah and obey the messenger. But if ye turn away, then (it is) for him (to do) only that wherewith he hath been charged, and for you (to do) only that wherewith ye have been charged. If ye obey him, ye will go aright. But the messenger hath no other charge than to convey (the message), plainly.

قل اطيعوا الله واطيعوا الرسول فان تولوا فانما
عليه ما حمل وعليكم ما حملتم وان تطيعوه
تهتدوا وما على الرسول الا البلغ المبين ﴿٥٤﴾

55. Allah hath promised such of you as believe and do good works that He will surely make them to succeed (the present rulers) in the earth even as He caused those who were before them to succeed (others); and that He will surely establish for them their religion which He hath approved for them, and will give them in exchange safety after their fear. They serve Me. They ascribe nothing as partner unto Me. Those who disbelieve henceforth, they are the miscreants.

وعد الله الذين امنوا منكم وعملوا الصلحت ليستخلفنهم
في الارض كما استخلف الذين من قبلهم وليمكنن
لهم دينهم الذي ارتضى لهم وليبدلنهم من بعد
خوفهم امنا يعبدونني لا يشركون بي شيئا ومن
كفر بعد ذلك فاولئك هم الفسقون ﴿٥٥﴾

56. Establish worship and pay the poor-due and obey the messenger, that haply ye may find mercy.

واقيموا الصلوة واتوا الزكوة واطيعوا الرسول
لعلكم ترحمون ﴿٥٦﴾

57. Think not that the disbelievers can escape in the land. Fire will be their home—a hapless journey's end!

لا تحسبن الذين كفروا معجزين في الارض
ع ومأوىهم النار ولبئس المصير ﴿٥٧﴾

58. O ye who believe ! Let your slaves, and those of you who have not come to puberty, ask leave of you at three times (before they come into your presence): Before the prayer of dawn, and when ye lay aside your raiment for the heat of noon, and after the prayer of night,[1] Three times of privacy for you. It is no sin for them or for you at other times, when some of you go round attendant upon others (if they come into your presence without leave). Thus Allah maketh clear the revelations for you. Allah is Knower, Wise.

59. And when the children among you come to puberty then let them ask leave even as those before them used to ask it. Thus Allah maketh clear His revelations for you. Allah is knower Wise.

60. As for women past child-bearing, who have no hope of marriage, it is no sin for them if they discard their (outer) clothing in such a way as not to show adornment. But to refrain is better for them. Allah is Hearer, Knower.

61. No blame is there upon the blind nor any blame upon the lame nor any blame upon the sick nor on yourselves if ye eat from your houses, or the houses of your fathers, or the houses of your mothers, or the houses of your brothers or the houses of your sisters, or the houses of your fathers's brothers, or the houses of your father's sisters, or the houses of your mother's brothers, or the houses of your mother's sisters or (form that) whereof ye hold the keys, or (from the house) of a friend. No sin shall it be for you whether ye eat together or apart. But when ye enter houses, salute one another with a greeting from Allah, blessed and sweet. Thus Allah maketh clear His revelations for you, that haply ye may understand.

يٰٓاَيُّهَا الَّذِيْنَ اٰمَنُوْا لِيَسْتَاْذِنْكُمُ الَّذِيْنَ مَلَكَتْ
اَيْمَانُكُمْ وَالَّذِيْنَ لَمْ يَبْلُغُوا الْحُلُمَ مِنْكُمْ ثَلٰثَ مَرّٰتٍ
مِنْ قَبْلِ صَلٰوةِ الْفَجْرِ وَحِيْنَ تَضَعُوْنَ ثِيَابَكُمْ مِّنَ
الظَّهِيْرَةِ وَمِنْۢ بَعْدِ صَلٰوةِ الْعِشَآءِ ثَلٰثُ عَوْرٰتٍ
لَّكُمْ لَيْسَ عَلَيْكُمْ وَلَا عَلَيْهِمْ جُنَاحٌۢ بَعْدَهُنَّ
طَوّٰفُوْنَ عَلَيْكُمْ بَعْضُكُمْ عَلٰى بَعْضٍ كَذٰلِكَ يُبَيِّنُ
اللّٰهُ لَكُمُ الْاٰيٰتِ وَاللّٰهُ عَلِيْمٌ حَكِيْمٌ ﴿٥٨﴾
وَاِذَا بَلَغَ الْاَطْفَالُ مِنْكُمُ الْحُلُمَ فَلْيَسْتَاْذِنُوْا كَمَا
اسْتَاْذَنَ الَّذِيْنَ مِنْ قَبْلِهِمْ كَذٰلِكَ يُبَيِّنُ اللّٰهُ لَكُمْ
اٰيٰتِهٖ وَاللّٰهُ عَلِيْمٌ حَكِيْمٌ ﴿٥٩﴾
وَالْقَوَاعِدُ مِنَ النِّسَآءِ الّٰتِيْ لَا يَرْجُوْنَ نِكَاحًا فَلَيْسَ
عَلَيْهِنَّ جُنَاحٌ اَنْ يَّضَعْنَ ثِيَابَهُنَّ غَيْرَ مُتَبَرِّجٰتٍۢ بِزِيْنَةٍ
وَاَنْ يَّسْتَعْفِفْنَ خَيْرٌ لَّهُنَّ وَاللّٰهُ سَمِيْعٌ عَلِيْمٌ ﴿٦٠﴾
لَيْسَ عَلَى الْاَعْمٰى حَرَجٌ وَّلَا عَلَى الْاَعْرَجِ حَرَجٌ وَّلَا
عَلَى الْمَرِيْضِ حَرَجٌ وَّلَا عَلٰٓى اَنْفُسِكُمْ اَنْ تَاْكُلُوْا مِنْۢ بُيُوْتِكُمْ
اَوْ بُيُوْتِ اٰبَآئِكُمْ اَوْ بُيُوْتِ اُمَّهٰتِكُمْ اَوْ بُيُوْتِ اِخْوَانِكُمْ
اَوْ بُيُوْتِ اَخَوٰتِكُمْ اَوْ بُيُوْتِ اَعْمَامِكُمْ اَوْ بُيُوْتِ عَمّٰتِكُمْ
اَوْ بُيُوْتِ اَخْوَالِكُمْ اَوْ بُيُوْتِ خٰلٰتِكُمْ اَوْ مَا مَلَكْتُمْ مَّفَاتِحَهٗٓ
اَوْ صَدِيْقِكُمْ لَيْسَ عَلَيْكُمْ جُنَاحٌ اَنْ تَاْكُلُوْا جَمِيْعًا اَوْ
اَشْتَاتًا فَاِذَا دَخَلْتُمْ بُيُوْتًا فَسَلِّمُوْا عَلٰٓى اَنْفُسِكُمْ
تَحِيَّةً مِّنْ عِنْدِ اللّٰهِ مُبٰرَكَةً طَيِّبَةً كَذٰلِكَ يُبَيِّنُ
اللّٰهُ لَكُمُ الْاٰيٰتِ لَعَلَّكُمْ تَعْقِلُوْنَ ﴿٦١﴾

1. the prayer to be offered when the night has fully come.

62. They only are the true believers who believe in Allah and His messenger and, when they are with him on some common errand, go not away until they have asked leave of him. Lo! those who ask leave of thee, those are they who believe in Allah and His messenger. So, if they ask thy leave for some affair of theirs, give leave to whom thou wilt of them, and ask for them forgiveness of Allah. Lo! Allah is Forgiving, Merciful.

63. Make not the calling of the messenger among you as your calling one of another. Allah knoweth those of you who steal away, hiding themselves. And let those who conspire to evade orders beware lest grief or painful punishment befall them.

64. Lo! verily unto Allah belongeth whatsoever is in the heavens and the earth. He knoweth your condition. And (He knoweth) the Day when they are returned unto Him so that He may inform them of what they did. Allah is Knower of all things.

إِنَّمَا الْمُؤْمِنُونَ الَّذِينَ آمَنُوا بِاللَّهِ وَرَسُولِهِ وَإِذَا كَانُوا
مَعَهُ عَلَىٰ أَمْرٍ جَامِعٍ لَمْ يَذْهَبُوا حَتَّىٰ يَسْتَأْذِنُوهُ إِنَّ
الَّذِينَ يَسْتَأْذِنُونَكَ أُولَٰئِكَ الَّذِينَ يُؤْمِنُونَ بِاللَّهِ
وَرَسُولِهِ فَإِذَا اسْتَأْذَنُوكَ لِبَعْضِ شَأْنِهِمْ فَأْذَنْ
لِمَنْ شِئْتَ مِنْهُمْ وَاسْتَغْفِرْ لَهُمُ اللَّهَ إِنَّ اللَّهَ
غَفُورٌ رَحِيمٌ ٦٢
لَا تَجْعَلُوا دُعَاءَ الرَّسُولِ بَيْنَكُمْ كَدُعَاءِ بَعْضِكُمْ
بَعْضًا قَدْ يَعْلَمُ اللَّهُ الَّذِينَ يَتَسَلَّلُونَ مِنْكُمْ لِوَاذًا ع
فَلْيَحْذَرِ الَّذِينَ يُخَالِفُونَ عَنْ أَمْرِهِ أَنْ تُصِيبَهُمْ
فِتْنَةٌ أَوْ يُصِيبَهُمْ عَذَابٌ أَلِيمٌ ٦٣
أَلَا إِنَّ لِلَّهِ مَا فِي السَّمَاوَاتِ وَالْأَرْضِ قَدْ يَعْلَمُ مَا
أَنْتُمْ عَلَيْهِ وَيَوْمَ يُرْجَعُونَ إِلَيْهِ فَيُنَبِّئُهُمْ بِمَا
عَمِلُوا وَاللَّهُ بِكُلِّ شَيْءٍ عَلِيمٌ ٦٤

Al-Furqān, "The Criterion," takes its name from a word occurring in v. 1. The subject is the folly of superstition and the craving for miraculous events in face of the wonders of God's creation.

It belongs to the middle group of Meccan Sūrahs, except vv. 68-70 which were revealed at Al-Madînah.

THE CRITERION (OF RIGHT AND WRONG)

Revealed at Mecca

In the name of Allah, the Beneficent, the Merciful.

1. Blessed is He Who hath revealed unto His slave the Criterion (of right and wrong), that he may be a warner to the peoples:

2. He unto Whom belongeth the sovereignty of the heavens and the earth, He hath chosen no son nor hath He any partner in the sovereignty. He hath created everything and hath meted out for it a measure.

3. Yet they choose beside Him other gods who create naught but are themselves created, and possess not hurt nor profit for themselves, and possess not death nor life, nor power to raise the dead.

4. Those who disbelieve say: This is naught but a lie that he hath invented, and other folk have helped him with it, so that they have produced a slander and a lie.

5. And they say: Fables of the men of old which he hath had written down so that they are dictated to him morn and evening.

6. Say (unto them, O Muhammad): He Who knoweth the secret of the heavens and the earth hath revealed it. Lo! He is ever Forgiving, Merciful.

7. And they say: What aileth this messenger (of Allah) that he eateth food and walketh in the markets? Why is not an angel sent down unto him, to be a warner with him?

اٰياتها ٧٧ (٢٥) سُوْرَةُ الْفُرْقَانِ مَكِّيَّةٌ ركوعاتها ٦

بِسْمِ اللّٰهِ الرَّحْمٰنِ الرَّحِيْمِ

تَبٰرَكَ الَّذِيْ نَزَّلَ الْفُرْقَانَ عَلٰى عَبْدِهٖ لِيَكُوْنَ
لِلْعٰلَمِيْنَ نَذِيْرًا ﴿١﴾
الَّذِيْ لَهٗ مُلْكُ السَّمٰوٰتِ وَالْاَرْضِ وَلَمْ يَتَّخِذْ
وَلَدًا وَّلَمْ يَكُنْ لَّهٗ شَرِيْكٌ فِي الْمُلْكِ وَخَلَقَ كُلَّ
شَيْءٍ فَقَدَّرَهٗ تَقْدِيْرًا ﴿٢﴾
وَاتَّخَذُوْا مِنْ دُوْنِهٖٓ اٰلِهَةً لَّا يَخْلُقُوْنَ شَيْئًا وَّهُمْ
يُخْلَقُوْنَ وَلَا يَمْلِكُوْنَ لِاَنْفُسِهِمْ ضَرًّا وَّلَا
نَفْعًا وَّلَا يَمْلِكُوْنَ مَوْتًا وَّلَا حَيٰوةً وَّلَا
نُشُوْرًا ﴿٣﴾
وَقَالَ الَّذِيْنَ كَفَرُوْٓا اِنْ هٰذَآ اِلَّآ اِفْكُ ِۨافْتَرٰىهُ وَ
اَعَانَهٗ عَلَيْهِ قَوْمٌ اٰخَرُوْنَ فَقَدْ جَآءُوْ ظُلْمًا وَّ
زُوْرًا ﴿٤﴾
وَقَالُوْٓا اَسَاطِيْرُ الْاَوَّلِيْنَ اكْتَتَبَهَا فَهِيَ تُمْلٰى عَلَيْهِ
بُكْرَةً وَّاَصِيْلًا ﴿٥﴾
قُلْ اَنْزَلَهُ الَّذِيْ يَعْلَمُ السِّرَّ فِي السَّمٰوٰتِ وَالْاَرْضِ
اِنَّهٗ كَانَ غَفُوْرًا رَّحِيْمًا ﴿٦﴾
وَقَالُوْا مَالِ هٰذَا الرَّسُوْلِ يَاْكُلُ الطَّعَامَ وَيَمْشِيْ
فِي الْاَسْوَاقِ لَوْلَآ اُنْزِلَ اِلَيْهِ مَلَكٌ فَيَكُوْنَ مَعَهٗ
نَذِيْرًا ﴿٧﴾

8. Or (why is not) a treasure thrown down unto him, or why hath he not a paradise from whence to eat? And the evil-doers say: Ye are but following a man bewitched.

أَوْ يُلْقَىٰ إِلَيْهِ كَنْزٌ أَوْ تَكُونُ لَهُ جَنَّةٌ يَأْكُلُ
مِنْهَا ۚ وَقَالَ الظَّالِمُونَ إِنْ تَتَّبِعُونَ إِلَّا رَجُلًا
مَسْحُورًا ﴿٨﴾

9. See how they coin similitudes for thee, so that they are all astray and cannot find a road!

انْظُرْ كَيْفَ ضَرَبُوا لَكَ الْأَمْثَالَ فَضَلُّوا فَلَا يَسْتَطِيعُونَ
سَبِيلًا ﴿٩﴾ ع

10. Blessed is He Who, if He will, will assign thee better than (all) that -- Gardens underneath which rivers flow -- and will assign thee mansions.

تَبَارَكَ الَّذِي إِنْ شَاءَ جَعَلَ لَكَ خَيْرًا مِنْ ذَٰلِكَ
جَنَّاتٍ تَجْرِي مِنْ تَحْتِهَا الْأَنْهَارُ وَيَجْعَلْ لَكَ
قُصُورًا ﴿١٠﴾

11. Nay, but they deny (the coming of) the Hour, and for those who deny (the coming of) the Hour We have prepared a flame.

بَلْ كَذَّبُوا بِالسَّاعَةِ ۖ وَأَعْتَدْنَا لِمَنْ كَذَّبَ
بِالسَّاعَةِ سَعِيرًا ﴿١١﴾

12. When it seeth them from afar, they hear the crackling and the roar thereof.

إِذَا رَأَتْهُمْ مِنْ مَكَانٍ بَعِيدٍ سَمِعُوا لَهَا تَغَيُّظًا
وَزَفِيرًا ﴿١٢﴾

13. And when they are flung into a narrow place thereof, chained together, they pray for destruction there.

وَإِذَا أُلْقُوا مِنْهَا مَكَانًا ضَيِّقًا مُقَرَّنِينَ دَعَوْا هُنَالِكَ
ثُبُورًا ﴿١٣﴾

14. Pray not that day for one destruction, but pray for many destructions!

لَا تَدْعُوا الْيَوْمَ ثُبُورًا وَاحِدًا وَادْعُوا ثُبُورًا كَثِيرًا ﴿١٤﴾

15. Say: Is that (doom) better or the Garden of Immortality which is promised unto those who ward off (evil)? It will be their reward and journey's end.

قُلْ أَذَٰلِكَ خَيْرٌ أَمْ جَنَّةُ الْخُلْدِ الَّتِي وُعِدَ الْمُتَّقُونَ ۚ
كَانَتْ لَهُمْ جَزَاءً وَمَصِيرًا ﴿١٥﴾

16. Therein abiding, they have all that they desire. It is for thy Lord a promise that must be fulfilled.

لَهُمْ فِيهَا مَا يَشَاءُونَ خَالِدِينَ ۚ كَانَ عَلَىٰ رَبِّكَ وَعْدًا
مَسْئُولًا ﴿١٦﴾

17. And on the day when He will assemble them and that which they worship instead of Allah and will say: Was it ye who misled these My slaves or did they (themselves) wander from the way?

وَيَوْمَ يَحْشُرُهُمْ وَمَا يَعْبُدُونَ مِنْ دُونِ اللَّهِ فَيَقُولُ
أَأَنْتُمْ أَضْلَلْتُمْ عِبَادِي هَٰؤُلَاءِ أَمْ هُمْ ضَلُّوا
السَّبِيلَ ﴿١٧﴾

18. They will say: Be Thou glorified! It was not for us to choose any protecting friends beside Thee; but Thou didst give them and their fathers ease till they forgot the warning and became lost folk.

قَالُوا سُبْحٰنَكَ مَا كَانَ يَنۢبَغِي لَنَآ أَنْ نَّتَّخِذَ مِنْ
دُونِكَ مِنْ أَوْلِيَآءَ وَلٰكِنْ مَّتَّعْتَهُمْ وَءَابَآءَهُمْ حَتّٰى
نَسُوا الذِّكْرَ وَكَانُوا قَوْمًۢا بُورًا ﴿١٨﴾

19. Thus they will give you the lie regarding what ye say, then ye can neither avert (the doom) nor obtain help. And whoso among you doth wrong, We shall make him taste great torment.

فَقَدْ كَذَّبُوكُمْ بِمَا تَقُولُونَ فَمَا تَسْتَطِيعُونَ صَرْفًا
وَلَا نَصْرًا وَمَنْ يَّظْلِمْ مِّنْكُمْ نُذِقْهُ عَذَابًا كَبِيرًا ﴿١٩﴾

20. We never sent before thee any messengers but lo! they ate food and walked in the markets. And We have appointed some of you a test for others: Will ye be steadfast? And thy Lord is ever Seer.

وَمَآ أَرْسَلْنَا قَبْلَكَ مِنَ الْمُرْسَلِينَ إِلَّآ إِنَّهُمْ
لَيَأْكُلُونَ الطَّعَامَ وَيَمْشُونَ فِي الْأَسْوَاقِ وَجَعَلْنَا
بَعْضَكُمْ لِبَعْضٍ فِتْنَةً أَتَصْبِرُونَ وَكَانَ رَبُّكَ
بَصِيرًا ﴿٢٠﴾

21. And those who look not for a meeting with Us say: Why are angels not sent down unto us and (why) do we not see our Lord? Assuredly they think too highly of themselves and are scornful with great pride.

وَقَالَ الَّذِينَ لَا يَرْجُونَ لِقَآءَنَا لَوْلَآ أُنْزِلَ عَلَيْنَا
الْمَلٰٓئِكَةُ أَوْ نَرٰى رَبَّنَا لَقَدِ اسْتَكْبَرُوا فِيٓ أَنْفُسِهِمْ
وَعَتَوْ عُتُوًّا كَبِيرًا ﴿٢١﴾

22. On the day when they behold the angels, on that day there will be no good tidings for the guilty; and they will cry: A forbidding ban!

يَوْمَ يَرَوْنَ الْمَلٰٓئِكَةَ لَا بُشْرٰى يَوْمَئِذٍ لِّلْمُجْرِمِينَ
وَيَقُولُونَ حِجْرًا مَّحْجُورًا ﴿٢٢﴾

23. And We shall turn unto the work they did and make it scattered motes.

وَقَدِمْنَآ إِلٰى مَا عَمِلُوا مِنْ عَمَلٍ فَجَعَلْنٰهُ هَبَآءً
مَّنْثُورًا ﴿٢٣﴾

24. Those who have earned the Garden on that day will be better in their home and happier in their place of noonday rest;

أَصْحٰبُ الْجَنَّةِ يَوْمَئِذٍ خَيْرٌ مُّسْتَقَرًّا وَّأَحْسَنُ
مَقِيلًا ﴿٢٤﴾

25. A day when the heaven with the clouds will be rent asunder and the angels will be sent down, a grand descent.

وَيَوْمَ تَشَقَّقُ السَّمَآءُ بِالْغَمٰمِ وَنُزِّلَ الْمَلٰٓئِكَةُ
تَنْزِيلًا ﴿٢٥﴾

26. The Sovereignty on that day will be the True (Sovereignty) belonging to the Beneficent One, and it will be a hard day for disbelievers.

الْمُلْكُ يَوْمَئِذٍ الْحَقُّ لِلرَّحْمٰنِ وَكَانَ يَوْمًا عَلَى
الْكٰفِرِينَ عَسِيرًا ﴿٢٦﴾

27. On the day when the wrong-doer gnaweth his hands, he will say: Ah, would that I had chosen a way together with the messenger (of Allah)!

وَيَوْمَ يَعَضُّ الظَّالِمُ عَلَىٰ يَدَيْهِ يَقُولُ يَٰلَيْتَنِي اتَّخَذْتُ
مَعَ الرَّسُولِ سَبِيلًا ٢٧

28. Alas for me! Ah, would that I had never taken such an one for friend!

يَٰوَيْلَتَىٰ لَيْتَنِي لَمْ أَتَّخِذْ فُلَانًا خَلِيلًا ٢٨

29. He verily led me astray from the Reminder after it had reached me. Satan was ever man's deserter in the hour of need.

لَقَدْ أَضَلَّنِي عَنِ الذِّكْرِ بَعْدَ إِذْ جَاءَنِي ۗ وَكَانَ
الشَّيْطَٰنُ لِلْإِنسَٰنِ خَذُولًا ٢٩

30. And the messenger saith: O my Lord! Lo! mine own folk make this Qur'ān of no account.

وَقَالَ الرَّسُولُ يَٰرَبِّ إِنَّ قَوْمِي اتَّخَذُوا هَٰذَا
الْقُرْءَانَ مَهْجُورًا ٣٠

31. Even so have We appointed unto every Prophet an opponent from among the guilty; but Allah sufficeth for a Guide and Helper.

وَكَذَٰلِكَ جَعَلْنَا لِكُلِّ نَبِيٍّ عَدُوًّا مِّنَ الْمُجْرِمِينَ ۗ
وَكَفَىٰ بِرَبِّكَ هَادِيًا وَنَصِيرًا ٣١

32. And those who disbelieve say: Why is the Qur'ān not revealed unto him all at once? (It is revealed) thus that We may strengthen thy heart therewith; and We have arranged it in right order.

وَقَالَ الَّذِينَ كَفَرُوا لَوْلَا نُزِّلَ عَلَيْهِ الْقُرْءَانُ جُمْلَةً
مع وَٰحِدَةً ۚ كَذَٰلِكَ لِنُثَبِّتَ بِهِ فُؤَادَكَ ۖ وَرَتَّلْنَٰهُ
تَرْتِيلًا ٣٢

33. And they bring thee no similitude but We bring thee the Truth (as against it), and better (than their similitude) as argument.

وَلَا يَأْتُونَكَ بِمَثَلٍ إِلَّا جِئْنَٰكَ بِالْحَقِّ وَأَحْسَنَ
تَفْسِيرًا ٣٣

34. Those who will be gathered on their faces unto Hell: such are worse in plight and further from the right road.

الَّذِينَ يُحْشَرُونَ عَلَىٰ وُجُوهِهِمْ إِلَىٰ جَهَنَّمَ أُولَٰئِكَ
ع ٣ شَرٌّ مَّكَانًا وَأَضَلُّ سَبِيلًا ٣٤

35. We verily gave Moses the Scripture and placed with him his brother Aaron as his wazir.

وَلَقَدْ ءَاتَيْنَا مُوسَى الْكِتَٰبَ وَجَعَلْنَا مَعَهُ أَخَاهُ
هَٰرُونَ وَزِيرًا ٣٥

36. Then We said: Go together unto the folk who have denied Our revelations. Then We destroyed them, a complete destruction.

فَقُلْنَا اذْهَبَا إِلَى الْقَوْمِ الَّذِينَ كَذَّبُوا بِـَٔايَٰتِنَا فَدَمَّرْنَٰهُمْ
تَدْمِيرًا ٣٦

37. And Noah's folk, when they denied the messengers, We drowned them and made of them a portent for mankind. We have prepared a painful doom for evil-doers.

وَقَوْمَ نُوحٍ لَّمَّا كَذَّبُوا الرُّسُلَ أَغْرَقْنَٰهُمْ وَجَعَلْنَٰهُمْ
لِلنَّاسِ ءَايَةً ۖ وَأَعْتَدْنَا لِلظَّٰلِمِينَ عَذَابًا أَلِيمًا ٣٧

38. And (the tribes of) 'Aād and Thamūd, and the dwellers in Ar-Rass,[1] and many generations in between.

وَعَادًا وَّثَمُوْدَا۟ وَاَصْحٰبَ الرَّسِّ وَقُرُوْنًا بَيْنَ ذٰلِكَ
كَثِيْرًا ﴿٣٨﴾

39. Each (of them) We warned by examples, and each (of them) We brought to utter ruin.

وَكُلًّا ضَرَبْنَا لَهُ الْاَمْثَالَ وَكُلًّا تَبَّرْنَا تَتْبِيْرًا ﴿٣٩﴾

40. And indeed they have passed by the township whereon was rained the fatal rain.[2] Can it be that they have not seen it? Nay, but they hope for no resurrection.

وَلَقَدْ اَتَوْا عَلَى الْقَرْيَةِ الَّتِيْٓ اُمْطِرَتْ مَطَرَ السَّوْءِ
اَفَلَمْ يَكُوْنُوْا يَرَوْنَهَا بَلْ كَانُوْا لَا يَرْجُوْنَ
نُشُوْرًا ﴿٤٠﴾

41. And when they see thee (O Muhammad) they treat thee only as a jest (saying): Is this he whom Allah sendeth as a messenger?

وَاِذَا رَاَوْكَ اِنْ يَّتَّخِذُوْنَكَ اِلَّا هُزُوًا اَهٰذَا الَّذِيْ
بَعَثَ اللّٰهُ رَسُوْلًا ﴿٤١﴾

42. He would have led us far away from our gods if we had not been staunch to them. They will know, when they behold the doom, who is more astray as to the road.

اِنْ كَادَ لَيُضِلُّنَا عَنْ اٰلِهَتِنَا لَوْلَآ اَنْ صَبَرْنَا عَلَيْهَا
وَسَوْفَ يَعْلَمُوْنَ حِيْنَ يَرَوْنَ الْعَذَابَ مَنْ اَضَلُّ
سَبِيْلًا ﴿٤٢﴾

43. Hast thou seen him who chooseth for his god his own lust? Wouldst thou then be guardian over him?

اَرَءَيْتَ مَنِ اتَّخَذَ اِلٰهَهٗ هَوٰىهُ اَفَاَنْتَ تَكُوْنُ
عَلَيْهِ وَكِيْلًا ﴿٤٣﴾

44. Or deemest thou that most of them hear or understand? They are but as the cattle—nay, but they are farther astray!

اَمْ تَحْسَبُ اَنَّ اَكْثَرَهُمْ يَسْمَعُوْنَ اَوْ يَعْقِلُوْنَ اِنْ هُمْ
اِلَّا كَالْاَنْعَامِ بَلْ هُمْ اَضَلُّ سَبِيْلًا ﴿٤٤﴾ ع

45. Hast thou not seen how thy Lord hath spread the shade—And if He willed He could have made it still—then We have made the sun its pilot;

اَلَمْ تَرَ اِلٰى رَبِّكَ كَيْفَ مَدَّ الظِّلَّ وَلَوْ شَآءَ لَجَعَلَهٗ
سَاكِنًا ثُمَّ جَعَلْنَا الشَّمْسَ عَلَيْهِ دَلِيْلًا ﴿٤٥﴾

46. Then We withdraw it unto Us, a gradual withdrawal?

ثُمَّ قَبَضْنٰهُ اِلَيْنَا قَبْضًا يَّسِيْرًا ﴿٤٦﴾

47. And He it is Who maketh night a covering for you, and sleep a repose, and maketh day a resurrection.

وَهُوَ الَّذِيْ جَعَلَ لَكُمُ الَّيْلَ لِبَاسًا وَّالنَّوْمَ سُبَاتًا
وَّجَعَلَ النَّهَارَ نُشُوْرًا ﴿٤٧﴾

48. And He it is Who sendeth the winds, glad tidings heralding His mercy, and We send down purifying water from the sky,

وَهُوَ الَّذِيْٓ اَرْسَلَ الرِّيٰحَ بُشْرًا بَيْنَ يَدَيْ رَحْمَتِهٖ
وَاَنْزَلْنَا مِنَ السَّمَآءِ مَآءً طَهُوْرًا ﴿٤٨﴾

1. Said to have been a town in Yamamah.
2. The great trade caravans from Mecca into Syria passed by the Dead Sea.

49. That We may give life thereby to a dead land, and We give many beasts and men that We have created to drink thereof.

لِّنُحْـِۧيَ بِهٖ بَلْدَةً مَّيْتًا وَّنُسْقِيَهٗ مِمَّا خَلَقْنَآ اَنْعَامًا
وَّاَنَاسِيَّ كَثِيْرًا ﴿٤٩﴾

50. And verily We have repeated it among them that they may remember, but most of mankind begrudge aught save ingratitude.

وَلَقَدْ صَرَّفْنٰهُ بَيْنَهُمْ لِيَذَّكَّرُوْا ۖ فَاَبٰىٓ اَكْثَرُ النَّاسِ
اِلَّا كُفُوْرًا ﴿٥٠﴾

51. If We willed, We could raise up a warner in every village.

وَلَوْ شِئْنَا لَبَعَثْنَا فِيْ كُلِّ قَرْيَةٍ نَّذِيْرًا ﴿٥١﴾

52. So obey not the disbelievers, but strive against them herewith with a great endeavour.

فَلَا تُطِعِ الْكٰفِرِيْنَ وَجَاهِدْهُمْ بِهٖ جِهَادًا كَبِيْرًا ﴿٥٢﴾

53. And He it is Who hath given independence to the two seas[1] (though they meet); one palatable, sweet, and the other saltish, bitter; and hath set a bar and a forbidding ban between them.

وَهُوَ الَّذِيْ مَرَجَ الْبَحْرَيْنِ هٰذَا عَذْبٌ فُرَاتٌ وَّ
هٰذَا مِلْحٌ اُجَاجٌ ۚ وَجَعَلَ بَيْنَهُمَا بَرْزَخًا وَّحِجْرًا
مَّحْجُوْرًا ﴿٥٣﴾

54. And He it is Who hath created man from water, and hath appointed for him kindred by blood and kindred by marriage: for thy Lord is ever Powerful.

وَهُوَ الَّذِيْ خَلَقَ مِنَ الْمَآءِ بَشَرًا فَجَعَلَهٗ نَسَبًا
وَّصِهْرًا ۗ وَكَانَ رَبُّكَ قَدِيْرًا ﴿٥٤﴾

55. Yet they worship instead of Allah that which can neither benefit them nor hurt them. The disbeliever was ever a partisan against his Lord.

وَيَعْبُدُوْنَ مِنْ دُوْنِ اللّٰهِ مَا لَا يَنْفَعُهُمْ وَلَا
يَضُرُّهُمْ ۗ وَكَانَ الْكَافِرُ عَلٰى رَبِّهٖ ظَهِيْرًا ﴿٥٥﴾

56. And We have sent thee (O Muhammad) only as a bearer of good tidings and a warner.

وَمَآ اَرْسَلْنٰكَ اِلَّا مُبَشِّرًا وَّنَذِيْرًا ﴿٥٦﴾

57. Say: I ask of you no reward for this, save that whoso will may choose a way unto his Lord.

قُلْ مَآ اَسْـَٔلُكُمْ عَلَيْهِ مِنْ اَجْرٍ اِلَّا مَنْ شَآءَ اَنْ
يَّتَّخِذَ اِلٰى رَبِّهٖ سَبِيْلًا ﴿٥٧﴾

58. And trust thou in the Living One Who dieth not, and hymn His praise. He sufficeth as the Knower of His bondmen's sins.

وَتَوَكَّلْ عَلَى الْحَيِّ الَّذِيْ لَا يَمُوْتُ وَسَبِّحْ بِحَمْدِهٖ ؕ
مع وَكَفٰى بِهٖ بِذُنُوْبِ عِبَادِهٖ خَبِيْرًا ﴿٥٨﴾

59. Who created the heavens and the earth and all that is between them in six Days,[2] then He mounted the Throne. The Beneficent! Ask any one informed concerning Him!

الَّذِيْ خَلَقَ السَّمٰوٰتِ وَالْاَرْضَ وَمَا بَيْنَهُمَا فِيْ سِتَّةِ اَيَّامٍ
ثُمَّ اسْتَوٰى عَلَى الْعَرْشِ ۛ اَلرَّحْمٰنُ فَسْـَٔلْ بِهٖ خَبِيْرًا ﴿٥٩﴾

60. And when it is said unto them: Adore the Beneficent! they say: And what is the Beneficent? Are we to adore whatever thou (Muhammad) biddest us? And it increaseth aversion in them.

وَاِذَا قِيْلَ لَهُمُ اسْجُدُوْا لِلرَّحْمٰنِ قَالُوْا وَمَا الرَّحْمٰنُ ق
ع اَنَسْجُدُ لِمَا تَاْمُرُنَا وَزَادَهُمْ نُفُوْرًا ﴿٦٠﴾ السجدة

1. *i.e.* the two kinds of the earth.
2. See XXII 47, XXXII 5, and LXX 4.

61. Blessed be He Who hath placed in the heaven mansions of the stars, and hath placed therein a great lamp and a moon giving light!

تَبٰرَكَ الَّذِيْ جَعَلَ فِي السَّمَآءِ بُرُوْجًا وَّجَعَلَ فِيْهَا
سِرٰجًا وَّقَمَرًا مُّنِيْرًا ﴿٦١﴾

62. And He it is Who hath appointed night and day in succession, for him who desireth to remember, or desireth thankfulness.

وَهُوَ الَّذِيْ جَعَلَ الَّيْلَ وَالنَّهَارَ خِلْفَةً لِّمَنْ اَرَادَ
اَنْ يَّذَّكَّرَ اَوْ اَرَادَ شُكُوْرًا ﴿٦٢﴾

63. The (faithful) slaves of the Beneficent are they who walk upon the earth modestly, and when the foolish ones address them answer: Peace!

وَعِبَادُ الرَّحْمٰنِ الَّذِيْنَ يَمْشُوْنَ عَلَى الْاَرْضِ هَوْنًا
وَّاِذَا خَاطَبَهُمُ الْجٰهِلُوْنَ قَالُوْا سَلٰمًا ﴿٦٣﴾

64. And who spend the night before their Lord, prostrate and standing,

وَالَّذِيْنَ يَبِيْتُوْنَ لِرَبِّهِمْ سُجَّدًا وَّقِيَامًا ﴿٦٤﴾

65. And who say: Our Lord! Avert from us the doom of hell; lo! the doom thereof is anguish;

وَالَّذِيْنَ يَقُوْلُوْنَ رَبَّنَا اصْرِفْ عَنَّا عَذَابَ جَهَنَّمَ
اِنَّ عَذَابَهَا كَانَ غَرَامًا ﴿٦٥﴾

66. Lo! it is wretched as abode and station;

اِنَّهَا سَآءَتْ مُسْتَقَرًّا وَّمُقَامًا ﴿٦٦﴾

67. And those who, when they spend, are neither prodigal nor grudging; and there is ever a firm station between the two;

وَالَّذِيْنَ اِذَآ اَنْفَقُوْا لَمْ يُسْرِفُوْا وَلَمْ يَقْتُرُوْا وَكَانَ
بَيْنَ ذٰلِكَ قَوَامًا ﴿٦٧﴾

68. And those who cry not unto any other god along with Allah, nor take the life which Allah hath forbidden save in (course of) justice, nor commit adultery—and whoso doth this shall pay the penalty;

وَالَّذِيْنَ لَا يَدْعُوْنَ مَعَ اللّٰهِ اِلٰهًا اٰخَرَ وَلَا يَقْتُلُوْنَ
النَّفْسَ الَّتِيْ حَرَّمَ اللّٰهُ اِلَّا بِالْحَقِّ وَلَا يَزْنُوْنَ ۚ وَ
مَنْ يَّفْعَلْ ذٰلِكَ يَلْقَ اَثَامًا ﴿٦٨﴾

69. The doom will be doubled for him on the Day of Resurrection, and he will abide therein disdained for ever;

يُّضٰعَفْ لَهُ الْعَذَابُ يَوْمَ الْقِيٰمَةِ وَيَخْلُدْ فِيْهٖ
مُهَانًا ﴿٦٩﴾

70. Save him who repenteth and believeth and doth righteous work; as for such, Allah will change their evil deeds to good deeds. Allah is ever Forgiving, Merciful.

اِلَّا مَنْ تَابَ وَاٰمَنَ وَعَمِلَ عَمَلًا صَالِحًا فَاُولٰٓئِكَ
يُبَدِّلُ اللّٰهُ سَيِّاٰتِهِمْ حَسَنٰتٍ ۭ وَكَانَ اللّٰهُ غَفُوْرًا
رَّحِيْمًا ﴿٧٠﴾

71. And whosoever repenteth and doth good, he verily repenteth toward Allah with true repentance—

وَمَنْ تَابَ وَعَمِلَ صَالِحًا فَاِنَّهٗ يَتُوْبُ اِلَى اللّٰهِ
مَتَابًا ﴿٧١﴾

72. And those who will not witness vanity, but when they pass near senseless play, pass by with dignity.

وَالَّذِينَ لَا يَشْهَدُونَ الزُّورَ وَإِذَا مَرُّوا بِاللَّغْوِ
مَرُّوا كِرَامًا ﴿٧٢﴾

73. And those who, when they are reminded of the revelations of their Lord, fall not deaf and blind thereat.

وَالَّذِينَ إِذَا ذُكِّرُوا بِآيَاتِ رَبِّهِمْ لَمْ يَخِرُّوا عَلَيْهَا
صُمًّا وَعُمْيَانًا ﴿٧٣﴾

74. And who say: Our Lord! Vouchsafe us comfort of our wives and of our offspring, and make us patterns for (all) those who ward off (evil).

وَالَّذِينَ يَقُولُونَ رَبَّنَا هَبْ لَنَا مِنْ أَزْوَاجِنَا وَ
ذُرِّيَّاتِنَا قُرَّةَ أَعْيُنٍ وَاجْعَلْنَا لِلْمُتَّقِينَ إِمَامًا ﴿٧٤﴾

75. They will be awarded the high place forasmuch as they were steadfast, and they will meet therein with welcome and the word of peace,

أُولَٰئِكَ يُجْزَوْنَ الْغُرْفَةَ بِمَا صَبَرُوا وَيُلَقَّوْنَ فِيهَا
تَحِيَّةً وَسَلَامًا ﴿٧٥﴾

76. Abiding there for ever. Happy is it as abode and station!

خَالِدِينَ فِيهَا حَسُنَتْ مُسْتَقَرًّا وَمُقَامًا ﴿٧٦﴾

77. Say (O Muhammad, unto the disbelievers); My Lord would not concern Himself with you but for your prayer. But now ye have denied (the Truth), therefor there will be judgement.

قُلْ مَا يَعْبَأُ بِكُمْ رَبِّي لَوْلَا دُعَاؤُكُمْ فَقَدْ كَذَّبْتُمْ
فَسَوْفَ يَكُونُ لِزَامًا ﴿٧٧﴾ ع

Ash-Shu'arā, "The Poets," takes its title from v. 224 ff., where the difference between poets and a Prophet is tersely pointed out; poets being those who say what they do not mean, while a Prophet always practises what he preaches. The pagan Arabs and their poets believed the poetic inspiration to be the work of Jinn.

The story of a number of former Prophets is here given to console the believers at a time of persecution, with the assurance that it is no new thing for a messenger of God to be persecuted, but that the persecutors always suffer in the end. It shows also that all the messengers of God came with the same message.

It belongs to the middle group of Meccan Sūrahs, with the exception of vv. 224-227, which were revealed at Al-Madīnah.

THE POETS

Revealed at Mecca

In the name of Allah, the Beneficent, the Merciful.

1. Ṭā. Sīn. Mīm.[1]

2. These are revelations of the Scripture that maketh plain.

3. It may be that thou tormentest thyself (O Muhammad) because they believe not.

4. If We will, We can send down on them from the sky a portent so that their necks would remain bowed before it.

5. Never cometh there unto them a fresh reminder from the Beneficent One but they turn away from it.

6. Now they have denied (the Truth); but there will come unto them tidings of that whereat they used to scoff.

7. Have they not seen the earth, how much of every fruitful kind We make to grow therein?

8. Lo! herein is indeed a portent; yet most of them are not believers.

9. And lo! thy Lord! He is indeed the Mighty, the Merciful.

10. And when thy Lord called Moses, saying: Go unto the wrongdoing folk,

11. The folk of Pharaoh. Will they not ward off (evil)?

12. He said: My Lord! Lo! I fear that they will deny me,

13. And I shall be embarrassed, and my tongue will not speak plainly, therefor send for Aaron (to help me).

14. And they have a crime against me, so I fear that they will kill me.

15. He said: Nay, verily. So go ye twain with Our tokens. Lo! We shall be with you, Hearing.

1. See Sûr. II. v. 1, footnote.

اياتها ٢٢٧ (٢٦) سورة الشعراء مكية ركوعاتها ١١

بسم الله الرحمن الرحيم

المنزل ٥

طسٓمٓ ﴿١﴾

تلك آيات الكتاب المبين ﴿٢﴾

لعلك باخع نفسك ألا يكونوا مؤمنين ﴿٣﴾

إن نشأ ننزل عليهم من السماء آية فظلت

أعناقهم لها خاضعين ﴿٤﴾

وما يأتيهم من ذكر من الرحمن محدث إلا

كانوا عنه معرضين ﴿٥﴾

فقد كذبوا فسيأتيهم أنبؤا ما كانوا به يستهزءون ﴿٦﴾

أولم يروا إلى الأرض كم أنبتنا فيها من كل زوج

كريم ﴿٧﴾

إن في ذلك لآية وما كان أكثرهم مؤمنين ﴿٨﴾

ع وإن ربك لهو العزيز الرحيم ﴿٩﴾

وإذ نادى ربك موسى أن ائت القوم الظالمين ﴿١٠﴾

قوم فرعون ألا يتقون ﴿١١﴾

قال رب إني أخاف أن يكذبون ﴿١٢﴾

ويضيق صدري ولا ينطلق لساني فأرسل إلى

هارون ﴿١٣﴾

ولهم علي ذنب فأخاف أن يقتلون ﴿١٤﴾

قال كلا فاذهبا بآياتنا إنا معكم مستمعون ﴿١٥﴾

16. And come together unto Pharaoh and say: Lo! we bear a message of the Lord of the Worlds,

17. (Saying): Let the Children of Israel go with us.

18. (Pharaoh) said (unto Moses): Did we not rear thee among us as a child? And thou didst dwell many years of thy life among us,

19. And thou didst that thy deed which thou didst, and thou wast one of the ingrates,

20. He said: I did it then, when I was of those who are astray.

21. Then I fled from you when I feared you, and my Lord vouchsafed me a command and appointed me (of the number) of those sent (by Him).

22. And this is the past favour wherewith thou reproachest me: that thou hast enslaved the Children of Israel.

23. Pharaoh said: And what is the Lord of the Worlds?

24. (Moses) said: Lord of the heavens and the earth and all that is between them, if ye had but sure belief.

25. (Pharaoh) said unto those around him: Hear ye not?

26. He said: Your Lord and the Lord of your fathers.

27. (Pharaoh) said: Lo! your messenger who hath been sent unto you is indeed a madman!

28. He said: Lord of the East and the West and all that is between them, if ye did but understand.

29. (Pharaoh) said: If thou choosest a god other than me, I assuredly shall place thee among the prisoners.

30. He said: Even though I show thee something plain?

31. (Pharaoh) said: Produce it then, if thou art of the truthful!

32. Then he flung down his staff and it became a serpent manifest,

فأتيا فرعون فقولا إنا رسول رب العلمين ﴿١٦﴾

أن أرسل معنا بني إسرآءيل ﴿١٧﴾

قال ألم نربك فينا وليدا ولبثت فينا من عمرك سنين ﴿١٨﴾

وفعلت فعلتك التي فعلت وأنت من الكفرين ﴿١٩﴾

قال فعلتها إذا وأنا من الضالين ﴿٢٠﴾

ففررت منكم لما خفتكم فوهب لي ربي حكما وجعلني من المرسلين ﴿٢١﴾

وتلك نعمة تمنها علي أن عبدت بني إسرآءيل ﴿٢٢﴾

قال فرعون وما رب العلمين ﴿٢٣﴾

قال رب السموت والأرض وما بينهما إن كنتم موقنين ﴿٢٤﴾

قال لمن حوله ألا تستمعون ﴿٢٥﴾

قال ربكم ورب آبآئكم الأولين ﴿٢٦﴾

قال إن رسولكم الذي أرسل إليكم لمجنون ﴿٢٧﴾

قال رب المشرق والمغرب وما بينهما إن كنتم تعقلون ﴿٢٨﴾

قال لئن اتخذت إلها غيري لأجعلنك من المسجونين ﴿٢٩﴾

قال أولو جئتك بشيء مبين ﴿٣٠﴾

قال فأت به إن كنت من الصدقين ﴿٣١﴾

فألقى عصاه فإذا هي ثعبان مبين ﴿٣٢﴾

33. And he drew forth his hand and lo! it was white to the beholders.

34. (Pharaoh) said unto the chiefs about him: Lo, this is verily a knowing wizard,

35. Who would drive you out of your land by his magic. Now what counsel ye?

36. They said: Put him off, (him) and his brother, and send them into the cities summoners

37. Who shall bring unto thee every knowing wizard.

38. So the wizards were gathered together at a set time on a day appointed.

39. And it was said unto the people: Are ye (also) gathering?

40. (They said): Aye, so that we may follow the wizards if they are the winners.

41. And when the wizards came they said unto Pharaoh: Will there surely be a reward for us if we are the winners?

42. He said: Aye, and ye will then surely be of those brought near (to me).

43. Moses said unto them: Throw what ye are going to throw!

44. Then they threw down their cords and their staves and said: By Pharaoh's might, lo! we verily are the winners.

45. Then Moses threw his staff and lo! it swallowed that which they did falsely show:

46. And the wizards were flung prostrate,

47. Crying: We believe in the Lord of the Worlds,

48. The Lord of Moses and Aaron.

49. (Pharaoh) said: Ye put your faith in him before I give you leave? Lo! he doubtless is your chief who taught you magic! But verily ye shall come to know. Verily I will cut off your hands and your feet alternately, and verily I will crucify you every one.

وَنَزَعَ يَدَهُ فَإِذَا هِيَ بَيْضَاءُ لِلنّٰظِرِينَ ﴿٣٣﴾

قَالَ لِلْمَلَإِ حَوْلَهُ إِنَّ هٰذَا لَسٰحِرٌ عَلِيمٌ ﴿٣٤﴾

يُرِيدُ أَنْ يُخْرِجَكُمْ مِنْ أَرْضِكُمْ بِسِحْرِهِ فَمَاذَا

تَأْمُرُونَ ﴿٣٥﴾

قَالُوا أَرْجِهْ وَأَخَاهُ وَابْعَثْ فِي الْمَدَائِنِ حٰشِرِينَ ﴿٣٦﴾

يَأْتُوكَ بِكُلِّ سَحَّارٍ عَلِيمٍ ﴿٣٧﴾

فَجُمِعَ السَّحَرَةُ لِمِيقَاتِ يَوْمٍ مَعْلُومٍ ﴿٣٨﴾

وَقِيلَ لِلنَّاسِ هَلْ أَنْتُمْ مُجْتَمِعُونَ ﴿٣٩﴾

لَعَلَّنَا نَتَّبِعُ السَّحَرَةَ إِنْ كَانُوا هُمُ الْغٰلِبِينَ ﴿٤٠﴾

فَلَمَّا جَاءَ السَّحَرَةُ قَالُوا لِفِرْعَوْنَ أَئِنَّ لَنَا لَأَجْرًا

إِنْ كُنَّا نَحْنُ الْغٰلِبِينَ ﴿٤١﴾

قَالَ نَعَمْ وَإِنَّكُمْ إِذًا لَمِنَ الْمُقَرَّبِينَ ﴿٤٢﴾

قَالَ لَهُمْ مُوسٰى أَلْقُوا مَا أَنْتُمْ مُلْقُونَ ﴿٤٣﴾

فَأَلْقَوْا حِبَالَهُمْ وَعِصِيَّهُمْ وَقَالُوا بِعِزَّةِ فِرْعَوْنَ

إِنَّا لَنَحْنُ الْغٰلِبُونَ ﴿٤٤﴾

فَأَلْقٰى مُوسٰى عَصَاهُ فَإِذَا هِيَ تَلْقَفُ مَا يَأْفِكُونَ ﴿٤٥﴾

فَأُلْقِيَ السَّحَرَةُ سٰجِدِينَ ﴿٤٦﴾

قَالُوا آمَنَّا بِرَبِّ الْعٰلَمِينَ ﴿٤٧﴾

رَبِّ مُوسٰى وَهٰرُونَ ﴿٤٨﴾

قَالَ آمَنْتُمْ لَهُ قَبْلَ أَنْ آذَنَ لَكُمْ إِنَّهُ لَكَبِيرُكُمُ الَّذِي

عَلَّمَكُمُ السِّحْرَ فَلَسَوْفَ تَعْلَمُونَ لَأُقَطِّعَنَّ أَيْدِيَكُمْ

وَأَرْجُلَكُمْ مِنْ خِلَافٍ وَلَأُصَلِّبَنَّكُمْ أَجْمَعِينَ ﴿٤٩﴾

50. They said: It is no hurt, for lo! unto our Lord we shall return.

51. Lo! we ardently hope that our Lord will forgive us our sins because we are the first of the believers.

52. And We inspired Moses, saying: Take away My slaves by night, for ye will be pursued.

53. Then Pharaoh sent into the cities summoners,

54. (Who said): Lo! these indeed are but a little troop,

55. And lo! they are offenders against us.

56. And lo! we are a ready host.

57. Thus did We take them away from gardens and watersprings,

58. And treasures and a fair estate.

59. Thus (were those things taken from them) and We caused the Children of Israel to inherit them.

60. And they overtook them at sunrise.

61. And when the two hosts saw each other, those with Moses said: Lo! we are indeed caught.

62. He said: Nay, verily! for lo! my Lord is with me. He will guide me.

63. Then We inspired Moses, saying: Smite the sea with thy staff. And it parted, and each part was as a mountain vast.

64. Then brought We near the others to that place.

65. And We saved Moses and those with him, every one;

66. We drowned the others.

67. Lo! herein is indeed a portent, yet most of them are not believers.

68. And lo, thy Lord! He is indeed the Mighty, the Merciful.

قالوا لا ضير إنا إلى ربنا منقلبون ٥٠

إنا نطمع أن يغفر لنا ربنا خطايانا أن كنا أول
المؤمنين ٥١

وأوحينا إلى موسى أن أسر بعبادي إنكم متبعون ٥٢

فأرسل فرعون في المدائن حاشرين ٥٣

إن هؤلاء لشرذمة قليلون ٥٤

وإنهم لنا لغائظون ٥٥

وإنا لجميع حاذرون ٥٦

فأخرجناهم من جنات وعيون ٥٧

وكنوز ومقام كريم ٥٨

كذلك وأورثناها بني إسرائيل ٥٩

فأتبعوهم مشرقين ٦٠

فلما تراءى الجمعان قال أصحاب موسى إنا
لمدركون ٦١

قال كلا إن معي ربي سيهدين ٦٢

فأوحينا إلى موسى أن اضرب بعصاك البحر فانفلق
فكان كل فرق كالطود العظيم ٦٣

وأزلفنا ثم الآخرين ٦٤

وأنجينا موسى ومن معه أجمعين ٦٥

ثم أغرقنا الآخرين ٦٦

إن في ذلك لآية وما كان أكثرهم مؤمنين ٦٧

وإن ربك لهو العزيز الرحيم ٦٨

69. Recite unto them the story of Abraham:

70. When he said unto his father and his folk: What worship ye?

71. They said: We worship idols, and are ever devoted unto them.

72. He said: Do they hear you when ye cry?

73. Or do they benefit or harm you?

74. They said: Nay, but we found our fathers acting on this wise.

75. He said: See now that which ye worship,

76. Ye and your forefathers!

77. Lo! they are (all) an enemy unto me, save the Lord of the Worlds,

78. Who created me, and He doth guide me,

79. And Who feedeth me and watereth me.

80. And when I sicken, then He healeth me,

81. And Who causeth me to die, then giveth me life (again),

82. And Who, I ardently hope, will forgive me my sin on the Day of Judgement.

83. My Lord! Vouchsafe me wisdom and unite me to the righteous,

84. And give unto me a good report in later generations,

85. And place me among the inheritors of the Garden of Delight.

86. And forgive my father. Lo! he is of those who err,

87. And abase me not on the day when they are raised,

88. The day when wealth and sons avail not (any man)

89. Save him who bringeth unto Allah a whole heart.

90. And the Garden will be brought nigh for those who ward off (evil).

وقف لازم
وَاتْلُ عَلَيْهِمْ نَبَأَ إِبْرٰهِيمَ ٦٩
إِذْ قَالَ لِأَبِيهِ وَقَوْمِهِ مَا تَعْبُدُونَ ٧٠
قَالُوا نَعْبُدُ أَصْنَامًا فَنَظَلُّ لَهَا عٰكِفِينَ ٧١
قَالَ هَلْ يَسْمَعُونَكُمْ إِذْ تَدْعُونَ ٧٢
أَوْ يَنْفَعُونَكُمْ أَوْ يَضُرُّونَ ٧٣
قَالُوا بَلْ وَجَدْنَا آبَاءَنَا كَذٰلِكَ يَفْعَلُونَ ٧٤
قَالَ أَفَرَءَيْتُمْ مَا كُنْتُمْ تَعْبُدُونَ ٧٥
أَنْتُمْ وَآبَاؤُكُمُ الْأَقْدَمُونَ ٧٦
فَإِنَّهُمْ عَدُوٌّ لِي إِلَّا رَبَّ الْعٰلَمِينَ ٧٧
الَّذِي خَلَقَنِي فَهُوَ يَهْدِينِ ٧٨
وَالَّذِي هُوَ يُطْعِمُنِي وَيَسْقِينِ ٧٩
وَإِذَا مَرِضْتُ فَهُوَ يَشْفِينِ ٨٠
وَالَّذِي يُمِيتُنِي ثُمَّ يُحْيِينِ ٨١
وَالَّذِي أَطْمَعُ أَنْ يَغْفِرَ لِي خَطِيئَتِي يَوْمَ الدِّينِ ٨٢
رَبِّ هَبْ لِي حُكْمًا وَأَلْحِقْنِي بِالصّٰلِحِينَ ٨٣
وَاجْعَلْ لِي لِسَانَ صِدْقٍ فِي الْآخِرِينَ ٨٤
وَاجْعَلْنِي مِنْ وَرَثَةِ جَنَّةِ النَّعِيمِ ٨٥
وَاغْفِرْ لِأَبِي إِنَّهُ كَانَ مِنَ الضَّالِّينَ ٨٦
وَلَا تُخْزِنِي يَوْمَ يُبْعَثُونَ ٨٧
يَوْمَ لَا يَنْفَعُ مَالٌ وَلَا بَنُونَ ٨٨
إِلَّا مَنْ أَتَى اللّٰهَ بِقَلْبٍ سَلِيمٍ ٨٩
وَأُزْلِفَتِ الْجَنَّةُ لِلْمُتَّقِينَ ٩٠

91. And hell will appear plainly to the erring,

وَبُرِّزَتِ الْجَحِيمُ لِلْغَاوِينَ ﴿٩١﴾

92. And it will be said unto them: Where is (all) that ye used to worship

وَقِيلَ لَهُمْ أَيْنَمَا كُنتُمْ تَعْبُدُونَ ﴿٩٢﴾

93. Instead of Allah? Can they help you or help themselves?

مِن دُونِ اللَّهِ هَلْ يَنصُرُونَكُمْ أَوْ يَنتَصِرُونَ ﴿٩٣﴾

94. Then they will be hurled therein, they and the seducers

فَكُبْكِبُوا فِيهَا هُمْ وَالْغَاوُونَ ﴿٩٤﴾

95. And the hosts of Iblis, together.

وَجُنُودُ إِبْلِيسَ أَجْمَعُونَ ﴿٩٥﴾

96. And they will say, when they are quarrelling therein:

قَالُوا وَهُمْ فِيهَا يَخْتَصِمُونَ ﴿٩٦﴾

97. By Allah, of a truth we were in error manifest

تَاللَّهِ إِن كُنَّا لَفِي ضَلَالٍ مُّبِينٍ ﴿٩٧﴾

98. When we made you equal with the Lord of the Worlds.

إِذْ نُسَوِّيكُم بِرَبِّ الْعَالَمِينَ ﴿٩٨﴾

99. It was but the guilty who misled us.

وَمَا أَضَلَّنَا إِلَّا الْمُجْرِمُونَ ﴿٩٩﴾

100. Now we have no intercessors

فَمَا لَنَا مِن شَافِعِينَ ﴿١٠٠﴾

101. Nor any loving friend.

وَلَا صَدِيقٍ حَمِيمٍ ﴿١٠١﴾

102. Oh, that we had another turn (on earth), that we might be of the believers!

فَلَوْ أَنَّ لَنَا كَرَّةً فَنَكُونَ مِنَ الْمُؤْمِنِينَ ﴿١٠٢﴾

103. Lo! herein is indeed a portent, yet most of them are not believers!

إِنَّ فِي ذَٰلِكَ لَآيَةً وَمَا كَانَ أَكْثَرُهُم مُّؤْمِنِينَ ﴿١٠٣﴾

104. And lo, thy Lord! He is indeed the Mighty, the Merciful.

ع وَإِنَّ رَبَّكَ لَهُوَ الْعَزِيزُ الرَّحِيمُ ﴿١٠٤﴾

105. Noah's folk denied the messengers (of Allah).

كَذَّبَتْ قَوْمُ نُوحٍ الْمُرْسَلِينَ ﴿١٠٥﴾

106. When their brother Noah said unto them: Will ye not ward off (evil)?

إِذْ قَالَ لَهُمْ أَخُوهُمْ نُوحٌ أَلَا تَتَّقُونَ ﴿١٠٦﴾

107. Lo! I am a faithful messenger unto you,

إِنِّي لَكُمْ رَسُولٌ أَمِينٌ ﴿١٠٧﴾

108. So keep your duty to Allah, and obey me.

فَاتَّقُوا اللَّهَ وَأَطِيعُونِ ﴿١٠٨﴾

109. And I ask of you no wage therefor; my wage is the concern only of the Lord of the Worlds.

وَمَا أَسْأَلُكُمْ عَلَيْهِ مِنْ أَجْرٍ إِنْ أَجْرِيَ إِلَّا عَلَىٰ
رَبِّ الْعَالَمِينَ ﴿١٠٩﴾

110. So keep your duty to Allah, and obey me.

فَاتَّقُوا اللَّهَ وَأَطِيعُونِ ﴿١١٠﴾

111. They said: Shall we put faith in thee, when the lowest (of the people) follow thee?

قَالُوا أَنُؤْمِنُ لَكَ وَاتَّبَعَكَ الْأَرْذَلُونَ ﴿١١١﴾

112. He said: And what knowledge have I of what they may have been doing (in the past)?

113. Lo! their reckoning is my Lord's concern, if ye but knew;

114. And I am not (here) to repulse believers.

115. I am only a plain warner.

116. They said: If thou cease not, O Noah, thou wilt surely be among those stoned (to death).

117. He said: My Lord! Lo! my own folk deny me.

118. Therefor judge Thou between us, a (conclusive) judgement, and save me and those believers who are with me.

119. And We saved him and those with him in the laden ship.

120. Then afterward We drowned the others.

121. Lo! herein is indeed a portent, yet most of them are not believers.

122. And lo, thy Lord, He is indeed the Mighty, the Merciful.

123. (The tribe of) 'Aād denied the messengers (of Allah),

124. When their brother Hūd said unto them: Will ye not ward off (evil)?

125. Lo! I am a faithful messenger unto you,

126. So keep your duty to Allah and obey me.

127. And I ask of you no wage therefor; my wage is the concern only of the Lord of the Worlds.

128. Build ye on every high place a monument for vain delight?

129. And seek ye out strongholds, that haply ye may last for ever?

130. And if ye seize by force, seize ye as tyrants?

131. Rather keep your duty to Allah, and obey me.

قَالَ وَمَا عِلْمِي بِمَا كَانُوا يَعْمَلُونَ ﴿١١٢﴾
إِنْ حِسَابُهُمْ إِلَّا عَلَىٰ رَبِّي لَوْ تَشْعُرُونَ ﴿١١٣﴾
وَمَا أَنَا بِطَارِدِ الْمُؤْمِنِينَ ﴿١١٤﴾
إِنْ أَنَا إِلَّا نَذِيرٌ مُبِينٌ ﴿١١٥﴾
قَالُوا لَئِنْ لَمْ تَنْتَهِ يَا نُوحُ لَتَكُونَنَّ مِنَ الْمَرْجُومِينَ ﴿١١٦﴾
النصف
قَالَ رَبِّ إِنَّ قَوْمِي كَذَّبُونِ ﴿١١٧﴾
فَافْتَحْ بَيْنِي وَبَيْنَهُمْ فَتْحًا وَنَجِّنِي وَمَنْ مَعِيَ
مِنَ الْمُؤْمِنِينَ ﴿١١٨﴾
فَأَنْجَيْنَاهُ وَمَنْ مَعَهُ فِي الْفُلْكِ الْمَشْحُونِ ﴿١١٩﴾
ثُمَّ أَغْرَقْنَا بَعْدُ الْبَاقِينَ ﴿١٢٠﴾
إِنَّ فِي ذَٰلِكَ لَآيَةً وَمَا كَانَ أَكْثَرُهُمْ مُؤْمِنِينَ ﴿١٢١﴾
وَإِنَّ رَبَّكَ لَهُوَ الْعَزِيزُ الرَّحِيمُ ﴿١٢٢﴾
كَذَّبَتْ عَادٌ الْمُرْسَلِينَ ﴿١٢٣﴾
إِذْ قَالَ لَهُمْ أَخُوهُمْ هُودٌ أَلَا تَتَّقُونَ ﴿١٢٤﴾
إِنِّي لَكُمْ رَسُولٌ أَمِينٌ ﴿١٢٥﴾
فَاتَّقُوا اللَّهَ وَأَطِيعُونِ ﴿١٢٦﴾
وَمَا أَسْأَلُكُمْ عَلَيْهِ مِنْ أَجْرٍ إِنْ أَجْرِيَ إِلَّا عَلَىٰ
رَبِّ الْعَالَمِينَ ﴿١٢٧﴾
أَتَبْنُونَ بِكُلِّ رِيعٍ آيَةً تَعْبَثُونَ ﴿١٢٨﴾
وَتَتَّخِذُونَ مَصَانِعَ لَعَلَّكُمْ تَخْلُدُونَ ﴿١٢٩﴾
وَإِذَا بَطَشْتُمْ بَطَشْتُمْ جَبَّارِينَ ﴿١٣٠﴾
فَاتَّقُوا اللَّهَ وَأَطِيعُونِ ﴿١٣١﴾

132. Keep your duty toward Him Who hath aided you with (the good things) that ye know,

133. Hath aided you with cattle and sons

134. And gardens and watersprings.

135. Lo! I fear for you the retribution of an awful Day.

136. They said: It is all one to us whether thou preachest or art not of those who preach;

137. This is but a fable of the men of old,

138. And we shall not be doomed.

139. And they denied him; therefor We destroyed them. Lo! herein is indeed a portent, yet most of them are not believers.

140. And lo! thy Lord, He is indeed the Mighty, the Merciful.

141. (The tribe of) Thamūd denied the messengers (of Allah)

142. When their brother Ṣāliḥ said unto them: Will ye not ward off (evil)?

143. Lo! I am a faithful messenger unto you,

144. So keep your duty to Allah and obey me.

145. And I ask of you no wage therefor; my wage is the concern only of the Lord of the Worlds.

146. Will ye be left secure in that which is here before us,

147. In gardens and watersprings

148. And tilled fields and heavy-sheathed palm-trees,

149. Though ye hew out dwellings in the mountain, being skilful?

150. Therefor keep your duty to Allah and obey me,

151. And obey not the command of the prodigal,

وَاتَّقُوا الَّذِيْٓ اَمَدَّكُمْ بِمَا تَعْلَمُوْنَ ﴿١٣٢﴾

اَمَدَّكُمْ بِاَنْعَامٍ وَّبَنِيْنَ ﴿١٣٣﴾

وَجَنّٰتٍ وَّعُيُوْنٍ ﴿١٣٤﴾

اِنِّيْٓ اَخَافُ عَلَيْكُمْ عَذَابَ يَوْمٍ عَظِيْمٍ ﴿١٣٥﴾

قَالُوْا سَوَآءٌ عَلَيْنَآ اَوَعَظْتَ اَمْ لَمْ تَكُنْ مِّنَ الْوٰعِظِيْنَ ﴿١٣٦﴾

اِنْ هٰذَآ اِلَّا خُلُقُ الْاَوَّلِيْنَ ﴿١٣٧﴾

وَمَا نَحْنُ بِمُعَذَّبِيْنَ ﴿١٣٨﴾

فَكَذَّبُوْهُ فَاَهْلَكْنٰهُمْ ۭ اِنَّ فِيْ ذٰلِكَ لَاٰيَةً ۭ وَمَا كَانَ
اَكْثَرُهُمْ مُّؤْمِنِيْنَ ﴿١٣٩﴾

ع وَاِنَّ رَبَّكَ لَهُوَ الْعَزِيْزُ الرَّحِيْمُ ﴿١٤٠﴾

كَذَّبَتْ ثَمُوْدُ الْمُرْسَلِيْنَ ﴿١٤١﴾

اِذْ قَالَ لَهُمْ اَخُوْهُمْ صٰلِحٌ اَلَا تَتَّقُوْنَ ﴿١٤٢﴾

اِنِّيْ لَكُمْ رَسُوْلٌ اَمِيْنٌ ﴿١٤٣﴾

فَاتَّقُوا اللّٰهَ وَاَطِيْعُوْنِ ﴿١٤٤﴾

وَمَآ اَسْـَٔلُكُمْ عَلَيْهِ مِنْ اَجْرٍ ۚ اِنْ اَجْرِيَ اِلَّا عَلٰى
رَبِّ الْعٰلَمِيْنَ ﴿١٤٥﴾

اَتُتْرَكُوْنَ فِيْ مَا هٰهُنَآ اٰمِنِيْنَ ﴿١٤٦﴾

فِيْ جَنّٰتٍ وَّعُيُوْنٍ ﴿١٤٧﴾

وَّزُرُوْعٍ وَّنَخْلٍ طَلْعُهَا هَضِيْمٌ ﴿١٤٨﴾

وَتَنْحِتُوْنَ مِنَ الْجِبَالِ بُيُوْتًا فٰرِهِيْنَ ﴿١٤٩﴾

فَاتَّقُوا اللّٰهَ وَاَطِيْعُوْنِ ﴿١٥٠﴾

وَلَا تُطِيْعُوْٓا اَمْرَ الْمُسْرِفِيْنَ ﴿١٥١﴾

152. Who spread corruption in the earth, and reform not.

الَّذِيْنَ يُفْسِدُوْنَ فِى الْاَرْضِ وَلَا يُصْلِحُوْنَ ۝

153. They said: Thou art but one of the bewitched;

قَالُوْا اِنَّمَا اَنْتَ مِنَ الْمُسَحَّرِيْنَ ۝

154. Thou art but a mortal like us. So bring some token if thou art of the truthful.

مَآ اَنْتَ اِلَّا بَشَرٌ مِّثْلُنَا فَاْتِ بِاٰيَةٍ اِنْ كُنْتَ مِنَ الصّٰدِقِيْنَ ۝

155. He said: (Behold) this she-camel. She hath the right to drink (at the well), and ye have the right to drink, (each) on an appointed day.

قَالَ هٰذِهٖ نَاقَةٌ لَّهَا شِرْبٌ وَّلَكُمْ شِرْبُ يَوْمٍ مَّعْلُوْمٍ ۝

156. And touch her not with ill lest there come on you the retribution of an awful Day.

وَلَا تَمَسُّوْهَا بِسُوْٓءٍ فَيَاْخُذَكُمْ عَذَابُ يَوْمٍ عَظِيْمٍ ۝

157. But they hamstrung her, and then were penitent,

فَعَقَرُوْهَا فَاَصْبَحُوْا نٰدِمِيْنَ ۝

158. So the retribution came on them. Lo! herein is indeed a portent, yet most of them are not believers.

فَاَخَذَهُمُ الْعَذَابُ اِنَّ فِىْ ذٰلِكَ لَاٰيَةً وَّمَا كَانَ اَكْثَرُهُمْ مُّؤْمِنِيْنَ ۝

159. And lo! thy Lord! He is indeed the Mighty, the Merciful.

وَاِنَّ رَبَّكَ لَهُوَ الْعَزِيْزُ الرَّحِيْمُ ۝

160. The folk of Lot denied the messengers (of Allah),

كَذَّبَتْ قَوْمُ لُوْطِ الْمُرْسَلِيْنَ ۝

161. When their brother Lot said unto them: Will ye not ward off (evil)?

اِذْ قَالَ لَهُمْ اَخُوْهُمْ لُوْطٌ اَلَا تَتَّقُوْنَ ۝

162. Lo! I am a faithful messenger unto you,

اِنِّىْ لَكُمْ رَسُوْلٌ اَمِيْنٌ ۝

163. So keep your duty to Allah and obey me.

فَاتَّقُوا اللّٰهَ وَاَطِيْعُوْنِ ۝

164. And I ask of you no wage therefor; my wage is the concern only of the Lord of the Worlds.

وَمَآ اَسْئَلُكُمْ عَلَيْهِ مِنْ اَجْرٍ اِنْ اَجْرِيَ اِلَّا عَلٰى رَبِّ الْعٰلَمِيْنَ ۝

165. What! Of all creatures do ye come unto the males,

اَتَاْتُوْنَ الذُّكْرَانَ مِنَ الْعٰلَمِيْنَ ۝

166. And leave the wives your Lord created for you? Nay, but ye are froward folk.

وَتَذَرُوْنَ مَا خَلَقَ لَكُمْ رَبُّكُمْ مِّنْ اَزْوَاجِكُمْ بَلْ اَنْتُمْ قَوْمٌ عٰدُوْنَ ۝

167. They said: If thou cease not, O Lot, thou wilt soon be of the outcast.

قَالُوْا لَئِنْ لَّمْ تَنْتَهِ يٰلُوْطُ لَتَكُوْنَنَّ مِنَ الْمُخْرَجِيْنَ ۝

168. He said: I am in truth of those who hate your conduct.

قَالَ اِنِّىْ لِعَمَلِكُمْ مِّنَ الْقَالِيْنَ ۝

169. My Lord! Save me and my household from what they do.

رَبِّ نَجِّنِيْ وَاَهْلِيْ مِمَّا يَعْمَلُوْنَ ۝

170. So We saved him and his household, every one,

فَنَجَّيْنٰهُ وَاَهْلَهٗۤ اَجْمَعِيْنَ ۝

171. Save an old woman among those who stayed behind.

اِلَّا عَجُوْزًا فِي الْغٰبِرِيْنَ ۝

172. Then afterward We destroyed the others.

ثُمَّ دَمَّرْنَا الْاٰخَرِيْنَ ۝

173. And We rained on them a rain. And dreadful is the rain of those who have been warned.

وَاَمْطَرْنَا عَلَيْهِمْ مَّطَرًا ۚ فَسَآءَ مَطَرُ الْمُنْذَرِيْنَ ۝

174. Lo! herein is indeed a portent, yet most of them are not believers.

اِنَّ فِيْ ذٰلِكَ لَاٰيَةً ۚ وَمَا كَانَ اَكْثَرُهُمْ مُّؤْمِنِيْنَ ۝

175. And lo! thy Lord, He is indeed the Mighty, the Merciful.

وَاِنَّ رَبَّكَ لَهُوَ الْعَزِيْزُ الرَّحِيْمُ ۝

176. The dwellers in the wood (of Midian) denied the messengers (of Allah),

كَذَّبَ اَصْحٰبُ لْئَيْكَةِ الْمُرْسَلِيْنَ ۝

177. When Shu'eyb said unto them: Will ye not ward off (evil)?

اِذْ قَالَ لَهُمْ شُعَيْبٌ اَلَا تَتَّقُوْنَ ۝

178. Lo! I am a faithful messenger unto you,

اِنِّيْ لَكُمْ رَسُوْلٌ اَمِيْنٌ ۝

179. So keep your duty to Allah and obey me.

فَاتَّقُوا اللّٰهَ وَاَطِيْعُوْنِ ۝

180. And I ask of you no wage for it; my wage is the concern only of the Lord of the Worlds.

وَمَاۤ اَسْـَٔلُكُمْ عَلَيْهِ مِنْ اَجْرٍ ۚ اِنْ اَجْرِيَ اِلَّا عَلٰى رَبِّ الْعٰلَمِيْنَ ۝

181. Give full measure, and be not of those who give less (than the due).

اَوْفُوا الْكَيْلَ وَلَا تَكُوْنُوْا مِنَ الْمُخْسِرِيْنَ ۝

182. And weigh with the true balance.

وَزِنُوْا بِالْقِسْطَاسِ الْمُسْتَقِيْمِ ۝

183. Wrong not mankind in their goods, and do not evil, making mischief, in the earth.

وَلَا تَبْخَسُوا النَّاسَ اَشْيَآءَهُمْ وَلَا تَعْثَوْا فِي الْاَرْضِ مُفْسِدِيْنَ ۝

184. And keep your duty unto Him Who created you and the generations of the men of old.

وَاتَّقُوا الَّذِيْ خَلَقَكُمْ وَالْجِبِلَّةَ الْاَوَّلِيْنَ ۝

185. They said: Thou art but one of the bewitched;

قَالُوْۤا اِنَّمَاۤ اَنْتَ مِنَ الْمُسَحَّرِيْنَ ۝

186. Thou art but a mortal like us, and lo! we deem thee of the liars.

وَمَاۤ اَنْتَ اِلَّا بَشَرٌ مِّثْلُنَا وَاِنْ نَّظُنُّكَ لَمِنَ الْكٰذِبِيْنَ ۝

187. Then make fragments of the heaven fall upon us, if thou art of the truthful,

فَاَسْقِطْ عَلَيْنَا كِسَفًا مِّنَ السَّمَآءِ اِنْ كُنْتَ مِنَ الصّٰدِقِيْنَ ۝

188. He said: My Lord is best aware of what ye do.

قَالَ رَبِّيْ اَعْلَمُ بِمَا تَعْمَلُوْنَ ۝

189. But they denied him, so there came on them the retribution of the day of gloom. Lo! it was the retribution of an awful Day.

فَكَذَّبُوْهُ فَاَخَذَهُمْ عَذَابُ يَوْمِ الظُّلَّةِ ۚ اِنَّهٗ كَانَ عَذَابَ يَوْمٍ عَظِيْمٍ ۝

190. Lo! herein is indeed a portent; yet most of them are not believers.

اِنَّ فِيْ ذٰلِكَ لَاٰيَةً ۚ وَمَا كَانَ اَكْثَرُهُمْ مُّؤْمِنِيْنَ ۝

191. And lo! thy Lord! He is indeed the Mighty, the Merciful.

وَاِنَّ رَبَّكَ لَهُوَ الْعَزِيْزُ الرَّحِيْمُ ۝

192. And lo! it is a revelation of the Lord of the Worlds,

وَاِنَّهٗ لَتَنْزِيْلُ رَبِّ الْعٰلَمِيْنَ ۝

193. Which the True Spirit hath brought down

نَزَلَ بِهِ الرُّوْحُ الْاَمِيْنُ ۝

194. Upon thy heart, that thou mayest be (one) of the warners,

عَلٰى قَلْبِكَ لِتَكُوْنَ مِنَ الْمُنْذِرِيْنَ ۝

195. In plain Arabic speech.

بِلِسَانٍ عَرَبِيٍّ مُّبِيْنٍ ۝

196. And lo, it is in the Scriptures of the men of old.

وَاِنَّهٗ لَفِيْ زُبُرِ الْاَوَّلِيْنَ ۝

197. Is it not a token for them that the doctors of the Children of Israel[1] know it?

اَوَلَمْ يَكُنْ لَّهُمْ اٰيَةً اَنْ يَّعْلَمَهٗ عُلَمٰٓؤُا بَنِيْٓ اِسْرَآءِيْلَ ۝

198. And if We had revealed it unto one of any other nation than the Arabs,

وَلَوْ نَزَّلْنٰهُ عَلٰى بَعْضِ الْاَعْجَمِيْنَ ۝

199. And he had read it unto them, they would not have believed in it.

فَقَرَاَهٗ عَلَيْهِمْ مَّا كَانُوْا بِهٖ مُؤْمِنِيْنَ ۝

200. Thus do We make it traverse the hearts of the guilty.

كَذٰلِكَ سَلَكْنٰهُ فِيْ قُلُوْبِ الْمُجْرِمِيْنَ ۝

201. They will not believe in it till they behold the painful doom,

لَا يُؤْمِنُوْنَ بِهٖ حَتّٰى يَرَوُا الْعَذَابَ الْاَلِيْمَ ۝

202. So that it will come upon them suddenly, when they perceive not.

فَيَاْتِيَهُمْ بَغْتَةً وَّهُمْ لَا يَشْعُرُوْنَ ۝

203. Then they will say: Are we to be reprieved?

فَيَقُوْلُوْا هَلْ نَحْنُ مُنْظَرُوْنَ ۝

204. Would they (now) hasten on Our doom?

اَفَبِعَذَابِنَا يَسْتَعْجِلُوْنَ ۝

205. Hast thou then seen, if We content them for (long) years,

اَفَرَءَيْتَ اِنْ مَّتَّعْنٰهُمْ سِنِيْنَ ۝

206. And then cometh that which they were promised,

ثُمَّ جَآءَهُمْ مَّا كَانُوْا يُوْعَدُوْنَ ۝

207. (How) that wherewith they were contented naught availeth them?

مَاۤ اَغْنٰى عَنْهُمْ مَّا كَانُوْا يُمَتَّعُوْنَ ۝

1. The Jews knew, from their Scripture, that a Prophet had been promised to the Arabs.

208. And We destroyed no township but it had its warners

209. For reminder, for We never were oppressors.

210. The devils did not bring it down.

211. It is not meet for them, nor is it in their power,

212. Lo! verily they are banished from the hearing.

213. Therefor invoke not with Allah another god lest thou be one of the doomed.

214. And warn thy tribe of near kindred,

215. And lower thy wing (in kindness) unto those believers who follow thee.

216. And if they (thy kinsfolk) disobey thee, say: Lo! I am innocent of what they do.

217. And put thy trust in the Mighty, the Merciful,

218. Who seeth thee when thou standest up (to pray)

219. And (seeth) thine abasement among those who fall prostrate (in worship).

220. Lo! He, only He, is the Hearer, the Knower.

221. Shall I inform you upon whom the devils descend?

222. They descend on every sinful, false one.

223. They listen eagerly, but most of them are liars.

224. As for poets, the erring follow them.

225. Hast thou not seen how they stray in every valley,

226. And how they say that which they do not?

227. Save those who believe and do good works, and remember Allah much, and vindicate themselves after they have been wronged. Those who do wrong will come to know by what a (great) reverse they will be overturned!

وَمَآ أَهْلَكْنَا مِن قَرْيَةٍ إِلَّا لَهَا مُنذِرُونَ ﴿٢٠٨﴾
ذِكْرَىٰ وَمَا كُنَّا ظَٰلِمِينَ ﴿٢٠٩﴾
وَمَا تَنَزَّلَتْ بِهِ ٱلشَّيَٰطِينُ ﴿٢١٠﴾
وَمَا يَنۢبَغِى لَهُمْ وَمَا يَسْتَطِيعُونَ ﴿٢١١﴾
إِنَّهُمْ عَنِ ٱلسَّمْعِ لَمَعْزُولُونَ ﴿٢١٢﴾
فَلَا تَدْعُ مَعَ ٱللَّهِ إِلَٰهًا ءَاخَرَ فَتَكُونَ مِنَ ٱلْمُعَذَّبِينَ ﴿٢١٣﴾
وَأَنذِرْ عَشِيرَتَكَ ٱلْأَقْرَبِينَ ﴿٢١٤﴾
وَٱخْفِضْ جَنَاحَكَ لِمَنِ ٱتَّبَعَكَ مِنَ ٱلْمُؤْمِنِينَ ﴿٢١٥﴾
فَإِنْ عَصَوْكَ فَقُلْ إِنِّى بَرِىٓءٌ مِّمَّا تَعْمَلُونَ ﴿٢١٦﴾
وَتَوَكَّلْ عَلَى ٱلْعَزِيزِ ٱلرَّحِيمِ ﴿٢١٧﴾
ٱلَّذِى يَرَىٰكَ حِينَ تَقُومُ ﴿٢١٨﴾
وَتَقَلُّبَكَ فِى ٱلسَّٰجِدِينَ ﴿٢١٩﴾
إِنَّهُۥ هُوَ ٱلسَّمِيعُ ٱلْعَلِيمُ ﴿٢٢٠﴾
هَلْ أُنَبِّئُكُمْ عَلَىٰ مَن تَنَزَّلُ ٱلشَّيَٰطِينُ ﴿٢٢١﴾
تَنَزَّلُ عَلَىٰ كُلِّ أَفَّاكٍ أَثِيمٍ ﴿٢٢٢﴾
يُلْقُونَ ٱلسَّمْعَ وَأَكْثَرُهُمْ كَٰذِبُونَ ﴿٢٢٣﴾
وَٱلشُّعَرَآءُ يَتَّبِعُهُمُ ٱلْغَاوُۥنَ ﴿٢٢٤﴾
أَلَمْ تَرَ أَنَّهُمْ فِى كُلِّ وَادٍ يَهِيمُونَ ﴿٢٢٥﴾
وَأَنَّهُمْ يَقُولُونَ مَا لَا يَفْعَلُونَ ﴿٢٢٦﴾
إِلَّا ٱلَّذِينَ ءَامَنُوا۟ وَعَمِلُوا۟ ٱلصَّٰلِحَٰتِ وَذَكَرُوا۟ ٱللَّهَ
كَثِيرًا وَٱنتَصَرُوا۟ مِنۢ بَعْدِ مَا ظُلِمُوا۟ ۗ وَسَيَعْلَمُ
ٱلَّذِينَ ظَلَمُوٓا۟ أَىَّ مُنقَلَبٍ يَنقَلِبُونَ ﴿٢٢٧﴾

An-Naml, "The Ant," takes its name from the ant mentioned in v. 18. Some commentators, objecting to the miraculous, seek to explain the ants, in the story of Solomon, as an old Arab tribe, the birds as cavalry, Hudhud (the hoopoe) as a man's name, and the Jinn as foreign troops. It belongs to the middle group of Meccan Sūrahs.

THE ANT

Revealed at Mecca

In the name of Allah, the Beneficent, the Merciful.

1. Tā. Sīn.[1] These are revelations of the Qur'ān and a Scripture that maketh plain;

2. A guidance and good tidings for believers

3. Who establish worship and pay the poor-due and are sure of the Hereafter.

4. Lo! as for those who believe not in the Hereafter, We have made their works fair-seeming unto them so that they are all astray.

5. Those are they for whom is the worst of punishment, and in the Hereafter they will be the greatest losers.

6. Lo! as for thee (Muhammad), thou verily receivest the Qur'ān from the presence of One Wise, Aware.

7. (Remember) when Moses said unto his household: Lo! I spy afar off a fire; I will bring you tidings thence, or bring to you a borrowed flame that ye may warm yourselves.

8. But when he reached it, he was called, saying: Blessed is whosoever is in the fire and whosoever is round about it! And glorified be Allah, the Lord of the Worlds!

9. O Moses! Lo! it is I, Allah, the Mighty, the Wise:

10. And throw down thy staff! But when he saw it writhing as it were a demon, he turned to flee headlong; (but it was said unto him): O Moses! Fear not! Lo! the emissaries fear not in My presence.

11. Save him who hath done wrong and afterward hath changed evil for good.[2] And lo! I am Forgiving, Merciful.

1. See Sūr. II. v. 1, footnote.
2. Moses had been guilty of a crime in Egypt.

آياتها ٩٣ (٢٧) سورة النمل مكية ركوعاتها ٧

بسم الله الرحمن الرحيم

طس تلك آيات القرآن وكتاب مبين ①

هدى وبشرى للمؤمنين ②

الذين يقيمون الصلوة ويؤتون الزكوة وهم
بالآخرة هم يوقنون ③

إن الذين لا يؤمنون بالآخرة زينا لهم أعمالهم
فهم يعمهون ④

أولئك الذين لهم سوء العذاب وهم في
الآخرة هم الأخسرون ⑤

وإنك لتلقى القرآن من لدن حكيم عليم ⑥
إذ قال موسى لأهله إني آنست نارا سآتيكم منها
بخبر أو آتيكم بشهاب قبس لعلكم تصطلون ⑦
فلما جاءها نودي أن بورك من في النار ومن
حولها وسبحان الله رب العلمين ⑧
يموسى إنه أنا الله العزيز الحكيم ⑨
وألق عصاك فلما رآها تهتز كأنها جان ولى
مدبرا ولم يعقب يموسى لا تخف إني لا يخاف
لدي المرسلون ⑩

إلا من ظلم ثم بدل حسنا بعد سوء فإني
غفور رحيم ⑪

12. And put thy hand into the bosom of thy robe, it will come forth white but unhurt. (This will be one) among nine tokens unto Pharaoh and his people. Lo! they were ever evil-living folk.

13. But when Our tokens came unto them, plain to see, they said: This is mere magic.

14. And they denied them, though their souls acknowledged them, for spite and arrogance. Then see the nature of the consequence for the wrong-doers!

15. And We verily gave knowledge unto David and Solomon, and they said: Praise be to Allah, Who hath preferred us above many of His believing slaves!

16. And Solomon was David's heir. And he said: O mankind! Lo! we have been taught the language of birds, and have been given (abundance) of all things. This surely is evident favour.

17. And there were gathered together unto Solomon his armies of the jinn and humankind, and of the birds, and they were set in battle order;

18. Till, when they reached the Valley of the Ants, an ant exclaimed: O ants! Enter your dwellings lest Solomon and his armies crush you, unperceiving.

19. And (Solomon) smiled, laughing at her speech, and said: My Lord, arouse me to be thankful for Thy favour wherewith Thou hast favoured me and my parents, and to do good that shall be pleasing unto Thee, and include me in (the number of) Thy righteous slaves.

وَاَدْخِلْ يَدَكَ فِيْ جَيْبِكَ تَخْرُجْ بَيْضَآءَ مِنْ غَيْرِ
سُوْٓءٍ فِيْ تِسْعِ اٰيٰتٍ اِلٰى فِرْعَوْنَ وَقَوْمِهٖ اِنَّهُمْ
كَانُوْا قَوْمًا فٰسِقِيْنَ ﴿١٢﴾
فَلَمَّا جَآءَتْهُمْ اٰيٰتُنَا مُبْصِرَةً قَالُوْا هٰذَا سِحْرٌ
مُّبِيْنٌ ﴿١٣﴾
وَجَحَدُوْا بِهَا وَاسْتَيْقَنَتْهَآ اَنْفُسُهُمْ ظُلْمًا وَّعُلُوًّا
فَانْظُرْ كَيْفَ كَانَ عَاقِبَةُ الْمُفْسِدِيْنَ ﴿١٤﴾
وَلَقَدْ اٰتَيْنَا دَاوٗدَ وَسُلَيْمٰنَ عِلْمًا وَقَالَا الْحَمْدُ
لِلّٰهِ الَّذِيْ فَضَّلَنَا عَلٰى كَثِيْرٍ مِّنْ عِبَادِهِ
الْمُؤْمِنِيْنَ ﴿١٥﴾
وَوَرِثَ سُلَيْمٰنُ دَاوٗدَ وَقَالَ يٰٓاَيُّهَا النَّاسُ عُلِّمْنَا
مَنْطِقَ الطَّيْرِ وَاُوْتِيْنَا مِنْ كُلِّ شَيْءٍ اِنَّ هٰذَا لَهُوَ
الْفَضْلُ الْمُبِيْنُ ﴿١٦﴾
وَحُشِرَ لِسُلَيْمٰنَ جُنُوْدُهٗ مِنَ الْجِنِّ وَالْاِنْسِ وَ
الطَّيْرِ فَهُمْ يُوْزَعُوْنَ ﴿١٧﴾
حَتّٰٓى اِذَآ اَتَوْا عَلٰى وَادِ النَّمْلِ قَالَتْ نَمْلَةٌ يّٰٓاَيُّهَا
النَّمْلُ ادْخُلُوْا مَسٰكِنَكُمْ لَا يَحْطِمَنَّكُمْ سُلَيْمٰنُ
وَجُنُوْدُهٗ وَهُمْ لَا يَشْعُرُوْنَ ﴿١٨﴾
فَتَبَسَّمَ ضَاحِكًا مِّنْ قَوْلِهَا وَقَالَ رَبِّ اَوْزِعْنِيْٓ
اَنْ اَشْكُرَ نِعْمَتَكَ الَّتِيْٓ اَنْعَمْتَ عَلَيَّ وَعَلٰى وَالِدَيَّ
وَاَنْ اَعْمَلَ صَالِحًا تَرْضٰىهُ وَاَدْخِلْنِيْ بِرَحْمَتِكَ
فِيْ عِبَادِكَ الصّٰلِحِيْنَ ﴿١٩﴾

20. And he sought among the birds and said: How is it that I see not the hoopoe, or is he among the absent?

21. I verily will punish him with hard punishment or I verily will slay him, or he verily shall bring me a plain excuse.

22. But he was not long in coming, and he said: I have found out (a thing) that thou apprehendest not, and I come unto thee from Sheba with sure tidings.

23. Lo! I found a woman ruling over them, and she hath been given (abundance) of all things, and hers is a mighty throne.

24. I found her and her people worshipping the sun instead of Allah; and Satan maketh their works fair-seeming unto them, and debarreth them from the way (of Truth), so that they go not aright:

25. So that they worship not Allah, Who bringeth forth the hidden in the heavens and the earth, and knoweth what ye hide and what ye proclaim,

26. Allah; there is no God save Him, the Lord of the tremendous Throne.

27. (Solomon) said: We shall see whether thou speakest truth or whether thou art of the liars.

28. Go with this my letter and throw it down unto them; then turn away and see what (answer) they return.

29. (The Queen of Sheba) said (when she received the letter): O chieftains! Lo! there hath been thrown unto me a noble letter.

30. Lo! it is from Solomon, and lo! it is: In the name of Allah the Beneficent, the Merciful;

31. Exalt not yourselves against me, but come unto me as those who surrender.

32. She said: O chieftains! Pronounce for me in my case. I decide no case till ye are present with me.

وتفقد الطير فقال ما لي لا أرى الهدهد أم
كان من الغائبين ﴿٢٠﴾
لأعذبنه عذابا شديدا أو لأاذبحنه أو ليأتيني
بسلطن مبين ﴿٢١﴾
فمكث غير بعيد فقال أحطت بما لم تحط به و
جئتك من سبإ بنبإ يقين ﴿٢٢﴾
إني وجدت امرأة تملكهم وأوتيت من كل
شيء ولها عرش عظيم ﴿٢٣﴾
وجدتها وقومها يسجدون للشمس من دون
الله وزين لهم الشيطن أعملهم فصدهم
عن السبيل فهم لا يهتدون ﴿٢٤﴾
ألا يسجدوا لله الذي يخرج الخبء في السموت
والأرض ويعلم ما تخفون وما تعلنون ﴿٢٥﴾
الله لا إله إلا هو رب العرش العظيم ﴿٢٦﴾
قال سننظر أصدقت أم كنت من الكذبين ﴿٢٧﴾
اذهب بكتبي هذا فألقه إليهم ثم تول عنهم
فانظر ماذا يرجعون ﴿٢٨﴾
قالت يأيها الملؤا إني ألقي إلي كتب كريم ﴿٢٩﴾
إنه من سليمن وإنه بسم الله الرحمن الرحيم ﴿٣٠﴾
ألا تعلوا علي وأتوني مسلمين ﴿٣١﴾
قالت يأيها الملؤا أفتوني في أمري ما كنت
قاطعة أمرا حتى تشهدون ﴿٣٢﴾

33. They said: We are lords of might and lords of great prowess, but it is for thee to command; so consider what thou wilt command.

34. She said: Lo! kings, when they enter a township, ruin it and make the honour of its people shame. Thus will they do.

35. But lo! I am going to send a present unto them, and to see with what (answer) the messengers return.

36. So when (the envoy) came unto Solomon, (the King) said: What! Would ye help me with wealth? But that which Allah hath given me is better than that which He hath given you. Nay it is ye (and not I) who exult in your gift.

37. Return unto them. We verily shall come unto them with hosts that they cannot resist, and we shall drive them out from thence with shame, and they will be abased.

38. He said: O chiefs! Which of you will bring me her throne before they come unto me, surrendering?

39. A stalwart of the Jinn said: I will bring it thee before thou canst rise from thy place. Lo! I verily am strong and trusty for such work.

40. One with whom was knowledge of the Scripture said: I will bring it thee before thy gaze returneth unto thee. And when he saw it set in his presence, (Solomon) said: This is of the bounty of my Lord, that He may try me whether I give thanks or am ungrateful. Whosoever giveth thanks he only giveth thanks for (the good of) his own soul: and whosoever is ungrateful (is ungrateful only to his own soul's hurt). For lo! my Lord is Absolute in independence, Bountiful.

41. He said: Disguise her throne for her that we may see whether she will go aright or be of those not rightly guided.

قالوا نحن اولوا قوة واولوا بأس شديد ۵ و
الامر اليك فانظري ماذا تأمرين ٣٣
قالت ان الملوك اذا دخلوا قرية افسدوها و
جعلوا اعزة اهلها اذلة وكذلك يفعلون ٣٤
واني مرسلة اليهم بهدية فنظرة بم يرجع
المرسلون ٣٥
فلما جاء سليمن قال اتمدونن بمال فما
اتىن الله خير مما اتىكم بل انتم بهديتكم
تفرحون ٣٦
ارجع اليهم فلنأتينهم بجنود لا قبل لهم بها
ولنخرجنهم منها اذلة وهم صغرون ٣٧
قال يايها الملؤا ايكم يأتيني بعرشها قبل ان
يأتوني مسلمين ٣٨
قال عفريت من الجن انا اتيك به قبل ان
تقوم من مقامك واني عليه لقوي امين ٣٩
قال الذي عنده علم من الكتب انا اتيك به
قبل ان يرتد اليك طرفك فلما راه مستقرا
عنده قال هذا من فضل ربي ليبلوني ءاشكر
ام اكفر ومن شكر فانما يشكر لنفسه ومن كفر
فان ربي غني كريم ٤٠
قال نكروا لها عرشها ننظر اتهتدي ام تكون
من الذين لا يهتدون ٤١

42. So, when she came. it was said (unto her): Is thy throne like this? She said : (It is) as though it were the very one. And (Solomon said): We were given the knowledge before her and we had surrendered (to Allah).

فَلَمَّا جَآءَتْ قِيْلَ اَهٰكَذَا عَرْشُكِ قَالَتْ كَاَنَّهٗ هُوَ وَاُوْتِيْنَا الْعِلْمَ مِنْ قَبْلِهَا وَكُنَّا مُسْلِمِيْنَ ۝

43. And (all) that she was wont to worship instead of Allah hindered her, for she came of disbelieving folk.

وَصَدَّهَا مَا كَانَتْ تَعْبُدُ مِنْ دُوْنِ اللّٰهِ اِنَّهَا كَانَتْ مِنْ قَوْمٍ كٰفِرِيْنَ ۝

44. It was said unto her: Enter the hall. And when she saw it she deemed it a pool and bared her legs. (Solomon) said: Lo! it is a hall, made smooth, of glass. She said: My Lord! Lo! I have wronged myself, and I surrender with Solomon unto Allah, the Lord of the Worlds.

قِيْلَ لَهَا ادْخُلِى الصَّرْحَ فَلَمَّا رَاَتْهُ حَسِبَتْهُ لُجَّةً وَّكَشَفَتْ عَنْ سَاقَيْهَا قَالَ اِنَّهٗ صَرْحٌ مُّمَرَّدٌ مِّنْ قَوَارِيْرَ قَالَتْ رَبِّ اِنِّى ظَلَمْتُ نَفْسِى وَاَسْلَمْتُ مَعَ سُلَيْمٰنَ لِلّٰهِ رَبِّ الْعٰلَمِيْنَ ۝

45. And We verily sent unto Thamūd their brother Sālih, saying: Worship Allah. And lo! they (then) became two parties quarrelling.

وَلَقَدْ اَرْسَلْنَا اِلٰى ثَمُوْدَ اَخَاهُمْ صٰلِحًا اَنِ اعْبُدُوا اللّٰهَ فَاِذَا هُمْ فَرِيْقٰنِ يَخْتَصِمُوْنَ ۝

46. He said: O my people! Why will ye hasten on the evil rather than the good? Why will ye not ask pardon of Allah, that ye may receive mercy?

قَالَ يٰقَوْمِ لِمَ تَسْتَعْجِلُوْنَ بِالسَّيِّئَةِ قَبْلَ الْحَسَنَةِ لَوْلَا تَسْتَغْفِرُوْنَ اللّٰهَ لَعَلَّكُمْ تُرْحَمُوْنَ ۝

47. They said: We augur evil of thee and those with thee. He said: Your evil augury is with Allah. Nay, but ye are folk that are being tested.

قَالُوا اطَّيَّرْنَا بِكَ وَبِمَنْ مَّعَكَ قَالَ طٰٓئِرُكُمْ عِنْدَ اللّٰهِ بَلْ اَنْتُمْ قَوْمٌ تُفْتَنُوْنَ ۝

48. And there were in the city nine persons who made mischief in the land and reformed not.

وَكَانَ فِى الْمَدِيْنَةِ تِسْعَةُ رَهْطٍ يُّفْسِدُوْنَ فِى الْاَرْضِ وَلَا يُصْلِحُوْنَ ۝

49. They said: Swear one to another by Allah that we verily will attack him and his household by night, and afterward we will surely say unto his friend: We witnessed not the destruction of his household. And lo! we are truthtellers.

قَالُوا تَقَاسَمُوْا بِاللّٰهِ لَنُبَيِّتَنَّهٗ وَاَهْلَهٗ ثُمَّ لَنَقُوْلَنَّ لِوَلِيِّهٖ مَا شَهِدْنَا مَهْلِكَ اَهْلِهٖ وَاِنَّا لَصٰدِقُوْنَ ۝

50. So they plotted a plot: and We plotted a plot, while they perceived not.

وَمَكَرُوْا مَكْرًا وَّمَكَرْنَا مَكْرًا وَّهُمْ لَا يَشْعُرُوْنَ ۝

51. Then see the nature of the consequence of their plotting, for lo! We destroyed them and their people, every one.

فَانْظُرْ كَيْفَ كَانَ عَاقِبَةُ مَكْرِهِمْ اَنَّا دَمَّرْنٰهُمْ وَقَوْمَهُمْ اَجْمَعِيْنَ ۝

52. See, yonder are their dwellings empty and in ruins because they did wrong. Lo! herein is indeed a portent for a people who have knowledge.

53. And We saved those who believed and used to ward off (evil).

54. And Lot! when he said unto his folk: will ye commit abomination knowingly?

55. Must ye needs lust after men instead of women? Nay, but ye are folk who act senselessly.

56. But the answer of his folk was naught save that they said: Expel the household of Lot from your township, for they (forsooth) are folk who would keep clean!

57. Then We saved him and his household save his wife; We destined her to be of those who stayed behind.

58. And We rained a rain upon them. Dreadful is the rain of those who have been warned.

59. Say (O Muhammad): Praise be to Allah, and peace be on His slaves whom He hath chosen! Is Allah best, or (all) that ye ascribe as partners (unto Him)?

60. Is not He (best) Who created the heavens and the earth, and sendeth down for you water from the sky wherewith We cause to spring forth joyous orchards, whose trees it never hath been yours to cause to grow. Is there any God beside Allah? Nay, but they are folk who ascribe equals (unto Him)!

61. Is not He (best) Who made the earth a fixed abode, and placed rivers in the folds thereof, and placed firm hills therein, and hath set a barrier between the two seas? Is there any God beside Allah? Nay, but most of them know not!

فَتِلْكَ بُيُوتُهُمْ خَاوِيَةً بِمَا ظَلَمُوا ۗ إِنَّ فِي ذَٰلِكَ
لَآيَةً لِقَوْمٍ يَعْلَمُونَ ﴿٥٢﴾
وَأَنْجَيْنَا الَّذِينَ آمَنُوا وَكَانُوا يَتَّقُونَ ﴿٥٣﴾
وَلُوطًا إِذْ قَالَ لِقَوْمِهِ أَتَأْتُونَ الْفَاحِشَةَ وَأَنْتُمْ
تُبْصِرُونَ ﴿٥٤﴾
أَئِنَّكُمْ لَتَأْتُونَ الرِّجَالَ شَهْوَةً مِنْ دُونِ النِّسَاءِ ۚ
بَلْ أَنْتُمْ قَوْمٌ تَجْهَلُونَ ﴿٥٥﴾
فَمَا كَانَ جَوَابَ قَوْمِهِ إِلَّا أَنْ قَالُوا أَخْرِجُوا آلَ
لُوطٍ مِنْ قَرْيَتِكُمْ ۖ إِنَّهُمْ أُنَاسٌ يَتَطَهَّرُونَ ﴿٥٦﴾
فَأَنْجَيْنَاهُ وَأَهْلَهُ إِلَّا امْرَأَتَهُ قَدَّرْنَاهَا مِنَ
الْغَابِرِينَ ﴿٥٧﴾
ع ٤ ١٩ وَأَمْطَرْنَا عَلَيْهِمْ مَطَرًا ۖ فَسَاءَ مَطَرُ الْمُنْذَرِينَ ﴿٥٨﴾
قُلِ الْحَمْدُ لِلَّهِ وَسَلَامٌ عَلَىٰ عِبَادِهِ الَّذِينَ اصْطَفَىٰ ۗ
آللَّهُ خَيْرٌ أَمَّا يُشْرِكُونَ ﴿٥٩﴾
الجزء ٢٠ أَمَّنْ خَلَقَ السَّمَاوَاتِ وَالْأَرْضَ وَأَنْزَلَ لَكُمْ مِنَ
السَّمَاءِ مَاءً فَأَنْبَتْنَا بِهِ حَدَائِقَ ذَاتَ بَهْجَةٍ مَا
كَانَ لَكُمْ أَنْ تُنْبِتُوا شَجَرَهَا ۗ أَإِلَٰهٌ مَعَ اللَّهِ ۚ بَلْ
هُمْ قَوْمٌ يَعْدِلُونَ ﴿٦٠﴾
أَمَّنْ جَعَلَ الْأَرْضَ قَرَارًا وَجَعَلَ خِلَالَهَا أَنْهَارًا
وَجَعَلَ لَهَا رَوَاسِيَ وَجَعَلَ بَيْنَ الْبَحْرَيْنِ
حَاجِزًا ۗ أَإِلَٰهٌ مَعَ اللَّهِ ۚ بَلْ أَكْثَرُهُمْ لَا
يَعْلَمُونَ ﴿٦١﴾

62. Is not He (best) Who answereth the wronged one when he crieth unto Him and removeth the evil, and hath made you viceroys of the earth? Is there any God beside Allah? Little do they reflect!

63. Is not He (best) Who guideth you in the darkness of the land and the sea, He Who sendeth the winds as heralds of His mercy? Is there any God beside Allah? High exalted be Allah from all that they ascribe as partner (unto Him)!

64. Is not He (best) Who produceth creation, then reproduceth it, and Who provideth for you from the heaven and the earth? Is there any God beside Allah? Say: Bring your proof, if ye are truthful!

65. Say (O Muhammad): None in the heavens and the earth knoweth the Unseen save Allah; and they know not when they will be raised (again).

66. Nay, but doth their knowledge reach to the Hereafter? Nay, for they are in doubt concerning it. Nay, for they cannot see it.

67. Yet those who disbelieve say: When we have become dust like our fathers, shall we verily be brought forth (again)?

68. We were promised this, forsooth, we and our fathers. (All) this is naught but fables of the men of old.

69. Say (unto them, O Muhammad): Travel in the land and see the nature of the sequel for the guilty!

70. And grieve thou not for them, nor be in distress because of what they plot (against thee).

71. And they say: When (will) this promise (be fulfilled), if ye are truthful?

72. Say: It may be that a part of that which ye would hasten on is close behind you.

أَمَّنْ يُجِيبُ الْمُضْطَرَّ إِذَا دَعَاهُ وَيَكْشِفُ السُّوٓءَ
وَيَجْعَلُكُمْ خُلَفَآءَ الْأَرْضِ ۗ أَءِلَٰهٌ مَّعَ اللَّهِ ۚ قَلِيلًا
مَّا تَذَكَّرُونَ ﴿٦٢﴾
أَمَّنْ يَهْدِيكُمْ فِي ظُلُمَٰتِ الْبَرِّ وَالْبَحْرِ وَمَنْ يُرْسِلُ
الرِّيَٰحَ بُشْرًا بَيْنَ يَدَيْ رَحْمَتِهِۦ ۗ أَءِلَٰهٌ مَّعَ اللَّهِ ۚ
تَعَٰلَى اللَّهُ عَمَّا يُشْرِكُونَ ﴿٦٣﴾
أَمَّنْ يَبْدَؤُا الْخَلْقَ ثُمَّ يُعِيدُهُۥ وَمَنْ يَرْزُقُكُمْ مِّنَ
السَّمَآءِ وَالْأَرْضِ ۗ أَءِلَٰهٌ مَّعَ اللَّهِ ۚ قُلْ هَاتُوا بُرْهَٰنَكُمْ
إِنْ كُنتُمْ صَٰدِقِينَ ﴿٦٤﴾
قُلْ لَّا يَعْلَمُ مَنْ فِي السَّمَٰوَٰتِ وَالْأَرْضِ الْغَيْبَ
إِلَّا اللَّهُ ۚ وَمَا يَشْعُرُونَ أَيَّانَ يُبْعَثُونَ ﴿٦٥﴾
بَلِ ادَّٰرَكَ عِلْمُهُمْ فِي الْآخِرَةِ ۚ بَلْ هُمْ فِي شَكٍّ
ع مِّنْهَا ۖ بَلْ هُمْ مِّنْهَا عَمُونَ ﴿٦٦﴾
وَقَالَ الَّذِينَ كَفَرُوٓا أَءِذَا كُنَّا تُرَٰبًا وَءَابَآؤُنَآ أَئِنَّا
لَمُخْرَجُونَ ﴿٦٧﴾
لَقَدْ وُعِدْنَا هَٰذَا نَحْنُ وَءَابَآؤُنَا مِنْ قَبْلُ ۙ إِنْ
هَٰذَآ إِلَّآ أَسَٰطِيرُ الْأَوَّلِينَ ﴿٦٨﴾
قُلْ سِيرُوا فِي الْأَرْضِ فَانْظُرُوا كَيْفَ كَانَ عَٰقِبَةُ
الْمُجْرِمِينَ ﴿٦٩﴾
وَلَا تَحْزَنْ عَلَيْهِمْ وَلَا تَكُنْ فِي ضَيْقٍ مِّمَّا يَمْكُرُونَ ﴿٧٠﴾
وَيَقُولُونَ مَتَىٰ هَٰذَا الْوَعْدُ إِنْ كُنتُمْ صَٰدِقِينَ ﴿٧١﴾
قُلْ عَسَىٰٓ أَنْ يَكُونَ رَدِفَ لَكُمْ بَعْضُ الَّذِي تَسْتَعْجِلُونَ ﴿٧٢﴾

73. Lo! thy Lord is full of bounty for mankind, but most of them do not give thanks.

74. Lo! thy Lord knoweth surely all that their bosoms hide, and all that they proclaim.

75. And there is nothing hidden in the heaven or the earth but it is in a clear Record.

76. Lo! this Qur'ān narrateth unto the Children of Israel most of that concerning which they differ.

77. And lo! it is a guidance and a mercy for believers.

78. Lo! thy Lord will judge between them of His wisdom, and He is the Mighty, the Wise.

79. Therefor (O Muhammad) put thy trust in Allah, for thou (standest) on the plain Truth.

80. Lo! thou canst not make the dead to hear, nor canst thou make the deaf to hear the call when they have turned to flee;

81. Nor canst thou lead the blind out of their error. Thou canst make none to hear, save those who believe Our revelations and who have surrendered.

82. And when the word is fulfilled concerning them, We shall bring forth a beast of the earth to speak unto them because mankind had not faith in Our revelations.

83. And (remind them of) the Day when We shall gather out of every nation a host of those who denied Our revelations, and they will be set in array;

84. Till, when they come (before their Lord), He will say: Did ye deny My revelations when ye could not compass them in knowledge, or what was it that ye did?

وَإِنَّ رَبَّكَ لَذُو فَضْلٍ عَلَى النَّاسِ وَلٰكِنَّ أَكْثَرَهُمْ
لَا يَشْكُرُونَ ﴿٧٣﴾
وَإِنَّ رَبَّكَ لَيَعْلَمُ مَا تُكِنُّ صُدُورُهُمْ وَمَا يُعْلِنُونَ ﴿٧٤﴾
وَمَا مِنْ غَائِبَةٍ فِي السَّمَاءِ وَالْأَرْضِ إِلَّا فِي كِتٰبٍ
مُبِينٍ ﴿٧٥﴾
إِنَّ هٰذَا الْقُرْاٰنَ يَقُصُّ عَلٰى بَنِي إِسْرَاءِيلَ أَكْثَرَ
الَّذِي هُمْ فِيهِ يَخْتَلِفُونَ ﴿٧٦﴾
وَإِنَّهُ لَهُدًى وَرَحْمَةٌ لِلْمُؤْمِنِينَ ﴿٧٧﴾
إِنَّ رَبَّكَ يَقْضِي بَيْنَهُمْ بِحُكْمِهِ ۚ وَهُوَ الْعَزِيزُ
الْعَلِيمُ ﴿٧٨﴾
فَتَوَكَّلْ عَلَى اللّٰهِ ۖ إِنَّكَ عَلَى الْحَقِّ الْمُبِينِ ﴿٧٩﴾
إِنَّكَ لَا تُسْمِعُ الْمَوْتٰى وَلَا تُسْمِعُ الصُّمَّ الدُّعَاءَ إِذَا
وَلَّوْا مُدْبِرِينَ ﴿٨٠﴾
وَمَا أَنْتَ بِهٰدِي الْعُمْيِ عَنْ ضَلٰلَتِهِمْ ۖ إِنْ تُسْمِعُ
إِلَّا مَنْ يُؤْمِنُ بِاٰيٰتِنَا فَهُمْ مُسْلِمُونَ ﴿٨١﴾
وَإِذَا وَقَعَ الْقَوْلُ عَلَيْهِمْ أَخْرَجْنَا لَهُمْ دَابَّةً
مِنَ الْأَرْضِ تُكَلِّمُهُمْ أَنَّ النَّاسَ كَانُوا بِاٰيٰتِنَا
لَا يُوقِنُونَ ﴿٨٢﴾ ع
وَيَوْمَ نَحْشُرُ مِنْ كُلِّ أُمَّةٍ فَوْجًا مِمَّنْ يُكَذِّبُ
بِاٰيٰتِنَا فَهُمْ يُوزَعُونَ ﴿٨٣﴾
حَتّٰى إِذَا جَاءُو قَالَ أَكَذَّبْتُمْ بِاٰيٰتِي وَلَمْ تُحِيطُوا
بِهَا عِلْمًا أَمَّاذَا كُنْتُمْ تَعْمَلُونَ ﴿٨٤﴾

85. And the Word will be fulfilled concerning them because they have done wrong, and they will not speak.

86. Have they not seen how We have appointed the night that they may rest therein, and the day sight-giving? Lo! therein verily are portents for a people who believe.

87. And (remind them of) the Day when the Trumpet will be blown, and all who are in the heavens and the earth will start in fear, save him whom Allah willeth. And all come unto Him, humbled.

88. And thou seest the hills thou deemest solid flying with the flight of clouds; the doing of Allah Who perfecteth all things. Lo! He is Informed of what ye do.

89. Whoso bringeth a good deed will have better than its worth; and such are safe from fear that Day.

90. And whoso bringeth an ill deed, such will be flung down on their faces in the Fire. Are ye rewarded aught save what ye did?

91. (Say): I (Muhammad) am commanded only to serve the Lord of this land which He hath hallowed, and unto Whom all things belong. And I am commanded to be of those who surrender (unto Him),

92. And to recite the Qur'ān. And whoso goeth right, goeth right only for (the good of) his own soul; and as for him who goeth astray—(unto him) say: Lo! I am only a warner.

93. And say: Praise be to Allah Who will show you His portents so that ye shall know them. And thy Lord is not unaware of what ye (mortals) do.

وَوَقَعَ الْقَوْلُ عَلَيْهِمْ بِمَا ظَلَمُوْا فَهُمْ لَا يَنْطِقُوْنَ ۞

اَلَمْ يَرَوْا اَنَّا جَعَلْنَا الَّيْلَ لِيَسْكُنُوْا فِيْهِ وَالنَّهَارَ مُبْصِرًا ۖ اِنَّ فِيْ ذٰلِكَ لَاٰيٰتٍ لِّقَوْمٍ يُّؤْمِنُوْنَ ۞

وَيَوْمَ يُنْفَخُ فِي الصُّوْرِ فَفَزِعَ مَنْ فِي السَّمٰوٰتِ وَمَنْ فِي الْاَرْضِ اِلَّا مَنْ شَآءَ اللّٰهُ ۖ وَكُلٌّ اَتَوْهُ دٰخِرِيْنَ ۞

وَتَرَى الْجِبَالَ تَحْسَبُهَا جَامِدَةً وَّهِيَ تَمُرُّ مَرَّ السَّحَابِ ۚ صُنْعَ اللّٰهِ الَّذِيْ اَتْقَنَ كُلَّ شَيْءٍ ۚ اِنَّهٗ خَبِيْرٌۢ بِمَا تَفْعَلُوْنَ ۞

مَنْ جَآءَ بِالْحَسَنَةِ فَلَهٗ خَيْرٌ مِّنْهَا ۚ وَهُمْ مِّنْ فَزَعٍ يَّوْمَئِذٍ اٰمِنُوْنَ ۞

وَمَنْ جَآءَ بِالسَّيِّئَةِ فَكُبَّتْ وُجُوْهُهُمْ فِي النَّارِ ۚ هَلْ تُجْزَوْنَ اِلَّا مَا كُنْتُمْ تَعْمَلُوْنَ ۞

اِنَّمَآ اُمِرْتُ اَنْ اَعْبُدَ رَبَّ هٰذِهِ الْبَلْدَةِ الَّذِيْ حَرَّمَهَا وَلَهٗ كُلُّ شَيْءٍ ۖ وَاُمِرْتُ اَنْ اَكُوْنَ مِنَ الْمُسْلِمِيْنَ ۞

وَاَنْ اَتْلُوَا الْقُرْاٰنَ ۚ فَمَنِ اهْتَدٰى فَاِنَّمَا يَهْتَدِيْ لِنَفْسِهٖ ۚ وَمَنْ ضَلَّ فَقُلْ اِنَّمَآ اَنَا مِنَ الْمُنْذِرِيْنَ ۞

وَقُلِ الْحَمْدُ لِلّٰهِ سَيُرِيْكُمْ اٰيٰتِهٖ فَتَعْرِفُوْنَهَا ۚ وَمَا رَبُّكَ بِغَافِلٍ عَمَّا تَعْمَلُوْنَ ۞

Al-Qasas, "The Story," takes its name from a word in v. 25. The name is moreover justified by the nature of the Sūrah, which consists mostly of the story of Moses, his early struggles and ultimate triumph, revealed at a time when the Prophet's case seemed desperate. It is one of the last Meccan Sūrahs. Some Arabic writers even say that it was revealed during the Hijrah, while others are of opinion that v. 85 only was revealed during the flight.

A late Meccan Sūrah, except v. 85 revealed during the Prophet's flight from Mecca to Al-Madînah, and vv. 52-55 revealed at Al-Madînah.[1]

1. *Tafsir al-Jalâleyn.*

THE STORY

Revealed at Mecca

In the name of Allah, the Beneficent, the Merciful.

1. Tā. Sīn. Mīm.[1]

2. These are revelations of the Scripture that maketh plain.

3. We narrate unto thee (somewhat) of the story of Moses and Pharaoh with truth, for folk who believe.

4. Lo! Pharaoh exalted himself in the earth and made its people castes. A tribe among them he oppressed, killing their sons and sparing their women. Lo! he was of those who work corruption.

5. And We desired to show favour unto those who were oppressed in the earth, and to make them examples and to make them the inheritors,

6. And to establish them in the earth, and to show Pharaoh and Haman and their hosts that which they feared from them.

7. And We inspired the mother of Moses, saying: Suckle him and, when thou fearest for him, then cast him into the river and fear nor grieve. Lo! We shall bring him back unto thee and shall make him (one) of Our messengers.

8. And the family of Pharaoh took him up, that he might become for them an enemy and a sorrow. Lo! Pharaoh and Haman and their hosts were ever sinning.

9. And the wife of Pharaoh said: (He will be) a consolation for me and for thee. Kill him not. Peradventure he may be of use to us, or we may choose him for a son. And they perceived not.

1. See Sūr. II, v. I, footnote.

اٰیاتها ٨٨ (٢٨) سورة القصص مكية ركوعاتها ٩

بسم الله الرحمٰن الرحيم ○

طسٓمٓ ①
تلك اٰيٰت الكتٰب المبين ②
نتلوا عليك من نبا موسٰى وفرعون بالحق
لقوم يؤمنون ③
ان فرعون علا فى الارض وجعل اهلها شيعا
يستضعف طآئفة منهم يذبح ابنآءهم و
يستحى نسآءهم انه كان من المفسدين ④
ونريد ان نمن على الذين استضعفوا فى الارض
ونجعلهم ائمة ونجعلهم الوٰرثين ⑤
ونمكن لهم فى الارض ونرى فرعون وهامٰن
وجنودهما منهم ما كانوا يحذرون ⑥
واوحينآ الى ام موسٰى ان ارضعيه فاذا خفت
عليه فالقيه فى اليم ولا تخافى ولا تحزنى انا
رآدوه اليك وجاعلوه من المرسلين ⑦
فالتقطه اٰل فرعون ليكون لهم عدوا وحزنا ان
فرعون وهامٰن وجنودهما كانوا خٰطـٔين ⑧
وقالت امرات فرعون قرت عين لى ولك لا
تقتلوه عسٰى ان ينفعنا او نتخذه ولدا وهم
لا يشعرون ⑨

10. And the heart of the mother of Moses became void, and she would have betrayed him if We had not fortified her heart, that she might be of the believers.

وَأَصْبَحَ فُؤَادُ أُمِّ مُوسَىٰ فَارِغًا إِن كَادَتْ لَتُبْدِي بِهِ
لَوْلَا أَن رَّبَطْنَا عَلَىٰ قَلْبِهَا لِتَكُونَ مِنَ الْمُؤْمِنِينَ ﴿١٠﴾

11. And she said unto his sister: Trace him. So she observed him from afar, and they perceived not.

وَقَالَتْ لِأُخْتِهِ قُصِّيهِ فَبَصُرَتْ بِهِ عَن جُنُبٍ وَّ
هُمْ لَا يَشْعُرُونَ ﴿١١﴾

12. And We had before forbidden foster-mothers for him, so she said: Shall I show you a household who will rear him for you and take care of him?

وَحَرَّمْنَا عَلَيْهِ الْمَرَاضِعَ مِن قَبْلُ فَقَالَتْ هَلْ أَدُلُّكُمْ
عَلَىٰ أَهْلِ بَيْتٍ يَكْفُلُونَهُ لَكُمْ وَهُمْ لَهُ نَاصِحُونَ ﴿١٢﴾

13. So We restored him to his mother that she might be comforted and not grieve, and that she might know that the promise of Allah is true. But most of them know not.

فَرَدَدْنَاهُ إِلَىٰ أُمِّهِ كَيْ تَقَرَّ عَيْنُهَا وَلَا تَحْزَنَ وَلِتَعْلَمَ أَنَّ
وَعْدَ اللَّهِ حَقٌّ وَلَٰكِنَّ أَكْثَرَهُمْ لَا يَعْلَمُونَ ﴿١٣﴾ ع

14. And when he reached his full strength and was ripe, We gave him wisdom and knowledge. Thus do We reward the good.

وَلَمَّا بَلَغَ أَشُدَّهُ وَاسْتَوَىٰ آتَيْنَاهُ حُكْمًا وَعِلْمًا وَ
كَذَٰلِكَ نَجْزِي الْمُحْسِنِينَ ﴿١٤﴾

15. And he entered the city at a time of carelessness of its folk, and he found therein two men fighting, one of his own caste, and the other of his enemies; and he who was of his caste asked him for help against him who was of his enemies. So Moses struck him with his fist and killed him. He said: This is of the devil's doing. Lo! he is an enemy, a mere misleader.

وَدَخَلَ الْمَدِينَةَ عَلَىٰ حِينِ غَفْلَةٍ مِّنْ أَهْلِهَا فَوَجَدَ
فِيهَا رَجُلَيْنِ يَقْتَتِلَانِ هَٰذَا مِن شِيعَتِهِ وَهَٰذَا مِنْ
عَدُوِّهِ فَاسْتَغَاثَهُ الَّذِي مِن شِيعَتِهِ عَلَى الَّذِي مِنْ
عَدُوِّهِ فَوَكَزَهُ مُوسَىٰ فَقَضَىٰ عَلَيْهِ قَالَ هَٰذَا مِنْ
عَمَلِ الشَّيْطَانِ إِنَّهُ عَدُوٌّ مُّضِلٌّ مُّبِينٌ ﴿١٥﴾

16. He said: My Lord! Lo! I have wronged my soul, so forgive me. Then He forgave him. Lo! He is the Forgiving, the Merciful.

قَالَ رَبِّ إِنِّي ظَلَمْتُ نَفْسِي فَاغْفِرْ لِي فَغَفَرَ لَهُ
إِنَّهُ هُوَ الْغَفُورُ الرَّحِيمُ ﴿١٦﴾

17. He said: My Lord! Forasmuch as Thou hast favoured me, I will nevermore be a supporter of the guilty.

قَالَ رَبِّ بِمَا أَنْعَمْتَ عَلَيَّ فَلَنْ أَكُونَ ظَهِيرًا
لِّلْمُجْرِمِينَ ﴿١٧﴾

18. And morning found him in the city, fearing, vigilant, when behold! he who had appealed to him the day before cried out to him for help. Moses said unto him: Lo! thou art indeed a mere hothead.

فَأَصْبَحَ فِي الْمَدِينَةِ خَائِفًا يَتَرَقَّبُ فَإِذَا الَّذِي
اسْتَنصَرَهُ بِالْأَمْسِ يَسْتَصْرِخُهُ قَالَ لَهُ مُوسَىٰ
إِنَّكَ لَغَوِيٌّ مُّبِينٌ ﴿١٨﴾

19. And when he would have fallen upon the man who was an enemy unto them both, he said: O Moses! wouldst thou kill me as thou didst kill a person yesterday? Thou wouldst be nothing but a tyrant in the land, thou wouldst not be of the reformers.

فَلَمَّآ اَنۡ اَرَادَ اَنۡ يَّبۡطِشَ بِالَّذِىۡ هُوَ عَدُوٌّ لَّهُمَا ۙ
قَالَ يٰمُوۡسٰٓى اَتُرِيۡدُ اَنۡ تَقۡتُلَنِىۡ كَمَا قَتَلۡتَ
نَفۡسًۢا بِالۡاَمۡسِ ۖ اِنۡ تُرِيۡدُ اِلَّاۤ اَنۡ تَكُوۡنَ جَبَّارًا
فِى الۡاَرۡضِ وَمَا تُرِيۡدُ اَنۡ تَكُوۡنَ مِنَ
الۡمُصۡلِحِيۡنَ ﴿۱۹﴾

20. And a man came from the uttermost part of the city, running. He said: O Moses! Lo! the chiefs take counsel against thee to slay thee; therefor escape. Lo! I am of those who give thee good advice.

وَجَآءَ رَجُلٌ مِّنۡ اَقۡصَا الۡمَدِيۡنَةِ يَسۡعٰى قَالَ
يٰمُوۡسٰٓى اِنَّ الۡمَلَاَ يَاۡتَمِرُوۡنَ بِكَ لِيَقۡتُلُوۡكَ فَاخۡرُجۡ
اِنِّىۡ لَكَ مِنَ النّٰصِحِيۡنَ ﴿۲۰﴾

21. So he escaped from thence, fearing, vigilant. He said: My Lord! Deliver me from the wrongdoing folk.

فَخَرَجَ مِنۡهَا خَآئِفًا يَّتَرَقَّبُ قَالَ رَبِّ نَجِّنِىۡ مِنَ
ع الۡقَوۡمِ الظّٰلِمِيۡنَ ﴿۲۱﴾

22. And when he turned his face toward Midian, he said: Peradventure my Lord will guide me in the right road.

وَلَمَّا تَوَجَّهَ تِلۡقَآءَ مَدۡيَنَ قَالَ عَسٰى رَبِّىۡۤ اَنۡ
يَّهۡدِيَنِىۡ سَوَآءَ السَّبِيۡلِ ﴿۲۲﴾

23. And when he came unto the water of Midian he found there a whole tribe of men, watering. And he found apart from them two women keeping back (their flocks). He said: What aileth you? The two said: We cannot give (our flocks) to drink till the shepherds return from the water; and our father is a very old man.

وَلَمَّا وَرَدَ مَآءَ مَدۡيَنَ وَجَدَ عَلَيۡهِ اُمَّةً مِّنَ النَّاسِ
يَسۡقُوۡنَ ۖ وَوَجَدَ مِنۡ دُوۡنِهِمُ امۡرَاَتَيۡنِ تَذُوۡدٰنِ ۚ
قَالَ مَا خَطۡبُكُمَا ؕ قَالَتَا لَا نَسۡقِىۡ حَتّٰى يُصۡدِرَ الرِّعَآءُ
وَاَبُوۡنَا شَيۡخٌ كَبِيۡرٌ ﴿۲۳﴾

24. So he watered (their flock) for them. Then he turned aside into the shade, and said: My Lord! I am needy of whatever good thou sendest down for me.

فَسَقٰى لَهُمَا ثُمَّ تَوَلّٰٓى اِلَى الظِّلِّ فَقَالَ رَبِّ اِنِّىۡ لِمَاۤ
اَنۡزَلۡتَ اِلَىَّ مِنۡ خَيۡرٍ فَقِيۡرٌ ﴿۲۴﴾

25. Then there came unto him one of the two women, walking shyly. She said: Lo! my father biddeth thee, that he may reward thee with a payment for that thou didst water (the flock) for us. Then, when he came unto him and told him the (whole) story, he said: Fear not! Thou hast escaped from the wrongdoing folk.

فَجَآءَتۡهُ اِحۡدٰىهُمَا تَمۡشِىۡ عَلَى اسۡتِحۡيَآءٍ قَالَتۡ اِنَّ
اَبِىۡ يَدۡعُوۡكَ لِيَجۡزِيَكَ اَجۡرَ مَا سَقَيۡتَ لَنَا ؕ فَلَمَّا
جَآءَهٗ وَقَصَّ عَلَيۡهِ الۡقَصَصَ ۙ قَالَ لَا تَخَفۡ
نَجَوۡتَ مِنَ الۡقَوۡمِ الظّٰلِمِيۡنَ ﴿۲۵﴾

26. One of the two women said: O my father! Hire him! For the best (man) that thou canst hire is the strong, the trustworthy.

27. He said: Lo! I fain would marry thee to one of these two daughters of mine on condition that thou hirest thyself to me for (the term of) eight pilgrimages. Then if thou completest ten it will be of thine own accord, for I would not make it hard for thee. Allah willing, thou wilt find me of the righteous.

28. He said: That (is settled) between thee and me. Whichever of the two terms I fulfil, there will be no injustice to me, and Allah is Surety over what we say.

29. Then, when Moses had fulfilled the term, and was travelling with his housefolk, he saw in the distance a fire and said unto his housefolk: Bide ye (here). Lo! I see in the distance a fire; peradventure I shall bring you tidings thence, or a brand from the fire that ye may warm yourselves.

30. And when he reached it, he was called from the right side of the valley in the blessed field, from the tree: O Moses! Lo! I, even I, am Allah, the Lord of the Worlds;

31. Throw down thy staff. And when he saw it writhing as it had been a demon, he turned to flee headlong, (and it was said unto him): O Moses! Draw nigh and fear not. Lo! thou art of those who are secure.

32. Thrust thy hand into the bosom of thy robe, it will come forth white without hurt. And guard thy heart from fear. Then these shall be two proofs from your Lord unto Pharaoh and his chiefs: Lo! they are evil-living folk.

قَالَتْ إِحْدَاهُمَا يَا أَبَتِ اسْتَأْجِرْهُ إِنَّ خَيْرَ مَنِ
اسْتَأْجَرْتَ الْقَوِيُّ الْأَمِينُ ﴿٢٦﴾
قَالَ إِنِّي أُرِيدُ أَنْ أُنكِحَكَ إِحْدَى ابْنَتَيَّ هَاتَيْنِ
عَلَىٰ أَن تَأْجُرَنِي ثَمَانِيَ حِجَجٍ فَإِنْ أَتْمَمْتَ عَشْرًا
فَمِنْ عِندِكَ وَمَا أُرِيدُ أَنْ أَشُقَّ عَلَيْكَ سَتَجِدُنِي
إِن شَاءَ اللَّهُ مِنَ الصَّالِحِينَ ﴿٢٧﴾
قَالَ ذَٰلِكَ بَيْنِي وَبَيْنَكَ أَيَّمَا الْأَجَلَيْنِ قَضَيْتُ فَلَا
عُدْوَانَ عَلَيَّ وَاللَّهُ عَلَىٰ مَا نَقُولُ وَكِيلٌ ﴿٢٨﴾ ع ٣ ٦
فَلَمَّا قَضَىٰ مُوسَى الْأَجَلَ وَسَارَ بِأَهْلِهِ آنَسَ مِن جَانِبِ
الطُّورِ نَارًا قَالَ لِأَهْلِهِ امْكُثُوا إِنِّي آنَسْتُ نَارًا لَّعَلِّي
آتِيكُم مِّنْهَا بِخَبَرٍ أَوْ جَذْوَةٍ مِّنَ النَّارِ لَعَلَّكُمْ
تَصْطَلُونَ ﴿٢٩﴾
فَلَمَّا أَتَاهَا نُودِيَ مِن شَاطِئِ الْوَادِ الْأَيْمَنِ فِي
الْبُقْعَةِ الْمُبَارَكَةِ مِنَ الشَّجَرَةِ أَن يَا مُوسَىٰ إِنِّي أَنَا
اللَّهُ رَبُّ الْعَالَمِينَ ﴿٣٠﴾
وَأَنْ أَلْقِ عَصَاكَ فَلَمَّا رَآهَا تَهْتَزُّ كَأَنَّهَا جَانٌّ
وَلَّىٰ مُدْبِرًا وَلَمْ يُعَقِّبْ يَا مُوسَىٰ أَقْبِلْ وَلَا تَخَفْ
إِنَّكَ مِنَ الْآمِنِينَ ﴿٣١﴾
اسْلُكْ يَدَكَ فِي جَيْبِكَ تَخْرُجْ بَيْضَاءَ مِنْ غَيْرِ سُوءٍ
وَاضْمُمْ إِلَيْكَ جَنَاحَكَ مِنَ الرَّهْبِ فَذَانِكَ
بُرْهَانَانِ مِن رَّبِّكَ إِلَىٰ فِرْعَوْنَ وَمَلَئِهِ إِنَّهُمْ كَانُوا
قَوْمًا فَاسِقِينَ ﴿٣٢﴾

33. He said: My Lord! Lo! I killed a man among them and I fear that they will kill me.

34. My brother Aaron is more eloquent than me in speech. Therefor send him with me as a helper to confirm me. Lo! I fear that they will give the lie to me.

35. He said: We will strengthen thine arm with thy brother, and We will give unto you both power so that they cannot reach you for Our portents. Ye twain, and those who follow you, will be the winners.

36. But when Moses came unto them with Our clear tokens, they said: This is naught but invented magic. We never heard of this among our fathers of old.

37. And Moses said: My Lord is best aware of him who bringeth guidance from His presence, and whose will be the sequel of the Home (of bliss). Lo! wrong-doers will not be successful.

38. And Pharaoh said: O chiefs! I know not that ye have a god other than me, so kindle for me (a fire), O Haman, to bake the mud; and set up for me a lofty tower in order that I may survey the god of Moses; and lo! I deem him of the liars.

39. And he and his hosts were haughty in the land without right, and deemed that they would never be brought back to Us.

40. Therefor We seized him and his hosts, and abandoned them unto the sea. Behold the nature of the consequence for evil-doers!

41. And We made them patterns that invite unto the Fire, and on the Day of Resurrection they will not be helped.

قَالَ رَبِّ اِنِّىۡ قَتَلۡتُ مِنۡهُمۡ نَفۡسًا فَاَخَافُ اَنۡ يَّقۡتُلُوۡنِ ۝٣٣

وَاَخِىۡ هٰرُوۡنُ هُوَ اَفۡصَحُ مِنِّىۡ لِسَانًا فَاَرۡسِلۡهُ مَعِىَ

رِدۡاً يُّصَدِّقُنِىۡۤ اِنِّىۡۤ اَخَافُ اَنۡ يُّكَذِّبُوۡنِ ۝٣٤

قَالَ سَنَشُدُّ عَضُدَكَ بِاَخِيۡكَ وَنَجۡعَلُ لَـكُمَا سُلۡطٰنًا

فَلَا يَصِلُوۡنَ اِلَيۡكُمَا ۚ بِاٰيٰتِنَاۤ ۚ اَنۡتُمَا وَمَنِ اتَّبَعَكُمَا

الۡغٰلِبُوۡنَ ۝٣٥

فَلَمَّا جَآءَهُمۡ مُّوۡسٰى بِاٰيٰتِنَا بَيِّنٰتٍ قَالُوۡا مَا هٰذَاۤ

اِلَّا سِحۡرٌ مُّفۡتَـرًى وَّمَا سَمِعۡنَا بِهٰذَا فِىۡۤ اٰبَآئِنَا

الۡاَوَّلِيۡنَ ۝٣٦

وَقَالَ مُوۡسٰى رَبِّىۡۤ اَعۡلَمُ بِمَنۡ جَآءَ بِالۡهُدٰى مِنۡ

عِنۡدِهٖ وَمَنۡ تَكُوۡنُ لَهٗ عَاقِبَةُ الدَّارِ ؕ اِنَّهٗ لَا يُفۡلِحُ

الظّٰلِمُوۡنَ ۝٣٧

وَقَالَ فِرۡعَوۡنُ يٰۤاَيُّهَا الۡمَلَاُ مَا عَلِمۡتُ لَـكُمۡ مِّنۡ

اِلٰهٍ غَيۡرِىۡ ۚ فَاَوۡقِدۡ لِىۡ يٰهَامٰنُ عَلَى الطِّيۡنِ فَاجۡعَلۡ

لِّىۡ صَرۡحًا لَّعَلِّىۡۤ اَطَّلِعُ اِلٰۤى اِلٰهِ مُوۡسٰى ۙ وَاِنِّىۡ

لَاَظُنُّهٗ مِنَ الۡكٰذِبِيۡنَ ۝٣٨

وَاسۡتَكۡبَرَ هُوَ وَجُنُوۡدُهٗ فِى الۡاَرۡضِ بِغَيۡرِ الۡحَـقِّ وَ

ظَنُّوۡۤا اَنَّهُمۡ اِلَيۡنَا لَا يُرۡجَعُوۡنَ ۝٣٩

فَاَخَذۡنٰهُ وَجُنُوۡدَهٗ فَنَبَذۡنٰهُمۡ فِى الۡيَمِّ ۚ فَانۡظُرۡ

كَيۡفَ كَانَ عَاقِبَةُ الظّٰلِمِيۡنَ ۝٤٠

وَجَعَلۡنٰهُمۡ اَئِمَّةً يَّدۡعُوۡنَ اِلَى النَّارِ ۚ وَيَوۡمَ الۡقِيٰمَةِ

لَا يُنۡصَرُوۡنَ ۝٤١

42. And We made a curse to follow them in this world, and on the Day of Resurrection they will be among the hateful.

43. And We verily gave the Scripture unto Moses after We had destroyed the generations of old; clear testimonies for mankind, and a guidance and a mercy, that haply they might reflect.

44. And thou (Muhammad) wast not on the western side (of the Mount) when We expounded unto Moses the commandment, and thou wast not among those present;

45. But We brought forth generations, and their lives dragged on for them. And thou wast not a dweller in Midian, reciting unto them Our revelations, but We kept sending (messengers to men).

46. And thou wast not beside the Mount when We did call; but (the knowledge of it is) a mercy from thy Lord that thou mayest warn a folk unto whom no warner came before thee, that haply they may give heed.

47. Otherwise, if disaster should afflict them because of that which their own hands have sent before (them), they might say: Our Lord! Why sentest Thou no messenger unto us, that we might have followed Thy revelations and been of the believers?

48. But when there came unto them the Truth from Our presence, they said: Why is he not given the like of what was given unto Moses? Did they not disbelieve in that which was given unto Moses of old? They say: Two magics[1] that support each other; and they say: Lo! in both we are disbelievers.

49. Say (unto them, O Muhammad): Then bring a Scripture from the presence of Allah that giveth clearer guidance than these two (that) I may follow it, if ye are truthful.

وَأَتْبَعْنٰهُمْ فِي هٰذِهِ الدُّنْيَا لَعْنَةً ۚ وَيَوْمَ الْقِيٰمَةِ هُمْ
مِّنَ الْمَقْبُوحِينَ ﴿٤٢﴾ ع ٤ ٧
وَلَقَدْ آتَيْنَا مُوسَى الْكِتٰبَ مِنْ بَعْدِ مَا أَهْلَكْنَا
الْقُرُونَ الْأُولٰى بَصَائِرَ لِلنَّاسِ وَهُدًى وَّرَحْمَةً
لَّعَلَّهُمْ يَتَذَكَّرُونَ ﴿٤٣﴾
وَمَا كُنْتَ بِجَانِبِ الْغَرْبِيِّ إِذْ قَضَيْنَا إِلٰى مُوسَى
الْأَمْرَ وَمَا كُنْتَ مِنَ الشّٰهِدِينَ ﴿٤٤﴾
وَلٰكِنَّا أَنْشَأْنَا قُرُونًا فَتَطَاوَلَ عَلَيْهِمُ الْعُمُرُ ۚ وَمَا
كُنْتَ ثَاوِيًا فِي أَهْلِ مَدْيَنَ تَتْلُوا عَلَيْهِمْ آيٰتِنَا ۙ
وَلٰكِنَّا كُنَّا مُرْسِلِينَ ﴿٤٥﴾
وَمَا كُنْتَ بِجَانِبِ الطُّورِ إِذْ نَادَيْنَا وَلٰكِنْ رَّحْمَةً مِّنْ
رَّبِّكَ لِتُنْذِرَ قَوْمًا مَّا أَتٰهُمْ مِّنْ نَّذِيرٍ مِّنْ قَبْلِكَ
لَعَلَّهُمْ يَتَذَكَّرُونَ ﴿٤٦﴾
وَلَوْلَا أَنْ تُصِيبَهُمْ مُّصِيبَةٌ بِمَا قَدَّمَتْ أَيْدِيهِمْ
فَيَقُولُوا رَبَّنَا لَوْلَا أَرْسَلْتَ إِلَيْنَا رَسُولًا فَنَتَّبِعَ آيٰتِكَ
وَنَكُونَ مِنَ الْمُؤْمِنِينَ ﴿٤٧﴾
فَلَمَّا جَاءَهُمُ الْحَقُّ مِنْ عِنْدِنَا قَالُوا لَوْلَا أُوتِيَ
مِثْلَ مَا أُوتِيَ مُوسَى ۚ أَوَلَمْ يَكْفُرُوا بِمَا أُوتِيَ مُوسَى
مِنْ قَبْلُ ۚ قَالُوا سِحْرٰنِ تَظٰهَرَا ۖ وَقَالُوا إِنَّا بِكُلٍّ
كٰفِرُونَ ﴿٤٨﴾
قُلْ فَأْتُوا بِكِتٰبٍ مِّنْ عِنْدِ اللّٰهِ هُوَ أَهْدٰى مِنْهُمَا
أَتَّبِعْهُ إِنْ كُنْتُمْ صٰدِقِينَ ﴿٤٩﴾

1. *i.e.* the Scripture of Moses and the Koran.

50. And if they answer thee not, then know that what they follow is their lusts. And who goeth farther astray than he who followeth his lust without guidance from Allah? Lo! Allah guideth not wrongdoing folk.

فإن لم يستجيبوا لك فاعلم أنما يتبعون أهواءهم
ومن أضل ممن اتبع هوىه بغير هدى من الله
إن الله لا يهدي القوم الظلمين ﴿٥٠﴾

51. And now verily We have caused the Word to reach them, that haply they may give heed.

ولقد وصلنا لهم القول لعلهم يتذكرون ﴿٥١﴾

52. Those unto whom We gave the Scripture before it, they believe in it.

الذين ءاتينهم الكتب من قبله هم به يؤمنون ﴿٥٢﴾

53. And when it is recited unto them, they say: We believe in it. Lo! it is the Truth from our Lord. Lo! even before it we were of those who surrender (unto Him).

وإذا يتلى عليهم قالوا ءامنا به إنه الحق من ربنا
إنا كنا من قبله مسلمين ﴿٥٣﴾

54. These will be given their reward twice over, because they are steadfast and repel evil with good, and spend of that wherewith We have provided them.

أولئك يؤتون أجرهم مرتين بما صبروا ويدرءون
بالحسنة السيئة ومما رزقنهم ينفقون ﴿٥٤﴾

55. And when they hear vanity, they withdraw from it and say: Unto us our works and unto you your works. Peace be unto you! We desire not the ignorant.

وإذا سمعوا اللغو أعرضوا عنه وقالوا لنا أعملنا
ولكم أعملكم سلم عليكم لا نبتغي الجهلين ﴿٥٥﴾

56. Lo! thou (O Muhammad) guidest not whom thou lovest, but Allah guideth whom He will. And He is best aware of those who walk aright.

إنك لا تهدي من أحببت ولكن الله يهدي من
يشاء وهو أعلم بالمهتدين ﴿٥٦﴾

57. And they say: If we were to follow the Guidance with thee we should be torn out of our land. Have We not established for them a sure sanctuary,[1] whereunto the produce of all things is brought (in trade), a provision from Our presence? But most of them know not.

وقالوا إن نتبع الهدى معك نتخطف من أرضنا
أولم نمكن لهم حرما ءامنا يجبى إليه ثمرت كل
شيء رزقا من لدنا ولكن أكثرهم لا يعلمون ﴿٥٧﴾

58. And how many a community have We destroyed that was thankless for its means of livelihood! And yonder are their dwellings, which have not been inhabited after them save a little. And We, even We, were the inheritors.

وكم أهلكنا من قرية بطرت معيشتها فتلك
مسكنهم لم تسكن من بعدهم إلا قليلا و
كنا نحن الورثين ﴿٥٨﴾

59. And never did thy Lord destroy the townships, till He had raised up in their mother (-town) a messenger reciting unto them Our revelations. And never did We destroy the townships unless the folk thereof were evil-doers.

وما كان ربك مهلك القرى حتى يبعث في أمها
رسولا يتلوا عليهم ءايتنا وما كنا مهلكي القرى إلا
وأهلها ظلمون ﴿٥٩﴾

1. The sacred territory of Mecca.

60. And whatsoever ye have been given is a comfort of the life of the world and an ornament thereof; and that which Allah hath is better and more lasting. Have ye then no sense?

61. Is he whom We have promised a fair promise which he will find (true) like him whom We suffer to enjoy awhile the comfort of the life of the world, then on the Day of Resurrection he will be of those arraigned?

62. On the Day when He will call unto them and say: Where are My 'partners whom ye imagined?

63. Those concerning whom the Word will have come true will say: Our Lord! These are they whom we led astray. We led them astray even as we ourselves were astray. We declare our innocence before Thee: us they never worshipped.

64. And it will be said: Cry unto your (so-called) partners (of Allah). And they will cry unto them, and they will give no answer unto them, and they will see the Doom. Ah, if they had but been guided!

65. And on the Day when He will call unto them and say: What answer gave ye to the messengers?

66. On that Day (all) tidings will be dimmed for them, nor will they ask one of another.

67. But as for him who shall repent and believe and do right, he haply may be one of the successful.

68. Thy Lord bringeth to pass what He willeth and chooseth. They have never any choice. Glorified be Allah and exalted above all that they associate (with Him)!

69. And thy Lord knoweth what their breasts conceal, and what they publish.

70. And He is Allah; there is no God save Him. His is all praise in the former and the latter (state), and His is the command, and unto Him ye will be brought back.

وَمَآ أُوتِيتُم مِّن شَيْءٍ فَمَتَاعُ الْحَيٰوةِ الدُّنْيَا وَ
زِينَتُهَا ۚ وَمَا عِندَ اللّٰهِ خَيْرٌ وَّأَبْقَىٰ ۚ أَفَلَا تَعْقِلُونَ ﴿٦٠﴾ ع ٦ ٩
أَفَمَن وَّعَدْنٰهُ وَعْدًا حَسَنًا فَهُوَ لَاقِيهِ كَمَن مَّتَّعْنٰهُ
مَتَاعَ الْحَيٰوةِ الدُّنْيَا ثُمَّ هُوَ يَوْمَ الْقِيٰمَةِ مِنَ الْمُحْضَرِينَ ﴿٦١﴾
وَيَوْمَ يُنَادِيهِمْ فَيَقُولُ أَيْنَ شُرَكَآءِيَ الَّذِينَ
كُنتُمْ تَزْعُمُونَ ﴿٦٢﴾
قَالَ الَّذِينَ حَقَّ عَلَيْهِمُ الْقَوْلُ رَبَّنَا هٰٓؤُلَآءِ الَّذِينَ
أَغْوَيْنَا ۚ أَغْوَيْنٰهُمْ كَمَا غَوَيْنَا ۚ تَبَرَّأْنَآ إِلَيْكَ ۖ مَا
كَانُوٓا إِيَّانَا يَعْبُدُونَ ﴿٦٣﴾
وَقِيلَ ادْعُوا شُرَكَآءَكُمْ فَدَعَوْهُمْ فَلَمْ
يَسْتَجِيبُوا لَهُمْ وَرَأَوُا الْعَذَابَ ۚ لَوْ أَنَّهُمْ كَانُوا
يَهْتَدُونَ ﴿٦٤﴾
وَيَوْمَ يُنَادِيهِمْ فَيَقُولُ مَاذَآ أَجَبْتُمُ الْمُرْسَلِينَ ﴿٦٥﴾
فَعَمِيَتْ عَلَيْهِمُ الْأَنۢبَآءُ يَوْمَئِذٍ فَهُمْ لَا
يَتَسَآءَلُونَ ﴿٦٦﴾
فَأَمَّا مَن تَابَ وَاٰمَنَ وَعَمِلَ صَالِحًا فَعَسٰٓى أَن
يَّكُونَ مِنَ الْمُفْلِحِينَ ﴿٦٧﴾
وَرَبُّكَ يَخْلُقُ مَا يَشَآءُ وَيَخْتَارُ ۗ مَا كَانَ لَهُمُ الْخِيَرَةُ ۚ
سُبْحٰنَ اللّٰهِ وَتَعٰلَىٰ عَمَّا يُشْرِكُونَ ﴿٦٨﴾
وَرَبُّكَ يَعْلَمُ مَا تُكِنُّ صُدُورُهُمْ وَمَا يُعْلِنُونَ ﴿٦٩﴾
وَهُوَ اللّٰهُ لَآ إِلٰهَ إِلَّا هُوَ ۖ لَهُ الْحَمْدُ فِي الْأُولَىٰ وَ
الْاٰخِرَةِ ۖ وَلَهُ الْحُكْمُ وَإِلَيْهِ تُرْجَعُونَ ﴿٧٠﴾

71. Say: Have ye thought, if Allah made night everlasting for you till the Day of Resurrection, who is a God beside Allah who could bring you light? Will ye not then hear?

قُلْ أَرَءَيْتُمْ إِن جَعَلَ اللّٰهُ عَلَيْكُمُ الَّيْلَ سَرْمَدًا
إِلَىٰ يَوْمِ الْقِيٰمَةِ مَنْ إِلٰهٌ غَيْرُ اللّٰهِ يَأْتِيكُم بِضِيَآءٍ
أَفَلَا تَسْمَعُونَ ﴿٧١﴾

72. Say: Have ye thought, if Allah made day everlasting for you till the Day of Resurrection, who is a God beside Allah who could bring you night wherein ye rest? Will ye not then see?

قُلْ أَرَءَيْتُمْ إِن جَعَلَ اللّٰهُ عَلَيْكُمُ النَّهَارَ سَرْمَدًا إِلَىٰ
يَوْمِ الْقِيٰمَةِ مَنْ إِلٰهٌ غَيْرُ اللّٰهِ يَأْتِيكُم بِلَيْلٍ
تَسْكُنُونَ فِيهِ أَفَلَا تُبْصِرُونَ ﴿٧٢﴾

73. Of His mercy hath He appointed for you night and day, that therein ye may rest, and that ye may seek His bounty, and that haply ye may be thankful.

وَمِن رَّحْمَتِهِ جَعَلَ لَكُمُ الَّيْلَ وَالنَّهَارَ
لِتَسْكُنُوا فِيهِ وَلِتَبْتَغُوا مِن فَضْلِهِ وَلَعَلَّكُمْ
تَشْكُرُونَ ﴿٧٣﴾

74. And on the Day when He shall call unto them and say: Where are My partners whom ye pretended?

وَيَوْمَ يُنَادِيهِمْ فَيَقُولُ أَيْنَ شُرَكَآءِيَ الَّذِينَ
كُنتُمْ تَزْعُمُونَ ﴿٧٤﴾

75. And We shall take out from every nation a witness and We shall say: Bring your proof. Then they will know that Allah hath the Truth, and all that they invented will have failed them.

وَنَزَعْنَا مِن كُلِّ أُمَّةٍ شَهِيدًا فَقُلْنَا هَاتُوا بُرْهَانَكُمْ
فَعَلِمُوا أَنَّ الْحَقَّ لِلّٰهِ وَضَلَّ عَنْهُم مَّا كَانُوا
يَفْتَرُونَ ﴿٧٥﴾ ع

76. Now Korah was of Moses' folk, but he oppressed them; and We gave him so much treasure that the stores thereof would verily have been a burden for a troop of mighty men. When his own folk said unto him: Exult not; lo! Allah loveth not the exultant;

إِنَّ قَارُونَ كَانَ مِن قَوْمِ مُوسَىٰ فَبَغَىٰ عَلَيْهِمْ وَ
ءَاتَيْنَٰهُ مِنَ الْكُنُوزِ مَا إِنَّ مَفَاتِحَهُ لَتَنُوٓأُ بِالْعُصْبَةِ
أُولِي الْقُوَّةِ إِذْ قَالَ لَهُ قَوْمُهُ لَا تَفْرَحْ إِنَّ اللّٰهَ
لَا يُحِبُّ الْفَرِحِينَ ﴿٧٦﴾

77. But seek the abode of the Hereafter in that which Allah hath given thee and neglect not thy portion of the world, and be thou kind even as Allah hath been kind to thee, and seek not corruption in the earth; lo! Allah loveth not corrupters,

وَابْتَغِ فِيمَآ ءَاتَىٰكَ اللّٰهُ الدَّارَ الْءَاخِرَةَ وَلَا تَنسَ
نَصِيبَكَ مِنَ الدُّنْيَا وَأَحْسِن كَمَآ أَحْسَنَ اللّٰهُ
إِلَيْكَ وَلَا تَبْغِ الْفَسَادَ فِي الْأَرْضِ إِنَّ اللّٰهَ لَا يُحِبُّ
الْمُفْسِدِينَ ﴿٧٧﴾

78. **He said**: I have been given it only on account of knowledge I possess. Knew he not that Allah had destroyed already of the generation before him men who were mightier than him in strength and greater in respect of following? The guilty are not questioned of their sins.

79. Then went he forth before his people in his pomp. Those who were desirous of the life of the world said: Ah, would that unto us had been given the like of what hath been given unto Korah! Lo! he is lord of rare good fortune.

80. But those who had been given knowledge said. Woe unto you! the reward of Allah for him who believeth and doth right is better, and only the steadfast will obtain it.

81. So we caused the earth to swallow him and his dwelling place. Then he had no host to help him against Allah , nor was he of those who can save themselves.

82. And morning found those who had coveted his place but yesterday crying: Ah, welladay! Allah enlargeth the provision for whom He will of His slaves and straiteneth it (for whom He will). If Allah had not been gracious unto us He would have caused it to swallow us (also). Ah, welladay! The disbelievers never prosper.

83. As for that abode of the Hereafter We assign it unto those who seek not oppression in the earth, nor yet corruption. The sequel is for those who ward off (evil).

84. Whoso bringeth a good deed, he will have better than the same; while as for him who bringeth an ill deed, those who do ill deeds will be requited only what they did.

85. Lo! He who hath given thee the Qur'an for a law will surely bring thee home again.[1] Say: My Lord is best aware of him who bringeth guidance and him who is in error manifest.

قَالَ إِنَّمَآ أُوتِيتُهُۥ عَلَىٰ عِلْمٍ عِندِىٓ ۚ أَوَلَمْ يَعْلَمْ أَنَّ
ٱللَّهَ قَدْ أَهْلَكَ مِن قَبْلِهِۦ مِنَ ٱلْقُرُونِ مَنْ هُوَ أَشَدُّ
مِنْهُ قُوَّةً وَأَكْثَرُ جَمْعًا ۚ وَلَا يُسْـَٔلُ عَن ذُنُوبِهِمُ
ٱلْمُجْرِمُونَ ﴿٧٨﴾
فَخَرَجَ عَلَىٰ قَوْمِهِۦ فِى زِينَتِهِۦ ۖ قَالَ ٱلَّذِينَ يُرِيدُونَ
ٱلْحَيَوٰةَ ٱلدُّنْيَا يَـٰلَيْتَ لَنَا مِثْلَ مَآ أُوتِىَ قَـٰرُونُ
إِنَّهُۥ لَذُو حَظٍّ عَظِيمٍ ﴿٧٩﴾
وَقَالَ ٱلَّذِينَ أُوتُوا۟ ٱلْعِلْمَ وَيْلَكُمْ ثَوَابُ ٱللَّهِ خَيْرٌ لِّمَنْ
ءَامَنَ وَعَمِلَ صَـٰلِحًا ۚ وَلَا يُلَقَّىٰهَآ إِلَّا ٱلصَّـٰبِرُونَ ﴿٨٠﴾
فَخَسَفْنَا بِهِۦ وَبِدَارِهِ ٱلْأَرْضَ فَمَا كَانَ لَهُۥ مِن فِئَةٍ
يَنصُرُونَهُۥ مِن دُونِ ٱللَّهِ وَمَا كَانَ مِنَ ٱلْمُنتَصِرِينَ ﴿٨١﴾
وَأَصْبَحَ ٱلَّذِينَ تَمَنَّوْا۟ مَكَانَهُۥ بِٱلْأَمْسِ يَقُولُونَ وَيْكَأَنَّ
ٱللَّهَ يَبْسُطُ ٱلرِّزْقَ لِمَن يَشَآءُ مِنْ عِبَادِهِۦ وَيَقْدِرُ ۖ
لَوْلَآ أَن مَّنَّ ٱللَّهُ عَلَيْنَا لَخَسَفَ بِنَا ۖ وَيْكَأَنَّهُۥ لَا يُفْلِحُ
ٱلْكَـٰفِرُونَ ﴿٨٢﴾ ع
تِلْكَ ٱلدَّارُ ٱلْءَاخِرَةُ نَجْعَلُهَا لِلَّذِينَ لَا يُرِيدُونَ عُلُوًّا
فِى ٱلْأَرْضِ وَلَا فَسَادًا ۚ وَٱلْعَـٰقِبَةُ لِلْمُتَّقِينَ ﴿٨٣﴾
مَن جَآءَ بِٱلْحَسَنَةِ فَلَهُۥ خَيْرٌ مِّنْهَا ۖ وَمَن جَآءَ بِٱلسَّيِّئَةِ
فَلَا يُجْزَى ٱلَّذِينَ عَمِلُوا۟ ٱلسَّيِّـَٔاتِ إِلَّا مَا كَانُوا۟ يَعْمَلُونَ ﴿٨٤﴾
إِنَّ ٱلَّذِى فَرَضَ عَلَيْكَ ٱلْقُرْءَانَ لَرَآدُّكَ إِلَىٰ مَعَادٍ ۚ
قُل رَّبِّىٓ أَعْلَمُ مَن جَآءَ بِٱلْهُدَىٰ وَمَنْ هُوَ فِى
ضَلَـٰلٍ مُّبِينٍ ﴿٨٥﴾

1. A tradition says that this verse was revealed during the prophet's flight from Makkah to Al-Madinah.

86. Thou hadst no hope that the Scripture would be inspired in thee; but it is a mercy from thy Lord, so never be a helper to the disbelievers.

87. And let them not divert thee from the revelations of Allah after they have been sent down unto thee; but call (mankind) unto thy Lord, and be not of those who ascribe partners (unto Him).

88. And cry not unto any other god along with Allah. There is no God save him. Everything will perish save His countenance. His is the command, and unto Him ye will be brought back.

وَمَا كُنْتَ تَرْجُوْٓا اَنْ يُّلْقٰٓى اِلَيْكَ الْكِتٰبُ اِلَّا رَحْمَةً
مِّنْ رَّبِّكَ فَلَا تَكُوْنَنَّ ظَهِيْرًا لِّلْكٰفِرِيْنَ ﴿٨٦﴾
وَلَا يَصُدُّنَّكَ عَنْ اٰيٰتِ اللّٰهِ بَعْدَ اِذْ اُنْزِلَتْ اِلَيْكَ
وَادْعُ اِلٰى رَبِّكَ وَلَا تَكُوْنَنَّ مِنَ الْمُشْرِكِيْنَ ﴿٨٧﴾
وَلَا تَدْعُ مَعَ اللّٰهِ اِلٰهًا اٰخَرَ لَآ اِلٰهَ اِلَّا هُوَ كُلُّ شَيْءٍ
هَالِكٌ اِلَّا وَجْهَهٗ لَهُ الْحُكْمُ وَاِلَيْهِ تُرْجَعُوْنَ ﴿٨٨﴾

Al-'Ankabūt, "The Spider," takes its name from v. 41 where false beliefs are likened to the spider's web for frailty. Most of this Sūrah belongs to the middle or last Meccan period. Some authorities consider vv. 7 and 8, others the whole latter portion of the Sūrah,[1] to have been revealed at Al-Madînah. It gives comfort to the Muslims in a time of persecution.

A late Meccan Sūrah.

1. *An-Nāsikh wal-Mansūkh* by Ibn Salāmah.

THE SPIDER

Revealed at Mecca

In the name of Allah, the Beneficent, the Merciful.

1. Alif. Lām. Mīm.[1]

2. Do men imagine that they will be left (at ease) because they say, We believe, and will not be tested with affliction?

3. Lo! We tested those who were before you. Thus Allah knoweth those who are sincere, and knoweth those who feign.

4. Or do those who do ill-deeds imagine that they can outstrip Us? Evil (for them) is that which they decide.

5. Whoso looketh forward to the meeting with Allah (let him know that) Allah's reckoning is surely nigh, and He is the Hearer, the Knower.

6. And Whosoever striveth, striveth only for himself, for lo! Allah is altogether Independent of (His) creatures.

7. And as for those who believe and do good works, We shall remit from them their evil deeds and shall repay them the best for that they did.

8. We have enjoined on man kindness to parents; but if they strive to make thee join with Me that of which thou hast no knowledge, then obey them not. Unto Me is your return and I shall tell you what ye used to do.

9. And as for those who believe and do good works, We verily shall make them enter in among the righteous.

1. See Sūr. II, v. 1, footnote.

آياتها ٦٩ (٢٩) سُورَةُ الْعَنْكَبُوتِ مَكِّيَّةٌ رُكُوعَاتُهَا ٧

بِسْمِ اللّٰهِ الرَّحْمٰنِ الرَّحِيْمِ ○

الٓمّٓ ﴿١﴾

أَحَسِبَ النَّاسُ أَنْ يُتْرَكُوا أَنْ يَقُولُوا آمَنَّا وَهُمْ
لَا يُفْتَنُونَ ﴿٢﴾

وَلَقَدْ فَتَنَّا الَّذِينَ مِنْ قَبْلِهِمْ فَلَيَعْلَمَنَّ اللّٰهُ
الَّذِينَ صَدَقُوا وَلَيَعْلَمَنَّ الْكٰذِبِينَ ﴿٣﴾

أَمْ حَسِبَ الَّذِينَ يَعْمَلُونَ السَّيِّاٰتِ أَنْ يَّسْبِقُونَا
سَآءَ مَا يَحْكُمُونَ ﴿٤﴾

مَنْ كَانَ يَرْجُوا لِقَآءَ اللّٰهِ فَإِنَّ أَجَلَ اللّٰهِ لَاٰتٍ
وَهُوَ السَّمِيعُ الْعَلِيمُ ﴿٥﴾

وَمَنْ جَاهَدَ فَإِنَّمَا يُجَاهِدُ لِنَفْسِهٖ إِنَّ اللّٰهَ لَغَنِيٌّ
عَنِ الْعٰلَمِينَ ﴿٦﴾

وَالَّذِينَ اٰمَنُوا وَعَمِلُوا الصّٰلِحٰتِ لَنُكَفِّرَنَّ عَنْهُمْ
سَيِّاٰتِهِمْ وَلَنَجْزِيَنَّهُمْ أَحْسَنَ الَّذِي كَانُوا
يَعْمَلُونَ ﴿٧﴾

وَوَصَّيْنَا الْإِنْسَانَ بِوَالِدَيْهِ حُسْنًا وَإِنْ جَاهَدٰكَ
لِتُشْرِكَ بِي مَا لَيْسَ لَكَ بِهٖ عِلْمٌ فَلَا تُطِعْهُمَا إِلَيَّ
مَرْجِعُكُمْ فَأُنَبِّئُكُمْ بِمَا كُنْتُمْ تَعْمَلُونَ ﴿٨﴾

وَالَّذِينَ اٰمَنُوا وَعَمِلُوا الصّٰلِحٰتِ لَنُدْخِلَنَّهُمْ فِي
الصّٰلِحِينَ ﴿٩﴾

10. Of mankind is he who saith: We believe in Allah, but, if he be made to suffer for the sake of Allah, he mistaketh the persecution of mankind for Allah's punishment; and then, if victory cometh from thy Lord, will say: Lo! we were with you (all the while). Is not Allah best aware of what is in the bosoms of (His) creatures?

11. Verily Allah knoweth those who believe, and verily He knoweth the hypocrites.

12. Those who disbelieve say unto those who believe: Follow our way (of religion) and we verily will bear your sins (for you). They cannot bear aught of their sins. Lo! they verily are liars.

13. But they verily will bear their own loads and other loads beside their own, and they verily will be questioned on the Day of Resurrection concerning that which they invented.

14. And verily We sent Noah (as Our messenger) unto his folk, and he continued with them for a thousand years save fifty years; and the flood engulfed them, for they were wrongdoers.

15. And We rescued him and those with him in the ship, and made of it a portent for the peoples.

16. And Abraham! (Remember) when he said unto his folk: Serve Allah, and keep your duty unto Him; that is better for you if ye did but know.

17. Ye serve instead of Allah only idols, and ye only invent a lie. Lo! those whom ye serve instead of Allah own no provision for you. So seek your provision from Allah, and serve Him, and give thanks unto Him, (for) unto Him ye will be brought back.

18. But if ye deny, then nations have denied before you. The messenger is only to convey (the Message) plainly.

وَمِنَ النَّاسِ مَنْ يَّقُوْلُ اٰمَنَّا بِاللّٰهِ فَاِذَآ اُوْذِيَ فِي اللّٰهِ
جَعَلَ فِتْنَةَ النَّاسِ كَعَذَابِ اللّٰهِ ؕ وَلَئِنْ جَآءَ نَصْرٌ
مِّنْ رَّبِّكَ لَيَقُوْلُنَّ اِنَّا كُنَّا مَعَكُمْ ؕ اَوَلَيْسَ اللّٰهُ بِاَعْلَمَ
بِمَا فِيْ صُدُوْرِ الْعٰلَمِيْنَ ﴿١٠﴾
وَلَيَعْلَمَنَّ اللّٰهُ الَّذِيْنَ اٰمَنُوْا وَلَيَعْلَمَنَّ الْمُنٰفِقِيْنَ ﴿١١﴾
وَقَالَ الَّذِيْنَ كَفَرُوْا لِلَّذِيْنَ اٰمَنُوا اتَّبِعُوْا سَبِيْلَنَا
وَلْنَحْمِلْ خَطٰيٰكُمْ ؕ وَمَا هُمْ بِحٰمِلِيْنَ مِنْ خَطٰيٰهُمْ
مِّنْ شَيْءٍ ؕ اِنَّهُمْ لَكٰذِبُوْنَ ﴿١٢﴾
وَلَيَحْمِلُنَّ اَثْقَالَهُمْ وَاَثْقَالًا مَّعَ اَثْقَالِهِمْ ؗ وَلَيُسْـَٔلُنَّ
يَوْمَ الْقِيٰمَةِ عَمَّا كَانُوْا يَفْتَرُوْنَ ﴿١٣﴾ ع ١٢
وَلَقَدْ اَرْسَلْنَا نُوْحًا اِلٰى قَوْمِهٖ فَلَبِثَ فِيْهِمْ اَلْفَ
سَنَةٍ اِلَّا خَمْسِيْنَ عَامًا ؕ فَاَخَذَهُمُ الطُّوْفَانُ وَ
هُمْ ظٰلِمُوْنَ ﴿١٤﴾
فَاَنْجَيْنٰهُ وَاَصْحٰبَ السَّفِيْنَةِ وَجَعَلْنٰهَآ اٰيَةً لِّلْعٰلَمِيْنَ ﴿١٥﴾
وَاِبْرٰهِيْمَ اِذْ قَالَ لِقَوْمِهِ اعْبُدُوا اللّٰهَ وَاتَّقُوْهُ ؕ
ذٰلِكُمْ خَيْرٌ لَّكُمْ اِنْ كُنْتُمْ تَعْلَمُوْنَ ﴿١٦﴾
اِنَّمَا تَعْبُدُوْنَ مِنْ دُوْنِ اللّٰهِ اَوْثَانًا وَّتَخْلُقُوْنَ اِفْكًا ؕ
اِنَّ الَّذِيْنَ تَعْبُدُوْنَ مِنْ دُوْنِ اللّٰهِ لَا يَمْلِكُوْنَ لَكُمْ
رِزْقًا فَابْتَغُوْا عِنْدَ اللّٰهِ الرِّزْقَ وَاعْبُدُوْهُ وَاشْكُرُوْا
لَهٗ ؕ اِلَيْهِ تُرْجَعُوْنَ ﴿١٧﴾
وَاِنْ تُكَذِّبُوْا فَقَدْ كَذَّبَ اُمَمٌ مِّنْ قَبْلِكُمْ ؕ وَمَا عَلَى
الرَّسُوْلِ اِلَّا الْبَلٰغُ الْمُبِيْنُ ﴿١٨﴾

19. See they not how Allah produceth creation, then reproduceth it? Lo! for Allah that is easy.

20. Say (O Muhammad): Travel in the land and see how He originated creation, then Allah bringeth forth the late growth. Lo! Allah is Able to do all things.

21. He punisheth whom He will and showeth mercy unto whom He will, and unto Him ye will be turned.

22. Ye cannot escape (from Him) in the earth or in the sky, and beside Allah there is for you no friend nor helper.

23. Those who disbelieve in the revelations of Allah and in (their) meeting with Him, such have no hope of My mercy. For such there is a painful doom.

24. But the answer of his folk was only that they said: "Kill him" or "Burn him." Then Allah saved him from the fire. Lo! herein verily are portents for folk who believe.

25. He said: Ye have chosen idols instead of Allah. The love between you is only in the life of the world. Then on the Day of Resurrection ye will deny each other and curse each other, and your abode will be the Fire, and ye will have no helpers.

26. And Lot believed him, and said: Lo! I am a fugitive unto my Lord. Lo! He, only He, is the Mighty, the Wise.

27. And We bestowed on him Isaac and Jacob, and We established the Prophethood and the Scripture among his seed, and We gave him his reward in the world, and lo! in the Hereafter he verily is among the righteous.

أَوَلَمْ يَرَوْا كَيْفَ يُبْدِئُ اللّٰهُ الْخَلْقَ ثُمَّ يُعِيدُهُ ط
إِنَّ ذٰلِكَ عَلَى اللّٰهِ يَسِيرٌ ﴿١٩﴾
قُلْ سِيرُوا فِي الْأَرْضِ فَانْظُرُوا كَيْفَ بَدَأَ الْخَلْقَ
ثُمَّ اللّٰهُ يُنْشِئُ النَّشْأَةَ الْآخِرَةَ إِنَّ اللّٰهَ عَلٰى كُلِّ
شَيْءٍ قَدِيرٌ ﴿٢٠﴾
يُعَذِّبُ مَنْ يَشَاءُ وَيَرْحَمُ مَنْ يَشَاءُ وَإِلَيْهِ تُقْلَبُونَ ﴿٢١﴾
وَمَا أَنْتُمْ بِمُعْجِزِينَ فِي الْأَرْضِ وَلَا فِي السَّمَاءِ وَ
مَا لَكُمْ مِنْ دُونِ اللّٰهِ مِنْ وَلِيٍّ وَلَا نَصِيرٍ ﴿٢٢﴾
وَالَّذِينَ كَفَرُوا بِآيَاتِ اللّٰهِ وَلِقَائِهِ أُولٰئِكَ يَئِسُوا
مِنْ رَحْمَتِي وَأُولٰئِكَ لَهُمْ عَذَابٌ أَلِيمٌ ﴿٢٣﴾
فَمَا كَانَ جَوَابَ قَوْمِهِ إِلَّا أَنْ قَالُوا اقْتُلُوهُ أَوْ حَرِّقُوهُ
فَأَنْجَاهُ اللّٰهُ مِنَ النَّارِ إِنَّ فِي ذٰلِكَ لَآيَاتٍ لِقَوْمٍ
يُؤْمِنُونَ ﴿٢٤﴾
وَقَالَ إِنَّمَا اتَّخَذْتُمْ مِنْ دُونِ اللّٰهِ أَوْثَانًا مَوَدَّةَ
بَيْنِكُمْ فِي الْحَيٰوةِ الدُّنْيَا ثُمَّ يَوْمَ الْقِيٰمَةِ يَكْفُرُ
بَعْضُكُمْ بِبَعْضٍ وَيَلْعَنُ بَعْضُكُمْ بَعْضًا وَمَأْوٰىكُمُ
النَّارُ وَمَا لَكُمْ مِنْ نٰصِرِينَ ﴿٢٥﴾
فَآمَنَ لَهُ لُوطٌ وَقَالَ إِنِّي مُهَاجِرٌ إِلٰى رَبِّي إِنَّهُ هُوَ
الْعَزِيزُ الْحَكِيمُ ﴿٢٦﴾
وَوَهَبْنَا لَهُ إِسْحٰقَ وَيَعْقُوبَ وَجَعَلْنَا فِي ذُرِّيَّتِهِ
النُّبُوَّةَ وَالْكِتٰبَ وَآتَيْنٰهُ أَجْرَهُ فِي الدُّنْيَا وَإِنَّهُ فِي
الْآخِرَةِ لَمِنَ الصّٰلِحِينَ ﴿٢٧﴾

28. And Lot! (Remember) when he said unto his folk: Lo! ye commit lewdness such as no creature did before you.

29. For come ye not in unto males, and cut ye not the road (for travellers), and commit ye not abomination in your meetings? But the answer of his folk was only that they said: Bring Allah's doom upon us if thou art a truth-teller!

30. He said: My Lord! Give me victory over folk who work corruption.

31. And when Our messengers brought Abraham the good news, they said:[1] Lo! we are about to destroy the people of that township, for its people are wrongdoers.

32. He said: Lo! Lot is there. They said: We are best aware of who is there. We are to deliver him and his household, all save his wife, who is of those who stay behind.

33. And when Our messengers came unto Lot, he was troubled upon their account, for he could not protect them; but they said: Fear not, nor grieve! Lo! we are to deliver thee and thy household, (all) save thy wife, who is of those who stay behind.

34. Lo! we are about to bring down upon folk of this township a fury from the sky because they are evil-livers.

35. And verily of that We have left a clear sign for people who have sense.

36. And unto Midian We sent Shu'eyb, their brother. He said: O my people! Serve Allah, and look forward to the Last Day, and do not evil, making mischief in the earth.

وَلُوطًا إِذْ قَالَ لِقَوْمِهِ إِنَّكُمْ لَتَأْتُونَ الْفَاحِشَةَ مَا
سَبَقَكُمْ بِهَا مِنْ أَحَدٍ مِنَ الْعَالَمِينَ ﴿٢٨﴾
أَئِنَّكُمْ لَتَأْتُونَ الرِّجَالَ وَتَقْطَعُونَ السَّبِيلَ وَ
تَأْتُونَ فِي نَادِيكُمُ الْمُنْكَرَ فَمَا كَانَ جَوَابَ قَوْمِهِ
إِلَّا أَنْ قَالُوا ائْتِنَا بِعَذَابِ اللَّهِ إِنْ كُنْتَ مِنَ
الصَّادِقِينَ ﴿٢٩﴾
ع قَالَ رَبِّ انْصُرْنِي عَلَى الْقَوْمِ الْمُفْسِدِينَ ﴿٣٠﴾
وَلَمَّا جَاءَتْ رُسُلُنَا إِبْرَاهِيمَ بِالْبُشْرَى قَالُوا إِنَّا
مُهْلِكُو أَهْلِ هَذِهِ الْقَرْيَةِ إِنَّ أَهْلَهَا كَانُوا
ظَالِمِينَ ﴿٣١﴾
قَالَ إِنَّ فِيهَا لُوطًا قَالُوا نَحْنُ أَعْلَمُ بِمَنْ فِيهَا
لَنُنَجِّيَنَّهُ وَأَهْلَهُ إِلَّا امْرَأَتَهُ كَانَتْ مِنَ
الْغَابِرِينَ ﴿٣٢﴾
وَلَمَّا أَنْ جَاءَتْ رُسُلُنَا لُوطًا سِيءَ بِهِمْ وَضَاقَ بِهِمْ
ذَرْعًا وَقَالُوا لَا تَخَفْ وَلَا تَحْزَنْ إِنَّا مُنَجُّوكَ وَأَهْلَكَ
إِلَّا امْرَأَتَكَ كَانَتْ مِنَ الْغَابِرِينَ ﴿٣٣﴾
إِنَّا مُنْزِلُونَ عَلَى أَهْلِ هَذِهِ الْقَرْيَةِ رِجْزًا مِنَ
السَّمَاءِ بِمَا كَانُوا يَفْسُقُونَ ﴿٣٤﴾
وَلَقَدْ تَرَكْنَا مِنْهَا آيَةً بَيِّنَةً لِقَوْمٍ يَعْقِلُونَ ﴿٣٥﴾
وَإِلَى مَدْيَنَ أَخَاهُمْ شُعَيْبًا فَقَالَ يَا قَوْمِ اعْبُدُوا
اللَّهَ وَارْجُوا الْيَوْمَ الْآخِرَ وَلَا تَعْثَوْا فِي الْأَرْضِ
مُفْسِدِينَ ﴿٣٦﴾

1. That he was to have a son.

37. But they denied him, and the dreadful earthquake took them, and morning found them prostrate in their dwelling-place!

فَكَذَّبُوهُ فَأَخَذَتْهُمُ الرَّجْفَةُ فَأَصْبَحُوا فِي دَارِهِمْ
جَاثِمِينَ ٣٧

38. And (the tribes of) 'Aād and Thamūd! (Their fate) is manifest unto you from their (ruined and deserted) dwellings. Satan made their deeds seem fair unto them and so debarred them from the Way, though they were keen observers.

وَعَادًا وَثَمُودَا وَقَدْ تَبَيَّنَ لَكُمْ مِنْ مَسَاكِنِهِمْ وَزَيَّنَ
لَهُمُ الشَّيْطَانُ أَعْمَالَهُمْ فَصَدَّهُمْ عَنِ السَّبِيلِ
وَكَانُوا مُسْتَبْصِرِينَ ٣٨

39. And Korah, Pharaoh and Haman! Moses came unto them with clear proofs (of Allah's sovereignty), but they were boastful in the land. And they were not winners (in the race).

وَقَارُونَ وَفِرْعَوْنَ وَهَامَانَ وَلَقَدْ جَاءَهُمْ مُوسَىٰ
بِالْبَيِّنَاتِ فَاسْتَكْبَرُوا فِي الْأَرْضِ وَمَا كَانُوا سَابِقِينَ ٣٩

40. So We took each one in his sin; of them was he on whom We sent a hurricane, and of them was he who was overtaken by the (Awful) Cry, and of them was he whom We caused the earth to swallow, and of them was he whom We drowned. It was not for Allah to wrong them, but they wronged themselves.

فَكُلًّا أَخَذْنَا بِذَنْبِهِ فَمِنْهُمْ مَنْ أَرْسَلْنَا عَلَيْهِ حَاصِبًا
وَمِنْهُمْ مَنْ أَخَذَتْهُ الصَّيْحَةُ وَمِنْهُمْ مَنْ خَسَفْنَا
بِهِ الْأَرْضَ وَمِنْهُمْ مَنْ أَغْرَقْنَا وَمَا كَانَ اللَّهُ
لِيَظْلِمَهُمْ وَلَٰكِنْ كَانُوا أَنْفُسَهُمْ يَظْلِمُونَ ٤٠

41. The likeness of those who choose other patrons than Allah is as the likeness of the spider when she taketh unto herself a house, and lo! the frailest of all houses is the spider's house, if they but knew.

مَثَلُ الَّذِينَ اتَّخَذُوا مِنْ دُونِ اللَّهِ أَوْلِيَاءَ كَمَثَلِ
الْعَنْكَبُوتِ اتَّخَذَتْ بَيْتًا وَإِنَّ أَوْهَنَ الْبُيُوتِ
لَبَيْتُ الْعَنْكَبُوتِ لَوْ كَانُوا يَعْلَمُونَ ٤١

42. Lo! Allah knoweth what thing they invoke instead of Him. He is the Mighty, the Wise.

إِنَّ اللَّهَ يَعْلَمُ مَا يَدْعُونَ مِنْ دُونِهِ مِنْ شَيْءٍ
وَهُوَ الْعَزِيزُ الْحَكِيمُ ٤٢

43. As for these similitudes, We coin them for mankind, but none will grasp their meaning save the wise.

وَتِلْكَ الْأَمْثَالُ نَضْرِبُهَا لِلنَّاسِ وَمَا يَعْقِلُهَا إِلَّا الْعَالِمُونَ ٤٣

44. Allah created the heavens and the earth with truth. Lo! therein is indeed a portent for believers.

خَلَقَ اللَّهُ السَّمَاوَاتِ وَالْأَرْضَ بِالْحَقِّ إِنَّ فِي ذَٰلِكَ
لَآيَةً لِلْمُؤْمِنِينَ ٤٤

45. Recite that which hath been inspired in thee of the Scripture, and establish worship. Lo! worship preserveth from lewdness and iniquity, but verily remembrance of Allah is more important. And Allah knoweth what ye do.

اتْلُ مَا أُوحِيَ إِلَيْكَ مِنَ الْكِتَابِ وَأَقِمِ الصَّلَاةَ
إِنَّ الصَّلَاةَ تَنْهَىٰ عَنِ الْفَحْشَاءِ وَالْمُنْكَرِ وَلَذِكْرُ
اللَّهِ أَكْبَرُ وَاللَّهُ يَعْلَمُ مَا تَصْنَعُونَ ٤٥

46. And argue not with the People of the Scripture unless it be in (a way) that is better, save with such of them as do wrong; and say: We believe in that which hath been revealed unto us and revealed unto you; our God and your God is One, and unto Him we surrender.

47. In like manner We have revealed unto thee the Scripture, and those unto whom We gave the Scripture aforetime will believe therein; and of these (also)[1] there are some who believe therein. And none deny Our revelations save the disbelievers.

48. And thou (O Muhammad) wast not a reader of any Scripture before it, nor didst thou write it with thy right hand, for then might those have doubted who follow falsehood.

49. But it is clear revelations in the hearts of those who have been given knowledge, and none deny our revelations save wrongdoers.

50. And they say: Why are not portents sent down upon him from his Lord? Say: Portents are with Allah only, and I am but a plain warner.

51. Is it not enough for them that We have sent down unto thee the Scripture which is read unto them? Lo! herein verily is mercy, and a reminder for folk who believe.

52. Say (unto them, O Muhammad): Allah sufficeth for witness between me and you. He knoweth whatsoever is in the heavens and the earth. And those who believe in vanity and disbelieve in Allah, they it is who are the losers.

53. They bid thee hasten on the doom (of Allah). And if a term had not been appointed, the doom would assuredly have come unto them (ere now). And verily it will come upon them suddenly when they perceive not.

54. They bid thee hasten on the doom, when lo! Hell verily will encompass the disbelievers

1. *i.e.* the people of Mecca.

ولا تجادلوا اهل الكتب الا بالتي هي احسن الا
الذين ظلموا منهم وقولوا امنا بالذي انزل
الينا وانزل اليكم والهنا والهكم واحد و
نحن له مسلمون ﴿٤٦﴾
وكذلك انزلنا اليك الكتب فالذين اتينهم الكتب
يؤمنون به ومن هؤلاء من يؤمن به وما يجحد
بايتنا الا الكفرون ﴿٤٧﴾
وما كنت تتلوا من قبله من كتب ولا تخطه
بيمينك اذا لارتاب المبطلون ﴿٤٨﴾
بل هو ايت بينت في صدور الذين اوتوا العلم
وما يجحد بايتنا الا الظلمون ﴿٤٩﴾
وقالوا لولا انزل عليه ايت من ربه قل انما
الايت عند الله وانما انا نذير مبين ﴿٥٠﴾
اولم يكفهم انا انزلنا عليك الكتب يتلى عليهم
ان في ذلك لرحمة وذكرى لقوم يؤمنون ﴿٥١﴾
قل كفى بالله بيني وبينكم شهيدا يعلم ما في
السموت والارض والذين امنوا بالباطل و
كفروا بالله اولئك هم الخسرون ﴿٥٢﴾
ويستعجلونك بالعذاب ولولا اجل مسمى لجاءهم
العذاب وليأتينهم بغتة وهم لا يشعرون ﴿٥٣﴾
يستعجلونك بالعذاب وان جهنم لمحيطة
بالكفرين ﴿٥٤﴾

55. On the Day when the doom will overwhelm them from above them and from underneath their feet, and He will say: Taste what ye used to do!

يَوْمَ يَغْشٰهُمُ الْعَذَابُ مِنْ فَوْقِهِمْ وَمِنْ تَحْتِ
اَرْجُلِهِمْ وَيَقُوْلُ ذُوْقُوْا مَا كُنْتُمْ تَعْمَلُوْنَ ﴿٥٥﴾

56. O my bondmen who believe! Lo! My earth is spacious. Therefor serve Me only.

يٰعِبَادِيَ الَّذِيْنَ اٰمَنُوْٓا اِنَّ اَرْضِيْ وَاسِعَةٌ فَاِيَّايَ
فَاعْبُدُوْنِ ﴿٥٦﴾

57. Every soul will taste of death. Then unto Us ye will be returned.

كُلُّ نَفْسٍ ذَآئِقَةُ الْمَوْتِ ثُمَّ اِلَيْنَا تُرْجَعُوْنَ ﴿٥٧﴾

58. Those who believe and do good works, them verily We shall house in lofty dwellings of the Garden underneath which rivers flow. There they will dwell secure. How sweet the guerdon of the toilers,

وَالَّذِيْنَ اٰمَنُوْا وَعَمِلُوا الصّٰلِحٰتِ لَنُبَوِّئَنَّهُمْ مِّنَ
الْجَنَّةِ غُرَفًا تَجْرِيْ مِنْ تَحْتِهَا الْاَنْهٰرُ خٰلِدِيْنَ
فِيْهَا نِعْمَ اَجْرُ الْعٰمِلِيْنَ ﴿٥٨﴾

59. Who persevere, and put their trust in their Lord!

الَّذِيْنَ صَبَرُوْا وَعَلٰى رَبِّهِمْ يَتَوَكَّلُوْنَ ﴿٥٩﴾

60. And how many an animal there is that beareth not its own provision! Allah provideth for it and for you. He is the Hearer, the Knower.

وَكَاَيِّنْ مِّنْ دَآبَّةٍ لَّا تَحْمِلُ رِزْقَهَا اللّٰهُ يَرْزُقُهَا وَ
اِيَّاكُمْ وَهُوَ السَّمِيْعُ الْعَلِيْمُ ﴿٦٠﴾

61. And if thou wert to ask them: Who created the heavens and the earth, and constrained the sun and the moon (to their appointed work)? they would say: Allah. How then are they turned away?

وَلَئِنْ سَاَلْتَهُمْ مَّنْ خَلَقَ السَّمٰوٰتِ وَالْاَرْضَ وَسَخَّرَ
الشَّمْسَ وَالْقَمَرَ لَيَقُوْلُنَّ اللّٰهُ فَاَنّٰى يُؤْفَكُوْنَ ﴿٦١﴾

62. Allah maketh the provision wide for whom He will of His bondmen, and straiteneth it for whom (He will). Lo! Allah is Aware of all things.

اَللّٰهُ يَبْسُطُ الرِّزْقَ لِمَنْ يَّشَآءُ مِنْ عِبَادِهٖ وَيَقْدِرُ
لَهٗ اِنَّ اللّٰهَ بِكُلِّ شَيْءٍ عَلِيْمٌ ﴿٦٢﴾

63. And if thou wert to ask them: Who causeth water to come down from the sky, and therewith reviveth the earth after its death? they verily would say: Allah. Say: Praise be to Allah! But most of them have no sense.

وَلَئِنْ سَاَلْتَهُمْ مَّنْ نَّزَّلَ مِنَ السَّمَآءِ مَآءً فَاَحْيَا بِهِ
الْاَرْضَ مِنْ بَعْدِ مَوْتِهَا لَيَقُوْلُنَّ اللّٰهُ قُلِ الْحَمْدُ
لِلّٰهِ بَلْ اَكْثَرُهُمْ لَا يَعْقِلُوْنَ ﴿٦٣﴾ ع

64. This life of the world is but a pastime and a game. Lo! the home of the Hereafter that is Life, if they but knew.

وَمَا هٰذِهِ الْحَيٰوةُ الدُّنْيَآ اِلَّا لَهْوٌ وَّلَعِبٌ وَاِنَّ الدَّارَ
الْاٰخِرَةَ لَهِيَ الْحَيَوَانُ لَوْ كَانُوْا يَعْلَمُوْنَ ﴿٦٤﴾ وقف لازم

65. And when they mount upon the ships they pray to Allah, making their faith pure for Him only, but when He bringeth them safe to land, behold! they ascribe partners (unto Him),

فَاِذَا رَكِبُوْا فِي الْفُلْكِ دَعَوُا اللّٰهَ مُخْلِصِيْنَ لَهُ الدِّيْنَ
فَلَمَّا نَجّٰىهُمْ اِلَى الْبَرِّ اِذَا هُمْ يُشْرِكُوْنَ ﴿٦٥﴾

66. That they may disbelieve in that which We have given them, and that they may take their ease. But they will come to know.

لِيَكْفُرُوا بِمَا آتَيْنَاهُمْ وَلِيَتَمَتَّعُوا فَسَوْفَ
يَعْلَمُونَ ٦٦

67. Have they not seen that We have appointed a sanctuary immune (from violence),[1] while mankind are ravaged all around them? Do they then believe in falsehood and disbelieve in the bounty of Allah?

أَوَلَمْ يَرَوْا أَنَّا جَعَلْنَا حَرَمًا آمِنًا وَيُتَخَطَّفُ النَّاسُ
مِنْ حَوْلِهِمْ أَفَبِالْبَاطِلِ يُؤْمِنُونَ وَبِنِعْمَةِ اللَّهِ
يَكْفُرُونَ ٦٧

68. Who doth greater wrong than he who inventeth a lie concerning Allah, or denieth the truth when it cometh unto him? Is not there a home in hell for disbelievers?

وَمَنْ أَظْلَمُ مِمَّنِ افْتَرَىٰ عَلَى اللَّهِ كَذِبًا أَوْ كَذَّبَ
بِالْحَقِّ لَمَّا جَاءَهُ أَلَيْسَ فِي جَهَنَّمَ مَثْوًى لِلْكَافِرِينَ ٦٨

69. As for those who strive in Us, We surely guide them to Our paths, and lo! Allah is with the good.

وَالَّذِينَ جَاهَدُوا فِينَا لَنَهْدِيَنَّهُمْ سُبُلَنَا وَإِنَّ اللَّهَ
لَمَعَ الْمُحْسِنِينَ ٦٩ ع

1. The territory of Mecca.

Ar-Rūm, "The Romans," takes its name from a word in the first verse.

The armies of the Eastern Roman Empire had been defeated by the Persians in all the territories near Arabia. In the year A.D. 613 Jerusalem and Damascus fell, and in the following year Egypt. A Persian army invaded Anatolia and was threatening Constantinople itself in the year A.D. 615 or 616 (the sixth or seventh year before the Hijrah) when, according to the best authorities, this Sūrah was revealed at Mecca. The pagan Arabs triumphed in the news of Persian victories over the Prophet and his little band of followers, because the Christian Romans were believers in the One God, whereas the Persians were not. They argued that the power of Allah could not be supreme and absolute, as the Prophet kept proclaiming it to be, since the forces of a pagan empire had been able to defeat His worshippers.

The Prophet's answer was provided for him in this grand assertion of Theocracy, which shows the folly of all those who think of Allah as a partisan. It opens with two prophecies: that the Romans would be victorious over the Persians, and that the little persecuted company of Muslims in Arabia would have reason to rejoice, "within ten years."[1] In fact, in A.D. 624 the Roman armies entered purely Persian territory, and in the same year a little army of Muslims, led by the Prophet, overthrew the flower of Arab chivalry upon the field of Badr.

But the prophecies are only the prelude to a proclamation of God's universal kingdom, which is shown to be an actual Sovereignty. The laws of nature are expounded as the laws of Allah in the physical sphere, and in the moral and political spheres mankind is informed that there are similar laws of life and death, of good and evil, action and inaction, and their consequences—laws which no one can escape by wisdom or by cunning. His mercy, like His law, surrounds all things, and the standard of His judgment is the same for all. He is not remote or indifferent, partial or capricious. Those who do good earn His favour, and those who do ill earn His wrath, no matter what may be their creed or race; and no one, by the lip profession of a creed, is able to escape His law of consequences.

It belongs to the middle group of Meccan Sūrahs.

1. The word in the Arabic ((*bida'*) implies a space of not less than three, and not more than nine, years.

THE ROMANS

Revealed at Mecca

In the name of Allah, the Merciful, the Beneficent.

1. Alif. Lām. Mīm.[1]

2. The Romans have been defeated

3. In the nearer land, and they, after their defeat, will be victorious

4. Within ten years Allah's is the command in the former case and in the latter and in that day believers will rejoice

5. In Allah's help to victory. He helpeth to victory whom He will. He is the Mighty, the Merciful:

6. It is a promise of Allah. Allah faileth not His promise, but most of mankind know not.

7. They know only some appearance of the life of the world, and are heedless of the Hereafter.

8. Have they not pondered upon themselves? Allah created not the heavens and the earth, and that which is between them, save with truth and for a destined end. But truly many of mankind are disbelievers in the meeting with their Lord.

9. Have they not travelled in the land and seen the nature of the consequence for those who were before them?[2] They were stronger than these in power, and they dug the earth and built upon it more than these have built. Messengers of their own came unto them with clear proofs (of Allah's Sovereignty). Surely Allah wronged them not, but they did wrong themselves.

ایاتها ٦٠ (٣٠) سورة الروم مكية ركوعاتها ٦

بسم الله الرحمن الرحيم

الم (١)

غلبت الروم (٢)

في أدنى الأرض وهم من بعد غلبهم سيغلبون (٣)

في بضع سنين لله الأمر من قبل ومن بعد

ويومئذ يفرح المؤمنون (٤)

بنصر الله ينصر من يشاء وهو العزيز الرحيم (٥)

وعد الله لا يخلف الله وعده ولكن أكثر الناس

لا يعلمون (٦)

يعلمون ظاهرا من الحيوة الدنيا وهم عن

الآخرة هم غفلون (٧)

أولم يتفكروا في أنفسهم ما خلق الله

السموت والأرض وما بينهما إلا بالحق و

أجل مسمى وإن كثيرا من الناس بلقاي ربهم

لكفرون (٨)

أولم يسيروا في الأرض فينظروا كيف كان عاقبة

الذين من قبلهم كانوا أشد منهم قوة وأثاروا

الأرض وعمروها أكثر مما عمروها وجاءتهم

رسلهم بالبينت فما كان الله ليظلمهم ولكن

كانوا أنفسهم يظلمون (٩)

1. See Sūr. II, v. 1, footnote.
2. To those who journeyed out from Mecca, northward into Mesopotamia and Syria, or southward to the Yaman and Hadramaut, appeared the ruins of old civilisations which, tradition said, had been destroyed on account of their corruption and disobedience to the will of God.

10. Then evil was the consequence to those who dealt in evil, because they denied the revelations of Allah and made a mock of them.

11. Allah produceth creation, then He reproduceth it, then unto Him ye will be returned.

12. And in the Day when the Hour riseth the unrighteous will despair.

13. There will be none to intercede for them of those whom they made equal with Allah. And they will reject their partners (whom they ascribed unto Him).

14. In the Day when the Hour cometh, in that Day they will be sundered.

15. As for those who believed and did good works, they will be made happy in a Garden.

16. But as for those who disbelieved and denied Our revelations, and denied the meeting of the Hereafter, such will be brought to doom.

17. So glory be to Allah when ye enter the night and when ye enter the morning—

18. Unto Him be praise in the heavens and the earth—and at the sun's decline and in the noonday!

19. He bringeth forth the living from the dead, and He bringeth forth the dead from the living, and He reviveth the earth after her death. And even so will ye be brought forth.

20. And of His signs is this: He created you of dust, and behold you human beings, ranging widely!

21. And of His signs is this: He created for you helpmates from yourselves that ye might find rest in them, and He ordained between you love and mercy. Lo, herein indeed are portents for folk who reflect.

ثُمَّ كَانَ عَاقِبَةَ الَّذِينَ أَسَاءُوا السُّوأَىٰ أَن كَذَّبُوا
ع بِآيَاتِ اللَّهِ وَكَانُوا بِهَا يَسْتَهْزِئُونَ ١٠
اللَّهُ يَبْدَأُ الْخَلْقَ ثُمَّ يُعِيدُهُ ثُمَّ إِلَيْهِ تُرْجَعُونَ ١١
وَيَوْمَ تَقُومُ السَّاعَةُ يُبْلِسُ الْمُجْرِمُونَ ١٢
وَلَمْ يَكُن لَّهُم مِّن شُرَكَائِهِمْ شُفَعَاءُ وَكَانُوا بِشُرَكَائِهِمْ
كَافِرِينَ ١٣
وَيَوْمَ تَقُومُ السَّاعَةُ يَوْمَئِذٍ يَتَفَرَّقُونَ ١٤
فَأَمَّا الَّذِينَ آمَنُوا وَعَمِلُوا الصَّالِحَاتِ فَهُمْ فِي رَوْضَةٍ
يُحْبَرُونَ ١٥
وَأَمَّا الَّذِينَ كَفَرُوا وَكَذَّبُوا بِآيَاتِنَا وَلِقَاءِ الْآخِرَةِ
فَأُولَٰئِكَ فِي الْعَذَابِ مُحْضَرُونَ ١٦
فَسُبْحَانَ اللَّهِ حِينَ تُمْسُونَ وَحِينَ تُصْبِحُونَ ١٧
وَلَهُ الْحَمْدُ فِي السَّمَاوَاتِ وَالْأَرْضِ وَعَشِيًّا وَحِينَ
تُظْهِرُونَ ١٨
يُخْرِجُ الْحَيَّ مِنَ الْمَيِّتِ وَيُخْرِجُ الْمَيِّتَ مِنَ
الْحَيِّ وَيُحْيِي الْأَرْضَ بَعْدَ مَوْتِهَا وَكَذَٰلِكَ
ع تُخْرَجُونَ ١٩
وَمِنْ آيَاتِهِ أَنْ خَلَقَكُم مِّن تُرَابٍ ثُمَّ إِذَا أَنتُم
بَشَرٌ تَنتَشِرُونَ ٢٠
وَمِنْ آيَاتِهِ أَنْ خَلَقَ لَكُم مِّنْ أَنفُسِكُمْ أَزْوَاجًا
لِّتَسْكُنُوا إِلَيْهَا وَجَعَلَ بَيْنَكُم مَّوَدَّةً وَرَحْمَةً
إِنَّ فِي ذَٰلِكَ لَآيَاتٍ لِّقَوْمٍ يَتَفَكَّرُونَ ٢١

22. And of His signs is the creation of the heavens and the earth, and the difference of your languages and colours. Lo! herein indeed are portents for men of knowledge.

23. And of His signs is your slumber by night and by day, and your seeking of His bounty. Lo! herein indeed are portents for folk who heed.

24. And of His signs is this: He showeth you the lightning for a fear and for a hope, and sendeth down water from the sky, and thereby quickeneth the earth after her death. Lo! herein indeed are portents for folk who understand.

25. And of His signs is this: The heavens and the earth stand fast by His command, and afterward, when He calleth you, lo! from the earth ye will emerge.

26. Unto Him belongeth whosoever is in the heavens and in the earth. All are obedient unto Him.

27. He it is Who produceth creation, then reproduceth it, and it is easier for Him. His is the Sublime Similitude in the heavens and in the earth. He is the Mighty, the Wise.

28. He coineth for you a similitude of yourselves. Have ye, from among those whom your right hands possess,[1] partners in the wealth We have bestowed upon you, equal with you in respect thereof, so that ye fear them as ye fear each other (that ye ascribe unto Us partners out of that which We created)? Thus We display the revelations for people who have sense.

29. Nay, but those who do wrong follow their own lusts without knowledge. Who is able to guide him whom Allah hath sent astray? For such there are no helpers.

1. *i.e.* the slaves.

وَمِنْ اٰيٰتِهٖ خَلْقُ السَّمٰوٰتِ وَالْاَرْضِ وَاخْتِلَافُ
اَلْسِنَتِكُمْ وَاَلْوَانِكُمْ ؕ اِنَّ فِيْ ذٰلِكَ لَاٰيٰتٍ
لِّلْعٰلِمِيْنَ ﴿٢٢﴾
وَمِنْ اٰيٰتِهٖ مَنَامُكُمْ بِالَّيْلِ وَالنَّهَارِ وَابْتِغَآؤُكُمْ
مِّنْ فَضْلِهٖ ؕ اِنَّ فِيْ ذٰلِكَ لَاٰيٰتٍ لِّقَوْمٍ
يَّسْمَعُوْنَ ﴿٢٣﴾
وَمِنْ اٰيٰتِهٖ يُرِيْكُمُ الْبَرْقَ خَوْفًا وَّطَمَعًا وَّيُنَزِّلُ
مِنَ السَّمَآءِ مَآءً فَيُحْيٖ بِهِ الْاَرْضَ بَعْدَ مَوْتِهَا ؕ
اِنَّ فِيْ ذٰلِكَ لَاٰيٰتٍ لِّقَوْمٍ يَّعْقِلُوْنَ ﴿٢٤﴾
وَمِنْ اٰيٰتِهٖ اَنْ تَقُوْمَ السَّمَآءُ وَالْاَرْضُ بِاَمْرِهٖ ؕ
ثُمَّ اِذَا دَعَاكُمْ دَعْوَةً ۖ مِّنَ الْاَرْضِ ۖ اِذَا اَنْتُمْ
تَخْرُجُوْنَ ﴿٢٥﴾
وَلَهٗ مَنْ فِي السَّمٰوٰتِ وَالْاَرْضِ ؕ كُلٌّ لَّهٗ قٰنِتُوْنَ ﴿٢٦﴾
وَهُوَ الَّذِيْ يَبْدَؤُا الْخَلْقَ ثُمَّ يُعِيْدُهٗ وَهُوَ اَهْوَنُ
عَلَيْهِ ؕ وَلَهُ الْمَثَلُ الْاَعْلٰى فِي السَّمٰوٰتِ وَالْاَرْضِ ۚ
وَهُوَ الْعَزِيْزُ الْحَكِيْمُ ﴿٢٧﴾ ع
ضَرَبَ لَكُمْ مَّثَلًا مِّنْ اَنْفُسِكُمْ ؕ هَلْ لَّكُمْ مِّنْ مَّا
مَلَكَتْ اَيْمَانُكُمْ مِّنْ شُرَكَآءَ فِيْ مَا رَزَقْنٰكُمْ فَاَنْتُمْ
فِيْهِ سَوَآءٌ تَخَافُوْنَهُمْ كَخِيْفَتِكُمْ اَنْفُسَكُمْ ؕ كَذٰلِكَ
نُفَصِّلُ الْاٰيٰتِ لِقَوْمٍ يَّعْقِلُوْنَ ﴿٢٨﴾
بَلِ اتَّبَعَ الَّذِيْنَ ظَلَمُوْٓا اَهْوَآءَهُمْ بِغَيْرِ عِلْمٍ ۚ فَمَنْ
يَّهْدِيْ مَنْ اَضَلَّ اللّٰهُ ؕ وَمَا لَهُمْ مِّنْ نّٰصِرِيْنَ ﴿٢٩﴾

30. So set thy purpose (O Muhammad) for religion as a man by nature upright—the nature (framed) of Allah, in which He hath created man. There is no altering (the laws of) Allah's creation. That is the right religion, but most men know not—

31. Turning unto Him (only); and be careful of your duty unto Him, and establish worship, and be not of those who ascribe partners (unto Him):

32. Of those who split up their religion and became schismatics, each sect exulting in its tenets.

33. And when harm toucheth men they cry unto their Lord, turning to Him in repentance; then, when they have tasted of His mercy, behold! some of them attribute partners to their Lord

34. So as to disbelieve in that which We have given them. (Unto such it is said): Enjoy yourselves awhile, but ye will come to know.

35. Or have We revealed unto them any warrant which speaketh of that which they associate with Him?

36. And when We cause mankind to taste of mercy they rejoice therein; but if an evil thing befall them as the consequence of their own deeds, lo! they are in despair!

37. See they not that Allah enlargeth the provision for whom He will, and straiteneth (it for whom He will). Lo! herein indeed are portents for folk who believe.

38. So give to the kinsman his due, and to the needy, and to the wayfarer. That is best for those who seek Allah's countenance. And such are they who are successful.

39. That which ye give in usury in order that it may increase on (other) people's property hath no increase with Allah; but that which ye give in charity, seeking Allah's countenance, hath increase manifold.

فَأَقِمْ وَجْهَكَ لِلدِّينِ حَنِيفًا فِطْرَتَ اللَّهِ الَّتِي فَطَرَ
النَّاسَ عَلَيْهَا لَا تَبْدِيلَ لِخَلْقِ اللَّهِ ذَٰلِكَ الدِّينُ
الْقَيِّمُ وَلَٰكِنَّ أَكْثَرَ النَّاسِ لَا يَعْلَمُونَ ﴿٣٠﴾
مُنِيبِينَ إِلَيْهِ وَاتَّقُوهُ وَأَقِيمُوا الصَّلَاةَ وَلَا تَكُونُوا
مِنَ الْمُشْرِكِينَ ﴿٣١﴾
مِنَ الَّذِينَ فَرَّقُوا دِينَهُمْ وَكَانُوا شِيَعًا كُلُّ
حِزْبٍ بِمَا لَدَيْهِمْ فَرِحُونَ ﴿٣٢﴾
وَإِذَا مَسَّ النَّاسَ ضُرٌّ دَعَوْا رَبَّهُمْ مُنِيبِينَ إِلَيْهِ
ثُمَّ إِذَا أَذَاقَهُمْ مِنْهُ رَحْمَةً إِذَا فَرِيقٌ مِنْهُمْ بِرَبِّهِمْ
يُشْرِكُونَ ﴿٣٣﴾
لِيَكْفُرُوا بِمَا آتَيْنَاهُمْ فَتَمَتَّعُوا فَسَوْفَ تَعْلَمُونَ ﴿٣٤﴾
أَمْ أَنْزَلْنَا عَلَيْهِمْ سُلْطَانًا فَهُوَ يَتَكَلَّمُ بِمَا كَانُوا بِهِ يُشْرِكُونَ ﴿٣٥﴾
وَإِذَا أَذَقْنَا النَّاسَ رَحْمَةً فَرِحُوا بِهَا وَإِنْ تُصِبْهُمْ
سَيِّئَةٌ بِمَا قَدَّمَتْ أَيْدِيهِمْ إِذَا هُمْ يَقْنَطُونَ ﴿٣٦﴾
أَوَلَمْ يَرَوْا أَنَّ اللَّهَ يَبْسُطُ الرِّزْقَ لِمَنْ يَشَاءُ وَيَقْدِرُ
إِنَّ فِي ذَٰلِكَ لَآيَاتٍ لِقَوْمٍ يُؤْمِنُونَ ﴿٣٧﴾
فَآتِ ذَا الْقُرْبَىٰ حَقَّهُ وَالْمِسْكِينَ وَابْنَ السَّبِيلِ
ذَٰلِكَ خَيْرٌ لِلَّذِينَ يُرِيدُونَ وَجْهَ اللَّهِ وَأُولَٰئِكَ
هُمُ الْمُفْلِحُونَ ﴿٣٨﴾
وَمَا آتَيْتُمْ مِنْ رِبًا لِيَرْبُوَ فِي أَمْوَالِ النَّاسِ فَلَا
يَرْبُو عِنْدَ اللَّهِ وَمَا آتَيْتُمْ مِنْ زَكَاةٍ تُرِيدُونَ
وَجْهَ اللَّهِ فَأُولَٰئِكَ هُمُ الْمُضْعِفُونَ ﴿٣٩﴾

40. Allah is He Who created you and then sustained you, then causeth you to die, then giveth life to you again. Is there any of your (so-called) partners (of Allah) that doth aught of that? Praised and exalted be He above what they associate (with Him)!

41. Corruption doth appear on land sea because of (the evil) which men's hands have done, that He may make them taste a part of that which they have done, in order that they may return.

42. Say (O Muhammad, to the disbelievers): Travel in the land, and see the nature of the consequence for those who were before you! Most of them were idolaters.

43. So set thy purpose resolutely for the right religion, before the inevitable Day cometh from Allah. On that Day mankind will be sundered—

44. Whoso disbelieveth must (then) bear the consequences of his disbelief, while those who do right make provision for themselves—

45. That He may reward out of His bounty those who believe and do good works. Lo! He loveth not the disbelievers (in His guidance).

46. And of His signs is this: He sendeth herald winds to make you taste His mercy, and that the ships may sail at His command, and that ye may seek His grace, and that haply ye may be thankful.

47. Verily We sent before thee (Muhammad) messengers to their own folk. They brought them clear proofs (of Allah's Sovereignty). Then We took vengeance upon those who were guilty (in regard to them). To help believers is incumbent upon Us.

اَللّٰهُ الَّذِیْ خَلَقَكُمْ ثُمَّ رَزَقَكُمْ ثُمَّ یُمِیْتُكُمْ ثُمَّ
یُحْیِیْكُمْ ؕ هَلْ مِنْ شُرَكَآىِٕكُمْ مَّنْ یَّفْعَلُ
مِنْ ذٰلِكُمْ مِّنْ شَیْءٍ ؕ سُبْحٰنَهٗ وَتَعٰلٰی عَمَّا
ع یُشْرِكُوْنَ ﴿٤٠﴾
ظَهَرَ الْفَسَادُ فِی الْبَرِّ وَالْبَحْرِ بِمَا كَسَبَتْ اَیْدِی
النَّاسِ لِیُذِیْقَهُمْ بَعْضَ الَّذِیْ عَمِلُوْا لَعَلَّهُمْ
یَرْجِعُوْنَ ﴿٤١﴾
قُلْ سِیْرُوْا فِی الْاَرْضِ فَانْظُرُوْا كَیْفَ كَانَ عَاقِبَةُ
الَّذِیْنَ مِنْ قَبْلُ ؕ كَانَ اَكْثَرُهُمْ مُّشْرِكِیْنَ ﴿٤٢﴾
فَاَقِمْ وَجْهَكَ لِلدِّیْنِ الْقَیِّمِ مِنْ قَبْلِ اَنْ
یَّاْتِیَ یَوْمٌ لَّا مَرَدَّ لَهٗ مِنَ اللّٰهِ یَوْمَىِٕذٍ
یَّصَّدَّعُوْنَ ﴿٤٣﴾
مَنْ كَفَرَ فَعَلَیْهِ كُفْرُهٗ ۚ وَمَنْ عَمِلَ صَالِحًا
فَلِاَنْفُسِهِمْ یَمْهَدُوْنَ ﴿٤٤﴾
لِیَجْزِیَ الَّذِیْنَ اٰمَنُوْا وَعَمِلُوا الصّٰلِحٰتِ مِنْ
فَضْلِهٖ ؕ اِنَّهٗ لَا یُحِبُّ الْكٰفِرِیْنَ ﴿٤٥﴾
وَمِنْ اٰیٰتِهٖٓ اَنْ یُّرْسِلَ الرِّیَاحَ مُبَشِّرٰتٍ وَّلِیُذِیْقَكُمْ
مِّنْ رَّحْمَتِهٖ وَلِتَجْرِیَ الْفُلْكُ بِاَمْرِهٖ وَلِتَبْتَغُوْا
مِنْ فَضْلِهٖ وَلَعَلَّكُمْ تَشْكُرُوْنَ ﴿٤٦﴾
وَلَقَدْ اَرْسَلْنَا مِنْ قَبْلِكَ رُسُلًا اِلٰی قَوْمِهِمْ فَجَآءُوْهُمْ
بِالْبَیِّنٰتِ فَانْتَقَمْنَا مِنَ الَّذِیْنَ اَجْرَمُوْا ؕ وَكَانَ حَقًّا
عَلَیْنَا نَصْرُ الْمُؤْمِنِیْنَ ﴿٤٧﴾

48. Allah is He Who sendeth the winds so that they raise clouds, and spreadeth them along the sky as pleaseth Him, and causeth them to break and thou seest the rain downpouring from within them. And when He maketh it[a] to fall on whom He will of His bondmen, lo! they rejoice;

اَللّٰهُ الَّذِيْ يُرْسِلُ الرِّيٰحَ فَتُثِيْرُ سَحَابًا فَيَبْسُطُهٗ
فِي السَّمَآءِ كَيْفَ يَشَآءُ وَيَجْعَلُهٗ كِسَفًا فَتَرَى الْوَدْقَ
يَخْرُجُ مِنْ خِلٰلِهٖ ۚ فَاِذَآ اَصَابَ بِهٖ مَنْ يَّشَآءُ مِنْ
عِبَادِهٖٓ اِذَا هُمْ يَسْتَبْشِرُوْنَ ﴿٤٨﴾

49. Though before that, even before it was sent down upon them, they were in despair.

وَاِنْ كَانُوْا مِنْ قَبْلِ اَنْ يُّنَزَّلَ عَلَيْهِمْ مِّنْ قَبْلِهٖ
لَمُبْلِسِيْنَ ﴿٤٩﴾

50. Look, therefor, at the prints of Allah's mercy (in creation): how He quickeneth the earth after her death. Lo! He verily is the Quickener of the Dead, and He is Able to do all things.

فَانْظُرْ اِلٰٓى اٰثٰرِ رَحْمَتِ اللّٰهِ كَيْفَ يُحْيِ الْاَرْضَ
بَعْدَ مَوْتِهَا ۭ اِنَّ ذٰلِكَ لَمُحْيِ الْمَوْتٰى ۚ وَهُوَ عَلٰى
كُلِّ شَيْءٍ قَدِيْرٌ ﴿٥٠﴾

51. And if We sent a wind and they beheld it yellow, they verily would still continue in their disbelief.

وَلَىِٕنْ اَرْسَلْنَا رِيْحًا فَرَاَوْهُ مُصْفَرًّا لَّظَلُّوْا مِنْۢ بَعْدِهٖ
يَكْفُرُوْنَ ﴿٥١﴾

52. For verily thou (Muhammad) canst not make the dead to hear, nor canst thou make the deaf to hear the call when they have turned to flee.

فَاِنَّكَ لَا تُسْمِعُ الْمَوْتٰى وَلَا تُسْمِعُ الصُّمَّ الدُّعَآءَ اِذَا وَلَّوْا مُدْبِرِيْنَ ﴿٥٢﴾

53. Nor canst thou guide the blind out of their error. Thou canst make none to hear save those who believe in Our revelations so that they surrender (unto Him).

وَمَآ اَنْتَ بِهٰدِ الْعُمْيِ عَنْ ضَلٰلَتِهِمْ ۭ اِنْ تُسْمِعُ اِلَّا
مَنْ يُّؤْمِنُ بِاٰيٰتِنَا فَهُمْ مُّسْلِمُوْنَ ﴿٥٣﴾

54. Allah is He Who shaped you out of weakness, then appointed after weakness strength, then, after strength, appointed weakness and grey hair. He createth what He will. He is the Knower, the Mighty.

اَللّٰهُ الَّذِيْ خَلَقَكُمْ مِّنْ ضُعْفٍ ثُمَّ جَعَلَ مِنْۢ بَعْدِ
ضُعْفٍ قُوَّةً ثُمَّ جَعَلَ مِنْۢ بَعْدِ قُوَّةٍ ضُعْفًا وَّ
شَيْبَةً ۭ يَخْلُقُ مَا يَشَآءُ ۚ وَهُوَ الْعَلِيْمُ الْقَدِيْرُ ﴿٥٤﴾

55. And on the Day when the Hour riseth the guilty will vow that they did tarry but an hour—thus were they ever deceived!

وَيَوْمَ تَقُوْمُ السَّاعَةُ يُقْسِمُ الْمُجْرِمُوْنَ ڏ مَا لَبِثُوْا
غَيْرَ سَاعَةٍ ۭ كَذٰلِكَ كَانُوْا يُؤْفَكُوْنَ ﴿٥٥﴾

56. But those to whom knowledge and faith are given will say: The truth is, ye have tarried, by Allah's decree, until the Day of Resurrection. This is the Day of Resurrection, but ye used not to know.

وَقَالَ الَّذِيْنَ اُوْتُوا الْعِلْمَ وَالْاِيْمَانَ لَقَدْ لَبِثْتُمْ
فِيْ كِتٰبِ اللّٰهِ اِلٰى يَوْمِ الْبَعْثِ ۡ فَهٰذَا يَوْمُ الْبَعْثِ
وَلٰكِنَّكُمْ كُنْتُمْ لَا تَعْلَمُوْنَ ﴿٥٦﴾

57. In that Day their excuses will not profit those who did injustice, nor will they be allowed to make amends.

58. Verily We have coined for mankind in the Qur'ān all kinds of similitudes; and indeed if thou camest unto them with a miracle, those who disbelieve would verily exclaim: Ye are but tricksters!

59. Thus doth Allah seal the hearts of those who know not.

60. So have patience (O Muhammad)! Allah's promise is the very truth, and let not those who have no certainty make thee impatient.

فيومئذ لا ينفع الذين ظلموا معذرتهم ولا هم
يستعتبون ﴿٥٧﴾

ولقد ضربنا للناس في هذا القرآن من كل
مثل ولئن جئتهم بآية ليقولن الذين كفروا
إن أنتم إلا مبطلون ﴿٥٨﴾

كذلك يطبع الله على قلوب الذين لا يعلمون ﴿٥٩﴾

فاصبر إن وعد الله حق ولا يستخفنك الذين
لا يوقنون ﴿٦٠﴾ ع ٦

Luqmān takes its name from v. 12 ff., which contain mention of the wisdom of Luqmān, a sage whose memory the Arabs reverenced, but who is unknown to Jewish Scripture. He is said to have been a negro slave and the fables associated with his name are so like those of Aesop that the usual identification seems justified. The Sūrah conveys assurance of success to the Muslims at a time of persecution.

It belongs to the middle or last group of Meccan Sūrahs; except vv. 27 and 28 which were revealed at Al-Madînah.

LUQMĀN

Revealed at Mecca

In the name of Allah, the Beneficent, the Merciful.

1. Alif. Lām. Mīm.[1]

2. These are revelations of the wise Scripture,

3. A guidance and a mercy for the good,

4. Those who establish worship and pay the poor-due and have sure faith in the Hereafter.

5. Such have guidance from their Lord. Such are the successful.

6. And of mankind is he who payeth for mere pastime of discourse, that he may mislead from Allah's way without knowledge, and maketh it the butt of mockery. For such there is a shameful doom.

7. And when Our revelations are recited unto him he turneth away in his pride as if he heard them not, as if there were a deafness in his ears. So give him tidings of a painful doom.

8. Lo! those who believe and do good works, for them are gardens of delight,

9. Wherein they will abide. It is a promise of Allah in truth. He is the Mighty, the Wise.

10. He hath created the heavens without supports that ye can see, and hath cast into the earth firm hills, so that it quake not with you; and He hath dispersed therein all kinds of beasts. And We send down water from the sky and We cause (plants) of every goodly kind to grow therein.

1. See Sûr. II, v. 1, footnote.

ايٰاتها ٣٤ (٣١) سورة لقمٰن مكية ركوعاتها ٤

بسم الله الرحمٰن الرحيم ۝

الٓمّٓ ۝١

تلك ايٰت الكتٰب الحكيم ۝٢

هدى ورحمة للمحسنين ۝٣

الذين يقيمون الصلوٰة ويؤتون الزكوٰة وهم
بالاخرة هم يوقنون ۝٤

اولٰئك على هدى من ربهم واولٰئك هم
المفلحون ۝٥

ومن الناس من يشتري لهو الحديث ليضل
عن سبيل الله بغير علم ويتخذها هزوا
اولٰئك لهم عذاب مهين ۝٦

واذا تتلى عليه ايٰتنا ولى مستكبرا كان لم يسمعها
كان في اذنيه وقرا فبشره بعذاب اليم ۝٧

ان الذين امنوا وعملوا الصلحٰت لهم
جنٰت النعيم ۝٨

خلدين فيها وعد الله حقا وهو العزيز الحكيم ۝٩

خلق السمٰوٰت بغير عمد ترونها والقى في
الارض رواسي ان تميد بكم وبث فيها من كل
دابة وانزلنا من السماء ماء فانبتنا فيها من
كل زوج كريم ۝١٠

11. This is the Creations of Allah. Now show me that which those (ye worship) besides Him have created. Nay, but the wrongdoers are in error manifest!

هٰذَا خَلْقُ اللّٰهِ فَاَرُوْنِیْ مَاذَا خَلَقَ الَّذِیْنَ مِنْ دُوْنِهٖ ؕ
بَلِ الظّٰلِمُوْنَ فِیْ ضَلٰلٍ مُّبِیْنٍ ﴿۱۱﴾

12. And verily We gave Luqman wisdom, saying: Give thanks unto Allah: and whosoever giveth thanks, he giveth thanks for (the good of) his soul. And whosoever refuseth -- Lo! Allah is absolute, owner of Praise.

وَلَقَدْ اٰتَیْنَا لُقْمٰنَ الْحِكْمَةَ اَنِ اشْكُرْ لِلّٰهِ ؕ وَمَنْ
یَّشْكُرْ فَاِنَّمَا یَشْكُرُ لِنَفْسِهٖ ۚ وَمَنْ كَفَرَ فَاِنَّ اللّٰهَ غَنِیٌّ
حَمِیْدٌ ﴿۱۲﴾

13. And (remember) when Luqman said unto his son when he was exhorting him; o my dear son! ascribe partners (unto Him) is a tremendous wrong.

وَاِذْ قَالَ لُقْمٰنُ لِابْنِهٖ وَهُوَ یَعِظُهٗ یٰبُنَیَّ لَا تُشْرِكْ
بِاللّٰهِ ؔ اِنَّ الشِّرْكَ لَظُلْمٌ عَظِیْمٌ ﴿۱۳﴾

14. And we have enjoined upon man concerning his parents. His mother beareth him in weakness upon weakness and his weaning is in two years -- Give thanks unto Me and unto thy parents. Unto Me is the journeying.

وَوَصَّیْنَا الْاِنْسَانَ بِوَالِدَیْهِ ۚ حَمَلَتْهُ اُمُّهٗ وَهْنًا عَلٰی
وَهْنٍ وَّفِصٰلُهٗ فِیْ عَامَیْنِ اَنِ اشْكُرْ لِیْ وَلِوَالِدَیْكَ ؕ
اِلَیَّ الْمَصِیْرُ ﴿۱۴﴾

15. But if they strive with thee to make thee ascribe unto Me as partner that of which thou hast no knowledge, then obey them not. consort with them in the world kindly, and follow the path of him who repenteth unto Me. Then unto Me will be your return, and I shall tell you what ye used to do--

وَاِنْ جَاهَدٰكَ عَلٰۤی اَنْ تُشْرِكَ بِیْ مَا لَیْسَ لَكَ بِهٖ
عِلْمٌ فَلَا تُطِعْهُمَا وَصَاحِبْهُمَا فِی الدُّنْیَا مَعْرُوْفًا ؗ
وَّاتَّبِعْ سَبِیْلَ مَنْ اَنَابَ اِلَیَّ ۚ ثُمَّ اِلَیَّ مَرْجِعُكُمْ
فَاُنَبِّئُكُمْ بِمَا كُنْتُمْ تَعْمَلُوْنَ ﴿۱۵﴾

16. O my dear son! Lo! though it be but the weight of a grain of mustard seed, and though it be in a rock, or in the heavens, or in the earth, Allah will bring it forth. Lo! Allah is Subtile, Aware.

یٰبُنَیَّ اِنَّهَاۤ اِنْ تَكُ مِثْقَالَ حَبَّةٍ مِّنْ خَرْدَلٍ فَتَكُنْ فِیْ
صَخْرَةٍ اَوْ فِی السَّمٰوٰتِ اَوْ فِی الْاَرْضِ یَاْتِ بِهَا اللّٰهُ ؕ
اِنَّ اللّٰهَ لَطِیْفٌ خَبِیْرٌ ﴿۱۶﴾

17. O my dear son! Establish worship and enjoin kindness and forbid iniquity, and persevere whatever may befall thee, Lo! that is of the steadfast heart of things.

یٰبُنَیَّ اَقِمِ الصَّلٰوةَ وَاْمُرْ بِالْمَعْرُوْفِ وَانْهَ عَنِ الْمُنْكَرِ
وَاصْبِرْ عَلٰی مَاۤ اَصَابَكَ ؕ اِنَّ ذٰلِكَ مِنْ عَزْمِ
الْاُمُوْرِ ﴿۱۷﴾

18. Turn not thy check in scorn toward folk nor walk with pertness in the land. Lo! Allah loveth not each braggart boaster.

وَلَا تُصَعِّرْ خَدَّكَ لِلنَّاسِ وَلَا تَمْشِ فِی الْاَرْضِ
مَرَحًا ؕ اِنَّ اللّٰهَ لَا یُحِبُّ كُلَّ مُخْتَالٍ فَخُوْرٍ ﴿۱۸﴾

19. Be modest in thy bearing and subdue the voice. Lo! the harshest of all voices is the voice of the ass.

وَاقْصِدْ فِي مَشْيِكَ وَاغْضُضْ مِنْ صَوْتِكَ إِنَّ أَنْكَرَ
ع الْأَصْوَاتِ لَصَوْتُ الْحَمِيرِ ﴿١٩﴾

20. See ye not how Allah hath made serviceable unto you whatsoever is in the skies and whatsoever is in the earth and hath loaded you with His favours both without and within? Yet of mankind is he who disputeth concerning Allah, without knowledge or guidance or a Scriputre giving light.

أَلَمْ تَرَوْا أَنَّ اللّٰهَ سَخَّرَ لَكُمْ مَا فِي السَّمٰوٰتِ وَمَا فِي
الْأَرْضِ وَأَسْبَغَ عَلَيْكُمْ نِعَمَهُ ظَاهِرَةً وَبَاطِنَةً وَ
مِنَ النَّاسِ مَنْ يُجَادِلُ فِي اللّٰهِ بِغَيْرِ عِلْمٍ وَلَا
هُدًى وَلَا كِتٰبٍ مُنِيرٍ ﴿٢٠﴾

21. And if it be said unto them: Follow that which Allah hath revealed, they say: Nay, but we follow that wherein we found our fathers. What! Even though the devil were inviting them unto the doom of flame?

وَإِذَا قِيلَ لَهُمُ اتَّبِعُوا مَا أَنْزَلَ اللّٰهُ قَالُوا بَلْ نَتَّبِعُ
مَا وَجَدْنَا عَلَيْهِ آبَاءَنَا أَوَلَوْ كَانَ الشَّيْطٰنُ
يَدْعُوهُمْ إِلَىٰ عَذَابِ السَّعِيرِ ﴿٢١﴾

22. Whosoever surrendereth his purpose to Allah while doing good, he verily hath grasped the firm hand-hold. Unot Allah belongeth the sequel of all things.

وَمَنْ يُسْلِمْ وَجْهَهُ إِلَى اللّٰهِ وَهُوَ مُحْسِنٌ فَقَدِ
اسْتَمْسَكَ بِالْعُرْوَةِ الْوُثْقَىٰ وَإِلَى اللّٰهِ عَاقِبَةُ
الْأُمُورِ ﴿٢٢﴾

23. And whosoever disbelieveth, let not his disbelief afflict thee (O Muhammad). Unto us is their return, and we shall tell them what they did. Lo! Allah is Aware of what is in the breasts (of men).

وَمَنْ كَفَرَ فَلَا يَحْزُنْكَ كُفْرُهُ إِلَيْنَا مَرْجِعُهُمْ فَنُنَبِّئُهُمْ
بِمَا عَمِلُوا إِنَّ اللّٰهَ عَلِيمٌ بِذَاتِ الصُّدُورِ ﴿٢٣﴾

24. We give them comfort for a little, and then We drive them to a heavy doom.

نُمَتِّعُهُمْ قَلِيلًا ثُمَّ نَضْطَرُّهُمْ إِلَىٰ عَذَابٍ غَلِيظٍ ﴿٢٤﴾

25. If thou shouldst ask them: Who created the heavens and the earth? they would answer: Allah. Say: Praise be to Allah! But most of them know not.

وَلَئِنْ سَأَلْتَهُمْ مَنْ خَلَقَ السَّمٰوٰتِ وَالْأَرْضَ لَيَقُولُنَّ
اللّٰهُ قُلِ الْحَمْدُ لِلّٰهِ بَلْ أَكْثَرُهُمْ لَا يَعْلَمُونَ ﴿٢٥﴾

26. Unto Allah belongeth whatsoever is in the heavens and the earth. Lo! Allah, He is the Absolute, the owner of Praise.

لِلّٰهِ مَا فِي السَّمٰوٰتِ وَالْأَرْضِ إِنَّ اللّٰهَ هُوَ الْغَنِيُّ
الْحَمِيدُ ﴿٢٦﴾

27. And if all the trees in the earth were pens, and the sea, with seven more seas to help it. (were ink), the words of Allah could not be exhausted, lo! Allah is Mighty, Wise.

وَلَوْ أَنَّ مَا فِي الْأَرْضِ مِنْ شَجَرَةٍ أَقْلَامٌ وَالْبَحْرُ
يَمُدُّهُ مِنْ بَعْدِهِ سَبْعَةُ أَبْحُرٍ مَا نَفِدَتْ كَلِمٰتُ
اللّٰهِ إِنَّ اللّٰهَ عَزِيزٌ حَكِيمٌ ﴿٢٧﴾

28. Your creation and your raising (from the dead) are only as (the creation and the raising of) a single soul, Lo! Allah is Hearer, Knower.

ما خلقكم ولا بعثكم إلا كنفس واحدة إن الله
سميع بصير ﴿٢٨﴾

29. Hast thou not seen how Allah causeth the night to pass into the day and causeth the day to pass into the night and hath subdued the sun and the moon (to do their work), each running unto an appointed term; and that Allah is Informed of what ye do?

ألم تر أن الله يولج الليل في النهار ويولج النهار
في الليل وسخر الشمس والقمر كل يجري إلى
أجل مسمى وأن الله بما تعملون خبير ﴿٢٩﴾

30. That (is so) because Allah. He is the True, and that which they invoke besides Him is the False, and because Allah, He is the Sublime, the Great.

ذلك بأن الله هو الحق وأن ما يدعون من دونه
الباطل وأن الله هو العلي الكبير ﴿٣٠﴾

31. Hast thou not seen how the ships glide on the sea by Allah's grace, that He may show you of His wonders? Lo! therein indeed are portents for every steadfast, grateful (heart).

ألم تر أن الفلك تجري في البحر بنعمت الله ليريكم
من آيته إن في ذلك لآيت لكل صبار شكور ﴿٣١﴾

32. And if a wave enshroudeth them like awnings, they cry unto Allah, making their faith pure for Him only. But when He bringeth them safe to land, some of them compromise. None denieth Our signs save every traitor ingrate.

وإذا غشيهم موج كالظلل دعوا الله مخلصين
له الدين فلما نجىهم إلى البر فمنهم مقتصد
وما يجحد بآيتنا إلا كل ختار كفور ﴿٣٢﴾

33. O mankind! Keep your duty to your Lord and fear a Day when the parent will not be able to avail the child in aught, nor the child to avail the parent. Lo! Allah's promise is the very truth. Let not the life of the world beguile you, nor let the deceiver beguile you, in regard to allah.

يأيها الناس اتقوا ربكم واخشوا يوما لا يجزي
والد عن ولده ولا مولود هو جاز عن والده
شيئا إن وعد الله حق فلا تغرنكم الحيوة الدنيا
ولا يغرنكم بالله الغرور ﴿٣٣﴾

34. Lo! Allah! With Him is knowledge of the Hour. He sendeth down the rain, and knoweth that which is in the wombs. No soul knoweth what it will earn tomorrow, and no soul knoweth in what land it will die. Lo! Allah is Knower, Aware.

إن الله عنده علم الساعة وينزل الغيث و
يعلم ما في الأرحام وما تدري نفس ماذا تكسب
غدا وما تدري نفس بأي أرض تموت إن الله
عليم خبير ﴿٣٤﴾

As-Sajdah, "The Prostration," takes its name from a word in v. 15.

It belongs to the middle group of Meccan Sūrahs.

THE PROSTRATION

Revealed at Mecca

In the name of Allah, the Beneficent, the Merciful.

1. Alif. Lām. Mīm.[1]

2. The revelation of the Scripture whereof there is no doubt is from the Lord of the Worlds.

3. Or say they: He hath invented it? Nay, but it is the Truth from thy Lord, that thou mayst warn a folk to whom no warner came before thee, that haply they may walk aright.

4. Allah it is Who created the heavens and the earth, and that which is between them, in six Days. Then He mounted the throne. Ye have not, beside Him, a protecting friend or mediator. Will ye not then remember?

5. He directeth the ordinance from the heaven unto the earth; then it ascendeth unto Him in a Day, whereof the measure is a thousand years of that ye reckon.

6. Such is the Knower of the invisible and the visible, the Mighty the Merciful,

7. Who made all things good which He created, and He began the creation of man from clay;

8. Then He made his seed from a draught of despised fluid;

9. Then He fashioned him and breathed into him of His spirit; and appointed for you hearing and sight and hearts. Small thanks give ye!

10. And they say: When we are lost in the earth, how can we then be re-created? Nay but they are disbelievers in the meeting with their Lord.

آياتها ٣٠ (٣٢) سُورَةُ السَّجْدَةِ مَكِّيَّةٌ رُكُوعَاتُهَا ٣

بِسْمِ اللّٰهِ الرَّحْمٰنِ الرَّحِيْمِ

الٓمٓ ﴿١﴾
تَنْزِيْلُ الْكِتٰبِ لَا رَيْبَ فِيْهِ مِنْ رَّبِّ الْعٰلَمِيْنَ ﴿٢﴾
اَمْ يَقُوْلُوْنَ افْتَرٰىهُ ۚ بَلْ هُوَ الْحَقُّ مِنْ رَّبِّكَ لِتُنْذِرَ
قَوْمًا مَّآ اَتٰىهُمْ مِّنْ نَّذِيْرٍ مِّنْ قَبْلِكَ لَعَلَّهُمْ
يَهْتَدُوْنَ ﴿٣﴾
اَللّٰهُ الَّذِيْ خَلَقَ السَّمٰوٰتِ وَالْاَرْضَ وَمَا بَيْنَهُمَا فِيْ
سِتَّةِ اَيَّامٍ ثُمَّ اسْتَوٰى عَلَى الْعَرْشِ ۗ مَا لَكُمْ مِّنْ
دُوْنِهٖ مِنْ وَّلِيٍّ وَّلَا شَفِيْعٍ ۗ اَفَلَا تَتَذَكَّرُوْنَ ﴿٤﴾
يُدَبِّرُ الْاَمْرَ مِنَ السَّمَآءِ اِلَى الْاَرْضِ ثُمَّ يَعْرُجُ
اِلَيْهِ فِيْ يَوْمٍ كَانَ مِقْدَارُهٗۤ اَلْفَ سَنَةٍ مِّمَّا
تَعُدُّوْنَ ﴿٥﴾
ذٰلِكَ عٰلِمُ الْغَيْبِ وَالشَّهَادَةِ الْعَزِيْزُ الرَّحِيْمُ ﴿٦﴾
الَّذِيْۤ اَحْسَنَ كُلَّ شَيْءٍ خَلَقَهٗ وَبَدَاَ خَلْقَ الْاِنْسَانِ
مِنْ طِيْنٍ ﴿٧﴾
ثُمَّ جَعَلَ نَسْلَهٗ مِنْ سُلٰلَةٍ مِّنْ مَّآءٍ مَّهِيْنٍ ﴿٨﴾
ثُمَّ سَوّٰىهُ وَنَفَخَ فِيْهِ مِنْ رُّوْحِهٖ وَجَعَلَ لَكُمُ السَّمْعَ
وَالْاَبْصَارَ وَالْاَفْـِٕدَةَ ۗ قَلِيْلًا مَّا تَشْكُرُوْنَ ﴿٩﴾
وَقَالُوْۤا ءَاِذَا ضَلَلْنَا فِي الْاَرْضِ ءَاِنَّا لَفِيْ خَلْقٍ جَدِيْدٍ ۬ؕ
بَلْ هُمْ بِلِقَآئِ رَبِّهِمْ كٰفِرُوْنَ ﴿١٠﴾

1. See Sūr. II, v. 1, footnote.

11. Say: The angel of death, who hath charge concerning you, will gather you, and afterward unto your Lord ye will be returned.

قُلْ يَتَوَفّٰكُمْ مَّلَكُ الْمَوْتِ الَّذِيْ وُكِّلَ بِكُمْ ثُمَّ
اِلٰى رَبِّكُمْ تُرْجَعُوْنَ ﴿۱۱﴾

12. Couldst thou but see when the guilty hang their heads before their Lord, (and say): Our Lord! We have now seen and heard, so send us back; we will do right, now we are sure!

وَلَوْ تَرٰۤى اِذِ الْمُجْرِمُوْنَ نَاكِسُوْا رُءُوْسِهِمْ عِنْدَ
رَبِّهِمْ رَبَّنَاۤ اَبْصَرْنَا وَسَمِعْنَا فَارْجِعْنَا نَعْمَلْ صَالِحًا
اِنَّا مُوْقِنُوْنَ ﴿۱۲﴾

13. And if We had so willed, We could have given every soul its guidance, but the word from Me concerning evil-doers took effect: that I will fill hell with the jinn and mankind together.

وَلَوْ شِئْنَا لَاٰتَيْنَا كُلَّ نَفْسٍ هُدٰىهَا وَلٰكِنْ حَقَّ
الْقَوْلُ مِنِّيْ لَاَمْلَئَنَّ جَهَنَّمَ مِنَ الْجِنَّةِ وَالنَّاسِ
اَجْمَعِيْنَ ﴿۱۳﴾

14. So taste (the evil of your deeds). Forasmuch as ye forgot the meeting of this your day, lo! We forget you. Taste the doom of immortality because of what ye used to do.

فَذُوْقُوْا بِمَا نَسِيْتُمْ لِقَآءَ يَوْمِكُمْ هٰذَا ۚ اِنَّا نَسِيْنٰكُمْ
وَذُوْقُوْا عَذَابَ الْخُلْدِ بِمَا كُنْتُمْ تَعْمَلُوْنَ ﴿۱۴﴾

15. Only those believe in Our revelations who, when they are reminded of them, fall down prostrate and hymn the praise of their Lord, and they are not scornful:

اِنَّمَا يُؤْمِنُ بِاٰيٰتِنَا الَّذِيْنَ اِذَا ذُكِّرُوْا بِهَا خَرُّوْا سُجَّدًا
وَّسَبَّحُوْا بِحَمْدِ رَبِّهِمْ وَهُمْ لَا يَسْتَكْبِرُوْنَ ﴿۱۵﴾

16. Who forsake their beds to cry unto their Lord in fear and hope. and spend of what We have bestowed on them.

تَتَجَافٰى جُنُوْبُهُمْ عَنِ الْمَضَاجِعِ يَدْعُوْنَ رَبَّهُمْ خَوْفًا
وَّطَمَعًا ۡ وَّمِمَّا رَزَقْنٰهُمْ يُنْفِقُوْنَ ﴿۱۶﴾

17. No soul knoweth what is kept hid for them of joy, as a reward for what they used to do.

فَلَا تَعْلَمُ نَفْسٌ مَّاۤ اُخْفِيَ لَهُمْ مِّنْ قُرَّةِ اَعْيُنٍ ۚ
جَزَآءًۢ بِمَا كَانُوْا يَعْمَلُوْنَ ﴿۱۷﴾

18. Is he who is a believer like unto him who is an evil-liver? They are not alike.

اَفَمَنْ كَانَ مُؤْمِنًا كَمَنْ كَانَ فَاسِقًا ؕ لَا يَسْتَوٗنَ ﴿۱۸﴾

19. But as for those who believe and do good works, for them are the Gardens of Retreat—a welcome (in reward) for what they used to do.

اَمَّا الَّذِيْنَ اٰمَنُوْا وَعَمِلُوا الصّٰلِحٰتِ فَلَهُمْ جَنّٰتُ
الْمَاْوٰى ۫ نُزُلًۢا بِمَا كَانُوْا يَعْمَلُوْنَ ﴿۱۹﴾

20. And as for those who do evil, their retreat is the Fire. Whenever they desire to issue forth from thence, they are brought back thither. Unto them it is said: Taste the torment of the Fire which ye used to deny!

وَاَمَّا الَّذِيْنَ فَسَقُوْا فَمَاْوٰىهُمُ النَّارُ ؕ كُلَّمَاۤ اَرَادُوْۤا اَنْ
يَّخْرُجُوْا مِنْهَاۤ اُعِيْدُوْا فِيْهَا وَقِيْلَ لَهُمْ ذُوْقُوْا عَذَابَ
النَّارِ الَّذِيْ كُنْتُمْ بِهٖ تُكَذِّبُوْنَ ﴿۲۰﴾

21. And verily We make them taste the lower punishment[1] before the greater, that haply they may return.

22. And who doth greater wrong than he who is reminded of the revelations of his Lord, then turneth from them? Lo! We shall requite the guilty.

23. We verily gave Moses the Scripture; so be not ye in doubt of his receiving it; and We appointed it a guidance for the Children of Israel.

24. And when they became steadfast believing firmly in Our revelations, We appointed from among them leaders who guided by Our command.

25. Lo! thy Lord will judge between them on the Day of Resurrection concerning that wherein they used to differ.

26. Is it not a guidance for them (to observe) how many generations We destroyed before them, amid whose dwelling places they do walk? Lo, therein verily are portents! Will they not then heed?

27. Have they not seen how We lead the water to the barren land and therewith bring forth crops whereof their cattle eat, and they themselves? Will they not then see?

28. And they say: When cometh this victory (of yours) if ye are truthful?

29. Say (unto them): On the day of the victory the faith of those who disbelieve (and who then will believe) will not avail them, neither will they be reprieved.

30. So withdraw from them (O Muhammad) and await (the event). Lo! they (also) are awaiting (it).

1. *i.e.* **punishment in this world.**

وَلَنُذِيقَنَّهُم مِّنَ الْعَذَابِ الْأَدْنَىٰ دُونَ الْعَذَابِ
الْأَكْبَرِ لَعَلَّهُمْ يَرْجِعُونَ ﴿٢١﴾

وَمَنْ أَظْلَمُ مِمَّن ذُكِّرَ بِآيَاتِ رَبِّهِ ثُمَّ أَعْرَضَ عَنْهَا
إِنَّا مِنَ الْمُجْرِمِينَ مُنتَقِمُونَ ﴿٢٢﴾

وَلَقَدْ آتَيْنَا مُوسَى الْكِتَابَ فَلَا تَكُن فِي مِرْيَةٍ مِّن
لِّقَائِهِ وَجَعَلْنَاهُ هُدًى لِّبَنِي إِسْرَائِيلَ ﴿٢٣﴾

وَجَعَلْنَا مِنْهُمْ أَئِمَّةً يَهْدُونَ بِأَمْرِنَا لَمَّا صَبَرُوا
وَكَانُوا بِآيَاتِنَا يُوقِنُونَ ﴿٢٤﴾

إِنَّ رَبَّكَ هُوَ يَفْصِلُ بَيْنَهُمْ يَوْمَ الْقِيَامَةِ فِيمَا كَانُوا
فِيهِ يَخْتَلِفُونَ ﴿٢٥﴾

أَوَلَمْ يَهْدِ لَهُمْ كَمْ أَهْلَكْنَا مِن قَبْلِهِم مِّنَ الْقُرُونِ
يَمْشُونَ فِي مَسَاكِنِهِمْ إِنَّ فِي ذَٰلِكَ لَآيَاتٍ أَفَلَا
يَسْمَعُونَ ﴿٢٦﴾

أَوَلَمْ يَرَوْا أَنَّا نَسُوقُ الْمَاءَ إِلَى الْأَرْضِ الْجُرُزِ
فَنُخْرِجُ بِهِ زَرْعًا تَأْكُلُ مِنْهُ أَنْعَامُهُمْ وَأَنفُسُهُمْ
أَفَلَا يُبْصِرُونَ ﴿٢٧﴾

وَيَقُولُونَ مَتَىٰ هَٰذَا الْفَتْحُ إِن كُنتُمْ صَادِقِينَ ﴿٢٨﴾

قُلْ يَوْمَ الْفَتْحِ لَا يَنفَعُ الَّذِينَ كَفَرُوا إِيمَانُهُمْ وَلَا
هُمْ يُنظَرُونَ ﴿٢٩﴾

فَأَعْرِضْ عَنْهُمْ وَانتَظِرْ إِنَّهُم مُّنتَظِرُونَ ﴿٣٠﴾

Al-Ahzāb, "The Clans," takes its name from the army of the allied clans which came against Yathrib (Al-Madinah) in the fifth year of the Hijrah (vv. 9-25). Certain of the Bani Naḍir, a Jewish tribe whom the Prophet had expelled from Yathrib on the ground of treason (see Sūrah LIX), went first to the leaders of Qureysh in Mecca and then to the chiefs of the great desert tribe of Ghaṭafān, urging them to extirpate the Muslims and promising them help from the Jewish population of Yathrib. As a result of their efforts, Qureysh with all their clans, and Ghaṭafān with all their clans marched to destroy Yathrib.

When the Prophet had news of their design, he ordered a trench to be dug before the city and himself led the work of digging it. The trench was finished when the clans arrived, 10,000 strong. The Prophet went out against them with his army of 3000, the trench being between the two armies. For nearly a month the Muslims were exposed to showers of arrows, in constant expectation of attack by much superior forces; and, to make matters worse, news came that the Jewish tribe of Bani Qureyẓah in their rear had broken their alliance with the Muslims and made common cause with Qureysh.

The women and children had been put in strongholds—towers like the peel-towers of Northern England, of which every family of note had one for refuge in time of raids. These were practically unguarded, and some of the Muslims asked permission of the Prophet to leave the battle front and go to guard them, though they were not then in danger because the Banî Qureyẓah were not likely to show their treachery until the victory of the clans was certain.

The case of the Muslims seemed, humanly speaking, hopeless. But a secret sympathiser in the enemy camp managed to sow distrust between the Banî Qureyẓah and the chiefs of the clans, making both feel uneasy. The obstacle of the trench was unexpected and seemed formidable; and when a fierce, bitter wind from the sea blew for three days and nights so furiously that they could not keep a shelter up, or light a fire, or boil a pot, Abū Sufiān, the leader of Qureysh, raised the siege in disgust. And when Ghaṭafān one morning found Qureysh had gone, they too departed for their homes.

On the very day when the Muslims returned from the trench, began the siege of the traitorous Bani Qureyẓah in their towers of refuge. It lasted for twenty-five days. When they at length surrendered some of the tribe of Aus, whose adherents they were, asked the Prophet to show them the same grace that he had shown to the tribe of Khazraj, in the case of Bani Naḍir, in allowing them to intercede for their dependents.

The Prophet said: "Would you like that one of you should decide concerning them?" They said: "Yes," and he appointed Sa'd ibn Mu'ādh, a great chief of Aus, who had been wounded and was being cared for in the Mosque. Sa'd was sent for and he ordered their men to be put to death, their women and children to be made captive, and their property to be divided among the Muslims at the Prophet's will.

I have taken this account from the narrative of Ibn Khaldūn, which is concise, rather than from that in Ibn Hishām, which is exceedingly diffuse, the two accounts being in absolute agreement. Vv. 26 and 27 refer to the punishment of Banî Qureyẓah.

In v. 37 the reference is to the unhappy marriage of Zeyd, the Prophet's freedman and adopted son, with Zeynab, the Prophet's cousin, a proud lady of Qureysh. The Prophet had arranged the marriage with the idea of breaking down the old barrier of pride of caste, and had shown but little consideration for Zeynab's feelings. Tradition says that both she and her brother were averse to the match, and that she had always wished to marry the Prophet. For Zeyd, the marriage was nothing but a cause of embarrassment and humiliation. When the Prophet's attention was first called to their unhappiness, he urged Zeyd to keep his wife and not divorce her, being apprehensive of the talk that would arise if it became known that a marriage arranged by him had proved unhappy. At last, Zeyd did actually divorce Zeynab, and the Prophet was commanded to marry her in order, by his example, to disown the superstitious custom of the pagan Arabs, in such matters, of treating their adopted sons as their real sons, which was against the laws of God (*i.e.* the laws of nature); whereas in arranging a marriage, the woman's inclinations ought to be considered. Unhappy marriage was no part of Allah's ordinance, and was not to be held sacred in Islām.

The Sūrah contains further references to the wives of the Prophet in connection with which it may be mentioned that from the age of twenty-five till the age of fifty he had only one wife, Khadîjah, fifteen years his senior, to whom he was devotedly attached and whose memory he cherished till his dying day. With the exception of 'Ayeshah, the daughter of his closest friend, Abū Bakr, whom he married at her father's request when she was still a minor, all his later marriages were with widows whose state was pitiable for one reason or another. Some of them were widows of men killed in war. One was a captive, when he made the marriage the excuse for emancipating all the conquered tribe and restoring their property. Two were daughters of his enemies, and his alliance with them was a cause of peace. It is noteworthy that the period of these marriages was also the period of his greatest activity, when he had little rest from campaigning, and was always busy with the problems of a growing empire.

The period of revelation is between the end of the fifth and the end of the seventh year of the Hijrah.

THE CLANS

Revealed at Al-Madīnah

In the name of Allah, the Beneficent, the Merciful.

1. O Prophet! Keep thy duty to Allah and obey not the disbelievers and the hypocrites. Lo! Allah is Knower, Wise.

2. And follow that which is inspired in thee from thy Lord. Lo! Allah is Aware of what ye do.

3. And put thy trust in Allah, for Allah is sufficient as Trustee.

4. Allah hath not assigned unto any man two hearts within his body, nor hath he made your wives whom ye declare (to be your mothers) your mothers,[1] nor hath he made those whom ye claim (to be your sons) your sons. This is but a saying of your mouths. But Allah sayeth the truth and He showeth the way.

5. Proclaim their real parentage. That will be more equitable in the sight of Allah. And if ye know not their fathers, then (they are) your brethren in the faith, and your clients. And there is no sin for you in the mistakes that ye make unintentionally, but what your hearts purpose (that will be a sin for you). Allah is Forgiving, Merciful.

6. The Prophet is closer to the believers than their selves, and his wives are (as) their mothers. And the owners of kinship are closer one to another in the ordinance of Allah than (other) believers and the fugitives (who fled from Mecca), except that ye should do kindness to your friends.[2] This is written in the Book (of nature).

اٰیاتها ٧٣ (٣٣) سُوْرَةُ الْاَحْزَابِ مَدَنِيَّةٌ ٩٠ رُكُوْعَاتُهَا ٩

بِسْمِ اللّٰهِ الرَّحْمٰنِ الرَّحِيْمِ

يٰۤاَيُّهَا النَّبِيُّ اتَّقِ اللّٰهَ وَلَا تُطِعِ الْكٰفِرِيْنَ وَالْمُنٰفِقِيْنَ ؕ
اِنَّ اللّٰهَ كَانَ عَلِيْمًا حَكِيْمًا ۙ ﴿١﴾

وَّاتَّبِعْ مَا يُوْحٰۤى اِلَيْكَ مِنْ رَّبِّكَ ؕ اِنَّ اللّٰهَ كَانَ بِمَا
تَعْمَلُوْنَ خَبِيْرًا ۙ ﴿٢﴾

وَّتَوَكَّلْ عَلَى اللّٰهِ ؕ وَكَفٰى بِاللّٰهِ وَكِيْلًا ﴿٣﴾

مَا جَعَلَ اللّٰهُ لِرَجُلٍ مِّنْ قَلْبَيْنِ فِيْ جَوْفِهٖ ۚ وَمَا جَعَلَ
اَزْوَاجَكُمُ الّٰٓـِٔيْ تُظٰهِرُوْنَ مِنْهُنَّ اُمَّهٰتِكُمْ ۚ وَمَا جَعَلَ
اَدْعِيَآءَكُمْ اَبْنَآءَكُمْ ؕ ذٰلِكُمْ قَوْلُكُمْ بِاَفْوَاهِكُمْ ؕ وَاللّٰهُ
يَقُوْلُ الْحَقَّ وَهُوَ يَهْدِي السَّبِيْلَ ﴿٤﴾

اُدْعُوْهُمْ لِاٰبَآئِهِمْ هُوَ اَقْسَطُ عِنْدَ اللّٰهِ ۚ فَاِنْ لَّمْ
تَعْلَمُوْۤا اٰبَآءَهُمْ فَاِخْوَانُكُمْ فِي الدِّيْنِ وَمَوَالِيْكُمْ ؕ
وَلَيْسَ عَلَيْكُمْ جُنَاحٌ فِيْمَاۤ اَخْطَاْتُمْ بِهٖ ۙ وَلٰكِنْ
مَّا تَعَمَّدَتْ قُلُوْبُكُمْ ؕ وَكَانَ اللّٰهُ غَفُوْرًا
رَّحِيْمًا ﴿٥﴾

اَلنَّبِيُّ اَوْلٰى بِالْمُؤْمِنِيْنَ مِنْ اَنْفُسِهِمْ وَاَزْوَاجُهٗۤ
اُمَّهٰتُهُمْ ؕ وَاُولُوا الْاَرْحَامِ بَعْضُهُمْ اَوْلٰى بِبَعْضٍ
فِيْ كِتٰبِ اللّٰهِ مِنَ الْمُؤْمِنِيْنَ وَالْمُهٰجِرِيْنَ اِلَّاۤ اَنْ
تَفْعَلُوْۤا اِلٰۤى اَوْلِيٰٓئِكُمْ مَّعْرُوْفًا ؕ كَانَ ذٰلِكَ فِي الْكِتٰبِ
مَسْطُوْرًا ﴿٦﴾

1. The reference is to a custom of the pagan Arabs by which a man could put away his wife by merely saying: "Thy back is as my mother's back for me."

2. The Prophet had ordained brotherhood between individuals of the Ansār (Muslims of Al-Madinah) and the Muhājirīn (fugitives from Mecca), a brotherhood which was closer than kinship by blood. This verse abolished such brotherhood, in so far as inheritance was concerned.

7. And when We exacted a covenant from the Prophets, and from thee (O Muhammad) and from Noah and Abraham and Moses and Jesus son of Mary, We took from them a solemn covenant;

8. That He may ask the loyal of their loyalty. And He hath prepared a painful doom for the unfaithful.

9. O ye who believe! Remember Allah's favour unto you when there came against you hosts, and We sent against them a great wind and hosts ye could not see. And Allah is ever Seer of what ye do.

10. When they came upon you from above you and from below you, and when eyes grew wild and hearts reached to the throats, and ye were imagining vain thoughts concerning Allah:

11. There were the believers sorely tried, and shaken with a mighty shock.

12. And when the hypocrites, and those in whose hearts is a disease, were saying: Allah and His messenger promised us naught but delusion.

13. And when a party of them said: O folk of Yathrib! There is no stand (possible) for you, therefor turn back. And certain of them (even) sought permission of the Prophet, saying: Our homes lie open (to the enemy). And they lay not open. They but wished to flee.

14. If the enemy had entered from all sides and they had been exhorted to treachery, they would have committed it, and would have hesitated thereupon but little.

15. And verily they had already sworn unto Allah that they would not turn their backs (to the foe). An oath to Allah must be answered for.

وَاِذْ اَخَذْنَا مِنَ النَّبِيِّنَ مِيْثَاقَهُمْ وَمِنْكَ وَمِنْ نُّوحٍ وَّاِبْرٰهِيْمَ وَمُوْسٰى وَعِيْسَى ابْنِ مَرْيَمَ وَاَخَذْنَا مِنْهُمْ مِّيْثَاقًا غَلِيْظًا ۙ ۞

لِّيَسْـَٔلَ الصّٰدِقِيْنَ عَنْ صِدْقِهِمْ ۚ وَاَعَدَّ لِلْكٰفِرِيْنَ عَذَابًا اَلِيْمًا ۞

يٰٓاَيُّهَا الَّذِيْنَ اٰمَنُوا اذْكُرُوْا نِعْمَةَ اللّٰهِ عَلَيْكُمْ اِذْ جَآءَتْكُمْ جُنُوْدٌ فَاَرْسَلْنَا عَلَيْهِمْ رِيْحًا وَّجُنُوْدًا لَّمْ تَرَوْهَا ۚ وَكَانَ اللّٰهُ بِمَا تَعْمَلُوْنَ بَصِيْرًا ۞

اِذْ جَآءُوْكُمْ مِّنْ فَوْقِكُمْ وَمِنْ اَسْفَلَ مِنْكُمْ وَاِذْ زَاغَتِ الْاَبْصَارُ وَبَلَغَتِ الْقُلُوْبُ الْحَنَاجِرَ وَتَظُنُّوْنَ بِاللّٰهِ الظُّنُوْنَا ۞

هُنَالِكَ ابْتُلِيَ الْمُؤْمِنُوْنَ وَزُلْزِلُوْا زِلْزَالًا شَدِيْدًا ۞

وَاِذْ يَقُوْلُ الْمُنٰفِقُوْنَ وَالَّذِيْنَ فِيْ قُلُوْبِهِمْ مَّرَضٌ مَّا وَعَدَنَا اللّٰهُ وَرَسُوْلُهٗٓ اِلَّا غُرُوْرًا ۞

وَاِذْ قَالَتْ طَّآئِفَةٌ مِّنْهُمْ يٰٓاَهْلَ يَثْرِبَ لَا مُقَامَ لَكُمْ فَارْجِعُوْا ۚ وَيَسْتَاْذِنُ فَرِيْقٌ مِّنْهُمُ النَّبِيَّ يَقُوْلُوْنَ اِنَّ بُيُوْتَنَا عَوْرَةٌ ۛ وَمَا هِيَ بِعَوْرَةٍ ۛ اِنْ يُّرِيْدُوْنَ اِلَّا فِرَارًا ۞

وَلَوْ دُخِلَتْ عَلَيْهِمْ مِّنْ اَقْطَارِهَا ثُمَّ سُئِلُوا الْفِتْنَةَ لَاٰتَوْهَا وَمَا تَلَبَّثُوْا بِهَآ اِلَّا يَسِيْرًا ۞

وَلَقَدْ كَانُوْا عَاهَدُوا اللّٰهَ مِنْ قَبْلُ لَا يُوَلُّوْنَ الْاَدْبَارَ ۚ وَكَانَ عَهْدُ اللّٰهِ مَسْـُٔوْلًا ۞

16. Say: Flight will not avail you if ye flee from death or killing, and then ye dwell in comfort but a little while.

قُل لَّن يَنفَعَكُمُ الْفِرَارُ إِن فَرَرْتُم مِّنَ الْمَوْتِ أَوِ
الْقَتْلِ وَإِذًا لَّا تُمَتَّعُونَ إِلَّا قَلِيلًا ﴿١٦﴾

17. Say: Who is he who can preserve you from Allah if He intendeth harm for you, or intendeth mercy for you? They will not find that they have any friend or helper other than Allah.

قُلْ مَن ذَا الَّذِي يَعْصِمُكُم مِّنَ اللَّهِ إِنْ أَرَادَ بِكُمْ
سُوءًا أَوْ أَرَادَ بِكُمْ رَحْمَةً ۚ وَلَا يَجِدُونَ لَهُم مِّن
دُونِ اللَّهِ وَلِيًّا وَلَا نَصِيرًا ﴿١٧﴾

18. Allah already knoweth those of you who hinder, and those who say unto their brethren: "Come ye hither unto us!" and they come not to the stress of battle save a little,

قَدْ يَعْلَمُ اللَّهُ الْمُعَوِّقِينَ مِنكُمْ وَالْقَائِلِينَ
لِإِخْوَانِهِمْ هَلُمَّ إِلَيْنَا ۖ وَلَا يَأْتُونَ الْبَأْسَ إِلَّا
قَلِيلًا ﴿١٨﴾

19. Being sparing of their help to you (believers). But when the fear cometh, then thou (Muhammad) seest them regarding thee with rolling eyes like one who fainteth unto death. Then, when the fear departeth, they scold you with sharp tongues in their greed for wealth (from the spoil). Such have not believed. Therefor Allah maketh their deeds fruitless. And that is easy for Allah.

أَشِحَّةً عَلَيْكُمْ ۖ فَإِذَا جَاءَ الْخَوْفُ رَأَيْتَهُمْ
يَنظُرُونَ إِلَيْكَ تَدُورُ أَعْيُنُهُمْ كَالَّذِي يُغْشَىٰ
عَلَيْهِ مِنَ الْمَوْتِ ۖ فَإِذَا ذَهَبَ الْخَوْفُ سَلَقُوكُم
بِأَلْسِنَةٍ حِدَادٍ أَشِحَّةً عَلَى الْخَيْرِ ۚ أُولَٰئِكَ لَمْ
يُؤْمِنُوا فَأَحْبَطَ اللَّهُ أَعْمَالَهُمْ ۚ وَكَانَ ذَٰلِكَ عَلَى
اللَّهِ يَسِيرًا ﴿١٩﴾

20. They hold that the clans have not retired (for good); and if the clans should advance (again), they would fain be in the desert with the wandering Arabs, asking for the news of you; and if they were among you, they would not give battle, save a little.

يَحْسَبُونَ الْأَحْزَابَ لَمْ يَذْهَبُوا ۖ وَإِن يَأْتِ الْأَحْزَابُ
يَوَدُّوا لَوْ أَنَّهُم بَادُونَ فِي الْأَعْرَابِ يَسْأَلُونَ عَنْ
ع ۲ ۱۸ أَنبَائِكُمْ ۖ وَلَوْ كَانُوا فِيكُم مَّا قَاتَلُوا إِلَّا قَلِيلًا ﴿٢٠﴾

21. Verily in the messenger of Allah ye have a good example for him who looketh unto Allah and the Last Day, and remembereth Allah much.

لَّقَدْ كَانَ لَكُمْ فِي رَسُولِ اللَّهِ أُسْوَةٌ حَسَنَةٌ لِّمَن كَانَ
يَرْجُو اللَّهَ وَالْيَوْمَ الْآخِرَ وَذَكَرَ اللَّهَ كَثِيرًا ﴿٢١﴾

22. And when the true believers saw the clans, they said: This is that which Allah and His messenger promised us. Allah and His messenger are true. It did but confirm them in their faith and resignation.

وَلَمَّا رَأَى الْمُؤْمِنُونَ الْأَحْزَابَ قَالُوا هَٰذَا مَا وَعَدَنَا
اللَّهُ وَرَسُولُهُ وَصَدَقَ اللَّهُ وَرَسُولُهُ ۚ وَمَا زَادَهُمْ
إِلَّا إِيمَانًا وَتَسْلِيمًا ﴿٢٢﴾

23. Of the believers are men who are true to that which they covenanted with Allah. Some of them have paid their vow by death (in battle), and some of them still are waiting; and they have not altered in the least:

مِنَ الْمُؤْمِنِيْنَ رِجَالٌ صَدَقُوْا مَا عَاهَدُوا اللّٰهَ عَلَيْهِ
فَمِنْهُمْ مَّنْ قَضٰى نَحْبَهٗ وَمِنْهُمْ مَّنْ يَّنْتَظِرُ ۖ وَمَا
بَدَّلُوْا تَبْدِيْلًا ﴿٢٣﴾

24. That Allah may reward the true men for Their truth, and punish the hypocrites if He will, or relent toward them (if He will). Lo! Allah is Forgiving. Merciful.

لِّيَجْزِيَ اللّٰهُ الصّٰدِقِيْنَ بِصِدْقِهِمْ وَيُعَذِّبَ
الْمُنٰفِقِيْنَ اِنْ شَآءَ اَوْ يَتُوْبَ عَلَيْهِمْ ۭ اِنَّ اللّٰهَ كَانَ
غَفُوْرًا رَّحِيْمًا ﴿٢٤﴾

25. And Allah repulsed the disbelievers in their wrath; they gained no good. Allah averted their attack from the believers. Allah is Strong, Mighty.

وَرَدَّ اللّٰهُ الَّذِيْنَ كَفَرُوْا بِغَيْظِهِمْ لَمْ يَنَالُوْا خَيْرًا ۭ
وَكَفَى اللّٰهُ الْمُؤْمِنِيْنَ الْقِتَالَ ۭ وَكَانَ اللّٰهُ قَوِيًّا
عَزِيْزًا ﴿٢٥﴾

26. And He brought those of the People of the Scripture who supported them down from their strongholds, and cast panic into their hearts. Some ye slew, and ye made captive some.

وَاَنْزَلَ الَّذِيْنَ ظَاهَرُوْهُمْ مِّنْ اَهْلِ الْكِتٰبِ مِنْ
صَيَاصِيْهِمْ وَقَذَفَ فِيْ قُلُوْبِهِمُ الرُّعْبَ فَرِيْقًا
تَقْتُلُوْنَ وَتَاْسِرُوْنَ فَرِيْقًا ﴿٢٦﴾

27. And He caused you to inherit their land and their houses and their wealth, and land ye have not trodden. Allah is Able to do all things.

وَاَوْرَثَكُمْ اَرْضَهُمْ وَدِيَارَهُمْ وَاَمْوَالَهُمْ وَاَرْضًا
ع ١٩ لَّمْ تَطَــُٔوْهَا ۭ وَكَانَ اللّٰهُ عَلٰى كُلِّ شَيْءٍ قَدِيْرًا ﴿٢٧﴾

28. O Prophet! Say unto thy wives: If ye desire the world's life and its adornments, come! I will content you and will release you with a fair release.

يٰٓاَيُّهَا النَّبِيُّ قُلْ لِّاَزْوَاجِكَ اِنْ كُنْتُنَّ تُرِدْنَ الْحَيٰوةَ
الدُّنْيَا وَزِيْنَتَهَا فَتَعَالَيْنَ اُمَتِّعْكُنَّ وَاُسَرِّحْكُنَّ
سَرَاحًا جَمِيْلًا ﴿٢٨﴾

29. But if ye desire Allah and His messenger and the abode of the Hereafter, then lo! Allah hath prepared for the good among you an immense reward.

وَاِنْ كُنْتُنَّ تُرِدْنَ اللّٰهَ وَرَسُوْلَهٗ وَالدَّارَ الْاٰخِرَةَ
فَاِنَّ اللّٰهَ اَعَدَّ لِلْمُحْسِنٰتِ مِنْكُنَّ اَجْرًا عَظِيْمًا ﴿٢٩﴾

30. O ye wives of the Prophet! Whosoever of you committeth manifest lewdness, the punishment for her will be doubled, and that is easy for Allah.

يٰنِسَآءَ النَّبِيِّ مَنْ يَّاْتِ مِنْكُنَّ بِفَاحِشَةٍ مُّبَيِّنَةٍ
يُّضٰعَفْ لَهَا الْعَذَابُ ضِعْفَيْنِ ۭ وَكَانَ ذٰلِكَ عَلَى
اللّٰهِ يَسِيْرًا ﴿٣٠﴾

31. And whosoever of you is submissive unto Allah and His messenger and doth right, We shall give her reward twice over, and We have prepared for her a rich provision.

32. O ye wives of the Prophet! Ye are not like any other women. If ye keep your duty (to Allah), then be not soft of speech, lest he in whose heart is a disease aspire (to you), but utter customary speech.

33. And stay in your houses. Bedizen not yourselves with the bedizenment of the Time of Ignorance. Be regular in prayer, and pay the poor-due, and obey Allah and His messenger. Allah's wish is but to remove uncleanness far from you, O Folk of the Household, and cleanse you with a thorough cleansing.

34. And bear in mind that which is recited in your houses of the revelations of Allah and wisdom. Lo! Allah is Subtile, Aware.

35. Lo! men who surrender unto Allah, and women who surrender, and men who believe and women who believe, and men who obey and women who obey, and men who speak the truth and women who speak the truth, and men who persevere (in righteousness) and women who persevere, and men who are humble and women who are humble, and men who give alms and women who give alms, and men who fast and women who fast, and men who guard their modesty and women who guard (their modesty), and men who remember Allah much and women who remember—Allah hath prepared for them forgiveness and a vast reward.

36. And it becometh not a believing man or a believing woman, when Allah and His messenger have decided an affair (for them), that they should (after that) claim any say in their affair; and whoso is rebellious to Allah and His messenger, he verily goeth astray in error manifest.

الجزء ٢٢
وَمَنْ يَّقْنُتْ مِنْكُنَّ لِلّٰهِ وَرَسُوْلِهٖ وَتَعْمَلْ
صَالِحًا نُّؤْتِهَآ اَجْرَهَا مَرَّتَيْنِ ۙ وَاَعْتَدْنَا لَهَا
رِزْقًا كَرِيْمًا ﴿٣١﴾
يٰنِسَآءَ النَّبِيِّ لَسْتُنَّ كَاَحَدٍ مِّنَ النِّسَآءِ اِنِ اتَّقَيْتُنَّ فَلَا
تَخْضَعْنَ بِالْقَوْلِ فَيَطْمَعَ الَّذِيْ فِيْ قَلْبِهٖ مَرَضٌ
وَّقُلْنَ قَوْلًا مَّعْرُوْفًا ﴿٣٢﴾
وَقَرْنَ فِيْ بُيُوْتِكُنَّ وَلَا تَبَرَّجْنَ تَبَرُّجَ الْجَاهِلِيَّةِ
الْاُوْلٰى وَاَقِمْنَ الصَّلٰوةَ وَاٰتِيْنَ الزَّكٰوةَ وَاَطِعْنَ
اللّٰهَ وَرَسُوْلَهٗ ؕ اِنَّمَا يُرِيْدُ اللّٰهُ لِيُذْهِبَ عَنْكُمُ
الرِّجْسَ اَهْلَ الْبَيْتِ وَيُطَهِّرَكُمْ تَطْهِيْرًا ﴿٣٣﴾
وَاذْكُرْنَ مَا يُتْلٰى فِيْ بُيُوْتِكُنَّ مِنْ اٰيٰتِ اللّٰهِ وَالْحِكْمَةِ ؕ
ع ٤ اِنَّ اللّٰهَ كَانَ لَطِيْفًا خَبِيْرًا ﴿٣٤﴾
اِنَّ الْمُسْلِمِيْنَ وَالْمُسْلِمٰتِ وَالْمُؤْمِنِيْنَ وَالْمُؤْمِنٰتِ وَ
الْقٰنِتِيْنَ وَالْقٰنِتٰتِ وَالصّٰدِقِيْنَ وَالصّٰدِقٰتِ وَ
الصّٰبِرِيْنَ وَالصّٰبِرٰتِ وَالْخٰشِعِيْنَ وَالْخٰشِعٰتِ وَ
الْمُتَصَدِّقِيْنَ وَالْمُتَصَدِّقٰتِ وَالصَّآئِمِيْنَ وَالصّٰٓئِمٰتِ
وَالْحٰفِظِيْنَ فُرُوْجَهُمْ وَالْحٰفِظٰتِ وَالذّٰكِرِيْنَ اللّٰهَ
كَثِيْرًا وَّالذّٰكِرٰتِ ۙ اَعَدَّ اللّٰهُ لَهُمْ مَّغْفِرَةً وَّاَجْرًا
عَظِيْمًا ﴿٣٥﴾
وَمَا كَانَ لِمُؤْمِنٍ وَّلَا مُؤْمِنَةٍ اِذَا قَضَى اللّٰهُ وَرَسُوْلُهٗٓ
اَمْرًا اَنْ يَّكُوْنَ لَهُمُ الْخِيَرَةُ مِنْ اَمْرِهِمْ ؕ وَمَنْ يَّعْصِ
اللّٰهَ وَرَسُوْلَهٗ فَقَدْ ضَلَّ ضَلٰلًا مُّبِيْنًا ﴿٣٦﴾

37. And when thou saidst unto him on whom Allah hath conferred favour and thou hast conferred favour: Keep thy wife to thyself, and fear Allah. And thou didst hide in thy mind that which Allah was to bring to light, and thou didst fear mankind whereas Allah had a better right that thou shouldst fear Him. So when Zeyd had performed the necessary formality (of divorce) from her, We gave her unto thee in marriage, so that (henceforth) there may be no sin for believers in respect of wives of their adopted sons, when the latter have performed the necessary formality (of release) from them. The commandment of Allah must be fulfilled.

38. There is no reproach for the Prophet in that which Allah maketh his due. That was Allah's way with those who passed away of old—and the commandment of Allah is certain destiny—

39. Who delivered the messages of Allah and feared Him, and feared none save Allah, Allah keepeth good account.

40. Muhammad is not the father of any man among you, but he is the messenger of Allah and the Seal of the Prophets; and Allah is Aware of all things.

41. O ye who believe! Remember Allah with much remembrance,

42. And glorify Him early and late.

43. He it is Who blesseth you, and His angels (bless you), that He may bring you forth from darkness unto light: and He is Merciful to the believers.

44. Their salutation on the Day when they shall meet Him will be: Peace! And He hath prepared for them a goodly recompense.

45. O Prophet! Lo! We have sent thee as a witness and a bringer of good tidings and a warner.

46. And as a summoner unto Allah by His permission, and as a lamp that giveth light.

وَاِذْ تَقُوْلُ لِلَّذِىٓ اَنْعَمَ اللّٰهُ عَلَيْهِ وَاَنْعَمْتَ عَلَيْهِ اَمْسِكْ عَلَيْكَ زَوْجَكَ وَاتَّقِ اللّٰهَ وَتُخْفِىْ فِىْ نَفْسِكَ مَا اللّٰهُ مُبْدِيْهِ وَتَخْشَى النَّاسَ ۚ وَاللّٰهُ اَحَقُّ اَنْ تَخْشٰهُ ۚ فَلَمَّا قَضٰى زَيْدٌ مِّنْهَا وَطَرًا زَوَّجْنٰكَهَا لِكَىْ لَا يَكُوْنَ عَلَى الْمُؤْمِنِيْنَ حَرَجٌ فِىٓ اَزْوَاجِ اَدْعِيَآئِهِمْ اِذَا قَضَوْا مِنْهُنَّ وَطَرًا ۚ وَكَانَ اَمْرُ اللّٰهِ مَفْعُوْلًا ۝

مَا كَانَ عَلَى النَّبِىِّ مِنْ حَرَجٍ فِيْمَا فَرَضَ اللّٰهُ لَهٗ ۚ سُنَّةَ اللّٰهِ فِى الَّذِيْنَ خَلَوْا مِنْ قَبْلُ ۚ وَكَانَ اَمْرُ اللّٰهِ قَدَرًا مَّقْدُوْرَا ۝ۙ

الَّذِيْنَ يُبَلِّغُوْنَ رِسٰلٰتِ اللّٰهِ وَيَخْشَوْنَهٗ وَلَا يَخْشَوْنَ اَحَدًا اِلَّا اللّٰهَ ۚ وَكَفٰى بِاللّٰهِ حَسِيْبًا ۝

مَا كَانَ مُحَمَّدٌ اَبَآ اَحَدٍ مِّنْ رِّجَالِكُمْ وَلٰكِنْ رَّسُوْلَ اللّٰهِ وَخَاتَمَ النَّبِيّٖنَ ۚ وَكَانَ اللّٰهُ بِكُلِّ شَىْءٍ عَلِيْمًا ۝

يٰٓاَيُّهَا الَّذِيْنَ اٰمَنُوا اذْكُرُوا اللّٰهَ ذِكْرًا كَثِيْرًا ۝ۙ

وَّسَبِّحُوْهُ بُكْرَةً وَّاَصِيْلًا ۝

هُوَ الَّذِىْ يُصَلِّىْ عَلَيْكُمْ وَمَلٰٓئِكَتُهٗ لِيُخْرِجَكُمْ مِّنَ الظُّلُمٰتِ اِلَى النُّوْرِ ۚ وَكَانَ بِالْمُؤْمِنِيْنَ رَحِيْمًا ۝

تَحِيَّتُهُمْ يَوْمَ يَلْقَوْنَهٗ سَلٰمٌ ۚ وَاَعَدَّ لَهُمْ اَجْرًا كَرِيْمًا ۝

يٰٓاَيُّهَا النَّبِىُّ اِنَّآ اَرْسَلْنٰكَ شَاهِدًا وَّمُبَشِّرًا وَّنَذِيْرًا ۝ۙ

وَّدَاعِيًا اِلَى اللّٰهِ بِاِذْنِهٖ وَسِرَاجًا مُّنِيْرًا ۝

47. And announce unto the believers the good tidings that they will have great bounty from Allah.

48. And incline not to the disbelievers and the hypocrites. Disregard their noxious talk, and put thy trust in Allah. Allah is sufficient as Trustee.

49. O ye who believe! If ye wed believing women and divorce them before ye have touched them, then there is no period that ye should reckon. But content them and release them handsomely.

50. O Prophet! Lo! We have made lawful unto thee thy wives unto whom thou hast paid their dowries, and those whom thy right hand possesseth of those whom Allah hath given thee as spoils of war, and the daughters of thine uncle on the father's side and the daughters of thine aunts on the father's side, and the daughters of thine uncles on the mother's side and the daughters of thine aunts on the mother's side who emigrated with thee, and a believing woman if she give herself unto the Prophet and the Prophet desire to ask her in marriage—a privilege for thee only, not for the (rest of) believers—We are aware of that which We enjoined upon them concerning their wives and those whom their right hands possess—that thou mayst be free from blame, for Allah is Forgiving, Merciful.

51. Thou canst defer whom thou wilt of them and receive unto thee whom thou wilt, and whomsoever thou desirest of those whom thou hast set aside (temporarily), it is no sin for thee (to receive her again); that is better; that they may be comforted and not grieve, and may all be pleased with what thou givest them. Allah knoweth what is in your hearts (O men) and Allah is Forgiving, Clement.

52. It is not allowed thee to take (other) women henceforth, nor that thou shouldst change them for other wives even though their beauty pleased thee, save those whom thy right hand possesseth. And Allah is Watcher over all things.

وبشر المؤمنين بأن لهم من الله فضلا كبيرا ﴿٤٧﴾
ولا تطع الكافرين والمنافقين ودع أذاهم وتوكل
على الله وكفى بالله وكيلا ﴿٤٨﴾
يا أيها الذين آمنوا إذا نكحتم المؤمنات ثم طلقتموهن
من قبل أن تمسوهن فما لكم عليهن من عدة
تعتدونها فمتعوهن وسرحوهن سراحا جميلا ﴿٤٩﴾
يا أيها النبي إنا أحللنا لك أزواجك اللاتي آتيت
أجورهن وما ملكت يمينك مما أفاء الله عليك
وبنات عمك وبنات عماتك وبنات خالك وبنات
خالاتك اللاتي هاجرن معك وامرأة مؤمنة إن
وهبت نفسها للنبي إن أراد النبي أن يستنكحها
خالصة لك من دون المؤمنين قد علمنا ما
فرضنا عليهم في أزواجهم وما ملكت أيمانهم لكيلا
يكون عليك حرج وكان الله غفورا رحيما ﴿٥٠﴾
ترجي من تشاء منهن وتؤوي إليك من تشاء ومن
ابتغيت ممن عزلت فلا جناح عليك ذلك أدنى
أن تقر أعينهن ولا يحزن ويرضين بما آتيتهن
كلهن والله يعلم ما في قلوبكم وكان الله عليما
حليما ﴿٥١﴾
لا يحل لك النساء من بعد ولا أن تبدل بهن
من أزواج ولو أعجبك حسنهن إلا ما ملكت
يمينك وكان الله على كل شيء رقيبا ﴿٥٢﴾ ع

53. O ye who believe! Enter not the dwellings of the Prophet for a meal without waiting for the proper time, unless permission be granted you. But if ye are invited, enter, and, when your meal is ended, then disperse. Linger not for conversation. Lo! that would cause annoyance to the Prophet, and he would be shy of (asking) you (to go); but Allah is not shy of the truth. And when ye ask of them (the wives of the Prophet) anything, ask it of them from behind a curtain. That is purer for your hearts and for their hearts. And it is not for you to cause annoyance to the messenger of Allah, nor that ye should ever marry his wives after him. Lo! that in Allah's sight would be an enormity.

54. Whether ye divulge a thing or keep it hidden, lo! Allah is ever Knower of all things.

55. It is no sin for them (thy wives) (to converse freely) with their fathers, or their sons, or their brothers, or their brothers' sons, or the sons of their sisters or of their own women, or their slaves. O women! Keep your duty to Allah. Lo! Allah is Witness over all things.

56. Lo! Allah and His angels shower blessings on the Prophet. O ye who believe! Ask blessings on him and salute him with a worthy salutation.

57. Lo! those who malign Allah and His messenger, Allah hath cursed them in the world and the Hereafter, and hath prepared for them the doom of the disdained.

58. And those who malign believing men and believing women undeservedly, they bear the guilt of slander and manifest sin.

يٰۤاَيُّهَا الَّذِيْنَ اٰمَنُوْا لَا تَدْخُلُوْا بُيُوْتَ النَّبِيِّ اِلَّاۤ اَنْ
يُّؤْذَنَ لَكُمْ اِلٰى طَعَامٍ غَيْرَ نٰظِرِيْنَ اِنٰىهُ ۙ وَلٰكِنْ
اِذَا دُعِيْتُمْ فَادْخُلُوْا فَاِذَا طَعِمْتُمْ فَانْتَشِرُوْا وَلَا
مُسْتَاْنِسِيْنَ لِحَدِيْثٍ ؕ اِنَّ ذٰلِكُمْ كَانَ يُؤْذِي النَّبِيَّ
فَيَسْتَحْيٖ مِنْكُمْ ۫ وَاللّٰهُ لَا يَسْتَحْيٖ مِنَ الْحَقِّ ؕ وَاِذَا
سَاَلْتُمُوْهُنَّ مَتَاعًا فَسْـَٔلُوْهُنَّ مِنْ وَّرَآءِ حِجَابٍ ؕ
ذٰلِكُمْ اَطْهَرُ لِقُلُوْبِكُمْ وَقُلُوْبِهِنَّ ؕ وَمَا كَانَ لَكُمْ اَنْ
تُؤْذُوْا رَسُوْلَ اللّٰهِ وَلَاۤ اَنْ تَنْكِحُوْۤا اَزْوَاجَهٗ مِنْۢ بَعْدِهٖۤ
اَبَدًا ؕ اِنَّ ذٰلِكُمْ كَانَ عِنْدَ اللّٰهِ عَظِيْمًا ﴿۵۳﴾
اِنْ تُبْدُوْا شَيْـًٔا اَوْ تُخْفُوْهُ فَاِنَّ اللّٰهَ كَانَ بِكُلِّ
شَيْءٍ عَلِيْمًا ﴿۵۴﴾
لَا جُنَاحَ عَلَيْهِنَّ فِيْۤ اٰبَآئِهِنَّ وَلَاۤ اَبْنَآئِهِنَّ وَلَاۤ
اِخْوَانِهِنَّ وَلَاۤ اَبْنَآءِ اِخْوَانِهِنَّ وَلَاۤ اَبْنَآءِ اَخَوٰتِهِنَّ
وَلَا نِسَآئِهِنَّ وَلَا مَا مَلَكَتْ اَيْمَانُهُنَّ ۚ وَاتَّقِيْنَ
اللّٰهَ ؕ اِنَّ اللّٰهَ كَانَ عَلٰى كُلِّ شَيْءٍ شَهِيْدًا ﴿۵۵﴾
اِنَّ اللّٰهَ وَمَلٰٓئِكَتَهٗ يُصَلُّوْنَ عَلَى النَّبِيِّ ؕ
يٰۤاَيُّهَا الَّذِيْنَ اٰمَنُوْا صَلُّوْا عَلَيْهِ وَسَلِّمُوْا
تَسْلِيْمًا ﴿۵۶﴾
اِنَّ الَّذِيْنَ يُؤْذُوْنَ اللّٰهَ وَرَسُوْلَهٗ لَعَنَهُمُ اللّٰهُ فِي
الدُّنْيَا وَالْاٰخِرَةِ وَاَعَدَّ لَهُمْ عَذَابًا مُّهِيْنًا ﴿۵۷﴾
وَالَّذِيْنَ يُؤْذُوْنَ الْمُؤْمِنِيْنَ وَالْمُؤْمِنٰتِ بِغَيْرِ مَا
ع اكْتَسَبُوْا فَقَدِ احْتَمَلُوْا بُهْتَانًا وَّاِثْمًا مُّبِيْنًا ﴿۵۸﴾

59. O Prophet! Tell thy wives and thy daughters and the women of the believers to draw their cloaks close round them (when they go abroad). That will be better, so that they may be recognised and not annoyed. Allah is ever Forgiving, Merciful.

60. If the hypocrites, and those in whose hearts is a disease, and the alarmists in the city do not cease, We verily shall urge thee on against them, then they will be your neighbours in it but a little while.

61. Accursed, they will be seized wherever found and slain with a (fierce) slaughter:

62. That was the way of Allah in the case of those who passed away of old; thou wilt not find for the way of Allah aught of power to change.

63. Men ask you of the Hour. Say: The knowledge of it is with Allah only. What can convey (the knowledge) unto thee? It may be that the Hour is nigh.

64. Lo! Allah hath cursed the disbelievers, and hath prepared for them a flaming fire,

65. Wherein they will abide for ever. They will find (then) no protecting friend nor helper.

66. On the Day when their faces are turned over in the fire, they say: Oh, would that we had obeyed Allah and had obeyed His messenger!

67. And they say: Our Lord! Lo! we obeyed our princes and great men, and they misled us from the Way.

68. Our Lord! Oh, give them double torment and curse them with a mighty curse.

69. O ye who believe! Be not as those who slandered Moses, but Allah proved his innocence of that which they alleged, and he was well esteemed in Allah's sight.

70. O ye who believe! Guard your duty to Allah, and speak words straight to the point;

يا أيها النبي قل لأزواجك وبناتك ونساء المؤمنين
يدنين عليهن من جلابيبهن ذلك أدنى أن
يعرفن فلا يؤذين وكان الله غفورا رحيما ٥٩
لئن لم ينته المنافقون والذين في قلوبهم
مرض والمرجفون في المدينة لنغرينك بهم
ثم لا يجاورونك فيها إلا قليلا ٦٠
ملعونين أينما ثقفوا أخذوا وقتلوا تقتيلا ٦١
سنة الله في الذين خلوا من قبل ولن تجد
لسنة الله تبديلا ٦٢
يسئلك الناس عن الساعة قل إنما علمها عند
الله وما يدريك لعل الساعة تكون قريبا ٦٣
إن الله لعن الكافرين وأعد لهم سعيرا ٦٤
خالدين فيها أبدا لا يجدون وليا ولا نصيرا ٦٥
يوم تقلب وجوههم في النار يقولون يا ليتنا
أطعنا الله وأطعنا الرسولا ٦٦
وقالوا ربنا إنا أطعنا سادتنا وكبراءنا فأضلونا
السبيلا ٦٧
ربنا آتهم ضعفين من العذاب والعنهم لعنا
كبيرا ٦٨
يا أيها الذين آمنوا لا تكونوا كالذين آذوا موسى
فبرأه الله مما قالوا وكان عند الله وجيها ٦٩
يا أيها الذين آمنوا اتقوا الله وقولوا قولا سديدا ٧٠

71. He will adjust your works for you and will forgive you your sins. Whosoever obeyeth Allah and His messenger, he verily hath gained a signal victory.

72. Lo! We offered the trust unto the heavens and the earth and the hills, but they shrank from bearing it and were afraid of it. And man assumed it. Lo! he hath proved a tyrant and a fool:

73. So Allah punisheth hypocritical men and hypocritical women, and idolatrous men and idolatrous women. But Allah pardoneth believing men and believing women, and Allah is Forgiving, Merciful.

يُصْلِحْ لَكُمْ أَعْمَالَكُمْ وَيَغْفِرْ لَكُمْ ذُنُوبَكُمْ ۗ وَمَنْ
يُطِعِ اللّٰهَ وَرَسُولَهُ فَقَدْ فَازَ فَوْزًا عَظِيمًا ﴿٧١﴾
إِنَّا عَرَضْنَا الْأَمَانَةَ عَلَى السَّمٰوٰتِ وَالْأَرْضِ وَ
الْجِبَالِ فَأَبَيْنَ أَنْ يَحْمِلْنَهَا وَأَشْفَقْنَ مِنْهَا وَحَمَلَهَا
الْإِنْسَانُ ۖ إِنَّهُ كَانَ ظَلُومًا جَهُولًا ﴿٧٢﴾
لِيُعَذِّبَ اللّٰهُ الْمُنٰفِقِينَ وَالْمُنٰفِقٰتِ وَالْمُشْرِكِينَ
وَالْمُشْرِكٰتِ وَيَتُوبَ اللّٰهُ عَلَى الْمُؤْمِنِينَ وَالْمُؤْمِنٰتِ ۗ
ع وَكَانَ اللّٰهُ غَفُورًا رَحِيمًا ﴿٧٣﴾

Saba, "Sheba," takes its name from v. 15 ff., where Sheba (*Saba*), a region in the Yaman, is mentioned as having been devastated by a flood. It warns of the effects of luxury.

An early Meccan Sūrah.

SABA
Revealed at Mecca

In the name of Allah, the Beneficent, the Merciful.

1. Praise be to Allah, unto Whom belongeth whatsoever is in the heavens and whatsoever is in the earth. His is the praise in the Hereafter, and He is the Wise, the Aware.

2. He knoweth that which goeth down into the earth and that which cometh forth from it, and that which descendeth from the heaven and that which ascendeth into it. He is the Merciful, the Forgiving.

3. Those who disbelieve say: The Hour will never come unto us. Say: Nay, by my Lord, but it is coming unto you surely. (He is) the Knower of the Unseen. Not an atom's weight, or less than that or greater, escapeth Him in the heavens or in the earth, but it is in a clear Record,

4. That He may reward those who believe and do good works. For them is pardon and a rich provision.

5. But those who strive against Our revelations, challenging (Us), theirs will be a painful doom of wrath.

6. Those who have been given knowledge see that what is revealed unto thee from thy Lord is the truth and leadeth unto the path of the Mighty, the Owner of Praise.

7. Those who disbelieve say: Shall we show you a man who will tell you (that) when ye have become dispersed in dust with most complete dispersal, still, even then, ye will be created anew?

اٰياتها ٥٤ (٣٤) سُوْرَةُ سَبَاٍ مَّكِّيَّةٌ رُكُوْعَاتُهَا ٦

بِسْمِ اللّٰهِ الرَّحْمٰنِ الرَّحِيْمِ

اَلْحَمْدُ لِلّٰهِ الَّذِيْ لَهٗ مَا فِي السَّمٰوٰتِ وَمَا فِي الْاَرْضِ وَلَهُ الْحَمْدُ فِي الْاٰخِرَةِ ؕ وَهُوَ الْحَكِيْمُ الْخَبِيْرُ ①

يَعْلَمُ مَا يَلِجُ فِي الْاَرْضِ وَمَا يَخْرُجُ مِنْهَا وَمَا يَنْزِلُ مِنَ السَّمَآءِ وَمَا يَعْرُجُ فِيْهَا ؕ وَهُوَ الرَّحِيْمُ الْغَفُوْرُ ②

وَقَالَ الَّذِيْنَ كَفَرُوْا لَا تَاْتِيْنَا السَّاعَةُ ؕ قُلْ بَلٰى وَرَبِّيْ لَتَاْتِيَنَّكُمْ ۙ عٰلِمِ الْغَيْبِ ۚ لَا يَعْزُبُ عَنْهُ مِثْقَالُ ذَرَّةٍ فِي السَّمٰوٰتِ وَلَا فِي الْاَرْضِ وَلَاۤ اَصْغَرُ مِنْ ذٰلِكَ وَلَاۤ اَكْبَرُ اِلَّا فِيْ كِتٰبٍ مُّبِيْنٍ ۙ③

لِّيَجْزِيَ الَّذِيْنَ اٰمَنُوْا وَعَمِلُوا الصّٰلِحٰتِ ؕ اُولٰٓئِكَ لَهُمْ مَّغْفِرَةٌ وَّرِزْقٌ كَرِيْمٌ ④

وَالَّذِيْنَ سَعَوْ فِيْۤ اٰيٰتِنَا مُعٰجِزِيْنَ اُولٰٓئِكَ لَهُمْ عَذَابٌ مِّنْ رِّجْزٍ اَلِيْمٌ ⑤

وَيَرَى الَّذِيْنَ اُوْتُوا الْعِلْمَ الَّذِيْۤ اُنْزِلَ اِلَيْكَ مِنْ رَّبِّكَ هُوَ الْحَقَّ ۙ وَيَهْدِيْۤ اِلٰى صِرَاطِ الْعَزِيْزِ الْحَمِيْدِ ⑥

وَقَالَ الَّذِيْنَ كَفَرُوْا هَلْ نَدُلُّكُمْ عَلٰى رَجُلٍ يُّنَبِّئُكُمْ اِذَا مُزِّقْتُمْ كُلَّ مُمَزَّقٍ ۙ اِنَّكُمْ لَفِيْ خَلْقٍ جَدِيْدٍ ۚ⑦

8. Hath he invented a lie concerning Allah, or is there in him a madness? Nay, but those who disbelieve in the Hereafter are in torment and far error.

أَفْتَرَىٰ عَلَى اللَّهِ كَذِبًا أَمْ بِهِ جِنَّةٌ ۗ بَلِ الَّذِينَ لَا
يُؤْمِنُونَ بِالْآخِرَةِ فِي الْعَذَابِ وَالضَّلَالِ
الْبَعِيدِ ٨

9. Have they not observed what is before them and what is behind them of the sky and the earth? If We will, We can make the earth swallow them, or cause obliteration from the sky to fall on them. Lo! herein surely is a portent for every slave who turneth (to Allah) repentant.

أَفَلَمْ يَرَوْا إِلَىٰ مَا بَيْنَ أَيْدِيهِمْ وَمَا خَلْفَهُمْ مِنَ
السَّمَاءِ وَالْأَرْضِ ۚ إِنْ نَشَأْ نَخْسِفْ بِهِمُ الْأَرْضَ
أَوْ نُسْقِطْ عَلَيْهِمْ كِسَفًا مِنَ السَّمَاءِ ۚ إِنَّ فِي ذَٰلِكَ لَآيَةً
ع لِكُلِّ عَبْدٍ مُنِيبٍ ٩

10. And assuredly We gave David grace from Us, (saying): O ye hills and birds, echo his psalms of praise! And We made the iron supple unto him,

وَلَقَدْ آتَيْنَا دَاوُودَ مِنَّا فَضْلًا ۖ يَا جِبَالُ أَوِّبِي مَعَهُ
وَالطَّيْرَ ۖ وَأَلَنَّا لَهُ الْحَدِيدَ ١٠

11. Saying: Make thou long coats-of-mail and measure the links (thereof). And do ye right. Lo! I am Seer of what ye do.

أَنِ اعْمَلْ سَابِغَاتٍ وَقَدِّرْ فِي السَّرْدِ ۖ وَاعْمَلُوا صَالِحًا ۖ
إِنِّي بِمَا تَعْمَلُونَ بَصِيرٌ ١١

12. And unto Solomon (We gave) the wind, whereof the morning course was a month's journey and the evening course a month's journey, and We caused the fount of copper to gush forth for him, and (We gave him) certain of the jinn who worked before him by permission of his Lord. And such of them as deviated from Our command, them We caused to taste the punishment of flaming fire.

وَلِسُلَيْمَانَ الرِّيحَ غُدُوُّهَا شَهْرٌ وَرَوَاحُهَا شَهْرٌ ۖ وَ
أَسَلْنَا لَهُ عَيْنَ الْقِطْرِ ۖ وَمِنَ الْجِنِّ مَنْ يَعْمَلُ بَيْنَ
يَدَيْهِ بِإِذْنِ رَبِّهِ ۖ وَمَنْ يَزِغْ مِنْهُمْ عَنْ أَمْرِنَا نُذِقْهُ
مِنْ عَذَابِ السَّعِيرِ ١٢

13. They made for him what he willed: synagogues and statues, basins like wells and boilers built into the ground. Give thanks, O house of David! Few of My bondmen are thankful.

يَعْمَلُونَ لَهُ مَا يَشَاءُ مِنْ مَحَارِيبَ وَتَمَاثِيلَ وَ
جِفَانٍ كَالْجَوَابِ وَقُدُورٍ رَاسِيَاتٍ ۚ اعْمَلُوا آلَ دَاوُودَ
شُكْرًا ۚ وَقَلِيلٌ مِنْ عِبَادِيَ الشَّكُورُ ١٣

14. And when We decreed death for him, nothing showed his death to them save a creeping creature of the earth which gnawed away his staff. And when he fell the jinn saw clearly how, if they had known the unseen, they would not have continued in despised toil.

فَلَمَّا قَضَيْنَا عَلَيْهِ الْمَوْتَ مَا دَلَّهُمْ عَلَىٰ مَوْتِهِ إِلَّا
دَابَّةُ الْأَرْضِ تَأْكُلُ مِنْسَأَتَهُ ۖ فَلَمَّا خَرَّ تَبَيَّنَتِ
الْجِنُّ أَنْ لَوْ كَانُوا يَعْلَمُونَ الْغَيْبَ مَا لَبِثُوا
فِي الْعَذَابِ الْمُهِينِ ١٤

15. There was indeed a sign for Sheba in their dwelling-place: Two gardens on the right hand and the left (as who should say): Eat of the provision of your Lord and render thanks to Him. A fair land and an indulgent Lord!

16. But they were froward, so We sent on them the flood of 'Arim, and in exchange for their two gardens gave them two gardens bearing bitter fruit, the tamarisk and here and there a lote-tree.

17. This We awarded them because of their ingratitude. Punish We ever any save the ingrates?

18. And We set, between them and the towns which We had blessed, towns easy to be seen, and We made the stage between them easy, (saying): Travel in them safely both by night and day.

19. But they said: Our Lord! Make the stage between our journeys longer. And they wronged themselves, therefore We made them bywords (in the land) and scattered them abroad, a total scattering. Lo! herein verily are portents for each steadfast, grateful (heart).

20. And Satan indeed found his calculation true concerning them, for they follow him, all save a group of true believers.

21. And he had no warrant whatsoever against them, save that We would know him who believeth in the Hereafter from him who is in doubt thereof; and thy Lord (O Muhammad) taketh note of all things.

22. Say (O Muhammad): Call upon those whom ye set up beside Allah! They possess not an atom's weight either in the heavens or the earth, nor have they any share in either, nor hath He an auxiliary among them.

لَقَدْ كَانَ لِسَبَإٍ فِي مَسْكَنِهِمْ آيَةٌ ۚ جَنَّتَانِ عَنْ يَمِينٍ
وَشِمَالٍ ۚ كُلُوا مِنْ رِزْقِ رَبِّكُمْ وَاشْكُرُوا لَهُ ۚ بَلْدَةٌ
طَيِّبَةٌ وَرَبٌّ غَفُورٌ ﴿١٥﴾
فَأَعْرَضُوا فَأَرْسَلْنَا عَلَيْهِمْ سَيْلَ الْعَرِمِ وَبَدَّلْنَاهُمْ
بِجَنَّتَيْهِمْ جَنَّتَيْنِ ذَوَاتَيْ أُكُلٍ خَمْطٍ وَأَثْلٍ وَشَيْءٍ
مِنْ سِدْرٍ قَلِيلٍ ﴿١٦﴾
ذَٰلِكَ جَزَيْنَاهُمْ بِمَا كَفَرُوا ۖ وَهَلْ نُجْزِي إِلَّا
الْكَفُورَ ﴿١٧﴾
وَجَعَلْنَا بَيْنَهُمْ وَبَيْنَ الْقُرَى الَّتِي بَارَكْنَا فِيهَا
قُرًى ظَاهِرَةً وَقَدَّرْنَا فِيهَا السَّيْرَ ۖ سِيرُوا فِيهَا
لَيَالِيَ وَأَيَّامًا آمِنِينَ ﴿١٨﴾
فَقَالُوا رَبَّنَا بَاعِدْ بَيْنَ أَسْفَارِنَا وَظَلَمُوا أَنْفُسَهُمْ
فَجَعَلْنَاهُمْ أَحَادِيثَ وَمَزَّقْنَاهُمْ كُلَّ مُمَزَّقٍ ۚ إِنَّ
فِي ذَٰلِكَ لَآيَاتٍ لِكُلِّ صَبَّارٍ شَكُورٍ ﴿١٩﴾
وَلَقَدْ صَدَّقَ عَلَيْهِمْ إِبْلِيسُ ظَنَّهُ فَاتَّبَعُوهُ إِلَّا
فَرِيقًا مِنَ الْمُؤْمِنِينَ ﴿٢٠﴾
وَمَا كَانَ لَهُ عَلَيْهِمْ مِنْ سُلْطَانٍ إِلَّا لِنَعْلَمَ مَنْ
يُؤْمِنُ بِالْآخِرَةِ مِمَّنْ هُوَ مِنْهَا فِي شَكٍّ ۗ وَرَبُّكَ
عَلَىٰ كُلِّ شَيْءٍ حَفِيظٌ ﴿٢١﴾ ع ٢ ٨
قُلِ ادْعُوا الَّذِينَ زَعَمْتُمْ مِنْ دُونِ اللَّهِ ۖ لَا يَمْلِكُونَ
مِثْقَالَ ذَرَّةٍ فِي السَّمَاوَاتِ وَلَا فِي الْأَرْضِ وَمَا لَهُمْ
فِيهِمَا مِنْ شِرْكٍ وَمَا لَهُ مِنْهُمْ مِنْ ظَهِيرٍ ﴿٢٢﴾

23. No intercession availeth with Him save for him whom He permitteth. Yet, when fear is banished from their hearts, they say: What was it that your Lord said? They say: The Truth. And He is the Sublime, the Great.

24. Say: Who giveth you provision from the sky and the earth? Say: Allah. Lo! we or you assuredly are rightly guided or in error manifest.

25. Say: Ye will not be asked of what we committed, nor shall we be asked of what ye do.

26. Say: Our Lord will bring us all together, then He will judge between us with truth. He is the All-knowing Judge.

27. Say: Show me those whom ye have joined unto Him as partners. Nay (ye dare not)! For He is Allah, the Mighty, the Wise.

28. And We have not sent thee (O Muhammad) save as a bringer of good tidings and a warner unto all mankind; but most of mankind know not.

29. And they say: When is this promise (to be fulfilled) if ye are truthful?

30. Say (O Muhammad): Yours is the promise of a Day which ye cannot postpone nor hasten by an hour.

31. And those who disbelieve say: We believe not in this Qur'ān nor in that which was before it; but oh, if thou couldst see, when the wrong-doers are brought up before their Lord, how they cast the blame one to another; how those who were despised (in the earth) say unto those who were proud: But for you, we should have been believers!

32. And those who were proud say unto those who were despised: Did we drive you away from the guidance after it had come unto you? Nay, but ye were guilty.

ولا تنفع الشفاعة عنده الا لمن اذن له حتى
اذا فزع عن قلوبهم قالوا ماذا قال ربكم قالوا
الحق وهو العلي الكبير ﴿٢٣﴾
قل من يرزقكم من السموت والارض قل الله و
انا او اياكم لعلى هدى او في ضلل مبين ﴿٢٤﴾
قل لا تسئلون عما اجرمنا ولا نسئل عما تعملون ﴿٢٥﴾
قل يجمع بيننا ربنا ثم يفتح بيننا بالحق و
هو الفتاح العليم ﴿٢٦﴾
قل اروني الذين الحقتم به شركاء كلا بل هو
الله العزيز الحكيم ﴿٢٧﴾
وما ارسلنك الا كافة للناس بشيرا ونذيرا و
لكن اكثر الناس لا يعلمون ﴿٢٨﴾
ويقولون متى هذا الوعد ان كنتم صدقين ﴿٢٩﴾
قل لكم ميعاد يوم لا تستاخرون عنه ساعة
ولا تستقدمون ﴿٣٠﴾
وقال الذين كفروا لن نؤمن بهذا القران ولا
بالذي بين يديه ولو ترى اذ الظلمون موقوفون
عند ربهم يرجع بعضهم الى بعض القول
يقول الذين استضعفوا للذين استكبروا لولا
انتم لكنا مؤمنين ﴿٣١﴾
قال الذين استكبروا للذين استضعفوا انحن صددنكم
عن الهدى بعد اذ جاءكم بل كنتم مجرمين ﴿٣٢﴾

33. Those who were despised say unto those who were proud: Nay, but (it was your) scheming night and day, when ye commanded us to disbelieve in Allah and set up rivals unto Him. And they are filled with remorse when they behold the doom; and We place carcans on the necks of those who disbelieved. Are they requited aught save what they did?

34. And We sent not unto any township a warner, but its pampered ones declared: Lo! we are disbelievers in that which ye bring unto us.

35. And they say: We are more (than you) in wealth and children. We are not the punished!

36. Say (O Muhammad): Lo! my Lord enlargeth the provision for whom He will and narroweth it (for whom He will). But most of mankind know not.

37. And it is not your wealth nor your children that will bring you near unto Us, but he who believeth and doth good (he draweth near). As for such, theirs will be twofold reward for what they did, and they will dwell secure in lofty halls.

38. And as for those who strive against Our revelations, challenging, they will be brought to the doom.

39. Say: Lo! my Lord enlargeth the provision for whom He will of His bondmen, and narroweth (it) for him. And whatsoever ye spend (for good) He replaceth it. And He is the Best of Providers.

40. And on the day when He will gather them all together, He will say unto the angels: Did these worship you?

وقال الذين استضعفوا للذين استكبروا بل مكر
اليل والنهار اذ تامروننا ان نكفر بالله ونجعل له
اندادا واسروا الندامة لما راوا العذاب و
جعلنا الاغلل في اعناق الذين كفروا هل
يجزون الا ما كانوا يعملون ٣٣

وما ارسلنا في قرية من نذير الا قال مترفوها
انا بما ارسلتم به كفرون ٣٤

وقالوا نحن اكثر اموالا واولادا وما نحن
بمعذبين ٣٥

قل ان ربي يبسط الرزق لمن يشاء ويقدر و
ع لكن اكثر الناس لا يعلمون ٣٦

وما اموالكم ولا اولادكم بالتي تقربكم عندنا
زلفى الا من امن وعمل صالحا فاولئك
لهم جزاء الضعف بما عملوا وهم في الغرفت
امنون ٣٧

والذين يسعون في ايتنا معجزين اولئك
في العذاب محضرون ٣٨

قل ان ربي يبسط الرزق لمن يشاء من عباده و
يقدر له وما انفقتم من شيء فهو يخلفه و
هو خير الرزقين ٣٩

ويوم يحشرهم جميعا ثم يقول للملئكة اهؤلاء
اياكم كانوا يعبدون ٤٠

41. They will say: Be Thou glorified. Thou art our Protector from them! Nay, but they worshipped the jinn; most of them were believers in them.

42. That day ye will possess no use nor hurt one for another. And We shall say unto those who did wrong: Taste the doom of the Fire which ye used to deny.

43. And if Our revelations are recited unto them in plain terms, they say: This is naught else than a man who would turn you away from what your fathers used to worship; and they say: This is naught else than an invented lie. Those who disbelieve say of the truth when it reacheth them: This is naught else than mere magic.

44. And We have given them no Scriptures which they study, nor sent We unto them, before thee, any warner.

45. Those before them denied, and these have not attained a tithe of that which We bestowed on them (of old); yet they denied My messengers. How intense then was My abhorrence (of them)!

46. Say (unto them, O Muhammad): I exhort you unto one thing only: that ye awake, for Allah's sake, by twos and singly, and then reflect: There is no madness in your comrade. He is naught else than a warner unto you in face of a terrific doom.

47. Say: Whatever reward I might have asked of you is yours. My reward is the affair of Allah only. He is Witness over all things.

48. Say: Lo! my Lord hurleth the truth. (He is) the Knower of Things Hidden.

49. Say: The truth hath come, and falsehood showeth not its face and will not return.

50. Say: If I err, I err only to my own loss, and if I am rightly guided it is because of that which my Lord hath revealed unto me. Lo! He is Hearer, Nigh.

قَالُوْا سُبْحٰنَكَ اَنْتَ وَلِيُّنَا مِنْ دُوْنِهِمْ ۚ بَلْ كَانُوْا
يَعْبُدُوْنَ الْجِنَّ ۚ اَكْثَرُهُمْ بِهِمْ مُّؤْمِنُوْنَ ﴿٤١﴾
فَالْيَوْمَ لَا يَمْلِكُ بَعْضُكُمْ لِبَعْضٍ نَّفْعًا وَّلَا ضَرًّا ۗ
وَنَقُوْلُ لِلَّذِيْنَ ظَلَمُوْا ذُوْقُوْا عَذَابَ النَّارِ الَّتِيْ
كُنْتُمْ بِهَا تُكَذِّبُوْنَ ﴿٤٢﴾
وَاِذَا تُتْلٰى عَلَيْهِمْ اٰيٰتُنَا بَيِّنٰتٍ قَالُوْا مَا هٰذَآ اِلَّا
رَجُلٌ يُّرِيْدُ اَنْ يَّصُدَّكُمْ عَمَّا كَانَ يَعْبُدُ اٰبَآؤُكُمْ ۚ
وَقَالُوْا مَا هٰذَآ اِلَّآ اِفْكٌ مُّفْتَرًى ۗ وَقَالَ الَّذِيْنَ كَفَرُوْا
لِلْحَقِّ لَمَّا جَآءَهُمْ ۙ اِنْ هٰذَآ اِلَّا سِحْرٌ مُّبِيْنٌ ﴿٤٣﴾
وَمَآ اٰتَيْنٰهُمْ مِّنْ كُتُبٍ يَّدْرُسُوْنَهَا وَمَآ اَرْسَلْنَآ
اِلَيْهِمْ قَبْلَكَ مِنْ نَّذِيْرٍ ﴿٤٤﴾
وَكَذَّبَ الَّذِيْنَ مِنْ قَبْلِهِمْ ۙ وَمَا بَلَغُوْا مِعْشَارَ
مَآ اٰتَيْنٰهُمْ فَكَذَّبُوْا رُسُلِيْ ۫ فَكَيْفَ كَانَ نَكِيْرِ ﴿٤٥﴾
قُلْ اِنَّمَآ اَعِظُكُمْ بِوَاحِدَةٍ ۚ اَنْ تَقُوْمُوْا لِلّٰهِ مَثْنٰى
وَفُرَادٰى ثُمَّ تَتَفَكَّرُوْا ۫ مَا بِصَاحِبِكُمْ مِّنْ جِنَّةٍ ۭ اِنْ
هُوَ اِلَّا نَذِيْرٌ لَّكُمْ بَيْنَ يَدَيْ عَذَابٍ شَدِيْدٍ ﴿٤٦﴾
قُلْ مَا سَاَلْتُكُمْ مِّنْ اَجْرٍ فَهُوَ لَكُمْ ۭ اِنْ اَجْرِيَ اِلَّا عَلَى
اللّٰهِ ۚ وَهُوَ عَلٰى كُلِّ شَيْءٍ شَهِيْدٌ ﴿٤٧﴾
قُلْ اِنَّ رَبِّيْ يَقْذِفُ بِالْحَقِّ ۚ عَلَّامُ الْغُيُوْبِ ﴿٤٨﴾
قُلْ جَآءَ الْحَقُّ وَمَا يُبْدِئُ الْبَاطِلُ وَمَا يُعِيْدُ ﴿٤٩﴾
قُلْ اِنْ ضَلَلْتُ فَاِنَّمَآ اَضِلُّ عَلٰى نَفْسِيْ ۚ وَاِنِ اهْتَدَيْتُ
فَبِمَا يُوْحِيْٓ اِلَيَّ رَبِّيْ ۭ اِنَّهٗ سَمِيْعٌ قَرِيْبٌ ﴿٥٠﴾

51. Couldst thou but see when they are terrified with no escape, and are seized from near at hand,

وَلَوْ تَرَىٰ إِذْ فَزِعُوا فَلَا فَوْتَ وَأُخِذُوا مِن مَّكَانٍ
قَرِيبٍ ﴿٥١﴾

52. And say: We (now) believe therein. But how can they reach (faith) from afar off,

وَقَالُوا آمَنَّا بِهِ وَأَنَّىٰ لَهُمُ التَّنَاوُشُ مِن مَّكَانٍ
بَعِيدٍ ﴿٥٢﴾

53. When they disbelieved in it of yore! They aim at the unseen from afar off.

وَقَدْ كَفَرُوا بِهِ مِن قَبْلُ وَيَقْذِفُونَ بِالْغَيْبِ
مِن مَّكَانٍ بَعِيدٍ ﴿٥٣﴾

54. And a gulf is set between them and that which they desire, as was done for people of their kind of old. Lo! they were in hopeless doubt.

وَحِيلَ بَيْنَهُمْ وَبَيْنَ مَا يَشْتَهُونَ كَمَا فُعِلَ
بِأَشْيَاعِهِم مِّن قَبْلُ إِنَّهُمْ كَانُوا فِي شَكٍّ مُّرِيبٍ ﴿٥٤﴾

Al-Malā'ikah, "The Angels," also called *Al-Fāṭir,* "The Creator," takes its name in either case from a word in verse 1.

An early Meccan Sūrah.

THE ANGELS

Revealed at Mecca

In the name of Allah, the Beneficent, the Merciful.

1. Praise be to Allah, the Creator of the heavens and the earth, Who appointeth the angels messengers having wings two, three and four. He multiplieth in creation what He will. Lo! Allah is Able to do all things.

2. That which Allah openeth unto mankind of mercy none can withhold it; and that which He withholdeth none can release thereafter. He is the Mighty, the Wise.

3. O mankind! Remember Allah's grace toward you! Is there any creator other than Allah Who provideth for you from the sky and the earth? There is no God save Him. Whither then are ye turned?

4. And if they deny thee, (O Muhammad), messengers (of Allah) were denied before thee. Unto Allah all things are brought back.

5. O mankind! Lo! the promise of Allah is true. So let not the life of the world beguile you, and let not the (avowed) beguiler beguile you with regard to Allah.

6. Lo! the devil is an enemy for you, so treat him as an enemy. He only summoneth his faction to be owners of the flaming Fire.

7. Those who disbelieve, theirs will be an awful doom; and those who believe and do good works, theirs will be forgiveness and a great reward.

اٰياتها ٤٥ (٣٥) سُوْرَةُ فَاطِرٍ مَكِّيَّةٌ ركوعاتها ٥

بِسْمِ اللّٰهِ الرَّحْمٰنِ الرَّحِيْمِ

اَلْحَمْدُ لِلّٰهِ فَاطِرِ السَّمٰوٰتِ وَالْاَرْضِ جَاعِلِ
الْمَلٰٓئِكَةِ رُسُلًا اُولِيْٓ اَجْنِحَةٍ مَّثْنٰى وَثُلٰثَ وَرُبٰعَ
يَزِيْدُ فِي الْخَلْقِ مَا يَشَآءُ اِنَّ اللّٰهَ عَلٰى كُلِّ
شَيْءٍ قَدِيْرٌ ①
مَا يَفْتَحِ اللّٰهُ لِلنَّاسِ مِنْ رَّحْمَةٍ فَلَا مُمْسِكَ لَهَا
وَمَا يُمْسِكْ فَلَا مُرْسِلَ لَهٗ مِنْ بَعْدِهٖ وَهُوَ الْعَزِيْزُ
الْحَكِيْمُ ②
يٰٓاَيُّهَا النَّاسُ اذْكُرُوْا نِعْمَتَ اللّٰهِ عَلَيْكُمْ هَلْ مِنْ
خَالِقٍ غَيْرُ اللّٰهِ يَرْزُقُكُمْ مِّنَ السَّمَآءِ وَالْاَرْضِ لَآ
اِلٰهَ اِلَّا هُوَ فَاَنّٰى تُؤْفَكُوْنَ ③
وَاِنْ يُّكَذِّبُوْكَ فَقَدْ كُذِّبَتْ رُسُلٌ مِّنْ قَبْلِكَ وَ
اِلَى اللّٰهِ تُرْجَعُ الْاُمُوْرُ ④
يٰٓاَيُّهَا النَّاسُ اِنَّ وَعْدَ اللّٰهِ حَقٌّ فَلَا تَغُرَّنَّكُمُ
الْحَيٰوةُ الدُّنْيَا وَلَا يَغُرَّنَّكُمْ بِاللّٰهِ الْغَرُوْرُ ⑤
اِنَّ الشَّيْطٰنَ لَكُمْ عَدُوٌّ فَاتَّخِذُوْهُ عَدُوًّا اِنَّمَا يَدْعُوْا
حِزْبَهٗ لِيَكُوْنُوْا مِنْ اَصْحٰبِ السَّعِيْرِ ⑥
اَلَّذِيْنَ كَفَرُوْا لَهُمْ عَذَابٌ شَدِيْدٌ وَالَّذِيْنَ
اٰمَنُوْا وَعَمِلُوا الصّٰلِحٰتِ لَهُمْ مَّغْفِرَةٌ وَّاَجْرٌ
كَبِيْرٌ ⑦

8. Is he, the evil of whose deeds is made fair-seeming unto him so that he deemeth it good, (other than Satan's dupe)? Allah verily sendeth whom He will astray, and guideth whom He will; so let not thy soul expire in sighings for them. Lo! Allah is Aware of what they do!

9. And Allah it is Who sendeth the winds and they raise a cloud; then We lead it unto a dead land and revive therewith the earth after its death. Such is the Resurrection.

10. Whoso desireth power (should know that) all power belongeth to Allah. Unto Him good words ascend, and the pious deed doth He exalt; but those who plot iniquities, theirs will be an awful doom; and the plotting of such (folk) will come to naught.

11. Allah created you from dust, then from a little fluid, then He made you pairs (the male and female). No female beareth or bringeth forth save with His knowledge. And no one groweth old who groweth old nor is aught lessened of his life, but it is recorded in a Book. Lo! that is easy for Allah.

12. And two seas[1] are not alike: this, fresh, sweet, good to drink, this (other) bitter, salt. And from them both ye eat fresh meat and derive the ornament that ye wear. And thou seest the ship cleaving them with its prow that ye may seek of His bounty, and that haply ye may give thanks.

13. He maketh the night to pass into the day and He maketh the day to pass into the night. He hath subdued the sun and moon to service. Each runneth unto an appointed term. Such is Allah, your Lord; His is the Sovereignty; and those unto whom ye pray instead of Him own not so much as the white spot on a date-stone.

1. *i.e.* the two kinds of water in the earth.

أَفَمَنْ زُيِّنَ لَهُ سُوٓءُ عَمَلِهِ فَرَاٰهُ حَسَنًا ۭ فَاِنَّ اللّٰهَ
يُضِلُّ مَنْ يَّشَآءُ وَيَهْدِيْ مَنْ يَّشَآءُ ڮ فَلَا تَذْهَبْ
نَفْسُكَ عَلَيْهِمْ حَسَرٰتٍ ۭ اِنَّ اللّٰهَ عَلِيْمٌۢ بِمَا يَصْنَعُوْنَ ﴿٨﴾
وَاللّٰهُ الَّذِيْٓ اَرْسَلَ الرِّيٰحَ فَتُثِيْرُ سَحَابًا فَسُقْنٰهُ
اِلٰى بَلَدٍ مَّيِّتٍ فَاَحْيَيْنَا بِهِ الْاَرْضَ بَعْدَ مَوْتِهَا ۭ
كَذٰلِكَ النُّشُوْرُ ﴿٩﴾
مَنْ كَانَ يُرِيْدُ الْعِزَّةَ فَلِلّٰهِ الْعِزَّةُ جَمِيْعًا ۭ اِلَيْهِ
يَصْعَدُ الْكَلِمُ الطَّيِّبُ وَالْعَمَلُ الصَّالِحُ يَرْفَعُهٗ ۭ
وَالَّذِيْنَ يَمْكُرُوْنَ السَّيِّاٰتِ لَهُمْ عَذَابٌ شَدِيْدٌ ۭ
وَمَكْرُ اُولٰۗىِٕكَ هُوَ يَبُوْرُ ﴿١٠﴾
وَاللّٰهُ خَلَقَكُمْ مِّنْ تُرَابٍ ثُمَّ مِنْ نُّطْفَةٍ ثُمَّ جَعَلَكُمْ
اَزْوَاجًا ۭ وَمَا تَحْمِلُ مِنْ اُنْثٰى وَلَا تَضَعُ اِلَّا بِعِلْمِهٖ ۭ
وَمَا يُعَمَّرُ مِنْ مُّعَمَّرٍ وَّلَا يُنْقَصُ مِنْ عُمُرِهٖٓ اِلَّا
فِيْ كِتٰبٍ ۭ اِنَّ ذٰلِكَ عَلَى اللّٰهِ يَسِيْرٌ ﴿١١﴾
وَمَا يَسْتَوِي الْبَحْرٰنِ ڰ هٰذَا عَذْبٌ فُرَاتٌ سَاۗىِٕغٌ شَرَابُهٗ
وَهٰذَا مِلْحٌ اُجَاجٌ ۭ وَمِنْ كُلٍّ تَاْكُلُوْنَ لَحْمًا طَرِيًّا وَّ
تَسْتَخْرِجُوْنَ حِلْيَةً تَلْبَسُوْنَهَا ۚ وَتَرَى الْفُلْكَ فِيْهِ
مَوَاخِرَ لِتَبْتَغُوْا مِنْ فَضْلِهٖ وَلَعَلَّكُمْ تَشْكُرُوْنَ ﴿١٢﴾
يُوْلِجُ الَّيْلَ فِي النَّهَارِ وَيُوْلِجُ النَّهَارَ فِي الَّيْلِ ۙ وَ
سَخَّرَ الشَّمْسَ وَالْقَمَرَ ڮ كُلٌّ يَّجْرِيْ لِاَجَلٍ مُّسَمًّى ۭ
ذٰلِكُمُ اللّٰهُ رَبُّكُمْ لَهُ الْمُلْكُ ۭ وَالَّذِيْنَ تَدْعُوْنَ مِنْ
دُوْنِهٖ مَا يَمْلِكُوْنَ مِنْ قِطْمِيْرٍ ﴿١٣﴾

14. If ye pray unto them they hear not your prayer, and if they heard they could not grant it you. On the Day of Resurrection they will disown association with you. None can inform you like Him Who is Aware.

اِنْ تَدْعُوْهُمْ لَا يَسْمَعُوْا دُعَآءَكُمْ وَلَوْ سَمِعُوْا مَا اسْتَجَابُوْا لَكُمْ وَيَوْمَ الْقِيٰمَةِ يَكْفُرُوْنَ بِشِرْكِكُمْ وَلَا يُنَبِّئُكَ مِثْلُ خَبِيْرٍ ۝

15. O mankind! Ye are the poor in your relation to Allah. And Allah! He is the Absolute, the Owner of Praise.

يٰٓاَيُّهَا النَّاسُ اَنْتُمُ الْفُقَرَآءُ اِلَى اللّٰهِ وَاللّٰهُ هُوَ الْغَنِيُّ الْحَمِيْدُ ۝

16. If He will, He can be rid of you and bring (instead of you) some new creation.

اِنْ يَّشَأْ يُذْهِبْكُمْ وَيَأْتِ بِخَلْقٍ جَدِيْدٍ ۝

17. That is not a hard thing for Allah.

وَمَا ذٰلِكَ عَلَى اللّٰهِ بِعَزِيْزٍ ۝

18. And no burdened soul can bear another's burden, and if one heavy laden crieth for (help with) his load, naught of it will be lifted even though he (unto whom he crieth) be of kin. Thou warnest only those who fear their Lord in secret, and have established worship. He who groweth (in goodness), groweth only for himself, (he cannot by his merit redeem others). Unto Allah is the journeying.

وَلَا تَزِرُ وَازِرَةٌ وِّزْرَ اُخْرٰى وَاِنْ تَدْعُ مُثْقَلَةٌ اِلٰى حِمْلِهَا لَا يُحْمَلْ مِنْهُ شَيْءٌ وَّلَوْ كَانَ ذَا قُرْبٰى اِنَّمَا تُنْذِرُ الَّذِيْنَ يَخْشَوْنَ رَبَّهُمْ بِالْغَيْبِ وَ اَقَامُوا الصَّلٰوةَ وَمَنْ تَزَكّٰى فَاِنَّمَا يَتَزَكّٰى لِنَفْسِهٖ وَاِلَى اللّٰهِ الْمَصِيْرُ ۝

19. The blind man is not equal with the seer;

وَمَا يَسْتَوِى الْاَعْمٰى وَالْبَصِيْرُ ۝

20. Nor is darkness (tantamount to) light;

وَلَا الظُّلُمٰتُ وَلَا النُّوْرُ ۝

21. Nor is the shadow equal with the sun's full heat;

وَلَا الظِّلُّ وَلَا الْحَرُوْرُ ۝

22. Nor are the living equal with the dead. Lo! Allah maketh whom He will to hear. Thou canst not reach those who are in the graves.

وَمَا يَسْتَوِى الْاَحْيَآءُ وَلَا الْاَمْوَاتُ اِنَّ اللّٰهَ يُسْمِعُ مَنْ يَّشَآءُ وَمَا اَنْتَ بِمُسْمِعٍ مَّنْ فِى الْقُبُوْرِ ۝

23. Thou art but a warner.

اِنْ اَنْتَ اِلَّا نَذِيْرٌ ۝

24. Lo! We have sent thee with the Truth, a bearer of glad tidings and a warner; and there is not a nation but a warner hath passed among them.

اِنَّا اَرْسَلْنٰكَ بِالْحَقِّ بَشِيْرًا وَّنَذِيْرًا وَّاِنْ مِّنْ اُمَّةٍ اِلَّا خَلَا فِيْهَا نَذِيْرٌ ۝

25. And if they deny thee, those before them also denied. Their messengers came unto them with clear proofs (of Allah's sovereignty), and with the Psalms and the Scripture giving light.

وَاِنْ يُّكَذِّبُوْكَ فَقَدْ كَذَّبَ الَّذِيْنَ مِنْ قَبْلِهِمْ جَآءَتْهُمْ رُسُلُهُمْ بِالْبَيِّنٰتِ وَبِالزُّبُرِ وَبِالْكِتٰبِ الْمُنِيْرِ ۝

26. Then seized I those who disbelieved, and how intense was My abhorrence!

27. Hast thou not seen that Allah causeth water to fall from the sky, and We produce therewith fruit of divers hues; and among the hills are streaks white and red, of divers hues, and (others) raven-black;

28. And of men and beasts and cattle, in like manner, divers hues? The erudite among His bondmen fear Allah alone. Lo! Allah is Mighty, Forgiving.

29. Lo! those who read the Scripture of Allah, and establish worship, and spend of that which We have bestowed on them secretly and openly, they look forward to imperishable gain,

30. That He will pay them their wages and increase them of His grace. Lo! He is Forgiving, Responsive.

31. As for that which We inspire in thee of the Scripture, it is the Truth confirming that which was (revealed) before it. Lo! Allah is indeed Observer, Seer of His slaves.

32. Then We gave the Scripture as inheritance unto those whom We elected of Our bondmen. But of them are some who wrong themselves and of them are some who are lukewarm, and of them are some who outstrip (others) through good deeds, by Allah's leave. That is the great favour!

33. Gardens of Eden! They enter them wearing armlets of gold and pearl and their raiment therein is silk.

34. And they say: Praise be to Allah Who hath put grief away from us. Lo! Our Lord is Forgiving, Bountiful,

ثُمَّ اَخَذْتُ الَّذِيْنَ كَفَرُوْا فَكَيْفَ كَانَ نَكِيْرِ ﴿٢٦﴾ ع ٣ ١٥
اَلَمْ تَرَ اَنَّ اللّٰهَ اَنْزَلَ مِنَ السَّمَآءِ مَآءً ۚ فَاَخْرَجْنَا بِهٖ
ثَمَرٰتٍ مُّخْتَلِفًا اَلْوَانُهَا ؕ وَمِنَ الْجِبَالِ جُدَدٌۢ بِيْضٌ
وَّحُمْرٌ مُّخْتَلِفٌ اَلْوَانُهَا وَغَرَابِيْبُ سُوْدٌ ﴿٢٧﴾
وَمِنَ النَّاسِ وَالدَّوَآبِّ وَالْاَنْعَامِ مُخْتَلِفٌ اَلْوَانُهٗ
كَذٰلِكَ ؕ اِنَّمَا يَخْشَى اللّٰهَ مِنْ عِبَادِهِ الْعُلَمٰٓؤُا ؕ اِنَّ
اللّٰهَ عَزِيْزٌ غَفُوْرٌ ﴿٢٨﴾
اِنَّ الَّذِيْنَ يَتْلُوْنَ كِتٰبَ اللّٰهِ وَاَقَامُوا الصَّلٰوةَ وَ
اَنْفَقُوْا مِمَّا رَزَقْنٰهُمْ سِرًّا وَّعَلَانِيَةً يَّرْجُوْنَ تِجَارَةً
لَّنْ تَبُوْرَ ۙ ﴿٢٩﴾
لِيُوَفِّيَهُمْ اُجُوْرَهُمْ وَيَزِيْدَهُمْ مِّنْ فَضْلِهٖ ؕ اِنَّهٗ
غَفُوْرٌ شَكُوْرٌ ﴿٣٠﴾
وَالَّذِيْۤ اَوْحَيْنَاۤ اِلَيْكَ مِنَ الْكِتٰبِ هُوَ الْحَقُّ مُصَدِّقًا
لِّمَا بَيْنَ يَدَيْهِ ؕ اِنَّ اللّٰهَ بِعِبَادِهٖ لَخَبِيْرٌۢ بَصِيْرٌ ﴿٣١﴾
ثُمَّ اَوْرَثْنَا الْكِتٰبَ الَّذِيْنَ اصْطَفَيْنَا مِنْ عِبَادِنَا ۚ
فَمِنْهُمْ ظَالِمٌ لِّنَفْسِهٖ ۚ وَمِنْهُمْ مُّقْتَصِدٌ ۚ وَمِنْهُمْ
سَابِقٌۢ بِالْخَيْرٰتِ بِاِذْنِ اللّٰهِ ؕ ذٰلِكَ هُوَ الْفَضْلُ
الْكَبِيْرُ ﴿٣٢﴾
جَنّٰتُ عَدْنٍ يَّدْخُلُوْنَهَا يُحَلَّوْنَ فِيْهَا مِنْ اَسَاوِرَ
مِنْ ذَهَبٍ وَّلُؤْلُؤًا ۚ وَلِبَاسُهُمْ فِيْهَا حَرِيْرٌ ﴿٣٣﴾
وَقَالُوا الْحَمْدُ لِلّٰهِ الَّذِيْۤ اَذْهَبَ عَنَّا الْحَزَنَ ؕ اِنَّ
رَبَّنَا لَغَفُوْرٌ شَكُوْرُ ۙ ﴿٣٤﴾

35. Who, of His grace, hath installed us in the mansion of eternity, where toil toucheth us not nor can weariness affect us.

36. But as for those who disbelieve, for them is fire of hell; it taketh not complete effect upon them so that they can die, nor is its torment lightened for them. Thus We punish every ingrate.

37. And they cry for help there, (saying): Our Lord! Release us; we will do right, not (the wrong) that we used to do. Did not We grant a life long enough for him who reflected to reflect therein? And the warner came unto you. Now taste (the flavour of your deeds), for evil-doers have no helper.

38. Lo! Allah is the Knower of the Unseen of the heavens and the earth. Lo! He is Aware of the secret of (men's) breasts.

39. He it is Who hath made you regents in the earth; so he who disbelieveth, his disbelief be on his own head. Their disbelief increaseth for the disbelievers, in their Lord's sight, naught save abhorrence. Their disbelief increaseth for the disbelievers naught save loss.

40. Say: Have ye seen your partner-gods to whom ye pray beside Allah? Show me what they created of the earth! Or have they any portion in the heavens? Or have We given them a Scripture so that they act on clear proof therefrom? Nay, the evil-doers promise one another only to deceive.

41. Lo! Allah graspeth the heavens and the earth that they deviate not, and if they were to deviate there is not one that could grasp them after Him. Lo! He is ever Clement, Forgiving.

الَّذِىٓ اَحَلَّنَا دَارَ الْمُقَامَةِ مِنْ فَضْلِهٖ ۚ لَا يَمَسُّنَا
فِيْهَا نَصَبٌ وَّلَا يَمَسُّنَا فِيْهَا لُغُوْبٌ ﴿٣٥﴾
وَالَّذِيْنَ كَفَرُوْا لَهُمْ نَارُ جَهَنَّمَ ۚ لَا يُقْضٰى عَلَيْهِمْ
فَيَمُوْتُوْا وَلَا يُخَفَّفُ عَنْهُمْ مِّنْ عَذَابِهَا ۭ كَذٰلِكَ
نَجْزِىْ كُلَّ كَفُوْرٍ ﴿٣٦﴾
وَهُمْ يَصْطَرِخُوْنَ فِيْهَا ۚ رَبَّنَآ اَخْرِجْنَا نَعْمَلْ صَالِحًا
غَيْرَ الَّذِىْ كُنَّا نَعْمَلُ ۭ اَوَلَمْ نُعَمِّرْكُمْ مَّا يَتَذَكَّرُ فِيْهِ
مَنْ تَذَكَّرَ وَجَآءَكُمُ النَّذِيْرُ ۭ فَذُوْقُوْا فَمَا لِلظّٰلِمِيْنَ
ع مِنْ نَّصِيْرٍ ﴿٣٧﴾
اِنَّ اللّٰهَ عٰلِمُ غَيْبِ السَّمٰوٰتِ وَالْاَرْضِ ۭ اِنَّهٗ عَلِيْمٌۢ
بِذَاتِ الصُّدُوْرِ ﴿٣٨﴾
هُوَ الَّذِىْ جَعَلَكُمْ خَلٰۗىِٕفَ فِى الْاَرْضِ ۭ فَمَنْ كَفَرَ
فَعَلَيْهِ كُفْرُهٗ ۭ وَلَا يَزِيْدُ الْكٰفِرِيْنَ كُفْرُهُمْ عِنْدَ
رَبِّهِمْ اِلَّا مَقْتًا ۚ وَلَا يَزِيْدُ الْكٰفِرِيْنَ كُفْرُهُمْ اِلَّا
خَسَارًا ﴿٣٩﴾
قُلْ اَرَءَيْتُمْ شُرَكَاۗءَكُمُ الَّذِيْنَ تَدْعُوْنَ مِنْ دُوْنِ اللّٰهِ ۭ
اَرُوْنِىْ مَاذَا خَلَقُوْا مِنَ الْاَرْضِ اَمْ لَهُمْ شِرْكٌ فِى
السَّمٰوٰتِ ۚ اَمْ اٰتَيْنٰهُمْ كِتٰبًا فَهُمْ عَلٰى بَيِّنَتٍ مِّنْهُ ۚ بَلْ
اِنْ يَّعِدُ الظّٰلِمُوْنَ بَعْضُهُمْ بَعْضًا اِلَّا غُرُوْرًا ﴿٤٠﴾
اِنَّ اللّٰهَ يُمْسِكُ السَّمٰوٰتِ وَالْاَرْضَ اَنْ تَزُوْلَا ڬ وَ
لَىِٕنْ زَالَتَآ اِنْ اَمْسَكَهُمَا مِنْ اَحَدٍ مِّنْۢ بَعْدِهٖ ۭ اِنَّهٗ
كَانَ حَلِيْمًا غَفُوْرًا ﴿٤١﴾

42. And they swore by Allah, their most binding oath, that if a warner came unto them they would be more tractable than any of the nations; yet, when a warner came unto them it aroused in them naught save repugnance,

43. (Shown in their) behaving arrogantly in the land and plotting evil; and the evil plot encloseth but the men who make it. Then, can they expect aught save the treatment of the folk of old? Thou wilt not find for Allah's way of treatment any substitute, nor wilt thou find for Allah's way of treatment aught of power to change.

44. Have they not travelled in the land and seen the nature of the consequence for those who were before them, and they were mightier than these in power? Allah is not such that aught in the heavens or in the earth escapeth Him. Lo! He is the Wise, the Mighty.

45. If Allah took mankind to task by that which they deserve, He would not leave a living creature on the surface of the earth; but He reprieveth them unto an appointed term, and when their term cometh—then verily (they will know that) Allah is ever Seer of His slaves.

وَأَقْسَمُوا بِاللَّهِ جَهْدَ أَيْمَانِهِمْ لَئِن جَاءَهُمْ نَذِيرٌ
لَّيَكُونُنَّ أَهْدَىٰ مِنْ إِحْدَى الْأُمَمِ ۖ فَلَمَّا جَاءَهُمْ
نَذِيرٌ مَّا زَادَهُمْ إِلَّا نُفُورًا ﴿٤٢﴾

اسْتِكْبَارًا فِي الْأَرْضِ وَمَكْرَ السَّيِّئِ ۚ وَلَا يَحِيقُ الْمَكْرُ
السَّيِّئُ إِلَّا بِأَهْلِهِ ۚ فَهَلْ يَنظُرُونَ إِلَّا سُنَّتَ الْأَوَّلِينَ ۚ
فَلَن تَجِدَ لِسُنَّتِ اللَّهِ تَبْدِيلًا ۖ وَلَن تَجِدَ لِسُنَّتِ
اللَّهِ تَحْوِيلًا ﴿٤٣﴾

أَوَلَمْ يَسِيرُوا فِي الْأَرْضِ فَيَنظُرُوا كَيْفَ كَانَ عَاقِبَةُ
الَّذِينَ مِن قَبْلِهِمْ وَكَانُوا أَشَدَّ مِنْهُمْ قُوَّةً ۚ وَمَا
كَانَ اللَّهُ لِيُعْجِزَهُ مِن شَيْءٍ فِي السَّمَاوَاتِ وَلَا فِي
الْأَرْضِ ۚ إِنَّهُ كَانَ عَلِيمًا قَدِيرًا ﴿٤٤﴾

وَلَوْ يُؤَاخِذُ اللَّهُ النَّاسَ بِمَا كَسَبُوا مَا تَرَكَ عَلَىٰ
ظَهْرِهَا مِن دَابَّةٍ وَلَٰكِن يُؤَخِّرُهُمْ إِلَىٰ أَجَلٍ
مُّسَمًّى ۖ فَإِذَا جَاءَ أَجَلُهُمْ فَإِنَّ اللَّهَ كَانَ بِعِبَادِهِ
ع ٥ ١٧ بَصِيرًا ﴿٤٥﴾

Yā Sīn takes its name from the two letters of the Arabic alphabet which stand as the first verse and are generally held to signify *Yā Insān* ("O Man"). This Sūrah is regarded with special reverence, and is recited in times of adversity, illness, fasting and on the approach of death.

It belongs to the middle group of Meccan Sūrahs.

YĀ SĪN

Revealed at Mecca

In the name of Allah, the Beneficent, the Merciful.

1. Yā Sīn.

2. By the wise Qur'ān,

3. Lo! thou art of those sent

4. On a straight path,

5. A revelation of the Mighty, the Merciful,

6. That thou mayst warn a folk whose fathers were not warned, so they are heedless.

7. Already hath the word proved true of most of them, for they believe not.

8. Lo! We have put on their necks carcans reaching unto the chins, so that they are made stiff-necked.

9. And We have set a bar before them and a bar behind them, and (thus) have covered them so that they see not.

10. Whether thou warn them or thou warn them not, it is alike for them, for they believe not.

11. Thou warnest only him who followeth the Reminder and feareth the Beneficent in secret. To him bear tidings of forgiveness and a rich reward.

12. Lo! We it is Who bring the dead to life. We record that which they send before (them), and their footprints. And all things We have kept in a clear register.

ایاتها ٨٣ (٣٦) سورة يس مكية ٤١ ركوعاتها ٥

بسم الله الرحمن الرحيم

يس ١

والقرآن الحكيم ٢

إنك لمن المرسلين ٣

على صراط مستقيم ٤

تنزيل العزيز الرحيم ٥

لتنذر قوما ما أنذر آباؤهم فهم
غافلون ٦

لقد حق القول على أكثرهم فهم لا
يؤمنون ٧

إنا جعلنا في أعناقهم أغلالا فهي إلى الأذقان
فهم مقمحون ٨

وجعلنا من بين أيديهم سدا ومن خلفهم
سدا فأغشيناهم فهم لا يبصرون ٩

وسواء عليهم أأنذرتهم أم لم تنذرهم لا
يؤمنون ١٠

إنما تنذر من اتبع الذكر وخشي الرحمن بالغيب
فبشره بمغفرة وأجر كريم ١١

إنا نحن نحي الموتى ونكتب ما قدموا وآثارهم
وكل شيء أحصيناه في إمام مبين ١٢ ع

13. Coin for them a similitude: The people of the city when those sent (from Allah) came unto them;

وَاضْرِبْ لَهُمْ مَّثَلًا اَصْحٰبَ الْقَرْيَةِ اِذْ جَآءَهَا الْمُرْسَلُوْنَ ﴿١٣﴾

14. When We sent unto them twain, and they denied them both, so We reinforced them with a third, and they said: Lo! we have been sent unto you.

اِذْ اَرْسَلْنَآ اِلَيْهِمُ اثْنَيْنِ فَكَذَّبُوْهُمَا فَعَزَّزْنَا بِثَالِثٍ فَقَالُوْٓا اِنَّآ اِلَيْكُمْ مُّرْسَلُوْنَ ﴿١٤﴾

15. They said: Ye are but mortals like unto us. The Beneficent hath naught revealed. Ye do but lie!

قَالُوْا مَآ اَنْتُمْ اِلَّا بَشَرٌ مِّثْلُنَا وَمَآ اَنْزَلَ الرَّحْمٰنُ مِنْ شَيْءٍ اِنْ اَنْتُمْ اِلَّا تَكْذِبُوْنَ ﴿١٥﴾

16. They answered: Our Lord knoweth that we are indeed sent unto you,

قَالُوْا رَبُّنَا يَعْلَمُ اِنَّآ اِلَيْكُمْ لَمُرْسَلُوْنَ ﴿١٦﴾

17. And our duty is but plain conveyance (of the message).

وَمَا عَلَيْنَآ اِلَّا الْبَلٰغُ الْمُبِيْنُ ﴿١٧﴾

18. (The people of the city) said: We augur ill of you. If ye desist not, we shall surely stone you, and grievous torture will befall you at our hands.

قَالُوْٓا اِنَّا تَطَيَّرْنَا بِكُمْ لَئِنْ لَّمْ تَنْتَهُوْا لَنَرْجُمَنَّكُمْ وَلَيَمَسَّنَّكُمْ مِّنَّا عَذَابٌ اَلِيْمٌ ﴿١٨﴾

19. They said: Your evil augury be with you! Is it because ye are reminded (of the truth)? Nay, but ye are froward folk?

قَالُوْا طَآئِرُكُمْ مَّعَكُمْ اَئِنْ ذُكِّرْتُمْ بَلْ اَنْتُمْ قَوْمٌ مُّسْرِفُوْنَ ﴿١٩﴾

20. And there came from the uttermost part of the city a man running. He cried: O my people! Follow those who have been sent!

وَجَآءَ مِنْ اَقْصَا الْمَدِيْنَةِ رَجُلٌ يَّسْعٰى قَالَ يٰقَوْمِ اتَّبِعُوا الْمُرْسَلِيْنَ ﴿٢٠﴾

21. Follow those who ask of you no fee, and who are rightly guided.

اتَّبِعُوْا مَنْ لَّا يَسْـَٔلُكُمْ اَجْرًا وَّهُمْ مُّهْتَدُوْنَ ﴿٢١﴾

22. For what cause should I not serve Him Who hath created me, and unto Whom ye will be brought back?

وَمَا لِيَ لَآ اَعْبُدُ الَّذِيْ فَطَرَنِيْ وَاِلَيْهِ تُرْجَعُوْنَ ﴿٢٢﴾

23. Shall I take (other) gods in place of Him when, if the Beneficent should wish me any harm, their intercession will avail me naught, nor can they save?

ءَاَتَّخِذُ مِنْ دُوْنِهٖٓ اٰلِهَةً اِنْ يُّرِدْنِ الرَّحْمٰنُ بِضُرٍّ لَّا تُغْنِ عَنِّيْ شَفَاعَتُهُمْ شَيْـًٔا وَّلَا يُنْقِذُوْنِ ﴿٢٣﴾

24. Then truly I should be in error manifest.

اِنِّيْٓ اِذًا لَّفِيْ ضَلٰلٍ مُّبِيْنٍ ﴿٢٤﴾

25. Lo! I have believed in your Lord, so hear me!

اِنِّيْٓ اٰمَنْتُ بِرَبِّكُمْ فَاسْمَعُوْنِ ﴿٢٥﴾

26. It was said (unto him): Enter Paradise. He said: Would that my people knew

27. With what (munificence) my Lord hath pardoned me and made me of the honoured ones!

28. We sent not down against his people after him a host from heaven, nor do We ever send.

29. It was but one Shout, and lo! they were extinct.

30. Ah, the anguish for the bondmen! Never came there unto them a messenger but they did mock him!

31. Have they not seen how many generations We destroyed before them, which indeed return not unto them;

32. But all, without exception, will be brought before Us?

33. A token unto them is the dead earth. We revive it, and We bring forth from it grain so that they eat thereof;

34. And We have placed therein gardens of the date-palm and grapes, and We have caused springs of water to gush forth therein,

35. That they may eat of the fruit thereof, and their hands made it not. Will they not, then, give thanks?

36. Glory be to Him Who created all the sexual pairs, of that which the earth groweth, and of themselves, and of that which they know not!

37. A token unto them is night. We strip it of the day, and lo! they are in darkness:

38. And the sun runneth on unto a resting-place for him. That is the measuring of the Mighty, the Wise.

قيل ادخل الجنة قال يليت قومي يعلمون ۲۶
بما غفر لي ربي وجعلني من المكرمين ۲۷
وما انزلنا على قومه من بعده من جند من
السماء وما كنا منزلين ۲۸
ان كانت الا صيحة واحدة فاذا هم خمدون ۲۹
يحسرة على العباد ما ياتيهم من رسول الا
كانوا به يستهزءون ۳۰
الم يروا كم اهلكنا قبلهم من القرون انهم
اليهم لا يرجعون ۳۱
وان كل لما جميع لدينا محضرون ۳۲
واية لهم الارض الميتة احيينها واخرجنا
منها حبا فمنه ياكلون ۳۳
وجعلنا فيها جنت من نخيل واعناب وفجرنا
فيها من العيون ۳۴
لياكلوا من ثمره وما عملته ايديهم افلا
يشكرون ۳۵
سبحن الذي خلق الازواج كلها مما تنبت
الارض ومن انفسهم ومما لا يعلمون ۳۶
واية لهم اليل نسلخ منه النهار فاذا هم
مظلمون ۳۷
والشمس تجري لمستقر لها ذلك تقدير
العزيز العليم ۳۸

39. And for the moon We have appointed mansions till she return like an old shrivelled palm-leaf.

40. It is not for the sun to overtake the moon, nor doth the night outstrip the day. They float each in an orbit.

41. And a token unto them is that We bear their offspring in the laden ship,

42. And have created for them of the like thereof whereon they ride.

43. And if We will, We drown them, and there is no help for them, neither can they be saved;

44. Unless by mercy from Us and as comfort for a while.

45. When it is said unto them: Beware of that which is before you and that which is behind you, that haply ye may find mercy (they are heedless).

46. Never came a token of the tokens of their Lord to them, but they did turn away from it!

47. And when it is said unto them: Spend of that wherewith Allah hath provided you, those who disbelieve say unto those who believe, Shall we feed those whom Allah, if He willed, would feed? Ye are in naught else than error manifest.

48. And they say: When will this promise be fulfilled, if ye are truthful?

49. They await but one Shout, which will surprise them while they are disputing.

50. Then they cannot make bequest, nor can they return to their own folk.

51. And the trumpet is blown and lo! from the graves they hie unto their Lord,

وَالْقَمَرَ قَدَّرْنٰهُ مَنَازِلَ حَتّٰى عَادَ كَالْعُرْجُوْنِ
الْقَدِيْمِ ٣٩
لَا الشَّمْسُ يَنْۢبَغِيْ لَهَآ اَنْ تُدْرِكَ الْقَمَرَ وَلَا
الَّيْلُ سَابِقُ النَّهَارِ ۚ وَكُلٌّ فِيْ فَلَكٍ يَّسْبَحُوْنَ ٤٠
وَاٰيَةٌ لَّهُمْ اَنَّا حَمَلْنَا ذُرِّيَّتَهُمْ فِي الْفُلْكِ الْمَشْحُوْنِ ٤١
وَخَلَقْنَا لَهُمْ مِّنْ مِّثْلِهٖ مَا يَرْكَبُوْنَ ٤٢
وَاِنْ نَّشَاْ نُغْرِقْهُمْ فَلَا صَرِيْخَ لَهُمْ وَلَا هُمْ
يُنْقَذُوْنَ ٤٣
اِلَّا رَحْمَةً مِّنَّا وَمَتَاعًا اِلٰى حِيْنٍ ٤٤
وَاِذَا قِيْلَ لَهُمُ اتَّقُوْا مَا بَيْنَ اَيْدِيْكُمْ وَمَا
خَلْفَكُمْ لَعَلَّكُمْ تُرْحَمُوْنَ ٤٥
وَمَا تَاْتِيْهِمْ مِّنْ اٰيَةٍ مِّنْ اٰيٰتِ رَبِّهِمْ اِلَّا كَانُوْا
عَنْهَا مُعْرِضِيْنَ ٤٦
وَاِذَا قِيْلَ لَهُمْ اَنْفِقُوْا مِمَّا رَزَقَكُمُ اللّٰهُ ۙ قَالَ
الَّذِيْنَ كَفَرُوْا لِلَّذِيْنَ اٰمَنُوْٓا اَنُطْعِمُ مَنْ لَّوْ يَشَآءُ
اللّٰهُ اَطْعَمَهٗٓ ۖ اِنْ اَنْتُمْ اِلَّا فِيْ ضَلٰلٍ مُّبِيْنٍ ٤٧
وَيَقُوْلُوْنَ مَتٰى هٰذَا الْوَعْدُ اِنْ كُنْتُمْ صٰدِقِيْنَ ٤٨
مَا يَنْظُرُوْنَ اِلَّا صَيْحَةً وَّاحِدَةً تَاْخُذُهُمْ وَهُمْ
يَخِصِّمُوْنَ ٤٩
فَلَا يَسْتَطِيْعُوْنَ تَوْصِيَةً وَّلَآ اِلٰٓى اَهْلِهِمْ يَرْجِعُوْنَ ٥٠ ع
وَنُفِخَ فِي الصُّوْرِ فَاِذَا هُمْ مِّنَ الْاَجْدَاثِ اِلٰى رَبِّهِمْ
يَنْسِلُوْنَ ٥١

وقف لازم
وقف منزل
وقف غفران

52. Crying: Woe upon us! Who hath raised us from our place of sleep? This is that which the Beneficent did promise, and the messengers spoke truth.

قَالُوا يٰوَيْلَنَا مَنْ بَعَثَنَا مِنْ مَّرْقَدِنَا ۜ هٰذَا مَا
وَعَدَ الرَّحْمٰنُ وَصَدَقَ الْمُرْسَلُوْنَ ﴿٥٢﴾

53. It is but one Shout, and behold them brought together before Us!

اِنْ كَانَتْ اِلَّا صَيْحَةً وَّاحِدَةً فَاِذَا هُمْ جَمِيْعٌ
لَّدَيْنَا مُحْضَرُوْنَ ﴿٥٣﴾

54. This day no soul is wronged in aught; nor are ye requited aught save what ye used to do.

فَالْيَوْمَ لَا تُظْلَمُ نَفْسٌ شَيْـًٔا وَّلَا تُجْزَوْنَ اِلَّا مَا
كُنْتُمْ تَعْمَلُوْنَ ﴿٥٤﴾

55. Lo! those who merit Paradise this day are happily employed,

اِنَّ اَصْحٰبَ الْجَنَّةِ الْيَوْمَ فِيْ شُغُلٍ
فٰكِهُوْنَ ﴿٥٥﴾

56. They and their wives, in pleasant shade, on thrones reclining;

هُمْ وَاَزْوَاجُهُمْ فِيْ ظِلٰلٍ عَلَى الْاَرَآئِكِ
مُتَّكِـُٔوْنَ ﴿٥٦﴾

57. Theirs the fruit (of their good deeds) and theirs (all) that they ask;

لَهُمْ فِيْهَا فَاكِهَةٌ وَّلَهُمْ مَّا يَدَّعُوْنَ ﴿٥٧﴾

58. The word from a Merciful Lord (for them) is: Peace!

سَلٰمٌ قَوْلًا مِّنْ رَّبٍّ رَّحِيْمٍ ﴿٥٨﴾

59. But avaunt ye, O ye guilty, this day!

وَامْتَازُوا الْيَوْمَ اَيُّهَا الْمُجْرِمُوْنَ ﴿٥٩﴾

60. Did I not charge you, O ye sons of Adam, that ye worship not the devil— Lo! he is your open foe!—

اَلَمْ اَعْهَدْ اِلَيْكُمْ يٰبَنِيْۤ اٰدَمَ اَنْ لَّا تَعْبُدُوا
الشَّيْطٰنَ ۚ اِنَّهٗ لَكُمْ عَدُوٌّ مُّبِيْنٌ ﴿٦٠﴾

61. But that ye worship Me? That was the right path.

وَّاَنِ اعْبُدُوْنِيْ ۚ هٰذَا صِرَاطٌ مُّسْتَقِيْمٌ ﴿٦١﴾ وقف غفران

62. Yet he hath led astray of you a great multitude. Had ye then no sense?

وَلَقَدْ اَضَلَّ مِنْكُمْ جِبِلًّا كَثِيْرًا ۚ اَفَلَمْ تَكُوْنُوْا
تَعْقِلُوْنَ ﴿٦٢﴾

63. This is hell which ye were promised (if ye followed him).

هٰذِهٖ جَهَنَّمُ الَّتِيْ كُنْتُمْ تُوْعَدُوْنَ ﴿٦٣﴾

64. Burn therein this day for that ye disbelieved.

اِصْلَوْهَا الْيَوْمَ بِمَا كُنْتُمْ تَكْفُرُوْنَ ﴿٦٤﴾

65. This day We seal up mouths, and hands speak out and feet bear witness as to what they used to earn.

اَلْيَوْمَ نَخْتِمُ عَلٰۤى اَفْوَاهِهِمْ وَتُكَلِّمُنَاۤ اَيْدِيْهِمْ
وَتَشْهَدُ اَرْجُلُهُمْ بِمَا كَانُوْا يَكْسِبُوْنَ ﴿٦٥﴾

66. And had We willed, We verily could have quenched their eyesight so that they should struggle for the way. Then how could they have seen?

وَلَوْ نَشَآءُ لَطَمَسْنَا عَلٰٓى اَعْيُنِهِمْ فَاسْتَبَقُوا الصِّرَاطَ
فَاَنّٰى يُبْصِرُوْنَ ﴿٦٦﴾

67. And had We willed, We verily could have fixed them in their place, making them powerless to go forward or turn back.[1]

وَلَوْ نَشَآءُ لَمَسَخْنٰهُمْ عَلٰى مَكَانَتِهِمْ فَمَا اسْتَطَاعُوْا
مُضِيًّا وَّلَا يَرْجِعُوْنَ ﴿٦٧﴾

68. He whom We bring unto old age, We reverse him in creation (making him go back to weakness after strength) Have ye then no sense?

وَمَنْ نُّعَمِّرْهُ نُنَكِّسْهُ فِى الْخَلْقِ ۚ اَفَلَا يَعْقِلُوْنَ ﴿٦٨﴾

69. And We have not taught him (Muhammad) poetry, nor is it meet for him. This is naught else than a Reminder and a Lecture[2] making plain,

وَمَا عَلَّمْنٰهُ الشِّعْرَ وَمَا يَنْۢبَغِىْ لَهٗ ۚ اِنْ هُوَ اِلَّا ذِكْرٌ
وَّقُرْاٰنٌ مُّبِيْنٌ ﴿٦٩﴾

70. To warn whosoever liveth, and that the word may be fulfilled against the disbelievers.

لِّيُنْذِرَ مَنْ كَانَ حَيًّا وَّيَحِقَّ الْقَوْلُ عَلَى الْكٰفِرِيْنَ ﴿٧٠﴾

71. Have they not seen how We have created for them of Our handiwork the cattle, so that they are their owners,

اَوَلَمْ يَرَوْا اَنَّا خَلَقْنَا لَهُمْ مِّمَّا عَمِلَتْ اَيْدِيْنَآ اَنْعَامًا
فَهُمْ لَهَا مٰلِكُوْنَ ﴿٧١﴾

72. And have subdued them unto them, so that some of them they have for riding, some for food?

وَذَلَّلْنٰهَا لَهُمْ فَمِنْهَا رَكُوْبُهُمْ وَمِنْهَا يَاْكُلُوْنَ ﴿٧٢﴾

73. Benefits and (divers) drinks have they from them. Will they not then give thanks?

وَلَهُمْ فِيْهَا مَنَافِعُ وَمَشَارِبُ ؕ اَفَلَا يَشْكُرُوْنَ ﴿٧٣﴾

74. And they have taken (other) gods beside Allah, in order that they may be helped.

وَاتَّخَذُوْا مِنْ دُوْنِ اللّٰهِ اٰلِهَةً لَّعَلَّهُمْ
يُنْصَرُوْنَ ﴿٧٤﴾

75. It is not in their power to help them; but they (the worshippers) are unto them a host in arms.

لَا يَسْتَطِيْعُوْنَ نَصْرَهُمْ ۙ وَهُمْ لَهُمْ جُنْدٌ
مُّحْضَرُوْنَ ﴿٧٥﴾

76. So let not their speech grieve thee (O Muhammad). Lo! We know what they conceal and what proclaim.

فَلَا يَحْزُنْكَ قَوْلُهُمْ ۘ اِنَّا نَعْلَمُ مَا يُسِرُّوْنَ وَمَا
يُعْلِنُوْنَ ﴿٧٦﴾

77. Hath not man seen that We have created him from a drop of seed? Yet lo! he is an open opponent.

اَوَلَمْ يَرَ الْاِنْسَانُ اَنَّا خَلَقْنٰهُ مِنْ نُّطْفَةٍ فَاِذَا
هُوَ خَصِيْمٌ مُّبِيْنٌ ﴿٧٧﴾

78. And he hath coined for Us a similitude, and hath forgotten the fact of his creation, saying: Who will revive these bones when they have rotted away?

وَضَرَبَ لَنَا مَثَلًا وَّنَسِىَ خَلْقَهٗ ؕ قَالَ مَنْ يُّحْىِ
الْعِظَامَ وَهِىَ رَمِيْمٌ ﴿٧٨﴾

1. But they have sight and power of motion so can choose their way.
2. Ar. *Qur'ān*.

79. Say: He will revive them Who produced them at the first, for He is Knower of every creation,

قُلْ يُحْيِيهَا الَّذِيٓ اَنْشَاَهَآ اَوَّلَ مَرَّةٍ ۖ وَهُوَ بِكُلِّ
خَلْقٍ عَلِيمٌ ﴿٧٩﴾

80. Who hath appointed for you fire from the green tree, and behold! ye kindle from it.

الَّذِي جَعَلَ لَكُمْ مِّنَ الشَّجَرِ الْاَخْضَرِ نَارًا فَاِذَآ
اَنْتُمْ مِّنْهُ تُوقِدُونَ ﴿٨٠﴾

81. Is not He Who created the heavens and the earth, Able to create the like of them? Aye, that He is! for He is the All-Wise Creator,

اَوَلَيْسَ الَّذِي خَلَقَ السَّمٰوٰتِ وَالْاَرْضَ بِقٰدِرٍ
عَلٰٓى اَنْ يَّخْلُقَ مِثْلَهُمْ ۚ بَلٰى ۚ وَهُوَ الْخَلّٰقُ الْعَلِيمُ ﴿٨١﴾ وقف غفران

82. But His command, when He intendeth a thing, is only that he saith unto it: Be! and it is.

اِنَّمَآ اَمْرُهٗٓ اِذَآ اَرَادَ شَيْـًٔا اَنْ يَّقُولَ لَهٗ كُنْ
فَيَكُونُ ﴿٨٢﴾

83. Therefor glory be to Him in Whose hand is the dominion over all things! Unto Him ye will be brought back.

فَسُبْحٰنَ الَّذِي بِيَدِهٖ مَلَكُوتُ كُلِّ شَيْءٍ وَّاِلَيْهِ
تُرْجَعُونَ ﴿٨٣﴾ ع ٥

As-Ṣāffāt takes its name from a word in the first verse. The reference in the first three verses is to the angels, as is made clear by vv. 164-166, where the revealing angel speaks in person. Tradition says that soothsayers and astrologers throughout the East were bewildered at the time of the Prophet's coming by the appearance in the heavens of a comet and many meteors which baffled all their science and made them afraid to sit at nights on high peaks to watch the stars, as was their general custom. They told enquirers that their familiars could no longer guide them, being themselves completely at a loss and terrified. This is the explanation usually given of vv. 7-9, and of a passage of similar import in Sūrah LXXII, vv. 8-10.

It stands early in the middle group of Meccan Sūrahs.

THOSE WHO SET THE RANKS

Revealed at Mecca

In the name of Allah, the Beneficent, the Merciful.

1. By those who set the ranks in battle order

2. And those who drive away (the wicked) with reproof

3. And those who read (the Word) for a reminder,

4. Lo! thy Lord is surely One:

5. Lord of the heavens and of the earth and all that is between them, and Lord of the sun's risings.

6. Lo! We have adorned the lowest heaven with an ornament, the planets;

7. With security from every froward devil.

8. They cannot listen to the Highest Chiefs for they are pelted from every side,

9. Outcast, and theirs is a perpetual torment:

10. Save him who snatcheth a fragment, and there pursueth him a piercing flame.[1]

11. Then ask them (O Muhammad): Are they stronger as a creation, or those (others) whom We have created? Lo! We created them of plastic clay.

12. Nay, but thou dost marvel when they mock

13. And heed not when they are reminded,

14. And seek to scoff when they behold a portent,

15. And they say: Lo! this is mere magic:

1. LXXII, 8-10; LXVII, 5.

اٰياتها ١٨٢ (٣٧) سورة الصّٰفّٰت مكية ركوعاتها ٥

بسم الله الرحمٰن الرحيم

والصّٰفّٰت صفًّا ①

فالزّٰجرٰت زجرًا ②

فالتّٰليٰت ذكرًا ③

إنّ إلٰهكم لواحد ④

ربّ السمٰوٰت والأرض وما بينهما وربّ المشارق ⑤

إنّا زيّنّا السماء الدنيا بزينة الكواكب ⑥

وحفظًا من كلّ شيطٰن مارد ⑦

لا يسّمّعون إلى الملإ الأعلى ويقذفون من كلّ جانب ⑧

دحورًا ولهم عذاب واصب ⑨

إلّا من خطف الخطفة فأتبعه شهاب ثاقب ⑩

فاستفتهم أهم أشدّ خلقًا أم من خلقنا إنّا خلقنٰهم من طين لازب ⑪

بل عجبت ويسخرون ⑫

وإذا ذكّروا لا يذكرون ⑬

وإذا رأوا اٰية يستسخرون ⑭

وقالوا إن هٰذا إلّا سحر مبين ⑮

16. When we are dead and have become dust and bones, shall we then, forsooth, be raised (again)?

17. And our forefathers?

18. Say (O Muhammad): Yea, in truth: and ye will be brought low.

19. There is but one Shout, and lo! they behold,

20. And say: Ah, woe for us! This is the Day of Judgement.

21. This is the Day of Separation, which ye used to deny.

22. (And it is said unto the angels): Assemble those who did wrong, together with their wives and what they used to worship

23. Instead of Allah, and lead them to the path to hell;

24. And stop them, for they must be questioned:

25. What aileth you that ye help not one another?

26. Nay, but this day they make full submission.

27. And some of them draw near unto others, mutually questioning.

28. They say: Lo! ye used to come unto us, imposing, (swearing that ye spoke the truth).

29. They answer: Nay, but ye (yourselves) were not believers.

30. We had no power over you, but ye were wayward folk.

31. Now the Word of our Lord hath been fulfilled concerning us. Lo! we are about to taste (the doom).

32. Thus we misled you. Lo! we were (ourselves) astray.

33. Then lo! this day they (both) are sharers in the doom.

34. Lo! thus deal We with the guilty.

35. For when it was said unto them, There is no god save Allah, they were scornful

ءَاِذَا مِتْنَا وَكُنَّا تُرَابًا وَّعِظَامًا ءَاِنَّا لَمَبْعُوْثُوْنَ ۙ ﴿۱۶﴾

اَوَ اٰبَآؤُنَا الْاَوَّلُوْنَ ؕ ﴿۱۷﴾

قُلْ نَعَمْ وَاَنْتُمْ دَاخِرُوْنَ ۚ ﴿۱۸﴾

فَاِنَّمَا هِيَ زَجْرَةٌ وَّاحِدَةٌ فَاِذَا هُمْ يَنْظُرُوْنَ ﴿۱۹﴾

وَقَالُوْا يٰوَيْلَنَا هٰذَا يَوْمُ الدِّيْنِ ﴿۲۰﴾

ع هٰذَا يَوْمُ الْفَصْلِ الَّذِيْ كُنْتُمْ بِهٖ تُكَذِّبُوْنَ ﴿۲۱﴾

اُحْشُرُوا الَّذِيْنَ ظَلَمُوْا وَاَزْوَاجَهُمْ وَمَا كَانُوْا
يَعْبُدُوْنَ ۙ ﴿۲۲﴾

مِنْ دُوْنِ اللّٰهِ فَاهْدُوْهُمْ اِلٰى صِرَاطِ الْجَحِيْمِ ﴿۲۳﴾

وَقِفُوْهُمْ اِنَّهُمْ مَّسْئُوْلُوْنَ ۙ ﴿۲۴﴾

مَا لَكُمْ لَا تَنَاصَرُوْنَ ﴿۲۵﴾

بَلْ هُمُ الْيَوْمَ مُسْتَسْلِمُوْنَ ﴿۲۶﴾

وَاَقْبَلَ بَعْضُهُمْ عَلٰى بَعْضٍ يَّتَسَآءَلُوْنَ ﴿۲۷﴾

قَالُوْا اِنَّكُمْ كُنْتُمْ تَاْتُوْنَنَا عَنِ الْيَمِيْنِ ﴿۲۸﴾

قَالُوْا بَلْ لَّمْ تَكُوْنُوْا مُؤْمِنِيْنَ ۚ ﴿۲۹﴾

وَمَا كَانَ لَنَا عَلَيْكُمْ مِّنْ سُلْطٰنٍ ۚ بَلْ كُنْتُمْ قَوْمًا طٰغِيْنَ ﴿۳۰﴾

فَحَقَّ عَلَيْنَا قَوْلُ رَبِّنَآ ۖ اِنَّا لَذَآئِقُوْنَ ﴿۳۱﴾

فَاَغْوَيْنٰكُمْ اِنَّا كُنَّا غٰوِيْنَ ﴿۳۲﴾

فَاِنَّهُمْ يَوْمَئِذٍ فِي الْعَذَابِ مُشْتَرِكُوْنَ ﴿۳۳﴾

اِنَّا كَذٰلِكَ نَفْعَلُ بِالْمُجْرِمِيْنَ ﴿۳۴﴾

اِنَّهُمْ كَانُوْا اِذَا قِيْلَ لَهُمْ لَآ اِلٰهَ اِلَّا اللّٰهُ ۙ
يَسْتَكْبِرُوْنَ ۙ ﴿۳۵﴾

36. And said: Shall we forsake our gods for a mad poet?

ويقولون ائنا لتاركوا الهتنا لشاعر مجنون ٣٦

37. Nay, but he brought the Truth, and he confirmed those sent (before him).

بل جاء بالحق وصدق المرسلين ٣٧

38. Lo! (now) verily ye taste the painful doom—

انكم لذائقوا العذاب الاليم ٣٨

39. Ye are requited naught save what ye did—

وما تجزون الا ما كنتم تعملون ٣٩

40. Save single-minded slaves of Allah;

الا عباد الله المخلصين ٤٠

41. For them there is a known provision,

اولئك لهم رزق معلوم ٤١

42. Fruits. And they will be honoured

فواكه وهم مكرمون ٤٢

43. In the Gardens of delight,

في جنت النعيم ٤٣

44. On couches facing one another;

على سرر متقبلين ٤٤

45. A cup from a gushing spring is brought round for them,

يطاف عليهم بكاس من معين ٤٥

46. White, delicious to the drinkers,

بيضاء لذة للشربين ٤٦

47. Wherein there is no headache nor are they made mad thereby.

لا فيها غول ولا هم عنها ينزفون ٤٧

48. And with them are those of modest gaze, with lovely eyes,

وعندهم قصرت الطرف عين ٤٨

49. (Pure) as they were hidden eggs (of the ostrich).

كانهن بيض مكنون ٤٩

50. And some of them draw near unto others, mutually questioning.

فاقبل بعضهم على بعض يتساءلون ٥٠

51. A speaker of them saith: Lo! I had a comrade

قال قائل منهم اني كان لي قرين ٥١

52. Who used to say: Art thou in truth of those who put faith (in his words)?

يقول ائنك لمن المصدقين ٥٢

53. Can we, when we are dead and have become mere dust and bones can we (then) verily be brought to book?

ءاذا متنا وكنا ترابا وعظاما ءانا لمدينون ٥٣

54. He saith: Will ye look?

قال هل انتم مطلعون ٥٤

55. Then looketh he and seeth him in the depth of Hell.

فاطلع فراه في سواء الجحيم ٥٥

56. He saith: By Allah, thou verily didst all but cause my ruin,

قال تالله ان كدت لتردين ٥٦

57. And had it not been for the favour of my Lord, I too had been of those haled forth (to doom).

وَلَوْلَا نِعْمَةُ رَبِّيْ لَكُنْتُ مِنَ الْمُحْضَرِيْنَ ۝

58. Are we then not to die

اَفَمَا نَحْنُ بِمَيِّتِيْنَ ۝

59. Saving our former death, and are we not to be punished?

اِلَّا مَوْتَتَنَا الْاُوْلٰى وَمَا نَحْنُ بِمُعَذَّبِيْنَ ۝

60. Lo! this is the supreme triumph.

اِنَّ هٰذَا لَهُوَ الْفَوْزُ الْعَظِيْمُ ۝

61. For the like of this, then, let the workers work.

لِمِثْلِ هٰذَا فَلْيَعْمَلِ الْعٰمِلُوْنَ ۝

62. Is this better as a welcome, or the tree of Zaqqūm?[1]

اَذٰلِكَ خَيْرٌ نُّزُلًا اَمْ شَجَرَةُ الزَّقُّوْمِ ۝

63. Lo! We have appointed it a torment for wrong-doers.

اِنَّا جَعَلْنٰهَا فِتْنَةً لِّلظّٰلِمِيْنَ ۝

64. Lo! it is a tree that springeth in the heart of hell,

اِنَّهَا شَجَرَةٌ تَخْرُجُ فِيْۤ اَصْلِ الْجَحِيْمِ ۝

65. Its crop is as it were the heads of devils.

طَلْعُهَا كَاَنَّهٗ رُءُوْسُ الشَّيٰطِيْنِ ۝

66. And lo! they verily must eat thereof, and fill (their) bellies therewith.

فَاِنَّهُمْ لَاٰكِلُوْنَ مِنْهَا فَمَالِـُٔوْنَ مِنْهَا الْبُطُوْنَ ۝

67. And afterward, lo! thereupon they have a drink of boiling water

ثُمَّ اِنَّ لَهُمْ عَلَيْهَا لَشَوْبًا مِّنْ حَمِيْمٍ ۝

68. And afterward, lo! their return is surely unto hell.

ثُمَّ اِنَّ مَرْجِعَهُمْ لَاِلَى الْجَحِيْمِ ۝

69. They indeed found their fathers astray,

اِنَّهُمْ اَلْفَوْا اٰبَآءَهُمْ ضَآلِّيْنَ ۝

70. But they make haste (to follow) in their footsteps.

فَهُمْ عَلٰۤى اٰثٰرِهِمْ يُهْرَعُوْنَ ۝

71. And verily most of the men of old went astray before them,

وَلَقَدْ ضَلَّ قَبْلَهُمْ اَكْثَرُ الْاَوَّلِيْنَ ۝

72. And verily We sent among them warners.

وَلَقَدْ اَرْسَلْنَا فِيْهِمْ مُّنْذِرِيْنَ ۝

73. Then see the nature of the consequence for those warned,

فَانْظُرْ كَيْفَ كَانَ عَاقِبَةُ الْمُنْذَرِيْنَ ۝

74. Save single-minded slaves of Allah.

اِلَّا عِبَادَ اللّٰهِ الْمُخْلَصِيْنَ ۝

75. And Noah verily prayed unto Us, and gracious was the Hearer of his prayer

وَلَقَدْ نَادٰىنَا نُوْحٌ فَلَنِعْمَ الْمُجِيْبُوْنَ ۝

76. And We saved him and his household from the great distress,

وَنَجَّيْنٰهُ وَاَهْلَهٗ مِنَ الْكَرْبِ الْعَظِيْمِ ۝

77. And made his seed the survivors,

وَجَعَلْنَا ذُرِّيَّتَهٗ هُمُ الْبَاقِيْنَ ۝

78. And left for him among the later folk (the salutation):

وَتَرَكْنَا عَلَيْهِ فِي الْاٰخِرِيْنَ ۝

79. Peace be unto Noah among the peoples! — سَلَامٌ عَلَىٰ نُوحٍ فِي الْعَالَمِينَ ٧٩

80. Lo! thus do We reward the good. — إِنَّا كَذَٰلِكَ نَجْزِي الْمُحْسِنِينَ ٨٠

81. Lo! he is one of Our believing slaves. — إِنَّهُ مِنْ عِبَادِنَا الْمُؤْمِنِينَ ٨١

82. Then We did drown the others. — ثُمَّ أَغْرَقْنَا الْآخَرِينَ ٨٢

83. And lo! of his persuasion verily was Abraham — وَإِنَّ مِنْ شِيعَتِهِ لَإِبْرَاهِيمَ ٨٣

84. When he came unto his Lord with a whole heart; — إِذْ جَاءَ رَبَّهُ بِقَلْبٍ سَلِيمٍ ٨٤

85. When he said unto his father and his folk: What is it that ye worship? — إِذْ قَالَ لِأَبِيهِ وَقَوْمِهِ مَاذَا تَعْبُدُونَ ٨٥

86. Is it a falsehood--gods beside Allah—that ye desire? — أَئِفْكًا آلِهَةً دُونَ اللَّهِ تُرِيدُونَ ٨٦

87. What then is your opinion of the Lord of the Worlds? — فَمَا ظَنُّكُمْ بِرَبِّ الْعَالَمِينَ ٨٧

88. And he glanced a glance at the stars — فَنَظَرَ نَظْرَةً فِي النُّجُومِ ٨٨

89. Then said: Lo! I feel sick! — فَقَالَ إِنِّي سَقِيمٌ ٨٩

90. And they turned their backs and went away from him. — فَتَوَلَّوْا عَنْهُ مُدْبِرِينَ ٩٠

91. Then turned he to their gods and said: Will ye not eat? — فَرَاغَ إِلَىٰ آلِهَتِهِمْ فَقَالَ أَلَا تَأْكُلُونَ ٩١

92. What aileth you that ye speak not? — مَا لَكُمْ لَا تَنْطِقُونَ ٩٢

93. Then he attacked them, striking with his right hand. — فَرَاغَ عَلَيْهِمْ ضَرْبًا بِالْيَمِينِ ٩٣

94. And (his people) came toward him, hastening. — فَأَقْبَلُوا إِلَيْهِ يَزِفُّونَ ٩٤

95. He said: Worship ye that which ye yourselves do carve — قَالَ أَتَعْبُدُونَ مَا تَنْحِتُونَ ٩٥

96. When Allah hath created you and what ye make? — وَاللَّهُ خَلَقَكُمْ وَمَا تَعْمَلُونَ ٩٦

97. They said: Build for him a building and fling him in the red-hot fire. — قَالُوا ابْنُوا لَهُ بُنْيَانًا فَأَلْقُوهُ فِي الْجَحِيمِ ٩٧

98. And they designed a snare for him, but We made them the undermost. — فَأَرَادُوا بِهِ كَيْدًا فَجَعَلْنَاهُمُ الْأَسْفَلِينَ ٩٨

99. And he said: Lo! I am going unto my Lord Who will guide me. — وَقَالَ إِنِّي ذَاهِبٌ إِلَىٰ رَبِّي سَيَهْدِينِ ٩٩

100. My Lord! Vouchsafe me of the righteous. — رَبِّ هَبْ لِي مِنَ الصَّالِحِينَ ١٠٠

1. XLIV, 43; LVI, 52.

101. So We gave him tidings of a gentle son.

102. And when (his son) was old enough to walk with him, (Abraham) said: O my dear son, I have seen in a dream that I must sacrifice thee. So look, what thinkest thou? He said: O my father! Do that which thou art commanded. Allah willing, thou shalt find me of the steadfast.

103. Then, when they had both surrendered (to Allah), and he had flung him down upon his face,

104. We called unto him: O Abraham!

105. Thou hast already fulfilled the vision. Lo! thus do We reward the good.

106. Lo! that verily was a clear test.

107. Then We ransomed him with a tremendous victim.

108. And We left for him among the later folk (the salutation):

109. Peace be unto Abraham!

110. Thus do We reward the good.

111. Lo! he is one of Our believing slaves.

112. And We gave him tidings of the birth of Isaac, a Prophet of the righteous.

113. And We blessed him and Isaac. And of their seed are some who do good, and some who plainly wrong themselves.

114. And We verily gave grace unto Moses and Aaron,

115. And saved them and their people from the great distress,

116. And helped them so that they became the victors.

117. And We gave them the clear Scripture

118. And showed them the right path.

فَبَشَّرْنٰهُ بِغُلٰمٍ حَلِيْمٍ ١٠١

فَلَمَّا بَلَغَ مَعَهُ السَّعْيَ قَالَ يٰبُنَيَّ اِنِّيْۤ اَرٰى فِي
الْمَنَامِ اَنِّيْۤ اَذْبَحُكَ فَانْظُرْ مَاذَا تَرٰى ؕ قَالَ
يٰۤاَبَتِ افْعَلْ مَا تُؤْمَرُ ؗ سَتَجِدُنِيْۤ اِنْ شَآءَ اللّٰهُ مِنَ
الصّٰبِرِيْنَ ١٠٢

فَلَمَّاۤ اَسْلَمَا وَتَلَّهٗ لِلْجَبِيْنِ ١٠٣

وَنَادَيْنٰهُ اَنْ يّٰۤاِبْرٰهِيْمُ ١٠٤

قَدْ صَدَّقْتَ الرُّءْيَا ۚ اِنَّا كَذٰلِكَ نَجْزِي الْمُحْسِنِيْنَ ١٠٥

اِنَّ هٰذَا لَهُوَ الْبَلٰٓؤُا الْمُبِيْنُ ١٠٦

وَفَدَيْنٰهُ بِذِبْحٍ عَظِيْمٍ ١٠٧

وَتَرَكْنَا عَلَيْهِ فِي الْاٰخِرِيْنَ ١٠٨

سَلٰمٌ عَلٰۤى اِبْرٰهِيْمَ ١٠٩

كَذٰلِكَ نَجْزِي الْمُحْسِنِيْنَ ١١٠

اِنَّهٗ مِنْ عِبَادِنَا الْمُؤْمِنِيْنَ ١١١

وَبَشَّرْنٰهُ بِاِسْحٰقَ نَبِيًّا مِّنَ الصّٰلِحِيْنَ ١١٢

وَبٰرَكْنَا عَلَيْهِ وَعَلٰۤى اِسْحٰقَ ؕ وَمِنْ ذُرِّيَّتِهِمَا مُحْسِنٌ
ع وَّظَالِمٌ لِّنَفْسِهٖ مُبِيْنٌ ١١٣

وَلَقَدْ مَنَنَّا عَلٰى مُوْسٰى وَهٰرُوْنَ ١١٤

وَنَجَّيْنٰهُمَا وَقَوْمَهُمَا مِنَ الْكَرْبِ الْعَظِيْمِ ١١٥

وَنَصَرْنٰهُمْ فَكَانُوْا هُمُ الْغٰلِبِيْنَ ١١٦

وَاٰتَيْنٰهُمَا الْكِتٰبَ الْمُسْتَبِيْنَ ١١٧

وَهَدَيْنٰهُمَا الصِّرَاطَ الْمُسْتَقِيْمَ ١١٨

119. And We left for them among the later folk (the salutation):

120. Peace be unto Moses and Aaron!

121. Lo! thus do We reward the good.

122. Lo! they are two of our believing slaves.

123. And Lo! Elias was of those sent (to warn).

124. When he said unto his folk: will ye not ward off (evil)?

125. Will ye cry unto Baal and forsake the best of Creators.

126. Allah, your Lord and Lord of your forefathers?

127. But they denied him, so they surely will be haled forth (to the doom).

128. Save single minded slaves of Allah.

129. And we left for him among the later folk (the salutation):

130. Peace be unto Elias!

131. Lo! thus do we reward the good.

132. Lo! he is one of Our believing slaves.

133. And Lo! Lot verily was of those sent (to warn).

134. When We saved him and his household, every one.

135. Save an old woman among those who stayed behind;

136. Then We destroyed the others.

137. And Lo! ye verily pass by (the runs of) them in the morning.

138. And at night-time; have ye then no sense?

139. And Lo! Jonah verily was of those sent (to warn).

140. When he fled unto the laden ship.

وَتَرَكْنَا عَلَيْهِمَا فِي الْاٰخِرِيْنَ ﴿۱۱۹﴾

سَلٰمٌ عَلٰى مُوْسٰى وَهٰرُوْنَ ﴿۱۲۰﴾

اِنَّا كَذٰلِكَ نَجْزِي الْمُحْسِنِيْنَ ﴿۱۲۱﴾

اِنَّهُمَا مِنْ عِبَادِنَا الْمُؤْمِنِيْنَ ﴿۱۲۲﴾

وَاِنَّ اِلْيَاسَ لَمِنَ الْمُرْسَلِيْنَ ﴿۱۲۳﴾

اِذْ قَالَ لِقَوْمِهٖٓ اَلَا تَتَّقُوْنَ ﴿۱۲۴﴾

اَتَدْعُوْنَ بَعْلًا وَّتَذَرُوْنَ اَحْسَنَ الْخَالِقِيْنَ ﴿۱۲۵﴾

اللّٰهَ رَبَّكُمْ وَرَبَّ اٰبَآئِكُمُ الْاَوَّلِيْنَ ﴿۱۲۶﴾

فَكَذَّبُوْهُ فَاِنَّهُمْ لَمُحْضَرُوْنَ ﴿۱۲۷﴾

اِلَّا عِبَادَ اللّٰهِ الْمُخْلَصِيْنَ ﴿۱۲۸﴾

وَتَرَكْنَا عَلَيْهِ فِي الْاٰخِرِيْنَ ﴿۱۲۹﴾

سَلٰمٌ عَلٰٓى اِلْ يَاسِيْنَ ﴿۱۳۰﴾

اِنَّا كَذٰلِكَ نَجْزِي الْمُحْسِنِيْنَ ﴿۱۳۱﴾

اِنَّهٗ مِنْ عِبَادِنَا الْمُؤْمِنِيْنَ ﴿۱۳۲﴾

وَاِنَّ لُوْطًا لَّمِنَ الْمُرْسَلِيْنَ ﴿۱۳۳﴾

اِذْ نَجَّيْنٰهُ وَاَهْلَهٗٓ اَجْمَعِيْنَ ﴿۱۳۴﴾

اِلَّا عَجُوْزًا فِي الْغٰبِرِيْنَ ﴿۱۳۵﴾

ثُمَّ دَمَّرْنَا الْاٰخَرِيْنَ ﴿۱۳۶﴾

وَاِنَّكُمْ لَتَمُرُّوْنَ عَلَيْهِمْ مُّصْبِحِيْنَ ﴿۱۳۷﴾

وَبِالَّيْلِ اَفَلَا تَعْقِلُوْنَ ﴿۱۳۸﴾ ع

وَاِنَّ يُوْنُسَ لَمِنَ الْمُرْسَلِيْنَ ﴿۱۳۹﴾

اِذْ اَبَقَ اِلَى الْفُلْكِ الْمَشْحُوْنِ ﴿۱۴۰﴾

141. And they drew lots and was of those rejected;

فَسَاهَمَ فَكَانَ مِنَ الْمُدْحَضِيْنَ ۞

142. And the fish swallowed him while he was blameworthy;

فَالْتَقَمَهُ الْحُوْتُ وَهُوَ مُلِيْمٌ ۞

143. And had he not been one of those who glorify (Allah)

فَلَوْلَا اَنَّهُ كَانَ مِنَ الْمُسَبِّحِيْنَ ۞

144. He would have tarried in its belly till the day when they are raised;

لَلَبِثَ فِيْ بَطْنِهِ اِلٰى يَوْمِ يُبْعَثُوْنَ ۞

145. Then We cast him on a desert shore while he was sick;

فَنَبَذْنٰهُ بِالْعَرَآءِ وَهُوَ سَقِيْمٌ ۞

146. And We caused a tree of gourd to grow above him;

وَاَنْبَتْنَا عَلَيْهِ شَجَرَةً مِّنْ يَّقْطِيْنٍ ۞

147. And We sent him to a hundred thousand (folk) or more

وَاَرْسَلْنٰهُ اِلٰى مِائَةِ اَلْفٍ اَوْ يَزِيْدُوْنَ ۞

148. And they believed, therefore We gave them comfort for a while.

فَاٰمَنُوْا فَمَتَّعْنٰهُمْ اِلٰى حِيْنٍ ۞

149. Now ask them (O Muhammad): Hath thy Lord daughters whereas they have sons?

فَاسْتَفْتِهِمْ اَلِرَبِّكَ الْبَنَاتُ وَلَهُمُ الْبَنُوْنَ ۞

150. Or created We the angels females while they were present?

اَمْ خَلَقْنَا الْمَلٰئِكَةَ اِنَاثًا وَّهُمْ شٰهِدُوْنَ ۞

151. Lo! it is of their falsehood that they say:

اَلَا اِنَّهُمْ مِّنْ اِفْكِهِمْ لَيَقُوْلُوْنَ ۞

152. Allah hath begotten. And lo! verily they tell a lie.

وَلَدَ اللّٰهُ وَاِنَّهُمْ لَكٰذِبُوْنَ ۞

153. (And again of their falsehood): He hath preferred daughters to sons.

اَصْطَفَى الْبَنَاتِ عَلَى الْبَنِيْنَ ۞

154. What aileth you? How judge ye?

مَا لَكُمْ كَيْفَ تَحْكُمُوْنَ ۞

155. Will ye not then reflect?

اَفَلَا تَذَكَّرُوْنَ ۞

156. Or have ye a clear warrant?

اَمْ لَكُمْ سُلْطٰنٌ مُّبِيْنٌ ۞

157. Then produce your writ, if ye are truthful.

فَأْتُوْا بِكِتٰبِكُمْ اِنْ كُنْتُمْ صٰدِقِيْنَ ۞

158. And they imagine kinship between him and the jinn, whereas the jinn know well that they will be brought before (Him).

وَجَعَلُوْا بَيْنَهُ وَبَيْنَ الْجِنَّةِ نَسَبًا وَلَقَدْ عَلِمَتِ الْجِنَّةُ اِنَّهُمْ لَمُحْضَرُوْنَ ۞

159. Glorified be Allah from that which they attribute (unto Him),

سُبْحٰنَ اللّٰهِ عَمَّا يَصِفُوْنَ ۞

160. Save single-minded slaves of Allah!

اِلَّا عِبَادَ اللّٰهِ الْمُخْلَصِيْنَ ۞

161. Lo! verily, ye and that which ye worship,

فَاِنَّكُمْ وَمَا تَعْبُدُوْنَ ۞

162. Ye cannot excite (anyone) against Him

163. Save him who is to burn in hell.

164. There is not one of Us[1] but hath his known position

165. Lo! We, even We are they who set the ranks.

166. Lo! We, even We are they who hymn His praise

167 And indeed they used to say:

168. If we had but a reminder from the men of old

169. We would be single-minded slaves of Allah.

170. Yet (now that it is come) they disbelieve therein; but they will come to know.

171. And verily Our word went forth of old unto Our bondmen sent (to warn)

172. That they verily would be helped.

173. And that Our host, they verily would be the victors.

174. So withdraw from them (O Muhammad) awhile,

175. And watch, for they will (soon) see.

176. Would they hasten on Our doom?

177. But when it cometh home to them, then it will be a hapless morn for those who have been warned.

178. Withdraw from them awhile

179. And watch, for they will (soon) see.

180. Glorified be thy Lord, the Lord of Majesty, from that which they attribute (unto Him)

181. And peace be unto those sent (to warn).

182. And praise be to Allah, Lord of the Worlds!

مَآ اَنْتُمْ عَلَيْهِ بِفٰتِنِيْنَ ﴿١٦٢﴾

اِلَّا مَنْ هُوَ صَالِ الْجَحِيْمِ ﴿١٦٣﴾

وَمَا مِنَّآ اِلَّا لَهٗ مَقَامٌ مَّعْلُوْمٌ ﴿١٦٤﴾

وَّاِنَّا لَنَحْنُ الصَّآفُّوْنَ ﴿١٦٥﴾

وَاِنَّا لَنَحْنُ الْمُسَبِّحُوْنَ ﴿١٦٦﴾

وَاِنْ كَانُوْا لَيَقُوْلُوْنَ ﴿١٦٧﴾

لَوْ اَنَّ عِنْدَنَا ذِكْرًا مِّنَ الْاَوَّلِيْنَ ﴿١٦٨﴾

لَكُنَّا عِبَادَ اللّٰهِ الْمُخْلَصِيْنَ ﴿١٦٩﴾

فَكَفَرُوْا بِهٖ فَسَوْفَ يَعْلَمُوْنَ ﴿١٧٠﴾

وَلَقَدْ سَبَقَتْ كَلِمَتُنَا لِعِبَادِنَا الْمُرْسَلِيْنَ ﴿١٧١﴾

اِنَّهُمْ لَهُمُ الْمَنْصُوْرُوْنَ ﴿١٧٢﴾

وَاِنَّ جُنْدَنَا لَهُمُ الْغٰلِبُوْنَ ﴿١٧٣﴾

فَتَوَلَّ عَنْهُمْ حَتّٰى حِيْنٍ ﴿١٧٤﴾

وَّاَبْصِرْهُمْ فَسَوْفَ يُبْصِرُوْنَ ﴿١٧٥﴾

اَفَبِعَذَابِنَا يَسْتَعْجِلُوْنَ ﴿١٧٦﴾

فَاِذَا نَزَلَ بِسَاحَتِهِمْ فَسَآءَ صَبَاحُ الْمُنْذَرِيْنَ ﴿١٧٧﴾

وَتَوَلَّ عَنْهُمْ حَتّٰى حِيْنٍ ﴿١٧٨﴾

وَّاَبْصِرْ فَسَوْفَ يُبْصِرُوْنَ ﴿١٧٩﴾

سُبْحٰنَ رَبِّكَ رَبِّ الْعِزَّةِ عَمَّا يَصِفُوْنَ ﴿١٨٠﴾

وَسَلٰمٌ عَلَى الْمُرْسَلِيْنَ ﴿١٨١﴾

وَالْحَمْدُ لِلّٰهِ رَبِّ الْعٰلَمِيْنَ ﴿١٨٢﴾

1. Here the revealing angel speaks in person.

Ṣād. This Sūrah takes its name from the letter of the Arabic Alphabet which stands alone as the first verse. Tradition says that the first ten verses were revealed when the leaders of Qureysh tried to persuade Abū Talib to withdraw his protection from the Prophet, or when Abū Talib died. The former is the more probable.

Its place is in the middle group of Meccan Sūrahs.

SAD

Revealed at Makkah

In the name of Allah, the beneficent, the Merciful.

1. Sad, By the renowned Qur'an.

2. Nay, but those who disbelieve are in false pride and schism.

3. How many a generation we destroyed before them, and they cried out when it was no longer the time for escape!

4. And they marvel that a warner from among themselves hath come unto them, and the disbelievers say: This is a wizard, a charlatan.

5. Maketh he the gods one God? Lo! that is an astounding thing.

6. The chiefs among them go about, exhorting: Go and be staunch to your gods! Lo! this is a thing designed.

7. We have not heard of this in later religion. This is naught but an invention.

8. Hath the reminder been revealed unto him (alone) among us? Nay, but they are in doubt concerning My reminder; nay but they have not yet tasted My doom.

9. Or are theirs the treasures of the mercy of the Lord, the Mighty, the Bestower?

10. Or is the kingdom of the heavens and the earth and all that is between them theirs? Then let them ascend by ropes!

11. A defeated host are (all) the factions that are there.

اٰيَاتُهَا ٨٨ (٣٨) سُوْرَةُ صٓ مَكِّيَّةٌ رُكُوْعَاتُهَا ٥

بِسْمِ اللّٰهِ الرَّحْمٰنِ الرَّحِيْمِ

صٓ وَالْقُرْاٰنِ ذِي الذِّكْرِ ١

بَلِ الَّذِيْنَ كَفَرُوْا فِيْ عِزَّةٍ وَّشِقَاقٍ ٢

كَمْ اَهْلَكْنَا مِنْ قَبْلِهِمْ مِّنْ قَرْنٍ فَنَادَوْا وَّلَاتَ
حِيْنَ مَنَاصٍ ٣

وَعَجِبُوْٓا اَنْ جَآءَهُمْ مُّنْذِرٌ مِّنْهُمْ وَقَالَ
الْكٰفِرُوْنَ هٰذَا سٰحِرٌ كَذَّابٌ ٤

اَجَعَلَ الْاٰلِهَةَ اِلٰهًا وَّاحِدًا اِنَّ هٰذَا لَشَيْءٌ
عُجَابٌ ٥

وَانْطَلَقَ الْمَلَاُ مِنْهُمْ اَنِ امْشُوْا وَاصْبِرُوْا عَلٰٓى
اٰلِهَتِكُمْ اِنَّ هٰذَا لَشَيْءٌ يُّرَادُ ٦

مَا سَمِعْنَا بِهٰذَا فِي الْمِلَّةِ الْاٰخِرَةِ اِنْ هٰذَآ اِلَّا
اخْتِلَاقٌ ٧

ءَاُنْزِلَ عَلَيْهِ الذِّكْرُ مِنْۢ بَيْنِنَا بَلْ هُمْ فِيْ شَكٍّ
مِّنْ ذِكْرِيْ بَلْ لَّمَّا يَذُوْقُوْا عَذَابِ ٨

اَمْ عِنْدَهُمْ خَزَآئِنُ رَحْمَةِ رَبِّكَ الْعَزِيْزِ
الْوَهَّابِ ٩

اَمْ لَهُمْ مُّلْكُ السَّمٰوٰتِ وَالْاَرْضِ وَمَا بَيْنَهُمَا
فَلْيَرْتَقُوْا فِي الْاَسْبَابِ ١٠

جُنْدٌ مَّا هُنَالِكَ مَهْزُوْمٌ مِّنَ الْاَحْزَابِ ١١

12. The folk of Noah before them denied (their messenger) and (so did the tribe of) 'Aād, and Pharaoh firmly planted,

كَذَّبَتْ قَبْلَهُمْ قَوْمُ نُوحٍ وَّعَادٌ وَّفِرْعَوْنُ ذُو الْأَوْتَادِ ﴿١٢﴾

13. And (the tribe of) Thamūd, and the folk of Lot, and the dwellers in the wood[1]: these were the factions.

وَثَمُودُ وَقَوْمُ لُوطٍ وَّأَصْحٰبُ لْـَٔيْكَةِ أُولٰٓئِكَ الْأَحْزَابُ ﴿١٣﴾

14. Not one of them but did deny the messengers, therefore My doom was justified,

إِنْ كُلٌّ إِلَّا كَذَّبَ الرُّسُلَ فَحَقَّ عِقَابِ ﴿١٤﴾

15. These wait for but one Shout, there will be no second thereto.

وَمَا يَنْظُرُ هٰٓؤُلَآءِ إِلَّا صَيْحَةً وَّاحِدَةً مَّا لَهَا مِنْ فَوَاقٍ ﴿١٥﴾

16. They say: Our Lord! Hasten on for us our fate before the Day of Reckoning.

وَقَالُوا رَبَّنَا عَجِّلْ لَّنَا قِطَّنَا قَبْلَ يَوْمِ الْحِسَابِ ﴿١٦﴾

17. Bear with what they say, and remember Our bondman David, lord of might. Lo! he was ever turning in repentance (toward Allah).

اِصْبِرْ عَلٰى مَا يَقُولُونَ وَاذْكُرْ عَبْدَنَا دَاوٗدَ ذَا الْأَيْدِ إِنَّهٗٓ أَوَّابٌ ﴿١٧﴾

18. Lo! We subdued the hills to hymn the praises (of their Lord) with him at nightfall and sunrise,

إِنَّا سَخَّرْنَا الْجِبَالَ مَعَهٗ يُسَبِّحْنَ بِالْعَشِيِّ وَالْإِشْرَاقِ ﴿١٨﴾

19. And the birds assembled; all were turning unto Him

وَالطَّيْرَ مَحْشُورَةً كُلٌّ لَّهٗٓ أَوَّابٌ ﴿١٩﴾

20. We made his kingdom strong and gave him wisdom and decisive speech.

وَشَدَدْنَا مُلْكَهٗ وَاٰتَيْنٰهُ الْحِكْمَةَ وَفَصْلَ الْخِطَابِ ﴿٢٠﴾

21. And hath the story of the litigants come unto thee? How they climbed the wall into the royal chamber!

وَهَلْ أَتٰىكَ نَبَؤُا الْخَصْمِ إِذْ تَسَوَّرُوا الْمِحْرَابَ ﴿٢١﴾

22. How they burst in upon David, and he was afraid of them! They said: Be not afraid! (We are) two litigants, one of whom hath wronged the other, therefor judge aright between us; be not unjust; and show us the fair way.

إِذْ دَخَلُوا عَلٰى دَاوٗدَ فَفَزِعَ مِنْهُمْ قَالُوا لَا تَخَفْ خَصْمٰنِ بَغٰى بَعْضُنَا عَلٰى بَعْضٍ فَاحْكُمْ بَيْنَنَا بِالْحَقِّ وَلَا تُشْطِطْ وَاهْدِنَآ إِلٰى سَوَآءِ الصِّرَاطِ ﴿٢٢﴾

23. Lo! this my brother hath ninety and nine ewes while I had one ewe; and he said: Entrust it to me, and he conquered me in speech.

إِنَّ هٰذَآ أَخِي لَهٗ تِسْعٌ وَّتِسْعُونَ نَعْجَةً وَّلِيَ نَعْجَةٌ وَّاحِدَةٌ فَقَالَ أَكْفِلْنِيهَا وَعَزَّنِي فِي الْخِطَابِ ﴿٢٣﴾

1. Midian.

24. (David) said: He hath wronged thee in demanding thine ewe in addition to his ewes, and lo! many partners oppress one another, save such as believe and do good works, and they are few. And David guessed that We had tried him, and he sought forgiveness of his Lord, and he bowed himself and fell down prostrate and repented.

قَالَ لَقَدْ ظَلَمَكَ بِسُؤَالِ نَعْجَتِكَ إِلَىٰ نِعَاجِهِ
وَإِنَّ كَثِيرًا مِّنَ الْخُلَطَاءِ لَيَبْغِي بَعْضُهُمْ عَلَىٰ
بَعْضٍ إِلَّا الَّذِينَ آمَنُوا وَعَمِلُوا الصَّالِحَاتِ وَ
قَلِيلٌ مَّا هُمْ ۗ وَظَنَّ دَاوُودُ أَنَّمَا فَتَنَّاهُ فَاسْتَغْفَرَ
رَبَّهُ وَخَرَّ رَاكِعًا وَأَنَابَ ۩ ٢٤

25. So We forgave him that; and lo! he had access to Our presence and a happy journey's end.

فَغَفَرْنَا لَهُ ذَٰلِكَ ۖ وَإِنَّ لَهُ عِندَنَا لَزُلْفَىٰ وَحُسْنَ
مَآبٍ ٢٥

26. (And it was said unto him): O David! Lo! We have set thee as a viceroy in the earth; therefor judge aright between mankind, and follow not desire that it beguile thee from the way of Allah. Lo! those who wander from the way of Allah have an awful doom, forasmuch as they forgot the Day of Reckoning.

يَا دَاوُودُ إِنَّا جَعَلْنَاكَ خَلِيفَةً فِي الْأَرْضِ فَاحْكُم بَيْنَ
النَّاسِ بِالْحَقِّ وَلَا تَتَّبِعِ الْهَوَىٰ فَيُضِلَّكَ عَن
سَبِيلِ اللَّهِ ۚ إِنَّ الَّذِينَ يَضِلُّونَ عَن سَبِيلِ اللَّهِ
لَهُمْ عَذَابٌ شَدِيدٌ بِمَا نَسُوا يَوْمَ الْحِسَابِ ٢٦

27. And We created not the heaven and the earth and all that is between them in vain. That is the opinion of those who disbelieve. And woe unto those who disbelieve from the Fire!

وَمَا خَلَقْنَا السَّمَاءَ وَالْأَرْضَ وَمَا بَيْنَهُمَا بَاطِلًا ۚ
ذَٰلِكَ ظَنُّ الَّذِينَ كَفَرُوا ۚ فَوَيْلٌ لِّلَّذِينَ كَفَرُوا
مِنَ النَّارِ ٢٧

28. Shall We treat those who believe and do good works as those who spread corruption in the earth; or shall We treat the pious as the wicked?

أَمْ نَجْعَلُ الَّذِينَ آمَنُوا وَعَمِلُوا الصَّالِحَاتِ كَالْمُفْسِدِينَ
فِي الْأَرْضِ أَمْ نَجْعَلُ الْمُتَّقِينَ كَالْفُجَّارِ ٢٨

29. (This is) a Scripture that We have revealed unto thee, full of blessing, that they may ponder its revelations, and that men of understanding may reflect.

كِتَابٌ أَنزَلْنَاهُ إِلَيْكَ مُبَارَكٌ لِّيَدَّبَّرُوا آيَاتِهِ وَلِيَتَذَكَّرَ
أُولُو الْأَلْبَابِ ٢٩

30. And We bestowed on David, Solomon. How excellent a slave! Lo! he was ever turning in repentance (toward Allah).

وَوَهَبْنَا لِدَاوُودَ سُلَيْمَانَ ۚ نِعْمَ الْعَبْدُ ۖ إِنَّهُ أَوَّابٌ ٣٠

31. When there were shown to him at eventide lightfooted coursers

إِذْ عُرِضَ عَلَيْهِ بِالْعَشِيِّ الصَّافِنَاتُ الْجِيَادُ ٣١

32. And he said: Lo! I have preferred the good things (of the world) to the remembrance of my Lord; till they were taken out of sight behind the curtain.

فَقَالَ إِنِّي أَحْبَبْتُ حُبَّ الْخَيْرِ عَن ذِكْرِ رَبِّي حَتَّىٰ
تَوَارَتْ بِالْحِجَابِ ٣٢

33. (Then he said): Bring them back to me, and fell to slashing (with his sword their) legs and necks.

34. And verily We tried Solomon, and set upon his throne a (mere) body. Then did he repent.

35. He said: My Lord! Forgive me and bestow on me sovereignty such as shall not belong to any after me. Lo! Thou art the Bestower.

36. So We made the wind subservient unto him, setting fair by his command whithersoever he intended.

37. And the unruly,[1] every builder and diver (made We subservient),

38. And others linked together in chains,

39. (Saying): This is Our gift, so bestow thou, or withhold, without reckoning.

40. And lo! he hath favour with Us, and a happy journey's end.

41. And make mention (O Muhammad) of Our bondman Job, when he cried unto his Lord (saying): Lo! the devil doth afflict me with distress and torment.

42. (And it was said unto him): Strike the ground with thy foot. This (spring) is a cool bath and a refreshing drink.

43. And We bestowed on him (again) his household and therewith the like thereof, a mercy from Us, and a memorial for men of understanding.

44. And (it was said unto him): Take in thine hand a branch and smite therewith, and break not thine oath. Lo! We found him steadfast, how excellent a slave! Lo! he was ever turning in repentance (to his Lord).

45. And make mention of our bondmen, Abraham, Isaac and Jacob, men of parts and vision.

46. Lo! We purified them with a pure thought, remembrance of the Home (of the Hereafter).

47. Lo! in Our sight they are verily of the elect, the excellent.

1. Lit. *devils*.

رُدُّوهَا عَلَيَّ فَطَفِقَ مَسْحًا بِالسُّوقِ وَالْأَعْنَاقِ ﴿٣٣﴾

وَلَقَدْ فَتَنَّا سُلَيْمٰنَ وَأَلْقَيْنَا عَلٰى كُرْسِيِّهٖ جَسَدًا
ثُمَّ أَنَابَ ﴿٣٤﴾

قَالَ رَبِّ اغْفِرْ لِي وَهَبْ لِي مُلْكًا لَّا يَنْبَغِي لِأَحَدٍ
مِّنْ بَعْدِي إِنَّكَ أَنْتَ الْوَهَّابُ ﴿٣٥﴾

فَسَخَّرْنَا لَهُ الرِّيحَ تَجْرِي بِأَمْرِهٖ رُخَاءً حَيْثُ
أَصَابَ ﴿٣٦﴾

وَالشَّيٰطِينَ كُلَّ بَنَّاءٍ وَّغَوَّاصٍ ﴿٣٧﴾

وَّاٰخَرِينَ مُقَرَّنِينَ فِي الْأَصْفَادِ ﴿٣٨﴾

هٰذَا عَطَاؤُنَا فَامْنُنْ أَوْ أَمْسِكْ بِغَيْرِ حِسَابٍ ﴿٣٩﴾

وَإِنَّ لَهُ عِنْدَنَا لَزُلْفٰى وَحُسْنَ مَاٰبٍ ﴿٤٠﴾

وَاذْكُرْ عَبْدَنَا أَيُّوبَ إِذْ نَادٰى رَبَّهُ أَنِّي مَسَّنِيَ
الشَّيْطٰنُ بِنُصْبٍ وَّعَذَابٍ ﴿٤١﴾

ارْكُضْ بِرِجْلِكَ هٰذَا مُغْتَسَلٌ بَارِدٌ وَّشَرَابٌ ﴿٤٢﴾

وَوَهَبْنَا لَهُ أَهْلَهُ وَمِثْلَهُمْ مَّعَهُمْ رَحْمَةً مِّنَّا وَ
ذِكْرٰى لِأُولِي الْأَلْبَابِ ﴿٤٣﴾

وَخُذْ بِيَدِكَ ضِغْثًا فَاضْرِبْ بِّهٖ وَلَا تَحْنَثْ إِنَّا
وَجَدْنٰهُ صَابِرًا نِعْمَ الْعَبْدُ إِنَّهُ أَوَّابٌ ﴿٤٤﴾

وَاذْكُرْ عِبٰدَنَا إِبْرٰهِيمَ وَإِسْحٰقَ وَيَعْقُوبَ أُولِي
الْأَيْدِي وَالْأَبْصَارِ ﴿٤٥﴾

إِنَّا أَخْلَصْنٰهُمْ بِخَالِصَةٍ ذِكْرَى الدَّارِ ﴿٤٦﴾

وَإِنَّهُمْ عِنْدَنَا لَمِنَ الْمُصْطَفَيْنَ الْأَخْيَارِ ﴿٤٧﴾

48. And make mention of Ishmael and Elisha and Dhū'l-Kifl.[1] All are of the chosen.

وَاذْكُرْ إِسْمٰعِيلَ وَالْيَسَعَ وَذَا الْكِفْلِ وَكُلٌّ مِّنَ
الْأَخْيَارِ ﴿٤٨﴾

49. This is a reminder. And lo! for those who ward off (evil) is a happy journey's end,

هٰذَا ذِكْرٌ وَإِنَّ لِلْمُتَّقِينَ لَحُسْنَ مَاٰبٍ ﴿٤٩﴾

50. Gardens of Eden, whereof the gates are opened for them,

جَنّٰتِ عَدْنٍ مُّفَتَّحَةً لَّهُمُ الْأَبْوَابُ ﴿٥٠﴾

51. Wherein, reclining, they call for plenteous fruit and cool drink (that is) therein.

مُتَّكِـِٕينَ فِيهَا يَدْعُونَ فِيهَا بِفَاكِهَةٍ كَثِيرَةٍ وَّ
شَرَابٍ ﴿٥١﴾

52. And with them are those of modest gaze, companions.

وَعِنْدَهُمْ قٰصِرٰتُ الطَّرْفِ أَتْرَابٌ ﴿٥٢﴾

53. This it is that ye are promised for the Day of Reckoning.

هٰذَا مَا تُوعَدُونَ لِيَوْمِ الْحِسَابِ ﴿٥٣﴾

54. Lo! this in truth is Our provision, which will never waste away.

إِنَّ هٰذَا لَرِزْقُنَا مَا لَهُ مِنْ نَّفَادٍ ﴿٥٤﴾

55. This (is for the righteous). And lo! for the transgressors there will be an evil journey's end,

هٰذَا وَإِنَّ لِلطّٰغِينَ لَشَرَّ مَاٰبٍ ﴿٥٥﴾

56. Hell, where they will burn, an evil resting place.

جَهَنَّمَ يَصْلَوْنَهَا فَبِئْسَ الْمِهَادُ ﴿٥٦﴾

57. Here is a boiling and an ice-cold draught, so let them taste it,

هٰذَا فَلْيَذُوقُوهُ حَمِيمٌ وَّغَسَّاقٌ ﴿٥٧﴾

58. And other (torment) of the kind in pairs (the two extremes)!

وَّاٰخَرُ مِنْ شَكْلِهِ أَزْوَاجٌ ﴿٥٨﴾

59. Here is an army rushing blindly with you. (Those who are already in the fire say): No word of welcome for them. Lo! they will roast at the Fire.

هٰذَا فَوْجٌ مُّقْتَحِمٌ مَّعَكُمْ لَا مَرْحَبًا بِهِمْ إِنَّهُمْ
صَالُوا النَّارِ ﴿٥٩﴾

60. They say: Nay, but you (misleaders), for you there is no word of welcome. Ye prepared this for us (by your misleading). Now hapless is the plight.

قَالُوا بَلْ أَنْتُمْ لَا مَرْحَبًا بِكُمْ أَنْتُمْ قَدَّمْتُمُوهُ
لَنَا فَبِئْسَ الْقَرَارُ ﴿٦٠﴾

61. They say: Our Lord! Whoever did prepare this for us, oh, give him double portion of the Fire!

قَالُوا رَبَّنَا مَنْ قَدَّمَ لَنَا هٰذَا فَزِدْهُ عَذَابًا ضِعْفًا
فِي النَّارِ ﴿٦١﴾

62. And they say: What aileth us that we behold not men whom we were wont to count among the wicked?

وَقَالُوا مَا لَنَا لَا نَرٰى رِجَالًا كُنَّا نَعُدُّهُمْ مِّنَ
الْأَشْرَارِ ﴿٦٢﴾

63. Did we take them (wrongly) for a laughing-stock, or have our eyes missed them?

أَتَّخَذْنٰهُمْ سِخْرِيًّا أَمْ زَاغَتْ عَنْهُمُ الْأَبْصَارُ ﴿٦٣﴾

1. A prophet of the Arabs whose story is like that of Ezekiel.

64. Lo! that is very truth: the wrangling of the dwellers in the Fire.

65. Say (unto them, O Muhammad) I am only a warner, and there is no God save Allah, the One, the Absolute.

66. Lord of the heavens and the earth and all that is between them, the Mighty, the Pardoning.

67. Say: It is tremendous tidings

68. Whence ye turn away!

69. I had no knowledge of the Highest Chiefs when they disputed;

70. It is revealed unto me only that I may be a plain warner.

71. When thy Lord said unto the angels: lo! I am about to create a mortal out of mire,

72. And when I have fashioned him and breathed into him of My spirit, then fall down before him prostrate.

73. The angels fell down prostrate, every one.

74. Saving Iblis; he was scornful and became one of the disbelievers.

75. He said: O Iblis! What hindereth thee from falling prostrate before that which I have created with both My hands?[1] Art thou too proud or art thou of the high exalted?

76. He said: I am better than him. Thou createdst me of fire, whilst him Thou didst create of clay.

77. He said: Go forth from hence, for lo! thou art outcast.

78. And lo! My curse is on thee till the Day of Judgement.

ع إن ذلك لحق تخاصم أهل النار ٦٤
قل إنما أنا منذر وما من إله إلا الله الواحد
القهار ٦٥
رب السموت والأرض وما بينهما العزيز
الغفار ٦٦
قل هو نبؤا عظيم ٦٧
أنتم عنه معرضون ٦٨
ما كان لي من علم بالملإ الأعلى إذ
يختصمون ٦٩
إن يوحى إلي إلا أنما أنا نذير مبين ٧٠
إذ قال ربك للملئكة إني خالق بشرا من
طين ٧١
فإذا سويته ونفخت فيه من روحي فقعوا
له سجدين ٧٢
فسجد الملئكة كلهم أجمعون ٧٣
إلا إبليس استكبر وكان من الكفرين ٧٤
قال يإبليس ما منعك أن تسجد لما خلقت
بيدي أستكبرت أم كنت من العالين ٧٥
قال أنا خير منه خلقتني من نار وخلقته
من طين ٧٦
قال فاخرج منها فإنك رجيم ٧٧
وإن عليك لعنتي إلى يوم الدين ٧٨

1. The Muslim mystics explain this as meaning with both the glorious and the terrific attributes of God, whereas the angels were created by the exercise of only one class of attributes.

79. He said: My Lord! Reprieve me till the day when they are raised.

قَالَ رَبِّ فَأَنْظِرْنِيٓ إِلَىٰ يَوْمِ يُبْعَثُونَ ﴿٧٩﴾

80. He said: Lo! thou art of those reprieved

قَالَ فَإِنَّكَ مِنَ الْمُنْظَرِينَ ﴿٨٠﴾ لا

81. Until the day of the time appointed.

إِلَىٰ يَوْمِ الْوَقْتِ الْمَعْلُومِ ﴿٨١﴾

82. He said: Then, by Thy might, I surely will beguile them every one,

قَالَ فَبِعِزَّتِكَ لَأُغْوِيَنَّهُمْ أَجْمَعِينَ ﴿٨٢﴾ لا

83. Save Thy single-minded slaves among them.

إِلَّا عِبَادَكَ مِنْهُمُ الْمُخْلَصِينَ ﴿٨٣﴾

84. He said: The Truth is, and the Truth I speak,

قَالَ فَالْحَقُّ وَالْحَقَّ أَقُولُ ﴿٨٤﴾ ج

85. That I shall fill hell with thee and with such of them as follow thee, together.

لَأَمْلَأَنَّ جَهَنَّمَ مِنْكَ وَمِمَّنْ تَبِعَكَ مِنْهُمْ
أَجْمَعِينَ ﴿٨٥﴾

86. Say (O Muhammad, unto mankind): I ask of you no fee for this, and I am no impostor.

قُلْ مَآ أَسْـَٔلُكُمْ عَلَيْهِ مِنْ أَجْرٍ وَمَآ أَنَا۠ مِنَ
الْمُتَكَلِّفِينَ ﴿٨٦﴾

87. Lo! it is naught else than a reminder for all peoples

إِنْ هُوَ إِلَّا ذِكْرٌ لِلْعٰلَمِينَ ﴿٨٧﴾

88. And ye will come in time to know the truth thereof.

ع وَلَتَعْلَمُنَّ نَبَأَهُۥ بَعْدَ حِينٍۭ ﴿٨٨﴾

Az-Zumar, "The Troops," takes its name from a peculiar word, meaning troops or companies, which occurs in v. 71, and again in v. 73. Some authorities think that vv. 53 and 54 were revealed at Al-Madînah.

It seems manifestly to belong to the middle group of Meccan Sūrahs, though Nöldeke places it in his last group.

THE TROOPS

Revealed at Mecca

In the name of Allah, the Beneficent, the Merciful.

1. The revelation of the Scripture is from Allah, the Mighty, the Wise.

2. Lo! We have revealed the Scripture unto thee (Muhammad) with truth; so worship Allah, making religion pure for Him (only).

3. Surely pure religion is for Allah only. And those who choose protecting friends beside Him (say): We worship them only that they may bring us near unto Allah. Lo! Allah will judge between them concerning that wherein they differ. Lo! Allah guideth not him who is a liar, an ingrate.

4. If Allah had willed to choose a son, he could have chosen what he would of that which He hath created. Be He glorified! He is Allah, the One, the Absolute.

5. He hath created the heavens and the earth with truth. He maketh night to succeed day, and He maketh day to succeed night, and He constraineth the sun and the moon to give service, each running on for an appointed term. Is not He the Mighty, the Forgiver?

6. He created you from one being, then from that (being) He made its mate; and He hath provided for you of cattle eight kinds. He created you in the wombs of your mothers, creation after creation, in a three-fold gloom. Such is Allah, your Lord. His is the Sovereignty. There is no God save Him. How then are ye turned away?

آياتها ٧٥ (٣٩) سُورَةُ الزُّمَرِ مَكِّيَّةٌ رُكُوعَاتُهَا ٨

بِسْمِ اللّٰهِ الرَّحْمٰنِ الرَّحِيْمِ

تَنْزِيْلُ الْكِتٰبِ مِنَ اللّٰهِ الْعَزِيْزِ الْحَكِيْمِ ①
اِنَّآ اَنْزَلْنَآ اِلَيْكَ الْكِتٰبَ بِالْحَقِّ فَاعْبُدِ اللّٰهَ
مُخْلِصًا لَّهُ الدِّيْنَ ②
اَلَا لِلّٰهِ الدِّيْنُ الْخَالِصُ ۭ وَالَّذِيْنَ اتَّخَذُوْا مِنْ
دُوْنِهٖٓ اَوْلِيَاۗءَ ۘ مَا نَعْبُدُهُمْ اِلَّا لِيُقَرِّبُوْنَآ اِلَى
اللّٰهِ زُلْفٰى ۭ اِنَّ اللّٰهَ يَحْكُمُ بَيْنَهُمْ فِيْ مَا هُمْ
فِيْهِ يَخْتَلِفُوْنَ ڛ اِنَّ اللّٰهَ لَا يَهْدِيْ مَنْ هُوَ
كٰذِبٌ كَفَّارٌ ③
لَوْ اَرَادَ اللّٰهُ اَنْ يَّتَّخِذَ وَلَدًا لَّاصْطَفٰى مِمَّا يَخْلُقُ
مَا يَشَاۗءُ ۙ سُبْحٰنَهٗ ۭ هُوَ اللّٰهُ الْوَاحِدُ الْقَهَّارُ ④
خَلَقَ السَّمٰوٰتِ وَالْاَرْضَ بِالْحَقِّ ۚ يُكَوِّرُ الَّيْلَ
عَلَي النَّهَارِ وَيُكَوِّرُ النَّهَارَ عَلَي الَّيْلِ وَسَخَّرَ الشَّمْسَ
وَالْقَمَرَ ۭ كُلٌّ يَّجْرِيْ لِاَجَلٍ مُّسَمًّى ۭ اَلَا هُوَ
الْعَزِيْزُ الْغَفَّارُ ⑤
خَلَقَكُمْ مِّنْ نَّفْسٍ وَّاحِدَةٍ ثُمَّ جَعَلَ مِنْهَا زَوْجَهَا
وَاَنْزَلَ لَكُمْ مِّنَ الْاَنْعَامِ ثَمٰنِيَةَ اَزْوَاجٍ ۭ يَخْلُقُكُمْ
فِيْ بُطُوْنِ اُمَّهٰتِكُمْ خَلْقًا مِّنْۢ بَعْدِ خَلْقٍ فِيْ ظُلُمٰتٍ
ثَلٰثٍ ۭ ذٰلِكُمُ اللّٰهُ رَبُّكُمْ لَهُ الْمُلْكُ ۭ لَآ اِلٰهَ اِلَّا هُوَ ۚ
فَاَنّٰى تُصْرَفُوْنَ ⑥

وقف لازم

7. If ye are thankless, yet Allah is Independent of you, though He is not pleased with thanklessness of His bondmen: and if ye are thankful He is pleased therewith for you. No laden soul will bear another's load. Then unto you Lord is your return; and He will tell you what ye used to do. Lo! he knoweth what is in the breasts (of men).

8. And when some hurt toucheth man, he crieth unto his Lord, turning unto Him (repentant). then, when He granteth Him a boon from Him , he forgetteth that for which he cried unto Him before, and setteth up rivals to Allah that he may beguile (men) from His way. Say (O Muhammad, unto such an one): Take pleasure in thy disbelief a while. Lo! thou art of the owners of the Fire.

9. Is he who payeth adoration in the watches of the night, prostrate and standing, bewaring of the Hereafter and hoping for the mercy of his Lord, (to be accounted equal with a disbeliver)? Say (unto them, O Muhammad): Are those who know equal with those who know not? But only men of understanding will pay heed.

10. Say: O My bondmen who believe ! observe your duty to your Lord. For those who do good in this world there is good, and Allah's earth is spacious. Verily the steadfast will be paid their wages without stint.

11. Say (O Mahammad): Lo! I am commanded to worship Allah, making religion pure for Him (only).

12. And I am commanded to be the first of those wo surrender[1] (unto Him).

13. Say: Lo! if I should disobey my Lord. I fear the doom of a tremendous Day.

14. Say: Allah I Worship, making my religion pure for Him (only).

1. Ar. Muslimun.

اِنْ تَكْفُرُوْا فَاِنَّ اللّٰهَ غَنِيٌّ عَنْكُمْ وَلَا يَرْضٰى لِعِبَادِهِ الْكُفْرَ ۚ وَاِنْ تَشْكُرُوْا يَرْضَهُ لَكُمْ ۚ وَلَا تَزِرُ وَازِرَةٌ وِّزْرَ اُخْرٰى ۚ ثُمَّ اِلٰى رَبِّكُمْ مَّرْجِعُكُمْ فَيُنَبِّئُكُمْ بِمَا كُنْتُمْ تَعْمَلُوْنَ ۚ اِنَّهُ عَلِيْمٌ بِذَاتِ الصُّدُوْرِ ۞

وَاِذَا مَسَّ الْاِنْسَانَ ضُرٌّ دَعَا رَبَّهُ مُنِيْبًا اِلَيْهِ ثُمَّ اِذَا خَوَّلَهُ نِعْمَةً مِّنْهُ نَسِيَ مَا كَانَ يَدْعُوْا اِلَيْهِ مِنْ قَبْلُ وَجَعَلَ لِلّٰهِ اَنْدَادًا لِّيُضِلَّ عَنْ سَبِيْلِهِ ۚ قُلْ تَمَتَّعْ بِكُفْرِكَ قَلِيْلًا ۛ اِنَّكَ مِنْ اَصْحٰبِ النَّارِ ۞

اَمَّنْ هُوَ قَانِتٌ اٰنَآءَ الَّيْلِ سَاجِدًا وَّقَآئِمًا يَّحْذَرُ الْاٰخِرَةَ وَيَرْجُوْا رَحْمَةَ رَبِّهِ ۚ قُلْ هَلْ يَسْتَوِى الَّذِيْنَ يَعْلَمُوْنَ وَالَّذِيْنَ لَا يَعْلَمُوْنَ ۚ اِنَّمَا يَتَذَكَّرُ اُولُوا الْاَلْبَابِ ۞

قُلْ يٰعِبَادِ الَّذِيْنَ اٰمَنُوا اتَّقُوْا رَبَّكُمْ ۚ لِلَّذِيْنَ اَحْسَنُوْا فِيْ هٰذِهِ الدُّنْيَا حَسَنَةٌ ۚ وَاَرْضُ اللّٰهِ وَاسِعَةٌ ۚ اِنَّمَا يُوَفَّى الصّٰبِرُوْنَ اَجْرَهُمْ بِغَيْرِ حِسَابٍ ۞

قُلْ اِنِّيْ اُمِرْتُ اَنْ اَعْبُدَ اللّٰهَ مُخْلِصًا لَّهُ الدِّيْنَ ۞ وَاُمِرْتُ لِاَنْ اَكُوْنَ اَوَّلَ الْمُسْلِمِيْنَ ۞

قُلْ اِنِّيْ اَخَافُ اِنْ عَصَيْتُ رَبِّيْ عَذَابَ يَوْمٍ عَظِيْمٍ ۞

قُلِ اللّٰهَ اَعْبُدُ مُخْلِصًا لَّهُ دِيْنِيْ ۙ ۞

15. Then worship what ye will beside Him. Say: The losers will be those who lose themselves and their housefolk on the Day of Resurrection. Ah, that will be the manifest loss!

فَاعْبُدُوا مَا شِئْتُمْ مِّنْ دُوْنِهٖ ۚ قُلْ اِنَّ الْخٰسِرِيْنَ الَّذِيْنَ خَسِرُوْۤا اَنْفُسَهُمْ وَاَهْلِيْهِمْ يَوْمَ الْقِيٰمَةِ ؕ اَلَا ذٰلِكَ هُوَ الْخُسْرَانُ الْمُبِيْنُ ۞

16. They have an awning of fire above them and beneath them a dais (of fire). With this doth Allah appal His bondmen. O My bondmen, therefor fear Me!

لَهُمْ مِّنْ فَوْقِهِمْ ظُلَلٌ مِّنَ النَّارِ وَمِنْ تَحْتِهِمْ ظُلَلٌ ؕ ذٰلِكَ يُخَوِّفُ اللّٰهُ بِهٖ عِبَادَهٗ ؕ يٰعِبَادِ فَاتَّقُوْنِ ۞

17. And those who put away false gods lest they should worship them and turn to Allah in repentance, for them there are glad tidings. Therefor give good tidings (O Muhammad) to my bondmen

وَالَّذِيْنَ اجْتَنَبُوا الطَّاغُوْتَ اَنْ يَّعْبُدُوْهَا وَاَنَابُوْۤا اِلَى اللّٰهِ لَهُمُ الْبُشْرٰى ۚ فَبَشِّرْ عِبَادِ ۞

18. Who hear advice and follow the best thereof. Such are those whom Allah guideth, and such are men of understanding.

الَّذِيْنَ يَسْتَمِعُوْنَ الْقَوْلَ فَيَتَّبِعُوْنَ اَحْسَنَهٗ ؕ اُولٰٓئِكَ الَّذِيْنَ هَدٰىهُمُ اللّٰهُ وَاُولٰٓئِكَ هُمْ اُولُوا الْاَلْبَابِ ۞

19. Is he on whom the word of doom is fulfilled (to be helped), and canst thou (O Muhammad) rescue him who is in the Fire?

اَفَمَنْ حَقَّ عَلَيْهِ كَلِمَةُ الْعَذَابِ ؕ اَفَاَنْتَ تُنْقِذُ مَنْ فِى النَّارِ ۞

20. But those who keep their duty to their Lord, for them are lofty halls with lofty halls above them, built (for them), beneath which rivers flow. (It is) a promise of Allah. Allah faileth not His promise.

لٰكِنِ الَّذِيْنَ اتَّقَوْا رَبَّهُمْ لَهُمْ غُرَفٌ مِّنْ فَوْقِهَا غُرَفٌ مَّبْنِيَّةٌ ۙ تَجْرِيْ مِنْ تَحْتِهَا الْاَنْهٰرُ ؕ وَعْدَ اللّٰهِ ؕ لَا يُخْلِفُ اللّٰهُ الْمِيْعَادَ ۞

21. Hast thou not seen how Allah hath sent down water from the sky and hath caused it to penetrate the earth as watersprings, and afterward thereby produceth crops of divers hues; and afterward they wither and thou seest them turn yellow; then He maketh them chaff. Lo! herein verily is a reminder for men of understanding.

اَلَمْ تَرَ اَنَّ اللّٰهَ اَنْزَلَ مِنَ السَّمَآءِ مَآءً فَسَلَكَهٗ يَنَابِيْعَ فِى الْاَرْضِ ثُمَّ يُخْرِجُ بِهٖ زَرْعًا مُّخْتَلِفًا اَلْوَانُهٗ ثُمَّ يَهِيْجُ فَتَرٰىهُ مُصْفَرًّا ثُمَّ يَجْعَلُهٗ حُطَامًا ؕ اِنَّ فِيْ ذٰلِكَ لَذِكْرٰى لِاُولِى الْاَلْبَابِ ۞

22. Is he whose bosom Allah hath expanded for the Surrender[1] (unto Him), so that he followeth a light from His Lord, (as he who disbelieveth)? Then woe unto those whose hearts are hardened against remembrance of Allah. Such are in plain error.

اَفَمَنْ شَرَحَ اللّٰهُ صَدْرَهٗ لِلْاِسْلَامِ فَهُوَ عَلٰى نُوْرٍ مِّنْ رَّبِّهٖ ؕ فَوَيْلٌ لِّلْقٰسِيَةِ قُلُوْبُهُمْ مِّنْ ذِكْرِ اللّٰهِ ؕ اُولٰٓئِكَ فِيْ ضَلٰلٍ مُّبِيْنٍ ۞

2. Ar. *Al-Islám.*

23. Allah hath (now) revealed the fairest of statements, a Scripture consistent, (wherein promises of reward are) paired (with threats of punishment), whereat doth creep the flesh of those who fear their Lord, so that their flesh and their hearts soften to Allah's reminder. Such is Allah's guidance, wherewith He guideth whom He will. And him Whom Allah sendeth astray, for him there is no guide.

24. Is he then, who will strike his face against the awful doom upon the Day of Resurrection (as he who doth right)? And it will be said unto the wrong-doers: Taste what ye used to earn.

25. Those before them denied, and so the doom came on them whence they knew not.

26. Thus Allah made them taste humiliation in the life of the world, and verily the doom of the Hereafter will be greater if they did but know.

27. And verily We have coined for mankind in this Qur'ān all kinds of similitudes, that haply they may reflect;

28. A Lecture[1] in Arabic, containing no crookedness, that haply they may ward off (evil).

29. Allah coineth a similitude: A man in relation to whom are several part-owners, quarrelling, and a man belonging wholly to one man. Are the two equal in similitude? Praise be to Allah! But most of them know not.

30. Lo! thou wilt die, and lo! they will die;

31. Then lo! on the Day of Resurrection, before your Lord ye will dispute.

32. And who doth greater wrong than he who telleth a lie against Allah, and denieth the truth when it reacheth him? Will not the home of disbelievers be in hell?

1. Ar. *Qurān.*

اَللّٰهُ نَزَّلَ اَحۡسَنَ الۡحَدِيۡثِ كِتٰبًا مُّتَشَابِهًا مَّثَانِيَ
تَقۡشَعِرُّ مِنۡهُ جُلُوۡدُ الَّذِيۡنَ يَخۡشَوۡنَ رَبَّهُمۡ ثُمَّ
تَلِيۡنُ جُلُوۡدُهُمۡ وَقُلُوۡبُهُمۡ اِلٰى ذِكۡرِ اللّٰهِ ؕ ذٰلِكَ
هُدَى اللّٰهِ يَهۡدِىۡ بِهٖ مَنۡ يَّشَآءُ ؕ وَمَنۡ يُّضۡلِلِ
اللّٰهُ فَمَا لَهٗ مِنۡ هَادٍ ﴿۲۳﴾
اَفَمَنۡ يَّتَّقِىۡ بِوَجۡهِهٖ سُوۡٓءَ الۡعَذَابِ يَوۡمَ الۡقِيٰمَةِ ؕ
وَقِيۡلَ لِلظّٰلِمِيۡنَ ذُوۡقُوۡا مَا كُنۡتُمۡ تَكۡسِبُوۡنَ ﴿۲۴﴾
كَذَّبَ الَّذِيۡنَ مِنۡ قَبۡلِهِمۡ فَاَتٰٮهُمُ الۡعَذَابُ
مِنۡ حَيۡثُ لَا يَشۡعُرُوۡنَ ﴿۲۵﴾
فَاَذَاقَهُمُ اللّٰهُ الۡخِزۡىَ فِى الۡحَيٰوةِ الدُّنۡيَا ۚ وَ
لَعَذَابُ الۡاٰخِرَةِ اَكۡبَرُ ۘ لَوۡ كَانُوۡا يَعۡلَمُوۡنَ ﴿۲۶﴾
وَلَقَدۡ ضَرَبۡنَا لِلنَّاسِ فِىۡ هٰذَا الۡقُرۡاٰنِ مِنۡ كُلِّ
مَثَلٍ لَّعَلَّهُمۡ يَتَذَكَّرُوۡنَ ﴿۲۷﴾
قُرۡاٰنًا عَرَبِيًّا غَيۡرَ ذِىۡ عِوَجٍ لَّعَلَّهُمۡ يَتَّقُوۡنَ ﴿۲۸﴾
ضَرَبَ اللّٰهُ مَثَلًا رَّجُلًا فِيۡهِ شُرَكَآءُ مُتَشٰكِسُوۡنَ
وَرَجُلًا سَلَمًا لِّرَجُلٍ ؕ هَلۡ يَسۡتَوِيٰنِ مَثَلًا ؕ اَلۡحَمۡدُ
لِلّٰهِ ۚ بَلۡ اَكۡثَرُهُمۡ لَا يَعۡلَمُوۡنَ ﴿۲۹﴾
اِنَّكَ مَيِّتٌ وَّاِنَّهُمۡ مَّيِّتُوۡنَ ﴿۳۰﴾
ثُمَّ اِنَّكُمۡ يَوۡمَ الۡقِيٰمَةِ عِنۡدَ رَبِّكُمۡ تَخۡتَصِمُوۡنَ ﴿۳۱﴾
فَمَنۡ اَظۡلَمُ مِمَّنۡ كَذَبَ عَلَى اللّٰهِ وَكَذَّبَ
بِالصِّدۡقِ اِذۡ جَآءَهٗ ؕ اَلَيۡسَ فِىۡ جَهَنَّمَ مَثۡوًى
لِّلۡكٰفِرِيۡنَ ﴿۳۲﴾

33. And whoso bringeth the truth and believeth therein—Such are the dutiful.

والذی جاء بالصدق وصدق به اولئك هم
المتقون ﴿٣٣﴾

34. They shall have what they will of their Lord's bounty. That is the reward of the good:

لهم ما يشاءون عند ربهم ذلك جزؤا
المحسنين ﴿٣٤﴾

35. That Allah will remit from them the worst of what they did, and will pay them reward for the best they used to do.

ليكفر الله عنهم اسوا الذی عملوا ويجزيهم
اجرهم باحسن الذی كانوا يعملون ﴿٣٥﴾

36. Will not Allah defend His slave? Yet they would frighten thee with those beside Him. He whom Allah sendeth astray, for him there is no guide.

اليس الله بكاف عبده ويخوفونك بالذين
من دونه ومن يضلل الله فما له من هاد ﴿٣٦﴾

37. And he whom Allah guideth, for him there can be no misleader. Is not Allah Mighty, Able to Requite (the wrong)?

ومن يهد الله فما له من مضل اليس الله
بعزيز ذی انتقام ﴿٣٧﴾

38. And verily, if thou shouldst ask them: Who created the heavens and the earth? they will say: Allah. Say: Bethink you then of those ye worship beside Allah, If Allah willed some hurt for me, could they remove from me His hurt; or if He willed some mercy for me, could they restrain His mercy? Say: Allah is my all. In Him do (all) the trusting put their trust.

ولئن سالتهم من خلق السموت والارض
ليقولن الله قل افرءيتم ما تدعون من دون
الله ان ارادنی الله بضر هل هن كشفت ضره
او ارادنی برحمة هل هن ممسكت رحمته قل
حسبی الله عليه يتوكل المتوكلون ﴿٣٨﴾

39. Say: O my people! Act in your manner. I too am acting. Thus ye will come to know

قل يقوم اعملوا علی مكانتكم انی عامل فسوف
تعلمون ﴿٣٩﴾

40. Who it is unto whom cometh a doom that will abase him, and on whom there falleth everlasting doom.

من ياتيه عذاب يخزيه ويحل عليه عذاب
مقيم ﴿٤٠﴾

41. Lo! We have revealed unto thee (Muhammad) the Scripture for mankind with truth. Then whosoever goeth right it is for his soul, and whosoever strayeth, strayeth only to its hurt. And thou art not a warder over them.

انا انزلنا عليك الكتب للناس بالحق فمن
اهتدی فلنفسه ومن ضل فانما يضل
عليها وما انت عليهم بوكيل ﴿٤١﴾

42. Allah receiveth (men's) souls at the time of their death, and that (soul) which dieth not (yet) in its sleep. He keepeth that (soul) for which He hath ordained death and dismisseth the rest till an appointed term. Lo! herein verily are portents for people who take thought.

43. Or choose they intercessors other than Allah? Say: What! Even though they have power over nothing and have no intelligence?

44. Say: Unto Allah belongeth all intercession. His is the Sovereignty of the heavens and the earth. And afterward unto Him ye will be brought back.

45. And when Allah alone is mentioned, the hearts of those who believe not in the Hereafter are repelled, and when those (whom they worship) beside Him are mentioned, behold! they are glad.

46. Say: O Allah! Creator of the heavens and the earth! Knower of the invisible and the visible! Thou wilt judge between Thy slaves concerning that wherein they used to differ.

47. And though those who do wrong possess all that is in the earth, and therewith as much again, they verily will seek to ransom themselves therewith on the Day of Resurrection from the awful doom; and there will appear unto them, from their Lord, that wherewith they never reckoned.

48. And the evils that they earned will appear unto them, and that whereat they used to scoff will surround them.

49. Now when hurt toucheth a man he crieth unto Us, and afterward when We have granted him a boon from Us, he saith: Only by force of knowledge I obtained it. Nay, but it is a test. But most of them know not.

اَللّٰهُ يَتَوَفَّى الْاَنْفُسَ حِيْنَ مَوْتِهَا وَالَّتِيْ لَمْ تَمُتْ
فِيْ مَنَامِهَا ۚ فَيُمْسِكُ الَّتِيْ قَضٰى عَلَيْهَا الْمَوْتَ
وَيُرْسِلُ الْاُخْرٰٓى اِلٰٓى اَجَلٍ مُّسَمًّى ؕ اِنَّ فِيْ ذٰلِكَ
لَاٰيٰتٍ لِّقَوْمٍ يَّتَفَكَّرُوْنَ ﴿٤٢﴾
اَمِ اتَّخَذُوْا مِنْ دُوْنِ اللّٰهِ شُفَعَآءَ ؕ قُلْ اَوَلَوْ كَانُوْا لَا
يَمْلِكُوْنَ شَيْـًٔا وَّلَا يَعْقِلُوْنَ ﴿٤٣﴾
قُلْ لِّلّٰهِ الشَّفَاعَةُ جَمِيْعًا ؕ لَهٗ مُلْكُ السَّمٰوٰتِ وَ
الْاَرْضِ ؕ ثُمَّ اِلَيْهِ تُرْجَعُوْنَ ﴿٤٤﴾
وَاِذَا ذُكِرَ اللّٰهُ وَحْدَهُ اشْمَاَزَّتْ قُلُوْبُ الَّذِيْنَ لَا
يُؤْمِنُوْنَ بِالْاٰخِرَةِ ۚ وَاِذَا ذُكِرَ الَّذِيْنَ مِنْ دُوْنِهٖٓ
اِذَا هُمْ يَسْتَبْشِرُوْنَ ﴿٤٥﴾
قُلِ اللّٰهُمَّ فَاطِرَ السَّمٰوٰتِ وَالْاَرْضِ عٰلِمَ الْغَيْبِ
وَالشَّهَادَةِ اَنْتَ تَحْكُمُ بَيْنَ عِبَادِكَ فِيْ مَا كَانُوْا
فِيْهِ يَخْتَلِفُوْنَ ﴿٤٦﴾
وَلَوْ اَنَّ لِلَّذِيْنَ ظَلَمُوْا مَا فِي الْاَرْضِ جَمِيْعًا وَّمِثْلَهٗ
مَعَهٗ لَافْتَدَوْا بِهٖ مِنْ سُوْٓءِ الْعَذَابِ يَوْمَ الْقِيٰمَةِ ؕ
وَبَدَا لَهُمْ مِّنَ اللّٰهِ مَا لَمْ يَكُوْنُوْا يَحْتَسِبُوْنَ ﴿٤٧﴾
وَبَدَا لَهُمْ سَيِّاٰتُ مَا كَسَبُوْا وَحَاقَ بِهِمْ مَّا كَانُوْا
بِهٖ يَسْتَهْزِءُوْنَ ﴿٤٨﴾
فَاِذَا مَسَّ الْاِنْسَانَ ضُرٌّ دَعَانَا ۫ ثُمَّ اِذَا خَوَّلْنٰهُ
نِعْمَةً مِّنَّا ۙ قَالَ اِنَّمَآ اُوْتِيْتُهٗ عَلٰى عِلْمٍ ؕ بَلْ هِيَ
فِتْنَةٌ وَّلٰكِنَّ اَكْثَرَهُمْ لَا يَعْلَمُوْنَ ﴿٤٩﴾

50. Those before them said it, yet (all) that they had earned availed them not;

51. But the evils that they earned smote them; and such of these as do wrong, the evils that they earn will smite them; they cannot escape.

52. Know they not that Allah enlargeth providence for whom He will, and straiteneth if (for whom He will). Lo! herein verily are portents for people who believe.

53. Say: O My slaves who have been prodigal to their own hurt! Despair not of the mercy of Allah, Who forgiveth all sins. Lo! He is the Forgiving, the Merciful.

54. Turn unto Him repentant, and surrender unto Him, before there come unto you the doom, when ye cannot be helped.

55. And follow the better (guidance) of that which is revealed unto you from your Lord, before the doom cometh on you suddenly when ye know not,

56. Lest any soul should say: Alas, my grief that I was unmindful of Allah, and I was indeed among the scoffers!

57. Or should say: if Allah had but guided me I should have been among the dutiful!

58. Or should say, when it seeth the doom: Oh, that I had but a second chance that I might be among the righteous!

59. (But now the answer will be): Nay, for My revelations came unto thee, but thou didst deny them and wast scornful and wast among the disbelievers.

قَدْ قَالَهَا الَّذِينَ مِنْ قَبْلِهِمْ فَمَآ اَغْنٰى عَنْهُمْ مَّا
كَانُوْا يَكْسِبُوْنَ ﴿٥٠﴾
فَاَصَابَهُمْ سَيِّاٰتُ مَا كَسَبُوْا ؕ وَالَّذِيْنَ ظَلَمُوْا
مِنْ هٰٓؤُلَآءِ سَيُصِيْبُهُمْ سَيِّاٰتُ مَا كَسَبُوْا ؕ وَمَا
هُمْ بِمُعْجِزِيْنَ ﴿٥١﴾
اَوَلَمْ يَعْلَمُوْٓا اَنَّ اللّٰهَ يَبْسُطُ الرِّزْقَ لِمَنْ يَّشَآءُ
ع وَيَقْدِرُ ؕ اِنَّ فِيْ ذٰلِكَ لَاٰيٰتٍ لِّقَوْمٍ يُّؤْمِنُوْنَ ﴿٥٢﴾
قُلْ يٰعِبَادِيَ الَّذِيْنَ اَسْرَفُوْا عَلٰٓى اَنْفُسِهِمْ لَا
تَقْنَطُوْا مِنْ رَّحْمَةِ اللّٰهِ ؕ اِنَّ اللّٰهَ يَغْفِرُ الذُّنُوْبَ
جَمِيْعًا ؕ اِنَّهٗ هُوَ الْغَفُوْرُ الرَّحِيْمُ ﴿٥٣﴾
وَاَنِيْبُوْٓا اِلٰى رَبِّكُمْ وَاَسْلِمُوْا لَهٗ مِنْ قَبْلِ اَنْ يَّاْتِيَكُمُ
الْعَذَابُ ثُمَّ لَا تُنْصَرُوْنَ ﴿٥٤﴾
وَاتَّبِعُوْٓا اَحْسَنَ مَآ اُنْزِلَ اِلَيْكُمْ مِّنْ رَّبِّكُمْ مِّنْ
قَبْلِ اَنْ يَّاْتِيَكُمُ الْعَذَابُ بَغْتَةً وَّاَنْتُمْ لَا
تَشْعُرُوْنَ ﴿٥٥﴾
اَنْ تَقُوْلَ نَفْسٌ يّٰحَسْرَتٰى عَلٰى مَا فَرَّطْتُّ فِيْ
جَنْبِ اللّٰهِ وَاِنْ كُنْتُ لَمِنَ السّٰخِرِيْنَ ﴿٥٦﴾
اَوْ تَقُوْلَ لَوْ اَنَّ اللّٰهَ هَدٰىنِيْ لَكُنْتُ مِنَ الْمُتَّقِيْنَ ﴿٥٧﴾
اَوْ تَقُوْلَ حِيْنَ تَرَى الْعَذَابَ لَوْ اَنَّ لِيْ كَرَّةً فَاَكُوْنَ
مِنَ الْمُحْسِنِيْنَ ﴿٥٨﴾
بَلٰى قَدْ جَآءَتْكَ اٰيٰتِيْ فَكَذَّبْتَ بِهَا وَاسْتَكْبَرْتَ وَكُنْتَ
مِنَ الْكٰفِرِيْنَ ﴿٥٩﴾

60. And on the Day of Resurrection thou (Muhammad) seest those who lied concerning Allah with their faces blackened. Is not the home of the scorners in hell?

61. And Allah delivereth those who ward off (evil) because of their deserts. Evil toucheth them not, nor do they grieve.

62. Allah is Creator of all things, and He is Guardian over all things.

63. His are the keys of the heavens and the earth, and they who disbelieve the revelations of Allah—such are they who are the losers.

64. Say (O Muhammad, to the disbelievers): Do ye bid me serve other than Allah? O ye fools!

65. And verily it hath been revealed unto thee as unto those before thee (saying): If thou ascribe a partner to Allah thy work will fail and thou indeed wilt be among the losers.

66. Nay, but Allah must thou serve, and be among the thankful!

67. And they esteem not Allah as He hath the right to be esteemed, when the whole earth is His handful on the Day of Resurrection, and the heavens are rolled in His right hand. Glorified is He and High Exalted from All that they ascribe as partner (unto Him).

68. And the Trumpet is blown, and all who are in the heavens and the earth swoon away, save him whom Allah willeth. Then it is blown a second time, and behold them standing waiting!

69. And the earth shineth with the light of her Lord, and the book is set up, and the Prophets and the witnesses are brought, and it is judged between them with truth, and they are not wronged.

70. And each soul is paid in full for what it did. And He is best Aware of what they do.

وَيَوْمَ الْقِيٰمَةِ تَرَى الَّذِيْنَ كَذَبُوْا عَلَى اللّٰهِ وُجُوْهُهُمْ
مُّسْوَدَّةٌ ۚ اَلَيْسَ فِيْ جَهَنَّمَ مَثْوًى لِّلْمُتَكَبِّرِيْنَ ﴿٦٠﴾
وَيُنَجِّي اللّٰهُ الَّذِيْنَ اتَّقَوْا بِمَفَازَتِهِمْ ۫ لَا يَمَسُّهُمُ
السُّوْٓءُ وَلَا هُمْ يَحْزَنُوْنَ ﴿٦١﴾
اَللّٰهُ خَالِقُ كُلِّ شَيْءٍ ۫ وَّهُوَ عَلٰى كُلِّ شَيْءٍ وَّكِيْلٌ ﴿٦٢﴾
لَهٗ مَقَالِيْدُ السَّمٰوٰتِ وَالْاَرْضِ ۭ وَالَّذِيْنَ كَفَرُوْا
بِاٰيٰتِ اللّٰهِ اُولٰٓئِكَ هُمُ الْخٰسِرُوْنَ ﴿٦٣﴾ ع
قُلْ اَفَغَيْرَ اللّٰهِ تَاْمُرُوْٓنِّيْٓ اَعْبُدُ اَيُّهَا الْجٰهِلُوْنَ ﴿٦٤﴾
وَلَقَدْ اُوْحِيَ اِلَيْكَ وَاِلَى الَّذِيْنَ مِنْ قَبْلِكَ ۚ لَىِٕنْ اَشْرَكْتَ
لَيَحْبَطَنَّ عَمَلُكَ وَلَتَكُوْنَنَّ مِنَ الْخٰسِرِيْنَ ﴿٦٥﴾
بَلِ اللّٰهَ فَاعْبُدْ وَكُنْ مِّنَ الشّٰكِرِيْنَ ﴿٦٦﴾
وَمَا قَدَرُوا اللّٰهَ حَقَّ قَدْرِهٖ ۖ وَالْاَرْضُ جَمِيْعًا
قَبْضَتُهٗ يَوْمَ الْقِيٰمَةِ وَالسَّمٰوٰتُ مَطْوِيّٰتٌ ۢ بِيَمِيْنِهٖ ۭ
سُبْحٰنَهٗ وَتَعٰلٰى عَمَّا يُشْرِكُوْنَ ﴿٦٧﴾
وَنُفِخَ فِي الصُّوْرِ فَصَعِقَ مَنْ فِي السَّمٰوٰتِ وَمَنْ فِي
الْاَرْضِ اِلَّا مَنْ شَاۗءَ اللّٰهُ ۭ ثُمَّ نُفِخَ فِيْهِ اُخْرٰى فَاِذَا
هُمْ قِيَامٌ يَّنْظُرُوْنَ ﴿٦٨﴾
وَاَشْرَقَتِ الْاَرْضُ بِنُوْرِ رَبِّهَا وَوُضِعَ الْكِتٰبُ وَجِايْۗءَ
بِالنَّبِيّٖنَ وَالشُّهَدَاۗءِ وَقُضِيَ بَيْنَهُمْ بِالْحَقِّ وَهُمْ
لَا يُظْلَمُوْنَ ﴿٦٩﴾
وَوُفِّيَتْ كُلُّ نَفْسٍ مَّا عَمِلَتْ وَهُوَ اَعْلَمُ بِمَا
يَفْعَلُوْنَ ﴿٧٠﴾ ع

71. And those who disbelieve are driven unto hell in troops till, when they reach it and the gates thereof are opened, and the warders thereof say unto them: Came there not unto you messengers of your own, reciting unto you the revelations of your Lord and warning you of the meeting of this your Day? they say: Yea, verily. But the word of doom for disbelievers is fulfilled.

72. It is said (unto them): Enter ye the gates of hell to dwell therein. Thus hapless is the journey's end of the scorners.

73. And those who keep their duty to their Lord are driven unto the Garden in troops till, when they reach it, and the gates thereof are opened, and the warders thereof say unto them: Peace be unto you! Ye are good, so enter ye (the Garden of delight), to dwell therein;

74. They say: Praise be to Allah, Who hath fulfilled His promise unto us and hath made us inherit the land, sojourning in the Garden where we will! So bounteous is the wage of workers.

75. And thou (O Muhammad) seest the angels thronging round the Throne, hymning the praises of their Lord. And they are judged aright. And it is said: Praise be to Allah, the Lord of the Worlds!

وَسِيقَ الَّذِينَ كَفَرُوا إِلَىٰ جَهَنَّمَ زُمَرًا ۖ حَتَّىٰ إِذَا
جَاءُوهَا فُتِحَتْ أَبْوَابُهَا وَقَالَ لَهُمْ خَزَنَتُهَا أَلَمْ
يَأْتِكُمْ رُسُلٌ مِّنكُمْ يَتْلُونَ عَلَيْكُمْ آيَاتِ رَبِّكُمْ
وَيُنذِرُونَكُمْ لِقَاءَ يَوْمِكُمْ هَٰذَا ۚ قَالُوا بَلَىٰ وَلَٰكِنْ
حَقَّتْ كَلِمَةُ الْعَذَابِ عَلَى الْكَافِرِينَ ﴿٧١﴾
قِيلَ ادْخُلُوا أَبْوَابَ جَهَنَّمَ خَالِدِينَ فِيهَا ۖ فَبِئْسَ
مَثْوَى الْمُتَكَبِّرِينَ ﴿٧٢﴾
وَسِيقَ الَّذِينَ اتَّقَوْا رَبَّهُمْ إِلَى الْجَنَّةِ زُمَرًا ۖ حَتَّىٰ
إِذَا جَاءُوهَا وَفُتِحَتْ أَبْوَابُهَا وَقَالَ لَهُمْ خَزَنَتُهَا
سَلَامٌ عَلَيْكُمْ طِبْتُمْ فَادْخُلُوهَا خَالِدِينَ ﴿٧٣﴾
وَقَالُوا الْحَمْدُ لِلَّهِ الَّذِي صَدَقَنَا وَعْدَهُ وَأَوْرَثَنَا
الْأَرْضَ نَتَبَوَّأُ مِنَ الْجَنَّةِ حَيْثُ نَشَاءُ ۖ فَنِعْمَ
أَجْرُ الْعَامِلِينَ ﴿٧٤﴾
وَتَرَى الْمَلَائِكَةَ حَافِّينَ مِنْ حَوْلِ الْعَرْشِ يُسَبِّحُونَ
بِحَمْدِ رَبِّهِمْ ۖ وَقُضِيَ بَيْنَهُم بِالْحَقِّ وَقِيلَ
الْحَمْدُ لِلَّهِ رَبِّ الْعَالَمِينَ ﴿٧٥﴾ ع

Al-Mū'min, "The Believer," takes its name from vv. 28-45, which describe the attempt of a believer, in the house of Pharaoh, to dissuade his people from opposing Moses and Aaron. It is the first of seven Sūrahs beginning with the Arabic letters Ḥā Mîm, all of which are sometimes referred to as Ḥā, Mîm.

It belongs to the middle group of Meccan Sūrahs. Some authorities hold vv. 56 and 57 to have been revealed at Al-Madînah.

THE BELIEVER

Revealed at Mecca

In the name of Allah, the Beneficent, the Merciful.

1. Hā. Mīm.[1]

2. The revelation of the Scripture is from Allah, the Mighty, the Knower,

3. The Forgiver of sin, the Accepter of repentance, the Stern in punishment, the Bountiful. There is no God save Him. Unto Him is the journeying.

4. None argue concerning the revelations of Allah save those who disbelieve, so let not their turn of fortune in the land deceive thee (O Muḥammad).

5. The folk of Noah and the factions after them denied (their messengers) before these, and every nation purposed to seize their messenger and argued falsely, (thinking) thereby to refute the Truth. Then I seized them, and how (awful) was My punishment!

6. Thus was the word of thy Lord concerning those who disbelieve fulfilled: that they are owners of the Fire.

7. Those who bear the Throne, and all who are round about it, hymn the praises of their Lord and believe in Him and ask forgiveness for those who believe (saying): Our Lord! Thou comprehendest all things in mercy and knowledge, therefor forgive those who repent and follow Thy way: Ward off from them the punishment of hell!

8. Our Lord! And make them enter the Gardens of Eden which Thou hast promised them, with such of their fathers and their wives and their descendants as do right. Lo! Thou, only Thou, art the Mighty, the Wise:

1. See Sūr. II, v. 1, footnote.

اياتها ٨٥ (٤٠) سُوْرَةُ الْمُؤْمِنِ مَكِّيَّةٌ ركوعاتها ٩

بِسْمِ اللّٰهِ الرَّحْمٰنِ الرَّحِيْمِ

حٰمٓ ﴿١﴾

تَنْزِيْلُ الْكِتٰبِ مِنَ اللّٰهِ الْعَزِيْزِ الْعَلِيْمِ ﴿٢﴾

غَافِرِ الذَّنْۢبِ وَقَابِلِ التَّوْبِ شَدِيْدِ الْعِقَابِ

ذِي الطَّوْلِ لَآ اِلٰهَ اِلَّا هُوَ اِلَيْهِ الْمَصِيْرُ ﴿٣﴾

مَا يُجَادِلُ فِيْٓ اٰيٰتِ اللّٰهِ اِلَّا الَّذِيْنَ كَفَرُوْا فَلَا

يَغْرُرْكَ تَقَلُّبُهُمْ فِي الْبِلَادِ ﴿٤﴾

كَذَّبَتْ قَبْلَهُمْ قَوْمُ نُوْحٍ وَّالْاَحْزَابُ مِنْۢ بَعْدِهِمْ

وَهَمَّتْ كُلُّ اُمَّةٍۢ بِرَسُوْلِهِمْ لِيَاْخُذُوْهُ وَجٰدَلُوْا

بِالْبَاطِلِ لِيُدْحِضُوْا بِهِ الْحَقَّ فَاَخَذْتُهُمْ فَكَيْفَ

كَانَ عِقَابِ ﴿٥﴾

وَكَذٰلِكَ حَقَّتْ كَلِمَتُ رَبِّكَ عَلَى الَّذِيْنَ كَفَرُوْٓا

اَنَّهُمْ اَصْحٰبُ النَّارِ ﴿٦﴾

اَلَّذِيْنَ يَحْمِلُوْنَ الْعَرْشَ وَمَنْ حَوْلَهٗ يُسَبِّحُوْنَ بِحَمْدِ

رَبِّهِمْ وَيُؤْمِنُوْنَ بِهٖ وَيَسْتَغْفِرُوْنَ لِلَّذِيْنَ اٰمَنُوْا

رَبَّنَا وَسِعْتَ كُلَّ شَيْءٍ رَّحْمَةً وَّعِلْمًا فَاغْفِرْ لِلَّذِيْنَ

تَابُوْا وَاتَّبَعُوْا سَبِيْلَكَ وَقِهِمْ عَذَابَ الْجَحِيْمِ ﴿٧﴾

رَبَّنَا وَاَدْخِلْهُمْ جَنّٰتِ عَدْنِ ِۨالَّتِيْ وَعَدْتَّهُمْ

وَمَنْ صَلَحَ مِنْ اٰبَآئِهِمْ وَاَزْوَاجِهِمْ وَذُرِّيّٰتِهِمْ

اِنَّكَ اَنْتَ الْعَزِيْزُ الْحَكِيْمُ ﴿٨﴾

وقف النبي صلى الله عليه وسلم

وقف لازم

9. And ward off from them ill deeds; and he from whom Thou wardest off ill deeds that day, him verily hast Thou taken into mercy. That is the supreme triumph.

10. Lo! (on that day) those who disbelieve are informed by proclamation: Verily Allah's abhorrence is more terrible than your abhorrence one of another, when ye were called unto the faith but did refuse.

11. They say: Our Lord! Twice hast Thou made us die, and twice hast Thou made us live. Now we confess our sins. Is there any way to go out?

12. (It is said unto them): This is (your plight) because when Allah only was invoked, ye disbelieved, but when some partner was ascribed to Him ye were believing. But the command belongeth only to Allah, the Sublime, the Majestic.

13. He it is Who showeth you His portents, and sendeth down for you provision from the sky. None payeth heed save him who turneth (unto Him) repentant.

14. Therefore (O believers) pray unto Allah, making religion pure for Him (only), however much the disbelievers be averse—

15. The Exalter of Ranks, the Lord of the Throne. He casteth the Spirit of His command upon whom He will of His slaves, that He may warn of the Day of Meeting—

16. The day when they come forth, nothing of them being hidden from Allah. Whose is the sovereignty this Day? It is Allah's the One, the Almighty.

17. This Day is each soul requited that which it hath earned: no wrong (is done) this Day. Lo! Allah is Swift at reckoning.

وَقِهِمُ السَّيِّاٰتِ ؕ وَمَنْ تَقِ السَّيِّاٰتِ يَوْمَئِذٍ
ع فَقَدْ رَحِمْتَهٗ ؕ وَذٰلِكَ هُوَ الْفَوْزُ الْعَظِيْمُ ﴿٩﴾
اِنَّ الَّذِيْنَ كَفَرُوْا يُنَادَوْنَ لَمَقْتُ اللّٰهِ اَكْبَرُ
مِنْ مَّقْتِكُمْ اَنْفُسَكُمْ اِذْ تُدْعَوْنَ اِلَى الْاِيْمَانِ
فَتَكْفُرُوْنَ ﴿١٠﴾
قَالُوْا رَبَّنَآ اَمَتَّنَا اثْنَتَيْنِ وَاَحْيَيْتَنَا اثْنَتَيْنِ
فَاعْتَرَفْنَا بِذُنُوْبِنَا فَهَلْ اِلٰى خُرُوْجٍ مِّنْ
سَبِيْلٍ ﴿١١﴾
ذٰلِكُمْ بِاَنَّهٗۤ اِذَا دُعِيَ اللّٰهُ وَحْدَهٗ كَفَرْتُمْ ۚ
وَاِنْ يُّشْرَكْ بِهٖ تُؤْمِنُوْا ؕ فَالْحُكْمُ لِلّٰهِ الْعَلِيِّ
الْكَبِيْرِ ﴿١٢﴾
هُوَ الَّذِيْ يُرِيْكُمْ اٰيٰتِهٖ وَيُنَزِّلُ لَكُمْ مِّنَ السَّمَآءِ
رِزْقًا ؕ وَمَا يَتَذَكَّرُ اِلَّا مَنْ يُّنِيْبُ ﴿١٣﴾
فَادْعُوا اللّٰهَ مُخْلِصِيْنَ لَهُ الدِّيْنَ وَلَوْ كَرِهَ
الْكٰفِرُوْنَ ﴿١٤﴾
رَفِيْعُ الدَّرَجٰتِ ذُو الْعَرْشِ ۚ يُلْقِي الرُّوْحَ مِنْ
اَمْرِهٖ عَلٰى مَنْ يَّشَآءُ مِنْ عِبَادِهٖ لِيُنْذِرَ يَوْمَ
التَّلَاقِ ﴿١٥﴾
يَوْمَ هُمْ بٰرِزُوْنَ ۚ لَا يَخْفٰى عَلَى اللّٰهِ مِنْهُمْ شَيْءٌ ؕ
لِمَنِ الْمُلْكُ الْيَوْمَ ؕ لِلّٰهِ الْوَاحِدِ الْقَهَّارِ ﴿١٦﴾
اَلْيَوْمَ تُجْزٰى كُلُّ نَفْسٍ بِمَا كَسَبَتْ ؕ لَا ظُلْمَ الْيَوْمَ ؕ
اِنَّ اللّٰهَ سَرِيْعُ الْحِسَابِ ﴿١٧﴾

18. Warn them (O Muhammad) of the Day of the approaching (doom), when the hearts will be choking the throats, (when) there will be no friend for the wrong-doers, nor any intercessor who will be heard.

وَأَنْذِرْهُمْ يَوْمَ الْأَزِفَةِ إِذِ الْقُلُوبُ لَدَى الْحَنَاجِرِ كَظِمِيْنَ ۚ مَا لِلظّٰلِمِيْنَ مِنْ حَمِيْمٍ وَّلَا شَفِيْعٍ يُّطَاعُ ۟

19. He knoweth the traitor of the eyes, and that which the bosoms hide.

يَعْلَمُ خَآئِنَةَ الْأَعْيُنِ وَمَا تُخْفِي الصُّدُوْرُ ۟

20. Allah judgeth with truth, while those to whom they cry instead of Him judge not at all. Lo! Allah, He is the Hearer, the Seer.

وَاللّٰهُ يَقْضِيْ بِالْحَقِّ ۗ وَالَّذِيْنَ يَدْعُوْنَ مِنْ دُوْنِهٖ لَا يَقْضُوْنَ بِشَيْءٍ ۗ اِنَّ اللّٰهَ هُوَ السَّمِيْعُ الْبَصِيْرُ ۟

21. Have they not travelled in the land to see the nature of the consequence for those who disbelieved before them? They were mightier than these in power and (in the) traces (which they left behind them) in the earth. Yet Allah seized them for their sins, and they had no protector from Allah.

أَوَلَمْ يَسِيْرُوْا فِي الْأَرْضِ فَيَنْظُرُوْا كَيْفَ كَانَ عَاقِبَةُ الَّذِيْنَ كَانُوْا مِنْ قَبْلِهِمْ ۚ كَانُوْا هُمْ أَشَدَّ مِنْهُمْ قُوَّةً وَّآثَارًا فِي الْأَرْضِ فَأَخَذَهُمُ اللّٰهُ بِذُنُوْبِهِمْ وَمَا كَانَ لَهُمْ مِنَ اللّٰهِ مِنْ وَّاقٍ ۟

22. That was because their messengers kept bringing them clear proofs (of Allah's Sovereignty) but they disbelieved; so Allah seized them. Lo! He is Strong, Severe in punishment.

ذٰلِكَ بِأَنَّهُمْ كَانَتْ تَّأْتِيْهِمْ رُسُلُهُمْ بِالْبَيِّنَاتِ فَكَفَرُوْا فَأَخَذَهُمُ اللّٰهُ ۚ اِنَّهٗ قَوِيٌّ شَدِيْدُ الْعِقَابِ ۟

23. And verily We sent Moses with Our revelations and a clear warrant

وَلَقَدْ أَرْسَلْنَا مُوْسٰى بِآيٰتِنَا وَسُلْطٰنٍ مُّبِيْنٍ ۟

24. Unto Pharaoh and Haman and Korah, but they said: A lying sorcerer!

إِلٰى فِرْعَوْنَ وَهَامٰنَ وَقَارُوْنَ فَقَالُوْا سٰحِرٌ كَذَّابٌ ۟

25. And when he brought them the Truth from Our Presence, they said: Slay the sons of those who believe with him, and spare their women. But the plot of disbelievers is in naught but error.

فَلَمَّا جَآءَهُمْ بِالْحَقِّ مِنْ عِنْدِنَا قَالُوا اقْتُلُوْا أَبْنَآءَ الَّذِيْنَ اٰمَنُوْا مَعَهٗ وَاسْتَحْيُوْا نِسَآءَهُمْ ۚ وَمَا كَيْدُ الْكٰفِرِيْنَ اِلَّا فِيْ ضَلٰلٍ ۟

26. And Pharaoh said: Suffer me to kill Moses, and let him cry unto his Lord. Lo! I fear that he will alter your religion or that he will cause confusion in the land.

وَقَالَ فِرْعَوْنُ ذَرُوْنِيْ أَقْتُلْ مُوْسٰى وَلْيَدْعُ رَبَّهٗ ۚ اِنِّيْ أَخَافُ أَنْ يُّبَدِّلَ دِيْنَكُمْ أَوْ أَنْ يُّظْهِرَ فِي الْأَرْضِ الْفَسَادَ ۟

27. Moses said: Lo! I seek refuge in my Lord and your Lord from every scorner who believeth not in a Day of Reckoning.

28. And a believing man of Pharaoh's family, who hid his faith, said: Would ye kill a man because he saith: My Lord is Allah, and hath brought you clear proofs from your Lord? If he is lying, then his lie is upon him; and if he is truthful, then some of that wherewith he threateneth you will strike you. Lo! Allah guideth not one who is a prodigal, a liar.

29. O my people! Yours is the kingdom to-day, ye being uppermost in the land. But who would save us from the wrath of Allah should it reach us? Pharaoh said: I do but show you what I think, and I do but guide you to a wise policy.

30. And he who believed said: O my people! Lo! I fear for you a fate like that of the factions (of old);

31. A plight like that of Noah's folk, and 'Aād and Thamūd, and those after them, and Allah willeth no injustice for (His) slaves.

32. And, O my people! Lo! I fear for a Day of Summoning,—

33. A Day when ye will turn to flee, having no preserver from Allah, and he whom Allah sendeth astray, for him there is no guide.

34. And verily Joseph brought you of old clear proofs, yet ye ceased not to be in doubt concerning what he brought you till, when he died, he said: Allah will not send any messenger after him. Thus Allah deceiveth him who is a prodigal, a doubter.

وَقَالَ مُوسَىٰٓ إِنِّي عُذْتُ بِرَبِّي وَرَبِّكُم مِّن كُلِّ

ع ٣ ٨ مُتَكَبِّرٍ لَّا يُؤْمِنُ بِيَوْمِ الْحِسَابِ ٢٧

وَقَالَ رَجُلٌ مُّؤْمِنٌ مِّنْ آلِ فِرْعَوْنَ يَكْتُمُ إِيمَانَهُ

أَتَقْتُلُونَ رَجُلًا أَن يَقُولَ رَبِّيَ اللَّهُ وَقَدْ جَاءَكُم

بِالْبَيِّنَاتِ مِن رَّبِّكُمْ وَإِن يَكُ كَاذِبًا فَعَلَيْهِ كَذِبُهُ

وَإِن يَكُ صَادِقًا يُصِبْكُم بَعْضُ الَّذِي يَعِدُكُمْ

إِنَّ اللَّهَ لَا يَهْدِي مَنْ هُوَ مُسْرِفٌ كَذَّابٌ ٢٨

يَا قَوْمِ لَكُمُ الْمُلْكُ الْيَوْمَ ظَاهِرِينَ فِي الْأَرْضِ

فَمَن يَنصُرُنَا مِن بَأْسِ اللَّهِ إِن جَاءَنَا قَالَ

فِرْعَوْنُ مَا أُرِيكُمْ إِلَّا مَا أَرَىٰ وَمَا أَهْدِيكُمْ إِلَّا

سَبِيلَ الرَّشَادِ ٢٩

وَقَالَ الَّذِي آمَنَ يَا قَوْمِ إِنِّي أَخَافُ عَلَيْكُم مِّثْلَ

يَوْمِ الْأَحْزَابِ ٣٠

مِثْلَ دَأْبِ قَوْمِ نُوحٍ وَعَادٍ وَثَمُودَ وَالَّذِينَ

مِن بَعْدِهِمْ وَمَا اللَّهُ يُرِيدُ ظُلْمًا لِّلْعِبَادِ ٣١

وَيَا قَوْمِ إِنِّي أَخَافُ عَلَيْكُمْ يَوْمَ التَّنَادِ ٣٢

يَوْمَ تُوَلُّونَ مُدْبِرِينَ مَا لَكُم مِّنَ اللَّهِ مِنْ عَاصِمٍ

وَمَن يُضْلِلِ اللَّهُ فَمَا لَهُ مِنْ هَادٍ ٣٣

وَلَقَدْ جَاءَكُمْ يُوسُفُ مِن قَبْلُ بِالْبَيِّنَاتِ فَمَا زِلْتُمْ

فِي شَكٍّ مِّمَّا جَاءَكُم بِهِ حَتَّىٰ إِذَا هَلَكَ قُلْتُمْ

لَن يَبْعَثَ اللَّهُ مِن بَعْدِهِ رَسُولًا كَذَٰلِكَ يُضِلُّ

اللَّهُ مَنْ هُوَ مُسْرِفٌ مُّرْتَابٌ ٣٤

35. Those who wrangle concerning the revelations of Allah without any warrant that hath come unto them, it is greatly hateful in the sight of Allah and in the sight of those who believe. Thus doth Allah print on every arrogant, disdainful heart.

36. And Pharaoh said: O Haman! Build for me a tower that haply I may reach the roads,—

37. The roads of the heavens, and may look upon the God of Moses, though verily I think him a liar. Thus was the evil that he did made fair-seeming unto Pharaoh, and he was debarred from the (right) way. The plot of Pharaoh ended but in ruin.

38. And he who believed said: O my people! Follow me. I will show you the way of right conduct.

39. O my people! Lo! this life of the world is but a passing comfort, and lo! the Hereafter, that is the enduring home.

40. Whoso doth an ill-deed, he will be repaid the like thereof, while whoso doth right, whether male or female, and is a believer, (all) such will enter the Garden, where they will be nourished without stint.

41. And, O my people! What aileth me that I call you unto deliverance when ye call me unto the Fire?

42. Ye call me to disbelieve in Allah and ascribe unto Him as partners that whereof I have no knowledge, while I call you unto the Mighty, the Forgiver.

الَّذِينَ يُجَادِلُونَ فِي آيَاتِ اللَّهِ بِغَيْرِ سُلْطَانٍ أَتَاهُمْ
كَبُرَ مَقْتًا عِنْدَ اللَّهِ وَعِنْدَ الَّذِينَ آمَنُوا كَذَٰلِكَ
يَطْبَعُ اللَّهُ عَلَىٰ كُلِّ قَلْبِ مُتَكَبِّرٍ جَبَّارٍ ﴿٣٥﴾
وَقَالَ فِرْعَوْنُ يَا هَامَانُ ابْنِ لِي صَرْحًا لَعَلِّي
أَبْلُغُ الْأَسْبَابَ ﴿٣٦﴾
أَسْبَابَ السَّمَاوَاتِ فَأَطَّلِعَ إِلَىٰ إِلَٰهِ مُوسَىٰ وَإِنِّي
لَأَظُنُّهُ كَاذِبًا ۚ وَكَذَٰلِكَ زُيِّنَ لِفِرْعَوْنَ سُوءُ
عَمَلِهِ وَصُدَّ عَنِ السَّبِيلِ ۚ وَمَا كَيْدُ فِرْعَوْنَ
إِلَّا فِي تَبَابٍ ﴿٣٧﴾ ع ٤ ٩
وَقَالَ الَّذِي آمَنَ يَا قَوْمِ اتَّبِعُونِ أَهْدِكُمْ سَبِيلَ
الرَّشَادِ ﴿٣٨﴾
يَا قَوْمِ إِنَّمَا هَٰذِهِ الْحَيَاةُ الدُّنْيَا مَتَاعٌ وَإِنَّ
الْآخِرَةَ هِيَ دَارُ الْقَرَارِ ﴿٣٩﴾
مَنْ عَمِلَ سَيِّئَةً فَلَا يُجْزَىٰ إِلَّا مِثْلَهَا ۖ وَمَنْ
عَمِلَ صَالِحًا مِنْ ذَكَرٍ أَوْ أُنْثَىٰ وَهُوَ مُؤْمِنٌ
فَأُولَٰئِكَ يَدْخُلُونَ الْجَنَّةَ يُرْزَقُونَ فِيهَا بِغَيْرِ
حِسَابٍ ﴿٤٠﴾
وَيَا قَوْمِ مَا لِي أَدْعُوكُمْ إِلَى النَّجَاةِ وَتَدْعُونَنِي
إِلَى النَّارِ ﴿٤١﴾ النصف
تَدْعُونَنِي لِأَكْفُرَ بِاللَّهِ وَأُشْرِكَ بِهِ مَا لَيْسَ
لِي بِهِ عِلْمٌ وَأَنَا أَدْعُوكُمْ إِلَى الْعَزِيزِ
الْغَفَّارِ ﴿٤٢﴾

43. Assuredly that whereunto ye call me hath no claim in the world or in the Hereafter, and our return will be unto Allah, and the prodigals will be owners of the fire.

44. And ye will remember what I say unto you. I confide my cause unto Allah. Lo! Allah is Seer of (His) slaves.

45. So Allah warded off from him the evils which they plotted, while a dreadful doom encompassed Pharaoh's folk.

46. The Fire; they are exposed to it morning and evening; and on the day when the Hour upriseth (it is said): Cause Pharaoh's folk to enter the most awful doom.

47. And when they wrangle in the fire, the weak say unto those who were proud: Lo! we were a following unto you: will ye therefor rid us of a portion of the Fire?

48. Those who were proud say: Lo! we are all (together) herein. Lo! Allah hath judged between (His) slaves.

49. And those in the Fire say unto the guards of hell: Entreat your Lord that He relieve us of a day of the torment.

50. They say: Came not your messengers unto you with clear proofs? They say: Yea, verily. They say: Then do ye pray, although the prayer of disbelievers is in vain.

51. Lo! We verily do help Our messengers, and those who believe, in the life of the world and on the Day when the witnesses arise,—

لَا جَرَمَ أَنَّمَا تَدْعُونَنِي إِلَيْهِ لَيْسَ لَهُ دَعْوَةٌ فِي
الدُّنْيَا وَلَا فِي الْآخِرَةِ وَأَنَّ مَرَدَّنَا إِلَى اللّٰهِ وَأَنَّ
الْمُسْرِفِينَ هُمْ أَصْحٰبُ النَّارِ ﴿٤٣﴾
فَسَتَذْكُرُونَ مَا أَقُولُ لَكُمْ وَأُفَوِّضُ أَمْرِي إِلَى
اللّٰهِ إِنَّ اللّٰهَ بَصِيرٌ بِالْعِبَادِ ﴿٤٤﴾
فَوَقٰهُ اللّٰهُ سَيِّاٰتِ مَا مَكَرُوا وَحَاقَ بِاٰلِ فِرْعَوْنَ
سُوْءُ الْعَذَابِ ﴿٤٥﴾
اَلنَّارُ يُعْرَضُونَ عَلَيْهَا غُدُوًّا وَعَشِيًّا وَيَوْمَ
تَقُومُ السَّاعَةُ أَدْخِلُوا اٰلَ فِرْعَوْنَ أَشَدَّ
الْعَذَابِ ﴿٤٦﴾
وَإِذْ يَتَحَاجُّونَ فِي النَّارِ فَيَقُولُ الضُّعَفٰؤُا لِلَّذِينَ
اسْتَكْبَرُوا إِنَّا كُنَّا لَكُمْ تَبَعًا فَهَلْ أَنْتُمْ مُغْنُونَ
عَنَّا نَصِيبًا مِنَ النَّارِ ﴿٤٧﴾
قَالَ الَّذِينَ اسْتَكْبَرُوا إِنَّا كُلٌّ فِيهَا إِنَّ اللّٰهَ قَدْ
حَكَمَ بَيْنَ الْعِبَادِ ﴿٤٨﴾
وَقَالَ الَّذِينَ فِي النَّارِ لِخَزَنَةِ جَهَنَّمَ ادْعُوا
رَبَّكُمْ يُخَفِّفْ عَنَّا يَوْمًا مِنَ الْعَذَابِ ﴿٤٩﴾
قَالُوا أَوَلَمْ تَكُ تَأْتِيكُمْ رُسُلُكُمْ بِالْبَيِّنٰتِ قَالُوا
بَلٰى قَالُوا فَادْعُوا وَمَا دُعٰؤُا الْكٰفِرِينَ إِلَّا فِي
ضَلٰلٍ ﴿٥٠﴾ ع
إِنَّا لَنَنْصُرُ رُسُلَنَا وَالَّذِينَ اٰمَنُوا فِي الْحَيٰوةِ الدُّنْيَا
وَيَوْمَ يَقُومُ الْأَشْهَادُ ﴿٥١﴾

52. The Day when their excuse availeth not the evil-doers, and theirs is the curse, and theirs the ill abode.

53. And We verily gave Moses the guidance, and We caused the Children of Israel to inherit the Scripture,

54. A guide and a reminder for men of understanding.

55. Then have patience (O Muhammad). Lo! the promise of Allah is true. And ask forgiveness of thy sin, and hymn the praise of thy Lord at fall of night and in the early hours.

56. Lo! those who wrangle concerning the revelations of Allah without a warrant having come unto them, there is naught else in their breasts save pride which they will never attain. So take thou refuge in Allah. Lo! He, only He, is the Hearer, the Seer.

57. Assuredly the creation of the heavens and the earth is greater than the creation of mankind; but most of mankind know not.

58. And the blind man and the seer are not equal, neither are those who believe and do good works (equal with) the evil-doer. Little do ye reflect!

59. Lo! the Hour is surely coming, there is no doubt thereof; yet most of mankind believe not.

60. And your Lord hath said: Pray unto Me and I will hear your prayer. Lo! those who scorn My service, they will enter hell, disgraced.

61. Allah it is Who hath appointed for you night that ye may rest therein, and day for seeing. Lo! Allah is a Lord of bounty for mankind, yet most of mankind give not thanks.

يَوْمَ لَا يَنْفَعُ الظّٰلِمِيْنَ مَعْذِرَتُهُمْ وَلَهُمُ اللَّعْنَةُ
وَلَهُمْ سُوْٓءُ الدَّارِ ﴿٥٢﴾
وَلَقَدْ اٰتَيْنَا مُوْسَى الْهُدٰى وَاَوْرَثْنَا بَنِيْٓ
اِسْرَآءِيْلَ الْكِتٰبَ ﴿٥٣﴾
هُدًى وَّذِكْرٰى لِاُولِي الْاَلْبَابِ ﴿٥٤﴾
فَاصْبِرْ اِنَّ وَعْدَ اللّٰهِ حَقٌّ وَّاسْتَغْفِرْ لِذَنْۢبِكَ وَ
سَبِّحْ بِحَمْدِ رَبِّكَ بِالْعَشِيِّ وَالْاِبْكَارِ ﴿٥٥﴾
اِنَّ الَّذِيْنَ يُجَادِلُوْنَ فِيْٓ اٰيٰتِ اللّٰهِ بِغَيْرِ سُلْطٰنٍ
اَتٰىهُمْ اِنْ فِيْ صُدُوْرِهِمْ اِلَّا كِبْرٌ مَّا هُمْ بِبَالِغِيْهِ
فَاسْتَعِذْ بِاللّٰهِ اِنَّهٗ هُوَ السَّمِيْعُ الْبَصِيْرُ ﴿٥٦﴾
لَخَلْقُ السَّمٰوٰتِ وَالْاَرْضِ اَكْبَرُ مِنْ خَلْقِ النَّاسِ
وَلٰكِنَّ اَكْثَرَ النَّاسِ لَا يَعْلَمُوْنَ ﴿٥٧﴾
وَمَا يَسْتَوِي الْاَعْمٰى وَالْبَصِيْرُ وَالَّذِيْنَ اٰمَنُوْا
وَعَمِلُوا الصّٰلِحٰتِ وَلَا الْمُسِيْٓءُ قَلِيْلًا مَّا
تَتَذَكَّرُوْنَ ﴿٥٨﴾
اِنَّ السَّاعَةَ لَاٰتِيَةٌ لَّا رَيْبَ فِيْهَا وَلٰكِنَّ اَكْثَرَ
النَّاسِ لَا يُؤْمِنُوْنَ ﴿٥٩﴾
وَقَالَ رَبُّكُمُ ادْعُوْنِيْٓ اَسْتَجِبْ لَكُمْ اِنَّ الَّذِيْنَ
ع ٦ يَسْتَكْبِرُوْنَ عَنْ عِبَادَتِيْ سَيَدْخُلُوْنَ جَهَنَّمَ دٰخِرِيْنَ ﴿٦٠﴾
اَللّٰهُ الَّذِيْ جَعَلَ لَكُمُ الَّيْلَ لِتَسْكُنُوْا فِيْهِ وَالنَّهَارَ
مُبْصِرًا اِنَّ اللّٰهَ لَذُوْ فَضْلٍ عَلَى النَّاسِ وَلٰكِنَّ اَكْثَرَ
النَّاسِ لَا يَشْكُرُوْنَ ﴿٦١﴾

62. Such is Allah, your Lord, the Creator of all things. There is no God save Him. How then are ye perverted?

63. Thus are they perverted who deny the revelations of Allah.

64. Allah it is Who appointed for you the earth for a dwelling-place and the sky for a canopy, and fashioned you and perfected your shapes, and hath provided you with good things. Such is Allah, your Lord. Then blessed be Allah, the Lord of the Worlds!

65. He is the Living One. There is no God save Him. So pray unto Him, making religion pure for Him (only). Praise be to Allah, the Lord of the Worlds!

66. Say (O Muhammad): I am forbidden to worship those unto whom ye cry beside Allah since there have come unto me clear proofs from my Lord, and I am commanded to surrender to the Lord of the Worlds.

67. He it is Who created you from dust, then from a drop (of seed), then from a clot, then bringeth you forth as a child, then (ordaineth) that ye attain full strength and afterward that ye become old men—though some among you die before—and that ye reach an appointed term, that haply ye may understand.

68. He it is Who quickeneth and giveth death. When He ordaineth a thing, He saith unto it only: Be! and it is.

69. Hast thou not seen those who wrangle concerning the revelations of Allah, how they are turned away!—

70. Those who deny the Scripture and that wherewith We send Our messengers. But they will come to know,

ذٰلِكُمُ اللّٰهُ رَبُّكُمْ خَالِقُ كُلِّ شَيْءٍ لَّآ اِلٰهَ اِلَّا هُوَ فَاَنّٰى وقف لازم
تُؤْفَكُوْنَ ٦٢
كَذٰلِكَ يُؤْفَكُ الَّذِيْنَ كَانُوْا بِاٰيٰتِ اللّٰهِ يَجْحَدُوْنَ ٦٣
اَللّٰهُ الَّذِيْ جَعَلَ لَكُمُ الْاَرْضَ قَرَارًا وَّالسَّمَآءَ
بِنَآءً وَّصَوَّرَكُمْ فَاَحْسَنَ صُوَرَكُمْ وَرَزَقَكُمْ
مِّنَ الطَّيِّبٰتِ ذٰلِكُمُ اللّٰهُ رَبُّكُمْ فَتَبٰرَكَ اللّٰهُ رَبُّ
الْعٰلَمِيْنَ ٦٤
هُوَ الْحَيُّ لَآ اِلٰهَ اِلَّا هُوَ فَادْعُوْهُ مُخْلِصِيْنَ لَهُ
الدِّيْنَ اَلْحَمْدُ لِلّٰهِ رَبِّ الْعٰلَمِيْنَ ٦٥
قُلْ اِنِّيْ نُهِيْتُ اَنْ اَعْبُدَ الَّذِيْنَ تَدْعُوْنَ مِنْ
دُوْنِ اللّٰهِ لَمَّا جَآءَنِيَ الْبَيِّنٰتُ مِنْ رَّبِّيْ وَاُمِرْتُ
اَنْ اُسْلِمَ لِرَبِّ الْعٰلَمِيْنَ ٦٦
هُوَ الَّذِيْ خَلَقَكُمْ مِّنْ تُرَابٍ ثُمَّ مِنْ نُّطْفَةٍ ثُمَّ
مِنْ عَلَقَةٍ ثُمَّ يُخْرِجُكُمْ طِفْلًا ثُمَّ لِتَبْلُغُوْٓا اَشُدَّكُمْ
ثُمَّ لِتَكُوْنُوْا شُيُوْخًا وَمِنْكُمْ مَّنْ يُّتَوَفّٰى مِنْ قَبْلُ وَ
لِتَبْلُغُوْٓا اَجَلًا مُّسَمًّى وَّلَعَلَّكُمْ تَعْقِلُوْنَ ٦٧
هُوَ الَّذِيْ يُحْيٖ وَيُمِيْتُ فَاِذَا قَضٰٓى اَمْرًا فَاِنَّمَا
يَقُوْلُ لَهٗ كُنْ فَيَكُوْنُ ٦٨ ع ٧ ٨ ١٢
اَلَمْ تَرَ اِلَى الَّذِيْنَ يُجَادِلُوْنَ فِيْٓ اٰيٰتِ اللّٰهِ اَنّٰى
يُصْرَفُوْنَ ٦٩
الَّذِيْنَ كَذَّبُوْا بِالْكِتٰبِ وَبِمَآ اَرْسَلْنَا بِهٖ رُسُلَنَا
فَسَوْفَ يَعْلَمُوْنَ ٧٠

71. When carcans are about their necks and chains. They are dragged

72. Through boiling waters; then they are thrust into the Fire.

73. Then it is said unto them: Where are (all) that ye used to make partners (in the Sovereignty)

74. Beside Allah? They say: They have failed us; but we used not to pray to anything before. Thus doth Allah send astray the disbelievers (in His guidance).

75. (And it is said unto them): This is because ye exulted in the earth without right, and because ye were petulant.

76. Enter ye the gates of Hell, to dwell therein. Evil is the habitation of the scornful.

77. Then have patience (O Muhammad). Lo! the promise of Allah is true. And whether we let thee see a part of that which We promise them, or (whether) We cause thee to die, still unto Us they will be brought back.

78. Verily We sent messengers before thee, among them those of whom We have told thee, and some of whom We have not told thee; and it was not given to any messenger that he should bring a portent save by Allah's leave, but when Allah's commandment cometh (the cause) is judged aright, and the followers of vanity will then be lost.

79. Allah it is Who hath appointed for you cattle, that ye may ride on some of them, and eat of some—

80. (Many) benefits ye have from them—and that ye may satisfy by their means a need that is in your breasts, and may be borne upon them as upon the ship.

81. And He showeth you His tokens. Which, then, of the tokens of Allah do ye deny?

اذ الاغلل في اعناقهم والسلسل يسحبون ﴿٧١﴾
في الحميم ثم في النار يسجرون ﴿٧٢﴾
ثم قيل لهم اين ما كنتم تشركون ﴿٧٣﴾
من دون الله قالوا ضلوا عنا بل لم نكن
ندعوا من قبل شيئا كذلك يضل الله
الكفرين ﴿٧٤﴾
ذلكم بما كنتم تفرحون في الارض بغير
الحق وبما كنتم تمرحون ﴿٧٥﴾
ادخلوا ابواب جهنم خلدين فيها فبئس
مثوى المتكبرين ﴿٧٦﴾
فاصبر ان وعد الله حق فاما نرينك بعض
الذي نعدهم او نتوفينك فالينا يرجعون ﴿٧٧﴾
ولقد ارسلنا رسلا من قبلك منهم من قصصنا
عليك ومنهم من لم نقصص عليك وما كان
لرسول ان يأتي باية الا باذن الله فاذا
جاء امر الله قضي بالحق وخسر هنالك
المبطلون ﴿٧٨﴾ ع ٨ ١٢
الله الذي جعل لكم الانعام لتركبوا منها و
منها تأكلون ﴿٧٩﴾
ولكم فيها منافع ولتبلغوا عليها حاجة في
صدوركم وعليها وعلى الفلك تحملون ﴿٨٠﴾
ويريكم ايته فاي ايت الله تنكرون ﴿٨١﴾

82. Have they not travelled in the land to see the nature of the consequence for those before them? They were more numerous than these, and mightier in power and (in the) traces (which they left behind them) in the earth. But all that they used to earn availed them not.

83. And when their messengers brought them clear proofs (of Allah's Sovereignty) they exulted in the knowledge they (themselves) possessed. And that which they were wont to mock befell them.

84. Then, when they saw Our doom, they said: We believe in Allah only and reject (all) that we used to associate (with Him)!

85. But their faith could not avail them when they saw Our doom. This is Allah's law which hath ever taken course for His bondsmen. And then the disbelievers will be ruined.

أَفَلَمْ يَسِيرُوا فِي الْأَرْضِ فَيَنظُرُوا كَيْفَ كَانَ عَاقِبَةُ
الَّذِينَ مِن قَبْلِهِمْ ۚ كَانُوا أَكْثَرَ مِنْهُمْ وَأَشَدَّ قُوَّةً
وَآثَارًا فِي الْأَرْضِ فَمَا أَغْنَىٰ عَنْهُم مَّا كَانُوا
يَكْسِبُونَ ﴿٨٢﴾
فَلَمَّا جَاءَتْهُمْ رُسُلُهُم بِالْبَيِّنَاتِ فَرِحُوا بِمَا
عِندَهُم مِّنَ الْعِلْمِ وَحَاقَ بِهِم مَّا كَانُوا
بِهِ يَسْتَهْزِئُونَ ﴿٨٣﴾
فَلَمَّا رَأَوْا بَأْسَنَا قَالُوا آمَنَّا بِاللَّهِ وَحْدَهُ وَكَفَرْنَا
بِمَا كُنَّا بِهِ مُشْرِكِينَ ﴿٨٤﴾
فَلَمْ يَكُ يَنفَعُهُمْ إِيمَانُهُمْ لَمَّا رَأَوْا بَأْسَنَا ۖ
سُنَّتَ اللَّهِ الَّتِي قَدْ خَلَتْ فِي عِبَادِهِ ۖ وَخَسِرَ
هُنَالِكَ الْكَافِرُونَ ﴿٨٥﴾ ع ٩ ١٤

Fuṣilat, "They Are Expounded," derives its title from a word in v. 2. It is also often called *Ḥā, Mîm, As-Sajdah*, from a word in v. 37, *Ḥā Mîm* being added to distinguish it from Sūrah XXXII, which is called As-Sajdah.

It belongs to the middle group of Meccan Sūrahs.

FUŞILAT ("THEY ARE EXPOUNDED")

Revealed at Mecca

In the name of Allah, the Beneficent, the Merciful.

1. Hā. Mīm.[1]
2. A revelation from the Beneficent, the Merciful.
3. A Scripture whereof the verses are expounded, a Lecture[2] in Arabic for people who have knowledge.
4. Good tidings and a warning. But most of them turn away so that they hear not.
5. And they say: Our hearts are protected from that unto which thou (O Muhammad) callest us, and in our ears there is a deafness, and between us and thee there is a veil. Act, then. Lo! we also shall be acting.
6. Say (unto them O Muhammad): I am only a mortal like you. It is inspired in me that your God is One God, therefor take the straight path unto Him and seek forgiveness of Him. And woe unto the idolaters,
7. Who give not the poor-due, and who disbelieve in the Hereafter.
8. Lo! as for those who believe and do good works, for them is a reward enduring.
9. Say (O Muhammad, unto the idolaters): Disbelieve ye verily in Him Who created the earth in two Days,[1] and ascribe ye unto Him rivals? He (and none else) is the Lord of the Worlds.
10. He placed therein firm hills rising above it, and blessed it and measured therein its sustenance in four Days, alike for (all) who ask ;

1. See Sûr. II, v. 1, footnote.
2. Ar. *Qur'ān.*

اياتها ٥٤ (٤١) سورة حم السجدة مكية (٦١) ركوعاتها ٦

بِسْمِ اللّٰهِ الرَّحْمٰنِ الرَّحِيْمِ

حٰمٓ ﴿١﴾

تَنْزِيْلٌ مِّنَ الرَّحْمٰنِ الرَّحِيْمِ ﴿٢﴾

كِتٰبٌ فُصِّلَتْ اٰيٰتُهٗ قُرْاٰنًا عَرَبِيًّا لِّقَوْمٍ يَّعْلَمُوْنَ ﴿٣﴾

بَشِيْرًا وَّنَذِيْرًا فَاَعْرَضَ اَكْثَرُهُمْ فَهُمْ لَا
يَسْمَعُوْنَ ﴿٤﴾

وَقَالُوْا قُلُوْبُنَا فِيْٓ اَكِنَّةٍ مِّمَّا تَدْعُوْنَآ اِلَيْهِ وَفِيْٓ
اٰذَانِنَا وَقْرٌ وَّمِنْۢ بَيْنِنَا وَبَيْنِكَ حِجَابٌ فَاعْمَلْ
اِنَّنَا عٰمِلُوْنَ ﴿٥﴾

قُلْ اِنَّمَآ اَنَا بَشَرٌ مِّثْلُكُمْ يُوْحٰٓى اِلَيَّ اَنَّمَآ اِلٰهُكُمْ
اِلٰهٌ وَّاحِدٌ فَاسْتَقِيْمُوْٓا اِلَيْهِ وَاسْتَغْفِرُوْهُ وَوَيْلٌ
لِّلْمُشْرِكِيْنَ ﴿٦﴾

الَّذِيْنَ لَا يُؤْتُوْنَ الزَّكٰوةَ وَهُمْ بِالْاٰخِرَةِ هُمْ كٰفِرُوْنَ ﴿٧﴾

اِنَّ الَّذِيْنَ اٰمَنُوْا وَعَمِلُوا الصّٰلِحٰتِ لَهُمْ اَجْرٌ
غَيْرُ مَمْنُوْنٍ ﴿٨﴾

قُلْ اَئِنَّكُمْ لَتَكْفُرُوْنَ بِالَّذِيْ خَلَقَ الْاَرْضَ فِيْ
يَوْمَيْنِ وَتَجْعَلُوْنَ لَهٗٓ اَنْدَادًا ذٰلِكَ رَبُّ الْعٰلَمِيْنَ ﴿٩﴾

وَجَعَلَ فِيْهَا رَوَاسِيَ مِنْ فَوْقِهَا وَبٰرَكَ فِيْهَا
وَقَدَّرَ فِيْهَآ اَقْوَاتَهَا فِيْٓ اَرْبَعَةِ اَيَّامٍ سَوَآءً
لِّلسَّآئِلِيْنَ ﴿١٠﴾

11. Then turned He to the heaven when it was smoke, and said unto it and unto the earth: Come both of you, willingly or loth. They said: We come, obedient.

12. Then He ordained them seven heavens in two Days[1] and inspired in each heaven its mandate; and We decked the nether heaven with lamps, and rendered it inviolable[2]. That is the measuring of the Mighty, the Knower.

13. But if they turn away, then say: I warn you of a thunderbolt like the thunderbolt (which fell of old upon the tribes) of 'Aād and Thamūd;

14. When their messengers came unto them from before them and behind them, saying: Worship none but Allah! they said: If our Lord had willed, He surely would have sent down angels (unto us), so lo! we are disbelievers in that wherewith ye have been sent.

15. As for 'Aād, they were arrogant in the land without right, and they said: Who is mightier than us in power? Could they not see that Allah Who created them, He was mightier than them in power? And they denied Our revelations.

16. Therefor We let loose on them a raging wind in evil days, that We might make them taste the torment of disgrace in the life of the world. And verily the doom of the Hereafter will be more shameful, and they will not be helped.

17. And as for Thamūd, We gave them guidance, but they preferred blindness to the guidance, so the bolt of the doom of humiliation overtook them because of what they used to earn.

1. XXII, 47; XXXII, 5; LXX, 4.
2. XXVII, 6-10: LXXII, 8-10.

ثُمَّ اسْتَوٰٓى اِلَى السَّمَآءِ وَهِىَ دُخَانٌ فَقَالَ لَهَا
وَلِلْاَرْضِ ائْتِيَا طَوْعًا اَوْ كَرْهًا ۭ قَالَتَآ اَتَيْنَا
طَآئِعِيْنَ ﴿١١﴾
فَقَضٰىهُنَّ سَبْعَ سَمٰوٰتٍ فِىْ يَوْمَيْنِ وَاَوْحٰى
فِىْ كُلِّ سَمَآءٍ اَمْرَهَا ۭ وَزَيَّنَّا السَّمَآءَ الدُّنْيَا
بِمَصَابِيْحَ ۖ وَحِفْظًا ۭ ذٰلِكَ تَقْدِيْرُ الْعَزِيْزِ
الْعَلِيْمِ ﴿١٢﴾
فَاِنْ اَعْرَضُوْا فَقُلْ اَنْذَرْتُكُمْ صٰعِقَةً مِّثْلَ
صٰعِقَةِ عَادٍ وَّثَمُوْدَ ﴿١٣﴾
اِذْ جَآءَتْهُمُ الرُّسُلُ مِنْ بَيْنِ اَيْدِيْهِمْ وَمِنْ
خَلْفِهِمْ اَلَّا تَعْبُدُوْٓا اِلَّا اللّٰهَ ۭ قَالُوْا لَوْ شَآءَ رَبُّنَا
لَاَنْزَلَ مَلٰٓئِكَةً فَاِنَّا بِمَآ اُرْسِلْتُمْ بِهٖ كٰفِرُوْنَ ﴿١٤﴾
فَاَمَّا عَادٌ فَاسْتَكْبَرُوْا فِى الْاَرْضِ بِغَيْرِ الْحَقِّ وَ
قَالُوْا مَنْ اَشَدُّ مِنَّا قُوَّةً ۭ اَوَلَمْ يَرَوْا اَنَّ اللّٰهَ
الَّذِىْ خَلَقَهُمْ هُوَ اَشَدُّ مِنْهُمْ قُوَّةً ۭ وَكَانُوْا
بِاٰيٰتِنَا يَجْحَدُوْنَ ﴿١٥﴾
فَاَرْسَلْنَا عَلَيْهِمْ رِيْحًا صَرْصَرًا فِىْٓ اَيَّامٍ نَّحِسَاتٍ
لِّنُذِيْقَهُمْ عَذَابَ الْخِزْىِ فِى الْحَيٰوةِ الدُّنْيَا ۭ
وَلَعَذَابُ الْاٰخِرَةِ اَخْزٰى وَهُمْ لَا يُنْصَرُوْنَ ﴿١٦﴾
وَاَمَّا ثَمُوْدُ فَهَدَيْنٰهُمْ فَاسْتَحَبُّوا الْعَمٰى عَلَى
الْهُدٰى فَاَخَذَتْهُمْ صٰعِقَةُ الْعَذَابِ الْهُوْنِ
بِمَا كَانُوْا يَكْسِبُوْنَ ﴿١٧﴾

18. And We delivered those who believed and used to keep their duty to Allah.

19. And (make mention of) the Day when the enemies of Allah are gathered unto the Fire, they are driven on—

20. Till, when they reach it, their ears and their eyes and their skins testify against them as to what they used to do.

21. And they say unto their skins: Why testify ye against us? They say: Allah hath given us speech Who giveth speech to all things, and Who created you at the first, and unto Whom ye are returned.

22. Ye did not hide yourselves lest your ears and your eyes and your skins should testify against you but ye deemed that Allah knew not much of what ye did!

23. That, your thought which ye did think about your Lord, hath ruined you; and ye find yourselves (this day) among the lost.

24. And though they are resigned, yet the Fire is still their home; and if they ask for favour, yet they are not of those unto whom favour can be shown.

25. And We assigned them comrades (in the world), who made their present and their past fair-seeming unto them. And the Word concerning nations of the jinn and humankind who passed away before them hath effect for them. Verily they are the losers.

26. Those who disbelieve say: Heed not this Qur'ān, and drown the hearing of it; haply ye may conquer.

٢ ع ١٦ وَنَجَّيْنَا الَّذِينَ آمَنُوا وَكَانُوا يَتَّقُونَ ﴿١٨﴾
وَيَوْمَ يُحْشَرُ أَعْدَاءُ اللَّهِ إِلَى النَّارِ فَهُمْ
يُوزَعُونَ ﴿١٩﴾
حَتَّىٰ إِذَا مَا جَاءُوهَا شَهِدَ عَلَيْهِمْ سَمْعُهُمْ
وَأَبْصَارُهُمْ وَجُلُودُهُمْ بِمَا كَانُوا
يَعْمَلُونَ ﴿٢٠﴾
وَقَالُوا لِجُلُودِهِمْ لِمَ شَهِدْتُمْ عَلَيْنَا قَالُوا أَنْطَقَنَا
اللَّهُ الَّذِي أَنْطَقَ كُلَّ شَيْءٍ وَهُوَ خَلَقَكُمْ أَوَّلَ
مَرَّةٍ وَإِلَيْهِ تُرْجَعُونَ ﴿٢١﴾
وَمَا كُنْتُمْ تَسْتَتِرُونَ أَنْ يَشْهَدَ عَلَيْكُمْ سَمْعُكُمْ
وَلَا أَبْصَارُكُمْ وَلَا جُلُودُكُمْ وَلَٰكِنْ ظَنَنْتُمْ أَنَّ
اللَّهَ لَا يَعْلَمُ كَثِيرًا مِمَّا تَعْمَلُونَ ﴿٢٢﴾
وَذَٰلِكُمْ ظَنُّكُمُ الَّذِي ظَنَنْتُمْ بِرَبِّكُمْ أَرْدَاكُمْ
فَأَصْبَحْتُمْ مِنَ الْخَاسِرِينَ ﴿٢٣﴾
فَإِنْ يَصْبِرُوا فَالنَّارُ مَثْوًى لَهُمْ وَإِنْ يَسْتَعْتِبُوا
فَمَا هُمْ مِنَ الْمُعْتَبِينَ ﴿٢٤﴾
وَقَيَّضْنَا لَهُمْ قُرَنَاءَ فَزَيَّنُوا لَهُمْ مَا بَيْنَ
أَيْدِيهِمْ وَمَا خَلْفَهُمْ وَحَقَّ عَلَيْهِمُ الْقَوْلُ
فِي أُمَمٍ قَدْ خَلَتْ مِنْ قَبْلِهِمْ مِنَ الْجِنِّ وَالْإِنْسِ
٣ ع ١٧ إِنَّهُمْ كَانُوا خَاسِرِينَ ﴿٢٥﴾
وَقَالَ الَّذِينَ كَفَرُوا لَا تَسْمَعُوا لِهَٰذَا الْقُرْآنِ
وَالْغَوْا فِيهِ لَعَلَّكُمْ تَغْلِبُونَ ﴿٢٦﴾

27. But verily We shall cause those who disbelieve to taste an awful doom, and verily We shall requite them the worst of what they used to do.

28. That is the reward of Allah's enemies: the Fire. Therein is their immortal home, payment forasmuch as they denied Our revelations.

29. And those who disbelieve will say: Our Lord! Show us those who beguiled us of the jinn and humankind. We will place them underneath our feet that they may be among the nethermost.

30. Lo! those who say: Our Lord is Allah, and afterward are upright, the angels descend upon them, saying: Fear not nor grieve, but hear good tidings of the Paradise which ye are promised.

31. We are your protecting friends in the life of the world and in the Hereafter. There ye will have (all) that your souls desire, and there ye will have (all) for which ye pray.

32. A gift of welcome from the Forgiving, the Merciful.

33. And who is better in speech than him who prayeth unto his Lord and doth right, and saith: Lo! I am of those who surrender[1] (unto Him)!

34. The good deed and the evil deed are not alike. Repel the evil deed with one which is better, then lo! he, between whom and thee there was enmity, (will become) as though he was a bosom friend.

35. But none is granted it save those who are steadfast, and none is granted it save the owner of great happiness.[2]

فلنذيقن الذين كفروا عذابا شديدا و
لنجزينهم اسوا الذي كانوا يعملون ﴿٢٧﴾
ذلك جزاء اعداء الله النار لهم فيها دار
الخلد جزاء بما كانوا بايتنا يجحدون ﴿٢٨﴾
وقال الذين كفروا ربنا ارنا الذين اضلنا
من الجن والانس نجعلهما تحت اقدامنا
ليكونا من الاسفلين ﴿٢٩﴾
ان الذين قالوا ربنا الله ثم استقاموا
تتنزل عليهم الملئكة الا تخافوا ولا
تحزنوا وابشروا بالجنة التي كنتم
توعدون ﴿٣٠﴾
نحن اولياؤكم في الحيوة الدنيا وفي الاخرة
ولكم فيها ما تشتهي انفسكم ولكم فيها ما
تدعون ﴿٣١﴾
نزلا من غفور رحيم ﴿٣٢﴾ ع ١٨
ومن احسن قولا ممن دعا الى الله وعمل
صالحا وقال انني من المسلمين ﴿٣٣﴾
ولا تستوي الحسنة ولا السيئة ادفع بالتي
هي احسن فاذا الذي بينك وبينه عداوة
كانه ولي حميم ﴿٣٤﴾
وما يلقىها الا الذين صبروا وما يلقىها الا
ذو حظ عظيم ﴿٣٥﴾

1. Ar. *Muslimin.*
2. *i.e.* not everyone is able to practise such forgiveness.

36. And if a whisper from the devil reach thee (O Muhammad) then seek refuge in Allah. Lo! He is the Hearer, the Knower.

37. And of His portents are the night and the day and the sun and the moon. Adore not the sun nor the moon; but adore Allah Who created them, if it is in truth Him Whom ye worship.

38. But if they are too proud—still those who are with thy Lord glorify Him night and day, and tire not.

39. And of His portents (is this): that thou seest the earth lowly, but when We send down water thereon it thrilleth and groweth. Lo! He Who quickeneth it is verily the Quickener of the dead. Lo! He is Able to do all things.

40. Lo! those who distort Our revelations are not hid from Us. Is he who is hurled into the Fire better, or he who cometh secure on the Day of Resurrection? Do what ye will. Lo! He is Seer of what ye do.

41. Lo! those who disbelieve in the Reminder when it cometh unto them (are guilty), for lo! it is an unassailable Scripture.

42. Falsehood cannot come at it from before it or behind it. (It is) a revelation from the Wise, the Owner of Praise.

43. Naught is said unto thee (Muhammad) save what was said unto the messengers before thee. Lo! thy Lord is owner of forgiveness, and owner (also) of dire punishment.

وَإِمَّا يَنزَغَنَّكَ مِنَ الشَّيْطٰنِ نَزْغٌ فَاسْتَعِذْ بِاللّٰهِ ۚ
إِنَّهُ هُوَ السَّمِيعُ الْعَلِيمُ ﴿٣٦﴾
وَمِنْ اٰيٰتِهِ الَّيْلُ وَالنَّهَارُ وَالشَّمْسُ وَالْقَمَرُ ۚ
لَا تَسْجُدُوا لِلشَّمْسِ وَلَا لِلْقَمَرِ وَاسْجُدُوا
لِلّٰهِ الَّذِي خَلَقَهُنَّ إِن كُنتُمْ إِيَّاهُ
تَعْبُدُونَ ﴿٣٧﴾
فَإِنِ اسْتَكْبَرُوا فَالَّذِينَ عِندَ رَبِّكَ يُسَبِّحُونَ لَهُ
بِالَّيْلِ وَالنَّهَارِ وَهُمْ لَا يَسْأَمُونَ ﴿٣٨﴾ السجدة
وَمِنْ اٰيٰتِهِ أَنَّكَ تَرَى الْأَرْضَ خَاشِعَةً فَإِذَا
أَنزَلْنَا عَلَيْهَا الْمَاءَ اهْتَزَّتْ وَرَبَتْ ۚ إِنَّ
الَّذِي أَحْيَاهَا لَمُحْيِ الْمَوْتَىٰ ۚ إِنَّهُ عَلَىٰ كُلِّ شَيْءٍ
قَدِيرٌ ﴿٣٩﴾
إِنَّ الَّذِينَ يُلْحِدُونَ فِي اٰيٰتِنَا لَا يَخْفَوْنَ عَلَيْنَا ۗ
أَفَمَن يُلْقَىٰ فِي النَّارِ خَيْرٌ أَم مَّن يَأْتِي اٰمِنًا
يَوْمَ الْقِيٰمَةِ ۚ اعْمَلُوا مَا شِئْتُمْ ۙ إِنَّهُ بِمَا
تَعْمَلُونَ بَصِيرٌ ﴿٤٠﴾
إِنَّ الَّذِينَ كَفَرُوا بِالذِّكْرِ لَمَّا جَاءَهُمْ ۖ وَإِنَّهُ
لَكِتٰبٌ عَزِيزٌ ﴿٤١﴾
لَّا يَأْتِيهِ الْبٰطِلُ مِن بَيْنِ يَدَيْهِ وَلَا مِنْ خَلْفِهِ ۖ
تَنزِيلٌ مِّنْ حَكِيمٍ حَمِيدٍ ﴿٤٢﴾
مَّا يُقَالُ لَكَ إِلَّا مَا قَدْ قِيلَ لِلرُّسُلِ مِن قَبْلِكَ ۚ
إِنَّ رَبَّكَ لَذُو مَغْفِرَةٍ وَذُو عِقَابٍ أَلِيمٍ ﴿٤٣﴾

44. And if We had appointed it a Lecture[1] in a foreign tongue they would assuredly have said: If only its verses were expounded (so that we might understand)! What! A foreign tongue and an Arab?—Say unto them (O Muhammad): For those who believe it is a guidance and a healing; and as for those who disbelieve, there is a deafness in their ears, and it is blindness for them. Such are called to from afar.

45. And We verily gave Moses the Scripture, but there hath been dispute concerning it; and but for a Word that had already gone forth by thy Lord, it would ere now have been judged between them; but lo! they are in hopeless doubt concerning it.

46. Whoso doth right it is for his soul, and whoso doth wrong it is against it. And thy Lord is not at all a tyrant to His slaves.

47. Unto Him is referred (all) knowledge of the Hour. And no fruits burst forth from their sheaths, and no female carrieth or bringeth forth but with His knowledge. And on the day when He calleth unto them: Where are now My partners? they will say: We confess unto Thee, not one of us is a witness (for them).

48. And those to whom they used to cry of old have failed them, and they perceive they have no place of refuge.

49. Man tireth not of praying for good, and if ill toucheth him, then he is disheartened, desperate.

50. And verily, if We cause him to taste mercy after some hurt that hath touched him, he will say: This is my own; and I deem not that the Hour will ever rise, and if I am brought back to my Lord, I surely shall be better off with Him—But We verily shall tell those who disbelieve (all) that they did, and We verily shall make them taste hard punishment.

1. Ar. *Qur'ān.*

وَلَوْ جَعَلْنٰهُ قُرْاٰنًا اَعْجَمِيًّا لَّقَالُوْا لَوْلَا فُصِّلَتْ اٰيٰتُهٗ
ءَاَعْجَمِيٌّ وَّعَرَبِيٌّ قُلْ هُوَ لِلَّذِيْنَ اٰمَنُوْا هُدًى وَّ
شِفَآءٌ وَالَّذِيْنَ لَا يُؤْمِنُوْنَ فِيْٓ اٰذَانِهِمْ وَقْرٌ وَّهُوَ
عَلَيْهِمْ عَمًى اُولٰٓئِكَ يُنَادَوْنَ مِنْ مَّكَانٍ بَعِيْدٍ ﴿٤٤﴾
وَلَقَدْ اٰتَيْنَا مُوْسَى الْكِتٰبَ فَاخْتُلِفَ فِيْهِ وَلَوْلَا
كَلِمَةٌ سَبَقَتْ مِنْ رَّبِّكَ لَقُضِيَ بَيْنَهُمْ وَاِنَّهُمْ
لَفِيْ شَكٍّ مِّنْهُ مُرِيْبٍ ﴿٤٥﴾
مَنْ عَمِلَ صَالِحًا فَلِنَفْسِهٖ وَمَنْ اَسَآءَ فَعَلَيْهَا
وَمَا رَبُّكَ بِظَلَّامٍ لِّلْعَبِيْدِ ﴿٤٦﴾
اِلَيْهِ يُرَدُّ عِلْمُ السَّاعَةِ وَمَا تَخْرُجُ مِنْ ثَمَرٰتٍ
مِّنْ اَكْمَامِهَا وَمَا تَحْمِلُ مِنْ اُنْثٰى وَلَا تَضَعُ اِلَّا
بِعِلْمِهٖ وَيَوْمَ يُنَادِيْهِمْ اَيْنَ شُرَكَآءِيْ قَالُوْٓا
اٰذَنّٰكَ مَا مِنَّا مِنْ شَهِيْدٍ ﴿٤٧﴾
وَضَلَّ عَنْهُمْ مَّا كَانُوْا يَدْعُوْنَ مِنْ قَبْلُ وَظَنُّوْا
مَا لَهُمْ مِّنْ مَّحِيْصٍ ﴿٤٨﴾
لَا يَسْئَمُ الْاِنْسَانُ مِنْ دُعَآءِ الْخَيْرِ وَاِنْ مَّسَّهُ
الشَّرُّ فَيَئُوْسٌ قَنُوْطٌ ﴿٤٩﴾
وَلَئِنْ اَذَقْنٰهُ رَحْمَةً مِّنَّا مِنْ بَعْدِ ضَرَّآءَ مَسَّتْهُ
لَيَقُوْلَنَّ هٰذَا لِيْ وَمَآ اَظُنُّ السَّاعَةَ قَآئِمَةً وَّلَئِنْ
رُّجِعْتُ اِلٰى رَبِّيْٓ اِنَّ لِيْ عِنْدَهٗ لَلْحُسْنٰى فَلَنُنَبِّئَنَّ
الَّذِيْنَ كَفَرُوْا بِمَا عَمِلُوْا وَلَنُذِيْقَنَّهُمْ مِّنْ عَذَابٍ
غَلِيْظٍ ﴿٥٠﴾

51. When We show favour unto man, he withdraweth and turneth aside, but when ill toucheth him then he aboundeth in prayer.

52. Bethink you: If it is from Allah and ye reject it—who is further astray than one who is at open feud (with Allah)?

53. We shall show them Our portents on the horizons and within themselves until it will be manifest unto them that it is the Truth. Doth not thy Lord suffice, since He is Witness over all things?

54. How! Are they still in doubt about the meeting with their Lord? Lo! Is not He surrounding all things?

وَاِذَآ اَنْعَمْنَا عَلَى الْاِنْسَانِ اَعْرَضَ وَنَاٰ بِجَانِبِهٖ ۚ
وَاِذَا مَسَّهُ الشَّرُّ فَذُوْ دُعَآءٍ عَرِيْضٍ ﴿۵۱﴾
قُلْ اَرَءَيْتُمْ اِنْ كَانَ مِنْ عِنْدِ اللّٰهِ ثُمَّ كَفَرْتُمْ
بِهٖ مَنْ اَضَلُّ مِمَّنْ هُوَ فِيْ شِقَاقٍ بَعِيْدٍ ﴿۵۲﴾
سَنُرِيْهِمْ اٰيٰتِنَا فِي الْاٰفَاقِ وَفِيْٓ اَنْفُسِهِمْ حَتّٰى
يَتَبَيَّنَ لَهُمْ اَنَّهُ الْحَقُّ ۭ اَوَلَمْ يَكْفِ بِرَبِّكَ اَنَّهٗ
عَلٰى كُلِّ شَيْءٍ شَهِيْدٌ ﴿۵۳﴾
اَلَآ اِنَّهُمْ فِيْ مِرْيَةٍ مِّنْ لِّقَآءِ رَبِّهِمْ ۭ اَلَآ اِنَّهٗ بِكُلِّ
شَيْءٍ مُّحِيْطٌ ﴿۵۴﴾

Ash-Shūrā, "Counsel," takes its name from a word in v. 38. It belongs to the middle group of Meccan Sūrahs.

COUNSEL

Revealed at Mecca

In the name of Allah, the Beneficent, the Merciful.

1. Ḥā. Mîm.[1]

2. ʻAin. Sîn. Qāf.

3. Thus Allah the Mighty, the Knower inspireth thee (Muhammad) as (He inspired) those before thee.

4. Unto Him belongeth all that is in the heavens and all that is in the earth, and He is the Sublime, the Tremendous.

5. Almost might the heavens above be rent asunder while the angels hymn the praise of their Lord and ask forgiveness for those on the earth. Lo! Allah is the Forgiver, the Merciful.

6. And as for those who choose protecting friends beside Him, Allah is Warden over them, and thou art in no wise a guardian over them.

7. And thus We have inspired in thee a Lecture[2] in Arabic, that thou mayest warn the mother-town[3] and those around it, and mayest warn of a day of assembling whereof there is no doubt. A host will be in the Garden, and a host of them in the Flame.

8. Had Allah willed, He could have made them one community, but Allah bringeth whom He will into His mercy. And the wrong-doers have no friend nor helper.

9. Or have they chosen protecting friends besides Him? But Allah, He (alone) is the Protecting Friend. He quickeneth the dead, and He is Able to do all things.

اٰیاتها ٥٣ (٤٢) سُورَةُ الشُّورٰى مَكِّيَّةٌ (٤) رکوعاتها ٥

بِسْمِ اللّٰهِ الرَّحْمٰنِ الرَّحِيْمِ

حٰمٓ ﴿١﴾

عٓسٓقٓ ﴿٢﴾

كَذٰلِكَ يُوْحِيْٓ اِلَيْكَ وَاِلَى الَّذِيْنَ مِنْ قَبْلِكَ

اللّٰهُ الْعَزِيْزُ الْحَكِيْمُ ﴿٣﴾

لَهٗ مَا فِي السَّمٰوٰتِ وَمَا فِي الْاَرْضِ وَهُوَ الْعَلِيُّ

الْعَظِيْمُ ﴿٤﴾

تَكَادُ السَّمٰوٰتُ يَتَفَطَّرْنَ مِنْ فَوْقِهِنَّ وَالْمَلٰٓئِكَةُ

يُسَبِّحُوْنَ بِحَمْدِ رَبِّهِمْ وَيَسْتَغْفِرُوْنَ لِمَنْ فِي

الْاَرْضِ اَلَآ اِنَّ اللّٰهَ هُوَ الْغَفُوْرُ الرَّحِيْمُ ﴿٥﴾

وَالَّذِيْنَ اتَّخَذُوْا مِنْ دُوْنِهٖٓ اَوْلِيَآءَ اللّٰهُ حَفِيْظٌ

عَلَيْهِمْ وَمَآ اَنْتَ عَلَيْهِمْ بِوَكِيْلٍ ﴿٦﴾

وَكَذٰلِكَ اَوْحَيْنَآ اِلَيْكَ قُرْاٰنًا عَرَبِيًّا لِّتُنْذِرَ اُمَّ

الْقُرٰى وَمَنْ حَوْلَهَا وَتُنْذِرَ يَوْمَ الْجَمْعِ لَا رَيْبَ فِيْهِ

فَرِيْقٌ فِي الْجَنَّةِ وَفَرِيْقٌ فِي السَّعِيْرِ ﴿٧﴾

وَلَوْ شَآءَ اللّٰهُ لَجَعَلَهُمْ اُمَّةً وَّاحِدَةً وَّلٰكِنْ

يُّدْخِلُ مَنْ يَّشَآءُ فِيْ رَحْمَتِهٖ وَالظّٰلِمُوْنَ مَا لَهُمْ

مِّنْ وَّلِيٍّ وَّلَا نَصِيْرٍ ﴿٨﴾

اَمِ اتَّخَذُوْا مِنْ دُوْنِهٖٓ اَوْلِيَآءَ فَاللّٰهُ هُوَ الْوَلِيُّ

وَهُوَ يُحْيِ الْمَوْتٰى وَهُوَ عَلٰى كُلِّ شَيْءٍ قَدِيْرٌ ﴿٩﴾ ع

1. See Sûr. II, v. 1, footnote.
2. Ar. *Qur'ân*.
3. *I.e.* Mecca.

10. And in whatsoever ye differ, the verdict therein belongeth to Allah. Such is my Lord, in Whom I put my trust, and unto Whom I turn:

11. The Creator of the heavens and the earth. He hath made for you pairs of yourselves, and of the cattle also pairs, whereby He multiplieth you. Naught is as His likeness; and He is the Hearer, the Seer.

12. His are the keys of the heavens and the earth. He enlargeth providence for whom He will and straiteneth (it for whom He will). Lo! He is Knower of all things.

13. He hath ordained for you that religion which He commended unto Noah, and that which We inspire in thee (Muhammad), and that which We commended unto Abraham and Moses and Jesus, saying: Establish the religion, and be not divided therein. Dreadful for the idolaters is that unto which thou callest them. Allah chooseth for Himself whom He will, and guideth unto Himself him who turneth (toward Him).

14. And they were not divided until after the knowledge came unto them, through rivalry among themselves; and had it not been for a Word that had already gone forth from thy Lord for an appointed term, it surely had been judged between them. And those who were made to inherit the Scripture after them are verily in hopeless doubt concerning it.

15. Unto this, then, summon (O Muhammad). And be thou upright as thou art commanded, and follow not their lusts, but say: I believe in whatever Scripture Allah hath sent down, and I am commanded to be just among you. Allah is our Lord and your Lord. Unto us our works and unto you your works; no argument between us and you. Allah will bring us together, and unto Him is the journeying.

وَمَا اخْتَلَفْتُمْ فِيهِ مِنْ شَيْءٍ فَحُكْمُهُ إِلَى اللَّهِ
ذَٰلِكُمُ اللَّهُ رَبِّي عَلَيْهِ تَوَكَّلْتُ وَإِلَيْهِ أُنِيبُ ﴿١٠﴾
فَاطِرُ السَّمٰوٰتِ وَالْأَرْضِ جَعَلَ لَكُمْ مِنْ أَنْفُسِكُمْ
أَزْوَاجًا وَمِنَ الْأَنْعَامِ أَزْوَاجًا يَذْرَؤُكُمْ فِيهِ
لَيْسَ كَمِثْلِهِ شَيْءٌ وَهُوَ السَّمِيعُ الْبَصِيرُ ﴿١١﴾
لَهُ مَقَالِيدُ السَّمٰوٰتِ وَالْأَرْضِ يَبْسُطُ الرِّزْقَ لِمَنْ
يَشَاءُ وَيَقْدِرُ إِنَّهُ بِكُلِّ شَيْءٍ عَلِيمٌ ﴿١٢﴾
شَرَعَ لَكُمْ مِنَ الدِّينِ مَا وَصَّىٰ بِهِ نُوحًا وَالَّذِي
أَوْحَيْنَا إِلَيْكَ وَمَا وَصَّيْنَا بِهِ إِبْرٰهِيمَ وَمُوسَىٰ وَ
عِيسَىٰ أَنْ أَقِيمُوا الدِّينَ وَلَا تَتَفَرَّقُوا فِيهِ كَبُرَ عَلَى
الْمُشْرِكِينَ مَا تَدْعُوهُمْ إِلَيْهِ اللَّهُ يَجْتَبِي إِلَيْهِ
مَنْ يَشَاءُ وَيَهْدِي إِلَيْهِ مَنْ يُنِيبُ ﴿١٣﴾
وَمَا تَفَرَّقُوا إِلَّا مِنْ بَعْدِ مَا جَاءَهُمُ الْعِلْمُ
بَغْيًا بَيْنَهُمْ وَلَوْلَا كَلِمَةٌ سَبَقَتْ مِنْ رَبِّكَ
إِلَىٰ أَجَلٍ مُسَمًّى لَقُضِيَ بَيْنَهُمْ وَإِنَّ الَّذِينَ
أُورِثُوا الْكِتٰبَ مِنْ بَعْدِهِمْ لَفِي شَكٍّ مِنْهُ
مُرِيبٍ ﴿١٤﴾
فَلِذَٰلِكَ فَادْعُ وَاسْتَقِمْ كَمَا أُمِرْتَ وَلَا تَتَّبِعْ
أَهْوَاءَهُمْ وَقُلْ آمَنْتُ بِمَا أَنْزَلَ اللَّهُ مِنْ كِتٰبٍ
وَأُمِرْتُ لِأَعْدِلَ بَيْنَكُمُ اللَّهُ رَبُّنَا وَرَبُّكُمْ لَنَا
أَعْمَالُنَا وَلَكُمْ أَعْمَالُكُمْ لَا حُجَّةَ بَيْنَنَا وَبَيْنَكُمُ
اللَّهُ يَجْمَعُ بَيْنَنَا وَإِلَيْهِ الْمَصِيرُ ﴿١٥﴾

16. And those who argue concerning Allah after He hath been acknowledged, their argument hath no weight with their Lord, and wrath is upon them and theirs will be an awful doom.

17. Allah it is Who hath revealed the Scripture with Truth, and the Balance. How canst thou know? It may be that the Hour is nigh.

18. Those who believe not therein seek to hasten it, while those who believe are fearful of it and know that it is the Truth. Are not they who dispute, in doubt concerning the Hour, far astray?

19. Allah is gracious unto His slaves. He provideth for whom He will. And He is the Strong, the Mighty.

20. Whoso desireth the harvest of the Hereafter, We give him increase in its harvest. And Whoso desireth the harvest of the world, We give him thereof, and he hath no portion in the Hereafter.

21. Or have they partners (of Allah) who have made lawful for them in religion that which Allah allowed not? And but for a decisive word (gone forth already), it would have been judged between them. Lo! for wrong-doers is a painful doom.

22. Thou seest the wrong-doers fearful of that which they have earned, and it will surely befall them: while those who believe and do good works (will be) in flowering meadows of the Gardens, having what they wish from their Lord. This is the great preferment.

والذين يحاجون في الله من بعد ما استجيب
له حجتهم داحضة عند ربهم وعليهم غضب
ولهم عذاب شديد ﴿١٦﴾
الله الذي انزل الكتب بالحق والميزان وما
يدريك لعل الساعة قريب ﴿١٧﴾
يستعجل بها الذين لا يؤمنون بها والذين
امنوا مشفقون منها ويعلمون انها الحق
الا ان الذين يمارون في الساعة لفي ضلل
بعيد ﴿١٨﴾
الله لطيف بعباده يرزق من يشاء وهو
ع ٢ القوي العزيز ﴿١٩﴾
من كان يريد حرث الاخرة نزد له في حرثه
ومن كان يريد حرث الدنيا نؤته منها وما له
في الاخرة من نصيب ﴿٢٠﴾
ام لهم شركؤا شرعوا لهم من الدين
ما لم يأذن به الله ولولا كلمة الفصل
لقضي بينهم وان الظلمين لهم عذاب
اليم ﴿٢١﴾
ترى الظلمين مشفقين مما كسبوا وهو واقع
بهم والذين امنوا وعملوا الصلحت في روضت
الجنت لهم ما يشاءون عند ربهم ذلك هو
الفضل الكبير ﴿٢٢﴾

23. This it is which Allah announceth unto His bondmen who believe and do good works. Say (O Muhammad, unto mankind): I ask of you no fee therefor, save loving kindness among kinsfolk. And whoso scoreth a good deed We add unto its good for him. Lo! Allah is Forgiving, Responsive.

24. Or say they: He hath invented a lie concerning Allah? If Allah willed, He could have sealed thy heart (against them). And Allah will wipe out the lie and will vindicate the truth by His words. Lo! He is Aware of what is hidden in the breasts (of men).

25. And He it is Who accepteth repentance from His bondmen, and pardoneth the evil deeds, and knoweth what ye do;

26. And accepteth those who do good works, and giveth increase unto them of His bounty. And as for disbelievers, theirs will be an awful doom.

27. And if Allah were to enlarge the provision for His slaves they would surely rebel in the earth, but He sendeth down by measure as He willeth. Lo! He is Informed, a Seer of His bondmen.

28. And He it is Who sendeth down the saving rain after they have despaired, and spreadeth out His mercy. He is the Protecting Friend, the Praiseworthy.

29. And of His portents is the creation of the heaven and the earth, and of whatever beasts He hath dispersed therein. And He is Able to gather them when He will.

30. Whatever of misfortune striketh you, it is what your right hands have earned. And He forgiveth much.

ذَٰلِكَ الَّذِي يُبَشِّرُ اللَّهُ عِبَادَهُ الَّذِينَ آمَنُوا وَ
عَمِلُوا الصَّالِحَاتِ ۗ قُل لَّا أَسْأَلُكُمْ عَلَيْهِ أَجْرًا إِلَّا
الْمَوَدَّةَ فِي الْقُرْبَىٰ ۗ وَمَن يَقْتَرِفْ حَسَنَةً نَّزِدْ لَهُ
فِيهَا حُسْنًا ۚ إِنَّ اللَّهَ غَفُورٌ شَكُورٌ ﴿٢٣﴾
أَمْ يَقُولُونَ افْتَرَىٰ عَلَى اللَّهِ كَذِبًا ۖ فَإِن يَشَإِ اللَّهُ
يَخْتِمْ عَلَىٰ قَلْبِكَ ۗ وَيَمْحُ اللَّهُ الْبَاطِلَ وَيُحِقُّ الْحَقَّ
بِكَلِمَاتِهِ ۚ إِنَّهُ عَلِيمٌ بِذَاتِ الصُّدُورِ ﴿٢٤﴾
وَهُوَ الَّذِي يَقْبَلُ التَّوْبَةَ عَنْ عِبَادِهِ وَيَعْفُوا
عَنِ السَّيِّئَاتِ وَيَعْلَمُ مَا تَفْعَلُونَ ﴿٢٥﴾
وَيَسْتَجِيبُ الَّذِينَ آمَنُوا وَعَمِلُوا الصَّالِحَاتِ
وَيَزِيدُهُم مِّن فَضْلِهِ ۚ وَالْكَافِرُونَ لَهُمْ عَذَابٌ
شَدِيدٌ ﴿٢٦﴾
وَلَوْ بَسَطَ اللَّهُ الرِّزْقَ لِعِبَادِهِ لَبَغَوْا فِي الْأَرْضِ
وَلَٰكِن يُنَزِّلُ بِقَدَرٍ مَّا يَشَاءُ ۚ إِنَّهُ بِعِبَادِهِ خَبِيرٌ
بَصِيرٌ ﴿٢٧﴾
وَهُوَ الَّذِي يُنَزِّلُ الْغَيْثَ مِن بَعْدِ مَا قَنَطُوا
وَيَنشُرُ رَحْمَتَهُ ۚ وَهُوَ الْوَلِيُّ الْحَمِيدُ ﴿٢٨﴾
وَمِنْ آيَاتِهِ خَلْقُ السَّمَاوَاتِ وَالْأَرْضِ وَمَا بَثَّ
فِيهِمَا مِن دَابَّةٍ ۚ وَهُوَ عَلَىٰ جَمْعِهِمْ إِذَا يَشَاءُ
قَدِيرٌ ﴿٢٩﴾
وَمَا أَصَابَكُم مِّن مُّصِيبَةٍ فَبِمَا كَسَبَتْ أَيْدِيكُمْ
وَيَعْفُوا عَن كَثِيرٍ ﴿٣٠﴾

31. Ye cannot escape in the earth, for besides Allah ye have no protecting friend nor any helper.

32. And of His portents are the ships, like banners on the sea;

33. If He will, He calmeth the wind so that they keep still upon its surface -- Lo! herein verily are signs for every steadfast, grateful (heart).

34. Or He causeth them to perish on account of that which they have earned- And He forgiveth much.

35. And that those who argue concerning Our revelations may know they have no refuge.

36. Now whatever ye have been given is but a passing confort for the life of the world, and that which Allah hath is better and more lasting for those who believe and put their trust in their Lord.

37. And those who shun the worst of sins and indecencies and, when they are wroth, forgive.

38. And those who answer the call of their Lord and establish worship, and whose affairs are a matter of counsel, and who spend of what We have bestowed on them,

39. And those who, when great wrong is done to them, defend themselves.

40. The guerdon of an ill deed is an ill the like thereof. But whosoever pardoneth and amendeth, his wage is the affair of Allah. Lo! He loveth not wrongdoers.

41. And whoso defendeth himself after he hath suffered wrong -- for such, there is no way (of blame) against them.

42. The way (of blame) is only against those who oppress mankind, and wrongfully rebel in the earth. For such there is a painful doom.

وَمَآ أَنتُم بِمُعْجِزِينَ فِى ٱلْأَرْضِ ۖ وَمَا لَكُم مِّن
دُونِ ٱللَّهِ مِن وَلِىٍّ وَلَا نَصِيرٍ ٣١
وَمِنْ ءَايَٰتِهِ ٱلْجَوَارِ فِى ٱلْبَحْرِ كَٱلْأَعْلَٰمِ ٣٢
إِن يَشَأْ يُسْكِنِ ٱلرِّيحَ فَيَظْلَلْنَ رَوَاكِدَ عَلَىٰ ظَهْرِهِۦٓ ۚ
إِنَّ فِى ذَٰلِكَ لَءَايَٰتٍ لِّكُلِّ صَبَّارٍ شَكُورٍ ٣٣
أَوْ يُوبِقْهُنَّ بِمَا كَسَبُوا۟ وَيَعْفُ عَن كَثِيرٍ ٣٤
وَيَعْلَمَ ٱلَّذِينَ يُجَٰدِلُونَ فِىٓ ءَايَٰتِنَا مَا لَهُم مِّن
مَّحِيصٍ ٣٥
فَمَآ أُوتِيتُم مِّن شَىْءٍ فَمَتَٰعُ ٱلْحَيَوٰةِ ٱلدُّنْيَا ۖ
وَمَا عِندَ ٱللَّهِ خَيْرٌ وَأَبْقَىٰ لِلَّذِينَ ءَامَنُوا۟ وَعَلَىٰ
رَبِّهِمْ يَتَوَكَّلُونَ ٣٦
وَٱلَّذِينَ يَجْتَنِبُونَ كَبَٰٓئِرَ ٱلْإِثْمِ وَٱلْفَوَٰحِشَ وَ
إِذَا مَا غَضِبُوا۟ هُمْ يَغْفِرُونَ ٣٧
وَٱلَّذِينَ ٱسْتَجَابُوا۟ لِرَبِّهِمْ وَأَقَامُوا۟ ٱلصَّلَوٰةَ وَ
أَمْرُهُمْ شُورَىٰ بَيْنَهُمْ وَمِمَّا رَزَقْنَٰهُمْ يُنفِقُونَ ٣٨
وَٱلَّذِينَ إِذَآ أَصَابَهُمُ ٱلْبَغْىُ هُمْ يَنتَصِرُونَ ٣٩
وَجَزَٰٓؤُا۟ سَيِّئَةٍ سَيِّئَةٌ مِّثْلُهَا ۖ فَمَنْ عَفَا وَأَصْلَحَ
فَأَجْرُهُۥ عَلَى ٱللَّهِ ۚ إِنَّهُۥ لَا يُحِبُّ ٱلظَّٰلِمِينَ ٤٠
وَلَمَنِ ٱنتَصَرَ بَعْدَ ظُلْمِهِۦ فَأُو۟لَٰٓئِكَ مَا عَلَيْهِم مِّن
سَبِيلٍ ٤١
إِنَّمَا ٱلسَّبِيلُ عَلَى ٱلَّذِينَ يَظْلِمُونَ ٱلنَّاسَ وَيَبْغُونَ
فِى ٱلْأَرْضِ بِغَيْرِ ٱلْحَقِّ ۚ أُو۟لَٰٓئِكَ لَهُمْ عَذَابٌ أَلِيمٌ ٤٢

43. And verily whoso is patient and forgiveth—lo! that, verily, is (of) the steadfast heart of things.

44. He whom Allah sendeth astray, for him there is no protecting friend after Him. And thou (Muhammad) wilt see the evil-doers when they see the doom, (how) they say: Is there any way of return?

45. And thou wilt see them exposed to (the Fire), made humble by disgrace, and looking with veiled eyes. And those who believe will say: Lo! the (eternal) losers are they who lose themselves and their housefolk on the Day of Resurrection. Lo! are not the wrong-doers in perpetual torment?

46. And they will have no protecting friends to help them instead of Allah. He whom Allah sendeth astray, for him there is no road.

47. Answer the call of your Lord before there cometh unto you from Allah a Day which there is no averting. Ye have no refuge on that Day, nor have ye any (power of) refusal.

48. But if they are averse, We have not sent thee as a warder over them. Thine is only to convey (the message). And lo! when We cause man to taste of mercy from Us he exulteth therefor. And if some evil striketh them because of that which their own hands have sent before, then lo! man is an ingrate.

49. Unto Allah belongeth the sovereignty of the heavens and the earth. He createth what He will. He bestoweth female (offspring) upon whom He will, and bestoweth male (offspring) upon whom He will;

50. Or He mingleth them, males and females, and He maketh barren whom He will. Lo! He is Knower, Powerful.

وَلَمَن صَبَرَ وَغَفَرَ إِنَّ ذَٰلِكَ لَمِنْ عَزْمِ الْأُمُورِ ﴿٤٣﴾
وَمَن يُضْلِلِ اللَّهُ فَمَا لَهُ مِن وَلِيٍّ مِّن بَعْدِهِ
وَتَرَى الظَّالِمِينَ لَمَّا رَأَوُا الْعَذَابَ يَقُولُونَ هَلْ
إِلَىٰ مَرَدٍّ مِّن سَبِيلٍ ﴿٤٤﴾
وَتَرَاهُمْ يُعْرَضُونَ عَلَيْهَا خَاشِعِينَ مِنَ الذُّلِّ
يَنظُرُونَ مِن طَرْفٍ خَفِيٍّ وَقَالَ الَّذِينَ آمَنُوا
إِنَّ الْخَاسِرِينَ الَّذِينَ خَسِرُوا أَنفُسَهُمْ وَأَهْلِيهِمْ
يَوْمَ الْقِيَامَةِ أَلَا إِنَّ الظَّالِمِينَ فِي عَذَابٍ مُّقِيمٍ ﴿٤٥﴾
وَمَا كَانَ لَهُم مِّنْ أَوْلِيَاءَ يَنصُرُونَهُم مِّن دُونِ
اللَّهِ وَمَن يُضْلِلِ اللَّهُ فَمَا لَهُ مِن سَبِيلٍ ﴿٤٦﴾
اسْتَجِيبُوا لِرَبِّكُم مِّن قَبْلِ أَن يَأْتِيَ يَوْمٌ لَّا مَرَدَّ
لَهُ مِنَ اللَّهِ مَا لَكُم مِّن مَّلْجَإٍ يَوْمَئِذٍ وَمَا لَكُم
مِّن نَّكِيرٍ ﴿٤٧﴾
فَإِنْ أَعْرَضُوا فَمَا أَرْسَلْنَاكَ عَلَيْهِمْ حَفِيظًا إِنْ عَلَيْكَ
إِلَّا الْبَلَاغُ وَإِنَّا إِذَا أَذَقْنَا الْإِنسَانَ مِنَّا رَحْمَةً فَرِحَ
بِهَا وَإِن تُصِبْهُمْ سَيِّئَةٌ بِمَا قَدَّمَتْ أَيْدِيهِمْ
فَإِنَّ الْإِنسَانَ كَفُورٌ ﴿٤٨﴾
لِّلَّهِ مُلْكُ السَّمَاوَاتِ وَالْأَرْضِ يَخْلُقُ مَا يَشَاءُ
يَهَبُ لِمَن يَشَاءُ إِنَاثًا وَيَهَبُ لِمَن يَشَاءُ
الذُّكُورَ ﴿٤٩﴾
أَوْ يُزَوِّجُهُمْ ذُكْرَانًا وَإِنَاثًا وَيَجْعَلُ مَن يَشَاءُ
عَقِيمًا إِنَّهُ عَلِيمٌ قَدِيرٌ ﴿٥٠﴾

51. And it was not (vouchsafed) to any mortal that Allah should speak to him unless (it be) by revelation or from behind a veil, or (that) He sendeth a messenger to reveal what He will by His leave. Lo! He is Exalted, Wise.

52. And thus have We inspired in thee (Muhammad) a Spirit of Our command. Thou knewest not what the Scripture was, nor what the Faith. But We have made it a light whereby We guide whom We will of Our bondmen. And lo! thou verily dost guide unto a right path—

53. The path of Allah, unto Whom belongeth whatsoever is in the heavens and whatsoever is in the earth. Do not all things reach Allah at last?

وَمَا كَانَ لِبَشَرٍ أَنْ يُكَلِّمَهُ اللّٰهُ إِلَّا وَحْيًا أَوْ مِنْ
وَرَآئِ حِجَابٍ أَوْ يُرْسِلَ رَسُولًا فَيُوحِيَ بِإِذْنِهِ
مَا يَشَآءُ إِنَّهُ عَلِيٌّ حَكِيمٌ ﴿٥١﴾
وَكَذٰلِكَ أَوْحَيْنَآ إِلَيْكَ رُوحًا مِنْ أَمْرِنَا مَا كُنْتَ
تَدْرِي مَا الْكِتٰبُ وَلَا الْإِيمَانُ وَلٰكِنْ جَعَلْنٰهُ
نُورًا نَهْدِي بِهِ مَنْ نَشَآءُ مِنْ عِبَادِنَا وَإِنَّكَ
لَتَهْدِيٓ إِلٰى صِرَاطٍ مُسْتَقِيمٍ ﴿٥٢﴾
صِرَاطِ اللّٰهِ الَّذِي لَهُ مَا فِي السَّمٰوٰتِ وَمَا فِي
الْأَرْضِ أَلَآ إِلَى اللّٰهِ تَصِيرُ الْأُمُورُ ﴿٥٣﴾ ع

Az-Zukhruf, "Ornaments of Gold." is the fourth of the Ḥā. Mīm. Sūrahs. It takes its name from a word meaning golden ornaments which occurs in v. 35.

It belongs to the middle group of Meccan Sūrahs.

ORNAMENTS OF GOLD

Revealed at Makkah

In the name of Allah, the Beneficent, the Merciful.

1. Ha.Mim.[1]

2. By the Scripture which maketh plain.

3. Lo! We have appointed it a Lecture[2] in Arabic that haply ye may understand.

4. And lo! in the source of Decrees, which We possess, it is indeed sublime, decisive,

5. Shall we uterly ignore you because ye are wanton folk?

6. How many a Prophet did we send among the men of old!

7. And never came there unto them a Prophet but they used to mock him.

8. Then We destroyed men mightier than these in prowess; and the example of the men of old hath gone (before them).

9. And if thou (Muhammad) ask them: who created the heavens and the earth, they will surely answer:The Mighty, the Knower created them;

10. Who made the earth a resting place for you, and placed roads for you therein, that haply ye may find your way;

11. And Who sendeth down water from the sky in (due) measure, and we revive a dead land therewith. Even so will ye be brought forth;

12. He who created all the pairs and appointed for you ships and cattle whereupon ye ride:

13. That ye may mount upon their backs, and may remember your Lord's favour when ye mount thereon, and may say: Glorified be He who hath subdued these unto us, and we were not capable (of subduing them):

1. See Sur, II, v.1, footnote.
2. Ar. *Qur'an.*

آياتها ٨٩ (٤٣) سورة الزخرف مكية ركوعاتها

بسم الله الرحمن الرحيم

حم ۝١

والكتاب المبين ۝٢

إنا جعلناه قرآنا عربيا لعلكم تعقلون ۝٣

وإنه في أم الكتاب لدينا لعلي حكيم ۝٤

أفنضرب عنكم الذكر صفحا أن كنتم قوما مسرفين ۝٥

وكم أرسلنا من نبي في الأولين ۝٦

وما يأتيهم من نبي إلا كانوا به يستهزئون ۝٧

فأهلكنا أشد منهم بطشا ومضى مثل الأولين ۝٨

ولئن سألتهم من خلق السماوات والأرض
ليقولن خلقهن العزيز العليم ۝٩

الذي جعل لكم الأرض مهدا وجعل لكم
فيها سبلا لعلكم تهتدون ۝١٠

والذي نزل من السماء ماء بقدر فأنشرنا
به بلدة ميتا كذلك تخرجون ۝١١

والذي خلق الأزواج كلها وجعل لكم من الفلك
والأنعام ما تركبون ۝١٢

لتستووا على ظهوره ثم تذكروا نعمة ربكم إذا
استويتم عليه وتقولوا سبحان الذي سخر
لنا هذا وما كنا له مقرنين ۝١٣

14. And lo! unto our Lord we are returning.

وانا الى ربنا لمنقلبون ﴿١٤﴾

15. And they allot to Him a portion of His bondmen! Lo! man is verily a mere ingrate.

وجعلوا له من عباده جزءا ان الانسان لكفور
مبين ﴿١٥﴾

16. Or chooseth He daughters of all that He hath created, and honoureth He you with sons?

ام اتخذ مما يخلق بنت واصفكم بالبنين ﴿١٦﴾

17. And if one of them hath tidings of that which he likeneth to the Beneficent One,[1] his countenance becometh black and he is full of inward rage.

واذا بشر احدهم بما ضرب للرحمن مثلا
ظل وجهه مسودا وهو كظيم ﴿١٧﴾

18. (Liken they then to Allah) that which is bred up in outward show, and in dispute cannot make itself plain?

اومن ينشؤا في الحلية وهو في الخصام غير
مبين ﴿١٨﴾

19. And they make the angels, who are the slaves of the Beneficent, females. Did they witness their creation? Their testimony will be recorded and they will be questioned.

وجعلوا الملئكة الذين هم عبد الرحمن اناثا
اشهدوا خلقهم ستكتب شهادتهم ويسئلون ﴿١٩﴾

20. And they say: If the Beneficent One had (so) willed, we should not have worshipped them. They have no knowledge whatsoever of that. They do but guess.

وقالوا لو شاء الرحمن ما عبدنهم ما لهم
بذلك من علم ان هم الا يخرصون ﴿٢٠﴾

21. Or have We given them any Scripture before (this Qur'ān) so that they are holding fast thereto?

ام اتينهم كتبا من قبله فهم به مستمسكون ﴿٢١﴾

22. Nay, for they say only: Lo! we found our fathers following a religion, and we are guided by their footprints.

بل قالوا انا وجدنا اباءنا على امة وانا على
اثرهم مهتدون ﴿٢٢﴾

23. And even so We sent not a warner before thee (Muhammad) into any township but its luxurious ones said: Lo! we found our fathers following a religion, and we are following their footprints.

وكذلك ما ارسلنا من قبلك في قرية من نذير
الا قال مترفوها انا وجدنا اباءنا على امة و
انا على اثرهم مقتدون ﴿٢٣﴾

24. (And the warner) said: What! Even though I bring you better guidance than that ye found your fathers following? They answered: Lo! in what ye bring we are disbelievers.

قل اولو جئتكم باهدى مما وجدتم عليه
اباءكم قالوا انا بما ارسلتم به كفرون ﴿٢٤﴾

25. So We requited them. Then see the nature of the consequence for the rejecters!

فانتقمنا منهم فانظر كيف كان عاقبة
المكذبين ﴿٢٥﴾

1. *i.e.* tidings of the birth of a girl-child.

26. And when Abraham said unto his father and his folk: Lo! I am innocent of what ye worship

27. Save Him Who did create me, for He will surely guide me.

28. And he made it a word enduring among his seed, that haply they might return.

29. Nay, but I let these and their fathers enjoy life (only) till there should come unto them the Truth and a messenger making plain.

30. And now that the Truth hath come unto them they say: This is mere magic, and lo! we are disbelievers therein.

31. And they say: If only this Qur'ān had been revealed to some great man of the two towns[1]!

32. Is it they who apportion their Lord's mercy? We have apportioned among them their livelihood in the life of the world, and raised some of them above others in rank that some of them may take labour from others; and the mercy of thy Lord is better than (the wealth) that they amass.

33. And were it not that mankind would have become one community[2], We might well have appointed, for those who disbelieve in the Beneficent, roofs of silver for their houses and stairs (of silver) whereby to mount,

34. And for their houses doors (of silver) and couches of silver whereon to recline,

35. And ornaments of gold. Yet all that would have been but a provision of the life of the world. And the Hereafter with your Lord would have been for those who keep from evil.

36. And he whose sight is dim to the remembrance of the Beneficent, We assign unto him a devil who becometh his comrade:

1. The two towns were Mecca and Tā'if.
2. Through love of riches.

وَإِذْ قَالَ إِبْرٰهِيمُ لِأَبِيهِ وَقَوْمِهِ إِنَّنِي بَرَآءٌ
مِّمَّا تَعْبُدُونَ ﴿٢٦﴾
إِلَّا الَّذِي فَطَرَنِي فَإِنَّهُ سَيَهْدِينِ ﴿٢٧﴾
وَجَعَلَهَا كَلِمَةً بَاقِيَةً فِي عَقِبِهِ لَعَلَّهُمْ يَرْجِعُونَ ﴿٢٨﴾
بَلْ مَتَّعْتُ هٰؤُلَآءِ وَآبَآءَهُمْ حَتّٰى جَآءَهُمُ الْحَقُّ
وَرَسُولٌ مُّبِينٌ ﴿٢٩﴾
وَلَمَّا جَآءَهُمُ الْحَقُّ قَالُوا هٰذَا سِحْرٌ وَّإِنَّا بِهِ
كٰفِرُونَ ﴿٣٠﴾
وَقَالُوا لَوْلَا نُزِّلَ هٰذَا الْقُرْاٰنُ عَلٰى رَجُلٍ مِّنَ
الْقَرْيَتَيْنِ عَظِيمٍ ﴿٣١﴾
أَهُمْ يَقْسِمُونَ رَحْمَتَ رَبِّكَ نَحْنُ قَسَمْنَا بَيْنَهُمْ
مَّعِيشَتَهُمْ فِي الْحَيٰوةِ الدُّنْيَا وَرَفَعْنَا بَعْضَهُمْ فَوْقَ
بَعْضٍ دَرَجٰتٍ لِّيَتَّخِذَ بَعْضُهُمْ بَعْضًا سُخْرِيًّا وَّ
رَحْمَتُ رَبِّكَ خَيْرٌ مِّمَّا يَجْمَعُونَ ﴿٣٢﴾
وَلَوْلَآ أَنْ يَّكُونَ النَّاسُ أُمَّةً وَّاحِدَةً لَّجَعَلْنَا
لِمَنْ يَّكْفُرُ بِالرَّحْمٰنِ لِبُيُوتِهِمْ سُقُفًا مِّنْ فِضَّةٍ
وَّمَعَارِجَ عَلَيْهَا يَظْهَرُونَ ﴿٣٣﴾
وَلِبُيُوتِهِمْ أَبْوَابًا وَّسُرُرًا عَلَيْهَا يَتَّكِـُٔونَ ﴿٣٤﴾
وَزُخْرُفًا وَإِنْ كُلُّ ذٰلِكَ لَمَّا مَتَاعُ الْحَيٰوةِ الدُّنْيَا
وَالْاٰخِرَةُ عِنْدَ رَبِّكَ لِلْمُتَّقِينَ ﴿٣٥﴾ ع ٣
وَمَنْ يَّعْشُ عَنْ ذِكْرِ الرَّحْمٰنِ نُقَيِّضْ لَهُ شَيْطٰنًا
فَهُوَ لَهُ قَرِينٌ ﴿٣٦﴾

37. And lo! they surely turn them from the way of Allah, and yet they deem that they are rightly guided;

38. Till, when he cometh unto Us, he said (unto his comrade): Ah, would that between me and thee there were the distance of the two horizons[1] —an evil comrade!

39. And it profiteth you not this day, because ye did wrong, that ye will be sharers in the doom.

40. Canst thou (Muhammad) make the deaf to hear, or canst thou guide the blind or him who is in error manifest?

41. And if We take thee away, We surely shall take vengeance on them :

42. Or (if) We show thee that wherewith We threaten them; for lo! We have complete command of them.

43. So hold thou fast to that which is inspired in thee, Lo! thou art on a right path.

44. And lo! it is in truth a Reminder for thee and for thy folk: and ye will be questioned.

45. And ask those of Our messengers whom We sent before thee: Did We ever appoint gods to be worshipped beside the Beneficent?

46. And verily We sent Moses with Our revelations unto Pharaoh and his chiefs, and he said: I am a messenger of the Lord of the Worlds.

47. But when he brought them Our tokens, behold! they laughed at them.

48. And every token that We showed them was greater than its sister (token), and We grasped them with the torment, that haply they might turn again.

49. And they said: O wizard! Entreat thy Lord for us by the pact the He hath made with thee, Lo! we verily will walk aright.

1. Lit. the two Easts

وَإِنَّهُمْ لَيَصُدُّونَهُمْ عَنِ السَّبِيلِ وَيَحْسَبُونَ
أَنَّهُمْ مُهْتَدُونَ ﴿٣٧﴾
حَتَّىٰ إِذَا جَاءَنَا قَالَ يَا لَيْتَ بَيْنِي وَبَيْنَكَ بُعْدَ
الْمَشْرِقَيْنِ فَبِئْسَ الْقَرِينُ ﴿٣٨﴾
وَلَنْ يَنْفَعَكُمُ الْيَوْمَ إِذْ ظَلَمْتُمْ أَنَّكُمْ فِي الْعَذَابِ
مُشْتَرِكُونَ ﴿٣٩﴾
أَفَأَنْتَ تُسْمِعُ الصُّمَّ أَوْ تَهْدِي الْعُمْيَ وَمَنْ كَانَ
فِي ضَلَالٍ مُبِينٍ ﴿٤٠﴾
فَإِمَّا نَذْهَبَنَّ بِكَ فَإِنَّا مِنْهُمْ مُنْتَقِمُونَ ﴿٤١﴾
أَوْ نُرِيَنَّكَ الَّذِي وَعَدْنَاهُمْ فَإِنَّا عَلَيْهِمْ مُقْتَدِرُونَ ﴿٤٢﴾
فَاسْتَمْسِكْ بِالَّذِي أُوحِيَ إِلَيْكَ إِنَّكَ عَلَىٰ صِرَاطٍ
مُسْتَقِيمٍ ﴿٤٣﴾
وَإِنَّهُ لَذِكْرٌ لَكَ وَلِقَوْمِكَ وَسَوْفَ تُسْأَلُونَ ﴿٤٤﴾
وَاسْأَلْ مَنْ أَرْسَلْنَا مِنْ قَبْلِكَ مِنْ رُسُلِنَا أَجَعَلْنَا
ع مِنْ دُونِ الرَّحْمَٰنِ آلِهَةً يُعْبَدُونَ ﴿٤٥﴾
وَلَقَدْ أَرْسَلْنَا مُوسَىٰ بِآيَاتِنَا إِلَىٰ فِرْعَوْنَ وَمَلَئِهِ
فَقَالَ إِنِّي رَسُولُ رَبِّ الْعَالَمِينَ ﴿٤٦﴾
فَلَمَّا جَاءَهُمْ بِآيَاتِنَا إِذَا هُمْ مِنْهَا يَضْحَكُونَ ﴿٤٧﴾
وَمَا نُرِيهِمْ مِنْ آيَةٍ إِلَّا هِيَ أَكْبَرُ مِنْ أُخْتِهَا وَ
أَخَذْنَاهُمْ بِالْعَذَابِ لَعَلَّهُمْ يَرْجِعُونَ ﴿٤٨﴾
وَقَالُوا يَا أَيُّهَ السَّاحِرُ ادْعُ لَنَا رَبَّكَ بِمَا عَهِدَ عِنْدَكَ
إِنَّنَا لَمُهْتَدُونَ ﴿٤٩﴾

50. But when We eased them of the torment, behold! they broke their word.

فلما كشفنا عنهم العذاب إذا هم ينكثون ٥٠

51. And Pharaoh caused a proclamation to be made among his people saying: O my people! Is not mine the sovereignty of Egypt and these rivers flowing under me? Can ye not then discern?

ونادى فرعون في قومه قال يقوم أليس لي
ملك مصر وهذه الأنهر تجري من تحتي
أفلا تبصرون ٥١

52. I am surely better than this fellow, who is despicable, and can hardly make (his meaning) plain!

أم أنا خير من هذا الذي هو مهين ولا يكاد
يبين ٥٢

53. Why, then, have armlets of gold not been set upon him or angels sent along with him?

فلولا ألقي عليه أسورة من ذهب أو جاء معه
الملئكة مقترنين ٥٣

54. Thus he persuaded his people to make light (of Moses), and they obeyed him, Lo! they were a wanton folk.

فاستخف قومه فأطاعوه إنهم كانوا قوما فسقين ٥٤

55. So, when they angered Us, We punished them and drowned them every one.

فلما ءاسفونا انتقمنا منهم فأغرقنهم أجمعين ٥٥

56. And We made them a thing past, and an example for those after (them).

ع فجعلنهم سلفا ومثلا للآخرين ٥٦

57. And when the son of Mary is quoted as an example, behold! the folk laugh out.

ولما ضرب ابن مريم مثلا إذا قومك منه
يصدون ٥٧

58. And say: Are our gods better, or is he? They raise not the objection save for argument, Nay! but they are a contentious folk.

وقالوا ءألهتنا خير أم هو ما ضربوه لك إلا
جدلا بل هم قوم خصمون ٥٨

59. He is nothing but a slave[1] on whom We bestowed favour, and We made him a pattern for the Children of Israel.

إن هو إلا عبد أنعمنا عليه وجعلنه مثلا لبني
إسراءيل ٥٩

60. And had We willed We could have set among you angels to be viceroys in the earth.

ولو نشاء لجعلنا منكم ملئكة في الأرض
يخلفون ٦٠

61. And lo! verily there is knowledge of the Hour. So doubt ye not concerning it, but follow Me. This is the right path.

وإنه لعلم للساعة فلا تمترن بها واتبعون
هذا صراط مستقيم ٦١

62. And let not Satan turn you aside. Lo! he is open enemy for you.

ولا يصدنكم الشيطن إنه لكم عدو مبين ٦٢

1. 'Abd Allah, "slave of God." is a proud designation with the Muslims, bondage to Allah implying liberation from all earthly servitudes.

63. When Jesus came with clear proofs (of Allah's sovereognty), he said: I have come unto you with wisdom, and to make plain some of that concerning which ye differ. So keep your duty to Allah, and obey me.

وَلَمَّا جَاءَ عِيسَىٰ بِالْبَيِّنَاتِ قَالَ قَدْ جِئْتُكُمْ
بِالْحِكْمَةِ وَلِأُبَيِّنَ لَكُمْ بَعْضَ الَّذِي تَخْتَلِفُونَ
فِيهِ ۖ فَاتَّقُوا اللَّهَ وَأَطِيعُونِ ﴿٦٣﴾

64. Lo! Allah, He is my Lord and your Lord. So worship Him. This is a right path.

إِنَّ اللَّهَ هُوَ رَبِّي وَرَبُّكُمْ فَاعْبُدُوهُ ۚ هَٰذَا صِرَاطٌ
مُسْتَقِيمٌ ﴿٦٤﴾

65. But the factions among them differed. Then woe unto those who do wrong from the doom of a painful day.

فَاخْتَلَفَ الْأَحْزَابُ مِنْ بَيْنِهِمْ ۖ فَوَيْلٌ لِلَّذِينَ
ظَلَمُوا مِنْ عَذَابِ يَوْمٍ أَلِيمٍ ﴿٦٥﴾

66. Await they aught save the Hour, that it shall come upon them suddenly, when they know not.

هَلْ يَنْظُرُونَ إِلَّا السَّاعَةَ أَنْ تَأْتِيَهُمْ بَغْتَةً وَ
هُمْ لَا يَشْعُرُونَ ﴿٦٦﴾

67. Friends on that Day will be foes one to another, save those who kept their duty (to Allah).

الْأَخِلَّاءُ يَوْمَئِذٍ بَعْضُهُمْ لِبَعْضٍ عَدُوٌّ إِلَّا
ع ٦ ١٢ الْمُتَّقِينَ ﴿٦٧﴾

68. O My slaves! For you there is no fear this Day, nor is it ye who grieve;

يَا عِبَادِ لَا خَوْفٌ عَلَيْكُمُ الْيَوْمَ وَلَا أَنْتُمْ تَحْزَنُونَ ﴿٦٨﴾

69. (Ye) who believed Our revelation and were self-surrendered.

الَّذِينَ آمَنُوا بِآيَاتِنَا وَكَانُوا مُسْلِمِينَ ﴿٦٩﴾

70. Enter the Garden, ye and your wives, to be made glad.

ادْخُلُوا الْجَنَّةَ أَنْتُمْ وَأَزْوَاجُكُمْ تُحْبَرُونَ ﴿٧٠﴾

71. Therein are brought round for them trays of gold and goblets, and therein is all that souls desire and eyes find sweet. And ye are immortal therein.

يُطَافُ عَلَيْهِمْ بِصِحَافٍ مِنْ ذَهَبٍ وَأَكْوَابٍ ۖ وَ
فِيهَا مَا تَشْتَهِيهِ الْأَنْفُسُ وَتَلَذُّ الْأَعْيُنُ ۖ وَأَنْتُمْ
فِيهَا خَالِدُونَ ﴿٧١﴾

72. This is the Garden which ye are make to inherit because of what ye used to do.

وَتِلْكَ الْجَنَّةُ الَّتِي أُورِثْتُمُوهَا بِمَا كُنْتُمْ تَعْمَلُونَ ﴿٧٢﴾

73. Therein for you is fruit in plenty whence to eat.

لَكُمْ فِيهَا فَاكِهَةٌ كَثِيرَةٌ مِنْهَا تَأْكُلُونَ ﴿٧٣﴾

74. Lo! the guilty are immortal in hell's torment.

إِنَّ الْمُجْرِمِينَ فِي عَذَابِ جَهَنَّمَ خَالِدُونَ ﴿٧٤﴾

75. It is not relaxed for them, and they depspair therein.

لَا يُفَتَّرُ عَنْهُمْ وَهُمْ فِيهِ مُبْلِسُونَ ﴿٧٥﴾

76. We wronged them not, but they it was who did the wrong.

وَمَا ظَلَمْنَاهُمْ وَلَٰكِنْ كَانُوا هُمُ الظَّالِمِينَ ﴿٧٦﴾

77. And they cry: O master! Let thy Lord make an end of us. He saith: Lo! here ye must remain.

78. We verily brought the Truth unto you, but ye were, most of you, averse to the Truth.

79. Or do they determine any thing (against the Prophet)? Lo! We (also) are determining.

80. Or deem they that We cannot hear their secret thoughts and private confidences? Nay, but Our envoys, present with them, do record.

81. Say (O Muhammad); The Beneficent One hath no son. I am first among the worshippers.

82. Glorified be the Lord of the heavens and the earth, the Lord of the Throne, from that which they ascribe (unto Him)!

83. So let them flounder (in their talk) and play until they meet the Day which they are promised.

84. And He it is Who in the heaven is God, and in the earth God. He is the Wise, the Knower.

85. And blessed be He unto Whom belongeth the Sovereignty of the heavens and the earth and all that is between them, and with Whom is knowledge of the Hour, and unto Whom ye will be returned.

86. And those unto whom they cry instead of Him possess no power of intercession, saving him who beareth witness unto the Truth knowingly.

87. And if thou ask them who created them, they will surely say: Allah. How then are they turned away?

88. And he saith: O my Lord! Lo! those are a folk who believe not.

89. Then bear with them (O Muhammad) and say: Peace! But they will come to know.

وَنَادَوْا يٰمٰلِكُ لِيَقْضِ عَلَيْنَا رَبُّكَ قَالَ اِنَّكُمْ مّٰكِثُوْنَ ﴿٧٧﴾
لَقَدْ جِئْنٰكُمْ بِالْحَقِّ وَلٰكِنَّ اَكْثَرَكُمْ لِلْحَقِّ كٰرِهُوْنَ ﴿٧٨﴾
اَمْ اَبْرَمُوْٓا اَمْرًا فَاِنَّا مُبْرِمُوْنَ ﴿٧٩﴾
اَمْ يَحْسَبُوْنَ اَنَّا لَا نَسْمَعُ سِرَّهُمْ وَنَجْوٰىهُمْ بَلٰى
وَرُسُلُنَا لَدَيْهِمْ يَكْتُبُوْنَ ﴿٨٠﴾
قُلْ اِنْ كَانَ لِلرَّحْمٰنِ وَلَدٌ فَاَنَا اَوَّلُ الْعٰبِدِيْنَ ﴿٨١﴾
سُبْحٰنَ رَبِّ السَّمٰوٰتِ وَالْاَرْضِ رَبِّ الْعَرْشِ
عَمَّا يَصِفُوْنَ ﴿٨٢﴾
فَذَرْهُمْ يَخُوْضُوْا وَيَلْعَبُوْا حَتّٰى يُلٰقُوْا يَوْمَهُمُ
الَّذِيْ يُوْعَدُوْنَ ﴿٨٣﴾
وَهُوَ الَّذِيْ فِي السَّمَآءِ اِلٰهٌ وَّفِي الْاَرْضِ اِلٰهٌ وَ
هُوَ الْحَكِيْمُ الْعَلِيْمُ ﴿٨٤﴾
وَتَبٰرَكَ الَّذِيْ لَهٗ مُلْكُ السَّمٰوٰتِ وَالْاَرْضِ وَمَا
بَيْنَهُمَا وَعِنْدَهٗ عِلْمُ السَّاعَةِ وَاِلَيْهِ تُرْجَعُوْنَ ﴿٨٥﴾
وَلَا يَمْلِكُ الَّذِيْنَ يَدْعُوْنَ مِنْ دُوْنِهِ الشَّفَاعَةَ
اِلَّا مَنْ شَهِدَ بِالْحَقِّ وَهُمْ يَعْلَمُوْنَ ﴿٨٦﴾
وَلَئِنْ سَاَلْتَهُمْ مَّنْ خَلَقَهُمْ لَيَقُوْلُنَّ اللّٰهُ فَاَنّٰى
يُؤْفَكُوْنَ ﴿٨٧﴾
وَقِيْلِهٖ يٰرَبِّ اِنَّ هٰٓؤُلَآءِ قَوْمٌ لَّا يُؤْمِنُوْنَ ﴿٨٨﴾
فَاصْفَحْ عَنْهُمْ وَقُلْ سَلٰمٌ فَسَوْفَ يَعْلَمُوْنَ ﴿٨٩﴾

Ad-Dukhān, "The Smoke", takes its name from a word in v. 10. Tradition says that smoke here refers prophetically to the haze of dust which surrounded Mecca at the time of the great drought and famine which preceded the Muslim conquest of Mecca and facilitated it.

It belongs to the middle group of Meccan Sūrahs.

SMOKE

Revealed at Mecca

In the name of Allah, the Beneficent, the Merciful.

1. Ḥā. Mīm.[1]

2. By the Scripture that maketh plain

3. Lo! We revealed it on a blessed night —Lo! We are ever warning—

4. Whereupon every wise command is made clear

5. As a command from Our Presence— Lo! We are ever sending—

6. A mercy from thy Lord. Lo! He is the Hearer, the Knower:

7. Lord of the heavens and the earth and all that is between them, if ye would be sure.

8. There is no God save Him. He quickeneth and giveth death; your Lord and Lord of your forefathers.

9. Nay, but they play in doubt.

10. But watch thou (O Muhammad) for the Day when the sky will produce visible smoke

11. That will envelop the people.[2] This will be a painful torment.

12. (Then they will say): Our Lord, relieve us of the torment! Lo! we are believers.

13. How can there be remembrance for them, when a messenger making plain (the truth) had already come unto them,

14. And they had turned away from him and said: One taught (by others), a madman?

15. Lo! We withdraw the torment a little. Lo! ye return (to disbelief).

16. On the Day when We shall seize them with the greater seizure (then), in truth We shall punish.

17. And verily We tried before them Pharaoh's folk, when there came unto them a noble messenger,

اٰياتها ٥٩ (٤٤) سُورَةُ الدُّخَانِ مَكِّيَّةٌ رُكُوعَاتُهَا ٣

بِسْمِ اللّٰهِ الرَّحْمٰنِ الرَّحِيْمِ

حٰمٓ ﴿١﴾

وَالْكِتٰبِ الْمُبِيْنِ ﴿٢﴾

اِنَّآ اَنْزَلْنٰهُ فِيْ لَيْلَةٍ مُّبٰرَكَةٍ اِنَّا كُنَّا مُنْذِرِيْنَ ﴿٣﴾

فِيْهَا يُفْرَقُ كُلُّ اَمْرٍ حَكِيْمٍ ﴿٤﴾

اَمْرًا مِّنْ عِنْدِنَا اِنَّا كُنَّا مُرْسِلِيْنَ ﴿٥﴾

رَحْمَةً مِّنْ رَّبِّكَ اِنَّهٗ هُوَ السَّمِيْعُ الْعَلِيْمُ ﴿٦﴾

رَبِّ السَّمٰوٰتِ وَالْاَرْضِ وَمَا بَيْنَهُمَا اِنْ كُنْتُمْ مُّوْقِنِيْنَ ﴿٧﴾

لَآ اِلٰهَ اِلَّا هُوَ يُحْيٖ وَيُمِيْتُ رَبُّكُمْ وَرَبُّ اٰبَآئِكُمُ

الْاَوَّلِيْنَ ﴿٨﴾

بَلْ هُمْ فِيْ شَكٍّ يَّلْعَبُوْنَ ﴿٩﴾

فَارْتَقِبْ يَوْمَ تَاْتِي السَّمَآءُ بِدُخَانٍ مُّبِيْنٍ ﴿١٠﴾

يَّغْشَى النَّاسَ هٰذَا عَذَابٌ اَلِيْمٌ ﴿١١﴾

رَبَّنَا اكْشِفْ عَنَّا الْعَذَابَ اِنَّا مُؤْمِنُوْنَ ﴿١٢﴾

اَنّٰى لَهُمُ الذِّكْرٰى وَقَدْ جَآءَهُمْ رَسُوْلٌ مُّبِيْنٌ ﴿١٣﴾

ثُمَّ تَوَلَّوْا عَنْهُ وَقَالُوْا مُعَلَّمٌ مَّجْنُوْنٌ ﴿١٤﴾

اِنَّا كَاشِفُوا الْعَذَابِ قَلِيْلًا اِنَّكُمْ عَآئِدُوْنَ ﴿١٥﴾

يَوْمَ نَبْطِشُ الْبَطْشَةَ الْكُبْرٰى اِنَّا مُنْتَقِمُوْنَ ﴿١٦﴾

وَلَقَدْ فَتَنَّا قَبْلَهُمْ قَوْمَ فِرْعَوْنَ وَجَآءَهُمْ رَسُوْلٌ

كَرِيْمٌ ﴿١٧﴾

1. See Sûr. II, v. 1, footnote.

2. Of Mecca.

18. Saying: Give up to me the slaves of Allah. Lo! I am a faithful messenger unto you.

اَنْ اَدُّوْٓا اِلَیَّ عِبَادَ اللّٰهِ ؕ اِنِّیْ لَكُمْ رَسُوْلٌ اَمِیْنٌ ۙ

19. And saying: Be not proud against Allah. Lo! I bring you a clear warrant.

وَّ اَنْ لَّا تَعْلُوْا عَلَی اللّٰهِ ؕ اِنِّیْۤ اٰتِیْكُمْ بِسُلْطٰنٍ مُّبِیْنٍ ۚ

20. And lo! I have sought refuge in my Lord and your Lord lest ye stone me to death.

وَ اِنِّیْ عُذْتُ بِرَبِّیْ وَ رَبِّكُمْ اَنْ تَرْجُمُوْنِ ۙ

21. And if ye put no faith in me, then let me go.

وَ اِنْ لَّمْ تُؤْمِنُوْا لِیْ فَاعْتَزِلُوْنِ ۞

22. And he cried unto his Lord (saying): These are guilty folk.

فَدَعَا رَبَّهٗۤ اَنَّ هٰۤؤُلَآءِ قَوْمٌ مُّجْرِمُوْنَ ۞

23. Then (his Lord commanded): Take away My slaves by night. Lo! ye will be followed;

فَاَسْرِ بِعِبَادِیْ لَیْلًا اِنَّكُمْ مُّتَّبَعُوْنَ ۙ

24. And leave the sea behind at rest, for lo! they are a drowned host.

وَ اتْرُكِ الْبَحْرَ رَهْوًا ؕ اِنَّهُمْ جُنْدٌ مُّغْرَقُوْنَ ۞

25. How many were the gardens and the water-springs that they left behind,

كَمْ تَرَكُوْا مِنْ جَنّٰتٍ وَّ عُیُوْنٍ ۙ

26. And the cornlands and the goodly sites

وَّ زُرُوْعٍ وَّ مَقَامٍ كَرِیْمٍ ۙ

27. And pleasant things wherein they took delight!

وَّ نَعْمَةٍ كَانُوْا فِیْهَا فٰكِهِیْنَ ۙ

28. Even so (it was), and We made it an inheritance for other folk;

كَذٰلِكَ ۟ وَ اَوْرَثْنٰهَا قَوْمًا اٰخَرِیْنَ ۞

29. And the heaven and the earth wept not for them, nor were they reprieved.

فَمَا بَكَتْ عَلَیْهِمُ السَّمَآءُ وَ الْاَرْضُ وَ مَا كَانُوْا مُنْظَرِیْنَ ۞

30. And We delivered the Children of Israel from the shameful doom;

وَ لَقَدْ نَجَّیْنَا بَنِیْۤ اِسْرَآءِیْلَ مِنَ الْعَذَابِ الْمُهِیْنِ ۙ

31. (We delivered them) from Pharaoh. Lo! he was a tyrant of the wanton ones.

مِنْ فِرْعَوْنَ ؕ اِنَّهٗ كَانَ عَالِیًا مِّنَ الْمُسْرِفِیْنَ ۞

32. And We chose them, purposely, above (all) creatures.

وَ لَقَدِ اخْتَرْنٰهُمْ عَلٰی عِلْمٍ عَلَی الْعٰلَمِیْنَ ۚ

33. And We gave them portents wherein was a clear trial.

وَ اٰتَیْنٰهُمْ مِّنَ الْاٰیٰتِ مَا فِیْهِ بَلٰٓؤٌا مُّبِیْنٌ ۞

34. Lo! these, forsooth, are saying:

اِنَّ هٰۤؤُلَآءِ لَیَقُوْلُوْنَ ۙ

35. There is naught but our first death, and we shall not be raised again.

اِنْ هِیَ اِلَّا مَوْتَتُنَا الْاُوْلٰی وَ مَا نَحْنُ بِمُنْشَرِیْنَ ۞

36. Bring back our fathers, if ye speak the truth!

فَاْتُوْا بِاٰبَآئِنَاۤ اِنْ كُنْتُمْ صٰدِقِیْنَ ۞

37. Are they better, or the folk of Tubb'a[1] and those before them? We destroyed them, for surely they were guilty.

اَهُمْ خَیْرٌ اَمْ قَوْمُ تُبَّعٍ ۙ وَّ الَّذِیْنَ مِنْ قَبْلِهِمْ ؕ اَهْلَكْنٰهُمْ ۫ اِنَّهُمْ كَانُوْا مُجْرِمِیْنَ ۞

38. And We created not the heavens and the earth, and all that is between them, in play.

وَ مَا خَلَقْنَا السَّمٰوٰتِ وَ الْاَرْضَ وَ مَا بَیْنَهُمَا لٰعِبِیْنَ ۞

1. A name for many kings of Himyar (the South Arabians), each of whom was called Tubb'a just as every king of Egypt was called Pharaoh.

39. We created them not save with truth; but most of them know not.

مَا خَلَقْنَاهُمَا إِلَّا بِالْحَقِّ وَلَٰكِنَّ أَكْثَرَهُمْ لَا يَعْلَمُونَ ٣٩

40. Assuredly the Day of Decision is the term of all of them,

إِنَّ يَوْمَ الْفَصْلِ مِيقَاتُهُمْ أَجْمَعِينَ ٤٠

41. A day when friend can in naught avail friend, nor can they be helped,

يَوْمَ لَا يُغْنِي مَوْلًى عَنْ مَوْلًى شَيْئًا وَلَا هُمْ يُنْصَرُونَ ٤١

42. Save him on whom Allah hath mercy. Lo! He is the Mighty, the Merciful.

إِلَّا مَنْ رَحِمَ اللَّهُ إِنَّهُ هُوَ الْعَزِيزُ الرَّحِيمُ ٤٢

43. Lo! the tree of Zaqqūm,[1]

إِنَّ شَجَرَتَ الزَّقُّومِ ٤٣

44. The food of the sinner!

طَعَامُ الْأَثِيمِ ٤٤

45. Like molten brass, it seetheth in their bellies

كَالْمُهْلِ يَغْلِي فِي الْبُطُونِ ٤٥

46. As the seething of boiling water.

كَغَلْيِ الْحَمِيمِ ٤٦

47. (And it will be said): Take him and drag him to the midst of hell,

خُذُوهُ فَاعْتِلُوهُ إِلَىٰ سَوَاءِ الْجَحِيمِ ٤٧

48. Then pour upon his head the torment of boiling water.

ثُمَّ صُبُّوا فَوْقَ رَأْسِهِ مِنْ عَذَابِ الْحَمِيمِ ٤٨

49. (Saying): Taste! Lo! thou wast forsooth the mighty, the noble!

ذُقْ إِنَّكَ أَنْتَ الْعَزِيزُ الْكَرِيمُ ٤٩

50. Lo! this is that whereof ye used to doubt.

إِنَّ هَٰذَا مَا كُنْتُمْ بِهِ تَمْتَرُونَ ٥٠

51. Lo! those who kept their duty will be in a place secure

إِنَّ الْمُتَّقِينَ فِي مَقَامٍ أَمِينٍ ٥١

52. Amid gardens and water-springs,

فِي جَنَّاتٍ وَعُيُونٍ ٥٢

53. Attired in silk and silk embroidery, facing one another.

يَلْبَسُونَ مِنْ سُنْدُسٍ وَإِسْتَبْرَقٍ مُتَقَابِلِينَ ٥٣

54. Even so (it will be). And We shall wed them unto fair ones with wide lovely eyes.

كَذَٰلِكَ وَزَوَّجْنَاهُمْ بِحُورٍ عِينٍ ٥٤

55. They call therein for every fruit in safety:

يَدْعُونَ فِيهَا بِكُلِّ فَاكِهَةٍ آمِنِينَ ٥٥

56. They taste not death therein, save the first death. And He hath saved them from the doom of hell,

لَا يَذُوقُونَ فِيهَا الْمَوْتَ إِلَّا الْمَوْتَةَ الْأُولَىٰ
وَوَقَاهُمْ عَذَابَ الْجَحِيمِ ٥٦

57. A bounty from thy Lord. That is the Supreme triumph.

فَضْلًا مِنْ رَبِّكَ ذَٰلِكَ هُوَ الْفَوْزُ الْعَظِيمُ ٥٧

58. And We have made (this Scripture) easy in thy language only that they may heed.

فَإِنَّمَا يَسَّرْنَاهُ بِلِسَانِكَ لَعَلَّهُمْ يَتَذَكَّرُونَ ٥٨

59. Wait then (O Muhammad). Lo! they (too) are waiting.

فَارْتَقِبْ إِنَّهُمْ مُرْتَقِبُونَ ٥٩

1. XXVII, 62; LVI, 52.

Al-Jāthiyah, "Crouching," takes its name from a word in v. 28. It belongs to the middle group of Meccan Sūrahs.

CROUCHING

Revealed at Mecca

In the name of Allah, the Beneficent, the Merciful.

1. Ḥā. Mīm.[1]

2. The revelation of the Scripture is from Allah, the Mighty, the Wise.

3. Lo! in the heavens and the earth are portents for believers.

4. And in your creation, and all the beasts that He scattereth in the earth, are portents for a folk whose faith is sure.

5. And the difference of night and day and the provision that Allah sendeth down from the sky and thereby quickeneth the earth after her death, and the ordering of the winds, are portents for a people who have sense.

6. These are the portents of Allah which We recite unto thee (Muhammad) with truth. Then in what fact, after Allah and His portents, will they believe?

7. Woe unto each sinful liar!

8. Who heareth the revelations of Allah receive unto him, and then continueth in pride as though he heard them not. Give him tidings of a painful doom.

9. And when he knoweth aught of Our revelations he maketh it a jest. For such there is a shameful doom.

10. Beyond them there is hell, and that which they have earned will naught avail them, nor those whom they have chosen for protecting friends beside Allah. Theirs will be an awful doom.

11. This is guidance. And those who disbelieve the revelations of their Lord, for them there is a painful doom of wrath.

1. See Sūr. II, v. 1, footnote.

اياتها ٣٧ (٤٥) سُورَةُ الْجَاثِيَةِ مَكِّيَّةٌ رُكُوعَاتُهَا ٤

بِسْمِ اللّٰهِ الرَّحْمٰنِ الرَّحِيْمِ

حٰمٓ ١

تَنْزِيْلُ الْكِتٰبِ مِنَ اللّٰهِ الْعَزِيْزِ الْحَكِيْمِ ٢

اِنَّ فِي السَّمٰوٰتِ وَالْاَرْضِ لَاٰيٰتٍ لِّلْمُؤْمِنِيْنَ ٣

وَفِيْ خَلْقِكُمْ وَمَا يَبُثُّ مِنْ دَآبَّةٍ اٰيٰتٌ لِّقَوْمٍ يُّوْقِنُوْنَ ٤

وَاخْتِلَافِ الَّيْلِ وَالنَّهَارِ وَمَآ اَنْزَلَ اللّٰهُ مِنَ السَّمَآءِ

مِنْ رِّزْقٍ فَاَحْيَا بِهِ الْاَرْضَ بَعْدَ مَوْتِهَا وَتَصْرِيْفِ

الرِّيٰحِ اٰيٰتٌ لِّقَوْمٍ يَّعْقِلُوْنَ ٥

تِلْكَ اٰيٰتُ اللّٰهِ نَتْلُوْهَا عَلَيْكَ بِالْحَقِّ فَبِاَيِّ حَدِيْثٍۢ

بَعْدَ اللّٰهِ وَاٰيٰتِهِ يُؤْمِنُوْنَ ٦

وَيْلٌ لِّكُلِّ اَفَّاكٍ اَثِيْمٍ ٧

يَّسْمَعُ اٰيٰتِ اللّٰهِ تُتْلٰى عَلَيْهِ ثُمَّ يُصِرُّ مُسْتَكْبِرًا كَاَنْ

لَّمْ يَسْمَعْهَا فَبَشِّرْهُ بِعَذَابٍ اَلِيْمٍ ٨

وَاِذَا عَلِمَ مِنْ اٰيٰتِنَا شَيْئَا اِتَّخَذَهَا هُزُوًا اُولٰٓئِكَ

لَهُمْ عَذَابٌ مُّهِيْنٌ ٩

مِنْ وَّرَآئِهِمْ جَهَنَّمُ وَلَا يُغْنِيْ عَنْهُمْ مَّا كَسَبُوْا

شَيْئًا وَّلَا مَا اتَّخَذُوْا مِنْ دُوْنِ اللّٰهِ اَوْلِيَآءَ وَلَهُمْ

عَذَابٌ عَظِيْمٌ ١٠

هٰذَا هُدًى وَالَّذِيْنَ كَفَرُوْا بِاٰيٰتِ رَبِّهِمْ لَهُمْ

ع ١٧ عَذَابٌ مِّنْ رِّجْزٍ اَلِيْمٌ ١١

12. Allah it is Who hath made the sea of service unto you that the ships may run thereon by His command, and that ye may seek of His bounty, and that haply ye may be thankful;

13. And hath made of service unto you whatsoever is in the heavens and whatsoever is in the earth; it is all from Him. Lo! herein verily are portents for people who reflect.

14. Tell those who believe to forgive those who hope not for the days of Allah; in order that He may requite folk what they used to earn.

15. Whoso doth right, it is for his soul, and whoso doth wrong, it is against it. And afterward unto your Lord ye will be brought back.

16. And verily We gave the Children of Israel the Scripture and the Command and the Prophethood, and provided them with good things and favoured them above (all) peoples;

17. And gave them plain commandments. And they differed not until after the knowledge came unto them, through rivalry among themselves. Lo! thy Lord will judge between them on the Day of Resurrection concerning that wherein they used to differ.

18. And now have We set thee (O Muhammad) on a clear road of (Our) commandment; so follow it, and follow not the whims of those who know not.

19. Lo! they can avail thee naught against Allah. And lo! as for the wrong-doers, some of them are friends of others; and Allah is the Friend of those who ward off (evil).

20. This is clear indication for mankind, and a guidance and a mercy for a folk whose faith is sure.

21. Or do those who commit ill-deeds suppose that We shall make them as those who believe and do good works, the same in life and death? Bad is their judgement!

اللَّهُ الَّذِي سَخَّرَ لَكُمُ الْبَحْرَ لِتَجْرِيَ الْفُلْكُ فِيهِ بِأَمْرِهِ
وَلِتَبْتَغُوا مِنْ فَضْلِهِ وَلَعَلَّكُمْ تَشْكُرُونَ ﴿١٢﴾
وَسَخَّرَ لَكُمْ مَا فِي السَّمَاوَاتِ وَمَا فِي الْأَرْضِ جَمِيعًا
مِنْهُ إِنَّ فِي ذَٰلِكَ لَآيَاتٍ لِقَوْمٍ يَتَفَكَّرُونَ ﴿١٣﴾
قُلْ لِلَّذِينَ آمَنُوا يَغْفِرُوا لِلَّذِينَ لَا يَرْجُونَ أَيَّامَ
اللَّهِ لِيَجْزِيَ قَوْمًا بِمَا كَانُوا يَكْسِبُونَ ﴿١٤﴾
مَنْ عَمِلَ صَالِحًا فَلِنَفْسِهِ وَمَنْ أَسَاءَ فَعَلَيْهَا
ثُمَّ إِلَىٰ رَبِّكُمْ تُرْجَعُونَ ﴿١٥﴾
وَلَقَدْ آتَيْنَا بَنِي إِسْرَائِيلَ الْكِتَابَ وَالْحُكْمَ وَالنُّبُوَّةَ
وَرَزَقْنَاهُمْ مِنَ الطَّيِّبَاتِ وَفَضَّلْنَاهُمْ عَلَى الْعَالَمِينَ ﴿١٦﴾
وَآتَيْنَاهُمْ بَيِّنَاتٍ مِنَ الْأَمْرِ فَمَا اخْتَلَفُوا إِلَّا مِنْ
بَعْدِ مَا جَاءَهُمُ الْعِلْمُ بَغْيًا بَيْنَهُمْ إِنَّ رَبَّكَ
يَقْضِي بَيْنَهُمْ يَوْمَ الْقِيَامَةِ فِيمَا كَانُوا فِيهِ يَخْتَلِفُونَ ﴿١٧﴾
ثُمَّ جَعَلْنَاكَ عَلَىٰ شَرِيعَةٍ مِنَ الْأَمْرِ فَاتَّبِعْهَا وَلَا
تَتَّبِعْ أَهْوَاءَ الَّذِينَ لَا يَعْلَمُونَ ﴿١٨﴾
إِنَّهُمْ لَنْ يُغْنُوا عَنْكَ مِنَ اللَّهِ شَيْئًا وَإِنَّ الظَّالِمِينَ
بَعْضُهُمْ أَوْلِيَاءُ بَعْضٍ وَاللَّهُ وَلِيُّ الْمُتَّقِينَ ﴿١٩﴾
هَٰذَا بَصَائِرُ لِلنَّاسِ وَهُدًى وَرَحْمَةٌ لِقَوْمٍ
يُوقِنُونَ ﴿٢٠﴾
أَمْ حَسِبَ الَّذِينَ اجْتَرَحُوا السَّيِّئَاتِ أَنْ نَجْعَلَهُمْ
كَالَّذِينَ آمَنُوا وَعَمِلُوا الصَّالِحَاتِ سَوَاءً مَحْيَاهُمْ
وَمَمَاتُهُمْ سَاءَ مَا يَحْكُمُونَ ﴿٢١﴾ ع ٢ ١٨

22. And Allah hath created the heavens and the earth with truth, and that every soul may be repaid what it hath earned. And they will not be wronged.

وَخَلَقَ اللّٰهُ السَّمٰوٰتِ وَالْاَرْضَ بِالْحَقِّ وَلِتُجْزٰى
كُلُّ نَفْسٍۭ بِمَا كَسَبَتْ وَهُمْ لَا يُظْلَمُوْنَ ﴿٢٢﴾

23. Hast thou seen him who maketh his desire his god, and Allah sendeth him astray purposely, and sealeth up his hearing and his heart, and setteth on his sight a covering? Then who will lead him after Allah (hath condemned him)? Will ye not then heed?

اَفَرَءَيْتَ مَنِ اتَّخَذَ اِلٰهَهٗ هَوٰىهُ وَاَضَلَّهُ اللّٰهُ
عَلٰى عِلْمٍ وَّخَتَمَ عَلٰى سَمْعِهٖ وَقَلْبِهٖ وَجَعَلَ عَلٰى
بَصَرِهٖ غِشٰوَةً ۗ فَمَنْ يَّهْدِيْهِ مِنْۢ بَعْدِ اللّٰهِ ۗ اَفَلَا
تَذَكَّرُوْنَ ﴿٢٣﴾

24. And they say: There is naught but our life of the world; we die and we live, and naught destroyeth us save time; when they have no knowledge whatsoever of (all) that; they do but guess.

وَقَالُوْا مَا هِيَ اِلَّا حَيَاتُنَا الدُّنْيَا نَمُوْتُ وَنَحْيَا
وَمَا يُهْلِكُنَآ اِلَّا الدَّهْرُ ۚ وَمَا لَهُمْ بِذٰلِكَ مِنْ
عِلْمٍ ۚ اِنْ هُمْ اِلَّا يَظُنُّوْنَ ﴿٢٤﴾

25. And when Our clear revelations are recited unto them their only argument is that they say: Bring (back) our fathers then, if ye are truthful.

وَاِذَا تُتْلٰى عَلَيْهِمْ اٰيٰتُنَا بَيِّنٰتٍ مَّا كَانَ حُجَّتَهُمْ
اِلَّآ اَنْ قَالُوا ائْتُوْا بِاٰبَآئِنَآ اِنْ كُنْتُمْ صٰدِقِيْنَ ﴿٢٥﴾

26. Say (unto them, O Muhammad): Allah giveth life to you, then causeth you to die, then gathereth you unto the Day of Resurrection whereof there is no doubt. But most of mankind know not.

قُلِ اللّٰهُ يُحْيِيْكُمْ ثُمَّ يُمِيْتُكُمْ ثُمَّ يَجْمَعُكُمْ اِلٰى يَوْمِ
الْقِيٰمَةِ لَا رَيْبَ فِيْهِ وَلٰكِنَّ اَكْثَرَ النَّاسِ
لَا يَعْلَمُوْنَ ﴿٢٦﴾ ع ٣ ١٩

27. And unto Allah belongeth the Sovereignty of the heavens and the earth; and on the day when the Hour riseth, on that day those who follow falsehood will be lost.

وَلِلّٰهِ مُلْكُ السَّمٰوٰتِ وَالْاَرْضِ ۚ وَيَوْمَ تَقُوْمُ
السَّاعَةُ يَوْمَئِذٍ يَّخْسَرُ الْمُبْطِلُوْنَ ﴿٢٧﴾

28. And thou wilt see each nation crouching, each nation summoned to its record. (And it will be said unto them): This day ye are requited what ye used to do.

وَتَرٰى كُلَّ اُمَّةٍ جَاثِيَةً ۫ كُلُّ اُمَّةٍ تُدْعٰٓى اِلٰى
كِتٰبِهَا ۗ اَلْيَوْمَ تُجْزَوْنَ مَا كُنْتُمْ تَعْمَلُوْنَ ﴿٢٨﴾

29. This Our Book pronounceth against you with truth. Lo! We have caused (all) that ye did to be recorded.

هٰذَا كِتٰبُنَا يَنْطِقُ عَلَيْكُمْ بِالْحَقِّ ۗ اِنَّا كُنَّا نَسْتَنْسِخُ
مَا كُنْتُمْ تَعْمَلُوْنَ ﴿٢٩﴾

30. Then, as for those who believed and did good works, their Lord will bring them in unto His mercy. That is the evident triumph.

فَاَمَّا الَّذِيْنَ اٰمَنُوْا وَعَمِلُوا الصّٰلِحٰتِ فَيُدْخِلُهُمْ
رَبُّهُمْ فِيْ رَحْمَتِهٖ ۗ ذٰلِكَ هُوَ الْفَوْزُ الْمُبِيْنُ ﴿٣٠﴾

31. And as for those who disbelieved (it will be said unto them): Were not Our revelations recited unto you? But ye were scornful and became a guilty folk.

وأما الذين كفروا أفلم تكن آيتي تتلى عليكم
فاستكبرتم وكنتم قوما مجرمين ٣١

32. And when it was said: Lo! Allah's promise is the truth, and there is no doubt of the Hour's coming, ye said: We know not what the Hour is. We deem it naught but a conjecture, and we are by no means convinced.

وإذا قيل إن وعد الله حق والساعة لا ريب
فيها قلتم ما ندري ما الساعة إن نظن إلا
ظنا وما نحن بمستيقنين ٣٢

33. And the evils of what they did will appear unto them, and that which they used to deride will befall them.

وبدا لهم سيات ما عملوا وحاق بهم ما كانوا
به يستهزءون ٣٣

34. And it will be said: This day We forget you, even as ye forgot the meeting of this your day; and your habitation is the Fire, and there is none to help you.

وقيل اليوم ننسكم كما نسيتم لقاء يومكم هذا
ومأوكم النار وما لكم من نصرين ٣٤

35. This, forasmuch as ye made the revelations of Allah a jest, and the life of the world beguiled you. Therefor this day they come not forth from thence, nor can they make amends.

ذلكم بأنكم اتخذتم ايت الله هزوا وغرتكم
الحيوة الدنيا فاليوم لا يخرجون منها ولا
هم يستعتبون ٣٥

36. Then praise be to Allah, Lord of the heavens and Lord of the earth, the Lord of the Worlds!

فلله الحمد رب السموت ورب الأرض رب
العلمين ٣٦

37. And unto Him (alone) belongeth majesty in the heavens and the earth, and He is the Mighty, the Wise.

وله الكبرياء في السموت والأرض وهو
العزيز الحكيم ٣٧

Al-Aḥqāf, "The Wind-Curved Sandhills" (a formation which will be familiar to all desert travellers, and which especially characterised the region in which the tribe of 'Aād were said originally to have lived), takes its name from a word in v. 21 and is the last of the *Ḥā Mîm* group.

It belongs to the middle group of Meccan Sūrahs, with the exception of v. 10, vv. 15-18, and v. 35, which were revealed at Al-Madînah.

THE WIND-CURVED SANDHILLS

Revealed at Mecca

In the name of Allah, the Beneficent, the Merciful.

1. Ḥā. Mîm.[1]

2. The revelation of the Scripture is from Allah, the Mighty, the Wise.

3. We created not the heavens and the earth and all that is between them save with truth, and for a term appointed. But those who disbelieve turn away from that whereof they are warned.

4. Say (unto them, O Muhammad): Have ye thought on all that ye invoke beside Allah? Show me what they have created of the earth. Or have they any portion in the heavens? Bring me a Scripture before this (Scripture), or some vestige of knowledge (in support of what ye say), if ye are truthful.

5. And who is further astray than those who, instead of Allah, pray unto such as hear not their prayer until the Day of Resurrection, and are unconscious of their prayer,

6. And when mankind are gathered (to the Judgement) will become enemies for them, and will become deniers of having been worshipped.

7. And when Our clear revelations are recited unto them, those who disbelieve say of the Truth when it reacheth them: This is mere magic.

8. Or say they: He hath invented it? Say (O Muhammad): If I have invented it, shall ye have no power to support me against Allah? He is best aware of what ye say among yourselves concerning it. He sufficeth for a witness between me and you And He is the Forgiving, the Merciful.

1. See Sûr. II, v. 1, footnote.

الجزء ٢٦

آياتها ٣٥ (٤٦) سُورَةُ الْأَحْقَافِ مَكِّيَّةٌ رُكُوعَاتُهَا ٤

بِسْمِ اللّٰهِ الرَّحْمٰنِ الرَّحِيْمِ ○

حٰمٓ ﴿١﴾

تَنْزِيْلُ الْكِتٰبِ مِنَ اللّٰهِ الْعَزِيْزِ الْحَكِيْمِ ﴿٢﴾

مَا خَلَقْنَا السَّمٰوٰتِ وَالْاَرْضَ وَمَا بَيْنَهُمَآ اِلَّا بِالْحَقِّ

وَاَجَلٍ مُّسَمًّى ۚ وَالَّذِيْنَ كَفَرُوْا عَمَّآ اُنْذِرُوْا

مُعْرِضُوْنَ ﴿٣﴾

قُلْ اَرَءَيْتُمْ مَّا تَدْعُوْنَ مِنْ دُوْنِ اللّٰهِ اَرُوْنِيْ

مَاذَا خَلَقُوْا مِنَ الْاَرْضِ اَمْ لَهُمْ شِرْكٌ فِي

السَّمٰوٰتِ ۖ اِيْتُوْنِيْ بِكِتٰبٍ مِّنْ قَبْلِ هٰذَآ اَوْ اَثٰرَةٍ

مِّنْ عِلْمٍ اِنْ كُنْتُمْ صٰدِقِيْنَ ﴿٤﴾

وَمَنْ اَضَلُّ مِمَّنْ يَّدْعُوْا مِنْ دُوْنِ اللّٰهِ مَنْ

لَّا يَسْتَجِيْبُ لَهٗٓ اِلٰى يَوْمِ الْقِيٰمَةِ وَهُمْ عَنْ دُعَآئِهِمْ

غٰفِلُوْنَ ﴿٥﴾

وَاِذَا حُشِرَ النَّاسُ كَانُوْا لَهُمْ اَعْدَآءً وَّكَانُوْا

بِعِبَادَتِهِمْ كٰفِرِيْنَ ﴿٦﴾

وَاِذَا تُتْلٰى عَلَيْهِمْ اٰيٰتُنَا بَيِّنٰتٍ قَالَ الَّذِيْنَ كَفَرُوْا

لِلْحَقِّ لَمَّا جَآءَهُمْ ۙ هٰذَا سِحْرٌ مُّبِيْنٌ ﴿٧﴾

اَمْ يَقُوْلُوْنَ افْتَرٰىهُ ۖ قُلْ اِنِ افْتَرَيْتُهٗ فَلَا تَمْلِكُوْنَ

لِيْ مِنَ اللّٰهِ شَيْـًٔا ۖ هُوَ اَعْلَمُ بِمَا تُفِيْضُوْنَ فِيْهِ ۖ كَفٰى بِهٖ

شَهِيْدًا ۢ بَيْنِيْ وَبَيْنَكُمْ ۖ وَهُوَ الْغَفُوْرُ الرَّحِيْمُ ﴿٨﴾

9. Say: I am no new thing among the messengers (of Allah), nor know I what will be done with me or with you. I do but follow that which is inspired in me, and I am but a plain warner.

10. Bethink you: If it is from Allah and ye disbelieve therein, and a witness of the Children of Israel[1] hath already testified to the like thereof and hath believed, and ye are too proud (what plight is yours)? Lo! Allah guideth not wrongdoing folk.

11. And those who disbelieve say of those who believe: If it had been (any) good, they would not have been before us in attaining it. And since they will not be guided by it, they say: This is an ancient lie;

12. When before it there was the Scripture of Moses, an example and a mercy; and this is a confirming Scripture in the Arabic language, that it may warn those who do wrong and bring good tidings for the righteous.

13. Lo! those who say: Our Lord is Allah, and thereafter walk aright, there shall no fear come upon them neither shall they grieve.

14. Such are rightful owners of the Garden, immortal therein, as a reward for what they used to do.

15. And We have commended unto man kindness toward parents. His mother beareth him with reluctance, and bringeth him forth with reluctance, and the bearing of him and the weaning of him is thirty months, till, when he attaineth full strength and reacheth forty years, he saith: My Lord! Arouse me that I may give thanks for the favour wherewith Thou hast favoured me and my parents, and that I may do right acceptable unto Thee. And be gracious unto me in the matter of my seed. Lo! I have turned unto Thee repentant, and lo! I am of those who surrender[2] (unto Thee).

قُلْ مَا كُنْتُ بِدْعًا مِّنَ الرُّسُلِ وَمَآ اَدْرِيْ مَا يُفْعَلُ
بِيْ وَلَا بِكُمْ ۭ اِنْ اَتَّبِعُ اِلَّا مَا يُوْحٰٓى اِلَيَّ وَمَآ اَنَا اِلَّا
نَذِيْرٌ مُّبِيْنٌ ۝٩
قُلْ اَرَءَيْتُمْ اِنْ كَانَ مِنْ عِنْدِ اللّٰهِ وَكَفَرْتُمْ بِهٖ وَ
شَهِدَ شَاهِدٌ مِّنْۢ بَنِيْٓ اِسْرَاۗءِيْلَ عَلٰي مِثْلِهٖ فَاٰمَنَ
وَاسْتَكْبَرْتُمْ ۭ اِنَّ اللّٰهَ لَا يَهْدِي الْقَوْمَ الظّٰلِمِيْنَ ۝١٠
وَقَالَ الَّذِيْنَ كَفَرُوْا لِلَّذِيْنَ اٰمَنُوْا لَوْ كَانَ خَيْرًا مَّا
سَبَقُوْنَآ اِلَيْهِ ۭ وَاِذْ لَمْ يَهْتَدُوْا بِهٖ فَسَيَقُوْلُوْنَ
هٰذَآ اِفْكٌ قَدِيْمٌ ۝١١
وَمِنْ قَبْلِهٖ كِتٰبُ مُوْسٰٓى اِمَامًا وَّرَحْمَةً ۭ وَهٰذَا
كِتٰبٌ مُّصَدِّقٌ لِّسَانًا عَرَبِيًّا لِّيُنْذِرَ الَّذِيْنَ ظَلَمُوْا ڰ
وَبُشْرٰى لِلْمُحْسِنِيْنَ ۝١٢
اِنَّ الَّذِيْنَ قَالُوْا رَبُّنَا اللّٰهُ ثُمَّ اسْتَقَامُوْا فَلَا خَوْفٌ
عَلَيْهِمْ وَلَا هُمْ يَحْزَنُوْنَ ۝١٣
اُولٰۗىِٕكَ اَصْحٰبُ الْجَنَّةِ خٰلِدِيْنَ فِيْهَا ۚ جَزَاۗءًۢ بِمَا
كَانُوْا يَعْمَلُوْنَ ۝١٤
وَوَصَّيْنَا الْاِنْسَانَ بِوَالِدَيْهِ اِحْسٰنًا ۭ حَمَلَتْهُ اُمُّهٗ
كُرْهًا وَّوَضَعَتْهُ كُرْهًا ۭ وَحَمْلُهٗ وَفِصٰلُهٗ ثَلٰثُوْنَ
شَهْرًا ۭ حَتّٰٓى اِذَا بَلَغَ اَشُدَّهٗ وَبَلَغَ اَرْبَعِيْنَ سَنَةً ۙ قَالَ
رَبِّ اَوْزِعْنِيْٓ اَنْ اَشْكُرَ نِعْمَتَكَ الَّتِيْٓ اَنْعَمْتَ عَلَيَّ وَعَلٰي
وَالِدَيَّ وَاَنْ اَعْمَلَ صَالِحًا تَرْضٰىهُ وَاَصْلِحْ لِيْ فِيْ
ذُرِّيَّتِيْ ڔ اِنِّىْ تُبْتُ اِلَيْكَ وَاِنِّىْ مِنَ الْمُسْلِمِيْنَ ۝١٥

1. Abdullah ibn Salam, a learned Jew of Al-Madinah, who became a devout Muslim. This is the usual explanation though the verse is still considered as of Meccan revelation.
2. Ar. *Muslimīn.*

16. Those are they from whom We accept the best of what they do, and overlook their evil deeds. (They are) among the owners of the Garden. This is the true promise which they were promised (in the world).

أولئك الذين نتقبل عنهم أحسن ما عملوا
ونتجاوز عن سيئاتهم في أصحاب الجنة وعد
الصدق الذي كانوا يوعدون ١٦

17. And whoso saith unto his parents: Fie upon you both! Do ye threaten me that I shall be brought forth (again) when generations before me have passed away? And they twain cry unto Allah for help (and say): Woe unto thee! Believe! Lo! the promise of Allah is true. But he saith: This is naught save fables of the men of old:

والذي قال لوالديه أف لكما أتعدانني أن
أخرج وقد خلت القرون من قبلي وهما
يستغيثان الله ويلك آمن إن وعد الله حق
فيقول ما هذا إلا أساطير الأولين ١٧

18. Such are those on whom the Word concerning nations of the Jinn and mankind which have passed away before them hath effect. Lo! they are the losers.

أولئك الذين حق عليهم القول في أمم قد
خلت من قبلهم من الجن والإنس إنهم
كانوا خاسرين ١٨

19. And for all there will be ranks from what they do, that He may pay them for their deeds! and they will not be wronged.

ولكل درجات مما عملوا وليوفيهم أعمالهم
وهم لا يظلمون ١٩

20. And on the day when those who disbelieve are exposed to the Fire (it will be said): Ye squandered your good things in the life of the world and sought comfort therein. Now this day ye are rewarded with the doom of ignominy because ye were disdainful in the land without a right, and because ye used to transgress.

ويوم يعرض الذين كفروا على النار أذهبتم
طيباتكم في حياتكم الدنيا واستمتعتم بها فاليوم
تجزون عذاب الهون بما كنتم تستكبرون في
الأرض بغير الحق وبما كنتم تفسقون ٢٠

21. And make mention (O Muhammad) of the brother of 'Aād[1] when he warned his folk among the wind-curved sandhills—and verily warners came and went before and after him—saying: Serve none but Allah. Lo! I fear for you the doom of a tremendous Day.

واذكر أخا عاد إذ أنذر قومه بالأحقاف وقد
خلت النذر من بين يديه ومن خلفه ألا
تعبدوا إلا الله إني أخاف عليكم عذاب
يوم عظيم ٢١

22. They said: thou hast come to turn us away from our gods? Then bring upon us that wherewith thou threatenest us, if thou art of the truthful.

قالوا أجئتنا لتأفكنا عن آلهتنا فأتنا بما
تعدنا إن كنت من الصادقين ٢٢

1. The prophet Hūd.

23. He said: The knowledge is with Allah only. I convey unto you that wherewith I have been sent, but I see you are a folk that know not.

24. Then, when they beheld it as a dense cloud coming toward their valleys, they said: Here is a cloud bringing us rain. Nay, but it is that which ye did seek to hasten, a wind wherein is painful torment,

25. Destroying all things by commandment of its Lord. And morning found them so that naught could be seen save their dwellings. Thus do We reward the guilty folk.

26. And verily We had empowered them with that wherewith We have not empowered you, and had assigned them ears and eyes and hearts; but their ears and eyes and hearts availed them naught since they denied the revelations of Allah; and what they used to mock befell them.

27. And verily We have destroyed townships round about you, and displayed (for them) Our revelations, that haply they might return.

28. Then why did those whom they had chosen for gods as a way of approach (unto Allah) not help them? Nay, but they did fail them utterly. And (all) that was their lie, and what they used to invent.

29. And when We inclined toward thee (Muhammad) certain of the Jinn, who wished to hear the Qur'ān and, when they were in its presence, said: Give ear! and, when it was finished, turned back to their people, warning.

قَالَ اِنَّمَا الْعِلْمُ عِنْدَ اللّٰهِ ۖ وَاُبَلِّغُكُمْ مَّاۤ اُرْسِلْتُ
بِهٖ وَلٰكِنِّيْۤ اَرٰىكُمْ قَوْمًا تَجْهَلُوْنَ ﴿٢٣﴾
فَلَمَّا رَاَوْهُ عَارِضًا مُّسْتَقْبِلَ اَوْدِيَتِهِمْ ۙ قَالُوْا
هٰذَا عَارِضٌ مُّمْطِرُنَا ۚ بَلْ هُوَ مَا اسْتَعْجَلْتُمْ
بِهٖ ۚ رِيْحٌ فِيْهَا عَذَابٌ اَلِيْمٌ ﴿٢٤﴾
تُدَمِّرُ كُلَّ شَيْءٍۭ بِاَمْرِ رَبِّهَا فَاَصْبَحُوْا لَا يُرٰۤى
اِلَّا مَسٰكِنُهُمْ ۚ كَذٰلِكَ نَجْزِي الْقَوْمَ
الْمُجْرِمِيْنَ ﴿٢٥﴾
وَلَقَدْ مَكَّنّٰهُمْ فِيْمَاۤ اِنْ مَّكَّنّٰكُمْ فِيْهِ وَ
جَعَلْنَا لَهُمْ سَمْعًا وَّاَبْصَارًا وَّاَفْـِٕدَةً ۖ فَمَاۤ
اَغْنٰى عَنْهُمْ سَمْعُهُمْ وَلَاۤ اَبْصَارُهُمْ
وَلَاۤ اَفْـِٕدَتُهُمْ مِّنْ شَيْءٍ اِذْ كَانُوْا يَجْحَدُوْنَ ۙ
بِاٰيٰتِ اللّٰهِ وَحَاقَ بِهِمْ مَّا كَانُوْا بِهٖ
يَسْتَهْزِءُوْنَ ﴿٢٦﴾ ع
وَلَقَدْ اَهْلَكْنَا مَا حَوْلَكُمْ مِّنَ الْقُرٰى وَصَرَّفْنَا
الْاٰيٰتِ لَعَلَّهُمْ يَرْجِعُوْنَ ﴿٢٧﴾
فَلَوْلَا نَصَرَهُمُ الَّذِيْنَ اتَّخَذُوْا مِنْ دُوْنِ اللّٰهِ
قُرْبَانًا اٰلِهَةً ۚ بَلْ ضَلُّوْا عَنْهُمْ ۚ وَذٰلِكَ اِفْكُهُمْ
وَمَا كَانُوْا يَفْتَرُوْنَ ﴿٢٨﴾
وَاِذْ صَرَفْنَاۤ اِلَيْكَ نَفَرًا مِّنَ الْجِنِّ يَسْتَمِعُوْنَ
الْقُرْاٰنَ ۚ فَلَمَّا حَضَرُوْهُ قَالُوْۤا اَنْصِتُوْا ۚ فَلَمَّا قُضِيَ
وَلَّوْا اِلٰى قَوْمِهِمْ مُّنْذِرِيْنَ ﴿٢٩﴾

30. They said: O our people! Lo! we have heard a Scripture which hath been revealed after Moses,[1] confirming that which was before it, guiding unto the truth and a right road.

قَالُوْا يٰقَوْمَنَآ اِنَّا سَمِعْنَا كِتٰبًا اُنْزِلَ مِنْ بَعْدِ مُوْسٰى
مُصَدِّقًا لِّمَا بَيْنَ يَدَيْهِ يَهْدِيْٓ اِلَى الْحَقِّ وَاِلٰى
طَرِيْقٍ مُّسْتَقِيْمٍ ﴿٣٠﴾

31. O our people! respond to Allah's summoner and believe in Him. He will forgive you some of your sins and guard you from a painful doom.

يٰقَوْمَنَآ اَجِيْبُوْا دَاعِيَ اللّٰهِ وَاٰمِنُوْا بِهٖ يَغْفِرْ لَكُمْ
مِّنْ ذُنُوْبِكُمْ وَيُجِرْكُمْ مِّنْ عَذَابٍ اَلِيْمٍ ﴿٣١﴾

32. And whoso respondeth not to Allah's summoner he can nowise escape in the earth, and ye (can find) no protecting friends instead of Him. Such are in error manifest.

وَمَنْ لَّا يُجِبْ دَاعِيَ اللّٰهِ فَلَيْسَ بِمُعْجِزٍ فِي
الْاَرْضِ وَلَيْسَ لَهٗ مِنْ دُوْنِهٖٓ اَوْلِيَآءُ اُولٰٓئِكَ فِيْ
ضَلٰلٍ مُّبِيْنٍ ﴿٣٢﴾

33. Have they not seen that Allah, Who created the heavens and the earth and was not wearied by their creation, is Able to give life to the dead? Aye, He verily is Able to do all things.

اَوَلَمْ يَرَوْا اَنَّ اللّٰهَ الَّذِيْ خَلَقَ السَّمٰوٰتِ وَالْاَرْضَ
وَلَمْ يَعْيَ بِخَلْقِهِنَّ بِقٰدِرٍ عَلٰٓى اَنْ يُّحْيِۦَ الْمَوْتٰى
بَلٰٓى اِنَّهٗ عَلٰى كُلِّ شَيْءٍ قَدِيْرٌ ﴿٣٣﴾

34. And on the day when those who disbelieve are exposed to the Fire (they will be asked). Is not this real? They will say: Yea, by our Lord. He will say: Then taste the doom for that ye disbelieved.

وَيَوْمَ يُعْرَضُ الَّذِيْنَ كَفَرُوْا عَلَى النَّارِ اَلَيْسَ
هٰذَا بِالْحَقِّ قَالُوْا بَلٰى وَرَبِّنَا قَالَ فَذُوْقُوا
الْعَذَابَ بِمَا كُنْتُمْ تَكْفُرُوْنَ ﴿٣٤﴾

35. Then have patience (O Muhammad) even as the stout of heart among the messengers (of old) had patience, and seek not to hasten on the doom for them. On the day when they see that which they are promised (it will seem to them) as though they had tarried but an hour of daylight. A clear message. Shall any be destroyed save evil-living folk?

فَاصْبِرْ كَمَا صَبَرَ اُولُوا الْعَزْمِ مِنَ الرُّسُلِ وَلَا
تَسْتَعْجِلْ لَّهُمْ كَاَنَّهُمْ يَوْمَ يَرَوْنَ مَا يُوْعَدُوْنَ لَمْ
يَلْبَثُوْٓا اِلَّا سَاعَةً مِّنْ نَّهَارٍ بَلٰغٌ فَهَلْ يُهْلَكُ
اِلَّا الْقَوْمُ الْفٰسِقُوْنَ ﴿٣٥﴾

1. From the mention of Moses it has been conjectured by some commentators that these Jinn were foreign (*i.e* non-Arabian) Jews, the word *Jinn* in old Arabic being often applied to clever foreigners.

Muḥammad. This Sūrah takes its name from the mention of the Prophet by name in v. 2. Most commentators agree that v. 18 was revealed when the Prophet, forced to flee from Mecca, looked back, weeping, for a last sight of his native city. Some have considered the whole Sūrah to be a Meccan revelation, but with no good reason.

It belongs to the first and second years after the Hijrah, with the exception of v. 18, which was revealed during the Hijrah.

MUHAMMAD

Revealed Al-Madinah

In the name of Allah, the Beneficent, the Merciful.

1. Those who disbelieve and turn (men) from the way of Allah, He rendereth their actions vain.

2. And those who believe and do good works and believe in that which is revealed unto Muhammad—and it is the truth from their Lord—He riddeth them of their ill-deeds and improveth their state.

3. That is because those who disbelieve follow falsehood and because those who believe follow the truth from their Lord. Thus Allah coineth their similitudes for mankind.

4. Now when ye meet in battle those who disbelieve, then it is smiting of the necks until, when ye have routed them, then making fast of bonds; and afterward either grace or ransom till the war lay down its burdens. That (is the ordinance). And if Allah willed He could have punished them (without you) but (thus it is ordained) that He may try some of you by means of others. And those who fought in the way of Allah, He rendereth not their actions vain.

5. He will guide them and improve their state,

6. And bring them in unto the Garden which He hath made known to them.

7. O ye who believe! If ye help Allah's cause, He will help you and will make your foothold firm.

8. And those who disbelieve, perdition is for them, and He will make their actions vain.

9. That is because they are averse to that which Allah hath revealed, therefor maketh He their actions fruitless.

ایاتها ٣٨ (٤٧) سُورَةُ مُحَمَّدٍ مَدَنِيَّةٌ رکوعاتها ٤

بِسْمِ اللّٰهِ الرَّحْمٰنِ الرَّحِيْمِ ○

اَلَّذِيْنَ كَفَرُوْا وَصَدُّوْا عَنْ سَبِيْلِ اللّٰهِ اَضَلَّ
اَعْمَالَهُمْ ①

وَالَّذِيْنَ اٰمَنُوْا وَعَمِلُوا الصّٰلِحٰتِ وَاٰمَنُوْا بِمَا
نُزِّلَ عَلٰى مُحَمَّدٍ وَّهُوَ الْحَقُّ مِنْ رَّبِّهِمْ كَفَّرَ
عَنْهُمْ سَيِّاٰتِهِمْ وَاَصْلَحَ بَالَهُمْ ②

ذٰلِكَ بِاَنَّ الَّذِيْنَ كَفَرُوا اتَّبَعُوا الْبَاطِلَ وَاَنَّ
الَّذِيْنَ اٰمَنُوا اتَّبَعُوا الْحَقَّ مِنْ رَّبِّهِمْ كَذٰلِكَ
يَضْرِبُ اللّٰهُ لِلنَّاسِ اَمْثَالَهُمْ ③

فَاِذَا لَقِيْتُمُ الَّذِيْنَ كَفَرُوْا فَضَرْبَ الرِّقَابِ حَتّٰى اِذَا
اَثْخَنْتُمُوْهُمْ فَشُدُّوا الْوَثَاقَ فَاِمَّا مَنًّا بَعْدُ وَاِمَّا
فِدَاءً حَتّٰى تَضَعَ الْحَرْبُ اَوْزَارَهَا ذٰلِكَ وَلَوْ يَشَاءُ
اللّٰهُ لَانْتَصَرَ مِنْهُمْ وَلٰكِنْ لِّيَبْلُوَا بَعْضَكُمْ بِبَعْضٍ وَ
الَّذِيْنَ قُتِلُوْا فِيْ سَبِيْلِ اللّٰهِ فَلَنْ يُّضِلَّ اَعْمَالَهُمْ ④
سَيَهْدِيْهِمْ وَيُصْلِحُ بَالَهُمْ ⑤

وَيُدْخِلُهُمُ الْجَنَّةَ عَرَّفَهَا لَهُمْ ⑥

يٰاَيُّهَا الَّذِيْنَ اٰمَنُوْا اِنْ تَنْصُرُوا اللّٰهَ يَنْصُرْكُمْ وَ
يُثَبِّتْ اَقْدَامَكُمْ ⑦

وَالَّذِيْنَ كَفَرُوْا فَتَعْسًا لَّهُمْ وَاَضَلَّ اَعْمَالَهُمْ ⑧

ذٰلِكَ بِاَنَّهُمْ كَرِهُوْا مَا اَنْزَلَ اللّٰهُ فَاَحْبَطَ اَعْمَالَهُمْ ⑨

رکوع ١٢ وقد يبتدأ بقوله ذلك ولكن حسن اتصاله بما قبله ويوقف على ذلك ١٢

10. Have they not travelled in the land to see the nature of the consequence for those who were before them? Allah wiped them out. And for the disbelievers there will be the like thereof.

11. That is because Allah is patron of those who believe, and because the disbelievers have no patron.

12. Lo! Allah will cause those who believe and do good works to enter Gardens underneath which rivers flow; while those who disbelieve take their comfort in this life and eat even as the cattle eat, and the Fire is their habitation.

13. And how many a township stronger than thy township (O Muhammad) which hath cast thee out, have We destroyed, and they had no helper!

14. Is he who relieth on a clear proof from his Lord like those for whom the evil that they do is beautified while they follow their own lusts?

15. A similitude of the Garden which those who keep their duty (to Allah) are promised: Therein are rivers of water unpolluted, and rivers of milk whereof the flavour changeth not, and rivers of wine delicious to the drinkers, and rivers of clear-run honey; therein for them is every kind of fruit, with pardon from their Lord. (Are those who enjoy all this) like those who are immortal in the Fire and are given boiling water to drink so that it teareth their bowels?

16. Among them are some who give ear unto thee (Muhammad) till, when they go forth from thy presence, they say unto those who have been given knowledge: What was that he said just now? Those are they whose hearts Allah hath sealed, and they follow their own lusts.

17. While as for those who walk aright, He addeth to their guidance, and giveth them their protection (against evil).

أَفَلَمْ يَسِيرُوا فِي الْأَرْضِ فَيَنظُرُوا كَيْفَ كَانَ عَاقِبَةُ
الَّذِينَ مِن قَبْلِهِمْ ۚ دَمَّرَ اللَّهُ عَلَيْهِمْ ۖ وَلِلْكَافِرِينَ أَمْثَالُهَا ﴿١٠﴾
ذَٰلِكَ بِأَنَّ اللَّهَ مَوْلَى الَّذِينَ آمَنُوا وَأَنَّ الْكَافِرِينَ
ع لَا مَوْلَىٰ لَهُمْ ﴿١١﴾
إِنَّ اللَّهَ يُدْخِلُ الَّذِينَ آمَنُوا وَعَمِلُوا الصَّالِحَاتِ جَنَّاتٍ
تَجْرِي مِن تَحْتِهَا الْأَنْهَارُ ۖ وَالَّذِينَ كَفَرُوا يَتَمَتَّعُونَ وَ
يَأْكُلُونَ كَمَا تَأْكُلُ الْأَنْعَامُ وَالنَّارُ مَثْوًى لَّهُمْ ﴿١٢﴾
وَكَأَيِّن مِّن قَرْيَةٍ هِيَ أَشَدُّ قُوَّةً مِّن قَرْيَتِكَ
الَّتِي أَخْرَجَتْكَ أَهْلَكْنَاهُمْ فَلَا نَاصِرَ لَهُمْ ﴿١٣﴾
أَفَمَن كَانَ عَلَىٰ بَيِّنَةٍ مِّن رَّبِّهِ كَمَن زُيِّنَ لَهُ سُوءُ
عَمَلِهِ وَاتَّبَعُوا أَهْوَاءَهُم ﴿١٤﴾
مَّثَلُ الْجَنَّةِ الَّتِي وُعِدَ الْمُتَّقُونَ ۖ فِيهَا أَنْهَارٌ مِّن
مَّاءٍ غَيْرِ آسِنٍ وَأَنْهَارٌ مِّن لَّبَنٍ لَّمْ يَتَغَيَّرْ طَعْمُهُ
وَأَنْهَارٌ مِّنْ خَمْرٍ لَّذَّةٍ لِّلشَّارِبِينَ وَأَنْهَارٌ مِّنْ
عَسَلٍ مُّصَفًّى ۖ وَلَهُمْ فِيهَا مِن كُلِّ الثَّمَرَاتِ وَ
مَغْفِرَةٌ مِّن رَّبِّهِمْ ۖ كَمَنْ هُوَ خَالِدٌ فِي النَّارِ وَ
سُقُوا مَاءً حَمِيمًا فَقَطَّعَ أَمْعَاءَهُمْ ﴿١٥﴾
وَمِنْهُم مَّن يَسْتَمِعُ إِلَيْكَ حَتَّىٰ إِذَا خَرَجُوا مِنْ
عِندِكَ قَالُوا لِلَّذِينَ أُوتُوا الْعِلْمَ مَاذَا قَالَ آنِفًا ۚ
أُولَٰئِكَ الَّذِينَ طَبَعَ اللَّهُ عَلَىٰ قُلُوبِهِمْ وَاتَّبَعُوا
أَهْوَاءَهُمْ ﴿١٦﴾
وَالَّذِينَ اهْتَدَوْا زَادَهُمْ هُدًى وَآتَاهُمْ تَقْوَاهُمْ ﴿١٧﴾

18. Await they aught save the Hour, that it should come upon them unawares? And the beginnings thereof have already come. But how, when it hath come upon them, can they take their warning?

19. So know (O Muhammad) that there is no God save Allah, and ask forgiveness for thy sin and for believing men and believing women. Allah knoweth (both) your place of turmoil and your place of rest.

20. And those who believe say: If only a Sūrah were revealed! But when a decisive Sūrah is revealed and war is mentioned therein, thou seest those in whose hearts is a disease looking at thee with the look of men fainting unto death. Therefor woe unto them!

21. Obedience and a civil word. Then, when the matter is determined, if they are loyal to Allah it will be well for them.

22. Would ye then, if ye were given the command, work corruption in the land and sever your ties of kinship?

23. Such are they whom Allah curseth so that he deafeneth them and maketh blind their eyes.

24. Will they then not meditate on the Qur'ān, or are there locks on the hearts?

25. Lo! those who turn back after the guidance hath been manifested unto them, Satan hath seduced them, and He giveth them the rein.

26. That is because they say unto those who hate what Allah hath revealed: We will obey you in some matters; and Allah knoweth their secret talk.

27. Then how (will it be with them) when the angels gather them, smiting their faces and their backs!

28. That will be because they followed that which angereth Allah, and hated that which pleaseth Him. Therefor He hath made their actions vain.

فهل ينظرون إلا الساعة أن تأتيهم بغتة فقد
جاء أشراطها فأنى لهم إذا جاءتهم ذكراهم ١٨
فاعلم أنه لا إله إلا الله واستغفر لذنبك وللمؤمنين
٢ ع ٦ والمؤمنات والله يعلم متقلبكم ومثواكم ١٩
ويقول الذين آمنوا لولا نزلت سورة فإذا
أنزلت سورة محكمة وذكر فيها القتال رأيت
الذين في قلوبهم مرض ينظرون إليك نظر
المغشي عليه من الموت فأولى لهم ٢٠
طاعة وقول معروف فإذا عزم الأمر فلو
صدقوا الله لكان خيرا لهم ٢١
فهل عسيتم إن توليتم أن تفسدوا في الأرض
وتقطعوا أرحامكم ٢٢
أولئك الذين لعنهم الله فأصمهم وأعمى أبصارهم ٢٣
أفلا يتدبرون القرآن أم على قلوب أقفالها ٢٤
إن الذين ارتدوا على أدبارهم من بعد ما تبين
لهم الهدى الشيطان سول لهم وأملى لهم ٢٥
ذلك بأنهم قالوا للذين كرهوا ما نزل الله سنطيعكم
في بعض الأمر والله يعلم إسرارهم ٢٦
فكيف إذا توفتهم الملائكة يضربون وجوههم
وأدبارهم ٢٧
ذلك بأنهم اتبعوا ما أسخط الله وكرهوا
٣ ع ٧ رضوانه فأحبط أعمالهم ٢٨

29. Or do those in whose hearts is a disease deem that Allah will not bring to light their (secret) hates?

30. And if We would, We could show them unto thee (Muhammad) so that thou shouldst know them surely by their marks. And thou shalt know them by the burden of their talk. And Allah knoweth your deeds.

31. And verily We shall try you till We know those of you who strive hard (for the cause of Allah) and the steadfast, and till We test your record.

32. Lo! those who disbelieve and turn from the way of Allah and oppose the messenger after the guidance hath been manifested unto them, they hurt Allah not a jot, and He will make their actions fruitless.

33. O ye who believe! Obey Allah and obey the messenger, and render not your actions vain.

34. Lo! those who disbelieve and turn from the way of Allah and then die disbelievers, Allah surely will not pardon them.

35. So do not falter and cry out for peace when ye (will be) the uppermost, and Allah is with you, and He will not grudge (the reward of) your actions.

36. The life of the world is but a sport and a pastime. And if ye believe and ward off (evil), He will give you your wages, and will not ask of you your worldly wealth.

37. If He should ask it of you and importune you, ye would hoard it, and He would bring to light your (secret) hates.

38. Lo! ye are those who are called to spend in the way of Allah, yet among you there are some who hoard. And as for him who hoardeth, he hoardeth only from his soul. And Allah is the Rich, and ye are the poor. And if ye turn away He will exchange you for some other folk, and they will not be the likes of you.

أَمْ حَسِبَ الَّذِينَ فِي قُلُوبِهِم مَّرَضٌ أَن لَّن يُخْرِجَ
اللَّهُ أَضْغَانَهُمْ ٢٩
وَلَوْ نَشَاءُ لَأَرَيْنَاكَهُمْ فَلَعَرَفْتَهُم بِسِيمَاهُمْ وَ
لَتَعْرِفَنَّهُمْ فِي لَحْنِ الْقَوْلِ وَاللَّهُ يَعْلَمُ أَعْمَالَكُمْ ٣٠
وَلَنَبْلُوَنَّكُمْ حَتَّىٰ نَعْلَمَ الْمُجَاهِدِينَ مِنكُمْ وَ
الصَّابِرِينَ وَنَبْلُوَ أَخْبَارَكُمْ ٣١
إِنَّ الَّذِينَ كَفَرُوا وَصَدُّوا عَن سَبِيلِ اللَّهِ وَ
شَاقُّوا الرَّسُولَ مِن بَعْدِ مَا تَبَيَّنَ لَهُمُ الْهُدَىٰ
لَن يَضُرُّوا اللَّهَ شَيْئًا وَسَيُحْبِطُ أَعْمَالَهُمْ ٣٢
يَا أَيُّهَا الَّذِينَ آمَنُوا أَطِيعُوا اللَّهَ وَأَطِيعُوا الرَّسُولَ
وَلَا تُبْطِلُوا أَعْمَالَكُمْ ٣٣
إِنَّ الَّذِينَ كَفَرُوا وَصَدُّوا عَن سَبِيلِ اللَّهِ ثُمَّ
مَاتُوا وَهُمْ كُفَّارٌ فَلَن يَغْفِرَ اللَّهُ لَهُمْ ٣٤
فَلَا تَهِنُوا وَتَدْعُوا إِلَى السَّلْمِ وَأَنتُمُ الْأَعْلَوْنَ
وَاللَّهُ مَعَكُمْ وَلَن يَتِرَكُمْ أَعْمَالَكُمْ ٣٥
إِنَّمَا الْحَيَاةُ الدُّنْيَا لَعِبٌ وَلَهْوٌ وَإِن تُؤْمِنُوا وَ
تَتَّقُوا يُؤْتِكُمْ أُجُورَكُمْ وَلَا يَسْأَلْكُمْ أَمْوَالَكُمْ ٣٦
إِن يَسْأَلْكُمُوهَا فَيُحْفِكُمْ تَبْخَلُوا وَيُخْرِجْ أَضْغَانَكُمْ ٣٧
هَا أَنتُمْ هَٰؤُلَاءِ تُدْعَوْنَ لِتُنفِقُوا فِي سَبِيلِ اللَّهِ فَمِنكُم
مَّن يَبْخَلُ وَمَن يَبْخَلْ فَإِنَّمَا يَبْخَلُ عَن نَّفْسِهِ وَ
اللَّهُ الْغَنِيُّ وَأَنتُمُ الْفُقَرَاءُ وَإِن تَتَوَلَّوْا يَسْتَبْدِلْ قَوْمًا
غَيْرَكُمْ ثُمَّ لَا يَكُونُوا أَمْثَالَكُمْ ٣٨

Al-Fatḥ takes its name from the word *Fatḥ* meaning "Victory" which occurs several times, and refers, not to the conquest of Mecca but to the truce of Al-Ḥudeybîyeh, which, though at the time it seemed a set-back to the Muslims, proved in fact the greatest victory for Al-Islām.

In the sixth year of the Hijrah, the Prophet set out with some 1400 Muslims from Al-Madînah and the country around, in the garb of pilgrims, not for war but to visit the Ka'bah. When they drew near Mecca, they were warned that Qureysh had gathered their allies against them, and that their cavalry under Khālid ibn Al-Walîd was on the road before them. Making a detour through gullies of the hills, they escaped the cavalry and, coming into he valley of Mecca, encamped at Al-Ḥudeybîyeh below the city. The Prophet resolutely refused to give battle and persisted in attempts to parley with Qureysh who had sworn not to let him reach the Ka'bah. The Muslims were all the while in a position of some danger. Finally Othmān ibn 'Affān was sent into the city, as the man most likely to be well received on account of his relationships. Othmān was detained by the Meccans, and news that he had been murdered reached the Muslims in their camp.[1]

It was then that the Prophet, sitting under a tree, took from his comrades the oath (referred to in v. 18) that they would hold together and fight to the death.[2] Then it became known that the rumour of Othmān's death was false, and Qureysh at length agreed to a truce of which the terms were favourable to them. The Prophet and his multitude were to give up the project of visiting the sanctuary for that year, but were to make the pilgrimage the following year when the idolaters undertook to evacuate Mecca for three days to allow them to do so. Fugitives from Qureysh to the Muslims were to be returned, but not fugitives from the Muslims to Qureysh; and there was to be no hostility between the parties for ten years.

"And there was never a victory," says Ibn Khaldûn, "greater than this victory; for, as Az-Zuhrî says, when it was war the people did not meet, but when the truce came and war laid down its burdens and people felt safe one with another, then they met and indulged in conversation and discussion. And no man spoke of Al-Islām to another but the latter espoused it, so that there entered Al-Islām in those two years (*i.e.*, between Al-Ḥudeybîyeh and the breaking of the truce by Qureysh) as many as all those who had entered it before, or more."[3]

The date of revelation is the sixth year of the Hijrah.

1. Ibn Hishām, Part II, pp. 176-178.
2. Ibn Hishām Part II, p. 179.
3. Ibn Khaldûn, *Tārīkh.* Supplement to Part II, II, *Būlāq* 1824 A.H. He follows Ibn Hishām.

VICTORY

Revealed at Al-Madīnah

In the name of Allah, the Beneficent, the Merciful.

1. Lo! We have given thee (O Muhammad) a signal victory,

2. That Allah may forgive thee of thy sin that which is past and that which is to come, and may perfect His favour unto thee, and may guide thee on a right path,

3. And that Allah may help thee with strong help—

4. He it is Who sent down peace of reassurance into the hearts of the believers that they might add faith unto their faith. Allah's are the hosts of the heavens and the earth, and Allah is ever Knower, Wise—

5. That He may bring the believing men and the believing women into Gardens underneath which rivers flow, wherein they will abide, and may remit from them their evil deeds—That, in the sight of Allah, is the Supreme triumph—

6. And may punish the hypocritical men and the hypocritical women, and the idolatrous men and the idolatrous women, who think an evil thought concerning Allah. For them is the evil turn of fortune, and Allah is wroth against them and hath cursed them, and hath made ready for them hell, a hapless journey's end.

7. Allah's are the hosts of the heavens and the earth, and Allah is ever Mighty, Wise.

8. Lo! We have sent thee (O Muhammad) as a witness and a bearer of good tidings and a warner,

اٰيَاتُهَا (٤٨) سُوْرَةُ الْفَتْحِ مَدَنِيَّةٌ رُكُوْعَاتُهَا

بِسْمِ اللّٰهِ الرَّحْمٰنِ الرَّحِيْمِ

اِنَّا فَتَحْنَا لَكَ فَتْحًا مُّبِيْنًا ﴿١﴾

لِّيَغْفِرَ لَكَ اللّٰهُ مَا تَقَدَّمَ مِنْ ذَنْۢبِكَ وَمَا تَاَخَّرَ وَيُتِمَّ نِعْمَتَهٗ عَلَيْكَ وَيَهْدِيَكَ صِرَاطًا مُّسْتَقِيْمًا ﴿٢﴾

وَّيَنْصُرَكَ اللّٰهُ نَصْرًا عَزِيْزًا ﴿٣﴾

هُوَ الَّذِيْٓ اَنْزَلَ السَّكِيْنَةَ فِيْ قُلُوْبِ الْمُؤْمِنِيْنَ لِيَزْدَادُوْٓا اِيْمَانًا مَّعَ اِيْمَانِهِمْ ؕ وَلِلّٰهِ جُنُوْدُ السَّمٰوٰتِ وَالْاَرْضِ ؕ وَكَانَ اللّٰهُ عَلِيْمًا حَكِيْمًا ﴿٤﴾

لِّيُدْخِلَ الْمُؤْمِنِيْنَ وَالْمُؤْمِنٰتِ جَنّٰتٍ تَجْرِيْ مِنْ تَحْتِهَا الْاَنْهٰرُ خٰلِدِيْنَ فِيْهَا وَيُكَفِّرَ عَنْهُمْ سَيِّاٰتِهِمْ ؕ وَكَانَ ذٰلِكَ عِنْدَ اللّٰهِ فَوْزًا عَظِيْمًا ﴿٥﴾

وَّيُعَذِّبَ الْمُنٰفِقِيْنَ وَالْمُنٰفِقٰتِ وَالْمُشْرِكِيْنَ وَالْمُشْرِكٰتِ الظَّآنِّيْنَ بِاللّٰهِ ظَنَّ السَّوْءِ ؕ عَلَيْهِمْ دَآئِرَةُ السَّوْءِ ۚ وَغَضِبَ اللّٰهُ عَلَيْهِمْ وَلَعَنَهُمْ وَاَعَدَّ لَهُمْ جَهَنَّمَ ؕ وَسَآءَتْ مَصِيْرًا ﴿٦﴾

وَلِلّٰهِ جُنُوْدُ السَّمٰوٰتِ وَالْاَرْضِ ؕ وَكَانَ اللّٰهُ عَزِيْزًا حَكِيْمًا ﴿٧﴾

اِنَّآ اَرْسَلْنٰكَ شَاهِدًا وَّمُبَشِّرًا وَّنَذِيْرًا ﴿٨﴾

9. That ye (mankind) may believe in Allah and His messenger, and may honour Him, and may revere Him, and may glorify Him at early dawn and at the close of day.

10. Lo! those who swear allegiance unto thee (Muhammad), swear allegiance only unto Allah. The Hand of Allah is above their hands. So whosoever breaketh his oath, breaketh it only to his soul's hurt; while whosoever keepeth his covenant with Allah, on him will He bestow immense reward.

11. Those of the wandering Arabs who were left behind will tell thee: Our possessions and our households occupied us, so ask forgiveness for us! They speak with their tongues that which is not in their hearts. Say: Who can avail you aught against Allah, if he intend you hurt or intend you profit? Nay, but Allah is ever Aware of what ye do.

12. Nay, but ye deemed that the messenger and the believers would never return to their own folk, and that was made fair-seeming in your hearts, and ye did think an evil thought, and ye were worthless folk.

13. And as for him who believeth not in Allah and His messenger—Lo! We have prepared a flame for disbelievers.

14. And Allah's is the Sovereignty of the heavens and the earth. He forgiveth whom He will, and punisheth whom He will. And Allah is ever Forgiving, Merciful.

لِتُؤْمِنُوْا بِاللّٰهِ وَرَسُوْلِهٖ وَتُعَزِّرُوْهُ وَتُوَقِّرُوْهُ ؕ وَ
تُسَبِّحُوْهُ بُكْرَةً وَّاَصِيْلًا ﴿٩﴾
اِنَّ الَّذِيْنَ يُبَايِعُوْنَكَ اِنَّمَا يُبَايِعُوْنَ اللّٰهَ ؕ
يَدُ اللّٰهِ فَوْقَ اَيْدِيْهِمْ ۚ فَمَنْ نَّكَثَ
فَاِنَّمَا يَنْكُثُ عَلٰى نَفْسِهٖ ۚ وَمَنْ اَوْفٰى
بِمَا عٰهَدَ عَلَيْهُ اللّٰهَ فَسَيُؤْتِيْهِ اَجْرًا
عَظِيْمًا ﴿١٠﴾ ع
سَيَقُوْلُ لَكَ الْمُخَلَّفُوْنَ مِنَ الْاَعْرَابِ شَغَلَتْنَآ
اَمْوَالُنَا وَاَهْلُوْنَا فَاسْتَغْفِرْ لَنَا ۚ يَقُوْلُوْنَ
بِاَلْسِنَتِهِمْ مَّا لَيْسَ فِيْ قُلُوْبِهِمْ ؕ قُلْ فَمَنْ
يَّمْلِكُ لَكُمْ مِّنَ اللّٰهِ شَيْئًا اِنْ اَرَادَ بِكُمْ ضَرًّا
اَوْ اَرَادَ بِكُمْ نَفْعًا ؕ بَلْ كَانَ اللّٰهُ بِمَا تَعْمَلُوْنَ
خَبِيْرًا ﴿١١﴾
بَلْ ظَنَنْتُمْ اَنْ لَّنْ يَّنْقَلِبَ الرَّسُوْلُ وَ
الْمُؤْمِنُوْنَ اِلٰٓى اَهْلِيْهِمْ اَبَدًا وَّزُيِّنَ ذٰلِكَ
فِيْ قُلُوْبِكُمْ وَظَنَنْتُمْ ظَنَّ السَّوْءِ ۖۚ وَكُنْتُمْ
قَوْمًا بُوْرًا ﴿١٢﴾
وَمَنْ لَّمْ يُؤْمِنْ بِاللّٰهِ وَرَسُوْلِهٖ فَاِنَّآ اَعْتَدْنَا
لِلْكٰفِرِيْنَ سَعِيْرًا ﴿١٣﴾
وَلِلّٰهِ مُلْكُ السَّمٰوٰتِ وَالْاَرْضِ ؕ يَغْفِرُ لِمَنْ
يَّشَآءُ وَيُعَذِّبُ مَنْ يَّشَآءُ ؕ وَكَانَ اللّٰهُ غَفُوْرًا
رَّحِيْمًا ﴿١٤﴾

15. Those who were left behind will say, when ye set forth to capture booty: Let us go with you. They fain would change the verdict of Allah. Say (unto them, O Muhammad): Ye shall not go with us. Thus hath Allah said beforehand. Then they will say: Ye are envious of us. Nay, but they understand not, save a little.

سيقول المخلفون إذا انطلقتم إلى مغانم
لتأخذوها ذرونا نتبعكم يريدون أن يبدلوا
كلم الله قل لن تتبعونا كذلكم قال الله
من قبل فسيقولون بل تحسدوننا بل
كانوا لا يفقهون إلا قليلا ١٥

16. Say unto those of the wandering Arabs who were left behind: Ye will be called against a folk of mighty prowess,[1] to fight them until they surrender; and if ye obey, Allah will give you a fair reward; but if ye turn away as ye did turn away before, He will punish you with a painful doom.

قل للمخلفين من الأعراب ستدعون إلى
قوم أولي بأس شديد تقاتلونهم أو يسلمون
فإن تطيعوا يؤتكم الله أجرا حسنا وإن
تتولوا كما توليتم من قبل يعذبكم عذابا
أليما ١٦

17. There is no blame for the blind, nor is there blame for the lame, nor is there blame for the sick (that they go not forth to war). And whoso obeyeth Allah and His messenger, He will make him enter Gardens underneath which rivers flow; and whoso turneth back, him will He punish with a painful doom.

ليس على الأعمى حرج ولا على الأعرج
حرج ولا على المريض حرج ومن يطع الله
ورسوله يدخله جنت تجري من تحتها
الأنهر ومن يتول يعذبه عذابا أليما ١٧

18. Allah was well pleased with the believers when they swore allegiance unto thee beneath the tree, and He knew what was in their hearts, and He sent down peace of reassurance on them, and hath rewarded them with a near victory:

لقد رضي الله عن المؤمنين إذ يبايعونك
تحت الشجرة فعلم ما في قلوبهم فأنزل
السكينة عليهم وأثابهم فتحا قريبا ١٨

19. And much booty that they will capture. Allah is ever Mighty, Wise.

ومغانم كثيرة يأخذونها وكان الله عزيزا
حكيما ١٩

20. Allah promiseth you much booty that ye will capture, and hath given you this in advance, and hath withheld men's hands from you, that it may be a token for the believers, and that He may guide you on a right path:

وعدكم الله مغانم كثيرة تأخذونها فعجل
لكم هذه وكف أيدي الناس عنكم ولتكون
آية للمؤمنين ويهديكم صراطا مستقيما ٢٠

1. This prophecy is taken to refer to the war with the Persian or the Byzantine empire.

21. And other (gain), which ye have not been able to achieve, Allah will compass it. Allah is Able to do all things.

وَأُخْرَىٰ لَمْ تَقْدِرُوا عَلَيْهَا قَدْ أَحَاطَ اللَّهُ بِهَا ۚ
وَكَانَ اللَّهُ عَلَىٰ كُلِّ شَيْءٍ قَدِيرًا ﴿٢١﴾

22. And if those who disbelieve join battle with you they will take to flight, and afterward they will find no protecting friend nor helper.

وَلَوْ قَاتَلَكُمُ الَّذِينَ كَفَرُوا لَوَلَّوُا الْأَدْبَارَ ثُمَّ لَا
يَجِدُونَ وَلِيًّا وَلَا نَصِيرًا ﴿٢٢﴾

23. It is the law of Allah which hath taken course aforetime. Thou wilt not find for the law of Allah aught of power to change.

سُنَّةَ اللَّهِ الَّتِي قَدْ خَلَتْ مِنْ قَبْلُ ۖ وَلَنْ تَجِدَ
لِسُنَّةِ اللَّهِ تَبْدِيلًا ﴿٢٣﴾

24. And He it is Who hath withheld men's hands from you, and hath withheld your hands from them, in the valley of Mecca, after He had made you victors over them. Allah is Seer of what ye do.

وَهُوَ الَّذِي كَفَّ أَيْدِيَهُمْ عَنْكُمْ وَأَيْدِيَكُمْ
عَنْهُمْ بِبَطْنِ مَكَّةَ مِنْ بَعْدِ أَنْ
أَظْفَرَكُمْ عَلَيْهِمْ ۚ وَكَانَ اللَّهُ بِمَا تَعْمَلُونَ
بَصِيرًا ﴿٢٤﴾

25. These it was who disbelieved and debarred you from the Inviolable Place of Worship, and debarred the offering from reaching its goal. And if it had not been for believing men and believing women, whom ye know not—lest ye should tread them underfoot and thus incur guilt for them unknowingly; that Allah might bring into His mercy whom He will—If (the believers and the disbelievers) had been clearly separated We verily had punished those of them who disbelieved with painful punishment.

هُمُ الَّذِينَ كَفَرُوا وَصَدُّوكُمْ عَنِ الْمَسْجِدِ
الْحَرَامِ وَالْهَدْيَ مَعْكُوفًا أَنْ يَبْلُغَ مَحِلَّهُ ۚ وَلَوْ
لَا رِجَالٌ مُؤْمِنُونَ وَنِسَاءٌ مُؤْمِنَاتٌ لَمْ تَعْلَمُوهُمْ
أَنْ تَطَئُوهُمْ فَتُصِيبَكُمْ مِنْهُمْ مَعَرَّةٌ بِغَيْرِ
عِلْمٍ ۖ لِيُدْخِلَ اللَّهُ فِي رَحْمَتِهِ مَنْ يَشَاءُ ۚ
لَوْ تَزَيَّلُوا لَعَذَّبْنَا الَّذِينَ كَفَرُوا مِنْهُمْ
عَذَابًا أَلِيمًا ﴿٢٥﴾

26. When those who disbelieve had set up in their hearts zealotry, the zealotry of the Age of Ignorance, then Allah sent down His peace of reassurance upon His messenger and upon the believers and imposed on them the word of self-restraint, for they were worthy of it and meet for it. And Allah is Aware of all things.

إِذْ جَعَلَ الَّذِينَ كَفَرُوا فِي قُلُوبِهِمُ الْحَمِيَّةَ
حَمِيَّةَ الْجَاهِلِيَّةِ فَأَنْزَلَ اللَّهُ سَكِينَتَهُ عَلَىٰ
رَسُولِهِ وَعَلَى الْمُؤْمِنِينَ وَأَلْزَمَهُمْ كَلِمَةَ التَّقْوَىٰ
وَكَانُوا أَحَقَّ بِهَا وَأَهْلَهَا ۚ وَكَانَ اللَّهُ بِكُلِّ
شَيْءٍ عَلِيمًا ﴿٢٦﴾ ع ٣

27. Allah hath fulfilled the vision[1] for His messenger in very truth. Ye shall indeed enter the Inviolable Place of Worship, if Allah will, secure, (having your hair) shaven and cut, not fearing. But He knoweth that which ye know not, and hath given you a near victory beforehand.

لَقَدْ صَدَقَ اللّٰهُ رَسُوْلَهُ الرُّءْيَا بِالْحَقِّ لَتَدْخُلُنَّ
الْمَسْجِدَ الْحَرَامَ اِنْ شَآءَ اللّٰهُ اٰمِنِيْنَ مُحَلِّقِيْنَ
رُءُوْسَكُمْ وَمُقَصِّرِيْنَ لَا تَخَافُوْنَ فَعَلِمَ مَا لَمْ
تَعْلَمُوْا فَجَعَلَ مِنْ دُوْنِ ذٰلِكَ فَتْحًا قَرِيْبًا ﴿٢٧﴾

28. He it is Who hath sent His messenger with the guidance and the religion of Truth, that He may cause it to prevail over all religion. And Allah sufficeth as a witness.

هُوَ الَّذِيْٓ اَرْسَلَ رَسُوْلَهُ بِالْهُدٰى وَدِيْنِ
الْحَقِّ لِيُظْهِرَهُ عَلَى الدِّيْنِ كُلِّهٖ وَكَفٰى بِاللّٰهِ
شَهِيْدًا ﴿٢٨﴾

29. Muhammad is the messenger of Allah. And those with him are hard against the disbelievers and merciful among themselves. Thou (O Muhammad) seest them bowing and falling prostrate (in worship), seeking bounty from Allah and (His) acceptance. The mark of them is on their foreheads from the traces of prostration. Such is their likeness in the Torah and their likeness in the Gospel—like as sown corn that sendeth forth its shoot and strengtheneth it and riseth firm upon its stalk, delighting the sowers—that He may enrage the disbelievers with (the sight of) them. Allah hath promised, unto such of them as believe and do good works, forgiveness and immense reward.

مُحَمَّدٌ رَّسُوْلُ اللّٰهِ وَالَّذِيْنَ مَعَهٗٓ اَشِدَّآءُ عَلَى
الْكُفَّارِ رُحَمَآءُ بَيْنَهُمْ تَرٰىهُمْ رُكَّعًا سُجَّدًا يَّبْتَغُوْنَ
فَضْلًا مِّنَ اللّٰهِ وَرِضْوَانًا سِيْمَاهُمْ فِيْ وُجُوْهِهِمْ
مِّنْ اَثَرِ السُّجُوْدِ ذٰلِكَ مَثَلُهُمْ فِي التَّوْرٰىةِ
وَمَثَلُهُمْ فِي الْاِنْجِيْلِ كَزَرْعٍ اَخْرَجَ شَطْئَهٗ
فَاٰزَرَهٗ فَاسْتَغْلَظَ فَاسْتَوٰى عَلٰى سُوْقِهٖ يُعْجِبُ
الزُّرَّاعَ لِيَغِيْظَ بِهِمُ الْكُفَّارَ وَعَدَ اللّٰهُ الَّذِيْنَ
اٰمَنُوْا وَعَمِلُوا الصّٰلِحٰتِ مِنْهُمْ مَّغْفِرَةً
ع وَّاَجْرًا عَظِيْمًا ﴿٢٩﴾

1. The Prophet had had a vision that he was entering the Sanctuary at Mecca in peace and safety.

Al-Hujurāt takes its name from v. 4, which, with the following verse, is said to refer to the behaviour of a deputation at a time when deputations from all parts of Arabia were coming to Al-Madīnah to profess allegiance to the Prophet. The whole Sūrah, dealing as it does with manners, and particularly with behaviour toward the Prophet, evidently belongs to a period when there were many seeking audience, among them many who were quite uncivilised.

The date of revelation is the ninth year of the Hijrah, "the year of deputations," as it is called.

THE PRIVATE APARTMENTS

Revealed at Al-Madīnah

In the name of Allah, the Beneficent, the Merciful.

1. O ye who believe! Be not forward in the presence of Allah and His messenger, and keep your duty to Allah. Lo! Allah is Hearer, Knower.

2. O ye who believe! Lift not up your voices above the voice of the Prophet, nor shout when speaking to him as ye shout one to another, lest your works be rendered vain while ye perceive not.

3. Lo! they who subdue their voices in the presence of the messenger of Allah, those are they whose hearts Allah hath proven unto righteousness. Theirs will be forgiveness and immense reward.

4. Lo! those who call thee from behind the private apartments, most of them have no sense.

5. And if they had had patience till thou camest forth unto them, it had been better for them. And Allah is Forgiving, Merciful.

6. O ye who believe! If an evil-liver bring you tidings,[1] verify it, lest ye smite some folk in ignorance and afterward repent of what ye did.

7. And know that the messenger of Allah is among you. If he were to obey you in much of the government, ye would surely be in trouble; but Allah hath endeared the faith to you and hath beautified it in your hearts, and hath made disbelief and lewdness and rebellion hateful unto you. Such are they who are rightly guided:

اٰيَاتُهَا ١٨ (٤٩) سُوْرَةُ الْحُجُرٰتِ مَدَنِيَّةٌ رُكُوْعَاتُهَا ٢

بِسْمِ اللّٰهِ الرَّحْمٰنِ الرَّحِيْمِ

يٰٓاَيُّهَا الَّذِيْنَ اٰمَنُوْا لَا تُقَدِّمُوْا بَيْنَ يَدَيِ اللّٰهِ
وَرَسُوْلِهٖ وَاتَّقُوا اللّٰهَ ؕ اِنَّ اللّٰهَ سَمِيْعٌ عَلِيْمٌ ﴿١﴾
يٰٓاَيُّهَا الَّذِيْنَ اٰمَنُوْا لَا تَرْفَعُوْٓا اَصْوَاتَكُمْ فَوْقَ صَوْتِ
النَّبِيِّ وَلَا تَجْهَرُوْا لَهٗ بِالْقَوْلِ كَجَهْرِ بَعْضِكُمْ
لِبَعْضٍ اَنْ تَحْبَطَ اَعْمَالُكُمْ وَاَنْتُمْ لَا تَشْعُرُوْنَ ﴿٢﴾
اِنَّ الَّذِيْنَ يَغُضُّوْنَ اَصْوَاتَهُمْ عِنْدَ رَسُوْلِ اللّٰهِ
اُولٰٓئِكَ الَّذِيْنَ امْتَحَنَ اللّٰهُ قُلُوْبَهُمْ لِلتَّقْوٰى ؕ
لَهُمْ مَّغْفِرَةٌ وَّاَجْرٌ عَظِيْمٌ ﴿٣﴾
اِنَّ الَّذِيْنَ يُنَادُوْنَكَ مِنْ وَّرَآءِ الْحُجُرٰتِ
اَكْثَرُهُمْ لَا يَعْقِلُوْنَ ﴿٤﴾
وَلَوْ اَنَّهُمْ صَبَرُوْا حَتّٰى تَخْرُجَ اِلَيْهِمْ لَكَانَ
خَيْرًا لَّهُمْ ؕ وَاللّٰهُ غَفُوْرٌ رَّحِيْمٌ ﴿٥﴾
يٰٓاَيُّهَا الَّذِيْنَ اٰمَنُوْٓا اِنْ جَآءَكُمْ فَاسِقٌۢ بِنَبَاٍ
فَتَبَيَّنُوْٓا اَنْ تُصِيْبُوْا قَوْمًاۢ بِجَهَالَةٍ فَتُصْبِحُوْا
عَلٰى مَا فَعَلْتُمْ نٰدِمِيْنَ ﴿٦﴾
وَاعْلَمُوْٓا اَنَّ فِيْكُمْ رَسُوْلَ اللّٰهِ ؕ لَوْ يُطِيْعُكُمْ فِيْ كَثِيْرٍ
مِّنَ الْاَمْرِ لَعَنِتُّمْ وَلٰكِنَّ اللّٰهَ حَبَّبَ اِلَيْكُمُ الْاِيْمَانَ
وَزَيَّنَهٗ فِيْ قُلُوْبِكُمْ وَكَرَّهَ اِلَيْكُمُ الْكُفْرَ وَالْفُسُوْقَ
وَالْعِصْيَانَ ؕ اُولٰٓئِكَ هُمُ الرّٰشِدُوْنَ ﴿٧﴾

1. The reference is to a man who brought false news of a revolt of the subject Jews at Kheyber.

8. (It is) a bounty and a grace from Allah; and Allah is Knower, Wise.

9. And if two parties of believers fall to fighting, then make peace between them. And if one party of them doth wrong to the other, fight ye that which doth wrong till it return unto the ordinance of Allah; then, if it return, make peace between them justly, and act equitably. Lo! Allah loveth the equitable.

10. The believers are naught else than brothers. Therefore make peace between your brethren and observe your duty to Allah that haply ye may obtain mercy.

11. O ye who believe! Let not a folk deride a folk who may be better than they (are), nor let women (deride) women who may be better than they are; neither defame one another, nor insult one another by nicknames. Bad is the name of lewdness after faith. And whoso turneth not in repentance, such are evil-doers.

12. O ye who believe! Shun much suspicion; for lo! some suspicion is a sin. And spy not, neither backbite one another. Would one of you love to eat the flesh of his dead brother? Ye abhor that (so abhor the other)! And keep your duty (to Allah). Lo! Allah is Relenting, Merciful.

13. O mankind! Lo! We have created you male and female, and have made you nations and tribes that ye may know one another. Lo! the noblest of you, in the sight of Allah, is the best in conduct. Lo! Allah is Knower, Aware.

فَضْلًا مِّنَ اللّٰهِ وَنِعْمَةً ۚ وَاللّٰهُ عَلِيْمٌ حَكِيْمٌ ۝

وَاِنْ طَآئِفَتٰنِ مِنَ الْمُؤْمِنِيْنَ اقْتَتَلُوْا فَاَصْلِحُوْا بَيْنَهُمَا ۚ فَاِنْۢ بَغَتْ اِحْدٰىهُمَا عَلَى الْاُخْرٰى فَقَاتِلُوا الَّتِيْ تَبْغِيْ حَتّٰى تَفِيْٓءَ اِلٰٓى اَمْرِ اللّٰهِ ۚ فَاِنْ فَآءَتْ فَاَصْلِحُوْا بَيْنَهُمَا بِالْعَدْلِ وَاَقْسِطُوْا ۚ اِنَّ اللّٰهَ يُحِبُّ الْمُقْسِطِيْنَ ۝

اِنَّمَا الْمُؤْمِنُوْنَ اِخْوَةٌ فَاَصْلِحُوْا بَيْنَ اَخَوَيْكُمْ وَاتَّقُوا اللّٰهَ لَعَلَّكُمْ تُرْحَمُوْنَ ۝

يٰٓاَيُّهَا الَّذِيْنَ اٰمَنُوْا لَا يَسْخَرْ قَوْمٌ مِّنْ قَوْمٍ عَسٰٓى اَنْ يَّكُوْنُوْا خَيْرًا مِّنْهُمْ وَلَا نِسَآءٌ مِّنْ نِّسَآءٍ عَسٰٓى اَنْ يَّكُنَّ خَيْرًا مِّنْهُنَّ ۚ وَلَا تَلْمِزُوْٓا اَنْفُسَكُمْ وَلَا تَنَابَزُوْا بِالْاَلْقَابِ ۚ بِئْسَ الِاسْمُ الْفُسُوْقُ بَعْدَ الْاِيْمَانِ ۚ وَمَنْ لَّمْ يَتُبْ فَاُولٰٓئِكَ هُمُ الظّٰلِمُوْنَ ۝

يٰٓاَيُّهَا الَّذِيْنَ اٰمَنُوا اجْتَنِبُوْا كَثِيْرًا مِّنَ الظَّنِّ ۖ اِنَّ بَعْضَ الظَّنِّ اِثْمٌ ۖ وَّلَا تَجَسَّسُوْا وَلَا يَغْتَبْ بَّعْضُكُمْ بَعْضًا ۚ اَيُحِبُّ اَحَدُكُمْ اَنْ يَّأْكُلَ لَحْمَ اَخِيْهِ مَيْتًا فَكَرِهْتُمُوْهُ ۚ وَاتَّقُوا اللّٰهَ ۚ اِنَّ اللّٰهَ تَوَّابٌ رَّحِيْمٌ ۝

يٰٓاَيُّهَا النَّاسُ اِنَّا خَلَقْنٰكُمْ مِّنْ ذَكَرٍ وَّاُنْثٰى وَجَعَلْنٰكُمْ شُعُوْبًا وَّقَبَآئِلَ لِتَعَارَفُوْا ۚ اِنَّ اَكْرَمَكُمْ عِنْدَ اللّٰهِ اَتْقٰىكُمْ ۚ اِنَّ اللّٰهَ عَلِيْمٌ خَبِيْرٌ ۝

14. The wandering Arabs say: We believe. Say (unto them, O Muhammad): Ye believe not, but rather say "We submit," for the faith hath not yet entered into your hearts. Yet, if ye obey Allah and His messenger, He will not withhold from you aught of (the reward of) your deeds. Lo! Allah is Forgiving, Merciful.

15. The (true) believers are those only who believe in Allah and His messenger and afterward doubt not, but strive with their wealth and their lives for the cause of Allah. Such are the sincere.

16. Say (unto them, O Muhammad): Would ye teach Allah your religion, when Allah knoweth all that is in the heavens and all that is in the earth, and Allah is Aware of all things?

17. They make it a favour unto thee (Muhammad) that they have surrendered (unto Him). Say: Deem not your Surrender a favour unto me; nay, but Allah doth confer a favour on you, inasmuch as He hath led you to the Faith, if ye are earnest.

18. Lo! Allah knoweth the Unseen of the heavens and the earth. And Allah is Seer of what ye do.

قَالَتِ الْأَعْرَابُ آمَنَّا ۖ قُلْ لَّمْ تُؤْمِنُوا وَلٰكِنْ قُولُوْٓا
أَسْلَمْنَا وَلَمَّا يَدْخُلِ الْإِيْمَانُ فِيْ قُلُوْبِكُمْ ۖ وَإِنْ
تُطِيْعُوا اللّٰهَ وَرَسُوْلَهٗ لَا يَلِتْكُمْ مِّنْ أَعْمَالِكُمْ شَيْـًٔا ۚ
إِنَّ اللّٰهَ غَفُوْرٌ رَّحِيْمٌ ﴿١٤﴾
إِنَّمَا الْمُؤْمِنُوْنَ الَّذِيْنَ اٰمَنُوْا بِاللّٰهِ وَرَسُوْلِهٖ ثُمَّ
لَمْ يَرْتَابُوْا وَجٰهَدُوْا بِأَمْوَالِهِمْ وَأَنْفُسِهِمْ فِيْ
سَبِيْلِ اللّٰهِ ۚ أُولٰٓئِكَ هُمُ الصّٰدِقُوْنَ ﴿١٥﴾
قُلْ أَتُعَلِّمُوْنَ اللّٰهَ بِدِيْنِكُمْ ۚ وَاللّٰهُ يَعْلَمُ مَا
فِي السَّمٰوٰتِ وَمَا فِي الْأَرْضِ ۚ وَاللّٰهُ بِكُلِّ شَيْءٍ
عَلِيْمٌ ﴿١٦﴾
يَمُنُّوْنَ عَلَيْكَ أَنْ أَسْلَمُوْا ۖ قُلْ لَّا تَمُنُّوْا عَلَيَّ
إِسْلَامَكُمْ ۚ بَلِ اللّٰهُ يَمُنُّ عَلَيْكُمْ أَنْ هَدٰىكُمْ
لِلْإِيْمَانِ إِنْ كُنْتُمْ صٰدِقِيْنَ ﴿١٧﴾
إِنَّ اللّٰهَ يَعْلَمُ غَيْبَ السَّمٰوٰتِ وَالْأَرْضِ ۚ وَاللّٰهُ
ع ١٤ بَصِيْرٌ بِمَا تَعْمَلُوْنَ ﴿١٨﴾

Takes its name from the letter of the Arabic alphabet which stands alone at the beginning of the first verse

It belongs to the middle group of Meccan Sūrahs.

QĀF

Revealed at Mecca

In the name of Allah, the Beneficent, the Merciful.

1. Qāf. By the glorious Qur'ān,

2. Nay, but they marvel that a warner of their own hath come unto them; and the disbelievers say: This a strange thing:

3. When we are dead and have become dust (shall we be brought back again)? That would be a far return!

4. We know that which the earth taketh of them[1], and with Us is a recording Book.

5. Nay, but they have denied the truth when it came unto them, therefor they are now in troubled case.

6. Have they not then observed the sky above them, how We have constructed it and beautified it, and how there are no rifts therein!

7. And the earth have We spread out, and have flung firm hills therein, and have caused of every lovely kind to grow thereon,

8. A vision and a reminder for every penitent slave.

9. And We send down from the sky blessed water whereby We give growth unto gardens and the grain of crops,

10. And lofty date-palms with ranged clusters,

11. Provision (made) for men; and therewith We quicken a dead land. Even so will be the resurrection of the dead.

12. The folk of Noah denied (the truth) before them, and (so did) the dwellers at Ar-Rass and (the tribe of) Thamūd,

13. And (the tribe of) 'Aād, and Pharaoh, and the brethren of Lot,

اياتها (٥٠) سورة ق مكية ركوعاتها

بسم الله الرحمن الرحيم

ق والقرآن المجيد ١

بل عجبوا أن جاءهم منذر منهم فقال
الكافرون هذا شيء عجيب ٢

أإذا متنا وكنا ترابا ذلك رجع بعيد ٣

قد علمنا ما تنقص الأرض منهم وعندنا
كتاب حفيظ ٤

بل كذبوا بالحق لما جاءهم فهم في أمر مريج ٥

أفلم ينظروا إلى السماء فوقهم كيف بنيناها و
زيناها وما لها من فروج ٦

والأرض مددناها وألقينا فيها رواسي وأنبتنا
فيها من كل زوج بهيج ٧

تبصرة وذكرى لكل عبد منيب ٨

ونزلنا من السماء ماء مباركا فأنبتنا به جنات
وحب الحصيد ٩

والنخل باسقات لها طلع نضيد ١٠

رزقا للعباد وأحيينا به بلدة ميتا كذلك
الخروج ١١

كذبت قبلهم قوم نوح وأصحاب الرس وثمود ١٢

وعاد وفرعون وإخوان لوط ١٣

1. *i.e.* those of them who die and are buried in the earth.

14. And the dwellers in the wood,[1] and the folk of Tubb'a:[2] every one denied their messengers, therefor My threat took effect.

15. Were We then worn out by the first creation? Yet they are in doubt about a new creation.

16. We verily created a man and We know what his soul whispereth to him and We are nearer to him than his jugular vein.

17. When the two Receivers receive (him), seated on the right hand and on the left,

18. He uttereth no word but there is with him an observer ready.

19. And the agony of death cometh in truth. (And it is said unto him): This is that which thou wast wont to shun.

20. And the trumpet is blown. This is the threatened Day.

21. And every soul cometh, along with it a driver and a witness

22. (And unto the evil-doer it is said): Thou wast in heedlessness of this. Now We have removed from thee thy covering, and piercing is thy sight this day.

23. And (unto the evil-doer) his comrade saith: This is that which I have ready (as testimony).

24. (And it is said): Do ye twain[3] hurl to hell each rebel ingrate,

25. Hinderer of good, transgressor, doubter,

26. Who setteth up another god along with Allah. Do ye twain hurl him to the dreadful doom.

27. His comrade saith: Our Lord! I did not cause him to rebel, but he was (himself) far gone in error.

28. He saith: Contend not in My presence, when I had already proffered unto you the warning.

29. The sentence that cometh from Me cannot be changed, and I am in no wise a tyrant unto the slaves.

وَّأَصْحٰبُ الْأَيْكَةِ وَقَوْمُ تُبَّعٍ ۚ كُلٌّ كَذَّبَ الرُّسُلَ
فَحَقَّ وَعِيدِ ﴿١٤﴾
أَفَعَيِينَا بِالْخَلْقِ الْأَوَّلِ ۚ بَلْ هُمْ فِي لَبْسٍ مِّنْ
خَلْقٍ جَدِيدٍ ﴿١٥﴾
وَلَقَدْ خَلَقْنَا الْإِنسٰنَ وَنَعْلَمُ مَا تُوَسْوِسُ بِهِ
نَفْسُهُ ۖ وَنَحْنُ أَقْرَبُ إِلَيْهِ مِنْ حَبْلِ الْوَرِيدِ ﴿١٦﴾
إِذْ يَتَلَقَّى الْمُتَلَقِّيٰنِ عَنِ الْيَمِينِ وَعَنِ الشِّمَالِ قَعِيدٌ ﴿١٧﴾
مَا يَلْفِظُ مِن قَوْلٍ إِلَّا لَدَيْهِ رَقِيبٌ عَتِيدٌ ﴿١٨﴾
وَجَاءَتْ سَكْرَةُ الْمَوْتِ بِالْحَقِّ ۖ ذٰلِكَ مَا كُنتَ
مِنْهُ تَحِيدُ ﴿١٩﴾
وَنُفِخَ فِي الصُّورِ ۚ ذٰلِكَ يَوْمُ الْوَعِيدِ ﴿٢٠﴾
وَجَاءَتْ كُلُّ نَفْسٍ مَّعَهَا سَائِقٌ وَشَهِيدٌ ﴿٢١﴾
لَقَدْ كُنتَ فِي غَفْلَةٍ مِّنْ هٰذَا فَكَشَفْنَا عَنكَ
غِطَاءَكَ فَبَصَرُكَ الْيَوْمَ حَدِيدٌ ﴿٢٢﴾
وَقَالَ قَرِينُهُ هٰذَا مَا لَدَيَّ عَتِيدٌ ﴿٢٣﴾
أَلْقِيَا فِي جَهَنَّمَ كُلَّ كَفَّارٍ عَنِيدٍ ﴿٢٤﴾
مَّنَّاعٍ لِّلْخَيْرِ مُعْتَدٍ مُّرِيبٍ ﴿٢٥﴾
الَّذِي جَعَلَ مَعَ اللَّهِ إِلٰهًا آخَرَ فَأَلْقِيَاهُ فِي
الْعَذَابِ الشَّدِيدِ ﴿٢٦﴾
قَالَ قَرِينُهُ رَبَّنَا مَا أَطْغَيْتُهُ وَلٰكِن كَانَ فِي ضَلٰلٍ بَعِيدٍ ﴿٢٧﴾
قَالَ لَا تَخْتَصِمُوا لَدَيَّ وَقَدْ قَدَّمْتُ إِلَيْكُم بِالْوَعِيدِ ﴿٢٨﴾
مَا يُبَدَّلُ الْقَوْلُ لَدَيَّ وَمَا أَنَا بِظَلّٰمٍ لِّلْعَبِيدِ ﴿٢٩﴾

1. Midian.
2. The name of a famous dynasty in Al-Yaman.
3. The driver and the witness (v. 21) or the two Receivers (v. 17).

30. On the day when We say unto hell: Art thou filled? and it saith: Can there be more to come?

31. And the Garden is brought nigh for those who kept from evil, no longer distant.

32. (And it is said): That is that which ye were promised. (It is) for every penitent and heedful one,

33. Who feareth the Beneficent in secret and cometh with a contrite heart.

34. Enter it in peace. This is the day of Immortality.

35. There they have all that they desire, and there is more with Us.

36. And how many a generation We destroyed before them, who were mightier than these in prowess so that they overran the lands! Had they any place of refuge (when the judgement came)?

37. Lo! therein verily is a reminder for him who hath a heart, or giveth ear with full intelligence.

38. And verily We created the heavens and the earth, and all that is between them, in six Days,[1] and naught of weariness touched Us.

39. Therefor (O Muhammad) bear with what they say, and hymn the praise of thy Lord before the rising and before the setting of the sun;

40. And in the night-time hymn His praise, and after the (prescribed) prostrations.

41. And listen on the day when the crier crieth from a near place,

42. The day when they will hear the (Awful) Cry in truth. That is the day of coming forth (from the graves).

43. Lo! We it is Who quicken and give death, and unto Us is the journeying.

44. On the day when the earth splitteth asunder from them, hastening forth (they come). That is a gathering easy for Us (to make).

45. We are best aware of what they say, and thou (O Muhammad) art in no wise a compeller over them. But warn by the Qur'ān him who feareth My threat.

يَوْمَ نَقُولُ لِجَهَنَّمَ هَلِ امْتَلَأْتِ وَتَقُولُ هَلْ
مِن مَّزِيدٍ ٣٠
وَأُزْلِفَتِ الْجَنَّةُ لِلْمُتَّقِينَ غَيْرَ بَعِيدٍ ٣١
هَٰذَا مَا تُوعَدُونَ لِكُلِّ أَوَّابٍ حَفِيظٍ ٣٢
مَّنْ خَشِيَ الرَّحْمَٰنَ بِالْغَيْبِ وَجَاءَ بِقَلْبٍ مُّنِيبٍ ٣٣
ادْخُلُوهَا بِسَلَامٍ ذَٰلِكَ يَوْمُ الْخُلُودِ ٣٤
لَهُم مَّا يَشَاءُونَ فِيهَا وَلَدَيْنَا مَزِيدٌ ٣٥
وَكَمْ أَهْلَكْنَا قَبْلَهُم مِّن قَرْنٍ هُمْ أَشَدُّ مِنْهُم
بَطْشًا فَنَقَّبُوا فِي الْبِلَادِ هَلْ مِن مَّحِيصٍ ٣٦
إِنَّ فِي ذَٰلِكَ لَذِكْرَىٰ لِمَن كَانَ لَهُ قَلْبٌ أَوْ أَلْقَى
السَّمْعَ وَهُوَ شَهِيدٌ ٣٧
وَلَقَدْ خَلَقْنَا السَّمَاوَاتِ وَالْأَرْضَ وَمَا بَيْنَهُمَا فِي
سِتَّةِ أَيَّامٍ وَمَا مَسَّنَا مِن لُّغُوبٍ ٣٨
فَاصْبِرْ عَلَىٰ مَا يَقُولُونَ وَسَبِّحْ بِحَمْدِ رَبِّكَ قَبْلَ
طُلُوعِ الشَّمْسِ وَقَبْلَ الْغُرُوبِ ٣٩
وَمِنَ اللَّيْلِ فَسَبِّحْهُ وَأَدْبَارَ السُّجُودِ ٤٠
وَاسْتَمِعْ يَوْمَ يُنَادِ الْمُنَادِ مِن مَّكَانٍ قَرِيبٍ ٤١
يَوْمَ يَسْمَعُونَ الصَّيْحَةَ بِالْحَقِّ ذَٰلِكَ يَوْمُ الْخُرُوجِ ٤٢
إِنَّا نَحْنُ نُحْيِي وَنُمِيتُ وَإِلَيْنَا الْمَصِيرُ ٤٣
يَوْمَ تَشَقَّقُ الْأَرْضُ عَنْهُمْ سِرَاعًا ذَٰلِكَ حَشْرٌ عَلَيْنَا يَسِيرٌ ٤٤
نَّحْنُ أَعْلَمُ بِمَا يَقُولُونَ وَمَا أَنتَ عَلَيْهِم بِجَبَّارٍ
فَذَكِّرْ بِالْقُرْآنِ مَن يَخَافُ وَعِيدِ ٤٥

1. XXII, 47: XXXII, 5: LXX, 4.

Adh-Dhāriyāt, "The Winnowing Winds," takes its name from a word in V. 1. I have followed the usual interpretation of the first four verses, but they may also be taken as all referring to winds or to angels.

An early Meccan Sūrah.

THE WINNOWING WINDS

Revealed at Mecca

In the name of Allah, the Beneficent, the Merciful.

1. By those that winnow with a winnowing

2. And those that bear the burden (of the rain)

3. And those that glide with ease (upon the sea)

4. And those who distribute (blessings) by command,

5. Lo! that wherewith ye are threatened is indeed true,

6. And lo! the judgement will indeed befall.

7. By the heaven full of paths,

8. Lo! ye, forsooth, are of various opinion (concerning the truth).

9. He is made to turn away from it who is (himself) averse.

10. Accursed be the conjecturers

11. Who are careless in an abyss!

12. They ask: When is the Day of Judgement?

13. (It is) the day when they will be tormented at the Fire,

14. (And it will be said unto them): Taste your torment (which ye inflicted). This is what ye sought to hasten.

15. Lo! those who keep from evil will dwell amid gardens and watersprings,

16. Taking that which their Lord giveth them; for lo! aforetime they were doers of good;

17. They used to sleep but little of the night,

18. And ere the dawning of each day would seek forgiveness,

اياتها (٥١) سُوْرَةُ الذّٰرِيٰتِ مَكِّيَّةٌ رُكُوْعَاتُهَا ٣

بِسْمِ اللّٰهِ الرَّحْمٰنِ الرَّحِيْمِ ○

وَالذّٰرِيٰتِ ذَرْوًا ﴿١﴾

فَالْحٰمِلٰتِ وِقْرًا ﴿٢﴾

فَالْجٰرِيٰتِ يُسْرًا ﴿٣﴾

فَالْمُقَسِّمٰتِ اَمْرًا ﴿٤﴾

اِنَّمَا تُوْعَدُوْنَ لَصَادِقٌ ﴿٥﴾

وَّاِنَّ الدِّيْنَ لَوَاقِعٌ ﴿٦﴾

وَالسَّمَآءِ ذَاتِ الْحُبُكِ ﴿٧﴾

اِنَّكُمْ لَفِيْ قَوْلٍ مُّخْتَلِفٍ ﴿٨﴾

يُّؤْفَكُ عَنْهُ مَنْ اُفِكَ ﴿٩﴾

قُتِلَ الْخَرّٰصُوْنَ ﴿١٠﴾

الَّذِيْنَ هُمْ فِيْ غَمْرَةٍ سَاهُوْنَ ﴿١١﴾

يَسْـَٔلُوْنَ اَيَّانَ يَوْمُ الدِّيْنِ ﴿١٢﴾

يَوْمَ هُمْ عَلَى النَّارِ يُفْتَنُوْنَ ﴿١٣﴾

ذُوْقُوْا فِتْنَتَكُمْ هٰذَا الَّذِيْ كُنْتُمْ بِهٖ تَسْتَعْجِلُوْنَ ﴿١٤﴾

اِنَّ الْمُتَّقِيْنَ فِيْ جَنّٰتٍ وَّعُيُوْنٍ ﴿١٥﴾

اٰخِذِيْنَ مَآ اٰتٰىهُمْ رَبُّهُمْ اِنَّهُمْ كَانُوْا قَبْلَ ذٰلِكَ مُحْسِنِيْنَ ﴿١٦﴾

كَانُوْا قَلِيْلًا مِّنَ الَّيْلِ مَا يَهْجَعُوْنَ ﴿١٧﴾

وَبِالْاَسْحَارِ هُمْ يَسْتَغْفِرُوْنَ ﴿١٨﴾

19. And in their wealth the beggar and the outcast had due share.

20. And in the earth are portents for those whose faith is sure,

21. And (also) in yourselves. Can ye then not see?

22. And in the heaven is your providence and that which ye are promised;

23. And by the Lord of the heaven and the earth, it is the truth, even as (it is true) that ye speak.

24. Hath the story of Abraham's honored guests reached thee (O Muhammad)?

25. When they came in unto him and said: Peace! he answered, Peace! (and thought): Folk unknown (to me).

26. Then he went apart unto his housefolk so that they brought a fatted calf;

27. And he set it before them, saying: Will ye not eat?

28. Then he conceived a fear of them. They said: Fear not! and gave him tidings of (the birth of) a wise son.

29. Then his wife came forward, making moan, and smote her face, and cried: A barren old woman!

30. They said: Even so saith thy Lord. Lo! He is the Wise, the Knower.

31. (Abraham) said: And (afterward) what is your errand, O ye sent (from Allah)?

32. They said: Lo! we are sent unto a guilty folk,

33. That we may send upon them stones of clay,

34. Marked by thy Lord for (the destruction of) the wanton.

35. Then We brought forth such believers as were there.

وَفِيٓ اَمْوَالِهِمْ حَقٌّ لِّلسَّآئِلِ وَالْمَحْرُوْمِ ﴿١٩﴾

وَفِي الْاَرْضِ اٰيٰتٌ لِّلْمُوْقِنِيْنَ ﴿٢٠﴾

وَفِيٓ اَنْفُسِكُمْ اَفَلَا تُبْصِرُوْنَ ﴿٢١﴾

وَفِي السَّمَآءِ رِزْقُكُمْ وَمَا تُوْعَدُوْنَ ﴿٢٢﴾

فَوَرَبِّ السَّمَآءِ وَالْاَرْضِ اِنَّهٗ لَحَقٌّ مِّثْلَ مَآ
اَنَّكُمْ تَنْطِقُوْنَ ﴿٢٣﴾

هَلْ اَتٰىكَ حَدِيْثُ ضَيْفِ اِبْرٰهِيْمَ الْمُكْرَمِيْنَ ﴿٢٤﴾

اِذْ دَخَلُوْا عَلَيْهِ فَقَالُوْا سَلٰمًا قَالَ سَلٰمٌ قَوْمٌ
مُّنْكَرُوْنَ ﴿٢٥﴾

فَرَاغَ اِلٰٓى اَهْلِهٖ فَجَآءَ بِعِجْلٍ سَمِيْنٍ ﴿٢٦﴾

فَقَرَّبَهٗٓ اِلَيْهِمْ قَالَ اَلَا تَاْكُلُوْنَ ﴿٢٧﴾

فَاَوْجَسَ مِنْهُمْ خِيْفَةً قَالُوْا لَا تَخَفْ وَبَشَّرُوْهُ
بِغُلٰمٍ عَلِيْمٍ ﴿٢٨﴾

فَاَقْبَلَتِ امْرَاَتُهٗ فِيْ صَرَّةٍ فَصَكَّتْ وَجْهَهَا وَقَالَتْ
عَجُوْزٌ عَقِيْمٌ ﴿٢٩﴾

قَالُوْا كَذٰلِكِ قَالَ رَبُّكِ اِنَّهٗ هُوَ الْحَكِيْمُ
الْعَلِيْمُ ﴿٣٠﴾

قَالَ فَمَا خَطْبُكُمْ اَيُّهَا الْمُرْسَلُوْنَ ﴿٣١﴾

قَالُوْٓا اِنَّآ اُرْسِلْنَآ اِلٰى قَوْمٍ مُّجْرِمِيْنَ ﴿٣٢﴾

لِنُرْسِلَ عَلَيْهِمْ حِجَارَةً مِّنْ طِيْنٍ ﴿٣٣﴾

مُّسَوَّمَةً عِنْدَ رَبِّكَ لِلْمُسْرِفِيْنَ ﴿٣٤﴾

فَاَخْرَجْنَا مَنْ كَانَ فِيْهَا مِنَ الْمُؤْمِنِيْنَ ﴿٣٥﴾

36. But We found there but one house of those surrendered[1] (to Allah).

37. And We left behind therein a portent for those who fear a painful doom.

38. And in Moses (too, there is a portent) when We sent him unto Pharaoh with clear warrant,

39. But he withdrew (confiding) in his might, and said: A wizard or a madman!

40. So We seized him and his hosts and flung them in the sea, for he was reprobate.

41. And in (the tribe of) 'Aād (there is a portent) when We sent the fatal wind against them.

42. It spared naught that it reached, but made it (all) as dust.

43. And in (the tribe of) Thamūd (there is a portent) when it was told them: Take your ease awhile.

44. But they rebelled against their Lord's decree, and so the thunderbolt overtook them even while they gazed;

45. And they were unable to rise up, nor could they help themselves:

46. And the folk of Noah aforetime. Lo! they were licentious folk.

47. We have built the heaven with might, and We it is who make the vast extent (thereof).

48. And the earth have We laid out, how gracious is the Spreader (thereof)!

49. And all things We have created by pairs, that haply ye may reflect.

فَمَا وَجَدْنَا فِيهَا غَيْرَ بَيْتٍ مِّنَ الْمُسْلِمِينَ ﴿٣٦﴾
وَتَرَكْنَا فِيهَا آيَةً لِّلَّذِينَ يَخَافُونَ الْعَذَابَ
الْأَلِيمَ ﴿٣٧﴾
وَفِي مُوسَىٰ إِذْ أَرْسَلْنَاهُ إِلَىٰ فِرْعَوْنَ بِسُلْطَانٍ
مُّبِينٍ ﴿٣٨﴾
فَتَوَلَّىٰ بِرُكْنِهِ وَقَالَ سَاحِرٌ أَوْ مَجْنُونٌ ﴿٣٩﴾
فَأَخَذْنَاهُ وَجُنُودَهُ فَنَبَذْنَاهُمْ فِي الْيَمِّ وَهُوَ
مُلِيمٌ ﴿٤٠﴾
وَفِي عَادٍ إِذْ أَرْسَلْنَا عَلَيْهِمُ الرِّيحَ الْعَقِيمَ ﴿٤١﴾
مَا تَذَرُ مِن شَيْءٍ أَتَتْ عَلَيْهِ إِلَّا جَعَلَتْهُ
كَالرَّمِيمِ ﴿٤٢﴾
وَفِي ثَمُودَ إِذْ قِيلَ لَهُمْ تَمَتَّعُوا حَتَّىٰ حِينٍ ﴿٤٣﴾
فَعَتَوْا عَنْ أَمْرِ رَبِّهِمْ فَأَخَذَتْهُمُ الصَّاعِقَةُ وَهُمْ
يَنظُرُونَ ﴿٤٤﴾
فَمَا اسْتَطَاعُوا مِن قِيَامٍ وَمَا كَانُوا
مُنتَصِرِينَ ﴿٤٥﴾
وَقَوْمَ نُوحٍ مِّن قَبْلُ إِنَّهُمْ كَانُوا قَوْمًا
فَاسِقِينَ ﴿٤٦﴾ ع ٢
وَالسَّمَاءَ بَنَيْنَاهَا بِأَيْدٍ وَإِنَّا لَمُوسِعُونَ ﴿٤٧﴾
وَالْأَرْضَ فَرَشْنَاهَا فَنِعْمَ الْمَاهِدُونَ ﴿٤٨﴾
وَمِن كُلِّ شَيْءٍ خَلَقْنَا زَوْجَيْنِ لَعَلَّكُمْ
تَذَكَّرُونَ ﴿٤٩﴾

1. Ar. *Muslimīn.*

50. Therefor flee unto Allah; lo! I[1] am a plain warner unto you from Him

فَفِرُّوٓا إِلَى اللّٰهِ ۖ إِنِّي لَكُم مِّنْهُ نَذِيرٌ مُّبِينٌ ﴿٥٠﴾

51. And set not any other God along with Allah; lo! I am a plain warner unto you from Him.

وَلَا تَجْعَلُوا مَعَ اللّٰهِ إِلٰهًا اٰخَرَ ۖ إِنِّي لَكُم مِّنْهُ نَذِيرٌ مُّبِينٌ ﴿٥١﴾

52. Even so there came no messenger unto those before them but they said: A wizard or a madman!

كَذٰلِكَ مَا أَتَى الَّذِينَ مِن قَبْلِهِم مِّن رَّسُولٍ إِلَّا قَالُوا سَاحِرٌ أَوْ مَجْنُونٌ ﴿٥٢﴾

53. Have they handed down (the saying as an heirloom one unto another? Nay, but they are froward folk.

أَتَوَاصَوْا بِهِ ۚ بَلْ هُمْ قَوْمٌ طَاغُونَ ﴿٥٣﴾

54. So withdraw from them (O Muhammad), for thou art in no wise blameworthy,

فَتَوَلَّ عَنْهُمْ فَمَا أَنتَ بِمَلُومٍ ﴿٥٤﴾

55. And warn, for warning profiteth believers.

وَذَكِّرْ فَإِنَّ الذِّكْرٰى تَنفَعُ الْمُؤْمِنِينَ ﴿٥٥﴾

56. I created the jinn and humankind only that they might worship Me.

وَمَا خَلَقْتُ الْجِنَّ وَالْإِنسَ إِلَّا لِيَعْبُدُونِ ﴿٥٦﴾

57. I seek no livelihood from them, nor do I ask that they should feed Me.

مَا أُرِيدُ مِنْهُم مِّن رِّزْقٍ وَمَا أُرِيدُ أَن يُطْعِمُونِ ﴿٥٧﴾

58. Lo! Allah! He it is that giveth livelihood, the Lord of Unbreakable might.

إِنَّ اللّٰهَ هُوَ الرَّزَّاقُ ذُو الْقُوَّةِ الْمَتِينُ ﴿٥٨﴾

59. And lo! for those who (now) do wrong there is an evil day like unto the evil day (which came for) their likes (of old); so let them not ask Me to hasten on (that day).

فَإِنَّ لِلَّذِينَ ظَلَمُوا ذَنُوبًا مِّثْلَ ذَنُوبِ أَصْحٰبِهِمْ فَلَا يَسْتَعْجِلُونِ ﴿٥٩﴾

60. And woe unto those who disbelieve from (that) their day which they are promised.

فَوَيْلٌ لِّلَّذِينَ كَفَرُوا مِن يَوْمِهِمُ الَّذِي يُوعَدُونَ ﴿٦٠﴾

1. The revealing angel, it would appear.

At-Tūr, "The Mount," takes name from the opening verse.

An early Meccan Sūrah.

THE MOUNT

Revelated at Makkah

In the name of Allah, the Beneficent, the Merciful.

1. By the mount.

2. And a Scripture inscribed.

3. On fine parchment unrolled.

4. And the House frequented.

5. And the roof exalted.

6. And the sea kept filled.

7. Lo! the doom of thy Lord will surely come to pass;

8. There is none that can ward it off.

9. On the day when the heaven will heave with (awful) heaving.

10. And the mountains move away with (awful) movement.

11. Then woe that day unto the deniers.

12. Who play in talk of grave matters:

13. The day when they are thrust with a (disdainful) thrust, into the fire of hell.

14. (And it is said unto them); this is the Fire which ye were wont to deny.

15. Is this magic, or do ye not see?

16. Endure the heat thereof, and whether ye are patient of it or impatient of it is all one for you. Ye are only being paid for what ye used to do.

17. Lo! those who kept their duty dwell in gardens and delight.

18. Happy because of what their Lord hath given them, and (because) their Lord hath warded off from them the torment of hell-fire.

اٰياتها ٤٩ (٥٢) سُوْرَةُ الطُّوْرِ مَكِّيَّةٌ رُكُوْعَاتُهَا ٢

بِسْمِ اللّٰهِ الرَّحْمٰنِ الرَّحِيْمِ

وَالطُّوْرِ ﴿١﴾
وَكِتٰبٍ مَّسْطُوْرٍ ﴿٢﴾
فِيْ رَقٍّ مَّنْشُوْرٍ ﴿٣﴾
وَّالْبَيْتِ الْمَعْمُوْرِ ﴿٤﴾
وَالسَّقْفِ الْمَرْفُوْعِ ﴿٥﴾
وَالْبَحْرِ الْمَسْجُوْرِ ﴿٦﴾
اِنَّ عَذَابَ رَبِّكَ لَوَاقِعٌ ﴿٧﴾
مَّا لَهٗ مِنْ دَافِعٍ ﴿٨﴾
يَّوْمَ تَمُوْرُ السَّمَآءُ مَوْرًا ﴿٩﴾
وَّتَسِيْرُ الْجِبَالُ سَيْرًا ﴿١٠﴾
فَوَيْلٌ يَّوْمَئِذٍ لِّلْمُكَذِّبِيْنَ ﴿١١﴾
الَّذِيْنَ هُمْ فِيْ خَوْضٍ يَّلْعَبُوْنَ ﴿١٢﴾
يَوْمَ يُدَعُّوْنَ اِلٰى نَارِ جَهَنَّمَ دَعًّا ﴿١٣﴾
هٰذِهِ النَّارُ الَّتِيْ كُنْتُمْ بِهَا تُكَذِّبُوْنَ ﴿١٤﴾
اَفَسِحْرٌ هٰذَآ اَمْ اَنْتُمْ لَا تُبْصِرُوْنَ ﴿١٥﴾
اِصْلَوْهَا فَاصْبِرُوْٓا اَوْ لَا تَصْبِرُوْا سَوَآءٌ عَلَيْكُمْ
اِنَّمَا تُجْزَوْنَ مَا كُنْتُمْ تَعْمَلُوْنَ ﴿١٦﴾
اِنَّ الْمُتَّقِيْنَ فِيْ جَنّٰتٍ وَّنَعِيْمٍ ﴿١٧﴾
فٰكِهِيْنَ بِمَآ اٰتٰهُمْ رَبُّهُمْ وَوَقٰهُمْ رَبُّهُمْ عَذَابَ الْجَحِيْمِ ﴿١٨﴾

19. (And it is said unto them): Eat and drink in health (as reward) for what ye used to do,

20. Reclining on ranged couches. And We wed them unto fair ones with wide, lovely eyes.

21. And they who believe and whose seed follow them in faith, We cause their seed to join them (there), and We deprive them of naught of their (life's) work. Every man is a pledge for that which he hath earned.

22. And We provide them with fruit and meat such as they desire.

23. There they pass from hand to hand a cup wherein is neither vanity nor cause of sin.

24. And there go round, waiting on them menservants of their own, as they were hidden pearls.

25. And some of them draw near unto others, questioning:

26. Saying: Lo! of old, when we were with our families, we were ever anxious;

27. But Allah hath been gracious unto us and hath preserved us from the torment of the breath of Fire.

28. Lo! we used to pray unto Him of old. Lo! He is the Benign, the Merciful.

29. Therefor warn (men, O Muhammad). By the grace of Allah thou art neither soothsayer nor madman.

30. Or say they: (he is), a poet, (one) for whom we may expect the accident of time?

31. Say (unto them): Expect (your fill)! Lo! I am with you among the expectant.

32. Do their minds command them to do this, or are they an outrageous folk?

33. Or say they: He hath invented it? Nay, but they will not believe!

34. Then let them produce speech the like thereof, if they are truthful.

35. Or were they created out of naught? Or are they the creators?

كُلُوا وَاشْرَبُوا هَنِيٓـًٔا بِمَا كُنْتُمْ تَعْمَلُونَ ﴿١٩﴾
مُتَّكِـِٔينَ عَلٰى سُرُرٍ مَّصْفُوفَةٍ وَزَوَّجْنٰهُمْ بِحُورٍ
عِينٍ ﴿٢٠﴾
وَالَّذِينَ اٰمَنُوا وَاتَّبَعَتْهُمْ ذُرِّيَّتُهُمْ بِإِيمَانٍ اَلْحَقْنَا
بِهِمْ ذُرِّيَّتَهُمْ وَمَآ اَلَتْنٰهُمْ مِّنْ عَمَلِهِمْ مِّنْ
شَيْءٍ كُلُّ امْرِئٍ بِمَا كَسَبَ رَهِينٌ ﴿٢١﴾
وَاَمْدَدْنٰهُمْ بِفَاكِهَةٍ وَّلَحْمٍ مِّمَّا يَشْتَهُونَ ﴿٢٢﴾
يَتَنَازَعُونَ فِيهَا كَاْسًا لَّا لَغْوٌ فِيهَا وَلَا تَاْثِيمٌ ﴿٢٣﴾
وَيَطُوفُ عَلَيْهِمْ غِلْمَانٌ لَّهُمْ كَاَنَّهُمْ لُؤْلُؤٌ
مَّكْنُونٌ ﴿٢٤﴾
وَاَقْبَلَ بَعْضُهُمْ عَلٰى بَعْضٍ يَّتَسَآءَلُونَ ﴿٢٥﴾
قَالُوٓا اِنَّا كُنَّا قَبْلُ فِيٓ اَهْلِنَا مُشْفِقِينَ ﴿٢٦﴾
فَمَنَّ اللّٰهُ عَلَيْنَا وَوَقٰىنَا عَذَابَ السَّمُومِ ﴿٢٧﴾
اِنَّا كُنَّا مِنْ قَبْلُ نَدْعُوهُ اِنَّهُ هُوَ الْبَرُّ الرَّحِيمُ ﴿٢٨﴾ ع
فَذَكِّرْ فَمَآ اَنْتَ بِنِعْمَتِ رَبِّكَ بِكَاهِنٍ وَّلَا مَجْنُونٍ ﴿٢٩﴾
اَمْ يَقُولُونَ شَاعِرٌ نَّتَرَبَّصُ بِهٖ رَيْبَ الْمَنُونِ ﴿٣٠﴾
قُلْ تَرَبَّصُوا فَاِنِّي مَعَكُمْ مِّنَ الْمُتَرَبِّصِينَ ﴿٣١﴾
اَمْ تَاْمُرُهُمْ اَحْلَامُهُمْ بِهٰذَآ اَمْ هُمْ قَوْمٌ
طَاغُونَ ﴿٣٢﴾
اَمْ يَقُولُونَ تَقَوَّلَهٗ بَلْ لَّا يُؤْمِنُونَ ﴿٣٣﴾
فَلْيَاْتُوا بِحَدِيثٍ مِّثْلِهٖٓ اِنْ كَانُوا صٰدِقِينَ ﴿٣٤﴾
اَمْ خُلِقُوا مِنْ غَيْرِ شَيْءٍ اَمْ هُمُ الْخٰلِقُونَ ﴿٣٥﴾

36. Or did they create the heavens and the earth? Nay, but they are sure of nothing!

37. Or do they own the treasures of thy Lord? Or have they been given charge (thereof)?

38. Or have they any stairway (unto heaven) by means of which they overhear (decrees)? Then let their listeners produce some warrant manifest!

39. Or hath He daughters whereas ye have sons?

40. Or askest thou (Muhammad) a fee from them so that they are plunged in debt?

41. Or possess they the Unseen so that they can write (it) down?

42. Or seek they to ensnare (the messenger)? But those who disbelieve, they are the ensnared!

43. Or have they any god beside Allah? Glorified be Allah from all that they ascribe as partner (unto Him)!

44. And if they were to see a fragment of the heaven falling, they would say: A heap of clouds!

45. Then let them be (O Muhammad), till they meet their day, in which they will be thunder-stricken,—

46. A day in which their guile will naught avail them, nor will they be helped.

47. And verily, for those who do wrong, there is a punishment beyond that. But most of them know not.

48. So wait patiently (O Muhammad) for thy Lord's decree, for surely thou art in Our sight; and hymn the praise of thy Lord when thou uprisest,

49. And in the night-time also hymn His praise, and at the setting of the stars.

اَمْ خَلَقُوا السَّمٰوٰتِ وَالْاَرْضَ ۚ بَلْ لَّا يُوْقِنُوْنَ ﴿٣٦﴾

اَمْ عِنْدَهُمْ خَزَآئِنُ رَبِّكَ اَمْ هُمُ الْمُصَيْطِرُوْنَ ﴿٣٧﴾

اَمْ لَهُمْ سُلَّمٌ يَّسْتَمِعُوْنَ فِيْهِ ۚ فَلْيَاْتِ مُسْتَمِعُهُمْ

بِسُلْطٰنٍ مُّبِيْنٍ ﴿٣٨﴾

اَمْ لَهُ الْبَنٰتُ وَلَكُمُ الْبَنُوْنَ ﴿٣٩﴾

اَمْ تَسْـَٔلُهُمْ اَجْرًا فَهُمْ مِّنْ مَّغْرَمٍ مُّثْقَلُوْنَ ﴿٤٠﴾

اَمْ عِنْدَهُمُ الْغَيْبُ فَهُمْ يَكْتُبُوْنَ ﴿٤١﴾

اَمْ يُرِيْدُوْنَ كَيْدًا ۚ فَالَّذِيْنَ كَفَرُوْا هُمُ الْمَكِيْدُوْنَ ﴿٤٢﴾

اَمْ لَهُمْ اِلٰهٌ غَيْرُ اللّٰهِ ۚ سُبْحٰنَ اللّٰهِ عَمَّا يُشْرِكُوْنَ ﴿٤٣﴾

وَاِنْ يَّرَوْا كِسْفًا مِّنَ السَّمَآءِ سَاقِطًا يَّقُوْلُوْا

سَحَابٌ مَّرْكُوْمٌ ﴿٤٤﴾

فَذَرْهُمْ حَتّٰى يُلٰقُوْا يَوْمَهُمُ الَّذِيْ فِيْهِ

يُصْعَقُوْنَ ﴿٤٥﴾

يَوْمَ لَا يُغْنِيْ عَنْهُمْ كَيْدُهُمْ شَيْـًٔا وَّلَا هُمْ

يُنْصَرُوْنَ ﴿٤٦﴾

وَاِنَّ لِلَّذِيْنَ ظَلَمُوْا عَذَابًا دُوْنَ ذٰلِكَ وَلٰكِنَّ

اَكْثَرَهُمْ لَا يَعْلَمُوْنَ ﴿٤٧﴾

وَاصْبِرْ لِحُكْمِ رَبِّكَ فَاِنَّكَ بِاَعْيُنِنَا وَسَبِّحْ

بِحَمْدِ رَبِّكَ حِيْنَ تَقُوْمُ ﴿٤٨﴾

وَمِنَ الَّيْلِ فَسَبِّحْهُ وَاِدْبَارَ النُّجُوْمِ ﴿٤٩﴾ ع

An-Najm, "The Star," takes its name from a word in the first verse.

An early Meccan Sūrah.

THE STAR

Revealed at Makkah

In the name of Allah, the Beneficent the Merciful.

1. By the Star when it setteth.

2. Your comrade erreth not, nor is deceived;

3. Nor doth he speak of (his own) desire.

4. It is naught save an inspiration that is inspired.

5. Which one of mighty powers hath taught him.

6. One vigorous: and he grew clear to view.[1]

7. When he was on the uppermost horizon.

8. Then he drew nigh and came down

9. Till he was (distant) two bows length or even nearer.

10. And He revealed unto His slave that which He revealed.

11. The heart lied not (in seeing) what it saw.

12. Will ye then dispute with him concerning what he seeth?

13. And verily he saw him yet another time.[2]

14. By the lote-tree of the utmost boundary.

15. Nigh unto which is the Garden of Abode.

16. When that which shroudeth did enshroud the lote-tree.

17. The eye turned not aside nor yet was overbold.

18. Verily he saw one of the greater revelations of his Lord.

19. Have ye thought upon Al-Lat and Al-Uzza.[3]

اٰياتها ٦٢ (٥٣) سُوْرَةُ النَّجْمِ مَكِّيَّةٌ رُكُوْعَاتُهَا ٣

بِسْمِ اللّٰهِ الرَّحْمٰنِ الرَّحِيْمِ

وَالنَّجْمِ اِذَا هَوٰى ۝١

مَا ضَلَّ صَاحِبُكُمْ وَمَا غَوٰى ۝٢

وَمَا يَنْطِقُ عَنِ الْهَوٰى ۝٣

اِنْ هُوَ اِلَّا وَحْيٌ يُّوْحٰى ۝٤

عَلَّمَهٗ شَدِيْدُ الْقُوٰى ۝٥

ذُوْ مِرَّةٍ فَاسْتَوٰى ۝٦

وَهُوَ بِالْاُفُقِ الْاَعْلٰى ۝٧

ثُمَّ دَنَا فَتَدَلّٰى ۝٨

فَكَانَ قَابَ قَوْسَيْنِ اَوْ اَدْنٰى ۝٩

فَاَوْحٰى اِلٰى عَبْدِهٖ مَا اَوْحٰى ۝١٠

مَا كَذَبَ الْفُؤَادُ مَا رَاٰى ۝١١

اَفَتُمٰرُوْنَهٗ عَلٰى مَا يَرٰى ۝١٢

وَلَقَدْ رَاٰهُ نَزْلَةً اُخْرٰى ۝١٣

عِنْدَ سِدْرَةِ الْمُنْتَهٰى ۝١٤

عِنْدَهَا جَنَّةُ الْمَاْوٰى ۝١٥

اِذْ يَغْشَى السِّدْرَةَ مَا يَغْشٰى ۝١٦

مَا زَاغَ الْبَصَرُ وَمَا طَغٰى ۝١٧

لَقَدْ رَاٰى مِنْ اٰيٰتِ رَبِّهِ الْكُبْرٰى ۝١٨

اَفَرَءَيْتُمُ اللّٰتَ وَالْعُزّٰى ۝١٩

1. This and the five following verses are generally accepted as referring to the Prophet's vision on Mt. Hira.
2. This is generally accepted as a reference to the Prophet's vision in which he ascended through the seven heavens.
3. An idol of the pagan Arabs.

20. And Manāt,[1] the third, the other?

21. Are yours the males and His the females?[2]

22. That indeed was an unfair division!

23. They are but names which ye have named, ye and your fathers, for which Allah hath revealed no warrant. They follow but a guess and that which (they) themselves desire. And now the guidance from their Lord hath come unto them.

24. Or shall man have what he coveteth?

25. But unto Allah belongeth the after (life), and the former.

26. And how many angels are in the heavens whose intercession availeth naught save after Allah giveth leave to whom He chooseth and accepteth!

27. Lo! it is those who disbelieve in the Hereafter who name the angels with the names of females.

28. And they have no knowledge thereof. They follow but a guess, and lo! a guess can never take the place of the truth.

29. Then withdraw (O Muhammad) from him who fleeth from Our remembrance and desireth but the life of the world.

30 Such is their sum of knowledge. Lo! thy Lord is best aware of him who strayeth, and He is best aware of him who goeth right.

31. And unto Allah belongeth whatsoever is in the heavens and whatsoever is in the earth, that He may reward those who do evil with that which they have done, and reward those who do good with goodness.

وَمَنٰوةَ الثَّالِثَةَ الْأُخْرٰى ﴿٢٠﴾

أَلَكُمُ الذَّكَرُ وَلَهُ الْأُنْثٰى ﴿٢١﴾

تِلْكَ إِذًا قِسْمَةٌ ضِيزٰى ﴿٢٢﴾

إِنْ هِيَ إِلَّا أَسْمَاءٌ سَمَّيْتُمُوهَا أَنْتُمْ وَآبَاؤُكُمْ
مَا أَنْزَلَ اللّٰهُ بِهَا مِنْ سُلْطٰنٍ إِنْ يَتَّبِعُونَ إِلَّا
الظَّنَّ وَمَا تَهْوَى الْأَنْفُسُ وَلَقَدْ جَاءَهُمْ مِنْ
رَبِّهِمُ الْهُدٰى ﴿٢٣﴾

أَمْ لِلْإِنْسَانِ مَا تَمَنّٰى ﴿٢٤﴾

ع فَلِلّٰهِ الْآخِرَةُ وَالْأُولٰى ﴿٢٥﴾

وَكَمْ مِنْ مَلَكٍ فِي السَّمٰوٰتِ لَا تُغْنِي شَفَاعَتُهُمْ
شَيْئًا إِلَّا مِنْ بَعْدِ أَنْ يَأْذَنَ اللّٰهُ لِمَنْ يَشَاءُ
وَيَرْضٰى ﴿٢٦﴾

إِنَّ الَّذِينَ لَا يُؤْمِنُونَ بِالْآخِرَةِ لَيُسَمُّونَ الْمَلٰئِكَةَ
تَسْمِيَةَ الْأُنْثٰى ﴿٢٧﴾

وَمَا لَهُمْ بِهِ مِنْ عِلْمٍ إِنْ يَتَّبِعُونَ إِلَّا الظَّنَّ
وَإِنَّ الظَّنَّ لَا يُغْنِي مِنَ الْحَقِّ شَيْئًا ﴿٢٨﴾

فَأَعْرِضْ عَنْ مَنْ تَوَلّٰى عَنْ ذِكْرِنَا وَلَمْ يُرِدْ
إِلَّا الْحَيٰوةَ الدُّنْيَا ﴿٢٩﴾

ذٰلِكَ مَبْلَغُهُمْ مِنَ الْعِلْمِ إِنَّ رَبَّكَ هُوَ أَعْلَمُ
بِمَنْ ضَلَّ عَنْ سَبِيلِهِ وَهُوَ أَعْلَمُ بِمَنِ اهْتَدٰى ﴿٣٠﴾

وَلِلّٰهِ مَا فِي السَّمٰوٰتِ وَمَا فِي الْأَرْضِ لِيَجْزِيَ الَّذِينَ
أَسَاءُوا بِمَا عَمِلُوا وَيَجْزِيَ الَّذِينَ أَحْسَنُوا بِالْحُسْنَى ﴿٣١﴾

1. The pagan Arabs pretended that their idols were daughters of Allah.

32. Those who avoid enormities of sin and abominations, save the unwilled offences-(for them) Lo! thy lord is of vast mercy. He is best aware of you (from the time) when He created you from the earth, and when ye were hidden in the bellies of your mothers. Therefore ascribe not purity unto yourselves. He is best aware of him who wardeth off (evil).

33. Didst thou (O Muhammad) observe him who turned away,

34. And gave a little, then was grudging?

35. Hath he knowledge of the Unseen so that he seeth?

36. Or hath he not had news of what is in the books of moses.

37. And Abraham who paid his debts;

38. That no laden one shall bear another's load.

39. And that man hath only that for which he maketh effort,

40. And that his effort will be seen.

41. And afterward he will be repaid for it with fullest payment:

42. And that thy Lord, He is the Goal;

43. And that He it is Who maketh laugh, and maketh weep.

44. And that He it is Who giveth death and giveth life:

45. And that He createth the two spouses, the male and the female:

46. From a drop (of seed) when it is poured forth:

47. And that He hath ordained the Second bringing forth.

48. And that He is Who enricheth and contenteth.

49. And that He it is who is the Lord of Sirius;

الَّذِينَ يَجْتَنِبُونَ كَبٰٓئِرَ الْاِثْمِ وَالْفَوَاحِشَ اِلَّا
اللَّمَمَ ؕ اِنَّ رَبَّكَ وَاسِعُ الْمَغْفِرَةِ ؕ هُوَ اَعْلَمُ بِكُمْ
اِذْ اَنْشَاَكُمْ مِّنَ الْاَرْضِ وَاِذْ اَنْتُمْ اَجِنَّةٌ فِىْ
بُطُوْنِ اُمَّهٰتِكُمْ ۚ فَلَا تُزَكُّوْٓا اَنْفُسَكُمْ ؕ هُوَ اَعْلَمُ
ع بِمَنِ اتَّقٰى ﴿۳۲﴾
اَفَرَءَيْتَ الَّذِىْ تَوَلّٰى ﴿۳۳﴾ لا
وَاَعْطٰى قَلِيْلًا وَّاَكْدٰى ﴿۳۴﴾
اَعِنْدَهٗ عِلْمُ الْغَيْبِ فَهُوَ يَرٰى ﴿۳۵﴾
اَمْ لَمْ يُنَبَّاْ بِمَا فِىْ صُحُفِ مُوْسٰى ﴿۳۶﴾ لا
وَاِبْرٰهِيْمَ الَّذِىْ وَفّٰٓى ﴿۳۷﴾
اَلَّا تَزِرُ وَازِرَةٌ وِّزْرَ اُخْرٰى ﴿۳۸﴾ لا
وَاَنْ لَّيْسَ لِلْاِنْسَانِ اِلَّا مَا سَعٰى ﴿۳۹﴾ لا
وَاَنَّ سَعْيَهٗ سَوْفَ يُرٰى ﴿۴۰﴾
ثُمَّ يُجْزٰىهُ الْجَزَآءَ الْاَوْفٰى ﴿۴۱﴾ لا
وَاَنَّ اِلٰى رَبِّكَ الْمُنْتَهٰى ﴿۴۲﴾ لا
وَاَنَّهٗ هُوَ اَضْحَكَ وَاَبْكٰى ﴿۴۳﴾ لا
وَاَنَّهٗ هُوَ اَمَاتَ وَاَحْيَا ﴿۴۴﴾ لا
وَاَنَّهٗ خَلَقَ الزَّوْجَيْنِ الذَّكَرَ وَالْاُنْثٰى ﴿۴۵﴾ لا
مِنْ نُّطْفَةٍ اِذَا تُمْنٰى ﴿۴۶﴾ ص
وَاَنَّ عَلَيْهِ النَّشْاَةَ الْاُخْرٰى ﴿۴۷﴾ لا
وَاَنَّهٗ هُوَ اَغْنٰى وَاَقْنٰى ﴿۴۸﴾ لا
وَاَنَّهٗ هُوَ رَبُّ الشِّعْرٰى ﴿۴۹﴾ لا

50. And that He destroyed the former (tribe of) 'Aād.[1]

وَاَنَّهٗۤ اَهۡلَكَ عَادَا ۨالۡاُوۡلٰى ۝٥٠

51. And (the tribe of) Thamūd He spared not:

وَثَمُوۡدَاۡ فَمَاۤ اَبۡقٰى ۝٥١

52. And the folk of Noah aforetime, lo! they were more unjust and more rebellious:

وَقَوۡمَ نُوۡحٍ مِّنۡ قَبۡلُ ؕ اِنَّهُمۡ كَانُوۡا هُمۡ اَظۡلَمَ وَاَطۡغٰى ۝٥٢

53. And Al-Mu'tafikah[2] He destroyed

وَالۡمُؤۡتَفِكَةَ اَهۡوٰى ۝٥٣

54. So that there covered them that which did cover.

فَغَشّٰٮهَا مَا غَشّٰى ۝٥٤

55. Concerning which then, of the bounties of thy Lord, canst thou dispute?

فَبِاَىِّ اٰلَاۤءِ رَبِّكَ تَتَمَارٰى ۝٥٥

56. This is a warner of the warners of old.

هٰذَا نَذِيۡرٌ مِّنَ النُّذُرِ الۡاُوۡلٰى ۝٥٦

57. The threatened Hour is nigh.

اَزِفَتِ الۡاٰزِفَةُ ۝٥٧

58. None beside Allah can disclose it.

لَيۡسَ لَهَا مِنۡ دُوۡنِ اللّٰهِ كَاشِفَةٌ ۝٥٨

59. Marvel ye then at this statement,

اَفَمِنۡ هٰذَا الۡحَدِيۡثِ تَعۡجَبُوۡنَ ۝٥٩

60. And laugh and not weep,

وَتَضۡحَكُوۡنَ وَلَا تَبۡكُوۡنَ ۝٦٠

61. While ye amuse yourselves?

وَاَنۡتُمۡ سٰمِدُوۡنَ ۝٦١

62. Rather prostrate yourselves before Allah and serve Him.

فَاسۡجُدُوۡا لِلّٰهِ وَاعۡبُدُوۡا ۝٦٢ ۩

1. There was still in existence a tribe of that name.
2. Generally supposed to be a name for the villages of the people of Lot.

Al-Qamar, "The Moon," takes its name from the first verse: "The hour drew nigh and the moon was rent in twain." A strange appearance of the moon in the sky, as if it had been torn asunder, is recorded in the traditions of several Companions of the Prophet as having astonished the people of Mecca about the time when the idolaters were beginning to persecute the Muslims.

An early Meccan Sūrah.

THE MOON

Revealed at Makkah

In the name of Allah, the Beneficent, the Merciful.

1. The hour drew nigh and the moon was rent in twain.

2. And if they behold a portent they turn away and say: Prolonged illusion!

3. They denied (the Truth) and followed their own lusts. Yet everything will come to a decision.

4. And surely there hath come unto them news whereof the purport should deter,

5. Effective wisdom: but warnings avail not

6. So withdraw from them (O Muhammad) on the day when the summoner summoneth unto a painful thing.

7. With downcast eyes, they come forth from the graves as they were locusts spread abroad.

8. Hastening toward the Summoner; the disbelievers say: This is a hard day.

9. The folk of Noah denied before them, yea, they denied our slave[1] and said: A madman; and he was repulsed.

10. So he cried unto his Lord, saying; I am vanquished, so give help!

11. Then opened We the gates of heaven with pouring water.

12. And caused the earth to gush forth springs, so that the waters met for a predestined purpose.

13. And we carried him upon a thing of planks and nails.

14. That ran (upon the waters) in Our sight, as a reward for him who was rejected.

15. And verily we left it as a token; but is there any that remembereth?

ایاتها ٥٥ (٥٤) سورة القمر مكية ركوعاتها ٣

بسم الله الرحمن الرحيم

اقتربت الساعة وانشق القمر (١)

وان يروا اية يعرضوا ويقولوا سحر مستمر (٢)

وكذبوا واتبعوا اهواءهم وكل امر مستقر (٣)

ولقد جاءهم من الانباء ما فيه مزدجر (٤)

حكمة بالغة فما تغن النذر (٥)

فتول عنهم يوم يدع الداع الى شيء نكر (٦)

خشعا ابصارهم يخرجون من الاجداث كانهم
جراد منتشر (٧)

مهطعين الى الداع يقول الكفرون هذا
يوم عسر (٨)

كذبت قبلهم قوم نوح فكذبوا عبدنا وقالوا
مجنون وازدجر (٩)

فدعا ربه اني مغلوب فانتصر (١٠)

ففتحنا ابواب السماء بماء منهمر (١١)

وفجرنا الارض عيونا فالتقى الماء على امر
قد قدر (١٢)

وحملنه على ذات الواح ودسر (١٣)

تجري باعيننا جزاء لمن كان كفر (١٤)

ولقد تركنها اية فهل من مدكر (١٥)

1. To be'abd Allah' a slave of God," is the proudest rank the Muslim can claim, bondage to Allah implying liberation from all other servitudes. All especially devoted men, all the chosen ones, are called slaves of Allah in the koran.

16. Then see how (dreadful) was My punishment after My warnings!

17. And in truth We have made the Qur'ān easy to remember;[1] but is there any that remembereth?

18. (The tribe of) 'Aād rejected warnings. Then how (dreadful) was My punishment after My warnings.

19. Lo! We let loose on them a raging wind on a day of constant calamity,

20. Sweeping men away as though they were uprooted trunks of palm-trees.

21. Then see how (dreadful) was My punishment after My warnings!

22. And in truth We have made the Qur'ān easy to remember; but is there any that remembereth?

23. (The tribe of) Thamūd rejected warnings

24. For they said: Is it a mortal man, alone among us, that we are to follow? Then indeed we should fall into error and madness.

25. Hath the remembrance been given unto him alone among us? Nay, but he is a rash liar.

26. (Unto their warner it was said): To-morrow they will know who is the rash liar!

27. Lo! We are sending the she-camel as a test for them; so watch them and have patience;

28. And inform them that the water is to be shared between (her and) them. Every drinking will be witnessed.

29. But they called their comrade and he took and hamstrung (her).

30. Then see how (dreadful) was My punishment after My warnings!

31. Lo! We sent upon them one Shout, and they became as the dry twigs (rejected by) the builder of a cattle-fold.

32. And in truth We have made the Qur'ān easy to remember; but is there any that remembereth?

33. The folk of Lot rejected warnings.

34. Lo! We sent a storm of stones upon them (all) save the family of Lot, whom We rescued in the last watch of the night,

فَكَيْفَ كَانَ عَذَابِي وَنُذُرِ ﴿١٦﴾

وَلَقَدْ يَسَّرْنَا الْقُرْآنَ لِلذِّكْرِ فَهَلْ مِنْ مُدَّكِرٍ ﴿١٧﴾

كَذَّبَتْ عَادٌ فَكَيْفَ كَانَ عَذَابِي وَنُذُرِ ﴿١٨﴾

إِنَّا أَرْسَلْنَا عَلَيْهِمْ رِيحًا صَرْصَرًا فِي يَوْمِ نَحْسٍ مُسْتَمِرٍّ ﴿١٩﴾

تَنْزِعُ النَّاسَ كَأَنَّهُمْ أَعْجَازُ نَخْلٍ مُنْقَعِرٍ ﴿٢٠﴾

فَكَيْفَ كَانَ عَذَابِي وَنُذُرِ ﴿٢١﴾

ع وَلَقَدْ يَسَّرْنَا الْقُرْآنَ لِلذِّكْرِ فَهَلْ مِنْ مُدَّكِرٍ ﴿٢٢﴾

كَذَّبَتْ ثَمُودُ بِالنُّذُرِ ﴿٢٣﴾

فَقَالُوا أَبَشَرًا مِنَّا وَاحِدًا نَتَّبِعُهُ إِنَّا إِذًا لَفِي ضَلَالٍ وَسُعُرٍ ﴿٢٤﴾

أَأُلْقِيَ الذِّكْرُ عَلَيْهِ مِنْ بَيْنِنَا بَلْ هُوَ كَذَّابٌ أَشِرٌ ﴿٢٥﴾

سَيَعْلَمُونَ غَدًا مَنِ الْكَذَّابُ الْأَشِرُ ﴿٢٦﴾

إِنَّا مُرْسِلُو النَّاقَةِ فِتْنَةً لَهُمْ فَارْتَقِبْهُمْ وَاصْطَبِرْ ﴿٢٧﴾

وَنَبِّئْهُمْ أَنَّ الْمَاءَ قِسْمَةٌ بَيْنَهُمْ كُلُّ شِرْبٍ مُحْتَضَرٌ ﴿٢٨﴾

فَنَادَوْا صَاحِبَهُمْ فَتَعَاطَى فَعَقَرَ ﴿٢٩﴾

فَكَيْفَ كَانَ عَذَابِي وَنُذُرِ ﴿٣٠﴾

إِنَّا أَرْسَلْنَا عَلَيْهِمْ صَيْحَةً وَاحِدَةً فَكَانُوا كَهَشِيمِ الْمُحْتَظِرِ ﴿٣١﴾

وَلَقَدْ يَسَّرْنَا الْقُرْآنَ لِلذِّكْرِ فَهَلْ مِنْ مُدَّكِرٍ ﴿٣٢﴾

كَذَّبَتْ قَوْمُ لُوطٍ بِالنُّذُرِ ﴿٣٣﴾

إِنَّا أَرْسَلْنَا عَلَيْهِمْ حَاصِبًا إِلَّا آلَ لُوطٍ نَجَّيْنَاهُمْ بِسَحَرٍ ﴿٣٤﴾

1. It is a fact that the Koran is marvellously easy for believers to commit to memory. Thousands of people in the East know the whole Book by heart. The translator, who finds great difficulty in remembering well-known English quotations accurately, can remember page after page of the Koran in Arabic with perfect accuracy.

35. As grace from Us. Thus We reward him who giveth thanks.

36. And he indeed had warned them of Our blow, but they did doubt the warnings.

37. They even asked him of his guests for an ill purpose. Then We blinded their eyes (and said): Taste now My punishment after My warnings!

38. And in truth the punishment decreed befell them early in the morning.

39. Now taste My punishment after My warnings!

40. And in truth We have made the Qur'ān easy to remember; but is there any that remembereth?

41. And warnings came in truth unto the house of Pharaoh

42. Who denied Our revelations, every one. Therefore We grasped them with the grasp of the Mighty, the Powerful.

43. Are your disbelievers better than those, or have ye some immunity in the Scriptures?

44. Or say they: We are a host victorious?

45. The hosts will all be routed and will turn and flee.

46. Nay, but the Hour (of doom) is their appointed tryst, and the Hour will be more wretched and more bitter (than their earthly failure).

47. Lo! the guilty are in error and madness.

48. On the day when they are dragged into the Fire upon their faces (it is said unto them): Feel the touch of hell.

49. Lo! We have created every thing by measure.

50. And Our commandment is but one (commandment), as the twinkling of an eye.

51. And verily We have destroyed your fellows; but is there any that remembereth?

52. And every thing they did is in the Scriptures,

53. And every small and great thing is recorded.

54. Lo! the righteous will dwell among gardens and rivers,

55. Firmly established in the favour of a Mighty King.

نِعْمَةً مِّنْ عِنْدِنَا كَذٰلِكَ نَجْزِيْ مَنْ شَكَرَ ﴿٣٥﴾

وَلَقَدْ اَنْذَرَهُمْ بَطْشَتَنَا فَتَمَارَوْا بِالنُّذُرِ ﴿٣٦﴾

وَلَقَدْ رَاوَدُوْهُ عَنْ ضَيْفِهٖ فَطَمَسْنَا اَعْيُنَهُمْ

فَذُوْقُوْا عَذَابِيْ وَنُذُرِ ﴿٣٧﴾

وَلَقَدْ صَبَّحَهُمْ بُكْرَةً عَذَابٌ مُّسْتَقِرٌّ ﴿٣٨﴾

فَذُوْقُوْا عَذَابِيْ وَنُذُرِ ﴿٣٩﴾

ع وَلَقَدْ يَسَّرْنَا الْقُرْاٰنَ لِلذِّكْرِ فَهَلْ مِنْ مُّدَّكِرٍ ﴿٤٠﴾

وَلَقَدْ جَآءَ اٰلَ فِرْعَوْنَ النُّذُرُ ﴿٤١﴾

كَذَّبُوْا بِاٰيٰتِنَا كُلِّهَا فَاَخَذْنٰهُمْ اَخْذَ عَزِيْزٍ مُّقْتَدِرٍ ﴿٤٢﴾

اَكُفَّارُكُمْ خَيْرٌ مِّنْ اُولٰٓئِكُمْ اَمْ لَكُمْ بَرَآءَةٌ فِي الزُّبُرِ ﴿٤٣﴾

اَمْ يَقُوْلُوْنَ نَحْنُ جَمِيْعٌ مُّنْتَصِرٌ ﴿٤٤﴾

سَيُهْزَمُ الْجَمْعُ وَيُوَلُّوْنَ الدُّبُرَ ﴿٤٥﴾

بَلِ السَّاعَةُ مَوْعِدُهُمْ وَالسَّاعَةُ اَدْهٰى وَاَمَرُّ ﴿٤٦﴾

اِنَّ الْمُجْرِمِيْنَ فِيْ ضَلٰلٍ وَّسُعُرٍ ﴿٤٧﴾

يَوْمَ يُسْحَبُوْنَ فِي النَّارِ عَلٰى وُجُوْهِهِمْ ذُوْقُوْا مَسَّ سَقَرَ ﴿٤٨﴾

اِنَّا كُلَّ شَيْءٍ خَلَقْنٰهُ بِقَدَرٍ ﴿٤٩﴾

وَمَآ اَمْرُنَآ اِلَّا وَاحِدَةٌ كَلَمْحٍ بِالْبَصَرِ ﴿٥٠﴾

وَلَقَدْ اَهْلَكْنَآ اَشْيَاعَكُمْ فَهَلْ مِنْ مُّدَّكِرٍ ﴿٥١﴾

وَكُلُّ شَيْءٍ فَعَلُوْهُ فِي الزُّبُرِ ﴿٥٢﴾

وَكُلُّ صَغِيْرٍ وَّكَبِيْرٍ مُّسْتَطَرٌ ﴿٥٣﴾

اِنَّ الْمُتَّقِيْنَ فِيْ جَنّٰتٍ وَّنَهَرٍ ﴿٥٤﴾

ع فِيْ مَقْعَدِ صِدْقٍ عِنْدَ مَلِيْكٍ مُّقْتَدِرٍ ﴿٥٥﴾

Ar-Rahmān-takes its name from the first verse. In the refrain: "Which is it, of the favours of your Lord, that ye deny?" *ye* and the verb are in the dual form, and the question is generally believed to be addressed to mankind and the Jinn. Some have held that vv. 46-76 refer, not to the paradise hereafter but to the later conquests of the Muslims, the four gardens being Egypt, Syria, Mesopotamia and Persia. There may well be a double meaning.

An early Meccan Sūrah.

THE BENEFICENT

Revealed at Mecca

In the name of Allah, the Beneficent, the Merciful,

1. The Beneficent

2. Hath made known the Qur'ān.

3. He hath created men,

4. He hath taught him utterance.

5. The sun and the moon are made punctual.

6. The stars and the trees adore.

7. And the sky He hath uplifted; and He hath set the measure,

8. That ye exceed not the measure,

9. But observe the measure strictly, nor fall short thereof.

10. And the earth hath He appointed for (His) creatures,

11. Wherein are fruit and sheathed palm-trees,

12. Husked grain and scented herb.

13. Which is it, of the favours of your Lord, that ye deny?

14. He created man of clay like the potter's,

15. And the Jinn did He create of smokeless fire.

16. Which is it, of the favours of your Lord, that ye deny?

17. Lord of the two Easts,[1] and Lord of the two Wests![2]

18. Which is it, of the favours of your Lord, that ye deny?

19. He hath loosed the two seas.[3] They meet.

اٰياتها ٧٨ (٥٥) سُوْرَةُ الرَّحْمٰنِ مَدَنِيَّةٌ رُكُوْعَاتُهَا ٣

بِسْمِ اللّٰهِ الرَّحْمٰنِ الرَّحِيْمِ

اَلرَّحْمٰنُ ۙ﴿١﴾

عَلَّمَ الْقُرْاٰنَ ؕ﴿٢﴾

خَلَقَ الْاِنْسَانَ ۙ﴿٣﴾

عَلَّمَهُ الْبَيَانَ ﴿٤﴾

اَلشَّمْسُ وَالْقَمَرُ بِحُسْبَانٍ ۙ﴿٥﴾

وَّالنَّجْمُ وَالشَّجَرُ يَسْجُدٰنِ ﴿٦﴾

وَالسَّمَآءَ رَفَعَهَا وَوَضَعَ الْمِيْزَانَ ۙ﴿٧﴾

اَلَّا تَطْغَوْا فِي الْمِيْزَانِ ﴿٨﴾

وَاَقِيْمُوا الْوَزْنَ بِالْقِسْطِ وَلَا تُخْسِرُوا الْمِيْزَانَ ﴿٩﴾

وَالْاَرْضَ وَضَعَهَا لِلْاَنَامِ ۙ﴿١٠﴾

فِيْهَا فَاكِهَةٌ ۙ وَّالنَّخْلُ ذَاتُ الْاَكْمَامِ ۖ﴿١١﴾

وَالْحَبُّ ذُو الْعَصْفِ وَالرَّيْحَانُ ۚ﴿١٢﴾

فَبِاَيِّ اٰلَآءِ رَبِّكُمَا تُكَذِّبٰنِ ﴿١٣﴾

خَلَقَ الْاِنْسَانَ مِنْ صَلْصَالٍ كَالْفَخَّارِ ۙ﴿١٤﴾

وَخَلَقَ الْجَآنَّ مِنْ مَّارِجٍ مِّنْ نَّارٍ ۚ﴿١٥﴾

فَبِاَيِّ اٰلَآءِ رَبِّكُمَا تُكَذِّبٰنِ ﴿١٦﴾

رَبُّ الْمَشْرِقَيْنِ وَرَبُّ الْمَغْرِبَيْنِ ۚ﴿١٧﴾

فَبِاَيِّ اٰلَآءِ رَبِّكُمَا تُكَذِّبٰنِ ﴿١٨﴾

مَرَجَ الْبَحْرَيْنِ يَلْتَقِيٰنِ ۙ﴿١٩﴾

1. The two points where the sun rises in winter and in summer.
2. The two points where the sun sets in winter and in summer.
3. *i.e* the salt water and the sweet.

20. There is a barrier between them. They encroach not (one upon the other).

21. Which is it, of the favours of your Lord, that ye deny?

22. There cometh forth from both of them the pearl and coral-stone.

23. Which is it, of the favours of your Lord, that ye deny?

24. His are the ships displayed upon the sea, like banners.[1]

25. Which is it, of the favours of your Lord, that ye deny?

26. Everyone that is thereon will pass away;

27. There remaineth but the Countenance of thy Lord of Might and Glory.

28. Which is it, of the favours of your Lord, that ye deny?

29. All that are in the heavens and the earth entreat Him. Every day He exerciseth (universal) power.

30. Which is it, of the favours of your Lord, that ye deny?

31. We shall dispose of you, O ye two dependents (man and jinni).

32. Which is it, of the favours of your Lord, that ye deny?

33. O company of jinn and men, if ye have power to penetrate (all) regions of the heavens and the earth, then penetrate (them)! Ye will never penetrate them save with (Our) sanction.

34. Which is it, of the favours of your Lord, that ye deny?

35. There will be sent, against you both, heat of fire and flash of brass, and ye will not escape.

36. Which is it, of the favours of your Lord, that ye deny?

37. And when the heaven splitteth asunder and becometh rosy like red hide—

بينهما برزخ لا يبغيان ﴿٢٠﴾
فبأي آلاء ربكما تكذبان ﴿٢١﴾
يخرج منهما اللؤلؤ والمرجان ﴿٢٢﴾
فبأي آلاء ربكما تكذبان ﴿٢٣﴾
وله الجوار المنشئت في البحر كالأعلام ﴿٢٤﴾
فبأي آلاء ربكما تكذبان ﴿٢٥﴾
كل من عليها فان ﴿٢٦﴾
ويبقى وجه ربك ذو الجلل والإكرام ﴿٢٧﴾
فبأي آلاء ربكما تكذبان ﴿٢٨﴾
يسئله من في السموت والأرض كل يوم
هو في شأن ﴿٢٩﴾
فبأي آلاء ربكما تكذبان ﴿٣٠﴾
سنفرغ لكم أيه الثقلن ﴿٣١﴾
فبأي آلاء ربكما تكذبان ﴿٣٢﴾
يمعشر الجن والإنس إن استطعتم أن تنفذوا
من أقطار السموت والأرض فانفذوا لا
تنفذون إلا بسلطن ﴿٣٣﴾
فبأي آلاء ربكما تكذبان ﴿٣٤﴾
يرسل عليكما شواظ من نار ونحاس فلا
تنتصران ﴿٣٥﴾
فبأي آلاء ربكما تكذبان ﴿٣٦﴾
فإذا انشقت السماء فكانت وردة كالدهان ﴿٣٧﴾

1. The usual explanation of the commentators is "built into the sea like mountains."

38. Which is it, of the favours of your Lord, that ye deny?

39. On that day neither man nor jinni will be questioned of his sin.

40. Which is it, of the favours of your Lord, that ye deny?

41. The guilty will be known by their marks, and will be taken by the forelocks and the feet.

42. Which is it, of the favours of your Lord, that Ye deny?

43. This is Hell which the guilty deny.

44. They go circling round between it and fierce, boiling water.

45. Which is it, of the favours of your Lord, that Ye deny?

46. But for him who feareth the standing before his Lord there are two gardens.

47. Which is it, of the favours of your Lord, that ye deny?

48. Of spreading branches.

49. Which is it, of the favours of your lord, that ye deny?

50. Wherein are two fountains flowing.

51. Which is it, of the favours of your Lord, that ye deny?

52. Wherein is every kind of fruit in pairs.

53. Which is it, of the favours of your Lord, that Ye deny?

54. Reclining upon couches lined with silk brocade, the fruit of both gardens near to hand.

55. Which is it, of the favours of your Lord, that ye deny?

56. Therein are those of modest gaze. Whom neither man nor jinni will have touched before them.

فَبِاَيِّ اٰلَآءِ رَبِّكُمَا تُكَذِّبٰنِ ﴿٣٨﴾

فَيَوْمَئِذٍ لَّا يُسْـَٔلُ عَنْ ذَنْۢبِهٖٓ اِنْسٌ وَّلَا جَآنٌّ ﴿٣٩﴾

فَبِاَيِّ اٰلَآءِ رَبِّكُمَا تُكَذِّبٰنِ ﴿٤٠﴾

يُعْرَفُ الْمُجْرِمُوْنَ بِسِيْمٰهُمْ فَيُؤْخَذُ بِالنَّوَاصِيْ
وَالْاَقْدَامِ ﴿٤١﴾

فَبِاَيِّ اٰلَآءِ رَبِّكُمَا تُكَذِّبٰنِ ﴿٤٢﴾

هٰذِهٖ جَهَنَّمُ الَّتِيْ يُكَذِّبُ بِهَا الْمُجْرِمُوْنَ ﴿٤٣﴾

يَطُوْفُوْنَ بَيْنَهَا وَبَيْنَ حَمِيْمٍ اٰنٍ ﴿٤٤﴾

فَبِاَيِّ اٰلَآءِ رَبِّكُمَا تُكَذِّبٰنِ ﴿٤٥﴾

وَلِمَنْ خَافَ مَقَامَ رَبِّهٖ جَنَّتٰنِ ﴿٤٦﴾

فَبِاَيِّ اٰلَآءِ رَبِّكُمَا تُكَذِّبٰنِ ﴿٤٧﴾

ذَوَاتَآ اَفْنَانٍ ﴿٤٨﴾

فَبِاَيِّ اٰلَآءِ رَبِّكُمَا تُكَذِّبٰنِ ﴿٤٩﴾

فِيْهِمَا عَيْنٰنِ تَجْرِيٰنِ ﴿٥٠﴾

فَبِاَيِّ اٰلَآءِ رَبِّكُمَا تُكَذِّبٰنِ ﴿٥١﴾

فِيْهِمَا مِنْ كُلِّ فَاكِهَةٍ زَوْجٰنِ ﴿٥٢﴾

فَبِاَيِّ اٰلَآءِ رَبِّكُمَا تُكَذِّبٰنِ ﴿٥٣﴾

مُتَّكِـِٕيْنَ عَلٰى فُرُشٍۢ بَطَآئِنُهَا مِنْ اِسْتَبْرَقٍ ۚ وَ
جَنَا الْجَنَّتَيْنِ دَانٍ ﴿٥٤﴾

فَبِاَيِّ اٰلَآءِ رَبِّكُمَا تُكَذِّبٰنِ ﴿٥٥﴾

فِيْهِنَّ قٰصِرٰتُ الطَّرْفِ لَمْ يَطْمِثْهُنَّ اِنْسٌ
قَبْلَهُمْ وَلَا جَآنٌّ ﴿٥٦﴾

57. Which is it, of the favours of your Lord, that ye deny?

58. (In beauty) like the jecynth and the coral-stone.

59. Which is it, of the favours of your Lord, that ye deny ?

60. Is the reward of goodness aught save goodness?

61. Which is it, of the favours of your Lord, that ye deny?

62. And beside them are two other gardens.

63. Which is it, of the favours or your Lord, that ye deny?

64. Dark green with foliage.

65. Which is it, of the favours of your Lord, that ye deny?

66. Wherein are two abundant springs.

67. Which is it, of the favours of your Lord, that ye deny?

68. Wherein is fruit, the date palm and pomegranate.

69. Which is it, of the favours of your Lord, that ye deny?

70. Wherein (are found) the good and beautiful.

71. Which is it, of the favours of your Lord, that ye deny ?

72. Fair ones, close guarded in pavilions.

73. Which is it, of the favours of your Lord, that ye deny?

74. Whom neither man nor jinni will have touched before them.

75. Which is it, of the favours of your Lord, that ye deny?

76. Reclining on green cushions and fair carpets.

77. Which is it, of the favours of your Lord, that ye deny?

78. Blesse be the name of thy Lord, Mighty and Glorious.

فَبِاَيِّ اٰلَآءِ رَبِّكُمَا تُكَذِّبٰنِ ۝٥٧

كَاَنَّهُنَّ الْيَاقُوْتُ وَالْمَرْجَانُ ۝٥٨

فَبِاَيِّ اٰلَآءِ رَبِّكُمَا تُكَذِّبٰنِ ۝٥٩

هَلْ جَزَآءُ الْاِحْسَانِ اِلَّا الْاِحْسَانُ ۝٦٠

فَبِاَيِّ اٰلَآءِ رَبِّكُمَا تُكَذِّبٰنِ ۝٦١

وَمِنْ دُوْنِهِمَا جَنَّتٰنِ ۝٦٢

فَبِاَيِّ اٰلَآءِ رَبِّكُمَا تُكَذِّبٰنِ ۝٦٣

مُدْهَآمَّتٰنِ ۝٦٤

فَبِاَيِّ اٰلَآءِ رَبِّكُمَا تُكَذِّبٰنِ ۝٦٥

فِيْهِمَا عَيْنٰنِ نَضَّاخَتٰنِ ۝٦٦

فَبِاَيِّ اٰلَآءِ رَبِّكُمَا تُكَذِّبٰنِ ۝٦٧

فِيْهِمَا فَاكِهَةٌ وَّنَخْلٌ وَّرُمَّانٌ ۝٦٨

فَبِاَيِّ اٰلَآءِ رَبِّكُمَا تُكَذِّبٰنِ ۝٦٩

فِيْهِنَّ خَيْرٰتٌ حِسَانٌ ۝٧٠

فَبِاَيِّ اٰلَآءِ رَبِّكُمَا تُكَذِّبٰنِ ۝٧١

حُوْرٌ مَّقْصُوْرٰتٌ فِى الْخِيَامِ ۝٧٢

فَبِاَيِّ اٰلَآءِ رَبِّكُمَا تُكَذِّبٰنِ ۝٧٣

لَمْ يَطْمِثْهُنَّ اِنْسٌ قَبْلَهُمْ وَلَا جَآنٌّ ۝٧٤

فَبِاَيِّ اٰلَآءِ رَبِّكُمَا تُكَذِّبٰنِ ۝٧٥

مُتَّكِـِٕيْنَ عَلٰى رَفْرَفٍ خُضْرٍ وَّعَبْقَرِيٍّ حِسَانٍ ۝٧٦

فَبِاَيِّ اٰلَآءِ رَبِّكُمَا تُكَذِّبٰنِ ۝٧٧

تَبٰرَكَ اسْمُ رَبِّكَ ذِى الْجَلٰلِ وَالْاِكْرَامِ ۝٧٨

Al-Wāqi'ah, "The Event," takes its name from a word in I. V.

An early Meccan Sūrah.

THE EVENT

Revealed at Mecca

In the name of Allah, the Beneficent, the Merciful.

1. When the event befalleth-

2. There is no denying that it will befall

3. Abasing (some), exalting (others);

4. When the earth is shaken with a shock

5. And the hills are ground to powder

6. So that they become a scattered dust,

7. And ye will be three kinds:

8. (First) those on the right hand; what of those on the right hand?

9. And (then) those on the left hand; what of those on the left hand?

10. And the foremost in the race, the foremost in the race;

11. Those are they who will be brought nigh

12. In gardens of delight;

13. A multitude of those of old

14. And a few of those of later time,

15. On lined couches,

16. Reclining therein face to face.

17. There wait on them immortal youths

18. With bowls and ewers and a cup from a pure spring

19. Wherefrom they get no aching of the head nor any madness,

اٰيَاتُهَا ٩٦ (٥٦) سُوْرَةُ الْوَاقِعَةِ مَكِّيَّةٌ ٤٦ رُكُوْعَاتُهَا ٣

بِسْمِ اللّٰهِ الرَّحْمٰنِ الرَّحِيْمِ

إِذَا وَقَعَتِ الْوَاقِعَةُ ﴿١﴾

لَيْسَ لِوَقْعَتِهَا كَاذِبَةٌ ﴿٢﴾

خَافِضَةٌ رَّافِعَةٌ ﴿٣﴾

إِذَا رُجَّتِ الْأَرْضُ رَجًّا ﴿٤﴾

وَّبُسَّتِ الْجِبَالُ بَسًّا ﴿٥﴾

فَكَانَتْ هَبَآءً مُّنْۢبَثًّا ﴿٦﴾

وَّكُنْتُمْ أَزْوَاجًا ثَلٰثَةً ﴿٧﴾

فَأَصْحٰبُ الْمَيْمَنَةِ مَآ أَصْحٰبُ الْمَيْمَنَةِ ﴿٨﴾

وَأَصْحٰبُ الْمَشْـَٔمَةِ مَآ أَصْحٰبُ الْمَشْـَٔمَةِ ﴿٩﴾

وَالسّٰبِقُوْنَ السّٰبِقُوْنَ ﴿١٠﴾

أُولٰٓئِكَ الْمُقَرَّبُوْنَ ﴿١١﴾

فِيْ جَنّٰتِ النَّعِيْمِ ﴿١٢﴾

ثُلَّةٌ مِّنَ الْأَوَّلِيْنَ ﴿١٣﴾

وَقَلِيْلٌ مِّنَ الْاٰخِرِيْنَ ﴿١٤﴾

عَلٰى سُرُرٍ مَّوْضُوْنَةٍ ﴿١٥﴾

مُّتَّكِـِٔيْنَ عَلَيْهَا مُتَقٰبِلِيْنَ ﴿١٦﴾

يَطُوْفُ عَلَيْهِمْ وِلْدَانٌ مُّخَلَّدُوْنَ ﴿١٧﴾

بِأَكْوَابٍ وَّأَبَارِيْقَ ۙ وَكَأْسٍ مِّنْ مَّعِيْنٍ ﴿١٨﴾

لَّا يُصَدَّعُوْنَ عَنْهَا وَلَا يُنْزِفُوْنَ ﴿١٩﴾

20. And fruit that they prefer

وَفَاكِهَةٍ مِّمَّا يَتَخَيَّرُونَ ٢٠

21. And flesh of fowls that they desire.

وَلَحْمِ طَيْرٍ مِّمَّا يَشْتَهُونَ ٢١

22. And (there are) fair ones with wide, lovely eyes,

وَحُورٌ عِينٌ ٢٢

23. Like unto hidden pearls,

كَأَمْثَالِ اللُّؤْلُؤِ الْمَكْنُونِ ٢٣

24. Reward for what they used to do.

جَزَآءً بِمَا كَانُوا يَعْمَلُونَ ٢٤

25. There hear they no vain speaking nor recrimination

لَا يَسْمَعُونَ فِيهَا لَغْوًا وَلَا تَأْثِيمًا ٢٥

26. (Naught) but the saying: Peace, (and again) Peace.

إِلَّا قِيلًا سَلٰمًا سَلٰمًا ٢٦

27. And those on the right hand: what of those on the right hand?

وَأَصْحٰبُ الْيَمِينِ مَآ أَصْحٰبُ الْيَمِينِ ٢٧

28. Among thornless lote-trees

فِي سِدْرٍ مَّخْضُودٍ ٢٨

29. And clustered plantains,

وَطَلْحٍ مَّنضُودٍ ٢٩

30. And spreading shade,

وَظِلٍّ مَّمْدُودٍ ٣٠

31. And water gushing,

وَمَآءٍ مَّسْكُوبٍ ٣١

32. And fruit in plenty

وَفَاكِهَةٍ كَثِيرَةٍ ٣٢

33. Neither out of reach nor yet forbidden,

لَّا مَقْطُوعَةٍ وَلَا مَمْنُوعَةٍ ٣٣

34. And raised couches.

وَفُرُشٍ مَّرْفُوعَةٍ ٣٤

35. Lo! We have created them a (new) creation

إِنَّآ أَنشَأْنٰهُنَّ إِنشَآءً ٣٥

36. And made them virgins,

فَجَعَلْنٰهُنَّ أَبْكَارًا ٣٦

37. Lovers, friends,

عُرُبًا أَتْرَابًا ٣٧

38. For those on the right hand;

لِّأَصْحٰبِ الْيَمِينِ ٣٨

39. A multitude of those of old

ثُلَّةٌ مِّنَ الْأَوَّلِينَ ٣٩

40. And a multitude of those of later time.[1]

وَثُلَّةٌ مِّنَ الْآخِرِينَ ٤٠

41. And those on the left hand: What of those on the left hand?

وَأَصْحٰبُ الشِّمَالِ مَآ أَصْحٰبُ الشِّمَالِ ٤١

1. This verse is said to have been revealed at Al-Madinah.

42. In scorching wind and scalding water

فِىۡ سَمُوۡمٍ وَّحَمِيۡمٍۙ

43. And shadow of black smoke,

وَّظِلٍّ مِّنۡ يَّحۡمُوۡمٍۙ

44. Neither cool nor refreshing.

لَّا بَارِدٍ وَّلَا كَرِيۡمٍ

45. Lo! heretofore they were effete with luxury

اِنَّهُمۡ كَانُوۡا قَبۡلَ ذٰلِكَ مُتۡرَفِيۡنَۚ

46. And used to persist in the awful sin.

وَكَانُوۡا يُصِرُّوۡنَ عَلَى الۡحِنۡثِ الۡعَظِيۡمِۚ

47. And they used to say: When we are dead and have become dust and bones, shall we then, forsooth, be raised again,

وَكَانُوۡا يَقُوۡلُوۡنَ ۙ اَئِذَا مِتۡنَا وَكُنَّا تُرَابًا وَّعِظَامًا ءَاِنَّا لَمَبۡعُوۡثُوۡنَۙ

48. And also our forefathers?

اَوَاٰبَآؤُنَا الۡاَوَّلُوۡنَ

49. Say (unto them, O Muhammad): Lo! those of old and those of later time

قُلۡ اِنَّ الۡاَوَّلِيۡنَ وَالۡاٰخِرِيۡنَۙ

50. Will all be brought together to the tryst of an appointed day.

لَمَجۡمُوۡعُوۡنَ ۙ اِلٰى مِيۡقَاتِ يَوۡمٍ مَّعۡلُوۡمٍ

51. Then lo! ye, the erring, the deniers,

ثُمَّ اِنَّكُمۡ اَيُّهَا الضَّآلُّوۡنَ الۡمُكَذِّبُوۡنَۙ

52. Ye verily will eat of a tree called Zaqqūm

لَاٰكِلُوۡنَ مِنۡ شَجَرٍ مِّنۡ زَقُّوۡمٍۙ

53. And will fill your bellies therewith;

فَمَالِـُٔوۡنَ مِنۡهَا الۡبُطُوۡنَۚ

54. And thereon ye will drink of boiling water,

فَشَارِبُوۡنَ عَلَيۡهِ مِنَ الۡحَمِيۡمِۚ

55. Drinking even as the camel drinketh.

فَشَارِبُوۡنَ شُرۡبَ الۡهِيۡمِ

56. This will be their welcome on the Day of Judgement.

هٰذَا نُزُلُهُمۡ يَوۡمَ الدِّيۡنِ

57. We created you. Will ye then admit the truth?

نَحۡنُ خَلَقۡنٰكُمۡ فَلَوۡلَا تُصَدِّقُوۡنَ

58. Have ye seen that which ye emit?

اَفَرَءَيۡتُمۡ مَّا تُمۡنُوۡنَ

59. Do ye create it or are We the Creator?

ءَاَنۡتُمۡ تَخۡلُقُوۡنَهٗٓ اَمۡ نَحۡنُ الۡخٰلِقُوۡنَ

60. We mete out death among you, and We are not to be outrun,

نَحۡنُ قَدَّرۡنَا بَيۡنَكُمُ الۡمَوۡتَ وَمَا نَحۡنُ بِمَسۡبُوۡقِيۡنَۙ

61. That We may transfigure you and make you what ye know not.

عَلٰٓى اَنۡ نُّبَدِّلَ اَمۡثَالَكُمۡ وَنُنۡشِئَكُمۡ فِىۡ مَا لَا تَعۡلَمُوۡنَ

62. And verily ye know the first creation. Why, then, do ye not reflect?

ولقد علمتم النشأة الأولى فلولا تذكرون ﴿٦٢﴾

63. Have ye seen that which ye cultivate?

أفرءيتم ما تحرثون ﴿٦٣﴾

64. Is it ye who foster it, or are We the Fosterer?

ءأنتم تزرعونه أم نحن الزرعون ﴿٦٤﴾

65. If We willed, We verily could make it chaff, then would ye cease not to exclaim:

لو نشاء لجعلنه حطما فظلتم تفكهون ﴿٦٥﴾

66. Lo! we are laden with debt!

إنا لمغرمون ﴿٦٦﴾

67. Nay, but we are deprived!

بل نحن محرومون ﴿٦٧﴾

68. Have ye observed the water which ye drink?

أفرءيتم الماء الذى تشربون ﴿٦٨﴾

69. Is it ye who shed it from the raincloud, or are We the shedder?

ءأنتم أنزلتموه من المزن أم نحن المنزلون ﴿٦٩﴾

70. If We willed We verily could make it bitter. Why, then, give ye not thanks?

لو نشاء جعلنه أجاجا فلولا تشكرون ﴿٧٠﴾

71. Have ye observed the fire which ye strike out;

أفرءيتم النار التى تورون ﴿٧١﴾

72. Was it ye who made the tree thereof to grow, or were We the grower?

ءأنتم أنشأتم شجرتها أم نحن المنشئون ﴿٧٢﴾

73. We, even We, appointed it a memorial and a comfort for the dwellers in the wilderness.

نحن جعلنها تذكرة ومتاعا للمقوين ﴿٧٣﴾

74. Therefore (O Muhammad), praise the name of thy Lord, the Tremendous.

فسبح باسم ربك العظيم ﴿٧٤﴾

75. Nay, I swear by the places of the stars—

فلا أقسم بموقع النجوم ﴿٧٥﴾

76. And lo! that verily is a tremendous oath, if ye but knew

وإنه لقسم لو تعلمون عظيم ﴿٧٦﴾

77. That (this) is indeed a noble Qur'ān

إنه لقرءان كريم ﴿٧٧﴾

78. In a Book kept hidden

فى كتب مكنون ﴿٧٨﴾

79. Which none toucheth save the purified,

لا يمسه إلا المطهرون ﴿٧٩﴾

80. A revelation from the Lord of the Worlds.

تنزيل من رب العلمين ﴿٨٠﴾

81. Is it this Statement that ye scorn,

أفبهذا الحديث أنتم مدهنون ﴿٨١﴾

82. And make denial thereof your livelihood?

83. Why, then, when (the soul) cometh up to the throat (of the dying)

84. And ye are at that moment looking

85. —And We are nearer unto him than ye are, but ye see not—

86. Why then, if ye are not in bondage (unto Us),

87. Do ye not force it back, if ye are truthful?

88. Thus if he is of those brought nigh,

89. Then breath of life, and plenty, and a Garden of delight.

90. And if he is of those on the right hand,

91. Then (the greeting) "Peace be unto thee" from those on the right hand.

92. But if he is of the rejecters, the erring,

93. Then the welcome will be boiling water

94. And roasting at hell-fire.

95. Lo! this is certain truth.

96. Therefor (O Muhammad) praise the name of thy Lord, the Tremendous.

وَتَجْعَلُونَ رِزْقَكُمْ أَنَّكُمْ تُكَذِّبُونَ ﴿٨٢﴾
فَلَوْلَآ إِذَا بَلَغَتِ الْحُلْقُومَ ﴿٨٣﴾
وَأَنْتُمْ حِينَئِذٍ تَنْظُرُونَ ﴿٨٤﴾
وَنَحْنُ أَقْرَبُ إِلَيْهِ مِنْكُمْ وَلٰكِنْ لَا
تُبْصِرُونَ ﴿٨٥﴾
فَلَوْلَآ إِنْ كُنْتُمْ غَيْرَ مَدِينِينَ ﴿٨٦﴾
تَرْجِعُونَهَآ إِنْ كُنْتُمْ صٰدِقِينَ ﴿٨٧﴾
فَأَمَّآ إِنْ كَانَ مِنَ الْمُقَرَّبِينَ ﴿٨٨﴾
فَرَوْحٌ وَرَيْحَانٌ وَجَنَّتُ نَعِيمٍ ﴿٨٩﴾
وَأَمَّآ إِنْ كَانَ مِنْ أَصْحٰبِ الْيَمِينِ ﴿٩٠﴾
فَسَلٰمٌ لَكَ مِنْ أَصْحٰبِ الْيَمِينِ ﴿٩١﴾
وَأَمَّآ إِنْ كَانَ مِنَ الْمُكَذِّبِينَ الضَّآلِّينَ ﴿٩٢﴾
فَنُزُلٌ مِنْ حَمِيمٍ ﴿٩٣﴾
وَتَصْلِيَةُ جَحِيمٍ ﴿٩٤﴾
إِنَّ هٰذَا لَهُوَ حَقُّ الْيَقِينِ ﴿٩٥﴾
فَسَبِّحْ بِاسْمِ رَبِّكَ الْعَظِيمِ ﴿٩٦﴾ ع

Al-Ḥadid, "Iron," takes its name from a word in v. 25.

The reference in the word "victory" in v. 10, is undoubtedly to the conquest of Mecca, though Nöldeke[1] takes it to refer to the battle of Badr, and so would place the Sūrah in the fourth or fifth year of the Hijrah. The words of the verse are against such an assumption since no Muslims "spent and fought" before the battle at Badr, which was the beginning of their fighting.

The date of revelation must be the eighth or ninth year of the Hijrah.

1. Th. Nöldeke, *Geschichte der Qorâns* 2nd Ed., Part I, Leipzig, 1909, p. 195.

IRON

Revealed at Al-Madinah

In the name of Allah, the Beneficent, the Merciful.

1. All that is in the heavens and the earth glorifieth Allah; and He is the Mighty, the Wise.

2. His is the Sovereignty of the heavens and the earth; He quickeneth and He giveth death; and He is Able to do all things.

3. He is the First and the Last, and the Outward and the Inward; and He is the Knower of all things.

4. He it is Who created the heavens and the earth in six Days;[1] then He mounted the Throne. He knoweth all that entereth the earth and all that emergeth therefrom and all that cometh down from the sky and all that ascendeth therein; and He is with you wheresoever ye may be. And Allah is Seer of what ye do.

5. His is the Sovereignty of the heavens and the earth, and unto Allah (all) things are brought back.

6. He causeth the night to pass into the day, and He causeth the day to pass into the night, and He is Knower of all that is in the breasts.

7. Believe in Allah and His messenger, and spend of that whereof He hath made you trustees; and such of you as believe and spend (aright), theirs will be a great reward.

1. XXII. 47; XXXII. 5; LXX, 4.

اياتها ٢٩ (٥٧) سُورَةُ الْحَدِيدِ مَدَنِيَّةٌ رُكُوعَاتُهَا ٤

بِسْمِ اللّٰهِ الرَّحْمٰنِ الرَّحِيْمِ

سَبَّحَ لِلّٰهِ مَا فِي السَّمٰوٰتِ وَالْاَرْضِ ۚ وَهُوَ
الْعَزِيْزُ الْحَكِيْمُ ﴿١﴾
لَهٗ مُلْكُ السَّمٰوٰتِ وَالْاَرْضِ ۚ يُحْيٖ وَيُمِيْتُ ۚ
وَهُوَ عَلٰى كُلِّ شَيْءٍ قَدِيْرٌ ﴿٢﴾
هُوَ الْاَوَّلُ وَالْاٰخِرُ وَالظَّاهِرُ وَالْبَاطِنُ ۚ وَهُوَ
بِكُلِّ شَيْءٍ عَلِيْمٌ ﴿٣﴾
هُوَ الَّذِيْ خَلَقَ السَّمٰوٰتِ وَالْاَرْضَ فِيْ سِتَّةِ
اَيَّامٍ ثُمَّ اسْتَوٰى عَلَى الْعَرْشِ ۚ يَعْلَمُ مَا يَلِجُ
فِي الْاَرْضِ وَمَا يَخْرُجُ مِنْهَا وَمَا يَنْزِلُ مِنَ
السَّمَآءِ وَمَا يَعْرُجُ فِيْهَا ۚ وَهُوَ مَعَكُمْ
اَيْنَ مَا كُنْتُمْ ۚ وَاللّٰهُ بِمَا تَعْمَلُوْنَ
بَصِيْرٌ ﴿٤﴾
لَهٗ مُلْكُ السَّمٰوٰتِ وَالْاَرْضِ ۚ وَاِلَى اللّٰهِ تُرْجَعُ
الْاُمُوْرُ ﴿٥﴾
يُوْلِجُ الَّيْلَ فِي النَّهَارِ وَيُوْلِجُ النَّهَارَ فِي الَّيْلِ ۚ
وَهُوَ عَلِيْمٌ ۢبِذَاتِ الصُّدُوْرِ ﴿٦﴾
اٰمِنُوْا بِاللّٰهِ وَرَسُوْلِهٖ وَاَنْفِقُوْا مِمَّا جَعَلَكُمْ
مُّسْتَخْلَفِيْنَ فِيْهِ ۚ فَالَّذِيْنَ اٰمَنُوْا مِنْكُمْ وَاَنْفَقُوْا
لَهُمْ اَجْرٌ كَبِيْرٌ ﴿٧﴾

8. What aileth you that ye believe not in Allah, when the messenger calleth you to believe in your Lord, and He hath already made a covenant with you, if ye are believers?

9. He it is Who sendeth down clear revelations unto His slave, that He may bring you forth from darkness unto light; and lo! for you, Allah is Full of Pity, Merciful.

10. And what aileth you that ye spend not in the way of Allah, when unto Allah belongeth the inheritance of the heavens and the earth? Those who spent and fought before the victory are not upon a level (with the rest of you). Such are greater in rank than those who spent and fought afterwards. Unto each hath Allah promised good. And Allah is Informed of what ye do.

11. Who is he that will lend unto Allah a goodly loan,[1] that He may double it for him and his may be a rich reward?

12. On the day when thou (Muhammad) wilt see the believers, men and women, their light shining forth before them and on their right hands, (and wilt hear it said unto them): Glad news for you this day: Gardens underneath which rivers flow, wherein ye are immortal. That is the Supreme triumph.

13. On the day when the hypocritical men and the hypocritical women will say unto those who believe: Look on us that we may borrow from your light! It will be said: Go back and seek for light! Then there will separate them a wall wherein is a gate, the inner side whereof containeth mercy, while the outer side thereof is toward the doom.

وَمَا لَكُمْ لَا تُؤْمِنُونَ بِاللَّهِ ۚ وَالرَّسُولُ يَدْعُوكُمْ
لِتُؤْمِنُوا بِرَبِّكُمْ وَقَدْ أَخَذَ مِيثَاقَكُمْ إِنْ كُنْتُمْ
مُؤْمِنِينَ ﴿٨﴾
هُوَ الَّذِي يُنَزِّلُ عَلَىٰ عَبْدِهِ آيَاتٍ بَيِّنَاتٍ لِيُخْرِجَكُمْ
مِنَ الظُّلُمَاتِ إِلَى النُّورِ ۚ وَإِنَّ اللَّهَ بِكُمْ لَرَءُوفٌ
رَحِيمٌ ﴿٩﴾
وَمَا لَكُمْ أَلَّا تُنْفِقُوا فِي سَبِيلِ اللَّهِ وَلِلَّهِ مِيرَاثُ
السَّمَاوَاتِ وَالْأَرْضِ ۚ لَا يَسْتَوِي مِنْكُمْ مَنْ أَنْفَقَ
مِنْ قَبْلِ الْفَتْحِ وَقَاتَلَ ۚ أُولَٰئِكَ أَعْظَمُ دَرَجَةً
مِنَ الَّذِينَ أَنْفَقُوا مِنْ بَعْدُ وَقَاتَلُوا ۚ وَكُلًّا وَعَدَ
ع اللَّهُ الْحُسْنَىٰ ۚ وَاللَّهُ بِمَا تَعْمَلُونَ خَبِيرٌ ﴿١٠﴾
مَنْ ذَا الَّذِي يُقْرِضُ اللَّهَ قَرْضًا حَسَنًا فَيُضَاعِفَهُ
لَهُ وَلَهُ أَجْرٌ كَرِيمٌ ﴿١١﴾
يَوْمَ تَرَى الْمُؤْمِنِينَ وَالْمُؤْمِنَاتِ يَسْعَىٰ نُورُهُمْ
بَيْنَ أَيْدِيهِمْ وَبِأَيْمَانِهِمْ بُشْرَاكُمُ الْيَوْمَ جَنَّاتٌ
تَجْرِي مِنْ تَحْتِهَا الْأَنْهَارُ خَالِدِينَ فِيهَا ۚ ذَٰلِكَ
هُوَ الْفَوْزُ الْعَظِيمُ ﴿١٢﴾
يَوْمَ يَقُولُ الْمُنَافِقُونَ وَالْمُنَافِقَاتُ لِلَّذِينَ آمَنُوا
انْظُرُونَا نَقْتَبِسْ مِنْ نُورِكُمْ قِيلَ ارْجِعُوا وَرَاءَكُمْ
فَالْتَمِسُوا نُورًا فَضُرِبَ بَيْنَهُمْ بِسُورٍ لَهُ بَابٌ
بَاطِنُهُ فِيهِ الرَّحْمَةُ وَظَاهِرُهُ مِنْ قِبَلِهِ
الْعَذَابُ ﴿١٣﴾

3. A loan without interest or any thought of gain or loss.

14. They will cry unto them (saying): Were we not with you? They will say: Yea, verily; but ye tempted one another, and hesitated, and doubted, and vain desires beguiled you till the ordinance of Allah came to pass; and the deceiver deceived you concerning Allah;

15. So this day no ransom can be taken from you nor from those who disbelieved. Your home is the Fire; that is your patron, and a hapless journey's end.

16. Is not the time ripe for the hearts of those who believe to submit to Allah's reminder and to the truth which is revealed, that they become not as those who received the Scripture of old but the term was prolonged for them and so their hearts were hardened, and many of them are evil-livers.

17. Know that Allah quickeneth the earth after its death. We have made clear Our revelations for you, that haply ye may understand.

18. Lo! those who give alms, both men and women, and lend unto Allah a goodly loan, it will be doubled for them, and theirs will be a rich reward.

19. And those who believe in Allah and His messengers, they are the loyal; and the martyrs are with their Lord; they have their reward and their light; while as for those who disbelieve and deny Our revelations, they are owners of hell-fire.

20. Know that the life of this world is only play, and idle talk, and pageantry, and boasting among you, and rivalry in respect of wealth and children; as the likeness of vegetation after rain, whereof the growth is pleasing to the husbandman, but afterward it drieth up and thou seest it turning yellow, then it becometh straw. And in the Hereafter there is grievous punishment, and (also) forgiveness from Allah and His good pleasure, whereas the life of the world is but matter of illusion.

يُنَادُونَهُمْ أَلَمْ نَكُن مَّعَكُمْ قَالُوا بَلَىٰ وَلَٰكِنَّكُمْ
فَتَنتُمْ أَنفُسَكُمْ وَتَرَبَّصْتُمْ وَارْتَبْتُمْ وَغَرَّتْكُمُ
الْأَمَانِيُّ حَتَّىٰ جَاءَ أَمْرُ اللَّهِ وَغَرَّكُم بِاللَّهِ الْغَرُورُ ﴿١٤﴾
فَالْيَوْمَ لَا يُؤْخَذُ مِنكُمْ فِدْيَةٌ وَلَا مِنَ الَّذِينَ كَفَرُوا
مَأْوَاكُمُ النَّارُ هِيَ مَوْلَاكُمْ وَبِئْسَ الْمَصِيرُ ﴿١٥﴾
أَلَمْ يَأْنِ لِلَّذِينَ آمَنُوا أَن تَخْشَعَ قُلُوبُهُمْ لِذِكْرِ
اللَّهِ وَمَا نَزَلَ مِنَ الْحَقِّ وَلَا يَكُونُوا كَالَّذِينَ
أُوتُوا الْكِتَابَ مِن قَبْلُ فَطَالَ عَلَيْهِمُ الْأَمَدُ
فَقَسَتْ قُلُوبُهُمْ وَكَثِيرٌ مِّنْهُمْ فَاسِقُونَ ﴿١٦﴾
اعْلَمُوا أَنَّ اللَّهَ يُحْيِي الْأَرْضَ بَعْدَ مَوْتِهَا قَدْ
بَيَّنَّا لَكُمُ الْآيَاتِ لَعَلَّكُمْ تَعْقِلُونَ ﴿١٧﴾
إِنَّ الْمُصَّدِّقِينَ وَالْمُصَّدِّقَاتِ وَأَقْرَضُوا اللَّهَ
قَرْضًا حَسَنًا يُضَاعَفُ لَهُمْ وَلَهُمْ أَجْرٌ كَرِيمٌ ﴿١٨﴾
وَالَّذِينَ آمَنُوا بِاللَّهِ وَرُسُلِهِ أُولَٰئِكَ هُمُ الصِّدِّيقُونَ
وَالشُّهَدَاءُ عِندَ رَبِّهِمْ لَهُمْ أَجْرُهُمْ وَنُورُهُمْ وَالَّذِينَ
ع كَفَرُوا وَكَذَّبُوا بِآيَاتِنَا أُولَٰئِكَ أَصْحَابُ الْجَحِيمِ ﴿١٩﴾
اعْلَمُوا أَنَّمَا الْحَيَاةُ الدُّنْيَا لَعِبٌ وَلَهْوٌ وَزِينَةٌ وَ
تَفَاخُرٌ بَيْنَكُمْ وَتَكَاثُرٌ فِي الْأَمْوَالِ وَالْأَوْلَادِ كَمَثَلِ
غَيْثٍ أَعْجَبَ الْكُفَّارَ نَبَاتُهُ ثُمَّ يَهِيجُ فَتَرَاهُ
مُصْفَرًّا ثُمَّ يَكُونُ حُطَامًا وَفِي الْآخِرَةِ عَذَابٌ
شَدِيدٌ وَمَغْفِرَةٌ مِّنَ اللَّهِ وَرِضْوَانٌ وَمَا الْحَيَاةُ
الدُّنْيَا إِلَّا مَتَاعُ الْغُرُورِ ﴿٢٠﴾

21. Race one with another for forgiveness from your Lord and a Garden whereof the breadth is as the breadth of the heavens and the earth, which is in store for those who believe in Allah and His messengers. Such is the bounty of Allah. which He bestoweth upon whom He will. and Allah is of Infinite bounty.

سابقوا الى مغفرة من ربكم وجنة
عرضها كعرض السماء والارض اعدت
للذين امنوا بالله ورسله ذلك فضل
الله يؤتيه من يشاء والله ذو الفضل
العظيم ﴿٢١﴾

22. Naught of disaster befalleth in the earth or in yourselves but it is in a Book before We bring it into being—Lo! that is easy for Allah—

ما اصاب من مصيبة في الارض ولا في انفسكم
الا في كتب من قبل ان نبراها ان ذلك على
الله يسير ﴿٢٢﴾

23. That ye grieve not for the sake of that which hath escaped you. nor yet exult because of that which hath been given. Allah loveth not all prideful boasters,

لكيلا تاسوا على ما فاتكم ولا تفرحوا بما اتىكم
والله لا يحب كل مختال فخور ﴿٢٣﴾

24. Who hoard and who enjoin upon the people avarice. And whosoever turneth away, still Allah is the Absolute, the Owner of Praise.

الذين يبخلون ويامرون الناس بالبخل
ومن يتول فان الله هو الغني
الحميد ﴿٢٤﴾

25. We verily sent Our messengers with clear proofs, and revealed with them the Scripture and the Balance, that mankind may observe right measure; and He revealed iron. wherein is mighty power and (many) uses for mankind. and that Allah may know him who helpeth Him and His messengers. though unseen. Lo! Allah is Strong. Almighty.

لقد ارسلنا رسلنا بالبينت وانزلنا معهم
الكتب والميزان ليقوم الناس بالقسط
وانزلنا الحديد فيه باس شديد
ومنافع للناس وليعلم الله من
ينصره ورسله بالغيب ان الله قوي
عزيز ﴿٢٥﴾

26. And We verily sent Noah and Abraham and placed the Prophethood and the Scripture among their seed. and among them there is he who goeth right, but many of them are evil-livers.

ولقد ارسلنا نوحا وابرهيم وجعلنا في
ذريتهما النبوة والكتب فمنهم مهتد
وكثير منهم فسقون ﴿٢٦﴾

27. Then we caused Our messengers to follow in their footsteps; and We caused Jesus, son of Mercy, to follow, and gave him the Gospel, and placed compassion and mery in the hearts of those who followed him. But monasticism they invented -- we ordained it not for them -- only seeking Allah's pleasure, and they observed it not with right observance. So we give those of them who believe their reward, but many of them are evil-livers.

ثُمَّ قَفَّيْنَا عَلَىٰٓ آثَارِهِمْ بِرُسُلِنَا وَقَفَّيْنَا بِعِيسَى
ابْنِ مَرْيَمَ وَآتَيْنَاهُ الْإِنْجِيلَ ۙ وَجَعَلْنَا فِي
قُلُوبِ الَّذِينَ اتَّبَعُوهُ رَأْفَةً وَرَحْمَةً ۚ وَرَهْبَانِيَّةً
ابْتَدَعُوهَا مَا كَتَبْنَاهَا عَلَيْهِمْ إِلَّا ابْتِغَاءَ
رِضْوَانِ اللَّهِ فَمَا رَعَوْهَا حَقَّ رِعَايَتِهَا ۖ فَآتَيْنَا
الَّذِينَ آمَنُوا مِنْهُمْ أَجْرَهُمْ ۖ وَكَثِيرٌ مِنْهُمْ
فَاسِقُونَ ﴿٢٧﴾

28. O ye who believe ! Be mindful of your duty to Allah and put faith in His messenger. He will give you twofold of His mercy and will appoint for you a light wherein ye shall walk, and will forgive you. Allah is Forgiving,-- Merciful;

يَا أَيُّهَا الَّذِينَ آمَنُوا اتَّقُوا اللَّهَ وَآمِنُوا بِرَسُولِهِ
يُؤْتِكُمْ كِفْلَيْنِ مِنْ رَحْمَتِهِ وَيَجْعَلْ لَكُمْ
نُورًا تَمْشُونَ بِهِ وَيَغْفِرْ لَكُمْ ۚ وَاللَّهُ غَفُورٌ
رَحِيمٌ ﴿٢٨﴾

29. That the People of the Scripture[1] may know that they control naught of the bounty of Allah, but that the bounty in Allah's hand to give whom He will. And Allah is of infinite bounty.

لِئَلَّا يَعْلَمَ أَهْلُ الْكِتَابِ أَلَّا يَقْدِرُونَ عَلَىٰ
شَيْءٍ مِنْ فَضْلِ اللَّهِ ۙ وَأَنَّ الْفَضْلَ بِيَدِ
اللَّهِ يُؤْتِيهِ مَنْ يَشَاءُ ۚ وَاللَّهُ ذُو الْفَضْلِ
الْعَظِيمِ ﴿٢٩﴾

1. i.e., Jews and Christians

Al-Mujādilah, "She That Disputeth," takes its name from a word in verse 1.

A woman had complained to the Prophet that her husband had put her away for no good reason by employing an old formula of the pagan Arabs, saying that her back was for him as the back of his mother, and she "disputed" with the Prophet because he would take no action against the man before this revelation came to him. There is a brief reference to the same method of getting rid of wives in Sūrah XXXIII, v. 4. This Sūrah must therefore have been revealed before Sūrah XXXIII.

The date of revelation is the fourth or fifth year of the Hijrah.

SHE THAT DISPUTETH

Revealed at Al-Madinah

In the name of Allah, the Beneficent, the Merciful.

1. Allah hath heard the saying of her that disputeth with thee (Muhammad) concerning her husband, and complaineth unto Allah. And Allah heareth your colloquy. Lo! Allah is Hearer, Knower.

2. Such of you as put away your wives (by saying they are as their mothers)—They are not their mothers;[1] none are their mothers except those who gave them birth—they indeed utter an ill word and a lie. And lo! Allah is Forgiving, Merciful.

3. Those who put away their wives (by saying they are as their mothers)[1] and afterward would go back on that which they have said, (the penalty) in that case (is) the freeing of a slave before they touch one another. Unto this ye are exhorted; and Allah is Informed of what ye do.

4. And he who findeth not (the wherewithal), let him fast for two successive months before they touch one another; and for him who is unable to do so (the penance is) the feeding of sixty needy ones. This, that ye may put trust in Allah and His messenger. Such are the limits (imposed by Allah); and for disbelievers is a painful doom.

5. Those who oppose Allah and His messenger will be abased even as those before them were abased; and We have sent down clear tokens, and for disbelievers is a shameful doom

6. On the day when Allah will raise them all together and inform them of what they did. Allah hath kept account of it while they forgot it. And Allah is Witness over all things.

1. XXXIII, 4.

اٰياتها ٢٢ (٥٨) سُوْرَةُ الْمُجَادَلَةِ مَدَنِيَّةٌ رُكُوْعَاتُهَا ٣

بِسْمِ اللّٰهِ الرَّحْمٰنِ الرَّحِيْمِ

الجزء ٢٨ قَدْ سَمِعَ اللّٰهُ قَوْلَ الَّتِيْ تُجَادِلُكَ فِيْ زَوْجِهَا
وَتَشْتَكِيْٓ اِلَى اللّٰهِ ۖ وَاللّٰهُ يَسْمَعُ تَحَاوُرَكُمَا ۭ اِنَّ
اللّٰهَ سَمِيْعٌۢ بَصِيْرٌ ①
اَلَّذِيْنَ يُظٰهِرُوْنَ مِنْكُمْ مِّنْ نِّسَآئِهِمْ مَّا هُنَّ
اُمَّهٰتِهِمْ ۭ اِنْ اُمَّهٰتُهُمْ اِلَّا الّٰۗـِٔيْ وَلَدْنَهُمْ ۭ وَ
اِنَّهُمْ لَيَقُوْلُوْنَ مُنْكَرًا مِّنَ الْقَوْلِ وَزُوْرًا ۭ وَاِنَّ
اللّٰهَ لَعَفُوٌّ غَفُوْرٌ ②
وَالَّذِيْنَ يُظٰهِرُوْنَ مِنْ نِّسَآئِهِمْ ثُمَّ يَعُوْدُوْنَ
لِمَا قَالُوْا فَتَحْرِيْرُ رَقَبَةٍ مِّنْ قَبْلِ اَنْ يَّتَمَآسَّا ۭ
ذٰلِكُمْ تُوْعَظُوْنَ بِهٖ ۭ وَاللّٰهُ بِمَا تَعْمَلُوْنَ خَبِيْرٌ ③
فَمَنْ لَّمْ يَجِدْ فَصِيَامُ شَهْرَيْنِ مُتَتَابِعَيْنِ مِنْ
قَبْلِ اَنْ يَّتَمَآسَّا ۚ فَمَنْ لَّمْ يَسْتَطِعْ فَاِطْعَامُ
سِتِّيْنَ مِسْكِيْنًا ۭ ذٰلِكَ لِتُؤْمِنُوْا بِاللّٰهِ وَرَسُوْلِهٖ ۭ
وَتِلْكَ حُدُوْدُ اللّٰهِ ۭ وَلِلْكٰفِرِيْنَ عَذَابٌ اَلِيْمٌ ④
اِنَّ الَّذِيْنَ يُحَآدُّوْنَ اللّٰهَ وَرَسُوْلَهٗ كُبِتُوْا كَمَا
كُبِتَ الَّذِيْنَ مِنْ قَبْلِهِمْ وَقَدْ اَنْزَلْنَآ اٰيٰتٍۢ
بَيِّنٰتٍ ۭ وَلِلْكٰفِرِيْنَ عَذَابٌ مُّهِيْنٌ ⑤
يَوْمَ يَبْعَثُهُمُ اللّٰهُ جَمِيْعًا فَيُنَبِّئُهُمْ بِمَا عَمِلُوْا ۭ
ع اَحْصٰىهُ اللّٰهُ وَنَسُوْهُ ۭ وَاللّٰهُ عَلٰى كُلِّ شَيْءٍ شَهِيْدٌ ⑥

7. Hast thou not seen that Allah knoweth all that is in the heavens and all that is in the earth? There is no secret conference of three but He is their fourth, nor of five but He is their sixth, nor of less than that or more but He is with them wheresoever they may be; and afterward, on the Day of Resurrection, He will inform them of what they did. Lo! Allah is Knower of all things.

8. Hast thou not observed those who were forbidden conspiracy and afterward returned to that which they had been forbidden, and (now) conspire together for crime and wrongdoing and disobedience toward the Messenger? And when they come unto thee they greet thee with a greeting wherewith Allah greeteth thee not, and say within themselves; why should Allah punish us for what we say ? Hell will suffice them; they will feel the heat thereof -- a hapless journey's end!

9. O ye who believe! When ye conspire together, conspire not together for crime and wrongdoing and disobedience toward the Messenger, but conspire together for righteousness and piety, and keep your duty toward Allah, unto whom ye will be gathered.

10. Lo! Conspiracy is only of the devil, that he may vex those who believe; but he can harm them not at all unless by Allah's leave. In Allah let believers put their trust.

11. O ye who believe! When it is said: Make room in assemblies, then make room; Allah will make way for you (hereafter) and when it is said: Come up higher; Allah will exalt those who believe among you, and those who have knowledge, to high ranks. Allah is informed of what ye do.

الم تر ان الله يعلم ما في السموت وما في الارض ط
ما يكون من نجوى ثلثة الا هو رابعهم ولا
خمسة الا هو سادسهم ولا ادنى من ذلك و
لا اكثر الا هو معهم اين ما كانوا ثم ينبئهم بما
عملوا يوم القيمة ان الله بكل شيء عليم ⑦
الم تر الى الذين نهوا عن النجوى ثم يعودون
لما نهوا عنه ويتنجون بالاثم والعدوان و
معصيت الرسول واذا جاءوك حيوك بما لم
يحيك به الله ويقولون في انفسهم لولا يعذبنا
الله بما نقول حسبهم جهنم يصلونها
فبئس المصير ⑧
يايها الذين امنوا اذا تناجيتم فلا تتناجوا بالاثم
والعدوان ومعصيت الرسول وتناجوا بالبر و
التقوى واتقوا الله الذي اليه تحشرون ⑨
انما النجوى من الشيطن ليحزن الذين امنوا
وليس بضارهم شيئا الا باذن الله وعلى الله
فليتوكل المؤمنون ⑩
يايها الذين امنوا اذا قيل لكم تفسحوا في
المجلس فافسحوا يفسح الله لكم واذا قيل
انشزوا فانشزوا يرفع الله الذين امنوا منكم
والذين اوتوا العلم درجت والله بما تعملون
خبير ⑪

12. O ye who believe! When ye hold conference with the messenger, offer an alms before your conference. That is better and purer for you. But if ye cannot find (the wherewithal) then lo! Allah is Forgiving, Merciful.

13. Fear ye to offer alms before your conference? Then, when ye do it not and Allah hath forgiven you, establish worship and pay the poor-due and obey Allah and His messenger. And Allah is Aware of what ye do.

14. Hast thou not seen those who take for friends a folk with whom Allah is wroth? They are neither of you nor of them, and they swear a false oath knowingly.

15. Allah hath prepared for them a dreadful doom. Evil indeed is that which they are wont to do.

16. They make a shelter of their oaths and turn (men) from the way of Allah: so theirs will be a shameful doom.

17. Their wealth and their children will avail them naught against Allah. Such are rightful owners of the Fire: they will abide therein.

18. On the day when Allah will raise them all together, then will they swear unto Him as they (now) swear unto you, and they will fancy that they have some standing. Lo! is it not they who are the liars?

19. The devil hath engrossed them and so hath caused them to forget remembrance of Allah. They are the devil's party. Lo! is it not the devil's party who will be the losers?

يٰۤاَيُّهَا الَّذِيْنَ اٰمَنُوْۤا اِذَا نَاجَيْتُمُ الرَّسُوْلَ فَقَدِّمُوْا
بَيْنَ يَدَيْ نَجْوٰىكُمْ صَدَقَةً ۚ ذٰلِكَ خَيْرٌ لَّكُمْ وَاَطْهَرُ ۚ
فَاِنْ لَّمْ تَجِدُوْا فَاِنَّ اللّٰهَ غَفُوْرٌ رَّحِيْمٌ ﴿١٢﴾
ءَاَشْفَقْتُمْ اَنْ تُقَدِّمُوْا بَيْنَ يَدَيْ نَجْوٰىكُمْ
صَدَقٰتٍ ۚ فَاِذْ لَمْ تَفْعَلُوْا وَتَابَ اللّٰهُ عَلَيْكُمْ
فَاَقِيْمُوا الصَّلٰوةَ وَاٰتُوا الزَّكٰوةَ وَاَطِيْعُوا اللّٰهَ وَ
رَسُوْلَهٗ ۚ وَاللّٰهُ خَبِيْرٌۢ بِمَا تَعْمَلُوْنَ ﴿١٣﴾ ع ٢ ٢
اَلَمْ تَرَ اِلَى الَّذِيْنَ تَوَلَّوْا قَوْمًا غَضِبَ اللّٰهُ عَلَيْهِمْ ۗ
مَا هُمْ مِّنْكُمْ وَلَا مِنْهُمْ ۙ وَيَحْلِفُوْنَ عَلَى الْكَذِبِ
وَهُمْ يَعْلَمُوْنَ ﴿١٤﴾
اَعَدَّ اللّٰهُ لَهُمْ عَذَابًا شَدِيْدًا ۗ اِنَّهُمْ سَآءَ مَا
كَانُوْا يَعْمَلُوْنَ ﴿١٥﴾
اِتَّخَذُوْۤا اَيْمَانَهُمْ جُنَّةً فَصَدُّوْا عَنْ سَبِيْلِ
اللّٰهِ فَلَهُمْ عَذَابٌ مُّهِيْنٌ ﴿١٦﴾
لَنْ تُغْنِيَ عَنْهُمْ اَمْوَالُهُمْ وَلَاۤ اَوْلَادُهُمْ مِّنَ اللّٰهِ
شَيْـًٔا ۗ اُولٰٓئِكَ اَصْحٰبُ النَّارِ ۗ هُمْ فِيْهَا خٰلِدُوْنَ ﴿١٧﴾
يَوْمَ يَبْعَثُهُمُ اللّٰهُ جَمِيْعًا فَيَحْلِفُوْنَ لَهٗ كَمَا
يَحْلِفُوْنَ لَكُمْ وَيَحْسَبُوْنَ اَنَّهُمْ عَلٰى شَيْءٍ ۗ اَلَاۤ
اِنَّهُمْ هُمُ الْكٰذِبُوْنَ ﴿١٨﴾
اِسْتَحْوَذَ عَلَيْهِمُ الشَّيْطٰنُ فَاَنْسٰىهُمْ ذِكْرَ اللّٰهِ ۗ
اُولٰٓئِكَ حِزْبُ الشَّيْطٰنِ ۗ اَلَاۤ اِنَّ حِزْبَ الشَّيْطٰنِ
هُمُ الْخٰسِرُوْنَ ﴿١٩﴾

20. Lo! those who oppose Allah and His messenger, they will be among the lowest.

21. Allah hath decreed: Lo! I verily shall conquer, I and My messengers. Lo! Allah is Strong, Almighty.

22. Thou wilt not find folk who believe in Allah and the Last Day loving those who oppose Allah and His messenger, even though they be their fathers or their sons or their brethren or their clan. As for such, He hath written faith upon their hearts and hath strengthened them with a Spirit from Him, and He will bring them into Gardens underneath which rivers flow, wherein they will abide. Allah is well pleased with them, and they are well pleased with Him. They are Allah's party. Lo! is it not Allah's party who are the successful?

اِنَّ الَّذِيۡنَ يُحَآدُّوۡنَ اللّٰهَ وَرَسُوۡلَهٗۤ اُولٰٓئِكَ فِى الۡاَذَلِّيۡنَ ۞

كَتَبَ اللّٰهُ لَاَغۡلِبَنَّ اَنَا وَرُسُلِىۡ ؕ اِنَّ اللّٰهَ قَوِىٌّ عَزِيۡزٌ ۞

لَا تَجِدُ قَوۡمًا يُّؤۡمِنُوۡنَ بِاللّٰهِ وَالۡيَوۡمِ الۡاٰخِرِ يُوَآدُّوۡنَ مَنۡ حَآدَّ اللّٰهَ وَرَسُوۡلَهٗ وَلَوۡ كَانُوۡۤا اٰبَآءَهُمۡ اَوۡ اَبۡنَآءَهُمۡ اَوۡ اِخۡوَانَهُمۡ اَوۡ عَشِيۡرَتَهُمۡ ؕ اُولٰٓئِكَ كَتَبَ فِىۡ قُلُوۡبِهِمُ الۡاِيۡمَانَ وَاَيَّدَهُمۡ بِرُوۡحٍ مِّنۡهُ ؕ وَيُدۡخِلُهُمۡ جَنّٰتٍ تَجۡرِىۡ مِنۡ تَحۡتِهَا الۡاَنۡهٰرُ خٰلِدِيۡنَ فِيۡهَا ؕ رَضِىَ اللّٰهُ عَنۡهُمۡ وَرَضُوۡا عَنۡهُ ؕ اُولٰٓئِكَ حِزۡبُ اللّٰهِ ؕ اَلَاۤ اِنَّ حِزۡبَ اللّٰهِ هُمُ الۡمُفۡلِحُوۡنَ ۞

Al-Ḥashr, "Exile," takes its name from vv. 2-17, which refer to the exile of the Banî Naḍir, a Jewish tribe of Al-Madînah (for treason and projected murder of the Prophet) and the confiscation of their property. The "Hypocrites," as the lukewarm Muslims were called, had secretly symphathised with these Jews, whose opposition had grown strong since the Muslim reverse at Mt. Uḥud, and had promised to side with them if it came to a collision with the Muslims; and to emigrate with them if they were forced to emigrate. But when the Muslims marched against the Banî Naḍir, and the latter took refuge in their strong towers, the Hypocrites did nothing. And when at length they were reduced and exiled, the Hypocrites did not go with them into exile.

The date of revelation is the fourth year of the Hijrah.

EXILE

Revealed at Al-Madīnah

In the name of Allah, the Beneficent, the Merciful.

1. All that is in the heavens and all that is in the earth glorifieth Allah, and He is the Mighty, the Wise.

2. He it is Who hath caused those of the People of the Scripture[1] who disbelieved to go forth from their homes unto the first exile. Ye deemed not that they would go forth, while they deemed that their strongholds would protect them from Allah. But Allah reached them from a place whereof they recked not, and cast terror in their hearts so that they ruined their houses with their own hands and the hands of the believers. So learn a lesson, O ye who have eyes!

3. And if Allah had not decreed migration for them, He verily would have punished them in this world, and theirs in the Hereafter is the punishment of the Fire.

4. That is because they were opposed to Allah and His messenger; and whoso is opposed to Allah, (for him) verily Allah is stern in reprisal.

5. Whatsoever palm-trees ye cut down or left standing on their roots, it was by Allah's leave, in order that He might confound the evil-livers.

6. And that which Allah gave as spoil unto His messenger from them, ye urged not any horse or riding-camel for the sake thereof, but Allah giveth His messenger lordship over whom He will. Allah is Able to do all things.

أياتها ٢٤ (٥٩) سُورَةُ الْحَشْرِ مَدَنِيَّةٌ ركوعاتها ٣

بِسْمِ اللهِ الرَّحْمٰنِ الرَّحِيْمِ ○

سَبَّحَ لِلّٰهِ مَا فِي السَّمٰوٰتِ وَمَا فِي الْأَرْضِ ۚ وَ
هُوَ الْعَزِيْزُ الْحَكِيْمُ ①

هُوَ الَّذِيْٓ اَخْرَجَ الَّذِيْنَ كَفَرُوْا مِنْ اَهْلِ الْكِتٰبِ
مِنْ دِيَارِهِمْ لِاَوَّلِ الْحَشْرِ ؕ مَا ظَنَنْتُمْ اَنْ
يَّخْرُجُوْا وَظَنُّوْٓا اَنَّهُمْ مَّانِعَتُهُمْ حُصُوْنُهُمْ مِّنَ
اللهِ فَاَتٰىهُمُ اللهُ مِنْ حَيْثُ لَمْ يَحْتَسِبُوْا ۖ وَ
قَذَفَ فِيْ قُلُوْبِهِمُ الرُّعْبَ يُخْرِبُوْنَ بُيُوْتَهُمْ
بِاَيْدِيْهِمْ وَاَيْدِي الْمُؤْمِنِيْنَ ۗ فَاعْتَبِرُوْا
يٰٓاُولِي الْاَبْصَارِ ②

وَلَوْلَآ اَنْ كَتَبَ اللهُ عَلَيْهِمُ الْجَلَآءَ لَعَذَّبَهُمْ
فِي الدُّنْيَا ۖ وَلَهُمْ فِي الْاٰخِرَةِ عَذَابُ النَّارِ ③

ذٰلِكَ بِاَنَّهُمْ شَآقُّوا اللهَ وَرَسُوْلَهٗ ۚ وَمَنْ يُّشَآقِّ
اللهَ فَاِنَّ اللهَ شَدِيْدُ الْعِقَابِ ④

مَا قَطَعْتُمْ مِّنْ لِّيْنَةٍ اَوْ تَرَكْتُمُوْهَا قَآئِمَةً عَلٰٓى
اُصُوْلِهَا فَبِاِذْنِ اللهِ وَلِيُخْزِيَ الْفٰسِقِيْنَ ⑤

وَمَآ اَفَآءَ اللهُ عَلٰى رَسُوْلِهٖ مِنْهُمْ فَمَآ اَوْجَفْتُمْ
عَلَيْهِ مِنْ خَيْلٍ وَّلَا رِكَابٍ وَّلٰكِنَّ اللهَ يُسَلِّطُ
رُسُلَهٗ عَلٰى مَنْ يَّشَآءُ ۚ وَاللهُ عَلٰى كُلِّ شَيْءٍ
قَدِيْرٌ ⑥

1. The term for Jews and Christians. In this case it refers to Jews.

7. That which Allah giveth as spoil unto His messenger from the people of the townships, it is for Allah and His messenger[1] and for the near of kin and the orphans and the needy and the wayfarer, that it become not a commodity between the rich among you. And whatsoever the messenger giveth you, take it. And whatsoever he forbiddeth, abstain (from it). And keep your duty to Allah. Lo! Allah is stern in reprisal.

مَآ أَفَآءَ اللّٰهُ عَلٰى رَسُوْلِهٖ مِنْ أَهْلِ الْقُرٰى فَلِلّٰهِ
وَلِلرَّسُوْلِ وَلِذِى الْقُرْبٰى وَالْيَتٰمٰى وَالْمَسٰكِيْنِ
وَابْنِ السَّبِيْلِ كَىْ لَا يَكُوْنَ دُوْلَةً بَيْنَ الْأَغْنِيَآءِ
مِنْكُمْ وَمَآ اٰتٰىكُمُ الرَّسُوْلُ فَخُذُوْهُ وَمَا نَهٰىكُمْ
عَنْهُ فَانْتَهُوْا وَاتَّقُوا اللّٰهَ إِنَّ اللّٰهَ شَدِيْدُ
الْعِقَابِ ﴿٧﴾

8. And (it is) for the poor fugitives who have been driven out from their homes and their belongings, who seek bounty from Allah and help Allah and His messenger. They are the loyal.

لِلْفُقَرَآءِ الْمُهٰجِرِيْنَ الَّذِيْنَ أُخْرِجُوْا مِنْ دِيَارِهِمْ
وَأَمْوَالِهِمْ يَبْتَغُوْنَ فَضْلًا مِّنَ اللّٰهِ وَرِضْوَانًا وَّ
يَنْصُرُوْنَ اللّٰهَ وَرَسُوْلَهٗ أُولٰٓئِكَ هُمُ الصّٰدِقُوْنَ ﴿٨﴾

9. Those who entered the city and the faith before them love those who flee unto them for refuge, and find in their breasts no need for that which hath been given them, but prefer (the fugitives) above themselves though poverty become their lot. And whoso is saved from his own avarice--such are they who are successful.

وَالَّذِيْنَ تَبَوَّؤُ الدَّارَ وَالْإِيْمَانَ مِنْ قَبْلِهِمْ يُحِبُّوْنَ
مَنْ هَاجَرَ إِلَيْهِمْ وَلَا يَجِدُوْنَ فِىْ صُدُوْرِهِمْ حَاجَةً
مِّمَّآ أُوْتُوْا وَيُؤْثِرُوْنَ عَلٰٓى أَنْفُسِهِمْ وَلَوْ كَانَ بِهِمْ
خَصَاصَةٌ وَمَنْ يُّوْقَ شُحَّ نَفْسِهٖ فَأُولٰٓئِكَ
هُمُ الْمُفْلِحُوْنَ ﴿٩﴾

10. And those who came (into the faith) after them say: Our Lord! Forgive us and our brethren who were before us in the faith, and place not in our hearts any rancour toward those who believe. Our Lord! Thou art Full of Pity, Merciful.

وَالَّذِيْنَ جَآءُوْ مِنْ بَعْدِهِمْ يَقُوْلُوْنَ رَبَّنَا اغْفِرْ
لَنَا وَلِإِخْوَانِنَا الَّذِيْنَ سَبَقُوْنَا بِالْإِيْمَانِ وَلَا
تَجْعَلْ فِىْ قُلُوْبِنَا غِلًّا لِّلَّذِيْنَ اٰمَنُوْا رَبَّنَآ إِنَّكَ
رَءُوْفٌ رَّحِيْمٌ ﴿١٠﴾

11. Hast thou not observed those who are hypocrites, (how) they tell their brethren who disbelieve among the People of the Scripture: If ye are driven out, we surely will go out with you, and we will never obey anyone against you, and if ye are attacked we verily will help you. And Allah beareth witness that they verily are liars.

أَلَمْ تَرَ إِلَى الَّذِيْنَ نَافَقُوْا يَقُوْلُوْنَ لِإِخْوَانِهِمُ الَّذِيْنَ
كَفَرُوْا مِنْ أَهْلِ الْكِتٰبِ لَئِنْ أُخْرِجْتُمْ لَنَخْرُجَنَّ
مَعَكُمْ وَلَا نُطِيْعُ فِيْكُمْ أَحَدًا أَبَدًا وَّإِنْ قُوْتِلْتُمْ
لَنَنْصُرَنَّكُمْ وَاللّٰهُ يَشْهَدُ إِنَّهُمْ لَكٰذِبُوْنَ ﴿١١﴾

1. i.e. for the State.

12. (For) indeed if they are driven out they go not out with them, and indeed if they are attacked they help not, and indeed if they had helped them they would have turned and fled, and then they would not have been victorious.

13. Ye are more awful as a fear in their bosoms than Allah. That is because they are a folk who understand not.

14. They will not fight against you in a body save in fortified villages or from behind walls. Their adversity among themselves is very great. Ye think of them as a whole whereas their hearts are divers. That is because they are a folk who have no sense.

15. On the likeness of those (who suffered) a short time before them, they taste the ill-effects of their conduct, and theirs is painful punishment.

16. (And the hypocrites are) on the likeness of the devil when he telleth man to disbelieve, then, when he disbelieveth saith: Lo! I am quit of thee. Lo! I fear Allah, the Lord of the Worlds.

17. And the consequence for both will be that they are in the Fire, therein abiding. Such is the reward of evil-doers.

18. O ye who believe! Observe your duty to Allah. And let every soul look to that which it sendeth on before for the morrow. And observe your duty to Allah! Lo! Allah is Informed of what ye do.

19. And be not ye as those who forgot Allah, therefore He caused them to forget their souls. Such are the evil-doers.

20. Not equal are the owners of the Fire and the owners of the Garden. The owners of the Garden, they are the victorious.

لَىِٕنْ اُخْرِجُوْا لَا يَخْرُجُوْنَ مَعَهُمْ ۚ وَلَىِٕنْ قُوْتِلُوْا لَا يَنْصُرُوْنَهُمْ ۚ وَلَىِٕنْ نَّصَرُوْهُمْ لَيُوَلُّنَّ الْاَدْبَارَ ۫ ثُمَّ لَا يُنْصَرُوْنَ ۝

لَاَنْتُمْ اَشَدُّ رَهْبَةً فِيْ صُدُوْرِهِمْ مِّنَ اللّٰهِ ۚ ذٰلِكَ بِاَنَّهُمْ قَوْمٌ لَّا يَفْقَهُوْنَ ۝

لَا يُقَاتِلُوْنَكُمْ جَمِيْعًا اِلَّا فِيْ قُرًى مُّحَصَّنَةٍ اَوْ مِنْ وَّرَآءِ جُدُرٍ ۚ بَأْسُهُمْ بَيْنَهُمْ شَدِيْدٌ ۚ تَحْسَبُهُمْ جَمِيْعًا وَّقُلُوْبُهُمْ شَتّٰى ۚ ذٰلِكَ بِاَنَّهُمْ قَوْمٌ لَّا يَعْقِلُوْنَ ۝

كَمَثَلِ الَّذِيْنَ مِنْ قَبْلِهِمْ قَرِيْبًا ذَاقُوْا وَبَالَ اَمْرِهِمْ ۚ وَلَهُمْ عَذَابٌ اَلِيْمٌ ۝

كَمَثَلِ الشَّيْطٰنِ اِذْ قَالَ لِلْاِنْسَانِ اكْفُرْ ۚ فَلَمَّا كَفَرَ قَالَ اِنِّيْ بَرِيْٓءٌ مِّنْكَ اِنِّيْٓ اَخَافُ اللّٰهَ رَبَّ الْعٰلَمِيْنَ ۝

فَكَانَ عَاقِبَتَهُمَآ اَنَّهُمَا فِي النَّارِ خَالِدَيْنِ فِيْهَا ۚ وَذٰلِكَ جَزٰٓؤُا الظّٰلِمِيْنَ ۝

يٰٓاَيُّهَا الَّذِيْنَ اٰمَنُوا اتَّقُوا اللّٰهَ وَلْتَنْظُرْ نَفْسٌ مَّا قَدَّمَتْ لِغَدٍ ۚ وَاتَّقُوا اللّٰهَ ۚ اِنَّ اللّٰهَ خَبِيْرٌ بِمَا تَعْمَلُوْنَ ۝

وَلَا تَكُوْنُوْا كَالَّذِيْنَ نَسُوا اللّٰهَ فَاَنْسٰهُمْ اَنْفُسَهُمْ ۚ اُولٰٓئِكَ هُمُ الْفٰسِقُوْنَ ۝

لَا يَسْتَوِيْٓ اَصْحٰبُ النَّارِ وَاَصْحٰبُ الْجَنَّةِ ۘ اَصْحٰبُ الْجَنَّةِ هُمُ الْفَآئِزُوْنَ ۝

21. If We had caused this Qur'ān to descend upon a mountain, thou (O Muhammad) verily hadst seen it humbled, rent asunder by the fear of Allah. Such similitudes coin We for mankind that haply they may reflect.

22. He is Allah, than Whom there is no other God, the Knower of the invisible and the visible. He is the Beneficent, the Merciful.

23. He is Allah, than Whom there is no other God, the Sovereign Lord, the Holy One, Peace, the Keeper of Faith, the Guardian, the Majestic, the Compeller, the Superb. Glorified be Allah from all that they ascribe as partners (unto Him)!

24. He is Allah, the Creator, the Shaper out of naught, the Fashioner. His are the most beautiful names. All that is in the heavens and the earth glorifieth Him, and He is the Mighty, the Wise.

لَوْ اَنْزَلْنَا هٰذَا الْقُرْاٰنَ عَلٰى جَبَلٍ لَّرَاَيْتَهٗ خَاشِعًا
مُّتَصَدِّعًا مِّنْ خَشْيَةِ اللّٰهِ ؕ وَتِلْكَ الْاَمْثَالُ نَضْرِبُهَا
لِلنَّاسِ لَعَلَّهُمْ يَتَفَكَّرُوْنَ ﴿٢١﴾
هُوَ اللّٰهُ الَّذِيْ لَآ اِلٰهَ اِلَّا هُوَ ۚ عٰلِمُ الْغَيْبِ وَ
الشَّهَادَةِ ۚ هُوَ الرَّحْمٰنُ الرَّحِيْمُ ﴿٢٢﴾
هُوَ اللّٰهُ الَّذِيْ لَآ اِلٰهَ اِلَّا هُوَ ۚ اَلْمَلِكُ الْقُدُّوْسُ
السَّلٰمُ الْمُؤْمِنُ الْمُهَيْمِنُ الْعَزِيْزُ الْجَبَّارُ الْمُتَكَبِّرُ ؕ
سُبْحٰنَ اللّٰهِ عَمَّا يُشْرِكُوْنَ ﴿٢٣﴾
هُوَ اللّٰهُ الْخَالِقُ الْبَارِئُ الْمُصَوِّرُ لَهُ الْاَسْمَآءُ
الْحُسْنٰى ؕ يُسَبِّحُ لَهٗ مَا فِي السَّمٰوٰتِ وَالْاَرْضِ ۚ
وَهُوَ الْعَزِيْزُ الْحَكِيْمُ ﴿٢٤﴾ ع ٣

Al-Mumtaḥanah, "She that is to be Examined," takes its name from v. 10, where the believers are told to examine women who come to them as fugitives from the idolaters and, if they find them sincere converts to Al-Islām, not to return them to the idolaters. This marked a modification in the terms of the Truce of Ḥudeybiyah, by which the Prophet had engaged to return all fugitives, male and female, while the idolaters were not obliged to give up renegades from Al-Islām. The more terrible persecution which women had to undergo, if extradited, and their helpless social condition were the causes of the change. Instead of giving up women refugees who were sincere, and not fugitives on account of crime or some family quarrel, the Muslims were to pay an indemnity for them; while as for Muslim husbands whose wives might flee to Qureysh, no indemnity was to be paid by the latter but, when some turn of fortune brought wealth to the Islāmic State, they were to be repaid by the State what their wives had taken of their property. In v. 12 is the pledge which was to be taken from the women refugees after their examination.

The date of revelation is the eighth year of the Hijrah.

SHE THAT IS TO BE EXAMINED

Revealed at Al-Madinah

In the name of Allah, the Beneficent, the Merciful.

1. O ye who believe! Choose not My enemy and your enemy for friends. Do ye give them friendship when they disbelieve in that Truth which hath come unto you, driving out the messenger and you because ye believe in Allah, your Lord? If ye have come forth to strive in My way and seeking My good pleasure, (show them not friendship). Do ye show friendship unto them in secret, when I am best Aware of what ye hide and what ye proclaim? And whosoever doth it among you, he verily hath strayed from the right way.

2. If they have the upperhand of you, they will be your foes, and will stretch out their hands and their tongues toward you with evil (intent), and they long for you to disbelieve.

3. Your ties of kindred and your children will avail you naught upon the Day of Resurrection. He will part you. Allah is Seer of what ye do.

4. There is a goodly pattern for you in Abraham and those with him, when they told their folk: Lo! we are guiltless of you and all that ye worship beside Allah. We have done with you. And there hath arisen between us and you hostility and hate for ever until ye believe in Allah only—save that which Abraham promised his father (when he said): I will ask forgiveness for thee, though I own nothing for thee from Allah—our Lord! In Thee we put our trust, and unto Thee we turn repentant, and unto Thee is the journeying.

آياتها ١٣ (٦٠) سُورَةُ الْمُمْتَحِنَةِ مَدَنِيَّةٌ رُكُوعَاتُهَا ٢

بِسْمِ اللَّهِ الرَّحْمَٰنِ الرَّحِيمِ

يَا أَيُّهَا الَّذِينَ آمَنُوا لَا تَتَّخِذُوا عَدُوِّي وَعَدُوَّكُمْ
أَوْلِيَاءَ تُلْقُونَ إِلَيْهِمْ بِالْمَوَدَّةِ وَقَدْ كَفَرُوا بِمَا
جَاءَكُمْ مِنَ الْحَقِّ يُخْرِجُونَ الرَّسُولَ وَإِيَّاكُمْ أَنْ
تُؤْمِنُوا بِاللَّهِ رَبِّكُمْ إِنْ كُنْتُمْ خَرَجْتُمْ جِهَادًا فِي سَبِيلِي
وَابْتِغَاءَ مَرْضَاتِي تُسِرُّونَ إِلَيْهِمْ بِالْمَوَدَّةِ وَأَنَا
أَعْلَمُ بِمَا أَخْفَيْتُمْ وَمَا أَعْلَنْتُمْ وَمَنْ يَفْعَلْهُ
مِنْكُمْ فَقَدْ ضَلَّ سَوَاءَ السَّبِيلِ ﴿١﴾
إِنْ يَثْقَفُوكُمْ يَكُونُوا لَكُمْ أَعْدَاءً وَيَبْسُطُوا إِلَيْكُمْ
أَيْدِيَهُمْ وَأَلْسِنَتَهُمْ بِالسُّوءِ وَوَدُّوا لَوْ
تَكْفُرُونَ ﴿٢﴾
لَنْ تَنْفَعَكُمْ أَرْحَامُكُمْ وَلَا أَوْلَادُكُمْ يَوْمَ الْقِيَامَةِ
يَفْصِلُ بَيْنَكُمْ وَاللَّهُ بِمَا تَعْمَلُونَ بَصِيرٌ ﴿٣﴾
قَدْ كَانَتْ لَكُمْ أُسْوَةٌ حَسَنَةٌ فِي إِبْرَاهِيمَ وَالَّذِينَ
مَعَهُ إِذْ قَالُوا لِقَوْمِهِمْ إِنَّا بُرَآءُ مِنْكُمْ وَمِمَّا
تَعْبُدُونَ مِنْ دُونِ اللَّهِ كَفَرْنَا بِكُمْ وَبَدَا بَيْنَنَا
وَبَيْنَكُمُ الْعَدَاوَةُ وَالْبَغْضَاءُ أَبَدًا حَتَّىٰ تُؤْمِنُوا
بِاللَّهِ وَحْدَهُ إِلَّا قَوْلَ إِبْرَاهِيمَ لِأَبِيهِ لَأَسْتَغْفِرَنَّ
لَكَ وَمَا أَمْلِكُ لَكَ مِنَ اللَّهِ مِنْ شَيْءٍ رَبَّنَا عَلَيْكَ
تَوَكَّلْنَا وَإِلَيْكَ أَنَبْنَا وَإِلَيْكَ الْمَصِيرُ ﴿٤﴾

معانقة ٣ السماع الوقف عن القبلة ٣

5. Our Lord! Make us not a prey for those who disbelieve, and forgive us, our Lord! Lo! Thou, only Thou, art the Mighty, the Wise.

6. Verily ye have in them a goodly pattern for everyone who looketh to Allah and the Last Day. And whosoever may turn away, lo! still Allah, He is the Absolute, the Owner of Praise.

7. It may be that Allah will ordain love between you and those of them with whom ye are at enmity. Allah is Mighty, and Allah is Forgiving, Merciful.

8. Allah forbiddeth you not those who warred not against you on account of religion and drove you not out from your homes, that ye should show them kindness and deal justly with them. Lo! Allah loveth the just dealers.

9. Allah forbiddeth you only those who warred against you on account of religion and have driven you out from your homes and helped to drive you out, that ye make friends of them. Whosoever maketh friends of them—(All) such are wrong-doers.

10. O ye who believe! When believing women come unto you as fugitives, examine them. Allah is best aware of their faith. Then, if ye know them for true believers, send them not back unto the disbelievers. They are not lawful for the disbelievers, nor are the disbelievers lawful for them. And give the disbelievers that which they have spent (upon them). And it is no sin for you to marry such women when ye have given them their dues. And hold not to the ties of disbelieving women; and ask for (the return of) that which ye have spent; and let the disbelievers ask for that which they have spent. That is the judgement of Allah. He judgeth between you. Allah is Knower, Wise.

ربنا لا تجعلنا فتنة للذين كفروا واغفر لنا
ربنا إنك أنت العزيز الحكيم ٥
لقد كان لكم فيهم أسوة حسنة لمن كان
يرجوا الله واليوم الآخر ومن يتول فإن الله
ع هو الغني الحميد ٦
عسى الله أن يجعل بينكم وبين الذين عاديتم
منهم مودة والله قدير والله غفور رحيم ٧
لا ينهكم الله عن الذين لم يقاتلوكم في الدين
ولم يخرجوكم من دياركم أن تبروهم وتقسطوا
إليهم إن الله يحب المقسطين ٨
إنما ينهكم الله عن الذين قتلوكم في الدين
وأخرجوكم من دياركم وظهروا على إخراجكم
أن تولوهم ومن يتولهم فأولئك هم الظلمون ٩
يأيها الذين آمنوا إذا جاءكم المؤمنت مهجرت
فامتحنوهن الله أعلم بإيمانهن فإن علمتموهن
مؤمنت فلا ترجعوهن إلى الكفار لا هن حل
لهم ولا هم يحلون لهن وآتوهم ما أنفقوا
ولا جناح عليكم أن تنكحوهن إذا آتيتموهن
أجورهن ولا تمسكوا بعصم الكوافر وسئلوا
ما أنفقتم وليسئلوا ما أنفقوا ذلكم
حكم الله يحكم بينكم والله عليم
حكيم ١٠

11. And if any of your wives have gone from you unto the disbelievers and afterward ye have your turn (of triumpn), then give unto those whose wives have gone the like of that which they have spent, and keep your duty to Allah in whom ye are believers.

12. O Prophet! If believing women come unto thee, taking oath of allegiance unto thee that they will ascribe nothing as partner unto Allah, and will neither steal nor commit adultery nor kill their children, nor produce any lie that they have devised between their hands and feet, nor disobey thee in what is right,[1] then accept their allegiance and ask Allah to forgive them. Lo! Allah is Forgiving, Merciful.

13. O ye who believe! Be not friendly with a folk with whom Allah is wroth, (a folk) who have despaired of the Hereafter as the disbelievers despair of those who are in the graves.

وَإِنْ فَاتَكُمْ شَيْءٌ مِّنْ أَزْوَاجِكُمْ إِلَى الْكُفَّارِ
فَعَاقَبْتُمْ فَآتُوا الَّذِينَ ذَهَبَتْ أَزْوَاجُهُم مِّثْلَ
مَا أَنفَقُوا ۚ وَاتَّقُوا اللَّهَ الَّذِي أَنتُم بِهِ مُؤْمِنُونَ ﴿١١﴾
يَا أَيُّهَا النَّبِيُّ إِذَا جَاءَكَ الْمُؤْمِنَاتُ يُبَايِعْنَكَ
عَلَىٰ أَن لَّا يُشْرِكْنَ بِاللَّهِ شَيْئًا وَلَا يَسْرِقْنَ وَلَا
يَزْنِينَ وَلَا يَقْتُلْنَ أَوْلَادَهُنَّ وَلَا يَأْتِينَ بِبُهْتَانٍ
يَفْتَرِينَهُ بَيْنَ أَيْدِيهِنَّ وَأَرْجُلِهِنَّ وَلَا يَعْصِينَكَ
فِي مَعْرُوفٍ ۙ فَبَايِعْهُنَّ وَاسْتَغْفِرْ لَهُنَّ اللَّهَ ۖ إِنَّ
اللَّهَ غَفُورٌ رَّحِيمٌ ﴿١٢﴾
يَا أَيُّهَا الَّذِينَ آمَنُوا لَا تَتَوَلَّوْا قَوْمًا غَضِبَ
اللَّهُ عَلَيْهِمْ قَدْ يَئِسُوا مِنَ الْآخِرَةِ كَمَا يَئِسَ
الْكُفَّارُ مِنْ أَصْحَابِ الْقُبُورِ ﴿١٣﴾

1. This is called the women's oath of allegiance. It was the oath exacted from men also until the second pact of Al-'Aqabah when the duty of defence was added to the men's oath.

As-Saff, "The Ranks," takes its name from a word in v. 4. In the copy of the Koran which I have followed, it is stated to have been revealed at Mecca, though its contents evidently refer to the Madînah period. It may have been revealed while the Prophet and his companions were encamped in the valley of Mecca during the negotiations of the Truce of Ḥudeybîyah, with which some of its verses are associated by tradition.

In that case the date of revelation would be the sixth year of the Hijrah.

THE RANKS

Revealed at Al-Madīnah

In the name of Allah, the Beneficent, the Merciful.

1. All that is in the heavens and all that is in the earth glorifieth Allah, and He is the Mighty, the Wise.

2. O ye who believe! Why say ye that which ye do not?

3. It is most hateful in the sight of Allah that ye say that which ye do not.

4. Lo! Allah loveth those who battle for His cause in ranks, as if they were a solid structure.

5. And (remember) when Moses said unto his people: O my people! Why persecute ye me, when ye well know that I am Allah's messenger unto you? So when they went astray Allah sent their hearts astray. And Allah guideth not the evil-living folk.

6. And when Jesus son of Mary said: O Children of Israel Lo! I am the messenger of Allah unto you, confirming that which was (revealed) before me in the Torah[1], and bringing good tidings of a messenger who cometh after me, whose name is the Praised One.[2] Yet when he hath come unto them with clear proofs, they say: This is mere magic.

7. And who doth greater wrong than he who inventeth a lie against Allah when he is summoned unto Al-Islām?[3] and Allah guideth not wrongdoing folk.

8. Fain would they put out the light of Allah with their mouths, but Allah will perfect His light, however much the disbelievers are averse.

آياتها ١٤ (٦١) سُورَةُ الصَّفِّ مَدَنِيَّةٌ رُكُوعَاتُهَا ٢

بِسْمِ اللّٰهِ الرَّحْمٰنِ الرَّحِيمِ

سَبَّحَ لِلّٰهِ مَا فِي السَّمٰوٰتِ وَمَا فِي الْأَرْضِ وَهُوَ
الْعَزِيزُ الْحَكِيمُ ①
يَا أَيُّهَا الَّذِينَ آمَنُوا لِمَ تَقُولُونَ مَا لَا تَفْعَلُونَ ②
كَبُرَ مَقْتًا عِنْدَ اللّٰهِ أَنْ تَقُولُوا مَا لَا تَفْعَلُونَ ③
إِنَّ اللّٰهَ يُحِبُّ الَّذِينَ يُقَاتِلُونَ فِي سَبِيلِهِ صَفًّا
كَأَنَّهُمْ بُنْيَانٌ مَرْصُوصٌ ④
وَإِذْ قَالَ مُوسَىٰ لِقَوْمِهِ يَا قَوْمِ لِمَ تُؤْذُونَنِي وَقَدْ
تَعْلَمُونَ أَنِّي رَسُولُ اللّٰهِ إِلَيْكُمْ فَلَمَّا زَاغُوا أَزَاغَ
اللّٰهُ قُلُوبَهُمْ وَاللّٰهُ لَا يَهْدِي الْقَوْمَ الْفَاسِقِينَ ⑤
وَإِذْ قَالَ عِيسَى ابْنُ مَرْيَمَ يَا بَنِي إِسْرَائِيلَ إِنِّي
رَسُولُ اللّٰهِ إِلَيْكُمْ مُصَدِّقًا لِمَا بَيْنَ يَدَيَّ مِنَ
التَّوْرَاةِ وَمُبَشِّرًا بِرَسُولٍ يَأْتِي مِنْ بَعْدِي
اسْمُهُ أَحْمَدُ فَلَمَّا جَاءَهُمْ بِالْبَيِّنَاتِ قَالُوا هٰذَا
سِحْرٌ مُبِينٌ ⑥
وَمَنْ أَظْلَمُ مِمَّنِ افْتَرَىٰ عَلَى اللّٰهِ الْكَذِبَ وَهُوَ
يُدْعَىٰ إِلَى الْإِسْلَامِ وَاللّٰهُ لَا يَهْدِي الْقَوْمَ
الظَّالِمِينَ ⑦
يُرِيدُونَ لِيُطْفِئُوا نُورَ اللّٰهِ بِأَفْوَاهِهِمْ وَاللّٰهُ مُتِمُّ
نُورِهِ وَلَوْ كَرِهَ الْكَافِرُونَ ⑧

1. Books of Moses.
2. Ar. *Aḥmad.* A name of the Prophet of Arabia. The promised "Comforter" was believed by many Christian communities of the East to be a Prophet yet to come, and most of them accepted Muhammad as that Prophet.
3. Lit. "The Surrender."

9. He it is Who hath sent His messenger with the guidance and the religion of truth, that He may make it conqueror of all religion, however much idolaters may be averse.

10. O ye who believe! Shall I show you a commerce that will save you from a painful doom?

11. Ye should believe in Allah and His messenger, and should strive for the cause of Allah with your wealth and your lives. That is better for you, if ye did but know.

12. He will forgive you your sins and bring you into Gardens underneath which rivers flow, and pleasant dwellings in Gardens of Eden. That is the Supreme triumph.

13. And (He will give you) another blessing which ye love: help from Allah and present victory. Give good tidings (O Muhammad) to believers.

14. O ye who believe! Be Allah's helpers, even as Jesus son of Mary said unto the disciples: Who are my helpers for Allah? They said: We are Allah's helpers. And a party of the Children of Israel believed, while a party disbelieved. Then We strengthened those who believed against their foe, and they became the uppermost.

هُوَ الَّذِیۡۤ اَرۡسَلَ رَسُوۡلَہٗ بِالۡہُدٰی وَ دِیۡنِ الۡحَقِّ
ع لِیُظۡہِرَہٗ عَلَی الدِّیۡنِ کُلِّہٖ وَ لَوۡ کَرِہَ الۡمُشۡرِکُوۡنَ ﴿۹﴾
یٰۤاَیُّہَا الَّذِیۡنَ اٰمَنُوۡا ہَلۡ اَدُلُّکُمۡ عَلٰی تِجَارَۃٍ تُنۡجِیۡکُمۡ
مِّنۡ عَذَابٍ اَلِیۡمٍ ﴿۱۰﴾
تُؤۡمِنُوۡنَ بِاللّٰہِ وَ رَسُوۡلِہٖ وَ تُجَاہِدُوۡنَ فِیۡ سَبِیۡلِ
اللّٰہِ بِاَمۡوَالِکُمۡ وَ اَنۡفُسِکُمۡ ؕ ذٰلِکُمۡ خَیۡرٌ لَّکُمۡ اِنۡ کُنۡتُمۡ
تَعۡلَمُوۡنَ ﴿ۙ۱۱﴾
یَغۡفِرۡ لَکُمۡ ذُنُوۡبَکُمۡ وَ یُدۡخِلۡکُمۡ جَنّٰتٍ تَجۡرِیۡ مِنۡ
تَحۡتِہَا الۡاَنۡہٰرُ وَ مَسٰکِنَ طَیِّبَۃً فِیۡ جَنّٰتِ عَدۡنٍ ؕ
ذٰلِکَ الۡفَوۡزُ الۡعَظِیۡمُ ﴿ۙ۱۲﴾
وَ اُخۡرٰی تُحِبُّوۡنَہَا ؕ نَصۡرٌ مِّنَ اللّٰہِ وَ فَتۡحٌ قَرِیۡبٌ ؕ
وَ بَشِّرِ الۡمُؤۡمِنِیۡنَ ﴿۱۳﴾
یٰۤاَیُّہَا الَّذِیۡنَ اٰمَنُوۡا کُوۡنُوۡۤا اَنۡصَارَ اللّٰہِ کَمَا قَالَ
عِیۡسَی ابۡنُ مَرۡیَمَ لِلۡحَوَارِیّٖنَ مَنۡ اَنۡصَارِیۡۤ اِلَی
اللّٰہِ ؕ قَالَ الۡحَوَارِیُّوۡنَ نَحۡنُ اَنۡصَارُ اللّٰہِ فَاٰمَنَتۡ
طَّآئِفَۃٌ مِّنۡۢ بَنِیۡۤ اِسۡرَآءِیۡلَ وَ کَفَرَتۡ طَّآئِفَۃٌ ۚ
فَاَیَّدۡنَا الَّذِیۡنَ اٰمَنُوۡا عَلٰی عَدُوِّہِمۡ فَاَصۡبَحُوۡا
ع ظٰہِرِیۡنَ ﴿۱۴﴾

Al-Jum'ah, "The Congregation," takes it name from a word in v. 9, where obedience to the call to congregational prayer is enjoined. Tradition says that vv. 9-11 refer to an occasion when a caravan entered Al-Madinah with beating of drums at the time when the Prophet was preaching in the mosque, and that the congregation broke away to look at it except twelve men. If, as one version of the tradition says, the caravan was that of Daḥyah al-Kalbi, the incident must have occurred before the fifth year of the Hijrah, because Daḥyah was a Muslim in the fifth year A.H. The date of revelation is between the years 2 and 4 A.H.

THE CONGREGATION

Revealed at Al-Madinah

In the name of Allah, the Beneficent, the Merciful.

1. All that is in the heavens and all that is in the earth glorifieth Allah, the Sovereign Lord, the Holy One, the Mighty, the Wise.

2. He it is Who hath sent among the unlettered ones a messenger of their own, to recite unto them His revelations and to make them grow, and to teach them the Scripture and Wisdom, though heretofore they were indeed in error manifest,

3. Along with others of them who have not yet joined them. He is the Mighty, the Wise.

4. That is the bounty of Allah; which He giveth unto whom he will. Allah is of Infinite bounty.

5. The likeness of those who are entrusted with the Law of Moses, yet apply it not, is as the likeness of the ass carrying books. Wretched is the likeness of folk who deny the revelations of Allah. And Allah guideth not wrongdoing folk.

6. Say (O Muhammad): O ye who are Jews! If ye claim that ye are favoured of Allah part from (all) mankind, then long for death if ye are truthful.

7. But they will never long for it because of all that their own hands have sent before, and Allah is Aware of evildoers.

اٰياتها ١١ (٦٢) سُوْرَةُ الْجُمُعَةِ مَدَنِيَّةٌ ركوعاتها ٢

بِسْمِ اللّٰهِ الرَّحْمٰنِ الرَّحِيْمِ ○

يُسَبِّحُ لِلّٰهِ مَا فِي السَّمٰوٰتِ وَمَا فِي الْاَرْضِ الْمَلِكِ
الْقُدُّوْسِ الْعَزِيْزِ الْحَكِيْمِ ①

هُوَ الَّذِيْ بَعَثَ فِي الْاُمِّيّٖنَ رَسُوْلًا مِّنْهُمْ يَتْلُوْا
عَلَيْهِمْ اٰيٰتِهٖ وَيُزَكِّيْهِمْ وَيُعَلِّمُهُمُ الْكِتٰبَ
وَالْحِكْمَةَ ۗ وَاِنْ كَانُوْا مِنْ قَبْلُ لَفِيْ ضَلٰلٍ
مُّبِيْنٍ ②

وَّاٰخَرِيْنَ مِنْهُمْ لَمَّا يَلْحَقُوْا بِهِمْ ۗ وَهُوَ الْعَزِيْزُ
الْحَكِيْمُ ③

ذٰلِكَ فَضْلُ اللّٰهِ يُؤْتِيْهِ مَنْ يَّشَآءُ ۗ وَاللّٰهُ ذُو
الْفَضْلِ الْعَظِيْمِ ④

مَثَلُ الَّذِيْنَ حُمِّلُوا التَّوْرٰىةَ ثُمَّ لَمْ يَحْمِلُوْهَا
كَمَثَلِ الْحِمَارِ يَحْمِلُ اَسْفَارًا ۗ بِئْسَ مَثَلُ
الْقَوْمِ الَّذِيْنَ كَذَّبُوْا بِاٰيٰتِ اللّٰهِ ۗ وَاللّٰهُ لَا يَهْدِي
الْقَوْمَ الظّٰلِمِيْنَ ⑤

قُلْ يٰاَيُّهَا الَّذِيْنَ هَادُوْٓا اِنْ زَعَمْتُمْ اَنَّكُمْ
اَوْلِيَآءُ لِلّٰهِ مِنْ دُوْنِ النَّاسِ فَتَمَنَّوُا الْمَوْتَ اِنْ
كُنْتُمْ صٰدِقِيْنَ ⑥

وَلَا يَتَمَنَّوْنَهٗٓ اَبَدًا ۢ بِمَا قَدَّمَتْ اَيْدِيْهِمْ ۗ وَاللّٰهُ
عَلِيْمٌۢ بِالظّٰلِمِيْنَ ⑦

8. Say (unto them, O Muhammad): Lo! the death from which ye shrink will surely meet you, and afterward ye will be returned unto the Knower of the invisible and the visible, and He will tell you what ye used to do.

9. O ye who believe! When the call is heard for the prayer of the day of congregation, haste unto remembrance of Allah and leave your trading. That is better for you if ye did but know.

10. And when the prayer is ended, then disperse in the land and seek of Allah's bounty, and remember Allah much, that ye may be successful.

11. But when they spy some merchandise or pastime they break away to it and leave thee standing. Say: That which Allah hath is better than pastime and than merchandise, and Allah is the best of providers.

قُلْ اِنَّ الْمَوْتَ الَّذِیْ تَفِرُّوْنَ مِنْهُ فَاِنَّهٗ مُلٰقِیْكُمْ
ثُمَّ تُرَدُّوْنَ اِلٰى عٰلِمِ الْغَیْبِ وَالشَّهَادَةِ فَیُنَبِّئُكُمْ
بِمَا كُنْتُمْ تَعْمَلُوْنَ ﴿٨﴾ ع
یٰۤاَیُّهَا الَّذِیْنَ اٰمَنُوْۤا اِذَا نُوْدِیَ لِلصَّلٰوةِ مِنْ یَّوْمِ
الْجُمُعَةِ فَاسْعَوْا اِلٰى ذِكْرِ اللّٰهِ وَذَرُوا الْبَیْعَ ذٰلِكُمْ
خَیْرٌ لَّكُمْ اِنْ كُنْتُمْ تَعْلَمُوْنَ ﴿٩﴾
فَاِذَا قُضِیَتِ الصَّلٰوةُ فَانْتَشِرُوْا فِی الْاَرْضِ
وَابْتَغُوْا مِنْ فَضْلِ اللّٰهِ وَاذْكُرُوا اللّٰهَ كَثِیْرًا
لَّعَلَّكُمْ تُفْلِحُوْنَ ﴿١٠﴾
وَاِذَا رَاَوْا تِجَارَةً اَوْ لَهْوَا انْفَضُّوْۤا اِلَیْهَا وَ
تَرَكُوْكَ قَآىِٕمًا قُلْ مَا عِنْدَ اللّٰهِ خَیْرٌ مِّنَ
اللَّهْوِ وَمِنَ التِّجَارَةِ وَاللّٰهُ خَیْرُ الرّٰزِقِیْنَ ﴿١١﴾ ع

Al-Munāfiqūn, "The Hypocrites," takes its name from a word occurring in the first verse. V. 8 refers to a remark of Abdullah ibn Ubeyy, the "Hypocrite" leader, expressing the desire that the old aristocracy of Yathrib, of which he had been the acknowledged chief, might regain the ascendancy and turn out the refugees from Mecca, whom he regarded as intruders.

The date of the revelation is the fourth year of the Hijrah.

THE HYPOCRITES

Revealed at Al-Madinah

In the name of Allah, the Beneficent, the Merciful.

1. When the hypocrites come unto thee (O Muhammad), they say: We bear witness that thou art indeed Allah's messenger. And Allah knoweth that thou art indeed His messenger, and Allah beareth witness that the Hypocrites are speaking falsely.

2. They make their faith a pretext so that they may turn (men) from the way of Allah. Verily evil is that which they are wont to do,

3. That is because they believed, then disbelieved, therefore their hearts are sealed so that they understand not.

4. And when thou seest them their figures please thee; and if they speak thou givest ear unto their speech. (They are) as though they were blocks of wood in striped cloaks.[1] They deem every shout to be against them. They are the enemy, so beware of them. Allah confound them! How they are perverted!

5. And when it is said unto them: Come! The messenger of Allah will ask forgiveness for you! they avert their faces and thou seest them turning away, disdainful.

6. Whether thou ask forgiveness for them or ask not forgiveness for them, Allah will not forgive them. Lo! Allah guideth not the evil-living folk.

7. They it is who say: Spend not on behalf of those (who dwell) with Allah's messenger that they may disperse (and go away from you); when Allah's are the treasures of the heavens and the earth; but the hypocrites comprehend not.

1. Or *propped-up blocks of wood*.

اياتها ١١ (٦٣) سورة المنافقون مدنية ركوعاتها ٢

بسم الله الرحمن الرحيم ○

إذا جاءك المنافقون قالوا نشهد إنك لرسول
الله والله يعلم إنك لرسوله والله يشهد إن
المنافقين لكاذبون ①
اتخذوا أيمانهم جنة فصدوا عن سبيل الله
إنهم ساء ما كانوا يعملون ②
ذلك بأنهم آمنوا ثم كفروا فطبع على قلوبهم
فهم لا يفقهون ③
وإذا رأيتهم تعجبك أجسامهم وإن يقولوا
تسمع لقولهم كأنهم خشب مسندة يحسبون
كل صيحة عليهم هم العدو فاحذرهم قاتلهم
الله أنى يؤفكون ④
وإذا قيل لهم تعالوا يستغفر لكم رسول الله لووا
رءوسهم ورأيتهم يصدون وهم مستكبرون ⑤
سواء عليهم أستغفرت لهم أم لم تستغفر
لهم لن يغفر الله لهم إن الله لا يهدي
القوم الفاسقين ⑥
هم الذين يقولون لا تنفقوا على من عند
رسول الله حتى ينفضوا ولله خزائن السماوات
والأرض ولكن المنافقين لا يفقهون ⑦

وقف لازم

8. They say: Surely, if we return to Al-Madīnah the mightier will soon drive out the weaker; when might belongeth to Allah and to His messenger and the believers; but the hypocrites know not.

9. O ye who believe! Let not your wealth nor your children distract you from remembrance of Allah. Those who do so, they are the losers.

10. And spend of that wherewith We have provided you before death cometh unto one of you and he saith: My Lord! If only Thou wouldst reprieve me for a little while, then I would give alms and be among the righteous.

11. But Allah reprieveth no soul when its term cometh, and Allah is Aware of what ye do.

يَقُولُونَ لَئِنْ رَّجَعْنَآ اِلَى الْمَدِيْنَةِ لَيُخْرِجَنَّ الْاَعَزُّ مِنْهَا الْاَذَلَّ ۚ وَلِلّٰهِ الْعِزَّةُ وَلِرَسُولِهٖ وَلِلْمُؤْمِنِيْنَ وَلٰكِنَّ الْمُنَافِقِيْنَ لَا يَعْلَمُوْنَ ۟

يٰۤاَيُّهَا الَّذِيْنَ اٰمَنُوْا لَا تُلْهِكُمْ اَمْوَالُكُمْ وَلَاۤ اَوْلَادُكُمْ عَنْ ذِكْرِ اللّٰهِ ۚ وَمَنْ يَّفْعَلْ ذٰلِكَ فَاُولٰٓئِكَ هُمُ الْخٰسِرُوْنَ ۟

وَاَنْفِقُوْا مِنْ مَّا رَزَقْنٰكُمْ مِّنْ قَبْلِ اَنْ يَّاْتِيَ اَحَدَكُمُ الْمَوْتُ فَيَقُوْلَ رَبِّ لَوْلَاۤ اَخَّرْتَنِيْ اِلٰۤى اَجَلٍ قَرِيْبٍ ۙ فَاَصَّدَّقَ وَاَكُنْ مِّنَ الصّٰلِحِيْنَ ۟

وَلَنْ يُّؤَخِّرَ اللّٰهُ نَفْسًا اِذَا جَآءَ اَجَلُهَا ۚ وَاللّٰهُ خَبِيْرٌ ۢ بِمَا تَعْمَلُوْنَ ۟

At-Taghābun, "Mutual Disillusion," takes its name from a word in v. 9.

The date of revelation is possibly the year 1 A.H., though it is generally regarded as a late Meccan Sūrah, vv. 14 ff. being taken as referring to the pressure brought to bear by wives and families to prevent Muslims leaving Mecca at the time of the Hijrah.

MUTUAL DISILLUSION

Revealed at Mekkah

In the name of Allah, te Beneficent, the Merciful.

1. All that is in the heavens and all that is in the earth glorifieth Allah; unto Him belongeth sovereignty and unto Him belongeth praise, and He is Able to do all things.

2. He it is who created you, but one of you is a disbeliever and one of you is a believer, and Allah is Seer of what ye do.

3. He careated the heavens and the earth with truth, and He shaped you and made good your shapes, and unto him is the journeying.

4. He knoweth all that is in the heavens and all that is in the earth, and He knoweth what ye conceal and what ye publish, And Allah is aware of what is in the breasts (of men).

5. Hath not the story reached you of those who disbelieved of old and so did taste the illefects of their conduct, and theirs will be a painful doom.

6. That was because their messengers (from Allah) kept coming unto them with clear proofs (of Allah's sovereignty), but they said: shall mere mortals guide us? So they disbelieved and turned away, and Allah, was independent (of them). allah is Absolute, Owner of Praise.

7. Those who disbelive assert that they will not be raised again. Say (unto them, O Muhammad): Yea, verily, by my Lord! ye will be raised again and then ye will be informed of what ye did; and that is easy for Allah.

8. So believe in allah and His messenger and the light which We have revealed. and Allah is Aware of what ye do.

اياتها ١٨ (٦٤) سُوْرَةُ التَّغَابُنِ مَدَنِيَّةٌ ركوعاتها ٢

بِسْمِ اللّٰهِ الرَّحْمٰنِ الرَّحِيْمِ

يُسَبِّحُ لِلّٰهِ مَا فِي السَّمٰوٰتِ وَمَا فِي الْاَرْضِ لَهُ
الْمُلْكُ وَلَهُ الْحَمْدُ وَهُوَ عَلٰى كُلِّ شَيْءٍ قَدِيْرٌ ١
هُوَ الَّذِيْ خَلَقَكُمْ فَمِنْكُمْ كَافِرٌ وَّمِنْكُمْ مُّؤْمِنٌ
وَاللّٰهُ بِمَا تَعْمَلُوْنَ بَصِيْرٌ ٢
خَلَقَ السَّمٰوٰتِ وَالْاَرْضَ بِالْحَقِّ وَصَوَّرَكُمْ
فَاَحْسَنَ صُوَرَكُمْ وَاِلَيْهِ الْمَصِيْرُ ٣
يَعْلَمُ مَا فِي السَّمٰوٰتِ وَالْاَرْضِ وَيَعْلَمُ مَا
تُسِرُّوْنَ وَمَا تُعْلِنُوْنَ وَاللّٰهُ عَلِيْمٌ بِذَاتِ
الصُّدُوْرِ ٤
اَلَمْ يَاْتِكُمْ نَبَؤُا الَّذِيْنَ كَفَرُوْا مِنْ قَبْلُ فَذَاقُوْا
وَبَالَ اَمْرِهِمْ وَلَهُمْ عَذَابٌ اَلِيْمٌ ٥
ذٰلِكَ بِاَنَّهُ كَانَتْ تَّاْتِيْهِمْ رُسُلُهُمْ بِالْبَيِّنٰتِ
فَقَالُوْا اَبَشَرٌ يَّهْدُوْنَنَا فَكَفَرُوْا وَتَوَلَّوْا وَّاسْتَغْنَى
اللّٰهُ وَاللّٰهُ غَنِيٌّ حَمِيْدٌ ٦
زَعَمَ الَّذِيْنَ كَفَرُوْا اَنْ لَّنْ يُّبْعَثُوْا قُلْ بَلٰى وَرَبِّيْ
لَتُبْعَثُنَّ ثُمَّ لَتُنَبَّؤُنَّ بِمَا عَمِلْتُمْ وَذٰلِكَ عَلَى
اللّٰهِ يَسِيْرٌ ٧
فَاٰمِنُوْا بِاللّٰهِ وَرَسُوْلِهِ وَالنُّوْرِ الَّذِيْٓ اَنْزَلْنَا وَ
اللّٰهُ بِمَا تَعْمَلُوْنَ خَبِيْرٌ ٨

9. The day when He shall gather you unto the Day of Assembling, that will be a day of mutual disillusion. And whoso believeth in Allah and doth right, He will remit from him his evil deeds and vill bring him into Gardens underneath which rivers flow, therein to abide for ever. That is the Supreme triumph.

10. But those who disbelieve and deny Our revelations, such are owners of the Fire; they will abide therein—a hapless journey's end!

11. No calamity befalleth save by Allah's leave. And whosoever believeth in Allah, He guideth his heart. And Allah is Knower of all things.

12. Obey Allah and obey His messenger; but if ye turn away, then the duty of Our messenger is only to convey (the message) plainly.

13. Allah! There is no God save Him. In Allah, therefore, let believers put their trust.

14. O ye who believe! Lo! among your wives and your children there are enemies for you, therefore beware of them. And if ye efface and overlook and forgive, then lo! Allah is Forgiving, Merciful.

15. Your wealth and your children are only a temptation, whereas Allah! with Him is an immense reward.

16. So keep your duty to Allah as best ye can, and listen, and obey, and spend; that is better for your souls. And whoso is saved from his own greed, such are the successful.

17. If ye lend unto Allah a goodly loan,[1] He will double it for you and will forgive you, for Allah is Responsive, Clement,

18. Knower of the invisible and the visible, the Mighty, the Wise.

يَوْمَ يَجْمَعُكُمْ لِيَوْمِ الْجَمْعِ ذٰلِكَ يَوْمُ التَّغَابُنِ
وَمَنْ يُؤْمِنْ بِاللّٰهِ وَيَعْمَلْ صَالِحًا يُكَفِّرْ عَنْهُ سَيِّاٰتِهٖ
وَيُدْخِلْهُ جَنّٰتٍ تَجْرِيْ مِنْ تَحْتِهَا الْاَنْهٰرُ
خٰلِدِيْنَ فِيْهَآ اَبَدًا ذٰلِكَ الْفَوْزُ الْعَظِيْمُ ﴿٩﴾
وَالَّذِيْنَ كَفَرُوْا وَكَذَّبُوْا بِاٰيٰتِنَآ اُولٰٓئِكَ اَصْحٰبُ
ع النَّارِ خٰلِدِيْنَ فِيْهَا وَبِئْسَ الْمَصِيْرُ ﴿١٠﴾
مَآ اَصَابَ مِنْ مُّصِيْبَةٍ اِلَّا بِاِذْنِ اللّٰهِ وَمَنْ يُّؤْمِنْ
بِاللّٰهِ يَهْدِ قَلْبَهٗ وَاللّٰهُ بِكُلِّ شَيْءٍ عَلِيْمٌ ﴿١١﴾
وَاَطِيْعُوا اللّٰهَ وَاَطِيْعُوا الرَّسُوْلَ فَاِنْ تَوَلَّيْتُمْ فَاِنَّمَا
عَلٰى رَسُوْلِنَا الْبَلٰغُ الْمُبِيْنُ ﴿١٢﴾
اَللّٰهُ لَآ اِلٰهَ اِلَّا هُوَ وَعَلَى اللّٰهِ فَلْيَتَوَكَّلِ الْمُؤْمِنُوْنَ ﴿١٣﴾
يٰٓاَيُّهَا الَّذِيْنَ اٰمَنُوْٓا اِنَّ مِنْ اَزْوَاجِكُمْ وَاَوْلَادِكُمْ
عَدُوًّا لَّكُمْ فَاحْذَرُوْهُمْ وَاِنْ تَعْفُوْا وَتَصْفَحُوْا وَ
تَغْفِرُوْا فَاِنَّ اللّٰهَ غَفُوْرٌ رَّحِيْمٌ ﴿١٤﴾
اِنَّمَآ اَمْوَالُكُمْ وَاَوْلَادُكُمْ فِتْنَةٌ وَاللّٰهُ عِنْدَهٗٓ
اَجْرٌ عَظِيْمٌ ﴿١٥﴾
فَاتَّقُوا اللّٰهَ مَا اسْتَطَعْتُمْ وَاسْمَعُوْا وَاَطِيْعُوْا وَ
اَنْفِقُوْا خَيْرًا لِّاَنْفُسِكُمْ وَمَنْ يُّوْقَ شُحَّ نَفْسِهٖ
فَاُولٰٓئِكَ هُمُ الْمُفْلِحُوْنَ ﴿١٦﴾
اِنْ تُقْرِضُوا اللّٰهَ قَرْضًا حَسَنًا يُّضٰعِفْهُ لَكُمْ وَ
يَغْفِرْ لَكُمْ وَاللّٰهُ شَكُوْرٌ حَلِيْمٌ ﴿١٧﴾
ع عٰلِمُ الْغَيْبِ وَالشَّهَادَةِ الْعَزِيْزُ الْحَكِيْمُ ﴿١٨﴾

1. *i.e.* a loan without interest or any thought of gain or loss.

At-Talāq, "Divorce," is so called from vv. 1-7, which contain an amendment to the laws of divorce which are set forth in Sūrah II. This is generally referred traditionally to a mistake made by Ibn 'Umar in divorcing his wife, which is said to have happened in the 6th year of the Hijrah. But others relate that the Prophet on that occasion only quoted this verse which had already been revealed.

The date of revelation is the sixth year of the Hijrah or a little earlier.

DIVORCE

Revealed at Al-Madinah

In the name of Allah, the Beneficent, the Merciful.

1. O Prophet! When ye (men) put away women, put them away for their (legal) period and reckon the period, and keep your duty to Allah, your Lord. Expel them not from their houses nor let them go forth unless they commit open immorality. Such are the limits (imposed by) Allah: and whoso transgresseth Allah's limits, he verily wrongeth his soul. Thou knowest not: it may be that Allah will afterward bring some new thing to pass.

2. Then, when they have reached their term, take them back in kindness or part from them in kindness, and call to witness two just men among you, and keep your testimony upright for Allah. Whoso believeth in Allah and the Last Day is exhorted to act thus. And whosoever keepeth his duty to Allah, Allah will appoint a way out for him:

3. And will provide for him from (a quarter) whence he hath no expectation. And whosoever putteth his trust in Allah, He will suffice him. Lo! Allah bringeth His command to pass. Allah hath set a measure for all things.

4. And for such of your women as despair of menstruation, if ye doubt, their period (of waiting) shall be three months, along with those who have it not. And for those with child, their period shall be till they bring forth their burden. And whosoever keepeth his duty to Allah, He maketh his course easy for him.

5. That is the commandment of Allah which He revealeth unto you. And whoso keepeth his duty to Allah, He will remit from him his evil deeds and magnify reward for him.

آياتها ١٢ (٦٥) سورة الطلاق مدنية ركوعاتها ٢

بسم الله الرحمن الرحيم

يا أيها النبي إذا طلقتم النساء فطلقوهن لعدتهن
وأحصوا العدة واتقوا الله ربكم لا تخرجوهن
من بيوتهن ولا يخرجن إلا أن يأتين بفاحشة
مبينة وتلك حدود الله ومن يتعد حدود
الله فقد ظلم نفسه لا تدري لعل الله
يحدث بعد ذلك أمرا (١)
فإذا بلغن أجلهن فأمسكوهن بمعروف أو
فارقوهن بمعروف وأشهدوا ذوي عدل منكم
وأقيموا الشهادة لله ذلكم يوعظ به من كان يؤمن
بالله واليوم الآخر ومن يتق الله يجعل له مخرجا (٢)
ويرزقه من حيث لا يحتسب ومن يتوكل على
الله فهو حسبه إن الله بالغ أمره قد جعل
الله لكل شيء قدرا (٣)
واللائي يئسن من المحيض من نسائكم إن ارتبتم
فعدتهن ثلاثة أشهر واللائي لم يحضن وأولات
الأحمال أجلهن أن يضعن حملهن ومن يتق
الله يجعل له من أمره يسرا (٤)
ذلك أمر الله أنزله إليكم ومن يتق الله يكفر
عنه سيئاته ويعظم له أجرا (٥)

6. Lodge them where ye dwell, according to your wealth, and harass them not so as to straiten life for them. And if they are with child, then spend for them till they bring forth their burden. Then, if they give suck for you, give them their due payment and consult together in kindness; but if ye make difficulties for one another, then let some other woman give suck for him (the father of the child).

7. Let him who hath abundance spend of his abundance, and he whose provision is measured, let him spend of that which Allah hath given him. Allah asketh naught of any soul save that which He hath given it. Allah will vouchsafe, after hardship, ease.

8. And how many a community revolted against the ordinance of its Lord and His messengers, and we called it to a stern account and punished it with dire punishment,

9. So that it tasted the ill-effects of its conduct, and the consequence of its conduct was loss.

10. Allah hath prepared for them stern punishment; so keep your duty to Allah, O men of understanding! O ye who believe! Now Allah hath sent down unto you a reminder,

11. A messenger reciting unto you the revelations of Allah made plain, that He may bring forth those who believe and do good works from darkness unto light. And whosoever believeth in Allah and doth right, He will bring him into Gardens underneath which rivers flow, therein to abide for ever. Allah hath made good provision for him.

12. Allah it is Who hath created seven heavens, and of the earth the like thereof. The commandment cometh down among them slowly, that ye may know that Allah is able to do all things, and that Allah surroundeth all things in knowledge.

أَسْكِنُوهُنَّ مِنْ حَيْثُ سَكَنْتُمْ مِنْ وُجْدِكُمْ وَلَا
تُضَآرُّوهُنَّ لِتُضَيِّقُوا عَلَيْهِنَّ ۚ وَإِنْ كُنَّ أُولَاتِ حَمْلٍ
فَأَنْفِقُوا عَلَيْهِنَّ حَتَّىٰ يَضَعْنَ حَمْلَهُنَّ ۚ فَإِنْ أَرْضَعْنَ
لَكُمْ فَآتُوهُنَّ أُجُورَهُنَّ ۖ وَأْتَمِرُوا بَيْنَكُمْ بِمَعْرُوفٍ ۖ
وَإِنْ تَعَاسَرْتُمْ فَسَتُرْضِعُ لَهُ أُخْرَىٰ ﴿٦﴾
لِيُنْفِقْ ذُو سَعَةٍ مِنْ سَعَتِهِ ۖ وَمَنْ قُدِرَ عَلَيْهِ رِزْقُهُ
فَلْيُنْفِقْ مِمَّا آتَاهُ اللَّهُ ۚ لَا يُكَلِّفُ اللَّهُ نَفْسًا إِلَّا مَا
ع آتَاهَا ۚ سَيَجْعَلُ اللَّهُ بَعْدَ عُسْرٍ يُسْرًا ﴿٧﴾
وَكَأَيِّنْ مِنْ قَرْيَةٍ عَتَتْ عَنْ أَمْرِ رَبِّهَا وَرُسُلِهِ
فَحَاسَبْنَاهَا حِسَابًا شَدِيدًا وَعَذَّبْنَاهَا عَذَابًا نُكْرًا ﴿٨﴾
فَذَاقَتْ وَبَالَ أَمْرِهَا وَكَانَ عَاقِبَةُ أَمْرِهَا خُسْرًا ﴿٩﴾
أَعَدَّ اللَّهُ لَهُمْ عَذَابًا شَدِيدًا ۖ فَاتَّقُوا اللَّهَ يَا أُولِي الْأَلْبَابِ ۚ
الَّذِينَ آمَنُوا ۚ قَدْ أَنْزَلَ اللَّهُ إِلَيْكُمْ ذِكْرًا ﴿١٠﴾
رَسُولًا يَتْلُو عَلَيْكُمْ آيَاتِ اللَّهِ مُبَيِّنَاتٍ لِيُخْرِجَ الَّذِينَ
آمَنُوا وَعَمِلُوا الصَّالِحَاتِ مِنَ الظُّلُمَاتِ إِلَى النُّورِ ۚ
وَمَنْ يُؤْمِنْ بِاللَّهِ وَيَعْمَلْ صَالِحًا يُدْخِلْهُ جَنَّاتٍ
تَجْرِي مِنْ تَحْتِهَا الْأَنْهَارُ خَالِدِينَ فِيهَا أَبَدًا ۖ قَدْ
أَحْسَنَ اللَّهُ لَهُ رِزْقًا ﴿١١﴾
اللَّهُ الَّذِي خَلَقَ سَبْعَ سَمَاوَاتٍ وَمِنَ الْأَرْضِ مِثْلَهُنَّ
يَتَنَزَّلُ الْأَمْرُ بَيْنَهُنَّ لِتَعْلَمُوا أَنَّ اللَّهَ عَلَىٰ كُلِّ
ع شَيْءٍ قَدِيرٌ وَأَنَّ اللَّهَ قَدْ أَحَاطَ بِكُلِّ شَيْءٍ عِلْمًا ﴿١٢﴾

At-Taḥrīm, "Banning," takes its name from a word in v. 1.

There are three traditions as to the occasion of vv. 1-4:

(1) The Prophet was very fond of honey. One of his wives received a present of honey from a relative and by its means inveigled the Prophet into staying with her longer than was customary. The others felt aggrieved, and Ayeshah devised a little plot. Knowing the Prophet's horror of unpleasant smells, she arranged with two other wives that they should hold their noses when he came to them after eating the honey, and accuse him of having eaten the produce of a very rank-smelling tree. When they accused him of having eaten *Maghāfīr* the Prophet said that he had eaten only honey. They said: "The bees had fed on Maghāfīr." The Prophet was dismayed and vowed to eat no more honey.

(2) Ḥafṣah found the Prophet in her room with Mārya—the Coptic girl, presented to him by the ruler of Egypt, who became the mother of his only male child, Ibrāhim—on a day which custom had assigned to Ayeshah. Moved by Ḥafṣah's distress, the Prophet vowed that he would have no more to do with Mārya, and asked her not to tell Ayeshah. But Ḥafaṣh's distress had been largely feigned. No sooner had the Prophet gone than she told Ayeshah with glee how easily she had got rid of Mārya.

(3) Before Al-Islām women had had no standing in Arabia. The Koran gave them legal rights and an assured position, which some of them were inclined to exaggerate. The Prophet was extremely kind to his wives. One day Omar had to rebuke his wife for replying to him in a tone which he considered disrespectful. She assured him it was the tone in which his own daughter Ḥafṣah, Ayeshah and others of the Prophet's wives answered the Prophet. Omar went at once and remonstrated with Ḥafṣah and with another of the Prophet's wives to whom he was related. He was told to mind his own business, which increased his horror and dismay. Soon afterwards the Prophet separated from his wives for a time, and it was thought that he was going to divorce them. Then Omar ventured to tell the story of his own vain effort to reform them, at which the Prophet laughed heartily.

Traditions (1) and (3) are the better authenticated and are alone adduced by the great traditionists. But the commentators generally prefer (2) as more explanatory of the text. All allude to a tendency on the part of some of the wives of the Prophet to presume on their new status and the Prophet's well-known kindness—a tendency so marked that, if allowed to continue, it would have been of bad example to the whole community. The Koran first rebukes the Prophet for yielding to their desires to the extent of undertaking to forgo a thing which Allah had made lawful for him—in the case of (2), fulfilment of his vow involved a wrong to Mārya—and then reproves the women for their double-dealing and intrigue.

The above traditions have been made by some non-Muslim writers the text for strictures which appear irrelevant because their ideology is altogether un-Islamic. The Prophet has never been regarded by Muslims as other than a human messenger of God; sanctity has never been identified with celibacy. For Christendom the strictest religious ideal has been celibacy, monogamy is already a concession to human nature. For Muslims, monogamy is the ideal, polygamy the concession to human nature. Polygamy is of the nature of some men in all countries, and of all men in some countries. Having set a great example of monogamic marriage, the Prophet was to set a great example of polygamic marriage, by following which men of that temperament could live righteous lives. He encountered all the difficulties inherent in the situation, and when he made mistakes the Koran helped him to retrieve them. Al-Islām did not institute polygamy. It restricted an existing institution by limiting the number of a man's legal wives, by giving to every woman a legal personality and legal rights which had to be respected, and making every man legally responsible for his conduct towards every woman. Whether monogamy or polygamy should prevail in a particular country or period is a matter of social and economic convenience. The Prophet himself was permitted to have more wives than were allowed to others because, as head of the State, he was responsible for the support of women who had no other protector. With the one exception of Ayeshah, all his wives had been widows.

BANNING

Revealed at Mecca

In the name of Allah, the Beneficent, the Merciful.

1. O Prophet! Why bannest thou that which Allah hath made lawful for thee, seeking to please thy wives? And Allah is Forgiving, Merciful.

2. Allah hath made lawful for you (Muslims) absolution from your oaths (of such a kind), and Allah is your Protector. He is the Knower, Wise.

3. When the Prophet confided a fact unto one of his wives and when she afterward divulged it and Allah apprised him thereof, he made known (to her) part thereof and passed over part. And when he told it her she said: Who hath told thee? He said: The Knower, the Aware hath told me.

4. If ye twain turn unto Allah repentant, (ye have cause to do so) for your hearts desired (the ban); and if ye aid one another against him (Muhammad) then lo! Allah, even He, is his protecting Friend, and Gabriel and the righteous among the believers; and furthermore the angels are his helpers.

5. It may happen that his Lord, if he divorce you, will give him in your stead wives better than you, submissive (to Allah), believing, pious, penitent, inclined to fasting, widows and maids.

6. O ye who believe! Ward off from yourselves and your families a Fire whereof the fuel is men and stones, over which are set angels strong, severe, who resist not Allah in that which He commandeth them, but do that which they are commanded.

اٰياتها ١٢ (٦٦) سُوْرَةُ التَّحْرِيْمِ مَدَنِيَّةٌ رُكُوْعَاتُهَا ٢

بِسْمِ اللّٰهِ الرَّحْمٰنِ الرَّحِيْمِ ○

يٰۤاَيُّهَا النَّبِيُّ لِمَ تُحَرِّمُ مَاۤ اَحَلَّ اللّٰهُ لَكَ ۚ تَبْتَغِيْ
مَرْضَاتَ اَزْوَاجِكَ ۗ وَاللّٰهُ غَفُوْرٌ رَّحِيْمٌ ﴿١﴾

قَدْ فَرَضَ اللّٰهُ لَكُمْ تَحِلَّةَ اَيْمَانِكُمْ ۚ وَاللّٰهُ مَوْلٰىكُمْ ۚ
وَهُوَ الْعَلِيْمُ الْحَكِيْمُ ﴿٢﴾

وَاِذْ اَسَرَّ النَّبِيُّ اِلٰى بَعْضِ اَزْوَاجِهٖ حَدِيْثًا ۚ فَلَمَّا
نَبَّاَتْ بِهٖ وَاَظْهَرَهُ اللّٰهُ عَلَيْهِ عَرَّفَ بَعْضَهٗ وَ
اَعْرَضَ عَنْۢ بَعْضٍ ۚ فَلَمَّا نَبَّاَهَا بِهٖ قَالَتْ مَنْ
اَنْۢبَاَكَ هٰذَا ۗ قَالَ نَبَّاَنِيَ الْعَلِيْمُ الْخَبِيْرُ ﴿٣﴾

اِنْ تَتُوْبَاۤ اِلَى اللّٰهِ فَقَدْ صَغَتْ قُلُوْبُكُمَا ۚ وَاِنْ
تَظٰهَرَا عَلَيْهِ فَاِنَّ اللّٰهَ هُوَ مَوْلٰىهُ وَجِبْرِيْلُ وَ
صَالِحُ الْمُؤْمِنِيْنَ ۚ وَالْمَلٰۤئِكَةُ بَعْدَ ذٰلِكَ
ظَهِيْرٌ ﴿٤﴾

عَسٰى رَبُّهٗۤ اِنْ طَلَّقَكُنَّ اَنْ يُّبْدِلَهٗۤ اَزْوَاجًا خَيْرًا
مِّنْكُنَّ مُسْلِمٰتٍ مُّؤْمِنٰتٍ قٰنِتٰتٍ تٰۤئِبٰتٍ عٰبِدٰتٍ
سٰۤئِحٰتٍ ثَيِّبٰتٍ وَّاَبْكَارًا ﴿٥﴾

يٰۤاَيُّهَا الَّذِيْنَ اٰمَنُوْا قُوْۤا اَنْفُسَكُمْ وَاَهْلِيْكُمْ نَارًا
وَّقُوْدُهَا النَّاسُ وَالْحِجَارَةُ عَلَيْهَا مَلٰۤئِكَةٌ
غِلَاظٌ شِدَادٌ لَّا يَعْصُوْنَ اللّٰهَ مَاۤ اَمَرَهُمْ وَ
يَفْعَلُوْنَ مَا يُؤْمَرُوْنَ ﴿٦﴾

7. (Then it will be said): O ye who disbelieve! Make no excuses for yourselves this day. Ye are only being paid for what ye used to do.

8. O ye who believe! Turn unto Allah in sincere repentance! It may be that your Lord will remit from you your evil deeds and bring you into Gardens underneath which rivers flow, on the day when Allah will not abase the Prophet and those who believe with him. Their light will run before them and on their right hands: they will say: Our Lord! Perfect our light for us, and forgive us! Lo! Thou art Able to do all things.

9. O Prophet! Strive against the disbelievers and the hypocrites, and be stern with them. Hell will be their home, a hapless journey's end.

10. Allah citeth an example for those who disbelieve: the wife of Noah and the wife of Lot, who were under two of Our righteous slaves yet betrayed them so that they (the husbands) availed them naught against Allah and it was said (unto them): Enter the Fire along with those who enter.

11. And Allah citeth an example for those who believe: the wife of Pharaoh when she said: My Lord! Build for me a home with thee in the Garden, and deliver me from Pharaoh and his work, and deliver me from evildoing folk;

12. And Mary, daughter of 'Imrān, whose body was chaste, therefor We breathed therein something of Our Spirit. And she put faith in the words of her Lord and His Scriptures, and was of the obedient.

يَا أَيُّهَا الَّذِينَ كَفَرُوا لَا تَعْتَذِرُوا الْيَوْمَ إِنَّمَا تُجْزَوْنَ
مَا كُنتُمْ تَعْمَلُونَ ﴿٧﴾ ع ١٩
يَا أَيُّهَا الَّذِينَ آمَنُوا تُوبُوا إِلَى اللَّهِ تَوْبَةً نَّصُوحًا
عَسَىٰ رَبُّكُمْ أَن يُكَفِّرَ عَنكُمْ سَيِّئَاتِكُمْ وَيُدْخِلَكُمْ
جَنَّاتٍ تَجْرِي مِن تَحْتِهَا الْأَنْهَارُ يَوْمَ لَا يُخْزِي
اللَّهُ النَّبِيَّ وَالَّذِينَ آمَنُوا مَعَهُ نُورُهُمْ يَسْعَىٰ
بَيْنَ أَيْدِيهِمْ وَبِأَيْمَانِهِمْ يَقُولُونَ رَبَّنَا أَتْمِمْ
لَنَا نُورَنَا وَاغْفِرْ لَنَا إِنَّكَ عَلَىٰ كُلِّ شَيْءٍ قَدِيرٌ ﴿٨﴾
يَا أَيُّهَا النَّبِيُّ جَاهِدِ الْكُفَّارَ وَالْمُنَافِقِينَ وَاغْلُظْ
عَلَيْهِمْ وَمَأْوَاهُمْ جَهَنَّمُ وَبِئْسَ الْمَصِيرُ ﴿٩﴾
ضَرَبَ اللَّهُ مَثَلًا لِّلَّذِينَ كَفَرُوا امْرَأَتَ نُوحٍ وَ
امْرَأَتَ لُوطٍ كَانَتَا تَحْتَ عَبْدَيْنِ مِنْ عِبَادِنَا
صَالِحَيْنِ فَخَانَتَاهُمَا فَلَمْ يُغْنِيَا عَنْهُمَا مِنَ اللَّهِ
شَيْئًا وَقِيلَ ادْخُلَا النَّارَ مَعَ الدَّاخِلِينَ ﴿١٠﴾
وَضَرَبَ اللَّهُ مَثَلًا لِّلَّذِينَ آمَنُوا امْرَأَتَ فِرْعَوْنَ وقف لازم
إِذْ قَالَتْ رَبِّ ابْنِ لِي عِندَكَ بَيْتًا فِي الْجَنَّةِ وَ
نَجِّنِي مِن فِرْعَوْنَ وَعَمَلِهِ وَنَجِّنِي مِنَ الْقَوْمِ
الظَّالِمِينَ ﴿١١﴾
وَمَرْيَمَ ابْنَتَ عِمْرَانَ الَّتِي أَحْصَنَتْ فَرْجَهَا
فَنَفَخْنَا فِيهِ مِن رُّوحِنَا وَصَدَّقَتْ بِكَلِمَاتِ رَبِّهَا
وَكُتُبِهِ وَكَانَتْ مِنَ الْقَانِتِينَ ﴿١٢﴾ ع ٢٠

Al-Mulk, takes its name from a word in the first verse. It belongs to the middle group of Meccan Sūrahs.

THE SOVEREIGNTY

Revealed at Mecca

In the name of Allah, the Beneficent, the Merciful.

1. Blessed is He in Whose hand is the Sovereignty, and He is Able to do all things—

2. Who hath created life and death that He may try you, which of you is best in conduct; and He is the Mighty, the Forgiving,

3. Who hath created seven heavens in harmony. Thou (Muhammad) canst see no fault in the Beneficent One's creation; then look again: Canst thou see any rifts?

4. Then look again and yet again, thy sight will return unto thee weakened and made dim.

5. And verily We have beautified the world's heaven with lamps, and We have made them missiles for the devils[1] and for them We have prepared the doom of flame.

6. And for those who disbelieve in their Lord there is the doom of hell, a hapless journey's end!

7. When they are flung therein they hear its roaring as it boileth up,

8. As it would burst with rage. Whenever a (fresh) host is flung therein the wardens thereof ask them: Came there unto you no warner?

9. They say: Yea, verily, a warner came unto us; but we denied and said: Allah hath naught revealed; ye are in naught but a great error.

1. On the authority of a tradition going back to Ibn 'Abbās, the allusion is to the soothsayers and astrologers who saw the source of good and evil in the stars. See LXXII, v. 9, footnote.

اٰياتها ٣٠ (٦٧) سُوْرَةُ الْمُلْكِ مَكِّيَّةٌ رُكُوعاتها ٢

بِسْمِ اللّٰهِ الرَّحْمٰنِ الرَّحِيْمِ

الجزء ٢٩

تَبٰرَكَ الَّذِيْ بِيَدِهِ الْمُلْكُ وَهُوَ عَلٰى كُلِّ شَيْءٍ
قَدِيْرُ ﴿١﴾
الَّذِيْ خَلَقَ الْمَوْتَ وَالْحَيٰوةَ لِيَبْلُوَكُمْ اَيُّكُمْ
اَحْسَنُ عَمَلًا وَهُوَ الْعَزِيْزُ الْغَفُوْرُ ﴿٢﴾
الَّذِيْ خَلَقَ سَبْعَ سَمٰوٰتٍ طِبَاقًا مَا تَرٰى فِيْ
خَلْقِ الرَّحْمٰنِ مِنْ تَفٰوُتٍ فَارْجِعِ الْبَصَرَ هَلْ
تَرٰى مِنْ فُطُوْرٍ ﴿٣﴾
ثُمَّ ارْجِعِ الْبَصَرَ كَرَّتَيْنِ يَنْقَلِبْ اِلَيْكَ الْبَصَرُ
خَاسِئًا وَّهُوَ حَسِيْرٌ ﴿٤﴾
وَلَقَدْ زَيَّنَّا السَّمَآءَ الدُّنْيَا بِمَصَابِيْحَ وَجَعَلْنٰهَا
رُجُوْمًا لِّلشَّيٰطِيْنِ وَاَعْتَدْنَا لَهُمْ عَذَابَ السَّعِيْرِ ﴿٥﴾
وَلِلَّذِيْنَ كَفَرُوْا بِرَبِّهِمْ عَذَابُ جَهَنَّمَ وَبِئْسَ
الْمَصِيْرُ ﴿٦﴾
اِذَآ اُلْقُوْا فِيْهَا سَمِعُوْا لَهَا شَهِيْقًا وَّهِيَ تَفُوْرُ ﴿٧﴾
تَكَادُ تَمَيَّزُ مِنَ الْغَيْظِ كُلَّمَآ اُلْقِيَ فِيْهَا فَوْجٌ سَاَلَهُمْ
خَزَنَتُهَآ اَلَمْ يَاْتِكُمْ نَذِيْرٌ ﴿٨﴾
قَالُوْا بَلٰى قَدْ جَآءَنَا نَذِيْرٌ فَكَذَّبْنَا وَقُلْنَا
مَا نَزَّلَ اللّٰهُ مِنْ شَيْءٍ اِنْ اَنْتُمْ اِلَّا فِيْ ضَلٰلٍ
كَبِيْرٍ ﴿٩﴾

10. And they say: Had we been wont to listen or have sense, we had not been among the dwellers in the flames.

11. So they acknowledge their sins; but far removed (from mercy) are the dwellers in the flames.

12. Lo! those who fear their Lord in secret, theirs will be forgiveness and a great reward.

13. And keep your opinion secret or proclaim it, lo! He is Knower of all that is in the breasts (of men).

14. Should He not know what He created? And He is the Subtile, the Aware.

15. He it is Who hath made the earth subservient unto you, so walk in the paths thereof and eat of His providence. And unto Him will be the resurrection (of the dead).

16. Have ye taken security from Him Who is in the heaven that He will not cause the earth to swallow you when lo! it is convulsed?

17. Or have ye taken security from Him Who is in the heaven that He will not let loose on you a hurricane? But ye shall know the manner of My warning.

18. And verily those before them denied, then (see) the manner of My wrath (with them)!

19. Have they not seen the birds above them spreading out their wings and closing them? Naught upholdeth them save the Beneficent. Lo! He is Seer of all things.

20. Or who is he that will be an army unto you to help you instead of the Beneficent? The disbelievers are in naught but illusion.

21. Or who is he that will provide for you if He should withhold His providence? Nay, but they are set in pride and frowardness.

وَقَالُوا لَوْ كُنَّا نَسْمَعُ أَوْ نَعْقِلُ مَا كُنَّا فِي أَصْحٰبِ
السَّعِيرِ ﴿١٠﴾
فَاعْتَرَفُوا بِذَنْبِهِمْ فَسُحْقًا لِأَصْحٰبِ السَّعِيرِ ﴿١١﴾
إِنَّ الَّذِينَ يَخْشَوْنَ رَبَّهُمْ بِالْغَيْبِ لَهُمْ مَغْفِرَةٌ
وَأَجْرٌ كَبِيرٌ ﴿١٢﴾
وَأَسِرُّوا قَوْلَكُمْ أَوِ اجْهَرُوا بِهِ إِنَّهُ عَلِيمٌ
بِذَاتِ الصُّدُورِ ﴿١٣﴾
أَلَا يَعْلَمُ مَنْ خَلَقَ وَهُوَ اللَّطِيفُ الْخَبِيرُ ﴿١٤﴾
هُوَ الَّذِي جَعَلَ لَكُمُ الْأَرْضَ ذَلُولًا فَامْشُوا فِي
مَنَاكِبِهَا وَكُلُوا مِنْ رِزْقِهِ وَإِلَيْهِ النُّشُورُ ﴿١٥﴾
ءَأَمِنْتُمْ مَنْ فِي السَّمَاءِ أَنْ يَخْسِفَ بِكُمُ الْأَرْضَ
فَإِذَا هِيَ تَمُورُ ﴿١٦﴾
أَمْ أَمِنْتُمْ مَنْ فِي السَّمَاءِ أَنْ يُرْسِلَ عَلَيْكُمْ
حَاصِبًا فَسَتَعْلَمُونَ كَيْفَ نَذِيرِ ﴿١٧﴾
وَلَقَدْ كَذَّبَ الَّذِينَ مِنْ قَبْلِهِمْ فَكَيْفَ كَانَ
نَكِيرِ ﴿١٨﴾
أَوَلَمْ يَرَوْا إِلَى الطَّيْرِ فَوْقَهُمْ صٰٓفّٰتٍ وَيَقْبِضْنَ مَا وقف لازم اخلاف وقف غفران وقف منزل
يُمْسِكُهُنَّ إِلَّا الرَّحْمٰنُ إِنَّهُ بِكُلِّ شَيْءٍ بَصِيرٌ ﴿١٩﴾
أَمَّنْ هٰذَا الَّذِي هُوَ جُنْدٌ لَكُمْ يَنْصُرُكُمْ مِنْ دُونِ
الرَّحْمٰنِ إِنِ الْكٰفِرُونَ إِلَّا فِي غُرُورٍ ﴿٢٠﴾
أَمَّنْ هٰذَا الَّذِي يَرْزُقُكُمْ إِنْ أَمْسَكَ رِزْقَهُ
بَلْ لَجُّوا فِي عُتُوٍّ وَنُفُورٍ ﴿٢١﴾

22. Is he who goeth groping on his face more rightly guided, or he who walketh upright on a beaten road?

23. Say (unto them, O Muhammad): He it is Who gave you being, and hath assigned unto you ears and eyes and hearts. Small thanks give ye!

24. Say: He it is Who multiplieth you in the earth, and unto Whom ye will be gathered.

25. And they say: When (will) this promise (be fulfilled), if ye are truthful?

26. Say: The knowledge is with Allah only, and I am but a plain warner;

27. But when they see it nigh, the faces of those who disbelieve will be awry, and it will be said (unto them): This is that for which ye used to call.

28. Say (O Muhammad): Have ye thought: Whether Allah causeth me (Muhammad) and those with me to perish or hath mercy on us, still, who will protect the disbelievers from a painful doom?

29. Say: He is the Beneficent. In Him we believe and in Him we put our trust. And ye will soon know who it is that is in error manifest.

30. Say: Have ye thought: If (all) your water were to disappear into the earth, who then could bring you gushing water?

أَفَمَنْ يَمْشِي مُكِبًّا عَلَىٰ وَجْهِهِ أَهْدَىٰ أَمَّنْ
يَمْشِي سَوِيًّا عَلَىٰ صِرَاطٍ مُسْتَقِيمٍ ﴿٢٢﴾
قُلْ هُوَ الَّذِي أَنْشَأَكُمْ وَجَعَلَ لَكُمُ السَّمْعَ وَ
الْأَبْصَارَ وَالْأَفْئِدَةَ ۖ قَلِيلًا مَا تَشْكُرُونَ ﴿٢٣﴾
قُلْ هُوَ الَّذِي ذَرَأَكُمْ فِي الْأَرْضِ وَإِلَيْهِ
تُحْشَرُونَ ﴿٢٤﴾
وَيَقُولُونَ مَتَىٰ هَٰذَا الْوَعْدُ إِنْ كُنْتُمْ صَادِقِينَ ﴿٢٥﴾
قُلْ إِنَّمَا الْعِلْمُ عِنْدَ اللَّهِ وَإِنَّمَا أَنَا نَذِيرٌ
مُبِينٌ ﴿٢٦﴾
فَلَمَّا رَأَوْهُ زُلْفَةً سِيئَتْ وُجُوهُ الَّذِينَ كَفَرُوا
وَقِيلَ هَٰذَا الَّذِي كُنْتُمْ بِهِ تَدَّعُونَ ﴿٢٧﴾
قُلْ أَرَأَيْتُمْ إِنْ أَهْلَكَنِيَ اللَّهُ وَمَنْ مَعِيَ أَوْ
رَحِمَنَا فَمَنْ يُجِيرُ الْكَافِرِينَ مِنْ عَذَابٍ
أَلِيمٍ ﴿٢٨﴾
قُلْ هُوَ الرَّحْمَٰنُ آمَنَّا بِهِ وَعَلَيْهِ تَوَكَّلْنَا ۖ
فَسَتَعْلَمُونَ مَنْ هُوَ فِي ضَلَالٍ مُبِينٍ ﴿٢٩﴾
قُلْ أَرَأَيْتُمْ إِنْ أَصْبَحَ مَاؤُكُمْ غَوْرًا فَمَنْ
يَأْتِيكُمْ بِمَاءٍ مَعِينٍ ﴿٣٠﴾ ع

Al-Qalam, "The Pen," takes its name from a word in the first verse. A very early Meccan Sūrah.

THE PEN

Revealed at Mecca

In the name of Allah, the Beneficent, the Merciful.

1. Nūn.[1] By the pen and that which they write (therewith),

2. Thou art not, for thy Lord's favour unto thee, a madman.

3. And lo! thine verily will be a reward unfailing.

4. And lo! thou art of a tremendous nature.

5. And thou wilt see and they will see

6. Which of you is the demented.

7. Lo! thy Lord is best aware of him who strayeth from his way, and He is best aware of those who walk aright.

8. Therefor obey not thou the rejecters

9. Who would have had thee compromise, that they may compromise.

10. Neither obey thou each feeble oath-monger,

11. Detractor, spreader abroad of slanders,

12. Hinderer of the good, transgressor, malefactor

13. Greedy, therewithal, intrusive.

14. It is because he is possessed of wealth and children

15. That, when Our revelations are recited unto him, he saith: Mere fables of the men of old.

16. We shall brand him on the nose.

17. Lo! We have tried them as We tried the owners of the garden when they vowed they would pluck its fruit next morning.

آياتها ٥٢ (٦٨) سورة القلم مكية ركوعاتها ٢

بسم الله الرحمن الرحيم ○

ن والقلم وما يسطرون ①

ما أنت بنعمة ربك بمجنون ②

وإن لك لأجرا غير ممنون ③

وإنك لعلى خلق عظيم ④

فستبصر ويبصرون ⑤

بأييكم المفتون ⑥

إن ربك هو أعلم بمن ضل عن سبيله و
هو أعلم بالمهتدين ⑦

فلا تطع المكذبين ⑧

ودوا لو تدهن فيدهنون ⑨

ولا تطع كل حلاف مهين ⑩

هماز مشاء بنميم ⑪

مناع للخير معتد أثيم ⑫

عتل بعد ذلك زنيم ⑬

أن كان ذا مال وبنين ⑭

إذا تتلى عليه آياتنا قال أساطير الأولين ⑮

سنسمه على الخرطوم ⑯

إنا بلوناهم كما بلونا أصحاب الجنة إذ أقسموا
ليصرمنها مصبحين ⑰

1. See Sûr. II, v. 1, footnote.

18. And made no exception (for the will of Allah);[1]

19. Then a visitation came upon it while they slept.

20. And in the morning it was as if plucked,

21. And they cried out one unto another in the morning,

22. Saying: Run unto your field if ye would pluck (the fruit).

23. So they went off, saying one unto another in low tones:

24. No needy man shall enter it to-day against you.[2]

25. They went betimes, strong in (this) purpose.

26. But when they saw it, they said: Lo! we are in error!

27. Nay, but we are desolate!

28. The best among them said: Said I not unto you: Why glorify ye not (Allah)?

29. They said: Glorified be our Lord! Lo! we have been wrong-doers.

30. Then some of them drew near unto others, self-reproaching.

31. They said: Alas for us! In truth we were outrageous.

32. It may be that our Lord will give us better than this in place thereof. Lo! we beseech our Lord.

33. Such was the punishment. And verily the punishment of the Hereafter is greater if they did but know.

34. Lo! for those who keep from evil are gardens of bliss with their Lord.

35. Shall We then treat those who have surrendered[3] as We treat the guilty?

36. What aileth you? How foolishly ye judge!

37. Or have ye a Scripture wherein ye learn

وَلَا يَسْتَثْنُونَ ﴿١٨﴾

فَطَافَ عَلَيْهَا طَآئِفٌ مِّن رَّبِّكَ وَهُمْ نَآئِمُونَ ﴿١٩﴾

فَأَصْبَحَتْ كَالصَّرِيمِ ﴿٢٠﴾

فَتَنَادَوْا مُصْبِحِينَ ﴿٢١﴾

أَنِ اغْدُوا عَلَىٰ حَرْثِكُمْ إِن كُنتُمْ صَارِمِينَ ﴿٢٢﴾

فَانطَلَقُوا وَهُمْ يَتَخَافَتُونَ ﴿٢٣﴾

أَن لَّا يَدْخُلَنَّهَا الْيَوْمَ عَلَيْكُم مِّسْكِينٌ ﴿٢٤﴾

وَغَدَوْا عَلَىٰ حَرْدٍ قَادِرِينَ ﴿٢٥﴾

فَلَمَّا رَأَوْهَا قَالُوا إِنَّا لَضَالُّونَ ﴿٢٦﴾

بَلْ نَحْنُ مَحْرُومُونَ ﴿٢٧﴾

قَالَ أَوْسَطُهُمْ أَلَمْ أَقُل لَّكُمْ لَوْلَا تُسَبِّحُونَ ﴿٢٨﴾

قَالُوا سُبْحَانَ رَبِّنَا إِنَّا كُنَّا ظَالِمِينَ ﴿٢٩﴾

فَأَقْبَلَ بَعْضُهُمْ عَلَىٰ بَعْضٍ يَتَلَاوَمُونَ ﴿٣٠﴾

قَالُوا يَا وَيْلَنَا إِنَّا كُنَّا طَاغِينَ ﴿٣١﴾

عَسَىٰ رَبُّنَا أَن يُبْدِلَنَا خَيْرًا مِّنْهَا إِنَّا إِلَىٰ رَبِّنَا
رَاغِبُونَ ﴿٣٢﴾

كَذَٰلِكَ الْعَذَابُ وَلَعَذَابُ الْآخِرَةِ أَكْبَرُ لَوْ
كَانُوا يَعْلَمُونَ ﴿٣٣﴾

إِنَّ لِلْمُتَّقِينَ عِندَ رَبِّهِمْ جَنَّاتِ النَّعِيمِ ﴿٣٤﴾

أَفَنَجْعَلُ الْمُسْلِمِينَ كَالْمُجْرِمِينَ ﴿٣٥﴾

مَا لَكُمْ كَيْفَ تَحْكُمُونَ ﴿٣٦﴾

أَمْ لَكُمْ كِتَابٌ فِيهِ تَدْرُسُونَ ﴿٣٧﴾

1. *i.e.* they forgot to say: "If God wills."
2. It was a custom throughout the East to allow the poor a gleaning of all harvests.
3. Ar. *Muslimîn.*

38. That ye shall indeed have all that ye choose?

اِنَّ لَكُمْ فِيْهِ لَمَا تَخَيَّرُوْنَ ۟

39. Or have ye a covenant on oath from Us that reacheth to the Day of Judgement, that yours shall be all that ye ordain?

اَمْ لَكُمْ اَيْمَانٌ عَلَيْنَا بَالِغَةٌ اِلٰى يَوْمِ الْقِيٰمَةِ اِنَّ لَكُمْ لَمَا تَحْكُمُوْنَ ۟

40. Ask them (O Muhammad) which of them will vouch for that!

سَلْهُمْ اَيُّهُمْ بِذٰلِكَ زَعِيْمٌ ۟

41. Or have they other gods? Then let them bring their other gods if they are truthful.

اَمْ لَهُمْ شُرَكَاءُ ۚ فَلْيَأْتُوْا بِشُرَكَائِهِمْ اِنْ كَانُوْا صٰدِقِيْنَ

42. On the day when it befalleth in earnest, and they are ordered to prostrate themselves but are not able,

يَوْمَ يُكْشَفُ عَنْ سَاقٍ وَّيُدْعَوْنَ اِلَى السُّجُوْدِ فَلَا يَسْتَطِيْعُوْنَ ۟

43. With eyes downcast, abasement stupefying them. And they had been summoned to prostrate themselves while they were yet unhurt.

خَاشِعَةً اَبْصَارُهُمْ تَرْهَقُهُمْ ذِلَّةٌ ۚ وَقَدْ كَانُوْا يُدْعَوْنَ اِلَى السُّجُوْدِ وَهُمْ سٰلِمُوْنَ ۟

44. Leave Me (to deal) with those who give the lie to this pronouncement. We shall lead them on by steps from whence they know not.

فَذَرْنِيْ وَمَنْ يُّكَذِّبُ بِهٰذَا الْحَدِيْثِ ۚ سَنَسْتَدْرِجُهُمْ مِّنْ حَيْثُ لَا يَعْلَمُوْنَ ۟

45. Yet I bear with them, for lo! My scheme is firm.

وَاُمْلِيْ لَهُمْ ۚ اِنَّ كَيْدِيْ مَتِيْنٌ ۟

46. Or dost thou (Muhammad) ask a fee from them so that they are heavily taxed?

اَمْ تَسْأَلُهُمْ اَجْرًا فَهُمْ مِّنْ مَّغْرَمٍ مُّثْقَلُوْنَ ۟

47. Or is the Unseen theirs that they can write (thereof)?

اَمْ عِنْدَهُمُ الْغَيْبُ فَهُمْ يَكْتُبُوْنَ ۟

48. But wait thou for thy Lord's decree, and be not like him of the fish[1], who cried out in despair.

فَاصْبِرْ لِحُكْمِ رَبِّكَ وَلَا تَكُنْ كَصَاحِبِ الْحُوْتِ ۘ اِذْ نَادٰى وَهُوَ مَكْظُوْمٌ ۟

49. Had it not been that favour from his Lord had reached him he surely had been cast into the wilderness while he was reprobate.

لَوْلَا اَنْ تَدَارَكَهُ نِعْمَةٌ مِّنْ رَّبِّهِ لَنُبِذَ بِالْعَرَاءِ وَهُوَ مَذْمُوْمٌ ۟

50. But his Lord chose him and placed him among the righteous.

فَاجْتَبٰهُ رَبُّهُ فَجَعَلَهُ مِنَ الصّٰلِحِيْنَ ۟

51. And lo! those who disbelieve would fain disconcert thee with their eyes when they hear the Reminder, and they say: Lo! he is indeed mad;

وَاِنْ يَّكَادُ الَّذِيْنَ كَفَرُوْا لَيُزْلِقُوْنَكَ بِاَبْصَارِهِمْ لَمَّا سَمِعُوا الذِّكْرَ وَيَقُوْلُوْنَ اِنَّهُ لَمَجْنُوْنٌ ۟

52. When it is naught else than a Reminder to creation.

وَمَا هُوَ اِلَّا ذِكْرٌ لِّلْعٰلَمِيْنَ ۟

1. *i.e.* Jonah.

Al-Ḥāqqah, takes its name from a word recurring in the first three verses.

It belongs to the middle group of Meccan Sūrahs.

THE REALITY

Revealed at Mecca

In the name of Allah, the Beneficent, the Merciful.

1. The Reality!

2. What is the Reality?

3. Ah, what will convey unto thee what the reality is!

4. (The tribes of) Thamūd and 'Aād disbelieved in the Judgement to come.

5. As for Thamūd, they were destroyed by the lightning.

6. And as for 'Aād, they were destroyed by a fierce roaring wind,

7. Which He imposed on them for seven long nights and eight long days so that thou mightest have seen men lying overthrown, as they were hollow trunks of palm-trees.

8. Canst thou (O Muhammad) see any remnant of them?

9. And Pharaoh and those before him, and the communities that were destroyed, brought error,

10. And they disobeyed the messenger of their Lord, therefor did He grip them with a tightening grip.

11. Lo! when the waters rose, We carried you upon the ship

12. That We might make it a memorial for you, and that remembering ears (that heard the story) might remember.

13. And when the Trumpet shall sound one blast

14. And the earth with the mountains shall be lifted up and crushed with one crash,

15. Then, on that day will the Event befall.

16. And the heaven will split asunder, for that day it will be frail:

اٰياتها (٦٩) سُوْرَةُ الْحَاقَّةِ مَكِّيَّةٌ رُكُوْعَاتُهَا ٢

بِسْمِ اللّٰهِ الرَّحْمٰنِ الرَّحِيْمِ

اَلْحَاقَّةُ ۙ ١

مَا الْحَاقَّةُ ۚ ٢

وَمَآ اَدْرٰىكَ مَا الْحَاقَّةُ ۗ ٣

كَذَّبَتْ ثَمُوْدُ وَعَادٌۢ بِالْقَارِعَةِ ٤

فَاَمَّا ثَمُوْدُ فَاُهْلِكُوْا بِالطَّاغِيَةِ ٥

وَاَمَّا عَادٌ فَاُهْلِكُوْا بِرِيْحٍ صَرْصَرٍ عَاتِيَةٍ ۙ ٦

سَخَّرَهَا عَلَيْهِمْ سَبْعَ لَيَالٍ وَّثَمٰنِيَةَ اَيَّامٍ ۙ حُسُوْمًا

فَتَرَى الْقَوْمَ فِيْهَا صَرْعٰى ۙ كَاَنَّهُمْ اَعْجَازُ

نَخْلٍ خَاوِيَةٍ ۚ ٧

فَهَلْ تَرٰى لَهُمْ مِّنْۢ بَاقِيَةٍ ٨

وَجَآءَ فِرْعَوْنُ وَمَنْ قَبْلَهٗ وَالْمُؤْتَفِكٰتُ

بِالْخَاطِئَةِ ۚ ٩

فَعَصَوْا رَسُوْلَ رَبِّهِمْ فَاَخَذَهُمْ اَخْذَةً رَّابِيَةً ١٠

اِنَّا لَمَّا طَغَا الْمَآءُ حَمَلْنٰكُمْ فِي الْجَارِيَةِ ۙ ١١

لِنَجْعَلَهَا لَكُمْ تَذْكِرَةً وَّتَعِيَهَآ اُذُنٌ وَّاعِيَةٌ ١٢

فَاِذَا نُفِخَ فِي الصُّوْرِ نَفْخَةٌ وَّاحِدَةٌ ۙ ١٣

وَّحُمِلَتِ الْاَرْضُ وَالْجِبَالُ فَدُكَّتَا دَكَّةً وَّاحِدَةً ۙ ١٤

فَيَوْمَئِذٍ وَّقَعَتِ الْوَاقِعَةُ ۙ ١٥

وَانْشَقَّتِ السَّمَآءُ فَهِيَ يَوْمَئِذٍ وَّاهِيَةٌ ۙ ١٦

17. And the angels will be on the sides thereof, and eight will uphold the Throne of their Lord that day, above them.

18. On that day ye will be exposed; not a secret of you will be hidden.

19. Then, as for him who is given his record in his right hand, he will say: Take, read my book!

20. Surely I knew that I should have to meet my reckoning.

21. Then he will be in blissful state

22. In a high Garden

23. Whereof the clusters are in easy reach.

24. (And it will be said unto those therein): Eat and drink at ease for that which ye sent on before you in past days.

25. But as for him who is given his record in his left hand, he will say: Oh, would that I had not been given my book

26. And knew not what my reckoning!

27. Oh, would that it had been death!

28. My wealth hath not availed me,

29. My power hath gone from me.

30. (It will be said): Take him and fetter him

31. And then expose him to hell-fire

32. And then insert him in a chain whereof the length is seventy cubits.

33. Lo! he used not to believe in Allah the Tremendous,

34. And urged not on the feeding of the wretched,

وَّالْمَلَكُ عَلٰٓى اَرْجَآىِٕهَا ؕ وَيَحْمِلُ عَرْشَ رَبِّكَ
فَوْقَهُمْ يَوْمَىِٕذٍ ثَمٰنِيَةٌ ؕ ﴿١٧﴾
يَوْمَىِٕذٍ تُعْرَضُوْنَ لَا تَخْفٰى مِنْكُمْ خَافِيَةٌ ﴿١٨﴾
فَاَمَّا مَنْ اُوْتِىَ كِتٰبَهٗ بِيَمِيْنِهٖ ۙ فَيَقُوْلُ هَآؤُمُ
اقْرَءُوْا كِتٰبِيَهْ ﴿١٩﴾
اِنِّىْ ظَنَنْتُ اَنِّىْ مُلٰقٍ حِسَابِيَهْ ﴿٢٠﴾
فَهُوَ فِىْ عِيْشَةٍ رَّاضِيَةٍ ﴿٢١﴾
فِىْ جَنَّةٍ عَالِيَةٍ ﴿٢٢﴾
قُطُوْفُهَا دَانِيَةٌ ﴿٢٣﴾
كُلُوْا وَاشْرَبُوْا هَنِيْٓـًٔا بِمَآ اَسْلَفْتُمْ فِى الْاَيَّامِ
الْخَالِيَةِ ﴿٢٤﴾
وَاَمَّا مَنْ اُوْتِىَ كِتٰبَهٗ بِشِمَالِهٖ ۙ فَيَقُوْلُ يٰلَيْتَنِىْ
لَمْ اُوْتَ كِتٰبِيَهْ ﴿٢٥﴾
وَلَمْ اَدْرِ مَا حِسَابِيَهْ ﴿٢٦﴾
يٰلَيْتَهَا كَانَتِ الْقَاضِيَةَ ﴿٢٧﴾
مَآ اَغْنٰى عَنِّىْ مَالِيَهْ ﴿٢٨﴾
هَلَكَ عَنِّىْ سُلْطٰنِيَهْ ﴿٢٩﴾
خُذُوْهُ فَغُلُّوْهُ ﴿٣٠﴾
ثُمَّ الْجَحِيْمَ صَلُّوْهُ ﴿٣١﴾
ثُمَّ فِىْ سِلْسِلَةٍ ذَرْعُهَا سَبْعُوْنَ ذِرَاعًا فَاسْلُكُوْهُ ﴿٣٢﴾
اِنَّهٗ كَانَ لَا يُؤْمِنُ بِاللّٰهِ الْعَظِيْمِ ﴿٣٣﴾
وَلَا يَحُضُّ عَلٰى طَعَامِ الْمِسْكِيْنِ ﴿٣٤﴾

35. Therefor hath he no lover here this day,	فَلَيْسَ لَهُ الْيَوْمَ هٰهُنَا حَمِيمٌ ﴿٣٥﴾
36. Nor any food save filth	وَلَا طَعَامٌ إِلَّا مِنْ غِسْلِينٍ ﴿٣٦﴾
37. Which none but sinners eat.	لَا يَأْكُلُهُ إِلَّا الْخَاطِئُونَ ﴿٣٧﴾
38. But nay! I swear by all that ye see	فَلَا أُقْسِمُ بِمَا تُبْصِرُونَ ﴿٣٨﴾
39. And all that ye see not	وَمَا لَا تُبْصِرُونَ ﴿٣٩﴾
40. That it is indeed the speech of an illustrious messenger.	إِنَّهُ لَقَوْلُ رَسُولٍ كَرِيمٍ ﴿٤٠﴾
41. It is not poet's speech—little is it that ye believe!	وَمَا هُوَ بِقَوْلِ شَاعِرٍ قَلِيلًا مَا تُؤْمِنُونَ ﴿٤١﴾
42. Nor diviner's speech—little is it that ye remember!	وَلَا بِقَوْلِ كَاهِنٍ قَلِيلًا مَا تَذَكَّرُونَ ﴿٤٢﴾
43. It is a revelation from the Lord of the Worlds.	تَنْزِيلٌ مِنْ رَبِّ الْعٰلَمِينَ ﴿٤٣﴾
44. And if he had invented false sayings concerning Us,	وَلَوْ تَقَوَّلَ عَلَيْنَا بَعْضَ الْأَقَاوِيلِ ﴿٤٤﴾
45. We assuredly had taken him by the right hand	لَأَخَذْنَا مِنْهُ بِالْيَمِينِ ﴿٤٥﴾
46. And then severed his life-artery,	ثُمَّ لَقَطَعْنَا مِنْهُ الْوَتِينَ ﴿٤٦﴾
47. And not one of you could have held Us off from him.	فَمَا مِنْكُمْ مِنْ أَحَدٍ عَنْهُ حٰجِزِينَ ﴿٤٧﴾
48. And lo! it is a warrant unto those who ward off (evil).	وَإِنَّهُ لَتَذْكِرَةٌ لِلْمُتَّقِينَ ﴿٤٨﴾
49. And lo! We know that some among you will deny (it).	وَإِنَّا لَنَعْلَمُ أَنَّ مِنْكُمْ مُكَذِّبِينَ ﴿٤٩﴾
50. And lo! it is indeed an anguish for the disbelievers.	وَإِنَّهُ لَحَسْرَةٌ عَلَى الْكٰفِرِينَ ﴿٥٠﴾
51. And lo! it is absolute truth.	وَإِنَّهُ لَحَقُّ الْيَقِينِ ﴿٥١﴾
52. So glorify the name of thy Tremendous Lord.	فَسَبِّحْ بِاسْمِ رَبِّكَ الْعَظِيمِ ﴿٥٢﴾

Al-Ma'ārij takes its name from a word in verse 3. An early Meccan Sūrah.

THE ASCENDING STAIRWAYS

Revealed at Mecca

In the name of Allah, the Beneficent, the Merciful.

1. A questioner questioned concerning the doom about to fall
2. Upon the disbelievers, which none can repel,
3. From Allah, Lord of the Ascending Stairways
4. (Whereby) the angels and the Spirit ascend unto Him in a Day whereof the span is fifty thousand years.
5. But be patient (O Muhammad) with a patience fair to see.
6. Lo! they behold it afar off
7. While We behold it nigh:
8. The day when the sky will become as molten copper,
9. And the hills become as flakes of wool,
10. And no familiar friend will ask a question of his friend
11. Though they will be given sight of them. The guilty man will long be able to ransom himself from the punishment of that day at the price of his children
12. And his spouse and his brother
13. And his kin that harboured him
14. And all that are in the earth, if then it might deliver him.
15. But nay! for lo! it is the fire of hell
16. Eager to roast;
17. It calleth him who turned and fled (from truth),

اٰياتها ٤٤ (٧٠) سُوْرَةُ الْمَعَارِجِ مَكِّيَّةٌ رُكُوْعَاتُهَا ٢

بِسْمِ اللّٰهِ الرَّحْمٰنِ الرَّحِيْمِ

سَاَلَ سَآئِلٌۢ بِعَذَابٍ وَّاقِعٍ ﴿١﴾

لِّلْكٰفِرِيْنَ لَيْسَ لَهٗ دَافِعٌ ﴿٢﴾

مِّنَ اللّٰهِ ذِى الْمَعَارِجِ ﴿٣﴾

تَعْرُجُ الْمَلٰٓئِكَةُ وَالرُّوْحُ اِلَيْهِ فِىْ يَوْمٍ كَانَ
مِقْدَارُهٗ خَمْسِيْنَ اَلْفَ سَنَةٍ ﴿٤﴾

فَاصْبِرْ صَبْرًا جَمِيْلًا ﴿٥﴾

اِنَّهُمْ يَرَوْنَهٗ بَعِيْدًا ﴿٦﴾

وَّنَرٰىهُ قَرِيْبًا ﴿٧﴾

يَوْمَ تَكُوْنُ السَّمَآءُ كَالْمُهْلِ ﴿٨﴾

وَتَكُوْنُ الْجِبَالُ كَالْعِهْنِ ﴿٩﴾

وَلَا يَسْـَٔلُ حَمِيْمٌ حَمِيْمًا ﴿١٠﴾

يُّبَصَّرُوْنَهُمْ ۗ يَوَدُّ الْمُجْرِمُ لَوْ يَفْتَدِىْ مِنْ عَذَابِ
يَوْمِئِذٍۢ بِبَنِيْهِ ﴿١١﴾

وَصَاحِبَتِهٖ وَاَخِيْهِ ﴿١٢﴾

وَفَصِيْلَتِهِ الَّتِىْ تُـْٔوِيْهِ ﴿١٣﴾

وَمَنْ فِى الْاَرْضِ جَمِيْعًا ۙ ثُمَّ يُنْجِيْهِ ﴿١٤﴾

كَلَّا ۗ اِنَّهَا لَظٰى ﴿١٥﴾

نَزَّاعَةً لِّلشَّوٰى ﴿١٦﴾

تَدْعُوْا مَنْ اَدْبَرَ وَتَوَلّٰى ﴿١٧﴾

18. And hoarded (wealth) and withheld it.

19. Lo! man was created anxious,

20. Fretful when evil befalleth him

21. And, when good befalleth him, grudging;

22. Save worshippers

23. Who are constant at their worship

24. And in whose wealth there is a right acknowledged

25. For the beggar and the destitute;

26. And those who believe in the Day of Judgement,

27. And those who are fearful of their Lord's doom—

28. Lo! the doom of their Lord is that before which none can feel secure—

29. And those who preserve their chastity

30. Save with their wives and those whom their right hands possess, for thus they are not blameworthy;

31. But whoso seeketh more than that, those are they who are transgressors;

32. And those who keep their pledges and their covenant,

33. And those who stand by their testimony

34. And those who are attentive at their worship,

35. These will dwell in Gardens, honoured.

36. What aileth those who disbelieve, that they keep staring toward thee (O Muhammad), open-eyed,

37. On the right and on the left, in groups?

وَجَمَعَ فَأَوْعٰى ⑱

إِنَّ الْإِنْسَانَ خُلِقَ هَلُوعًا ⑲

إِذَا مَسَّهُ الشَّرُّ جَزُوعًا ⑳

وَّإِذَا مَسَّهُ الْخَيْرُ مَنُوعًا ㉑

إِلَّا الْمُصَلِّيْنَ ㉒

الَّذِيْنَ هُمْ عَلٰى صَلَاتِهِمْ دَآئِمُوْنَ ㉓

وَالَّذِيْنَ فِيْٓ أَمْوَالِهِمْ حَقٌّ مَّعْلُوْمٌ ㉔

لِّلسَّآئِلِ وَالْمَحْرُوْمِ ㉕

وَالَّذِيْنَ يُصَدِّقُوْنَ بِيَوْمِ الدِّيْنِ ㉖

وَالَّذِيْنَ هُمْ مِّنْ عَذَابِ رَبِّهِمْ مُّشْفِقُوْنَ ㉗

إِنَّ عَذَابَ رَبِّهِمْ غَيْرُ مَأْمُوْنٍ ㉘

وَالَّذِيْنَ هُمْ لِفُرُوْجِهِمْ حٰفِظُوْنَ ㉙

إِلَّا عَلٰٓى أَزْوَاجِهِمْ أَوْ مَا مَلَكَتْ أَيْمَانُهُمْ فَإِنَّهُمْ غَيْرُ مَلُوْمِيْنَ ㉚

فَمَنِ ابْتَغٰى وَرَآءَ ذٰلِكَ فَأُولٰٓئِكَ هُمُ الْعٰدُوْنَ ㉛

وَالَّذِيْنَ هُمْ لِأَمٰنٰتِهِمْ وَعَهْدِهِمْ رٰعُوْنَ ㉜

وَالَّذِيْنَ هُمْ بِشَهٰدٰتِهِمْ قَآئِمُوْنَ ㉝

وَالَّذِيْنَ هُمْ عَلٰى صَلَاتِهِمْ يُحَافِظُوْنَ ㉞

أُولٰٓئِكَ فِيْ جَنّٰتٍ مُّكْرَمُوْنَ ㉟

فَمَالِ الَّذِيْنَ كَفَرُوْا قِبَلَكَ مُهْطِعِيْنَ ㊱

عَنِ الْيَمِيْنِ وَعَنِ الشِّمَالِ عِزِيْنَ ㊲

38. Doth every man among them hope to enter the Garden of Delight?

39. Nay, verily. Lo! We created them from what they know.

40. But nay! I swear by the Lord of the rising-places and the setting-places of the planets that We are Able

41. To replace them by (others) better than them. And We are not to be outrun.

42. So let them chat and play until they meet their Day which they are promised--

43. The Day when they come forth from the graves in haste, as racing to a goal,

44. With eyes aghast, abasement stupefying them: such is the Day which they are promised.

أَيَطْمَعُ كُلُّ امْرِئٍ مِّنْهُمْ أَنْ يُّدْخَلَ جَنَّةَ
نَعِيْمٍ ﴿٣٨﴾
كَلَّا ۖ إِنَّا خَلَقْنٰهُمْ مِّمَّا يَعْلَمُوْنَ ﴿٣٩﴾
فَلَآ أُقْسِمُ بِرَبِّ الْمَشٰرِقِ وَالْمَغٰرِبِ إِنَّا
لَقٰدِرُوْنَ ﴿٤٠﴾
عَلٰٓى أَنْ نُّبَدِّلَ خَيْرًا مِّنْهُمْ ۙ وَمَا نَحْنُ
بِمَسْبُوْقِيْنَ ﴿٤١﴾
فَذَرْهُمْ يَخُوْضُوْا وَيَلْعَبُوْا حَتّٰى يُلٰقُوْا يَوْمَهُمُ
الَّذِيْ يُوْعَدُوْنَ ﴿٤٢﴾
يَوْمَ يَخْرُجُوْنَ مِنَ الْأَجْدَاثِ سِرَاعًا كَأَنَّهُمْ
إِلٰى نُصُبٍ يُّوْفِضُوْنَ ﴿٤٣﴾
خَاشِعَةً أَبْصَارُهُمْ تَرْهَقُهُمْ ذِلَّةٌ ۗ ذٰلِكَ
الْيَوْمُ الَّذِيْ كَانُوْا يُوْعَدُوْنَ ﴿٤٤﴾

Takes its name from its subject, which is the preaching of the prophet Noah. An early Meccan Sūrah.

NOAH

Revealed at Mecca

In the name of Allah, the Beneficent, the Merciful.

1. Lo! We sent Noah unto his people (saying): Warn thy people ere the painful doom come unto them.

2. He said: O my people! Lo! I am a plain warner unto you

3. (Bidding you): Serve Allah and keep your duty unto Him and obey me,

4. That He may forgive you somewhat of your sins and respite you to an appointed term. Lo! the term of Allah, when it cometh, cannot be delayed, if ye but knew.

5. He said: My Lord! Lo! I have called unto my people night and day

6. But all my calling doth but add to their repugnance;

7. And lo! whenever I call unto them that Thou mayest pardon them they thrust their fingers in their ears and cover themselves with their garments and persist (in their refusal) and magnify themselves in pride.

8. And lo! I have called unto them aloud,

9. And lo! I have made public proclamation unto them, and I have appealed to them in private.

10. And I have said: Seek pardon of your Lord. Lo! He was ever Forgiving.

11. He will let loose the sky for you in plenteous rain,

12. And will help you with wealth and sons, and will assign unto you Gardens and will assign unto you rivers.

13. What aileth you that ye hope not toward Allah for dignity

14. When He created you by (divers) stages?

أياتها ٢٨ (٧١) سورة نوح مكية ٧١ ركوعاتها ٢

بِسْمِ اللّٰهِ الرَّحْمٰنِ الرَّحِيْمِ ○

إِنَّآ أَرْسَلْنَا نُوْحًا إِلٰى قَوْمِهٖٓ أَنْ أَنْذِرْ قَوْمَكَ مِنْ
قَبْلِ أَنْ يَّأْتِيَهُمْ عَذَابٌ أَلِيْمٌ ①
قَالَ يٰقَوْمِ إِنِّيْ لَكُمْ نَذِيْرٌ مُّبِيْنٌ ②
أَنِ اعْبُدُوا اللّٰهَ وَاتَّقُوْهُ وَأَطِيْعُوْنِ ③
يَغْفِرْ لَكُمْ مِّنْ ذُنُوْبِكُمْ وَيُؤَخِّرْكُمْ إِلٰٓى أَجَلٍ مُّسَمًّى إِنَّ
أَجَلَ اللّٰهِ إِذَا جَآءَ لَا يُؤَخَّرُ لَوْ كُنْتُمْ تَعْلَمُوْنَ ④ وقف لازم
قَالَ رَبِّ إِنِّيْ دَعَوْتُ قَوْمِيْ لَيْلًا وَّنَهَارًا ⑤
فَلَمْ يَزِدْهُمْ دُعَآءِيْٓ إِلَّا فِرَارًا ⑥
وَإِنِّيْ كُلَّمَا دَعَوْتُهُمْ لِتَغْفِرَ لَهُمْ جَعَلُوْٓا أَصَابِعَهُمْ
فِيْٓ اٰذَانِهِمْ وَاسْتَغْشَوْا ثِيَابَهُمْ وَأَصَرُّوْا وَ
اسْتَكْبَرُوا اسْتِكْبَارًا ⑦
ثُمَّ إِنِّيْ دَعَوْتُهُمْ جِهَارًا ⑧
ثُمَّ إِنِّيْٓ أَعْلَنْتُ لَهُمْ وَأَسْرَرْتُ لَهُمْ إِسْرَارًا ⑨
فَقُلْتُ اسْتَغْفِرُوْا رَبَّكُمْ إِنَّهٗ كَانَ غَفَّارًا ⑩
يُّرْسِلِ السَّمَآءَ عَلَيْكُمْ مِّدْرَارًا ⑪
وَّيُمْدِدْكُمْ بِأَمْوَالٍ وَّبَنِيْنَ وَيَجْعَلْ لَّكُمْ
جَنّٰتٍ وَّيَجْعَلْ لَّكُمْ أَنْهٰرًا ⑫
مَا لَكُمْ لَا تَرْجُوْنَ لِلّٰهِ وَقَارًا ⑬
وَقَدْ خَلَقَكُمْ أَطْوَارًا ⑭

15. See ye not how Allah hath created seven heavens in harmony,

16. And hath made the moon a light therein, and made the sun a lamp?

17. And Allah hath caused you to grow as a growth from the earth,

18. And afterward He maketh you return thereto, and He will bring you forth again, a (new) forthbringing.

19. And Allah hath made the earth a wide expanse for you

20. That ye may thread the valley-ways thereof.

21. Noah said: My Lord! Lo! they have disobeyed me and followed one whose wealth and children increase him in naught save ruin;

22. And they have plotted a mighty plot,

23. And they have said: Forsake not your gods. Forsake not Wadd, nor Suwā, nor Yaghūth and Ya'ūq and Nasr.[1]

24. And they have led many astray, and Thou increasest the wrong-doers in naught save error.

25. Because of their sins they were drowned, then made to enter a Fire. And they found they had no helpers in place of Allah.

26. And Noah said: My Lord! Leave not one of the disbelievers in the land.

27. If Thou shouldst leave them, they will mislead Thy slaves and will beget none save lewd ingrates.

28. My Lord! Forgive me and my parents and him who entereth my house believing, and believing men and believing women, and increase not the wrong-doers in aught save ruin.

أَلَمْ تَرَوْا كَيْفَ خَلَقَ اللَّهُ سَبْعَ سَمٰوٰتٍ طِبَاقًا ﴿١٥﴾
وَجَعَلَ الْقَمَرَ فِيهِنَّ نُورًا وَجَعَلَ الشَّمْسَ سِرَاجًا ﴿١٦﴾
وَاللَّهُ أَنْبَتَكُمْ مِنَ الْأَرْضِ نَبَاتًا ﴿١٧﴾
ثُمَّ يُعِيدُكُمْ فِيهَا وَيُخْرِجُكُمْ إِخْرَاجًا ﴿١٨﴾
وَاللَّهُ جَعَلَ لَكُمُ الْأَرْضَ بِسَاطًا ﴿١٩﴾
لِتَسْلُكُوا مِنْهَا سُبُلًا فِجَاجًا ﴿٢٠﴾
قَالَ نُوحٌ رَبِّ إِنَّهُمْ عَصَوْنِي وَاتَّبَعُوا مَنْ لَمْ يَزِدْهُ مَالُهُ وَوَلَدُهُ إِلَّا خَسَارًا ﴿٢١﴾
وَمَكَرُوا مَكْرًا كُبَّارًا ﴿٢٢﴾
وَقَالُوا لَا تَذَرُنَّ آلِهَتَكُمْ وَلَا تَذَرُنَّ وَدًّا وَلَا سُوَاعًا وَلَا يَغُوثَ وَيَعُوقَ وَنَسْرًا ﴿٢٣﴾
وَقَدْ أَضَلُّوا كَثِيرًا وَلَا تَزِدِ الظّٰلِمِينَ إِلَّا ضَلَالًا ﴿٢٤﴾
مِمَّا خَطِيئٰتِهِمْ أُغْرِقُوا فَأُدْخِلُوا نَارًا فَلَمْ يَجِدُوا لَهُمْ مِنْ دُونِ اللَّهِ أَنْصَارًا ﴿٢٥﴾
وَقَالَ نُوحٌ رَبِّ لَا تَذَرْ عَلَى الْأَرْضِ مِنَ الْكٰفِرِينَ دَيَّارًا ﴿٢٦﴾
إِنَّكَ إِنْ تَذَرْهُمْ يُضِلُّوا عِبَادَكَ وَلَا يَلِدُوا إِلَّا فَاجِرًا كَفَّارًا ﴿٢٧﴾
رَبِّ اغْفِرْ لِي وَلِوَالِدَيَّ وَلِمَنْ دَخَلَ بَيْتِيَ مُؤْمِنًا وَلِلْمُؤْمِنِينَ وَالْمُؤْمِنٰتِ وَلَا تَزِدِ الظّٰلِمِينَ إِلَّا تَبَارًا ﴿٢٨﴾

1. Idols of the pagan Arabs.

Al-Jinn takes its name from a word in the first verse, and also from the subject of verses 1-18. The meaning of the word jinn in the Koran has exercised the minds of Muslim commentators, ancient and modern. Mr. Ya'qūb Hasan of Madras, in the first volume of a remarkable work in Urdu, *Kitābu'l-Hudā*, shows that it has at least three meanings in the Koran and that one of those meanings is something akin to "clever foreigners" as in the case of the Jinn who worked for Solomon. But undoubtedly the first and obvious meaning is "elemental spirits," to whom, as to mankind, the Koran came as a guidance. The incident is said to have occurred during the Prophet's return from his unsuccessful missionary journey to Ṭā'īf.

A late Meccan Sūrah.

THE JINN

Revealed at Mecca

In the name of Allah, the Beneficent, the Merciful.

1. Say (O Muhammad): It is revealed unto me that a company of the Jinn gave ear, and they said: Lo! it is a marvellous Qur'ān,

2. Which guideth unto righteousness, so we believe in it and we ascribe no partner unto our Lord:

3. And (we believe) that He—exalted be the glory of our Lord!—hath taken neither wife nor son,

4. And that the foolish ones among us used to speak concerning Allah an atrocious lie,

5. And lo! we had supposed that humankind and Jinn would not speak a lie concerning Allah—

6. And indeed (O Muhammad) individuals of humankind used to invoke the protection of individuals of the Jinn, so that they increased them in revolt (against Allah);

7. And indeed they supposed, even as ye suppose, that Allah would not raise anyone (from the dead)—

8. And (the Jinn who had listened to the Qur'ān said): We had sought the heaven but had found it filled with strong warders and meteors.

9. And we used to sit on places (high) therein to listen. But he who listened now findeth a flame in wait for him;[1]

10. And we know not whether harm is boded unto all who are in the earth, or whether their Lord intendeth guidance for them;

11. And among us there are righteous folk and among us there are far from that. We are sects having different rules.

12. And we know that we cannot escape from Allah in the earth, nor can we escape by flight.

13. And when we heard the guidance, we believed therein, and Whoso believeth in his Lord, he feareth neither loss nor oppression.

اٰياتها ٢٨ (٧٢) سورة الجن مكية ركوعاتها ٢

بسم الله الرحمٰن الرحيم ۝

قل اوحي الي انه استمع نفر من الجن فقالوا
انا سمعنا قراٰنا عجبا ۙ ①
يهدي الى الرشد فاٰمنا به ولن نشرك بربنا احدا ۙ ②
وانه تعٰلى جد ربنا ما اتخذ صاحبة ولا ولدا ۙ ③
وانه كان يقول سفيهنا على الله شططا ۙ ④
وانا ظننا ان لن تقول الانس والجن على الله كذبا ۙ ⑤
وانه كان رجال من الانس يعوذون برجال من
الجن فزادوهم رهقا ۙ ⑥
وانهم ظنوا كما ظننتم ان لن يبعث الله احدا ۙ ⑦
وانا لمسنا السماء فوجدنٰها ملئت حرسا شديدا
وشهبا ۙ ⑧
وانا كنا نقعد منها مقاعد للسمع فمن يستمع
الاٰن يجد له شهابا رصدا ۙ ⑨
وانا لا ندري اشر اريد بمن في الارض ام اراد
بهم ربهم رشدا ۙ ⑩
وانا منا الصٰلحون ومنا دون ذٰلك كنا طرائق قددا ۙ ⑪
وانا ظننا ان لن نعجز الله في الارض ولن نعجزه هربا ۙ ⑫
وانا لما سمعنا الهدٰى اٰمنا به فمن يؤمن بربه
فلا يخاف بخسا ولا رهقا ۙ ⑬

1. About the time of the Prophet's mission there were many meteors and other strange appearances in the heavens, which, tradition says, frightened the astrologers from the high observatories where they used to watch at night, and threw out all their calculations.

14. And there are among us some who have surrendered (to Allah) and there are among us some who are unjust. And whoso hath surrendered to Allah, such have taken the right path purposefully.

15. And as for those who are unjust, they are firewood for hell.

16. If they (the idolaters) tread the right path, We shall give them to drink of water in abundance

17. That We may test them thereby, and whoso turneth away from the remembrance of his Lord; He will thrust him into ever-growing torment:

18. And the places of worship are only for Allah, so pray not unto anyone along with Allah:

19. And when the slave of Allah[1] stood up in prayer to Him, they crowded on him, almost stifling.[2]

20. Say (unto them, O Muhammad): I pray unto Allah only, and ascribe unto Him no partner.

21. Say: Lo! I control not hurt nor benefit for you.

22. Say: Lo! none can protect me from Allah, nor can I find any refuge beside Him

23. (Mine is) but conveyance (of the truth) from Allah, and His messages; and whoso disobeyeth Allah and His messenger, lo! his is fire of hell, wherein such dwell for ever.

24. Till (the day) when they shall behold that which they are promised (they may doubt); but then they will know (for certain) who is weaker in allies and less in multitude.

25. Say (O Muhammad, unto the disbelievers): I know not whether that which ye are promised is nigh, or if my Lord hath set a distant term for it.

26. (He is) the Knower of the Unseen, and He revealeth unto none His secret,

27. Save unto every messenger whom He hath chosen, and then He maketh a guard to go before him and a guard behind him

28. That He may know that they have indeed conveyed the messages of their Lord. He surroundeth all their doings, and He keepeth count of all things.

وَّاَنَّا مِنَّا الْمُسْلِمُوْنَ وَمِنَّا الْقٰسِطُوْنَ فَمَنْ اَسْلَمَ
فَاُولٰٓئِكَ تَحَرَّوْا رَشَدًا ﴿١٤﴾
وَاَمَّا الْقٰسِطُوْنَ فَكَانُوْا لِجَهَنَّمَ حَطَبًا ﴿١٥﴾
وَّاَنْ لَّوِ اسْتَقَامُوْا عَلَى الطَّرِيْقَةِ لَاَسْقَيْنٰهُمْ مَّآءً غَدَقًا ﴿١٦﴾
لِّنَفْتِنَهُمْ فِيْهِ وَمَنْ يُّعْرِضْ عَنْ ذِكْرِ رَبِّهٖ يَسْلُكْهُ
عَذَابًا صَعَدًا ﴿١٧﴾
وَّاَنَّ الْمَسٰجِدَ لِلّٰهِ فَلَا تَدْعُوْا مَعَ اللّٰهِ اَحَدًا ﴿١٨﴾
وَّاَنَّهٗ لَمَّا قَامَ عَبْدُ اللّٰهِ يَدْعُوْهُ كَادُوْا يَكُوْنُوْنَ عَلَيْهِ لِبَدًا ﴿١٩﴾
قُلْ اِنَّمَآ اَدْعُوْا رَبِّيْ وَلَآ اُشْرِكُ بِهٖٓ اَحَدًا ﴿٢٠﴾
قُلْ اِنِّيْ لَآ اَمْلِكُ لَكُمْ ضَرًّا وَّلَا رَشَدًا ﴿٢١﴾
قُلْ اِنِّيْ لَنْ يُّجِيْرَنِيْ مِنَ اللّٰهِ اَحَدٌ وَّلَنْ اَجِدَ
مِنْ دُوْنِهٖ مُلْتَحَدًا ﴿٢٢﴾
اِلَّا بَلٰغًا مِّنَ اللّٰهِ وَرِسٰلٰتِهٖ وَمَنْ يَّعْصِ اللّٰهَ وَرَسُوْلَهٗ
فَاِنَّ لَهٗ نَارَ جَهَنَّمَ خٰلِدِيْنَ فِيْهَآ اَبَدًا ﴿٢٣﴾
حَتّٰٓى اِذَا رَاَوْا مَا يُوْعَدُوْنَ فَسَيَعْلَمُوْنَ مَنْ اَضْعَفُ
نَاصِرًا وَّاَقَلُّ عَدَدًا ﴿٢٤﴾
قُلْ اِنْ اَدْرِيْٓ اَقَرِيْبٌ مَّا تُوْعَدُوْنَ اَمْ يَجْعَلُ لَهٗ رَبِّيْٓ اَمَدًا ﴿٢٥﴾
عٰلِمُ الْغَيْبِ فَلَا يُظْهِرُ عَلٰى غَيْبِهٖٓ اَحَدًا ﴿٢٦﴾
اِلَّا مَنِ ارْتَضٰى مِنْ رَّسُوْلٍ فَاِنَّهٗ يَسْلُكُ مِنْ بَيْنِ
يَدَيْهِ وَمِنْ خَلْفِهٖ رَصَدًا ﴿٢٧﴾
لِّيَعْلَمَ اَنْ قَدْ اَبْلَغُوْا رِسٰلٰتِ رَبِّهِمْ وَاَحَاطَ بِمَا
لَدَيْهِمْ وَاَحْصٰى كُلَّ شَيْءٍ عَدَدًا ﴿٢٨﴾

1. *i.e.* the Prophet.
2. Generally taken to be an allusion to the rough treatment which the Prophet received at the hands of the people of Tā'if.

Al-Muzammil takes its title from a word in verse 1. After his first trance and vision, the Prophet went to his wife Khadîjah and told her to wrap him up in cloaks, and that was afterwards his habit on such occasions, at any rate, in the early days at Mecca.

A very early Meccan revelation with the exception of the last verse, which all authorities assign to Al-Madînah.

THE ENSHROUDED ONE

Revealed at Makkah

In the name of Allah, the Beneficent, the Merciful.

1. O thou wrapped up in thy raiment!

2. Keep vigil the night, long, save a little—

3. A half thereof, or abate a little thereof

4. Or add (a little) thereto and chant the Qur'ān in measure,

5. For We shall charge thee with a word of weight.

6. Lo! the vigil of the night is (a time) when impression is more keen and speech more certain.

7. Lo! thou hast by day a chain of business.

8. So remember the name of thy Lord and devote thyself with a complete devotion—

9. Lord of the East and the West; there is no God save Him; so choose thou Him alone for thy defender—

10. And bear with patience what they utter, and part from them with a fair leave-taking.

11. Leave Me to deal with the deniers, lords of ease and comfort (in this life); and do thou respite them awhile.

12. Lo! with Us are heavy fetters and a raging fire,

13. And food which choketh (the partaker), and a painful doom

14. On the day when the earth and the hills rock, and the hills become a heap of running sand.

15. Lo! We have sent unto you a messenger as witness against you, even as We sent unto Pharaoh a messenger.

اٰيَاتُهَا (٧٣) سُوْرَةُ الْمُزَّمِّلِ مَكِّيَّةٌ رُكُوْعَاتُهَا

بِسْمِ اللّٰهِ الرَّحْمٰنِ الرَّحِيْمِ

يٰٓاَيُّهَا الْمُزَّمِّلُ ﴿١﴾

قُمِ الَّيْلَ اِلَّا قَلِيْلًا ﴿٢﴾

نِّصْفَهٗٓ اَوِ انْقُصْ مِنْهُ قَلِيْلًا ﴿٣﴾

اَوْ زِدْ عَلَيْهِ وَرَتِّلِ الْقُرْاٰنَ تَرْتِيْلًا ﴿٤﴾

اِنَّا سَنُلْقِيْ عَلَيْكَ قَوْلًا ثَقِيْلًا ﴿٥﴾

اِنَّ نَاشِئَةَ الَّيْلِ هِيَ اَشَدُّ وَطْاً وَّاَقْوَمُ قِيْلًا ﴿٦﴾

اِنَّ لَكَ فِي النَّهَارِ سَبْحًا طَوِيْلًا ﴿٧﴾

وَاذْكُرِ اسْمَ رَبِّكَ وَتَبَتَّلْ اِلَيْهِ تَبْتِيْلًا ﴿٨﴾

رَبُّ الْمَشْرِقِ وَالْمَغْرِبِ لَآ اِلٰهَ اِلَّا هُوَ فَاتَّخِذْهُ

وَكِيْلًا ﴿٩﴾

وَاصْبِرْ عَلٰى مَا يَقُوْلُوْنَ وَاهْجُرْهُمْ هَجْرًا جَمِيْلًا ﴿١٠﴾

وَذَرْنِيْ وَالْمُكَذِّبِيْنَ اُولِي النَّعْمَةِ وَمَهِّلْهُمْ

قَلِيْلًا ﴿١١﴾

اِنَّ لَدَيْنَآ اَنْكَالًا وَّجَحِيْمًا ﴿١٢﴾

وَّطَعَامًا ذَا غُصَّةٍ وَّعَذَابًا اَلِيْمًا ﴿١٣﴾

يَوْمَ تَرْجُفُ الْاَرْضُ وَالْجِبَالُ وَكَانَتِ الْجِبَالُ

كَثِيْبًا مَّهِيْلًا ﴿١٤﴾

اِنَّآ اَرْسَلْنَآ اِلَيْكُمْ رَسُوْلًا ۙ شَاهِدًا عَلَيْكُمْ كَمَآ

اَرْسَلْنَآ اِلٰى فِرْعَوْنَ رَسُوْلًا ﴿١٥﴾

16. But Pharaoh rebelled against the messenger, whereupon We seized him with no gentle grip.

17. Then how, if ye disbelieve, will ye protect yourselves upon the day which will turn children grey,

18. The very heaven being then rent asunder. His promise is to be fulfilled.

19. Lo! This is a Reminder. Let him who will, then, choose a way unto his Lord.

20. Lo! thy Lord knoweth how thou keepest vigil sometimes nearly two-thirds of the night, or (sometimes) half or a third thereof, as do a party of those with thee. Allah measureth the night and the day. He knoweth that ye count it not, and turneth unto you in mercy. Recite, then, of the Qur'ān that which is easy for you. He knoweth that there are sick folk among you, while others travel in the land in search of Allah's bounty, and others (still) are fighting for the cause of Allah. So recite of it that which is easy (for you), and establish worship and pay the poor-due, and (so) lend unto Allah a goodly loan.[1] Whatsoever good ye send before you for your souls, ye will surely find it with Allah, better and greater in the recompense. And seek forgiveness of Allah. Lo! Allah is Forgiving, Merciful.

فَعَصٰى فِرْعَوْنُ الرَّسُوْلَ فَاَخَذْنٰهُ اَخْذًا وَّبِيْلًا ﴿١٦﴾
فَكَيْفَ تَتَّقُوْنَ اِنْ كَفَرْتُمْ يَوْمًا يَّجْعَلُ الْوِلْدَانَ
شِيْبَا ۖ ﴿١٧﴾
السَّمَآءُ مُنْفَطِرٌۢ بِهٖ ۚ كَانَ وَعْدُهٗ مَفْعُوْلًا ﴿١٨﴾
اِنَّ هٰذِهٖ تَذْكِرَةٌ ۚ فَمَنْ شَآءَ اتَّخَذَ اِلٰى رَبِّهٖ
ع ١٣ سَبِيْلًا ﴿١٩﴾
اِنَّ رَبَّكَ يَعْلَمُ اَنَّكَ تَقُوْمُ اَدْنٰى مِنْ ثُلُثَيِ الَّيْلِ
وَنِصْفَهٗ وَثُلُثَهٗ وَطَآئِفَةٌ مِّنَ الَّذِيْنَ مَعَكَ ؕ
وَاللّٰهُ يُقَدِّرُ الَّيْلَ وَالنَّهَارَ ؕ عَلِمَ اَنْ لَّنْ تُحْصُوْهُ
فَتَابَ عَلَيْكُمْ فَاقْرَءُوْا مَا تَيَسَّرَ مِنَ الْقُرْاٰنِ ؕ
عَلِمَ اَنْ سَيَكُوْنُ مِنْكُمْ مَّرْضٰى ۙ وَاٰخَرُوْنَ يَضْرِبُوْنَ
فِى الْاَرْضِ يَبْتَغُوْنَ مِنْ فَضْلِ اللّٰهِ ۙ وَاٰخَرُوْنَ
يُقَاتِلُوْنَ فِىْ سَبِيْلِ اللّٰهِ ۖ فَاقْرَءُوْا مَا تَيَسَّرَ مِنْهُ ۙ
وَاَقِيْمُوا الصَّلٰوةَ وَاٰتُوا الزَّكٰوةَ وَاَقْرِضُوا اللّٰهَ
قَرْضًا حَسَنًا ؕ وَمَا تُقَدِّمُوْا لِاَنْفُسِكُمْ مِّنْ خَيْرٍ
تَجِدُوْهُ عِنْدَ اللّٰهِ هُوَ خَيْرًا وَّاَعْظَمَ اَجْرًا ؕ
ع ١٤ وَاسْتَغْفِرُوا اللّٰهَ ؕ اِنَّ اللّٰهَ غَفُوْرٌ رَّحِيْمٌ ﴿٢٠﴾

1. *i.e.* a loan without interest or any thought of gain or loss.

Al-Mudath-thir takes its name from a word in verse 1. The Prophet was accustomed to wrap himself in his cloak at the time of his trances. A tradition says that some time —about six months—elapsed between the first revelation (Sūrah XCVI, vv. 1-5) and the second revelation in this Sūrah. Then the Prophet suddenly again beheld the angel who had appeared to him on Mt. Ḥirā, and wrapped himself in his cloak, whereupon this Sūrah was revealed to him. Another opinion is that by this Sūrah the Prophet was ordered to begin the public preaching of Al-Islām, his preaching having until then been done privately among his family and intimates. He is said to have begun his public preaching three years after his call.

In either case this is a very early Meccan Sūrah.

THE CLOAKED ONE

Revealed at Mekkah

In the name of Allah, the Beneficent, the Merciful.

1. O thou enveloped in thy cloak,

2. Arise and warn!

3. Thy Lord magnify,

4. Thy raiment purify,

5. Pollution shun!

6. And show not favour, seeking worldly gain!

7. For the sake of thy Lord, be patient!

8. For when the trumpet shall sound,

9. Surely that day will be a day of anguish,

10. Not of ease, for disbelievers.

11. Leave Me (to deal) with him whom I created lonely,

12. And then bestowed upon him ample means,

13. And sons abiding in his presence

14. And made (life) smooth for him,

15. Yet he desireth that I should give more.

16. Nay! For lo! he hath been stubborn to Our revelations.

17. On him I shall impose a fearful doom.

18. For lo! he did consider; then he planned—

19. (Self-) destroyed is he, how he planned!

اياتها ٥٦ (٧٤) سُورَةُ الْمُدَّثِّرِ مَكِّيَّةٌ (٤) رُكُوعَاتُهَا ٢

بِسْمِ اللّٰهِ الرَّحْمٰنِ الرَّحِيْمِ ○

يٰٓاَيُّهَا الْمُدَّثِّرُ ۝١

قُمْ فَاَنْذِرْ ۝٢

وَرَبَّكَ فَكَبِّرْ ۝٣

وَثِيَابَكَ فَطَهِّرْ ۝٤

وَالرُّجْزَ فَاهْجُرْ ۝٥

وَلَا تَمْنُنْ تَسْتَكْثِرُ ۝٦

وَلِرَبِّكَ فَاصْبِرْ ۝٧

فَاِذَا نُقِرَ فِي النَّاقُوْرِ ۝٨

فَذٰلِكَ يَوْمَئِذٍ يَّوْمٌ عَسِيْرٌ ۝٩

عَلَى الْكٰفِرِيْنَ غَيْرُ يَسِيْرٍ ۝١٠

ذَرْنِيْ وَمَنْ خَلَقْتُ وَحِيْدًا ۝١١

وَّجَعَلْتُ لَهٗ مَالًا مَّمْدُوْدًا ۝١٢

وَّبَنِيْنَ شُهُوْدًا ۝١٣

وَّمَهَّدْتُّ لَهٗ تَمْهِيْدًا ۝١٤

ثُمَّ يَطْمَعُ اَنْ اَزِيْدَ ۝١٥

كَلَّا ۭ اِنَّهٗ كَانَ لِاٰيٰتِنَا عَنِيْدًا ۝١٦

سَاُرْهِقُهٗ صَعُوْدًا ۝١٧

اِنَّهٗ فَكَّرَ وَقَدَّرَ ۝١٨

فَقُتِلَ كَيْفَ قَدَّرَ ۝١٩

20. Again (self) destroyed is he, how he planned;

21. Then looked he,

22. Then frowned he and showed displeasure.

23. Then turned he away in pride.

24. And said: this is naught else than magic from of old;

25. This is naught else than speech of mortal man.

26. Him shall I fling unto the burning.

27. Ah, what will convey unto thee what that burning is;

28. It leaveth naught; it spareth naught

29. It shrivellth the man.

30. Above it are nineteen.

31. We have appointed only angels to be wardens of the fire, and their number have We made to be a stumbling block for those who disbelieve; that those to whom the scripture hath been given may have certainty, and that believers may increase in faith; and that those to whom the Scriputre hath been given and believers may not doubt. and that those in whose hearts there is disease, and disbelievers, may say: what meaneth Allah by this smilitude? Thus Allah sendeth astray whom He will, and whom He will He guideth. None knoweth the hosts of thy Lord save Him. This is naught else than a Reminder unto mortals.

32. Nay, by the Moon

33. And the night when it withdraweth.

34. And the dawn when it shineth forth.

ثُمَّ قُتِلَ كَيْفَ قَدَّرَ (٢٠)

ثُمَّ نَظَرَ (٢١)

ثُمَّ عَبَسَ وَبَسَرَ (٢٢)

ثُمَّ أَدْبَرَ وَاسْتَكْبَرَ (٢٣)

فَقَالَ إِنْ هٰذَآ إِلَّا سِحْرٌ يُؤْثَرُ (٢٤)

إِنْ هٰذَآ إِلَّا قَوْلُ الْبَشَرِ (٢٥)

سَأُصْلِيهِ سَقَرَ (٢٦)

وَمَآ أَدْرٰكَ مَا سَقَرُ (٢٧)

لَا تُبْقِي وَلَا تَذَرُ (٢٨)

لَوَّاحَةٌ لِّلْبَشَرِ (٢٩)

عَلَيْهَا تِسْعَةَ عَشَرَ (٣٠)

وَمَا جَعَلْنَآ أَصْحٰبَ النَّارِ إِلَّا مَلٰٓئِكَةً ۙ وَمَا جَعَلْنَا
عِدَّتَهُمْ إِلَّا فِتْنَةً لِّلَّذِينَ كَفَرُوا لِيَسْتَيْقِنَ الَّذِينَ
أُوتُوا الْكِتٰبَ وَيَزْدَادَ الَّذِينَ اٰمَنُوٓا إِيمَانًا ۙ وَلَا يَرْتَابَ
الَّذِينَ أُوتُوا الْكِتٰبَ وَالْمُؤْمِنُونَ ۙ وَلِيَقُولَ الَّذِينَ
فِي قُلُوبِهِم مَّرَضٌ وَّالْكٰفِرُونَ مَاذَآ أَرَادَ اللّٰهُ
بِهٰذَا مَثَلًا ۚ كَذٰلِكَ يُضِلُّ اللّٰهُ مَن يَشَآءُ وَيَهْدِي
مَن يَشَآءُ ۚ وَمَا يَعْلَمُ جُنُودَ رَبِّكَ إِلَّا هُوَ ۚ وَمَا
هِيَ إِلَّا ذِكْرٰى لِلْبَشَرِ (٣١) ع ١٥

كَلَّا وَالْقَمَرِ (٣٢)

وَالَّيْلِ إِذْ أَدْبَرَ (٣٣)

وَالصُّبْحِ إِذَآ أَسْفَرَ (٣٤)

35. Lo! this is one the greatest (portents)

إنها لإحدى الكبر ٣٥

36. As a warning unto men,

نذيرا للبشر ٣٦

37. Unto him of you who will advance or hang back.

لمن شاء منكم أن يتقدم أو يتأخر ٣٧

38. Every soul is a pledge for its own deeds;

كل نفس بما كسبت رهينة ٣٨

39. Save those who will stand on the right hand.

إلا أصحب اليمين ٣٩

40. In gardens they will ask one another

مع في جنت يتساءلون ٤٠

41. Concerning the guilty:

عن المجرمين ٤١

42. What hath brought you to this burning?

ما سلككم في سقر ٤٢

43. They will answer: We were not of those who prayed.

قالوا لم نك من المصلين ٤٣

44. Nor did we feed the wretched.

ولم نك نطعم المسكين ٤٤

45. We used to wade (in vain dispute) with (all) waders.

وكنا نخوض مع الخائضين ٤٥

46. And we used to deny the Day of Judgement.

وكنا نكذب بيوم الدين ٤٦

47. Till the inevitable came unto us.

حتى أتىنا اليقين ٤٧

48. The mediation of no mediators will avail them then.

فما تنفعهم شفاعة الشفعين ٤٨

49. Why now turn they away from the Admonishment.

فما لهم عن التذكرة معرضين ٤٩

50. As they were frightened asses.

كأنهم حمر مستنفرة ٥٠

51. Fleeing from a lion!

فرت من قسورة ٥١

52. Nay, but everyone of them desireth that he should be given open pages (from Allah).

بل يريد كل امرئ منهم أن يؤتى صحفا منشرة ٥٢

53. Nay, verily. They fear not the Hereafter.

كلا بل لا يخافون الآخرة ٥٣

54. Nay, verily Lo! this is an admonishment.

كلا إنه تذكرة ٥٤

55. So whosoever will may heed.

فمن شاء ذكره ٥٥

56. And they will not heed unless Allah willeth (it). He is the fount of fear. He is the fount of Mercy.

ع وما يذكرون إلا أن يشاء الله هو أهل التقوى وأهل المغفرة ٥٦

Al-Qiyāmah takes its name from a word in the first verse. An early Meccan Sūrah.

THE RISING OF THE DEAD

Revealed at Mecca

In the name of Allah, the Beneficent, the Merciful.

1. Nay, I swear by the Day of Resurrection;

2. Nay, I swear by the accusing soul (that this Scripture is true).

3. Thinketh man that We shall not assemble his bones?

4. Yea, verily. Yea, We are able to restore his very fingers!

5. But man would fain deny what is before him.

6. He asketh: When will be this Day of Resurrection?

7. But when sight is confounded

8. And the moon is eclipsed

9. And sun and moon are united,

10. On that day man will cry: Whither to flee!

11. Alas! No refuge!

12. Unto thy Lord is the recourse that day.

13. On that day man is told the tale of that which he hath sent before and left behind.

14. Oh, but man is a telling witness against himself,

15. Although he tender his excuses.

16. Stir not thy tongue herewith to hasten it.[1]

17. Lo! upon Us (resteth) the putting together thereof and the reading thereof.

18. And when We read it, follow thou the reading;

19. Then lo! upon Us (resteth) the explanation thereof.

ايٰتها ٤٠ (٧٥) سُوْرَةُ الْقِيٰمَةِ مَكِّيَّةٌ رُكُوْعَاتُهَا ٢

بِسْمِ اللّٰهِ الرَّحْمٰنِ الرَّحِيْمِ

لَآ اُقْسِمُ بِيَوْمِ الْقِيٰمَةِ ﴿١﴾

وَلَآ اُقْسِمُ بِالنَّفْسِ اللَّوَّامَةِ ﴿٢﴾

اَيَحْسَبُ الْاِنْسَانُ اَلَّنْ نَّجْمَعَ عِظَامَهٗ ﴿٣﴾

بَلٰى قٰدِرِيْنَ عَلٰٓى اَنْ نُّسَوِّيَ بَنَانَهٗ ﴿٤﴾

بَلْ يُرِيْدُ الْاِنْسَانُ لِيَفْجُرَ اَمَامَهٗ ﴿٥﴾

يَسْـَٔلُ اَيَّانَ يَوْمُ الْقِيٰمَةِ ﴿٦﴾

فَاِذَا بَرِقَ الْبَصَرُ ﴿٧﴾

وَخَسَفَ الْقَمَرُ ﴿٨﴾

وَجُمِعَ الشَّمْسُ وَالْقَمَرُ ﴿٩﴾

يَقُوْلُ الْاِنْسَانُ يَوْمَئِذٍ اَيْنَ الْمَفَرُّ ﴿١٠﴾

كَلَّا لَا وَزَرَ ﴿١١﴾

اِلٰى رَبِّكَ يَوْمَئِذِ نِ الْمُسْتَقَرُّ ﴿١٢﴾

يُنَبَّؤُا الْاِنْسَانُ يَوْمَئِذٍ بِمَا قَدَّمَ وَاَخَّرَ ﴿١٣﴾

بَلِ الْاِنْسَانُ عَلٰى نَفْسِهٖ بَصِيْرَةٌ ﴿١٤﴾

وَّلَوْ اَلْقٰى مَعَاذِيْرَهٗ ﴿١٥﴾

لَا تُحَرِّكْ بِهٖ لِسَانَكَ لِتَعْجَلَ بِهٖ ﴿١٦﴾

اِنَّ عَلَيْنَا جَمْعَهٗ وَقُرْاٰنَهٗ ﴿١٧﴾

فَاِذَا قَرَاْنٰهُ فَاتَّبِعْ قُرْاٰنَهٗ ﴿١٨﴾

ثُمَّ اِنَّ عَلَيْنَا بَيَانَهٗ ﴿١٩﴾

1. *i.e.* the Koran, which was revealed gradually, piece by piece.

20. Nay, but ye do love the fleeting Now

كلا بل تحبون العاجلة ﴿٢٠﴾

21. And neglect the Hereafter.

وتذرون الآخرة ﴿٢١﴾

22. That day will faces be resplendent,

وجوه يومئذ ناضرة ﴿٢٢﴾

23. Looking toward their Lord;

إلى ربها ناظرة ﴿٢٣﴾

24. And that day will other faces be despondent,

ووجوه يومئذ باسرة ﴿٢٤﴾

25. Thou wilt know that some great disaster is about to fall on them.

تظن أن يفعل بها فاقرة ﴿٢٥﴾

26. Nay, but when the life cometh up to the throat

كلا إذا بلغت التراقي ﴿٢٦﴾

27. And men say: Where is the wizard (who can save him now)?

وقيل من راق ﴿٢٧﴾

28. And he knoweth that it is the parting;

وظن أنه الفراق ﴿٢٨﴾

29. And agony is heaped on agony;

والتفت الساق بالساق ﴿٢٩﴾

30. Unto thy Lord that day will be the driving.

إلى ربك يومئذ المساق ﴿٣٠﴾

31. For he neither trusted, nor prayed.

فلا صدق ولا صلى ﴿٣١﴾

32. But he denied and flouted.

ولكن كذب وتولى ﴿٣٢﴾

33. Then went he to his folk with glee.

ثم ذهب إلى أهله يتمطى ﴿٣٣﴾

34. Nearer unto thee and nearer,

أولى لك فأولى ﴿٣٤﴾

35. Again nearer unto thee and nearer (is the doom).

ثم أولى لك فأولى ﴿٣٥﴾

36. Thinketh man that he is to be left aimless?

أيحسب الإنسان أن يترك سدى ﴿٣٦﴾

37. Was he not a drop of fluid which gushed forth?

ألم يك نطفة من مني يمنى ﴿٣٧﴾

38. Then he became a clot; then (Allah) shaped and fashioned

ثم كان علقة فخلق فسوى ﴿٣٨﴾

39. And made of him a pair, the male and female.

فجعل منه الزوجين الذكر والأنثى ﴿٣٩﴾

40. Is not He (Who doth so) able to bring the dead to life?

أليس ذلك بقادر على أن يحيي الموتى ﴿٤٠﴾

Ad-Dahr, *Al-Insān* or is, in either case, so called from a word in the first verse. An early Meccan Sūrah.

"TIME" OR "MAN"

Revealed at Makkah

In the name of Allah, the Beneficent, the Merciful.

1. Hath there come upon man (ever) any period of time in which he was a thing unremembered?

2. Lo! We create man from a drop of thickened fluid to test him; so We make him hearing, knowing.

3. Lo! We have shown him the way whether he be grateful or disbelieving.

4. Lo! We have prepared for disbelievers manacles and carcans and a raging fire.

5. Lo! the righteous shall drink of a cup whereof the mixture is of water of Kāfūr,

6. A spring wherefrom the slaves of Allah drink, making it gush forth abundantly,

7. (Because) they perform the vow and fear a day whereof the evil is wide-spreading,

8. And feed with food the needy wretch, the orphan and the prisoner, for love of Him,

9. (Saying): We feed you, for the sake of Allah only. We wish for no reward nor thanks from you;

10. Lo! we fear from our Lord a day of frowning and of fate.

11. Therefor Allah hath warded off from them the evil of that day, and hath made them find brightness and joy;

12. And hath awarded them for all that they endured, a Garden and silk attire;

13. Reclining therein upon couches, they will find there neither (heat of) a sun nor bitter cold.

14. The shade thereof is close upon them and the clustered fruits thereof bow down.

15. Goblets of silver are brought round for them, and beakers (as) of glass

آياتها ٣١ (٧٦) سُورَةُ الدَّهْرِ مَدَنِيَّةٌ ركوعاتها ٢

بِسْمِ اللّٰهِ الرَّحْمٰنِ الرَّحِيْمِ ۝

هَلْ اَتٰى عَلَى الْاِنْسَانِ حِيْنٌ مِّنَ الدَّهْرِ لَمْ يَكُنْ
شَيْئًا مَّذْكُوْرًا ۝١
اِنَّا خَلَقْنَا الْاِنْسَانَ مِنْ نُّطْفَةٍ اَمْشَاجٍ نَّبْتَلِيْهِ
فَجَعَلْنٰهُ سَمِيْعًا بَصِيْرًا ۝٢
اِنَّا هَدَيْنٰهُ السَّبِيْلَ اِمَّا شَاكِرًا وَّاِمَّا كَفُوْرًا ۝٣
اِنَّا اَعْتَدْنَا لِلْكٰفِرِيْنَ سَلٰسِلَاۡ وَاَغْلٰلًا وَّسَعِيْرًا ۝٤
اِنَّ الْاَبْرَارَ يَشْرَبُوْنَ مِنْ كَاْسٍ كَانَ مِزَاجُهَا كَافُوْرًا ۝٥
عَيْنًا يَّشْرَبُ بِهَا عِبَادُ اللّٰهِ يُفَجِّرُوْنَهَا تَفْجِيْرًا ۝٦
يُوْفُوْنَ بِالنَّذْرِ وَيَخَافُوْنَ يَوْمًا كَانَ شَرُّهٗ مُسْتَطِيْرًا ۝٧
وَيُطْعِمُوْنَ الطَّعَامَ عَلٰى حُبِّهٖ مِسْكِيْنًا وَّيَتِيْمًا وَّاَسِيْرًا ۝٨
اِنَّمَا نُطْعِمُكُمْ لِوَجْهِ اللّٰهِ لَا نُرِيْدُ مِنْكُمْ جَزَآءً وَّلَا
شُكُوْرًا ۝٩
اِنَّا نَخَافُ مِنْ رَّبِّنَا يَوْمًا عَبُوْسًا قَمْطَرِيْرًا ۝١٠
فَوَقٰهُمُ اللّٰهُ شَرَّ ذٰلِكَ الْيَوْمِ وَلَقّٰىهُمْ نَضْرَةً وَّسُرُوْرًا ۝١١
وَجَزٰىهُمْ بِمَا صَبَرُوْا جَنَّةً وَّحَرِيْرًا ۝١٢
مُّتَّكِـِٕيْنَ فِيْهَا عَلَى الْاَرَآئِكِ لَا يَرَوْنَ فِيْهَا شَمْسًا
وَّلَا زَمْهَرِيْرًا ۝١٣
وَدَانِيَةً عَلَيْهِمْ ظِلٰلُهَا وَذُلِّلَتْ قُطُوْفُهَا تَذْلِيْلًا ۝١٤
وَيُطَافُ عَلَيْهِمْ بِاٰنِيَةٍ مِّنْ فِضَّةٍ وَّاَكْوَابٍ كَانَتْ قَوَارِيْرَا۠ ۝١٥

16. (Bright as) glass but (made) of silver, which they (themselves have measured to the measure (of their deeds).

17. There are they watered with a cup whereof the mixture is of Zanjabîl,

18. The water of a spring therein, named Salsabîl.

19. There serve them youths of everlasting youth, whom, when thou seest, thou wouldst take for scattered pearls.

20. When thou seest, thou wilt see there bliss and high estate.

21. Their raiment will be fine green silk and gold embroidery. Bracelets of silver will they wear. Their Lord will slake their thirst with a pure drink.

22. (And it will be said unto them): Lo! this is a reward for you. Your endeavour (upon earth) hath found acceptance.

23. Lo! We, even We, have revealed unto thee the Qur'ān, a revelation;

24. So submit patiently to thy Lord's command, and obey not of them any guilty one or disbeliever.

25. Remember the name of thy Lord at morn and evening.

26. And worship Him (a portion) of the night. And glorify Him through the livelong night.

27. Lo! these love fleeting life, and put behind them (the remembrance of) a grievous day.

28. We, even We created them, and strengthened their frame. And when We will, We can replace them, bringing others like them in their stead.

29. Lo! this is an Admonishment, that whosoever will may choose a way unto his Lord.

30. Yet ye will not, unless Allah willeth. Lo! Allah is Knower, Wise.

31. He maketh whom He will to enter His mercy, and for evil-doers hath prepared a painful doom.

قواريرا من فضة قدروها تقديرا ﴿١٦﴾
ويسقون فيها كاسا كان مزاجها زنجبيلا ﴿١٧﴾
عينا فيها تسمى سلسبيلا ﴿١٨﴾
ويطوف عليهم ولدان مخلدون اذا رايتهم
حسبتهم لؤلؤا منثورا ﴿١٩﴾
واذا رايت ثم رايت نعيما وملكا كبيرا ﴿٢٠﴾
عليهم ثياب سندس خضر واستبرق وحلوا
اساور من فضة وسقهم ربهم شرابا طهورا ﴿٢١﴾
ان هذا كان لكم جزاء وكان سعيكم مشكورا ﴿٢٢﴾
انا نحن نزلنا عليك القران تنزيلا ﴿٢٣﴾
فاصبر لحكم ربك ولا تطع منهم اثما او كفورا ﴿٢٤﴾
واذكر اسم ربك بكرة واصيلا ﴿٢٥﴾
ومن اليل فاسجد له وسبحه ليلا طويلا ﴿٢٦﴾
ان هؤلاء يحبون العاجلة ويذرون وراءهم
يوما ثقيلا ﴿٢٧﴾
نحن خلقنهم وشددنا اسرهم واذا شئنا بدلنا
امثالهم تبديلا ﴿٢٨﴾
ان هذه تذكرة فمن شاء اتخذ الى ربه سبيلا ﴿٢٩﴾
وما تشاءون الا ان يشاء الله ان الله كان عليما
حكيما ﴿٣٠﴾
يدخل من يشاء في رحمته والظلمين اعد
لهم عذابا اليما ﴿٣١﴾

Al-Mursalāt takes its name from a word in the first verse. Verses 1, 2 and 3 are taken to refer to winds, verses 4 and 5 to angels. An early Meccan Sūrah.

THE EMISSARIES

Revealed at Mecca

In the name of Allah, the Beneficent, the Merciful.

1. By the emissary winds, (sent) one after another

2. By the raging hurricanes,

3. By those which cause earth's vegetation to revive;

4. By those who winnow with a winnowing,

5. By those who bring down the Reminder,

6. To excuse or to warn,

7. Surely that which ye are promised will befall.

8. So when the stars are put out,

9. And when the sky is riven asunder,

10. And when the mountains are blown away,

11. And when the messengers are brought unto their time appointed—

12. For what day is the time appointed?

13. For the Day of Decision.

14. And what will convey unto thee what the Day of Decision is!—

15. Woe unto the repudiators on that day!

16. Destroyed We not the former folk,

17. Then caused the latter folk to follow after?

18. Thus deal We ever with the guilty.

19. Woe unto the repudiators on that day!

اٰياتها ٥٠ (٧٧) سُوْرَةُ الْمُرْسَلٰتِ مَكِّيَّةٌ (٣٣) رُكُوْعَاتُهَا ٢

بِسْمِ اللّٰهِ الرَّحْمٰنِ الرَّحِيْمِ

وَالْمُرْسَلٰتِ عُرْفًا ﴿١﴾

فَالْعٰصِفٰتِ عَصْفًا ﴿٢﴾

وَّالنّٰشِرٰتِ نَشْرًا ﴿٣﴾

فَالْفٰرِقٰتِ فَرْقًا ﴿٤﴾

فَالْمُلْقِيٰتِ ذِكْرًا ﴿٥﴾

عُذْرًا اَوْ نُذْرًا ﴿٦﴾

اِنَّمَا تُوْعَدُوْنَ لَوَاقِعٌ ﴿٧﴾

فَاِذَا النُّجُوْمُ طُمِسَتْ ﴿٨﴾

وَاِذَا السَّمَآءُ فُرِجَتْ ﴿٩﴾

وَاِذَا الْجِبَالُ نُسِفَتْ ﴿١٠﴾

وَاِذَا الرُّسُلُ اُقِّتَتْ ﴿١١﴾

لِاَيِّ يَوْمٍ اُجِّلَتْ ﴿١٢﴾

لِيَوْمِ الْفَصْلِ ﴿١٣﴾

وَمَآ اَدْرٰىكَ مَا يَوْمُ الْفَصْلِ ﴿١٤﴾

وَيْلٌ يَّوْمَئِذٍ لِّلْمُكَذِّبِيْنَ ﴿١٥﴾

اَلَمْ نُهْلِكِ الْاَوَّلِيْنَ ﴿١٦﴾

ثُمَّ نُتْبِعُهُمُ الْاٰخِرِيْنَ ﴿١٧﴾

كَذٰلِكَ نَفْعَلُ بِالْمُجْرِمِيْنَ ﴿١٨﴾

وَيْلٌ يَّوْمَئِذٍ لِّلْمُكَذِّبِيْنَ ﴿١٩﴾

20. Did We not create you from a base fluid

21. Which We laid up in a safe abode

22. For a known term?

23. Thus We arranged. How excellent is Our arranging!

24. Woe unto the repudiators on that day!

25. Have We not made the earth a receptacle

26. Both for the living and the dead,

27. And placed therein high mountains and given you to drink sweet water therein?

28. Woe unto the repudiators on that day!

29. (It will be said unto them): Depart unto that (doom) which ye used to deny;

30. Depart unto the shadow falling threefold.

31. (Which yet is) no relief nor shelter from the flame.

32. Lo! it throweth up sparks like the castles,

33. (Or) as it might be camels of bright yellow hue.

34. Woe unto the repudiators on that day!

35. This is a day wherein they speak not,

36. Nor are they suffered to put forth excuses.

37. Woe unto the repudiators on that day!

38. This is the Day of Decision. We have brought you and the men of old together.

39. If now ye have any wit, outwit Me.

40. Woe unto the repudiators on that day!

أَلَمْ نَخْلُقكُّم مِّن مَّآءٍ مَّهِينٍ ﴿٢٠﴾

فَجَعَلْنٰهُ فِى قَرَارٍ مَّكِينٍ ﴿٢١﴾

إِلٰى قَدَرٍ مَّعْلُومٍ ﴿٢٢﴾

فَقَدَرْنَا فَنِعْمَ الْقٰدِرُوْنَ ﴿٢٣﴾

وَيْلٌ يَّوْمَئِذٍ لِّلْمُكَذِّبِيْنَ ﴿٢٤﴾

أَلَمْ نَجْعَلِ الْأَرْضَ كِفَاتًا ﴿٢٥﴾

أَحْيَآءً وَّأَمْوَاتًا ﴿٢٦﴾

وَّجَعَلْنَا فِيْهَا رَوَاسِىَ شٰمِخٰتٍ وَّأَسْقَيْنٰكُم
مَّآءً فُرَاتًا ﴿٢٧﴾

وَيْلٌ يَّوْمَئِذٍ لِّلْمُكَذِّبِيْنَ ﴿٢٨﴾

اِنْطَلِقُوْٓا إِلٰى مَا كُنْتُمْ بِهٖ تُكَذِّبُوْنَ ﴿٢٩﴾

اِنْطَلِقُوْٓا إِلٰى ظِلٍّ ذِىْ ثَلٰثِ شُعَبٍ ﴿٣٠﴾

لَّا ظَلِيْلٍ وَّلَا يُغْنِىْ مِنَ اللَّهَبِ ﴿٣١﴾

إِنَّهَا تَرْمِىْ بِشَرَرٍ كَالْقَصْرِ ﴿٣٢﴾

كَأَنَّهٗ جِمٰلَتٌ صُفْرٌ ﴿٣٣﴾

وَيْلٌ يَّوْمَئِذٍ لِّلْمُكَذِّبِيْنَ ﴿٣٤﴾

هٰذَا يَوْمُ لَا يَنْطِقُوْنَ ﴿٣٥﴾

وَلَا يُؤْذَنُ لَهُمْ فَيَعْتَذِرُوْنَ ﴿٣٦﴾

وَيْلٌ يَّوْمَئِذٍ لِّلْمُكَذِّبِيْنَ ﴿٣٧﴾

هٰذَا يَوْمُ الْفَصْلِ جَمَعْنٰكُمْ وَالْأَوَّلِيْنَ ﴿٣٨﴾

فَإِنْ كَانَ لَكُمْ كَيْدٌ فَكِيْدُوْنِ ﴿٣٩﴾

ع وَيْلٌ يَّوْمَئِذٍ لِّلْمُكَذِّبِيْنَ ﴿٤٠﴾

41. Lo! those who kept their duty are amid shade and fountains,

إِنَّ الْمُتَّقِينَ فِي ظِلَٰلٍ وَعُيُونٍ ﴿٤١﴾

42. And fruits such as they desire.

وَفَوَٰكِهَ مِمَّا يَشْتَهُونَ ﴿٤٢﴾

43. (Unto them it is said): Eat, drink and welcome, O ye blessed, in return for what ye did.

كُلُوا وَاشْرَبُوا هَنِيٓـًٔا بِمَا كُنتُمْ تَعْمَلُونَ ﴿٤٣﴾

44. Thus do We reward the good.

إِنَّا كَذَٰلِكَ نَجْزِي الْمُحْسِنِينَ ﴿٤٤﴾

45. Woe unto the repudiators on that day!

وَيْلٌ يَوْمَئِذٍ لِّلْمُكَذِّبِينَ ﴿٤٥﴾

46. Eat and take your ease (on earth) a little. Lo! ye are guilty.

كُلُوا وَتَمَتَّعُوا قَلِيلًا إِنَّكُم مُّجْرِمُونَ ﴿٤٦﴾

47. Woe unto the repudiators on that day!

وَيْلٌ يَوْمَئِذٍ لِّلْمُكَذِّبِينَ ﴿٤٧﴾

48. When it is said unto them: Bow down, they bow not down!

وَإِذَا قِيلَ لَهُمُ ارْكَعُوا لَا يَرْكَعُونَ ﴿٤٨﴾

49. Woe unto the repudiators on that day!

وَيْلٌ يَوْمَئِذٍ لِّلْمُكَذِّبِينَ ﴿٤٩﴾

50. In what statement, after this, will they believe?

فَبِأَيِّ حَدِيثٍ بَعْدَهُۥ يُؤْمِنُونَ ﴿٥٠﴾

ع ٢ ٢٢

An-Nabā' **takes its name from a word in the second verse. An early Meccan Sūrah.**

THE TIDINGS

Revealed at Mecca

In the name of Allah, the Beneficent, the Merciful.

1. Whereof do they question one another?

2. (It is) of the awful tidings,

3. Concerning which they are in disagreement.

4. Nay, but they will come to know!

5. Nay, again, but they will come to know!

6. Have We not made the earth an expanse,

7. And the high hills bulwarks?

8. And We have created you in pairs.

9. And have appointed your sleep for repose,

10. And have appointed the night as a cloak,

11. And have appointed the day for livelihood.

12. And We have built above you seven strong (heavens),

13. And have appointed a dazzling lamp,

14. And have sent down from the rainy clouds abundant water,

15. Thereby to produce grain and plant,

16. And gardens of thick foliage.

17. Lo! the Day of Decision is a fixed time,

18. A day when the trumpet is blown, and ye come in multitudes,

19. And the heaven is opened and becometh as gates,

اٰياتها ٤٠ (٧٨) سُوْرَةُ النَّبَاِ مَكِّيَّةٌ رُكُوْعَاتُهَا ٢

بِسْمِ اللّٰهِ الرَّحْمٰنِ الرَّحِيْمِ ○

الجزء ٣٠

عَمَّ يَتَسَآءَلُوْنَ ۝١

عَنِ النَّبَاِ الْعَظِيْمِ ۝٢

الَّذِيْ هُمْ فِيْهِ مُخْتَلِفُوْنَ ۝٣

كَلَّا سَيَعْلَمُوْنَ ۝٤

ثُمَّ كَلَّا سَيَعْلَمُوْنَ ۝٥

اَلَمْ نَجْعَلِ الْاَرْضَ مِهٰدًا ۝٦

وَّالْجِبَالَ اَوْتَادًا ۝٧

وَّخَلَقْنٰكُمْ اَزْوَاجًا ۝٨

وَّجَعَلْنَا نَوْمَكُمْ سُبَاتًا ۝٩

وَّجَعَلْنَا الَّيْلَ لِبَاسًا ۝١٠

وَّجَعَلْنَا النَّهَارَ مَعَاشًا ۝١١

وَّبَنَيْنَا فَوْقَكُمْ سَبْعًا شِدَادًا ۝١٢

وَّجَعَلْنَا سِرَاجًا وَّهَّاجًا ۝١٣

وَّاَنْزَلْنَا مِنَ الْمُعْصِرٰتِ مَآءً ثَجَّاجًا ۝١٤

لِّنُخْرِجَ بِهٖ حَبًّا وَّنَبَاتًا ۝١٥

وَّجَنّٰتٍ اَلْفَافًا ۝١٦

اِنَّ يَوْمَ الْفَصْلِ كَانَ مِيْقَاتًا ۝١٧

يَوْمَ يُنْفَخُ فِي الصُّوْرِ فَتَاْتُوْنَ اَفْوَاجًا ۝١٨

وَّفُتِحَتِ السَّمَآءُ فَكَانَتْ اَبْوَابًا ۝١٩

20. And the hills are set in motion and become as a mirage

21. Lo! hell lurketh in ambush,

22. A home for the rebellious.

23. They will abide therein for ages.

24. Therein taste they neither coolness nor (any) drink

25. Save boiling water and a paralysing cold:

26. Reward proportioned (to their evil deeds).

27. For lo! they looked not for a reckoning;

28. They called Our revelations false with strong denial.

29. Everything have We recorded in a Book.

30. So taste (of that which ye have earned). No increase do We give you save of torment.

31. Lo! for the duteous is achievement—

32. Gardens enclosed and vineyards,

33. And maidens for companions,

34. And a full cup.

35. There hear they never vain discourse, nor lying

36. Requital from thy Lord—a gift in payment—

37. Lord of the heavens and the earth, and (all) that is between them, the Beneficent; with Whom none can converse.

38. On the day when the angels and the Spirit stand arrayed, they speak not, saving him whom the Beneficent alloweth and who speaketh right.

39. That is the True Day. So whoso will should seek recourse unto his Lord.

40. Lo! We warn you of a doom at hand, a day whereon a man will look on that which his own hands have sent before, and the disbeliever will cry: "Would that I were dust!"

وَسُيِّرَتِ الْجِبَالُ فَكَانَتْ سَرَابًا ٢٠

اِنَّ جَهَنَّمَ كَانَتْ مِرْصَادًا ٢١

لِّلطّٰغِيْنَ مَاٰبًا ٢٢

لّٰبِثِيْنَ فِيْهَآ اَحْقَابًا ٢٣

لَا يَذُوْقُوْنَ فِيْهَا بَرْدًا وَّلَا شَرَابًا ٢٤

اِلَّا حَمِيْمًا وَّغَسَّاقًا ٢٥

جَزَآءً وِّفَاقًا ٢٦

اِنَّهُمْ كَانُوْا لَا يَرْجُوْنَ حِسَابًا ٢٧

وَّكَذَّبُوْا بِاٰيٰتِنَا كِذَّابًا ٢٨

وَكُلَّ شَيْءٍ اَحْصَيْنٰهُ كِتٰبًا ٢٩

ع فَذُوْقُوْا فَلَنْ نَّزِيْدَكُمْ اِلَّا عَذَابًا ٣٠

اِنَّ لِلْمُتَّقِيْنَ مَفَازًا ٣١

حَدَآئِقَ وَاَعْنَابًا ٣٢

وَّكَوَاعِبَ اَتْرَابًا ٣٣

وَّكَاْسًا دِهَاقًا ٣٤

لَا يَسْمَعُوْنَ فِيْهَا لَغْوًا وَّلَا كِذّٰبًا ٣٥

جَزَآءً مِّنْ رَّبِّكَ عَطَآءً حِسَابًا ٣٦

رَّبِّ السَّمٰوٰتِ وَالْاَرْضِ وَمَا بَيْنَهُمَا الرَّحْمٰنِ لَا يَمْلِكُوْنَ مِنْهُ خِطَابًا ٣٧
يَوْمَ يَقُوْمُ الرُّوْحُ وَالْمَلٰٓئِكَةُ صَفًّا لَّا يَتَكَلَّمُوْنَ
اِلَّا مَنْ اَذِنَ لَهُ الرَّحْمٰنُ وَقَالَ صَوَابًا ٣٨
ذٰلِكَ الْيَوْمُ الْحَقُّ فَمَنْ شَآءَ اتَّخَذَ اِلٰى رَبِّهٖ مَاٰبًا ٣٩
اِنَّآ اَنْذَرْنٰكُمْ عَذَابًا قَرِيْبًا يَّوْمَ يَنْظُرُ الْمَرْءُ مَا قَدَّمَتْ
ع يَدٰهُ وَيَقُوْلُ الْكٰفِرُ يٰلَيْتَنِيْ كُنْتُ تُرٰبًا ٤٠

An-Nāzi'āt takes its name from a word in the first verse. An early Meccan Sūrah.

"THOSE WHO DRAG FORTH"

Revealed at Mecca

آياتها ٤٦ (٧٩) سُورَةُ النّٰزِعٰتِ مَكِّيَّةٌ رُكُوعَاتُهَا ٢

In the name of Allah, the Beneficent, the Merciful.

بِسْمِ اللّٰهِ الرَّحْمٰنِ الرَّحِيْمِ

1. By those who drag forth to destruction,

وَالنّٰزِعٰتِ غَرْقًا ①

2. By the meteors rushing,

وَّالنّٰشِطٰتِ نَشْطًا ②

3. By the lone stars floating,[1]

وَّالسّٰبِحٰتِ سَبْحًا ③

4. By the angels hastening,

فَالسّٰبِقٰتِ سَبْقًا ④

5. And those who govern the event,

فَالْمُدَبِّرٰتِ اَمْرًا ⑤ وقف لازم

6. On the day when the first trump resoundeth

يَوْمَ تَرْجُفُ الرَّاجِفَةُ ⑥

7. And the second followeth it,

تَتْبَعُهَا الرَّادِفَةُ ⑦

8. On that day hearts beat painfully

قُلُوْبٌ يَّوْمَئِذٍ وَّاجِفَةٌ ⑧

9. While eyes are downcast

اَبْصَارُهَا خَاشِعَةٌ ⑨ وقف لازم

10. (Now) they are saying: Shall we really be restored to our first state

يَقُوْلُوْنَ ءَاِنَّا لَمَرْدُوْدُوْنَ فِي الْحَافِرَةِ ⑩

11. Even after we are crumbled bones?

ءَاِذَا كُنَّا عِظَامًا نَّخِرَةً ⑪

12. They say: Then that would be a vain proceeding.

قَالُوْا تِلْكَ اِذًا كَرَّةٌ خَاسِرَةٌ ⑫ وقف لازم

13. Surely it will need but one shout,

فَاِنَّمَا هِيَ زَجْرَةٌ وَّاحِدَةٌ ⑬

14. And lo! they will be awakened.

فَاِذَا هُمْ بِالسَّاهِرَةِ ⑭

15. Hath there come unto thee the history of Moses?

هَلْ اَتٰىكَ حَدِيْثُ مُوْسٰى ⑮ وقف لازم

16. How his Lord called him in the holy vale of Ṭuwa,

اِذْ نَادٰىهُ رَبُّهٗ بِالْوَادِ الْمُقَدَّسِ طُوًى ⑯

17. (Saying): Go thou unto Pharaoh—Lo! he hath rebelled—

اِذْهَبْ اِلٰى فِرْعَوْنَ اِنَّهٗ طَغٰى ⑰

18. And say (unto him): Hast thou (will) to grow (in grace)?

فَقُلْ هَلْ لَّكَ اِلٰى اَنْ تَزَكّٰى ⑱

19. Then I will guide thee to thy Lord and thou shalt fear (Him).

وَاَهْدِيَكَ اِلٰى رَبِّكَ فَتَخْشٰى ⑲

1. Some commentators take vv. 2 and 3 also as referring to angels and explain them thus: "By those who console (the spirits of the righteous) tenderly." "By those who come floating (down from heaven with their Lord's command)." The rendering given in the text above is the more obvious.

20. And he showed him the tremendous token.

فأريه الآية الكبرى ٢٠

21. But he denied and disobeyed,

فكذب وعصى ٢١

22. Then turned he away in haste,

ثم أدبر يسعى ٢٢

23. Then gathered he and summoned

فحشر فنادى ٢٣

24. And proclaimed: "I (Pharaoh) am your Lord the Highest."

فقال أنا ربكم الأعلى ٢٤

25. So Allah seized him (and made him) an example for the after (life) and for the former.

فأخذه الله نكال الآخرة والأولى ٢٥

26. Lo! herein is indeed a lesson for him who feareth.

إن في ذلك لعبرة لمن يخشى ٢٦

27. Are ye the harder to create, or is the heaven that He built?

ءأنتم أشد خلقا أم السماء بنيها ٢٧

28. He raised the height thereof and ordered it;

رفع سمكها فسويها ٢٨

29. And He made dark the night thereof, and He brought forth the morn thereof.

وأغطش ليلها وأخرج ضحيها ٢٩

30. And after that He spread the earth,

والأرض بعد ذلك دحيها ٣٠

31. And produced therefrom the water thereof and the pasture thereof,

أخرج منها ماءها ومرعيها ٣١

32. And He made fast the hills,

والجبال أرسيها ٣٢

33. A provision for you and for your cattle.

متاعا لكم ولأنعامكم ٣٣

34. But when the great disaster cometh,

فإذا جاءت الطامة الكبرى ٣٤

35. The day when man will call to mind his (whole) endeavour,

يوم يتذكر الإنسان ما سعى ٣٥

36. And hell will stand forth visible to him who seeth,

وبرزت الجحيم لمن يرى ٣٦

37. Then, as for him who rebelled

فأما من طغى ٣٧

38. And chose the life of the world,

وآثر الحيوة الدنيا ٣٨

39. Lo! hell will be his home.

فإن الجحيم هي المأوى ٣٩

40. But as for him who feared to stand before his Lord and restrained his soul from lust,

وأما من خاف مقام ربه ونهى النفس عن الهوى ٤٠

41. Lo! the Garden will be his home.

فَإِنَّ الْجَنَّةَ هِيَ الْمَأْوٰى ﴿٤١﴾

42. They ask thee of the Hour: when will it come to port?

يَسْـَٔلُوْنَكَ عَنِ السَّاعَةِ أَيَّانَ مُرْسٰىهَا ﴿٤٢﴾

43. Why (ask they)? What hast thou to tell thereof?

فِيْمَ أَنْتَ مِنْ ذِكْرٰىهَا ﴿٤٣﴾

44. Unto thy Lord belongeth (knowledge of) the term thereof.

إِلٰى رَبِّكَ مُنْتَهٰىهَا ﴿٤٤﴾

45. Thou art but a warner unto him who feareth it.

إِنَّمَا أَنْتَ مُنْذِرُ مَنْ يَّخْشٰىهَا ﴿٤٥﴾

46. On the day when they behold it, it will be as if they had but tarried for an evening or the morn thereof.

كَأَنَّهُمْ يَوْمَ يَرَوْنَهَا لَمْ يَلْبَثُوْا إِلَّا عَشِيَّةً أَوْ ضُحٰىهَا ﴿٤٦﴾ ع

'*Abasa*, "He Frowned," takes its name from the first word. One day when the Prophet was in conversation with one of the great men of Qureysh (his own tribe), seeking to persuade him of the truth of Al-Islām, a blind man came and asked a question concerning the faith. The Prophet was annoyed at the interruption, frowned and turned away from the blind man. In this Sūrah he is told that a man's importance is not to be judged from his appearance or wordly station.

An early Meccan Sūrah.

"HE FROWNED"
Revealed at Mecca

آياتها ٤٢ (٨٠) سُورَةُ عَبَسَ مَكِّيَّةٌ رُكُوعُهَا ١

In the name of Allah, the Beneficent, the Merciful.	بِسْمِ اللّٰهِ الرَّحْمٰنِ الرَّحِيْمِ
1. He frowned and turned away	عَبَسَ وَتَوَلّٰىٓ ﴿١﴾
2. Because the blind man came unto him.	اَنْ جَآءَهُ الْاَعْمٰى ﴿٢﴾
3. What could inform thee but that he might grow (in grace)	وَمَا يُدْرِيْكَ لَعَلَّهٗ يَزَّكّٰىٓ ﴿٣﴾
4. Or take heed and so the reminder might avail him?	اَوْ يَذَّكَّرُ فَتَنْفَعَهُ الذِّكْرٰى ﴿٤﴾
5. As for him who thinketh himself independent,	اَمَّا مَنِ اسْتَغْنٰى ﴿٥﴾
6. Unto him thou payest regard.	فَاَنْتَ لَهٗ تَصَدّٰى ﴿٦﴾
7. Yet it is not thy concern if he grow not (in grace).	وَمَا عَلَيْكَ اَلَّا يَزَّكّٰى ﴿٧﴾
8. But as for him who cometh unto thee with earnest purpose	وَاَمَّا مَنْ جَآءَكَ يَسْعٰى ﴿٨﴾
9. And hath fear,	وَهُوَ يَخْشٰى ﴿٩﴾
10. From him thou art distracted.	فَاَنْتَ عَنْهُ تَلَهّٰى ﴿١٠﴾
11. Nay, but verily it is an Admonishment,	كَلَّآ اِنَّهَا تَذْكِرَةٌ ﴿١١﴾
12. So let whosoever will pay heed to it,	فَمَنْ شَآءَ ذَكَرَهٗ ﴿١٢﴾ وقف لازم
13. On honoured leaves,	فِيْ صُحُفٍ مُّكَرَّمَةٍ ﴿١٣﴾
14. Exalted, purified,	مَّرْفُوْعَةٍ مُّطَهَّرَةٍ ﴿١٤﴾
15. (Set down) by scribes	بِاَيْدِيْ سَفَرَةٍ ﴿١٥﴾
16. Noble and righteous.	كِرَامٍ بَرَرَةٍ ﴿١٦﴾
17. Man is (self-) destroyed: how ungrateful!	قُتِلَ الْاِنْسَانُ مَآ اَكْفَرَهٗ ﴿١٧﴾
18. From what thing doth He create him?	مِنْ اَيِّ شَيْءٍ خَلَقَهٗ ﴿١٨﴾
19. From a drop of seed. He createth him and proportioneth him,	مِنْ نُّطْفَةٍ خَلَقَهٗ فَقَدَّرَهٗ ﴿١٩﴾
20. Then maketh the way easy for him,	ثُمَّ السَّبِيْلَ يَسَّرَهٗ ﴿٢٠﴾

English	Arabic
21. Then causeth him to die, and burieth him;	ثُمَّ أَمَاتَهُۥ فَأَقْبَرَهُۥ ﴿٢١﴾
22. Then, when He will, He bringeth him again to life.	ثُمَّ إِذَا شَآءَ أَنشَرَهُۥ ﴿٢٢﴾
23. Nay, but (man) hath not done what He commanded him.	كَلَّا لَمَّا يَقْضِ مَآ أَمَرَهُۥ ﴿٢٣﴾
24. Let man consider his food:	فَلْيَنظُرِ الْإِنسَانُ إِلَىٰ طَعَامِهِۦٓ ﴿٢٤﴾
25. How We pour water in showers	أَنَّا صَبَبْنَا الْمَآءَ صَبًّا ﴿٢٥﴾
26. Then split the earth in clefts	ثُمَّ شَقَقْنَا الْأَرْضَ شَقًّا ﴿٢٦﴾
27. And cause the grain to grow therein	فَأَنۢبَتْنَا فِيهَا حَبًّا ﴿٢٧﴾
28. And grapes and green fodder	وَعِنَبًا وَقَضْبًا ﴿٢٨﴾
29. And olive-trees and palm-trees	وَزَيْتُونًا وَنَخْلًا ﴿٢٩﴾
30. And garden-closes of thick foliage	وَحَدَآئِقَ غُلْبًا ﴿٣٠﴾
31. And fruits and grasses:	وَفَاكِهَةً وَأَبًّا ﴿٣١﴾
32. Provision for you and your cattle.	مَّتَاعًا لَّكُمْ وَلِأَنْعَامِكُمْ ﴿٣٢﴾
33. But when the Shout cometh	فَإِذَا جَآءَتِ الصَّآخَّةُ ﴿٣٣﴾
34. On the Day when a man fleeth from his brother	يَوْمَ يَفِرُّ الْمَرْءُ مِنْ أَخِيهِ ﴿٣٤﴾
35. And his mother and his father	وَأُمِّهِۦ وَأَبِيهِ ﴿٣٥﴾
36. And his wife and his children,	وَصَاحِبَتِهِۦ وَبَنِيهِ ﴿٣٦﴾
37. Every man that day will have concern enough to make him heedless (of others).	لِكُلِّ امْرِئٍ مِّنْهُمْ يَوْمَئِذٍ شَأْنٌ يُغْنِيهِ ﴿٣٧﴾
38. On that day faces will be bright as dawn,	وُجُوهٌ يَوْمَئِذٍ مُّسْفِرَةٌ ﴿٣٨﴾
39. Laughing, rejoicing at good news;	ضَاحِكَةٌ مُّسْتَبْشِرَةٌ ﴿٣٩﴾
40. And other faces, on that day, with dust upon them,	وَوُجُوهٌ يَوْمَئِذٍ عَلَيْهَا غَبَرَةٌ ﴿٤٠﴾
41. Veiled in darkness,	تَرْهَقُهَا قَتَرَةٌ ﴿٤١﴾
42. Those are the disbelievers, the wicked.	ع أُولَٰٓئِكَ هُمُ الْكَفَرَةُ الْفَجَرَةُ ﴿٤٢﴾

At-Takwīr takes its name from a word in verse 1. Verses 8 and 9 contain an allusion to the practice of the pagan Arabs of burying alive girl-children whom they deemed superfluous. An early Meccan Sūrah.

THE OVERTHROWING

Revealed at Mecca

In the name of Allah, the Beneficent, the Merciful.

1. When the sun is overthrown,

2. And when the stars fall,

3. And when the hills are moved,

4. And when the camels big with young are abandoned,

5. And when the wild beasts are herded together,

6. And when the seas rise,

7. And when souls are reunited,

8. And when the girl-child that was buried alive is asked

9. For what sin she was slain.

10. And when the pages are laid open,

11. And when the sky is torn away,

12. And when hell is lighted,

13. And when the garden is brought nigh,

14. (Then) every soul will know what it hath made ready.

15. Oh, but I call to witness the planets,

16. The stars which rise and set,

17. And the close of night,[1]

18. And the breath of morning[2]

19. That this is in truth the word of an honoured messenger,

اياتها (٨١) سُورَةُ التَّكْوِيرِ مَكِّيَّةٌ رُكُوعُهَا

بِسْمِ اللّٰهِ الرَّحْمٰنِ الرَّحِيْمِ ○

إِذَا الشَّمْسُ كُوِّرَتْ ﴿١﴾

وَإِذَا النُّجُوْمُ انْكَدَرَتْ ﴿٢﴾

وَإِذَا الْجِبَالُ سُيِّرَتْ ﴿٣﴾

وَإِذَا الْعِشَارُ عُطِّلَتْ ﴿٤﴾

وَإِذَا الْوُحُوْشُ حُشِرَتْ ﴿٥﴾

وَإِذَا الْبِحَارُ سُجِّرَتْ ﴿٦﴾

وَإِذَا النُّفُوْسُ زُوِّجَتْ ﴿٧﴾

وَإِذَا الْمَوْءٗدَةُ سُئِلَتْ ﴿٨﴾

بِأَيِّ ذَنْۢبٍ قُتِلَتْ ﴿٩﴾

وَإِذَا الصُّحُفُ نُشِرَتْ ﴿١٠﴾

وَإِذَا السَّمَآءُ كُشِطَتْ ﴿١١﴾

وَإِذَا الْجَحِيْمُ سُعِّرَتْ ﴿١٢﴾

وَإِذَا الْجَنَّةُ أُزْلِفَتْ ﴿١٣﴾

عَلِمَتْ نَفْسٌ مَّآ أَحْضَرَتْ ﴿١٤﴾

فَلَآ أُقْسِمُ بِالْخُنَّسِ ﴿١٥﴾

الْجَوَارِ الْكُنَّسِ ﴿١٦﴾

وَالَّيْلِ إِذَا عَسْعَسَ ﴿١٧﴾

وَالصُّبْحِ إِذَا تَنَفَّسَ ﴿١٨﴾

إِنَّهٗ لَقَوْلُ رَسُوْلٍ كَرِيْمٍ ﴿١٩﴾

1. Lit. "And the night when it closeth."
2. Lit. "And the morning when it breathes."

20. Mighty, established in the presence of the Lord of the Throne,

21. (One) to be obeyed, and trustworthy;

22. And your comrade is not mad.

23. Surely he beheld him on the clear horizon.[1]

24. And he is not avid of the Unseen.

25. Nor is this the utterance of a devil worthy to be stoned:

26. Whither then go ye?

27. This is naught else than a reminder unto creation,

28. Unto whomsoever of you willeth to walk straight.

29. And ye will not, unless (it be) that Allah, the Lord of Creation, willeth.

ذِي قُوَّةٍ عِنْدَ ذِي الْعَرْشِ مَكِينٍ ۙ ﴿٢٠﴾

مُطَاعٍ ثَمَّ أَمِينٍ ۗ ﴿٢١﴾

وَمَا صَاحِبُكُمْ بِمَجْنُونٍ ۚ ﴿٢٢﴾

وَلَقَدْ رَآهُ بِالْأُفُقِ الْمُبِينِ ۚ ﴿٢٣﴾

وَمَا هُوَ عَلَى الْغَيْبِ بِضَنِينٍ ۚ ﴿٢٤﴾

وَمَا هُوَ بِقَوْلِ شَيْطٰنٍ رَجِيمٍ ۙ ﴿٢٥﴾

فَأَيْنَ تَذْهَبُونَ ۗ ﴿٢٦﴾

إِنْ هُوَ إِلَّا ذِكْرٌ لِلْعٰلَمِينَ ۙ ﴿٢٧﴾

لِمَنْ شَآءَ مِنْكُمْ أَنْ يَسْتَقِيمَ ۗ ﴿٢٨﴾

وَمَا تَشَآءُونَ إِلَّا أَنْ يَشَآءَ اللّٰهُ رَبُّ
الْعٰلَمِينَ ﴿٢٩﴾ ع

1. The reference is to the Prophet's vision at Mt. Hira.

Al-Infiṭār **takes its name from a word in verse 1. An early Meccan Sūrah.**

THE CLEAVING

Revealed at Mecca

In the name of Allah, the Beneficent, the Merciful.

1. When the heaven is cleft asunder,

2. When the planets are dispersed,

3. When the seas are poured forth,

4. And the sepulchres are overturned,

5. A soul will know what it hath sent before (it) and what left behind.

6. O man! What hath made thee careless concerning thy Lord, the Bountiful,

7. Who created thee, then fashioned, then proportioned thee?

8. Into whatsoever form He will, He casteth thee.

9. Nay, but they deny the Judgement:

10. Lo! there are above you guardians,

11. Generous and recording,

12. Who know (all) that ye do.

13. Lo! the righteous verily will be in delight.

14. And lo! the wicked verily will be in hell;

15. They will burn therein on the Day of Judgement,

16. And will not be absent thence.

17. Ah, what will convey unto thee what the Day of Judgement is!

18. Again, what will convey unto thee what the Day of Judgement is!

19 A day on which no soul hath power at all for any (other) soul. The (absolute) command on that day is Allah's.

ایاتها ١٩ (٨٢) سُوْرَةُ الْاِنْفِطَارِ مَكِّيَّةٌ رکوعها ١

بِسْمِ اللّٰهِ الرَّحْمٰنِ الرَّحِيْمِ

اِذَا السَّمَآءُ انْفَطَرَتْ ۝١

وَاِذَا الْكَوَاكِبُ انْتَثَرَتْ ۝٢

وَاِذَا الْبِحَارُ فُجِّرَتْ ۝٣

وَاِذَا الْقُبُوْرُ بُعْثِرَتْ ۝٤

عَلِمَتْ نَفْسٌ مَّا قَدَّمَتْ وَاَخَّرَتْ ۝٥

يٰٓاَيُّهَا الْاِنْسَانُ مَا غَرَّكَ بِرَبِّكَ الْكَرِيْمِ ۝٦

الَّذِيْ خَلَقَكَ فَسَوّٰىكَ فَعَدَلَكَ ۝٧

فِيْٓ اَيِّ صُوْرَةٍ مَّا شَآءَ رَكَّبَكَ ۝٨

كَلَّا بَلْ تُكَذِّبُوْنَ بِالدِّيْنِ ۝٩

وَاِنَّ عَلَيْكُمْ لَحٰفِظِيْنَ ۝١٠

كِرَامًا كَاتِبِيْنَ ۝١١

يَعْلَمُوْنَ مَا تَفْعَلُوْنَ ۝١٢

اِنَّ الْاَبْرَارَ لَفِيْ نَعِيْمٍ ۝١٣

وَاِنَّ الْفُجَّارَ لَفِيْ جَحِيْمٍ ۝١٤

يَّصْلَوْنَهَا يَوْمَ الدِّيْنِ ۝١٥

وَمَا هُمْ عَنْهَا بِغَآئِبِيْنَ ۝١٦

وَمَآ اَدْرٰىكَ مَا يَوْمُ الدِّيْنِ ۝١٧

ثُمَّ مَآ اَدْرٰىكَ مَا يَوْمُ الدِّيْنِ ۝١٨

يَوْمَ لَا تَمْلِكُ نَفْسٌ لِّنَفْسٍ شَيْـًٔا وَالْاَمْرُ يَوْمَئِذٍ لِّلّٰهِ ۝١٩

At-Taṭfīf, "Defrauding," takes its name from a word in verse 1. An early Meccan Sūrah.

DEFRAUDING

Revealed at Mecca

In the name of Allah, the Beneficent, the Merciful.

1. Woe unto the defrauders:

2. Those who when they take the measure from mankind demand it full,

3. But if they measure unto them or weigh for them, they cause them loss.

4. Do such (men) not consider that they will be raised again

5. Unto an awful Day:

6. The day when (all) mankind stand before the Lord of the Worlds?

7. Nay, but the record of the vile is in Sijjīn—

8. Ah! what will convey unto thee what Sijjīn is!—

9. A written record.

10. Woe unto the repudiators on that day!

11. Those who deny the Day of Judgement

12. Which none denieth save each criminal transgressor,

13. Who, when thou readest unto him Our revelations, saith: (Mere) fables of the men of old.

14. Nay, but that which they have earned is rust upon their hearts.

15. Nay, but surely on that day they will be covered from (the mercy of) their Lord.

16. Then lo! they verily will burn in hell,

17. And it will be said (unto them): This is that which ye used to deny.

18. Nay, but the record of the righteous is in 'Iliyīn—

19. Ah, what will convey unto thee what 'Iliyīn is!—

ایاتها ٣٦ (٨٣) سُورَةُ الْمُطَفِّفِينَ مَكِّيَّةٌ ركوعها ١

بِسْمِ اللّٰهِ الرَّحْمٰنِ الرَّحِيْمِ ○

وَيْلٌ لِّلْمُطَفِّفِيْنَ ①

الَّذِيْنَ إِذَا اكْتَالُوْا عَلَى النَّاسِ يَسْتَوْفُوْنَ ②

وَإِذَا كَالُوْهُمْ أَوْ وَّزَنُوْهُمْ يُخْسِرُوْنَ ③

أَلَا يَظُنُّ أُولٰٓئِكَ أَنَّهُمْ مَّبْعُوْثُوْنَ ④

لِيَوْمٍ عَظِيْمٍ ⑤

يَّوْمَ يَقُوْمُ النَّاسُ لِرَبِّ الْعٰلَمِيْنَ ⑥

كَلَّآ إِنَّ كِتٰبَ الْفُجَّارِ لَفِيْ سِجِّيْنٍ ⑦

وَمَآ أَدْرٰىكَ مَا سِجِّيْنٌ ⑧

كِتٰبٌ مَّرْقُوْمٌ ⑨

وَيْلٌ يَّوْمَئِذٍ لِّلْمُكَذِّبِيْنَ ⑩

الَّذِيْنَ يُكَذِّبُوْنَ بِيَوْمِ الدِّيْنِ ⑪

وَمَا يُكَذِّبُ بِهٖٓ إِلَّا كُلُّ مُعْتَدٍ أَثِيْمٍ ⑫

إِذَا تُتْلٰى عَلَيْهِ اٰيٰتُنَا قَالَ أَسَاطِيْرُ الْأَوَّلِيْنَ ⑬

كَلَّا بَلْ ٚ رَانَ عَلٰى قُلُوْبِهِمْ مَّا كَانُوْا يَكْسِبُوْنَ ⑭

كَلَّآ إِنَّهُمْ عَنْ رَّبِّهِمْ يَوْمَئِذٍ لَّمَحْجُوْبُوْنَ ⑮

ثُمَّ إِنَّهُمْ لَصَالُوا الْجَحِيْمِ ⑯

ثُمَّ يُقَالُ هٰذَا الَّذِيْ كُنْتُمْ بِهٖ تُكَذِّبُوْنَ ⑰

كَلَّآ إِنَّ كِتٰبَ الْأَبْرَارِ لَفِيْ عِلِّيِّيْنَ ⑱

وَمَآ أَدْرٰىكَ مَا عِلِّيُّوْنَ ⑲

20. A written record.

كِتٰبٌ مَّرْقُوْمٌ ﴿٢٠﴾

21. Attested by those who are brought near (unto their Lord).

يَّشْهَدُهُ الْمُقَرَّبُوْنَ ﴿٢١﴾

22. Lo! the righteous verily are in delight,

اِنَّ الْاَبْرَارَ لَفِيْ نَعِيْمٍ ﴿٢٢﴾

23. On couches, gazing.

عَلَى الْاَرَآئِكِ يَنْظُرُوْنَ ﴿٢٣﴾

24. Thou wilt know in their faces the radiance of delight.

تَعْرِفُ فِيْ وُجُوْهِهِمْ نَضْرَةَ النَّعِيْمِ ﴿٢٤﴾

25. They are given to drink of a pure wine, sealed.

يُسْقَوْنَ مِنْ رَّحِيْقٍ مَّخْتُوْمٍ ﴿٢٥﴾

26. Whose seal is musk—For this let (all) those strive who strive for bliss—

خِتٰمُهٗ مِسْكٌ وَفِيْ ذٰلِكَ فَلْيَتَنَافَسِ الْمُتَنٰفِسُوْنَ ﴿٢٦﴾

27. And mixed with water of Tasnim,

وَمِزَاجُهٗ مِنْ تَسْنِيْمٍ ﴿٢٧﴾

28. A spring whence those brought near to Allah drink.

عَيْنًا يَّشْرَبُ بِهَا الْمُقَرَّبُوْنَ ﴿٢٨﴾

29. Lo! the guilty used to laugh at those who believed.

اِنَّ الَّذِيْنَ اَجْرَمُوْا كَانُوْا مِنَ الَّذِيْنَ اٰمَنُوْا يَضْحَكُوْنَ ﴿٢٩﴾

30. And wink one to another when they passed them;

وَاِذَا مَرُّوْا بِهِمْ يَتَغَامَزُوْنَ ﴿٣٠﴾

31. And when they returned to their own folk, they returned jesting;

وَاِذَا انْقَلَبُوْٓا اِلٰٓى اَهْلِهِمُ انْقَلَبُوْا فَكِهِيْنَ ﴿٣١﴾

32. And when they saw them they said: Lo! these have gone astray.

وَاِذَا رَاَوْهُمْ قَالُوْٓا اِنَّ هٰٓؤُلَآءِ لَضَآلُّوْنَ ﴿٣٢﴾

33. Yet they were not sent as guardians over them.

وَمَآ اُرْسِلُوْا عَلَيْهِمْ حٰفِظِيْنَ ﴿٣٣﴾

34. This day it is those who believe who have the laugh of disbelievers,

فَالْيَوْمَ الَّذِيْنَ اٰمَنُوْا مِنَ الْكُفَّارِ يَضْحَكُوْنَ ﴿٣٤﴾

35. On high couches, gazing.

عَلَى الْاَرَآئِكِ يَنْظُرُوْنَ ﴿٣٥﴾

36. Are not the disbelievers paid for what they used to do?

هَلْ ثُوِّبَ الْكُفَّارُ مَا كَانُوْا يَفْعَلُوْنَ ﴿٣٦﴾

Al-Inshiqāq, "The Sundering," takes its name from a word in verse 1. An early Meccan Sūrah.

THE SUNDERING

Revealed at Mecca

In the name of Allah, the Beneficent, the Merciful.

1. When the heaven is split asunder

2. And attentive to her Lord in fear,

3. And when the earth is spread out

4. And hath cast out all that was in her, and is empty

5. And attentive to her Lord in fear!

6. Thou, verily, O man, art working toward thy Lord a work which thou wilt meet (in His presence).

7. Then whoso is given his account in his right hand

8. He truly will receive an easy reckoning

9. And will return unto his folk in joy.

10. But whoso is given his account behind his back,

11. He surely will invoke destruction

12. And be thrown to scorching fire.

13. He verily lived joyous with his folk.

14. He verily deemed that he would never return (unto Allah).

15. Nay, but lo! his Lord is ever looking on him!

16. Oh, I swear by the afterglow of sunset,

17. And by the night and all that it enshroudeth,

18. And by the moon when she is at the full,

آياتها (٨٤) سُورَةُ الانْشِقَاقِ مَكِّيَّةٌ رُكُوعُهَا

بِسْمِ اللّٰهِ الرَّحْمٰنِ الرَّحِيْمِ

إِذَا السَّمَآءُ انْشَقَّتْ ﴿١﴾

وَأَذِنَتْ لِرَبِّهَا وَحُقَّتْ ﴿٢﴾

وَإِذَا الْأَرْضُ مُدَّتْ ﴿٣﴾

وَأَلْقَتْ مَا فِيْهَا وَتَخَلَّتْ ﴿٤﴾

وَأَذِنَتْ لِرَبِّهَا وَحُقَّتْ ﴿٥﴾

يٰأَيُّهَا الْإِنْسَانُ إِنَّكَ كَادِحٌ إِلٰى رَبِّكَ كَدْحًا

فَمُلٰقِيْهِ ﴿٦﴾

فَأَمَّا مَنْ أُوْتِيَ كِتٰبَهُ بِيَمِيْنِهِ ﴿٧﴾

فَسَوْفَ يُحَاسَبُ حِسَابًا يَّسِيْرًا ﴿٨﴾

وَّيَنْقَلِبُ إِلٰى أَهْلِهِ مَسْرُوْرًا ﴿٩﴾

وَأَمَّا مَنْ أُوْتِيَ كِتٰبَهُ وَرَآءَ ظَهْرِهِ ﴿١٠﴾

فَسَوْفَ يَدْعُوْا ثُبُوْرًا ﴿١١﴾

وَّيَصْلٰى سَعِيْرًا ﴿١٢﴾

إِنَّهُ كَانَ فِيْ أَهْلِهِ مَسْرُوْرًا ﴿١٣﴾

إِنَّهُ ظَنَّ أَنْ لَّنْ يَّحُوْرَ ﴿١٤﴾

بَلٰى إِنَّ رَبَّهُ كَانَ بِهِ بَصِيْرًا ﴿١٥﴾

فَلَا أُقْسِمُ بِالشَّفَقِ ﴿١٦﴾

وَالَّيْلِ وَمَا وَسَقَ ﴿١٧﴾

وَالْقَمَرِ إِذَا اتَّسَقَ ﴿١٨﴾

19. That ye shall journey on from plane to plane.

لَتَرْكَبُنَّ طَبَقًا عَنْ طَبَقٍ ١٩

20. What aileth them, then, that they believe not

فَمَا لَهُمْ لَا يُؤْمِنُونَ ٢٠

21. And, when the Qur'ān is recited unto them, worship not (Allah)?

وَإِذَا قُرِئَ عَلَيْهِمُ الْقُرْآنُ لَا يَسْجُدُونَ ٢١ السجدة

22. Nay, but those who disbelieve will deny;

بَلِ الَّذِينَ كَفَرُوا يُكَذِّبُونَ ٢٢

23. And Allah knoweth best what they are hiding.

وَاللَّهُ أَعْلَمُ بِمَا يُوعُونَ ٢٣

24. So give them tidings of a painful doom,

فَبَشِّرْهُمْ بِعَذَابٍ أَلِيمٍ ٢٤

25. Save those who believe and do good works, for theirs is a reward unfailing.

إِلَّا الَّذِينَ آمَنُوا وَعَمِلُوا الصَّالِحَاتِ لَهُمْ أَجْرٌ غَيْرُ مَمْنُونٍ ٢٥

Al-Buruj takes its name from a word in verse 1 which I have translated "mansions of the stars." The word has the meaning of towers or mansions and is applied to the signs of the Zodiac. Verses 4 to 7 are generally taken to refer to the massacre of the Christians of Najrān in Al-Yaman by a Jewish king Dhū Nawās, an event of great historical importance since it caused the intervention of the Negus and led to the Abyssinian supremacy in the Yaman which lasted until the War of the Elephant (Sūrah CV) in the Prophet's year of birth. Professor Horowitz thinks that the words "owners of the ditch, of the fuel-fed fire" refer not to any historical event but to the condition of all persecutors in the hereafter.[1]

An early Meccan Sūrah.

1. See "Islamic Culture" (Hyderabad, Deccan), April 1929.

THE MANSIONS OF THE STARS

Revealed at Mecca

اٰيَاتُهَا (٨٥) سُوْرَةُ الْبُرُوْجِ مَكِّيَّةٌ رُكُوْعُهَا

In the name of Allah, the Beneficent, the Merciful.

بِسْمِ اللّٰهِ الرَّحْمٰنِ الرَّحِيْمِ ○

1. By the heaven, holding mansions of the stars,

وَالسَّمَآءِ ذَاتِ الْبُرُوْجِ ﴿١﴾

2. And by the Promised Day,

وَالْيَوْمِ الْمَوْعُوْدِ ﴿٢﴾

3. And by the witness and that whereunto he beareth testimony,

وَشَاهِدٍ وَّمَشْهُوْدٍ ﴿٣﴾

4. (Self-) destroyed were the owners of the ditch

قُتِلَ اَصْحٰبُ الْاُخْدُوْدِ ﴿٤﴾

5. Of the fuel-fed fire,

النَّارِ ذَاتِ الْوَقُوْدِ ﴿٥﴾

6. When they sat by it,

اِذْ هُمْ عَلَيْهَا قُعُوْدٌ ﴿٦﴾

7. And were themselves the witnesses of what they did to the believers.[1]

وَّهُمْ عَلٰى مَا يَفْعَلُوْنَ بِالْمُؤْمِنِيْنَ شُهُوْدٌ ﴿٧﴾

8. They had naught against them save that they believed in Allah, the Mighty, the Owner of Praise,

وَمَا نَقَمُوْا مِنْهُمْ اِلَّآ اَنْ يُّؤْمِنُوْا بِاللّٰهِ الْعَزِيْزِ الْحَمِيْدِ ﴿٨﴾

9. Him unto Whom belongeth the Sovereignty of the heavens and the earth; and Allah is of all things the Witness.

الَّذِيْ لَهٗ مُلْكُ السَّمٰوٰتِ وَالْاَرْضِ ؕ وَاللّٰهُ عَلٰى كُلِّ شَيْءٍ شَهِيْدٌ ﴿٩﴾

10. Lo! they who persecute believing men and believing women and repent not, theirs verily will be the doom of hell, and theirs the doom of burning.

اِنَّ الَّذِيْنَ فَتَنُوا الْمُؤْمِنِيْنَ وَالْمُؤْمِنٰتِ ثُمَّ لَمْ يَتُوْبُوْا فَلَهُمْ عَذَابُ جَهَنَّمَ وَلَهُمْ عَذَابُ الْحَرِيْقِ ﴿١٠﴾

11. Lo! those who believe and do good works, theirs will be Gardens underneath which rivers flow. That is the Great Success.

اِنَّ الَّذِيْنَ اٰمَنُوْا وَعَمِلُوا الصّٰلِحٰتِ لَهُمْ جَنّٰتٌ تَجْرِيْ مِنْ تَحْتِهَا الْاَنْهٰرُ ؕ ذٰلِكَ الْفَوْزُ الْكَبِيْرُ ﴿١١﴾

12. Lo! the punishment of thy Lord is stern.

اِنَّ بَطْشَ رَبِّكَ لَشَدِيْدٌ ﴿١٢﴾

13. Lo! He it is Who produceth, then reproduceth.

اِنَّهٗ هُوَ يُبْدِئُ وَيُعِيْدُ ﴿١٣﴾

1. Or it might be: "(Self-)destroyed were the owners of the trench of fuel-fed fire (*i.e.* hell) when they took their ease on earth and were themselves the witnesses," etc.

14. And He is the Forgiving, the Loving

وَهُوَ الْغَفُورُ الْوَدُودُ ﴿١٤﴾

15. Lord of the Throne of Glory,

ذُو الْعَرْشِ الْمَجِيدُ ﴿١٥﴾

16. Doer of what He will.

فَعَّالٌ لِّمَا يُرِيدُ ﴿١٦﴾

17. Hath there come unto thee the story of the hosts

هَلْ أَتَاكَ حَدِيثُ الْجُنُودِ ﴿١٧﴾

18. Of Pharaoh and (the tribe of) Thamūd?

فِرْعَوْنَ وَثَمُودَ ﴿١٨﴾

19. Nay, but those who disbelieve live in denial

بَلِ الَّذِينَ كَفَرُوا فِي تَكْذِيبٍ ﴿١٩﴾

20. And Allah, all unseen, surroundeth them.

وَاللَّهُ مِن وَرَائِهِم مُّحِيطٌ ﴿٢٠﴾

21. Nay, but it is a glorious Qur'ān.

بَلْ هُوَ قُرْآنٌ مَّجِيدٌ ﴿٢١﴾

22. On a guarded tablet.

فِي لَوْحٍ مَّحْفُوظٍ ﴿٢٢﴾

At-Tāriq takes its name from a word in verse 1. There are other meanings to the word *Tāriq*, but I have chosen that which must have occurred to every hearer of this Sūrah, especially as in verse 3 it is stated that a star is meant. The Morning Star has here a mystic sense, and is taken to refer to the Prophet himself. Some have thought that it refers to a comet which alarmed the East about the time of the Prophet's call. Others believe that this and other introductory verses, hard to elucidate, hide scientific facts unimagined at the period of revelation, and are related to the verses following them. Ghamrāwi Bey, my collaborator in the revision of this work, informed me that the late Dr. Sidqi among others considered that the reference here is to the fertilising germ penetrating the ovary, the subject being the same as vv. 5-7.

An early Meccan Sūrah.

THE MORNING STAR

Revealed at Mecca

آياتها ١٧ (٨٦) سُورَةُ الطَّارِقِ مَكِّيَّةٌ رُكُوعُهَا ١

In the name of Allah, the Beneficent, the Merciful.

بِسْمِ اللَّهِ الرَّحْمَٰنِ الرَّحِيمِ

1. By the heaven and the Morning Star

وَالسَّمَاءِ وَالطَّارِقِ ﴿١﴾

2. —Ah, what will tell thee what the Morning Star is!

وَمَا أَدْرَاكَ مَا الطَّارِقُ ﴿٢﴾

3. —The piercing Star!

النَّجْمُ الثَّاقِبُ ﴿٣﴾

4. No human soul but hath a guardian over it.

إِنْ كُلُّ نَفْسٍ لَمَّا عَلَيْهَا حَافِظٌ ﴿٤﴾

5. So let man consider from what he is created.

فَلْيَنْظُرِ الْإِنْسَانُ مِمَّ خُلِقَ ﴿٥﴾

6. He is created from a gushing fluid

خُلِقَ مِنْ مَاءٍ دَافِقٍ ﴿٦﴾

7. That issued from between the loins and ribs.

يَخْرُجُ مِنْ بَيْنِ الصُّلْبِ وَالتَّرَائِبِ ﴿٧﴾

8. Lo! He verily is Able to return him (unto life)

إِنَّهُ عَلَىٰ رَجْعِهِ لَقَادِرٌ ﴿٨﴾

9. On the day when hidden thoughts shall be searched out.

يَوْمَ تُبْلَى السَّرَائِرُ ﴿٩﴾

10. Then will he have no might nor any helper.

فَمَا لَهُ مِنْ قُوَّةٍ وَلَا نَاصِرٍ ﴿١٠﴾

11. By the heaven which giveth the returning rain,

وَالسَّمَاءِ ذَاتِ الرَّجْعِ ﴿١١﴾

12. And the earth which splitteth (with the growth of trees and plants)

وَالْأَرْضِ ذَاتِ الصَّدْعِ ﴿١٢﴾

13. Lo ! this (Qur'ān) is a conclusive word,

إِنَّهُ لَقَوْلٌ فَصْلٌ ﴿١٣﴾

14. It is no pleasantry.

وَمَا هُوَ بِالْهَزْلِ ﴿١٤﴾

15. Lo! they plot a plot (against thee, O Muhammad)

إِنَّهُمْ يَكِيدُونَ كَيْدًا ﴿١٥﴾

16. And I plot a plot (against them).

وَأَكِيدُ كَيْدًا ﴿١٦﴾

17. So give a respite to the disbelievers. Deal thou gently with them for a while.

فَمَهِّلِ الْكَافِرِينَ أَمْهِلْهُمْ رُوَيْدًا ﴿١٧﴾

1. The Arabic word means originally "that which comes at night" or "one who knocks at the door."

Al-A'ala takes its name from a word in verse 1. An early Meccan Sūrah.

THE MOST HIGH

Revealed at Mecca

In the name of Allah, the Beneficent, the Merciful.

1. Praise the name of thy Lord the Most High,

2. Who createth, then disposeth;

3. Who measureth, then guideth;

4. Who bringeth forth the pasturage,

5. Then turneth it to russet stubble.

6. We shall make thee read (O Muhammad) so that thou shalt not forget

7. Save that which Allah willeth. Lo! He knoweth the disclosed and that which still is hidden;

8. And We shall ease thy way unto the state of ease.

9. Therefor remind (men), for of use is the reminder.

10. He will heed who feareth,

11. But the most hapless will flout it,

12. He who will be flung to the great fire

13. Wherein he will neither die nor live.

14. He is successful who groweth,

15. And remembereth the name of his Lord, so prayeth.

•16. But ye prefer the life of the world

17. Although the Hereafter is better and more lasting.

18. Lo! This is in the former scrolls,

19. The Books of Abraham and Moses.

آياتها ١٩ (٨٧) سورة الأعلى مكية ركوعها ١

بسم الله الرحمن الرحيم

سبح اسم ربك الأعلى ﴿١﴾

الذي خلق فسوى ﴿٢﴾

والذي قدر فهدى ﴿٣﴾

والذي أخرج المرعى ﴿٤﴾

فجعله غثاء أحوى ﴿٥﴾

سنقرئك فلا تنسى ﴿٦﴾

إلا ما شاء الله إنه يعلم الجهر وما يخفى ﴿٧﴾

ونيسرك لليسرى ﴿٨﴾

فذكر إن نفعت الذكرى ﴿٩﴾

سيذكر من يخشى ﴿١٠﴾

ويتجنبها الأشقى ﴿١١﴾

الذي يصلى النار الكبرى ﴿١٢﴾

ثم لا يموت فيها ولا يحيى ﴿١٣﴾

قد أفلح من تزكى ﴿١٤﴾

وذكر اسم ربه فصلى ﴿١٥﴾

بل تؤثرون الحيوة الدنيا ﴿١٦﴾

والآخرة خير وأبقى ﴿١٧﴾

إن هذا لفي الصحف الأولى ﴿١٨﴾

صحف إبراهيم وموسى ﴿١٩﴾

Al-Ghāshiyah takes its name from a word in verse 1. An early Meccan Sūrah.

THE OVERWHELMING

Revealed at Mecca

اياتها (٨٨) سورة الغاشية مكية ركوعها

In the name of Allah, the Beneficent, the Merciful.

بسم الله الرحمن الرحيم

1. Hath there come unto thee tidings of the Overwhelming?

هل أتاك حديث الغاشية ﴿١﴾

2. On that day (many) faces will be downcast,

وجوه يومئذ خاشعة ﴿٢﴾

3. Toiling, wary,

عاملة ناصبة ﴿٣﴾

4. Scorched by burning fire,

تصلى نارا حامية ﴿٤﴾

5. Drinking from a boiling spring,

تسقى من عين آنية ﴿٥﴾

6. No food for them save bitter thorn-fruit

ليس لهم طعام إلا من ضريع ﴿٦﴾

7. Which doth not nourish nor release from hunger.

لا يسمن ولا يغني من جوع ﴿٧﴾

8. On that day other faces will be calm,

وجوه يومئذ ناعمة ﴿٨﴾

9. Glad for their effort past,

لسعيها راضية ﴿٩﴾

10. In a high garden

في جنة عالية ﴿١٠﴾

11. Where they hear no idle speech.

لا تسمع فيها لاغية ﴿١١﴾

12. Wherein is a gushing spring,

فيها عين جارية ﴿١٢﴾

13. Wherein are couches raised

فيها سرر مرفوعة ﴿١٣﴾

14. And goblets set at hand

وأكواب موضوعة ﴿١٤﴾

15. And cushions ranged

ونمارق مصفوفة ﴿١٥﴾

16. And silken carpets spread.

وزرابي مبثوثة ﴿١٦﴾

17. Will they not regard the camels how they are created?

أفلا ينظرون إلى الإبل كيف خلقت ﴿١٧﴾

18. And the heaven, how it is raised?

وإلى السماء كيف رفعت ﴿١٨﴾

19. And the hills, how they are set up?

وإلى الجبال كيف نصبت ﴿١٩﴾

20. And the earth, how it is spread?

وإلى الأرض كيف سطحت ﴿٢٠﴾

21. Remind them, for thou art but a remembrancer,

فذكر إنما أنت مذكر ﴿٢١﴾

22. Thou art not at all a warder over them.

لست عليهم بمصيطر ﴿٢٢﴾

23. But whoso is averse and disbelieveth,

إلا من تولى وكفر ﴿٢٣﴾

24. Allah will punish him with direst punishment.

فيعذبه الله العذاب الأكبر ﴿٢٤﴾

25. Lo! unto Us is their return

إن إلينا إيابهم ﴿٢٥﴾

26. And Ours their reckoning.

ثم إن علينا حسابهم ﴿٢٦﴾

Al-Fajr takes its name from verse 1. A very early Meccan Sūrah.

THE DAWN

Revealed at Mekkah

In the name of Allah, the Beneficent, the Mereiful.

1. By the Dawn

2. And ten nights

3. And the Even and the Odd

4. And the night when it departeth.

5. There surely is an oath for thinking man.

6. Dost thou not consider how thy Lord dealt with (the tribe of) 'Aad,

7. With many columned Iram,

8. The like of which was not created in the lands;

9. And with (the tribe of) Thamud, who clove the rocks in the valley;

10. And with Pharaoh, firm of might,

11. Who (all) were rebellious (to Allah) in these lands,

12. And multiplied iniquity therein?

13. Therefor thy Lord poured on them the disaster of His punishment.

14. Lo! thy Lord is ever watchful.

15. As for man, whenever his Lord trieth him by honouring him, and is gracious unto him, he saith: My Lord honoureth me.

16. But whenever He trieth him by straitening his means of life, he saith: My Lord despiseth me.

17 Nay, but ye (for your part) honour bot the orphean.

آياتها (٨٩) سُوْرَةُ الْفَجْرِ مَكِّيَّةٌ رُكُوعُهَا

بِسْمِ اللّٰهِ الرَّحْمٰنِ الرَّحِيْمِ

وَالْفَجْرِ ﴿١﴾

وَلَيَالٍ عَشْرٍ ﴿٢﴾

وَّالشَّفْعِ وَالْوَتْرِ ﴿٣﴾

وَالَّيْلِ إِذَا يَسْرِ ﴿٤﴾

هَلْ فِيْ ذٰلِكَ قَسَمٌ لِّذِيْ حِجْرٍ ﴿٥﴾

أَلَمْ تَرَ كَيْفَ فَعَلَ رَبُّكَ بِعَادٍ ﴿٦﴾

إِرَمَ ذَاتِ الْعِمَادِ ﴿٧﴾

الَّتِيْ لَمْ يُخْلَقْ مِثْلُهَا فِي الْبِلَادِ ﴿٨﴾

وَثَمُوْدَ الَّذِيْنَ جَابُوا الصَّخْرَ بِالْوَادِ ﴿٩﴾

وَفِرْعَوْنَ ذِي الْأَوْتَادِ ﴿١٠﴾

الَّذِيْنَ طَغَوْا فِي الْبِلَادِ ﴿١١﴾

فَأَكْثَرُوْا فِيْهَا الْفَسَادَ ﴿١٢﴾

فَصَبَّ عَلَيْهِمْ رَبُّكَ سَوْطَ عَذَابٍ ﴿١٣﴾

إِنَّ رَبَّكَ لَبِالْمِرْصَادِ ﴿١٤﴾

فَأَمَّا الْإِنْسَانُ إِذَا مَا ابْتَلٰىهُ رَبُّهٗ فَأَكْرَمَهٗ وَ
نَعَّمَهٗ فَيَقُوْلُ رَبِّيْ أَكْرَمَنِ ﴿١٥﴾

وَأَمَّا إِذَا مَا ابْتَلٰىهُ فَقَدَرَ عَلَيْهِ رِزْقَهٗ فَيَقُوْلُ
رَبِّيْ أَهَانَنِ ﴿١٦﴾

كَلَّا بَلْ لَّا تُكْرِمُوْنَ الْيَتِيْمَ ﴿١٧﴾

1. Of the month of pilgrimage.

2. I had written Many columned," following the run of commentators, who take the word 'mad' to mean columns, pillars, when I happened upon ibn Khaldun's diatribe against that rendering and all the legends to which it has given rise, in the preface to the *prolegomena*. The word meant " tent-poles" to the Arabs of the Prophet's day. as Ibn Khaldun points out. In view of recent discoveries in the Yaman, however, I prefer the usual rendering.

18. And urge not on the feeding of the poor,

وَلَا تَحٰٓضُّوْنَ عَلٰى طَعَامِ الْمِسْكِيْنِ ۝١٨

19. And ye devour heritages with devouring greed

وَتَاْكُلُوْنَ التُّرَاثَ اَكْلًا لَّمًّا ۝١٩

20. And love wealth with abounding love.

وَّتُحِبُّوْنَ الْمَالَ حُبًّا جَمًّا ۝٢٠

21. Nay, but when the earth is ground to atoms, grinding, grinding,

كَلَّآ اِذَا دُكَّتِ الْاَرْضُ دَكًّا دَكًّا ۝٢١

22. And thy Lord shall come with angels, rank on rank,

وَّجَآءَ رَبُّكَ وَالْمَلَكُ صَفًّا صَفًّا ۝٢٢

23. And hell is brought near that day; on that day man will remember, but how will the remembrance (then avail him)?

وَجِايْٓءَ يَوْمَئِذٍۢ بِجَهَنَّمَ ۙ يَوْمَئِذٍ يَّتَذَكَّرُ
الْاِنْسَانُ وَاَنّٰى لَهُ الذِّكْرٰى ۝٢٣

24. He will say: Ah, would that I had sent before me (some provision) for my life!

يَقُوْلُ يٰلَيْتَنِيْ قَدَّمْتُ لِحَيَاتِيْ ۝٢٤

25. None punisheth as He will punish on that day!

فَيَوْمَئِذٍ لَّا يُعَذِّبُ عَذَابَهٗٓ اَحَدٌ ۝٢٥

26. None bindeth as He then will bind.

وَّلَا يُوْثِقُ وَثَاقَهٗٓ اَحَدٌ ۝٢٦

27. But ah! thou soul at peace!

يٰٓاَيَّتُهَا النَّفْسُ الْمُطْمَئِنَّةُ ۝٢٧

28. Return unto thy Lord, content in His good pleasure!

ارْجِعِيْٓ اِلٰى رَبِّكِ رَاضِيَةً مَّرْضِيَّةً ۝٢٨

29. Enter thou among My bondmen!

فَادْخُلِيْ فِيْ عِبٰدِيْ ۝٢٩

30. Enter thou My Garden!

وَادْخُلِيْ جَنَّتِيْ ۝٣٠

Al-Balad takes its name from a word in verse 1. A very early Meccan Sūrah.

THE CITY

Revealed at Mecca

In the name of Allah, the Beneficent, the Merciful.

1. Nay, I swear by this city—

2. And thou art an indweller of this city[1]—

3. And the begetter and that which he begat,

4. We verily have created man in an atmosphere:[2]

5. Thinketh he that none hath power over him?

6. And he saith: I have destroyed vast wealth:

7. Thinketh he that none beholdeth him?

8. Did We not assign unto him two eyes

9. And a tongue and two lips,

10. And guide him to the parting of the mountain ways?

11. But he hath not attempted the Ascent—

12. Ah, what will convey unto thee what the Ascent is!—

13. (It is) to free a slave,

14. And to feed in the day of hunger

15. An orphan near of kin,

16. Or some poor wretch in misery,

17. And to be of those who believe and exhort one another to perseverance and exhort one another to pity.

18. Their place will be on the right hand.

19. But those who disbelieve Our revelations, their place will be on the left hand.

20. Fire will be an awning over them.

اياتها (٩٠) سورة البلد مكية ركوعها ١

بِسْمِ اللّٰهِ الرَّحْمٰنِ الرَّحِيْمِ

لَآ اُقْسِمُ بِهٰذَا الْبَلَدِ ①

وَاَنْتَ حِلٌّۢ بِهٰذَا الْبَلَدِ ②

وَوَالِدٍ وَّمَا وَلَدَ ③

لَقَدْ خَلَقْنَا الْاِنْسَانَ فِيْ كَبَدٍ ④

اَيَحْسَبُ اَنْ لَّنْ يَّقْدِرَ عَلَيْهِ اَحَدٌ ⑤

يَقُوْلُ اَهْلَكْتُ مَالًا لُّبَدًا ⑥

اَيَحْسَبُ اَنْ لَّمْ يَرَهٗٓ اَحَدٌ ⑦

اَلَمْ نَجْعَلْ لَّهٗ عَيْنَيْنِ ⑧

وَلِسَانًا وَّشَفَتَيْنِ ⑨

وَهَدَيْنٰهُ النَّجْدَيْنِ ⑩

فَلَا اقْتَحَمَ الْعَقَبَةَ ⑪

وَمَآ اَدْرٰىكَ مَا الْعَقَبَةُ ⑫

فَكُّ رَقَبَةٍ ⑬

اَوْ اِطْعٰمٌ فِيْ يَوْمٍ ذِيْ مَسْغَبَةٍ ⑭

يَّتِيْمًا ذَا مَقْرَبَةٍ ⑮

اَوْ مِسْكِيْنًا ذَا مَتْرَبَةٍ ⑯

ثُمَّ كَانَ مِنَ الَّذِيْنَ اٰمَنُوْا وَتَوَاصَوْا بِالصَّبْرِ وَتَوَاصَوْا بِالْمَرْحَمَةِ ⑰

اُولٰٓئِكَ اَصْحٰبُ الْمَيْمَنَةِ ⑱

وَالَّذِيْنَ كَفَرُوْا بِاٰيٰتِنَا هُمْ اَصْحٰبُ الْمَشْئَمَةِ ⑲

عَلَيْهِمْ نَارٌ مُّؤْصَدَةٌ ⑳

1. Or "when thou hast control over this city" (prophetically).
2. Or "in affliction."

Ash-Shams takes its name from a word in verse 1. A very early Meccan Sūrah.

THE SUN

Revealed at Mecca

In the name of Allah, the Beneficent, the Merciful.

1. By the sun and his brightness,

2. And the moon when she followeth him,

3. And the day when it revealeth him,

4. And the night when it enshroudeth him,

5. And the heaven and Him Who built it,

6. And the earth and Him Who spread it,

7. And a soul and Him Who perfected it

8. And inspired it (with conscience of) what is wrong for it and (what is) right for it.

9. He is indeed successful who causeth it to grow,

10. And he is indeed a failure who stunteth it.

11. (The tribe of) Thamūd denied (the truth) in their rebellious pride.

12. When the basest of them broke forth

13. And the messenger of Allah said: It is the she-camel of Allah, so let her drink!

14. But they denied him, and they hamstrung her, so Allah doomed them for their sin and rased (their dwellings).

15. He dreadeth not the sequel (of events).

اٰیاتُہا ١٥ (٩١) سُوْرَةُ الشَّمْسِ مَكِّيَّةٌ رکوعُہا ١

بِسْمِ اللّٰهِ الرَّحْمٰنِ الرَّحِيْمِ ○

وَالشَّمْسِ وَضُحٰىهَا ﴿١﴾

وَالْقَمَرِ اِذَا تَلٰىهَا ﴿٢﴾

وَالنَّهَارِ اِذَا جَلّٰىهَا ﴿٣﴾

وَالَّيْلِ اِذَا يَغْشٰىهَا ﴿٤﴾

وَالسَّمَآءِ وَمَا بَنٰىهَا ﴿٥﴾

وَالْاَرْضِ وَمَا طَحٰىهَا ﴿٦﴾

وَنَفْسٍ وَّمَا سَوّٰىهَا ﴿٧﴾

فَاَلْهَمَهَا فُجُوْرَهَا وَتَقْوٰىهَا ﴿٨﴾

قَدْ اَفْلَحَ مَنْ زَكّٰىهَا ﴿٩﴾

وَقَدْ خَابَ مَنْ دَسّٰىهَا ﴿١٠﴾

كَذَّبَتْ ثَمُوْدُ بِطَغْوٰىهَآ ﴿١١﴾

اِذِ انْۢبَعَثَ اَشْقٰىهَا ﴿١٢﴾

فَقَالَ لَهُمْ رَسُوْلُ اللّٰهِ نَاقَةَ اللّٰهِ وَسُقْيٰهَا ﴿١٣﴾

فَكَذَّبُوْهُ فَعَقَرُوْهَا فَدَمْدَمَ عَلَيْهِمْ رَبُّهُمْ

بِذَنْۢبِهِمْ فَسَوّٰىهَا ﴿١٤﴾

ع ١٦ وَلَا يَخَافُ عُقْبٰهَا ﴿١٥﴾

Al-Leyl takes its name from a word in verse 1. A very early Meccan Sūrah.

THE NIGHT
Revealed at Mecca

اياتها ٢١ سورة اليل مكية ركوعها

In the name of Allah, the Beneficent, the Merciful.

بِسْمِ اللهِ الرَّحْمٰنِ الرَّحِيمِ

1. By the night enshrouding

وَالَّيْلِ اِذَا يَغْشٰى ۙ

2. And the day resplendent

وَالنَّهَارِ اِذَا تَجَلّٰى ۙ

3. And Him Who hath created male and female,

وَمَا خَلَقَ الذَّكَرَ وَالْاُنْثٰى ۙ

4. Lo! your effort is dispersed (toward divers ends).

اِنَّ سَعْيَكُمْ لَشَتّٰى ۙ

5. As for him who giveth and is dutiful (toward Allah)

فَاَمَّا مَنْ اَعْطٰى وَاتَّقٰى ۙ

6. And believeth in goodness;

وَصَدَّقَ بِالْحُسْنٰى ۙ

7. Surely We will ease his way unto the state of ease.

فَسَنُيَسِّرُهٗ لِلْيُسْرٰى ۙ

8. But as for him who hoardeth and deemeth himself independent,

وَاَمَّا مَنْۢ بَخِلَ وَاسْتَغْنٰى ۙ

9. And disbelieveth in goodness;

وَكَذَّبَ بِالْحُسْنٰى ۙ

10. Surely We will ease his way unto adversity.

فَسَنُيَسِّرُهٗ لِلْعُسْرٰى ۙ

11. His riches will not save him when he perisheth.

وَمَا يُغْنِيْ عَنْهُ مَالُهٗۤ اِذَا تَرَدّٰى ۙ

12. Lo! Ours it is (to give) the guidance

اِنَّ عَلَيْنَا لَلْهُدٰى ۙ

13. And lo! unto Us belong the latter portion and the former.

وَاِنَّ لَنَا لَلْاٰخِرَةَ وَالْاُوْلٰى ۙ

14. Therefor have I warned you of the flaming Fire

فَاَنْذَرْتُكُمْ نَارًا تَلَظّٰى ۙ

15. Which only the most wretched must endure,

لَا يَصْلٰىهَاۤ اِلَّا الْاَشْقَى ۙ

16. He who denieth and turneth away.

الَّذِيْ كَذَّبَ وَتَوَلّٰى ۙ

17. Far removed from it will be the righteous

وَسَيُجَنَّبُهَا الْاَتْقَى ۙ

18. Who giveth his wealth that he may grow (in goodness),

الَّذِيْ يُؤْتِيْ مَالَهٗ يَتَزَكّٰى ۙ

19. And none hath with him any favour for reward,

وَمَا لِاَحَدٍ عِنْدَهٗ مِنْ نِّعْمَةٍ تُجْزٰى ۙ

20. Except as seeking (to fulfil) the purpose of his Lord Most High.

اِلَّا ابْتِغَاۤءَ وَجْهِ رَبِّهِ الْاَعْلٰى ۙ

21. He verily will be content.

وَلَسَوْفَ يَرْضٰى ۞

Ad-Duhā, "The Morning Hours," takes its name from the first verse. There was an interval during which the Prophet received no revelation and the idolaters mocked him, saying: "Allah, of whom we used to hear so much, has forsaken poor Muhammad and now hates him." Then came this revelation. The Prophet had been a leading citizen of Mecca until he received his call. Now he was regarded as a madman. He was a man near fifty, and the prophecy in this Sūrah that "the latter portion would be better for him than the former" must have seemed absurd to those who heard it. Yet the latter portion of the Prophet's life, the last ten years, is the most wonderful record of success in human history.

An early Meccan Sūrah.

SŪRAH XCIV *Solace*

Al-Inshirāḥ, "Solace," takes its name from a word in verse 1, and also from its subject, which is relief from anxiety. It was probably revealed upon the same occasion as Sūrah XCIII; and, at a time when the Prophet was derided and shunned after having been respected and courted, must have struck the disbelievers as ridiculous. It refers to the inward assurance which the Prophet had received by revelation, and speaks of future events as accomplished, as is usual in the Koran, the revelation coming from a plane where time is not. Verse 4, speaking of his fame as exalted, must have seemed particularly absurd at that time of humiliation and persecution. But today, from every mosque in the world, the Prophet's name is cried, as that of the messenger of God, five times a day, and every Muslim prays for blessings on him when his name is mentioned.

An early Meccan Sūrah.

THE MORNING HOURS
Revealed at Mecca

اٰياتها (٩٣) سُورَةُ الضُّحٰى مَكِّيَّةٌ رُكُوعُها

In the name of Allah, the Beneficent, the Merciful.

بِسْمِ اللّٰهِ الرَّحْمٰنِ الرَّحِيْمِ

1. By the morning hours

وَالضُّحٰى ①

2. And by the night when it is stillest,

وَالَّيْلِ اِذَا سَجٰى ②

3. Thy Lord hath not forsaken thee nor doth He hate thee,

مَا وَدَّعَكَ رَبُّكَ وَمَا قَلٰى ③

4. And verily the latter portion will be better for thee than the former,

وَلَلْاٰخِرَةُ خَيْرٌ لَّكَ مِنَ الْاُوْلٰى ④

5. And verily thy Lord will give unto thee so that thou wilt be content.

وَلَسَوْفَ يُعْطِيْكَ رَبُّكَ فَتَرْضٰى ⑤

6. Did He not find thee an orphan and protect (thee)?

اَلَمْ يَجِدْكَ يَتِيْمًا فَاٰوٰى ⑥

7. Did He not find thee wandering and direct (thee)?

وَوَجَدَكَ ضَآلًّا فَهَدٰى ⑦

8. Did He not find thee destitute and enrich (thee)?

وَوَجَدَكَ عَآئِلًا فَاَغْنٰى ⑧

9. Therefor the orphan oppress not,

فَاَمَّا الْيَتِيْمَ فَلَا تَقْهَرْ ⑨

10. Therefor the beggar drive not away,

وَاَمَّا السَّآئِلَ فَلَا تَنْهَرْ ⑩

11. Therefor of the bounty of thy Lord be thy discourse.

وَاَمَّا بِنِعْمَةِ رَبِّكَ فَحَدِّثْ ⑪ ع

SŪRAH XCIV *Solace*

SOLACE
Revealed at Mecca

اٰياتها (٩٤) سُورَةُ اَلَمْ نَشْرَحْ مَكِّيَّةٌ رُكُوعُها

In the name of Allah, the Beneficent, the Merciful.

بِسْمِ اللّٰهِ الرَّحْمٰنِ الرَّحِيْمِ

1. Have We not caused thy bosom to dilate,

اَلَمْ نَشْرَحْ لَكَ صَدْرَكَ ①

2. And eased thee of the burden

وَوَضَعْنَا عَنْكَ وِزْرَكَ ②

3. Which weighed down thy back;

الَّذِيْٓ اَنْقَضَ ظَهْرَكَ ③

4. And exalted thy fame?

وَرَفَعْنَا لَكَ ذِكْرَكَ ④

5. But lo! with hardship goeth ease,

فَاِنَّ مَعَ الْعُسْرِ يُسْرًا ⑤

6. Lo! with hardship goeth ease;

اِنَّ مَعَ الْعُسْرِ يُسْرًا ⑥

7. So when thou art relieved, still toil

فَاِذَا فَرَغْتَ فَانْصَبْ ⑦

8. And strive to please thy Lord.

وَاِلٰى رَبِّكَ فَارْغَبْ ⑧ ع

At-Tīn, **"The Fig," takes its name from a word in verse 1. The sense is mystical, referring to man in relation to the revealed Law of God and His judgement.**

A very early Meccan Sūrah.

THE FIG

Revealed at Mecca

اٰياتها (٩٥) سُورَةُ التِّينِ مَكِّيَّةٌ رُكُوعُهَا

In the name of Allah, the Beneficent, the Merciful.

بِسْمِ اللّٰهِ الرَّحْمٰنِ الرَّحِيْمِ ○

1. By the fig and the olive,

وَالتِّيْنِ وَالزَّيْتُوْنِ ۙ ①

2. By Mount Sinai,

وَطُوْرِ سِيْنِيْنَ ۙ ②

3. And by this land made safe;

وَهٰذَا الْبَلَدِ الْاَمِيْنِ ۙ ③

4. Surely We created man of the best stature

لَقَدْ خَلَقْنَا الْاِنْسَانَ فِيْٓ اَحْسَنِ تَقْوِيْمٍ ④

5. Then We reduced him to the lowest of the low,

ثُمَّ رَدَدْنٰهُ اَسْفَلَ سٰفِلِيْنَ ۙ ⑤

6. Save those who believe and do good works, and theirs is a reward unfailing.

اِلَّا الَّذِيْنَ اٰمَنُوْا وَعَمِلُوا الصّٰلِحٰتِ فَلَهُمْ اَجْرٌ غَيْرُ مَمْنُوْنٍ ۭ ⑥

7. So who henceforth will give the lie to thee about the judgement?

فَمَا يُكَذِّبُكَ بَعْدُ بِالدِّيْنِ ۭ ⑦

8. Is not Allah the most conclusive of all judges?

اَلَيْسَ اللّٰهُ بِاَحْكَمِ الْحٰكِمِيْنَ ۧ ⑧

Al-'Alaq takes its name from a word in verse 2. Verses 1-5 are the words which the Prophet received in the vision at Ḥirā, therefore the first of the Koran to be revealed.

A very early Meccan Sūrah.

THE CLOT

Revealed at Mecca

اٰیَاتُهَا ١٩ (٩٦) سُوْرَةُ الْعَلَقِ مَكِّیَّةٌ رُكُوْعُهَا ١

In the name of Allah, the Beneficent, the Merciful.

بِسْمِ اللّٰهِ الرَّحْمٰنِ الرَّحِیْمِ ○

1. Read: In the name of thy Lora who createeth,

اِقْرَاْ بِاسْمِ رَبِّكَ الَّذِیْ خَلَقَ ۚ ﴿١﴾

2. Createth man from a clot.

خَلَقَ الْاِنْسَانَ مِنْ عَلَقٍ ۚ ﴿٢﴾

3. Read: And thy Lord is the Most Bounteous,

اِقْرَاْ وَرَبُّكَ الْاَكْرَمُ ۙ ﴿٣﴾

4. Who teacheth by the pen,

الَّذِیْ عَلَّمَ بِالْقَلَمِ ۙ ﴿٤﴾

5. Teacheth man that which he knew not.

عَلَّمَ الْاِنْسَانَ مَا لَمْ یَعْلَمْ ؕ ﴿٥﴾

6. Nay, but verily man is rebellious

كَلَّاۤ اِنَّ الْاِنْسَانَ لَیَطْغٰۤی ۙ ﴿٦﴾

7. That he thinketh himself independent!

اَنْ رَّاٰهُ اسْتَغْنٰی ؕ ﴿٧﴾

8. Lo! unto thy Lord is the return.

اِنَّ اِلٰی رَبِّكَ الرُّجْعٰی ؕ ﴿٨﴾

9. Hast thou seen him who dissuadeth

اَرَءَیْتَ الَّذِیْ یَنْهٰی ۙ ﴿٩﴾

10. A slave when he prayeth?

عَبْدًا اِذَا صَلّٰی ؕ ﴿١٠﴾

11. Hast thou seen if he (relieth) on the guidance (of Allah)

اَرَءَیْتَ اِنْ كَانَ عَلَی الْهُدٰۤی ۙ ﴿١١﴾

12. Or enjoineth piety?

اَوْ اَمَرَ بِالتَّقْوٰی ؕ ﴿١٢﴾

13. Hast thou seen if he denieth (Allah's guidance) and is froward?

اَرَءَیْتَ اِنْ كَذَّبَ وَتَوَلّٰی ؕ ﴿١٣﴾

14. Is he then unaware that Allah seeth?

اَلَمْ یَعْلَمْ بِاَنَّ اللّٰهَ یَرٰی ؕ ﴿١٤﴾

15. Nay, but if he cease not, We will seize him by the forelock—

كَلَّا لَئِنْ لَّمْ یَنْتَهِ ۙ لَنَسْفَعًا بِالنَّاصِیَةِ ۙ ﴿١٥﴾

16. The lying, sinful forelock—

نَاصِیَةٍ كَاذِبَةٍ خَاطِئَةٍ ۚ ﴿١٦﴾

17. Then let him call upon his henchmen!

فَلْیَدْعُ نَادِیَهٗ ۙ ﴿١٧﴾

18. We will call the guards of hell.

سَنَدْعُ الزَّبَانِیَةَ ۙ ﴿١٨﴾

19. Nay! Obey not thou him. But prostrate thyself, and draw near (unto Allah).

كَلَّا ؕ لَا تُطِعْهُ وَاسْجُدْ وَاقْتَرِبْ ۩ ﴿١٩﴾

Al-Qadr takes its name from a word in verse 1. It refers to the night (one of the last nights of Ramaḍān) on which the Prophet received his Call and the first verses of the Koran were revealed in the vision of Mt. Ḥirā. It is said to be the night on which God's decrees for the year are brought down to the earthly plane.

A very early Meccan Sūrah.

SŪRAH XCVIII *The Clear Proof*

Al-Beyyinah takes its name from a word in the first verse. There is no certainty as to the period of revelation. Many regard it as a late Meccan Sūrah. I follow the attribution in the *Musḥaf* which I have followed throughout.

The probable date of revelation is the year 1 A.H.

POWER

Revealed at Makkah

In the name of Allah, the beneficent, the merciful.

1. Lo! We revealed it on the Night of Power.

2. Ah, what will convey unto thee what the Night of Power is!

3. The Night of Power is better than a thousand months.

4. The angels and the spirit[1] descend therein, by the permission of their Lord, with all decrees.

5. (That night is) Peace until the rising of the dawn.

SURAH XCVIII *THE CLEAR PROOF*

REVEALED AT AL-MADINAH

In the name of Allah, the Beneficent, the Merciful.

1. Those who disbelieve among the people of the Scripture and the idolaters could not have left off (erring) till the clear proof came unto them.

2. A messenger from Allah, reading purified pages.

3. Containing correct scriptures.

4. Nor were the People of the Scripture divided until after the clear proof came unto them.

5. And they are ordained naught else than to serve Allah, keeping religion pure for Him, as men by nature upright, and to establish worship, and to pay the poor due. That is true religion.

6. Lo! those who disbelieve, among the People of the Scripture and the Idolaters, will abide in fire of hell. They are the worst of created beings.

7. (And) Lo! those who believe and do good works are the best of created beings.

8. Their reward is with their Lord: Gardens of Eden underneath which rivers flow. Wherein they dwell for ever. Allah hath pleasure in them and they have pleasure in Him. This is (in store) for him who feareth his Lord.

أياتها (٩٧) سورة القدر مكية ركوعها

بسم الله الرحمن الرحيم

إنا أنزلنه في ليلة القدر ﴿١﴾

وما أدرىك ما ليلة القدر ﴿٢﴾

ليلة القدر خير من ألف شهر ﴿٣﴾

تنزل الملئكة والروح فيها بإذن ربهم من كل أمر ﴿٤﴾

سلم هي حتى مطلع الفجر ﴿٥﴾ ع ٢٢

أياتها (٩٨) سورة البينة مدنية ركوعها

بسم الله الرحمن الرحيم

لم يكن الذين كفروا من أهل الكتب و
المشركين منفكين حتى تأتيهم البينة ﴿١﴾
رسول من الله يتلوا صحفا مطهرة ﴿٢﴾
فيها كتب قيمة ﴿٣﴾
وما تفرق الذين أوتوا الكتب إلا من بعد ما جاءتهم البينة ﴿٤﴾
وما أمروا إلا ليعبدوا الله مخلصين له الدين حنفاء
ويقيموا الصلوة ويؤتوا الزكوة وذلك دين القيمة ﴿٥﴾
إن الذين كفروا من أهل الكتب والمشركين في نار
جهنم خلدين فيها أولئك هم شر البرية ﴿٦﴾
إن الذين آمنوا وعملوا الصلحت أولئك هم خير البرية ﴿٧﴾
جزاؤهم عند ربهم جنت عدن تجري من تحتها
الأنهر خلدين فيها أبدا رضي الله عنهم و
رضوا عنه ذلك لمن خشي ربه ﴿٨﴾ ع ٢٣

1. i.e., Gabriel or, as some commentators think, a general term for angels of the highest rank.

Az-Zilzāl takes its name from a word in verse 1. A very early Meccan Sūrah.

SŪRAH C The Coursers

Al-'Aādiyāt takes its name from a word in the first verse. A very early Meccan Sūrah.

THE EARTHQUAKE
Revealed at Mecca

In the name of Allah, the Beneficent, the Merciful.

1. When Earth is shaken with her (final) earthquake

2. And Earth yieldeth up her burdens,

3. And man saith: What aileth her?

4. That day she will relate her chronicles,

5. Because thy Lord inspireth her.

6. That day mankind will issue forth in scattered groups to be shown their deeds.

7. And whoso doth good an atom's weight will see it then,

8. And whoso doth ill an atom's weight will see it then.

اٰیاتہا ٨ (٩٩) سُوْرَةُ الزَّلْزَالِ مَدَنِيَّةٌ رُكُوعُهَا ١

بِسْمِ اللّٰهِ الرَّحْمٰنِ الرَّحِيْمِ ۝

اِذَا زُلْزِلَتِ الْاَرْضُ زِلْزَالَهَا ۝١

وَاَخْرَجَتِ الْاَرْضُ اَثْقَالَهَا ۝٢

وَقَالَ الْاِنْسَانُ مَا لَهَا ۝٣

يَوْمَئِذٍ تُحَدِّثُ اَخْبَارَهَا ۝٤

بِاَنَّ رَبَّكَ اَوْحٰى لَهَا ۝٥

يَوْمَئِذٍ يَّصْدُرُ النَّاسُ اَشْتَاتًا ۙ لِّيُرَوْا اَعْمَالَهُمْ ۝٦

فَمَنْ يَّعْمَلْ مِثْقَالَ ذَرَّةٍ خَيْرًا يَّرَهٗ ۝٧

وَمَنْ يَّعْمَلْ مِثْقَالَ ذَرَّةٍ شَرًّا يَّرَهٗ ۝٨

SŪRAH C
THE COURSERS
Revealed at Mecca

In the name of Allah, the Beneficent, the Merciful.

1. By the snorting coursers.

2. Striking sparks of fire

3. And scouring to the raid at dawn,

4. Then, therewith, with their trail of dust,

5. Cleaving, as one, the centre (of the foe),[1]

6. Lo! man is an ingrate unto his Lord

7. And lo! he is a witness unto that:

8. And lo! in the love of wealth he is violent.

9. Knoweth he not that, when the contents of the graves are poured forth

10. And the secrets of the breasts are made known.

11. On that day will their Lord be perfectly informed concerning them.

اٰیاتہا ١١ (١٠٠) سُوْرَةُ الْعٰدِيٰتِ مَكِّيَّةٌ رُكُوعُهَا ١

بِسْمِ اللّٰهِ الرَّحْمٰنِ الرَّحِيْمِ ۝

وَالْعٰدِيٰتِ ضَبْحًا ۝١

فَالْمُوْرِيٰتِ قَدْحًا ۝٢

فَالْمُغِيْرٰتِ صُبْحًا ۝٣

فَاَثَرْنَ بِهٖ نَقْعًا ۝٤

فَوَسَطْنَ بِهٖ جَمْعًا ۝٥

اِنَّ الْاِنْسَانَ لِرَبِّهٖ لَكَنُوْدٌ ۝٦

وَاِنَّهٗ عَلٰى ذٰلِكَ لَشَهِيْدٌ ۝٧

وَاِنَّهٗ لِحُبِّ الْخَيْرِ لَشَدِيْدٌ ۝٨

اَفَلَا يَعْلَمُ اِذَا بُعْثِرَ مَا فِى الْقُبُوْرِ ۝٩

وَحُصِّلَ مَا فِى الصُّدُوْرِ ۝١٠

اِنَّ رَبَّهُمْ بِهِمْ يَوْمَئِذٍ لَّخَبِيْرٌ ۝١١

1. The meaning of the first five verses is by no means clear. The above is a probable rendering.

Al-Qāri'ah takes its name from a word in verse 1 recurring in the next two verses.

SŪRAH CII *Rivarly in Worldly Increase*

At-Takāthur takes its name from a word in the first verse. A very early Meccan Sūrah.

THE CALAMITY
Revealed at Mecca

In the name of Allah, the Beneficent, the Merciful.

1. The Calamity!

2. What is the Calamity?

3. Ah, what will convey unto thee what the Calamity is!

4. A day wherein mankind will be as thickly-scattered moths

5. And the mountains will become as carded wool.

6. Then, as for him whose scales are heavy (with good works),

7. He will live a pleasant life.

8. But as for him whose scales are light,

9. The Bereft and Hungry One will be his mother.

10. Ah, what will convey unto thee what she is!

11. Raging fire,

SŪRAH CII
RIVALRY IN WORLDLY INCREASE
Revealed at Mecca

In the name of Allah, the Beneficent, the Merciful.

1. Rivalry in worldly increase distracteth you

2. Until ye come to the graves.

3. Nay, but ye will come to know!

4. Nay, but ye will come to know!

5. Nay, would that ye knew (now) with a sure knowledge!

6. For ye will behold hell-fire.

7. Aye, ye will behold it with sure vision.

8. Then, on that day, ye will be asked concerning pleasure.

آياتها ١١ (١٠١) سُورَةُ الْقَارِعَةِ مَكِّيَّةٌ رُكُوعُهَا ١

بِسْمِ اللّٰهِ الرَّحْمٰنِ الرَّحِيْمِ ○

اَلْقَارِعَةُ ۙ ①

مَا الْقَارِعَةُ ۚ ②

وَمَآ اَدْرٰىكَ مَا الْقَارِعَةُ ؕ ③

يَوْمَ يَكُوْنُ النَّاسُ كَالْفَرَاشِ الْمَبْثُوْثِ ۙ ④

وَتَكُوْنُ الْجِبَالُ كَالْعِهْنِ الْمَنْفُوْشِ ؕ ⑤

فَاَمَّا مَنْ ثَقُلَتْ مَوَازِيْنُهٗ ۙ ⑥

فَهُوَ فِيْ عِيْشَةٍ رَّاضِيَةٍ ؕ ⑦

وَاَمَّا مَنْ خَفَّتْ مَوَازِيْنُهٗ ۙ ⑧

فَاُمُّهٗ هَاوِيَةٌ ؕ ⑨

وَمَآ اَدْرٰىكَ مَا هِيَهْ ؕ ⑩

نَارٌ حَامِيَةٌ ۠ ⑪ ع

آياتها ٨ (١٠٢) سُوْرَةُ التَّكَاثُرِ مَكِّيَّةٌ رُكُوعُهَا ١

بِسْمِ اللّٰهِ الرَّحْمٰنِ الرَّحِيْمِ ○

اَلْهٰىكُمُ التَّكَاثُرُ ۙ ①

حَتّٰى زُرْتُمُ الْمَقَابِرَ ؕ ②

كَلَّا سَوْفَ تَعْلَمُوْنَ ۙ ③

ثُمَّ كَلَّا سَوْفَ تَعْلَمُوْنَ ؕ ④

كَلَّا لَوْ تَعْلَمُوْنَ عِلْمَ الْيَقِيْنِ ؕ ⑤

لَتَرَوُنَّ الْجَحِيْمَ ۙ ⑥

ثُمَّ لَتَرَوُنَّهَا عَيْنَ الْيَقِيْنِ ۙ ⑦

ثُمَّ لَتُسْـَٔلُنَّ يَوْمَىِٕذٍ عَنِ النَّعِيْمِ ۠ ⑧ ع

Al-'Asr takes its name from a word in verse 1.

A very early Meccan Sūrah.

SŪRAH CIV *The Traducers*

Al-Humazah takes its name from a word in verse 1. The idolaters waylaid all newcomers to Mecca and warned them against the Prophet, in order to prevent their listening to his preaching.

An early Meccan Sūrah.

THE DECLINING DAY

Revealed at Mecca

ايَاتُهَا ٣ (١٠٣) سُوْرَةُ الْعَصْرِ مَكِّيَّةٌ رُكُوْعُهَا ١

In the name of Allah, the Beneficent, the Merciful.

بِسْمِ اللّٰهِ الرَّحْمٰنِ الرَّحِيْمِ

1. By the declining day,

وَالْعَصْرِ ۙ﴿١﴾

2. Lo! man is in a state of loss,

اِنَّ الْاِنْسَانَ لَفِيْ خُسْرٍ ۙ﴿٢﴾

3. Save those who believe and do good works, and exhort one another to truth exhort one another to endurance.

اِلَّا الَّذِيْنَ اٰمَنُوْا وَعَمِلُوا الصّٰلِحٰتِ وَتَوَاصَوْا

بِالْحَقِّ ۙ وَتَوَاصَوْا بِالصَّبْرِ ﴿٣﴾

SŪRAH CIV

THE TRADUCER

Revealed at Mecca

ايَاتُهَا ٩ (١٠٤) سُوْرَةُ الْهُمَزَةِ مَكِّيَّةٌ رُكُوْعُهَا ١

In the name of Allah, the Beneficent the Merciful.

بِسْمِ اللّٰهِ الرَّحْمٰنِ الرَّحِيْمِ

1. Woe unto every slandering traducer,

وَيْلٌ لِّكُلِّ هُمَزَةٍ لُّمَزَةِ ۙ﴿١﴾

2. Who hath gathered wealth (of this world) and arranged it.

الَّذِيْ جَمَعَ مَالًا وَّعَدَّدَهٗ ۙ﴿٢﴾

3. He thinketh that his wealth will render him immortal.

يَحْسَبُ اَنَّ مَالَهٗٓ اَخْلَدَهٗ ۚ﴿٣﴾

4. Nay, but verily he will be flung to the Consuming One,

كَلَّا لَيُنْۢبَذَنَّ فِي الْحُطَمَةِ ۖ﴿٤﴾

5. Ah, what will convey unto thee what the Consuming One is!

وَمَآ اَدْرٰىكَ مَا الْحُطَمَةُ ۗ﴿٥﴾

6. (It is) the fire of Allah, kindled,

نَارُ اللّٰهِ الْمُوْقَدَةُ ۙ﴿٦﴾

7. Which leapeth up over the hearts (of men)

الَّتِيْ تَطَّلِعُ عَلَى الْاَفْـِٕدَةِ ۗ﴿٧﴾

8. Lo! it is closed in on them

اِنَّهَا عَلَيْهِمْ مُّؤْصَدَةٌ ۙ﴿٨﴾

9. In outstreched columns.

فِيْ عَمَدٍ مُّمَدَّدَةٍ ﴿٩﴾

Al-Fīl, "The Elephant," takes its name from a word in the first verse. The allusion is to the campaign of Abraha, the Abyssinian ruler of Al-Yaman, against Mecca, with the purpose of destroying the Ka'bah in the year of the Prophet's birth. He had with him an elephant which much impressed the Arabs. Tradition says that the elephant refused to advance on the last stage of the march, and that swarms of flying creatures pelted the Abyssinians with stones. Another tradition says that they retired in disorder owing to an outbreak of smallpox in the camp. At the time when this Sūrah was revealed, many men in Mecca must have known what happened. Dr. Krenkow, a sound Arabic scholar, is of opinion that the flying creatures may well have been swarms of insects carrying infection. In any case the Ka'bah was saved from destruction after its defenders had despaired.

A very early Meccan Sūrah.

SŪRAH CVI *"Winter" or "Qureysh"*

Ash-Shitā is so called from a word occurring in verse 2. It is also often called *Qureysh*. A very early Meccan Sūrah.

SŪRAH CVII *Small Kindnesses*

Al Ma'ūn takes its name from a word in the last verse.

An early Meccan revelation.

THE ELEPHANT

Revealed at Mecca

In the name of Allah, the Beneficent the Merciful.

1. Hast thou not seen how thy Lord dealt with the owners of the Elephant?
2. Did He not bring their stratagem to naught,
3. And send against them swarms of flying creatures,
4. Which pelted them with stones of baked clay,
5. And made them like green crops devoured (by cattle)?

آياتها ٥ (١٠٥) سورة الفيل مكية ركوعها ١

بسم الله الرحمن الرحيم

ألم تر كيف فعل ربك بأصحاب الفيل ١

ألم يجعل كيدهم في تضليل ٢

وأرسل عليهم طيرا أبابيل ٣

ترميهم بحجارة من سجيل ٤

فجعلهم كعصف مأكول ٥

SŪRAH CVI

"WINTER" OR "QUREYSH"

Revealed at Mecca

In the name of Allah, the Beneficent, the Merciful.

1. For the taming[1] of Qureysh
2. For their taming (We cause) the caravans to set forth in winter and summer.
3. So let them worship the Lord of this House,
4. Who hath fed them against hunger
5. And hath made them safe from fear.

آياتها ٤ (١٠٦) سورة قريش مكية ركوعها ١

بسم الله الرحمن الرحيم

لإيلاف قريش ١

إيلافهم رحلة الشتاء والصيف ٢

فليعبدوا رب هذا البيت ٣

الذي أطعمهم من جوع وآمنهم من خوف ٤

SŪRAH CVII

SMALL KINDNESSES

Revealed at Mecca

In the name of Allah, the Beneficent, the Merciful.

1. Hast thou observed him who belieth religion?
2. That is he who repelleth the orphan,
3. And urgeth not the feeding of the needy.
4. Ah, woe unto worshippers
5. Who are heedless of their prayer;
6. Who would be seen (at worship)
7. Yet refuse small kindnesses!

آياتها ٧ (١٠٧) سورة الماعون مكية ركوعها ١

بسم الله الرحمن الرحيم

أرأيت الذي يكذب بالدين ١

فذلك الذي يدع اليتيم ٢

ولا يحض على طعام المسكين ٣

فويل للمصلين ٤

الذين هم عن صلاتهم ساهون ٥

الذين هم يراءون ٦

ويمنعون الماعون ٧

1. *i.e.* "*civilising*"

Al-Kauthar takes its name from a word in the first verse. The disbelievers used to taunt the Prophet with the fact that he had no son, and therefore none to uphold his religion after him.

SŪRAH CIX *The Disbelievers*

Al-Kāfirūn takes its name from a word in verse 1. It was revealed at a time when the idolaters had asked the Prophet to compromise in matters of religion.

SŪRAH CX *Succour*

An-Nasr takes its name from a word in the first verse. It is one of the very last revelations, having come to the Prophet only a few weeks before his death. Though ascribed always to Al-Madînah, tradition says that it was actually revealed at Mecca during the days the Prophet spent there when he made his farewell pilgrimage. It is described in Ibn Hishām and elsewhere as the first announcement that the Prophet received of his approaching death.

The date of revelation is the tenth year of the Hijrah.

ABUNDANCE

Revealed at Mecca

اٰياتها ٣ (١٠٨) سُوْرَةُ الْكَوْثَرِ مَكِّيَّةٌ رُكُوعُها ١

In the name of Allah, the Beneficent, the Merciful.

بِسْمِ اللّٰهِ الرَّحْمٰنِ الرَّحِيْمِ ○

1. Lo! We have given thee Abundance;

اِنَّآ اَعْطَيْنٰكَ الْكَوْثَرَ ۝١

2. So pray unto thy Lord, and sacrifice.

فَصَلِّ لِرَبِّكَ وَانْحَرْ ۝٢

3. Lo! It is thy insulter (and not thou) who is without posterity.

اِنَّ شَانِئَكَ هُوَ الْاَبْتَرُ ۝٣ ع

SŪRAH CIX

THE DISBELIEVERS

Revealed at Mecca

اٰياتها ٦ (١٠٩) سُوْرَةُ الْكٰفِرُوْنَ مَكِّيَّةٌ رُكُوعُها ١

In the name of Allah, the Beneficent, the Merciful.

بِسْمِ اللّٰهِ الرَّحْمٰنِ الرَّحِيْمِ ○

1. Say: O disbelievers!

قُلْ يٰۤاَيُّهَا الْكٰفِرُوْنَ ۝١

2. I worship not that which ye worship;

لَآ اَعْبُدُ مَا تَعْبُدُوْنَ ۝٢

3. Nor worship ye that which I worship.

وَلَآ اَنْتُمْ عٰبِدُوْنَ مَآ اَعْبُدُ ۝٣

4. And I shall not worship that which ye worship.

وَلَآ اَنَا عَابِدٌ مَّا عَبَدْتُّمْ ۝٤

5. Nor will ye worship that which I worship.

وَلَآ اَنْتُمْ عٰبِدُوْنَ مَآ اَعْبُدُ ۝٥

6. Unto you your religion, and unto me my religion.

لَكُمْ دِيْنُكُمْ وَلِيَ دِيْنِ ۝٦ ع

SŪRAH CX

SUCCOUR

Revealed at Al-Madinah

اٰياتها ٣ (١١٠) سُوْرَةُ النَّصْرِ مَدَنِيَّةٌ رُكُوعُها ١

In the name of Allah, the Beneficent, the Merciful.

بِسْمِ اللّٰهِ الرَّحْمٰنِ الرَّحِيْمِ ○

1. When Allah's succour and the triumph cometh

اِذَا جَآءَ نَصْرُ اللّٰهِ وَالْفَتْحُ ۝١

2. And thou seest mankind entering the religion of Allah in troops,

وَرَاَيْتَ النَّاسَ يَدْخُلُوْنَ فِيْ دِيْنِ اللّٰهِ اَفْوَاجًا ۝٢

3. Then hymn the praises of thy Lord, and seek forgiveness of Him. Lo! He is ever ready to show mercy.

فَسَبِّحْ بِحَمْدِ رَبِّكَ وَاسْتَغْفِرْهُ ۗ اِنَّهٗ كَانَ تَوَّابًا ۝٣ ع

Al-Masad takes its name from a word (to the Arabs a very homely word) in the last verse. It is the only passage in the whole Koran where an opponent of the Prophet is denounced by name. Abu Lahab (The Father of Flame), whose real name was Abdul 'Uzzā, was an uncle of the Prophet and was the only member of his own clan who bitterly opposed the Prophet. He made it his business to torment the Prophet, and his wife took a pleasure in carrying thorn bushes and strewing them in the sand where she knew that the Prophet was sure to walk barefooted.

An early Meccan revelation.

SŪRAH CXII *The Unity*

At-Tauḥid, "The Unity," takes its name from its subject. It has been called the essence of the Koran, of which it is really the last Sūrah. Some authorities ascribe this Sūrah to the Madînah period, and think that it was revealed in answer to a question of some Jewish doctors concerning the nature of God.

It is generally held to be an early Meccan Sūrah.

SŪRAH CXIII *The Daybreak*

Al-Falaq, "The Daybreak", takes its name from a word in the first verse. This and the following Sūrah are prayers for protection, this one being for protection from fears proceeding from the unknown. The two Sūrahs are known as *Al-Mu'awwadhateyn*, the two cries for refuge and protection.

An early Meccan Sūrah.

PALM FIBRE

Revealed at Mecca

In the name of Allah, the Beneficent, the Merciful.

1. The power of Abū Lahab will perish, and he will perish.

2. His wealth and gains will not exempt him.

3. He will be plunged in flaming fire,

4. And his wife, the wood-carrier,

5. Will have upon her neck a halter of palm-fibre.

اٰيَاتُهَا (١١١) سُوْرَةُ اللَّهَبِ مَكِّيَّةٌ رُكُوْعُهَا

بِسْمِ اللّٰهِ الرَّحْمٰنِ الرَّحِيْمِ ○

تَبَّتْ يَدَآ اَبِيْ لَهَبٍ وَّتَبَّ ①

مَآ اَغْنٰى عَنْهُ مَالُهٗ وَمَا كَسَبَ ②

سَيَصْلٰى نَارًا ذَاتَ لَهَبٍ ③

وَّامْرَاَتُهٗ ۭ حَمَّالَةَ الْحَطَبِ ④

فِيْ جِيْدِهَا حَبْلٌ مِّنْ مَّسَدٍ ⑤ ع ٢٦

SŪRAH CXII

THE UNITY

Revealed at Mecca

In the name of Allah, the Beneficent, the Merciful.

1. Say: He is Allah, the One!

2. Allah, the eternally Besought of all!

3. He begetteth not nor was begotten.

4. And there is none comparable unto Him.

اٰيَاتُهَا (١١٢) سُوْرَةُ الْاِخْلَاصِ مَكِّيَّةٌ رُكُوْعُهَا

بِسْمِ اللّٰهِ الرَّحْمٰنِ الرَّحِيْمِ ○

قُلْ هُوَ اللّٰهُ اَحَدٌ ①

اَللّٰهُ الصَّمَدُ ②

لَمْ يَلِدْ ڏ وَلَمْ يُوْلَدْ ③

وَلَمْ يَكُنْ لَّهٗ كُفُوًا اَحَدٌ ④ ع ٢٧

SŪRAH CXII

THE DAYBREAK

Revealed at Mecca

In the name of Allah, the Beneficent, the Merciful.

1. Say: I seek refuge in the Lord of Daybreak

2. From the evil of that which He created;

3. From the evil of the darkness when it is intense,

4. And from the evil of malignant witchcraft,[1]

5. And from the evil of the envier when he envieth.

اٰيَاتُهَا (١١٣) سُوْرَةُ الْفَلَقِ مَكِّيَّةٌ رُكُوْعُهَا

بِسْمِ اللّٰهِ الرَّحْمٰنِ الرَّحِيْمِ ○

قُلْ اَعُوْذُ بِرَبِّ الْفَلَقِ ①

مِنْ شَرِّ مَا خَلَقَ ②

وَمِنْ شَرِّ غَاسِقٍ اِذَا وَقَبَ ③

وَمِنْ شَرِّ النَّفّٰثٰتِ فِي الْعُقَدِ ④

وَمِنْ شَرِّ حَاسِدٍ اِذَا حَسَدَ ⑤ ع ٢٨

1. Lit. "from the evil of blowers (feminine) upon knots," it having been a common form of witchcraft in Arabia for women to tie knots in a cord and blow upon them with an imprecation.

An-Nās, the second of the two cries for refuge and protection, takes its name from a recurring word which marks the rhythm in the Arabic. In this case protection is sought especially from the evil in a man's own-heart and in the hearts of other men.

An early Meccan revelation.

MANKIND

Revealed at Mecca

In the name of Allah, the Beneficent, the Merciful.

1. Say: I seek refuge in the Lord of mankind,

2. The King of mankind,

3. The God of mankind,

4. From the evil of the sneaking whisperer,

5. Who whispereth in the hearts of mankind,

6. Of the jinn and of mankind.

اٰيَاتُهَا ٦ (١١٤) سُوْرَةُ النَّاسِ مَكِّيَّةٌ رُكُوْعُهَا ١

بِسْمِ اللّٰهِ الرَّحْمٰنِ الرَّحِيْمِ ○

قُلْ اَعُوْذُ بِرَبِّ النَّاسِ ۙ ﴿١﴾

مَلِكِ النَّاسِ ۙ ﴿٢﴾

اِلٰهِ النَّاسِ ۙ ﴿٣﴾

مِنْ شَرِّ الْوَسْوَاسِ ۙ الْخَنَّاسِ ۪ۙ ﴿٤﴾

الَّذِيْ يُوَسْوِسُ فِيْ صُدُوْرِ النَّاسِ ۙ ﴿٥﴾

ع ٢٩ مِنَ الْجِنَّةِ وَالنَّاسِ ﴿٦﴾

PRAYER

To be used after reading the Holy Qur'an

O Allah! change my fear in my grave into love! O Allah! have mercy on me in the name of the Great Qur'an; and make it for me a Guide and Light and Guidance and Mercy; O Allah! Make me remember what of it I have forgotten; make me know of it that which I have become ignorant of; and make me recite it in the hours of the night and the day; and make it an argument for me O Thou Sustainer of (all) the worlds! Amen!

دُعَاءُ خَتْمِ الْقُرْاٰنِ

اَللّٰهُمَّ اٰنِسْ وَحْشَتِيْ فِيْ قَبْرِيْ اَللّٰهُمَّ ارْحَمْنِيْ
بِالْقُرْاٰنِ الْعَظِيْمِ وَاجْعَلْهُ لِيْ اِمَامًا وَّنُوْرًا وَّ
هُدًى وَّرَحْمَةً اَللّٰهُمَّ ذَكِّرْنِيْ مِنْهُ مَا نَسِيْتُ
وَعَلِّمْنِيْ مِنْهُ مَا جَهِلْتُ وَارْزُقْنِيْ تِلَاوَتَهٗ اٰنَاءَ
الَّيْلِ وَاٰنَاءَ النَّهَارِ وَاجْعَلْهُ لِيْ حُجَّةً يَّا
رَبَّ الْعٰلَمِيْنَ

Muhammad the Prophet of Islam ISBN 81-7101-000-8 PP 120

Hazrat MOHAMMAD

The Prophet of Islam

(PBUH)

By: Prof. FAZL AHMAD

A biographical account of the pious life of the Holy Prophet, which narrates in simple style the grand saga of the spiritual and social revolution brought about by the divine mission the Last postle of Allah was sent with. One finds in these pages an attempt to unravel the mystery of what made the uncultured namadic tribes of Arabia to be tansformed into the architects of the most powerful civilisations of the world. The book is also best suited for the Non-Muslims to have a correct understanding of all that the Benefactor of Humanity stood for.

The Noble Qur'an (Tafseer-e-Usmani)

ISBN 81-7101-140-3 (VOL. I) ISBN 81-7101-141-1 (VOL. II)
ISBN 81-7101-142-X (VOL. III) ISBN 81-7101-143-8 (Set)

The Urdu translation of the Nobel Quran which forms the base of this English Translation and commentary was undertaken by the great Muslim Scholar popularly known as Shaikh-ul-Hind Maulana Mahmood-ul-Hassan. He completed the transalation of Arabic verses and also wrote commentary for the first 3 Parts (Fatiha, Baqara & Aal-e Imran).

The commentary of the rest of the Noble Quran was written by Sheikh-ul-Islam Allama Shabbir Ahmed Usmani, by whose name base of this commentry in urdu language is known.

Now this commentary alongwith Arabic Text & its English Translation is completed in 3 Volumes.

Eli Franco, Isabelle Ratié (Eds.)

Around Abhinavagupta

Around Abhinavagupta

Aspects of the Intellectual History of Kashmir from the Ninth to the Eleventh Century

edited by

Eli Franco and Isabelle Ratié

LIT

Front cover: Annotated manuscript of Abhinavagupta's *Īśvarapratyabhijñāvimarśinī*, © SOAS Library, London.

Back cover: Goddess (possibly Śāradā), Kashmir, late 9th century, © Metropolitan Museum of Art, New York (www.metmuseum.org).

Bibliographic information published by the Deutsche Nationalbibliothek
The Deutsche Nationalbibliothek lists this publication in the Deutsche Nationalbibliografie; detailed bibliographic data are available on the Internet at http://dnb.d-nb.de.

ISBN 978-3-643-90697-7

Verlagskontakt:
Fresnostr. 2 D-48159 Münster
Tel. +49 (0) 2 51-62 03 20
E-Mail: lit@lit-verlag.de http://www.lit-verlag.de

Auslieferung:

Deutschland: LIT Verlag Fresnostr. 2, D-48159 Münster
Tel. +49 (0) 2 51-620 32 22, E-Mail: vertrieb@lit-verlag.de

E-Books sind erhältlich unter www.litwebshop.de

Contents

Introduction

ELI FRANCO AND ISABELLE RATIÉ

Abhinavagupta (fl. ca. 975-1025) is arguably the most famous figure among Kashmirian medieval intellectuals, and rightly so: the length, number, diversity and refinement of his works deserve to be qualified as exceptional. The crucial importance of his contributions to Indian aesthetics – which include a treatise on histrionics[1] and another on poetics[2] – has long been acknowledged, but he has also authored, among many theological works, a huge summa on Śaiva rituals and metaphysics[3] that constitutes an unparalleled source for the history of Śaiva religions, as well as two particularly brilliant philosophical works[4] expounding one of the most complex, subtle and original philosophical systems ever produced in India, the Pratyabhijñā ("Recognition") system of Utpaladeva (fl. ca. 925-975).

Some of the contributions to the present volume specifically deal with one or several of Abhinavagupta's works;[5] yet this book is not meant as a collection of studies devoted to the great Śaiva polymath. For however exceptional Abhinavagupta's works may be, they are grounded in a specific historical, social, artistic, religious and philosophical context, and it is this context that we had set out to explore when, in June 2013, we held at the University of Leipzig an international conference entitled *Around Abhinavagupta. Aspects of the Intellectual History of Kashmir from the 9th to the 11th Century*. Our ambition was to highlight the intellectual background against which Abhinavagupta's figure has emerged – a background no less exceptional than Abhinavagupta himself. We

---

1 The *Abhinavabhāratī*, a commentary on the *Nāṭyaśāstra* attributed to Bharata.

2 The *Dhvanyālokalocana*, a commentary on Ānandavardhana's *Dhvanyāloka*.

3 The *Tantrāloka*.

4 The *Īśvarapratyabhijñāvimarśinī* and *Īśvarapratyabhijñāvivṛtivimarśinī*.

5 See in particular those by L. BANSAT-BOUDON, E. GANSER, A. GRAHELI, L. MCCREA, D. SHULMAN and J. TÖRZSÖK.

were hoping to show how the works of the great Śaiva author, far from being an isolated phenomenon, can be seen as an accomplished expression of a unique intellectual milieu, that of Kashmir in the 9th, 10th and 11th centuries. The present volume gathers many revised versions of the presentations given during the conference[6] as well as a few additional articles.[7]

[6] The conference included the following presentations. 08/06/2013: M. WITZEL, "Kashmiri Brahmins under the Karkota, Utpala and Lohara Dynasties, 625-1101 CE" (9^{30}-10^{15}); L. BANSAT-BOUDON, "The World on Show, or Sensibility in Disguise: Philosophical and Aesthetic Issues in a Stanza by Abhinavagupta (*Tantrāloka* I 332, *Locana* ad I 13)" (10^{15}-11^{00}); R. TORELLA, "A Vaiṣṇava Paramādvaita in Tenth-Century Kashmir? Vāmanadatta and his *Saṃvitprakāśa*" (11^{30}-12^{15}); J. NEMEC, "*Amūrtatva* and Materiality in Pratyabhijñā Philosophy" (12^{15}-13^{00}); M. KAUL, "Can a Reflected Image Exist Separately Outside the Mirror? An Exploration into Abhinavagupta's Theory of Reflection" (15^{00}-15^{45}); S. VASUDEVA, "*Lakṣaṇam aparyālocitābhidhānam*: The Dispute Between Śobhākara and Ruyyaka" (15^{45}-16^{30}); D. CUNEO, "The Culmination of 'Kashmirian' Sanskrit Aesthetics: Jayaratha's *Vimarśinī* on Ruyyaka's *Alaṃkārasarvasva*" (17^{00}-17^{45}). 09/06/2013: D. SHULMAN, "Ānandavardhana and Abhinavagupta on the Limits of *Rasadhvani*: A Reading of DhvĀ 3.43" (09^{30}-10^{15}, in absentia); Y. BRONNER, "Udbhaṭa and the Dawn of Kashmiri Poetics" (10^{15}-11^{00}); J. TÖRZSÖK, "Theatre, Acting and the Image of the Actor in Abhinavagupta's Tantric Sources" (11^{30}-12^{15}); E. GANSER, "Elements of Ritual Speculation in the *Abhinavabhāratī*" (12^{15}-13^{00}); L. MCCREA, "Abhinavagupta as an Intellectual Historian of Buddhism" (15^{00}-15^{45}); V. ELTSCHINGER, "Whose Insight did Śaṅkaranandana Provide with Adornment? More light on the *Prajñālaṅkāra*" (15^{45}-16^{30}). 10/06/2013: A. GRAHELI, "Jayanta and Abhinavagupta on the Contextual Principle of *Tātparya*" (09^{30}-10^{15}); S. MORIYAMA, "Utpaladeva and Bhāsarvajña: A Comparison Between their Refutations of the Sāṃkhya Theory of Causation and Soteriology" (10^{15}-11^{00}); E. FRANCO, "Why Isn't Comparison a Means of Knowledge? Bhāsarvajña on *Upamāna*" (11^{30}-12^{15}); V. VERGIANI, "Canonising the *Vākyapadīya*: The Sense and Purpose of Helārāja's Commentarial Project" (12^{15}-13^{00}); C. YOSHIMIZU, "The Transmission of the *Mūlamadhyamakakārikā* and the *Prasannapadā* to Tibet from Kashmir" (15^{00}-15^{45}); O. ALMOGI, "Tantric Scriptures in the *rNying ma rgyud 'bum* Believed to Have Been Transmitted by Kashmirian Paṇḍitas: A Preminary Survey" (15^{45}-16^{30}); D. WANGCHUK, "The *Nine-Dimensional Magical Mirror*: A Philosophical Work Ascribed to the Kashmirian Paṇḍita Vimalamitra" (17^{00}-17^{45}).

[7] These include the contributions by Y. MUROYA and I. RATIÉ.

ARTS AND AESTHETICS, GRAMMAR, RELIGION AND PHILOSOPHY, HISTORIOGRAPHY IN ABHINAVAGUPTA'S KASHMIR

Of course the following pages are not the first to tackle the cultural history of Kashmir, which has long attracted scholarly attention, and there is hardly any need to say that this volume is in countless ways indebted to earlier publications on this topic. Yet so far such studies have either focused on one specific component (Buddhist,[8] Hindu,[9] linguistic,[10] poetic,[11] historiographic,[12] artistic,[13] etc.) of Kashmir's cultural wealth, or they have endeavoured to give a glimpse of the entire history of Kashmiri culture as a whole up to its most recent developments.[14] To the best of our knowledge, however, no attempt has ever been made to study the many-faceted outburst of intellectual creativity that occurred in Kashmir around Abhinavagupta's time; and the goal of this book is to try and map out the extraordinary cultural efferverscence that took place then in the little kingdom.

Not only did poetical and theatrical traditions flourish: Kashmiri authors elaborated theories on poetry and theatre that were to spread far beyond the borders of the valley and are widely regarded as an important revolution in the history of Indian aesthetics. Several chapters in this volume are devoted to aesthetics in Kashmir; while reflecting the paramount importance of this discipline in the intellectual landscape of Abhinavagupta's time, they offer fresh insights on its history. Y. BRONNER's contribution focuses on the origins of a distinctly Kashmiri aesthetics and the early figure of Udbhaṭa (fl. ca. 800); L. BANSAT-BOUDON, E. GANSER, D. SHULMAN and J. TÖRZSÖK examine Abhinavagupta's aesthetics and its sources; D. CUNEO and S. VASUDEVA, for their part, have chosen to explore the late developments (12th-13th centuries) of Kashmiri

---

8 See e.g. NAUDOU 1968.

9 See IKARI ED. 1994; SANDERSON 2007 and 2009.

10 See KAUL AND AKLUJKAR EDS. 2008.

11 See MCCREA 2008.

12 See e.g. SLAJE 2004, COX ED. 2013 and SLAJE 2014.

13 For recent publications on Kashmiri plastic arts and crafts in particular (and for further bibliography on this vast topic) see e.g. PAL 2007, SIUDMAK 2013 and LINROTHE 2014.

14 See RAO ED. 2008; see also STEINER ED. 2012, which gathers contributions on various Kashmiri texts.

aesthetics in the works of Ruyyaka, Śobhākara and Jayaratha, the famous commentator of Abhinavagupta's *Tantrāloka*.

The grammatical science and the philosophical-grammatical tradition also had brilliant representatives such as Helārāja – a commentator on Bhartṛhari's *Vākyapadīya* who might have been the son of a master of Abhinavagupta's, and who might even have been himself one of Abhinavagupta's masters. V. VERGIANI shows that Helārāja's work, which has been paid little scholarly attention so far except as a key to understanding Bhartṛhari's philosophy, deserves to be studied for its own merits.

As for Buddhism, it had been present in the valley since ancient times.[15] L. MCCREA discusses the views of various Buddhist philosophers as reported by Abhinavagupta in his commentaries on the Pratyabhijñā treatise – in particular those of two famous Kashmiri Buddhist authors, namely Dharmottara (a prominent thinker of the so-called "logico-epistemological school" who probably died at the very beginning of the 9th century) and Śaṅkaranandana (who seems to have been an older contemporary of Abhinavagupta, and whom the latter often quotes with admiration). Recent scholarship has established that Śaṅkaranandana was a propounder of the Buddhist idealistic current known as the Vijñānavāda,[16] and L. MCCREA's contribution shows that Dharmottara, for his part, must have been the champion of a famous Buddhist theory traditionally ascribed to the Sautrāntikas, according to which we must infer that objects exist outside of consciousness.

Two contributions also focus on the important role played by Kashmiri pandits in the transition of Buddhism from India to Tibet. So far the details of this transition have been known mainly through later Tibetan historiographies and the colophons of canonical texts. O. ALMOGI's contribution to this volume presents a preliminary survey of an extra-canonical collection of texts (the *rNying ma rgyud 'bum*, or the *Collection of Ancient Tantras*), the

---

[15] As shown in SANDERSON 2009, pp. 101-104, despite claims by Brahmanical and Śaiva sources to the effect that the presence of their movements in the valley dates back to a greater antiquity than that of Buddhism, textual and archeological evidence of Brahmanical Kashmir "does not take us back as far as our earliest evidence of Kashmirian Buddhism." Besides, the decline of Buddhism happened relatively late in Kashmir (Buddhism was still flourishing in Kalhaṇa's time), and as shown in SLAJE 2007, in the 15th century CE, some Hindu authors at least were still well acquainted with Buddhist terminology.

[16] See ELTSCHINGER 2015.

claimed origin of these works (many of them were allegedly transmitted by Kashmiri pandits or at least with their help), and the figures presumably involved in their transmission. As for C. YOSHIMIZU, she presents newly discovered works by Tibetan witnesses of the transmission of Buddhism from Kashmir to Tibet that shed a particularly interesting light on the influence of Kashmir regarding the formation of the Tibetan monastic and scholastic system.

Brahmanical authors were no less active in the valley, and two brilliant Kashmiri representatives of the Nyāya tradition wrote important works during this period: Bhaṭṭa Jayanta (a 9th-century philosopher as well as a fiercely funny satirist who authored the *Āgamaḍambara*,[17] a play on religious politics set during the reign of king Śaṅkaravarman) and Bhāsarvajña (the author of the *Nyāyabhūṣaṇa*, whose originality is pointed out by Abhinavagupta himself).[18] E. FRANCO offers an analysis of one of Bhāsarvajña's most conspicuous departures from his own Naiyāyika tradition, namely his refusal to acknowledge analogy (*upamāna*) as a valid means of knowledge. A. GRAHELI examines the positions held by Bhaṭṭa Jayanta and Abhinavagupta in a debate on verbal signification, and shows that the latter is likely to have been influenced by the former in this controversy. Y. MUROYA, for his part, examines how later Naiyāyikas knew and understood Jayanta's thought by analyzing the way in which the 14th-century Navya-Nyāya philosopher Gaṅgeśa refers to Jayanta in the context of a debate on analogy; his contribution shows that Gaṅgeśa's view of Jayanta's position was certainly mediated by Vācaspatimiśra's and Udayana's interpretations.

The valley also hosted many Hindu heterodox movements, both Vaiṣṇava and Śaiva. Their exegetical and philosophical literature – particularly rich in the case of Śaiva traditions – remains partly unavailable to date, and two of the contributions present some hitherto unpublished material pertaining to that literature: R. TORELLA gives an overview of a Vaiṣṇava text that he is currently editing and translating, the *Saṃvitprakāśa* – a unique 10th-century text by Vāmanadatta; and I. RATIÉ offers an edition and translation of a thus far unknown fragment of the detailed commentary (*Vivṛti*) that the Śaiva nondualist philosopher Utpaladeva wrote on his own *Īśvarapratyabhijñā* treatise. S. MORIYAMA explores another work

---

17 See DEZSŐ 2005.

18 See RATIÉ 2011, pp. 88-91.

by Utpaladeva that remains little studied to date, namely the *Īśvarasiddhi*, and examines in this connection the Śaiva nondualists' criticism of the Sāṅkhya theory of causation. J. NEMEC tackles the evolution of the notion of materiality in the Pratyabhijñā system and endeavours to highlight the different positions adopted by Somānanda, Utpaladeva and Abhinavagupta in this regard; as for J. TÖRZSÖK, she shows how Abhinavagupta's theatrical notions are in part grounded in his tantric sources.

Finally, this creative ferment also resulted in a remarkable historiographical perspective expressed in the 12th-century *Rājataraṅgiṇī*, a chronicle of the kings of Kashmir written by Kalhaṇa. M. WITZEL's contribution highlights the extraordinary wealth of information contained in this source and largely draws on it to depict the social status and learning of the Brahmins of Kashmir. This historiographical approach is in many respects consonant with Abhinavagupta's tendency, emphasized by L. MCCREA, to replace the abstracted, depersonalized presentation of debates usually found in Indian philosophical literature with a historicized account of his Buddhist opponents' various positions.

UNDERSTANDING THE "KASHMIRI MIRACLE"

Recent studies have pointed out that this period of intense creativity can only be understood as the outcome of a series of dynamic interactions between different communities, and we hope that the present book, which gathers contributions by scholars working on religious, philosophical, literary, social and historical aspects of medieval Kashmir, can help draw an overall picture of these interactions.

In the field of philosophy as well as in that of religious exegesis, the works written in medieval Kashmir cannot be properly understood without taking into account the constant interaction between various competing traditions. It is the case of the Pratyabhijñā system of the Śaiva non-dualist philosophers, which, somewhat paradoxically, is permeated with notions borrowed from the very Buddhist rivals whom these Śaivas claim to refute.[19] This dialectic of criticism and appropriation of Buddhist notions is so pervasive in Śaiva philosophical texts that nowadays this Śaiva corpus constitutes a crucial source for the history of late Indian philosophical

---

[19] See in particular TORELLA 1992, RATIÉ 2010 and 2011b.

Buddhism.[20] In this respect it is certainly no coincidence that the *Vivṛti* fragment studied in I. RATIÉ's contribution happens to deal with a Buddhist thesis (on the nature of memory) and quotes a passage from Dharmakīrti's *Pramāṇaviniścaya*; and L. MCREA's contribution shows that Abhinavagupta's longest commentary on the Pratyabhijñā treatise, the *Īśvarapratyabhijñāvivṛtivimarśinī*, affords the historians of Buddhism a complex and precise overview of the relationship between the great Buddhist philosophers of the time. The Buddhists, however, were by no means the Śaivas' sole interlocutors: the Pratyabhijñā system is the result of a constant polemical dialogue with many different schools of thought, and the contributions by S. MORIYAMA and A. GRAHELI examine the reaction of Śaiva authors to ideas elaborated by non-Buddhist trends such as the Sāṅkhya and Nyāya.

As for the close relationship between Vaiṣṇava and Śaiva traditions, it is highlighted here by R. TORELLA, who points out that the teachings of the Pāñcarātrin Vāmanadatta were held in great esteem by Śaiva authors (Abhinavagupta even mentions him reverently as a *guru* – perhaps one of his own masters?). R. TORELLA further shows that the numerous striking similarities between Vāmanadatta's metaphysical views and Utpaladeva's Śaiva nondualistic system are in all probability the result of a strong influence of Utpaladeva's metaphysics on Vāmanadatta's thought.[21]

These fruitful interactions tend to transcend the categories in which the various types of Indian literature are usually compartmentalized: it has recently been argued for instance that the Kashmiri aesthetic revolution is at least in part the result of what John Pocock – following Thomas Kuhn – would call a "paradigm transfer," in the field of aesthetics, of a model first developed in the field of Vedic exegesis by the Mīmāṃsakas.[22] A. GRAHELI's con-

---

20 See e.g. RATIÉ 2014 and 2015, pp. 43-44.

21 These similarities are briefly mentioned in SANDERSON 2009, p. 108; the latter notes that Vāmanadatta's philosophical position "can barely be distinguished from the dynamic nondualism of consciousness propagated [...] by Utpaladeva [...]." However, A. Sanderson does not pass any judgement on what must have been the direction of influence (ibid.: "It is not at all clear to me, however, that Vāmanadatta's thought was inspired by Utpaladeva's. The reverse may well have been the case.").

22 See MCCREA 2008. See also, however, Y. BRONNER's contribution to this volume, which places this Kashmiri aesthetic revolution earlier and draws a somewhat more complex picture of it.

tribution to this volume also shows how Abhinavagupta imports in the field of aesthetics a notion first developed by the Naiyāyika Jayanta in the context of an epistemological debate on verbal testimony and scriptural authority. V. VERGIANI, for his part, points out that Helārāja was influenced by various trends outside of his Bhartṛharian grammatical tradition and endeavoured to provide an interpretation of Bhartṛhari's work compatible with the Nyāya's theistic views and opposed to the Mīmāṃsakas' epistemological and metaphysical tenets.

Furthermore, scholars have already pointed out that there are many points of contact between the aesthetics elaborated by the Kashmiri poeticians and the metaphysics of Kashmiri Śaiva nondualism;[23] but the exact nature of this complex relationship remains to be determined. While E. GANSER offers a fresh analysis of the elements of ritual speculation found in Abhinavagupta's work on the aesthetics of theatre, J. TÖRZSÖK studies mentions of theatre and actors in tantric texts that were familiar to Abhinavagupta; her contribution shows that these texts certainly played an essential role in Abhinavagupta's conception of theatre and that they constitute an important source for the historians of Indian theatre and aesthetics. L. BANSAT-BOUDON, for her part, focuses on the relationship between Abhinavagupta's philosophy and his aesthetics by unravelling the various meanings of a stanza from the *Tantrāloka* that Abhinavagupta himself quotes in his work on poetics.

The dynamics of the various interactions that made Kashmir such a lively intellectual center are also to be understood in view of the valley's peculiar geographical and geo-political position. Not only did medieval Kashmir profoundly influence South Indian Śaivism;[24] the valley also played a crucial role during the so-called "second wave" of transmission of Buddhism into Tibet (11th-12th centuries) that was to have far-reaching consequences for the history of Buddhism throughout Asia – an aspect of Kashmiri creativity explored by O. ALMOGI and C. YOSHIMIZU. The latter shows how Kashmir, and in particular the Kashmiri scholar Mahāsumati, had a decisive impact on the history of the Tibetan Madhyamaka

---

23 See e.g. GNOLI 1956, pp. XXXIXff.; MASSON AND PATWARDHAN 1969; BANSAT-BOUDON 1992, pp. 341 ff.; and GEROW 1994.

24 On this still little-studied influence see e.g. SANDERSON 1990, pp. 80-83; TORELLA 1994, pp. xxxvi-xxxvii; and COX 2006, pp. 173-240.

tradition, by reinstating Candrakīrti's *Prasannapadā* as the main hermeneutical tool for the study of Nāgārjuna's *Mūlamadhyamakakārikā*. O. ALMOGI, for her part, points out that some of the texts belonging to the extra-canonical collection that she studies only have a doubtful connection to Kashmir, despite claims to the contrary by the editors and compilers of the collection. This suggests that the role of Kashmiri pandits in the transmission of Buddhism from India to Tibet might have been at times imaginary – but it also illustrates the remarkable prestige enjoyed by Kashmiris in Tibet, and it shows how Kashmir, whether real or fantasized, had a significant impact on Tibetan Buddhism.

By enabling specialists of different fields (religious and social studies, history, philosophy, grammar, aesthetics), linguistic domains (Sanskrit, Tibetan) and geographical areas (Tibet) to share the latest results of their research, we have thus tried not only to provide an overview of the Kashmiri "golden age," but also to trace its genesis, dynamics and impact on neighbouring areas. We are of course fully aware that much remains to be done in this respect and we certainly make no claim to exhaustivity; but we hope that however incomplete, our attempt can draw attention to what we see as the main feature of this Kashmiri intellectual and artistic blossoming. It seems to us, in sum, that if the valley around Abhinavagupta's time can be seen as a "Kashmiri miracle" – to paraphrase an expression once coined for Athens in Pericles' time –, this is so primarily thanks to Kashmir's great variety of different communities and their complex interactions, not only in religious matters, but also across secular or semi-secular intellectual disciplines such as poetry, poetics, logic, epistemology, grammar or visual arts. This is not to say – far from that – that Abhinavagupta's Kashmir was a haven of tolerance and that these communities fully accepted each other by embracing a peaceful and universalistic ecumenism: the naïveté of such a view has often been rightfully pointed out.[25] But while fighting each other or at least competing (sometimes fiercely) with each other, these communities learnt a great deal about each other, borrowed from their opponents while claiming to defeat them, transformed their rivals' thought, terminology and traditions while appropriating them, and it seems to us

---

25 See e.g., on Jayanta's so-called tolerance, WEZLER 1976; on that of the *Yogavāsiṣṭha* (the earliest nucleus of which, the *Mokṣopāya*, is a Kashmiri text), SLAJE 1993; and on tolerance in Kalhaṇa's *Rājataraṅginī*, TÖRZSÖK forthcoming.

that this constant circulation and metamorphosis of ideas and practices is first and foremost what has made Abhinavagupta's Kashmir such a fascinating place and time.

Finally, we would like to thank all those who participated in the conference of which the present volume is the outcome, as well as those who could not attend but nonetheless sent written contributions, and the institutions whose help made the conference and the book possible – above all the Deutsche Forschungsgemeinschaft (DFG) for its important financial contribution in the form of a grant (FR 2531/3-1), but also the Academy of Korean Studies (KSPS) for its continuous support and generous grant (AKS-2012-AAZ-104), the Sächsische Akademie der Wissenschaften, the University of Leipzig and the Unité Mixte de Recherche (UMR) 7528 "Mondes iranien et indien." We are particularly indebted to our friend Adelheid Buschner, whose help in organizing the conference proved (as ever) invaluable; and to Simon Ratié, who, despite being only seven weeks old at the time of the conference, attended some of the presentations in his mother's arms with remarkable composure – and even, at times, with what appeared to be a mildly amused interest.

Leipzig/Paris, 15/07/2016

REFERENCES

BANSAT-BOUDON 1992
L. Bansat-Boudon, *Poétique du théâtre indien. Lectures du Nāṭyaśāstra*, Paris: Publications de l'École Française d'Extrême-Orient 169, 1992

COX 2006
W. Cox, *Making a Tantra in Medieval South India: the Mahārthamañjarī and the Textual Culture of Cola Cidambaram*, 2 vols., unpublished Doctoral Thesis, Department of South Asian Languages and Civilisations, University of Chicago, 2006

COX ED. 2013
W. Cox (ed.), Special Issue *Kalhaṇa's Rājataraṅgiṇī and Its Inheritors* of the *Indian Economic and Social History Review* 50(2), 2013

DEZSŐ 2005
C. Dezső, *Much ado about religion*, ed. and transl., New York: New York University Press/JJC Foundation, 2005

ELTSCHINGER 2015
V. Eltschinger, "Latest News from a Kashmirian 'Second Dharmakīrti,'" in P. Mc Allister, C. Scherrer-Schaub and H. Krasser (eds.), *Cultural Flows across the Western Himalaya*, Wien: Verlag der Österreichischen Akademie der Wissenschaften, 2015, pp. 303-364

GEROW 1994
E. Gerow, "Abhinavagupta's Aesthetics as a Speculative Paradigm," *Journal of the Oriental American Society* 114(2), 1994, pp. 186-208

GNOLI 1956
R. Gnoli, *The Aesthetic Experience according to Abhinavagupta*, [Rome: Istituto Italiano per il Medio ed Estremo Oriente, 1956] Varanasi: Chowkhamba Sanskrit Studies 62, 1985

IKARI ED. 1994
Y. Ikari (ed.), *A Study of the Nīlamata. Aspects of Hinduism in Ancient Kashmir*, Kyoto: Institute for Research in Humanities, Kyoto University, 1994

KAUL AND AKLUJKAR EDS. 2008
M. Kaul and A. Aklujkar (eds.), *Linguistic Traditions of Kashmir. Essays in Memory of Paṇḍit Dinanath Yaksha*, Delhi: D.K. Printworld, 2008

R. LINROTHE 2014
R. Linrothe, *Collecting Paradise. Buddhist Art of Kashmir and its Legacies*, with essays by M.R. Kerin and C. Luczanits, New York: Rubin Museum of Arts, 2014

MASSON AND PATWARDHAN 1969
J.L. Masson and M.V. Patwardhan, *Śāntarasa and Abhinavagupta's Philosophy of Aesthetics*, Poona: Bhandarkar Oriental Research Institute, [1969] 1985

MCCREA 2008
L. McCrea, *The Teleology of Poetics in Medieval Kashmir*, Cambridge (Mass.): Harvard University Press, Harvard Oriental Series 71, 2008

NAUDOU 1968
J. Naudou, *Les Bouddhistes Kaśmīriens au Moyen-Âge*, Paris: Presses Universitaires de France, 1968

PAL 2007
P. Pal, *The Arts of Kashmir*, with contributions by F. Ames, S. Digby, G.J. Larson and J. Siudmak, Florence: Asia Society/5 Continents, 2007

RAO 2008
A. Rao (ed.), *The Valley of Kashmir. The Making and Unmaking of a Composite Culture?*, Delhi: Manohar, 2008

RATIÉ 2010
I. Ratié, "The Dreamer and the Yogin – on the Relationship between Buddhist and Śaiva Idealisms," *Bulletin of the School of Oriental and African Studies* 73(3), 2010, pp. 437-478

RATIÉ 2011
I. Ratié, *Le Soi et l'Autre: Identité, différence et altérité dans la philosophie de la Pratyabhijñā*, Leiden/Boston: Brill, 2011

RATIÉ 2011b
I. Ratié, "Can One Prove that Something Exists Beyond Consciousness? A Śaiva Criticism of the Sautrāntika Inference of External Objects," *Journal of Indian Philosophy* 39, 2011, pp. 479-501

RATIÉ 2014
I. Ratié, "On the distinction between epistemic and metaphysical Buddhist idealisms: a Śaiva perspective," *Journal of Indian Philosophy* 42, 2014, pp. 353-375

RATIÉ 2015
I. Ratié, "Śivaïsme et boudddhisme philosophiques: une influence réciproque?", *Bulletin d'Études Indiennes* 33, 2015, pp. 39-57

SANDERSON 1990
A. Sanderson, "The Visualization of the Deities of the Trika," in A. Padoux (ed.), *L'Image divine. Culte et méditation dans l'hindouisme*, Paris: Éditions du Centre National de la Recherche Scientifique, 1990, pp. 31-88

SANDERSON 2007
A. Sanderson, "The Śaiva Exegesis of Kashmir," in D. Goodall and A. Padoux (eds.), *Mélanges tantriques à la mémoire d'Hélène Brunner*, Pondicherry: Institut Français de Pondichéry/École Française d'Extrême-Orient, 2007, pp. 231-442 [and bibliography, pp. 551-582]

SANDERSON 2009
A. Sanderson, "Kashmir," in K.A. Jacobsen (ed.), *Brill's Encyclopedia of Hinduism*, vol. I: *Regions, Pilgrimage, Deities*, Leiden/Boston: Brill, pp. 99-126

SIUDMAK 2013
J. Siudmak, *The Hindu-Buddhist Sculpture of Ancient Kashmir and its Influences*, Leiden/Boston: Brill, 2013

SLAJE 1993
W. Slaje, "*sarvasiddhāntasiddhānta*. On 'Tolerance' and 'Syncretism' in the *Yogavāsiṣṭha*," *Wiener Zeitschrift für die Kunde Südasiens* 36 (Supplementband), 1993, pp. 307-322

SLAJE 2004
W. Slaje, *Medieval Kashmir and the Science of History*, Austin: South Asia Institute, The University of Texas at Austin, Madden Lecture 2003-2004

SLAJE 2007
W. Slaje, "The Last Buddhist of Kashmir as Recorded by Jonarāja," in W. Shukla (ed.), *Sanskrit Studies*, vol. II, New Delhi: 2007, pp. 185-193

SLAJE 2014
W. Slaje, *Kingship in Kaśmīr (AD 1148-1459), From the Pen of Jonarāja, Court Paṇḍit to Sulṭān Zayn al-'Ābidīn*, critically edited with an annotated translation, indexes and maps, Halle: Universitätsverlag Halle-Wittenberg

STEINER ED. 2012
R. Steiner (ed.), *Highland Philology. Results of a Text-Related Kashmir Panel at the 31st DOT, Marburg 2010*, Halle: Studia Indologica Universitatis Halensis 4, Universitätsverlag Halle-Wittenberg, 2012

TORELLA 1992
R. Torella, "The Pratyabhijñā and the Logico-Epistemological School of Buddhism," in GOUDRIAAN (ed.), *Ritual and Speculation in Early Tantrism, Studies in Honor of André Padoux*, Albany: SUNY Press, SUNY Series in Tantric Studies, 1992, pp. 327-345

TORELLA 1994
R. Torella, *Īśvarapratyabhijñākārikā of Utpaladeva with the Author's Vṛtti*, ed. and transl., [Roma: 1994] corrected ed., Delhi: Motilal Banarsidass, 2002

TÖRZSÖK forthcoming
J. Törzsök, "Tolerance and its limits in twelfth-century Kashmir: tantric elements in Kalhaṇa's *Rājataraṅginī*," *Indologica Taurinensia*

WEZLER 1976
A. Wezler, "Zur Proklamation religiös-weltanschaulicher Toleranz bei dem indischen Philosophen Jayantabhaṭṭa," *Saeculum, Jahrbuch für Universalgeschichte* 27, 1976, pp. 329-347

Tantric Scriptures in the *rNying ma rgyud 'bum* Believed to Have Been Transmitted to Tibet by Kashmiris: A Preliminary Survey*

ORNA ALMOGI

1. INTRODUCTORY REMARKS

The extra-canonical collection known as the *rNying ma rgyud 'bum*, or the *Collection of Ancient Tantras*, contains numerous texts claimed to have been transmitted to Tibet by or with the help of Kashmiri personages. One of the best-known Kashmiri Buddhist masters in the Tibetan tradition, particularly the one associated with the early transmission of Buddhism in Tibet, is no doubt Vimalamitra, who is mostly associated with texts belonging to the Atiyoga (or rDzogs chen) and Mahāyoga classes of rNying ma *tantra*s. And indeed, numerous texts contained in the *rNying ma rgyud 'bum* are said to have been transmitted with his help, which mainly took the form of working on their translation into Tibetan, though he also expounded them to Indians and Tibetans and engaged in related activities. Another figure mentioned in the colophons of several Mahāyoga *tantra*s found in the collection is a certain Kashmiri translator named Ānanda. Furthermore, in one case Kashmir is explicitly mentioned as the place of translation, and thus perhaps was the place of origin of the *tantra* or Tantric cycle in question. In the present paper I shall attempt to present a preliminary survey of these *tantra*s, and briefly

* The publication of this article has been enabled thanks to the generous support of the German Research Foundation (DFG) between the years 2011 and 2015 (SFB 950). Thanks are also due to Philip Pierce (Kathmandu) for proofreading my English.

refer to the doctrinal cycles they belong to, the individuals presumably involved in their transmission, and the authenticity of these ascribed transmissions.[1]

At first, however, a few words should be perhaps said about the *rNying ma rgyud 'bum* itself. The *rNying ma rgyud 'bum* is a collection of Tantric scriptures believed by the followers of the rNying ma school to have been transmitted to Tibet from India – either directly or via other places, including Nepal, China, and Central Asia – mainly during the first period of dissemination of Buddhism in Tibet. Most of these texts have been, however, regarded as spurious by the followers of what is referred to as the New Schools and thus were, apart from a few exceptions, excluded from the Tibetan Buddhist canon, while those that have been included were not put in the Tantra (rGyud) section, but compiled in a separate section called "Ancient Tantras" (rNying rgyud). The by and large exclusion of these *tantra*s from the canon has thus led to the formation of the para-canonical collection known as the *rNying ma rgyud 'bum*. The need to compile this collection had become particularly urgent owing to the constant growth in the number of these "Ancient Tantras" – growth, that is, mainly due to the activities of those persons known as treasure revealers (*gter ston*).

We still do not have a complete picture regarding the formation of this collection and its various versions, but what is quite certain is that small collections of these texts had existed from quite early on – perhaps already as early as the eleventh century – and were later formed into bigger collections. The *rNying ma rgyud 'bum* edition prepared at the behest of the fifteen-century Tibetan master Ratna gling pa (1403-1479, P470)[2] is commonly considered to be the first systematic attempt to compile a *rNying ma rgyud 'bum* edition, and there is no doubt that this edition has had a great influence on the history of the transmission of the collection, including its form and content. However, we have sufficient historical evidence that

---

1 For a discussion of the authenticity of titles and colophons of Tantric texts in the Tibetan canon, see ALMOGI 2008. Authentication strategies relating to rNying ma scriptures pursued in the colophons of the *rNying ma rgyud 'bum* will be discussed in a separate article.

2 The dates of Tibetan figures given in the present paper are based on the TBRC and are followed by the TBRC resource ID number. Likewise, place names are identified by their TBRC resource ID number, when possible.

there were other large-scale compilations of these scriptures even earlier.[3]

A number of editions of the collection are accessible, and for the present study I have consulted selected ones from various lines of transmission, including what I refer to as the "Central Bhutanese Group" (Tb, Gt), "South-Western Tibetan Group" (Tk, Tn), "Tibetan-Nepalese Borderlands Group" (Nu, Na), and the "(Central)-Eastern Tibetan Group" (Dg).[4] In addition, I have also consulted the collection known as the *Bai ro rgyud 'bum* (Bg). (The total number of texts referred to in each of the cases discussed below, however, is based on the editions from the Central Bhutanese Group, which contain the largest number of texts. The text titles and colophons provided are primarily based on the Tb edition.)

2. KASHMIR AS THE PLACE OF TRANSLATION

First I would like to discuss the one case in which Kashmir is explicitly mentioned as the place of translation (and by extension perhaps as the place of origin). The *tantra* is titled *dPal rdo rje gzhon nu thugs rje khros pa rtsa ba'i rgyud kyi bshad pa* ("*The Explanatory* [*Tantra*] *of the Basic Tantra* [*of*] **Vajrakumāra, the One Endowed with Wrathful Compassion*"), is 13 chapters long, and is found, in all versions consulted, in the Mahāyoga section. The colophon reads as follows:[5]

> The *Explanatory* [*Tantra*] *of the Basic Tantra of the Wrathful Vajra* (*dPal rdo rje khros pa'i rtsa ba'i rgyud kyi bshad pa*) is [herewith] concluded. Near the self-arisen *stūpa* [located at] a cemetery [called] Bi sa ka (=*Viśākha?) in Kashmir, India, the Venerable Lady *Sattvavajrī (rDo rje sems ma), endowed with supernatural powers, and the translator 'Gar Shes [rab?] rang 'byung translated [the *tantra*], and [then] proofread and finalized [the translation]. Later, that Venerable Lady and 'Brom ston rGyal ba['i 'byung gnas?] revised and finalized [the translation once

3 See ALMOGI forthcoming.

4 Text catalogue numbers given for Tb are based on the online catalogue found in *The Tibetan & Himalayan Library*. Likewise, existing catalogues for Gt, Tn, Tk, and Dg have also been consulted. For publication details of these catalogues, see the bibliography, under the respective sigla. References to the Tibetan-Nepalese Borderlands Group (Nu and Na) are based on the comparative catalogue prepared in ALMOGI forthcoming.

5 For the Tibetan text, see the appendix, § I, no. 1.

> again]. If the reading [here in this version] is wrong, may the Venerable Lady forgive [me]!

The two translators said to have been involved in the initial translation, the Venerable Lady *Sattvavajrī and the translator 'Gar Shes [rab?] rang 'byung, seem to be rather unknown figures, and this appears to be the only time they are mentioned as translators in the numerous colophons of the various *rNying ma rgyud 'bum* editions. To be sure, they seem to be mentioned as a translation team in the colophon of a single text in the Tibetan Buddhist canon, a *dhāraṇī* titled *'Phags pa spyan ras gzigs dbang phyug seng ge sgra'i gzungs* (**Ārya-Avalokiteśvarasiṃhanāda-nāma-dhāraṇī*), which is found in the Tantra section of the *bKa' 'gyur* (P386/T656). There, however, the Tibetan translator is named Shes rab 'byung gnas (i.e. *'byung gnas* instead of *rang byung*, which latter has indeed more of a rNying ma ring to it). It seems, then, that this is the only translation of a canonical text that our translators were involved in, since neither of them is mentioned as a translator elsewhere, not even in collaboration with other translators.

Interestingly, the *bKa' 'gyur* colophon reads almost identically with the first part of the colophon of our text in the *rNying ma rgyud 'bum*, the main difference being the slight variation in the name of the Tibetan translator, and in addition two further minor differences, one in the spelling of the name of the cemetery and one in the omission of the word *rgya gar* for India:[6]

> The **Ārya-Avalokiteśvarasiṃhanāda-nāma-dhāraṇī* is [herewith] concluded. Near the self-arisen *stūpa* [located at] a cemetery [called] 'Bri sa ka (=*Viśākha?) in Kashmir the Venerable Lady *Sattvavajrī (rDo rje sems ma), endowed with supernatural powers, and the translator 'Gar Shes rab 'byung gnas translated [the *tantra*], and [then] proofread and finalized [the translation].

One indeed may wonder whether our colophon has been copied from the canonical *dhāraṇī*, with the addition of a new passage in which a revision of the translation is reported, perhaps in order to strengthen the impression of authenticity. The mention of someone

[6] P386 (55b1-3); T656 (SKORUPSKI 1985, p. 291): *'phags pa spyan ras gzigs dbang phyug seng ge sgra zhes bya ba'i gzung rdzogs sho || || kha che'i yul dur khrod 'bri sa ka rang byung gi mchod rten tsar* [T *rtsar*] *dngos grub brnyes* [T *brnyed*] *pa'i rje btsun ma rdo rje sems ma dang | sgra bsgyur gyi lo tstsha* [T *tsā*] *ba 'gar shes rab 'byung gnas zhes bya bas bsgyur cing zhus te gtan la phab pa'o ||*.

– to all appearances 'Brom ston rGyal ba'i 'byung gnas (1004/05-1064, P2557), the famous student of Atiśa – as having cooperated with *Sattvavajrī (the same Indian female adept stated as having been involved in the initial translation) on the revision and finalization of the Tibetan version clearly places our alleged translator team in the eleventh century. 'Brom ston rGyal ba'i 'byung gnas's involvement in the translation of an Ancient *tantra* is, however, doubtful. The modern anthology of short biographies, the *mKhas grub rim byon*, provides a brief biography of mGar (a variant of 'Gar) Shes rab 'byung gnas. According to this source, he was born around the mid-eleventh century and did his initial studies in Tibet. Then he travelled to Kashmir, other parts of India, Nepal, and other places, where he met numerous accomplished Indian scholars, under whose guidance he deepened his studies of Indian scriptures and treatises, and of Sanskrit as well. He is further said to have merely translated into Tibetan one text (the text is specified as a *bstan bcos*, usually meaning *śāstra*, but this is obviously a reference to the canonical *dhāraṇī* just mentioned).[7] Unfortunately, the *mKhas grub rim byon* does not specify its source for this report. The place in Kashmir named as where the translation was done has so far not been identified.

3. TANTRAS WHOSE TRANSLATION IS ASCRIBED TO THE KASHMIRI ĀNANDA

There are six translation colophons in the *rNying ma rgyud 'bum* in which the Kashmiri Ānanda (*kha che a/ā nan ta*) is mentioned as the translator, in all cases in collaboration with Padmasambhava, and in one of these cases (no. 6), in addition, with the famed early Tibetan translator Vairocana (Bai ro tsa na) as a third member. In three of these cases (nos. 2, 5, 6) he is simply referred to as the Kashmiri Ānanda, but in two cases (no. 3, 4) he is given the title *lo tsā ba*, commonly reserved for the Tibetans in translation teams, and in one case (no. 1) he is even explicitly designated as a "Tibetan translator" (*bod kyi lo tsa ba*).

7 *Mkhas grub rim byon* (335-336): mGar shes rab 'byung gnas: *khong ni spyi lo'i dus rabs bcu gcig pa'i dus dkyil tsam du sku 'khrungs pa'i lo tsā ba zhig yin | khong gis thog mar bod yul nas slob gnyer mdzad cing | de nas kha che dang | bal yul | rgya gar sogs su phebs te paṇ grub mang po'i zhabs la gtugs shing rgya gzhung dang legs sbyar gyi skad la phul du phyin pa sbyangs nas bstan bcos gcig tsam bod yig tu bskyur ba mdzad | khong gi bsgyur rtsom ni bka' 'gyur las spyan ras gzigs dbang phyug seng ge sgra'i gzungs zhes bya ba bzhungs so ||*.

So who is the Kashmiri Ānanda? In the following, I shall attempt to answer this question in brief. An earlier mention of this translator is found perhaps in the *dBa'/sBa bzhed*, one of the earliest historical documents narrating the early dissemination of Buddhism in Tibet.[8] There it is reported that after the arrival in Tibet of mKhan po Bo dhi sa twa, the son of the Za hor king (i.e. Śāntarakṣita), in response to an invitation by the Tibetan king (*btsan po*), the king sent three of his ministers to meet him in the lHa sa temple where he was residing to find out whether there was any danger of black magic or evil spirits from his side. For this purpose the markets of Lhasa were searched for a translator from either Kashmir or Yang le (i.e. probably Pharphing in Nepal). One of the three Kashmiris found was the Kashmiri Ānanda who was the only one able to serve as a translator of doctrinal matters, thanks to his education, which included Brahmin sacred scriptures, Sanskrit grammar, and medicine. (He is, by the way, said to have been the son of one sKyes bzang, a Brahmin who had been exiled to Tibet for having committed a crime.) Consequently, Ānanda is reported to have become a translator for Śāntarakṣita. However, no translation in the Tibetan canon is ascribed to him, so it seems that his translation activities – if we take this report at face value – were confined to oral teachings. As pointed out by Pasang Wangdu and Hildegard Diemberger in their translation of the *dBa' bzhed*, he is mentioned as a translator in all versions of the work, and also in the *Bu ston chos 'byung* (referred to there as either Paṇḍita Ānanda, the Kashmiri Ānanda, or the Brahmin Ānanda), which considers him an important translator, placing him twelfth in the list of scholars and translators. However, as pointed out by Wangdu and Dimberger, there also exist other, conflicting reports: according to the *lDe'u chos 'byung*, he was invited to Tibet during the last part of the reign of Khri srong lde btsan in order to translate doctrinal texts, and in the *rGyal rabs gsal ba'i me long* he is mentioned in connection with the Bon po–Buddhist controversy.[9] The reference to him as (*bod kyi*) *lo tsā ba* clearly reflects the fact that he – as a translator (or rather interpreter) having knowledge of Sanskrit and at the same time good command of Tibetan – assumed the role commonly reserved to Tibetans in the translator teams.

---

8 On the *dBa' bzhed*, see WANGDU AND DIEMBERGER 2000. For a brief discussion of the dating of the this historical work, see MARTIN 1997, no. 1.

9 WANGDU AND DIEMBERGER 2000, pp. 44-45.

All of the six Tantric scriptures included in the *rNying ma rgyud 'bum* said to have been translated by him belong to the cycle of the deity Padma dbang chen (a form of Hayagrīva), which is included in the Mahāyoga section. All six translation colophons are short and, except for the names of the translators, do not provide any additional information, for example, regarding the time or place or any other circumstances surrounding the translation. It is thus unclear why the Kashmiri Ānanda should have been the translator of this specific cycle.

4. TANTRAS STATED AS HAVING BEEN TRANSLATED OR TRANSMITTED BY VIMALAMITRA

There seem to be altogether fifty-seven *tantra*s in the *rNying ma rgyud 'bum* (i.e. in the larger editions of the Central Bhutanese Group) in whose transmission Vimalamitra (b. 8th cent.) – generally believed to have been born in Kashmir, but according to some historical sources in one of the neighbouring areas – is said to have been involved in one way or another. It is impossible to discuss in detail the role of Vimalamitra in the transmission of Buddhism into Tibet within the framework of this paper, and I shall merely outline here some of the highlights of his activities from the point of view of the rNying ma tradition, mainly in order to provide a general background to my discussion below. According to traditional sources, Vimalamitra was involved in the transmission of various scriptures, mainly of the Atiyoga and Mahāyoga classes. bDud 'joms rin po che 'Jigs bral ye shes rdo rje (1904-1988, P736) – according to whom Vimalamitra was born in Glang po'i tshal (*Hastivana) or Glang po'i sgang (*Hastisthala) in Western India to the householder Sukhacakra and his wife Ātmaprakāśā[10] – outlines his involvement in the transmission of Tantric teachings as follows:

- Of the Sādhana section of the Mahāyoga teachings, he was entrusted with the cycle of Vajrāmṛta, one of the five "pronouncements" of this section.[11]

---

[10] NSTB, pp. 481 and 498, respectively (Sanskrit reconstructions are as offered by Gyurme Dorji and Matthew Kapstein, the translators-cum-editors of the NSTB). According to *ibid*, p. 462, s.v. Hastisthala, the place is "probably to be identified with Hastināpura in modern Himachal Pradesh," which shares its northern borders with the modern state of Jammu and Kashmir. Regarding the circumstances of Vimalamitra's invitation to Tibet, see *ibid*, p. 555.

[11] NSTB, p. 480.

- Another part of the Sādhana section, the treasure consisting in the **Mahottara* (*Che mchog*), one of the eight "concealed treasures" of this section, was also entrusted to him.[12]
- All instructions relating to the Aural Lineage (*snyan brgyud*) of the rDzogs chen teachings were given to him by the masters Śrī Siṃha and Jñānasūtra.[13]
- Regarding the Māyājāla cycle of Mahāyoga, the composition of several treatises is attributed to him.[14] In Tibet he is believed to have expounded what is referred to as the Eighteen Māyājāla *tantra*s to rMa Rin chen mchog, in cooperation with whom he then also translated them into Tibetan.[15] He is also said to have taught the Vajrāmṛta cycle to gNyags Jñānakumāra and others.[16] Furthermore, he supposedly translated (with the help of gNyags Jñānakumāra and g.Yu sgra snying po) thirteen texts of the Eighteen Sems sde *tantra*s (*sems sde bco brgyad*) of the Atiyoga class, which are known as the "later translations" (*phyi 'gyur*) – the first five, known as the "early translations," having purportedly been translated by Vairocana. He is also reported to have given the highly esoteric teachings of the *sNying thig* cycle to the king Khri srong lde btsan and to Nyang Ting 'dzin bzang po. Subsequently, believing that there were no other worthy recipients, he concealed the books at dGe gong in mChims pu, the famed retreat centre near bSam yas monastery.[17] These concealed treasures are said to have been later on discovered by the twelfth-century master Zhang ston (1097-1167).[18]

Of the fifty-seven *tantra*s in the *rNying ma rgyud 'bum* whose transmission or translation is attributed to Vimalamitra, thirty belong to the Atiyoga (or rDzogs chen) class, one to the Anuyoga class, and,

---

12 NSTB, pp. 482-483.

13 NSTB, pp. 498-499, 501. Vimalamitra is said here to have concealed three copies of the most secret books in as many places, one of them being the district Suvarṇadvīpa of Kashmir.

14 NSTB, p. 481 (listing several treatises, mainly related to the Māyājāla cycles, that were composed by Vimalamitra).

15 On the Māyājāla *tantra*s, see ALMOGI 2014, passim, where this cluster of *tantra*s is briefly discussed within the framework of the Eighteen Mahāyoga Tantric Cycles.

16 NSTB, pp. 534-535.

17 NSTB, p. 555.

18 NSTB, p. 561.

finally, twenty-six to the Mahāyoga class. In fifty cases Vimalamitra is mentioned as being involved in the translation (*bsgyur pa, bsgyur zhing gtan la phab pa, zhus shing gtan la phab pa*) as follows (the numbers within brackets are the numbers of the corresponding titles as listed in section III of the appendix):

- twenty-seven texts in collaboration with gNyags Jñānakumāra (nos. 1, 5, 6, 7, 8, 14, 19, 24, 29, 30, 34, 35, 37, 39, 41, 42, 43, 44, 47, 48, 49, 50, 51, 52, 53, 54, 55);
- one with gNyags Jñānakumāra, sKa ba dpal brtsegs, and Cog ro Klu'i rgyal mtshan (no. 20);
- one with gNyags Jñānakumāra and rMa Rin chen mchog (no. 38);
- three with g.Yu sgra snying po (nos. 2, 3, 4);
- five with Ācārya Dran pa ye shes (nos. 9, 10, 11, 12, 15);
- four with sKa ba dpal brtsegs (nos. 16, 26, 27, 28);
- three with sKa ba dpal brtsegs, Cog ro Klu'i rgyal mtshan, and Zhang Ye shes sde (nos. 22, 23, 32);
- one with sNubs Nam mkha'i snying po (no. 31);
- one with Dharmaśrīprabha and Ratna a gra (no. 33);
- one with rMa Rin chen mchog (no. 36);
- two with Vairocana (nos. 18, 45);
- one with mChims mDzid gsal 'bar (no. 46).

In seven cases he is mentioned as being involved in the transmission of the scripture in question in one way or another other than translation: for example, by way of bestowing teachings and empowerments (nos. 13, 17, 21, 25, 40, 56, 57). Four of the *tantra*s in question are connected with what is known as the Aural Lineage of rDzogs chen (nos. 5, 11, 12, 21), and eight of them are said to have been concealed (nos. 10, 14, 15, 21, 22, 25, 40, 56), of which six belong to the Atiyoga (or rDzogs chen) class and two to the Mahāyoga class. While many of the colophons are rather short, some of them are quite long, describing the transmission lineage and at times also the circumstances surrounding the transmission. However, these descriptions appear to be rather legendary. Only in three cases is the place of translation mentioned: once Bre'u dge 'u of 'Chims phu (TBRC: G3528) (no. 8), and twice 'Phan yul (TBRC: G1116), an area north of Lhasa (nos. 42, 43).

Now, bearing in mind the fact that a greater part of the rNying ma *tantras* are considered revealed treasures (*gter ma*), the first question that arises is how many of the scriptures said to have been transmitted or translated by Vimalamitra are authentic; in other words, how many of them are indeed of Indic origin and how true are the reports of Vimalamitra's involvement. We will of course not be able to provide wholly clear answers to these questions. What we can do is discuss some aspects of the transmission of these *tantras* that promise to shed some light on their authenticity.

Since we know that the corpus of rNying ma *tantras* constantly grew due to the activities of the treasure revealers (*gter ston*), we could perhaps attempt in the first place to try to find early evidence of the existence of the texts we are concerned with:

- Of the thirty Atiyoga texts in question, thirteen (nos. 1, 10, 12, 14, 16, 17, 18, 20, 21, 22, 23, 29, 32) seem to have existed already during the twelfth century, inasmuch as they are found in the collection known as the *Bai ro rgyud 'bum*, which is believed to have been compiled sometime in the second half of that century, and which mainly includes texts of the Sems sde section of the Atiyoga class (it is, to be sure, unclear how many texts were included in this early compilation and how many texts were added to it later). Interestingly, further two of the Mahāyoga texts in our list (no. 38, 40) are included in the *Bai ro rgyud 'bum*.
- Furthermore, of the twenty-six Mahāyoga *tantras*, at least two are explicitly referred to by or cited in texts found in Dunhuang (nos. 35, 36), and there appears to be an indirect reference to one more *tantra* in the same material (no. 34). One *tantra* appears to be mentioned in the famed eleventh-century *bKa' shog* by Zhi ba 'od (no. 55), and two further ones to be implied there (nos. 36, 37). At least two texts (nos. 35, 36) are mentioned in the ninth century by gNubs gSang rgyas ye shes (P2885) in his *bSam gtan mig sgron* and in the eleventh century by Rong zom Chos kyi bzang po (P3816) in various of his works. (These last two sources have not been exhaustively examined in this regard, and it is thus very possible that references to some more of the texts in question are made by them.) Significantly, merely four of the twenty-six *tantras* under discussion could be confirmed to have been admitted into the widely circulated editions of the *bKa' 'gyur* (nos. 35, 36, 37, 44), while the connection between text nos. 46-53 and P464/D841 is yet to be studied. Two further texts have been admitted into the O rgyan gling *bKa' 'gyur* (nos. 27,

45). (It is very possible that a few more may be found in these editions of the *bKa' 'gyur* under slightly different titles, but further investigation is required. The same applies to some of the other so-called "local *bKa' 'gyur*" editions.)

The sources considered here are of course not exhaustive, and several others should certainly be looked into as well. However, the picture gained so far may give us a general idea of how things stand.

Another point that could be considered is the alleged collaboration of Vimalamitra with the individual Tibetan translators just mentioned. There are altogether twenty-five texts in the Tibetan Buddhist canon with which Vimalamitra is associated:

- Interestingly, merely two *tantra*s whose translation is attributed to Vimalamitra are included in the *bKa' 'gyur* (P456/D833, P464/D841), both of which are found in the rNying rgyud section. As already stated, while P456/D833 is found in our list (no. 44), the identity of P464/ D841 with eight texts in our list (nos. 46-53) is yet to be examined. The colophons of both canonical texts name gNyags Jñānakumāra as the Tibetan translator, in conformity with the corresponding texts in the *rNying ma rgyud 'bum*, except in one case (no. 46), where mChims mDzid gsal 'bar is named as Vimalamitra's Tibetan collaborator.
- The remaining twenty-three canonical texts are found in the *bsTan 'gyur*. In twenty cases Vimalamitra is merely mentioned as the author (rGyud 'grel: P2941/D2092, P3505/D2681, P3506/D2682, P3931/D3112, P4724, P4725, P4732, P4738, P4740, P4746, P4747, P4764, P4772, P4774, P4776, P4780; Sher phyin: P5214/D3814; dBu ma: P5306/D3910, P5334/ D3938, P5367/D3972), in two cases as both author and translator (rGyud 'grel: P4755; Sher phyin: P5217/D3818), and in a further single case only as a translator (Sher phyin: P5215/ D3815). I am not able to go at present into the question of whether all of these cases refer to one and the same Vimalamitra, and would merely like to mention that only seventeen of the twenty-three texts are Tantric treatises (only four of them, significantly, have been admitted into the sDe dge edition of the *bsTan 'gyur*), while the other six are Sūtric – three in the Sher phyin section and a further three in the dBu ma section. Of the three treatises whose translation is attributed to Vimalamitra, only one is Tantric (P4755), in cooperation with rMa Rin chen mchog, and two are classified as Sher phyin (P5215/D3815, P5217/D3818), both in collaboration with Nam mKha'

(skyong), while in the last case the Indian Jñānagarbha is also mentioned as a collaborator.

Thus, of all translators named in the *rNying ma rgyud 'bum* as having collaborated with Vimalamitra, only Jñānakumāra is named in the canonical colophons in this capacity.[19] However, one should bear in mind that the doctrinal cycles in question have been excluded altogether from the *bKa' 'gyur*, so that it is not surprising that we find no records or evidence of Vimalamitra's alleged collaboration with the other translators named in the *rNying ma rgyud 'bum* colophons or rNying ma historical sources. By contrast, most of the remaining Tibetan translators mentioned as his collaborators are very well known, while only Ratna a gra and mChims mDzid gsal 'bar seem not to be known otherwise.

5. CONCLUDING REMARKS

In this paper I have attempted to present a preliminary survey of texts found in the *rNying ma rgyud 'bum* collection stated as having been transmitted to Tibet from Kashmir or via Kashmiri personages. At the same time, however, I have also attempted to demonstrate that many of these claimed transmissions are doubtful. Nonetheless, in some of the cases where a link to Kashmir has been suggested (or imagined) by the "treasure revealers" or the compilers and editors of the collection one can find, at least in rNying ma historical sources, evidence of some connection between the cycle to which the text in question belongs and Kashmir or Kashmiri personages. While in most cases this does not actually reflect the actual state of affairs, the connection to Kashmir having probably been alleged arbitrarily (or else wrongly imagined), in some instances the historicity of the reports is yet to be examined.

APPENDIX

The following sections provide the titles and colophons of the *tantra*s claimed to have a connection with Kashmir or Kashmiri Buddhist masters. The titles and colophons cited here are based on the mTshams brag edition (Tb). No attempt has been made to systematically collate the titles and colophons with other *rNying ma rgyud*

---

19 Dharmaśrīprabha is mentioned in three canonical colophons as a fellow translator (P1035/D6, P5430/D4517 and P5936/D4392), but none of the works are Tantric.

'bum editions and, accordingly, critically edit them. In obviously erroneous cases, however, emendations were suggested (within square brackets). Note, however, that no attempt to emend erroneously transliterated Sanskrit words has been made. Likewise, no editorial glosses have been recorded. Also to be noted is that in some cases the titles given in the various versions slightly vary. Occasionally, the titles and colophons in Tb have been compared with those found in Gt (as recorded in CANTWELL ET AL. 2006) to clarify doubtful readings. In some other cases the number of chapters varies among the various editions of the *rNying ma rgyud 'bum* as well. These differences, however, have no relevance to this paper and therefore will not be discussed here.

The catalogue numbers and the location of the texts in the mTshams brag edition of the *rNying ma rgyud 'bum* are provided in the respective footnotes, together with early references to the works when applicable. In most cases the texts listed are included in all *rNying ma rgyud 'bum* editions, from all lines of transmission. In cases where they are not included in one or more of the editions consulted or from an entire line altogether, a remark is made to that effect. Cases in which the texts are included in the *Bai ro rgyud 'bum* are likewise noted. In cases of admission into the *bKa' 'gyur*, the Peking (and if applicable also the sDe dge) catalogue numbers are provided. Similarly, texts that have been admitted only into the O rgyan gling *bKa' 'gyur* are identified as such. Occasionally, early references to individual texts are recorded, including ones in the Dunhuang material, the ninth-century *bSam gtan mig sgron*, and the works of Rong zom Mahāpaṇḍita (eleventh century).

I. Tantras Whose Translation Is Said to Have Been Executed In Kashmir

1) *dPal rdo rje gzhon nu thugs rje khros pa rtsa ba'i rgyud kyi bshad pa*[20]

> Colophon: *dpal rdo rje khros pa rtsa ba'i rgyud kyi bshad pa zhes bya ba rdzogs s.ho* || || *rgya gar kha che'i yul* | *dur khrod bi sa ka'i rang 'byung mchod rten tsar rtsar* | *dngos grub brnyes pa'i rje btsun rdo rje sems ma dang* || [=|] *sgra bsgyur lo tstsha ba 'gar shes* [*rab*?] *rang 'byung zhes bya bas bsgyur cing zhus te gtan la phab pa'o* || *slad nas rje btsun ma de nyid*

[20] Tb.674, vol. XXXVII (*ji*), pp. 2[l. 1]-102[l. 6]. For an English translation, see above, § 2.

dang 'brom ston rgyal bas bcos te gtan la phab pa'o || sgra log na rje btsun mas bzod [=*bzos*] *par mdzod cig || ||*

II. Tantras Whose Translation Is Ascribed to the Kashmiri Ānanda

1) *dPal padma dbang chen dregs pa bsrung bzlog yon tan gyi rgyud*[21]

Colophon: *padma dbang chen dregs pa bsrung bzlog gi rgyud rdzogs so || || rgya gar gyi paṇḍi ta padma sam bha wa dang | bod kyi lo tsa ba kha che a nan tas bsgyur ba'o || ||*

2) *dPal padma dbang chen | padma gar gyi dbang phyug gi | dregs pa can gzan la 'bebs pa 'phrin las kyi rgyud pa'i rgyud*[22]

Colophon: *padma dbang chen dregs pa gzan 'bebs kyi rgyud rdzogs so || || padma 'byung gnas dang | kha che a nan tas bsgyur ba'o || ||*

3) *dPal padma dbang chen dregs pa gnas* [=*gnad*] *'bebs kyi rgyud*[23]

Colophon: *padma dbang chen dregs pa gnad 'bebs kyi rgyud rdzogs so || || paṇ ḍi ta padma sam bha ba dang | lo tsa ba kha che a nan tas bsgyur ba'o || ||*

4) *dPal padma dbang chen dregs pa zil gnon gyi rgyud*[24]

Colophon: *dbang chen dregs pa zil gnon gyi rgyud rdzogs so || || paṇḍi ta padma 'byung gnas dang | lo tsa ba kha che a nan tas bsgyur ba'o || ||*

5) *dPal padma dbang chen dregs pa dbang sdud kyi rgyud*[25]

Colophon: *dbang chen dregs pa dbang sdud kyi rgyud rdzogs so || | gu ru padma dang kha che a nan tas bsgyur ba'o ||*

6) *De bzhin gshegs pa thams cad kyi dgongs pa'i khro bo 'dus pa | bde gshegs spyir dril | rta mgrin rngog ma le brgan gyi rgyud*[26]

---

[21] Tb.560, vol. XXXI (*ki*), pp. 74[l. 7]-111[l. 4].

[22] Tb.561, vol. XXXI (*ki*), pp. 111[l. 4]-149[l. 4].

[23] Tb.562, vol. XXXI (*ki*), pp. 149[l. 4]-191[l. 2].

[24] Tb.564, vol. XXXI (*ki*), pp. 245[l. 7]-308[l. 1].

[25] Tb.565, vol. XXXI (*ki*), pp. 308[l. 1]-356[l. 3].

[26] Tb.570, vol. XXXI (*ki*), pp. 489[l. 3]-616[l. 7].

Colophon: *padma dbang chen bde gshegs 'dus pa'i rgyud rdzogs so || || slob dpon chen po padma 'byung gnas dang | kha ches a nan ta dang | bai ro tsa na* [=*nas*] *bsgyur ba'o || sā mā yā rgya rgya rgya ||*

III. Tantras Said to Have Been Transmitted or Translated by Vimalamitra

1) *Byang chub kyi sems rmad du byung ba | byang chub sems rmad du byung ba'i le'u*[27]

Colophon: *rmad du byung ba rdzogs so || || rgya gar gyi mkhan po bi ma la mi tra dang | lo tsa ba gnyags dznyā na ku* [*ma*] *ras bsgyur nas gtan la phab pa'o || shrī singha dang | bai ro tsa nas sngar yang bsgyur || ||*

2) *rDzogs pa chen po chos nyid byang chub kyi sems bkra shis mi 'gyur ba gsal bar gnas pa'i rgyud*[28]

Colophon: *rdzogs pa chen po chos nyid byang chub kyi sems bkra shis mi 'gyur ba gsal bar gnas pa'i rgyud ces bya ba rdzogs so || || rgya gar gyi mkhan po bi ma la mi tra dang | sgra bsgyur gyi lo tsa ba chen po g.yu sgra snying pos bsgyur ba'i 'grel pa dang bcas par bshad pa'o || ||*

3) *rDzogs pa chen po byang chub kyi sems kun la 'jug pa rnam dag ston pa'i rgyud*[29]

Colophon: *rdzogs pa chen po chos nyid byang chub kyi sems kun la 'jug pa rnam dag ston pa'i rgyud ces bya ba rdzogs so || || rgya gar gyi mkhan po bi ma la mi tra dang | bod kyi sgra bsgyur gyi lo tsa ba g.yu sgra snying pos bsgyur cing gtan la phab pa'o || ||*

4) *rDzogs pa chen po chos nyid byang chub kyi sems thig le rgya mtsho gnas la 'jug pa zhes bya ba'i rgyud*[30]

Colophon: *rdzogs pa chen po chos nyid byang chub kyi sems thig le rgya mtsho gnas la 'jug pa'i rgyud ces bya ba rdzogs so || || rgya gar gyi mkhan po bi ma la mi tra dang | sgra bsgyur gyi lo tsa ba chen po g.yu sgras zhus shing gtan la phab pa'o ||*

5) *Rin po che snang byed kyi rgyud*[31]

---

27 Tb.56, vol. II (*kha*), pp. 774[l. 1]-856[l. 1]. Found in Bg.

28 Tb.122, vol. V (*ca*), pp. 2[l. 1]-71[l. 5].

29 Tb.123, vol. V (*ca*), pp. 71[l. 5]-100[l. 5]. Probably missing in Na.

30 Tb.124, vol. V (*ca*), pp. 100[l. 5]-127[l. 2].

31 Tb.128, vol. V (*ca*), pp. 222[l. 1]-257[l. 4]. Not found in Tn, Tk.

Colophon: *rin po che snang byed ces bya ba'i rgyud rdzogs so || || slob dpon bi ma la mi tra dang | lo tsa ba gnyags dznyā na ku mā ras bsgyur zhing gtan la phab pa'o || khri srong lde btsan byang chub sems dpa'i rigs || ting 'dzin bzang po snod dang skal bar ldan || 'khrul rtsad chod nas ldog pa'i thabs dang ldan || lta ba rtogs nas sgro 'dogs chod pa'i tshe || snyan brgyud gdams pa skal ldan dag la brgyud || rtsa rgyud bshad rgyud ma bu la sogs rnams || snang dang mi snang bdag med dbyings su sba || skal ldan las 'phro can gyis rnyed par smon lam gdab || ces gdams so || nam zhig skal ldan gang zag gis || snyan brgyud bshad rgyud 'dzom par shog || ithi | dngos grub dam pa sems la chongs ||*

6) *Byang chub sems kyi man ngag | rin po che sgron ma 'bar ba'i rgyud*[32]

Colophon: *rin po che sgron ma 'bar ba'i rgyud rdzogs so || || rgya gar gyi mkhan po bi ma la mi tra dang | zhu chen gyi lo tsa ba gnyags dznyā nas dbu tshal gser khang du rgyal po yon mchod kyi don du bsgyur cing gtan la phab pa'o ||*

7) *Rin po che sgron ma zhes bya ba'i rgyud*[33]

Colophon: *rin po che sgron ma zhes bya ba'i rgyud rdzogs so || || slob dpon bi ma la mi tra dang | lo tsa ba gnyags ku mā ras rgyal po yon mchod kyi don du dbu tshal gser khang du bsgyur ba'o || chos skor mda' 'ug 'dod pa dang || rgyal po grong sprang byed pa dang || chos gos 'og tu gri 'dzugs dang || che btsun dug la spyod pa'i tshe | nyi zla'i 'od ltar 'byung bar 'gyur ||*

8) *rDzogs pa chen po sku gsum ye shes lnga'i don bshad pa nyi zla kha sbyor seng ge sgra yi dgongs pa bshad pa'i rgyud*[34]

Colophon: *paṇḍi ta bi ma la dang lo tsa ba gnyags ku mā ras 'chings [='chims] phu bre'u dge 'ur bsgyur cing zhus te gtan la phab pa'i rgyud | seng ge sgra'i dgongs pa nyi zla kha sbyor zhes bya ba'i rgyud | yang gsang rmad du byung ba bklags pas go ba'i bshad rgyud rdzogs so || || gsang | gsang | gsang rgya rtags || ||*

---

32 Tb.130, vol. V (*ca*), pp. 267[l. 1]-338[l. 6]. Not found in Tn, Tk. Whether the texts found in Nu and Na and bear similar titles are identical with our text is yet to be verified.

33 Tb.131, vol. V (*ca*), pp. 338[l. 6]-365[l. 4]. Not found in Tn, Tk.

34 Tb.136, vol. V (*ca*), pp. 440[l. 5]-596[l. 2]. Not found in Tn, Tk.

9) *rDzogs pa chen po 'khor ba rtsad nas gcod pa chos sku skye med rig pa'i rgyud*[35]

Colophon: *rdzogs pa chen po 'khor ba rtsad nas gcod pa chos sku skye med rig pa'i rgyud las | rin po che gter gyi 'byung gnas zhes bya ba rdzogs so || || rgya gar gyi mkhan po bi ma la mi tra dang | a tsarya dran pa ye shes kyis rang 'gyur byas te gtan la phab pa'o || ||*

10) *rDzogs pa chen po lta ba'i yang snying | sangs rgyas thams cad kyi dgongs pa | nam mkha' klong yangs kyi rgyud*[36]

Colophon: *rdzogs pa chen po lta ba'i yang snying rdzogs so || rdzogs pa chen po lta ba'i yang snying | sangs rgyas thams cad kyi dgongs pa | nam mkha' glong* [=*klong*] *yangs kyi rgyud ces bya ba | gser gyi dril shing can 'di | dang po ngo bo nyid kyi skus rgyal ba kun tu bzang po la bshad | des rdo rje sems dpa' la bshad | des dga' rab rdo rje la bshad | des bram ze bde mchog snying po la bshad | des shrī sing ha la bshad | des bi ma la mi tra la bshad | des myang ting 'dzin bzang po la bshad | des gter du sbas pa 'brom ye shes bla ma'i bu | 'brom ye shes snying pos bton nas | des myang shes rab mchog gi sras | des shangs kyi ston pa lce chung ba ye shes rgyal mtshan la bshad | des bla ma gnyan chung ba la gnang ba'o | rgya gar gyi mkhan po bi ma la mi tra dang | bod kyi lo tsa ba dran pa ye shes kyis bsgyur cing gtan la phab nas | myang ting 'dzin bzang pos lcags sgrom nag po'i nang du bri ze'i rgyud drug gdams pa dang bcas pa bse sgrom smug por bcug nas | dbu ru bzong phug mo'i brag la mkha' 'gro ma rdo rje rgyan gcig ma dang | badzra sā dhu legs pa rtsal la gtad nas sbas pa rdzogs so ||*

11) *rDzogs pa chen po sangs rgyas thams cad kyi dgongs pa chos sku gcig tu 'dus par bka' bgros pa'i don rin po che 'byung gnas kun 'byung gi rgyud*[37]

Colophon: *rdzogs pa chen po sangs rgyas thams cad kyi dgongs pa chos sku gcig tu 'dus par bka' bgros pa'i don rin po che yon tan kun 'byung gi rgyud las | dharmma kā ya sadhi pa ya | gu ru te tsu dznyā na ke tu tsitta sa ma ya gu hya ya rdzogs so || || rgya gar gyi mkhan po bi ma la mi tra dang | zhu chen gyi lo tsa ba dran pa ye shes kyis bsgyur cing gtan la phab nas | myang ting nge 'dzin la gdams | des sbas | mo rgyal le 'tsho la gdams| des sbas | blo gros seng ge la gdams | des 'brom ye shes bla ma la gdams | des sras rgyal ba'i shes rab la gdams | des zhang dar ma ye shes la gdams | des shangs pa lce chung ba ye shes rgyal mtshan la gdams so || snyan*

---

[35] Tb.142, vol. VI (*cha*), pp. 162[l. 1]-194[l. 7].

[36] Tb.143, vol. VI (*cha*), pp. 194[l. 7]-307[l. 3]. Found in Bg.

[37] Tb.144, vol. VI (*cha*), pp. 307[l. 4]-414[l. 7].

brgyud nges pa gdam [=gdams] ngag gi lde mig | po ti se ru mthing shog can gyi rgyud rdzogs so || ||

12) *Byang chub sems yid skyob pa*[38]

Colophon: *rgya gar gyi mkhan po bi ma la mi tra dang | zhu chen gyi lo tsa ba dran pa'i ye shes kyis bsgyur cing zhus te gtan la phab nas | nyang ting 'dzin la gdams | des sba mo rgya le mtsho la gdams || [=|] des sba blo gros dbang phyug la gdams | des 'brom ye shes bla ma la gdams | des sras rgyal ba'i shes rab la gdams | des zhang dar ma ye shes la gdams | des shangs pa lce chung ba ye shes rgyal mtshan la gdams | des shud kye ston pa mi' 'jigs la gdams | des sngog [=rngog] ston rgyal mtshan la gdams | de lce ston rdo rje gzungs la gdams so || snyan rgyud [=brgyud] nges pa'i lde mig | po ti se ru mthing shog can gyi rgyud rdzogs so ||*

13) *rDzogs pa chen po don 'dus rig pa'i gsung rang byung bde ba'i 'khor lo*[39]

Colophon: *gser gyis dril | bi ma las a tsarya la | des myang la | des gzod [=gzong] phug mor gdam [=gdams] ngag 'di ye shes snying po la | ston kyang des kas ston | des myang dbang phyug rgya mtsho la | des shangs pa la | des gtsang gi bgrod ston la | des ra ston la | des byang chub rgyan la | rdzogs so || ||*

14) *rDzogs pa chen po rmad byung don gyi snying po rang byung bde ba'i 'khor lo'i rgyud*[40]

Colophon: *rdzogs pa chen po rmad byung don gyi snying po rang byung bde ba'i 'khor lo'i rgyud gser gyi 'khril shing can zhes bya ba rdzogs so || || rgya gar gyi mkhan po bi ma la mi tra dang | bod kyi lo tsa ba gnyag dznyā na ku ma ras bsgyur cing zhus te gtan la phab pa'o || myang ting 'dzin bzang po la bshad | des gter du man ngag dang bcas pa bcug | mgon po nag po rdo rje legs pa dang | rdo rje rgyan gcig ma la gtad | dbu ru gzong phug mo'i brag la sbas | 'brom ye shes snying pos bton nas | sras dbang phyug rgya mtsho la bshad | des sras ye shes seng ge la gtad | des rngog ston 'od 'bar la gtad | des rong pa snubs chung ba dang | myang rin chen gtsug tor la gtad pa'o ||*

15) rDzogs pa chen po ma rig mun pa rab tu sel bar byed pa'i lta ba ye shes gting nas rdzogs pa'i rgyud[41]

---

38 Tb.145, vol. VI (*cha*), pp. 415[l. 1]-464[l. 5]. Found in Bg.

39 Tb.146, vol. VI (*cha*), pp. 464[l. 5]-520[l. 6].

40 Tb.147, vol. VI (*cha*), pp. 520[l. 6]-570[l. 3]. Found in Bg.

41 Tb.153, vol. VII (*ja*), pp. 433[l. 5]-497[l. 3].

Colophon: *rdzogs pa chen po ma rig mun pa sel bar byed pa'i lta ba ye shes gting nas rdzogs pa'i rgyud rdzogs so || || rin po che dngul gyi dril shing can 'di rgya gar gyi mkhan po bi ma la mi tra dang | bod kyi lo tsa ba ā tsarya dran pa'i ye shes kyis skad dang rgyud kyis bsgyur nas gtan la phab nas | myang ting 'dzin bzang pos lcags sgrom nag po'i nang du | bse sgrom smug po'i nang du bcug ste dbu ru gzong phug mo'i brag tu bcug ste | mkha' 'gro ma rdo rje rgyan cig ma dang | badzra sā dhu legs pa rtsal [la] gtad nas sbas pa | 'brom ye shes snying pos bton nas myang dbang phyug rgya mtsho la gtad pa | shangs pa lce chung ba ye shes la gtad pa rdzogs so || ||*

16) *Rin po che 'khor lo rtsegs pa'i rgyud*[42]

Colophon: *rin po che 'khor lo rtsegs pa'i rgyud ces bya ba thun mong ma yin pa'i rgyud chen po rdzogs so || || bi ma la dang dpal brtsegs kyis bsgyur ||*

17) *Dur khrod phung po 'bar ba man ngag gi rgyud*[43]

Colophon: *dur khrod phung po 'bar ba'i man ngag gi rgyud rdzogs so || || slob dpon bi ma las mnga' bdag la gdams pa | gzhan la bstan par gyur na sgrol byed chen pos snying khrag 'jib | ces gdams so ||*

18) *Byang chub kyi sems nya mo bag la nyal*[44]

Colophon: *bi ma la dang bai ro'i 'gyur ||*

19) *'Phags pa gsang sngags chen po bsam gyis mi khyab pa'i mdo*[45]

Colophon: *byang chub kyi sems ting nge 'dzin drug pa zhes kyang bya | man ngag gi dgongs pa la bzla zhes kyang bya'o || 'phags pa gsang sngags chen po bsam gyis mi khyab pa zhes bya ba theg pa chen po'i mdo rdzogs so || || rgya gar gyi mkhan po bi ma la mi tra dang | bod kyi lo tstsha ba snyāgs dznyā na ku ma ras bsgyur cing zhus te gtan la phab | slad kyis a tsarya bai ro tsa na dang | snubs sangs rgyas ye shes kyis bsgyur te gtan la phab | ithi ||*[46]

---

42 Tb.156, vol. VII (*ja*), pp. 588[l. 1]-624[l. 1]. Found in Bg.

43 Tb.163, vol. VII (*ja*), pp. 816[l. 5]-839[l. 2]. Found in Bg.

44 Tb.167, vol. VII (*ja*), pp. 883[l. 6)-919[l. 6]. Found in Bg. Tb does not provide a title, the above title being taken from the phrase following the homage. Tk provides the title *Nya mo bag la nyal gyi rgyud.*

45 Tb.190, vol. VIII (*nya*), pp. 616[l. 3]-630[l. 1]. Found only in the Central Bhutanese Group.

46 It seems that we here have two translation colophons, the connection between them being unclear; that is, it is unclear whether the present version is a revised

20) *rDzogs pa chen po byang chub kyi sems mdzod kyi chos | rtsa ba nam mkha' gnyis pa las | ye shes nam mkha'*[47]

Colophon: *ye shes nam mkha' mdzod kyi rgyud rdzogs so || || rgya gar gyi paṇḍi ta bi ma la mi tra dang | lo tsa ba snyags dznya na ku mā ra dang | ka cog gis bsgyur ba'o || ||*

21) *Ye shes bla ma chen po'i rgyud*[48]

Colophon: *'og min gi gnas chos kyi dbyings kyi pho brang du | sangs rgyas 'od srungs chen pos gsungs | zhu ba po lag na rdo rjes zhus | sdud pa po dga' rab rdo rje bsdus nas | sa non pa'i byang chub sems dpa' mi gzhi la lag brgyud de | 'jig rten du ma 'phel lo || rgyud kyi snying po ye shes bla ma'i rgyud || bskal pa thog ma med pa'i sngon rol nas || bskal pa bzang po'i byang chub sems dpa'i thugs nas thugs brgyud | snyan nas snyan du bsgrags || phyag nas phyag tu gtad de rgya yis btab || rgya gar ngan sngags 'bru gsum 'phyod du rtags || ra chod gzu lums byed pa'i slob ma la || sdig la mi 'dzem gnag pa'i las la sbyar || gu lang rin chen gser gyi rtags btsugs kyang || gnag pa'i ngan sngags 'bru gsum shor re skan || bi ma mi tra mkhas pa'i skye [=skyes] mchog khyod || sangs rgyas thugs kyi dgongs pa rgyud bdun po || rdo rje dbyings kyi pho brang dbyings su sbos || | zhes shrī sing has gsungs nas rgya yis btab bo || rdzogs so || || de nas bi ma la mi tra bod du byon nas | dbang bskur chos bshad nas || rje 'bangs gnyis la bka' gdams pa | sangs rgyas thugs kyi dgongs pa nyung rgyud pa || rdo rje gdan gyi 'og nas seng ge ma smad dgu || stobs chung rnams kyis seng ge mi thub kyis || rgyal blon phyag tu gtad kyis shor ra re || rgyal po snyan khung chung ba dang || blon po gdud [=gdug] pa che ba dang || chos pa dam la mi gnas pas | thugs la chongs la gter du sbos || zhes gsungs nas || slar gter du sbas so ||*

22) *dBang bskur bla ma rin po che'i rgyud*[49]

Colophon: *ā tsarya bi ma la mi tra dang | bod kyi lo tsa ba ska cog zhang gsum gyis bsgyur cing zhus te gtan la phab pa'o || || rdzogs so || || tha ras rgya yis btab bo || sngon du 'gro ba'i bsten pa ste || sta gon cho ga rdzogs pa'o || dang po la ni sgrub pa 'byung || ting 'dzin sngags dang 'phro 'du*

---

translation by Vairocana and sNubs Sangs rgyas ye shes of Vimalamitra's and sNyags dznya na ku ma ra's translation, or whether it is a wholly independent translation prepared by the former team.

47 Tb.203, vol. VIII (*nya*), pp. 905[l. 3]-933[l. 2]. Found in Bg. Found only in the Central Bhutanese Group.

48 Tb.235, vol. IX (*ta*), pp. 399[l. 2]-415[l. 4]. Found in Bg.

49 Tb.236, vol. IX (*ta*), pp. 415[l. 5]-437[l. 3]. Found in Bg. Found only in the Central Bhutanese and the Tibetan-Nepalese Borderlands Groups.

bya || gnyis pa tshe dbang bskur bar bya || gsum pa ye shes spyi blugs dang || bzhi pa sangs rgyas rab bdun dang || lnga pa rig pa rtsal gyi dbang || rim pa bzhin du las la sbyar || rdzogs dang rgyud lung man ngag bshad || nga yis bstan pa'i tshe dbang 'di || ma bskur bar du bshad pa min || ces dga' rab rdo rjes 'jam dpal la gdams pa'o | zhes ye shes bla ma'i le'u lag rdzogs so || || ithi | gter rgya ||

23) *Lha mo 'od zer can gyi rgyud*[50]

Colophon: *rgya gar gyi slob dpon bi ma la mi tra dang | bod kyi lo tsa ba ska cog [zhang] gsum gyis bsgyur cing zhus te gtan la phab pa | lha mo 'od zer can gyi rgyud rdzogs so || ||*

24) *'Phags pa 'jam dpal gyi bshad rgyud rin po che'i 'phreng ba*[51]

Colophon: *le'u dgu yis bstan pa'o || mtshan yang dag par brjod pa'i bshad rgyud rin po che'i 'phreng ba zhes bya ba rdzogs so || || 'phags pa 'jam dpal gyi mtshan yang dag par brjod pa'i bshad rgyud rin po che'i 'phreng ba zhes pa | khog don gyi bka' tshoms rnam par bshad pa | rgya gar gyi mkhan po bi ma la mi tra dang | bod kyi lo tsa ba gnyags dznyā na ku ma ras bsgyur zhing [=cing] zhus te gtan la phab nas | bod kyi yon bdag rje rgyal po la gtad pa'o || dpe myang ting 'dzin la gnang ba lags so ||*

25) *De bzhin gshegs pa thams cad kyi ting nge 'dzin dngos su bshad pa ye shes 'dus pa'i mdo | theg pa chen po gsang ba bla na med pa'i rgyud | chos thams cad kyi 'byung gnas | sangs rgyas thams cad kyi dgongs pa | gsang sngags gcig pa'i ye shes | rdzogs pa chen po don gsal bar byed pa'i rgyud | rig pa rang shar chen po'i rgyud |*[52]

Colophon: *ston pa gzhon nu dpa' bo stobs ldan gyis | dur khrod me ri 'bar bar 'khor rnams kyi rtog pa bsal ba | ye shes lag phrad du bstan pa'i rgyud rig pa rang shar chen po'i rgyud ces bya ba | man ngag gi bshad rgyud chen po rdzogs so || ||* [...] *dpal gsang sngags kyi srung ma lcam dral gyis bka'i bya ra gyis shig | dam tshig nyams pa thams cad kyi snying khrag 'jibs la srog chod cig | dpal sngags kyi srung ma smug nag khros pa'i rgyal mo e ka rtsa [=dza] tis bka'i bya ra gyis shig | dpal zhwa'i mgon po dam tshig gi bdag po| dam tshig la mi gnas pa rnams la zhags pas chings la sgrol cig | dam tshig nyams pa rnams la byin na | mkha' 'gro sde chen bco brgyad kyis chad pa chod cig | man ngag gi rgyud dam pa 'di ni slob dpon bi ma las sgra mi mthun pa gsum las bsgyur ba lags so || des rje blon gnyis*

---

[50] Tb.237, vol. IX (*ta*): pp. 437[l. 3]-446[l. 1]. Found in Bg. Found only in the Central Bhutanese and Tibetan-Nepalese Borderlands Group.

[51] Tb.271, vol. X (*tha*), pp. 671[l .6]-709[l. 6].

[52] Tb.286, vol. XI (*da*): pp. 323[l. 1]-699[l. 1]. Not found in Tn.

la snang [=gnang] ste | rgyud chen po 'di nam [=nas] | rje las myang ban la yang med par | rin po che shel gyi glegs shing du bsdams nas | rin po che dngul gyi ga'u'i nang du bcug nas | gzer chen po bzhis gdams nas | myang ban la | rje'i zhal nas 'di bod phung bar byed pa'i ngan sngags yin gyis | 'dis bod phung nas 'gro bas | 'di yang khyed kyis de tsho'i zla la sbos shig | ces bsdams nas re [=ras] nag la dril nas | myang ban la'ang cha med par | rje la snang [=gnang] ba lags so || de nas myang ban chen po des zhwa'i lha khang du mgon po gres thag can la gnyer du gtad nas sbas pa lags so || rje'i gsang ba'i thugs dam nyid ma nor ba lags so || de nas gnas brtan ldan mas | lce btsun seng ge dbang phyug la gnang ba lags so || lha rjes nyams su blangs pa'i man ngag shin tu zab par bstan pa || [=|] gang dang yang mi 'dra bar nyams su blangs par bstan pa'i gsang ba'i man ngag dam pa 'di gud du sbas pa lags so || rgyud kyi rgyal po 'di ni 'dzam bu'i gling gzhan na med par yid ches so || nyan mi dgos dpe lung thob pas chog go || man ngag rnams kyi rgyal po 'di || [=|] snod med pa la byin na gnyis ka 'tshig | las can sbyangs pa'i stobs kyis rnyed par shog | de nas gsang sngags bstan pa yun rings gnas par shog | ces gsungs so || 'gro rnams ma rig mun sel 'gyur || bdag 'dra smyon pa lce btsun gyis || yang dag don gyi man ngag zab mo 'di || rgya gar mkhas pa'i bka' rgyud [=brgyud] bdag la babs || kun la dkon pa'i man ngag zab mo 'di || kun gyis ma tshoms sa yi gter du sbas || las kyi 'phro can cig gis rnyed par shog || ces smon lam btab nas | lha rjes sa'i gter du sbas so || man ngag zab mo yang dag pa'o || dad med log lta can dang las 'brel med pa'i spyod yul min | [...] sang kri ta'i dha ka la | [sang] skri ta'i yi gi [=ge] las bsgyur ba lags so || [...] spu ta spu ta tra sa yi yis | o rgyan gyi yi ge las bsgyur ba lags so || [...] bag ta shud dha ri pa ta yan | rgya nag po'i yi ge las bsgyur ba lags so || slob dpon chen po bhi ma las sgra gsum las bsgyur ba lags so || ithi gsang ngo | rgya rgya rgya ||

26) *Rin po che spungs pa'i yon tan chen po ston pa'i rgyud kyi rgyal po chen po*[53]

Colophon: *rin po che spungs pa zhes bya ba'i rgyud kyi rgyal po | 'bum phrag drug cu rtsa bzhi'i bcud phyung ba rdzogs so || || rgya gar gyi mkhan po bi ma la dang| bod kyi lo tsa ba ka ba dpal brtsegs kyis bsgyur ba'o ||*

27) *dPal nam mkha' med pa sku gdung 'bar ba chen po'i rgyud*[54]

Colophon: *zhes dpal nam mkha' med pa'i rgyud rin po che sku gdung 'bar ba'i rgyud chen po gsang ba yang bsdus kyi snying po | rang bzhin rdzogs*

---

[53] Tb.288, vol. XI (*da*), pp. 757[l. 3]-788[l. 2]. Not found in Tn.

[54] Tb.289, vol. XI (*da*), pp. 788[l. 2]-815[l. 7]. Not found in Tn. Admitted into the O rgyan gling *bKa' 'gyur* (O36).

pa chen po'i rgyud | sho lo ka 'bum phrag brgya rtsa bzhi las khyad par du byung ba rdzogs so || ithi || rgya rgya rgya | rgya gar gyi mkhan po bi ma la mi tra dang | bod kyi lo tstsha ba ka ba dpal brtsegs kyis bsgyur cing gtan la phab pa'o ||

28) *Ngo sprod rin po che spras pa'i zhing khams bstan pa'i rgyud*[55]

Colophon: *gsang ba ngo sprod rin po che spras pa'i rgyud ces bya ba | rang bzhin rdzogs pa chen po 'bum phrag drug cu rtsa bzhi'i bcud rang byung ba rdzogs so || || rgya gar gyi mkhan po bi ma la dang | bod kyi lo tsa ba ka ba dpal brtsegs kyis bsgyur ba'o || dpal sngags kyi srung mas srungs shig |*

29) *Thig le gsang ba'i brda rgyud*[56]

Colophon: *rdzogs so || || rgya gar gyi mkhan po bi ma la mi tra dang | bod kyi lo tsha ba snyag* [=*snyags*] *dznyā na ku mā ras bsgyur ba'o ||*

30) *gSang ba rgya mtsho'i rgyud dam pa'i dam pa | rnal 'byor gyi rnal 'byor | gsang ba thams cad kyi tig ka rgyud kyi rgyal po*[57]

Colophon: *de bzhin gshegs pa thams cad kyi rang bzhin | gsang ba rgya mtsho zhes bya ba | shin tu rnal 'byor dam pa rdzogs so || || rgya gar gyi paṇḍi ta bi ma la mi tra dang | lo tshtsa* [=*tstsha*] *ba snyags dznyā na ku ma ras bsgyur ||*

31) *Thugs rje chen po'i gtor ma sha khrag rus pa'i gtor rgyud chen po*[58]

Colophon: *gtor rgyud chen po rdzogs so || || bstan pas mi rtogs pas gter du bcang | bcom ldan 'das kun tu bzang po la phyag 'tshal lo || lung 'di bka' thams cad kyi dam | rgyud thams cad kyi spyod 'grel | man ngag thams cad kyi snying khu | dgongs pa thams cad kyi zhe phugs | rnal 'byor pa thams cad kyi lta phugs su gyur pa 'di ni | kun mkhyen sems kyi ston pa zhes bya ba de yin par shes par bya'o || lta ba mdor bsdus pa zhes de la bgyi'o || man ngag thams cad kyi lta ba mdor bsdus pa zhes bya ba rdzogs so || || rgya gar gyi mkhan po padma sam bha ba dang | bi ma la mi tra dang | bod kyi lo tsa ba snubs nam mkha'i snying pos bsgyur ba'o || phyis bal po bā su bha ra dang | snubs sangs rgyas ye shes kyis zhus gtugs so || thugs rje chen po'i gtor rgyud rdzogs so ||*

---

55 Tb.294, vol. XII (*na*), pp. 280[l. 1]-304[l. 7].

56 Tb.306, vol. XIII (*pa*), pp. 528[l. 2]-540[l. 4]. Found in Bg.

57 Tb.313, vol. XIII (*pa*), pp. 621[l. 1]-641[l. 2]. Found only in the Central Bhutanese and Tibetan-Nepalese Borderlands Groups.

58 Tb.380, vol. XVII (*tsa*), pp. 2[l. 1]-176[l. 4].

32) *rDo rje rtse mo 'dus pa'i rgyud*[59]

Colophon: *gsung gi rgyud rdo rje rtse mo 'dus pa zhes bya ba | slob dpon bi ma la dang | lo tsa ba ka cog [zhang] gsum gyis bsgyur cing zhus te gtan la phab pa rdzogs so || ||*

33) *rGyud kyi rgyal po chen po las kyi 'phreng ba*[60]

Colophon: *lung chen bshad pa'i rgyud karma mā le rdzogs so | rgya gar gyi slob dpon dharmma shrī pra bha dang | ārya bi ma la la sogs pa'i paṇḍi ta la | ratna a grags bsgyur cing gtan la phab pa'o || ||*

34) *Dam tshig thams cad kyi nyams chag skong ba'i lung lnga | bshags pa thams cad kyi rgyud dri ma med pa'i rgyal po*[61]

Colophon: *nyams chag thams cad skong ba'i rgyud kyi rgyal po | bshags pa thams cad kyi rgyud dri ma med pa'i rgyal po zhes bya ba rdzogs so || || rgya gar gyi mkhan po bi ma la mi tra dang | bod kyi lo tsa ba snyags dznyā na ku ma ras bsgyur zhing zhus te gtan la phab pa'o ||*

35) *'Phags pa thabs kyi zhags pa padmo 'phreng gi don bsdus pa*[62]

Colophon: *'phags pa thabs kyi zhags pa padmo 'phreng ba las | rtog pa'i rgyal po'i don bsdus pa zhes bya ba rdzogs so || || rgya gar gyi paṇḍi ta bi ma la mi tra dang | lo tsa ba snyags dznyā na ku ma ras dpal gyi bsam yas su bsgyur cing zhus te gtan la phab pa'o ||*

36) *gSang ba'i snying po de kho na nyid nges pa*[63]

---

59 Tb.408, vol. XVIII (*tsha*), pp. 717[l. 7]-752[l. 3]. Found in Bg.

60 Tb.413, vol. XIX (*dza*), pp. 579[l. 6]-785[l. 7].

61 Tb.415, vol. XX (*wa*), pp. 2[l. 1]-123[l. 5]. A prayer linked by Kapstein to this *tantra* is found in the Dunhuang manuscript IOL TIB J 584. Most of the lines of the prayer are found in the *tantra* (chaps. 4, 5 and 6), which forms a part of the *Na rak dong sprugs* cycle of the *bKa' ma*. Kapstein has also linked IOL Tib J 318 to this cycle. See DALTON AND VAN SCHAIK 2006, p. 288.

62 Tb.416, vol. XX (*wa*), pp. 123[l. 6]-152[l. 6]. The basic *tantra* (*mūla*: *rtsa ba*) **Upāyapāśatantra* was found in Dunhuang and has been cited, referred to, and partially transmitted in several other Dunhuang documents. See DALTON AND VAN SCHAIK 2006, pp. 196-197. It is also mentioned by gNubs Sangs rgyas ye shes and Rong zom Chos kyi bzang po. See ALMOGI 2014, p. 73, n. 59. The *tantra* was admitted, too, into the *bKa' 'gyur* (P458/D835).

63 Tb.417, vol. XX (*wa*), pp. 152[l. 6]-218[l. 7]. The *tantra* is cited in documents found in Dunhuang, including IOL TIB J 332/1 and IOL TIB J 437/2; the mantra for the peaceful *maṇḍala* is found in IOL TIB J 540. See DALTON AND VAN SCHAIK 2006, pp. 61, 183 and 250-251, respectively. The *tantra* is possibly implied by the word "etc." (*la sogs pa*) in Zhi ba 'od's *bKa' shog*, in its listing of apparently syncretic (*'dres ma*) Māyājālatantras (*sgyu 'phrul gyi rgyud*). See

Colophon: *rdzogs so || rgya gar gyi paṇḍi ta bi ma la mi tra dang | lo tsa ba rma rin chen mchog gis bsgyur ba'o ||*

37) *gSang ba'i snying po de kho na nyid nges pa sgyu 'phrul dra ba bla ma chen po*[64]

Colophon: *rtog pa'i sgyu 'phrul dra ba'i le'u stong phrag brgya pa las | lung gi spyi sangs rgyas thams cad kyi gsang ba | gsang ba'i snying po de kho na nyid nges pa'i bla ma chen po'i le'u las | thams cad ma lus par 'phros pa rdzogs so || rgya gar gyi paṇḍi ta ā tsarya bi ma la mi tra dang | bod kyi lo tsa ba gnyag* [=*gnyags*] *dznyā na ku ma ras bsgyur ba'o ||*

38) *rGyas pa chen po'i rgyud phyi ta don 'dzin pa*[65]

Colophon: *rgyas pa chen po'i rgyud phyi ta don 'dzin pa rdzogs so || rgya gar gyi paṇṭi* [=*paṇḍi ta*] *bi ma la mi tra dang | bod kyi lo tsa ba rma rin chen mchog dang | snyags dznyā na ku ma ras bsgyur cing gtan la phab pa'o ||*

39) *Chos nyid zhi ba'i lha rgyud*[66]

Colophon: *rgyud kyi rgyal po chen po chos nyid zhi ba'i lha rgyud rdzogs so || || rgya gar gyi paṇḍi ta bi ma mi tra dang | bod kyi lo tsa ba gnyags dznyā na ku ma ras bsgyur cing zhus te gtan la phab pa'o || ||*

40) *rDo rje srin po rno ba rdo rje mchu can gyi rgyud ces bya ba| rgyud thams cad kyi snying po 'khor ba dong sprugs chen po'i rgyud*[67]

Colophon: *mkhas pa'i mkhas pa bla ma dam pa'i gdam ngag la | bka' dang sdod nas* [=*gnas*?] *don gyi man ngag btsal || rdo rje gdan nas shri sing ha ngas gnang || rang gi rgyud sbyangs 'gro ba'i don byas nas || sangs rgyas thugs kyi dgongs pas ma nor rgyud || thugs kyi klong nas bcud gsum spros pa ni || byang chub sems dpa' re re'i don du bzhag || rgyud kyi snying po*

KARMAY 1998, p. 31, no. 2. It is also mentioned by gNubs Sangs rgyas ye shes and Rong zom Chos kyi bzang po. See ALMOGI 2014, p. 77, n. 83. It has likewise been admitted into the *bKa' 'gyur* (P455/D832).

64 Tb.419, vol. XX (*wa*), pp. 337[l. 6]-417[l. 2]. The *tantra* is possibly implied by the word "etc." (*la sogs pa*) in Zhi ba 'od's *bKa' shog*, in its listing of apparently syncretic (*'dres ma*) Māyājālatantras (*sgyu 'phrul gyi rgyud*). See KARMAY 1998, p. 31, no. 2. It is also mentioned by gNubs Sangs rgyas ye shes. See ALMOGI 2014, p. 77, n. 85. The *tantra* has been admitted into the *bKa' 'gyur* (P460/D837).

65 Tb.427, vol. XXI (*zha*), pp. 476[l. 2]-477[l. 3]. Found in Bg.

66 Tb.433, vol. XXI (*zha*), pp. 610[l. 3]-622[l. 3].

67 Tb.436, vol. XXI (*zha*), pp. 697[l. 4]-715[l. 5]. Found in Bg.

man ngag gzer bzhi po || sde dang tshoms bu gcad nas rgya yis btab || 'chi med bdud rtsi thig le nyag gcig go || rdo rje gdan gyi 'og nas bzhengs pa 'di || spu rgyal rtsad po'i don du shri singha ngas gnang ba sku drin che || bod kyi chos lugs ngan pas slar gter du sbos | zhes bi ma la mi tras gdams so rdzogs so || ||

41) *sGyu 'phrul rgya mtsho zhes bya ba'i rgyud*[68]

Colophon: *sgyu 'phrul rgya mtsho'i rgyud chen po rdzogs so || || rgya gar gyi mkhan po bi ma mi tra dang | snyags dznā na ku ma ras bsgyur ba'o ||*

42) *sGyu 'phrul thal ba'i rgyud*[69]

Colophon: *sgyu 'phrul thal ba'i rgyud rdzogs so || || rgya gar gyi mkhan po bi ma la mi tra dang | dznā na ku mā ras 'phan yul du bsgyur cing gtan la phab pa'o ||*

43) *sGyu 'phrul thal ba'i rgyud chen po*[70]

Colophon: *sgyu 'phrul thal ba'i rgyud chen po zhes bya ba rdzogs so || || rgya gar gyi mkhan po bi ma la mi tra dang | dznā na ku mā ras 'phan yul du bsgyur cing zhus te gtan la phab pa'o || ||*

44) *rDo rje sems dpa'i sgyu 'phrul dra ba gsang ba thams cad kyi me long zhes bya ba'i rgyud*[71]

Colophon: *rdo rje sems dpa' sgyu 'phrul dra ba gsang ba me long gi rgyud chen po rdzogs so || || rgya gar gyi mkhan po bi ma la mi tra dang | ban dhe dznā na ku ma ras bsgyur cing zhus te gtan la phab pa'o ||*

45) *gSang ba'i snying po de kho na nyid nges pa'i khro bo chen po'i stobs kyi rnal 'byor dbang phyug sgrub pa'i sgyu 'phrul dra ba'i rgyud*[72]

Colophon: *gsang ba'i snying po de kho na nyid nges pa | khro bo chen po stobs kyi rnal 'byor dbang phyug sgrub pa'i sgyu 'phrul dra ba'i rgyud*

---

68 Tb.437, vol. XXII (*za*), pp. 2[l. 1]-103[l. 1].

69 Tb.438, vol. XXII (*za*), pp. 103[l. 1]-186[l. 4]. Found only in the Central Bhutanese Group.

70 Tb.439, vol. XXII (*za*), pp. 186[l. 5]-322[l. 2].

71 Tb.441, vol. XXII (*za*), pp. 480[l. 6]-692[l. 6]. The *tantra* has been admitted into the *bKa' 'gyur* (P456/D833).

72 Tb.442, vol. XXII (*za*), pp. 692[l. 7]-699[l. 2]. The *tantra* has been admitted into the O rgyan gling *bKa' 'gyur* (O17).

rdzogs so || || rgya gar gyi mkhan po bi ma la mi tra dang | lo tsa ba slob dpon bai ro tsa nas bsgyur cing zhus te gtan la phab pa'o ||

46) *bDud rtsi 'khyil ba 'chi med tshe'i rgyud*[73]

Colophon: *bdud rtsi 'khyil ba 'chi med tshe'i rgyud ces bya ba rdzogs so || || 'di chig rgyud yin bas spel na | dam can chos skyong dang | mkha' 'gro rnams kyi bka' chad yong bas | lung m thob pa la thos par mi bya ste | mthong ba lya cis smo so || rgya gar gyi mkhan po paṇḍita bi ma mi tra la | bod kyi lo tstsha ba mchims mdzid gsal 'bar gyis zhus te | bsgyur nas gtan la phab po ||*

47) *bDud rtsi chen po chos nyid gsang ba'i rgyud*[74]

Colophon: *bdud rtsi chen po chos nyid gsang ba'i rgyud rdzogs so || || rgya gar gyi mkhas pa bi ma la mi tra dang | bod kyi lo tsha ba gnyags snya* [=*dznyā*] *na ku ma ras bsgyur ba'o || ||*

48) *bDud rtsi las rgya mtsho'i rgyud*[75]

Colophon: *bdud rtsi las rgya mtsho'i rgyud ces bya ba rdzogs so || || rgya gar gyi mkhan po bi ma la mi tra dang | bod kyi lo tsa snyag dznyā na ku ma ras bsgyur ba'o ||*

49) *bDud rtsi chen po 'khor lo 'bar ba'i rgyud*[76]

Colophon: *bdud rtsi chen po 'khor lo 'bar ba'i rgyud rdzogs so || || rgya gar gyi mkhan po bi ma la mi tra dang | bod kyi lotstsha ba gnyags dznyā na ku ma ras bsgyur ba'o ||*

50) *Thams cad bdud rtsi lnga'i rang bzhin | rin ba* [=*po*] *che 'phreng ba'i rgyud*[77]

Colophon: *bdud rtsi gsung gi rgyud rin po che 'phreng ba rdzogs so || || rgya gar gyi paṇḍi ta bi ma la mi tra dang | bod kyi lo tstsha ba gnyags dznyā na ku ma ras bsgyur ro || ||*

51) *bDud rtsi bde ba chen po'i rgyud*[78]

---

[73] Tb.627, vol. XXXIV (*ngi*), pp. 98[l. 3]-147[l. 4]. The connection of text nos. 46-53 with the canonical work P464/D841 is yet to be studied.

[74] Tb.628, vol. XXXIV (*ngi*), pp. 147[l. 4]-206[l. 6]. See above, n. 73.

[75] Tb.630, vol. XXXIV (*ngi*), pp. 359[l. 3]-476[l. 1]. See above, n. 73.

[76] Tb.631, vol. XXXIV (*ngi*), pp. 476[l. 1]-528[l. 7]. See above, n. 73.

[77] Tb.632, vol. XXXIV (*ngi*), pp. 528[l. 7]-593[l. 4]. See above, n. 73.

[78] Tb.633, vol. XXXIV (*ngi*), pp. 593[l. 4]-647[l. 1]. See above, n. 73.

Colophon: *bdud rtsi bde ba chen po'i rgyud rdzogs so || || rgya gar gyi paṇ ḍi ta bi ma la mi tra dang | bod kyi lo tsha ba gnyags dznyā nas bsgyur ro ||*

52) *bDud rtsi rin po che ye shes gsang ba'i 'khor lo'i rgyud*[79]

Colophon: *ye shes gsang ba 'khor lo'i rgyud rdzogs so || || rgya gar gyi mkhan po bi ma la mi tra dang | zhu chen gyi lo tstsha ba zhang dznyā nas gtan la phab pa las | phyis ka ba dpal brtsegs la stsogs pas yongs su gtan la phab pa'o ||*

53) *Thams cad bdud rtsi lnga'i rang bzhin du 'khrungs shing skye bar byed pa'i 'bras bu rin po che'i 'od ltar bstan pa'i rgyud*[80]

Colophon: *'og min du grags pa tshe rdzogs so || || lha yul du grags par yang 'gro'o || mi yul du grags par yang rgyud cig bzhugs so || rgya gar gyi mkhan po bi ma la mi tra dang | snyags dznyā nas bsgyur ba'o || ||*

54) *'Phrin las phun sum tshogs pa'i rgyud*[81]

Colophon: *rgya gar gyi mkhan po bi ma la mi tra dang | lo tstsha ba ā tsarya dznyā nas gtan la phab pa las | rtag pa phyogs gcig pa rdzogs so ||*

55) *Phur ba bcu gnyis 'byung ba'i rgyud chung ngu bstan pa'o*[82]

Colophon: *phur ba bcu gnyis 'byung ba'i rgyud chung ngu | bcom ldan 'das rdo rje gzhon nus gsungs pa rdzogs s.hyo || || rgya gar gyi slob dpon bi ma la mi tra dang | lo tstsha ba gnyags dznyā na ku mā ras bsgyur cing zhus te gtan la phab pa'o || ||*

56) *gNod sbyin nor bdag gsang ba'i rgyud*[83]

Colophon: *gnod sbyin a pa ra tsitta gsang ba'i rgyud ces bya ba rdzogs so || || gu ru padmas bi ma la bshad | des gnyags dznyā na la bshad | des rdo rje yang dbang gter la bshad | des gter du sbas so || man ngag la dam tshig snying po rtsa ba'i sngags kyi dza dza'i gong du gzhug | dngos grub blang ba yang de ltar shes par bya | gtor ma'i snying po dza dza 'og tu*

---

[79] Tb.634, vol. XXXIV (*ngi*), pp. 647[l. 2]-714[l. 1]. See above, n. 73.

[80] Tb.635, vol. XXXIV (*ngi*), pp. 714[l. 1]-808[l. 5]. See above, n. 73.

[81] Tb.672, vol. XXXVI (*chi*): pp. 1008[l. 6]-1052[l. 3].

[82] Tb.684, vol. XXXVII (*ji*), pp. 1003[l. 3]-1030[l. 2]. A text titled *Ki la ya tan tra chung ngu* is mentioned in Zhi ba 'od's *bKa' shog* as spurious text. See KARMAY 1998, p. 33, no. 19.

[83] Tb.812, vol. XLIII (*pi*), pp. 322[l. 5]-328[l. 2]. Found only in the Central Bhutanese Group.

gdags | *kun dka'* [=*dga'*] *rtsa ba'i sngags la sbyar zhes gu ru bi ma las gsungs so* || ||

57) *sNying lung chen po'i rgyud*[84]

Colophon: *bi ma la mi tras sbrang gi btsas su bzhag pa rdzogs so* || ||

REFERENCES

ALMOGI forthcoming
O. Almogi, *The Collection of the Ancient Tantras (rNying ma rgyud 'bum): The History of Its Formation, Production, and Transmission*, Hamburg: University of Hamburg, Indian and Tibetan Studies Series

ALMOGI 2008
O. Almogi, "How Authentic Are Titles and Colophons of Tantric Works in the Tibetan Canon? The Case of Three Works and Their Authors and Translators," in O. Almogi (ed.), *Contributions to Tibetan Buddhist Literature. Proceedings of the Eleventh Seminar of the International Association for Tibetan Studies, Königswinter 2006*, Halle: International Institute for Tibetan and Buddhist Studies, Beiträge zur Zentralasienforschung 14, 2008, pp. 87-124

ALMOGI 2014
O. Almogi, "The Eighteen Mahāyoga Tantric Cycles: A Real Canon or the Mere Notion of One?" *Revue d'Études Tibétaines* 30, 2014, pp. 47-110

Bg
The Bai ro rgyud 'bum. The rGyud 'bum of Vairocana. A collection of ancient tantras and esoteric instructions compiled and translated by the eighth century Tibetan master, reproduced from the rare manuscript belonging to the Venerable Tokden Rimpoche of Gangon, 8 vols., Lch: Tashi Y. Tashigangpa, 1971; catalogue: *The Tibetan and Himalayan Digital Library* (THL), the University of Virginia, at http://www.thlib.org/encyclope dias/ literary/canons/ngb/

CANTWELL ET AL. 1999-2003
C. Cantwell, R. Mayer and M. Fisher, *The Rig 'dzin Tshe dbang nor bu Edition of the rNying ma'i rgyud 'bum: An Illustrated Inventory*, 1999-2003, http://ngb.csac-.anthropology.ac.uk/index.html

CANTWELL ET AL. 2006
C. Cantwell, R. Mayer, M. Kowalewski and J.-L. Achard, *The sGang steng-b rNying ma'i rGyud 'Bum Manuscript from Bhutan*, *Revue d'Études Tibétaines* 11, 2006

[84] Tb.853, vol. XLIV (*phi*), pp. 81[l. 5]-102[l. 2]. Found only in the Central Bhutanese Group.

D
The Tibetan Buddhist Canon (*bKa' 'gyur* and *bsTan 'gyur*), sDe dge edition; catalogue: *Peking Tripitaka Online Search*, at http://web1.otani.ac.jp/cri/ twrpe/peking/

DALTON AND VAN SCHAIK 2006
J. Dalton and S. van Schaik, *Tibetan Tantric Manuscripts from Dunhuang: A Descriptive Catalogue of the Stein Collection at the British Library*, Leiden: Brill, 2006

dBa' bzhed
See WANGDU AND DIEMBERGER 2000

Dg
sDe dge Xylograph Edition of the *rNying ma rgyud 'bum*, 25+1 vols.; scans: TBRC W21939; catalogue: *The Tibetan & Himalayan Library*, at http://www.thlib.org/encyclopedias/literary/canons/ngb/

Gt
sGang steng Ms Edition of the *rNying ma rgyud 'bum* B, 46 vols.; digitisation: Karma Phuntsho in cooperation with The British Library; catalogue: see CANTWELL ET AL. 2006

JAMPA SAMTEN 1994
Jampa Samten, "Notes on the bKa' 'gyur of O rgyan gling, the Family Temple of the Sixth Dalai Lama (1683-1706)," in *Tibetan Studies. Proceedings of the 6th Seminar of the International Association for Tibetan Studies, Fragernes 1992*, Oslo: The Institute for Comparative Research in Human Culture, vol. I, 1994, pp. 393-402

KARMAY 1998
S.G. Karmay, *The Arrow and the Spindle: Studies in History, Myths, Rituals and Beliefs in Tibet*, Kathmandu: Mandala Book Point, 1998

MARTIN 1997
D. Martin (in collaboration with Y. Bentor), *Tibetan Histories: A Bibliography of Tibetan-Language Historical Works*, London: Serindia Publications, 1997

mKhas grub rim byon
Ko zhul grags pa 'byung gnas and rGyal ba blo bzang mkhas grub, *Gangs can mkhas grub rim byon ming mdzod*, Lanzhuo: Kan su'u mi rigs dpe skrun khang, 1992

Na
National Archives Ms. Edition of the *rNying ma rgyud 'bum*, 37(?) vols. (incomplete); microfilm: Nepal-German Manuscript Preservation Project (NGMPP), Reel No. AT 1/1-AT 25; catalogue: see ALMOGI forthcoming

NSTB
G. Dorje and M. Kapstein (transl.), *The Nyingma School of Tibetan Buddhism: Its Fundamentals and History*, Boston: Wisdom Publications, 1991

Nu
Nubri Ms. Edition of the *rNying ma rgyud 'bum*, 37 vols.; microfilm: Nepal-German Manuscript Preservation Project (NGMPP), Reel No. L 426/4-L 448/1; catalogue: see ALMOGI forthcoming

O
O rgyan gling *bKa' 'gyur* (text nos. according to JAMPA SAMTEN 1994)

P
The Tibetan Buddhist Canon (*bKa' 'gyur* and *bsTan 'gyur*), Peking edition; catalogue: *Peking Tripitaka Online Search*, at http://web1.otani.ac.jp/cri/twrpe/peking/

rNying ma rgyud 'bum
See Tb, Gt, Tk, Tn, Nu, Na, Dg

SKORUPSKI 1985
T. Skorupski, *A Catalogue of the sTog Palace Kanjur*, Tokyo: The International Institute for Buddhist Studies, Bibliographia Philologica Buddhica, Series Maior 4, 1985

T
sTog *bKa' 'gyur*; scans: TBRC W22083; catalogue: see SKORUPSKI 1985

Tb
mTshams brag Ms. Edition of the *rNying ma rgyud 'bum*, Thimphu: National Library, 1982, 46 vols.; scans: TBRC: W21521; catalogue: *The Tibetan & Himalayan Library*, at http://www.thlib.org/encyclopedias/literary/canons/ngb/

Tk
gTing skyes Ms. Edition of the *rNying ma rgyud 'bum*, Thimphu: Dingo Khyentse Rimpoche, 1973-1975, 33+3 vols.; scans: TBRC: W21598; catalogue: *The Tibetan & Himalayan Library*, at http://www.thlib.org/encyclopedias/literary/canons/ngb/

Tn
Rig 'dzin Tshe dbang nor bu Ms. Edition of the *rNying ma rgyud 'bum*; catalogue: see CANTWELL ET AL. 1999-2003

WANGDU AND DIEMBERGER 2000
P. Wangdu and H. Diemberger (transl.), *dBa' bzhed: The Royal Narrative Concerning the Bringing of the Buddha's Doctrine to Tibet*, Vienna: Österreichische Akademie der Wissenschaften, 2000

The World on Show, or Sensibility in Disguise.

Philosophical and Aesthetic Issues in a Stanza by Abhinavagupta (*Tantrāloka* I 332, *Locana* ad *Dhvanyāloka* I 13)*

LYNE BANSAT-BOUDON

The stanza I examine here belongs to two texts by Abhinavagupta: the *Tantrāloka* (henceforth TĀ) and the *Dhvanyālokalocana* (henceforth *Locana*). It is amenable to different interpretations according to the text in which it appears, its context and its exegesis. The stanza must have been famous, since it is quoted again by Bhāskara, commenting on Abhinavagupta's *Īśvarapratyabhijñāvimarśinī* (henceforth ĪPV) ad *Īśvarapratyabhijñākārikā* (henceforth ĪPK) I 1, 14.[1]

Jayaratha, the author of the *Viveka* (henceforth TĀV), comments on the stanza in the TĀ. In the *Locana* [ad *Dhvanyāloka* I 13], it is Abhinavagupta who offers a self-exegesis of it. I give here a provisional translation, in conformity with the context in which it is employed as well as with the analysis of the TĀV:[2]

* I wish to express my deep gratitude to David Shulman whose paper, published in this volume, has inspired the last section of my contribution and whose careful reading of my first draft has significantly improved its English wording. I am likewise indebted to Yigal Bronner for his insightful comments on the question of the *aprastutapraśaṃsā* and to Yves Codet for a thorough discussion on several points of interpretation. I am also extremely grateful to Christophe Valia-Kollery for his final reading of the English text and, needless to say, to Isabelle Ratié for her rigorous and generous work on the final editing.

1 *Bhāskarī* ad ĪPV I 1, 4; see Appendix-4.

2 See below, § 1, for the detail of Jayaratha's analysis.

bhāvavrāta haṭhāj janasya hṛdayāny ākramya yan nartayan bhaṅgībhir vividhābhir ātmahṛdayaṃ pracchādya saṃkrīḍase |
yas tvām āha jaḍaṃ jaḍaḥ sahṛdayaṃmanyatvaduḥśikṣito manye 'muṣya jaḍātmatā stutipadaṃ tvatsāmyasaṃbhāvanāt ||[3]

O whole of things! Since you play at forcibly[4] grabbing hold of the hearts of men, as does an actor with his various costumes, and at hiding your heart that is the Self, he who calls you unconscious is himself unconscious: wrongly believing that he is endowed with a heart (*sahṛdaya*), he has not completed his education. Nevertheless, his very unconsciousness, I think,[5] is praiseworthy, since we do imagine him (*saṃbhāvana*) as identical to you.

The stanza is explicitly organized by the theatrical metaphor. We will see how remarkable it is in its complex construction and in the different levels of meaning that inform it.[6]

Being an apostrophe to the *bhāvavrāta*, the "whole of things," or phenomenal diversity, the stanza appears as a drama with three characters: the *bhāvavrāta*, the *jana* (the ordinary man whom the TĀV turns into a *vādin*, an "interlocutor," that is, here an adversary; see below, p. 38), and the "I" of the main verb, *manye*, through which Abhinavagupta, exponent of the Trika, makes his voice heard. The "I" of *manye* thus adresses phenomenal diversity as he would the deity – this is the interpretation of both the TĀV (below, pp. 40, 45-47) and the *Locana* (below, p. 60) – and introduces an effect of *mise en abyme* with the reported speech attributed to the *jana*.

The meter is *śārdūlavikrīḍita*, frequent in lyrical poetry, and such is indeed the tone of this address to the *bhāvavrāta*, which amounts to a celebration – a lyricism that again expresses itself through the "I" of *manye*, in which Abhinavagupta manifests himself as the representative of the Śaivas.

---

3 Sanskrit texts are quoted as they appear in the reference edition – I have not corrected the *sandhi*.

4 Note that *haṭhāt* has the double meaning: "by force" and "invincibly."

5 Compare D. Shulman's paper in this volume on the use of *jāne*: according to Abhinavagupta (commenting on a verse quoted in the *Dhvanyālokavṛtti* ad III 43), *jāne* "is often a marker of the figure *utprekṣā*, 'flight of fancy,' but [...] here [...] its litteral meaning is what matters."

6 For examples of Tantric usages of the theatrical analogy, see J. Törzsök's contribution to this volume.

Moreover, as Jayaratha observes as if in passing, the stanza is organized by the *aprastutapraśaṃsā* figure. This is a remark that Jayaratha exploits only partially, focussing on the denoted meaning, which is the *aprastuta*, or non-pertinent topic, whereas the *Locana* gives the *aprastutapraśaṃsā* all its meaning and weight, as we shall see (see below, pp. 48ff.).

Among figures of speech, the *aprastutapraśaṃsā* is one of those in which suggestion is in operation: while something non-pertinent or irrelevant (*aprastuta*) to the speaker and the listener is being described (*praśaṃsā*),[7] what is really meant, that is, the suggested meaning, is something pertinent or relevant (*prastuta*) to them; besides, the relationship between the non-pertinent and the pertinent can be of three types[8] (in the case of our stanza, similarity – *sārūpya*).

That stanza (as well as its commentaries by Abhinavagupta, Jayaratha or Bhāskara) plays, in particular, on the polysemy of the adjective *jaḍa*, since *jaḍa* means, among several equivocations i) insentient, ii) unconscious (Jayaratha glosses it by *acetana*), iii) devoid of reason, that is stupid, or even iv) insane (as we shall see about the *Locana*'s analysis).

In the light of its commentaries, the stanza appears as a remarkable illustration of the way Śaiva thought merges philosophical and aesthetic registers within one another. One can see here a movement, a turn of mind, inherent in that system of thought which offers us the essential lineaments of Indian aesthetic theory.

I would like to show that, in the two occurrences of the stanza, aesthetics and poetics (to which the *Locana* explicitly refers) serve as a speculative paradigm for the doctrine of which Abhinavagupta is one of the foremost exponents.

Jayaratha goes no further than a philosophical interpretation of the stanza, which coincides with the expressed meaning alone: everything is sentient. And in order to establish that fundamental truth of Kashmirian non-dualist Śaivism, Jayaratha develops the dramatic metaphor of the first hemistich.

---

7 See GEROW 1971, p. 317: "mention made of a topic irrelevant to the subject" and INGALLS ET AL. 1990, who understands: "praise by means of the extraneous," and identifies it as the allegory.

8 The three types of relationship between *aprastuta* and *prastuta* being that of cause and effect, general and particular and similarity; see *Dhvanyāloka* I 13 and *Locana*.

The *Locana* proposes the same reading of the stanza: everything is sentient, including, first and foremost, the object wrongly said to be insentient, but the *Locana* goes beyond this statement by hinting at a second meaning, more esoteric, and for that very reason only suggested, thus taking the *aprastutapraśaṃsā* as an example of *dhvani*, specially, *vastudhvani* (see below, p. 50).

Nevertheless, since Jayaratha identifies the stanza as an *aprastutapraśaṃsā*, there should be a suggested meaning, which would be the *prastuta*. Although Jayaratha does not emphasize it, I propose to find that suggested meaning in the *avataraṇikā* to the exegetical passage and in its conclusion (see below, p. 37). On the basis of an understanding of that *aprastutapraśaṃsā* as organized by similarity (as shown by the *Locana*, which gives two examples of the figure and refers to our stanza as a case of *aprastutapraśaṃsā* based on similarity; see below, p. 48), the expressed *aprastuta* would be, beyond the apostrophe to the *bhāvavrāta*, the postulation of the equal sentience of the subject (here the *paśu*) and the object (in the form of all the objects, the *bhāvavrāta*). The suggested *prastuta* would be – by means of Jayaratha's rather unexpected identification of the *paśu* with the *vādin*, the "opponent" – the Śaivas' non-dualist attack against all opponents of their doctrine, with the ultimate intention of ridiculing all of them and establishing the Śaiva non-dualism as supreme.

Now, the question remains that, in the TĀ's context and according to Jayaratha's exegesis (who cares little, it seems, for the subtleties of Abhinavagupta's reasonings in the *Locana*), the *aprastutapraśaṃsā* is here to be understood as a mere figure of speech, and not as a case of *vastudhvani*, as claimed by Abhinavagupta in his *Locana* quoting the same verse. If one follows Ānandavardhana's exposition in the *vṛtti* ad I 13[9] and Abhinavagupta's commentary thereon, this means that, in the context of the TĀ, the direct expressed meaning (the apostrophe to the *bhāvavrāta*) is considered predominant (the criterium for such a distinction being that it is the expressed meaning that, in this case, creates *camatkāra*, "wonderment"), whereas the suggested meaning (the ridiculing and defeat of the adversaries) is subordinated. We shall see the whole process in detail further on (pp. 48ff.).

[9] I admit, with Ingalls, that Ānandavardhana is as well the author of the *vṛtti*; see INGALLS ET AL. 1990, pp. 25-27.

Thus, in the TĀ, the *aprastutapraśaṃsā* is considered as a mere figure of speech and mainly serves a polemical purpose.

It is in this way that we can understand Jayaratha's *avataraṇikā*:

> *idānīm asya śāstrasya paraṃ gāmbhīryaṃ manyamāno granthakṛt, etad-arthasatattvam ajānānair api anyair anyathābodhena yatkiṃcid uttānam eva anyathā ucyate, tān prati aprastutapraśaṃsayā upahasitum āha...*,
>
> Now, considering the extreme depth of the [preceeding] teaching, [and, also,] that others, though ignorant of its essential meaning, persist in making erroneous and non-sensical pronouncements, as an effect of an understanding itself erroneous, the author of the treatise contradicts them, using the [following] *aprastutapraśaṃsā*, for ridiculing them [...],

as well as the conclusion, in which sarcasm intends to denounce any other system of thought as erroneous, and to reaffirm the infaillibility of the non-dualist Śaiva doctrine:

> *evaṃ prakṛte 'pi asya granthasya yas tattvaṃ na jānāti mā jñāsīt, pratyuta anyathāpi yatkiṃcana vakti ity asāv eva jaḍo, na punar asya granthasya kaścid doṣaḥ ity arthaḥ* |
>
> In order to come back to our subject, such is its meaning: the one who does not know the truth [expounded] in this treatise – let him not know it! And even more if he utters nonsense and falsehood, it is he himself who is the unconscious idiot; this treatise is not at fault in any way. This is the meaning.

1. THE *TANTRĀLOKAVIVEKA* AD *TANTRĀLOKA* I 332

I will limit myself to a synthesis of the analysis of the TĀV, whose text I give in Appendix-1.

The reasoning of the stanza is tightly woven and plays with paradox, as so often in this system of thought:

1. Everything is sentient. This is why (*yat*)...
2. ... the one who says phenomenal diversity is insentient and stupid is himself insentient and stupid, blinded by his very ignorance, that is, by his being unable to recognize the identity of the subject and the object;
3. Nevertheless, since we Śaivas imagine – by virtue of the principle of non-duality – that such an ignorant fool is similar to you, O *bhāvavrāta*, the blame that he puts on you and that we

have just transferred to him (since he is the fool) turns to praise.

The entire philosophical point of the stanza lies in this last statement, the locus of a paradoxical mockery: it is because the *jana* partakes of this consciousness which he wrongly believes to be unconscious that he is really a *sahṛdaya*,[10] not for the reason he thinks (his sentience contrasting with the insentience of the objects).

The TĀV develops this line of thought and makes it clear that the stanza is a formulation of the non-dualism of the doctrine, which is precisely the main issue of the first chapter of the TĀ where our stanza appears.

The novelty of the TĀV's interpretation consists in reading, under the *jana* of the stanza (who appears again in the relative clause: *yas tvām āha...*), a *vādin*, that is, an "interlocutor" and therefore an opponent of Trika monism (note that the term *vādin* appears three times in the TĀV ad I 332; see Appendix-1, in bold). Jayaratha gives the content of the experience, inner struggles and impotence of that *vādin*, through a rather enigmatic (and unidentified[11]) stanza showing him doing battle with the dualizing thoughts (*vikalpa*s), whatever the school in which they have been theorized:

adyāsmān asataḥ kariṣyati sataḥ kiṃ nu dvidhā vāpy ayaṃ
kiṃ sthāsnūn uta naśvarān uta mithobhinnān abhinnān uta |
itthaṃ sadvadanāvalokanaparair bhāvair jagadvartibhir
manye maunaniruddhyamānahṛdayair duḥkhena taiḥ sthīyate ||

Now, will it [dialectics (according to the context of the stanza in the ĪPVV)] make us existent or nonexistent, or even both? Will it make us permanent or destructible, different from each other or nondifferent? In my view, thus [confronted with such dilemmas], beings remain in pain: they who live in this world, immersed in contemplating the face of the Being, have their hearts closed by the silence [to which they are reduced,

---

[10] On this reasoning, see the *Locana* ad *Dhvanyālokavṛtti* I 13 quoted below, p. 61. On the notion of *sahṛdaya(tā)* in the aesthetic register, see esp. BANSAT-BOUDON 1992a, pp. 148-149, 151; also (for its use in both aesthetic and spiritual registers), 2012a, pp. 225-233; and below, n. 33.

[11] Although Abhinavagupta could well be its author, due to the similarity of structure with TĀ I 332 (stanza organized by "*manye*"), as well as to the presence of the same stanza in another text by Abhinavagupta, namely the *Īśvarapratyabhijñāvivṛtivimarśinī* (henceforth ĪPVV); see the following §.

unable as they are to see that the opposition *sat-asat* is meant to dissolve in the awareness of the supreme Self (*paramātman*)[12]].

Let us note that the ĪPVV I 1, 1, Abhinavagupta's commentary on Utpaladeva's *Vivṛti* (most of which has been lost), has already cited this stanza in a condensed form, in an extremely sarcastic passage denying dialectics (*tarka*) the power of attaining supreme Reality.[13] Only "Recognition" (*pratyabhijñā*) of one's identity with the supreme principle or reality can ensure one's access to it, hence to liberation.

Thus every dualist doctrine is reduced to the level of inferior thought, tinged with very ordinary prejudices, characterizing the common man who knows nothing at all (*akiṃcijjña*), says the TĀV, and who can be shown to be a fool of the first order.[14] And yet one

---

12 On this implied meaning, see ĪPVV I 1, 1 (translated below) and *Bhagavadgītā* [BhG] II 16 [= II 17, in the Kaśmīr recension] and Abhinavagupta's commentary thereon (in particular his gloss for *antaḥ*).

13 ĪPVV, vol. I, p. 9: *evaṃ parameśvarasvarūpe samāviśya granthakāraḥ sūtravṛttyarthaṃ pūrvapakṣottarapakṣaiḥ samudghāṭayiṣyan tarko 'pratiṣṭhaḥ iti apratiṣṭhatā, adyāsmān asataḥ kariṣyati sataḥ sthāsnūn atho naśvarān iti, svaśaktipradarśanamātrasāratayā gomayapāyasīyanyāyopahāsena paramārthānupayogitā* | *aho dhig vyākhyātṛgraham itarahevākabhṛtakam aho tarkasyāntaḥ kvacid api na labhyaś ca vibudhaiḥ* |. "Having thus immersed himself in the nature of *parameśvara* and preparing to reveal the meaning of the verse and its commentary through a series of *prima facie* views and established conclusions, the author [Utpaladeva] says: 'Dialectics has no foundation.' The lack of foundation [of dialectics is explicit in the verse]: 'Now, will it [dialectics] make us existent or nonexistent? [...] Will it make us permanent or destructible?' [Trying to express] the supreme meaning [through logical terms] is pointless, according to [the verse]: 'Alas! The understanding of dialecticians [only] results in another whim [to analyze]! Alas! For scholars, there is no end to dialectics!' [Here the emphasis is on] the derisory nature [of dialectics when employed for the purpose of attaining the supreme meaning; it is as absurd as the reasoning criticized] in the saying that assimilates 'the cowpat and the milk' [on the basis that they both have a bovine origin], given that the essence [of the supreme principle can only be perceived] when one sees its energy [at work behind the products that constitute empiric reality]."

14 See in particular Abhinavagupta's *Paramārthasāra* (henceforth PS) 27, which presents other systems of thought as mere practical and provisional truths (*vyavahāramātram etat paramārthena tu na santy eva*, for which Yogarāja glosses *vyavahāramātram* by *saṃvṛtyartham*) and as such inferior to Abhinavagupta's doctrine (see BANSAT-BOUDON AND TRIPATHI 2011, p. 152, n. 656). See also the famous analogy used by Kṣemarāja in his PH 8 (BANSAT-BOUDON AND TRIPATHI 2011, pp. 160-161, n. 689), where the different schools are described as

sees the final pirouette which consists in the reversal of blame into praise.

Already, in the *avataraṇikā*, as we have seen, the TĀV shows how the stanza partakes of the polemic construction of the Traika system. Not only does this polemical tone persist throughout the commentary, but Jayaratha shows a violence which is foreign to the stanza itself and which culminates in the final condemnation, almost an imprecation (see above, p. 37).

Thus there is no way out for the cornered adversary. And if, despite everything, he resists – so what! His position, now ruined, is of no consequence.

I would have liked to show how, in the context of such a general attack on all dualism, one could read at least a partial refutation of the Sāṃkhya. But this it is not the place for such a digression, nor for comparing the way both Trika and Sāṃkhya use the theatrical metaphor. I shall limit myself to reminding the reader of *Sāṃkhyakārikā* (henceforth SK) 59, 61, 65-66, where *prakṛti*, unconscious yet active, is said to be playing before the *puruṣa*, conscious yet inactive – it is indeed an actress (*nartakī*; SK 59), since the *Gauḍapādīyabhāṣya* speaks of the *rasa*s she is enacting.

Intent upon his demonstration of non-dualism, Jayaratha unfolds the dramatic metaphor of the first hemistich, showing how the analogy at work in the stanza poetically condenses the underlying argument of the passage: objects are sentient (*ajaḍa*), but the deity which presides over their manifestation disguises that sentience as make-believe insentience (*jaḍatva*), so much so that it succeeds in deceiving the insensitive man (*ahṛdaya*): the world displays its splendors to the finite being who is its deluded and impotent spectator. Thus Jayaratha unfolds the web of significations associated with the notion of *sahṛdayatā*, "sensibility," understood as an aesthetic notion.

One should observe, however, that Jayaratha forces the meaning of the stanza by making it serve his exegetic project, infringing on its morphology and syntax, and even on its metrics.

---

the many "roles" (as well as "levels" of realization of the ultimate truth, *bhūmikā*) taken on by the Supreme Lord as an actor and are seen as hierarchical levels arranged along the scale of the *tattva*s – culminating with the eleventh and highest *bhūmikā* or *sthiti*, which is that of Trika philosophers.

It seems, for instance, that he understands the present participle *nartayan* not as a causative, but as a sort of denominative (the equivalent of a *nartāyate*), inasmuch as *nartayan* is glossed by *naṭavat*. Similarly, he dislocates the syntax by making *nartayan* govern the group in the instrumental: *vividhābhir bhaṅgībhiḥ*, when one expects that an instrumental accompanying *pracchādya* might more naturally express *means* (unless the instrumental is considered as the complement of means applied to both gerunds and also to *nartayan*); moreover, the expected syntactic order would thus coincide with the metrical organization of the stanza, namely, with the second *pāda*, whereas *nartayan*, at the end of the first *pāda*, would take a direct object: *janasya hṛdayāni*, which is shared with the gerund *ākramya*.[15]

Jayaratha persists in his bold interpretation, since the syntactic segment thus reorganized is again glossed by an equivalent one: *vividhābhir bhaṅgībhiḥ nartayan yat saṃkrīḍase – naṭavat atāttvikena rūpeṇa samullasasi*. Thus, *vividhābhir bhaṅgībhiḥ* is explained as *atāttvikena rūpeṇa* ("taking on a non-real form"), *nartayan* as *naṭavat*, " in the way of an actor," and *saṃkrīḍase* as *samullasasi* ("he plays").[16]

In the same vein, the term *bhaṅgī* is to be understood here more as "costumes" (one of its meanings) than as "twists" or "bends"[17] (or emotional "modes," as understood in the *Locana*; see below, p. 61) – such costumes representing the various roles played by the actor. Let us remember that the *āhāryābhinaya* – costume and make-up – although it has "to be borrowed" (*āhārya*) from the external world before the actor enters the stage, is conceived as a full-fledged register of acting (*abhinaya*).[18]

---

15 This will be the syntactical order of the stanza in Abhinavagupta's self-exegesis of the same verse in the *Locana*; see below, p. 58: *haṭhād eva lokaṃ yathecchaṃ vikārakāraṇābhir nartayati*.

16 Lit., "Since (*yat*) you play (*saṃkrīḍase* = *samullasasi*), in the way of an actor (*nartayan* = *naṭavat*), with various costumes, i.e. with a form that is not real (*vividhābhir bhaṅgībhiḥ* = *atāttvikena rūpeṇa*)."

17 Cf. Padoux's translation: "O Totalité des choses! De force, Tu t'empares des cœurs humains et Tu joues, tel un acteur, à *cacher sous de multiples détours* (my emphasis) le cœur du Soi [...]"; transl. SILBURN AND PADOUX 1998, p. 126.

18 On the four registers of *abhinaya*, see BANSAT-BOUDON 1990; also BANSAT-BOUDON 1992, pp. 145-155, 341-387.

The verb itself, *saṃkrīḍase* (glossed as *samullasasi*), is also to be understood in the sense of dramatic acting, when it evokes the divine actor, the *naṭarāja* – or his *śakti*, as we shall see.

We should note with what coherence the stanza and its commentary spin out the metaphor, in conformity with the essential lineaments of the aesthetic theory defended by Abhinavagupta and the Śaiva tradition, including the key notion of *sahṛdayatā* and its antonym, *ahṛdayatā*.

Both texts manifest the tension between the two protagonists of the aesthetic experience as lived out in the theatre, that is, the actor and the spectator. Nothing is left out of the process. On one side, the actor, master of himself and of the universe (if I can borrow from Corneille, *Cinna*, Vth act!), that is, master of the splendors lucidly displayed to the spectator's eyes (since, like the divine actor, he *causes* the objective world *to be* on stage);[19] master also of that spectator's heart, which he moves "forcibly" (*haṭhāt*), that is, "at will" (*yatheccham*, as we shall see in the *Locana* quoted below, p. 61), and who hides his Self in order to assume the variety of his roles. On the other side, the spectator, more specifically the unqualified spectator, the *ahṛdaya*, who sees nothing but the diversity of the world in the variety of those roles.

Such a spectator – who is a figure of the opponent in the interpretation of the TĀV – is, in fact, deceived, unable to discern the reality beneath appearances. And he is all the more deceived since he overestimates himself – wrongy believing, due to his presumptuousness (a way of translating the philosophical notion the Trika inherits from the Sāṃkhya, namely *abhimāna*,[20] the sentiment of the ego, and not of the Self), that he is a *sahṛdaya*.

On the philosophical level, the insensibility (*ahṛdayatā*) of that deceived spectator represents *avidyā* (or *ajñāna*), metaphysical ignorance, as it manifests itself in a double error (*bhrānti*) consisting, in Śaiva reasonings and particularly in Abhinavagupta's PS (30-31 and 39-40), in taking the Self for the non-Self, that is, in forgetting the unity of the Self and in placing before itself the object, namely phenomenal diversity (to which also belong the multiplicity of the

---

[19] On Śiva as the unique Agent and Actor and the reasonings on the "beingness" (*astitva*) of the phenomenal world, see BANSAT-BOUDON 2014, pp. 64-73.

[20] See PS 19 in BANSAT-BOUDON AND TRIPATHI 2011, pp. 138ff.

paśus[21]), before just as wrongly taking the non-Self (the body, the breath, etc.) as the Self – which amounts to being an error heaped upon error, "darkness upon darkness" (*timirād api timiram idam*), or a "great pustule upon a boil" (*gaṇḍasyopari mahān ayaṃ sphoṭaḥ*), as PS 31 says.[22]

Incidentally, it is interesting to note that at some point in the ĪPVV (ad II 4 19, vol. III, p. 244)[23] it is the error itself (*bhrama*)[24] which plays on the stage:

> *sa ca bhramo nāṭyatulyasya aparamārthasato 'tyaktasvarūpāvaṣṭambhananaṭakalpena parameśvaraprakāśena pratītigocarīkṛtasya saṃsārasya nāyakaḥ sūtradhāraḥ pradhānabhūtaḥ pravartayitā itivṛtte nāyako vā, yallagnaṃ viśvetivṛttam ābhāti; tata eva prathamaḥ* |

---

[21] On this point, see especially *Spandanirṇaya* I 1 (quoted and translated in BANSAT-BOUDON AND TRIPATHI 2011, pp. 330-331) which states that Śiva takes on the role of the seven *pramātṛ*s and of the objects which they bring into being.

[22] On the double error, see BANSAT-BOUDON AND TRIPATHI 2011, pp. 24-25, 161-169, 191-192 and n. 848; also, below, n. 24.

[23] Quoted in RATIÉ 2011, pp. 559; see also J. Törzsök's contribution to this volume.

[24] Here "*bhrama*" must be construed as "*bhrānti*," "error," and refers to the Traika conception of a two-levelled error. According to Abhinavagupta and his commentator in the PS, the first level of error is to mistake the Self for the non-Self, i.e., in forgetting one's own plenitude and in apprehending oneself as a finite subject, defined in relation to an object (see PS 25 and 30 in BANSAT-BOUDON AND TRIPATHI 2011). Thereupon intervenes the second level of error: taking the non-Self (body, *buddhi*, etc.) to be the Self, that is, predicating the Self of the non-Self, so that we assert 'I am fat,' 'I am intelligent,' etc. (see PS 31 in BANSAT-BOUDON AND TRIPATHI 2011). On the interpretation of *bhrama* here, in the ĪPVV, as an error on two levels – of which the first, more fundamental one is to mistake the Self for the non-Self – I somewhat differ from Ratié and Törzsök (see above, n. 23). See, for instance, Yogarāja's *Paramārthasāravivṛti* (henceforth PSV) ad 61: *bhrāntiḥ dvayarūpo bhramaḥ*, "the 'error,' i.e., the illusion formed of duality," and PSV 39, who describes how the dissolution of the second level of error is the condition for the vanishing of the first and main grade of error: *yāvad anātmani dehādāv ātmābhimāno na galitas tāvat svātmaprathārūpe 'pi jagati bhedaprathāmoho na vilīyate*. "As long as the conceit that locates the Self in the non-Self – the body, etc. – does not dissipate, so long does the delusion not dissolve that consists in valorizing difference (lit. 'display of difference') in this world, [the things of] which are even so but the display of one's own Self." (Transl. BANSAT-BOUDON AND TRIPATHI 2011, p. 192.) Here that first grade of error is described as *bhedaprathāmohaḥ*, the "delusion that consists in valorizing difference."

> The drama (*nāṭya*) that the world of transmigration is [i.e. the phenomenal world subjected to the cycle of rebirth] (*saṃsāra*),[25] though ultimately deprived of reality, can only be experienced insofar as it is the manifestation of the supreme Lord who, like the actor (*naṭa*), never gives up his own, immutable nature. [Metaphysical] error[26] is the hero (*nāyaka*)[27] of the drama; in other words, it is the *sūtradhāra*, the leader of the company, whose preeminent function is both that of instigator of the plot (*itivṛtta*) and protagonist of the play. It is in its close connection with metaphysical error that the plot of the universe (*viśvetivṛtta*) appears. This is why metaphysical error is "primary."

Error here is nothing but nescience (*avidyā*), namely the mistaking of the Self for the non-Self which in turn will lead to an even deeper error, that of mistaking the non-Self for the Self. Like the *sūtradhāra*, both the leader and first actor of a theatre group who plays the main role (*nāyaka*), *avidyā* leads the plot of the universe (*viśvetivṛtta*) on the stage of the world of transmigration (*saṃsāra*). Better than *viśva* in the alternative analogy, that of the drama of the universe (*viśvetivṛtta*), *saṃsāra* is able to represent the target in the metaphor of the "world as a theatre": in the endless flow of reincarnations, empirical beings take on one role after another. And although, in Śaiva terms, the play (*nāṭya*) is not ultimately "true" (*aparamārthasat*),[28] it has enough power of illusion to fool the spectators, so long as these remain in the condition of *paśu*. At the source of this dramatic illusion is Parameśvara, the Supreme Agent[29] and Supreme

---

[25] Lit. "the world of transmigration comparable to a play."

[26] "Error" here is in the sense of nescience (*avidyā*); see below.

[27] With a play on the word *nāyaka*, "the one who leads," which in dramaturgy also refers to the "hero." So error leads the dramatic plot of the universe in the same way as the *sūtradhāra* leads it on the stage: it is both its instigator and main protagonist. For the *sūtradhāra* is the character *de rigueur* in the prologue which introduces the dramatic fiction as well as the first protagonist of the play (see LÉVI 1890, p. 378 and BANSAT-BOUDON 1992, p. 83 et 219). He is also the true incarnation of theatricality in that he appears as the very figure of the Actor in the *pūrvaraṅga*, the half-ritualistic and half-dramatical "preliminaries" to the performance of the dramatic fiction which are described in the fifth chapter of the *Nāṭyaśāstra* (see BANSAT-BOUDON 1992, pp. 74-76).

[28] Cf. above, p. 41, Jayaratha's notation: *atāttvikena rūpeṇa*, "taking on a non-real form."

[29] On Śiva as the Agent *par excellence*, see BANSAT-BOUDON 2014, pp. 65-71. See also ĪPV II 4 19 (vol. II, p. 200): *iti cidrūpasyaiva kartṛtvam upapannam abhinnasya bhedāveśasahiṣṇutvena kriyāśaktyāveśasaṃbhavāt*, "Thus, only what is

actor, who, in disguising himself, plays at being other than himself without ever being affected by it (*atyaktasvarūpāvaṣṭambhanaṭa*).[30] This is possible because such a change of appearance, far from being due to particular circumstances, stems from Parameśvara's power to hide at will. This ability is one of his *śakti*s, his *tirodhānaśakti*, his concealment energy.[31] Thus the disguisement of the Self is a correlate of its sovereign freedom, its *svātantryaśakti*, the first of its energies.[32] The notation "*ātmahṛdayaṃ pracchādya*" (TĀ I 332) is therefore an essential element of the playful process of self-subjugation which can be read between the lines of the stanza.

One can see that the stanza and its commentaries transpose metaphysical ignorance to the aesthetic register: thus the TĀV conceives of *ajñāna* as *ahṛdayatā*, which implies an imperfect education (*duḥśikṣita*), as opposed to the perfect education that characterizes

undivided consciousness can be an Agent, for, being capable of taking on different forms, it can exercize the power of action."

30 On the main characteristic of the Lord, i.e. that his essential nature cannot be altered whatever form he takes on, see in particular PSV 1 quoting *Spandakārikā* (henceforth SpK) I 3 (see BANSAT-BOUDON AND TRIPATHI 2011, pp. 66-67, and n. 253); also PS 34 (and PSV ad loc.) and PS 36. This is also the case with ordinary, empirical, actors who never forget that they themselves are not the characters or at least not fundamentally so. This they never – or should never – ignore, since they would otherwise risk being possessed by the deity whose role they are playing or start doing for real what should remain fiction, for example killing a fellow actor who happens to be playing the part of an enemy (see the anecdotes in TARABOUT 1998, pp. 296ff.). See also ĪPV II 4 19 (quoted above, n. 29) which asserts that, although capable of being many, the Lord (or consciousness, *cit*) remains one and unaffected by the multiplicity he himself creates. It is in this context that the passage of the ĪPVV (vol. III, p. 244) quoted above, p. 43, uses the metaphor of the error as *sūtradhāra*.

31 See HULIN 1978, p. 308, n. 5, who translates by "énergie de cèlement." The *tirodhānaśakti* is one of the *pañcakṛtya*, Śiva's five cosmic functions (see BANSAT-BOUDON AND TRIPATHI 2011, p. 100, n. 413).

32 See PSV 5 commenting on "Śiva himself, who takes on the condition of a fettered soul": "Thus, that Lord who has been described above as a uniform mass of blissful consciousness, and whose nature is freedom (*svātantrya*), Śiva himself, whose essence is now the veiling of his own true nature (*svarūpagopana*), takes on the role (*bhūmikā*) of a cognizer endowed with a body, according to his own will, as though he were an actor (*naṭa*) and, since he is [henceforth] to be maintained and treated as a domestic animal [that is, as a tethered beast], he is now distinguished by his existence as a fettered subject (*paśu*)"; on *svarūpagopana*, see also also PS 15 (on *māyāśakti*) and PSV ad loc.: BANSAT-BOUDON AND TRIPATHI 2011, pp. 126-129, and n. 529.

the *sahṛdaya*, in aesthetics.[33] The height of ignorance and bewilderment (*moha*) is to think of oneself as sensible and sensitive, as well as perfectly educated.

On the one hand, therefore, we have that deceived spectator; on the other, the sovereign actor. But who is this actor who is the object of comparison for the *bhāvavrāta*? "He" is, in fact, an actress, even if in veiled terms. Abhinavagupta himself gives this interpretative key in his ĪPV ad ĪPK I 1, 4:[34] the actor *par excellence*, that is, the agent of phenomenal manifestation, is the *māyāśakti*, herself an hypostasis of Śiva's Śakti, therefore indissociable from him:[35]

> ... *teṣāṃ "jaḍabhūtānāṃ" cinmayatve 'pi māyākhyayā īśvaraśaktyā jāḍyaṃ prāpitānāṃ jīvantaṃ pramātāram āśritya pratiṣṭhā...* |
>
> [...] Although made of consciousness, the "insentient entities" are made insentient by the work of the Lord's Śakti named *māyā*. Their foundation depends on the living being, that is, on the cognizing subject [...].

It is that *māyāśakti* (who "measures" out the empirical world) that the Śaiva doctrine presents, with the organization of the thirty-six *tattva*s, as governing the phenomenal manifestation, called *meya* – a derivative of the same root *mā*, "to measure," "to construct."

In this respect, and in this respect only, *māyā* is comparable to the *prakṛti* of the Sāṃkhya, who shows herself on the stage of the world[36] by assuming, one after the other, those roles that are her "evolutes" or "products," the remaining twenty-three *tattva*s – the difference consisting in that *prakṛti* is unconscious, whereas *māyā*,

---

33 See Abhinavagupta's famous definition of the *sahṛdaya* in *Locana* ad *Dhvanyāloka*, *vṛtti* ad I 1 (CSS ed., pp. 38-39; INGALLS ET AL. 1990, p. 70): *yeṣāṃ kāvyānuśīlanābhyāsavaśād viśadībhūte manomukure varṇanīyatanmayībhavanayogyatā te svahṛdayasaṃvādabhājaḥ sahṛdayāḥ*; for the use of *sahṛdayatā* in both aesthetic and spiritual registers, see BANSAT-BOUDON 2012a, pp. 225-233.

34 See the text of the stanza, ĪPK I 1, 4, in Appendix-3.

35 See, for instance, Abhinavagupta's *maṅgala* to his *Locana* on Ānandavardhana's *avataraṇikā* to III 1 (CSS ed., p. 288; INGALLS ET AL. 1990, p. 369): *smarāmi smarasaṃhāralīlāpāṭavaśālinaḥ* | *prasahya śambhor dehārdhaṃ harantīṃ parameśvarīm* ||. "I remember the Supreme Goddess who stole half of Śambhu's body after he had shown his effortless skill in playing at annihilating Smara himself."

36 See SK 59 and above, p. 40; also BANSAT-BOUDON AND TRIPATHI 2011, pp. 52-53.

Śiva's hypostasis[37] (in other words, the hypostasis of Consciousness), is conscious throughout.

This is the reason why the stanza is a hymn to the deity which sets in motion the *bhāvavrāta*. Besides, in this non-dualism, it makes little difference whether it is an actor (Śiva) or an actress (*māyā*).[38]

It is worth noting that the passage of the ĪPV I 1, 4 that offers that interpretative key to TĀ I 332 is precisely the one a propos of which Bhāskara, commenting on it, in his turn, several centuries later, finds it appropriate to cite the same stanza, although with a tiny variant (see Appendix-4). Thus the philosophical point of the stanza, in the TĀ, at least, is strengthened by the usage Bhāskara makes of it.

Let us come back to the long-drawn-out metaphor. When it is said of this actor, or this actress, that he/she hides his/her Self, one cannot help seeing here a reference to the notion of *sākṣātkārakalpapratīti* (or *pratyakṣakalpapratīti*) a "quasi direct perception,"[39] essential to the success of the aesthetic process meant to culminate in *rasa*.

In effect, *sākṣātkārakalpapratīti* is a way to condense in one term the complex process that manifests on the stage a person (or a fancy) who, being neither entirely the actor nor entirely the character, allows the spectator to see everything with impunity, in a distanciated rapture. As such, the "quasi direct perception" governs the next step of the aesthetical process when considered from the point of view of the audience, namely *sādhāraṇīkaraṇa* or "generalization." *Sādhāraṇīkaraṇa*, the depersonalization of emotions free of any reference to a specific ego (and thus their universalization), enables the audience to enjoy a controlled and purified identification (*tanmayībhāva*), the source of delight and bliss.[40]

As for the influence cast over the hearts of men, it is a way of alluding to *rasa*, the irresistible aesthetic rapture which, when transposed onto the ontological level, merges with the beatific experience

---

37 See PS 15 in BANSAT-BOUDON AND TRIPATHI 2011, pp. 126-129, where *māyā* is described as *devī māyāśaktiḥ*; also BANSAT-BOUDON 2008, pp. 60-62.

38 See TĀV VIII 333: *devīti devābhinnatvāt*.

39 The notion is found at several places in the *Abhinavabhāratī* ad *Nāṭyaśāstra*; see BANSAT-BOUDON 1992, pp. 150-152; 2012, pp. 224-225.

40 On the stages of the aesthetic process as analyzed by Abhinavagupta in his *Abhinavabhāratī*, see BANSAT-BOUDON 1992, pp. 152-155, 1992a and 2012, pp. 214-215.

of "repose in the Self" (*ātmaviśrānti*)[41] preliminary to the experience of "liberation in this life" (*jīvanmukti*). I have shown several times how the aesthetic experience works as a propaedeutics to the spiritual.[42] I shall thus not linger on this question, but we will return to it a propos the *Locana* (see below, pp. 50-55).

To conclude this part: phenomenal diversity in the form of the *māyāśakti* plays *before* the spectator, and plays *with* him as well, if he happens not to be a *sahṛdaya*, making him wrongly believe in the dichotomy subject/object.

2. THE *LOCANA*[43] AD *DHVANYĀLOKAVṚTTI* I 13[44]

Let us come to the *Locana*. The broader context is that of the exposition of *dhvani*; the narrower context, that of the definition of the *aprastutapraśaṃsā*, more precisely, of the third category of *aprastutapraśaṃsā*, based on the similarity of the expressed (which is, in this case, *aprastuta* – what is non-pertinent to the speaker and the listener) and the suggested (which is *prastuta* – what is pertinent to them), in order to establish where and when the figure works as such or as a case of *dhvani*.

What Ānandavardhana wants to show is that he has discovered something new, not a new name for categories already recognized, and so he goes through a number of such well-known categories – *alaṃkāras* that involve an element of suggestion (including the *aprastutapraśaṃsā*) – and shows that they are not at all identical with his new concept of *dhvani*. He is thus led to defend his new theory, namely that the *ālaṃkārika* register is delimited by the predominance of the literal meaning, whereas that of the *dhvani* is defined by the predominance of the suggested meaning. Therefore, taking the *aprastutapraśaṃsā* as an example, he concludes (CSS ed., pp. 126-129; INGALLS ET AL. 1990, p. 159):

---

41 On the notion of *ātmaviśrānti*, see below, p. 72 and n. 100; also BANSAT-BOUDON AND TRIPATHI 2011, pp. 56, 71, 321.

42 See, esp., BANSAT-BOUDON 2004, pp. 280-283; 2012, pp. 231-233.

43 CSS ed., pp. 127-132; INGALLS ET AL. 1990, pp.160-163, 165-167.

44 CSS ed., pp. 125-132; INGALLS ET AL. 1990, pp. 158-165.

... yadā tu sārūpyamātravaśenāprastutapraśaṃsāyām aprakṛtaprakṛtayoḥ saṃbandhas tadāpy aprastutasya sarūpyābhidhīyamānasya prādhānyenāvivakṣāyāṃ dhvanāv evāntarbhāvaḥ | itarathā tv alaṃkārāntaratvam eva | tad ayam atra saṃkṣepaḥ –
vyaṅgyasya yatrāprādhānyaṃ vācyamātrānuyāyinaḥ |
samāsoktyādayas tatra vācyālaṅkṛtayaḥ sphuṭāḥ ||
vyaṅgyasya pratibhāmātre vācārthānugame 'pi vā |
na dhvanir yatra vā tasya prādhānyaṃ na pratīyate ||
tatparāv eva śabdārthau yatra vyaṅgyaṃ prati sthitau |
dhvaneḥ sa eva viṣayo mantavyaḥ saṅkarojjhitaḥ ||

[...]. But when, in an *aprastutapraśaṃsā*, the relation of extraneous and germane is based only on similarity, then, if the extraneous expressed idea (*aprastuta*) bearing similarity is not intended to be predominant, the case falls in the area of *dhvani*. Otherwise,[45] it will just be one of the figures.[46] Here then is the summary of the matter:
"Wherever the suggested meaning (*vyaṅgya*) does not predominate, but is merely ancillary to the literal sense (*vācya*), it is clear that such instances are only figures of the literal sense, such as *samāsokti* and others,"
"In places where there is just a glimmer of the suggested or where the suggested is just subservient to the expressed, or where its preeminence is not clearly discernible, there is no *dhvani*,"
"Only those instances wherein word and meaning are solely directed towards the suggested should be regarded as the area of *dhvani* – which admits no admixture of [any figure of speech]."[47]

In his *Locana*,[48] Abhinavagupta goes further (CSS ed., pp. 127-128; INGALLS ET AL. 1990, pp. 162-163). For some reason, he considers that the capacity to arouse wonder (*camatkārakāritva*) in the listener is the criterion for determining which of the explicit or suggested meanings prevails. Moreover, he seems to link or even subordinate the ability to create a sense of wonder in the listener with the plausibility of the meaning, be it literal or suggested.

---

45 I.e., if it is the *aprastuta* that is intended to be predominant.

46 Transl. INGALLS ET AL. 1990, p. 159 (slightly modified).

47 My translation; see *Locana* ad loc., where *anupraveśa* comments on *saṅkara*: *saṅkareṇālaṅkārānupraveśasaṃbhāvanayā ujjhita ity arthaḥ*. Ānandavardhana and his exegete will take up the question again, in *Dhvanyālokavṛtti* ad III 40 and *Locana* thereon; see below, § 3.

48 *Locana* ad the *vṛtti* (CSS ed., pp. 126ff.): *yadā tu sārūpyamātravaśenāprastutapraśaṃsāyām...*

Giving the example of a stanza whose protagonist is a *vetāla*, Abhinavagupta argues that the believability of the literal meaning – which seems to be the source of the listener's sense of wonder – is a factor in the decision to consider it predominant.[49] That first segment of the passage (see complete text in Appendix-2) reads as follows:

> *atra yady api sārūpyavaśena kṛtaghnaḥ kaścid anyaḥ prastuta ākṣipyate, tathāpy aprastutasyaiva vetālavṛttāntasya camatkāra-kāritvam | na hy acetanopālambhavad asaṃbhāvyamāno 'yam artho na ca na hṛdya iti vācyasyātra pradhānatā | ...*
>
> Here, although some other ingrate is suggested as the pertinent subject (*prastuta*), by the power of similarity, the capacity of causing wonder[50] lies in the story of the *vetāla*, which is extraneous. The sense is not impossible as would be a reproach against an insentient being, and it is not without attraction. So the predominance here lies in the literal sense.[51]

However, says the second segment of the *Locana*, if the literal meaning is entirely implausible, that goes hand in hand with a suggested meaning that is the source of the verse's main charm – which would then make it a *vastudhvani*, namely the "suggestion of some narrative item or 'content.'" This is where (CSS ed., p. 127; INGALLS ET AL. 1990, p. 162) Abhinavagupta makes a self-citation of his own stanza ("*bhāvavrāta haṭhāj...*," already present in TĀ I 332):

> *... yadi punar acetanādinātyantāsambhāvyamānatadarthaviśeṣaṇenāprastutena varṇitena prastutam ākṣipyamāṇaṃ camatkārakāri tadā vastudhvanir asau | yathā mamaiva – "bhāvavrāta haṭhāj..." |*
>
> But if the pertinent subject [of the utterance] (*prastuta*) [i.e., the speaker's intention which he wants to convey to the listener, therefore, the suggested meaning he has in his mind] is a source of wonder (*camatkārakārin*), [although] suggested (*ākṣipyamāṇa*) by means of [another] that is non-pertinent (or irrelevant) (*aprastuta*) to the speaker and the listener – insofar as that [other irrelevant subject] is insentient, etc., or described in such a way that its particularities are entirely unimaginable (*atyantāsaṃbhāvyamāna*) for such a result [namely, suggesting the real meaning] – then, we have a

---

[49] The point is further discussed below, *Dhvanyālokavṛtti* III 40; see below, p. 67, and n. 91.

[50] Underlined passages are my emphasis.

[51] Transl. INGALLS ET AL. 1990, p. 162 (slightly modified).

case of *vastudhvani*, as in this verse of my own: "O whole of things, forcibly..."[52]

Let us examine these two stanzas, which Abhinavagupta gives as examples of the category of *aprastutapraśaṃsā* based on similarity.[53]

1. The first one, which shows a *vetāla* killing his benefactor, ironically celebrates the former as the Prince of gratitude. That is the expressed/explicit meaning. The suggested meaning aims at some other ingrate, of whom we know nothing in the absence of context, or at any other ingrate.[54] Nevertheless, it is the expressed meaning, the colourful story of the *vetāla*, which is a cause of wonder (*camatkārakārin*), while it is all the more credible (hence convincing) as *vetāla*s' stories are a recurrent motive in narrative literature.

Thus, as one may infer from the next passage of the *Locana*, one can recognize here an instance of *aprastutapraśaṃsā*, since ingratitude is common to the explicit and implicit subjects of the utterance, but it is an *aprastutapraśaṃsā* pertaining to the *ālaṃkārika* register, since there is something striking and convincing in the description of the non-pertinent *vetāla*, which makes that literal meaning predominant (*vācyasyātra pradhānatā*).

2. The second stanza given as an example, which Abhinavagupta says that he composed himself, without giving its source, is the stanza under examination: "*bhāvavrāta haṭhāj...*" Abhinavagupta explains that, the expressed meaning being completely impossible, i.e., implausible (how to address the mass of the objects and to consider them as sentient?),[55] the suggested meaning prevails over it, thus creating wonder and establishing the stanza as a case of *vastudhvani*.

---

52 My translation. See below, p. 57, for an extended translation of the same passage, which applies to the verse itself ("*bhāvavrāta*," etc.) and shows its implications once the suggested meaning has been identified.

53 Ānandavardhana and Abhinavagupta will take up the question again in III 40; see below, § 3.

54 The verse, which addresses the *vetāla* (a *śārdūlavikrīḍita*, with two irregularities: the 8th syllable is long; there is one syllable too many, at the beginning of the second *pāda*; it should read "*kandhe*" instead of "*svakandhe*"), reads as follows: *prāṇā yena samarpitās tatra balād yena tvam utthāpitaḥ svakandhe yasya ciraṃ sthito 'si vidadhe yas te saparyām api | tasyāsya smitamātrakeṇa janayan prāṇāpahārikriyāṃ bhrātaḥ pratyupakāriṇāṃ dhuri paraṃ vetāla līlāyase ||*.

55 See the passage of the *Locana* quoted immediately above, which emphasizes that the "particularities" ascribed to the *aprastuta* (the *bhāvavrāta*) are "entirely unimaginable" (*atyantāsaṃbhāvyamāṇa*).

Otherwise, it would indeed be a case of *aprastutapraśaṃsā* based on similarity, but this *aprastutapraśaṃsā* would pertain to the rhetorical register alone (as in the stanza of the *vetāla*).

This is what Ānandavardhana teaches (CSS ed., pp. 128-129, quoted above, p. 49). It is, as well, what Abhinavagupta develops (CSS ed., p. 128; INGALLS ET AL. 1990, p. 163):

> *"itharathā tv iti" | itarathaiva punar alaṅkārāntaratvam alaṅkāraviśeṣatvaṃ na vyaṅgyasya kathaṃ cid api prādhānya iti bhāvaḥ |*
>
> "But, otherwise..." – Otherwise, it will just be another figure of speech, that is, the particular figure of speech [named *aprastutapraśaṃsā*]; but this is not the case when the suggested meaning is prevalent in any way whatsoever. Such is the deeper meaning.[56]

Now, what is this suggested meaning? Abhinavagupta reveals it first, immediately after quoting his stanza: under the description of the *bhāvavrāta*, one should read the detailed and very lively evocation of a *mahāpuruṣa*, a "great being" – a "great being" who puzzles Ingalls (see, below, p. 63), and in whom I propose to recognize the figure of the *jīvanmukta*, who is "liberated while living." In effect, all the epithets qualifying that *mahāpuruṣa* might apply to the *jīvanmukta*.

Here comes the third part of the passage, which deals with the figure of the *jīvanmukta*, i.e., the unfolding of the suggested meaning:

> *... kaścin mahāpuruṣo vītarāgo 'pi sarāgavad iti nyāyena gāḍhavivekālokatiraskṛtatimirapratāno 'pi lokamadhye svātmānaṃ pracchādayaṃl lokaṃ ca vācālayann ātmany apratibhāsam evāṅgīkurvaṃs tenaiva lokena mūrkho 'yam iti yad avajñāyate tadā tadīyaṃ lokottaraṃ caritaṃ prastutaṃ vyaṅgyatayā prādhānyena prakāśyate...*

I summarize the passage, which is given entirely in the Appendix. The statement that first gives the key to such correspondences is that the *mahāpuruṣa*, "although living in this world" (*lokamadhye*; precisely what makes the *jīvanmukta* a living oxymoron), has dispelled the darkness of metaphysical ignorance (*gāḍhavivekālokatiraskṛtatimirapratāno 'pi*). He nonetheless hides his Self (*svātmānaṃ pracchādayan*), in conformity with the modes of life of a renunciate: although dispassionnate (*vītarāgo 'pi*), he behaves as if still in the grip

[56] My translation. Note that the topic will be taken up again by Ānandavardhana and his exegete in III 40, and further clarified (see below, § 3).

of ordinary passions (*sarāgavad*); by so doing he is the object of innumerable comments and gossips (*lokaṃ ca vācālayan*), which he accepts without trying to deny them (*ātmany apratibhāsam evāṅgīkurvan*). This is why people regard him as a fool or madman (*mūrkha*) and despise him (*avajñāyate*) for it. Such is, Abhinavagupta concludes, the extraordinary, supra-mundane conduct (*lokottaraṃ caritam*) of so extraordinary (*kaścit*)[57] a man.

This is a remarkable text, probably one of the most complete descriptions of the *jīvanmukta*, whose main feature is that he is *lokottara*. In which way? Although living in this phenomenal world, *he sees through it* and accedes to ultimate reality, as taught by *Bhagavadgītā* (henceforth BHG) II 71 (according to the numbering of the Kashmirian version; see Lakshman Joo's edition), which Ānandavardhana quotes as an example for *Dhvanyālokavṛtti* ad III 1 (see below, p. 56):

yā niśā sarvabhūtānāṃ tasyāṃ jāgarti saṃyamī |
yasyāṃ jāgrati bhūtāni sā rātriḥ paśyato muneḥ ||

That which is night[58] for all beings, in that the self-controlled ascetic is awake. That which all beings are awake is night for the sage who sees.

In this way, "supramundanity" is associated with supralucidity,[59] with the result that the *jīvanmukta* remains indifferent to the ordinary world, its affects, prescriptions and prohibitions. We observe many ways of referring to the *jīvanmukta*'s *alaukika* or *lokottara* character, besides the use of the term itself, among which are the recourse to paradox, as in the verse of the BHG just quoted, and such exclamations as "*iti citram*," "how wonderful!", by which the *Gītārthasaṃgraha* comments on it[60] – another way of expressing that everpresent *camatkāra*, "wonder," "wonderment," which is also a criterion, as we have seen, for determining which of the explicit or

---

57 On this connotation of *kaścit*, see notably D. Shulman's paper in this volume.

58 "Night" is a metaphor for *māyā*, as explained by the *Gītārthasaṃgraha*. See the entire passage ad loc.

59 See also *Locana* on *Dhvanyālokavṛtti* ad III 1 (quoted below, p. 56), commenting on BHG II 71.

60 *Gītārthasaṃgraha* ad BHG II 71: ... *paśyata eva sā rātrir iti citram | vidyāyāṃ cāvadhatte yogī yatra sarvo vimūḍhaḥ | avidyāyāṃ tv abuddhaḥ yatra janaḥ prabuddhaḥ – ity api citram.*

suggested meanings prevails, hence, whether the verse belongs to the *dhvani* register or to that of the *alaṃkāras*.[61]

All similar features specific to the *jīvanmukta* are variously emphasized in the texts, especially in Śaiva texts.

The way the *jīvanmukta* makes others talk about him (*lokaṃ ca vācālayan*), without trying to explain himself – so much so that he is, for ordinary men, an object of scandal and contempt – is described in *Gītārthasaṃgraha* ad BHG XIV 26:

> *yas tu phalaṃ kiṃcid apy anabhilaṣyan kim etad alīkam anutiṣṭhasi iti paryanuyujyamāno 'pi nirantarabhagavadbhaktivedhavidrutāntaḥkaraṇatayā kaṇṭakitaromavān vepamānatanur visphāritanayanayugalaparivartamānasalilasaṃpātaḥ tūṣṇiṃbhavenaivottaraṃ prayacchati* |

Harassed by his circle, who cannot bear not to understand him: "Why such an untrue behaviour?" (which is in some way an echo of "hiding his Self" – *svātmānaṃ pracchādayan* – of the *Locana*), the yogin answers through silence to the crowd of the *paśu*s, immersed as he is in the mystical experience of *bhakti*, whose symptoms are thrilling with joy, quivering and an uninterrupted flow of tears from his wide open eyes.

This is of course more than what the common man can understand and tolerate. Therefore the *jīvanmukta* is harassed, mocked and despised for being stupid (*mūrkha*), insensible or insentient (*jaḍa*), or even insane (*unmatta*).[62]

Similarly, *kārikā* 71 (an *āryā*) in the PS, also a work of Abhinavagupta, asserts:

> *madaharṣakopamanmathaviṣādabhayalobhamohaparivarjī* |
> *niḥstotravaṣaṭkāro jaḍa iva vicared avādamatiḥ* ||

> Living without self-deception, excitement, anger, infatuation, dejection, fear, greed, or delusion; uttering neither praises [of the gods] nor ritual formulae and having no opinions whatever, he should behave as one insensible (*jaḍa*).

This vision of the *jīvanmukta* is the same as in the *Locana* and the *Gītārthasaṃgraha*. It is worth noting that the "*jaḍa*" of the stanza is glossed by Yogarāja as "*unmatta*" – "insane" in the eyes of the world

---

[61] On *camatkāra*, see BANSAT-BOUDON ANDTRIPATHI 2011, p. 320.

[62] See below.

– which implies that "having effectively conquered himself, considering that all is *brahman*, he should disport himself for purposes of play."[63]

Such a description of the *jīvanmukta*, although marked as Śaiva, is nonetheless shared by other schools, as the Vedāntic *Āgamaśāstra* (II 36b-37) clearly shows.[64]

In the same vein, the *Bālapriyā* subcommentary of the *Locana* cites a stanza, probably a proverb, which describes the way the world (or the common man) and the *jīvanmukta* (here the "one who knows the reality" – *jñātatattva*) consider each other as a *piśāca*, conventionally perceived as insentient (*jaḍa*) and insane (*unmatta*):

> *jñātatattvasya loko 'yaṃ jaḍonmattapiśācavat* |
> *jñātatattvo 'pi lokasya jaḍonmattapiśācavat* ||
>
> For the one who knows the reality, this world is like an insentient and insane *piśāca*, but, for this world, it is the one who knows the reality who is like an insentient and insane *piśāca*.[65]

---

63 Commenting on PS 71: *jaḍa iva vicared avādamatiḥ*, "He should just behave as one insensible, having no opinions whatever," Yogarāja observes: *pūrṇatvād ākāṅkṣāvirahāc conmatta ivetikartavyatārūpe śāstrīye karmaṇi pramāṇopapanne vā prameyasatattve pramātṛbhiḥ sahedam upapannam idaṃ neti vicārabahiṣkṛtabuddhir... iti dāntaprāyo bhūtvā sarvaṃ brahmāvalokayan krīḍārthaṃ vihared eveti jaḍatvena nirūpitaḥ* |. "Since he is himself replete, due to the absence of all expectations, he is like one at a loss (*unmatta*); his mind has banished considerations having to do with actions taught in the injunctive treatises, such as those that specify the manner of accomplishing [rituals, etc.] or [those that involve] the existence of something to be apprehended in conformity with some mode of correct apprehension (*pramāṇa*) and requiring an accompanying apprehender (*pramātṛ*), such as 'this [conclusion] is proven, this [one] is not' [...]. Thus, having effectively conquered himself, considering that all is *brahman*, he should disport himself for purposes of play. For this reason, he has been described here as insensible (or insane)." On the ascetic seen as *unmatta* in Tantric texts, see J. Törzsök's contribution to this volume.

64 *Āgamaśāstra* II 36cd-37: ... *advaitaṃ samanuprāpya jaḍaval lokam ācaret* || *nistutir nirnamaskāro niḥsvadhākāra eva ca* | *calācalaniketaś ca yatir yādṛcchiko bhavet* ||. "Having realized nonduality, one should behave as a fool among people. Giving no praise, paying no homage, nor pronouncing *svadhā* [i.e., not offering libations to the Manes/Ancestors], with an unfixed home, and acting spontaneously [without willing anything] (*yādṛcchika*), one should become an ascetic." (Transl. BHATTACHARYA 1989, modified as to the meaning of *yādṛcchika*.)

65 Same quote in *Jñānaśrīmitranibandhāvali*, *pariccheda* 3, p. 419.

Nevertheless, that so-called insentience and stupidity of the *jīvanmukta*, as he appears in the eyes of the uncomprehending common man, is but the corollary of the "supramundanity" (*lokottaratva/alaukikatva*) that is the very mark of the accomplished yogin, the *jīvanmukta*. This runs like a red thread in Abhinavagupta's works. In his *Gītārthasaṃgraha*, he interprets BHG II 66-70 (according to the numbering of the Kashmirian version) as referring to the *sthitaprajña*, himself portrayed as the *jīvanmukta*, as made obvious by the quotation (from an unidentified source): "*yogī ca sarvavyavahārān kurvāṇo 'pi lokottaraḥ*" – "Extraordinary is the yogin, even when he attends to worldly transactions" –, which qualifies such a yogin as *lokottara*, as is the case in the passage of the *Locana* we are dealing with.[66]

That "supramundanity" (*lokottaratva/alaukikatva*) appears again in the *Locana* commenting on *Dhvanyālokavṛtti* ad III 1. In his *vṛtti*, Ānandavardhana deals with the type of *dhvani* where the literal sense is not intended (*avivakṣitavācya*) – that is, where it is entirely set aside,[67] and cites precisely the same BHG II 71 which Abhinavagupta comments upon in his *Gītārthasaṃgraha* (see above, p. 53, and n. 60). Ānandavardhana's *vṛtti* (CSS ed., p. 294; INGALLS ET AL. 1990, p. 376) reads as follows:

> *anena hi vākyena niśārtho na ca jāgaraṇārthaḥ kaścid vivakṣitaḥ | kiṃ tarhi? tattvajñānāvahitatvam atattvaparāṅmukhatvaṃ ca muneḥ pratipādyata iti tiraskṛtavācyasyāsya vyañjakatvam |*
>
> For in this sentence the meanings "night" and "waking" are not at all intended. What then? What is communicated is rather the attention of the sage to the knowledge of ultimate reality and his disregard for what is not

---

66 *Gītārthasaṃgraha* ad BHG II 66-70: [*rāgadveṣetyādi pratiṣṭhitety antam*] *yas tu manaso niyāmakaḥ sa viṣayān sevamāno 'pi na krodhādikallolair abhibhūyate iti sa eva sthitaprajño yogīti tātparyam | "yogī ca sarvavyavahārān kurvāṇo 'pi lokottaraḥ" – iti nirūpayatā parameśvareṇa saṃkṣipyāsya svarūpaṃ kathyate*. "He who controls his mind is not thrown about by the waves of wrath, etc., even when he perceives the sense-objects; hence he alone is a yogin, a man-of-stabilized-intellect; such is the intended meaning. As has been said: 'Extraordinary is the yogin, even when he attends to worldly transactions.'"

67 See also, in this volume, D. Shulman's paper, examining *Dhvanyāloka* III 40 and III 43.

that reality. Thus the subjective force is of [the sub-type where] the literal meaning is entirely set aside.[68]

Here is another opportunity for Abhinavagupta to comment again on BHG II 71, this time in the context of the *dhvani* exposition, and to focus on the same *lokottaratā* to which he refers in his *Gītārtha-saṃgraha* on this verse. His *Locana* on *Dhvanyālokavṛtti* ad III 1 thus reads (CSS ed., p. 294; INGALLS ET AL. 1990, p. 376):

tasmād bādhitasvārtham etad vākyaṃ saṃyamino lokottaratālakṣaṇena nimittena tattvadṛṣṭāv avadhānaṃ mithyādṛṣṭau ca parāṅmukhatvaṃ dhvanati |

Therefore this sentence, its primary meaning being obstructed,[69] suggests that the self-controlled ascetic, because of his extraordinary nature, is attentive to the perception [lit. "vision"] of ultimate reality and disregards false perception.[70]

Let us come back to *Locana* ad I 13, which cites our stanza: "*bhāvavrāta*, etc." It is that extraordinary conduct of the yogin which is a source of wonder (see also the use of *kaścit* qualifying *mahāpuruṣa*), and it is why the suggested meaning (the *jīvanmukta*) prevails over the expressed one (the *bhāvavrāta*), thus making the *aprastutapraśaṃsā* a case of *dhvani*. Such is the meaning of Abhinavagupta's *avataraṇikā* to his exegesis of his own stanza ("*bhāvavrāta*, etc."), as we have seen.[71]

Although the passage has already been quoted (above, p. 50), I come back to its interpretation, whose implications may be further developed now that the suggested meaning has been identified:

But if the true subject [of the utterance] (*prastuta*) [i.e., the speaker's intention which he wants to convey to the listener, therefore, the suggested meaning he has in his mind, namely, the evocation of the *jīvanmukta*] is a source of wonder, [although] suggested (*ākṣipyamāṇa*) by means of [another subject] that is non-pertinent or irrelevant (*aprastuta*) [to the speaker

---

[68] Transl. INGALLS ET AL. 1990, p. 376 (slightly modified). A similar eviction of the litteral meaning, in order to establish a suggestion based on metaphoric usage, is found in *Meghadūta* 31, quoted by the *vṛtti* ad III 43, in which the word *maitrī*, "friendship," applied to the breeze, must be taken metaphorically, since no breeze is ever literally "friendly" (see, in the volume, D. Shulman's analysis of the verse).

[69] Since "night" and "waking" must not be taken literally here.

[70] Transl. INGALLS ET AL. 1990, p. 376 (slightly modified).

[71] Note a variant, *pāda* c: sa tvām āha jaḍaṃ tataḥ...

and the listener, namely, the *bhāvavrāta*] – that other subject being insentient, etc., or described in such a way that its particularities are entirely unimaginable for such a result [namely, suggesting the real meaning and thus arousing a sense of wonder, as does the *prastuta*, i.e., the portrayal of the *jīvanmukta*] – then, we have a case of *vastudhvani*.

Now that the *mahāpuruṣa* is identified as a *jīvanmukta*, let us come to the functioning of the figure, based on the similarity of the "suggested" meaning, pertinent or relevant (*prastuta*) to the speaker and listener, and the "suggesting" (or "expressed") meaning that is not pertinent to them (*aprastuta*), and to the examination of the expressed meaning, which consists in the description of the *bhāvavrāta*.

The next segment of the *Locana* reads as follows:

> *... jaḍo 'yam iti hy udyānendūdayādir bhāvo lokenāvajñāyate, sa ca pratyuta kasyacid virahiṇa autsukyacintādūyamānamānasatāṃ anyasya praharṣaparavaśatāṃ karotīti haṭhād eva lokaṃ yathecchaṃ vikārakāraṇābhir nartayati* | ...

In Jayaratha's TĀV (and in Abhinavagupta's ĪPV ad I 1, 4, as we have seen, p. 46), the *bhāvas* of the *bhāvavrāta* denote the objects of experience (apparently external and internal) that are "blue" (and "pleasure," according to the pan-Indian definition).[72] Hence, the so-called materiality of the empirical world is at stake – which is the point of departure for Jayaratha's demonstration of what is, in Śaiva doctrine, the ultimate reality: the non-duality of the subject and the object.

For its part (see the Sanskrit text quoted immediately above), the *Locana* limits the notion of *bhāva*(s) to the class of entities, apparently insentient, which are called *vibhāvas*, "determinants" or "stimulants" in aesthetic theory. The examples given by Abhinavagupta, the garden (*udyāna*) or moonrise (*indūdaya*), belong to the subcategory named *uddīpanavibhāvas*, "inflaming causes." The *uddīpanavibhāvas* arouse such and such *vyabhicāribhāvas*, "transitory

---

[72] See (Appendix-1) TĀV I 332: *he bhāvavrāta nīlādyartha*[*ḥ*]. "Blue" [or "yellow" (*pīta*), etc.] is the standard example of the external form grasped by the sense-organs, whereas *sukha*, "pleasure," is that of the internal, grasped by the *antaḥkaraṇa*. Therefore, the syntagm *nīlasukhādi* represents the "knowable" (*vedya*), or "objectivity" insofar as it is an object of consciousness, whether external or internal. Such reasonings are common to Buddhist idealists and to the Trika, even though the latter (see SPK I 4) reaches the opposite conclusion: the existence of a permanent Subject, a substratum for the impermanent, incidental experiences of pleasure and pain, etc.

affects." In other words, as taught in the *rasasūtra* (*Nāṭyaśāstra* VI),[73] a given combination of *vibhāva*s (or "determinants"), *anubhāva*s (or "consequents") and *vyabhicāribhāva*s ("transitory affects"), constitutive of a given *sthāyibhāva*, "permanent affect" (although the *sthāyibhāva* is not mentioned in the *rasasūtra*), culminates in the advent of a given *rasa*.[74]

For this very reason, not all *vibhāva*s are a source of delight, as Abhinavagupta underlines it (here and at other places),[75] since the same garden and the same moonrise are capable of arousing two opposite emotions, nostalgia or exultation, according to the condition of the lover who contemplates them, that is, according to the emotional status of the *ālambanavibhāva*, the "substantial cause" that is the hero himself – whether he is sepatated from (*virahin*) his

---

73 *Nāṭyaśāstra* VI, *rasasūtra*, vol. I, pp. 271ff.: *vibhāvānubhāvavyabhicārisaṃyogād rasaniṣpattiḥ*, "*rasa* is the result of the combination of 'determinants,' 'consequents' and 'transitory affects.'"

74 On all these categories and the way they contribute to the whole of the aesthetic process, see BANSAT-BOUDON 1992, pp. 109-117; 1992a, pp. 141-145. On *ālambanavibhāva*s and *uddīpanavibhāva*s, see below, n. 75; also BANSAT-BOUDON 1992, p. 113, 1992a, pp. 141-142; and, in this volume, D. Shulman's paper.

75 *Abhinavabhāratī* ad *Nāṭyaśāstra* VI, *rasasūtra*, vol. I, p. 282 (including the corrections made by GNOLI 1968, p. 20): *tatrānubhāvānāṃ vibhāvānāṃ vyabhicāriṇāṃ ca pṛthak sthāyini niyamo nāsti | bāṣpāder ānandākṣirogādijatvadarśanāt | vyāghrādeś ca krodhabhayādihetutvāt śramacintāder utsāhabhayādyanekasahacaratvāvalokanāt | sāmagrī tu na vyabhicāriṇī | tathā hi bandhuvināśo yatra vibhāvaḥ paridevitāśrupātādis tv anubhāvaś cintādainyādiś ca vyabhicārī so 'vaśyaṃ śoka eveti.* "The *anubhāva*s, *vibhāvas*, *vyabhicārin*s, taken separately, are not restricted to a particular *sthāyin*, as one sees, for instance, tears caused by happincss or an eye disease; since, for instance, a tiger may create anger or fear; since one notices that fatigue and restlessness can accompany more than one *sthāyin*, such as ardour or fear. However, any given combination [of these three factors] is necessarily associated to one specific *sthāyin* [lit. "does not deviate from the *sthāyin*."] Thus, when the death of a relative is the "determinant," when lamentations and tears are the "consequents," when anxiety and despondency are the "transitory affects," it is necessarily the [*sthāyin* that is] sorrow which is at stake." Such psychological considerations are so widespread as to be almost conventions, or *topoi*, as shown, for instance, by Gauḍapāda's commentary ad SK 12: a beautiful and virtuous woman (here an *ālambanavibhāva*) is a source of joy to all, but a source of sorrow to her co-wives and of stupefaction to passionate beings; a dharmic king (also an *ālambanavibhāva*) inspires happiness in the good and unhappiness in the wicked; clouds (an *uddīpanavibhāva*), although inanimate, generate joy in the world, when they bring rain and thus urge the ploughman to plough, but they produce stupefaction in separated lovers (... *meghāḥ... jagataḥ sukham utpādayanti te vṛṣṭyā karṣakāṇāṃ karṣaṇodyogaṃ janayanti virahiṇāṃ moham*).

beloved or not (CSS ed., p. 128: ... *sa ca pratyuta kasyacid virahiṇa autsukyacintādūyamānamānasatām anyasya praharṣaparavaśatāṃ karotīti*...).[76]

This is how the essential features of Indian aesthetic and dramatic theory come through in the exegesis Abhinavagupta proposes for the expressed meaning of his own stanza.

The *Locana* thus presents the same scheme of interpretation as does the TĀV, namely, the exploitation of the dramatic analogy, but at the cost of a slight shift from the evocation of Śakti, the divine actress, to that of the *vibhāva*s and their "powers."

It is nonetheless possible to recognize the figure of the deity as an actor/actress, in a more subtle way, under the web of meanings that implies, in a Śaiva context, the metaphoric notion of *hṛdaya*, the Heart – in other words the supreme and unique principle of phenomenal manifestation. I shall come back to this.

For this is not all. Such an aesthetic interpretation of the *bhāvavrāta* is subordinated to a superior ambition, of a philosophical order.

As is the case in the TĀV, the *Locana* wants to show that it is wrong to ascribe the status of an insentient, therefore stupid, entity to phenomenal diversity. This is demonstrated by the fact that those *bhāva*s, understood as apparently insentient *vibhāva*s (here *uddīpanavibhāva*s), have a complete and irresistible (*haṭhāt*) hold over the ordinary man. Thus the dramatic metaphor is again entirely applicable here. These all-powerful *vibhāva*s cause men (the hearts of men) to play as they wish, as does an actor (*haṭhād eva lokaṃ yathecchaṃ vikārakāraṇābhir nartayati*). They are the source of men's emotions. They move them. One thinks of Zola's statement in *La faute de l'Abbé Mouret* : "Ils cédèrent aux exigences du jardin" – "They gave in to the demands of the garden." There is nothing more sentient, more sensible and more intelligent than these *vibhāva*s.

Here, Abhinavagupta introduces an amazing development, in the form of a digression, about the "heart" (*hṛdaya*) of the *bhāva*s, which, in his first comment of the text, he had described as the "wordly objects" of the *bhāvavrāta*, the "totality" of them; here however *bhāva* is understood in the limited sense of the *vibhāva*s of the *uddīpana* category, i.e. gardens, moonrises and so on.

---

[76] Compare Ingalls' analysis, below, p. 64.

> ... *na ca tasya hṛdayaṃ kenāpi jñāyate kīdṛg ayam iti, pratyuta mahāgambhīro 'tividagdhaḥ suṣṭhugarvahīno 'tiśayena krīḍācaturaḥ...*

The ordinary man does not know anything about their hearts, since he is still unaware that they have one, whereas he allows himself a heart, convinced that he is a *sahṛdaya*, "endowed with a heart." However, the Śaiva thinker and mystic knows well that the object also is "endowed with a heart."

The passage in which Abhinavagupta describes that heart, which he has the privilege to know, is of great beauty, perhaps also by virtue of its paradoxical character. That heart is "most deep" (*mahāgambhīra*), "very intelligent" (*atividagdha*), "entirely devoid of conceit" (*suṣṭhugarvahīna*) – the conceit, *abhimāna*, that characterizes the common man who claims to be a *sahṛdaya* – and "skillful at play" (*krīḍācatura*). In the final analysis, it means that the object is not different from consciousness, hence, not different from Śiva, himself "most deep," etc., and "skillful at play," just like an actor. We have come full circle.

Let us observe also that Abhinavagupta undoubtedly understands the present participle *nartayan* as a fullfledged causative that governs *janasya hṛdayāni* in the stanza[77] – he comments on "*haṭhāj janasya hṛdayāni nartayan*" of his verse as: "*haṭhād eva lokaṃ yathecchaṃ vikārakāraṇābhir nartayati.*"

The "whole of things" (here understood as the totality of the *vibhavas*) *causes* the hearts of men *to play*, just as it deceives or dupes them, making them feel the entire range of emotions. This is the reason why I propose, in this context, a slightly different translation of the stanza, of which I give only the first hemistich here:

> O whole of things [such as the "determinants" that are gardens or moonrise]! Since, hiding your heart that is the Self [as does an actor], you play, while you forcibly grab hold of the hearts of men, by causing them to enact (*nartayan*) the variety of [emotional] modes,[78] he who calls you unconscious is himself unconscious, etc. [...]"

The preeminence of suggestion (the evocation of the *jīvanmukta*) does not prevent the expressed meaning from being tightly coherent

---

77 Contrary to Jayaratha, who understands it as a kind of denominative; see above, p. 41.

78 Lit., "by causing them to enact (*nartayan*) through the variety of [emotional] modes...", unless one considers the instrumental as being the complement of means applying to the gerund *ākramya*.

and articulated. It is even a *sine qua non* condition for establishing a term-by-term correspondence between what suggests and what is suggested. The stanza is indeed built on an *aprastutapraśaṃsā* of the third category, that of the relationship of similarity between the non-pertinent and the pertinent; yet, if one follows Ānandavardhana and his exegete, since the aesthetic balance is tilted towards the suggested meaning, it is not the mere figure of speech known as "*aprastutapraśaṃsā*," but a case of *vastudhvani*. The following chart shows the symetry of the two meanings (denoted and suggested; non-pertinent and pertinent):

BHĀVAVRĀTA: THE *APRASTUTA*	*JĪVANMUKTA*: THE *PRASTUTA*
ātmahṛdayaṃ pracchādya (in the verse)	*svātmānaṃ pracchādayan*
The series of epithets qualifying the heart of the *bhāvavrāta*: "very deep," "very intelligent"... (in the exegesis of the verse)	*gāḍhavivekāloka°*...
"skillful at play" (*krīḍācatura*) in the exegesis of the verse + *haṭhāj janasya hṛdayāni... nartayan* (in the verse) and *haṭhād eva lokaṃ yatheccham vikārakāraṇābhir nartayati* (in the exegesis of the verse)	*lokaṃ vācālayan*
The consequence being that such *bhāva*s are regarded as insentient and foolish, and despised for it: *jaḍo 'yam iti... bhāvo lokenāvajñāyate*... (in the exegesis of the verse)	With the same consequence: *tenaiva lokena mūrkho 'yam iti yad avajñāyate*

I leave aside the rest of the exegesis (see complete text in Appendix-2) that focusses on the paradoxical mockery, already emphasized in the TĀV, by means of which the accusation of insentience made against phenomenal diversity discredits the accuser, who is in his turn accused of being more than stupid:

> *... sa yadi lokena jaḍa iti tata eva kāraṇāt pratyuta vaidagdhyasambhāvananimittāt sambhāvitaḥ | ātmā ca yata eva kāraṇāt pratyuta jāḍyena sambhāvyas tata eva sahṛdayaḥ sambhāvitas tad asya lokasya jaḍo 'sīti yad ucyate tadā jāḍyam* [*jāḍyam* corr. : *jaḍyam* CSS ed.] *evaṃvidhasya bhāvavrātasyāvidagdhasya prasiddham iti sā pratyuta stutir iti* | *jaḍād api pāpīyān ayaṃ loka iti dhvanyate* |

Moreover, in the reversal of blame into praise, the dichotomy of subject and object dissolves.

Indeed, I am tempted to say, distancing myself from Ānandavardhana's theory and Abhinavagupta's exegesis, that in the *Locana* it is not only the suggested meaning which is *camatkārakārin*, but the articulation of both the suggested and expressed meanings. By means of this articulation, the deceived spectator – namely, the common man who is the subject of the directly expressed meaning (as also analyzed in the TĀV) – and the emancipated spectator[79] – namely, the *jīvanmukta* evoked through the suggested meaning unveiled in the *Locana* – are turned into symmetrical figures, actually mirroring one another.[80]

Thus my interpretation differs from that of Ingalls, who does not seem to have understood who that *mahāpuruṣa* really is, except when, almost without realizing it, he identifies the *mahāpuruṣa* as a Pāśupata, basing himself on the sole evidence of the syntagm *lokaṃ vācālayan* ("making people speak") which qualifies the *mahāpuruṣa*. According to Ingalls, this *mahāpuruṣa* deliberately makes ordinary men talk about him, seeking to arouse their disapproval, as a provocative Pāśupata will do.[81]

Ingalls shows his uneasiness, or even his irritation, in his note (n. 4, pp. 163-164), which seems to miss the point, if only for the reason that he refers to a "second meaning" without identifying it explicitly:

---

[79] Phrase borrowed from the title of RANCIÈRE 2008, although Rancière's perspective is different.

[80] See BANSAT-BOUDON AND TRIPATHI 2011, pp. 55-56.

[81] INGALLS ET AL. 1990, p. 164: "But the great man does conceal his thoughts. His causing the tongues of men to wag, in the case of the Pāśupatas and I dare say of any Tantrics, was a premeditated instigation of reproach" – and, for that, Ingalls refers to INGALLS 1962. See also J. Törzsök's contribution to this volume.

> What is one to make of Abhinava's account of his own verse ? The literal meaning of the stanza is not difficult. "Men who decry, as do the non-Tantric philosophers, the delights of love and of the senses, calling them brute pleasures, are really stupider than the pleasure they run down. So I will not copy them by calling names. To call them stupid would be to compliment them." Now it is true that the literal meaning is impossible from the realistic point of view [...]. Neither garden nor moonrise, being insentient, actually makes the heart dance, nor do they conceal their own heart, for they have none. So one is forced to look for a second meaning. To pass to that second meaning is more difficult. Abhinavagupta has thrown what seems to me a needless stumbling block in our way by the discrepancy between the plurality of delights (or stimulants, *bhāvavrāta*) and the singularity of the great man (*mahāpuruṣa*).[82]

I would object to Ingalls' observations that i) the *Locana* asserts that those insentient objects do have a heart and ii) there is no discrepancy between a plural and a singular, since the term *bhāvavrāta* is a neuter singular, working as a collective name.

In any case, it seems to me that one can give credit to Abhinavagupta. Exegete of the *Dhvanyāloka* and author of several fundamental texts of his school, he knows what he wants to say, and his exegesis is perfectly articulated. Needless to say, one is free not to always agree with Abhinavagupta's position. Nevertheless, in my view, the question is not whether we agree or not with Abhinavagupta's interpretation, but how to understand and convey it as that of an important witness, testifying, not only to a given current of thought at a given time, but also to the way that thought results from previous debates. Hence it seems necessary to try to understand Abhinavagupta's sometimes intricate thought.

Moreover – would it be an irrefutable argument?[83] – he, *as author of the stanza*, certainly knows best what he speaks of. He is surely the most authorized to know the *tātparya*, the author's intention.

---

[82] My emphasis.

[83] For there is scope as well for an antagonist position, as hold by the Telugu *cāṭu* verse mentioned to me by David Shulman in a private correspondence – a very contemporary position, indeed, quite in tune with the theory of literature: 'The beauties of a poem,/ are best known by a critic./ What does the author knows ?/ The beauties of a woman are known/ only to her husband./ What does a father know?/'. Yet such emphasis on the preeminent role of the reader (a *sahṛdaya* compared to a husband), the Telugu verse is less radical than the view expressed by Mallarmé (*Quant au livre*), who goes so far as to deny any hermeneutic authority to both author and reader: "Impersonnifié, le volume, autant qu'on s'en

As to Ingalls' interpretation of our stanza, I would add that it is a bit hasty to liken those *bhāvas* that are *vibhāvas* to "delights" alone – which contradicts both the theory expounded in the *Nāṭyaśāstra* and the *Locana* itself: not all *vibhāvas* are a source of delight, as we have seen (see above, p. 59).

Thus it seems to me that Ingalls goes astray when he suggests that the stanza refers to a liberation to be obtained by the path of *bhoga,* "enjoyment." Rather, in my view, and in the light of Abhinavagupta's self-exegesis, the stanza implicitly refers to the kind of *mukti* which is *jīvanmukti*, a central notion in Kashmirian non-dualist Śaivism.[84] After all, Abhinavagupta's point of view is that of the Trika, not of the Pāśupata doctrine.

At the end, let us reconsider a question of chronology. Pandey asserted that Abhinavagupta's philosophical works predated his aesthetic texts, his main reason being a reference to the TĀ in the *Locana.* Ingalls (p. 32) refutes Pandey's opinion by showing that this so-called reference to the TĀ is in fact a corrupt reading: the correct reading, according to Ingalls, is *Tattvāloka* instead of *Tantrāloka*. In any case, however we resolve thc question of the reading, the stanza under examination ("*bhāvavrāta*, etc.") proves that Abhinavagupta cites his own TĀ, which thus must be prior to his *Locana.* For it would be difficult to reverse the reasoning, namely, that a stanza, composed ad hoc by Abhinavagupta for his commentary on *Dhvanyāloka*, would have been reused in the TĀ, in such a manner as to fit so perfectly into it.[85]

---

sépare comme auteur, ne réclame approche de lecteur. Tel, sache, entre les accessoires humains, il a lieu tout seul : fait, étant. Le sens enseveli se meut et dispose, en chœur, des feuillets." ("Disembodied, the book, inasmuch as the author detaches himself from it, does not require a reader's approach. Thus of all human accessories, it happens by itself: once made, there it is. Know: the buried meaning is moving and altogether arranges the pages.").

84 On *jīvanmukti* as the main goal and concern of the non-dualist Śaiva doctrine, see BANSAT-BOUDON AND TRIPATHI 2011, pp. 32-37.

85 Isabelle Ratié has suggested (personal communication) that the huge TĀ might not have been composed in one go but that here and there Abhinavagupta might have incorporated parts of his early works, possibly including one that contained the *bhāvavrāta* stanza; see, for instance, RATIÉ 2011, p. 329, about the existence of an early *Bhedavādavidāraṇa*, now lost, of which a segment of Chapter 10 of the TĀ seems to be a paraphrasis. Obviously one cannot be categorical on this.

3. *DHVANYĀLOKAVṚTTI* III 40[86] AND *LOCANA* THEREON,[87] OR FURTHER OBSERVATIONS ON THE QUESTION OF THE *DHVANI*

Allow me a last point: the text which David Shulman has given to this volume mainly deals with the *Dhvanyāloka* theory of subordinate suggestion and considers as well the symmetrical case of subordinate denotation and enhanced suggestion. In a post-script, the paper refers, apropos *Dhvanyālokavṛtti* III 40, to Dharmakīrti's two stanzas cited and commented by Ānandavardhana (CSS ed., pp. 487-490; INGALLS ET AL. 1990, pp. 625-626) – which announce the autobiographical verse he gives in his *vṛtti* ad III 43: *yā vyāpāravatī...* (CSS ed., pp. 507-510; INGALLS ET AL. 1990, pp. 653; see D. Shulman's contribution to this volume).

In effect, *Dhvanyāloka* III 40[88] and its *vṛtti* give Ānandavardhana an opportunity to come back to the *aprastutapraśaṃsā*, in this case the *aprastutapraśaṃsā* belonging to the same category as the one which characterizes our stanza, that is, an *aprastutapraśaṃsā* based on the similarity of *prastuta* and *aprastuta* (CSS ed., pp. 487-489; INGALLS ET AL. 1990, pp. 625-626).

Here is the first stanza (a *śārdūlavikrīḍita*) ascribed to Dharmakīrti,[89] which Ānandavardhana quotes in support of his demonstration:

> *lāvaṇyadraviṇavyayo na gaṇitaḥ kleśo mahān arjitaḥ*
> *svacchandaṃ carato janasya hṛdaye cintājvaro nirmitaḥ* |
> *eṣāpi svayam eva tulyaramaṇābhāvād varākī hatā*

---

[86] CSS ed., pp. 483-494; INGALLS ET AL. 1990, pp. 624-634.

[87] CSS ed., pp. 483-494; INGALLS ET AL. 1990, pp. 628-631, 634-635.

[88] The text of the *kārikā* is given below, p. 68.

[89] As pointed out by Isabelle Ratié (personal communication), modern philology considers that the first stanza is only "hypothetically ascribed to Dharmakīrti" (see STCHERBATSKY 1930-1932, vol. I, pp. 35-36), since it is nowhere to be found in any of Dharmakīrti's known works, whereas the second stanza, which has long been well-known, appears in the reference edition of the *Pramāṇavārttika* by Miyasaka (see PV, *Parārthānumāna* 286). That the first stanza should only be "hypothetically ascribed to Dharmakīrti" seems to have been a point of contention at the time of Ānandavardhana and Abhinavagupta: in his *vṛtti*, Ānanda describes it as "commonly ascribed to Dharmakīrti" (see below) whereas for Abhinavagupta it is "indubitably (*nirvivāda*) [the work of Dharmakīrti]". However, it is obvious that for both the two stanzas are by Dharmakīrti, since this is the key argument in their demonstration that the second stanza is a direct expression of the first, itself a case of *dhvani*.

ko 'rthaś cetasi vedhasā vinihitas tanvyās tanuṃ tanvatā ||

Since David Shulman has translated this intricate (and somewhat enigmatic) stanza,[90] I will only summarize its meaning: what was the creator's/Brahman's goal when he formed such a matchless girl? For, not only have such perfections created a feverish anxiety in the hearts of men, but the girl herself, not having found a lover worthy of her, is left to languish, unrecognized and unattended.

Ānandavardhana, in his *vṛtti* (*loc. cit.*, CSS ed., pp. 487-488), reveals the suggested meaning to be read beneath the expressed one, which is described as highly implausible: such words can neither be those of a lover (*rāgin* – since a lover could not regard himself as inferior to his beloved) nor of the symmetrical figure of the ascetic (*nīrāga* – since love and beauty are none of his concerns).[91]

And Ānandavardhana concludes (CSS ed., p. 489; INGALLS ET AL. 1990, p. 625):

> ... *tasmād aprastutapraśaṃseyam* | *yasmād anena vācyena guṇībhūtātmanā nissāmānyaguṇāvalepādhmātasya nijamahimotkarṣajanitasamatsarajanajvarasya viśeṣajñam ātmano na kañcid evāparaṃ paśyataḥ paridevitam etad iti prakāśyate* |
>
> Therefore, it must be an *aprastutapraśaṃsā*, for by the subordination of the literal sense there appears [the suggestion] of a lament (*paridevita*) by a man puffed up with pride in his uncommon talents (*nissāmānyaguṇa*°), on seeing that others fail to recognize his qualities (*viśeṣajñam ātmano na kañcid evāparaṃ paśyataḥ*) because he has fired their jealousy by the degree of his brilliance (*nijamahimotkarṣa*°).[92]

Thus is the *aprastutapraśaṃsā* clearly established. Moreover, according to the theorization and examplification at work in the *vṛtti* ad *Dhvanyāloka* I 13, that particular use of the *aprastutapraśaṃsā*

---

[90] See his contribution to this volume: "It was a huge effort, and he spared no expense./ A hungry fire now burns in the hearts of men/ who were happy before./ And as for her, poor girl, she's left to languish/ because no lover could ever/ be her equal. So what was God thinking/ when he turned his mind/ to fashioning **her** body?"

[91] On this important factor of the plausibility of the *aprastuta*, see above, p. 50. Nevertheless, Abhinavagupta ad loc. (CSS ed., p. 488; INGALLS ET AL. 1990, pp. 630-631) – *nanu ca rāgino 'pi...* – raises possible objections to this line of argument, but only to explain the reason why Ānandavardhana in his *vṛtti* unveils the implicit meaning of Dharmakīrti's verse.

[92] Transl. INGALLS ET AL. 1990, p. 626, with my suppletions.

in Dharmakīrti's first stanza should constitute a case of *dhvani*, in the manner of the stanza "*bhāvavrāta*, etc.": in both cases, the suggested meaning prevails over the literal sense.

Nevertheless, here (*Dhvanyāloka* III 40, with its *vṛtti*), Ānandavardhana's point about the status of the *aprastutapraśaṃsā* is not explicitly stated, for *Dhvanyāloka* III 40 adopts a somewhat different perspective, which is that of subordinate suggestion, and refers to *dhvani* in this context alone:

> *prakāro 'yaṃ guṇībhūtavyaṅgyo 'pi dhvanirūpatām* |
> *dhatte rasāditātparyaparyalocanayā punaḥ* ||
>
> This type of poetry also, where the suggestion is subordinated, may take on the nature of *dhvani* when regarded from the viewpoint of its final meaning, if that meaning is *rasa*, etc.[93]

Yet, in the course of his demonstration (CSS ed., pp. 486-487; INGALLS ET AL. 1990, p. 625), Ānandavardhana comes to deal with a more general statement, which invites the *sahṛdaya* to distinguish between the three areas of i) mere rhetoric, namely, the figures of speech, ii) *dhvani* and iii) subordinate suggestion (*guṇībhūtavyaṅgya*):

> *vācyavyaṅgyayoḥ prādhānyāprādhānyaviveke paraḥ prayatno vidhātavyaḥ, yena dhvaniguṇībhūtavyaṅgyayor* [*dhvaniguṇībhūtavyaṅgyayor* corr. : *dhvanir guṇībhūtavyaṅgyayor* CSS ed.] *alaṅkārāṇāṃ cāsaṅkīrṇo viṣayaḥ sujāto bhavati* |

It is in that general context that Ānandavardhana cites Dharmakīrti's first verse as a case of *dhvani* (although the term *dhvani* is not mentioned, it is undoubtedly what Ānandavardhana means, since he shows that the literal sense is subordinated to the suggested one), and not as a case of a mere ("pure" – *śuddha* – as stated by Abhinavagupta thereon) *alaṃkāra*.[94] Moreover, the force of the previous definitions (*vṛtti* ad *Dhvanyāloka* I 13; see CSS ed., pp. 125-132; INGALLS ET AL. 1990, pp. 158-165 and above, pp. 49ff.) allows the

---

[93] *Dhvanyāloka* III 40 (transl. INGALLS ET AL. 1990, p. 624).

[94] *Locana* ad *vṛtti* on III 40 (CSS ed., p. 486; INGALLS ET AL. 1990, p. 629): *yatra vyaṅgyaṃ nāsty eva tatra teṣāṃ śuddhānāṃ prādhānyam* |. "Where there is no suggested element at all, the predominance is of pure figures of speech." (Transl. Ingalls et al.)

reader of the *Dhvanyāloka* to come to the conclusion that Dharmakīrti's stanza, as an *aprastutapraśaṃsā*, is indeed a case of *vastudhvani*.

This is confirmed by Abhinavagupta who, in his turn, goes even farther in demonstrating the soundness of Ānandavardhana's exegesis: Dharmakīrti's first stanza, being an example of *aprastutapraśaṃsā* in which the suggested meaning is made predominant, is to be seen as a case of *dhvani* (as in the stanza "*bhāvavrāta*, etc."). Commenting on *kārikā* 40, he observes in the first place (CSS ed., p. 483; INGALLS ET AL. 1990, p. 628):

> *etad eva nirvāhayan kāvyātmatvaṃ dhvaner eva paridīpayati* |
>
> Carrying this line of argument to its conclusion, he [Ānanda] brings into full light the doctrine that *dhvani* is the soul of poetry. (Transl. Ingalls et al.)

For, as emphasized by Abhinavagupta, Ānandavardhana's *vṛtti* makes clear that the accomplished yet neglected girl is none other than the metaphoric transposition of a man immensely talented yet entirely misunderstood as such. Methodically, Abhinavagupta relates each of the four notions forged by Ānandavardhana with each of the four *pāda*s of the verse in order to show a term-by-term correspondence between the denoted meaning (which is anyway *aprastuta*) and the suggested meaning (which is *prastuta*).

Thus, the four *pāda*s hint respectively at i) the uncommon perfection (*nissāmānya*) of that great man, *for which the creator has spared no effort, nor expenses* (*pāda* 1); ii) his extreme brilliance (*nijamahimā*), *of which other men are jealous* (= *pāda* 2); iii) therefore, due to this very jealousy, the non-recognition of his merits (*viśeṣajñam* [*ātmano na kañcid evāparaṃ paśyataḥ*]), which turns his glory into *a miserable fate* (= *pāda* 3: *vārakī hatā*, with the necessary transposition of the expressed feminine to the suggested masculine); iv) the bitter lament (*paridevita*) of such a man, *who rebels against the Creator himself* (= *pāda* 4: *ko 'rthaś cetasi vedhasā...*).[95] This shows that the suggested meaning is to be considered as prevalent.

---

95 *Locana* (CSS ed., p. 489; INGALLS ET AL. 1990, p. 630): *nissāmānyeti nijamahimeti viśeṣajñam iti paridevitam ity etaiś caturbhir vākyakhaṇḍaiḥ krameṇa pādacatuṣṭayasya tātparyaṃ vyākhyātam* |. "By the four sentence-elements *niḥsāmānya* (uncommon), *nijamahimā* (his brilliance), *viśeṣajñam* [*na paśyataḥ*] ([seeing that others fail] to recognize his qualities), and *paridevitam* (a lament), our author explains the [suggested] meaning of each successive line in the stanza." (Transl. Ingalls et al.) Compare Ānandavardhana's analysis, above, p. 67.

Let us come back to the *vṛtti*. Ānandavardhana (CSS ed., p. 489; INGALLS ET AL. 1990, pp. 625-626) immediately validates his interpretation by means of a second stanza by Dharmakīrti, which, according to him, directly expresses the suggested meaning of the first, namely the bitter and candid complaint of a man considering himself a misunderstood genius – and, what is more, that complaint is that of Dharmakīrti himself, speaking in the first person:

tathā cāyaṃ dharmakīrteḥ śloka iti prasiddhiḥ | sambhāvyate ca tasyaiva | yasmāt –
anadhyavasitāvagāhanam analpadhīśaktināpy adṛṣṭaparamārthatattvam adhikābhiyogair api |
mataṃ mama jagaty alabdhasadṛśapratigrāhakaṃ prayāsyati payonidheḥ paya iva svadehe jarām ||
ity anenāpi ślokenaivaṃvidho 'bhiprāyaḥ prakāśita eva |

Moreover, the [first] verse is commonly ascribed to Dharmakīrti and this is just as one might expect, for in the [following] other verse he reveals the same (*evaṃvidha*) intention (*abhiprāya*):[96]
No one in this world
has fathomed my thought.
Even the best minds that engaged with it
with all their strength
failed to see my truth.
Not even one worthy reader
really got it.
Like water in the ocean,
my ideas will grow old
inside my body.[97]

Therefore, not only does the second stanza work as an exegesis of the first, but it is a self-exegesis, hence unquestionable (*nirvivāda*°), as says Abhinavagupta in his *Locana* thereon.

For Abhinavagupta again supports Ānandavardhana's demonstration (CSS ed., p. 489; INGALLS ET AL. 1990, p. 630). It is in order to contradict a fancied objector asking: "what proof is there of this interpretation?", and again: "what if the stanza *is* [commonly ascribed to Dharmakīrti]?", that "with this in mind, he [Ānanda] shows the meaning of *this* stanza [the first one] by means of the meaning

[96] Transl. INGALLS ET AL. 1990, p. 625.

[97] The meter is *pṛthivī*. Transl. D. Shulman (see his contribution to this volume).

furnished by *that* [other] verse [the second one], which is indubitably [the work of Dharmakīrti]."[98]

By quoting the two stanzas of Dharmakīrti, Ānandavardhana thus gives, so to speak, the "proof by author," even though here the exegete and the author called in to help are two – himself and Dharmakīrti. So does Abhinavagupta with the "*bhāvavrāta*" stanza, in his *Locana* ad I 13, and all the more convincingly so since the author of the commentary and that of the stanza are one and the same person.

Then, commenting on the *evaṃvidho 'bhiprāyaḥ* of the *vṛtti* on the second stanza, Abhinavagupta (CSS ed., p. 490; INGALLS ET AL. 1990, p. 631) offers a very lucid interpretation of the respective ultimate issues of the two stanzas, showing that the first stanza belongs to the *dhvani* register, the second to that of the *alaṃkāras*. Moreover he gives a stunning description of the *dhvani* process that makes us fully grasp in which way the *aprastutapraśaṃsā* he quoted in I 13 ("*bhāvavrāta*, etc.") is a case of *vastudhvani* – in other words, how *dhvani* is at work there, as it is at work here:

> *"evaṃvidha" iti | paridevitam viṣaya ity arthaḥ | iyati cārthe aprastutapraśaṃsopamālakṣaṇam alaṅkāradvayam | anantaraṃ tu svātmani vismayadhāmatayādbhute viśrāntiḥ | parasya ca... svātmani kuśalakāritāpradarśanayā dharmavīrasparśena vīrarase viśrāntir iti mantavyam |*
>
> By "the same [intention]," he means that the object [of the second stanza] is [explicitly] a "lament" [which gives the clue to the first one]. The literal sense so far [in Dharmakīrti's two stanzas] is a couple of figures, namely *aprastutapraśaṃsā* [in the first] and simile (*upamā*) [in the second]. But [in the case of the first stanza], immediately after [apprehending the figure of speech as an *aprastutapraśaṃsā*], there is [for the listener] repose in one's own self (*svātmani viśrāntiḥ*), that is, in the *adbhuta* [*rasa*], the "Marvelous," for he is filled with wonder (*vismaya*) [at the advent of the suggested meaning, which prevails on the literal]. As for the other [stanza], one should understand that there occurs [the listener's] repose in one's own self (*svātmani viśrāntiḥ*), that is, in the *vīrarasa*, the "Heroic," for [the stanza] is concerned with [lit., "is touched by"] the [subcategory of *vīrarasa* which is the] *dharmavīra*[*rasa*],[99] the heroic sentiment arising

---

98 *Locana* (CSS ed., p. 489; INGALLS ET AL. 1990, p. 630) – following): *nanv atrāpi kiṃ pramāṇam ity āśaṅkyāha – "tathā ceti" | nanu kiṃ iyatety āśaṅkya tadāśayena nirvivādatadīyaślokārpitenāsyāśāyaṃ saṃvadati – "saṃbhāvyata iti"* |. (My translation.)

99 Note the implicit play on words: Dharmakīrti is by his very name destined to incarnate the *dharmavīrarasa*, the heroic *rasa* based on observing *dharma*.

from *dharma*, by showing [Dharmakīrti's] benevolence [towards men to be instructed in the ultimate reality].[100]

However, it is noteworthy that the statement remains somewhat elliptical since, in this passage, Abhinavagupta does not explain (contrary to his exegesis of "*bhāvavrāta*, etc.") that, if the listener of Dharmakīrti's first stanza experiences the *adbhutarasa*, and thus *ātmaviśrānti*, it is due to that capacity of "creating wonderment" (*camatkārakāritva*) in the listener which characterizes the suggested meaning of the verse. For this very reason, the statement also implies that the suggested meaning prevails over the literal – a scheme that we have seen at play in the "*bhāvavrāta*" verse quoted in the *Locana* ad I 13, in which the emphasis was, however, put on the *dhvani* process rather than on the *rasa* process, as is the case here. Moreover, such an ellipsis is quite appropriate in connection with a commentary (ad III 40) that refers to *rasa*s (see the text above, p. 68).

Symmetrically, the second stanza is to be read as a mere figure of speech (an *upamā*, in which the *target* is Dharmakīrti himself, the *ground* the ocean, where the same water flows through water, endlessly and in vain), in which no suggested meaning is to be found and therefore, neither any predominance of a suggested meaning, nor any *dhvani*, but only a candidly direct expression of a lament. It nevertheless leads to the experience of a given *rasa*, here the *vīrarasa*.

Thus, my investigation has taken the paths of intertextuality and intratextuality. On the one hand, Abhinagagupta's *bhāvavrāta* stanza is reproduced by Bhāskara, several centuries later, whereas Jayaratha's TĀV quotes the full text of a stanza of which Abhinavagupta's ĪPVV gives only the first hemistich in a condensed form (see above, p. 39 and n. 13). On the other hand, the *bhāvavrāta* stanza, originally a part of the TĀ, is later on quoted by Abhinavagupta in

---

Indeed Dharmakīrti, although he is in despair at being underestimated, does not swerve from his dharmic duty which is to enlighten men.

100 My translation. It seems that Ingalls misses the point by failing to recognize the key notion of *ātmaviśrānti* in *svātmani... viśrāntiḥ*. Moreover the process of aestheticization which turns the *sthāyibhāva* named *vismaya* into the corresponding *rasa* called *adbhuta* is misunderstood; this is apparent in the awkwardness of Ingall's translation which seems to omit *svātmani*: "one becomes filled with amazement at the speaker himself, and so the aesthetic sense [of the reader] comes to rest in the *rasa* of wonder" (unless *svātmani* is rendered as "... with amazement *at the speaker himself*," which is not acceptable).

his *Locana* ad I 13, that too, with a self-exegesis rather different from that offered by Jayaratha. Thus a web of analogies, characteristic of all Sanskrit literature, and of Sanskrit exegetical literature in particular, has taken shape. In this respect, it is a happy coincidence that David Shulman's contribution to this volume and mine should enter into consonance with one another.

In conclusion, I would say that the question of *sahṛdayatā*, to be taken in its aesthetic as well as philosophical acceptation, has proved to be central in the whole discussion. It follows from comparing the TĀV with the *Locana* on the same stanza that the difference of interpretation has something to do with the "taste" of the listener, that is, with his degree of *sahṛdayatā* – itself, in Śaiva reasonings, the expression of one's sovereign freedom, *svātantrya*. Thus, one is free to consider the literal meaning as preeminent, like Jayaratha in support of the doctrinal (and polemical) point which he is making, or on the contrary, like Abhinavagupta, to regard the implicit sense as prevalent over the literal, thereby taking the reader into the ever-resounding domain of the *dhvani* and giving him access to an even deeper philosophical and spiritual meaning.

APPENDIX

1. TĀV ad I 332 (KSTS 23, pp. 305-307)

idānīm asya śāstrasya paraṃ gāmbhīryaṃ manyamāno granthakṛt, etadarthasatattvam ajānānair apy anyair anyathābodhena yatkiṃcit uttānam eva anyathā ucyate, tān prati aprastutapraśaṃsayā upahasitum āha –

> *bhāvavrāta haṭhāj janasya hṛdayāny ākramya yan nartayan bhaṅgībhir vividhābhir ātmahṛdayaṃ pracchādya saṃkrīḍase* |
> *yas tvām āha jaḍaṃ jaḍaḥ sahṛdayaṃmanyatvaduḥśikṣito manye 'muṣya jaḍātmatā stutipadaṃ tvatsāmyasambhāvanāt* ||

he bhāvavrāta nīlādyartha | *ātmano hṛdayaṃ tena ātmatathyaṃ rūpaṃ gopayitvā janasya* ***sarvasyaiva vādino*** *hṛdayāni āśayān balātkāreṇa ākramya –*

> *adyāsmān asataḥ kariṣyati sataḥ kiṃ nu dvidhā vāpy ayaṃ kiṃ sthāsnūn uta naśvarān uta mithobhinnān abhinnān uta* |
> *itthaṃ sadvadanāvalokanaparair bhāvair jagadvartibhir manye maunaniruddhyamānahṛdayair duḥkhena taiḥ sthīyate* ||

ityādisthityā vividhābhir bhaṅgībhiḥ nartayan yat saṃkrīḍase – naṭavat atāttvikena rūpeṇa samullasasi, ataḥ sa ***sarvo vādī*** *asahṛdayam api ātmānaṃ sahṛdayatvena manyamāno 'ta eva duḥśikṣito mithyābhimānāt akiṃciñjñaḥ, tvām bhāvavrātam, jaḍam – acetanam āha, ato 'smābhir utprekṣyate – yat* ***amuṣya vādino*** *vastutaś caitanyasvabhāvena bhavatā yat sāmyaṃ tasya saṃbhāvanāt bhāvavattvam eva jaḍātmā iti yady ucyate sā asya nindāsthāne stutiḥ | bhāvānāṃ hi vastutaś caitanyam eva rūpam acetyamānatve hi teṣāṃ na kiṃcidrūpaṃ syāt, atas tad eva ye na jānate te jaḍebhyo 'pi jaḍāḥ iti kathaṃ ca teṣāṃ cetanātmakair bhāvaiḥ nindāparyavasāyi sāmyaṃ syāt iti bhāvaḥ | evaṃ prakṛte 'pi asya granthasya yas tattvaṃ na jānāti mā jñāsīt, pratyuta anyathāpi yatkiṃcana vakti ity asāv eva jaḍo, na punar asya granthasya kaścid doṣaḥ ity arthaḥ ||*

2. Locana ad Dhvanyālokavṛtti I 13
(CSS ed., pp. 127-128)

atra yady api sārūpyavaśena kṛtaghnaḥ kaścid anyaḥ prastuta ākṣipyate, tathāpy aprastutasyaiva vetālavṛttāntasya camatkārakāritvam | na hy acetanopālambhavad asaṃbhāvyamāno 'yam artho na ca na hṛdya iti vācyasyātra pradhānatā | yadi punar acetanādinātyantāsambhāvyamānatadarthaviśeṣaṇenāprastutena varṇitena prastutam ākṣipyamāṇaṃ camatkārakāri tadā vastudhvanir asau | yathā mamaiva –

> *bhāvavrāta haṭhāj janasya hṛdayāny ākramya yan nartayan bhaṅgībhir vividhābhir ātmahṛdayaṃ pracchādya saṃkrīḍase |*
> *sa tvām āha jaḍaṃ tataḥ sahṛdayaṃmanyatvaduḥśikṣito manye 'muṣya jaḍātmatā stutipadaṃ tvatsāmyasambhāvanāt ||*

kaścin mahāpuruṣo vītarāgo 'pi sarāgavad iti nyāyena gāḍhavivekālokatiraskṛtatimirapratāno 'pi lokamadhye svātmānaṃ pracchādayaṃl lokaṃ ca vācālayann ātmany apratibhāsam evāṅgīkurvaṃs tenaiva lokena mūrkho 'yam iti yad avajñāyate tadā tadīyaṃ lokottaraṃ caritaṃ prastutaṃ vyaṅgyatayā prādhānyena prakāśyate | jaḍo 'yam iti hy udyānendūdayādir bhāvo lokenāvajñāyate, sa ca pratyuta kasyacid virahiṇa autsukyacintādūyamānamānasatām anyasya praharṣaparavaśatāṃ karotīti haṭhād eva lokaṃ yathecchaṃ vikārakāraṇābhir nartayati | na ca tasya hṛdayaṃ kenāpi jñāyate kīdṛg ayam iti, pratyuta mahāgambhīro 'tividagdhaḥ suṣṭhugarvahīno 'tiśayena krīḍācaturaḥ sa yadi lokena jaḍa iti tata eva kāraṇāt pratyuta vaidagdhyasambhāvananimittāt sambhāvitaḥ | ātmā ca yata eva kāraṇāt pratyuta jāḍyena sambhāvyas tata eva sahṛdayaḥ sambhāvitas tad asya lokasya jaḍo 'sīti yad ucyate tadā jāḍyam[101] *evaṃvidhasya bhāvavrātasyāvidagdhasya prasiddham iti sā pratyuta stutir iti | jaḍād api pāpīyān ayaṃ loka iti dhvanyate | tad āhā – "yadā tv" iti | "itarathā tv" iti | itarathaiva punar alaṃkārāntaratvam alaṃkāraviśeṣatvaṃ na vyaṅgyasya kathaṃcid api prādhānya iti bhāvaḥ ||*

3. ĪPK I 1, 4

tathā hi jaḍabhūtānāṃ pratiṣṭhā jīvadāśrayā |
jñānaṃ kriyā ca bhūtānāṃ jīvatāṃ jīvanaṃ matam ||

4. Bhāskarī ad ĪPV I 1, 4

antaryāmiśuddhacittattvavaśenendriyāṇāṃ sā śaktir astīti cet satyam, sarvatra tadvaśenaiva sāstīti sarvaṃ jaḍam evocyatām, ajaḍam eva veti kiṃ viśeṣakalpanābhiḥ | paramārthavicāre tu,

> *bhāvavrāta haṭhāj janasya hṛdayāny ākramya yan nartayan bhaṅgībhir vividhābhir ātmahṛdayaṃ pracchādya saṃkrīḍase |*
> *yas tvām āha jaḍaṃ svayaṃ sahṛdayaṃmanyatvaduḥśikṣito manye 'muṣya jaḍātmatā stutipadaṃ tvatsāmyasambhāvanāt ||*

iti nītyā sarveṣāṃ bhāvānāṃ svarūpam api cinmayam eveti ekaprakāśavād eva sarvatra supratiṣṭhitaḥ | yas tu granthakṛtā viśeṣa uktaḥ sasphuṭatvāsphuṭatvakṛtaḥ, athavā jaḍānām upadeśānahatvam apekṣyaivam uktam iti na virodha ity alam |

REFERENCES

Abhinavabhāratī
See *Nāṭyaśāstra*

Āgamaśāstra
See BHATTACHARYA 1989

BANSAT-BOUDON 1990
L. Bansat-Boudon, "The *Sāmānyābhinaya* or How to Play the Game," *Indologica Taurinensia* 15-16, [1989-1990] 1990, pp. 67-77

---

[101] Typo in CSS ed.: *jaḍyam.*

BANSAT-BOUDON 1992
L. Bansat-Boudon, *Poétique du théâtre indien. Lectures du Nāṭyaśāstra*, Paris: École française d'Extrême-orient, Publications de l'École française d'Extrême-orient 169, 1992

BANSAT-BOUDON 1992a
L. Bansat-Boudon, "Le cœur-miroir. Remarques sur la théorie indienne de l'expérience esthétique et ses rapports avec le théâtre," *Les Cahiers de Philosophie* 14, 1992, pp. 133-154

BANSAT-BOUDON 2004
L. Bansat-Boudon, *Pourquoi le théâtre ? La réponse indienne*, Paris: Mille et une nuits, 2004

BANSAT-BOUDON 2008
L. Bansat-Boudon, "Introduction au śivaïsme non dualiste du Cachemire. Lectures du *Paramārthasāra* (2002-2007)," *Annuaire de l'École pratique des hautes études, Section des sciences religieuses, Résumé des conférences et travaux (2006-2007)* 115, 2008, pp. 57-65

BANSAT-BOUDON AND TRIPATHI 2011
L. Bansat-Boudon and K. Tripathi, *An Introduction to Tantric Philosophy: The Paramārthasāra of Abhinavagupta with the Commentary of Yogarāja* [translated by L. Bansat-Boudon and K. Tripathi. Introduction, notes, critically revised Sanskrit text, appendix, indices by L. Bansat-Boudon], London/New York: Routledge, Studies in Tantric Traditions 3, 2011

BANSAT-BOUDON 2012
L. Bansat-Boudon, "Aesthetica in nuce dans le mythe d'origine du théâtre indien," in S. D'Intino and C. Guenzi (eds.), *Aux abords de la clairière. Études indiennes et comparées en l'honneur de Charles Malamoud*, Turnhout: Brepols, Bibliothèque de l'École des hautes études, Sciences religieuses 154, 2012, pp. 213-238

BANSAT-BOUDON 2012a
L. Bansat-Boudon, "L'Inde et l'impératif théâtral," in E. Feuillebois-Pierunek (ed.), *Théâtres d'Asie et d'Orient: traditions, rencontres, métissages*, Bruxelles: PIE Peter Lang, 2012, pp. 165-192

BANSAT-BOUDON 2014
L. Bansat-Boudon, "On Śaiva Terminology: Some Key Issues of Understanding," *Journal of Indian Philosophy* 42(1), 2014, pp. 39-97

BHATTACHARYA 1989
V. Bhattacharya, *The Āgamaśāstra of Gauḍapāda, edited, translated and annotated*, [Calcutta: 1943] Delhi: Motilal Banarsidass, 1989

BHG
[*Bhagavadgītā*] *Śrīmad Bhagavad Gītā with Commentary by Mahāmaheśvara Rājānaka Abhinavagupta*, ed. Lakshman Raina [Lakshman Joo], Srinagar: Kashmir Pratap Steam Press, 1933

Bhāskarī
Īśvara-Pratyabhijñā-Vimarśinī of Abhinavagupta: Doctrine of Divine Recognition, vols. I and II: *Sanskrit Text with the Commentary Bhāskarī*, eds. K.A.S. Iyer and K.C. Pandey, [Allahabad/Lucknow: 1930-1954] Delhi: Motilal Banarsidass, 1986

Dhvanyāloka
The Dhvanyāloka, with the Locana & Bālapriyā Commentaries by Abhinavagupta & Śrī Rāmaśāraka, with the Divyañjana Notes by Śrī Mahādeva Śāstrī, ed. P. Śāstrī, Benares: Chowkhamba Sanskrit Series Office, Kashi Sanskrit Series 135, 1940

Gītārthasaṃgraha
See BHG

GEROW 1971
E. Gerow, *A Glossary of Indian Figures of Speech*, The Hague: Mouton, Publications in Near and Middle East Studies Series A, 1971

GNOLI 1968
R. Gnoli, *The Aesthetic Experience According to Abhinavagupta*, [Rome: Istituto per lo studio del Medio ed Estremo Oriente, 1956] Benares: Chowkhamba Sanskrit Series Office, Chowkhamba Sanskrit Studies 62, 1968

HULIN 1978
M. Hulin, *Le Principe de l'ego dans la pensée indienne classique. La notion d'ahaṃkāra*, Paris: De Boccard, Publications de l'Institut de civilisation indienne 44, 1978

INGALLS 1962
D.H.H. Ingalls, "Cynics and Pāśupatas: The Seeking of Dishonor," *Harvard Theological Review* 55, 1962, pp. 281-298

INGALLS ET AL. 1990
D.H.H. Ingalls, J.M. Masson and M.V. Pathwardhan, *The Dhvanyāloka of Ānandavardhana, with the Locana of Abhinavagupta*, Cambridge (Mass.)/London: Harvard University Press, Harvard Oriental Series 49, 1990

ĪPK
The Īśvarapratyabhijñākārikā of Utpaladeva with the author's Vṛtti, ed. and transl. R. Torella, Rome: Istituto per lo studio del Medio ed Estremo Oriente, Serie Orientale Roma 71, 1994

ĪPV
[*Īśvarapratyabhijñāvimarśinī*] *The Īshvara-Pratyabhijñā Vimarshinī of Utpaladeva with Commentary by Abhinava Gupta*, vol. I, ed. M. Rāma Shāstri, Srinagar: Research Department, Jammu & Kashmir State, Kashmir Series of Texts and Studies

22, 1918; vol. II (*The Īśwarapratyabhijñā of Utpaladeva with the Vimarśinī by Abhinavagupta*), ed. M. Kaul Shāstrī, Srinagar: Research Department, Jammu & Kashmir State, Kashmir Series of Texts and Studies 33, 1921

ĪPVV
[*Īśvarapratyabhijñāvivṛtivimarśinī*] *Īśvarapratyabhijñā Vivṛtivimarśini by Abhinavagupta*, ed. M. Kaul Shāstrī, 3 vols., Srinagar: Research Department, Jammu & Kashmir Government, Kashmir Series of Texts and Studies 60, 62, 65, 1938-1943

Jñānaśrīmitranibandhāvali
Jñānaśrīmitranibandhāvali, ed. A. Thakur, Patna: Kashi Prasad Jayaswal Research Institute, Tibetan Sanskrit Works Series 5, 1959

LÉVI 1890
S. Lévi, *Le Théâtre indien*, [Paris: Honoré Champion, 1890] 2nd ed. Paris: Bibliothèque de l'École des Hautes Études, Sciences philologiques et historiques 83, 1963

Locana
[*Dhvanyālokalocana*] See *Dhvanyāloka*

Nāṭyaśāstra
Nāṭyaśāstra of Bharatamuni with the Commentary Abhinavabhāratī, ed. R.S. Nagar, Delhi/Ahmedabad: Parimal Publications, Parimal Sanskrit Series 4, 1981-1984

PS
[*Paramārthasāra*] See BANSAT-BOUDON AND TRIPATHI 2011

PSV
[*Paramārthasāravivṛti*] See PS

PV
Pramāṇavārttika-kārikā (Sanskrit and Tibetan), ed. Y. Miyasaka, *Acta Indologica* 2, 1971-1972, pp. 1-206

RANCIÈRE 2008
J. Rancière, *Le spectateur émancipé*, Paris: La Fabrique, 2008

RATIÉ 2011
I. Ratié, *Le Soi et l'Autre. Identité, différence et altérité dans la philosophie de la Pratyabhijñā*, Leiden/Boston: Brill, 2011

SK
Sāṃkhyakārikā of Īśvarakṛṣṇa with the Commentary of Gauḍapāda, ed. T.G. Mainkar, Poona: [1964] Oriental Book Agency, 1972 [enlarged ed.]

SILBURN AND PADOUX 1998
L. Silburn† and A. Padoux, *Abhinavagupta, La Lumière sur les Tantras. Chapitres 1 à 5 du Tantrāloka, traduits et commentés*, Paris: De Boccard, Publications de l'Institut de civilisation indienne 66, 1998

SPK
[*Spandakārikā*] *The Spandakarikas of Vasugupta, with the Nirnaya by Ksemaraja*, ed. and transl. M. Kaul Shāstrī, Srinagar: Research Department, Jammu & Kashmir State, Kashmir Series of Texts and Studies 42, 1925

Spandanirṇaya
See SPK

STCHERBATSKY 1930-1932
F.T. Stcherbatsky, *Buddhist Logic*, 2 vols., [Leningrad: 1930-1932], New Delhi: Munshiram Manoharlal, 1986

TĀ
The Tantrāloka of Abhinava Gupta with Commentary by Rājānaka Jayaratha, ed. M. Kaul Shāstrī, 12 vols., Srinagar: Research Department, Jammu & Kashmir State, Kashmir Series of Texts and Studies 23, 28, 29, 30, 35, 36, 41, 47, 52, 57, 58, 59, 1918-1938

TARABOUT 1998
G. Tarabout, "Notes sur théâtre et possession, ou petite collection d'historiettes," in L. Bansat-Boudon (ed.), *Puruṣārtha* 20: *Théâtres indiens*, Paris: Éditions de l'École des Hautes Études en Sciences Sociales, 1998, pp. 295-297

TĀV
[*Tantrālokaviveka*] See TĀ

Understanding Udbhaṭa:

The Invention of Kashmiri Poetics in the Jayāpīḍa Moment*

YIGAL BRONNER

According to the standard account of the Kashmiri school of literary theory and of the history of Sanskrit poetics more generally, the work of Ānandavardhana (c. 850), typically read together with that of his important commentator Abhinavagupta (c. 1000), is the tradition's only watershed. Whatever preceded it was primitive in comparison to Ānanda's sophisticated theory of suggestion and the nondualist inflection it received at Abhinava's hands, and everything that followed was a secondary formulation at best. This account is problematic even aside from its strong bias in favor of Kashmiri theorists, who never enjoyed the almost sacred aura that some Indologists grant them. Indeed, various misconceptions that mire our understanding of the evolution of literary thinking within Kashmir itself hinder a more accurate appreciation of its legacy. The purpose of this essay is to correct one such misconception and to show that, contrary to the prevailing view, the big breakthrough of Kashmiri poetics took place, or at the very least decisively began, a generation or two before Ānanda. This breakthrough was led by Udbhaṭa (c. 800) and, to a lesser extent, Vāmana, his colleague at the court of Jayāpīḍa (r. 776-807), and Rudraṭa, who must have followed them by no more than a couple of decades. It was during this important phase that all the building blocks of Ānanda's theory were introduced and Sanskrit poetics dramatically changed its course, as voices within the tradition testify. The genius of Ānanda's *Dhvanyāloka* (*Light on Suggestion*, henceforth DhvĀ), I argue, was in his perfect

* For the comments, suggestions, and encouragement, I am grateful to Lawrence McCrea, Andrew Ollett, Sheldon Pollock, and David Shulman. I also want to express my gratitude to Eli Franco and Isabelle Ratié for inviting me to participate in the conference that led to this collection, for their patience and continued support, and for their extremely helpful observations and advice.

combination of his predecessors' building blocks in a uniquely coherent and hence uniquely powerful – some would say too powerful – package or framework.

I should note that scholars have already realized several significant aspects of this thesis, even if strangely in isolation from one another, and I will highlight their insights in the course of my discussion. In this sense, this article may be read as a review essay that pieces together evidence from earlier works. From these and other evidentiary pieces, however, a new picture emerges, namely, that Sanskrit poetics underwent its pivotal turning point during Jayāpīḍa's reign and under Udbhaṭa's lead. It is this thinker whom Indologists have most misunderstood and neglected, partly, of course, because of the loss of the bulk of his corpus. But enough has been preserved or quoted to at least begin to understand his true impact.

1. THE JAYĀPĪḌA MOMENT AND THE ACADEMIZATION OF SANSKRIT POETICS

In an earlier essay I argued that from the vantage point of Kalhaṇa, Kashmir's towering twelfth-century chronicler, Jayāpīḍa's reign was seen as a defining moment in the kingdom's attitude to learning and the arts. Kalhaṇa describes Jayāpīḍa as inaugurating and personally overseeing a great intellectual renaissance and suggests that in doing so, he was trying to emulate the vast but short-lived political hegemony of Kashmir of his grandfather, Lalitāditya, with a cultural hegemony that was just as impressive and far more enduring. Moreover, I argued that central to this king's intellectual makeover was his investment in poetry and poetic theory. According to Kalhaṇa's account, which is unique in its wealth of details, the king appointed numerous poets laureate and even assigned some of them to high government posts. Indeed, the two highest offices went to the literary theorists who are the focus of this essay: Vāmana, who was made a minister or councilor to the king (*mantrin*), and Udbhaṭa, who was installed as the chief scholar in his assembly (*sabhāpati*), the highest academic placement in the kingdom. Kalhaṇa even mentions Udbhaṭa's astronomical remuneration in the only report in his chronicle of the wages paid to an academic: the extraordinary sum of 100,000 dinars per diem.[1]

---

1 The description of Jayāpīḍa's cultural makeover is found in Kalhaṇa, *Rājataraṅgiṇī* (henceforth RT) 4.486-499, where 4.495 and 4.497 mention Udbhaṭa and Vāmana, respectively. For a discussion of this passage and its significance,

I do not think that I am reading too much into the text by suggesting that Kalhaṇa was consciously evoking here a dramatic change in the prestige and institutional support enjoyed by the study of poetry. In this connection, a comparison with his account of the relevant record of King Avantivarman (r. 855-883), under whose auspices Ānanda worked, is revealing. In three short verses Kalhaṇa reports that Śūra, Avantivarman's minister, made new appointments to the assembly, thereby causing the sciences to reappear in the country after a period of neglect; that these scholars received wealth and honor and were carried around in royal palanquins; and that four poets gained fame during Avantivarman's reign, one of whom was Ānanda.[2] There is no mention of poets being appointed to high cabinet posts, no word of the king's direct involvement in the project (or, indeed, of actually sponsoring Ānanda and his colleagues), and nothing to suggest that literary theory was the target of special attention. To judge from a comparison of Kalhaṇa's two passages, then, the Jayāpīḍa era plausibly represents a major turning point for Sanskrit poetics in Kashmir, while Avantivarman's reign marked a secondary and partial revival.

To realize why Kalhaṇa may have held this view, compare the state of Sanskrit poetics when it was entering the Jayāpīḍa moment with that of contemporary knowledge systems. By the close of the eighth century, many of Sanskrit's scientific disciplines and philosophical schools boasted long-standing and prestigious textual traditions. These traditions were usually well defined and well structured, so that new contributions were easily contextualized vis-à-vis an ancient core text and its established interpretations and in contrast to rival disciplines. In grammar, for instance, the triad of a core text by Pāṇini, a supplement by Vātsyāyana, and an authoritative, vast exposition by Patañjali had been in place since the beginning of the Common Era. In the field of Vedic hermeneutics (Mīmāṃsā), the seventh century CE witnessed a major rift between Kumārilabhaṭṭa, whose influence on poetics in the Jayāpīḍa moment I address later, and Prabhākara, both of whom expressed their views in expositions of Śabara's authoritative commentary (c. 400) on the foundational

see BRONNER 2013, pp. 167-176 (for payments of 100,000 dinars, see p. 174, n. 38).

2 Kalhaṇa, RT 5.32-34. The trope of reinstating a discipline after a period of neglect is common in the chronicle and is said also apropos of Jayāpīḍa; RT 4.486-488. For the trope of revival as used specifically apropos of grammar, see AKLUJKAR 2008, pp. 42, 71.

Sūtra by Jaimini (second century BCE). In the field of logic, the sixth century saw Uddyotakara's elucidation of Vātsyāyana's commentary (c. 450) on Akṣapada Gotama's core dicta (second century CE? The text's final redaction must have taken place later). The logicians and the Mīmāṃsakas often argued with one another (and occasionally with the grammarians), as well as with an equally long line of Buddhist thinkers. Thus, when Dharmakīrti in the seventh century presented his ideas on the nature of valid knowledge, he contrasted them with those of the logicians of Gotama's line while at the same time placing himself in a parallel Buddhist textual tradition by composing a commentary on the earlier work of Diṅnāga, naturally inviting later Buddhist thinkers to comment on his works.[3] Even discourses on more mundane and practical topics, such as statecraft, archery, architecture, and lovemaking, all had a claim by 750 CE to a core *sūtra* text, written in elliptical style and archaic language and often claiming a divine origin.[4] And although this cannot be documented in every case, it can be assumed that these academic disciplines came to enjoy regular support from royal courts throughout South Asia.[5]

Literature, by contrast, could lay claim to no comparable scholarly tradition. Despite centuries of composing and appreciating poems in literary gatherings, and despite a long-standing agreement about the nature of a core of poetic devices, by 750 CE this tradition possessed no more than a handful of manuals for aspiring poets. Two such works, Bhāmaha's *Kāvyālaṃkāra* (early or mid-seventh century, henceforth KAl) and Daṇḍin's *Kāvyādarśa* (c. 700, henceforth KĀ), have survived, and we know of a handful of other such texts that are no longer extant.[6] But there was no foundational, au-

---

3 Obviously, the organization of these discourses was not always so neat. Bhartṛhari's fifth-century treatise on the philosophy of language had close ties with grammar, Mīmāṃsā, and Vedānta but is not easily defined as belonging to any of these lines. Likewise, in grammar there were texts that competed with Pāṇini's for authority, and in Mīmāṃsā, Śabara "worked in a field where there were many rival interpreters of the *Mīmāṃsāsūtra*" (MCCREA 2013, p. 128). But such competition only serves to highlight the prestige of these academic disciplines.

4 On the ideology and structure of such *śāstra*s, see POLLOCK 1985. For a good discussion of the different kinds of *sūtra* texts, see HOUBEN 1997.

5 For a detailed discussion of royal investment in grammar, for instance, see POLLOCK 2006, pp. 162-184.

6 For the relative chronology of Bhāmaha and Daṇḍin, see BRONNER 2012.

thoritative text for this tradition, let alone a single learned commentary. The bulk of the discussion must have been oral, and the discussants were not professional *ālaṃkārikas* but poets and lay connoisseurs of the verbal art.[7] In short, this tradition was not a full-fledged academic discourse carried out by scholiasts, and it had nothing like the shelf space, patronage, respectability, and court visibility of its sibling disciplines.

All this changed rapidly and dramatically during the three decades of Jayāpīḍa's reign. First, note the marked shift in the pattern of institutional support enjoyed by literary experts, which, as we have seen, Kalhaṇa recorded; it is clear from his account that poetics is treated on a par with such senior and far more prestigious scholarly disciplines as grammar and logic. Second, there is the volume of production. The corpus of Vāmana's and Udbhaṭa's works alone is as large as all earlier works on poetics combined. This is primarily the result of the productivity of Udbhaṭa, who authored four works in the field.[8] Third, there is the change in the nature of the works produced. What these leading theorists of Jayāpīḍa's court were actively seeking to create was precisely a well-defined starting point necessary for an aspiring academic discipline, namely, a core text followed by a succession of commentaries. In fact, they produced two alternative and hence competing such beginnings. Udbhaṭa identified an existing text, Bhāmaha's KAl, as a worthy starting point and presented his work as expanding and continuing it. He thus composed an extensive scholastic commentary on Bhāmaha, the first such learned treatise in this tradition. Vāmana, by contrast, composed a *sūtra* text in clear imitation of Pāṇini's aphorisms and supplied them with a self-written commentary, surely hoping that additional subcommentaries would follow.

Even before I address the main innovations of these works, it is important to notice what immediately changed with the shift in

---

7 Bhāmaha's text, with its implied and at times expressed hostility to kings, does not give the impression of a work sponsored by a court (BRONNER 2009, pp. 182-184). Daṇḍin's work, however, was almost certainly produced at the Pallava court in Kanchipuram (BRONNER 2012, pp. 70-78).

8 These are his short textbook, the KAlSS; his accompanying *Kumārasambhava*, a poem on the theme of the marriage of Śiva and Pārvatī that exemplifies the ornaments discussed in the textbook; his mostly lost *Vivaraṇa* on Bhāmaha; and his commentary on the *Nāṭyaśāstra*, now lost but amply quoted and unambiguously cited in later literature. It is arguable that the second of these is not an entirely independent work, but even so, the volume of production is entirely unprecedented in the earlier history of Sanskrit poetics.

genre and style. Udbhaṭa and Vāmana no longer presented their works as meant for poets in the making, as Bhāmaha and Daṇḍin had done before them.[9] Rather, they were writing for, and thereby cultivating, a readership of fellow literary scholars. This meant, among other things, a move from a writer-oriented perspective to a reader-oriented one. Such a move is usually associated with Ānanda or Bhaṭṭa Nāyaka,[10] but in fact, it originated in the Jayāpīḍa moment.

Think, in this context, of the question of illustrations. Bhāmaha and Daṇḍin were, for the most part, content to make up their own examples, which lent their manuals a consistent and easy style in the simple *anuṣṭubh* meter and helped impart the art of poesy to aspiring poets. Of course, educated readers could detect in these examples echoes of famous couplets and art-prose passages, and some of the illustrations were not without charm, Daṇḍin's in particular. Occasionally, a real verse from the praxis also made its way into these books.[11] But on the whole, the works of Bhāmaha and Daṇḍin had, by design, a textbookish texture. Things could not have been more different in Jayāpīḍa's court. True, to accompany his *Kāvyālaṃkārasārasaṃgraha* (henceforth KAlSS), a simpler work that presents the gist of his worldview, Udbhaṭa produced a *Kumārasambhava*, an entire poem made of illustrations in *anuṣṭubh* (although now with their own narrative integrity). But his extensive *Vivaraṇa* was simply packed with examples that demonstrated how the theory applied to actual poetic praxis. As K. Krishnamoorthy has shown, cited excerpts from the *Vivaraṇa* show that Udbhaṭa was engaged in close reading and criticism of the very sort we find later in Ānanda and Abhinava.[12] This new orientation toward the practice is, moreover, clearly demonstrable even in the work's few surviving fragments, as Biswanath Bhattacharya has shown in a series of short publications. Indeed, this was no secret in the tradition, as Ānanda and

[9] See, for example, Bhāmaha, KAl 6.3-4; Daṇḍin, KĀ 1.12.

[10] See McCREA 2008, pp. 220-259; and POLLOCK 2010.

[11] These rare instances include Bhāmaha's example of *paryāyokta* (KAl 3.9; originally from the now-lost *Ratnāharaṇa*) and Daṇḍin's example of *utprekṣā* (KĀ 2.224; the verse is found in both the *Mṛcchakaṭika* and the *Cārudatta*), both of which were originally in *anuṣṭubh*. Some illustrations, such as Daṇḍin's examples of *yamaka*s, are in more complex meters and were possibly, even if unlikely, the work of another hand.

[12] KRISHNAMOORTHY 1979b, pp. 310-311.

Abhinava were the first to acknowledge.[13] And Udbhaṭa was not alone. In his commentary on his own aphorisms, Vāmana made a point of giving extensive examples from a large variety of works with which his readers were familiar, called explicit attention to this feature of his work,[14] and clearly tried, like many subsequent writers, to choose examples that were popular or striking.

One result of this new textual practice was that, almost overnight, Sanskrit poetics produced its first official canon, showcasing luminaries such as Kālidāsa, Māgha, and Bhavabhūti, to mention only a few, and a sizable corpus of beautiful and memorable stanzas, many of which continued to be cited and anthologized time and again.[15] Even more significant is the change in the treatment that these verses received. The emphasis was no longer on the way poetry could be composed, as in the works of Bhāmaha and Daṇḍin, but on the processes through which it was cognized and appreciated, analyses that are crucial, as we shall see, to the attempts of Udbhaṭa and his colleagues to systematize their tradition and turn it into a respectable knowledge system. As Daniel Ingalls has aptly put it, "It was under King Jayāpīḍa that the school of literary criticism in Kashmir originated."[16]

2. STRIVING FOR SYSTEMATIZATION

The intellectual heritage of the early poetic tradition, that is, before the Jayāpīḍa moment, has nothing like a coherent conceptual system. The main analytic categories of flaws (*doṣa*), virtues (*guṇa*), and ornaments (*alaṃkāra*) were loosely connected through the metaphor of a poem's body, which they served to ornament, flaw, or be virtues of, but, as Edwin Gerow has noted, they seemed to require

---

13 See, for example, BHATTACHARYA 1978, for Udbhaṭa's supplementing of one of Bhāmaha's made-up examples for *yamaka* with one penned by Māgha (for more such studies, see n. 15). As for Ānanda, he refers to the fact that Udbhaṭa – the citation is anonymous, but Abhinava supplies the identification in his commentary on the passage – showed how *guṇavṛtti* operates in poetic practice (*amukhyavṛttyā kāvyeṣu vyavahāraṃ darśayatā*, [Abhinava:] *darśayatā bhaṭṭodbhaṭavāmanādinā*; Ānandavardhana, DhvĀ, pp. 31-32). I will come back to the implications of this quote.

14 Vāmana, *Kāvyālaṃkārasūtrāṇi* (henceforth KAlSū) ad 4.3.33: *ebhir nidarśanaiḥ svīyaiḥ parakīyaiś ca puṣkalaiḥ.*

15 See BHATTACHARYA 1973 and BHATTACHARYA 1977, where at least fifteen later repetitions of an example cited by Udbhaṭa are recorded.

16 INGALLS 1990, p. 5.

no universal theory.[17] Thus it was never entirely clear how these categories worked in relation to one another. What, for example, was the division of labor between ornaments and virtues, and how were virtues related to flaws? It was likewise not a priority rigorously to differentiate one category from another even within the discussion of ornaments, the topic that received the bulk of attention. Thus, Daṇḍin seems undisturbed by the fact that some of his examples for "dismissal" (*ākṣepa*) are remarkably similar to those he provides for "denial" (*apahnuti*).[18] Finally, the order in which ornaments were addressed was rather haphazard, so that similar devices were often grouped and discussed separately, without any apparent analytic criterion.

We should be careful not to overstate this seeming anarchy, both in absolute and relative terms. It is not as if Bhāmaha and Daṇḍin lacked aesthetic tenets altogether. Bhāmaha strongly believed that counterfactual speech (*vakrokti*), which he further modified as entailing intensification (*atiśaya*), is a criterion to which one should hold every ornament and every poem, and this sometimes led him to negate the aesthetic value of ornamental devices recognized by other thinkers if not entire poetic genres, whereas Daṇḍin had a more complex and holistic understanding of ornaments as disguising and revealing one another, even if this vision was never fully spelled out.[19] Likewise, the prestigious sciences, and especially the triad of grammar, Mīmāṃsā, and logic, had their own fair share of ad hoc procedures that resisted theorization, and the order in which topics were addressed in the core texts of these disciplines was also not always thematic. Pāṇini's *sūtra*s, where economy overrides other organizing criteria, are a particular case in point.

Still, the senior knowledge systems always possessed sets of guidelines, stipulations that operated in tandem and, very often, hierarchically. These disciplines offered elaborate operations to create a word from morphemes, to realize the meaning of a sentence, or to come to possess valid knowledge: there were procedures that had to be activated before others could take place, and these often governed

---

[17] GEROW 1977, p. 235.

[18] Compare Daṇḍin, KĀ 2.121, 123, and 127 (*ākṣepa*), with 2.203, 205, and 207 (*apahnuti*).

[19] On Bhāmaha, see BRONNER 2012, p. 111; on Daṇḍin, see Bronner 2010, pp. 214-230.

additional, subordinate procedures. Thus arriving at the correct declension of a noun, for example, required an intricate flowchart that was theorized as such, with metarules governing the application of ordinary rules, the relationship between general cases and exceptions, and the hierarchy between subordinate and superordinate cases. True, not every outcome was arrived at through such detailed flowcharts, not all the sequences were necessarily structured or theorized hierarchically, and there was not always a consensus about the nature of the sequence in question, as in the Mīmāṃsā debate about the production of sentence meaning as either a top-down or bottom-up process, or in the argument about the relative importance and even the validity of certain means of valid knowledge in logic. But we can say with confidence that the senior South Asian academic disciplines were used to thinking about their procedures as interrelated and hierarchical structures.

Nothing of the sort existed for the early tradition of poetics. Not only were the different types of aesthetic elements and ornamental devices often based on entirely independent principles, sometimes ironically because they were originally modeled after tools from a diversity of other disciplines,[20] but also there was hardly any attempt to theorize the way in which they could be combined. A case in point is Daṇḍin's approach to the interaction among ornaments as a modular and hence endlessly open system, in which each device could interact with any other to create a new subtype.[21] Other examples are Bhāmaha's mixture (*saṃsṛṣṭi*) of ornaments and Daṇḍin's idea about the combination of virtues; as Lawrence McCrea has shown, such amalgamations often came with no guidelines other than "the more, the merrier."[22]

Let me clarify that there is no necessity to think of such elasticity as a problem in discussing poetry. In fact, I believe that the open-endedness and modularity of Daṇḍin's approach were key to his work's breathtaking success in the southern peninsula and then far beyond the confines of the Indian subcontinent, in Sri Lanka, Southeast Asia, Tibet, Mongolia, and possibly China, beginning in the

---

20 For example, simile varieties of doubt (*saṃśaya*) and its resolution (*nirṇaya*) were modeled after steps in the logician's syllogism (Daṇḍin, KĀ 2.26-27), and the *rasa*-related ornaments, as is well known, reflected insights from dramaturgy.

21 I intend to write about this feature of Daṇḍin's work elsewhere.

22 MCCREA 2008, p. 39.

ninth century, that is, shortly after the Jayāpīḍa moment.[23] My argument is rather that from the vantage point of thinkers working within the Jayāpīḍa moment, this state of affairs was seen as one of the reasons that barred Sanskrit poetics from the coveted status of a respected academic discipline, and hence they sought to transform it radically.

It is hard to miss some of these efforts, and even scholars who were not very appreciative of the work of Udbhaṭa and Vāmana grudgingly recognized them.[24] Udbhaṭa sought to create a coherent model for the different aesthetic elements in poetry and, at the very least, to explain how virtues (*guṇa*) and ornaments related to and differed from one another. K. Krishnamoorthy offers a very useful elucidation of this attempt. He shows, on the basis of explicit references from the works of Ānanda, Abhinava, Ruyyaka, and Hemacandra, that while the job of virtues and ornaments is basically identical in Udbhaṭa's vision, they are distinct in their scope: the former are grounded in the arrangement (*saṃghaṭanā*) of materials rather than the materials themselves, which are the scope of the latter.[25] Vāmana, too, clearly took the seeming disarray of poetic categories as a priority and tried to rectify it on several levels. First, he envisioned virtues, flaws, and ornaments as part of a hierarchical universe, at the top of which stood the soul (*ātman*) of a poem, an organizing principle that he identified with *rīti*, poetic diction or style. This allowed him to turn the rather vague metaphor of a poem's body into an ordered one, at least in theory, and as is well known, Ānanda followed exactly the same basic scheme. Second, he tried to clarify the relationship between flaws and virtues as opposites and, somewhat more subtly, like Udbhaṭa he strove to differentiate between virtues and ornaments.[26] Third, he tried to show that ornaments are not as unruly as they seem and that, in fact, they are all

[23] This vast and hardly studied phenomenon is the topic of *A Lasting Vision: Daṇḍin's Mirror in the World of Asian Letters*, a research group held at the Institute of Advanced Studies in Jerusalem between September 2015 and January 2016.

[24] "In different ways Udbhaṭa and Vāmana present the first efforts that have survived to encompass or organize the theory of poetic diction under a principle. Both authors, however, continue the major thrust of the *alaṃkāra* or *kāvya*-oriented tradition of speculation" (GEROW 1977, p. 234).

[25] KRISHNAMOORTHY 1979b, pp. 308-309.

[26] For discussions of Vāmana's overall system, see LAHIRI 1933. For his theorization of *guṇa* and its distinction from and hierarchical relation to *alaṃkāra*, see RAGHAVAN 1978, pp. 278-284 and 289-291, respectively.

analyzable as permutations of one device: the simile. Possibly as a reaction to this last move, which many must have viewed as too extreme, Rudraṭa suggested a fourfold categorization of ornaments into those based on factuality (*vāstava*), similitude (*aupamya*), intensification (*atiśaya*), and textual embrace (*śleṣa*), which is one reason that Edwin Gerow dubbed him "the first successful systematist."[27]

But the elegant superstructures suggested by these thinkers are in some sense incidental to their efforts. Their main thrust for systematization is located elsewhere, namely, in their effort to explain poetry's aesthetic effects as deriving from the semantic and cognitive processes that underlie them, with the help of a massive importation of tools and procedures from the senior academic disciplines, particularly Mīmāṃsā. This has been one of Lawrence McCrea's major insights into the nature of Ānanda's work as a paradigm shift, but here, too, the shift happened or at least began earlier.[28] As we shall see, both Vāmana and Rudraṭa were fascinated by such semantic-cognitive theoretical possibilities, and in doing so they were following Udbhaṭa, supposedly "the least theoretical *ālaṃkārika*."[29]

---

27 For a discussion of Rudraṭa's efforts, see GEROW 1977, pp. 238-245. The quote is from page 239.

28 Although McCrea acknowledges that Udbhaṭa and Vāmana "on a few occasions drew on the concepts and terminology of linguistic philosophy (chiefly grammar and Mīmāṃsā) in explaining the non-literal meaning in various *alaṃkāras*," he believes that "these forays into the theory of non-literary language are for the most part incidental and do not play a major role in the aesthetic theory of these authors" (MCCREA 2008, p. 118).

29 GEROW 1977, p. 235. To be fair, it should be noted that Gerow said this "on the basis of [Udbhaṭa's] extant work," that is, the KAlSS, at a time when the authenticity of the fragments of the *Vivaraṇa* was still being debated. As I will show, however, even Udbhaṭa's extant work is filled with theoretical innovations. Let me note, by the way, that my working assumption here is that Udbhaṭa was Vāmana's senior, on four grounds. First, a verse from his commentary on Bhāmaha praising King Lalitāditya, Jayāpīḍa's grandfather and predecessor, suggests that Udbhaṭa may have begun his career under Lalitāditya and was already a veteran and renowned scholar by Jayāpīḍa's time (Udbhaṭa, *Vivaraṇa*, frag. 97, ll. 1-5; see BHATTACHARYA 1979). Second, his appointment as the president of Jayāpīḍa's academy also points to his seniority, especially when compared with Kalhaṇa's less detailed reference to Vāmana (RT 4.495, 497). Third, later references to these two scholars typically discuss Udbhaṭa before Vāmana (e.g., Abhinavagupta, *Locana*, p. 32; Ruyyaka, *Alaṃkārasarvasva*, pp. 6-11; I come back to these citations later). Fourth, a comparison of their works on certain points (for example, *rūpaka*, discussed in section 3 of this essay) makes it likelier that Vāmana was familiar with Udbhaṭa's ideas rather than the other

3. RETHINKING *RŪPAKA*: THE FIRST THEORY OF METAPHOR IN SANSKRIT POETICS

Consider, in this context, *rūpaka*, the first meaning-based ornament (*arthālaṃkāra*) listed in the oldest texts on poetics and clearly one of the most important devices throughout the history of this tradition.[30] In its original conception, *rūpaka* was understood as a statement of identity between a pair of entities, in which one (e.g., the moon) lends its shape or form (*rūpa*) to another (e.g., a face). The analysis of *rūpaka* was accordingly focused on the relationship of sameness between the equated pair, in contrast to mere resemblance in simile (*upamā*), and on the propositional structure of equating rather than of comparing them. Bhāmaha's definition of *rūpaka* uses the simile's pair of basic building blocks, the subject and the standard of comparison (*upameya*, *upamāna*), and he clearly thought of the two ornaments in close relation to each other. *Rūpaka*, he said, is the identity (*tattva*) with which the standard shapes (*rūpyate*) the subject, "based on an observed sameness in attributes" (*guṇānāṃ samatāṃ dṛṣṭvā*), whereas in simile the standard remains distinct (*viruddhenopamānena*) because the relationship is based on a partial set of attributes (*guṇaleśena*).[31] Or, to follow Daṇḍin's succinct formulation, *rūpaka* is "nothing but a simile wherein difference is obscured."[32]

Note that there is also a grammatical undercurrent to this discussion. The grammarians analyzed simile in the context of two types of nominal compounds, where either the entities themselves, as in the tiger-man (noun-noun) variety, or their attributes, as in compounds of the snow-white (noun-adjective) type, are likened.[33] The early discussion of *rūpaka* drew on this analysis, even though Pāṇini never sanctioned a *rūpaka*-specific compound (*rūpakasamāsa*). This created a problem for those who wanted to analyze *rūpaka* as a variation on simile while remaining faithful to Pāṇini, and it led to a

way around. None of this, of course, is conclusive proof, but I will follow this relative chronology as a working assumption.

30 It is listed as the first ornament of sense in Bhāmaha, KAl 2.4 (after *yamaka* and *anuprāsa*).

31 Bhāmaha, KAl 2.21, 2.30.

32 Daṇḍin, KĀ 2.66: *upamaiva tirobhūtabhedā rūpakam ucyate.*

33 See *Aṣṭādhyāyī*, 2.1.56 and 2.1.55, respectively.

spectrum of unhappy solutions. Bhāmaha treated *rūpaka* as if it existed solely within the confines of nominal compounds that were identical in form to the tiger-man variety discussed by Pāṇini apropos of simile, presumably in order to lend the analysis a Pāṇinian authority, although the poetic praxis offered many examples outside compounds.[34] But Vāmana, already in the Jayāpīḍa moment, denied outright that *rūpaka* could even exist inside compounds, despite overwhelming evidence to the contrary, presumably precisely for the same reason: the absence of an explicit Pāṇinian decree.[35]

This makes it even clearer that whatever the linguistic environment in which early ornamentalists spotted *rūpaka*s, they were modeling their analysis on that of simile and were basically defining the two devices in tandem: stating a resemblance between X and Y was a simile; equating or identifying them was a *rūpaka*. Likening and equating were understood as closely related propositions, even if each had its distinct aesthetic charm. What is entirely absent from this early phase is any attempt to understand *rūpaka* in terms of its special mode of signification, in which a *word* Y applies to the meaning of a *signified* X. This analysis, integral to the Western understanding of metaphor, was not part of the early study of *rūpaka* (or, for that matter, of any of its sister ornaments, like *utprekṣā*), despite the fact that it was available and even prominent in all the senior disciplines. Indeed, it can be stated more generally that although different strands of Sanskrit thought had produced highly sophisticated theories of semantics and had paid much attention to the role of figurative language (*lakṣaṇā*, *guṇavṛtti*, *upacāra*) in the process, the early texts on poetics happily ignored these as irrelevant for their purposes. All this was to change with Udbhaṭa, so it is perhaps not a coincidence that it was also he who decisively cut the Gordian grammatical knot that tied *rūpaka* to compounds express-

---

34 See Bhāmaha, KAl 2.23-24, where all the examples are of compounds. Bhāmaha famously identified himself as a staunch follower of Pāṇini (see, for example, KAl 4.22, 6.36-37).

35 Vāmana, KAlSū ad 4.3.6: *mukhacandrādīnāṃ tūpamā. samāsān na candrādīnāṃ rūpatvaṃ yuktam iti*. Another possible explanation is that Vāmana, like Udbhaṭa, was already silently moving away from the simile paradigm for analyzing *rūpaka*. Note that Daṇḍin, eyeing practice more than any readymade grammatical category, had no problem in identifying *rūpaka*s either outside, inside, or partly inside and partly outside the confines of compounds in the context of his astonishingly detailed formal analysis of this ornament (Daṇḍin, KĀ 2.68).

ing similitude by identifying a different Pāṇinian noun-noun compound type, the *mayūra-vyaṃsaka* or "picaroon-peacock" variety, as its locus.[36] This certainly helped him move away from the question of *rūpaka*'s syntactic environment and concentrate, instead, on its mode of signification.

Here, then, is Udbhaṭa's definition of *rūpaka*:

> *śrutyā saṃbandhavirahād yat padena padāntaram |*
> *guṇavṛtti pradhānena yujyate rūpakaṃ tu tat ||*[37]

> *Rūpaka* is a word that is connected to a predominant word in its secondary-attributive capacity because a connection based on its explicit meaning is impossible.

Udbhaṭa, we will see later, has more to say about *rūpaka*, but even this brief statement in and of itself is a revolution in the discourse on ornaments. Indeed, it does not bear even the slightest resemblance to Bhāmaha's definition. Recall that by virtue of composing a vast commentary on Bhāmaha's work, Udbhaṭa basically installed his predecessor as the tradition's founding father and tried, if possible, to retain his language. But when true innovation was called for, as was often the case, he signaled this by scrapping the older language altogether and introducing an entirely different statement. What, then, is the nature of the innovation in this case? First, note that Udbhaṭa no longer refers to the entities in *rūpaka* but to the words that denote them. Second, *rūpaka* is no longer seen as a relationship of identity (or heightened resemblance, or simile in disguise) but as a specific semantic process called *guṇavṛtti*, or the secondary-attributive capacity. Third, and this is something that is not entirely apparent from the definition itself but can be demonstrated with the help of other sources, this semantic operation is understood in terms of its relatively recent analysis by the seminal scholar Kumārilabhaṭṭa, who redefined *guṇavṛtti* in his *Tantravārttika*

---

[36] Udbhaṭa, *Vivaraṇa*, frag. 22b, l. 8. Sahadeva attacks this position (*Kāvyālaṃkārasūtraṭippana*, henceforth KAlSūṬ, folios 65-66), and later thinkers, such as Hemacandra, know it to be based on the *Vivaraṇa* (BHATTACHARYYA 1962, pp. 80-81). Judging from Udbhaṭa's discussion of *upamā* in his KAlSS (1.15-21) and Indurāja's elucidation thereof, the introduction of *mayūra-vyaṃsaka* as the category of compound underlying *rūpaka* was part of a systematic analysis of the use of compounds in such statements. Pāṇini mentions this compound in *Aṣṭādhyāyī* 2.1.72 as the first of a larger list of miscellanea compounds that he does not further discuss and is, hence, very useful for Udbhaṭa's purposes.

[37] KAlSS 1.11.

(henceforth TV), a subcommentary on Śabara's exegesis on the *Mīmāṃsāsūtra* of Jaimini.

Before I address Kumārila's specific understanding of this term, let us appreciate the profound innovation in stating that *rūpaka* means the semantic process of *guṇavṛtti*. Authors of earlier texts on ornaments were obviously well versed in semantics. Bhāmaha even dedicated one full chapter out of six in his book to various aspects of language, where, among other topics, he directly discussed the relationship between words and the knowledge they produce. Here he endorsed the theory that words signify abstract universals (the word "cow" signifies cowness) and rejected the Buddhist theory of *apoha*, according to which a word communicates its referent through the elimination of everything other than it ("cow" eliminates everything that is noncow).[38] But nowhere in this earliest extant work on Sanskrit poetics is there even a mention of figurative language, let alone an explanation of its aesthetic potential or its being operative in the ornamental devices to which much of the remaining text is devoted. For Bhāmaha, it seems, the semantic and the aesthetic were mutually exclusive ways of approaching language: the former had to do with the movement from signifier to signified; the latter hinged on the counterfactual expressivity (*vakratā*) of poetry. The situation is only slightly different in Daṇḍin, who mentions the term *gauṇavṛtti*, a synonym of *guṇavṛtti*, twice in his book. The first is when he defines the poetic virtue of *samādhi*, which consists, for him, of the artful attribution of traits that really belong in one entity (X) to another (Y).[39] Although *samādhi* is defined in terms of the logical (or propositional) relationship between the entities rather than its underlying semantic operations, Daṇḍin's examples and analysis actually imply an emphasis on figurative speech, and he concludes his short discussion by recommending, in this context, the use of words such as "vomit," ordinarily vulgar, "if employed figuratively" (*gauṇavṛttivyapāśraya*).[40] The second instance is the only mention of figurative language in the entire chapter on poetic ornaments, the main and longest chapter in the book. Here Daṇḍin notes that some of the more colorful (*citra*) varieties

---

38 Bhāmaha, KAl 6. 17-19. See also Śāntarakṣita, *Tattvasaṃgraha* 912-914 (quote) and 1019-1021 (refutation); BRONNER 2012, pp. 89-90.

39 KĀ 1.93: *anyadharmas tato 'nyatra lokasīmānurodhinā | samyag ādhīyate yatra sa samādhiḥ smṛto yathā ||*.

40 Ibid., 1.95.

of causation (*hetu*), where the effect is far removed from, is simultaneous with, or even precedes the cause, "are based on figurative usage" (*gauṇavṛttivyapāśraya*).[41] This should be seen primarily in the context of his attack on Bhāmaha's refusal to accept *hetu* as an ornament precisely on the ground that, according to Bhāmaha, stating a relationship of cause and effect is prosaic.[42] Other than this, Daṇḍin has nothing to say about figurative language in his long primer on poetics, and it seems that for him, the role of figurative language in producing aesthetic enjoyment is, at best, incidental.[43]

It is against this background that Udbhaṭa's move is so dramatic. With no known precedent, he defines *rūpaka* as a word used in its specific semantic process of figuration, on the charm of which this all-important ornament now rests. Moreover, his reliance on the discipline of Mīmāṃsā in this analysis is unmistakable and, indeed, outspoken. As noted, Kumārila had influentially redefined *guṇavṛtti* in his TV, a move that, for the first time in the history of Sanskrit thinking, sought to clarify the difference between the two main terms for the figurative function, *lakṣaṇā* and *guṇavṛtti*, which up to that time had been used rather indistinguishably. For Kumārila, *lakṣaṇā* is a nonmetaphorical transference of meaning, as in a metonym or synecdoche ("the podiums are yelling"; *mañcāḥ krośanti*), whereas *guṇavṛtti* is a metaphorical transference based on a two-phase process. First, a word Y, for example, "fire," when applied to a predominant word X, for example, "boy," is blocked from conveying its normal referent and signifies, instead, its attributes (*guṇa*), such as being vibrant and quick to flare up. Second, this word Y (fire) comes to signify attributes similar to those that exist in X (boy), so that we come to realize that the boy is vibrant and fiery.[44] This is

---

41 Ibid., 2.252.

42 Compare Bhāmaha, KAl 2.86-87, with Daṇḍin KĀ 2.233-242; see BRONNER 2012, pp. 102-104.

43 Note that the term *gauṇa* appears in Daṇḍin's definition of a pair of subtypes of *rūpaka*, *upamārūpaka* and *vyatirekarūpaka*, which runs as follows: *iṣṭaṃ sādharmyavaidharmyadarśanād gauṇamukhyayoḥ | upamāvyatirekākhyaṃ rūpakadvitayaṃ yathā* ‖ (KĀ 2.88). However, as the commentator Ratnaśrījñāna explains (and as Daṇḍin's following examples demonstrate), the pair of *mukhya* and *gauṇa* refers here not to semantic operations but to the primary element (the beloved's face-moon) and a secondary one (the moon) in a proposition that depicts them as either similar or dissimilar.

44 TV 354: *abhidheyāvinābhūte pravṛttir lakṣaṇeṣyate | lakṣyamāṇaguṇair yogād vṛtter iṣṭā tu gauṇatā* ‖. "The use [of a word] in a meaning necessarily connected with its literal meaning is called "figurative expression"; but usage arising from

exactly how Udbhaṭa understood *guṇavṛtti* in his brief definition of *rūpaka* in the KAlSS and precisely the manner in which his commentator Indurāja further explained the process in detail. Even more important, Udbhaṭa deliberately cites a key phrase from Kumārila's new definition in a surviving fragment of his *Vivaraṇa*, just at the point when he is discussing *rūpaka*.[45]

Udbhaṭa, in other words, used a cutting-edge analysis of figurative semantics from Mīmāṃsā to rethink *rūpaka* and define it, for the first time in the tradition's history, more like what we would call a metaphor. Several scholars have already identified key aspects of this move and have appreciated its innovativeness. Sivaprasad Bhattacharyya has noted that "the term *guṇavṛtti* at least in this form of the word as in Udbhaṭa (and in Ānandavardhana who criticises his view) was not in vogue in earlier literature" and was newly imported from other disciplines.[46] Chitta Ranjan Basistha dubbed Udbhaṭa's definition of *rūpaka* a "complete departure" from the work of all his predecessors.[47] Daniel Ingalls argued that the early tradition lacked a concept parallel to the Greek metaphor,[48] and that Udbhaṭa's definition of *rūpaka* introduced "a distinction that was new to Sanskrit poetics and that was destined ultimately to transform the analysis of all the figures. This is a distinction between the furnishing of a meaning *śrutyā*, that is, explicitly, and furnishing it *arthena*, that is, by the power of the contextual facts, or implicitly."[49] Similarly, Gnoli maintained that "Udbhaṭa, by introducing into poetry the secondary function of words... let open the door to the conception of a third potency of language, the *vyañjanāvṛtti*," thus implying that this definition eventually led the way to Ānanda's theory of suggestion.[50]

---

attributes that are figuratively indicated is defined "secondary-attributive." See also the surrounding discussion. See MCCREA 2008, p. 91, n. 61, from where the translation is borrowed with slight modifications.

45 *Vivaraṇa*, frag. 22b, l. 5, *svābhidheyāvinā(bhūtagu)ṇavṛtti(tām)*; see GNOLI 1962, p. xxxiv, where the reminiscence of Kumārila is noted.

46 BHATTACHARYYA 1962, p. 75.

47 BASISTHA 2003, p. 139.

48 INGALLS 1990, p. 8, n. 10: "*Rūpaka* is not what a Greek would have called a metaphor, but that translation has come to be used by every Sanskritist. *Rūpaka* is actually a simile in which the particle of assimilation has been omitted, e.g., 'her moon face, her cherry lip.' In a Greek metaphor the object as well as the particle is missing: 'her stars shone upon my face,' meaning that her eyes looked at me. The distinction is noted by Gero Jenner."

49 Ibid., p. 8.

50 GNOLI 1962, pp. xxiii-xxiv.

But what scholars have not fully appreciated is how pervasive this trend was already in Udbhaṭa's thinking and in the Jayāpīḍa moment at large.[51] It is not so much that the figures were about to be transformed, but that the whole analytic paradigm was already radically altered, as I will try to demonstrate with several case studies later. Note, by the way, that Udbhaṭa was not alone in this move. Vāmana, too, defined *rūpaka* using the semantic capacity of *guṇavṛtti*, a fact that has been entirely overlooked. This neglect may be due to the fact that Vāmana's actual definition of *rūpaka* does not highlight this move and, in fact, is worded in a way that is closely reminiscent of older and more traditional definitions.[52] However, two *sūtra*s later, in introducing his newly minted ornament, *vakrokti*, Vāmana notes: "The following *sūtra* shows that just as *gauṇa* [a synonym of *guṇavṛtti*] is its own ornament, so is the case with *lākṣaṇika* [= *lakṣaṇā*]."[53] In other words, Vāmana advances the discussion a step further. If Udbhaṭa identified *rūpaka* with *guṇavṛtti* as distinct from *lakṣaṇā*, Vāmana concurs and adds, as if completing an imaginary grid, an ornament that is based on this other main mode of figurative speech. It should be noted that, unlike Udbhaṭa, Vāmana does not seem to follow Kumārila's distinction between the two modes. Although his notion of *guṇavṛtti*, like Udbhaṭa's, clearly implies the transference of attributes, his concept of *lakṣaṇā* accommodates resemblance (*sādṛśya*) as well as metonymy – here he perhaps takes a cue from Bhartṛmitra[54] – and the new ornament of *vakrokti* is, in fact, based on *lakṣaṇā* involving resemblance (like all of Vāmana's figures). This new classification, moreover, allowed Vāmana to further tidy up the distinction between ornaments and virtues (*guṇa*) in

---

51 Ingalls did point in this direction, though, at least in the case of Udbhaṭa: "To follow the concern for the implied or suggested sense through the whole of Udbhaṭa's book would require a much more detailed exposition than is justified in this Introduction. It appears in his definition of *paryāyokta*, *aprastutapraśaṃsā*, *sandeha*, and elsewhere" (INGALLS 1990, p. 8).

52 KAlSū 4.3.6: *upamānopameyasya guṇasāmyāt tattvāropo rūpakam.*

53 Ibid., before 4.3.8: *yathā ca gauṇasyārthālaṃkāratvaṃ tathā lākṣaṇikasyāpīti darśayitum āha.* As the Kashmiri commentator Sahadeva observes, Vāmana refers here to *rūpaka* and its kin ornaments: *yathā ca gauṇasyeti, rūpakādisthitasya rūpakādiṣu guṇāt puraskṛtya pravṛttaḥ* (KAlSūṬ, f. 68).

54 Sahadeva quotes a classical list of the five types of relationships in *lakṣaṇā*, and the verse he cites (*abhidheyena sambandhāt sādṛśyāt samavāyataḥ* | *vaiparītyāt kriyāyogāl lakṣaṇā pañcadhā smṛtā* ||; KAlSūṬ, f. 68) is attributed by Mukulabhaṭṭa to Bhartṛmitra (*Abhidhāvṛttimātṛkā*, p. 17). For more on this list of five, see KUNJUNNI RAJA 1977, pp. 238-239.

that it helped him incorporate Daṇḍin's aforementioned virtue of *samādhi*, which had figurative language built into it, into ornament land. It is no coincidence that he begins his long list of examples for his new *vakrokti*, which includes citations from canonical works such as the *Meghadūta* and the *Śiśupālavadha*, with a slight reworking of Daṇḍin's example for the virtue of *samādhi*: "The pond's day lotus opened his eyes just as the night lotus shut his."[55]

In all of this discussion, it is important not to lose sight of the forest for the trees. Whatever the exact analyses of figurative processes they followed, the crucial thing about Udbhaṭa and Vāmana's relevant discussions is that they both equated *rūpaka* (and in Vāmana's case, also *vakrokti*) with what they identified as their underlying semantic processes, which so far had had no place whatsoever in the analysis of ornaments, and that for this purpose they were borrowing their terminology and analyses from other disciplines. For these theoreticians, what was charming or ornamental about such poetic ornaments was precisely their underlying semantics, and Vāmana even added, apropos of *vakrokti*, that the special cognitive process that was unique to this ornament was essential to its aesthetic experience: "The secret here is the swiftness with which such metaphors convey their meanings."[56] As we shall see, such attempts to ground ornaments in specific semantic operations and cognitive scenarios pervade and define the Jayāpīḍa moment.

4. *ŚLIṢṬA* AND ITS COMPLEX SEMANTIC-COGNITIVE SCENARIOS

Take, for example, *śliṣṭa* (later known as *śleṣa*), another case where Udbhaṭa discarded Bhāmaha's definition altogether and came up with a radically new one. Bhāmaha saw *śliṣṭa* as a footnote to *rūpaka*, and he used the same analytic tools to define both. *Śliṣṭa*, too, he

55 Compare *unmimīla kamalaṃ sarasīnāṃ kairavaṃ ca nimimīla muhūrtāt* (Vāmana, KAlSū ad 4.3.8) with: *kumudāni nimīlanti kamalāny unmiṣanti ca* (Daṇḍin, KĀ 1.94). These examples state only that the respective flowers "opened" and "shut," but in doing so they use verbs that apply to the eyes only (no comparable verbs exist in English). In the translation, however, the noun "eye" had to be added. To get a better sense of the metaphor Vāmana has in mind, read instead "The day lotus woke up just as the night lotus fell asleep." But the problem with this translation is that it lacks the similarity between flowers and eyes that is key for him.

56 KAlSū ad 4.3.8: *ity evamādiṣu lakṣaṇārtho nirūpyata iti lakṣaṇāyāṃ jhaṭity arthapratipattikṣamatvaṃ rahasyam ācakṣata iti.*

said, is a case of identity between a subject and a standard of comparison but not as a result of a genuine, empirically observed sameness between them; rather, the identity in *śliṣṭa* is manufactured (*sādhyate*) by adjectives, verbs, and nouns that apply simultaneously (*yugapad*, *samam*) to both. Even this characterization, he conceded, may be true of *rūpaka* as well, so he made a further stipulation: what ultimately sets *śliṣṭa* apart from *rūpaka* is its "embrace" (*śleṣa*) of either meaning(s) or sound(s) (*arthavacasoḥ*).[57] Thus Bhāmaha acknowledged that the ornament involves a linguistic manipulation, namely, simultaneity, and makes a reference, vague though it may be, to "sense and sound." But his definition is still phrased primarily as the logical relationship (an identity, manufactured though it may be) between two entities and has nothing to say about the semantic-cognitive processes that underlie it. This is why it had to go.

Here, instead, is Udbhaṭa's alternative definition:

> *ekaprayatnoccāryāṇāṃ tacchāyāṃ caiva bibhratām* |
> *svaritādiguṇair bhinnair bandhaḥ śliṣṭam ihocyate* ||
> *alaṃkārāntaragatāṃ pratibhāṃ janayat padaiḥ* |
> *dvividhair arthaśabdoktiviśiṣṭaṃ tat pratīyatām* ||[58]

> An arrangement of [words] that could be pronounced in the same articulatory effort, as well as of those that merely appear like them but differ in their phonetic aspects from the level of the accent on, is called *śliṣṭa*. It is labeled as either "sound" or "sense" depending on [its employment of such] twofold words, and it produces the impression that falls under the scope of some other ornament.

We are clearly in a very different world than Bhāmaha's, one that is dense and complex and requires considerable unpacking, which is why we are lucky to have Indurāja's detailed commentary. But even before we turn to his illuminating exposition – and this is another case where a close affinity between Indurāja's commentary and a fragment that survived from Udbhaṭa's *Vivaraṇa* can be demonstrated – what is absent from Udbhaṭa's definition is immediately clear:

---

57 KAl 3.14-17b: *upamānena yat tattvam upameyasya sādhyate* | *guṇakriyābhyāṃ nāmnā ca śliṣṭaṃ tad abhidhīyate* || *lakṣaṇaṃ rūpake 'pīdaṃ lakṣyate kāmam atra tu* | *iṣṭaḥ prayogo yugapad upamānopameyayoḥ* || *śīkarāmbhomadasṛjas tuṅgā jaladadantinaḥ* | *ity atra meghakariṇāṃ nirdeśaḥ kriyate samam* || *śleṣād evārthavacasor asya ca kriyate bhidā* |.

58 KAlSS 4.9-10.

there is no mention of a subject and a standard of comparison. Udbhaṭa frees *śliṣṭa* from the confines of *rūpaka* (or, for that matter, simile), in which Bhāmaha (and Vāmana after him) toiled to keep it, and on this issue he is closer to Daṇḍin's understanding of this device as freely associating with any ornament in the book.[59] But unlike any literary thinker before him, Udbhaṭa is first and foremost concerned with understanding how *śliṣṭa*'s special verbal arrangement (*bandha*) leads from two sets of signifiers to two sets of signifieds and then to the cognition of some other ornament.

Here is where we ought to follow the lead of Indurāja, a keen reader of Udbhaṭa who also had in front of him his voluminous *Vivaraṇa*. Indurāja first makes clear that Udbhaṭa subscribes to the one-word, one-meaning axiom. According to this worldview, which originated in Mīmāṃsā, the multivalence of language is not the result of true polysemy of any single word because signifiers, by definition, each have one signified. Rather, it is a special combination of two sets of entirely monosemic signifiers that creates semantic proliferation.[60] If the two sets consist of words that are entirely identical in form, then they can be uttered concurrently, and presumably their meanings are simultaneously activated; Indurāja, perhaps in agreement with the *Vivaraṇa*, explains this using the Mīmāṃsā term *tantra*, which applies to cases where one ritual act serves two ritual goals simultaneously. Here, it would seem, a single articulatory effort serves two simultaneous semantic goals. But if the words differ in any audible way, beginning with accent, and are made to sound alike only through the poet's crafty way of embracing them together, then only one set of signifiers is uttered, and its signified is initially grasped (meaning 1), leading to an activation through resemblance of a second set of signfieds (meaning 2), whose signifiers are nonetheless not pronounced. The first semantic-cognitive scenario, which consists of true homophony even outside the context of a *śliṣṭa* arrangement, is labeled "sense based," while the second, consisting of manufactured homophony, is the ornament's "sound-based" variety.[61]

---

59 KĀ 2.360ab: *śleṣaḥ sarvāsu puṣṇāti prāyo vakroktiṣu śriyam* |; see BRONNER 2010, pp. 214-230.

60 Indurāja, *Laghuvṛtti*, p. 58: *arthabhedena tāvac chabdā bhidyanta iti bhaṭṭodbhaṭasya siddhāntaḥ*. For a discussion of the Mīmāṃsā view on this and of Udbhaṭa as adhering to it, see KUNJUNNI RAJA, pp. 42-45.

61 Indurāja, *Laghuvṛtti*, pp. 58-59: *tatrārthabhedena bhidyamānāḥ śabdāḥ kecit*

And this is not all. What, one may ask, is this second meaning, and how does it relate to the first? Udbhaṭa is very clear about this point in his *Vivaraṇa*. The second meaning can be either another sentence or another ornament (*vākyāntare alaṃkārāntare vā pratibhotpadyate*).[62] This paves the way to another semantic phase where the relationship between meaning 1 and meaning 2 is itself the scope of reflection and comprehension (meaning 3), and as Udbhaṭa indicates in the *Vivaraṇa*, this further reflection takes into account which of the first two meanings was contextual and which was not rooted in the context.[63] Moreover, Udbhaṭa indicates (and Indurāja explains when discussing his examples) that the content of this further reflection (meaning 3) belongs not in *śliṣṭa* per se but in some other ornament, be it simile, *rūpaka*, or *virodha* (antithesis), to give the examples that Udbhaṭa himself supplies in the KAlSS. Udbhaṭa is nonetheless very explicit, both here and in the surviving fragments

---

tantreṇa prayoktuṃ śakyāḥ kecin na. yeṣāṃ halsvarasthānaprayatnādīnāṃ sāmyaṃ te tantreṇa prayoktuṃ śakyante. yatra tu halām ekatvānekatvarūpatvāt... bhedas teṣāṃ tantreṇa prayogaḥ kartum aśakyaḥ sādhāraṇarūpatvāt tantrasya. tad uktaṃ sādhāraṇaṃ bhavet tat tantram iti. evaṃ cāvasthite ye tantreṇoccārayituṃ śakyante ta ekaprayatnoccāryāḥ. tadbandhe saty arthaśleṣo bhavati. tad uktam ekaprayatnoccāryāṇām iti. tathā ye teṣām evaikaprayatnoccāryāṇāṃ śabdānāṃ chāyāṃ sādṛśyaṃ bibhrati tadupanibandhe ca śabdaśliṣṭam, śabdāntara uccāryamāṇe sādṛśyavaśenānuccāritasyāpi śabdāntarasya śliṣṭatvāt. Note that Vāmana, too, uses the Mīmāṃsā term *tantra* in his discussion of *śliṣṭa*, and that his language is closely reminiscent of what we find in Indurāja: *tantraprayoge tantreṇoccāraṇe sati śleṣa* (KAlSū ad 4.3.7). All this suggests that Udbhaṭa's *Vivaraṇa* included a longer discussion of *tantra* in this context. For close similarities between Indurāja's comments on *śliṣṭa* and the relevant surviving fragment of the *Vivaraṇa*, see BASISTHA 2003, pp. 182-184.

62 *Vivaraṇa*, frag. 39b, ll. 7-8. For a useful reconstruction of this passage based on its citation in later works, see KULKARNI 1983, p. 131. If one compares this reconstructed *Vivaraṇa* citation with Indurāja's exposition on the KAlSS, it is palpably clear that the latter is based on the former. Compare, for example, *Vivaraṇa*, frag. 39b, l. 6: *dantyauṣṭhyalaghupra[yatnatarālaghuprayatnatarakṛte ca bhede]* (reconstruction based on Hemacandra), to Indurāja, *Laghuvṛtti*, p. 58: *sthānānāṃ cauṣṭhyadantauṣṭhyatvādinā prayatnānāṃ ca laghutvālaghutvādinā bhedaḥ.*

63 *Vivaraṇa*, frag. 39b, l. 5: ... *pratipādakabhāvaḥ kintu tābhyāṃ prākaraṇikāprākaraṇika*... (see also frag. 39b, l. 2, and frag. 40a, l. 3). Udbhaṭa is generally interested in the semantic consequences of context relatedness when two meanings are involved. See, for example, his new definition of *samāsokti* (*prakṛtārthena vākyena*...; KAlSS 2.10).

of the *Vivaraṇa*, that this further ornamental relationship is not another full-blown ornament but rather the "impression" (*pratibhā*) thereof.[64]

All this is quite confusing and complicated, and to better appreciate the detailed theorization of the semantic-cognitive scenario in question, let us examine more closely one of Udbhaṭa's illustrations:

indukāntamukhī snigdhamahānīlaśiroruhā |
muktāśrīs trijagadratnaṃ padmarāgāṅghripallavā ||[65]

Her face is dear to the moon,
her tresses, shiny black sapphires,
and her delicate toes, crimson rubies –
she's our mother of pearl,
the one gem
of the three worlds.

This is part of a longer description of Pārvatī, whom Śiva will eventually marry. My translation tries to re-create at least something of the simultaneity of the original, although in following Indurāja's analysis, we will have to stay closer to the Sanskrit and its language-specific puns. As Indurāja explains, the verse has several semantic layers. In the first, the modifications of Pārvatī enhance the beauty of her various body parts: her face is dear to the moon in the sense that it is moon-like; her tresses are long and shiny black; her toes (or, more accurately, her feet) are like red lotuses (the compound word for ruby, *padma-rāga*, can also mean "lotus-red"); and finally – and this is absent from my translation – she is free of anything that is nonradiant (*mukta-aśrīḥ*). All this substantiates her supreme beauty as "the one gem / of the three worlds." A second layer of meaning stems from an added set of signifiers that are embraced into the verse: her face is a moonstone (the stone that is "dear to the moon"), her tresses are black sapphires, her toes are rubies, and her radiance is that of a pearl, or "mother of pearl," in my translation (now reading *muktā-śrīḥ*). This level of signification, with its identification of the body parts with various precious stones, further explains why Pārvatī is in the end *identified* with a unique, marvelous jewel, "the one gem / of the three worlds." So the final, third meaning is *rūpaka*,

---

64 Udbhaṭa, *Vivaraṇa*, frag. 39b, l. 7: ... *āntarapratibhā. tayālaṅkārāntare vākyāntare vā pratibhotpadyate*; Indurāja, *Laghuvṛtti*, p. 59: *alaṃkārāntarāṇām atra pratibhāmātraṃ na tu padabandha ity arthaḥ.*

65 KAlSS, example 4.16.

an identification of the wholes (Pārvatī and this gem of the three worlds) that is based on that of the parts. Yet presumably because it is based on this unique linguistic embrace, this is not a full-blown instance of *rūpaka* but merely an impression thereof.[66] Note, by the way, that this is mostly a sound-based embrace, because most pairs of signifiers are for various reasons not homo-articulable.[67]

I should say that this semantic-cognitive scenario is not without problems. It is not always easy to understand why its different phases should follow this sequence: why, for example, context alone should determine which meaning gets to be articulated and cognized first, and why *śliṣṭa* is more present in our mind than *rūpaka* and not the other way around. Indeed, these issues were the focus of criticism by later thinkers such as Mammaṭa in a debate that received significant scholarly attention.[68] For the purpose of this essay, however, we can ignore most aspects of this dispute and focus on the important pattern it embodies, namely, that thinkers like Udbhaṭa and his followers are suddenly focusing, like their colleagues from the senior disciplines, on explaining the different aesthetic elements (*śliṣṭa*, *rūpaka*, *virodha*, *upamā*) as constituting flowcharts and hierarchies: a system that is now organized and analyzable thanks to the multilayered semantic-cognitive processes underlying it. In the case of the *śliṣṭa* scenario, what Udbhaṭa is doing is mapping a series of meaning moments, cataloging them, and explaining the way earlier meaning moments lead the way to later ones.

This is even more manifest in Rudraṭa's discussion of *śleṣa* (his name for *śliṣṭa*). Rudraṭa differs from Udbhaṭa in several key aspects in defining this ornament. He accepts the possibility of homonymy in language (thus rejecting the one-word, one-meaning axiom), and he thus identifies sound-based embraces with cases of manufactured homophony but sense-based embraces with true homonymy. But

---

66 Indurāja, *Laghuvṛtti*, p. 60: *indukāntamukhīty atra bhagavatī candravatsundaraṃ mukhaṃ yasyāḥ sā tathāvidhā. tathā snigdhadīrghakṛṣṇakeśī. muktā parityaktāśrīr aśobhā yayā sā tathāvidhā. trailokyotkṛṣṭā ca. tathā padmavat kamalavat rāgo lauhityaṃ yayos tathāvidhau pādapallavau yasyās tadrūpā. yadā tv asau bhagavatī rūpakapratibhotpattinibandhanena śleṣeṇa trailokyādaravartimāṇikyasaṃbhārarūpatayā rūpyate tadā prakṛto 'rthaś candrakāntendranīlamauktikaśobhāpadmarāgair avacchāditarūpatayā pratīyate sākṣād evaṃvidharatnamayāvayavayogitvāt tribhuvanodarāntargataratnasamṛddhirūpeti.*

67 Ibid., p. 60, ll. 22-27.

68 Mammaṭa, *Kāvyaprakāśa*, pp. 520-529. See AGRAWAL 1975; and ROODBERGEN 1984.

just like Udbhaṭa's and, indeed, more so, his discussion is focused on the way one meaning can lead to the cognition (*gamayet*, *avagamayet*, and so on) of another, and it is this movement from one sense layer to another that he views as the defining characteristic of a sense-based "embrace."[69] Rudraṭa goes on to list ten scenarios in which one meaning (meaning 1) can produce another (meaning 2) and a relationship between the two (meaning 3). Meaning 2 can be an unrelated piece of information, in which case, as the commentator Namisādhu explains, what readers cherish is precisely their unrelatedness, as in the speech of a madman.[70] But this is only a rather generic (*aviśeṣa*) version, a first step, and from here on things become considerably more complicated. A second meaning may be the ornament of antithesis (*viruddhaśleṣa*) that adds to the power of the verse; it may enhance the first, as when a description of an ideal king is amplified by a second reading that modifies Śiva (Rudraṭa calls this type *adhika*); it may supply a proverb (*ukti*) that complements the first sense; it may sum in toto (*tattva*) what is first stated in parts (*avayava*); it may supplement the emotional flavor (*rasa*) of the first with another, appropriate one, as when a verse refers to both a king's military and his erotic conquests; or it may ironically contradict and thus supplant the first, as when we understand that a woman's praise for her go-between's selfless dedication really amounts to blaming her for betraying her and jumping into bed with her beloved (*vyāja*).[71] In such and similar cases, meaning 2 can be either a mere statement, an ornament, or an emotional flavor, and the different aesthetic effects involved are the results of distinct cognitive scenarios in which the second meaning either supplements or supplants the first. Those familiar with Ānanda's analyses of suggestion by content (*vastu*, *alaṃkāra*, *rasa*) and by cognitive scenario will at once see that these analytic tools are already all present in Rudraṭa's extensive analysis of *śleṣa*, and to some extent also in Udbhaṭa's analysis of the same ornament.

There is much more that could be said about this discussion, but for my purposes it suffices to say that at the hands of Udbhaṭa and

---

[69] KAl 10.1: *yatraikam anekārthair vākyaṃ racitaṃ padair anekasmin | arthe kurute niścayam arthaśleṣaḥ sa vijñeyaḥ ||*. For his definition of *śabdaśleṣa*, see ibid., 4.1.

[70] *Ṭippaṇaka* ad 10.3: *nanu prakṛtānupayogyarthāntaram unmattavākyavad asaṃbaddham avagatam api kvopayujyate. satyam. etad evāsyālaṃkāratvam. evaṃ hi sahṛdayāvarjakatvam asya.*

[71] KAl 10.1-23.

his followers the analysis of *śliṣṭa/śleṣa* changed dramatically. From an ornament Bhāmaha analyzed very much like an identification (*rūpaka*), involving a manufactured identity between the subject and the standard of comparison, it became a locus for startlingly complex analyses of semantic and cognitive scenarios, where a series of additional statements and ornaments (for Udbhaṭa) and also emotional flavors (for Vāmana[72] and Rudraṭa), appeared in layered structures, each with a distinct aesthetic feel. One could argue that such cognitive-aesthetic layered structures are unique to the special effects of *śleṣa* and are not found elsewhere in the works produced in the Jayāpīḍa moment. But nothing can be further from the truth. To realize this, let us first return to Udbhaṭa's discussion of *rūpaka*, which I have only very briefly sampled.

5. *RŪPAKA*'S MULTILAYERED ORNAMENTAL PROCESSES

Here is Udbhaṭa's first example of *rūpaka* in the KAlSS:

> *jyotsnāmbunendukumbhena tārākusumaśāritam* |
> *kramaśo rātrikanyābhir vyomodyānam asicyata* ||[73]

> Pouring moonlight-spray
> from their Luna-jar,
> the night-maidens gradually
> watered the sky-garden,
> whose blossoms are stars.

This is a description of nightfall, wherein the night's gradual overtaking of the sky is described as an act of irrigating a garden, bit by bit. According to Indurāja's explanation, the comprehension of such a poem involves two distinct stages. The first takes place within compounds such as "moonlight-spray" (*jyotsnāmbu*), where the word "spray" is applied to "moonlight." Here we see the semantic process of *guṇavṛtti* in operation: "moonlight," which is the predominant word insofar as it is contextual (this, after all, is part of a longer description of nightfall), blocks "spray" (the subordinate word)

---

72 This is not a topic Vāmana discusses, but his example beautifully "embraces" the fearsomeness of veteran soldiers and the charms of skilled courtesans – the heroic and the erotic – who both fail to disturb the Buddha's calm (KAlSū ad 4.3.7).

73 KAlSS, example 1.11.

from conveying its literal meaning. "Spray" thus comes to denote not some liquid but "brightness," "delightfulness," "shimmer," and so on, attributes that belong in it but also in "moonlight." In the second stage, the word "spray," now figuratively signifying (and thus consisting of) "moonlight," becomes an implement in an act of irrigation insofar as it is construed with the overall syntax. Indurāja's crucial point is that these two semantic-cognitive stages correspond, just as we have seen in the case of *śliṣṭa*, to two different ornaments and hence two distinct aesthetic experiences: only the first, which involves the figurative capacity (*guṇavṛtti*) of words like "spray," is considered *rūpaka* because, as we have seen, *rūpaka* is now by definition identified with this semantic process. Yet in the second stage, the "spray" – now made of moonlight and used for irrigation – involves no *rūpaka* but rather a "touch of intensification" (*atiśayokticchāyāṃ bhajate*).[74]

A certain pattern begins to emerge: different ornaments are identified with distinct semantic operations and are understood to occupy analytically distinguishable moments in a multilayered but interconnected cognitive-aesthetic sequence. The one possible problem in applying this pattern to the example just discussed is that our understanding of it is based entirely on Indurāja, writing more than a century after the Jayāpīḍa moment: unlike the previous examples discussed, here we have no direct way of knowing whether his explanation replicates Udbhaṭa's extremely fragmented *Vivaraṇa*. I am not particularly troubled by this problem. Indurāja was a very keen observer with an excellent grasp of Udbhaṭa's stance, and both he and his intended readers had the full *Vivaraṇa* in front of them. Moreover, I find support for Indurāja's take on the first example of

---

74 *Laghuvṛtti*, pp. 11-12: *atra khalu dve 'vasthe vidyete. ekā tāvaj jyotsnāyā ambūkaraṇāvasthā. aparā tv ambutvam āpāditāyā jyotsnāyāḥ sekasaṃbandharūpā. tatra yadā tāvaj jyotsnāmburūpatvam āpadyate tadā prākaraṇikatvāj jyotsnā pradhānam ambu ca tadviparyayād guṇas tadānīṃ cāmbuśabdo jyotsnāśabdānurodhenāmbugataśauklyādiguṇasadṛśaguṇayogāl lakṣaṇayā jyotsnāyāṃ vṛttim anubhavati. tadā ca tasya pradhānārthānurodhād guṇavṛttitvena rūpakatvam uktam. yadā tv asau ambuśabda āpāditāmbubhāvajyotsnābhidhāyī san sekakriyayā samanvayam āpadyamāno yad etad atra sekasādhanatvenāmbūpayujyate taj jyotsnaiveti jyotsnayā viśiṣyate tadā tasya na rūpakāvasthā, pūrvāvasthāyām evānubhūtaguṇavṛttitvāt. atas tasyām avasthāyām asau atiśayokticchāyāṃ bhajate. pūrvāvasthāpekṣayā tv etad rūpakam uktam. pradhānānurodhena tatra guṇeṣu vartamānatvāt. rūpakatvaṃ cātrādhyāropyamāṇagatena rūpeṇādhyāropaviṣayasya vastuno rūpavataḥ kriyamāṇatvād anvartham draṣṭavyam.*

rūpaka from his discussion of the fourth, where a quote from the *Vivaraṇa* is found.

Udbhaṭa lists four types of *rūpaka* in the KAlSS. The first two, the complete-set (*samastavastuviṣaya*) and the partial (*ekadeśavivartin*) *rūpaka*, are borrowed from Bhāmaha, but the third and the fourth are Udbhaṭa's own invention, and he relates each of the new pair to one of Bhāmaha's original duo. This is easy enough in the case of his *mālārūpaka*, where a string of standards is serially identified with a single subject (Bhāmaha's complete-set identification restated repeatedly).[75] More mysterious is the category of *ekadeśavṛtti*, whose name is intentionally similar to Bhāmaha's *ekadeśavivartin* and whose definition is opaque.[76] Udbhaṭa's example clarifies things at least somewhat:

> *āsāradhārāviśikhair nabhobhāgaprabhāsibhiḥ* |
> *prasādhyate sma dhavalair āśārājyaṃ balāhakaiḥ* ||[77]

> Then the white clouds
> illuminating the horizon
> poured a rain of arrows
> to redeem
> the kingdom of the sky.

The sky's turn to autumn is described with a martial metaphor. It is easy to see that this is not a complete-set *rūpaka*: while the rain pour (*āsāradhārā*) is equated with arrows (*viśikha*) and the sky (*āśā*) with a kingdom (*rājya*), the white clouds (*balāhaka*) and the horizon (*nabhobhāga*) are not matched with an explicit standard of identification, such as warriors and the front line, respectively. But what sets this *ekadeśavṛtti* apart from the older and similarly named *ekadeśavivartin*? The explanation must lie in the "embrace" (*śliṣṭa*) in the verb *prasādhyate*, which refers both to the clouds' act of beautifying the sky in this season and to a forceful "seizing" of the heavenly "kingdom" (my translation tries to capture this duality with the verb "redeem"). This verb, too, thus supports the martial metaphor, although in a different and more tangible way than, say, the warriors, who are implied as the standard of the clouds but are never explicitly mentioned. The verb *prasādhyate* presumably allows the contextual operation of beautifying the sky to take place first, in connection

---

75 KAlSS 1.13ab: *samastavastuviṣayaṃ mālārūpakam ucyate* |.

76 KAlSS 1.13cd: *yad vaikadeśavṛtti syāt pararūpeṇa rūpaṇāt* |.

77 KAlSS, example 1.14.

with all the other beautifying aspects that are mentioned, and then, thanks to its polysemy (or, as Udbhaṭa would probably explain this, the perfect "embrace" of two verbs, one meaning "beautifying" and another "conquering"), it fits in with the military metaphor for capturing the kingdom, along with its other necessary implements, agents, and loci, some of which are only implied. It is the partial (*ekadeśa*) semantic operation (*vṛtti*, as in *guṇavṛtti*) – partial in the sense that it is limited to one cognitive moment resulting from this verb – that explains why Udbhaṭa's *ekadeśavṛtti* variety of *rūpaka* supplements Bhāmaha's *ekadeśavivartin*.

This, indeed, is what Indurāja maintains, and he caps his explanation with a surprising gloss on the word *ekadeśa* in the variety's name. He understands this seemingly straightforward nominal combination of the words *eka* (one) and *deśa* (place) as instead consisting of *ekadā* (at one point in time) and *īśa* (powerful), which *sandhi* resolution also allows and which supports his reading of the second semantic-cognitive operation here as a matter of temporal sequence: initially, the meaning that agrees with the verb *prasādhyate* is the one that fits with the contextual description of the beautiful autumnal sky, but then a second realization of the various semantic elements as construing with the verb in its martial sense becomes powerful. The first moment, Indurāja maintains, leads to *rūpaka* (of the partial-set type, with its explicit and implied identifications), but the second, if I understand him correctly, brings in a touch or shadow of *śliṣṭa* (*śleṣacchāyā*). So here, too, we have a multiphase semantic-cognitive sequence, and again each phase in this sequence seems responsible for a different aesthetic effect. But in an exact reversal of what we have seen in the previous section, here *rūpaka* comes in first, as the main ornament, and *śliṣṭa* dovetails in a partial, shadowy form. The reader may be right to be skeptical about Indurāja's unusual gloss on *ekadeśa*, and he, too, felt a need to cite a precedent from a particularly relevant and authoritative source to substantiate his gloss: Udbhaṭa's own *Vivaraṇa*. It is taken, of course, not from Udbhaṭa's commentary on the category of *ekadeśavṛtti*, because such a category did not yet exist in Bhāmaha, but from his gloss on Bhāmaha's definition of *viśeṣokti*, where Udbhaṭa analyzed Bhāmaha's *ekadeśa* as made of *ekadā* and *īśa*, and where he was clearly interested in precisely this same sort of cognitive alternation between two different meaning moments.[78] It is worth noting that the

[78] *Laghuvṛtti*, pp. 14-15: *atra prasādhyata ity ayaṃ śabdaḥ śleṣacchāyayā dvayor arthayor vartate bhūṣaṇa upārjane ca. tatra bhūṣaṇaṃ prakṛtam. śaratsamayo*

other Kashmiri commentator on Udbhaṭa, Tilaka, also follows this ingenious gloss,[79] and I believe that both have correctly captured Udbhaṭa's understanding of *ekadeśavṛttirūpaka* as a *rūpaka* that is in control in the first meaning moment.

To summarize what we have seen so far: Udbhaṭa silently rejects Bhāmaha's approach to both *śliṣṭa* and *rūpaka* as logical relationships between an X (*upameya*) and a Y (*upamāna*) and instead adopts a radically different analysis that is rooted in a nuanced attention to the context-governed semantic processes that each is now understood to entail, and which he borrows from other disciplines, particularly Mīmāṃsā. Moreover, in both *śliṣṭa* (as Udbhaṭa explained it) and *rūpaka* (as explained by his trustworthy commentator Indurāja), the semantic-cognitive operation is multiphase, so that each phase is responsible for a different aesthetic effect or ornament. Put differently, *śliṣṭa* and *rūpaka*, as they are now understood, each correspond to one semantic-cognitive step in a chain of reactions, wherein they can be either the trigger or the triggered, and which involves aesthetic hierarchy: the initial impression is a full-blown ornament, while the later one, which also seems necessarily to involve a reflection on the former, tends to have a more shadowy presence (*pratibhā*, *chāyā*). Nothing of this has any precedent in older discussions of ornaments, and we begin to realize the dramatic theoretical breakthrough in the Jayāpīḍa moment.

6. MULTIPHASE MIXTURES AND THE AESTHETICS OF COGNITIVE MISSTEPS

Many more examples of this trend could be supplied. There is, for instance, the entire rethinking of mixtures in this period along the

---

hy atra prastutaḥ. tatra ca śuklair balāhakair diśo bhūṣyante. yad upārjanaṃ tad aprakṛtatvād atra param anyat. tasya ca parasyāprakṛtasyopārjanasya yat tadrūpaṃ kārakakadambakaṃ yena tad rūpavat kriyate nṛpaviśikharājyasaṅgrāmabhūmyātmakaṃ tenātra yathākramaṃ balāhakāsāradhārādiṅnabhobhāgānāṃ rūpyatvenābhimatānāṃ rūpaṇā vihitā. tenātraikadeśavṛttitvam. ekadeśavṛttīty atra hy ekadānyadeśaḥ prabhaviṣṇur yo 'sau vākyārthas tadvṛttitvaṃ rūpakasyābhimatam. viśeṣoktilakṣaṇe ca bhāmahavivaraṇe bhaṭṭodbhaṭena ekadeśaśabda evaṃ vyākhyāto yathehāsmābhir nirūpitaḥ. tatra viśeṣoktilakṣaṇam "ekadeśasya vigame yā guṇāntarasaṃstutiḥ | viśeṣaprathanāyāsau viśeṣoktir matā yathā ||." iti tenātra viśeṣoktilakṣaṇavad ekadeśaśabdena anyadā prabhaviṣṇur vākyārtha ucyate. anyatra cānyadā prabhaviṣṇūpārjanam aprakṛtaṃ hi tac chleṣavaśenātra nītam. tenātraikadeśavṛttitā.

79 *Vivṛti*, p. 10.

lines we have just seen. The mixture (*saṃsṛṣṭi*) of ornaments is traditionally thought of as an ornamental variety in its own right. Bhāmaha defined it as the mere coexistence of several ornaments, regardless of possible interrelations.[80] This must have troubled Daṇḍin, because he insisted in his corresponding discussion on the possibility of hierarchy among the ornamental devices involved. Mixtures, he said, can be of two kinds, "depending on whether one component is deemed primary (*aṅgin*) and the other supportive (*aṅga*), or whether they are seen as equivalent in terms of their relative importance."[81] This stipulation, however, has more to do with the logical or aesthetic relations between the ornaments than with the semantic operations and temporal cognitive scenarios they entail, and in any case Daṇḍin had his reasons not to expand on the topic of mixtures more than was absolutely necessary.[82]

All this changed quite dramatically during the Jayāpīḍa moment, in which mixtures and their cognition become a major topic of attention. Udbhaṭa has no less than four categories of what he calls "fusion" (*saṃkara*) on top of Bhāmaha's mixture (*saṃsṛṣṭi*), and his analysis is all about semantic and mental scenarios. Take, for example, the first subcategory of fusion, where the charm is in the fact that the reader is left in some kind of aesthetic limbo about the operating ornament in a given passage. This sort of fusion, which Indurāja dubbed "doubt," is defined as "the impression of a plurality of ornaments, when they cannot operate simultaneously, and when the grasping of any one of them involves neither a decisive reason in its

---

80 KAl 3.49: *varā vibhūṣā saṃsṛṣṭir bahvalaṃkārayogataḥ | racitā ratnamāleva sā caivam uditā yathā ||*.

81 KĀ 2.357cd-358: *nānālaṃkārasaṃsṛṣṭiḥ saṃsṛṣṭis tu nigadyate || aṅgāṅgibhāvāvasthānaṃ sarveṣāṃ samakakṣatā | ity alaṃkārasaṃsṛṣṭer lakṣaṇīyā dvayī gatiḥ ||*.

82 Consistent with his emphasis on ornaments' subtypes as the main arena for creative variation, Daṇḍin begins this discussion by reminding his readers that he has already dealt with the devices that are appended to Bhāmaha's list, where they are seen as either independent ornaments (e.g., *ananvaya*) or mixtures thereof (e.g., *upamārūpaka*), as subtypes of their respective parent ornaments, where, he believes, they truly belong. He then proceeds to curtail the importance of Bhāmaha's "best embellishment," so that where Bhāmaha gave a pair of examples of his one type of "mixture," Daṇḍin uncharacteristically supplies only a single example even though he insists that there are two methods for mixing ornaments (KĀ 2.356-359). In addition, Daṇḍin silently appropriates at least one of Bhāmaha's "mixtures" into the fold of his ornamental subtypes. Compare, for example, KAl 3.50 with KĀ 2.179 f.

favor nor any counterreason against it."[83] Indurāja explains in some detail how this is a case where several ornaments vie for our attention at successive cognitive moments without allowing us to reach a conclusive decision.[84] We need not follow every particular of Indurāja's fascinating discussion to realize that all the aspects we have been examining are prominently manifested in it and also in Udbhaṭa's own words: the focus on semantic operations (*vṛtti*); the importance of sequence (*samam... asaṃbhave*); the close attention to what goes on in the mind of the listener, where various inferential signs are sought in order to corroborate or eliminate the individual ornaments (*ekasya ca grahe nyāyadoṣābhāve*); and the regard for the more shadowy impressions (*ullekha*) ornaments may leave in the mind.

Vāmana was perhaps trying to take the discussion one step further by ignoring amalgamations of independent ornaments in the way Bhāmaha understood them and most of Udbhaṭa's varieties of fusion and by arguing, instead, that mixtures should be understood purely as hierarchical relations among aesthetic devices, each embodying a separate cognitive moment. Thus he was trying to limit mixture to just one semantic-cognitive scenario of succession and subordination, as his definition succinctly states: "Mixture is an ornament that begets an ornament."[85] Indeed, Sahadeva, in a lengthy miniessay that he appends to his commentary on Vāmana's section on ornaments, systematically refutes all of Udbhaṭa's categories of mixture and fusion but one and concludes by stating that it is only Udbhaṭa's last type of fusion, dubbed the "assisted-assistant" type by Indurāja (*anugrāhyānugrāhaka*), that Vāmana accepted when speaking of "mixtures."[86] Rudraṭa, for his part, was less restrictive and may have been leaning more toward Udbhaṭa, if we are to judge by the terminology he uses (*saṃkara* rather than *saṃsṛṣṭi*). But it is palpably clear that he, too, like the other thinkers in the Jayāpīḍa moment, was interested in mixtures from the listener's cognitive-

---

83 KAlSS 5.11: *anekālaṃkriyollekhe samaṃ tadvṛttyasaṃbhave | ekasya ca grahe nyāyadoṣābhāve ca saṃkaraḥ* ||.

84 *Laghuvṛtti*, pp. 68-69.

85 KAlSū 4.3.30: *alaṃkārasyālaṃkārayonitvaṃ saṃsṛṣṭiḥ*. Vāmana goes on to show that ornaments found in Bhāmaha, such as *upamārūpaka* and *utprekṣāvayava*, are really instances or subtypes of mixture thus defined, thereby using his new definition of mixtures to lend the ornamental tools in his box added coherence.

86 KAlSūṬ, f. 89: *anugrāhyānugrāhakasaṃkaras tu gṛhīta eva*.

aesthetic perspective. Thus he divided fusions into two types, based on whether the components of the blending remain distinct in our mind, as in mixtures of rice and sesame, or become indistinguishable from one another, as in the water-and-milk variety.[87]

Udbhaṭa's assigning a unique aesthetic pleasure to a reflection on ambiguous ornamental cocktails and Rudraṭa's water-and-milk metaphor for a similar sense of inconclusiveness call to mind a related mode of analysis that is particularly prominent in the Jayāpīḍa moment: the grounding of ornaments in scenarios that entail, first, a cognitive misstep and, second, a subsequent realization of it as such. Consider Udbhaṭa's ornament of apparent redundancy, *punaruktavadābhāsa*. It has already been recognized that Udbhaṭa's removal of Bhāmaha's *yamaka* (twinning) and placing, in its stead, this newly coined ornament at the very beginning of his KAlSS, where he generally follows Bhāmaha's list and its arbitrary order very closely, was a bold and deliberate statement that was meant to call attention to its innovativeness.[88] The boldness did not end there: Udbhaṭa also used his commentary on Bhāmaha's text for a lengthy discussion and a tripartite illustration of *punaruktavadābhāsa*, despite the fact that Bhāmaha knew nothing of this ornament.[89] But what was the reason for this move, which does not seem to be motivated solely (if at all) by observation of the poetic praxis and cannot be reduced to some aversion to *yamaka*?[90] Could it be that Udbhaṭa wanted to signal the importance of aesthetic pleasure as rooted in semantic-cognitive scenarios of the sort discussed earlier? After all, the charm of *punaruktavadābhāsa* rests undeniably in the fact that the reader, at first blush (*upakramāvasthā*), misjudges words such as *nāga* and *kuñjara* as both denoting "elephant" (*gajavācitvenaikārthatvaṃ pratibhāti*), and then this initial impression is blocked by further consideration of the way the signifieds are construed together (*padārthā-*

---

87 *Kāvyālaṅkāra* 10.25: *yogavaśād eteṣāṃ tilataṇḍulavac ca dugdhajalavac ca* | *vyaktāvyaktāṃśatvāt saṃkara utpadyate dvedhā* ||.

88 Basistha perceptively compared this move to Daṇḍin's topping of the traditional set of devices with *svabhāvokti*, an ornament the aesthetic merit of which Bhāmaha had explicitly denied (BASISTHA 2003, p. 116).

89 *Vivaraṇa*, frag. 19. For a good discussion of this passage, see KRISHNAMOORTHY 1979a. See also BASISTHA 2003, pp. 116-120.

90 Krishnamoorthy maintains that this figure was nonexistent in pre-Udbhaṭa poetry, and that one of the first poets to actually use it after Udbhaṭa was Ānandavardhana himself (KRISHNAMOORTHY 1979a, pp. 31-32).

nvayaparyālocanayā tu tad bādhyate) – a very Kumārila-like scenario.[91] And surely, this second cognitive moment, when the reader realizes that the word *kuñjara* here modifies the elephant (*nāga*) as "fabulous" or "preeminent," is followed by a third, where the falseness of the initial impression is realized as such and the craftiness of the poet is cherished. This further realization is the key to the charm of the new ornament and the reason for the presence of the word "apparent" (*ābhāsa*) in its name. The pages of the KAlSS are full of cases where such appearances (*ābhāsa*), impressions (*ullekha*), and shadowy presences or mental impression (*chāyā*, *pratibhā*) are recorded in the mind, are recognized as such, and cause aesthetic pleasure, and it may well be that to call attention to this new notion of the aesthetic Udbhaṭa began his book with *punaruktavadābhāsa* instead of *yamaka*, or, in fact, as a new framework within which to explain *yamaka*, hitherto analyzed only in formal-structural terms, as an ornament whose charm is based on exactly this sort of cognitive scenario.[92] And as we shall see in the next section, *ābhāsa*s and other misconceptions are a trademark of poetics in the Jayāpīḍa moment.

7. *UTPREKṢĀ*, *ADHYAVASĀNA*, AND VĀMANA'S THEORIZATION OF ORNAMENTS

The clearest example of this tendency is Vāmana's crucial and entirely overlooked redefinition of *utprekṣā*, for which the common translation is "poetic fancy," but which I prefer to call "seeing as." *Utprekṣā* has always been understood as entailing an act of fictive-creative imagination, as in seeing darkness as rubbing the body with a thick black ointment.[93] As in other instances I have examined, ear-

---

91 This is the explanation given in Indurāja, *Laghuvṛtti*, p. 3, apropos of Udbhaṭa's example.

92 In his *Vivaraṇa*, Udbhaṭa suggests that *yamaka* should be seen as just one instance of the more expansive and hitherto unknown *punaruktavadābhāsa* (see frag. 1, l. 5, where he considers and rejects an objection arguing for a categorical distinction between the two). If this is correct, the reanalysis of *yamaka*, too, is entirely based on the cognitive sequence it entails: how it looks to us redundant at first, and how we go on to resolve the evident redundancy it contains. I am grateful to Lawrence McCrea for calling my attention to this line in the *Vivaraṇa* and its significance.

93 The example, which is cited and discussed in KĀ 2.224-232, is actually far more complex, and it is not simple to decide what is imagined as what, as is

ly writers felt no need to relate such imaginative moments to theories of erroneous perceptions and cognitive blunders that were abundantly available in other *śāstra*s. But this theoretical freedom was precisely what literary thinkers in the Jayāpīḍa moment were willing to sacrifice in order to make Sanskrit poetics an academic discipline. It is in this context that we must understand Vāmana's identification of *utprekṣā* with *adhyavasāna* or its close synonym *adhyavasāya*,[94] which, as in the case of Udbhaṭa's rethinking of *rūpaka*, is an innovation that is closely modeled on a recent development in another field.

This field is logic, and more precisely Buddhist epistemology. As McCrea and Patil explain in an excellent essay, the meaning of *adhyavasāna* underwent important developments in the line of thinkers following Dharmakīrti. For Dharmakīrti, they show, it was an inferential determination – useful and indeed necessary from a pragmatic point of view, but nonetheless erroneous – that our mental concepts and images are identical with external objects. The usefulness of such a misidentification is evident in the successful equation of the particulars with our mental universals for them, or in inferring fire from smoke. As McCrea and Patil demonstrate, for Dharmakīrti, this was but one cognitive misstep in a whole palette of inferential and perceptual misjudgments, leading to "the misidentification of our own conceptual images with objects that are not perceptually available to us at all."[95] McCrea and Patil also show that Dharmakīrti's notion of *adhyavasāna* was significantly expanded by his commentator Dharmottara, who took it to be a necessary feature in every act of perceptual awareness: "For Dharmottara, an episode of valid awareness, whether perceptual or inferential, is not a single event, but a process made up of two stages. In the first stage, an object is grasped – that is, its image is directly presented to awareness. In the second stage, we determine a second and distinct object

---

shown in a pair of excellent forthcoming essays by Gary Tubb (TUBB forthcoming a and b).

94 KAlSū 4.3.9: *atadrūpasyānyathādhyavasānam atiśayārtham utprekṣā*. That the two terms are synonyms for Vāmana is made clear in his immediate glossing of one with the other: *adhyavasānam adhyavasāyaḥ*.

95 MCCREA AND PATIL 2006, p. 313.

that can be attained – that is, an object upon which we may act." This second step is *adhyavasāna*.[96]

There are several features of Dharmottara's rethinking of *adhyavasāna* that make it particularly handy and attractive for Vāmana's purposes. First, there is the immediate availability of his innovation: Dharmottara was Vāmana's colleague at Jayāpīḍa's court, another stellar intellectual in this king's galaxy of scholars, as Kalhaṇa reports in the passage with which this essay began.[97] Second, Dharmottara's two-phase understanding of perception and the role of *adhyavasāna* therein fit the new general interest in Jayāpīḍa-moment poetics in the aesthetics of multiphase cognitive sequences, not unlike Kumārila's two-phase notion of *guṇavṛtti*, which became the basis of Udbhaṭa's *rūpaka*. Third, and more specifically, applying *adhyavasāna* to the *perception* of one object as another, which has long been the understanding of *utprekṣā*, or seeing as, allowed Vāmana to explain this ornament accurately while using cutting-edge theories from the highly respected discipline of logic. Note, by the way, that Vāmana's quick adoption of the revised *adhyavasāna*, if I am right in making this link, indicates that the innovation that McCrea and Patil identified in Dharmottara was immediately noticed in wider intellectual circles, beyond the epistemological discourse per se.

Even more important, *adhyavasāna* helped Vāmana organize ornaments as occupying a spectrum of increasing imaginative-cognitive fictitiousness. First, as Vāmana explains, *utprekṣā* goes beyond *rūpaka*, which is based on the superimposition (*adhyāropa*) of the traits of one entity on another, and *vakrokti*, based as it is on *lakṣaṇā*, in that it alone involves the further step of perceptual misidentification (*adhyavasāna*). Second, the long-recognized ornaments of "doubt" (*sandeha*, which is different from the doubt type of fusion discussed earlier) and "antithesis" (*virodha*) are now seen as part of the same spectrum: doubt (*sandeha*), says Vāmana, is an inconclusive knowledge, whereas seeing-as (*utprekṣā*) entails an erroneous knowledge, and antithesis (*virodha*) is for the first time defined as the false impression of something as antithetical (*viruddhābhāsatva*)

---

[96] Ibid., p. 326. See also RATIÉ 2010 for further analysis of Dharmottara's notion of *adhyavasāna* in ordinary perception and imagination and the fascinating legacy of *utprekṣā* in later Kashmiri thinking. See also Somdev Vasudeva's contribution in this volume.

[97] RT 4.498.

– another of Vāmana's key innovations and a further example of the growing interest in the Jayāpīḍa moment in the aesthetic value of apparent cognitive certainties and the realization of them as such.[98] In other words, the importation of concepts from logic, and in particular the new notion of *adhyavasāna*, allowed Vāmana to turn a bunch of ornaments that tradition had handed to him as unrelated devices into a far more coherent set of aesthetic tools that were based on a series of interrelated fictive or fictitious cognitive moments; it also allowed him, for the first time in the history of the tradition, to reorder the hitherto rather random list of ornaments in a way that reflected his new theoretical understanding of them.[99]

Take, for example, Vāmana's fascinating insight into the key distinction between *utprekṣā* (seeing as) and *atiśayokti* (intensification).[100] For him, the first of this newly conceived pair involves only one fictitious determination (*adhyavasāna*), while the second is a more layered imaginative act: "Intensification is the imagining of a conceived attribute [followed by] the imagining of its eminence."[101] In other words, Vāmana was reinterpreting the traditional *atiśayokti* as an even more complex cognitive scenario – an act consisting of multiple imaginative moments. Think, in this context, of Daṇḍin's illustration of this ornament: a verse that depicts women who set out at night to meet their lovers and, given the whiteness of their clothes, become invisible in the moonlight.[102] Vāmana replaces Daṇḍin's illustration, in the simple *anuṣṭubh* meter, with one that expands on the same theme in the far more complex, rare *pādākulaka* meter – it is hard to say whether this verse is inspired by Daṇḍin or is the original on which Daṇḍin's textbook example was based – and the verse is now understood as entailing a twofold act of imagination: first,

---

98 KAlSū, before 4.3.11: *yathā bhrāntijñānasvarūpotprekṣā tathā saṃśayajñānasvarūpo sandeho 'pīti darśayitum āha*. On antithesis, see 4.3.12 and its introduction: *sandehavad virodho 'pi prāptāvasara ity āha: viruddhābhāsatvaṃ virodhaḥ*.

99 Daṇḍin and Udbhaṭa, while occasionally highlighting their differences from Bhāmaha in a pinpointed change in the list of devices and its order, nonetheless adhered to its otherwise mostly arbitrary order. But after Vāmana's radical revision and attempt to organize the list in a way that was theory-based, there was no looking back.

100 KAlSū, introduction to 4.3.10: *utprekṣaivātiśayoktir iti kecit. tannirāsārtham āha.*

101 Ibid., 4.3.10: *sambhāvyadharmatadutkarṣakalpanātiśayoktiḥ*.

102 KĀ 2.293. The verse itself is an echo of Bhāmaha's example of the excessive whiteness of the *saptacchada* blossom, also invisible in moonlight (KAl 2.82).

of the extraordinary whiteness of the women's apparel and complexion, and second, based on it, of their disappearance in broad moonlight.[103]

The verse depicting the women at night is Vāmana's second example of *atiśayokti*. Before this he supplies an illustration from Māgha that involves imagining, first, the Gaṅgā falling in two streams from heaven rather than in one, and second, that heaven, now supplied with its imagined two-pronged Gaṅgā, is comparable to Kṛṣṇa's Tamāla-dark chest with its bright, pearl strings.[104] One interesting thing about this illustration of *atiśayokti* is that it is already cited in Udbhaṭa's *Vivaraṇa*, also while discussing *atiśayokti*, even though Udbhaṭa's understanding of this figure may well have been different.[105] Thus Vāmana's short discussion, with its brief definition and two illustrations, is carefully tied to a coherent spectrum of ornaments, is rich in echoes and citations from the praxis, and engages other treatises in the discipline of poetics. In all of this it clearly led the way for later discussions of ornaments. Indeed, although I do not have the space here to discuss the full implications of Vāmana's rethinking of *utprekṣā* and its related devices, let me briefly note that this move was the basis of the subsequent theoretical revolution in thinking about ornaments in Kashmir. Ruyyaka, the great twelfth-century Kashmiri theoretician, identified *utprekṣā* with *adhyvasāna* and understood *atiśayokti* as a further step in the same fictitious determination of things as they are not, a part of his even more thoroughgoing rethinking of ornaments as imaginatively engaging with the real.[106] It has been said that "Ruyyaka is the first author to introduce *adhyavasāya* in *utprekṣā*," but in fact he is deeply and openly indebted to Vāmana in this and in his larger attempt to theorize ornaments.[107]

---

[103] KAlSū, second example after 4.3.10.

[104] KAlSū, after 4.3.10; cf. Māgha, *Śiśupālavadha* 3.8.

[105] *Vivaraṇa*, frag. 37b, ll. 6-7.

[106] For Ruyyaka, *utprekṣā* is *adhyvasāya* with an emphasis on the process (*adhyavasāye vyāpāraprādhānye*), and *atiśayokti* is an *adhyvasāya* with an emphasis on the product (*adhyavāsitaprādhānye*; *Alaṃkārasarvasva* 22-23). For a fascinating essay on Ruyyaka's understanding of *utprekṣā*, see SHULMAN 2012, pp. 55-62.

[107] It is thus not a coincidence that Ruyyaka's first example for *utprekṣā* (*sa vaḥ pāyād induḥ*; *Alaṃkārasarvasva*, p. 71) is the same one given by Vāmana and becomes a standard example in later discourse. The quote is from JANAKI 1965,

8. UDBHAṬA'S RETHINKING OF *PARYĀYOKTA*

Although Vāmana's reformulation of *utprekṣā* fits well with the attempts to rethink ornaments along the lines of semantic-cognitive theories from other fields, it is a detour for us in that it came to full fruition not in Ānanda's essay on suggestion but with Ruyyaka in a much later moment in the discourse on ornaments. Given my interest in the more immediate impact of the Jayāpīḍa moment, let us return to Udbhaṭa and to one final example from his work, that of *paryāyokta*, or "speaking around," a device that he rethought in a way that importantly prefigured Ānanda's notion of *dhvani*.

Both Bhāmaha and Daṇḍin understood *paryāyokta* as a case in which a speaker indirectly refers to something the direct mention of which is better avoided. The examples of both authors make it clear that what is spoken around in *paryāyokta* is some truth, presumably known to both speaker and listener, that is replaced with some obvious pretext because of considerations of decorum. Bhāmaha cites the now-lost *Ratnāharaṇa*, where Kṛṣṇa refuses Śiśupāla's offering of food he knows is poisoned by citing the custom of eating only what was first offered to Brahmins.[108] Daṇḍin's example, wherein a speaker has arranged a rendezvous of two lovers and dismisses herself by a transparent pretext, has a similar logic, albeit in a very different context and mood: what the friend wants to convey to the pair of lovers is that this is the time to consummate their love (*tadrasotsavaṃ nirvartayitum*), but she does so by telling them to wait while she tends to an urgent and entirely bogus gardening activity. As Daṇḍin explains in his definition, speaking around is "when one avoids stating one's desired goal directly and, instead, comes up with a speech in a different fashion that accomplishes this very goal."[109] This is probably meant to elaborate on Bhāmaha's definition, which is little more than a tautological gloss on the ornament's name ("*paryāyokta* is that which is said in a different fashion"; *paryāyoktaṃ yad anyena prakāreṇābhidhīyate*).[110] Clearly, both au-

p. 107, although the misperception is widespread and although Janaki's introduction is an outstanding piece of scholarship.

108 KAl 3.8cd-9: *uvāca ratnāharaṇe caidyaṃ śārṅgadhanur yathā* ‖ *gṛheṣv adhvasu vā nānnaṃ bhuñjmahe yad adhītinaḥ* | *na bhuñjate dvijās tac ca rasadānanivṛttaye* ‖.

109 KĀ 2.293: *artham iṣṭam anākhyāya sākṣāt tasyaiva siddhaye* | *yat prakārāntarākhyānaṃ paryāyoktaṃ tad īdṛśam* ‖.

110 KAl 3.8.

thors understood this ornament as a relationship between two meanings, one expressed and another intended, but neither was particularly interested in exploring the process leading from one to the other.

Turning to Udbhaṭa we immediately realize that he does not see *paryāyokta* as confined merely to cases of white lies. His example depicts Śiva as having the wives of the demon Gajāsura wear their hair disheveled, cry, pound their breasts, and break their bangles. In this way, Śiva's slaying of Gajāsura is insinuated or "spoken around."[111] Udbhaṭa thus vastly expands *paryāyokta* into a more general mode of indirect speech. And as we have come to expect, the aesthetic effect of this device is grounded in a specific, multi-phase semantic-cognitive scenario:

> *paryāyoktaṃ yad anyena prakāreṇābhidhīyate* |
> *vācyavācakavṛttibhyāṃ śūnyenāvagamātmanā* ||[112]

> *Paryāyokta* is what is said in a different fashion, namely, in a way that is cognized in a process that is different from the operations of the signifiers and signifieds.

This definition, which reshaped the discussion of this ornament in later centuries,[113] consists of two distinct halves: in the first, Udbhaṭa repeats Bhāmaha's words verbatim, a point I will return to later, but the second is entirely new and signature Udbhaṭa. *Paryāyokta*, we learn, entails three stages. First, there is the operation of the individual signifiers (*vācaka*), each of which signifies its own signified.[114] This is followed by the operation of the signifieds (*vācya*) themselves when they are construed with one another. For Mīmāṃsakas of the Bhāṭṭa school, this is a straightforward explanation of meaning production along the lines of the "from signified to syntax" theorem (*abhihitānvaya*), and indeed, Indurāja, in explaining the passage,

---

111 KAlSS, example 4.6: *yena lambālakaḥ sāsraḥ karaghātāruṇastanaḥ* | *akāri bhagnavalayo gajāsuravadhūjanaḥ* ||.

112 KAlSS 4.6.

113 It is repeated by Abhinavagupta as the ornament's definition (see *Locana*, p. 117) and then used as the basis for some rewording by both Mammaṭa (*paryāyoktaṃ vinā vācyavācakatvena yad vacaḥ*; *Kāvyaprakāśa*, p. 680) and Ruyyaka (*gamyasyāpi bhaṅgyantareṇābhidhānaṃ paryāyoktam*; *Alaṃkārasarvasva*, p. 141).

114 As Indurāja explains: *vācakasyābhidhāyakasya svaśabdasya vṛttir vyāpāro vācyārthapratyāyanam* (*Laghuvṛtti*, p. 55).

echoes the words of Kumārila, Udbhaṭa's likely inspiration here as well.[115] From the point of view of Sanskrit poetics, this Mīmāṃsā speak is radically new. But what may have come as news to literary specialists and Mīmāṃsakas alike was Udbhaṭa's introduction of a third and independent semantic-cognitive phase, when the intended meaning is finally cognized or, indeed, suggested (*avagamātmanā*), which is how Abhinava himself glossed the term.[116] It is this phase alone that Udbhaṭa identified with the aesthetic effect of *paryāyokta*.

What exactly happens in this phase? In his KAlSS, Udbhaṭa characterizes it only negatively, as separate from the first two phases, and the relevant portion of his *Vivaraṇa*, where he might have explained this in more detail, is now lost. Indurāja, in his commentary on this passage, adds only that this phase's different expressivity is a cognition or insinuation (*avagamanasvabhāvena*) that comes about through (overall?) semantic implication (*arthasāmarthyātmanā*), and that, at least in the illustration, the cause (Gajāsura's death) is insinuated by its effect (his wives' intense lamentation).[117] But Indurāja returns to this topic in an epilogue to his commentary in which he tries to convince his readers that every aesthetic effect that Ānandavardhana attributed to suggestion could be explained as the doing of ornaments as analyzed by Udbhaṭa. *Paryāyokta* figures prominently in this discussion (as does *śliṣṭa*). Indeed, Indurāja begins his epilogue by quoting a very similar verse to the one Udbhaṭa has given, which clearly involves *paryāyokta* in the way Udbhaṭa defined and illustrated it, but which was explained by Ānanda as involving suggestion as well. In this verse Viṣṇu's beheading of Rāhu, which did away with this demon's body but still left him with his head (the cause), is intimated by stating that from the elaborate love life of this demon's wives, kissing alone remained (the effect).[118] For Ānanda, this is a case where the intended suggested

---

115 *Laghuvṛtti*, p. 55: *vāc[yas]ya tv abhidheyasya vyāpāro vācyāntareṇa sahākāṅkṣāsaṃnidhiyogyatāmāhātmyāt saṃsargagamanam.* Cf. Kumārilabhaṭṭa, TV 455: *ākāṅkṣā saṃnidhānaṃ ca yogyatā ceti ca trayam | saṃbandhakāraṇatvena kḷptaṃ nāntaraśrutiḥ ||*.

116 *Locana*, p. 118: *avagamātmanā vyaṅgyena*. I come back to Abhinava's discussion of this definition in n. 133 below.

117 *Laghuvṛtti*, p. 55: *atra lambālakatvādayaḥ kāryarūpatvāt kāraṇabhūtaṃ gajāsuravadhaṃ vācyavācakavyāpārāspṛṣṭam api gamayanti.*

118 *Laghuvṛtti*, p. 86: *cakrābhighātaprasabhājñayaiva cakāra yo rāhuvadhūjanasya | āliṅganoddāmavilāsavandhyaṃ ratotsavaṃ cumbanamātraśeṣam ||*. Cf. Ānandavardhana, DhvĀ, p. 225.

meaning is the emotional flavor (*rasa*) of Viṣṇu's heroism, and *paryāyokta* is a humble sidekick (although, as has been pointed out, Ānanda seemed concerned that the sidekick outshone the hero here).[119] Indurāja, however, points out that what is suggested in this case, as in Udbhaṭa's very similar example, is neither an ornament nor a *rasa* but merely a piece of narrative content (*vastumātra*): the fact that Rāhu was beheaded and his head lived on. Indurāja reminds his readers that Ānanda himself divided suggestion according to the suggested content: a bare narrative fact (*vastumātra*), an ornament, or an emotional component (*rasādi*). And the suggestion of bare narrative facts, he maintains, requires no new theorization of the sort Ānanda proposed, since it is exactly what Udbhaṭa called *paryāyokta*.[120]

In this manner Indurāja systematically shows that all the other categories Ānanda devised for suggestion are nothing but the workings of the different ornaments in Udbhaṭa's book.[121] Indurāja, of course, had an axe to grind. But it is clear that thinkers in the Jayāpīḍa moment prefigured Ānanda's ideas and analyses of suggestion in speaking, for example, of what "is cognized in a process that is different from the operations of the signifiers and signifieds" (as in Udbhaṭa's definition of *paryāyokta*),[122] or of one meaning as enabling the understanding of another (as in Rudraṭa's thorough analysis

---

119 DhvĀ, p. 225: *atra hi paryāyoktasyāṅgitvena vivakṣā rasāditātparye saty apīti*. For a discussion of this passage and the problem of the sidekick, see INGALLS ET AL. 1990, pp. 276-277.

120 For a comprehensive discussion of this passage in Indurāja, see MCCREA 2008, pp. 312-316.

121 Later in the passage Indurāja also argues that a further ornament, such as *rūpaka*, could also be insinuated through either *paryāyokta* or *śliṣṭa*, in the way Udbhaṭa understood them, and *rasādi* through a variety of other ornaments, and he goes through Ānanda's other subtypes for suggestion, showing that all of them can be found in Udbhaṭa's ornaments. For more, see MCCREA 2008, pp. 311-330.

122 Thus, although Ingalls believes that Indurāja's conclusion is exaggerated, he concedes that Udbhaṭa "speaks of a meaning being understood (*pratīyamāna*), or implied (*gamyate*), or of its being included (*antargata*) in another meaning," even though "he avoids using the more technical terms *vyajyate* or *dhvanyate* for 'is suggested.'" Ingalls, moreover, believes on the basis of Ānanda's quote of Manoratha's criticism of those who understood *dhvani* but failed to explain it, that Udbhaṭa was already familiar with this terminology. Indeed, he says, "Indurāja's remark is justified to this extent: Udbhaṭa was fully aware of the

of *śleṣa*), and, more generally, in grounding the discussion on poetics in semantic-cognitive scenarios. It is no wonder that Ānanda often had to bend over backward to distinguish between his notion of suggestion and ornaments such as *paryāyokta* and *śliṣṭa*.[123]

9. *ABHIDHĀ* AND *RASA*: UDBHAṬA'S THEORY?

More examples can be easily provided,[124] but I think that the picture is clear enough. Thinkers of the Jayāpīḍa moment were hard at work revolutionizing the discourse on ornaments and making it academic. They each sought to produce a foundational text for the nascent discipline and a scholastic-commentarial tradition in the pattern of the senior *śāstra*s; they turned their attention from textbook examples to actual praxis and from the writer to the reader; they grounded aesthetic effects in semantic capacities (*vṛtti*s) and complex and often reflexive cognitive scenarios, with hierarchies that regularly culminated in implied meanings of various sorts (narrative contents, ornaments, and emotional flavors); and, precisely for this purpose, they extensively borrowed models, terminology, and analytic modes

type of semantic operation that Ānanda was later to call suggestiveness (*vyañjakatva*, *dhvani*) and of the importance to poetry of the suggestions which it could bring about." INGALLS 1990, p. 9.

123 "In *paryāyokta* (statement of periphrasis), if the suggestion is predominant we may include it in *dhvani*. But by no means may we include *dhvani* in it, for as we shall demonstrate, *dhvani* is of much wider range and is always the predominant element. Furthermore, in the examples such as adduced by Bhāmaha, the suggestion is *not* predominant, because there is no intention there of subordinating the literal sense" (*paryāyokte 'pi yadi prādhānyena vyaṅgyatvaṃ tad bhavatu nāma tasya dhvanāv antarbhāvaḥ. na tu dhvanes tatrāntarbhāvaḥ. tasya mahāviṣayatvenāṅgitvena ca pratipādayiṣyamāṇatvāt. na punaḥ paryāyokte bhāmahodāhṛtasadṛśe vyaṅgyasyaiva prādhānyam, vākyasya tatropasarjanābhāvenāvivakṣitatvāt*; DhvĀ, pp. 118-119; transl. INGALLS ET AL. 1990, pp. 149-150). Note that Ānanda finds it more convenient here to mention Bhāmaha's example and gloss over Udbhaṭa's.

124 I will briefly mention only two additional and particularly understudied examples from a much longer list of candidates. The first is Udbhaṭa's *kāvyaliṅga*, a new ornament defined as the understanding that X is a cause for recollection or direct experience of Y (KAlSS 6.7: *śrutam ekaṃ yad anyatra smṛter anubhavasya vā | hetutāṃ pratipadyeta kāvyaliṅgaṃ tad ucyate* ||). I mention this ornament briefly later. The second is Vāmana's *ākṣepa*, which he defined as two ways of suggesting a simile: negatively, by dismissing the standard as useless, but also through a more positive route of suggestion that is strongly reminiscent of Ānanda's *dhvani* (*upamānasyākṣepataḥ pratipattiḥ... upamānāni gamyante*; KAlSū ad 4.3.27).

from other disciplines, particularly Mīmāṃsā (e.g., *guṇavṛtti*, *lakṣaṇā*, *tantra*, *abhihitānvaya*, and the one-word, one-meaning axiom), but also epistemology (*adhyavasāna*) and grammar (*mayūravyaṃsaka*). All these developments shaped the discussion on poetics in the coming centuries, and all are highly visible in Ānanda's seminal essay on suggestion, with its Mīmāṃsā-based semantic-hierarchical model and the various cognitive scenarios it identifies with different aesthetic responses. In trying to evaluate Ānanda's innovativeness more accurately in the context of these earlier changes, two crucial questions merit further examination: did thinkers like Udbhaṭa have a comprehensive and coherent semantic-aesthetic theory of which the preceding instances were part, and, if so, what place did *rasa* play in it?

These questions were already raised and given surprising answers several decades ago, but with little or no following. The most important and largely ignored attempt to answer the first is an essay by Sivaprasad Bhattacharyya, "Abhidhāvṛtti in Udbhaṭa," which appeared in 1962, the same year in which Raniero Gnoli published the surviving fragments from the *Vivaraṇa*. Bhattacharyya pieced together some of the just-published fragments with a vast number of citations of or allusions to Udbhaṭa's work in later tradition and made several bold arguments about his vision (although it is easy to lose sight of some of them in his dense prose style): (1) Udbhaṭa did have a comprehensive semantic theory of poetry. (2) This theory was based on a layered notion of *abhidhā*, a broad semantic capacity that included literal (*śruti* or *mukhyavṛtti*), figurative (*guṇavṛtti*), and suggestive operations. (3) Later thinkers were well aware of and strongly indebted to Udbhaṭa's theory of *abhidhā* and, in the case of Ānanda and Abhinava, struggled to show how *dhvani* differed from it. (4) Udbhaṭa also had a complete and related aesthetic theory that, like Ānanda's model, included all known poetic elements: ornaments, virtues (*guṇa*s), and emotional factors, such as *bhāva* and *rasa*.[125]

It is not easy to assess Bhattacharyya's arguments, but it is clear that *abhidhā* and its synonym *abhidhāna* were extremely important to Udbhaṭa, and that his notion of these terms was far broader than what we typically tend to associate with them today. Consider, in this context, a partially preserved discussion from an early passage

---

125 BHATTACHARYYA 1962.

in the *Vivaraṇa* apropos of a verse wherein Bhāmaha, when introducing poetry, provides a seemingly straightforward list of the fields of knowledge it presupposes. The third in this list – after grammar and prosody and before historical narratives, worldly wisdom, logic, and the arts – is *abhidhānārthāḥ*, a compound that consists of *abhidhāna*, probably in the sense of "words," and *artha*, "meanings," thus referring quite naturally in the context of this list to words and their meanings, word meanings, or perhaps lexicography.[126] Interestingly, however, Udbhaṭa seizes on this compound to introduce a notion of semantics that has no precedent in the actual text of Bhāmaha or, indeed, in any early text on poetics. For him, the compound refers to the literal and figurative capacities of *abhidhāna* as a unified semantic model (*śabdānām abhidhānam abhidhāvyāpāro mukhyo guṇavṛttiś ca*), for which he immediately provides a detailed discussion.[127] He goes on to demonstrate this broad notion of *abhidhā* by showing, for example, how the verb "goes" (*eti*) may be used literally, in a sentence such as "Devadatta goes to the mountain," but also figuratively, in a *Rāmāyaṇa* verse describing how happiness "goes" to a man.[128] The idea is that both instances fall under the same semantic theory of *abhidhāna* that poetry presupposes. All this, moreover, comes on the heels of an earlier discussion of *abhidhāvyāpāra* in fragment 9, the context and contents of which are not fully clear, but which is rather lengthy and involves citations of famous verses from the poetic praxis.[129]

---

[126] KAl 1.9: *śabdaś chando 'bhidhānārthā itihāsāśrayāḥ kathāḥ | loko yuktiḥ kalāś ceti mantavyāḥ kāvyahetavaḥ* ‖ (I emend the last word on the basis of Gnoli's suggestion; *Vivaraṇa*, frag. 10a, l. 2). For different ways of understanding *abhidhānārthāḥ*, see MASSON 1972, pp. 252-253.

[127] The quoted clause is not preserved in Gnoli's fragments but is cited in Abhinavagupta and elsewhere (*Locana*, p. 32; see n. 131). Gnoli believes that its place was in l. 4 of fragment 10a of his manuscript (GNOLI 1962, p. xviii).

[128] *Vivaraṇa*, frags. 10a-b. This passage is discussed in MASSON 1972, p. 253, but Masson is mainly interested in arguing that the attribution of the fragments to Udbhaṭa is inconclusive, a view that no longer seems plausible. The *Rāmāyaṇa* verse (*eti jīvantam ānando*; 6.114.2) is cited in the grammatical literature (e.g., Patañjali, *Vyākaraṇamahābhāṣya* 3.1.67), but probably in different contexts, as noted in BHATTACHARYYA 1962, p. 76, n. 11.

[129] *Vivaraṇa*, frag. 9. The verses are *na dānena na mānena*, which appears in the *Hitopadeśa* and elsewhere (see GNOLI 1962, p. 6, n. 21), and *namas tuṅgaśiraścumbi*, the famous opening verse of Bāṇa's *Harṣacarita* and one of the most popular *kāvya* stanzas ever (on this verse, see TUBB 2014, pp. 311-314). At the presumed end of this passage (frag. 10, l. 1), Udbhaṭa says *alaṃ vistareṇa*, indicating that the preceding discussion was not short.

So at the very least we can say that Udbhaṭa was eager to introduce his innovative agenda about the relevance of semantics to poetics in general and, more specifically, to showcase a notion of *abhidhāna* or *abhidhā* and its various layers as underpinning poetry, even if this meant hijacking an innocent item in Bhāmaha's list of poetry's presupposed fields of knowledge. It is also clear that this notion of *abhidhā* and similar semantic insights of the Jayāpīḍa moment are the context in which Ānanda formulated his theory of *dhvani* and from which he wished to differentiate it. Indeed, in quoting the relevant passage from Udbhaṭa's *Vivaraṇa*, Abhinava was primarily concerned with explaining and defending Ānanda's nuanced claim that, on the one hand, others had already equated the soul of poetry, which he identified with *dhvani*, with figurative language and, in doing so, had tangentially touched (*manākspṛṣṭa*) on *dhvani*, but that, on the other, they had failed to name, let alone define, *dhvani*.[130] Abhinava identified those "others" as the main theoreticians of the Jayāpīḍa moment, Udbhaṭa and Vāmana; credited each of them with his distinctive innovation in this area (*guṇavṛtti* and *lakṣaṇā*, respectively); and provided a short quote from each of their main texts. For Vāmana he cited the identification of *vakrokti* with *lakṣaṇā*, and for Udbhaṭa, the just-mentioned line on *abhidhāna* that appears as a gloss on Bhāmaha's list of presupposed areas of knowledge.[131]

---

130 DhvĀ, pp. 28-32: *bhāktam āhus tam anye. anye taṃ dhvanisaṃjñitaṃ kāvyātmānaṃ guṇavṛttir ity āhuḥ. yady api ca dhvaniśabdasaṃkīrtanena kāvyalakṣaṇavidhāyibhir guṇavṛttir anyo vā na kaścit prakāraḥ prakāśitaḥ, tathāpy amukhyavṛttyā kāvyeṣu vyavahāraṃ darśayatā dhvanimārgo manākspṛṣṭo 'pi na lakṣita iti parikalpyaivam uktam bhāktam āhus tam anye 'ti.* "'Others say that it is an associated meaning (*bhākta*).' Others say that this soul of poetry which we call *dhvani* is [merely] secondary usage (*guṇavṛtti*). And although the authors for definitions for poetry have not given the specific name *dhvani* to secondary usage nor to any other sort of thing, still, in showing how secondary usage is employed in poetry, they have at least touched on the process of *dhvani* even if they have not actually defined it." (Transl. INGALLS ET AL. 1990, p. 64.)

131 *Locana*, p. 32: *darśayateti bhaṭṭodbhaṭavāmanādinā. bhāmahenoktaṃ śabdāś chando 'bhidhānārthāḥ, ity abhidhānasya śabdād bhedaṃ vyākhyātuṃ bhaṭṭodbhaṭo babhāṣe 'śabdānām abhidhānam abhidhāvyāpāro mukhyo guṇavṛttiś ca' iti. vāmano 'pi 'sādṛśyāl lakṣaṇā vakrokti' iti.* "He is referring to such authors as Bhaṭṭodbhaṭa and Vāmana. For where Bhāmaha says, 'Words, meters, designations (*abhidhāna*), meanings,' Bhaṭṭodbhaṭa explains the difference between words and designations as follows: 'Designation means the denotative function of words, which may be either primary or secondary (*guṇavṛtti*).' And Vāmana has said, '*Vakrokti* is secondary usage (*lakṣaṇā*) based on similarity.'"

So in the eyes of thinkers like Ānanda and Abhinava, at least, *abhidhā/abhidhāna* was elevated to soul-like importance in the eyes of Udbhaṭa, it included both denotation and figurative language, and it "touched on" *dhvani* without calling it so. Indeed, I believe that Udbhaṭa's *abhidhā* also included, in addition to the primary and secondary functions, a third operation of suggestion of the sort we have seen in the case of *paryāyokta*. I find support for this argument in the fact that Udbhaṭa supplemented Bhāmaha's definition of this ornament rather than supplanted it, even though he had no qualms about discarding a characterization of his enshrined predecessor when he was revising its accepted understanding, as we have seen with *rūpaka* and *śliṣṭa*. I believe that he nonetheless embedded Bhāmaha's original language in his definition of *paryāyokta*, however opaque and tautological the original was, because it allowed him to get added mileage from the verb *abhidhīyate*, which Bhāmaha used and which is derived from the same verbal root and prefix as *abhidhā/abhidhāna*. Note that derivations from *abhi* and *dhā* appear frequently in Bhāmaha's text, although in a nontechnical sense of "communicating," "stating," "naming," or "describing."[132] In the case of *paryāyokta*, for example, Bhāmaha must have had in mind not the particular semantic capacity though which Kṛṣṇa conveyed his message to Śiśupāla, but merely the fact that it was "communicated" (*abhidhīyate*) in some other way (*anyena prakāreṇa*). For Udbhaṭa, by contrast, *abhidhā* was a technical term that was key to his project of semanticizing poetics, and thus there was added value

(Transl. INGALLS ET AL. 1990, p. 66.) Abhinava explains Udbhaṭa's commentarial move as motivated by the need to differentiate two items on the list, *śabdaḥ* and *abhidhāna*, but I wonder whether he is not also gently insinuating that Udbhaṭa hijacked Bhāmaha's text to introduce notions that were really his own. See also BHATTACHARYYA 1962, p. 73.

132 I have counted thirty-two occurrences of various derivations from *abhi+dhā* in Bhāmaha: *abhidhā*, in the sense of "name" or "statement" (3.21, 3.25); *abhidhāna*, in the sense of "word," "utterance," "communication," or "mention" (1.9, 1.21, 1.37, 1.41, 1.59, 2.18, 2.34, 2.86, 3.25, 5.56); *abhidhāyin*, in the sense of "expressing" (6.13); *abhidhāsyate*, in the sense of "saying" (4.13); *abhidhitsā*, "the intention to say" or "the intention to communicate" (1.22, 2.2, 2.68); *abhidhīyate*, in the sense of what is "said," "named," or "labeled," (2.33, 2.37, 2.42, 2.65, 3.8, 3.14, 4.12, 6.8); and *abhidheya*, in the sense of "signified," "sense," or a meaning that is distinct from the word signifying it (1.10, 1.15, 1.36, 2.17, 2.86, 4.34, 6.8). In none of these occurrences, as far as I can see, did Bhāmaha use the verb in its technical sense of direct, nonfigurative denotation, let alone in the expanded sense it had for Udbhaṭa.

in retaining it despite everything else that had changed in *paryāyokta*: it helped driving the point home that this third *vṛtti*, beyond those of the signifiers and the signifieds, was still part of *abhidhā/abhidhāna*, now seen as the underlying semantic function of poetry as such, and it allowed him to imply, as we have seen that he did in his gloss on *abhidhānārthāḥ* in the *Vivaraṇa*, that this was really Bhāmaha's position.[133]

So I am inclined to agree with Bhattacharyya that Udbhaṭa had a sweeping notion of *abhidhā* that included a variety of semantic-cognitive scenarios and was responsible for a diversity of aesthetic effects in poetry. It is also clear that later writers, both inside and outside Kashmir, gave Udbhaṭa due credit for this vision and were influenced by it. A case in point is the late ninth-century *Hṛdayadarpaṇa* of Bhaṭṭa Nāyaka, another lost masterpiece of Sanskrit poetics. In an excellent essay that pieces together the views of Bhaṭṭa Nāyaka from quotations of his work that survived in other works, Sheldon Pollock shows, among other things, that "for Bhaṭṭa Nāyaka, *abhidhā* does not have its usual sense of direct denotation" and is "constantly essential" to the aesthetic process, leading the way to the complex process of *bhāvanā* (which Bhaṭṭa Nāyaka creatively borrowed from Mīmāṃsā). In fact, "*abhidhā* in Bhaṭṭa Nāyaka's usage is best understood or even translated as 'literary language,' something 'completely different' from the language of scripture and everyday discourse, as Abhinavagupta describes it."[134] It seems more than likely that Bhaṭṭa Nāyaka, like Mukulabhaṭṭa and others who shared

---

133 Abhinavagupta later argued, somewhat heavy-handedly, that this retained verb proves that *paryāyokta* and *dhvani* are distinct phenomena: *ata eva paryāyeṇa prakārāntareṇāvagamanātmanā vyaṅgyenopalakṣitaṃ sad yad abhidhīyate tad abhidhīyamānam uktam eva sat paryāyoktam ity abhidhīyata iti lakṣaṇapadam, paryāyoktam iti lakṣyapadam, arthālaṃkāratvaṃ sāmānyalakṣaṇaṃ ceti sarvaṃ yujyate* (*Locana*, p. 118). "When what is said is distinguished by a *paryāya* (periphrasis), that is, speaking in a different manner, which consists in giving to understand, [that is, when it is distinguished] by a suggestion, then the literally used words themselves form a *paryāyokta* (statement of periphrasis). Here 'when something is said' forms the definition, 'statement of periphrasis' is the thing to be defined, and the general characteristic of this thing is as a figure of speech based on meaning (*arthālaṃkāra*). And so everything here is in order." (Transl. INGALLS ET AL. 1990, p. 150.)

134 POLLOCK 2010, pp. 147, 153; for his discussion of Bhaṭṭa Nāyaka's date, see p. 144. It was Bhattacharyya who dubbed the *Hṛdayadarpaṇa* and the *Vivaraṇa*, together with the *Kāvyakautuka* of Bhaṭṭa Tota, as "lost masterpieces" of the discipline (BHATTACHARYYA 1981).

this view, was following Udbhaṭa in this approach, as already suggested by Bhattacharyya, and that Udbhaṭa's theory of *abhidhā* preceded, led the way to, and for a long time continued to compete with Ānanda's theory of *dhvani*.[135]

What is less clear is how detailed and systematic this *abhidhā* theory was, both in its analysis of language and in its application to ornaments. First, did Udbhaṭa have a complete linguistic model of *abhidhā* that explained how words are analyzed from the level of word bases and case endings up (as Bhattacharyya takes a quote of Udbhaṭa's *Vivaraṇa* from Rājaśekhara to imply),[136] and did he provide a detailed description of the various meaning moments, from the literal and the figurative to the suggested, or was he merely content with seeing *abhidhā* as coterminous with poetic language and its various semantic-cognitive effects? Second, how consistent was Udbhaṭa in applying *abhidhā* to every ornament in the book? Did he keep coming back to this notion in his *Vivaraṇa*, explaining the semantic path of every aesthetic device, or did he do so only in cases that involved some sort of indirection, as in the cases I discussed earlier? To answer these questions, we would require a far better copy of the *Vivaraṇa* than we now have.

Let us now turn to the second query, regarding the role of *rasa* in Udbhaṭa's thinking. It should be stated at the outset that Udbhaṭa was a groundbreaking and influential *rasa* theorist. Udbhaṭa was the author of the earliest known commentary on the *Nāṭyaśāstra*, the root text on dramaturgy ascribed to Bharata, and in this now-lost commentary he introduced key *rasa*-related innovations. For example, as V. Raghavan showed long ago, Udbhaṭa was the first author in this tradition to expand the list of eight emotional flavors by introducing peace (*śānta*), a ninth *rasa*, possibly emending the *Nāṭyaśāstra*'s text in the process. This most likely meant that Udbhaṭa also theorized the emotional basis (*bhāva*) and other psychoaesthetic factors that give rise to peace, and that this theorization served as the basis for later discussions of the topic.[137] Udbhaṭa was also the first to coin and conceptualize *rasābhāsa*, a scenario of *rasa* production that cannot be completed because of social impropriety and is hence

135 BHATTACHARYYA 1962, pp. 73-74.

136 BHATTACHARYYA 1962, pp. 77-78.

137 RAGHAVAN 1975, 13, 47, 71.

a mere "semblance of *rasa*."[138] This, again, is a mode of analysis that played an important role in later *rasa* theory.

Moreover, Udbhaṭa was, as far as we know, "the first person to write on both Alaṃkāraśāstra and Nāṭyaśāstra,"[139] and in doing so he began to think the two together. More specifically, Udbhaṭa was the first to account for the fact that poetic language, and not just dramatic action, can convey *rasa* and its associated elements. There are two main steps in Udbhaṭa's groundbreaking theorization of *rasa* in poetry. The first is his understanding that poetry can bring about the entire range of *rasa* experience, from its nascent state to maturation and then to cessation. To demonstrate this, Udbhaṭa kept the names of the five content-related ornaments that he inherited from his predecessors (with the unrelated *paryāyokta* inexplicably inserted in their midst), but he used them as empty bottles into which he poured new *rasa* wine. The old ornaments were now defined not according to the randomly chosen emotional and narrative contents after which they were still named – joy in "joyous" (*preyas*), emotional flavor in "flavored" (*rasavat*), pride in "prideful" (*ūrjasvin*), a lucky coincidence in "coincidence" (*samāhita*), and opulence in "magnificence" (*udātta*)[140] – but as different stages in the evolution of emotional flavors as understood in dramaturgy or, more precisely, in dramaturgy as Udbhaṭa theorized it. *Preyasvat* (his name for *preyas*) was now taken to express basic emotions (*bhāva*) that did not evolve to full-blown *rasa*; *rasavat* was fully evolved *rasa*; *ūrjasvin* became a case of *rasa* whose production was hampered by a socially inappropriate excess of emotions; *samāhita* was the cessation of emotion, *rasa*, or their incomplete imitations; and *udātta* (or at least one variety thereof) was a case of emotional description that played a supportive aesthetic role but did not dominate the poem.[141] Second, Udbhaṭa explained that these emotional-aesthetic states are poetically communicated by up to five types of indicators: "the proper term, as well as the [depiction of] stable emotions, transitory emotions, stimulant factors, and gestures."[142] Udbhaṭa's view that

---

[138] POLLOCK 2016, p. 11.

[139] MCCREA 2008, p. 44.

[140] My translation of the original ornaments reflects my understanding of them as used in Daṇḍin, as I intend to explain elsewhere.

[141] KAlSS 4.2-5, 7-8; see MCCREA 2008, pp. 44-50.

[142] KAlSS 4.3: *svaśabdasthāyisaṃcārivibhāvābhinayāspadam*. Or, as Indurāja points out, likely quoting one of Udbhaṭa's lost texts, "For Udbhaṭa, *rasa* was

the mere mention of the name of a certain *rasa* ("proper term") could give rise to its experience has often been criticized, but what the critics have overlooked is the big picture: Udbhaṭa was the first to theorize, under the heading of ornaments such as *rasavat*, a spectrum of linguistic means for evoking *rasa*, from the literal to the suggested, as Indurāja explains in detail.[143]

Thus Udbhaṭa found a clever way to import the dramatic theory of *rasa* evocation into poetics. It has been said time and again that his solution, involving the analysis of *rasa* as an ornament (or, rather, a set of ornaments), is unsatisfactory, but the problem with this criticism is, first, that it overlooks Udbhaṭa's vastly expanded understanding of ornaments. As we have seen, he no longer viewed ornaments as isolated devices defined by formal structures or the contents they conveyed, but as grounded, instead, in the poetic language of *abhidhā*, which covered everything from the literal to the suggested semantic-cognitive operations. Consistent with this analysis of ornaments, Udbhaṭa understood *rasa* as the result of the effect, or perhaps the cumulative effect, of all these capacities; this is also consistent with the way dramaturgy understood *rasa* production as the combination of all its underlying indicators.[144] Then there is the argument that viewing *rasa* as an ornament contradicts its status as the very soul (*ātman*) of poetry, because the soul is not an ornamental device but the very essence of the poetic body that ornaments are supposed to ornament. The problem with this criticism is that it is based anachronistically on Ānanda's later formulation of *rasa* as poetry's soul, its sole telos and the one element to which all others must be subordinated, and on the assumption that Udbhaṭa must have shared this model.

I will return shortly to Indurāja's struggle to harmonize the worldviews of these two thinkers, also quite anachronistically. But note that for all the criticism, the majority of later thinkers accepted Udbhaṭa's radically new and highly sophisticated understanding of the *rasa* ornaments. This is true even of Ānanda and Abhinava, although they were hard at work to differentiate these ornaments from what they saw as *rasa* as manifested through *dhvani*. And the irony is that even the basis for this differentiation was likely borrowed

---

brought about in five ways" (*yad uktaṃ bhaṭṭodbhaṭena pañcarūpāḥ rasā iti*, followed by a detailed exposition of each of the five; *Laghuvṛtti*, p. 53).

143 *Laghuvṛtti*, pp. 51-55. See the repeated use of the verb *gamayati*, "causes to understand" or "suggests," in this exposition.

144 As suggested by KRISHNAMOORTHY 1979b, p. 307.

from Udbhaṭa himself. As Krishnamoorthy has pointed out, Udbhaṭa's distinction between predominant *rasa* in *rasavat* and subordinate *rasa* (*upalakṣaṇatāṃ prāptam*) in *udātta* was understood at least by the anonymous author of the *Kalpalatāviveka* (henceforth KLV) to have paved the way for Ānanda's differentiation between *guṇībhūtavyaṅgya*, where the element (whether *rasa* or not) is aesthetically subordinate, and *dhvani* poetry, where suggestion is predominant.[145]

It is thus clear that Udbhaṭa gave a great deal of thought to *rasa*, a topic that was central to his work as both a dramatist and a poetician, and that he was concerned with newly theorizing the role of *rasa*, originally theorized in the context of drama, in nondramatic poetry. His answer was to make *rasa* part of his overall semantic-aesthetic model now standing at the base of his new notion of ornaments, and to maintain, in all likelihood, that as with *rūpaka*, *śliṣṭa*, and *paryāyokta*, *rasa* was based on several layers of semantic operations (from the explicit mention of the proper term to various indirect indicators) and a whole spectrum of cognitive scenarios in the reader's mind (from rising to cessation). If we examine this solution on its own terms, without viewing it through the eyes of posterity, we must admit its elegance and parsimony precisely because it requires no new semantic theorization beyond what Udbhaṭa took to be the linguistic basis of aesthetics. Yet it is also true that this was not the view of many of his junior contemporaries and immediate

---

145 "Udbhaṭa and his followers maintained that when *rasa* becomes the meaning of the passage, it is a case of the ornament *rasavat*. The proponent who taught [the distinction between] *dhvani* and *guṇībhūtavyaṅgya* [Mammaṭa] responded to this by saying: 'This [*rasa* etc. as a primary suggested meaning] is different than the ornament for conveying *rasa* etc.,' and 'These are ornaments such as *rasavat*.' And to support his opinion, he spoke about the criterion of an existence that is meant for the support of another. But this is what was meant by [Udbhaṭa's definition of *udātta*] as secondary, that is, as *rasa* that has not become the meaning of the passage in the sense that it is not predominant. So the ornament of *udātta* is based only on the literal meaning, and, as such, it is not an exception to the rule of *rasavat*. So much was the opinion of Udbhaṭa and his followers" (KLV, p. 280: *rasasya vākyārthībhāve ye rasavadalaṃkāram udbhaṭādayaḥ pratipannās tān prati dhvaniguṇībhūtavyaṅgyavādinācāryeṇa 'bhinno rasādyalaṃkārād' ity 'ete ca rasavadādyalaṃkārā' iti ca vadatā svābhiprāyapratipādanaṃ yad vihitaṃ tad upajīvyaparasyeyam uktiḥ. upalakṣaṇībhūtam iti. vākyārthībhāvam anāpannam aṅgabhūtam apradhānam iti yāvat. tena mukhyavṛttyaivodāttam etat, na rasavadalaṃkārāpavādatvenety arthaḥ. anyatra tu rasavad iti. etatparyantā bhaṭṭodbhaṭādīnām uktiḥ*). For a discussion of this passage, see KRISHNAMOORTHY 1979b, pp. 304-305.

successors. Vāmana, for example, removed *rasa* from the domain of ornaments altogether and viewed its evocation as the doing of poetic virtues; Rudraṭa discussed it in a way that was simply unrelated to either ornaments or virtues; and Ānanda postulated it as a distinct goal of poetry that virtues and ornaments both enhance, but that necessitates the separate and hitherto-unknown semantic model of suggestion in order to be realized.[146]

What we cannot say on the basis of the available textual evidence is whether Udbhaṭa privileged *rasa* in relation to other aesthetic factors (as Lala Ramayadupala Simha and Krishnamoorthy maintain, but without sufficiently conclusive evidence),[147] or at least explained how *rasa* and other literary devices work in tandem, and Indurāja's contradictory attempts to deal with this question suggest that he, too, found it difficult. The topic comes up three times in his commentary. First, apropos of *rasavat*, Indurāja raises the objection that the status of *rasa* and *bhāva* as ornaments of poetry (*kāvyālaṃkāratva*) contradicts their nature as its very life breath (*kāvyajīvitatva*). His response is that Udbhaṭa did not address this question because this would have forced him into a lengthy digression, suggesting, at the very least, that he believed this question was not germane to Udbhaṭa's efforts in this book.[148]

---

146 For a discussion of this evolution, see McCREA 2008, pp. 50-54. For a later direct attack on the notion that *rasavat* and its sister devices can even be considered ornaments, see Kuntaka, *Vakroktijīvita* 3.11-15.

147 This argument has a long and twisted history. It begins with a mistaken transliteration of Udbhaṭa's KAlSS by Jacob, where a verse that Indurāja cites about *rasa* as the soul of poetry (*Laghuvṛtti*, p. 83: *rasādyadhiṣṭhitaṃ kāvyaṃ jīvadrūpatayā yataḥ | kathyate tad rasādīnāṃ kāvyātmatvaṃ vyavasthitam ||*) appears as part of the root text (JACOB 1897, p. 847; cf. JACOBI 1902-1903, p. 396). P.V. Kane and others have pointed out this mistake and argued that the entire argument is anachronistic (KANE 1951, p. 137; INGALLS 1990, p. 7). But Simha nonetheless believed that the verse, although clearly part of the commentary, could have been a citation from one of Udbhaṭa's lost texts and concluded that "Udbhaṭa is to be regarded as one of the great pioneers of Rasavāda holding Rasa to be the soul of poetry in the most unequivocal, unambiguous and unfeigned terminology," and Krishnamoorthy thought that Simha "rightly holds these verses are from the pen of Udbhaṭa himself" (SIMHA 1958, p. 126; KRISHNAMOORTHY 1979b, p. 307). But although Simha is right that there is nothing in the citational practices of Indurāja to prevent this from being the case, the positive evidence he marshals in favor of this strong argument is far from conclusive.

148 *Laghuvṛtti*, p. 54: *rasānāṃ bhāvānāṃ ca kāvyaśobhātiśayahetutvāt kiṃ kāvyālaṃkāratvam uta kāvyajīvitatvam iti na tāvad vicāryate granthagauravabhayāt. rasabhāvasvarūpaṃ cātra na vivecitam aprakṛtatvād bahuvaktavyatvāc ca.* See

Indurāja returns to this issue later in two independent essays that are found at the end of his commentary, and in which he propagates views that seem contradictory. The first of these is in the context of Udbhaṭa's innovative *kāvyahetu* ornament (also named *kāvyaliṅga*). This ornament involves reasoning that is poetic rather than logical, and for Indurāja this is an excuse to probe at length the nature of poetry and ask whether it even requires ornaments in order to be poetic. Here he approvingly quotes Vāmana's position that poetry necessitates only virtues and not ornaments because it is the former that (according to Vāmana) evoke *rasa*, the very soul of poetry. To support this view, he cites a verse by Amaru that involves the following scenario: a woman has accepted her lover after suffering long in his absence; they begin to make love; he mistakenly calls her by the name of another, but after quickly ascertaining that this slip was not overheard by anyone, she ignores it and resumes lovemaking. The point of the example is that it involves no ornament whatsoever (*na khalv atrārthālaṃkāraḥ kaścit paridṛśyate*), and that what makes it poetic is the virtue (*guṇa*) of clarity, amplified by those of sweetness and forcefulness (*atha mādhuryaujobhyāṃ paribṛṃhitasya prasādasya vidyamānatvāt kāvyarūpatā*). Indurāja then raises a lengthy objection that this verse lends itself to being cataloged as an instance of the ornament of *rasavat*, and it seems that this would likely have been Udbhaṭa's position. But Indurāja flatly rejects this objection in favor of a combination of the views of Vāmana and Ānanda: *rasa*, being the soul of poetry, cannot ornament it (*na khalu kāvyasya rasānāṃ cālaṃkāryālaṃkārabhāvaḥ, kiṃ tv ātmaśarīrabhāvaḥ*), and hence the verse proves that a poem needs virtues but can do without ornaments (*yuktam idam uktaṃ niralaṃkāram api kāvyaṃ saguṇaṃ dṛśyate*).[149] The logical implication of this discussion is that Indurāja rejected Udbhaṭa's analysis of *rasa* through *rasavat* and similar ornaments precisely because it contradicted Vāmana's and Ānanda's.

However, in the concluding passages of his book, Indurāja revisits this issue in the process of arguing that all of Ānanda's categories of suggestion are compatible with ornaments the way Udbhaṭa

---

also McCREA 2008, pp. 323-324.

149 *Laghuvṛtti*, pp. 82-84. Abhinava later quotes the same Amaru verse as an example of *rasa* in short, single-stanza poems (*Locana*, p. 325).

analyzed them.[150] Interestingly, his example involving the suggestion of *rasa* through an ornament is very similar to the one just cited: a woman is making love to a man, he calls her by the name of another, and yet she cannot bring herself to draw away from him. Here Indurāja analyzes the verse in a way that is closely reminiscent of the view of the objector he just refuted, and he concludes that since *rasa* is suggested here through the ornament of *rasavat*, this, too, is a case where Ānanda's notion of suggestion is in agreement with Udbhaṭa's analysis of ornaments (*ato 'tra saṃbhogaśṛṅgārasyerṣyāvipralambhaśṛṅgāratirodhānahetoḥ pratīyamānatā. tatra ca pūrvaṃ rasavattvalakṣaṇo 'laṃkāraḥ pratipādito rasavaddarśitetyādinā. evaṃ rasāntareṣv api vācyam*).[151] This implies that for Indurāja, Ānanda's notion of *rasadhvani* was not entirely incompatible with Udbhaṭa's *rasavat*. It is possible, perhaps, to make sense of Indurāja's apparently contradictory views if we understand that what he was trying to do here was to harmonize the views of all the leading voices of the field, Udbhaṭa, Vāmana, and Ānanda (perhaps with a special inclination to Vāmana, a favorite of his teacher Mukula Bhaṭṭa),[152] although what is sacrificed in this effort is precisely how these scholars differed. In short, here Indurāja does not prove particularly helpful for the attempt to uncover Udbhaṭa's precise position on *rasa* in relation to other aesthetic factors, even if the very fact that he struggled to harmonize this position with those of Udbhaṭa's successors strongly suggests that they were not identical.

To conclude, my discussion so far leaves some questions unanswered but also leads to some surprising realizations. It turns out that Udbhaṭa, in pioneering the semanticization of poetics, offered what may have been a comprehensive linguistic model for poetry that was based on a broad vision of *abhidhāna* or *abhidhāvyāpāra* as he understood it. Taking inspiration from Mīmāṃsā models in general and Kumārila in particular, he explained how poetry worked on the basis of the various semantic capacities of this expanded

---

150 *Laghuvṛtti*, p. 85: *nanu yatra kāvye sahṛdayahṛdayāhlādinaḥ pradhānabhūtasya svaśabdavyāpārāspṛṣṭatvena pratīyamānaikarūpasyārthasya sadbhāvas tatra tathāvidhārthābhivyaktihetuḥ kāvyajīvitabhūtaḥ kaiścit sahṛdayair dhvanir nāma vyañjakatvabhedātmā kāvyadharmo 'bhihitaḥ sa kasmād iha nopadiṣṭaḥ? ucyate. eṣv evālaṃkāreṣv antarbhāvāt.*

151 *Laghuvṛtti*, p. 88.

152 MCCREA 2008, pp. 265-266, n. 11. I am grateful to Lawrence McCrea for sharing with me his insights about Indurāja's possible Vāmana inclinations.

abhidhā, from the literal to the metaphoric and the implied, in a layered process that necessitated the description and analysis of various cognitive phases. And he was keenly interested in grounding the aesthetic effects of many, if not all, ornaments in their specific semantic processes and cognitive scenarios. It is this new analysis – the reconceptualization of ornaments as grounded in a spectrum of semantic-cognitive scenarios – that enabled him to take account, for the first time in the history of Sanskrit poetics, of the way *rasa*, up to then seriously dealt with only in dramaturgy, was realized in poetry as well. *Rasa* and its related factors were now seen as aesthetic responses that poetry could partly evoke, fully evoke, evoke in a way that might be mitigated by socioaesthetic considerations, evoke and then put to rest, and evoke in a way that supported but did not dominate the main action of the poem. All this was done through a set of literal and suggested semantic capacities and under the heading of a radically new subset of ornaments or, more precisely, old ornaments of which only the name remained. We know that *rasa* was an important topic in Udbhaṭa's thinking, both as a drama theorist and as a literary theorist, and thus his revolution of the *rasa* ornaments must have been central to his work as he saw it. And although we do not know whether Udbhaṭa also privileged *rasa* in relation to other ornaments, there is no reason to think that his analysis of it was in any way inconsistent or contradictory. True, his successors moved to extricate *rasa* from the realm of ornaments and eventually to make it altogether independent from ornamental processes, borrowing a great deal from him in the process. But when his model is evaluated in its own right and not through later prisms, it is easy to see why Udbhaṭa believed that he had the problem solved.

10. CONCLUDING REMARKS

What, we may now ask, was the precise nature of Ānandavardhana's innovation? He was not the first to turn the attention of Sanskrit literati from the poet to the reader. He was not the first to semanticize literary theory and connect poetry's aesthetic effects, on the one hand, and the layered modes of signification and cognition it necessitated, on the other. He was not the first to suggest sweeping aesthetic models that had hierarchy built into them and to import rather massively from Mīmāṃsā in the process. He was not the first to rethink the roles of *guṇa* and *alaṃkāra* in a single coherent theory. And he was not the first to turn his attention to *rasa* and *rasa*-related elements within such a model and to discuss how poetry can convey them in ways that are distinct from drama. All these innovations belong, as I hope I have shown, in a short period of great creativity and investment in poetics as an academic discipline under the auspices of Jayāpīḍa or shortly after his reign. Ānanda's distinct innovation was to take these ideas and tendencies, all introduced a generation or two before him, and push them further, arguably to their logical conclusion, thereby creating a semantic-aesthetic model that was even more sweeping, even more hierarchical, and even more indebted to Mīmāṃsā.

Ānanda's key move was to postulate the existence of suggestion, an autonomous capacity of language that was distinct from *abhidhā*, and to argue that although it was operative in ornaments as well, it was also to be understood as separate and aesthetically superior. It was in suggestion, he famously asserted, that connoisseurs found the highest pleasures of poetry and, most important, the savoring of *rasa*, which he dubbed the soul of poetry, a process that happened independently of ornaments. Ānanda maintained, moreover, that his new, thoroughgoing model explained what poets had done all along, despite the fact that it had escaped the attention of theorists, even as under the various types of *dhvani* he often appropriated what his predecessors from the Jayāpīḍa moment had analyzed as ornaments or explained through their own semantic models.[153] And it was this last claim, as McCrea has convincingly demonstrated, that Ānanda's critics heatedly challenged in a debate that flared for two centuries. What the critics of Ānanda objected to – and this is criticism that he anticipated or perhaps had already faced – was his insistence that poetry's aesthetic effect necessitated the theorization of a new semantic-cognitive process outside the existing models of *alaṃkāra*, *abhidhā*, *guṇavṛtti*, *lakṣaṇā*, *adhyavasāna*, or even *anumāna*.[154]

I take this later criticism of Ānanda to further substantiate my claim that the first main breakthrough of Sanskrit poetics took place before him, and that it was on the heels of it that he proposed his important secondary breakthrough. For it was during the Jayāpīḍa moment that all these semantic-cognitive models – from which Ānanda tried to distance himself and to which his critics tried to hold him – were first applied to the analysis of poetry, and unlike that of Ānanda, this earlier paradigm shift was not at all heralded by any

153 For an example of this in the case of *śleṣa*, see BRONNER 2010, pp. 211-212.

154 For an excellent study of this controversy, see MCCREA 2008, pp. 260-448.

prior development in the field. Moreover, against the standard deterministic approach to the history of Sanskrit poetics, it is important to stress that this initial breakthrough was not a natural event, somehow necessitated by an inherent potential or trajectory within the tradition, as the continued popularity of the alternative text of Daṇḍin throughout the Indian subcontinent and south, east, and far north of its borders can attest: the discourse on poetry did not have to be semanticized, and a dominant branch of it continued to thrive without this added theoretical burden. The same hindsight determinism also requires us to believe that the efforts of Ānanda and Abhinava were somehow bound to happen, and to ignore the opponents of Ānanda from within the tradition as petty critics who presumably failed to recognize this historical inevitability. It is high time that we move away from this partisan and deterministic view of Sanskrit poetics and approach its intellectual history with new questions and fresh eyes.

For example, we can try to historicize the dramatic changes that took place in Kashmiri poetics during the ninth century and the great influence literary thinkers from this small Himalayan valley later came to exercise far and wide. We may ask, for instance, what was so unusual about the court of Jayāpīḍa that it fueled a sudden investment in poetics, and what propelled it along a path modeled after other academic disciplines? These are questions that require more research, but I would like to point attention to one aspect of Jayāpīḍa's investments in the arts and the learning that seems particularly relevant. His court, as we learn from Kalhaṇa's report, actively recruited intellectuals who belonged to a vast range of disciplines and philosophical schools in a way that may have encouraged an interdisciplinary approach. Indeed, the court was highly tolerant of these scholars' denominations, if not actively encouraging diversity in this area. Remember, for example, that the list of pandits of this king ends, or culminates, with the rising sun of the Buddhist scholar Dharmottara, whom we have seen directly influenced Vāmana's rethinking of ornaments. It is perhaps not a coincidence that it was here, in this fertile setting that invited thinking across schools and theologies, that the erosion of boundaries between poetics and dramaturgy began, and that models from Mīmāṃsā, Buddhist epistemology, and other disciplines began to be applied to the study of poetry.

In this context it is particularly tempting to postulate that the various Udbhaṭas who worked in Kashmir at the turn of the ninth century – the grammarian, the logician, the Cārvāka scholar, the drama specialist, and the literary theorist – were a single person with multiple scholarly identities. There are three aspects of the preceding discussion that make this hypothesis particularly attractive. First, even if installing him as the president of the royal academy and making him the highest paid-academic in Kashmir's history were primarily tied to his literary activities, as the immediate context of the list provided by Kalhaṇa suggests, the sectarian-theological identity of "this partisan of this-wordliness alone who considers himself the world's greatest Cārvāka" as Vādi Devasūri has called him, did not stand in the way.[155] Thus this identity, if it is indeed confirmed, could validate the particularly open and tolerant atmosphere of Jayāpīḍa's intellectual assembly. Second, as a writer on an astonishingly broad spectrum of disciplines who constantly strove to merge them – we know that he tried to combine logic with Cārvāka philosophy[156] – Udbhaṭa would have been the very epitome of the interdisciplinary ideal of the Jayāpīḍa moment, perhaps supplying us with yet another reason for his status as *sabhāpati*. Finally, and perhaps most intriguing, from the little we know about the works of the various Udbhaṭas from later citations, a surprisingly similar intellectual profile emerges of a bold innovator cloaked in the rather thin guise of a traditionalist. Udbhaṭa the grammarian, for example, was a "non-orthodox" Pāṇinian who suggested derivations that "strike us through their audacity": he "does not hesitate to split a rule," "reckless changes in some rules do not deter him," and "he felt almost completely free from the traditional interpretations of Pāṇini's grammar, most notably Patañjali and the author of the *Kāśikā*."[157] As a Cārvāka, he "deserted the traditional explanation" and "had given a different interpretation altogether" for the first two aphorisms of the *Bṛhaspatisūtra*, then turned the long-accepted interpretation of another key dictum about the relationship between material objects and consciousness on its head (arguing that *bhūtebhyaḥ* in *bhūtebhyaś caitanyam* is in the dative rather than in the ablative case), and even went as far as propagating an unseen property of the material elements that underlies the human experiences of pleasure

---

155 *paramalokāyatamanyena lokavyavahāraikapakṣapatinā*. This is from Vādi Devasūri's *Syādvādaratnākara*, quoted in SOLOMON 1977-1978, p. 987.

156 SOLOMON 1977-1978, p. 992; BHATTACHARYA 2010, p. 421.

157 BRONKHORST 2008, pp. 293-296.

and pain – positions that have earned him the nickname "cunning/ fraudulent Cārvāka" (*cārvākadhūrta*).[158] Indeed, R. Bhattacharya even doubts Udbhaṭa's Cārvāka leanings altogether, saying that "there is every reason to believe that he had hammered out a philosophical system of his own but instead of writing a new *sūtra* work... he had manipulated the Cārvāka aphorisms to present his singularly distinct point of view."[159] In his commentary on Bharata's *Nāṭyaśāstra*, Udbhaṭa may have taken the license to emend the root text so as to introduce, for the first time in the history of this discourse, a new *rasa* on top of the original group of eight.[160] And in the field of poetics, as this essay demonstrates, he wore the mantle of a conservative who sought to enshrine Bhāmaha's KAl as the tradition's foundational text but had no qualms about radically and repeatedly redefining his predecessor's concepts. Thus, while limiting himself to the basic set of ornaments supplied by Bhāmaha and following rather faithfully their original, unsystematic order in his KAlSS, Udbhaṭa unceremoniously nixed the very first device in Bhāmaha's list (*yamaka*) and replaced it with a different ornament of his own invention (*punaruktavadābhāsa*), dramatically changed the understanding of the remaining ornaments (as we have seen in every case I have looked at), added others that directly contradicted his predecessor's view (*kāvyahetu* is the most blatant example, given Bhāmaha's stark opposition to the ornament *hetu*), and he had no problem, in his *Vivaraṇa*, with hijacking Bhāmaha's root text to have it serve his own purposes and support his notions of semantic models (*abhidhāna*) and cognitive scenarios (*ekadeśa*). Many of these moves have been noted by later commentators from within the respective traditions.

In fact, it may not be entirely a coincidence that none of the prose treatises that had an Udbhaṭa as their author have survived: some of them may have seemed simply too provocative in later generations. After all, as Bronkhorst has noted, "Udbhaṭa united in his person two intellectual traditions which were both destined to disappear

---

[158] Jayanta Bhaṭṭa uses the term anonymously in the *Nyāyamañjarī*, but the commentator Cakradhara makes the identification (*cārvākadhūrtas tv iti udbhaṭa*). For more, see SOLOMON 1977-1978, pp. 988-989 and FRANCO 2011, p. 638. As Franco notes, Udbhaṭa, "the most innovative Cārvāka," was also ironically referred to in this text as "the well-instructed Cārvāka" (ibid., the quote is from p. 637).

[159] BHATTACHARYA 2010, pp. 421-422.

[160] RAGHAVAN 1975, p. 13.

from Indian soil during the following centuries," namely, the Cārvāka philosophy and "freethinking" grammar that did not accept Patañjali as an authority.[161] Whatever the truth of this may be, and regardless of the still-open question of the identity of the various Udbhaṭas, it is clear that history has not been particularly kind to the literary theorist of this name, whose seminal contribution was eclipsed by that of followers who were heavily influenced by him and the bulk of whose corpus was lost. Further understanding of this prolific, original, and influential thinker depends to a large extent on the prospects of its recovery in the future. But it is important to remember that his now-lost works remained available for centuries to scholars inside and well beyond Kashmir, and their massive reliance on his works on poetics and dramaturgy, together with the information provided by Kalhaṇa, supports the main argument of this essay. Kashmiri thinkers like Bhaṭṭa Nāyaka, Abhinavagupta, Mukula Bhaṭṭa, Mahima Bhaṭṭa, Mammaṭa, Tilaka, Ruyyaka, Indurāja, and Sahadeva and non-Kashmirians such as Hemacandra, Rājaśekhara, Bhoja, the author of the KLV, and many others all quoted Udbhaṭa extensively, and many of them credited him for his discoveries and explicitly viewed his contribution as a turning point in the tradition's thinking. It is hard to imagine the further evolution of Sanskrit poetics, including but by no means limited to the DhvĀ of Ānanda, who was also influenced by Udbhaṭa even in his *Devīśataka*, without understanding the seminal contribution of Udbhaṭa and the Jayāpīḍa moment more generally.

REFERENCES

Abhidhāvṛttimātrikā
Mukulabhaṭṭa, *Abhidhāvṛttimātrikā*, ed. M.R. Telang, Bombay: Nirnaya Sagara Press, 1916

AGRAWAL 1975
M.M. Agrawal, "Some Problems of Śleṣa-Alaṅkāra in Indian Poetics," *Annals of the Bhandarkar Oriental Research Institute* 56, 1975, pp. 93-103

AKLUJKAR 2008
A. Aklujkar, "Patañjali's *Mahābhāṣya* as a Key to Happy Kashmir," in M. Kaul and A. Aklujkar (eds.), *Linguistic Traditions of Kashmir: Essays in Memory of Paṇḍit Dinanath Yaksha*, New Delhi: D.K. Printworld, 2008, pp. 41-87

[161] BRONKHORST 2008, p. 297.

Alaṃkārasarvasva
Ruyyaka, *Alaṃkārasarvasva*, with the commentary of Vidyācakravartin, ed. S.S. Janaki and V. Raghavan, Delhi: Meharchand Lachmandas, 1965

Aṣṭādhyāyī
[Pāṇini, *Aṣṭādhyāyī*] See *Vyākaraṇamahābhāṣya*

BASISTHA 2003
C.R. Basistha, *Alaṃkāra School of Poetics and Bhaṭṭa Udbhaṭṭa: A Study*, Kolkata: Sanskrit Pustak Bhandar, 2003

BHATTACHARYA 1973
B. Bhattacharya, "Identification of a Citation in Udbhaṭa's Bhāmaha Vivaraṇa Fragments," *Journal of the Ganganatha Jha Kendriya Sanskrit Vidyapeetha* 29(1-4), 1973, pp. 141-143

BHATTACHARYA 1977
B. Bhattacharya, "A Supplementary Note on the Identification of a Citation in Udbhaṭa's Bhāmaha-Vivaraṇa Fragments," *Journal of the Ganganatha Jha Kendriya Sanskrit Vidyapeetha* 33(3), 1977, pp. 15-17

BHATTACHARYA 1978
B. Bhattacharya, "Identification of a Citation from Māgha's *Śiśupāla-Vadha* in Udbhaṭa's *Bhāmaha-Vivaraṇa* Fragment," *Mysore Orientalist* 11, 1978, pp. 21-22

BHATTACHARYA 1979
B. Bhattacharya, "Critical Observations on an Overlooked Reference to King Lalitāditya of Kāśmīra in Udbhaṭa's *Bhāmaha-Vivaraṇa*," *Vishveshvaranand Indological Journal* 17(1-2), 1979, pp. 53-59

BHATTACHARYA 2010
R. Bhattacharya, "Commentators of the *Cārvākasūtra*: A Critical Survey," *Journal of Indian Philosophy* 38, 2010, pp. 419-430

BHATTACHARYYA 1962
S. Bhattacharyya, "Abhidhāvṛtti in Udbhaṭa," *Our Heritage* 10(2), 1962, pp. 73-89

BHATTACHARYYA 1981
S. Bhattacharyya, "Three Lost Masterpieces of the Alaṃkāra Śāstra," in *Studies in Indian Poetics*, Calcutta: Firma KLM, 1981, pp. 29-37

BRONKHORST 2008
J. Bronkhorst, "Udbhaṭa, a Grammarian and Cārvāka," in M. Kaul and A. Aklujkar (eds.), *Linguistic Traditions of Kashmir: Essays in Memory of Paṇḍit Dinanath Yaksha*, New Delhi: D.K. Printworld, 2008, pp. 281-299

BRONNER 2009
Y. Bronner, "Change in Disguise: The Early Discourse on *Vyājastuti*," *Journal of the American Oriental Society* 129(2), 2009, pp. 179-198

BRONNER 2010
Y. Bronner, *Extreme Poetry: The South Asian Movement of Simultaneous Narration*, New York: Columbia University Press, 2010

BRONNER 2012
Y. Bronner, "A Question of Priority: Revisiting the Debate on the Relative Chronology of Daṇḍin and Bhāmaha," *Journal of Indian Philosophy* 40(1), 2012, pp. 67-118

BRONNER 2013
Y. Bronner, "From Conqueror to Connoisseur: Kalhaṇa's Account of Jayapīḍa and the Fashioning of Kashmir as the Kingdom of Learning," *Indian Economic and Social History Review* 50(2), 2013, pp. 161-177

DhvĀ
Ānandavardhana, *Dhvanyāloka*, with commentaries by Abhinavagupta and Śrīrāmaśāraka, ed. Pt. P. Śāstrī, Varanasi: Chowkhamba Sanskrit Series Office, Kashi Sanskrit Series 135, 1940

FRANCO 2011
E. Franco, "Lokāyata,", in K.A. Jacobsen, H. Basu, A. Malinar and V. Narayanan (eds.), *Brill's Encyclopedia of Hinduism*, vol. III, Leiden: Brill, 2011, pp. 629-642

GEROW 1977
E. Gerow, *Indian Poetics*, vol. V.2, fasc. 3 of *A History of Indian Literature*, ed. Jan Gonda, Wiesbaden: Otto Harrassowitz, 1977

GNOLI 1962
R. Gnoli, *Udbhaṭa's Commentary on the Kāvyālaṃkāra of Bhāmaha*, Rome: Istituto Italiano per il Medio ed Estremo Oriente, 1962

HOUBEN 1997
J. Houben, "Sūtra and Bhāṣyasūtra in Bhartṛhari's *Mahābhāṣya Dīpikā*: On the Theory and Practice of a Scientific and Philosophical Genre," in D. van der Meij (ed.), *India and Beyond: Aspects of Literature, Meaning, Ritual and Thought: Essays in Honour of Frits Staal*, London: Kegan Paul International, 1997, pp. 271-305

INGALLS 1990
D.H.H. Ingalls, "Introduction," in INGALLS ET AL. 1990, pp. 1-39

INGALLS ET AL. 1990
D.H.H. Ingalls, J.M. Masson and M.V. Patwardhan (transl.), *The Dhvanyāloka of Ānandavardhana with the Locana of Abhinavagupta*, Cambridge (MA): Harvard University Press, Harvard Oriental Series 49, 1990

JACOB 1897
G.A. Jacob, "Notes on Alaṅkāra Literature," *Journal of the Royal Asiatic Society*, 1897, pp. 829-853

JACOBI 1902-1903
H. Jacobi, "Ānandavardhana's *Dhvanyāloka*" [German transl.], *Zeitschrift der Deutschen Morgenländischen Gesellschaft* 56, 1902, pp. 392-410, 582-615, 760-789; 57, 1903, pp. 18-60, 311-343, repr. in H. Jacobi, *Schriften zur indischen Poetic und Asthetik,* Darmstadt: Wissenschaftliche Buchgessellschaft, 1969, pp. 2-161

JANAKI 1965
S.S. Janaki, "Introduction," see *Alaṃkārasarvasva*

KĀ
Daṇḍin, *Kāvyādarśa* [*Kāvyalakṣaṇa*], with the commentary of Ratnaśrījñāna, ed. A. Thakur and U. Jha, Darbhanga: Mithila Institute of Post Graduate Studies, 1957

KAl (of Bhāmaha)
Bhāmaha, *Kāvyālaṃkāra*, ed. B.N. Śarmā and B. Upādhyāya, [Varanasi: Kāśī Sanskrit Series 61, 1928] repr. Varanasi: Chaukhambha Sanskrit Sansthan, 1981

KAl (of Rudrata)
Rudraṭa, *Kāvyālaṃkāra*, with commentaries by Namisādhu and Satyadev Chowdhri, ed. R. Śukla, Delhi: Vāsudev Prakāśan, [1965] repr. 1990

KAlSS
Udbhaṭa, *Kāvyālaṃkārasārasaṃgraha*, with the *Laghuvṛtti* of Indurāja, ed. N.D. Banhatti, 2nd ed., Poona: Bhandrakar Oriental Research Institute, Bombay Sanskrit and Prakrit Series 79, 1982

KAlSū
Vāmana, *Kāvyālaṃkārasūtrāṇi*, with the *Kāmadhenu* Commentary of Gopendra Tripurahar Bhupal, ed. H. Shastri, 2nd ed., Varanasi: Chaukhamba, 1995

KAlSūṬ
Sahadeva, *Kāvyālaṃkārasūtraṭippana*, Manuscript T.316, University of Kerala Oriental Manuscript Library

KANE 1951
V.P. Kane, *History of Sanskrit Poetics*, 2nd ed., Bombay: Nirnaya Sagara Press, 1951

Kāvyaprakāśa
Mammaṭa, *Kāvyaprakāśa*, ed. V. Jhalakikar, Poona: Bhandarkar Oriental Research Institute, 1965, repr. 1983

KLV
Kalpalatāviveka (anonymous), ed. M.L. Nagar and H. Shastry, with an English introduction by P.R. Vora, Ahmedabad: Lalbhai Dalpatbhai Bharatiya Sanskriti Vidyamandira, 1968

KRISHNAMOORTHY 1979a
K. Krishnamoorthy, "Punaruktavadābhāsa and the Genuineness of the Published Fragments from Udbhaṭa's Bhāmahavivaraṇa," in *Studies in Indian Aesthetics and Criticism*, Mysore: D.V.K. Murthy, 1979, pp. 29-33

KRISHNAMOORTHY 1979b
K. Krishnamoorthy, "Udbhaṭa's Original Contribution to Sanskrit Literary Theory," in J.P. Sinha (ed.), *Ludwik Sternbach Felicitation Volume*, Lucknow: Akhila Bharatiya Sanskrit Parishad, 1979, pp. 303-311

KULKARNI 1983
V.M. Kulkarni, "Fresh Light on Bhāmaha-Vivaraṇa," in *Studies in Sanskrit Sāhitya-Śāstra: A Collection of Selected Papers Relating to Sanskrit Poetics and Aesthetics*, Patan: B.L. Institute of Technology, 1983, pp. 130-133

KUNJUNNI RAJA 1977
K. Kunjunni Raja, *Indian Theories of Meaning*, 2nd ed., Madras: Adyar Library and Research Center, 1977

Laghuvṛtti
[Indurāja, *Laghuvṛtti*] See KAlSS

LAHIRI 1933
P.C. Lahiri, "Vāmana's Theory of Rīti and Guṇa," *Indian Historical Quarterly* 9, 1933, pp. 835-853

Locana
[*Dhvanyālokalocana* of Abhinavagupta] See DhvĀ

MASSON 1972
J.L. Masson, "A Note on the Authenticity of the *Bhāmahavivaraṇa* Attributed to Udbhaṭa," *Indo-Iranian Journal* 13, 1972, pp. 250-254

MCCREA 2008
L. McCrea, *The Teleology of Poetics in Medieval Kashmir*, Cambridge (MA): Harvard University Press, 2008

MCCREA 2013
L. McCrea, "The Transformations of Mīmāṃsā in the Larger Context of Indian Philosophical Discourse," in E. Franco (ed.), *Historiography and Periodization of Indian Philosophy*, Vienna: Verein Sammlung de Nobili, Publications of the De Nobili Research Library 37, 2013, pp. 127-143

MCCREA AND PATIL 2006
L. McCrea and P. Patil, "Traditionalism and Innovation: Philosophy, Exegesis, and Intellectual History in Jñānaśrīmitra's *Apohaprakaraṇa*," *Journal of Indian Philosophy* 34(4), 2006, pp. 303-366

Mīmāṃsāsūtra
Jaimini, *Mīmāṃsādarśanam*, with the *Śabarabhāṣya* of Śabara, the *Prabhā* of Sri Vaidyanāthaśāstrī (Adhyāya 1, Pāda 1 only), and the *Tantravārttika* and *Ṭupṭīkā* of Kumārilabhaṭṭa, ed. K.V. Abhyankar and G.A. Joshi, 7 vols, Trivandrum: Ānandāśrama Sanskrit Series 97, [1930-1934] 1970-1976

POLLOCK 1985
S. Pollock, "The Theory of Practice and the Practice of Theory in Indian Intellectual History," *Journal of the American Oriental Society* 105, 1985, pp. 499-519

POLLOCK 2006
S. Pollock, *The Language of the Gods in the World of Men: Sanskrit, Culture, and Power in Premodern India*, Berkeley: University of California Press, 2006

POLLOCK 2010
S. Pollock, "What Was Bhaṭṭa Nāyaka Saying?", in S. Pollock (ed.), *Epic and Argument in Sanskrit Literary History: Essays in Honor of Robert P. Goldman*, pp. 143-184, Delhi: Manohar, 2010

POLLOCK 2016
S. Pollock, *A Rasa Reader: Classical Indian Aesthetics*, New York: Columbia University Press, 2016

RAGHAVAN 1975
V. Raghavan, *The Number of Rasas*, 3rd ed., Madras: Adyar Library and Research Center, 1975

RAGHAVAN 1978
V. Raghavan, *Bhoja's Śṛṅgāra Prakāśa*, Madras: Vasanta Press, 1978

RATIÉ 2010
I. Ratié, "A Five-Trunked, Four-Tusked Elephant Is Running in the Sky: How Free is Imagination According to Utpaladeva and Abhinavagupta?", *Asiatische Studien/Études Asiatiques* 64(2), 2010, pp. 341-385

ROODBERGEN 1984
J.A.F. Roodbergen, "Śleṣa: The Construction of an Argument," in S.D. Joshi (ed.), *Amṛtadhārā: Professor R.N. Dandekar Felicitation Volume*, Delhi: Ajanta Publications, 1984, pp. 359-369

RT
Kalhaṇa, *Rājataraṅgiṇī*, ed. V. Bandhu, 2 vols., Hoshiarpur: Woolner Indological Series 8, 1963-1965

SHULMAN 2012
D. Shulman, *More than Real: A History of Imagination in South India*, Cambridge (Mass.): Harvard University Press, 2012

SIMHA 1958
L.R. Simha, "Udbhaṭa and the Rasavāda," *Annals of the Bhandarkar Oriental Research Institute* 39, 1958, pp. 118-126

Śiśupālavadha
Māgha, *Śiśupālavadha*, with commentary by Vallabhadeva, ed. R.C. Kak and H. Shastri, Delhi: Bharatiya Book Corporation, 1990

SOLOMON 1977-1978
E.A. Solomon, "Bhaṭṭa Udbhaṭa," *Annals of the Bhandarkar Oriental Research Institute* 58-59, 1977-1978, pp. 985-992

Tattvasaṃgraha
Śāntarakṣīta, *Tattvasaṃgraha*, with the commentary of Kamalaśīla, ed. E. Krishnamacharya with a foreword by V. Bhattacharyya, vol. I, Baroda: Oriental Institute, 1984

Ṭippaṇaka
[Namisādhu, *Ṭippaṇaka*] See *Kāvyālaṃkāra*

TUBB 2014
G. Tubb, "On the Boldness of Bāṇa," in Y. Bronner, D. Shulman and G. Tubb (eds.), *Innovations and Turning Points: Toward a History of Kāvya Literature*, Delhi: Oxford University Press, 2014, pp. 308-354

TUBB forthcoming a
G. Tubb, "*Aupamyotprekṣā*: Poetic Fancy Based on Similitude"

TUBB forthcoming b
G. Tubb, "Theories of Semantics and the Analysis of Poetic Fancy in the Sanskrit Tradition"

TV
[Kumārilabhaṭṭa, *Tantravārttika*] See *Mīmāṃsāsūtra*

Vakroktijīvita
Kuntaka, *Vakroktijīvita*, ed. R. Miśra, Varanasi: Chaukhambha Sanskrit Sansthan, 1990

Vivaraṇa
[Udbhaṭa, *Vivaraṇa*] See GNOLI 1962

Vivṛti
[Tilaka, *Vivṛti*] *Kāvyālaṃkārasārasaṃgraha*, with the *Vivṛti* of Tilaka, ed. K.S.R. Sastri, Baroda: Oriental Institute, Gaekwad's Oriental Series 55, 1931

Vyākaraṇamahābhāṣya
Patañjali, *Vyākaraṇamahābhāṣya*, ed. B. Śāstrī Jośī, 6 vols., Delhi: Chaukhamba Sanskrit Pratishthan, Vrajajīvan Prācyabhāratī Granthamālā 23, 1992 [repr.]

The Culmination of Sanskrit Aesthetics in Kashmir: A Hypothesis on Ruyyaka's *Alaṃkārasarvasva* in the Light of Jayaratha's *Vimarśinī*[*]

DANIELE CUNEO

INTRODUCTION

The present paper is an attempt at provisionally fleshing out a working hypothesis on the historical and cultural position of Ruyyaka (first half of the 12th century) and his *Alaṃkārasarvasva* (henceforth AS) – especially in the light of its earliest commentary, Jayaratha's 13th-century *Vimarśinī* – within both the knowledge system of *alaṃkāraśāstra* in Kashmir and the history of *alaṃkāraśāstra tout court.*[1] The hypothesis consists in considering Ruyyaka as the culmination, both historical and theoretical, of the great period of cultural revolutions that Kashmir witnessed in Sanskrit literary studies and as the harbinger of a renovated way of "practicing the profession" of an

---

* I am deeply grateful to Eli Franco, Elisa Ganser, Charles Li and Isabelle Ratié for their precious remarks and suggestions. All mistakes, of course, are mine alone.

1 On Ruyyaka, beside the classical histories of Sanskrit poetics (DE 1960, KANE 1961, GEROW 1977), it is worth mentioning the study and the outstanding German translation of the *Alaṃkārasarvasva* by Jacobi (JACOBI 1908a and 1908b). Ruyyaka is the author of numerous other works, some extant and some yet untraced. In order to complete the research started with the present paper, an exhaustive analysis of the whole material by Ruyyaka is an obvious *desideratum*. In particular, one should focus first on the *Kāvyaprakāśasaṅketa*, Ruyyaka's commentary on Mammaṭa's *magnum opus*, and the *Vyaktivivekavicāra*, Ruyyaka's commentary on Mahimabhaṭṭa's 11th-century polemical masterpiece against the already established mainstream of Sanskrit poetics, Ānandavardhana's *dhvani* theory (see below, n. 33).

ālaṃkārika, namely a rekindled interest in the classification, definition and analysis of the ever-increasing multitude of figures of speech (*alaṃkāras*). This postulated position of culmination, as I will argue, allowed Ruyyaka to see the development of his discipline from a historically and theoretically privileged perspective and therefore enabled him to implicitly identify the theoretical issues and turning points that had been the object of the most heated debate in the previous centuries in Kashmir, but that could now be considered settled and agreed upon. Only after this self-aware meta-theoretical move could he confidently move on to more pressing, contemporary issues. The once debated and then agreed upon topics I am referring to are the objects of two veritable Kuhnian paradigm shifts that the valley of Kashmir witnessed from the end of the 9th to the beginning of the 11th century, which gave rise to a hornets' nest of more or less indignant oppositions.

As compellingly argued in MCCREA 2008, the "first revolution" consisted in the change from the formalist theory of poetics propounded by the earlier authors (Bhāmaha, Daṇḍin, Vāmana, Udbhaṭa and Rudraṭa) to the essentialist and functionalist theory of poetics centred on *dhvani* "implicature" as the true essence of poetry (Ānandavardhana and his followers), especially under the influence of Mīmāṃsā-like hermeneutics. As I have argued elsewhere (CUNEO 2013), a second paradigm shift occurred by the hand of Abhinavagupta (and possibly of Bhaṭṭa Nāyaka [POLLOCK 2010], before him): a transition from a conception of aesthetic experience (*rasa*) that does not account for the ontological difference between the universe experienced in ordinary reality and the universe created by and experienced in art, to a conception of aesthetic experience (*rasa*, again) that does account for such a difference and makes it the crucial speculative argument justifying and legitimizing the intrinsically pleasurable nature of the emotions aroused by an artwork. Ruyyaka takes stock of the changed theoretical scenario of his system of knowledge and takes it then from there to a direction that will be followed by most *ālaṃkārikas* in the following centuries.

In order to flesh out this working hypothesis, three pieces of evidence, or sets of clues, so to say, will be assessed. First, the introductory section[2] of the AS will be scrutinised in the attempt to interpret it as the first detailed account and value-laden emic narrative of Kaśmīri *alaṃkāraśāstra*, which is actively being spun by Ruyyaka

---

2 In Jayaratha's words, that portion is indeed called *avataraṇikā* (AS, p. 7).

and his first commentator Jayaratha – the same author of the massive *Tantrālokaviveka* on Abhinavagupta's religio-philosophical masterpiece –, especially in their position as the last heirs of the *dhvani* poetics that was started by Ānandavardhana, perfected by Abhinavagupta and normalized by Mammaṭa.[3] Second, two theoretical issues (the existence of *tātparyaśakti* and the sub-classifications of *lakṣaṇā*) will be dealt with, especially insofar as Ruyyaka positions himself in a dialogue with, and sometimes in a constructive opposition to, his immediate predecessors, Mammaṭa and Abhinavagupta. Thirdly, a passage that among many others Jayaratha's commentary borrows from Abhinavagupta's main work on poetics, the *Dhvanyālokalocana* (henceforth *Locana*), will be analysed as a clever attempt at redirecting a traditional argument to fit a new context, that is, the justification of the renovated interest in poetical figuration, now that the issues concerning the conveyance of poetic meaning (*dhvani*) and the import and epistemology of the emotional component in poetry (*rasa*) have been settled and have therefore lost some of their theoretical appeal.

THE TELEOLOGICAL NARRATIVE

The "first" doxographical account of Sanskrit poetics, the introductory portion of Ruyyaka's AS, has a well-known antecedent in the most celebrated passage of Abhinavagupta's *Abhinavabhāratī* (henceforth ABH), i.e., his commentary on the *rasasūtra* of Bharata's *Nāṭyaśāstra* (henceforth NŚ). The succession of authors arguing about the essence of *rasa* and progressively refuting each other in a ever-ascending ladder of discrimination provides Ruyyaka with a concrete instance of a multi-doctrinal narrative in which – in particular – the opinions of various *ālaṃkārika*s on the ontology of *rasa* are strung together in order to give an account of the topic in a full-fledged way that is both historical and teleological, as it culminates in the *siddhānta*, the final view upheld by Abhinavagupta.[4] However, unlike the characters in Abhinavagupta's narrative, whose works are now lost to us, the protagonists of Ruyyaka's account are

3 It is noteworthy that such a doxographical account has been and partly still is one of the models – I do not know whether explicitly or implicitly – for the historical and theoretical subdivision of the schools of poetics used in the standard works on the history of Sanskrit Poetics.

4 In a previous paper (CUNEO forthcoming), I have analyzed the passage in some detail especially with regard to Abhinavagupta's attitude towards history, tradition, novelty and narrative.

well known, as their works survived the ravages of time. The contemporary reader is thus allowed to assume a critical viewpoint on the rhetorical strategies by which Ruyyaka constructs his own version of the story, which is the history of *alaṃkāraśāstra*.

After the *maṅgala* verse to Vāk, the goddess of speech,[5] the AS starts off *in medias res* by stating that:

> *iha hi tāvad bhāmahodbhaṭaprabhṛtayaś cirantanālaṅkārakārāḥ pratīyamānam artham vācyopaskārakatayālaṅkārapakṣanikṣiptaṃ manyante* | (AS, p. 3.)
>
> To start with, in fact, Bhāmaha, Udbhaṭa and the other ancient authors of *alaṃkāraśāstra* maintain that the implied meaning is apportioned to the sphere of the figures of speech by being a supporting element of the expressed meaning.[6]

Since the very first sentence of his work, Ruyyaka posits the existence of a *pratīyamānārtha*, an "implied meaning," otherwise known as the *vyaṅgyārtha*, the "manifested" or "suggested" meaning, first introduced in the revolutionary, essentialistic and functionalistic theory propounded by Ānandavardhana's *Dhvanyāloka* (henceforth DhvĀ) in order to account for all the poetical meanings that could not be explained – so it was claimed and argued for – by the preceding linguistic and poetical theories. By the very insertion of the suggested meaning within the theory of the authors who long

---

[5] It is interesting to note that in commenting on the *maṅgala* Jayaratha refers *en passant* to the metaphysics of so-called Kashmir Śaivism, without the need of any explanation, especially relying on the doctrine of the levels of the word as expounded in Bhartṛhari's *Vākyapadīya* (for instance, 1. 1 and 1. 167 are quoted) as well as quoting analogous verses of a clear Bhartṛharian or *śaivādvaita* flavor that I could not identify, such as this one: *yeyaṃ vimarśarūpaiva paramārthacamatkṛtiḥ* | *saiva sāraṃ padārthānāṃ parā vāg abhidhīyate* || (p. 1). Along the lines of the connection between *alaṃkāraśāstra* and *śaivādvaita*, an interesting issue is the relative paucity of hard-core *śaiva* theological and metaphysical speculations on the part of the renowned *śaivādvaitin* Jayaratha in his exposition of the AS. Reasons for absences are often doomed to remain speculative. My current hypothesis, however, is that Ruyyaka followed Abhinavagupta also in what I have tentatively called his ecumenical attitude, i.e. a conscious attempt to underplay the "sectarian" aspects of his thought while commenting on works of a "trans-sectarian" discipline such as *alaṃkāraśāstra* (CUNEO 2016).

[6] The striking absence of Daṇḍin here as well as in the worldview of Kashmirian *alaṃkāraśāstra*, if we exclude a handful of quotations, has been often noted. For the most recent and complete remarks, see Bronner (2012, 71).

predated Ānandavardhana's system, Ruyyaka is rigging the game from the start and is thereby spinning a teleological narrative that already contains its final outcome in its very premises. As already hinted at before, such a teleological account of the schools predating the revolution of *dhvani* is precisely the one that has been recounted by most of the 20th-century scholars on Sanskrit poetics and that has been heavily criticized in recent scholarship, already starting with Gerow's work and culminating with the "Chicago school of *alaṃkāraśāstra*," if I can gather under a single label the pioneering works of Pollock, McCrea and Bronner, among others. According to such a teleological account, the *dhvani*-theory and its "discovery" of the suggested meaning as the soul of true poetry is "the highest point reached by Sanskrit literary criticism (KRISHNAMOORTHY 1964, p. 62 [quoted in MCCREA 2008, p. 2])" and all the thinkers that predated Ānandavardhana are just an imperfect version of it or rungs of a speculative ladder, to use Abhinavagupta's metaphor, that cannot but climax in the perfection of the poetics of suggestion (*dhvani*).

With this framework in mind, Ruyyaka's narrative can be even more revealing. After the general statement that the manifested meaning is subsumed under the label of the figures of speech, Ruyyaka elaborates further by stating which specific figures of speech can subsume the three well-known possible varieties of *vyaṅgyārtha* (the *vastudhvani*, the manifestation of a narrative element, the *alaṃkāradhvani*, the manifestation of a figure of speech and the *rasadhvani*, the manifestation of an aesthetic emotion).

Without delving into the details of this passage, for our present purpose it is crucial to note that, although all the varieties of *dhvani* were treated by the ancient school within the purview of some or other figure of speech – so argues Ruyyaka –, they were always considered as a secondary element, an *upaskāraka*, a supporting element, an ornament, that is exactly an *alaṃkāra*. Consequently, the passage finishes with these words:

> Therefore, in this way, the threefold implied meaning in its totality has been so declared as an ornament [on the part of the ancient authors of *alaṃkārśāstra*].[7]

Then, the text continues and mentions Vāmana and then again Udbhaṭa, in order to highlight their differences within the general scope

---

7 *tad itthaṃ trividham api pratīyamānam alaṅkāratayā khyāpitam eva* (AS, p. 6).

of the theory of the ancients. However, a decisive clue in this tentative reconstruction of Ruyyaka's teleological narrative is a mere *tu-śabda*, a "but" in the text, which follows the name of Vāmana. Jayaratha takes the hint given by this particle to reveal the direction of a theoretical improvement in the progression towards *dhvani*-theory, a progression that Vāmana is made to embody by Ruyyaka's text. Jayaratha affirms:

> Even though Vāmana declares the implied meaning to be included in the figures of speech, he has stated that there exists some sort of soul [of poetry] that is supported by those [figures of speech].[8]

The soul of poetry for Vāmana is *rīti*, "style," qualified as *viśiṣṭā padaracanā*, "a specific composition of words."[9] So, in Jayaratha's understanding of Ruyyaka's reconstruction, Vāmana does fail to recognize the existence of *dhvani*, "suggestion," but he is accorded the merit of focusing the discourse on an *ātman*, a soul, an enlivening entity that inheres in the body of poetry and is different from the mere ornaments, the figures of speech. With a fully teleological move, his work is therefore implicitly portrayed as a closer prefiguration of Ānandavardhana's forthcoming innovation. Anyways, in order to summarise the first part of his account, Ruyyaka concludes:

> Therefore, such is the opinion of the ancients: it is the figures of speech that are the main thing in poetry.[10]

As further proof of the teleological nature of Ruyyaka's reconstruction of the "history" of his discipline, the continuation of the narrative is not at all chronological. His attention is now turned towards the opponents of *dhvani*, Kuntaka and Bhaṭṭa Nāyaka. Whereas, showing a fair degree of historical awareness and scrupulousness, Jayaratha feels the need to justify their anachronistic treatment before the actual exposition of *dhvani* by stating:

> Although the authors of the *Vakroktijīvita* and of the *Hṛdayadarpaṇa* also indeed predate Ānandavardhana, their opinion has been stated first because they follow the opinion of the ancients.[11]

---

8 *vāmanena pratīyamānasyālaṅkārāntarbhāvam abhidadhatāpi tadupaskārya ātmā kaścid uktaḥ* (*Alaṃkārasarvasvavimarśinī*, p. 7).

9 Cf. Vāmana, *Kāvyālaṃkārasūtra* 1.2.6: *rītir ātmā kāvyasya* and 1. 2. 7: *viśiṣṭā padaracanā rītiḥ*.

10 *tad evam alaṅkārā eva kāvye pradhānam iti prācyānāṃ matam* (AS, p. 7).

11 *yady api vakroktijīvitahṛdayadarpaṇakārāv api dhvanikārānantarabhāvāv eva,*

So, with regard to Kuntaka, Ruyyaka explains:

> As to the author of the *Vakroktijīvita*, he stated that, on account of its predominance, the life of poetry is the multifarious obliqueness of speech, whose essence is the curved expression of [the poet's] dexterity.[12]

After this general statement, Ruyyaka explains further that according to Kuntaka the most important factor is nothing but the activity of the poet and that all kinds of *dhvani* are included in *vakrokti* as the result of such activity.[13]

Bhaṭṭa Nāyaka is also treated in some brief lines and portrayed as the exponent of the centrality of *rasa*-enjoyment, again with a *vyāpāra*, an "activity" or a "function" being at the centre. It is not, however, the activity of the poet, but a function of poetry itself, an enjoyment-capacity (*bhoga*) that characterizes poetry as the entity that triggers an enjoyment, similar to the enjoyment of the absolute, as Bhaṭṭa Nāyaka famously stated.[14]

---

tathāpi tau cirantanamatānuyāyināv eveti tanmataṃ pūrvam evoddiṣṭam (*Alaṃkārasarvasvavimarśinī*, p. 12).

12 *vakroktijīvitakāraḥ punar vaidagdhyabhaṅgībhaṇitisvabhāvāṃ bahuvidhāṃ vakroktim eva prādhānyāt kāvyajīvitam uktavān* (AS, p. 8).

13 Considering the importance of the concept of *pratibhā*, "poetic genius," in Kuntaka's work, Jayaratha quite appropriately comments that this activity is an act shaped by the genius of the poet (*vyāparasyeti kavipratibhollikhitasya karmaṇaḥ* [*Alaṃkārasarvasvavimarśinī*, p. 8]).

14 As an interesting aside, Bhaṭṭa Nāyaka was probably one of the first authors in the history of *alaṃkāraśastra* to formulate the comparison between the aesthetic and the mystical experience. For Bhaṭṭa Nāyaka's own words, see *Locana* ad DhvĀ 1. 6, pp. 91-92: *vāgdhenur dugdha etaṃ hi rasaṃ yad bālatṛṣṇayā* | *tena nāsya samaḥ sa syād duhyate yogibhir hi yaḥ* ||. In Ingalls' translation (INGALLS 1990, p. 120), "Prompted by the thirst of these children, the cow of speech gives forth this *rasa* as milk; to which the experience milked by yogis bears no comparison." On Bhaṭṭa Nāyaka, in general, see POLLOCK 2010. Abhinavagupta often lingers on the comparison between the aesthetic and mystical experience both in his *Locana* on Ānandavardhana's DhvĀ (for instance, see *Locana* ad DhvĀ 1. 18, p. 160; ad DhvĀ 2. 4, p. 183; ad DhvĀ 2. 4, p. 190; ad DhvĀ 3. 43; p. 510; translated in INGALLS 1990, pp. 194, 222, 226 and 655, respectively) and in his commentary on Bharata's NŚ (for instance, see ABH ad NŚ 6, prose after 31, *rasasūtra*, vol. I, p. 277; p. 285; p. 290; translated in GNOLI 1968, pp. 45-48, 82-85 and 83, n. 4, respectively). Along very similar lines, the standard reformulation of the comparison between aesthetic and mystical experience is probably the very late one by Viśvanātha, in his *Sāhityadarpaṇa* 3.2, namely that the savouring of *rasa* is "*brahmāsvādasahodaraḥ*." Among the abundant secondary literature, see LARSON 1976, PATNAKAR 1993, BÄUMER 1997, KUNJUNNI RAJA 2000 and FERNÀNDEZ 2001.

The narrative ends with the ascertainment of suggestion (*asti tāvad vyaṅgyaniṣṭho vyañjanāvyāpāraḥ*) and the detailed exposition of all its subcategories.[15] The details of the theory of *dhvani* have been retold again and again so many times that there is no need to linger on them in the present context. However, as a conclusion of the narration of Ruyyaka's narrative, it might be useful to try and make better sense of it with the help of another commentator of the AS, the southerner Samudrabandha.[16] At the end of this introductory section, he summarises and typologizes the different opinions about *kāvya* that Ruyyaka states. Samudrabandha writes:

> *iha viśiṣṭau śabdārthau kāvyam – tayoś ca vaiśiṣṭyaṃ dharmamukhena vyāpāramukhena vyaṅgyamukhena veti trayaḥ pakṣāḥ | ādyo 'py alaṅkārato guṇato veti dvaividhyam | dvitīyo 'pi bhaṇitivaicitryeṇa bhogakṛttvena veti dvaividhyam |* (*Alaṃkārasarvasvavyākhyā*, p. 11.)
>
> Here [in Ruyyaka's account], poetry is word and meaning made distinctive [or qualified]. And their distinctiveness is with regard to a property, with regard to a function or with regard to the manifested meaning. These are the three opinions. The first one is further twofold, with respect to the figures of speech and with respect to the qualities. The second is twofold as well, with respect to the multifariousness of expression and the capacity of enjoyment.

Therefore, according to Samudrabandha there are five theoretical views regarding *kāvya* as Ruyyaka has exposed them. Accordingly, the specificity of poetry lies in 1) the figures of speech (*alaṃkāra*), according to the old school of Bhāmaha and so forth, in 2) the qualities (*guṇa*), the position of Vāmana and its style as fundamentally consisting of qualities,[17] in 3) the multifariousness of expression, i.e. the obliqueness (*vakrokti*) propounded by Kuntaka, in 4) the capacity of enjoyment (*bhokṛttva*), i.e. the centrality of the apperception of *rasa* advocated by Bhaṭṭa Nāyaka, and in 5) the suggested meaning (*vyaṅgya*) as maintained by Ānandavardhana and accepted by Ruyyaka himself.

---

15 The quick dismissal-cum-refutation of Mahima Bhaṭṭa's *Vyaktiviveka* that precedes the final remark on the establishment of suggestion is not of present concern.

16 On Samudrabandha, see NARAYANAN 2002.

17 Cf. Vāmana, *Kāvyālaṃkārasūtra* 1. 2. 7: *viśiṣṭā padaracanā rītiḥ* and 1. 2. 8: *viśeṣo guṇātmā*.

Now, coming back to the text of Ruyyaka from our own perspective, it is striking but maybe understandable that the two greatest exponents of *dhvani* before him, i.e. Abhinavagupta and Mammaṭa, are not mentioned in the narrative. One might argue that they have not been included because they do not maintain any new theory of their own and they just improve the *dhvani*-theory laid out by Ānandavardhana. However, one might reasonably speculate that they are not mentioned exactly because they were Ruyyaka's immediate predecessors and thus his writing could be interpreted as a form of confrontation with them and, possibly, a summation of their own contributions. The rest of the paper runs along the lines of these speculations.

THE ECLECTICISM

Arguably, an additional reason for considering Ruyyaka's contribution as a culmination in the history of Kashmiri aesthetics is his way of combining the views of his two major predecessors, Mammaṭa and Abhinavagupta. In particular, my focus will be turned towards the inclusion of *tātparyaśakti* as part of the epistemological understanding of linguistic signification, a case in point where Ruyyaka follows Abhinavagupta against Mammaṭa, and Ruyyaka's understanding of the subdivisions of secondary signification (*lakṣaṇā*), a clear instance where Mammaṭa's elaborations are preferred over Abhinavagupta's.

The concept of *tātparyaśakti* itself is in all likelihood an innovation by Jayanta Bhaṭṭa, the famous 9th-century Kashmirian logician.[18] For the time being and our present purpose, suffice it to say that Ānandavardhana never mentions the concept of *tātparyaśakti*, while Abhinavagupta includes it in a fourfold subdivision of the process of linguistic signification that is thoroughly treated in his *Locana*, a commentary to the DhvĀ.[19] The four phases (*kākṣyas*) are *abhidhā*, *tātparya*, *lakṣaṇā* and *vyañjanā*. On hearing any sentence, we at first understand the separate meanings, as the single words can only signify the respective universals (*sāmānya*), in accordance with the early Mīmāṃsaka understanding of the issue.[20] This is where the

---

[18] For a detailed treatment of the concept of *tātparyaśakti* in both Jayanta and Abhinavagupta, see the article by Graheli in the present volume.

[19] See, in particular, the long discussion in *Locana* ad DhvĀ 1. 4.

[20] *Śābarabhāṣya* ad *Mīmāṃsāsūtra* 1. 1. 24, p. 112: *sāmānye hi padaṃ pravartate*.

functioning of *abhidhā*, "denotation," ends.[21] Then, a unified sentence meaning is obtained thanks to *tātparyaśakti*, which communicates the individual meanings connected in a particularized sentence meaning. Then, only in the case of some obstacle in signification such as the famous impossibility of having a village right upon the Ganges (*gaṅgāyāṃ ghoṣaḥ*), one resorts to *lakṣaṇā*, "indication," and a related meaning is understood to account for the difficulty in a literal interpretation: in the famous example, it is the bank of the Ganges that is actually to be understood as the substratum for the village (*gaṅgātīre ghoṣaḥ*). Finally, the fourth phase: it is only through *vyañjanā*, the "suggestive capacity," that one comes to understand, if present at all, the implied meanings – often, but not always poetic meanings –, among which we find for instance any possible reason and purpose (*prayojana*) for the particular use of secondary signification, *lakṣaṇā*: in the case of the example, one says "the village is on the Ganges," and so uses a figurative expression, in order to implicitly convey that the settlement possesses some of the good qualities associated with the sacred river, such as its coolness and holiness.

This bird's eye view on Abhinavagupta's philosophy of linguistic signification is of present concern, because Mammaṭa – who follows Abhinava in multiple respects, most famously in the analysis of the ontology of *rasa* – does not seem to accept the principle of *tātparyaśakti*, as he mentions it only once in the *kārikās* as the opinion of others,[22] and only *en passant* in a couple of passages of his *svavṛtti*.[23]

---

21 Again, in accordance with (at least one interpretation of) Śabara, *padāni hi svaṃ svam artham abhidhāya nivṛttavyāpārāṇi* (*Śābarabhāṣya* ad *Mīmāṃsāsūtra* 1. 1. 25, p.116).

22 In *Kāvyaprakāśa* (henceforth KP) 6: *syād vācako lākṣaṇikaḥ śabdo 'tra vyañjakas tridhā* | *vācyādayas tadarthāḥ syus tātparyārtho 'pi keṣucit* ||. "Language here is threefold: denotative, indicative and suggestive. Its meaning is respectively denoted and so forth. According to some, there is also the meaning of *tātparya*." The *vṛtti* by Mammaṭa himself attributes *tātparyaśakti* to Bhāṭṭa Mīmāṃsā. For an understanding of this attribution, most probably unwarranted, see again Graheli's contribution to the present volume.

23 *Svavṛtti* ad KP 6, p. 9, the passage related to the *kārikā* treated in the previous note; *Svavṛtti* ad KP 18, p. 34: *taṭādau viśeṣāḥ pāvanatvādayas te cābhidhātātparyalakṣaṇābhyo vyāpārāntareṇa gamyāḥ* |. "In the case of the 'bank' and the like [understood in cases such as 'the village on the Ganges' (*gaṅgāyāṃ ghoṣaḥ*) and the like], qualifications such as 'holiness' and the like are understood by means of a function that is different from denotation, *tātparya* and indica-

Ruyyaka, on the other hand, clearly states –anachronistically – that it was accepted by the *dhvanikāra*, i.e., by Ānandavardhana. He writes: ... *abhidhātātparyalakṣaṇākhyavyāpāratrayottīrṇasya... vyañjanāvyāparasya...* Therefore, in this case, Ruyyaka sides with Abhinavagupta and against Mammaṭa.

However, in other cases such as in his understanding of "secondary signification," *lakṣaṇā*, or – as he calls it in this case – *bhaṅgī*, he follows the system followed by Mammaṭa as opposed to Abhinavagupta's theories. More specifically, in the opening of the AS, as Ruyyaka is explaining that in the view of the "ancients" the *pratīyamānārtha*, the "implied meaning," is considered to fall under the purview of *alaṃkāras*, he specifies that this happens by way of a "twofold indirection" (*dvividhayā bhaṅgyā*) in accordance with the tenth *kārikā* of Mammaṭa's KP that is partially quoted in that very junction: *svasiddhaye parākṣepaḥ parārthe svasamarpaṇaṃ*, "a further [meaning] is supplied in order to account for the realization of its own [primary meaning]. Its [primary meaning] is abandoned for the sake of a further meaning." Accordingly, as amply illustrated in Jayaratha's commentary, thc various *alaṃkāras* (*paryāyokta*, *aprastutapraśaṃsā*, etc.) are understood to convey an indirect meaning along these two modalities of signification (the suppletion of a further meaning or the complete abandonment of the primary meaning). In its non-poetic embodiment, the first modality is exemplified by the example *kuntāḥ praviśanti* "the spears are entering," in which the meaning can be accounted for only if one implies that the soldiers that carry the spears are entering as well. The second is exemplified by the time-honoured *gaṅgāyāṃ ghoṣaḥ*, in which the meaning "Ganges" has to be abandoned to leave the room for the meaning

tion"; *Svavṛtti* ad KP 47, p. 155: *ity abhidhātātparyalakṣaṇātmakavyāpāratrayātivartī dhvananādiparyāyo vyāpāro 'napahnavanīya eva* |. "Consequently, it is surely not possible to reject the function called 'suggesting' and so forth [i.e., called with other names] as exceeding the three functions of denotation, *tātparya* and indication." My contention is that, on the evidence of the previously quoted *kārikā*, Mammaṭa does not seem to accept *tātparyaśakti*, although he does mention it twice in his *vṛtti* together with the other functions, but only in order to stress that suggestion is a different, further function of linguistic signification. From this unfortunately scanty evidence, it is also possible to argue that Mammaṭa had a noncommittal attitude toward the existence of *tātparyaśakti*. It is worth noting that the order in which he mentions the three functions of *abhidhā*, *tātparya* and *lakṣaṇā* is in accordance with Abhinavagupta's understanding of *tātparyaśakti* as the second phase of linguistic signification, and therefore it seems most probable, if not certain, that it is his theory that Mammaṭa has in mind.

"bank."[24] What is of present concern is the fact that this subdivision of *lakṣaṇā* is not at all found in Abhinavagupta's works.[25]

To wrap up the import of this second twofold clue, Ruyyaka's eclecticism within the purview of the *dhvani*-theory with regard to his two immediate predecessors could well be regarded as one more aspect of his work that hints at his liminality, his borderline role, as one of the last exponents of Kashmirian *alaṃkāraśāstra*.

SERVANT OF TWO MASTERS?

By focusing on the first few pages of Ruyyaka's AS, the teleological narrative of the discipline, and the minor points of its understanding of the functions of language, the central feature of the work has so far remained untouched: its being for the most part a comprehensive treatment of figures of speech. Ruyyaka's best efforts, in other words, cannot but be in his sophisticated analysis of poetic figuration in all its varieties and his at least implicit attempt to logically categorize the various figures of speech and the principles that inform them. Ruyyaka's system of classification is followed by GEROW 1971 in his own masterful attempt to find a *ratio* in both the history and the system(s) of *alaṃkāras*. In Gerow's words (ibid., p. 21):

> Not until the close of the early figurative period [in the history of *alaṃkāraśāstra*], in the works of certain of the encyclopedists, is there any

---

[24] It is interesting to note that Mammaṭa borrowed this subdivision of *lakṣaṇā* and in general his understanding of secondary signification at large – including in contemporary parlance both metaphorical and metonymical meanings – from the relatively understudied *Abhidhāvṛttimātṛkā* of Mukula (first half of the 10th century, Kashmir), arguably the first author to challenge Ānandavardhana's *dhvani* theory. See, for instance, Mukula's formulation of the first modality, i.e., the suppletion of a further meaning (*Abhidhāvṛttimātṛkā* 3ab): *svasiddhyarthatayākṣepo yatra vastvantarasya tat*. On Mukula, see VENUGOPALAN 1977, MCCREA 2008, pp. 260-310, AGRAWAL 2008, KEATING 2013a and 2013b. Moreover, Mammaṭa devoted an entire short work to the functions of language, the *Śabdavyāpāravicāra*, in which he quotes even more extensively from Mukula's work. I am presently working on an article focused on an in-depth investigation of the relation between Mukula and Mammaṭa.

[25] The reason why Abhinavagupta does not seem to be aware of – or does not seem to care about – the theory of secondary signification devised by Mukula, then adopted by Mammaṭa, and subsequently well attested in many authors of *alaṃkāraśāstra*, is a really difficult question to answer and lies way beyond the scope of the present article.

really serious attempt to make the outward presentation of the figures conform to their inner logic. Ruyyaka must be mentioned as the writer who has gone the farthest in this direction. Much of our argument is based on his system.

Therefore, the aspects treated so far in the present essay might be indeed regarded as somewhat marginal. However, the link between the marginality to Ruyyaka's work of aspects that were central to a couple of centuries of speculation in Kashmir and the main topic of the AS, i.e. *alaṃkāra*s, is the very last clue that I tried to identify (or maybe to conjecture, if one can conjecture a clue) in order to interpret the figure of Ruyyaka as the hinge between two worlds, the momentous character that sets a before and an after.

My hypothesis is that this link can be found in the reply that Jayaratha gives to an implicit question on the part of Ruyyaka's to the *ālaṃkārika*s who came after the speculative earthquakes that Kashmir witnessed in the period between Ānandavardhana and Mahimabhaṭṭa, so to say. The query would be something like: "why should we *ālaṃkārika*s now keep bothering to catalogue the various figures of speech and to fine-tune their individual definitions, if it has been now long proved and established that the soul of poetry is *dhvani*, the suggested meaning, and even more so in Abhinavagupta's extremization of the theory, according to which the real soul of poetry is only *rasa*, an aesthetic emotion that seems to have little to do with tropes and figuration?" The centrality of this question is supported by the definition of poetry given in the standard textbook of *alaṃkāraśāstra*, the already mentioned KP. There Mammaṭa affirms:

tad adoṣau śabdārthau saguṇāv analaṃkṛtī punaḥ kvāpi | (KP 4ab.)

It [i.e. poetry] consists of word and meaning, without defects and with qualities, and sometimes without figures of speech.

It is clear from this definition that *alaṃkāra*s are not an essential element of poetry. This marginality of poetic figuration is perfectly in tune with the essentialistic and functionalistic revolution propounded by Ānandavardhana, for which every element should be aiming at the revelation of a manifested meaning, and no formal element is essential for this to occur. Thus, the change of focus of the AS – not *dhvani* but the figures of speech, although *dhvani* is clearly advocated in the beginning and somewhat taken for granted now – might indeed be interpreted as an attempt of reconciliation between the view of the "ancients" and the view of the "contemporary" *ālaṃ-*

kārikas. The AS itself does not seem to offer more than that. However, a definition of the central concept of *alaṃkāra* found in the *Vyaktivivekavicāra* by the same Ruyyaka could provide important clues in this direction. He writes:

> *tathā ca śabdārthayor vicchittir alaṃkāraḥ | vicchittiś ca kavipratibhollāsarūpatvāt kavipratibhollāsasya ānantyād anantatvaṃ bhajamāno na paricchettuṃ śakyate |*
>
> And, in this way, ornamentation is the charm of word and meaning. Moreover, it is not possible to accurately define charm, because it is infinite, as it consists of the play of the poet's imagination, which is in its turn infinite in scope.[26]

In the words of a famous article by Jacobi (JACOBI 1908a), *vicchitti* becomes the test of poetic figurativeness. The use of the term *vicchitti* directly refers to the poetological discourse advocated by Kuntaka regarding the centrality of *vakrokti*, also called *bhaṅgī*, *bhaṇiti*, *vaicitrya* or, indeed, *vicchitti*. This stress on figuration betrays once more Ruyyaka's closeness to the theoretical position of the "ancients," although through the doorway of Kuntaka's reformulation of it, as well as its emphasis on the importance of poetic imagination. Once more, one might feel the need for a justification of Ruyyaka's being a servant of two masters, of his being both an exponent of the *dhvani*-school and yet so close to the position and the interests of the school of the "ancients." It is Jayaratha who comes to the rescue by providing the text with a clear theoretical reason for the essentiality of figuration and, in general, of the formal, "physical" aspects of poetry. Jayaratha argues:

> *nanu yady evaṃ tarhi "gaṅgāyāṃ ghoṣaḥ" ity atrāpi vyaṅgyasya sadbhāvāt kāvyatvaṃ prasajyate | naitat | iha yadvad ātmano vyāpakatvāc charīre ghaṭādau (ca) vartamānatve 'pi karaṇādiviśiṣṭe śarīra eva jīvavyavahāro na ghaṭādau tadvad asyāpi vividhaguṇālaṃkāraucityacārutvaśabdārthaśarīragatvenaivātmatvavyavahāro nānyatreti na kaścid doṣaḥ |*
>
> Someone might object: if this were the case [the objector has in mind the presence of *dhvani* in common, worldly expressions], then the very notion of poetry would be unwarrantedly applicable also to cases such as "the village is on the Ganges," because of the presence of a suggested meaning. It is not like that. In this regard, although the soul is present in both a body and a pot [or any other insentient object], as it is omni-pervasive, we can

26 *Vyaktivivekavicāra*, p. 44.

> only talk of a living being in the case of a body qualified by sense organs and the like and not in the case of pots and so on. In the very same way, even that [suggested meaning] can be said to be the soul [of poetry] only insofar as it is found in a body of word and meaning [endowed with] beauty, propriety and various qualities and figures of speech, and in no other case. Therefore, there is no defect [in the definition].[27]

Along the lines of this powerful argument, the *alaṃkāra*s (and *guṇa*s) are indeed a *condition sine qua non* of *kāvya*, just as much as *dhvani* is. As a soul can only vivify a body endowed with the characteristics of a living body, in the very same way *dhvani* can only vivify a linguistic body endowed with the time-honoured characteristics described by the ancient authors since the very beginning of the tradition of *alaṃkāraśāstra*. We can only talk of poetry if both *dhvani* and some degree of beauty and figuration are present at the same time. Such an argument based on the long-established master-metaphor of the body-soul image can very well be regarded as an implicit answer to the question "why should we still be bothered by tropology and figuration in a poetic culture where suggestiveness is the only soul of poetry?" What is even more striking is that Jayaratha is here actually just re-using an argument that Abhinavagupta levied in his *Locana*,[28] but my contention is that this reasoning is repurposed in Jayaratha's text in order to meet the new needs of a time when the existence of *dhvani* is commonly accepted, but the importance of *alaṃkāra*s is under theoretical threat at the very least.

---

27 *Alaṃkārasarvasvavimarśinī*, p. 11.

28 *Locana* ad DhvĀ 1.4, p. 59: *nanv evaṃ "siṃho vaṭuḥ" ity atrāpi kāvyarūpatā syāt, dhvananalakṣaṇasyātmano 'trāpi samanantaraṃ vakṣyamāṇatayā bhāvāt | nanu ghaṭe 'pi jīvavyavahāraḥ syāt, ātmano vibhutvena tatrāpi bhāvāt | śarīrasya khalu viśiṣṭādhiṣṭānayuktasya saty ātmani jīvavyavahāraḥ, na yasya kasyacid iti cet – guṇālaṅkāraucityasundaraśabdārthaśarīrasya sati dhvananākhyātmani kāvyarūpatāvyavahāraḥ | na cātmano 'sāratā kācid iti ca samānam |*. INGALLS 1990 translates (p. 86): "Our opponent might object: 'If this were so, such examples as 'The boy is a lion' would be poetry, because, as you will shortly say, the soul of poetry, which you define as suggestion, is found in such examples as well [as in poems which exhibit *rasa*].' To which we answer no; one might as readily say that a clay pot is alive, because, as the soul is omnipresent, it must be in the pot as well. Should you try to reply to this answer by saying that it is only when the soul is present in a body that serves as basis for particular [sense faculties and the like], and not when the soul is present in any other sort of locus, that we speak of life, very well, we will employ the title 'poetry' only when *dhvani* is embodied in a composition containing *guṇa*s, figures of speech, propriety, and beautiful words and meanings. But in neither case does the soul [or *dhvani*] lose its precious nature."

In fact, Jayaratha is here commenting the portion of the AS, in which Ruyyaka explains how the *dhvanikāraḥ*, i.e. Ānandavardhana, accepted the function of suggestion as the soul of poetry, "because [– among other reasons –] only the meaning of the sentence that is suggested is its main element, *insofar as qualities and figures of speech are its supporting elements* (emphasis mine)."[29] Figuration has now outspokenly become part and parcel of the justification of poetry as a mode of signification sui generis, in a way that might have been implicitly understood in Abhinavagupta's poetological synthesis, for instance,[30] but surely did not come to the surface of his theoretical discourse, focused as it was on the wide-ranging defence and rationalization of a *dhvani*-centered epistemology[31] and on his understanding of the psychology and ontology of *rasa*.[32]

On account of my avowedly interpretive reading of Ruyyaka and Jayaratha, it might not seem implausible to state that Ruyyaka is indeed trying to combine and to an extent reconcile the views of Ānandavardhana and his followers with the view of the ancients. *Vicchitti* and *vyaṅgya*, just to use the terms he prefers, are body and soul of poetry and one cannot seem to live without the other. To sum up, one might say that Jayaratha, borrowing Abhinavagupta's words, offers a sound legitimisation for Ruyyaka's enterprise and also for "the mainstay of Sanskrit Literary theory throughout its history," as it was happily put in MCCREA 2008 (p. 6), that is, a justification for the endless, minute and hair-splitting treatment, classification and exemplification of figures of speech.

---

29 *vākyārthasyaiva ca vyaṅgyarūpasya guṇālaṃkāropaskartavyatvena prādhānyād* (AS, p. 10).

30 One might well argue that the centrality of figuration is apparent in Mammaṭa's work too, as a good portion of it is devoted to the analysis of *alaṃkāra*s and other formal aspects of poetry, but the KP is a manual that attempts to deal with all the aspects of the poetic event, while in the case of Ruyyaka's AS the figures of speech retake centre stage by becoming *the* topic of an independent work, which had not happened in Kashmir for more than two centuries, if one excludes the purposively backward-looking efforts of Pratihārendurāja's *Kāvyālaṃkārasārasaṃgrahalaghuvṛtti* (first half of the 10th century), Sahadeva's *Kāvyālaṃkārasūtravṛttiṭippaṇa* (first half of the 10th century) – anyway, commentaries to older, "classical" works – and Kuntaka's *Vakroktijīvita* (second half of the 10th century).

31 For the most recent treatment of Abhinavagupta's repurposing of *dhvani* epistemology, see POLLOCK 2012.

32 For an analysis of the specificity of Abhinavagupta's understanding of *rasa* as opposed to his predecessors, see CUNEO 2013.

CONCLUSIONS

As a way of a tentative conclusion, it is worth recapitulating my points regarding Ruyyaka and Jayaratha as the possible culmination of Kashmirian Sanskrit aesthetics. First of all, in the introductory portion of the AS, by postulating since the very beginning the existence of the implied meaning, the *pratīyamānārtha*, within the theories of authors who could have no knowledge of it, Ruyyaka spins a narrative that is already in itself a conscious teleology of speculative positions and an a priori and ad hoc legitimisation of his final viewpoint. The recounting of such a teleological doxography is only possible in an extremely self-aware scholarly tradition that is thereby giving an account of itself, so to say. The second reason is Ruyyaka's theoretical blend of the positions of Abhinavagupta and Mammaṭa, the two greatest exponents of *dhvani*-poetics before him. In particular, I mentioned the issue of *tātparyaśakti* along with Ruyyaka's appropriation of Abhinavagupta's fourfold model of linguistic signification in opposition to Mammaṭa's seeming non-acceptance of it and the internal subdivisions of the function of *lakṣaṇā* that Ruyyaka borrows from Mammaṭa in opposition to Abhinavagupta's silence on the matter. The third reason is the implicit justification he gives – and the explicit justification that Jayaratha gives – for continuing to deal with *alaṃkāra*s and for writing a whole work dedicated to them, although the soul of poetry is firmly established as suggestion and the focus on *alaṃkāra*s might not strike one as warranted anymore. His and Jayaratha's solution of the co-dependence of suggestion and figuration, already found in Abhinavagupta's refunctionalization of the great master-metaphor that is the soul-body image, seems to reach a higher theoretical scope and purpose in the hands of authors deeply interested in both sides of the poetological spectrum. In the expert hands of Ruyyaka and Jayaratha, the conciliation of the old school who focused on *alaṃkāra* and the like and the new school of *dhvani* and *rasa* might therefore be said to have reached its historical and theoretical culmination.[33]

---

[33] As it has been often repeated throughout this essay, I do not claim to offer knockout historical arguments, if anything like that can ever be found. But I am accumulating pointers to a possible interpretation of Ruyyaka's historical and cultural role. As pointed out at the beginning, in order to establish this interpretation on a firmer ground, it would be necessary to thoroughly investigate not only the whole of the AS with Jayaratha's commentary, but also Ruyyaka's commentary on the KP, especially with regards to his seeming disagreements with Mammaṭa, and his commentary on Mahima Bhaṭṭa's *Vyaktiviveka*, especially with regard to his understanding of the relation between figuration and

REFERENCES

ABH
[*Abhinavabhāratī*] See NŚ

Abhidhāvṛttimātṛkā
Abhidhāvṛttimātṛkā of Mukulabhaṭṭa and Śabdavyāpāravicāra of Rājānaka Mammaṭācārya, ed. M.R. Telang, Bombay: Nirnaya Sagar Press, 1916

AGRAWAL 2008
M.M. Agrawal, "Mukulabhaṭṭa and Vyañjanā," in M. Kaul and A. Aklujkar (eds.), *Linguistic Traditions of Kashmir. Essays in Memory of Paṇḍit Dinanath Yaksha*, New Delhi/Jammu: D.K. Printworld/The Harabhatta Shastri Indological Research Institute, 2008, pp. 28-40

Alaṃkārasarvasvavyākhyā
Alaṃkārasarvasva of Ruyyaka, with the commentary of Samudrabandha, ed. T.G. Śāstrī, Trivandrum: Travancore Government Press, Trivandrum Sanskrit Series 40, 1915

Alaṃkārasarvavimarśinī
See AS

AS
Alaṃkārasarvasva of Ruyyaka, with the commentary Alaṃkāravimarśinī of Jayaratha, ed. MM. Paṇḍit D. Prasād and K.P. Parab, [Bombay: Nirnaya Sagar Press, 1893] Delhi: Bhāratiya Vidyā Prakaśana, 1982

BÄUMER 1997
B. Bäumer, "Aesthetics of Mysticism or Mysticism of Aesthetics? The Approach of Kashmir Śaivism," in B. Bäumer (ed.), *Mysticism in Shaivism and Christianity*, Delhi: Abhishiktananda Society, 1997, pp. 329-349

BRONNER 2004
Y. Bronner, "Back to the Future. Appaya Dīkṣita's Kuvalayānanda and the Rewriting of Sanskrit Poetics," *Wiener Zeitschrift für die Kunde Südasiens* 48, 2004, pp. 47-79

---

suggestion as well as their relative importance and centrality as minimal requirements for poetry to be poetry. A further avenue of research worth investigating in this regard is the influence of Ruyyaka's work on the later *ālaṃkārikas*. For instance, the influence of Ruyyaka on Appaya Dīkṣita has been party studied in BRONNER 2004. Useful discussions on Ruyyaka's stance within the history of the development of some *alaṃkāras*' definitions are to be found in TUBB AND BRONNER 2008.

BRONNER 2012
Y. Bronner, "A Question of Priority: Revisiting the Bhāmaha-Daṇḍin Debate," *Journal of Indian Philosophy* 40, 2012, pp. 67-118

CUNEO 2008-2009
D. Cuneo, *Emotions without Desire. An Interpretive Appraisal of Abhinavagupta's Rasa Theory. Annotated Translation of the First, Sixth and Seventh Chapters of Abhinavagupta's Abhinavabhāratī*, Unpublished PhD Thesis, Rome: "Sapienza" University of Rome, 2008-2009

CUNEO 2013
D. Cuneo, "Unfuzzying the fuzzy. The distinction between *rasa*s and *bhāva*s in Bharata and Abhinavagupta," in N. Mirnig, P.-D. Szántò and M. Williams (eds.), *Puṣpikā: Tracing Ancient India through Texts and Traditions. Contributions to Current Research in Indology*, vol. I, Oxford: Oxbow books, 2013, pp. 50-75

CUNEO 2016
D. Cuneo, "Detonating or Defusing Desire. From Utpaladeva's Ecstatic Aesthetics to Abhinavagupta's Ecumenical Art Theory," in B. Bäumer and R. Torella (eds.), *Utpaladeva, Philosopher of Recognition*, Delhi: DK Printworld, 2016, pp. 31-76

CUNEO forthcoming
D. Cuneo, "'This is Not a Quote.' Quotation Emplotment, Quotational Hoax and Other Unusual Cases of Textual Reuse in Sanskrit Poetics and Dramaturgy," in E. Freschi and P. Maas (eds.), *Adaptive Reuse in Premodern South Asian Texts and Contexts*, Harrassowitz: Wiesbaden, pp. 219-253

DE 1960
S.K. De, *History of Sanskrit Poetics*, Calcutta: Firma K.L.M., 1960

DhvĀ
Dhvanyāloka of Ānandavardhana with the Locana of Abhinavagupta, the Bālapriyā subcommentary of Rāmaśāraka, and the Divyāñjana notes of Pt. Mahādeva Śāstri, ed. P. Śāstri, Benares: Kashi Sanskrit Series 135, 1940

FERNÀNDEZ 2001
R. Fernàndez, "The Play of Freedom: An Aesthetic approach to Kashmir Śaivism," in MARCHIANÒ AND MILANI 2001, pp. 125-134

GEROW 1977
E. Gerow, *Indian Poetics*, Wiesbaden: Otto Harrassowitz, 1977

GNOLI 1968
R. Gnoli, *The Aesthetic Experience according to Abhinavagupta*, 2nd ed., Varanasi: Chowkamba Sanskrit Studies 72, 1968

INGALLS 1990
D.H.H. Ingalls (ed.), *The Dhvanyāloka of Ānandavardhana with the Locana of Abhinavagupta*, transl. D.H.H. Ingalls, J.M. Masson and M.V. Patwardan, London: Harvard Oriental Series 49, 1990

JACOBI 1908a
H. Jacobi, "Über Begriff und Wesen der poetischen Figuren in der indischen Poetik," Göttingen: Nachrichten von der Königlichen Gesellschaft der Wissenschaften zu Göttingen, Philosogisch-Historische Klasse, 1980

JACOBI 1908b
H. Jacobi, "Ruyyaka's *Alaṃkārasarvasva*," *Zeitschrift der Morgenlandische Gesellschaft* 62, 1980, pp. 392-410, 582-615, 760-789

KANE 1961
P.V. Kane, *History of Sanskrit Poetics*, Delhi: Motilal Banarsidass, 1961

Kāvyālaṃkārasūtra
Kāvyālaṃkārasūtra of Vāmana, with the Kāmadhenu of Gopendra Tripurahara Bhūpāla, ed. Bechana Jha, Varanasi: Chaukhamba, 1989

Kāvyaprakāśasaṅketa
Kāvyaprakāśā of Mammaṭa, with the Saṃketa by Māṇikyacandra, ed. V.S. Abhyankar, Poona: Ānandāśrama Publisher, 1921

KEATING 2013a
M. Keating, "'The Cow is to be Tied up': Sort-Shifting in Classical Indian Philosophy of Language," *History of Philosophy Quarterly* 30(4), 2013, pp. 311-333

KEATING 2013b
M. Keating, "Mukulabhaṭṭa's Defense of *Lakṣaṇā*: How We Use Words to Mean Something Else, But Not Everything Else," *Journal of Indian Philosophy* 41, 2013, pp. 439-461

KP
Kāvyaprakāśa of Mammaṭa, ed. and transl. MM. G. Jha, revised ed., Varanasi: Bharatiya Vidya Prakasan, 1985

KRISHNAMOORTHY 1964
K. Krishnamoorthy, *Essays in Sanskrit Criticism*, Dharwar: Karnatak University, 1964

KUNJUNNI RAJA 2000
K. Kunjunni Raja, "Experience of Aesthetic Rapture," *Adyar Library Bulletin* 64, 2000, pp. 89-102

LARSON 1976
G.J. Larson, "The aesthetic (*rasāsvāda*) and the religious (*brahmāsvāda*) in Abhinavagupta's Kashmirian Shaivism," *Philosophy East and West* 26, 1976, pp. 371-387

Locana
[*Dhvanyālokalocana*] See DhvĀ

MARCHIANÒ AND MILANI 2001
G. Marchianò and R. Milani (eds.), *Frontiers of Transculturality in Contemporary Aesthetics*, Torino: Trauben, 2001

MCCREA 2008
L.J. McCrea, *The Teleology of Poetics in Medieval Kashmir*, Cambridge (Mass.)/London: Harvard University Press, Harvard Oriental Series 71, 2008

NARAYANAN 2002
C. Narayanan, *A Study of Samudrabandha's Commentary on Alaṅkārasarvasva*, Calicut: Publication Division, University of Calicut, 2002

NŚ
Nāṭyaśāstra of Bharatamuni with the Commentary Abhinavabhāratī by Abhinavaguptācārya, ed. M.R. Kavi, Baroda: [1926-1964] Gaekwad's Oriental Series, vol. I, 2nd ed., revised and critically edited by K.S.R. Sastri, 1956; vol. II, 1934; vol. III, 1954; vol. IV, 1964

PATNAKAR 1993
R.B. Patnakar, "Rasānubhava and Brahmānubhava," *Journal of the Asiatic Society of Bombay* 64-66, 1993, pp. 168-178

POLLOCK 2010
S. Pollock, "What was Bhaṭṭa Nāyaka saying? The Hermeneutical Trans-formation of Indian Aesthetics," in S. Pollock (ed.), *Epic and Argument in Indian Literary History. Essays in Honor of Robert P. Goldman*, Delhi: Manohar, 2010, pp. 143-183

POLLOCK 2012
S. Pollock, "Vyakti and the History of Rasa," *Saṃskṛtavimarśaḥ* 6, 2012, pp. 232-253

Śābarabhāṣya
Śābarabhāṣya of Śabara Svāmin, in *Mīmāṃsāsarśana*, ed. K.V. Abhyaṅkara and G.S.A. Joshi, Poona: Ānandāśramasaṃskṛtagranthāvaliḥ, 1970-1976

Sāhityadarpaṇa
Sāhityadarpaṇa of Viśvanātha, ed. Śālagrāma Śāstri, Delhi: Motilal Banarsidass, 1982

TUBB AND BRONNER 2008
G.A. Tubb and Y. Bronner, "*Vastutas tu*: Methodology and the New School of Sanskrit Poetics," *Journal of Indian Philosophy* 36, 2008, pp. 619-632

Vākyapadīya
Vākyapadīya of Bhartṛhari with the Commentaries Vṛtti and the Paddhati of Vṛṣabhadeva. Kāṇḍa I, ed. K.A. Subramania Iyer, Poona, Deccan College Monograph Series 32, 1966

VENUGOPALAN 1977
K. Venugopalan, "Mukula Bhaṭṭa. *Abhidhāvṛttimātṛkā* (Edited and translated)," *Journal of Indian Philosophy* 4, 1977, pp. 203-264

Vyaktiviveka
Vyaktiviveka of Rājānaka Mahimabhaṭṭa and its commentary of Rājānaka Ruyyaka, ed. T.G. Śāstrī, Trivandrum: Travancore Government Press, Trivandrum Sanskrit Series 5, 1909

Vyaktivivekavicāra
See *Vyaktiviveka*

Why Isn't "Comparison" a Means of Knowledge? Bhāsarvajña on *Upamāna**

ELI FRANCO

The inclusion of a paper on Bhāsarvajña's *Nyāyabhūṣaṇa* (hereafter NBhū) in this volume requires a word of justification. The evidence that ties Bhāsarvajña to Kashmir is wafer-thin[1] and in fact we do not know where he lived. On the other hand, there are very close affinities between the NBhū and the *Nyāyamañjarī* (hereafter NM) and thus the relevance of the former to the Nyāya philosophy of Kashmir is undeniable. Further, the NBhū was well known in Kashmir and our oldest manuscript of it, in Śāradā script, comes from the Kashmiri region. Furthermore, Bhāsarvajña's NBhū represents the most thorough response to the Kashmiri Buddhist philosopher Prajñākaragupta. Thus, even if Bhāsarvajña himself was not a Kashmiri, his work certainly played an important role in the region. Last but not least, Bhāsarvajña was known to and referred to by Abhinavagupta.

Bhāsarvajña is one of the most important and most fascinating philosophers of classical India and his magnum opus, the *Nyāyabhūṣaṇa*, deserves far more attention than it has received so far. The work was thought to be lost for a long time and its first (and so far only) edition was published in 1968 by Swami Yogīndrānanda.[2] Since then, only a single book-length study and a handful of papers

---

* I am grateful to my Naiyāyikī, Karin Preisendanz, for several discussions on *upamāna* and the materials presented here.

1 See the discussion in JOSHI 1986, pp. 1-3.

2 The edition is a small miracle. It is based on a single manuscript which the editor was not permitted to consult directly; instead a transcript was prepared for his perusal. The fact that the edition is nevertheless quite readable testifies to the accuracy of the single manuscript, the modern transcript, and the editor's capacity. However, at least two more manuscripts of the text have been discovered and a new edition is certainly a desideratum. Even in the small section translated below, a few significant improvements could be made.

have been devoted to it.[3] This is indeed surprising, for Bhāsarvajña is an unusual figure in the Nyāya tradition inasmuch as he did not hesitate to reject some of the most fundamental doctrines of his tradition. Mostly his new tenets relate to the metaphysics of the Vaiśeṣika. He unified the categories of qualities and motions and reduced the number of qualities[4]; he changed the doctrine of liberation in arguing that *mokṣa* is not a neutral state but a blissful one, and he considered God, time and space to be a single entity. In the area of *pramāṇas,* Bhāsarvajña's most conspicuous departure from the Nyāya tradition is that he accepted only three means of knowledge, perception, inference and verbal communication, and denied *upamāna* an independent status. It is on this rejection of *upamāna* that I would like to expand here today.

Upamāna, often translated as "analogy" or "comparison," is one of the minor means of knowledge. Only three philosophical traditions accepted it as an independent means, that is, assumed that it cannot be included in one of the other means of knowledge or reduced to a combination thereof: Nyāya (but not Vaiśeṣika), Mīmāṃsā and Vedānta. The Vedānta theory merely repeats that of the Mīmāṃsā and thus there are basically only two theories of *upamāna* in

---

3 Potter's bibliography mentions the following: (494.2.1) A. Thakur, "*Nyāyabhūṣaṇa*: a lost work of medieval Indian logic," JBRS 45, 1959, pp. 89-101; (494.2.2) G. Oberhammer, "Der Worterkenntnis bei Bhāsarvajña," Offenbarung, pp. 107-120; (494.2.3) G. Oberhammer, "Bhāsarvajñas Lehre von der Offenbarung," WZKSOA 18, 1974, pp. 131-182; (494.2.4) Summarized by B.K. Matilal, EnIndPh2, 1977, pp. 410-424; (494.2.5) T. Kumare, "*Sakalajagadvidhātranumānam* (I) – the proof of the God Śiva by Bhāsarvajña," JIBSt 28(1), 1979, pp. 7-10; 30(2), 1982, 26-29; (494.2.6) L.V.Joshi, *A Critical Study of the Pratyakṣa Pariccheda of Bhāsarvajña's Nyāyabhūṣaṇa*, Ahmedabad: 1986; (494.2.7) E. Franco, "Bhāsarvajña and Jayarāśi: the refutation of skepticism in the *Nyāyabhūṣaṇa*," BerlinIndStud 3, 1987, pp. 23-50; (494.2.8) P.K. Sen, "Some textual problems in *Nyāyabhūṣaṇa*," Prajnajyoti, pp. 199-205; (494.2.11) P. Haag-Bernede with K. Venugopaladas, "Une vue dissidente sur le nombre: le *Nyāyabhūṣaṇa* de Bhāsarvajña", BEFEO 88, 2001, pp. 125-159. To these and MUROYA 2011, a considerable number of studies in Japanese, notably by Shodo Yamakami, could be added. See http://www.cc.kyotosu.ac.jp/~yamakami/publication. html.

4 He denied that numbers, size (*parimāṇa*), separeteness, disjunction, farness, nearness and impetus (*vega*) are qualities. He also denied that viscosity (*sneha*) belongs to water alone.

classical Indian philosophy, namely, of the Mīmāṃsā[5] and the Nyāya. In the pre-classical period, certain Buddhists, probably of the Sarvāstivāda tradition, also accepted it.[6] However, already Vasubandhu accepted only three means of knowledge (perception, inference, and verbal testimony), and Dignāga, followed by the entire Epistemological Tradition, only two (perception and inference).

The minor position of *upamāna* in philosophical texts can be contrasted with its prominent position in Alaṅkāraśāstra. As GEROW 1971 (p. 140) points out, among the hundred or so known *alaṃkāras*, about half are reducible to a basic simile.[7] One author, Vāmana, even attempted, albeit not convincingly, to reduce all figures involving meaning (*arthālaṅkāra*) to *upamā*. Unlike what one may expect, the reason why *upamāna* was rejected as an independent means of knowledge, or even when accepted, hardly ever used in philosophical discourse, is not that arguments based on analogy or comparison were considered uncertain. Rather, *upamāna* in philosophical texts means something different; it cannot be understood as analogy or comparison in the usual meaning of these terms, and it is, if its definition is followed, quite useless.

Bhāsarvajña's main thesis on *upamāna* is that it is included in verbal communication and thus does not constitute an independent means of knowledge. The discussion is divided into two parts, the first directed against the Mīmāṃsā, the second against the Nyāya. One has to note perhaps that he does not identify his opponents by name or school affiliation, but their identity is clear.

That Bhāsarvajña's first opponent is a Mīmāṃsaka is obvious already from the terms of discussion. For instance, he refers to the division of Vedic sentences into injunctions, narrations and repetitions (*vidhi, arthavāda* and *anuvāda*, NBhū, p. 417, ll. 23-24), uses the typical Mīmāṃsā example for verbal communication (in a context of sacrifice) "Bring fire" (p. 417, l. 24), brings presumption (*arthāpatti*) into play, and mentions the typical Mīmāṃsā pair of terms *niyoga* and *pratiṣedha* (p. 419, l. 12).

Bhāsarvajña presents his argument as a formal inference:[8]

---

5 Within the Mīmāṃsā there is a minor variation on the status of similarity (*sādṛśya*), which according to Prabhākara forms a category in itself.

6 See *Upāyahṛdaya* 13.3-4; see also FRANCO 2004, pp. 486-487.

7 On *upamā* in Alaṅkāraśāstra see also PORCHER 1978, pp. 23-58.

8 NBhū, p. 417, l. 22: *yathā gaus tathā gavaya ity upamānaṃ śabdāntarbhūtaṃ, vākyarūpatvād, agnim ānayetyādivākyavat.*

Thesis: the *upamāna* "the gayal is like a cow" is included in verbal communication (*śabda*),
Reason: because it has the form/nature of a statement,
Example: like the statement "Bring fire."

If the Mīmāṃsaka would claim that the special form of *upamāna* justifies its being considered a separate means of knowledge, the same would apply to the injunctions, narrations, etc., and there would be no end to the number of *pramāṇas*.

Before we consider Bhāsarvajña's argument, it would be useful to take a brief look at the Mīmāṃsā theory of *upamāna*. Śabara himself does not mention *upamāna*. As is the case with other means of knowledge, he contents himself with citing an earlier commentary by an anonymous Vṛttikāra. For the latter too, *upamāna* does not seem to have been a major concern and in the quoted passage it is only briefly defined and illustrated (ŚBh 32.4-5):

> *upamānam api sādṛśyam asannikṛṣṭe 'rthe buddhim utpādayati, yathā gavayadarśanam gosmaraṇasya.*
>
> *Upamāna*, [i.e.] similarity, produces a cognition with respect to an object that is not in contact [with the senses].[9] For instance, seeing a gayal for someone who remembers a cow (*gosmaraṇasya*).

No matter whether *gosmaraṇa* in this sentence is taken as a *bahuvrīhi* or not,[10] it is clear that the word *smaraṇa* posed a problem to the later Mīmāṃsakas, for recollection is not accepted as a means of knowledge. Although it is not quite clear what the Vṛttikāra meant, the later Mīmāṃsā tradition (both Bhāṭṭa and Prābhākara, and the Vedānta as well)[11] is unanimous that he could not have meant that *smaraṇa* simply means recollecting. Kumārila, who is probably[12] Bhāsarvajña's main adversary in this section, gives two interpretations: the object cognized by *upamāna* is either the cow qualified by the similarity to the gayal, or the similarity qualified by the cow.[13]

---

9 Or perhaps: *upamāna* is similarity; it produces a cognition with respect to an object that is not in contact [with the senses].

10 It is not entirely certain that *gosmaraṇa* has to be taken as a *bahuvrīhi*. Thus, one can also translate it "for the recollection of a cow."

11 BHATT 1962, p. 290.

12 Note that the discussion does not follow closely the one in the ŚV. Contrast for instance with the discussion in NM.

13 ŚV, Upamāna 36: *tasmād yat smaryate tat syāt sādṛśyena viśeṣitam | prameyam upamānasya sādṛśyam vā tadanvitam ||*. See also Jha's translation (JHA 1909, p.

Now, the Mīmāṃsakas argue that a cognition which has the form "my cow is similar to this gayal" cannot be subsumed under any other acceptable means of knowledge. It is not perception because the person in the forest who has this cognition cannot perceive his cow at home. Bhāsarvajña is not explicit as to why the opponent considers that the cognition cannot be inference or verbal communication, but this is clear. It cannot be subsumed under inference because is not conditioned by concomitance (*vyāpti*) and so on. Nor does one need a previous verbal communication in order to see the similarity between the two animals. This is, of course, one of the main differences between the Mīmāṃsā and Nyāya theories of *upamāna*.

Thus, the Mīmāṃsā objection against Bhāsarvajña's inclusion of *upamāna* in verbal communication amounts to a denial that the reason "having the form/nature of a statement" occurs in the subject of inference (technically, the inference contains the fallacy *svarūpāsiddha-hetu* or *āśrayāsiddha-hetu*). *Upamāna* is something completely different, as is apparent from the following illustration: someone who owns a cow goes to the forest and encounters a gayal. He sees the similarity of the gayal to his cow, and has the cognition "my cow is similar to this gayal." Verbal communication plays no role in this example.

Bhāsarvajña rejects the Mīmāṃsā claim at first appearance by a surprising move. The cognition "the cow is similar to this gayal" was experienced before and is therefore nothing but recollection. And of course recollection cannot be the result of a means of knowledge. This point is generally accepted,[14] but the Mīmāṃsakas are especially sensitive to it because of its ramifications to the relationship between *smṛti* and *śruti*.

The opponent retorts that the cow was seen, but the similarity[15] between the two was not seen before. However, this is precisely what Bhāsarvajña claims. The cow was already perceived with its similarity to a gayal (even before the gayal was seen!) because this similarity is something visible (i.e., a visible property of the cow).

227).

14 The only philosophical tradition that admits memory as means of knowledge is that of the Jainas.

15 This clearly refers to the definition of *upamāna* in ŚV, Upamāna 36 quoted above.

Or if it were not visible, it would never be perceived, even after the gayal is seen.

Further, the reverse cognition (i.e., the *upamāna* as means) is also produced: "This gayal is similar to my cow." But such a cognition is not produced by the sense faculty alone or assisted by a recollection of any old thing. So there must be something already perceived in the cow that triggers its recollection when the gayal is seen. If the Mīmāṃsaka admits that the *upamāna* is produced by a sense faculty assisted by a recollection of something specific, he must admit that the cow was seen as similar to a gayal. Otherwise one would not recollect the cow rather than, say, a buffalo. The recollection presupposes that something specific was perceived in the cow which was not perceived in buffaloes, etc. So the similarity to the gayal was perceived before. Thus, both *upamāna* (the gayal is similar to the cow) and *upamiti* (the cow is similar to the gayal) are rejected as recollection.

But how is it possible to perceive the similarity to the gayal before perceiving the gayal itself?

It is possible because this perception does not mean that one can ascertain the similarity to a gayal. Rather, when the cow is perceived for the first time by a non-conceptual cognition, that is, in an undifferentiated manner, its similarity to the gayal is also perceived, more precisely, what is later called the similarity to a gayal is also perceived, we would say intuitively, just as the universal cow-ness is perceived when seeing a cow for the first time (even though it can only be ascertained upon the perception of further individuals of the same species).

The upshot of the argument is this: similarity means to have a common property, and this (exact same) common property resides in both the cow and the gayal. Therefore, even though the gayal itself is seen for the first time, its similarity to the cow is not perceived for the first time because it was perceived when the cow was perceived. Thus, its similarity is recollected. Bhāsarvajña construes an analogous case to the perception of universals. Once the universal cow-ness or bovinity is seen, even when an individual cow is seen for the first time, the bovinity that resides in it cannot be said to be perceived for the first time because it was perceived before in other cows (otherwise one would not recognize the cow as cow).[16]

---

[16] In other words, when one sees a cow etc., for the first time, one perceives the

The opponent continues: the cognition that qualifies[17] the gayal, "the cow is similar to it,"[18] cannot be a recollection because it arises for the first time when the gayal is seen. Otherwise the conceptual cognition (which associates a perceived individual with a concept) would also be recollection.

Bhāsarvajña replies that this cognition can be proved by two other means of knowledge: *arthāpatti* and inference.

The proof by *arthāpatti* (NBhū, p. 418, l. 23) is this: if the cow were not similar to this gayal, it would not have been perceived as similar to it because the similarity resides in both. But the gayal is perceived as similar to the cow, therefore, the cow too is similar to it.[19]

Bhāsarvajña also formulates an inference to the same effect that could have been lifted straight from a Navya Nyāya text:

> The cow is similar to this gayal because the gayal is delimited by the similarity of the cow. (NBhū, p. 418, l. 26: *prayogo 'pi: anena sadṛśī gauḥ, svasādṛśyenāsyāvacchedakatvāt.*)
>
> *Vyāpti*: whatever A delimits B by its own similarity (i.e., by the similarity of A), that A is seen as similar to B, for instance, one brother to another. (NBhū, p. 418, l. 27: *yat svasādṛśyena yasyāvacchedakaṃ, tat tena sadṛśaṃ dṛṣṭaṃ, yathā bhrātrā bhrātrantaram.*)

A complicated statement, but trivial when understood. It amounts to an assertion that if A and B share a common property, that property resides also in B.

Further, if a different *pramāṇa* is assumed for such a case, this will lead to the assumption of an indefinite number of *pramāṇas*. Consider the following cognition: "Something seen before is longer

---

universal cow-ness too, but one is not aware of it as such. However, after perceiving further cows, one becomes aware of it as well as of the fact that it was already seen when perceiving the first individual cow.

17 The qualification is understood to be already verbal/conceptual. In *nirvikalpaka-pratyakṣa* the differentiation between the qualified and the qualifications is not yet done.

18 Should one expect, "the gayal is similar to the cow"? According to Bhāsarvajña, this same content can be a qualification of the cow or the gayal.

19 I am not sure about the purpose of this statement. Perhaps Bhāsarvajña tries to show that both *pramāṇas* make *upamāna* superfluous.

than this object seen now."[20] This cognition is not *upamāna* because its object is not similarity. Nor is it perception, inference, etc., for the same reasons that the opponent refuses to subsume *upamāna* in them. Thus, a further *pramāṇa* would have to be assumed for such cognitions. This example is important because it clearly shows that the translation of *upamāna* as comparison is inaccurate.

When someone is asked, "how do you know that the cow that is at home is similar to the gayal present here?", he answers: "I saw the cow before by perception." For the same reason cognitions such as "this is bigger than that" should be considered as recollections, that is, because the size was perceived before, albeit in a non-differentiated manner by a non-conceptual cognition.

A final attempt is made by the Mīmāṃsaka to save his position by pointing out that inasmuch as the recollection imitates the experience, one cannot have a conceptual recollection on the basis of a non-conceptual and non-differentiated experience. But Bhāsarvajña denies that. One observes that conceptual recollection arises also from non-conceptual experience. (Although it is not stated here, recollection is generally considered to be always conceptual). That's the way things are and one cannot forbid them to be so.

This concludes Bhāsarvajña's arguments against the Mīmāṃsā. He now turns to his main or more important adversary, the Nyāya. The Nyāya defines the object, i.e., the result, of *upamāna* as the cognition of the relation between a term and a designated object (*saṃjñāsaṃjñisambandha*). Consider the following situation: one learns that for a certain sacrifice a gayal is required. The person who wants to obtain this animal hears a forest inhabitant saying: "The gayal is like a cow," and goes to the forest to look for a gayal. He sees an animal similar to a cow, but with a round neck, i.e., without the dewlap, and understands: "This is a gayal." In the same manner, someone is sent to the forest by a physician to bring some medicinal plants he has never seen before and is told for instance, "the plant called pea-leafed (*māṣaparṇī*) is like the sheaf of peas."[21] One goes to the forest, finds the plant and brings it to the physician. So *upamāna* as means is the cognition of similarity produced by a sense

---

20 Cf. NBhū, p. 418, ll. 28-29: *pūrvadṛṣṭaṃ vastu etasmāt sthūlam, etasmād dīrgham, etasmād hrasvam.*

21 I am not sure what the word *stamba* in NBhū, p. 419, l. 18 means. A similar example appears in NBh on 1.1.6., but the word *stamba* does not appear in it.

faculty, assisted by recollection produced by mnemonic traces, produced by a cognition, produced by a statement (NBhū, p. 419, ll. 20-21): *vākyajajñānajanitasaṃskārajanitasmṛtisahakāriṇendriyeṇa janitaṃ sārūpyajñānam upamānam*).[22] The result (*phala*) of *upamāna*, as just mentioned, is the cognition of the relation between a word or a term and the object it designates.

But that is not correct, says Bhāsarvajña. The relation between a term and a designated object is known from the moment one hears the statement. When the gayal is seen, the relation is only remembered. Again, if asked "How do you know that this is a gayal?", one would answer: "I understood it from the statement of the forester." One would not answer: I know it from *upamāna*. In everyday practice we see only three *pramāṇas* being used, for instance, "I see a pot by perception," "I infer fire from smoke" and "I know about heaven from sacred writings." One never sees anyonc saying "I know this by *upamāna*." Indeed, one should add here, that in philosophical texts too, *upamāna* is, to my knowledge, never used. I'll return to this point below.

Now, the opponent argucs, of course, that as long as the gayal is not seen, the relation between the term and the designated object is not perceived or understood (for one cannot perceive a relation, if one of the relata is not perceived). That, says Bhāsarvajña, is simply not true. For instance, one apprehends a relation between an invisible god like Indra and his name Śakra. Another example: one can name a child before it is born.

Now the Naiyāyika objects that in these examples there is a cause of linguistic understanding (I understand *nimitta* here as in *vyutpattinimitta*) which allows the understanding of a term such as "thousand-eyes" in respect to Indra, but this is not the case for gayals etc.

Bhāsarvajña retorts that in such cases too there is a *nimitta*, namely, the similarity to the cow. The word "gayal" (*gavaya*) is understood by having recourse to a *nimitta*, namely, the similarity to the cow.

The opponent objects that the similarity is not the *nimitta*. Rather gayal-ness or being a gayal (*gavayatva*) is the *nimitta* for the usage (*pravṛtti*) of the term gayal. When the latter is not apprehended, one cannot use the term.

---

22 This seems like a modification of Vātsyāyana's statement in NBh, for whom *upamāna* seems to be the statement.

Bhāsarvajña retorts that this is not a problem because the gayalness too is understood from the statement that the gayal is similar to a cow. For instance, by showing a form in a picture, someone can explain: this is a camel, this is an elephant, and so forth. Or one can explain by words. One can explain a camel by saying that his neck has a special form and so forth, an elephant by saying that it has special teeth, and so on. Thus, from words alone one can understand the camel-ness and elephant-ness. When explaining the words camel and elephant by means of neck, teeth, etc., one can make them known, and no other means of knowledge is possible in this case.

Now, the Naiyāyika has to consent to that, but objects that the cognition that arises from a statement is afflicted, *upapluta*. This is a rather unusual term, but interestingly also used by Jayanta in the NM in the same context.[23] However, we cannot assume that Bhāsarvajña refers to Jayanta. It seems rather that both use the same earlier source, undoubtedly lost now, Jayanta adopting it, Bhāsarvajña rejecting it. It is also clear that the relationship between the cognition that arises from the statement and the one that arises when seeing the gayal was perceived as a problem before Bhāsarvajña and Jayanta dealt with it, and one of the former Naiyāyikas must have suggested that the cognition based on the verbal communication is in some way defective or flawed, and that it becomes "corrected" only upon the actual seeing of the individual. Only when the relation between the term and the object is apprehended from *upamāna*, it is established in respect to a particular individual and the cognition stops being "afflicted."

But what could this affliction be?[24] It is not the falsity of cognition, because the cognition is not false. Nor is it a doubt, because the cognition does not take the form of an alternative such as "is it a man or a pillar?". As the cognition "the gayal is similar to a cow" is actually a *pramāṇa*, there can be no affliction. The fact that the cognition is not related to an individual animal cannot be considered an affliction. Otherwise, the cognition of the fundamental entities of the Nyāya-Vaiśeṣika, which are known only from inference or sacred

---

[23] E.g. NM, vol. I, p. 389: *yathā naiyāyikānām atideśavākyavelāyāṃ sopaplavā saṃjñāsaṃjñisamandhabuddhir upamānān nirupaplavībhavati*... On *upamāna* in the NM see also BIJALWAN 1977, pp. 187-213.

[24] As far as I understand, the "affliction" is a somewhat metaphorical way to say that the cognition based on verbal communication is not as clear and distinct (*vispaṣṭa*, cf. NM, vol. I, p. 379, l. 2) as the one that arises when the gayal is in front of one's eyes.

writings, would be afflicted, for instance, the Self, the mind (*manas*), *dharma* and *adharma*, and so on. They too are not related to an individual entity perceived by the faculty of vision, for instance, the Self is that in which desires inhere; the atom is the smallest thing; the mind exists because two cognitions do not arise at the same time.

Bhāsarvajña looks at the problem from another perspective. What is the difference between *upamāna* and a convention (*saṃketa*) that a certain word designates a certain object (i.e., when one learns the word gayal for the first time)? The Naiyāyika opponent agrees that when there is a verbal convention, the *upamāna*, i.e., the statement on the similarity, is not a different *pramāṇa* (i.e., is included in *śabda*).[25] In the convention one says "the gayal is that in which there is similarity to a cow[26]; the term gayal [is used] for that [animal]." However, when one hears "the gayal is like a cow," mere similarity is perceived, not the relation of the term with the designated object.[27] For this reason *upamāna* is accepted as having this relation as its object.

The argument seems almost gratuitous. Bhāsarvajña says that if the relation is not perceived from the statement, the statement is superfluous. Mere similarity is perceived even by someone who does not hear the statement.[28] Therefore, one and the same thing is perceived in statements such as "the gayal is similar to a cow," "such an animal is called gayal," or "the term gayal is used for such an animal." Otherwise one would need two different *pramāṇas* when saying in *saṃketa* "this is a cow" and "the word cow is used for this animal."

---

[25] The convention here seems to be done without seeing the animal. The term *saṃketa* is usually used for the initial agreement, often attributed to God or the Rishis, which fixes the usage of words. But here it seems to refer to a situation where one learns a new word.

[26] Of course, *saṃketa* usually does not involve similarity, but a direct indication: this word designates that object present here.

[27] It is not clear to me what the difference, if any, should be between the two formulations: *yatra gosādṛśyam asti sa gavayaḥ*, and *yādṛśo gaus tādṛśo gavayaḥ*. The first formulation looks more like a definition, but since the definition is based on similarity, it is not clear why the opponent claims that in the one case *upamāna* is not another *pramāṇa* and in the other it is. Perhaps what the opponent means is that in *saṃketa*, in addition to the statement of similarity, there is also a statement about the word applying to its object, and that this additional element is lacking in *upamāna*.

[28] Indeed for the Mīmāṃsaka hearing the statement is not necessary for *upamāna*; cf. above.

One may object: when one understands in the forest that the word gayal is the term for this animal, one perceives an individual. Before that, the perception of the individual does not arise. But if so, one would not be able to apply the convention to further individuals of the same species, and a new *pramāṇa* would have to be assumed each time a new individual cow is recognized. But this is not the case. Even without saying it in so many words, the speaker intends and the hearer understands that the word cow is applied to every such individual.

The opponent attempts to save his position by claiming that this is understood by implication (*sāmarthya*). But the same would apply to the so-called *upamāna*. One says that the gayal is similar to a cow and one understands by implication that the term gayal applies to such an animal. Even when what is said explicitly differs from the intention, one understands from the context what is meant. For instance, sayings "eat poison; don't eat at his house." One understands that this is not an invitation to eat poison, but a warning that eating in that house is to be avoided at all costs. In the same manner, even though it is not explicitly stated, when one says that the gayal is similar to a cow, one also understands that the word gayal designates an object similar to a cow.

This brings to a close Bhāsarvajña's arguments against *upamāna*. His next task is to show that the Sūtrakāra also did not accept *upamāna* as *pramāṇa*, in spite of very clear statements to the contrary. But I will not go into that here.

Bhāsarvajña's argument against the Nyāya and Mīmāṃsā is basically the same: in both cases *upamāna* and its result are nothing but recollection, that is, a mere repetition of a previous experience. As the theories of the two schools differ, so do the relevant recollections. For the Mīmāṃsā it is a recollection of a previous perception, for the Nyāya of a statement by a trustworthy person. But in both cases, Bhāsarvajña claims, they bring nothing new. It seems to me that we have to agree with this opinion as far as the Mīmāṃsā is concerned. It is less obvious about the Nyāya.[29]

For the Mīmāṃsā, as we have seen, *upamāna* is reduced to a trivial inference based on the reversibility of the relation of similarity,

[29] This is not necessarily Bhāsarvajña's original opinion. He certainly relies on Mīmāṃsā arguments against the Nyāya and vice versa. Since this is often the case, and given that most philosophical texts of classical India are lost, the original contribution of individual authors is difficult to ascertain.

namely, if A is similar to B, B is similar to A. The perception of the similarity of the gayal to the cow brings about the apprehension that the cow is similar to the gayal. Our understanding of the Mīmāṃsā *upamāna* as a trivial inversion is hardly new. As Govardhan Bhatt has pointed out in his foundational study of Kumārila (BHATT 1962, pp. 294, 304): "In Mīmāṃsā *upamāna* is a form of immediate inference in which from the similarity of A to B we infer the similarity of B to A. [...] The conclusion 'the cow is similar to the *gavaya*' follows from a single premise, viz. 'the *gavaya* is similar to the cow'[...]." Hardly something to write home about. And it is clear that *upamāna* cannot be translated as an "analogy" or "comparison" in this context; indeed Bhatt leaves it untranslated throughout the discussion.

When we come to the Nyāya theory of *upamāna*, things do not look much brighter. For the Nyāya, *upamāna* has to do with an identification of an object, but it is identification under extremely narrow conditions. It has to be based on a statement by a reliable person, the statement has to express similarity between two objects, one of the objects has to be unknown, and the identification should consist in relating a certain word to that unknown object.[30] Furthermore, even though it is not stated explicitly, there is some evidence to suggest that the object has to belong to an unknown species.[31] In other words, if I point out to the way to identify Yigal to someone who has never seen him before, by saying "Yigal is similar to Clark Gable," that would not count as *upamāna*, because the species of being human has already been seen by that person. But even if we ignore such doubtful cases, it is clear that the requirements of *upamāna* make extreme restrictions on its use as identification. It is for this reason that Uddyotakara suggested that dissimilarity[32] too should be included in *upamāna*.

---

30 That the identification is required to be based on similarity clearly limits its use, and in fact leads to unreasonable distinctions. If I say, for instance, the plant whose leafs form perfect triangles is called X, that would not count as *upamāna*. I would have to say "the plant whose leafs are like the perfect triangles that you see here." Further, an identification can also be done by having recourse to dissimilarity and other means. These too cannot count as *upamāna*. To avoid this corset, some have attempted to include "dissimilarity" under similarity. See BHATT 1962, p. 297.

31 Cf. ŚV, Upamāna 13.

32 That is, when one is informed: A is dissimilar (or in some respect opposite) to B.

The story of *upamāna* in philosophical literature is a sad one. Even the few schools that accepted it trivialized it and narrowed its scope to such an extent as to make it useless. It is, therefore, not surprising that *upamāna* was never actually used in the Indian philosophical discourse; at least I cannot recall even a single case. When Kumārila once attempted to show that *upamāna*, in the true sense of analogy, could actually be used in reasoning about Vedic ritual, the Naiyāyikas were quick to point out that such a usage of *upamāna* goes well beyond its definition (see NM, vol. I, pp. 392-395, see also BHATT 1962, p. 307). To use Bhatt's example again (ibid., p. 308), from the fact that I perceive a woman to be similar to my wife, I can conclude by *upamāna* that my wife is also similar to her, but I cannot conclude that I can use that woman as a substitute to my wife.

In trivialising *upamāna* and taking it away from its original meaning of analogy and comparison, Indian philosophy deprived itself of a most powerful tool of thought. We all know how persuasive analogies and comparisons can be. We know how a new example can open up a stilted discussion, give it a new perspective, lead to unexpected developments, or make things vivid and accessible (think of Plato's cave or Wittgenstein's family resemblance[33] or Chuang Tzu's butterfly and fish, or, to take at least one example of the Indian tradition, Dharmakīti's glow of the jewel through the keyhole[34]).

Of course, it is not the failure to develop *upamāna* into a significant means of knowledge that can account for the poverty of examples in Indian philosophy (examples in inference are not really examples, but instantiations of the property to be proved; they require neither creativity nor imagination, and indeed some logicians maintain that they are superfluous and argue that they should not be stated). But perhaps had it been developed, it could have facilitated the development of philosophy in India in more original directions. Actually, the treatment of *upamāna* itself is symptomatic to a more general avoidance in the Indian philosophical tradition of using new examples. It is disconcerting to observe that the example of the cow

---

33 To respond to a question by one of the participants in the conference, the example of the two brothers above has nothing to do with Wittgenstein's family resemblance.

34 On the way this example prompted Śākyabuddhi to further philosophical developments see FRANCO 2014, pp. 22-23.

and the gayal appears already in relation to *upamāna* in the *Mahābhāṣya* of Patañjali,[35] and it is being repeated literally for more than two thousand years, while further examples are hardly ever mentioned or thought about seriously. And there is no doubt that the thinking always along the lines of this single example of the cow and the gayal has not facilitated creative philosophical developments. In addition, the adherence to the old definitions in the *Nyāyasūtra* or *Śābarabhāṣya*, that are clearly inappropriate to capture the breadth of comparisons and analogies, has further contributed to a reduction of the scope of *upamāna* and prevented its interpretation and development as real analogy or comparison. Perhaps the most regrettable point in relying on these definitions is that they prevented many employments of analogies or comparisons in respect to well-known things, but nevertheless expressing something genuinely new, unexpected, illuminating a subject matter from a different perspective. This does not mean of course that Indian philosophers have, in practice, forgone analogies altogether, but they certainly used them to a smaller degree than in European and Chinese philosophy, and a theoretical reflection about them has not been developed.[36] The Ālaṅkārikas have far surpassed them in their insightful analysis of analogy.

REFERENCES

BIJALWAN 1977

C.D. Bijalwan, *Indian Theories of Knowledge, based upon Jayanta's Nyāyamañjarī*, Delhi, 1977

BHATT 1962

G.P. Bhatt, *Epistemology of the Bhāṭṭa school of Pūrva Mīmāṃsā*, Vārāṇasī: Chowkhamba Sanskrit Series Office, 1962

FRANCO 1987

E. Franco, "Bhāsarvajña and Jayarāśi: the refutation of skepticism in the *Nyāyabhūṣaṇa*," *Berliner Indologische Studien* 3, 1987, pp. 23-50

FRANCO 2004

E. Franco, *The Spitzer Manuscript – The Oldest Philosophical Manuscript in Sanskrit*, Wien: Österreichischen Akademie der Wissenschaften, 2004

---

35 See also OBERHAMMER ET AL. 1991-2006, s.v. *upamāna*.

36 Interestingly, the fallacy of tu quoque, known also as the douchebag fallacy (i.e., I can be an idiot because you are an idiot), is not seldom used in Indian texts and to my knowledge has not been recognized as false.

FRANCO 2014
E. Franco, "Introduction," in E. Franco and M. Notake, *Dharmakīrti on the Duality of the Object. Pramāṇavārttika III 1-63*, Berlin: 2014

GEROW 1971
E. Gerow, *A Glossary of Indian Figures of Speech*, The Hague-Paris: Mouton, 1971

JHA 1909
G. Jha, *Mīmāṃsāslokavārtika, translated from the original Sanskrit with extracts from the commentaries of Sucarita Miśra (the Kāśikā) and Pārthasārathi Miśra (the Nyāyaratnākara)*, Calcutta: Asiatic Society, 1909

JOSHI 1986
L.V. Joshi, *A Critical Study of the Pratyakṣa Pariccheda of Bhāsarvajña's Nyāyabhūṣaṇa*, Ahmedabad, 1986

MUROYA 2011
Y. Muroya, "Bhāsarvajña's interpretation of *bhāva eva nāśaḥ* and a related chronological problem," in H. Krasser, H. Lasic, E. Franco and B. Kellner (eds.), *Religion and Logic in Buddhist Philosophical Analysis. Proceedings of the Fourth International Dharmakīrti Conference, Vienna, August 23-27, 2005*, Wien: Verlag der österreichischen Akademie der Wissenschaften, 2011, pp. 341-361

NBh
Nyāyadarśana. Gautamīyanyāyadarśana with Bhāṣya of Vātsyāyana, ed. A. Thakur, Delhi: Indian Council of Philosophical Research, 1997

NBhū
Nyāyabhūṣaṇa of Bhāsarvajña, ed. Yogīndrananda, Vārāṇasī: 1968

NM
Nyāyamañjarī of Jayanta, with editor's *Nyāyasaurabha*, ed. K.S. Varadacarya, 2 vols., Mysore: 1969-1983

OBERHAMMER ET AL. 1991-2006
G. Oberhammer et al., *Terminologie der frühen philosophischen Scholastik in Indien*, 3 vols., Wien: Verlag der Österreichischen Akademie der Wissenschaften, 1991-2006

PORCHER 1978
M.-C. Porcher, *Figures de style en sanskrit*, Paris: 1978

Potter, Bibliography
K.H. Potter, *Bibliography of Indian Philosophies*, available online at http://faculty.washington.edu/kpotter/ckeyt/home.htm

ŚBh
[*Śābarabhāṣya*, in] E. Frauwallner, *Materialien zur ältesten Erkenntnislehre der Karmamīmāṃsā*, Wien: Verlag der Österreichischen Akademie der Wissenschaften, 1968

ŚV
Ślokavārttika of Kumārila, ed. D. Śāstrī, Vārāṇasī: 1978

Upāyahṛdaya
[*Upāyahṛdaya*, in] G. Tucci, *Pre-Diṅnāga Buddhist Texts on Logic from Chinese Sources*, Baroda: Oriental Institute, 1929

Elements of Ritual Speculation in the *Abhinavabhāratī*: Abhinavagupta on the Visible and Invisible Purposes of the *Pūrvaraṅga*[*]

ELISA GANSER

INTRODUCTION, OR WHY THEATRE CANNOT BE EASILY REDUCED TO A LITERARY WORK

As far as Abhinavagupta's aesthetic theory is concerned, both the *Dhvanyālokalocana* and the *Abhinavabhāratī* (end of the tenth/beginning of the eleventh c.) have been privileged grounds of enquiry in modern scholarship over the past century.[1] In the *Locana*, Abhinavagupta examines the aesthetic process taking place through the medium of poetry, while in the *Abhinavabhāratī* (henceforth ABh) this process has been analyzed taking into account the dramatic medium. This last includes not only the text of the play, but the whole array of spectacular devices and arts ancillary to theatre. In both cases – poetry and drama – the final aim of the work of art is to provoke an aesthetic experience in the reader or spectator, namely the savouring of the *rasa*, the "flavour" or "essence" of the literary

* This article is an outcome of the project "Theatre and ritual in Abhinavagupta's *Abhinavabhāratī*," started in Paris at the École Pratique des Hautes Études (Section des sciences religieuses). Drafts of this paper in its different stages have been carried out with the generous support of the Gonda Foundation in Leiden, as well as of the URPP Asia and Europe, University of Zürich. I wish to express my gratitude to Lyne Bansat-Boudon, Daniele Cuneo, Hugo David, Robert Leach, Angelika Malinar, and the participants of Research Field 1 of the URPP Asia and Europe, for their criticism and feedback on earlier drafts of this paper. Many thanks also to the editors, Eli Franco and Isabelle Ratié, for their careful reading and insightful comments.

1 Among seminal studies on Abhinavagupta's aesthetic theory one may recall DE 1922, MUKHERJEE 1926, RAGHAVAN 1940, GNOLI 1956, MASSON AND PATWARDHAN 1970, INGALLS ET AL. 1990, BANSAT-BOUDON 1992, MCCREA 2008 and CUNEO 2009.

work.[2] Originally the object of two distinct intellectual disciplines or "sciences" (*śāstra*), the "Science of Poetic Ornaments" (Alaṃkāraśāstra), or poetics, and the "Science of Theatre" (Nāṭyaśāstra), or dramaturgy, the two art forms of poetry and drama started to merge in the work of Vāmana (beginning of the ninth c.), and were finally conflated into a single theory of the literary text with Ānandavardhana (second half of the ninth c.). Confined to its literary dimension, theatre began to be treated in the scholarly treatises like a poetic text (*kāvya*). As a consequence, excerpts from the famous medieval plays began to be counted among the repertoire of poetic examples. Poetry, which had until then been the object of formal analysis in the work of the first Ālaṃkārikas, came to be attributed with the capacity, formerly exclusive to theatre, of provoking one of the eight (or nine) aestheticized emotions (*rasa*) in its reader.[3]

The new approach to literary theory inaugurated by Ānandavardhana brought poetry and drama together as part of the same literary discourse centred on *rasa*, and superseded the old model of formalist poetics. As convincingly argued by MCCREA 2008, this presupposed the application of a model of text analysis originally extraneous to Alaṃkāraśāstra. It incorporated, namely, the theory developed in Vedic exegesis (Mīmāṃsā) according to which a text (paradigmatically the Veda) must have a single overriding purpose around which the other components are hierarchically arranged. *Rasa* was recognized as the single overriding goal of poetry by Ānandavardhana and his epigones. Such a way of interpreting a text, which McCrea calls "teleological text analysis," entails that the role of every poetic sentence, literary figure or dramatic segment, must be reassessed in terms of its subordination to the realization of the main *rasa* of the literary composition, be it a poem or a play.[4]

---

2 The eight *rasas* first canonized in the *Nāṭyaśāstra* (henceforth NŚ) are the amorous (*śṛṅgāra*), the comic (*hāsya*), the pathetic (*karuṇa*), the furious (*raudra*), the heroic (*vīra*), the fearsome (*bhayānaka*), the loathsome (*bībhatsa*) and the wondrous (*adbhuta*). To these eight the later tradition adds a ninth flavour, the pacified (*śānta*). On the shift of the meaning of *rasa* from "flavour" to "essence," see CUNEO 2013.

3 On the two opposed models of literary analysis and their conflation in the work of Ānandavardhana, see MCCREA 2008, pp. 99ff.

4 For the Vedic exegetes, this single and overriding goal was to convey, through the Vedic text, an injunction (*codanā*) to undertake a sacrifice, accompanied by other subordinated injunctions describing its details.

This process reached its culmination in Alaṃkāraśāstra with Abhinavagupta's sub-commentary on Ānandavardhana's *Dhvanyāloka* (henceforth DhĀ), called the *Locana*. In Nāṭyaśāstra, the "teleological" analysis of the various components of a theatrical representation, as helpers in conveying a given *rasa* to the spectator, was brought to an end with the ABh.[5] The ABh is the last extant commentary on the whole of Bharata's NŚ, the seminal text on dramatic theory composed around the beginning of the Common Era. It knows no rivals in the breadth of the topics it combines into a unified coherent theory: its topics range from the composition of the dramatic text, its representation by means of the various arts ancillary to theatre, i.e. histrionics (*abhinaya*), instrumental music (*vādya*), vocal music (*gīta*) and dance (*nṛtta*), its aesthetic appreciation, up to the series of preliminary actions that precede every performance of a play (*pūrvaraṅga*). Abhinavagupta's approach to the work of art in his two major theoretical texts on literary criticism may be considered along the same paradigm: the teleological model of text interpretation, first devised by the Mīmāṃsakas and later applied by Ānandavardhana to the poetic or dramatic work, made it necessary to rethink the features of a poem or a play as fitting into the new model. But while most of the elements of a dramatic performance could be straightforwardly analyzed in connection with the main *rasa* of the work, just like in poetry, a certain number of theatrical components could be less easily subsumed under a strict *rasa*-oriented scheme.

In the work of the Kashmiri Ālaṃkārikas starting with Ānandavardhana, in effect, the *rasa* is conceived primarily as a literary category: it is a meaning, i.e. the meaning which is the very "soul" or essence of a poetic text,[6] an uncommon meaning communicated through a specific function of language called *vyañjanā*, "suggestion." Translated into theatrical terms, this means that the *rasa* is first of all the concern of the playwright: the depiction of the characters, the conception of the plot-structure with its principal and

---

5 Already in Bharata's NŚ (first centuries AD?) many elements are organized around *rasa*s and *bhāva*s as the factors lending cohesion to the various dramatic elements and techniques of representation forming a play, but as the theory of *rasa* evolved into a clear "reception theory" some of the tenets of the NŚ had to be re-interpreted to suit the new paradigm. On this shift, see POLLOCK 2010. For a plea for caution in the interpretation of Bharata's *rasa*, see CUNEO 2013, p. 59, n. 28.

6 See DhĀ 1.5: *kāvyāsyātmā sa evārtha*, and *Vṛtti*.

secondary articulations – the *sandhis* and *sandhyaṅgas* to which I shall return later – the choice of the poetic embellishments including a repertoire of figures of speech, all of which is analyzed in poetics and in dramatics for the sake of the poet's instruction.

Despite the primary importance it enjoys in conveying the *rasa*, the dramatic text is but a part of the whole process that a theatrical production entails, for the theatrical process is much more complex than the poetical one: it consists of a mixture of different arts, each of which exists independently even outside of the theatre; it involves a plurality of agents acting at different times and pursuing different aims; it has to appeal to a variety of spectators through its universalistic character.[7] Moreover, not all of the elements involved in a theatrical production participate in the literary process, or can even boast of a discursive nature.[8] Dance and instrumental music, for instance, are non-linguistic in character, and yet they may appear at times so closely intermingled with a poetic text as to give the impression that they communicate a certain emotional meaning, as if they were a second language, or a poetic embellishment. In reality, as Abhinavagupta puts it in the case of dancing, it is only metaphorically that we can attribute some meaning to dance,[9] its main purpose in the performance being to charm the audience and thus aid

---

7 While poetry is, according to the *Locana*, an activity which involves a high degree of literary cultivation through the assiduous study of poetic compositions, an activity reserved, therefore, to a restricted circle of connoisseurs or sensitive readers (*sahṛdaya*, "those endowed with heart"), theatre is regarded since its beginnings, and at least in theory, as an art equally accessible to the members of the highest classes, as well as to those less exposed to Sanskrit education, including women, children and the feeble-minded (*strībālamūrkha°*, cf. NŚ 34.222).

8 This is not to say that the oral or performative dimension of poetry was not taken into account by Ānandavardhana, just as it had not been neglected by the earlier Ālaṃkarikas who dealt with both the "embellishments of speech" (*śabdālaṃkāra*), such as alliteration and the like, and the "embellishments of meaning" (*arthālaṃkāra*), such as metaphor, simile, etc. However, this distinction between prosodic and semantic features had no special role to play for Indian theoreticians in the critical evaluation of poetry, neither according to the earlier criterion of poetic beauty, nor in the *rasa*-focused analysis fostered by Ānandavardhana.

9 See ABh ad NŚ 4.261bc-263ab, vol. I, p. 176: *kalahāntariteyaṃ khaṇḍiteyaṃ nṛtyatīti vyavahāra aupacārikaḥ, tadarthagīyamānarūpakagatagītavādyānusāritvāt tannṛttasya.* "The common way of saying that 'this distanced woman (*kalahāntaritā*), [or] this deceived woman (*khaṇḍitā*), is dancing' is metaphorical, since her dance [merely] follows the vocal and instrumental music inherent in

the appreciation of the *rasa*.[10] Through similar interpretative procedures, non-linguistic elements or elements exclusively belonging to (in L. Bansat-Boudon's words[11]) the "spectacular dimension" of theatre, can fruitfully be connected to the overall goal of the performance.

In other phases of the theatrical spectacle, however, the same elements look totally unconnected to the dramatic text and to its emotional core. Think, in particular, of the series of songs and ritual actions, the execution of which the theory prescribes before the performance of each and every play, in order to propitiate the deities and thus ensure the success of the performance. How can one account for these disparate elements as being part of one and the same "expressive" unit, i.e. the theatrical performance, especially when this unit is thought to have a single goal, i.e. the *rasa*, which is linguistic in nature? The present article is an attempt to uncover some of the interpretative strategies devised by Abhinavagupta in order to address this complex issue. Its main focus will be the preliminaries that take place in India before the performance of a play, collectively called "*pūrvaraṅga*." The *pūrvaraṅga* offers a particularly good example by which to illustrate the challenge posed by the analysis of theatre as part of a larger literary discourse – a discourse that had already partly adopted and adapted a model developed by ritual exegetes – for three reasons: first, because it was conceptualized since the first definitions of the NŚ as a ritual, i.e. the worship (*pūjā*) of the deities of the stage;[12] second, because it comprises a series of operations that are not easily connected to the rest of the performance; and third, because it does not appear in the text of the transmitted plays but is the exclusive work of theatre practitioners.

---

the sung composition having such a meaning." On dance and its role in conveying meaning "figuratively" or "by reflection," see BANSAT-BOUDON 1992, pp. 399-404 and BANSAT-BOUDON 2004, pp. 193-198, and n. 57.

[10] I have dealt in detail with the function of dance within the aesthetic process taking place through a dramatic performance in a previous article (GANSER 2013).

[11] See, for instance, BANSAT-BOUDON 1992, p. 9.

[12] See for instance NŚ 5.55: *sarvadaivatapūjārhaṃ sarvadaivatapūjanam | dhanyaṃ yaśasyam āyuṣyaṃ pūrvaraṅgapravartanam ||*. "The execution of the *pūrvaraṅga*, the worship of all the deities, which deserves to be worshipped by all the deities, bestows wealth, confers renown and ensures a long life." (I am following the ABh in my reading of the first compound, cf. ABh ad NŚ 5.55, vol. I, p. 225: *sarvair daivataiḥ pūjārhaṃ praśaṃsanīyam*).

THE *PŪRVARAṄGA*: RITUAL THEATRE OR THEATRICAL RITUAL?

The study of the *pūrvaraṅga* has been marked, in modern scholarship, by a recurring concern with the origins of Indian theatre: the rituals that are described by Bharata in the *pūrvaraṅga* chapter of the NŚ in fact betray, according to some, the ritual origins of the dramatic art. No doubt, the *pūrvaraṅga* displays a strong ritual character, which has puzzled many scholars since the discovery of Bharata's NŚ, and has given rise to a cluster of distinct arguments in connection with the "quest for the origins." However, the gap between this ritualistic interpretation of drama and the greater concern with aesthetics displayed both in the earliest dramatic works as well as in the technical treatises, does not allow us to rule out at once the hypothesis that the *pūrvaraṅga* is not primarily a ritual, but an already dramatized version of a ritual.[13]

As the NŚ describes it, the *pūrvaraṅga* is a ritual worship (*pūjā*) made up of eighteen or nineteen parts (up to twenty in the later treatises) – technically called limbs (*aṅga*) – which is invariably carried out on stage at the beginning of a theatrical performance, insofar as a theatrical performance is conceived as the unit of the preliminaries (*pūrvaraṅga*) and the play (*nāṭya*, or one of the ten dramatic genres called *daśarūpaka*). The limbs of the *pūrvaraṅga* are divided into two groups, the first being performed behind a stage curtain, the second after its removal and directly in front of the audience. The first group consists of a series of technical preparations such as arranging the orchestra on the stage, tuning the instruments, training the voice etc., and ends with a complete musical piece. The second part of the *pūrvaraṅga* includes not only musical pieces, dances, circumambulations on the stage, salutations to the deities that preside over it, a benedictory verse and other actions that we can easily regard as being part of a ritual, but also the first hints at histrionics, as well as a direct reference to the topic of the following play.

The nine limbs performed behind the stage curtain (*antaryavanikāṅga*) are:[14]

---

13 For a partial review of the different ritualistic and aesthetic interpretations of Indian drama in modern scholarship and a bibliography thereon, see GITOMER 1994.

14 The list of the limbs is given in NŚ 5.9-15 and their definitions in NŚ 5.17-29.

	NAME	DESCRIPTION
1.	*pratyāhāra*	disposition of the orchestra on stage
2.	*avataraṇa*	entrance of the female singers
3.	*ārambha*	act of training the voice through vocalizing
4.	*āśrāvaṇā*	entertainment through musical instrumentation
5.	*vaktrapāṇi*	rehearsing the styles of playing
6.	*parighaṭṭanā*	playing on the strings
7.	*saṃghoṭanā*	playing on drums
8.	*mārgāsārita*	playing together strings and drums
9.	*āsārita*	playing and singing on different rhythmical structures

The ten limbs performed after the removal of the stage curtain (*bahiryavanikāṅga*) are:

1.	*gītaka/vardhamāna*	song in praise of the gods (without or with dance)
2.	*utthāpana*	establishment of the performance on stage
3.	*parivartana*	circumambulation and praise of the protectors of the directions
4.	*nāndī*	verses eulogizing gods, Brahmins and kings
5.	*śuṣkāvakṛṣṭa*	song with meaningless syllables and praise of Indra's staff (*jarjara*)
6.	*raṅgadvāra*	first representation by means of the voice and bodily gestures
7.	*cārī*	bodily movements expressing the amorous *rasa*
8.	*mahācārī*	bodily movements expressing the furious *rasa*
9.	*trigata*	humorous conversation between the jester, the theatre director and an assistant
10.	*prarocanā*	invitation to the audience to watch the play by alluding to its contents

A very influential interpretation of the *pūrvaraṅga* was advanced by J.F. Kuiper. Neglecting altogether the first phase of the preliminaries, Kuiper saw in the practice around the erection of the staff representing Indra's banner – the *jarjaraprayoga*, which he equated with the second phase of the *pūrvaraṅga* – the kernel of the whole practice of the preliminaries. He therefore proceeded to connect the *pūrvaraṅga*, or at least its second part performed in front of the public, to the Vedic cosmogonic rite of New Year which is the festival of Indra's banner called Indradhvajamaha, thus claiming Vedic origins for Sanskrit theatre.[15] In Kuiper's view, the *pūrvaraṅga* is a ritual comparable to a Vedic sacrifice, which would give to the theatrical performance following it a ritual character: all theatrical performances, in fact, would be meant to commemorate the first play that took place in the times of yore in occasion of the festival of Indra's banner.[16] This interpretation of the *pūrvaraṅga* as a ritual was preceded and followed by concurring interpretations along the ritualistic model, all marked by a similar concern for the origins of Indian theatre.[17]

As should be clear by now, Kuiper's interpretation was based on the recognition of a distinction between the function of the first and the second phase of the *pūrvaraṅga*. Nevertheless, the very heterogeneity of the single elements within the second phase alone had not passed unnoticed in early studies on Indian theatre. Just like Kuiper, Feistel did not pay much attention to the first phase of the *pūrvaraṅga*, whose elements he regarded as "purely technical preparations for the musical accompaniment of the second part of the preliminaries" (FEISTEL 1972, p. 3).[18] As for the second phase, he considered it religiously relevant, despite his remark that the last two limbs, i.e. the *trigata* and the *prarocanā*, constituted exceptions, since these are directly connected to the following play (ibid., p. 2, and KUIPER 1979, p. 171). The focus, however, remained for him mainly on the problem of the origins of the theatrical art taught by Bharata. In effect, following GONDA 1943 and THIEME 1966, Feistel tried to connect the *trigata* and the *prarocanā* to the popular mimic theatre and

---

15 See KUIPER 1977, especially pp. 166-171.

16 KUIPER 1979, p. 170. See also BIARDEAU 1981 and, for some caution about Kuiper's conclusions, BANSAT-BOUDON 1992, pp. 69ff.

17 See, for instance, GONDA 1943, THIEME 1969, FEISTEL 1972 and LIDOVA 1994.

18 The article by Feistel on which I am basing my observations is an English summary, published in 1972, of his German thesis discussed in 1969.

to the shadow play respectively, while the other limbs of the *pūrvaraṅga* he linked to cult dances.

In a more recent study, BANSAT-BOUDON 1992, the heterogeneity of the various limbs that make up the preamble to a theatrical performance is given full attention, not so much in terms of "origins" (of the whole theatrical practice in India, of the preliminaries or of different sections of the preliminaries), but with regard to their coherence as distinct members forming the unitary entity which is the *pūrvaraṅga*, and at the same time as parts of the same theatrical event consisting of the *pūrvaraṅga* and the play together. In this analysis, both the commentary by Abhinavagupta and a broad understanding of the wider cultural context in which Sanskrit theatre is inscribed are relied upon. Differently from Kuiper and his predecessors, Bansat-Boudon considers the *pūrvaraṅga* a continuum where the ritual, whose elements are still dominant in the first phase, gradually gives way to the theatre in the second phase, through the successive introduction of theatrical elements which give theatre its peculiar identity:

> [Le *pūrvaraṅga*] se présente comme un rituel théâtralisé destiné, par là-même, à fonder la théâtralité de l'événement qui doit suivre. De fait, rituel et théâtre se trouvent si étroitement associés qu'il est parfois difficile de les distinguer l'un de l'autre (BANSAT-BOUDON 1992, p. 70).

Rather than there being a clear cut between an essentially sacred rite (the *pūrvaraṅga*) and a profane event (the play) (cf. KUIPER 1979, p. 169), there is a kind of twilight zone (the *purvaraṅga*), marking the transition from the ritual, i.e. the rite of installation and worship of the deities of the stage (the *raṅgadaivatapūjana* described in NŚ, ch. 2), to the theatre (the play following the *pūrvaraṅga*) (BANSAT-BOUDON 1992, p. 79 and n. 154).

The present paper takes its cues from the acknowledgement of the twofold nature of the *pūrvaraṅga* as highlighted by Bansat-Boudon, but looks particularly at the exegetical strategies devised by Abhinavagupta to explain this double nature, taking into account McCrea's views concerning the "teleological turn" in poetic theory. By looking at Abhinavagupta's ABh not exclusively as a text on aesthetics or as an instrument to better understand Bharata's instructions on staging, but as a work also concerned with problems of hermeneutics in general and of ritual hermeneutics in particular,[19] this

---

[19] On some of the exegetical sources of Abhinavagupta's aesthetics, see DAVID 2014, who also argues that at least one passage of the ABh, concerned with the

article is meant as a contribution to the study of the intellectual history of medieval Kashmir, and to the study of concepts travelling across what we often regard as self-contained compartments of scholarly investigation.[20] In order to identify if not the direct sources for some concepts originally extraneous to poetic and dramatic theory, at least a possible context common to other exegetical traditions, I will concentrate, in what follows, on Abhinavagupta's use of the two concepts of *dṛṣṭa* and *adṛṣṭa* (lit. "seen" and "unseen") in his analysis of the purposes of the different parts of the *pūrvaraṅga*, a topic which has received very little attention so far in studies on Indian theatre and aesthetics.[21]

THE PURPOSE OF THE LIMBS OF THE *PŪRVARAṄGA*: THE *LOCANA* PASSAGE

An enquiry into whether Abhinavagupta uses concepts that issue from speculations on ritual cannot but take as its starting point the *Locana*, Abhinavagupta's first work on literary criticism.[22] There

"generalisation" of emotions operated by art, might suggest "an original statement as to the nature of religious Scriptures themselves."

20 As many of the papers presented on the occasion of the conference "Around Abhinavagupta" showed, texts belonging to different "disciplines" or "domains of knowledge" were widely circulating around the turn of the millennium in Kashmir, and were not at any rate bound to be read only by the exponents of one particular scholastic or religious tradition.

21 The concepts of *dṛṣṭa* and *adṛṣṭa* are mentioned by LATH 1978, pp. 82-85 with reference to Gāndharva, the music used in the *pūrvaraṅga*. He considers "*adṛṣṭa*" as the transcendental merit resulting from ritual, and equals it to the Mīmāṃsaka's *apūrva*, a position I do not share. RAMANATHAN 1999 also speaks of Abhinavagupta's use of *adṛṣṭaphala* and *adṛṣṭaprayojana* with regard to Gāndharva. However, no attempt is made to find a *ratio* behind the use of this terminology. INGALLS ET AL. 1990 (cf. below) recur to the oft invoked analogy of the *pūrvaraṅga* as a Vedic sacrifice. His conclusions about the meaning of *dṛṣṭa* and *adṛṣṭa* in the *pūrvaraṅga*, are only partly in agreement with the analysis conducted here.

22 Besides the greater sophistication of Abhinavagupta's aesthetic theory in his commentary on Bharata's NŚ, the chronological priority of the *Locana* is confirmed by Abhinavagupta's references, in the ABh, to theoretical developments already expounded in his commentary on Ānandavardhana's work, to whom he refers three times: twice under the name *Sahṛdayālokalocana* (ABh ad NŚ 7.1, vol. I, p. 343 and ABh ad NŚ 16.5, vol. II, p. 300), and simply as *Vivaraṇa* in the third instance (ABh ad NŚ 19.76a, vol. III, p. 42). On the chronology of Abhinavagupta's works on literary criticism, see also INGALLS 1992, p. 31.

Abhinavagupta acknowledges for the first time the fundamental alterity of the various parts making up the *pūrvaraṅga*, with respect to other parts of the play subsumed under the dominant *rasa*-centred analysis of theatre. I consider this an early, and not yet fully developed, attempt to account for the arrangement of disparate elements into a single theatrical performance.

In the long commentary on DhĀ 3.10-14 – a pentad of stanzas meant to explain how a poet should achieve the suggestion of the *rasa* through the literary work as a whole – Abhinavagupta points out a difference between the purpose (*prayojana*) of the *sandhyaṅgas* (lit. "the limbs or subsidiary divisions (*aṅga*) of the joints (*sandhi*)"), i.e. the subdivisions of the successive stages of plot development in a story, and that of the *pūrvaraṅgāṅgas*, (lit. "the limbs or subsidiary divisions of the *pūrvaraṅga*"), i.e. the different parts of the preliminaries to a dramatic performance. Now, we have seen above that the *pūrvaraṅga* is described in the NŚ as the ordered sequence of a given number of elements, or *aṅgas*. The name *sandhyaṅga* refers, similarly, to a technical category that stems from the NŚ, where it is treated immediately after the category called *sandhi*.[23] The relevant passage in DhĀ 3.10-14 lists the *sandhyaṅgas* together with the *sandhis* as one of the five means by which a literary work as a whole becomes capable of conveying the main aesthetic emotion to the spectator:

> The arrangement of *sandhis* and *sandhyaṅgas* should be done with regard to the manifestation of *rasa*, [and] not out of the mere wish to carry out a practice prescribed by a treatise (*śāstra*). [...] These are [the five] causes that make a literary work capable of suggesting the *rasa*.[24]

Before proceeding to Abhinavagupta's remarks on *sandhis* and *sandhyaṅgas*, it is necessary to say something about the explanation of

---

23 On *sandhis* and *sandhyaṅgas*, see BANSAT-BOUDON 1992, pp. 132-137. As Bansat-Boudon remarks, more than junctures, as the term *sandhi* is literally translated, *sandhis* and *sandhyaṅgas* are segments, and are defined in the ABh as parts of the subject matter (*arthāvayava*, *arthabhāgarāśi*, *kathāvayava*, *kathābhāga*) (ibid., p. 132, n. 240).

24 *sandhisandhyaṅgaghaṭanaṃ rasābhivyaktyapekṣayā | na tu kevalayā śāstrasthitisampādanecchayā* ‖ DhĀ 3.12 ‖ ... *prabandhasya rasādīnāṃ vyañjakatve nibandhanam* ‖ DhĀ 14cd |. Transl. based on INGALLS ET AL. 1990, p. 428.

this passage as found in the *Vṛtti* (Ānandavardhana's auto-commentary on the DhĀ,[25] of which Abhinavagupta's *Locana* is a commentary). First of all, the examples taken to illustrate the point at stake are all borrowed from dramatic literature: Harṣa's *Ratnāvalī* is the perfect illustration of a play where plot elements and their subsidiaries (*sandhi*s and *sandhyaṅga*s) are properly composed according to the main *rasa*, the amorous (*śṛṅgāra*), while Bhaṭṭanārāyaṇa's *Veṇīsaṃhāra* provides the paradigmatic example of a play where a blind reliance on the rules of plot composition provokes a failure in the effective communication of the appropriate *rasa*. In the second act of this play, the author has shown Duryodhana suddenly in love, in accordance with Bharata's rule that the second act should display the *sandhyaṅga* called *vilāsa* ("playful amorousness"), notwithstanding the inappropriateness and incompatibility of this emotion to the overall tone of the act, otherwise centred on the theme of war and vengeance. Secondly, and not really unexpectedly, the treatise (*śāstra*) mentioned in DhĀ 3.12 as the basis for plot composition is none other than Bharata's NŚ (*śāstrasthitisampādanecchayā* is glossed in the *Vṛtti* as *bharatamatānusaraṇamātrecchayā* "out of the wish merely to follow Bharata's opinion"), since this is the authority to be followed in matters of dramatics. Abhinavagupta's sub-commentary, on the other hand, gives an unexpected twist to the passage, turning an apparently straightforward question – can the plot be creatively constructed in spite of the rules, provided it highlights the dominant *rasa*? – into a true problem of textual exegesis.

On DhĀ 3.12, the *Locana* comments:

> [Ānandavardhana] uses the word "mere" and the word "wish" [in the *kārikā*] with the following intention: the sage Bharata has taught that the purpose of the *sandhyaṅga*s is to bring about the excellence of the plot, which is instrumental in [the arousal of] *rasa* (*rasāṅgabhūta*), and not to produce an invisible [result] (*adṛṣṭasampādana*) or (*vā*) to prevent the obstacles etc. (*vighnādivāraṇa*) [from arising], as in the case of the limbs of the *pūrvaraṅga*.[26]

---

[25] On the much debated question of the authorship of the *Vṛtti*, see INGALLS 1990, pp. 26-27.

[26] *Locana* ad DhĀ 3.12, p. 340: *kevalaśabdam icchāśabdaṃ ca prayuñjānasyāyam āśayaḥ. bharatamuninā sandhyaṅgānāṃ rasāṅgabhūtam itivṛttaprāśastyotpādanam eva prayojanam uktam. na tu pūrvaraṅgāṅgavad adṛṣṭasampādanaṃ vighnādivāraṇaṃ vā*. Transl. based on INGALLS ET AL. 1990, p. 440. The text of the Nirnaya Sagar Edition (p. 185) reads *adṛṣṭasampādanaṃ vighnavāraṇam*

Such a view is further supported by a quotation from the NŚ, which supplies the definition of the purpose of *sandhyaṅga*s given by Bharata:

> As [Bharata] has taught [in NŚ 19.51-52]: "The purpose of the [*sandhy*]*aṅga*s is observed to be sixfold in the *śāstra*: 1) developing the desired topic [of the play][27], 2) preserving the plot from decay, 3) enabling the performance to please [the audience], 4) concealing what has to be concealed, 5) expressing [the subject matter] in an outstanding way, 6) revealing what has to be revealed.[28]

If we follow Abhinavagupta's commentary on DhĀ 3.12, it is clear that the sense we should give to NŚ 19.51-52 is that the sixfold purpose of the *sandhyaṅga*s coincides with the production of an excellent plot, which is instrumental for *rasa*-appreciation. The use of this very quotation shows that Abhinavagupta is not completely keen on interpreting DhĀ 3.12 in terms of a conflict between rule-reliance and poetic sensitivity, because the production of a good plot leading to *rasa* is indeed what he believes Bharata teaches to be the purpose of the *sandhyaṅga*s. Consequently, compliance with the *rasa* in the creation of a good plot-sequence is itself subject to regulation and is not a matter of individual taste. The quotation of NŚ 19.51-52 could then possibly be regarded as supporting an interpretation of the DhĀ passage in terms of conflicting rules and the hierarchy between different rules. For instance, in case of conflict between the given succession of the stages of the plot and the *rasa* one wishes to bring about, the *rasa* will be the leading factor in plot-composition, and

---

instead of *adṛṣṭasampādanaṃ vighnādivāraṇaṃ vā*. The translation would then be "[...] not the production of an unseen [result], i.e. the prevention from obstacles (*vighnāvāraṇa*), [which is the purpose of the limbs of the *pūrvaraṅga*]." Although this reading cannot be completely ruled out prior to a detailed examination of the manuscripts of the *Locana*, as I try to show in this paper the production of an invisible result (*adṛṣṭa*) is not co-extensive with the protection from obstacles, since it refers, in the first place, to the satisfaction of the gods.

27 I follow Abhinavagupta's commentary on Bharata's passage to interpret the first purpose, in ABh ad NŚ 19.51, vol. III, p. 32: *abhīṣṭasya prayojanasya rasāsvādakṛtā* [°*kṛtā* conj. : °*kṛto* ABh] *racanā vistāraṇā*: "Developing, i.e. expanding, according to the *rasa* to be relished, the purpose aimed at [by the literary composition]."

28 *Locana* ad DhĀ 3.12, p. 340: *yathoktam: iṣṭasyārthasya racanā vṛttāntasyānupakṣayaḥ | rāgaprāptiḥ prayogasya guhyānāṃ caiva gūhanam || āścaryavad abhikhyānaṃ prakāśyānāṃ prakāśanam | aṅgānāṃ ṣaḍvidhaṃ hy etad dṛṣṭaṃ śāstre prayojanam ||* (NŚ 19.51-52). Transl. INGALLS ET AL. 1990, p. 440, modified.

some of the subsidiary stages of the plot could be omitted without any transgression of the primary rule taking place. However, the contrastive category introduced by Abhinavagupta at this point of his commentary on DhĀ 3.10-14, namely the "invisible" (*adṛṣṭa*) (lit. the "unseen," i.e. what is beyond the range of the senses because of its supersensible nature), as well as in his own commentary on NŚ 19.51-52 in the ABh, make this interpretation rather weak.

Now, Abhinavagupta does not comment directly on the compound *śāstrasthiti°* of DhĀ 3.12 as the *Vṛtti* did, since both the distribution of the *sandhyaṅga*s according to a given sequence in the various acts of a play (as the *aṅga vilāsa* in the second act), and compliance with the dominant *rasa* of the play, are the object of rules prescribed by Bharata, as it is made explicit through the quotation of NŚ 19.51-52. It therefore makes no sense for him to say that one has to harmonize his plot with the *rasa*, rather than with the rules stipulated by a treatise. The expression "not out of the mere wish to carry out a practice prescribed by a treatise (*śāstra*)" must therefore point to a difference in the purpose following which one carries out a certain rule-bound activity, as indicated by the contrastive category of the *aṅga*s of the *pūrvaraṅga*. The latter are said to have a different purpose, in that they aim to produce something invisible (*adṛṣṭa*), or to prevent the obstacles from hindering the performance, which implies that they do not primarily help in conveying the *rasa*. The failure of the author of the *Veṇīsaṃhāra* in conveying the heroic *rasa* (*vīra*) is not due to his failure to understand that, although it is prescribed by Bharata, the *sandhyaṅga* called *vilāsa* should be avoided under specific circumstances, but to his failure to interpret Bharata's teachings in the proper way. On the proper use of *sandhyaṅga*s, the *Locana* concludes:

> And later, in defining *vilāsa* (amourousness) as a component of the *pratimukhasandhi*, he [i.e. Bharata] says: "*Vilāsa* is said to be a yearning for the enjoyment of *rati*" [NŚ 19.76]. The term "enjoyment of *rati*" is used to imply such *vibhāva*s and the like as shall suggest the basic emotional drive (*sthāyibhāva*) of the main *rasa* of the play. [The author of the *Veṇīsaṃhāra*] *has failed to understand the meaning properly*, for in that play the *rasa* in question is the heroic (*vīra*).[29] (Transl. INGALLS ET AL. 1990, p. 440, emphasis mine.)

---

29 *Locana* ad DhĀ 3.12, p. 340: *tataś ca – samīhā ratibhogārthā vilāsaḥ parikīrtitaḥ* | (NŚ 19.76) *iti pratimukhasandhyaṅgavilāsalakṣaṇe. ratibhogaśabda ādhikārikarasasthāyibhāvopavyañjaka-vibhāvādyupalakṣaṇārthatvena prayuktaḥ,*

Thus, the sense given by Abhinavagupta to DhĀ 3.12 (see n. 24) could be supplied as follows:

> The arrangement of *sandhi*s and *sandhyaṅga*s should be done with regard to the manifestation of *rasa*, [and] not out of the mere wish to carry out a practice prescribed by a treatise (*śāstra*) [*without applying any reasoning concerning the very purpose of those rules*].

Why is it not the case for the limbs of the *pūrvaraṅga*? Going back to the aim of these limbs, this is the only occasion where an invisible result is mentioned in the *Locana*, and it is no accident that it should be mentioned not in connection to poetic elements, but rather to purely theatrical ones: the *pūrvaraṅgāṅga*s are in fact exclusively found in theatre. They find no place in poetic theory, for they are part of the spectacular or performative dimension of the play, not of the literary or dramatic one. But if the *aṅga*s of the *pūrvaraṅga* are said to result in the production of something unseen (*adṛṣṭa*), should we assume that what the *sandhyaṅga*s bring about, namely "excellence of the plot" (*itivṛttaprāśastya*), has to be considered, by contrast, to be a visible effect (*dṛṣṭa*)? I will elaborate on this hypothesis shortly. With regard to the second aim of the limbs of the *pūrvaraṅga* referred to, it is no surprise that the obstacles threatening the successful accomplishment of a given activity – be it literary or not – should be warded off at the very beginning of the activity in question.[30] Moreover, the beginnings of Indian theatre are mythically marked by the occurrence of obstacles, personified by demonic beings who impeded the first performance to take place in front of an assembly of gods.[31] What the causal link between the performance of the *pūrvaraṅga* and the elimination of the obstacles is will be clarified in what follows.

To sum up, in the *Locana* we find the following opposition:

---

yathātattvaṃ nādhigatārtha iti, prakṛto hy atra vīrarasaḥ. See also INGALLS ET AL. 1990, p. 442, n. 17.

30 On the difficulty of beginnings in India, see Malamoud as quoted in BANSAT-BOUDON 1992, pp. 69-70. On beginnings in treatises and on the need of an auspicious verse or act (*maṅgala*) in order to ward off potential obstacles, see SLAJE 2008 on *Śāstrārambha*.

31 On the accounts of the origins of the theatrical art in the NŚ and its commentary, see BANSAT-BOUDON 1992, pp. 54-61, BANSAT-BOUDON 1997 and BANSAT-BOUDON 2004, pp. 50-53, 63-77. For an accurate analysis of the aesthetic failure of the first performance, see BANSAT-BOUDON 2012.

	PURPOSE (*prayojana*)	RESULT (*phala*)
*sandhyaṅga*s	→ *itivṛttaprāśastyotpādana/ rasāṅgabhūta*	→ [*dṛṣṭa*?]
≠		
*pūrvaraṅgāṅga*s	→ *adṛṣṭasaṃpādana*	→ *adṛṣṭa*
	→ *vighnādivāraṇa*	→ ?

In medieval models of practical rationality, the actions of a rational person generally imply a purpose (*prayojana*) which ultimately corresponds to the expected result of that action (*phala*) provided no obstruction occurs. A farmer, for instance, will undertake to plant a seed in order to obtain crops, which will eventually be obtained provided no heavy rains or draught takes place between the time of sowing and that of the harvest. The farmer, who is a rational agent, acts on the basis of the empirical observation of the said causal relation. There are actions, however, whose results are invisible to the ordinary man, as for instance ritual actions or actions having an ethical bearing. The unseen results of these actions arc taught by scripture, as for instance in the famous Vedic formula: "A man desirous of heaven should perform the fire oblation" (*agnihotraṃ juhuyāt svargakāmaḥ*). The causal link between the invisible object "heaven" and the action of sacrificing into the fire, which is the means to obtain it, cannot be known through empirical means, but only through scripture, since such objects lie beyond the range of the senses.[32] In the same way, in the *Locana* passage (see n. 26), the implication seems to be that one has to follow the prescriptions of the *śāstra* alone when performing the limbs of the *pūrvaraṅga* if one wants to obtain an invisible result, since there is no other way to know empirically that one's performance of them will lead to the expected result.

Two questions should concern us here. First of all, what exactly is the double purpose of the limbs of the *pūrvaraṅga*, and how are the two purposes connected to one another? Secondly, can the result of the *pūrvaraṅga* called "invisible" (*adṛṣṭa*) be conceived as endowed with a "visible" (*dṛṣṭa*) counterpart? In order to solve these,

---

[32] On the medieval model of "practical rationality" in its different Brahmanical and Buddhist versions, and its epistemic limits regarding actions undertaken for the sake of invisible realities, see BIARDEAU 1969, pp. 83-85, DAVID 2013, pp. 273-274 and ELTSCHINGER 2013, pp. 103-134.

it is now necessary to delve into Abhinavagupta's second major work on literary theory, the ABh.

THE PURPOSE OF THE LIMBS OF THE *PŪRVARAṄGA*: THE *ABH* PASSAGE

As already noted by Ingalls in a note to his translation of the passage of the *Locana* seen above (see n. 26) (INGALLS ET AL. 1990, p. 442, n. 14), the opposition between elements having an invisible result and elements aiming at a visible one, only suggested by way of a cursory remark in the *Locana*, is more accurately dealt with in the ABh and, we can add, it undergoes a major development there. Let us now turn to ABh ad NŚ 19.51-52, the passage dealing with the purpose of plot subdivisions (*sandhyaṅgas*):

> The purpose of the [*sandhy*]*aṅgas* is observed to be sixfold in the *śāstra*. [NŚ 19.52cd]

Abhinavagupta comments:

> As to the first purpose [of *sandhyaṅgas*], [i.e developing the desired topic of the play (*iṣṭārthasya racanā*)], it is based on aesthetic relishing (*camatkārakṛta*), [thus] it is validated just through a particular direct perception although it is seen in a *smṛti*[-text]. It is not something invisible (*adṛṣṭa*), like [the purpose of] the twilight-worship (*sandhyopāsana)* and other [permanent rites], or a [purpose] having both natures (*ubhayarūpa*)[, i.e. visible and invisible,] as in the case of the limbs of the *pūrvaraṅga*. This is the sense. [The expression] "in [the] *śastra*" [used by Bharata] means: "in the Veda which is theatre."[33]

We are now faced with a threefold type of purpose (*prayojana*) concerning:

1. The subdivisions of the successive stages of plot development, or *sandhyaṅgas*.
2. The twilight worship or *sandhyopāsana* and other permanent rites.
3. The limbs of the preliminary rite, or *pūrvaraṅgāṅgas*.

---

[33] ABh ad NŚ 19.52, vol. III, p. 32: *ādyaṃ tu prayojanaṃ camatkārakṛtaṃ smṛtidṛṣṭam api pratyakṣaviśeṣasiddham eva, na tu sandhyopāsanādivad adṛṣṭaṃ, nāpi pūrvaraṅgāṅgavad ubhayarūpam ity arthaḥ. śāstra iti nāṭyātmake veda ity arthaḥ.*

In terms of category of purpose we can schematize:

			PRAYOJANA
1.	*saṅdhyāṅgas*	→	*camatkārakṛta* (*rasāṅgabhūta* = [*dṛṣṭa*])[34]
2.	*sandhyopāsanādi*	→	*adṛṣṭa*
3.	*pūrvaraṅgāṅgas*	→	*ubhayarūpa* (=*dṛṣṭa*+*adṛṣṭa*)

If, as this passage seems to confirm, the *sandhyaṅgas* have a visible purpose (*dṛṣṭa*), which coincides with their being subservient to the aesthetic experience of *rasa*, and if religious rites such as the twilight worship have an invisible one, what would then be the twofold purpose of the limbs of the *pūrvaraṅga*, having an observable and unobservable nature at the same time? One possibility would be to connect this statement to the *Locana* passage, and thus read back the twofold-purpose assigned to the limbs of the *pūrvaraṅga* here, into the two purposes listed there:

	PRAYOJANA	PHALA
pūrvaraṅgāṅgas	→ production of something invisible (*adṛṣṭasampādana*)	→ *adṛṣṭa*
	→ protection from the obstacles (*vighnādivāraṇa* [=*dṛṣṭa*?])	→ [*dṛṣṭa*?]

However tempting such equation might look, it is not always necessarily sound to superimpose a scheme developed by an author in a later text on a previous work by the same author. According to Ingalls, the contrast drawn by Abhinavagupta between the limbs of the *pūrvaraṅga* and the limbs of the *sandhi* is one between things having a religious purpose (*adṛṣṭa*, "invisible"), which would in turn give the *pūrvaraṅga* the character of a ritual similar to a Vedic sacrifice, and things having a purely secular one (*dṛṣṭa*, "visible"), which he

[34] I take the first purpose of *sandhyaṅgas* alone as paradigmatic for the group of six purposes listed by Bharata, since no separate explanation of the other five purposes is provided by Abhinavagupta, and since I take the compound *camatkārakṛta* ("based on aesthetic relishing") as a synonym of *rasāṅgabhūta* ("instrumental in [the arousal of] *rasa*"), which the *Locana* passage ad DhĀ 3.12 recognizes as the property of the overall purpose of *sandhyaṅgas*, i.e. the production of the "excellence of the plot."

identifies with the beautification of the play. As he further explains on the basis of the ABh passage, the effect of the *pūrvaraṅga* is not completely religious, but it is partly visible due to this same beautifying character: "After all, the *pūrvaraṅga* too can be beautiful." (INGALLS ET AL. 1990, p. 442, n. 14). In my opinion, "religious" vs. "secular=beautiful," are probably not the best candidates to make full sense of the terms *dṛṣṭa* and *adṛṣṭa* with relation to the double purpose of the limbs of the *pūrvaraṅga*. Their meaning needs to be ascertained through a closer analysis of the ABh passage, and by looking at other usages of the same words, and at the concepts they convey. In effect, this twofold scheme of visible and invisible purposes, to which correspond visible and invisible results, is one which is employed to a great extent by Abhinavagupta in the ABh, although its origin has to be searched for outside the realm of poetic theory since, as noticed above, it is neither used in the DhĀ and *Vṛtti*, nor is it fully developed in the *Locana*. Its systematic application to dramatic theory appears to be an innovation of the ABh.[35]

A closer analysis of the three paradigmatic elements said to serve different sets of purposes reveals a clue about the possible sources for the concepts of visible and invisible purposes and results, borrowed by Abhinavagupta while making sense of the *pūrvaraṅga*.

---

[35] The concept is indeed totally absent from the NŚ. Of course it is not possible to completely rule out the possibility that other commentators on Bharata's NŚ applied the concepts of *dṛṣṭa* and *adṛṣṭa* to dramatic theory. However, this does not seem to be the case if we judge from the extant fragments of these commentaries as known to us from the ABh. As for the use of *dṛṣṭa* and *adṛṣṭa* concepts in poetic theory, the terminology is not completely absent. We find it, namely in the work of Ānandavardhana's predecessor Vāmana. In *Kāvyālaṃkārasūtra* 1.5, poetry is given a double aim: "Good poetry has two purposes, an observable one and an unobservable one: it produces pleasure [for its appreciator] and renown [for its composer]" (*kāvyaṃ sad dṛṣṭādṛṣṭārtham, prītikīrtihetutvāt*). This means, according to the auto-commentary: "The observable purpose [of poetry] is beauty, since it produces pleasure [in the reader], while [its] unobservable purpose is due to the fact that it causes the renown [of the poet] (*cāru dṛṣṭaprayojanaṃ, prītihetutvāt. adṛṣṭaprayojanaṃ kīrtihetutvāt*). Note that pleasure and renown are listed already in Bhāmaha's (7th c.) *Kāvyālaṃkāra* 1.2cd as the two effects of poetry: "The composition of good poetry imparts fame and pleasure" (*karoti kīrtiṃ prītiṃ ca sādhukāvyanibandhanam*). As far as I can judge, Vāmana speaks of observable and unobservable aims of poetry with reference to the immediacy of the results: beauty is a visible purpose of poetry, since its result, i.e. the pleasure caused in the reader, can be immediately verified. Fame or renown, on the other hand, is not visible as such. This acceptation of *dṛṣṭa/adṛṣṭa* is known to Abhinavagupta, but it is not exactly the model he has in mind here, as we shall see.

1. Sandhyaṅgas and Dṛṣṭaprayojana

Apart from their being construed in accordance with the aesthetic emotion, a piece of information already provided in the *Locana*, the *sandhyaṅga*s, says Abhinavagupta in the ABh (see n. 33), have their purpose observed in a *smṛti*-text and validated through a special kind of direct perception. The *smṛti*-text invoked here is, I believe, none other than the NŚ, as the authoritative treatise where the rules of theatre are laid down. This conforms to the classification of *śruti* and *smṛti* under the same category of *śāstra* (as opposed to *itihāsa* "history" and *kāvya* "poetry"), discussed by Abhinavagupta in his commentary on *sandhi*s and *sandhyaṅga*s in the *Locana* passage ad DhĀ 3.12.[36] It moreover agrees with the widespread medieval meaning of *smṛti* as a codified non-Vedic scripture.[37] According to the analysis carried out by Mīmāṃsakas and Dharmaśāstra authors, *smṛti*-texts contain regulations pertaining to both domains, the empirical and the ethical-ritual. Some regulations have a purpose that is visible (*dṛṣṭa*), for they clearly serve some practical transaction, such as the rules about inter-caste marriage, food consumption, etc., while others have an invisible purpose (*adṛṣṭa*), insofar as no result can be empirically observed from their performance, as for instance in the case of the Aṣṭaka, a ceremony performed for the ancestors. One would not know about the causal relation between ethical-ritual actions and their unseen results if they were not laid down in a scripture. As a consequence, when the purpose of an action prescribed

---

[36] *Locana* ad DhĀ 3.12: *iha prabhusammitebhyaḥ śrutismṛtiprabhṛtibhyaḥ kartavyam idam ity ājñāmātraparamārthebhyaḥ śāstrebhyo ye na vyutpannāḥ, na cāpy asyedaṃ vṛttam amuṣmāt karmaṇa ity evaṃ yuktiyuktakarmaphalasambandhaprakaṭanakārikebhyo mitrasammitebhya itihāsaśāstrebhyo labdhavyutpattayaḥ, atha cāvaśyaṃ vyutpādyāḥ prajārthasampādanayogyatākrāntā rājaputraprāyās teṣāṃ hṛdayānupraveśamukhena caturvargopāyavyutpattir ādheyā. hṛdayānupraveśaś ca rasāsvādamaya eva.* "Princes, who are not educated in scripture – those works of *śruti*, *smṛti*, etc. which consist in commands, like those of a master, to do this or that – and who have not received instruction from history, which like a friend reveals to us the connection of cause and effect as endowed with reasoning such as 'this result came from such an act,' and who are therefore in pressing need of instruction, for they are given the power to accomplish the wants of their subjects, can be given instruction in the four goals of man only by entering into their hearts. And what enters into the heart is the relish of *rasa* (*rasāsvāda*)." (Transl. INGALLS ET AL. 1990, p. 437, slightly modified.)

[37] On the shift of the meaning of "*smṛti*" from memorized traditional customs to non-Vedic normative texts, see BRICK 2006 and YOSHIMIZU 2012, pp. 643-647.

by a scripture is not seen, one is allowed to infer that the rule for the performance of the action in question must have an invisible purpose and therefore an expected invisible result. However, according to a principle of economy, when the purpose is empirically ascertainable there is no need to search further for an invisible purpose.[38] To say that the purpose of the *sandhyaṅga*s which is the development of the desired subject matter of a play is contained in a *smṛti*-text, and that this purpose is ascertained through a particular perception, suggests in my view an analogous kind of rule analysis: a rule has a visible purpose when a result is directly observed as caused by the performance of the action they prescribe, which is the means of realization of that expected result. In the case of the *sandhyaṅga*s, we can certainly ascertain a causal link between the proper arrangement of the plot-segments in a play, and the development of the desired topic of the play, namely when we savour the emotion that is conveyed by the literary composition. This savouring or delectation (*camatkāra*) is, according to the aesthetic theory propounded by Abhinavagupta, a kind of perceptive knowledge, a perception sui generis.[39]

2. *Sandhyopāsana and Adṛṣṭaprayojana*

As its name indicates, the *sandhyopāsana* is worship (*upāsana*) performed in the morning and evening twilight (*sandhyā*) through a sequence of fixed actions.[40] According to a well-known classification, first laid down by Mīmāṃsakas and largely adopted by the other schools and in Dharmaśāstras, religious acts or rites can be divided into three broad categories: obligatory regular rites performed on

---

38 This principle, known as the rule of economy in postulating something invisible (*adṛṣṭakalpanālpīyasī nyāyyā*), or Ockham's razor (KATAOKA 2010, p. 137), is already laid down in the *Śābarabhāṣya* (ad 2.1.7), and becomes very widespread within and beyond ritual exegesis. That it was known and used by Abhinavagupta in the ABh is testified by a variation on the same theme in a passage of the first chapter, ABh ad NŚ 1.84-86, vol. I, p. 31: *evaṃ sarvatra dṛṣṭam api sadṛśopalakṣaṇāntaṃ prayojanam utprekṣyam. sarvathā tadalābhe niyamādṛṣṭam eva.* "Similarly, some visible purpose as well has to be imagined for each and every [element of the theatrical performance], through the indirect mention of similar [things]. And in every case, if a [visible purpose] is not obtainable, an invisible [one based on] restriction [in performance has to be] necessarily [postulated]."

39 See GNOLI 1968, p. xxxv.

40 On *sandhyā* worship, see for instance KANE 1941, vol. II.1, pp. 312-321.

fixed occasions (*nitya*), occasional rites (*naimittika*) and rites performed to obtain a certain desired result (*kāmya*). *Sandhyā* worship is considered to belong to the first group of obligatory rites, as stated also in Abhinavagupta's *Tantrāloka* (TĀ 26.12-13). Although Mīmāṃsakas do not, as far as I am aware, directly connect the three categories of rituals with rules aiming at visible or invisible results, Kane quotes a text belonging to the corpus of juridical literature, namely Aparārka's (12th c.) commentary on the *Yājñavalkyasmṛti*, in which the content of *smārta* rules is divided into various categories on the basis of a previous text, the *Bhaviṣyapurāṇa*. Among these types of purposes for *smārta* rules are found the very three used by Abhinavagupta in the passage under discussion: those having a visible purpose (*dṛṣṭa*), those having an invisible one (*adṛṣṭa*), and those having both (*dṛṣṭādṛṣṭa*). The example for a purely *adṛṣṭārthasmṛti* is, according to this source, none other than the twilight worship.[41] Following the type of analysis implemented by both Mīmāṃsakas and jurists, such a rule would have the Veda as the source of its validity, since its purpose is not seen, and it has a result which we could call "religious."[42]

3. *Pūrvarāṅgāṅgas and Dṛṣṭādṛṣṭaprayojana*

As in the other two cases, it may be useful to look at similar types of rule-analysis discussed by Mīmāṃsāka and Dharmaśāstra authors. Again, the quotation by Aparārka might be of help since, despite the fact that his work is later than Abhinavagupta, and its source, the *Bhaviṣyapurāṇa*, was possibly unknown to Bharata's commentator, the two share a very similar conception of rules having a twofold purpose (*dṛṣṭādṛṣṭārtharūpa*, *ubhayarūpa*), and could thus be thought to reflect a common view. Moreover, the idea that rules can have more than one purpose goes back to older Mīmāṃsā sources. The example provided by the *Bhaviṣyapurāṇa* is the rule according to which a brahmanical student should carry a staff made

---

41 KANE 1946, p. 840, n.1634. I am not certain about what Mīmāṃsakas would regard as the result of the particular rite of *sandhyā*. It could be noted here that in Manu 2.101 *sandhyā*s are said to purify one from the sins committed during night and day. The discussion about *nitya* rites in general and their result, developed in his various works by Kumārila, has been analyzed in detail in YOSHIMIZU 2007.

42 See YOSHIMIZU 2012, pp. 667-669, with "religious" meaning "pertaining to the sphere of *dharma*, which is the domain of the Veda."

of *palāśa*-wood. This rule clearly has as its purpose the protection of the student. However, the restriction that the staff should be made of *palāśa* and not of some other material, has an invisible purpose. The idea that, within a rule having a visible purpose, the restriction to perform an action in a particular manner aims at an invisible result, is already present in Kumārila's discussion of *smārta* rules, at *Tantravārttika* 1.3.2. The principle is called "restrictive injunction" (*niyamavidhi*) and it allows the Mīmāṃsā thinker to preserve the religious function of some rules and their consequent basis in the Veda, despite their clearly visible purpose. The paradigmatic example in the context of *smārta* rules[43] is that a student should obey his teacher. Following common sense, showing obeisance to a master has the visible purpose of pleasing him and thus prompting him to teach. However, the restriction concerning obedience to one's teacher as the preferred procedure over other means, such as making donations and the like, which are amenable to the same result, has an invisible purpose (*adṛṣṭārtha*), namely to establish an "invisible potency" (*apūrva*) leading the student to the completion of his studies bereft of obstacles.[44] In this light and despite the fact that Abhinavagupta never uses the term *apūrva*, unlike Kumārila and his successors, the purpose of the limbs of the *pūrvaraṅga*, which is the prevention from obstacles, can be considered to be equally invisible. Should then the particle *vā* in the *Locana* passage "*na tu pūrvaraṅgāṅgavad adṛṣṭasampādanaṃ vighnādivāraṇaṃ vā*" (see

---

43 Within Vedic exegesis and in the work of later Mīmāṃsā authors, the typical example of a restrictive injunction is that which enjoins the sacrificer to beat the unhusked rice with a mortar and pestle before preparing the sacrificial cake. This injunction has the observable (*dṛṣṭa*) purpose of having the rice husked in order to prepare the cake, but it aims at the same time at an unobservable (*adṛṣṭa*) effect through a restriction in the means of obtaining husked rice, namely by using a mortar and pestle and not, say, one's fingernails. See KANE 1962, vol. V.2, pp. 1229-1230 and YOSHIMIZU 2012, p. 669.

44 *Tantravārttika* 1.3.2: *tasmāt saty api dṛṣṭārthatve sambhāvyate vedamūlatvaṃ niyamādṛṣṭasiddher ananyapramāṇakatvāt. ... dṛṣṭaṃ ca prīto gurur adhyāpayiṣyatīty evam ādi niṣpadyate. niyamāc cāvighnasamāptyarthāpūrvasiddhiḥ.* "Even if serving an observable purpose, (the obedience to one's teacher) can be regarded as based on the Veda because the establishment of an invisible [purpose] through restriction has no other means of knowledge [except the Veda]. [...] It is true that we observe that a teacher is willing to teach (his student) if pleased (by any means); but (if the student always obeys his teacher) following the [*smārta*] restriction, he establishes an *apūrva* [i.e., unobservable potency] that leads to the completion (of his study) without interruption." (Text and transl. YOSHIMIZU 2012, p. 670, n. 26, modified.) "Without interruption" translates here the term *avighna*°, literally "without obstacles."

n. 26) be intended as pointing out an option rather than an exclusive alternative? What would then be the visible purpose of the limbs of the *pūrvaraṅga* advocated in the ABh though absent in the *Locana* passage?

For the time being, to our initial scheme the following can be added:

	PRAYOJANA	PHALA
*pūrvaraṅgāṅga*s	→ *adṛṣṭasaṃpādana*	→ *adṛṣṭa*
	→ *vighnādivāraṇa* [=*adṛṣṭa*]	→ [*adṛṣṭa*]
	→ ?	→ *dṛṣṭa*

In order to supply the missing elements, I will next look at other statements in the ABh regarding the twofold purpose of the limbs of the *pūrvaraṅga*. In the analysis Abhinavagupta pursues in the fifth chapter of his commentary devoted to the *pūrvaraṅga*, and partly in the fourth chapter as well, the distinction between elements performed behind the curtain and elements performed in front of the spectators becomes relevant, not so much in terms of their being directly performed in front of an audience or not, but in terms of the variety in the type of rule analysis implemented for them. Both phases of the *pūrvaraṅga*, to be sure, are grasped by the audience through direct perception, though by different sense faculties (music being the object of hearing, and dance of sight). However, their purpose as objects of rule regulation can be known either through direct perception or through other epistemic means, i.e. scripture.

"*ADṚṢṬA*" AS THE PURPOSE OF RULE RESTRICTION (*NIYAMĀDṚṢṬA*)

As mentioned above, the first phase of the *pūrvaraṅga* is performed behind a curtain, thus hidden from the spectators. It consists mainly of a musical phase, and includes nine limbs, from the arrangement of the orchestra on stage (*pratyāhāra*) to the rendering of the first musical piece combining singing and instrument playing (*āsārita*). In the fifth chapter of the ABh, Abhinavagupta regards this group of limbs to be performed behind the curtain as having a visible purpose (*dṛṣṭārtha*), i.e. an empirically ascertainable goal: without the arrangement of the orchestra on stage, without tuning the instruments and training the voice, in other words without the raw material or the causal complex necessary for the production of a performance, how can a play ever take place?[45] However, despite the fact that the limbs performed behind the stage curtain have such an evident role to play in the theatrical performance, and although they take place hidden from the eyes of the spectators, the actions prescribed for those limbs have to be executed exactly in the way taught by the *śāstra*, and in no other way. This explains why they can be considered to have an additional invisible purpose, which is expressed through a double analogy:

> In the absence of the *pratyāhāra* (i.e. the arrangement of the musical instruments on stage) and the other limbs [performed behind the curtain], in fact, the causal complex (*sāmagrī*) consisting in [the arrangement of the group of] the singers, and other [preliminary actions that are necessary for a theatrical performance], remains incomplete. How, then, can a theatrical performance take place? Indeed, it is certainly not possible to make a cloth without threads, brush, loom etc. [The same applies to the *pratyāhāra* etc. as well,] with the exception that, as we will teach, [their performance according to the rules laid down in the *Naṭyaśāstra*] has an additional purpose, due to the restriction (*niyamaprayojana*)[in performance intended for an invisible result], just as the act of eating while facing the east.[46]

The analogy of the cloth is commonly used in Nyāya-Vaiśeṣika to illustrate the conditional complex (*sāmagrī*) which is necessary to bring about an effect.[47] Just as a cloth cannot be produced without the threads, the brush, the loom and the other causes, so a theatrical performance cannot be produced if the musical orchestra is not sitting on stage, if the singers have not warmed up their voices and if the musicians have not tuned their instruments, i.e. if the group of limbs performed behind the curtain have not been executed. This purpose alone would have been sufficient to justify the performance of these *aṅga*s as part of the *pūrvaraṅga*. However, an additional

---

45 ABh ad NŚ 5.17-20, vol. I, p. 214: *evaṃ tāvad antaryavanikāṅgānāṃ dṛṣṭārtha eva prayogaḥ, tāny antareṇa prayogasyaivāsampatteḥ*. "In this way, the performance of the elements behind the curtain has first of all an observable aim, in that a performance cannot be produced without them."

46 ABh ad NŚ 5.5-7, vol. I, p. 209: *pratyāhārādikena hy aṅgena vinā gāyanādisāmagryasampatteḥ kathaṃ nātyaprayogaḥ. na hy aho kila tantuturīvemāder vinā* (*vinā* conj. Ed., om. mss.) *śakyaḥ paṭaḥ kartum. kevalaṃ prāṅmukhānnabhojanavan niyamaprayojanatvam apīti* (conj. Ed., *niyojanatve 'pīti* mss.) *vakṣyate*.

47 See for instance FOUCHER 1949, pp. 103-106.

element is brought in by Abhinavagupta through the second analogy. It is not completely evident from this terse passage what Abhinavagupta has in mind when he talks about the purpose due to restriction as the additional purpose of the limbs of the *pūrvaraṅga* performed behind the curtain. The maxim which is the source of his analogy is a common one and, in its classical phrasing, the rule that "one should eat food facing the east" (*prāṅmuko 'nnāni bhuñjīta*) is quoted in many different contexts, including Dharmaśāstra and Mīmāṃsā sources.[48]

In order to understand how the second analogy works in the context of the ABh, we therefore need to look closer at both internal and external evidence. To be sure, the same analogy of eating towards the east is used in two other instances in the ABh. Both instances make it clear that a restriction (*niyama*), concerning the way of performing an action that has already a visible purpose, aims at "the unseen" (*adṛṣṭa*).[49] The idea is therefore quite similar to the Mīmāṃsaka "restrictive injunction" (*niyamavidhi*) seen above, by which *smārta* rules can acquire a double purpose and result in both seen

---

[48] According to BENSON 2010, p. 526, the source of this principle is to be found in juridical texts, namely the *dharmasūtras*. The *Kūrmapurāṇa* quotes it twice (*Kūrmapurāṇa* 2.12.63.1 and 2.19.1.2: *prāṅmuko 'nnāni bhuñjīta sūryābhimukha eva vā* |). In *Mānavadharmaśāstra* (henceforth MDhŚ) 2.51-52, the same principle is found with a slightly different formulation: *samāhṛtya tu tad bhaikṣaṃ yāvad artham amāyayā | nivedya gurave 'śnīyād ācamya prāṅmukhaḥ śuciḥ || āyuṣyaṃ prāṅmukho bhuṅkte yaśasyaṃ dakṣiṇāmukhaḥ | śriyaṃ pratyaṅmukho bhuṅkte ṛtaṃ bhuṅkta udaṅmukhaḥ ||*. "After collecting as much almsfood as he needs without guile, he should present it to his teacher, purify himself by sipping some water, and eat it facing the east. Facing the east while eating procures long life; facing the south procures fame; facing the west procures prosperity; and facing the north procures truth." (Text and transl. by Olivelle.)

[49] ABh ad NŚ 33.1, vol. IV, p. 396. *anena ca phalavailakṣaṇyam api vyākhyātam. gāndharvasya prayoktari prādhānyenādṛṣṭaphalatvād* [*prādhānyenādṛṣṭaphalatvād* conj.: *prādhānyena dṛṣṭaphalatvād* Ed.]. *gānasya tu... dṛṣṭaṃ mukhyaṃ phalaṃ prāṅmukhabhojanavat tv adṛṣṭam apy astu.* "By this [reasoning], we have explained even the difference in the result [of *gāndharva* and *gāna* music], since the result of *gāndharva* is mainly an invisible one and it concerns the performer. [The music added to drama and called] (*gāna*), on the contrary, [...] has as its main result (*phala*) something visible (*dṛṣṭa*). However, just like in taking food facing eastwards, it also has an invisible (*adṛṣṭa*) [result]." ABh ad NŚ 32.421, vol. IV, p. 389: *anye tu dṛṣṭaprayojane 'pi niyamād adṛṣṭaṃ* [*niyamād adṛṣṭaṃ* conj. : *niyamād adṛṣṭaprayojane 'pi niyamād adṛṣṭaṃ* Ed.] *bhojanaprāṅmukhatvavad iti*. "Others [maintain that] although there is a visible result (*dṛṣṭaprayojana*), an invisible result is also [attained] because of a restriction, just as in facing the east while eating."

and unseen fruits. For the Mīmāṃsā thinker Kumārila, however, the particular restriction prescribed for the performance of a certain action has an invisible result (*adṛṣṭa*) which coincides with an *apūrva* and helps in the production of the final result of the whole sacrifice, a position which is not found as such in the ABh.

The closest parallel to Abhinavagupta's formulation of the analogy of eating while facing the east, functioning as a typical illustration of an action producing an invisible result (*adṛṣṭa*) through a restriction (*niyama*), is found in Candrānanda's (7th-8th c.?)[50] commentary on *Vaiśeṣikasūtra* 6.2.2. The *mūla* text has established that the result of actions prescribed by the *śāstra* is ripened by the performer of that action (VS 6.1.5). It then proceeds to establish that the performance of those actions aims at felicity (*abhyudaya*), when they are not performed with a view to their visible goal (VS 6.2.1). *Vaiśeṣikasūtra* 6.2.2 provides a list of those actions aiming at the unseen (*adṛṣṭa*), among which are actions for which the *śāstra* prescribes various restrictions in performance. According to the commentator, an example of an action with a special restriction concerning direction (*diṅniyama*), is that of consuming one's meal facing the east. If one does not perform eating with its visible result, i.e. satiety, in mind, then the performance aims at religious merit (*dharma*).[51]

---

[50] About the date of Candrānanda there is little certainty. Abhinavagupta likely knew his commentary on the VS, as he quotes a lost work by one Bhaṭṭa Candrānanda in one of his own works. This might be the same person as Candrānanda the VS commentator, who is moreover believed to have lived in Kashmir (see ISAACSON 1995, pp. 141-142). I thank Isabelle Ratié for this reference.

[51] VS 6.2.2.: *abhiṣecanopavāsabrahmacaryagurukulavāsavānaprasthyayajñadānaprokṣaṇadiṅnakṣatramantrakālaniyamāś cādṛṣṭāya* |. "Ablution, fast, abstinence, residence in the house of the preceptor, life in the state of an anchorite, sacrifice, gifts donation, consecration by sprinkling, restrictions concerning direction, constellation, ritual formula and time, [all these] aim at the invisible." *Vṛtti* ad VS 6.2.2, p. 48: *diṅniyamaḥ – 'prāṅmukho 'nnāni bhuñjīta.' ... evaṃ etat sarvaṃ dṛṣṭaprayojanatiraskāreṇa prayujyamānaṃ dharmāya saṃpadyata iti.* "A restriction about spatial direction [is to be found, for instance, in the rule] 'one should take food facing the East.' [...] Thus all these [actions], which are performed without resorting to their visible purpose, are produced in view of religious merit (*dharma*)." Note that other commentators take *niyama* as a separate element of the long coordinative compound in VS 6.2.2, with the meaning of "religious observance," while Candrānanda takes *niyama* separately with all the elements starting with direction (*diś-*), so that there are restrictions concerning direction (*diṅniyama*), constellation (*nakṣatraniyama*), ritual formula (*mantraniyama*) and time (*kālaniyama*).

Despite the great conceptual and semantic similarity between Abhinavagupta's and Candrānanda's formulations, the former does not explicitly equate the invisible result achieved through rule restrictions (*niyamādṛṣṭa*) to *dharma*, while the latter does not seem to acknowledge a double purpose for those restricted actions when he says that the visible purpose is set aside (*tiraskāra*), probably following the *sūtra*'s formulation that the visible purpose is absent (*dṛṣṭābhāve*, in VS 6.2.1) for them. Is it then legitimate to consider Abhinavagupta's *niyamādṛṣṭa* as an equivalent of the *apūrva* invoked by Kumārila in TV 1.3.2, the invisible purpose aimed at through the restriction about paying obeisance to one's master and resulting in the absence of obstacles? This might not be the case: first of all, Abhinavagupta never uses the term "*apūrva*" as a synonym of "*adṛṣṭa*"; second, and more crucially, it seems to me that that the kind of causality implied by Kumārila's analysis of *niyamādṛṣṭa* would be far too mechanical for Abhinavagupta who is, unlike the champion of Vedic exegesis Kumārila, reluctant to deny any kind of agency to the deities in the attainment of a religious result.[52] It should also be pointed out that for Abhinavagupta the production of an invisible result through restrictive rules is not the only possible way to achieve an "*adṛṣṭa*," and certainly not the only way for the limbs of the *pūrvaraṅga*. Other kinds of causalities are envisaged by the author of the ABh between the performance of the limbs of the *pūrvaraṅga* and the "unseen," "*adṛṣṭa*."

"*ADṚṢṬA*" AS THE RESULT KNOWN THROUGH A SCRIPTURE: WARDING OFF THE DEMONS WHILE PLEASING THE GODS

Far from consigning the production of *adṛṣṭa* in the *pūrvaraṅga* to a strict adherence to the rules, which automatically brings about some invisible result, as in the Mīmāṃsaka analysis of ritual action, Abhinavagupta has demons and gods also play a role in the preliminaries of Sanskrit theatre. After all, as we saw earlier in the *Locana* passage, the *pūrvaraṅga* aims at removing potential obstacles that may hinder the performance and that actually disturbed the first mythical representation. However, a direct causal link between the production of an *adṛṣṭa* (or *apūrva*) and the removal of obstacles such

52 As is well known, the gods play a minor role in the analysis of sacrificial action conducted by Mīmāṃsā authors. They are considered, namely, as nothing but names constituting the addressee of the sacrificial oblation. See CLOONEY 1997.

as the one advocated by Kumārila is never called for in Abhinavagupta's analysis.[53] The obstacles imagined as demons threatening a Sanskrit play are, in effect, not really destroyed; they are appeased insofar as they are, just like the gods, satisfied by the performance of the *pūrvaraṅga*. The pacification of the obstacles can be considered an invisible purpose of the limbs of the *pūrvaraṅga*, since this purpose is known only through the *śāstra*, and not through any other means of knowledge. Abhinavagupta explains it in his commentary on NŚ 4.271cd-272ab. The relevant verse in the NŚ reads:

> After the orchestra has been properly arranged [on stage], o best among the twice-borns, the practitioners (understand "the musicians and the singers") should perform the song called *āsārita*.[54]

In order to justify the absence of the intermediate elements between the *pratyāhāra* (first limb) and *āsārita* (last limb), Abhinavagupta takes the verse to refer to the entire group of limbs performed in the first phase of the *pūrvaraṅga*:

> By this [verse], the following is taught: this injunction to perform [the *āsārita* applies] once the whole collection of limbs [of the *pūrvaraṅga*] occurring behind the curtain has been executed. The visible result (*dṛṣṭaphala*) of this [group of limbs], whose essence if the singing of meaningless syllables, consists in an introduction to the performance of instrumental music that will follow [in the second phase of the *pūrvaraṅga*]. Moreover, it has a result that is [known only] through the *śāstra*, i.e. the pacification of the obstacles by satisfying the *daitya*s etc.[55]

In this passage, a visible result is contrasted to a scriptural one (*śāstrīyaphala*) that coincides with the pacification of the obstacles. This agrees in principle with what was stated above with regard to

---

53 The direct causality between the production of an *adṛṣṭa* and the removal of obstacles was also advocated by some early Buddhist authors to explain the practice of composing an auspicious verse (*maṅgala*) before the beginning of a treatise. This *adṛṣṭa* corresponds to merit (*puṇya*), which is regarded as the direct cause of the removal of obstacles, as for instance in Sthiramati's commentary on Vasubandhu's *Madhyāntavibhāga*, and in Yaśomitra on Vasubandhu's *Abhidharmakośabhāṣya* (cf. SLAJE 2007, p. 17, and n. 27).

54 NŚ 4.271cd-272ab: *kṛtvā kutapavinyāsaṃ yathāvad dvijasattamāḥ* ‖ *āsāritaprayogas tu tataḥ kāryaḥ prayoktṛbhiḥ* |.

55 ABh ad NŚ 4.271cd-272ab, vol. I, p. 184: *tena tad uktaṃ bhavati – antaryavanikāgate śuṣkākṣaraprayogaprāṇabhaviṣyadātodyaprayogaprastāvanātmake dṛṣṭaphale* [*dṛṣṭaphale* conj. : *dṛṣṭaphala°* Ed.] *daityādiparitoṣaṇayā tadvighnaśamanaśāstrīyaphale ca prayukte 'ṅgakalāpe 'yaṃ prayogavidhiḥ.*

Kumārila's analysis of *smārta* rules: warding off the obstacles to ensure a successful performance is an invisible purpose that we can only learn about through scripture (here through *śāstra*, i.e. the NŚ).[56] However, it would be a mistake to consider Abhinavagupta's analysis a direct application of the Mīmāṃsaka model, since the obstacles are prevented only insofar as they get satisfied by the performance of music in the *pūrvaraṅga*, and not by means of an impersonal potency that is produced through strict rule observance. This, in fact, is not a case of restrictive injunction leading to an invisible result.

Now, to please the obstacles or demons is the invisible aim of the first phase of the *pūrvaraṅga*, and this is what the *śāstra* tells us. Yet, demons are neither the only category of beings that have to be satisfied through the *pūrvaraṅga*, nor the main one.[57] Quoting his master Bhaṭṭa Tauta, whose opinions Abhinavagupta usually makes his own, he says:

> Our teacher [Bhaṭṭa Tauta] maintains: unless the demons are acting as obstacles and [other obstructive means], what is the need for a *pūrvaraṅga* [to be performed] on the basis of rules? The [*pūrvaraṅga*], in fact, is mainly the cause of satisfaction of the deities installed in the [various] parts of the playhouse, because of [their] action[s] protecting against the obstacles. And it is only due to invariable connection (*nāntarīyaka*) that demons are satisfied. Once the obstacles have occurred, [it makes sense to perform the] *pūrvaraṅga*.[58]

---

56 Here the opposition between *dṛṣṭa* and *adṛṣṭa* is definitely of an epistemological order. In his translation of the *Codanāsūtra* of the *Ślokavārttika*, K. Kataoka explains the dichotomy of the "seen" (*dṛṣṭa*) vs. the "heard" (*śruta*), parallel to the one between the "perceptible world" (*dṛṣṭa*) and the "imperceptible one" (*adṛṣṭa*), common in the *Śābarabhāṣya*, as originating from a contrast between *pramāṇa*s in terms of their objects, namely direct perception (*pratyakṣa*) vs. scriptural teaching (*upadeśa*). Religiously, the same dichotomy is configured in terms of the worldly vs. the dharmic (KATAOKA 2010, p. 343, n. 287).

57 This is in accordance with NŚ 5.45-52, which provides a list of all the various semi-divine and divine beings that are satisfied by the performance of the various limbs of the *pūrvaraṅga*.

58 ABh ad NŚ 1.56cd-57ab, vol. I, p. 25 : *asmadupādhyāyās tu – yāvad daityais tatra vighnādyācaraṇaṃ na kṛtaṃ tāvat pūrvaraṅgasya vidhipūrvakasya ko 'vakāśaḥ. sa hi vighnarakṣākaraṇena maṇḍapabhāganiveśitadevatāparitoṣahetuḥ prādhānyena, nāntarīyakatayā ca daityaparitoṣakāraṇaṃ. vighnās tu yadā jātās tataḥ prabhṛti pūrvaraṅgaḥ.*

The causal sequence outlined in this passage has the action of the obstacles as the main reason for doing the *pūrvaraṅga*: actors perform the *pūrvaraṅga* in order to protect the performance against obstacles. This, however, is not an automatic process, nor does it explain the particular chain of actions performed in the *pūrvaraṅga*. Since the gods appointed to the various parts of theatre[59] exercise a protective action against the obstacle, they have to be satisfied, or propitiated, so that they bestow their protection as a result. How do they get pleased? Through the various songs, dances etc., occurring in the limbs of the *pūrvaraṅga*. As a by-product, or secondary result, the demons are also pleased through the songs of the first part of the *pūrvaraṅga*. Here, the aesthetic quality of the *pūrvaraṅga* definitely plays a role, but this is certainly not a visible purpose, as Ingall's equation "*dṛṣṭa*=secular=beautiful" would imply. We know that the gods are pleased through beautiful dances and songs not because we can directly cognize it, but because the scriptures tell us so. If it were not for the mythical account recalled in the NŚ, and for a direct injunction to do so, no one would perform the *pūrvaraṅga*, let alone in a way conforming to a scripture!

I will now look at the third qualification of the couple "*dṛṣṭa*"/"*adṛṣṭa*" in the context of the purpose of the limbs of the *pūrvaraṅga*.

"*ADṚṢṬA*" AS A RESULT BROUGHT ABOUT BY AN EXTRAORDINARY BEAUTY

Concerning the twofold result of the limbs occurring in the second phase of the *pūrvaraṅga*, their observable result mainly consists in introducing the common spectator to the theatrical reality and its dimension, as well as to some of the specific features of the forthcoming play. Abhinavagupta cleverly creates a series of correspondences between these limbs of the *pūrvaraṅga* and some effect helpful to the play. Thus the benediction (*nāndī*) attracts the attention of the spectators, while the *cārī* and *mahācārī* introduce the amorous and the heroic *rasa*s, and the *trigata* the comic, a *rasa* appealing even to the uneducated audience. One by one, the elements of the second phase of the *pūrvaraṅga* are connected to a result which is

---

59 The installation of deities in the various parts of the auditorium, following the construction of a playhouse, is rendered necessary in order to protect the performance against obstacles. This installation is accompanied by a ceremony of worship, which forms the topic of the third chapter of the NŚ.

called "visible" since it can be directly verified for every performance. Although elements of the second phase of the *pūrvaraṅga* are more easily linked with the forthcoming play and its literary dimension, and consequently with the savouring of *rasa*, the function of the so-called *bahiryavanikāṅga*s does not exhaust itself in it. Says Abhinavagupta:

> In this way, [the group of limbs] at the beginning of a theatrical performance, starting with the *gītaka* song and the *piṇḍī* dances and ending with the *prarocanā*, indeed conforms to the ways of the world (*laukikānusārin*). In this regard, one should not raise the question whether any of these limbs has the capacity [to produce something] (*sāmarthya*), whether [something] has to be achieved (*lakṣyatva*) [through them], etc., because their performance concerns the unsophisticated [spectators]. Therefore, this [group of limbs] has nothing extra-worldly (*alaukika*) in itself. It is only because theatre has mainly the nature of a composition [that some *alaukika* components] have to be added, in order to provide variety [in the performance of the *pūrvaraṅga*], and so as to produce an invisible [result]. This has to be borne in mind, so let us not run on at too great length with it.[60]

The opposition *laukika*/*alaukika* ("worldly"/"extra-worldly") fostered in this passage is not the same as the one seen above, i.e. *laukika* vs. *śāstrīya* as "actions motivated by worldly purposes" and "actions whose motive we can only know through a scripture." The motive of this second series of limbs is indeed visible since their use is self-evident: they help the unsophisticated ones, by preparing and introducing them gradually to the spectacle they are going to witness. This alone would be enough to justify their performance before a play. However, to this phase of the *pūrvaraṅga* are added elements which do not seem to have any practical aim other than charming the spectator. These elements are often called *alaukika* in the ABh, not because they are of a suprasensitive or otherworldly nature, but since they belong to the sphere of theatre, which is different from the mundane sphere albeit not totally divorced from it.[61]

---

60 ABh ad NŚ 5.26-29, vol. I, p. 220: *tathaiva nāṭyārambhe gītakapiṇḍyādiprarocanāntaṃ laukikānusāry eva. nātra kasyacid aṅgasya sāmarthyalakṣyatvādi codanīyam, sukumārajanaviṣayatvād asya prayogasya. tasmān nālaukikaṃ kiñcid etad. kevalaṃ nāṭyasya racanāprādhānyād vaicitryeṇa yojanīyam adṛṣṭasampattaye ceti mantavyam ity alaṃ bahunā.*

61 I am currently preparing an article dealing with the status of "artifice" and its relation to the "natural" in Indian theatre (see GANSER forthcoming).

A typical example of an extraordinary element would be dance, whose insertion in the *pūrvaraṅga* occurs as an addition to an already existent whole.[62] However, even other elements of the *pūrvaraṅga* such as songs, or instrumental music may be considered *alaukika*, in the sense that they do not occur as such in the ordinary world. These elements are said to introduce variety (*vaicitrya*), seen as a beautifying factor, into the performance. This same beauty charms the spectator and entices him into the performed events he is attending.[63] Since this adherence to the performance is necessary for the appreciation of the *rasa*, the purpose which is variety can be considered a visible one, akin to that of the *sandhyaṅgas*. At the same time, these elements produce an unspecified unobservable result, possibly again through the intermediary of the gods' satisfaction, although we would have liked Abhinavagupta to linger somewhat longer on the connection between *alaukika* elements and invisible purposes.[64]

CONCLUSION

To sum up, different but connected values are assigned to the opposite concepts of "seen" or (*dṛṣṭa*) and "unseen" (*adṛṣṭa*), in the performance of the different phases that make up the preliminaries of a play in Indian theatre. The concept of visible purpose (*dṛṣṭaprayojana*) in the context of the *pūrvaraṅga* always refers to the fact that certain actions regulated by text-bound rules aim at directly perceivable results, i.e. they have an evident usefulness for the theatrical performance: they either enable the performance to take place at all, or help the audience to connect to the future play and appreciate it aesthetically. This kind of purpose can be verified though direct experience, and in this sense it is "seen," as it can be experientially verified by everyone. The concept of unseen or invisible purpose

62 The account about the introduction of dance in the *pūrvaraṅga* is given in NŚ 4.1-18ab.

63 See GANSER 2013.

64 If we are to read between the lines, we know at least from the fourth chapter of the ABh that an invisible purpose is given to some of the danced sequences in the *pūrvaraṅga*: since the movements reproduce the attributes of the different deities, the various dance patterns are supposed to please them. See for instance ABh ad NŚ 4.259-260, vol. I, p. 169: *ata evānayā kevalasyāpi karaṇasya devatāparitoṣaṇenādṛṣṭārthaṃ prayogaḥ.* "Therefore, this [indicates] that even a single dance unit (*karaṇa*) can be performed in view of an invisible [result], by pleasing the deities."

(*adṛṣṭaprayojana*), on the other hand, is somewhat more problematic, and varies considerably according to the function of the different phases of the *pūrvaraṅga*. It can refer to the purpose of rule restriction, to the purpose which is cognized through an authoritative scripture, or to the purpose of extraordinary elements.

This ambiguity probably has to do with the complex history of the concept of *adṛṣṭa* outside literary theory. Here is not the place to reconstruct the semantic, linguistic, or textual history of the "unseen," a history that already stretches for over a millennium by the time of Abhinavagupta. Several modern studies inform us about its developments in the different domains of Indian scholarly investigation.[65] The original conceptual unity of the early uses of *adṛṣṭa* is itself a matter of debate, let alone its incorporation and adaptation in the various scholarly systems of medieval India! Abhinavagupta's use of *adṛṣṭa* can be regarded as a sophisticated adoption and adaptation of a concept, developed elsewhere, for his own purposes. Just as, to echo Halbfass, the development of the concept of *apūrva* (or *adṛṣṭa*) in Mīmāṃsā is the encounter of Vedic exegesis and of the theory of sacrifice with a general theory of *karma*, and the concept of *adṛṣṭa* in classical Vaiśeṣika is the encounter of a system of cosmology with soteriological ideas and the theory of *karma*, Abhinavagupta's concept of *adṛṣṭa* in the ABh may be regarded as the encounter of Indian aesthetics – itself already an encounter of formalistic Alaṃkaraśāstra and Nāṭyaśāstra with the Mīmāṃsā theory of the unitary text – with a theory of ritual and Vedic exegesis.

In this connection, rather than trying to give a "closed" meaning to the concepts of *dṛṣṭa* and *adṛṣṭa* used by Abhinavagupta, or to refer them to definite and circumscribed realities, I deem it more useful to consider them to be principles of textual hermeneutics. Given the paucity of systematic explanations of these two concepts in the ABh, despite their frequent recurrence throughout the text, and given the total absence of a context of reference within the poetic tradition as a whole for interpreting them satisfactorily in the domain of this discipline, it has been necessary to look for different models of textual interpretation outside the confines of the literary discourse. A comparison with some of the procedures developed in the exegetical tradition by Mīmāṃsā (especially Kumārila) and Dharmaśāstra authors (Aparārka, but certainly others before him)

---

65 See HALBFASS 1980 and WEZLER 1983.

has highlighted the fact that, in looking for the sources of Abhinavagupta's concepts of *dṛṣṭa* and *adṛṣṭa*, the domain of ritual speculation is a good candidate.

The comparison with the analysis of *smārta* rules has shown that visible and invisible purposes in the domain of theatre can safely be connected with worldly and ethical-ritual goals, something already suggested by Ingalls et al. However, the equation between the visible purposes of the *pūrvaraṅga* and an aesthetic concern for beauty has to be rejected: visible purposes are not necessarily linked with beauty, as for instance in the whole series of limbs occurring behind a curtain. Conversely, an extraordinary beauty can well have an invisible purpose if it results in the satisfaction of the gods and therefore contributes to the attainment of an imperceptible result such as the removal of the obstacles to the performance. The adjunction of some extraordinary elements in the second phase of the *pūrvaraṅga* aims, in effect, at satisfying the gods, while giving pleasure at the same time to even the less refined spectator, thus enabling the whole audience to savour the *rasa* of the play. The use of this exegetical model thus allows Abhinavagupta to connect elements that are not easily linked with one another, and to subordinate disparate elements to wider goals. But there is, I believe, another reason why such a model has been applied in the first instance to the analysis of the *pūrvaraṅga*, namely its primarily ritual nature, as the scheme of twofold results of the preliminaries as a whole demonstrates.

Applying a twofold purpose to the limbs of the *pūvaraṅga* thus entails two different operations. First of all, it connects in a meaningful and coherent way the different parts of the preliminaries between them, as well as to the theatrical performance as a single unit with a single overriding goal. Secondly, it preserves the identity of the *pūrvaraṅga* as a specific kind of ritual, the worship of the deities of the stage through songs and dances, a rite altogether different from the Vedic sacrifice around which ritual exegesis traditionally revolves.

If the context from which Abhinavagupta's analysis of the *pūrvaraṅga* stems is, as suggested in this essay, one of ritual exegesis closely linked with the hermeneutics of scriptural rules, we must admit that Abhinavagupta was looking at the NŚ not merely as a manual for actors, but as a scripture containing rules of performance hierarchically organized and analysable through the same tools developed by the Brahmanical exegetes for the analysis of the Vedic and non-Vedic sources of *dharma*.[66] Such a model requires, in my view, an even deeper appropriation of the exegetical paradigm than the one applied by Ānandavardhana to the analysis of a poetic text, since it does not only take into account the teleological organization of the minimal elements of poetics into one and the same literary work, but it also elaborates, just as the ritual exegetes had done in the case of Vedic rituals and the text enjoining them, a close parallelism between the elements of a theatrical composition (here both the *pūrvaraṅga* and the play), and the scripture prescribing their performance, the NŚ.[67]

In conclusion, I regard the transition from the single, invisible purpose of the limbs of the *pūrvaraṅga* in the *Locana* passage, to the twofold model of visible and invisible purposes presented in the ABh, and implemented throughout the text, as an actual refinement in Abhinavagupta's aesthetic thought triggered by the challenge posed by the complex phenomenon that is theatre, as well as a personal contribution to ritual speculation by an original Śaiva philosopher.

REFERENCES

ABh
See NŚ

BANSAT-BOUDON 1992
L. Bansat-Boudon, *Poétique du théâtre indien. Lectures du Nāṭyaśāstra*, Paris:

---

[66] On this distinction, see YOSHIMIZU 1992.

[67] This development in the appropriation of the model of ritual exegesis in the ABh is reflected also by the fact that Abhinavagupta considers not only a play or a poem as a single complex sentence (*mahāvākya*) (cf., for instance, ABh ad NŚ 1.107: *rāmāyaṇaprāyād ekasmān mahāvākyād*; and Abh ad NŚ 19.37, vol. III, p. 23: *mahāvākyārtharūpasya rūpakārthasya pañcāṃśāḥ*), but also the NŚ, a large sentence of 6.000 verses (ABh ad NŚ 1.6, vol. I, p. 9: *mahāvākyātmanā ṣaṭsahasrīrūpeṇa... śāstreṇa tattvaṃ nirṇīyate.* "The true essence [of theatre] is established by the treatise in form of a large utterance of six thousand verses"). The idea of a single "large sentence" (*mahāvākya*), with the unity of purpose that such a single complex sentence should have, again has its origins in Mīmāṃsā. The fact that the whole tradition stemming from the NŚ considers theatre to be a fifth Veda could have played a role in the parallelism with ritual speculation. However, a closer investigation into the status of Ālaṃkāraśāstra and Nāṭyaśāstra within Brahmanical knowledge classification, and into the place assigned to the *śāstras* of poetics and dramatics by the exponents of the poetic and aesthetic tradition, is still a desideratum.

École Française d'Extrême-Orient, Publications de l'École Française d'Extrême-Orient 169, 1992

BANSAT-BOUDON 1997
L. Bansat-Boudon, "Conférence de Mme Lyne Bansat-Boudon. Le rite, le théâtre et l'ordre du monde: lectures du *Nāṭyaśāstra* (1996-1998)," *Annuaire de l'École Pratique des Hautes Études, Section des Sciences Religieuses* 106, 1997-1998, pp. 165-171

BANSAT-BOUDON 2001
L. Bansat-Boudon, "*Nāndyante sūtradhāraḥ*: Contribution d'Abhinavagupta à la question de la bénédiction liminaire dans le théâtre," in R. Torella (ed.), *Le parole e i marmi: Studi in onore di Raniero Gnoli nel suo 70. compleanno*, vol. II, Roma: Istituto Italiano per l'Africa e l'Oriente, 2001, pp. 37-84

BANSAT-BOUDON 2004
L. Bansat-Boudon, *Pourquoi le Théâtre? Le réponse indienne*, Paris: Mille et une nuits, 2004

BANSAT-BOUDON 2012
L. Bansat-Boudon, "Aesthetica *in nuce* dans le mythe d'origine du théâtre indien," in S. D'Intino and C. Guenzi (eds.), *Aux abords de la clairière. Études indiennes et comparées en l'honneur de Charles Malamoud*, Paris: Brepols, Bibliothèque de l'École des Hautes Études, 2012, pp. 209-234

BENSON 2010
J. Benson, *Mahādeva Vedāntin. Mīmāṃsānyāyasaṃgraha. A Compendium of the Principles of Mīmāṃsā* (ed. and transl.), Wiesbaden: Harrassowitz Verlag, Ethno-Indology, Heidelberg Studies in South Asian Rituals 5, 2010

BIARDEAU 1969
M. Biardeau, *La philosophie de Maṇḍana Miśra vue à partir de la Brahmasiddhi*, Paris: École Française d'Extrême-Orient, Publications de l'École Française d'Extrême-Orient 76, 1969

BIARDEAU 1981
M. Biardeau, [Review of KUIPER 1979] "F.B.J. Kuiper *Varuṇa and Vidūṣaka. On the origin of the Sanskrit drama*," *Indo-Iranian Journal* 23, 1981, pp. 293-318

BRICK 2006
D. Brick, "Transforming tradition into texts: The early development of *smṛti*," *Journal of Indian Philosophy* 34, 2006, pp. 287-302

CLOONEY 1997
F.X. Clooney, "What's a god? The quest for the right understanding of *devatā* in Brāhmaṇical ritual theory (*mīmāṃsā*)," *International Journal of Hindu Studies* 1(2), 1997, pp. 337-385

CUNEO 2009
D. Cuneo, *Emotions without Desire. An Interpretive Appraisal of Abhinavagupta's Rasa Theory. Annotated Translation of the First, Sixth and Seventh Chapters of Abhinavagupta's Abhinavabhāratī*, Unpublished PhD Thesis, Rome: "Sapienza" University of Rome, 2009

CUNEO 2013
D. Cuneo, "Unfuzzying the fuzzy. The distinction between *rasa*s and *bhāva*s in Bharata and Abhinavagupta," in N. Mirnig, P.-D. Szántò and M. Williams (eds.), *Puṣpikā: Tracing Ancient India through Texts and Traditions. Contributions to Current Research in Indology*, vol. I, Oxford: Oxbow books, 2013, pp. 50-75

DAVID 2013
H. David, "Action theory and scriptural exegesis in early Advaita-Vedānta (1): Maṇḍana Miśra on *upadeśa* and *iṣṭasādhanatā*," in V. Eltschinger and H. Krasser (eds.), *Scriptural Authority, Reason and Action. Proceedings of a Panel at the 14th World Sanskrit Conference, Kyoto September 1st-5th 2009*, Vienna: Verlag der österreichischen Akademie der Wissenschaften, Beitrage zur Kultur- und Geistesgeschichte Asiens 79, 2013, pp. 271-318

DAVID 2014
H. David, "Time, Action and Narration. On Some Exegetical Sources of Abhinavagupta's Aesthetic Theory," *Journal of Indian Philosophy* 44, 2014, pp. 125-154

DE 1959
S.K. De, "The Theory of Rasa in Sanskrit Poetics," in *Some Problems of Sanskrit Poetics*, [1st ed. in Sir Asutosh Mookerjee Silver Jubile Volume III (Orientalia), part II] Calcutta: Mukhopaghyay, 1959, pp. 177-235

DhĀ
Dhvanyāloka of Ānandavardhana with the226Locana of Abhinavagupta, the Bālapriyā subcommentary of Rāmaśāraka, and the Divyāñjana notes of Pt. Mahādeva Śāstri, ed. P. Śāstri, Benares: 1940, Kashi Sanskrit Series 135

DhĀ (Nirnaya Sagar ed.)
Dhvanyāloka of Ānandavardhana with the Locana of Abhinavagupta, ed. D. and K. Pāṇḍuraṅg Parab (revised by V.L. Śāstrī Paṃśikar), [Bombay: 1935, Nirnaya Sagar Press, Kāvyamālā 25] New Delhi: Munshiram Manoharlal Publishers, 1983

Locana
[*Dhvanyālokalocana*] See DhĀ

ELTSCHINGER 2013
V. Eltschinger, "Turning hermeneutics into apologetics. Reasoning and rationality under changing historical circumstances," in V. Eltschinger and H. Krasser (eds.), *Scriptural Authority, Reason and Action. Proceedings of a Panel at the 14th World*

Sanskrit Conference, Kyoto September 1st-5th 2009, Vienna: Verlag der österreichischen Akademie der Wissenschaften, Beitrage zur Kultur- und Geistesgeschichte Asiens 79, 2013, pp. 71-145

FEISTEL 1969
H.O. Feistel, *Das Vorspiel auf dem Theater: ein Beitrag zur Frühgeschichte des klassischen indischen Schauspiels*, Tübingen: Eberhard-Karls Universität, 1969

FEISTEL 1972
H.O. Feistel, "The *pūrvaraṅga* and the chronology of pre-classical Sanskrit theatre," *Samskrita Ranga annual* 6 (Special felicitation volume in honour of dr. V. Raghavan), 1972, pp. 1-26

FOUCHER 1949
A. Foucher, *Le compendium des Topiques (Tarka Samgraha) d'Annambhaṭṭa. Avec des extraits de trois commentaires indiens. Texte et traduction. Éléments de systématique et de logique indiennes*, Paris: Adrien Maisonneuve, 1949

GANSER 2010
E. Ganser, *Theatre and its Other. The irresistible alterity of dance in Abhinavagupta's theory of drama. A Study, Annotated Translation and Edition of Selected Portions from the Fourth Chapter of Abhinavagupta's Abhinavabhāratī*, Unpublished PhD Thesis, Rome: "Sapienza" University of Rome, 2010

GANSER 2013
E. Ganser, "Trajectories of dance on the surface of theatrical meanings. A contribution to the theory of *rasa* from the fourth chapter of the *Abhinavabhāratī*," in N. Mirnig, P.-D. Szántò and M. Williams (eds.), *Puṣpikā: Tracing Ancient India through Texts and Traditions. Contributions to Current Research in Indology*, vol. I, Oxford: Oxbow books, 2013, pp. 173-202

GANSER forthcoming
E. Ganser, "Poetic convention, theatrical artifice and the place of nature in Indian dramatic theory"

GITOMER 1994
D.L. Gitomer, "Whither the thick sweetness of their passion?", in L. Patton (ed.), *Authority, Anxiety, and Canon. Essays in Vedic Interpretation*, New York: SUNY Press, 1994, pp. 171-198

GNOLI 1968
R. Gnoli, *The aesthetic experience according to Abhinavagupta*, [Rome: Istituto Italiano per il Medio ed Estremo Oriente, Serie Orientale Roma 11, 1956] Varanasi: Chowkhamba Sanskrit Series Office, 1968

GONDA 1943
J. Gonda, *Zur Frage nach dem Ursprung und Wesen des Indischen Dramas*, Leiden: Brill, Acta Orientalia 19, 1943

HALBFASS 1980
W. Halbfass, "Karma, *apūrva*, and 'natural' causes. Observations on the growth and limits of the theory of *saṃsāra*," in W. Doniger O'Flaherty (ed.), *Karma and rebirth in classical Indian traditions*, Berkeley/London: University of California Press, 1980, pp. 268-302

INGALLS ET AL. 1990
D.H.H. Ingalls, J.M. Masson and M.V. Patwardhan, *The Dhvanyāloka of Ānandavardhana, with the Locana of Abhinavagupta*, Cambridge (Mass.)/London: Harvard University Press, Harvard Oriental Series 49, 1990

ISAACSON 1995
H. Isaacson, *Materials for the Study of the Vaiśeṣika System*, Unpublished PhD Thesis, Leiden: University of Leiden, 1995

KANE 1941
P.V. Kane, *History of Dharmaśāstra: Ancient and mediaeval religious and civil law in India*, vol. II, part 1, Poona: Bhandarkar Oriental Research Institute, Government Oriental Series, Class B, 6.2.1, 1941

KANE 1962
P.V. Kane, *History of Dharmaśāstra: Ancient and mediaeval religious and civil law in India*, vol. V.2, Poona: Bhandarkar Oriental Research Institute, Government Oriental Series, Class B, 6.5.2, 1962

KATAOKA 2011
K. Kataoka, *Kumārila on truth, omniscience, and killing*, vol. II: *An annotated translation of Mīmāṃsāślokavārttika ad 1.1.2 (Codanāsūtra)*, Vienna: Österreichische Akademie der Wissenschaften, Beiträge zur Kultur- und Geistesgeschichte Asiens 68, 2011

Kāvyālaṃkārasūtra
Kāvyālaṃkārasūtra of Vāmana, with the Kāmadhenu of Gopendra Tripurahara Bhūpāla, ed. B. Jha, Varanasi: Chaukhamba, 1989

KUIPER 1979
F.B.J. Kuiper, *Varuṇa and Vidūṣaka. On the origin of the Sanskrit drama*, Amsterdam: North-Holland Publishing Company, Verhandelingen der Koninklijke Nederlandse Akademie van Wetenschappen, Afd. Letterkunde, Nieuwe reeks 100, 1979

LATH 1978
M. Lath, *A Study of Dattilam. A Treatise on the Sacred Music of Ancient India*, New Delhi: Impex India, 1978

LIDOVA 1994
N. Lidova, *Drama and ritual of early Hinduism,* Delhi: Motilal Banarsidass Publishers Private Limited, Performing Arts Series 4, 1994

MASSON AND PATWARDHAN 1970
J.M. Masson and M.V. Patwardhan, *Aesthetic rapture: The Rasādhyāya of the Nāṭyaśāstra*, 2 vols., Poona: Deccan College, 1970

MCCREA 2008
L.J. McCrea (2008), *The teleology of poetics in medieval Kashmir*, Cambridge (Mass.)/London: Harvard University Press, Harvard Oriental Series 71, 2008

MDhŚ
[*Mānavadharmaśāstra*] See OLIVELLE 2005

Mīmāṃsādarśana
Mīmāṃsādarśana of Maharṣi Jaimini, with Śābarabhāṣya of Śabaramuni, with the Commentary Tantravārtika of Kumārila Bhaṭṭa, Nyāyasudhā Commentary of Bhaṭṭa Someśvara, Bhāṣyavivaraṇa Bhāvaprakāśikā by Mahāprabhulāl Gosvāmī, ed. M. Gosvāmī, 4 vols., Benares: 1984, Tārā Printing Works, Prācyabhāratī Series 16

MUKHERJEE 1926
S.C. Mukherjee, *Le rasa: Essai sur l'esthétique indienne*, Paris: Libraire Félix Alcan, 1926

NŚ
Nāṭyaśāstra of Bharatamuni with the Commentary Abhinavabhāratī by Abhinavaguptācārya, ed. M.R. Kavi, Baroda: 1926-1960, Gaekwad's Oriental Series 36, 68, 124, 145; vol. I (2nd ed.) revised and ed. R. Sastri, 1956; vol. II, 1934; vol. III, 1954; vol. IV, 1964

OLIVELLE 2005
P. Olivelle, *Manu's Code of Law. A Critical Edition and Translation of the Mānava-Dharmaśāstra*, New York: Oxford University Press, 2005

POLLOCK 2010
S. Pollock, "What was Bhaṭṭa Nāyaka saying? The Hermeneutical Trans-formation of Indian Aesthetics," in S. Pollock (ed.), *Epic and Argument in Indian Literary History. Essays in Honor of Robert P. Goldman*, Delhi: Manohar, 2010, pp. 143-83

RAGHAVAN 1940
V. Raghavan, *The Number of Rasas*, Adyar: Adyar Library and Research Centre, Adyar Library Series 23, 1940

RAMANATHAN 1999
N. Ramanathan, *Musical forms in Saṅgītaratnākara*, Chennai: Sampradaya, 1999

SLAJE 2008
W. Slaje (ed.), *Śāstrārambha: Inquiries into the Preamble in Sanskrit*, Wiesbaden: Harrassowitz Verlag, Abhandlungen für die Kunde des Morgenlandes 62, 2008

TĀ
Tantrāloka of Abhinavagupta with commentary by Rājānaka Jayaratha, ed. M.K. Shāstrī, 12 vols., Allahabad-Srinagar-Bombay: 1918-1938, Kashmir Series of Texts and Studies

THIEME 1966
P. Thieme, "Das indische Theater," in H. Kindermann (ed.), *Fernöstliches Theater*, Stuttgart: Alfred Kröner Verlag, 1966, pp. 21-120

TV
[*Tantravārttika*] See *Mīmāṃsādarśana*

VS
Vaiśeṣikasūtra of Kaṇāda, with the commentary of Candrānanda, ed. Muni Śri Jambuvijayaji, Baroda: 1961, Oriental Institute, Gaekwad Oriental Series 136

WEZLER 1983
A. Wezler, "A note on concept *adṛṣṭa* as used in the Vaiśeṣikasūtra," in *Aruṇabhāratī: Professor A.N. Jaini felicitation volume. Essays in contemporary Indological research*, Baroda: Oriental Institute, 1983, pp. 35-58

YOSHIMIZU 2007
K. Yoshimizu, "Kumārila's Reevaluation of the Sacrifice and the Veda from a Vedānta Perspective," in J. Bronkhorst (ed.), *Mīmāṃsā and Vedānta. Interaction and Continuity*, Delhi: Motilal Banarsidass, 2007, pp. 201-253

YOSHIMIZU 2012
K. Yoshimizu, "Kumārila and Medhātithi on the Authority of Codified Sources of *dharma*," in F. Voegeli, V. Eltschinger, D. Feller, M.P. Candotti, B. Diaconescu and M. Kulkarni (eds.), *Devadattīyam: Johannes Bronkhorst Felicitation Volume*, Bern/Oxford: Peter Lang, Worlds of South and Inner Asia 5, 2012, pp. 643-681

The Force of *Tātparya*: Bhaṭṭa Jayanta and Abhinavagupta*

ALESSANDRO GRAHELI

1. INTRODUCTION

In India, most theories of meaning have hinged on two distinct capacities of language to convey meanings, *abhidhā* and *lakṣaṇā*. The two, respectively, have been widely used to explain direct, primary meanings, and secondary, implied, and metaphorical meanings. INGALLS 1990 (p. 14) writes that, in addition to these two,

> the school of ritualists founded by Kumārila held that there existed a third power which furnished a "final meaning" to the sentence as a whole. They called this the *tātparyaśakti*, and defended its reality against their opponents, the Prābhākara ritualists, who claimed that the designative force in each word kept on operating until at the conclusion of the sentence it worked automatically in harmony with the other words.

Here, Ingalls evokes the Bhāṭṭa theory of sentence signification, *abhihitānvaya* ("correlation of designated meanings"), and the Prā bhākara one, *anvayābhidhāna*, "designation of correlated [words]."[1] The notion of *tātparyaśakti*, however, is not found in Kumārila's

---

* This paper is based on the material gathered for the forthcoming critical edition of the sixth chapter of the *Nyāyamañjarī* of Bhaṭṭa Jayanta, researched during the FWF (Fonds zur Förderung der wissenschaftlichen Forschung) project M-1160 G-15, July 2009 to June 2011. Manuscript material used in this paper was provided by the *Nyāyabhāṣya* projects at the ISTB (FWF Projects P-17244, P-19328 and P-24388). Special thanks are due to Elisa Freschi, who read an early draft of the paper and enhanced its value with insightful remarks.

[1] Details on the *abhihitānvaya* and *anvitābhidhāna* theories, seen from different angles, can be found in BROUGH 1953, KUNJUNNI RAJA 1963, pp. 189-227, SIDERITS 1985, TABER 1989, MATILAL 1990, pp. 106-119, and PRASAD 1994, pp. 331-338, among others. SIDERITS 1985, p. 96, rendered *abhihitānvaya* as the "designated relation theory"; MATILAL AND SEN 1988, p. 73, as "signification before connection," and MATILAL 1990, pp. 107ff., as "designation before connection"; PRASAD 1994, p. 331, as "theory of compositional significance."

works nor in other early Bhāṭṭa sources. Ingalls is not alone in attributing the *tātparyaśakti* idea to the Bhāṭṭas, as noticed also by KUNJUNNI RAJA 1963, p. 221:

> Some of the ancient commentators, and modern scholars following them, have thus associated *tātparyavṛtti* with the Bhāṭṭa school of Mīmāṃsā. But there is one difficulty in such an assumption which many of the scholars have not noticed. All the great authoritative writers on Bhāṭṭa Mīmāṃsā like Kumārilabhaṭṭa, Pārthasārathimiśra, Vācaspatimiśra, Cidānanda and Nārāyaṇabhaṭṭa have unequivocally stated that according to the *abhihitānvaya* theory advocated by them the syntactically unified sentence-meaning is to be conveyed through the secondary power, *lakṣaṇā*.

Long after Kumārila (7th c. CE), the *tātparyaśakti* became a common feature in explanations of the process of sentence signification, particularly in Navyanyāya and Ālaṅkāra treatises, two of Ingalls's interests that justify his assumption in the above-quoted passage. In Nyāya sources, the earliest use of *tātparyaśakti* is found at the end of the 9th c., in Bhaṭṭa Jayanta's *Nyāyamañjarī* (henceforth NM), while in poetics the first occurrence is, to my knowledge, in Abhinavagupta's *Dhvanyālokalocana* (10th-11th c., henceforth *Locana*). Both Jayanta and Abhinavagupta, in fact, appear to have adopted a form of *abhihitānvaya* in which the role of *lakṣaṇā* is covered by that of *tātparya*.

The theme of this paper is a comparison of Jayanta's and Abhinavagupta's version of *abhihitānvaya*. I will try to find answers to three main questions:

- What is the import of the term *tātparya* in Jayanta's expression *tātparyaśakti*?
- What were the reasons behind Jayanta's modification of the Bhāṭṭa theory of *abhihitānvaya*, which brought about the replacement of *lakṣaṇā* with *tātparyaśakti*?
- Is there a connection between Jayanta's and Abhinavagupta's views on sentence signification and the use of *tātparyaśakti*?

To do this, I will sketch relevant traits of the Bhāṭṭa theory of *abhihitānvaya*. I will then discuss differences in Jayanta's adaptation of the theory, and focus on the *tātparyaśakti* concept. Lastly, I will describe Abhinavagupta's version of the theory, trying to detect possible links with Jayanta's and Kumārila's ideas.

2. JAYANTA AND THE MĪMĀṂSAKAS

2.1. Designation of Word-Meanings

2.1.1. From Phonemes to Words

Jayanta's theory of meaning evolved from a criticism of the Vyākaraṇa and Mīmāṃsā positions, particularly Bhartṛhari's *sphoṭavāda*, the Bhāṭṭa theory of *abhihitānvaya*, and the Prābhākara *anvitābhidhāna*. In the first part of NM 6, Jayanta concludes that phonemes are the cause of word-meanings (*padārtha*), polemizing with the Sphoṭavādins and in agreement with the Mīmāṃsakas: a string of phonemic sounds in a fixed sequence, i.e., a word, causes the cognition of the meaning in the hearer, in a psychological process that involves perceptions (*anubhava*), dispositions (*saṃskāra*) and recollections (*smaraṇa*).

In this paper I will render *artha* with "meaning," and *śabda*, occasionally, with "words," to simplify the exposition and the linguistic scope of the paper. Yet, translations such as "sound," "word," "language," "linguistic expression," "verbal testimony," are all in some way too narrow, and the same is true of "thing," "object," "thing-meant," "referent," "reference," "sense," "meaning," etc., for *artha*. The main difficulty is the conflation of the linguistic, epistemic, and ontological senses in the two Sanskrit words. Also, these English words are for the most part loaded terms that carry the inheritance of centuries of philosophical speculations, not necessarily reflected in the Sanskrit milieu. For instance, see NM^{Va}, vol. II, p. 540, l. 16, where Jayanta distinguishes the teleological from the ontological use of the word *artha*.[2]

For passages of the NM and the *Nyāyamañjarīgranthibhaṅga* (henceforth GBh) quoted in this paper, I will supply substantive variants from the relevant manuscript materials and occasionally re-edit the text. A list of available manuscripts of the NM can be found in GRAHELI 2012a, and the criteria used in the choice of the best readings are discussed in GRAHELI 2012b and GRAHELI 2015b, ch. 5.

The process of word-signification is debated in depth in NM^{Va}, vol. II, pp. 143-184. Jayanta's position on this issue is summed up in Figure 1. In this diagram, as well as in the following ones, the

---

2 *arthaḥ arthyamānaḥ ucyate, na vasturūpa eva, abhāvasyāpi prayojanatvasaṃbhavāt.*

designative causation is indicated by a straight arrow, and phonemic expressions are in italics (e.g., *g au ḥ*). In Figure 1, specifically, the object of designation is indicated in single quotation marks.

Figure 1: Signification of phonemes

g–au–ḥ

↓

'gauḥ'

Words, which are constituted of phonemes, convey word-meanings by direct designation (*abhidhā*). Jayanta largely quotes from and adheres to the Mīmāṃsā atomistic and compositional view, but while Mīmāṃsakas speak of *abhidhāvyāpāra*, "designative operativity," Jayanta calls it *abhidhātrī śakti*, "designative capacity."

2.1.2. Jayanta on śakti

Jayanta does not use the term *śakti* casually. He glosses *śakti* as "that which has the nature of contributing to the own form [of something],"[3] and he frequently resorts to this term when discussing causal relations. A *śakti* is not a property-possessor, but rather a property inhering in a property-possessor: *śakti*s and other properties are considered by him as distinguishing factors that prove the plurality of entities (*dharmin*; see NM^{Va}, vol. II, p. 42, l. 15-p. 43, l. 2).[4] Hence, *śakti*s are counted as delimiting properties (*avacchedā dharmāḥ*, see GBh, p. 136, ll. 11-17). This means that *abhidhā* and *tātparya* are understood by Jayanta as properties of linguistic expressions.

In a general discussion on causality, Jayanta distinguishes two types of *śakti*, fixed (*avasthitā*) and situational (*āgantukī*): in the production of a clay-pot, an example of the first type is the *śakti* of clay, and of the second that of the combination of stick, wheel, etc. (NM^{Va}, vol. II, p. 403, ll. 8-10)[5]. If we apply this distinction to the two *śakti*s

---

3 E.g., NM^{Va}, vol. I, p. 182, l. 11: *svarūpasahakārisvabhāvaiva*; NM^{Va}, vol. I, p. 403, l. 8: *yogyatāvacchinnasvarūpasahakārisannidhānam eva*. See also *Nyāyakośa*, s.v. *kāraṇaniṣṭhaḥ kāryotpādanayogyo dharmaviśeṣaḥ*.

4 *api cāsmanmate bhinnaiḥ dharmair yuktasya dharmiṇaḥ | dharmo 'sya kenacit kaścit pratyayena grahīṣyate || vicitrasahakāryādiśaktibhedaś ca dharmiṇaḥ | nānopādhyupakārāṅgaśaktyabhinnātmatā kutaḥ ||*.

5 *saiveyaṃ dvividhā śaktir ucyate avasthitā āgantukī ca. mṛttvādyavacchinnaṃ svarūpaṃ avasthitā śaktiḥ. āgantukī ca daṇḍacakrādisaṃgarūpā.*

under discussion, it is possible that Jayanta either considered *abhidhāśakti* to be a fixed *śakti*, and *tātparyaśakti* a situational one, or that he took them both as situational ones, although he does not explicitly say so.

Whatever the case, Jayanta contrasted his own notion of *vācakaśakti* with that of the Mīmāṃsakas, who thought of it as permanent and natural (e.g., NM^{Va}, vol. I, p. 591, ll. 1-3; vol. II, p. 403, l. 6). In Nyāya, indeed, signification is based on a convention (*samaya*, *saṅketa*), so *abhidhāśakti* must either be situational, or "fixed" after the *saṅketa,* but certainly not "permanent" in the Mīmāṃsaka sense. Therefore, to understand the signifier-signified relation as a natural or permanent *śakti* is not acceptable for Jayanta (NM^{Va}, vol. II, p. 596, ll. 16-10).[6] The conventional nature of the signifier-signified relation is a necessary assumption in the Nyāya epistemology of *śabda*, which is founded on the trustworthiness of the speaker (*āptavācakatva*) and, consequently, on the authorship of the Veda (*pauruṣeyatā*). In the NM, the *abhidhātrī śakti* seems indeed to be linked to the very definition of *śabda* in *Nyāyasūtra* (henceforth NS) 1.1.7, *āptopadeśaḥ śabdaḥ*, since Jayanta glosses *upadeśaḥ* with *abhidhānakriyā* (NM^{Va}, vol. I, p. 399, ll. 1-2).

Here I will render *abhidhāna* with "designation" and *śakti*, or its synonym *sāmarthya*, with "capacity," meaning that the combined phonemes of a word have the potentiality to cause a word-meaning. In Figure 1 and the following diagrams, therefore, the straight arrow shows the actualization of the designative capacity.

A compositional theory of sentence signification is necessarily influenced by the implied theory of word signification, namely whether the *artha* of the word is considered as a particular (*vyakti*), a configuration (*ākṛti*), or a natural kind (*jāti*), the three options contemplated in NS 2.2.66.

2.1.3. Mīmāṃsakas on word-meanings

Śabara distinguished the meaning of a word from that of a sentence, thus establishing a general principle that would become central in the formulation of later Mīmāṃsā theories: "The word functions in relation to the natural kind, the sentence in relation to the particular" (*Śābarabhāṣya* [henceforth ŚBh] ad *Mīmāṃsāsūtra* [henceforth MSū] 1.1.24, p. 112, l.1).[7] Kumārila elaborates on this rule in the

---

6 *iti na śaktirūpaḥ śabdārthayoḥ sambandhaḥ.*

7 *sāmānye hi padaṃ pravartate viśeṣe vākyam.*

Tantravārttika (henceforth TV). It is clear, from the observation of its practical usage, that in language we have sentence-meanings that must be particulars, because the force of an injunctive sentence such as "Bring the white cow!" produces a specific act of bringing a particular cow. Each word-meaning is a natural kind (*ākṛti* or *jāti*, the two terms being used interchangeably by Kumārila, unlike in Nyāya). By mutual specification among the word-meanings, the particular sentence-meaning is produced. More precisely, the mutual specification is the sentence-meaning (TV 2.1.46, pp. 436-437):

> In the theory that the word-meaning is the natural kind (*ākṛti*), the sentence-meaning is the mutual influence caused by the contiguity of the naturally (*svarūpeṇa*) designated "whiteness" and "cowness," in which the difference of meanings is [already] accomplished. This correlation of whiteness with cowness, or of cowness with whiteness, is grasped as a collection from the sum of the single entities [i.e., of the single word-meanings].[8]

2.1.4. *Jayanta on word-meanings*

According to Jayanta (NM^{Va}, vol. II, p. 59, l. 4-p. 60, l. 7), instead, what is designated by a word is not just a generality (a natural kind), nor a particular, as in Vyāḍi's theory (see GANERI 1995, p. 410), but rather a *tadvat* (*tad asyāstīti*), a property-possessor, in which general and particular aspects are predominant according to the specific applications. This theory of meaning allows the Naiyāyika the necessary flexibility to account for both types of reference.[9] In the following diagrams, I have inscribed a particular in a circle, and a natural kind in a dashed circle. The kind-possessing particular (or particular-possessing kind) is inscribed in both a dashed and a continuous circle (see Figure 2).

---

8 *ākṛtipadārthapakṣe śuklatvagotvayoḥ svarūpeṇābhihitayoḥ saṃnidhānād itaretarānurañjanam arthasiddhabhedaṃ vākyārthaḥ. sa ca gotve śuklatvasaṃsargaḥ śuklatve vā gotvasaṃsargaḥ sāmastyenaikaikavyaktyupasaṃhārād upalabhyata iti.*

9 See GANERI 1999, pp. 102-104, for the philosophical implications of this concept. The tadvat theory was already in existence before Jayanta's time, since it is mentioned in the *Nyāyavārttika* ad NS 1.1.1, p. 4, l. 16; ad NS 1.1.3, p. 28, l. 3; ad NS 1.1.29, p. 100, l. 3; ad NS 2.2.66, pp. 306-312.

Figure 2: Three views on word-meaning: Vyāḍi, Śabara, Jayanta

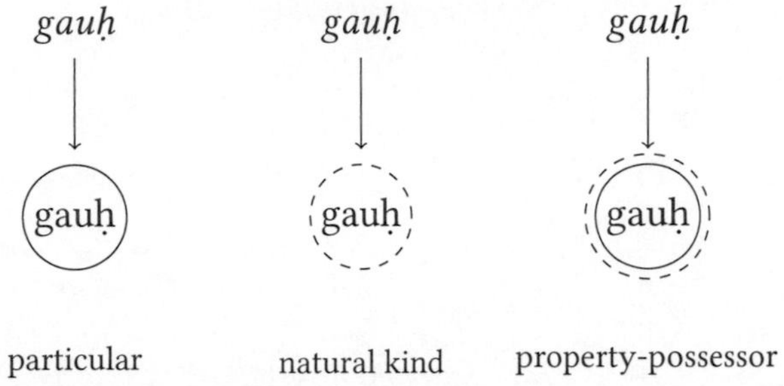

Leaving aside the particularistic position, which is of no direct relevance here, the ontological difference between the Mīmāṃsā and the Nyāya versions of direct designation is an important factor in the development of the two parallel theories.

2.2. Signification of Sentence-Meanings

I will now consider a recurrent example of injunctive sentence, *gām abhyāja kṛṣṇāṃ daṇḍena*, "Bring the black cow, by means of the stick," used in the NM as well (NM^{Va}, vol. I, p. 695, l. 17, NM 4). The single words designate their own meanings, which in Jayanta's view are neither merely natural kinds, nor particulars, but rather property-possessors. Up to this point, as far as the designation of word-meanings is concerned, there is no disagreement with the Bhāṭṭas's *abhihitānvaya*, except for the ontological quality of the word-meanings. But what about the step from the word-meanings to the sentence-meaning, i.e., the *anvaya*? Here, too, the Bhāṭṭas and Jayanta share the view that the sentence-meaning is the correlation of word-meanings. This correlation is indicated by the horizontal line connecting the word-meanings in Figure 3.

Figure 3: Correlation of word-meanings

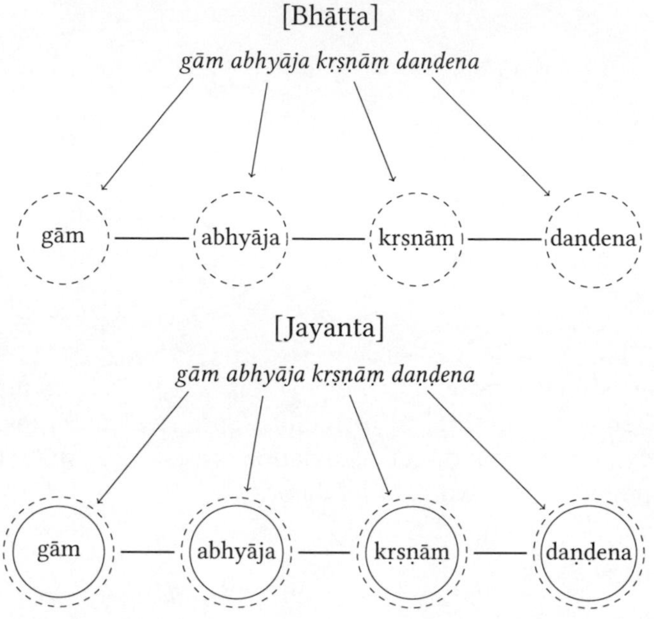

2.2.1. The Bhāṭṭas on the correlation of word-meanings

In the Bhāṭṭa version of *abhihitānvaya*, the correlation of the word-meanings is derived by *lakṣaṇāvyāpāra*, an indirect significatory process that needs some explanation. The recurrent passage in support of *lakṣaṇāvyāpāra* is found in *Prakaraṇapañcikā*, *vākyārthamātṛkā*, p. 396, l. 6 and *Tattvabindu*, p. 153): "Our position is that in every case that the sentence-meaning is indirectly indicated (*lakṣyamāṇaḥ*)." Both Śālikanātha and Vācaspati ascribe it to Kumārila, although I could not find it in his extant works.[10]

In the mainstream Bhāṭṭa theory, *lakṣaṇā* should be understood in the general sense of "indication" or "implication"[11] as opposed to

---

10 *vākyārtho lakṣyamāṇo hi sarvatraiveti naḥ sthitiḥ.* Interestingly, with rare exceptions, *abhihitānvaya* has been mostly studied on the basis of an opponent's presentation, that of Śālikanātha, a very detailed and lucid presentation, but not necessarily an unbiased one. A historical reconstruction of the Bhāṭṭa theory is not within the scope of this paper. However, the role of *lakṣaṇā* is confirmed in later Bhāṭṭa sources, e.g, in the *Mānameyodaya*, p. 94, l. 5: *vayaṃ tu padārthā lakṣaṇayaiva vākyārthaṃ bodhayantīti brūmaḥ.*

11 See TABER 1989, p. 426, n. 10, and PRASAD 1994, p. 333. FUJII 2001, p. 14, renders it as "metaphor."

"direct designation" (*abhidhā*). Nārayaṇa Bhaṭṭa, in the *Mānameyodaya* (p. 94, l. 6-p. 95, l. 2) explains that such an implication (*lakṣaṇā*) is obtained by a presumptive inference (*arthāpātti*). The argument runs as follows:

> If in the *gām ānaya* sentence the word-meanings "cow" and "bring," evoked by the words [*gām* and *ānaya*], remained in their general form of natural kind without a mutual relation, this [general notion] would contradict the words' purpose (*tātparya*) of making known a single, specified meaning, [a purpose that is] fixed at the time of language acquisition. Since a signified [sentence-meaning] in the form of natural kind is not possible, the word-meanings must culminate in a particular constituted of their mutual relation. Thus, this [particular] cow must be brought, and [the natural kind] "bringing" is related to [this] "cow": so, once this mutual relation is achieved, the sentence-meaning constituted of "cow" and "bringing" is realized.[12]

In the Bhāṭṭa view, there are three necessary conditions that must be met for a successful correlation of word-meanings: mutual expectancy (*ākāṅkṣā*), proximity (*saṃnidhāna*, *sannidhi*, or *āsatti*), and suitability (*yogyatā*).[13] Whether these conditions can pertain to word-meanings, as apparently implied in the Bhāṭṭa theory, is a debated issue that I will not enter here. In short, however, we can say that mutual expectancy answers the need of a syntactical relation among word-meanings; suitability relates to word-meanings, too, and guarantees the semantic coherence of the sentence-meaning; proximity, however, seems to belong to the sphere of words, since it guarantees the compactness and unity of a sentence.

In this way the individual word-meanings – i.e., the natural kinds designated by the individual words – mutually specify each other and thus compose a unitary sentence-meaning, a particular, according to the principle stated in ŚBh ad MSū 1.1.24, p. 112, l. 1: "The word functions in relation to the natural kind, the sentence in relation to the particular" (*sāmānye hi padaṃ pravartate viśeṣe vākyam*). This correlation of word-meanings is indirectly assumed, because

---

12 *atra ca padaiḥ smāryamāṇā gavādipadārthā yady anyonyānvayaṃ vinā sāmānyarūpā evāvatiṣṭheran tarhi padānāṃ vyutpattisamayāvadhṛtam ekaviśiṣṭārthabodhatātparyaṃ virudhyeta iti sāmānyarūpasya vācyasyānupapatter anyonyānvayarūpe viśeṣe eva padārthāḥ paryavasyanti. tataś ca gaur iyam ānīyamānaiva ānayanaṃ ca gosaṃbaddham eva iti parasparānvayalābhāt gavānayanarūpavākyārthasiddhiḥ.*

13 TV 2.1.48: *ākāṅkṣā saṃnidhānaṃ ca yogyatā ceti ca trayam | saṃbandhakāraṇatvena kḷptaṃ nānantaraśrutiḥ ||.*

the pragmatic use of language would not be explainable otherwise, as shown by means of dotted arrows in Figure 4.

Figure 4: The Bhāṭṭa theory

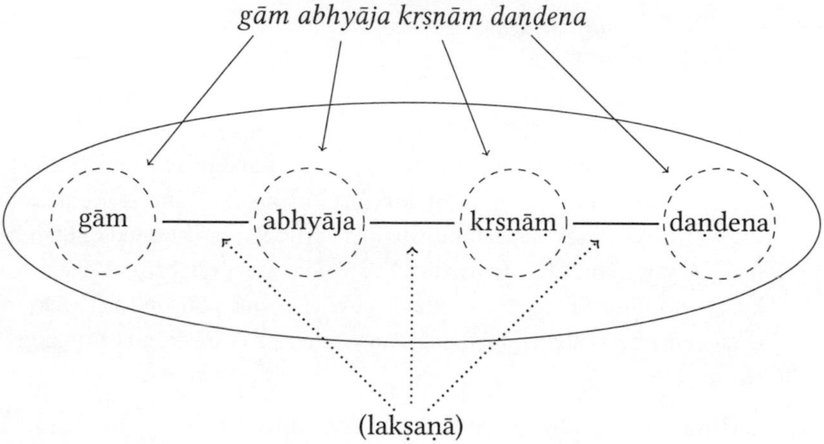

2.2.2. Jayanta on the correlation of word-meanings

The notion of the sentence-meaning as a correlation (*saṃsarga*) of word-meanings is introduced by Jayanta in NM 5, after a thorough discussion on the ontological nature of word-meanings (*padārtha*s). Although such a correlation is not designated by words, we still know it because of them.[14]

This correlation among word-meanings, i.e., the sentence-meaning, is possible due to the conjoined action (*saṃhatyakāritva*) of words. Thus, words uttered together in a sentence convey a single sentence-meaning (NM^{Va}, vol. II, p. 216, ll. 6-7).[15] To explain the phenomenon, Jayanta uses the argument of *Ślokavārttika* (henceforth ŚV), *vākyādhikaraṇa* 272: a root and a suffix designate an individual meaning, but simultaneously depend on each other, because they are never used in isolation.[16] The meaning of the suffix of an optative verb is not designated by the root, because the injunctive force is not expressed by the verbal root; neither is the meaning of

---

[14] *nanu saṃsargo 'pi na śabdārthaḥ. satyam. sa hi śabdasyābhidheyo na bhavati, na tu tato na pratīyate. anabhidheyaḥ kathaṃ pratīyate iti cet etad agre nirṇīṣyate.*

[15] *saṃhatyakārīṇi hi padānīty uktam. samuditaiḥ padair eko vākyārthaḥ pratyāyyate.*

[16] *prakṛtipratyayau yadvat apekṣete parasparam | padaṃ padāntaraṃ tadvat vākyaṃ vākyāntaraṃ tathā ||.*

the root expressed by the suffix, because it is impossible, for the optative endings, to express the meaning of the verb *yāji* by themselves; nor can they produce their respective effect independently from each other. In the same way, also words produce their effect in mutual dependence, while still designating their individual meaning (NM^{Va}, vol. II, p. 217, l. 14-p. 218, l. 7).[17]

2.2.3. Jayanta on the capacity of tātparya

In NM 6 (NM^{Va}, vol. II, pp. 202-219) Jayanta resumes the topic of the relation among word-meanings, already introduced in previous parts of the NM. By analyzing the contrasting theories of *abhihitā-nvaya* and *anvitābhidhāna* he develops a sui generis explanation to suit the needs of his own school (NM^{Va}, vol. II, p. 190, ll. 8-10):

> Words have two capacities, designative and *tātparya*. Of these, the designative capacity serves the word-meanings, and the *tātparya* capacity culminates in the sentence-meaning.[18]

In other words, the *tātparya* capacity is the cause of knowledge of the correlation of the word-meanings (NM^{Va}, vol. II, p. 218, ll. 9-10).[19]

If the sentence is composed of single words that designate their respective meanings, to account for a unitary meaning by tracing it back to the phonemic segments is problematic, because to postulate two quite different capacities of one same linguistic expression raises issues of theoretical parsimony.[20] Words, i.e. phonemic strings, have exhausted their role in the designation of the word-meaning. Hence, commenting on MSū 1.1.25, Śabara (ŚBh, p. 116, ll. 5-6) maintains that there cannot be a meaning of the sentence independently of the meanings of the words composing it:

---

17 *api ca prakṛtipratyayau parasparāpekṣam artham abhidadhāte. na ca prakṛtyā pratyayārtho 'bhidhīyate, niyogasyādhātuvācyatvāt. na ca pratyayena prakṛty-artho 'bhidhīyate yajyāder* (*yajyāder*] P K; *niyogāder* NM^{Va}) *liṅvācyatvānupa-patteḥ. na ca tau pṛthak pṛthak svakāryaṃ kurutaḥ. evaṃ padāny api parasparāpekṣīṇi saṃhatyakāryaṃ kariṣyanti.*

18 *padānāṃ hi dvayī śaktir abhidhātrī ca* (*ca*] P K; om. NM^{Va}) *tātparyaśaktiś ca. tatra abhidhātrī śaktir eṣāṃ padārtheṣūpayuktā | tātparyaśaktiś ca* (*ca*] P NM^{Va}; *tu* K) *vākyārthe paryavasyatīti.*

19 *teṣāṃ tātparyaśaktis tu saṃsargāvagamāvadhiḥ.*

20 SIDERITS 1985 (pp. 262-265, 287-288) eloquently deals with the pros and cons of the parsimony argument.

> Words, having designated their respective meanings, cease to function. Then the word-meanings, at that point already known, convey the meaning of the sentence.[21]

But this, for Jayanta, is not acceptable.

> The cognition of a sentence-meaning is not produced by word-meanings, but rather by the sentence itself. That is why the expression "meaning of the sentence" is used, and not "meaning of the word-meanings." Just as a word, constituted by a conceptual group of phonemes, produces the cognition of the word-meaning, so a sentence, constituted by a conceptual group of words, will produce the cognition of the sentence-meaning (NM[Va], vol. II, p. 188, ll. 2-3).[22]

Here Jayanta wants to safeguard the epistemological autonomy of *śabdapramāṇa*, the epistemic instrument of verbal testimony. Linguistic communication happens mostly by means of sentences, so if word-meanings were accepted as the cause of sentence-meaning, word-meanings would themselves be *śabdapramāṇa*, which is not the case. A word-meaning would be an object of knowledge (*prameya*) when designated by a word, and subsequently become an instrument of knowledge (*pramāṇa*) to convey a sentence-meaning, akin to smoke, when it is in a first moment the object of perception, and later generates inferential knowledge of fire. Echoing the Bhāṭṭa usage of the term *tātparya*, as shown below, Jayanta says that those very words that have designated their meanings fulfil their role in the cognition of the sentence-meaning by conveying their word-meanings (NM[Va], vol. II, p. 189, l. 20-p. 190, l. 2).[23]

Thus debating with the Bhāṭṭas, Jayanta at this point of the discussion quotes in his favor ŚV, *vākyādhikaraṇa* 343, and accuses them of misunderstanding their very source:

---

21 *padāni hi svaṃ svam artham abhidhāya nivṛttavyāpārāṇi. athedānīṃ padārthā avagatāḥ santo vākyārtham avagamayanti.*

22 *na padārthebhyo vākyārthāvagatiḥ api tu vākyād eva. tathā cāyaṃ vākyārtha iti prasiddho* (*prasiddho*] P K; *prasiddhiḥ* NM[Va]) *na padārthārtha iti. yathā hi kālpanikavarṇasamūhātmakaṃ padaṃ padārthapratipattim ādadhāti tathā kālpanikapadasamūhātmakaṃ vākyaṃ vākyārthapratipattim ādhāsyati.*

23 *kiṃ tu viratavyāpāre cakṣuṣīva śabde dhūmādivat prameyāt padārthāt agner iva vākyārthasyāvagamo nāsti. na hi padārthāḥ prameyībhūya dhūmavat punaḥ pramāṇībhavitum arhanti. kiṃ tu padāny eva tatpratipādanadvāreṇa vākyārthapratipattau paryavasyanti.*

> Their [i.e. the phonemes'] activity of conveying the word-meaning is inseparable (*nāntarīyaka*) from their activity of producing knowledge of the sentence-meaning, just as it happens with the activity of fuel producing flames while cooking [food].[24]

If one looks at the immediate context of the ŚV, Jayanta's reasons to see this stanza as conducive to his case are even clearer (ŚV, *vākyādhikaraṇa* 342): "Even if they directly convey the word-meanings, phonemes do not turn sterile (*niṣphale*)."[25]

Jayanta understands the production of the word-meanings and of the sentence-meaning as two distinct processes (*vyāpāra*s) carried on by the very same words. These two processes, the intermediate (*avāntara*) and the final one (*pradhāna*), do not hamper each other, and are explained by postulating two distinct capacities of words, *abhidhātrī śakti* and *tātparyaśakti*. The first conveys the word-meanings, the second the sentence-meanings (NM^{Va}, vol. II, p. 190, ll. 7-10).[26]

Interestingly, even Pārthasārathi utilizes the term *tātparya* while commenting on these very ŚV verses, where he asserts that even if words complete their designative operation with the word-meanings, at that moment the *tātparya* of the words is not completed, because *tātparya* concerns the knowledge of the sentence-meaning.[27] There are some parallels with Jayanta's explanation:

- Both Jayanta and Pārthasārathi speak of *tātparya* in the context of the same ŚV stanza.
- Śabara's principle that words cease to function with the designation of the word-meanings is interpreted analogously: what ceases is *abhidhā*, while their *tātparya* is not yet completed.
- Designation is understood as an intermediate, propaedeutic operation.

---

24 *vākyārthamataye* (*mataye*] P K; *pratyaye* NM^{Va}) *teṣāṃ pravṛttau nāntarīyakam* | *pāke jvāleva kāṣṭhānāṃ padārthapratipādanam* ||.

25 *sākṣād yady api kurvanti padārthapratipādanam* | *varṇās tathāpi naitasmin paryavasyanti niṣphale* ||.

26 *avāntaravyāpāro hi na kārakasya pradhānavyāpāre* (*pradhāna-*] P K; *pradhāne* NM^{Va}) *kārakatāṃ vihanti* (*vihanti*] P K; *vyāhanti* NM^{Va}) *padānāṃ hi dvayī śaktiḥ abhidhātrī tātparyaśaktiś ca. tatra abhidhātrī śaktir eṣāṃ padārtheṣūpayuktā. tātparyaśaktiś ca vākyārthe paryavasyatīti.*

27 *ataḥ padārthāvasitābhidhāvyāpārāṇām api padānāṃ tatrānavasitatātparyāṇāṃ vākyārthāvagatāv eva tātparyam iti.*

- The *tātparya* is that of words, not of the word-meanings. The integrity of *śabda* as an independent means of knowledge, is thus guaranteed.

In this particular passage, the word *tātparya* does not occur in the ŚV itself, and while I think that Pārthasārathi uses the term in a general sense of "purpose,"[28] it is also possible that the *tātparya* concept was evoked in the same context of ŚV, *vākyādhikaraṇa* 342-343, by some Mīmāṃsā source available to both Jayanta and Pārthasārathi, but no longer extant. Umbeka's *Ślokavārttikatātparyaṭīkā* is a prime suspect, since we know that Jayanta was familiar with it.[29] Unfortunately, at present, there are no known manuscripts that cover the *vākyādhikaraṇa* portion of the ŚV.

Jayanta's theory of *tātparyaśakti* is sketched in Figure 5.

Figure 5: Jayanta's tātparyaśakti theory

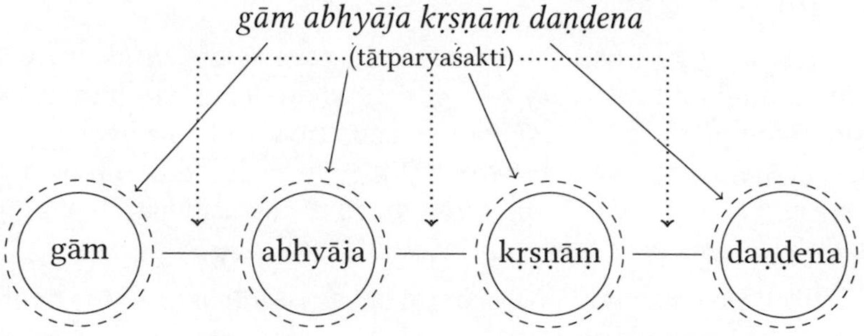

2.2.4. What does tātparya mean in the NM?

The term *tātparya* is frequently found in Mīmāṃsā, Nyāya, and Alaṅkāra works, but with different shades of sense.[30]

Tātparya is often understood, quite simply, as "speaker's intention."[31] Yet, the word is certainly not used in this sense by Mīmāṃsākas in the ritual context, where it is derived from *tatpara*, and

---

[28] See also his commentary ad ŚV, *vākyādhikaraṇa* 230.

[29] Evidence of Jayanta's re-use of Umbeka's commentary is discussed in GRAHELI 2015a.

[30] A reliable historical account of the development of the concept was sketched by KUNJUNNI RAJA 1963, pp. 213-224. PRASAD 1994 also added thought-provoking reflections, but he largely focused on the later reception and implementation of the term.

[31] See e.g. STAAL 1966, p. 308: "The term *tātparya*, lastly, refers to the speaker's

where *tat* is taken as referring to *kārya*, the ultimate purpose of a Vedic ritual.[32] "According to the Prābhākaras, on the other hand, the *tātparya* makes the primary significatory power itself capable of conveying not only the individual word-meanings, but their mutual connection as well. Thus even when *tātparya* is not taken as a separate *vṛtti*, it could be referred to as the motive force conveying the syntactic relation" (KUNJUNNI RAJA 1963, p. 223). There certainly cannot be any speaker's intention in a Vedic injunction, since the Veda is by definition authorless (*apauruṣeya*).[33]

It is helpful to observe the context in which the expression *tātparyaśakti* is used in the NM. Its first occurrence is in NM^{Va}, p. 696, l. 1 (NM 4), in the context of the polemic, against the Mīmāṃsakas, on the authorlessness of the Veda. In Nyāya, even the Veda has an author, albeit a divine one, and not a common human being. The Prābhākaras' idea that Vedic injunctions are *kāryapara*, and consequently their usage of the term *tātparya* (from *tatpara*) in reference to *kāryapara*, is not applicable to Jayanta's position (NM^{Va}, vol. I, p. 695, ll. 13-14).[34]

Most interestingly, in the same context Jayanta rejects the idea that the sentence-meaning is the speaker's intention and gives two examples in support of his argument. With the first, "Hey Devadatta, bring the white cow by means of the stick," he shows that if the sentence-meaning were the speaker's intention, there would be no sentence-meaning in this case, because there is no word designating

---

intention."

32 See e.g. *Prakaraṇapañcikā*, p. 378, l. 9: *tena tatraiva tātparyam*, where *tatra* clearly refers to *kārya* in the immediate context.

33 PRASAD 1994, p. 321, perhaps in an attempt to find a synthesis of the two different applications, wrote that it is also used to mean "an intention, in the form of a demand, of a word in order to complete the sentence in which it occurs. Anything which is intended, such as explicit or inexplicit contests, background assumptions, demands for incomplete expressions to be completed, and the volitional attitude or state of the speaker, is covered by intention (*tātparya*)." Moreover, "[...] a theory of meaning is a theory of understanding, which takes 'intention' in its broadest sense. Therefore, the speaker's intention is one of the meaning contents. But if he intends his utterance 'to be understood' by the hearer with all the meaning contents, then his intention must be taken in the broadest sense" (PRASAD 1994, p. 341, n. 22).

34 *... vaidikāni punar apauruṣeyatayā kāryaparāṇy eva vākyānīti etad api na peśalam. apauruṣeyasya vacasaḥ pratikṣiptatvāt, vede 'pi kartur īśvarasya sādhitatvāt.*

the speaker's intention, and one cannot say that the sentence-meaning is indicated by a nonexistent word-meaning. In a second example, Jayanta shows that the *tātparya* capacity is not capable of conveying the speaker's intention of the prohibition implied in the statement that eating poison is better than eating in someone else's house. The speaker's intention, in fact, is not to enjoin actual poisoning, and it can be guessed only in a second moment, once the sentence-meaning is known. It is not that the *tātparya* function can be stretched to every case by ignoring the *abhidhātrī* function. Therefore, the purpose of language is not to convey the speaker's intention (NM^{Va}, vol. I, p. 695, l. 16-p. 696, l. 3).[35]

Commenting on this very passage, Cakradhara underlines the necessity of the *abhidhātrī* function:

> The designative capacity of words relates to word-meanings. The *tātparya* capacity relates to sentence-meaning, the correlation of word-meanings. How could the sentence-meaning, the correlation of word-meanings, be known without the word-meanings?[36]

Furthermore, *tātparya* cannot mean "speaker's intention" (*vivakṣā*), also because it is consistently used as a property of words, and not of the speaker. Elsewhere Jayanta declares that the knowledge of the speaker's intention is the result of an inference, not of verbal testimony.[37]

In sum, my hypothesis is that *tātparya* is intended by Jayanta as deriving from *tatpara* in the sense of "with the purpose of the sentence-meaning" (*vākyārthapara*), as in the Bhāṭṭa tradition. However, with the *tātparyaśakti* compound Jayanta has used the term in

---

35 ... *na ca puruṣavacanam api vivakṣāparam iti darśitam. tathā hi, na vivakṣā vākyārthaḥ. "devadatta gām abhyāja śuklaṃ* (*śuklaṃ*] P K; *kṛṣṇāṃ* NM^{Va}) *daṇḍena" iti padagrāme vivakṣāvācinaḥ padasyāśravaṇāt apadārthasya ca* (*ca*] P K; om. NM^{Va}) *vākyārthatvānupapatteḥ | na ca viṣabhakṣaṇavākyasyeva paragṛhe bhojananivṛttau pauruṣeyavacaso vivakṣāyāṃ tātparyaśaktir api prabhavati | na hi sarvātmanā 'bhidhātrīṃ śaktim avadhīryaiva tātparyaśaktiḥ prasaratīti na vivakṣāparatvam.*

36 GBh, pp. 123, ll. 22-24: *na hi sarvātmanābhidhātrīm iti | padānāṃ hi padārthe 'bhidhātrī śaktiḥ, padārthasaṃsargātmake vākyārthe tātparyaśaktiḥ, padārthābhāve ca kathaṃ tatsaṃsargātmakavākyārthalābhaḥ.*

37 See NM^{Va}, vol. I, p. 696, ll. 4-5: *kathaṃ tarhi puruṣavacanād uccāritāt vivakṣāvagama iti cet, anumānād iti brūmaḥ.* On the speaker's intention as an object of inference, see TABER 1996 and GRAHELI forthcoming.

a wider sense that embraces both the syntactical and semantic correlation among word-meanings and the context in which a sentence happens to be used. This context may also include considerations on the reliability of the speaker, a crucial factor in Nyāya epistemology.

3. ABHINAVAGUPTA

KUNJUNNI RAJA 1963 (p. 219) suggests that Abhinavagupta may have taken the idea of *tātparyaśakti* from Jayanta himself, with the intention of adjusting the theory to the particular needs of the Ālaṃkārikas:

> What prompted Abhinavagupta to accept Jayanta's modified form of *abhihitānvaya* theory and not that of the real followers of the Bhāṭṭa school seems to be the fact that the Ālaṃkārikas of the *dhvani* school could not accept *lakṣaṇā* to explain the syntactic relation among the word-meanings, since they accepted it only in cases of *anvayānupapatti* and not in cases of *tātparyānupapatti.*

Before turning to Abhinavagupta's views on sentence signification, however, it is necessary to look at Ānandavardhana's ideas on this matter.

3.1. Ānandavardhana and the Dhvani Theory

Ānandavardhana (*Dhvanyāloka* [henceforth DhvĀ] 1.2) classified two possible types of meanings in poetry, directly expressed (*vācya*) and implied (*pratīyamāna*). He called the latter one "suggestion" (*dhvani*), a meaning produced by words, and even by meanings of words, when the primary meaning becomes marginal (DhvĀ 1.13).[38]

The *dhvani* theory built a bridge between pre-existing theories of sentence signification and the aesthetic theory of *rasa*. It was presented in an inclusivistic spirit, explaining other approaches as partial representations of the complete picture. Ānandavardhana also tried to fence arguments against the postulation of *dhvani*, such as those of the Mīmāṃsakas and of the Naiyāyikas, which are here reflected in Jayanta's dismissal of *dhvani*.[39]

---

[38] *yatrārthaḥ śabdo vā tam artham upasarjanīkṛtasvārthau | vyaṅktaḥ kāvyaviśeṣaḥ sa dhvanir iti sūribhiḥ kathitaḥ ||*.

[39] For a general introduction to the criticism and defense of the *dhvani*, see KUNJUNNI RAJA 1963, pp. 277-315.

The first exemplification of *dhvani* is found in DhvĀ 1.4, where an often-quoted verse of the *Sattasaī* (2.75) is used as an instance in which the literal meaning (*vācya*) is a positive request and the suggested meaning (*pratīyamāna*) is a prohibition:

> Go your rounds freely, gentle monk;
> the little dog is gone.
> Just today from the thickets by the Godā
> came a fearsome lion and killed him.[40]

3.1.1. *Jayanta and the DhvĀ*

In the NM, Jayanta cites this very passage when referring to the *dhvani* theory and, probably, to Ānandavardhana. Jayanta dismisses the necessity of postulating *dhvani*, and reduces poetic suggestions to the larger domain of sentence signification, which he discusses in NM 5 and 6. Abhinavagupta, in turn, discusses the mainstream theories of sentence signification while commenting on this same passage of the DhvĀ.

In the context of the discussion on *arthāpatti*, which is used by Mīmāṃsakas to explain elliptic sentences,[41] Jayanta summarily brushes aside the *dhvani* theory as follows:

> Another self-fancied scholar resorted to a certain *dhvani*, which is also encompassed by the capacity (*sāmārthya*) of *śabda*. Knowledge of a prohibition comes from an injunction, and knowledge of an injunction from a prohibition, as in "Go freely, gentle monk" and "Do not enter the house, traveller." [Yet,] this is the capacity of the very words, which express the form of things delimited by other instruments of knowledge, in various ways and circumstances. Actually such a discussion with poets does not

---

[40] Transl. INGALLS 1990, p. 83. DhvĀ, p. 16: *bhama dhammia vīsattho so suṇao ajja mārio teṇa | golāṇaikacchaku aṅgavāsiṇā dariasīheṇa ||* (*chāyā*: *bhrama dhārmika viśrabdha sa śunako 'dya māritas tena | godāvarīnadīkulalatāgahanavāsinā dṛptasiṃhena ||*). In the NM editions there is a substantive variant in the citation of this *gāthā*: Varadacarya (NM[Va], vol. I, p. 129, l. 13) reads *bhava dhammiya* in place of *bhama dhammia*. The reading *bhava* is also found in J (fol. 29v, 3), although Shah (GBh, p. 32) emends it into *bhama*. As for the NM text, however, the main manuscript evidence has *bhama*, including K, 50r,6 and P, 37r,11. For other variant readings, see *Sattasaī* 175, p. 63.

[41] On *arthāpatti* in relation to elliptic sentences, see KUNJUNNI RAJA 1963, pp. 169-174.

> even look good. Even scholars are perplexed in the impervious path (*adhvani*) of *vākyārtha*.[42]

The "mighty capacity of *śabda*," which for Jayanta can encompass also the suggestive meanings in poetry, refers to its capacities of designation and *tātparya*, the two causes of knowledge of the sentence-meaning.

3.2. *Abhinavagupta on Tātparya and Lakṣaṇā*

In the context of the *bhama dhammiya* verse, and for that matter in the whole introductory section of the DhvĀ, there is no discussion on word-meanings and sentence-meanings, as frequently done in later treatises on poetics such as the *Kāvyaprakāśa* and the *Sāhityadarpaṇa*. A lengthy discussion on these issues is found in the *vṛtti* of DhvĀ 3.32-33, although even there the *abhihitānvaya* theory is not explained in detail, and *tātparyaśakti* is not mentioned at all. For the present purpose, it is sufficient to say that the signification of word- and sentence-meanings, as explained by the Mīmāṃsakas and the Naiyāyikas, was considered inadequate by Ānandavardhana, because it could not do justice to the expressed/suggested dichotomy of poetical meanings.

Unlike Ānandavardhana, Abhinavagupta chose to discuss the Bhāṭṭa, Prābhākara and Vaiyākaraṇa views on signification exactly in his commentary on DhvĀ 1.4, pp. 16ff. Abhinavagupta's discussion stems from the conflict of injunction and prohibition which characterizes the verse. He analyzes the verse in the light of four capacities of words: *abhidhā*, *tātparya*, *lakṣaṇā* and *vyañjanā*.

Abhinavagupta, in the first mention of *tātparyaśakti*, presents it as an objector's view, which could well be referring to Jayanta's (*Locana* ad DhvĀ 1.4, p. 16):

> One may object that the non-exhausted *tātparyaśakti* – by means of the intention of the speaker (*vivakṣayā*), and by means of the inverse meta-

---

42 NM^{Va}, vol. I, p. 129, l. 7-p. 130, l. 2: *etena śabdasāmarthyamahimnā so 'pi vāritaḥ | yam anyaḥ paṇḍitaṃmanyaḥ prapede kaṃcana dhvanim || vidher niṣedhāvagatir vidhibuddhir niṣedhataḥ | yathā | bhava dhammiya vīsattho mā sma pāntha gṛhaṃ viśa* (vl. *viśaḥ* K, 20r,5) *|| mānāntaraparicchedyavasturūpopadeśinām* (vl. *vasturūpāpadeśinām* P) *| śabdānām eva sāmarthyaṃ tatra tatra tathā tathā || athavā nedṛśī carcā kavibhiḥ saha śobhate | vidvāṃso 'pi vimuhyanti vākyārthagahane 'dhvani ||*.

> phor (*viparītalakṣaṇā*) caused by a contradiction on the strength of an obstruction of the primary meaning which has the form of a disconnection of word-meanings such as *dṛpta*, *dhārmika*, *tat*, etc. – generates the cognition of a prohibition, which becomes the sentence-meaning (*vākyārthībhūtaniṣedhapratītim*): this meaning is based only on the [regular] signification capacity of language (*śabdaśakti*).[43]

Indeed, this seems to partially represent Jayanta's view, seen above (see § 3.1.1). Jayanta did maintain that the Śabara principle that words exhaust their capacity is limited to the designation of word-meanings, leaving room for the other capacity of words, i.e., *tātparya*. And in the above criticism of the *dhvani* theory, he wrote that the suggested meanings are explainable by this very capacity of words (*śabdānām eva sāmarthyaṃ*), a view that seems mirrored here by Abhinavagupta (*śabdaśaktimūla eva so 'rthaḥ*).

This explanation, however, is not accepted by Abhinavagupta. In general, he conceives four powers of signification, *abhidhā*, *tātparya*, *lakṣaṇā* and *vyañjana*. Three of these, *abhidhā*, *tātparya*, and *vyañjana*, are at play in the case of the *bhama dhammiya* verse.

The step of designation is limited to the signification of natural kinds. The designation is based on a convention (*samaya*), which concerns only natural kinds and not particulars (*Locana* ad DhvĀ 1.4, p. 16).[44] As for the reasons behind the notion of word-meanings as natural kinds, the principle is clearly derived from Śabara's and Kumārila's explanations discussed above (see § 2.1.4), unlike the conventional nature of signification, which is a Nyāya-Vaiśeṣika tenet.

Once the designation of the natural kinds is completed, the syntactic correlation of word-meanings, i.e. the particular sentence-meaning, can be grasped. Here Abhinavagupta explicitly resorts to

---

43 *nanu tātparyaśaktir aparyavasitā* (*aparyavasitā*] Kri Pa; *paryavasitā* Ja) *vivakṣayā dṛptadhārmikatadādipadārthānanvaya(padārthānanvaya*] Kri Pa; *padārthānvaya* Ja)*rūpamukhyārthabādhaka* (*bādhaka*] Ja Kri; *bādha* Pa)*balena virodhanimittayā viparītalakṣaṇayā ca vākyārthībhūtaniṣedhapratītim abhihitānvayadṛśā karotīti śabdaśaktimūla eva so 'rthaḥ*. This and the following passages from the Locana are based on three editions, DhvĀL[Ja], DhvĀL[Kri], and DhvĀL[Pa] (respectively, Ja, Kri and Pa in the attribution of the variant readings).

44 *naitat. trayo hy atra vyāpārāḥ* (*vyāpārāḥ*] Kri Ja Pa; *vyavahārāḥ* Ja v.l.) *saṃvedyante – padārtheṣu sāmānyātmasv abhidhāvyāpāraḥ, samayāpekṣayārthāva* (*samayāpekṣayārthāva*] Kri Pa; *samayāpekṣārthāva* Ja)*gamanaśaktir hi* (*hi*] Kri Pa; om. Ja) *abhidhā. samayaś ca tāvaty eva, na viśeṣāṃśe.*

the Mīmāṃsaka principle that the natural kinds, i.e., the word-meanings, convey knowledge of the particular, i.e. the sentence-meaning, by quoting from ŚV, *arthāpatti* 70cd (*Locana* ad DhvĀ, 1.4, p. 16).[45]

To analyze the processes at play in the *Sattasaī* verse, I shall reduce the wording to the bare essence. In Figure 6 Abhinavagupta's description of the process is sketched. The word-meanings, i.e., the natural kinds, are generated by each individual word by designation, and the particular meanings of the two sentences involved, *bhrama dhārmika* and *śunakaḥ māritaḥ siṃhena*, are due to the *tātparya-śakti*. The remarkable difference with the Bhāṭṭa theory, however, is that Abhinavagupta does not mention *lakṣaṇā* as the process that causes the sentence-meaning. Rather, like Jayanta, he resorts to *tātparyaśakti*, although he assigns to it the same role played by *lakṣaṇā* in the Bhāṭṭa view. The expression *tātparyaśakti* is not found in the DhvĀ, although the word *tātparya* is frequently used in its generic sense, e.g. twice in the stanzas (2.22 and 3.40) or DhvĀ 3.42, *vṛtti*, p. 221 (*rasādiṣu vivakṣā tu syāt tātparyavatī yadā*), and mostly in connection with *vivakṣā*, "the speaker's intention," and related terms. Therefore, in its technical application to poetics, it could well be Abhinavagupta's own coinage.[46] While commenting on the *vṛtti* of DhvĀ 3.33, where an objection attributed by Abhinavagupta to the Mīmāṃsakas is raised, Abhinavagupta characterizes again the *abhihitānvaya* process without mentioning *lakṣaṇāvyāpāra*. After quoting ŚV, *vākyādhikaraṇa* 343, he adds (*Locana* ad DhvĀ, 3.33, p. 188): "The meaning generated through *tātparya* by the word-meanings known from the words is itself the sentence-meaning, and it is expressed (i.e., it is not suggested)."[47]

---

[45] *tato viśeṣarūpe vākyārthe tātparyaśaktiḥ parasparānvite, "sāmānyāny anyathā-siddher viśeṣaṃ gamayanti hi" iti nyāyāt.*

[46] In the same period, the expression *tātparyaśakti* is also found in Dhanika's commentary to the *Daśarūpaka*, 4.37, p. 211, l. 15, *kāryaparyavasāyitvāt tātparya-śakteḥ*. In this passage, Dhanika explicitly adopted the Prābhākara usage of *tāt-parya* as derived from *tatpara* in the *kāryapara* sense. He elaborated further on the technical use of *tātparya* in a string of *Kāvyanirṇaya* stanzas (*Daśarūpaka*, p. 212).

[47] *śabdāvagataiḥ padārthais tātparyeṇa yo'rtha utthāpyate sa eva vākyārthaḥ sa eva ca vācya iti.*

Figure 6: Designation and tātparyaśakti in the bhama dhammiya verse

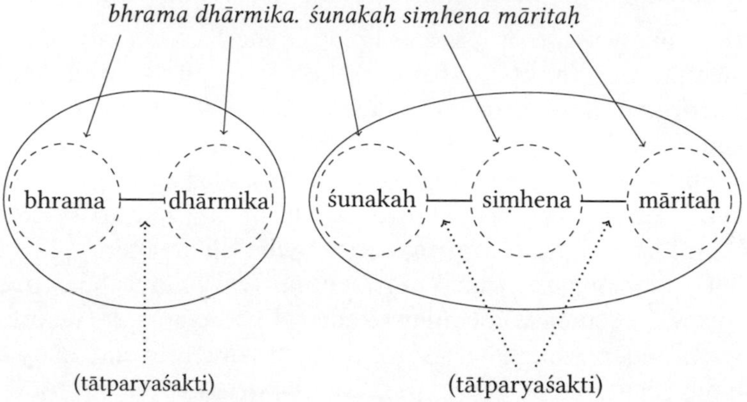

These two stages of expression of general word-meanings and signification of the particular, however, do not generate any poetical meaning. What is conveyed so far is merely an injunction, "Go freely, gentle monk," and a description, "the dog was killed by a lion" (*Locana* ad DhvĀ 1.4, p. 16).[48] Yet, the implicit message is obviously the negation of an injunction, which cannot be appreciated without the power of poetical suggestion (*dhvani*).

Besides designation and *tātparya*, Abhinavagupta conceives a third power, *lakṣaṇāśakti*, "metaphor," but he explains that in the instance of the *Sattasaī* verse it does not apply, because there are no problems of semantic coherence that require the intervention of this metaphoric power. Here the primary meaning – "the dog that was impeding your movement has been killed by a lion, so now you are allowed to move around, since the cause of impediment is gone" – is perfectly congruous, so there is no scope for the metaphoric power (*Locana* ad DhvĀ 1.4, p. 16).[49]

The third power, *lakṣaṇaśakti*, applies instead to cases such as "there is a hamlet on the Ganges," where the primary meaning is

---

48 *tatra ca dvitīyakakṣāyāṃ bhrameti vidhyatiriktaṃ na kiṃcit pratīyate, anvayamātrasyaiva pratipannatvāt.*

49 *... yogyatāvirahāt. tathā tava bhramaṇaniṣeddhā sa śvā siṃhena hataḥ. tad idānīṃ bhramaṇaniṣedhakakāraṇavaikalyād bhramaṇam tavocitam ity anvayasya na kācit kṣatiḥ. ata eva mukhyārthabādhā nātra śaṅkyeti na viparītalakṣaṇāyā avasaraḥ.*

nonsensical and a secondary meaning, "there is a hamlet on the Ganges's bank," is implied (see Figure 7).

Figure 7: Application of designation, tātparya, and metaphor

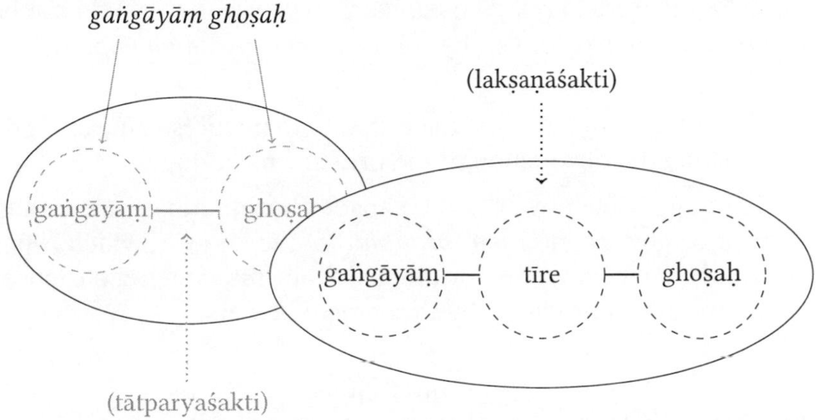

Abhinavagupta's main purpose here is to defend Ānandavardhana's postulation of *dhvani* or *vyañjanāśakti*, the fourth stage of signification in Abhinavagupta's scheme. The idea is that "there is a hamlet on the bank of the Ganges" conveys a subtler message, that such a hamlet is pure, cooled by the river's breeze, sanctified by the holy river, etc. These notions are not automatically generated by designation, nor by the correlation of the word-meanings, nor by metaphorical usages. Also, they are not produced by other epistemic instruments, such as perception or inference. Therefore, a fourth level of signification must be accepted (*Locana* ad DhvĀ 1.4, p. 18).[50]

In *Locana* ad DhvĀ 1.4, p. 18, Abhinavagupta sums up the topic of signification by giving an eloquent definition of the four stages:[51]

---

50 *yat tv idaṃ ghoṣasyātipavitratvaśītalatvasevyatvādikaṃ prayojanam aśabda*(*aśabda*] Kri; *aśabdāntara* Ja Pa)*vācyaṃ pramāṇāntarāpratipannam... tasmād abhidhātātparyalakṣaṇā*(*lakṣaṇā*] Kri Pa; *lakṣaṇa* Ja)*vyatiriktaś caturtho 'sau vyāpāro dhvananadyotanavyañjanapratyāyanāvagamanādisodaravyapadeśanirūpito 'bhyupagantavyaḥ.*

51 *tena samayāpekṣā vācyārthāvagamana*(*vācyārthāvagamana*] Kri; *vācyāvagama* Ja Pa)*śaktir abhidhāśaktiḥ. tadanyathānupapattisahāyārthāvabodhanaśaktiḥ tātparyaśaktiḥ. mukhyārthabādhādisahakāryapekṣārthapratibhāsanaśaktir lakṣaṇāśaktiḥ. tacchaktitrayopajanitārthāvagamamūlajātatatpratibhāsa*(*pratibhāsa*] Kri *Pa*; *pratibhā* Ja)*pavitritapratipattṛpratibhāsahāyārthadyotanaśaktir dhvananavyāpāraḥ.*

1. The designative power is the capacity to designate expressed meanings on the basis of the conventional relation among words and meanings.
2. The *tātparya* power is the capacity to convey the meaning assisting those [expressed meanings], because they would not be possible otherwise, i.e., by implication (*anyathānupapatti*, i.e., *arthāpatti*).
3. The metaphoric power is the capacity to manifest a meaning by assisting the obstruction of the primary meaning.
4. The suggestive power is the capacity to illuminate a meaning by assisting the intuition (*pratibhā*) of the knower, which is purified by the reflection originated from the comprehension of the meanings produced by these three powers.

4. CONCLUSIONS

In the NM the discussion on sentence signification takes place in the larger picture of the epistemological investigation on *śabda*, verbal testimony, as an instrument to know reality, and the same applies to the Mīmāṃsaka sources. Before Jayanta, in extant Pracīna Nyāya works, not only was the concept of *tātparyaśakti* not used, but there was hardly any elaboration on the process of sentence signification, with linguistic discussions focusing on word signification rather than sentence signification. This void was well known to Jayanta, who, after discussing the different Mīmāṃsaka positions on sentence signification, explained why he could not count on his own tradition on this matter (NM^{Va}, vol. II, p. 135, l. 15-p. 136, l. 10; NM 5):

> The authors of the *sūtra* and of the *bhāṣya* did not provide clues on sentence-meanings anywhere. Wherefrom shall we learn about the nature of the sentence-meaning, before discussing it [here]? One may ask why they did not provide clues, and the answer is that these sciences deal with something different: *ānvīkṣikī* (i.e., Nyāya) is the science of epistemology, not the science of sentence-meanings (i.e., Mīmāṃsā). One may further ask why was then word-meaning taught at all, [by the *sūtra*] "the word-meaning, however, is the particular, the configuration, the universal character," and this is a good question. That endeavour, however, was undertaken by the author of the *sūtra* in order to establish the epistemic validity of *śabda*, and to put to rest the Buddhist (*bhadanta*) who asserts the absence of contact among words and meanings.

> One may then argue that, if this is so, the epistemic foundation of verbal testimony would be weakened, without the sentence-meaning as a real external object, so an effort should be made in that area as well. This is true. The author of the *sūtra*, by teaching only word-meanings, thought that he had covered also that [area of sentence-meanings], and thus he did not teach sentence-meanings separately. Therefore, his purport is that the word-meaning itself is the sentence-meaning. [...] It is not that the sentence-meaning is a single word-meaning; rather, it is constituted by multiple word-meanings.[52]

On this topic, therefore, Jayanta largely drew from Mīmāṃsā theories, his sympathy clearly leaning towards the Bhāṭṭa version of these. He could not accept, however, Mīmāṃsaka views in conflict with basic Nyāya tenets:

- the fixed nature of the word-meaning relation, opposed to the Nyāya idea of a conventional relation;
- the notion of word-meaning as "natural kind," opposed to that of "property-possessor";
- explaining the knowledge of the sentence-meaning, i.e. the correlation of word-meanings, as an inferential process, thus undermining the autonomy of *śabdapramāṇa*;
- limiting epistemically valid *śabda* to injunctions, and deriving the term *tātparya* from *tatpara* in the sense of *kāryapara*.

Consequently, it was necessary for Jayanta to devise a new theory, enriched by the Mīmāṃsaka scholarship, but not incompatible with the axioms of his tradition. Hence, his theory contains elements of

---

52 *vākyārthas tu na kvacid api sūtrakārabhāṣyakārābhyāṃ sūcita iti kutaḥ śikṣitvā vākyārthasvarūpaṃ vayam ācakṣmahe | kim iti tābhyām asau na sūcita* (*sūcita*] P NM^{Va}; *sūtrita* K) *iti cet pṛthakprasthānā imā* (*-prasthānā imā*] P; *-prasthānā hīmā* NM^{Va}; *-prasthānāgamā* K) *vidyāḥ. pramāṇavidyā ceyam ānvīkṣikī na vākyārthavidyeti || yady evaṃ padārtho 'pi kasmād iha darśitaḥ* (*darśitaḥ*] P NM^{Va}; *pradarśito* K) *"vyaktyākṛtijātayas tu padārthaḥ" iti sthāne praśnaḥ. sa tu śabdānām arthāsaṃsparśitāṃ vadantaṃ bhadantaṃ* (*bhadantaṃ*] K P; *rudantaṃ ca* NM^{Va}) *śamayituṃ śabdaprāmāṇyasiddhaye sūtrakṛtā* (*sūtrakṛtā*] P NM^{Va}; om. K) *yatnaḥ kṛtaḥ. yady evaṃ vākyārtham api bāhyaṃ* (*bāhyaṃ*] P NM^{Va}; *sāhyāṃ* K) *vāstavam antareṇa śabda*(*śabda-*] K P; *śāstrasya* NM^{Va}) *pramāṇatā na pratiṣṭhāṃ labhata iti tatrāpi prayatnaḥ kartavya eva. satyam. padārthapratipādanayatnenaiva tu kṛtena tatra yatnaṃ kṛtaṃ manyate sūtrakāraḥ, yad ayaṃ pṛthak padārthebhyo na vākyārtham upadiśati sma. tasmād ayam asyāśayaḥ padārtha eva vākyārthaḥ iti... kiṃ tu naikaḥ padārtho vākyārthaḥ. anekas tu padārtho vākyārthaḥ.*

the *abhihitānvaya* theory, some correctives derived from the Prābhākaras's criticism, and adaptations to the Naiyāyikas's needs.

In the light of the material gathered so far, it is likely that Abhinavagupta knew Jayanta and was influenced by his use of the term *tātparyaśakti.* Abhinavagupta's theory was based on ideas derived not only from Mīmāṃsā, as is most obvious, but also from the Nyāya tradition, such as the conventional relation between words and meanings, and the use of the term *śakti* in the causal sense of contributory cause.

The term *tātparya* would later acquire more specific and technical usages in Nyāya and poetics. For instance, it was glossed in *Kārikāvali* 84cd as "the speaker's intention" (*vaktur icchā*), and the awareness of the speaker's intention was listed (ibid., 82cd) – along with knowledge of words' contiguity, consistency, and mutual expectancy – as the cause of knowledge resulting from language (*āsattijñānaṃ yogyatājñānam ākāṅkṣājñānaṃ tātparyajñānaṃ ca śābdabodhe kāraṇam*).

In *ālaṅkārika* theories of signification, too, *tātparya* has often been an object of the discussion. For instance, to quote two of the most widely used manuals of poetics, at the beginning of the second *ullāsa* of *Kāvyaprakāśa* 6 (p. 24), Mammaṭa explained that "*śabda* is of three types, directly designative, indirectly indicative, and suggestive, and its *artha*s are [respectively] directly designated, etc. According to some, it is also the *artha* of *tātparya*."[53] And in the *vṛtti* he explained, in the context of *abhihitānvaya*, that the *tātparyārtha* is the *artha* of the sentence, and not of individual words. Mammaṭa's addition of *tātparya* was noticed and reiterated also by Viśvanātha in *Sāhityadarpaṇa* 27 (p. 66), at the end of the second *pariccheda*.[54]

Such explanations and usages of the term *tātparya*, however, are not found in Nyāya and poetics before Jayanta and Abhinavagupta. As for Abhinavagupta, it is possible that his idea of *tātparya* as the second step in sentence signification came from reading, directly or indirectly, either Jayanta's work or a common source. After weighing Jayanta's criticism of the dhvani theory, comparing Jayanta's and Abhinavagupta's discussions on sentence signification, and considering their geographical and chronological proximity, one

---

[53] *syād vācako lākṣaṇikaḥ śabdo 'tra vyañjakas tridhā | vācyādayas tadarthāḥ syuḥ tātparyārtho 'pi keṣucit* ||.

[54] *tātparyākhyāṃ vṛttim āhuḥ padārthānvayabodhane | tātparyārthaṃ tadarthaṃ ca vākyaṃ tadbodhakaṃ pare* ||.

may reasonably assume a direct influence of Jayanta's work on Abhinavagupta's.. Although the creativity and literary skill of these two luminaries seem to occasionally hide re-uses and quotations, there still is a strong impression of a thread connecting them.[55]

REFERENCES

BROUGH 1953
J. Brough, "Some Indian Theories of Meaning," *Transactions of the Philological Society* 52(1), 1953, pp. 161-176

DhvĀ
[*Dhvanyāloka*] See DhvĀL[Ja]

DhvĀL[Ja]
The Dhvanyāloka of Ānandavardhanāchārya. With the Commentary of Abhinavaguptāchārya, ed. Pandit Durgaprasad and V.L. Shastri Pansikar, 3rd revised ed., Bombay: Pandurang Jawaji, Kāvyamālā 25, 1928

DhvĀL[Pa]
The Dhvanyāloka of Śrī Ānandavardhanācārya with the Locana Sanskrit Commentary of Śrī Abhinavagupta, With the Prakāśa Hindi translation of both the texts and exhaustive notes, ed. Acharya J. Pathak, Kashi: Chowkhamba Vidyabhawan, The Vidyabhawan Sanskrit Granthamala 97, 1965

DhvĀL[Kri]
Abhinavagupta's Dhvanyāloka-Locana, With an Anonymous Sanskrit Commentary, Chapter First, ed. K. Krishnamurthy, New Delhi: Meharchand Lachmandas Publications, 1988

Daśarūpaka
The Daśarūpaka of Dhanaṃjaya: with the Commentary Avaloka by Dhanika and the Sub-Commentary Laghuṭīkā by Bhaṭṭanṛsiṃha, ed. T. Venkatacharya, Adyar, Madras: The Adyar Library and Research Center, The Adyar Library Series 97, 1969

FUJII 2001
T. Fujii, "Jayantabhaṭṭa on *tātparyaśakti*-theory," *Journal of Indian and Buddhist Studies* 49(2), 2001, pp. 14-16

GANERI 1995
J. Ganeri, "Vyāḍi and the Realist Theory of Meaning," *Journal of Indian Philosophy* 23, 1995, pp. 403-428

---

55 Abhinavagupta seems to have borrowed from Jayanta also in his criticism of *vijñānavāda* Buddhism, as noticed in RATIÉ 2010, p. 460, n. 66.

GANERI 1999
J. Ganeri, *Semantic Powers*, New York: Oxford University Press, 1999

GBh
Cakradhara's Nyāyamañjarīgranthibhaṅga, ed. N.J. Shah, Ahmedabad: L.D. Institute of Indology, Lalbhai Dalpatbhai series 35, 1972

GRAHELI 2012a
A. Graheli, "A Preliminary List and Description of the *Nyāyamañjarī* Manuscripts," *Journal of Indian Philosophy* 40, 2012, pp. 317-337

GRAHELI 2012b
A. Graheli, "The choice of the best reading in Jayanta Bhaṭṭa's *Nyāyamañjarī*," in E. Freschi et al. (eds.), *The Study of Asia between Antiquity and Modernity*, Rome: *Rivista degli Studi Orientali* 84, 2012, pp. 107-122

GRAHELI 2015a
A. Graheli, "Epistemology of Textual Re-use in the *Nyāyamañjarī*," *Journal of Indian Philosophy* 43, 2015, pp. 137-170

GRAHELI 2015b
A. Graheli, *History and Transmission of the Nyāyamañjarī, Critical Edition of the Section on the Sphoṭa,* Wien: Verlag der Österreichischen Akademie der Wissenschaften, 2015

GRAHELI forthcoming
A. Graheli, "Bhaṭṭa Jayanta: Comprehension, Knowledge, and the Reduction of Testimony to Inference," in D. Cuneo, C. Formigatti and E. Freschi (eds.), *Constructing Sexuality, Conceptualising the Philosophy of Testimony, Thinking Manuscripts Across Media: South Asian Perspectives. A Coffee Break Project.* Special issue of *Kervan, Rivista Internazionale di Studii Afroasiatici* (Turin)

INGALLS 1990
D.H.H. Ingalls (ed.), *The Dhvanyāloka of Ānandavardhana with the Locana of Abhinavagupta*, transl. D.H.H. Ingalls, J.M. Masson and M.V. Patwardhan, Cambridge (MA): Harvard University Press, Harvard Oriental Series 49, 1990

J
"Jaisalmer, Jinabhadrasūri Tāḍaprakriya Grantha Bhaṇḍāra, ms. 386"; probably 13th c.; foll. 186; palm leaf; Jaina Devanagari; contains *āhnika*s 1-6 of the GBh

K
"Thenjipalam (Malappuram District), Malayalam Department of the University of Calicut, ms. 2606"; undated; foll. 188; cm. 5 × 48 ca.; palm-leaf; Malayalam; contains the complete NM 1-6 and about one third of NM 7; in the original foliation, the first leaf is foliated as *śrī*, and is followed by foll. 1-187 in letter numerals

Kārikāvali
The Kārikāvali of Vishwanātha Panchānana Bhatta. With the Commentary Siddhānta Muktāvali, ed. M.G. Shastri Bakre, Bombay: Pāndurang Jāwajī, Proprietor of the Nirnaya Sagar Press, 1934

Kāvyaprakāśa
Kāvyaprakāśa of Mammaṭācārya, With Uddyota of Nāgeśa Bhaṭṭa and Pradīpa of Govinda Ṭhakkura, ed. Upadhyaya Shri Shivaji, Varanasi: Sampūrṇānanda Saṃskṛta Viśvavidyālaya, Sarasvatī Bhavana Granthamālā 143, 2002

KUNJUNNI RAJA 1963
K. Kunjunni Raja, *Indian Theories of Meaning*, Madras: Adyar Library and Research Centre, 1963

Locana
[*Dhvanyālokalocana*] See DhvĀL

MATILAL 1990
B.K. Matilal, *The Word and the World*, Oxford: Oxford University Press, 1990

MATILAL AND SEN 1988
B.K. Matilal and P.K. Sen, "The Context Principle and Some Indian Controversies over Meaning," *Mind* 97(385), New Series, 1988, pp. 73-97

MD
Mīmāṃsādarśana, ed. K.V. Abhyankar and G.S.A. Joshi, 7 vols., [1930-1933] 2nd ed., Pune: Anandasrama, Ānandāśramasaṃskṛtagranthāvāli 97, 1970-1974

Mānameyodaya
Mānameyodaya, an Elementary Treatise of Mīmāṃsā by Nārāyaṇa, ed. C. Kunhan Raja and S.S. Suryanarayana Sastri, Madras: Theosophical Publishing House, 1933

MSū
[*Mīmāṃsāsūtra*] See MD

NM^Va^
Nyāyamañjarī: with Ṭippaṇī Nyāyasaurabha, ed. K.S. Varadacarya, 2 vols., Mysore: Oriental Research Institute, 1969-1983

NS
[*Nyāyasūtra*] *Gautamīyanyāyadarśana with Bhāṣya of Vātsyāyana. Nyāyacaturgranthikā 1*, ed. A. Thakur, [Darbhanga: Mithila Institute Series Ancient Text 20, 1967] revised ed., New Delhi: Indian Council of Philosophical Research, 1997

Nyāyakośa
Nyāyakośa or Dictionary of technical terms of Indian Philosophy by Mahāmahopādhyāya Bhīmācārya Jhalakīkara [1874], ed. V.S. Abhyankar, Pune: Bhandarkar Oriental Research Institute, 1996

Nyāyavārttika
Nyāyabhāṣyavārttika of Bhāradvāja Uddyotakara. Nyāyacaturgranthikā 2, ed. A. Thakur, Indian Council of Philosophical Research, 1997

P
"Pune, Bhandarkar Oriental Research Institute, ms. 390/1875-76"; Saka 1394 [CE 1472]; foll. 432; mm. 130 × 130; birch-bark, bound; Śāradā; the manuscript is presently constituted of 432 leaves (435 according to Cat. Report 1875, p. XXV); the original foliation runs up to NM 3 and restarts from NM 4: 3-149 (= NM 1-3) + 1-270 (= NM 4-12) + 282-286 (an unidentified work) + 7 (parts of *Raghuvaṃśa* 15.11-78); except for occasional missing leaves, the NM is complete; the first two folios are lost

PRASAD 1994
H.S. Prasad, "The Context Principle of Meaning in Prābhākara Mīmāṁsā," *Philosophy East and West* 44(2), 1994, pp. 317-346

Prakaraṇapañcikā
Prakaraṇa Pañcikā of Śālikanātha Miśra with the Nyāya-Siddhi of Jaipuri Nārāyaṇa Bhaṭṭa, ed. A.S. Sastri, Benares: Benares Hindu University, Darśana Series 4, 1961

RATIÉ 2010
I. Ratié, "The Dreamer and the Yogin: on the Relationship between Buddhist and Śaiva Idealisms," Bulletin of SOAS 73(3), 2010, pp. 437-478

Sattasaī
[*Sattasaī*] *Über das SaptaÇataka des Hāla*, ed. A. Weber, Leipzig: Abhandlungen für die Kunde des Morgenlandes, 1870

ŚBh
[*Śābarabhāṣya*] See MD

Sāhityadarpaṇa
Sāhityadarpaṇa of Kavirāja Viśvanātha, ed. Maheshwara Bhattacharya, Delhi: Bharatiya Book Corporation, 1988

SIDERITS 1985
M. Siderits, "The Prābhākara Mīmāṃsā Theory of Related Designation," in B.K. Matilal and J.L. Shaw, *Analytical Philosophy in Comparative Perspective*, Dordrecht: Reidel, Synthese Library, Studies in Epistemology, Logic, Methodology, and Philosophy of Science, 1985

STAAL 1966
J.F. Staal, "Indian Semantics, I," *Journal of the American Oriental Society* 86(3), 1966, pp. 304-311

ŚV
Ślokavārttika of Śrī Kumārila Bhaṭṭa with the Commentary Nyāyaratnākara of Śrī Pārthasārathi Miśra, ed. Śāstrī Dvārikādāsa, Varanasi: Prāchyabhārati Series 10, 1978

TABER 1989
J. Taber, "The Theory of the Sentence in Pūrva Mīmāṃsā and Western Philosophy," *Journal of Indian Philosophy* 17, 1989, pp. 407-430

TABER 1996
J. Taber, "is Verbal Testimony a Form of Inference?", *Studies in Humanities and Social Sciences* 3(2), 1996, pp. 19-31

Tattvabindu
Tattvabindu by Vācaspatimiśra with Tattvavibhāvanā by Ṛṣiputra Parameśvara, ed. V.A. Ramaswami Sastri, Madras: Annamalai University, 1936

TV
[*Tantravartika*] See MD

Abhinavagupta as Intellectual Historian of Buddhism

LAWRENCE MCCREA

The importance of Buddhist philosophy, and specifically the Buddhist epistemological tradition of Dharmakīrti, in the development of the Pratyabhijnā tradition initiated by Somānanda and further developed by Utpaladeva and Abhinavagupta has long been recognized and subjected to serious scrutiny (e.g. TORELLA 1992, RATIÉ 2010 and 2011b). But, though Buddhist terminology and modes of argument exercised a pervasive influence on Pratyabhijnā philosophical and discursive practice throughout its history, the type of influence displayed in Abhinavagupta's magnum opus, his *Īśvarapratyabhijnāvivṛtivimarśinī* (henceforth ĪPVV), is of an altogether different scale and character from anything seen earlier in the Pratyabhijñā literature. This work, a long and extremely elaborate commentary on Utpala's own (now only partly extant) *Īśvarapratyabhijñāvivṛti*, is arguably Abhinavagupta's magnum opus, and certainly represents his fullest exploration of the Pratyabhijñā tradition. Closely as Abhinavagupta follows Utpala in the theory of consciousness and reality he elaborates there, I think that the ĪPVV represents in certain key respects a major departure from any earlier work in the Pratyabhijñā tradition, and even from Abhinavagupta's own treatment in his shorter *Īśvarapratyabhijñāvimarśinī* (henceforth ĪPV).

What I want to draw attention to here is not any major doctrinal innovation on Abhinavagupta's part. I think it is right to say that the essentials of the Pratyabhijñā philosophical stance are there in Utpaladeva's work (insofar as the available fragments of his *Īśvarapratyabhijñāvivṛti* allow us to judge). Rather, I want to show how Abhinavagupta's highly detailed, sophisticated, and bibliographically ambitious analysis of the Pratyabhijñā position and, even more so, of the Buddhist epistemological tradition it both draws on and seeks to refute, broke important new ground in the analysis and presentation of Buddhist thought and its relation to his own and Utpala's theories and, in doing so, quite transformed the nature of the argument between these competing forces, in effect replacing a clash of abstracted, depersonalized and dehistoricized philosophical positions with a *narrative* account, in which the proponents of the various Buddhist positions each develops his own view through the analysis and critique of his predecessors, and in which the Prātyabhijñānika Utpala, latest in the historical sequence of positions on display here, is shown to be historically as well as philosophically conclusive.

To explore in somewhat more detail Abhinavagupta's methods and the picture they allow him to develop of the wealth of Buddhist thought that forms the historical background for his own and Utpala's theorizing, I would like to examine in particular the arguments for and against the existence of external or extra-mental objects – *bāhyārtha*s – given in section 1.5 of the *Īśvarapratyabhijñākārikā* (henceforth ĪPK) and its commentaries. The section begins, in verses 1-3, with a general case made for an idealist view – that "objects" can in no way exist independent of or separate from awareness. In verses 4-5, an opponent's arguments for the reality of mind-independent objects is raised, and in verses 6 and following these arguments are rejected and the specific Pratyabhijñā argument that "objects" can only exist as part of the awareness of a single permanent knower is explained and defended.

The objection raised against the idealist view in ĪPK 1.5.4-5 is not a generic or "common sense" realist view, but represents a specific philosophical position well known in the time Utpala and Abhinavagupta were working. This is the *anumeyabāhyārtha* or "inferable external object view," labeled by Abhinavagupta himself, as by many other doxographers of the period, as the view of the "Sautrāntikas."[1] This view holds that, even though all that appears to us in any mental episodes are the images – *ākāra*s – that form the content of our awareness, we can infer that, because particular images occur only at some times and not at others, and because there is no apparent cause for this variation in one's own consciousness stream, there must be some cause external to our consciousness stream that causes us, for example, to have the awareness "blue" at a particular

[1] See, for example, *Tarkabhāṣā* (henceforth TBh), pp. 34-36, KAJIYAMA 1998, pp. 139-144, DREYFUS 1997, pp. 103-105, and RATIÉ 2011b, pp. 481-482.

moment – this inferred external cause is, they claim, the "object" of the awareness.

The chapter which outlines this theory and the responses made to it is an interesting one for exploring Abhinavagupta's knowledge of and attitude toward the Buddhists, as it is centrally concerned with two different groups of Buddhist philosophers who are at odds with one another, as well as with the Pratyabhijñā Śaiva who critiques them. The philosophical arguments between the Buddhist externalist view and the anti-externalist views of both the Buddhist idealists and the Pratyabhijñā theorists have already been explored in some detail by Isabelle Ratié in several recent publications.[2] One thing her work on this topic has made very clear is the complex interplay Utpala creates between the two different Buddhist views under consideration here and his own position, which both he and his commentator Abhinavagupta describe as the *īśvara-advaya-vāda*, the "belief in non-duality in (or as) God." Utpala obviously is unwilling to accept the *bāhyārthavādin* view of the Sautrāntika, but also wishes to differentiate his position from that of the Buddhist *vijñānavādin*, showing in effect that the non-dualist Śaiva is able to formulate an effective rejoinder to the Buddhist *bāhyārthavādin*, while the Buddhist idealist or *vijñānavādin* cannot do so. There are times, then, when Utpala appears to endorse the *bāhyārthavādin*'s attacks against the *vijñānavādin* (though not against his own view, of course).

While it is obvious from his arguments that he was closely familiar with both older and more nearly contemporary Buddhist philosophical works, Utpala very rarely quotes or names his Buddhist interlocutors. There are two quotations of Dharmakīrti's *Pramāṇaviniścaya* (henceforth PVin) known to date, but these seem to be rare exceptions.[3] In marked contrast to this nearly citation-free exposition of the various Buddhist positions in Utpala's works, we see in Abhinavagupta's commentaries on Utpala (to some extent in the ĪPV, but much more so in the ĪPVV) an extraordinarily thorough and exacting effort to match up the positions Utpala ascribes to the Buddhist *vijñānavādin*s and *bāhyārthavādin*s with citations from actual Buddhist texts. (Students of the Buddhist epistemological tradition, many with little or no interest in Pratyabhijñā for its own sake,

2 RATIÉ 2010, RATIÉ 2011b.

3 *Vivṛti* on ĪPK 1.5.3 (see TORELLA 2007d, pp. 928 and 937) and 1.3.5 (see I. Ratié's contribution to the present volume).

have long appreciated the value of the ĪPVV precisely as a treasury of quotations from lost Buddhist works – even now when some of these lost works have recently become accessible). But what I want to explore here, at least in the first instance, is what this massive citational apparatus tells us about Abhinavagupta's own picture of Buddhist intellectual history as it bears on his larger project – not only who held what view, and who Utpala is referring to, borrowing from, and reacting against, but how Abhinavagupta sees the representatives of various positions interacting and reacting against one another (a topic that greatly interests him, as it happens).

This strong interest of Abhinavagupta in mapping the specific Buddhist texts in which these rival views are embedded is one thing that sets his work very much apart from that of Utpala – even from his most elaborate exposition of his views in the *Vivṛti*, to judge from the surviving fragments of that text. Quite apart from whatever value it may have as a philosophical or theological work in its own right, or as an exegesis of the complicated and fragmentary work of Utpala, Abhinavagupta's ĪPVV tells us a complex and carefully documented story about several major strands in the history of Buddhist thought in India from Vasubandhu's time to his own – a story which, as I hope to show here, departs in some rather striking ways from the picture of this history developed by scholars over the past century, and which is at least in some cases based in textual materials no longer available to us. Whether or not we conclude on further reflection that his account is accurate, it seems that it is at the very least worth paying attention to, and what I would like to do here is to offer a preliminary account of some of the more noteworthy features of Abhinavagupta's reconstruction of the history of Buddhist philosophy, particularly as it bears on the arguments over the status of objects in section 1.5 of the ĪPVV.

WHO ARE ABHINAVAGUPTA'S *BĀHYĀRTHAVĀDIN*S?

One of the most obvious features of historical interest in Abhinavagupta's account is that, where Utpala usually leaves his Buddhist opponents and interlocutors anonymous, Abhinavagupta often puts names to them. For example, at the end of the preliminary rejoinder to the *bāhyārthavādin* view in 1.5.6, Utpala reviews with approval a set of arguments against external objects already set forth, as he puts it, "by the *vijñānavādin*s," by which, it is clear, he specifically means to refer to Buddhist opponents of the external-object view.

Abhinavagupta, in commenting on the passage, supplies us with a list:

> "**By the *vijñānavādins***" – This matter has been stated at length in Dignāga's *Ālambanaparīkṣā* and other works, in Vasubandhu's *Vijñaptimātratāsiddhi* [i.e. the *Viṃsikā*], here and there in the works of Bhaṭṭa [Śaṅkaranandana] such as the *Prajñālaṃkāra*, and elsewhere.[4]

So Abhinavagupta names the Buddhist *vijñānavādin*s whose views he is considering, as well as giving the titles of their works, in contrast to Utpala, who was content to retain a generic label. And, in the same way, where Utpala was content to leave unnamed the Buddhist *bāhyārthavādin*s who attack both Buddhist and Śaiva idealism in ĪPK 1.5.4-5, Abhinavagupta here too supplies us with the identity of at least one of them. Near the conclusion of the presentation of the *bāhyārthavādin* view in *kārikā* 5, Utpala apparently presents a supplemental argument in favor of the reality of extramental objects propounded, as he simply puts it "by the *bāhyārthavādin*s themselves" ("*bāhyārthavādibhir eva*").[5] True to his usual form, he seems to have left these *bāhyārthavādin*s unnamed, just as he did in the case of the vijñānavādins referred to above. And Abhinavagupta, in commenting on this passage in the ĪPVV, follows just the same pattern as before, specifying the unnamed *bāhyārthavādin*s:

> He says, "**By the *bāhyārthavādin*s themselves.**" For here a new argument is stated. And an effort respecting this has been made by those such as the Teacher Dharmottara, in works such as the *Proof of External Objects* [*Bāhyārthasiddhi*].[6]

Here Abhinavagupta makes it quite plain that he believes Dharmottara to have written a work called the *Proof of External Objects* in which he argued for a *bāhyārthavādin* position. The mention here of "those *such as* the teacher Dharmottara" (*upādhyāyadharmottarādibhiḥ*), and of "works *such as* the *Bāhyārthasiddhi*" (*bāhyārthasiddhyādau*) might be seen as leaving open at least the possibility that the *Bāhyārthasiddhi* was not written by Dharmottara but by one of

---

4 ĪPVV, vol. II, p. 144: *"vijñānavādibhiḥ" iti. ālambanaparīkṣādau daiṅnāge, vijñaptimātratāsiddhau vāsabandhavyāṃ* [*vijñaptimātratāsiddhau vāsabandhavyāṃ* corr. : *vijñaptimātrādisiddhāvāsabandhanyāṃ* Ed.] *prajñālaṃkārādiṣu bhāṭṭadarśaneṣu tatra tatra cānyatra vitatyāyam artha ukta iti.*

5 ĪPVV, vol. II, p. 128.

6 ĪPVV, vol. II, p. 128: *āha "bāhyārthavādibhir eva" iti. apūrvaṃ hy atrocyate. kṛtaś cātra prayāso bāhyārthasiddhyādāv upādhyāyadharmottarādibhiḥ.*

the other, unnamed *bāhyārthavādin*s – though this would constitute a fairly dramatic violation of standard citational practice if it were so. But, in any case, there is a second reference later in the ĪPVV (vol. II, p. 394) to a position "shown at length in the *Bāhyārthasiddhi* by the teacher Dharmottara" (*pradarśitaṃ vitatya bāhyārthasiddhāv upādhyāyadharmottareṇa*), leaving no room whatsoever for doubt. Whether or not Abhinavagupta actually had access to this work of Dharmottara's or knew it merely by hearsay is more open to doubt, though he seems to have some fairly specific information regarding its contents and does include at least one likely quotation of the work which I shall examine shortly.[7]

It is worth noting here parenthetically that Abhinavagupta's attempt to pin down the identity of the *bāhyārthavādin*s referred to by Utpala, and his discussion of Buddhist *bāhyārthavāda* in general, reveals an interesting lacuna in his otherwise seemingly very broad knowledge of Buddhist arguments and texts. Abhinavagupta shows no sign whatever that he is familiar with the works of Śubhagupta who is, from our point of view at least, the most famous and widely known post-Dharmakīrtian Buddhist advocate of the reality of extra-mental objects, as argued in his oft-quoted *Bāhyārthasiddhikārikā*.[8] Abhinavagupta never names Śubhagupta, or (so far as I can determine) quotes him, and none of his references to Buddhist *bāhyārthavāda* show any specific features which indicate that he knew his work. There is one passage in which Abhinavagupta refers to a specific doctrine associated with Śubhagupta. In explaining the *bāhyārthavādin*'s response to the challenge of explaining how macroscopic (*sthūla*) objects can appear in our awareness, even though no such objects can exist externally, Abhinavagupta quotes a *bāhyārthavādin* claim to the effect that "macroscopicness is a property of *appearance*" (*pratibhāsadharmaḥ sthūlatā* – ĪPVV, vol. II, p. 85). This might seem like a reference to Śubhagupta, who famously argued in in his *Bāhyārthasiddhikārikā* that "blue" atoms, even though they are infinitesimally small and individually imperceptible, can produce in us an awareness of an apparently macroscopic object; the macroscopic size, *sthūlatā*, belongs to the perceptual image, not to

7 These two mentions in the ĪPVV would appear to be the only known references to Dharmottara's *Bāhyārthasiddhi*. The work appears not to have been recognized ot mentioned in any of the secondary literature on the Buddhist epistemological tradition (apart from a brief reference in MCCREA AND PATIL 2010, p. 143).

8 See, principally, HATTORI 1960 and SASTRI 1967.

the atoms which cause it to arise.[9] But in fact the very words quoted here by Abhinavagupta – *pratibhāsadharmaḥ sthūlatā* – are quoted (with only the minor variant reading *sthaulyam* for *sthūlatā*) by Mokṣākaragupta in his TBh, where they are ascribed not to Śubhagupta, but to *Dharmottara*. And, incidentally, they are quoted as representative of what Mokṣākara explicitly labels as the "Sautrāntika" view, which would seem to be an independent confirmation of Abhinavagupta's apparent assignment of Dharmottara to the Sautrāntika camp.[10]

Abhinavagupta's two references to the *Bāhyārthasiddhi* should in themselves be sufficient to establish that, whether rightly or wrongly, Abhinavagupta at least regarded Dharmottara as a proponent of the reality of extra-mental objects, and therefore as a representative of what he terms the "Sautrāntika" view. But, if anyone were still in doubt on this point, there are in fact clear confirmations of this view in several of Abhinavagupta's other named references to Dharmottara in the ĪPVV. Several of the passages where Abhinavagupta juxtaposes the views of Śaṅkaranandana against those of Dharmottara clearly indicate that Dharmottara was a believer in external objects, and that Śaṅkaranandana repeatedly criticized him on this basis. I will cite here two brief examples. The first occurs in the ĪPVV on ĪPK 1.5.2, during the initial presentation of the idealist position, and before the onset of the major *bāhyārthavādin pūrvapakṣa* in 1.5.4-5. After presenting the basic view that consciousness can have no "object" outside of itself, since anything that appears to consciousness must itself have the form of conscious illumination (*prakāśamānatā*), Abhinavagupta considers and rejects a secondary argument in the following terms:

> In just the same way even pragmatic effect [*arthakriyā*] exists only insofar as it is apparent to consciousness [*prathamāna*]. Hence the very same principle applies to it as well. Thus he [Utpala] has used the word "**object**" [*artha*] in the expression "**a determinate object,**"[11] in order to explain

---

[9] See HATTORI 1960, pp. 11-12, DREYFUS 1997, pp. 363-364, as well as Kamalaśīla's description and critique of Śubhagupta's position in his comment on *Tattvasaṃgraha* 1973-1979, pp. 552-553.

[10] See TBh, p. 36; also KAJIYAMA 1998, p. 144.

[11] See TORELLA 2007d, p. 935 for the relevant passage of Utpala's *Vivṛti*. (*na hi yathāṅkurasya ghaṭasyaiva vā sattā nijātmamātrapariniṣṭhitā bhavati. prathate cāparanirākāṅkṣaiva tathā ghaṭaḥ prakāśamāno devadattasya prathamāna iti pramātṛsaṃlagna eva paryavasitārtho bhavati.*)

> that one cannot establish externality [*bāhyatā*] by means of pragmatic effect [*arthakriyā*] in accordance with the view of Dharmottara [*dharmottaradṛśā*]. And this is what the Master [*bhaṭṭa*, i.e. Śaṅkaranandana] says: "A distinct thing exists via its properties, which are invariably associated with conscious illumination and whose nature is linked with its existence; [but] this does not lead to a proof of anything external." [*Prajñālaṃkāra*][12]

Here the argument being rejected – that *arthakriyā* can serve as a reliable indicator of the real existence of a mind-independent object – is specifically ascribed to Dharmottara, and is presented as a target of criticism by both Utpala and Śaṅkaranandana, who are shown to make the same point in attacking it.

A similar dynamic is seen in the next quotation, which comes from the previous chapter of the ĪPVV on ĪPK 1.4.1:

> So, what the Master Śaṅkaranandana says in order to refute Dharmottara when he says that "Conceptual awarenesses are transformed into experiences" [*anubhavāyante vikalpāḥ*] – namely, that "It is established that a thing is discerned as something established [*siddha*], but it is not therefore the case that it *is* so"[13] – this shows that nothing external [*bāhya*] to one's own experience need be accepted.[14]

Here again Śaṅkaranandana is presented as specifically setting out to refute Dharmottara, and this refutation is shown to be striking a blow at the externalist, *bāhyārthavādin* position. The words here ascribed to Dharmottara – that "conceptual awarenesses are transformed into experiences" [*anubhavāyante vikalpāḥ*] are cited repeatedly, with minor variations, throughout the ĪPVV.[15] Though no such formulation is to be found in any of Dharmottara's extant Sanskrit works, the view it expresses is very much in keeping with what Dharmottara says about what he takes to be the necessary role of

---

12 ĪPVV, vol. II, p. 71: *arthakriyāpi prathamānaiva tathā bhavatīti tatrāpy ayam eva vidhir ity arthakriyayāpi na bāhyatā siddhyati dharmottaradṛśeti vaktuṃ "paryavasitārthaḥ" ity arthapadam. tad āha bhaṭṭaḥ: "prakāśenāvinābhūtaiḥ sattāyāṃ niyatātmabhiḥ | dharmair bhāvaḥ pṛthagbhāvo na bāhyasiddhim ṛcchati ||" iti.* (*Prajñālaṃkāra* – see BÜHNEMANN 1980, p. 195.)

13 A quotation from the *Prajñālaṃkāra* – see BÜHNEMANN 1980, p. 196.

14 ĪPVV, vol. II, p. 16: *tena yad āha bhaṭṭaśāṅkaranandanaḥ "anubhavāyante vikalpāḥ" iti dharmottaraṃ dūṣayituṃ "siddhaṃ siddhatayā vastu nirūpyaṃ na tathā tataḥ |" iti, tat svānubhavabāhyam anoṃkāryam iti darśayati.*

15 ĪPVV, vol. I, p. 271 (*vikalpāḥ pratyakṣāyante*), vol. II, p. 219 (*pratyakṣāyante hi vikalpāḥ*), p. 228 (*vikalpāḥ hi pratyakṣāyante*), p. 277 (*darśanāyante vikalpāḥ*).

determination, *adhyavasāya*, in perception, as for example, most famously, in his *Nyāyabinduṭīkā* (henceforth NBṬ), where he says that "determination produced by the force of perception determines the object *as something seen*"[16] and "only insofar as it produces *adhyavasāya* is perception a *pramāṇa*."[17] As we shall see below, Śaṅkaranandana's attack on Dharmottara's theory of *adhyavasāya* as Abhinavagupta understands it is intimately linked to his attack on the theory of extra-mental objects.

I would like to quote one more, rather lengthy, passage reflecting Dharmottara's *bāhyārthavāda* at this point – one which may carry more evidentiary weight, as in contains what certainly appears to be a quotation of Dharmottara's own words. The passage begins with an objection to the idealist view raised by a Buddhist *bāhyārthavādin* opponent:

> But external objects are established by perception itself, their real existence or non-existence being determined through their coherence with their pragmatic effects [or the lack thereof]; and these very [external objects], insofar as they form part of the unified set of causal factors, will be the causes of those appearances whose nature is invariably linked to the establishment of an object, which are awarenesses, and which arise in a sequence.[18]

Abhinavagupta then explains Utpala's response in this manner:

> Having considered this [view] of Dharmottara [*dharmottarīya*], he [Utpala] says "**No...**" "**According to the principle stated previously**" – i.e. in the previous two *sūtra*s. For there it was said that "Perception itself has the form of consciousness; how could it serve to manifest something that does not have the form of consciousness?" Therefore, what has been said by the teacher Dharmottara – namely that "The object's difference [from

---

16 NBṬ, p. 85: *pratyakṣabalotpannenādhyavasāyena dṛśyatvenārtho 'vasīyate*. See also McCREA AND PATIL 2006, p. 330. Dharmottara's claim here, as explained in McCREA AND PATIL 2006, pp. 330-331, is that the determination that immediately follows a perceptual awareness presents its own (conceptually constructed) object *as if it were something actually perceived*. This tracks very closely with the claim made here that "conceptual awarenesses are transformed into experiences."

17 NBṬ, p. 84: *adhyavasāyaṃ kurvad eva pratyakṣaṃ pramāṇaṃ bhavati*. See also McCREA AND PATIL 2006, p. 320.

18 ĪPVV, vol. II, pp. 82-83: *nanu pratyakṣasiddhā evārthakriyāsaṃvādapratilabdhasatyabhāvābhāvā bāhyāḥ, ta evābhāsānāṃ viṣayavyavasthāniyatasvabhāvānāṃ bodhānāṃ krameṇodbhavatām ekasāmagrīrūpatānupātena hetavo bhaviṣyanti.*

consciousness] is established [*siddha*] by experience; its non-difference is not based on experience, but is conditionally established [*vyavasthāpyamāna*][19] through the reasoning that 'Since every awareness is similar to every other insofar as it has the nature of mere experience, it must have some feature which differentiates it according to each object' [quoting *Pramāṇavārttika* (henceforth PV), *pratyakṣa* 302]" – [this] is shown to be unreasonable [*ayuktīkṛtam*].[20]

The passage begins with a restatement of the basic *bāhyārthavādin* or "Sautrāntika" position, as already outlined by Utpala: that it can only be "external objects" that account for the different appearances that periodically arise and disappear in our stream of consciousness. And this position is explicitly labeled as "belonging to Dharmottara" (*dharmottarīya*). Furthermore, the *pratīka*s encapsulating Utpala's response to this argument are followed by what is presented as Dharmottara's own statement, seemingly an extended quotation (possibly from the aforementioned *Bāhyārthasiddhi*, though one cannot be certain of this). The quotation too clearly represents the *bāhyārthavādin* position, and is said by Abhinavagupta to have been effectively refuted by Utpala's argument against the possibility of extra-mental objects. Furthermore, the citation of the PV as an authority within this apparent quotation of Dharmottara suggests not only that Abhinavagupta took Dharmottara himself to be arguing from a Sautrāntika point of view, but believed that Dharmottara wished to read Dharmakīrti as supporting this position as well.

DHARMAKĪRTI'S CONTESTED ROLE

This line of inquiry leads directly into a second, perhaps even more surprising, element in Abhinavagupta's reconstruction of the history of Buddhist thought on objects – the question of Dharmakīrti's own position on the matter. Recall that, in the passage quoted above, Abhinavagupta specified the "*vijñānavādin*s" referred to by Utpala

---

19 For the translation of √*vyavasthā* as "conditionally establish," see MCCREA AND PATIL 2006, pp. 340ff.

20 ĪPVV, vol. II, p. 83: *iti dharmottarīyam āśaṅkyāha "na ca" iti. "uktanyāyena" iti pūrvasūtradvaye. tatra hi "pratyakṣam eva prakāśātmakam aprakāśarūpabhāvane kathaṃ syāt" ity uktam. tena yad āhācāryadharmottaraḥ – "anubhavasiddho bhāvasya bhedaḥ, yas tv abhedaḥ sa "tatrānubhavamātreṇa jñānasya sadṛśātmanaḥ* [*sadṛśātmanaḥ* corr. : *sadṛśātmanā* Ed. – see PVV, cf. ĪPVV, vol. II, p. 79] | *bhāvyaṃ tenātmanā yena pratikarma vibhajyate* ‖" [PV 2.302] *iti yuktibalena vyavasthāpyamāno 'nānubhavika" iti tad ayuktīkṛtam.*

in the concluding *Vivṛti* on 1.5.6 – Diṅnāga, Vasubandhu, and Śaṅkaranandana. Conspicuous by his absence in that list is Dharmakīrti. And this, I believe, is not a mere oversight, or the result of some deliberately restricted subgrouping of Buddhist idealists. Rather, I think it can be clearly shown that, as far as Abhinavagupta is concerned, and in terms of his and Utpala's doxography, Dharmakīrti cannot be definitively classified as either a *vijñānavādin* or a *bāhyārthavādin*, but must be seen as a *neutral*, or at least as someone whose real views on the question of external objects cannot be conclusively determined.

It is true that we do find here many of the standard quotations of Dharmakīrti offered up in support of the *vijñānavādin* position, such as the ever popular *sahopalambhaniyamād abhedo nīlataddhiyoḥ* – "Because of necessary co-apprehension, there is no difference between 'blue' and the awareness of it."[21] But, in addition to these, there are quite a few passages of Dharmakīrti quoted in support of the externalist stance as well. At least in Abhinavagupta's reconstruction, the *vijñānavādin*s and *bāhyārthavādin*s dealt with in ĪPK 1.5 are *both* committed, card-carrying Dharmakīrtians, and they both freely and extensively quote from the master's works in support of their own positions.

I will cite here just two examples of the *bāhyārthavādin*'s use of quotations from Dharmakīrti specifically in support of his own externalist position. Explaining the relation between the image that immediately appears in our awareness and the external object he insists we must infer as its cause, the *bāhyārthavādin* states as follows:

> If you ask how something not grasped [i.e. the inferable external object] can be determined [*adhyavasita*] as something seen, he replies, "**Because of similarity.**" Whatever variation there is of form, together with time and place, for the "blue" which exists in an awareness, all of it, without exception, belongs to that [object] which imparts its form to it. And thus, like the mixing up of foods served up together, a determination [*adhyavasāya*], springing from an error caused by similarity, and having the *awareness's* form as its object, arises, having this form: "I am determining the form *of an object*, distinct from my awareness, fit to be designated as 'this.'" And this determination, even though it springs from an error, is not like the determination of "silver" as applied to mother-of-pearl.[22] It

---

21 ĪPVV, vol. II, p. 78.

22 One of the standard examples of perceptual error. One at first sees a shiny bit of mother-of-pearl, and mistakes it for a piece of silver, but then upon closer

takes the form of error, certainly, since it determines an external object when it is really the form of an awareness that is grasped, but, insofar as, on the basis of invariable connection with an object, it determines an object which is the root of that awareness, which is capable of imparting form to the awareness, and which is its cause, it displays in itself that it is the function of a *pramāṇa*, on the principle that "Even error can be a *pramāṇa*, on the basis of a connection" [*bhrāntir api saṃbandhataḥ pramā* – quoting PVin 2.1].[23] As [Dharmakīrti] says: "Even in the case of perception, it is a *pramāṇa* because it does not arise when the object does not exist. Both [*pramāṇa*s] are alike in that they are caused by something that has an invariable connection with them." [Quoting PVin 1.3.] [*The bāhyārthavādin continues*:] and this "function of the *pramāṇa*," arising from the power of sight, takes on the form of a determination through perception etc., and treats the perception that assists it as the grasper of the object (so that one thinks to oneself, "I see"), in the same way that a minister acts toward a king who is subject to his will. Thereby one conforms to the everyday notion that the external object is grasped by perception itself. [Pūrvapakṣin:] *Then what is it that the inference operates on?* He [Utpala] says: "**With agreement**" [***sasaṃvāda***]. [That is to say,] the object, which is the root cause, and which imparts forms to the cognition, is similar in form to it. It is *this* that the inference operates upon.[24]

---

examination realizes one's error. The "error" in question here is not of the same sort, as (at least for the non-epistemologist) there is no moment when one discovers one's mistake, no "blocking awareness" (as it is usually described). For more on this, see MCCREA AND PATIL 2010, pp. 164-165.

23 See p. 46.

24 ĪPVV, vol. II, pp. 90-91: *agṛhītaḥ kathaṃ dṛṣṭatvenāvasita iti ced āha "sārūpyāt" iti. yāvat kiṃcid deśakālasahacārisvarūpavaicitryaṃ* [*°sahacārisvarūpa°* corr. : *°sahacāri svarūpa°* Ed.] *jñānānta*[*r*]*vṛtter nīlasya, tāvat sarvam avikalaṃ tadarpakasyeti samānābhihāramelananyāyena jñānīyākāraviṣayo 'dhyavasāya utpannaḥ sārūpyakṛtād vibhramāj jñānabhinnam arthākāram idaṃtocitam adhyavasyāmīty evam upajāyate, na cāsau vibhramajo 'py adhyavasāyo gṛhītāyāṃ śuktikāyāṃ rūpyādhyavasāya iva gṛhīte jñānākāre bāhye 'vasāyatayā bhramamātrasvabhāvaḥ, kiṃtv arthapratibandhanān maulikaṃ jñānākārārpaṇasamartham arthaṃ kāraṇabhūtam adhyavasyan "bhrāntir api sambandha*[*ta*]*ḥ pramā" iti nyāyena pramāṇavyāpāratām ātmany ādarśayati. yad āha "arthasyāsaṃbhave 'bhāvāt pratyakṣe 'pi pramāṇatā | pratibaddhasvabhāvasya taddhetutve samaṃ dvayam ||" iti. pramāṇavyāpāraś cāyaṃ bhavan darśanabalāt paśyāmīty evaṃ pratyakṣādinādhyavasāyarūpatāṃ gṛhṇan pratyakṣam anugrāhakam arthasyāmātya iva paravaśīkṛtaṃ rājānaṃ grāhakatvena vyavaharati, tataḥ pratyakṣagṛhīta eva bāhyo 'rtha iti laukikam anusṛtaṃ bhavati. tarhy anumānasya kutra vyāpāraḥ. āha "sasaṃvāda" iti mūlakāraṇabhūtaḥ samarpaka ākārāṇām asty arthas tadākārasadṛśa iti. etāvati vyāpāro 'numānasya.*

It is perfectly clear that the *bāhyārthavādin* portrayed here sees himself as a Dharmakīrtian, and quotes two passages from the PVin in support of his argument for the reality of external objects, in the evident belief that Dharmakīrti's statements are not only consistent with but actually advocate an externalist position.

The second passage I wish to examine here comes at the very end of Abhinavagupta's commentary on *Īśvarapratyabhijñāvivṛti* 1.5.5, as the very culmination of the *bāhyārthavādin pūrvapakṣa*. (It follows directly on the first of the two *Bāhyārthasiddhi* references given above, and may be meant as a recapitulation of an argument actually made by Dharmottara.) Here Abhinavagupta, apparently following Utpala's lead, recapitulates the *bāhyārthavādin* argument earlier advanced in 1.5.4 – that the occasional occurrence of particular awarenesses such as "blue" in our stream of consciousness cannot be accounted for from any cause internal to the consciousness stream, and that we must therefore infer some external object whose presence or absence causes us to be aware of blue at some times but not others:[25]

> It is not only the argument just stated that applies here, since there is this argument as well – that is, the one stated in the previous *sūtra*: something additional must be postulated, just as the sense-capacity [*indriya*] must be postulated, and that thing *is* the external object. As the Noble One [Dharmakīrti] has said: "There can be proof of the external object through disjunction" [*bāhyasiddhiḥ syāt vyatirekataḥ* – quoting PVin 1.58cd].[26]

Here again Dharmakīrti is treated by the *bāhyārthavādin* as a supporter of his own position, and the quotation of the PVin is presented

---

25 See ĪPVV vol. II, p. 128: *tathā hy ahaṃkārātmakamanaḥsaptamānāṃ śabdādisukhādijñānānāṃ janikā yāḥ śaktayo vāsanās tadādhārabhūtam ekam ālayavijñānaṃ svāpamadādau pravṛttijñānasaptakābhāve 'pi santānavṛttyā vartamānaṃ tat svasantānavartino nimittasyābhāvāt parasantānānāṃ ca sadāsannidhānāt* [*sadāsannidhānāt* corr. : *sadā sannidhānāt* Ed.] *kathaṃ krameṇa pravṛttijñānāni kuryāt.* ("That is to say: how can the single 'storehouse consciousness' that is the substratum for the [various] traces which are the capacities that produce the six kinds of awareness, sound etc., plus such things as pleasure, along with the 'mind' – i.e. the sense of self – as a seventh, which [storehouse consciousness] exists even in states such as sleep or madness, when none of the seven types of occurrent awareness are present, [how can it] produce the occurrent awarenesses in sequence, since no cause for this exists in one's own consciousness stream, and since other consciousness streams are always remote?")

26 ĪPVV, vol. II, pp. 128-129: *na kevalaṃ pūrvokto 'trābhiprāyaḥ, yāvad ayam apīti pūrvasūtre ya ukto nyāya indriyavad adhikaṃ kiṃcit kalpanīyaṃ sa bāhyo 'rthaḥ. yad āryaḥ – ... bāhyasiddhiḥ syād vyatirekataḥ* ‖ [PVin 1.58cd.]

not only as backing the *bāhyārthavādin* position, but as the very culmination and summation of it. There is no question that both the *vijñānavādin* and the *bāhyārthavādin* presented by Abhinavagupta see themselves as followers of Dharmakīrti and wish to invoke his words as an authority in support of their views. And, as far as I can determine, Abhinavagupta has no interest in attempting to adjudicate this question; he does not appear to make any effort to declare whether he finds the *vijñānavādin* or the *bāhyārthavādin* reading of Dharmakīrti to be the more plausible.

Neither the *bāhyārthavādin* nor the *vijñānavādin* Dharmakīrtians as portrayed by Abhinavagupta in the ĪPVV reflect extensively on the tension between the seemingly pro- and anti-externalist statements found in different parts of Dharmakīrti's works. But there is one particularly striking passage where the *bāhyārthavādin* does directly confront the hermeneutic issue. It reflects the *bāhyārthavādin*'s response to a *vijñānavādin* opponent, who points to Dharmakīrti's own writings, in particular his *Santānāntarasiddhi*, as evidence for his advocacy of the "mind only" position:

> [Pūrvapakṣin:] But the Teacher [Dharmakīrti] has himself raised this doubt and rejected it, so how is this question raised? – To enlighten the one who suffers from this confusion, he[, the *bāhyārthavādin*,] after repeating his text, refutes its meaning, with the passage beginning "**What**" and ending "**As if it were not described by him**" [***atadvarṇitam iva***]. By saying "**As if it were not described by him**" the *bāhyārthavādin* makes this clear: even though he is authoritative, the teacher Dharmakīrti, out of conformity with the works of the teacher Diṅnāga, due to his partiality toward him, speaks in this way, but this is not his own inclination. The meaning of his work, the *Santānāntarasiddhi*, is as follows: just as, on the theory of external objects, the intentionality of other people is inferred from speech belonging to another body, in just the same way, on the theory of [mere] awareness, [it is inferred] from the appearance of speech belonging to the appearance of a body.[27]

---

27 ĪPVV, vol. II, p. 111: *nanu parihṛtam etad ācāryena svayam eva śaṅkitvā, tat kim idaṃ codyata iti yasya bhramaḥ syāt taṃ pratyāyayituṃ tadgranthapāṭhapūrvakaṃ tadarthaṃ dūṣayati "yad api" ityādinā "atadvarṇitam iva" ityantena. "atadvarṇitam" iti vacasā bāhyārthavādīdam āviṣkaroti – prāmāṇiko 'py ācāryadharmakīrtir ācāryadiṅnāgagranthānurodhāt tatpakṣapātād evam abhidhatte, na punar asya svarucir eṣeti. asya santānāntarasiddhigranthasyārthaḥ – yathaiva bāhyanaye vyāhārāt parakāyagatāt parasamīhānumīyate, tathaiva vijñānanaye vyāhārābhāsāt parakāyābhāsagatād iti.*

The passage is tantalizing for several reasons. Judging from the available *pratīkas* and from Abhinavagupta's comment "after repeating his text" (*tadgranthapāṭhapūrvakam*), it would appear that Utpala, speaking in the voice of the *bāhyārthavādin*, actually quotes a text which purports to show Dharmakīrti's advocacy to *vijñānavāda* and prompts his attempt at reinterpretation – possibly a quotation from the *Santānāntarasiddhi* itself. But it also represents a kind of discussion we do not very often find about mechanisms of interpretation, about the role of context, and about assessing the motivations of authors in a way that opens up questions of sincerity or hidden motivation. It engages directly with a question that is still very much a live one – why is it that Dharmakīrti seems to write sometimes in a way that seems to presuppose the existence of mind-independent objects while at other times writing from what seems to be an idealistic position? Whether or not one finds this reading of the *Santānāntarasiddhi*, or this account of Dharmakīrti's intention in writing it, to be at all convincing (as many, I imagine, will not), it is clear in any case that the *bāhyārthavādin* wishes to support the view that Dharmakīrti was a consistent and principled upholder of a materialist position, and that apparent indications to the contrary in his work can be explained away. The *bāhyārthavādin*'s point about the actual argument of the *Santānāntarasiddhi* seems, to me at least, to be well taken. It does not in fact offer a positive argument for an idealistic stance; rather it removes one potential obstacle to such a stance. It aims to show that one can establish the existence of other minds just as easily on an idealist view as on an externalist one, but this is not in itself inconsistent with a belief in extra-mental objects. So the *bāhyārthavādin*'s reading of the text may not be as untenable as would at first appear to be the case; though the motive for writing it if one were a committed believer in external objects (as the *bāhyārthavādin* plainly supposes Dharmakīrti to be) would remain something of a puzzle, as his own admittedly somewhat strained rationalization itself suggests. It is not at all clear whether Abhinavagupta is paraphrasing an argument actually made by a Buddhist *bāhyārthavādin* here or simply engaging in a bit of creative rational reconstruction of his own, but in any case it is certainly plain that he understands the Buddhist *bāhyārthavādin*/Sautrāntika as an adherent of Dharmakīrti, and that the *bāhyārthavādin* as portrayed by him believes Dharmakīrti to have been a *bāhyārthavādin* himself. The contest between Abhinavagupta's *vijñānavādin* and *bāhyārthavādin* is then not simply a philosophical dispute over which view is more workable, but a struggle over the intellectual legacy and the interpretation of Dharmakīrti's works as well.

ADHYAVASĀYA AND *BĀHYĀRTHAVĀDA*

The third component of Abhinavagupta's reconstruction of the intra-Buddhist debate over objects I want to consider here concerns another aspect of the confrontation between Dharmottara and Śaṅkaranandana, already referred to above. We have seen that Abhinavagupta presents Śaṅkaranandana as criticizing Dharmottara in his works, and criticizing him specifically as an upholder of the Sautrāntika theory of inferred external objects. But there is a second axis to Śaṅkaranandana's criticism which is linked to the first. Śaṅkaranandana is regularly portrayed not only as a critic of the Buddhist *bāhyārthavādin*s, but also as a critic of "those who believe that validity is dependent on determination" (*adhyavasāyāpekṣaprāmāṇyavādin*s). Neither Śaṅkaranandana (in the relevant passages quoted from his works) nor Abhinavagupta specifies who is referred to by this phrase, but it is not at all difficult to determine; there are significant indications that point to the fact that here too the real opponent is Dharmottara. This label will not, I imagine, seem inappropriate to anyone at all familiar with Dharmottara's work. It may come as a surprise to hear Dharmottara described as a *bāhyārthavādin*, but no one should be at all surprised to find him labeled an *adhyavasāyāpekṣaprāmāṇyavādin*; "belief that validity is dependent on determination" is in fact as succinct and clear a description as one could wish of Dharmottara's principal and distinctive contribution to Buddhist epistemology.

What is more surprising is that Śaṅkaranandana openly and specifically attacks this doctrine. Among post-Dharmottaran Indian Buddhist authors, he is the only one I know of to do so. Dharmottara's epistemic revolution and his dramatic elevation of the status of determination as a crucial element of perception, radical as it was when he advanced it, seems quickly to have gained near-universal acceptance among Dharmakīrtians – even those who were strongly critical of Dharmottara in other areas. Śaṅkaranandana's position on this question, then, seems quite distinctive, and acquiring a clearer picture of how exactly he understands perception to function as a *pramāṇa* without allowing any role for *adhyavasāya* is, for me at least, one of the more enticing hopes raised by the recent recovery of many of Śaṅkaranandana's *prakaraṇa* texts.

Abhinavagupta's many critical remarks on *adhyavasāya* and its controversial role in Buddhist epistemology are widely scattered throughout his work, and often embedded in rather complex chains of argument which are hard to disentangle. I will mention here only two brief passages which show the linkages between the *bāhyārtha* issue and that of *adhyavasāya*. In the first, the relation between the contents of conceptual awareness and external objects is under discussion, and the following view is advanced:

> ... For the Buddhists who hold that validity arises by force of determination, even inference has an external object, as has been said [by Dharmakīrti]: "The validity of both [*pramāṇa*s] has the real thing [*vastu*] as its object." [Quoting PVin 2.7ab.][28]

This shows the link between *bāhyārthavāda* and belief in the importance of *adhyavasāya*, and, incidentally, provides another instance of the *bāhyārthavādin*'s invocation of Dharmakīrti. Abhinavagupta's criticism of this argument revolves around the impossibility of any awareness having as its "object" something which is not itself directly manifest to consciousness and therefore having the form of illumination (*prakāśa*). And here again, as in one of the passages I quoted above, the argument turns to the proposed role of *arthakriyā* in accrediting the linkage of conceptual awarenesses to their associated external objects. It is at this point that Śaṅkaranandana is brought into the conversation once again. To quote:

> And *arthakriyā* as well, insofar as it is phenomenally apparent, culminates in mere appearance. Hence the external object cannot be proven even on the basis of that. As the Master [Śaṅkaranandana] has said. Beginning by saying, "If the appearance is different, what does the object matter... ?" and concluding by saying "If you think it is for some purpose, the knowledge will serve that purpose; so what recourse is there?", he shows that what supports worldly activity is nothing but a chain of appearances. So, as for the claim that the external object is established precisely through its general acceptance [*prasiddhi*] – it is actually just the opposite that is true.[29]

---

28 ĪPVV, vol. II, p. 131: *saugatais tāvad adhyavasāyabalāt prāmāṇyaṃ vadadbhir anumānam api bāhyaviṣayam evety uktam "prāmāṇyaṃ vastuviṣayaṃ dvayor api... ||"* [*Pramāṇaviniścaya* 2.7ab]

29 ĪPVV, vol. II, p. 132: *arthakriyāpi cābhāsamānatayaivābhāsaviśrānteti tato 'pi na bāhyasiddhiḥ. yathā ca bhaṭṭaḥ "ābhāsabhede tv arthaḥ kaḥ... |" ity upakramya "yatphalāyeti cej jñānaṃ tatphalāyeti kā gatiḥ |"* [quoting *Prajñālaṃ-*

This recapitulates the argument against the *bāhyārthavādin* given above (in which Abhinavagupta similarly invoked Śaṅkaranandana in support of his attack), but here the attack is pressed against an opponent named as the "*adhyavasāyāpekṣaprāmāṇyavādin*." The same linkage between the *bāhyārtha* and *adhyavasāyāpekṣaprāmāṇyavāda* arguments is made clear by another passage, in which a quotation from Śaṅkaranandana's *Prajñālaṃkāra* earlier cited as a critique of *bāhyārthavāda* is pressed into service as an attack on *adhyavasāya*:

> It is for this very reason that the Master [Śaṅkaranandana] does not accept that validity is dependent on *adhyavasāya*. As he says: "It is established that a visible thing is discerned as something established [*siddha*], but it is not therefore the case that it *is* so."[30]

So to challenge the dependence of validity on *adhyavasāya* and to attack the reality of extra-mental objects are apparently seen as more or less equivalent tasks. It is clear that Śaṅkaranandana and, implicitly, Abhinavagupta as well accepted that these doctrines were so closely linked that an attack on one amounted to an attack on the other.

Śaṅkaranandana's and (apparently) Abhinavagupta's acceptance of a hard and fast link between denying the reality of external objects and rejecting the necessary role of *adhyavasāya* in all *pramāṇa*s would appear to shed some light on another important and rather surprising lacuna in Abhinavagupta's survey of Buddhist opinion on objects – namely on Abhinavagupta's total failure to engage with what was arguably the dominant stance on both issues in tenth and eleventh century Buddhist philosophy in India, that of Prajñākaragupta. Prajñākaragupta and his followers were adamant advocates of the "mind only" theory, and totally rejected the existence of extra-mental objects. But they also fully endorsed the need for *adhyavasāya* in all valid awareness, both perceptual and inferential, and later followers of Prajñākaragupta such as Jñānaśrīmitra and Ratnakīrti

---

kāra – see BÜHNEMANN 1980, p. 195] *ity ābhāsaparamparām eva vyavahāropakaraṇabhūtām avādīt. tataś ca prasiddhyaiva bāhyaḥ siddhyatīti pratyuta viparītam etat...*

[30] ĪPVV, vol. II, p. 250: *bhaṭṭas tv adhyavasāyāpekṣām etadartham eva prāmāṇyasya necchati. tad āha "siddhaṃ siddhatayā rūpaṃ nirūpyaṃ na tathā tataḥ |" iti.*

explicitly model their account of *adhyavasāya* on that of Dharmottara.[31] Abhinavagupta was aware of Prajñākaragupta's work. He nowhere quotes him, as far as I can determine, and he refers to him by name only once – as the upholder of the *bhāvikāraṇatāvāda*, the belief that future objects can act as causes for events that precede them.[32] This interesting and distinctive doctrine of Prajñākara's, which Eli Franco has investigated in some detail,[33] is fairly recondite, and Abhinavagupta's familiarity with it suggests that he had more than a casual, second-hand awareness of Prajñākaragupta's work and most likely had access to his *Pramāṇavārttikālaṃkāra*. Yet, if so, it is surprising that he altogether overlooks Prajñākara's synthesis of the anti-*bāhyārtha* and pro-*adhyavasāya* positions. Abhinavagupta seems to accept without question the assumption that support of *adhyavasāya* as a criterion for *prāmāṇya* and belief in external objects naturally and inevitably go together – an assumption he apparently shares with and presumably derives from Śaṅkaranandana who, as we have seen, stresses the linkage between these two views in his criticisms of each (at least as Abhinavagupta explains his position). This represents a rather serious gap in his attempt to displace all of the various Buddhist positions and show the superiority of the Pratyabhijñā view, as it leaves unaddressed what had already become by his time arguably the dominant Buddhist view, even though the most important text arguing for that view was apparently known to him. This shows that, immensely erudite and sophisticated as Abhinavagupta's reconstruction of Buddhist philosophical opinion may be, it is neither all encompassing nor free from distortions and biases. Whether we attribute this oversight on Abhinavagupta's part to his uncritical adoption of Śaṅkaranandana's polemical lens or to some other factor, it does give us a significant sense of the limits of his vision in these matters.

CONCLUSION

Much of Abhinavagupta's reconstruction of the history of the Buddhist debate over objects is based on texts he apparently had access to that we, at least for the time being, do not – Dharmottara's *Bā-*

---

31 For Prajñākaragupta's views on *adhyavasāya*, see MCCREA 2011. For Jñānaśrīmitra, see MCCREA AND PATIL 2006, pp. 333-336.

32 ĪPVV, vol. II, p. 227.

33 See FRANCO 2007.

hyārthasiddhi, the *Prajñālaṃkāra* and other *prakaraṇa* texts by Śaṅkaranandana, as well as the full text of Utpala's *Vivṛti*. Much uncertainty must therefore remain in any attempt to make sense of and to evaluate the story Abhinavagupta is telling here – in particular, in determining how accurate is his depiction of the various players' views, and how much it may be distorted or obscured by his own agenda, or by that of Śaṅkaranandana, the latest in Abhinavagupta's array of Buddhist luminaries, and the one to whose views he seems most sympathetic. Some important gaps in our knowledge of the background here have recently been filled, and others certainly will be filled in the near future. Several important fragments of Utpala's *Vivṛti* have now been recovered and edited by Professor Torella and Professor Ratié, and it is at least possible that more will come to light in time.[34] Many of Śaṅkaranandana's works, including the *Prajñālaṃkāra*, are now available in manuscript and, as these begin to make their way into print, it is virtually certain that a clearer picture will emerge of the ways in which Abhinavagupta responds to, uses, and is perhaps in some ways co-opted by Śaṅkaranandana's work in his writings. Also, one imagines, a clearer picture will emerge of how Śaṅkaranandana builds on and responds to the work of Dharmakīrti and, one hopes, Dharmottara. All this being said, the main contours of Abhinavagupta's reconstruction of the previous half-millennium of Buddhist thought on objects are crystal clear, and I believe are very unlikely to be altered materially by any new discoveries. That he (1) regarded Vasubandhu and Diṅnāga as unambiguous advocates of *vijñānavāda*, (2) that he took Dharmakīrti's stance on the question of external objects to be inconclusive, or at least contested by his followers, (3) that he took Dharmottara and Śaṅkaranandana to be, respectively, the chief post-Dharmakīrtian advocates of the Buddhist *bāhyarthavādin* and *vijñānavādin* positions, (4) that he believed Śaṅkaranandana's arguments against *bāhyārthavāda* to be at least in part specifically directed against Dharmottara, and (5) that he understood Śaṅkaranandana's critique of Dharmottara's *bāhyārthavāda* to be crucially linked to his attack on Dharmottara's belief in the constitutive role of *adhyavasāya* in all *pramāṇa*s, such that attacking the latter was crucial to, and perhaps sufficient for, undermining the other – all this seems to be fairly certain.

---

[34] TORELLA 1988, 2007a, 2007b, 2007c, 2007d, RATIÉ 2015, forthcoming, and I. Ratié's contribution to the present volume.

Whether he is correct or incorrect in these suppositions is of course more difficult to determine, and judgement on this point will certainly be much affected by reflection especially on the works of Śaṅkaranandana as they come to light. In particular, the question of how much Abhinavagupta's picture of the constellation of Buddhist opinions of the issue is borrowed from or shaped by Śaṅkaranandana's own polemical concerns remains a pressing one. It seems likely that Abhinavagupta's overlooking of Prajñākaragupta's anti-*bāhyārtha* but pro-*adhyavasāya* position can be accounted for at least in part by Śaṅkaranandana's own linking of the two issues in his attack on Dharmottara, and access to Śaṅkaranandana's *Prajñālaṃkāra* and other works may well serve to illuminate the issue.

It would seem vain to hope for any further data on Dharmottara's lost *Bāhyārthasiddhi*, but it is possible of course that the portions of his *Pramāṇaviniścayaṭīkā* soon to become available may shed some further light on his position on the *bāhyārtha* question.

In any case, all potential doubts regarding the accuracy of his reconstruction aside, Abhinavagupta's bibliographically ambitious and historically nuanced recapitulation of Buddhist thought on the *bāhyārtha* issue, and on many others of course, forms one of the central components of what is arguably his magnum opus, and is one of the features that most obviously sets it apart from both earlier and later works in the Pratyabhijñā tradition. Abhinavagupta's turn toward intellectual history should itself be seen as a noteworthy historical event in Kashmiri intellectual and cultural life at the turn of the millennium, and richly deserves to be made the subject of long and searching scrutiny.

REFERENCES

BÜHNEMANN 1980

G. Bühnemann, "Identifizierung von Sanskrittexten Śaṅkaranandanas," *Wiener Zeitschrift für die Kunde Südasiens* 24, 1980, pp. 191-198

DREYFUS 1997

G. Dreyfus, *Recognizing Reality: Dharmakīrti's Philosophy and its Tibetan Interpretations*, Albany: SUNY Press, 1997

FRANCO 2007

E. Franco, "Prajñākaragupta on Pratītyasamutpāda and Reverse Causation," in B. Kellner et al. (eds.), *Pramāṇakīrti. Papers Dedicated to Ernst Steinkellner on the Occasion of his 70th Birthday*, Wien: Arbeitskreis für Tibetische und Buddhistische

Studien Universität Wien, Wiener Studien zur Tibetologie und Buddhismuskunde 70.1, 2007, pp. 163-185

HATTORI 1960
M. Hattori, "*Bāhyārthasiddhikārikā* of Śubhagupta," Indogaku Bukkyogaku Kenkyu 8(1), 1960, pp. 9-14

ĪPK
Īśvarapratyabhijñākārikā of Utpaladeva with the Author's Vṛtti, ed. and transl. R. Torella, [Roma: 1994] corrected ed., Delhi: Motilal Banarsidass, 2002

ĪPV
Īśvarapratyabhijñāvimarśinī, ed. M.R. Shāstrī/M.K. Shāstrī, 2 vols., Srinagar: Nirnaya Sagar Press, Kashmir Series of Texts and Studies 22 and 33, 1918-1921

ĪPVV
Īśvarapratyabhijñāvivṛtivimarśinī by Abhinavagupta, ed. M.K. Sastri, 3 vols., Bombay: Kashmir Series of Texts and Studies 60, 62 and 65, 1938-1943

KAJIYAMA 1998
Y. Kajiyama, *An Introduction to Buddhist Philosophy: An Annotated Translation of the Tarkabhāṣā of Mokṣākaragupta, Reprint with Corrections in the Author's Hand*, Wien: Arbeitskreis für Tibetische und Buddhistische Studien Universität Wien, 1998

MCCREA 2011
L. McCrea, "Prajnākaragupta on the Pramāṇas and their Objects," in H. Krasser, H. Lasic, E. Franco, and B. Kellner (eds.), *Religion and Logic in Buddhist Philosophical Analysis: Proceedings of the Fourth International Dharmakīrti Conference*, Wien: Verlag der Österreichischen Akademie der Wissenschaften, 2011, pp. 319-328

MCCREA AND PATIL 2006
L. McCrea and P. Patil, "Traditionalism and Innovation: Philosophy, Exegesis, and Intellectual History in Jnānaśrīmitra's *Apohaprakaraṇa*," *Journal of Indian Philosophy* 34(4), 2006, pp. 303-366

MCCREA AND PATIL 2010
L. McCrea and P. Patil, *Buddhist Philosophy of Language in India: Jñānaśrīmitra on Exclusion*, New York: Columbia University Press, 2010

NBṬ
Dharmottarapradīpa (being a sub-commentary on Dharmottara's Nyāyabinduṭīkā, a commentary on Dharmakīrti's Nyāyabindu), ed. D. Malvania, Patna: Kashi Prasad Jayaswal Research Institute, 1955

PV
"*Pramāṇavārttika-kārikā* (Sanskrit and Tibetan)," ed. Y. Miyasaka, *Acta Indologica* 2, 1972, pp. 1-206

PVin
Dharmakīrti's Pramāṇaviniścaya, Chapters 1 and 2, ed. E. Steinkellner, Beijing/ Vienna: China Tibetology Publishing House/Austrian Academy of Sciences Press, 2007

PVV
"Dharmakīrti's *Pramāṇavārttika* with Commentary by Manorathanandin," ed. R. Sāṅkṛtyāyana, *Journal of the Bihar and Orissa Research Society* 24-26, 1938-1940, Appendix

RATIÉ 2010
I. Ratié, "The Dreamer and the Yogin – on the Relationship between Buddhist and Śaiva Idealisms," *Bulletin of the School of Oriental and African Studies* 73(3), 2010, pp. 437-478

RATIÉ 2011a
I. Ratié, *Le Soi et l'Autre. Identité, différence et altérité dans la philosophie de la Pratyabhijñā*, Leiden-Boston: Brill, Jerusalem Studies in Religion and Culture 13, 2011

RATIÉ 2011b
I. Ratié, "Can One Prove that Something Exists Beyond Consciousness? A Śaiva Criticism of the Sautrāntika Inference of External Objects," *Journal of Indian Philosophy* 39(4-5), 2011, pp. 479-501

RATIÉ 2015
I. Ratié, "Some Hitherto Unknown Fragments of Utpaladeva's *Vivṛti* (I): On the Buddhist Controversy Over the Existence of Other Conscious Streams," in B. Bäumer & R. Torella (eds.), *Utpaladeva, Philosopher of Recognition*, Delhi: DK Printworld, 2015

RATIÉ forthcoming
I. Ratié, "Some Hitherto Unknown Fragments of Utpaladeva's *Vivṛti* (II): against the existence of external objects," in D. Goodall, S. Hatley, H. Isaacson, S. Raman (eds.), *Śaivism and the Tantric Traditions. Volume in Honour of Alexis G.J.S. Sanderson*

SASTRI 1967
N.A. Sastri, "Bāhyārtha Siddhi Kārikā," *Bulletin of Tibetology* 4(2), 1967, pp. 1-96

Tattvasaṃgraha
The Tattvasaṃgraha of Śāntarakṣita with the Commentary of Kamalaśīla, ed. E. Krishnamacharya, Baroda: Central Library, 1926

TBh
Tarkabhāṣā of Mokṣākaragupta, ed. E. Krishnamacharya, Baroda: Oriental Institute, Gaekwad's Oriental Series 94, 1942

TORELLA 1988
R. Torella, "A Fragment of Utpaladeva's *Īśvarapratyabhijnā-vivṛti*," *East and West* 38, 1988, pp. 137-174

TORELLA 1992
R. Torella, "The Pratyabhijnā and the Logical-Epistemological School of Buddhism," in T. Goudriaan (ed.), *Ritual and Speculation in Early Tantrism, Studies in Honor of André Padoux*, Albany: SUNY Press, SUNY Series in Tantric Studies, 1992, pp. 327-345

TORELLA 2007a
R. Torella, "Studies on Utpaladeva's *Īśvarapratyabhijnā-vivṛti*. Part I: *anupalabdhi* and *apoha* in a Śaiva Garb," in K. Preisendanz (ed.), *Expanding and Merging Horizons. Contributions to South Asian and Cross-Cultural Studies in Commemoration of Wilhelm Halbfass*, Wien: Verlag der Österreichischen Akademie der Wissenschaften, 2007, pp. 473-490

TORELLA 2007b
R. Torella, "Studies on Utpaladeva's *Īśvarapratyabhijnā-vivṛti*. Part II: What is memory?," in K. Klaus & J.-U. Hartmann (eds.), *Indica et Tibetica. Festschrift fur Michael Hahn zum 65. Geburtstag von Freunden und Schülern überreicht*, Wien: Arbeitskreis fur tibetische und buddhistische Studien Universität Wien, Wiener Studien zur Tibetologie und Buddhismuskunde 66, 2007, pp. 539-563

TORELLA 2007c
R. Torella, "Studies on Utpaladeva's *Īśvarapratyabhijnā-vivṛti*. Part III. Can a Cognition Become the Object of Another Cognition?," in D. Goodall and A. Padoux (eds.), *Mélanges tantriques à la mémoire d'Hélène Brunner*, Pondichéry: Institut Français de Pondichéry/École Française d'Extrême-Orient, Collection Indologie 106, 2007, pp. 475-484

TORELLA 2007d
R. Torella, "Studies on Utpaladeva's *Īśvarapratyabhijnā-vivṛti*. Part IV. Light of the Subject, Light of the Object," in B. Kellner, H. Krasser et al. (eds.), *Pramāṇakīrtiḥ. Papers dedicated to Ernst Steinkellner on the Occasion of his 70th Birthday*, Wien: Arbeitskreis fur tibetische und buddhistische Studien Universitat Wien, Wiener Studien zur Tibetologie und Buddhismuskunde 70.2, 2007, pp. 925-940

A Note on the Sāṅkhya Theory of Causation in Utpaladeva's *Īśvarasiddhi*[*]

SHINYA MORIYAMA

The aim of this paper is to shed new light on Utpaladeva's *Īśvarasiddhi* (henceforth ĪS). This 10th-century work is important for considering the intellectual links in that period between Kashmir Śaivism and Sāṅkhya philosophy. As earlier studies have shown, the great philosopher Utpaladeva, who was a member of the Pratyabhijñā school of Kashmir Śaivism, composed the *Īśvarasiddhi* to establish God's existence on the basis of a classical proof by the Nyāya philosopher Aviddhakarṇa, whose original text of the proof is now lost. After presenting Aviddhakarṇa's proof of God's existence[1] and defending it against Mīmāṃsā and Buddhist criticism, Utpaladeva continues with a long discussion that presents the Sāṅkhya's and Nyāya-Vaiśeṣika school's theories of causation and liberation. TABER 1986 (pp. 128-129) finds the discussion in this final section peculiar, as has been summarized by Ratié in the following way:

> John Taber finds rather strange the length of this discussion with Sāṃkhya (which spreads over about two thirds of Utpaladeva's tract), since according to him, Utpaladeva's zeal in attacking the Sāṃkhya position contrasts with the Nyāya's relative indifference to this opponent, and since the Sāṃkhya does not seem to have been an influential school in Utpaladeva's time. (RATIÉ 2015, pp. 289-290)

But, of course, it is unsure whether the Nyāya were really indifferent to the Sāṅkhya position. As Ratié has pointed out, Uddyotakara's

* I would like to thank Dr. Hayato Kondo and Dr. Yohei Kawajiri for their valuable comments on an earlier draft of this essay, as well as Ms. Cynthia Peck-Kubaczek for correcting my English.

1 See ĪS, p. 1, ll. 9-12. For details on Utpaladeva's proof, see RATIÉ 2015, pp. 259-265. For Aviddhakarṇa's proof, see KRASSER 2002, pp. 150ff. and MORIYAMA forthcoming.

criticism of the Sāṅkhya can be seen as an "embryonic form" of Utpaladeva's sophisticated discussion. In addition, Ratié also mentions Bhāsarvajña, a contemporary of Utpaladeva, as a Naiyāyika who presented an elaborate criticism of the Sāṅkhya philosophy. However, since the chronological order of these two authors is uncertain, Ratié carefully avoids concluding that Bhāsarvajña had an impact on Utpaladeva's argument. Instead, she moves to the more promising idea that Utpaladeva's *Īśvarasiddhi* was motivated by Sadyojyotis' *Nareśvaraparīkṣā*, an important work on Śaiva dualism. She writes:

> [...] although Utpaladeva's criticism of the Sāṃkhya argument often seems more refined than Sadyojyotis', both refutations focus on the idea that a complex effect can only be the product of a conscious entity, and that intellect, if conceived as a material entity, cannot account for the universe. Utpaladeva's treatise thus seems to emphasize a principle shared by both dualist and nondualist Śaivas, namely the idea that only the conscious is independent (*svatantra*) and therefore capable of action, whereas unconscious entities only seem to act insofar as their actions are always prompted by consciousness. (RATIÉ 2015, p. 321)

In this manner, Ratié regards the aim of Utpaladeva's treatise as being "to show to the Saiddhāntikas that Śaiva nondualists too can appropriate the Nyāya inference of the Lord."

Ratié's conclusion is quite convincing. Nevertheless, there still remain some unanswered questions about this unique controversy on the theories of causation and liberation between the Sāṅkhya and the Nyāya-Vaiśeṣika schools.[2] Of them, our following examination

---

[2] It is also remarkable that Utpaladeva criticizes the Sāṅkhya theory of liberation, seemingly by using some Nyāya-Vaiśeṣika materials of the same content. In my symposium presentation upon which the present paper is based, I pointed out that the discussion in ĪS, p. 25, l. 18-p. 27, l. 16 is in part comparable to Vyomaśiva's argument against the Sāṅkhya soteriology (Vyom, p. 7, ll. 8-24) and to Bhāsarvajña's discussion in NBhūṣ, p. 570, l. 23-p. 574, l. 10. In addition, I also discussed the difference in their approaches to the Sāṅkhya notion of *buddhi*: whereas the Nyāya-Vaiśeṣika authors, who accept *buddhi* as an impermanent quality (*guṇa*) of the permanent soul, Utpaladeva repeatedly questions the perceptibility (*saṃvedyatva*) of the *buddhi* because for the Śaivas the idea of a *buddhi*, if it has any role in cognitive processes, has to be of a conscious nature. Although a further comparison between Utpaladeva's criticism against the Sāṅkhya soteriology and parallel arguments by contemporary authors of the Nyāya-Vaiśeṣika school would allow a better understanding of Utpaladeva's perspective on this topic (for a chronology of these authors, including Bhaṭṭa Jayanta, see SLAJE 1986), I will not include this incomplete examination in this paper.

concerns a question about Utpaladeva's knowledge of Sāṅkhya philosophy, especially the material he used for reconstructing the Sāṅkhya theory of causation.[3]

***

In the first place, we shall review Utpaladeva's modification of the Sāṅkhya theory of causation, in particular, the concept of *sahakārin* (auxiliary cause), which is rarely found in Sāṅkhya literature. Utpaladeva's Sāṅkhya classifies *sahakārin* into two types, namely, those that, "uniting with the material cause, give rise to the effect through transformation of the material cause" (TABER 1986, p. 120), and those that "do not unite with the material cause but operate externally to it, e.g., the stick and wheel a potter uses to fashion clay." Let us look at Utpaladeva's explanations of these two types of *sahakārin*:

The first type of *sahakārin* is described as follows:

> [1a] ĪS, p. 10, ll. 4-7: *tataś ca ye te sahabhāvam āpannāḥ kāryam āvirbhāvayanti te parasparayoge vicitravṛttayo dṛśyante. tathā hi – bījāntargamanena bījabhūtā jalabhūmyādayo rasādipariṇāmāt dīrghapracitasaṃniveśam aṅkuraṃ sahakāritayā kurvanti.*
>
> And therefore, those which come into co-existence [with the material cause] and make the effect manifest are seen as possessing various functions when they unite with each other. To explain: as auxiliary causes, [entities] like water and earth, which have become [part of] the seed by penetrating into it, cause a sprout that has a [certain] configuration accumulated over a long time, due to [their] transformation into flavor, etc.
>
> [1b] ĪS, p. 11, ll. 8-11: *hetum antaḥ praviśyānye prāpyopādānarūpatām | citrayanti hi kāryāṇi bhaumodakarasā iva ||16||*
>
> The other [auxiliary causes] like earthy water and flavor, having entered a [material] cause (e.g., a seed) and taken on the material form, produce a variety of effects.[4]
>
> [1c] ĪS, p. 19, ll. 16-18: *na cāpi sahakāriṇām upādānakāraṇasyāntaḥ praveśamātrād upayogaviśeṣānusandhānavataḥ kasyacid avyāpāre 'pi vicitrā puruṣārthopayoginī racanā upakalpyate.*

---

[3] For the relation of Sāṅkhya to Śaiva Tantrism, see TORELLA 1999. For Rāmakaṇṭha's reaction to the Sāṅkhya theory of *buddhi* and liberation, which is also comparable to Utpaladeva's argument, see WATSON 2006, pp. 95ff.

[4] See also TABER 1986, p. 136, n. 30.

Moreover, [the following Sāṅkya opinion is] not accepted: even if there is no activity of a certain [agent, i.e., God] who would possess the synthetic awareness of [each] specific contribution [of each effect for the benefit of souls], there is a variety of configurations that serve for the benefit of souls merely due to the penetration of auxiliary causes into the material cause.

The second type of *sahakārin* is described as follows:

[2a] ĪS, p. 10, ll. 21-24: *yatra punaḥ sahakāriṇo bahiḥ svadeśasanniviṣṭā eva kāryeṣu upayujyante, yathā mṛtpiṇḍacakrādayaḥ, tatropādānasanniveśavaisādṛśye syād avasaro buddhimataḥ kumbhakārasyeva.*

On the other hand, when auxiliary causes contribute to their effects while being arranged in their respective places, outside [of the material cause], like a wheel and such like for a lump of clay, then, there can be room for an intelligent [cause, i.e. *nimittakāraṇa*] like a potter as regards dissimilar configurations of the material cause.

[2b] ĪS, p. 11, ll. 12-15: *anye punar upādāne bahir viparivartinaḥ | rūpavaicitryayogāya kāryeṣu na tathā kṣamāḥ* ||17||

On the other hand, the other [auxiliary causes], which operate on the material cause from outside, are not capable [of producing] effects suitable for the variety of forms [and other qualities] likewise (i.e., the second type of auxiliary cause allows the necessity of God differently from its first type).

By relying on the operation of the first type of *sahakārin*, the Sāṅkhya opponent thus explains that the arising of a specific configuration (*sanniveśaviśeṣa*) such as a sprout can be fully explained, even without an intelligent agent, within the schema of their causality, which ultimately presupposes a single material cause called primordial matter (*pradhāna*/*prakṛti*). This position is the opposite of the Nyāya-Vaiśeṣika account, which accepts an intelligent agent as the regulative cause (*nimittakāraṇa*) and atoms as the basic components of the variety of the universe. But, were there really any Sāṅkhya authors who held such a well-ordered view of causation?

On this point, Taber has assumed that it is "a somewhat Buddhist formation of the Sāṅkhya," whereby he quotes Dharmakīrti's *Pramāṇavārttika* 2.24-25:

yeṣu satsu bhavaty eva yat tebhyo 'nyasya kalpane |
taddhetutvena sarvatra hetūnām anavasthitiḥ ||
svabhāvapariṇāmena hetur aṅkurajanmani |

> *bhūmyādis tasya saṃskāre tadviśeṣasya darśanāt* ||
>
> If one assumes that the [effect's] cause is something different than those things which are present when the [effect] arises, everything will have an infinite number of causes. The earth and such like become the cause for the arising of a sprout by undergoing a special transformation of its own nature. For it is observed that when it is perfected (by plowing, manuring, etc.), the [sprout] has special properties.[5]

Because these two verses are quoted in Sadyojotis' *Nareśvaraparīkṣā* (p. 120, ll. 1-4), they were certainly known to Utpaladeva as well. Moreover, the terms *svabhāvapariṇāma* and *viśeṣa*, which Dharmakīrti uses for illustrating the arising of sprout from a seed together with earth, etc., are similar to the terms Utpaladeva uses in his exposition. Although Dharmakīrti does not use the term *sahakārin* here, elsewhere he explains the two functions of *sahakārin*, namely, operating together to accomplish a single effect (*ekārthakriyā*) and producing difference (*viśeṣotpādana*) in the continuity of the material cause.[6] The latter function obviously corresponds to Utpaladeva's first type of *sahakārin*. However, unlike Dharmakīrti, Utpaladeva's Sāṅkhya opponent emphasizes the *sahakārin*'s "penetration" (*praveśa*) into the material cause. In this sense, Taber's assumption does not fit well with Utpaladeva's description of the first type of *sahakārin*.

***

When we focus on the "penetration of *sahakārin*," another passage comes to mind, namely, a reference to this concept in the *Yuktidīpikā* (henceforth YD). To my limited knowledge, this is the only instance of such a reference in the extant Sāṅkhya literature. The concept appears in its commentary on *Sāṅkhyakārikā* (henceforth SK) 9c as follows:

> YD 123.1-11 (ad SK 9c): *syān matam – yathāpo bījād aṅkurasyotpattau* [*aṅkurasyotpattau* A : *bījāṅkurasyotpattau* ed.] *samarthā bhavanti na kāṣṭhād agner vā, ubhayaṃ ca tat tāsu na vidyate bījād apāṃ vicchinnatvāt, ... tathā ca tantvādīnāṃ paṭasyaiva śaktiniyamaḥ syāt, na ca paṭasya tantuṣu sattvaṃ syād iti. etat cāyuktam. kasmāt. sādhyatvāt. aṅkurādayo 'pi kāryam abādīnām. ... yat tūktam – apāṃ vicchinnatvān na tāsv aṅkuro*

---

5 The above translation basically follows FRANCO forthcoming, pp. 304-305. For another translation, see TABER 1986, p. 136, n. 28.

6 Cf. HB, p. 11*, ll. 12-23; p. 15*, ll. 7-14.

'stīti tatrāpi yāsām apāṃ bījānuprvaveśād aṅkurabhāvena vipariṇāmaḥ, tābhyas tasyānanyatvaṃ [*tasyānanyatvaṃ* A : *tasyānyatvaṃ* ed.] *sādhyam. ato na kiṃcid etat.*[7]

[Objection:] One might argue: for instance, [a *sahakārin* like] water is capable of producing a sprout from its seed, but not [capable of producing] fire from pieces of wood, and the two [i.e., both a sprout and fire] do not exist in this [water] because [the *sahakārin* like] water is different from [a material cause like] a seed. [...] Likewise, the causal power of threads for instance must be restricted to the [production of] the cloth only [and not to the production of anything else], and the cloth cannot exist in the threads [because the cloth and threads are different from each other]. [Reply:] This is not correct. [Objection:] Why? [Reply:] Because [the effect] is accomplished [by *sahakārin*]. [The effects] like a sprout, too, are [accepted as] the effect of water. [...] On the other hand, with regard to [the objection] that a sprout does not exist in [water] because water is different from [a sprout], too, [the following is replied:] "It is established that [a sprout] is not different from the water that transforms [itself] into a sprout by penetrating into the seed." Thus, the [objection] carries no weight.

Here the author of the YD explains the manner in which the notion of *sahakārin* is fully compatible with the Sāṅkhya's *satkāryavāda*. Even though the effect (a sprout) does not exist in a *sahakārin*, such as water, which is a different entity than the material cause (a seed), inasmuch as the water penetrates into the seed, one can see the sprout as a transformation of the water. This corresponds precisely to Utpaladeva's presentation of the first type of *sahakārin*. But is there any evidence for Utpaladeva's familiarity with the YD? The latter is not unimaginable when considering Kashmir Śaivism's close relation to the Sāṅkhya text. For instance, with regard to the above term *sādhyatvāt*, Wezler and Motegi have documented a marginal note found in a Kashmir manuscript of the YD as follows:

YD, p. 123, marginal note (5): ***sādhyatvād*** *iti. na hi sarvathaivāpsu na vidyate 'ṅkuraḥ. yā hy āpo bījadeśānupraveśenāsīnād upādānād antarviparivarttitayāṅkuraṃ janayantīti tāsv apy aṅkuro 'sty eveti.*

According to the editors' introduction (YD, pp. xxiv-xxv), "[t]he author, or one of the authors, ... was remarkably familiar with Mahāyāna Buddhism, a fact that would suggest that he/they may have lived before the extinction of Buddhism in Kashmir, i.e. in the 14th

7 Against the edition of the YD, I prefer to read these two parts as found in the manuscript A mentioned in the footnotes of the edition.

century A.D." There is also another marginal note where we find the words "Abhinavagupta's *Sāṃkhyanirṇaya*," which A. Sanderson has identified as a section of the *Tantrāloka* (YD, p. xxv). From such information, it is at least possible to say that this unique Sāṅkhya text had a certain impact in the Kashmir region, where it was studied together with Kashmir Śaiva texts.[8]

***

In this connection, it is also remarkable that Utpaladeva's grand-disciple Abhinavagupta mentions this type of *sahakārin* in his commentary (*Īśvarapratyabhijñāvivṛtivimarśinī*, henceforth ĪPVV) on Utpaladeva's *Īśvarapratyabhijñāvivṛti*, a work of which most is lost. In one section of his commentary, Abhinavagupta refutes the Sāṅkhya dualism, especially the difference between the soul (*puruṣa/ātman*) as a conscious being and the intellect (*buddhi*) as a product of primordial matter. Here, the Sāṅkhya opponent claims that a pot arises from a lump of clay as its material cause, and its specific features (*viśeṣa/śeṣa*)[9] are given by *sahakārin*s like a stick, a wheel, and a potter; in the same manner, the soul takes the role of a *sahakārin* as a co-operating factor for the arising of various things from primordial matter. But if this is so, Abhinavagupta says, the Sāṅkhya should accept causality based on a "causal complex" (*sāmagrī*) rather than a "single material cause" (*ekopādāna*).[10] Against this, the Sāṅkhya opponent claims the following:

> ĪPVV, vol. I, p. 171, l. .22-p. 172, l. 4: *nanu kānicit sahakārīṇi upādānarūpam āviśanty eva kāraṇatāṃ pratipadyante. jalabhūmyoḥ pariṇāmiko hi*

---

8 With regard to this, Dr. Yohei Kawajiri kindly informed me about an important marginal note in a manuscript of the *Īśvarapratyabhijñākārikā*: *anyā ca vṛttiḥ pariṇāmāt pariṇāmo hi pūrvasvabhāvatirodhānenaiva yathā ghaṭasya kāpālānivṛttis tu tasyaiva rūpasyāpratyastamitasya yathā bhūtenaiva parāmṛśamānasya yathā tathā vattena tadyathā devadattasya gamana ghaṭasyodakāharaṇaṃ tadvṛttibhedānutattvabhedo bhavati tenaiva rūpeṇāvādhitapratyajñāviṣayatvāt iti ca nṛpativārtikaṭīkāyām* ||. This marginal note describes the distinction between the concept of *vṛtti* and that of *pariṇāma* on the basis of a text called *Nṛpativārt(t)ikaṭīkā*. The name "Nṛpativārttika" reminds us of *Rājavārttika*, another name of the YD (see "Introduction" of the YD, pp. xxv-xxvii). Thus this might be another piece of evidence for the popularity of the YD in Kashmir.

9 Cf. ĪPVV, vol. I, p. 171, l. 11: *śeṣaśabdavācyaṃ viśeṣamātram*. Thus, in the following, I choose to translate the term *śeṣa* as "specific feature."

10 See ĪPVV, vol. I, p. 171, ll. 8-22. I would read *ekopādāna-* for *ekakopādāna-* (p. 171, l. 22).

> *rasa ūṣmaṇo vegavatā kālaprabhāvitena bījāntarvartitām eva upayāti, tāvatā vicitrasya aṅkurasya svarūpalābhāt. anyāni tu dharmādharmapuruṣārthaprabhṛtīni abhivyaktimātre vyāpriyante. teṣu kā kāryaśeṣāntargamanacintā. yady evam, abhivyaktir na kāryaśeṣa iti tatra vyāpriyamāṇānām eṣāṃ dīpacakṣurādīnām iva kathaṃkāraṃ kāraṇatāpariganaṇanaṃ bhavet. kāryaśeṣaḥ seti cet, tarhi asatī saiva. enāṃ tāni yathā utthāpayanti, tathā upādānam api mukhyakāryam utthāpayet.*
>
> [Objection:] Only certain auxiliary causes entering into the nature of a material cause become the [material] cause, for the flavor as a transformation of water and earth comes into existence exactly inside of the seed, through the heat that has strengthened during the time, and to this extent, a variety of sprouts arise. On the other hand, other [auxiliary causes] such as merit, demerit, and the soul's purpose operate on the mere manifestation [of the effect] (*abhivyaktimātra*). With regard to those [auxiliary causes like merit], what is the point of considering [their] entering into the specific features of the effect?
>
> [Reply:] If so, since manifestation is not a specific feature of the effect, how could one consider as causes these [auxiliary causes] operating on the [manifestation], such as light and the visual organ? [If they do not operate on the specific features of the effect, they are not the cause]. If the [manifestation] is [also] a specific feature of the effect, then the [manifestation] itself is non-existent [at the moment of the cause]. Just as those [auxiliary causes] produce a [non-existent] manifestation, likewise the material cause, too, would produce a [non-existent] primary effect (*mukhyakārya*). [Thus, the Sāṅkhya's *satkāryavāda* is rejected].

In this manner, Abhinavagupta introduces the Sāṅkhya claim by using the notion of "penetration of *sahakārin*," according to which he is able to explain how various specific features can arise from a single material cause. However, the Sāṅkhya opponent also insists on another kind of *sahakārin* that operates only for the manifestation of the effect. If we compare the two kinds of *sahakārin* with the previous explanation of Utpaladeva, we soon notice that Abhinavagupta strongly criticizes "manifestation" as the effect of the second type of *sahakārin*,[11] which Utpaladeva explained in another way. But what is more important for us is that both philosophers describe the first type of *sahakārin* as a factor that can enter into a material

[11] For more details about the concept of *abhivyakti* in the Pratyabhijñā school, see RATIÉ 2014.

cause and that they do not criticize this unique concept. Why were they indifferent to the Sāṅkhya claim?

***

To close this short essay, I would like to present my tentative thoughts on this question. This Sāṅkhya concept of "penetration of the *sahakārin*" was probably acceptable for the Pratyabhijñā philosophers when both the material cause and auxiliary causes were regarded as "manifestations" (*ābhāsa*) of Śiva's consciousness. For instance, Utpaladeva's passage, *śaukalyamahattvapaṭatvādyavabhāsāḥ parasparānupraveśakṣamāḥ* (*Vṛtti* on ĪPK II.3.7) and that of Abhinavagupta, *sarvapadārthānupraveśanāt prakāśa ity etāvanmātram abhinnaṃ tattvam avaśiṣyate* (ĪPVV, vol. II, p. 76, ad ĪPK I.5.3) give a significant role to "penetration" (*anupraveśa*) in their presentation of the non-dualism of Śiva's consciousness or illumination (*prakāśa*). As is well known, the Sāṅkhya theory of causation is compatible with Śaiva philosophy, even though Utpaladeva gave a sharp criticism against the Sāṅkhya concept of *buddhi*.[12] Just as the Sāṅkhya explains the evolution of the world from a single, material cause, the Śaiva maintains the manifestation of the world from Śiva's consciousness; just as the Sāṇkhya accepts the nature of primordial matter as existing in every material thing, the Śaiva claims the omnipresence of Śiva's nature in this world. Taking such a Śaiva schema of causality into consideration, it is no wonder that both Utpaladeva and Abhinavagupta focused on the Sāṅkhya idea of the *sahakārin*'s penetration into the material cause, which is easily adopted for an exposition of the dynamic relation between various manifest things that are capable of entering each other through the single, divine nature of Śiva. This is possibly the reason that the two philosophers of the Pratyabhijñā school did not come up with any objections to the Sāṅkhya theory of the first type of *sahakārin*.

---

[12] Cf. TORELLA 1994, p. 185, n. 31. For Utpaladeva's specific notion of the soul as the agent and the cognizer in comparison with its Sāṅkhya ideas, see BRONKHORST 1996. For more details of Utpaladeva's argument that adjusts the Sāṅkhya theory of causation to his own system, see RATIÉ 2014. For the lengthy criticism of the Sāṅkhya notion of *buddhi* in the Pratyabhijñā treatise, see RATIÉ 2011, pp. 94-106 and 276-289. In Utpaladeva's short treatise, APS, too, there is a brief criticism against the Sāṅkhya notion of *buddhi*, see LAWRENCE 2009, p. 638.

REFERENCES

APS
Ajaḍapramātṛsiddhi of Utpaladeva, ed. M.K. Shastri, Srinagar: Kashmir Series of Texts and Studies 34, 1921

BRONKHORST 1996
J. Bronkhorst, "The Self as Agent: A Review Article," *Asiatische Studien/Études Asiatiques* 50(3), 1996, pp. 603-621

FRANCO forthcoming
E. Franco, Summary of the *Pramāṇasiddhi*-chapter of the *Pramāṇavārttika*, in *Encyclopedia of Indian Philosophy*

HB
[*Hetubindu* of Dharmakīrti] E. Steinkellner, *Dharmakīrti's Hetubinduḥ. Teil I: Tibetischer Text und rekonstruierter Sanskrit Text*, Vienna: 1967

ĪPK
[*Īśvarapratyabhijñākārikā* of Utpaladeva] See TORELLA 1994

ĪPV
Īśvarapratyabhijñāvimarśinī of Abhinavagupta, ed. M.R. Shāstrī and M.K. Shāstrī, Srinagar: Kashmir Series of Texts and Studies 22 and 33, 1918-1921

ĪPVV
Īśvarapratyabhijñāvivṛtivimarśinī of Abhinavagupta, ed. M.K. Shāstrī, Bombay: Kashmir Series of Texts and Studies 60, 62 and 65, 1938-1943

ĪS
Īśvarasiddhi of Utpaladeva, ed. M.K. Shastri, Srinagar: Kashmir Series of Texts and Studies 34, 1921

KRASSER 2002
H. Krasser, *Śaṅkaranandanas Īśvarāpākaraṇasaṅkṣepa. Teil 2: Annotierte Übersetzungen und Studie zur Auseinandersetzung über die Existenz Gottes*, Wien: 2002

LAWRENCE 2009
D.P. Lawrence, "Proof of a Sentient Knower: Utpaladeva's *Ajaḍapramātṛsiddhi* with the *Vṛtti* of Harabhatta Shastri," *Journal of Indian Philosophy* 37, 2009, pp. 627-653

MORIYAMA forthcoming
S. Moriyama, "Another look at a fragment of Aviddhakarṇa's proof of God"

NBhūṣ
Nyāyabhūṣaṇa of Bhāsarvajña, ed. S. Yogīndrānanda, Varanasi: 1968

NP
Nareśvaraparīkṣā of Sadyojotis, ed. M.K. Shastri, [Srinagar: Kashmir Series of Texts and Studies 45, 1926] repr. New Delhi: 1989

PV 2
Pramāṇavārttika of Dharmakīrti, chapter 2, in Y. Miyasaka, "*Pramāṇavārttika-kārikā* (Sanskrit and Tibetan)," *Acta Indologica* II, 1971-1972, pp. 1-206

RATIÉ 2011
I. Ratié, *Le Soi et l'Autre. Identité, différence et altérité dans la philosophie de la Pratyabhijñā*, Leiden-Boston: Brill, 2011

RATIÉ 2014
I. Ratié, "A Śaiva interpretation of the *Satkāryavāda*: The Sāṃkhya Notion of *Abhivyakti* and Its Transformation in the Pratyabhijñā Treatise," *Journal of Indian Philosophy* 42, 2014, pp. 127-172

RATIÉ 2015
I. Ratié, "Utpaladeva's proof of God: on the purpose of the *Īśvarasiddhi*," in B. Bäumer and R. Torella (eds.), *Utpaladeva, Philosopher of Recognition*, Delhi: DK Printworld, 2015, pp. 254-337

SK
[*Sāṅkhyakārikā* of Īśvarakṛṣṇa] See YD

SLAJE 1986
W. Slaje, "Untersuchungen zur Chronologie einiger Nyāya-Philosophen," *Studien zur Indologie und Iranistik* 11-12, 1986, pp. 245-278

TABER 1986
J. Taber, "Utpaladeva's *Īśvarasiddhi*," *The Adyar Library Bulletin* 52, 1986, pp. 106-137

TORELLA 1994
R. Torella, *The Īśvarapratyabhijñākārikā of Utpaladeva with the Author's Vṛtti*, Roma: 1994

TORELLA 1999
R. Torella, "Sāṃkhya as *sāmānyaśāstra*," *Asiatische Studien* 53, 1999, pp. 553-562

Vyom
Vyomavatī of Vyomaśiva, ed. G. Sastri, 2 vols., Varanasi: 1983

WATSON 2006
A. Watson, *The Self's Awareness of Itself: Bhaṭṭa Rāmakaṇṭha's Arguments against the Buddhist Doctrine of No-self*, Wien: 2006

YD
Yuktidīpikā, eds. A. Wezler and Sh. Motegi, Stuttgart: 1998

Jayanta as Referred to by Udayana and Gaṅgeśa*

YASUTAKA MUROYA

INTRODUCTION

It is well known that the Navya-Nyāya author Gaṅgeśa, or Gaṅgeśvara Upādhyāya (ca. 14th century CE), refers to an author he calls "Jayanta." It has been held that this reference is to Bhaṭṭa Jayanta (ca. 9th c.), the Kashmiri Nyāya philosopher, also known as the "Commentator" (*vṛttikāra*).[1] Gaṅgeśa's historically interesting reference is found in the *upamāna* chapter (*upamānakhaṇḍa*) of his

* Research on this paper has been made possible through the generous support of the German Research Foundation (DFG) in the context of a research project (Grant No. FR 2531/4-1 "Logic, Dialectics and Epistemology of the Nyāya Tradition") at the Institute for South and Central Asian Studies, Leipzig University. I gratefully acknowledge my indebtedness to the late H.H. Muni Shree Jambuvijayaji, Jaisalmer Lodravapur Parsvanath Jain Svetambara Trust (Jaisalmer), Oriental Research Library, Libraries & Research Department of Jammu & Kashmir Government (Srinagar), Oriental Research Institute, University of Mysore (Mysore), Department of Malayalam and Kerala Studies, University of Calicut (Thenjipalam), Mumbai University Library (Mumbai), Bhandarkar Oriental Research Institute (Pune), Oriental Research Institute & Manuscripts Library, University of Kerala (Thiruvananthapuram) for granting access to their manuscript materials, and to an Austrian FWF project (Grant No. P24388 "Metaphysics and Epistemology of the Nyāya Tradition III"), as well as to Hiroko Matsuoka, Mai Miyo and Masahiro Ueda for utilizing their copies of the relevant manuscripts.

1 For two of the most recent investigations on the background of Jayanta's ancestors and his composition of the NM, including the relevant bibliographical information up to date, see DEZSŐ 2004 (Part I, Introduction, Chapter 1 "Bhaṭṭa Jayanta's life") and SLAJE 2012. On his designation as the *vṛttikāra* (cf. RAGHAVAN 1960; DEZSŐ 2004, p. vii), cf., e.g., NM, vol. II, p. 718, ll. 5-6 (*pāda*s a-b of Śārdūlavikrīḍita): *vādeṣv āpta*[a]*jayo jayanta iti yaḥ khyātaḥ satām agraṇīr anvarthena ca vṛtti*[b]*kāra iti yaṃ śaṃsanti nāmnā budhāḥ* | (v.l.: a. *āpta-*] P; *ātta* ed. – b. *anvarthena ca vṛtti-*] P; *anvarthe navavṛtti* ed.). The hitherto known reading *navavṛttikāra* is not supported by one of the best manuscripts from Pune; for a survey of the known mss. of the NM and on their genealogical relationship in the sixth chapter, see GRAHELI 2012 and 2011, pp. 113-114. For

Tattvacintāmaṇi (TC), an investigation into comparison, identification or analogy (*upamāna*), where Jayanta and others are given the epithet "old Naiyāyikas" (*jarannaiyāyikā jayantaprabhṛtayaḥ*).[2] In the first English translation of the entire analogy chapter, published in 2012, Stephen Phillips remarks that "rival Naiyāyika positions are sometimes aired, and often he [Gaṅgeśa (YM)] distinguishes his contemporary or "New" (*navya*) Nyāya from that of "Old" Nyāya, as he does in one place in this chapter, even mentioning one philosopher of Old Nyāya by name (Jayanta Bhaṭṭa)."[3] The present article is a preliminary attempt to examine a possible link between Jayanta and Gaṅgeśa, a point that as yet scholars have left open.

1.

In his introduction to the monumental *editio princeps* of Jayanta's *Nyāyamañjarī* (NM) published in 1895, the editor Gaṅgādhara Śāstrī Tailaṅga already calls attention to the fact mentioned above:[4]... *jayantabhaṭṭo nāma, yaṃ jarannaiyāyikapadena vyapadideśa nyāyacintāmaṇāv upamānakhaṇḍe gaṅgeśopādhyāyaḥ*. The renowned professor of the Benares Sanskrit College then turns to the issue of Jayanta's dates, examining in particular his chronological relation to another representative of Nyāya, Vācaspati Miśra I (ca. 10th c.), arguing that Vācaspati predates Jayanta.[5] The Benares paṇḍit, who also published the first edition of the *Nyāyavārttikatātparyaṭīkā*

another text-critical problem regarding the printed edition of the NM, cf. n. 91 below.

2 TC (C), p. 61, ll. 2-3 = TC (D) = TC (V), p. 19, l. 2.

3 PHILLIPS 2012, p. 106. In the appendix to his translation, Phillips renders *jarannaiyāyikā jayantaprabhṛtayaḥ* as "the Old Naiyāyikas, Jayanta and the rest" (p. 121).

4 Cf. NM (V), *nyāyamañjarībhūmikā*, p. 1, with the reference "*kalikātāsosāiṭīmudritapustake* 61 pṛ."

5 Śāstrī identifies the *ācāryāḥ* mentioned by Jayanta as Vācaspatimiśra (n. *: *tātparyaṭīkāyāṃ vācaspatimiśrāḥ*) in a famous passage discussing the *pratyakṣasūtra* (NS 1.1.4). See NM (V), p. 78, l. 5 = NM, vol. I, p. 204, l. 2: *avyapadeśyapadasya varṇāyāṃ cakrur ācāryāḥ*; cf. VON STIETENCRON 1970, p. 216. Varadacarya, the editor of the NM Mysore edition, appears to follow Śāstrī's identification in structuring the relevant portion. See e.g., NM, vol. I, p. 175, l. 1: *vācaspatimatam* for NM, vol. I, p. 175, l. 2 (*atrācāryās tāvad ācakṣate*). Marui supposes that the Varanasi paṇḍit is the first to mention the relative chronology of Jayanta and Vācaspati; see MARUI 2001, p. 443 = MARUI 2014, p. 98. On designations such as *ācārya* and *vyākhātṛ*, including relevant, up-to-date bibliographical information, see MARUI 2006 and 2014, pp. 231-299.

(NVTṬ), is not the only one to have associated Jayanta with Vācaspati in terms of relative chronology. The dating of Vācaspati in particular has often been discussed in relation to the controversy concerning the famous *Nyāyasūcīnibandha* (NSN), which is to have been composed in the year 898 (*vasvaṅkavasuvatsare*), albeit of an unspecified era, and is ascribed to an author named Vācaspati.[6] In 1936 there was a turning point in the discussion. Erich Frauwallner, reviewing Gopinath Kaviraj's evaluation made in 1924,[7] took recourse in a comparative method based on the two Nyāya philosophers' theoretical development to determine their relative chronology. Against the earlier premise of Śāstrī, he concluded that Jayanta preceded Vācaspati.[8] But this was not the end of the controversy.

1.1. A new piece of information found in a work by Udayana prompted a new historical examination of the timeline of the Nyāya au-

---

[6] For an important investigation on the relative chronology of Vācaspati and Jayanta in relation to the NSN, see HACKER 1951; for a systematic overview of the controversy among scholars, see MARUI 2001 (=MARUI 2014, pp. 96-113) and ACHARYA 2006, Introduction, pp. xviii-xx. On the problematic identity of the author of the published version of the NSN edited by Dvivedin (in the Bibliotheca Indica edition of the NV, Calcutta 1887-1914), as well as its text-critical and genealogical features related to fourteen categorically selected *Nyāyasūtrapāṭha* mss., see MUROYA 2006. The hitherto only known ms. that could be identified as a NSN is found in the I.S. Desai collection (Acc. No. 99.12) at the Mumbai University Library; see VELANKAR 1953, p. 146 (Ser. No. 753, Devanagari, 14 fols.). My recent, albeit not yet completed examination of the ms. shows that it is not Dvivedin's exemplar; for instance, a worm-eaten portion (MUROYA 2006, p. 421) found in his exemplar is lacking; and where the Mumbai ms. reads *trayodaśabhiḥ* exactly as Dvivedin's ms. (MUROYA 2006, pp. 420 f.), there appears an additional passage, NS (R) 2.2.13a (= NBh, p. 104, l. 15), which is even wrongly allocated at the end of the *catuṣṭvaprakaraṇa*, and not at the beginning of the next *prakaraṇa* (see Ruben's remark in NS [R], p. 43). Furthermore, it retains NS (R) 2.1.30 against the printed NSN as well as Vācaspati's identification of it as the text of the NBh; see Ruben's remark in NS (R), p. 29 and 187, n. 122; cf. MARUI 2001, pp. 453-454 (=MARUI 2014, p. 110) and MUROYA 2006, pp. 406-407. Inasmuch as the Mumbai ms. assigns the structural relationship *upodghāta* to NS 3.2.10-17 just as the Dvivedin's NSN and other mss. examined (MUROYA 2006, pp. 410-416 and 424), I estimate that their genealogically reconstructed archetype could "hardly have been established in, or before, the period of Keśavamiśra," the author of the *Gautamīyasūtraprakāśa* (ca. 16th c.); see MUROYA 2006, p. 427.

[7] For Kaviraj's counterargument, see KAVIRAJ 1924, p. 104 and FRAUWALLNER 1936, pp. 149-150 = 1982, pp. 267-268.

[8] FRAUWALLNER 1936. For a summary of Frauwallner's arguments, see MARUI 2001, p. 443 = MARUI 2014, pp. 99-100.

thors of the early medieval period. Eight years before the publication, in 1967, of Udayana's *Nyāyavārttikatātparyapariśuddhi* (NVTP) on the first book of the *Nyāyasūtra* (NS), Anantalal Thakur disclosed a profoundly interesting reference to Jayanta,[9] writing:

> Udayana shows that Vācaspati refers to the view of Jayanta – the "Old Logician." This reference is highly important for determining the date of Vācaspati. [...] The reference makes Vācaspati at least a younger contemporary of Jayanta.[10]

1.2. The passage in question runs:

> *upamānasya phale vipratipadyamānān prati sāśaṅkaṃ jarannaiyāyikajayantaprabhṛtīnāṃ parihāram āha – yady apīti.*[11]

The *pratīka* "*yady api*" extracted by Udayana refers to Vācaspati's NVTṬ. Thakur makes a reference to p. 170 of the Calcutta edition of the NVTṬ, unfortunately without specification or further explanation. Ever since Thakur's edition of the NVTP in 1967, the relevant passage has been accessible to the scholarly world; in fact it appears in the commentary on the definition *sūtra* of analogy (NS 1.1.6: *prasiddhasādharmyāt sādhyasādhanam upamānam*). The analysis of this passage by modern scholars has varied.

---

9 Thakur must have recognized this at the latest in 1953. According to the preface of the NVTṬ and NVTP, Thakur started with the editorial work of the various NS commentaries in 1953 on the basis of the Jaisalmer mss. supplied by P.L. Vaidya and J.S. Jetly; see also the preface in ND (M) and NA.

10 THAKUR 1959, Introduction, p. 21 (elision by YM). Thakur's information is briefly reviewed by Svāmī Yogīndrānanda, the editor of the NBhūṣ; see his prāgbandha, p. 14. See also Thakur's similar remarks in THAKUR 1974, p. 403 ("Udayana shows that Vācaspati refers to the view of Jayanta, the old Logician"), and his introduction to the NVTP, Preface, p. viii ("The *Pariśuddhi* says that Vācaspati reproduces the views of old logicians including Jayantabhaṭṭa of Kashmir"). Later than Thakur, but independently, Umesha Mishra records (MISHRA 1966, p. 199) the various philosophical figures mentioned by name by Udayana, consulting a ms. of the NVTP (altogether 1215 pages [sic]) most of which was then unpublished. Among them is found a mention of "Jarannaiyāyika Jayanta-prabhṛtīnām," albeit without any concrete information about the context or the relation to the NS.

11 See THAKUR 1959, Introduction, p. 21, n. 1. The passage corresponds to NVTP, p. 215, ll. 20-21 = ND (M), p. 362, ll. 3-4. The editor records *phalaiḥ* in "J." This refers to a highly faithful and precise 15th-century transcript, NVTP (J2) in my abbreviation, but its 13th-century exemplar NVTP (J1) clearly reads *phale*; cf. NVTP (J1), f. 229r,1.

1.3. The first issue to be clarified may be reduced to answering the following questions: (1) which passage does the *pratīka* "*yady api*" refer to in the NVTṬ? (2) What is the implication of the *parihāra* ("refutation") intended by Vācaspati? (3) Where are Jayanta's views found in the text of the NVTṬ? (4) Reversely, which are the actual passages of the NM that Vācaspati seems to refer to?

1.4. Regarding question (2), it was noted by Matilal that "Vācaspati Miśra I refuted a view of Jayanta. Thus, accepting the authority of Udayana, we place Jayanta prior to Vācaspati. [...] This also explains why Gaṅgeśa referred to Jayanta as 'the old Naiyāyika' (*jaran-naiyāyika*)."[12] Matilal does not refer to the other three points above.

1.4.1. Regarding question (1), Bruce Perry and Diwakar Acharya, independently of one another, have identified the *pratīka* with the *yady api* occurring in the following passage:[13]

> ***yady api*** *prasiddhasādharmyam upamānam ity ucyamāne pramāṇaviśeṣābhidhāyyupamānapadasāmānādhikaraṇyāt karaṇatvalābhaḥ, tathāpi tadābhāsanirākaraṇāya* ***sādhyasādhana****padopādānam. tenopamānābhāsam apākṛtaṃ bhavati* [emphasis by YM].

Both hold that it is concerned with the gloss validating *sādhyasādhana*, a term that appears in the analogy *sūtra*. Perry suggests that "a close examination of Jayanta Bhaṭṭa's treatment of *upamāna* might corroborate the accuracy of Udayana's presentation." He renders *jarannaiyāyika* as "old-fashioned Naiyāyika."[14]

1.4.2. Acharya notes, with pertinent reservations about Udayana's reliability (pp. xxvii-xxviii):

> [...] Udayana, commenting upon *Nyāyasūtra* I.1.6, makes a remark that the view there that Vācaspatimiśra refuted is the view of Jayanta and the other *jarannaiyāyikas* [...]. Even if we set aside the question whether Udayana was right in assigning the view Vācaspatimiśra criticised to Jayanta and other *jarannaiyāyikas*, it can be deduced from Udayana's remarks that

---

12 MATILAL 1977, pp. 93-94.

13 The indication in PERRY 1995, p. 20, n. 46 is made in regard to ND (M), p. 357, ll. 6-8 with further references ("cf. also NVT, p. 357, ll. 15ff. and NVTP, p. 362, ll. 22-23, NVT, p. 358, ll. 20 ff and NVTP, p. 364, l. 12"). ACHARYA 2006, Introduction, p. xxvii quotes the whole text of NVTṬ, p. 162, ll. 13-15, equivalent to ND (M), p. 357, ll. 6-8 in the edition used by Perry.

14 PERRY 1995, pp. 19-20, n. 46 and n. 47, respectively.

> Jayanta was regarded as anterior to Vācaspatimiśra in the early half of the eleventh century [elision by YM].

Furthermore, Acharya specifies the relevant passage in question in the NM:

> *prasiddhasādharmyajñānam upamānam, phalaṃ sañjñāsañjñisambandhajñānam ity uktaṃ bhavati.*[15]

Although Acharya has basically clarified all four questions mentioned above, the exact correlation between the passages in the NVTṬ and the NM remains to be examined.

1.5. Voicing his doubts about Matilal's analysis of an alleged antagonism between Jayanta and Vācaspati, Hiroshi Marui has presented a new interpretation. Marui provides a different identification of the *pratīka* "*yady api*" than that of the scholars mentioned above, namely, with "NVTṬ, [p.] 163, [ll.] 8ff.":

> ***yady api*** *yathā gaur evaṃ gavaya ity etasmād api gosādṛśyasya gavayaśabdaḥ samākhyeti śakyam avagantum. na khalu pratyakṣa eva sañjñākarma, samānajātīyavyavacchinne hi tad bhavati* [The text as such is not quoted by him; emphasis by YM].[16]

This passage is connected with Vācaspati's explanation of the concept of *prasiddhi* as contained in *prasiddhasādharmyāt* in the analogy *sūtra* (cf. § 1.2 above).[17] Marui's interpretation of Udayana's remark suggests a new perspective:

> Vācaspati introduces here the refutation of (or as the text may alternatively mean: made by) old scholars of Nyāya beginning with Jayanta who refuted the opponents' rejection of the *upamāna* as another means of cognition [English rendering by YM].[18]

The alternative possibility reflected in the above translation is pointed out by Marui. In addition, Marui remarks that a comparison of the relevant portion in the NM and NVTṬ does not show their clear correspondence, and cautions against relying blindly upon Udayana's information.

---

15 NM, vol. I, p. 382, ll. 7-8; p. 205 in Gaurinath Sastri's edition of the NM (3 vols., Varanasi 1982-1984) used by Acharya.

16 NVTṬ, p. 163, ll. 8-10.

17 On Vācaspati's concept of *prasiddhi*, see n. 73 below; cf. § 3.5.

18 The original is in Japanese. See MARUI 2001, p. 446 = MARUI 2014, p. 102.

2.

As shown above (§§ 1.4-1.5), there are different opinions about the identification of the *pratīka* "*yady api*" in the NVTṬ. Udayana's commentary NVTP reveals another significant piece of information on this point. Immediately after his reference to Jayanta, Udayana paraphrases the expression *sañjñākarma* ("naming action") as *sañjñākaraṇa* ("naming"). The immediate vicinity of the two expressions (*yady api* and *sañjñākarma*) leads us to identify Udayana's *sañjñākarma* with the same term that appears in a sentence of the NVTṬ: *na khalu pratyakṣa eva* ***sañjñākarma*** ("As you should know, the naming action is not [applied] only to the perceptible object").[19] This corroborates Marui's identification, and is confirmed by the sequence of the *pratīka* immediately preceding.[20]

2.1. There is a further textual source of relevance. Let us turn our attention to Vardhamāna's commentary on Udayana's NVTP, the so-called *Nyāyanibandhaprakāśa* (NNP). The printed editions of this work by Gaṅgeśa's son cover the commentary incompletely, the first one up to NVTP, p. 210, l. 12 on NS 1.1.5 (ed. V.P. Dvivedin and L.S. Dravida, Calcutta: 1911-1924) and the second, the *Trisūtrī* section (ed. S.K. Sadhukhan, Kolkata: 2009). A critical edition of the commentary, including the portion of the analogy *sūtra* in question, has been announced by Sadhukhan as in preparation. Accordingly, the following information is based on a paper ms. from Mysore made available to me recently.

2.2. There is a relevant gloss by Vardhamana on Udayana's mention of *jayantaprabhṛtīnāṃ parihāraḥ*, a gloss which supports Marui's identification of the *yady api* in question. It runs as follows:

> *sāśaṃkaṃ pūsarvvapakṣaṃ* (recte: *sapūrvapakṣaṃ*) *yady apītyādinā'vagatagavaya* (recte: *'vagaṃtuṃ gavayaḥ*) *ity aṃtena pūrvvapakṣaḥ tathāpītyādinā pramāṇāṃtaram āstheyam ity aṃtena jayantaprabhṛtīnāṃ parihāra ity arthaḥ* (transliteration of NNP Ms., f. 67r,8-9, without recording scribal correction).

According to Vardhamāna, the relevant portion of the NVTṬ is divided into two parts. The first part – from *yady api* to *avagantuṃ gavayaḥ* – is attributed to the *pūrvapakṣa*, as implied by *sāśaṅkam*

---

19 NVTP, p. 215, l. 21 and NVTṬ, p. 163, ll. 9-10.

20 The preceding *pratīka* in NVTP, p. 215, l. 19, namely, *prasiddhasādharmyād ity atra*, corresponds to NVTṬ, p. 163, ll. 5-6.

("accompanied by a doubt or objection," if it is a *bahuvrīhi* compound[21]), and the second – from *tathāpi* through *pramāṇāntaram āstheyam* – to *jayantaprabhṛtīnāṃ parihāraḥ*. Vardhamāna appears to render the second part as the *uttarapakṣa* presented by Jayanta and others.

2.3. In the following reproduction of the relevant text of the NVTṬ, the aforementioned information by Vardhamāna is incorporated:

NVTṬ, p. 163, ll. 8-13 [= Pūrvapakṣa]:

yady api *yathā gaur evaṃ gavaya ity asmād*[a] *api gosadṛśasya*[b] *gavaya*[c]*samākhyeti śakyam avagantum. na khalu pratyakṣa eva sañjñākarma. samānāsamāna*[d]*jātīyavyavacchinne hi tad bhavati. tac ca yadi mānāntareṇāpi tathāvagamyate, kas tatra*[e] *sañjñākarma nivārayet. gosādṛśyena copalakṣitaḥ piṇḍo ya iti sarvanāmnā parāmṛṣṭaḥ*[f] *śakyo ghaṭādibhyo 'samānajātīyebhyo*[g] *mahiṣādi*[h]*bhyaś ca samānajātīyebhyo vyavacchinno 'vagantuṃ gavayaḥ,*

NVTṬ, p. 163, ll. 13-17 [= Jayantaprabhṛtīnāṃ parihāraḥ]:

tathāpi *yāvad ayam asau gavaya iti sākṣāt pratīte sambandhini sañjñāṃ na niveśayati*[i] *tāvad ayaṃ pariplutamatiḥ pramātā "kaccit*[j] *khalu drakṣyāmi tādṛśaṃ piṇḍaṃ yatra gavayasañjñāṃ pratipatsye*[k]*" iti pramotsuka evodīkṣate. na cāsau vākyamātrasahāyo 'pratyakṣīkṛtagosadṛśagavayatvajātimatpiṇḍaḥ*[l] *"ayam asau gavayākhyaḥ" iti pratipattum arhati, na ca vākyaṃ vinā pratyakṣamātrāt. tasmād āgamapratyakṣābhyām anyad evedam āgamasmṛtisahitaṃ sādṛśyajñānam upamānākhyaṃ pramāṇam āstheyam.*[22]

---

21 Otherwise, if an *avyayībhāva* compound, this would carry the sense of "apprehensively."

22 NVTṬ, p. 163, ll. 8-17 = ND (C), p. 170, ll. 13-22 = ND (M), p. 357, l. 23-p. 358, l. 6. v.l.: a. *asmād*] J1; *etasmād* ed., C, M – b. *-sadṛśasya*] J1, C, M; *sādṛśyasya* ed. – c. *gavaya-*] J1; *gavayaḥ* ed. ("J"), M ("J"); *gavayaśabdaḥ* ed., C, M – d. *samānāsamāna-*] J1; *samāna* ed., C, M – e. *kas tatra*] ed., J1, M; om. C – f. *parāmṛṣṭaḥ*] J1, C, M; *pararāmṛṣṭaḥ* ed. – g. *-jātīyebhyo*] J1, C; *jātiyebhyo* M; *jātibhyo* ed. – h. *mahiṣādi-*] ed., C, M; *mahiṣyādi* J1, ed. ("J"), M ("J") – i. *niveśayati*] J1, C, M; *niveśyati* ed. – j. *kaccit*] ed., J1, M; *kañcid* C (see also the corresponding *pratīka* in NVTP, p. 216, l. 6: *enam evārthaṃ kañcid ityādinā darśitavān*; however, NVTP [J1] reads *kaccit*) – k. *pratipatsye*] J1; *pratipatsya* ed., C, M – l. *-sadṛśagavayatvajātimatpiṇḍaḥ "ayam asau*] J1; *sadṛśagavayatvajātimatpiṇḍo 'sau* ed., M; *sadṛśagavayapiṇḍam asau* C; *sadṛśe piṇḍe 'yam asau* ed. ("C Var"; however, the Calcutta edition records "*gosadṛśe piṇḍo yam asau*" as the reading of "kha-pu-pāṭhaḥ," the text of a manuscript of the "Asiatic Society Bengal Calcutta"; cf. ND [C], p. 170, n. 3), M ("C var"). Due to the

Vardhamāna's analysis leaves the impression that one can take the concessive conjunctive *yady api* as syntactically connected to the *tathāpi*, with both parts constituting a single very long main sentence with several subordinate sentences.[23]

2.4. Vardhamāna's gloss indirectly corroborates the following two points: (1) the *pratīka* "*yady api*" refers to NVTṬ, p. 163, l. 8, and (2) the refutation *by* Jayanta and others comprises a response to the objection. This implies that the view introduced by Vācaspati is not his own refutation of Jayanta's theory, but Jayanta's argumentation against those who disprove the *upamāna* theory of Nyāya (*vipratipadyamānān prati* in the NVTP; cf. § 1.2 above).[24] Of course, if one does not take the genitive of the *jayantaprabhṛtīnām* in the NVTP in the subjective sense, but in the objective, one can still suppose, for instance, that the *pūrvapakṣa* portion corresponds to the objection as represented, or treated, by Jayanta, and the *uttarapakṣa* portion to Vācaspati's refutation of Jayanta's objection, or counterargument, against his opponent.

2.5. It seems unlikely, however, that this latter supposition is the understanding purported by Vardhamāna, when we look at his father's reference to the theory of "Jayanta and others." Gaṅgeśa makes an unacknowledged quotation of the last sentence of the passage adduced above from the NVTṬ (*tasmād... āstheyam*) and subsequently concludes his presentation by saying "thus say the old Naiyāyikas headed by Jayanta" (*iti jarannaiyāyikā jayantaprabhṛtayaḥ*). This treatment by the 14th-century philosopher suggests that the last sentence in question still belongs to Jayanta and others. The table below shows possible sources used by Gaṅgeśa. For purposes of analysis, the relevant portion of the TC is divided into nine parts.[25]

---

significance of the cited passage, the collation of the Calcutta edition (C) and Thakur's earlier one (M) is noted here.

23 The Calcutta edition (ND [C], p. 170, ll. 13-20) only places commas between *yady api* and *evodīkṣate* which ends with a *daṇḍa* (... *śakyam avagantum*, ... *saṃjñākarma*, ... *tad bhavati*, ... *nivārayet*, ... *'vagantuṃ gavayaḥ*, ...). Thakur's punctuation for the same portion (NVTṬ, p. 163, ll. 8-15) is different (... *śakyam avagantum*. ... *sañjñākarma*, ... *tad bhavati*. ... *tathāvagamyate*, ... *nivārayet*? ...*'vagantuṃ gavayaḥ*, ...). Thakur's earlier punctuation for the same portion (ND [M], p. 357, l. 23-p. 358, l. 3) is again different (... *śakyam avagantum*, ... *sañjñākarma*, ... *tad bhavati*. ... *tathāvagamyate*, ... *nivārayet*? ...*'vagantuṃ gavayaḥ*, ... *niveśayati*, ...).

24 Both points are in accordance with Marui's interpretation (cf. § 1.5 above).

25 In the context of the TC, according to Phillips's structural analysis (PHILLIPS 2012, pp. 120-121), parts 1 to 5 pertain to the discourse by "Jayanta Bhaṭṭa and

Table 1: Gaṅgeśa's Presentation and His Sources[26]

TC *upamāna*	**Sources**
1. C, p. 56, ll. 2-5 = D, p. 26, ll. 11-13 = V, p. 17, ll. 8-10: "*kīdṛśo*[a] *gavayaḥ*" *iti jijñāsāyāṃ* "*yathā gaus tathā*[b] *gavayaḥ*" *iti śrutottaravākyasya*[c] *tathābhūte piṇḍe dṛṣṭe* "*tathā'yam*[d]" *ity atideśavākyārthānusandhāne* "*ayaṃ gavayaśabda*[e]*vācyaḥ*" *iti matir upamānaphalam.*[27]	NKus, p. 377, ll. 4-5: "*yathā gaus tathā gavayaḥ*" *iti śrutātideśavākyasya gosadṛśaṃ piṇḍam anubhavataḥ smarataś ca vākyārtham* "*ayam asau gavayaśabdavācyaḥ*" *iti bhavati matiḥ.*
2. C, p. 56, l. 5-p. 57, l. 1 = D, p. 26, ll. 13-15 = V, p. 17, l. 10-p. 18, l. 1: *na ceyaṃ vākyamātrāt, apratyakṣīkṛtapiṇḍasyāpi prasaṅgāt. nāpi pratyakṣamātrāt, aśrutavākyasyāpi prasaṅgāt.*	NKus, p. 377, ll. 5-7: *seyaṃ na tāvad vākyamātraphalam, anupalabdhapiṇḍasyāpi prasaṅgāt. nāpi pratyakṣaphalam, aśrutavākyasyāpi prasaṅgāt.*
3. C, p. 57, l. 1-p. 58, l. 1= D, p. 26, ll. 15-18 = V, p. 18, ll. 1-4: *nāpi tayoḥ samāhārāt. sa hi pramāṇasamāhāro vā phalasamāhāro vā? ādye pramāṇatve sati samāhāraḥ, samāhṛta-*	NVTP, p. 216, ll. 9-12: *etena vākyapratyakṣasamāhāro 'pi nirastaḥ. sa hi pramāṇasamāhāro vā syāt, phalasamāhāro vā? ādye 'pi pramāṇatve sati samāhāraḥ, samāhṛtayor vā prāmāṇyam iti? na tāvat prathamaḥ, phalānekatve sati samāhārānupapatteḥ*[a],

company." Parts 6 and 7 are attributed to "Objection" and "Old Nyāya," respectively. As for Part 8, he seemingly attributes it to "Old Nyāya." Part 9 is Gaṅgeśa's response. The text subsequent to part 9, which is not reproduced here, is the articulation of "a fully adequate view in a *siddhānta* of New Nyāya"; see PHILLIPS 2012, p. 156, n. 17.

[26] For an English translation of the relevant portion of the TC, see PHILLIPS 2012, Appendix, pp. 120-121 and notes (p. 156). I have tentatively edited the text quoted in the table on the basis of the corresponding text in the right column. Selection of variant readings in the TC can be reasonably modified in accordance with the selection of available textual variations in the right column. In particular, the text of the NKus has not been compared with other editions of the work. It is to be noted that the variant readings marked by "kha" in the Calcutta edition of the TC correspond in some crucial cases to the readings of the Jaisalmer mss. of the NVTṬ and NVTP.

[27] v.l.: a. *kīdṛśo*] V; *kīdṛśa* C, D – b. *tathā*] C, V; *tadvad* C (kha), D – c. *śrutottaravākyasya*] C (kha), D; *śrutottarasya* C, V – d. *tathā'yam*] C, D, V; *tathā gavaya ity* C (kha) – e. *-śabda-*] C, D; *pada* V.

yor vā prāmāṇyam[a]*? nādyaḥ, phalānekatve samāhārānupapatteḥ, tasya parasparasahakārirūpatvāt.*[28]	*tasyaikaphalaṃ prati parasparādhipatyarūpatvāt.*[29]
4. C, p. 58, l. 1-p. 58, l. 3 = D p. 26, ll. 19-21 = V, p. 18, ll. 4-5: *nāntyaḥ, vākyapratyakṣayor bhinnakālatvāt, vākyatadarthayoḥ smṛtidvāropanaye 'pi gavayapiṇḍasambandhenāpīndriyādinā tadgatasādṛśyānupanaye*[a] *samayaparicchedāsiddheḥ.*[30]	NVTP, p. 216, ll. 12-14: *nāpi dvitīyaḥ, vākyapratyakṣayor bhinnakālatvāt, vākyatadarthayoḥ smṛtidvāropanītāv api gavayapiṇḍasambaddhenāpīndriyādinā tadgatasādṛśyānupanaye samayaparicchedāsiddheḥ.* NKus, p. 377, ll. 7-9: *nāpi samāhāraphalam, vākyapratyakṣayor bhinnakālatvāt, vākyatadarthayoḥ smṛtidvāropanītāv api gavayapiṇḍasambandhenāpīndriyeṇa tadgatasādṛśyānupalambhe samayaparicchedāsiddheḥ.*
5. C, p. 58, l. 3-p. 59, l. 1 = D, p. 26, ll. 21-22 = V, p. 18, ll. 5-6: *phalasamāhāre ca tadantarbhāve śabdānumānayor api pratyakṣatvaprasaṅgaḥ.*	NVTP, p. 216, ll. 14-15: *phalasamāhāre tu tadantarbhāve 'numānaśabdayor api pratyakṣatvaprasaṅgaḥ.* NKus, p. 377, ll. 9-10: *phalasamāhāre tu tadantarbhāve 'numānāder api pratyakṣatvaprasaṅgaḥ.*
6. C, p. 59, l. 2-p. 60, l. 1 = D p. 26, l.22-p. 27, l. 2 = V, p. 18, ll. 6-7: *tat kiṃ tatphalasya pramāṇabahirbhāva eva? antarbhāve vā kiyatī sīmā*[a]*? tattadasādhāraṇendriyādisāhityam?*[31]	NVTP, p. 216, ll. 15-16: *tat kiṃ tatphalasya tatpramāṇabahirbhāva eva? antarbhāve vā kiyatī sīmā? tattadasādhāraṇendriyādisāhityam.* NKus, p. 377, ll. 10-11: *tat kiṃ tatphalasya tatpramāṇabahirbhāva eva? antarbhāve vā kiyatī sīmā? tattadasādhāraṇendriyādisāhityam?*
7. C, p. 60, l. 1-p. 61, l. 1 = D p. 27, ll. 2-6 = V, p. 18, ll. 7-10: *asti tarhi sādṛśyajñāne 'pi visphāritasya cakṣu-*	NVTP, p. 216, ll. 16-19: *asti tarhi sādṛśyādijñānakāle 'pi visphāritasya cakṣuṣo vyāpāraḥ. na*[a]*, tasmin sati ta-*

[28] v.l.: a. *prāmāṇyam*] C, V; *pramāṇatvam* C (kha), D.

[29] v.l.: a. *-papatteḥ*] J1; *papatte* ed.

[30] v.l.: a. *gavayapiṇḍasambandhenāpīndriyādinā tadgatasādṛśyānupanaye*] C (kha), D; om. C, V.

[31] v.l.: a. *sīmā*] C (kha), D; *sā matiḥ* C, V.

ṣo vyāpāraḥ. tasmin[a] *sati tasyānupayogāt. upalabdhagosādṛśyaviśiṣṭagavayapiṇḍasya vākyārthasmṛtimataḥ kālāntare 'pi tadanusandhānabalāt samaya*[b]*paricchedopapatteḥ*[c].[32]

syānupayogāt, upalabdhagosādṛśyaviśiṣṭagavayapiṇḍasya vākyasmṛtimataḥ kālāntare 'py anusandhānabalāt samayaparicchedopapatter[b] *iti*.[33]

NKus, p. 378, ll. 1-3: *asti tarhi sādṛśyādijñānakāle visphāritasya cakṣuṣo vyāpāraḥ. na, upalabdhagosādṛśyaviśiṣṭagavayapiṇḍasya vākyatadarthasmṛtimataḥ kālāntare 'py anusandhānabalāt samayaparicchedopapatteḥ.*

8. C, p. 61, ll. 1-3 = D, p. 27, ll. 6-7 = V, p. 19, ll. 1-2: *tasmād āgamapratyakṣābhyām anyad evedam āgamasmṛtisahitaṃ sādṛśyajñānam upamānapramāṇam iti jarannaiyāyikā jayantaprabhṛtayaḥ.*

NVTṬ, p. 163, ll. 17-18: *tasmād āgamapratyakṣābhyām anyad evedam āgamasmṛtisahitaṃ sādṛśyajñānam upamānākhyaṃ pramāṇam āstheyam.*

9. C, p. 61, l. 3-p. 62, l. 5 = D, p. 30, ll. 6-11 = V, p. 19, ll. 3-7: *tan na. vaidharmyāvyāpteḥ. yadodīcyena*[a] *kramelakaṃ*[b] *nindatoktam*[c] *– dhik karabham atidīrghagrīvaṃ pralambacapalauṣṭhaṃ kaṭhoratīkṣṇakaṇṭakāśinam*[d] *kutsitāvayavasanniveśam apasadaṃ paśūnām iti, tad upaśrutya dā-*

NVTṬ, p. 163, ll. 19-22: *nanu yadodīcyena kramelakaṃ nindatoktam – dhik karabham atidīrghavakragrīvaṃ pralamboṣṭhaṃ kaṭhoratīkṣṇakaṇṭakāśinaṃ kutsitāvayavasanniveśam apasadaṃ paśūnām iti, tad upaśrutya dākṣiṇātya uttarāpathaṃ gatas tādṛśaṃ vastūpalabhya "nūnam ayam*[a]

---

32 v.l.: a. *tasmin*] V; *asmin* C, D – b. *samaya-*] C, V; *sama* D – c. *-cchedopapatteḥ*] C (kha); *cchedotpatteḥ* C, D, V. The word *asti* at the beginning is placed in all three editions as part of the previous sentence and syntactically connected to -*sāhityam*; cf. also Kṛṣṇakānta's (ca. 1800; cf. EIPh, vol. I, p. 732, no. 1476) *Dīpanī* in TC (C), p. 60, l. 5: *samādhatte – tarhīti*. However, Pragalbha (ca. 1470; cf. EIPh, vol. I, p. 535, no. 901) and Gokulanātha (ca. 1645; cf. EIPh, vol. I, p. 644, no. 1186), commentators of the TC's analogy chapter, begin a new sentence with *asti*; see the former's *Pragalbhī* or *Upamānasaṅgraha* in TC (V), p. 18, l. 23 (*kvacid aṃśe vyāpāraṃ dṛṣṭvā śaṅkate – astīti*) and the latter's *Raśmicakra* in TC (D), p. 29, ll. 25-26 (*śaṅkottarābhyām āha – astītyādi*). This interpretation is attested to by Varadarāja (ca. 12th c.) in his commentary on the NKus; cf. *Bodhanī* in NKus, p. 378, l. 11: ... *samayaparicchedo 'pi pratyakṣaphala*(!) *syād ity āha – asti tarhīti*.

33 v.l.: a. *na*] ed., J1 (added by a second hand); om. J1 (thus in the main text) – b. -*papatter*] J1 (added by the second hand); *papattir* ed.

kṣiṇātya uttarāpathaṃ gatvā[e] *tādṛśaṃ vastūpalabhya "nūnam asau karabhaḥ" iti pratyeti. tatra kiṃ mānam? na tāvad upamānam, sādṛśyābhāvāt. na ca pramāṇā*[f]*ntaraṃ sambhavati.*[34]

asau karabhaḥ" iti pratyeti. tat katamad eteṣu pramāṇam? na tāvad upamānam, sādharmyābhāvāt. nāpi pañcamaṃ pramāṇam upeyate[b].[35]

2.6. The textual parallels identified in the table above reveal how well thought out Gaṅgeśa's composition is. He may have been inspired by Udayana's specification of "*jarannaiyāyika-jayanta-prabhṛtīnāṃ parihāraḥ.*" His description of the *upamāna* theory of the old Nyāya basically follows the presentation and structure of Udayana's NKus, but another work by Udayana, the NVTP, and its target, the NVTṬ, have also been carefully studied, passages put together and incorporated. It is possible that Gaṅgeśa shared his view of the structure of the NVTṬ and NVTP passages with his son.

2.7. Udayana's additional gloss is also highly relevant: parts 3 to 7 are not found in the NVTṬ, but this text was introduced by Udayana into the NVTP to clarify the coherence and background of part 9 beginning with *nanu* (originally presented by Vācaspati). Udayana identifies the passage (parts 3-7) as the theory of old Naiyāyikas (*jarannaiyāyikamata*) that was attacked by some opponent (part 9) in the NVTṬ.[36] This opponent, who advocated subsuming *upamāna* under verbal testimony, presents a deviating case of analogical identification with the example of an abusive or censuring statement (*nindatokta*) made by a northerner (*udīcya*), where an analogical statement as intended by the Nyāya plays no role, because the statement does not involve any indication of the similarity or homogeneity (*sādharmya*) between a thing already known and something still unknown. This northerner merely adduces the distinctive character

---

[34] v.l.: a. *yadodīcyena*] C, D; *yadā audīcyena* V – b. *kramelakaṃ*] C (kha), V; *krameṇa kaṃ* C, D – c. *nindatoktam*] C (kha); *ninditoktaṃ* V; *nirgatyoktaṃ* C, D – d. *-tīkṣṇakaṇṭakāśinam*] C (kha), D; *śūkāśinaṃ* C; *śukāśinaṃ* V – e. *gatvā*] C, D, V; *gata*(!) C (kha) – f. *pramāṇā-*] D, V; *pramānā* C.

[35] v.l.: a. *ayam*] J1; om. ed. – b. *upeyate*] J1; *upagamyate* ed. As paṇḍit Sukhlalji Sanghavi, one of the editors of Hemacandra's (1089-1172) PM, has already noted (p. 76, l. 16), this passage of the NVTṬ (p. 163, ll. 19-21) is silently quoted in the PM with some modifications, where the reading *nindatoktam* is confirmed, while the corresponding text in the TC varies among the mss.; cf. PM, p. 34, l.25-p. 35, l. 3 (*yathā vā audīcyena... karabhaśabdasya' iti*).

[36] Cf. NVTP, p. 216, l. 19: *tad etaj jarannaiyāyikamatam āskandati – nanv iti.*

of a camel (*karabha*), whereupon a southerner (*dākṣiṇātya*) hears this and identifies an animal encountered on his way with the name "camel" at a later point in time. Udayana appears to call the opponent responsible for part 9 "*pūrve*" ("the former, or elder"), although his identity is open to further examination.[37] A detailed analysis of parts 3-7, especially in regard to Udayana's understanding of the theory of old Naiyāyikas, is beyond the scope of the present examination.

2.7.1. Whichever philosophical tradition the opponent may have belonged to, Gaṅgeśa, who understands the coherence of the discussion in the NVTṬ and NVTP, inserts parts 3-7 between part 2 and 8. Gaṅgeśa's presentation in its totality is the result of his editorial rearrangement of the extant sources.

2.7.2. Vācaspati, in turn, responds to the opponent by interpreting the term *sādharmya* in the *upamāna-sūtra* as indicating attributes in general (*dharmamātropalakṣaṇa*), an interpretation by which the fault of non-pervasion or narrow application (*avyāpti*) of the *sūtra*'s definition can be avoided.[38] This maneuver opens up a historically important dimension. After this synecdochic interpretation by Vācaspati, the idea that analogical reasoning is based on "attributes in general" is incorporated into the interpretation of the *sūtra* as conforming to the Nyāya tenets.[39] This interpretation seems to have been unknown to Uddyotakara and Jayanta. Nevertheless, it may not

---

[37] Cf. NVTP, p. 216, ll. 19-21, and p. 217, l. 1: *pūrve hi yathā gaus tathety eva vākyaṃ gavayapadenāpratītasamayenāpi prayogamātropayoginā sahitaṃ sambandhapratipattihetuḥ... ity āhuḥ*. Curiously enough, Abhayatilaka glosses *pūrve* as *jaradvaiśeṣikāḥ*; he appears not to follow the classical theory recognizing only two means of valid cognition; see NA, p. 127, ll. 18-19: *une* [= Udayane]. *pūrve iti. pratyakṣānumānaśābdapramāṇatrayavādinaḥ, śābde copamānam antarbhāvayanto jaradvaiśeṣikāḥ*. For a type of analogy adduced by those who deny the independence or distinctness of *upamāna* as a *pramāṇa* on the basis of the description or indication of some distinctive characters or attributes of something unknown, see NM, vol. I, p. 378, ll. 3-9 (on *ruru* "deer" and *caitra*; the latter is partly quoted in PM, p. 34, ll. 18-19), NBhūṣ, p. 420, ll. 18-22 (on *uṣṭra* "camel" and *gaja* "elephant") and PM, p. 34, ll. 20-23 (on *haṃsa* "goose"). Cf. also n. 25 above.

[38] Cf. NVTṬ, p. 16, ll. 6-7: *sādharmyagrahaṇaṃ ca dharmamātropalakṣaṇam iti karabhasañjñāpratītiphalam apy upamānam eveti nāvyāptiḥ*.

[39] On the three kinds of analogy in Varadarāja's TR (*k*. 1.22) and its TRSS (p. 87, l. 12-p. 88, l. 3), see BIJALWAN 1977, pp. 204-205 and KUMAR 1994, pp. 20-21. The instance adduced by Varadarāja in the case of *dharmamātropamāna* is based on that of the NVTṬ (part 9 in table 1); see KUMAR 1994, p. 19.

necessarily be Vācaspati's creation. Indeed, it appears to be a slight improvement on an idea presented by his probable predecessor, Bhaṭṭa Vāgīśvara (ca. 10th c.) in his commentary *Nyāyasūtratātparyadīpikā* (NTD).[40]

2.7.3. Gaṅgeśa's reference to Jayanta was obviously influential in the later tradition of the NS commentaries. The 15th-century "Naiyāyika and Dharmaśāstrin Vācaspati Miśra of Mithilā" also presents the theory advocated by the "old Jayanta and others" (*jaranto jayantādayaḥ*).[41] Although his description basically runs along the lines of Gaṅgeśa's, to a certain extent it shows reformulations and additions.[42]

2.8. In the table below, a comparison of the structure of the passage in the NVTṬ, NVTP, NKus and TC is made in accordance with the sequence found in the NVTṬ.

Table 2: Division of the NVTṬ into Five Parts from A to E and Their Correspondence to Other Works

NVTṬ (Vardhamāna's gloss)	NVTP	NKus	TC
(n.c.)		Part 1	Part 1
Part A: Pūrvapakṣa (*yady api... avagantum gavayaḥ*)	(cf. p. 215, l. 21-p. 216, l. 4)		
Part B: Jayantaprabhṛtīnāṃ parihāraḥ (*tathāpi yāvad... evodīkṣate*)	(cf. p. 216, ll. 5-6)		

40 Vāgīśvara already mentions the possibility of interpreting the term *sādharmya* in the analogy *sūtra* as the indication of attributes (*dharmopalakṣaṇa*); cf. NTD, p. 37, ll. 4-5 on NS (NTD) 2.1.47 = NS 2.1.44: *lakṣaṇasūtragatasya sādharmyaśabdasya dharmopalakṣaṇatvena vyākhyānāt*. Even the term *dharmamātra* appears in the NTD; cf. NTD, p. 37, l. 15, and 25. On the doctrinal and chronological relationship of Vācaspati and Vāgīśvara, see MUROYA 2013, forthcoming a and b, where I have put forward the hypothesis that Vāgīśvara predates Vācaspati.

41 On Vācaspati Miśra II, see PREISENDANZ 2005, pp. 70-73.

42 Cf. NTĀ, p. 82, ll. 3-15.

Part C: Jayantaprabhṛtīnāṃ parihāraḥ (*na cāsau... pratyakṣamātrāt*)	(cf. p. 216, ll. 7-8)	≈ Part 2	≈ Part 2
(n.c.)	Parts 3-7 (*jarannaiyāyikamata*)	Parts 4-7	Parts 3-7
Part D: Jayantaprabhṛtīnāṃ parihāraḥ (*tasmād ... āstheyam*)			Part 8 (*jarannaiyāyikā jayantaprabhṛtayaḥ*)
Part E: (*nanu... upeyate*)	= Pūrve (cf. *jarannaiyāyikamatam āskandati*)		Part 9

2.9. In the NVTṬ, there is a portion where Vācaspati presents his own theory, as introduced with the expression "*atrocyate*" (NVTṬ, p. 164, l. 10-p. 165, l. 6). This is a reply to the opponents whose theories appear in part 9 (NVTṬ, p. 163, l. 19-p. 164, l. 9) and a subsequent part (NVTṬ, p. 164, ll. 1-9, which is not reproduced here). Udayana's characterization of Vācaspati's response is noteworthy, because he calls Vācaspati the "quite new, or modern Naiyāyika" (NVTP, p. 217, l. 13: *atrocyate 'bhinavanaiyāyikaiḥ*).[43] And, as Thakur's *index nominum* "Viśiṣṭanāmasūcī" of the NVTP confirms, this is the only occurrence of the epithet in the NVTP, just as there is only one mention of Jayanta. The unmistakably sharp contrast between the two epithets, *jarannaiyāyika* and *abhinavanaiyāyika*, is probably not merely coincidental, especially in the work of such a rigorous thinker. In Udayana's historicist view, the philosophical, and perhaps temporal, distance between Jayanta and Vācaspati is evident and probably significant. Udayana's distinction

---

[43] Cf. ACHARYA 2006, Introduction, p. xxvii: "he [Udayana; YM] takes Vācaspatimiśra's concluding remarks on the topic as the view of the *abhinavanaiyāyikas* or *ādhunikas*, situating himself among them." As regards the latter epithet, however, Abhayatilaka understands it as designating contemporary Vaiśeṣikas (*nūtanavaiśeṣika*); see NA, p. 127, ll. 24-25: *ādhunikā iti. pratyakṣānumānapramāṇadvayavādino 'numāne ca śābdam upamānaṃ cāntarbhāvayanto nūtanavaiśeṣikāḥ*. On the views of *ādhunika*s in the context of Udayana's description, see CHATTOPADHYAY 2007, pp. 75-76.

explicitly supports Vācaspati's superiority in theoretical construction and systematization – a superiority that might have been acknowledged and prevalent at the time, and possibly region, of Udayana's activity. It may not be unrealistic to assume that Udayana recognized, or intended to proclaim, the emergence of the "new period" of the Nyāya tradition by underlining the alleged novelty of Vācaspati's theory (cf. § 2.10.3 below).[44]

2.10. What is then Vācaspati's own theory?[45] His main justification of analogy as an independent means of valid cognition is presented in the classical framework of the theory of analogy, but appears to be closely related to the theory of the synthetic process of cognitions originating from verbal testimony (*śrutamayī*) and perception (*pratyakṣamayī*).[46] Vācaspati provides an analytical description of the process in which a word's relation to its initially unknown referent is determined through analogy (cf. NVTṬ, p. 164, l. 17: *vācyavācakasambandhāvasāya*).[47] This aspect illustrates the goal of analogy, which is the resultant cognition of analogy (*upamiti* or *upamānaphala*), namely, the determination of the relation between a word and its referent (*sañjñāsañjñisambandhapariccheda*; cf. *samayapariccheda* in the NVTP, NKus and TC). This analogical result is proclaimed to be the objective of analogy, as is already found in the classical theory.[48]

---

[44] On Udayana's crucial role as the founder of the Navya-Nyāya, see WADA 2007, pp. 9-23 (chapter 1).

[45] For an account of Vācaspati's theory of analogy, see, e.g., BHATTACHARYA 2004, pp. 288-289.

[46] Cf. n. 73 below.

[47] Udayana classifies the establishment of the relation of a word and its referent (*vācyavācakabhāvavyavasthā*) into five cases; see NVTP, p. 217, ll. 13-17. His fivefold classification is mentioned by Pragalbha, but in a different manner and order; cf. *Pragalbhī* in TC (V), p. 19, ll. 21-22: *pañcadhā hi sañjñā*: *śṛṅgagrāhikā, pāribhāṣikī, aupādhikī, nimittasaṅkocavatī, naimittikī ceti*. On the fivefold classification of the names or terms (*sañjñā*) in the Navya-Nyāya period, see, e.g., EIPh, vol. VI, p. 416 (in reference to Śaṅkaramiśra's [15th c.] *Vādivinoda*, summarized by V. Varadachari): "Words operate in five ways to give their meaning;" or ibid., p. 327 for a fourfold classification (in reference to Vardhamāna's *Kiraṇāvalīprakāśa*, summarized by Nani Lal Sen and V. Varadachari); or EIPh, vol. XIII, pp. 385-386 for a threefold classification (in reference to Jagadīśa Bhaṭṭācārya's [ca. 17th c.] *Śabdaśaktiprakāśikā*, summarized by B.K. Matilal).

[48] See NVTṬ, p. 363, ll. 11-12 on NS 2.1.47: *tasmāt pratyakṣa eva gavaye gavayatvasya pratyakṣatvāt sañjñāsañjñisambandhaparicchedaḥ pramāṇārthaḥ*.

2.10.1. In this context, Vācaspati's focus is to clarify the mutual relationship of each term involved, such as *sañjñā*, *sañjñin*, and *sambandha*. According to Vācaspati, the word *gavaya* does not directly denote a thing (*piṇḍa*) as its object; its denotative application to the target object is mediated by *gavaya*-hood (*gavayatvaṃ nimittīkṛtya*).[49] This is for him reality or the ultimate state of affairs (*paramārtha*).[50]

2.10.2. Since Vācaspati describes the theoretical details mostly in an indirect and deductive manner, an overview of his theoretical construction can only be tentative. The presupposition that the universal (*gavaya*-hood) is the basis for the usage of a word (*gavaya*) appears to be closely linked to the conceptualization of the "object characterized by a name" (*sañjñin*),[51] or the object to be denoted (*vācya*) in analogical cognition. For Vācaspati, this is *gavaya*-hood, and not (solely) its substratum. An implicitly presupposed condition may be that (1) the denotative application of a word must be preceded by the perception of the thing (such as an animal) which is to be taken for its referent (cf. n. 48 above). Vācaspati practically holds that (2) the knowledge of an analogical statement such as "a *gavaya* is like a cow" is not sufficient, in terms of conclusive causal efficacy, to enable the denotative application of a word. What is required for the application, in addition to (1) the perception of its referent, is a coherently connected complex of three more elements, namely, in our case (3) the perception of the animal's *gavaya*-hood as the specific

For classical expressions, see nn. 68 and 72; for the theory in the Spitzer manuscript, see FRANCO 2010, pp. 132-136.

49 See NVTṬ, p. 164, ll. 10-11: *atrocyate. na tāvad ākāśādiśabdavad eṣa gavayaśabdaḥ sākṣāt piṇḍasya vācakaḥ, kintu gavayatvaṃ nimittīkṛtya piṇḍe vartata iti paramārthaḥ*. In response to his opponent, Bhāsarvajña illustrates that the *gavayatva* as the *pravṛttinimitta* is understood by means of a verbal statement; cf. NBhūṣ, p. 420, ll. 14-16: *gavayatvam eva gavayasañjñāpravṛttau nimittaṃ tadagrahaṇe kathaṃ tatsañjñāpravṛttir iti cet, nanu gavayatvam api tata eva vākyāt pratipadyate*; cf. Kumar 1994, p. 43. On Gaṅgeśa's "best (analysis of the) meaning" (*paramārtha*), as translated by PHILLIPS 2012, p. 122, see TC (C), p. 65, l. 3-p. 66, l. 1 = TC (D), p. 30, l. 21-p. 31, l. 2 = TC (V), p. 20, ll. 6-8: *ato gandhādyupalakṣitena pṛthivītvena nimittena pṛthivyādipadavat sādṛśyādyupalakṣite gavayatvādau gavayādipadānāṃ śaktir iti tu paramārthataḥ*; cf. n. 53 below. On the role of *gavayatva* in the NKus, see CHATTOPADHYAY 2007, pp. 77-79. On the view of Navya-Nyāya philosophers that "an individual entity qualified by a universal is the meaning of a word," see WADA 2006.

50 Udayana paraphrases this word with *vastugati* ("apprehension of reality"); see NVTP, p. 217, l. 20: *paramārtho vastugatiḥ*.

51 See NVTṬ, p. 363, l. 9 on NS 2.1.47: *gavayatvaṃ hi sañjñi*.

universal (*sāmānya-viśeṣa*), (4) the perceptual determination about the relation of the *gavaya* and *gavaya*-hood, and (5) the connection of the *gavaya*-hood with the *gavaya*'s similarity to a cow (*gosādṛśya*). The "similarity" in the fifth element is regarded as an indication (*upalakṣaka*) of *gavaya*-hood.[52] The totality of the above elements would justify the epistemological independence of an analogy.

2.10.3. While it is possible that Vācaspati's idea that an analogy must have a linguistic and semantic basis is indirectly represented in his formulation of the resultant cognition of analogy (cf. § 3.4.3 below), it is nonetheless clearly discernible from Jayanta's less explicit and more classical formulation (cf. § 3.1.1 below). Vācaspati formulates his own understanding of analogy as follows:

> NVTṬ, p. 164, ll. 20-21: *vākyārthasmaraṇasahakāri gavayatvajātimataḥ piṇḍasya gosādṛśyadarśanam eva tarkasahāyaṃ gavayatvābhidhāne pramāṇam.*[53]

Not only does Vācaspati's formulation contain the classical elements such as the auxiliary function of recollection and perception of similarity (cf. n. 72 below), it also reflects a more advanced stage of theoretical development, such as the specification by *gavaya*-hood, as described above. Vācaspati sheds fresh light upon the supporting and mediating function of suppositional reasoning (*tarkasahāya*), which excludes, on the grounds of theoretical cumbersome-

---

[52] Cf. NVTṬ, p. 164, ll. 11-15: *na ca yathā gaur evaṃ gavaya iti vākyād gavayatvam avagatam. na hy anavagatasambandhaṃ gavayapadam etad avabodhayati. tatas tadavagamāt tu sambandhavedane parasparāśrayaprasaṅgaḥ. na ca gosādṛśyenopalakṣyate gavayatvam. na khalv anupalabdhacareṇa gavayatvena gosādṛśyaṃ sambaddhaṃ dṛṣṭam. na cādṛṣṭasambandham upalakṣakam. na hi puruṣeṇādṛṣṭasambandho daṇḍaḥ puruṣam upalakṣayitum arhati.* For another point of view on this text, see KUMAR 1994, p. 40.

[53] Translation: "Precisely the perception of the similarity of the thing possessing the universal *gavaya*-hood with the cow, inasmuch as [the perception is] assisted by the recollection of the meaning of the verbal testimony, is the means of valid cognition [called analogy] with regard to the designation of *gavaya*-hood, while [it is] accompanied by suppositional reasoning." For a similar formulation by Gaṅgeśa emphasizing the corroborative and subsidiary role of *tarka*, see TC (C), p. 86, l. 5-p. 87, l. 3 = TC (D), p. 53, ll. 20-22 = TC (V), p. 27, ll. 8-10: *paścāc ca dṛṣṭe 'pi piṇḍe 'tideśavākyārthaṃ smaratas tarkasahakārāt "gavayatvaviśiṣṭo dharmī gavayaśabdavācyaḥ" iti pravṛttinimittaviśeṣaparicchittir upamānaphalam*; for an English translation, see PHILLIPS 2012, pp. 128-129; cf. also n. 49 above.

ness (*kalpanāgaurava*), the view that similarity (*sādṛśya*) is a qualifier of the object designated by a word.[54] For Vācaspati, similarity, which is the object of perception required for an analogical cognition, remains an element indicative of, for example, *gavaya*-hood, but not necessarily the qualifier of the target thing. It is of interest to observe that this latter position, deemed "heavy" or theoretically cumbersome by Vācaspati, corresponds to the one adopted by Jayanta's "contemporaries," as will be shown below (cf. §§ 3.1.2 and 3.3).

Vācaspati's theoretical elaborations and sophistication appear to be the basis for the emerging development of the theory of analogy put forth by Udayana through Gaṅgeśa (cf. § 2.9 above). A further investigation of the relevant portion of their theories is, however, beyond the scope of the present paper.

3.

What, then, is Jayanta's description and could the presentation by Vācaspati under investigation (cf. table 2 above) be connected to it?[55] Vācaspati's literary style as well as his philosophical tendency to integrate earlier thoughts in ingenious ways makes it difficult to prove this conclusively[56] – a frequent methodological difficulty when examining Vācaspati's indebtedness to his predecessors. Although it is admitted that there is no compelling evidence (such as evident textual parallels or quotations) on either side, Udayana's historical information justifies the following investigation. As for general *points d'appui* indicative of Vācaspati alluding to Jayanta, there are two terms that appear in the relevant portions in the NVTṬ and NM. One is the relation of the "naming action" (*sañjñākarma*)

---

54 On Vācaspati's description of the reasoning process based on *tarka*, see NVTṬ, p. 134, l. 19-p. 135, l. 6 on NS 1.1.6. In particular, for his concluding remark in terms of logical economy (*lāghava*), see NVTṬ, p. 165, ll. 5-6: *gavayatvajātimatpiṇḍābhidhāne tu lāghavam*. On Vācaspati's denial of similarity as a qualifier, see NVTṬ, p. 164, l. 22: *tarkaś ca gosādṛśyaviśiṣṭapiṇḍābhidhāne kalpanāgauravaprasaṅgaḥ*; and on the denial of it as *sañjñin*, see NVTṬ, p. 363, l. 11 on NS 2.1.47: *na ca sādṛśyaṃ sañjñi* ≈ NTD, p. 38, l. 31 on NS (NTD ed.) 2.1.51: *na ca... sādṛśyam eva sañjñi* [elision by YM]. On the role of "belief-warranting *tarka*" after Udayana, see PHILLIPS 2012, e.g., pp. 30-32.

55 For an account of Jayanta's theory of analogy, cf., e.g., BHATTACHARYA 2004, pp. 233-237.

56 For very detailed and helpful observations on Vācaspati's style, see ACHARYA 2006, pp. lxiii-lxvii.

to a perception (*pratyakṣa*). The other is the distinctive role of *upaplava* ("clouding, covering, obscuring,"[57] or "disturbance, obstacle"). I shall examine this connection in the following sections.

3.1. While in the NVTṬ an opponent denies that there is an exclusive relationship between the action of naming and something actually visible (cf. *na khalu pratyakṣa eva sañjñākarma* in § 2 above),[58] this is treated positively, though with a different implication, by the Naiyāyika proponent in the NM and illustrated as a doctrinally crucial component of analogy. It is referred to thrice in the NM: (1) *ata eva pratyakṣapūrvakaṃ sañjñākarmety ācakṣate* (NM, vol. I, p. 377, l. 2);[59] (2) *pratyakṣapūrvakaṃ sañjñākarmeti na hi vaidikī | codanā* (in a stanza; NM, vol. I, p. 377, ll. 11-12); and (3) *pratyakṣapūrvakaṃ tasmāt sañjñākarmeti gīyate*[60] (in a stanza; NM, vol. I, p. 380, l. 1).

---

[57] In addition to lexicographically known meanings such as "*Störung*" (PW, vol. I, p. 960), my tentative renderings are derived from the meaning of the verb *upa-plu* (PW, vol. IV, p. 1191: "*überziehen*"; and "*getrübt, bezogen*" for *upapluta* used in some compounded words).

[58] Bhāsarvajña, who, as a Naiyāyika, is well known for his exceptional rejection of analogy as an independent means of valid cognition, and insists upon the analogy's inclusion in verbal testimony (see Eli Franco's contribution to the present volume), appears to advocate a similar objection; see NSāra, p. 422, ll. 5-6: *na ca pratyakṣa evārthe sañjñāsañjñisambandhapratipattiḥ, apratyakṣe 'pi śakrādau sañjñāsañjñisambandhapratipattidarśanāt*; cf. NBhūṣ, p. 420, ll. 10-11. Svāmī Yogīndrānanda, the editor of the NBhūṣ, believes that the *uttarapakṣa* part in the NVTṬ (parts B-D in table 2) as identified by Vardhamāna is refuted by Bhāsarvajña, and quotes the texts of NBhūṣ, p. 420, ll. 10-11 and 24-25 to compare them; see the editor's *prāgbandha*, p. 11, item (4): *tad etad nyāyabhūṣaṇakāro nirākaroti*. However, parts from B to D, including part A, are basically to be traced back to the NM, as the present paper will show. For a hint of allusions to Jayanta in Bhāsarvajña's presentation, see nn. 78, 81 and 82 in relation to the concept of *upaplava*. On Bhāsarvajña's anteriority to Vācaspati, see MUROYA 2011.

[59] K.S. Varadacharya, the editor of the NM, connects this statement to Vācaspati's formulation (in my division it is part B in table 2; cf. § 3.3 below) and probably to a passage in Kumārila's *Ślokavārttika*, *upamāna* section, *k.* 9 as quoted by Jayanta (NM, vol. I, p. 389, ll. 15-17: *yathā bhavadbhir naiyāyikā uktāḥ – atha tv adhikatā kācit pratyakṣād eva sā bhaved iti*). See Varadacharya's *ṭippaṇī*, NM, vol. I, p. 377, ll. 17-20 (*etattattvaṃ tu uttaratra* [389 *puṭe*] *vyaktībhaviṣyati. ācakṣate – tathā ca vācaspatimiśrāḥ...*); cf. KUMAR 1994, p. 24.

[60] Apart from this, Jayanta associates the action of "singing, praising" ($\sqrt{}$*gī*) with *pravaramuni* ("eminent sage") at the end of the analogy section (NM, vol. I, p. 395, l. 7: *parigrāhyaṃ tasmāt pravaramunigītaṃ sumatibhiḥ ||*), but this sage's identity is not clear from Jayanta's ambiguous formulation. SHAH 1978, p. 189 holds that he is referring to Akṣapāda. Jayanta's use of the epithet *muni* to refer

The first statement is placed at the end of introducing the position of Naiyāyika "contemporaries" (*adyatanāḥ*), the second in their opponent's criticism and the third in the response by Jayanta's "contemporaries." The aspect centered upon perception is also advocated by presumably Naiyāyika opponents ("*anye*"[61]) introduced by the Vaiśeṣika philosopher Vyomaśiva (ca. 10th c.), probably the learned Śaiva guru Vyomaśiva of Araṇipadra (modern Ranod), in his *Vyomavatī*.[62] These Naiyāyika opponents, reminiscent of Jayanta's description of his "contemporaries," adduce an alleged *sūtra* "*pratyakṣaṃ sañjñākarma*" as authenticating evidence for acknowledging analogy as an independent means of valid cognition.[63]

3.1.1. What is the theory of Jayanta's "contemporaries"? To begin with their stock example, there is a creature (*prāṇin*) which is not known to a city-dweller, featured as the cognizing subject (*pramātṛ*); this city-dweller has heard a statement of extension (*atideśavākya*)[64] such as "a *gavaya* is like a cow" (*yathā gaus tathā gavayaḥ*)

---

to the legendary author of the NS is found in the NM several times (e.g., *akṣapādamuni* in NM, vol. I, p. 2, l. 6 and p. 282, l. 3; *akṣapādo muniḥ* in NM, vol. II, p. 718, l. 4; or *munir akṣapādaḥ* in NM, vol. I, p. 614, l. 4; *mahānuni* in NM, vol. I, p. 71, l. 14), in addition to *vyāsamuni* in NM, vol. II, p. 453, l. 18 or *kapilamuni* in NM, vol. I, p. 70, l. 18.

61 See Vyo, p. 588, l. 28.

62 On this identity, including bibliographical information, see DEZSŐ 2004, Notes, pp. 58-60. I am grateful to Professor Alexis Sanderson for initially drawing my attention to this identity and allowing me to access valuable extracts from his "prosopographical file" (dated 27 April 2012). On different possibilities including bibliographical information, see, e.g., EIPh, vol. II, pp. 424-425; PATIL 2013, p. 97, n. 16.

63 See Vyo, p. 589, ll. 2-3: *na ca vākyād eva saṅketapratipattiḥ, gavayapiṇḍasya parokṣatvāt, pratyakṣaṃ sañjñākarmeti sūtravyāghātāc ca*; the edition appears to disconnect *sañjñākarmeti* from *sūtravyāghātāc* by placing a comma in between, which I do not adopt here. In his summary of the Vyo, V. Varadachari regards this *sūtra* as *Vaiśeṣikasūtra* (VS) 2.1.19 (*pratyakṣapūrvakatvāt sañjñākarmaṇaḥ*), and includes the relevant portion in Vyomaśiva's response to the presumably Naiyāyika opponent, with which my above description is not compatible; cf. EIPh, vol. II, p. 448. On Śaṅkaramiśra's different transmission of VS 2.1.19, cf. VS, *prathamaṃ pariśiṣṭam*, p. 81.

64 The term *atideśavākya* is variously rendered by modern scholarship. On its usage in the context of analogy, see NTD, p. 38, l. 13 on NS (ed. NTD) 2.1.51 = NS 2.1.48: *tatheti sādṛśyābhidhānam upasaṃhāraḥ, atra sthitasyānyatrātideśaḥ* ("The *upasaṃhāra* ['application' as mentioned in the *sūtra*] means the statement of similarity such as '[it is] like this,' [and is] the extension of something subsisting in this [object] to a different [object]."). For a detailed account of its general usage in philosophical contexts, see OBERHAMMER, PRETS AND

from a forester; wandering about in a forest, the city-dweller notices a creature similar to a cow; recalling the above statement, he understands that "this is that which is designated by the word *gavaya*" (*ayaṃ sa gavayaśabdavācyaḥ*).[65] In this process of identifying the formerly unknown animal with the specific name *gavaya*, according to Jayanta's "contemporaries," analogy (1) is the cognition of the creature's resemblance to a thing already well known (*prasiddhapiṇḍasārūpyajñāna*), (2) arises from the perception (*indriyaja*) of the creature and (3) brings about the understanding of the relation between the name and the thing denoted by it (*sañjñāsañjñisambandhapratipattiphala*).[66]

3.1.2. How much does Jayanta's own theory comply with these three aspects focused upon by his "contemporaries"? His acceptance of the third aspect is roughly confirmed in the description (underlined as [3'] below) given in his *Nyāyakalikā* (NKal).[67]

> NKal, p. 3, ll. 12-14 = NKal (K), p. 216, ll. 3-5: *yathā gaus tathā gavaya ity āṭavikaprayuktātideśavākyasaṃskṛtamater aṭavīṃ paryaṭato* (a)*gopiṇḍasārūpyāvacchinnagavayapiṇḍajñānaṃ* (3')*sañjñāsañjñisambandhaparicchedaphalam upamānam*.[68]

PRANDSTETTER 1991, pp. 22-24 ("Einbeziehendes Hinweisen").

65 See NM, vol. I, p. 376, ll. 5-8: *śrutātideśavākyo hi nāgarakaḥ*[a] *kānane paribhramāṇo*[b] *gosadṛśaṃ prāṇinam avalokayati*[c]. *tato vanecarapuruṣakathitaṃ "yathā gaus tathā gavayaḥ" iti vacanam anusmarati. smṛtvā ca pratipadyate – ayaṃ sa*[d] *gavayaśabdavācya iti*. (v.l.: a. *nāgarakaḥ*] ed., P, S; *nāgarikaḥ* C – b. *paribhramāṇo*] C, P; *paribhraman* ed., S – c. *avalokayati*] C, P; *avagacchati* ed., S – d. *sa*] C, P, S; om. ed.)

66 NM, vol. I, p. 376, ll. 1-3: *adyatanās tu vyācakṣate*: *śrutātideśavākyasya pramātur aprasiddhe piṇḍe* (1) *prasiddhapiṇḍasārūpyajñānam* (2) *indriyajaṃ* (3) *sañjñāsañjñisambandhapratipattiphalam upamānam*. Cf. BIJALWAN 1977, p. 188.

67 On Jayanta's authorship of the NKal, see MARUI 2000, 2008 and 2014, pp. 59-95.

68 From a terminological point of view, the expression *sañjñāsañjñisambandhaparicchedaphala* is used in the NM by an opponent of the elder Naiyāyikas; see NM, vol. I, p. 374, ll. 10-11: *na ca sañjñāsañjñisambandhaparicchedaphalatvena pramāṇāntaratā vaktavyā*; at the same time, a similar expression, *sañjñāsañjñisambandhaparicche da*, appears in Vācaspati's own formulation of analogy's objective, as in n. 48 above; see also Udayana's NKus, *k.* 3.10: *sambandhasya paricchedaḥ sañjñāyāḥ sañjñinā saha* | *patyakṣāder asādhyatvād upamānaphalaṃ viduḥ* ‖ (cited in TRSS, p. 89, ll. 10-11 as *udayanasammati* "Udayana's view"); cf. BIJALWAN 1997, p. 196. Expressions such as *-sambandhapratipatti* (see n. 66 above) or *-sambandhabodha* (NM, vol. I, p. 381, l. 1) appear in the position Jayanta supports.

NM, vol. I, p. 380, ll. 15-16: (a')*gosārūpya*[a]*viśeṣitavipinagatagavayapiṇḍa-darśanam* (2')*adhyakṣa*[b]*phalam api tadanavagata*[c]*sañjñāsañjñisambandhabodhavidhānād*[d] *upamānam ucyate.*[69]

The expression underlined with (a) in the NKal does not fully correspond to the first aspect indicated by Jayanta's "contemporaries" (cf. § 3.1.1), but rather to the expression underlined as (a') in the passage quoted here from the NM.

Yet, the correspondence between (a) and (a') is not free of uncertainty. The usage of *gavayapiṇḍajñāna* in the NKal is slightly ambiguous in relation to its equivalent *gavayapiṇḍadarśana* in the NM, since the former does not specify the perceptional aspect of analogy (the aspect listed as [2] above) as clearly as Jayanta's "contemporaries" do. The above passage of the NM shows up in the counterargument by Jayanta's "contemporaries" against their opponent, where they establish analogy's status, admitting that (2') it is in effect the result of perception (*pratyakṣaphala*, *adhyakṣaphala*).[70]

As mentioned above (cf. § 2.10.3), the aspect of the *gavaya* being qualified by its similarity to a cow (cf. *avacchinna*, a slightly strong term, in the NKal, and *viśeṣita* in the NM) as formulated in (a) and (a') is regarded by Vācaspati as theoretically cumbersome.

3.1.3. K.S. Varadacharya, the editor of the NM, calls the position of Jayanta's "contemporaries" *upamānasvarūpe vārttikapakṣaḥ*.[71] The paṇḍit from Mysore appears to ascribe the position to Uddyotakara. This position can be in essence traced back to Uddyotakara's prototypical formulation.[72] As mentioned above (cf. § 3.1.2), however,

---

69 v.l.: a. *gosārūpya-*] ed., C, S; *gosādṛśya* P – b. *adhyakṣa-*] ed., P, S; *apy akṣa* C – c. *tadanavagata-*] ed., P, S; *tadavagata* C – d. *-dhānād*] ed., P, S; *dhānām* C.

70 Gaurinath Sastri, the editor of the TC (V), includes the above passage of the NM in Jayanta's own opinion: *jayantabhaṭṭais tu svamatavarṇanāvasare kathitaṃ...* [elision by YM]; cf. his *prāstāvika*, p. (ca). Such being the case, the *vayam* ("we") in NM, vol. I, p. 380, l. 13 can be rendered as referring also to Jayanta himself: *tasyaiva ca vayaṃ brūma upamānapramāṇatām* ||. "And we claim that precisely this [result of perception] is the means of valid cognition [called] analogy."

71 For this designation, see NM, vol. I, p. 376, l. 1.

72 See NV, p. 54, ll. 2-3 on NS 1.1.6: *āgamāhitasaṃskārasmṛtyapekṣaṃ sārūpyajñānam upamānam* ("Analogy is the cognition of resemblance on the basis of the recollection [arising] from the impression left by verbal testimony."); cf. ibid., p. 245, ll. 8-9 on NS 2.1.48: *āgamāhitasaṃskārasmṛtyapekṣaṃ sārūpyapratyakṣam upamānam*. On Uddyotakara's formulation, see, e.g., KUMAR 1994,

the primary definition of analogy by Jayanta's "contemporaries" explicitly states that it arises from perception (*indriyaja*, *indriyajanita*), showing a relatively more advanced stage of theoretical development.[73]

3.1.4. One might mention in passing that the theory of the elder Naiyāyikas, who clearly advocate analogy as being a "statement of extension" (*atideśavākya*),[74] is not mentioned in the NKal. In the

---

p. 17, OBERHAMMER, PRETS AND PRANDSTETTER 1996, p. 47 (containing a German translation of the second passage) and BHATTACHARYA 2004, p. 178). For Vācaspati's re-formulation, see NVTṬ, p. 163, ll. 3-4 on NS 1.1.6: *etad uktaṃ bhavati – na kevalaṃ sārūpyajñānaṃ samākhyāsambandhapratipattihetuḥ, api tv āgamārthasmṛtyapekṣam iti*; cf. ibid., p. 361, ll. 15-16 on NS 2.1.44: *yathā gaur evaṃ gavaya ity atideśavākyārthasmṛtisahakāri sārūpyajñānaṃ sādhyasya gavayo 'yam iti sañjñāsañjñisambandhasya sādhanam upamānam.* Uddyotakara's formulation is closely related to a definition referred to by Jinendrabuddhi (ca. 8th c.), the commentator on Dignāga's *Pramāṇasamuccaya* and its *vṛtti*, as pertaining to some Pakṣila: see PIND 2009, A29 (*pakṣilas tv āha – āgamāhitasaṃskārasmṛtyapekṣāt sādharmyajñānāt samākhyāsambandhapratipattir upamānārtha iti*). The first half of this definition by Pakṣila is found nowhere in the current version of Vātsyāyana's NBh.

73 A specific mention of the aspect of perception in the analogical process is also made by other Naiyāyikas, as is shown in their definition of *upamāna*: NBhūṣ, p. 419, ll. 20-21 (*vākyajajñānajanitasaṃskārajanitasmṛtisahakāriṇendriyeṇa janitaṃ sārūpyajñānam upamānaṃ*) ≈ NMuk, vol. II, p. 36, l. 22 (*vākyajanitajñānāhitasaṃskārasamudbhūtasmaraṇasahakārīndriyajanitaṃ sārūpyasaṃvedanam upamānam*); NTD, p. 37, ll. 3-4 (*vākyārthasmaraṇasahakāri pratyakṣajanitadharmajñānaṃ sañjñāsañjñisambandhapratītiphalakam upamānam*; cf. also NTD, p. 4, ll. 3-4 and p. 39, ll. 3-5). Vācaspati holds that analogy is preceded by perception and verbal testimony: *upamānaṃ tu pratyakṣapūrvakam api śabdapūrvakam evety asyānumānād apakarṣaḥ* (NVTṬ, p. 84, ll. 8-9 on NS 1.1.3). While keeping the same theoretical focus, Vācaspati also adopts other terminologies. He divides the analogical process, more precisely the establishment (*prasiddhi*) of similarity, into the two aspects, one by verbal testimony (*śrutamayī* "born of verbal testimony") and the other by perception (*pratyakṣamayī* "born of perception"); see NVTṬ, p. 163, ll. 5-6 (*prasiddhasādharmyād ity atra prasiddhir ubhayī: śrutamayī pratyakṣamayī ca*); see also KUMAR 1994, p. 18. Bhaṭṭa Vāgīśvara's similar formulation as edited by Kishore Nath Jha (NTD, p. 4, l. 22: *prasiddhiś cobhayī. pratyakṣamayy anumānamayī ca*) is not supported by the manuscript NTD (T) from Trivandrum, whereas its transcript NTD (M), utilized for the printed edition, reads as reproduced by Jha; see NTD (M), p. 6, l. 13. The manuscript points to a lacuna due to the presence of the second *ca*: *prasiddhiś cobhayī patyakṣamayī ca* (NTD [T], f. 3v,1), which is most probably to be reconstructed together with *śrutamayī* as Vācaspati transmits it: *prasiddhiś cobhayī ⟨śrutamayī⟩ pratyakṣamayī ca.*

74 See NM, vol. I, p. 374, ll. 1-2: *atra vṛddhanaiyāyikās tāvad evam upamānasvarūpam ācakṣate – sañjñāsañjñisambandhapratītiphalaṃ prasiddhetarayoḥ*

NM, for its part, the elder's position is characterized as reflected in the Bhāṣyakāra's words and is not explicitly denied by Jayanta.[75]

3.2. If we return to the issue of the relationship between Jayanta's presentation and that of Vācaspati, the criticism of the opponent in the NVTṬ that perception is not exclusively in charge of an action of naming (cf. § 2 above) may be regarded as standing in affinity with the objection by the opponent in the NM. The following passages in the discourse of Jayanta's opponent may also be of relevance for a comparison with the text of part A in the NVTṬ:

> NM, vol. I, p. 378, ll. 1-2: *sa tu pratyakṣato vāstu pramāṇāntarato 'pi vā* | *smaryamāṇe 'pi cārthe 'sti saṅketakaraṇaṃ kvacit* ||; ibid., l. 14: *pratyakṣāgamasiddhe 'rthe tasmān mānāntareṇa kim* ||.[76]
>
> NVTṬ, p. 163, ll. 10-11: *tac ca yadi mānāntareṇāpi tathāvagamyate, kas tatra sañjñākarma nivārayet.*[77]

The main argument by both opponents is that the objective of analogical cognition, which is the act assigning or establishing a verbal convention (*saṅketakaraṇa* in the NM) or the action of naming (*sañjñākarma* in the NVTṬ), is realized by a means of cognition other than analogy, as acknowledged in the Nyāya tradition. This shows that the Naiyāyika's analogy is superfluous.

3.3. Furthermore, the opponent of Jayanta's "contemporaries" analyzes the psychological state and process that occurs during analo-

---

sārūpyapratipādakam atideśavākyam evopamānam ≈ NKC, vol. II, p. 497, ll. 9-10. For a German translation of this passage, see OBERHAMMER, PRETS AND PRANDSTETTER 1996, p. 47.

75 See NM, vol. I, p. 375, l. 16: *bhāṣyākṣarāṇy apy etat*[a]*pakṣasākṣyacchāyām iva vahanti*[b] *lakṣyante* (v.l.: a. *etat-*] C, P; *caitat* ed., S – b. *vahanti*] P; *vadanti* ed., S; *dadhantī* C).

76 Translation: "But let it [i.e., the determination of the object to be named (*avacchedaḥ sañjñinaḥ*)] be either due to perception or to some other means of valid cognition. Furthermore, one conventionally assigns [a name to its object] in reference to a particular thing when the object is recollected. [...] Therefore, when an object is established by perception and verbal testimony, there is no use of another means of valid cognition [such as analogy]."

77 Translation: "And if it [i.e., the naming action (*sañjñākarma*)] is also apprehended by some other means [of valid cognition that is not analogy] in this manner [i.e., if it is applied to the thing as excluded from the homogenous and heterogeneous (*samānāsamānajātīyavyavacchinna*)], who could suppress the naming action regarding this [kind of thing]?"

gical reasoning. He holds that even if a cognizing subject's awareness of a yet unidentified animal *gavaya* remains "covered" or "obscured/fuzzy" (*sa-upaplavā*), on the mere basis of verbal testimony about the *gavaya*'s likeness to cow, the connection between the name *gavaya* and the animal denoted by it is not obscured at all.[78] Jayanta's "contemporaries" deny this. Their response suggests a possible affinity with the idea presented by Vācaspati (part B in table 2):

> NM, vol. I, p. 379, ll. 2-3: *atrāhuḥ – nāṭavikaraṭitād vākyād vispaṣṭaḥ*[a] *sañjñāsañjñisambandhapratyayo bhavitum arhati, sañjñinas tadānīm apratyakṣatvāt. yady api ca*[b] *gosārūpyaviśiṣṭatayā tadavaccheda*[c] *upapāditaḥ, tathāpi sopaplavaiva tadānīṃ bhavati*[d] *buddhiḥ.*[79]

> NVTṬ, p. 163, ll. 13-15: *tathāpi yāvad "ayam asau gavayaḥ" iti sākṣāt pratīte sambandhini sañjñāṃ na niveśayati, tāvad ayaṃ pariplutamatiḥ pramātā "kaccit khalu drakṣyāmi tādṛśaṃ piṇḍaṃ yatra gavayasañjñāṃ pratipatsye" iti pramotsuka evodīkṣate.*[80]

---

78 NM, vol. I, p. 378, ll. 10-11: *atha sopaplavā vākyād buddhir ity abhidhīyate* ‖ *upaplavo 'pi sambandhe na kaścid anubhūyate* |. As regards this passage, Yogīndrānanda, the editor of the NBhūṣ, refers to a passage by an opponent appearing in the NBhūṣ (p. 420, l. 24: *nanu vākyād upaplutā pratipattir āsīt*) as evidence for Bhāsarvajña's reproduction of Jayanta's views (prāgbandha, p. 15, no. 5: *bhāsarvajñas tu jayantavādān anuvādītīti vidyate*); cf. his prāgbandha, p. 16, item (ca) under no. 5; see also n. 58 above.

79 v.l.: a. *vispaṣṭaḥ*] ed., P, S; *vispaṣṭaṃ* C – b. *ca*] C, P; om. ed., S – c. *-avaccheda*] C, P, S; *avagama* ed. – d. *tadānīṃ bhavati*] C, P; *bhavati tadānīṃ* ed., S. Translation: "They reply to this [objection]. An awareness of the relation between a name and its object cannot become vivid on the [mere] basis of a statement shouted by a forester, because the object denoted by the name is not cognized by perception at that time [of the cognizer's hearing the statement]. And even if the determination of this [object], as qualified by [its] similarity to a cow, is established [by the statement], even in this way the awareness [of the cognizer] remains obscured at that time." For an account of this passage, see BIJALWAN 1977, p. 201.

80 Translation: "Even in this manner, as long as he does not apply a name to the object that is related [to the name and] is cognized directly in this way: 'This is that *gavaya*,' this cognizer, whose awareness is thoroughly obscured, is [still] expectant [of the following], just striving after true cognition: 'I really hope that I will see such a kind of thing for which I will understand the name *gavaya*.'" I have understood *kaccit* as an interrogative in the sense of *kāmapravedana* (*Amarakośa*) or *iṣṭaparipraśna* (*Medinīkośa*), an aspect which is implied by *-utsuka*; cf. PW, vol. II, p. 47, s.v. "*kad* mit *cit*." The editor of the NM reads *kaścit* instead of *kaccit*; cf. n. 59 above.

Despite the differences in rhetoric and theoretical details, the above comparison shows that their main argument is grounded in the idea that for the city-dweller, the cognizing subject, the awareness (*buddhi* or *pratyaya* in the NM, or *mati* in the NVTṬ) of the *gavaya* remains obscured (*sa-upaplava* in the NM or *paripluta* in the NVTṬ) until the actual connection of the name with its object, or the actual application of the name to its object, takes place. This becomes possible only after the target object is perceived on the spot. In Jayanta's work the concept of *upaplava* recurrently appears in the justification of analogy by his "contemporaries," in sharp contrast to the unique mention in the NVTṬ.[81] Expressions standing in contradistinction to it in the NM are, for instance, *vispaṣṭa* (see the above quotation), *nirupaplava* and *nirākāṅkṣā*.[82]

3.4. The passage in part C (table 2) ≈ part 2 (table 1), a portion ascribed by Vardhamāna to Jayanta and others (cf. §§ 2.2-3 above), calls for some explanation. The content is concerned with the operability of verbal testimony (*vākya*) and perception (*pratyakṣa*) if analogy is not approved as an independent means of valid cognition but is included in one or the other. It is possible to compare Vācaspati's formulation with certain passages of the NM as they are reproduced by Prabhācandra (ca. 11th c.) in his NKC with additional phrases, but also, stylistically, with Udayana's concise formulation. The renowned paṇḍit and editor Mahendra Kumar has already noted the relation of the passage in the NKC to the NM and NKus.[83] Let me compare the relevant passages:

---

[81] See, for instance, NM, vol. I, p. 378, ll. 10-11 (*sopaplavā... buddhir iti... upaplavo 'pi...*); p. 379, ll. 12 (*buddhyupaplavaḥ*) and 13 (*dadhāti śyāmalāṃ dhiyam*; the editor's *ṭippaṇī*: *sakalaṅkāṃ* "stained," *sopaplavām*); p. 380, ll. 5-7 (*na nivartata evopaplavaḥ*) and 9-10 (*sa upaplavo viraṃsyati*); p. 389, ll. 11-12 (*sopaplavā... upamānān nirupaplavībhavati*); cf. KUMAR 1994, pp. 46-47. Cf. also NBhūṣ, p. 420, l. 25 (*ko 'yam upaplavaḥ*) and NVTP, p. 217, l. 5 (*kaḥ pariplavārthaḥ*). Cakradhara (ca. 11th c.) explains *sopaplavā* with *anirākāṅkṣā*; cf. NMGBh, p. 68, l. 13.

[82] See NM, vol. I, p. 379, l. 6 (*na nirākāṅkṣatā puṃsas... upajāyate*; the BORI ms. [P] reads *puṃsas* instead of *-buddhis* given in the edition); p. 381, ll. 4-6 (*buddhir... nirupaplavā jāyate*). The editor of the NM paraphrases *vispaṣṭa* with *nirupaplava*; see his *ṭippaṇī* on NM, vol. I, p. 379, l. 14. For a similar position on the psychological transition from obscurity to clarity or settlement, as presented by an opponent of Bhāsarvajña, see NBhūṣ, p. 420, ll. 24-25: *nanu vākyād upaplutā pratipattir āsīt, upamānāt tu sañjñiviśeṣāvacchedena vyavasthitā bhavati*; see also n. 78 above, where the first half of the text has already been quoted.

[83] See the editor's note in NKC, vol. II, p. 497, n. 1.

NVTṬ, p. 163, ll. 16-17: *na cāsau vākyamātrasahāyo 'pratyakṣīkṛtagosadṛśagavayatvajātimatpiṇḍaḥ "ayam asau gavayākhyaḥ" iti pratipattum arhati, na ca vākyaṃ vinā pratyakṣamātrāt.*[84]

NKC, vol. II, p. 497, ll. 4-6: *nāpy āgamasya tatphalam. na khalu nāgarakaḥ pratipattā* [sic] *āraṇyakavākyād evāraṇyasthaprāṇinaṃ gavayaśabdavācyatayā pratipadyate, kintu sārūpyaṃ prasiddhena gavā tasya paśyan.*[85] ≈ NM, vol. I, p. 375, ll. 10-11.[86]

NKC, vol. II, p. 497, ll. 2-3: *na hi pratyakṣasya tatphalam, vanasthagavayākāramātraparicchedaphalatvāt tasya.*[87] ≈ NM, vol. I, p. 376, ll. 10-11.[88]

NKus, p. 377, ll. 5-7: *seyaṃ na tāvad vākyamātraphalam, anupalabdhapiṇḍasyāpi prasaṅgāt. nāpi pratyakṣaphalam, aśrutavākyasyāpi prasaṅgāt.*[89]

---

84 Translation: "But that [cognizer], who is supported merely by a verbal statement, [but] has not yet perceived the thing which possesses the universal '*gavaya*-hood' and is similar to the cow, is not able to understand that 'this is that which is called *gavaya*.' And [this understanding does] not [occur to him, either,] due to mere perception, without the verbal statement."

85 Translation: "Nor does its (the analogy's) result pertain to verbal testimony. As you should know, the city-dweller who is the subject of understanding does not understand the creature in the forest as designated by the word *gavaya* exclusively on the basis of the forester's statement, but rather [he can understand it thus only] as the one who is [actually] perceiving the similarity of this [*gavaya*] with the cow already known." In the NKC, the text is continued with a passage on *atiprasaṅga* that is not clearly identified in the NM; see NKC, vol. II, p. 497, ll. 6-7: *na hi gavayādarśane "ayaṃ sa gavayaśabdavācyaḥ" iti sañjñāsañjñisambandhapratītir yuktā, atiprasaṅgāt.*

86 NM, vol. I, p. 375, ll. 10-11: *pratipattā hi*[a] *nāgarako*[b] *nāraṇyakavākyād eva taṃ prāṇinaṃ gavayaśabdavācyatayā budhyate, kintu sārūpyaṃ*[c] *prasiddhena gavā tasya paśyann*[d] *iti* (v.l.: a. *hi*] P; *'pi* ed., C, S – b. *nāgarako*] P, S; *nāgariko* ed., C – c. *sārūpyaṃ*] ed., C, P; om. S – d. *paśyann iti*] C, P; *paśyati* ed., S).

87 Translation: "For, its (the analogy's) result does not pertain to perception, because its (the perception's) result is the determination of the mere form of a *gavaya* in the forest."

88 NM, vol. I, p. 376, ll. 10-11: *pratyakṣaṃ tāvad etasmin viṣaye na kṛtaśramam* | *vanasthagavayākāraparicchedaphalaṃ hi tat* ||. Cf. KUMAR 1994, p. 35.

89 Translation: "First, this [awareness (*mati*), i.e., 'This is that which is designated by the word *gavaya*'] here is not the result of mere statement, because it would [otherwise] occur, as an undesirable consequence, even to him who has not perceived the [target] thing. Nor is it the result of perception, because it would [otherwise] occur, as an undesirable consequence, even to him who has not heard the statement." For another English translation, see DRAVID 1996, p. 264; see also KUMAR 1994, p. 47.

3.4.1. From the viewpoint of the main assertion presented here, the passages all point out the theoretical insufficiency and restriction of a position that subsumes analogy either under verbal testimony or under perception. Vācaspati's justification is not as explicit as Jayanta's explanation or Udayana's unitary argument resorting to the two undesirable consequences (*prasaṅga*).

3.4.2. The position held by Jayanta's "contemporaries" is given a still more elaborate and broader description. Between the two passages quoted above from the NKC (cf. § 3.4), Prabhācandra inserts an argument against the reduction of analogy to inference, making again an unacknowledged citation from the NM.[90] A set of three counterarguments occurs in Jayanta's description. One of the Naiyāyikas' intentions in this controversy is to establish that analogy is distinct not only from perception and verbal testimony, but also from other candidates such as inference and recollection. Their emphasis on the specificity of analogy is densely expressed by such terms as *ananyajanya*, *ananyakāraṇaka*,[91] *upamānaikajanyā*, or *na pramāṇāntarodbhavā*.[92] The absence of the counterargument against

---

[90] See NKC, vol. II, p. 497, ll. 3-4: *nāpy anumānasya, pakṣadharmānvayavyatirekādisāmagrīm antareṇāpi sañjñāsañjñisambandhapratipatter utpādapratīteḥ.* ≈ NM, vol. I, p. 381, ll. 8-9 (*na caitāvatā*[a] "*anumānam evedam*" *ity āśaṅkanīyam, anapekṣitapakṣadharmānvayavyatirekādisāmagrīkasya tatpratyayotpādāt* [v.l.: a. *na caitāvatā*] C, P; *naitāvatā* ed., S]).

[91] There is a text-critical problem in the manuscript transmission of the NM with regard to *ananyajanya* ("something that does not arise from any other [means of cognition than analogy]") and *ananyakāraṇaka* ("something that does not have any other [cognitive] cause [than analogy]"). The printed editions do not record these important terms in Jayanta's description. The two most reliable manuscripts of the NM, one (BORI) written in Śāradā and the other (University of Calicut) in Malayalam script, retain the superior text which qualifies the resultant cognition of analogy (*upamānaphala* or *upamiti*). My reconstruction of the relevant portion, NM, vol. I, p. 376, ll. 8-10, is as follows: *tad etat sañjñāsañjñisambandhavijñānam*[a] *ananyajanyam*[b] *ity upamānaphalam ucyate*[c]. *katham punar idam ananyakāraṇakaṃ jñānam ucyate*[d]. (v.l.: a. *-vijñānam*] C, P; *jñānaṃ* ed., S – b. *ananyajanyam*] C, P; *tajjanyam* ed., S – c. *ucyate*] C, P; *ity ucyate* ed., S – d. *kathaṃ... ucyate*] C, P [*-karaṇa-*]; om. ed., S). Prabhācandra's allusion to the first half of this text, especially, *pratyakṣādyajanya-*, confirms my reconstruction; see NKC, vol. II, p. 497, ll. 1-2: *tad etat sañjñāsañjñisambandhajñānaṃ pratyakṣādyajanyatvād upamānaphalam.* On Prabhācandra's quotation of the NM, see n. 96 below.

[92] On *upamānaikajanyā* ("something [i.e., the awareness] which arises exclusively from analogy") and *na pramāṇāntarodbhavā* ("something [i.e., the awareness] which does not originate from any other means of cognition [than analo-

the reduction of analogy to inference in the NVTṬ renders doubtful the assumption that part C specifically alludes to Jayanta's text in the NM, unless it refers to Jayanta's NKal (cf. *pratyakṣāgamābhyām anyatarasmād api*).[93] In fact, Uddyotakara had already been confronted by some opponent unable to distinguish analogy from perception and verbal testimony.[94] With reservations, accordingly, the first half of part D (*āgamapratyakṣābhyām anyad evedam*) can be regarded as a generalizing echo of the theoretical and argumentative preoccupation observed in the NV on which Vācaspati comments.

3.4.3. In the description of the NVTṬ, the target animal *gavaya* is dealt with as something qualified by a specific qualifier, "possessing the universal *gavaya*-hood" (*gavayatvajātimant-*), whereas this component is not explicit in the NM. Rather, it is assumed that this additional component is required by Vācaspati's own theory of analogy (cf. §§ 2.10-2.10.2 above).[95]

3.4.4. It is worthy to note that the first passage quoted above from the NKC (cf. § 3.4) is not found in the theory of Jayanta's "contemporaries," whom Prabhācandra calls the "modern Naiyāyikas" (*abhinavanaiyāyika*).[96] It is rather found in Jayanta's presentation of

---

gy]"), see NM, vol. I, p. 381, ll. 10-11: *tasmād ayaṃ sa gavayo nāmety evaṃvidhā matiḥ | upamānaikajanyaiva na pramāṇāntarodbhavā ||*.

93 See NKal, p. 3, ll. 14-16 = NKal (K), p. 216, ll. 5-7: *gopiṇḍasārūpyaviśiṣṭagavayapiṇḍasya sañjñāsañjñisambandhapratīteḥ pratyakṣāgamābhyām anyatarasmād apy asiddheḥ*. The description in the NKal focuses on distinguishing analogy from perception and/or verbal testimony. This twofold alternative is not clearly identified in the NM; the fact that the dual case presumably expresses the duality of perception and verbal testimony reminds me of Udayana's presentation of the old Naiyāyika's theory about *vākyapratyakṣasamāhāra* ("aggregation of statement and perception"; cf. parts 3-5 in table 1 in § 2.5 above).

94 For Uddyotakara's opponent, see NV, p. 54, l. 6 on NS 1.1.6: *pratyakṣāgamābhyāṃ nopamānaṃ bhidyate*. The NS itself is preoccupied with rejecting the opinion that analogy is included in inference (NS 2.1.46: *pratyakṣeṇāpratyakṣasiddheḥ*). Cf. KUMAR 1994, p. 39.

95 In a gloss by Vācaspati on the NBh, a similar formulation (*gavayatvasāmānyaviśeṣavant-*) occurs; see NVTṬ, p. 162, ll. 6-7 on NS 1.1.6: *prajñāpanīyasya gavayaśabdavācyatayā pratyakṣadṛśyamānagosādṛśyasya gavayatvasāmānyaviśeṣavataḥ piṇḍasya prajñāpanam upamānam*. Cf. BIJALWAN 1977, p. 189.

96 NKC, vol. II, p. 497, l. 14: *atrocyate. yat tāvad abhinavanaiyāyikair abhihitam – śrutātideśavākyasyetyādi*. The *pratīka* "*śrutātideśavākyasya*" introduces the text of NKC, vol. II, p. 496, l. 8-p. 497, l. 2 (≈ NM, vol. I, p. 376, ll. 2-9) which Prabhācandra quotes after adducing the *upamāna-sūtra* (NKC, vol. II, p. 496, ll. 4-5 = e.g., NM, vol. I, p. 381, l. 14) as the tenet of Naiyāyikas on analogy, as well as its gloss made by Jayanta (NKC, vol. II, p. 496, ll. 6-8 ≈ NM, vol. I, p.

the theory of the elder Naiyāyikas (*vṛddhanaiyāyikāḥ*), more precisely, in the part beginning with *ucyate* as a response to the refutation of the elders' theory.[97] Why Prabhācandra does not refer to a relevant passage stated by Jayanta's "contemporaries,"[98] and how he analyzes the textual structure and relationship between these two groups of Naiyāyikas, deserves another, independent study.

3.5. Likewise, the remaining half of part D (*tasmād... āgamasmṛtisahitaṃ sādṛśyajñānam upamānākhyaṃ pramāṇam āstheyam*) in the NVTṬ may be regarded as a corroborative justification of Uddyotakara's definition of analogy (*āgamāhitasaṃskārasmṛtyapekṣaṃ sārūpyajñānam upamānam*).[99] In a wider context, this justification may be implicitly connected with Vācaspati's terse gloss on Uddyotakara's definition and the subsequent division into two types of *prasiddhi* as one of the key concepts expressed in the analogy *sūtra* (cf. § 2.10 and n. 73 above). These two are presented before part A and may supply the whole complex of passages in question (parts A to C) with the larger framework of Vācaspati's exegetical strategy of supporting Uddyotakara. The above last line of part D is probably not forcibly associated with the views of Jayanta's "contemporaries." This analysis is different from the account by Vardhamāna, who unanimously ascribes parts B-D to the refutation by the Naiyāyikas beginning with Jayanta. Consequently it can be cautiously assumed that Vācaspati might have inserted the discussion undertaken by Jayanta's "contemporaries" as a corroborative proof of Uddyotakara's theory, inasmuch as the former's discussion fortifies the latter's theory.

CONCLUSION

The investigations conducted in the present paper have aimed at evaluating the historicity of Gaṅgeśa's reference to Jayanta, a topic

382, ll. 4-6); cf. the editor's corresponding notes, where he refers to the NV and NVTṬ instead of Jayanta's gloss.

97 For the epithet *vṛddhanaiyāyika*, see NM, vol. I, p. 374, l. 1 = NKC, vol. II, p. 497, l. 9 = NKC, vol. II, p. 500, l. 14; for the response, see NM, vol. I, pp. 374-375, where the expression *ucyate* is used (p. 374, l. 14).

98 For instance, NM, vol. I, p. 376, ll. 14-15: *āgamād api tatsiddhir na vanecarabhāṣitāt* | *tatkāle*[a] *sañjñino nāsti gavayasya hi darśanam* ‖ (v.l.: a. *-kāle*] C, P; *kālaṃ* ed., S).

99 On Uddyotakara's definition and Vācaspati's division, see nn. 72 and 73 above, respectively.

which so far had not been concretely clarified on a philological basis. I have also offered a preliminary investigation to clarify another largely unexplored issue, namely Udayana's identification of Jayanta as Vācaspati's source.

4.1. These two points of investigation are inseparably linked. A comparative analysis of the relevant textual materials written by Gaṅgeśa's predecessors such as Vācaspati and Udayana shows that Gaṅgeśa's presentation of what is allegedly Jayanta's theory is substantially biased by the texts of Vācaspati and Udayana. The present paper was initially based upon the explicit information given by Vardhamāna – Gaṅgeśa's son – about the structure in the NVTṬ, but the estimation presented here does not entirely agree with Vardhamāna's structural analysis.

If my hypothesis holds good, it is likely that Vardhamāna, and probably Gaṅgeśa as well, was not in a position to examine the relevant passages in the NM directly, at least regarding analogy, and thus drew upon Udayana's gloss. If they had had direct access to the NM, it is hardly imaginable that they would have overlooked the function of part D and, in the case of Gaṅgeśa, Udayana's addition of parts 3-7.

4.2. The analysis in this paper, in its attempt to find possible traces of the sources used by Vācaspati, gives Udayana's testimony a certain level of plausibility. Furthermore, Udayana's interpretation of Vācaspati's commentary is reflected in the various designations of his predecessors such as *jarannaiyāyika* including Jayanta, another *jarannaiyāyika* (in parts 3-7, which have not been investigated in this paper), *ādhunika* (controversial and as yet unidentified), and *abhinavanaiyāyika* referring to Vācaspati.[100] Udayana's clearly historicist consciousness as shown in his use of such labels stratifies the development and controversy of the theory of analogy (see §§ 2.9 and 2.10.3 above).

What Udayana has offered to his readers is a rather scanty and cryptic gloss on the issue of Vācaspati's allusion to Jayanta. Consequently, what Udayana recognizes as Jayanta's text remains hypothetical. However, if my analysis with regard to parts B-D in table 2

---

[100] On the usage of expressions "indicative of the new intellectual climate of the period, in which one's own position within a scholarly tradition is conceptualized in a historicist manner," see PREISENDANZ 2005, pp. 71-72; see also POLLOCK 2001, pp. 5-15. For a critical review of Pollock's thesis, cf. PATIL 2013, pp. 102-105.

(cf. §§ 3.3-5 above) holds good, it follows that Udayana's description in his NKus basically does not touch on the psychological argumentation illustrated in part B (cf. §§ 3.1-2 above), which can be traced back to Jayanta's presentation. It remains undecided whether Udayana made a distinction between the theory as formulated by Uddyotakara and the Kashmiri philosopher's conspicuous presentation, choosing to adopt only the former for the sake of his own systematization. It also remains open how Udayana distinguished the theory of "old Naiyāyikas" from Jayanta's presentation. Due to the preliminary character of the present paper, an attempt to contextualize the treated materials in a wider perspective is still needed.

REFERENCES

ACHARYA 2006

D. Acharya, *Vācaspatimiśra's Tattvasamīkṣā. The Eearliest Commentary on Maṇḍanamiśra's Brahmasiddhi*, Critically Edited with an Introduction and Critical Notes, Stuttgart: Franz Steiner, Nepal Research Centre Publications 25, 2006

BHATTACHARYA 2004

S. Bhattacharya, *Development of Nyāya Philosophy and Its Social Context*, in D.P. Chattopadhyaya (ed.), *History of Science, Philosophy and Culture in Indian Civilization*, vol. III.3, Delhi: Centre for Students in Civilizations, 2004

BIJALWAN 1977

C.D. Bijalwan, *Indian Theory of Knowledge based upon Jayanta's Nyāyamañjarī*, New Delhi: Heritage Publishers, 1977

CHATTOPADHYAY 2007

U. Chattopadhyay, "Udayanācārya on Upamāna (Knowledge by Analogy)," *Journal of the Asiatic Society* 49(4), 2007, pp. 58-82

DEZSŐ 2004

C. Dezső, "*Much Ado About Religion.*" *A Critical Edition and Annotated Translation of the Āgamaḍambara, a Satirical Play by the Ninth Century Kashmirian Philosopher Bhaṭṭa Jayanta*, PhD Dissertation (Balliol College, Oxford), 2004; see "Much Ado About Religion" under "Book Extras, Clay Sanskrit Library," http://www.claysanskritlibrary.org/extras.php

DRAVID 1996

N.S. Dravid, *Nyāyakusumāñjali of Udayanācārya*, vol. I, New Delhi: Indian Council of Philosophical Research, 1996

EIPh

Encyclopedia of Indian Philosophies, ed. K.H. Potter, vol. I: *Bibliography*, Section I [Delhi: 1970] 3rd revised ed., Delhi: Motilal Banarsidass Publishers, 1995; vol. II:

Indian Metaphysics and Epistemology: The Tradition of Nyāya-Vaiśeṣika up to Gaṅgeśa, [Delhi: 1977] Delhi: Motilal Banarsidass Publishers, 1995; vol. VI: *Indian Philosophical Analysis Nyāya-Vaiśeṣika from Gaṅgeśa to Raghunātha Śiromaṇi*, Delhi: Motilal Banarsidass, 1993; vol. XIII: *Nyāya-Vaiśeṣika Philosophy from 1515 to 1660*, Delhi: Motilal Banarsidass, 2011

FRANCO 2010
E. Franco, "The Discussion of *pramāṇa*s in the Spitzer Manuscript," in B.S. Gillon (ed.), *Logic in Earliest Classical India, Papers of the 12th World Sanskrit Conference, Vol. 10.2*, Delhi: Motilal Banarsidass Publishers, 2010, pp. 121-138

FRAUWALLNER 1936
E. Frauwallner, "Beiträge zur Geschichte des Nyāya. I. Jayanta and seine Quellen," *Wiener Zeitschrift für die Kunde des Morgenlandes* 43, 1936, pp. 263-278 = G. Oberhammer and E. Steinkellner (eds.), *Kleine Schriften. Erich Frauwallner*, Wiesbaden: Steiner, Glasenapp-Stiftung 22, 1982, pp. 145-160

GRAHELI 2011
A. Graheli, "The Choice of the Best Reading in Bhaṭṭa Jayanta's *Nyāyamañjarī*," *Rivista Degli Studi Orientali* (Nuova Serie), 2011 [published in 2012] 84(1-4), pp. 107-122

GRAHELI 2012
A. Graheli, "A Preliminary List and Description of the Nyāyamañjarī Manuscripts," *Journal of Indian Philosophy* 40, 2012, pp. 317-337

HACKER 1951
P. Hacker, "Jayantabhaṭṭa und Vācaspatimiśra, ihre Zeit und ihre Bedeutung für die Chronologie des Vedānta," in *Beiträge zur indischen Philologie und Altertumskunde: Walther Schubring zum 70. Geburtstag dargebracht von der deutschen Indologie*, Hamburg: Cram, De Gruyter & Co., Alt- und Neu-Indische Studien 7, 1951, pp. 160-169 = L. Schmithausen (ed.), *Kleine Schriften. Paul Hacker*, Wiesbaden: Steiner, Glasenapp-Stiftung 15, 1978, pp. 110-119

KAVIRAJ 1924
G. Kaviraj, "IV. Gleanings from the History and Bibliography of Nyāya Vaiśeṣika Literature," in G.N. Kaviraja (ed.), *The Princess of Wales Sarasvati Bhavana Studies*, vol. III, Benares: Government Sanskrit Library, 1924, pp. 79-157

KUMAR 1994
S. Kumar, *Upamāna in Indian Philosophy*, [Delhi: 1980] 2nd revised ed., Delhi: Eastern Book Linkers, 1994

MARUI 2000
H. Marui, "Some Remarks on Jayanta's Writings: Is Nyāyakalikā His Authentic Work?," in S. Mayeda (ed.), *The Way to Liberation. Indological Studies in Japan*, Delhi: Manoharlal Publishers, 2000, pp. 91-106

MARUI 2001
H. Marui, "On the chronological order of Jayanta Bhaṭṭa and Vācaspatimiśra" (Jayanta Bhaṭṭa to Vācaspatimiśra no sengo-kankei wo megutte), in *Emptiness and Reality, Collected Papers in Memory of Dr. Yasunori Ejima*, Tokyo: Shunjusha Publishing Company, 2001 [in Japanese]

MARUI 2006
H. Marui, "Some notes on the controversies between the '*ācāryāḥ*' and the '*vyākhyātāraḥ*' in the *Nyāyamañjarī*," *Journal of Indian and Buddhist Studies* 54(3), 2006, pp. 1145-1153 = (33)-(41)

MARUI 2008
H. Marui, "On the Authorship of the *Nyāyakalikā* Again," *Journal of Indian and Buddhist Studies* 56(3), 2008, pp. 1063-1071 = (27)-(35)

MARUI 2014
H. Marui, *A Study of Jayanta: The Nyāya Philosophy as Described by a Medieval Kashmirian Poet*, Tokyo: Sankibo Busshorin, 2014 [in Japanese]

MATILAL 1977
B.K. Matilal, *Nyāya-Vaiśeṣika*, in J. Gonda (ed.), *A History of Indian Literature*, vol. VI.2, Wiesbaden: Otto Harrassowitz, 1977

MISHRA 1966
U. Mishra, *History of Indian Philosophy*, vol. II, Allahabad: Tirabhukti, 1966

MUROYA 2006
Y. Muroya, "Apropos the *Nyāyasūcīnibandha*: Some Historical Problems and the Manuscript Transmission of the *Nyāyasūtra*," *Journal of the Ganganatha Jha Kendriya Sanskrit Vidyapeetha* 62(1-4), 2006 [published in 2007], pp. 405-432

MUROYA 2011
Y. Muroya, "Bhāsarvajña's Interpretation of *bhāva eva nāśaḥ* and a Related Chronological Problem," in H. Krasser, H. Lasic, E. Franco and B. Kellner (eds.), *Religion and Logic in Buddhist Philosophical Analysis, Proceedings for the 4th International Dharmakīrti Conference* (*August 23-27, 2005*), Wien: Verlag der Österreichischen Akademie der Wissenschaften, Österreichische Akademie der Wissenschaften, Philologisch-historische Klasse 424, 2011, pp. 341-365

MUROYA 2013
Y. Muroya, "On the *Nyāyasūtratātparyadīpikā*," *Journal of Indian and Buddhist Studies* 62(1), 2013, pp. 288-282 = (241)-(247) [in Japanese]

MUROYA forthcoming a
Y. Muroya, "Aniruddha's reference to 'Mañjarīkāra' fragments and their relation to Vācaspati Miśra and Bhaṭṭa Vāgīśvara," *Proceedings of the Japan-Austria International Symposium on Transmission an Tradition, The Meaning and the Role of "Fragments" in Indian Philosophy, 20-24 Agusut 2012, Matsumoto*

MUROYA forthcoming b
Y. Muroya, "On Parallel Passages in the Commentaries of Vācaspati Miśra and Bhaṭṭa Vāgīśvara," in E. Freschi and P.A. Maas (eds.), *Proceedings of the Panel "Adaptive Reuse of Texts, Ideas and Images" at the 32nd Deutscher Orientalistentag*

NA
Nyāyālaṅkāra (Pañcaprasthānanyāyamahātarkaviṣamapadavyākhyā). A Commentary on the Five Classical Texts of the Nyāya Philosophy of Abhayatilaka Upādhyāya, ed. A. Thakur and J.S. Jetly, Baroda: Oriental Institute, Gaekwad Oriental Series 169, 1981

NBh
Gautamīyanyāyadarśana with Bhāṣya of Vātsyāyana, ed. A. Thakur, New Delhi: Indian Council of Philosophical Research, Nyāyacaturgranthikā 1, 1997

NBhūṣ
Śrīmadācāryabhāsarvajñapraṇītasya Nyāyasārasya svopajñaṃ vyākhyānaṃ Nyāyabhūṣaṇam, ed. Svāmī Yogīndrānanda, Varanasi: Caukhambā Saṃskṛta Pratiṣṭhāna, Vrajajīvana Prācyabhāratī Granthamālā 13, 1968

ND (C)
Nyāyadarśanam with Vātsyāyana's Bhāṣya, Uddyotakara's Vārttika, Vācaspati Miśra's Tātparyaṭīkā & Viśvanātha's Vṛtti, ed. T. Nyaya-Tarkatirtha, A. Tarkatirtha and H. Tarkatirtha, 2 vols., [Calcutta: Metropolitan Printing & Publishing House, Calcutta Sanskrit Series 18 and 19, 1936-1944; Kyoto: Rinsen, 1982; New Delhi 1985] New Delhi: Munshiram Manoharlal Publishers, 2003

ND (M)
Nyāyadarśana of Gautama with the Bhāṣya of Vātsyāyana, the Vārttika of Uddyotakara, the Tātparyaṭīkā of Vācaspati & the Pariśuddhi of Udayana. [Volume I Chapter I], ed. A. Thakur, Darbhanga: Mithila Institute of Post-Graduate Studies and Research in Sanskrit Learning, Mithila Institute Series, Ancient Text 20, 1967

NKal
The Nyāya Kalikā, ed. G.N. Kaviraja, Benares: Vidya Vilas Press, Princess of Wales Sarasvati Bhavana Texts 17, 1925

NKal (K)
"A Critical Edition of Bhaṭṭa Jayanta's *Nyāyakalikā* (Part 1)," ed. K. Kataoka, *The Memoirs of the Institute for Advanced Studies on Asia* 163 (2013), pp. 236-184 = (1)-(53)

NKC
Nyāya-Kumuda-Candra of Śrīmat Prabhācandrācārya. A Commentary on Bhaṭṭākalaṅkadeva's Laghīyastraya, ed. M.K. Nyāyācārya, 2 vols., [Bombay: Sri Garib Dass Oriental Series 121-122, 1938-1941,] Delhi: Sri Satguru Publications, 1991

NM
Nyāyamañjarī of Jayantabhaṭṭa, with Ṭippaṇī – Nyāyasaurabha by the Editor, ed. K.S. Varadacharya, Mysore: Oriental Research Institute, University of Mysore, Oriental Research Institute Series 116 and 139, 1969-1983

NM (C)
Manuscript of the NM, Department of Malayalam and Kerala Studies, University of Calicut, "Nyāya-mañjarī-nyāyasūtra," Ms. No. 2606, Sl. No. 3912, palm-leaf, 188 leaves, Malayalam

NM (P)
Manuscript of the NM, Bhandarkar Oriental Research Institute, "Nyāyamañjarī," Ms. No. 390/1875-76, birchbark, "435" leaves (however, 432 available leaves), Śāradā, dated 1472 CE

NM (S)
Manuscript of the NM, Oriental Research Library, Libraries & Research Department J&K Govt., "Nyāyamañjarī," Ms. No. 1088, paper, "168" leaves (however, ff. 2-189), Śāradā

NM (V)
The Nyāyamañjarī of Jayanta Bhaṭṭa, ed. MM. G.S. Tailanga, Benares: E.J. Lazarus & Co., *Vizianagram Sanskrit Series* 10, 1895

NMGBh
Cakradhara's Nyāyamañjarī-Granthibhaṅga, ed. N.J. Shah, Ahmedabad: L.D. Institute of Indology, L.D. Series 35, 1972

NMuk
Nyāyasāraḥ of Bhāsarvajña with the Commentaries, Nyāyamuktāvaḷī of Aparārkadeva and Nyāyakalānidhi of Ānandānubhavācārya, ed. S.S. Sastri and V.S. Sastri, Madras: Government Oriental Manuscripts Library, 1961

NNP
[*Nyāyanibandhaprakāśa* of Vardhamāna] See NNP (ms.)

NNP (ms.)
Manuscript of the NNP, Oriental Research Institute, University of Mysore, "Nyāyavārtikatātparyapariśuddhi Prakāśa," Acc. No. C. 1378, Devanagari, paper, 243 leaves

NS
[*Nyāyasūtra*] See NBh

NS (R)
Die Nyāyasūtra's. Text, Übersetzung, Erläuterung und Glossar, ed. W. Ruben, Leipzig: Deutsche Morgenländische Gesellschaft, Abhandlungen für die Kunde des Morgenlandes 18(2), 1928

NSāra
[*Nyāyasāra* of Bhāsarvajña] See NBhūṣ

NSN
[*Nyāyasūcīnibandha* ascribed to Vācaspati Miśra] See NSN (ms.)

NSN (ms.)
Manuscript of the NSN, Mumbai University Library, "*Nyāyasūcīnibandha* of Vācaspati," Acc. No. 99.12, paper, 14 leaves, Devanagari

NTĀ
Nyāyatattvāloka. A Commentary on the Nyāyasūtras of Gautama by Vācaspati Miśra (Junior), ed. K.N. Jha, Allahabad: Ganganatha Jha Kendriya Sanskrit Vidyapitha, Ganganatha Jha Kendriya Sanskrit Vidyapitha Text Series 33, 1992

NTD
Bhaṭṭavāgīśvarapraṇītā Nyāyatātparyadīpikā, ed. K.N. Jha, Allahabad: Gaṅgānāth Jhā Kendrīya Saṃskṛta Vidyāpīṭham, 1979

NTD (M)
Manuscript of the NTD, Government Oriental Manuscripts Library, Chennai, Ms. R. 3405 ("Nyāyasūtratātparyadīpikā"), paper, 198 pages, Devanagari, copied in 1920-1921

NTD (T)
Manuscript of the NTD, Oriental Research Institute & Manuscripts Library, University of Kerala, Ms. 14670 ("Nyāyasūtratātparyadīpikā"), palm leaf, 92 leaves, Malayalam, undated

NV
Nyāyabhāṣyavārttika of Bhāradvāja Uddyotakara, ed. A. Thakur, New Delhi: Indian Council of Philosophical Research, Nyāyacaturgranthikā 2, 1997

NVTP
Nyāyavārttikatātparyapariśuddhi of Udayanācarya, ed. A. Thakur, New Delhi: Indian Council of Philosophical Research, Nyāyacaturgranthikā 4, 1996

NVTP (J1)
Manuscript of the NVTP, Jain Jñānabhaṇḍār (Baḍā Bhaṇḍār), Collection of Jinabhadrasūri, Jaisalmer, "Tātparyapariśuddhi ṭippaṇī saha apūrṇa," Ms. No. ji. kā. 1275/2, paper, 169 leaves (ff. 157,v-325), Devanagari, incomplete (up to 5.1.1), dated ca. 1222 CE

NVTP (J2)
Manuscript of the NVTP, Jain Jñānabhaṇḍār (Baḍā Bhaṇḍār), Collection of Jinabhadrasūri, Jaisalmer, "Tātparyapariśuddhi ṭippaṇī saha apūrṇa," Ms. No. ji. kā. 70, paper, 163 leaves (ff. 402-566; ff. 540, 549 missing), Devanagari, date ca. 1444 CE

NVTṬ
Nyāyavārttikatātparyaṭīkā of Vācaspatimiśra, ed. A. Thakur, New Delhi: Indian Council of Philosophical Research, Nyāyacaturgranthikā 3, 1996

NVTṬ (J1)
Manuscript of the NVTṬ, Jain Jñānabhaṇḍār (Baḍā Bhaṇḍār), Collection of Jinabhadrasūri, Jaisalmer, "Nyāyatātparyaṭīkā ṭippaṇī saha," Ms. No. ji. kā. 1274/1-2, paper, 276 leaves (ff. 5-280; f. 37 is missing), Devanagari, dated 1222 CE

OBERHAMMER, PRETS AND PRANDSTETTER 1991-1996
G. Oberhammer, E. Prets and J. Prandstetter, *Terminologie der frühen philosophischen Scholastik in Indien. Ein Begriffswörterbuch zur alt-indischen Dialektik, Erkenntnislehre und Methodologie*, Band 1: A-I. Wien, Österreichische Akademie der Wissenschaften, Philosophisch-Historische Klasse Denkschriften, 223. Band, 1991; Band 2: U-Pū. Wien: Verlag der Österreichischen Akademie der Wissenschaften, Österreichische Akademie der Wissenschaften, Philosophisch-Historische Klasse Denkschriften, 248. Band, 1996

PATIL 2013
P. Patil, "The Historical Rhythms of the Nyāya-Vaiśeṣika Knowledge System," in E. Franco (ed.), *Periodization and Historiography of Indian Philosophy*, Wien: Verein Sammlung de Nobili – Arbeitsgemeinschaft für Indologie und Religionsforschung, 2013, pp. 91-126

PERRY 1995
B.M. Perry, *An Introduction to the Nyāyacaturgranthikā: With English Translations*, PhD Dissertation, University of Pennsylvania, 1995 (UMI No. 9532256)

PHILLIPS 2012
S. Phillips, *Epistemology in Classical India. The Knowledge Sources of the Nyāya School*, New York/London: Routledge, 2012

PIND 2009
O.H. Pind, *Dignāga's Philosophy of Language. Dignāga on anyāpoha. Pramāṇasamuccaya V.* Texts, Transl., and Annotation, PhD Dissertation, Universität Wien, 2009 (http://othes.univie.ac.at/8283/1/2009-12-03_0507516.pdf, accessed on April 14, 2014)

PM
Pramāṇa Mīmāṃsā of Kalikāla Sarvajña Śrī Hemacandrācārya with Bhāṣā Tippaṇa of Pandita Sukhlalji Saṅghvi, ed. S. Sanghavi, M. Kumar and D. Malvania, Ahmedabad/Calcutta: The Sancalaka-Singhi Jaina Granthamala, 1939

POLLOCK 2001
S. Pollock, "New Intellectuals in Seventeenth-Century India," *Indian Economic Social History Review* 38(3), 2001, pp. 3-31

PREISENDANZ 2005
K. Preisendanz, "The Production of Philosophical Literature in South Asia during the Pre-colonial Period (15th to 18th Centuries): The Case of the *Nyāyasūtra* Commentarial Tradition," *Journal of Indian Philosophy* 33, 2005, pp. 55-94

PW
Sanskrit-Wörterbuch, hrsg. von der Kaiserlichen Akademie der Wissenschaften, bearbeitet von Otto Böhtlingk und Rudoph Roth. Theil I-VII, St. Petersburg 1855(1852)-1875

RAGHAVAN 1960
V. Raghavan, "Why was Jayanta Bhaṭṭa Known as Vṛttikāra?," in H.L. Hiriyappa and M.M. Patkar (eds.), *Professor P.K. Gode Commemoration Volume*, 3 Parts, Poona: Oriental Book Agency, Poona Oriental Series 93, Part 3, 1960, pp. 173-174

SHAH 1978
N.J. Shah, *Jayanta Bhaṭṭa's Nyāyamañjarī* [*Dvitīya Ahnika*] *with Gujarati Translation*, Ahmedabad: L.D. Institute of Indology, L.D. Series 67, 1978

SLAJE 2012
W. Slaje, "Wann, wo und weshalb schrieb Bhaṭṭa Jayanta seine 'Blütenrispe am Baum des Nyāya,'" in R. Steiner (ed.), *Highland Philology. Results of a Text-Related Kashmir Panel at the 31st DOT, Marburg 2010*, Halle (Saale): Universitätsverlag Halle-Wittenberg, 2012, pp. 121-142

TC
[*Tattvacintāmaṇi* of Gaṅgeśa] See TC (C), (D) and (V)

TC (C)
Tattvacintāmaṇau Upamānakhaṇḍaṃ. Śrīmadgaṅgeśopādhyāyaviracitaṃ. Śrīkṛṣṇakāntavidyāvāgīśaviracitadīpanyākhyaṭīkāsahitaṃ. (*The Tattva-Chintāmaṇi by Gaṅgeśa Upādhyāya. Part III. Upamāna Khaṇḍa with the commentary of Krisṇakānta Vidyāvāgīça*), ed. K.N. Tarka-vāgīśa, Calcutta: The Baptist Mission Press, Bibliotheca Indica, New Series 844, 1897

TC (D)
Mahāmahopādyāyagaṅgeśaviracitatattvacintāmaṇau upamānakhaṇḍam Mahāmahopādhyāyagokulanāthopādhyāyaviracitaraśmicakravyākhyāsahitam, ed. R. Jhā and D. Jhā, Darbhanga: Kāmeśvarasasiṃha-Darabhaṅgā-Saṃskṛta-Viśvavidyālayaḥ, Mm. Gokulanāthagranthāvalī 7, 1983

TC (V)
Tattvacintāmaṇi of Gaṅgeśopādhyāya [*Upamāna*] *with Pragalbhī by Pragalbhācārya*, ed. G. Sastri, Varanasi: Sampurnanand Sanskrit Vishvavidyalaya, M.M. Śivakumāraśāstri-Granthamālā 7, 1983

THAKUR 1959
Jñānaśrīmitranibandhāvali (Buddhist Philosophical Works of Jñānaśrīmitra), ed. A. Thakur, Patna: Kashi Prasad Jayaswal Research Institute, Tibetan Sanskrit Works Series 5, 1959

THAKUR 1974
A. Thakur, "Udayanācārya and His Contribution," in C.D. Shastri Felicitation Committee (eds.), *Charudeva Shastri Felicitation Volume, Presented to Prof. Charudeva Shastri on the Occasion of His Seventy-fifth Anniversary by His Friends and Admirers*, Delhi: 1974, pp. 400-406

TR
Tārkikarakṣā. ŚrīmadācāryaVaradarājaviracitā, tatkṛtaSārasaṅgrahābhidhavyākhyāsahitā, mahopādhyāyakolācalaśrīMallināthasūriviracitayā Niṣkaṇṭakākhyayā vyākhyayā Jñānapūrṇanirmitayā Laghudīpikākhyayā ṭīkayā ca samanvitā, ed. V.P. Dvivedin [repr. from the Pandit], Varanasi: Medical Hall, 1903

TRSS
[Varadarāja's autocommentary *Sārasaṅgraha* to the TR] See TR

VELANKAR 1953
H.D. Velankar (compl.), *A Descriptive Catalogue of the Sanskrit Manuscripts in "The Itchharam Suryaram Desai Collection" in the Library of the University of Bombay*, Bombay: The University of Bombay, 1953

VON STIETENCRON 1970
H. von Stietenkron, Review of "Brahmānanda Gupta: Die Wahrnehmungslehre in der Nyāyamañjarī," *Zeitschrift der Deutschen Morgenländischen Gesellschaft* 119, 1970, pp. 215-216

VS
Vaiśeṣikasūtra of Kaṇāda with the Commentary of Candrānanda, ed. Muni Shri Jambuvijayaji, Baroda: Oriental Institute, Gaekwad's Oriental Series 136, 1961

Vyo
Praśastapādabhāṣyam of Praśasta Devāchārya, with Commentaries (up to Dravya) Sūkti by Jagadiśa Tarkālaṅkāra, Setu by Padmanābha Miśra and Vyomavatī by Vyomaśivāchārya (to the end), ed. G. Kaviraj and D. Shastri, Varanasi: Chaukhamba Amarabharati Prakashan, Chowkhamba Sanskrit Series 61, 1925

WADA 2006
T. Wada, "A Navya-nyāya Presupposition in Determining the Meaning of Words," *Acta Asiatica/Bulletin of the Institute of Eastern Culture* 90, 2006, pp. 71-91

WADA 2007
T. Wada, *The Analytical Method of Navya-Nyāya*, Groningen: Egbert Forsten, Gonda Indological Studies 14, 2007

Realism and the Pratyabhijñā: Influences on and Legacies of Somānanda's Conception of Materiality*

JOHN NEMEC

1. INTRODUCTION

Somānanda, who is the founding author of the Pratyabhijñā, makes the case for a thoroughly disembodied form of being, as I have argued elsewhere.[1] This is exhibited in his conception of the nature of apparently physical entities, which he describes as *amūrta* or as possessed of an *amūrtatva* – as ever and completely without a form.[2] Moreover, because all entities are in his view nothing but consciousness, they cannot but function as consciousness does, this being conceived by Somānanda as the capacity of the divine yogin – Śiva – to create phenomena at will, without any recourse to extrinsic means in doing so;[3] and, as such, his conception of causality

---

* I thank Eli Franco and Isabelle Ratié for inviting me to the conference, "Around Abhinavagupta," at which I presented an earlier version of this essay, and for their editorial comments on this essay. The present work reflects the content of the conference presentation but also incorporates several lines of thinking inspired by the feedback of colleagues at the Leipzig meeting. I would like to thank Eli Franco for his comments at the conference regarding the use of *mūrtatva* and related terms in Nyāya and Vaiśeṣika writings, and Lawrence McCrea for bringing to my attention a discussion in Mīmāṃsā sources of the figurative use of the desiderative, a discussion of which Somānanda was very possibly aware.

1 The nature and functioning of Śiva as consciousness, as Somānanda conceives of it, is the subject of a forthcoming essay and is detailed therein. See NEMEC forthcoming.

2 Everything, in fact, is described as *amūrta*. See *Śivadṛṣṭi* (ŚD) 5.4cd-5: *icchāvantaḥ sarva eva vyāpakāś ca samastakāḥ* ‖ *amūrtāś ca tathā sarve sarve jñānakriyātmakāḥ* | *prabhavaś ca tathā sarva icchāmarśās tathākhilāḥ* ‖. These and related passages are examined in NEMEC forthcoming.

3 See ŚD 1.44-45ab: *yoginām icchayā yadvan nānārūpopapattitā* | *na cāsti sā-*

stands in clear contrast to those that take into consideration the real functioning of physical, material substances.[4]

Somānanda's discussion of *amūrta*(*tva*) calls into question the treatment in the ŚD of the realist ontology of the Naiyāyikas and Vaiśeṣikas, as well as in the writings of those who follow Somānanda in the Pratyabhijñā lineage. Indeed, to explain the appearance and functioning of apparently distinct, material entities is a – perhaps *the* – fundamental philosophical challenge facing the nondualist idealist; for the common-sense realist can claim that discrete, material phenomena are proven to exist externally to consciousness simply by dint of the fact that they appear as such in the ken.[5] In the present essay, I wish to suggest that Somānanda had precisely this type of concern in mind when articulating his theory of consciousness, and his associated asseveration of the formlessness of all entities.

Indeed, Somānanda measures his own ontological formulations against the realists' views of the nature of substances (*dravya*s), as they are articulated by various Nyāya-Vaiśeṣika authors and works; and it is in opposition to them (in part, at least) that he fashions his own ontology, for he can be understood to take the *ātmadravya* as the model for his ubiquitous agent, Śiva, though he significantly modifies the Vaiśeṣika formulation by in effect collapsing all the various *padārtha*s into a singular entity in doing so. This also leads him to challenge notions of agency in a radical manner (as is by now well known[6]), and in doing so he invokes, in perhaps a playful manner, a discussion of figurative uses of the desiderative found in grammatical works and in Kumārila's *Tantravārttika* (TV).

---

dhanaṃ kiñcin mṛdādīcchāṃ vinā prabhoḥ ‖ *tathā bhagavadicchaiva tathātvena prajāyate* |. This passage is also examined in NEMEC forthcoming.

4 See ŚD 2.53-54, which suggests that a unitary consciousness cannot function as would a fully embodied, physical agent – Devadatta – who is an *avayavin*: *ātmānam ātmanā hanti devadatto yathā tathā* | *bhaviṣyaty atra tatrāsya svāṅgair eva vibhāgitā* ‖ *hastādeḥ karaṇatvaṃ hi mastakādeś ca karmatā* | *kartā manaḥsvāvayavī nāmūrtāyā idaṃ punaḥ* ‖. (This passage is also examined in NEMEC forthcoming.) Consider the same in light of *Vaiśeṣikasūtra* (VS) 10.11, which allows for the existence of distinct components of the individual body: *śiraḥ pṛṣṭam udaraṃ pāṇir iti tadviśeṣebhyaḥ.*

5 In fact, something similar to this is suggested in the first *pāda* of the third *adhyāya* of the VS, for which see n. 16, below.

6 See, e.g., NEMEC 2014, especially pp. 104ff.

In what follows, I will first offer an analysis of the ways in which Somānanda apparently modifies – or at least has in mind – Nyāya-Vaiśeṣika ontology in the formulation of his theory of the self or *ātman*, conceived of as conterminal with Śiva in the form of consciousness, after which I will illustrate the ways in which Somānanda's simple denial of the existence of materiality is qualified and transformed in Utpaladeva's articulation of the Pratyabhijñā. This Utpaladeva accomplishes by explicitly incorporating the *padārtha*s into Pratyabhijñā ontology, albeit in a subordinated position in the hierarchy of being. Specifically, he suggests that the *padārtha*s are dependent on the prior existence of the *ātman*, who serves as their basis, and who stands as the preeminent *dravya* in a manner that mirrors Somānanda's apparent view of the same; and in doing so Utpaladeva adopts an approach that is clearly influenced by the *Vākyapadīya* (VP) and its commentaries, even while Somānanda's views of immateriality were first directed against Bhartṛhari.

Finally, I will briefly examine selected passages of the *Īśvarapratyabhijñāvimarśinī* (ĪPV) and *Īśvarapratyabhijñāvivṛtivimarśinī* (ĪPVV), where one finds Abhinavagupta not only clarifying the views of his *paramaguru*, but also synthesizing them with those of his *parameṣṭhiguru*.

2. SOMĀNANDA'S *AMŪRTATVA* IN LIGHT OF NYĀYA-VAIŚEṢIKA FORMULATIONS

Though he refers by name to the Nyāya and Vaiśeṣika schools only occasionally in the ŚD,[7] it is evident that Somānanda has their ideas in mind when formulating his understanding of Śiva's nature as consciousness. One can know this, firstly, because Somānanda signals his concern with Nyāya-Vaiśeṣika lines of thinking at the opening of the sixth chapter of the ŚD, where he suggests that his system must account for the nature of agency and action without distinguishing *dravya* from *karman*:

> 6.1. *atha śakteḥ śaktimato na bhedo dravyakarmavat* |
> *sthāpito dravyato bhinnā kriyā no na ca nāsti sā* ||

---

[7] See ŚD 6.28cd: *nyāyavaiśeṣikāṇāṃ tu bandhamokṣau pṛthaksthitī*. Somānanda's criticism is here limited, as is evident, to the fact that Naiyāyikas and Vaiśeṣikas draw a sharp distinction between bondage and liberation, a duality proscribed in the ŚD (at, e.g., 3.72). See also ŚD 4.38c, where the Vaiśeṣikas are named; and ŚD 1.28a, where reference is made to the Nyāya, etc.

6.2. *evaṃ tathā śaktimataḥ śaktasya samavasthitā |*
jagadvicitratā śaive na punar darśanāntare ||

Now, no [ontological] distinction is established [in our view] between the power and the possessor of the power just as [we make no such distinction] between substance (*dravya*) and action (*karman*). Action (*kriyā*) is not different from substance (*dravyatas*), nor is it the case that [action] does not exist. And in this way the variegation of the world is fully established for the empowered possessor of power in Śaivism [alone], but not in any other philosophical system.

The mutual distinction of *dravya* and *karman* is of course a basic feature of Nyāya-Vaiśeṣika ontology, as is well known.[8] Somānanda, however, denies the possibility of distinguishing the agent of action (viz., the *ātman* or *ātmadravya*) from the action itself (*karman*), this in his affirmation of the Śaiva identification of the power or *śakti* and the possessor of the power in question (*śaktimat*).

The context in which this statement is found further suggests that Somānanda, implicitly or self-consciously, measured his formulation of the individual agent, of Śiva-as-consciousness, against the Vaiśeṣika categories that undoubtedly would have been known to him, and his response to them (for I would argue that one of the projects of the ŚD is indeed to respond to – to reformulate – precisely such a realist ontology) involves a rather more comprehensive intervention than merely to deny the distinction of *dravya* from *karman*. Indeed, to read Somānanda in light of the *padārtha*s is to understand him in effect to identify everything with a single entity, the *ātman*, the agent *par excellence* that is (in his well-known

---

8 *Dravya* and *karman* are of course counted as two among the six mutually distinct *padārtha*s. See, e.g., Kaṇāda's VS 1.1.4-6. See also, e.g., Praśastapāda's *Padārthadharmasaṃgraha* (PDhSaṃ) in its opening lines: *dravyaguṇakarmasāmānyaviśeṣasamavāyānāṃ ṣaṇṇāṃ padārthānāṃ sādharmyavaidharmyatattvajñānaṃ niḥśreyasahetuḥ*. HALBFASS 1992 (pp. 69-87, esp. 75-76) outlines why it might be the case that the six-fold schema of *padārtha*s was not at first to be found in Kaṇāda's text, however, suggesting as he does that it possibly was a subsequent addition thereto; and, as is well known, Bhāsarvajña (himself a Kashmiri who possibly was an early contemporary of Somānanda's but who could also possibly have lived at a time closer to Abhinavagupta than to him) rather counts *karman* as another of the *guṇa*s. Somānanda seems to have the VS, perhaps along with the commentary on it by Candrānanda, and probably the PDhSaṃ in mind when formulating his position. On the other hand, there is a Vaiśeṣika precedent to the identification of *śakti* and *śaktimat*, for which see FRANCO 1987, pp. 325-326.

view) identical with Śiva.[9] He does so, of course, in an effort to identify all entities as entirely and utterly singular in nature, this in pursuit of a strategy of understanding consciousness, also conterminal with Śiva, as *the* foundational entity, the singular type of *dravya*, as it were, one that is fully active and, indeed, volitional.

The context in which the first and third of the six *padārtha*s were mentioned is therefore of no coincidence. For, Somānanda mentions *dravya* and *karman* immediately following an astounding passage at the close of the fifth chapter of the ŚD, in which all the world's various entities and agents, both apparently animate and inanimate, are mutually identified.

> 5.105. *sarve bhāvāḥ svam ātmānaṃ jānantaḥ sarvataḥ sthitāḥ* |
> *madātmanā ghaṭo vetti vedmy ahaṃ vā ghaṭātmanā* ||
> 5.106. *sadāśivātmanā vedmi sa vā vetti madātmanā* |
> *śivātmanā yajñadatto yajñadattātmanā śivaḥ* ||
> 5.107. *sadāśivātmanā vetti ghaṭaḥ sa ca ghaṭātmanā* |
> *sarve sarvātmakā bhāvāḥ sarvasarvasvarūpataḥ* ||
> 5.108. *sarvasya sarvam astīha nānābhāvātmarūpakaiḥ* |
> *madrūpatvaṃ ghaṭasyāsti mamāsti ghaṭarūpatā* ||
> 5.109. *nānābhāvaiḥ svam ātmānaṃ jānann āste svayaṃ śivaḥ* |
> *cidvyaktirūpakaṃ nānābhedabhinnam anantakam* ||
> 5.110. *evaṃ sarveṣu bhāveṣu sarvasāmye vyavasthite* |
> *tena sarvagataṃ sarvaṃ śivarūpaṃ nirūpitam* ||

> All entities, being aware of their own nature, exist as all others. The pot knows by way of my nature, or I know by way of the pot's. I know by dint of Sadāśiva's, or he by mine, Yajñadatta by Śiva's, [and] Śiva by Yajñadatta's. The pot knows by dint of Sadāśiva's nature, and he by the pot's. All entities consist of everything, since everything is of the nature of everything. Everything exists here as everything by having the nature and form of [all] the various entities. The pot has my nature, and I have that of the pot. Śiva exists autonomously as one who is aware, by way of the various entities, of his own nature as the form of the manifestation of consciousness, which is differentiated by the various entities, [and] is endless. Thus, given that all [entities] are equally present in all entities, it therefore follows that we have ascertained that Śiva's form is omnipresent, is [itself] everything.

The passage in question, first noted and paraphrased (in a manner that is reflected in the translation here offered) by Torella, certain-

---

[9] So much is articulated explicitly in, e.g., ŚD 1.2 and the ŚDVṛ thereon.

ly offers what that scholar has labeled a "visionary crescendo," a culminating point in Somānanda's description of the nature of self.[10]

Yet, the author of the ŚD very possibly also had a more specific, and technical, concern in mind when he composed this passage. For, with it he explicitly eliminates the very distinctions that serve to distinguish the Vaiśeṣika *padārtha*s in their various forms. To wit, no distinction is here permitted between entities that act and those that do not, or between material and immaterial entities;[11] nor is a distinction drawn between sentient agents and insentient entities.[12] Neither is any distinction permitted between omnipresent and spatially delimited entities (about which, see below),[13] nor apparently is any absolute distinction of *nitya* from *anitya* evinced.[14] All entities are ubiquitous (*sarve bhāvāḥ... sarvataḥ sthitāḥ*), Somānanda here declares, in an affront to both the realism

---

[10] See TORELLA 1994, pp. xv-xvi, who also links it to the *sarvasarvātmakatvavāda* (alluded to most explicitly at ŚD 5.107cd).

[11] The distinction is drawn in numerous places in the VS, and a full survey of the matter lies beyond the scope of the present essay. See VS 5.2.23, to offer but one example, where three *dravya*s – *dik*, *kāla*, and *ākāśa* – are said to be inactive, because they differ from those entities that do have *karman*s associated with them: *dikkālāv ākāśaṃ ca kriyāvadbhyo vaidharmyān niṣkriyāṇi*. Candrānanda's commentary on the same reads as follows: *ākāśakāladiśo 'mūrtāḥ kriyāvataḥ pṛthivyāder amūrtatayā vaidharmyān niṣkriyāḥ, caśabdād ātmāpi niṣkriyaḥ*. See also, e.g., VS 7.1.24, where actions (*karman*s) themselves are said to be devoid of actions, and qualities (*guṇa*s) of qualities: *karmabhiḥ karmāṇi guṇair guṇāḥ*. (Cf. VS 7.2.5.)

[12] These types of distinctions are made in VS 3.1.1ff., where the agency of the *ātman* is established insofar as it is distinguishable from both the *indriya*s and the objects known by them. A real object is said to exist, and instruments are known to perceive them, and thus there must be an agent who is distinguishable from and who deploys the instruments in coming to know the objects. This is the *ātman*, and not some material entity like the body, or the senses themselves, or some inanimate object, like a pot. See n. 16, below.

[13] See, e.g., VS 7.1.28-29, where *ākāśa* and *ātman* are said to be infinitely large: *vibhavād mahān ākāśaḥ. tathā cātmā*. Cf. VS 7.1.30, where the *manas* is said to be atomic in size, because it is unlike *ākāśa* and *ātman*: *tadabhāvād aṇu manaḥ*.

[14] VS 4.1.1 defines *nitya* as that which is existent (*sat*) and without a cause (*akāraṇa*): *sad akāraṇavat tan nityam*. The non-eternal (*anitya*) is defined as its opposite at VS 4.1.4: *anityam iti ca viśeṣapratiṣedha-bhāvaḥ*. The question of the eternality or non-eternality of various *padārtha*s is dealt with throughout the text. VS 7.1.4-9 identify which of the *guṇa*s are *nitya* and which *anitya*, for example.

and dualism mapped by the *padārtha*s, and everything is "equally present in all entities" (*sarveṣu bhāveṣu sarvasāmye vyavasthite*). This is to say that Śiva's form is omnipresent – *sarvagata* –, identical with everything that exists in or as the universe.

Thus, what is offered here is precisely the mirror opposite of the ontological account found in VS 3.1.4-6, where we are told that the consciousness that can be aware of the objects of sense must belong to the *ātman* and not to the senses or the body – the material entities associated with individual persons –, because otherwise the effects, which like the body are held to be comprised of material *paramāṇu*s, would also have to be understood to be conscious, a phenomenon that Kaṇāda suggests is unknown in the world. Candrānanda's *Vaiśeṣikasūtravṛtti* (VSVṛ) ad VS 3.1.5,[15] moreover, offers the pot (*ghaṭādivat*) as an example of an entity that is comprised of the *aṇu*s and is clearly insentient.[16] Clearly, this is precisely

---

15 POTTER 1977 (p. 685) lists Candrānanda as an "undatable writer," noting Sandesara's suggestion of the 7th century along with Hattori's suspicion that he postdates Gaṅgeśa (and the period covered by the volume in which Potter reports this assessment). While some questions remains as to precisely when Candrānanda lived and wrote, he is by no means an undatable writer. Indeed, the VSVṛ is, according to Halbfass, a work probably of 900 C.E. or earlier. See HALBFASS 1992, pp. 79-80 and, especially, 237. Halbfass, furthermore, isolates (ibid., pp. 237 and 262, n. 2) the *terminus post quem* by identifying a passage (at VSVṛ ad VS 3.2.4) that shows Candrānanda knew Uddyotakara's *Nyāyavārttika* (a "probably seventh century" product), and, following AKLUJKAR 1969-1970, he notes that Helārāja probably knew the VSVṛ. (Aklujkar identifies four places where Helārāja quotes Candrānanda's *vṛtti* in his commentary ad VP 3.6.2-3. Isaacson, in turn, accepts 600 C.E. as the *terminus post quem* and, while he is not fully confident in the evidence, accepts the tenth century as the *terminus ante quem*, noting along the way Aklujkar's evidence, even as he suggests that it is possible that both Candrānanda and Helārāja were drawing from a common source, rather than the former from the latter. See ISAACSON 1995, pp. 140-143.

16 The *sūtra*s in question are, as noted above, found at VS 3.1.4-6. These explain why the *indriya*s and the body cannot be the agent of perception. The context is as follows: VS 3.1.1 suggests that the existence of the objects of sense are well known: *prasiddhā indriyārthāḥ* ("The objects of the senses are well known"). VS 3.1.2 suggests that it must be the *ātman*, viz., some agent apart from the *indriya*s and their objects, who knows the perceptions furnished by the *indriya*s: *indriyārthaprasiddhir indriyārthebhyo 'rthāntarasya hetuḥ* ("That the objects of the senses are well known is the reason [for inferring the existence] of an object that is different from the *indriya*s and their objects"). VS 3.1.3 denies the possibility that the experience of the objects of the senses can be attributed to the body or the *indriya*s themselves. Following this are the reasons. VS 3.1.4 states that there is no consciousness in the causes of the per-

the argument rejected by Somānanda, and I would propose that the example in the ŚD of the knowing pot is self-consciously offered to counter precisely the line of argument found in the VS, and the other works that are related to it. Perhaps Somānanda even had Candrānanda's VSVṛ in mind, for if Isaacson's suspicions are justified, this Vaiśeṣika author was himself a Kashmiri, as of course was Somānanda.[17]

That we are to take Somānanda literally when he both identifies individual human agents with one another – Devadatta *is* Yajñadatta, and vice versa – *and* with apparently inanimate enti-

---

ceptions: *kāraṇājñānāt* ("Because there is no consciousness in the causes [of the perceptions, i.e., the *indriyas*, or the body]"). VS 3.1.5 explains why this must be so. This is so, because if it were otherwise, the effects would similarly be conscious, this because both are made up of the same material *dravyas*, earth, water, fire, and air: *kāryeṣu jñānāt* ("Because [there would be] consciousness in the effects [as well]"). Finally, VS 3.1.6 closes the argument by suggesting that such awareness does not exist in the effects: *ajñānāc ca* ("And [this cannot be so,] because so much is not known [in the world]"). The VSVṛ clarifies the concern here addressed as follows: (ad 3.1.4:) *bhūtānām indriyakāraṇānām ajñatvāt tat kāryāṇīndriyāṇy apy ajñāni.* (ad 3.1.5:) *anyasya bhūtakāryasya ghaṭāder ajñatvād bhūtāny apy ajñāni.* (ad 3.1.6:) *bhūtānām ajñānād indriyāṇy apy ajñāny ity upasaṃhārārtham idaṃ sūtram.* Similarly, one may find reference in the germane context to the lack of such agency in the operative example – the *ghaṭa* – in the PDhSaṃ, where in describing the nature of the *ātman* Praśastapāda (see PDhSaṃ, pp. 167ff.) offers the mundane pot as a contrasting example to it, this insofar as it is insentient: *ātmatvābhisambandhād ātmā. tasya saukṣmyād apratyakṣatve sati karaṇaiḥ śabdādyupalabdhyanumitaiḥ śrotrādibhiḥ samadhigamaḥ kriyate. vāsyādīnāṃ karaṇānāṃ kartṛprayojyatvadarśanāc chabdādiṣu prasiddhyā ca prasādhako 'numīyate. na śarīrendriyamanasām ajñatvāt. na śarīrasya caitanyaṃ ghaṭādivadbhūtakāryatvāt, mṛte cāsambhavāt. nendriyāṇāṃ karaṇatvāt...* See also VS 3.1.13, which indicates that contact of the *ātman*, the senses, and the objects of sense produces knowledge different from what was previously described, that is, it produces valid knowledge: *ātmendriyamano 'rthasannikarṣād yan niṣpadyate tad anyat*. Finally, cf. NS 2.1.22: *nātmamanasos sannikarṣābhāve pratyakṣotpattiḥ*. (Note, however, that this *sūtra* comes in the form of an objection to the definition of perception offered at NS 1.1.4, which reads: *indriyārthasannikarṣotpannaṃ jñānam avyapadeśyam avyabhicāri vyavasāyātmakaṃ pratyakṣam*. The reply to this objection, however, suggests that contact with the *ātman* is presumed in the definition offered at 1.1.4, invalidating the objection thereby. See NS 2.1.24: *jñānaliṅgatvād ātmano nānavarodhaḥ*.)

17 While ISAACSON 1995 (p. 141) suggests the Candrānanda may well have been a Kashmiri, he does not insist unequivocally that he must have been so, due to a lack of conclusive evidence: "As to the geographical region in which Candrānanda lived and wrote, the indications, admittedly not conclusive, that we have point clearly to Kashmir."

ties, such as the simple water-pot, is further underscored by the fact that the ŚD also makes reference in the fifth chapter to a discussion regarding the figurative use of the desiderative, a discussion that is first found in Patañjali's *Mahābhāṣya* (MBh) and subsequently is adopted by Kumārila. The passage of the ŚD in question again invokes the agency and self-awareness of a pot, and goes on to suggest that even the apparently inanimate bank of the river has volition, may "wish" to collapse.

> 5.16. *jānan kartāram ātmānaṃ ghaṭaḥ kuryāt svakāṃ kriyām |*
> *ajñāte svātmakartṛtve na ghaṭaḥ sampravartate ||*
> 5.17. *svakarmaṇi mamaitat tad ity ajñānān na ceṣṭanam |*
> *kūlaṃ pipatiṣati...*

> Cognizing itself as the agent, the pot may perform its own action. If it were not aware of its own agency, the pot would not undertake an action. There would be no performance of its own action if it were not aware that it was its own.[18] The bank [of the river] wishes to collapse...[19]

We here are told not only that the apparently inanimate *ghaṭa* is in fact a conscious agent, but something else is also added in the suggestion that "the bank [of the river] wishes to collapse," for with this expression, Somānanda evokes the aforementioned discussions of the use of the desiderative in a figurative manner of speech.

The expression – *kūlaṃ pipatiṣati* – first appears (with the word order reversed) in the MBh ad *Aṣṭādhyāyī* 3.1.7, and in the corresponding passage of the *Kāśikāvṛtti* (KāVṛ). The Pāṇinian *sūtra* in question of course falls within the (vast) section of the *Aṣṭādhyāyī* that deals with suffixation (beginning with A 3.1.1: *pratyayaḥ*) and allows for the use of the suffix *saN* following verbal roots that refer to an object of an action that is wished for by the agent of the action in question.[20] This results in the production of the desidera-

---

18 That is, it would not be able to do its own work, of carrying water, for example, if it were not aware of itself as the agent of the action in question. This is how Chaturvedi understands the passage, as well, for which see CHATURVEDI 1986, p. 180.

19 See also ŚD 1.23 and the *Vṛtti* on the same, as well as ŚD 3.62.

20 A 3.1.7, which reads *dhātoḥ karmaṇaḥ samānakartṛkād icchāyāṃ vā*, may be translated as follows: "Optionally (*vā*), [the affix *saN* is applied] in the sense of a wish (*icchāyām*) following a verbal root (*dhātoḥ*) that refers to the object [that is wished for] (*karmaṇaḥ*) and has the same agent of action [as the agent who wishes for the object in question] (*samānakartṛkād*)." The KāVṛ on this passage reads, in part: *iṣikarmako yo dhātur iṣiṇaiva samānakartṛkaḥ, tasmād*

tive, as in *cikīrṣati* (optionally) for *kartum icchati*, or *jihīrṣati* (optionally) for *hartum icchati*.

Following this is a pair of *vārttika*s that further define the scope of the *sūtra*, and it is the first of these that is of concern here. It reads: *āśaṅkāyām upasaṃkhyānam* ("there is [optionally] the addition [of the affix *saN*] when there is fear/apprehension"), suggesting thereby that the affix *saN* can optionally be used when there is an immanent danger of the action in question occurring. Three examples are given. The first pair includes the one that is here in question (as Vāmana and Jayāditya telegraph it): *śaṅke patiṣyati kūlam. pipatiṣati kūlam.* That is, one can say that the bank of the river "wishes" to collapse in instances in which there is a fear of the event occurring, as opposed to on occasions when the agent of the action desires as much. The line thus would better be rendered "the bank [of the river] is in danger of collapsing" or "the bank [of the river] is about to collapse." (Similar expressions, of course, are found in English – one may say that "the wall threatens to collapse," for example – as well as in a host of other languages.) Patañjali further clarifies that the meaning of *pipatiṣati kūlam* is not to be taken literally, this by underscoring that a riverbank, being insentient, cannot wish for any particular action or result.

> *āśaṅkāyām acetaneṣūpasaṅkhyānaṃ kartavyam. aśmā luluṭhiṣate. kūlaṃ pipatiṣatīti. kiṃ punaḥ kāraṇaṃ na sidhyati. evaṃ manyate. cetanāvata etat bhavatīccheti. kūlaṃ cācetanam. acetanagrahaṇena nārthaḥ. āśaṅkāyām ity eva.*
>
> It [i.e., the desiderative] may be deployed when there is fear/apprehension as regards insensible entities (*acetana*). One says (*iti*): "The stone is on the point of rolling" (*aśmā luluṭhiṣate*); "the bank [of the river] is about to collapse" (*kūlaṃ pipatiṣati*). [Objection:] But why does the cause [for the use of the desiderative] not [otherwise] avail itself [in these instances]?[21] [Reply:] Think of it this way: this [i.e., the cause of the use of the desiderative] comes to fruition for one who is conscious; [and] it is referred to as (*iti*) will (*icchā*); yet, the bank [of the river] is not conscious. No meaning [of the desiderative] is yielded by mentioning an unconscious [entity]. This is precisely why [the *vārttika*] says

---

icchāyām arthe vā san pratyayo bhavati. "A verbal root that is associated with the object of wishing and has the same agent as that of the act of wishing optionally may take following it the suffix *saN* when its meaning is the wish."

21 This is to ask why a *vārttika* is here called for. What does it do to clarify the scope of the *sūtra*?

[that the desiderative affix *saN* may optionally be affixed] "when there is fear/apprehension."

Patañjali, in a manner that reflects the sort of common-sense (or, if one prefers, naïve) realism that is evident in the VS (and NS), thus takes it as obvious and axiomatic that an apparently inanimate entity has no volition whatever (not entirely without reason, it may be added), and it is on the basis of this presumption that Kātyāyana furnishes the *vārttika* in question. What the *vārttika* adds, that is, is precisely the occasion for using the desiderative when insentient entities are involved, a use not made evident by the *sūtra* itself given its reference to the wishing or volition of the (sentient) agent of the verbal action in question.[22]

It is quite likely that Somānanda had precisely the present passage of the MBh in mind when deploying the example of the riverbank, for, to reiterate, he offers the line in a context that demands we read it as a direct repudiation of the position explicitly articulated by Patañjali (as well by Kaṇāda), namely, that inanimate entities have no consciousness or volition of their own, requiring thereby that the meaning of the expression in question be taken figuratively.

It is also possible that Somānanda had in mind another occurrence of the same expression, once again offered by a realist, this time the Mīmāṃsaka Kumārila, who utters precisely the same line in his TV ad *Mīmāṃsāsūtra* 3.1.13.[23] There, Kumārila adduces three ways one can speak of the intention (*vivakṣā*) expressed by a Vedic injunction. Such utterances can be taken metaphorically, or the intentionality may be ascribed to Mīmāṃsakas and practitioners of the ritual, or, finally, one could even maintain that the Vedic texts themselves are literally conscious, able to hold their own intentions.[24] In charting the first of these options, Kumārila quotes the expression under consideration – *kūlaṃ pipatiṣati* – exemplify-

---

[22] Patañjali offers yet another example: *śvā mumūrṣati*. Meaning literally "the dog wishes to die," one should understand the utterance to suggest "the dog is about to die," for while being conscious, no dog would have the desire to see its own demise. This, at least, is how the *Pradīpa* explains the example: *śunaś caitanye 'pi jīvitasya priyatvād vyādhyādyabhibhave 'pi tiryaktvān martum icchā nāsti*.

[23] See TV ad MS 3.1.13, vol. IV, pp. 65-70. I am grateful to Larry McCrea for referring me to the passage in question.

[24] Lawrence McCrea reviews the relevant passage in MCCREA 2000, p. 456, n. 61. A more detailed discussion is also found in YOSHIMIZU 2008, pp. 53-58.

ing thereby the metaphorical use of language in expressing the intention of the agent in question. Again, we see that the very unconsciousness of the agent renders the expression of necessity a metaphorical one. Yet, Somānanda deploys the selfsame expression in a context that demands we rather take it literally, as we have seen. In a perhaps playful manner, then, Somānanda seems to wish to suggest that his interlocutors simply err in what he would undoubtedly deem to be their naïvely and erroneously conceived realism.

Returning now to the passage that closes the fifth chapter of the ŚD, I would add that one should perhaps further understand Somānanda's reference to Śiva as *sarvagata* (ŚD 5.110c) not as so much of a boiler-plate description of the ubiquity of an omnipresent deity as it is an effort to differentiate the view of the ŚD from that of the realists, who distinguish omnipresent from spatially circumscribed entities in the VS, NS, and elsewhere. For, not only is it the case that the VS understands only spatially limited entities to be capable of performing actions (*karmans*)[25] – precisely not the position taken in the ŚD, which not only identifies *karman* with *dravya*, as we have seen, but also identifies both with an *ubiquitous* agent, Śiva, conterminal with the *ātman* and existing in the form of consciousness –, but Somānanda elsewhere explicitly challenged the notion that consciousness is spatially delimited, and he did so precisely in the context of denying the very existence of material entities, that is, in describing all of existence as *amūrta*:[26]

> 2.76cd. *asarvagapramāṇaṃ hi mūrtir no lakṣyate citaḥ* |
>
> For, consciousness does not appear as having a limited measure,[27] or as having a form (*mūrti*).

In glossing this passage, itself offered in the context of Somānanda's critique of the description of Brahman found in the *maṅgala* verse of what Somānanda identifies as the (*Śabdadhātu*)*samīkṣā*,[28]

---

[25] This is of necessity so, given the purely physical nature of action as it is defined in the VS. See VS 1.1.6: *utkṣepaṇam avakṣepaṇam ākuñcanaṃ prasāraṇaṃ gamanam iti karmāṇi* ("The actions are: moving upward, moving downward, bending, extending, and moving").

[26] See ŚD 2.73cd and following for the beginning of this critique.

[27] Note that Utpaladeva glosses °*pramāṇa* in ŚD 2.76c with °*parimāṇa*, and my translation here follows his gloss.

[28] Torella has suggested that one should rather understand the title of this work

a *maṅgala* that is identical to that of the *Nītiśataka*,[29] Utpaladeva further clarifies that consciousness cannot be understood (as Somānanda says Bhartṛhari wrongly does) in terms that suggest it is something that has a form, is something solid:[30]

> *upacāre ca kiṃ prayojanam. asarvagatadravyaparimāṇaṃ mūrtiḥ kāṭhinyaṃ vā na cid bhavati, tat kathaṃ cinmūrtaya iti.*
>
> What, moreover, is the motivation for using figurative speech? Consciousness is not a substance of a limited measure, nor is it that which has a form, i.e., a solid entity. So, why does [Bhartṛhari] say "[homage] to the one whose form is [pure, endless] consciousness"?

In doing so, one can well see that the language used to describe materiality in the ŚD (*asarvagapramāṇa*) and the ŚDVṛ (*asarvagataparimāṇa*) echoes that of Praśastapāda's PDhSaṃ (which reads, in part: *mūrtir asarvagatadravyaparimāṇam*), for we are told that four of the nine *dravya*s – *ākāśa*, *kāla*, *diś*, and *ātman* – are possessed of an *amūrtatva*, this insofar as they cannot be said to be *dravya*s of circumscribed size:[31]

> *ākāśakāladigātmanāṃ saty api dravyabhāve niṣkriyatvaṃ sāmānyādivad amūrtatvāt. mūrtir asarvagatadravyaparimāṇaṃ tadanuvidhāyinī ca kriyā sā cākāśādiṣu nāsti tasmān na teṣāṃ kriyāsambandho 'stīti.*
>
> Even though ether (*ākāśa*), time (*kāla*), space (*diś*), and self (*ātman*) are *dravya*s, they are devoid of action, as are *sāmānya*, etc., this due to their not having a form (*amūrtatva*). That which has a form (*mūrti*) has the measure of a non-ubiquitous substance (*asarvagatadravyaparimāṇa*), and action conforms to that; and since [action] does not exist in ether and the rest, it follows that they are not connected to action.

Here, and elsewhere,[32] the *dravya*s in question are said both not to have a form and to be omnipresent.

---

to be the *Ṣaḍdhātusamīkṣā*. (See TORELLA 2008, p. 513, nn. 7 and 8; cf. TORELLA 1994, pp. xxvi-xxvii, n. 39).

29 On this identification, and the question of the attribution of the authorship of the three *śataka* works to Bhartṛhari, see IYER 1969, pp. 10-13, esp. p. 13.

30 See ŚDVṛ ad ŚD 2.74cd-76.

31 See PDhSaṃ, pp. 734ff.

32 See also, e.g., NS 4.2.19, where the omnipresence of *ākāśa* is again noted: *ākāśāsarvagatatvaṃ vā* ("Otherwise, the ether would not be omnipresent"). The context of the statement involves an objection by an opponent who denies the possibility that *aṇu*s can be infinitesimally small in size, because if they were, the Naiyāyika could not claim that *ākāśa* is *sarvagata/vibhu*. This is so,

Moreover, while as an idealist he understands apparently external, material entities to be of a nature that is rather different from what his realist counterparts would suggest it is, what is here offered is something that Somānanda, too, accepts. That is, Somānanda, too, holds that an immaterial entity – indeed, the one and only immaterial entity, Śiva-as-consciousness – is omnipresent and is thus not moved by any sort of *physical* activity. Further, he quite willingly accepts the definition of materiality here offered – that that which is *mūrta* is circumscribed, is *asarvagata* –, even though it is on the basis of this definition that he denies, *tout court*, the very existence of materiality, this on the grounds that consciousness – the one and only form of existence, in his view – is by nature precisely not such a circumscribed and discrete entity.[33]

To sum up: one can see that while Somānanda diverges from the Nyāya-Vaiśeṣika (and related realist views) in understanding *dravya* and *karman* to be mutually identifiable, in understanding an ubiquitous and not a spatially delimited entity to act, and in under-

---

the objector claims, because to have the ether reside within the *aṇu*s requires them to have parts – a "within" and a "without" – and so the Naiyāyika must either maintain that the *aṇu*s are divisible in this manner, or they must forego their claim that *ākāśa* is omnipresent. The objection begins at NS 4.2.18: *ākāśavyatibhedāt tadanupapattiḥ* ("There is an impossibility of that [i.e., of the indivisibility of the atom], because it is penetrated by the ether"). The *Nyāyasūtrabhāṣya* (NSBh) of Vātsyāyana (a.k.a. Pakṣilasvāmin) ad NS 4.2.18 clarifies the objection: *tasyāṇor niravayavasya nityasyānupapattiḥ. kasmāt. ākāśavyatibhedāt. antar bahiś cāṇur ākāśena samāviṣṭo vyatibhinnaḥ, vyatibhedāt sāvayavaḥ sāvayavatvād anitya iti.* "It is not possible for an eternal, partless *aṇu* to exist. Why? Because it is penetrated by the ether. The *aṇu* is penetrated (*samāviṣṭa* = *vyatibhinna*) internally and externally by the ether; because it is penetrated, it has parts; [and] because it has parts, it is not eternal." Cf. NSBh ad 4.2.19, which reads in part: *paramāṇor antar nāsty ākāśam ity asarvagatatvam prasajyata iti.* "The unwanted consequence that *ākāśa* is not omnipresent results from it not existing within the *paramāṇu*." By contrast, material entities are said to be tangible and divisible – not omnipresent. See NS 4.2.23, where the opponent suggests that *aṇu*s must have parts, because they have a material form, which by definition means they must have some sort of physical shape: *mūrtimatāñ ca saṃsthānopapatter avayavasadbhāvaḥ* ("[Atoms] really do have parts, moreover, because that which has a form (*mūrtimat*) must have a physical shape").

33 This may be seen in the fact that he criticizes Bhartṛhari for, he suggests, understanding the agent to function as if he were an *avayavin*, performing discrete actions with discrete parts of his body, each part independent of the other. See ŚD 2.53-54, found in n. 4, above. This and related passages are also examined in more detail in NEMEC forthcoming.

standing apparently inanimate entities to be fully conscious and volitional – indeed to be identified with Śiva, and the *ātman* – it is nevertheless the case that the *dravya*s, and the *ātmadravya* in particular, can be read as a model, a key point of reference, in Somānanda's construction of his notion of being and agency. For, to put matters negatively, the very realist principles that he challenges – those regarding the existence of insentient, discrete, material entities – are precisely those articulated in the VS (and NS), and confirmed by Patañjali, and Kumārila; and, to put matters positively, much can be said for taking the *dravya* of the same name in the standard Nyāya-Vaiśeṣika formulation as an important point of reference for Somānanda's understanding of the *ātman*, because his notion of the self – identical as it is with Śiva – is similar to its Nyāya-Vaiśeṣika counterpart in being conceived of as eternal (*nitya*), all pervasive (*vibhu*, *sarvagata*), immaterial (*amūrta*), and – what is key – as the volitional agent.[34] Indeed, to fuse the natures of *dravya* and *karman* is precisely the move by which Somānanda could logically conceive of a volitional agent who is at the same time active and ubiquitous. The ubiquitousness and volitional quality of the Nyāya-Vaiśeṣika *ātman* is thus preserved in Somānanda's view, though it is combined with a capacity for action (*karman*s), while simultaneously understood to stand as the basis for the appearance of the various phenomena appearing in the world, this perhaps in a manner that is analogous to the role of *dravya*s in the VS, where the balance of the *padārtha*s are said to appear in consonance with the first among them.[35]

Somānanda's apparent, deep criticism of the realists simultaneously evinces an accommodation of a basic feature of their sys-

---

34 On this formulation, see, e.g. POTTER 1977, p. 99: "There is practical unanimity among our philosophers that the self is the agent of our actions. There is no question that selves do not move. The theory is rather that agency does not require mobility. Kaṇāda, for a start, in inferring the existence of other selves from their bodies' activity, suggests that selves are agents of their bodies' actions. Vātsyāyana is quite explicit: he argues that moral responsibility requires a locus which persists, and that the self is the locus. Thus selves are responsible agents of the activities which breed *karma* and bondage. Vātsyāyana by no means limits the function of the self to a witnessing consciousness. Praśastapāda also speaks of selves as agents." So much is precisely what we find in Pratyabhijñā theology: a self that does not (physically) move, it being consciousness only, but which is ever and always the (albeit fully active) agent of action.

35 See reference to Śaṅkara's critique of the Vaiśeṣika, below, and n. 37.

tem, therefore, this in the form of the recognition of the existence of a ubiquitous agent who interacts with an apparently diverse universe, but without compromising its ubiquity in doing so. For, indeed, while Somānanda clearly would have had access to other models of the self – in scriptural sources, for one, and in the Sāṅkhya,[36] which had a profound influence on Śaiva philosophy and their understanding of the order of the *tattva*s in particular – there can be little doubt that he measured his own conception of the *ātman* in relation to Nyāya-Vaiśeṣika formulations, and was concerned with refuting their views in the course of articulating his own. It therefore requires perhaps no great stretch of the imagination to conjecture that Somānanda modelled his notion of (a ubiquitous, volitional) self in part on – and in opposition to – that of his realist counterparts.

3. THE CATEGORIES (*PADĀRTHAS*) AS A MEASURE OF BEING, AND AGENCY

Somānanda is not alone either in his manner of critiquing Nyāya-Vaiśeṣika ontology or in measuring his view of agency and external reality against Nyāya-Vaiśeṣika formulations. For, not only were these philosophical schools highly influential in premodern South Asia – we know of the significant presence of the Nyāya (and Vaiśeṣika) in the Kashmir Valley at the time when Somānanda, Utpaladeva, and Abhinavagupta were active, for example, this being one of the key philosophical traditions that can be found to have flourished "around Abhinavagupta" –, but other philosophical idealists also took up, and took issue with, the realists' ontology. Śaṅkara, for example, challenges the Vaiśeṣika in a manner that is similar to Somānanda's apparent critique: he suggests that all the *padārtha*s may be subsumed under the first among them – *dravya* – insofar as the others only appear when the former is present and never in its absence. He further argues that the differ-

---

36 Of course, the *puruṣatattva* of the Sāṅkhya is incorporated into Śaiva ontology as the twelfth of thirty-six *tattva*s. Somānanda's understanding of the nature of the *ātman* also shares many qualities (though not all of them, as has been made evident) with the eternal, all-pervasive, independent, partless, unchanging, and utterly inactive *puruṣa* of the Sāṅkhya. This is to say that the Sāṅkhya formulation, too, would have been a point of reference for Somānanda and the authors of the Pratyabhijñā, even if the relationship of *puruṣa* to *prakṛti* in the Sāṅkhya is one of proximity rather than direct interaction and even while the Sāṅkhya, like the Nyāya-Vaiśeṣika, presents a dualistic philosophical model.

ences among the *padārtha*s amount only to a difference of nomenclature, leading thereby to an accordion-like collapsing of the Vaiśeṣika ontological categories into the first of the six *padārthas*.[37]

---

[37] See Śaṅkara's *Brahmasūtrabhāṣya* ad BS 2.2.17 (*aparigrahāc cātyantam anapekṣā)*, p. 235, ll. 24 to p. 236, l. 12ff.: *api ca vaiśeṣikās tantrārthabhūtān ṣaṭpadārthān dravyaguṇakarmasāmānyaviśeṣasamavāyākhyān atyantabhinnān bhinnalakṣaṇān abhyupagacchanti. yathā manuṣyo 'śvaḥ śaśa iti. tathātvaṃ cābhyupagamya tadviruddhaṃ dravyādhīnatvaṃ śeṣāṇām abhyupagacchanti. tan nopapadyate. katham. yathā hi loke śaśakuśapalāśaprabhṛtīnām atyantabhinnānāṃ satāṃ netaretarādhīnatvaṃ bhavati, evaṃ dravyādīnām atyantabhinnatvān naiva dravyādhīnatvaṃ guṇādīnāṃ bhavitum arhati. atha bhavati dravyādhīnatvaṃ guṇādīnāṃ tato dravyabhāve bhāvād dravyābhāve 'bhāvād dravyam eva saṃsthānādibhedād anekaśabdapratyayabhāg bhavati. yathā devadatta eka eva sann avasthāntarayogād anekaśabdapratyayabhāg bhavati tadvat. tathā sati sāṅkhyasiddhāntaprasaṅgaḥ svasiddhāntavirodhaś cāpadyeyātām. nanv agner anyasyāpi sato dhūmasyāgnyadhīnatvaṃ dṛśyate. satyaṃ dṛśyate. bhedapratītes tu tatrāgnidhūmayor anyatvaṃ niścīyate. iha tu śuklaḥ kambalo rohiṇī dhenur nīlam utpalam iti dravyasyaiva tasya tasya tena tena viśeṣaṇena pratīyamānatvān naiva dravyaguṇayor agnidhūmayor iva bhedapratītir asti. tasmād dravyātmakatā guṇasya. etena karmasāmānyaviśeṣasamavāyānāṃ dravyātmakatā vyākhyātā.* "The Vaiśeṣikas assume six categories, which constitute the subject-matter of their system, viz. substance, quality, action, generality, particularity, and inherence. These six categories they maintain to be absolutely different from each other, and to have different characteristics; just as a man, a horse, a hare differ from one another. Side by side with this assumption they make another which contradicts the former one, viz. that quality, action, &c. have the attribute of depending on substance. But that is altogether inappropriate. How so? Well, just as ordinary things in the world, such as animals, grass, trees, and the like, being absolutely different from each other do not depend on each other, so the qualities, &c. also being absolutely different from substance, cannot depend on the latter. Or else let the qualities, &c. depend on substance; then it follows that, as they are present where substance is present, and absent where it is absent, substance only exists, and, according to its various structures, etc., becomes the object of different terms and conceptions (such as quality, action, &c.); just as Devadatta, for instance, [although] being absolutely unitary is the object of various conceptions and names according to the conditions in which he finds himself. But this latter alternative would involve the acceptance of the Sāṅkhya doctrine and the contradiction of their own (i.e., the Vaiśeṣika) standpoint. – But (the Vaiśeṣika may say) smoke also is different from fire and yet it is dependent on it. – True, we reply; but we ascertain the difference of smoke and fire from the fact of their being apperceived in separation. Substance and quality, on the other hand, are not so apperceived; for when we are conscious of a white blanket, or a red cow, or a blue lotus, the substance is in each case cognized by means of the quality; the latter therefore has its Self in the substance. The same reasoning applies to action, generality, particularity, and inherence." (Transl. a modification of Thibaut's, emphasis mine.) See THIBAUT 1890, pp. 394-396. HALBFASS 1992, pp. 79 and 86, n. 47 also makes reference to the passage in

Returning now to the Pratyabhijñā: as is not infrequently the case,[38] what is somewhat inchoate in the ŚD is rather more clearly and fully articulated in the ĪPK. So much is the case with the Pratyabhijñā's treatment of the self, for we find explicit evidence in Utpaladeva's writings for precisely what is apparently evident in the ŚD, namely, the apparent modelling (not without significant modifications) of the Śaiva notion of the *ātman* on the Vaiśeṣika *ātmadravya*. Indeed, while Somānanda is often indirect in his manner of engagement with the realists, Utpaladeva is rather more direct and open in identifying the *ātman* with the *dravya* of the same name.

I note, firstly, that Utpaladeva suggests that the activity of consciousness is found precisely in, or rather as, the very nature of the *ātman*:[39]

> *ātmāta eva caitanyaṃ citkriyācitikartṛtā* |
> *tātparyeṇoditas tena jaḍāt sa hi vilakṣaṇaḥ* ||
>
> Precisely for this reason the self has been defined as "sentience" (*caitanyam*) meaning by this the activity of consciousness in the sense of being the subject of this activity. It is thanks to sentiency, in fact, that the self differs from insentient reality. (Transl. Torella.)

One here sees reiterated Somānanda's identification of the agent of action with the action itself, though the matter is expressed in different terms (for no reference to the *śakti* and the *śaktimat* are here offered). This of course signals a marked departure from Nyāya-Vaiśeṣika formulations; and yet, the *svopajñavṛtti* associates the

---

question. What Śaṅkara had in mind is exemplified in, e.g., VS 1.1.14, where the nature of the *dravya*s (apart from *ākāśa*, *diś*, *kāla*, and *ātman*) is defined as being endowed with actions (*kriyā* = *karman*) and qualities (*guṇa*), and where it is defined as a *samavāyikāraṇa*: *kriyāvad guṇavat samavāyikāraṇam iti dravyalakṣaṇam*. VS 1.1.15, in turn, marks the *guṇa*s as inhering in substances (i.e., as being *dravyāśrayin*s), while VS 1.1.16 suggests that an action has a single *dravya* as its *āśraya*; and, finally, VS 1.1.17 (*dravyaguṇakarmaṇāṃ dravyaṃ kāraṇaṃ sāmānyam*) states that *dravya*, *guṇa*, and *karman* equally are caused by substance.

38 See NEMEC 2012 for an example of this, where we see Utpaladeva articulating in greater detail a critique of the Buddhist epistemologists that is found in a telegraphed and truncated form in the ŚD.

39 See ĪPK 1.5.12.

present formulation with the Vaiśeṣika categories, this by identifying the *ātman* with the *ātmadravya*:[40]

> *ātmadravyasya bhāvātmakam apy etaj jaḍād bhedakatayā vimarśākhyaṃ mukhyaṃ rūpam uktaṃ caitanyaṃ dṛśiśaktiś citir iti. sā cetanakriyā citikartṛtaiva.*
>
> Sentience – that is, the power of consciousness, perceiving – though an abstract (*bhāva°*), has been said to be the primary nature – the reflective awareness (*vimarśa°*) – of the substance self, being that which distinguishes it from insentient reality. This activity of being conscious means precisely being the subject of such activity. (Transl. Torella.)

Abhinavagupta, quoting both the *Śivasūtra*s and Patañjali's *Yogasūtra*s in supporting the identification of consciousness with the *ātman*, makes it clear that the entity in question – the *ātmadravya* – is modelled on the Vaiśeṣika formulation, though the Pratyabhijñā view of the *ātman* differs from the Vaiśeṣika counterpart insofar as the Śaiva *ātman* is held to be the source or basis of all entities:[41]

> *yato vimarśa eva pradhānam ātmano rūpam amum eva hetuṃ prayojanarūpam uddiśya ātmā dharmisvabhāvo dravyabhūto 'pi, caitanyam iti dharmivācinā śabdena sāmānādhikaraṇyam āśritya uditaḥ kathitaḥ, bhagavatā śivasūtreṣu "caitanyam ātmā"* (ŚSū 1.1) *iti paṭhitam, caitanyam iti hi dharmavācakopalakṣaṇam, "citiśaktir apariṇāminī" "... taddṛśeḥ kaivalyam"* (YS 2.25) *"draṣṭā dṛśimātraḥ..."* (YS 2.20) *ityādāv api hi dharmaśabdena sāmānādhikaraṇyam ātmano darśitaṃ guruṇānantena, dravyaṃ hi tad ucyate – yadviśrāntaḥ padārthavargaḥ sarvo bhāti cārthyate cārthakriyāyai tad yadi na kupyate tat sakalo 'yaṃ tattvabhūtabhāvabhuvanasaṃbhāraḥ saṃvidi viśrāntaḥ tathā bhavatīti. sa eva guṇakarmādidharmāśraya-bhūtapadārthāntarasvabhāvaḥ tām eva mukhyadravyarūpām āśrayata iti saiva dravyam.*
>
> Because free consciousness (*vimarśa*) is itself the chief nature of self; therefore, with a view to represent it as such, the Self, though a substance and substratum of attributes, is put in the same case as that of sentiency (*caitanya*), though the latter stands for an attribute, in the *Śivasūtra* "*caitanyam ātmā*" by the glorious one (sic). The word "sentiency" (*caitanya*) stands for any word, which means the essential characteristic

---

[40] TORELLA 1994 (pp. 119-120, nn. 24 and 25) makes no reference to the Nyāya-Vaiśeṣika in his extended notes on the present passage of the ĪPKVṛ, though he does refer (in n. 25) to the *ātmadravya* as being "the *dravya par excellence*, because everything without distinction rests on him."

[41] See ĪPV ad ĪPK 1.5.12, vol. I, p. 200, l. 7-p. 201, l. 9.

> [of self]. For, the teacher [Patañjali], in (I) "the power of sentiency is unchanging," (II) "that is the perfect isolation (*kaivalya*) of consciousness (*dṛśi*) (YS 2.25), and (III) "the subject is nothing more than consciousness" (YS 2.20), has put the Self in the same case as that of the word, which stands for the essential nature. The substance is that, resting on which everything shines and is desired for practical purposes. Therefore, if you do not get angry [I would say that] the entire mass of categories, elements, objects and worlds shines as such only resting on the universal consciousness (*saṃvid*): and because this mass, including the categories, such as quality, action, etc., essential nature and such other categories are the substrata, rests on that (*saṃvid*) which is the most important of all substances; therefore, that (*saṃvid*) alone is the true substance. (Transl. Pandey.)

Here, one is witness to Abhinavagupta's effort definitively to redefine the nature of the *dravya* in question in a Śaiva mold, suggesting that consciousness (*saṃvid*) alone is the primary substance (*mukhyadravya*) in doing so, because, he says, the mass of *padārtha*s (*padārthavarga*), including qualities, action, etc., rests on it. This is to say that Abhinavagupta's sub-commentary confirms that, in his view at least, the Pratyabhijñā view of the *ātman*, itself existing as or in the form of consciousness, is the preeminent *dravya*, that on which all entities depend – Abhinava says: *ātmā dharmisvabhāvo dravyabhūto 'pi caitanyam* –, a view that parallels Śaṅkara's critique of the Vaiśeṣikas and confirms that the Pratyabhijñā theory of self is, if not modeled on, at the least measured against the realists' formulations (or at least this is so in Abhinavagupta's view of the matter). This is so even as he and Utpaladeva part ways with the view of material entities propounded by the founding author of the Pratyabhijñā, as we shall see, when they show themselves to be more amenable to acknowledging the (relative) existence of (apparently) material entities than was Somānanda.

4. A COMPARISON OF UTPALADEVA'S APPROACH TO MATERIALITY WITH SOMĀNANDA'S

Turning now to a comparison of Utpaladeva's treatment of materiality with Somānanda's, we find the two authors pursuing differing strategies for explaining the appearance in the world of apparently distinct, material entities. Somānanda is entirely dismissive of the very possibility of the existence of any material entity, as has been shown; Utpaladeva's treatment of the matter is rather more nuanced. This is not to say that Utpala discards the basic framework offered by the ŚD, for he does not: like Somānanda (and as is well known) Utpaladeva, too, identifies Śiva with the *ātman* and both with consciousness, and sees this divine agent as the primary, indeed the only, entity in existence, the one from which all others are derived and on which they all rest.[42] Yet, Utpaladeva also simultaneously allows greater scope for the existence of apparently material entities than does Somānanda, and in doing so he largely adopts the model of another idealist, that of Bhartṛhari, against whom Somānanda directed his vociferous arguments opposing the very existence of materiality.

I note, firstly, that Utpaladeva incorporates realist categories, and the *padārtha*s in particular, into his system, albeit by placing them in a subordinated position in his overarching ontology:[43]

> *kriyāsaṃbandhasāmānyadravyadikkālabuddhayaḥ* |
> *satyāḥ sthairyopayogābhyām ekānekāśrayā matāḥ* ||

> The ideas of action, relation, universal, substance, space and time, which are based on unity and multiplicity, are to be considered real (*satyāḥ*), because of their permanence and efficacy (*sthairyopayogābhyām*). (Transl. Torella.)

Note that the list here offered is not precisely that of the six *padārtha*s, which should include *dravya*, *guṇa*, *karman*, *sāmānya*, *viśeṣa*, and *samavāya*. *Dik* and *kāla*, moreover, are of course counted as two of the nine *dravya*s in the Vaiśeṣika formulation. What is offered here is something of a hybrid list, then, one that I suspect shows the influence of Bhartṛhari's formulations, which also influenced Utpaladeva, as we shall see momentarily. (*Dik* and *kāla* are important categories in the VP and its commentaries.) Nevertheless, it is probably safe enough here to agree with Torella, who summarizes the contents of ĪPK 2.2 as follows: "This second *āhnika* aims at establishing that the categories acknowledged by the *bāhyavādin*s (the reference is particularly to the Nyāya-Vaiśeṣika) are acceptable only if seen from the Śaiva viewpoint."[44]

---

42 Guided by Abhinava's ĪPV ad ĪPK 1.5.12, reviewed above, I mean by this in particular that Utpaladeva understands the *ātman* to be the *dravya* par excellence, that on which all other entities depend and from which they can emerge.

43 See ĪPK 2.2.1.

44 See TORELLA 1994, p. 157, n. 1. It may be worth reiterating that Abhinavagupta makes explicit reference to the six *padārtha*s (and their inherent, though

If the *padārtha*s, or the bulk of them anyway, are explicitly incorporated into the ĪPK and ĪPKVṛ, it stands to reason that they must have some real ontological standing in Utpaladeva's system, even if they are comprehensible only in the context of a Śaiva idealism. And, indeed, this is precisely what is found in his writings, where one witnesses Utpala following Bhartṛhari in incorporating materiality into his ontology. This he does by explicitly acceding to the existence of *mūrti*s, entities with form, at ĪPK 2.1.5:

> *mūrtivaicitryato deśakramam ābhāsayaty asau* |
> *kriyāvaicitryanirbhāsāt kālakramam apīśvaraḥ* ||
>
> Through the variety of physical forms he causes spatial succession to appear; through the manifestation of the variety of actions the Lord also causes temporal successions to appear. (Transl. Torella.)

Since the "variety of physical forms," as Torella translates *mūrtivaicitrya*, serves as a means for manifesting differences in spatial location, they of necessity appear in a form real enough to validate the existence of spatial extension. So much is also confirmed in the *svopojñavṛtti*, where Utpaladeva states that *deśakrama* exists as a result of the appearance of the mutual distinction of many entities (*anekasyānyonyabhedābhāsād deśakramaḥ*). Not incidentally, as we shall see presently, Utpaladeva also indicates in both the *mūla* and the *Vṛtti* that temporal sequence (*kālakrama*) is dependent on action (*kriyā*).[45]

Of course, the context for such statements is clearly that of the appearance of mundane existence, the actions and entities of the everyday world, as is made clear in the present *āhnika* itself:[46]

---

subordinated, place within the hierarchy of being) in his ĪPV ad ĪPK 1.5.12, as was shown, above.

45 See ĪPKVṛ ad ĪPK 2.1.5: *anekasyānyonyabhedābhāsād deśakramaḥ kriyāmukhena kālakramo 'pi. ekasya tu bhāvasya tattajjanmasattāvipariṇāmādikriyābhedāt kālakrama eva.* "In the case of many entities, there is spatial succession through the manifestation of mutual diversity and temporal succession through actions. However, with reference to a single entity there is only temporal succession due to different actions such as birth, existence, change, etc." (Transl. Torella.)

46 See also the *svopajñavṛtti* on the same verse (ĪPK 2.1.2): *māyāśakter bhinnabhāvāvabhāsānāṃ kriyā kālaśaktivaśāt sakramā na tv ātmavimarśarūpānādinidhanā prabhoḥ svabhāvabhūtā.* "The action of entities that, due to the power of *māyā*, appear differentiated, is successive, being dependent on the power of Time; but that action, informed by the awareness of the self, without beginning or end, which is the very essence of the Lord, is not." (Transl. Torella.)

2.1.2. *sakramatvaṃ ca laukikyāḥ kriyāyāḥ kālaśaktitaḥ* |
ghaṭate na tu śāśvatyāḥ prābhavyāḥ syāt prabhor iva ||

Succession pertains to ordinary action, which is dependent on the power of Time; it is not, however, admissible for divine eternal action, as it is not for the Lord. (Transl. Torella.)

There is a distinction to be made between worldly (*laukikī*) action, on the one hand, and the "eternal (*śāśvatī*) action" of the Lord, on the other. Indeed, Utpaladeva surely would not wish to suggest that the objects of cognition exist as they are conceived by the naïve realist: fully real, material entities that exist outside of consciousness and entirely independently of the agent's capacity to cognize them. As an epistemic and metaphysical idealist, he of course understands them rather to be the very contents of consciousness and as such entirely dependent upon it.[47]

Utpaladeva nevertheless does allow scope for the manifestation of *mūrti*s at this subordinated level, and he does so in a manner that is not expressed in the ŚD: there is no denial of their very existence in the ĪPK as there is asseverated in the ŚD. Utpaladeva further parts ways with his teacher in making reference to the *deśa*- and *kāla-krama*s, corresponding as they do with *mūrti* and *kriyā*, respectively, allowing thereby for the appearance of (real) temporal and spatial distinctions at the mundane level of existence. In doing so, he again follows the model of the grammarians, this being evident because a closely similar formulation to Utpaladeva's is found in Harivṛṣabha's *Vākyapadīyavṛtti* (VPVṛ), where two types of *vivarta* are described, one related to *mūrti*, the other to *kriyā*:[48]

mūrtikriyāvivartāv avidyāśaktipravṛttimātram. tau vidyātmani tattvānyatvābhyām anākhyeyau. etad dhy avidyāyā avidyātvam.

---

[47] Utpaladeva is of course equally the non-dualist as is his teacher, and he wishes his view of materiality to be contextualized by the fact that it pertains only to the apparent diversity of a subordinated, merely mundane or worldly, level of being. On the other hand, Somānanda nowhere deals with matters in this way, by distinguishing worldly from transcendent forms of action. He rather imagines all entities and beings equally to function in the same manner, as is evident in his mutual identification of Yajñadatta, Devadatta, and the *ghaṭa*. See NEMEC forthcoming for a further description of the nature of Śiva's action as the agent *par excellence*. Cf. NEMEC 2011, pp. 31-34 and 100-104. See also TORELLA 1994, p. xxvii.

[48] See VPVṛ ad VP 1.1, vol I, p. 9, ll. 1-3.

> Spatial (*mūrti*) and temporal (*kriyā*) manifestations are nothing but the functioning of the powers of nescience (*avidyā*). The two cannot be expressed as either identical with nor different from the one whose nature is *vidyā*. For, the fact of being nescience consists in just that. (Transl. an adaptation from Iyer's.)

Elsewhere, in the commentary of Helārāja on verse 14 of the *dravyasamuddeśa* (=VP 3.2.14), *kriyā* is associated with the power of time (*kālaśakti*), while *mūrti* is associated with the power of space (*dikśakti*):[49]

> *kālaśaktyavacchinno hi kriyāvivartaḥ dikśaktyavacchinnaś ca mūrtivivarta iti mūrtikriyāvivartarūpaṃ viśvaṃ pratipāditam.*

> For, the transformation of action (*kriyāvivarta*) is circumscribed by the power of time (*kālaśakti*), while the transformation of form (*mūrtivivarta*) is circumscribed by the power of space (*dikśakti*). Therefore, the universe (*viśva*) is taught to have the transformation of form and of action as its nature.

Of course, this offers a formulation that is very close to the one propounded by Utpaladeva and stands, I propose, as the model for what is stated in the ĪPK. Somānanda, on the other hand, never so much as utters the term *kālaśakti* (nor *dikśakti*) and nowhere mentions their relation to *kriyā* and *mūrti*, respectively; nor even does he anywhere offer *kriyā* and *mūrti* as a paired concept.[50] What is instead presented, as we have seen, is a single model for being, and for agency, one that renders the activity of the mundane (apparently material) water-pot identical both to that of the monadic agent – Devadatta or Yajñadatta – *and* to that of the divine agent, Śiva.

It is evident, then, that while Somānanda bluntly dealt with the idealist's challenge – that of explaining the apparent existence of apparently distinct, material entities –, Utpaladeva, following the VP and its commentaries, finessed the question: for, while he placed the *ātman*, conterminal with Śiva, at the top of his ontological hierarchy, he did not simply deny the existence of discrete, materi-

---

49 See Helārāja's commentary on VP 3.2.14 (in the *dravyasamuddeśa*), vol. III.1, p. 117, ll. 8-11.

50 Utpaladeva, in turn, nowhere in the ĪPK speaks of Somānanda's rather detailed treatment of the immaterial nature of the *functioning* of Śiva's powers (for more about which see NEMEC forthcoming). So, different approaches are here offered in treating the nature of physical, material entities, even if (I would reiterate) they are philosophically compatible and theologically consonant.

al entities (remembering here that by definition a *mūrti* is *asarvagataparimāṇa*, the very measure of a delimited entity), but rather subordinated and relativized them, rendering them merely mundane (yet nevertheless extant) phenomena – and (distant) derivatives of the *ātman*, the preeminent *dravya*, at that.

5. ABHINAVAGUPTA'S SYNTHESIS

Finally, I turn very briefly to Abhinavagupta's treatment of materiality, or more specifically to a single instance thereof, found in his ĪPV and ĪPVV as they comment on ĪPK 2.1.5 (which itself was reviewed above). First, the relevant passage of the ĪPV:[51]

> *padārthasya svaṃ rūpaṃ mūrtiḥ tasyā yat vaicitryaṃ vibhedaḥ tadyathā gṛham iti anyat svarūpaṃ prāṅgaṇam iti anyat vipaṇir iti anyad devakulam ity aparam udyānam ity anyad araṇyam iti taditarat; tasmād vaicitryād ābhāsyamānād deśarūpo dūrādūravitatatvāvitatatvādiḥ kramo bhagavatāvabhāsyate. yadā tu gāḍhapratyabhijñāprakāśabalāt tad evedaṃ hastasvarūpam iti pratipattau mūrter na bhedo 'tha cānyānyarūpatvaṃ bhāti tadaikasmin svarūpe yad anyat anyat rūpaṃ tad virodhavaśād asahabhavat kriyety ucyate. tasyā yat vaicitryaṃ parimitāparimitarūpatātmakaṃ tadekānusaṃdhānena phalasiddhyādinibandhanavaśād yathāruci carcitena nirbhāsayan kālarūpaṃ kramam eva bhāsayati.*

> Here the word "*mūrti*" means the body of the object; and *vaicitrya* means variety. Thus, by means of manifestation of the variety of external bodies such as house, courtyard, market, temple, garden and forest, each of which is different from the rest, the spatial successions such as distant and near, wide and narrow, etc., are made manifest by the Lord. But when, because of the strong recognition, the experience, "this is essentially the same hand," arises and though there is no essential change in the body, yet formal differences appear; then the variety of forms, which cannot coexist in the same body, because the forms are contrary to one another, is spoken of as action. He makes the temporal succession manifest, through manifestation of variety of forms, involved in action, limited or unlimited in their nature, as related to one, that is freely constructed in imagination, because the fruition, etc., of action are related to it. (Transl. Pandey.)[52]

---

[51] See ĪPV, vol. II, p. 13, ll. 9-p. 15, l. 3 (the same appears in PANDEY 1954, vol. II, p. 17, ll. 1-10).

[52] See also the translation of Isabelle Ratié, found at RATIÉ 2011, p. 202, n. 67.

Much is embedded in the present passage (including, e.g., the *vigraha* of *mūrtivaicitryatas*, found at ĪPK 2.1.5a), and Abhinavagupta's commentaries engage many concerns that lie beyond the scope of the present essay. They deal, for one, with the issue of *anusaṃdhāna*,[53] discussed also by Utpaladeva (though elsewhere), but not by Somānanda, who never uses the term; for another, Abhinavagupta here articulates, in a formulation that is to my knowledge unattested in the surviving writings of Utpaladeva, a sophisticated understanding of action (*kriyā*), envisioning it as depending on the manifestation of a marked recognition (*gāḍhapratyabhijñāprakāśabalāt*) of the identity of a single entity that appears, nevertheless, in distinguishable, nay contradictory, forms. Yet, apart from these notable flourishes, Abhinavagupta here offers what is ultimately a sophisticated reiteration of the ideas expressed in the passages of the ĪPK and ĪPKVṛ with which the present excerpt corresponds. In fact, Abhinavagupta's ĪPV ad 2.1.5 limits itself to an affirmation of the place of *mūrtivaicitrya* in the manifested universe, an affirmation that fully reflects the fact that Utpaladeva adopted the formulation of the VP and its commentaries.

The ĪPVV, too, reflects the same position, as well as the influence of the Grammarians.[54] Yet, it adds something to it, as well, and in noting as much I wish to indicate that the selected commentarial excerpts illustrate Abhinavagupta's synthetic method, his capacity fluidly to synchronize the sometimes differing (not to say contradictory) philosophical formulations found in the writings of his *paramaguru* and his *parameṣṭhiguru*, Utpaladeva and Somānanda. For, if one looks across the extensive commentary of the ĪPVV ad 2.1.5, one notices Abhinavagupta incorporate, subtly and

---

53 This concept is dealt with at length in, e.g., RATIÉ 2011, pp. 143-168, 184-212, 265-270, and *passim*.

54 See, e.g., ĪPVV ad ĪPK 2.1.5 (vol. III, p. 12, ll. 4-7 and 9-13 of the KSTS edition): *mūrtīnāṃ saṃvedyarūpāṇāṃ bhāvānāṃ yat vaicitryaṃ gṛhaprāṅgaṇavipaṇidevakulārāmāraṇyādibhedena, tato hetos tat vaicitryam ābhāsayan parameśvaro deśakramaṃ vaitatyāvaitatyātmakam avabhāsayati. ekapratyabhijñābalāt tu yat svarūpeṇābhinnaṃ hastādi... tasya yad anyānyadeśatvam anyānyadharmatvaṃ svarūpaikatām abādhamānaṃ – gacchati caitraḥ, pacyate phalam, – ityevaṃbhūtaṃ kriyāvaicitryaṃ, tasya nirbhāsanād hetor īśvaro virodham avirodhaṃ ca svātantryāt nirbhāsayan kālākhyaṃ kramam ekasya viruddharūpatayānucitam api avabhāsayatīti sūtrārthaḥ.*

without comment, the language found in the ŚD the ŚDVṛ describing the nature of a material entity or *mūrti*:[55]

... *na tv asarvagatadravyaparimāṇam iha mūrtiḥ kāṭhinyaṃ vety āśayaḥ.*

Here we find the material entity, the *mūrti*, described as it is in Somānanda's masterwork and in the ŚDVṛ, as *asarvagatadravyaparimāṇa* and as *kāṭhinya*, for the language here deployed precisely reflects the description of material entities found at ŚD 2.74cd-76 and the *Vṛtti* thereupon.

More generally, the spirit of the ĪPVV ad 2.1.5, when viewed in a more comprehensive manner, may be said to offer a rather thoroughgoing synthesis of the two ideas – of *mūrti* as being the product of nothing but consciousness itself – that is, as it being an entity entirely dependent on the *ātmadravya* as its basis or source – and of *mūrtis* as apparently physical entities that exist on a mundane level and serve as the very measure of what appears to be real physical extension.

To reiterate, the views are by no means incompatible; but they are distinguishable. And Somānanda nowhere shows any cognizance of, or interest in supporting, the position (articulated first in the ĪPK and ĪPKVṛ) that shows itself to be influenced by the writings of the VP and its commentaries, favoring instead the view that all that appears to be material is in fact nothing but consciousness. The point, then, is not merely to note that the ĪPVV explicitly engages the views found in both the ŚD and ŚDVṛ, on the one hand, and the ĪPK and ĪPKVṛ, on the other; it is further to suggest, albeit in the telegraphed form here offered, that to do so is a sort of hallmark of the longer of Abhinavagupta's two sub-commentaries. Whether so much reflects a practice of synthesis found in Utpaladeva's *Īśvarpratyabhijñāvivṛti* I cannot say, since the vast majority of this work is lost. Yet, the present offers, I submit, but one example of many acts of integration found in the longer of Abhinavagupta's two sub-commentaries.[56]

---

55 See ĪPVV ad ĪPK 2.1.5 (vol. III, p. 13, ll. 4-5). There is much else in the ĪPVV that refers to the formulations of the Nyāya-Vaiśeṣika, often in a manner that serves more fully to flesh out the accommodation by Utpaladeva of *mūrtis*, as conceived by the realists, at a subordinated ontological level. See, e.g., ĪPVV ad ĪPK 2.1.5, vol. III, p. 13, ll. 20ff.

56 One may also add that, from an emic perspective, a difference in perspective on the divine defines the differences of expression of the ŚD, on the one hand, and the ĪPK (and ĪPKVṛ), on the other. The former speaks the language of id-

6. CONCLUSION

The materials here reviewed evince a complex history of engagement by Pratyabhijñā authors with the realist *āstika* schools and the Vaiśeṣika in particular. They present on the one hand an instance of philosophical continuity, for while Somānanda's critique is in various places implicit or indirect, it is evident that he both formulated his theory of Śiva-as-consciousness with the measure of the Vaiśeṣika *padārtha*s in mind and that he likely modelled, in part at least, his conception of the *ātman* on the Vaiśeṣika *dravya* of the same name. Precisely the same is evident in the ĪPK (and especially the ĪPKVṛ) and is confirmed in the corresponding passages of the ĪPV and ĪPVV. We have, then, a continuity of approach in dealing with realist ontology from roughly 900-950 C.E. (when Somānanda flourished) to Abhinavagupta's day (c. 975-1025 C.E.).

On the other hand, the texts evince a real development in the Pratyabhijñā treatment of the basic question to hand –namely, the reality or otherwise of apparently discrete, material entities. This is evident first and foremost in the form of Utpaladeva's reorientation of the Pratyabhijñā treatment of material entities (*mūrti*s), which sets aside the more extreme implications of Somānanda's vociferous, even truculent, denial of their very existence – a position that might aptly be described as a sort of naïve idealism –, opting instead for a moderated position admitting of a worldly or relative reality of *mūrti*s while borrowing substantially from the VP and its commentaries in formulating such a view. As is to be expected, Abhinavagupta offers a scholastic, inclusive account of the matter to hand, and it is one that synchronizes the arguments of his *parama-* and *parameṣṭhi-guru*s while serving more clearly to de-

entification with Śiva from the first lines, while the latter speaks of Utpala "somehow" coming to recognize his identity with the divine. (Compare ŚD 1.1, and 1.2, with ĪPK 1.1.1.) Utpala, in other words, shows a perspective of climbing to the transcendent, Somānanda of standing within it, or, perhaps, of being aware of it from the first. Abhinavagupta moves fluidly between such positions. Finally, I note that it is possible that Utpaladeva's perspective is implicitly exemplified in the patterned organization of the *āhnika*s of the ĪPK, which ascend, as it were, toward oneness: the four *adhikāra*s of the ĪPK show a regular pattern of successively reducing the number of *āhnika*s found in each by half: there are 8 *āhnika*s in the first *adhikāra*, four in the second, two in the third, and a single *āhnika* in the last *adhikāra*. One may speculate that so much is symbolic of the movement toward unity for which Utpaladeva promises to offer assistance in ĪPK 1.1.1.

fine and elaborate upon Utpaladeva's account, exhibiting a significant fidelity to that author's philosophical formulations along the way. All of this is accomplished in a manner that exhibits the possibility of philosophical innovation in the context of a certain continuity of tradition, even, it must be noted, where Utpaladeva adopts the thinking of the very opponents against whom Somānanda argues most vociferously, Bhartṛhari and the grammarians.

It should come as no great surprise that a competing Hindu school that held currency in the Kashmir Valley at the time of the flourishing of the Pratyabhijñā held the attention of these authors. Indeed, that the authors of the Pratyabhijñā would adopt elements of Nyāya-Vaiśeṣika ontology for their own purposes, despite the fact that these opponents were both philosophical realists and dualists, involves them in perhaps no greater a philosophical accommodation than what was needed to incorporate major elements of the idealist, but *nāstika*, epistemology of the Vijñānavāda, as well it is known they did (Utpaladeva and Abhinavagupta in particular). The dualism of the former is rejected and the ontology modified, adapted, while the theory of agency (one involving the denial of the existence of the *ātman*) of the latter is rejected while the epistemology is modified, adapted, to the theistic and Self-affirming position of the Śaivas. Vaiśeṣika ontological categories, moreover, were similarly of concern to other idealists, such as Śaṅkara. The present study thus may stand as but one exemplar not only of the complex patterns of influence among the various śāstric schools of learning in premodern South Asia, but also of the extensive work that remains to be completed in the course of developing a thoroughgoing intellectual history of Kashmir in and around the time of Abhinavagupta.

REFERENCES

A
[*Aṣṭādhyāyī*] See KāVṛ

AKLUJKAR 1969-1970
A. Aklujkar, "Candrānanda's Date," *Journal of the Oriental Institute* (Baroda) 19(4), 1969-1970, pp. 340-341

Brahmasūtrabhāṣya
Brahmasūtrabhāṣya, ed. W.L. Shāstrī Pansīkar, Bombay: Nirnaya Sagar Press, 1915

CHATURVEDI 1986
R. Chaturvedi, *The Śivadṛṣṭi of Śri Somānanda Nātha, with the Vṛtti of Śri Utpaladeva: Edited with the Saṅskrita Commentary and Hindi Translation*, Varanasi: Varanaseya Sanskrit Sansthan, 1986

FRANCO 1987
E. Franco, *Perception, Knowledge and Disbelief: A Study of Jayaśrī's Scepticism*, Stuttgart: Franz Steiner Verlag, 1987

HALBFASS 1992
W. Halbfass, *On Being and What There Is: Classical Vaiśeṣika and the History of Indian Ontology*, New York: SUNY Press, 1992

ĪPK
[*Īśvarapratyabhijñākārikā*] See TORELLA 1994

ĪPKVṛ
[*Īśvarapratyabhijñākārikāvṛtti*] See TORELLA 1994

ĪPV
The Īśvarapratyabhijñā of Utpaladeva with the Vimarśinī by Abhinavagupta, ed. M.K. Shāstrī, Bombay: Nirnaya Sagar Press, Kashmir Series of Texts and Studies 22 and 23, 1918-1921

ĪPVV
The Īśvarapratyabhijñā Vivṛtivimarśinī by Abhinavagupta, ed. M.K. Shāstrī, 3 vols., Bombay: Nirnaya Sagar Press, Kashmir Series of Texts and Studies 60, 62 and 65, 1938, 1941, and 1943

ISAACSON 1995
H. Isaacson, "Materials for the Study of the Vaiśeṣika System," Ph.D. Dissertation, Leiden University, 1995

IYER 1969
K.A.S. Iyer, *Bhartṛhari: A Study of the Vākyapadīya in Light of the Ancient Commentaries*, Poona: Deccan College Postgraduate and Research Institute, [1969] 1992

KāVṛ
The Kāśikāvṛtti of Vāmana-Jayāditya, with the Nyāsa or Pañcikā of Jinendrabuddhipāda and the Padamañjarī of Haradatta Miśra, ed. Swami D. Shastri and Pt. K. Shukla, 6 vols., Varanasi: Pracya Bharati Prakashan, Prachya Bharati Series 2-7, 1965

MBh
Vyākaraṇa-mahābhāṣya of Patañjali with the Commentary Bhāṣyapradīpa of Kayaṭa Upādhyāya and the Supercommentary Bhāṣyapradīpoddyota of Nāgeśa Bhaṭṭa, ed. Pt. D. Sharma, 6 vols, repr., Delhi: Chaukhamba Sanskrit Pratishthan, Vrajajivan Prachyabharati Granthamala 23, 1988

McCREA 2000
L. McCrea, "The Hierarchical Organization of Language in Mīmāṃsā Interpretive Theory," *Journal of Indian Philosophy* 28(5-6), 2000, pp. 429-459

MS
[*Mīmāṃsāsūtra*, in] *Mīmāṃsādarśana*, ed. K.V. Abhyankar and J.A. Joshi, 7 vols., Trivandrum: Ānandāśrama Sanskrit Series 97, 1970-1976

NEMEC 2012
J. Nemec, "The Two Pratyabhijñā Theories of Error," *Journal of Indian Philosophy* 40(2), 2012, pp. 225-257

NEMEC 2014
"The Evidence for Somānanda's Pantheism," *Journal of Indian Philosophy* 42(1), 2014, pp. 99-114

NEMEC forthcoming
J. Nemec, "The Body and Consciousness in Early Pratyabhijñā Philosophy: *amurtatva* in Somānanda's *Śivadṛṣṭi*"

NS
Nyāyadarśanam, with Vātsyāyana's Bhāṣya, Uddyotakara's Vārttika, Vācaspati Miśra's Tātparyaṭīkā & Viśvanatha's Vṛtti, ed. T. Nyaya-Tarkatirtha and A. Tarkatirtha, [1936-1944] 2nd ed., New Delhi: Munshiram Manoharlal, 1985

NSBh
[*Nyāyasūtrabhāṣya*] See NS

PANDEY 1954
K.C. Pandey, *Bhāskarī. An English Translation of the Īśvara Pratyabhijñā Vimarśinī in the Light of the Bhāskarī with an Outline of the History of Śaiva Philosophy*, 3 vols., Lucknow: Princess of Wales Saraswati Bhavana Texts 84, 1954

PDhSaṃ
[*Padārthadharmasaṃgraha*] *Praśastapādabhasya with the Commentary Nyāyakandalī of Śrīdharabhaṭṭa*, ed. and transl. (Hindi) Śrīdurgādharajhā Śarma, Varanasi: Vidya Mandir Press, Gaṅgānātha-Jhā-Granthamālā 1, 1963

POTTER 1977
K.H. Potter (ed.), *Encyclopedia of Indian Philosophies, vol. II. Indian Metaphysics and Epistemology: The Tradition of Nyāya-Vaiśeṣika up to Gaṅgeśa*, Princeton: Princeton University Press, 1977

Pradīpa
See MBh

RATIÉ 2011
I. Ratié, *Le Soi et l'Autre: Identité, différence et altérité dans la philosophie de la Pratyabhijñā*, Leiden-Boston: Brill, Jerusalem Studies in Religion and Culture 13, 2011

ŚD
[*Śivadṛṣṭi* 1-3] The *Ubiquitous Śiva: Somānanda's Śivadṛṣṭi and His Tantric Interlocutors*, ed. and transl. J. Nemec, New York: Oxford University Press, 2011

ŚD (KSTS ed.)
The Śivadṛṣṭi of Somānandanātha with the Vṛtti by Utpaladeva, ed. M.K. Shastri, Pune: Aryabhushan Press, Kashmir Series of Texts and Studies 54, 1934

ŚDVṛ
[*Śivadṛṣṭivṛtti*] See ŚD

THIBAUT 1890-1896
G. Thibaut, *The Vedāntasūtras, with the Shankara-bhasya*, Oxford: Oxford University Press, Sacred Books of the East Series 34 and 38, 1890-1896

TORELLA 1994
R. Torella, *The Īśvarapratyabhijñākārikā of Utpaladeva with the Author's Vṛtti: Critical Edition and Annotated Translation*, Rome: IsMEO, 1994

TORELLA 2008
R. Torella, "From an Adversary to the Main Ally: The Place of Bhartṛhari in the Kashmirian Śaiva Advaita," in M. Kaul and A. Aklujkar (eds.), *The Linguistic Traditions of Kashmir: Essays in Memory of Pandit Dinanath Yaksha*, Delhi: D.K. Printworld, 2008, pp. 508-524

TV
[*Tantravārttika*, in] *Mīmāṃsādarśana*, ed. K.V. Abhyankar and J.A. Joshi, 7 vols., Trivandrum: Ānandāśrama Sanskrit Series 97, 1970-1976

VP, vol. I
Vākyapadīya of Bhartṛhari with the Commentaries Vṛtti and Paddhati of Vṛṣabhadeva, Kāṇḍa I, ed. K.A.S. Iyer, Pune: Deccan College, Deccan College Monograph Series 32, 1966

VP, vol. III.1
Vākyapadīya with the Commentary of Helārāja, Kāṇḍa III, Part 1, ed. K.A.S. Iyer, Pune: Deccan College, 1963

VPVṛ
[*Vākyapadīyavṛtti*] See VP 1

VS
The Vaiśeṣikasūtra of Kaṇāda with the Commentary of Candrānanda, ed. Muni Śrī Jambuvijayaji, Baroda: Baroda Oriental Institute, Gaekwad Oriental Series 136, 1961

VSVṛ
[*Vaiśeṣikasūtravṛtti*] See VS

YOSHIMIZU 2008
K. Yoshimizu, "The intention of Expression (*vivakṣā*), the Expounding (*vyākhyā*) of a text, and the Authorlessness of the Veda," *Zeitschrift der Deutschen Morgenländischen Gesellschaft* 158, 2008, pp. 51-71

YS
[*Yogasūtra*] *Sāṃkhyadarśana or Yogadarśana of Patañjali with the Scholium of Vyāsa and the Commentaries Tattva Vaiśāradī, Pātañjala Rahasya, Yogavārttika and Bhāsvatī of Vācaspati Miśra, Rāghavānanda Sarasvatī, Vijñāna Bhikṣu and Hariharānandāraṇya*, ed. G.D. Śāstrī, [1935] 2nd ed., Varanasi: Chaukhambha Sanskrit Sansthan, The Kashi Sanskrit Series 110, 1989

Some Hitherto Unknown Fragments of Utpaladeva's *Vivṛti* (III): On Memory and Error*

ISABELLE RATIÉ

FRAGMENTS OF UTPALADEVA'S *VIVṚTI* IN MARGINAL ANNOTATIONS

As is now well known, Utpaladeva's detailed commentary (the *Vivṛti* or *Ṭīkā*) on his own Pratyabhijñā treatise (the *Īśvarapratyabhijñākārikā*s, hereafter ĪPK) was certainly the most important philosophical text of the Pratyabhijñā corpus;[1] yet unfortunately, to date we only have access to a few fragments of this work. A particularly lengthy one was edited and translated by Raffaele Torella[2] on the basis of a unique, very incomplete manuscript[3] now preserved in the National Archives of India (Delhi). But more *Vivṛti* fragments have recently come to light. The latter do not come, however, from any newly discovered *Vivṛti* manuscript, but from annotations written in the margins of manuscripts containing other Pratyabhijñā texts.[4] The present article is the continuation of a series of papers devoted to the edition, translation and explanation of

---

* I am very grateful to Vincent Eltschinger and Eli Franco for reading a previous version of this essay and making insightful remarks.

1 See TORELLA 2014.

2 See TORELLA 1988, 2007a, 2007b, 2007c, 2007d and 2012. The following pages owe much to these remarkable studies.

3 It covers 13 verses out of the 190 that constitute the ĪPK.

4 For a diplomatic edition of a few brief fragments found in a manuscript of Utpaladeva's short commentary (*Vṛtti*) see KAWAJIRI 2015. For an edition, translation and analysis of lengthier fragments found in the margins of manuscripts containing Abhinavagupta's *Īśvarapratyabhijñāvimarśinī* (hereafter ĪPV), see RATIÉ 2016 and RATIÉ forthcoming a. On the recent discovery of what could be the lengthiest *Vivṛti* fragment known to date in the margins of a manuscript of Abhinavagupta's *Īśvarapratyabhijñāvivṛtivimarśinī* (hereafter ĪPVV), see RATIÉ forthcoming c.

fragments found in the margins of manuscripts containing Abhinavagupta's commentaries on the Pratyabhijñā treatise.[5] So far I have dealt with fragments commenting on ĪPK 1.5.4-9 and 1.8.10-11, that is, with passages that originally came after the part of the text edited by Raffaele Torella (which covers ĪPK 1.3.6 to ĪPK 1.5.3). This paper deals with a fragment of Utpaladeva's *Vivṛti* on ĪPK 1.3.5 that came immediately before the beginning of the *Vivṛti* codex unicus in its current state.

THE CONTEXT OF THE PRESENT FRAGMENT AND THE GOAL OF UTPALADEVA'S ARGUMENT

In the previous verses, Utpaladeva has endeavoured to show that memory can be satisfactorily explained only provided that we accept the existence of the Self (*ātman*), that is, an enduring conscious substance that ensures our continuous existence as sentient entities despite the constant changes undergone by our body and mind.[6]

The soundness of this argument is contested by a Buddhist opponent who sees consciousness as a series of discrete, purely momentary events rather than as a unitary, lasting entity. This Buddhist interlocutor claims that memories can be accounted for even if there is no such thing as an *ātman*. According to him, memories arise through a causal mechanism of residual traces (*saṃskāra*) or imprints (*vāsanā*). Such traces, left by past experiences, remain latent in the conscious stream until their "awakening" (*prabodha*) is triggered by the perception of an object related to the one perceived in the past (we remember seeing a pot yesterday if this memory is occasioned for instance by the sight of a similar pot). And this imprint theory does not necessarily lead to acknowledging the existence of a permanent substrate (the Self) in which the imprints would need to be stored, since we can understand the conscious stream as made of purely momentary events that are all different from each other but also causally linked to each other. A cognition X bearing a certain latent trace exists for a single moment, but

5 On the manuscripts bearing these marginal annotations and the difficulties involved in their edition see RATIÉ 2016 and RATIÉ forthcoming c.

6 The following lines only provide a very sketchy outline of Utpaladeva's position in the Indian debate over the Self's existence and role in memory (*smṛti*). For detailed accounts of this issue see RATIÉ 2006, TORELLA 2007b, RATIÉ 2011 (Chapters 1-4) and RATIÉ forthcoming b.

within that moment it contributes to the production of a momentary cognition Y. This cognition Y comes to exist a moment later, bears a latent trace similar to that of X because its nature has been causally determined to contain such a trace by X, and contributes to the production of a cognition Z – and so on.

Now, Utpaladeva has just shown that this well-known Buddhist explanation of memory makes no sense. According to him, the imprint theory might very well account for the fact that the remembered object bears some resemblance to the object that was perceived in the past (this likeness is insured by the residual trace); but it cannot explain the very nature of memories. For memories are not just cognitions of an object: what differentiates them from perceptions, imaginations, etc., is the fact that when remembering, we are aware not only of an object, but also of having perceived that object in the past. Remembering a pot is not just being aware of a pot, but rather, being aware of a pot *as something that we saw yesterday*. Memories involve the subjective awareness that the remembered object has already been experienced; but how can the Buddhist account for this? When remembering, we do not simply take our own past experience as the object of our cognition, since the object of our cognition is nothing but the object that we remember – that is, the pot. So how are we aware not only of the pot, but also *of the fact that we did perceive the pot in the past*?

According to Utpaladeva's Buddhist opponent, we are not aware of our own perceptions as we are aware of objects such as pots: we do not grasp cognitions as we grasp objects in perception, through a separate cognitive act. We become aware of our own consciousness in a much more immediate way, since any cognitive event involves a self-awareness (*svasaṃvedana*) through which we instantly know that we know a certain object without having to posit our own knowledge as a distinct entity to be known. And since the Buddhist must acknowledge that the awareness of our past experience cannot simply be the *object* of our memory, according to Utpaladeva, he can only explain this awareness if he concedes that we are aware of having experienced the object in the past through mere self-awareness. But by accepting such an explanation he seals his fate. For if we are aware of having previously perceived something through mere self-awareness, it must be the *same* lasting consciousness that experienced the object in the past and remembers it now: memory is nothing but the self-awareness of an enduring sentient entity that is aware of itself as having perceived something in the past. In other words, if the Buddhist is willing to give a rational account of memory, he must acknowledge the existence of the Self.

The Buddhist tries to escape the uncomfortable position in which the Śaiva has just put him by arguing that memories are not really about objects that have been previously perceived. They only *seem* to faithfully recall such things to consciousness because instead of being, as perception, the immediate experience of a given, they build or construct their object (which is absent since it belongs to the past) by shaping or determining (and thus distorting) the past perception and its objective content. Because memories consist in such a mental elaboration or determination (*avasāya*, *adhyavasāya*), they are in essence errors (*bhrānti*, *bhrama*).[7]

Utpaladeva replies that if such is the case, then the very essence of memory – which is traditionally defined as what prevents us from being entirely deprived of what we perceived before –[8] is completely lost. And this is a consequence that the Buddhist cannot afford, since he himself considers that only memory enables us to know which objects should be sought or shunned. Thus according to Dharmakīrti, the establishment (*vyavasthā*, *vyavasthiti*) of ob-

---

7 See ĪPK 1.3.3: *athātadviṣayatve 'pi smṛtes tadavasāyataḥ* | *dṛṣṭālambanatā bhrāntyā tad etad asamañjasam* ||. "[– The Buddhist:] But even though memory does not [really] have as its object the [past perception and its object], it erroneously (*bhrāntyā*) [appears] to have as its objective support the [previously] perceived [object], because [memory consists in] a determination (*avasāya*) of the [past perception and its object. – The Śaiva:] This [thesis of yours] is not consistent." Cf. ĪPV, vol. I, p. 98: *na tad darśanaṃ nāpi tadviṣayaḥ smṛter viṣayaḥ, tathāpi tūbhayam adhyavasīyate, bhramarūpatayā smṛteḥ*. "The object of memory is neither the [past] perception nor the object of that [past perception]; rather, both are [merely] determined [and not grasped as they really are], since memory consists in an error."

8 The Śaivas thus quote the definition of memory in *Yogasūtra* 1.11: *anubhūtaviṣayāsampramoṣaḥ smṛtiḥ*. "Memory is not being deprived of the object [previously] experienced." See TORELLA 2007b, p. 540, and RATIÉ 2011, pp. 132-133. In fact the term *sampramoṣa* was borrowed from a Buddhist context where it simply meant "forgetfulness" (see WUJASTYK forthcoming) and it is very likely that the *sūtra*'s original meaning was rather something along these lines: "Memory is not forgetting the [previously] experienced object." Nonetheless, the Śaivas (as well as other rather late authors such as Śaṅkara or Vācaspatimiśra) understand the term as meaning "taking away" or "stealing" (*apahāra*, *steya*), an interpretation according to which the *sūtra* basically means that memory consists in not being robbed or deprived of one's previous experiences.

jects, that is, our ability to ascertain that something exists as an object capable of bringing about a specific, desirable or undesirable effect, entirely rests on memory, so that all our wordly activities are grounded in our capacity to remember.[9] Besides, Utpaladeva remarks that considering memory as mistaken in essence is at odds with the Buddhist's contention that memory is based on residual traces:[10] the very purpose of this explanation is to account for memory's faithfulness,[11] so that doubting this faithfulness betrays a major inconsistency in the Buddhist's discourse.

Utpaladeva then turns to the notion of determination and shows that if memory is an error consisting in such a determination, it cannot tell us anything regarding the object (it is perfectly mute, *tūṣṇīka*,[12] with respect to that object), and as a consequence it cannot help us deal with objects in our everyday lives.

Admittedly, in the Buddhist perspective, an erroneous cognition is not entirely mute or unconscious. As any cognition, it is imme-

---

9 See e.g. *Pramāṇaviniścaya* (hereafter PVin) 1. 18: *taddṛṣṭāv eva dṛṣṭeṣu saṃvitsāmarthyabhāvinaḥ | smaraṇād abhilāṣeṇa vyavahāraḥ pravartate ||*. "Wordly activity (*vyavahāra*) occurs due to the desire of [things] that have been [previously] perceived; [this desire in turn arises] thanks to the memory [of these things] that takes place only once they have been perceived, thanks to the power [i.e. the imprint left by a former perceptual] cognition." On this passage see KELLNER 2001, p. 504 and ELTSCHINGER AND RATIÉ 2013, pp. 180-181.

10 See ĪPV, vol. I, p. 100: *na ca tadaprakāśane saṃskārajatvena kiṃcit kṛtyam. tad dhi sādṛśyaṃ labdhum avalambyate. na cānubhavena viṣayaprakāśanātmanā smṛtyabhidhānāyā bhrānteḥ kiṃcid api sādṛśyam asti, sarvathā viṣayam aspṛśyantyāḥ.* "And if[, as the Buddhist contends,] there is no manifestation of the [previously perceived object in memory, the Buddhist's assumption] that [memory] arises from a residual trace is perfectly useless! For [the Buddhist] clings to this [theory] so as to explain the similarity [of the remembered object with the previously perceived object]. But there is no similarity whatsoever between the [past] experience – which consists in the manifestation of the object – and the error that[, according to the Buddhist, we] call memory, since [an error can] have no contact at all with a [real] object."

11 See ĪPK 1.3.4: *smṛtitaiva kathaṃ tāvad bhrānteś cārthasthitiḥ katham | pūrvānubhavasaṃskārāpekṣā ca kim itīṣyate ||*. "To begin with, how could the very essence of memory [be preserved then]? And how could the object be established [in our worldly activities] thanks to an error? And [if memory is nothing but an error,] why does [the Buddhist] consider that [memory] depends on a residual trace [left] by some previous experience?" On my understanding of *tāvat* here, which follows Utpaladeva's and Abhinavagupta's commentaries, see RATIÉ 2011, p. 131, n. 48.

12 ĪPV, vol. I, p. 102; ĪPVV, vol. I, p. 250.

diately aware of itself (*svasaṃvedana*), so that at least it reveals its own conscious nature. Besides, as an erroneous cognition, it manifests what is in fact a mere aspect of itself (*svākāra*) as if it were an external object – so even an error can be said to be conscious both of itself and of its subjective aspect wrongly apprehended as an object.[13] For example, when we mistake mother-of-pearl for a piece of silver, our determination of mother-of-pearl as being silver involves the awareness of silver (which is in fact an internal aspect of our own consciousness wrongly considered as existing outside of us) as well as the awareness that we are conscious of silver (i.e. the self-awareness that characterizes any cognition). So the Buddhist might argue that although memory is in essence an error, it enables us to establish the objects of our daily activities, because contrary to what the Śaivas claim, even an error is not entirely unconscious (*jaḍa*) and can tell us something about reality.

To this objection, Utpaladeva replies that the erroneous cognition of mother-of-pearl mistaken for silver tells us absolutely nothing of the real object erroneously determined as silver: it is perfectly "mute" as regards the mother-of-pearl, it includes no awareness whatsoever of it. And if all memories amount to erroneous cognitions, they are in the same way incapable of helping us establish the existence and nature of the objects around us.

This Śaiva line of argument is summed up in ĪPK 1.3.5:

> And if the determination (*avasāya*) [in which memory supposedly consists] is an error, the establishment of the object cannot result from this [determination], which is unconscious [with respect to the real object; but even] if [one objects that this determination] is not unconscious [in all respects, then] the establishment of the object cannot result from the

---

[13] See e.g. ĪPV, vol. I, pp. 102-103: *atha tu taṃ avasāyarūpaṃ svasaṃvedanāṃśaṃ svākāraṃ vāvalambyājaḍatvam asyāḥ, evam apy ajāḍye nijaṃ svasaṃvedanam ullekhaś ca svākāra itīyaty eṣā pariniṣṭhitā smṛtiḥ.* "But [if the Buddhist replies that] the [memory cognition] is conscious with respect to what consists in determination [itself, that is], with respect to the part [of determination] that is aware of itself or the subjective aspect [of determination that is mistaken for an external object]; even so, [or, as Utpaladeva puts it in the verse, even] if [the Buddhist objects that in his system determination] 'is not unconscious,' this memory is confined to this only: its own self-awareness, and the representation [of itself] that is an aspect of itself [mistaken for an external object]."

[conscious part of determination,] which is confined to itself and the representation[14] [of itself as the external object].[15]

The *Vivṛti* fragment begins with an allusion to two theories of error that are traditionally regarded as Buddhist, namely the *asatkhyātivāda* and the *ātmakhyātivāda*, often respectively ascribed to Mādhyamikas and Vijñānavādins.[16] According to the first theory, in error consciousness manifests something nonexistent (*asat*), whereas according to the second, it manifests itself (*ātman*). Utpaladeva does not take the trouble of examining the first theory here. The reason for this is probably that if the Buddhist opponent adopts the *asatkhyātivāda*, he must admit that the remembered object is simply nonexistent,[17] which (at least in the Śaivas' eyes) renders null and void his claim that we constantly have recourse to memory so as to establish the existence and causal efficacy of currently existing wordly objects. The fragment therefore focuses on the Buddhist *ātmakhyātivāda*, that is, on the thesis that when we mistake a piece of mother-of-pearl for silver, silver is not a mere nonbeing, but rather, a subjective aspect (*svākāra*) of consciousness that consciousness mistakes for an objective entity existing outside of itself.

---

14 See ĪPVV, vol. I, p. 242: *nijollekha iti svātmollekha iti sūtravṛttyor dvandvasamāsaḥ.* "*nijollekha* means[, as specified in the *Vṛtti*,] 'itself and the representation'; in both the verse and the *Vṛtti*, it is a *dvandva* compound."

15 *bhrāntitve cāvasāyasya na jaḍād viṣayasthitiḥ | tato 'jāḍye nijollekhaniṣṭhān nārthasthitis tataḥ* ||. On Abhinavagupta's commentaries on this verse see RATIÉ 2011, pp. 130-142. Cf. *Vṛtti*, p. 13: *adhyavasāya eva bhrāntyā viṣayavyavasthāpako na tu svasaṃvit, sa ca jaḍaḥ katham arthavyavasthāyā hetuḥ. cidrūpo 'py atītārthamātram ābhāsayed abāhyasvātmollekhamātraprakāśo vā na taddhetuḥ.* "It is determination that[, according to you Buddhists, must] erroneously establish objects, and not self-awareness. And [since] this [determination] is unconscious [with respect to the object,] how could it be the cause of [our] establishing objects? Even [if you consider it as] having a conscious nature, [as a memory] it may only manifest the past object [that no longer exists according to you, and not the existing external object]; or it is the manifestation of a purely internal [reality, i.e.] itself and a representation [of an aspect of itself as being the object; so] it [can]not be the cause that [establishes the objects of our daily activities]." On this passage see TORELLA 1994, p. 102.

16 On these see e.g. BHATT 1962, pp. 98-101, SCHMITHAUSEN 1965, pp. 121-125 and MATILAL 1986, pp. 183-190. In fact a form of *asatkhyātivāda* was propounded in Advaita Vedānta too (see SCHMITHAUSEN 1965, pp. 234-239), but this is irrelevant here: Utpaladeva is merely mentioning his Buddhist opponent's two options when defining error.

17 See e.g. ĪPVV, vol. I, p. 236, quoted below, n. 58.

As emphasized by Utpaladeva in the fragment, this theory is based on the principle that error cannot consist in the *perception* of something as being different from what it really is.[18] According to the Buddhist this is impossible because perception, which immediately manifests a given, cannot distort what it manifests: faithful to Dignāga's classical dichotomy between perception and concept, Utpaladeva's opponent claims that only conceptual cognitions can be erroneous (*bhrānta*). And for this Buddhist this is true even in the case of so-called perceptual errors: even when, due to some eye disease, we *see* two moons instead of one, the error does not lie in the phenomenon of the double moon (since we are indeed aware of the double moon, which is immediately manifest to us and therefore really exists as a conscious manifestation). The mistake rather lies in the conceptual process through which we *judge* that this manifestation exists outside of us instead of being a mere internal aspect of our consciousness. It is this "determination as being external" (*bāhyatāvasāya*) that constitutes error. And that this is the very essence of error is shown by the fact that somebody afflicted with an eye disease ceases to be mistaken not when (s)he no longer *sees* the double moon, but rather, when (s)he, reflecting on his/her condition, understands that the double moon has no external existence.[19] This point was obviously defended at length by the Buddhist Vijñānavādin Śaṅkaranandana,[20] whom Abhinavagupta repeatedly mentions in the ĪPVV while explaining this *Vivṛti* passage.[21]

---

[18] This criticism of the thesis that error might be a distorted perception (*anyathāpratīti*) might be directed against the Naiyāyikas' *anyathākhyātivāda*. According to the latter, in error we do not just conceptually construct an object that would be either nonexistent or a mere internal aspect of consciousness; rather, we *perceive* that object, which is real and belongs to the external world, although we do not perceive it as it really is, that is, in the place and time where it rightly belongs. On *anyathākhyātivāda* see e.g. MATILAL 1986, pp. 201-208. Note that the Bhāṭṭa Mīmāṃsakas' theory (often designated as a *viparītakhyātivāda*) is very close (see e.g. BHATT 1962, pp. 96-98) and that Maṇḍanamiśra defends a version of the *anyathākhyātivāda* (see SCHMITHAUSEN 1965, pp. 100-137).

[19] Cf. Abhinavagupta's commentary quoted below, n. 65.

[20] On Śaṅkaranandana's commitment to the Vijñānavāda see ELTSCHINGER 2015 and Lawrence McCrea's contribution to the present volume.

[21] See below, n. 66.

As the rest of the fragment makes clear, this is not Utpaladeva's own theory regarding error,[22] and the whole point of thus expounding the Buddhist position is to show that given the way the Vijñānavādin understands error, if he defines memories as errors, he ends up contradicting his own principles. Utpaladeva thus quotes Dharmakīrti (and this is a particularly interesting aspect of this fragment, since verbatim quotations are quite rare in the *Vivṛti* passages known to date)[23] to the effect that only consciousness can es-

---

22 See the translation below and n. 66. As for the theory of error defended by Utpaladeva and Abhinavagupta, see RASTOGI 1986 and NEMEC 2012, although the findings of these studies are somewhat debatable. This is the case in particular of the main thesis in NEMEC 2012, namely the idea that Abhinavagupta introduced the *apūrṇakhyāti* theory so as to unify two incompatible theories developed in two distinct works by Utpaladeva (i.e. his commentary on Somānanda's *Śivadṛṣṭi* and his Pratyabhijñā treatise). It seems to me that the hypothesis, presented as a fact, lacks textual support and is actually very unlikely, because (1), we do not possess the greater part of Utpaladeva's *Vivṛti* (where Utpaladeva may well have expounded and united the various aspects of his doctrine regarding error); (2), I cannot think of any other conceptual gap of this magnitude in Utpaladeva's otherwise so tightly organized system; (3), Abhinavagupta's developments on *apūrṇakhyāti* occur precisely in the context of an explanation of the *Vivṛti*, and comparisons between known fragments of the *Vivṛti* and the corresponding ĪPVV passages have shown that ideas which might be considered at first sight as innovations on Abhinavagupta's part are in fact already found in Utpaladeva's magnum opus (see TORELLA 1994, p. xliii and RATIÉ 2016, p. 222). Besides, one should also be wary of assuming that it was a mere coincidence if the Śaivas used the term *akhyāti* that traditionally designates the Prābhākaras' definition of error (on this "apparent similarity of names" see RASTOGI 1986, p. 4; cf. NEMEC 2012, p. 241, who considers that "despite the similarity in nomenclature," Utpaladeva had "apparently no intention of referring explicitly" to Prabhākara's theory). The Śaiva nondualists demonstrably had in-depth knowledge not only of the Bhāṭṭa Mīmāṃsaka literature but also of the Prābhākara tradition (see RATIÉ 2011, pp. 326-337; note also that Abhinavagupta explicitly mentions the Prābhākaras in the ĪPVV: see e.g. vol. I, pp. 219-220), and I can see no good reason allowing to consider that the use of such a specific and well-known terminology is purely coincidental, especially since Abhinavagupta clearly alludes to the Prābhākaras' peculiar definition of error in the ĪPVV (see e.g. vol. III, p. 154 on *smṛtitvākhyāti*).

23 Apart from the quotation of a Śaiva source that Abhinavagupta identifies as two (now lost) commentaries on the *Śivasūtra*s by Bhaṭṭa Kallaṭa (ĪPVV, vol. II, p. 30, see TORELLA 2007b, n. 112, p. 561), the only quotations known so far in the *Vivṛti* were *Bhagavadgītā* 15.15 (in fact quoted in the *Vṛtti* on ĪPK 1.3.7 but partially repeated in the *Vivṛti* ad loc., see TORELLA 2007a, p. 480), *Bhagavadgītā* 7.12 (see TORELLA 2007d, p. 928) and the PVin (see ibid., p. 937).

tablish the existence of an object. But if memory is a mere error, according to the *ātmakhyātivāda* it is only conscious of itself and of its own internal appearance in the form of an object, so that it can tell us nothing of external reality. The conclusion (which remains implicit in the fragment) is that our ability to remember, which makes all our worldly activities possible, would remain inexplicable if there were no enduring Self.

THE *VIVṚTI* FRAGMENT ON ĪPK 1.3.5: TEXT[24]

[§ A][25] ***asato*** *vātmano vā*[26] *prathamānasyānyathā* ***sattvenārthatvena*** *vā*[27] *pratītir* ***bhramaḥ***. ***na ca***[28] *niyatākārasya prathamānasyānyathāpratītiḥ*[29] *sambhavatīti prathamānarūpātiviparītāvasāya****pratītyantaram*** *eva bhrāntaṃ vaktavyam.* ***tac ca*** *vikalparūpam eva, nirvikalpakasyābhāsamātraniṣṭhatvād aparārthapātitvam ayuktam.* ***vikalpanātmanas tv***[30] *avabhāsena*[31] *saha vikalpyaikīkāriṇaḥ parā-*

[24] I have taken the liberty of standardizing the *sandhi* and spellings; the words quoted in Abhinavagupta's ĪPVV are underlined and in bold. See the Appendix for the manuscripts' references.

[25] § A is found in S2 (folio 14b, top margin), S3 (folio 23a, bottom and right margins), S7 (folio 15b, bottom margin), S9 (folio 29a, bottom margin) and J[R] (folio 50b, bottom margin). It is found neither in SOAS nor in D2 (which are now known to bear marginal annotations containing *Vivṛti* fragments: see RATIÉ 2016 and RATIÉ forthcoming a). The corresponding *pratīka*s are found in ĪPVV, vol. I, p. 246.

[26] *vā* S2, S3, S7, J[R] : om. S9.

[27] On the basis of Abhinavagupta's commentary (ĪPVV, vol. I, p. 246, quoted below, n. 58), which bears *yā pratītiḥ sa bhrama iti*, one could suspect that this *vā* is a corruption for *yā*. This would conveniently solve the difficulty involved in the sentence (see below, ibid.). However, not to mention that the use of a relative without a correlative in the *Vivṛti* seems somewhat odd, all the consulted manuscripts (S2, S3, S7, S9, J[R]) read *vā*, and Abhinavagupta seems to interpret this third *vā* in the sentence as expressing a disjunction between *sattvena* and *arthatvena*. In other words, as far as I understand, according to him this *vā* means that the object presented in an erroneous cognition is manifest *either* as an existing entity (according to the *asatkhyāti* theory) *or* as an object (according to the *ātmakhyāti* thesis). See below, n. 58.

[28] The words ***tataś ceti*** given as a quotation by the ĪPVV editors and not found in this passage could arouse the suspicion that a sentence is missing here, but in fact they belong to the sentence that preceded the beginning of this fragment, as is obvious from Abhinavagupta's commentary (ibid, vol. I, p. 246).

[29] S2 bears two dots after *prathamānasyānyathāpratītiḥ.*

[30] ***vikalpanātmanas tv*** S3, S7, J[R] : *vikalpātmanas tv* S2, ĪPVV. The words °*pāti-*

rthābhipātād[32] ***bhrāntitvaṃ yuktam***...[33] *arthe dvicandre bāhyatāvasāya eva bhrāntir na dvicandrābhāso nāpi dvicandrāvasāyaḥ.* ***bāhyatāvasāyo 'pi ca*** *timirakāraṇatvāvicārasamutthas*[34] *tadvicārān nivartata iti* ***tāvad*** *bhrāntitattvaṃ*[35] ***bhavatām****, tad āha vṛttau.*[36]

[§ B][37] ***smṛtijñānaṃ hi***[38] *pratibhāsamānarūpe svasaṃvedanam, adhyavasīyamāne punar pūrvānubhūte 'rthe*[39] *vikalpa iti* ***sa*** *svasaṃvedanāṃśo 'sya*[40] *na bhrānto nāpy anubhūtārthavyavasthāhetus tasyābhinnatvāt, vikalpādhyavasāyas*[41] *tu syād arthavya-*

---

tvam ayuktam and ***vikalpanātmanas tu*** are illegible in S9 (the lower edge is damaged). Note also that at this point a blank space was left in S3 and S7 bears 3 dots. S2 has no such dots, but the scribe had to go on with the rest of the text somewhat further up and on the right (to avoid writing on a gloss of the ĪPV), and traced a line to indicate the continuity of the text.

31 *avabhāsena* conj. : *avasāyena* S3, S7, S9, J^R : *ayasāyena* S2. The word *avasāyena* is odd here given the context, and in light of Abhinavagupta's explanation of the passage (see below, n. 64) one would rather expect *dṛśyena*, but I cannot see how the latter could have been corrupted into *avasāyena.*

32 *parārthābhipātād* S3, S7, S9, J^R : *paramārthābhipātād* S2.

33 It seems that a part of the text is missing here since Abhinavagupta gives several *pratīka*s not found in marginal annotations (ĪPVV, vol. I, p. 247: ***dṛśya*** *iti...* ***viparīta*** *iti...* ***ata*** *iti...*). Nothing in the marginal annotations indicates that there might be a lacuna.

34 *timirakāraṇatvāvicārasamutthas* S3, S7, S9 : *timirakāraṇatvāvicarasamutthas* S2 : *timirakāraṇatvāvicārāsamutthas* J^R.

35 *bhrāntitattvaṃ* S3, S7, J^R : *bhrāntitvaṃ* S2, S9.

36 From this point onwards the marginal annotations quote the *Vṛtti* on ĪPK 1.3.5 (see above, n. 15). S3 and J^R quote it entirely; S7 quotes it up to *saṃvit*, while S2 and S9 only give the first word (*adhyavasāya ity ādi*).

37 § B is found in S3 (folio 23a, top and right margins), S7 (folio 15b, top margin), S9 (folio 29a, left, bottom and right margins), J^R (folio 50a, left margin) and in nn. 17 and 18 of the ĪPV edition, p. 101, vol. I. It is not found in D2, SOAS and S2 (although the latter bears § A). In S3, S7 and J^R, the passage is introduced with the words *asya vṛttipadānāṃ ṭīkā* (not found in S9 or in ĪPV, vol. I, n. 17, p. 101; the words *asya vṛtti°* are no longer legible in J^R). The corresponding *pratīka*s are found in ĪPVV, vol. I, pp. 249-251, and it can be assumed from Abhinavagupta's commentary that § B followed § A.

38 ***hi*** S3, S7, J^R : om. S9, n. 17 ĪPV (vol. I, p. 101).

39 *pūrvānubhūte 'rthe* S7 : *pūrvānubhūto 'rtho* S3, S9, J^R : *pūrvānubhūtārtho* n. 17 ĪPV (vol. I, p. 101).

40 *svasaṃvedanāṃśo 'sya* conj. : *svasaṃvedanaṃ so 'sya* S3, S7, S9, n. 17 ĪPV (vol. I, p. 101). The *akṣara* preceding *sya* is no longer legible in J^R. Cf. ĪPVV, vol. I, p. 249 : ***sa*** *iti – yo 'ṃśo...*

41 *vikalpādhyavasāyas* S7, S9 : *vikalpo 'dhyavasāyas* J^R : *vikalpe adhyavasāyas* n. 17 ĪPV (vol. I, p. 101). The *akṣara*s *°lpādhya°* are illegible in S3 (damaged

vasthāpanaṃ[42] ***yāvatā*** *bhrāntir asau,* ***bhrāntasyāpy*** *avasāyasya viṣayavyavasthā na yuktety āha*[43] *bhrāntitve ceti. bhrāntasyādhyavasāyasya*[44] ***jaḍatvād*** *viṣayavyavasthāpakatvaṃ na yujyate.* ***vyavasthāpanaṃ hi*** *vastunaḥ*[45] ***saṃvedanam ātmani*** *tadvācakaśabdodīraṇe* ***ca*** *śrotṛṣu tathābhūtārthākārasaṃvedanotpādanārtham.*[46] *tathācāryadharmakīrtiḥ:*[47]

> *saṃvinniṣṭhā hi viṣayavyavasthitayas tāḥ katham acetano 'rtho vyavasthāpayed*[48] *iti.*[49]

pratipramātṛ *vyavasthitatvaṃ tāvad*[50] *bhidyate, tasya bhāvasvarūpatve bhedo na syāt,*[51] *pramātrā vyavasthāpito 'rthaḥ sarvān pra-*

---

upper right corner). Cf. ĪPVV, vol. I, p. 250: *yas tu vikalpanavyāpārātmādhyavasāyaḥ...*

42 *arthavyavasthāpanaṃ* S3, S9, J[R], n. 17 ĪPV (vol. I, p. 101) : *arthavyasthāpanaṃ* S7.

43 In S3 the words *'dhyavasāyas tu syād arthavyavasthāpanaṃ* ***yāvatā*** *bhrāntir asau,* ***bhrāntasyāpy*** *avasāyasya viṣayavyavasthā na yuktety āha* were first omitted and then added in the top right corner and right margin.

44 *bhrāntasyādhyavasāyasya* S3, S7, S9, J[R] : *tathā bhrāntasyāpy adhyavasāyasya* n. 17 ĪPV (vol. I, p. 101). °*dhyavasāyasya* is no longer legible in J[R].

45 *vastunaḥ* S3, S7 [but *na* and *ta* are virtually homographs in this *nāgarī*], S9, J[R] : *vastutaḥ naḥ* n. 17 ĪPV (vol. I, p. 101).

46 *tathābhūtārthākārasaṃvedanotpādanārtham* S9 : *tathābhūtārthākāre saṃvedanotpādanārtham* S3, S7, J[R], n. 17 ĪPV (vol. I, p. 101). Cf. the gloss in ĪPVV, vol. I, p. 250: *tatsadṛśasyārthākārasyādhyavasāyasya... jananārtham.*

47 Due to the *sandhi* ambiguity one could understand this passage either as *tathā ca+āryadharmakīrtiḥ* or as *tathā+ācāryadharmakīrtiḥ*, and I have no certainty as to which interpretation is to be preferred. The other known quotation from the PVin in the *Vivṛti* (see TORELLA 2007d, p. 937) is introduced with *tathā cācāryadharmakīrtiḥ*, which makes the second hypothesis more likely – hence my choice here (which has no bearing on the meaning of the passage anyway). Note, however, that if at least one passage in the ĪPVV involves a similar ambiguity (see ĪPVV, vol. I, p. 279: *tathācāryadharmakīrtiḥ*, understood as *tathā+ācāryadharmakīrtiḥ* by the KSTS editors), the other ĪPVV mentions of Dharmakīrti's name that I know of unambiguously refer to the Buddhist philosopher as *āryadharmakīrtiḥ* (see ĪPVV, vol. II, p. 46, pp. 111 and 174).

48 *vyavasthāpayed* S3, S7, J[R], n. 17 ĪPV (vol. I, p. 101) : *vyavasthāyed* S9.

49 PVin 1, pp. 24-25 (the edition has *saṃvinniṣṭhāś ca* instead of *saṃvinniṣṭhā hi*). Note that STERN 1991 had already spotted this quotation in n. 17 of ĪPV, vol. I, p. 101, and had remarked that the footnote was a passage from Utpaladeva's *Vivṛti* (see STERN 1991, p. 158 and n. 55).

50 *tāvad* n. 18 ĪPV (vol. I, p. 101) : *tā* S3 (with a blank left after *tā*), S7 (with 4 dots), S9 (with no mark indicating that something is missing), J[R] (something seems to have been deleted after *tā*).

mātṝn prati vyavasthitaḥ[52] *syāt. na caivam. tadā tathābhūta**vastu-saṃvedanarūpatvalābhaḥ***[53] ***pramātur*** *vyavasthāpanam. ato jaḍo 'dhyavasāyas tathā syāt tad āha na jaḍād viṣayasthitir iti.*[54]

[§ C][55] *nanu kenaivam uktaṃ jaḍo 'dhyavasāyaḥ, saṃvitsvabhāvo hy asau jñānāvyatirekāt.*[56] *tad āha tato 'jāḍya iti.*[57]

---

51 After *syāt* S3 has 3 dots, S7 has 5 dots, J^R has 4 dots. In S9, the sentence from *pramātrā...* was first omitted and the text went on directly with *na caivaṃ...*, but the missing text was added (with a mark indicating it) between lines of the ĪPV text.

52 *vyavasthitaḥ* S3, S7, S9, n. 18 ĪPV (vol. I, p. 101) : *vyavasthāpitaḥ* J^R.

53 The compound ***vastusaṃvedanarūpatvalābhaḥ*** is not quoted in the ĪPVV while Abhinavagupta is commenting on this passage (vol. I, p. 251). However, it is quoted earlier (vol. I, p. 250), and in that previous passage Abhinavagupta specifies that the compound only appears later in the *Vivṛti* by explaining that Utpaladeva will sum up (*upasaṃhariṣyati*) this point later.

54 *na jaḍād viṣayasthitir iti* S3, J^R, n. 18 ĪPV (vol. I, p. 101) : *na jaḍād ityādi* S9 : *na jaḍād viṣayavyavasthitir iti* S7.

55 § C is found in D2 (folio I 121, as an interlinear annotation that goes on in the right margin), S2 (folio 14b, top margin), S3 (folio 23a, left margin), S5 (folio 39b, as an interlinear annotation that goes on in the right margin), S7 (folio 15b, left margin), S9 (folio 29a, bottom margin), J^R (folio 50b, right margin) and in n. 21 of ĪPV, vol. I, p. 102. In S3 and S7 it is followed by the words *iti pratyabhijñāṭīkāyāṃ sūtrakārakṛtāyām*; these words are omitted in S2, S9 and the ĪPV n., and they are only partly legible in J^R. Determining the place of this passage with respect to the two others is no easy task because Abhinavagupta does not quote any word from it and because S3, S7 and S9 give a sequence (B-C-A) that is contradicted by Abhinavagupta's commentary, according to which § A clearly preceded § B (S2 only has C-A, and the ĪPV footnotes, B-C). Given Abhinavagupta's explanations immediately before § A, it also seems very unlikely that § C preceded § A. So we are left with two possible sequences: either A-C-B or A-B-C. The sequence A-C-B is neither infirmed nor confirmed by Abhinavagupta's commentary (which does not quote any word from the *Vivṛti* while making the transition from § A to § B), but the opponent in C criticizes the expression *jaḍo 'dhyavasāyaḥ* used by Utpaladeva in B, so it seems probable that § C originally followed § B, all the more since in the ĪPVV, immediately after commenting on § B, Abhinavagupta explains the passage of the *Vṛtti* beginning with *cidrūpo 'pi* (which is precisely an explanation of the words *tato 'jāḍye* in the verse) in the following way (ĪPVV, vol. I, p. 251): *apiśabdo vṛttau parābhyupagamasyāyuktatādyotakaḥ. yady api tvayā cidrūpo 'ṅgīkṛtas tathāpi na nirdoṣatvam iti.* "The word[s] 'even [if]' in the *Vṛtti* indicate that accepting the [Buddhist] opponent['s objection] is not sound. [It means the following:] 'Even if you[, our Buddhist opponent,] admit that [determination] consists in consciousness, [your position] is not without defects.'" So it seems likely that the original order of the fragment was A-B-C, and that the purpose of § C was to introduce the meaning of the second half of the verse after explaining the meaning of the first half at the end of § B.

THE *VIVṚTI* FRAGMENT ON ĪPK 1.3.5: ANNOTATED TRANSLATION

Error is the cognition of [something] that is being manifest as different [from what it really is; that is,] either [error is the cognition] of [something] nonexistent [that is being manifest] as if it existed, or [it is the cognition of the cognition] itself [that is being manifest] as if it were an object.[58] And there can be no cognition of a

---

[56] *jñānāvyatirekāt* D2, S3, S7, J[R], n. 21 ĪPV (vol. I, p. 102) : *jñānātirekāt* S2, S9.

[57] *tad āha tato 'jāḍya iti* S2, S7, S9 : *tad āha tato 'jāḍye i iti* S3 : *ity āha tata ityādi* D2, S5 : *ity āha tata ityādi* n. 21 ĪPV (vol. I, p. 102). In J[R] *āha tato 'jā°* is illegible, and followed by *°ḍye iti*. The text that follows in the ĪPV footnote (*nijaṃ collekhaś ceti dvandvaḥ, niṣṭhād iti tyablope pañcamī, tataḥ smṛtyadhyavasāyata iti*) is in fact made of short glosses explaining the ĪPV.

[58] This first sentence is difficult. At first sight one might assume that Utpaladeva is presenting here three rival definitions of error instead of two, namely the Mādhyamikas' (error is the cognition "of [something] nonexistent," *asataḥ*), the Vijñānavādins' (error is the cognition "of [the cognition] itself," *ātmanaḥ*), and the Naiyāyikas' (error is the cognition "of [something] that is manifest as being different [from what it is], as an object," *prathamānasyānyathāsattvenārthatvena*). Such an interpretation, however, is problematic for several reasons. First, the word *arthatvena* does not fit with this understanding, since according to the Naiyāyikas, in error what appears as being different from what it really is is not a subjective aspect of cognition: for them, when we mistake a piece of mother-of-pearl for silver, the silver of our erroneous cognition is not a purely internal aspect of our cognition that we would mistake for an object (as the Vijñānavādins believe), but a real object that we mistake for another real object, so that *arthatvena* would be at best pointless if Utpaladeva had the Naiyāyikas' theory in mind here. Besides, Abhinavagupta (who does not take *anyathā* and *sattvena* as forming a single compound) clearly understands the passage as an alternative between two options only. See ĪPVV, vol. I, p. 246: ***asata*** *ity anantarbahīrūpasya dvicandrasya prakāśamānasyaiva* ***sattvene****ti bahīrūpeṇa jñānākārasya v****ārthatvenā****nātmatvena yā pratītiḥ sa* ***bhrama*** *iti*. "Error is the cognition of [something] nonexistent[, that is,] of a double moon [for instance] that is neither internal nor external [to consciousness, and] that is nonetheless being manifest as if it existed, i.e. as external [to consciousness]; or [error is the cognition] of an aspect of cognition [that is nonetheless being manifest] as [if it were] an object, [that is,] as [if it were] not [consciousness] itself." So according to Abhinavagupta, here Utpaladeva is simply mentioning the two alternative Buddhist views on error so as to show that given these views, the Buddhist cannot define memory as a mere error. See also ĪPV, vol. I, p. 100 (commenting on ĪPK 1.3.4): *kiṃ ca bhrāntāv asad vātmākāro vā prakhyāti, na tu tayārthaḥ svīkriyate tasyāprakāśanād iti tayārtho na vyavasthāpita eva. prakāśanātmā hi vyavasthāpanā, tataś ca smaraṇād abhilāṣena* katham arthaviṣayo vyavahāraḥ.* [**abhilāṣeṇa* corr. RATIÉ 2011, p. 133 : *abhilāpena* ĪPV.] "Moreover, in an error, [what] is manifest (*prakhyāti*) is either

[given] specific aspect as being different [from what it really is] (*anyathāpratīti*) while [this specific aspect] is being manifest.[59] Therefore [we] may call "erroneous" only a cognition that is different [from nonconceptual cognition[60] and consists in] an entirely distorted (*ativiparīta*) determination of [something] whose form is being manifest.[61] And this [erroneous cognition can] only consist in a concept:[62] since a nonconceptual [cognition] exclusively rests

---

[something] nonexistent or an aspect [of the cognition] itself; but this [error] cannot appropriate the [real] object since it does not manifest this [object] – therefore [memory, if it is erroneous, can]not establish the object at all. For establishing [an object] consists in manifesting [it]; and therefore how could any wordly activity regarding objects [occur, as the Buddhists contend,] due to the desire [of previously perceived objects,] thanks to the memory [of these objects]?" This is an allusion to PVin 1.18 (see above, n. 9). See also ĪPVV, vol. I, p. 236 (commenting on ĪPK 1.4.3): *smṛtir asad eva asatkhyātipakṣa ālambate, vāsanopakalpitaṃ vā jñānākāram ātmākhyātipakṣa ābhāsayati...* "[If] memory [is an error, it] has as its objective support (*ālambate*) [something] purely nonexistent, according to the thesis of [error as] the manifestation of [something] nonexistent (*asatkhyāti*); or, according to the thesis of [error as] the manifestation of [cognition] itself (*ātmakhyāti*), it manifests an aspect of cognition that is conceptually constructed due to some imprint."

59 That is, if something is being immediately manifested – as in the first moment of perception, when we experience the mere presence of a given without any conceptual mediation – then this thing cannot appear as other than what it is; which means that pure perception cannot be erroneous.

60 See ĪPVV, vol. I, p. 246: *pratītyantaraṃ nirvikalpapratītivyatiriktam.* "Another cognition, [that is, a cognition] distinct from nonconceptual cognition."

61 See ĪPVV, vol. I, p. 246: *yat prathamānaṃ prakāśamānaṃ tad vastu. tan niyatākāraṃ yathaiva prakāśate tathaiva tat, anyathābhūtaṃ tan na bhavati. tatas tasya yā pratītir avikalpā prakāśarūpā sā sarvathaivānyathātvaṃ viparītavedanarūpatvaṃ na sahate...* "That which is being manifest, [i.e.] that which is appearing, is something real. That [real entity], which has a specific aspect, exists exactly in the way in which it is being manifest – it does not exist in a different way. Therefore the cognition of this [immediately manifest aspect], which is nonconceptual [and] consists in [nothing but] manifestation (*prakāśa*), cannot bear in any way to be other [than it is – that is, it cannot] consist in a distorted awareness."

62 See ĪPVV, vol. I, p. 246: *nanu nirvikalpakāntaram eva tathāstu. nety āha* ***tac ce****ti. avikalpakatvam etad eva yat prathāmātrarūpatvam, saṃyojanaviyojanādivyāpāras tu vikalpanam.* "[– Objection:] 'But [then] let [us admit] that another [type of cognition, i.e. the] nonconceptual [one], is in the same way [entirely distorted].' [To this objection Utpaladeva] replies that it is not [the case] with [the sentence beginning with] 'And this...' [That is to say:] being nonconceptual means nothing but consisting in a pure phenomenality (*prathā*), whereas conceptualization is an activity of uniting, separating, etc."

on a phenomenon, it cannot be aimed at[63] another object. On the contrary, [a cognition] that consists in conceptualization can be an error, because [such a cognition], which identifies a conceptualized object with a [perceived] phenomenon, can] be aimed at another object [...].[64] With respect to the object that is a double moon [seen

---

63 Literally, it cannot "fall" (*pātin*) to another object. Cf. Abhinavagupta's explanation of the word *pātin* in a different context (see ĪPV, vol. I, p. 286, commenting on ĪPK 1.7.4): *pātir jñāpanavācī patiś ca viśrāntivācī prayuktas tantreṇa.* "[The root] *pat-* in the causative expresses the act of making [something] known, and the root *pat* in its simple form, which expresses the fact of resting [on something], is [to be understood as] simultaneously employed [in the word *pātin*]."

64 The passage is difficult because there is a lacuna (see above, n. 33) and because the sentence seems to be somewhat corrupted (see above, n. 31). For the idea that determination identifies (literally, unites) a perceived object (*dṛśya*) with a conceptualized object (*vikalpya*), see e.g. ĪPVV, vol. I, p. 248, which defines the error sublated by a correcting awareness as "the determination of the identity of a perceived object with a conceptualized object" (*dṛśyavikalpyābhedādhyavasāya*). Abhinavagupta gives two different interpretations of this definition of erroneous determination (from ĪPVV, vol. I, p. 247, we may surmise that at least the second was summed up in the missing *Vivṛti* passage: *etad upasaṃharaty* ***ata*** *iti*...). According to the first one, determination is erroneous only insofar as the perceived object is identified with a conceptualized object *that differs from it* (e.g. when the perceived mother-of-pearl is identified with the object of the "silver" concept), whereas when the perceived object really corresponds to the conceptualized object, there is no error (ĪPVV, vol. I, p. 247): *śuktau dṛśyāyāṃ taddṛśyaviparītena rajatenādhyavasāya aikyaṃ yadā karoti tadā bhrāntatvam, nīle tu dṛśye nīlenaiva vikalpyenaikye kā bhrāntatā.* "When, whereas mother-of-pearl is the perceived object (*dṛśya*), a determination identifies [it] with silver, which is distorted with respect to that perceived object, there is an error. But when, whereas blue is the perceived object, [it] is identified with a conceptualized object (*vikalpya*) that is nothing but blue, what error could there be [in that identification]?" According to the other explanation, in fact every determination is erroneous insofar as it illegitimately identifies the content of a perception with a mentally constructed object, although in our worldly activities, we consider as pragmatically valid some of these determinations (i.e., those which enable us to reach our goals): *anye tu vyācakṣate dṛśye spaṣṭe vikalpyenāspaṣṭena yad aikyaṃ tad adhyavasyan sarvo vikalpo bhrāntaḥ, vastumūlatvena tu prāpakatvān na bhrāntitayā vyavahriyate, nīlasyaiva prāpyatvād arthakriyākāritvenābhimānāt spaṣṭāspaṣṭatādyavāntarānādaraṇāt. yas tu dṛśyenaikyaṃ nādhyavasyati, sa vikalpyarūpasvaviṣayamātraniṣṭhaḥ sarvathaivābhrānta iti.* "Others, however, explain that every concept is erroneous insofar as it determines the identity of a perceived [object] that is vivid[ly manifest] with a conceptualized object that is not vivid[ly manifest]. Nonetheless, [we] do not treat (*vyavahriyate*) [a given concept] as an error on the grounds that it [enables] us to reach [what we desire], since it is based on the real thing [although it does not grasp it directly];

by someone afflicted with an eye disease], the error is nothing but the determination [of the double moon] as being external: it is not the phenomenon of the double moon, nor is it the determination [of that phenomenon as being] the double moon. Moreover, the determination [of the double moon] as being external arises from a lack of reflection on the fact that [the double moon phenomenon] results from [the eye disease called] *timira*; [and] reflecting on this makes [this determination as an external entity] cease.[65] This,

---

because the [object that we] are trying to reach is precisely the blue, because [we] consider [that the concept of blue] has the efficacy [of enabling us to reach it, and] because [we] disregard the fact that [the perception and the concept of blue] are respectively vivid and not vivid, etc. On the other hand, a [concept] that does not determine the identity [of the conceptualized object] with a perceived [object and] exclusively rests on its own object, namely the conceptualized object, is absolutely devoid of error." This second Buddhist position is clearly reminiscent of Dharmakīrti's explanation of the error through which we come to wrongly identify mental constructs resulting from a process of exclusion (*apoha*, *vyāvṛtti*) with actually perceived entities. See *Pramāṇavārttikasvavṛtti*, p. 39: *nanu bāhyā vivekino na ca teṣu vikalpapravṛttir iti kathaṃ teṣu bhavati. vyākhyātāraḥ khalv evaṃ vivecayanti na vyavahartāraḥ. te tu svālambanam eva arthakriyāyogyaṃ manyamānā dṛśyavikalpyāv arthāv ekīkṛtya pravartante.* "[– Question:] But external [objects all] differ [from each other], and concepts[, which have universals as their objects, can]not apply to [them]; so how [is it that concepts] are [nonetheless said to apply] to them? [– Answer:] It is philosophers (*vyākhyātṛ*) who thus distinguish [particulars from conceptual objects], not the agents of everyday activity (*vyavahartṛ*). Rather, the [latter], believing that it is their [conceptual] object that is capable of the causal efficacy [which in fact belongs to the particular], act [on particulars] after identifying (*ekīkṛtya*) two [different] objects, [namely] the perceptible (*dṛśya*) and the conceptualized (*vikalpya*)." Cf. *Pramāṇavārttikasvavṛttiṭīkā*, p. 222, where someone asks: *yadi sāmānyabuddhir na svalakṣaṇapratibhāsinī, kathaṃ svalakṣaṇe lokaṃ pravartayati.* "If the [conceptual] cognition of a universal does not manifest a particular, how does it make people act on the particular?" Here is Dharmakīrti's answer according to Karṇakagomin: *asvalakṣaṇapratibhāsiny api svapratibhāse 'narthe 'rthādhyavasāyavibhramād dhetor vyavahārayati lokaṃ dṛśyavikalpyāv ekīkṛtya pravartayatīti yāvat.* "Although [a conceptual cognition] does not manifest the particular, due to an error (*vibhrama*) [consisting in] determining (*adhyavasāya*) as an object a manifestation of [consciousness] itself [whereas the latter] is not an object, it prompts people to act in their everyday activities (*vyavahārayati*) – that is, it prompts them to act after [wrongly] identifying a perceptible [object] with a conceptualized [one]."

65 See ĪPVV, vol. I, pp. 247-248: *tena dvicandranirvikalpakaṃ tathāvidhavikalpyamātraniṣṭhaś ca tadadhyavasāyo na bhrāntiḥ. na hy atrobhayatrāpi bādhakaṃ prabhavati. na hi nivṛtte 'pi timira evaṃ pratipattiḥ: na me dvicandraḥ pratibhāta iti. tatpratibhānād eva hi timiracikitsitādi*. yas tu dvicandro 'yaṃ bāhyaḥ sarvasādhāraṇa ity adhyavasāyaḥ, sa eva bhrānto bādhakena tathāve-*

[which is expounded] for now[, at this point of the treatise], is the essence of error for you [Buddhists][66] – this is what is said in the *Vṛtti*.

Since [it is so],[67] the memory cognition is a self-awareness (*svasaṃvedana*) with respect to [its own] form that is being [imme-

---

danāt. nivṛtte tāvat timira evaṃ pratipattiḥ: yo mayā dvicandro bāhyatvena sarvasādhāraṇyenādhyavasitaḥ sa tathā na pratibhātaḥ, pratibhātas tv abāhya evāsādhāraṇas timirādikāraṇāntarotthāpitas tadasādhāraṇapṛṣṭha eva tv abhyamaṃsi bāhyo 'yaṃ sarvasādhāraṇa iti na cāsau tatheti. [**timiracikitsitādi* corr. : *timiracikitsitādiḥ* ĪPVV.] "Therefore the nonconceptual [cognition] of the two moons is no illusion; neither is the determination of this [nonconceptual cognition insofar as it] exclusively rests on a conceptualized object of the same sort[, i.e. on a conceptualized object that is 'the double moon.'] For in these [two cases, namely perceiving a double moon and determining it as being a double moon], no refuting [means of knowledge] can prevail over any of the two [cognitions]. For even when the *timira* [condition] ceases [to affect someone, this person] does not think: '[While I was affected by this condition,] the double moon was not manifest to me'; for [we] administer some medicine against *timira* precisely because the manifestation of this [double moon indeed occurs to those who have this condition]. Rather, what is erroneous is the determination 'this double moon is external [to me and] common to all [perceiving subjects]'; because [later] one becomes aware that [this determination] is thus [erroneous] thanks to a [means of knowledge] that refutes it. Indeed, when the *timira* [condition] ceases [to affect someone, this person] thinks: 'The double moon that was determined by me as being an external [object and] as being common to all [perceiving subjects] was not manifest in that way; rather, it was manifest [as being] perfectly internal [and] not common [to other perceiving subjects]; it sprung from causes different [from those resulting in the perception of an external object,] such as the *timira* [condition]; but although it was not common [to any other perceiving subject], I considered that it was external [and] common to all, whereas it is not so.'"

66 See ĪPVV, vol. I, p. 249: ***tāvad*** *iti, iha tāvad upayogi darśitam, anyat tu darśayiṣyate.* ***bhavatām*** *iti svadarśane bhrāntitattvaṃ yat tad iha na tāvad darśitam iti yāvat.* "'For now' – [that is,] up to this point [this theory,] which is useful [to Utpaladeva's argumentation,] has been expounded, but a different [theory] will be expounded [in the sequel]. The implicit meaning with 'for you [Buddhists]' is that for now [Utpaladeva] has not shown what constitutes the essence of error according to his own system." Note that while commenting on this Buddhist theory of error Abhinavagupta mentions and quotes Śaṅkaranandana three times. See ĪPVV, vo. I, p. 247 (*tad vijñānaśūnyatā nītibāhyaiveti bhadraśaṅkaranandanaḥ*) ibid., p. 248 (*yad āha bhaṭṭaḥ: asaty asyābahirbhāvo bādhaḥ sattvam ato dvidhā | iti*) and ibid. (*āha: ābhāsabhede tv arthaḥ kas tatrābhedo bhramo 'vapuḥ | iti*). BÜHNEMANN 1980, p. 195, identifies the source of the last two quotations as the *Prajñālaṅkāra*.

67 On Abhinavagupta's explanation of *hi* here see ĪPVV, vol. I, p. 249: ***hīti*** *yasmād evambhūto 'tra vibhāgo 'stīti* tasmād viṣayavyavasthāpakatvam adhy-*

diately] manifest [when we remember]; but with respect to the object that was previously experienced and is being determined [when we remember], it is a [mere] concept. Therefore the part of it that is a self-awareness is not erroneous, [but] neither is [this part] the cause [enabling us] to establish the [previously] experienced object, because it is not distinct from the [cognition itself].[68] As for conceptual determination, it might be [considered at first sight as the cause of] the establishment of the object, but in fact (*yāvatā*) it is an error,[69] and establishing an object is not possible for an erroneous determination. This is what [the author of the verses][70] says with "And if [the determination] is an error..." An erroneous determination cannot be what establishes the object because it is not conscious[71] [with respect to that object]. For establishing

---

avasāyasya na yujyate yathā prakṛtasya smṛtijñānasyeti. [**vibhāgo 'stīti* conj. : *vibhāga itīti* ĪPVV.] "[The word] *hi* [means:] since in a[ny determination], the part [regarding which determination is conscious] is such, [i.e., is not external to consciousness], a determination such as the memory cognition, which is the subject at hand, cannot establish the object."

68 See Abhinavagupta's explanation of *tasyābhinnatvāt* in ĪPVV, vol. I, p. 249: *yato so 'ṃśaḥ pratibhāsamānaḥ svarūpasvābhāsasvabhāvas tasmāt smṛtijñānād abhinno na vyatirikto na bāhyasvabhāvaḥ...* "Since the part [of determination] that is being manifest consists in its own nature and in an aspect of itself [erroneously represented as external], it is not different – i.e. not distinct – from the memory cognition – [that is,] it does not have the nature of an external [object]."

69 See ĪPVV, vol. I, p. 250: *yas tu vikalpanavyāpārātmādhyavasāyaḥ, sa yady api svāṃśād avatīrṇa iva lakṣyata ity ato 'rthe vyavasthāpakatayā sambhāvayitum ārabdhaḥ, tathāpi na nirvahaty asya sambhāvanā. tad āha* ***yāvate****ti pūrvaprakrāntasambhāvanānirvāhābhāvadyotakam avyayam.* "As for the determination consisting in an activity of conceptualization, even though at first one may suppose that it establishes the object because it seems to reach beyond a [mere] part of itself, this supposition is doomed. This is what [Utpaladeva says with] *yāvatā*: the word [functioning here as an] indeclinable term indicates that the possibility first entertained is doomed." For a similar use of *yāvatā* in Utpaladeva's *Vivṛti* see RATIÉ 2016, p. 236.

70 In the known *Vivṛti* fragments, Utpaladeva systematically adopts the convention (widely followed among Sanskrit writers) of referring to himself in the third person.

71 See ĪPVV, vol. I, p. 250: *nanu bhrāntaṃ ca bhaviṣyati vyavasthāpakaṃ ca bhaviṣyati, duṣyati kiṃ hi tata iti bhrāntatvena saha samuccīyamānaṃ vyavasthāpakatvam āśaṅkitam niṣedhati* ***bhrāntasyāpī****ti. atra hetur* ***jaḍatvād*** *iti.* "'[– Objection:] But [this determination] can be erroneous while also being what establishes [the object]; what problem could arise from this?' [With the passage beginning with] *bhrāntasyāpi*, [Utpaladeva] refutes this objection that being what establishes [the object] might be compatible with being erroneous.

[an object] is being conscious (*saṃvedana*) of a real thing[, and this consciousness occurs] in oneself as well as in those who hear [us] when [we] utter words denoting this [thing] so as to produce [in them too] a consciousness having the aspect of such an object.[72] Thus the master Dharmakīrti [has said]:

> For the objects' [various] states (*vyavasthiti*) rest on consciousness: how could an unconscious thing establish them?[73]

To begin with, [for a given object,] being established [or not] varies according to each knowing subject. [Now,] if this [property of being established] belonged to the [very] nature of [objective] enti-

---

Here is the [logical] reason [for this refutation]: 'because it is not conscious.'"

[72] See ĪPVV, vol. I, p. 250: *nanu viṣayasya vyavasthāpaka iti ko 'rtho viṣayasya* vyavasthāṃ karoti. tatra yathā kāṣṭhasya ploṣaṃ karoty agnir ity ukte jāḍyam agner na pratibandhakam, tathaivāvasāyo vyavasthāṃ viṣayasya karotīti kim asya jāḍyājāḍyacintayety āśaṅkyāha* **vyavasthāpanaṃ hī***ti.* [**'rtho viṣayasya* conj. : *'rthaviṣayasya* ĪPVV.] "[– Objection]: 'But what is this thing that establishes the object and [is said to be] what causes the establishment of the object? In that regard, just as when one says that fire causes the combustion of wood, the fact that fire is not conscious does not prevent [fire from causing this combustion], in the same way, determination causes the establishment of the object, therefore what is the point of this quibble over [determination] being conscious or not?' Having anticipated this [objection, Utpaladeva says] 'For establishing...'." Utpaladeva's definition of the establishment of the object here is thus meant to show that it cannot be compared to a mere material transformation (undergone by the object) since this transformation rather affects the conscious subjects who are aware of it. See ibid.: *ity etad vyavasthāśabdavācyam, na tv arthasyāsau kāṣṭhasyeva kaścid vikāraḥ.* "This is what is expressed by the word 'establishment' [in this context], and [such an establishment] is not [just] some [material] transformation [within the object itself] as in the case of wood [being combusted by fire]."

[73] From ĪPVV, vol. I, p. 144, which glosses this quotation, it seems that Utpaladeva had already quoted this PVin passage earlier in the *Vivṛti*. My translation here follows Abhinavagupta's interpretation (ibid.): *saṃvidy anubhavaniścayarūpāyāṃ niṣṭhānyānapekṣiṇī viśrāntir yāsāṃ tā viṣayāṇāṃ nīlādīnāṃ vyavasthitayo vividhenāsaṅkīrṇenātmanāvasthānāni, tā vyavasthitīḥ katham acetano 'rtho nīlādiprāyaḥ prayuñjīta vyavasthāpayet...* "The [various] states of objects such as blue – [that is to say,] their existence as various distinct natures – rest on consciousness, which consists in experiences and [their] ascertainment, without being in need of any other [substratum; so] how could an unconscious thing, which is nothing more than [insentient objects] such as blue, establish these states?" This quotation seems to have been particularly in favour among Śaiva authors: it appears in shorter forms (and with slight variations) e.g. in works by Abhinavagupta (ĪPV, vol. I, p. 281; ĪPVV, vol. II, p. 341), Jayaratha (*Tantrālokaviveka* on *Tantrāloka* 4.185b, vol. III, p. 832) and Yogarāja (*Paramārthasāravivṛti* on *Paramārthasāra* 43, p. 62).

ties, there would be no [such] difference: an object established by one knowing subject would be established for all of them. But this is not the case.[74] So the establishment [of objects] is the fact that a knowing subject becomes conscious of[75] a real thing that is such[, i.e. that consists in a specific object]. Therefore the determination [in which memory supposedly consists] must be unconscious in this way[, i.e. with respect to the external object, which it cannot establish] – this is what [the author of the verse][76] expresses [in the first half of the verse] with [the words] "the establishment of the object cannot result from this [determination], which is unconscious [with respect to the real object]."

[– Objection:] But who is thus claiming that determination is unconscious? For [according to us Buddhists,] this [determination] has consciousness as its nature, since it is not distinct from a cogni-

---

[74] In other words, according to Abhinavagupta, a given object is established by some subjects and not by others (who happen not to perceive or notice it), which means that being established is not a mere property inherent in objects and must be grounded in subjectivity. See ĪPVV, vol. I, pp. 250-251*: nanu viṣayadharma eva vyavasthāstu bhāṭṭanyāyena. atrāha* ***pratipramātṛ*** *iti. viṣayadharmo hi pratipramātṛ na bhidyate. na hy ekasya śuklaḥ paṭaḥ, anyasya pītaḥ, anyasya na śuklo na pīta iti bhavati. iha punar ekasya spaṣṭaṃ pratibhāto 'parasyāpratibhāta eveti dṛṣṭam. viṣayadharmatāyāṃ tv idaṃ na ghaṭate. yaḥ pratipramātṛ bhidyate dharmaḥ, sa viṣayadharmo na bhavati sukhādir iva.* "[– Objection:] 'But let [us admit] that the establishment [of objects] is nothing but a property belonging to objects[, namely being manifest], according to the reasoning [put forward] by the followers of the [Mīmāṃsaka] master [Kumārila].' [Utpaladeva] responds to this [objection] with [the sentence beginning with] *pratipramātṛ*... For a property belonging to objects does not vary according to each knowing subject: it is not the case that a cloth is white for one [subject,] yellow for another [subject and] neither white nor yellow for [yet] another [subject]! On the contrary, in this [case, namely establishing objects, we] observe that what is vividly manifest for one [subject] is not manifest for [someone] else; but this is not possible if [the manifestation of objects to subjects is nothing but] a property belonging to objects. [Now,] a property that varies according to each knowing subject is not a property that belongs to objects, just as pleasure and so on [belong to subjects and not to objects]." On the Śaiva criticism of the *bhāṭṭa*s' theory of "manifestedness" (*prakaṭatā*) as a property belonging to objects, see RATIÉ 2011, pp. 316-325.

[75] Literally, it is the fact that the knowing subject "gets to consist in the consciousness of..."

[76] See above, n. 70.

tion. This is what [the author of the verse][77] expresses [in the second half of the verse] with [the words] *tato 'jāḍye...*[78]

APPENDIX: A LIST OF ANNOTATED ĪPV MANUSCRIPTS KNOWN TO CONTAIN *VIVṚTI* FRAGMENTS[79]

- D2: *Īśvarapratyabhijñāvimarśinī manuscript*, Delhi, National Archives of India (Manuscripts belonging to the Acheology and Research Department, Jammu and Kashmir Government, Srinagar, in "List of Gilgit Manuscripts and Sanskrit Mss"), no. 5, vol. II [paper, *śāradā* script]
- J[R:] *Īśvarapratyabhijñāvimarśinī* manuscript, Jammu, Rashtriya Sanskrit Sansthan, no. 47 (formerly no. 52A) and no. 70 (formerly no. 52B) [paper, *śāradā* script, incomplete]
- S2: *Īśvarapratyabhijñāvimarśinī* manuscript, Śrinagar, Oriental Research Library, no. 1035 [paper, *śāradā* script]
- S3: *Īśvarapratyabhijñāvimarśinī* manuscript, Śrinagar, Oriental Research Library, no. 838 ("*Īśvarapratyabhijñākaumudi*") [paper, *śāradā* script]
- S5: [*Īśvarapratyabhijñāvimarśinī* manuscript, catalogued as] *Sāṃkhyatattvakaumudī* by Vācaspati Miśra [Abhinavagupta's text is copied after the latter], Śrinagar, Oriental Research Library, no. 1212 [paper, *śāradā* script]
- S7: *Īśvarapratyabhijñāvimarśinī* manuscript, Śrinagar, Oriental Research Library, no. 2250 [paper, *nāgarī* script]
- S9: *Īśvarapratyabhijñāvimarśinī* manuscript, Śrinagar, Oriental Research Library, no. 1161 [paper, *śāradā* script]

---

77 See above, n. 70.

78 On this last paragraph see above, n. 55. Cf. the very similar objection mentioned by Abhinavagupta while he is summing up the meaning of the verse (ĪPVV, vol. I, p. 242): *nanu prakāśarūpatvam asti smṛtyadhyavasāyasya svasaṃvedane svākāre ca, tat katham asya jaḍatvam.* "[– The Buddhist:] But the determination that is memory consists in [a conscious] manifestation with respect to self-awareness and the aspect of itself [that it presents as an object]; so how can it [be said to] be unconscious?"

79 Note also that what appears to be a particularly lengthy *Vivṛti* fragment has recently been found in the margins of an ĪPVV manuscript (see RATIÉ forthcoming c).

- SOAS: *Īśvarapratyabhijñāvimarśinī* manuscript, London, School of Oriental and African Studies Library, no. 207 in R.C. Dogra, *A Handlist of the Manuscripts in South Asian Languages in the Library*, London: SOAS, 1978/no. 44255 ["*Pratyabhijñāsūtra* with Abhinavagupta's *Sūtrārthavimarśinī*," *śāradā* script]

REFERENCES

BHATT 1962
G. Bhatt, *The Basic Ways of Knowing. An In-depth Study of Kumārila's Contribution to Indian Epistemology*, [Varanasi: 1962] revised ed., Delhi: Motilal Banarsidass, 1989

BÜHNEMANN 1980
G. Bühnemann, "Identifizierung von Sanskrittexten Śaṅkaranandanas," *Wiener Zeitschrift für die Kunde Südasiens* 24, 1980, pp. 191-198

ELTSCHINGER 2015
V. Eltschinger, "Latest News from a Kashmirian 'Second Dharmakīrti,'" in P. Mc Allister, C. Scherrer-Schaub and H. Krasser (eds.), *Cultural Flows across the Western Himalaya*, Wien: Verlag der Österreichischen Akademie der Wissenschaften, 2015, pp. 303-364

ELTSCHINGER AND RATIÉ 2013
V. Eltschinger and I. Ratié, *Self, No-Self, and Salvation. Dharmakīrti's Critique of the Notions of Self and Person*, Wien: Verlag der Österreichischen Akademie der Wissenschaften, 2013

ĪPK
[*Īśvarapratyabhijñākārikā*] See TORELLA 1994

ĪPV
Īśvarapratyabhijñāvimarśinī, ed. M.R. Shāstrī/M.K. Shāstrī, 2 vols., Srinagar: Kashmir Series of Texts and Studies 22 & 33, Nirnaya Sagar Press, 1918-1921

ĪPVV
Īśvarapratyabhijñāvivṛtivimarśinī by Abhinavagupta, ed. M.K. Shāstrī, 3 vols., Bombay: Kashmir Series of Texts and Studies 60, 62 and 65, Nirnaya Sagar Press, 1938-1943

KAWAJIRI 2015
Y. Kawajiri, "New Fragments of the *Īśvarapratyabhijñā-Ṭīkā*," in B. Bäumer and R. Torella (eds.), *Utpaladeva, Philosopher of Recognition*, Delhi: DK Printworld, 2015, pp. 77-101

KELLNER 2001
B. Kellner, "Negation – Failure or Success? Remarks on an Allegedly Characteristic Trait of Dharmakīrti's *Anupalabdhi* Theory," *Journal of Indian Philosophy* 29, 2001, pp. 495-517

MATILAL 1986
B.K. Matilal, *Perception. An Essay on Classical Indian Theories of Knowledge*, Oxford: Clarendon Press, 1986

NEMEC 2012
J. Nemec, "The Two Pratyabhijñā Theories of Error," *Journal of Indian Philosophy* 40(2), 2002, pp. 225-257

Paramārthasāra
Paramārthasāra by Abhinavagupta with the commentary of Yogarāja, ed. J.C. Chatterji, Srinagar: Kashmir Series of Texts and Studies 7, 1916

Paramārthasāravivṛti
See *Paramārthasāra*

Pramāṇavārttikasvavṛtti
The Pramāṇavārttikam of Dharmakīrti. The First Chapter with the Autocommentary, ed. R. Gnoli, Rome: Serie Orientale Roma 23, Istituto Italiano per il Medio ed Estremo Oriente, 1960

Pramāṇavārttikasvavṛttiṭīkā
Karṇakagomin's Commentary on the Pramāṇavārttikavṛtti of Dharmakīrti, ed. R. Sāṅkṛtyāyana, [Allahabad: 1943] Kyoto: Rinsen Books Co., 1982

PVin 1
Dharmakīrti's Pramāṇaviniścaya, Chapters 1 and 2, ed. E. Steinkellner, Beijing/Vienna: China Tibetology Publishing House/Austrian Academy of Sciences Press, 2007

RASTOGI 1986
N. Rastogi, "Theory of Error according to Abhinavagupta," *Journal of Indian Philosophy* 14, 1986, pp. 1-33

RATIÉ 2006
I. Ratié, "La Mémoire et le Soi dans l'*Īśvarapratyabhijñāvimarśinī* d'Abhinavagupta," *Indo-Iranian Journal* 49, 2006, pp. 39-103

RATIÉ 2011
I. Ratié, *Le Soi et l'Autre. Identité, différence et altérité dans la philosophie de la Pratyabhijñā*, Leiden/Boston: Brill, 2011

RATIÉ 2016
I. Ratié, "Some hitherto unknown fragments of Utpaladeva's *Vivṛti* (I): on the Buddhist controversy over the existence of other conscious streams," in R. Torel-

la & B. Bäumer (eds.), *Utpaladeva, Philosopher of Recognition*, Delhi: DK Printworld, 2016, pp. 221-253

RATIÉ forthcoming a
I. Ratié, "Some hitherto unknown fragments of Utpaladeva's *Vivṛti* (II): against the existence of external objects," in D. Goodall, S. Hatley, H. Isaacson, S. Raman (eds.), *Śaivism and the Tantric Traditions. Volume in Honour of Alexis G.J.S. Sanderson*

RATIÉ forthcoming b
I. Ratié, "Utpaladeva and Abhinavagupta on the freedom of consciousness," in J. Ganeri (ed.), *Oxford Handbook of Indian Philosophy*, Oxford: Oxford University Press

RATIÉ forthcoming c
I. Ratié, "In search of Utpaladeva's lost *Vivṛti* on the Pratyabhijñā treatise: a report on the latest discoveries (with the *Vivṛti* on the end of Chapter 1.8)," *Journal of Indian Philosophy*

SCHMITHAUSEN 1965
L. Schmithausen, *Maṇḍanamiśra's Vibhramavivekaḥ, mit einer Studie zur Entwicklung der indischen Irrtumslehre*, Wien: Hermann Böhlaus Nachf./Kommissionsverlag der österreichischen Akademie der Wissenschaften, 1965

STERN 1991
E. Stern, "Additional fragments of *Pramāṇaviniścaya* I-II," *Wiener Zeitschrift für die Kunde Südasiens* 35, 1991, pp. 151-168

Tantrāloka
Tantrāloka of Abhinavagupta with commentary by Rājānaka Jayaratha, ed. M.K. Shāstrī, 12 vols., Allahabad/Srinagar/Bombay: Kashmir Series of Texts and Studies 23, 28, 29, 30, 35, 36, 41, 47, 52, 57, 58 & 59, 1918- 1938

Tantrālokaviveka
See *Tantrāloka*

TORELLA 1988
R. Torella, "A Fragment of Utpaladeva's *Īśvarapratyabhijñā-vivṛti*," *East and West* 38, 1988, pp. 137-174

TORELLA 1994
R. Torella, *Īśvarapratyabhijñākārikā of Utpaladeva with the Author's Vṛtti,* ed. and transl., [Roma: 1994] corrected ed., Delhi: Motilal Banarsidass, 2002

TORELLA 2007a
R. Torella, "Studies on Utpaladeva's *Īśvarapratyabhijñā-vivṛti*. Part I: *anupalabdhi* and *apoha* in a Śaiva Garb," in K. Preisendanz (ed.), *Expanding and Merging Horizons. Contributions to South Asian and Cross-Cultural Studies in Commemoration of Wilhelm Halbfass*, Wien: Verlag der Österreichischen Akademie der Wissenschaften, 2007, pp. 473-490

TORELLA 2007b
R. Torella, "Studies on Utpaladeva's *Īśvarapratyabhijñā-vivṛti*. Part II: What is memory?", in K. Klaus & J.-U. Hartmann (eds.), *Indica et Tibetica. Festschrift für Michael Hahn zum 65. Geburtstag von Freunden und Schülern überreicht*, Wien: Arbeitskreis für tibetische und buddhistische Studien Universität Wien, Wiener Studien zur Tibetologie und Buddhismuskunde 66, 2007, pp. 539-563

TORELLA 2007c
R. Torella, "Studies on Utpaladeva's *Īśvarapratyabhijñā-vivṛti*. Part III. Can a Cognition Become the Object of Another Cognition?", in D. Goodall and A. Padoux (eds.), *Mélanges tantriques à la mémoire d'Hélène Brunner*, Pondicherry: Institut Français de Pondichéry/École Française d'Extrême-Orient, Collection Indologie 106, 2007, pp. 475-484

TORELLA 2007d
R. Torella, "Studies on Utpaladeva's *Īśvarapratyabhijñā-vivṛti*. Part IV. Light of the Subject, Light of the Object," in B. Kellner, H. Krasser *et al.* (eds.), *Pramāṇakīrtiḥ. Papers dedicated to Ernst Steinkellner on the Occasion of his 70th Birthday*, Wien: Arbeitskreis für tibetische und buddhistische Studien Universität Wien, Wiener Studien zur Tibetologie und Buddhismuskunde 70.2, 2007, pp. 925-940

TORELLA 2012
R. Torella, "Studies in Utpaladeva's *Īśvarapratyabhijñā-vivṛti*. Part V: Self-awareness and yogic perception," in F. Voegeli et al. (eds.), *Devadattīyam. Johannes Bronkhorst Felicitation Volume*, Bern: Peter Lang, 2012, pp. 275-300

TORELLA 2014
R. Torella, "Utpaladeva's Lost *Vivṛti* on the *Īśvarapratyabhijñā-kārikā*," *Journal of Indian Philosophy* 42, 2014, pp. 115-126

WUJASTYK forthcoming
D. Wujastyk, "Some Problematic Yoga Sutras and their Buddhist Background," in P. Maas et al., *Yoga in Transformation. Historical and Contemporary Perspectives on a Global Phenomenon*, Vienna: Vienna University Press

Vṛtti
[*Īśvarapratyabhijñākārikāvṛtti*] See TORELLA 1994

Yogasūtra 1
[*Yogasūtra*, Chapter 1] *Samādhipāda. Das erste Kapitel des Pātañjalayogaśāstra*, ed. P.A. Maas, Aachen: Shaker Verlag, 2006

Ānandavardhana and Abhinavagupta on the Limits of *Rasa-Dhvani*: A Reading of DhvĀ 3.43

DAVID SHULMAN

1. *GUṆĪ-BHŪTA-VYAṄGYA* REVISITED: "MIXING IN" AND "COMBINING"

Any ramified system of classification will, if extended far enough, sooner or later hit its limit. Something always turns up to challenge the implicit axiology, or the systematicity, of the applied categories – something that eludes classification in the terms at hand. Such cases, as we know from Bateson and Russell, are often the most interesting and revealing for an observer not imprisoned by the categories in question. Subtle classificatory schemes may be resilient enough to survive such a challenge, but a residue of doubt or ambiguity, once articulated, never vanishes. Extreme cases may lead to apparent paradox: what, for example, are we to do with a set that is a member of itself?

One salient locus for such limit-cases in Kashmiri poetics is the remarkable, though at times neglected, third *uddyota* of the *Dhvanyāloka* (together with Abhinavagupta's commentary). I might as well confess at the outset that I find the third and fourth *uddyota*s more compelling, in many ways, than the first two. This short essay may explain why. There are both relatively superficial and even obvious reasons as well as some that may, I hope, have a certain complexity and depth. I'll begin with the former.

Kārikā 3.35 opens Ānanda's major discussion of *guṇī-bhūta-vyaṅgya-kāvya*, that is, poetry in which suggestion, *dhvani* or *vyañjanā*, is theoretically less powerful, or less beautiful (*cāru*), than the openly expressed meaning.[1] One particularly good kind of poe-

---

[1] *prakāro 'nyo guṇī-bhūta-vyaṅgyaḥ kāvyasya dṛśyate | yatra vyaṅgyânvaye vācya-cārutvaṃ syāt prakarṣavat* ||.

try, according to Ānanda, embodies suggestion as a primary aim and thus generates the *rasa*-experience. And yet we can confidently state, on empirical grounds, that poems of "subordinate suggestion" (PSS) are actually far more widespread in the Sanskrit literary corpus than Ānanda's preferred type of "dominant suggestion"; and aside from such statistical considerations, Ingalls is certainly right to say that PSS verses are "among the most beautiful stanzas in the whole book [that is, the *Dhvanyāloka*]."[2] Ingalls also correctly states that PSS verses are not, in Ānanda's view, inferior to the type he prefers, despite a long tradition, beginning with Mammaṭa[3] and continuing into modern commentators, that insists that PSS are indeed second-rate poems.[4] In any case, it is clear that PSS constitute a test-case for the *dhvani* theory in general; we shall see that Ānanda finds it necessary to assert the validity of his theory, indeed to strengthen his theoretical claim, precisely in the context of attempting to incorporate PSS in his wider scheme of poetic effects. At the same time, he is, one might say, driven to reflect, in an indirectly autobiographical and personal way, on the problem that has emerged. McCrea lucidly formulates the difficulty as follows:

> The great strength of Ānandavardhana's model of poetry is its ability to provide a general criterion for aesthetic value in literature, in terms of which particular prescriptions regarding composition may be explained and justified and existing compositions may be evaluated. But... in the case of poetry which does not have *rasa* as its telos, this explanatory and evaluative power simply evaporates.[5]

One can assume that Ānanda himself knew this and did what he could to stem the evaporation. We could also posit a related question that may have troubled him specifically: did Ānandavardhana feel that his sophisticated new theory was capable of explaining the expressive force of some (perhaps most) of his own poems?

There is no space, and no need, for us to re-examine here the entire gamut, or to restate the typology Ānanda offers and Abhinavagupta explains of *guṇī-bhūta-vyaṅgya-kāvya*. The discussion in *uddyota* 3 culminates, in my view, in the very striking verse *yā*

---

2 INGALLS ET. AL 1990, p. 23.

3 *Kāvya-prakāśa* 1.4-5.

4 INGALLS ET. AL. 1990, pp. 22-23.

5 MCCREA 2008, pp. 231-232.

vyāpāravatī inserted into the discussion of *kārikā* 43. In order to understand the full force of this autobiographical verse – which, I will argue, simply cannot be adequately defined or even addressed by *rasa-dhvani* theory, despite Abhinavagupta's valiant attempt to do just that – we will have to move backwards and forwards a bit through Ānanda's theoretical discussions, including early analyses of figuration in relation to suggestion in the second *uddyota*, which resurface in *uddyota* 3. One convenient point of departure is the distinction between types of suggestion that are "combined" or "associated" (*saṃsṛṣṭa*)[6] and those that are "mixed in" or "fused" (*saṅkīrṇa*).[7] This typological division is the substance of *kārikā* 3.43.

We are dealing not with the figure "Mixing" (*saṅkara*) but with a more general classificatory principle. "Combination" is often said to be like an assortment of sesamum and paddy (*tila-taṇḍula-vat*) – that is, one can still, with some effort, separate out the different grains. "Mixing in" is like water mixed with milk (*kṣīra-nīra-vat*); only a goose has the miraculous, inborn ability to distinguish the two components. Thc basic typology of *saṅkara*, the more important and far-reaching of the two terms, goes back to Udbhaṭa who, however, is primarily concerned with the figure.[8] Taken together, the two modes allow for a considerable proliferation of analytic types, as we will see. The third *uddyota* expands this earlier analytical frame exponentially. We will look at one of Ānanda's major examples of *saṅkara* and two particularly interesting ones of *saṃsṛṣṭi*.

Note, first, how 3.43 sets out the parameters of the discussion.

> *saguṇībhūta-vyaṅgyaiḥ sâlaṅkāraiḥ saha prabhedaiḥ svaiḥ* |
> *saṅkara-saṃsṛṣṭibhyāṃ punar apy uddyotate bahudhā* ||
>
> It [= *dhvani*] operates in various ways by mixing in and combining with subordinate suggestion, with figures, and with its own sub-categories.

If we read the DhvĀ in linear sequence, as a long, coherent essay in which certain themes and ideas develop and recur, then 3.43 can be seen to be a refinement and extension of 1.13, where the figure *saṅkara* is partially defined and only rather tentatively admitted

---

6 "Associated" is Ingalls' term.

7 Again, the latter translation is Ingalls'.

8 Discussion in DhvĀ 1.13 (see Ingall's discussion). See KRISHNAMOORTHY 1979.

into the overall category of potential suggestion. There, in *uddyota* 1, suggestion that counts has to be predominant within a given verse (and this can happen in *saṅkara* when a striking figure gives rise to suggestion that goes far beyond the literal sense). Here Abhinavagupta, citing Udbhaṭa, exemplifies four major types of *saṅkara* and effectively allows only instances of *alaṅkāra-dhvani*, where a figure is suggested, to be *saṅkara*-based *dhvani*. But by the time we reach 3.43, *saṅkara* as a poetic and analytical mode has been re-integrated into the domain of *dhvani*, which turns out to be far more flexible, comprehensive, and diverse than we might have suspected on the basis of earlier discussions in this same work. The *kārikā* tells us that we can find *dhvani* operating through both "mixing in" and "combination" in three major ways, depending upon whether the basis for either of these modes is a PSS, one or more figures of speech, or a sub-category of suggestion itself. Given this tripartite typology, Ānanda then spells out what he considers to be the three major categories of "mixing in." We need to take a moment to consider these, as they relate directly to Abhinavagupta's discussion of the verse that interests us most.

Again, let me emphasize that the types of "mixing in" are not new to the DhvĀ but rather derived from Udbhaṭa. What is important in this context is the fact that they have been upgraded to useful analytical descriptions of *dhvani* that falls outside, or on the margins, of the more clear-cut types that directly and unequivocally trigger the *rasa*-experience. These examples of "mixing in" thus include: 1) cases where one variety of suggestion feeds into and enhances another one and is in turn enhanced by the latter (*anugrāhyânugrāhaka-bhāva*), 2) instances where there is doubt as to which of two varieties of suggestion, or two suggestive figures, is primary (*sandehâspadatva*) and 3) the compounding of suggestiveness when two varieties are crammed together in the same, usually tightly compressed locus (*ekapadânupraveśa*). Note that there is a difference, in Ānanda's view, between the beauty that derives from the mutual enhancement of two distinct types flowing into or through one another and the vastly compounded and intensified state that comes from tasting two completely fused forms of *rasa*, especially if one of them is the kind that leaves no interval or space for reflection but rather floods the listener/spectator with immediate sensation (*asaṃlakṣya-krama*).[9] This third type of *saṅkara*,

[9] All this is spelled out in the *vṛtti* to 3.43.

by the way, can coexist with *saṃsṛṣṭi*, "combination," in the same verse, as Ānanda demonstrates through a well-known poem.[10]

It is not this scholastic classification per se that deserves our attention. What is striking is the language of intensification and enhancement precisely in the typological boundary zone where subordinate suggestion, along with other rather suspect poetic means and devices (perhaps even what Ānanda calls *citra*), struggles to be deemed effective *dhvani* – and even for that matter, *rasa-dhvani* – after all. The always present metaphorical register of cooking and tasting remains useful: a good poem tastes good, and the taste can be fully brought out by the skillful cook as he combines distinct condiments and flavors. At the same time, another set of images comes into play – images of suggestion as first enveloping or pervading all real poetic expression from within and then of turning or spinning inwards and moving through itself and its own parts and pieces (*aṅga*). In fact, Ānanda has explicitly stated the overwhelming accessibility of *rasa-dhvani* – for nearly all kinds of poetry – in the prose passage that immediately precedes *kārikā* 3.43: "There is simply no such thing as something that a poet entirely intent upon *rasa* cannot use as a component in generating the *rasa* he has chosen out of his desire for that *rasa* – and that will not, when so used, intensify the charm of the poem" (*tasmān nâsty eva tad vastu yat sarvātmanā rasa-tātparyavataḥ kaves tad-icchayā tad-abhimata-rasâṅgatāṃ na dhatte tathopanibadhyamānaṃ vā na cārutvâtiśayaṃ puṣṇāti*). He goes on to say, pointedly, that his own poetic works substantiate this claim here and there (*yathāyatham*).

But wait a minute. Haven't we been told already in *uddyota* 2 that an accomplished poet needs to exercise a certain caution or care (*samīkṣā*) if he wants to turn the various means at his disposal, in particular the figures of speech, to the purpose of producing *rasa-dhvani*?[11] What kind of care is Ānanda talking about? What actually allows a figure of speech to contribute to the emergence of *rasa*? (The context in these *kārikā*s is specifically *śṛṅgāra-rasa*, a test-case for the theory more generally.) A whole set of features are cited to qualify *samīkṣā*, including, first of all, the insistence that the figure itself never assume the foreground in the poem (*nâṅgitvena kathaṃ cana*). But the easiest way to follow Ānanda's

---

[10] *Snigdha-syāmala**, first cited in 2.1 and beautifully analyzed by Abhinavagupta there.

[11] DhvĀ 2.17-19.

line of thought is to study the first example he cites, the famous verse from *Abhijñānaśākuntala* 1.20, which we will have occasion to mention later as well:

calâpāṅgāṃ dṛṣṭiṃ spṛśasi bahuśo vepathumatīṃ
rahasyâkhyāyîva svanasi mṛdu karṇântikacaraḥ |
karaṃ vyādhunvatyāḥ pibasi rati-sarvasvam adharaṃ
vayaṃ tattvânveṣān madhukara hatās tvaṃ khalu kṛtī ||

Again and again you touch the tremulous edges
of her eyes. You murmur softly
in her ear, as if sharing some deep secret,
and though she waves her hand wildly,
you gobble up every bit of goodness
from her lips. You're just a bee, god damn it,
but you've got everything
you wanted, while I'm still busy trying
to figure things out.

Ānanda tells us that this poem is built around the figure of *svabhāvokti*, "naturalistic description," which, he says, is entirely in harmony with the rasa (*rasânuguṇa*).

Before we see what Abhinavagupta has to say about this verse, we should perhaps contextualize it rather than taking it as an isolated exemplum (like so many of the verses cited by the poeticians). This poem comes at a critical moment in the first act of the play. Duṣyanta, still hidden but already in love with the enchanting Śakuntalā, whom he has just seen for the first time, has overheard her girlfriends' teasing banter, which suggests that Śakuntalā would very much like to find a husband. This is good news. He is, however, slightly tormented about the question of her social origins – living in the ashram, she might be a Brahmin girl, thus ruled out as a possible wife for a king. On the other hand, he wants her, and he conveniently assumes that this fact alone probably means that she's available. While he's deliberating with himself in this vein, the bee closes in on her; in some distress, she calls for help, and now the king has the perfect entrance cue. With evident irony, on the verge of self-parody, he suddenly reveals himself as the great protector of the realm who is thus perfectly cast as this girl's savior. From this point on, their love can begin to develop openly. Note that from the point of view of emergent *śṛṅgāra-rasa*, this transition from a state of hidden desire to a tangible, visible presence signals a necessary development, thickening and intensifying the erotic mood by establishing mutuality and a whole series of immediate verbal and non-verbal effects.

Ānanda has nothing more to say about the verse, but we need to pay attention to Abhinavagupta's initial comments about it. He focuses, somewhat characteristically, on the particle *khalu*, the penultimate word in the verse. This *khalu*, he says, tells us that the bee has achieved his goal effortlessly (*ayatna-siddhaṃ tavaiva caritârthatvam*), in telling contrast to Duṣyanta, who is observing his rival rather helplessly – so that we have, on this level of deliberate semantic choice, a suggestiveness that requires a small gap for thought (*saṃlakṣya-krama*), though Abhinavagupta does not spell this out. In a world of continually compounded resonances such as that embodied in a good Sanskrit verse, no word, indeed no syllable, is likely to be entirely innocent. A further cognitively charged suggestion is noted in Abhinavagupta's comment on *pāda* 2: the fact that the bee keeps on buzzing around her ear (*karṇântika-caraḥ*) shows that it is caught up in the illusion that Śakuntalā's eyes are elongated blue nympheas (*nīlotpala*), that is, her eyes must reach all the way to her ears (*śravaṇâvakāśa-paryantatvāt*), as should be the case for every beautiful woman. Interestingly, Abhinavagupta has nothing explicit to say about the figure *bhrāntimat*, "cognitive error," which, if his reading is correct, must be active here.

However, on one level the identification of the various figures involved doesn't much matter, since the real point is that whatever they may be – and Ānanda has already pointed to the figure *svabhāvokti* as central – they are entirely at the service of the *rasa* of refined desire. Figuration, that is, helps primarily to enhance the *rasa* as it begins to rise and overflow (this is a paraphrase of Abhinavagupta's way of talking about *rasa*, not Ānanda's). But on another level, the definition of the figures involved does make a difference. Abhinavagupta concludes his comment on the verse by saying that some unspecified "others" read Ānanda's comment as pointing to a *rūpaka-vyatireka*, that is, the bee is metaphorically identified as a lover, and as such he obviously and, as Abhinavagupta has just told us, effortlessly supersedes the clumsy and hesitant human lover Duṣyanta. We thus have two perhaps not entirely incongruent readings: one in which the figure *svabhāvokti*, giving us the naturalistic observation of the bee's way of being and acting, "mixes in" with the dominant *rasa*, enveloping the entire verse and thus occupying the same locus as the *rasa* (*saṅkara* of type 3, as defined above), and one in which the figuration, specifically the *rūpaka-vyatireka*, assists and enhances the *rasa* (*saṅkara* of type 1). Abhinavagupta will state these two options with crystal clarity in his comment on *kārikā* 3.43, with reference to this same verse.

Interestingly, neither Ānanda nor Abhinavagupta address what seem to me, at least, to be the more pressing and impressive elements of Kālidāsa's verse – the fact, for example, that the tone is ironic and rather self-deprecating; Duṣyanta is playing with himself as he explores the new world of feeling he has discovered, and he sounds rather disgusted with his own propensity to a somewhat barren intellection at a moment where he needs and wants to act. Moreover, as so often in Kālidāsa, this verse, with its primary image, is meant to adumbrate and thus enhance a much later, thematically powerful moment in the play – in Act VI, where Duṣyanta, now consumed by remorse, has painted a picture of the absent Śakuntalā and, forgetting that this painting is only an artistic illusion, attempts to drive away a bee that is attracted to the face, and more specifically the lips, of the image (6.20). The Vidūṣaka, observing the scene, will have to disabuse the hapless king of his confusion, thus re-establishing an all-too-tenuous border between illusion and reality. But this fusing of visible reality with mental projection – a different sort of *saṅkara* than those spelled out by the DhvĀ and its great commentator, one that is far more far-reaching in its possible cognitive effects – also constitutes one of the latent, highly reflexive themes of the play as a whole. The appearance of the error-driven bee in both Act I and Act VI – probably the same bee – thus turns out to be rather crucial, even, we might say, over-determined. This is obviously not the kind of observation that either Ānanda or Abhinavagupta would be likely to make; they have more urgent tasks at hand. However, it is also worth stating that even if *svabhāvokti* can be identified here, it's a relatively pallid example of the figure, so conventional and predictable as to be almost silly. I'm afraid such a reading may well vitiate the *rasa*-driven analysis that Abhinavagupta, following Ānanda, is offering us.

And yet "mixing in" does have an honorable role in the theory of *dhvani*, including (especially) *rasa-dhvani*, and beyond it; there is good reason to take the time to understand it as it appears in both the DhvĀ and the *Locana*. Certain kinds of "mixing in" definitely serve specific aesthetic goals and can help characterize the sensitive listener's experience. In particular, what we might call "deep compounding" is clearly capable of working upon the awareness of the listener in unexpected ways. But what about *saṃsṛṣṭi*, "combination," *saṅkara*'s categorical sibling? Let us briefly consider two examples relevant to our discussion.

We began with 3.43, and it is in the *vṛtti* to that *kārikā* that we find, first, a prominent example of *saṃsṛṣṭi*, familiar from an earlier passage (2.5):

teṣāṃ gopa-vadhū-vilāsa-suhṛdāṃ rādhā-rahaḥ-sākṣiṇāṃ
kṣemaṃ bhadra kalinda-śaila-tanayā-tīre latā-veśmanām |
vicchinne smara-talpa-kalpana-mṛdu-cchedopayoge 'dhunā
te jāne jaraṭhī-bhavanti vigalan-nīla-tviṣaḥ pallavāḥ ||

How are they, my friend – the bowers of vines
on the banks of the river that are friends to the gopīs
and witnesses to *her*, Rādhā's, secrets? And the twigs and sprays
that we would cut to make a love-bed – we need them
no more. I know: they've now grown old and lost
their dark sheen.

Kṛṣṇa is speaking – either to himself (Abhinavagupta's theory about the second half of the verse) or, more likely, to a messenger from the herders of Braj who has sought him out in Mathurā. The meeting with the messenger has called up in Kṛṣṇa an overwhelming feeling of longing and nostalgia that is channeled into his question about the vines and the sprays. So is this longing the true subject of the *dhvani* active in the verse? Not quite. Abhinavagupta gives an extended interpretation in his comments on 2.5, which deals with cases where *rasa* is subordinate to some other expressive element in the statement and thus becomes the somewhat limited figure known as *rasavat*. We can summarize his analysis there together with his brief comments on 3.43 as follows:

1. Only bowers of vines can be true friends to the gopīs, since they can't speak and thus will certainly tell no one about the gopīs' secret love encounters. Similarly, such bowers witnessed Rādhā's meetings with Kṛṣṇa; hence Rādhā truly loves them (*rādhāyāś ca sâtiśayaṃ prema-sthānam*). However, vines and sprays are not, after all, really "friends" or "witnesses" – these words are used metaphorically, by *lakṣaṇā*, so we have two instances of *lakṣaṇā-mūla-dhvani* of the type where the literal meaning is transferred to another (*arthântara-saṅkramita*). There has to be some motive behind such a transfer, and in this case the *lakṣaṇā* indicates the ex-

treme affection Rādhā has for the vines and their benevolent presence in her life and the lives of her friends. (In fact, this articulation of the motivation seems to me rather weak.)

2. There are further suggestive usages of the kind that require thought and, thus, a short interval before the *rasa* kicks in. Kṛṣṇa, very sure of himself, thinks: "If I'm not somewhere close, why would the gopīs need a love-bed? (*mayy anāsīne kā smara-talpa-kalpaneti bhāvaḥ*)." In other words, he is certain that their love for him and his for them is perfectly mutual (*parasparânurāga-niścaya-garbha*). Also, the fact that the green sprays that have lined the bowers are now grey and old means that it must be quite a long time since he, Kṛṣṇa, left Braj, for if he had stayed there, he and the gopīs would have been making love continuously and the sprays would never have dried out and faded. Similarly, the final phrase, "lost their dark sheen," suggests that Kṛṣṇa is long gone and yet – remembering the sprays – filled with intense longing (*autsukya-nirbharatva*).

3. That longing, as already intimated, results from memories awakened by the sight of the messenger (*gopa-darśana-prabuddha-saṃskāra*), so that Kṛṣṇa now feels the pleasure of reawakening desire (*prabuddha-rati-bhāva*) on the basis of the conditioning factors (*vibhāva*) operating within his memory – specifically, the memory of Rādhā (the *ālambana* or foundational condition) and of the bowers (which are intensifiers, *uddīpana-vibhāva*s). Note that this anamnetic yearning takes place inside a character internal to the poem and not directly in someone listening to the poem outside.

4. Two words – *te*, "they," and *jāne*, "I know" (or perhaps, "I recall and therefore know") – operate in a very different manner from that of all three previous points. They are not devoid of *dhvani*, but they serve the literal (*vācya*) sense, which is in this case the real source of charm in the poem, a direct evocation of the emotional power of memory (*vācyasyaiva smaraṇasya prādhānyena cārutva-hetutvāt*). One could also say (pushing Abhinavagupta's statement a little further) that the image of the once-green, now pale and dying sprays is strong enough to override the existing instances of definable suggestion. The poet concretizes and highlights the stark image by starting the fourth *pāda* with this *te*: "they," "these" (very leaves and twigs and sprays) are what

> concern us. Abhinavagupta notes that *jāne* is often a marker of the figure *utprekṣā*, "flight of fancy," but that here, again, its literal meaning is what matters. That is: the actual content of Kṛṣṇa's knowing/remembering, a personal act, is of real interest to the listener.

This final comment by Abhinavagupta comes closest, in my view, to shedding light on the deeper mechanisms of this lovely verse. What does Kṛṣṇa, who happens to be God, actually know at any given moment? He can, it seems, forget rather important pieces of his life. Also, the anacolouthon, *jāne*, close to the start of *pāda* 4, brings this entire epistemic domain into focus as a subject. There is a subtle but marked transition from *te* to *jāne* that signals, as Abhinavagupta seems to propose, the return to the literal meaning as of primary interest. But to feel the true force of this transition one has to go back to *pāda* 3 with, first, its dense and profoundly expressive compound – *smara-talpa-kalpana-mṛdu-cchedopayoge* – and then its plaintive adverb at the end, *adhunā*, "now." The compound calls up, step by step, the sweet moments when the eager lovers cut leaves and sprays to make themselves a bed. This vivid memory then issues remorselessly into the brutal, lonely "now."

In fact, I think this loss of the green love-beds is the heart of the poem – and both Ānanda and Abhinavagupta are right in seeing the other forms of suggestion that may well be present as decidedly secondary. The torments of memory and, I suppose, of forgetting comprise another primary register. Seen in this light, the *lakṣaṇā* suddenly seems more powerful than it looked at first glance. The longing has been deftly transferred to, or projected on to, the mute vines and sprays. Indirection generates intensity in a good Sanskrit poem.[12]

Abhinavagupta's two, widely separated comments on this verse are differently focused: in 2.5 he is mostly interested in *saṃlakṣya-krama-vyaṅgya*, while in 3.43 he wants to highlight *guṇī-bhūta-vyaṅgya*. I have compounded his interpretative remarks. In both cases, however, whatever the emphasis, we can clearly see the difference between what we find here and the mode of "mixing in" studied earlier. The triggers of suggestion in this verse are distinct in type and situated at different points in the syntax. We don't see the mingling of figures that enhance one another mutually, nor do we see *dhvani* swerving back into itself and absorbing its own sub-

---

[12] My thanks to Yigal Bronner for discussing this poem with me.

types so as to generate much higher voltages. Instead, the suggested senses seem to dwell peacefully side by side. There is, in short, no fusion; the poem isn't intent on swallowing up its own tail. On the other hand, an emotional state, pregnant with highly specific cognitive themes, swells to the point where the listener can barely contain it. That progression, which depends on opening up a certain space for reflection, creates the poem and shapes the listener's experience. The first half, quizzical, almost innocuous, quietly sets the stage for the agony of the second half. No one, I think, gets lost to himself or herself, or finds his or her feelings "universalized," in the course of hearing this verse. If anything, the poem might be said to foster in every listener who has known love and the loss of love some form of radical "personalization." I'll return to this theme.

We're closing in, by now, on Ānanda's autobiographical *yā vyāpāravatī*, the verse I find so compelling. Before we turn to it, I want to examine one more, relatively simple example of *saṃsṛṣṭi* that follows immediately upon *yā vyāpāravatī*, thus effectively bracketing it together with the two poems we've already discussed. The verse is a famous one, from Kālidāsa's *Megha-dūta* (31):

dīrghī-kurvan paṭu mada-kalaṃ kūjitaṃ sārasānāṃ
pratyūṣeṣu sphuṭita-kamalâmoda-maitrī-kaṣāyaḥ |
yatra strīṇāṃ harati surata-glāniṃ aṅgânukūlaḥ
siprā-vātaḥ priyatama iva prârthanā-cāṭu-kāraḥ ||

Each morning at dawn
it draws out the cry of the cranes –
a little eerie, and exciting –
as, sharpened by the friendly fragrance
of lotus flowers unfolding, it soothes
the bodies of young women exhausted
after a night of long loving and makes them
ready for more. It's like a practiced lover,
begging, bantering, flattering,
this breeze blowing
from the Siprā River.

Ānanda introduces this verse as an example of *saṃsṛṣṭi* dependent upon a single word – or, more generally, where some variety of suggestion combines with an expressly stated (that is, not suggested) figure of speech (*vācyâlaṅkāra*). After citing the verse he notes that it, too (as in the previous example), contains one instance of suggestion based on metaphoric usage, where the literal meaning is put aside (*avivakṣita-vācya*): this is the word *maitrī*, "friendship," used to characterize the fragrant breeze as "friendly." No breeze is ever literally friendly. In addition, Ānanda says, other words in the verse contain various other figures. Abhinavagupta spells them out in one of his insightful interpretative passages.

For example, how is it that the breeze "draws out" the cranes' cry? There are three reasons: the sound carries over a long distance (*siprā-vātena hi dūram apy asau śabdo nīyate*); the cranes go on crying because they're so happy at the touch of the breeze (*tathā su-kumāra-pavana-sparśa-jāta-harṣāc ciraṃ kūjantīti*); and the cry mingles with the sound of the waves stirred by the breeze, thus becoming fuller and longer (*tat kūjitaṃ ca vātândolita-siprā-taraṅga-ja-madhura-śabda-miśraṃ bhavatīti dīrghatvam*). This naturalistic observation puts us in the domain of *svabhāvokti*, though Abhinavagupta doesn't say this.[13] Then there is something to be said about the word *kaṣāya* at the end of *pāda* b: it means, according to Abhinavagupta, both the reddish color of the pollen in the opening lotuses and "in love" (*uparakta*), the latter sense suited to the explicit simile – the wind as lover – in the final *pāda*. In fact, the word that modifies *kaṣāya* is that same *maitrī*, the metaphoric "friendship," which, Abhinavagupta asserts, suggests a mutual harmony derived from an exclusive and repeated connection (*anyâsaṅgâviyoge parasparānukūlya-lābha*).[14] In other words, the erotic register, which will become explicit at the end of the poem, is already suggested by the lexical choices in the first half.

But the explicit simile has its own suggestive power that can be paraphrased as follows: the breeze-as-lover –appearing as grammatical subject only at the start of *pāda* d, the neuralgic point of so many Sanskrit poems – is gentle, courteous, considerate, and skilled; it/he arouses the exhausted beloved by lightly massaging her body and, at the same time, whispering to her words of praise and endearment that make her beg for more loving; thus the wind becomes the very embodiment of pure desire that comes alive from equal and mutual affection (*parasparânurāga-prāṇa-śṛṅgāra-sarvasva-bhūto 'sau pavanaḥ*). And this, says Abhinavagupta, is only natural, since the breeze from the Siprā is surely a cultured, self-

---

[13] Ingalls (p. 662) rightly says that *svabhāvokti* pervades the entire stanza. By now we should have observed that *svabhāvokti* seems to have a particular association with *saṃsṛṣṭi*.

[14] V.l. *abhyāsâṅgâviyoga-parasparânukūlya-lābhaḥ*.

aware lover (*nāgarika*), not just any old village idiot (*na tv avidagdho grāmya-prāyaḥ*). And once we have reached this point, it is easy to go back and read the first half of the verse as adumbrating, or indeed already modifying, the culminating image, so that it is the breeze as lover who draws out the moans of his beloved and who is profoundly attached to her face, which is like the fragrant lotus opening at dawn. I think these points are well taken and do, indeed, partly explain how the verse thickens and refines the passionate tone it is seeking to establish by light touches of resonant suggestion.

And yet we are meant to see in this poem a clear case of *saṃsṛṣṭi*, despite the analytic drift toward what appears more like "mixing in," especially given the pervasiveness of the naturalistic description that thus occupies the same locus as the sequential suggestions. In fact, even the word *maitrī*, as Abhinavagupta unpacks it, now seems integral to the central metaphoric register with its underlying simile. We need only pry this word loose from the tight compound in which it appears – but without sacrificing its intrinsic relation to *kaṣāya* in the sense of "in love" – to see how suited it is to the mood of profoundly affectionate loving. So has the verse been misclassified by Ānanda and better defined by Abhinavagupta? Do we really care? It's all too easy to become trapped within the proliferating categorical niceties of this particular poetic theory.[15] When that happens, the whole point of the discussion, which – do we still remember this? – was once focused on substantial aesthetic effects and the mechanisms that generate them, tends to get lost. Ānanda himself, as we shall see, was well aware of this danger.

For the record, and for the purposes of this essay, let me summarize what has emerged from our reading of the *vṛtti* following this *kārikā* with Abhinavagupta's comment. There are two basic interpretative options. We can look at *maitrī* as an instance of metaphor-based suggestion, with a very limited range indeed – so limited as to separate the word off, more or less completely, from the other active suggestive images and lexemes in the verse. In this case we have, technically speaking, a case of *saṃsṛṣṭi*; but the result is a gap almost ludicrous in dimension between this restricted form of *dhvani* and the overall import and potential effect of the

---

15 See, for example, Patwardhan's learned comment on this passage in INGALLS ET AL., pp. 662-663.

poem. Or we can follow Abhinavagupta's hint and let *maitrī* do the work it is clearly capable of doing along with its figurative partners (*svabhāvokti* and *upamā*, at the least, but maybe also *rūpaka* and *utprekṣā*), in which case we are a) much closer to "mixing in," with its greater intensities and b) beautifully poised to deepen our exploration of the cognitive and logical processes that the verse naturally triggers, whether they lead to some kind of *rasa*-experience or not. In general, I find these processes – which Abhinavagupta begins to analyze with real insight – far more compelling than any universalized liquefaction.

2. AUTOBIOGRAPHY, CONFESSION, SUBVERSION

At last we come to the verse I've been wanting to read with you. Let me remind you that it appears in the DhvĀ between remarks on *teṣāṃ gopa-vadhū** ("How are they, my friend...") and *dīrghī-kurvan* ("Every morning at dawn..."), in the context of the attempt to make sense of PSS in the larger scheme of *dhvani*-oriented poetics and, more specifically, in relation to the two modes we have been studying, "mixing in" and "combining." We will see in a moment that our first example, *calâpāṅgāṃ dṛṣṭim* ("Again and again..."), is also explicitly drawn into discussion of this new verse. Here it comes:

yā vyāpāravatī rasān rasayituṃ kā-cit kavīnāṃ navā
dṛṣṭir yā pariniṣṭhitârtha-viṣayonmeṣā ca vaipaścitī |
te dve apy avalambya viśvam aniśaṃ nirvarṇayanto vayaṃ
śrāntā naiva ca labdham abdhi-śayana tvad-bhakti-tulyaṃ sukham ||

Poets have a special way of seeing
that is always new, and compelling,
that lets you taste
what can be tasted.
And there's the other way, too,
where you think and analyze
with an opening mind
until you know for sure
how things are.
I've tried them both, Lord
who sleeps on the sea,
and I'm so tired of always
working hard to define
the world, for nothing ever

even comes close
to the happiness I have
in loving you.

Ānanda tells us that he composed this verse.[16] In theory, it could be a statement projected on to some other literary persona (Ingalls reluctantly suggests Bhartṛhari or Dharmakīrti; the latter choice is, in fact, rather meaningful, as I hope to show). Yet the poem rings true as a personal statement, perhaps intertextually enhanced; and its placement at this point in *uddyota* 3, in the midst of the attempt to make sense of PSS as a workable category, supports, I think, this reading. The poem is introduced by a short statement about "mixing in" as frequently occurring when *rasa-dhvani* – *dhvani* of an imperceptible interval – mingles with explicitly stated figures of speech (*vācyâlaṅkāra*). This remark allows Abhinavagupta first to mention, once again, that we have three major forms of "mixing in" as well as the neighboring category of "combination," and then to call to mind the Kālidāsa verse about the lucky bee (*calâpāṅgāṃ dṛṣṭim*). We have already seen the two main interpretative options that Abhinavagupta offers for this verse. It's at least possible that Abhinavagupta wished to connect the naturalistic description of Kālidāsa's bee with Kālidāsa's meticulous, and also evocative, portrait of the morning breeze from the Siprā in the next verse to come up for analysis. Or perhaps he felt that the bee offers an indubitable example of successful "mixing in" of figures and *asaṃlakṣya-krama-vyaṅgya*. Whatever the case may be, both Ānanda's preface to the new verse and Abhinavagupta's explication of it set the stage for a second general remark, to the effect that we also find "mixing in" with other forms of suggestion – that is, those kinds that are not *rasa-dhvani*. It is to illustrate this statement that Ānanda quotes his own verse. At the very least, this means that *yā vyāpāravatī* leaves room for the reader to think, quite consciously, about what the poem is trying to say. This poem, according to its author, is not meant to spark off an immediate *rasa* experience, despite Ānanda's preface to this passage. It has another, apparently more urgent aim.

---

16 As has been noted before, by Raghavan, Ingalls, and Chakrabarti, the first three-quarters of the verse appear verbatim in *Yoga-vāsiṣṭha-mahā-rāmāyaṇa*, 6.1 – whose date, in the form of the text we now have, may be later than Ānanda's.

Ānanda comments only very briefly on the verse. He says it contains the kind of *dhvani* that is based on metaphor, *lakṣaṇā*, where the literal meaning is transferred (*saṅkramita*) to another object; and that the figure of speech *virodha*, "contradiction," comes in to assist the aesthetic process at this point. As in our previous example (centered on the transferred and suggestive meanings of the word *maitrī*), the discussion here begins with the single word "seeing" (*dṛṣṭi*). Put simply, you cannot "see" a taste, as Abhinavagupta makes clear in his comments. So the prominent use of *dṛṣṭi* (at the start of *pāda* b) sets up a tension in the mind that is resolved only when we understand the motivation behind the poet's choice: the "seeing" involved is not ordinary sensual perception but an imaginative act of the inner eye, which sees much farther and deeper than in ordinary vision (*loka-vārtâpatita-bodhâvasthā*, Abhinavagupta again). Moreover, the extraordinary nature of this imaginative vision (*pratibhā-rūpā dṛṣṭiḥ*) is explicitly signaled by the word "special" (*kā-cit*, in the sense of something wonderful, even ineffable, *nirvacanīya*). This extraordinary form of seeing is always fresh and new, "continuously, moment by moment, creating worlds by unexpected novelties" (*kṣaṇe kṣaṇe nūtanair nūtanair vaicitryair jaganti āsūtrayantī*).

Before we go any further, we should note how Ānanda's laconic and technical remark has been saved by Abhinavagupta's gloss. The *lakṣaṇā*-based *dhvani* does tell us something about the way a good poet works. But even so, there is, once again – as in the case of the Siprā breeze – a huge gap between the limited, almost mechanical treatment of a single word, here the suggestive word "seeing," and the dramatic import of the verse as a whole. What we have is a very direct statement, not meant to trigger any *rasa* (and what *rasa* would it be, anyway? We'd have to invent a new one, something like "exhaustion"), but powerfully formulated so as to allow any listener or reader to identify with the thought presented. That includes those among us who have specialized in the Kashmiri *alaṅkāra-śāstra*. Ānanda tells us that after long efforts at working at poetry and, apparently, poetics as well as at disciplined intellection that seeks to know things as they are, he's tired of it all. There's another, much more promising road to happiness.

Here is a moment where a ramified system of categories, replete with metaphysical assumptions, like all such systems, reveals to itself, and to us, its own insufficiency. I find the statement very moving. It also speaks to the natural resistance a sensitive reader may have to analytical dissection of a good poem, as when Mandelstam tells us, a millennium or so after Ānandavardhana, that when you can paraphrase a poem, you know that poetry "has not spent the night; the sheets have not been rumpled." We could also say that the extreme semanticization of Sanskrit poetics in the Kashmiri *śāstra*, to use Yigal Bronner's term, comes briefly face to face with what has been sacrificed and lost.

Yet if we seek to understand more deeply the drive to a metaphysical program internal to aesthetic theory, a program still latent in Ānanda but fully elaborated in Abhinavagupta[17] with features specific to Kashmiri erudition in the ninth to the eleventh centuries, then we have only to follow Abhinavagupta's lucid exposition of this same verse. Here is what he says:

> *kavīnām iti vaipaścitīti vacanena nâhaṃ kavir na paṇḍita ity ātmano 'nauddhatyam dhvanyate. an-ātmīyam api daridra-gṛha iva upakaraṇatayânyata āhṛtam etan mayā dṛṣṭi-dvayam ity arthaḥ. te dve apīti na hy ekayā dṛṣṭyā samyaṅ-nirvarṇanaṃ nirvahati... aniśam iti punaḥ punaḥ anavarataṃ nirvarṇayantaḥ varṇanayā tathā niścitârtham. idam ittham iti parāmarśânumānâdinā nirbhajya nirvarṇanaṃ kim atra sāraṃ syād iti tilaśas tilaśo vicayanam. yac ca nirvarṇyate tat khalu madhye vyāpāryamāṇayā madhye cârtha-viśeṣeṣu niścitonmeṣayā niścalayā dṛṣṭyā samyaṅ-nirvarṇitaṃ bhavati. vayam iti mithyā-tattva-dṛṣṭy-āharaṇa-vyasaninaḥ ity arthaḥ. śrāntā iti na kevalaṃ sāraṃ na labdhaṃ yāvat pratyuta khedaḥ prāpta iti bhāvaḥ... abdhi-śayaneti yoga-nidrayā tvam ata eva sāra-svarūpa-vedī svarūpâvasthita ity arthaḥ. śrāntasya śayana-sthitaṃ prati bahumāno bhavati.*
>
> *tvad-bhaktīti tvam eva paramâtma-sva-rūpaḥ viśva-sāraḥ bhakteḥ śraddhā-pūrvaka upâsana-krama-jaḥ tad-āveśaḥ. tena tulyam api na labhyam, āstāṃ tāvat taj-jātīyam.*
>
> *evam prathamam eva parameśvara-bhakti-bhājaḥ kutūhala-mātrâvalambita-kavi-prāmāṇikobhaya-vṛtteḥ punar api parameśvara-bhakti-viśrāntir eva yukteti manvānasyeyaṃ muktiḥ sakala-pramāṇa-pariniścita-dṛṣṭâdṛṣṭa-viśeṣa-jaṃ yat sukhaṃ yad api vā lokottaraṃ rasa-carvaṇâtmakaṃ tata ubhayato 'pi parameśvara-viśrānty-ānandaḥ prakṛṣyate. tad-ānanda-vipruṇ-mātrâvabhāso hi rasâsvāda ity uktam prāg asmābhiḥ. laukikaṃ tu sukhaṃ tato 'pi nikṛṣṭa-prāyaṃ bahutara-duḥkhânuṣaṅgād iti tātparyam.*

---

17 See SHULMAN 1988.

By the words "of poets" and "think and analyze," he suggests his lack of pretension, as if to say, "I'm neither a poet nor a scholar." That is: I took over these two ways of seeing, though they are not really mine, the way food is borrowed from elsewhere to serve in a poor man's home. Why "both"? Because neither one alone is enough to paint the world as it really is... "All the time": describing (literally: painting) over and over, without cease, in order to define everything as exactly as possible. That means dividing things up bit by bit through reflection (*parāmarśa*) and inference (*anumāna*), among other things, in order to find the essence; and also it means letting your eyes engage with it all while from time to time they stare steadily at some detail or another. "I": who am addicted both to false seeing[18] and to true seeing. "So tired": not only did I not find the essential truth, but I'm also exhausted... "Lord who sleeps on the sea": You who in your Yogic sleep know the real form of essential truth and who rest in your self. A person who is exhausted has respect for a person who is sleeping.

"In loving you": you are the self of the highest self and the inner essence of all that is. "Loving you" means complete immersion in that through a series of ritual acts informed by profound attentiveness. "Comes close": not only is there nothing equal to this, but there is nothing even remotely like it.

What he means is that he was first devoted to God, but out of passionate curiosity alone he took on the modes of life of the poet and the logician; then he realized once more that resting in love of God is the right way. That happiness that comes from analyzing whatever can be seen and what cannot be seen through logical means of knowing, and also that kind that is made up of an otherworldly tasting – the joy of resting in God is much better than either of these. For tasting *rasa* is but a pale reflection of a single drop of that joyfulness – as I have said elsewhere. As for ordinary happiness in the world, it's far worse than this, because so much unhappiness is inevitably mixed into it. That's what the verse means.

Ānanda's biographical moment inspires a personal echo in Abhinavagupta. We sometimes ask ourselves how Abhinavagupta's *rasa*-based poetics relates to his Śaiva ritual-based metaphysics.[19] Here we find one candid answer by the master himself. Rasa experience (*rasâsvāda*), to which he has devoted two massive commen-

---

18 *mithyā-dṛṣṭi*: that is, the poet's imagined reality.

19 See SHULMAN 2010; also the penetrating suggestions in Gnoli 1968, pp. xlii-l.

taries, turns out to be hardly more than a slight spray of real joyfulness. He knows a lot about such forms of intense and lasting happiness. Among other things, were we to tease out the full complement of components that make up such joy, we could extract from this passage the primary notion of deep resting – as when consciousness turns inward upon itself and finds repose in that self.[20] There would also be something to say about *āveśa*, "complete immersion" informed by attentiveness. This is not the place to attempt to define the nature of the awareness that emerges when one attains some such state. There is, however, in my view, a direct link between these statements and Abhinavagupta's own *stotra*s, which by no means lend themselves to being understood in terms of the theory proposed in the DhvĀ or, more to the point, in the *Locana*. These poems are, above all, personal, non-repeatable expressions in which complex cognitive and affective states merge to create a new aesthetic.

Having allowed himself this lyrical, yet straightforward, crescendo, Abhinavagupta returns one more time to the initial suggestion embodied in the word *dṛṣṭi*. He wants a more precise analysis of the *dhvani* involved – one that will make better sense of Ānanda's remark that his verse will serve to illustrate "mixing in" (and not "combination"). Patwardhan has lucidly articulated the argument here, and I see no reason to repeat it.[21] Abhinavagupta's need to revisit this issue is, however, more than a mere retreat from the candor that has informed his paraphrase of the verse. As we have seen, "mixing in" – especially when it involves the inward twist or turn of suggestiveness moving through its own, profoundly pervasive nature, joining with its own sub-categories or with figures that occupy the same locus that it inhabits in itself – is, indeed, a powerful conceptual tool. One might say that this mode exemplifies, on the level of poetic experience, something of the inward turn of awareness that is named "repose in self."

---

[20] See *Abhinavabhāratī*: *rasa-niṣpatti-sūtra*, summary of Bhaṭṭa Nāyaka's position (GNOLI 1968, p. 10); see comment by Gnoli, p. xxiii, n. 1; CHAKRABARTI 2005, pp. 27-36.

[21] INGALLS ET. AL. 1990, pp. 658-669.

3. POST-SCRIPT ON DHARMAKĪRTI

Before we let go of Ānanda's verse, and before we find ourselves immersed, again, not in real joyfulness but in the seductive ersatz variety of cataloguing and making lists, we might note that the verse we have studied could be seen as part of a small set. *Kārikā* 3.40, only a few pages back from 3.43, asserts, not surprisingly, that PSS can indeed fit the over-arching category of *dhvani* if the poet's intention is ultimately directed toward *rasa*. The rather extensive *vṛtti* closes with two autobiographical verses attributed – thus Ānanda – to Dharmakīrti.[22] *Yā vyāpāravatī* is thus by no means alone; the theoretical context helps explain why. Here are the two verses in question:

lāvaṇya-draviṇa-vyayo na gaṇitaḥ kleśo mahān arjitaḥ
svacchandaṃ carato janasya hṛdaye cintā-jvaro nirmitaḥ |
eṣâpi svayam eva tulya-ramaṇâbhāvād varākī hatā
ko 'rthaś cetasi vedhasā vinihitas tanvyās tanuṃ tanvatā ||

It was a huge effort, and he spared no expense.
A hungry fire now burns in the hearts of men
who were happy before.
And as for her, poor girl, she's left to languish
because no lover could ever
be her equal. So what was God thinking
when he turned his mind
to fashioning her body?

an-adhyavasitâvagāhanam an-alpa-dhī-śaktinâ-
py adṛṣṭa-paramârtha-tattvam adhikâbhiyogair api |
mataṃ mama jagaty alabdha-sadṛśa-pratigrāhakaṃ
prayāsyati payonidheḥ paya iva sva-dehe jarām ||

No one in this world
has fathomed my thought.
Even the best minds that engaged with it
with all their strength
failed to see my truth.
Not even one worthy reader
really got it.
Like water in the ocean,

---

22 Only the second is solidly attested in surviving works of Dharmakīrti, and there is reason to doubt the attribution to this poet-philosopher of the first. For present purposes, Ānanda's attribution remains of interest.

my ideas will grow old
inside my body.

The second verse makes explicit what is hinted at (through the figure *aprastuta-praśaṃsā*, according to Ānanda) in the first, very well-known poem.[23] The disgruntled tone is Dharmakīrti's signature. In the first verse he has displaced his complaint on to a young girl who will never find a lover worthy of her greatness. The second poem speaks to us directly in the first person: the great thinker will never be understood. A poet of genius, Dharmakīrti offers us an unsettling image of near-autistic, profoundly isolated self-containment: water – ever the same water – endlessly flows through water. Or is there something more to the image, a vision, perhaps, of the mind as restless, fluid, in movement, moving through itself and thus intensifying its own aliveness in the way *dhvani* "mixes in" with other instances of *dhvani*? And is there meaning to the fact that Ānanda has chosen three autobiographical verses, one of them his own, to illustrate just such points of intensified aesthetic experience where the system he has so rigorously developed pushes beyond its own premises?

REFERENCES

Alaṅkāra-sarvasva
Alaṅkāra-sarvasva of Ruyyaka, ed. S.S. Janaki, Delhi: Meharchand Lachhmandas, 1965

CHAKRABARTI 2005
A. Chakrabarti, Arindam, "The Heart of Repose, the Repose of the Heart: A Phenomenological Analysis of the Concept of Viśrānti," in S. Das and E. Fürlinger (eds.), *Sāmarasya: Studies in Indian Arts, Philosophy, and Interreligious Dialogue in Honor of Bettina Bäumer*, New Delhi: D.K. Printworld, 2005, pp. 27-36

DhvĀ
Dhvanyāloka of Ānandavardhana with the *Locana* of Abhinavagupta, ed. P. Ramacandrudu, Hyderabad: Sri Jayalaksmi Publications, 1998

GNOLI 1968
R. Gnoli, *The Aesthetic Experience according to Abhinavagupta*, 2nd ed., Varanasi: Chowkhambha, 1968

[23] Ruyyaka cites the verse under *atiśayokti* (*Alaṅkāra-sarvasva*, p. 82); Appayya Dīkṣita discusses it under *vyāja-nindā* (*Kuvalayânanda* 72).

INGALLS ET AL. 1990
D.H.H. Ingalls, J.M. Masson and M.V. Patwardhan, *The Dhvanyāloka of Ānandavardhana with the Locana of Abhinavagupta*, Cambridge (Mass.): Harvard University Press, 1990

Kāvya-prakāśa
Kāvya-prakāśa of Mammaṭa, Poona: Anandasrama Press, 1929

KRISHNAMOORTHY 1979
K. Krishnamoorthy, "Udbhaṭa's Original Contribution to Sanskrit Literary Theory," in *Ludwik Sternbach Felicitation Volume* 1, Lucknow: Akhila Bharatiya Sanskrit Parishad, 1979, pp. 303-311

Kuvalayânanda
Kuvalayânanda of Appayya Dīkṣita, Varanasi: Chokhamba, 1992

Locana
See DhvĀ

MCCREA 2008
L. McCrea, *The Teleology of Poetics in Medieval Kashmir*, Cambridge (Mass.): Harvard University Press, 2008

SHULMAN 2008
D. Shulman, "Sage, Poet, and Hidden Wisdom in Medieval India," *Cultural Traditions and Worlds of Knowledge: Explorations in the Sociology of Knowledge* 7, 2008, pp. 109-137

SHULMAN 2010
D. Shulman, "Notes on Camatkāra," in D. Shulman (ed.), *Language, Ritual and Poetics in Ancient India and Iran*, Jerusalem: Israel Academy of Sciences and Humanities, 2010, pp. 249-276

A Vaiṣṇava Paramādvaita in 10th-Century Kashmir?

The Work of Vāmanadatta

RAFFAELE TORELLA

Bhāgavatotpala, more widely known in Kashmir under the name Utpalavaiṣṇava,[1] scattered his commentary on the *Spandakārikā* (*Spandapradīpikā*, henceforth SpPr) with often striking quotations from a work entitled *Saṃvitprakāśa* (henceforth SP), sometimes paired with another work entitled *Ātmasaptati*, their tone and content looking closely related to each other. If we know the namc of author, which neither Bhāgavatotpala nor later authors ever mentioned, we owe it to Jayaratha, the diligent commentator of Abhinavagupta's *Tantrāloka* (henceforth TĀ). TĀ 5.154cd-155ab reads:

> *nīle pīte sukhe duḥkhe citsvarūpam akhaṇḍitam* |
> *gurubhir bhāṣitaṃ tasmād upāyeṣu vicitratā* ||

> In blue, yellow, plcasure and pain the very nature of consciousness remains undivided: this has been said by the master. Therefore, there is diversity as regards the means [only].

"By the master," Jayaratha says in his commentary (vol. III, p. 467), "namely by Vāmanadattācārya in the SP." This passage is not found in the mss. of the SP (see below), but we can still give credit to Jayaratha's attribution, since the *śloka*, this time in full, is quoted in SpPr p. 18 (Dyczkowski ed.) as belonging to the SP, and

[1] In the two printed editions of the SpPr (both not fully reliable) by Gopinātha Kavirāja and M. S. G. Dyczkowski, the name in the colophon is given as Bhagavatotpala and Bhagavadutpala, respectively. What most probably is the correct form (Bhāgavatotpala) is found in the colophon of two mss. of the SpPr in the Research Library, Srinagar (No. 861, *raciteyaṃ bhāgavatotpalena*; No. 829, *ity ācāryabhāgavato-utpalaviracitā*). These mss. belong to a group of four. Śāradā mss. of the SpPr which have not been used for the above editions (No. 2233 has *ity ācāryotpalaviracitā*; No. 994 ends abruptly while commenting on *śloka* 31).

moreover it recurs unchanged in the *Lakṣmītantra* (henceforth LT), which incorporates many verses from the SP (see below). The colophons of the *Ātmasaptati* and the other four Prakaraṇas which follow the SP in the extant mss. also mention his name as the author.

Vāmanadatta most probably lived around the middle of 10th century. The earliest authors to quote from him are the aforementioned Bhāgavatotpala, and Nārāyaṇakaṇṭha in the *Mṛgendravṛtti* (see below). Bhāgavatotpala, who quotes Utpaladeva (the *Īśvarapratyabhijñākārikā*, henceforth ĪPK)[2] but not Abhinavagupta, probably belongs to the second half of the 10th century. Nārāyaṇakaṇṭha belongs approximately to the same period, given that he also quotes Utpaladeva (the *Īśvarasiddhi*)[3] and that his son Rāmakaṇṭha is quoted by Abhinavagupta[4] (and Kṣemarāja – he is the *kairaṇavyākhyātṛ* referred to in the *Svacchandoddyota,* vol. I, p. 322).

The colophons of the SP and the other Prakaraṇas indicate that Vāmanadatta is from Kashmir and a brahmin, and they introduce us to his particular doctrinal position:

ekāyane prasūtasya kaśmīreṣu dvijātmanaḥ |
kṛtir vāmanadattasya... ||

The mention of the Ekāyana testifies to Vāmanadatta's affiliation to the Pāñcarātra. The followers of the Pāñcarātra refer to one Ekāyanaveda which they consider the essence and primordial source of the four Vedas and also call "secret tradition" (*Īśvarasaṃhitā* 21.531: *ādyam ekāyanaṃ vedaṃ rahasyāmnāyasaṃjñitam*). The lost *Kāśmirāgamaprāmāṇya* of Yāmuna, according to what the author himself says in his main work, the *Āgamaprāmāṇya* (p. 79), dealt with the non-human nature of the Ekāyana-branch. In another passage of the *Āgamaprāmāṇya* (p. 40) Yāmuna points out that the Ekāyanaśākhins upheld – against the Śaivas – the birth, i.e. the limited nature, of Rudra. By crossing the references given in the *Haravijaya* and the *Nareśvaraparīkṣā* (SANDERSON 2009, pp. 107-108), we have in Kashmir two subdivisions of Pāñcarātra: Ekāyanas and followers of Saṃkarṣaṇaśāstra, corresponding to Saṃhitā Pāñcarātra and Saṃkarṣaṇa Pāñcarātra, respectively. However, a

---

2 Pp. 3, 7, 17, 38-39, 53.

3 5. 55, quoted in *Mṛgendravṛtti* pp. 30-31 (ad vidyāpāda 1.11).

4 For a thorough assessment of Rāmakaṇṭha's date see GOODALL 1998, pp. xiii-xviii.

later Saṃhitā, the *Pārameśvarasaṃhitā,* links the Ekāyanaveda with Saṃkarṣaṇa (CZERNIAK-DROŻDŻOWICZ forthcoming), the Ekāyanas receiving the appellation of Āgamasiddhāntins, against the Vaidika termed Mantrasiddhāntins.[5] According to the *Pādmasaṃhitā*, the Ekāyanas are a very special kind of Bhāgavatas: they do not need initiation into Pāñcarātra, being so to speak born Pāñcarātrins (CZERNIAK-DROŻDŻOWICZ forthcoming).

The presence of Vaiṣṇavism in Kashmir from early times is extensively documented by archeological and literary evidence,[6] just as it seems probable that some of the Pāñcarātra Saṃhitās (cited apparently for the first time in the SpPr) were elaborated in Kashmir. Indeed, the SP is a *stuti* dedicated to Viṣṇu, and in it and the other Prakaraṇas several doctrinal references that are peculiar to the Pāñcarātra can be found, such as, for instance, the doctrine of the *vyūha*s in Prakaraṇa 4. However, as we shall see, this is a Pāñcarātra interpreted in a strictly non-dualistic sense, which makes it fully consonant with the contemporary schools of non-dual Śaivism. Many Śaiva masters do not hesitate to quote Vāmanadatta's work as an authority alongside other authoritative purely Śaiva texts and to support Śaiva doctrines. This gives the impression that the adhesion to a certain spiritual climate in the Kashmir of the time represented such a strong element of affinity, at the most elevated levels, that it succeeded in overcoming sectarian and doctrinal differences. One may also quote another example, that of Bhaṭṭa Divākaravatsa, belonging approximately to the same period (SANDERSON 2007, p. 255), and author of two works, the *Kakṣyāstotra* and the *Vivekāñjana*, which are quoted as authorities by Śaiva authors, like Abhinavagupta and Kṣemarāja, despite their Pāñcarātra contents. This may appear all the more surprising when one thinks that the relations between Śaivas and Vaiṣṇavas had often been – and were to become even more so in the future – such as to cast a shadow over the alleged tolerance of Hinduism (cf. DASGUPTA 1932, p. 18; GONDA 1970, pp. 93-94). Even when coexistence is, after all, peaceful, as in the Kashmir of the time, Śaivas and Vaiṣṇavas do not go beyond a generic acknowledgement of the limited and provisional truth of the other, which is only admitted if

---

5 On Āgamasiddhānta and Mantrasiddhānta (plus Tantra° and Tantrāntara°), see RASTELLI 2003.

6 The relevant passages from the *Rājataraṅgiṇī* have been collected and studied in RAI 1955, pp. 188-194. See SANDERSON 2009a, pp. 58-70; 2009b, pp. 107-109.

subordinated to the absolute truth represented by one's own creed. This is particularly evident in the Vaiṣṇavas, who are much more oriented than the Śaivas towards the *ekāntavāda* (cf. GONDA 1970, p. 93). Anyhow, we see that in India even when one religious community accepts the partial truth of another, the delimitation between the respective authoritative texts tends to remain rigid. Śaivas and Pāñcarātrins are no exception to this. In criticizing the validity of the scriptures belonging to the Pāśupatas, Kālamukhas, Kāpālikas and Śaivas (*Āgamaprāmāṇya* p. 44), Yāmuna says:

> As the authoritativeness of these Tantras is already vitiated by their mutual contradictions, it is not really necessary for them to be rejected with the stick of the Veda. [...] Let it not be said, how could Rudra, who is very trustworthy, promulgate such a vast collection of texts which are not authoritative ? [...] Or else one may reason that since Rudra may have composed such a system for the purpose of deceiving the world because he is known as a promulgator of deceitful doctrines, it is not even necessary to assume error on his part. (Transl. BUITENEN 1971, p. 71.)

It is known, on the other hand, that Kṣemarāja in the *Pratyabhijñāhṛdaya* relegates the Pāñcarātra to a very humble position on the scale of principles.[7]

The figure of Vāmanadatta does not have any place in the later Vaiṣṇava tradition, in which sectarian elements tend to prevail. He survives only indirectly since several stanzas of the SP are found to be incorporated or paraphrased in the LT (particularly in Chapter 14), a relatively late and eclectic text, which only begins to be considered an authority from the time of Vedāntadeśika onwards (GUPTA 1972, p. xx).[8] Bhāgavatotpala, an author whose doctrinal and religious affiliation is very close to Vāmanadatta's (and Pāñcarātra's),[9] and who quotes him so frequently, aims to illuminate and

---

7 See p. 17: *parā prakṛtir bhagavān vāsudevaḥ, tadvisphuliṅgaprāyā eva jīvāḥ iti pāñcarātrāḥ parasyāḥ prakṛteḥ pariṇāmābhyupagamād avyakte evābhiniviṣṭāḥ*. This does not prevent Maheśvarānanda from quoting as an authority a Pāñcarātra scripture like the LT (see below), most probably due to the emphasis this text places on the Goddess.

8 Some verses of the LT are cited in the *Mahārthamañjarīparimala* (henceforth MPP): 14.5cd-6, cit. p. 65; 22.7ab, cit. p. 175. The probable date of Maheśvarānanda is very close to Vedāntadeśika's (around the beginning of the 14th c.; cf. SANDERSON 2007, p. 412).

9 Quite unconvincingly, DYCZKOWSKI 1992 argues (p. 28) that Bhāgavatotpala was in fact a Śaiva as shown by his referring to Śiva as his *abhimatadevatā* (SpPr, p. 7). It is instead clear from the context that by saying so Bhāgavatot-

support the doctrine of the Spanda with an equal share of Vaiṣṇava and Śaiva authorities. He cites (p. 12) two passages, from a Śaiva and a Pāñcarātrin work, now both lost, that indicate the existence of a tolerant and all-comprehensive stratum of the two opposing schools that recognised each other as being united in non-duality. The Pāñcarātra text, the *Māyāvāmanasaṃhitā*, reads:

> *viṣṇuśivasūryabuddhādirūpatayā tattacchakticakraparivārayutas tatkāraṇaṃ bhagavān eka eva dhyānabhedenopāsyatvenābhihitaḥ.*
>
> In the form of Viṣṇu, Śiva, Sūrya, Buddha etc. and accompanied by the retinue of the various powers of which he is the sole cause, one is the Blessed One, variously named depending on the different kinds of meditation and the diverse rites.

And the Śaiva text, the *Kulayukti*:

> *vedānte vaiṣṇave śaive saure bauddhe 'nyato 'pi ca |*
> *eka eva paraḥ svātmā jñātā jñeyaṃ maheśvari ||*
>
> In Vedānta, in Viṣṇuism, in Śaivism, in the Saura sect, in Buddhism and so on, one is the supreme, the own self, the knower and the knowable, O Maheśvarī.[10]

No mention of Vāmanadatta and his works (or of Bhāgavatotpala) is to be found in the extant works of Yāmuna, the first great systemizer and defender of the Pāñcarātra tradition, who must have lived a little later than Vāmanadatta (we must however take into account that his *Kāśmīrāgamaprāmāṇya* has not come down to us); nor is it in Vedāntadeśika or in Rāmānuja. The later Pāñcarātra tradition, once it firmly turned towards the *viśiṣṭādvaita*, erased the memory not only of Vāmanadatta, but also of a whole series of Vaiṣṇava texts apparently grounded on non-duality, whose existence is testified by Bhāgavatotpala's quotations, for instance the *Jñānasaṃbodha*, the *Jābalīsūtra*, the *Ṣāḍguṇyaviveka* and others.

Vāmanadatta's teaching, on the contrary, was held in great respect by the Śaiva authors. Primarily by those who belonged to the great and variegated non-dual tradition, but not by them alone; in

---

pala is referring to the author of the *Spandakārikā*, not to himself. Then, the first part of his very name (Bhāgavata) leaves no doubt about his religious affiliation.

10 A verse from the SP (not extant in the mss.) cited in SpPr, p. 27 states that there is no difference between the qualities of Śiva and Viṣṇu (*bhedaḥ sarvajñatādīnāṃ jñānādīnāṃ ca nāsty amī | jñānasyaiva dharmatayā cidrūpasya sthitir yataḥ ||*).

fact, the first Śaiva to quote him is the *siddhāntin* Nārāyaṇakaṇṭha, who in the above-mentioned passage (*Mṛgendravṛtti*, vidyāpāda, p. 153) quotes with approval, without citing the author or the title, two verses belonging to Prakaraṇa 2 (6, 56). The first of these two verses is also quoted in the chapter of the *Sarvadarśanasaṃgraha* on the Śaivadarśana, but in order to forestall drawing the mistaken conclusion that the *Ātmasaptati* was known to Mādhava, it must be said, as I have shown elsewhere (TORELLA 1979), that the chapter on the Śaivadarśana is not much more than a clever collage of passages that Mādhava has taken from Nārāyaṇakaṇṭha's *Mṛgendravṛtti* and Aghoraśiva's *Tattvaprakāśavṛtti*.

The author who most extensively quotes from Vāmanadatta's works is Bhāgavatotpala. The total number of verses quoted is 42,[11] and they are all to be found in Prakaraṇa 1 (the SP), with the exception of six (five belonging to Prakaraṇa 2 and one to Prakaraṇa 5). Another literal quotation, this time from Prakaraṇa 2 (v. 30), can be found in Abhinavagupta's *Parātrīśikāvivaraṇa* (p. 214); a passage of his *Tantrasāra* (henceforth TS) may contain a reminiscence of a verse of SP.[12] Other quotations from Vāmanadatta's Prakaraṇas are found in Maheśvarānanda's MMP,[13] Śivopādhyāya's *Vijñānabhairavoddyota*,[14] Kṣemarāja's *Stavacintāmaṇivivṛti*[15] and Bhāskarakaṇṭha's commentary on the *Īśvarapratyabhijñāvimarśinī*.[16]

---

11 P. 3 (SP 107-8), p. 6 (SP 78-80), p. 8 (2.58), p. 9 (SP 24, 2.19, 5.26), p. 10 (SP 95), pp. 13-4 (SP 112-13), pp. 17-18 (SP 54-56), p. 18 (SP 49-50, 42-43, 45, one *śloka* from SP not found in the mss.), p. 19 (SP 53, 57, 59), p. 22 (SP 106), p. 23 (SP 103-4), p. 27 (SP 14, one *śloka* from SP not found in the mss.), p. 29 (SP 72), p. 31 (SP 27), p. 36 (SP 30), p. 37 (SP 31, 63, one *śloka* from SP not found in the mss., 12, 38-39ab), p. 38 (one *śloka* from *Ātmasaptati* not found in the mss., SP 10), p. 39 (1.92), p. 40 (2.47, 1.95), p. 41 (one *śloka* from *Ātmasaptati* not found in the mss), p. 47 (1.20), p. 48 (one *śloka* from SP not found in the mss.).

12 TS pp. 8-9: *cinmātratattvaṃ... upādhibhir amlānam* – SP 3cd: *yad upādhibhir amlānaṃ naumi tad vaiṣṇavaṃ padam.*

13 See p. 20 (not found in the mss; cf. below); p. 21 (2.58); p. 22 (not found in the mss.); p. 25 (3.27 and 3.2).

14 See p. 109 (SP 13).

15 See p. 83 (SP 13).

16 Vol. I, p. 48 (SP 13); vol. I, p. 93 (SP 20); vol. I, p. 64 (SP 31); vol. I, p.13, 302 (SP 36); vol. I, p. 71 (SP 39cd); vol. I, p. 72, 268, vol. II, p.137 (2.6); vol. I, p. 54, 248, 412, vol. II, p. 203 (2.19); vol. I, p. 53, 218 (2.30-31).

The passage from the TĀ cited above permits us to touch on another question to which, however, it is not possible to obtain a definite answer, namely whether Abhinavagupta had been a disciple of Vāmanadatta. The fact that Abhinavagupta calls him *gurubhiḥ* is not cogent in itself, since the term may have been used in a generic sense.

Of the SP and the other Prakaraṇas only three mss. have come down to us,[17] all of them incomplete. Two printed editions are available (only based on mss. A and B), one by M. Dyczkowski and one by Bh. P. Tripathi, both of them quite problematic with respect to the reading of the mss. and the emendations proposed.[18] As we have seen, the work is divided into Prakaraṇas. SP is the title of the first one[19] and was later extended by some, including the two editors referred to above, to the whole work. The SpPr, probably the oldest source for this collection of texts, uses the title *Saṃvitprakāśa* only for verses belonging to the first Prakaraṇa,[20] and *Ātmasaptati*[21] for closely related verses, quite similar both in content and style to the SP. All the latter verses come indeed from Prakaraṇa 2, entitled *Ātmasaptati*[22] in mss. B and C, and *Ātmasaṃstuti* in ms. A.[23] It is clear that Bhāgavatotpala considers the SP and

---

17 A: Research Library, Srinagar, No. 1371 (Kashmiri *devanāgarī*); B: Benares Hindu University Library, Varanasi, No. C4003 (*śāradā*); C: Niedersächsische Staats- und Universitätsbibliothek, Göttingen, Cod. Ms. Sanscr. Vish 5 (*śāradā*).

18 The two editions (both bearing the title of SP) are in fact only one as Tripathi's is virtually identical (including the typographical setting) to Dyczkowski's with the exception of a few corrections mainly of misprints. It would be possible to make some hypotheses about the reason why Dyczkowski decided to hand his edition over to Tripathi. About the "story" of Dyczkowski's edition see TORELLA 1994, p. 482.

19 In the three mss. the colophon reads: *saṃvitprakāśo nāma prathamaṃ prakaraṇam.*

20 Once he calls it *Saṃvitprakaraṇa* (p. 38); see below. There is only one exception: the quotation p. 9 from Prakaraṇa 5.26 is introduced by *uktaṃ saṃvitprakāśe* (see below).

21 On one occasion both editions of the SpPr (Kavirāja p. 112, Dyczkowski p. 37) have *uktaṃ hi svātmasaptatau*, which must be a mere mistake (at least, all the Srinagar mss. mentioned above read *uktaṃ hy ātmasaptatau*).

22 *ātmasaptatir nāma dvitīyaṃ prakaraṇam.*

23 According to the number recorded by the Srinagar ms. A (see below), the second Prakaraṇa should have had nineteen verses more than the 60 that have come down to us. Thus, *Ātmasaptati* might be either a mistake for *Ātmasaṃstuti* or (much more probably) an approximate reference to the number of the

Ātmasaptati as two distinct works.[24] Instead, Maheśvarānanda ascribes to SP one verse belonging to Prakaraṇa 2 (MMP, p. 21) and two verses belonging to Prakaraṇa 3 (ibid., p. 25).[25] Even admitting that it was Vāmanadatta himself that collected different treatises composed by him into a single work, he does not appear to have given this collection a particular title. Prakaraṇa 1 has the peculiar character of a philosophical *stuti* to Hari, also showing here and there subtle emotional nuances. The second mostly lacks these features, even though Vāmanadatta still calls it *saṃstuti*.[26] These features are altogether absent in the other Prakaraṇas, which makes rather unlikely the hypothesis that the Prakaraṇas as a whole might have had the collective title of *Viṣṇustuti*.[27] Of the 160 *śloka*s that Vāmanadatta himself mentions in one of the closing verses of Prakaraṇa 1[28] only 140 have survived. The title and the number of the extant verses of the other Prakaraṇas are as follows: *ātmasaptati* (vv. 60), *vikalpaviplava* (vv. 60), *vidyāviveka* (vv. 98), *varṇavicāra* (vv. 52), *paramārthaprakāśa* (vv. 27).[29] The Srinagar ms. A has seven and half more verses, belonging to a seventh Prakaraṇa, after which the ms. ends abruptly. B and C end with the colophon of

---

verses (79) that composed it. The confusion might have been caused by the previous part of the colophon of Prakaraṇa 2: *imaṃ vāmanadattena vihitām ātmasaṃstutim | adhigamya vimucyate jantavo bhavaviplavāt ||*.

24 See SpPr pp. 37-38: *uktaṃ hi svātmasaptatau* [*read: hy ātmasaptatau*] *yadvad vastu svabhāvena jñānena viṣayīkṛtam | tadvat tādātmyam āyāti jīvaḥ sarvamayo hy ataḥ || iti |* ***anyat*** *saṃvitprakaraṇe – yathāgninā samāviṣṭaṃ sarvaṃ tadrūpam īkṣyate | tathā jñānasamāviṣṭaṃ sarvaṃ tadrūpam īkṣyatām || iti.*

25 The fact that Maheśvarānanda uses a single title, i.e. the title of Prakaraṇa 1, also for verses coming from other Prakaraṇas, has only one precedent, but an important one, that of the SpPr referred to above, n. 20. One may surmise that, even though *Saṃvitprakāśa* is definitely the specific title only of Prakaraṇa 1, the intrinsic importance and renown of the latter and its occuring first in the collection of Prakaraṇas (and also being by far the longest) may have sporadically given the occasion of an extended appellation.

26 See n. 23 above.

27 Cf. SANDERSON 2009a, p. 108. On the only occasion Bhāgavatotpala identifies three verses quoted by him as *stutau* (p. 19) they all belong to Prakaraṇa 1. Once Vāmanadatta himself refers to one *Haristuti*, but this is a hymn composed by his daughter Vāmadevī (4.78cd).

28 SP 139: *ṣaṣṭyuttaraṃ ślokaśatam idaṃ bodhaṃ vināpi yaḥ | paṭhen madhuripor agre bhaktyā mokṣaṃ sa gacchati ||*.

29 After the colophon of each Prakaraṇa (except 1 and 4), the Srinagar ms. A records what was the original (?) number of verses: 79 (Prakaraṇa 2), 61 (Prakaraṇa 3), 52 (Prakaraṇa 5), 27 (Prakaraṇa 6).

Prakaraṇa 6, both having a lacuna between 4.90 and 6.22. The *devanāgarī* MS in the BORI Library bearing the title of SP has nothing to do with Vāmanadatta's work.

We are left with a preliminary question: what happened in the Vaiṣṇava circles immediately before the time of Abhinavagupta to make at least three significant Pāñcarātra authors – Vāmanadatta, Bhaṭṭa Divākaravatsa and Bhāgavatotpala – enter into the philosophical and spiritual orbit of their Śaiva adversaries? It has also been suggested the possibility of the inverted path (SANDERSON 2009a, p. 108), that is, the birth of the non-dual Śaiva philosophy from the influence of these eccentric Vaiṣṇava developments (*in primis,* Vāmanadatta's Prakaraṇas), a possibility that seems to me rather unlikely. It is not single points, but a whole constellation of typically Śaiva themes that can be found there, particularly linked to the complex philosophical world of Utpaladeva.

If, in this presentation of some aspects of Vāmanadatta's work, I mainly focus on Prakaraṇas 1 and 2 it is because, apart from their probably being in themselves his most significant texts, they are by far the most quoted by thc Śaiva authors. First of all, in the complex mosaic of a philosophical *stuti*, written in a refined *kāvya* style, the SP proper, we find, within an undoubtedly Pāñcaratra doctrinal framework, a fascinating blend of rigourous speculation and devotional poetry, which at first sight reminds us of the then rising star of Utpaladeva, the actual founder of Pratyabhijñā, more or less contemporary to Vāmanadatta (and also often referrred to by Bhāgavatotpala), with his collection of Śaiva *stotra*s. The other Prakaraṇas share the same philosophical and spiritual attitude as the SP without, however, the *bhakti* nuances of the latter and the sense of intimate dialogue with Hari, emphasized by the frequent vocatives (*nātha*, *prabhu*, *bhagavan*, etc.) and above all by the constant addressing him as *tvam*.[30]

Some of the fundamental themes of Utpaladeva – unobjectifibility of consciousness, subject/object relationship and problematicity of the very notion of *viṣaya* – recur in several stanzas of the SP and *Ātmasaptati*:[31]

---

30 Most of the *tvaṃ* of the SP turn to *ahaṃ* in the verses incorporated into the LT, where the Goddess herself is speaking.

31 The text and numeration of the stanzas is according to my forthcoming edition (see Appendix).

2.5. The self cannot be object of cognition for anybody, what is other than it is not logically admissible. From the differentiation of the knowable derives the differentiation of the means of knowledge. If there is no such differentiation, then what might produce the differentiation [of knowledge]?

2.6. If the self were knowable, its knower would be "other"; but then the self would be[come] "other." "Other," in fact, is what is the object of knowledge.

2.56. Consciousness alone shines; that which is other from it is illuminated. What is illuminated is the object, and how can the object subsist without a subject?

1.10. Just as whatever is penetrated by fire is seen as being of the same essence as fire, in the same manner whatever is penetrated by consciousness is to be seen as being of the same essence as consciousness.

1.11. An intrinsic and definite status is inconceivable for things, dependent as they are on a subject that knows them, and consequently they can only manifest themselves, by their very nature, as having the knower as their essence.

1.12. The fact that things have You as their essence, no one disputes. Their capacity of being known demonstrates this: indeed, only that which in itself is light may be made to shine.[32]

1.24. If knowledge (*vedanam*) knows something after bringing the knowable object to having knowledge as its own form, then how to speak of knowable object and knowing subject (*vedakatā*) as two distinct realities?[33]

2.8. "Making [something] an object of knowledge" – the wise ones say in this connection – is the same as "making [it] one's own." What is universally accepted for any other reality, why should it not be so for consciousness?

2.9. What has not been made its own by consciousness (*saṃvidāsvīkṛtaṃ*) cannot be termed "object of knowledge" (*viṣaya*).[34] [But] what has

---

[32] Cf. ĪPK 1.5.2 (cf. TORELLA 2002, pp. 111-112).

[33] The text remains doubtful owing to the oscillation in the mss. and old quotations between *vedanatā* and *vedakatā*; also the emendation of *vedanam* to *vedakaḥ* might be considered.

[34] Also the reading *saṃvidā svīkṛtaṃ* "what has been made its own by consciousness" could be considered (this would anticipate the conclusion made in

been made its own by a certain entity becomes identical with such entity. [Then,] how can the very designation of "object of knowledge" stand?[35]

2.35. While knowledge can shine autonomously being separated from the senses and without being muddied by the objects of knowledge, the same cannot be said of the object of knowledge.

2.36. It is said in this connection that in order to make known the objects of knowledge the three means of knowledge work separately being concerned with distinct classes of objects of knowledge. [But] the same does not hold for knowledge.

Another favourite topic of Utpaladeva's discourse is the alleged externality of the object of knowledge (ĪPK 1.8.5, 1.8.7; cf. TORELLA 2002, pp. 148-150). In the same vein, Vāmanadatta says:

2.32. Even establishing the other as other is not possible until the other is assimilated by the self, since only when it is known does the other become the other.

2.44. If it were possible to define an object as being external even when it has entered one's consciousness, then it would be external to consciousness itself, so how could it be said to be "its" [of consciousness]?

2.45. If, on the other hand, it has not entered one's consciousness, how can its existence be known, since only consciousness has the task of hunting down being and non-being?

The examination of the nature of relation is closely connected with Utpaladeva's treatment of the same topic in ĪPK 1.2.10-11 (TORELLA 2002, pp. 95-98), 2.4.14 (TORELLA 2002, p. 183) and the *Sambandhasiddhi*.

2.17. There can be no relationship between two things complete and realised in themselves (*siddha*), because all expectation is lacking between them; and not even between two that are not realised and established, because as such they would not exist. So any relationship in reality does not exist.

2.54. What is real/existing (*satāṃ*) is without any such "requiring" because it is already complete and realised in itself, nor conversely is "non-requiring" possible in what is non-existent owing to its non-realisa-

the following *ardhaśloka*).

35 Cf. e.g. Utpaladeva's *Īśvarapratyabhijñāvivṛti* ad 1.4.1 (TORELLA 2007b, p. 544).

tion. Things lacking "dependency" have neither the nature of the knower nor of the knowable.

The status of cause presupposes sentiency. Only the conscious agent subject can be a causal agent (ĪPK 2.4.1-21; cf. TORELLA 2002, pp. 175-188).

1.63. It is well known that everything has You as cause, since Your presence is apparent in everything. Given that everything shows the presence of consciousness, the cause [of everything] cannot be something without consciousness.

2.22. Whatever is denied the quality of active subject cannot assume the role of instrument, etc. [...]

Vāmanadatta appears also reminiscent of how Utpaladeva deals with the theme of memory in ĪPK 1.2.3, 1.3.1ff. (cf. TORELLA 2007b).

1.20. You, always omniscient, are present in the heart of everyone: if this were not so, how otherwise could one account for memory, whose object is something that no longer exists?

The presence of Bhartṛhari's teaching is evident at several places of Vāmanadatta's works, and, as is well known, it was through Utpaladeva that Bhartṛhari became one of the main pillars of nondual Śaiva philosophy (TORELLA 2009).

1.7. It is merely a question of the power of the word: that is, the fact that it brings about a fragmentation of the real, which itself would be unitary, by virtue of a multiplicity of functions.

5.26. The word is the cause of all human activities: this is what reason shows, it is not only scripture that says so. In fact, there is no operation whatsoever without the work of discursive thought, nor is there discursive thought without the word.

The concept of *pratibhā* as the ultimate ground for the means of knowledge appears to be nourished with Utpaladeva's ideas as expressed particularly in the *Īśvarapratyabhijñāvivṛti* (in turn, being a development of Bhartṛhari's doctrine):[36]

2.37. Sensorial knowledge derives directly from the object, inferential knowledge comes from the relation [between objects]; it has been said

[36] Cf. TORELLA 2013.

that they [sensorial knowledge and inferential knowledge] are the root of *āgama*. No other means of knowledge exists.

2.38. It is required that, in turn, these three means of knowledge have intuition as their own soul, otherwise it would impossible to account for ascertainment of truth and error.

2.39ab. Intuition is only known by introspective self-awareness; it is present in a form exempt from succession (*akramātmikā*) within the various activities.[37]

Just like Utpaladeva, Vāmanadatta makes frequent use of the simile of the mirror or crystal and the reflection on them to account for the relationship between consciousness and the images of the allegedly external objects.

1.51. Just as the child has no separate cognition of the mirror without his face [reflected in it], just so he who is not wise does not grasp the consciousness from which the knowable has been extracted.

1.54-56. Just as the true nature of a crystal continuously coloured by other things is not perceived owing to its excessive transparency, in the same way, O Blessed One, Your own body, which is united with the various beings, owing to its absolute limpidity is not perceived without them. Neither for this [reason] can we affirm that such a crystal does not exist separately from whatever colours it, or that the pure body of consciousness does not exist once liberated from the form of things.

1.57-59. Just as it is impossible to indicate separately the intrinsic existence of a universal from which all particulars have been removed – but this does not imply that it does not exist –, and just as it is impossible to indicate the intrinsic existence of gold once it has been freed from its various forms, such as earring, etc. – but this does not imply that it does not exist –, so be it said of Your permanent, intimate, pure nature, once pleasure and pain have been eliminated. It consists of consciousness, only knowable through introspective intimate awareness.

1.40. Pleasure and pain do not appear, discrimination has no firm ground: everything appears the same once You, the sun of consciousness, rise.

---

[37] If we accept the reading *kramātmikā*, transmitted in all the extant mss., the meaning does not change significantly: "it [only] appears in a successive form within... "

1.41. For the blind You are the one in whom there is no darkness, for the deaf You are the one in whom the Voice never disappears. Starting from Brahmā to the animals, You are the same in the knowledge of everybody.

Hari is present at all levels of ordinary reality. In fact, since everything is equally penetrated by Him, there is no real difference between *mokṣa* and *saṃsāra*. If the various ordinary reality can occur in its multifariousness it is precisely because of His constituting its permanent and undifferentiated basis (cf. ĪPK 2.3.15b *samabhittitalopame*; ĪPK 1.3.6-7, 2.4.19; cf. TORELLA 2002, pp.103-104, 186).

1.95. No ordinary activity – whether corporeal or verbal or mental – can take place if Thou, O Lord, art not already present in it and established beforehand.[38]

1.89. Two persons who meet and speak of ordinary things thereby express something that however has You as its final subject, [even] without speaking of You [directly]. [...]

1.36. Albeit directly perceptible, in that You transcend all conceptual processes, You are "forgotten" – like something in front of someone whose mind is elsewhere.

1.39. Lights do not shine if Your light does not rise. You are the only one that can truly be called light; all the others are like the darkness.

2.58. In actual fact, there is no bondage, and there being no bondage, there is no liberation either. These two entities are both fabricated by discursive thought and in themselves are nothing.

1.60. I bow to Brahman which is without specification, partless, outside space and time, light to itself, exclusively consisting of consciousness, perennially risen.

1.61. Were You not exempt from particularization among particulars, the comprehension of the particular would be impossible as everything resides in itself.

1.62. In You, Lord, who are the cause, there is no differentiation, then how could differentiation be in the effects forming this world? Therefore, o Padmanābha, the world is without differentiation.

---

[38] Cf. the so-called *ādisiddhasūtra* (1.1.2) of ĪPK.

1.64. You are the substratum of everything, made of everything and transcending everything. How is it possible that there be space and time in You, who are infinite and without action (*niṣkriyātmani*)?[39]

1.66. The wise ones know you to be what never declines from its own nature, what is not modified by other realities, what is not delimited by other realities, this permanent being You are.

1.67. Time, etc. arise from You with the aim of delimiting what can be delimited. But what can time etc. do to You, whose own form is immeasurable?

In the motif of the presence of Hari, or consciousness, in the empty space that separates two physical realities, or two thoughts or sensorial experiences, or two phonemes in a word, we can detect Vāmanadatta's acquaintance with the texts of the Spanda school and with Śaiva scriptures such as the *Vijñānabhairava*.[40]

1.4. The mind that, having expelled conceptual constructs, remains in the middle state, experiences there the immaculate flow of consciousness.

1.42. Always pure does this perception remain, albeit variegated according to the various forms. At the moment in which the passing from one form to another occurs, at that moment too perception is [fully] immaculate.

1.43. Just as a garment originally white and then dyed cannot take any other colour unless it first returns to its original white [...]

1.44. [Just as] he who pronounces a phrase, how could he pass from one phoneme to another, if in the interval, he did not repose in You, who are pure consciousness?

1.45. In the same way, consciousness, which is pure by nature and assumes one form or another, stays pure in the interval between abandoning one form and passing on to another.

***

---

[39] The absence of *kriyā* in Hari, stated also in SP 73b, as a point of apparent disagreement with the Śaiva *paramādvaita,* will be treated in my forthcoming edition and translation.

[40] Very intriguing is the mention of the Krama goddess Kālakarṣaṇī in 4.13d.

The season in which a few brilliant personalities of Pāñcarātra surrendered to the fascination by the philosophers and spiritual masters of the Śaiva *paramādvaita* was short, in any case lasting no more than three to four decades. All the same, the mainstream of Pāñcarātra never forgave them, and committed them to disdainful oblivion. Their memory however has survived for centuries in the Śaiva circles, proud perhaps of having attracted such brilliant outsiders.

APPENDIX

VĀMANADATTA'S VERSES QUOTED IN THE PAPER (ACCORDING TO R. TORELLA'S FORTHCOMING EDITION)

A = Kāśmīri Devanāgari Ms (Śrinagar); B =Śāradā Ms (Benares); C = Śāradā Ms (Göttingen); E = M.S.G. Dyczkowski edition; V = Bh.P. Tripathi (Vāgīśa Śāstrī) edition

1.4. *dūrāpāstavikalpena cetasā yo*[41] *'nubhūyate* |
madhyamāṃ vṛttim āsthāya sa saṃvitprasaro 'malaḥ ||
1.7. *kevalaṃ vākprabhāvo*[42] *'yaṃ yad abhinnam api svayam* |
vibhedayati sā vastu svetikartavyatāvaśāt[43] ||
1.10. *yathāgninā samāviṣṭaṃ sarvaṃ tadrūpam īkṣyate*[44] |
tathā jñānasamāviṣṭaṃ sarvaṃ tadrūpam īkṣyatām[45] ||[46]
1.11. *pramātrapekṣabhāveṣu*[47] *na hy avasthāvakalpate* |

41 °*na cetasā yo* ABC, *na cen māyā* EV. (LT 14.12b *cetasā yatra bhūyate*; the more correct *yena* is the reading of mss. ADEFG).

42 *vākprabhāvo* AC, *vākprabho* then corrected to *vākprabhāvo* B, *vākyabhāvo* EV.

43 *sā vastu svetikartavyatā*° ABC, *tad vastuṣv iti kartavyatā*° EV.

44 *īkṣyate* CEV, *īkṣyatām* corrected to *īkṣyate* B, *īkṣyatām* A (*īkṣyate* cit. in SpPr, p. 38).

45 *īkṣyatām* EV, *īkṣatām* C; *īkṣyatām* cit. in SpPr, p. 38 (cf. LT 14.14 *tathā saṃvitsamāviṣṭaṃ cetyaṃ saṃvittayekṣyate*).

46 The *ardhaśloka*, omitted in AB, has been added in both mss. in the margin, where however it is only partly legible (*sarvaṃ ta...kṣyate na sa...* A, *tathā jñā...rve*? *tadrūpaṃ ī...* B). It is quoted in full in SpPr, p. 38.

47 °*apekṣa*° em, °*apekṣā*° ABC (in AB the original *pramātṛ*° has been then cor-

yatas tataḥ prakāśantāṃ[48] *svayam eva tadātmanā* ‖
1.12. *tvadātmakatvaṃ bhāvānāṃ vivadante*[49] *na kecana* |
yat prakāśyadaśāṃ yātā nāprakāśaḥ[50] *prakāśyate*[51] ‖
1.20. *sarvajñaḥ sarvadaiva tvaṃ sarvasya hṛdaye na cet* |
kenānyathāsya[52] *saṃbhāvyā naṣṭārthaviṣayā smṛtiḥ* ‖
1.24. *vedyaṃ svarūpatāṃ nītvā yadā jānāti vedanam*[53] |
tadānīṃ vedyatā kā syāt kā vā vedakatāparā[54] ‖
1.36. *vikalpātītarūpatvāt pratyakṣo 'py asi vismṛtaḥ* |
puraḥsthito yathā bhāvaś cetaso 'nyābhilāṣiṇaḥ ‖
1.39. *na prakāśāḥ prakāśante*[55] *tvatprakāśodayaṃ vinā* |
prakāśākhyas tvam eko 'taḥ sarve 'nye tamasā samāḥ ‖
1.40. *sukhaduḥkhe na bhāsete*[56] *viveko nāvatiṣṭhate* |
sarvaṃ[57] *samaṃ samābhāti*[58] *cidbhānāv udite tvayi* ‖
1.41. *andhānām apy anandhas tvaṃ*[59] *mūkānām anapāyivāk* |
āviriñcāt tiryagantaṃ samaḥ[60] *sarvasya vedane* ‖
1.42. *sadaiva śuddho 'nubhavo 'yaṃ pratyākārakarburaḥ* |

---

rected to *pramātra°*), *pramātṛpakṣabhāveṣu* EV.

48 *prakāśantāṃ* ABC (*prakāśāntāṃ* corrected to *prakāśantāṃ* A), *prakāśase* EV.

49 *vivadante* EV (indeed, P 1.3.47 prescribes *ātmanepada*), *vivadanti* ABC; *vivadante* cit. SpPr, p. 37 (reading confirmed by the Srinagar mss. listed above).

50 *prakāśyadaśāṃ yātā nā°* A, *prakāśyadaśāya tanau* (*tā* in the margin seems to correct *ta-*) B, *prakāśyadaśāyāto nā°* C, *prakāśyadaśāṃ yāto nā°* EV. SpPr p. 37 has *prakāśyadaśāṃ yāto* (*prakāśyadaśāṃ yātā* ms. No. 829, 2233, *prakāśadaśāṃ yātā* ms. No. 861, *prakāśadaśāṃ yātaṃ* ms. No. 994).

51 *prakāśyate* C, *prakāśate* ABEV (this is also the reading in SpPr, p. 37, but mss. No.s 829 and 861 have *prakāśyate*).

52 *kenā°* ACEV, *kānā°* corrected to *kenā°* B.

53 *vedanam* AEV, *vedanām* C, *vedanām* corrected to *vedanam* B.

54 *vedakatā°* ABC, *vedanatā°* em. (EV); *vedanatā°* cit. in SpPr, p. 9, and all mss. (also possible).

55 *prakāśante* ABEV, *prakāśyante* C.

56 *sukhaduḥkhe na bhāsete* ABC, *akhandās te na bhāsante* EV.

57 *sarvaṃ* ABC, *sarve* EV.

58 *samābhāti* ABC, *samābhānti* EV.

59 *anandhas tvaṃ* ABC, *anandhatvaṃ* EV.

60 *āviriñcāt tiryagantaṃ samaḥ* ABC, *avacinvanti mārgaṃ taṃ samaṃ* EV.

ākārāntarasaṃcārakāle tadāpi[61] *nirmalaḥ* ||
1.43. *yathā jātyā sitaṃ vastraṃ raktaṃ rāgeṇa kenacit* |
na tad aprāpya[62] *śuklatvaṃ punā*[63] *rāgāntaram śrayet* ||
1.44. *ayam uccārayan vākyaṃ varṇād varṇaṃ kathaṃ vrajet* |
yāvan madhye na viśrāntas tvayi śuddhacidātmani ||
1.45. *evaṃ śuddhā citir jātyā*[64] *yadākāroparāgiṇī* |
tattyāgāparasaṃcāramadhye śuddhaiva tiṣṭhati ||
1.51. *mukhaṃ vinā yathādarśaṃ pṛthag bālo*[65] *na manyate* |
tathā samuddhṛtajñeyaṃ[66] *jñānaṃ nāvaity apaṇḍitaḥ*[67] ||
1.54. *atyantācchasvabhāvatvāt sphaṭikasya yathā svakam* |
rūpaṃ paroparaktasya nityaṃ naivopalabhyate[68] ||
1.55. *tathā bhāvasamāyuktaṃ bhagavaṃs tāvakaṃ vapuḥ* |
atyantanirmalatayā pṛthak tair nopalabhyate ||
1.56. *naitāvatāsau*[69] *sphaṭikaḥ pṛthaṅ nāsty eva*[70] *rañjanāt* |
bhāvarūpaparityaktā tava vā nirmalā tanuḥ ||
1.57. *yathoddhṛtaviśeṣasya sāmānyasya nijasthitiḥ*[71] |

---

61 *tadāpi* conj., *tasyāpi* ABCEV. The text remains doubtful (cf. LT 14.24 *sadaivāpratibaddhāyā bhāntyā eva vapur mama* | *pratyakṣaṃ cetyasaṃcārakāle 'pi vimalātmanām* (*viditātmanām* mss. ABCDG) ||.

62 *na tad aprāpya* ABC, *tatpadaprāpta*° EV (probably referring to the quotation in SpPr, p. 18 *tatpadaṃ prāpta*°, found in all mss.). Cf. LT 14.25c *punaḥ svavarṇam aprāpya*.

63 *punā* BEV, *puna* AC.

64 *citir jātyā* BCEV, *cinnirvṛttyā* A.

65 *bālo* ABC, *bimbo* EV.

66 *samuddhṛta*° BC, *samuddhṛtaṃ* AEV.

67 *jñānaṃ nāvaity* (*nāvety* C) *apaṇḍitaḥ* ABC, *jñātaṃ na dvaitapaṇḍitaiḥ* EV.

68 *naivo*° em. (cf. LT 4.36 *atyantācchasvabhāvatvāt sphaṭikādir yathā maṇiḥ* | *uparakto japādyais tu tena rūpeṇa nekṣyate* ||), *evo*° ABC (B has in the left margin: *nopalabhyate iti dvayor anuṣaṅgaḥ*, then cancelled) EV (*evo*° also in Sp.Pr, p. 17, and all mss.).

69 *naitāvatā*° CEV (cit. in SpPr, p. 18), *etāvatā* corrected to *naitāvatā*° B, *etāvatā*° A.

70 *nāsty eva* em. (cf. EV; cit. in SpPr, p. 18, and all mss.), *nāste na* ABC. Cf. LT 14.37cd *pṛthag janair na lakṣyāsmi naivāhaṃ nāsmi tāvatā*.

71 *nija*° ABC, *nijā* EV (*nijā* cit. in SpPr p. 19 and all mss.)

pṛthaṅ na śakyā nirdeṣṭuṃ na ca tan nāsti[72] *tāvatā* ||
1.58. *yathoddhṛtakuṇḍalādeḥ*[73] *kanakasya svayaṃ sthitiḥ* |
<*pṛthaṅ na śakyā nirdeṣṭuṃ na ca tan nāsti tāvatā*> ||[74]
1.59. *evaṃ nityā nijā śuddhā sukha*[75]*-duḥkhaniṣedhanāt*[76] |
svasaṃvedanasaṃvedyā tava saṃvinmayī sthitiḥ ||
1.60. *aviśeṣaṃ nirvibhāgam adeśaṃ kālavarjitam*[77] |
svajyotiś cidghanaikāntaṃ naumi brahma sadoditam ||
1.61. *nirviśeṣo viśeṣeṣu nābhaviṣyad bhavān yadi* |
viśeṣāvagatir na syāt sarvasya svātmani sthiteḥ ||
1.62. *tvayi nātha na bhedo 'sti kāraṇe tat*[78] *kuto bhidā* |
kārye 'smin syāt padmanābha nirviśeṣaṃ tato jagat ||
1.63. *tvatkāraṇatvaṃ*[79] *sarvasminn api jñātaṃ*[80] *tvadanvayāt*[81] |
saṃvitsamanvite viśve nāsaṃvit kāraṇaṃ bhavet ||[82]
1.64. *sarvādhāre sarvamaye sarvataś cātirekiṇi* |
tvayy anante ko nu deśaḥ[83] *kālo vā niṣkriyātmani* ||

---

72 *tan nāsti* ABC, *tatrāsti* EV (cit. in SpPr, p. 19, but all mss. have *tan nāsti*).

73 *yathoddhṛtakuṇḍalādeḥ* em. (cf. EV), *yathoddhṛtā kuṇḍalādeḥ* BC, *yathoddhṛtā kuṇḍalādiḥ* A (*yathoddhṛtā kuṇḍalādeḥ* is also in SpPr, p. 19; of the four mss. only ms. No. 861 has the *śloka*, in the latter form).

74 An *ardhaśloka* is omitted in the mss, probably due to homoteleuton; the *ardhaśloka* that I have tentatively added comes from the quotation of the *śloka* in SpPr, p. 19 (it occurs only in ms. No. 861); in fact, its being totally identical to 57cd makes its wording (not its meaning) somewhat suspicious. Cf. also LT 14.38: *kuṇḍalāder yathā bhinnā na lakṣyā kanakasthitiḥ* | *na ca śakyā vinirdeṣṭuṃ tatrāpy asty eva sā dhruvam* ||.

75 *sukha°* ABEV, *sukhaṃ* C.

76 *°niṣedhanāt* ABC, *°aviśeṣitā* EV (*°aviśeṣitā* cit. in SpPr, p. 19, and all mss. Cf. LT 14.39 *evaṃ nityā viśuddhā ca sukhaduḥkhādyabheditā* | *svasaṃvedanasaṃvedyā mama saṃvinmayī sthitiḥ* ||.

77 *nirvibhāgam adeśaṃ kālavarjitam* BC, *nirvibhāgapade ṣaṭkālavarjitam* A, *nirvibhāgapadaṃ saṅkaṭavarjitam* EV.

78 *tat* ABC, *yat* EV.

79 *tvatkāraṇatvaṃ* ABC, *tvatkāraṇe tvaṃ* EV.

80 *jñātaṃ* em. (cf. V), *jātaṃ* ABC, *jñāto* E.

81 *tvad°* C, *tad°* corrected to *tvad°* ABC, *yad°* EV.

82 The *ardhaśloka*, omitted in BC, in B has been later added in the margin.

83 *tvayy anante ko nu deśaḥ* ABC, *tvayy ante ko 'nudeśaḥ syāt* EV.

1.66. *yat svarūpān na cyavate yat*[84] *parair nopādhīyate* |
yad anyair aparicchedyaṃ tan nityaṃ tvāṃ vidur budhāḥ ||
1.67. *paricchedyaparicchittyai*[85] *tvattaḥ kālādisaṃbhavaḥ* |
aprameyasvarūpasya tava kālādayo nu ke[86] ||
1.73. *ity avajñātadeśāder akriyāj*[87] *jagadudbhavaḥ* |
tvatto vivṛttyā[88] *mantavyo na svarūpānyathāsthiteḥ* ||
1.89. *tvānuktvā*[89] *tvatparaṃ*[90] *brūtaḥ*[91] *saṃgatau*[92] *vyāvahārikam* |
.... ||[93]
1.95. *śarīrajo vā śābdo vā manaso*[94] *vā samudgataḥ* |
vyavahāro 'py asau nāsti yatra tvaṃ nātha nāgrataḥ ||

*

2.5. *ātmā na meyaḥ kasyāpi tadanyan nopapadyate* |
meyabhedān mānabhedas[95] *tasyābhāve sa kiṃkṛtaḥ* ||
2.6. *ātmā yadi bhaven meyas tasya mātā bhavet paraḥ* |
para ātmā[96] *tadānīṃ syāt sa paro yas tu mīyate* ||
2.8. *svīkāro viṣayīkāraḥ sa tatrodghoṣyate budhaiḥ* |
yad anyatra prasiddhaṃ tat saṃvidaḥ kim apohyate[97] ||
2.9. *saṃvidāsvīkṛtaṃ*[98] *yac ca na tad viṣayasaṃjñitam* |

---

84 *yat* ABC, *sat* EV.

85 °*paricchittyai* ABC, °*paricchinnais* EV.

86 *nu ke* BC, *na ke* A , *na vai* EV.

87 *ity avajñātadeśāder akriyāj* ABC, *ity eva jñātadeśāder akriyā*° EV.

88 *vivṛttyā* ABC, *vivṛtyā* EV.

89 *tvānuktvā* conj., *tvām uktvā* ABCEV.

90 *tvat*° conj., *tat*° ABCEV.

91 *brūtaḥ* ABC, *brūmaḥ* EV.

92 *saṃgatau* BC, *saṃghatau* A, *sadgatau* EV.

93 An *ardhaśloka* likely to have been omitted here.

94 *manaso* AC, *manaso* corrected to *mānaso* B, *mānaso* EV (cit. SpPr, p.10 *mānaso*, and all mss.).

95 *meyabhedān mānabhedas* ABC, *meyabhedātmāno bhedas* EV.

96 *para ātmā* ABC, *parānyātmā* EV.

97 *apohyate* AEV, *apodyate* C, *apodyate* corrected to *apohyate* B.

yatsvīkṛtaṃ[99] *tadātmaiva viṣayoktiḥ kva*[100] *tiṣṭhatām* ||
2.17. *saṃbandhaḥ siddhayor nāsti nairākāṅkṣyeṇa vṛttitaḥ* |
nāsiddhayor asattvena tenāsau syān na vastutaḥ ||
2.22ab. *nirastakartṛbhāveṣu*[101] *karaṇatvādyasaṃbhavaḥ*[102] |
.... ||
2.32. *paravyavasthāpi pare yāvan nātmīkṛtaḥ paraḥ* |
tāvan na śakyate kartuṃ yato buddhaḥ paraḥ paraḥ ||
2.35. *yathendriyair vinābhūtaṃ*[103] *viṣayair apy anāvilam* |
svataḥ prakāśate jñānaṃ viṣayo naivam iṣyate ||
2.36. *tatrāhur*[104] *viṣayajñaptyai yat pramāṇatrayaṃ pṛthak* |
pṛthagviṣayasaṃyogān na tad abhyeti vedanam ||
2.37. *sākṣāt samakṣadhīr arthāt saṃbandhād anumānadhīḥ* |
te mūlam āgamasyāhur iti nānyapramodbavaḥ ||
2.38. *trayāṇām api mānānāṃ pratibhāprāṇateṣyate* |
samyaṅmithyātvanirṇīter anyathānupapattitaḥ ||
2. 39. *svavittir eva pratibhā kartavyeṣv akramātmikā*[105] |
nirmalā kathitā tajjñair yayā jīvanti jantavaḥ ||
2.44. *jñāne 'py antaḥpraviṣṭasya bhāvasya yadi bāhyatā*[106] |
jñānād eva tadā bāhyaṃ svam idānīṃ kim ucyatām ||
2.45. *athāpraviṣṭo*[107] *vijñānaṃ sattāsya jñāyate kutaḥ* |
jñānasyaivādhikāro 'sti[108] *sadasanmārgaṇe yataḥ* ||
2.54. *anapekṣā satāṃ siddher asiddher api nāsatām* |

---

98 EV read *saṃvidā svīkṛtaṃ* (also possible).

99 *yat°* em., *tat°* ABC, *tat* EV.

100 *kva* BCEV, *ku* A.

101 °*bhāveṣu* ABC, °*bhāve tu* EV.

102 *karaṇatva°* BC, *kāraṇatva°* AEV.

103 EV read *vinā bhūtam*.

104 *tatrāhur* ABC, *tatrāṅga°* EV.

105 °*ṣv akrama°* em., °*ṣu krama°* ABCEV.

106 *bāhyataḥ* corrected to *bāhyatā* B, *bāhyataḥ* ACEV.

107 *athāpraviṣṭo* AC, *athāpravaṣṭo* B, *arthāpraviṣṭaṃ* EV.

108 *'sti* ABEV, *'pi* C.

nirapekṣeṣu bhāveṣu na mātṛtvaṃ na meyatā ‖
2.56. *prakāśate saṃvid ekā tadanyat tu prakāśyate* |
prakāśyaṃ[109] *ca bhavet karma tac ca kartrā*[110] *vinā katham* ‖
2.58. *vastusthityā na bando 'sti tadabhāvān*[111] *na muktatā* |
vikalpaghaṭitāv etāv ubhāv api na kiṃcana ‖

*

4.78cd. *tathā hy ukto madduhitrā*[112] *vāmadevyā haristutau* ‖

*

5.26. *vāg evāsyāḥ kāraṇaṃ viśvavṛtter nyāyyaṃ*[113] *caitan nāgamaḥ kevalo 'yam* |
nāsaṃkalpaṃ kiṃcid astīha kāryaṃ vācaṃ vinā na vikalpo 'sti kaścit ‖

REFERENCES

Āgamaprāmāṇya
See VAN BUITENEN 1971

Bhāskarī
Bhāskarī. A Commentary on the Īśvarapratyabhijñāvimarśinī of Abhinavagupta, vols. I-II, ed. K.A.S. Iyer and K.C. Pandey, Allahabad: The Princess of Wales Sarasvati Bhavana Texts 70 and 83, 1938-1950

VAN BUITENEN 1971
J.A.B. van Buitenen, *Yāmuna's Āgamaprāmāṇyam or Treatise on the Validity of Pañcarātra*, ed. and transl., Madras: Rāmānuja Research Society, 1971

CZERNIAK-DROŻDŻOWICZ forthcoming
M. Czerniak-Drożdżowicz, "*Ekāyanaveda* – in Search of the Roots," in M.S.G. Dyczkowski, N. Rastogi and R. Torella (eds.), *Proceedings of the XIV World Sanskrit Conference, Delhi Jan. 2012, Tantra-Āgama Section*, New Delhi: D.K. Printworld

---

[109] *prakāśyaṃ* A, *prakāśye* BCEV.

[110] *kartrā* AEV, *kartā* BC.

[111] *tadabhāvān* ACEV, *tadā bhāvan* B.

[112] *tathā hy ukto madduhitrā* AB, *tathādyuktaṃ madduhitryā* EV.

[113] *nyāyyaṃ* em. (cf. EV), *nyāyaṃ* A (*nyāyyaṃ* cit. SpPr, p. 9; the mss. oscillate between *nyāyaṃ* and *nyāyyaṃ*).

DASGUPTA 1932
S. Dasgupta, *A History of Indian Philosophy*, vol. III, [Cambridge: 1932] Delhi: 1975

DYCZKOWSKI 1992
M.S.G. Dyczkowski, *The Stanzas on Vibration: the Spandakārikā with four commentaries* [...], transl. with an introduction and exposition, Albany: SUNY Press, 1992

GNOLI 1985
R. Gnoli, *Il Commento di Abhinavagupta alla Parātriṃśikā (Parātriṃśikātattvavivaraṇam),* traduzione e testo, Roma: IsMEO, Serie Orientale Roma 58, 1985

GONDA 1970
J. Gonda, *Viṣṇuism and Śaivism: A Comparison*, London: School of Oriental and African Studies, 1970

GOODALL 1998
D. Goodall, *Bhaṭṭa Rāmakaṇṭha's Commentary on the Kiraṇatantra. Vol. I: chapters 1-6*, ed. and transl., Pondichéry: Institut Français de Pondichéry, Publications du Départment d'Indologie 86.1, 1998

GUPTA 1972
S. Gupta, *Lakṣmītantra. A Pāñcarātra text*, transl. and notes, Leiden: Orientalia Rheno-Traiecticina 15, 1972

ĪPK
[*Īśvarapratyabhijñākārikā*] See TORELLA 2002

Īśvarasiddhi
See *Sambandhasiddhi*

LT
Lakṣmī-tantra: A Pāñcarātra Āgama, ed. (with Sanskrit gloss) Pandit V. Krishnamacharya, Adyar: The Adyar Library and Research Centre, The Adyar Library Series 87, 1959

MMP
[*Mahārthamañjarīparimala*] *Mahārthamañjarī with the Autocommentary Parimala,* ed. Pt. V.V. Dvivedi, Varanasi: Yogatantra-Ratnamālā 5, 1972

Mṛgendravṛtti
Mṛgendratantra (vidyāpāda and yogapāda) with commentary of Nārāyaṇakaṇṭha, ed. M.K. Shastri, Bombay: Kashmir Series of Texts and Studies 50, 1930

Parātrīśikāvivaraṇa
See GNOLI 1985

Pratyabhijñāhṛdaya
Pratyabhijñāhṛdayam, ed. M.R. Shastri, Srinagar: Kashmir Series of Texts and Studies 3, 1918

RAI 1955
S.C. Rai, "Studies on the history of religion in ancient Kāśmīra," *The Journal of the Bihar research Society* 41.2, 1955

RASTELLI 2003
M. Rastelli, "The Ekāyanaveda in the Pāñcarātra tradition," paper read at the 12th World Sanskrit Conference in Helsinki, July 2003 (unpublished)

Sambandhasiddhi
In *The Siddhitrayī and the Pratyabhijñā-kārikā-vṛtti*, ed. M.K. Shastri, Srinagar: Kashmir Series of Texts and Studies 34, 1921

SANDERSON 2007
A. Sanderson, "The Śaiva exegesis of Kashmir," in D. Goodall and A. Padoux (eds.), *Mélanges tantriques à la mémoire d'Hélène Brunner*, Pondichéry: Institut Français de Pondichéry, 2007, pp. 231-442

SANDERSON 2009a
A. Sanderson, "Kashmir," in K.A. Jacobsen (ed.), *Brill's Encyclopedia of Hinduism, Volume One: Regions, Pilgrimage, Deities*, Leiden/Boston: Brill, Handbuch der Orientalistik, Zweite Abteilung, Indien, vol. XXII, 2009, pp. 99-126

SANDERSON 2009b
A. Sanderson, "The Śaiva Age," in Sh. Einoo (ed.), *Genesis and Development of Tantrism*, Tokyo: Institute of Oriental Culture, University of Tokyo, 2009, pp. 41-349

SP (Dyczkowski ed.)
The Saṃvitprakāśa by Vāmanadatta, ed. M.S.G. Dyczkowski, with English introduction, Varanasi: Ratna Printing Works, 1990

SP (Tripathi's ed.)
Saṃvitprakāśa of Vāmanadatta, ed. B.P. Tripāṭhī 'Vāgīśa Śāstrī,' Varanasi: Sampurnanand Sanskrit University, Laghu-Granthamālā 51, 1993

SpPr (Dyczkowski ed.)
The Spandapradīpikā: a Commentary on the Spandakārikā, ed. M.S.G. Dyczkowski, Varanasi: Ratna Printing Works, 1990

SpPr (Kaviraja ed.)
Spandapradīpikā utpalācāryaviracitā, ed. M.M.G. Kaviraja, in *Tantrasaṅgraha*, part I, *Yogatantragranthamālā* 3, Varanasi: Varanaseya Sanskrit Vishvavidyalaya, 1970, pp. 83-128

Stavacintāmaṇi
Stavacintāmaṇi with vivṛti by Kṣemarāja, ed. M.R. Shastri, Srinagar: Kashmir Series of Texts and Studies 10, 1918

Svacchandoddyota
Svacchandatantra with commentary "Ud[d]yota" by Kṣemarāja, ed. V.V. Dwivedi, 2 vols., Delhi: Parimal Sanskrit Series 16, 1985

TORELLA 1979
R. Torella, "Due capitoli del Sarvadarśanasaṃgraha: Śaivadarśana e Pratyabhijñādarśana," *Rivista degli Studi Orientali* 53(3-4), 1979, pp. 361-410

TORELLA 1994
R. Torella, "On Vāmanadatta", in P.-S. Filliozat, C.P. Bhatta and S.P. Narang (eds.), *Pandit N.R. Bhatt Felicitation Volume*, Delhi: Motilal Banarsidass, 1994, pp. 481-498

TORELLA 2007a
R. Torella, "Studies in Utpaladeva's *Īśvarapratyabhijñā-vivṛti*. Part I. *Apoha* and *anupalabdhi* in a Śaiva garb," in K. Preisendanz (ed.), *Expanding and Merging Horizons. Contributions to South Asian and Cross-Cultural Studies in Commemoration of Wilhelm Halbfass,* Vienna: 2007, pp. 473-490

TORELLA 2007b
R. Torella, "Studies in Utpaladeva's *Īśvarapratyabhijñā-vivṛti*. Part II. What is memory?", in K. Klaus und J.-U. Hartmann (eds.), *Indica et Tibetica. Festschrift für Michael Hahn zum 65. Geburtstag von Freunden und Schülern überreicht*, Wien: Wiener Studien zur Tibetologie und Buddhismuskunde 66, Arbeitskreis für tibetische und buddhistische Studien Universität Wien, 2007, pp. 539-563

TORELLA 2009
R. Torella, "From an adversary to the main ally: The place of Bhartṛhari in the Kashmirian Śaivādvaita," in M. Chaturvedi (ed.), *Bhartṛhari: Language, Thought and Reality*. Delhi: 2009, pp. 343-354

TORELLA 2013
R. Torella, "Inherited cognitions: *prasiddhi*, *āgama*, *pratibhā*, *śabdana* (Bhartṛhari, Utpaladeva, Abhinavagupta, Kumārila and Dharmakīrti in dialogue)," in V. Eltschinger and H. Krasser (eds.), *Scriptural Authority, Reason and Action, Proceedings of a Panel at the XIV World Sanskrit Conference, Kyoto, September 1st-5th 2009*, Wien: Verlag der Österreichischen Akademie der Wissenschaften, 2013, pp. 455-480

TĀ
Tantrāloka Twith Commentary by Rājānaka Jayaratha, ed. M.K. Shastri, 12 vols., Allahabad/Srinagar/Bombay: Kashmir Series of Texts and Studies 23, 28, 29, 30, 35, 36, 41, 47, 52, 57, 58, 59, 1918-1938

TS
Tantrasāra, ed. M.R. Shastri, Srinagar: Kashmir Series of Text and Studies 17, 1918

Vijñānabhairava
Vijñānabhairava with the commentary partly by Kṣemarāja and partly by Śivopādhyāya, ed. M.R. Shastri, Bombay: Kashmir Series of Texts and Studies 8, 1918; *with commentary Kaumudī by Ānanda Bhaṭṭa*, Bombay: Kashmir Series of Texts and Studies 9, 1918

Theatre, Acting and the Image of the Actor in Abhinavagupta's Tantric Sources*

JUDIT TÖRZSÖK

A considerable number of Sanskrit plays that depict *śaiva* tantric practitioners have been subject to detailed analysis to obtain more information about tantric currents in classical India. This is perhaps particularly true for *kāpālika*s, who figure conspicuously in several classical plays.[1] This paper proposes to look at the question the other way round and show how *śaiva* tantric sources use theatrical terms and the image of the actor and how they incorporate theatre or some form of acting in their rituals. For, rather surprisingly, a number of *śaiva* tantric passages show awareness of the classical theatrical tradition and theory of drama. I shall focus on sources available to Abhinavagupta, whose major works treat theoretical questions concerning both tantra and drama. In fact, Abhinavagupta himself is the most important link between these two areas, for he is an exceptional author in that he produced original and influential works on both subjects. It is to be hoped that by studying points of contact between these fields we shall better understand the intellectual history of Kashmir in the early middle ages

---

* I am greatly indebted to Prof. Lyne Bansat-Boudon for her corrections, suggestions and critical remarks as well as for her prompt help at various stages during the writing of this paper. I would also like to thank Csaba Kiss for his corrections of the final text and for his remarks concerning the general argument. I am very grateful to the editors, Prof. Eli Franco and Prof. Isabelle Ratié, whose suggestions, corrections and insightful remarks greatly improved this paper, both in content and form. All the remaining errors are mine, of course.

1 For some general information and debate on the identity of *kāpālika*s, see SANDERSON 2011 and TÖRZSÖK 2011. The most important and well-known classical plays studied in this context are Mahendravikramavarman's *Mattavilāsaprahasana* and Bhavabhūti's *Mālatīmādhava*.

and the cultural background in which Abhinavagupta wrote his masterpieces.

In what follows, I shall first look at some examples of how dance is used in imagery and ritual, for, although dancing and acting cannot be identified, they often overlap in the Indian tradition, and dance forms an integral part of Indian theatre. After this partial detour, I shall analyse the image of the actor (*naṭa*) in scriptures (*tantra*s/*āgama*s) as well as in some exegetical works and attempt to understand the theoretical implications it entails in different contexts. This analysis is followed by a presentation of ritual observances, *vrata*s, which may involve some form of role playing. While the mere identification of the practitioner with the deity cannot be called role playing, the vocabulary used in these *vrata*s (e.g. *nepathya* for the costume to be worn, *rasa* for the dominant sentiment) often evokes the world of theatre. Finally, a short passage prescribing the offering of a dramatic representation (*nāṭaka*) is focused on.

1. SETTING THE MOOD: DANCING DEITIES, DANCING DEVOTEES

Śiva's association with theatre and dance[2] is a commonplace. The appearance of dancing forms of Śiva is also unexceptional in tantras and cannot be taken to bear any significance in itself. However, a pantheon in which dancing deities figure prominently, especially if they are described using some technical terms, may reflect a closer acquaintance with dancing and acting, or at least shows an attempt to associate such deities with the actual art. Similarly, it is

---

2 Here, I only wish to point out that I do not intend to discuss the concept and treatment of dance and theatre as overlapping but distinct notions in the Indian tradition. The terminology in Sanskrit is often ambiguous, or rather, the inseparable nature of the two is also reflected in that it is often not possible to translate certain terms as either denoting pure dance or pure theatre. For a detailed discussion of the terms *nṛtta, nāṭya* and *nṛtya*, see BANSAT-BOUDON 1992, pp. 408ff. It must be remarked that these distinctions may not always be applied systematically in the non-technical literature (when dealing with the goddess Naṭṭeśvarī/Nāṭyeśvarī, shall we translate her name as "Mistress of Dance" or "Mistress of Theatre"?). Nevertheless, in what follows, it is mainly the role of dance that is discussed in Part 1, before turning to acting and theatre proper (Parts 2-4), an order which reproduces (unintentionally) Bharata's order of discussion (whose internal logic is pointed out in BANSAT-BOUDON 1992, p. 96).

also prescribed sometimes that practitioners themselves should dance. Such dance may simply indicate happiness metaphorically, as, for instance, when the practitioner dances "out of joy" – these instances are irrelevant in the present context. It is, however, also enjoined occasionally that he should worship the deity with dancing, and, at least in some instances, his dance appears to conform (or is supposed to conform) to rules of the *Nāṭyaśāstra* (henceforth NŚ). Although the presence of these dancing deities and devotees may not have a direct bearing on how theatre is perceived or represented in the tantras, they form a background that cannot be neglected.

A Pantheon of Dancing Goddesses

The *Jayadrathayāmala* (henceforth JY)[3] in particular mentions a number of dancing Kālīs, whose description sometimes evokes more than just their association with Śiva destroying the universe at the end of each cosmic aeon. In the following passage, reference seems to be made to the various styles of poetic or dramatic composition (*vṛtti*) and "the power of speech" or "command of language" (*vāgvibhava*) is also mentioned.

> *naumi kālīṃ karālāsyāṃ pradhānāvaṇibhakṣyaṇī[ṃ]*[4] ||
> *krīḍārthaṃ yā kare citrabrahmāṇḍārbudamālikam* |
> *etā[ṃ] natvā pravakṣyāmi rahasyam idam adbhutam* ||
> *na mayā kasyacit khyātaṃ tvadṛte surasundari* |
> *sarvapralayasaṃsthāne jagad etat samāharet* ||
> *narttanti*[5] *ghoracaṇḍākṣī vṛttirājavilāyakī* |
> *sā kalākālanilayā tasyāṃ kālaḥ pralīyate* ||
> *cidacidvyaktimadhyasthā sā mahābhairavātmikā* |
> *anasyutā*[6] *vāgvibhave prajñāyogagatā yadā* ||
> *tadā yogeśvarī jñeyā sarvakālīśvareśvarī* | (2.17.772cd-777ab)

---

[3] I am grateful to Olga Serbaeva for making her e-text of the JY available to me.

[4] Letters or syllables in square brackets have been added by the present author.

[5] I have left this form as it stands in the MS, for it is unclear whether it is meant to be an irregular verb form (for *nṛtyati*, which would create an unmetrical *pāda*) or a present participle (for *nṛtyantī*).

[6] This is meant to stand for the adjective *anasūyā*. Given that *anasūyā* is almost always used as a noun, the author(s) may have preferred creating a form which resembles a past participle ending with *-ta*.

> I pay obeisance to Kālī,[7] whose mouth is gaping wide, who devours *prakṛti* and the earth [i.e. the universe from the *tattva* of Earth up to *prakṛti*] and who [holds] a colourful garland of ten million eggs of Brahmā in her hand,[8] to play with. After paying obeisance to her, I shall explain this miraculous secret. I have never told it to anyone apart from you, o beautiful goddess. When the dissolution of everything takes place, she withdraws this world, dancing, with terrible and frightening eyes, destroying[9] the King of [Poetic] Styles.[10] Time/Death and energy[11] reside in her, and time dissolves in her. She stands between the manifestation of consciousness and non-consciousness, she is of the nature of Mahābhairava/of a very frightening nature. When she practices her [transcendental] wisdom/when she is absorbed in [transcendental] wisdom, without envying the power of speech [of anyone], she is known as Yogeśvarī, the ruler of all Kālī rulers.

However, rather than using the *vṛtti*s and linguistic skills as tools, this Kālī does not appear to need them: she destroys the King of Styles and does not envy [anybody's] power of speech. The image suggests that her knowledge is beyond what can be expressed ver-

---

7 I do not comment on particularities of tantric or Aiśa Sanskrit here, unless they result in problems of interpretation.

8 Alternatively: she [holds] a garland of hundreds of millions of parts [which form] the manifold egg of Brahmā. In both interpretations, emphasis is laid on the fact that she holds the world in her hand, to play with.

9 Lit. "who makes him dissolve." However, it is likely that she is visualized as trampling on a male figure, as is common in visualisations and iconography.

10 The compound *vṛttirāja* could be interpreted in other ways, for instance as the King of Existence/Subsistence. However, a passage from the *Kubjikāmata* (6.29-33), in which this word also figures, suggests that a *vṛttirāja* possesses mastery of poetic and śāstric composition: *anena jñātamātreṇa pratyayān kurute bahūn | vṛttirājā varārohe niveśya cakramadhyataḥ || vṛttihīnas tatas tatra kāvyakartā na saṃśayaḥ | cakramadhye ca sañcintya suśuklāṃ ca parāparām || pustakavyagrahastāṃ ca jñānamudrādharāṃ tathā | sphāṭikenākṣasūtreṇa sarvābharaṇabhūṣitām || ... udgirantī[ṃ] mahaughena śāstrakoṭīr anekaśaḥ | evaṃ dhyānasamāviṣṭaḥ sākṣād vāgīśvaro bhavet ||*. For the place and importance of the four *vṛtti*s in the context of drama, see BANSAT-BOUDON 1995. It is also possible that both meanings are intended: being beyond what can be expressed, she tramples on the King of Styles, and representing Time and Death, she crushes the King of Existence.

11 The word *kalā* can be interpreted in several ways in tantric contexts and it may also be used here to achieve a certain poetic effect. Apart from "energy" it could also denote "limited power to act" or "principle(s) constituting the universe" etc., see the entry *kalā* in TAK II.

bally, and her performance cannot be controlled by the prescribed rules.

While it may be forced to see allusions to aesthetic experience and theatre in the descriptions of various dancing Kālīs,[12] it may be of some interest to point out the existence of a so-called "Dancer-Goddess": Naṭṭeśvarī[13] or Nāṭyeśvarī. At least three *śaiva* sources mention this goddess,[14] whose name appears alternatively as Naṭṭeśvarī (JY chapter 4.64), Nāṭeśvarī (*Agnipurāṇa* 1.50.32b) and Nāṭyeśvarī (*Pratiṣṭhālakṣaṇasārasamuccaya* 6.171).[15] The earliest source, the JY, clearly names her Naṭṭeśvarī[16] and describes her as a dancing goddess dominating the cycle of withdrawal (*saṃhāra-cakra*) and wearing bone ornaments or being skeleton-like (*karaṅkiṇī*). The other two sources first identify her with Cāmuṇḍā (*rudra-cāmuṇḍā*), suggesting that she has this name because she holds severed heads (*śiras/muṇḍa*); but they also give her the name Naṭeśvarī or Nṛtyatī, apparently because she also holds a *ḍamaru* drum.[17] In all these sources, she seems to be the female equivalent

---

12 One of them may still be worth mentioning, for it uses the word *rasa*, although it is possible that no allusion to the term *rasa* describing aesthetic experience is meant: *kālī karālā kalanapratṛptā cakrakṣayākāramahograrūpā* || *narttanti sarvagrasanodbhaṭākṣī kṣībā parānandarasāsavena* | (JY 2.5.15cd-16ab)."The terrible Kālī has been satisfied by seizing (*kal-*) [the world], has the very fierce form of the destruction of the multitude [of the world]/of the wheel [of time/of deities] (*cakra*), she is dancing with eyes eager to devour the universe and drunken with the nectar (*rasa*) of supreme joy." As suggested by Lyne Bansat-Boudon (personal communication), both meaning of *rasa* may be used here: intoxicating liquor and aesthetic enjoyment; similarly to *Paramārthasāra* (henceforth PS) 79-80 (for which see BANSAT-BOUDON AND TRIPATHI 2011, pp. 265-270).

13 The word *naṭṭa-* seems to come from Middle Indic *ṇaṭṭa-*, which can be derived from *naṭa, nṛtya* or *nāṭya*, cf. the entry *naṭṭa-* in the *Pāia-sadda-mahaṇṇavo* (SHETH 1928). Judging from the Sanskrit forms, the last derivation may be the most likely.

14 These parallels have been pointed out by Olga Serbaeva in her personal notes to the e-text of the JY.

15 The last of these sources was certainly not available to Abhinavagupta, but it includes a close parallel to the *Agnipurāṇa* passage.

16 *evaṃ tava samākhyātā nāmnā naṭṭeśvarī śivā* 4.64.36cd; and the name also figures in the colophon.

17 This appears to be the implication in the following verse: *sā caivāṣṭabhujā devī śiroḍamarukānvitā* | *tena sā rudracāmuṇḍā naṭeśvary atha nṛtyatī* || *Agnipurāṇa* 1.50.31cd-32ab.

of Śiva destroying the universe as the Lord of Dance (*naṭeśa*).[18]

Dancing as an Offering in Pretantric and Tantric Worship

The act of dancing can be part of prescribed *śaiva* worship, at least from the *pāśupata*s onwards. The first passage to prescribe the offering of dancing is perhaps the well-known *Pāśupatasūtra* (henceforth PSū)[19] 1.8: "One should serve [the Lord] with the offerings of laughing, dancing, making the sound *huḍuk*, making obeisance and mantra recitations."[20] However, such an offering was probably not a *pāśupata* oddity for it is also to be found in lay contexts, in the *Skandapurāṇa* for instance. To cite but one example (26.37), when people of Benares worship the *gaṇa* Nikumbha, they also sing and dance, among other things:

> Some did pilgrimage, others undertook fasts, fire rituals, mantra recitations, yet others, wishing their desire to be fulfilled, performed worship, or made offerings,[21] yet some others offered songs and dances.[22]

---

[18] Let us remark here that while the South Indian bronze image of a gracefully dancing Śiva has always dominated Western secondary literature, the earliest North Indian images of the dancing Śiva (from the 6th-7th centuries CE) seem to be bhairavic forms, carrying perhaps a skull-staff, such as the famous image (the west panel of the north entrance) in Elephanta (see e.g. COLLINS 1988, p. 24 and BURGESS 1871, p. 41).

[19] The date of this text is uncertain, as is that of its commentator, Kauṇḍinya. The latter's dating, based on scanty evidence, is usally given between 400 and 600 CE, while the founder of the *pāśupata* movement, Lakulīśa, may have lived near the beginning of the Christian era (see e.g. HARA 2002, pp. 198-199). Inscriptions confirm that *pāśupata*s were actively involved in public religion by the fourth century CE (see e.g. RĀMESH AND TEWARI 1990, pp. 4ff. and 21ff.)

[20] *hasitagītanṛttahuṃḍuṃkāranamaskārajapyopahāreṇopatiṣṭhet.* The odd word to be pronounced, which resembles the bull's cry according to Kauṇḍinya, is written in different forms *ḍuṃḍuṃ, huṃḍuṃ, huḍuṃ, huḍuk* in various sources. For a discussion, see HARA 2002, p. 216 and ACHARYA 2013.

[21] Note that here, *upahāra* clearly seems to refer to offerings, unlike in the PSū passage, at least if we follow Kauṇḍinya's interpretation. Dancing and singing is a very commonly cited *śaiva* way of worship from the earliest tantras onwards, see for instance, the way in which various semi-divine beings worship Śiva in *Niśvāsa Mūla* 1.4-6: *kecit stunvanti deveśaṃ kecin nṛtyanti cāgrataḥ* | *kecid gāyanti hṛṣṭās tu kecit praṇatamūrdhabhiḥ* ‖ *kecid ramanti gāyanti kecit puṣpaṃ kṣipanti ca* | *kecid dhyāyanti niratā vādyaṃ vādyanti cāpare* ‖ *siṃha-*

Turning back to *pāśupata* worship which includes singing and dancing, it seems to have been adopted and adapted in *śākta* tantric scriptural sources, such as the *Brahmayāmala* (henceforth BY) and the JY, often in sections concerning the *vidyāvrata* or *pūrvasevā*, the preliminary observance preceding *sādhana* proper.[23] However, occasionally it also pops up in other contexts in which one may not expect it to appear, such as in the following passage of the JY (2.17.252-8), in which it is integrated into a standard invocation of *yoginīs* that does not commonly involve such *pāśupata*-like elements.

atha melāpasaṃsiddho vidhānam idam ārabhet |
vīrabhūmau[24] *vīravapu[ḥ] smṛtim āsādya śobhanām*[25] ||
tatpratāpaprajaptāṅgo palālipravipūritaḥ |
stabdhātmā devadeveśīṃ japet saptaśatāni tu ||
yāvat tāvad devadevya āgacchanti samantataḥ |
nānārūpadharā bhīmā madaghūrṇitalocanā[ḥ][26] ||
dṛṣṭ[v]ā vāmāṅgasaṃbhūtam[27] *argham āsāṃ prakalpayet* |
datte [']rghe tāḥ pranṛtyanti mahātumulanādinaiḥ[28] ||
huḍukkārādivādyaiś[29] *ca karavaktre kṛtair api* |
tāsāṃ sārddham ato nartte[n] mahātāṇḍavayogataḥ ||
nṛttyamānaḥ sādhakendraḥ khetalaṃ yānti vegataḥ |
tābhiḥ sārddhaṃ rājamānas[30] *tārābhir iva candramā* ||
vaset kalpakṣayaṃ yāvad bahubhogabharāvṛtaḥ |
paryante devadeveśyā dehe nirvāṇam ety[31] *asau* ||

---

nādaṃ pramuñcanti garjante hy utpatanti ca | *hasante kilakilāyante nityapramuditendriyāḥ* ||.

22 *cakrur yātrās tathā kecid upavāsāṃs tathāpare* | *homaṃ japyaṃ tathaivānye pūjāṃ cānye varārthinaḥ* | *upahārāṃs tathaivānye gītanṛttaṃ tathāpare* |. Note that the NŚ (37.29) itself also attests that theatre was considered an offering to the gods: in fact, the text claims that they preferred it to garlands and incense (cited in BANSAT-BOUDON 1992, pp. 57-58).

23 See e.g. BY 21.

24 *vīrabhūmau* conj. : *cīrabhūmair* MS.

25 *śobhanām* em. : *śobhanāt* MS.

26 °*ghūrṇita*° em. : °*ghūrmita*° MS.

27 *vāmāṅga*° conj. : *nāmāṅga*° MS.

28 Understand or emend °*nādinaiḥ* to °*nādanaiḥ*.

29 *huḍuk*° conj. : *huhuk*° MS.

30 *rājamānas* em. : *rājapānas* MS.

31 *ety* em. : *aty* MS.

> The practitioner who is successful in meeting *yoginī*s should undertake the following rite. On a ground prescribed for heroes, having the body of a hero, he must mentally recite his auspicious [mantras], and having empowered his body by their force, being filled with meat and wine, he must paralyse his Self and repeat the mantra of the goddess of gods seven hundred times, until the divine goddesses arrive from all directions. They have different forms, are frightening, with their eyes rolling in intoxication. When he sees them, he should prepare a guest offering of blood taken from his left arm. After the offering, they will dance and shout loudly all around. He must make sounds such as *huḍuk* and the like with his hands and mouth; and then he will dance with them, performing a great *tāṇḍava* dance. The eminent *sādhaka*, while dancing, will suddenly fly up in the sky with them as their lord, shining just like the moon with the stars. He will then live till the end of a *kalpa* with them and enjoy multiple pleasures. In the end, he will reach final liberation in the body of the goddess of the gods.

The description of worship with dancing, the sound *huḍuk* and the like clearly echoes PSū 1.8, except that here the practitioner dances with the *yoginī*s, who are at the same time the objects of worship. Moreover, the dance is required to be performed *mahātāṇḍavayogataḥ*. The term *tāṇḍava* can have a more or less technical or general meaning according to context,[32] and here the short description does not allow us to determine the intended meaning. It is nevertheless probable that by this potentially technical precision, the dance prescribed is not simply jumping around in joy, but something more specific and structured.

The prescription of this structured or choreographed dance stands in contrast with another prescription of dance in the same text (albeit in another, independent section). The context of this passage is different, for what is prescribed is a unique *mudrā*. As this and other *mudrā*s of the JY show, they are not hand gestures but more complex performances involving the whole body. Their aim is to propitiate the deity, to obtain superhuman effects, and/or to induce possession. The *mudrā* in this case (4.2.407-411) is called the Mudrā of Dancing (*nṛttamudrā* or *nṛttanī*).

---

[32] It can be used in at least two different meanings: 1) Śiva's fierce dance as opposed to Pārvatī's graceful (*lāsya*) one (e.g. in NŚ 4.13-16 and *Daśarūpaka* 1.4, for which see also BANSAT-BOUDON 1992, pp. 22 and 285); 2) dance in general (*nṛtta*), see BANSAT-BOUDON 1992, p. 96 citing Abhinavagupta on NŚ 4.268: *tāṇḍavam iti sarvaṃ nṛttam ucyate*.

ataḥ paraṃ pravakṣyāmi nṛttanī nāma yā smṛtā |
mudrā sarvārthasampannā sādhakānāṃ mahātmanāṃ ||
unmattā[33] *ca pralāpī syād bālavat krī*[*ḍate*] *punaḥ* |
†*śiṣṭāla -- pravaddhāni*†[34] *mudreṣā samudāhṛtā* ||
tuṣyante devatās tasya deśalābhaś (?) *ca jāyate* |
bālava[*n nṛ*]*ttanaṅ kuryāt phatkāraravayojanaṃ* ||
nṛttanī nāma mudraiṣā sarvalokavaśaṃkarī |
mahāmelāpasaṃsiddhau nāsty asyāḥ sadṛśī priye ||
kim anyad vā samākhyātā vistareṇa sumadhyame |
na sā siddhir ihāstīti yā na vā naiva sidhyati ||
pūrvavīryasamāyuktā sarvākarṣakarī parā ||

I shall now teach you the *mudrā* traditionally called the "dancing one," which has everything an eminent *sādhaka* may desire. One must be intoxicated and babble, play like a child. [...] The deities will be satisfied and one shall obtain regions/places (?).[35] One must dance like a child and shout the sound *phat*[36] – this dancing *mudrā* will subjugate everybody. There is nothing comparable to it for obtaining an encounter with *yoginīs*, o my Beloved. What else shall I explain about it in more detail, o Beautiful Goddess? There is no supernatural effect that could not be obtained with it. This supreme *mudrā* has the power previously described and attracts everybody.

The dance prescribed is explicitly an unstructured, "child-like" one, although it also leads to encounter with *yoginīs* and is considered to be an offering, by which the deities will be propitiated.

The presence of wild, child-like or madman-like dancing on the one hand (*unmatta* above in 4.2.407-411) and that of more controlled or structured dance offerings on the other (*mahātāṇḍava* in

---

33 This may be corrupt for *unmatto* with a Middle Indic *-o* ending; or perhaps the word *mudrā* mentioned in the previous line attracted the feminine form here.

34 Cruxes are enclosed by cross signs.

35 This compound does not seem common and one feels tempted to conjecture something more usual such as *dravyalābha* (obtaining things), *dhanalābha* (obtaining wealth), *dhānyalābha* (obtaining grains/corn) or possibly *veśalābha* (gaining entry into someone or something). Alternatively, *deśalābha* could stand for *upadeśalābha* (obtaining instruction) or *samāveśalābha* (obtaining possession). If *deśalābha* is retained, it could perhaps also mean 'obtaining a country/countries', something that may be promised to kings. Finally, it could also mean the supernatural power of reaching a place (in an instant), but this magical power is not normally expressed in this way.

36 Perhaps this is corrupt for the more wide-spread mantric syllable *phaṭ*.

the preceding passage of 2.17.256), which occur in different parts of the JY, raises the question as to what kind of dance the *pāśupata* version was originally meant to be.

While the *sūtra*s themselves do not help to answer this question, Kauṇḍinya does deal with the problem. His text reads:

> And dancing is performed without being attached to the conventions of the *Nāṭyaśāstra* (*nāṭyaśāstrasamayānabhiṣvaṅgeṇa*), with [various] movements: throwing up or down hands and feet, contracting or extending them, moving without stopping.[37]

This is also how singing is understood to be performed by Kauṇḍinya: without attachment to the rules of the Science of music.[38]

However, at this crucial point, there is also an alternative manuscript reading concerning the use of the NŚ: *nāṭyaśāstrasamayānusāreṇa*, "according to the rules of the *Nāṭyaśāstra*." This reading was adopted by HARA 2002. According to HARA 2002, p. 216, even the reading *anabhiṣvaṅgena* (in the case of singing) should refer to conformity to śāstric prescriptions, which is nevertheless doubtful. What *anabhiṣvaṅga* could possibly denote is that dancing and singing are performed *without* applying the rules in a very strict manner.

More light may be shed on the question if Kauṇḍinya's description or gloss on *nṛtta* is better understood. HARA 2002 (p. 216) takes the upward and other movements (*utkṣepaṇādi*) to denote the five types of motion and refers to *Vaiśeṣikasūtra* 1.1.6,[39] whose list

---

37 *nṛttam api nāṭyaśāstrasamayānabhiṣvaṅgeṇa hastapādādīnām utkṣepaṇam avakṣepaṇam ākuñcanam prasāraṇaṃ calanam anavasthānam.* While the four elements *utkṣepaṇam, avakṣepaṇam, ākuñcanam, prasāraṇaṃ* must be construed with 'hands, feet etc.', the last two words cannot. I understand them to add a more general element of the definition of dance, namely the fact that it implies moving without stopping. I thank Prof. Eli Franco for calling my attention to the problem here, although his understanding is slightly different from mine in that he takes *anavasthānam* to qualify all the other movements. Note that the *Daśarūpaka* defines dance itself (*nṛtta*) as being "various ways of throwing the limbs" (*gātravikṣepa*, see BANSAT-BOUDON 1992, pp. 408-409). This dance must, of course, conform to rules (cf. NŚ, cg. 4 and BANSAT-BOUDON 1992, p. 40).

38 *gāndharvaśāstrasamayānabhiṣvaṅgena.* The term *gāndharva(śāstra)* refers in particular to the teaching of the NŚ on music, see BANSAT-BOUDON 1992, pp. 193ff.

39 This is cited as 1.1.7 by Hara, but editions of the text commonly number this *sūtra* as 1.1.6, including Jambuvijayaji's edition used by Hara.

indeed agrees with Kauṇḍinya's on the whole. What this betrays is not that Nāṭyaśāstric rules must be applied (as Hara takes it), but rather that Kauṇḍinya was not concerned at all with Nāṭyaśāstric conformity here – he allows the devotee's dance to involve any kind of movement. He allows similar freedom for singing, which does not conform to Gāndharvaśāstra and can be in Sanskrit or Prakrit, of the practitioner's own composition or someone else's. In fact, he even specifies ad loc. that for the sake of the observance, dancing (*nṛtta*) is to be performed together with singing.[40] Thus, unlike in a proper performance, the practitioner here acts as singer and dancer at the same time.[41]

From the *pāśupata*'s dance, the dancing *mudrā* and the dancing goddesses, the conclusion one can draw is that the dances described do not normally appear to conform to śāstric norms. The dance of the goddesses is meant to express their total freedom, which is not determined by śāstric prescriptions. This "wild dance" is in turn probably what is imitated by the dancing devotees, whether *pāśupata* or *śākta*, in order to strengthen their identity with the deity[42] and/or to enact possession by them (in the case of the *mudrā* at least). Accordingly, they may involve any kind of movement and are compared to the uncontrolled behaviour of children or madmen. However, one may occasionally encounter a more structured type of dance when the practitioner invokes *yoginī*s. Dancing with *yoginī*s seems to require a more controlled performance – perhaps so that the practitioner should remain the controller of these female powers, rather than abandon himself to them (and thus become their play-thing, *paśu*).

---

40 *niyamakāle niyamārthe geyasahakṛtaṃ nṛttaṃ prayoktavyam.*

41 Unless we assume that he asks someone else to sing for him, which is highly unlikely. However, the two may not be performed simultaneously.

42 On this idea in the *pāśupata* case, see HARA 2002, pp. 216ff.

2. LIKE AN ACTOR (*NAṬAVAT*)

One Actor Playing Many Roles[43]

More relevant to our investigation is the image of the actor (*naṭa*), who often figures in various comparisons. The most famous one, which also brings out several details of the image, is perhaps to be found in the *Śivasūtra*s (henceforth ŚS): the Self is an actor, the subtle body (*puryaṣṭaka*) is the stage and the sense organs are the spectators. As the commentaries further explain, the Self is identical with the godhead or consciousness (*cit*), who enacts a play, which is the phenomenal world. The roles he takes up are the limited individual subjects. Thus, the image, which is very wide-spread in different writings of Kashmirian nondualist Śaivism, conveniently explains the way in which one god or one soul becomes manifested as many.

This ontological image takes on an epistemological aspect in the writings of the exegetes. For the roles of the actor there, instead of being aspects of the phenomenal world, are identified with various philosophical and theological schools. This is the case in Kṣemarāja's *Pratyabhijñāhṛdaya* (henceforth PH) 8, in which the roles of the actor/consciousness are identified with the points of view of various schools[44] from the Cārvākas at the lowest level up to the Trika at the highest. The image relies on the same idea of representing how the One becomes many, but with a different emphasis: the One, which is perfect and omniscient, takes up various, imperfect forms which have limited knowledge. Consequently, in Kṣemarāja's description, various schools are further identified with the various, hierarchically arranged ontological principles or *tattva*s, from *buddhi* (representing several *darśana*s) up to Sadāśiva (grammarians following Bhartṛhari) for non-*śaiva* systems, with *śaiva*s being situated above them.

The idea of placing various religious systems in the hierarchy of *tattva*s seems to come from a scriptural source, as Kṣemarāja himself points out. The unidentified citation given by Kṣemarāja and

43 For another usage of the actor analogy, see Lyne Bansat-Boudon's article in this volume, in which she examines *Tantrāloka* (henceforth TĀ) 1.332 and the commentary thereon.

44 *tadbhūmikāḥ sarvadarśanasthitayaḥ.* On this passage and its commentary, see also BANSAT-BOUDON AND TRIPATHI 2011, p. 160, n. 689.

starting with "Buddhists are at the level of intellect (*buddhi*)" appears in slightly different forms in several exegetical works. The hierarchy it expresses is, however, the same: Buddhists are at the level of the intellect (*buddhi*), Jains are at the level of the [three] material strands of existence (*guṇa*),[45] at the top of the *guṇa*s are the Sāmkhyas, the Pāñcarātra is placed at the level of the material source of creation (*prakṛti/avyakta*), while the Veda-knowers (perhaps covering both Mīmāṃsā and Vedānta) are at the level of Puruṣa.[46] While the source is scriptural, seeing these systems as Śiva's roles seems to be Kṣemarāja's contribution to the idea. Kṣemarāja also includes several more systems into his account, which is another significant innovation.[47]

In addition to Śiva's roles being identified with schools, Kṣemarāja also hints at a further series of identifications between these schools and the sets of cognizing subjects (*pramātṛ*).[48] For in Kṣemarāja's above account, the Sāṃkhya and (some unidentified) others are said to be attached to the level (*bhūmi*) of the *vijñānakala*s. The *vijñānakala*s or *vijñānākala*s form a group of cognizing subjects who are "inert in gnosis" (SANDERSON 1986, p. 191), and are only tainted with the *āṇavamala* (impurity of believing one's self to be limited). They are one of the (usually) seven groups of cognizing subjects (*pramātṛ*). The identification of Śiva's roles and the seven cognizing subjects is brought out in Kṣemarāja's *Spandanirṇaya* 1.1.:

---

45 Note that *guṇa* or the *guṇa*s are not usually included in the standard list of *tattva*s, but they do figure among them in some scriptures, see the entry *guṇa* in TAK II.

46 The longest version of the quote is in *Nareśvaraparīkṣāprakāśa* ad 3.80: *buddhitattve sthitā bauddhā guṇeṣu tv arhatāḥ sthitāḥ | guṇamūrdhni sthitāḥ sāṃkhyā avyakte pāñcarātrikāḥ | sthitā vedavidaḥ puṃsi...* The *Īśvarapratyabhijñāvivṛtivimarśinī* (henceforth ĪPVV), vol. III, p. 98, gives only *buddhitattve sthitā bauddhā avyakte pāñcarātrikāḥ*, while Jayaratha ad TĀ 6.151 omits the Sāṃkhya: *buddhitattve sthitā bauddhā guṇeṣv apy ārhatāḥ sthitāḥ | sthitā vedavidaḥ puṃsi tv avyakte pāñcarātrikāḥ ||*. On the different conceptions of the Self, see also PS 33 (BANSAT-BOUDON AND TRIPATHI 2011, pp. 169-173 and 338-342).

47 In particular the inclusion of Bhartṛhari, who does not figure in the scriptural version at all, but who is placed very high in Kṣemarāja's hierarchy. On the importance of Bhartṛhari for Kashmirian nondualist Śaivism, see e.g. TORELLA 2008 and 2013, pp. 465ff. See also a possible reference to Bhartṛhari in PS 27 (in BANSAT-BOUDON AND TRIPATHI, p. 157, n. 675).

48 For discussions of the seven *pramātṛ*s, see BANSAT-BOUDON AND TRIPATHI 2011, pp. 330ff and VASUDEVA 2004, pp. 151ff.

> By his power of absolute freedom, the glorious Great Lord assumes [on the subjective level] the cognitive roles of Śiva, the Mantramaheśvaras, the Mantreśvaras, the Mantras, the Vijñānākalas, the Pralayākalas and the Sakalas[, whereas, on the objective level,] he assumes the roles [of the objects that are] made known thereby. (Transl. BANSAT-BOUDON AND TRIPATHI 2011, p. 331.)

A similar idea appears in Kṣemarāja's disciple's, Yogarāja's commentary on Abhinavagupta's PS.[49]

Although it is in Kṣemarāja's works that the epistemological aspect of Śiva's "roles" appears in the foreground, something of this shift is perceptible already in Abhinavagupta's TĀ 4.29ff. Without using the image of Śiva as actor, Abhinavagupta speaks of various theological and philosophical currents (*vaiṣṇava*s, *vedāntin*s, *vaibhāṣika*s) as being at different levels of the cognizing subject (*pramātṛ*),[50] in particular at the double level of *pralayākala*s ("those inert in dissolution"), which comprises *prāṇapramātṛ*s (those conceiving the self as inner breath) and *śūnyapramātṛ*s (those conceiving the self as void). In the same passage, he also cites the (lost) *Kāmika* and points out that the Sāṃkhya, Pāñcarātra, Buddhists and Jains are tainted by limited knowledge (*vidyā*) and passion (*rāga*), as well as by *niyati*. He gives us only a cursory account of where different schools are placed in the hierarchy of the universe and the cognizing subjects and does not elaborate on the question further; this short passage is nevertheless enlightening not only because of the placement of rival theories in the scheme of cognizing subjects, but also because of the context of this placement. For after explaining that all those following a [false, *asat*] master of these rival schools of thought are fettered by Māyā, he goes on to say that thanks to the practice of right reasoning (*sattarkayogena*), such a person will be led to a true master (*sadguru*). To support this, he cites *Mālinīvijayottara* 1.44, but with a slight alteration. The scriptural passage clearly states[51] that turning to the right *guru*

---

49 The hierarchy of schools is expounded in his commentary on Kārikā 27 (see BANSAT-BOUDON AND TRIPATHI 2011, pp. 152ff). However, the image of the actor appears only elsewhere, in his commentary on Kārikā 1 and 5 (BANSAT-BOUDON AND TRIPATHI 2011, pp. 68 and 87ff).

50 The cognizing subject (*pramātṛ*) and the subject of experience (*bhoktṛ*) is considered to be a knower (*jñātṛ*) in śaivism as well as in other systems, see e.g. VASUDEVA 2014, p. 15.

51 Note that Abhinavagupta cites the full *śloka* elsewhere (as in 13.202 or 13.249).

is the result of the descent of Rudra's *śakti*.[52] But in Abhinavagupta's description here, the descent of Rudra's power happens *after* such a person has already turned to a true *guru*. Thus, while scripture sees the descent of Śiva's power or his divine grace as the cause of turning to a *śaiva* guru for initiation, Abhinavagupta describes the path taken toward conversion as motivated primarily by reasoning.[53]

In this light, the passage preceding the verses about such a conversion gains more significance. By describing other religious currents in terms of variously limited cognizing subjects, their partial legitimacy is recognized by Abhinavagupta. For these limited ways of cognition can form a ladder to reach true (*śaiva*) cognition – in other words, conversion is possible, and it is possible through right argumentation (*sattarka*), even if one has a different theoretical background.[54]

Thus, it is potential conversion that forms the wider context of presenting religious currents as cognizing subjects in the TĀ. And conversion also seems to be the wider context of Kṣemarāja's PH and Yogarāja's commentary on the PS, in which similar passages are found. For both are short introductory texts, meant to explain the *śaiva* doctrine to those who are not yet initiated into its intrica-

---

52 The verse starts by saying that such a person is *rudraśaktisamāviṣṭo*, possessed by the Power of Rudra.

53 For the soteriological importance of *tarka* in the Pratyabhijñā, see RATIÉ 2013, pp. 425ff.

54 Abhinavagupta in fact goes even further than this: he claims that the person who realizes himself the *śaiva* truth or doctrine through right reasoning is superior to others and will have also mastered all the *śāstra*s, again thanks to his true reasoning. Here, he turns his scriptural source upside down again. For the *Mālinīvijayottara* describes someone possessed by *śakti* as suddenly (i.e. miraculously) becoming the master of all *śāstra*s (this is a sign or proof showing that he is really possessed); while Abhinavagupta attributes such knowledge to right reasoning (*sattarka*): *sa samastaṃ ca śāstrārthaṃ sattarkād eva manyate* (4.44cd). Abhinavagupta and his commentator painstakingly point out that when the *Mālinīvijayottara* says that such knowledge appears "suddenly" (*akasmāt*), it must be understood as a way of saying that ordinary people do not see where this knowledge comes from, rather than as really meaning "out of the blue."

cies,[55] therefore both may be used to introduce relative outsiders to *śaiva* thought.[56]

Having seen something of the later history of Śiva's or the Self's roles in the works of Pratyabhijñā authors, it may not be irrelevant to look back and identify the possible source of the image of the actor in theoretical writings. As pointed out above, the earliest *śaiva* source for this image, the ŚS, do not contain any reference to theological schools as roles: the Self is the dancer (*nartaka*) or perfected actor (*prauḍhanaṭa*, in Bhāskara's gloss), dancing (*nṛtyati*, in Kṣemarāja's commentary) in a play which is the world (*jagannāṭya*), on the inner-self as the stage. The *sūtra*s themselves do not mention the roles of this actor-dancer. Kṣemarāja does com-

55 Even if both texts contain arguments whose real understanding requires one to read and understand an impressive corpus, as the richly annotated translation of BANSAT-BOUDON AND TRIPATHI 2011 shows.

56 According to the introductory part of the PH, Kṣemarāja offers his work to those who are simple-minded, without much śāstric sophistication, but who desire the "entering into" Śiva, "entering" that the descent of Śiva's Power has already started to be bring about (*unmiṣita*). (*ye sukumāramatayo 'kṛtatīkṣṇatarkaśāstrapariśramāḥ śaktipātonmiṣitapārameśvarasamāveśābhilāṣiṇaḥ* ...). I understand this reference to "simpletons" (*sukumāramatayaḥ*) to imply that he intends to write for a wider public of little learning or insight and in particular for those who have been attracted to *śaiva* theology (through a "descent of *śakti*"), but are unable to guide themselves by their own reasoning (Abhinavagupta's *sattarka*) to discover *śaiva* doctrine in a spontaneous way, and therefore need guidance in the form of an introductory work. The text does not intend to convert those who have no inclination toward śaivism. But it tries to draw into śaivism those who have some interest in it, and in this sense its purpose is conversion. The PS does not name its target audience. However, being the *śaiva* rewriting of an originally *vaiṣṇava* work, it does not seem unreasonable to assume that the textual transformation was also intended to provide a model for the spiritual one, and that conversion was therefore one of the desired effects the work was expected to have. (On this work as the rewriting of Ādiśeṣa's original, see BANSAT-BOUDON AND TRIPATHI 2011, pp. 7ff.) Let us remark here that even Ādiśeṣa's original could be considered a "conversion text" to some extent, for, as noted in BANSAT-BOUDON AND TRIPATHI 2011, p. 4: "one has the feeling that the questions put by the disciple are principally framed in terms of Sāṃkhya, whereas the responses of the teacher are usually couched in advaitic terms, even though the latter continues to utilize (in order to make himself better understood?) several Sāṃkhya concepts." A possible conclusion one could draw from this is that the dialogue represents the conversion of a Sāṃkhya disciple to nondualist vaiṣṇavism. (Bansat-Boudon in BANSAT-BOUDON AND TRIPATHI 2011, pp. 4-6, considering the text more vedāntic than vaiṣṇava, concludes rather that it represents a transposition of dualism into nondualism.)

ment on them but without mentioning the line of reasoning about the roles as limited cognizing subjects. Here, he defines the roles of the Self as having the forms of the states of being awake etc.[57] and thus maintains the image as an ontological one.[58]

It may be difficult to identify the ultimate or earliest source of the image of the actor for the self. It is, however, quite possible that the idea comes from the Sāṃkhya, just as so many other elements in *śaiva* ontology, in spite of the fact that the Sāṃkhya presents it in a dualist system.[59] More precisely, the *Sāṃkhyakārikā*s speak of the subtle body taking up different forms or incarnations as an actor/dancer plays different roles:

> Caused in order to fulfill the aim of the Puruṣa/Spirit, and through the power of Prakṛti/Matter, this subtle body (*liṅgam*) [takes up forms] like an actor [takes up roles], which inevitably leads to a causal sequence.[60]

The idea or the comparison may have come from a yet different source. However, the same image is referred to around 700 CE in the *Bodhicaryāvatāra* (9.66) and it is taken to represent the Sāṃkhya view there. The fact that an outside source, a Buddhist text, mentions this image as that of the Sāṃkhya supports the hypothesis that around 700 CE, this simile was associated with the Sāṃkhya and its arguments.

The passage of the *Bodhicaryāvatāra* summarizes the debate between the Sāṃkhya and the Mādhyamaka on the individual soul.

> *tad evānyena rūpeṇa naṭavat so 'py aśāśvataḥ* |
> *sa evānyasvabhāvaś ced apūrveyaṃ tadekatā* ||
>
> [If you argue] it is the same thing taking on a different form, like an actor [we reply:] he too would not remain permanent. [If you say] it is the

---

[57] *tajjāgarādinānābhūmikāprapañcam.*

[58] Similarly, Maheśvarānanda follows this line of interpretation. For more details, see COX 2006, pp. 147 ff and 369ff.

[59] The parallel is remarked in BANSAT-BOUDON AND TRIPATHI 2011, p. 68. It must also be noted that the dancer is always female in the Sāṃkhya as opposed to the male one in the *śaiva* system, as Prof. Eli Franco pointed out to me (personal communication).

[60] *puruṣārthahetukam idaṃ nimittanaimittikaprasaṅgena* | *prakṛter vibhutvayogān naṭavad vyavatiṣṭhate liṅgam* || (42). The *Sāṃkhyakārikā*s also use the image of the female dancer (*nartakī*) for *prakṛti* in 59, 65 and 66. However, this usage cannot be the source of inspiration for the *śaiva* version.

same with different natures [we reply] its uniformity is then unprecedented.[61]

The image of the actor is again used to explain the identity of the one and the many, one identity existing behind numerous manifestations in the course of rebirths. In the argument of the Sāṃkhya, it is of course used in the framework of a dualist ontology, to explain the identity of the same soul in different rebirths. In this sense, a major shift occurs when the image is adopted in the ŚS, for there the Self is also the godhead.

To turn back again to Śaivism, when Abhinavagupta uses the image of the actor, although he maintains it as the metaphor of the Lord/Self, playing out the (phenomenal) word as the drama, he elaborates on it with very different details.

sa ca bhramo nāṭyatulyasya aparamārthasato 'tyaktasvarūpāvaṣṭambhanaṭakalpena parameśvaraprakāśena pratītigocarīkṛtasya saṃsārasya nāyakaḥ sūtradhāraḥ pradhānabhūtaḥ pravartayitā itivṛtte nāyako vā, yallagnaṃ viśvetivṛttam ābhāti; tata eva prathamaḥ.[62]

And this error [of identifying the body etc. with the subject of experience] is [called] the primary one. For the universe (*viśva*), [which can be identified with] the story of a play (*-itivṛttam*), manifests itself as depending on this leading (*nāyakaḥ*) [error], [just as the story of the play depends on] the Sūtradhāra, who is the main person, being the producer and (*vā*) the protagonist (*nāyaka*) in the story. [In the manner of a Sūtradhāra,] this error leads the world of transmigration (*saṃsārasya*), comparable to a play that is not ultimately true and which is made to be perceptible through the manifestation of the Supreme Lord, who is like an actor (*-naṭakalpena*) firmly relying on his nature he does not abandon.[63]

---

[61] I follow the interpretation of Prajñākara's *Ṭīkā* as edited by LA VALLÉE POUSSIN 1898 (p. 300), which agrees with Prof. Eli Franco's suggestions (personal communication). For a different understanding, cf. CROSBY-SKILTON 1996, p. 121: If you argue: it is the same thing taking on a different guise, like an actor. He too does not remain constant. The one thing has different natures. [We respond that] It has an unprecedented kind of uniformity.

[62] ĪPVV, vol. III, p. 244.

[63] See RATIÉ 2011, p. 559: "Et cette illusion (*bhrama*) [consistant à identifier le corps, etc. avec le sujet] est 'première' [selon Utpaladeva] parce que cette intrigue [théâtrale] (*itivṛtta*) qu'est l'univers (*viśva*) se manifeste en reposant [nécessairement] sur le '*nāyaka*' – c'est-à-dire le directeur de la troupe (*sūtradhāra*) qui, [parce qu'il en est le membre] le plus important, est celui qui met en branle l'action, ou le personnage principal de l'intrigue – du cycle des re-

The main point here is not the Lord/Self taking up roles and thus appearing in different ways, although this image is also present in the comparison of the Lord to the actor (*naṭakalpena*). The Sūtradhāra, who is both the "impeller" or producer and the protagonist, personifies the error of identifying the self with what it is not. It is thus this error that is responsible for our perception of multiplicity in the world, for the Lord/actor does not abandon his nature even as he plays multiple roles. By introducing the Sūtradhāra as Error personified here, Abhinavagupta keeps the original idea of the Soul/Lord taking up different roles or manifestations, but puts it in an epistemological perspective.

To summarize the changes this allegory of the actor/dancer undergoes in the course of several centuries, without positing a linear chronological development:

1. The Sāṃkhya uses the image of the actor as standing for the subtle body, which takes up various roles, i.e. various reincarnations. The image is used to express how the one becomes many, in a dualist system, and it is known as such by Buddhist opponents.
2. The ŚS take over the image, again to explain the transformation of one into many; but it is put in a nondualist context, in which the Self, identified with the godhead, takes up various manifestations, including the phenomenal world.
3. The philosophical tradition, notably Abhinavagupta, points out that the Supreme Self as the universal subject identical with the godhead manifests itself, with various degrees of limitation, as various cognizing subjects (*pramātṛ*). These limited cognizing subjects are in turn identified with various rival religious currents and their doctrines. This is done in a context that suggests that one can climb up this hierarchy of subjects and reach full understanding of the ultimate (*śaiva*) truth. This implies, as is explicitly stated, that conversion to śaivism through reasoning is possible.
4. Kṣemarāja synthesizes the image of the ŚS with the theory of the cognizing subjects. He describes the Self/godhead as tak-

naissances (*saṃsāra*), lequel, semblable à une pièce de théâtre (*nāṭya*), devient objet de cognition [alors qu'il n'est] pas réel au sens ultime, grâce à la manifestation du Seigneur Suprême (*parameśvara*) semblable à un acteur (*naṭa*) qui ne cesse pas de reposer dans sa nature propre [tout en interprétant tel ou tel rôle]."

ing up roles in the form of these cognizing subjects, which are in turn identified with schools of religious thought. Thus, all religious currents and philosophies are seen as lower manifestations of this divine Self. The context of this inclusivistic image remains potential conversion and emphasis is laid on the epistemological rather than the ontological problem the example of the actor represents.

5. Abhinavagupta himself also introduces an important innovation in the allegory: in addition to the Supreme Lord as actor (*naṭa*), he describes the Sūtradhāra as personifying the main error of the cognizing subject. The Sūtradhāra both participates in the play as the protagonist and directs or produces it, just as this fundamental error of cognition both participates in and puts into motion the world of transmigration. In this way, Abhinavagupta's elaboration provides an epistemic perspective while keeping the heritage of the ŚS.

This outline may well lack many important details and does not by any means have the ambition to write the full history of this image. It may, however, identify some significant changes, no matter how roughly, and provides a starting point to examine the occurrence of the image in *śaiva* scriptural sources available to the Kashmirian exegetes.

The Actor Image in Scriptural Sources

An early text (7th-9th cent. CE) in which several occurrences of the image can be found is the BY. This *śākta* text of the *yoginī* cult evokes the image of the actor to prescribe the way in which the practitioner must see himself. It insists in each case on non-duality – but this non-duality, as pointed out by SANDERSON 1992, p. 306 and as I have shown elsewhere (TÖRZSÖK 2013), refers to nondual practice, i.e. the non-distinction between what is pure and impure from the point of view of orthopraxy, and not to ontological non-duality.

evaṃ jñātvā parādvaitaṃ saṃstha[*ḥ*] *syāt sacarācaraṃ* |
sādhako [']*nilavad yathā krīḍann api na lipyate* ||[64]
aśucitvena deveśi yathārka[*ḥ*] *padmabodhane* |
sarvatattvakṛtātmā vai sa prapañcakṛtāspadā ||

[64] My conjectures. The MS reads *sādhako nilavadyandha krīḍānnapi na lipyate*.

naṭavat paśya -m- ātmānaṃ sarvabhakṣaḥ kṛtāntavat |
†*kharave -- yasvato*† *yukta[ḥ] kāmabhoktṛtvalakṣaṇaḥ* ||
saṃsakto 'pi na kāmī syā['] yathā bhāno[r] didhītayaḥ[65] |
śāpānugrahakarttāsau sarvaiśvaryapravarttakaḥ ||
bhuktvā tu vipulān bhogān etad vai tasya lakṣaṇam | (71.95-99ab)[66]

Knowing in this way the world to have this supreme nonduality,[67] the practitioner must be established [in this nonduality]. Just like the wind, he is not tainted by impurity even if he is playing, just as the sun is not tainted when it wakes up the lotuses. His self being made of all the levels of the universe, having the visible universe as his abode, he must see himself as an actor, while consuming everything like death. Even if he is attached [to things] and enjoys the objects of his desires (*kāmabhoktṛtva-lakṣaṇaḥ*), he will not covet anything, just as the rays of the sun [have no attachment to what they touch]. He will bestow his curse or grace and accomplish all acts of power, enjoying multiple pleasures – these will be his traits.

The image of the actor is employed to explain the practitioner's (ritually) nondualist attitude, which is prescribed in almost every chapter of this text. Although he is required to manipulate and consume impure substances, he must not be disgusted or feel impure. He must see himself as an actor in the sense that his real self is outside the reality of the play, which is the world. The same idea is expressed when he is compared to the sun or the rays of the sun and the wind: they can touch anything without being soiled.

This actor image is rather different from that of the Sāṃkhya. It does not intend to explain the dichotomy of the one and the many (as when one actor takes up several roles), but the detachment of the self. In this sense, it is perhaps closest to Abhinavagupta's example involving the Sūtradhāra and emphasizing that the actor/Self is both inside and outside the play/the multiplicity of the world, even if the BY does not describe the godhead but the individual

---

65 The MS reads *dīdhitayaḥ*, which is unmetrical.

66 Minor corrections I have made to the text are put between square brackets.

67 This translation attempts to follow the grammatical structure. It is, however, also possible that *sacarācaram* is not the object of *jñātvā*, but is corrupt for or to be understood as a locative ("he should be established in the world knowing supreme nonduality in this way"). The word *sa-* can also be the pronoun or the prefix to *carācara*. The word *saṃsthaḥ* is probably understood in a compound with *parādvaita-* (i.e. *parādvaita-* is to be read twice, once as the object of *jñātvā*, once in compound with *saṃsthaḥ*).

and does not imply or require an underlying nondualist ontology. Similarly, ritual nondualism is referred to in another occurrence (83.169) of the actor simile:

> *advaitabhāvasampannaḥ sarvabhakṣa[ḥ] kṛtāntavat |*
> *naṭavat paśya bhāvena ātmā vai sādhakeśvaraḥ ||*

> Endowed with non-duality and consuming everything like death, the eminent practitioner must see himself with the help of his imagination as an actor.[68]

Although the image itself is different from the actor of the Sāṃkhya, it echoes to some extent the Sāṃkhya idea of the self/Puruṣa as uninvolved witness (*sākṣin*),[69] who does not actively take part in any action, and is therefore never tainted. However, a major difference is that the BY's self actually participates in the action, and in spite of that, remains outside it. In this way, the Self as subject is active but without being involved in action, in a way similar to Abhinavagupta's conception.[70]

The closest early parallel to this view is then not found in the Sāṃkhya, but rather in the PSū (5.20), which insist on the fact that the perfected yogin is not tainted by any *karman* or sin: *siddhayogī*

---

68 I understand *paśya* as an imperative standing for the third person singular, or rather that the second and third persons are used alternatively in the prescription, which is meant for the *sādhaka*. It is also possible that *paśya* stands for *dṛṣṭvā*.

69 The idea certainly belongs to a kind of pan-Indian heritage or what TORELLA 1999 calls Sāṃkhya as *sāmānyaśāstra*; Torella mentions on the first page of his paper that the paradigm of spirit-consciousness-inactivity as opposed to matter-unconsciousness-productivity is wide-spread throughout Indian civilization. VASUDEVA 2014, p. 10 also mentions that what appears like a borrowing from the Sāṃkhya in Śaivism may often come from other schools which assimilated Sāṃkhya tenets in their own way. It must also be mentioned that Sāṃkhya itself appears in different forms and what appears in tantric sources may well be closer to various versions of what is called epic Sāṃkhya, which is often theistic. On the problem of epic Sāṃkhya, a discussion of which is beyond the scope of the present study, see for instance BROCKINGTON 1999, who also points out that some tenets we consider to belong to the Sāṃkhya may have been common currency already by the epic period (BROCKINGTON 1999, p. 489). Brockington 1999, p. 485 also mentions that in the *Mokṣadharma* the perceiving self is not the real doer and enjoyer but simply the pure witness-consciousness.

70 For the experiencer as an active entity in Abhinavagupta's works, see VASUDEVA 2014. For an analysis of Abhinavagupta's conception of the actor, who is a "receptacle" (*pātra*), see BANSAT-BOUDON 1992, p. 150 and 430.

na lipyate karmaṇā pātakena vā. This line in turn is also echoed in the *Skandapurāṇa* (52.24), which has a wording rather similar to the BY's (concerning the *sādhaka* who is not tainted even if he is playing): *yogī tu sarvapāpāni kurvann api na lipyate* ("the yogin is not tainted, even if he commits all kinds of sin").

Another scriptural occurrence, from the JY (1.30.19), also seems to stress "detachment in action" of the actor-self, even if in this case, the actor is said to be the "world" (*jagat*). It is less clear what theoretical implications are suggested, for after identifying the world with the actor and the stage with one's own nature, the rest of the image elaborates on the theatrical aspect. But it may not be too far-fetched to assume that, in addition to the actor's detachment, it stresses the multiplicity of the phenomenal world, which is probably understood as the play with various sentiments. Whatever is the case, the verse is unique in that it makes use of aesthetic terms, such as *vṛtti*, *bhāva* and *rasa*.

> *svabhāvaraṅgamadhye tu nṛtyate naṭavaj jagat* |
> *vṛttitraya[ṃ] samālambya nānābhāvarasāśrayaiḥ* ||
>
> The world dances like an actor on the stage, which is its nature, resorting to the three styles of composition and making use of the various feelings and dominant sentiments.

Such technical terms can also be found elsewhere, for instance the word *vibhāva* ("stimulants" which contribute to creating a particular aesthetic reaction)[71] in the following passage, taken from the lost *Triśirobhairava*. Here, however, the purpose of the demonstration is clearly to show the freedom of the enlightened actor-self in his play and suggests a nondualist conception of the self, which is identical with the godhead. In this light, it is possible that the above verse is also intended to stress the same freedom, in which case both citations would imply an underlying nondualist conception, whereby the enlightened Self is the omnipotent godhead playing at will. This enlightened and free actor-Self is contrasted below with the limited Self that does not recognize his identity with the godhead:[72]

---

[71] For more on *vibhāva*, translated into French as "déterminants," see BANSAT-BOUDON 1992, pp. 111-114.

[72] The passage is cited by Jayaratha ad TĀ 1.136. The source, the lost *Triśirobhairava*, was probably a Trika scripture prescribing the worship of a three-headed Bhairava. See TAK III at *trika* citing Sanderson.

anyathā svalpabodhas tu tantubhiḥ kīṭavad yathā |
malatantusamārūḍhaḥ krīḍate dehapañjare ||
samyagbuddhas tu vijñeyaḥ .... |
nānākārair vibhāvaiś ca bhramyate naṭavad yathā |
svabuddhibhāvarahitam icchākṣemabahiṣkṛtam ||

Otherwise, if one has little awareness, one plays in the cage of the body, locked up by one's [own] impurity, just like a silkworm, which is locked [in its cocoon] by its [own] silk threads.[73] But one who has right awareness whirls around like a dancer, with his various forms and conditions, without [being limited by] the [false] creations of his own mind, and being beyond volition or happiness.

In addition to emphasizing freedom, the passage also brings out the detachment of the Self by saying that he is beyond volition and happiness. In doing so, it presents this Self in a way similar to the BY's, albeit the detachment is described not from purity and impurity but from the act of attachment itself, since this divine Self is self-sufficient, being as it is the only truly existing entity.

3. "DRAMATIZED" OBSERVANCES

As pointed out above, the PSū already speak of the yogin as someone who is not tainted by any act or sin. This is an important statement, for several of the *pāśupata* observances involve contact with impure substances or impure acts. In this context, a later *pāśupata* text, the *Gaṇakārikāṭīkā* (1.7, p. 57), prescribes that the performer of the *pāśupata* observance must see himself as an actor, surrounded by other people as his public.

---

[73] It is not possible to retrace the development of the well-known example of the silk-worm. Two texts, however, should be mentioned here. The *Śāntiparvan* of the *Mahābhārata* may have the earliest two occurrences (12.2924-5b and 12.316.28) of this image. In both occurrences, the self locks itself in its own construction like a silk-worm, but in one case the threads represent *guṇa*s (*kośakāro yathātmānaṃ kīṭaḥ samanurundhati | sūtratantuguṇair nityaṃ tathāyam aguṇo guṇaiḥ || dvaṃdvam eti ca nirdvaṃdvas tāsu tāsv iha yoniṣu |*) and in the other, they represent ignorance (*saṃveṣṭyamānaṃ bahubhir mohatantubhir ātmajaiḥ | kośakāravad ātmānaṃ veṣṭayan nāvabudhyase ||*). Surprisingly, when the image appears in the *Svacchandatantra* (10.361), it is used to demonstrate that one cannot liberate one's self, so hard is the cocoon one has created that Śiva's intervention is needed to remove it (*kośakāro yathā kīṭa ātmānaṃ veṣṭayed dṛḍham | na codveṣṭayituṃ śakta ātmānaṃ sa punar yathā ||*).

evaṃ prathamāvasthāyāṃ vidhim anuṣṭhāya yadā khalu prāptajñānaḥ prakṣīṇakaluṣaḥ kṛtābhyanujñaś ca bhavati tadāvasthāntaraṃ gatvā raṅgavad avasthiteṣu janeṣu madhye naṭavad avasthito vivecya vivecya krāthanādīni kuryāt.

In this way, after performing what is prescribed in the first stage [of his observance], when he has obtained [*pāśupata*] knowledge [from his master] and his sins have been destroyed, after getting the authorisation [of his master], he should proceed to the next stage [of his observance]: in the middle of people around him, as if he were an actor on stage, gradually separating [himself from them],[74] he should snore etc.

Acting concerns the famous second stage of the *pāśupata* observance, in which the *pāśupata* behaves in an uncivilized way or "like a demon" (*pretavat*): snoring (PSū 3.12ff), pretending he is limp, making gestures of love (or perhaps sexual gestures), thus provoking slander and curse. In this way, he transfers the fruitions of his bad karma to passers-by and takes their good karmas. While doing so, however, he must remain detached: he must, according to the above passage, behave like an actor and provoke disgust in people as if he was acting in a play.

The *pāśupata*s were probably the first *śaiva*s who "acted" in their observance. They thus started a tradition of observances which involved a theatrical aspect or at least required the practitioner to disguise himself and play a role. He was always meant to do so in front of people surrounding him, in front of passers-by, he thus also demarked himself from society. The *pāśupata*s played to be repulsive in order to provoke an exchange of karma; but later tantrics appear to do role-playing rather in order to assimilate themselves to their deity. This imitation of the deity must of course be distinguished from other important techniques or ways of identification, such as ritual transformation of the body with mantras (*nyāsa/sakalīkaraṇa*), possession (*āveśa*) and complete merging into the god (at the time of final release, *mokṣa*).

There seem to be three particular roles prescribed in such ritual imitations: the goddess (*devī*), the god of love (*kāma*) and the madman (*unmatta*). These three are listed as three alternative vows in a passage of the JY (1.47.10cd-15ab), which gives a set of general rules to follow when impersonating a deity or a madman. In all

---

[74] My understanding of *vivecya vivecya* is tentative.

three cases, the disguised practitioner must behave in an uncontrolled manner and decorate himself excessively, like a woman.[75]

devīvratadharo mantrī nitya[ṃ] nepathyakādiṣu ||
unmattako [']*tha*[76] *śṛṅgārī cāpavratadharo* [']*thavā* |
gītālāpavilāsāḍhyo nānāvarṇoparañjitaḥ ||
vicitrāmbaramālāḍhyo mālāhastādyanekadhṛk |
grāmacatvararathyāsu prabhramet tvaritaḥ sadā ||
gāyan hasan paṭhan -- odaṃ nṛttaṃ[77] *valgan suharṣitaḥ*[78] |
†*vintryaurthy*†*āropitakaras* †*tadiṣṭakaḥ*†*karaḥ sadā* ||
samārañjitavaktraś ca raktasūtrāṅganāsadhṛk[79] |
†*viṣāṇāvaṣava*†*cchannaprakoṣṭhodantakarṇikaḥ* ||
svabhāvasthaś caran maunī kvacid bhāvaṃ samāśrayet |

The master of mantras may observe the Goddess-vow, the Madman(-like) vow or the vow of the Bow-[Carrying Kāma], in which he is in love,[80] always in a costume (*nepathyaka-*) and other [insignia]. He must sing, babble and play around a lot, wear various colours, adorn himself with coloured clothes and garlands and hold a garland and several other attributes in his hands. He should always wander around quickly in villages, crossroads and main roads (or: at crossroads and on main roads of villages), singing, laughing, reciting texts, [...] dancing, and bouncing very happily. [...][81] With his face coloured, he should look like a beautiful woman wearing a red thread [as decoration?]. He must have earrings

---

75 It is possible that the prescription here describes only the first one, the *devīvrata*. However, while one verse enjoins that one must be like a woman, the rest appears more appropriate for the other vows. Therefore, I understand these verses to describe the three *vrata*s in a general and not necessarily systematic way. Subsequently, each of the *vrata*s is described separately.

76 The MS reads *ṣa* for *tha*.

77 The MS reading *nṛttaṃ* is probably to be emended to *nṛtyan*.

78 The MS has *svaharṣitaḥ* for *suharṣitaḥ*.

79 Perhaps to be understood/emended to *raktasūtro* [']. The word *sadṛk* appears in the MS as *śadṛk*.

80 I understand the compound *cāpavratadharo* to stand for *cāpadhara-vratadharo*. The compound and the adjective *śṛṅgārī* suggest that Kāma is to be imitated here, for which there is indeed a prescription elsewhere, as will be shown.

81 The beginning of the line is corrupt and does not seem to yield sense as it stands, except that hand-held attributes are prescribed. The second compound may be corrupt for *śastrāṣṭakakaraḥ* "holding eight weapons in the hand" as in JY 1.15.86c: *śastrāṣṭakakarā devyaḥ*. There may be, however, some technical difficulties in carrying out this prescription with only two hands.

reaching down to his forearms [covered with...],[82] and observe his vow while staying in his own natural state or sometimes he may resort to [another] state.

The Goddess Vow

The detailed description of the goddess vow referred to above can be found under the heading of Cāmuṇḍā Vow (*cāmuṇḍāvrata*), in which the practitioner dresses up and behaves like the terrifying goddess (*Yoginīsaṃcāra* as transmitted in the JY 3.31.36cd-42ab, edited by Sanderson).

tataś cared vratavaraṃ triṣaṣṭikulasaṃbhavam ||
bhairavaṃ vā mahābhāge cāmuṇḍāvratam eva ca |
kṛṣṇāmbaradharo nityaṃ kṛṣṇagandhānulepanam ||
kṛṣṇamālāvalambī ca karṇālaṅkārabhūṣitaḥ |
valayābharaṇopetaṃ nūpuradhvanibhūṣitam ||
raktāmbaro raktapādo divyastrīrūpadhāriṇaḥ |
pracchanne nirjane deśe maunī vidyāvrataṃ caret ||
māsam ekaṃ caren mantrī dvādaśāṃ vā mahāvratām |
māsena tu mahāyogī yoginyāḥ paśyatecchayā ||
tair vṛtam tu caruṃ kṛtvā trailokye vicaret kṣaṇāt |
sarvajñaḥ sarvakarttā ca sṛṣṭisaṃhārakārakaḥ ||
yoginīnāṃ pade devi harttā karttā ca jāyate |

He must then observe the excellent vow of the 63 families also called Bhairava vow and the Cāmuṇḍā vow, o Fortunate One. [First the latter is described:][83] he must always wear black clothes and fragrant paste of black colour, with a black garland and decorated with earrings. He must have bracelets and [other] ornaments and jingling anklets. Dressed in

---

82 The text seems to be corrupt here and I cannot propose any convincing conjecture. The first word of the compound is *viṣāṇa* or *viṣāṇā*, which, provided the word is not entirely corrupt, would imply that the practitioner must wear a horn or a horn-like object.

83 I understand that only two observances are described in this chapter of the text: first the Cāmuṇḍāvrata (given here), and then the Bhairavavrata (also called Triṣaṣṭikula- or Kāpāla-vrata). SANDERSON 2009, p. 134, understands that the Bhairava-vrata and the Triṣaṣṭikula-vrata are two different observances, and that the practitioner can choose between altogether three *vrata*s. Since only two are described in the subsequent passage, I understand the *vā* above to refer to alternative names of the same observance; and since the Cāmuṇḍā-vrata is connected with a *ca*, I understand that both *vrata*s must be performed.

red, with red feet, having the form of a divine woman, he must perform his preliminary observance in a secret, solitary place. The master of mantras should perform [this] Great Observance for one or for twelve months.[84] After a month, the great yogi shall see the yoginīs if he wishes. Accompanied by them, he should make a rice offering [including the mingled sexual fluids] and wander in the three worlds in a second. He will become omniscient and omnipotent, performing creation and destruction. He will become the creator and the destroyer, o goddess, in the realm of yoginīs.

The prescription hesitates between prescribing the imitation of the terrifying black goddess or that of a beautiful, divine woman with red ornaments.[85] In any case, the observance is called a *vidyāvrata*, which is the preliminary observance commonly prescribed before the invocation of *yoginīs*.

The Observance of Kāma

Similarly, pretending to be Kāma is also part of the *vidyāvrata*s. I take the following *vrata*, which occurs in *Siddhayogeśvarīmata* (henceforth SYM)10.6cd-8, to be the same as the *śṛṅgārī cāpavrata,* lit. "the amourous observance of the bow" mentioned above in the JY, for the expression seems to suggest that Kāma must be imitated.

dhanurdhara[*ḥ*] *śarāṃś caiva pañca dikpālavat tataḥ* ||
raktena bhasmanā snāto raktayajñopavītinaḥ |
raktapuṣpadharo dhīmān hasantoccair japet tataḥ ||
śaram ekaṃ kare gṛhya maunī †neyāt†[86] *paribhramet* |
vrataṃ brahmaśirasyaita[*t*] *siddhidam parikīrtitam* ||

---

84 It is also possible to understand that the Cāmuṇḍā-vrata should be performed for one month and that the Mahāvrata (as a different observance, implying assimilation to Bhairava) is an alternative, but one which must be done for twelve months.

85 Let us note here that other *śākta* texts also prescribe that the practitioner should or can dress up as a woman. See e.g. *Devīpañcaśatikā* 5.54: *strīveśadhārī bhūtvāsau nagnavāso mahāmatiḥ* | *nirvikalpaḥ prasannātmā pūjākarmaviśāradaḥ.*

86 Perhaps one should understand *maunīneyāt* as a verb, some kind of irregular optative of a denominative from *mauna* or *maunī* – but this solution is highly conjectural.

> The practitioner should hold a bow and five arrows [and remain vigilant?] like a guardian of a direction.[87] He must be bathed in red ashes and should have a red sacred thread. Holding red flowers, the wise one should recite the mantras laughing loudly. Taking one arrow in his hand, he should remain silent [...] and wander about. This is the observance of the Brahma Head [a protection mantra], which is said to bestow success.

Although Kāma is not named here either, the prescription of the bow and the five arrows together with the red colour clearly imply the imitation of Kāma. Just as the goddess vow, this observance is also part of the *vidyāvrata* series, or preliminary mantra propitiation.

The Madman(-Like) Observance

This *vrata*, unlike the previous ones, goes back directly to a *pāśupata* prescription. In PSū 4.6, the practitioner is required to remain alone and act like a madman in the world or towards people (*unmattavad eko vicareta loke*). The commentator explains that it is again performed in order to mislead people about the real identity of the performer.[88]

The same *vrata* is also said to have been practiced by *lākula*s as pointed out in SANDERSON 2006, p. 209. Abhinavagupta mentions in his commentary on NŚ 12.85 that it existed for *lākula*s, in the so-called "stage of the highest yogi."[89] A similar *vidyāvrata*, under the name of *gaṇavrata*, but still with the prescription to behave like a madman, is also found in the earliest tantra, the *Niśvāsa*.[90] Subsequently, it becomes recurrent in *śākta* tantras, often echoing the PSū and their commentary,[91] as in the following passage of the BY

---

87 It is not clear to me what this comparison to a guardian of a direction implies. Since the practitioner takes on the appearance of Kāma, it is unlikely (but not impossible) that he should look menacing (like a guardian of a direction).

88 *laukikaparīkṣakāṇāṃ sammohanārtham uktam unmattavad iti.*

89 *paramayogyavasthāyāṃ lākuladarśanapratipannānām unmattavratam apy asti*. Cited in SANDERSON 2006, p. 209.

90 *nṛtyate gāyate caiva unmatto hasate bruvan ‖ bhasmāṅgī cīravāsaś ca gaṇavratam idaṃ smṛtam* | (*Niśvāsaguhya* 3.32cd-33ab). Note that the *Niśvāsaguhya* also has an observance in which one must be disguised as a woman, as in the *devīvrata: gāyate nṛtyate jāpī strīrūpī valabhūṣitaḥ* (3.35cd).

91 Cf. Kauṇḍinya on PSū 4.6 (*tato vaktavyaṃ māheśvaro 'haṃ kaumāro 'ham iti*) with verse 20 above. Parallel identified in KISS forthcoming, p. 30.

(21.18cd-27).[92] As Kiss points out, the aim here is nevertheless very different compared to the *pāśupata* version, for this prescription "seems to concentrate on the gradual adoption of non-conventional practices (*nirācāra*), which prepares the Sādhaka for the extreme rituals to be performed after this introductory test period" (KISS forthcoming, p. 33).

nagnarūpo bhaven nityaṃ muktakeśas tathaiva ca ||
rudate hasate caiva kvacid geyam udīrayet |
kvacin nṛtyaṃ kvacid valgaṃ kvacid dhāvati sādhakaḥ ||
brahmāhaṃ viṣṇurūpo 'haṃ īśvaro 'haṃ bravīti ca |
devāḥ prāptakarāsmākaṃ kiṅkaratvaṃ samāgatāḥ ||
airāvate samārūḍha indro 'haṃ paśya māṃ bravīt |
indrāṇī mama bhāryā ca śvāno 'haṃ sūkaraṃ hy ahaṃ ||
aśvamūrddho hy ahaṃ caiva ghoṭavigrahakam tathā |
rathyāyāṃ śayanaṃ kuryād uttiṣṭed dhāvate ti ca ||
yāgasthānaṃ na laṅgheta pūjayen manasāpi vā |
mūtreṇa vandayet saṃdhyāṃ kvacin mūrdhni tu prakṣipet ||
striyo dṛṣṭvā namaskṛtya mātā ca bhaginīti ca |
evaṃ saṃbhāṣayen mantrī kroṣaṇaṃ tu na kārayet ||
bhramaṇaṃ tu tathaiveha āhnikan tu tathaiva hi |
bhojanaṃ tu divā naiva unmatto 'pi samācaret ||
mastake tu tilāṃ kṣipya yūkaṃ kṛtvā tu bhakṣayet |
saśabdaṃ mārayed vātha lokasammohanaṃ prati ||
unmattakaṃ mahādevi evaṃ saṃcārya sādhakaḥ |
nānārūpābhi ceṣṭābhir yogināṃ tu hitāvahaṃ ||

He should always be naked, his hair unbound. He weeps, he laughs, sometimes he bursts out in song. Sometimes the Sādhaka dances, sometimes he jumps up, sometimes he runs [away]. He states, "I am Brahmā! I am Viṣṇu! I am Īśvara! The gods are in my hands! They have become my servants! Look at me – I am Indra, mounted on [his elephant] Airāvata!", he says. "Indrāṇī is my wife!". And, "I am a dog! I am a pig! I am horse-headed [?] and my body is that of a horse!". He should lie down on the road, then get up and run. He should not set foot on the site of pantheon-worship (*yāgasthāna*) and should not perform worship, not even mentally. He should salute the junctions of the day (*saṃdhyā*) by [offering his own] urine. He should sometimes pour some of it on his head. When seeing women, he should greet them thus: "Mother! Sister!". This is how the Mantrin should engage in conversation. He should not abuse [them]. Roaming (*bhramaṇa*) is [to be performed] in the same

[92] Edition and translation of this passage are taken from KISS forthcoming.

way in this case (*iha*) [as taught above], as [is the sequence of] the daily rituals (*āhnika*). He should not eat in the daytime, even though [he behaves like] a madman. He should throw sesamum seeds on his head and, pretending that they are (*kṛtvā*) lice, he should eat them. Or he should kill [the "lice"] with a big fuss in order to delude people. The Sādhaka should, O Mahādevī, pursue the Madman-like [observance] (*unmattaka*) thus, with different patterns of behaviour. This is for the benefit of yogins.

In this *vrata,* "acting" is described much more vividly than in the observances of the Goddess and Kāma. There is also a more detailed and elaborate version of this *vrata* in the JY (3.38.167cd-173cd) which brings out the theatrical aspect of the observance:

atha vonmattakaṃ kāryaṃ vrataṃ paramaśobhanam ||
asatyul[l]āpalāpī syād yena kena[93] *cid †ātaḥ†* |
digambaro muktakeśo sarvabhakṣo hy alolupaḥ ||
kṣaṇaṃ hase' kṣaṇaṃ gāye' kṣaṇaṃ rode' kṣaṇaṃ raṭet |
kṣaṇaṃ plavet kṣaṇaṃ nartte' kṣaṇaṃ dhāve' kṣaṇaṃ lalet ||
kṣaṇaṃ śāntaṃ kṣaṇaṃ vīraṃ kṣaṇaṃ[94] *bībhatsavad*[95] *bhavet* |
kṣaṇaṃ raudrarasāvastho kṣaṇam eva bhayānakam ||
kṣaṇaṃ śṛṅgāriṇaṃ devi kṣaṇaṃ hāsyaikatatparaḥ |
kṣaṇam adbhutasaṃrū ḍho kṣaṇaṃ kāruṇyam āsthitaḥ ||
nānārasasamāviṣṭo nānābhāvasamāsthitaḥ |
nānāvilāsasaṃyukto nānāgītaravākulaḥ ||
rathyāpatitanirmālyaṃ śavanirmālyam eva vā |
dhārayet satataṃ dehe sphuṭec ca bahubhāṣayā ||

Or he should perform the madman-like observance, which is particularly auspicious. He should babble lies [...][96] naked, with his hair undone, eating everything and not desiring anything, he must laugh for a second, then sing then cry and howl. One moment he must leap around, then dance, run or play around. For a moment he must resort to the [aesthetic experience of the] sentiment of tranquility,[97] then to the heroic one, to

93 The MS reads *keta*.

94 The MS reads *kṣaṭāṃ*.

95 The MS reads *bhītatsavad*.

96 The MS seems to be corrupt in several places here. The first word could also be considered a crux, but the meaning seems clear. Perhaps the latter half of the line means "he should speak with anyone [without distinction]."

97 It is notable that the text already knows of the *śāntarasa*, which appears perhaps only from Udbhaṭa onwards.

> that of disgust, wrath, terror, love, humour, marvel, and pathos.[98] Possessed by various aesthetic experiences and resorting to various dominant sentiments, playing various games and filled with the sound of multiple songs, he must always wear a garland that has either fallen on the road or a garland [that has come] from corpses on his body and express himself in several tongues.

The subsequent part of the text also prescribes that the practitioner must emit the cries of various animals and pretend to be a *kāpālika* and/or an outcaste *caṇḍāla*. Therefore, even though the theatrical aspect of the observance is very prominent here, the point remains the Sādhaka's preparation for impure rites through which he will become Bhairava himself as the master of the universe, both pure and impure. The list of *rasa*s must be understood in this light: they are all present in him, preparing him for the experience of totality.

4. THE GREAT PLAY OR MOCK PLAY (*MAHĀKRĪḌĀ*)

Thus far, we have seen various elements of theatre and dramatic theory appearing in tantric contexts. Occasionally, it also happens that the enactment of a play is prescribed in a ritual context. Such a prescription is found in the second half of the BY (54.93cdff.), which is chronologically somewhat later than the first half. The play itself or the rite in which the play is performed seems to be termed *mahākrīḍā* or "great play," which is an unusual name for a theatrical production. The word *krīḍā* is more often used in connection with Bhairava (or the practitioner who becomes Bhairava), who plays freely, at will in the world. It is therefore possible that this play to be performed for Bhairava is in some way related to this notion. However, *mahākrīḍā* may also be the term for the whole ritual that involves the play itself.

The ritual context of the performance is again an observance. Before the prescription of this *mahākrīḍā*, the BY first envisages a more common type of observance, in which the naked practitioner remains silent, wanders around at night in the cremation ground with various bhairavic weapons or attributes, eats meat and drinks alcohol. Then either an alternative is prescribed (in which he wears various clothes as opposed to being naked previously) or a continuation of the previous practice is given, in which he can wear va-

---

98 For *kāruṇya/karuṇā* meaning the pathetic sentiment, see BANSAT-BOUDON 2000, pp. 84ff.

rious clothes and ornaments, he plays drums, shouts and the like. The observance finishes with a drama (*nāṭya*), at the end of which the practitioner becomes a leader of *yoginīs*.

kṛṣṇāmbaro [']thavā raktā-[99] *vastraiś citrais tathā priye* | 93
bhasmasnāto [']thavā mantrī raktacandanacarccitaḥ
lalāṭe tilakaṃ kṛtvā pādau laktakarañjitau | 94
kaṇṭhe [ca] kaṇṭhikā[ṃ] dadyā' kiṅkiṇīśreṇimālinaḥ |
karṇe kare ca bāhubhyāṃ kaṭakābharaṇaṃ tathā | 95
javāmālāvṛto mantrī muṇḍamālāvalambakaiḥ |
ḍamarum vādayen mantrī paṭahikām vā mahātmanaḥ | 96
śivārāvaṃ prakurvīta kravyādāśabdam[100] *eva ca* ||
nṛtyārambhaṃ sabhāvātmā śabdāt tatra samārabhet | 97
yoginīsahitaṃ nāṭyaṃ vīrabhāvāvalambanaṃ ||

The master of mantras wears black or red clothes, or clothes of variegated colours, my Beloved, or he is bathed in ashes [and naked?], or covered with red sandalwood paste. He must make a *tilaka* on his forehead, put lac on his feet, a necklace around his neck with rows of jingling bells. He must also put jewels in his ears, on his hands, armlets on his arms and wear a garland of red *javā* flowers, which rests on a garland of heads.[101] The eminent master of mantras should play on an hourglass-shaped drum or a kettle drum and emit a jackal's cry or the sound of a demon. Then he should take up there, at the sound [of musical instruments] (*śabdāt*), the starting position in dance (*nṛtyārambham*),[102] while his self is infused with the [dominant] sentiment.[103] He must undertake the performance of a play (*nāṭyam*) with *yoginīs*, which is based on the heroic sentiment (*vīrabhāva-*).

The heroic sentiment is probably prescribed with reference to the Sādhaka as a "hero," who must be brave and fearless when he invokes *yoginīs* at night in the cremation ground and they suddenly arrive in hordes, with a frightening appearance. The text does not elaborate on the subject further and it remains a question what kind

---

99 This must be intended in the sense of *athavā raktāmbaro*.

100 This stands for *kravyādaśabdam metri causa*.

101 Because of the irregularities of the Sanskrit, this is a tentative interpretation.

102 For *nṛtyārambha* denoting a particular position (*avasthānaviśeṣa*) in dance, see e.g. the *Vikramacarita* Southern Recension F3b and the *Nṛtyaśāstra* it cites: *aṅgeṣu caturaśratvaṃ samapādau latākarau* | *prārambhe sarvanṛtyānām etat sāmānyam ucyate* ||.

103 Other interpretations of the compound are also possible, but this seemed to me the most appropriate in the context.

of play is to be performed with the *yoginīs* as actresses. The occurrence of the prescription is, however, not completely unparalleled. The short recension of the SYM (27.20) also enjoins that one must provide the god (Bhairava) with a play (*krīḍā*). Nothing is specified about this *krīḍā*, but it may well be the same play that the BY prescribes, for the BY also calls the whole ritual sequence involving the dramatic performance simply *krīḍana*.

CONCLUSION

Although theatre certainly cannot be considered a fundamental part of tantric prescriptions and texts, elements of acting and performance do appear in various ways as shown above. From the above investigations, it is possible to point out some major shifts as to how theatre and its image play a role in tantric texts. To summarize these changes:

1. The image of the actor, inherited from the Sāṃkhya (perhaps as *sāmānyaśāstra*) and identified there with the subtle body, becomes reinterpreted. The BY uses it not to explain the tension between the one and the many, but the detachment of the self from whatever it manipulates, in order to defend its ritual nondualism (without professing clear ontological nondualism). In this, it remains nevertheless close to the Sāṃkhya-like conception of the self as uninvolved witness (*sākṣin*). Later *śākta* tantras, however, use the image of Śiva as the actor or dancer to show the absolute freedom of the deity-self, as part of a nondualist ontology, in which creation or the phenomenal world is a product of the deity's play, but is identical with Him. This image of freedom, in turn, is reinforced by other images of dancing deities, in particular goddesses, whose dance also expresses their unrestrained character.

   At the exegetical level, the nondual image of the divine self as actor is the first to make an appearance (in the ŚS). However, its purpose is not to demonstrate the Self's or Śiva's freedom, but rather the unreal nature of multiplicity. This demonstration about the nature of being is then elaborated by the Kashmirian exegetes and developed into a demonstration about the nature of perception and knowledge. Rather than showing what there is, the image comes to show levels of knowledge: the roles of Śiva represent various cognizing subjects and thus various religious currents. This representation of rival schools of thought makes it possible to envisage their conversion, whereby they can ascend from their lower position until they reach true (*śaiva*) knowledge.

2. In the *pāśupata* system, observances that involved some form of acting or pretension did so in order to hide the identity of the practitioner and to provoke an exchange of karma between him and his spectators, i.e. passers-by. The aim is thus to mislead others, to elicit slander and curse. While some *pāśupata* observances were taken over in *śākta* Tantric sources, their purpose became different: they prepared the practitioner for the path of ritual non-duality because they required the use of impure substances; and they were one of the ways in which the practitioner enacted his identity with a/the deity. By the time of the JY, an awareness of the aesthetic aspects of this role playing seems to appear and the nine *rasa*s are referred to.
3. Contrary to the *pāśupata*s, whose dance (*nṛtta*) was probably unstructured and free, tantric sources also refer to structured dance and dramatic performance. The offering of a play (*nāṭya*) to Bhairava, although found in a unique prescription of the BY (and in a possible allusion in the SYM), may attest to a practice in which a play was performed as part of tantric ritual.

We cannot know what actual practice involved and some of these prescriptions could be just entirely fanciful, but there seems to be much more awareness of theatre and performing in the tantric sources than in pretantric *pāśupata* practice and particular effort seems to be made to integrate some aspects of theatre into religious practice. Whether this influenced Abhinavagupta or not, this is a remarkable feature in itself.

One of Abhinavagupta's major contributions to dramatic theory concerns the relationship between aesthetic relishing and *kaula* tantric experience, both of which require the suspension or obliteration of the ego. As far as I can see, this is not brought out anywhere in the scriptural sources, for *kaula* and *krama* texts proper I have been able to consult (omitting from this category the JY, which is very heterogeneous) do not appear to deal with *nāṭya* or related subjects, at least not directly. It would seem then that Abhinavagupta's theory of *carvaṇā* bringing together theatre and tantra is entirely his own, a fact that does not come as a surprise. It remains, however, to be seen whether (and how) the description of *kaula* experience in the scriptures is echoed in Abhinavagupta's writings on theatre.[104]

It also remains a question whether the above described use of theatre in tantras shows the increasing influence and importance of classical theatre, or rather, it betrays an attempt of the tantric authors to integrate their texts in the cultural framework of an elite. Whatever is the case, it reflects an increasing awareness of the dramatic tradition in an unexpected context: tantric scriptures. This fact in itself implies that theatre, although it was clearly destined to the elite in the form we know it from the classical sources, was perhaps less restricted to the royal court than our classical sources suggest. It is merely hypothetical of course, but more popular theatrical forms such as Mūṭiyeṭṭu in today's Kerala, which is some way between deity possession and theatre, may well have existed in the past elsewhere in India too, and stood as proof not only of the close relation of ritual and drama, but also of the universal appeal of theatre.

REFERENCES

ACHARYA 2013
D. Acharya, "How to Behave like a Bull? New Insight into the Origin and Religious Practice of Pāśupatas," *Indo-Iranian Journal* 56(2), 2013, pp. 101-131

Agnipurāṇa
Agnipurāṇa: a Collection of Hindu Mythology and Traditions, ed. R. Mitra, Calcutta: Asiatic Society of Bengal, Bibliotheca Indica 65, 1873-1879

BAKKER AND ISAACSON 2004
H.T. Bakker and H. Isaacson, *The Skandapurāṇa. Vol. IIA. Adhyāyas 26-31.14: The Vārāṇasī cycle. Critically edited with Prolegomena and English Synopsis*, Groningen: Egbert Forsten, 2004

BANSAT-BOUDON 1992
L. Bansat-Boudon, *Poétique du théâtre indien. Lectures du Nāṭyaśāstra*, Paris: École Française d'Extrême-Orient, 1992

---

104 For the way in which tantric ritual becomes "aestheticised" in Kaulism, see SANDERSON 1988, p. 680. A closer study of the *kaula* scriptures, many unedited, may reveal their influence on Abhinavagupta's aesthetic theory.

BANSAT-BOUDON 1995
L. Bansat-Boudon, "The Vṛttis or the Manners of Viṣṇu," in *International Conference on Sanskrit and Related Studies, September 23-26, 1993* (Proceedings), Cracow: Cracow Indological Studies 1, 1995, pp. 45-57

BANSAT-BOUDON 2000
L. Bansat-Boudon, "L'épopée mise en scène: l'*Uttararāmacarita*," *Journal Asiatique* 288(1), 2000, pp. 83-111

BANSAT-BOUDON AND TRIPATHI 2011
L. Bansat-Boudon and K.D. Tripathi, *An introduction to Tantric philosophy: the Paramārthasāra of Abhinavagupta with the commentary of Yogarāja*, London: Routledge, 2011

Bodhicaryāvatāra
[*Bodhicaryāvatāra*, in] *Prajñākaramati's Commentary to the Bodhicaryāvatāra of Śāntideva,* ed. L. de La Vallée Poussin, Calcutta: Asiatic Society, Bibliotheca Indica 983, 1031, 1090, 1126, 1139, 1305 and 1399, 1901-1914

BROCKINGTON 1999
J. Brockington, "Epic Sāṃkhya: texts, teachers, terminology," *Asiatische Studien/ Études asiatiques* 53, 1999, pp. 473-490

BURGESS 1871
J. Burgess, *The Rock Temples of Elephanta or Ghârâpurî*, Bombay: Sykes, 1871

BY
Brahmayāmala, National Archives, Kathmandu, Ms. No. 3-370; e-text by S. Hatley; working ed. of the first 49 chapters by Cs. Kiss[105]; for eds. of selected chapters see also KISS forthcoming

COLLINS 1988
C.D. Collins, *The Iconography and Ritual of Śiva at Elephanta*, Albany: SUNY Press, 1988

COX 2006
W. Cox, *Making a Tantra in Medieval South-India. The Mahārthamañjarī and the Textual Culture of Cōḻa Cidambaram*, Unpublished PhD thesis, University of Chicago, 2006

CROSBY AND SKILTON 1996
K. Crosby and A. Skilton, *Śāntideva The Bodhicaryāvatāra (translated with Introduction and Notes; with a general introduction by Paul Williams*), Oxford: Oxford University Press, 1996

[105] I am grateful to both authors for giving me access to their work. My references are to S. Hatley's transcription unless indicated otherwise.

Daśarūpaka
Daśarūpaka of Dhanaṃjaya with the commentary Avalokā By Dhanika and the sub-commentary Laghuṭīkā by Bhaṭṭanṛsiṃha, ed. T. Venkatacharya, Madras: The Adyar Library and Research Centre, 1969

Devīpañcaśatikā/Kālīkulapañcaśatikā
Devīpañcaśatikā/Kālīkulapañcaśatikā, MS K: National Archives, Kathmandu, MS no: 5-5183; MS Kh: National Archives, Kathmandu, MS no.: 5-358; MS G: National Archives, Kathmandu, MS no. 1 – 252; e-text Muktabodha Indological Research Institute (www.muktabodhalib.org), prepared under the supervision of M. Dyczkowski

Gaṇakārikā
Gaṇakārikā of Bhāsarvajña with the commentary Ratnaṭīkā, ed. C.D. Dalal, Baroda: Gaekwad's Oriental Series, 1920

HARA 2002
M. Hara, *Pāśupata Studies* (ed. J. Takashima), Vienna: De Nobili Research Library, 2002

ĪPVV
Īśvarapratyabhijñāvivṛtivimarśinī of Abhinavagupta, ed. M. Kaul, Srinagar: Research Department, Kashmir Series of Texts and Studies 60, 62 and 65, 1938-1943

JY
Jayadrathayāmala, National Archives, Kathmandu, 5-4650 (ṣaṭka 1 & 2); 5-722 (ṣaṭka 3); 1-1468 (ṣaṭka 4 A 151-16); e-text by Olga Serbaeva, draft version of 2004[106]

KISS forthcoming
Cs. Kiss, *The Brahmayāmala Tantra or Picumata vol II. The Religious Observances and Sexual Rituals of the Tantric Practitioner. Chapters 3, 21 and 45*

Kubjikāmata
Kubjikāmatatantra, ed. T. Goudriaan and J. Schoterman, Leiden: Brill, 1988[107]

LA VALLÉE POUSSIN 1898
L. de La Vallée Poussin, *Bouddhisme Études et matériaux Ādikarmapradīpa Bodhicaryāvatāraṭīkā*, London: Luzac & Co., 1898

Mattavilāsaprahasana
Mattavilāsaprahasana of Mahendravikramavarma, ed. G. Śāstrī, Trivandrum: Rājakīya Mudraṇayantrālaya, 1917

---

[106] I am grateful to Olga Serbaeva for making her transcription available to me.

[107] I am grateful to Somdev Vasudeva for making his electronic version of this text available.

Mahābhārata
Mahābhārata, ed. V.S. Sukthankar (1927-43) and S.K. Belvalkar (from 1943) with Shrimant Balasaheb Pant Pratinidhi, R.N. Dandekar, S.K. De, F. Edgerton, A.B. Gajendragadkar, P.V. Kane, R.D. Karmakar, V.G. Paranjpe, Raghu Vira, V.K. Rajavade, N.B. Utgikar, P.L. Vaidya, V.P. Vaidya, H.D. Velankar, M. Winternitz, R. Zimmerman *et al.*, 19 vols., Poona: Bhandarkar Oriental Research Institute, 1927-1959; e-text prepared under the supervision of J.D. Smith

Mālatīmādhava
Mālatīmādhava of Bhavabhūti with the commentary of Jagaddhara, ed. M.R. Kale, [1928] Delhi: Motilal Banarsidass, 1996

Mālinīvijayottara
Mālinīvijayottara, [ed. M. Kaul, Bombay: Kashmir Series of Texts and Studies 37, 1922] ed. Acharya K. Sagar, Varanasi: Krishnānand Sāgar, 1985; e-text by S. Vasudeva and Muktabodha Indological Research Institute (www.muktabodhalib.org)

Nareśvaraparīkṣāprakāśa
Nareśvaraparīkṣā of Sadyojyotis with the commentary -prakāśa by Bhaṭṭa Rāmakaṇṭha, ed. M. Kaul, [Śrinagar: Kashmir Series of Texts and Studies 45] New Delhi: Navrang, 1989

Niśvāsa(tattvasaṃhitā)
Niśvāsa(tattvasaṃhitā), National Archives, Kathmandu, 1-277; London, Wellcome Institute for the History of Medicine, Sanskrit MS I 33; e-text by D. Goodall, P. Bisschop, D. Acharya, and N. Kafle. *Mūla(sūtra), Naya(sūtra)* and *Uttara (sūtra)* ed. D. Goodall, forthcoming

NŚ
Nāṭyaśāstra of Bharatamuṇi with a commentary (Abhinavabhāratī) by Abhinavagupta, ed. M.R. Kavi, revised by K.S.R. Sastri, 2nd ed., Baroda: Oriental Institute, Gaekwad's Oriental Series 36, 68, 124, 145, 1954-1964

PH
Pratyabhijñāhṛdaya of Kṣemarāja, ed. J.C. Chatterji, Srinagar: Research Department, Kashmir Series of Texts and Studies 3, 1911

Pratiṣṭhālakṣaṇasārasamuccaya
Pratiṣṭhālakṣaṇasārasamuccaya, Paṇḍitabuddhisāgaraśarmaṇo 'dhyakṣatāyāṃ Vedācāryadāmodaraśarmaṇā saṃpāditaḥ, saṃpādakena Vedāntaśāstri Paṃ Bābukṛṣṇaśarmaṇā ca saṃśodhitaḥ, Nepālarājakīyapustakālayataḥ prakāśitaḥ; e-text Muktabodha Indological Research Institute (www. muktabodhalib.org), prepared under the supervision of M. Dyczkowski

PS
Paramārthasāra de Abhinavagupta, ed. J.C. Chatterji, Srinagar: Research Department, Kashmir Series of Texts and Studies 7, 1916

PSū
Pāśupatasūtra with the Pañcārthabhāṣya of Kauṇḍinya, ed. R.A. Sastri, Trivandrum: The Oriental Manuscripts Library of the University of Travancore, Trivandrum Sanskrit Series 143, 1940

RĀMESH AND TEWARI 1990
K.V. Rāmesh and S.P. Tewari, *A Copper-plate Hoard of the Gupta Period from Bagh, Madhya Pradesh*, New Delhi: Archaeological Survey of India, 1990

RATIÉ 2011
I. Ratié, *Le Soi et l'autre. Identité, différence et altérité dans la philosophie de la Pratyabhijñā*, Leiden/Boston: Brill, 2011

RATIÉ 2013
I. Ratié, "On reason and scripture in the Pratyabhijñā," in V. Eltschinger and H. Krasser (eds.), *Scriptural Authority, Reason and Action, Proceedings of a Panel at the 14th World Sanskrit Conference, Kyoto, September 1st-5th 2009* , Wien: ÖAW, 2013, pp. 375-454

Sāṃkhyakārikā
[*Sāṃkhyakārikā*, in] *Yuktidīpikā. The most significant commentary on the Sāṃkhyakārikā*, ed. A. Wezler and S. Motegi, vol. I, Stuttgart: Steiner, Alt- und New-Indische Studien 44, 1998

SANDERSON 1986
A. Sanderson, "Maṇḍala and Āgamic Idenity in the Trika of Kashmir," in A. Padoux (ed.), *Mantras et Diagrammes Rituels dans l'Hindouisme*, Paris: CNRS, 1986, pp. 169-213

SANDERSON 1988
A. Sanderson, "Śaivism and the Tantric Traditions," in S. Sutherland, L. Houlden, P. Clarke and F. Hardy (eds.), *The World's Religions*, London: Routledge, 1988, pp. 660-704

SANDERSON 1992
A. Sanderson, "The Doctrine of the Mālinīvijayottaratantra," in T. Goudriaan (ed.) *Ritual and Speculation in Early Tantrism: Studies in Honour of André Padoux*, Albany: SUNY Press, 1992, pp. 281-312

SANDERSON 2006
A. Sanderson, "The Lākulas: New Evidence of a System Intermediate between Pāñcārthika Pāśupatism and Āgamic Śaivism," *Indian Philosphical Annual* 24, 2006, pp. 143-217

SANDERSON 2009
A. Sanderson, "The Śaiva Age – The Rise and Dominance of Śaivism during the Early Medieval Period," in Sh. Einoo (ed.), *Genesis and Development of Tantrism*, Tokyo: Institute of Oriental Culture, University of Tokyo, Institute of Oriental Culture Special Series 23, 2009, pp. 41-350

SANDERSON 2011
A. Sanderson, Keynote lecture "The Rise of the Goddess in Early Medieval India," *OCHS conference on Śākta traditions, Oxford, 10 September 2011*; handout available at http://www.alexissanderson.com

SHETH 1928
H.D.T. Sheth, *Pāia-sadda-mahaṇṇavo: a comprehensive Prakrit Hindi Dictionary, with Sanskrit equivalents, quotations and complete references*, [Calcutta: 1923-8] Delhi: Motilal Banarsidass, 1986 (3rd repr.)

Skandapurāṇa
Skandapurāṇasya Ambikākhaṇḍaḥ, ed. Kṛṣṇaprasāda Bhaṭṭarāī, Kathmandu: Mahendrasaṃskṛtaviśvavidyālaya, 1988; see also BAKKER AND ISAACSON 2004

Spandanirṇaya
Spandanirṇaya, in *Spandakārikās of Vasugupta, with the Nirṇaya by Kṣemarāja,* ed. and transl. M.K. Shastri, Srinagar: Research Department, Kashmir Series of Texts and Studies 42, 1925

ŚS
Śivasūtras. The Shiva Sūtra Vimarśinī being the Sūtras of Vasu Gupta with the Commentary called Vimarshinī by Kṣemarāja, ed. J.C. Chatterji, Srinagar: Research Department, Kashmir Series of Texts and Studies 1, 1911

Svacchandatantra
Svacchandatantra with the commentary -uddyota of Kṣemarāja, ed. V.V. Dvivedi, 2 vols., Delhi: Parimal Publications, 1985

SYM
Siddhayogeśvarīmata, D = National Archives, Kathmandu, Ms. No. 5-2403; N = Asiatic Society of Bengal, Calcutta, 5465 (G); see TÖRZSÖK 1999 and TÖRZSÖK forthcoming

TĀ
Tantrāloka of Abhinavagupta, with a commentary -viveka by Jayaratha, ed. R.C. Dwivedi and N. Rastogi, 8 vols., [Śrinagar: Kashmir Series of Texts and Studies, 1918-1938] Delhi: Motilal Banarsidass: 1987, repr. with a new introduction; e-text Muktabodha Indological Research Institute (www.muktabodhalib.org)

TAK II
H. Brunner, G. Oberhammer and A. Padoux (eds.), *Tāntrikābhidhānakośa (Dictionary of Hindu Tantric Terms)*, vol. II, Vienna: ÖAW, 2004

TAK III
D. Goodall and M. Rastelli (eds.), *Tāntrikābhidhānakośa (Dictionary of Hindu Tantric Terms)*, vol. III, Vienna: ÖAW, 2014

TORELLA 1999
R. Torella, "Sāṃkhya as Sāmānyaśāstra," *Asiatische Studien/Études asiatiques* 53, 1999, pp. 553-562

TORELLA 2008
R. Torella, "From an Adversary to the Main Ally The Place of Bhartṛhari in the Kashmirian Śaiva Advaita," in A. Aklujkar and M. Kaul (eds.), *Linguistic Traditions of Kashmir: Essays in Memory of Pandit Dinanath Yaksh*, Delhi: D.K. Printworld, 2008, pp. 508-525

TORELLA 2013
R. Torella, "Inherited cognitions: *prasiddhi, āgama, pratibhā, śabdana* – Bhartṛhari, Utpaladeva, Abhinavagupta, Kumārila and Dharmakīrti in dialogue," in V. Eltschinger and H. Krasser (eds.), *Scriptural Authority, Reason and Action, Proceedings of a Panel at the 14th World Sanskrit Conference, Kyoto, September 1st-5th 2009*, Wien: ÖAW, 2013, pp. 455-480

TÖRZSÖK 1999
J. Törzsök, *The Doctrine of Magic Female Spirits – A critical edition of selected chapters of the Siddhayogeśvarīmata(tantra) with annotated translation and analysis*, Unpublished DPhil thesis, University of Oxford, 1999

TÖRZSÖK 2011
J. Törzsök, "Kāpālikas," in K. Jacobsen et al. (eds.), *Brill's Encyclopedia of Hinduism*, vol. III, Leiden: Brill, 2011, pp. 355-361

TÖRZSÖK 2013
J. Törzsök, "Nondualism in Early Śākta Tantras: Transgressive Rites and Their Ontological Justification in a Historical Perspective," *Journal of Indian Philosophy* 42 [2014], published online in 2013, pp. 195-223

TÖRZSÖK forthcoming
J. Törzsök, *The Teaching of Yoginīs. A critical edition of the Siddhayogeśvarīmata with an introduction and annotated translation*

VASUDEVA 2004
S. Vasudeva, *The Yoga of the Mālinīvijayottaratantra. Chapters 1-4, 7, 11-17. Critical Edition, Translation and Notes*, Pondichéry: IFP/EFEO, 2004

VASUDEVA 2014
S. Vasudeva, "The Unconscious Experiencer: Bhoktṛtva in the Pramātṛbheda of the Trika," *Journal of Indological Studies* 24, 2012-2014, pp. 203-230

Vaiśeṣikasūtra
Vaiśeṣikasūtras of Kaṇāda with the commentary of Candrānanda, ed. Muni Śrī Jambuvijayaji, Baroda: Oriental Institute, 1982

Vaiśeṣikadarśana of Kaṇāda with an anonymous commentary, ed. A. Thakur, Darbhanga: Mithila Institute, 1957

Vikramacarita
Vikrama's adventures or The Thirty-Two Tales of the Throne, ed. and transl. F. Edgerton, Part 2: Text, in Four Parallel Recensions, [Cambridge: 1926] Delhi: Motilal Banarsidass, 1993

Yoginīsaṃcāra
Yoginīsaṃcāra, transmitted as part of Ṣaṭka 3 of the *Jayadrathayāmala*, unpublished draft ed. by A. Sanderson, prepared in 2004[108]

[108] I am grateful to Prof. Sanderson for making his edition available to me in an electronic form.

Lakṣaṇam Aparyālocitābhidhānam – Śobhākara's Resistance to Ruyyaka*

SOMDEV VASUDEVA

The *Alaṅkāraratnākara*, or the "Treasury of Ornaments" (hereafter *AlRat*), of Śobhākareśvaramitra[1] (Śobhākara for short) is a Kashmirian work on *alaṅkāraśāstra* of the late twelfth to early thirteenth centuries that seeks to challenge innovations proposed in the *Alaṅkārasarvasva*, or the "Treasure of Ornaments" (hereafter *AlSar*), the most successful work of the Kashmirian rhetorician Ruyyaka, completed around 1150 AD. We may consider this a subgenre of response texts[2] the development of which can be traced throughout the history of *alaṅkāra* dialectics.[3] The nature of the intertextuality between Śobhākara's and Ruyyaka's works shows

* I would like to thank Isabelle Ratié and Eli Franco for their valuable corrections and comments.

1 Hitherto, the suffix *-īśvaramitra* has not been appended to Śobhākara's name. I do so on the strength of the early Kashmirian birchbark MS discussed below, which gives his name as *paṇḍitabhaṭṭaśrīśobhākareśvaramitra-*. That the suffix *-īśvaramitra* belongs to the proper name and is not a mere honorific title is made more likely by the fact that his father's name was Trayīśvaramitra (thus in Bodleian MS D87, though commonly given as Trayīśvaramiśra), where it is scarcely plausible to detach the suffix *-īśvaramitra* (KRISHNAMACHARIAR 1937 gives his father's name as Trayīśvaramiśra, the colophon of Devadhar's edition reads ... *bhaṭṭatrayīśvaramantriputrasya*..., making Śobhākara's father a minister). It appears to have been a practice in Kashmir to use a common suffix in naming successive generations, as can be seen in cases such as Bhaṭṭa Rāma**kaṇṭha**, son of Bhaṭṭa Nārāyaṇa**kaṇṭha**.

2 That is, rival texts teaching very similar doctrines within a short time of each other. This is a pattern comparable to what we see in other *śāstra*s, but it is also different as there exists no doctrinal framework provided by a Sūtra authored by an omniscient founder.

3 For example Bhāmaha and Daṇḍin, Ruyyaka and Śobhākareśvaramitra, Appayadīkṣita and Jagannātha, etc.

that their dispute is one that differs from earlier altercations, such as that between Bhāmaha and Daṇḍin (recently reevaluated in BRONNER 2011). Ruyyaka had reinvigorated *alaṅkāra* rhetorics by paying careful attention to implicit epistemological and ontological categories, and Śobhākara problematized this resystematisation. Both authors were writing after what MCCREA 1998 has identified as a Kuhnian paradigm shift introduced by the advent of the *dhvani* theory, a thesis to which both our authors subscribed.

In his *AlSar*, Ruyyaka introduces each *alaṅkāra* with a definition formulated as a Sūtra. He follows this with an explanatory Vṛtti auto-commentary into which he embeds and analyses verses drawn from a wide range of Kāvya literature. Since *alaṅkāra* rhetorics lacked a foundational Sūtra which could have given it a ready-made ontology and epistemology that commentators could build on, the ambition was probably to fill this perceived need, to become the Sūtrakāra of the *alaṅkāraśāstra*. At the same time, by adopting this particular format he consciously reverts to the formal style of presentation that the eminent authority Vāmana, a South Indian immigrant to Kashmir,[4] had introduced into *alaṅkāraśāstra* more than three hundred years earlier in his *Alaṅkārasūtravṛtti*.[5] In

---

4 As far as Vāmana's valuation of *rīti* is concerned, it may be significant that Vāmana was a South Indian immigrant to Kashmir, presumably conversant with some Dravidian language[s], and a man who had crossed a considerable part of India in search of patronage. This appears to imply that divergences in regional styles of Sanskrit might have been pronounced in the late eighth century.

5 Current narratives of the historical development of *alaṅkāraśāstra* credit Vāmana primarily with two things, the elaboration of *rīti*, or the Ways of Poetry, and the introduction of the notion of the soul of poetry (*kāvyasyātmā*) as a category of discussion. Arguably just as important, if not more important, was another legacy that Kashmirian rhetoricians such as Ruyyaka and Śobhākara inherited from their predecessors Vāmana and Bhāmaha (see BRONNER in this volume): an established canon of literary citations and the very idea of seeking out actual literary citations to exemplify figures of speech. This ensured that *alaṅkāraśāstra* would become firmly anchored in a living literary culture, eschewing the earlier model where literary theorists wrote their own examples to fit their theories. A format of Kārikā and Vṛtti, with specimen verses composed by the author himself is followed by Daṇḍin's *Kāvyādarśa*, Bhāmaha's *Kāvyālaṅkāra*, Udbhaṭa's *Kāvyālaṅkāra*, and Rudraṭa's *Kāvyālaṅkārasārasaṃgraha*. A format of Kārikā with Vṛtti, and verses excerpted from actual literature is adopted by Ānandavardhana's *Sahṛdayāloka* (or *Dhvanyāloka*), Mukulabhaṭṭa's *Abhidhāvṛttamātṛkā*, Mammaṭa's *Kāvyaprakāśa*, Kuntaka's *Vakroktijīvita*, and Mahimabhaṭṭa's *Vyaktiviveka*.

his introduction to the *AlSar,* Ruyyaka describes rhetorics as a *śāstra* that has undergone a process of evolution, where less precise theories of earlier authors are superseded by later ideas. Vāmana's Sūtras clearly were obsolete, and a new Sūtra was called for. Much as Ruyyaka styled his work on Vāmana, Śobhākara consciously styled his work in imitation of Ruyyaka, almost as if he intended it as a replacement, albeit with slightly longer prose passages to accommodate refutations of Ruyyaka's theories.

A striking feature is the vehemence with which Śobhākara attacks, without naming his opponent, nearly all the elements of Ruyyaka's treasure: definitions of *alaṅkāra*s, their classification into subtypes, the identification of *alaṅkāra*s in examples, and, significantly, the very epistemological basis upon which figures of speech can be differentiated. Even Śobhākara's choice of title *(-ratnākara)*, "storehouse of treasures" or "mine of treasures," is presumably intended as an upgrade of Ruyyaka's simpler title of "treasure."[6] Yet, while Śobhākara finds fault with many specific innovations Ruyyaka proposes, at the same time he is sympathetic to Ruyyaka's project of radically rethinking the semantic and epistemological foundations – imported from grammar and *pramāṇaśāstra* – upon which *alaṅkāraśāstra* was built. In this he can be quite innovative.[7] He is the first to insist, for example, that *rūpaka* metaphors must be based on *sāmānādhikaraṇya*. Śobhākara must therefore not be dismissed as a conservative voice trying to roll back Ruyyaka's new ideas.

An important third voice in this debate is Ruyyaka's commentator Jayaratha, who, in his *Vimarśinī,* takes it upon himself to shield the *AlSar* from Śobhākara's attacks. These three texts, the *AlSar*, the *AlRat*, and the *Vimarśinī,* provide us with an abundance of riches to explore the dynamics of an intense debate taking place towards the end of the Kashmirian hegemonic phase in the field of *alaṅkāra* rhetorics. In particular, they enable us to understand, at least provisionally, something about the underlying motivations and ideologies that steered the debate to assume the tone that it did.

---

6 As such, his work, in some passages appears more like a refutation, or a hostile commentary, such as the *Kāvyaprakāśakhaṇḍana* of the Jain scholar Siddhicandra Gaṇi, a refutation of Mammaṭa's *Kāvyaprakāśa*.

7 As I discuss below, even when he decides to return to *sambhāvanā* as the foundation of *utprekṣā* he does so with a markedly new perspective, one that goes to the heart of how a system of *alaṅkāras*, each with its own *vicchitti*, or strikingness, can be systematised.

The contemporary accounts of scholarly interactions in Kashmir that have come down to us shed only a little light on the matter, in no small part because they frequently contradict each other. The celebrated logician Bhaṭṭa Jayanta's (ca. 840-900) *Āgamaḍambara* describes heated theological and philosophical debates along sectarian lines, while a learned gathering of a different nature is described in the *Śrīkaṇṭhacarita* of Ruyyaka's disciple Maṅkha. While the first shows a world of intellectual hostility and rivalry the second portrays scholars gathered to have a good time. Such background information goes only part way in explaining the verse with which Jayaratha concludes his *Vimarśinī* commentary:

> Whatever here is correct or otherwise
> Has been stated in direct accordance with the system of rhetorics
> May the wise give it their regard for a moment
> Setting aside the anger of enmity
> With this much my task is achieved.[8]

What does he intend with this disclaimer? Why should enmity and anger be involved in a debate that seeks to establish workable definitions for figures of speech? It almost sounds as if he were describing a vendetta or a crime of passion, and he seems to be directing his words to Śobhākara, if he was still alive, or his followers.

Śobhākara introduces his work with a benediction verse that is borrowed from the *Nyāyamañjarī* of the Kashmirian logician Bhaṭṭa Jayanta. This raises the question of a possible connection between the *AlRat* and the *Nyāyamañjarī*. Is Śobhākara deliberately drawing attention to the fact that his ontology and epistemology are in some way related to the work of Bhaṭṭa Jayanta? Is his resistance to Ruyyaka part of a Kashmirian contest between realist Naiyāyikas and radical Śaiva Non-dualists to lay claim to the neutral domain of poetics and inscribe it with their own epistemologies and ontologies?

These questions can of course only be answered by tracing textual passages demonstrating Śobhākara's indebtedness to specific doctrines unique to Bhaṭṭa Jayanta. As such, the identification of these testimonia has become an important part of my ongoing project to critically re-edit the *AlRat*. The exact nature of the relation-

---

8 *Vimarśinī* (205 KM$_{Ed}$, 144^{r} K$_{R}$): *yan nāma kiṃ cid iha samyag athānyathā vā sākṣād alaṅkṛtinayocitam etad uktam* | *vidveṣaroṣam apasārya budhaiḥ kṣaṇasya tatrāvadheyam iyataiva vayaṃ kṛtārthāḥ* ||.

ship between the *AlRat* and the *Nyāyamañjarī* for now remains unclear, but some ideas are presented in the sequel.

Seen in this light, it is possible that Ruyyaka's paradigm of the gradual evolution of *alaṅkāra* rhetorics, evidencing historical awareness of progress within a *śāstra,* progressing from simple enumerative schemas to ever more refined epistemic analyses, might not have seemed to Śobhākara like a disinterested, objective sketch of the history of a neutral *śāstra*. Śobhākara may rather have perceived it as a transparent attempt to controvert established Naiyāyika tenets, and he may have tried to neutralize of Ruyyaka's attempts to move beyond Nyāya epistemology. *Alaṅkāra* epistemology might not have been the only thing Śobhākara believed to be at stake here, for Bhaṭṭa Jayanta upheld the primacy of the Nyāya as the main protection of the Veda against heretical doctrines.[9] This could explain why Śobhākara's debate with Ruyyaka seems at times as though it might be a scene in Bhaṭṭa Jayanta's *Āgamaḍambara.*

Before we look at this issue in detail, a few words about our sources are called for. Work on the *AlRat* has hitherto been hindered by the poor state of the editio princeps of Devadhar (who had access only to defective manuscript materials), published in 1942 in the Poona Oriental Series. There have been a few studies, the most notable of which is a precis by Parthasarathy Rao (PARTHASARATHY RAO 1992). Lallan Upadhyaya apparently also completed an unpublished new edition as a Ph.D. thesis at the University of Punjab in 1978, which I have not yet seen.[10] Fortunately, the situation can be improved substantially by making use of a Kashmirian birchbark manuscript in the Stein collection of the Bodleian library in Oxford (Bodleian MS Sansk D87), hereafter K_R. As far as I can tell, this manuscript has not, so far, been used to restore problematic passages in the *AlRat*.

This manuscript is not dated. The colophon on folio 156^r ll. 4-9 of K_R reads:

> *samāpto* [']*yam alaṅkāraratnākaraḥ* ‖ ‖ ‖ *kṛtir mahopādhyāyapaṇḍitabhaṭṭa**śrītrayīśvaramitra**putrasya tatrabhavataḥ paṇḍitabhaṭṭa**śrīśobhā-***

9 See KATAOKA 2007 for Jayanta's argument that the Nyāya is the only system which can establish the Veda's validity, since the Mīmāṃsā focuses on exegesis. See also HALBFASS 1986-1992, KATAOKA 2007, and FRESCHI AND KATAOKA 2012.

10 Two more theses I have not seen are SHARMA 1972 and DUBEY 1982.

> ***kareśvaramitrasya*** | || || *iti śubham śrīr astu* || || *aśuddhatvam ādarśadoṣāt* || || *śrīgaṇeśāya namaḥ* || || *oṃ namaḥ sarasvatyai* | ||

It is however bound in the same volume as a manuscript of the *Abhijñānaśakuntala*, written in a very similar (identical?) hand. This manuscript bears the following colophon:

> || *samāptam idam abhijñānaśakuntalam nāma nāṭakam* || || *iti śubham astu lekhakapāṭhakayoḥ* || || *śivaṃ ca sarvajagatām* || *aśuddhatvam ādarśadoṣāt* || *saṃ* 51 *pau śudi* 11 *gurau* || *śrīgaṇeśāya namaḥ* ||

The date should therefore be Thursday, the 11th lunar day of the waxing fortnight of the month Pauṣa in the year 51. As is common in Kashmirian dates, the first two digits of the Laukika (or Saptarṣi) era, the era usually used in Kashmirian manuscripts, are omitted. However, since the weekday is given, we are in a position to determine the century using the last two digits of the year, the weekday, and the lunar day of the month. Using M. Yano's *Pancanga* 3.14,[11] the only date in the last millennium where these conditions were fulfilled was January the 14th in AD 1677 (while Kashmir was under Mughal rule), a date which is also consistent with the Śāradā paleography. Given that the *AlRat* was bound with this manuscript, and given the codicological and paleographical similarities between the two manuscripts, it is likely that the *AlRat* was copied by the same scribe around the same time. For the text of Jayaratha's *Vimarśinī* I used Bodleian MS Stein Or d21, a later paper manuscript written in Śāradā, that for the sections consulted, proved superior to the Kāvyamālā edition (KM_{Ed}).

---

11 We add 47 years (see SEWELL AND BĀLKRIṢṆA DĪKṢIT 1896, p. 41) to arrive at a presumed Śaka year of ++98 where the 11th day of the month Pauṣa must be a Thursday. Consulting Yano's Pancanga on http://www.cc.kyotosu.ac.jp/~yanom/pancanga/, accessed on Sunday, July 17, 16, and considering the year Caitrādi and Pūrṇimānta, using the latitude and longitude of Srinagar, the full date correlation is Śaka 1598, Vikrama 1733. Pauṣa Śuklapakṣa 11, AD 1677-1-14 Thursday (=1677-1-4 in Julian).

Figure 1: Folio 101^{r} of K_R showing the end of the commentary on vibhāvanā (53 in P_{Ed}) and the definition of viśeṣokti (54 in P_{Ed}) on line 6

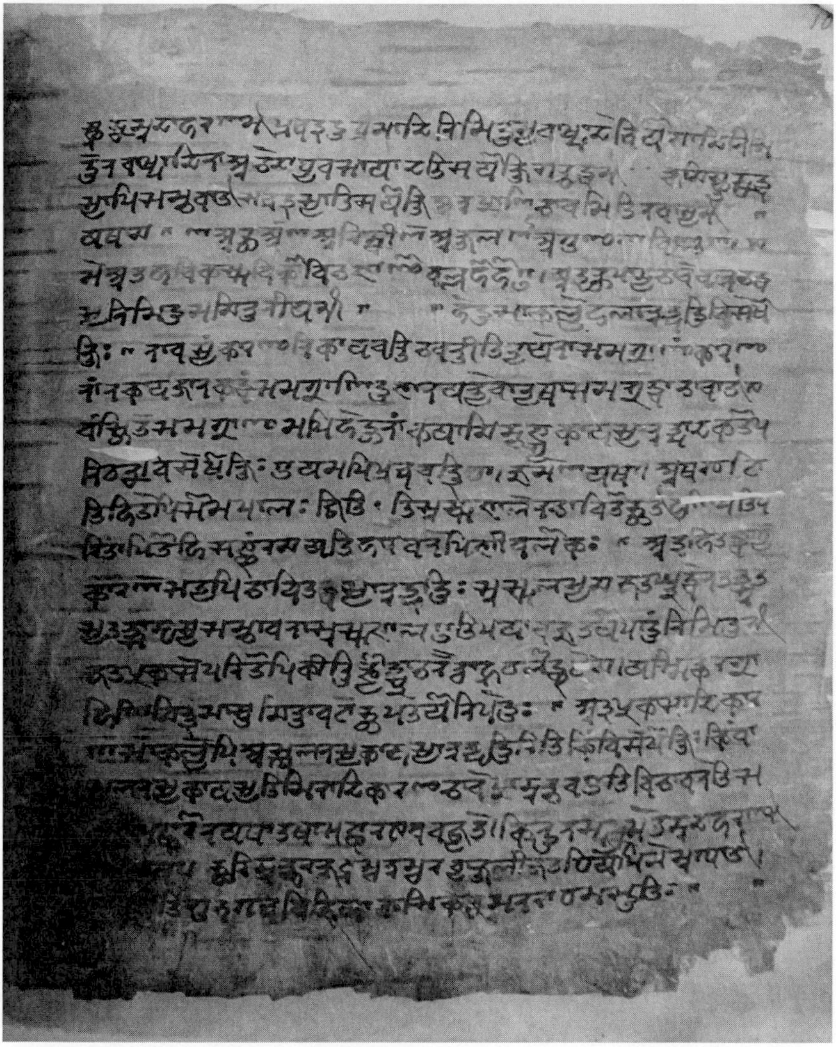

1. COGNITIVE ABERRATIONS

Śobhākara has composed a complex work on aesthetics. He shows little interest in engaging the theory of affective suggestion *(dhvani),* but instead analyses in detail the types of cognition affecting the reader, the poet, and the imaginary characters created by the poet in various figures of speech. This paper focuses on an issue that was central to his endeavour: the use of aberrant or deflected cognition to differentiate certain types of *alaṅkāra*s. We will limit our investigation to just three figures of speech in view of the prolixity of the arguments: the Erroneous (*bhrāntimat),* the Assumption (*utprekṣā)* and the Hyperbolic (*atiśayokti)*. In both Ruyyaka's and Śobhākara's works these three figures are introduced in a group of related figures of speech where similarly deflected cognitions are prominent[12] (summarized in the table below to show their relationship).[13]

Ornament	Śobhākara's Definition	Ruyyaka's Definition
Apahnuti The Concealed	29: *viṣayasya mukhyasya vāpahnave 'nyavidhiḥ,* An alternative mode when the target or the principal are concealed	20: *viṣayāpahnave,* When the target is concealed
Sandeha The Doubtful	30: *tasyāpi sandihyamānatve,* When the target is being doubted	17: *viṣayasya sandihyamānatve,* When the target is being doubted

---

[12] The important technical terms *viṣaya* and *viṣayin* are here translated as target and source. In a simple metaphor, for example: "Her face is the moon!", the face is the *viṣaya* or target, and the moon is the *viṣayin* or source.

[13] Ruyyaka does not see this as a discrete group. Rudraṭa, the first to classify figures according to underlying principles, had grouped them under the four headings [1.] *vāstava* (factuality), [2.] *aupamya* (similitude), [3.] *atiśaya* (hyperbole) and [4.] *śleṣa* (convergence of meaning). Ruyyaka classified figures of meaning into nine groups: [1.] *sādṛśya* (similarity), [2.] *gamyatva* (implication), [3.] *virodha* (contradiction), [4.] *śṛṅkhalābandha* (chain-like sequences), [5.] *tarkanyāya*, [6.] *kāvyanyāya*, [7.] *lokanyāya*, [8.] *gūḍhārthapratīti* (communicating a concealed meaning), [9.] *rasādayaḥ* (sentiment based).

Ornament	Śobhākara's Definition	Ruyyaka's Definition
Vitarka The Deliberation	31: *sambhāvitasambhāvyamānā-pohaḥ,* Exclusion of an entity that has been or is being suspected	—
Utprekṣā **The Assumption/ Identifying**	32: *viṣayitvena sambhāvanam,* Assuming of the target as the source	21: *adhyavasāye vyāpā-raprādhānye,* When the process of identifying ascertainment predominates
Bhrāntimat **The Erroneous**	33: *anyarūpatayā niścayaḥ,* Ascertainment of the target as something else	18: *sādṛśyād vastvanta-rapratītiḥ,* Cognition of something other due to similarity
Ullekha The Profiling	34: *ekasyānekadhā kalpanam,* Contrivancc of a single thing in many ways	19: *ekasyāpi nimittava-śād anekadhā graha-ṇam,* Perceiving a single thing as manifold because of an occasioning factor
Pratibhā The Intuition	35: *sambhāvyamānasya* [*kalpa-nam*], Hypothesis of an imagined entity	—
Kriyātipatti The Conditional	36: *yadyarthoktāv asambhāvya-mānasya* [*kalpanam*], [The hypothesis] of an unlikely thing conditioned by the statement of a word meaning "If"	—
Atiśayokti **The Hyperbolic**	37: *adhyavasānam,* Identifying ascertainment	22: *adhyavasitaprādhā-nye tu,* When, conversely [to 21], the identifyingly ascertained predominates

Ruyyaka's and Śobhākara's analysis of such deflected cognitions in poetry presupposes an intersubjectivity involving three different types of perceivers. [1.] The poet may imagine an agent who doubts, mistakes, or imagines etc. [2.] The poet himself or herself may doubt, imagine etc. [3.] The reader may doubt, imagine etc. To be able to analyse a poem along the lines of Ruyyaka or Śobhākara we therefore also need to know what each of these perceivers knows. That is to say, do they know what other agents know? What is their degree of positive and negative introspection, i.e., are the agents aware of what they themselves know or do not know? As I show below, Ruyyaka makes an essential distinction between epistemic and non-epistemic aberrant cognitions. He seeks to exclude the former, epistemic errors, from poetic discourse as too mundane: they do not inherently encapsulate the kind of strikingness *(vicchitti)* that arises from poetic insight. By non-epistemic he does not mean the ineffable qualia of cognition (*bhoga*), but rather doxastic or thetic types of cognition (*abhimāna*).

2. INTERSUBJECTIVITY, EPISTEMIC FAILURE AND DOXASTIC ERROR

Our authors agree that the figure of speech called the Erroneous is dependent on the first of the above mentioned three types of perceivers (i.e. an agent imagined by the poet), but disagree on whether epistemic errors can be allowed in *bhrāntimat*. *Bhrāntimat* (lit. "abounding in error")[14] was first defined by the Kashmirian *alaṅkārika* Rudraṭa. In his view, it requires a perceiver *(pratipattṛ)* who, when he is perceiving one thing, without doubting grasps instead another, similar thing.[15] Close to this is Mammaṭa's definition in the *Kāvyaprakāśa*, which may be approximated as: "Cognition of X when perceiving Y which is similar to X."[16] Ruyyaka

14 The suffix *matup* is added in the sense of plurality or abundance (*bhūman*). See the discussion in *Sarasvatīkaṇṭhābharaṇa* 3.38: ***bhrāntimān** iti bhūmni matup | bhūmārtho dvividho bahūnāṃ bhrāntīnām ekaviṣayato bhinnaviṣayāṇāṃ vā samānakartṛtā | ādyo bhrāntimato viṣayo, dvitīyo bhrāntimālāyāḥ |*.

15 *Kāvyālaṅkāra* 8.87: *arthaviśeṣaṃ paśyann avagacched anyam eva tatsadṛśaṃ | niḥsandehaṃ yasmin pratipattā bhrāntimān sa iti ||*.

16 *Kāvyaprakāśa* 10.132cd: *anyasaṃvit tattulyadarśane*. The perceiver making the error, however, need not be human, as Mammaṭa's example makes clear: *kapāle mārjāraḥ paya iti karān leḍhi śaśinas tarucchidraprotān bisam iti karī saṃkalayati | ratānte talpasthān harati vanitāpy aṃśukam iti prabhāmattaś candro jagad idam aho viplavayati ||552||*.

(*AlSar* 19) retains the centrality of similarity[17] in his definition: "The perception of a different thing due to similarity."[18] As an example he quotes a verse where parrots make a series of mistakes:[19]

Hoping the lips,
    of women whose eyes are like lily petals
    would be Bimba fruits
Believing their rich curls to be Utpākajambū [fruits][20]
Mistaking the red rubies in their earrings for pomegranate kernels
Your Majesty! The pet parrots of the Gūrjara king
Darting about repeatedly
Suddenly collapsed of thirst
In the desert.[21]

This verse expresses in evasive courtly circumlocution that the Gūrjara king is fleeing into the wilderness with his wives because of his defeat by the king who is being addressed. Ruyyaka expands on his definition in his prose auto-commentary with: "That mode of eloquent expression *(bhaṇiti)*, in which the property of the mind known as error exists, is called the Erroneous."[22] This clarifies that mere epistemic failure, which in itself is simply a property of the mind, is not intended to be an ornament of speech.[23] Ruyyaka specifically seeks to exclude epistemic errors resulting from common types of cognitive dysfunction such as those Dharmakīrti excludes in his definition of perception: "Error resulting from strong blows to the vitals etc. are not within the domain of this ornament."[24]

---

17 *AlSar* 19: *sādṛśyaprayuktā ca bhrāntir asya viṣayaḥ*, "Its domain is error employed [by the poet] due to similarity."

18 Ibid.: *sādṛśyād vastvantarapratītir bhrāntimān* ||.

19 Already Rudraṭa had introduced an additional perceiver (*pratipattṛ*), sometimes even an animal, who makes an error in *bhrāntimat*.

20 Ripe or cooked rose-apple fruits?

21 Ibid.: *oṣthe bimbaphalāśayālam alakeṣūtpākajambūdhiyā karṇālaṃkṛtibhāji dāḍimaphalabhrāntyā ca śoṇe maṇau* | *niṣpattyāsakṛdutpalacchadadṛśām āttaklamānāṃ marau rājan gūrjararājapañjaraśukaiḥ sadyastṛṣā mūrcchitam* ||.

22 Ibid.: *bhrāntiś cittadharmaḥ vidyate yasmin bhaṇitiprakāre sa bhrāntimān* |.

23 Jayaratha explains that therefore the presence of error in the ornament of speech is to be understood figuratively; *Vimarśinī* 19: *nanu bhrāntiś cittadharmaḥ sa yasyāsti sa bhrāntimān iti vaktuṃ nyāyyaṃ tat katham alaṃkārasyaitad abhidhānam ity āśaṅkya – āha* ***bhrāntir*** *ityādi* | *sa iti bhaṇitiprakāraḥ* | *ataś cālaṃkāre bhrāntisadbhāva* (*bhrāntisadbhāva*] KMED, *bhrāntimacchabdaḥ* Ka) *upacarita iti bhāvaḥ* |.

24 Ibid.: *gāḍhamarmaprahārādinā tu bhrāntir nāsyālaṅkārasya viṣayaḥ* |.

Among triggers for such mechanical dysfunction Dharmakīrti includes at *Nyāyabindu* 1.6 the *timira* eye-disease which distorts perceptions, rapid movement which makes a whirling firebrand appear like a circle, travelling on a boat which makes trees appear to move, and a disturbance of the humours *(saṃkṣobha)*.[25] Ruyyaka gives examples of the last of these, a misperception caused by a *gāḍhamarmaprahāra,*[26] a violent blow to the vitals.

Cāṇūramalla,
his whole chest smashed
by a punch from Kṛṣṇa
saw a hundred moons in the sky.[27]

We may compare this with a parallel idiom in English of "seeing stars." For Ruyyaka there is no outstanding artistic beauty *(vichitti)* in a depiction of such mechanically triggered misperception, and the above verse therefore does not exemplify the Erroneous. Rather, he emphasises the exigency of a remarkable error constructed by the imagination of a poet who has eloquently brought to light a similarity.

> On the other hand, an error which is also based on similarity, is perceived as arising directly from the poet's imagination for the sake of strikingness, as has been demonstrated [in the verse preceding the above verse]. But it is not so for a naturally arising (*svarasotthāpita-*) [epistemic error] as it occurs in the case of silver[28] and mother-of-pearl.[29]

---

25 *Nyāyabindu* 1.6: *tayā rahitaṃ timirāśubhramaṇanauyānasaṃkṣobhādyanāhitavibhramaṃ jñānaṃ pratyakṣam* |.

26 This is the exact phrase used to gloss *saṃkṣobha* in the *Tarkabhāṣā* 13.13: ***gāḍhamarmaprahārahatasya*** *jvalatstambhādi pratibhāsi jñānaṃ ca na pratyakṣam ity uktaṃ bhavati* | *nanu yadi nāma tajjñānaṃ na pratyakṣaṃ kathaṃ tato vastuprāptir iti cet, na tato vastuprāptiḥ* | *kiṃ tarhi, jñānāntarād eveti ke cit* || [so Dharmottara]. As we will see below, Jayaratha connects the exclusion rather to a discussion in *Pramāṇavārttika (pratyakṣapariccheda)* 3.282.

27 *AlSar* 19: *dāmodarakarāghātacūrṇitāśeṣavakṣasā* | *dṛṣṭaṃ cāṇūramallena śatacandraṃ nabhastalam* ||. Incidentally, the final *pāda* is also a famous *samasyāpūraṇa.*

28 Ruyyaka concludes the discussion by adding: *evaṃ sthāṇur vā syāt puruṣo vā syād iti saṃśaye 'pi boddhavyam* |. "This [principle] should be understood to extend also to doubt, which takes the form: 'Is this a man or a wooden post?'." This is a reference back to the definition of *sandeha*, the Dubious, at *AlSar* 18, where similarly only an imaginatively creative doubt is admitted, and not a mechanical failure due to poor lighting conditions or remoteness etc.

This introduces aspects of voluntarism (*svārasika* vs. *utpādya*) and doxastic conditions (*abhimāna*) into the investigation. For Śobhākara, aesthetic cognitions can be *svārasika (svarasataḥ, svarasotthāpita,* "naturally ocurring") or *utpādya, (utpādita, utthāpita, pratibhotthāpita, prayojanapara,* "intentionally evoked"). The *Alaṅkāraśāstra* usage[30] of these terms is probably indebted to Ānandavardhana's distinction of implicit *vākyārtha*s into either *svataḥsambhavin* or *kavipraudhoktimātrasiddha*.[31] A *vākyārtha* that reveals a second meaning (or situation) can be either inherently plausible *(svataḥsambhavin)*, or it can be imagined by a creative poet *kavipraudhoktimātrasiddha* (or, adding poetic intersubjectivity, imagined by a character imagined by the poet).[32] While discussing the figure of *ullekha*, Śobhākara predicates the *svārasika* and *utpādya* modes on cognition (*pratipatti*), and this draws a response from Jayaratha, who cites Bhaṭṭa Jayanta's theory of cognition. Generally, for Śobhākara, *svārasika* appears to denote involuntary, automatic, spontaneous, or invariable modes of cognition, whereas *utpādya* denotes volitional, intentionally evoked, telic or paratelic modes of cognition.

In his view, the Erroneous is not concerned with the mechanism of epistemic malfunction, but rather with the reader's appreciation of how the poet ventures to insinuate what the agent imagined in a poem believes to be happening. It is also important that the reader and the poet share the same degree of omniscience relative to the situation (we know what is really happening), whereas the imagined agent in the poem does not.

Śobhākara contests nearly everything of substance that Ruyyaka asserts about the Erroneous. It is he who first breaks with tradition and denies that similarity is necessary in the Erroneous. Let us

---

29 Ibid.: *sādṛśyahetukāpi bhrāntir vicchittyarthaṃ kavipratibhotthāpitaiva gṛhyate yathodāhṛtam | na svarasotthāpitā śuktikārajatavat |*.

30 For other usages see, e.g., FRESCHI 2012, p. 339 on the distinction between *svārasikākāṅkṣā* and *utthāpitākāṅkṣā*.

31 *Dhvanyāloka* 2.24: *prauḍhoktimātraniṣpannaśarīraḥ sambhavī svataḥ | artho 'pi dvividho jñeyo vastuno 'nyasya dīpakaḥ ||*.

32 *Dhvanyāloka* 2.24, *Vṛtti*: *svataḥsambhavī ya aucityena bahir api sambhāvyamānasadbhāvo na kevalaṃ bhaṇitivaśenaivābhiniṣpannaśarīraḥ |* Mammaṭa *Kāvyaprakāsa* 4.9: *svataḥsaṃbhavī na kevalaṃ bhaṇitimātraniṣpanno yāvad bahir apy aucityena saṃbhāvyamānaḥ | kavinā pratibhāṇamātreṇa bahir asann api nirmitaḥ kavinibaddhena vaktreti vā dvividho 'para iti trividhaḥ |*.

look at how he arrives at this conclusion. At first he appears to follow Ruyyaka's lead:

> *AlRat* (fol. 77ʳ K_R, 52 P_Ed): *anyarūpatayā niścayo bhrāntimān* ||33|| *viṣayasyānyarūpasyāpi rūpāntaratvenāsamyagabhimānarūpo niścayo bhrāntimān* | *udāharaṇam* –
>
> *pusiā kaṇṇāharaṇendaṇīla*[33]*kiraṇāhaā sasimaūhā*[34] |
> *māṇiṇivaäṇammi*[35] *sakajjalaṃsusaṅkāe*[36] *daïeṇa*[37] ||164||
>
> (*Gāhākosa* 302)[38]
> *atra sādṛśyahetukā bhrāntiḥ* |
>
> The Erroneous is the ascertainment [of the *viṣaya*] as having a different form [than its own]. The Erroneous is an ascertainment which is a non-veridical (*asamyag*), doxastic cognition (*abhimāna*)[39] of a target (*viṣaya*) as having a certain form even though it [factually] has another form. An example:
>
> Her lover wiped away the moonbeams
> darkened by sapphire rays from her earrings
> on the face of the sulking woman,
> in the belief that they were kohl-stained tears.
>
> Here we have a case of error caused by similarity.

In explaining the Erroneous as a non-veridical, doxastic alternative cognition that supplants a veridical cognition, Śobhākara uses the term *abhimāna* to designate a kind of make-believe that does not correspond to reality.[40] In this he appears to be following Ruyya-

---

33 °*ṇīla*°] P_Ed, °*nīla*° K_R.

34 *sasimaūhā*] P_Ed, *sasimarūhā* K_R.

35 °*vaäṇammi*] P_Ed, °*vaäṇāhi* K_R.

36 *saṅkāe*] P_Ed, *saṅkāï* K_R.

37 *Gāhākosa* 302: *pusiā kaṇṇāharaṇeṃdaṇīlakiraṇāhaā sasimaūhā* | *māṇiṇivaäṇammi sakajjalaṃsusaṃkāï daïeṇa* ||; *Vimarśinī* 19: *bimbapratibimbabhāvo yathā "pusiā kaṇṇāharaṇendaṇīlakiraṇāhaā sasima hā* | *māṇiṇivaäṇammi sakajjalaṃ susaṅkāe daïeṇa* ||*" (Chāyā: proñchitāḥ karṇābharaṇendranīlakiraṇāhṛtāḥ śaśimayūkhā* | *māninīvadane sakajjalāśruśaṅkayā dayitena) atra sakajjalatvendranīlakiraṇāhatatvayor bimbabhāvaḥ* | *sādṛśyanimittakatvam eva cāsya draḍhayituṃ pratyudāharati gāḍhetyādinā* |).

38 *Chāyā* (slightly modified): *proñchitāḥ karṇābharaṇendranīlakiraṇāhatāḥ śaśimayūkhāḥ* | *māninīvadane sakajjalāśruśaṅkayā dayitena* ||.

39 I.e., a non-veridical, doxastic cognition called an *abhimāna*.

40 That is, *abhimāna* is intended in the Naiyāyika sense of mistaken belief as explained in the commentaries to *Nyāyasūtra* 4.2.31: *svapnaviṣayābhimānavad ayam pramāṇaprameyābhimānaḥ*. For the likelihood that Śobhākara was a

ka's lead in shifting his focus beyond epistemic failure.[41] Ruyyaka would concur that the Prakrit verse exemplifies the Erroneous, for the similarity between the moonbeams and the tears is based on an imaginatively perceived similarity. Śobhākara proceeds, however, to argue that Ruyyaka's definition is too narrow, for neither is similarity a prerequisite, nor is intense emotional shock to be excluded.

AlRat (cont.): *tadanyanimittā yathā –*

> *prāsāde sā pathi pathi ca sā pṛṣṭhataḥ sā puraḥ sā*
> *paryaṅke sā diśi diśi ca sā tadviyogāturasya |*
> *haṃho cetaḥ prakṛtir aparā nāsti te*[42] *kāpi sā sā*
> *sā sā sā sā jagati sakale ko 'yam advaitavādaḥ* ||165||

(*Amaruśataka* 105)

atra[43] *gāḍharāgānubhavahetukaṃ*[44] *tanmayatānusaṃdhānaṃ prāsādāder vallabhārūpatvena pratītau nimittam* |

The Erroneous with a different cause is as follows:

> For him, anguished by separation from her –
> The terrace: She[45]
> Every path: She
> To the side: She
> Ahead: She
> The bed: She
> Everywhere: She
> Alas, O heart! There is no other material for you whatsoever
> The whole world: She she she she she she!

Naiyāyika, see below.

41 In the intellectual milieu of our Kashmirian authors, however, the term *abhimāna* does not come without its own baggage. For Ruyyaka and Jayaratha, as adherents of Śaiva non-dualism, *abhimāna* can in the context of ritual identification with a deity correspond to reality. Kṣemarāja commenting on *Svacchandatantra* 4.423 glosses *abhimāna* with "certain cognition" (*abhimānaṃ = niścitāṃ pratipattiṃ*). However, this is not an issue they would debate in a general śāstric discourse.

42 *te*] KR, *me* PEd.

43 *atra*] PEd, *atra ca* KR.

44 *gāḍharāgānubhavahetukaṃ*]. Cf. *AlSar: gāḍhamarmaprahārādinā tu bhrāntir nāsyālaṅkārasya viṣayaḥ; Cf. Pramāṇavārttika* (*pratyakṣapariccheda*) 3.282 cited by Jayaratha ad loc.: *kāmaśokabhayonmādacaurasvapnādyupaplutāḥ | abhūtān api paśyanti purato 'vasthitān iva* ||.

45 This translation follows Śobhākara's commentary that takes the speaker to be identifying the terrace etc. with his beloved.

What is this philosophy of non-dualism?
Here a cognitive synthesis of identity, caused by an experience of intense passion, functions as the occasioning cause for the cognition of the mansion etc. as having the form of the beloved.

Śobhākara interprets Amaru's verse – the final verse in most recensions – to be saying that the love-sick speaker actually misperceives completely unrelated everyday objects to be his beloved. This extreme cognitive deviancy is possible because of the derangement caused by the speaker's intense lovesickness, and the figure of speech remains, in contrast to Ruyyaka, the Erroneous. He continues with two further examples:

evaṃ ca – (P_{Ed} 53, K_R 77^v)
durjanadūṣitamanasāṃ puṃsāṃ sujane 'pi nāsti viśvāsaḥ |
bālaḥ pāyasadagdho dadhy api phūtkṛtya bhakṣayati ||166||[46]
"devam[47] *api harṣaṃ pitṛśokavihvalīkṛtaṃ śriyaṃ śāpa iti mahīṃ mahāpātakam iti rājyaṃ roga iti bhogān bhujagā*[48] *iti nilayaṃ niraya ityādi manyamānam" ityādau sādṛśyanimittavinābhāvisvaśokādinimittabhede*[49] *'pi nālaṅkārāntarabuddhiḥ kāryā* | *pratītibhede hy alaṅkārabhedo yukto na nimittabhede 'laṅkārānantyaprasaṅgāt* | *tadbhede tu kavipratibhotthāpitavicchittisadbhāve 'ntarbhāva eva nyāyyaḥ* |

Equally [not based on similarity is the following]:
People deceived by the wicked trust not even the good.
A child burnt by [hot] milk blows upon even yoghurt before eating.
In an example such as: "[Eminent persons surrounded] King Harṣa, who, overwhelmed by the grief of his father['s death], considered wealth to be a curse, the earth to be a great sin, sovereignty to be a disease, pleasures to be serpents, the palace to be a hell, and so on," even though there is a

---

46 This verse can be found in: *Subhāṣitaratnakośa* 38.12 (1265), *Subhāṣitāvali* 390, *Hitopadeśa* 4.110.

47 *Harṣacarita* 5, p.34 (28) [p. 239 (4)]: *devam api harṣaṃ tadavasthaṃ pitṛśokavihvalīkṛtam, śriyaṃ śāpa iti mahīṃ mahāpātakam iti rajyaṃ roga iti bhogān bhujaṅgā iti nilayaṃ niraya iti bandhuṃ bandhanam iti jīvitam ayaśa iti dehaṃ droha iti kalyatāṃ kalaṅka ity āyur apuṇyaphalam iti āhāraṃ viṣam iti viṣam amṛtam iti candanaṃ dahana iti kāmaṃ krakaca iti hṛdayasphoṭanam abhyudaya iti ca manyamānam... kulaputrāḥ... paurāṇikāḥ paryavārayan.* Śaṅkara ad loc: ***devam*** *ityādau devam api harṣam evaṃvidhā janāḥ paryavārayann iti sambandhaḥ* |.

48 *bhujagā*] P_{Ed}, *bhujaga* K_R.

49 °*nimittavinābhāvisva*°] conj., °*nimittāvinābhāvisva*° K_R, °*nimittaṃ vinā bhāvāvasāya*° (em.) P_{Ed}.

different type of occasioning cause,[50] namely personal grief etc., which does not presuppose causation by similarity, there should not arise the notion that it is a different figure of speech. A differentiation of figures of speech makes sense when there occurs a difference of cognition, not when a different occasioning cause occurs, because of the unwarranted consequence that an infinitude of figures of speech would arise. When there is such a difference [of cognition] then there is just cause for an inclusion in the proper category of strikingness contrived by the imagination of the poet.

In this example there is no immediate similarity between wicked people and good people, or between hot milk and yoghurt. In the second example too, similarity is not involved in the phenomena Harṣa mistakes for each other. Nevertheless, the rhetorical ornament still conforms, for Śobhākara, to the strictures laid down for the Erroneous. He therefore concludes that occasioning factors such as similarity should not be used to distinguish figures of speech. In any case, there are too many such factors in poetic language to make this a feasible undertaking. Rather, at least in the present context, he wishes to base separate figures of speech on different types of cognition.

Jayaratha endeavours to defend Ruyyaka by disputing that similarity can be absent in the Erroneous. Rather than *Nyāyabindu* 1.6, he takes Ruyyaka and Śobhākara to be referring to *Pramāṇavārtika* 3.282 (a much quoted verse originally intended to corroborate yogic perception) which he cites:[51]

---

50 "Occasioning cause" here translates *nimitta*. Śobhākara points out that it would be impossible to exhaustively enumerate all the occasioning factors that could generate a simile. Where the early *alaṅkārika* Daṇḍin (*Kāvyādarśa* 2.29-39 etc.) multiplies simile types, enumerating such types as: *samānopamā*, *nindopamā*, *praśaṃsopamā*, *ācikhyāsopamā*, *virodhopamā*, *pratiṣedhopamā*, *caṭūpamā*, *tattvākhyānopamā*, *asādhāraṇopamā*, *abhūtopamā*, *asaṃbhāvitopamā*, later rhetoricians such as Mammaṭa sought to find global categories to subsume such open-ended diversity.

51 *Vimarśinī* 19: ***sādṛśyaprayukte****ti* | *na tu "kāmaśokabhayonmādacaurasvapnādyupaplutāḥ* | *abhūtān api paśyanti purato 'vasthitān iva"* || (45). Cf. *Pramāṇavārttika* (*pratyakṣapariccheda*) 3.282 (=*Pramāṇaviniścaya* 1.29). Manorathanandin comments: *kāmaś ca śokaś ca bhayaṃ ca tair unmādāś caurasvapnādayaś ceti kāmaśokabhayonmādacaurasvapnādibhir upaplutā bhrāntās te 'bhūtān apy arthān bhāvanāvaśāt purato 'vasthitān iva paśyanti yasmāt tadanurūpaṃ pravṛttiṃ ceṣṭante* ||.

Those assailed by passion, grief, fear, drunkenness, dreams of(/or) thieves, and so on, perceive non-existent things as if they were right before them.

Jayaratha repeats Ruyyaka's judgment that misperceptions caused by intense conditions cannot be accommodated in the Erroneous, and he contradicts Śobhākara's interpretation of the final verse of the *Amaruśataka.* The poet, he claims, intended something quite different, and the figure of speech must be identified as the Particular *(viśeṣa),* where a single thing is perceived multiply, and not as the Erroneous. Rather than actually perceiving the beloved as being the terrace, the road etc., he intends that the lovesick speaker sees one woman in many places at once, we might say that he sees her everywhere.

Here an identifying cognitive synthesis of one finite woman, caused by intense passion, is the occasioning cause for [her] simultaneous perception on the terrace, [the road,] etc. Therefore it is not a case of the Erroneous, for that would involve a cognition of the terrace etc. as being the beloved. The Erroneous is defined as a non-ascertainment of the correct construal by taking X as Y. And since the terrace, and so on, are not perceived as the beloved, this is a clear case of the Particular (*viśeṣa*).[52] If one were to argue that there is a misperception due to seeing the beloved on the terrace and so on even though she is not there, then that is wrong. For in that case we would have here a bare epistemic mistake and not a figure of speech. There emerges a series of cognitions of a woman on the terrace etc., even though she is not there, by the force of intense passion as the occasioning cause, and this happens through inherent cognitive malfunction (*svarasataḥ*), because it is not contrived by the poet's imagination.[53]

---

[52] This is also what Ruyyaka identifies the ornament in this verse as in his discussion of the Particular (*AlSar* 50: *anādhāram ādheyam ekam anekagocaram aśakyavastvantarakaraṇaṃ viśeṣaḥ*), where it exemplifies a single thing having a multitude as its scope. He explains: *ekasyā eva yoṣitaḥ prāsādādau yugapadavasthānam.*

[53] *Vimarśinī* 19: *ity atraikasyā eva parimitāyā api yoṣito gāḍhānurāgahetukaṃ tanmayatānusaṃdhānaṃ prāsādādāv anekatra yugapatpratītau nimittam iti na bhrāntimadalaṃkāraḥ | sa hi prāsādāder vallabhārūpatvena pratītau syāt | anyasyānyarūpatvena samyagabhidhānātmāniścayo hi bhrāntimallakṣaṇam | na ca prāsādādir vallabhātvena pratīyate iti sphuṭa evāyaṃ viśeṣālaṅkārasya viṣayaḥ | atha prasādādāv abhūtāyā api vallabhāyā darśanād bhrāntir iti cet, naitat | evaṃ hy atra bhrāntimātraṃ syān nālaṃkāraḥ | gāḍhānurāgātmakanimittasāmarthyāt svarasata eva prāsādādāv asatyā api yuvatyāḥ pratītisamul-*

Yet this is exactly what Śobhākara had said is happening.[54] The lovesick speaker misperceives the terrace, etc., to be his beloved. Jayaratha does not address this other than by flatly denying that this is what the poet can have meant. Without a clear justification this remains just a personal opinion on the degree of derangement the speaker is experiencing, and Śobhākara could simply reply by stating his personal opinion to the contrary. Jayaratha finds similar tendentious faults of interpretation with the other examples Śobhākara's has provided. But let us return to Śobhākara's analysis of the Erroneous to see how he evaluates Ruyyaka's definition.

> *yadi ca "sādṛśyād vastvantarapratītir bhrāntimān"*[55] *ity avyāpakaṃ lakṣaṇaṃ tarhi vyāpakaṃ lakṣaṇāntaraṃ vidheyam, na tv alaṅkārāntaram upasaṅkhyeyam | sādṛśyavyatiriktanimittotthāpitāyāṃ ca bhrāntau vicchittiviśeṣasadbhāve*[56] *kathaṃ nāmānalaṃkāratā*[57] | *alaṅkāratve ca kim iti bhrāntimadbahirbhāvaḥ* |...
>
> And if the definition [provided by Ruyyaka]: "The Erroneous is the perception of a different thing due to similarity" is too narrow, then a different, wider definition must be provided, but one should not add another ornament [instead]. And when a specific strikingness is present in a misperception arising from an occasioning cause other than similarity, how could it not be a poetic ornament? And if it must be an ornament how could it be extraneous to the Erroneous?

After determining that similarity is not the only occasioning cause for the Erroneous, Śobhākara can criticize Ruyyaka's definition for being too limited. He reiterates that distinct cognitions must underlie individual figures of speech in two summary verses:

> *sandehasambhāvanayor yathāsti pratītibhedaḥ sphuṭa eva tadvat* | (fol. 78ʳ Kʀ)
> *sādṛśyahetvantarayor bhrameṣu na leśataḥ kvāpi viśeṣabuddhiḥ* ||
> *pratītibhedena vinā na vācyaḥ kutrāpy alaṅkāragataś ca bhedaḥ* |
> *nimittabhedena ca bhinnatāyāṃ prasajyate sā khalu saṃśayādau* ||

---

lāsāḥ kavipratibhānirvartitvābhāvāt |.

54 See above: ... *atra gāḍharāgānubhavahetukaṃ tanmayatānusaṃdhānaṃ prāsādāder vallabhārūpatvena pratītau nimittam* |.

55 Cit. *AlSar* 19.

56 °*sadbhāve*] Kʀ, °*sambhave* Pᴇᴅ.

57 *nāmānalaṃkāratā*] Pᴇᴅ, °*nalaṅkāratāpāṭhaḥ* Kʀ^mg, *nāmālaṃkārantatā* Kʀ^ac.

We have no cognition of a distinction whatsoever as regards errors, whether [their] cause is similarity or something else, in the way that we have a clear difference of cognition between doubt and assumption. Without a difference of cognition one can in no case assert a difference of a figure of speech. And if [there would be a] difference of cognitions due to difference in causes, this [having different cognitions] would apply to doubt and so on [as well].[58]

3. COMPETING TYPOLOGIES

The above discussion reveals that the main disagreement between Śobhākara and Ruyyaka concerns their rival typologies of cognition (*pratītibheda*). Under what headings can deflected cognitions be subsumed? Śobhākara lays out his schema as part of his definition of the figure of speech called the Assumption (*utprekṣā*). In agreement with earlier theorists, he sees this as grounded on a surmise (*saṃbhāvana*).[59] This reverts to an earlier consensus that Ruyyaka sought to overturn by claiming that the Assumption depends not on supposition, but that it arises rather when the predominant focus falls on the process of identifying ascertainment (*adhyavasāya*).[60] In the expression: "the anklet remained mute, as if in grief of separation from your foot,"[61] the target (*viṣaya)* is the anklet, and it is assumed, through a process of identification occurring as a part of cognition, that it is instead the source (*viṣayin*), in this case a conscious agent capable of speech, from whence derives its seeming ability to choose to remain mute. For Śobhākara the key feature of this cognitive deflection is an assumption (supposition, surmise) that the target is the source.

AlRat 32, P_{Ed} 47, K_R 74^v l. 3: *viṣayitvena saṃbhāvanam utprekṣā*[62] ||32||

---

[58] That is, doubt or imagination are different types of cognitions (*pratītibheda*), and each one of these is itself differentiated by occasioning factors (*nimittabheda*). For example, a doubt may arise from a similarity or from multiplicity.

[59] For an insightful recent discussion of this figure in the *AlSar* see SHULMAN 2012.

[60] *AlSar* 22: *adhyavasāye vyāpāraprādhānya utprekṣā.* On the Śaiva understanding of *adhyavasāya*, and how it differs from that of the Buddhists, see KAWAJIRI 2011.

[61] Śobhākara discusses the same standard example as Ruyyaka, *Raghuvaṃśa* 13.23.

[62] *utprekṣā*] P_{Ed}, *u*[*tpre*]+ K_R.

> *viṣayitvenārthād viṣayasya saṃbhāvanaṃ "bhavitavyam anena sthāṇunā" ityādyaniścayātmakohatarkādi*[63]*-śabdābhidheyasaṃbhāvanā*[64]*-pratyayaviṣayīkṛtatvam utprekṣā | ataś cāniścayātmakatayā saṃbhāvanāyāḥ saṃdehamūlatvaṃ na tv adhyavasāyagarbhatā |*
>
> Supposition [of the target] as the source is the Assumption. Surmise (*saṃbhāvanam*), that is to say of the target (*viṣaya*), as being the source (*viṣayin*), is the Assumption (*utprekṣā*). It is the condition of being made the object of a cognition that is a supposition, designated by words such as deliberation, speculation and so on,[65] which are not ascertainments, as in the example: "This must be a post." Therefore, *saṃbhāvanā* is based on doubt because it is a form of non-ascertainment, but it is not based on determination.

Śobhākara's main critique is that imagination cannot be based on a positive form of determining and ascertaining cognition as Ruyyaka claims, but that it must rather be based on doubt. An example of an ascertainment would be: "This is a post," and a doubt would be: "Is this a post or a man?". In a speculation, the situation is: "This surely must be a post!". Śobhākara would prefer to classify the Assumption as a form of doubt. He then contextualises this type of doubt further:

> *tathāhi saṃdehaniścayarūpatvena pratyayānāṃ dvaividhyam | niścayaś ca*[66] *yathārthāvyabhicārī*[67] *samyakpratyayaḥ | vyabhicārī tv asamyak | tatra tāvad utprekṣāyā*[68] *na samyaktvam*[69] *| arthāvyabhicārābhāvāt | nāpy asamyakpratyayarūpo viparyāsaḥ, tasya niścaya*[70]*rūpatvāt | asyāṃ ca śābdenāpi vṛttena bhrāntimadatiśayoktyādivad viṣayiṇo niścayābhāvāt |*

---

[63] °*niścayātmakohatarkādi*°] em., °++[*yā*]*tma*[*ko*]*hatarkādi*° KR, °*niścayātmakavitarkādi*° PEd.

[64] °*saṃbhāvanā*°] PEd, °*sambhavana*° KR.

[65] *ūhatarkādi-*] *Cf. Gītārthasaṃgraha* of Abhinavagupta 4.34 for a list of synonyms involving *ūha* and *tarka*: *...paripraśnena ūhāpohatarkavitarkādibhiḥ...* PEd in this place reads *vitarka*, a variant that is less plausible since Śobhākara accepts the existence of an independent *alaṅkāra* called *vitarka*. Cf. also e.g. ĪPVV, vol. I, p. 101: *...ūhanaṃ tarkaṇaṃ saṃbhāvanam iti...*

[66] *ca*] PEd, *cā*° KR.

[67] *yathārthāvyabhicārī*] PEd, ++[*rth*]*āvyabhicārī* KR.

[68] *tāvad utprekṣāyā*] KR^{pc}, *tāvad utprekṣā* PEd KR^{ac}.

[69] *samyaktvam*] PEd, *sa*[*myaktva*]*m* KR.

[70] *niścaya*°] PEd, *ni*[*śca*]*ya*° KR.

> *aniścitaṃ*[71] *ca*[72] *saṃdigdham evety avivādaḥ | ata eva nādhyavasāyamūlatvam asyāḥ | tasya viṣayanigaraṇaṃ viṣayiniścayaś ca*[73] *svarūpam | na cātraikam api saṃbhavati viṣayopādānāt, niścayābhāvāc ca*[74] *| tena "adhyavasāye vyāpāraprādhānya utprekṣā" iti lakṣaṇam aparyālocitābhidhānam eva |*
>
> To explain further, cognitions are twofold because they can take the form of doubt or ascertainment. Ascertainment, which does not deviate from factual reality, is veridical cognition. That which deviates is non-veridical. The Assumption is not veridical, because of the absence of non-deviation from factual reality. Nor is [the Assumption] a misperception in the form of a non-veridical cognition, because that consists in an ascertainment. But in the Assumption (*asyāṃ*) there is an absence of the ascertainment of the source (*viṣayin*) even verbally, just as there is in the Erroneous (*bhrāntimat*)[75] and the Hyperbole (*atiśayokti*). And nobody disputes that an uncertain cognition is doubtful. Therefore the Assumption cannot be based on identifying ascertainment (*adhyavasāya*), the essence of which is a devouring of the target and an ascertainment of the source. And in the present case not even one of these is possible, because the target is present and ascertainment is lacking. Therefore the definition: "The Assumption occurs when the process predominates in an identifying ascertainment," is ill-considered.

Śobhākara here makes the claim that it is universally accepted that uncertain cognition (*aniścita*) is doubtful.

---

[71] *aniścitaṃ*] KR, *aniścite* PEd.

[72] *ca*] PEd KR^pc, omitted KR^ac.

[73] °*niścayaś ca*] PEd KR^pc, °*niścaya*° KR.

[74] °*ābhāvāc ca*] PEd, °[*ā*]*bhā*+[*cca*] KR.

[75] In the Erroneous it is the target (*viṣaya*) that is misperceived as something else, but it is not mistaken for the source (*viṣayin*).

Figure 2: Śobhākara's typology of cognition

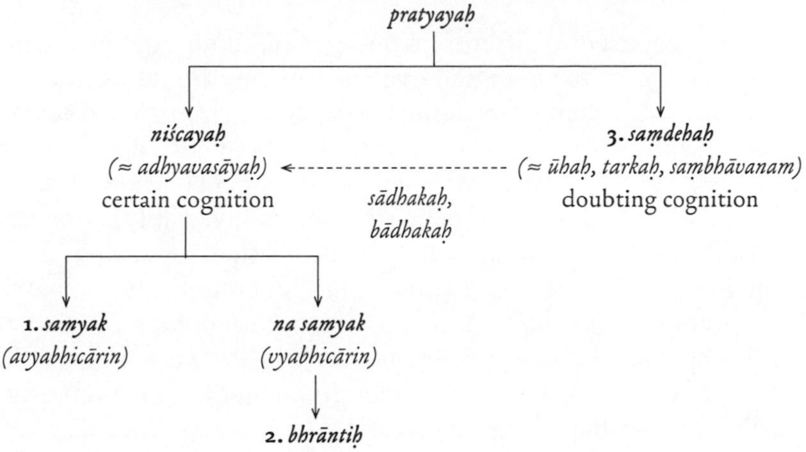

Given the importance epistemology plays in Śobhākara's system it is not surprising that Jayaratha subsequently singled out his cognitive typology for a detailed critique.[76] Jayaratha denies the introduction of veridicality, that is, the categories of *samyak* and *na samyak*, determined by the presence or absence of cognitive deviation (*vyabhicāra*), into this paradigm. He takes a step back and charges that Śobhākara has missed the bigger picture.[77] Ruyyaka's definition of the Assumption appeals not to the result of cognition, but rather to the underlying bare process of cognising (*pratītivṛttimātra*) that itself enables us to determine cognitive validity.

> *Vimarśinī* 54 KM, 78ᵛ l.14 K_{SV}: *iha hi niścayāniścayarūpatvena pratyayānāṃ dvaividhyam, niścayaś cārthāvyabhicārī samyag anyathā tv asamyag iti bhedo*[78] *na grāhyaḥ | pratītivṛttimātrasyaiveha vicārayitum upakrāntatvāt, tasya ca prāmāṇyavicāra upayogāt |*
>
> In this case one should not adopt a classification of cognitions into two kinds: ascertainment and non-ascertainment, nor [should one accept] that ascertainment is non-deviating and [hence] veridical, and otherwise [cognition] is non-veridical, because here we have begun to evaluate the

---

76 Abhinavagupta too considered *utprekṣā/utprekṣaṇa* as a particular category of cognition. See RATIÉ 2010, pp. 343-344.

77 Jayaratha does not, for example, engage Śobhākara in the *svataḥ/parataḥ* controversy of intrinsic or extrinsic validity, or any other argument that would even tacitly accept that validity is relevant here.

78 *bhedo*] KM$_{ED}$ K$_{SV}$, *bhedena* Kha.

bare process of cognition, and that [process itself] enables a deliberation on validity.

Jayaratha proposed a different paradigm of three cognitions that can, he claims, be experientially verified by any literary critic (*sahṛdayasākṣika*): ascertainment *(niścaya)*, doubt (*saṃśaya, sandeha*) and deliberation (*tarka, sambhāvanā*). The latter two he classifies under the heading of *aniścaya* (non-ascertainment). Therefore, Śobhākara's assertion that non-determination is invariably a doubtful cognition cannot be maintained. This means that for Jayaratha the distinction between doubting (*saṃdigdha*) cognitions and imaginative cognitions (*sambhāvita*), under which he includes conjectural (*tarkita*) cognitions, is much greater than in the paradigm of Śobhākara. Śobhākara does not consider doubt and imagination as identical, as Jayaratha seems to insinuate, he merely states that both belong under the heading of doubtful cognition. In his discussion of the Erroneous he even explicitly notes that there is a difference of cognition between doubt and imagination, and this is the reason why we may consider them as the bases of distinct figures of speech. Jayaratha continues:

> *Vimarśinī* cont.: *aniścayaś ca saṃśayatarkarūpatvena dvividhaḥ | ataś cāniścitaṃ ca saṃdigdham eveti na vācyam | tarkātmanaḥ saṃbhāvanāpratyayasyāpy aniścayātmakatve saṃdigdhatvābhāvāt | utprekṣā saṃbhāvanādiśabdābhidheyatarkapratītimūleti nāsyāḥ saṃdehamūlatvam | tasya bhinnalakṣaṇatvāt | athānavadhāraṇajñānaṃ*[79] *saṃśaya ity anavadhāraṇajñānatvāviśeṣāt saṃśayān nārthāntarabhāvas*[80] *tarkasyety asyāḥ saṃśayamūlatvam iti cet, naitat | anavadhāraṇajñānatvāviśeṣe 'pi saṃśayatarkayor bhinnarūpatvāt |*
>
> Non-ascertainment has two forms: doubt and deliberation. And therefore, it cannot be said that the non-ascertained is invariably doubtful, because an imaginative cognition that is a deliberation (*tarka*) is not doubtful while being a non-ascertainment. The Assumption is based on a cognition that is a deliberation and is designated by terms such as imagining etc., therefore it is not based on doubt, for that is defined differently. You may now argue as follows. Because doubt is a cognition which does not determine its object (*anavadhāraṇa*), therefore deliberation cannot be something different from doubt, since they both have in common that they do not determine their object. Therefore the Assumption is based on

---

79 °*jñānaṃ*] KSV, °*jñāna*° KMED.

80 *nārthāntarabhāvas*] KSV, *nārthāntarābhāvas* KMED.

doubt. This is wrong, because doubt and deliberation are different even though they are both non-determining cognitions.

The relevant part of the discussion simply confirms that both are in agreement that the Assumption is based on uncertain cognition. Jayaratha then analyses the standard śāstric examples of dubious cognitions.

> *tathāhi – sthāṇur vā puruṣo veti sāmyena*[81] *pakṣadvayollekhaḥ* (79ʳ) *saṃśayaḥ* | *puruṣeṇānena bhavitavyam ity ekatarapakṣānukūlakāraṇadarśanena pakṣāntarabādhanam iva tarkaḥ*[82] | *puruṣa evāyam iti pakṣāntarā*[83]*-saṃsparśenaikatarapakṣanirṇayo niścaya ity asti sahṛdayasākṣikaṃ pratyayānāṃ traividhyam* |

We can summarise this as follows. [1.] In an ascertainment: "This is precisely a man" one alternative is determined without any contact with an alternative. [2.] In a doubting cognition (*saṃśayaḥ*): "It is a post or it is a man" the two alternatives are equally vivid. [3.] In a deliberation *(tarkaḥ)*: "This must be a man" one alternative appears as if annulled by seeing a cause conformable to the other.

Figure 3: Jayarathas's typlogy of three cognitions

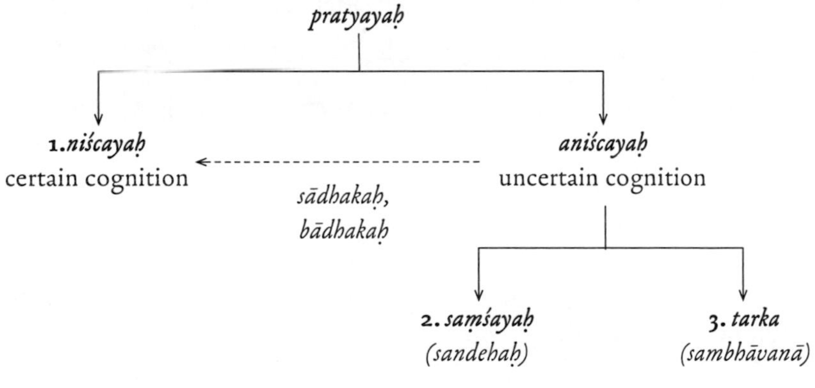

81 *sāmyena*] Ksv, *sāmānyena* KMed.

82 Cf. *Nyāyamañjarī*, vol. I, p. 18: *sandigdhe 'rthe 'nyatarapakṣānukūlakāraṇadarśanāt tasmin sambhāvanāpratyayas tarkaḥ* |.

83 *pakṣāntarā°*] Ksv, *pakṣāntara°* KMed.

The main disagreements are whether validity is relevant when a cognition is looked at as a bare process that is not yet complete, and whether surmise is a form of doubt or a category of its own.

For Śobhākara the Erroneous, as a form of identifying ascertainment, comes close to other figures of speech that involve ascertainment, most directly to the Hyperbolic (*atiśayokti*). He must therefore establish clear criteria to distinguish the two, and this sheds further light on how he understands his typology of cognitions.

> *AlRat* (80^r K$_R$) *adhyavasānam atiśayoktiḥ* ||37||
> *viṣayanigaraṇenābhedapratipattir viṣayiṇo 'dhyavasānam* | *iyaṃ*[84] *cābhedapratipattir viṣayānupādāne kevalaviṣayivācakaśabdaprayogabalena vākyāj jāyata iti śābdī* | *bhrāntimadādau tu nimittāntareṇātasmiṃs*[85] *tatpratītiḥ pramātrantarasyopajātā vaktrānūdyate na tu janyata*[86] *iti na pratipattiḥ śābdī* | *iha tu vaktrā supratītir eva tathāvidhā pratipādyata iti śābdī pratipattiḥ*[87] | *tenāsyās tato bhedaḥ* |
>
> Identifying ascertainment is the Hyperbolic. The cognition of the source (*viṣayin*) as non-different [from the target (*viṣaya*)], by the devouring of the target, is identifying ascertainment. And this cognition of non-difference is verbal (*śābdī*) because – given that the target is not [explicitly] stated – it is generated by the sentence through the force of an expression deployed to denote only the source. In the Erroneous etc., on the other hand, a perception of X with respect to not-X[88] being generated by some other occasioning factor for a different perceiver-agent [located in the text] is restated by the speaker but it is not produced, therefore the cognition is not verbal. But here, a clear cognition of this kind is articulated by the speaker, therefore it is a verbal perception. Thereby it (Hyperbole) is different from it (Erroneous).

It is important to Śobhākara that the doxastic error giving rise to the Erroneous is committed by an imagined character in the poem. It is this central feature that he recapitulates in his summary of the difference between the Erroneous and the Hyperbolic:

---

84 *iyaṃ*] P$_{Ed}$, *idaṃ* K$_R$.

85 *nimittāntareṇātasmiṃs*] K$_R$, *nimittāntareṇa tasmiṃs* P$_{Ed}$.

86 *na tu janyata*] P$_{Ed}$, *na++++* K$_R^{mg}$.

87 *pratipattiḥ*] P$_{Ed}$, *pra[tyā]pattis* K$_R^{mg}$.

88 The formulation *atasmiṃs tat* is widely cited as a definition for various kinds of error. *Cf. Nyāyamañjarī*, vol. I, p. 248: *atasmiṃs tadgraho bhavaty apramāṇatvakāraṇam...* etc. (a restatement of the *Nyāyabhāṣya* on 1.1.4).

pramātrantaradhīr bhrāntirūpā yasminn anūdyate | sa bhrāntimān svadhīr bhrāntā vaktrāsyāṃ tu nivedyate[89] || *iti saṃgrahaḥ* |

Summary: Where the mistaken cognition of another perceiver is restated it is the Erroneous, but in Hyperbole (*asyāṃ*) a speaker communicates his own mistaken cognition.

A differing poetic intersubjectivity is capable of altering the cognitive dynamics of the situation to such an extent that Śobhākara would identify a different ornament. If, for example, it were the poet who consciously and deliberately made an error in representing a situation in a very certain way, Śobhākara would identify the ornament as the Metaphor (*rūpaka*), provided that the error is one of verbal representation (*pratipādanabhrama*) as distinct from cognitive error (*bhrāntā pratipattiḥ*). In this he does not hesitate to go against Ruyyaka and all previous thinkers. For Śobhākara the target and the source are in that case related by *sāmānādhikaraṇyam,* that is, they are represented as collocated, as sharing a common substrate. This error must then also be shared by the reader, who sees two syntactically coordinated words sharing the same case-suffix, and therefore superimposes the source on the target.[90] The unusual doxastic error arising from unwarranted colocation, deliberately committed by the poet and willingly re-enacted by the reader, is what he calls a Metaphor.

4. *MAṄGALA* VERSES

While the preceding discussion attempts to clarify how Śobhākara deals with Ruyyaka's work, it does not tell us why the dispute appears so ardent. This a question that is much more difficult to answer, and only a few ideas may be offered at the present stage of research.

Both Ruyyaka and Śobhākara inherited a canon of example verses selected by their predecessors. When they do introduce new verses, therefore, it can be revealing to look at these more closely. Śobhākara, it turns out, introduces several new verses that happen to share a solar motif. This might be no more than a play on his name, but it is also possible that it intends to signal a religious affiliation. Can this possibly have played any role in defining his scho-

89 *nivedyate*] KR, *na vedyate* PEd.

90 Śobhākara adopts from Ruyyaka the idea that *rūpaka* is based on superimposition (*āropa*) but he redefines this as an extension of *sāmānādhikaraṇya*.

larly stance in his dispute with Ruyyaka? We have counter-evidence that suggests an author's religious affiliation was immaterial in a field such as *alaṅkāra*. Ānandavardhana was a (Pāñcarātrika?) Vaiṣṇava, and his almost reverential commentator Abhinavagupta was a Śaiva. Or, can we at least assume that religious affiliation might determine which teachers or *maṭha*s a student would seek out? While it certainly seems to be the normative case that, for example, Śaiva students would study with Śaiva teachers, that is not always the case. Nor does co-religiosity guarantee friendly relations between authors. The opposite may be the case, two students of the same teacher can plausibly become bitter rivals. A teacher's fame seems to have been even more important than sectarian bias. Abhinavagupta, again, studied with non-Śaiva teachers, and he taught Kṣemendra, who may have been, at that time already, a convert to Vaiṣṇavism. These contradictory trends mean that not much useful information can be added to what little we know about our authors' motivations. But still, it is worth factoring even such unsatisfactory information into our considerations. Consider the following list of *maṅgala* verses found in surviving works of Sanskrit rhetorics, identifying the main deity addressed or referenced:

- Daṇḍin, *Kāvyādarśa* 1: Sarasvatī
- Bhāmaha, *Kāvyālaṃkāra* 1: Sarvajña
- Vāmana, *Kāvyālaṅkārasūtravṛtti* 1: Paramaṃ Jyotis
- Udbhaṭa, *Kāvyālaṅkārasārasaṃgraha* 1: —
- Pratīhārendurāja, *Kāvyālaṅkārasārasaṃgrahalaghuvṛtti* 1: Śauri (here sun?), 2: two feet of Gaurī[91]
- Ānandavardhana, *Sahṛdayāloka* 1: Narasiṃha
- Kuntaka, *Vakroktijīvita* 1: Śiva
- Rudraṭa, *Kāvyālaṅkāra* 1: Gaṇādhipa, 2: Gaurī's two feet
- Mammaṭa, *Kāvyaprakāśa* 1: Kaveḥ Bhāratī
- Ruyyaka, *Alaṅkārasarvasva* 1: Parā Vāc
- Abhinavagupta, *Locanā* 1: Sarasvatyās tattvam
- *Locanāmaṅgalavivṛti**: Svacchanda[92]

---

91 Final verse: *mīmāṃsāsārameghāt padajaladhividhos tarkamāṇikyakośāt sāhityaśrīmurārer budhakusumamadhoḥ śauripādābjabhṛṅgāt* | *śrutvā saujanyasindhor dvijavaramukulatkīrtivallyālavālāt kāvyālaṅkārasāre laghuvivṛtim adhāt kauṅkaṇaḥ śrīndurājaḥ* ||.

92 *Locanāmaṅgalavivṛti* 1: *upāsmahe svānubhavaikavedyaṃ svacchandam ānan-*

- Mukulabhaṭṭa, *Abhidhāvṛttimātṛkā*: —
- Ratnākara, *Dhvanigāthāpañjikā* 1: Vāgdevī
- Mahimabhaṭṭa, *Vyaktiviveka* 1: Parā Vāc, [2: Sun, Jagatpradīpa[93]]
- Śāradātanaya, *Bhāvaprakāśana* 1: Karimukha (Gaṇeśa), 2: Govinda, 3: Śiva, 4: Śāradā

The *maṅgala* verse of *AlRat* is a special case. It is not a verse that Śobhākara composed himself. Dedicated to Gaṇeśa as the sun, worshipped by Gods and demons alike, dispelling the night of impediments, it signals to the reader that Śobhākara is seeking to place his work into the tradition of the Naiyāyika Bhaṭṭa Jayanta, for it is the third verse of the *Nyāyamañjarī*.[94]

> *surāsuraśiroratnamarīcikhacitāṅghraye* |
> *vighnāndhakārasūryāya gaṇādhipataye namaḥ* || (*AlRat*1.1 = *Nyāyamañjarī* 1.3)
>
> Homage to Gaṇeśa,
> The sun to the night that is impediments,
> His feet adorned with rays
> From the crest jewels of Gods and demons.

If it is additionally significant that Śobhākara chose a verse with a solar motif, we may need to question whether this could be indeed tied to his religious identity. Were some of these authors Sauras, Bhojakas, or Śaiva worshippers of Śivasūrya?[95] The sun as the light of the world is also the recipient of praise in the second verse of the *Vyaktiviveka* of Mahimabhaṭṭa, a work on which Ruyyaka wrote a hostile commentary. It may be significant, in this context, that both the names Mahiman and Śobhākara can be interpreted as denoting the sun. The suffix *-mitra* too is commonly found with

---

dasamudram īśam | *vyāptaṃ jagacchaktitarattaraṅgair adṛṣṭapāraṃ parameṣṭhināpi* ||.

93 The first verse contains a *vastunirdeśa* statement and a salutation to supreme speech. *Vyaktiviveka* 1-2: *anumāne 'ntarbhāvaṃ sarvasyaiva dhvaneḥ prakāśayitum* | *vyaktivivekaṃ kurute praṇamya mahimā parāṃ vācam* || *yukto 'yam ātmasadṛśān prati me prayatno nāsty eva taj jagati sarvamanoharaṃ yat* | *kecij jvalanti vikasanty apare nimīlanty anye yad abhyudayabhāji* ***jagatpradīpe*** ||.

94 I thank H. Isaacson for first drawing my attention to this fact.

95 See the original *Saurasaṃhitā*, recently discovered, and currently being edited by Diwakar Acharya, for one of the few remaining original sources of sun worship.

Bhojaka names.[96] In his *AlSar*, Ruyyaka accuses Mahimabhaṭṭa of making an ill-considered statement when he alleges that suggestion can be subsumed under inference. The expression he uses is not very common: *avicāritābhidhānam*.[97] Śobhākara, in an example of śāstric repartee, redirects the same insult back to Ruyyaka when he accuses him of failing to adequately define the Assumption: *lakṣaṇam aparyālocitābhidhānam*.[98] It is conceivable that we should interpret this data as support for a conflict between a realist Naiyāyika (and Mīmāṃsaka) faction, represented by Śobhākara, who draws on the work of Bhaṭṭa Jayanta, and a non-dualist Śaiva faction represented by Abhinavagupta, Ruyyaka and Jayaratha who engage in Śāstra on the basis of Utpaladeva's *Īśvarapratyabhijñā*. Though why Śobhākara would seem to be supporting Mahimabhaṭṭa remains unclear. Only more comparative research on specific doctrinal positions and intertextuality will enable us to determine the likelihood (or not) of this scenario.

In the dispute between Ruyyaka, Śobhākara, and Jayaratha, we see how fast *alaṅkāraśāstra* can change. Uninhibited by presence of an early founding text with authoritative commentaries, it had neither a given ontology nor an epistemology to call its own. This is not because it does not need either of these, to the contrary, *alaṅkārika*s unhesitatingly borrow terminology, categories, and even entire theoretical frameworks from other schools they studied.

---

96 A Bhojaka is usually identified as a Magabrāhmaṇa who serves as an officiant in the cult of Sūrya. See HUMBACH 1978 and VON STIETENCRON 1966. Their status seems to have been contested and renegotiated several times, for example in the *Śūdrācāraśiromaṇi* of Kṛṣṇa Śeṣa a Bhojaka is said to be a member of mixed castes to the second degree. BENKE 2010 translates (p. 98): "The son of a Brahmin and a woman called a Puṣpaśekhara, is a Bhojaka by *jāti* and makes a living from worship services for Sūrya." It remain unclear whether there were Magabrāhmaṇas in Kashmir, and if there were it remains equally unclear what relation these bear to the later threefold divison of Kashmirian Brāhmaṇas into Bhaṭṭa (Guru, Bāchabat), Kārkun and Joṣī (Jotish). See WITZEL 1994 for a detailed account of what we know about the Brāhmaṇas of Kashmir.

97 *AlSar* 1: *yat tu vyaktivivekakāro vācyasya pratīyamānaṃ prati liṅgatayā vyañjanasyānumānāntarbhāvam ākhyat tad vācyasya pratīyamānena saha* (*saha*] Ed, omitted T_1T_2) *tādātmyatadutpattyabhāvād* ***avicāritābhidhānam*** | *tad etat kuśāgradhiṣaṇaiḥ kṣodanīyam atigahanam iti neha pratanyate* |.

98 *AlRat* 32: *tenādhyavasāye vyāpāraprādhānya utprekṣeti* ***lakṣaṇam aparyālocitābhidhānam*** *eva* |.

ABBREVIATIONS

conj. = conjecture
corr. = correction
em. = emendation
om. = omitted
kiṃ{ci}t = deleted akṣaras
⟨*kiṃcit*⟩ = text supplied by editor
\+ = illegible akṣaras
kiṃ[ci]t = square brackets indicate partly legible akṣaras

REFERENCES

Āgamaḍambara 2005
Much ado about religion by Bhatta Jayánta, ed. and transl. Cs. Dezső, New York et al.: Clay Sanskrit Library, 2005

Abhidhāvṛttimātṛkā
Abhidhāvṛttimātṛkā, ed. and transl. K. Venugopalan, *Journal of Indian Philosophy* 4, 1977, pp. 203-264

AlRat
[*Alaṅkāraratnākara*] See P_{Ed} and K_R

AlSar
[*Alaṅkārasarvasva*] See KM_{ED}, K_{SV} and J_{ED}

BALA 2006
A. Bala, *The Dialogue of Civilizations in the Birth of Modern Science,* New York: Palgrave Macmillan, 2006

BENKE 2010
T. Benke, *The Śūdrācāraśiromaṇi of Kṛṣṇa Śeṣa: a 16th Century Manual of Dharma for Śūdras*, PhD dissertation, Philadelphia, 2010

BRONNER 2011
Y. Bronner, "A Question of Priority: Revisiting the Bhāmaha-Daṇḍin Debate," *Journal of Indian Philosophy* 40(1), 2011, pp. 67-118

CLAUSON 1912
G.L.M. Clauson, "Catalogue of the Stein Collection of Sanskrit mss. from Kashmir," *Journal of the Royal Asiatic Society*, 1912, pp. 587-627

DUBEY 1982
K. Dubey, *Śobhākara Mitra's Alaṅkāraratnākara: A Study*, PhD dissertation, Gorakhpur: 1982

FRESCHI AND KATAOKA 2012
E. Freschi and K. Kataoka, "Jayanta on the validity of sacred texts (other than the Veda)," *South Asian Classical Studies* 7, 2012, pp. 1-55

Gāhākosa
Gāhākosa: Das Saptaśatakam des Hāla, ed. A. Weber, Leipzig: Abhandlungen für die Kunde des Morgenlandes, Deutsche Morgenländische Gesellschaft 7(4), 1881

Gītārthasaṃgraha
Gītārthasaṃgraha. Śrībhagavadgītā with the Commentary by Abhinavagupta, ed. Lakṣmaṇa Raina Brahmacārī, Srinagar: Kashmir Pratap Steam Press, 1933

GNOLI 1962
R. Gnoli, *Udbhaṭa's commentary on the "Kāvyālaṃkāra" of Bhāmaha*, Rome: Istituto Italiano per il Medio ed Estremo Oriente, 1962

HALBFASS 1986-1992
W. Halbfass, "Observations on the Relationship between Vedic Exegesis and Philosophical Reflection," *Journal of Oriental Research* 56-62, 1986-1992, pp. 31-40

Harṣacarita
Śrīharṣacaritamahākāvyam, Bâṇabhaṭṭa's Biography of King Harshavardhana of Sthâṇîśvara, with Śaṅkara's commentary, Saṅketa, ed. A.A. Führer, Bombay: Government Central Press, Bombay Sanskrit and Prakrit Series 66, 1909

HUMBACH 1978
H. Humbach, "Mithra in India and the Hinduized Magi," in J. Duchesne-Guillemin (ed.), *Études mithriaques: Actes du 2e Congrès international [d'études mithriaques], Téhéran, du 1er au 8 septembre 1975*, Leiden: Brill, 1978, pp. 229-255

JED
Alaṅkārasarvasva of Ruyyaka, with Sañjīvanī Commentary of Vidyācakravartin, text and study S.S. Janaki, ed. V. Raghavan, Delhi: 1965

Ka
[Manuscript mentioned in KM_{Ed}] See KM_{Ed}

KATAOKA 2007
K. Kataoka, "Critical Edition of the *Śāstrārambha* Section of Bhaṭṭa Jayanta's *Nyāyamañjarī*," *The Memoirs of the Institute of Oriental Culture* 150, 2007, 204[123]-170[157]

Kāvyādarśa
Kāvyalakṣaṇa of Daṇḍin with the commentary Ratnaśrī of Ratnaśrījñāna, ed. A. Thakur and U. Jha, Darbhanga: Mithila Institute, 1957

Kāvyālaṅkāra (Bhāmaha)
Kāvyālaṃkāra of Bhāmaha, ed. B.N. Śarmā and B. Upādhyāya, [Varanasi: Kāśī Sanskrit Series 61, 1928] repr. Varanasi: Chaukhambha Sanskrit Sansthan, 1981

Kāvyālaṅkāra (Rudraṭa)
Rudraṭa's Kāvyālaṃkāra with Namisādhu's commentary, ed. Paṇḍita Durgāprasāda and K.P. Paraba, Bombay: Kāvyamālā 2, 1886

Kāvyālaṅkārasārasaṅgraha
Kāvyālaṅkārasārasaṅgraha of Udbhaṭa, with commentary by Indurāja, ed. N.D. Banhatti, 2nd ed., Poona: Bhandarkar Oriental Research Institute, Bombay Sanskrit and Prakrit Series 79, 1982

Kāvyaprakāśa
Śrīmammaṭabhaṭṭapraṇītaḥ Kāvyaprakāśaḥ, ed. R. Harihaśāstri, Trivandrum: Trivandrum Sanskrit Series 88, 1926

KAWAJIRI 2011
Y. Kawajiri, "A critique of the Buddhist theory of *adhyavasāya* in the Pratyabhijñā school," in H. Krasser, H. Lasic, E. Franco and B. Kellner (eds), *Religion and Logic in Buddhist Philosophical Analysis. Proceedings of the Fourth International Dharmakīrti Conference. Vienna, August 23-27, 2005,* Wien: Verlag der Österreichischen Akademie der Wissenschaften, 2011, pp. 255-269

Kha
[Manuscript mentioned in KMEd] See KMEd

KMEd
Alaṅkārasarvasva of Ruyyaka with the Vimarśinī commentary of Jayaratha, ed. G. Dvivedi, Bombay: Kāvyamālā 35, 1893

KR
[Manuscript] *Alaṅkāraratnākara* of Śobhākareśvaramitra, Śāradā on birchbark, ca. 17th cent. Digital color photographs of Bodleian library, Oxford, MS Sansk D87 (kindly provided by Michael Slouber)

KRISHNAMACHARYAR 1937
M. Krishnamacharyar, *History of classical Sanskrit literature* [Madras: 1937] Delhi: Motilal Banarsidass, 1970

KSV
[Manuscript] *Alaṅkārasarvasvavimarśinī*, Śāradā on paper, 19th cent. Digital color photographs of Bodleian library, Oxford, MS Sansk D21 (kindly provided by Michael Slouber)[99]

99 Bound in suede deerhide; ff. 38-144; ll. 24; *akṣaras* per line 25; 25.3*17.3cm; inscribed area 10.1* 18.5cm; rubrication; folios numbered in bottom left of the rectos; sometimes substantial marginal notes and corrections secunda manu upto *fol.* 86r; interlinear Sanskrit paraphrase *(chāyā)* for Prakrit passages; the *khaḍgabandha* is illustrated in the left margin of *fol.* 60r. Clauson records: "In Pt. Sāhibrā's handwriting. Purchased in 1894 from **Śaṅkara Rājānaka** [M.A.S.]. Explicit on fol. 144v l. 18: ‖ 87 ‖ *rājarāja iti bhūbhujām abhūd*

*Locanamaṅgalavivṛti**
[Manuscript] *Locanamaṅgalavivṛti**, MS Welcome MS No. δ 58, Śāradā on Kashmirian paper, Welcome Institute for the History of Medicine, London

McCREA 1998
L. McCrea, *The Teleology of Poetics in Medieval Kashmir*, [PhD Dissertation, University of Chicago, 1998] published version, Cambridge (Mass.): Harvard University Press, Harvard Oriental Series 71, 2009

Nyāyabindu
Dharmottarapradīpa (being a sub-commentary on Dharmottara's Nyāyabinduṭīkā, a commentary on Dharmakīrti's Nyāyabindu), ed. D. Malvania, Patna: Kashi Prasad Jayaswal Research Institute, 1955

Nyāyamañjarī
Nyāyamañjarī of Jayantabhaṭṭa, ed. K.S. Varadacharya, 2 vols., Mysore: Oriental Research Institute, 1969

Nyāyasūtra
Gautamīyanyāyadarśana with Bhāṣya of Vātsyāyana, Nyāyacaturgranthikā, volume I, ed. A. Thakur, New Delhi: Indian Council of Philosophical Research, 1997

PARTHASARATHY RAO 1992
G. Parthasarathy Rao, *Alankāraratnākara of Śobhākaramitra, a study,* New Delhi: Mittal Publications, 1992

P_{Ed}
Alaṅkāraratnākara of Śobhākaramitra, ed. C.R. Devadhar, Poona: Poona Oriental Series 77, 1942

Pramāṇavārttika
"*Pramāṇavārttika-kārikā (Sanskrit and Tibetan)*," ed. Y. Miyasaka, *Acta Indologica* 2, 1971-1972, pp. 1-206

Pramāṇavārttika (*svārthānumāna* chapter)
The Pramāṇavārttikam of Dharmakīrti. The First Chapter with the Autocommentary, ed. R. Gnoli, Roma: Istituto Italiano per il Medio ed Estremo Oriente, Serie Orientale Roma 23, 1960

---

agraṇīr guṇigaṇāśrayaḥ param tāṃsatī sarasirājahaṃsatāmātanotkalighanāgame pi vaḥ ‖ śaktādhikaśriyas tasya śrīśṛṅgāra iti śrutaḥ guṇātikrāntadhiṣaṇo mantriṇām agraṇīr abhūt ‖ tadātmajanmā vaidagdhyabandhur jayarathābhidhaḥ vyadhād idam asāmānyaṃ śravaṇābharaṇaṃ satām ‖ yan nāma kiñ cid iha samyag athānyathā vāmākṣādalaṅkṛtinayocitamateduktam vidveṣaroṣam apasārya budhaiḥ kṣaṇasya tatrāvadheyam iyataiva vayaṃ kṛtārthāḥ ‖ pūrṇeyam (fol. 144[r]) *alaṅkāravimarśinī kṛtis tatrabhavato rājānakaśrīśṛṅgāraputrarājānakaśrījayarathasyeti śubham ‖ ‖.*

Pramāṇavārttikavṛtti
Pramāṇavārttikam of ācārya Dharmakīrti, with the commentaries Svopajñavṛtti of the author and Pramāṇavārttikavṛtti of Manorathanandin, ed. R.C. Pandeya, Delhi: Motilal Banarsidass, 1989

Pramāṇaviniścaya
Dharmakīrti's Pramāṇaviniścaya, Chapters 1 and 2, ed. E. Steinkellner, Beijing/ Vienna: China Tibetology Publishing House/Austrian Academy of Sciences Press, 2007

RATIÉ 2010
I. Ratié, "'A five-trunked, four-tusked elephant is running is the sky' – How free is imagination according to Utpaladeva and Abhinavagupta?", *Études Asiatiques/ Asiatische Studien* 64(2), 2010, pp. 341-385

SEWELL AND BĀLKRIṢṆA DĪKṢIT 1896
R. Sewell and Ś. Bālkriṣṇa Dīkṣit, *The Indian Calendar, with tables for the conversion of Hindu and Muhammadan into A.D. dates, and vice versa*, London: Swan Sonnenschein & Co, 1896

SHARMA 1972
B. Sharma, *Traditions of Alaṅkāraśāstra: The Contribution of Śobhākaramitra*, PhD dissertation, Banaras: 1972

SHULMAN 2012
D. Shulman, *More Than Real: A History of the Imagination in South India*, Cambridge (Mass.): Harvard University Press, 2012

Śrīkaṇṭhacarita
Śrīkaṇṭhacarita of Maṅkhaka with the Commentary of Jonarāja, ed. Paṇḍita Durgâprasâda and Kâśînâtha Pâṇḍuranga Paraba, Bombay: Kāvyamālā 3, 1887

Subhāṣitaratnakośa
Subhāṣitaratnakośa of Vidyākara, ed. D.D. Kosambi and V.V. Gokhale, Cambridge (Mass.): Harvard Oriental Series 42, 1957

Subhāṣitāvali
Subhāṣitāvali of Vallabhadeva, ed. P. Peterson, Bombay: Bombay Sanskrit Series 31, 1886

Svacchandatantra
The Swacchanda-Tantra with commentary by Kshemarāja, ed. M.K. Shāstrī, 7 vols., Bombay: Kashmir Series of Texts and Studies, 1921-1935

Tarkabhāṣā
Tarkabhāṣā of Mokṣākaragupta, ed. E. Krishnamacharyya, Baroda: Oriental Institute, Gaekwad Oriental Series 94, 1942

Vākyapadīya
Bhartṛharis Vākyapadīya: Die Mūlakārikās nach den Handschriften herausgegeben und mit einem Pāda-Index versehen, ed. W. Rau, Wiesbaden: 1977

Vakroktijīvita
Vakroktijīvita of Kuntaka, ed. K. Krishnamoorthy, Dharwad: Karnatak University, 1977

Vimarśinī
[*Alaṅkārasarvasvavimarśinī*] See *AlSar*

Vyaktiviveka
Vyaktiviveka of Mahimabhaṭṭa, with the commentary of Ruyyaka, ed. R. Dwivedī, Varanasi: Chaukhambha Sanskrit Sansthan, Kashi Sanskrit Series 121, 1998

VON STIETENCRON 1966
H. von Stietencron, *Indische Sonnenpriester: Sāmba und die Śākadvīpīya-Brāhmaṇa: eine textkritische und religionsgeschichtliche Studie zum indischen Sonnenkult*, Wiesbaden: Otto Harrassowitz Schriftenreihe des Südasien-Instituts der Universität Heidelberg 3, 1966

WITZEL 1994
M. Witzel, "The Brahmins of Kashmir," in Y. Ikari, (ed.), *A Study of Nīlamata – Aspects of Hinduism in Ancient Kashmir*, Kyoto: Kyoto University, 1994, pp. 237-294

Helārāja on Omniscience, *Āgama*, and the Origin of Language*

VINCENZO VERGIANI

In the late first millennium CE, approximately at the same period that saw the rise of the Pratyabhijñā school of non-dualist Śaivism on the Indian philosophical scene, Kashmir was also home to Helārāja's composition of a complete commentary, consisting of two distinct works,[1] on Bhartṛhari's *Vākyapadīya* (henceforth, VP).[2] Only one of these survives, the *Prakīrṇaprakāśa* (henceforth, PrPr) on the third *kāṇḍa*.[3] As I have remarked in a recent publication,[4] it

---

* I touched on some of the issues discussed here in the paper I read at the conference "Around Abhinavagupta. Aspects of the Intellectual History of Kashmir from the 9th to the 11th Centuries," held in Leipzig in June 2013. I wish to thank the organisers, Eli Franco and Isabelle Ratié, for inviting me to that very stimulating event and for their warm hospitality. I also wish to express my gratitude to Raffaele Torella, Daniele Cuneo and Hugo David, who have provided helpful comments on an earlier draft of this article, and, in the case of Torella, also suggested an emendation to one of the passages I quote below. Needless to say, I alone am responsible for all remaining faults.

1 Or possibly three, because it is not clear whether the commentary on the first two books consisted of one or two distinct works. This text is now lost. As pointed out by Subramania Iyer (VP 3.1, p. xi), the *Śabdaprabhā*, to which Helārāja refers under *Jātisamuddeśa* 37 (VP 3.1, p. 45, l. 3), was his commentary on the first *kāṇḍa*. Another mention of the *Śabdaprabhā* (VP 3.1, p. 54, l. 9) is found in the commentary on *Jātisamuddeśa* 46, which I examine in detail here.

2 In the verses at the end of the *Prakīrṇaprakāśa* Helārāja himself says that he belongs to an illustrious lineage of Kashmiri Brahmins. See SUBRAMANIA IYER 1969, pp. 39-40.

3 Helārāja mentions his commentary on the first two *kāṇḍa*s of the VP in the second and third *maṅgalaśloka*s of PrPr: *kāṇḍadvaye yathāvṛtti siddhāntārthasatattvataḥ | prabandho vihito 'smābhir āgamārthānusāribhiḥ || taccheṣabhūte kāṇḍe 'smin saprapañce svarūpataḥ | ślokārthadyotanaparaḥ prakāśo 'yaṃ vidhīyate ||*. For a translation and discussion of these verses see VERGIANI 2014. I will examine the first *maṅgalaśloka* below, § 9.

4 See VERGIANI 2014.

seems likely that the appearance in mediaeval Kashmir of the first known complete commentary on the VP should be somehow linked to the key role that Bhartṛhari's views came to play in the philosophy of the Pratyabhijñā, and possibly to the change of fortune the grammarian-philosopher underwent, from an adversary for Somānanda to the main ally for Utpaladeva, to use Torella's phrase.[5] To what extent Helārāja shared the religious and philosophical outlook of Pratyabhijñā and consciously played a role in its appropriation of Bhartṛhari's ideas is unclear. In this article, I will examine one passage of Helārāja's only surviving work, the PrPr, in an effort to shed light on this somewhat elusive figure.[6]

The passage I examine in this article is Helārāja's commentary on VP 3.1.46, a verse of the *Jātisamuddeśa*, the first chapter of the third book of the VP. The PrPr on this *kārikā* contains an unusually extensive discussion of two topics – omniscience and scriptural authority – which at first sight may seem to be only tenuously related to the content of Bhartṛhari's verse. In dealing with these topics, which, as is known,[7] became pivotal to the Indian philosophical and religious debate in the second half of the first millennium CE, Helārāja literally packs the passage, which I will analyse in depth in the following pages, with quotations from various authoritative brahmanical works and indirect references to several others.[8]

The backdrop of Helārāja's treatment of these topics is the emergence, in the early first millennium CE, of two conflicting religio-philosophical visions within Brahmanism, one centred on the Veda and the other on a personal God. The former view, advocated by Mīmāṃsā, claims that the Veda is eternal and uncreated (*apau-*

---

5 On the Pratyabhijñā's reception of Bhartṛhari's ideas see TORELLA 2002, esp. p. xxv, and TORELLA 2008.

6 I will occasionally point to echoes and parallels between Helārāja's views and those found in the works of the Pratyabhijñā authors, but with no claim to being exhaustive or exploring them in depth. A systematic investigation of this theme will hopefully be the subject of a future publication.

7 In the centuries that lapsed between Bhartṛhari's and Helārāja's times the question of omniscience acquired great prominence in the religious and philosophical debates of early mediaeval India. On the significance of this important development, see e.g. FRANCO 2009, MCCLINTOCK 2010, TORELLA 2012, the various contributions in ELTSCHINGER AND KRASSER 2013, and MORIYAMA 2014.

8 Here I have tried to identify as many as possible of these allusions, but I am afraid that I may have missed just as many.

ruṣeya) and, precisely because of its total otherness from the world of men, it represents their only reliable guidance in the pursuit of transcendental goals – in short, the realisation of *dharma* through the correct performance of the prescribed rites. And, as a logical corollary of the eternality of the Veda, the Mīmāṃsakas claim that the language of the sacred texts (Sanskrit) is also eternal, namely, that there is a natural fixed relation between words and the objects or actions they designate. In their system there is no place for a creator God, since the universe is regarded as immutable, without beginning or end, and the righteousness of the customs and beliefs of the Āryas – in one word, the *varṇāśramadharma* – as codified in the traditional body of textual knowledge collectively known as Smṛti rests on the allegedly uninterrupted transmission of this knowledge, which claims to be based on the Vedas, from time immemorial through generation after generation of brahmins.

While similarly declaring its allegiance to the Veda, the other view, voiced by brahmanical systems such as Yoga and, notably, Nyāya-Vaiśeṣika,[9] attributes a central role to God (Īśvara), who is said to possess qualities such as knowledge (*jñāna*) and sovereignty (*aiśvarya*)[10] and is considered responsible for the periodical creation and destruction of the world. It is God who issues the Veda and, crucially, at the beginning of each creation cycle teaches it to the *ṛṣi*s who partake of his omniscience thanks to the merit they have gained through ascetic practices and meditation (presumably in previous lives). God is also responsible for instituting language, as it is he who establishes the convention (*samaya*) that links words to objects/meanings.

The above is a very broadly painted sketch of complex views with far-reaching religious and theoretical implications and much internal variation and has no claim to exhaustiveness. Nevertheless, it should help to situate Helārāja's ideas in a clearer historical

---

[9] As is known (see EIPh, p. 100), the seminal *sūtra*s of the latter two schools are distinctly non-theistic, but the shift towards theism is already evident in the works of the earliest commentators, namely Pakṣilasvāmin and Uddyotakara (Nyāya, probably 5th and 6th c. CE respectively) and Praśastapāda (Vaiśeṣika, 6th c. CE). On these developments in some brahmanical systems, see also MORIYAMA 2014, pp. 29f.

[10] On God's attributes according to Praśastapāda, see CHEMPARATHY 1968, pp. 72-73, which also contains the translation of a passage in the *Padārthadharmasaṃgraha* describing Īśvara's role in the creation and dissolution of the universe.

perspective. As I will show below, much of what he writes in the commentary on VP 3.1.46 can be traced back to Bhartṛhari's own work, but in other respects he is heavily indebted to ideas formulated by representatives of the two major theistic brahmanical schools of the time, Yoga and the already mentioned Nyāya-Vaiśeṣika, although he often reinterprets these ideas in his own original way. It seems to me, in fact, that Helārāja's commentary on VP 3.1.46, occurring as it does in the initial chapter of the PrPr, is a key passage (though undoubtedly not the only one) meant to establish the theoretical and ideological frame of the whole work and to demonstrate the possibility of incorporating Bhartṛhari's views into a theistic philosophical horizon, in contrast to Mīmāṃsā, whose positions on *āgama* and omniscience are explicitly challenged here by Helārāja.

In the next paragraph I will look at some of the evidence in the VP (especially in the first *kāṇḍa*) that testifies to Bhartṛhari's views on Vedic revelation and omniscience. Taken together, these passages, which Helārāja had certainly commented upon in the lost *Śabdaprabhā*, form the backbone of his argument in PrPr ad VP 3.1.46, and the foundation on which he builds the argument in order to promote his own philosophical agenda.

1. AN EARLY PHILOSOPHICAL ACCOUNT OF VEDIC REVELATION

The earliest non-mythological treatment of Vedic revelation is possibly found in *Nirukta* 1.20, a passage that is quoted in the *Vṛtti* on VP 1.5. These, together with another passage of the first *kāṇḍa* consisting of VP 1.173 with the *Vṛtti*, which also deals with Vedic revelation, the relation between Śruti and Smṛti, and the role of *ṛṣi*s in their transmission to mankind, are discussed in great depth by Aklujkar in an important article published in 2009. Even though Helārāja makes no direct reference to either VP passage, one may reasonably assume that he had them in mind when writing the commentary on VP 3.1.46 because he quotes the same passage from the *Nirukta* and further cites VP 1.172 (discussed below), a verse underscoring the uninterrupted transmission of both Śruti and Smṛti, which leads to the second VP passage that speaks of the Vedic revelation.

These VP passages predate most of (or possibly all) the other accounts of Vedic revelation to which Helārāja refers in the PrPr ad VP 3.1.46. It is worth presenting them in their entirety here (with Aklujkar's translations), since from a historical and theoretical vantage point they constitute the starting point of Helārāja's original synthesis.

The first passage, containing the *Nirukta* quotation, occurs in the VPVṛ ad 1.5,[11] and comments, or rather elaborates, on the term *anukāra* used in the verse:

> About to reveal to those others who have not discovered the [ordinarily imperceptible] properties[12] of things that subtle, eternal and sense-transcending [form of] speech which they [themselves] behold, the seers who have discovered the properties of things [and] to whom *mantras*[13] appear set down for transmission an image (*bilmam*), as they wish to convey, like something that happened in a dream, what they experienced through sighting and hearing. This is ancient [or traditionally handed down] lore.[14] Indeed, [another reliable or respectable source, the *Nirukta*] says: "There came about [or there were at a distant time] seers who had discovered the properties of things. Through instruction, they have entrusted *mantras* to others who had not discovered the properties of things. The others, experiencing fatigue toward instruction, have set down for transmission this corpus [i.e. the Nighaṇṭu, Nirukta, etc.] and the Veda and the Veda ancillaries in order to grasp the image. [The word] *bilma* is [to be thought of as] *bhilma* or [as] *bhāsana*."[15]

---

[11] The verse reads: *prāptyupāyo 'nukāraṃ ca tasya vedo maharṣibhiḥ | eko 'py anekavartmeva samāmnātaḥ pṛthak pṛthak* ||. "The means of reaching and the representative likeness of that [*śabda-tattva*] is Veda. It is set down for transmission severally by the great seers as if it has more than one path, although it is one." (Transl. AKLUJKAR 2009, p. 6.)

[12] For the translation of *dharma* in the compound *sākṣātkṛtadharmāṇo* with "property," see AKLUJKAR 2009, pp. 15f.

[13] I have taken the liberty to modify Aklujkar's translation in a few places (which I indicate in footnotes) for the sake of readability, but respecting the spirit of his renderings. Here I have re-introduced the Sanskrit term *mantra*, which for very good reasons Aklujkar translates with the phrase "materially effective speech formations." Despite the loss of accuracy, I think it safe to assume most Indologists know the meaning of *mantra*.

[14] Aklujkar translates *purākalpa* with "thought formulation (or systematized knowledge)." On *purākalpa* as the name of a text (or class of texts), see AKLUJKAR 2009, p. 24.

[15] *yāṃ sūkṣmāṃ nityām atīndriyāṃ vācam ṛṣayaḥ sākṣātkṛtadharmāṇo mantradṛśaḥ paśyanti tām asākṣātkṛtadharmabhyaḥ parebhyaḥ pravedayiṣyamāṇā bilmaṃ samāmananti, svapnavṛttam iva dṛṣṭasmṛtānubhūtam ācikhyāsanta ity eṣa purākalpaḥ. āha khalv api: "sākṣātkṛtadharmāṇa ṛṣayo babhūvuḥ. te 'pa-*

A very similar but somewhat more detailed account is found in VPVṛ 1.173.[16] The verse reads:

> *avibhāgād vivṛttānām abhikhyā svapnavac chrutau |*
> *bhāvatattvaṃ tu vijñāya liṅgebhyo vihitā smṛtiḥ ||*

> Those [*ṛṣi*s] who evolve from the [ultimate] unity [namely, *brahman*] come to know the Śruti as [ordinary persons come to know something] in a dream. As for the Smṛti, it is fashioned on the basis of the indications [in the Śruti] after knowing the real nature of things.

The *Vṛtti* remarks:

> The inherited view (*āgama*) of those who think that the [original] cause constantly [that is, again and again] proceeds forth [to create] in the manner of sleeping and waking up, fashioning itself after the individual persons [or the distinct *puruṣa*s] is this: some seers come about as a multiplicity in the unitary entity *pratibhā* [that is, at a stage which is just one step short of reaching *brahman* (...)]. They, seeing that [*pratibhātman* which is the same as] *mahat ātman*, the one characterized by Being [alone, that is, the one which is the undifferentiated or highest-level existence], matrix of nescience, join that [*pratibhātman*] through awakening [that is, through advanced awareness (...)]. Some [seers], on the other hand, come about as a multiplicity in *vidyā*. They, likewise, join the *ātman* that has the knot of the mind [that is, the *ātman* equipped and delimited for engagement with the world and that, yet, remains] pure [and] conception-free with respect to the elements ether etc., taken jointly or severally. Their adventitious,[17] nescience-based interaction [with the world] is not literally so [that is, it can be predicated of them only through a transfer of ordinary persons' attributes to them]. What is constant, intrinsic and primary [to them] is [their] *vidyā*-nature. They see [our] traditionally handed down text in its entirety with insight alone as one would hear in sleep a word [sound] inaccessible to the sense of hearing – [the text] having all the powers of differentiation and having the powers inseparable [from itself, i.e. the subtle form of the authoritative

---

rebhyo 'sākṣātkṛtadharmabhya upadeśena mantrān samprāduḥ. upadeśāya glāyanto 'pare bilmagrahaṇāyemaṃ granthaṃ samāmnāsiṣur vedaṃ ca vedāṅgāni ca. bilmaṃ bhilmaṃ bhāsanam iti veti. (Sanskrit text as given in AKLUJKAR 2008, p. 6; transl. ibid., pp. 24-26.)

[16] The following Sanskrit texts and translations (with a few minor modifications) are from AKLUJKAR 2009, pp. 29-31.

[17] Here the text in AKLUJKAR 2009, p. 30 reads "adventious," which I assume is a misprint for "adventitious" (Skt. *āgantu*).

> Veda]. Some [of them], additionally, having ascertained the nature of specific entities as it concerns the helping or harming of humans and having seen indications to that effect in some parts of the traditionally received texts, compose the Smṛti, meant for the mundane and non-mundane objects. As for the Śruti, they set [it] down for transmission as it was seen [in the experience described above], without a change of wording [or sound] whatsoever – initially, undivided [i.e. as a single corpus], later incorporating the *caraṇa* division.[18]

I need not go here into a detailed analysis of these passages (for which see AKLUJKAR 2009), but I would like to draw attention to a few points that are relevant to the topic of this article. While subscribing – as one would expect – to the dogma of the eternal and uncreated nature of the Veda, Bhartṛhari (following in the footsteps of the distant precedent set by Yāska and of countless mythological narratives) introduces a quasi historical dimension into the account of the rise and transmission of the brahmanical tradition by identifying a starting point for the process, in which the Vedic seers, the *ṛṣi*s, play the role first of recipients of the primordial Revelation (*śruti*) and then of authors of the *smṛti*s and teachers of later generations. In the case of the Śruti, they act as simple receptacles and transmitters of the Vedic text as it appears to them in their primordial experience (*śrutiṃ tu yathādarśanam avyabhicaritaśabdām eva... samāmananti*) without making any intervention of their own. On the contrary, their agency is a crucial element in the production of the Smṛti texts, which the *ṛṣi*s themselves compose on the basis of the indications they find in the Veda, and which rest on their perception of the true nature of things (*teṣāṃ teṣām arthānāṃ svabhāvam upalabhya*); their purpose is to help men pursue what is useful and avoid what is harmful (*puruṣānugrahopaghāta-*

---

18 *yeṣāṃ tu svapnaprabodhavṛttyā nityaṃ vibhaktapuruṣānukāritayā kāraṇaṃ pravartate teṣām ṛṣayaḥ kecit pratibhātmani vivartante. te* [*taṃ*] *sattālakṣaṇaṃ mahāntam ātmānam avidyāyoniṃ paśyantaḥ pratibodhenābhisambhavanti. kecit tu vidyāyāṃ vivartante. te manogranthim ātmānam ākāśādiṣu bhūteṣu, pratyekaṃ samuditeṣu vā, viśuddham anibaddhaparikalpaṃ tathaivābhisambhavanti. teṣāṃ cāgantur avidyāvyavahāraḥ sarva evaupacārikaḥ. vidyātmakatvaṃ tu nityam anāgantukaṃ mukhyam. te ca, svapna ivāśrotragamyaṃ śabdaṃ, prajñayaiva sarvam āmnāyaṃ sarvabhedaśaktiyuktam abhinnaśaktiyuktaṃ ca paśyanti. kecit tu puruṣānugrahopaghātaviṣayaṃ teṣāṃ teṣām arthānāṃ svabhāvam upalabhyāmnāyeṣu kvacit tadviṣayāṇi* </*tat-tad-*> *liṅgāni dṛṣṭvā ca dṛṣṭādṛṣṭārthāṃ smṛtim upanibadhnanti. śrutiṃ tu yathādarśanam avyabhicaritaśabdām eva, prathamam avibhaktāṃ punaḥ saṅgṛhītacaraṇavibhāgāṃ, samāmanantīty āgamaḥ.*

viṣayaṃ) for goals that, interestingly, may be either mundane or trans-empirical (*dṛṣṭādṛṣṭārthāṃ*). It is also remarkable that Bhartṛhari is completely silent on the process of creation or emanation of the physical world, and in particular of human beings. His narrative is really about the coming into being of the brahmanical tradition centred on the Veda. The beginning of VPVṛ 1.137 (*svapna-prabodhavṛttyā nityaṃ vibhaktapuruṣānukāritayā kāraṇaṃ pravartate*...) suggests that this process is repeated cyclically.[19] It is also worth noting that, despite the central place language occupies in his philosophy, not only epistemologically but also ontologically, Bhartṛhari makes no specific mention of the origin of the relation between words and meanings. This silence presumably implies that for him the relation linking certain sequences of sounds to certain objects in the universe is a given that the primordial sages "perceive" in the received text, and then they pass this knowledge to their descendants.

It is evident that in this account of Vedic revelation and the beginning of brahmanical tradition the extraordinary cognitive capacities of the seers play a key role. The manifestation of the Veda from the ultimate undivided *śabdabrahman* is an unexplained (and possibly, in Bhartṛhari's eyes, inexplicable) event that is not meant, ostensibly, for the instruction and salvation of creatures, since there is no subject intentionally acting as teacher. The seers, who themselves issue from the same ultimate reality, as pointed out in VP 1.173 (*avibhāgād vivṛttānām*), could not possibly receive the sacred text or draw the teachings they then hand down in the Smṛti if they were not endowed somehow with exceptional capacities. How did these capacities arise? A hemistich from the first kāṇḍa (VP 1.30cd), also quoted by Helārāja under VP 3.1.46,[20] suggests that the seers's knowledge is also founded on *āgama*: *ṛṣīṇām api yaj jñānaṃ tad apy āgamapūrvakam*, "Even in the case of seers, knowledge is preceded by inherited knowledge."[21] However, this is not purely intellectual knowledge, as is clarified in the *Vṛtti*:

---

[19] On Bhartṛhari's likely belief in the cyclical creation of the universe, see the remarks in AKLUJKAR 2009, p. 63.

[20] The context of the quotation in the PrPr (see PrPr 1, p. 54, ll. 23-24) is examined below, § 7.

[21] The text and translation of this verse and of the following *Vṛtti* are from AKLUJKAR 2010, pp. 405-406.

> Even in those mutually differing schools in which we hear the talk of some extraordinary human quality, impervious to reasoning,[22] the seers' knowledge of this or that thing, [to the extent it is] born of a mystical or transforming experience,[23] is said to occur when the seers' personalities are modified by a quality found [i.e. recommended for cultivation] in the *āgama*.[24]

Thus, the seers' superior (*anuttaraḥ*) kind of cognition is born from the cultivation of certain human qualities (*puruṣadharmaḥ*) with the support of traditional knowledge, and therefore, one can infer, it is not intrinsically different from ordinary cognition, but rather a potentiated version of the latter.[25] Significantly, in VP 1.172, quoted by Helārāja under VP 3.1.46,[26] Bhartṛhari refers to the hallowed authors of the Smṛti with the term *śiṣṭa*:

> *anādim avyavacchinnāṃ śrutim āhur akartṛkām |*
> *śiṣṭair nibadhyamānā tu na vyavacchidyate smṛtiḥ ||*

> They say that the Śruti is without beginning, uninterrupted, authorless, but the Smṛti, composed by *śiṣṭa*s, is [equally] unbroken.

No clear distinction is made, seemingly, between the two figures, but the role played by the former in the Vedic revelation and the association of the latter (for example in the *Mahābhāṣya*[27]) with

---

22 Aklujkar translates *tarkātītaḥ* with "impervious to (common) ways of making sense."

23 With the clause "to the extent it is born of a mystical or transforming experience" Aklujkar translates the single Sanskrit word *ārṣam* in an effort to capture its complex implications.

24 *yeṣv api tarkātītaḥ pṛthagvidyācaraṇaparigraheṣu kaścid anuttaraḥ puruṣadharmaḥ śrūyate, teṣv api* [*tat*]*tadarthajñānam ārṣam ṛṣīṇām āgamikenaiva dharmeṇa saṃskṛtātmanām āvirbhavatīty ākhyāyate.*

25 As will be shown below, this is one of the controversial issues that oppose Mīmāṃsā to those thinkers, such as Helārāja, who uphold the existence of omniscient beings.

26 Introduced with the words *uktaṃ brahmakāṇḍe* (see PrPr 1, p. 53, ll. 20-23; note that the verse number given there is wrong, since in Subramania Iyer's own edition of the first *kāṇḍa* the *kārikā* is numbered 136).

27 See MBh ad A. 6.3.109 (vol. III, p. 174, ll. 4-10): *ke punaḥ śiṣṭāḥ. vaiyākaraṇāḥ. kuta etat. śāstrapūrvikā hi śiṣṭir vaiyākaraṇāś ca śāstrajñāḥ. yadi tarhi śāstrapūrvikā śiṣṭiḥ śiṣṭipūrvakaṃ ca śāstraṃ tad itaretarāśrayaṃ bhavati. itaretarāśrayāṇi ca na prakalpante. evaṃ tarhi nivāsato ācārataś ca. sa cācāra āryāvartta eva. kaḥ punar āryāvarttaḥ. prāg ādarśāt pratyak kālakavanād dakṣiṇena himavantam uttareṇa pāriyātram. etasminn āryanivāse ye brāhmaṇāḥ*

contemporary brahmins excelling in virtue and learning – all the more idealised as they are vaguely identified – suggests that for Bhartṛhari omniscience is not just a quality associated with certain legendary individuals in a remote past but something that even his contemporary may possibly achieve. The same blurring of boundaries between *ṛṣi*s, yogis and *śiṣṭa*s is observed in other places in the VP that are discussed below, including VP 3.1.46, to which I now turn.

One caveat is required, however, before embarking on the examination of this *kārikā* and the commentary thereon. One of the challenging aspects of this passage is that often the philosophical and theological arguments voiced by Helārāja appear very terse or dense or both, and the logical links between one step in the reasoning and the next are not always as clear as one may wish because the author does not spell them out. The explanation for that is to be found in something Helārāja says towards the end of the passage, where he informs his readers that he has discussed the topic of omniscience in depth in his commentary on the first *kāṇḍa* and refers them back to it:

> Thus, by means of the first half [of the verse], [Bhartṛhari] has indicated here that omniscience has been proved on the basis of the authority of traditional sources. I have myself [dealt with and] settled [the topic of] the authority of *āgama* at length in the *Śabdaprabhā* on the first *kāṇḍa* of the VP, therefore one should draw the conclusion on the basis of that [discussion].[28]

In light of this statement, one should therefore regard PrPr on VP 3.1.46 as a kind of digest of a presumably much more articulated treatment of *āgama* and related topics that was found in Helārāja's earlier work, now unfortunately lost. Keeping this in mind, it is now time to examine the verse.

---

kumbhīdhānyā alolupā agṛhyamāṇakāraṇāḥ kiṃ cid antareṇa kasyāś cid vidyāyāḥ pāragās tatrabhavantaḥ śiṣṭāḥ.

28 PrPr 1, p. 54, ll. 7-9: *tad evam āgamaprāmāṇyam āśritya sarvajñasiddhir atra sūcitā pūrvārdhena. vistareṇāgamaprāmāṇyaṃ vākyapadīye 'smābhiḥ prathamakāṇḍe śabdaprabhāyāṃ nirṇītam iti tata evāvadhāryam.*

2. VP 3.1.46 IN LIGHT OF BHARTṚHARI'S VIEWS ON *YOGIPRATYAKṢA*

VP 3.1.46 occurs at the end of a portion of the *Jātisamuddeśa* (VP 3.1.40-45) in which the various universals are said to be differentiations of the one *mahāsattā* and are due to the latter's own powers.[29] It is observed that they persist even when their substratum is destroyed (v. 41), and this leads to a brief survey of different views about the events that happen at *pralaya*, the cyclical dissolution of the cosmos (vv. 42-43), and the relation between universals and particulars (vv. 44-45). The verse appeals to the experience of exceptional beings as proof of the existence of universals:

> *jñānaṃ tv asmadviśiṣṭānāṃ tāsu sarvendriyaṃ viduḥ* |
> *abhyāsān maṇirūpyādiviśeṣeṣv iva tadvidām* ||
>
> However, they state that the knowledge which those who are superior[30] to us have of these [universals] proceeds from all the senses through practice, just as the experts' [knowledge] of the characteristics of gems and precious metals.

Here Bhartṛhari appears to record an authoritative opinion which he apparently subscribes to: individuals with extraordinary powers, whose knowledge is not subject to the ordinary limitations of the senses, have a direct apprehension of universals (i.e. an apprehension that is not mediated through their substrata); and this kind of cognition is compared to the intuitive evaluation of the quality of gems and precious metals that jewellers and other such experts possess, sharpened by practice (*abhyāsāt*).

Who are these *asmadviśiṣṭa* individuals? Helārāja glosses the term with the phrase *pratiniyatapadārthadarśibhyo 'smadādibhyo viśiṣṭāḥ sarvadṛśa ādiguravaḥ* (PrPr 1, p. 51, l. 15), "the omniscient primeval teachers, who are superior to people like us who

---

[29] VP 3.1.40: *āśrayaḥ svātmamātrā vā bhāvā vā vyatirekiṇaḥ* | *svaśaktayo vā sattāyā bhedadarśanahetavaḥ* ||. Cf. ĪPK 1.5.14 and Torella's remarks thereon (TORELLA 2002, p. 121, n. 29).

[30] In translating *asmadviśiṣṭānām* with "superior to us" I follow Isaacson's translation of the same expression as found in Praśastapāda's PDhS (see ISAACSON 1990, p. 70), which I discuss below. However, note that in a discussion of *yogipratyakṣa*, Vyomaśiva's *Vyomavatī*, the earliest surviving commentary on PDhS (Vyomaśiva is dated to 900-960, see EIPh, p. 10, therefore roughly contemporaneous with Helārāja) employs the expression *asmadādivilakṣaṇā yoginīḥ* (vol. II, p. 145, ll. 9-12), where I think the term *vilakṣaṇa* puts the stress on difference rather than superiority.

[only] perceive objects restricted [to specific senses]," thus apparently identifying them with the *ṛṣis*. However, around the mid-first millennium CE the expression *asmadviśiṣṭa* is also found in the section on *pratyakṣa* of Praśastapāda's *Padārthadharmasaṅgraha* (henceforth, PDhS), where it refers to yogis who can have direct perceptual knowledge of universals and of other constituents of reality that are beyond the reach of normal human cognition. After dealing with ordinary perception (*asmadādīnāṃ pratyakṣam*, "the perceptual knowledge of [ordinary] people such as us"),[31] Praśastapāda goes on to present the phenomenon of yogic perception:

> But for yogis, who are superior to us (*asmadviśiṣṭānāṃ*), when [in the condition called] *yukta*, an unerring seeing of the object's own nature arises, by virtue of [their] internal organ [which is] assisted (*anugṛhīta*) by *dharma* arising from yoga, in regard to [the following substances:] their own *ātman* and the *ātman* of others, ether, space, time, atoms, the air and the internal organ, [as well as] in regard to the qualities, actions, universals and individuators which are inherent in these [substances], and in regard to [the category] inherence. Furthermore, for [yogis in the condition known as] *viyukta*, perceptual knowledge arises in regard to objects which are fine (*sūkṣma*), concealed [from sight], or at a [great] distance, because of contact between four [factors], in consequence of the assistance (*anugraha*) of *dharma* arising from yoga.[32]

In VP 3.1.46 Bhartṛhari is probably echoing a very similar theory of extraordinary perceptual knowledge, although he does not attribute the view to any particular school. It seems likely that these ideas were circulating in Vaiśeṣika circles before Praśastapāda's

---

[31] Transl. ISAACSON 1990, p. 70; the text of the whole section is given there on p. 61.

[32] *asmadviśiṣṭānāṃ tu yogināṃ yuktānāṃ yogajadharmānugṛhītena manasā svātmāntarākāśadikkālaparamāṇuvāyumanassu tatsamavetaguṇakarmasāmānyaviśeṣeṣu samavāye cāvitathaṃ svarūpadarśanam utpadyate. viyuktānāṃ punaś catuṣṭayasannikarṣād yogajadharmānugrahasāmarthyāt sūkṣmavyavahitaviprakṛṣṭeṣu pratyakṣam utpadyate*. (Transl. ISAACSON 1990, p. 71.) It is worth noting that there is a second occurrence of the phrase *asmadviśiṣṭānāṃ tu yogināṃ* in the *Viśeṣapadārthanirūpaṇa* of PDhS, where "Praśastapāda makes use of the concept of yogic perception in order to establish the existence of one of the fundamental categories of his system" (ISAACSON 1993, p. 154), namely *viśeṣa*.

time[33] and Bhartṛhari was acquainted with them. For the expression *asmadviśiṣṭa*, both authors have probably been inspired by *Vaiśeṣika Sūtra* (henceforth, VS) 2.18, *saṃjñākarma tv asmadviśiṣṭānām liṅgam* "The name-giving of those who are superior to us is the mark (of the existence of nine substances)."[34] This *sūtra* concludes a sequence of aphorisms dealing with air (*vāyu*) and its distinctive quality, touch (*sparśa*). As pointed out in MATILAL 1977, p. 56, "[s]ome difficulty is noticed in establishing the air as a substance, for it is not 'visible'. But the sense experience of touch [when air blows] establishes the external touch as a quality, and air is inferred as the bearer of this quality."[35] VS 2.1.16, *sāmānyatodṛṣṭāc cāviśeṣaḥ*, states that air is established to be a substance, having *sparśa* as its special quality, by analogy (*sāmānyatodṛṣṭāt*) with the other (visible) elements and their qualities; 2.1.17, *tasmād āgamikam*, records an objection declaring this conclusion to be based merely on traditional knowledge (*āgamikam*), to which the next *sūtra*, 2.1.18, *saṃjñākarma tv asmadviśiṣṭānāṃ liṅgam*, replies that the naming (*saṃjñākarma*) of things, in this case the name *vāyu* "air," is itself a sign that allows us to infer the existence of air because names were assigned by the one/s who is/are "superior to us."[36]

Another phrase used by Praśastapāda in the passage quoted above is *sūkṣmavyavahitaviprakṛṣṭa*, which also occurs in the VP.[37] But in this case, as Isaacson has noted, both probably borrow the

---

33 Praśastapāda is generally dated around 550 CE (for a brief assessment of this issue, see ISAACSON 1990, p. 10; see also EIPh, p. 282) and therefore supposedly later than Bhartṛhari.

34 Transl. NOZAWA 1993, p. 105. On the complex problem of identifying the various historical layers of the VS, and the probable relative lateness of those dealing with *yogipratyakṣa* see WEZLER 1982, and ISAACSON 1993, neither of which discusses VS 2.18 in particular.

35 See VS 2.1.10: *na ca dṛṣṭānāṃ sparśa ity adṛṣṭaliṅgo vāyuḥ.*

36 Near the end of the commentary on VP 3.1.46 Helārāja quotes another *sūtra* from this section, VS 2.1.19, echoing Candrānanda's *Vṛtti* thereon: see § 8 below.

37 See VPVṛ 1.81 (1.79 in Subramania Iyer's edition with the Vṛtti): *alaukikam api samādhānaṃ sūkṣmavyavahitaviprakṛṣṭopalabdhau cakṣur evānugṛhṇāti*, "Even supernormal concentration only benefits the sense of vision [not the object] in the perception of [objects that are] subtle, concealed or very distant." Helārāja also uses the phrase, with the additional reference to past and future objects, in the commentary on VP 3.1.46 (see § 8 below).

expression from YS 3.25,[38] *pravṛttyālokanyāsāt sūkṣmavyavahita-viprakṛṣṭajñānam,*[39] also dealing with yogic perception. While there is undoubtedly a tendency in all our texts to conflate *ṛṣi*s with yogis and *śiṣṭa*s, as I have noted above, it seems that in this case Bhartṛhari, engaged in a dialogue with other brahmanical thinkers, may have envisaged a larger and probably contemporaneous set of individuals than just the primordial seers understood by Helārāja.

In the second half of the verse, the comparison between yogic cognition and the expertise in gems and precious metals is clearly an intra-textual reference to a verse in the first *kāṇḍa,* VP 1.35:

> *pareṣām asamākhyeyam abhyāsād eva jāyate* |
> *maṇirūpyādivijñānaṃ tadvidāṃ nānumānikam* ||

> Those who know jewels, precious metals etc. perceive those objects in their distinctiveness [i.e. with their individual good features and bad features] only through constant practice. [If others ask them, "How did you figure out the merits or blemishes of this diamond, and so on?"] they cannot give expression to their [experience or process of] knowing. [This sort of knowing] is not an outcome of inference [it is like perception in its directness, but it is not ordinary perception either, as it perceives what most others cannot].[40]

VP 1.37-38 with the *Vṛtti* thereon further elaborate on the nature of the extraordinary cognition that allows certain individuals to have access to non-mundane truths. These individuals' superior faculties stem from their cultivation of a pure mind, which allows them to have direct knowledge – similar to perception in quality – of trans-empirical objects, and even see into the past and the future:

> *āvirbhūtaprakāśānāṁ anupaplutacetasām* |
> *atītānāgatajñānaṃ pratyakṣān na viśiṣyate* || (VP 1.37)

---

38 MAAS 2013 argues that the *sūtra* and *bhāṣya* portions of what he refers to as *Pātañjala Yogaśāstra* were composed as a unified whole and presents evidence from various ancient sources that support his hypothesis. The references Helārāja makes to this work in the passage examined here appear to confirm this. According to MAAS 2013, p. 65, "the work can be dated with some confidence to the period between 325 and 425 CE."

39 Cf. ISAACSON 1990, p. 71, n. 70.

40 Transl. AKLUJKAR 2010, p. 409 (see next note); in 1.35c Aklujkar suggests reading *maṇirūpyādiṣu jñānaṃ.*

The knowledge of the past and future [objects] of those whose insight has manifested itself and whose mind is in no way tainted differs in no way from perception.[41]

The *Vṛtti* explains that these are *śiṣṭa*s "whose flaws have been burnt out by ascetic practices and whose cognitions are unimpeded" (*tapasā nirdagdhadoṣā nirāvaraṇakhyātayaḥ śiṣṭāḥ*). Here, as in VP 1.35 and 3.1.46, it is emphasised that the extraordinary cognition of *śiṣṭa*s is the fruit of effort and practice (*abhyāsa*) and not inherently different from perception although, as AKLUJKAR 2010 puts it (p. 409), "it is like perception in its directness, but it is not ordinary perception either, as it perceives what most others cannot." These exceptional individuals see things, in fact, that are inaccessible to the senses of ordinary human beings, and their statements cannot be contradicted or invalidated by mere reasoning.[42] And in a different context, in the *Vṛtti* on VP 2.152,[43] which enumerates the possible sources of *pratibhā*, among which there is yoga, Bhartṛhari says that yogis can have a direct intuitive knowledge (*pratibhā*) even of other people's intentions (*tad yathā yogināṃ avyabhicāreṇa parābhiprāyajñānādiṣu*).[44]

As can be seen from this cursory survey of various passages in the VP where Bhartṛhari touches upon the topic of extraordinary cognition, he clearly admits of it but stops short of providing a systematic treatment. No clear-cut distinction is made between *ṛṣi*s, yogis and *śiṣṭa*s,[45] and there is no distinct theoretical treatment of omniscience in his epistemology, but the authoritativeness of the

41 Transl. SUBRAMANIA IYER 1965, p. 47. AKLUJKAR 2010 does not give a full translation of this verse.

42 VP 1.38: *atīndriyān asaṃvedyān paśyanty ārṣeṇa cakṣuṣā | ye bhāvān vacanaṃ teṣāṃ nānumānena bādhyate ||*.

43 VP 2.152: *svabhāvacaraṇābhyāsayogādṛṣṭopapāditām | viśiṣṭopahitāṃ ceti pratibhāṃ ṣaḍvidhāṃ viduḥ ||*.

44 On this passage, see the remarks in TORELLA 2012, p. 472, n. 9.

45 In this respect Bhartṛhari seems to anticipate the tendency to conflate these categories that will later become common (as reflected also in Helārāja's commentary on VP 3.1.46). ISAACSON 1993, p. 156 notes that "the vision of *ṛṣi*s, which is treated separately from yogic perception in the PDhS, and which is also mentioned separately in the VS, [...] in later times [...] seems to have usually been subsumed under *yogipratyakṣa*." See also TORELLA 2012, p. 471, n. 6): "when later speculation on this subject more and more shifts to its epistemological implications, *yogijñāna* and *ṛṣijñāna* will tend to be taken as mere synonyms."

*āgama*s, the foundational texts of Brahmanism, is explicitly related to their origination from exceptional and trustworthy individuals.

3. HELĀRĀJA'S COMMENTARY ON VP 3.1.46: GOD AS THE *ĀDIGURU*

The reference to extraordinary knowledge in VP 3.1.46 gives Helārāja the opportunity to discuss omniscience (*sarvajña*) at some length in his commentary, engaging with the debates on this and other related issues that had taken place since Bhartṛhari's time, and in particular allows him to introduce a theistic perspective that is notably absent in Bhartṛhari's work.

Helārāja reveals his philosophical agenda already in the introductory paragraph to VP 3.1.46, tackling the issue from the vantage point of the origin of language. As is known, in the *Jātisamuddeśa* Bhartṛhari examines the relation between word and meaning presupposing that words denote *jāti*, the universal. As shown above, in VP 3.1.46 he records an authoritative view according to which the universals of things can be directly perceived by exceptional beings, apparently implying that at least some *jāti*s are not just conceptual-linguistic constructs but are ontologically "real." On the basis of this premise, Helārāja introduces the verse considering a possible objection to the assertion that there is a fixed (*siddha*) or eternal (*nitya*) relation between word and meaning, as maintained by both the Grammarians and the Mīmāṃsakas:

> One may argue that, for someone who does not know the relation between the word [*go*] and its meaning, the nature ["cowness,"] distinct from other [natures] and recurring in [the individual] cows, [as evidenced in the individual cognitions] "[this is] a cow," "[this is also] a cow," does not manifest itself. And if that commonality [i.e. *gotva*] is manifested by the individual manifestations, how could there be no cognition of it [even for someone who does not know the relation between the word and the object]? If one will apprehend [it] learning (*vyutpanna*) from others, how did these others, and those before them [apprehend it]?[46]

---

[46] PrPr 1, p. 51, ll. 4-6: *nanv aviditaśabdārthasaṃbandhasyānyebhyo vyāvṛttaṃ goṣv anugataṃ rūpaṃ gaur gaur iti na pratibhāsate. yadi ca tābhir vyaktibhir abhivyaktaṃ tat sāmānyaṃ kathaṃ tatpratyayo na syāt. athānyebhyo vyutpannaḥ* pratipatsyate te 'pi kuta[ḥ]*... *Here I adopt the reading *vyutpannaḥ* found in R. Sharma's edition (VP 3.1, p. 95) instead of *'vyutpannaḥ* in Subramania Iyer's.

The objection points out that by itself the word – i.e. a phonic form (*rūpa*) such as *go* "cow" –, which the Mīmāṃsakas assume to be possessed with an innate capacity (*śakti*) of denotation, is unable to make the corresponding universal, e.g. "cowness" (*gotva*), known. First one has to learn the relation between that specific word and its object. The Mīmāṃsakas are ready to concede this, since it is a fact of ordinary experience that this is how children learn to speak. For example, in v. 41 of the *Sambandhākṣepaparihāra* (SAP) of the *Ślokavārttika* (henceforth, ŚlV), where many of the issues raised here by Helārāja are discussed, Kumārila remarks:

> *sarveṣām anabhijñānāṃ pūrvapūrvaprasiddhitaḥ* |
> *siddhaḥ sambandha ity evaṃ sambandhādir na vidyate* ||
>
> For all those who do not know it, the relation [between word and meaning] is fixed on the basis of the accepted usage of those before [them], and those [even] before, therefore in this way [one can conclude that] there is no beginning of the relation [i.e. it is eternal].

Thus, the word, the object and their relation are all eternal, but while the first two are accessible to the senses, the third has to be learnt afresh by each new member of the community. The uninstructed (*avyutpanna*) will learn the meaning of the word *go* – i.e. its regular association with the object "cow" – from the repeated observation of its use in different contexts on the part of knowledgeable speakers, normally one's elders.[47] However, as Helārāja points out, this explanation leads to a difficulty: each generation must have learnt the relation between words and meanings from the previous one in a chain of transmission that, although uninterrupted, is nevertheless made of ordinary human beings and therefore is not itself authoritative. The continuous practice of previous generations would be tantamount to a line of blind men[48] since it

---

47 The final verses of the SAP contain a more accurate description of the learning process (140cd-141ef): *śabdavṛddhābhidheyāṃś ca pratyakṣeṇātra paśyati* || *śrotuś ca pratipannatvam anumānena ceṣṭayā* || *anyathā 'nupapattyā ca budhyec chaktiṃ dvayāśritām* || *arthāpattyāvabuddhyante sambandhaṃ tripramāṇakam*.

48 In VP 1.42 (*hastasparśād ivāndhena viṣame pathi dhāvatā* | *anumānapradhānena vinipāto na durlabhaḥ* ||) Bhartṛhari compares a man who relies on reason alone to a blind man groping around while hurrying along an uneven path. The maxim of the blind men (see APTE, Appendix E, p. 53, s.v.) occurs e.g. in Kumārila's *Tantravārttika* (TV 1.3.1, p. 71): *puruṣāntareṣūtpadyamānaḥ kaiścid dṛśyata ity andhaparamparānyāyenāpramāṇatā*, where it refers to the transmission of *smṛtis*.

could not claim to stem from an unquestionably reliable source. As Helārāja puts it, drawing his conclusion,

> Therefore, unless [we assume that in the beginning there was] an omniscient seer (*draṣṭāram*) who had a direct vision [of the relation between *śabda* and *artha*], a succession of blind men would result. And in every case of relation between a word and an object, the so-called practice of the elders (*vṛddhavyavahāra*) would be generated through a succession of blind men, because it would have no foundation (*nirmūlatvāt*).[49]

In this way Helārāja claims that the assumption of the existence of an omniscient being who literally "saw" the relation between *śabda* and *artha* and transmitted its knowledge to later generations is the most logical explanation for the intrinsic stability and reliability of language – a claim, as we will see, that is reiterated at the end of the commentary on VP 3.1.46.

Furthermore, while in the case of cows and other similar material objects there is a visible configuration of features that is shared by all the individuals in which that given *jāti* inheres, in other cases, such as Brahmin-hood[50] (*brāhmaṇatva*) etc., this essence is much more elusive. Thus, it is harder to account for the relation between the word *brāhmaṇa* and its object:

> And, in the case of Brahmin-hood etc., there is no manifestation of a form that is recurring [in individuals of the same kind and] distinct [from that of individuals of a different kind, and which would be] also similar if it were cognised by a [small] child, or a mute person,[51] etc. because the form manifests [itself] in a similar way [to all people, since

---

49 PrPr 1, p. 51, ll. 6-8: ... *iti sākṣāddarśinaṃ sarvajñaṃ draṣṭāram antareṇāndhaparamparā prasajyate. sarvatra ca śabdārthasaṃbandhe 'ndhaparamparāyā eva vṛddhavyavahāra iti nāma kṛtaṃ syāt, nirmūlatvāt.*

50 Note that Helārāja appears to regard caste (which is one of the senses of the word *jāti*) as a "natural" kind rather than a socio-cultural construct. On the philosophical debate about the naturalness of social distinctions, see HALBFASS 1992, chapter 10.

51 That is, the direct perception of a cow is similar and similarly valid (*pramāṇa*) for everyone, whether the perceiving subject is an adult, a child or someone with mental or physical handicaps and regardless of their knowledge of the word *go*, but it was generally admitted that this does not hold in the case of Brahmins or other social types.

there are no external physical characteristics that can identify a Brahmin], as in the case of cow-hood etc.[52]

What guarantees the correct application of the word *brāhmaṇa* to certain individuals? Or, from a different angle, is there really a universal *brāhmaṇatva* the essence of which is captured by the word *brāhmaṇa*? The only way to explain the use of certain words to denote objects whose *jāti* has no uniform perceivable physical configuration is, according to Helārāja's conclusion, that "one must necessarily accept the existence of an omniscient being,"[53] someone who had a kind of direct "perception-like" apprehension of the *jāti*, of the word to express it, and of the relation between the two, and passed this knowledge on to ordinary human beings.

It seems likely that Helārāja was influenced by a similar argument already adumbrated in VS 6.1.3 and developed in Candrānanda's *Vṛtti* thereon.[54] Adhyāya 6 of the VS, which deals with qualities, begins its treatment with a discussion of *dharma*, which in Vaiśeṣika taxonomy is considered a quality. Introducing the first *sūtra* of the chapter, Candrānanda explains that the means for achieving *dharma* are the injunctions found in the Veda, and if one wonders about the source of the truthfulness of the Veda,[55] the answer is:

buddhipūrvā vākyakṛtir vede | (VS 6.1.1)

The composition of the sentences in the Veda is based on [the activity of] the intellect.

This pithy statement, claiming that the Veda is the product of some form of intelligence that is responsible for its composition, is one of the earliest attestations of a conception of the Veda radically different from the one upheld by Mīmāṃsā. In the *Vṛtti* Candrānanda elaborates on this idea, introducing the idea of *racanāvattva* of the

---

52 PrPr 1, p. 51, ll. 8-10: *brāhmaṇatvādīnāṃ rūpavyañjanasādṛśyād bālamūkādijñānasadṛśo 'py asau gotvādīnām ivāvṛttavyāvṛttarūpāvabhāso nāstīty avaśyam eva sarvajño 'bhyupagantavya iti.*

53 *avaśyam eva sarvajño 'bhyupagantavya(ḥ)* (PrPr 1, p. 51, ll. 9-10).

54 AKLUJKAR 1970, p. 340 has been the first, as far as I know, to point out that Helārāja seems to have known the work of Candrānanda, who was probably also a Kashmiri (ISAACSON 1995, pp. 141-142) and active in the 7th or 8th c. CE (CHEMPARATHY 1970, p. 48).

55 *tasya* [i.e. *dharmasya*] *vaidiko vidhiḥ sādhanam. vedasya satyatā kuta iti cet, yataḥ...* [the *sūtra* follows] (VSVṛ, p. 45, l. 3).

Veda that is also found in the work of Jayanta Bhaṭṭa[56] (and to which Helārāja himself refers below):

> A sentence such as *agnihotraṃ juhuyāt svargakāmaḥ* is a composition (*racanā*) issued from [the activity of] the intelligence of the venerable Maheśvara and therefore it is a valid source of knowledge, since truthfulness pervades the nature of what is composed by trustworthy (*āpta*) individuals.[57]

It is important to stress that, while the following *sūtra* states that the nature of the Veda is such as to point to the intervention of a seer/seers, using the word *ṛṣi* in line with traditional accounts of the self-revelation of the Veda (although perhaps suggesting a greater involvement of the seers in putting the sacred texts in a form accessible to human beings), already in the *Vṛtti* on VS 6.1.1 Candrānanda interprets it as a reference to God's authorship of the Veda. The following *sūtra* replies to the objection that *dharma* is not accessible to ordinary means of knowledge[58]:

> *na cāsmadbuddhibhyo liṅgam ṛṣeḥ* | (VS 6.1.2)

> And [since it could] not [have issued] from our intellects, it is an inferential sign of [the intervention of] a seer.

The *Vṛtti* explains:

> In fact, the knowledge of the Venerable One is not similar to our knowledge, whose domain are objects that are present, not concealed, and related (*sambaddha*) [to the senses]. Hence, the knowledge of the Venerable One can have as its domain objects that are beyond [the reach of] the senses.[59]

---

56 The relative chronology of Candrānanda and Jayanta Bhaṭṭa (9th c. CE) is uncertain as the former's date is not known but is certainly prior to Helārāja's. If Candrānanda is earlier than Jayanta Bhaṭṭa, as argued by Chemparathy (see n. 54 above), he may be recording an early version of a thesis that Jayanta fully expounds later in the *Nyāyamañjarī*.

57 *"agnihotraṃ juhuyāt svargakāmaḥ" ity evaṃbhūtā racanā bhagavato maheśvarasya buddhipūrvā sā tataḥ pramāṇam, āptapraṇītatvasya satyatāvyāpteḥ* (VSVṛ, p. 45, ll. 5-6).

58 Candrānanda introduces it with the words *atīndriyam aśakyaṃ jñātum iti cet* (VSVṛ, p. 45, l. 7) "If [one objects that] it is impossible to know what is beyond [the reach of] the senses."

59 VSVṛ, p. 45, ll. 9-11: *na hi yādṛśam asmadvijñānaṃ vartamānāvyavahitasambaddhārthaviṣayaṃ tādṛśam eva bhagavato vijñānam. ataḥ sambhavati bhaga-*

Similarly, one can infer that a superior being has assigned a name to Brahmins:

> *tathā brāhmaṇe saṃjñākarmasiddhir liṅgam* | (VS 6.1.3)
>
> In the same way, the consensus about the assignment of the name [*brāhmaṇa*] to a Brahmin is an inferential sign [of the intervention of a seer].

Candrānanda points out the implications of the *sūtra*:

> When we see objects such as Brahmins etc., the cognition "This is a Brahmin" does not arise for us through perception without [proper] instruction. And when someone has the perceptual knowledge of an object, then we see that a name is given (*saṃjñāpraṇayanam*), as in the case of [the naming of] a son etc. And they explain the meaning of the *sūtra* [saying] that names for "Brahmin," etc. are found [in use] that were composed by him [the Lord] after he directly saw [every] object.[60]

CHEMPARATHY 1970 has suggested (p. 50) that Candrānanda's idea that the existence of God can be inferred from the fact that things have names, as expressed in the passage quoted above, "may be deduced from an earlier proof of Praśastamati," i.e. Praśastapāda, as Candrānanda himself appears to indicate with the concluding words *iti sūtrārthaṃ varṇayanti*. As Chemparathy shows in another article (CHEMPARATHY 1968, p. 68), this earlier proof is found in a fragment of a lost work[61] of Praśastamati/Praśastapāda's quoted by Kamalaśīla in the *Tattvasaṅgrahapañjikā*, which is worth quoting in full as it seems to be one of the earliest sources for the theistic view on the origin of language embraced here by Helārāja (with some differences, as I will show below):

> However, Praśastamati has said: "At the beginning of creation the usage of words of men presupposes instruction by another; because, when they are awakened [from the state of dissolution] at a later time, [their usage of words] with regard to each object is fixed (*niyata*): just as in the case of children, whose usage of words is not yet established, the usage of words fixed for each object such as cow etc. presupposes the instruction of mother etc. He whose instruction of words is presupposed at the be-

---

vato 'tīndriyārthaviṣayaṃ vijñānam.

60 *vinopadeśena brāhmaṇādikam artham asmākam ālocayatāṃ pratyakṣeṇa na "brāhmaṇo'yam" iti jñānam utpadyate. pratyakṣeṇa cārtham ālocya saṃjñāpraṇayanaṃ dṛṣṭaṃ putrādiṣu. santi caitā brāhmaṇādisaṃjñās tā yena pratyakṣam artham ālocya praṇītā iti sūtrārthaṃ varṇayanti* (VSVṛ, p. 45, ll. 14-16).

61 Possibly a *Ṭīkā* on the VaiSū with the equally lost *Vākya* and *Bhāṣya* thereon: cf. Thakur in the Introduction to Jambuvijaya' edition of VS, pp. 12 and 14.

ginning of creation is the Īśvara, who possesses an abundance of knowledge that does not disappear even at the time of the dissolution."[62]

Needless to say, the language in question is not human speech in general in its innumerable varieties, but rather Sanskrit, the language par excellence in the eyes of all our authors. This view seems to imply that the fact Sanskrit is the language of the Vedic corpus is not enough to account for its *laukika* use. The Vedic revelation to the *ṛṣi*s is felt to be insufficient by itself to explain the origins of human language. Some further intervention is required. It is as if a link were missing between the highest truths embodied in the Veda and the dimension of *vyavahāra* and, as Helārāja sets out to establish in this passage, to a large extent following in the footsteps of various predecessors, this link is God.

As I mentioned above, Helārāja takes the term *asmadviśiṣṭa* as meaning "the omniscient primeval teachers." But these teachers, the *ṛṣi*s of yore, must have themselves received their knowledge from a previous source, and this can only be the Lord (*īśvara*) according to Helārāja, who quotes *Yogasūtra* (YS) 1.26 to support this view:

Thus Patañjali [says]: "He is the teacher even of the ancient [sages] because he is not limited by Time."[63]

Drawn from an authoritative brahmanical text such as the YS, the quotation allows Helārāja to bring God onto the stage (in the introduction to the verse, he had generically talked of a *sarvajñā*, an omniscient being), overstepping the non-dualist atheism of the VP. He then elaborates on the idea expressed in the *sūtra*:

The Lord is the teacher, i.e. the instructor (*upadeṣṭṛ*), of the omniscient beings. And his mind, senses and body are eternal because he is not li-

---

62 TSP p. 43, ll. 1-5: *praśastamatis tv āha sargādau puruṣāṇāṃ vyavahāro 'nyopadeśapūrvakaḥ, uttarakālaṃ prabuddhānāṃ pratyarthaniyatatvād aprasiddhavāgvyavahārāṇām kumārāṇāṃ gavādiṣu pratyarthaniyato vāgvyavahāro yathā mātrādyupadeśapūrvaka iti. yadupadeśapūrvakaḥ sargādau vyavahāraḥ sa īśvaraḥ pralayakāle 'py aluptajñānātiśaya.* Transl. CHEMPARATHY 1968, p. 68, with some minor modifications. Chemparathy points out (ibid., n. 15) that it is not sure whether the sentence after *iti* "is a continuation of Praśastamati's own argument or whether it is an additional concluding statement by Kamalaśīla himself."

63 PrPr 1, p. 51, ll. 16-17: *tathā ca patañjaliḥ: "sa pūrveṣām api guruḥ kālenānavacchedāt."* The pronoun *saḥ* refers back to Īśvara in YS 24: *kleśakarmavipākāśayair aparāmṛṣṭaḥ puruṣaviśeṣa īśvaraḥ.*

> mited by Time. Otherwise, once the dissolution [of the cosmos] has taken place, [and] Brahmā etc. have arisen again, who would be their teacher? And thus the world, having no normative knowledge (*śāstram*), no observance (*anuṣṭhānam*) of injunctions and interdictions, would be as good as blind and mute.[64]

The fact that the Creator is not under the sway of Time is shown by the fact that, after the *pralaya*, at the beginning of every new cosmic cycle, the divine beings who re-appear in the cosmos are once again taught its eternal law, *dharma*. Who else could be their teacher if not the Lord? They in turn hand down that knowledge to humans, as can be inferred from the remark that, if it were not so, the world would be bereft of *śāstra* (*niḥśāstram*), unaware of ritual and social obligations and taboos, and stumbling in the dark, as it were. Thus, in a few lines at the beginning of the PrPr on VP 3.1.46, Helārāja sketches an account of the spread of normative knowledge of cosmogonical proportions, tracing the contemporary views about matters that are beyond the reach of senses and reasoning (*dharma*, primarily, but also *ātman*, the constituents of the universe, etc.) to the seers who learn those truths directly from God at the dawn of time, when he also issues the Veda.

The historical antecedents of this position in philosophical texts are to be found especially in the works of the earliest Nyāya-Vaiśeṣika authors of the post-*sūtra* period. At the very beginning of PDhS (2, 1.7), for example, Praśastapāda states that *dharma* has been manifested in the Lord's injunctions.[65] And later, in the *Nyāyamañjarī* (henceforth, NM), Jayanta Bhaṭṭa (9th c. CE) argues for the existence of God responding to the criticisms levelled against theism by the Mīmāṃsakas, and in particular Kumārila. The latter were formidable opponents, whose opinions could not be ignored or easily dismissed. Having declared his theistic stance early in his commentary on VP 3.1.46, Helārāja himself feels obliged to take account of the Mīmāṃsakas' reaction to the theism of other brahmanical schools and explain their arguments, as a kind of *pūrvapa-*

---

[64] PrPr 1, p. 51, ll. 18-20: *sarvajñānām īśvaro gurur upadeṣṭā. tasya ca buddhīndriyadehānāṃ kālenānavacchedān nityatā. anyathā pralaye vṛtte punarutpanneṣu brahmādiṣu ka upadeṣṭā syāt. tataś ca niḥśāstraṃ niranuṣṭhānaṃ vidhiniṣedhayor andhamūkaprāyaṃ jagat syāt.*

[65] PDhS 2: *dravyaguṇakarmasāmānyaviśeṣasamavāyānāṃ ṣaṇṇām padārthānām sādharmyavaidharmyatattvajñānam niḥśreyasahetuḥ. tac ceśvaracodanābhivyaktād dharmād eva.*

kṣa that he then proceeds to confute, as I will show in the next section.

4. THE DISPUTE WITH MĪMĀṂSĀ ON *PRALAYA* AND THE PURPOSE OF *ARTHAVĀDAS*

Claiming that the Veda is issued from the Lord at the beginning of each new cosmic age, namely at each re-creation of the world after its periodical destruction, clearly clashes with the Mīmāṃsā's tenet of the eternal and uncreated nature of the Veda, which warrants its unique authority on transcendental matters. It is hardly surprising, therefore, that the Mīmāṃsakas oppose it, resolutely rejecting the idea of a cosmos subject to cyclic *pralaya* "dissolution" and *sṛṣṭi* "creation" under the impulsion of a creator God. What is at stake for them is not just the cyclicity of time or even the existence of God, for which they have little use, but the eternality of the words of the Veda[66] in which the injunctions for the realisation of *dharma* are formulated.

Much of the argument against the view that the relation between words and objects/meanings is based on a convention established by God at the beginning of creation is presented by Kumārila in the SAP of ŚlV ad *Jaiminisūtra* (henceforth, JS) 1.1.5, which is probably presupposed by Helārāja when he advances his counter-argument under VP 3.1.46.

Kumārila defines the terms of the dispute in SAP 12cd-13cd:

pratītiḥ samayāt puṃsāṃ bhaved akṣinikocavat |
samayaḥ pratimartyaṃ yā pratyuccāraṇam eva vā |
kriyate jagadādau vā sakṛd ekena kena cit ||

[Objection:] Comprehension [of the meaning of a verbal expression] will arise for human beings from a convention (*samayāt*) [linking a certain word to a certain object], like winking. [Reply:] Is this convention created [ad hoc] for each individual, or for each utterance, or does someone [create it] once [and for all] at the beginning of the world?

The answer, from a Mīmāṃsā perspective, is of course that the relation between word and meaning is eternal and uncreated. This is summarised in SAP 41ad (quoted above, § 3) and followed in SAP

66 And, to the extent that they are similar to Vedic words, of *laukika* words.

42cd-44cd by the dismissal of the opponents' thesis, which is briefly recalled and rejected:

sargādau ca kriyā nāsti, tādṛk kālo hi neṣyate |
yadi tv ādau jagat sṛṣṭvā dharmādharmau sasādhanau |
yathā śabdārthasambandhān vedān kaś cit pravartayet ||
jagaddhitāya vedasya tathā kiñ cin na duṣyati |
sarvajñavat tu duḥsādham ity atraitan na saṃśritam ||

And the making [of such a relation between word and meaning] does not happen at the beginning of creation, for we do not admit that there is such a time. [Objection:] But if someone, after creating the world, set *dharma* and *adharma* in motion, together with the means [to bring them about], and the Vedas, in which the relations between words and meanings are [instituted] for the sake of the world, in this way the Veda [itself] would not be diminished. [Reply:] But this is hard to prove, just like omniscience, therefore here [in the Mīmāṃsā system] we do not rely on this [idea].

In the following verses, Kumārila relentlessly attacks the thesis of the existence of a creator god deploying an array of arguments: how should one imagine the universe before the creation? And what would be the condition and nature of Prajāpati (the creator god of Vedic cosmogonies) himself prior to such an event? There would be no one to know him, who could then pass on the knowledge of God to future beings, and therefore, in the absence of a direct cognition of God, no way to ascertain his existence. Moreover, if God has no material body, how could he entertain the desire to create the world? And if God had a body, he could not have created it himself, therefore one should assume the existence of some other being who created him (and so on, in an infinite regress). If, on the other hand, it is maintained that the creator's body is eternal, what would it be made of, since earth etc. did not exist before he created them?[67]

Furthermore, it is difficult to account for the creation of a world in which misery prevails: how could God wish to create the world

---

[67] See SAP 45ab-49ab: *yadā sarvam idaṃ nāsīt kvāvasthā tatra gamyatām | prajāpateḥ kva vā sthānaṃ kiṃ rūpaṃ ca pratīyatām || jñātā ca kas tadā tasya yo janān bodhayiṣyati | upalabdher vinā caitat katham adhyavasīyatām || pravṛttiḥ katham ādyā ca jagataḥ sampratīyate | śarīrāder vinā cāsya katham icchāpi sarjane || śarīrādy atha tasya syāt, tasyotpattir na tatkṛtā | tadvad anyaprasaṅgo 'pi, nityaṃ yadi tad iṣyate || pṛthivyādāv anutpanne kimmayaṃ tat punar bhavet |*.

out of compassion before there were any beings to be compassionate about? And if compassion were his motive, surely he could make all creatures happy. And if it is argued that a world where there is no suffering is inconceivable, one can retort that this would imply that God is subject to a law above him, and consequently his alleged independence would be undermined.[68]

If, moreover, one argues that God creates the world out of desire, what is this desire that he cannot fulfil without creating the world? And without a purpose, not even a fool would act, therefore, what would be the point of God's intelligence?[69] Similarly, his desire to reabsorb the cosmos would be incomprehensible.[70]

If the Veda had been issued by a creator with such dubious motives, it would itself be unreliable and, therefore, not authoritative. If, on the other hand, the Veda is eternal, it cannot have any relation with events that took place at some point in time. Therefore, those Vedic passages that narrate the creation of the world should be construed as being meant to encourage others (*anyaprarocanā*) to engage in similar actions.[71]

With this last statement, Kumārila aims to preempt the inevitable objection that the Vedas themselves – as well as a myriad of other authoritative brahmanical works – contain accounts of the creation and destruction of the world by a creator God. The standard Mīmāṃsā position is that these are *arthavādas*,[72] namely Śruti and Smṛti passages of a varied nature – mythological accounts,

---

68 See SAP 49cd: *prāṇināṃ prāyaduḥkhā ca sisṛkṣāsya na yujyate* ‖; and SAP 52ab-54ab: *abhāvāc cānukampyānāṃ nānukampāsya jāyate* | *sṛjec ca śubham evaikam anukampāprayojitaḥ* ‖ *athāśubhād vinā sṛṣṭiḥ sthitir vā nopapadyate* | *ātmādhīnābhyupāye hi bhavet kiṃ nāma dṛṣkaram* | *tathā cāpekṣamāṇasya svātantryaṃ pratihanyate* ‖.

69 See SAP 54cd-55cd: *jagac cāsṛjatas tasya kiṃ nāmeṣṭaṃ na sidhyati* | *prayojanam anuddiśya na mando 'pi pravartate* | *evam eva pravṛttiś cec caitanyenāsya kiṃ bhavet* ‖.

70 See SAP 57ab: *saṃhārecchāpi caitasya bhaved apratyayāt punaḥ* |.

71 See SAP 61ab-62cd: *evaṃ vedo 'pi tatpūrvastatsadbhāvādibodhane* | *sāśaṅko na pramāṇaṃ syād nityasya vyāpṛtiḥ kutaḥ* ‖ *yadi prāg apy asau tasmād arthād āsīn na tena saḥ* | *sambaddha iti tasyānyas tadartho 'nyaprarocanā* ‖.

72 On the Mīmāṃsā theory of *arthavāda* and the slightly different views on the topic of the two major exegetical schools, the Bhāṭṭas and the Prābhākaras, see GERSCHHEIMER 1994. Helārāja's formulation here is vague enough to accommodate both, but his opponent seems to be Kumārila, who is quoted later in the passage.

descriptions, explanations, etc. – which are considered to have an auxiliary function with regard to actual direct teaching, as far as they praise certain beliefs, attitudes and conducts and disparage others, and in this way they encourage people to behave in certain ways, bolstering the normative teachings. Kumārila deals with the topic of *arthavāda* in great detail in the first three *adhikaraṇa*s of the TV; in the section of the SAP examined here he recalls it briefly in relation not only to the Veda but also to *smṛti*s such as the *Mahābhārata*, in particular in vv. 64ab-65cd:

> *upākhyānādirūpeṇa vṛttir vedavad eva naḥ |*
> *dharmādau bhāratādīnāṃ bhrāntis tebhyo 'py ato bhavet ||*
> *ākhyānānupayogitvāt teṣu sarveṣu vidyate |*
> *stutinindāśrayaḥ kaś cid vedas taccodito 'pi vā ||*

> According to us, the *Mahābhārata* etc. deal with [topics such as] *dharma* etc. in the form of stories etc., just like the Veda; therefore, [if taken at face value,] from these too one might be misled. Since narrations are of no use [by themselves], for all of these there is some [action enjoined by the] Veda that is the basis of the praise or blame [conveyed by the *arthavāda*], or even [some action] enjoined by them [i.e. the Smṛtis].

At the beginning of his riposte, Helārāja briefly recalls the Mīmāṃsā's stand on *pralaya* and quickly dismisses it as follows:

> But the Jaiminīyas maintain that there is no dissolution (*pralayaḥ*) at all – on the contrary, [they claim that] "the world is never different." This is not true, because the lore (*smṛteḥ*) of the dissolution [of the universe] is found in all the traditional texts (*sarvaśāstreṣu*).[73]

To begin with, Helārāja dismisses the Mīmāṃsā views on *pralaya* simply by invoking the consensus found "in all the traditional texts." The lapidary statement (*na kadācid anīdṛśaṃ jagat*) that in Helārāja's text[74] epitomises the Exegetes' view is not found in any surviving Mīmāṃsā work, but according to KATAOKA 2005 (p. 337) might be a quotation from Kumārila's lost *Bṛhaṭṭīkā*, since it

---

[73] PrPr 1, pp. 51[l. 20]-52[l. 1]: *atha pralayo naivāsti, api tu "na kadācid anīdṛśaṃ jagad" iti jaiminīyāḥ. tad etad asat sarvaśāstreṣu pralayasmṛteḥ.*

[74] Note that Helārāja quotes the same statement a few pages before our verse under VP 3.1.42, *anucchedyāśrayām eke sarvāṃ jātiṃ pracakṣate | na yaugapadyaṃ pralaye sarvasyeti vyavasthitāḥ ||*, where Bhartṛhari reports the opinion of some (*eke*) who believe that there is no simultaneous dissolution (*pralaya*) of the universe during which the *jāti*s are supposed to remain in existence without their substrata (see PrPr 1, p. 49, l. 1). Unlike here, though, Helārāja does not identify the upholders of this view.

is quoted by Śāntarakṣita.[75] The same sentence appears in NM, Āhnika 3, v. 158, at the very end of Jayanta Bhaṭṭa's long exposition of the views of those who deny the existence of God and, consequently, of the recurring dissolution of the world, and before he gives his reply. Like Helārāja – who I suspect may have been influenced by him – in vv. 157-158[76] Jayanta presents the belief in the cyclical destruction and re-creation of the world as a *prasiddhi*, a commonly accepted view that is opposed only by the *nītirahasyavedins*[77] (i.e. the Mīmāṃsakas).

However, Helārāja is not content with that, but proceeds to examine the Mīmāṃsā thesis on the nature and function of *arthavāda*s and refute it.

4.1. Helārāja's Exposition of the Mīmāṃsā View on Arthavādas

The goal of the Vedic tradition as understood by Mīmāṃsakas is to instruct about action, i.e. correct ritual practice – explains Helārāja – and, therefore, according to them, the narrations of past events, which do not contain any injunction or prohibition and do not teach anything new (*apūrva*), are not a *pramāṇa*, a source of valid knowledge:

> Then, since the purpose of the transmission [of the Vedas] is action [i.e. correct ritual practice],[78] a statement expressing an existing object is not a source of valid knowledge, they say. To explain: since one understands the origin of the relation between word and meaning from the practice of

---

[75] See KATAOKA 2005, p. 337, for the reference to the TS.

[76] NM 3.157-158 (vol. I, p. 491): *na ca prasiddhimātreṇa yuktam etasya kalpanam | nirmūlatvāt tathā coktaṃ prasiddhir vaṭayakṣavat || ata eva nirīkṣya durghaṭaṃ jagato janmavināśaḍambaram | na kadācid anīdṛśaṃ jagat kathitaṃ nītirahasyavedibhiḥ ||*. For a new critical edition of this section of NM, see KATAOKA 2005.

[77] I am not sure about the nuances of the expression *nītirahasyavedin*, literally "one who knows the secret of [proper ritual] conduct," but I suspect Jayanta Bhaṭṭa may have intended to be sarcastic.

[78] Cf. JS 1.2.1: *āmnāyasya kriyārthatvād ānarthakyam atadarthānāṃ tasmād anityam ucyate |*. "Because the tradition [, i.e. the Veda,] aims at ritual actions, those parts[, i.e. *arthavāda*, etc.,] which do not aim at such things are useless. Therefore [they are] said to be non-eternal." (Transl. KATAOKA 2011, p. 346, n. 388.)

> the elders as it is intended for some task to be done, and since the object of a word is what is intended [when the word is used], therefore, since there is no purpose in the expression of an object that is already realised, [e.g.] the telling of a mere story, a sentence whose object is existent [i.e. has already been realised] cannot be authoritative because it does not have the nature of a teaching (*aśāstratvāt*) insofar as nobody is teaching it, because it contains no incitation to [comply with] an injunction or a prohibition.[79]

Clearly, story-telling is not meant to prompt any course of action, and consequently, according to the Mīmāṃsakas, its words should be taken in a figurative sense. As shown above, they believe that such passages have an auxiliary function with regard to injunctions, insofar as they provide illustrations of beliefs, attitudes and conducts that are laudable and should be imitated, and conversely of others that are deplorable and should be avoided, thus bolstering the normative teachings:

> However, it becomes associated with the nature of an auxiliary (*aṅgabhāvena*) of a sentence prompting to action. The statements [known as] *arthavāda*s, having the nature of praise [of a given course of action], are in fact associated with the teaching (*śāstre*) [of a certain ritual operation] because they are understood to be auxiliary to the injunctive statements, since in this way the injunction is reinforced (*upodbalitaḥ*).[80]

---

79 PrPr 1, p. 52, ll. 1-5: *athāmnāyasya kriyārthatvād bhūtārthaprātipadikaṃ vākyam apramāṇam ity ucyate. tathā hi kāryaparatvenaiva vṛddhavyavahārāc chabdārthasaṃbandhavyutpattipratipatteḥ yatparaś ca śabdasya śabdārthaḥ ity ākhyāyikāmātravarṇane siddhārthābhidhāne prayojanābhāvād vidhiniṣedhacodanābhāvāt kasyacid apy aśāsanād bhūtārthaṃ vākyam aśāstratvād eva na pramāṇatām arhati.* Cf. *Śābarabhāṣya* ad JS 1.2.1, pp. 128-129: *kriyā katham anuṣṭheyā, iti tāṃ vadituṃ samāmnātāro vākyāni samāmananti. tad yāni vākyāni kriyāṃ nāvagamayanti, kriyāsambaddham vā kiñcit, evam eva bhūtam artham anvācakṣate... evañjātīyakāni tāni kaṃ dharmaṃ pramimīran.* "In order to state how an action should be performed, the transmitters [of traditional knowledge] hand down [certain] sentences. Now, there are sentences that do not inform about an action, or something connected with an action, [and] in this way indeed [only] tell about [some] past object – what *dharma* could such sentences institute?".

80 PrPr 1, p. 52, ll. 5-7: *pravartakavākyāṅgabhāvena tu samanvayam eti. śāstre stāvakatvena hy arthavādavākyāni vidhivākyāṅgabhāvagamanād anvayabhāñji bhavanti. evaṃ hi vidhir upodbalito bhavati.*

4.2. Critique of the Mīmāṃsā View

The *arthavāda* passages may well be meant mainly to encourage people to undertake certain actions, but does this mean that they should be discarded altogether as sources of valid knowledge? Helārāja concisely presents the two alternatives that arise with regard to the validity of *arthavāda*s. One view, upheld by the Mīmāṃsakas, maintains that they have no object of their own and are a subordinate element in complex sentences centred on an injunction;[81] the other view, to which Helārāja subscribes, starts from the observation that generally these texts do make sense even by themselves and argues that, only after they have fulfilled their communicative function and conveyed their object, they can assist in the achievement of further goals enjoined by other passages:

> With regard to this, we say: do the statements [known as] *arthavāda*s, [being] as meaningless as individual sounds, really become auxiliary in a prescriptive complex sentence (*mahāvākya*) that express the object to be realised? Or do they have some object of their own [and,] bringing an understanding of it, they turn out to be conducive to [the object] to be realised? These are the two alternative views.[82]

Helārāja explicitly rejects the first view with arguments that are at least partly borrowed from Mīmāṃsā itself. It cannot be denied, he points out, that these non-injunctive passages are independently meaningful, because if they were not, they could not be expected to play a supportive role to the prescriptive passages:

> The first view is not correct. Since [sentences] with established objects are seen to express their own object as is appropriate in each case, it should be considered whether such an expression [i.e. an *arthavāda*] is only authoritative with regard to its own object or otherwise, because it

---

[81] See Kumārila's conclusive remark in TV on JS 1.2.7 (for which see below), p. 23: *tasmād vidhinaikavākyatvāt tadanugraheṇārthavanto 'rthavādā iti.* "Therefore, because they form one sentence with an injunction, *arthavāda*s have a purpose insofar as they assist with it [i.e. the injunction]."

[82] PrPr 1, p. 52, ll. 8-10: *atra brūmaḥ. kim anarthakāni varṇavad evārthavādavākyāni mahāvākye vidhāyake kāryārthapratipādake 'ṅgabhāvam upayānti, āhosvid ātmīyaḥ kaścid eṣām artho 'sti yatra pratipattim ādadhati kāryaparāṇi saṃpadyanta iti pakṣadvayam.*

is not tenable that something having no function (*akiṃcitkarasya*), [i.e.] meaningless, can be an auxiliary in another context.[83]

Moreover, Mīmāṃsā subscribes to the principle of the intrinsic validity of cognitions (*svataḥ prāmāṇyam*), which is expounded by Kumārila in ŚlV 33-61 ad JS 1.1.2, according to which a cognition is inherently valid unless proven to be otherwise.[84] Therefore, argues Helārāja, if the sense of a statement in the non-prescriptive portions of the scriptures is not incongruous, namely contradicted by other valid means of knowledge or authoritative sources, there is no good reason to discard it. After recalling this principle, Helārāja applies it to the case of the existence of the omniscient Lord and other deities, who are frequently mentioned in traditional texts:

> When it is contradicted [by other *pramāṇa*s], it is not valid, but when it is not contradicted, it is indeed valid. For according to the views of the Jaiminīyas, a cognition that is not contradicted is self-validating. And we never descry anything contradicting [the existence of] the omniscient Lord and the deities apprehended from the *śāstra*.[85]

However, as pointed out above, the Mīmāṃsakas would retort that those passages, being of a non-injunctive nature, should be interpreted in a secondary or figurative sense. And, even regardless of the Mīmāṃsā's distinction between *vidhi* and *arthavāda*, it is a fact that *arthavāda* passages in the Vedic texts or the Smṛti generally contain numerous statements which are either mutually contradictory or contrary to ordinary experience. One of the arguments raised against their reliability (for example, by the Buddhists) is that, if

---

[83] PrPr 1, p. 52, ll. 10-12: *prathamaḥ pakṣo na yuktaḥ. yathāyathaṃ siddhārthānāṃ svārthapratipattidarśanād akiñcitkarasyānarthakasya paratrāṅgabhāvānupapatteḥ kevalaṃ sā pratipattiḥ tatra svārthe pramāṇabhūtā anyathā veti vicāryam.*

[84] See v. 47ab: *svataḥ sarvapramāṇānāṃ prāmāṇyam iti gamyatām* |. "It should be understood that the validity of every valid cognition is from itself," and the conclusion in v. 53: *tasmād bodhātmakatvena prāptā buddheḥ pramāṇatā* | *arthānyathātvahetūtthadoṣajñānād apodyate* ||. "Therefore, the validity of a cognition, which has resulted from its being a cognition, is [exceptionally] cancelled [only] when [one] finds that the object [of the cognition] is otherwise [than the way it was cognized] or that there are bad qualities in [its] cause." (Transl. KATAOKA 2011, vol. II, pp. 246-247 and 257-259.) For a recent extensive treatment of this theory, see ibid., esp. pp. 60-98.

[85] PrPr 1, p. 52, ll. 12-14: *yatra bādhaḥ tatrāpramāṇam. abādhe tu pramāṇam eva. abādhitā hi saṃvit svataḥ pramāṇam iti jaiminīyanayaḥ. sarvajñeśvaradevatānāṃ ca śāstrād adhigatānāṃ na kiñcana bādhakam utpaśyāmaḥ.*

they cannot be relied upon on issues that can be settled through ordinary *pramāṇa*s such as perception and inference, their reliability on trans-empirical topics is inevitably undermined too. Or, to put it differently, the dilemma is whether the authority of a traditional source is sufficient guarantee of the veridicity of *all* its contents – a problem to which Helārāja turns next.

4.3. On the Reliability of the Scriptures: The Example of Talking Cats

The example chosen by Helārāja to illustrate the objection that some scriptural passages are incongruous is quite unusual, as it refers to the fact that certain authoritative works (*śāstra*) refer to talking cats,[86] and I have not been able to find any precedent or parallel for it. In his defense of scriptural authority even on such matters, Helārāja resorts to the argument of omniscience:

> One may object that in the *śāstra* one hears [references to] the meaningful statements of cats etc., and this is incongruous [with common experience], therefore in the very same way any [statement] about [any] invisible [i.e. trans-empirical] object is not reliable. [Reply:] You cannot say that. The meaningfulness of the statements of omniscient beings is never

86 It is difficult to guess what authoritative text(s) Helārāja had in mind with this bizarre reference to talking cats. As far as I could ascertain, the few mentions of cats in Vedic texts (whether called *mārjāra* or *biḍāla*) never depict them speaking. However, in the *Mahābhārata* (12.136.18f.) there is a dialogue between a mouse called Palita, who is an expert on *arthaśāstra*, and a cat named Lomaśa. The two, finding themselves in a situation of danger, strike an unlikely alliance that allows both to save their lives, and in the course of the story they discuss at length issues such as trust, friendship, etc. The cat Lomaśa is said to be *buddhimān* "clever" and *vākyasampannaḥ* "possessed with eloquence." Since Itihāsa (the Epics) and Purāṇa were generally regarded as part of the Smṛti, and Helārāja mentions them a few lines below as a source of teachings on *dharma*, he may be alluding to this *Mahābhārata* episode or a similar story (I wish to thank Marco Franceschini for his help in checking the mentions of cats in Vedic texts and drawing my attention to the story of Lomaśa in the *Mahābhārata*). R. Śarmā does not say so explicitly, but after quoting the PrPr sentence about cats verbatim, he recalls that in the *Mahābhārata* one also finds a dialogue between a vulture and a jackal (AK, p. 98: *nanu ca mārjārādīnāṃ sārthakaṃ vacanaṃ śāstre śrūyate, mahābhārate ca gṛdhragomāyusaṃvādaḥ smaryate*).

> invalidated, [all the more so] when it is even seen to agree with other traditional sources (*āgama*).[87]

Thus, according to Helārāja one cannot dismiss the veridicity of a traditional source that mentions talking animals because the works in which they are found have been composed by omniscient beings. This seems to imply that these exceptional individuals have access to planes of experience that are beyond the reach of ordinary human cognition, and what sounds incongruous to us might be true on some other level of reality. Moreover, Helārāja points out that this skepticism is even less justified if several sources (*āgamāntareṇa*) agree on something that appears incomprehensible or even absurd to ordinary people.

With the example of talking animals apparently still on his mind, Helārāja appeals to an authoritative source, the YS:

> But ordinary people (*carmacakṣuṣaḥ*[88]) do not believe in this [sort of thing]. To illustrate [my point], the revered Patañjali taught: "Through the concentration upon word and meaning, there arises the knowledge of the cries of all beings" (YS 3.17).[89]

The quotation from the YS seems to have several implications. The *sūtra*, which Helārāja gives in a nonstandard form,[90] states that, while normally there is a superimposition or overlap between a word, the concept it expresses and the object it refers to, one can learn to discern one from the other with the help of meditation, thus achieving the super-natural power of understanding the meanings of the cries of all creatures. At one level, Helārāja seems to be arguing that, as far as matters accessible to the senses are concerned, the consensus of different authoritative texts is equivalent to

---

[87] PrPr 1, p. 52, ll. 15-17: *nanu ca mārjārādīnāṃ śāstre sārthakaṃ vacanaṃ śrūyate. na ca tatra saṃvādo 'stīty evam eva sarvam adṛṣṭārtham apramāṇam. maivaṃ vocaḥ. sarvajñabhūtānāṃ vacanasyāgamāntareṇāpi sārthakatvasya saṃvādopalabdher abādhitatvam eva.*

[88] Literally, "those who perceive with their skin," namely their senses alone.

[89] PrPr 1, p. 52, ll. 17-19: *carmacakṣuṣaḥ param etan na manyante. tathā hi bhagavān patañjaliḥ: "śabdārthasaṃyamanāt sarvabhūtarutajñānam" ādideśa.*

[90] As pointed out by SUBRAMANIA IYER (VP 3.1, p. 52, crit. app.), the *sūtra* usually reads as follows: *śabdārthapratyayānām itaretarādhyāsāt saṅkaras tas tatpravibhāgāsaṃyamāt sarvabhūtarutajñānam.* It is impossible to decide whether the discrepancy stems from the fact that Helārāja records a different version of it, or quotes it wrongly from memory, or abridges it intentionally.

the congruity of *āgama* with other *pramāṇa*s (such as perception and inference): the quote from YS may thus be construed as an example of another source subscribing to the idea that animals do communicate in their own way and therefore corroborating the mention of talking cats in other treatises.

Moreover, as a response to those who find the mention of talking animals absurd, the recourse to the YS quotation (and the YS itself) seems to imply that animals' cries are indeed a form of language with a communicative function; their meaning can become accessible to individuals who, with the help of meditative techniques, develop the ability to transcend the expressive (*vācaka*) level of language and grasp what is expressed (*vācya*) directly. In other words, the language of animals can become intelligible to individuals who do not rely just on their senses to understand the world around them, but also on their especially trained minds.

This also seems to be the intention behind the brief observation at the beginning of the passage just quoted. It is interesting to note that the term *carmacakṣus* also appears in Jayanta Bhaṭṭa's NM, in a section devoted to the refutation of Kumārila's objections against omniscience. After quoting ŚlV 112 ad JS 1.1.2 (for which see below), in vv. 127-128 Jayanta remarks:

> [Objection:] However, it is preposterous to claim that *dharma*, which consists in [the ritual duties] that ought to be fulfilled and is not affected by past, present and future, can be the object of perceptual cognition. [Reply:] True! This is [indeed] preposterous with regard to ordinary people (*carmacakṣuṣaḥ*) such as you or me, but it is not arduous for omniscient yogis to follow this path.[91]

The rationale behind the NM verses – and Helārāja's statement, possibly inspired by the former – seems to be that reality (both mundane, as in the case of the cries of animals, and ultra-mundane, as in the case of *dharma*) is far more complex than ordinary people even realise. Nevertheless, its aspects and dimensions that lie beyond the powers of human cognition are accessible to omniscient beings, so that if a *smṛti*, by definition the work of such an exceptional individual, contains statements that we do not understand or that seem to clash with our usual experience, we have to assume

[91] NM, Āhnika 2, pp. 270-271: *nanu kartavyatārūpaḥ trikālasparśavarjitaḥ | cakṣurviṣayatām eti dharma ity atisāhasam || satyaṃ sāhasam etat te mama vā carmacakṣuṣaḥ | na tv eṣa durgamaḥ panthā yogināṃ sarvadarśinām ||*.

that this is due to our limitations, rather than question the truthfulness of the text.

It is interesting to note that YS 3.17 is also quoted by Abhinavagupta in a passage of the *Parātriśikatattvavivaraṇa* and alluded to in another passage of the same work. The passages in question, discussed in TORELLA 2004 (esp. pp. 174-175), expound Abhinavagupta's view that phonemes (*varṇa*) possess denotative power (*vācakatva*)[92] and, if other sounds such as those produced by musical instruments or the cries of animals are also regarded as expressive in the broader sense of the word, "this simply means that all sounds, without distinction, must have phonemes as their ultimate stuff" (ibid., p. 175).

In Helārāja's passing mention of the cries of animals there is no trace of a speculation on the expressivity of individual phonemes (which, as noted by Torella, would be in conflict with Bhartṛhari's view according to which only *vākya*, the sentence, is the fundamental semantic unit of speech), or even less of the metaphysical implications of this notion as seen in Abhinavagupta's work. But from Helārāja's treatment of this topic it seems legitimate to draw the conclusion that, like Abhinavagupta, he sees the power to understand what animals say as the yogi's capacity of getting closer than ordinary humans to the essential unity of the single consciousness – or, even more to the point, the voice – of the whole universe.

4.4. Making the Case for the Validity of Non-Injunctive Texts

Helārāja's final position on non-prescriptive passages in scriptural sources appears to be that they are not always or exclusively subordinated to the teaching of ritual injunctions. If they appear to be invalidated (*asaṃvāditva*) by other statements or valid means of knowledge, they should be interpreted in a figurative way. But if a given statement is confirmed by other equally authoritative sources, it is definitely a *pramāṇa*. As Helārāja puts it:

---

[92] *varṇānām eva ca paramārthato...* "Ultimately, the power of verbal signification, consisting in the identification with meaning, only pertains to phonemes." (Transl. TORELLA 2004, p. 174.)

> Therefore, when in an *arthavāda* sentence there is no congruity [with other *pramāṇa*s, i.e.] when it results in a mere contradiction [of ordinary experience], then, since it expresses an unreal object, it will have to be [construed as] intended (*param*) for the expression of a [ritual] obligation (*kārya*, lit. "what has to be done"). But when there is no contradiction, [for example when] it agrees [with other traditional sources], [then] it is indeed a source of valid knowledge, and in that case it is not intended for any [ritual] obligation.[93]

What is the function, though, of the non-injunctive passages in scriptural sources, if it is admitted that at least some of them have a purpose of their own? Helārāja's opinion is that discursive texts, which often speak of past events and mention well-known objects (in contrast to injunctions, which prescribe actions that ought to be carried out), do indeed teach *dharma* in their own way. He illustrates his point with the example of Itihāsas and Purāṇas, whose authority is accepted by many currents within Brahmanism.[94] These famous works, basically consisting of narrations (like many of the Vedic *arthavāda*s), and often in the form of didactic dialogues (such as the one between Lomaśa and Palita!), also dispense teaching on religious and moral matters that cannot be settled by the simple recourse to reason:

> And in this [kind of sentence] there is nothing that is intended for [the reinforcement of a ritual] obligation, because, as the sentences in the Purāṇas and Itihāsa convey objects that are already realised, it is [generally] admitted that their knowledge alone is [sufficient] for *dharma* to arise since it is observed that the dialogues [contained in these works] fulfil [their function] merely by [doing] that[95].[96]

---

[93] PrPr 1, p. 52, ll. 19-21: *tasmād yatra nāsti saṃvādo bādhakamātraparyavasānam arthavādavākye, tad asatyārthapratipādanenāstu kāryamātrapratipādanaparam. yatra tu nāsti bādhaḥ śāstrāntareṇa saṃvādaḥ tat pramāṇam eva. na ca tatra kāryaparatā.*

[94] On the authority of *smṛti*s, see the following remark by Kumārila in TV (p. 79): *tena sarvasmṛtīnāṃ prayojanavato prāmāṇyasiddhiḥ. tatra yāvad dharmamokṣasambandhi tadvedaprabhavam. yat tv arthasukhaviṣayaṃ tallokavyavahārapūrvakam iti vivektavyam. eṣaivetihāsapurāṇayor apy upadeśavākyānāṃ gatiḥ. upākhyānāni tv arthavādeṣu vyākhyātāni.*

[95] The phrase "merely by doing that" translates *tāvati eva*, literally "to that extent alone." I take it to mean that they achieve their goal of teaching *dharma* merely by conveying *siddhārtha*s, accomplished objects and events, without having recourse to injunctions.

The religious perspective sketched in this passage is clearly a far cry from the Vedic orthodoxy advocated by Mīmāṃsā, as it pushes the boundaries of Brahmanism as narrowly defined by the latter to accommodate the beliefs and practices of what may be called in short "post-Vedic Brahmanism." Kumārila admits that the Smṛtis are authoritative, but applies the same distinction between injunctive and non-injunctive passages in them as in the Vedas. Commenting on JS 1.2.7, *vidhinā tv ekavākyatvāt stutyarthatvena vidhīnāṃ syuḥ*, "Because they [i.e. *arthavāda*s] form one sentence with an injunction, they should be [interpreted] as having the purpose of praising [the action prescribed by] the injunctions," he writes:

> The sentences of the *Mahābhārata* etc. should be explained in this way. [...] Some are direct injunctions concerning [matters such as] gifts, kingship, liberation, *dharma*, etc., while others are *arthavāda*s because they consist of traditional lore about the deeds of other people. And, as this is the intention in all the stories [narrated in these works], one should teach [them to people],[97] therefore, since [in such contexts] an injunction would be pointless, one has to admit that somehow the praise or blame [of certain actions] is being conveyed.[98]

According to Helārāja, however, the scope of the teachings imparted in these texts is much broader than the Vedic ritual arena, and even the passages dealing with established objects (*siddhārtha*s) may have a purpose of their own, for example teaching about appropriate objects of meditation, such as God (*īśvara*), as he argues in the continuation of the PrPr passage:

> Moreover, one can practise meditation etc. [only] when the object of meditation is well known, therefore even the texts that talk about the Lord etc. do have a purpose.[99] Thus, a scripture (*śāstram*) [states]: "It is the

96 PrPr 1, p. 52, ll. 21-22: *na ca tatra kāryaparatā siddhārthapratipādanena purāṇetihāsavākyānāṃ tāvaty eva praśnottarayoḥ samāptatvadarśanāt tatparijñānamātrāc ca dharmotpattyabhyupagamāt.*

97 A few lines above Kumārila specifies: *śrāvayec caturo varṇān*, "one should have the four *varṇa*s listen to them."

98 TV ad JS 1.2.7, p. 16: *evaṃ bhāratādivākyāni vyākhyeyāni. ... dānarājamokṣadharmādiṣu kecit sākṣād vidhayaḥ, kecit punaḥ parakṛtipurākalparūpeṇārthavādāḥ. sarvopākhyāneṣu ca tātparye sati śrāvayed iti vidher ānarthakyāt kathaṃcid gamyamānastutinindāparigrahaḥ.*

99 RATIÉ 2013 (pp. 433f., with n. 128) refers to Abhinavagupta's mention of the Purāṇas etc. as a source through which God becomes established (*siddha*) or well known (*prasiddha*), illustrating it with some passages from his commentaries on ĪPK, such as ĪPVV, vol. I, p. 32: *yad yaj jñānakriyāsvatantraṃ tad*

> self that should be known, considered and meditated upon" (BṛUp 2.4.5). Even Patañjali's treatise says: "The sacred syllable *oṃ* is his [the Lord's] sign; its repetition consists in the contemplation of the object signified; thence [arises] the knowledge of the inner consciousness and the absence of obstacles" (YS 27-29).[100]

Two sources are cited in support of this view. The first is a line found in a slightly different form in the *Bṛhadāraṇyaka Upaniṣad*, but clearly recognisable in Helārāja's quotation: *ātmā vā are draṣṭavyaḥ śrotavyo mantavyo nididhyāsitavyo maitreyi*. This often quoted line is the cornestone of all discussions on meditation in classical works of both Pūrva and Uttara Mīmāṃsā.[101] An abridgement of this consisting just in the two words *ātmā jñātavyaḥ* occurs in some of these texts prior or roughly contemporary to Helārāja,[102] who is possibly alluding to them by quoting the Upaniṣad in this form.

The second quotation consists of a string of three aphorisms from YS, in which the sacred syllable *oṃ* is said to be an expression or signifier (*vācakaḥ*) for God (which is its *artha* "object"), so that the recitation of *oṃ* is tantamount to the contemplation (*bhāvanam*) of the Lord and leads to the knowledge of the inner self, removing the obstacles on the path to realisation. Helārāja does not dwell on the two quotes, but their juxtaposition may be meant to remind the readers that while meditation, being necessarily confined to established objects (*siddha-/bhūta-artha*) such as *ātman, praṇava* or *īśvara*, cannot teach anything new or give access to higher truths, it can clear the way to self-realisation, since it trains the mind to discard the passions that are the obstacles (*antarāya*) on

---

īśvaraḥ purāṇāgamasiddha iva "Whatever is free as regards knowledge and action is a Lord, just as [the Lord] known (*siddha*) through Purāṇas and *āgamas*." (Transl. Ratié, ibid.)

100 PrPr 1, pp. 52[l. 22]-53[l. 5]: *kiñ ca dhyeye nirjñāte dhyānādir anuṣṭhātuṃ śakyate iti niṣprayojanatāpi nāstīśvarādipratipādakānāṃ vākyānām. tathā ca śāstram: "ātmā jñātavyo mantavyo nididhyāsitavyaḥ" iti. pātañjalam api: "tasya vācakaḥ praṇavaḥ, tajjapas tadarthabhāvanam, tataḥ pratyakcetanādhigamo 'ntarāyābhāvaś ca" iti.*

101 As pointed out to me by H. David, who also notes that the sentence *ātmā jñātavyaḥ* is the object of a debate regarding its status as an injunction (*vidhi*), which not all thinkers are willing to admit.

102 For example in ŚV, *Sambandhākṣepaparihāra* 103, quoted in RATIÉ 2014, p. 17, n. 58, where the author examines Kumārila's views on the knowledge of the self.

the way to liberation and, as suggested by some of the passages quoted above, it even provides a kind of direct experience of higher truths. Such an argument is found for example in NM (even though the wording of the latter does not suggest that in this case Jayanta's work was the direct source of inspiration of Helārāja), in the context of a discussion on the nature of *yogipratyakṣa* in contrast to divine omniscience:

> There is a difference, namely that the Lord's knowledge is such [i.e. embracing all objects in all three times] eternally, whereas that of yogis originates from the practice of yoga and meditation. [Objection:] But, nowhere is meditation [seen to focus] on a previously unknown object! What is then the use of meditation, since *dharma* is determined from the sacred texts? [Reply:] Only the injunctions [found in the Veda] are a means of valid knowledge with regard to *dharma*, therefore it is said that first the specific object to be proved [i.e. knowledge of *dharma*] can only come from traditional wisdom even for those yogis whose own nature consists in having apprehended *dharma* – this is indeed the way for yogis. Even later, when [their] perceptual cognition [capable of] apprehending *dharma* is active [thanks to meditation], only the [Vedic] injunctions [are authoritative on *dharma*], thus the distinction [between the two kinds of omniscience, divine and yogic,] becomes indeed blurred. Moreover we will explain that the Lord's knowledge, which is indeed connatural [to him] and has *dharma* as its object, is the cause of the Veda.[103]

The reply is that yogis are initially instructed about *dharma* from the Vedas, but then meditation allows them to "perceive" *dharma*. The ultimate source of *dharma* is God's knowledge of the Veda, as it emanates from him.

As a concluding remark on the validity of scriptural sources, Helārāja points out that one cannot pick and choose at will which

---

[103] NM, Āhnika 2, vol. I, pp. 279[l. 3]-280[l. 1]: *asti viśeṣaḥ īśvarasya tathāvidhaṃ nityam eva jñānaṃ yogināṃ tu yogabhāvanābhyāsaprabhavam iti. nanu nādṛṣṭapūrve arthe kvacid bhavati bhāvanā | āgamāt tu paricchinne dharme bhāvanayā 'pi kim ‖146‖ codanaiva dharme pramāṇam iti sāvadhāraṇapratijñārthaḥ prathamam āgamād avagatadharmasvarūpeṣu satsv api yogiṣu na viplavata eveti ucyate, yogiṣv asty evāyaṃ prakāraḥ. paścād api pravartamāne dharmagrāhiṇi pratyakṣe codanaivety avadhāraṇaṃ śithilībhavaty eva. api ceśvarajñānaṃ sāṃsiddhikam eva dharmaviṣayaṃ vedasya kāraṇabhūtaṃ vakṣyāmaḥ.*

passages to consider fully authoritative and which not.[104] If one unquestioningly admits the validity of some of the teachings of Smṛti authors such as Manu, one is logically obliged to admit it en bloc. In Helārāja's words:

> And it is biased (*pakṣapātaḥ*) to accept [the statements of] *smṛti* authors such as Manu etc. [on some issues] and reject [them when they are] about Mahendra, Rudra, etc., for it is not the case that Manu etc., the great *ṛṣi*s, are not omniscient or free from passions. If they were affected by passions or non-omniscient, how could their statements [ever] be authoritative?[105]

5. GOD AS THE AUTHOR OF BOTH ŚRUTI AND SMṚTI

Having rebutted the Mīmāṃsakas' views on Vedic *arthavāda*s and *smṛti*s, Helārāja can make full use of the innumerable texts of the brahmanic tradition that testify to the existence of omniscient beings and to their role in the transmission of traditional knowledge (*āgama*). First he quotes *Nirukta* 1.20.2, which has been discussed above (see § 1), and relying on its authority, he concludes that one should admit that omniscient beings do exist.[106] However, clearly Helārāja is not entirely satisfied with the account of Vedic revela-

---

[104] Cf. NM, Āhnika 3, p. 503, ll. 1-4: *na ca kārya evārthe vedāḥ pramāṇam iti mantrārthavādānām atatparatvam abhidhātum ucitam, kārya iva siddhe 'py arthe vedaprāmāṇyasya vakṣyamāṇatvāt.* "And the Vedas are not a source of valid knowledge only with regard to an object to be accomplished, therefore it is correct to say that mantras and *arthavāda*s are not [exclusively] meant for that [i.e. for an object to be accomplished], because we will explain that the Veda is an authority even with regard to established objects just as [it is] for objects to be accomplished."

[105] PrPr 1, p. 53, ll. 5-6: *smṛtikārāṇāṃ ca manvādīnām abhyupagamo mahendrarudrādīnāṃ pratyākhyānam iti pakṣapātaḥ. na hi manvādayo maharṣayo na sarvajñā vītarāgā vā. rāgādimattve 'jñatve vā teṣāṃ kathaṃ tadvacanaṃ pramāṇam.* Helārāja's statement is rather terse and potentially ambiguous. My translation is based on its interpretation found in R. Śarma's AK: *smṛtikārāṇāṃ ca manvādīnāṃ vacanāni bhavadbhir abhyupagamyante. mahendrarudrādidevatāpratipādakāni tu teṣāṃ vacanāni prakṣiptatvād yuktyā pratyākhyāyante.* "You accept the statements of the authors of the Smṛtis, such as Manu etc. But you reject their statements referring to deities such as Mahendra, Rudra, etc., because you argue that they are interpolated (*prakṣiptatvāt*)."

[106] The quotation of *Nirukta* 1.20 is followed by the words *ity āgamaprāmāṇyāt santi sarvajñāḥ* (PrPr 1, p. 53, l. 11; "based on the authority of this traditional source, omniscient beings do exist").

tion and the beginning of tradition found in the *Nirukta* – and, we have to assume, with Bhartṛhari's substantially analogous version of the same –, and he goes on to provide his own account of these processes, reclaiming a central role for God:

> These very [omniscient] sages (*munibhir*), whose primeval teacher was the Venerable One (*bhagavān*), [who taught them] so that there would not be a chain of blind men, have handed down that he is the expounder of all *śāstra*s (*sarvaśāstrapravaktā*). Even though the words of the *śāstra* are eternal, the *śāstra* was indeed composed by the Lord (*īśvarapraṇītatvam*) because it has the nature of [a work] comprised of compositions (*racanāvattvāt*). Accordingly, God is apprehended from the *śāstra*, [and] the *śāstra* proceeds from him, thus it has been said that "the cause of his [i.e. the Lord's apprehension] is the *śāstra*. But what is the cause of the *śāstra*? Its cause is the Lord. There is an eternal relation between *śāstra* and [the Lord's] excellence (*utkarṣa*), which are ever-present in the essence of the Lord" (YS-*Bhāṣya* 1.24)[107].[108]

In Helārāja's account Īśvara imparts the original teaching to the sages, here called *muni*s. God is said to be the "expounder of all *śāstra*s" (*sarvaśāstrapravaktā*);[109] his purpose is to provide mankind with guidance, namely the means to attain salvation, so that they will not stumble along in the darkness of ignorance. And while the words used in these works are eternal, since according to

---

107 The sentence (in inverted commas in the edition) is a quotation from YS-*Bhāṣya* 1.24, not identified in Subramania Iyer's edition of the PrPr. Cf. Vācaspatimiśra's *Tattvavaiśaradī* on YS 1.24 (p. 68): *so 'yam īdṛśa īśvarasya śāśvatka utkarṣaḥ* ***kiṃ sanimittaḥ*** *sapramāṇaka āhosvin* ***nirnimitto*** *niṣpramāṇaka iti? uttaram –* ***tasya śāstraṃ nimittam****. śrutismṛtītihāsapurāṇāni śāstram. codayati – śāstram punaḥ kiṃnimittam. ... pariharati – prakṛṣṭasattvanimittam,* "This is the eternal excellence of such a Lord – is there a cause [for admitting it], [i.e.] a valid proof [of it], or is it without a cause, [i.e.] without a proof? The answer is that *śāstra* is the cause [for admitting the excellence of the Lord]. *śāstra* comprises Śruti, Smṛti, Itihāsa and Purāṇa. He presents the objection: But what is the cause of *śāstra*? He replies: Its cause is the excellence of Being."

108 PrPr 1, p. 53, ll. 11-15: *yeṣām andhaparamparāvyudāsārtham ādigurur bhagavān sarvaśāstrapravaktā tair eva munibhir āgamyate. śāstrasya hi śabdanityatve 'pi racanāvattvād īśvarapraṇītatvam eva. tathā ca śāstrād īśvaraḥ samadhigamyate, tasmāc chāstraṃ pravṛttam iti "tasya śāstraṃ nimittam. śāstraṃ punaḥ kiṃnimittam? īśvaranimittam. tad etayoḥ śāstrotkarṣayor īśvarasattve vartamānayor anādiḥ saṃbandha" ity uktam.*

109 Among the earliest philosophical statements asserting God's authorship of the *śāstra*s are those found in the PDhS and the YS-*Bhāṣya*, for which see CHEMPARATHY 1968, pp. 73-74 and 76.

Bhartṛhari language is an integral part of the nature of the absolute, the form in which they are arranged as compositions (*racanā*) is proof that they have been created by God.

Helārāja's use of the expression *racanāvattva* reveals his indebtedness to Jayanta Bhaṭṭa's main argument (mostly developed in Āhnikas 3 and 4 of the NM[110]) for the existence of God, namely that the Veda, consisting of compositions, i.e. orderly sequences of words, must have an author, like any other text:

> Since [one has to admit that] sentences consist of arrangements of words, even according to the view that words are eternal, how can the Veda be uncreated, since one has to assume that an individual is its author? Accordingly, the Vedic compositions presuppose an author, because they have the nature of a composition, like worldly compositions.[111]

On the contrary, the Mīmāṃsakas argue that the uncreated eternal nature of the Veda is proven by the fact that no name has been handed down as that of its author, and they reject the theist argument that the existence of God can be asserted on the basis of *śāstra*, and the *śāstra* is authoritative because it is issued from God (an argument that Helārāja chooses to illustrate with the YS-*Bhāṣya* quote cited above), accusing it of circularity and questioning the interpretation of the scriptural sources mentioning a Creator God (see §§ 4.1 and 4.2 above).[112] Here is the summary of their position provided by Jayanta:

> However, it is clear that there is mutual dependence [of the two theses], since one understands that there is a creator [God] from the Veda: the authority of the Veda derives from him [i.e. God], and [the existence of]

---

[110] I am not aware of any translations or studies specifically devoted to these chapters of Jayanta Bhaṭṭa's major work, but there is a translation of the NM – rather free but helpful – in BHATTACHARYYA 1978 covering the first 5 *āhnikas*.

[111] NM, Āhnika 4, vol. I, p. 573, ll. 4-7: *padanityatvapakṣe 'pi vākye tadracanātmake, kartṛtvasaṃbhavāt puṃsaḥ vedaḥ katham akṛtrimaḥ. tathā ca vaidikyo racanāḥ kartṛpūrvikāḥ racanātvāt laukikaracanāvat.*

[112] Jayanta Bhaṭṭa responds to this allegation claiming that the existence of God is not only asserted on the basis of *āgama*, but can also be inferred from the orderly arrangement (*saṃniveśa*) of the universe, which must be the fruit of the design of an omniscient being (a claim that is of course rejected by Mīmāṃsā, as one could expect). On this inferential argument, which Helārāja only mentions in passing, see § 7 below.

> a creator is ascertained on the basis of the Veda! Consequently, this is a faulty reasoning stemming from [understanding] mantras and *arthavādas* literally (*yathāśruta*) without due consideration of the surrounding context. But, actually, no one has any memory of the author of the Veda. Therefore, the Veda is uncreated because there is no recollection of an author, even though he should definitely be remembered![113]

To this the Naiyāyika retorts:

> If one wonders which of these two arguments is invalid, the one [that the Veda has an author] because it has the nature of a composition or the one [that the Veda is uncreated] because there is no recollection of an author, only the argument of [the Veda] being a composition is said to be valid. Nowhere can it be admitted that syllables arrange themselves [orderly] without [the intervention of] an individual. Indeed, noble sir, where has this ever been seen or heard on earth, [namely] that words arrange [themselves] naturally in the texts? If the arrangement of words in the Veda were spontaneous, in fact, how could [the arrangement] of threads in a cloth not be spontaneous [too]?[114]

However, taking into account the unique character of the Veda, we have to assume that its author is also exceptional, in a different league from human authors. Only God possesses the exceptional qualities that one has to assume in the individual responsible for the creation of the text that shows the path to *dharma*:

> [Objection:] But, since the Veda teaches the relations between the means and the objectives for [the attainment] of the various results of [ritual] actions that are inaccessible to other means of valid knowledge, how can there be a teacher, an individual having direct knowledge of those objects? [Reply:] We say that the individual who is the author of the Veda is not a man like any other, but the supreme Lord who is competent to

---

113 NM, Āhnika 4, vol. I, p. 577, ll. 9-13: *vedāt kartravabodhe tu spaṣṭam anyonyasaṃśrayam. tato vedaprāmāṇatvaṃ vedāt kartuś ca niścayaḥ. tasmāt paurvāparyaparyālocanārahitayathāśrutamantrārthavādamūlā bhrāntir eṣā. na punaḥ paramārthataḥ kaścit kiñcit vedasya kartāraṃ smarati. tasmāt akṛtakā vedāḥ avaśyasmaraṇīyasyāpi kartuḥ asmaraṇāt.*

114 NM, Āhnika 4, vol. I, pp. 579[l. 13]-580[l. 2]: *nanu katarad anayoḥ sādhanayor aprayojakaṃ racanātvāt asmaryamāṇakartṛkatvād iti ca ucyate racanātvam eva prayojakam. na hi puruṣam antareṇa kvacid akṣaravinyāsa iṣṭavyaḥ. bho bhagavantaḥ sabhyāḥ kvedaṃ dṛṣṭaṃ kva vā śrutaṃ loke yad vākyeṣu padānāṃ racanā naisargikī bhavati. yadi svabhāvikī vede padānāṃ racanā bhavet paṭe hi hanta tantūnāṃ kathaṃ naisargikī na sā.*

create the three worlds. God is the supreme knower, perpetually blissful, [and] compassionate...[115]

In this account of the origin and transmission of the traditional body of knowledge, there is an intimate, co-substantive relation between God and the scriptures – a view expressed in the YS-*Bhāṣya* passage quoted by Helārāja and reiterated in another authoritative source he cites next, the *Bhagavadgītā*, introduced by the affirmation that Kṛṣṇa is an *avatāra* of Maheśvara:

> Similarly, the venerable incarnation (*avatāreṇa*) Kṛṣṇa, who is possessed (*āviṣṭa°*) with the nature of Maheśvara, has stated in the *Gītā*: "I am the author of the End of the Veda and the knower of the Veda" (BhGītā 15.15)[116].[117]

In this view, *śāstra*, the corpus of traditional brahmanical learning, exists within human time – history – and yet, at the same time, it transcends ordinary reality, as Helārāja explains in the following passage:

> Moreover, in this way the *śāstra*, being eternal, does not undergo destruction because it has the nature of the Lord's mind. And it has indeed been said that the Lord is eternal since he is not limited by Time.[118] The Veda itself, comprising specific compositions, always exists in the mind of the Lord, consisting of direct awareness (*darśanātmani*). Therefore, [in its case] there is definitely no [one who is the] author of the composition, like Manu etc. in the case of the Smṛti, [who composed their treatises] in the course of time. Thus, in the *Brahmakāṇḍa* [Bhartṛhari] has

---

115 NM, Āhnika 3, vol. I, p. 484, ll. 1-6: *nanu vede pramāṇāntarasaṃsparśarahitavicitrakarmaphalagatasādhyasādhanabhāvopadeśini katham tadarthasākṣāddarśī puruṣa upadeṣṭā bhavet. ucyate: vedasya puruṣaḥ kartā na hi yādṛśatādṛśaḥ | kintu trailokyanirmāṇanipuṇaḥ parameśvaraḥ || sa devaḥ paramo jñātā nityānandaḥ kṛpānvitaḥ |*.

116 The first half of the verse, not quoted by Helārāja but certainly known to his readers and resonating in their minds, reads: *vedaiś ca sarvair aham eva vedyo*, "I can be known through all the Vedas." Incidentally, in the *Īśvarapratyabhijñāvivṛti* Utpaladeva introduces a reference to the *Bhagavadgītā* with almost the same words used by Helārāja: ... *vikalpavyāpārāpohanaśaktir iti gītāsu bhagavatāviṣṭamaheśvarabhāvena parigaṇitā* (see TORELLA 2007, p. 480).

117 PrPr 1, p. 53, ll. 15-18: *tathā ca gītāsv āviṣṭamaheśvarabhāvena bhagavatā kṛṣṇāvatāreṇābhihitam: "vedāntakṛd vedavid eva cāham" iti.*

118 Cf. YS 1.26, quoted by Helārāja at the beginning of PrPr ad VP 3.1.46.

> stated: "They say that the Śruti is without beginning, uninterrupted, authorless, but the Smṛti, composed by *śiṣṭa*s, is [also] unbroken."[119]

Here Helārāja defends the usual distinction between Śruti and Smṛti, while reiterating that the Veda is made of compositions (and therefore, God's creation). The difference between the two classes of texts is that the Veda exists eternally in God's mind, while Smṛti works, even though they express eternal truths, are composed by human authors such as Manu at some point in historical time. From Helārāja's words this seems to imply that the ancient seers who had the revelation of the Veda passed it on without any intervention, in agreement with the view expressed by Bhartṛhari in VPVṛ 173 (quoted in § 1 above). In the case of the Smṛti, on the other hand, they distilled – as it were – the truths they had been taught to impart the same teachings to ordinary people. In both cases, however, the uninterrupted nature of the transmission is emphasised, an idea that is already found in the VP, as shown by the quotation of VP 1.172, and generally reiterated in the works of all brahmanical authors.

6. THE UNIQUE FEATURES OF *YOGIPRATYAKṢA*

In the final part of his articulate rebuttal of the Mīmāṃsakas' doctrines, Helārāja engages again with Kumārila's critique of omniscience, especially levelled at the idea that this form of cognition might include "direct" – i.e. perception-like – knowledge of *dharma,* which for the Exegetes is only possible through Vedic statements.[120] In ŚlV 1.1.2, v. 110cd-111, Kumārila seems to concede that an individual might be omniscient if he/she relied on all the

---

119 PrPr 1, p. 53, ll. 18-23: *evam api ca śāstrasya nityatve kṣatir nāstīśvarabuddhirūpatvāt tasya. īśvarasya nityatvaṃ kālenānavacchedād uktam eva. viśiṣṭaracanāvata eva vedasyeśvarabuddhau darśanātmani sadāvasthitatvam iti smṛtivad yathākālaṃ manvādivad asya racanākartāpi nāstīty uktaṃ brahmakāṇḍe: "anādim avyavacchinnāṃ śrutim āhur akartṛkām |. śiṣṭair nibadhyamānā tu na vyavacchidyate smṛtiḥ* ‖ (VP 1.172 [= SI 1.136]) *iti.*

120 See *Śābarabhāṣya* ad JS 1.1.2: *aśakyam hi tat puruṣeṇa jñātum ṛte vacanāt,* "For a human being cannot cognize that [heaven arises from the Agnihotra offering] without [resorting to] a [Vedic] statement" (transl. KATAOKA 2011) and the criticism of omniscience in ŚlV ad JS 1.1.2, vv. 110cd-114 (the last one partially quoted by Helārāja here), which is examined in depth in KATAOKA 2011 (in particular pp. 320-329), from which I borrow all the translations of ŚlV quoted in this section. On the Mīmāṃsa rejection of yogic perception, see also L. McCrea's contribution in FRANCO 2009, pp. 55-70.

pramāṇas, but he insists that *dharma* is the exclusive preserve of *śabda* (in the narrow sense of Vedic statements).[121] Claiming that *dharma* can be directly cognised through some kind of extraordinary perception is unacceptable to Kumārila, who points out that each *pramāṇa* has its own specific domain of operation, not unlike the senses, each of which has its own objects – form/colour for sight, sound for hearing, etc.:

> However, a man who postulates an omniscient being [who knows everything] through a single means of valid cognition surely understands everything, [even] taste and so on, with the eye [i.e. by seeing it]. But today people can cognize particular kinds of objects through particular means of valid cognition. The same was [the case] even in those days [of the Buddha and others]" (ŚlV ad 1.1.2, vv. 112-113).[122]

In fact, continues Kumārila in v. 114,

> Even [when] superiority of a particular [*pramāṇa*, e.g. a sense-faculty,] is seen, it [i.e. that superiority] should remain within the [same domain of] perceiving those things that are remote, subtle and so on, because [superiority can]not transgress the domain of that [*pramāṇa*]; it is not the case [that superiority is there] because the ear functions towards a color.[123]

Kumārila points out that each sense organ is only capable of grasping certain kinds of objects but not others. Yet, omniscient beings are supposed to have a simultaneous direct apprehension of all knowable objects in the universe – past, present and future. What is the nature of their cognition, then, since perception, the most obvious candidate among the *pramāṇas*, is not only subject to the

---

[121] ŚlV 1.1.2, v. 110cd-111: *nānena vacaneneha sarvajñatvanirākriyā* ‖ *vacanād ṛta ity evam apavādo hi saṃśritaḥ* ‖ *yadi ṣaḍbhiḥ pramāṇaiḥ syāt* | *sarvajñaḥ kena vāryate* ‖. "Here, with this statement, [Śabara] does not [intend to] deny [the possibility of] being omniscient; for [Śabara], stating [an exceptional condition] 'without a [Vedic] statement,' relies on an exception [and allows the general possibility that a person can know a *dharma* from a Vedic statement]. If [a person] knows everything through the six means of valid cognition, what would stop him [from being omniscient]?".

[122] *ekena tu pramāṇena sarvajño yena kalpyate* | *nūnaṃ sa cakṣuṣā sarvān rasādīn pratipadyate* ‖ *yajjātīyaiḥ pramāṇais tu yajjātīyārthadarśanam* | *bhaved idānīm lokasya tathā kālāntare 'py abhūt* ‖.

[123] ŚlV 114 ad JS 1.1.2: *yatrāpy atiśayo dṛṣṭaḥ sa svārthānatilaṅghanāt* | *dūrasūkṣmādidṛṣṭau syān na rūpe śrotravṛttitaḥ* ‖.

constraints mentioned above but also dependent on the presence of a perceivable object (and therefore confined to the present)?

Concluding the discussion on omniscience, Helārāja elaborates on the nature of extraordinary cognition and, contra Kumārila, he insists that omniscience is essentially perceptual in nature. His view appears to agree with some of Bhartṛhari's own statements on *yogipratyakṣa* quoted above. However, instead of relying on his *mūla* text, here Helārāja chooses to quote a passage of upaniṣadic flavour from an unnamed source in support of the idea that yogis can apprehend any object with any of the senses, or possibly all of them at once:

> Therefore, in this way, based on the authority of *āgama*, [we can affirm that] there are *śiṣṭa*s who see the real nature of things and perceive objects that are beyond the reach of the senses. Thus, they see universals such as cowness, brahmin-hood, etc., according to each case, as distinct from their substrata (*āśrayavivekena*). And the cognition of these *śiṣṭa*s employs all the senses because it does not suffer any limitation, for omniscient beings can carry out the activity of one sense even with another sense. Thus, a traditional source (*āgama*) declares: "Now they do not see with their senses alone: one hears sounds with the sense of smell, one sees colours behind the back, one can even perceive all the objects of the senses with the tip of a finger."[124] Alternatively, their cognition of the universal of brahmin-hood is not merely visual, but also related to other senses. It means that it is capable of ascertaining different subtle universals of sound etc. [125][126]

---

[124] The source of this passage is not known, and as far as I have been able to ascertain, no other author quotes it.

[125] I am not sure how to understand the final comment after the quote. Possibly, Helārāja is suggesting that yogis could tell a brahmin from his voice, etc. I suspect that the alternative interpretation he advances of the phenomenon in question reflects one of the positions in the debate, but I have not been able to identify its supporters.

[126] PrPr 1, pp. 53[l. 23]-54[l. 7]: *tad evam āgamaprāmāṇyād bhāvatattvadṛśaḥ śiṣṭāḥ santy atīndriyārthadarśina iti te yathāyathaṃ gotvabrāhmaṇatvādijātīr āśrayavivekenādhyakṣayanti. tac ca teṣāṃ śiṣṭānāṃ jñānaṃ sarvendriyaṃ pratiniyamānapekṣatvāt. sarvajñā hīndriyāntareṇāpīndriyāntaravyāpāraṃ kurvanti. tathā cāgamaḥ: "nedanīm indriyair eva paśyanti, ghrāṇataḥ śabdaṃ śṛṇoti, pṛṣṭhato rūpāṇi paśyati, apy aṅgulyagreṇa sarvendriyārthān upalabhate" iti. athavā na cākṣuṣam eva teṣāṃ viprādijātiviṣayaṃ vijñānam, api tv indriyāntarasaṃbandhy api. śabdādau sūkṣmajātiviśeṣāvadhāraṇakṣamam ity arthaḥ.* The first part of this passage, up to *kurvanti*, is translated in DESH-

After referring the readers to the discussion on *āgama* in the *Śabdaprabhā* (for which see § 1 above),[127] Helārāja goes on dealing with another aspect of Kumārila's argument against omniscience, namely, the limit of *atiśaya* ("excellence" or "superiority"). Turning to the second half of VP 3.1.46, he interprets it not just as a simple parallel between the expertise of jewellers and the omniscience of yogis, but also as rational proof of omniscience or, as he puts it, an "inference that corroborates it" (*anumānaṃ tadupodbalakam*).[128] The nature of this inference is explained as follows:

> In this world one sees particular men excel in knowledge, sovereignty, etc., thanks to practice (*abhyāsavaśāt*). Thus, jewellers have different degrees of excellence in inspecting the nature of gems, and treasurers (*rūpyatarkāṇām*) in distinguishing the quality of precious metals, on the basis of [the experience acquired through] practice. And when some [quality] is [capable] of excellence, it must necessarily be able to reach its highest level (*kāṣṭhāprāptam*) somewhere, like heat [is most powerful] in the sun, the capacity to burn in fire, or coolness in water. In the same way, one can observe superior qualities of knowledge, sovereignty, ability, strength and so forth in certain men; [these qualities,] showing excellence at the highest level [and] encompassing all objects of cognition, indeed allow us to infer a suitable substratum in which they all fully exist together (*pūrṇasamastasampatkam*) [i.e. God]. For it is this excellence that is the seed of omniscience inasmuch as it is observed thanks to the gradation of knowledge etc.[129]

PANDE 1994, pp. 109-110, together with a few more sentences from the end of the PrPr on VP 3.1.46.

[127] One can only speculate about the reason for the odd place of the reference to the *Śabdaprabhā*, in the middle of the discussion on the characteristics of *yogipratyakṣa*. It is possible that in his earlier work Helārāja had not dealt with the issue of *atiśaya*, on which he focuses below.

[128] PrPr 1, p. 54, ll. 9-10: *uttarārdhenāgamasiddhe sarvajñe 'trānumānaṃ tadupodbalakam āha.*

[129] PrPr 1, p. 54, ll. 10-16: *ihābhyāsavaśāj jñānaiśvaryādīnāṃ puruṣaviśeṣeṣv atiśayo dṛṣṭaḥ. yathā vaikaṭikānāṃ ratnatattvaparīkṣāyām, rūpyatarkāṇāṃ ca rūpyagatātiśayaparicchede yathābhyāsaṃ prakarṣatāratamyam. yac ca sātiśayaṃ tad avaśyaṃ kvacit kāṣṭhāprāptaṃ sambhāvyate. yathāditye tejaḥ, dāhakatvam agnau śaityam apsu. tathā jñānaiśvaryaśaktibalādayo guṇāḥ sātiśayāḥ puruṣeṣu dṛṣṭāḥ sarvajñeyavyāpikāṣṭhāprāptam atiśayam āvedayantaḥ tatsamucitam ādhāraṃ pūrṇasamastasampatkam anumāpayanty eva. atiśaya eva hi jñānādīnāṃ tāratamyena dṛśyamānaḥ sarvajñabījam.*

The gist of the inference is that, if a property can vary in degree at all, one can logically expect it to reach its peak somewhere. This reasoning is originally found in the *Bhāṣya* on YS 1.25, *tatra niratiśayaṃ sarvajñabījam*, "In him the seed of omniscience is above excellence" (both the *sūtra* and the *Bhāṣya* are quoted by Helārāja a few lines below):

> The cognition of [objects that are] beyond the reach of the senses, whether past, future or present, [taken] individually or together, be it small or big, is the seed of omniscience. [An individual] in whom this [cognition], as it grows, reaches its highest level, is omniscient. The seed of omniscience is able to reach the highest level because [cognition] is [associated] with excellence [i.e. it can vary in quantity/quality] just like size. The omniscient is someone in whom cognition has reached the highest level.[130]

In his refutation of Kumārila's arguments against omniscience, Jayanta Bhaṭṭa presents the *atiśaya*-based inference in a more articulated form, which may have inspired Helārāja:

> This is the excellence of cognition, which has different degrees (*tāratamya*) like the excellence of qualities such as white etc. Therefore, [this] suggests that excellence can also be absolute (*para*) maximum excellence (*niratiśaya*). And consequently, the yogis are extolled [as those] in whom the highest degree of that [i.e. cognition] is found. And the absolute maximum excellence of cognition is the capacity to apprehend objects that are subtle, hidden, very distant, past, future, etc.[131]

Jayanta considers Kumārila's objection to the idea of *atiśaya/niratiśaya*, quoting ŚlV 114 (see above) and a verse from Kumārila's lost *Bṛhaṭṭīkā* preserved in Śāntarakṣita's TS:

> [Objection:] But, let us admit this idea of the excellence of it [visual perception] when it does not transcend its own object. However, *dharma* is definitely not an object of visual perception! This has been said: ŚlVt 1.1.2.114 [see transl. above]; and also "Even those [people] who are

---

[130] YS-*Bhāṣya* 1.25: *yad idam atītānāgatapratyutpannapratyekasamuccayātīndriyagrahaṇam alpaṃ bahv iti sarvajñabījam. etad vivardhamānaṃ yatra niratiśayaṃ sa sarvajñaḥ. asti kāṣṭhāprāptiḥ sarvajñabījasya sātiśayatvāt parimāṇavad iti. yatra kāṣṭhāprāptir jñānasya sa sarvajñaḥ.*

[131] NM, Āhnika 2, vol. I, p. 268, ll. 7-11: *so 'yaṃ darśanātiśayaḥ śuklādiguṇātiśaya iva tāratamyasamanvita iti gamayati param api niratiśayam atiśayam. ataś ca yatrāsya paraḥ prakarṣaḥ te yogino gīyante. darśanasya ca paro 'tiśayaḥ sūkṣmavyavahitaviprakṛṣṭabhūtabhaviṣyadādiviṣayatvam.*

known among men[132] to be eminent in knowledge, intelligence and power are superior in small increments, not because they see imperceptible things" (TS 3159).[133]

Jayanta's reply is essentially that one should not assess yogic cognition according to the parameters of ordinary cognition:

This is not correct because, even if *dharma* is not an object of visual perception for people like us, nevertheless it will be cognisable to the senses of yogis.[134]

In the following lines Jayanta also argues that an ordinary person can neither prove nor disprove omniscience, because the yogi's experience is beyond the reach of ordinary cognition, therefore his Mīmāṃsaka opponent should not hastily dismiss it.[135] However, he does not insist on the superior perceptual faculties of yogis but suggests instead that the organ which is active in *yogipratyakṣa* is the mind, which unlike the sense organs is not dependent on the presence of the object in order to be able to cognise it.

Helārāja's argument is in many ways similar to Jayanta Bhaṭṭa's. He too quotes ŚlV 1.1.2.114 (partially) in order to refute it and then proceeds to present his view:

And one should not say that "even [when] superiority of a particular [*pramāṇa*, e.g. a sense faculty,] is seen, it [i.e. that superiority] should

---

132 The verse found in the NM contains two variants from the one cited in the TS: *nṛṇām* instead of *narāḥ* in b, which I tentatively take as a *nirdhāraṇaṣaṣṭhī* as shown by my translation, and *cātiśayā* in a, which is probably a mistake for *sātiśayā* found in the TS version. I borrow the translation (modifying it slightly to render *nṛṇām*) from KATAOKA 2011, pp. 327-328, where the section of TS in which this verse appears is compared to the corresponding section of ŚlV.

133 NM, Āhnika 2, vol. I, p. 269, ll. 1-6: *nanu svaviṣayānatikrameṇa bhavatu tadatiśayakalpanā. dharmas tu cakṣuṣo na viṣaya eva. tad uktam "yatrāpy atiśayo dṛṣṭaḥ sa svārthānatilaṅghanāt | dūrasūkṣmādidṛṣṭau syāt na rūpe śrotravṛttitā ||" api ca ye 'pi cātiśayā dṛṣṭā prajñāmedhābalair nṛṇām | stokastokāntaratvena na tv atīndriyadarśanāt || iti.*

134 NM, Āhnika 2, vol. I, p. 269, ll. 7-8: *etad ayuktam yataḥ yady api nāsmadādinayanaviṣayo dharmaḥ tathāpi yogīndriyagamyo bhaviṣyati.*

135 See NM, Āhnika 2, vol. I, p. 267, ll. 1-3: "You do not know that my perception is not capable of apprehending *dharma*; I do not know that your perception is not capable of apprehending *dharma*; neither of us knows if another's perception is unable to grasp *dharma*." (*matpratyakṣam akṣamaṃ dharmagrahaṇa iti bhavān na jānīte tvatpratyakṣam api na dharmagrāhīti nāhaṃ jāne anyasya pratyakṣam īdṛśam eveti ubhāv apy āvāṃ na jānīvahe.*)

remain within the [same domain of] perceiving [...] because [superiority can]not transgress the domain of that [*pramāṇa*]"[136] (ŚlV 114ab ad JS 1.1.2), because one cannot establish the proper domain [of a *pramāṇa* in that this is] in accordance with its substratum, and because one does see [properties such as] luminosity etc. in the sun that exceed their domain.[137] Consequently, [according to the second half of VP 3.1.46] one can adequately prove omniscience even through the inference [based on] its assumption[138] (*sambhāvanānumāna*). This has been said: "In him [i.e. God] the seed of omniscience is above excellence" (YS 1.25). This very seed of omniscience, characterised by the excellence of knowledge, etc., is above excellence in him. It means that "he in which it is above excellence is the omniscient"[139] (YS-*Bhāṣya* 1.25).[140]

Thus, according to Helārāja, a yogi may apprehend things in ways that are quite different from those of ordinary individuals and thus see invisible objects, hear inaudible sounds, etc., but also grasp things the senses are unable to grasp, such as past and future objects or trans-empirical entities such as *dharma*, because the scope of a capacity depends on the nature of its substratum. It is possible that Helārāja was also aware of – and responding to – the critique that Maṇḍana Miśra levels against the *niratiśaya* reasoning found

---

136 This quotation is not identified as such in Subramania Iyer's edition of the PrPr.

137 For the translation of the final remark I have relied on R. Śarma's interpretation. Cf. AK (p. 102): *svārthasya svāśrayānusāritvena niyantum aśakyatvāt. tad yathā – ādityasya dāhakatvaprakāśakatvādayo guṇāḥ sudūraviprakṛṣṭārthaviṣayakā dṛṣṭāḥ, naivam agnipradīpādeḥ,* "The reason is that one cannot limit the domain proper [to a certain property] in that this depends on its substratum. To explain: [certain] properties of the sun, such as the capacity to burn or to illuminate, are seen to affect objects that are very far removed [from it], but this is not so in the case of fires, lamps, etc."

138 Namely, the presumption of the existence of a substratum such that in it cognition can reach its acme, namely turn into omniscience.

139 This quotation is not identified as such in Subramania Iyer's edition of the PrPr.

140 PrPr 1, p. 54, ll. 17-22: *na ca yatrāpy atiśayo dṛṣṭaḥ sa svārthānatilaṅghanād iti vācyam. svārthasya svāśrayānusāreṇa vyavasthāpayitum aśakyatvāt, ādityādau ca prakāśakatvādeḥ svārthātilaṅghanena dṛṣṭatvāt. tasmāt saṃbhāvanānumānenāpi sarvajñasiddhir ucitā. tad uktam: "tatra niratiśayaṃ sarvajñabījam" iti. yad etat sarvajñabījaṃ jñānādīnām atiśayalakṣaṇaṃ tat tatra niratiśayam. "yatra niratiśayaṃ sa sarvajña" ity arthaḥ.*

in the YS-*Bhāṣya*, as his use of the expression *saṃbhāvanānumāna* may indicate.[141]

In the *Vidhiviveka* Maṇḍana considers two possibile interpretations of the argument in the YS-*Bhāsya* and points out its logical fallacy in either case. One may understand the notion of "highest level" (*kāṣṭhā*) as the objective limit (*avadhi*) of a substance or of a capacity,[142] or as the highest "conceivable" (*sambhāvanīya*) limit. In the former case, that can only suggest a level of cognition that is more powerful than the ordinary, but it does not establish that this kind of extraordinary cognition would be able to apprehend everything:

> If the highest level is that above which there is nothing, its attainment is indeed possible (*bhavatu*). However, it is not proved that by means of this [achievement] cognitions (*prājñānām*) can embrace all objects, but rather that most [but not all] objects will be apprehended.[143]

Alternatively, *niratiśaya* may be regarded as the highest "conceivable" (*atha yataḥ paraṃ na sambhāvyate*) level, but if this is a property of substances, Maṇḍana notes, the parallel with size made in the YS-*Bhāṣya* does not work, because the largest imaginable object would be one that takes up all the space (besides the absurdity of such a thing, the implication is possibly that there would be no comparable object).[144] If, on the other hand, *kāṣṭhā* is seen as a property of qualities, then the maximum conceivable level they can attain depends on the nature of the substratum so that, for instance, the effort required of different beings in order to cover a certain distance will differ greatly – and in any case, if the maximum dis-

---

141 On Maṇḍana Miśra's refutation of omniscience, see MORIYAMA 2014, p. 29, n. 5, and pp. 37f., and DAVID forthcoming.

142 ViV, p. 688 (1. 20): *kāṣṭhā yady avadhiḥ kāmaṃ paraṃ yasmād asambhavi* | *kāryadravyair anekānto guṇaiś ca garimādibhiḥ* ||. "If the highest level (*kāṣṭhā*) is the limit above which there can definitely be nothing, [such a limit is] uncertain with [regard to] substances that are produced and qualities such as weight etc."

143 ViV, pp. 688-689: *yadi yataḥ paraṃ nāsti sā kāṣṭhā bhavatu tatprāptiḥ, na tayā sarvaviṣayatvasiddhiḥ bhūyiṣṭhaviṣayatā tu bhavet prājñānāṃ...*

144 ViV, pp. 689-690: *atha yataḥ paraṃ na sambhāvyate. kāryadravyair vyabhicāraḥ, na hi sātiśayā api ghaṭādayaḥ parimāṇataḥ parāsambhāvanīyātiśayaśālinaḥ anyānavakāśaprasaṅgād ekenaiva sarvavyāpteḥ.*

tance one can conceive of is the end of the sky, since the sky is endless, who could ever achieve that level of capacity?[145]

Helārāja appears to overturn this argument (whether his response is triggered by Maṇḍana's treatment in the ViV or not). It is precisely because the power, intensity or scope of a quantifiable property depend on its substratum that it is possible to conceive some unique substance in which that property occurs at the highest level. It is well known that the cognitive capacities of different beings vary enormously. At the highest end of the spectrum there is God, who is omniscient. To express this idea, Helārāja has once again recourse to a quotation from an authoritative source, YS 1.25 with the *Bhāṣya* thereon (the same source that Maṇḍana attacks quite harshly[146]), where the being in which cognition achieves its apex, namely omniscience, is also said to be the fountainhead of the yogi's omniscience. As pointed out by KATAOKA 2011 (p. 326, n. 364), in the ŚlV Kumārila seems to allude to this *sūtra* "in the sense that one can reach the highest limit of human ability 'vertically', and not in the sense that one can transgress the natural demarcation of each *pramāṇa* 'horizontally.'" On the contrary, Helārāja seems to understand it as the affirmation of a divine power that cannot suffer any limitation whatsoever because – as he clarifies a few lines below – the world is its creation. Consequently, the omniscience of yogis, who partake of this aspect of God's nature,

[145] ViV, pp. 689-690: *na ca guṇadharmo 'yam iti sāmpratam tadgatānāṃ garimādīnāṃ tadavasthāsambhavāt sarvair gurutvavadbhir ekakāryārambhābhāvāt prayatnaviśeṣāc cāntikadūraprāpter manuṣyavātahariṇaharipatatriṇām. na ca tasyāsambhāvanīyaparāvastho 'tiśayaḥ anantatvān nabhasaḥ keṣāñcin niratiśayaprāptānām apātaprasaṅgāt. niravaśeṣagantavyadeśaprāptyā hi prayatno niratiśayaḥ syāt, tadanantatayā kuto 'sya niratiśayatā.*

[146] See the closing remark of this section of the ViV, where Maṇḍana questions the very notion of highest level or limit: if a property is measurable, any of its possible values or levels will be relative; if it is not measurable, the opponent's attempt to explain the yogi's omniscience as the result of the attainment of a level similar to God's is logically untenable, as no level can be determined. Maṇḍana certainly does not mince his words with the author of the YS-*Bhāṣya*: "What is this endlessness? [It is] the fact it cannot be determined [in any way]. [Objection: Being *niratiśaya*] is precisely this absence of a measure, since measure is the fact of having such and such an extent. And asserting that God's cognition has attained the highest level, this [man], who makes [corpses inhabited by] demons rise when he performs appeasing rites, [just] shows his ignorance!" (ViV, pp. 697-698: *kim idam ānantyam. aparicchinnatā. nanv eṣa parimāṇābhāva eva etāvattā hi parimāṇam, īdṛśīṃ ca kāṣṭāprāptim īśvarajñānasya vadann ajñānam āvirbhāvayati so 'yaṃ śāntikarmaṇi vetālodayaḥ.*).

is equally unbounded, to the extent that even the usual limitations of the human senses are overstepped.

7. THE NATURE OF ĪŚVARA

More than just omniscience is at stake, in fact, for Helārāja:

> And here the word "omniscience" (*sarvajña*) alludes to sovereignty (*aiśvarya*), therefore it is also established that the one in which sovereignty is above excellence is the lord of all things, the Supreme Lord, because one sees different degrees of sovereignty in kings etc. And thus it has been said that "Even the knowledge of the seers is based on tradition" (VP 1.30cd),[147] because it arises from the Lord who is the root [of their knowledge].[148]

Just as knowledge reaches its acme and is transfigured into divine omniscience, sovereignty, which is seen in different degrees in human beings, only fully exists in the Lord, as absolute independence and agency.[149] Here Helārāja argues that admitting the existence of a supreme God – Parameśvara – is a matter of reason, not just of belief and reliance on tradition. I think this is a crucial element of his discursive strategy in commenting on the VP, because it allows him to introduce God into Bhartṛhari's ontology through a philosophical argument. It is in this spirit, I believe, that Helārāja quotes the verse from the first *kāṇḍa*. In his vision the ancient sages who composed and handed down the traditional body of knowledge must have in turn received it from a pre-existing higher source, which cannot be anybody else but the omniscient God.[150] The nar-

---

[147] This half a verse is from one of the *kārikā*s in the first *kāṇḍa* that I mentioned in § 2 above as constituting some of the background of VP 3.1.46.

[148] PrPr 1, p. 54, ll. 22-23: *sarvajñagrahaṇaṃ cātraiśvaryopalakṣaṇam, tena yatra niratiśayam aiśvaryaṃ sa sarveśvaraḥ parameśvara ity api siddham, rājādīnām aiśvaryatāratamyadarśanāt. itthaṃ ca mūlabhūteśvarasambhavāt "ṛṣīṇām api yaj jñānaṃ tad api āgamapūrvakam."*

[149] Cf. YS-*Bhāṣya* 1.24: *tasmād yatra kāṣṭhāprāptir aiśvaryasya sa īśvara iti. na ca tatsamānam aiśvaryam asti.*

[150] A similar keenness to anchor human traditions in the higher reality of God's consciousness is seen in Abhinavagupta's view, as TORELLA 2013 (pp. 473-474) remarks: "Abhinavagupta agrees with a hypothetical objector saying that, if the *vyavahāra* is conceived of as based on increasingly older *prasiddhi*s, there would be the risk of a regressus ad infinitum and a cognitive chaos, unless, Abhinavagupta says, we recognize a single ultimate source for all *prasiddhi*s. In the Śaiva conception of the Absolute, such a standpoint is an all-

rative of Vedic revelation found in the *Nirukta* and subscribed to by Bhartṛhari is seemingly left untouched, but God is now firmly placed at its core.

Bhartṛhari defines *śabdabrahman* as light, consciousness, eternal, all-encompassing, etc., all qualifications that could equally apply to most descriptions of God, but his representation of the absolute is clearly too remote and impersonal for the religious sensibility of the 10th-c. Kashmiri Helārāja. Among the attributes of *śabdabrahman* are notably missing volition and agency. Bhartṛhari's ontology and cosmogony need to be complemented, as it were, by the divine will of a God who *chooses* to set the world in motion. The following paragraph of the PrPr ad VP 3.1.46 is particularly significant in this respect:

> However,[151] [unlike the *ṛṣi*s mentioned in VP 1.30,] Parameśvara, who is not limited by Time, is possessed with innate properties such as knowledge, sovereignty, etc. The insentient world is the body of that sentient [being], in conformity with his desire, comparable to [the physical body] of the individual self, therefore it is he, the knower of the connections etc. between [those] particular configurations [of parts, namely the phenomenal objects], [connections] that consist in the relations of [mutual] assistance [between the parts], who creates it.[152] Therefore, it has also been proved that all this [world] here also has an intelligent (*buddhimat*) creator – this is settled.[153]

---

knowing personal being in which the totality of the *prasiddhi*s are contained: this is Parameśvara, Bhairava, who also constitutes the inmost essence of all creatures. Or, [...] *prasiddhi* coincides with the very voice of the Lord."

151 The particle *tu* is meant to stress the contrast between the eternal nature of God's omniscience etc., and the acquired character of the seers', as they gain their superior qualities through a sustained effort.

152 The compound *upakāryopakārakabhāvasaṃsthānaviśeṣayogādi* may be construed in more than one way, and my interpretation should be seen as merely tentative. To begin with, the sense of *yogādi* is uncertain: the meaning "connection" for *yoga* is the only one that to me appears to suit the context, even though I am not sure what *ādi* can refer to. Moreover, I take the compound as a *ṣaṣṭhītatpuruṣa* (*saṃsthānaviśeṣāṇāṃ yogāḥ*), but it would also be possible to understand it as a *karmadhāraya*, meaning that the relations between the parts (namely the phenomenal objects) *are* that particular configuration that is the universe. Only a search for parallels within the PrPr and in other works of that time discussing the relation between God and the universe may hopefully shed light on this difficult expression.

153 PrPr 1, p. 55, ll. 1-3: *parameśvaras tu kālenānavacchinnaḥ sahajajñānaiśvaryādidharmayuktaḥ. tasya cetanasyācetanaṃ jagad icchānuvidhāyi pratyagāt-*

In this terse and dense passage Helārāja offers a glimpse into his theology. He begins by reiterating that, as he has shown in the previous pages through the recourse to scriptural sources and by means of reasoning, God's nature is eternal, and properties such as knowledge (*jñāna*) and sovereignty (*aiśvarya*) are inherent in it. As was argued above, they exist there in their highest, incommensurate form, namely as omniscience and omnipotence. Next, he compares God's relation with the material world to that between the body and the individual's inner self, in which the former is animated and controlled by the latter. The world, he says, exists and acts in conformity to God's will (*icchā*). Similarly, Helārāja refers to God's omniscience as the knowledge of the entities that populate the universe – the various specific arrangements (*saṃsthānaviśeṣa*) of parts – and the laws that govern their relations, concluding that he is the creator, for only a superior intelligent (*buddhimat*) being can be responsible for "all this here" (*idam atra viśvam*), namely, for the complexity and regularity of the universe. He also states that this has been proved (*siddham*), certainly an allusion to the classical naiyāyika proof of the existence of God – what TABER 1986 (p. 107) calls the "argument from design" and Potter "the cosmoteleological argument" (EIPh, p. 101) – as is found for instance epitomised in the following statement in NM (vol. I, p. 499, l. 2), *yad yat sanniveśaviśiṣṭaṃ tat tad buddhimatkartṛkaṃ*: in a nutshell, anything that consists in an orderly arrangement (*sanniveśa*) of parts must have an intelligent (*buddhimat*) creator. And in order to explain the wondrous complexity and endless variety of the world one can only assume the existence of an agent whose attributes are infinitely superior to those of ordinary agents, namely God. Interestingly, an elaborate discussion of the same proof is also the main topic of Utpaladeva's short theological treatise, the *Īsvarasiddhi*,[154] in which, as RATIÉ 2013 (pp. 390-391, n. 43) notes,

mana iva śarīram ity upakāryopakārakabhāvasaṃsthānaviśeṣayogādijñātā sa etan nirmimīta iti buddhimatkartṛkam apīdam atra viśvaṃ siddham iti sthitam.

[154] The initial lines of the *Īśvarasiddhi* after the opening verse read: *tanukaraṇādikāryaṃ buddhimatkartṛpūrvakaṃ saṃniveśaviśeṣavattvāt, yad yat saṃniveśaviśeṣavat tat tad buddhimatkartṛnirmitaṃ yathā ghaṭaḥ,* "Effects such as bodies, the organs, etc., presuppose an intelligent agent because they have a specific arrangement [of parts]: whatever shows a specific arrangement [of parts] has been created by an intelligent agent, for instance a pot." On the *Īśvarasiddhi* see TABER 1986 and, more recently, RATIÉ 2016.

"the Śaiva philosopher endeavours to prove the existence of *īśvara* merely from a Naiyāyika (and Saiddhāntika) point of view."[155]

However, there are implicit and explicit differences between Helārāja's views as presented here and the Naiyāyikas' classical position (without forgetting, of course, that on some issues there were different opinions even within Nyāya). The latter assume that the material causes of the creation, such as the atoms, exist independently of God, and have no unanimous opinion on whether God has a body, and if so, of what kind.[156] Helārāja's wording does not entirely clarify his stance on these questions. In the passage quoted above, it may also be possible to construe *icchānuvidhāyi* as the main predicate of the sentence outlining the relation between God and the world, which would thus emphasise the Lord's omnipotence; in this interpretation, Helārāja may not literally be saying that the world is God's body but simply illustrating their relation through the analogy with the relation between the physical body of ordinary creatures and the individual consciousness. Nor does he make any definite statement about the actual existence of the material world – however, since elsewhere he (like Bhartṛhari) resolutely advocates a non-dualist view of reality,[157] it seems legitimate to assume that for him the dichotomy consciousness/matter (which might indeed be suggested by the qualification of the world as *acetana*, "insentient") does not hold outside the plane of *vyavahāra*

---

155 Ultimately, though, as noted in RATIÉ 2016, p. 329, the non-dualist Śaivas "reject the very possibility of an *īśvarasiddhi* on the grounds that the Lord is 'always already established' (*ādisiddha*) in so far as the individual subject is always aware of his being the Lord through mere self-awareness (*svasaṃvedana*)."

156 On the various views held by different early Naiyāyikas on these and other theological issues, see Potter (EIPh, pp. 104-105).

157 It is worth recalling, for example, that one of Helārāja's lost works was called *Advayasiddhi*, the title of which already suggests that it was an apology of non-dualism. This is confirmed by the two contexts of the PrPr in which he refers to this work. See for instance PrPr on VP 3.2.15: "The power of consciousness of that [one reality] which has the nature of consciousness is not subject to change, therefore, since there is no [actual] modification, this is not a theory of *pariṇāma*, like the Sāṃkhya doctrine, but rather a theory of *vivarta*. [...] The rejection of [any] other cause has been expounded in the *Advayasiddhi*" (PrPr 1, p. 119, ll. 4-6: *tasya cidrūpasya cicchaktir apariṇāminīti vikārābhāvān nedaṃ sāṃkhyanayavat pariṇāmadarśanam, api tu vivartapakṣaḥ. viśeṣaś cānayor vākyapadīye 'smābhir vyākhyāta iti tata evāvadhāryam. ihāpi saṃbandhasamuddeśe vakṣyate. kāraṇāntaravyudāsaś cādvayasiddhāv abhihita*[*ḥ*]).

and, consequently, somehow God creates the world as an emanation of himself. The theological position that transpires from these few lines would thus appear to be not too distant from – or at least, not incompatible with – that of the Pratyabhijñā philosophers', according to whom the universe is the product of the externalisation of Śiva's consciousness.[158]

Helārāja's argument in favour of the existence of God appears in fact to be broadly similar to that made in the ĪS, which was likely known to him. His very mention of *icchā* as an attribute of God, in one breath with *jñāna* and *aiśvarya*,[159] absolute knowledge and unbounded agency, points to the affinity – if not the identity – with Śaiva theology, both non-dualist and dualist.[160] The crucial difference between these two groups, as RATIÉ 2016 (ibid., pp. 326-327) remarks, is that "the Saiddhāntikas hold a dualistic conception of cosmic creation somewhat similar to that of the Vaiśeṣikas" and identify the material cause of the universe with *māyā*, while for the non-dualists Śaivas "the consciousness presiding over the creation of the universe indeed acts out of mere will, but in the sense that it does not have recourse to any kind of matter that would exist apart from it." For example, in ĪPK 2.4.1 Utpaladeva explains that God's role as the creator consists in making things manifest *out of his volition* (*icchāvaśāt*), and the *Vṛtti* thereon reiterates that "it is precisely in this power of volition (*icchāśakti*) that his activity, that is, his being creator, consists" (*saiva cecchāśaktir nirmātṛtākhyā kriyā*

---

158 See for example ĪPK 3.2.3ab, *svāṅgarūpeṣu bhāveṣu pramātā kathyate patiḥ* |. "The cognizer is called 'lord' (*patiḥ*) when things appear to him as constituting his own body," and the *Vṛtti* thereon: *aiśvaryadaśāyāṃ pramātā viśvaṃ śārīratayā paśyan patiḥ*, "On the plane of sovereignty the cognizer who sees the universe as his body is 'lord.'" (Transl. TORELLA 2002, p. 198.) As Ratié remarks (RATIÉ 2013, pp. 379-380), "Far from being contingent, this ability of consciousness to grasp itself as being this or that constitutes its very essence and is fundamental to the [Pratyabhijñā] system in its epistemological as well as metaphysical and cosmological aspects, since the Śaiva non-dualists hold that there is nothing outside of Śiva understood as an all-encompassing consciousness, and that this unique consciousness creates the universe merely by grasping (*vimṛś-*) itself in the form of the universe."

159 Here one is reminded of the complex *icchā-jñāna-kriyā* as the *śaktitraya*, the triad of powers of the Trika current of Tantrism, on which see recently NEMEC 2011, pp. 39f.

160 For a discussion of the inferential proof of God in the work of the early Saiddhāntika author Sadyojyotis (7th-8th c.), see RATIÉ 2016, pp. 312ff., which points out the similarities with the argument found later in the ĪS.

tasya).[161] And in ĪPK 2.4.21 causality, agency and action belonging to the limited subjects on the plane of *vyavahāra* are said to be the manifestation of God's volition, which occurs when his consciousness chooses to project itself outwardly as the endless variety of the phenomenal world.[162]

In the passage quoted above Helārāja does not explicitly describe the creation of the world in unequivocally idealist terms as the manifestation of God's consciousness but – in light of the non-dualist views he advocates elsewhere[163] – his mention of the complex *jñāna-icchā-aiśvarya,* and his silence on the nature of the matter the world is made of, make an idealistic interpretation of his words here at least plausible, if not cogent.

Such an interpretation is further corroborated, I think, by his remark that, in creating the world, God knows the particular arrangements of various features that make up objects, and their connections, namely the relative place of things in a universe that for the limited subjects is an infinitely intricate network of such connections. This may be meant to suggest that at the cosmological level the relation of causality between objects that, in terms of *vyavahāra*, are self-contained, is established by God's principle of necessity (*niyati*). Admittedly, though, the passage is too short and ambiguous to allow a univocal interpretation of Helārāja's views. One regrets the loss of the *Śabdaprabhā* all the more.

---

161 ĪPK 2.4.1, *eṣa cānantaśaktitvād evam ābhāsayaty amūn | bhāvān icchāvaśād eṣā kriyā nirmātṛtāsya sā ||*. "And thus, his power being infinite, he makes those things manifest thanks to his volition; and this constitutes his activity, his being creator." (Transl. TORELLA 2002, p. 175.)

162 ĪPK 2.4.21: *itthaṃ tathā ghaṭapaṭādyābhāsajagadātmanā | tiṣṭhāsor evam icchaiva hetutā kartṛtā kriyā ||*. "Therefore, causality, agency, action are nothing but the will of Him who wishes to appear in the form of the universe, in the various manifestations of jar, cloth and so on." See also the *Vṛtti* thereon: *cidvapuṣaḥ svatantrasya viśvātmanā sthātum icchaiva jagat prati kāraṇatākartṛtārūpā saiva kriyāśaktiḥ.* "The very will of Him who is free and has consciousness as His nature to appear as universe constitutes His being cause as regards the universe, in the form of agency; and this is the power of Action." (Transl. TORELLA 2002, p. 187.)

163 See for instance his reference to the "rejection of [any] other cause" (contra Sāṃkhya dualism) in the passage quoted in n. 157 above.

8. THE ORIGIN OF LANGUAGE

In the final portion of his commentary on VP 3.1.46 Helārāja summarises his conclusions about omniscience, pointing to the role of the ancient seers in establishing language among humans but at the same time reconciling this narrative with the Grammarians' view:

> In this way, then, those who are superior to us have been proven by the tradition (*āgama*). And their cognition, which does not depend on the limitations of the senses, has the nature of direct experience (*sākṣātkārarūpa*) – therefore, yogis, who see the true nature of objects that are past or future, subtle, hidden, or very distant,[164] perceive all the universals such as cowness, brahmin-hood, etc., and start teaching them without confusion (*asaṅkareṇa*). However, in the case of brahmin-hood etc. there are some revealing clues (*upavyañjanam*) – having the [same] function as [the physical features such as] dewlap etc. [that characterise cows] – that for us are beyond the reach of the senses. After ascertaining those [clues], the *śiṣṭa*s instituted the names [of things]. This has been said: "The naming [of things] is preceded by perception" (VS 2.1.19). Thanks to the teaching of the venerable [seers] (*tatrabhavatām*), we too have a determinate knowledge of universals such as cowness etc., as is fit [in each case], through the uninterrupted transmission of the tradition. And the institution of names carried out by those [seers] who are superior to us is just the revelation of the existing relation of word and meaning as it stands (*yathāvasthita*) rather than the creation of an unprecedented convention (*apūrvasaṅketakaraṇam*), because the relation between word and meaning is natural (*svābhāvikatvāt*); therefore, distinct universals such as brahmin-hood etc. do exist on the basis of the authority of the *śiṣṭa*s and they are expressed by the suffixes for abstract nouns[165].[166]

---

[164] For a very similar list occurring in YS, VPVṛ and PDhS, see § 2, and especially n. 37 above. An identical list, adding past and future objects, is found in the expression *atītānāgatasūkṣmavyavahitādisamastavastuviṣaya* in NM, vol. I, p. 505, l. 13.

[165] This is an allusion to *Aṣṭādhyāyī* 5.1.119, *tasya bhāvas tvatalau*, prescribing the *taddhita* suffixes *tva* or *taL* (= -*tā*) "to form a derivate that denotes the property of being (*bhāva*) what the base of the *pada* denotes" (CARDONA 1997, p. 243). In this way Helārāja suggests that there is a correspondence between the structures of reality (in this case, the *jātis*) and the structures of the language (here, the *taddhita* suffixes), which is captured and revealed by Grammar.

[166] PrPr 1, p. 55, ll. 4-12: *tad evam āgamasiddhāḥ santy asmadviśiṣṭāḥ. indriyapratiniyamānapekṣaṃ ca sākṣātkārarūpaṃ teṣāṃ jñānam ity atītānāgatasū-*

In Helārāja's version of the original revelation, the seers (or *śiṣṭa*s, as he calls them here) play a key role in the origin of language. To corroborate this statement, Helārāja quotes VS 2.1.19.[167] Coming after 2.1.18, *saṃjñākarma tv asmadviśiṣṭānāṃ liṅgam*, which was briefly discussed above (see § 2), this *sūtra* adds that the seers' activity of name-giving (*saṃjñākarma*) was preceded by "perception" (*pratyakṣapūrvakaṃ*).

There is little doubt that in the intention of the author of VS 2.1.18 the expression *asmadviśiṣṭānāṃ* refers to seers or yogis, as shown above. However, in the *Vṛtti* Candrānanda takes it as an honorific plural[168] referring to God, in keeping with the Nyāya idea that the relation between *śabda* and *artha* is a convention originally established by the Lord,[169] as he clarifies in his commentary on VS 2.1.19:

> As they directly perceive the categories (*padārtha*), they create names, and [the same] is seen in the naming of a son, and the names [of things] have indeed been created, therefore we believe that there exists a venerable one, superior to us, who has a direct perception even of things that for us are imperceptible, [and] by whom names etc. were created."[170]

---

kṣmavyavahitaviprakṛṣṭārthasatattvadṛśo yoginaḥ sarvā gotvabrāhmaṇatvādijātīr adhyakṣayantaḥ tadupadeśam asaṅkareṇārabhante. brāhmaṇatvādiṣv asti kiñcit sāsnādisthānīyam upavyañjanam asmākaṃ param atīndriyam. śiṣṭais tad avadhārya saṃjñāḥ praṇītāḥ. tad uktaṃ: "pratyakṣapūrvakaṃ saṃjñākarma" iti. tatrabhavatām upadeśād vayam api sampradāyapāramparyād yathāyogaṃ gotvādijātīr adhyavasyāmaḥ. asmadviśiṣṭānāṃ cedaṃ saṃjñāpraṇayanaṃ yathāvasthitaśabdārthasaṃbandhaprakāśanamātraṃ, na tv apūrvasaṅketakaraṇaṃ svābhāvikatvāc chabdārthasaṃbandhasyeti śiṣṭaprāmāṇyāt santi brāhmaṇatvādijātayo viviktā yathāyathaṃ bhāvapratyayābhidheyāḥ.

167 This quotation is not identified as such in Subramania Iyer's edition of the PrPr, probably because it appears in a rather different form in Śaṅkara Miśra's version of the VS *sūtrapāṭha*, which was the only one available at the time he was preparing the edition.

168 VSVṛtti ad VS 2.1.18: *asmadviśiṣṭānām iti pūjāyāṃ bahuvacanam.*

169 The thesis of the conventional nature of the relation between word and meaning is first found in NS 2.1.55, *na, sāmāyikatvāc chabdārthasaṃpratyayasya.* For the idea that God is the "creator" of this relation, see e.g. Vācaspatimiśra's *Nyāyavārttikatātparyaṭīkā* thereon (p. 370): *abhidhānābhidheyayor niyamo gośabdasya sāsnādimān evārtha evam aśvaśabdasya keśarādimān eveti, tasmin niyogo boddhavya iti bhagavataḥ parameśvarasya sargādau, so 'yam samaya ity arthaḥ.*

170 *pratyakṣeṇa hi padārtham ālocayantaḥ saṃjñāḥ praṇayanti, dṛṣṭaṃ ca dārakasya nāmakaraṇe, praṇītāś cemāḥ khalu saṃjñāḥ, tasmān manyāmahe – asti*

Helārāja's version of the origin of language is slightly different from Candrānanda's. Having clearly stated earlier in the commentary that God is the seed or root of everything because the world is his creation, here he credits the *institution of language* to the primordial seers who are God's direct pupils. They are *sākṣātkṛtadharman*, that is, they "see" the true fabric of reality in all its aspects, from the minutest and subtlest to the largest, and they name things, actions and qualities accordingly, forging speech in such a way that it corresponds at some deep level with the phenomenal reality. From this angle, they act as intermediaries between God and ordinary humans in a much more fundamental way than in Bhartṛhari's account, where they just verbalise (or textualise) the *śāstra*s and teach them to later generations (or perhaps, the composition of *śāstra*s itself is the process through which they shape language).

However, there is a crucial difference between Candrānanda and Helārāja. The latter is keen to defend the Grammarians' doctrine of the eternal relation between *śabda* and *artha* epitomised in Kātyāyana's famous statement *siddhe śabdārthasambandhe*, and even more crucially, I think, Bhartṛhari's intuition that the absolute consciousness is essentially language. Having heavily relied on Nyāya-Vaiśeṣika theistic arguments throughout the commentary on VP 3.1.46, Helārāja now has to distance himself from their thesis that the relation between *śabda* and *artha* is a convention established by God at the beginning of each cosmic cycle. He therefore spells out clearly that the sages do not establish brand-new linguistic conventions (*apūrvasaṅketakaraṇam*), but rather they acknowledge the reality that has been revealed to them, of which the natural (*svābhāvika*) relation between *śabda* and *artha* is an integral part, and pass their knowledge on to the later generations. In his view, language and reality are God's co-extensive creations.

To sum up Helārāja's views about omniscience as laid down in the commentary on VP 3.1.46, knowledge is an inherent property of God, in which it exists in its incommensurate excellence (*niratiśaya*), namely omniscience. The latter is also found in human beings who can acquire it through the practice of meditation, etc. It is a direct cognition (*sākṣātkāra*), similar to ordinary perception, but

---

bhagavān asmadviśiṣṭo yo 'smadādiparokṣāṇām api bhāvānāṃ pratyakṣadarśī yenedaṃ saṃjñādi praṇītam iti. Transl. ISAACSON 1995, which provides an improved edition of this section of Candrānanda's *Vṛtti.*

it is not bound by any of its limitations: all the senses can synesthetically grasp all objects, whether perceivable but for some reason inaccessible (distant, hidden, infinitely small, etc.) or trans-empirical (*dharma*, *jāti*s, etc.) in the past, present and future. For this description of the nature of extraordinary cognition, it is worth stating once again that he essentially follows in Bhartṛhari's tracks, even though in his exposition he draws on a variety of brahmanical sources, many from Yoga and Nyāya-Vaiśeṣika. Helārāja is clearly aware of the previous debates on omniscience and presents two proofs of *sarvajña*, one based on *āgama*, the other based on inference. The former, which takes up most of the passage, appeals to the authority of traditional sources in two ways: first, there are numerous textual sources that mention omniscient beings, among whom God is foremost; second, the uncontested authority of scriptures and of all *śāstra*s derives from the fact that they have been composed (or at least, put in a form accessible to humans) and handed down by omniscient beings, whose teacher was God himself. In order to substantiate his claim that *āgama* proves omniscience, though, Helārāja has to engage with and respond to the Mīmāṃsakas' claim that *arthavāda*s, the non-injunctive portions of both Śruti and Smṛti, are not authoritative – which he does, resorting to a variety of arguments (consensus among scriptural sources; usefulness of passages on past events and well-known objects; etc.). The second kind of proof is the inference based on *atiśaya/niratiśaya*, which is given almost as an afterthought near the end of the passage, and as an explicit response to Kumārila's views (and possibly to Maṇḍana Miśra's). Remarkably, while much of what Helārāja writes can be understood in the context of the debates on omniscience that took place in the second half of the first millennium CE, in the PrPr on VP 3.1.46 there is no direct mention of or even allusion to the Buddhists, as far as I can tell, despite the fact they had been among the protagonists of the debate.[171] The controversy on omniscience as presented here by Helārāja is an entirely intra-brahmanical affair, opposing the atheistic Mīmāṃsā to the theistic schools. Less prominent, but still detectable, I think, is the contrast between pluralist and non-dualist views: only the latter, in Helārāja's eyes (and again, in line with Bhartṛhari), can really pro-

---

[171] And despite the fact that they are frequently referred to elsewhere in the PrPr. Helārāja even quotes Dharmakīrti's *Pramāṇavārttika* twice in the PrPr. I intend to discuss Helārāja's engagement with Buddhist thinkers, especially of the Pramāṇa tradition, in a future publication.

vide a satisfactory answer to all questions on the nature of cognition (including omniscience) and reality.

9. SITUATING HELĀRĀJA IN RELATION TO PRATYABHIJÑĀ

The conception of language as a fundamental dimension of reality that Helārāja presents in the final portion of PrPr ad VP 3.1.46 is undoubtedly resonant with Bhartṛhari's *śabdabrahman*. On the other hand, as I have noted above, Helārāja's belief in a supreme God who out of his volition (*icchā*) creates the universe is in strident contrast with Bhartṛhari's impersonal Brahman. Helārāja's theism, which – as he strives to show in the extensive passage I have examined here – has a long and respectable history within Vedic Brahmanism (*pace* Mīmāṃsā), is the expression of a religious sensibility that is a far cry from Bhartṛhari's and remarkably close to that of the non-dualist Śaivas of medieval Kashmir. One of the purposes of Helārāja's work may have been precisely to show that Bhartṛhari's theory of language and epistemology are in fact compatible with this radically different religious vision, that it is possible to accommodate most of the teachings found in the VP within a belief system centred on a personal God without incurring any unsolvable contradiction. To put it differently, in Helārāja's eyes, in order to embrace Bhartṛhari's intellectual mentorship one does not need to divorce it from his ontology – essentially, his idea of *śabdatattva* – but could instead appropriate the latter, drawing its full implications, and move beyond it, to a different conception of godhead.

Furthermore, while Helārāja appears to reassert the centrality of the Veda, there is little doubt that the theistic account of the revelation and the origin of *āgama* he advocates potentially opens the way to a relativisation of the importance of the Veda, which then facilitates the emergence of alternative narratives giving pre-eminence to other sets of "revealed" scriptures, such as the Tantric *āgama*s. The accounts of the transmission of scriptures (and of learning in general) found in the Pratyabhijñā literature are in fact structurally similar to Helārāja's and declare God (Śiva) to be their source – if not literally their "author."[172] For instance, in *Tantrālo-*

[172] For a discussion of the Śaiva revelation according to Abhinavagupta, see HANNEDER 1998, especially the Introduction; cf. also GNOLI 1999, TORELLA 2013, and RATIÉ 2013.

ka (henceforth, TĀ) 35, which deals with the "meeting of all scriptures" (*samastānāṃ śāstrāṇāṃ melanam*), Abhinavagupta begins with the following definition of *āgama*:

> In this world, all human activities hold in that they have as reference point an ancient complex of innate cognitions and beliefs (*prasiddhi*): this is what is called *āgama*.[173]

In TĀ 35.11b-12a (*pūrvapūrvopajīvitvamārgaṇe sā kvacit svayam* || *sarvajñarūpe hy ekasmin niḥśaṅkaṃ bhāsate purā* |) Abhinavagupta states that, tracing back this foundational knowledge (*prasiddhi*) to its origin, in the beginning it appears to belong without any doubt to one single inherently omniscient subject, namely Śiva:

> It is Bhairava, the Highest Lord, who consists in this realization (*vimarśa*) [and] is adorned with [all the] innumerable experiences, liberations, their causes and the a priori certainties.[174]

And in v. 30 he strongly reiterates the essential unity of the tradition (even including the Buddhists!):

> In fact *āgama* is one; therefore everything is included in it, from the mundane treatises to the Vaiṣṇava, Buddhist [and] Śaiva [treatises].[175]

In this final section I would like to present two more passages from different sections of the PrPr that appear to confirm Helārāja's affinity to the Pratyabhijñā system, not just culturally but philosophically.

The first is the opening *maṅgalaśloka* of the PrPr:

> *yasmin saṃmukhatāṃ prayāti ruciraṃ ko 'py antar ujjṛmbhate* |
> *nedīyān mahimā manasy abhinavaḥ puṃsaḥ prakāśātmanaḥ* |
> *tṛptiṃ yat paramāṃ tanoti viṣayāsvādaṃ vinā śāśvatīṃ* |
> *dhāmānandasudhāmayorjitavapus tat prātibhaṃ saṃstumaḥ* ||
>
> We praise that intuitive knowledge (*prātibham*), whose splendid body is full with the nectar of the bliss that is the light [of consciousness] – when

[173] TĀ 35 1cd-2ab: *iha tāvat samasto 'yaṃ vyavahāraḥ purātanaḥ* || *prasiddhim anusandhāya saiva cāgama ucyate* |. (Transl. TORELLA 2013, p. 458; on the notion of *prasiddhi* in the Pratyabhijñā philosophy, see TORELLA 2013.)

[174] TĀ 35.14: *bhogāpavargataddhetuprasiddhiśataśobhitaḥ* | *tadvimarśasvabhāvo 'sau bhairavaḥ parameśvaraḥ* ||. Transl. RATIÉ 2013, p. 388, n. 39.

[175] *eka evāgamas tasmāt tatra laukikaśāstrataḥ* | *prabhṛty ā vaiṣṇavād bauddhāc chaivāt sarvaṃ hi niṣṭhitam* ||. Transl. RATIÉ 2013, p. 415, n. 89. RATIÉ 2013 provides an insightful treatment of the concept of *āgama* in the works of Pratyabhijñā philosophers.

> that [intuitive knowledge] comes forth, a certain special new, intimate majesty (*mahimā*) unfolds brightly within, in the mind, for the individual soul (*puṃsaḥ*) whose nature is light [i.e. consciousness] – that [intuitive knowledge] which spreads supreme and eternal contentment without the savouring of sense objects (*viṣayāsvādam*).

Almost every word in this verse is reminiscent of the non-dualist śaiva imagery, even though the verse contains no direct reference to Śiva. The verse extols the breaking forth (*ujjṛmbhate*) of the light of consciousness in the mind of the individual subject (presumably, and implicitly, someone who has reached the appropriate level of spiritual advancement), who revels in the bliss resulting from the new profound realisation that the light was already inside him – that it was and is in fact his self (*prakāśātmanaḥ*) – and is pure self-awareness as it transcends the distinction between subject and object.

Two words in the verse are particularly noteworthy: *āsvāda* and *prātibha*. The former, literally meaning "tasting," occurs in the expression *viṣayāsvādaṃ vinā*, evoking the moment in which an individual becomes aware that the distinction between himself and the external world is fictitious and consciousness actually rests on itself, on its ever-lasting luminous nature. As pointed out by TORELLA 2002 (pp. 118f., n. 23), *āsvāda* is one of the common synonyms of *camatkāra* or *camatkṛti*, "one of the key words of this school," denoting the "savouring" of a cognition on the part of someone who, in Torella's words, "lets the experience rest on the cognizing subject, that is, makes the 'subject' part predominate over the 'object' part." A definition of this important notion is given by Abhinavagupta in ĪPVV (vol. II, p. 177, quoted in Torella, ibid.): *camatkṛtir hi bhuñjānasya yā kriyā bhogasamāpattimaya ānandaḥ*, "*camatkṛti* means the act of a person savouring (*bhuñjānasya*), that is, the bliss constituted by the full achievement of fruition" (Torella's transl.). Here one finds the same association of *camatkāra*, often glossed with *āsvāda* in the ĪPVV, with bliss and fulfilment as in Helārāja's opening verse of the PrPr. In the latter, though, the reference to a self-awareness stripped of the veil of any objective content points to the highest level of *camatkāra*, as described for example in ĪPVV (vol. III, p. 251):

> *prakāśasya ca paradaśāyāṃ camatkāramātrātmā yo vimarśas tad eva svātantryaṃ, na tu icchārūpaṃ... | camatkāro hi iti svātmani ananyāpekṣe viśramaṇam | evaṃ bhuñjānatārūpaṃ camattvaṃ, tad eva karoti, saṃ-*

> *rambheṇa*[176] *vimṛśati na anyatra anudhāvati | camad iti kriyāviśeṣaṇam, akhaṇḍa eva vā śabdo nirvighnāsvādanavṛttiḥ.*
>
> On the supreme plane [the plane of Parā], freedom (*svātantryam*) [of the Lord] is indeed that reflective awareness (*vimarśaḥ*) the essence of which is the mere savouring (*camatkāramātrātmā*) of the light [of consciousness], rather than the nature of volition. [...] For [what we call] *camatkāra* is [the fact of] resting on one's own self without relying on anything else: thus, wonderment (*camattvam*) is the condition of one who is relishing (*bhuñjānatārūpam*), this is what [the experience] causes;[177] it becomes intensely (*saṃrambheṇa*) aware (*vimṛśati*), it does not follow upon anything else. *camat* is an adverb [qualifying *kṛ*-], or the undivided expression [*camatkāra*] refers to unimpeded savouring (*nirvighnāsvādana*).

The word used by Helārāja to refer to this spiritually transforming experience of illumination is *prātibha*, "intuitive knowledge." Grammatically, this is a *taddhita* derivative from *pratibhā*, the unitary "flash" of understanding that according to Bhartṛhari guides all living beings – not just humans – in their daily life and initiates all actions (and, especially, all verbal exchanges). In that instantaneous insight – despite the fact that in everyday life it is coloured by the diversity of the phenomenal world – one can catch a glimpse of the *śabdatattva*, the word-principle that is universal consciousness.

One can plausibly assume that the use of *prātibha* in Helārāja's verse is meant to recall the centrality of the notion of *pratibhā* in Bhartṛhari's philosophy. However, as pointed out by TORELLA 2013 and RATIÉ 2013 from different but converging perspectives, the term *pratibhā* acquires an increased (if not entirely new) significance in the works of the Pratyabhijñā. It is the highest form of *prasiddhi*, that hard core of intuitive – and, to some extent, even instinctive – knowledge that is one of the major dimensions of *āgama*, "tradition" in its broadest – and literal – sense of that which is handed down from previous generations. However, besides the self-evident connection with *pratibhā*, the term *prātibha* has a long history of its own going back at least to YS 3.33 *prātibhād vā sar-*

---

[176] The printed edition of ĪPVV reads *saṃrambhe*. Torella (personal communication, March 2015) suggests emending it to *saṃrambheṇa* on the basis of a manuscript source available to him.

[177] The clause *tad eva karoti* is meant to gloss the element -*kāra* in the compound *camatkāra*.

vam,[178] where it refers to yogic knowledge, as is made clear by the YS-*Bhāṣya*, which defines it as the nascent moment of knowledge (*jñānasya pūrvarūpam*) and compares it to the light that precedes the rising of the sun (*yathodaye prabhā bhāskarasya*), adding that a yogi will be able to know anything – i.e. become omniscient – when this knowledge, called *prātibha*, arises (*tena vā sarvam eva jānāti yogī prātibhasya jñānasyotpattāv iti*).

It is precisely this *sūtra* that Abhinavagupta quotes in *āhnika* 13[179] of the TĀ, in the section that deals with the various kinds of *śaktipāta*, "descent of power." In relation to the second type of *śaktipāta*, called *madhyatīvra* "middle-violent," which dissipates ignorance,[180] it is said that "the knowledge thanks to which one knows one's own self as the source of bondage and liberation is intuitive knowledge (*prātibha*), the great knowledge, which is independent of scriptures and teachers."[181] A few verses later he states that nothing is unattainable with the help of this intuitive knowledge and then quotes YS 3.33 as an authoritative source in support of this view.[182]

Surely, the mention of *prātibha* in the initial verse of the PrPr is not sufficient in itself to clarify Helārāja's theological views and even less the extent to which they coincide with those expressed by Abhinavagupta in the TĀ. Despite these affinities, in fact, there is a conspicuous absence in the PrPr verse of any reference to Śiva (or any deity, for that matter), as I have mentioned above. In the following passage, however, which ends the commentary on the last two verses[183] of the *Dravyasamuddeśa*, Helārāja takes a further and decisive step:

---

178 The YS-*Bhāṣya* comments: *prātibhaṃ nāma tārakaṃ tadvivekajasya jñānasya pūrvarūpam. yathodaye prabhā bhāskarasya. tena vā sarvam eva jānāti yogī prātibhasya jñānasyotpattāv iti.*

179 The term *prātibha* recurs several times in this section but, oddly, it is hardly found elsewhere in the TĀ.

180 TĀ 13.131b: *madhyatīvrāt punaḥ sarvam ajñānaṃ vinivartate.*

181 TĀ 13.132: *svayam eva yato vetti bandhamokṣatayātmatām | tat prātibhaṃ mahājñānaṃ śāstrācāryānapekṣi yat ||.*

182 TĀ 13.146: *itthaṃ prātibhavijñānaṃ kiṃ kiṃ kasya na sādhayet | yat prātibhād vā sarvaṃ cety ūce śeṣamahāmuniḥ ||*. In his commentary Jayaratha remarks: *atraiva yad ityādipramāṇanirdeśaḥ. ūce iti pātañjalasūtreṣu.*

183 VP 3.2.17-18: *ātmā paraḥ priyo dveṣyo vaktā vācyaṃ prayojanam | viruddhāni yathaikasya svapne rūpāṇi cetasaḥ || ajanmani tathā nitye paurvāparyavivarjite | tattve janmādirūpatvaṃ viruddham upalabhyate ||*. "Just

> But for those who know the absolute reality, since the supreme Brahman, whose nature is consciousness and bliss, is free from birth and death, undivided, immutable, this whole world, consisting in the unfolding of material forms and actions, is unreal, whether in a state of wakefulness, sleep, etc. On the plane of absolute reality, though, it is established that there is nothing but the commonality of the connecting consciousness (*anvayicit*). By saying *viruddham upalabhyate,* [Bhartṛhari] admits that contradiction exists in [the state of] nescience. For it is [in] the very nature of nescience that, even though it is inexplicable, it leads to the visibility [of the phenomenal reality], [for] if it were explained, it would be nothing but knowledge.[184] Therefore, the power of Brahman to manifest the unreal proliferation [of the world], [a power] which has been established to be without beginning, having produced both the cognised object and the cognising subject in conformity with itself, unfolds the drama of the world. Therefore, those who see the true reality dismiss this [power] that is fine as long as it is not [critically] examined.[185]

An analysis of this passage and of its relation to the rest of the *Dravyasamuddeśa* would be beyond the scope of this paper. I will just draw attention to the final line, where Helārāja states that "the power of Brahman to manifest the unreal proliferation [of the world] [...] unfolds the drama of the world." The use of the phrase *jagannāṭyam ātanoti*, with its unmistakable śaiva connotations, is

---

as the self and the other, what is loved and what is hated, the speaker, the spoken and the purpose, are mutually contradictory natures [appearing] in the dreams of a single conscious mind, in the same way the fact of having the nature of [a being] subject to birth etc. is perceived as contradictory with regard to that reality that is unborn, eternal, and devoid of sequence."

184 Cf. the following passage in Maṇḍana Miśra's Bsi, p. 10: *anupapadyamānārthaiva hi māyā, upapadyamānārthatve yathārthabhāvān na māyā syāt...* "For illusion (*māyā*) has an object that is impossible to explain (*anupapadyamāna*): if it had an object that were possible to explain (*upapadyamāna*), it would not be an illusion since it would conform to its object..." I thank I. Ratié for bringing it to my attention.

185 PrPr 1, p. 121, ll. 10-16: *paramārthadṛśāṃ tu jananamaraṇarahite 'pravibhakte kūṭasthe parasmin brahmaṇi cidānandarūpe sarvam eva jagaj jāgratsvapnādyavasthāgataṃ mūrtikriyāvivartarūpam asatyam. anvayicitsāmānyamātraṃ tu paramārtha iti siddham. viruddham upalabhyate iti vadann avidyāyāṃ virodham abhyupaiti. etad eva hy avidyāyāḥ svarūpaṃ yad anupapadyamānam apy ābhāsopagamaṃ nayati, upapannatve vidyaiva syāt. tasmād asatyaprapañcaprakāśanaśaktir brahmaṇo 'nādisiddhā grāhyagrāhakayugalaṃ svānurūpam uparacayya jagannāṭyam ātanotīty avicāritaramaṇīyām imām apanayanti tattvadṛśaḥ.*

meant as a subtle clue, I think, suggesting that *brahman* may be seen as just another name of Śiva.

10. CONCLUSION

Much work remains to be done on Helārāja. From the main passage I have discussed here, Helārāja emerges as a refined, learned intellectual with a wide-ranging philosophical background. It is tempting, as suggested by SUBRAMANIA IYER 1969 (pp. 39-40), to identify him with the *bhūtirājatanaya* whom Abhinavagupta mentions more than once among his teachers, for example in the TĀ, and who may not be the same as Bhaṭṭendurāja, or simply Indurāja, also the son of a Bhūtirāja, who was the teacher of Abhinavagupta on Alaṃkāraśāstra (PANDEY 1963, pp. 142-143). The PrPr on VP 3.1.46 itself offers at least one – admittedly tenuous – trace that points in that direction, namely the attention that both Helārāja and Abhinavagupta pay to YS 3.17 (see § 4.3 above).

But even if Helārāja never was one of Abhinavagupta's teachers,[186] I think it very likely that his commentaries on Bhartṛhari's VP, probably composed in the first half of the 10th c. CE, reflected and facilitated the change in attitude towards Bhartṛhari that is first attested in Utpaladeva's work. It seems to me that Helārāja's effort aims to reclaim Bhartṛhari's philosophical legacy, showing that the latter's views on language and cognition are firmly rooted in the brahmanical tradition (perhaps partly as a reaction against the Buddhists's partial appropriation of some of Bhartṛhari's ideas). At the same time Helārāja emphasises that Bhartṛhari's Vedāntic monism – despite its atheism – stands apart from other Vedāntic trends that were gaining ground at the time because of its dynamic understanding of the relation between *brahman* and the world.[187] This may explain his critique of Mīmāṃsā, particularly conspicuous in the passage I have examined here. And, as the opportunity arises, Helārāja is also clearly eager to suggest that Bhartṛhari's vision is not only compatible with a theistic philosophical approach, but possibly can only be fully defended if it is embedded in a theistic interpretive frame. From this perspective, his work would have

---

[186] It may well prove impossible to ascertain the identity of Bhūtirāja's son.

[187] However, one important part in my future research on Helārāja's work will certainly be the investigation of possible connections with those currents of theistic Vedānta that emerged roughly at the same time (end of the first millennium CE), and which I have deliberately left aside in the present paper.

certainly influenced Abhinavagupta's philosophy, even if only indirectly.

On the other hand, it is difficult to pinpoint Helārāja's religious affiliation with any degree of certainty. The recurring references to God as Īśvara, or Maheśvara, or Parameśvara, in the PrPr on VP 3.1.46, might be explained by the use of the same terms in the Yoga, Nyāya and Vaiśeṣika sources that he quotes, but they strongly suggest that he was a śaiva, and this seems to be confirmed by the final lines of his commentary on the *Dravyasamuddeśa* (see § 9 above). However, nothing in these passages indicates that Helārāja was a Tantric devotee, although this could possibly be explained as the caution or even the reluctance of the commentator lest he should force a patently unjustified interpretation on the *mūla* text.

Militating against my hypothesis that Helārāja may have played an important role in the formation of Pratyabhijñā as a philosophical system is the fact that, as far as I know, no quotation or even direct mention of Helārāja has surfaced in Abhinavagupta's extensive oeuvre or generally the works of later śaiva authors and, vice versa, that so far no reference to early non-dualist śaiva texts has been found in the PrPr. He also seems to be scarcely mentioned by other authors in general, with the exception of Bhoja (see RAGHAVAN 1976, pp. 106f.). One could imagine that Helārāja was something of an outsider, an isolated intellectual unattached to any particular philosophical school or system and with his own unique religious vision, perhaps a form of non-Tantric śaiva monism, which might partly help to explain his scarce fortune.

However, the fact that so far little attention has been paid to Helārāja's work except as a key to understanding Bhartṛhari's philosophy could equally be responsible for the seemingly almost total oblivion of his name and, even more, his contribution. Only a systematic search of the considerable but not unwieldy bulk of texts involved will be able to confirm or disprove this dearth of cross-references, a search I am planning to carry out in the future.

In parallel, the scarce historical evidence on Helārāja's life and date needs to be re-examined critically and, if possible, expanded. And further research into the innumerable philosophical topics raised in his extensive commentary on the VP will certainly help to clarify his place in the philosophical debates of mediaeval Brahmanism and the history of Pratyabhijñā.

REFERENCES

AK
[*Ambākartrī*] *Vākyapadīyam* [Part III, vol. II] *(Bhūyodravya-Guṇa-Dik-Sādhana-Kriyā-Kāla-Puruṣa-Saṃkhyā-Upagraha- and Liṅga-Samuddeśa) with the commentary Prakāśa by Helārāja and Ambākartrī*, ed. Pt. R. Sharma, Varanasi: 1977, Sarasvatī Bhavana Granthamāla 91

AKLUJKAR 1970
A. Aklujkar, "Candrānanda's date," *Journal of the Oriental Institute* 19, 1970, pp. 340-341

AKLUJKAR 2009
A. Aklujkar, "Veda Revelation according to Bhartṛhari," in M. Chaturvedi (ed.), *Bhartṛhari. Language, Thought and Reality*, Delhi: Motilal Banarsidass, 2009, pp. 1-97

AKLUJKAR 2010
A. Aklujkar, "Grammarians' Leaving Logic at the Door," in P. Balcerowicz (ed.), *Logic and Belief in Indian Philosophy*, Delhi: Motilal Banarsidass, 2010, pp. 395-414

APTE 1912
V.S. Apte, *The Practical Sanskrit-English Dictionary*, [1912] 2nd revised and enlarged ed., Delhi: Sri Satguru Publications, 1989

BHATTACHARYYA 1978
J.V. Bhattacharyya, *Jayanta Bhaṭṭa's Nyāya-mañjarī: the compendium of Indian speculative logic*, vol. I, Delhi: Motilal Banarsidass, 1978

Bsi
Brahmasiddhi by Ācārya Maṇḍanamiśra with Commentary by Saṅkhapāni, Edited with Introduction, Appendices and Indexes, ed. K. Sastri, Madras: Madras Government Press, Madras Government Oriental Manuscripts 4, 1937

CARDONA 1997
G. Cardona, *Pāṇini: His Works and its Traditions,* Part I: *General Introduction and Background*, 2nd ed., revised and enlarged, Delhi: Motilal Banarsidass, 1997

CHEMPARATHY 1968
G. Chemparathy, "The Īśvara doctrine of Praśastapāda," *Vishveshvaranand Indological Journal* 6, 1968, pp. 65-87

CHEMPARATHY 1970
G. Chemparathy, "The Īśvara doctrine of the Vaiśeṣika commentator Candrānanda," *Ṛtam* 1(2), 1970, pp. 47-52

DAVID forthcoming
H. David, "Action Theory and Scriptural Exegesis in Early Advaita-Vedānta (2): Maṇḍana Miśra's Excursus on the Buddha's Omniscience"

DESHPANDE 1994
M.M. Deshpande, "The changing notion of *śiṣṭa* from Patañjali to Bhartṛhari," in S. Bhate and J. Bronkhorst (eds.), *Bhartṛhari, philosopher and grammarian: proceedings of the First International Conference on Bhartṛhari (University of Poona, January 6-8, 1992)*, Delhi: Motilal Banarsidass, 1994, pp. 95-115

ELTSCHINGER AND KRASSER 2013
V. Eltschinger and H. Krasser (eds.), *Scriptural Authority, Reason, and Action. Proceedings of a Panel at the 14th World Sanskrit Conference, Kyoto, September 1th-5th, 2009*, Wien: Verlag der Österreichischen Akademie der Wissenschaften, 2013

EIPh
[*Encyclopedia of Indian philosophies*, vol. II] K.H. Potter (ed.), *Indian metaphysics and epistemology: the tradition of Nyāya-Vaiśesika up to Gangeśa*, Delhi: Motilal Banarsidass, 1977

FRANCO 2009
E. Franco (ed.), *Yogic perception, meditation and altered states of consciousness*, Wien: Verlag der Österreichischen Akademie der Wissenschaften, 2009

GERSCHHEIMER 1994
G. Gerschheimer, "Le *Tripādīnītinayana* de Murāri Miśra: un texte d'obédience *prābhākara*?", in *Bulletin de l'École française d'Extrême-Orient* 81, 1994, pp. 295-326

GNOLI 1999
R. Gnoli, *Abhinavagupta. Luce dei Tantra*, Milano: Adelphi, 1999

HALBFASS 1992
W. Halbfass, *Tradition and Reflection. Explorations in Indian Thought*, Delhi: Sri Satguru Publications, 1992

HANNEDER 1998
J. Hanneder, *Abhinavagupta's Philosophy of Revelation. Mālinīślokavārttika I, 1-399*, Groningen: Egbert Forsten, 1998

ĪPK
Īśvarapratyabhijñākārikā with Vṛtti, ed. M.K. Shastri, Srinagar: Nirnaya Sagar Press, Kashmir Series of Texts and Studies 34, 1921; see also TORELLA 2002

ĪPV
Īśvarapratyabhijñāvimarśinī, ed. M.R. Śāstrī/M.K. Śāstrī, 2 vols., Srinagar: Nirnaya Sagar Press, Kashmir Series of Texts and Studies 22 & 33, 1918-1921

ĪPVV
Īśvarapratyabhijñāvivṛtivimarśinī, ed. M.K. Shāstrī, 3 vols., Bombay: Nirnaya Sagar Press, Kashmir Series of Texts and Studies 60, 62 & 65, 1938-1943

ISAACSON 1990
H. Isaacson, *A study of early Vaiśeṣika: the teachings on perception*, Unpublished MA Thesis, Groningen: University of Groningen, 1990

ISAACSON 1993
H. Isaacson, "Yogic Perception (*yogipratyakṣa*) in early Vaiśeṣika," *Studien zur Indologie und Iranistik* 18, 1993, pp. 139-160

ISAACSON 1995
H. Isaacson, *Materials for the Study of the Vaiśeṣika System*, Unpublished Doctoral Thesis, Leiden: University of Leiden, 1995

Īśvarasiddhi
In *Siddhitrayī and Pratyabhijñā-kārikā-vṛtti of Rajaka Utpala Deva*, ed. M.K. Shastri, Srinagar: Kashmir Series of Texts and Studies 34, 1921

JS
[*Jaiminisūtra* with *Śābarabhāṣya*] *Mīmāṃsādarśana,* ed. K.V. Abhyankar and G.A. Jośi, 7 vols., Poona: Ānandāśramasaṃskṛtagranthāvali 17, 1970-1976

KATAOKA 2005
K. Kataoka, "Critical Edition of the *Īśvarasiddhi* Section of Bhaṭṭa Jayanta's *Nyāyamañjarī*," *The Memoirs of the Institute of Oriental Culture* (University of Tokyo) 148, 2005, pp. 358-305 (57-110)

KATAOKA 2011
K. Kataoka, *Kumārila on truth, omniscience and killing*, Wien: Verlag der Österreichischen Akademie der Wissenschaften, 2011

MASS 2013
P.A. Maas, "A concise historiography of classical Yoga," in E. Franco (ed.), *Periodization and historiography of Indian philosophy*, Wien: Sammlung de Nobili, Arbeitsgemeinschaft für Indologie und Religionsforschung Universität Wien, 2013

MATILAL 1977
B.K. Matilal, *Nyāya-Vaiśeṣika* (*A history of Indian literature*, vol. VI.2), Wiesbaden: Harassowitz, 1977

MBh
Vyākaraṇa-Mahābhāṣya of Patañjali, ed. F. Kielhorn, 3 vols., [Bombay: Government Central Press, 1880-1885] 3rd ed. K.V. Abhyankar, Poona: BORI, 1962-1972

MCCLINTOCK 2010
S. McClintock, *Omniscience and the Rhetoric of Reason: Śāntarakṣita and Kamalaśīla on Rationality, Argumentation, and Religious Authority*, Boston: Wisdom Publications, 2010

MORIYAMA 2014
S. Moriyama, *Omniscience and Religious Authority. A Study on Prajñākaragupta's Pramāṇavārttikālaṅkārabhāṣya ad Pramāṇavārttika 2.8-10 and 29-33*, Berlin/Zürich: Leipziger Studien zu Kultur und Geschichte Süd- und Zentralasiens, 2014

NEMEC 2011
J. Nemec, *The Ubiquitous Śiva. Somānanda's Śivadṛṣṭi and his Tantric Interlocutors*, Oxford/New York: Oxford University Press, 2011

NM
Nyāyamañjarī of Jayantabhaṭṭa, with Ṭippaṇi-Nyāyasaurabha by the Editor, vol. I, ed. K.S. Varadacharya, Mysore: Oriental Research Institute, 1969

NOZAWA 1993
M. Nozawa, "The *Vaiśeṣikasūtra* with Candrānanda's Commentary (1), *Numazu Kōgyō Kōtō Senmon Gakkō Kenkyū Hōkoku* 27 [1992] 1993, pp. 97-116

NS
Nyāyasūtra. Gautamīyanyāyadarśana with Bhāṣya of Vātsyāyana, Nyāyacaturgranthikā, vol. I, ed. A. Thakur, New Delhi: Indian Council of Philosophical Research, 1997

Nyāyavārttikatātparyaṭīkā
Nyāyavārttikatātparyaṭīkā of Vācaspatimiśra, Nyāyacaturgranthikā, vol. III, ed. A. Thakur, New Delhi: Indian Council of Philosophical Research, 1996

PANDEY 1963
K.C. Pandey, *Abhinavagupta, an historical and philosophical study*, Varanasi: Chowkhamba, 1963

Parātrīśikātattvavivaraṇa
Parātrimshikā with commentary, the latter by Abhinavagupta, ed. M.R. Shāstrī, Bombay: Kashmir Series of Texts and Studies 18, 1918

PDhS
[*Padārthadharmasaṅgraha*] *The Praśastapādabhāṣya with the Commentary Nyāyakāndali of Sridhara*, ed. V.P. Dvivedin, [Benares: Vizianagram Sanskrit Series 6, 1895] Delhi: Sri Satguru Publications, Sri Garbi Dass Oriental Series 13, 1984

PrPr
[*Prakīrṇaprakāśa* 1 and 2] See VP 3.1 and 3.2

RAGHAVAN 1976
V. Raghavan, "The dates of Helarāja and Kaiyaṭa," in J.P. Sinha (ed.), *Prof. K.A. Iyer Felicitation Volume*, Lucknow: Akhila Bharatiya Sanskrit Parishad, 1976, pp. 105-109

RATIÉ 2011
I. Ratié, *Le Soi et l'Autre. Identité, différence et altérité dans la philosophie de la Pratyabhijñā*, Leiden/Boston: Brill, 2011

RATIÉ 2013
I. Ratié, "On reason and scripture in the Pratyabhijñā," in ELTSCHINGER AND KRASSER 2013, pp. 375-454

RATIÉ 2014
I. Ratié, *Une critique bouddhique du Soi selon la Mīmāṃsā: présentation, édition critique et traduction de la Mīmāṃsakaparikalpitātmaparīkṣā de Śāntarakṣita (Tattvasaṅgraha 222-284 et Pañjikā)*, Wien: Verlag der Österreichischen Akademie der Wissenschaften, 2014

RATIÉ 2016
I. Ratié, "Utpaladeva's Proof of God: On the Purpose of the *Īśvarasiddhi*," in R. Torella and B. Bäumer (eds.), *Utpaladeva, Philosopher of Recognition*, Delhi: DK Printworld, 2016, pp. 257-340

SAP
[*Sambandhākṣepaparihāra*] See ŚlV

ŚlV
Ślokavārttika of Śrī Kumārila Bhaṭṭa, ed. D. Śāstrī, Varanasi: Tara Publications, 1978

SUBRAMANIA IYER 1969
K.A. Subramania Iyer, *Bhartṛhari: a study of the Vākyapadīya in the light of ancient commentaries*, Poona: Deccan College, 1969

TĀ
Tantrāloka of Abhinavagupta with commentary by Rājānaka Jayaratha, ed. M.K. Shāstrī, 12 vols., Allahabad/Srinagar/Bombay: Kashmir Series of Texts and Studies 23, 28, 29, 30, 35, 36, 41, 47, 52, 57, 58 & 59, 1918-1938

TABER 1986
J.A. Taber, "Utpaladeva's *Īśvarasiddhi*," *The Adyar Library Bulletin* 52 (Golden Jubilee Volume), 1986, pp. 106-137

TORELLA 2001
R. Torella, "The Word in Abhinavagupta's *Bṛhadvimarśinī*," in R. Torella (ed.), *Le Parole e i Marmi, Studi in onore di Raniero Gnoli nel suo 70° compleanno*, 2 vols., Roma: IsIAO, Serie Orientale Roma, 2001

TORELLA 2002
R. Torella, *The Īśvarapratyabhijñākārikā of Utpaladeva with the Author's Vṛtti*, ed. and transl., Delhi: Motilal Banarsidass, 2002

TORELLA 2004
R. Torella, "How is verbal signification possible: understanding Abhinavagupta's reply," *Journal of Indian Philosophy* 32, 2004, pp. 173-178

TORELLA 2007
R. Torella, "Studies on Utpaladeva's *Īśvarapratyabhijñāvivṛti*: Part I: Anupalabdhi and Apoha in a Śaiva Garb," in K. Preisendanz (ed.), *Expanding and merging horizons. Contributions to South Asian and cross-cultural studies in commemoration of Wilhelm Halbfass*, Wien: Verlag der Österreichischen Akademie der Wissenschaften, 2007, pp. 473-490

TORELLA 2008
R. Torella, "From an Adversary to the Main Ally: The Place of Bhartṛhari in the Kashmirian Śaiva Advaita," in M. Kaul and A. Aklujkar (eds.), *Linguistic Traditions of Kashmir. Essays in Memory of Pandit Dinanath Yaksha*, New Delhi: DK Printworld, 2008, pp. 508-524

TORELLA 2012
R. Torella, "Observations on *yogipratyakṣa*," in Y. Honda, M. Desmarais, C. Watanabe (eds.), *Saṃskṛta-Sādhutā "Goodness of Sanskrit": Studies in Honour of Professor Ashok Aklujkar*, New Delhi: D.K. Printworld, 2012, pp. 470-487

TORELLA 2013
R. Torella, "Inherited cognitions: *prasiddhi*, *āgama*, *pratibhā*, *śabdana*. Bhartṛhari, Utpaladeva, Abhinavagupta, Kumārila and Dharmakīrti in dialogue," in ELTSCHINGER AND KRASSER 2013, pp. 455-480

TS
Tattvasaṅgraha of Shāntarakṣita, with the commentary of Kamalashīla, ed. E. Krishnamacharya, Baroda: Central Library, Gaekwad's Oriental Series 30-31, 1926

TV
The Tantravārttika, A gloss on Śabara Svāmi's commentary on the Mīmāṃsā Sūtras, by Bhaṭṭa Kumārila, ed. Pt. Ḍ. Panta, Benares: Benares Sanskrit Series, 1882

VERGIANI 2015
V. Vergiani, "*Āgamārthānusāribhiḥ*. Helārāja's use of quotations and other referential devices in his commentary on the *Vākyapadīya*," *Journal of Indian Philosophy* 43(2-3), 2015, pp. 191-217, DOI: 10.1007/s10781-014-9237-4

ViV
Vidhivivekaḥ of Maṇḍana Miśraḥ, with commentary Nyāyakaṇikā of Vācaspatimiśraḥ and supercommentaries Juṣadhvaṅkaraṇī and Svaditaṅkaraṇī of Parameśva-

raḥ. Critical and annotated edition: the pūrvapakṣaḥ [Sanskrit text], ed. E.M. Stern, Unpublished PhD Thesis, University of Pennsylvania, 1988

VP
Bhartṛharis Vākyapadīya. Die einem Pāda-Index versehen, ed. W. Rau, Wiesbaden: Franz Steiner, 1977

VP 1 (ed. SUBRAMANIA IYER)
Vākyapadīya of Bhartṛhari with the Commentaries Vṛtti and the Paddhati of Vṛṣabhadeva, Kāṇḍa I, ed. K.A. Subramania Iyer, Poona: Deccan College Monograph Series 32, 1966

VP 2 (ed. SUBRAMANIA IYER)
Vākyapadīya of Bhartṛhari (An ancient Treatise on the Philosophy of Sanskrit Grammar). Containing the Ṭīkā of Puṇyarāja and the Ancient Vṛtti, Kāṇḍa II, ed. K.A. Subramania Iyer, Delhi: Motilal Banarsidass, 1983

VP 3.1 (ed. SUBRAMANIA IYER)
Vākyapadīya of Bhartṛhari with the Commentary of Helārāja, Kāṇḍa III, Part I, ed. K.A. Subramania Iyer, Poona: Deccan College Monograph Series 21, 1963

VPVṛ
[*Vākyapadīyavṛtti*] See VP 1

VS
Vaiśeṣikaśutra of Kaṇāda with the commentary of Candrānanda, ed. Muni Jambuvijaya, Baroda: Oriental Institute, 1961

Vyomavatī
Vyomavatī of Vyomaśiva, ed. G. Shastri, Varanasi: Sampūrṇānanda Samskṛta Viśvavidyālaya, 1983-1984

WEZLER 1982
A. Wezler, "Remarks on the definition of '*yoga*' in the *Vaiśeṣikasūtra*," in L.A. Hercus et al. (eds.), *Indological and Buddhist Studies. Volume in Honour of Professor J.W. de Jong*, Canberra, 1982, pp. 643-686

YS
[*Yogasūtra*] *Vācaspatimiśraviracitaṭīkāsaṃvalitavyāsabhāṣyasametāni Pātañjalayogasūtrāṇi*, ed. K.Ś. Āgāśe, Pune: Ānandāśramamudraṇālaye, Ānandāśrama Sanskrit Series 47, 1904

YS-*Bhāṣya*
[*Yogasūtrabhāṣya*] See YS

Kashmiri Brahmins under the Kārkoṭa, Utpala and Lohara Dynasties, 625-1151 CE*

MICHAEL WITZEL

After the legends told in the *Nīlamata Purāṇa* of Kashmir and in the ahistorical early books of Kalhaṇa's *Rājataraṅgiṇī* (1150 CE, henceforth RT), "real" Kashmirian history starts with the Kārkoṭa dynasty of Kashmir (625-855 CE) – that is, if Kalhaṇa's calculation mistake of +25 years is corrected.[1]

The difference between Kalhaṇa's dates for the Kārkoṭa dynasty and that of Chinese travelers is due to the confusion between Laukika Samvat and Kali Samvat, both of which were used in medieval Kashmir. The beginning of Laukika Samvat equals Kali Samvat 25 (expired).[2] This discrepancy extends throughout Kalhaṇa's dates of the Kārkoṭa reign.[3] Apart from this problem, his dates are correct, down to the calendar day, for the period after 625 CE. The Kashmirian dynasties of the period treated in this paper thus are:

Kārkoṭa	625- 855 CE	RT IV
Utpala	855-939	RT V
Utpala interregnum	939-1003	RT VI
1st Lohara	1003-1101	RT VII

* In this paper there are some overlaps with my earlier ones on Kashmir (not indicated here); see WITZEL 1994 and 2008.

1 See WITZEL 1990. This mistake is due to Kalhaṇa's reliance on a Vaṃśāvalī, that he took for a list in Laukika Samvat, which was calculated in Kali Samvat.

2 Stein mentions the time difference, but did not recognize the reason for this confusion in Kārkoṭa dates. In STEIN 1900, vol. I, p. 69, he speculates about an "error in the record of several reigns attributed to this dynasty."

3 See STEIN 1900, vol. I, p. 96 (§ 91) on Cippanajayāpīda.

2nd Lohara 1001-1151 RT VIII

A skeleton overview of the fate of the Kashmirian Brahmins during the time of these dynasties is provided by Kalhaṇa's RT. It was written by him prior to 1070 Śaka = 1147 CE; the introduction was composed in 1148/1149, and the text was completed in 1150/1151. The time discrepancy between composition and final version is due to political reasons: Kalhaṇa's concern for his personal safety under a dynasty that he criticized.[4]

The most important factual data regarding Brahmins are those listed by him of land donations, *agrahāra*s. Here a list of those donations during the Kārkoṭa (625 CE-) and the following dynasties is given, neglecting a number of legendary donations mentioned since the beginning of Kaliyuga in RT I-III. Kalhaṇa provides the following list, until his time (1149/1150 CE):[5]

- 4.5: Durlabhavardhana, the first king of the Kārkoṭa dynasty (circa 625-637), gave the Village of Candragrāma Pāreviśoka-Koṭa (East of the Viśau river) and other places to the Brahmins;
- 4.9: several *agrahāra*s founded by Hanumant, son of Ūḍa (Oḍā, Aiḍa?), minister of king Durlabha-Pratāpāditya (circa 637-687);
- 4.12: Noṇa from the Rauhītaka country built the Noṇamaṭha for Brahmins born in Rauhītaka (modern Rohtak in Haryāṇa, or perhaps in the Multan area, see Stein ad loc.);[6]

---

4 He thus quickly wrote a new version of book VIII, one that favored the current king Jayasiṃha; the older version has been discovered by Hultzsch in a Kashmiri manuscript now in Berlin (as explained in KÖLVER 1971, pp. 79ff.) – Stein had an inkling of this state of affairs when he commented on the (unusual) deficiencies in RT VIII, see his Introduction, pp. 43f. However, Hultzsch came to the conclusion (p. 206) that the archetype perhaps represents the earlier version and the two additional manuscripts L and M (with 161 new verses), a later one; for trenchant arguments against this interpretation see KÖLVER 1971. For the Hultzsch data see now OBROCK ED. 2013, pp. 179-248; also cf. now on RT COX ED. 2013.

5 The numerous donations to various temples and Buddhist *vihāra*s are not mentioned here. The king reigning immediately before the Kārkoṭas, Bālāditya, is mentioned at 3.481 with a donation at Bheḍava (modern Biḍar, in Bring Pargaṇa) in Maḍavarājya (modern Maraz).

6 The name Nona occurs a few times in subsequent centuries, such as that of a Brahmin at RT 8.1328.

- 4.639: Jayāpīḍa (776/777-807/808) did not confiscate certain *agrahāra*s (at Tūlamūlya?) on the Candrabhāga (modern Tulamul, on a branch of the Sind river);
- 5.23: Khādhūyā, Hastikarṇa (modern Vāgahōm in Dachünpor Pargaṇ, on the Vitastā), under king Avantivarman, 855/856-883);
- 5.24: Pañcahastā (modern Pānzath, in Divasar Pargaṇa);
- 5.170: king Śaṅkaravarman (883-902) took back some *agrahāra*s;
- 5.397: <the village Helu given to a low caste man, Raṅga, by king Cakravarman, 936-937>;
- 5.403: Brahmins accepted *agrahāra*s from king Cakravarman;
- 5.442: Brahmins accepted *agrahāra*s from king Unmattāvanti (937-939);
- 6.87: king Yaśaskara (939-948 CE) built a *maṭha* for students from Āryadeśa;
- 6.89: 55 *agrahāra*s given by king Yaśaskara;
- 6.300: *maṭha* for persons from Madhyadeśa, Lāṭa and Suḍotra (Saurāṣṭra??) by Diḍḍā, grandmother of king Nandigupta (972-973 CE) (this is the modern Didmar);
- 6.304: *maṭha* for foreign Brahmins built by Nandigupta;
- 6.336: Brahmins holding the chief *agrahāra*s held a fast (prāyopaveśa)[7] under Queen Diddā (980/981-1003);
- 7.182: Āśācandra-agrahāra by queen Sūryamatī, queen of king Ananta (1028-1063), who built a *maṭha* with an *agrahāra* in the name of her brother Kallana (Āśācandra); another *maṭha* was built in the name of her brother Sillana, and Vijayeśvara *maṭha* in the name of her husband;
- 7.184: 108 *agrahāra*s by queen Sūryamatī;
- 7.185: in the name of king Ananta, queen Sūryamatī established *agrahāra*s at Amareśvara;
- 7.608: *agrahāra*s built by king Kalaśa (1063-1089);

---

[7] STEIN 1900, vol. I, pp. 36ff, refers to these fasts and Kalhaṇa's contempt for the *purohita*s who held them. "The solemn fasts or Prāyopaveśas to which they were apt to resort in critical circumstances, were evidently powerful means of coercion which weak rulers had reason to dread." Cf. now KÖLVER 1971, pp. 161ff., esp. p. 167, on suicide.

- 8.898: Akṣosuva plundered by Tilaka, the commander-in-chief, under king Bhikṣācara (1120-1121);
- 8.899-908: Brahmins holding *agrahāra*s and *pariṣādya*s held a fast in the Gokula.

Kalhaṇa has numerous references to various kinds of donations given under his contemporary king, Jayadeva (1128-1149). They include also those by his queens and officials, and gifts to Brahmins (*agrahāra*), temples, *maṭha*s and Buddhist *vihāra*s (traditionally, the latter frequently by queens): 8.3316-3370.

- 8.2408: numerous *agrahāra*s in Purāṇādhiṣṭhāna (Pandreṭhān) and Pravarapura (Srinagar), given for the upkeep of *maṭha*s built there;
- 8.2444: Brahmins from the Indus and Drāviḍa regions were settled;
- 8.2419: *maṭha*s and *agrahāra*s established by minister Dhanya;
- 8.2420: *maṭha*s and *agrahāra*s established by minister Udaya;
- 8.3355: *agrahāra*s granted by Sumanas, younger brother of Rilhaṇa, a minister of king Sussala, under the reign of king Jayasiṃha.

In India, such land grants were usually documented on copper plates. However, such copper plates have not been found so far in Kashmir. The reason might be that they were often issued on birchbark. This is proved by the story in Jonarāja's *Rājataraṇginī* of the forging of a document in the time of Zain ul Abidin.[8] (Similarly, in Nepal, land sales, mortgages etc. were documented on palm leaves.)[9] On the other hand, Kalhaṇa mentions (1.15) that the study of grants and inscriptions made him "overcome the trouble arising from many errors" (STEIN, see his note).

These notes of Kalhaṇa, which end in circa 1149/1150 CE, can be divided into several classes.

General grants by kings are numerous: here belong 3.481, 5.23-24, 5.403, 5.442, 5.448, 6.89, 7.608, 8.2408. The Brahmins thus settled and richly endowed, quickly gained considerable power. This has been described and characterized by Kalhaṇa and summ-

---

8 See now SLAJE 2004, pp. 15ff.

9 See KÖLVER AND ŚĀKYA 1985.

ed up by M.A. Stein.[10] Its effects can be seen at 6.336, 8.899, 8.908 where the Brahmins holding such grants organize a fast to put pressure on the king. Gandhi's "Satyāgraha" and some others of his methods have their predecessors... This kind of fast was often held at or in the Gokula, apparently a *maṭha*-like place where the Brahmins always assembled to discuss important religious and political issues.

Grants were also made by queens (7.182, 7.184-185) or by ministers (4.9, 8.2419, 8.2420, 8.335) throughout the period described by Kalhaṇa. Another case is of special interest: Noṇa from the Rauhītaka country built the Noṇamaṭha for Brahmins born in Rauhītaka (4.12). Stein identifies this country either with Multan or with modern Rohtak in Haryāṇa, which had been known since Vedic times as Rohītakakula. It is remarkable that a foreigner took the interest and was wealthy enough to execute a donation of this kind in another country. His action points to the close links between the two countries at a comparatively early period (circa 625-660 CE). This is not the only grant made on behalf of non-Kashmiris: there are those (6.87) for students (from Uttar Pradesh), and at 6.300 for Uttar Pradesh, Lāṭa (Southern Gujarat)[11] and Suḍotra (Saurāṣṭra?) people, or at 6.304, a more generally defined grant "for foreign Brahmins."

In spite of the general generosity of the kings, which usually was motivated by acute political interests, there also loomed a threat of confiscation of *agrahāra* land by certain kings (4.395 4.639, 5.170, cf. 6.175, 7.1091 etc.) and their generals. This contradicts the general rule that such donations are made "as long as the sun and moon last."

One the other hand, the usual inclusion of this phrase, in conjunction with the admonishment to future kings not to encroach on the grant is, taken by itself, evidence enough that such actions took place more or less regularly, particularly by new dynasties who redistributed older *agrahāra*s to Brahmins of their choice.

Examples of such threats in the RT are: 4.639 by Jayāpīḍa, 5.170 by Śaṅkaravarman. He resumed villages belonging to tem-

---

10 STEIN 1900, vol. I ad RT 2.132.

11 NAUDOU 1980, p. 56, n. 57 doubts that this is in southern Gujarat and thinks of a nearby (Khaśa) kingdom, Viṣalāṭā; however see above on king Bhoja, and cf. RT 8.1074.

ples (see below). Again, *agrahāra*s were actually plundered, against the common practice, by a king's general (8.898).

Kalhaṇa's knowledge about details on all these *agrahāra*s surprises. Apart from legendary information (in the entries before 625 CE) he must have gained definite data from copper plate and stone inscriptions recording such donations. In one case, this is clear: RT 1.344 (STEIN 1900, vol. I, Introduction, p. 26; cf. RT 5.397 on *praśasti*s, and 5.397 on granting a village). However, there also is direct mentioning of such inscriptions in Jonarāja's RT: an order of the king is incised on a copper plate (886), *tāmrapāttra,* next to birch bark documents (882), and in Śrīvara's RT (1.7.3). Copper plates are still mentioned by Akbar's historians as having been found in the ruins of the temples.

BUDDHIST ACCOUNTS

Since most of the Sanskrit literary texts of Kashmir were written by Hindus and stress the Hindu aspects of Kashmiri life, it is useful to turn, briefly, to the Buddhist accounts.

Early information is provided by the Chinese pilgrims whose accounts were translated in the 1800s, about the state of affairs in the 5th and the following centuries; they include: 404-424 CE Chemong,[12] 420- Fa-yong (Fa-Hian, Faxian),[13] 518 Sung-Yun and Hwei Sang,[14] 631-633 Hsuan-tsang[15] (Xuan Zang), 673-685 I-tsing,[16] 759-763 Wu k'ung[17] (Ou khong, Wukong 751-790),[18] 720

---

12 He crossed the Pamirs with a Kashmiri monk and stayed in Kashmir for a long time before visiting the holy places of India.

13 See BEAL 1884 pp. 1ff. He crossed over the Himalayas and Pamirs, with 20 monks, from Kashgar to the Gilgit Valley, stayed for one year, and then returned to China by sea. See also HU-VON HINÜBER 2016.

14 See BEAL 1884, pp. 55ff.

15 He stayed in Kashmir from May 631 to April 633; On Hsuan Tsang and other early Chinese travellers see BEAL 1884, 1908 and 1911. See also NAUDOU 1980, pp. 39ff.

16 TAKAKUSU 1896; further: CHAVANNES 1894.

17 LÉVI AND CHAVANNES 1895; cf. STEIN 1896 and 1900; his stay in Kashmir, 759-763 according to NAUDOU 1980, p. 56.

18 LÉVI AND CHAVANNES 1895, pp. 350ff.

Ambassador Ou-li-to,[19] 726 Huei-ch'ao[20] (Korean: Hyecho) (751-790), 747 Kao Sien-che (another Korean).

They report that in Kashmir there were *deva* and Buddhist temples. The Kashmiris cared more for the *deva* temples in Hsuan Tsang's time, which may point to the strong influence of the newly established Kārkoṭa dynasty and their restoration of Hinduism[21] after a period of strong Buddhist influence in the Valley. However, even at the time of Kalhaṇa (1150 CE), Buddhism flourished in the Valley.[22] The *Nīlamata* gives a detailed description of the festivities occurring at Buddha's birthday; according to M.A. Stein it is even retained today in the Brahmins' calendars. About a hundred years before Kalhaṇa, Kṣemendra still found it interesting to write a Sanskrit gist of the Avadāna stories (*Bauddhāvadānakalpalatā*). Even the late, post-Kalhaṇa *Rājataraṅgiṇī* of Jonarāja (circa 1459)[23] still mentions:

> The good country of Kashmira is adorned by the Vedas, [...] by the followers of Śiva and Viṣṇu, by the worshippers of the sun, by the Buddhists with their paintings, and Vihāra and Maṭhas.[24]

Due to the strong influence of Kashmir on early Tibetan Buddhism, Tibetan texts contain a lot of data on Kashmiri Buddhist monks and scholars, whose works were translated into Tibetan and many of whom actually traveled to Tibet, but hardly any information on non-Buddhist Kashmiri Brahmins.

J. Naudou's book[25] offers many pertinent details and discussions. This includes a few accounts of conversion to Buddhism. According to Taranātha, Dharmakīrti was converted to Buddhism

---

19 T'ang Shu, transl. NAUDOU 1980, p. 50: story of Mahāpadma (mohopotomo).

20 Transl. in FUCHS 1939; cf. also PELLIOT 1908, pp. 511-512; OTANI 1934, pp. 143-160.

21 See STEIN 1900 ad 1.179f. – a passage directed against the influence of the Buddhists: "When customs [...] had broken down [...] the Nāgas [...] sent down excessive snow to cause distress to the Bauddhas [...] every year [...]." The connection between snow and ice will be explored in a long paper on the 600 Kashmirian Nāgas. Cf. *Nīlamata* LR vv. 217ff., 465ff.

22 See STEIN 1900's summary on Buddhism in Kashmir, vol. I, pp. 8ff. See also SLAJE forthcoming.

23 See now SLAJE 2014.

24 However in a post-Jonarāja appendix (H) in KAUL 1966, p. 425, verse B 473. The idea goes back at least to Kṣemendra's *Lokaprakāśa,* no 139.

25 NAUDOU 1980.

by three Kashmiri Brahmins: Vidyāsiṃha, Devasīmha, Devavidyākara (NAUDOU 1980, p. 65). Śaṅkarānanda, a logician, called a *paramōpasaka mahāpaṇḍita brāhmaṇa,* is said to have been converted to Buddhism (ibid., p. 126).[26] Ratnavajra converted a Śaiva Brahmin, called the "red *ācārya*" (or Guhyaprajña; NAUDOU 1980, pp.169 and 172). A Brahmin called Śrībhadra or Sūryaketu was the teacher of Sajjana, grandson of Ratnavajra (NAUDOU 1980, p. 188). Somanātha (or Candranātha) of the early 11th century, was converted by his mother. He studied together with Sonasati, Lakṣmīkara, Dānaśrī/Danaśīla, Candrarāhula (NAUDOU 1980, p. 198).

BRAHMINS IN SANSKRIT TEXTS

Returning now to the notes on Brahmins in Sanskrit texts, we have to take into account a large number of texts with smaller or larger data sets on Brahmins. They cannot be dealt with here in any detail. However, there are but a few texts that may be as old or nearly as old as the *Nīlamata Purāṇa*[27] (circa 8th century), which basically is a Māhātmya of the Kashmir Valley. As such it contains materials on the sacred places but also incidental notices on groups of Brahmins, such as, surprisingly, the Taittirīya Yajurvedins[28] and the Pāñcarātrins.[29]

The Taittirīya school of the Black Yajurveda is found after the Vedic period, predominantly in South India, where according to the adage "every house cat knows the Yajurveda." Their appearance in Kashmir (and in Nepal)[30] during this early period surprises; however, it is another indication of early relations between South India and the Himalayas (see below). The Pāñcarātrins may be mentioned as they played an important role in the formation of the imperial Kashmir state under the late Kārkoṭas and early Utpala dynasties.[31] This included the composition of the *Viṣṇudharmottara Purāṇa* and the influence on the ritual of Rājābhiṣeka, the royal consecration.[32]

---

26 Much discussed, see now ELTSCHINGER 2015.

27 See *Nīlamata* LR and SR; see now IKARI ED. 1994.

28 *Nīlamata* LR 1202 = SR 1157.

29 See *Nīlamata* LR, vol. I, p. 156, v. 420.

30 See WITZEL 1980.

31 Note the military expansion especially under Lalitāditya and Jayāpīḍa.

32 However, INDEN ET AL. 2000, especially the second essay (INDEN 2000),

An important secular text from this period is that of the poet Dāmodaragupta; he was a minister of Jayāpīḍa (779-813 = rev. 804-839) and composed the *Kuṭṭanīmata* (mentioned in RT 4.496).[33] This may be an unlikely text to look for information on Brahmins as it deals with the "advice of a courtesan." However the Kashmiris always had a foible for texts dealing with the red light district.[34] "Although there is no direct reference to Kashmir, the poem gives a fairly accurate account of contemporary Kashmiri life."[35]

The more or less contemporary *Nyāyamañjarī* (henceforth NM) of Jayanta Bhaṭṭa (late 9th century) contains little of interest in this regard, however, it furnishes quite a lot of details on the Vedic and philosophical texts actually studied in Kashmir at the time. Occasionally, it also provides a sidelight on the actual religious conditions, such as on the commotion created by the arrival of a new Tantric sect, that of the Nīlāmbaras. Their story is further elaborated in Jayanta's philosophical, allegoric drama, the *Āgamaḍambara*, which indicates Jayanta's involvement in the political discussion of the time:[36] being "non-traditional" they were exiled from Kashmir

---

claims a "dialogical" reading of texts – notably the *Viṣṇudharmottara Purāṇa* as a Kashmirian Pāñcarātra text, composed by a "complex author" – that is "a world conquering monarch [with Candrāpīḍa and Muktāpīḍa as co-authors] and members of his court as well as adepts of the disciplinary order of Pāñcarātra Vaiṣṇavas." By his "intertextual reading" Inden sees the *Nīlamata*, the text preceding the *Viṣṇudharmottara Purāṇa*, as "a dialectical reworking of an earlier Śaiva vision of Kashmir, which in turn reworked a still older Buddhist vision." Cf. now SANDERSON 2007, p. 207. The rules for the royal *abhiṣeka* in *Nīlamata* (LR 854-866) concur with those of the Nepalese Rājyābhiṣeka, the *Viṣṇudharmottara Purāṇa* and the late *Agni Purāṇa*, see WITZEL 1987, and now CHAULAGAIN 2013.

33 See SHASTRI 1975; cf. RT 4.498, where the text is mentioned by name.

34 Such as the 5th century *Pādatāḍitaka* by Śyāmilaka, and Dāmodaragupta's *Kuṭṭanīmata*, Kṣemendra's *Samayamātṛkā* (1050 CE), *Deśopadeśa*, *Narmamāla* etc.

35 SHASTRI 1975, p. 41. This is to be contrasted with what is specifically said about the main location of the story, Benares, and also Pāṭaliputra, Mount Abu. See now the transl. in DEZSŐ AND GOODALL 2012.

36 WEZLER 1976; see however GRANOFF 1986-1992, esp. pp. 296-298. King Śaṅkaravarman (883-902 CE) installed a council deliberating the question; this is mentioned in NM itself (p. 363, transl. in BHATTACHARYA 1978 p. 562); it put a stop to the practices of the Nīlāmbaras. Jayanta has a long discussion on the validity of the Āgamas and Tantras (NM, transl. in BHATTACHARYA 1978, pp. 544-563. See now DEZSÖ 2015, Introduction.

by order of the king. Jayanta's son Abhinanda, however, describes him as a scholar of Veda and Vedānta, which is not unusual as people have multiple interests and "identities."[37]

More detailed information on the Brahmins of Kashmir is given in the somewhat later works of Albīrūnī, Bilhaṇa and Kalhaṇa. Albīrūnī, a Khvarezmian Muslim, provides a lot of detailed information in his *Tarīkh al Hind* (henceforth *India*) that was written in Arabic in 1030 CE. Not unlike present day anthropological field workers, he gained his information from local Panjabi and Kashmiri collaborators, and from various other sources, be it learned Brahmins or books, often acquired with difficulty.

Bilhaṇa (flourished circa 1050-1100 CE)[38] gives an account of the life of the Cālukya king Vikramāṅka or Vikramāditya VI (reigned until 1126 CE). Bilhaṇa was his court poet for some time, and wrote the *Vikramāṅkadevacarita*, an account of his life and deeds. In the last quarter of canto 18, Bilhaṇa describes his travels outside Kashmir, and towards the end his wish to return to Kashmir to spend his old age in Śaiva meditation. This includes a detailed description of his homeland, his village (Khonamuṣa near Srinagar), and an account of his family.

Kalhaṇa's RT was completed in 1149/1151.[39] The evidence from this text must be evaluated according to (1) his report of distant and more recent historical facts, (2) what he has to say about his own time, including references to earlier times expressed by contemporaneous similes.

DETAILS

In the *Kuṭṭanīmata*, the Brahmins play a conspicuous role. They adhere to the six duties: study, teaching, performing sacrifices for themselves, officiating for others, making gifts, and accepting gifts. Albirunī reports:

---

[37] Or as the late Robert Levy once told me (circa 1980) when asking the same question to a Bhaktapur (Nepal) resident, he quickly listed his multiple identities in Nepalese, Newar, *varṇa*, and caste society, his occupation and the various religio-cultural organizations (such as *sanā* Guṭhī) he was (or had to be) a member of.

[38] For Bilhaṇa, see SOLF 1886; cf. MISRA 1976, p. 115.

[39] See above, n. 4.

> He must continuously read, perform the sacrifices, take care of the fire which he lights, offer before it, worship it, and preserve it from being extinguished, that he may be burned by it after his death. It is called *homa*. (*India* II, 133)

The Brahmins receive the traditional designations *vipra, dvija, dvi-janman, agrajanman, bhūmideva, vasudhādeva*; their names end in *-sena*, *-svāmin*; and they have these titles: *-dīkṣita* (one initiated into the solemn Vedic sacrifices such as the Soma ritual), *-miśra, -bhaṭṭa*, (originally a Veda teacher), or *-bhāva* (a Śaiva teacher).[40] Albirunī, however, thinks that a brahmin is called in various ways:

> When he is busy with the service of one fire, he is called *iṣṭin*, if he serves three fires, he is called *agnihotrin*, if he besides offers an offering to the fire, he is called *dīkṣita*.

As for Veda learning, he reports that the Veda was allowed to be learnt only by the Brahmins[41] and Kṣatriyas (I, 104, 125). The latter, however, do not teach it (II, 125, 136). It was learnt[42] by rote and recited by heart by the Brahmins (I, 125) after having undergone initiation. Dāmodaragupta's descriptions are, again, largely traditional.[43] Only some Brahmins were skilled reciters of the Veda (414, 422).[44]

Similarly, Bilhaṇa's ancestors are described as follows: Muktikalaśa was "the abode of the four beloved Vedas" (v. 76). His son Rājakalaśa and Rājakalaśa's son Jyeṣṭhakalaśa also were learnt in

---

40 Bhaṭṭa also occurs in compounds indicating their sons: *bhaṭṭa-putra, bhaṭṭa-suta, bhaṭṭa-taneya, bhaṭṭa-dāyada*.

41 He also says that the study period extends until the 25th year for a young Brahmin (II 131), which again reminds of Kashmiri conceptions.

42 He expressively mentions the girdle (= *mekhalā*) next to two kinds of *yajñopavīta*, details that might point to Kashmiri informants, who followed prescriptions of the *Kāṭhaka Gṛhya Sūtra* II, 130. (The *mekhalā* still is worn today, also in Kerala.)

43 As all Vaidika families (420), his protagonist Purandhara studied with his teacher, wearing the deer skin and the (typical Kashmiri) girdle (*mekhalikā*) during his brahmacārin vow (197). When its breaks it is replaced (198). A Veda student is called *vaṭuka* (198). He cuts firewood for his teacher (414ff.) and *samidh*s – chores that Vaidika Brahmins learn early in their childhood (400, cf. 200). Pupils have to serve their teacher (421, 436), with whom they usually reside (433).

44 The incompatibility of Buddhism with Vedic *śākhā*s is seen at 266: *abhimata-sugatāvasthitir abhinandita-caraṇa-yugalaracanā ca*.

the Vedas. Bilhaṇa describes himself as having studied the Vedas and its Aṅgas, among other topics.[45]

We learn much more about the actual Vedic texts studied in Kashmir at the time of Jayanta Bhaṭṭa due to his numerous quotations contained in his NM. They include texts from all the four Vedas. The Ṛgveda was studied in the Śākala version, but in a slightly different sub-recension, that included a special recension of the Ṛgvedakhilas.

The Yajurveda of Kashmir is represented by the Kaṭha School, which still possessed, at the time, fragments of its *Śatādhyāya-Brāhmaṇa*, the *Śrautasūtra* and other now lost texts. The *Gṛhyasūtra*, under the name of *Kaṭha-* or *Laugākṣi-Sūtra*, has been the mainstay of Kashmiri ritual until today. (It has also influenced Śaiva ritual). There are several commentaries and numerous Paddhatis of this text. The Sāmaveda seems to have followed the usual Kauthuma tradition, traditionally linked with the Kaṭhas.[46]

The Atharvaveda was still very well known at the time, not in the Śaunaka Vulgate form but in the Paippalāda version. Apparently it still was recited with *svaras* at the time. Some of its later texts were also studied. The Atharvavedins were proud to have a special initiation; only someone having undergone it, was allowed to study their texts.

The only two passages in the RT, as far as I see, which refer to Vedic learning – though in rather conventional terms – are the interesting stanza 5.159: "In [charge of] these two temples of the lord of Gaurī, he placed the Brahman Nāyaka, who was versed in the four Vedas, and who was like a familiar dwelling-place to Sarasvatī" (see below); also, for a passing remark on Veda recitation see 8.2518.

Dāmodaragupta's *Kuṭṭanīmata* describes the further life of a Brahmin: after completing his studies, its protagonist Purandhara settled down as a householder and performed sacrifices (193) – for

---

45 For other *Kalaśas*, see RT 7.24 Rājakalaśa, 7.888 Praśastakalaśa, 7.1050 Kalaśarāja, 7.1286ff. King Kalaśa (1063-1089 CE, 7.232ff.); Tilakakalaśa (NAUDOU 1980, pp. 232-233, 240) Alaṅkārakalaśa (mid-12th century, reportedly a descendant of the grammarian Trilocana, NAUDOU 1980, pp. 240f.); for still another one of circa 800 CE, see http://east.uni-hd.de/buddh/ind/25/.

46 According to grammarians: e.g. Kaṭha-Kauthuma (Patañjali, *Mahābhāṣya* 2.4.3).

which one has to be married.[47] The solemn *śrauta* rituals[48] include the recitation of Vedic mantras and the use of sacrificial posts (*kratuyūpa,* 180). Vedic texts are popularly studied (419) and include many *vratas* (419); Manu is an author of the past (719).[49]

Veda recitation is mentioned by Kalhaṇa at RT 8.2518.

Bilhaṇa[50] too mentions the traditional Vedic and other rituals, e.g. at Kāṣṭhāla, which is "resonant with the exposition of the Śāstras" (25); the heads of its inhabitants are "grey by the smoke of the fire in which sacrifices are performed in the evening and in the morning," referring to Agnihotra or *sāndhya* type *homas* (25). His home village of Khonamuṣa is described as "having many sacrificial posts" (71). His family was "renowned and [...] inclined to Vedic studies (or meditation on Brahman)." They also were eager sacrificers whose "column of sacrificial smoke was filling the sky." (74)

Among his ancestors, Muktikalaśa's family is described as "perspiring [...] from the constant practice of Agnihotra sacrifices." Rājakalaśa was learned in the Vedas and a great sacrificer; his son Jyeṣṭhakalaśa also was "preoccupied in the performance of religious ceremonies" (80).

Among the rites of passage, marriage is mentioned in the *Kuṭṭanīmata* as *pariṇāya* (792) and *pāṇigraha* (167).[51] In connection with the funeral rituals, Agni is called *hutavahana* (489), *hutāśana* (491), *bhagavat* (489); the pyre of wood for cremation is mentioned at 491, 489. The *śrāddha* rituals are mentioned in connection with the prescription of securing rhinoceros meat, skin and horns (198). Purification with earth and water is mentioned by Kalhaṇa at 6.69.

The *Kuṭṭanīmata* already mentions the *deśaguṇa* of Kashmir of allowing to eat meat;[52] we find *māṃsarasa* (sauce) and also fish

---

47 They also include *japa*, and the customary rites for the ancestors (197).

48 For details on Vedic sacrifices see SHASTRI 1975, p. 85; Kalhaṇa mentions a "drinker of Soma" which, however, occurs in a simile (5.393).

49 An interesting passage (*Kuṭṭanīmata* 14) describes the annotation of a metrical text with marks indicating long and short syllables: *chandaḥ prastāravidhau guravo yasyām anārjava-sthitayaḥ*, see A.M. SHASTRI 1975, p. 176.

50 The translations quoted of Bilhaṇa's work are from BANERJI AND GUPTA 1965.

51 For example, Kalhaṇa ahistorically mentions a *jātakarma* for Gonanda II's son, soon after the beginning of Kaliyuga (1.759).

52 The custom still continues, as I witnessed in 1979. I also still saw meat used in

consumption. Kṣemendra (circa 1000-1070) describes, in his caricature work *Deśopadeśa*, how a Bengalī student, "a black skeleton monkeying about," is gradually enticed to eat meat and then becomes so fat that he takes away all too much room in front of his teacher to the detriment of his fellow students.

Wine, however, is not drunk by Brahmins, which is surprising in view of its frequent mentioning in the RT and in *Nīlamata*. It is to be consumed, according to *Nīlamata*, "by those who are wine drinkers" on the day of the first snow fall, while it remains unclear how far Brahmins were wine drinkers (*Kuṭṭanīmata* 14; contrast 395, 392, 351). Kṣemendra's *Deśopadeśa* describes, in a humorous way, the excesses of a Śaiva teacher (*śaivaguru*), who regularly gets drunk at nightly Tantric *kaula* sessions.[53] But this refers to the ritual consumption of alcohol.

The Kashmiris of this early period regarded leaving their country as polluting, and necessitating *prāyaścitta*s; they were actually carried out until at least the early 20th century when someone returned from outside the Valley.[54]

Tantric ritual makes its appearance already in the early parts of the RT, probably by retrofitting, see for example the *mātṛkacakra* and *devīcakra*, allegedly present right from early times of Kashmiri history.[55] Another Tantric ritual is the *samayācāra* (7.279-280). Kalhaṇa, just as Kṣemendra, and much earlier, Jayanta Bhaṭṭa, does not always speak favorably of Tantric adepts.

Kalhaṇa, however, respectfully mentions Bhaṭṭa Kallaṭa, the expounder of Śiva Sūtras.[56] But he derides the false *guru*s (7.278ff., 7.295ff., 7.523, 7.712); this is echoed by Kṣemendra in his *Narmamālā*, 8.11-13 where he describes, with many *śleṣa*s, the drunken excesses of a Śaiva Tantric (*kaula*), who nevertheless, next morning after a bath, walks innocently as a *bhaṭṭo 'nyabhaṭṭeṣu*.

---

*śrāddha*s.

53 Kṣemendra's *Narmamālā* 8.13 on *kaula* drinking and other excesses, cf. 3.81, and BALDISSERA 2005, pp. 130ff., with a detailed discussion of the *guru*'s and others' behaviors (esp. pp. 94f., 116f.).

54 STEIN 1900, n. ad 4.189. For purification with earth and water see RT 6.69.

55 The first ones were founded by the wife of Jalauka(s), the alleged son of Aśoka.

56 Cf. NAUDOU 1980, p. 119.

IMMIGRATION AND EMIGRATION

A typical feature of medieval state policies has been the strategy of inviting Brahmins from other, often very distant areas, so as to create a counterweight against the dominance of local Brahmins.[57] There is a record in the RT of an early invitation to Kashmir of a large number of Gandhāra Brahmins by a Hun king around 515 CE. However, mass immigration is not mentioned under the Kārkoṭas and their successors.

Individual immigration however, continued. This coincided with the stabilization of Hindu rule under the Kārkoṭas and the emergence of Kashmir as a cultural and scholarly center; similar developments are known from other outlying Indian areas. Rather, some new *maṭha*s and *agrahāra*s, mentioned by Kalhaṇa, seem to be meant for the temporary accommodation of foreigners during pilgrimages and periods of study.[58] The "Bengali student" in Kashmir has been well described, as a caricature, by Kṣemendra in his *Deśopadeśa*.[59] The popularity of Kashmir for Hindu studies is also indirectly testified by Albīrūnī when he says that Hindu learning had retreated, in his time and no doubt due to the two dozen incursions of his master, Muhammad of Ghazni, to Benares and Kashmir.

Immigration into Kashmir was usually well remembered by the descendants of the newcomers, and was present also in the general historical awareness of learned Kashmiris. A few better attested examples include the following.

Jayanta Bhaṭṭa (late 9th century) remembered his Bengali (*gauḍa*) ancestors of several centuries ago. His son Abhinanda(-paṇḍita) gives the lineage in his *Kādambarīkathāsāra*.[60] His ancestor Śakti, six generations before him, had immigrated to Darvābhisāra,

---

57 See WITZEL 1986.

58 And by foreigners, such as the Malwa king Bhoja, who commissioned a building at Kapaṭeśvara (7.190-193).

59 Similar color-based racist attitude at RT 4.329, and against "red-faced" Tibetans, 4.168.

60 Jayanta's father was Śrīcandra, belonging to the Bhāradvājagotra. The complete family line of descent is given by Jayanta's son Abhinanda in his *Kādambarīkathāsāra* 5-13 as: Śakti-Mitra-Śaktisvāmin-Kalyāṇasvāmin-(Kānta)(Śrī-)Candra-Jayanta "Vṛttikāra"; cf. STEIN 1900, 8.1861; BÜHLER 1873, pp. 102-106; further, introduction to the NM edition; NAGARAJAN 1970, p. 204, n. 1; BHATTACHARYA 1978, p. xxxiii; cf. JHA 1995. See now GRAHELI 2015, pp. 3ff.

the hill country south of Kashmir. According to family tradition, Śakti's grandson Śaktisvāmin was minister under the Kārkoṭa king Candrāpīḍa (r. 711-720 CE) while Jayanta wrote his *Āgamaḍambara* under the king Śaṅkaravarman (883-902).

Abhinavagupta's family, too, immigrated from Kanauj[61] under king Muktāpīḍa-Lalitāditya and settled in Paravarapura (Srinagar). He gives his ancestors as: Varāhagupta and Narahiṃhagupta (or Cukhulaka). His mother Vimalalakā and his father died when he was very young. His spiritual lineage and *guruparaṃparā* is given in *Tantrāloka* (37.37-64) and at the end of *Dhvanyāloka*.[62]

Abhinava's student Kṣemendra (circa 990-1070) and his son Somendra give their genealogy as:[63] Narendra-Bhogendra-Sindhu-Prakāśendra-Kṣemendra (brother: Cakrapāla)-Somendra. Kṣemendra's father was rich and a patron of Brahmins. His ancestor Narendra was a minister under king Jayāpīḍa.

Bilhaṇa's family belonged to the Kauśika gotra and had supposedly been brought from Madhyadeśa by the early, legendary king Gopāditya (RT 1.339). He lived in the late 11th/early 12th century, as is known from his stay at the court of Vikramāditya (ruled until 1126 CE; his son from 1126-1138).

Bilhaṇa left Kashmir under king Kalaśa (1063-1089, RT 7.935-937). He gives a detailed description of Khonamuṣa,[64] his home village near the capital of Pravarapura (*Vikramāṇkadevacarita* 18, 70-71)[65] which is described, still by Bühler in 1875, as producing saffron and grapes (72).

Immigration to Kashmir is also known to Albīrūni[66] (1030 CE); in fact it continued down to the Afghan period (1756-1819, from Panjab) to Sikh times (1819-1846), and to some extent also in the time of the Dogra rulers (1846-1947).

---

61 *Tantrāloka* 37.37-39 and passim to 37.64.

62 See NAGARAJAN 1970, p. 47; INGALLS 1990, pp. 30ff. and 726; cf. also NAUDOU 1980, p. 120.

63 See SŪRYAKĀNTA 1954, pp. 6ff. His *Bṛhatkathāmañjarī* was composed in 1039 CE, the *Avadānakalpalatā* in 1052, and the *Aucityavicāracarcā* in 1066.

64 Modern Khunmoh, 3 miles northwest of Pampar. For other (substrate) names in *-muṣa*, see RT 8.1011, 1133 *Manīmuṣa, Rāmuṣa* 8.2813; see discussion in WITZEL 1999.

65 See transl. in BANERJI AND GUPTA 1965.

66 See SACHAU 1910, vol. I, p. 22 and 173: Benares and Kashmir.

Thus, even around 1100 CE, one still remembered (or told legends about) the origin, several hundred years ago, of one's family. Under king Jayadeva (1122-1149) Brahmins from the Indus and Drāviḍa regions were settled (RT 8.244).

Emigration of Kashmiri Brahmins was not rare either at any stage in their history. However, we only have clear indications from the Middle Ages and from more recent times.[67] Exceptionally, we even hear of a reason, when Kalhaṇa reports that the Brahmins were threatened by king Jayāpīḍa (RT 4.631ff.) so that some of them emigrated, also due to his heavy taxation; those who remained behind complained loudly about their fate or committed suicide by fasting to death and by drowning (4.639). They also composed quite involved Sanskrit verses secretly criticizing the king under the mum of grammatical discussion (4.635-637).

At 6.45, a Brahmin says "after wandering about abroad, I have returned to my country on hearing of its good government," that is under Yaśaskara 939-948 CE. At RT 8.2227f., Vijayarāja, a descendent of the famous Bhaṭṭa Udbhaṭa, "being in great straits, was preparing to go abroad," which clearly shows the economic motive of emigration.

From outside the Valley evidence for Kashmiri emigration comes from the inscriptions at the Tiruvalleśvara temple, South of Madurai in Tamil Nadu, made already under the Pallavas.[68]

This movement was probably connected with the spread of Śaivism and the interrelations of Śaiva centers in the various parts of the subcontinent. It is notable, for example that the ritual handbook of the Śaivas, the *Karmakāṇḍakramāvalī*, is used both in Tamil Nadu and in Kashmir. Its author, Somaśambhu, is believed by some to have been a Kashmirian. The text is also thought to have been imported from South India in the second half of the 12th century. The earliest manuscript of this text, however, comes from Nepal.[69] This is not entirely surprising, for Nepal too has been a strong Śaiva center and its main Śiva shrine, Paśupatinātha, has

67 For the last circa 300 years, see SENDER 1988.

68 SWAMINATHAN 1990; cf. KULKE ET AL. 1982.

69 See BRUNNER-LACHAUX 1963-1998, vol. IV, p. liii: the earliest dated one (N_4) is dated 1151 CE, written in "Pāla script," however: the NGMCP catalog lists it as written in NS 279 = 1159 CE, Kesar Library no. 539, that is, only shortly after the time of the author; a slightly later one, NS 345, Kesar 370. See http://catalogue.ngmcp.uni-ham burg.de/.

been in existence since Licchavi times (circa 300-750 CE). Indeed, we find a Śaivaguru "*kāśmiradeśād āgataḥ*" in the colophon of a manuscript from Nepal dated 1184 CE.[70] In addition, Raniero Gnoli and then Alexis Sanderson have discovered quite a number of Kashmirian Śaiva texts in the Nepal Archives which were believed lost in Kashmir.[71]

Occasionally, we actually hear of a Kashmiri emigrant who had found success outside his homeland. A well known case it that of the poet Bilhaṇa, who lived around 1100 CE. He had travelled widely in Northern and Western India before finding a position with Vikramāditya, the Cālukya ruler of Kalyāṇa (died 1126 CE). A later successful emigrant who gained a high position at a foreign court was Soṭhala, the son of Bhāskara. He was the chief of the royal chancellary (*śrīkaraṇādhipā*) under the kings Jaitrapāla and Bhīllana of the Yādava dynasty at Devagiri (Daulatabad), at circa 1200 CE.

CONTACTS WITH THE REST OF INDIA AND STREAMS OF TRADITION

Other evidence for the emigration of Kashmiri Brahmins, or perhaps rather for intensive cultural relations,[72] can be seen in the several links established by exchanges of manuscripts. One stream of traditions seems to connect Kashmir and Gujarat, and then further down on the coast, even up to Kerala.

---

70 See REGMI 1955-1956, vol. I, p. 192; cf. WITZEL 1976.

71 The relationship with South India was kept up even under the Vijayanagara kings: an inscription made by one of the Vijayanagara generals states that he settled 60 Kashmirian Brahmins in his territory. Under the Sultans and under the Afghan occupation of Kashmir (1752-1812), large groups of Brahmins left the country for good and settled in towns all over Northern India, from Lahore to Lucknow and Benares.

72 Other sources for close cultural contacts with countries South of Kashmir include the reference (as mentioned) to a building donated by the Malwa king Bhoja at the sacred Pāpasūdana spring of Kapaṭeśvara (7.190-193). He also employed Padmarāja, a betel merchant, to regularly send him the water of this spring to his residence at Dhāra in Malwa (ibid.). This took place early in the 11th century. Earlier, as Kalhaṇa specifies, Kayya, the king of Lāṭa (S. Gujarat, 4.209), built the Viṣṇu Shrine of Kayyasvāmin (under Lalitāpīḍa, 783-795/808-817 CE). Under Nandigupta (972-973) a *maṭha* for people from Madhyadeśa, Lāṭa and Saudotra was built.

More than a hundred years ago G. Bühler[73] has already pointed out the use in Gujarati manuscripts of a verse written by an otherwise little known Kashmiri poet, Amṛtadatta, who lived under one of the early Muslim kings, Śāhāb ud-Dīn (1354-1373 CE).[74]

There also is the much earlier evidence gained from a study of the manuscript traditions of texts[75] such as the *Pāḍatāḍitaka*.[76] This is an early (5th century) classical Sanskrit text by the Kashmiri poet Śyāmilaka that is available in manuscripts in Malayalam script. However, as de Vreese has shown, the mistakes in the Malayalam manuscripts go back to misreadings of Śāradā script[77] (directly, or via Gujarat?).

As mentioned, South Indian Taittirīya Brahmins appear in Kashmir (and in Nepal)[78] around 700 CE, which is another indication of early relations between the extreme South and the Himalayas (see above). This has continued until today: the priests of the Paśupatināth temple in Kathmandu used to come from Kerala but were exchanged by Bhaṭṭas from Gokarṇa a few hundred years ago.[79]

Further evidence comes from Nepal,[80] where a Sanskrit version of the famous, lost *Bṛhatkathā* in Paiśācī, otherwise known in various versions from Kashmir,[81] has been written: Budhasvāmin's *Bṛhatkathāślokasaṃgraha*.

---

73 See KNAUER 1897, pp. ixf.

74 There is, however, some uncertainty on the date of Amṛtadatta. He could have lived before 1178.

75 See MEYER 1903; a Newari manuscript is dated NS 292 = 1172 CE. Cf. also the *Caurapañcāśikā* by Bilhaṇa, see SOLF 1886; cf. MISRA 1976, p. 115.

76 Ed. and transl. in SCHOKKER 1966-1976.

77 See DE VREESE 1971 on such misreadings. Such cases are not isolated. See the fate of the manuscripts in KUIPER 1987: Gujarati Nāgarī → Grantha → Devanāgari; cf. also WITZEL 2014a, 2014b.

78 See WITZEL 1980.

79 See MICHAELS 1994, and WITZEL 1976.

80 For the following section see details in WITZEL 1996.

81 Such as Kṣemendra's *Bṛhatkathāmañjari* (1037 CE) written while having access to the original in Paiśācī; further in retellings such as the *Pañcatantra*, *Hitopadeśa*, cf. also the *Tantrākhyāyikā, Kathāsaritsāgara* and now Salman Rushdie's *Haroon's Tales*. For the history of these texts see now NELSON 1978; TSUCHIDA 2002.

Again, in Nepal many important Kashmiri Śaiva texts have been discovered, and we also find such early copies of Kashmiri texts such as the *Somaśambhu Paddhati*[82] (late 11th century) and Dāmodaragupta's *Kuṭṭanīmata* (NS 292 = 1172 CE)[83] or the Śāradā manuscript of the *Kubjikāmata Tantra*;[84] Others include an early manuscript of the north Indian *Kṛtyakalpataru* with Śaradā annotations.[85] A Śāradā manuscript exists of an early version of the *Ādi Purāṇa* that is different from the *Brahma Purāṇa*.[86] The text is closely linked to the *Viṣṇudharmottara Purāṇa* (of Kashmir) and to the *Kṛtyakalpataru* (of 12th century, Kanauj): it contains a description of a *pūjā* only found in Kashmir, and it mentions wine drinking on the first day of snow, both highly unusual for a writer at Kanauj.

Another case which I can only report from hearsay concerns a manuscript written on birch bark that was kept at the National Archives office in the Singha Durbar Palace of Kathmandu but was burnt in the summer of 1973 in the great Darbar fire, a day before I could see it.[87] Finally, consider the manuscripts of the *Mañjuśrīmūlakalpa*, which is very well informed about 9th-century Nepali and Bengali dynasties but was found in Kerala in an old manuscript.[88]

Such "streams of tradition," frequently linking distant areas of the subcontinent, have been little studied so far but deserve much more attention in order to establish important traits of the cultural history of India.[89]

SCHOLARS

Under the Kārkoṭa and Utpala dynasties Kashmir saw a remarkable flowering of scholarship, which in part was due to the political stabilization, even an unprecedented expansion into north India under the kings Lalitāditya-Muktāpīḍa and Jayāpīḍa, and obviously

---

82 BRUNNER-LACHAUX 1963-1998.

83 MEYER 1903, see n. 76.

84 VAN KOOIJ 1985, pp. 881ff.

85 Discussion in WITZEL 1996.

86 See IKARI ED. 1994.

87 See description in WITZEL 1996.

88 Also, a Pāli manuscript in Gupta characters (National Archives, Kathmandu), edited by Oskar von Hinüber. See VON HINÜBER 1991, p. 48.

89 See WITZEL 2014a, 2014b.

the resources poured into cultural undertakings by the two dynasties.

The *Kuṭṭanīmata* (circa 779-813 CE) says that that one traveled for the sake of study,[90] and that both Pāṭaliputra and Kashmir were centers of learning,[91] while Benares was less so. However Albīrūnī, just two hundred years later (1030 CE), attests, instead, the prominence of Benares and Kashmir. In his time, "Hindu sciences have retired from those parts of the country conquered by us [the Muslims] and have fled to places which our hand cannot yet reach, to Kashmir, Benares and other places" (*India* I. 22).

Among the early scholars etc. mentioned by Kalhaṇa we find these poets and scholars:[92]

- 1.176: Candrācārya and others brought the *Mahābhāṣya* to Kashmir;[93]
- 1.177: Nagārjuna who already had become a "Bodhisattva" by the time of Kalhaṇa;
- 2.16: Kavi Candaka who composed a play;
- 4.144: Vākpatirāja, poet of Yaśovarman, Bhavabhūti, and other poets;
- 4.245: Muktāpīḍa brought wise men form various countries;
- 4.210: Buddhist scholar Sarvajñamitra (NAUDOU 1980, p. 73).

Jayāpīda:

- 4.488f.: restored study of *Mahābhāṣya*; grammarian Kṣīra;
- 4.493: brought scholars from various lands;
- 4.495: Bhaṭṭa Udbhaṭa, as *sabhāpati* (cf. 8.2227-2228);
- 4.496: Dāmodaragupta, author of *Kuṭṭanīmata*;
- 4.497: poets Manoratha, Śaṅkhadanta, Caṭaka, Saṃdhimat.

Ajitāpīḍa:

- 4.705: poet Śaṅkuka, his poem: *Bhuvanābhyudaya*.

Avantivarman:

---

90 See SHASTRI 1975, pp. 172ff.

91 See SHASTRI 1975, p. 172.

92 Cf. also STEIN 1900, p. 11.

93 Could this not just refer to the famous grammarian Candra, author of the *Candravyākaraṇa*? See also NAUDOU 1980, p. 48. On the reimport of the *Mahābhāṣya* see now the curious paper by AKLUJKAR 2008. Cf. BRONKHORST 2016.

- 5.28-29: Rāmaṭa, a grammarian, reciter at temple;
- 5.32f.: Śūra, minister of Avantivarman, furthered learning;
- 5.34: Muktākaṇa, Śivasvāmin, Ānandavardhana (author of *Dhvanyāloka*, cf. 8.1832), Ratnākara (author of *Haravijaya*);
- 5.66 Bhaṭṭa Kallata.

Śaṅkaravarman:

- 5.179: Nāyaka, learned in four Vedas (later reported a Alaṃkāra author?);
- 5.204: Bhallaṭa, Lavaṭa (poets).

Kalaśa:

- 7.258: reference to king Bhoja (of Dhāra) and contemporaneous poets.

Harṣa:

- 7.935: Bilhaṇa left under king Kalaśa, *vidyāpati* of king Parmāḍi of Karṇāṭa;
- 8. 2376ff., 2387ff.: under king Jayasiṃha (1128-1149), scholars and various Brahmins were supported.

From Bilhaṇa's description (*Vikramāṅkadevacarita*, canto 18)[94] of the capital of Kashmir, Pravarapura, and the surrounding villages we hear that Kashmir indeed was a center of learning: "In every house Sanskrit and Prakrit words sound charming like the mother tongue even of women" (6); "the unparalleled glory of the educational institution is cause for fame" (21); there is praise of theater performances (29). Kashmir is the home of Brahmins "of high scintillating spirit" (3). They live (e.g.) at Kāṣṭhāla which is "resonant with the exposition of the Śāstras" (25). One of Bilhaṇa's ancestors built "houses for the exposition (of Śāstras)." Another one, Jyeṣṭhakalaśa, wrote "a commentary on the *Mahābhāṣya* applauded by all" and consequently his estate "was always adorned by pupils" (79) (transl. BANERJI AND GUPTA 1965).

Bilhaṇa describes himself, not without pride, as one "in whose mouth lived the goddess of speech with the tinkle of her anklets inaudible ever since his *upanayana*" (81). He studied the Vedas, and the Aṅga, grammar, in the tradition of Patañjali (82). His eldest brother Iṣṭarāma and his younger brother Ānanda are described as poets, too (84-85). In vv. 86ff. Bilhaṇa describes his travels to Ma-

[94] For an edition, translation and discussion see n. 70, and BRONNER 2010.

thurā, Kānyakubja, Vārāṇasi, Ḍāhala (where he defeated the poet Gaṅgādhara), to Dhāra (unfortunately, he laments, after the death of king Bhoja), and to Somanātha (he did not like Gujarat), after which he "slowly proceeded in the southern direction" to king Vikramāṅka's court.

Maṅkha[95] (circa 1100-1150 CE), in his *Śrīkaṇṭhacarita*,[96] gives a detailed description of a *Sabhā* in the house of his brother Alaṃkāra (v. 15) that was assembled to discuss his work; it was attended by 33 local scholars, including poets and scholars such as grammarians, poeticians, philosophers, as well as two foreign ambassadors, etc. (25.25ff.). The list includes: Nandana, a Brahmavādin (vs. 25), Ruyya(ka), Maṅkha's guru (30, 135), Ramyadeva, a Vaidika and Vedāntin (31-33), Loṣṭadeva, a multilingual poet (36), Laṅkaka/Alaṃkāra, minister of king Jayasiṃha, Patañjali scholar and poet (36-47), Śrīgarbha, a poet and Mīmāṃsaka (48-50) Maṇḍana, descendant of Śrīgarbha, and friend of Maṅkha, learned in all 14 śāstras (51-53), Śrīkaṇṭha, brother of Śrīgarbha (54), Garga, a poet (55-60), Laṅkaka (59), Devadhara (57-59, 62), Alaṃkāra, minister of king Jayasiṃha of Kashmir (60-61), Devadhara (62), Nāga, a grammarian and specialist in alaṃkāraśāstra (62-64), Tutātita, a learned poet (65-60), Trailokya, a Mīmāṃsaka and Tārkika (66), Dāmodara, an official (67-68), Ṣaṣṭha, a learned scholar (69-70), Jinduka, a Mīmāṃsaka (71-72), Jalhaṇa, a poet, minister of the neighboring Rājapurī kingdom (73-75), Govinda, a poet-historian (76-77), Alakadatta, teacher of Kalyāṇa (= Kalhaṇa, author of the RT) (78-80), the poets Bhuḍḍa and Śrīvatsa (81-82), Ānanda, a Tārkika (Naiyāyika) (83-84), Padmarāja, a poet (86), Gunna, a Mīmāṃsaka (87-88), Lakṣmīdeva, a Vaidika (trivedin: pāṭhabodhi), Sāmavedin and Vedāntin (89-91), Janakarāja, a grammarian and Vaidika (92-93), Prakaṭa, a Śaiva philosopher (95), Ānandavardhana, son of the poet Śambhu, a medical doctor (vaidya) (96-97), Suhala, ambassador of king Govindacandra of Kānyakubja (100-102), Jogarāja, a teacher of poetry (106-107), Tejakaṇṭha, ambassador of king Aparāditya of Koṅkaṇa (110-111), Vāgīśvara, a poet (127), Paṭu, a learned poet (129-131), and Maṅkhaka himself (140).[97]

---

[95] See *Śrīkaṇṭhacarita*, cf. MANDAL 1991 and ZACHARIAE 1897.

[96] Details about his family are given at 3.63ff. See now SLAJE 2015, pp. 13ff.

[97] Cf. NAGARAJAN 1970, pp. 242f., based on BÜHLER 1877.

HIGH POSITIONS

Leaving aside scholars, such as those mentioned earlier, a few paragraphs can be added about the social status of medieval Brahmins and their livelihood.

It is Kalhaṇa who provides many more, tenable materials since he is, unlike Dāmodaragupta in his *Kuṭṭanīmata*, interested in recording historical events.

Some of the Brahmins received high positions in government: Mitraśarman was the chief minister (*sarvādhikāra*) of Lalitāditya, and Devaśarman, his grandson, that of Jayāpīḍa, while Bhaṭṭa Phālguṇa was the chief minister of the powerful queen Diddā (who ran Kashmir for 50 years circa 950-1003), first for her infant son, and finally in her own name).[98] Others were chief justices: *rājasthāna(-adhikāra)*; see also the list of participants in Maṅkha's Sabhā (above).

We do not hear about Buddhist officials in these records, but even the early Muslim king Zain ul Abidin (1420-1470) still had a Buddhist minister, Tilakācārya, (*Rājataraṅgiṇī* of Jonarāja, who died 1459, vv. 823ff.). This is the last time we hear about a (prominent) Buddhist in Kashmir in Brahmin writing.[99]

Brahmins also served in the military: Bujaṅga, son of a Brahmin Samānta, was a commander in Saṅgrāmarāja's army. Ajaka, a brahmin minister of king Salhaṇa, died in a battle, as well as the Brahmin soldiers Lavarāja and Yāśorāja (RT 8.1345). Other Brahmin soldiers, some killed in battles, occur at RT 8.1013, 1173 (killed by impaling!), 1868 (n.), 3018, cf. 8.2060. Campaka, Kalhaṇa's father, was a commander of forts under king Harṣa (RT 7.1177). Kalhaṇa says that it was only in such peaceful times as that of Yaśaskara that Brahmins laid down their arms.

SOCIAL POSITION OF BRAHMINS

Normally – as everywhere in India – Brahmins were not to be killed, as Jonarāja's *Rājataraṅgiṇī* (vv. 99ff.) tells referring to an incident in king Saṅgrāma's time (1236-1252): the sons of one Kalhaṇa where were thus spared by Saṅgrāma but as they later murdered

---

98 Even the official coins have the inscription *di-kṣe* (cf. RT 6.177), referring to queen Diddā and her first husband Kṣemagupta (RT 6.177ff.).

99 See now SLAJE 2006-2007. See however Śrīvara's RT 1.5.41, 1.5.62.

the king, they were nevertheless executed by Saṅgrāma's son, king Rāmadeva (1252-1286); Brahmins were killed (RT 8.2060), and Brahmin soldiers regularly died in battle (see above).

Some of the Brahmins function as royal priests, for example, ahistorically (by retrofitting)[100] at the *jātakarma* and coronation and of the legendary king Gonanda II (RT 1.75). They provide the water for inauguration (5.463), the *abhiṣeka* of Varṇaṭa, the successor of Yaśaskara (6.90-91); or, the local Brahmins of Hiraṇyapura assembled and quickly consecrated Uccala as king (7.1385). *Purohitas* with great endowments nevertheless were at the mercy of the landholding gentry, the Ḍāmaras.[101]

Other high government offices held by Brahmins include: Keśava, a Brahmin from Trigarta (Jammu) became a minister under king Ananta (1028-1063 CE, RT 7.204).

However, the relationship between Brahmins and the king has always been ambiguous. As mentioned, the Brahmins take action when they feel threatened or disturbed by royal politics: thus, the *pāriṣādya* and *purohitas* try to destroy Tuṅga by a fast (7.13ff.) and they often resort to fasts (*prayogopaveśana*).[102] At 6.85 the king bestows the royal insignia on a Brahmin (to keep their purity).

Land holding Brahmins and temple priests were organized in *parṣads*,[103] they and other *pāriṣadyas* of temples met, with music, in the *Gokula* for 5-6 days to elect the new king in 939 CE, after the end of the Utpala dynasty. This continued in Kalhaṇa's time,[104] and *parṣads* actualy existed even in Stein's time;[105] such priests arc called *thānapati*.[106]

---

100 Kalhaṇa merely fills in cultural details from his own period for a legendary king of the prehistorical period.

101 STEIN 1900, vol. I, Introduction, p. 19.

102 STEIN 1900 (vol. I, p. 19): "Kalhaṇa does not hide his contempt for this priestly class whose ignorance was equal to its arrogance, and bitterly condemns their baneful interference in affairs of state. In the humorous descriptions he gives of several great Purohita assemblies he freely ridicules their combined self-assertion and cowardice and shows scant respect for their sacred character (compare regarding Purohitas and their 'Prāyas' 5.465ff., 7.13ff., 8.901ff., 939ff.). [...] Various references show that whatever respect traditional notions demanded for the 'gods on earth' in abstracto, Kalhaṇa was not prepared to extend it to their claims as a political 'factor.'"

103 RT 5.171, 5.461-477.

104 See RT 8.900 on the Gokula and a *parṣad*.

105 STEIN 1900, vol. I, p. 67, n. ad 2.132, for example at Śārikā Devī on Hari

But in spite of the power of their assemblies and that which some Brahmins held individually, the opposite happens under a strong king. Brahmins were suppressed, for example, under king Tarāpīḍa (4.122) and subsequently killed him by magic. They are again threatened by Jayāpīḍa (4.631ff.) so that some emigrate; and again by Śaṅkaravarman (889-902 CE) who resumed villages belonging to temples, however, not without compensation (*pratikara*); he also reduced the *parṣad*'s allowances (5.170-171) and took over the direct management of the respective villages.

At the village level, the official (*sakandaka*) frequently was a Brahmin. However, the *sakandaka* was always appointed next to the *grāmakāyastha*, the official scribe. The *kāyastha*s suppressed the local population and have aptly been described by Kṣemendra in his *Deśopadeśa* as virtual devils with ink-pots. (cf. RT 5.175-181, 8.87-91).

Bilhaṇa mentions several of the Brahmins' land grants, e.g., at the confluence of the holy rivers, Vitastā and Sindhu,[107] there were landgrants made by Haladhara, a minister of king Ananta, (*Vikramāṅkadevacarita*, canto 18, v. 19; cf. RT 7.214); at Candrasīma, next to the temple built by king Saṃgrāmarāja on the banks of the Jhelum, there were land grants made by king Ananta (v. 24). Others were made at Vijayakṣetra (v. 39), a place already mentioned, for an earlier period, by Kalhaṇa. Anantadeva's wife Subhaṭā "proclaimed the free acceptance of land by Brāhmaṇas" (v. 45).

Bilhaṇa also mentions a foundation made by Brahmins themselves, namely his ancestor Muktikalaśa, who is described as "munificent and powerful" (77) and as having built "houses for the exposition (of Śāstras)."

Another possibility for Brahmins to gain income was to carry out rituals. According to Jonarāja's *Rājataraṅgiṇī*, king Siṃhadeva (1286-1301) performed an elaborate bathing ceremony of Vijayeśvara with the enormous expense of one lakh of gold *niṣka*s, under the guidance of the king's preceptor Śaṅkarasvāmin (v. 133), who then received the equally enormous income of 18 *maṭha*s from the king.

(recte: Hörī] Parvata.

106 In detail STEIN 1900 ad 2.182: cf. also on the corporations (*parṣad*) at pilgrimages places and their role in Kashmiri politics, and on *pāriṣadya*s, 5.171; 2.132.

107 This is a river in the Kashmir Valley, not the Indus river.

King Uccala (1101-1111) gave away thousands of cows, horses, gold, and other gifts to Brahmins who officiated at *śrāddhas* and at propitiatory rites in connection with bad omens, eclipse, comets, etc. (RT 8.76).

Kalhaṇa also mentions "learned *purohitas*" under king Yaśaskara and an astrologer, Rāmaṭa, working as a reciter (*vyākhyātṛ* 5.28-29) at a temple, who is also reported to be a grammarian (!). They could even gain income, as some still did in the early 1990s, from selling *pūjā* articles at temples (5.168).

Under king Jayasiṃha (1128-1149) various Brahmins were supported for their rituals and solemn sacrifices (RT 8. 2376ff., 2387ff.).

ESTEEM

In general, Kalhaṇa holds high regard for his fellow Brahmins, as Stein underlines; Kalhaṇa praises (4.631ff.) their courage against the king; similarly, at 5.16f. a brahmin addresses the king unceremoniously; at 5.48ff. the Brahmins show their need for money or land by some very meager offering they make to the gods; at 6.2ff. the Brahmins who had elected Yaśaskara are kept away from him immediately after his taking office.

His reign is described as ideal, with the following interesting details (6.9-13): Brahmins did not carry arms and only studied; Brahmin *gurus* did not drink spirits while chanting; ascetics did not get children, wives and crops; ignorant *gurus* did not perform the *matsyāpūpa* sacrifices; and they did not, by texts of their own composition, revise traditional doctrines. Housewives did not figure as divinities at the (Tantric) *gurudīkṣā*; and finally, minister, *purohita*, ambassador, judge and clerk were not without learning.

***

In sum, the major texts used here (RT, *Kuṭṭanīmata*, Albīrūnī's *India*, Bilhaṇa's *Vikramāṅkadevacarita*, Maṅkha's *Śrīkaṇṭhacarita* etc.) provide a mass of details on medieval Kashmiri Brahmins. The amount of information could still be substantially enlarged by using overlooked or stray references in other texts.[108]

---

[108] Much legendary information is contained in books such as WALI AND WALI 1916; KAUL 1924; KILAM 1955; SENDER 1988; cf. also MADAN 1965.

As the many references to individual authors mentioned in this paper indicate it would be a useful collaborative undertaking to produce a prosopography for Kashmiri authors, their works, and their contemporaries.[109]

REFERENCES

AKLUJKAR 2008
A. Aklujkar, "Patañjali's *Mahābhāṣya* as a key to happy Kashmir," in A. Aklujkar and M. Kaul (eds.), *Linguistic Traditions of Kashmir*, New Delhi: D.K. Printworld, 2008

BALDISSERA 2005
F. Baldissera, *The Narmamālā of Kṣemendra. Critical edition, study and translation*, Heidelberg: Ergon, 2005

BANERJI AND GUPTA 1965
S.C. Banerji and A.K. Gupta, *Bilhaṇa's Vikrāmaṅkadeva Caritam*, Calcutta: Sambodhi, 1965

BEAL 1884
S. Beal, *Chinese accounts of India*, vol. I, [London: 1884] repr. Calcutta: 1963

BEAL 1908
S. Beal, *Si-yu-ki. Buddhist Records of the western world. Translated from the Chinese of Hiuen Tsiang, AD 629*, London: 1908

BEAL 1911
S. Beal, *The Life of Hiuen-Tsiang by the shaman Hwui Li*, [London: 1911] repr. Delhi: Munshi Ram, 1973

BHATTACHARYA 1978
J.V. Bhattacharya, *Jayanta Bhaṭṭa's Nyāyamañjarī*, transl., Delhi: Motilal Banarsidass, 1978

BRONKHORST 2016
J. Bronkhorst, "Vedic schools in northwestern India," in J.E.M. Houben, J. Rotaru and M. Witzel (eds.), *Vedic Śākhās: Past, Present, Future: Proceedings of the Fifth International Vedic Workshop, Bucharest 2011*, Cambridge (Mass.): Harvard Oriental Series, Opera Minora, 2016, pp. 119-131

---

[109] Preferably in a WIKI-like website. I have drawn up a skeleton list, which I could share on request. (witzel@fas.harvard.edu).

BRONNER 2010
Y. Bronner, "The Poetics of ambivalence: Imagining and unimagining the political in Bilhaṇa's *Vikramāṅkadevacarita*," *Journal of Indian Philosophy* 38, 2010, pp. 457-483

BRUNNER-LACHAUX 1963-1998
H. Brunner-Lachaux, *Somaśambhupaddhati: Rituels dans la tradition śivaïte selon Somaśambhu*, 4 vols., Pondicherry: Institut Français de Pondichéry/École Française d'Extrême-Orient, 1963-1998

BÜHLER 1877
G. Bühler, *Detailed report of a tour in search of Sanskrit mss. made in Kasmir, Rajputana, and Central India*, extra number of the *Journal of the Bombay Branch of the Royal Asiatic Society*, 1877

BÜHLER 1873
G. Bühler, "Abhinanda the Gauda", *The Indian Antiquary* 2, 1873, pp. 102-106

CHAULAGAIN 2013
N. Chaulagain, *Hindu Kingship: Ritual, Power and History*, Unpublished PhD Dissertation, Harvard University, 2013

CHAVANNES 1894
É. Chavannes, *Mémoire composé à l'époque de la grande dynastie T'ang sur les Religieux Éminents qui allèrent chercher la loi dans les pays d'Occident par I-Tsing*, Paris: Ernest Leroux, 1894

COX ED. 2013
W. Cox (ed.), Special Issue *Kalhaṇa's Rājataraṅgiṇī and Its Inheritors* of the *Indian Economic and Social History Review* 50(2), 2013

DEZSŐ 2005
C. Dezső, *Much ado about religion*, ed. and transl., New York: New York University Press/JJC Foundation, 2005

DEZSŐ AND GODDALL 2012
C. Dezső and D. Goodall, *Dāmodaraguptaviracitaṃ kuṭṭanīmatam; The bawd's counsel: being a eighth-century verse novel in sanskrit by Dāmodaragupta*, Groningen: Forsten, 2012

DE VREESE 1971
K. de Vreese, Review of G.H. Schokker, *The Pādatāḍitaka of Śyāmilaka. A text-critical edition*, *Indo-Iranian Journal* 13, 1971, pp. 44-47

ELTSCHINGER 2015
V. Eltschinger, "Latest News from a Kashmirian 'Second Dharmakīrti,'" in P. Mc Allister, C. Scherrer-Schaub and H. Krasser, *Cultural Flows across the Western Himalaya*, Wien: Verlag der Österreichischen Akademie der Wissenschaften, 2015, pp. 303-364

FUCHS 1939
W. Fuchs, "Huei-ch'ao's Pilgerreise durch Nordwest-Indien und Zentral-Asien um 726", *Sonderausgabe aus den Sitzungsberichten der Preussischen Akademie der Wissenschaften, Phil.-hist. Kl.* 30 [1938] 1939, pp. 426-469, corr. p. 382

GRAHELI 2015
A. Graheli, *History and transmission of the Nyāyamañjarī. Critical edition of the section on the sphoṭa*, Wien: Verlag der Österreichischen Akademie der Wissenschaften, Beiträge zur Kultur- und Geistesgeschichte Asiens 91, 2015

GRANOFF 1986-1992
P. Granoff, "Tolerance in the Tantras: its form and function," *The Journal of Oriental Research Madras* 56-62, 1986-1992, pp. 284-302

HU-VON HINÜBER 2016
H. Hu-von Hinüber, "Grenzerfahrungen der chinesischen Indienpilger im 5. Jahrhundert," in H. von Senger and H. Hu-von Hinüber (eds.), *Der Weise geht leise. Im Gedenken an den Begründer der Freiburger Sinologie Professor Dr. Peter Greiser*, Wiesbanden: Harrassowitz, 2016, pp. 15-32

IKARI ED. 1994
Y. Ikari (ed.), *A study of the Nīlamata: Aspects of Hinduism in Ancient Kashmir*, Kyoto: Institute for Research in Humanities, Kyoto University, 1994

INDEN 2000
R. Inden, "Imperial Purāṇas: Kashmir as Vaiṣṇava center of the world," in INDEN ET AL. 2000, pp. 41-146

INDEN ET AL. 2000
R. Inden et al., *Querying the medieval: texts and the history of practices in South Asia*, New York: Oxford University Press, 2000

India
[*Tarīkh al Hind*] See SACHAU 1910

INGALLS 1990
D.H.H. Ingalls, *The Dhvanyāloka of Ānandavardhana with the Locana of Abhinavagupta*, Cambridge (Mass.): Harvard Oriental Series 49, 1990

JHA 1995
V.N. Jha, *Nyāyamañjarī of Jayanta Bhaṭṭa*, transl., Delhi: Sri Satguru, 1995

KAUL 1924
A. Kaul, *The Kashmiri Pandit*, Calcutta: Thacker, Spink and Co., 1924

KAUL 1966
S. Kaul, *Rājataraṅgiṇī of Jonarāja*, Hoshiarpur: Vishveshvaranand Institute, 1966

KILAM 1955
J.L. Kilam, *A history of Kashmiri Pandits*, Srinagar: Gandhi Memorial College, 1955

KNAUER 1897
F. Knauer, *Das Mānava-Gṛhya-Sūtra*, St. Petersburg: 1897

KÖLVER 1971
B. Kölver, *Textkritische und philologische Untersuchungen zur Rājataraṅgiṇī des Kalhaṇa*, Wiesbaden: F. Steiner, 1971

KÖLVER AND ŚĀKYA 1985
B. Kölver and H. Śākya, *Śrī Rudravarṇa Mahāvihāra (Pātan, Nepal) Documents from the Rudravarṇa-Mahāvihāra, Pāṭan*, Sankt Augustin: VGH Wissenschaftsverlag, 1985

KUIPER 1987
F.B.J. Kuiper, *Gopālakelicandrikā,* Amsterdam/New York: North-Holland Pub. Co., 1987

KULKE ET AL. 1982
H. Kulke, H.J. Leue, J. Lütt, D. Rothermund, *Historische Zeitschrift*, Sonderheft 10: *Indische Geschichte vom Altertum bis zur Gegenwart*, 1982

LÉVI AND CHAVANNES 1895
S. Lévi and É. Chavannes, "Voyages des pélerins bouddhistes. L'Itinéraire d'Ou-K'ong," *Journal Asiatique* 1895, pp. 341-384

MADAN 1975
T.N. Madan, *Family and Kinship, A study of the Pandits of rural Kashmir*, Bombay: 1975

MANDAL 1991
B.C. Mandal, *Śrīkaṇṭhacarita, a mahākāvya of Maṅkhaka: literary study with an analysis of social, political, and historical data of Kashmir of the 12th century A.D.*, Calcutta: Sanskrit Pustak Bhandar, 1991

MEYER 1903
J.J. Meyer, *Dāmodaragupta's Kuṭṭanīmatam – Lehren einer Kupplerin*, Leipzig: Lotus, 1903

MICHAELS 1994
A. Michaels, *Die Reisen der Götter. Der nepalische Paśupatinātha-Tempel und sein rituelles Umfeld*, Bonn: VGH Wissenschaftsverlag, 1994

MISRA 1976
B.N. Misra, *Studies on Bilhana and his Vikramankadevacarita*, New Delhi: K.B. Publication, 1976

NAGARAJAN 1970
K.S. Nagarajan, *Contribution of Kashmir to Sanskrit Literature*, Bangalore: 1970

NAUDOU 1980
J. Naudou, *Buddhists of Kaśmīr*, [French original published in Paris: 1968] Delhi: Agam, Kala Prakashan, 1980

Narmamālā
See BALDISSERA 2005

NELSON 1978
D. Nelson, "*Bṛhatkathā* Studies: The problem of an Ur-text," *Journal of Asian Studies* 37(4), 1978, pp. 663-676

Nīlamata LR
[*Nīlamata*, longer recension] *The Nīlamata Purāṇa,* ed. V.K. Ghai, 2 vols., Srinagar/Jammu: J. & K. Academy of Art, Culture and Languages, 1973

NĪLAMATA SR
[*Nīlamata,* shorter recension] *Nīlamata or Teaching of Nīla*, ed. K.S.J.M. de Vreese, Leiden: Brill, 1936

NM
Nyāyamañjarī, ed. Śrī S.N. Śukla, Benares: 1936

OBROCK ED. 2013
L. Obrock (ed.), in collaboration with K. Einike, *Marc Aurel Stein. Illustrated Rājataraṅgiṇī, together with Eugen Hultzsch' Critical Notes and Stein's Maps*, Halle: Universitätsverlag, 2013

OTANI 1934
Shōshin Otani, "chō-ōgotenjikukokuden chū no ichi-ni ni tsuite," ["On a few problems of the accounts in Huichao's *Wang Wu-Tianzhuguo zhuan*"], in R. Fujita, (ed.), *Oda-sensei Shōju-kinen Chōsen Ronshū* [*Festschrift for Prof. Oda Shōgo: papers on Korea*], Keijo-fu (Seoul): Keijō, 1934, pp. 143-160

PELLIOT 1908
P. Pelliot, "Une bibliothèque médiévale retrouvée au Kan-Sou," *Bulletin de l'École Française d'Extrême-Orient* 8, 1908, pp. 501-529

REGMI 1985-1986
D.R. Regmi, *Medieval Nepal*, Calcutta/Patna: 1965-1966

RT
Kalhana's Râjataranginî, or Chronicle of the kings of Kashmir, ed. M.A. Stein, vol. I, Bombay: Education Society's Press, 1892

SACHAU 1910
E.C. Sachau, *Alberuni's India. An English edition, with notes and indices,* 2 vols., London: Kegan Paul, Trench, Trübner & Co., 1910

SANDERSON 2007
A. Sanderson, "Atharvavedins in Tantric Territory: the Āṅgirasakalpa Texts of the Oriya Paippalādins and their Connection with the Trika and the Kālīkula, with critical editions of the *Parājapavidhi*, the *Parāmantravidhi*, and the **Bhadrakālīmantravidhiprakaraṇa*," in A. Griffiths and A. Schmiedchen (eds.), *The Atharvaveda and its Paippalādaśākhā*, Aachen: Shaker, 2007, pp. 195-311

SCHOKKER 1966-1976
G.H. Schokker, *The Pādatāḍitaka of Śyāmilaka. A text-critical edition*, The Hague: Mouton & Co., 1966-1976

SENDER 1988
H. Sender, *The Kashmiri Pandits. A Study of Cultural Choice in North India*, New York: Oxford University Press, 1988

SHASTRI 1975
A.M. Shastri, *India as seen in the Kuṭṭanī-mata of Dāmodaragupta*, Delhi: Motilal Banarsidass, 1975

SLAJE 2004
W. Slaje, *Medieval Kashmir and the Science of History*, Austin: South Asia Institute, University of Texas at Austin, 2004

SLAJE 2006-2007
W. Slaje, "The last Buddhist of Kashmir as recorded by Jonarāja," *Sanskrit Studies* 2, 2006-2007, pp. 185-193

SLAJE 2014
W. Slaje, *Kingship in Kaśmīr (AD 1148-1459). From the Pen of Jonarāja, Court Paṇḍit to Sulṭān Zayn al-'Ābidīn. Critically Edited with an Annotated Translation, Indexes and Maps*, Halle-Wittenberg: 2014

SLAJE 2015
W. Slaje, *Bacchanal im Himmel und andere Proben aus Maṅkha*, Mainz: Harrassowitz, 2015

SLAJE forthcoming
W. Slaje, *Buddhism and Islam in Kashmir as Represented by Rājataraṅgiṇī Authors*

SOLF 1886
W. Solf, *Die Kaśmīr-Recension der Pañcāśikā*, Kiel: Haeseler, 1886

Śrīkaṇṭhacarita
Śrīkaṇṭhacaritam of Maṅkhaka. With the commentary of Jonarāja, ed. Pandit Durgaprasada and K.P. Paraba, Delhi: Motilal, 1983

STEIN 1896
M.A. Stein, "Notes on Ou K'ong's account of Kashmir," *Sitzungsberichte der Kais. Akademie der Wissenschaften in Wien* 135, 1896, pp. 1-32

STEIN 1900
M.A. Stein, *Kalhaṇa's Rājataraṅgiṇī, a Chronicle of the Kings of Kaśmīr, translated with an introduction, commentary, and appendices*, 2 vols., Westminster: Archibald Constable and Company, 1900

SŪRYAKĀNTA 1954
Sūryakānta, *Kṣemendra Studies*, Poona: Oriental Book Agency, 1954

SWAMINATHAN 1990
K.D. Swaminathan, *Early South Indian temple architecture: study of Tiruvālīśvaram inscriptions*, Trivandrum: CBH Publications, 1990 [=*Tiruvalisvaram. A study of its history and inscriptions*, Dissertation, School of Oriental and African Studies, London, 1964]

TAKAKUSU 1896
J. Takakusu, *A record of the Buddhist religion as practised in India and the Malay Archipelago (A.D. 671-695) by I-Tsing*, Oxford: 1896

TSUCHIDA 2002
R. Tsuchida, "Über die direkte Quelle für die kaschmirischen Versionen der *Bṛhatkathā*," *Indologica Taurinensia* 28, 2002, pp. 211-250

VAN KOOIJ 1985
K. van Kooij, "Die sogenannte Gupta-Handschrift des *Kubjikāmatatantra*," *Zeitschrift der Deutschen Morgenländischen Gesellschaft*, Supplementband 1985

VON HINÜBER 1991
O. von Hinüber, *The Oldest Pāli Manuscript. Four Folios of the Vinaya-Piṭaka from the National Archives, Kathmandu*, Mainz/Stuttgart: Akademie der Wissenschaften und der Literatur, Mainz Abhandlungen der geistes- und sozialwissenschaftlichen Klasse 6, 1991

WALI AND WALI 1916
M.K.K. Wali and I.K.K. Wali, *A social survey of the Kashmiri Pandits*, Lahore: 1916

WEZLER 1976
A. Wezler, "Zur Proklamation religiös-weltanschaulicher Toleranz bei dem indischen Philosophen Jayantabhaṭṭa," *Saeculum* 27, 1976, pp. 329-347

WITZEL 1976
M. Witzel, "On the history and the present state of Vedic tradition in Nepal," *Vasudha* 15(12), 1976, pp. 17-24, 35-39; http://www.people.fas.harvard.edu/%7Ewitzel/Veda.in.Nepal.pdf

WITZEL 1980
M. Witzel, "On the location of the Licchavi capital of Nepal," *Studien zur Indologie und Iranistik* 5-6, 1980, pp. 311-336

WITZEL 1986
M. Witzel, "Regionale und überregionale Faktoren in der Entwicklung vedischer Brahmanengruppen (Materialien zu den vedischen Schulen, 5)", in H. Kulke and D. Rothermund (eds.), *Regionale Tradition in Südasien*, Heidelberg: Beiträge zur Südasienforschung 104, 1986, pp. 37-76

WITZEL 1987
M. Witzel, "The coronation rituals of Nepal, with special reference to the coronation of King Birendra in 1975," in N. Gutschow and A. Michaels (eds.), *Heritage of the Kathmandu Valley. Proceedings of an International Conference in Lübeck, June 1985*, St. Augustin: 1987, pp. 417-467

WITZEL 1990
M. Witzel, "On Indian historical writing: The case of the Vaṃśāvalīs," *Journal of the Japanese Association for South Asian Studies* 2, 1990, pp. 1-57

WITZEL 1994
M. Witzel, "The Brahmins of Kashmir," in IKARI ED. 1994, pp. 237-294

WITZEL 1996
M. Witzel, "Tantra and Dharma Teachers from Kashmir," *International Journal of Tantric Studies* 1-3, 1996

WITZEL 1999
M. Witzel, "Early Sources for South Asian Substrate Languages," *Mother Tongue* (extra number), October 1999, http://www.people.fas.harvard.edu/~witzel/MTSub strates.pdf

WITZEL 2008
M. Witzel, "The Brahmins of Kashmir," in A. Rao (ed.), *The Valley of Kashmir. The making and unmaking of a composite culture?*, New Delhi: Manohar, 2008, pp. 37-93

WITZEL 2014a
M. Witzel, "Textual Criticism in Indology and in European Philology during the 19th and 20th centuries," *Electronic Journal of Vedic Studies* 21(3), 2014, pp. 9-91

WITZEL 2014b
M. Witzel, "Ershi shiji de xifang wenxianxue – yi yinduxue wei zhongxin de heigu" ["Philology in the 19th and 20th centuries, with special reference to Indology"], *Gujing lunheng/Disquisitions on the Past and Present* [Academia Sinica] 26, 2014, pp. 116-150

ZACHARIAE 1897
T. Zachariae, *Maṅkhakośa*, Bombay: 1897

Transmission of the *Mūlamadhyamakakārikā* and *Prasannapadā* to Tibet from Kashmir

CHIZUKO YOSHIMIZU

INTRODUCTION

From the end of the tenth century up to the twelfth century, Tibetans revived Buddhist traditions that had deteriorated after the collapse of the ancient dynasty in Central Tibet by reintroducing scriptures, teachings, and monastic rules from their neighboring areas such as Northeast India, where the great Buddhist monasteries Nālandā and Vikramaśīla were located, Nepal, Kashmir, East Tibet, and Central Asia. Kashmir in particular was the favorite destination of Tibetan Buddhists. A considerable number of Buddhist exoteric as well as esoteric texts were introduced to Tibet from Kashmir by Tibetan translators and their Indian collaborators during this period called the "later diffusion" (*phyi dar*). The main sources of information about their translation activities before 2006 were later Tibetan historical literature and the colophons attached to Tibetan translations of canonical texts (*bka' 'gyur, bstan 'gyur*). Jean Naudou's illuminating book, *Les bouddhistes kaśmīriens au Moyen Âge* (Paris 1968),[1] was the most significant study based on these reference sources. He described the development of Buddhism in Kashmir and its impact on Tibetan Buddhism from the seventh to the fourteenth century. In particular, Tibetan history books such as the history of Buddhism (*Bu ston chos 'byung*) by Bu ston Rin chen grub (1290-1364) from the fourteenth century, and 'Gos gZhon nu dpal's (1392-1481) "Blue Annals" (*Deb ther sngon po*) from the fifteenth century have contributed a great deal to the knowledge of the later diffusion. They were, however, not composed by a person directly involved in translation projects of

---

[1] The English version, *Buddhists of Kaśmīr*, was published in 1980.

that period. A Buddhist history of old tradition (*rNying ma'i chos 'byung*) from the twelfth century provides only brief sketches of the early Tibetan translators and their translations.[2] Information in translation colophons of canonical texts was mostly added by later revisers of the translations or editors of each single version of canons.

Since the publication of newly discovered manuscripts from the tenth to thirteenth century begun in 2006 in China, a large number of textual witnesses that were once presumed to be lost have become available.[3] Today, voices of the time are made heard. Consulting some of these new materials, the present paper will examine how the most fundamental Madhyamaka treatises, i.e., Nāgārjuna's (second c.) *Mūlamadhyamakakārikā* (henceforth MMK) and Candrakīrti's (seventh c.) commentary on it named *Prasannapadā* (henceforth PsP), were studied, translated, and transmitted from Kashmir to Tibet or from teacher to student.

Nāgārjuna's masterpiece, the MMK, was translated into Tibetan from Sanskrit by the first quarter of the ninth century at the command of a Tibetan ruler. The translators were the Tibetan *lo tsā ba* Cog ro Klu'i rgyal mtshan and the Indian *paṇḍita* Jñānagarbha.[4] Towards the end of the eleventh century, this translation was revised by Pa tshab Nyi ma grags (1055?-1145?)[5] and his Indian collaborator Mahāsumati in Kashmir before it was further revised by Pa

2 This text was published in faximile edition in MEISEZAHL 1985. The author is Nyang ral Nyi ma 'od zer who lived either in 1124-1192 or 1136-1204 (see MEISEZAHL 1985, p. 9).

3 *bKa' gdams gsung 'bum*, vols. I-XXX (2006), vols. XXXI-LX (2007) and vols. LXI-XC (2009). *Bod kyi lo rgyus*, vols. I-XXX (2010), vols. XXXI-LX (2011).

4 This translator Jñānagarbha is supposed to have translated Śāntarakṣita's *Satyadvayavibhaṅgapañjikā* together with Ye shes sde. Therefore, as D. Seyfort Ruegg has pointed out (SEYFORT RUEGG 1981, p. 69, n. 224), it is unlikely that he is the same Jñānagarbha as the author of the *Satyadvayavibhaṅga* and its autocommentary (*vṛtti*).

5 Regarding his dates, see VAN DER KUIJP 1985, p. 4, VOSE 2009, p. 190, n. 20, YOSHIMIZU AND NEMOTO 2013, p. viii, n. 15 and p. xii, n. 30. 1055 was given for his birth date by 'Jam dbyangs bzhad pa Ngag dbang brtson 'grus (1648-1721) in his *bsTan rtsis re mig tu bkod pa* 2a, which was composed in 1716, and Sum pa mkhan po (1704-1788) in his *dPag bsam ljon bzang*, part III, p. 9, l. 2. Because it coincides with Atiśa's possible reincarnation (i.e., Atiśa died in 1054), van der Kuijp has cast doubt on it. His birth could be later than 1055.

tshab and Kanakavarman in lHa sa in the first half of the twelfth century. Pa tshab made these revisions of Klu'i rgyal mtshan's earlier translation in accordance with the *kārikā*s cited in the PsP.[6] Pa tshab also translated the PsP with Mahāsumati in Kashmir and revised it with Kanakavarman in lHa sa.[7] Several Tibetan history books have reported that Pa tshab Nyi ma grags resided in Kashmir for 23 years,[8] presumably from 1077 to 1100.[9] He was a contemporary of another well-known Tibetan translator who stayed in Kashmir from 1076 to ca. 1092, rNgog Blo ldan shes rab (1059-1109?). Ngog is also considered to have stayed in the same place as Pa tshab,[10] although there is no evidence that the two Tibetan translators knew each other.

---

6 MMK D19a3-6, P22a7-22b: *dbang phyug dam pa'i mnga' bdag rgyal po chen po dpal lha btsan po'i bka' lung gis | rgya gar gyi mkhan po chen po dbu ma pa | dznyā na garbha dang | zhu chen gyi lo tstshā ba dge slong cog ro klu'i rgyal mtshan gyis bsgyur cing zhus te gtan la phab pa | 'di la rab tu byed pa nyi shu rtsa bdun | shlauka bzhi brgya bzhi bcu rtsa dgu yod | bam po ni phyed dang gnyis su byas so || slad kyis kha che'i grong khyer dpe med kyi dbung | gtsug lag khang rin chen sbas pa'i dbus su | kha che'i mkhan po ha su ma ti dang | bod kyi sgra bsgyur gyi lo tstshā ba pa tshab nyi ma grags kyis mi'i bdag po 'phags pa lha'i sku ring la 'grel pa tshig gsal ba dang bstun nas bcos so || ||*slad kyis ra sa 'phrul snang gi gtsug lag khang du | rgya gar gyi mkhan po ka na ka dang | lo tstsha ba de nyid kyis hu chen bgyis pa'o ||*. *P omits the last sentence (*...*).

7 PsP D200a5ff., P225b4ff. (cited and translated in LANG 1990, p. 134, SEYFORT RUEGG 2000, p. 45, and YOSHIMIZU 2005, p. 132, n. 19): *kha che'i grong khyer dpe med kyi dbus || rin chen sbas pa'i gtsug lag khang gi 'dabs su || rgya gar gyi mkhan po rtog ge ba chen po || ma hā su ma ti'i zhal snga nas dang | bod kyi lo tsā ba pa tshab nyi ma grags kyis kha che'i dpe dang mthun pa ltar bsgyur || phyis ra sa ra mo che'i gtsug lag khang du kha che'i mkhan po ka na ka bar ma* (P: *ka na ka va rba*) *dang | bod kyi lo tsā ba de nyid kyis nyi 'og shar phyogs kyi dpe dang gtugs shing legs par bcos te gtan la phab pa'o ||*.

8 See *rNying ma'i chos 'byung* (MEISEZAHL 1985, Text 512a3f., Tafel 343.1), *Bu ston chos 'byung* 138b3 and *Deb ther sngon po, cha* 7b4 (BA 342).

9 LANG 1990 (p. 134) has inferred that he returned to Tibet by 1101, for the colophons of translations on which Pa tshab worked indicate that they were done during the reign of the Kashmiri King Harṣa (1089-1101). Cf. n. 13 below.

10 rNgog translated or revised numerous texts in *grong khyer dpe med* (*Anupamapura), Kashmir, where Pa tshab also worked, including the *Ratnagotravibhāga, Ratnagotravibhāgavyākhyā, Pramāṇavārttika, Pramāṇavārttikālaṃkāra, Pramāṇaviniścayaṭīkā, Anyāpohaprakaraṇa,* and *Anyāpohasiddhi* (see KRAMER 2007, pp. 61-67).

Neither Pa tshab nor his disciple left a biographical account of his activities in Kashmir.[11] Among newly discovered manuscripts, however, were three exegetical works attributed to Pa tshab Nyi ma grags, which are included in the eleventh volume of the *bKa' gdams gsung 'bum*: 1) "Commentary on Nāgārjuna's *Prajñā-nā-ma-Mūlamadhyamakakārikā* [entitled] the lamp that reveals the treatise" (*dBu ma rtsa ba'i shes rab kyi ti ka bstan bcos sgron ma gsal bar byed pa* 1a-52b); 2) "Pa tshab's instruction on the relation between the chapters" [of the *Mūlamadhyamakakārikā*] (*Le 'brel pa tshab kyi man ngag* 53a-54b); and 3) "explanation of difficult points in Candrakīrti's *Prasannapadā*" (*Tshig gsal ba'i dka' ba bshad pa* 55a-88a). The first and last one are to be regarded as the first commentarial works on the MMK and PsP respectively written in the Tibetan language.[12] They primarily provide explanations of the root texts, but they also contain some information about the transmission of the MMK and PsP, as will be seen below. The present paper is my first study of these three texts by Pa tshab Nyi ma grags. Because I focus on the historical background of his compositions, I will not deal with the content of his philosophical discussion.

1. TRANSMISSION OF THE MMK AND PSP TO PA TSHAB NYI MA GRAGS FROM KASHMIRI PAṆḌITAS

It is known from the colophons of the bsTan 'gyur versions of the MMK and PsP that the *paṇḍita-lo tsā ba* team, Mahāsumati-Pa tshab Nyi ma grags, worked on the revision of the MMK and the translation of the PsP during the reign of King Harṣa (1089-1101)[13]

---

[11] Pa tshab's short biography is included in *Deb ther sngon po, cha* 7b4-8a2 (BA 341f.). rNgog Blo ldan shes rab's biography by Gro lung pa Blo gros 'byung gnas (late eleventh to early twelfth centuries) does not provide much information about his stay in Kashmir. Cf. DRAM DUL 2004 and KRAMER 2007.

[12] For the outlines of the three texts, see DREYFUS AND TSERING 2010.

[13] King Harṣa is said to have been enthroned in 1089 and killed in 1101 in the age of forty-two years and eight months (RT 7.828-829, 1717). His name appears in the colophons of the Tibetan MMK cited above and the MA and MABh translated by Pa tshab and Tilakakalaśa (D219a5ff., D348a5ff.) as *'phags pa'i lha* (*Āryadeva). NAUDOU 1968, pp. 168-170, identifies him as Harṣa. The colophon of the Tibetan version of Dharmottara's *Paralokasiddhi* (D249a7f., P267b5f., cf. MEJOR 1991, p. 195), which was translated by Pa tshab and *Bhavyarāja (sKal ldan rgyal po), has recorded a king's name *śrī ha*

at *Rin chen sbas pa'i gtsug lag khang* (*Ratnagupta monastery) in *grong khyer dpe med* (*Anupamapura), which appears to be modern-day Srinagar.[14] 'Gos gZhon nu dpal cites later Tibetans' claims that their Madhyamaka lineage goes back to Indian masters including the Kashmiri Ratnavajra, Parahitabhadra, and Mahāsumati.[15] Although Ratnavajra's involvement in the Madhyamaka tradition is unclear, he is said to have been from a family of scholars with his grandson being the brahmin Sajjana and his great-grandson being the brahmin Sūkṣmajana with whom Pa tshab translated Āryadeva's *Catuḥśataka* and its *ṭīkā* by Candrakīrti at the *Ratnagupta monastery.[16] Ratnavajra's fame is based on his career in the Vikramaśīla monastery and his mastery of the tantric doctrines and practices.[17] Ratnavajra's student as well as Mahāsumati's teacher Parahitabhadra was known among later Tibetans as a great logician who collaborated with rNgog Blo ldan shes rab in translating, for example of the *Pramāṇaviniścaya* and *Nyāyabindu* of Dharmakīrti.[18] Although Parahitabhadra left a commentary on Nāgārjuna's *Śūnyatāsaptati*, there has been no evidence suggesting his further commitments to the transmission of Madhyamaka doctrines.[19] But at present, there is one small hint in Zhang Thang sag pa's commentary on the PsP. Zhang Thang sag pa is supposed to have been a direct disciple of Pa tshab Nyi ma grags.[20] Zhang him-

---

ri śa de ba (P) or *śrī ha ri sha de* (D).

14 NAUDOU 1968, pp. 168, 185 (1980, pp. 208ff.) has discussed the identification of these places.

15 *Deb ther sngon po, cha* 8b3f., BA 344 (cited in YOSHIMIZU AND NEMOTO 2013, p. x, n. 24), where 'Gos cites Thang sag seminary's allegation of their lineage.

16 CŚ D18a6f., P20a8: *kha che'i grong khyer dpe med kyi dbus* (D *dbung*) | (D omits |) *rin chen sbas pa'i kun dga' ra bar* | *rgya gar gyi mkhan po su smma dzā na* (D *su smra dzā na*) *dang* | *bod kyi lo tsā ba* (D *lo tstshā ba*) *pa tshab nyi ma grags kyis bsgyur cing zhus te gtan la phab pa'o* ||. Cf. CŚṬ P273b3-6, D239a5f. Cf. also LANG 1990, p. 133, 140, n. 20 and DIETZ 1984, p. 61, 273. Sajjana worked with rNgog Blo ldan shes rab.

17 See NAUDOU 1968, pp. 139ff.

18 See KRAMER 2007, pp. 61-67.

19 Parahitabhadra is also known as the author of the *Sūtrālaṃkārādiślokadvaya-vyākhyāna* (*mDo sde rgyan gyi tshigs su bcad pa dang po gnyis kyi bshad pa*, D4029, P5530), i.e., the commentary on the first two verses of the *Mahāyāna-sūtrālaṃkāra*.

20 For Zhang Thang sag pa 'Byung gnas ye shes *alias* Ye shes 'byung gnas, see YOSHIMIZU 2005 and YOSHIMIZU AND NEMOTO 2013, Introduction. It is most likely that he learned the PsP directly from his teacher Pa tshab (see YOSHI-

self or a scribe noted in the margin of the manuscript (*dBu ma tshig gsal gyi ti ka* 21a5) the name Parahita and identifies him as a follower of Bhāviveka (sixth c.).[21] If it was Zhang who inserted this note, Zhang possibly received this information from his teacher Pa tshab Nyi ma grags. Assuming that Parahita truly supported Bhāviveka's Madhyamaka thought, his student Mahāsumati took a different position.

Parahitabhadra's student Mahāsumati is also known as a great logician (**mahātārkika, rtog ge ba chen po*) according to the colophon of the PsP. The colophon of the MMK records his name as Hasumati.[22] This shortened name is often used by later Tibetans, although the way of abbreviation can hardly be explained.[23] Zhang Thang sag pa uses the even shorter version "Ha su," referring to a Kashmiri scholar who could be Hasumati.[24] Neither his own work nor any other translation work that bears his name survived. This scholar, however, played an important role in the transmission of the MMK and PsP: the colophon of Pa tshab's commentary on the MMK (i.e., *dBu ma rtsa ba'i shes rab kyi ti ka*) says: "This is a record of the explanation of *paṇḍita* Hasumati."[25] Although the colophon does not mention who recorded it, one may well assume that the person who received the explanation from Hasumati and wrote it down in the Tibetan language was Hasumati's student Pa tshab Nyi ma grags. Therefore, I have no reason to question his author-

---

MIZU forthcoming).

21 *dBu ma tshig gsal gyi ti ka* 21a5 (YOSHIMIZU AND NEMOTO 2013, p. 93, n. 1), where it is spelled *pha ra he ta* and said: *rgol ba 'di ni legs kyi phyogs pa* (a marginal note below the line shows that it is *pha ra he ta*) *zhig gam yang na gud na gnas pa zhig gis rgol ba'o* ||. The name *pha ra he ta* seems to have been mentioned as a representative of Bhāviveka's party, whom Pa tshab directly or indirectly knew.

22 See n. 6 above.

23 'Gos gZhon nu dpal also recorded his name as Hasumati (*Deb ther sngon po, cha* 8b4, BA 344). In some *gSan yig* literatures, the name Hasumati appears in the lineage of the Madhyamaka tradition (e.g., *gSan yig*s of Tsong kha pa Blo bzang grags pa and mKhas grub dGe legs dpal bzang po [see VAN DER KUIJP 1985, appendix]). Cf. also SEYFORT RUEGG 2000, p. 9, n. 10.

24 *dBu ma tshig gsal gyi ti ka* 24a2 (YOSHIMIZU AND NEMOTO 2013, p. 107, l. 3). Cf. also YOSHIMIZU forthcoming.

25 *dBu ma rtsa ba'i shes rab kyi ri ka* 55b22 (132): *dbu' ma rtsa ba'i shes rab kyi ti ga* | *bstan bcos sgron ma gsal bar byed pa zhes bya ba* | *pan ḍi ta ha su mati'i bshad lugs bris pa rdzogs sho* ||.

Here it is apparent that the author referred to two manuscripts from Kashmir and India. The Tibetan expression *rgya dpe* is often used for "original Sanskrit text" in contrast to "Tibetan text,"[38] but here it could refer to a Sanskrit manuscript from India compared to that from Kashmir (*kha che'i dpe*). Moreover, it is most likely identical with the manuscript from the "eastern borderland" (*nyi 'og shar phyogs*) mentioned above. The "eastern borderland" could be the border area between Tibet and East India or Bengal.[39] Although there is doubt about Pa tshab's authorship of this *Explanation of difficult points* because his name is merely inserted to the colophon in small letters,[40] I consider this work as his own composition. Who else but the translator, Pa tshab Nyi ma grags, was in a position to see the two manuscripts and indicate a minor difference between them? It is also evident that Pa tshab composed this work in Tibet after he and Kanakavarman had gained the second Sanskrit manuscript from India.

In the passage cited above, Pa tshab is pointing out a difference between the two manuscripts concerning the Sanskrit sentence, *tasya kāni saṃbandhābhidheyaprayojanāni* (PsP LVP, p. 2, l. 5ff., MACDONALD 2015, vol. I, p. 116), which asks about relation, subject matter, and purpose of the MMK. The Indian manuscript Pa tshab used adds to this compound *tatprayojana* in the sense of the

---

dpe kha cig las grags so || yang na don gyi ngag ni ngag gcig la don mang po 'dus pa la bya'o ||.

38 For instance, it appears in Zhang Thang sag pa's *dBu ma tshig gsal gyi ti ka* 5b1, 10a2, 10a4, 10a5 (YOSHIMIZU AND NEMOTO 2013, pp. 23, 45). It also appears in the colophon of the Tibetan version of the *Prajñāpāramitopadeśa* translated by rNgog Blo ldan shes rab (see KRAMER 2007, p. 57 and n. 56). For his translation of some Indian texts, rNgog used a manuscript from Magadha called *yul dbus kyi dpe* (KRAMER 2007, pp. 58, 67, nos. 27, 32 and 48).

39 In Tibetan literature, the expression "east" (*shar phyogs*) often intends East India, for instance, the expression "three [from] the East" (*shar gsum*) refers to three teachers or works from East India or Bengal.

40 *Tshig gsal ba'i dka' ba bshad pa* 88a9f. (203) cited below in n. 47. As seen there, this work had wrongly been attributed to Candrakīrti. The compiler or writer of the manuscript may have inserted Pa tshab's name, as DREYFUS AND TSERING 2010, p. 392 have speculated. Cf. also *dBu ma rtsa ba'i shes rab kyi ti ka* 1a (29), where, after the title, "here is the commentary on the Madhyamaka composed by the teacher Candrakīrti" (*slob dpon zla grags pas mdzad pa'i dbu ma'i 'grel pa zhes bya ba bzhugs so*), the compiler of the manuscript noted, "this is not composed by the teacher Candrakīrti but composed by the translator Pa tshab" (*'di slob dpon zla grags kyis mdzad pa min par pa tshab lo tsas mdzad yin 'dug*).

purpose of the purpose (*prayojanasya prayojana*), as some currently available manuscripts attest the reading *saṃbandhābhidheyaprayojanatatprayojanāni*.[41] In the above passage, Pa tshab seems to make good use of both manuscripts by interpreting the purpose of the purpose as not explicit but implicit in the text. Candrakīrti does not explicitly state the purpose of the purpose, so that the Kashmiri manuscript does not have it, whereas the Indian manuscript has it suggesting that Candrakīrti implies it. The second purpose must be implicit, because the fact is that he explicitly states one purpose alone, as will be seen below. This is Pa tshab's interpretation of why one manuscript has *tatprayojana* and another does not have it. Interestingly, however, Pa tshab implants in his own translation a different interpretation: what is implicit is the direct purpose of the treatise, whereas the purpose of the purpose is explicit. Pa tshab's solution is as follows: "What are relation, subject matter and the purpose of the purpose of [this treatise]?" (*'brel pa dang brjod bya dang dgos pa'i dgos pa gang yin*).[42] This Tibetan sentence includes *prayojanaprayojana* (i.e., *prayojanasya prayojana*), but, unlike the Sanskrit *saṃbandhābhidheyaprayojanatatprayojanāni,* it omits the first *prayojana* as an independent item. Pa tshab's intent here is, in my reading, that Candrakīrti explicitly states the *prayojanaprayojana* in his text, because Candrakīrti solely speaks of *nirvāṇa* as a purpose of the treatise (PsP LVP, p. 4, l. 1: *nirvāṇaṃ śāstrasya prayojanaṃ nirdiṣṭaṃ*), and because *nirvāṇa* is the final purpose of all other purposes, which must be the purpose of the purpose. The direct purpose of the treatise is implicit in the text. According to Pa tshab, it is "the purpose to make others understand [dependent origination (*pratītyasamutpāda*)]."[43] Pa tshab's student Zhang Thang sag pa follows his teacher in interpreting the text in a way to say

---

41 See TANJI 1988, p. 91, n. 13 and DE JONG 1978, p. 28, 2.6. As de Jong has indicated, "the purpose of the purpose" probably has been introduced by later scholars, who were familiar to setting forth the question about the four topics, *saṃbandha, abhidheya, prayojana* and *prayojanaprayojana*, not the first three only. According to MACDONALD 2015, vol. I, p. 116, n. 10, the Potala manuscript (Ms Q) reads *saṃbandhābhidheyaprayojanaprayojanāni*, while nine of the paper manuscripts attest *saṃbandhābhidheyaprayojanatatprayojanāni*. Cf. further ibid., vol. II, p. 10, n. 31.

42 PsP D2a1f., P2a6f.

43 *Tshig gsal ba'i dka' ba bshad pa* 56b16 (140): *dgos pa ni gzhan gyis khong du chud par bya ba'i phir ro* ‖.

that Candrakīrti presents the ultimate purpose rather than the purpose of the words (*sgra'i dgos pa*) of the treatise.[44]

This provides a good example of Pa tshab's emendation of his own earlier translation as a result of comparing the two manuscripts. Supposedly, he had first translated the sentence as having the three elements, i.e., *'brel pa, brjod bya* and *dgos pa* (**saṃbandhābhidheyaprayojanāni*) in accordance with the Kashmiri manuscript. He later replaced *dgos pa* (*prayojana*) with *dgos pa'i dgos pa* (**prayojanasya prayojana*), having looked at the manuscript from India. This is a well considered translation, for it entails both *prayojana* and *prayojanaprayojana*, and yet suggests that Candrakīrti explicitly states the final purpose alone, that is, *nirvāṇa*.

Pa tshab conducted the retranslation work of the PsP with the aid of Kanakavarman.[45] This scholar was probably engaged in teaching activities with Pa tshab, for Pa tshab's disciple Zhang Thang sag pa seems to have learned the MMK and PsP not only from Pa tshab but also from Kanakavarman. As I have previously discussed, Zhang cites the opinions of a *lo tsā ba* and a *paṇḍita* several times in his commentary on the PsP, who were to be identified as Pa tshab and Kanakavarman respectively.[46]

There is some information about Pa tshab's composition of the *Explanation of difficult points in the PsP*: this composition took place under a *paṇḍita*'s guidance. The colophon of this text says that it was composed on the basis of the instructions of the teacher *tshong dpon paṇḍita*.[47] Who is this enigmatic figure, *bla ma tshong*

---

44 *dBu ma tshig gsal gyi ti ka* 4a3 (YOSHIIMIZU AND NEMOTO 2013, p. 17): *dgos pa ni sgra'i dgos pa ma yin gyi nying dgos bla med kyi byang chub thob pa'o* ||.

45 Kanakavarman had a long career as a translator. He collaborated with Rin chen bzang po (958-1055) in the translation of the *Sarvadurgatipariśodhanapretahomavidhi*. He is also known for his translation with Mar thung Dad pa'i shes rab of Dignāga's (fifth c.) masterpieces of logic, the *Pramāṇasamuccaya* and its *vṛtti*. Cf. NAUDOU 1968, pp. 184f. Although Naudou identifies Kanakavarman as Kashmiri, Pa tshab is said to have met him at Vajrāsana (*rdo rje gdan*) of Bodhgayā and invited him to Tibet from there by an anonymous author in his composition based on the summary of Madhyamaka meanings in the way of inquiries and answers between Pa tshab lo tsā ba and Zhang Sha ra ba (*pa tshab lo tsa ba dang zhang sha ra ba gnyis kyi dri ba dri len gyi tshul du dbu ma'i don mdor bsdus pa*, manuscript 42a2-8). I am indebted to Leonard van der Kuijp for providing me with the pdf of the manuscript.

46 YOSHIMIZU forthcoming.

47 *Tshig gsal ba'i dka' ba bshad pa* 88a9f. (203): *slob dpon zla ba grags pa'i zhal snga nas kyis sbyar pa | tshig gsal ba'i dka' ba bshad pa | bla ma tshong*

dpon pan ḍi ta? The Tibetan word *tshong dpon* means "chief of traders" or "merchant," whose Sanskrit equivalent is *śreṣṭhin* or *vaṇij*. This term can also be understood to mean "distinguished man." Although it is hard to judge by this name even whether he is Indian or Tibetan, it seems natural to guess that this *paṇḍita* – from whom Pa tshab received oral instructions – was one of the Indian scholars who resided in Tibet while Pa tshab was working on the retranslation of the PsP. It could have been Pa tshab's collaborator, Kanakavarman.

CONCLUDING REMARKS

To summarize the transmission process of the MMK and PsP to Tibet from Kashmir and their dissemination into the Tibetan Buddhist scholastic circle through Pa tshab Nyi ma grags and his collaborators, the following phases may be assumed:

1. Pa tshab Nyi ma grags studied the MMK and PsP in Kashmir during his 23-year stay. He translated the PsP into the Tibetan language with the aid of the Kashmiri scholar Mahāsumati, using a Sanskrit manuscript accessible there. They also revised Klu'i rgyal mtshan's earlier translation of the MMK in accordance with the citations and interpretations of the MMK in the PsP. Since the earlier translation was based on Bhāviveka-Avalokitavrata's interpretation, their revision work of the MMK introduced a shift in authority for studying the MMK from Bhāviveka to Candrakīrti.
2. Pa tshab himself composed a commentary on the MMK relying on Mahāsumati's lectures who explained the MMK based on Candrakīrti's interpretation.
3. Pa tshab revised his translations of the PsP and the MMK with Kanakavarman in Tibet, referring to the second Sanskrit manuscript from a "borderland" of India.
4. Pa tshab composed a commentarial work to explain difficult points in the PsP on the basis of *Tshong dpon paṇḍita*'s guidance. Pa tshab himself left instructions on the relation between the chapters of the MMK for educational purposes (*Le 'brel pa tshab kyi man ngag*).[48]

---

dpon pan ḍi ta'i (88a10) *gtam ngag la brten* [insertion: *pa tsab kyis*] *sbyar ba'o* ‖.

[48] This short work seems to have been composed in order to help students me-

Thanks to the discovery of Pa tshab's works, there are now textual witnesses to confirm that these events actually took place in Kashmir and Tibet from the end of the eleventh century to the middle of the twelfth century. They undoubtedly are of particular significance for the history of the Indian and Tibetan Madhyamaka tradition because they reoriented the understanding of the MMK to Candrakīrti's interpretation.

REFERENCES

BA
The Blue Annals, transl. G. Rörich, Calcutta: The Asiatic Society, 1953

Bod kyi lo rgyus
Bod kyi lo rgyus rnam thar phyogs bsgrigs. 『藏族史記集成』dPal brtsegs bod kyi yig dpe rnying zhig 'jug khang. Si khron mi rigs dpe skrun khang (百慈藏文古籍研究室編、四川民族出版社、成都), 2010-2011

Bu ston chos 'byung
Bu ston rin chen grub, *bDe bar gshegs pa'i bstan pa'i gsal byed chos kyi 'byung gnas gsung rab rin po che'i mdzod ces bya ba*, in *the Collected Works of Bu ston*, ed. L. Chandra, pt. 24, New Delhi: Śaṭapiṭaka Series 64, 1971

dBu ma rtsa ba'i shes rab kyi ti ka
Pa tshab Nyi ma grags, *dBu ma rtsa ba'i shes rab kyi ti ka bstan bcos sgron ma gsal bar byed pa. bKa' gdams gsung 'bum*, vol. XI

dBu ma tshig gsal gyi ti ka
Zhang Thang sag pa 'Byung gnas ye shes/Ye shes 'byung gnas, manuscript; see YOSHIMIZU AND NEMOTO 2013

CŚ
Āryadeva, *Catuḥśataka*, D3846 (*dBu ma* 2), P5246 (vol. XCV)

CŚṬ
Candrakīrti, *Catuḥśatakaṭīkā*, D3865 (*dBu ma* 8), P5266 (vol. XCVIII)

DE JONG 1978
J.W. de Jong, "Textcritical Notes on the Prasannapadā," *Indo-Iranian Journal* 20, 1978, pp. 25-59

Deb ther sngon po
'Gos lo tsā ba gZhon nu dpal, *Bod kyi yul du chos dang chos smra ba ji ltar byung ba'i rim pa Deb ther sngon po*, ed. L. Chandra, New Delhi: Śaṭapiṭaka Series 212, 1974

---

morize chapter titles and contents of the MMK. For details, see YOSHIMIZU 2014.

DIETZ 1984
S. Dietz, *Die Buddhistische Briefliteratur Indiens nach dem tibetischen Tanjur herausgegeben, übersetzt und erläutert*, Wiesbaden: Asiatische Forschungen 84, 1984

DRAM DUL 2004
Dram Dul (ed.), *Biography of Blo ldan śes rab. The Unique Eye of the World by Gro luṅ pa Blo gros 'byuṅ gnas. The Xylograph Compared with a Bhutanese Manuscript*, Wien, 2004

DREYFUS AND TSERING 2010
G. Dreyfus and D. Tsering, "Pa tshab and the origin of Prāsaṅgika," in P. Hugon and K.A. Vose (eds.), *Journal of the International Association of Buddhist Studies* 32(1-2), [2009] 2010, pp. 387-417

EJIMA 1990
Y. Ejima, "Bhāvaviveka/Bhavya/Bhāviveka," *Journal of Indian and Buddhist Studies* (*Indogaku bukkyōgaku kenkyū*) 38(2), 1990, pp. 98-106

bKa' gdams gsung 'bum
『噶当文集』 dPal brtsegs bod kyi yig dpe rnying zhig 'jug khang. Si khron mi rigs dpe skrun khang (百慈蔵文古籍研究室編、四川民族出版社、成都), 2006-2011

KRAMER 2007
R. Kramer, *The Great Tibetan Translator. Life and Works of rNgog Blo ldan shes rab (1059-1109)*, München: 2007

VAN DER KUIJP 1985
L. van der Kuijp, "Notes on the Transmission of Nāgārjuna's *Ratnāvali* in Tibet," *Tibet Journal* 10(2), 1985, pp. 3-19

LANG 1990
K.C. Lang, "Pa tshab Nyi-ma-grags and the Introduction of Prāsaṅgika Madhyamaka into Tibet," in L. Epstein and R.F. Sherbourg (eds.), *Reflections on Tibetan Culture: Essays in Memory of Turrell V. Wylie*, Lewiston: 1990, pp. 127-141

Le 'brel pa tshab kyi man ngag
Pa tshab Nyi ma grags, *bKa' gdams gsung 'bum,* vol. XI

MA
Candrakīrti, *Madhyamakāvatāra*; see MABh

MABh
[Candrakīrti, *Madhyamakāvatārabhāṣya*] *Madhyamakāvatāra par Candrakīrti*, ed. L. de La Vallée Poussin, St. Pétersbourg: 1907-1912

MACDONALD 2015
A. MacDonald, *In Clear Words. The Prasannapadā: Chapter One*, 2 vols., Vienna: Austrian Academy of Sciences Press, 2015

MEISEZAHL 1985
R.O. Meisezahl (ed.), *Die große Geschichte des tibetischen Buddhismus nach alter Tradition rÑiṅ ma'i čhos 'byuṅ čhen mo*, Sankt Augustin: 1985

MEJOR 1991
M. Mejor, "On the Date of the Tibetan Translations of the *Pramāṇasamuccaya* and *Pramāṇavārttika*," in E. Steinkellner (ed.), *Studies in the Buddhist Epistemological Tradition: Proceedings of the Second International Dharmakīrti Conference, Vienna, June 11-16, 1989*, Wien: 1991, pp. 175-197

MMK
[Nāgārjuna, *Mūlamadhyamakakārikā*] *Mūlamadhyamakakārikāḥ.* ed. J.W. de Jong, Madras: Adyar Library and Research Center, 1977; Ye Shaoyong (叶少勇) ed., 『中論頌』 (*Mūlamadhyamakakārikā*), Zhongxi Book Company中西書局, Shanghai 2011; D3824, P5224

NAUDOU 1968
J. Naudou, *Les bouddhistes kaśmīriens au Moyen Âge*, Paris: 1968; [English transl.] *Buddhists in Kaśmīr*, Delhi: 1980

PsP
Candrakīrti, *Prasannapadā Madhyamakavṛtti*, D3860, P5260

PSP LVP
[Candrakīrti, *Prasannapadā Madhyamakavṛtti*] *Mūlamadhyamakakārikās de Nāgārjuna avec la Prasannapadā commentaire de Candrakīrti*, ed. L. de la Vallée Poussin, St. Pétersbourg: 1903-1913

dPag bsam ljon bzang
Sum pa mkhan po Ye shes dpal 'byor, ed. Sarat Chandra Das, part III, in R. Vira (ed.), *Indo-Asian Literatures*, vol. VIII, New Delhi: Śaṭapiṭaka Series, 1959

RT
Sir M.A. Stein, *Kalhaṇa's Rājataraṅgiṇī. A Chronicle of the Kings of Kaśmīr*, vol. III, Delhi: 1988 [repr.]

SAITO 1987
A. Saito, "*Konpon chūron* chibetto yaku hihan" [Criticism of the Tibetan translation of the *Mūlamadhyamakakārikā*], *Bukkyō kenkyū no shomondai*, Tokyo: The Sankibo Press, 1987, pp. 23-48

SAITO 1995
A. Saito, "Problems in Translating the *Mūlamadhyamakakikā* as Cited in its Commentaries," in D. Tulku (ed.), *Buddhist Translations, Problems and Perspectives*, Delhi: Manohar, 1995, pp. 87-96

SEYFORT RUEGG 1981
D. Seyfort Ruegg, *The Literature of the Madhyamaka School in India*, Wiesbaden: 1981

SEYFORT RUEGG 1990
D. Seyfort Ruegg, "On the authorship of some works ascribed to Bhāvaviveka/ Bhavya," in J. Bronkhorst (ed.), *Earliest Buddhism and Madhyamaka. Panels of the VIIth World Sanskrit Conference, Kern Institute, Leiden: August 23-29, 1987*, vol. II, Leiden: Brill, 1990, pp. 59-71

SEYFORT RUEGG 2000
D. Seyfort Ruegg, *Three Studies in the History of Indian and Tibetan Madhyamaka Philosophy. Studies in Indian and Tibetan Madhyamaka Thought, Part 1*, Wien: 2000

TANJI 1988
T. Tanji, *Chūronshaku akirakana kotoba I, Prasannapadā Madhyamakavṛtti I. Translated into Japanese with Notes*, Osaka, Kansai University Press: 1988

TAUSCHER 1983
H. Tauscher, "Some Problems of Textual History in Connection with the Tibetan Translations of the *Madhyamakāvatāra* and its Commentary," in E. Steinkellner and H. Tauscher (eds.), *Contributions on Tibetan and Buddhist Religion and Philosophy*, Wien: 1983, pp. 293-303

Tshig gsal ba'i dka' ba bshad pa
Pa tshab Nyi ma grags, *bKa' gdams gsung 'bum,* vol. XI

bsTan rtsis re mig tu bkod pa
'Jam dbyang bzhad pa Ngag dbang brtson 'grus, *bsTan rtsis re mig tu bkod pa'i tshegs chung rtogs byed gser gyi nyi ma'i 'od zer bkra ba*, in *the Collected Works of 'Jam dbyangs bzhad pa'i rdo rje Ngag dbang brtson 'grus (bKra shis 'khyil Blocks)*, ed. Ngawang Gelek Demo, vol. I, New Delhi: 1974

UEBACH 1987
H. Uebach, *Nel-pa Paṇḍitas Chronik Me-tog phreṅ-ba. Handschrift der Library of Tibetan Works and Archives. Tibetischer Text in Faksimile, Transkription und Übersetzung*, München: 1987

VOSE 2009
K. Vose, *Resurrecting Candrakīrti. Disputes in the Tibetan Creation of Prāsaṅgika*, Boston: 2009

YOSHIMIZU 2005
C. Yoshimizu, "A Tibetan Text from the Twelfth Century Unknown to Later Tibetans," *Cahiers d'Extrême-Asie* 15, 2005, pp. 125-163

YOSHIMIZU 2014
C. Yoshimizu, "Chapter Titles and Divisions of the *Mūlamadhyamakakārikā* in Early Tibetan Commentaries," *Journal of Tibetology* 『蔵学学刊』 9, Center for Tibetan Studies of Sichuan University, 2014, pp. 182-193

YOSHIMIZU forthcoming
C. Yoshimizu, "How did Tibetans learn a new text from the texts' translators and comment on it? The case of Zhang Thang sag pa (twelfth century)," in *The Proceedings of the Symposium: Cross-Cultural Transmission of Buddhist Texts: Theories and Practices of Translation, July 23-25, 2012, University of Hamburg*

YOSHIMIZU AND NEMOTO 2013
C. Yoshimizu and H. Nemoto, *Zhang Thang sag pa 'Byung gnas ye shes, dBu ma tshig gsal gyi ti ka, Part I, folios 1a-26a3 on Candrakīrti's Prasannapadā ad Mūlamadhyamakakārikā 1.1. Studies in Tibetan Religious and Historical Texts*, vol. I, Tokyo: The Toyo Bunko, 2013